SMITH, BAILEY & GUNN
ON
THE MODERN ENGLISH LEGAL
SYSTEM

AUSTRALIA
Law Book Co.
Sydney

CANADA and USA
Carswell
Toronto

HONG KONG
Sweet and Maxwell Asia

NEW ZEALAND
Brookers
Auckland

SINGAPORE and MALAYSIA
Sweet & Maxwell Asia
Singapore and Kuala Lumpur

SMITH, BAILEY AND GUNN
ON
THE MODERN ENGLISH LEGAL SYSTEM

Fourth Edition

by

S.H. BAILEY, M.A., LL.B.,

*Professor of Public Law and Pro-Vice-Chancellor at the
University of Nottingham*

JANE CHING, LL.B.,

*Solicitor and Principal Lecturer in Law at
Nottingham Trent University*

M.J. GUNN, LL.B.,

*Professor of Law and Head of the Department of Academic Legal Studies
at Nottingham Trent University*

and

DAVID ORMEROD, LL.B.,

Professor of Criminal Law, University of Leeds

LONDON
SWEET & MAXWELL
2002

First Edition 1984
Second Impression 1986
Third Impression 1987
Fourth Impression 1988
Second Edition 1991
Second Impression 1992
Third Impression 1994
Fourth Impression 1995
Third Edition 1996
Second Impression 1998
Third Impression 1999
Fourth Edition 2002

Published in 2002
Sweet & Maxwell Limited of
100 Avenue Road, Swiss Cottage, London NW3 3PF
http://www.sweetand maxwell.co.uk
Computerset by YHT Ltd, London
Printed By Clays Ltd., St Ives plc

A CIP Catalogue Record
for this book is available
from the British Library

ISBN 0421 741309
ISBN ISE Edition 0421 750804

PREFACE

The production of this new edition has necessitated more by way of revision and rewriting than any of its predecessors. The completion of this task has only been made possible by the addition to the team of authors of Jane Ching of Nottingham Trent University and David Ormerod of the University of Leeds. They have assumed responsibility for, respectively, the sections on civil and criminal procedure.

The constitutional and modernisation programmes of the Labour government have had and will continue to have enormous impact on the legal system. The enactment of the Human Rights Act 1998 is of such significance that an additional chapter has been devoted to it. Civil, criminal and tribunal processes have each been the subject of scrutiny by far-reaching reviews headed, respectively, by Lord Woolf, Sir Robin Auld and Sir Andrew Leggatt. The process of responding to and implementing such of their recommendations as commend themselves to government are at different stages. Other developments of particular note include the restructuring of administrative arrangements for magistrates' courts and of social security tribunals; the ongoing debate about judicial independence and (under the impact of ECHR) the requirements as to impartiality; revised arrangements for the appointment of the judiciary (yet to reach the goal of many of a fully independent judicial appointments commission); growing scepticism as to the value of the rule in *Pepper v. Hart*; changes in the structures of the European Union and the European Court of Human Rights; and the fundamental reorganisation of arrangements for the provision of publicly funded legal services. Unfortunately, many of the features of the changes share some virtues and vices with developments elsewhere in the public sector. These include, among many others, on the one hand a genuine concern to make processes more transparent and accessible to the public and more attuned to modern ways of doing business, but on the other a predilection for centralisation, a fatal attraction for expensive, unsuccessful IT projects, and an unwillingness to provide proper funding for new agencies.

The preface to the third edition of this text in 1996 incorporated, by way of "stop press", a brief summary of Lord Woolf's Final Report on the future of civil litigation in England and Wales. After some delays, a new system of civil litigation was introduced wholesale, on April 26, 1999, marked by the ceremonial issuing of the last "writ" in England and Wales the preceding Friday. In many ways, civil litigators entered a "year zero" of new rules, new procedures and vast uncertainty as to the continuing value, if any, of familiar precedent. The function of civil litigators changed and has continued to change in the three years that have passed since "Woolf Day". The focus of civil litigation is now intended to be, and perhaps is, equivalent to diplomacy rather than outright warfare. Concurrently, we have seen fundamental changes in the principles underlying the funding of civil (and criminal) litigation, the advent of the Human Rights Act 1998 and, perhaps in consequence of all of this, a significant decrease in civil litigation as an activity. Perhaps as a result, alternative dispute resolution (ADR) and, as technology becomes commonplace, even online dispute resolution (ODR) appear actively to be on the increase.

Since the last edition, the criminal process has seen both the enormous impact of the Human Rights Act 1998 and an annual series of major legislative changes, including the Criminal Procedures and Investigations Act 1996, the Crime and Disorder Act 1998, the Youth Justice and Criminal Evidence Act 1999, the Regulation of Investigatory Powers Act 2000 and the Criminal Justice and Police Act 2001.

The authors wish to thank a number of colleagues who have helped on particular points: W I Hooker, who helped with the Appeals Service tribunal papers, and M Mehan and P W Yong, who assisted David Ormerod with, respectively, research and proof reading.

Responsibility for the finished product rests with us.

We wish to thank the publishers for their support and for preparing the tables and index.

We have endeavoured to state the position as at the end of March 2002 although it has been possible to incorporate some later developments. Matters of particular note since the book went to press include the election of the first woman President of the Law Society (Carolyn Kirby); the publication of Judicial Statistics 2001 (LCD website), which shows a further drop of 20 per cent in the issue of civil proceedings; the publication of the 2001–2002 Report of the Court of Appeal (Criminal Division) and the Consolidated Criminal Practice Direction (Court Service website); the publication of the Court Service paper, *Modernising the Civil and Family Courts*, setting out a new business model for civil justice, and proposing that there should be 93 Primary Hearing Centres, 52 Local Hearing Venues (52 full time and 93 part-time) and 37 new proposed part-time Local Hearing Venues; and the LCD Consultation Paper following the OFT's report on Competition in the Professions: *In the Public Interest?* (LCD website).

The government's response to the Auld Report is the subject of a separate addendum by David Ormerod.

S H Bailey

JPL Ching

M J Gunn

D C Ormerod

August 15, 2002

Addendum

As occurred in the production the previous edition, the government has published a substantial report of far reaching consequences after the manuscript had been returned to the publishers. We can, at this late stage, offer only a short outline of the proposals.

The document – *Justice for All* (2002) Cm. 5563 – is available in full from the home office website. Many of the proposals in the Paper develop the recommendations of the *Auld Review* (Review *of the Criminal Courts* (2001)) the most significant of which have been referred to in the text of the relevant chapters (principally Chapters 14 and 17). In addition, many of the underlying themes of *Justice for All* have been introduced in the relevant chapters – notably the growing emphasis on victim's rights and the desire to increase the efficiency of the system through more effective management and coherence in the criminal process (see Chapter 14, Part C and Chapter 17, Part K.)

Many of the proposals have what might be regarded as extremely weak foundations, and many appear to be designed to meet populist concerns about the criminal justice system – e.g. disclosing previous convictions of the accused. These proposals are predictable, but no less palatable for that predictability given that they ignore established research findings on the dangers inherent in such reforms. Other proposals have their origin in the *Auld Review*, which was a hastily produced review by one eminent expert, but largely conducted without any empirical research. It is certainly questionable whether the methodology adopted by that Review is a strong enough base on which to found such radical amendments to the criminal process.

The Paper is critical of the existing criminal process suggesting that there are "too few criminals brought to justice; too many defendants who offend on bail; [a system that is] too slow to bring them to trial; too many guilty [who] go unconvicted; too many without the sentence they and society need." What of the too many suspects who are the victims of repeated stops and searches; the too many defendants who receive poor quality legal advice in the police station; the too many defendants who falsely confess; the too many innocent defendants who succumb to the lure of the sentencing discount to plead guilty; the too many defendants who do not receive the disclosure of evidence to guarantee true equality of arms?

The message in the Paper is explicitly one of crime control, in which the criminal justice system will be "effective in detecting crime, in bringing offenders to court, in convicting those who are guilty and in sentencing them properly". All of these are emphasised rather than the Due Process guarantees that are also crucial to the criminal justice system. This is also reflected in the language adopted to explain the need for efficiency in the system: "The process will be geared towards getting to the truth, convicting the offender as early as we possibly can, and minimising opportunities for anyone to impede efforts to achieve that."

Even where there appears to be strengthening of the defendant's position, this is often at some cost. As a particular example, the recent reviews of the disclosure regime have focused on the fact that its failings leave the potential for miscarriages of justice with convictions of innocent defendants (see Chapter 14, Part H), and yet the proposals relating to disclosure emphasize that "to convict more of the guilty, we will ensure that the case focuses on the relevant issues, and does not have any surprises, because the prosecution *and defence* will disclose their cases more fully pre-trial." (emphasis added). The principle of carrot and stick that has proved so unsuccessful in the Criminal Procedure and Investigation Act 1996 is adopted in proposals which seek to improve defence disclosure by increasing incentives and sanctions to ensure compliance. All of this will need to be examined closely in the context of the presumption of innocence and the right against self-incrimination. As will the removal of the restrictions on the jury being invited to draw inferences from discrepancies between the pre-trial defence statement and the defence case at trial, thus increasing the danger that the defendant will be convicted on the basis of lies rather than for the offence charged.

Other proposals also appear to ignore comprehensive research studies and earlier Royal Commission recommendations. For example, the fragile guarantee of (and appearance of) independence that exists between the police and the Crown Prosecution Service is jeopardized. In particular, the aim to produce the "closest possible working between the police and the Crown Prosecution Service to make sure that cases do not slip between the cracks because of poor case preparation or inadequate charging" poses a risk of blurring the crucial distinction between investigation and prosecution that was a valuable legacy of the *Royal Commission on Criminal Procedure* (1981 Cmnd. 8092), and endorsed by the Royal Commission on Criminal Justice (1993, Cm 2263). The C.P.S. will be given responsibility for determining the charge in cases other than for routine offences or where the police need to make a holding charge, and provide pre-charge advice to the police. The relationship will be further complicated by the continued scheme of co-locating the police and Crown Prosecution Service in joint Criminal Justice Units.

There are many major pre-trial changes that will have enormous impact especially those on bail which have the potential to remove the liberty of someone who is presumed to be innocent. The specific proposals include those to give the police power to impose conditions on a suspect's bail even before charge. In addition, there will be a fundamental challenge to the "right to bail" with the court's discretion being weighted *against* granting bail to a defendant who has been charged with an imprisonable offence committed whilst already on bail for another offence. The prosecution's right to appeal against bail decisions will be extended. In addition, in high crime areas there will be piloted a presumption of remand to custody if a suspect tests positive for Class A drugs at arrest but refuses treatment.

The impact of the proposals will be felt not only in the pre-trial process, but also in the criminal trial itself. In the magistrates' court, the proposals include extending sentencing powers of magistrates from 6 to 12 months and requiring them to sentence all those they have found guilty, rather than committing some to be sentenced in the Crown Court. There is the much anticipated move to create exceptions to the double jeopardy rule in serious cases where there is compelling new evidence. The proposals also include some very substantial changes to the rules of evidence in all courts so that a more inclusionary approach is taken including admitting relevant previous convictions and allowing witnesses to refer to their previous and original hearsay statements. Many proposals appear to be in direct conflict with the conclusions of the Law Commission Reports on which there has already been full public consultation. In addition, there are the anticipated recommendations to allow defendants to choose trial by judge alone in the Crown Court and to allow trial by judge alone in serious and complex fraud trials, lengthy trials, "or where the jury is at risk of intimidation."

In terms of sentencing, it is proposed to introduce several new sentences; again many would seem to have a populist flavour:

- to ensure that dangerous violent and sexual offenders stay in custody for as long as they present a risk to society

- intensive community sentences with multiple conditions such as tagging, reparation and drug treatment and testing

- "Custody Minus" – a community supervision backed by an automatic return to custody if the offender fails to comply with the conditions of his or her sentence

- "Custody Plus" – under which short sentence prisoners will be properly supervised and supported after release

- intermittent custody to enable use of weekend or night-time custody for low risk offenders

- fine enforcement schemes under which the fine will increase if the offender fails to pay

Broader themes

In *Justice for All*, the Government emphasizes that some of the key objectives of future reform will be to "rebalance" the criminal justice system "in favour of the victim." The victim's central role in the reform agenda is unmistakable. Even the introduction emphasizes that the focus of the system is on "fighting and reducing crime and delivering justice on *behalf of victims*, defendants and the community." This is echoed throughout:

> "we will put the victims, who suffer most from crime, at the heart of the system and do everything we can to support and inform them, and we will respect and protect the witnesses without whom the CJS would not function."

These objectives must be implemented with care if the delivery of justice to defendants is not to become subordinated to the needs of the victim.

Further explicitly victim orientated reforms will be to establish a "Victims' Commissioner", supported by a new "National Victims Advisory Panel". There will also be further legislation to introduce more measures for vulnerable and intimidated witnesses, such as screens, pre-recorded video evidence and TV links. In addition, it is intended that victims will be able to track the progress of their case online by 2005.

Other trends that are discussed in the main text also prevail, including the continued influence of managerialism with more targets and the "joining up" of the criminal justice agencies with "targets, delivery objectives, strategic plans" etc. (see Chapter 14, Part C).

Welcome Changes

It cannot be denied however that many of the proposals to improve the administration of the criminal justice system will be welcomed. In particular, investment in IT and the aim of ensuring that all CJS organisations will be able to exchange case file information electronically by 2005. In terms of structure, the most significant changes will be the new "National Criminal Justice Board" to support a new Cabinet Committee dedicated to the system, with 42 local Criminal Justice Boards being accountable to it. In addition there will be a new "Criminal Justice Council" to operate as a consultative body. There will also be a new Sentencing Guidelines Council designed to increase consistency in sentencing practice.

Justice for All includes many other welcome proposals. Some of the most obvious examples are the introduction of a Code for criminal evidence, criminal procedure (as advised by a new Criminal Procedures Rules Committee) and criminal law. Other uncontroversial measures will include, at trial, giving the prosecution the right of appeal against terminating rulings, extending the availability of preparatory hearings to ensure that serious cases such as drug trafficking as well as complex ones can be properly prepared.

ACKNOWLEDGEMENTS

The authors and publishers would like to thank the following for permission to reproduce materials from publications in which they have copyright.

Crown copyright. Reproduced with the permission of the Controller of HMSO.

Extracts from various law reports reproduced with kind permission of the Incorporated Council of Law Reporting for England and Wales.

While every care has been taken to establish and acknowledge copyright, and contact the copyright owners, the publishers tender their apologies for any accidental infringement. They would be pleased to come to a suitable arrangement with the rightful owners in each case.

CONTENTS

PART II: SOLVING LEGAL PROBLEMS

PART III: PRE-TRIAL PROCEDURE

PART IV: THE HEARING

TABLE OF CASES

xvii

TABLE OF STATUTES

TABLE OF STATUTORY INSTRUMENTS

RULES OF THE SUPREME COURT

COUNTY COURT RULES

PART I

COURTS, PERSONNEL AND
SOURCES OF LAW

CHAPTER 1

INTRODUCTION

A. THE ENGLISH LEGAL SYSTEM

THE study of the English legal system is a vital part of any law student's **1–001** course. Not only are the legal institutions and processes integral to every other legal course he or she will study, they are also the subject of necessary scrutiny for assessing how well the law provides solutions to the problems it is intended to meet.

Law students are not always aware of the social context in which the rules of law they learn about will actually operate. Some of their teachers are more enthusiastic than others about ensuring that their study is not directed solely to the rules of law contained in statutes or gleaned from the decisions of the superior courts. In respect of the institutions, processes and people of the English legal system in particular, some students affect impatience at the study of matters which they think are better left to social scientists. Some even have the misguided belief that the study of the institutions and processes of our law does not carry the intellectual challenge of other legal subjects. Yet a failure to understand the English legal system will make much of what the student learns of those other subjects either incomprehensible or misleading.

For example, those studying the law of negligence need to know the basic elements of the tort and their respective functions. They will discover that until comparatively recently its scope has been confined to cases of physical damage to person or property and that the great majority of cases actually brought arise out of accidents on the road or at work. Liability in tort will be compared with other sources of accident compensation, such as social security, and related to the insurance position. As regards a tort claim, however, the student should not only be aware of the rules which prescribe who has a right to bring a claim for damages, but also of the processes whereby legal rights are actually vindicated, and indeed the enormous practical difficulties that face potential claimants. These processes form an important part of the subject matter of this book.

Almost every aspect of life in the modern state is regulated or affected in some way by law. There are laws which provide for the remedying of defined grievances (*e.g.* by the payment of damages in respect of accidentally inflicted injuries), laws which prohibit anti-social activities and provide for the imposition of penal sanctions for breach (*e.g.* the criminal law of murder or theft), laws which regulate potentially harmful activities by, for example, systems for licensing, registration or inspection, usually in conjunction with

1.

the prescription of standards (*e.g.* liquor licensing, the protection of health and safety at work), laws which confer state benefits upon individuals (*e.g.* education, highways, social security, national health service) and laws which facilitate private arrangements (*e.g.* marriages, contracts, wills).[1] In a sense, the whole body of English law could be said to constitute the English legal system. However, we use the term in a narrower sense to cover the distinctive legal institutions and processes that come into operation when for some reason there is doubt or disagreement as to how the law applies in a given situation: there may be recourse to a lawyer or some other agency for legal advice, or, usually as a last resort, involvement in litigation before a court or tribunal.

The label "English legal system" is convenient, but has to be treated with a little care. For one thing, it extends to both England and Wales (Scotland, Northern Ireland, the Isle of Man and the Channel Islands have separate systems). For another, it is not as systematically organised as a "system" perhaps should be.

B. SOME BASIC CONCEPTS

1–002   There is not room here for an introduction to the theoretical background of the role of law in society.[2] There are, however, certain concepts that will appear at various points in this book and require some explanation here.

1. "Common Law" and "Civil Law"

1–003   The "common law" was the term that came to be used for the laws and customs applied by the royal courts which emerged after the Norman Conquest, and which progressively replaced local laws and customs applied in sundry local courts.[3] As the decisions of these courts came to be recorded and published, so the practice developed whereby past decisions would be cited in argument before the courts, and would be regarded as being of persuasive or even binding authority.[4] The point that decisions of the superior courts are a source of law in their own right is a distinctive feature of "common law systems", the term here being used to distinguish such systems from continental, "civil law",[5] systems based in origin upon Roman

---

[1] These five legal techniques were distinguished by R. Summers, "The Technique Element in Law," 59 Calif. L. R. 733 (1971). See also J. Farrar and A. M. Dugdale, *Introduction to Legal Method* (3rd ed., 1990), Chap. 2, who distinguish two further techniques: the "constitutive" technique whereby the law recognises a group of people as constituting a legal person (*e.g.* a company) and the "fiscal" technique whereby the government raises money by taxation.

[2] See B. Roshier and H. Teff, *Law and Society in England* (1980); P. S. Atiyah, *Law and Modern Society* (2nd ed., 1995); R. Cotterell, *The Sociology of Law: An Introduction* (2nd ed., 1992).

[3] See below, paras 2-003, 2-004 on the growth of the royal courts.

[4] See Chap. 7.

[5] This usage of the term "civil" should be distinguished from its uses "as opposed to (i) ecclesiastical; (ii) criminal; (iii) military": *Osborn's Concise Law Dictionary* (8th ed. 1993).

law but now upon a series of codes established in the nineteenth and twentieth centuries. The basic elements of English law have become established in a number of Commonwealth countries (most notably Australia, New Zealand and Canada, excluding Quebec) and the United States (except Louisiana).

2. "Common Law" and Statute

[handwritten annotation: → laws enacted by parliament.]

Apart from its use as a convenient label for one kind of legal system, the **1–004** term "common law" is used, in a narrower sense, for one of a number of distinct sources of law that exist within such a system. Laws enacted by the Queen in Parliament ("Acts of Parliament" or "statutes"), or made under delegated powers conferred by statute, have come to be of arguably greater significance than the decisions of the courts.[6] The common law has always been particularly associated with the protection of such matters as personal freedom, rights of property and contract, and individual interests in reputation and bodily security. However, the nineteenth and twentieth centuries have seen a substantial expansion of the accepted role of government to include the pursuit of such collective purposes as the protection of public health and welfare, and the direction of the economy. The National Health Service, state education and social security are all examples of services established and regulated by legislation. It has also come to be felt that important changes in areas still dominated by the common law are more legitimately made by statute than by judges, although the vein of judicial creativity is by no means exhausted.[7]

The term "common law" is thus used to denote rules derived from decisions of the superior courts in contrast to those derived from statute. There is, however, one usage that is narrower still. Only some judge-made rules are rules of the common law in this narrower sense—the others are rules of "equity" which are of distinct historical origin.

3. "Common Law" and "Equity"

By the thirteenth century, the Crown had, in effect, delegated its inherent **1–005** power to dispense justice to the judges of three royal courts: the Exchequer, the Common Bench—or as it came to be known in Tudor times, the Common Pleas—and the King's (or Queen's) Bench.[8] At this time, the Common Bench was by far the busiest court as regards civil cases, with jurisdiction over matters between subject and subject, such as disputes over rights to land and actions for debt.[9] Proceedings were commenced by the

---

[6] See Chaps 5 and 6.
[7] See paras 4-037—4-040.
[8] See further below, pp. on the development of these courts.
[9] The King's Bench shared with the Common Bench cases of "trespass" (the term then simply meaning "wrong" as in the Lord's Prayer) and heard proceedings to correct errors in the Common Bench and local courts. Its main function was to deal with what are now called criminal cases—pleas of the Crown. By the end of the sixteenth century it had by a series of procedural devices obtained a civil jurisdiction comparable with the Common Pleas.

plaintiff 's purchase of a writ from the Chancery.[10] The Chancery was originally the royal secretariat, the place where all kinds of royal documents were prepared and authenticated by the Great Seal. Its head was the Chancellor,[11] whose office came to be one of the great offices of state. In medieval times, most Chancellors were bishops and graduates in civil or canon law. Some holders of the office were in effect the King's chief minister.

The plaintiff was obliged to obtain a writ in a form appropriate to the claim. At first, if there was no precedent the Chancery would be prepared to draft a new one, but by the end of the thirteenth century this could no longer be done. Once the writ was obtained it governed the detailed form the action would take: if the wrong one had been chosen, the plaintiff was required to recommence proceedings.

Among the duties of the Chancellor were those of determining questions relating to Crown property, hearing common law actions concerning his clerks, servants and officials, and entertaining "petitions of right" (*i.e.* claims against the Crown). In addition, the Chancellor came to deal exclusively with petitions addressed to the King or the Council in respect of grievances which for some reason were not redressed or redressible by proceedings in the common law courts. This might be because of corruption or undue influence affecting proceedings (*e.g.* the bribery of jurors), or because in a particular case strict common law requirements for proof appeared to lead to injustice, or because the matter did not fall within the scope of writs recognised by the common law. The Chancellor would give relief in particular cases by an order directed to the parties, his intervention being based on the dictates of their consciences judged in accordance with his own view of what was just. Proceedings before the Chancellor were simpler, and were in other respects advantageous when compared with the procedures of the common law courts. Moreover, the Chancellor developed several remedies which were not available in other courts, most notably specific performance and the injunction—an order requiring the person to whom it is addressed to perform or to refrain from performing a stated act. When performing these judicial functions, the Chancellor came to be regarded as constituting a court, the Court of Chancery.

1–006 The standard illustration of how the Chancellor operated was provided by the person who borrowed money, acknowledged the debt by entering into a bond under seal, subsequently paid the debt, but failed to have the bond cancelled. For a common law court, the sealed bond provided incontrovertible proof of the existence of the debt: the court would enforce a second payment if proceedings were instituted by the creditor. However, the Chancellor could restrain such unconscionable action on the part of the creditor by an injunction directed to him, and order that the bond be cancelled.

At first it was not thought that there were separate systems of "law" and "equity". The Chancellor was frequently advised by the common law judges, and there were suggestions that the common law courts could take

---

[10] Proceedings in the King's Bench were commenced by a petition known as a "bill" addressed directly to the court by the plaintiff, a simpler and cheaper procedure.

[11] Where a Chancellor was not appointed, the Great Seal could be entrusted to temporary "Keepers of the Seal". Occasionally, a permanent appointment was made to the office of "Lord Keeper of the Great Seal" where it was wished not to make an appointment to the more dignified office of Lord Chancellor; the powers of the two offices were the same.

account of matters of conscience. However, tensions developed. The arguments on each side indeed reflected what is an inevitable dilemma in any system of law, the problem of reconciling the competing demands of justice and certainty. The more general a rule, the less likely it is to do justice in all the particular cases to which it applies; moreover, an attempt to construct in advance the qualifications to the rule necessary to do justice in all cases would lead to a system of rules of enormous complexity, even if all the problems could be foreseen. Hence the need for some means whereby particular cases could be dealt with justly. Ad hoc decision-making can however be unjust if like cases are treated differently and, in any event, tends to be unpredictable.[12] The Chancellors reacted to criticisms from common lawyers and to the need to introduce regularity into the processing of an increasing caseload by developing principles of "equity" or justice from their ad hoc interventions. At times, however, the tensions also reflected personal difficulties between the Chancellor and common lawyers. In the sixteenth century Cardinal Wolsey caused much discontent among common lawyers by his preference for his own robust "common sense" over legal learning, and in the early seventeenth century a dispute between Lord Chancellor Ellesmere and Sir Edward Coke, the Chief Justice of the King's Bench, was settled by King James I in favour of the former. The Chancellor's power to issue injunctions preventing a litigant from suing at common law or enforcing a judgment obtained at law was confirmed.[13] By the end of the century the common lawyers had given up the struggle. By this time it was also the established practice for lawyers rather than ecclesiastics to be appointed to the office of Lord Chancellor,[14] and, indeed, men trained in English common law and equity rather than civil law.

The principles of equity were progressively refined and developed, most **1–007** notably during the course of the seventeenth and eighteenth centuries. Of fundamental significance was the development of the concept of the "trust", whereby property could be legally owned by one person, but held by that person for the benefit of another, the latter's rights being recognised and enforced by the Court of Chancery. By the nineteenth century the organisation of the Court of Chancery was totally incapable of dealing with the business, and a series of reforms increased the number of judges sharing the work of the court with the Lord Chancellor. It was also obvious that the presence of two systems with separate courts was highly inconvenient for litigants. Further reforms in the middle of the century made some of the procedural devices of the Court of Chancery (discovery of documents, injunctions) available in the common law courts, allowed those courts to consider equitable defences, and empowered the Chancery to decide questions of common law, receive oral evidence, determine issues of

---

[12] This point was made in the 17th century by John Selden (*Table Talk*, edited by F. Pollock, 1927)—"Equity is a roguish thing, for law we have a measure, knowing what to trust to. Equity is according to the conscience of him that is Chancellor, and as it is larger or narrower so is equity. It is all one as if they should make the standard for the measure we call a foot to be the Chancellor's foot; what an uncertain measure would this be; one Chancellor has a long foot, another a short foot, a third an indifferent foot; it is the same thing in the Chancellor's conscience." These matters are considered further, below, paras 1-014—1-016.

[13] See J. H. Baker, "The Common Lawyers and the Chancery: 1616" (1969) 4 Ir. Jur. (N.S.) 368.

[14] It became customary for the Chancellor to be ennobled.

English court of chancery
↳ Equity → Injunction

fact by jury trial and award damages. One aspect of the general reorganisation of the superior courts by the Supreme Court of Judicature Acts 1873 and 1875[15] was the *procedural* fusion of law and equity. Matters of both law and equity can now be determined in the course of one set of proceedings: if there is any conflict between rules of law and rules of equity, the latter are to prevail.[16] In most instances there are differences between the operation of law and equity rather than conflict. For example, different remedies may be available in respect of what both systems acknowledge to be a wrong (*e.g.* damages (common law) and an injunction (equity) in respect of a nuisance). Equity may impose additional obligations on a person while recognising his or her rights at common law (*e.g.* by accepting that a trustee is the legal owner of property while requiring him or her to hold it for the benefit of another).

4. "LAW" AND "FACT"

(a) Historical background

1–008 Today, English law is expounded to law students as a system of substantive rules, derived from the common law and statute, which confer rights, impose obligations, create immunities, confer legal powers and so on. This is, however, a comparatively modern way of looking at the law.[17]

The earliest methods of conducting a law suit, adopted by royal courts from the practice of local courts, involved the intervention of the Almighty. The plaintiff was required to state his claim in the appropriate form. The defendant would make a formal denial of the claim. One of them, usually the defendant, would then be required to swear on oath that his cause was just, and the oath would be tested, or put to proof. This might be done by "compurgation", whereby a fixed number of persons (eventually 12) swore oaths in his support; by "battle" where a party or a person swearing an oath in his support could be compelled to prove his veracity by successfully defending himself in a fight, it being presumed that God would aid the righteous, or by "ordeal"—

> "we find that the person who can carry red-hot iron, who can plunge his hand or his arm into boiling water, who will sink when thrown into the water, is deemed to have right on his side".[18]

By the thirteenth century all these methods were regarded with disfavour although compurgation lingered on as the method of proof in actions of debt and detinue (*i.e.* actions to recover money owed or property) for several

---

[15] See below para. 2-003.
[16] 1873 Act, s.25(11). See now the Supreme Court Act 1981, s.49.
[17] On the historical background see J. H. Baker, *An Introduction to English Legal History* (3rd ed., 1990), Chaps 4, 5; S. F. C. Milsom, *Historical Foundations of the Common Law* (2nd ed., 1981), Chaps 2, 3.
[18] Sir William Holdsworth, *A History of English Law* (7th ed., 1956), Vol. 1, p. 310. The person who sunk in water was of course rescued—this was not a medieval "Catch-22" situation. See also R. Bartlett, *Trial by Fire and Water* (1986).

centuries beyond. In such systems there was comparatively little scope for legal learning outside the forms of writs and the correct formulation of claim and defence.

These modes of proof were replaced in both civil and criminal cases by trial by jury, whereby the sheriff (a local officer appointed by the Crown) was required to bring 12 men before the court to inquire into the disputed matter and state the truth of it. At first the "jurors" might be aware of this matter themselves or might be informed before they came to court, but it came to be the rule that they should only act upon evidence given in open court, and that their verdict should be unanimous. The development of the jury caused an elaboration of legal technique in disputes as to what was the material question to be put to the jury.

In civil cases, the material question would be an issue of fact, alleged in **1–009** pleadings on behalf of the plaintiff and denied by the defendant, which would decide the case one way or another. The lawyers appearing on behalf of each party could debate with the judges in court the appropriate wording of their pleas before they were formally enrolled in the court records. Furthermore, a party was entitled to admit all the facts alleged by his or her opponent but claim that they did not give rise to a good claim: this process of "demurrer" raised an issue of law for the judges to decide. Again, it was possible for tentative demurrers to be debated in court. These debates provided the opportunity for an increasing level of sophistication in legal argument. The judges were, however, reluctant to commit themselves to formal legal exceptions to general rules. Where possible, parties were encouraged to "plead the general issue", *i.e.* simply to deny all the allegations put forward by the opponent. This form of plea remains the standard form of plea in a criminal trial ("not guilty") but originally it was the norm in civil trials as well. This meant that many matters that today would be reflected in detailed rules of law were left to the jury for it to do justice on the facts of the particular case. The best example was the issue of whether a defendant was liable in trespass if he or she was not at fault. For a long time it was thought that the absence of any legal rule on the point meant that liability was strict—the better view held today is that the jury was entitled to acquit the defendant if he or she was not at fault, but that was never recorded as it was not then a matter for the lawyers. By contrast "special" pleas were only permitted where there was a serious chance that the jury was likely to go wrong if the "general issue" was left to it. Much of the lawyers' debate in court would, in practice, turn on whether a special plea was permitted in the given situation rather than on the substantive question of which of the parties in that situation ought to "win".

In the sixteenth century, the judges evinced a much greater willingness to **1–010** refine and determine questions of law. Pleadings became written rather than oral, and were entered before the appearance in court rather than at it. Informal, tentative discussions of pleas before formal enrolment were replaced by procedures that enabled matters of law to be raised at Westminster after the jury trial.[19] These procedures[20] enabled the lawyers to argue and the judges to determine the legal implications of facts that had

---

[19] The jury trial would normally be conducted away from Westminster: see below, para. 2-004.
[20] The defendant could enter a "motion in arrest of judgment" and the plaintiff a motion *non obstante verdicto*.

enumerate ; acquit

already been found: there could be, for example, an objection to the opponent's plea or to the direction on the law given by the judge for the guidance of the jury. The court at Westminster could order that the plaintiff or defendant should succeed notwithstanding the jury verdict against him or her. A later development was the power to order a new trial.[21] In the same period demurrers became much more common and the judges permitted greater use to be made of the "special verdict" whereby the jury would answer specific questions of fact put to them rather than return a general verdict for one or other of the parties, and the court would enter judgment in the light of these findings. Formal errors could be corrected by a "writ of error".[22]

The development of procedures such as these enabled attention to be switched from matters of form to matters of the substance of the law. The distinction between matters for the judge and matters for the jury now corresponded much more closely to the present day distinction between matters of "law" and matters of "fact".

In the nineteenth century the various procedures whereby decisions could be challenged on procedural or substantive legal grounds were replaced by appeals on points of law (and in some circumstances points of fact) to the High Court, the Court of Appeal and the House of Lords,[23] and as the decisions of these courts constitute precedents for the future,[24] it is in the course of such appeals that common law and equity can be developed.

In criminal cases, special pleading was virtually never permitted, and the general plea of "not guilty" has remained the standard form of pleading for the defendant. Questions of law concerning the indictment or the evidence could be raised informally at the trial, an indictment could be removed on a writ of certiorari into the Queen's Bench where the defendant could challenge it for insufficiency in form, and the trial judge could adjourn a difficult case for discussion in Serjeants' Inn or the Exchequer Chamber. This last procedure was only regularised in the nineteenth century. In 1908 it was replaced by a proper appeal to a Court of Criminal Appeal.[25] The scope for the systematic development of criminal law has thus, until comparatively recent times, been limited.

(b) The distinction today

1–011   A distinction between matters of "law" and matters of "fact" is drawn for a number of different purposes: one of the consequent difficulties is that it is possible for the line between "law" and "fact" to be drawn in slightly different places for each of these purposes. Three areas[26] where the distinction is of importance for the operation of the English legal system are (1) the division of function between judge and jury; (2) the rule that only a decision on a point of law can constitute a precedent that can be cited in

---

[21] This was of wider significance in that the court could quash a verdict that was against the weight of evidence or where there was a misdirection on a point of law.
[22] See below, paras 2-005, 18-001.
[23] See below, paras 2-005, 2-071—2-074
[24] See Chap. 7.
[25] See further below, para. 2-070.
[26] There are others, *e.g.* the effect of a misrepresentation in contract, estoppel and judicial review of administrative action under the *ultra vires* doctrine.

future cases; and (3) the question whether a particular point may be raised on an appeal limited to matters of law.

The first of these situations has declined in significance with the dramatic reduction over the last hundred years in the use of the jury in civil cases.[27] In all but a tiny proportion of cases the judge determines the facts in issue, states and applies the law and decides what remedy or remedies should be given. The discursive statement of reasons delivered by the judge may well contain a mixture of factual and legal determinations, and may be arranged for convenience of exposition rather than in clearly separated sections.[28] The components of the mixture will normally, however, be appropriately "labelled", and the precedent status and the scope of any further appeal will of course vary according to the true nature of the particular determination. The judge/jury distinction remains of significance in criminal cases where the mode of trial for the numerically small proportion of contested serious cases is still trial by jury.[29]

Rights of appeal can only be created by statute, and the grounds on which an appeal may be taken are almost invariably expressed in the statute. The commonest pattern is for a person aggrieved by the decision of a court, or, in numerous but certainly not all situations, a public authority, to be given one chance to appeal on a matter of fact but several chances to raise a matter of law.[30] Appeals from tribunals are normally limited to points of law.[31]

Some aspects of the law/fact distinction are fairly clear. An issue is one of fact where its resolution depends on the reliability or credibility of direct evidence such as a witness's testimony.[32] An issue whose resolution depends on probabilities, for example by way of inference from circumstantial evidence, is also one of fact.[33] These issues normally constitute answers to the question "what happened?" By contrast, if there is a dispute as to the existence or exact scope of a rule of the common law or a dispute over the meaning of the words of a statute, it is a dispute concerning a matter of law. This leaves one kind of issue that is difficult to classify: whether facts found fall within a common law rule or statutory description. This kind of question, one of "application",[34] has been variously characterised as "law", "fact", "mixed law and fact", "fact and degree", "degree" or *sui generis*. As a matter of theory it is difficult to resist the conclusion that this is really a question of law.[35] However, there have been many cases in which it has not been so categorised.

---

[27] See below para. 15-007.

[28] It is today much more common for judgments to be structured under headings (and sometimes sub-headings); all judgments are now given paragraph numbers: see below, para. 7-038.

[29] See below, paras 17-084—17-101. A few factual matters are determined by the judge, *e.g.* those relating to admissibility of evidence and those relating to mitigation.

[30] See generally Chap. 18.

[31] See below, para. 18-043.

[32] These are sometimes termed "primary facts". Such facts may be admitted, or "judicial" notice of them may be taken (*i.e.* the facts are of general knowledge or can easily be ascertained from standard reference works).

[33] These are sometimes termed "secondary facts". An example would be inferring the speed of a vehicle from tyre marks left on the road.

[34] The term used by E. Mureinik, "The Application of Rules: Law or Fact?" (1982) 98 L.Q.R. 587.

[35] *ibid. Cf.* G. J. Pitt, "Law, Fact and Casual Workers" (1985) 101 L.Q.R. 217.

1–012   A number of arguments have been advanced to support the classification
of a question of application as one of fact.

(1) The matter can as well be determined by a layman as by a trained
    lawyer.[36]

(2) The words to be applied are "ordinary words of the English language".
    This argument was used by the House of Lords in *Cozens v. Brutus*.[37]
    Here, the application of "insulting" in section 5 of the Public Order Act
    1936, which made it an offence to use threatening, abusive or insulting
    words or behaviour where that was conducive to a breach of the peace,
    was held to be a matter of fact for the magistrates. Lord Reid stressed
    the undesirability of courts providing definitions of "ordinary"
    statutory words, whether from dictionaries or otherwise:

    > "we have been warned time and again not to substitute other words
    > for the words of a statute. And there is very good reason for that. Few
    > words have exact synonyms. The overtones are almost always
    > different."[38]

    Similarly, it has been held that whether an appropriation is "dishonest"
    for the purpose of the law of theft is, within certain limits, a question of
    fact for the jury.[39]

(3) The rule in question sets a standard, such as one of "reasonableness".[40]
    The best example here is whether a defendant's conduct has been
    "unreasonable" and accordingly in breach of a duty to take care
    imposed by the law of negligence. This is clearly regarded as a question
    of fact.[41]

(4) The question is one of "degree". In *Edwards v. Bairstow*[42] the question
    was whether a particular transaction was an "adventure in the nature of
    trade". If it was, the profit was subject to tax. Lord Radcliffe stated that
    this matter was one "in which the facts warrant a determination either
    way" and "in which it could not be said to be wrong to arrive at a
    conclusion either way".[43] It was a question of degree and therefore a

---

[36] Denning L.J. in *British Launderers' Association v. Borough of Hendon* [1949] 1 K.B. 462.
[37] [1973] A.C. 854.
[38] *ibid.* p. 861.
[39] *R. v. Feely* [1973] Q.B. 530; *R. v. Ghosh* [1982] Q.B. 1053. See below, para. 17-073. In
    contrast, it has been held that whether an article is an "article which has a blade" is a
    question of law and not the interpretation of an ordinary English word: *R. v. Davis
    (Reginald)* (unreported, February 24, 1998, (CA (CrD)), *cf. R. v. Paul (Benjamin Michael
    Frederick), The Times*, September 17, 1998 (trial judge to determine meaning of "humane
    killer" in firearms certificate; for jury to apply that definition to the facts); *R. v. Criminal
    Injuries Compensation Board, ex p. M (a minor)* [2000] R.T.R. 21 ("ordinarily the true
    meaning of a public policy or scheme is for the court to decide").
[40] This is described by Glanville Williams as raising a question of "evaluative fact": [1976]
    Crim. L.R. 472.
[41] See *Qualcast (Wolverhampton) Ltd v. Haynes* [1959] A.C 743, below, para. 7-002.
[42] [1956] A.C. 14.
[43] *ibid.* p. 33.

question of fact.[44] In this situation it is held that Parliament intends the decision-maker to resolve difficulties of application, subject to control by the courts if the decision is irrational.[45]

Running through all these points is the wish to avoid the multiplication of   **1–013**
decisions that can be cited as a precedent, and an increase in the number of decisions that can be taken further on appeal.[46]

The view that some questions of application are to be classified as ones of fact is a classic illustration of the competing requirements of principle and pragmatism. On the one hand it is, for example, difficult to see that there is any clear distinction between matters requiring the attention of a "trained lawyer" and those that do not, or between English words that are "ordinary" and those that are not. The "ordinary English word" argument in particular has occasioned much academic criticism[47] and in practice has been ignored much more often than applied.[48] On the other hand it is equally possible to appreciate the dangers of excessive complexity. It would, for example, cause chaos, even (or, indeed especially) in an age of computerised legal databases, if every decision on whether a defendant had behaved "unreasonably" for the purposes of the law of negligence could potentially be cited as an authority.

Finally, there are two factors which further blur the distinction between law and fact. First, there may sometimes be a tendency for an appellate court, if it is satisfied that the decision on a point is wrong, to classify the point as one of law precisely to enable it to intervene. Secondly, if a decision on an undoubted question of fact is unsupported by any evidence, or is a decision which no reasonable person could have reached or is irrational it is regarded as erroneous in point of law.[49] This convenient fiction enables an appellate court to retain control over factual determinations that are palpably wrong.

5. "RULES" AND "DISCRETION"

As has already been touched upon, it is inherent in any decision-making   **1–014**
process that is required to handle more than a small number of cases (1) that

---

[44] For further examples, see *Ransom v. Higgs* [1974] 1 W.L.R. 1594 at 1618 (meaning of "trade" in a taxing statute); *IRC v. Scottish and Newcastle Breweries* [1982] 1 W.L.R. 322 at 327 (meaning of "plant" in a taxing statute); *Clark v. Perks* [2001] S.T.C. 1254 (meaning of "ship", also said to be "as ordinary an English word as one could imagine" (*per* Carnwath J. at para. [25])).

[45] *Edwards v. Bairstow*, above; *R. v. Monopolies and Mergers Commission, ex p. South Yorkshire Transport* [1993] 1 W.L.R. 23 at 32, *per* Lord Mustill; *R. v. Criminal Injuries Compensation Board, ex p. M (a minor)* [2000] R.T.R. 21.

[46] See, *e.g.* the statements in *Qualcast (Wolverhampton) Ltd v. Haynes*, below, para. 7-002, n. 12.

[47] See Glanville Williams, *Textbook of Criminal Law* (2nd ed., 1983), pp. 59–67 and [1976] Crim. L.R. 472 at 532; J. C. Smith and B. Hogan, *Criminal Law* (9th ed., 1999) pp., 499, 536–540. These authors point out that many apparently ordinary words have been the subject of judicial definition for the guidance of juries. Lord Woolf M.R. has stated that the relevant passage in Lord Reid's speech, "frequently the last resort of counsel appearing on behalf of respondents, has limitations" (*R. v. Radio Authority, ex p. Bull* [1997] 2 All E.R. 561 at 569).

[48] See D. W. Elliott, "Brutus v. Cozens: Decline and Fall" [1989] Crim.L.R. 323.

[49] See below, para. 18-043; *Edwards v. Bairstow*, above.

consistency and certainty are likely to be regarded as important objectives (albeit not the only ones) but (2) that their achievement is likely to be at the expense of an individualised consideration of and reaction to the merits of each case. This is as true of the handling of cases by courts and tribunals as it is of programmes established by government for the administration of, for example, state welfare benefits. In each of these situations it can loosely be said that the basic rules are made by Parliament (statute) or under the authority of Parliament (delegated legislation) or by certain senior judges (common law), and then put into effect by others (judges, magistrates, tribunal members, administrators in government offices and so on).[50]

It will be difficult, and usually impossible, for the "rulemaker" to draft a set of rules that covers all the possible cases that may arise, and indicate with precision the outcome desired in each of them. The consequence will be that a measure of "discretion" will be conferred on the "implementer": the word "discretion" being used here to mean an ability to choose among alternative courses of action or inaction. The inevitable imprecisions of language will be such that the persons charged with the task of implementation will have to interpret some of the words used and decide whether the words apply to the circumstances before them. Indeed, a measure of flexibility or uncertainty may be created deliberately to enable the rules to be applied to situations not anticipated by the rulemaker. This can be done by the use of words of general rather than particular meaning, or by the incorporation in the rules of a standard such as "reasonable", "fair" or "just". The element of choice that may be present here is limited.[51] The rulemaker may go further and *expressly* confer a discretion upon the implementer. This express discretion may to a greater or lesser extent be hedged around by restrictions or limits set by the rulemaker. It must be emphasised that it is not possible to draw a clear line between rule-based and discretion-based decision-making processes: the implementation of rules tends to involve the exercise of a measure of discretion, and discretions tend to be hedged around by rules. All that can be said is that the element of discretion may be weaker or stronger as the case may be.

1–015   These points may be illustrated by some examples, both real and hypothetical. Parliament, at the instigation of the government, has enacted that a person who is injured in an "accident arising out of and in the course of his employment" is entitled to certain welfare benefits.[52] This phrase, which first appeared in the Workmen's Compensation Act 1897, has to be applied by the DWP officer who decides in the first instance whether a particular claim for benefit is made out. The issue then may be taken on appeal to a Appeals Service appeal tribunal, then to a Social Security Commissioner and then to the courts.[53] The application of the phrase has

---

[50] The two groups overlap in the person of a High Court judge who can propound a rule of the common law and apply it in successive breaths.

[51] It is also less usual, although not incorrect, to use the term "discretion" here than in the situations about to be described.

[52] See Social Security Contributions and Benefits Act 1992, s.94. The range of benefits specially linked to this concept was reduced by the Social Security and Housing Benefits Act 1982 and subsequent legislation.

[53] See below, paras 2-037, 2-038.

indeed given rise to a vast number of cases.[54] It would clearly be absurd to expect any person to construct a set of rules which would cover in advance all the possible circumstances that might arise where there could be doubts as to the applicability of the phrase: even assuming a perfect set of rules *could* be constructed, it would be equally absurd to expect mere mortals to find their way around them, as the rules would be of great complexity. Moreover, an attempt to spell out in detail what would count as an "accident" and the "course of employment" might prevent the extension of the right to benefit to persons injured in novel ways or when employed in novel kinds of employment, where the extension would have been desired by the rulemaker. Accordingly, a certain measure of judgment has to be exercised by those determining the applicability of the statutory phrase, and in the sense that their task is not simple and mechanical they can be said to exercise a discretion.

It would, however, have been possible for an Act of Parliament to have provided that a sum of money should be allocated to a board, and that the board could "pay such sum as it thinks fit to any person who in the opinion of the board has suffered an accident at work". This would have entailed the delegation of a considerably greater measure of discretion than is inherent in the present statutory scheme. Moreover, the wording of the board's powers could have been varied so as to increase or decrease the area of choice open to it. The area of choice could be increased by, for example, deleting the words "at work". Conversely, it could be decreased by, for example, replacing "may" by "shall", by setting a limit to the sum payable in any one case, by deleting the words "in the opinion of the board" or by listing a number of factors that the board would be required to take into account. The wider the area of choice, the better able the board would be to reach the "right" or "most appropriate" decision in each individual case (according to its own concept of "rightness" or "propriety"). On the other hand, its greater freedom of action would enable it more easily to diverge from the rulemaker's conception of justice. Even if the board were comparatively free of fetters imposed by the rulemaker it might still have wished to develop policies for its own guidance to ensure a reasonable measure of flexibility.

A good example of a discretion-based decision making process concerned   **1–016** the "exceptional circumstances additions" and the "exceptional needs payments" which were formerly part of the supplementary benefits scheme. These provided, respectively, for an increase in the weekly payment, or a lump sum, in "exceptional cases" at the discretion of the Supplementary Benefits Commission. In practice, the Commission produced detailed codes for the guidance of the local officials who determined the claims on a day-to-day basis, although the codes were not published.[55] These arrangements

---

[54] See N. J. Wikely, *Ogus, Barendt and Wikeley's The Law of Social Security* (4th ed., 1994), pp. 306–323.

[55] See generally, J. A. Farmer, *Tribunals and Government* (1974), pp. 89–99; M. Adler and A. Bradley, *Justice, Discretion and Poverty* (1975).

contrasted with the rule-based system of national insurance, including those for industrial injuries. Following what was the classic "rules" v. "discretion" debate, these discretions were replaced by a rule-based structure,[56] although, more recently, the introduction of the Social Fund has seen in part a return to a discretion-based approach.[57]

Accordingly, among the advantages[58] of predetermined rules over discretions are that like cases will be treated alike (consistency), that persons will not in effect be punished by rules applied *ex post facto* (predictability), that the rule maker is more likely than a person exercising a discretion to be accountable to an electorate, that the implementer will have a more limited scope to deviate from the rulemaker's objective by arbitrary decision-making, that such divergent decisions can more easily be challenged, that the rules will normally be open to public criticism and that decision-making processes can more easily be planned and routinised. Conversely, rules can be inflexible, and can "permit unreasoned official behaviour"[59]

The "rules" v. "discretion" issue crops up at a number of points in the English legal system. The original development of equity was a discretionary case-by-case response to the generality or inadequacy of common law rules or procedures.[60] The subsequent development of rules of equity was a response to the arbitrariness of a system which could vary as the length of the Chancellor's foot.[61] The issue also arises in debates as to the extent to which courts and tribunals should be bound by precedent,[62] the comparative merits of different styles of statutory drafting,[63] whether it is proper for a jury to acquit a defendant who would by a strict application of the rules of criminal law be liable to be convicted, and the extent to which the discretion of a criminal court as to sentence should be limited or "structured" by the provision of guidelines.[64] As the widest discretionary powers are allocated to administrative bodies such as ministers, officials and local authorities, the extent to which the courts should control or review exercises or non-exercises of power is an important feature of administrative law[65]; however, analogous principles apply to the control by appellate courts of exercises of discretion by judges.[66] The "rules" v. "discretion" issue does not admit of easy or general solutions: the appropriate balance has to be sought depending upon the precise context in which the issue arises.

---

[56] See Wikely (1994), pp. 594–595. For a spirited defence of discretion see R. Titmuss, "Welfare 'Rights,' Law and Discretion" (1971) 42 *The Political Quarterly* 113; answered by R. White in P. Morris *et al., Social Needs and Legal Action* (1973), pp. 23–32; *cf.* M. Adler and S. Asquith (eds.), *Discretion and Welfare* (1981), especially Chaps 1, 7, 11.

[57] See below, para. 2-039.

[58] See generally J. Jowell, "The Legal Control of Administrative Discretion" [1973] P.L. 178, 184–194; the pioneering work in the field is K. C. Davis, *Discretionary Justice, A Preliminary Inquiry* (1969) and see P. P. Craig, *Administrative Law* (4th ed., 1999), pp. 392–399 and R. Baldwin, *Rules and Government* (1995), Chaps 1–3.

[59] [1973] P.L. 178 at p. 193.

[60] See above paras 1-005–1-007.

[61] See above para. 1-006.

[62] See below, paras 7-001–7-009.

[63] See below, para. 5-007.

[64] See below, para. 17-080.

[65] See below, para. 18-050.

[66] See below, para. 18-035.

C. THE BASIC INSTITUTIONS OF THE ENGLISH LEGAL SYSTEM

A number of institutions are of central importance to the creation of law. **1–017** Statute law is enacted by Parliament; a vast quantity of delegated legislation is made under powers conferred by Act of Parliament.[67] Both processes are heavily dominated by the government of the day; indeed, most of the delegated powers are exerciseable by government departments.[68] Legislative authority has also been accorded to institutions of the European Union: the Council of Ministers and the Commission.[69] Decisions of the superior courts may also constitute sources of law.[70]

The administration of the legal system, in the sense of the mechanisms for the provision of legal services, the courts and tribunals established for the resolution of legal disputes and the processes for effecting law reform, is almost entirely a matter for central government. In many countries, responsibility for legal affairs is exercised by a "Minister of Justice". However, in the United Kingdom, responsibility for different aspects of the legal system is divided among separate ministries or departments of state, the main ones being the Lord Chancellor's Department, the Home Office, the Law Officers' Departments and the Treasury.[71]

1. THE LORD CHANCELLOR'S DEPARTMENT[72]

As is mentioned elsewhere,[73] the Lord Chancellor exercises a wide range of **1–018** disparate functions, including those of judge, Speaker of the House of Lords, cabinet minister and government legal adviser. He also has extensive responsibilities concerning the administration of justice, including making or advising on judicial appointments,[74] and allowing or disallowing proposed Civil Procedure Rules and acting as chairman of the committee that makes procedural rules for the Crown Court.[75] He is responsible for the Court Service, which provides administrative support for the Court of Appeal, High Court, Crown Court and county courts,[76] and supervises the

---

[67] See Chaps 5 and 6.
[68] A detailed consideration of Parliament and government may be found in such works as S. A. de Smith and R. Brazier, *Constitutional and Administrative Law* (8th ed., 1998).
[69] See below, para. 5-039.
[70] See Chaps 2, 7.
[71] For a general survey, see R. Brazier, "Government and the Law: Ministerial Responsibility for Legal Affairs" [1989] P.L. 64 and *Ministers of the Crown* (1997). See also G. Zellick (ed.), *Law Reform and the Law Commission* (1988), Appendix 7.
[72] See P. Polden, *Guide to the Records of the Lord Chancellor's Department* (HMSO, 1988), which covers the development of the department from about 1870 (systematic record keeping started in 1889) to November 1951 and D. Woodhouse, *The Office of Lord Chancellor* (2001). See also R. B. Stevens, "A View from the Lord Chancellor's Office" (1987) 40 C.L.P. 181, "The Independence of the Judiciary: The View from the Lord Chancellor's Office" (1988) 8 O.J.L.S. 222 and *The Independence of the Judiciary* (1993); Sir D. Oulton, *Counsel*, Michaelmas 1986, p. 3; Lord Mackay of Clashfern, (1991) 44 C.L.P. 241.
[73] See below, para. 4-021.
[74] See below, para. 4-024.
[75] See below, para. 2-049, 2-070.
[76] See below, para. 2-055, 2-066.

schemes for the public funding and provision of legal services.[77]
Responsibility for overseeing the operations of magistrates' courts was
transferred to the Lord Chancellor's Department in 1992.[78] Under the
Courts and Legal Services Act 1990, the Lord Chancellor is responsible for
the appointment of a Legal Services Ombudsman, an Authorised
Conveyancing Practitioners Board and a Conveyancing Ombudsman.[79]
He is also generally responsible for law reform in civil matters, although
other government departments have their own specialised areas of concern.
For example, company law and employment law are within the province of
the Department of Trade and Industry. In 2001, lead responsibility for
human rights issues was transferred to him; and responsibility for data
protection and freedom of information has also been conferred upon him.
Finally, he has a number of miscellaneous responsibilities, for example for
the Land Registry,[80] the Public Record Office, the Official Receiver and the
Public Guardianship Office.

Since the Second World War the Lord Chancellor's Department has
grown from a small office of personal assistants and advisers to the Lord
Chancellor into a substantial government department employing a staff of
about 12,000. It has its headquarters in the House of Lords and at Selborne
House, Victoria Street, London. The most senior official holds the offices of
Permanent Secretary to the Lord Chancellor and Clerk of the Crown in
Chancery.[81] Within the Department, there is a Judicial Group (appointments and complaints); a Corporate Services Group (including finance,
personnel management, an IT Unit and the Statutory Publications Office); a
Communications Group; a Policy Group (with a criminal justice group, a
public and private rights directorate and a civil justice and legal services
directorate); a Legal Advisers Group; and the Court Service.[82] For the
purposes of courts administration the country is divided into six areas or
"Circuits", each controlled by a Circuit Administrator.[83] The Court Service
became an executive agency under the Next Steps programme from April 3,
1995[84]: the Lord Chancellor remains accountable to Parliament for the
Service, but decisions on day-to-day running are the responsibility of the

---

[77] See below Chaps 10, 11. The Lord Chancellor was responsible for civil legal aid from its
introduction, and responsibility for criminal legal aid was transferred from the Home
Secretary in July 1980.

[78] See (1992) *The Magistrate* 74.

[79] See below, paras 3-015, 3-043.

[80] Responsible for the compulsory registration of titles to land under the Land Registration
Act 2002, and the maintenance of a register of land charges under the Land Charges Act
1972. See National Audit Office, *Review of the Operations of H.M. Land Registry* (1986–87
H.C. 39). It became an executive agency in 1990 and achieved Trading Fund Status in 1993.

[81] By virtue of the Supreme Court (Offices) Act 1997, the holder need no longer be a lawyer
with a 10–year general qualification or civil servant with five years experience in the LCD.
The removal of these requirements, through a Bill that passed the Commons at one sitting,
attracted criticism from, amongst others, Lord Woolf M.R. (as he then was) on the ground
that the changes might weaken the link to the judiciary: Woodhouse (2001), pp. 59–61. In
1998, Sir Haydn Phillips, previously permanent secretary at the Department for Culture,
Media and Sport, became the first non-lawyer to hold the office.

[82] *Civil Service Yearbook 2001*, pp. 221–227.

[83] See below, paras 2-051, 2-055.

[84] See *LCD Court Service Annual Report 1994–95* (1994–95 H.C. 579), Chap. 13.

chief executive.[85] The Service adopted the *Court Service Charter for Court Users*, under the Citizens Charter, setting out standards of service users are entitled to expect, and explaining the complaints procedures.[86]

Since 1992 the Department has had a Parliamentary Secretary in the House of Commons,[87] ending the unsatisfactory arrangement whereby the Attorney-General, although not a member of the Department, acted as spokesman for the Lord Chancellor. The administrative functions of the Department in relation to courts and tribunals are now subject to review by the Parliamentary Commissioner for Administration,[88] and the Department's policy, administration and expenditure now fall within the remit of the Select Committee on Home Affairs.[89] **1–019**

For many years, government departments have been required to publish their aims and objectives. Following the 1998 Comprehensive Spending Review, key objectives have been turned into measurable Public Service Agreement targets, further refined following the 2000 Spending Review. For 2001–04, the "aim" of the LCD is simply stated as "justice".[90] To support that aim there are six "strategic objectives", which were revised in December 1999 as outcome measures. They are:

(1) To provide a fair, swift and effective system of justice which provides confidence in the rule of law; helps reduce crime, the fear of crime and the economic consequences of crime; and gives value for money.[91]

(2) To improve people's knowledge and understanding of their rights and responsibilities, including how to resolve disputes which affect them, in a way and at a cost proportionate to the issues at stake.[92]

(3) To improve the availability of affordable and good quality legal services so that the law underpins economic success at home and abroad, and

---

[85] The first chief executive was Michael Heubner, previously head of the Court Service at LCD Headquarters. See M. Heubner, *Counsel*, March–April 1995, pp. 27–28; R. Smith, *Legal Action*, May 1995, p. 26.

[86] Published in 1995. See also *The Citizen's Charter: Second Report: 1994* (Cm. 2540), noting improvements in the treatment of witnesses, victims, jurors and court users under the auspices of the Charter (pp. 62–65). The charter has been replaced by a series of more specific charters: see the Court Service website.

[87] See G. Drewry, (1992) 142 N.L.J. 50; J. Rozenberg, *The Search for Justice* (1994), p. 12. The first holder of the position was John M. Taylor M.P., a solicitor. There are currently three Parliamentary Secretaries: Baroness Scotland, Yvette Cooper M.P. and Rosie Winterton M.P.

[88] Courts and Legal Services Act 1990, s.110, providing that such functions are to be taken as the Department's functions, although there is an exception where action is taken at the direction or on the authority of a judicial officer.

[89] This development took place in 1991, having previously been resisted by the government on the unconvincing ground that such scrutiny might threaten the independence of the judiciary: see G. Drewry, (1983) 133 N.L.J. 959–960.

[90] Disappointingly for those interested in legal philosophy, the LCD does not define "justice".

[91] Associated targets are to improve user satisfaction levels by at least 5% by 2004; reduce the time from arrest to disposal to specified extents; improve the level of public confidence in the criminal justice system by March 31, 2004; and increase the number and proportion of recorded crimes for which an offender is brought to justice.

[92] The associated target is to reduce the proportion of disputes which are resolved by resort to the courts.

that the use of public funds secures greater social justice and reduces social exclusion.[93]

(4) To make civil and family law clearer and more easily enforceable giving priority to key government objectives in tackling social and economic issues.[94]

(5) To improve the lives of children and help build and sustain strong families through providing a legal and procedural framework which sustains family relationships, and, when they do break down, to resolve disputes with the least distress to those affected, especially the most vulnerable.[95]

(6) To uphold the independence of the judiciary – especially through the appointment of sufficient judges, magistrates and other judicial post holders of the right calibre to match needs, and through promoting a partnership with the judiciary for delivering justice effectively.

There is also a further target of securing year on year improvements in value for money in delivery of the Community Legal Service and the Criminal Defence Service.[96] These are broadly similar to the objectives previously formulated although the emphasis on securing value for money has replaced less subtle references to controlling costs. The increasingly visible emphasis by the Lord Chancellor's Department in previous plans on the containment of cost led to tensions between it and the judiciary, with arguments from leading judges that the quality of justice (and the independence of the judiciary) was threatened.[97]

The distinctive emphasis in the LCD's plans under the Labour government has been the recognition that justice has a part to play in supporting the achievement of the government's wider social and economic aims, including the combating of social exclusion. The new objectives "recognise the demands of a coherent, customer-facing, accessible and responsive justice system".[98–99] We deal elsewhere in this book with the radical changes to the civil justice system and publicly funded legal services and the possible future changes to the criminal justice and tribunal systems. Whether the ambitious and high-sounding aim and objectives can effectively be achieved within available resources is a recurrent tension. The explicit

---

[93] The associated target is to increase the number of people who receive suitable assistance in priority areas of law involving fundamental rights by 5% by 2004, and 5% p.a. increases in the number of international legal disputes resolved in the U.K.

[94] The associated target is to increase the enforceability of civil judgments by achieving a specified increase in the amount recovered per pound under executed warrants issued in the county courts.

[95] The associated target is to increase continued contact between children and the nonresident parent after a family breakdown, where this is in the best interests of the child.

[96] *The Lord Chancellor's Departments. Departmental Report, the Government's Expenditure Plans 2001–2002 to 2003–2004*, (Cm. 5107, 2001) pp. 4–5. The *Report* also contains information on progress against the objectives and targets as previously formulated. A separate, but overlapping PSA applies to the Criminal Justice System. An earlier strategic plan provided for one "fundamental aim", one "strategic priority", six "guiding principles" and six "key challenges". The simplification is to be welcomed.

[97] See below, para. 4-033.

[98–99] Cm. 5017, p. 22.

recognition in objective (3) that the justice system earns significant income from abroad is true, but sits rather oddly with the rest.

2. THE HOME OFFICE

The Home Secretary is responsible for the maintenance of law and order, and as a result performs various functions that might be regarded as those of a Minister of Justice. These include[1] overall responsibility for prisons and other aspects of the penal system, coroners' courts and the reform of the criminal law. The Home Secretary advises the Queen on the exercise of the royal prerogative of mercy to grant a free pardon in respect of a conviction or to remit all or part of a penalty.

1–020

3. THE LAW OFFICERS[2]

The Attorney-General and the Solicitor-General are the Law Officers of the Crown for England and Wales.[3] They are members of and the chief legal advisers to the government,[4] and are normally[5] members of the House of Commons. Occasionally the Attorney-General has been appointed to the cabinet. The Law Officers may appear on behalf of the Crown at the International Court in the Hague and the European Court of Human Rights in Strasbourg. In this country they may appear in civil litigation or conduct prosecutions. They may not, however, undertake private work.

1–021

In civil matters the Attorney may institute proceedings in the High Court for the enforcement of public rights[6] or on behalf of the interests of charity. His consent is required for the institution of criminal proceedings for a large

---

[1] For a full list see R. Brazier, [1989] P.L. 64 at 93.

[2] See J. Ll. J. Edwards, *The Law Officers of the Crown* (1964) and *The Attorney-General, Politics and the Public Interest* (1984); T. Daintith and A. Page, *The Executive in the Constitution* (1999), pp. 287–315; Sir Elwyn Jones, [1969] CLJ. 43; S. C. Silkin, (1980) 4 Trent LJ 21; Sir Michael Havers, (1984) 52 Medico-Legal Jo. 98. For a list of the Law Officers' functions see written answer by the Attorney-General; R. Brazier, [1989] PL 64 at 94.

[3] Since 1972, the Attorney has been Attorney-General for Northern Ireland (see Northern Ireland Constitution Act 1973, s.10). The Solicitor-General is authorised to act as his deputy *(ibid.)*. See Edwards (1984), Chap. 9. There are separate Law Officers for Scotland, the Lord Advocate and the Solicitor-General for Scotland: see Edwards (1984), Chap. 10; following devolution they are now members of the Scottish Executive and there is a new Scottish Law Officer to the U.K. government, the Advocate General for Scotland: Scotland Act 1998, ss. 48, 87.

[4] The settled constitutional practice that Law Officers' advice to government remains confidential was breached in the Westland affair: see R. Austin, (1986) 39 C.L.P. 269 at 277–278; M. Linklater and D. Leigh, *Not With Honour* (1986).

[5] Not invariably: the current Attorney is Lord Goldsmith Q.C., and his predecessor Lord Williams of Mostyn Q.C. The current Solicitor-General is Harriet Harman Q.C. M.P., formerly a cabinet minister, who succeeded Ross Cranston M.P., an academic lawyer before his election to Parliament. Ms. Harman is a solicitor, although not in practice as such at the time of her appointment, and was made a Q.C. on appointment.

[6] *e.g.* to seek injunction to restrain a public nuisance or to restrain repeated or threatened breaches of the criminal law.

number of criminal offences,[7] and he may stop trials on indictment by entering a *nolle prosequi*.[8] He superintends the work of the Queen's Proctor, who has certain duties in matrimonial cases. He exercises ministerial responsibility for the Director of Public Prosecutions, the Crown Prosecution Service and the Serious Fraud Office[9] and, from 1989, the Treasury Solicitor's Department.[10] The Law Officers are assisted by a small staff of civil servants, the Legal Secretariat to the Law Officers, based in the Attorney-General's chambers in the Royal Courts of Justice, and generally divide the duties between them according to their own preferences.[11] The Attorney is also the head of the Bar.[12]

When taking decisions in respect of criminal matters, the Attorney-General is expected to act independently of the government. While in an appropriate case he may seek the views of ministers as to the consequences of a prosecution, there should be no pressure from them in favour of or against a prosecution: the ultimate decision is his.[13] However, it has been asserted that the position is different where the government is acting as government in civil proceedings and the Attorney is the nominal plaintiff: here a decision whether to proceed is the government's collectively.[14]

4. THE DIRECTOR OF PUBLIC PROSECUTIONS, THE CROWN PROSECUTION SERVICE AND THE SERIOUS FRAUD OFFICE

1-022   In 1879 pressure for the introduction of a system of public prosecution led to the establishment of the office of Director of Public Prosecutions.[15] It was originally contemplated that he would be provided with a number of locally based assistants, but this development never took place. The Director and his or her staff have thus always been based in London. The first Director

---

[7] See below, paras 14-031, 14-036.

[8] *ibid.*

[9] See below.

[10] Following the recommendations of the *Review of Government Legal Services* by Sir Robert Andrew (HMSO, 1989). See Vol. 145 H.C. Deb., January 19, 1989, cols. 262–263, written answer by the Prime Minister. These departments, together with the Legal Secretariat to the Law Officers, are now collectively known as the Law Officers' Departments.

[11] Technically, the Solicitor-General is the Attorney-General's deputy, but it is now provided that any function of the Attorney-General may be exercised by the Solicitor-General: Law Officers Act 1997, s. 1; previously, the Solicitor-General could only act in the Attorney's place in specified circumstances: Law Officers Act 1944, s. 1, repealed by the 1997 Act.

[12] This caused some difficulty in 1989 when the Bar was severely critical of the Lord Chancellor's proposals for reform of the legal profession.

[13] The classic statement of principle was made by Sir Hartley Shawcross in 1951. H.C. Deb. January 29, 1951: see Edwards (1964), pp. 220–225 and (1984), pp. 318–324.

[14] Sir Michael Havers (H.C. Deb., December 1, 1986), referring to the decision not to seek an injunction to restrain publication of Chapman Pincher's book, *Their Trade is Treachery*, a decision to which he was not a party. Analogous decisions in the *Gouriet (Gouriet v. Union of Post Office Workers* [1978] A.C. 435) and *Crossman Diaries (Att.-Gen. v. Jonathan Cape Ltd.* [1976] Q.B. 752) cases had, by contrast, been taken independently by the Attorney: see J. Michael, "The Wright Case—The Attorney-General's Role" (1986) 136 N.L.J. 1199.

[15] Prosecution of Offences Act 1879. See generally J. Ll. J. Edwards, *The Law Officers of the Crown* (1964), Chaps 16, 17 and *The Attorney-General, Politics and the Public Interest* (1984), Chaps 1–5; G. Mansfield and J. Peay, *The Director of Public Prosecutions* (1987); J. Rozenberg, *The Case for the Crown* (1987); Thomas Hetherington, *Prosecution and the Public Interest* (1989).

took a narrow view of the scope of his functions, and between 1884 and 1908 the office was combined with that of Treasury Solicitor.

The Director's responsibilities are now set out in the Prosecution of Offences Act 1985. He or she is appointed by the Attorney-General and must be a person who has a 10-year general qualification.[16] Prior to the establishment of the Crown Prosecution Service the Director's main functions were to conduct prosecutions in serious cases and to give advice and assistance to chief officers of police respecting the conduct of other prosecutions. He was assisted by a Deputy Director and Assistant Directors, and had a headquarters staff of about 60.[17] The Director is now head of the Crown Prosecution Service,[18] which is responsible for the conduct of most proceedings instituted by the police. The Service is organised into 42 Areas,[19] each headed by a Chief Crown Prosecutor. It employs over 5,600 staff. It was subject to a review by Sir Iain Glidewell[20] which recommended extensive reform including the devolution and decentralisation of powers, a focus on the core business of prosecuting, with greater emphasis on the more serious cases and greater separation of management from legal work, and improved co-operation with other agencies. A Chief Executive was appointed in 1998. Also of significance has been the fact that in 2000–01

"it was publicly acknowledged that the Service has been chronically under resourced since its inception and had suffered as a result ever since".[21]

A Crown Prosecution Service Inspectorate became fully operational in 1997–98 and was placed on an independent statutory basis, reporting to the Attorney-General, from October 1, 2000.[22]

The Serious Fraud Office was established by the Criminal Justice Act 1987 with powers to investigate any suspected offence involving serious or complex fraud, and to institute and have the conduct of any criminal proceedings appearing to relate to such fraud.[23] Its operations extend to Northern Ireland, and are wider than that of the CPS, which is only

[16] 1985 Act, s.2, as amended. The current DPP is David Calvert-Smith Q.C., who was appointed in 1998. His immediate predecessors were Sir Theobald Mathew (1944–64), Sir Norman Skelhorn (1964–77), Sir Thomas Hetherington (1977–87), Allan Green Q.C. (1987–92) and Dame Barbara Mills (1992–98).

[17] See below, para. 14-031.

[18] Below, para. 14-033. The CPS has not become an executive agency but was to operate according to "Next Steps" principles from April 1996: *Department Reports of The Lord Chancellor's and Law Officers' Departments: The Government's Expenditure Plans 1996–97 to 1998–99* (Cm. 3209), p. 45. New corporate performance measures were introduced from May 1, 1996, and Public Service Agreements *published from December 1998*.

[19] Reduced from 31 to 13 in 1993: see *Annual Report of the Crown Prosecution Service 1993–94* (1993–94 H.C. 444), pp. 9–11, Annex B; but increased to 42 in 1999 coterminous with the areas of police authorities, except in London where the C.P.S. Area covers both Metropolitan and City police areas.

[20] *Review of the Crown Prosecution Service* (Cm. 3972, 1998).

[21] *Annual Report of the CPS, 2000–01* (2001–02 H.C. 138).

[22] Crown Prosecution Service Inspectorate Act 2000. It inspects each CPS Area on a two-year cycle and produces thematic reviews.

[23] s.1. See further below, p. On the work of the SFO, see D. N. Kirk and A. J. J. Woodcock, *Serious Fraud: Investigation and Trial* (2nd ed., 1997); M. Levi, *The Investigation, Prosecution and Trial of Serious Fraud* (RCCJ Research Study No. 14, 1993); JUSTICE, *Serious Fraud: Securing a fair trial* (1993).

responsible for the conduct of proceedings investigated and instituted by the police. It comprises lawyers and accountants, and works in close co-operation with police officers, seconded from a number of forces, who occupy the same building. There continues to be a Fraud Investigation Group attached to the headquarters of the CPS to deal with fraud cases not taken over by the SFO The SFO came under considerable criticism following a series of high profile cases where the defendants were acquitted, or only convicted on minor charges.[24] Nevertheless, in 1995 the government accepted the recommendation of a review group headed by Rex Davie that the SFO should not be merged with the Fraud Division of the CPS, but that the work should be restructured.[25] Under revised criteria for deciding which cases should go to the SFO, the key criterion is whether the suspected fraud was such that the direction of the investigation should be in the hands of those who would be responsible for the prosecution. Relevant factors include: cases in the order of at least £1 million; cases likely to give rise to national publicity and widespread public concern; cases requiring highly specialised knowledge of, for example, stock exchange practices or regulated markets; cases in which there is a significant international dimension; cases where legal, accountancy and investigative skills need to be brought together; cases which appear to be complex and in which the use of the SFO's special powers under section 2 of the 1987 Act might be appropriate. None of these factors, taken individually, is necessarily conclusive.[26] A Joint Vetting Committee has been established with the CPS to consider marginal cases referred to either organisation.

The DPP may be directed by the Divisional Court to appear for the prosecution on any criminal appeal to the House of Lords, and by the Court of Appeal (Criminal Division) to appear in appeals to that court from the Crown Court or from it to the House of Lords.[27] He also has the power to intervene in prosecutions.[28] This power is used rarely, for example where private prosecutions are instituted maliciously. It includes the right to discontinue proceedings.[29] Finally, the Director's consent to prosecution is required by statute in certain classes of case.[30]

---

[24] *e.g.* the failure of the prosecution in the *Blue Arrow* case, the acquittal of George Walker in a case arising out of the affairs of the Brent Walker group and the events that led to the passing of a non-custodial sentence on Roger Levitt: see (1993) 143 N.L.J. 1701. For the argument that the criticisms were exaggerated, see J. Bayes, (1994) 144 N.L.J. 1508. Over the first seven years of the SFO's existence, the overall conviction rate on a defendant-by-defendant basis was 62%, with one or more defendants convicted in over 75% of trials: *Annual Report of the Serious Fraud Office, 1994–95* (1994–95 H.C.589), p. 14. In 2000–01, 93% of defendants tried were convicted or pleaded guilty to one or more charges, with an average of 70% since the establishment of the SFO: *Annual Report, 2000–01*, Part I.

[25] Statement by the Attorney-General. Other recommendations for changes in working practices had previously been made in the Review of the Handling of Serious Fraud (the Graham Review, 1994: see *SFO Annual Report 1994–95*, pp. 21; R. Sarker, (1995) 16 Co.Law 56 at 213.

[26] *SFO Annual Report, 2000–01.*

[27] Prosecution of Offences Act 1985, s.3(2)(f). See below, para. 14-034.

[28] *ibid.* s.6. Below, para. 14-034.

[29] *Raymond v. Att.-Gen.* [1982] Q.B. 839, decided under the equivalent provision (s.4) of the Prosecution of Offences Act 1979.

[30] See below, para. 14-036.

5. THE TREASURY AND OTHER GOVERNMENT DEPARTMENTS

The Treasury is involved in the administration of justice at a number of **1–023** points. It has overall responsibilities for government expenditure and the organisation of the civil service. The parliamentary draftsmen are technically Parliamentary Counsel to the Treasury, reporting to the Prime Minister.[31]

The Treasury Solicitor heads a large legal department which does legal work for the Treasury and for other government departments.[32] She also presides over inter-departmental management machinery for civil service lawyers and was for many years and for most purposes the *de facto* head of the civil service Civil Legal Group in England and Wales.[33] In 1989 the government legal service was reorganised following a report by Sir Robert Andrew.[34] The Treasury Solicitor was recognised as head of the service, with the responsibility of advising on the personnel management of lawyers across departments and supported by the Government Legal Service Secretariat (formerly the Lawyers' Management Unit).[35] The European Division of the Department advises the European Secretariat of the Cabinet Office on Community law issues and conducts on behalf of the United Kingdom all litigation in the Court of Justice of the European Community.[36] Other Divisions undertake litigation, deal with *bona vacantia* (administering the estates of intestates), and advisory work for governmental departments. The Government Property Lawyers was established as a Next Steps executive agency of the Lord Chancellor's Department on April 1, 1993. It was located in Taunton and provided a conveyancing and lands advisory service for all government departments and other public bodies, but was closed in 1999 as declining workload had made the business non-viable.[37] The rest of the Department was established as an executive agency from 1996.[38] Legal services to government departments may be the subject of market testing in accordance with guidelines set by the Attorney-General.[39]

---

[31] *The Government's Expenditure Plans 1995–96 to 1997–98: Cabinet Office, Privy Council Office and Parliament* (Cm. 2820, 1995), p. 8.

[32] There are separate divisions for the Treasury, the Cabinet Office, Culture Media and Sport, Defence, and Education and Employment.

[33] See G. Drewry, "The Office of Treasury Solicitor" (1980) 130 N.L.J. 753 and "Lawyers in the U.K. Civil Service" (1981) 59 *Public Administration* 15; (1992) 136 S.J. 78 at 96.

[34] *Review of Government Legal Services* (HMSO, 1989). On the appointment of the inquiry see G. Drewry, "Government Lawyers under Scrutiny" (1988) 138 N.L.J. 219.

[35] H.C.Deb. January 19, 1989, written answer by the Prime Minister. See M. Mair, (1989) L.S.Gaz. March 22, 1989, pp. 12, 37: interview with the Treasury Solicitor, James Nurshaw.

[36] See T. Daintith and A. Page, *The Executive in the Constitution* (1999), pp. 317–319.

[37] *Law Officers' Departments Departmental Report, The Government's Expenditure Plans 1999–2000 to 2001–2002* (Cm. 4207, 1999), p. 42.

[38] *Departmental Report of The Lord Chancellor's and Law Officers' Departments: The Government's Expenditure Plans 1995–96 to 1997–98* (Cm. 2809, 1995), pp. 60–65. See Daintith and Page (1999), pp. 217–220.

[39] See (1992) 136 S.J. 663. The guidelines state that it is not appropriate to use the private sector for core governmental work where ministers and legal advisers need to maintain a close confidential relationship.

6. THE OFFICIAL SOLICITOR AND PUBLIC TRUSTEE; CAFCASS

1–024 While the Treasury Solicitor is concerned with the government's legal business, the Official Solicitor to the Supreme Court heads an office in that court. He is appointed by the Lord Chancellor and must be a person with a 10-year general qualification under section 71 of the Courts and Legal Services Act 1990.[40] His functions have broadly fallen into five categories[41]: the liberty of the subject (making bail applications for remand prisoners, reviewing the cases of persons committed to prison for contempt of court,[42] investigating applications for leave to issue a writ of habeas corpus); the paternalistic jurisdiction (representing wards of court in wardship proceedings, acting as guardian of a minor's estate, dealing with the affairs of mental patients); the conduct of litigation for children and mental patients; the administration of the estates of deceased persons when there is no-one else willing or able to do so; and assisting the court (investigating the conduct of litigation, briefing counsel to appear as *amicus curiae*).

The Office of Public Trustee was created under the Public Trustee Act 1906. From 1987, it had four main business areas. The Protection and Receivership Divisions of the Public Trust Office exercised functions under the Mental Health Act protecting the property and affairs of people with mental incapacity, the former providing administrative support to the Court of Protection. The Trust Division acted as executor or administrator of deceased persons estates or trustee of wills or settlements; in practice as an executor or trustee of last resort. Court Funds work involved managing money paid into court.[43] The Office became an executive agency within the LCD in 1994. There was some overlap with the role of the Official Solicitor's Office.

Significant changes have now been made,[44] effective from April 2001. The work of the Trust Division was transferred to the Official Solicitor and Court Funds work to the Court Service. Mental Health services were to be managed by a new executive agency within the Court of Protection, the Public Guardianship Office. The PGO took over the PTO's last resort receivership service on a reduced scale. Accordingly, the Public Trust Office was co-located with the Official Solicitor's office and the same individual holds the position of Official Solicitor and Public Trustee.

---

[40] Supreme Court Act 1981, s.90, as amended by the 1990 Act, Sched. 10, para. 49; on the meaning of "general qualification" see below, para. 4-023, n. 35. See N, Lowe and R. White, *Wards of Court* (2nd ed., 1986), Chap. 9; J. M. L. Evans, (1966) 63 L.S.Gaz. 270 at 335; C. Dyer, *The Law Magazine*, June 12, 1987, p. 27; D. Venables, (1990) 20 Fam. Law 53.

[41] M. Hinchliffe, (1989) J. of Child Law, pp. 64–67.

[42] It was in this capacity that the Official Solicitor came into prominence in 1972 in obtaining the release of trade unionists committed to prison for disobedience to orders of the National Industrial Relations Court in the course of a national dock strike: *Churchman v. Joint Shop Stewards Committee* [1972] I.C.R. 222; *Midland Cold Storage Ltd v. Turner, The Times*, July 27, 1972. See N. Lowe and B. Sufrin, *Borrie and Lowe's Law of Contempt* (3rd ed., 1996), pp. 633–635; B. A. Hepple, (1972) 1 I.L.J. 198; Lord Denning, *The Due Process of Law* (1980), pp. 36–39.

[43] See *Judicial Statistics 2000*, pp. 85–86.

[44] Following a *Quinquennial Review of the Public Trust Office* (1999); *Making Changes — The Future of the Public Trust Office* (LCD, April 2000); *The Way Forward and an Analysis of Consultation* (LCD, December 2000).

Also effective from April 2001, a new organisation, the Children and Family Court Advisory and Support Service (CAFCASS) was established to provide representation for children in family proceedings.[45] It took some responsibilities from the Official Solicitor's Office, the family court welfare function of the former 54 Probation Committees and the functions of the 57 Guardians *ad Litem* and Reporting Officer panels. The Official Solicitor continues to provide litigation friend (formerly guardian *ad litem*) services in proceedings other than under the Children Act 1989 and in certain circumstances also under the 1989 Act for parties under disability who are not the subject of proceedings.[46] Two important areas of work that involve the Official Solicitor are cases involving the sterilisation of a person who cannot consent to the operation and the discontinuance of nutrition and hydration for a patient in a vegetative state.[47] The launch of CAFCASS proved problematic, being described as "ill-planned and badly executed"[48] and having had "a diabolical start"[49] with a serious dispute with former guardians[50] and a significant budget deficit. Steps have been taken to address these problems.[51]

7. THE CRIMINAL JUSTICE CONSULTATIVE COUNCIL AND THE CRIMINAL JUSTICE SYSTEM

Communication among the various agencies involved in the criminal justice system is promoted by the Criminal Justice Consultative Council, established in 1991 on the recommendation of the Woolf Inquiry into the State of the Prisons. The Council's membership included (in 1995) three permanent secretaries, two judges, the DPP, a chief constable, a Q.C., a solicitor, a justices' clerk, a magistrate, a chief probation officer, the Director General of Prisons, the Chief Executive of the Court Service and senior Home Office representatives.[52] There are also now 42 Area Criminal Justice Strategy Committees (ACJSCs) with a corresponding range of

1–025

---

[45] Criminal Justice and Court Services Act 2000, ss. 11–17; N. Flicker, [2000] Farn. Law 102; G. Timmis, [2001] Fam. Law 280.

[46] Official Solicitor's Office website (*www.offsol.demon.co.uk*). On the division of responsibilities with CAFCASS, see *Practice Note (Officers of CAFCASS Legal Services and Special Casework: Appointment in Family Proceedings)* [2001] Fam. Law 249 and *Practice Note (The Official Solicitor: Appointment in Family Proceedings)* [2001] Fam. Law 307.

[47] *RF (Mental Patient: Sterilisation)* [1990] 2 A.C. 1: *Airedale NHS Trust v. Bland* [1993] A.C. 789; *Practice Note (Official Solicitor: Declaratory Proceedings: Medical and Welfare Decisions for Adults who lack capacity)* [2001] Fam. Law 551.

[48] M. Crisell, [2002] Fam. Law 310.

[49] S. Gerlis, [2002] Fam. Law 144.

[50] See V. Swenson, [2001] Fam. Law 708; *R. (on the application of National Association of Guardians ad Litem and Reporting Officers) v. Children and Family Court Advisory Service* [2001] EWHC Admin 693 (decision not to continue to offer the option of contracts for services (as distinct from contracts of employment) to existing guardians quashed as reasonable notice of this change of policy and an opportunity to make representations should have been afforded to the Association). Many former guardians and managers left the service, leading to increasing difficulties in handling the work: G. Timmis, [2002] Fam. Law 148.

[51] J. Tross (CAFCASS Acting Chief Executive), [2002] Fam. Law 318.

[52] *Criminal Justice Consultative Council: Summary of Activities 1994–95*, p. 16. See also Farquharson L.J., (1993) *The Magistrate* 26.

members. A range of other steps have over the years been taken to improve co-ordination within what is now formally termed (with its own website[53]) the Criminal Justice System. In 1998 a new national structure was put in place, with a Ministerial Steering Group on the Criminal Justice System,[54] a Strategic Planning Group of senior officials (SPG),[55] and a Criminal Justice Joint Planning Unit (CJJPU) with staff from the Home Office, LCD, CPS and the Treasury. There is also a Criminal Justice Integration Unit (CJIU) dealing with the better integration of information systems. Operational issues are reviewed by the Trial Issues Group (TIG), the successor to the Working Group on Pre-Trial Issues. Local TIGs were established in each of the 42 criminal justice areas. A Public Service Agreement for the whole of the CJS was published in December 1998, in addition to separate PSAs for the Home Office and LCD.[56] Sir Robin Auld[57] was highly critical of these arrangements: "the whole edifice is structurally inefficient, ineffective and wasteful".[58] His terms of reference precluded "a possible reordering of the great offices of State". However, there should be a single national body, a Criminal Justice Board, to plan and direct, local Criminal Justice Boards, and a statutory Criminal Justice Council as an advisory body. One significant task for the Criminal Justice Board should be to plan the production of an integrated IT system for the whole Criminal Justice System.

8. The Civil Justice Council

1–026   The Civil Justice Council was established in 1998 as part of the Woolf reforms.[59] Its functions are to keep the civil justice system under review, considering how to make the civil justice system more accessible, fair and efficient; advising the Lord Chancellor and the judiciary on the development of the civil justice system; referring proposal for changes in the system to the Lord Chancellor and the CPR committee; and making proposals for research.

---

[53] *www.criminal-justice-system.gov.uk.*
[54] Chaired by the Home Secretary and including Lord Chancellor, the Attorney General and the Chief Secretary to the Treasury.
[55] Senior officials from the LCD, Home Office, CPS and Treasury.
[56] See now the CJS Business Plan 2002–03.
[57] *Review of the Criminal Courts*, Chap. 8.
[58] Chap. 8, para. 14. A study of the Strategic Planning Group reported that the diagnosis of many was that it "is not strategic and it does not plan" (para. 25). The CJCC had succeeded in improving communication but was not routinely consulted and had no standing responsibility, staff or facilities (para. 31). Each agency (police, CPS, magistrates' courts, Crown Court, probation and prisons) had its own, quite separate, national information technology system (para. 98).
[59] Civil Procedure Act 1997, s. 6; *www.civiljusticecouncil.gov.uk.* It is chaired by the Master of the Rolls, its Vice Chairman is the Deputy Head of Civil Justice, and its other members include (in 2001) five judges, three solicitors, two barristers, two LCD civil servants, two academics (Professors R. Dingwall and M. Partington), and members from LAG, CA, NACAB, the TUC and the insurance industry.

D. LAW REFORM

It is inevitable that any legal system cannot be static: there will always be **1–027** aspects both of the substantive law and the institutional and procedural features of the system that require change. Many aspects of the common law are developed by the decisions of the superior courts. However, the judges seem generally to hold the view that this power should be exercised with caution, although this caution is from time to time thrown to the winds.[60] Commonly, a distinction is drawn between the application of an existing principle to new circumstances, which is regarded as a legitimate exercise for the judges, and the creation of a new principle, which is regarded as a matter for government and Parliament.[61]

Reform by the judges is further handicapped by the fact that the accidents of litigation may not throw up the right cases, that the precise issues in dispute are formulated by the parties (the opinions of the judges on other matters amounting to *obiter dicta* which are not binding in future cases),[62] and that the judges must normally confine themselves to the arguments and information presented by the parties. The judges cannot in any event commission empirical research and even the information derived from existing research is not admissible in evidence. Judicial reforms tend also to be retrospective in nature and hence potentially unfair.[63] Accordingly, most significant law reforms must be achieved by statute.

There are several mechanisms which exist or have existed to further the cause of law reform by statute, including one permanent body, the Law Commission, several part-time bodies, such as the Law Reform Committee and the Criminal Law Revision Committee, and any number of ad hoc Royal Commissions and departmental committees.

1. THE LAW COMMISSION[64]

Calls for a permanent law reform institution were answered in 1965 by the **1–028**

---

[60] See below, paras 4-037–4-040.
[61] See, *e.g.* Lord Pearson and Lord Salmon in *Launchbury v. Morgans* [1973] A.C. 127 at 142, 151.
[62] See below, para. 7-003.
[63] *Cf.* below, para. 7-027.
[64] See generally on the work of the Law Commission, J. H. Farrar, *Law Reform and the Law Commission* (1974); G. J. Zellick (ed.), *Law Reform and the Law Commission* (1988); N. Marsh, (1971) 13 William and Mary L.R. 263; L. C. B. Gower, (1973) 23 Univ. of Toronto L.J. 257; A. L. Diamond, (1976) 10 L.T. 11 and (1977) 51 A.L.J. 396; Sir Michael Kerr, (1980) 96 L.Q.R. 515; P. M. North, (1985) 101 L.Q.R. 338; S. Cretney, (1985) 48 M.L.R. 493; Sir Ralph Gibson, (1986) 39 C.L.P. 57; Sir Roy Beldam, (1987) 16 Kingston L.R. 21; Brooke J., (1995) 16 Stat. L.R. 1 and [1995] Crim. L.R. 911; Staughton L.J., (1995) 16 Stat. L.R. 7. For a discussion of the Law Commission's use of economic reasoning, see A.I. Ogus, "Economics and Law Reform; Thirty Years of Law Commission Endeavour" (1995) 111 L.Q.R. 407. The Commission reviewed the first 20 years of its operations in its 20th Annual Report, 1984–85 (Law Com. No. 155), Part I: see Editorial, (1986) 136 N.L.J. 201. For a critical account of its operations by a former member of its staff, see R. T. Oerton, *Lament for the Law Commission* (1987). For a proposal for its abolition, see A. Samuels, (1986) 136 N.L.J. 747; response by Oerton *ibid.* p. 1071.

establishment of two Law Commissions, one for England and Wales and one for Scotland.[65] This move was associated particularly with Lord Gardiner L.C.[66] The Law Commission for England and Wales comprises five "persons appearing ... to be suitably qualified by the holding of judicial office or by experience as a person having a general qualification (within the meaning of section 71 of the Courts and Legal Services Acts 1990) or as a teacher of law in a university".[67] In practice, the chairman has been a High Court judge, who works full-time for the Commission and normally subsequently receives promotion to the Court of Appeal. The pattern for the other appointments has become settled with a common law Q.C., a solicitor and two academics. There is a legal secretary, a staff of barristers and solicitors from the legal Civil Service and several parliamentary draftsmen.[68]

The Commission's task is:

> "to take and keep under review all the law with which [it is] concerned with a view to its systematic development and reform, including in particular the codification of such law, the elimination of anomalies, the repeal of obsolete and unnecessary enactments, the reduction of the number of separate enactments and generally the simplification and modernisation of the law".[69]

The topics investigated are either referred to it by the Lord Chancellor or are aspects of one of the programmes for examination of different branches of the law with a view to reform that have been approved by the Lord Chancellor and laid before Parliament.[70] The Commission is also required to provide advice and information to government and other bodies concerned with law reform.[71]

In the course of its existence the Law Commission has dealt with a large number of substantive legal topics and projects for the consolidation of

---

[65] Law Commissions Act 1965; Lord Chorley and G. Dworkin, (1965) 28 M.L.R. 675.

[66] He had argued the case for such a body in Chap. 1 of G. Gardiner and A. Martin (eds), *Law Reform NOW* (1963) and *cf.* (1953) 69 L.Q.R. 46.

[67] 1965 Act, s.l(2), as amended by the 1990 Act, Sched. 10, para. 25.

[68] Sir Michael Kerr, (1980) 96 L.Q.R. 515 at 523. Four of the five senior Civil Service legal posts were, however, abolished ((1984) 134 N.L.J. 467), the Law Commission relying instead on commissioning work from academic lawyers, some of whom join it on secondment (see 21st Annual Report, 1985–86 (Law Com. No. 159), pp. 1–2, 17). The Law Commission has also noted difficulties caused by delays in replacing staff who have moved elsewhere: 29th Annual Report, 1994 (Law Com. No. 232), pp. 58–59.

[69] 1965 Act, s.3(l).

[70] *ibid.* ss.3(l)(a)(b), (2). There have been eight general programmes (approved in 1965, 1968, 1973, 1989, 1991, 1995, 1999 and 2001) with major items on criminal law, family law and private international law. The programme arrangements are considered by S. Cretney in Zellick (1988), pp. 3–20. The most important criteria for the selection of projects are the importance of the issues, the availability of resources in terms of both expertise and funding and the suitability of the issues to be dealt with by the Commission: *Law Commission Eighth Programme of Law Report* (Law Com No. 274), para. 1.2. The Commission may also consider reform proposals from other quarters.

[71] The Commission publishes on its website (*www.lawcom.gov.uk*), three times a year, a bulletin, *Law Under Review*, giving details of the progress of government law reform projects.

statutes and the repeal of obsolete provisions ("Statute Law Reform").[72] It has also worked on the codification of the law of contract and of the law of landlord and tenant, although these tasks proved too onerous and the work has been suspended indefinitely.[73] The prospects for codification of the criminal law are brighter,[74] a draft code having been produced. However, it has been recognised that "the likelihood of Parliament being able to find time to consider, in a single Bill, a proposal as large as a complete Code is very remote".[75] Accordingly, the Commission aims to "progress in stages towards the long-term objective of the enactment of a complete Code", with further work on particular topics built into the base provided by the draft Code.[76] However, pressure for the introduction of a code has remained[77] and the government is now committed to codification as part of its criminal justice policy.[78] This would help to achieve "transparency and accessibility" and "certainty, speed and efficiency". This would be "a long-term commitment, not least because of the heavy demands it might make on Parliament's time".[79] The Commission now plans to draft a General Part of the Code covering general principles both as to the ingredients of specific offences (such as the meaning of intention) and free-standing matters (such as the defence of self-defence).[80]

A notable feature of the Law Commission's working methods in connection with the reform of a substantive legal topic is the circulation of a "working paper". This consists of a detailed statement of the present law on the topic, an account of the criticisms and supposed defects of the law, and a statement of the options for change. The Commission normally states a provisional view as to the option that should be preferred. The paper, in both full and summarised forms, is circulated widely and the views of interested parties sought.[81] Following consultation a final report is produced, which includes a draft Bill prepared by the parliamentary draftsmen seconded to the Commission. Overall, chances of implementation

---

[72] See below, para. 5-005.

[73] See A. L. Diamond, (1968) 31 M.L.R. 361; Sir Michael Kerr, (1980) 96 L.Q.R. 515 at 527–530.

[74] See J. C. Smith, [1984] Stat.L.R. 17 and [1987] Denning L.J. 137; I. Dennis, (1986) 50 J. of Crim. Law 161; *Codification of the Criminal Law: A Report to the Law Commission* (Law Com. No. 143, 1985); Symposium, [1986] Crim.L.R. 285–323; *Criminal Code for England and Wales* (Law Com. No. 177, 1989).

[75] 27th Annual Report, 1992 (Law Com. No. 210), p. 10.

[76] *ibid.* For the first steps, see the Reports under the general title *Legislating the Criminal Code, Offences against the Person and General Principles* (Law Com. No. 218, Cm. 2370, 1993); , *Intoxication and Criminal Liability* (Law Com. No. 229, 1995); *The Year and a Day Rule in Homicide* (Law Com. No. 230, 1995); *Involuntary Manslaughter* (Law Com. No. 237, 1996). For a vigorous rebuttal of criticisms of the drafting of the Code by F. A. R. Bennion ((1994) 15 Stat.L.R.108), see J. C. Smith (1995) 16 Stat.L.R.105.

[77] *e.g.* Lord Bingham, [1998] Crim. L.R. 694.

[78] White Paper, *Criminal Justice: The Way Ahead* (Cm. 5074, 2001).

[79] paras 3.57, 3.59.

[80] *Eighth Programme of Law Reform*, Item 5.

[81] See P. M. North, "Law Reform: the Consultation Process" (1982) 66 Trent L.J. 19 and (1985) 101 L.Q.R. 338 (expressing some scepticism as to the effectiveness of consultation). The Commission has not followed the example of the Australian Law Reform Commission and organised public meetings or hearings: see the paper by the ALRC Chairman, Mr Justice M. D. Kirby, "Reforming Law Reform: New Methods of Law Reform in Australia", to the 1979 Colloquium of the U.K. National Committee on Comparative Law, summarised in M. Zander, *The Law-Making Process* (4th ed., 1994), pp. 451–455.

are reasonably high, although they have less where the matter falls within the purview of a government department other than the Lord Chancellor's Department (most notably the Home Office and the Department of the Environment).[82] By 1994, of all the Commission's law reform reports, 78 had been implemented, 13 expressly or impliedly rejected and 32 remained outstanding. Of those 32, eight were due for presentation to Parliament in 1994–95, and nine were 1993 or 1994 reports.[83] However, these figures conceal the fact that lack of implementation of reports had reached crisis point by 1993. In that year, the Commission reported that only four of its reports since 1990 had been implemented, for lack of parliamentary time, with only one forming part of the government's legislative programme.[84] However, the introduction of new procedures and the end of a period of non-co-operation between government and opposition whips has enabled inroads to be made on the backlog, there having been a "sea-change in attitudes".[85] A record of nine reports were implemented in 1995 and eight in 1996; however, the next Parliament implemented only four.[86] There are also examples of the use of Law Commission proposals by the courts in developing the law.[87]

A Ministerial Committee on Law Reform has been established, chaired by a LCD minister, to develop and co-ordinate the government's interests in law reform, with particular reference to making effective use of the Law Commission, considering how implementation can be streamlined and considering outstanding Law Commission reports and the action to be taken on them.[88]

2. THE LAW REFORM COMMITTEE[89]

1–029   A part-time Law Revision Committee was appointed by Lord Sankey in 1934 and produced eight reports between then and 1939, most of which were implemented.[90] It was reconstituted by Lord Simonds in 1952 under the title of Law Reform Committee, and comprised judges, practising lawyers and academics. Its permanent secretariat was provided by the Lord Chancellor's Department, but it lacked research facilities and suffered from the inevitable problems of any part-time body. By 1982 it had produced 23 reports.

---

[82] See Lord Hailsham, "Obstacles to Law Reform" (1981) 34 C.L.P. 279; P. M. North, (1981) III (I) *Liverpool Law Review* 5 and (1985) 101 L.Q.R. 338 at 346–357; Lord Hooson Q.C., "Reform of the Legislative Process in the Light of the Law Commission's Work" (1983) 17 L.T. 67; S. Cretney, (1985) 48 M.L.R. 493; G. Drewry in Zellick (1988), pp. 28–43.

[83] 29th Annual Report, 1994 (Law Com. No.232), Appendix 6.

[84] 28th Annual Report, 1993 (Law Com. No.223), pp. 6–12.

[85] 29th Annual Report, Pt. V; below, para. 5-008.

[86] 36th Annual Report 2001 (Law Com. No. 275), p. 20.

[87] *e.g. Heil v. Rankin* [2001.] Q.B. 272 (appropriate levels of damages for non-pecuniary losses); *Kleinwort Benson v. Lincoln City Council* [1999] 2 A.C. 349 (abrogation of the rule that money was generally not recoverable in restitution on the ground that it was paid under a mistake of law): see further *Eighth Programme of Law Reform*, paras 2.11–2.21.

[88] 35th Annual Report 2000 (Law Com No. 268), p. 15.

[89] See E. C. S. Wade, (1961) 24 M.L.R. 3; J. H. Farrar, *Law Reform and the Law Commission* (1974), pp. 9–14, 133–137; M. C. Blair, (1982) 1 C.J.Q. 64.

[90] For an account of the one that was not (the 6th Interim Report on the Statute of Frauds and the Doctrine of Consideration (Cmd. 5549, 1937)), see J. Beatson, (1992) 45(2) C.L.P.1.

3. THE CRIMINAL LAW REVISION COMMITTEE

This committee, the counterpart to the Law Reform Committee, but **1–030**
responsible to the Home Secretary rather than the Lord Chancellor, was
established in 1959, and included judges, academics and the DPP[91] Its
reports have led to important reforming legislation, most notably the Theft
Acts 1968 and 1978. Perhaps the best known report was its llth Report on
Evidence, which aroused a storm of opposition, in part at least, according to
its defenders, based on the misrepresentation of some of its recommendations.[92] For the purposes of its review of sexual offences, the Committee was
advised by a Policy Advisory Committee comprising five members of the
CRLC and 10 members from other disciplines, including probation officers,
a consultant psychiatrist, a social worker and a sociologist. There was here a
greater potential for fundamental disagreement about what it is that the
law should be attempting to achieve than there had been on earlier
references to the CRLC[93] The Committee has not been convened since 1985,
but has not formally been abolished.

4. AD HOC COMMITTEES[94]

Investigations by Royal Commissions and departmental committees have **1–031**
long been a familiar feature of the law reform scene. They have the
advantage over part-time advisory committees of a much greater commitment of resources, both of the time of their members and in money for
research. They have the disadvantage when compared with permanent
bodies that, having accumulated a large amount of information and
expertise, their members disperse once the body has done its work. Other
points of contrast with the law reform bodies discussed above are that ad
hoc committees usually have a majority, or at least a large contingent, of
non-lawyers, and are more likely than those others to be employed in
connection with institutional reforms. Since 1960, there have been five
Royal Commissions of particular importance for the English legal system.
The Royal Commission on Assizes and Quarter Sessions,[95] chaired by Lord
Beeching, made proposals for the reorganisation of the criminal courts
(other than magistrates courts) which were speedily implemented.[96] The
Royal Commission on Civil Liability and Compensation for Personal Injury
reported in 1978.[97] It found the private law system for claiming damages in
tort to be too dependent on chance, unduly slow and expensive to operate,

---

[91] See generally, Glanville Williams, "The Work of Criminal Law Reform" (1975) 13
J.S.P.T.L. 183; J. C. Smith, "An Academic Lawyer and Law Reform" (1981) 1 L.S. 119.
[92] See the articles cited in the previous footnote and M. Zander in *Reshaping the Criminal Law*
(P. Glazebrook ed., 1978).
[93] Criminal Law Revision Committee, 15th Report on Sexual Offences (Cmnd. 9213, 1984), pp.
1, 100.
[94] A list of major reports of official committees and commissions on law reform is given in G.
Zellick (ed.), *Law Reform and the Law Commission* (1988), Appendix 6.
[95] Cmnd. 4153, 1969.
[96] See below, para. 2-051.
[97] Cmnd. 7054, Chairman: Lord Pearson.

but felt unable because of its terms of reference to recommend a comprehensive state scheme for the compensation of all accident victims. Such a scheme would have had serious implications for the large number of lawyers, particularly barristers, who specialise in tort work. In the event, the Commission made a large number of piecemeal proposals for reform, only some of which have been implemented.

The Royal Commission on Legal Services, chaired by an accountant, Sir Henry Benson, reported in 1979.[98] Its terms of reference were:

> "to inquire into the law and practice relating to the provision of legal services in England, Wales and Northern Ireland, and to consider whether any, and if so what, changes are desirable in the public interest in the structure, organisation, training, regulation of and entry to the legal profession, including the arrangements for determining its remuneration, whether from private sources or public funds, and in the rules which prevent persons who are neither barristers nor solicitors from undertaking conveyancing and other legal business on behalf of other persons".

The report was widely regarded as a disappointment.[99] It was criticised for its pedestrian style, its paucity of reasoning, the fact that only a limited amount of research[1] was commissioned and its apparent over-dependence on the information and arguments presented by the legal profession. The *Legal Action Group Bulletin* was tempted to ignore the report: it would certainly be kinder so shaky were its foundations.[2] Professor Zander, who had played a significant role in securing the establishment of the Commission and who had submitted a considerable body of evidence, was more welcoming: he counted well over a hundred recommendations that he thought would amount to valuable changes.[3] The only real enthusiasts were the two branches of the legal profession, which was unsurprising given that on many issues their position was endorsed by the Commission. Many of the recommendations directed at the profession were the subject of action; those directed at the government had little impact, except that responsibility for criminal legal aid was transferred from Home Secretary to Lord Chancellor.[4] Indeed, the government subsequently decided, contrary to the recommendation of a majority of members of the Royal Commission, to end the solicitors' conveyancing "monopoly", and fundamental changes followed the Lord Chancellor's White Paper, *Legal Services: A Framework for the Future*,[5] many comprised in the Courts and Legal Services Act 1990.

---

[98] Cmnd. 7648.

[99] See C. Glasser, *L.A.G. Bull*, September 1979, p. 201; (1979) 129 N.L.J. 1116–1122, 1131–1135, 1140–1146, 1223–1224; M. Elliott, (1980) J.S.W.L. 1; O. Hanson and J. Levin, (1979) *Yearbook of Social Policy*, Chap. 12; (1980) 43 M.L.R. 543–566; (1981) *Windsor Yearbook of Access to Justice* 121 (T. A. Downes, P. R. Hopkins and W. M. Rees) and 179 (P. A. Thomas); P. A. Thomas (ed.), *Law in the Balance* (1982).

[1] See C. Glasser, *op. cit.*

[2] November 1979, p. 246.

[3] (1980) 33 C.L.P. 33, 50.

[4] See *The Government Response to the Report of the Royal Commission on Legal Services* (Cmnd. 9077, 1983). The Law Society and the Bar also published their responses: see *L.A.G. Bulletin*, December 1983, pp. 3, 6.

[5] Cm. 740, 1989. See below, para. 3-006.

The Royal Commission on Criminal Procedure[6] provided an interesting **1–032** contrast. It was established in 1978 to consider the powers and duties of the police in respect of the investigation of criminal offences and the rights and duties of suspects and accused persons, the process of and responsibility for the prosecution of criminal offences and related matters. Three features of the report were especially noteworthy. First, the Commission was much more active than the Royal Commission on Legal Services in sponsoring research. Second, there was a clear intention to identify basic points of principle to which the specific recommendations were to be related.[7] Third, the report indicated the lines that reform should take, leaving the details to be worked out. In consequence, the Police and Criminal Evidence Bill was presented to Parliament in 1983, together with proposals for the establishment of a national prosecution service.

In the following decades, Royal Commissions and departmental committees were conspicuous by their absence. Questions of policy tended to be determined by government, with the use of teams of civil servants, perhaps with an independent chairman or advisers, to work out the details of implementation. Examples in the context of the law included the Civil Justice Review,[8] the Magistrates' Courts Scrutiny[9] and the Working Group on the Right of Silence.[10] The Green Papers on Reform of the Legal Profession were simply published as such. This kind of approach was certainly more convenient for government. It led to a speedier conclusion, and also avoided the risk of an independent body producing unwelcome recommendations. There were, however, corresponding doubts as to the quality of the reports produced.

Concerns over the series of widely publicised cases where there had been a miscarriage of justice[11] led to the appointment of the Royal Commission on Criminal Justice, chaired by Viscount Runciman. Its terms of reference were

"to examine the effectiveness of the criminal justice system in England and Wales in securing the conviction of those guilty of criminal offences and the acquittal of those who are innocent, having regard to the efficient use of resources"

and in particular to consider whether changes were needed in the conduct and supervision of police investigations, the role of the prosecutor, the disclosure of material, the role of experts, defence arrangements, the "right to silence", the role of trial courts and the Court of Appeal and arrangements for considering allegations of miscarriages of justice. It reported in 1993,[12] and made 352 detailed recommendations, many but not all of which were accepted. It commissioned a substantial body of

---

[6] Cmnd. 8092, 1981.

[7] The Commission applied three standards for judging both the existing system and its own recommendations: are the arrangements, actual or proposed, fair and clear; are they open, that is, not secret and is there accountability; are they workable and efficient?

[8] *Report of the Review Body on Civil Justice* (Cm. 394, 1988). See I. Ramsey, (1988) 15 J.L.S. 416.

[9] *Magistrates' Courts: Report of a scrutiny* (HMSO, 1989).

[10] *Report of the Working Group on the Right of Silence* (Home Office, 1989).

[11] See below, para. 14-001.

[12] Cm. 2263, 1993.

research.[13] However, the report received a largely critical response from academic commentators, who argued that significant findings of that research were ignored, that the report lacked a coherent or explicit theoretical base and that the thrust of the recommendations seemed to be in facilitating convictions rather than protecting the innocent.[14] Furthermore, by the time of the report, the government's major preoccupation was again the fight against crime, symbolised with the introduction, contrary to the RCCJ's recommendation, of provisions enabling inferences to be drawn from the silence of the accused, in the Criminal Justice and Public Order Act 1994.[15]

On the civil side, Lord Woolf was invited to conduct an inquiry on access to justice. His Interim Report on *Access to Justice*, published in June 1995, made 124 recommendations. The key feature was that there should be a fundamental transfer in the responsibility for the management of civil litigation from litigants and their legal advisers to the courts. These recommendations were confirmed and expanded in the Final Report on *Access to Justice*, and have generally been accepted and implemented.[16] Lord Justice Auld was commissioned on December 14, 1999, to conduct a Review of the Criminal Courts in England and Wales. The terms of reference were to inquire into:

"the practices and procedures of, and the rules of evidence applied by, the criminal courts at every level, with a view to ensuring that they deliver justice fairly, by streamlining all their processes, increasing their efficiency and strengthening the effectiveness of their relationships with others across the whole of the criminal justice system and having regard to the interests of all parties including victims and witnesses, thereby promoting public confidence in the rule of law".

He was not expected to (and did not) cost his proposals. The process adopted was not that of a Royal Commission. Sir Robin had 12 expert consultants, but appointed after the inquiry process had started. He sought and received many written submissions and held a very large series of consultation meetings. The voluminous report[17] was accordingly essentially his view of the necessary changes in the operation of the criminal courts. He commissioned relatively little research and has been criticised for making little use of previously published work.[18] The key recommendations were: that the criminal law should be codified (with codes of offences, procedure, evidence and sentencing); existing national planning and operational bodies should be replaced by a Criminal Justice Board, supported by local boards, and existing advisory and consultative bodies by a Criminal Justice Council; the Crown Court and magistrates' court should be replaced by a unified Criminal Court with three divisions; juries should be more widely representative of local communities; allocation of cases should be the

[13] It published 22 research studies (see list in Appendix 4).
[14] See below, para. 14-092.
[15] See below, para. 17-043–17-045.
[16] See below, Chap. 12.
[17] *Review of the Criminal Courts* (2001), *www.criminal-courts-review.org*.
[18] M. Zander, *Lord Justice Auld's Review of the Criminal Courts: A Response* (*www.lse.ac.uk/Depts/law*).

responsibility of the magistrates' court alone; there should be a significant shift of heavy work from High Court to Circuit judges; the prosecutor should assume responsibility for charges; the disclosure regime should be reformed; there should be a comprehensive review of the law of criminal evidence and reforms of the appellate structure.[19] The recommendations are under consideration by government; the report was, however, preceded by the publication of a White Paper, *Criminal Justice: The Way Ahead*.[20]

E. POSSIBLE INSTITUTIONAL REFORMS

Proposals have regularly been made for the establishment of a Ministry of Justice, performing all the functions concerning justice at present divided among separate ministries.[21] The calls have commonly been associated with demands for a more systematic approach to law reform,[22] and have equally commonly been resisted on the highly dubious ground that the establishment of such a ministry might pose a threat to the administration of justice. In 1918, the Machinery of Government Committee chaired by Lord Haldane[23] proposed a redistribution of functions between Lord Chancellor and Home Secretary. The former would cease to be Speaker of the House of Lords and to sit judicially, but would be responsible for all judicial appointments, would continue as chief constitutional adviser to the Crown and would "watch and master all questions relating to legislation". Other matters concerning the administration of justice would pass to the Home Secretary, who would be redesignated as Minister of Justice, and would probably sit in the Commons. These proposals were supported by the Law Society but opposed by the Bar. Four years later, the case against a Ministry of Justice (albeit a ministry on the continental pattern including responsibility for the judiciary) was powerfully made by Lord Birkenhead.[24] Some of the steam was taken out of the case for a Ministry by the establishment of the Law Commissions in 1965. More recently, the developments in the role of the Lord Chancellor's Department outlined above[25] have rendered it into a Ministry of Justice in all but name, with the significant qualifications that the ministerial head does not sit in the House of Commons and significant responsibilities remain with the Home Office.

  Proposals for change continue to be made. It has been suggested that the

1–033

---

[19] See further below, Chaps 14, 17.

[20] Cm. 5074 (2001).

[21] See JUSTICE Conference, *Do we Need a Ministry of Justice?* (1970); G. Drewry, "Ministry of Justice—a Matter of Meaning" (1982) 132 N.L.J. 602–603, "Lord Haldane's Ministry of Justice—Stillborn or Strangled at Birth?" (1983) 61 *Public Administration*, 396, "The Debate about a Ministry of Justice—a Joad's-Eye View" [1987] P.L.502 and "Justice and Public Administration" (1992) 45(2) C.L.P.187.

[22] See, *e.g.* Glanville Williams (ed.) *The Reform of the Law* (1951); *cf.* G. Gardiner and A. Martin (eds), *Law Reform NOW* (1963); P. Archer and A. Martin (eds), *More Law Reform NOW* (1983), pp. 15–20.

[23] Cd. 9230.

[24] *Points of View* (1922), Vol. I, p. 112. This was apparently prepared by Sir Claud Schuster, Permanent Secretary to the Lord Chancellor 1915–1944: Drewry (1983) *op. cit.*

[25] See para. 1-018.

LCD, possibly renamed the Department for Justice and Equality, should take over responsibility for criminal law reform from the Home Office and adopt a "cross-cutting role" in promoting good governance in the public sector.[26] Another model[27] would have the role of the LCD ("Department of Justice") refocused as "custodian of the principles of fairness and impartiality and now as the champion of the values of a rights-based society" and protector of "standards of justice which are, as far as possible, free from external pressures"; and the Lord Chancellor's role limited to acting as non-party political head of the judiciary, outside the cabinet and no longer head of the Department.[28] The Department, headed by a Secretary of State in the Commons, would take over responsibility for voluntary sector advice agencies currently funded by other government departments, and for criminal procedure and criminal law reform; and lose responsibility for the Land Registry and the Public Record Office. The Home Office would retain responsibility for crime prevention and law enforcement and the prison and probation services, and the Attorney-General, responsible for the CPS, would remain outside both departments. The desirability of such changes is corroborated by the stringent criticisms expressed by Lord Justice Auld of the current divisions of responsibility within the Criminal Justice system, although such structural changes lay beyond his terms of reference. If administrative efficiency and effectiveness were the sole criteria, then the case for combining responsibility for law making and law enforcement would be powerful; that proposals for change do not go as far as that rightly reflects the need for an appropriate level of separation between legislative and executive functions.

Finally, it may be noted that unlike the position in some other common law jurisdictions, the judges do not play a major role in supervising the administration of the courts.[29] A strong conception of the independence of judiciary would require the judiciary to assume administrative responsibility for the operation of the courts, including control over court buildings and facilities and the organisation of business. However, while there have been judicial expressions of concern that the decisions of civil servants are having an increasingly direct (and deleterious) effect on the work of the courts, what is sought for the judiciary is a position of greater influence, rather than a full transfer of responsibility.[30] Such a transfer would, moreover, in the opinion

---

[26] Sarah Spencer, *Time for Ministry of Justice? The future of the Home Office and the Lord Chancellor's Department* (IPPR, March 2001). The paper also favoured the LCD's assumption of responsibility for human rights issues; this step has been taken.

[27] N. Ardill, *Legal Action*, August 2001.

[28] It is difficult to imagine any incumbent of the office, least of all the current one, warming to this proposal; abolition of the office without replacement might be a kinder alternative.

[29] See I. R. Scott, "The Council of Judges in the Supreme Court of England and Wales"[1989] P.L. 379; Lord Mackay of Clashfern, (1991) 44 C. L. P. 241, 247–250; Mr Justice R. D. Nicholson (1993) 67 A.L.J. 404, 422–424. The judges are responsible for what happens in the court room and for "the administrative penumbra immediately surrounding the judicial process" (Lord Mackay, *op.cit.* at p. 247); presiding judges for each circuit and the senior presiding judge deal with the deployment and performance of the judiciary (below, para. 2-055.). Otherwise, administration is in the hands of the Court Service (above, para. 1-018.) and while the Lord Chancellor is ultimately accountable to Parliament for the service he is regarded by at least some of the judges as one of "them" rather than one of "us" for these purposes (below, para. 4-033.).

[30] See below, para. 4-033.

of Lord Mackay, be an "extremely retrograde step".[31] The current rhetoric is one of "partnership".[32]

F. INFORMATION ABOUT THE LEGAL SYSTEM

Statistical and factual information about the operation of the English legal system can be gleaned from various official sources. Official publications are grouped into a number of classes.[33] "Command papers" are "Presented to Parliament by Command of Her Majesty"[34] and include reports of Royal Commissions, departmental committees and the Law Commission. "House of Commons" and "House of Lords Papers" are published on behalf of the respective Houses of Parliament.[35] Other documents are published as "Non-Parliamentary Publications" by The Stationery Office[36] or by the department concerned.[37]

1–034

Statistical information may be found in the series of *Judicial Statistics* (1856–1922) published by the Home Office and covering both civil and criminal matters; and *Criminal Statistics* (1922 to date) also published by the Home Office. There are also Home Office Statistical Bulletins, which provide regular statistical information on some topics, such as the use of the Prevention of Terrorism Acts (now the Terrorism Act 2000), and occasional information on others, such as comparative figures on remands in custody by magistrates' courts in different areas. The Lord Chancellor's Department has published various series: *Civil Judicial Statistics* (1922–1974); *Statistics on Judicial Administration* (1972–1974) and *Judicial Statistics: England and Wales* (1975 to date). Information on legal services was given in the Annual Report of the Law Society and the Lord Chancellor's Advisory Committee, first issued in 1951 and from 1974–75 termed the *Legal Aid Annual Reports*, and is now found in the Annual Reports of the Legal Services Commission. The Lord Chancellor is required to publish annual reports on the business of the Supreme Court and county courts,[38] and the Master of the Rolls issues Annual Reviews of the work of the Court of Appeal (Civil Division).[39]

---

[31] *The Administration of Justice* (1994), p. 48. Lord Mackay argues that there is no way that a judge with security of tenure can be accountable to Parliament for the way in which money is spent and the courts are administered; as Lord Chancellor, he has no security of tenure: *ibid.*

[32] See also above, para. 1-019.

[33] See generally J. E. Pemberton, *British Official Publications* (2nd ed., 1973); D. Butcher, *Official Publications in Britain* (2nd ed., 1991).

[34] These papers are numbered in series and since 1870 have been prefixed by an abbreviation for "Command": 1st series [1]–[4222] 1833–1869; 2nd series [C.1]–[C.9550] 1870–1899; 3rd series [Cd.1]–[Cd.9239] 1900–1918; 4th series [Cmd.1–Cmd.9889], 1919–1956; 5th series [Cmnd.1–9927] 1956–1986; 6th series [Cm.1–] 1986–.

[35] These are numbered in the session of publication (*e.g.* 1983–84 H.C. or H.L. 1).

[36] TSO also publish Command Papers and Parliamentary Papers: see the daily, monthly and annual TSO lists.

[37] See the *Catalogue of British Official Publications Not Published by HMSO* (1980–).

[38] Courts and Legal Services Act 1990, s.l(12). See the Annual Reports of the Lord Chancellor's Department Court Service (LCD website).

[39] See *e.g.* below, para. 2-071.

Accessibility to this and other relevant information have been transformed by its availability on the internet.[40]

G. INTERNATIONAL STANDARDS

1–035   There has been an increasing awareness that minimum standards for the
operation of aspects of the legal system are set by international law,
enshrined in treaties to which the United Kingdom is a party. The most
important such treaties are the European Convention on Human Rights[41]
and the International Covenant on Civil and Political Rights.[42] Key articles
of the European Convention include Article 5 on the right to liberty and
security of person, Article 6 on the right to a fair trial, Article 7, prohibiting
retrospective criminal law, and Article 14, providing that the enjoyment of
Convention rights and freedoms shall be secured without discrimination on
any ground such as (for example) sex, race, colour, language or religion.
There have been an increasing number and variety of successful challenges
to the United Kingdom under these provisions in the context of the
administration of justice in England and Wales,[43] including a series of cases
concerning the rights of prisoners,[44] another series of cases that has required
the fundamental remodelling of arrangements for court martials in the
armed forces,[45] and cases concerning excessive delay in civil proceedings

---

[40] Good starting points are the Lord Chancellor's Department and Home Office websites.

[41] See below, para. 2-082.

[42] See S. H. Bailey, "Rights in the Administration of Justice" in D. J. Harris and S. Joseph
(eds), *The United Kingdom and the International Covenant on Civil and Political Rights*
(1995), Chap. 6.

[43] The lack of a right to legal representation for criminal appeals in Scotland has been held to
be unlawful: *Boner v. U.K.* (1995) 19 E.H.R.R. 246; *Maxwell v. U.K.* (1995) 19 E.H.R.R. 97

[44] Cases on prisoners' correspondence (*e.g. Golder v. U.K.* (1975) 1 E.H.R.R. 524; *Silver v. U.K.*
(1983) 5 E.H.R.R. 347); disciplinary proceedings (*Campbell and Fell v. U.K.* (1984) 7
E.H.R.R. 165), release of life sentence prisoners (*Weeks v. U.K.* (1987) 10 E.H.R.R. 293);
Oldham v. U.K., Judgment of September 26, 2000 (two-year delay between Parole Board
reviews not reasonable); *Curley v. U.K.* (2001) 31 E.H.R.R. 14 (inadequacy of review
arrangements); *Hirst v. U.K.*, Judgment of July 24, 2001 (21-month and two-year delays
between reviews not reasonable); *Thynne, Wilson and Gunnell v. U.K.* (1990) 13 E.H.R.R.
666; prisoners in psychiatric detention (*X v. U.K.* (1981) 4 E.H.R.R. 188); and persons
detained during Her Majesty's pleasure (*Hussein v. U.K.; Singh v. U.K.* (1996) 22 E.H.R.R.
1.

[45] *Findlav v. U.K.* (1997) 24 E.H.R.R. 221; *Coyne v. U.K.*, Judgment of 24 September, 1997;
Hood v. U.K. (2000) 29 E.H.R.R. 365; *Cable v. U.K.* (2000) 30 E.H.R.R. 1032; *Moore and
Gordon v. U.K.* (2001) 29 E.H. R.R. 729; *Stephen Jordan v. U.K.* (2001) 31 E.H.R.R. 6;
changes effected by the Armed Forces Act 1996 were held not fully to have secured trial by
an independent and impartial tribunal in *Morris v. U.K.*, Judgment of February 26, 2002
(Art. 6(1)).

(nine years),[46] the retrospective imposition of a confiscation order following conviction for drug offences,[47] violation of the right not to incriminate oneself, by the use at trial of statements obtained under legal compulsion,[48] the disproportionate use of a police power to enter a home,[49] the automatic refusal of bail in specified circumstances,[50] failure to disclose prosecution evidence,[51] inadequate jury directions concerning inferences from silence,[52] a lack of impartiality in proceedings where two jurors had allegedly made racist jokes,[53] and the degrading treatment of a disabled person held in custody.[54]

The necessity for a statutory regime to regulate covert surveillance by law enforcement authorities has been recognised.[55] Similarly, the Civil Procedure Rules[56] introduced as part of the Woolf reforms have been drafted to secure compliance with the requirement for a public hearing; the previous approach whereby small claims arbitrations were normally to be held in private were found to violate that requirement.[57] Challenges in high-profile cases concerning the right to silence and the abolition of the marital exemption from liability for rape[58] have failed.[59] Nevertheless, it has been argued that current trends in the criminal justice process render the United Kingdom increasingly vulnerable to challenge.[60] The implementation of the Human Rights Act 1998 has added to the pressures.[61]

---

[46] *Darnell v. U.K.*, (1994) 18 E.H.R.R. 205; *cf. Robins v. U.K.* (1997) 26 E.H.R.R. 527 (delay in decision concerning costs); *Howarth v. U.K.* (2000) 9 B.H.R.C. 253 (delay in Attorney-General's reference of a sentence to the Court of Appeal (Criminal Division) (Art. 6(1)).

[47] *Welch v. U.K.* (1995) 20 E.H.R.R. 247

[48] *Saunders v. U.K.* (1997) 23 E.H.R.R. 313; *IJL, GMR and AKP v. U.K.*, Judgment of September 19, 2000 (Art. 6(1)).

[49] *McLeod v. U.K.*, Judgment of 23 September 1998 (Art. 8).

[50] *Caballero v. U.K.* (2000) 30 E.H.R.R. 643; *S.B.C. v. U.K.*, Judgment of June 19, 2001 (violation of Art. 5(3) conceded; these cases concerned the Criminal Justice and Public Order Act 1994 s. 25, which prevented bail being granted in murder, manslaughter and rape cases (including attempts) to a person previously convicted of such an offence or culpable homicide; this was amended by the Crime and Disorder Act 1998, s. 56, enabling bail to be granted in exceptional circumstances).

[51] *Rowe and Davis v. U.K.* (2000) 20 E.H.R.R. 1; *Atlan v. U.K.* Judgment of June 19, 2001 (Art. 6(1)).

[52] *Condron v. U.K.*, Judgment of May 2, 2000 (Art. 6(1)).

[53] *Sander v. U.K.*, Judgment of May 9, 2000 (Art. 6(1)).

[54] *Price v. U.K.*, Judgment of July 14, 2001 Art. 3).

[55] Police Act 1997; Regulation of Investigatory Powers Act 2000; violations have been found in respect of covert police surveillance under the previous arrangements: *Khan v. U.K.* (2000) 8 B.H.R.C. 310; *P.G. and J.H. v. U.K.*, Judgment of September 25, 2001 (Art. 8).

[56] Below, p. 000.

[57] *Scarth v. U.K.*, Judgment of July 22, 1999 (Art. 6(1)).

[58] See below.

[59] See below.

[60] See Liberty, *Criminal Justice and Civil and Political Liberties* (1993).

[61] See generally, Chap. 8.

CHAPTER 2

COURTS AND TRIBUNALS

A. INTRODUCTION

2–001   THERE are several ways in which a legal dispute (which the parties also characterise as "legal") may be resolved. It may be settled by force or by agreement. The dispute may be referred informally or formally to a third party for him or her to arbitrate. Exceptionally, the dispute may be referred to one of the institutions established by the state expressly for the purpose of resolving such matters. Some of these institutions are termed "courts", others "tribunals". These terms cannot be defined with precision, and, for the most part, little turns on whether a particular institution is labelled a court or a tribunal, or whether an institution, however labelled, falls within the legal definition of a "court".

The term "tribunal" can be used very generally to mean any "judicial assembly",[1] including a court; in the present context it is commonly used for "judicial assemblies" other than courts. If established by the state they are generally described as "administrative tribunals" to distinguish them from "domestic tribunals" established by non-state institutions such as professional and sporting associations and trade unions as part of their disciplinary procedures. The label "administrative" reflects the fact that most such tribunals are established to perform judicial functions as part of the administration of some government scheme or programme.

Finally, it should be remembered that while the settlement of disputes is the main function of almost all courts and most tribunals, it is not the only one: a number of administrative functions have also been allocated to them.[2]

B. COURTS

1. SIGNIFICANCE

2–002   Apart from the police, the courts of law are perhaps the most visible feature of the English legal system. Only the courts have power to impose

---

[1] O.E.D.

[2] *e.g.* the licensing functions of magistrates and the discretionary powers of the High Court in relation to the administration of estates or the supervision of the affairs of children and mental patients; *cf.* below, para. 2-060.

punishment in criminal cases; reports of these, and important civil cases decided by the superior courts, commonly appear in the national and local press, and they may be covered by radio and television. Lawyers, and to an even greater extent, law students and lecturers place great emphasis on the decisions of the superior courts. It is, however, difficult to estimate the significance of the courts in the legal system as a whole. The number of cases determined by the courts is small, and by the superior courts[3] minute, in comparison with the number of disputes settled by other means. Moreover, in a high proportion of the cases dealt with by the magistrates' courts and county courts the proceedings are merely mechanical processes for, respectively, the fining of minor traffic offenders and the collection of debts, with no live issue to be determined.

On the other hand, the courts do have a much wider indirect impact, given, first, that the chances of success in legal proceedings will influence the settlement of disputes,[4] and, secondly, that the decisions of superior courts are a source of law.[5]

2. Historical Background[6]

(a) Courts of common law and equity

As we have said, the main function of almost all courts today is the adjudication of disputes. They can, however, trace their origins to local and central institutions in which no distinctions were drawn between the functions of administration, legislation and adjudication. At the local level in the Dark Ages there were community assemblies or "moots" which, *inter alia*, dealt with disputes according to local custom. These assemblies, apart from the smallest, village, assemblies, came to be based on administrative units established by the Crown, the shires, and their subdivisions, the hundreds and the boroughs. At the centre was the *Curia Regis* (King's Court).

2–003

Three related themes in early legal development can be discerned. First, the administration of justice came to be regarded as an adjunct of feudal lordship rather than a matter for the community as a whole. Then there was a further shift whereby it came in particular to be one of the prerogatives of the Crown. Thirdly, the administration of justice came to be differentiated from other functions of government. The strengthening of royal justice at the expense of local, communal, justice was a gradual process, and was neither intended nor planned, but it took place at all levels. This process involved the establishment of distinct royal courts, the placing of royal officials in the localities, whether temporarily or permanently, and the development of the supervisory jurisdiction of the royal courts over local courts.

At the centre, three common law courts evolved at different times out of

---

[3] See below, para. 2-017.
[4] See below, para. 11-025–11-031.
[5] See below, Chap. 7.
[6] See generally J. H. Baker, *An Introduction to Legal History* (3rd ed., 1990), Chaps 1–7.

the *Curia Regis*: the Exchequer,[7] the Common Pleas and the King's (or Queen's) Bench. They sat at Westminster Hall. The jurisdictional lines between these courts were complex. In theory, the Exchequer dealt with matters concerning the revenues of the Crown, the Common Pleas suits between subject and subject in which the Crown had no interest, and the King's Bench "pleas of the Crown" (*i.e.* criminal matters and civil cases involving a breach of the King's peace or some other royal interest). By the eighteenth century a variety of fictions had enabled each court to exercise a jurisdiction that was similar in substance although different in form to the others.

Parallel to the development of the common law courts at the centre was that of the Court of Chancery, and in particular its function of dealing with petitions.[8] For a time in the sixteenth and seventeenth centuries a number of "conciliar courts" also assumed importance, being courts established under the prerogative to handle judicial matters that came before the Privy Council but were not dealt with by the Chancellor. These included the Court of Star Chamber, which became notorious towards the end of its life for its handling of political crimes, the Court of Requests and several regional offshoots. They were looked on with suspicion by the common law courts and were abolished in the 1640s. The pattern of superior courts otherwise remained substantially unchanged until the nineteenth century, when some new courts were created, and there was subsequently a general reorganisation under the Supreme Court of Judicature Acts 1873–75.[9] In this reorganisation the various superior courts[10] were replaced by one Supreme Court of Judicature comprising the High Court (in five divisions) and the Court of Appeal. The intention initially was for the appellate jurisdiction of the House of Lords to be abolished, but a successful rearguard action was fought for its retention.[11]

2–004   Royal justices from the common law courts were also sent out to travel the country. Originally, they conducted all manner of governmental affairs, but they came to concentrate on judicial proceedings. There were two bases for their jurisdiction. In criminal and some civil cases they were given ad hoc commissions from the Crown. In other civil cases they sat with a jury to try issues that arose in litigation in the superior courts at Westminster: the juries technically were summoned to Westminster "unless before then (*nisi prius*) the King's justices have come" into the country. It was obviously more convenient to try the issues locally and transmit the result to London. The system came to be known as the "assize system" and continued until the 1970s,[12] and even the present arrangements have maintained the concept of High Court judges hearing cases in the provinces, albeit now reinforced by local judges.

---

[7] As well as a common law jurisdiction, this court had an established equity jurisdiction, which was transferred to the Court of Chancery as late as 1842.

[8] See above, paras 1-005–1-007.

[9] This followed the recommendations of the First Report of the Judicature Commission (HMSO, 1869).

[10] *i.e.* the Courts of Chancery, Queen's Bench, Common Pleas, Exchequer, Admiralty (see below, para. 2-006), Probate (*ibid.*), and Divorce and Matrimonial Causes (*ibid.*). The London Court of Bankruptcy, originally established by an Act of 1831 to relieve the Court of Chancery of some of its business, was incorporated in 1884.

[11] See below, para. 2-072.

[12] See below, para. 2-051.

The significant development in the handling of criminal cases less serious than those dealt with at the assizes was the appointment by the Crown of justices of the peace and the progressive widening of their criminal jurisdiction from the thirteenth century onwards.[13] Civil cases were heard by the successors of the old community assemblies, a variegated pattern of county, hundred, manorial and borough courts. These courts were subject to the supervisory jurisdiction of the superior royal courts and came to apply the common law. They declined for different reasons and at different times, although many were only formally abolished in the 1970s.[14] The important step in the establishment of a regular system of local civil courts was the creation of new, statutory, county courts in 1846.[15]

(b) Appeals[16]

Provision for appeals was complex. The record of a court's proceedings could be reviewed for error[17] by another common law court[18] or a special court, a number of which were established by statute at various times to sit in a room at Westminster Hall known as the Exchequer Chamber.[19] Error lay from the Courts of Exchequer Chamber to Parliament, this jurisdiction being exercised by the House of Lords. Another, informal, method of review was the practice of judges to reserve cases for the opinion of their brethren, expressed at meetings held in Serjeants' Inn or the Exchequer Chamber.[20] In Chancery proceedings, a case argued before the Master of the Rolls or a Vice-Chancellor[21] could be re-argued before the Chancellor, and the Chancellor could review his own previous decisions and those of his predecessors. In the seventeenth century it was established that proceedings in error lay from the Court of Chancery to the House of Lords. A Court of Appeal in Chancery with appellate judges (Lords Justices) specially appointed to it was created in 1851 to hear appeals from the Master of the Rolls and the Vice-Chancellors. This became the model for the Court of Appeal established by the Judicature Acts 1873–75. The nineteenth century also saw the replacement of proceedings in error by statutory appeals in the modern form.

2–005

---

[13] See below, para. 4-002. The justices also had many administrative responsibilities.

[14] Courts Act 1971, ss.42, 43; Administration of Justice Act 1977, s.23, Sched. 4.

[15] See below, para. 2-040: These must not be confused with the old shire or county courts presided over by the sheriff.

[16] See Baker (1990), Chap. 9.

[17] This process was more akin to the modern application for judicial review than statutory appeal: see Chap. 18.

[18] Proceedings in error lay from the Common Pleas to the King's Bench until 1830.

[19] (1) One was established in 1357 to hear error from the Exchequer. This comprised the Chancellor and the Treasurer with judges as assistants. (2) A second was established in 1585 to hear error from the Queen's Bench, this court comprising the justices of the Common Pleas and the barons of the Exchequer. (3) In 1830 a new Court of Exchequer Chamber was established to hear error from each of the common law courts. This comprised all the judges of the superior courts, error from one court being heard by the judges of the other two.

[20] In criminal cases such meetings became formalised with the creation of the Court for Crown Cases Reserved in 1848.

[21] See below para. 4-021.

(c) Other courts

2–006 Apart from the courts of common law and equity there were courts that followed civil law procedure: the High Court of Admiralty,[22] which dealt with maritime matters and the High Court of Chivalry,[23] a court of honour. Canon law was administered by archdeacons' courts, the bishops' consistory courts, each presided over by the chancellor of the diocese, and the archbishops' provincial courts, the Chancery Court of York and the Court of Arches.[24] Further appeals lay to the Pope or to Papal Delegates. Following the Reformation this jurisdiction passed to the Court of High Commission, which lapsed in the 1640s, and the Court of Delegates. The latter court was replaced by the Privy Council in 1832. The relationship between the ecclesiastical courts and the royal courts was stormy and complicated.[25] The jurisdiction of ecclesiastical courts over marriage, divorce and probate ended in 1857 with the creation of the Court of Divorce and Matrimonial Causes and the Court of Probate.[26] Since then, their jurisdiction has been confined to church matters. The present court structure was introduced by the Ecclesiastical Jurisdiction Measure 1963, which retained the consistory courts, but created an appellate system of gothic complexity, largely replacing the appellate jurisdiction of the Privy Council.[27] Appeals in matters of doctrine, ritual or ceremonial lie from the consistory courts to the Court of Ecclesiastical Causes Reserved, which comprises three bishops and two judges, appointed by the Queen.[28]

C. TRIBUNALS

1. INTRODUCTION

2–007 The significant role played by administrative tribunals in the adjudication of legal disputes is a development of the present century, although it is possible

---

[22] This court became part of the Supreme Court of Judicature in the 1873–75 reorganisation. See F. Wiswall, *The Development of Admiralty Jurisdiction and Practice Since 1800* (1971).

[23] This court has sat once since 1737: *Manchester Corporation v. Manchester Palace of Varieties Ltd* [1955] P. 133. See G. D. Squibb, *The High Court of Chivalry* (1959). It has jurisdiction over such questions as the right to arms, precedence and descent. In the 1955 case the corporation claimed successfully that the company should be prevented from using the former's arms in their seal and displayed above the main curtain at the Palace Theatre, Manchester.

[24] So called because it usually sat in the arched crypt of the church of St Mary le Bow in London. Its judge became known as the Dean of Arches.

[25] See Baker (1990), Chap. 8.

[26] These courts became part of the Supreme Court of Judicature in the 1873–75 reorganisation.

[27] See E. Garth Moore, *An Introduction to Canon Law* (1967), Chap. XIV; L. Leeder, *Ecclesiastical Law Handbook* (1997); M. Hill, *Ecclesiastical Law* (2nd ed., 2001); *Canons of the Church of England* (6th ed.), Section G *(www.cofe.anglican.org/legal/)*.

[28] The first two cases before this court were *In re St Michael and All Angels, Great Torrington* [1985] Fam. 81 and *In re St Stephen's, Walbrook* [1987] Fam. 146: see J. D. C. Harte, (1988) 2 Ecc-LJ. 22.

to find examples of similar institutions in earlier centuries.[29] For example, the General and Special Commissioners of Income Tax were established in 1799 and 1805 respectively, with both assessment and appellate functions. The Railway and Canal Commission was established in 1873, *inter alia*, to settle disputes between railway companies and between companies and their customers, and subsequently evolved into the Transport Tribunal.

The most important factors behind the expansion of the number of tribunals and the range of their work have been the advent of the welfare state and the development of state economic controls. The National Insurance Act 1911 set up the unemployment benefit scheme. All questions concerning claims to benefit were to be determined initially by an insurance officer. A workman dissatisfied with a determination could have it referred to a "court of referees" consisting of a chairman appointed by the Board of Trade, one member from an "employers' panel" and one from a "workmens' panel". A further right of appeal lay to an "umpire"—a national appellate authority appointed by the Crown. This arrangement proved superior to alternative methods of adjudication used in legislation of the period,[30] and was adopted as the general model for many of the new tribunals established in the following decades:

"The extension of governmental responsibility for welfare provision, regulation of the economy, employment policy and resource development has created new statutory rights, obligations and restraints. Consequently, new areas of potential dispute have opened up, the boundaries of which have been progressively extended, and which require legislative provision for adjudication. The tendency, for a variety of reasons, has been to use tribunals rather than ordinary courts for settling disputes of this kind."[31]

This is not to say that there have been clear principles governing either the decision to allocate a particular decision to a tribunal or the details of the machinery established:

"Parliament's selection of subjects to be referred to tribunals and inquiries does not form a regular pattern. Certain basic guidelines can be detected, but the choice is influenced by the interplay of various factors—the nature of the decisions, accidents of history, departmental preferences and political considerations—rather than by the application of a set of coherent principles."[32]

These tribunals commonly determine disputes between the citizen and the

---

[29] See R. E. Wraith and P. G. Hutchesson, *Administrative Tribunals* (1973), Chap. 1.
[30] *i.e.* Workmen's Compensation Act 1897: disputes concerning compensation for industrial injuries were supposed to be settled by arbitration but in practice went to county court judges and beyond on appeal; Old Age Pensions Act 1908: pensions were administered by pensions committees of local authorities, which also adjudicated disputes, with an appeal to the Local Government Board; National Insurance Act 1911, Part I: national health insurance was administered by friendly societies with an appeal to one of four Insurance Commissioners.
[31] *The Functions of the Council on Tribunals: Special Report by the Council* (Cmnd. 7805, 1980), p. 1.
[32] *ibid.* pp. 1–2.

state arising out of the administration of a statutory scheme.[33] In addition, some determine disputes between citizens, normally arising out of protective legislation enacted for the benefit of one of the parties.[34]

2. THE FRANKS REPORT

2–008   A significant landmark in the development of tribunals was the 1957 report of the Committee on Administrative Tribunals and Enquiries chaired by Sir Oliver Franks.[35] Part of the terms of reference required the Committee to review the constitution and working of tribunals other than the ordinary courts of law, constituted by a minister or for the purposes of a minister's functions.[36] Among the general points made by the Committee were, first, that the special procedures within their terms of reference should be marked by the characteristics of "openness, fairness and impartiality"[37]:

> "In the field of tribunals openness appears to us to require the publicity of proceedings and knowledge of the essential reasoning underlying the decisions; fairness to require the adoption of a clear procedure which enables parties to know their rights, to present their case fully and to know the case which they have to meet; and impartiality to require the freedom of tribunals from the influence, real or apparent, of Departments concerned with the subject matter of their decisions."[38]

Secondly, the Committee noted that tribunals as a system for adjudication had come to stay, and indeed that the tendency to refer issues arising from legislative schemes to special tribunals was likely to grow rather than to diminish.[39]

Thirdly, the Committee recommended the establishment of two permanent Councils on Tribunals, one for England and Wales and one for Scotland, to supervise tribunal and inquiry procedures.

In addition, the report made a whole series of detailed recommendations concerning both the constitution and procedures of tribunals generally and particular tribunals. Most of the proposals were implemented in the Tribunals and Inquiries Act 1958, subsequently consolidated in the Tribunals and Inquiries Acts 1971 and now 1992, and in changes of regulation and departmental practice.

---

[33] *e.g.* disputes concerning claims to welfare benefits.
[34] *e.g.* disputes between landlord and tenant arising out of rent controls, and between employer and employee concerning allegedly unfair dismissals and an expanding range of other employment matters.
[35] Cmnd. 218.
[36] The other part of the terms of reference concerned public inquiry procedures.
[37] Cmnd. 218, p. 5.
[38] *ibid.* p. 10.
[39] *ibid.* p. 8.

3. THE COUNCIL ON TRIBUNALS[40]

The 1958 Act established one Council on Tribunals, with a Scottish **2–009**
Committee. Its functions in respect of tribunals are:

"(a) to keep under review the construction and working of the
tribunals specified in Schedule 1 to the [1992] Act;
(b) to consider and report on particular matters referred to the
Council by the Lord Chancellor and the Lord Advocate with
respect to any tribunal other than a court of law whether or not
specified in Schedule 1; ... ."[41]

Thus, its powers are consultative and advisory. It was not given the
executive powers recommended by the Franks Report as to the appointment
of tribunal members, the review of remuneration and the formulation of
procedural codes.[42] Certainly it has no power to reverse or require
reconsideration of specific tribunal decisions. The Council has 15 members
appointed by the Lord Chancellor and the Lord Advocate, and the
Parliamentary Commissioner for Administration is a member *ex officio*. The
membership comprises a mixture of lawyers, both practising and academic,
and non-lawyers, with the latter predominating. The Council's requests for
additional powers, put forward in its Special Report of 1980, were generally
not accepted. A code for consultation with government departments has
been introduced,[43] but the Council still regularly complains that it is given
inadequate time to comment on draft regulations. The Council has done
much useful work in minor matters, securing, for example, many
amendments to draft Bills, rules and regulations, and some changes in
tribunal practice. It has published a Report on Model Rules for Tribunals,[44]
a Code of Practice on Access for Disabled People using the Tribunal
System[45] and (with Property Holdings) a Register of Tribunal Hearing
Accommodation.[46] However, its political position is weak, its resources are

---

[40] See *The Functions of the Council on Tribunals: Special Report by the Council* (Cmnd. 7805,
1980); the Council's Annual Reports; H. W. R. Wade, [1960] P.L. 351; J. F. Garner, [1965]
P.L. 321; D. G. T. Williams, [1984] P.L. 73 and (1990) 9 C.J.Q. 27; O. Lomas, (1985) 48
M.L.R. 694; C. Harlow and R. Rawlings, *Law and Administration* (2nd ed., 1997), Chap. 14.
[41] Special Report, p. 3. It has similar, although not identical, functions in respect of procedures
involving inquiries held on behalf of a minister.
[42] It must be consulted before procedural rules are made for Schedule 1 tribunals, but does not
make the rules itself: 1992 Act, s.8.
[43] See the Council's Annual Reports for 1980–81 (1981–82 H.C. 89), pp. 6–7 and 1981–82
(1982–83 H.C. 64), p. 8 and Appendix C. The Code was recirculated in 1986 and 1992:
Annual Report for 1991–92 (1992–93 H.C. 316), p. 50 and Appendix I and revised and
republished in January 2001 (*www.council-on-tribunals.gov.uk/consultcode*).
[44] An interim revised edition, taking account of jurisprudential developments on Article 6,
ECHR, was distributed to departments in 1999: Council on Tribunals Annual Reports for
1998–99, p. 7–8 and 1999–2000, para. 12.
[45] A Consultation Draft of Revised Guidance was issued in June 2002.
[46] See Annual Reports for 1990–91 (1991–92 H.C. 97), pp. 23–24 (and Cm.1434); 1992–93
(1993–94 H.C. 78), pp. 11–13 and Appendix A; and 1993–94 (1994–95 H.C. 22), pp. 11–12
and Appendix A. A second edition was published in 1995: Annual Report for 1994–95
(1995–96 H.C. 64), pp. 44–45.

inadequate[47] and it "remains an inconspicuous advisory committee".[48] It is still met from time to time by spurious arguments from departments why a proposed new tribunal should not be placed under its jurisdiction; it sometimes, but not always, succeeds in overcoming them.[49] Access to the deliberative stage of tribunal hearings is occasionally denied.[50]

4. THE LEGGATT REPORT

2–010   In 2000, the Lord Chancellor appointed Sir Andrew Leggatt, a former Lord Justice of Appeal,[51] to conduct a review of the delivery of justice through tribunals. This, the first major review since Franks, complemented Lord Woolf's review of civil justice[52] and Sir Robin Auld's examination of the criminal justice system.[53] Sir Andrew reported in March 2001.[54] The Review found that, since the Franks Report, the numbers of tribunals had increased considerably and their work had become more complex. They were "a substantial part of the system of justice" but "too often their methods are old fashioned and they are daunting to users". They were many and disparate, and achieved no economies of scale. "Most importantly, they are not independent of the departments that sponsor them." (Consideration of their compliance with the requirements of Article 6(1), ECHR was expressly made part of the Review's terms of reference.) Overall, the object of the review was to recommend a system that was "independent, coherent, professional, cost-effective and user-friendly".[55] The Review made a series of recommendations in respect of both the system as a whole and particular tribunals. Key points were these.[56]

First, responsibility for tribunals should not lie with those whose policies or decisions it is the tribunal's duty to consider, in order to promote the fact and appearance of independence. Accordingly, all tribunals should instead be supported by a Tribunals Service. This would also achieve economies of scale, particularly in the provision of premises, common basic training and the use of IT, and greater administrative efficiency. The Service should be

---

[47] The Lord Chancellor's Department took over two years to consider and reject a request for additional staff: Annual Report for 1985–86 (1986–87 H.C. 42), pp. 28–30. In the Council's expenditure was £780,271, and it had a staff of 13: see Annual Report for 2000–01, Part 10 and Appendix C.

[48] Sir William Wade and C. F. Forsyth, *Administrative Law* (8th ed., 2000), p. 904.

[49] Annual Reports for 1993–94 (1994–95 H.C. 22), pp. 6–8, 41–42 (supervisory jurisdiction over Police Appeal Tribunals eventually conceded). The Council's position is helped by the fact that its current chairman Lord Newton of Braintree is a member of the House of Lords, as was his predecessor, Lord Archer.

[50] *ibid.* pp. 9, 24–25 (industrial tribunals in Scotland).

[51] Assisted by Dame Valerie Strachan, former Chairman of the Board of H.M. Customs and Excise, Professors Carol Harlow, Martin Partington and Richard Susskind, David Hatch, Chairman of the National Consumer Council and then the Parole Board, and Mrs Doris Littlejohn, formerly President of the Employment Tribunals in Scotland.

[52] See Chap. 12.

[53] See para. 1-031.

[54] The report was actually published in August 2001. *Tribunals for Users: One System, One Service* (2001).

[55] p. 5.

[56] pp. 5–14.

part of the Lord Chancellor's Department.

Secondly, tribunals "should do all they can to render themselves understandable, unthreatening, and useful to users". Users should be able to obtain the information they need concerning venues, timetables and sources of professional advice. Decision-makers should produce reasoned decisions in plain English or Welsh and give a proper explanation of the appeal process. Every effort should be made to reduce the number of cases in which representation is needed. Voluntary and community bodies should be funded to provide legal representation for the residual category of complex cases where legal representation is necessary; legal aid should be available only as a last resort. The system required underpinning by "the judicious and well managed application of IT" (currently, in many tribunals, it is "primitive").

Finally, the position of the Council on Tribunals should be strengthened, with additional powers and a higher profile. Overall, there was a need for a "new culture, starting with improved recognition of just how daunting the tribunal experience usually is for first-time users, as most are".

Many of these recommendations, particularly those concerning structure and organisation, seem sensible in principle. It would seem right that the organisation of tribunals should be similar to that for courts given that the tasks they perform are broadly the same. Whether the costs of effecting structural changes can currently be justified is a separate matter.[57] However, it is submitted that one key element is questionable: the belief that the majority of proceedings can, through training, changes to procedures and otherwise, be made accessible to the (unrepresented) ordinary, first-time user. The fair resolution of disputes can only be based on the proper identification of the issues and the identification of the evidence that is relevant to those issues. This very commonly requires more than just the application of "common sense". We return to these matters elsewhere.[58]

The tone of the Consultation Paper on the Leggatt Report issued by the LCD[59] was largely sceptical. While the government was "determined to modernise tribunals" the report's recommendations, many of which were "controversial," would be judged "against the criterion of whether they will contribute to improving the service that users receive". This suggests that recommendations concerning service to users (*e.g.* improved access to information, adoption by tribunals of an enabling approach giving the parties confidence in their ability to participate, revised procedures, use of IT) are more likely to be endorsed than expensive structural changes. The government was satisfied that tribunals already complied with the requirement of independence and impartiality set out in Article 6(1), ECHR[60] and so structural changes needed justification by reference to the needs of users. Creation of a unified Tribunals Service would involve major

2–012

---

[57] See below on the government's view.
[58] Below, para. 16-021.
[59] August 2001, LCD website.
[60] The terms of appointment of part-time judicial tribunal members had been changed to ensure their independence following *Starrs and Chalmers v. Procurator Fiscal* (below, para. 4-020); employment tribunals and school admission and exclusion appeal tribunals met the required standards (*Link v. Secretary of State for Trade and Industry*, March 23, 2001 (employment tribunals); *R. (on the application of B) v. Alperton Community Schoo*, [2001] EWHC Admin 229 (Article 6(1) not applicable to these panels).

structural changes that would distract attention and resources from improving services; the breaking of links with departments could make it harder to manage the end-to-end process efficiently or draw on the tribunal's expertise when developing policy; there would be a lengthy period of change and uncertainty; a unified service could prove too large and cumbersome. Alternative, intermediate approaches might include the establishment of a portal linked to the IT systems of different tribunals, establishment of a common pool of suitable lawyers for judicial appointments, spread of good practice, enhanced roles for the Judicial Studies Board and the Council on Tribunals, and the establishment of further executive agencies to administer further tribunals or groups of tribunals. The government proposed to publish its views in summer 2002.

5. ADJUDICATION OR ADMINISTRATION

2–013 There has been some debate on whether tribunals are to be regarded as part of the machinery of justice or part of the machinery of administration. The Franks Committee stated[61]:

"Tribunals are not ordinary courts, but neither are they appendages of Government Departments. Much of the official evidence, including that of the Joint Permanent Secretary to the Treasury, appeared to reflect the view that tribunals should properly be regarded as part of the machinery of administration, for which the Government must retain a close and continuing responsibility. Thus, for example, tribunals in the social service field would be regarded as adjuncts to the administration of the services themselves. We do not accept this view. We consider that tribunals should properly be regarded as machinery provided by Parliament for adjudication rather than as part of the machinery of administration. The essential point is that in all these cases Parliament has deliberately provided for a decision outside and independent of the Department concerned, either at first instance (for example in the case of Rent Tribunals and the Licensing Authorities for Public Service and Goods Vehicles) or on appeal from a decision of a Minister or of an official in a special statutory position (for example a valuation officer or an insurance officer). Although the relevant statutes do not in all cases expressly enact that tribunals are to consist entirely of persons outside the Government service, the use of the term 'tribunal' in legislation undoubtedly bears this connotation, and the intention of Parliament to provide for the independence of tribunal is clear and unmistakable."

The extent to which tribunals are and should be "independent" has been much debated. Clearly it is necessary that the expression of the "departmental view" in an individual case should be confined to the representations made at the hearing itself.[62] However, in many respects the

---

[61] Cmnd. 218, p. 9.
[62] The Leggatt Report (above, para. 2-012) noted that "there is no question of the government improperly attempting to influence individual decisions. In that sense, tribunal decisions seem to us to be clearly impartial": para. 2.20.

departments retain a general influence over tribunal decision-making. They are responsible for the formulation of the relevant primary legislation and procedural rules, albeit in consultation with the Council on Tribunals, and indeed for the "detailed arrangements" for the working of tribunals.[63] There has, however, been a trend in recent years for the Lord Chancellor's Department to take over (or be given) responsibility for the operation of a growing list of tribunals. The Department is now responsible for the Lands Tribunal, the Special and General Commissioners of Income Tax, VAT and Duties Tribunals, the Social Security and Child Support Commissioners, Pensions Appeal Tribunals, the Transport Tribunal, and the Immigration Adjudicators and administrative responsibility for the immigration appellate authorities. The Council on Tribunals has set out some broad guidelines as to the allocation of administrative responsibility for tribunals, suggesting that the main consideration should be the independence of the tribunal and the public perception of that independence. It was necessary to show that there was real independence, especially where the outcome of a tribunal's hearings would affect the public purse on a policy seen by the government or a department as vitally important. There could be a long-term aim for the Lord Chancellor's Department to take over responsibility for all such tribunals, but this would not be realistic for the present. Other relevant factors were the tribunal's size and geographical spread, level and involvement with the law. The Council noted that most of the tribunals currently administered by the Department were relatively senior, relatively closely involved with specifically legal issues, and comparatively small, and only sat in a small number of places.[64]

A further aspect of the role of the Lord Chancellor's Department is that it is involved in the consideration of proposals to create new tribunals and provides advice and guidance to other departments on tribunal matters when so requested.[65]   **2–014**

The Franks view on this point has been criticised in two respects. First, it has been pointed out that some tribunals are "policy-oriented" rather than "court substitute":

> For instance, where there is a dispute about social security entitlement, tribunals are basically used in place of the ordinary courts because the latter have become too expensive, formal and technical in their procedure. On the other hand, many matters of planning, whether in transport, land use, or industrial expertise, are given to tribunals because of the lack of expertise and doctrinal flexibility, or policy consciousness, on the part of the courts. Thus different weaknesses in the courts give rise to different types of tribunals.[66]

---

[63] Annual Report of the Council on Tribunals for 1975–76 (1976–77 H.C. 236), p. 3. The Council recognises that it is not always practicable for a tribunal to use non-departmental staff and premises: Annual Report for 1981–82 (1982–83 H.C. 64), pp. 26–27.

[64] Annual Report for 1984–85 (1985–86 H.C. 54), pp. 13–14.

[65] Annual Report for 1986–87 (1987–88 H.C. 42), p. 13.

[66] B. Abel-Smith and R. Stevens, *In Search of Justice* (1968), p. 220; see J. A. Farmer, *Tribunals and Government* (1974), Chap. 8 for an argument in favour of the establishment of more policy-oriented tribunals as an alternative to ministerial decision-making.

Examples of policy-oriented tribunals include the Transport Tribunal[67] and the Civil Aviation Authority.[68] Secondly, it has been argued that even court-substitute tribunals should be seen as hybrid in nature; not only machinery for adjudication but, as well, "vital components of administration".[69]

On the other hand, the Leggatt Report[70] clearly favoured a sharp divide between policy development and adjudication with its proposals for the establishment of a unified Tribunals Service within the LCD. They argued that where tribunal members and managers were consulted as part of policy development,

> "a culture develops in which tribunal members can be seen by departments and ministers as an integral part of the process of development and its subsequent delivery by the policy department. This can compromise their independence severely."[71]

The government has, conversely, suggested that separation may make it more difficult to draw on the tribunal's expertise when developing policy.[72] Of themselves, these both seem weak arguments. On the one hand, there should be ways of changing the culture without an expensive structural change; on the other, tribunal chairmen and members can always respond to consultation on policy development without compromising their independence. The real danger is that the confidence of users is undermined by a perception that departments and tribunals are "common enterprises".[73] This has lain behind the steady expansion of the role of the LCD in respect of tribunals, and the continued extension of that role to more tribunals would be logical. Whether the upheaval of a structural change affecting all tribunals is justified is more debatable, particularly if the current arrangements are ECHR-compliant.

6. SUPPOSED ADVANTAGES OF TRIBUNALS AS COURT-SUBSTITUTES

2–015   The Franks Committee noted that tribunals have certain characteristics which often give them advantages over the courts: "cheapness, accessibility, freedom from technicality, expedition and expert knowledge of their particular subject".[74] Generally, tribunal proceedings are cheaper, speedier,[75] and more expert than courts of law. However, accessibility is hindered by the great complexity of the system of tribunals and the lack of

---

[67] Goods vehicle licensing appeals: Transport Act 1968, s.70, now the Goods Vehicles (Licensing of Operators) Act 1995, s.37.

[68] Air transport licensing: Civil Aviation Acts 1971, 1980, 1982: see R. Baldwin, *Regulating the Airlines* (1985). Other possible candidates were the Patents Appeal Tribunal (now the Patents Court), the Lands Tribunal and the Industrial Court (renamed the Industrial Arbitration Board in 1971 and the Central Arbitration Committee in 1976): Abel-Smith and Stevens (1968), p. 225.

[69] K. Hendry, "The Tasks of Tribunals: Some Thoughts" (1982) 1 C.J.Q. 253, 259; *cf.* J. A. G. Griffith, "Tribunals and Inquiries" (1959) 22 M.L.R. 125, 129.

[70] Above, para. 2-012.

[71] para. 2.21.

[72] Above, para. 2-012.

[73] Leggatt Report, para. 2.20.

[74] Cmnd. 218, p. 9.

[75] The problem of delays is, however, a frequently recurring theme of Annual Reports of the Council on Tribunals.

publicity given to their work. Moreover, the Council on Tribunals has stated that:

"Significant changes have ... taken place in the general constitutional and administrative climate. There is, for example, a movement towards greater formalism in procedures for settling disputes. The process started with reforms following the Franks Report which, in general, made tribunals more like courts. ... Since then the trend towards judicialisation has gathered momentum with the result that tribunals are becoming more formal, expensive and procedurally complex. Consequently they tend to become more difficult for an ordinary citizen to comprehend and cope with on his own."[76]

Associated with this movement are the Council's arguments in favour of the extension of legal aid to tribunals, the appointment of lawyer chairmen and the extension of rights of appeal to the courts. It has also been pointed out that, despite declarations by tribunals that they are not bound by precedent, the requirements of consistency and predictability of decision lead to the development of general principles and an informal *de facto* system of precedent,[77] especially as the decisions of certain tribunals are systematically reported.

Accordingly, it is perhaps more true today than ever that "such differences as there are between [courts and tribunals] are not in any sense fundamental but at most differences in degree ...."[78] In particular, it is not possible to argue that courts administer rules of law while tribunals administer both law and policy:

"[N]o such clear line can or should be drawn. Indeed it was the evolution of this myth which helped establish the tribunal system by convincing the judges of the ordinary courts that they were concerned with legal but not with policy questions. ... Properly understood, tribunals are a more modern form of court. In some cases they may have more discretion than the courts, and this is particularly true of the policy oriented tribunals. But certainly they have no more discretion than the Chancery Division has in handling trusts, wards or companies."[79]

Other, more pragmatic, reasons for establishing tribunals rather than entrusting matters to courts include the need not to overburden the judiciary,[80] the avoidance of ministerial responsibility for sensitive decisions

---

[76] *The Functions of the Council on Tribunals: Special Report by the Council* (Cmnd. 7805, 1980), p. 21.
[77] J. A. Farmer, *Tribunals and Government* (1974), pp. 174–180 and Chap. 3; below, para. 7-030.
[78] B. Abel-Smith and R. Stevens, *In Search of Justice* (1968), pp. 224, 228. This is perhaps not true of the policy-oriented tribunals: see Farmer (1974), p. 189.
[79] Abel-Smith and Stevens (1968), pp. 227–228.
[80] Franks Report, Cmnd. 218, p. 9. In evidence the Permanent Secretary to the Lord Chancellor had stated that the wholesale transfer of tribunal work to the courts would necessitate the creation of a large number of additional judges, particularly in the county courts. Much of the work did not need the services of a highly remunerated judge. Moreover, a dilution of the bench was undesirable. Since then, there has been a large increase in the number of such judges, but they have been directed towards criminal and not tribunal work: see below, para. 4-020.

and the easing of the workload of government departments.[81]

7. THE TRIBUNALS AND INQUIRIES ACT 1992

2–016   Apart from establishing the Council on Tribunals, the 1992 Act makes provision for the selection of chairmen of certain tribunals,[82] requires reasons to be given by Schedule 1 tribunals,[83] provides in many cases for an appeal on a point of law to the High Court[84] and renders inoperative most clauses in statutes passed before August 1, 1958 purporting to exclude judicial review.[85]

D. THE SYSTEM IN OUTLINE

1. COURTS

2–017   The courts structure is shown below in diagrammatic form, with a table showing the current workload. The main courts are considered in detail in section E.

2. TRIBUNALS

2–018   There are now approximately 70 types of tribunal within the jurisdiction of the Council on Tribunals,[86] and several others outside it. They may be roughly grouped according to subject matter.[87] The table below does not, however, purport to be a comprehensive list. Some tribunals are considered in detail in the next section.

     Other tribunals of note that were not included within the jurisdiction of the Council on Tribunals included the Criminal Injuries Compensation Board, set up under the royal prerogative to consider claims for *ex gratia*

---

[81] See K. Hendry, (1982) 1 C.J.Q. 253, 257–58, giving the immigration appeals system as an example. See also J. A. G. Griffith, (1959) 22 M.L.R. 125, 129 in relation to national insurance and rent tribunals: "the truth was that the Department did not wish to be bothered with these decisions. And this for the most obvious of reasons: that the Department did not mind what the decisions were, for no questions of policy were involved."

[82] s.6. See below, para. 4-016.

[83] s.10.

[84] s.11.

[85] Such clauses are not to prevent applications for certiorari or mandamus: see below, para. 18-053.

[86] An alphabetical list is published as an appendix to each Annual Report.

[87] See R. E. Wraith and P. G. Hutchesson, *Administrative Tribunals* (1973), Chap. 2. See also the table in Sir William Wade and C. F. Forsyth, *Administrative Law* (8th ed., 2000), pp. 929 *et seq.*

THE COURTS EXERCISING CRIMINAL JURISDICTION

HOUSE of LORDS

Appeal from the Divisional Court subject to the same conditions attached to appeal from the Court of Appeal.

Appeal from the Court of Appeal subject to the grant of a certificate by that court that a point of law of general public importance is involved, and to the granting of leave by that court or the House of Lords.

COURT of APPEAL
CRIMINAL DIVISION

Appeal from the Crown Court against conviction on indictment on a question of fact or law or against sentence. The leave of the Court of Appeal is normally needed.

QUEENS BENCH DIVISION
DIVISIONAL COURT

Appeal by way of Case Stated by prosecution or defence on a matter of law.

Appeal by way of Case Stated, on a question of law only, arising on appeal from the magistrates court.

CROWN COURT

Appeal from the magistrates court against conviction or sentence on a question of law or fact, or committal for sentence.

Committal for trial on indictment Jury trial in the Crown Court.

MAGISTRATES COURT

SUMMARY JURISDICTION

Trial of summary offences and other offences triable summarily with the consent of the accused.

COMMIT OR TRANSFER PROCEDURE

Initial procedural steps in respect of cases then committed or transferred for trial in the Crown Court.

THE PRINCIPAL COURTS EXERCISING CIVIL JURISDICTION

HOUSE of LORDS

Leapfrog appeal direct from the High Court provided (i)) all parties consent, and (ii) a point of law of general public importance is involved relating to the construction of an enactment or on a point on which the trial judge was bound by precedent. Certificate of trial judge and leave of House of Lords required.

Appeal from the Court of Appeal only by leave of that court or the House Lords

COURT of APPEAL
CIVIL DIVISION

Appeal from the High Court - permission normally required.

Appeal from the County Court - permission normally required.

HIGH COURT

Any division of the High Court may sit at any place in England or Wales, but sittings of the Queens Bench and Family Divisions are regularly held at the Crown Court first-tier centres.

QUEEN'S BENCH DIVISION

Trial of civil actions relating to contract and tort and other matters not within the scope of the Family and Chancery Divisions.

Claims for judicial review. Specialist courts: Admiralty, Commercial and Technology and Construction. Appeals from the final decisions of Circuit judge in county court (small-claims track and fast track).

FAMILY DIVISION

Trial of defended matrimonial proceedings, and actions relating to legitimacy, validity of marriage, the Married Woman's Property Act 1882 and other matters relating to matrimonial disputes and children.

Appeals from Family Proceedings Courts (Magistrates Courts) in family matters. (e.g. orders regarding children)

CHANCERY DIVISION

Trials of actions relating to mortgages, deeds, specific performance of contracts for the sale of land, partnerships, companies, bankruptcy, revenue matters and contentious probate business.

Divisional Court has certain limited jurisdiction consisting of appeals from the County Court in bankruptcy and land registration matters.

COUNTY COURT

JURISDICTION INCLUDES

(i)   Actions in contract or tort (except defamation);
(ii)   Equity matters (trusts, mortgages, partnerships etc.) where the value of the property does not exceed (30,000;
(iii) Actions for recovering land;
(iv)   Undefended and some defended matrimonial cases: proceedings under the Children Act 1989
(v)   Bankruptcy.

Workload of the courts: Proceedings commenced
Comparative Tables[88]

	1938	1963	1977	1982	1989	1995	2000
1. Appellate Courts							
Judicial Committee of							
the Privy Council	107	46	48	62	55	82	90
House of Lords:							
From courts in							
England & Wales	32	21	58	65	51	56	63
From elsewhere	11	18	6	6	12	16	16
Court of Appeal							
Civil Division	574	711	1,359	1,627	1,622	1,853	1,420
Criminal Division	—	2,065	6,399	6,674	7,076	8,187	7,740
High Court	263	484	1,029	1,482	2,535	4,674	4,897
2. Crown Court (disposals)							
Committals for trial	—	—	53,118	66,184	101,232	88,985	72,762
Committals for sentence	—	—	12,846	14,544	13,689	11,726	28,713
Appeals	—	—	15,497	20,775	16,860	26,062	14,359
3. High Court							
Chancery Division	9,826	16,137	14,651	17,119	30,813	42,251	37,333
Queen's Bench	83,641	123,998	176,128	164,396	288,287	153,624	26,876
4. Family matters							
(High Court, County Court							
and Family Proceedings							
Courts)							
Probate (grants issued)	149,752	—	251,703	279,127	231,883	248,947	264,397
Wardship	—	—	1,491	2,301	4,327	—	—
Adoption (orders made)	—	—	10,724	9,102	7,516	5,317	4,438
Public Law Applications	—	—	—	—	—	17,136	22,000
(Children)							
Private Law Applications	—	—	—	—	—	102,000	95,407
(Children)							
Dissolution of marriage	9,970	36,385	170,149	173,452	184,610	173,966	157,809
Nullity	263	919	1,095	921	478	881	452
Judicial separation	71	206	1,980	7,480	2,741	3,349	650
5. County courts							
Plaints entered/claims issued	1,262,402	1,543,324	1,673,966	2,048,568	2,615,508	2,445,248	1,871,923
Judgments on hearing	30,821	34,746	141,950	168,682	179,006	112,647	71,233
Trial	–	–	–	–	–	24,477	15,397
Arbitration/small claims	–	–	–	–	–	88,170	55,836
6. Magistrates' courts							
Indictable offences	—	—	470,000	539,000	449,000	497,000	493,000
Summary offences	—	—	458,000	469,000	568,000	587,000	627,000
(excluding motoring)							
Motoring offences	—	—	1,165,000	1,214,000	847,000	863,000	792,000
7. Other courts and tribunals							
Restrictive Practices Court	—	33	4	0	10	11	5
Employment Appeal	—	—	748	829	615	1,380	1,509
Tribunal							

[88] Based on *Judicial Statistics 2000* and earlier volumes, and (for magistrates' courts) *Criminal Statistics: England and Wales 2000* (Cm. 5312, 2001).

Table of Tribunals

General Subject Matter	Tribunal[89]	Jurisdiction	Cases decided in 2000 – England and Wales[90]	Judiciary[90]	Days sat/Hearings[90]	Success Rate[90]	Oral Hearings[90]
(a) *Social Administration*							
(1) Personal Welfare							
	Appeals Service Tribunals	See para. 2-037	178,521	2,002[91]	29,192[91]	40.8%[91]	85%[91]
	Social Security and Child Support Commissioners[92]	See para. 2-038	4,754	17	4,097	78%	9%
	Mental Health Review Tribunals	Applications for discharge by mental patients	11,266(E) / 567 (W)	672 (E) / 68 (W)	253 (E) / 220 (W)	7% (E) / 15% (W)	100%(E) / 55% (W)
(2) Education							
	Admission Appeal Panels[93]	Appeals against admission decisions	Community/Vol. 43,978 Controlled Foundation 11,443 Vol. Aided/Aided 7,234	–	–	38% / 23% / 27%	–
	Exclusion Appeal Panels[93]	Appeals against exclusion decisions	Parent 863 Governor 6	–	–	37% / 67%	–
	Independent Schools Tribunal	Complaints concerning regulation of independent schools	0	6	5	–	0%
	Registered Inspector of Schools Tribunal	Appeals in relation to registration of schools inspectors	0	–	0	–	–
	Schools Adjudicators	Adjudicators concerning school organisation plans, school establishment, closure or alteration and admissions arrangements	56	15	–	–	–

Special Educational Needs Tribunal[94]	Appeals in special educational needs cases	1,143	159	219	80%	100%
(3) Employment[95] Employment Tribunals	See para. 2-031	28,808	302	24,071	14%	100%
Police Appeals Tribunal	Appeals in police discipline cases	53	40	–	40%	30%
(4) National Health Service Health Authority Discipline Committees	Alleged breaches of terms of service	84	–	–	–	–
National Health Service Tribunal[96]	Appeals against a decision that a practitioner should be removed from the NHS	4	14	22	64% (E)	100% (E)
(5) Immigration/ Asylum[97] Asylum Support Adjudicators	Appeals concerning applications for support	69	–	69	44%	59%
Immigration Adjudicators[98]	Appeals against decisions of Immigration Officers to refuse leave to enter/ remain in the U.K. and in asylum cases	32,875	413	15,956	21%	98%
Immigration Appeal Tribunal	Appeals from Immigration Adjudicators and deportation orders	11,427	88	1,914	18%	–
(6) Residential Care Homes Registered Homes Tribunals[99]	Appeals concerning the registration of residential care, nursing and children's homes	25	45	92	32%	98%

General Subject Matter	Tribunal[89]	Jurisdiction	Cases decided in 2000 – England and Wales[90]	Judiciary[90]	Days Sat/Hearings[90]	Success Rate[90]	Oral Hearings[90]
(7) Criminal Injuries Compensation	Criminal Injuries Compensation Appeal Panel[1]	Appeals against review decisions of the Criminal Injuries Compensation Authority	8,109	158	570	40%	77%
(b) *Economic Matters* (8) Agriculture[2]	Agricultural Land Tribunals	Disputes between landlord and tenant in respect of notice to quit and bad husbandry and drainage disputes	65 (E) 9(W)	168 (E) 35(W)	24.5 (E) 10 (W)	– –	30.5% 15%
	Meat Hygiene Appeals Tribunals	Appeals relating to the licensing of premises	0	5	0	–	–
(9) Land/Housing[3]	Commons Commissioners	Determination of claims in respect of common land	218	1	1	–	100%
	Lands Tribunal	See para. 2-069	152	7	170	–	0%
	Rent Assessment Panels	Appeals concerning rents; disputes about leasehold valuation	8,185 (E) 267 (W)	382 (E) 37 (W)	– –	– –	– –
	Valuation Tribunals[4]	Rating and Council Tax Appeals	34,482 (E) 1,717 (W)	– (E) 234 (W)	– (E) 532 (W)	– –	– 95%
(10) Commerce[5]	Comptroller of Patents, Designs and Trade Marks	Adjudication in respect of patents, designs and trade marks	77 Patents *inter partes* 16 Patents *ex parte* 11 Designs *inter partes* 441 Trade marks *inter partes* 3,453 Trade marks *ex parte*	3 19 4 16 18	– – – – –	68% – 45% – –	– 100% 27% 92% 100%

Director General of Fair Trading[6]	Licensing decisions concerning consumer credit and estate agent activities	98	41	195	21%	33%
Copyright Tribunal	Disputes between citizens concerning licences for copyright material	0	10	0	–	–
Insolvency Practitioners Tribunal[7]	Disputes concerning authorisation of insolvency practitioners	1	20	5	0%	100%
Information Commissioner[8]	Complaints and registration concerning data controllers	4,039 (C) 33,421 (R)	–	–	–	–
Information Tribunal	Appeals from the Commissioner	–	5	–	–	–
(11) Transport[9] Civil Aviation Authority	Air transport and travel organisers licensing; air navigation order appeals	6	4	6	0%	100%
Parking Adjudicators (National Parking Adjudication Service)	Appeals against Penalty Charge Notices for unauthorised vehicle parking	1,371 (E) 90 (W)	19	– –	78% (E) 80% (W)	33% (E) 40% (W)
Parking Adjudicators (Parking and Traffic Appeals Service; London)	Appeals against Penalty Charge Notices for unauthorised vehicle parking	30,472	35	6	50%	28%

General Subject Matter	Tribunal[89]	Jurisdiction	Cases decided in 2000 – England and Wales[90]	Judiciary[90]	Days sat/Hearings[90]	Success Rate[90]	Oral Hearings[90]
	Traffic Commissioners	Licensing of public service passenger vehicles	7,899 (E) 605 (W)	13 (E) – (W)	1,507 (E) 125 (W)	90% 91%	6% 3%
	Transport Tribunal[10]	Appeals from Traffic Commissioners	46	8	19	–	100%
(c) Revenue	General Commissioners of Income Tax	Tax appeals	12,739 (E) 415 (W)	2,602 (E) 239 (W)	3,120 (E) 166(W)	– –	29% 23%
(12) Taxation	Special Commissioners of Income Tax	Tax appeals	174	15	133	–	98%
	Section 703 Tribunal	References concerning anti-avoidance provisions of the Income and Corporation Taxes Act 1988	14	7	14	–	0%
	VAT and Duties Tribunal	Appeals concerning VAT, customs and excise duties, landfill tax and insurance premium tax	604	123	1,531	–	–
	National Savings Bank and National Savings Stock Register Adjudicator	Determinations of cases where the right to a sum of money or a claim of financial loss is disputed	4	1	–	50%	50%

(d) *Pensions*						
(13) Pensions[11]						
Pensions Appeal Tribunals	Appeals from the Secretary of State	3,416	122	915	28%	100%
Occupational Pensions Regulatory Authority	Determinations concerning occupational and stakeholder pensions schemes	11	10	30	64%	18%
Pensions Compensation Board	Determination of applications for compensation where employer insolvent	0	–	2	–	–
Pensions Ombudsman	Complaints and disputes concerning occupational and personal pension schemes	185	–	–	–	–

89 Other miscellaneous tribunals include the Antarctic Act Tribunal, the Foreign Compensation Commission, the Horse Race Betting Levy Appeal Tribunal, Justice and Clerks Indemnification appointed person, the Mines and Quarries Tribunal, the Misuse of Drugs Tribunal, the Wireless Telegraphy Appeal Tribunal, and the National Lottery Commission (no cases in 2000).

90 Figures from Annual Report of the Council on Tribunals 2000–2001, Appendix A. Where a dash is shown data is either irrelevant or unavailable. "Judiciary": total number of Chairmen and members in the Tribunal's pool; "Days Sat/Hearings": total number of days that a panel or arbiter sat to consider cases; "Success Rate": % of total cases decided in sample period in which the Tribunal found in favour of the appeal or application either in whole or in part; "Oral Hearings": % of oral as opposed to "paper" hearings.

91 Figures include Scotland.

92 Figures are for England.

93 Figures relate to the 1999/2000 school year.

94 Reconstituted as the Special Educational Needs and Disability Tribunal by the Special Educational Needs and Disability Act 2001.

95 Other tribunals include the Industrial Arbitration Tribunal, the Industrial Training Levy Exemption Referees, the Reserve Forces Appeals Tribunals (no cases in 2000) and the Reserve Forces Reinstatement Committees and Umpires (2 hearings, no decisions in 2000).

96 Abolished by the Health and Social Care Act 2001 — with appeals lying to a Family Health Services Appeal Authority.

97 There is also an Immigration Services Tribunal.

98 Figures are from April 1, 2000 to March 31, 2001.

99 Replaced by Protection of Children Tribunals Act under the Care Standards Act 2000.

1 Figures include Scotland.

2 Other tribunals include agricultural arbitrators appointed under the Agricultural Holdings Act 1986 (no reliable figures for 2000); the Controller of Plant Variety Rights, the Plant Varieties and Seeds Tribunal, the Dairy Produce Quota Tribunal, Forestry Committees and the Sea Fish Licence Tribunal (no cases in 2000).

3 There are also London Building Acts Tribunals (no cases in 2000)

4 Figures are for England. One hearing may deal with many different cases, particularly where an individual's registration of common rights is concerned as these are each treated as one case.

5 Figures are for the fiscal year April 2000 — March 2001.

6 Figures include Scotland. There is also the Competition Commission Appeal Tribunal (no cases in 2000).

7 There is also a Banking Appeal Tribunal, a Building Societies Appeal Tribunal, a Financial Services Appeal Tribunal and a Friendly Societies Appeal Tribunal.

8 Figures are for April 1, 1999 to March 31, 2000.

9 There is also an Aircraft and Shipbuilding Industrial Arbitration Tribunal (no cases in 2000).

10 Figures include Scotland.

11 There are also Fire Service Pensions Appeal Tribunals and Police Pensions Appeal Tribunals (no cases in 2000).

compensation from the victims of crimes of violence,[12] and the Housing Benefit Review Boards set up[13] to hear appeals by claimants for rent or rates rebate or rent allowance (housing benefit) who remain dissatisfied with their local authority's determination of their claims.[14] Both areas now fall under the Council's jurisdiction. A Criminal Injuries Compensation Appeals Panel under the Council's jurisdiction was established by the Criminal Injuries Compensation Act 1995, and has dealt with applications from April 1, 1996, under a new statutory scheme.[15] The Board continued in parallel, dealing with cases arising earlier, until April 2000. Appeals in housing benefit cases have been transferred to Appeal Service tribunals,[16] a change long urged by the Council on Tribunals.

E. PARTICULAR COURTS AND TRIBUNALS

2–019 In this section we consider the courts and tribunals that feature most prominently in the English legal system, by virtue either of their status in the hierarchy or their caseload. For reasons of space it is not possible to cover all tribunals in detail. We have not divided this section into "courts" and "tribunals" but have incorporated coverage of certain tribunals approximately in accordance with their position in the overall hierarchy.

1. MAGISTRATES' COURTS

(a) Introduction

2–020 Magistrates' courts are the inferior criminal courts. In addition they exercise certain family law, administrative law and minor civil functions. England and Wales is divided into "commission areas" and there is a "commission of the peace" for each such area. The areas used to be specified in primary legislation, but this is now done by statutory instrument made by the Lord Chancellor.[17] The Justices of the Peace (Commission Areas) Order 1999[18]

---

[12] See the White Paper on Compensation for Victims of Crimes of Violence (Cmnd. 2323, 1964); Annual Reports of the Board; Review of the Criminal Injuries Compensation Scheme: Report of an Interdepartmental Working Party (HMSO, 1978). The Board was due to be reconstituted as a statutory tribunal under Part VII of the Criminal Justice Act 1988, and placed under the Council's jurisdiction, but implementation was delayed: see *R. v. Secretary of State for the Home Department, ex. p. Fire Brigades Union* [1995] 2 W.L.R. 464, below, para. 5-016, and Part VII ultimately repealed by the Criminal Inquiries Compensation Act 1995.

[13] Housing Benefits Regulations 1982 (S.I. 1982 No. 1124): see the Housing Benefits (General) Regulations 1987 (S.I. 1987, No. 1971), regs 81–87 and Sched. 7.

[14] These Boards comprise members of the authority whose officers' decisions are in question. The claim of such Boards to be independent was not supportable.

[15] Now the Criminal Injuries Compensation Scheme 2001: see *www.cica.gov.uk*.

[16] See below, para. 2-037.

[17] Justices of the Peace Act 1997, s.1, substituted by the Access to Justice Act 1999, s.74(1). An area may not consist of an area partly within and partly outside Greater London: s.1(2).

[18] S.I. 1999 No. 3010, as amended by S.I. 2000 Nos 677,1429, 2238, 3054, S.I. 2001 Nos 696, 2530.

provides for 40 areas in England (outside London), the City and five others in London and five in Wales, largely defined by reference to the areas of magistrates' courts committees. An area may be altered by the Lord Chancellor by statutory instrument, either acting of his own motion or at the request of a magistrates' courts committee.[19] England and Wales are also divided by orders made by the Lord Chancellor into "petty sessions areas" which either consist of the whole of a commission area or an area wholly included within a commission area. Their names are also specified by the Lord Chancellor.[20] A petty sessions area may be altered by the Lord Chancellor, normally on the basis of a draft order submitted by a magistrates' courts committee.[21] Each petty sessions area has its own "bench" of justices with an elected chairman and one or more deputy chairmen.[22] Each justice is a justice of the peace for the commission area and not merely for the petty session area in which he or she normally sits.[23]

(b) Criminal jurisdiction

Magistrates' courts are involved in some way in virtually all criminal prosecutions. Proceedings may be commenced by a summons or an arrest warrant issued by a justice of the peace.[24] Magistrates' courts try those offences triable only summarily, and have responsibilities in the procedure whereby persons charged with offences triable only on indictment are transferred for trial in the Crown Court. Where proceedings are brought in respect of the intermediate category of offences "triable either way", the court must decide whether the offence appears more suitable for summary trial or for trial on indictment. Once this is decided, and subject to the right of the accused to insist on trial by a jury, the court proceeds either to summary trial or the committal for trial procedure.[25]

A magistrates' court must be composed of at least two justices of the peace[26] unless there is express provision for a single justice to act,[27] as there is, for example, in the case of issuing a summons.[28] District Judges

2–021

---

[19] 1997 Act, s.32A, inserted by the 1999 Act, s.74(2).

[20] 1997 Act, s.4, substituted by the Access to Justice Act 1999, s.75(1). See the Petty Sessions Areas Order 1999 (S.I. 1999 No. 3009), as amended by S.I. 1999 No. 3220, S.I. 2000 Nos 515, 517, 628, 675, 694. See also the Petty Sessions Areas (Divisions and Names) Regulations 1988 (S.I. 1988 No. 1698), as amended by S.I. 1992 No. 709, S.I. 1996 No. 576 and S.I. 2001 No. 609.

[21] 1997 Act, s.33, as substituted by the 1999 Act, s.75(2), and 34, as amended by *ibid.* s.75(3).

[22] See the Justices of the Peace (Size and Chairmanship of Bench) Rules 1995 (S.I. 1995 No. 971), as amended by S.I. 1999 No. 2396. For proposals for amendments to these rules, *inter alia*, introducing postal voting and Bench Training and Development Committees, see LCD Consultation Paper (March 2001), LCD website.

[23] 1997 Act, s.5(1). This facilitates the cross-remanding of cases from one petty sessions area to another within the same commission area: see *R. v. Avon Magistrates' Courts Committee, ex p. Bath Law Society* [1988] Q.B. 409.

[24] Magistrates' Courts Act 1980, s.l. The other methods of commencing proceedings are by an arrest without warrant and by a voluntary bill of indictment: see below, Chap. 14. Only this last method bypasses the magistrates' court. As to the geographical limits of the jurisdiction of magistrates' courts, see the 1980 Act, s.2, as amended.

[25] These proceedings are explained more fully in the chapters on criminal procedure.

[26] The office of justice of the peace is considered below, Chap. 4.

[27] Magistrates' Courts Act 1980, s.121(1). Normally, three justices sit (three being the maximum: S.I. 1995 No. 971, r.3).

[28] *ibid.* s.26.

(magistrates' Courts) (formerly stipendiary magistrates)[29] normally sit alone.

(c) Criminal proceedings concerning children[30]

(i) Youth courts

2–022 A youth court[31] must be composed of not more than three justices, and must normally include a man and a woman.[32] The justices must be drawn from the youth court panel appointed by the justices for each petty sessions area at their annual meeting.[33] They must be "specially qualified for dealing with youth cases".[34] Each panel elects a chairman and deputy chairman, one of whom must normally preside over each youth court. A district Judge (magistrates' courts) is qualified to sit as a member of a youth court without being a member of the panel[35] and a youth court may consist of such a judge sitting alone.[36] If the court comprises a district Judge (magistrates' court) and other justices, the district Judge normally presides.[37] A court may be held in buildings set apart for the purpose, or, as is more usually the case, in a courtroom normally used for an adult magistrates' court.[38]

---

[29] See below, para. 4-013.

[30] For research into the "consumer's" view of the former juvenile justice system see H. Parker *et al., Receiving Juvenile Justice* (1981).

[31] Prior to October 1, 1992, youth courts were known as juvenile courts; the change of name was effected by the Criminal Justice Act 1991, s.70. See generally Home Office Circular 30/1992, *Criminal Justice Act 1991: Young People and the Youth Court.* The main changes were that the youth court, not the magistrates' court, now deals with 17-year-olds, and new sentencing powers were conferred: see B. Gibson, (1992) *The Magistrate* 109; W. Gordon *et al., Introduction to the Youth Court* (1996); T. Moore and T. Wilkinson, *Youth Court Guide* (2001).

[32] The Youth Courts (Constitution) Rules 1954 (S.I. 1954 No. 1711), as amended, r.12. References to juvenile courts are to be construed as references to youth courts: Criminal Justice Act 1991, s.70(2).

[33] Children and Young Persons Act 1933, Sched. 2, as amended. In London, the panels are appointed by the Lord Chancellor. In 1986, the Lord Chancellor, having accepted a recommendation from the Judicial Studies Board (see para. 4-029.), required a minimum of 12 sittings per annum for each panel member, with a suggested target of 15 sittings per annum.

[34] 1954 Rules, r.1. The rules do not specify any qualifications. The Home Secretary has suggested that they "should include some direct practical experience of dealing with young persons (*e.g.* through working with youth organisations, teaching or similar work) and a real appreciation of the surroundings and way of life of the children who are likely to come before courts". The most suitable age for first appointment would be between 30 and 40 and no one should normally be first appointed when over 50: Home Office Circular No. 138/1979, printed in *Clarke Hall and Morrison on Children* (10th ed., 1985), pp. E.390–399. See also Circulars 67/1982 (pp. E.514–523) and 61/1983 (pp. E.699–718).

[35] 1933 Act, Sched. 2, para. 2, as amended by the Access to Justice Act 1999, Sched. 11, para. 12.

[36] *ibid.* para. 2A, inserted by the 1999 Act, Sched. 11, para. 12.

[37] 1954 Rules, r.13, as amended by S.I. 2000 No. 1873, r.3.

[38] Guidance on the design of youth courts is given in *The Youth Court 2001: The Changing Culture of the Youth Court: Good Practice Guide* (HO/LCD, March 2001).

(ii) Jurisdiction

Criminal proceedings may not be instituted against children who are under **2–023** 10: it is conclusively presumed that they cannot be guilty of any offence.[39] Where children between 10 and 14 are prosecuted it must be proved that they were children of a "mischievous discretion", *i.e.* that they knew that what they were doing was, legally or morally seriously wrong.[40] Young persons of 14 and over are regarded as fully responsible for their acts.

The former juvenile courts had jurisdiction in both criminal cases and care proceedings. However, the Children Act 1989 transferred care proceedings to the family proceedings courts.[41] Criminal proceedings against children and young persons[42] must normally take place in a youth court. The main exceptions are that an adult magistrates' court *must* deal with children or young persons where they are charged jointly with an adult and *may* do so where different charges are made against an adult arising out of the same or connected circumstances or where either an adult or a child or young person is charged with aiding, abetting, causing, procuring, allowing or permitting the other's alleged offence.[43] The youth court must try the case summarily except (1) where the charge is homicide in which case the child or young person *must* be committed for trial in the Crown Court and (2) in the case of certain other offences where the court must commit for trial if specified conditions are established.[44]

Any person may institute criminal proceedings against a child or young person,[45] but they must notify the appropriate local authority.[46]

---

[39] Children and Young Persons Act 1933, s.50, as amended by the 1963 Act, s.16(1). At common law the relevant age was seven. Section 4 of the Children and Young Persons Act 1969 provided for the age to be raised to 14, but was repealed, unimplemented, by the Criminal Justice Act 1991, s.72.

[40] The presumption that a child of this age was incapable of committing an offence, confirmed as a continuing part of the common law by the House of Lords in *C (a minor) v. D.P.P.* [1995] 2 W.L.R. 383, was abolished by the Crime and Disorder Act 1998, s. 34. There is now an evidential burden on the defence to raise the issue.

[41] See below.

[42] This term applies to children and young persons under 18. For most purposes under the 1933 Act "child" is defined as a person under 14 and "young person" as a person of 14 or over but under 18. The term "child" is differently defined for other purposes: see *Halsbury's Laws of England* (4th ed.), Vol. 5(3), Reissue, para. 3.

[43] Children and Young Persons Act 1933, s.46, as extended by the 1963 Act, s.18. Applications for bail or for a remand may be heard by any justice or justices (1933 Act, s.46(2)). The adult magistrates' court will normally try the child or young person summarily but may or may be required to proceed with a view to committing him or her for trial in the Crown Court (Magistrates' Courts Act 1980, s.24, as amended) or remit for trial (*ibid.* s.29, as amended) or sentence (Children and Young Persons Act 1969, s.7(8), as amended) in the youth court.

[44] Magistrates' Courts Act 1980, s.24(1), as amended. These are: (1) that the offence is one in which the Crown Court can invoke the power under the Powers of Criminal Courts (Sentencing) Act 2000, s.91 to impose a long sentence of detention and the magistrates' or youth court considers that if the defendant is found guilty it ought to be possible for that power to be invoked; (2) that the defendant is charged jointly with an adult and the court considers it necessary in the interests of justice to commit them both for trial. There is also provision for committal of specified associated offences: s.24(1A) (inserted by the Crime and Disorder Act 1998, s.47(6)) and s.24(2), as amended.

[45] The provisions of section 5 of the Children and Young Persons Act 1969 which were to restrict private prosecutions were repealed, unimplemented, by the Criminal Justice Act 1991, s.72.

[46] 1969 Act, s.5(8), (9).

(iii) Procedure

2–024   The procedure of youth courts is less formal than for adult magistrates' courts.[47] Only members and officers of the court, the parties, their lawyers, witnesses and other persons directly concerned, press representatives, and other persons specially authorised may be present.[48] There are limits as to what may be reported.[49] In the case of children and young persons dealt with summarily the expression "finding of guilt" must be used instead of "conviction" and the expression "order made upon a finding of guilt" instead of "sentence".[50] Steps have been taken to change the culture of the youth court, with greater openness, engaging directly with the offender, feedback on the effectiveness of sentencing and a less adversarial setting.[51]

(d) Family proceedings

2–025   Magistrates have an extensive jurisdiction in family and child law matters.[52] The list includes powers to make orders for financial provision for, or the protection of, parties to a marriage and children of the family, orders under the Children Act 1989, the Child Support Act 1991, the Family Law Act 1996,[53] the Crime and Disorder Act 1998,[54] and adoption orders. Proceedings concerning these matters used to be termed "domestic proceedings" and the courts when hearing them "domestic courts", but they were renamed "family proceedings" and "family proceedings courts" by the Children Act 1989.[55] The court must be composed of two or three lay justices, or a district judge (magistrates' courts) sitting as chairman with one or two lay justices, or if neither of those is practicable, a district judge (magistrates' courts) sitting alone. In the case of the first two options, the court must, so far as practicable, include both a man and a woman.[56] Lay justices must be appointed from a family panel constituted on a similar basis to the youth court panel and district Judges must be nominated to sit as a

---

[47]   See the Magistrates' Courts (Children and Young Persons) Rules 1992 (S.I. 1992 No. 2071), as amended by S.I. 1997 No. 2420, S.I. 1998 No. 2167, S.I. 1999 No. 1343.

[48]   Children and Young Persons Act 1933, s.47(2) as amended by the Children and Young Persons Act 1963, s.17(2) and the Youth Justice and Criminal Evidence Act 1999, Sched. 4, para. 2(3).

[49]   1933 Act, s.49, as substituted by the Criminal Justice and Public Order Act 1994, s.49, and the Youth Justice and Criminal Evidence Act 1999, Sched. 2, para. 3. Reporting restrictions may be lifted in the public interest: subs. (4A), inserted by the Crime (Sentences) Act 1997, s.45; for government guidances see HO/LCD Circular, *Opening up Youth Court Proceedings* (June 1998); see also *McKerry v. Teesdale and Wear Valley JJ.* [2001] C.O.D. 199 (power to be exercised "with great care, caution and circumspection").

[50]   *ibid.* s.59.

[51]   See White Paper, *No More Excuses. A New Approach to Tackling Youth Crime in England* (Cm. 3809, 1997), Chap. 9; HO/LCD, *The Youth Court 2001: The Changing Culture of the Youth Court: Good Practice Guide* (2001).

[52]   Magistrates' Courts Act 1980, s.65, as amended.

[53]   Part IV, concerning family homes and domestic violence: see the Family Law Act 1996 (Part IV) (Allocation of Proceedings) Order 1997 (S.I. 1997 No. 1896).

[54]   ss.11 and 12 (child safety orders).

[55]   1980 Act, s.67(l), as amended by the 1989 Act, Sched. 11, Pt. II, para. 8.

[56]   *ibid.* s.66, substituted by the Access to Justice Act 1999, Sched. 11, paras 26, 27.

member of a family proceedings court by the Lord Chancellor.[57]

The law relating to child care was substantially altered by the 1989 Act, which re-stated the respective powers and responsibilities of parents, courts and local authorities. The courts have power to grant, *inter alia*, "contact orders" (replacing access orders) and "residence orders" (replacing custody orders) and a variety of emergency orders; the grounds on which care or supervision orders may be granted were simplified and narrowed.[58] The magistrates' courts, county courts and High Courts have concurrent jurisdiction under the 1989 Act and the Adoption Act 1976; the Lord Chancellor has power to make orders specifying the level of court and the description of court at which different classes of proceedings should be commenced, and makes provision for the transfer of proceedings.[59] Proceedings under the 1989 Act are normally to be commenced in the magistrates' court.[60] Most orders will, however, continue to be made in divorce or matrimonial proceedings which are commenced in the county court.[61]

The courts have power to make care or supervision orders in respect of children under 17 (16 if married), if they are satisfied that (a) the child is suffering or likely to suffer significant harm; and (b) this is attributable to (i) the care given to the child, or likely to be given to him or her if the order were not made, not being what it would be reasonable to expect a parent to give; or (ii) the child's being beyond parental control.[62] The welfare of the child is the paramount consideration, and the court must take other specified matters into account.[63] Under a care order, the child is taken into the care of the local authority; a supervision order places the child under the supervision of a designated local authority.[64]

(e) Civil jurisdiction

Apart from family proceedings, magistrates' courts have powers in relation to certain other civil matters, including enforcement of the payment of rates, the council tax, income tax and charges for supplies of gas, electricity and water. They also have an important jurisdiction in respect of the granting of liquor licences to public houses and clubs, and licences for bookmakers, betting offices, and premises for gaming and bingo. Finally, there is a vast

2–026

---

[57] *ibid.* s. 67, as amended by the Children Act 1989, Sched. 11, para. 8, and the Access to Justice Act 1999, Sched. 11, paras 26, 28; the Family Proceedings Courts (Constitution) Rules 1991 (S.I. 1991 No. 1405), as amended by S.I. 2000 No. 1873; the Family Proceedings Courts (Constitution) (Metropolitan Area) Rules 1991 (S.I. 1991 No. 1426), as amended by S.I. 2000 No. 1873.

[58] See below.

[59] Children Act 1989, s.92 and Sched. 11; Courts and Legal Services Act 1990, s.9.

[60] Children (Allocation of Proceedings) Order 1991 (S.I. 1991 No. 1677), as amended by S.I. 1993 No. 624, S.I. 1994 Nos 2164 and 3138, S.I. 1995 No. 1649, S.I. 1997 No. 1897, S.I. 1999 No. 2166, S.I. 1999 No. 524, S.I. 2001 No. 775.

[61] See below, para. 2-045.

[62] Children Act 1989, Part IV.

[63] *ibid.* s.l.

[64] *ibid.* s.31, as amended.

number[65] of statutory provisions enabling appeals to be brought against administrative decisions of various kinds.

(f) Appeals[66]

2–027 Appeals lie from a magistrates' court either as of right to the Crown Court,[67] where proceedings take the form of a complete rehearing, or to the High Court by a procedure whereby the magistrates state a case for the opinion of the High Court on a point of law. In family matters the appeal is heard by the Family Division, otherwise the appeal will lie to the Queen's Bench Division. Any further appeal from the High Court lies to the House of Lords in criminal cases and to the Court of Appeal and House of Lords in civil cases.

(g) Administration

2–028 Procedural rules are made by the Lord Chancellor after consultation with a Rule Committee, comprising the Lord Chief Justice, the President of the Family Division, the Senior District Judge (Chief Magistrate) and other persons appointed by the Lord Chancellor, who must include a justices' clerk, and specified lawyers.[68]

The administrative arrangements were substantially reformed by the Police and Magistrates' Courts Act 1994,[69] following the White Paper, *A New Framework for Local Justice*.[70] The previous arrangements were that there was a "Magistrates' Courts Committee" for each non-metropolitan county, metropolitan district and outer London borough, and in Inner London (105 in total). Each committee was responsible for (*inter alia*) the appointment of staff and the provision of courses of instruction; it also determined what accommodation and equipment should be provided, although the actual provision was made by the local authority. The local authority met the committee's expenses, including salary. The responsible Department was the Home Office, which provided an 80 per cent grant. In the 1980s the Home Office took a greater interest in the management of the service and instituted a number of measures to encourage greater economy and efficiency.[71]

There was some debate as to whether Magistrates' Courts Committees would be able to respond to the challenge of improving the management of

---

[65] D. Price, *Appeals* (1982) pp. 53–96, including appeals against refusal of a petshop licence, of a driving licence or a knacker's yard licence, a notice requiring a fire certificate and a notice requiring that an earth closet be replaced by a water closet. For discussion of the jurisdiction of magistrates to entertain appeals concerned with the licensing of pilots see G. Browne, "The Admiralty Jurisdiction of Inner London Magistrates" (1987) 151 J.P.N. 23.

[66] See generally, Chap. 18.

[67] See below, para. 2-051.

[68] Magistrates' Courts Act 1980, s.144, and see also ss.145–146; s.144, as amended by the Courts and Legal Services Act 1990, Sched. 18, para. 25(7), requires the appointment of one person with a Supreme Court qualification under s.71 of the 1990 Act, and one with the right to conduct litigation in the Supreme Court.

[69] ss.69–92.

[70] Cm. 1829, 1992.

[71] See generally, J. W. Raine, *Local Justice* (1989), Chap. 5.

the service.[72] A Home Office scrutiny[73] concluded that they would not, and recommended that they be replaced by a Magistrates' Courts Agency, an executive agency accountable to, but operationally independent of, the Home Office. The scrutiny found the present arrangements had led to a service which was highly fragmented, lacked a coherent management structure and failed to deliver value for money. Instead, there should be a national service, funded entirely by the government, but with maximum delegation of managerial responsibility and control of resources to the local level. Overall policy responsibility should rest with government, but the service should not be administered directly by a government department, so as to minimise the risk of government interference in judicial decision-making.

In the event, the government decided against establishing a national service, in view of the cost and the widespread opposition to the proposal among magistrates and court staff.[74] Instead, the White Paper proposed that responsibility for the service be transferred to the Lord Chancellor's Department (the Lord Chancellor already being responsible for the appointment of magistrates[75]). Magistrates' Courts Committees should have a more clearly defined management role, with a wider range of membership and effective administrative support. Area services should be combined, moving in due course from 105 to 50 or 60 management units. Committees should also be smaller in size; senior managers should have clearer personal accountability to committees for performance standards, in the context of systematic planning and performance review and a new overall policy framework. Finally, a magistrates' courts inspectorate should be established. Steps already in train were the introduction of cash limits to the grant from April 1992, a major programme of management training, the development of a standard court computer system, the formation of a best practice group to issue guidance and a review of court procedure.[76] Furthermore, committees would be encouraged to produce strategic plans.

The necessary legislative changes were made by the Police and Magistrates' Courts Act 1994.[77] There continued to be a Magistrates' Court Committee for each non-metropolitan county, metropolitan district and outer London borough, the Inner London area and the City of London.[78] However, the Lord Chancellor now had power, after consultation, to combine or otherwise alter committee areas (previously a "joint committee area" of two or more existing areas could be established but only

2–029

---

[72] J. W. Raine, (1986) 150 J.P.N. 260 at 280: J. Bowden and J. W. Raine, (1988) 152 J.P.N. 489 at 501, 521.

[73] *Magistrates' Courts: Report of a Scrutiny 1989* (HMSO, 1989 (the Le Vay Scrutiny)). For reactions, see (1989) 153 J.P.N. 489, 553, 627–8, 660–1; T. Kavanagh, *ibid.* p. 589; R. Burriss, *ibid.* p. 655; W. M. S. Tildesley, *ibid.* p. 670; J. W. Raine, *ibid.* p. 684; R. L. Jones, (1990) 154 J.P.N. 538. Coopers & Lybrand Deloitte were commissioned to cost the options for change: *ibid.* p. 666. *Cf.* the less radical proposals of the Justices' Clerks Society: *Administering Magistrates' Courts: The Role of the Justices' Clerk* (1989).

[74] See White Paper, Cm. 1829, p. 5.

[75] See below, para. 4-003.

[76] Cm.1829, pp. 3, 4.

[77] See S. Baker and J. English, *A Guide to the Police and Magistrates' Courts Act 1994* (1994).

[78] Justices of the Peace Act 1979, s.19, as amended by the Local Government Act 1985, s.12 and the 1994 Act, Sched. 8, para. 4.

on the application of the committees concerned.)[79] A substantial
programme of amalgamations followed. The legislative framework was
further changed by the Access to Justice Act 1999.[80]

Magistrates' Courts Committees have such functions as are conferred on
them by legislation and such other functions "relating to matters of an
administrative character" as are authorised by the Lord Chancellor.[81]
England and Wales outside Greater London is divided into areas specified
by the Lord Chancellor, with a committee for each area. An area must
consist of the whole of one or more commission areas or be included wholly
within one such area, and comprise the whole or one or more petty sessions
areas.[82] The Lord Chancellor may alter areas, on the basis of written
proposals from the relevant committee, or (after consultation) without such
proposals. The Lord Chancellor must be satisfied that the changes are likely
to contribute to an overall increase in the efficiency of the administration of
magistrates' courts.[83] Each committee is to comprise justices of the peace for
the area, chosen in accordance with regulations; it may also include persons
(who need not be justices of the peace) co-opted by the committee with the
Lord Chancellor's approval, or appointed by the Lord Chancellor.[84] The
relevant regulations[85] provide that a committee must consist of not more
than 12 members including (unless the Lord Chancellor directs otherwise)
any co-opted member or member appointed by the Lord Chancellor.
Members are appointed by a selection panel and serve for three year terms
(with a maximum of nine years); co-opted members serve for one year, but
can be reappointed, but not, unless there are exceptional circumstances, for
periods totalling more than three years. The committee must appoint its
own chairman, and must at least once a year meet in public.[86] In London,
the Greater London Magistrates' Courts Authority has been established as
the Magistrates' Court Committee for Greater London.[87]

Each committee is responsible for the efficient and effective administration of the magistrates' courts for its area. Committees may be given
directions by the Lord Chancellor and may be required to submit reports
and plans to him.[88] Each committee must appoint a justices' chief executive
from a short-list of one or more persons approved by the Lord Chancellor.
The justices' chief executive must make arrangements for the effective and
efficient administration of the magistrates' courts for the area. This includes
acting as clerk to the authority, exercising specific functions conferred by
legislation, allocating responsibilities among justices' clerks and committee
staff and determining the administrative procedures to be followed by

---

[79] 1994 Act, s.69.
[80] ss.81–83, substituting and inserting ss.27–30C in the Justices of the Peace Act 1997.
[81] 1997 Act, s.27.
[82] *ibid.* s.27A. See the Magistrates' Courts Committee Areas Order 1999 (S.I. 1999 No. 3008),
as amended by S.I. 2000 No. 676 and S.I. 2001 No. 695. There are 37 in England and four in
Wales.
[83] *ibid.* s.27B.
[84] *ibid.* s.28.
[85] Magistrates' Courts Committee (Constitution) Regulations 1999 (S.I. 1999 No. 2395), as
amended by S.I. 2001 No. 2711.
[86] *ibid.* s.30.
[87] *ibid.* ss. 30A, 30B.
[88] 1997 Act, ss.31, 37.

them.[89] He or she is also to be the collecting officer.[90] The committee also appoints one or more justices' clerks.[91]

Fears of a threat to judicial independence were met by the provision that when exercising any legal function[92] a justices' clerk is not subject to the direction of the justices' chief executive or any other person or body, and a member of staff of the magistrates' courts committee is not subject to the direction of any person or body other than a justices' clerk.[93]

Financial support is still to be provided by local authorities, with an 80 per cent grant from the Lord Chancellor's Department.[94] The "paying authority"[95] or authorities must provide the accommodation, and the goods and services, proper for the performance of the magistrates, the magistrates' courts committee or justices' clerks for the area, unless the committee gives notice that it intends to obtain any item(s) otherwise than from the authority (or authorities) or the committee is required by regulations[96] to obtain them elsewhere. The accommodation to be provided, the salaries to be paid and the nature and amount of expenses to be incurred are to be determined by the committee after consultation with the paying authority; a paying authority aggrieved by such a determination may appeal to the Lord Chancellor, whose decision is binding.

The Lord Chancellor appoints H.M. Inspectors of the Magistrates' Courts Service and has wide default powers.[97] The inspectorate has reported a substantial improvement in the performance of MCCs from 1997.　　**2–030**

Overall, the government intended to reinforce its key aims of "enhancing accountability, reducing idiosyncrasy, and increasing efficiency", by adopting the twin strategies of "curbing the autonomy of the professionals" by standardising procedures and "curbing the autonomy of the agencies" by forming them into amalgamated hierarchies and establishing systems of objectives and targets.[98] The effectiveness of these arrangements was, however, doubted by the Auld *Review of the Criminal Courts in England and Wales.*[99] The boundaries between the bench and the MCC were not clear; MCCs lacked budgetary control in that they simply bid each year to the maximum permitted by the Treasury; as budgets were effectively pre-

[89] Justices of the Peace Act 1997, ss. 40, 41, as amended by the Access to Justice Act 1999, ss. 83(3), 87, 88(3), Sched. 12, paras 9, 11, Sched. 15. See the Justices Chief Executives and Justices' Clerks (Appointment) Regulations 1999 (S.I. 1999 No. 2397) and further below, para. 4-011.

[90] 1997 Act, s.41A, inserted by the 1999 Act, s.91.

[91] 1997 Act, s. 42. See further below, para. 4-011.

[92] *i.e.* any function exercisable by one or more justices of the peace or the functions of advising justices about or bringing their attention to matters of law (including procedure and practice): s.48(2).

[93] s.48(1), substituted by the Access to Justice Act 1999, s.89(1), for a differently worded guarantee of independence originally set out in the Justices of the Peace Act 1979, s.30A, inserted by the 1994 Act, s.78.

[94] 1997 Act, ss. 55–57.

[95] *i.e.* any county, county borough or unitary district council whose area comprises all or part of the area to which the committee relates: 1997 Act, s.55 (10).

[96] Under the 1997 Act, s.59E (inserted by the 1999 Act, s.84), under which the Lord Chancellor may make regulations concerning the provision of standard goods and services.

[97] 1997 Act, ss. 38, 62, 63. See the Annual Reports of the Inspectorate. The Inspectorate carries out inspections of particular MCCs and conducts thematic reviews.

[98] J. W. Raine and M. J. Willson, *Managing Criminal Justice* (1993), p. 209 and *passim.*

[99] HMSO, 2001 Chap. 3 and 7.

determined by the cash limits, the paying local authorities had little incentive to monitor or challenge the budget-setting processes; accounting arrangements were unsatisfactory, particularly where a MCC fell in two local authority areas; audit arrangements were patchy; there were considerable variations in practice from area to area; co-operation with the Court Service, which administers the Crown Court, was poor. The Report had little difficulty in recommending the creation of a unified court supported by a single centrally funded executive agency, organised managerially within each circuit (if consistent with the efficient and effective operation of civil and family courts) on the basis of the 42 criminal justice areas. Implementation of national policy would be the responsibility of local managers working in close liaison with local judges and magistrates.

Justices form part of the membership of the local probation boards that are responsible, under the overall supervision of the Home Office, for the National Probation Service.[1] The objects of the Service are to assist the courts with sentencing and other decision-making in respect of persons charged or convicted of offences, and the supervision and rehabilitation of such persons. The former includes the preparation of bail information and pre-sentence reports. The latter includes giving effect to community orders, such as community rehabilitation orders (formerly probation orders), community punishment orders (formerly community service orders), supervising persons released from prison on licence, providing accommodation in probation hostels and other approved premises, and providing reports concerning the selection of persons for early release. A further object is that of giving information relating to the judicial and custodial process to victims.[2] Section 69 of the 2000 Act places a duty on local probation boards to ascertain whether victims of violent or sexual offences wish to make representations about any conditions or requirements that should be placed on the offender on his release.[3] Probation officers also work in prison establishments and with youth offending teams. The Service was previously a local service provided by probation committees. The Conservative government explored the possibility of establishing a national service, but ultimately decided that it should be retained as a local service.[4] The Labour government (now with full party support) established the National

---

[1] See the Criminal Justice and Court Services Act 2000, ss. 1–10; Local Probation Boards (Appointment) Regulations 2000 (S.I. 2000 No. 3342), Local Probation Boards (Miscellaneous Provisions) Regulations 2001 (S.I. 2001 No. 786), Local Probation Boards (Appointments and Miscellaneous Provisions) Regulations 2001 (S.I. 2001 No. 1035); F. V. Jarvis, *Probation Service Manual* (5th ed., 1993).

[2] 2000 Act, s.1; S.I. 2001 No. 786, reg. 2.

[3] Known as "Sarah's Law" as part of a package of measures introduced following the death of Sarah Payne: see Probation Circular 62/2001.

[4] See *Organising Supervision of Punishment in the Community: A Decision Document* (Home Office, HMSO, 1991), which followed a Green Paper, *Supervision and Punishment in the Community* (Cm. 966, 1990). The Green Paper had put forward for consultation the option of establishing a single, national, centrally run probation service, but the government ultimately decided "that for the time being the service will remain locally structured" noting the overwhelming view of respondents that the service can operate most effectively as a local service: *Decision Document*, pp. 2, 3.

Probation Service with effect from April 2001.[5] There is a National Directorate and 42 Probation Services, matching police force and CPS area boundaries throughout England and Wales, and grouped in 10 regions. The Service is subject to inspection by Her Majesty's Inspectorate of the National Probation Service,[6] first established by the Probation Services Act 1993. Its Strategic Framework for 2001–2004, entitled "The New Choreography" sets out nine "stretch objectives".[7] There is an increased emphasis on punishment and the protection of the public.[8] The 2000 Act separated out functions concerning the welfare of children and passed them to a new service, the Children and Family Courts Advisory and Support Service (CAFCASS).[9]

2. EMPLOYMENT TRIBUNALS[10]

Industrial tribunals (renamed employment tribunals in 1998[11]) were first established by the Industrial Training Act 1964 to hear appeals by employers assessed for levy payable to an industrial training board. They were then given jurisdiction over disputes about redundancy pay. The Royal Commission on Trade Unions and Employers' Associations[12] recommended that the tribunal's jurisdiction should be enlarged to comprise, subject to certain limitations, all disputes between the individual worker and employer,

2–031

---

[5] This followed the publication of figures that showed that less than half of persons who breached probation orders were returned to prison and wide variations in performance across the country. The new service would be a "unified centrally-driven service" that would develop evidence-based approaches to community punishment and public protection: Lord Bassam, H.L. Deb. July 3, 2000, col. 1286.

[6] 2000 Act, ss. 6, 7, formerly Her Majesty's Inspectorate of Probation. See *www.homeoffice.gov.uk/hmiprob*.

[7] More accurate and effective assessment and management of risk and dangerousness; more contact and involvement with the victims of serious sexual and other violent crime; the production and delivery of offender programmes which have a proven track record in reducing re-offending; interviewing early to take young people away from crime; enforcement; providing courts with good information and pre-trial services; valuing and achieving diversity in the NPS and the services it provides; building an excellent organisation that is fit for purpose; building an effective performance management framework. See the Home Office website.

[8] Probation officers, Boards and the Secretary of State must have regard to the aims of (a) the protection of the public, (b) the reduction of re-offending, (c) the proper punishment of offenders, (d) ensuring offenders' awareness of the effects of crime on victims and the public, and (e) the rehabilitation of offenders: *ibid.* s.2. Community sentences were re-named (see above) (requiring extensive amendment to the recent consolidation measure, the Powers of Criminal Courts (Sentencing) Act 2000). Community sentences "will no longer be a soft option": J. Straw M.P., H.C. Deb. March 28, 2000, col. 230.

[9] 2000 Act, ss. 11–17.

[10] See K. Whitesides and G. Hawker, *Industrial Tribunals* (1975); Sweet & Maxwell's *Encyclopedia of Employment Law*, Part A7; JUSTICE Report, *Industrial Tribunals* (1987); L. Dickens, *et al.*, *Dismissed: A Study of Unfair Dismissal and the Industrial Tribunal System* (1987); A. M. Leonard, *Judging Inequality* (Cobden Trust, 1987); B.J. Doyle, *Employment Tribunals: The New Law* (1998); J. MacMillan (1999) I.L.J. 33.

[11] By the Employment Rights (Dispute Resolution) Act 1998, s.l.

[12] Cmnd. 3623, 1968: Chairman: Lord Donovan.

the primary aim being to make available "a procedure which is easily accessible, informal, speedy and inexpensive, and which gives them the best possible opportunities of arriving at an amicable settlement of their differences".[13] To an extent this recommendation has been fulfilled and the jurisdiction of employment tribunals has steadily expanded. In addition to the points already mentioned employment tribunals have jurisdiction in respect of complaints of unfair dismissal,[14] questions as to terms required to be included in a contract of employment,[15] claims to equal pay,[16] failure to allow time off for specified purposes,[17] appeals against improvement notices or prohibition notices served by a health and safety inspector[18] and certain complaints relating to sex,[19] race[20] and disability[21] discrimination and a host of other matters between employer and employee. Apart from matters arising between employer and employee, they also handle claims by individuals against trade unions for unreasonable exclusion or expulsion in closed shop situations and claims for compensation in respect of pressure on the employer to take action against an individual by reason of membership or non-membership of a union.[22] An important development was the extension[23] and (long-delayed) implementation[24] of the Lord Chancellor's power to confer jurisdiction on employment tribunals in respect of claims for damages for breach of or for a sum due under a contract of employment or other contracts connected with employment.[25]

The tribunals sit at over 50 centres, grouped under 20 Regional Offices of Employment Tribunals and the Central Office of Employment Tribunals in London.[26] There is a President of Employment Tribunals (England and Wales) who both sits as a chairman and has important administrative responsibilities in relation to the system.[27] A fully-constituted tribunal has a legally qualified chairman and two "wing" members.[28] However, an

---

[13] Cmnd. 3623, 1968, para. 572.

[14] Employment Rights Act 1996, ss. 94–134.

[15] *ibid.* s.11, as amended.

[16] Equal Pay Act 1970, as amended.

[17] Trade Union and Labour Relations (Consolidation) Act 1992 ss. 168–169 (trade union duties), 170–171 (trade union activities); Employment Rights Act 1996, ss. 52–53 (to seek work during redundancy situation), 55–56 (ante natal care).

[18] Health and Safety at Work, etc, Act 1974, ss. 21–24.

[19] Sex Discrimination Act 1975, ss.63, 72, 73.

[20] Race Relations Act 1976, s.54.

[21] Disability Discrimination Act 1995, ss.4, 6.

[22] Trade Union and Labour Relations (Consolidation) Act 1992, ss.146, 150, 160.

[23] By the Trade Union and Labour Relations Act 1993, s.38. The only exclusion is a claim for damages or a sum due in respect of personal injuries.

[24] Industrial Tribunals Extension of Jurisdiction (England and Wales) Order 1994 (S.I. 1994 No.1623). An employment tribunal may not order the payment of an amount exceeding £25,000: *ibid.* Art. 10.

[25] Employment Protection (Consolidation) Act 1978, s.131, as amended; see now the Employment Tribunals Act 1996, s.3.

[26] Regional chairmen are based at 13 of these offices.

[27] See the Employment Tribunals (Constitution and Rules of Procedure) Regulations 2001 (S.I. 2001 No. 1171).

[28] See below, para. 4-016.

increasing range of cases can be heard by the chairman sitting alone[29] or by the chairman and one other member.[30] In deciding (which may be at any stage) whether a case should be heard by a fully constituted tribunal, the chairman must consider whether there is a likelihood of a dispute on the facts which makes that desirable, or, conversely, where there is a likelihood of an issue of law arising which would make it desirable for the chairman to sit alone, any views of the parties and whether there are other proceedings that might be heard concurrently.[31]

A common criticism of employment tribunals has been that they have become increasingly "legalistic":

> "First, it is observed that the immense quantity of case law reported and cited in the courts is complicating the work of tribunals. Secondly, statutes, which were intended to be straightforward enactments, are increasingly being subjected to subtle lawyers' reasoning."[32]

Lord Denning M.R. suggested that some limit be placed on the reporting of cases:

> "If we are not careful, we shall find the Industrial Tribunals bent down under the weight of the law books or, what is worse, asleep under them. Let principles be reported, but not particular instances."[33]

On the other hand, it has been suggested that growing "legalism" is inevitable given that the legislation is in fact complex and interpretative difficulties unavoidable, that there is a legally qualified chairman, that legal representation is increasingly common, that in practice litigants require consistency in decision-making, and that there must be a reliable yardstick for the conciliatory procedures incorporated in the legislation to work:

2–032

> "Naturally, tribunals will continue to dispense with the flummery and much of the procedural and evidential paraphernalia of the law courts—in this sense they are informal and comparatively free. But in most important respects, tribunals do closely resemble courts. Thus, if charges of legalism mean that they interpret the law in legal fashion, one would expect to find these charges fully proven for it is quite

---

[29] Employment Tribunals Act 1996, s.4, as amended by the Employment Rights (Disputes Resolution) Act 1998, s.3 (the powers having previously been extended by the Trade Union Reform and Employment Rights Act 1993, s.36): these include applications for interim relief in specified unfair dismissal cases; complaints under the Pension Schemes Act 1993, s.126; proceedings concerning deductions from pay; breach of contract claims; where the parties give written consent; where the respondent is not contesting the case; proceedings concerning redundancy payments; deductions of trade union subscription or political fund contributions from wages; failure to pay remuneration under a protective award; the right to secure written particulars of employment; guarantee payments; and other specified matters.

[30] 1996 Act, s.4(1)(b), as amended by the 1998 Act, s.4: this is possible (a) where such parties as are present at the beginning of the hearing in person or represented consent; or (b) where each of the parties consents.

[31] 1996 Act, s.4(5).

[32] R. Munday, "Tribunal Lore: Legalism and the Industrial Tribunals" (1981) 10 I.L.J. 146 at 147.

[33] *Walls Meat Co. Ltd v. Khan* [1979] I.C.R. 52 at 57, *cf.* Lawton L.J. in *Clay Cross (Quarry Services) Ltd v. Fletcher* [1979] 1 All E.R. 474 at 479.

impossible to see how else tribunals could be expected to behave."[34]

A JUSTICE Report on Industrial Tribunals[35] made a number of proposals for change. For the vast majority of cases the investigative approach should be improved, so as to reduce the need for representation, while, for a minority of cases, the adversarial system should be improved by providing legal aid for representation and establishing an upper tier Industrial Court, with senior chairmen and members, to hear them. The Industrial Court would also assume the appellate functions of the Employment Appeal Tribunal. The Committee confirmed that industrial tribunals did have a number of advantages over ordinary courts, being more accessible, less formal, more expeditious, less expensive and possessed of special expertise.[36] However, complaints of excessive "legalism" were to an extent justified. One cause was the present state of substantive employment law, which was in need of clarification and consolidation in a comprehensible form. The other main cause was the adversarial system which was a major obstacle to informality in the conduct of hearings.[37] The Committee also noted that research indicated that industrial tribunals were particularly weak in understanding and applying the legislation concerning complaints of sex or race discrimination.[38] Special training was necessary for chairmen and members who dealt with such cases.[39]

Some of those points were addressed in the Employment Rights (Dispute Resolution) Act 1998.[40] This renamed the tribunals, increased the range of cases that could be heard by the chairman alone, provided for the streamlining of the procedural rules and for the appointment of "legal officers" to carry out some of the functions of tribunal chairmen, empowered ACAS to establish an arbitration scheme for unfair dismissal disputes as a voluntary alternative to tribunal hearings and made it easier for compromise agreements to be reached. The arbitration service[41] commenced operation on May 21 and the new procedural rules[42] came into effect on July 16, 2001. Nevertheless, the government swiftly announced a further review.[43] The main proposals for change were the introduction of new procedural standards for handling disputes in the workplace, coupled with power for a tribunal to vary an award if such procedures were not in

[34] Munday, *op. cit.* p. 159. On the procedure of employment tribunals see below, paras 13-011, 16-003.
[35] Chairman: Bob Hepple (1987). See also R. Lewis and J. Clark, *Employment Rights, Industrial Tribunals and Arbitration* (1993), which argued the case for the introduction of voluntary arbitration as an option for unfair dismissal cases, as one response to the legalism of tribunals.
[36] pp. 7–9.
[37] Chap. 2.
[38] V. C. Kumar, *Industrial Tribunal Applicants under the Race Relations Act 1976* (Commission for Racial Equality 1986); A. Leonard, *Judging Inequality* (1987).
[39] pp. 35–38.
[40] Following the Green Paper, *Resolving Employment Rights Disputes: Options for Reform* (Cm. 2707, 1994): see D. Cockburn, (1995) 24 I.L.J. 285.
[41] See ACAS website *www.acas.org.uk.*
[42] Employment Tribunals (Constitution and Rules of Procedure) Regulations 2001 (S.I. 2001 No. 1171), as amended by S.I. 2001 No. 1459, *inter alia* introducing case management arrangements.
[43] *Routes to Resolution: Improving Dispute Resolution in Britain*: Consultation Document (July 2001), Government Response (November 2001); dti website, *www.dti.gov.uk/er.*

place or not used; the promotion of conciliation, introducing a fixed period for conciliation by ACAS; broadening the scope of compromise agreements and promoting the use of ADR; and the "modernisation" of employment tribunals by introducing a fast track for straightforward claims, including the possibility of a written determination, enabling the President to issue practice directions, providing clear guidance on costs, and making it easier for weak claims or responses to be struck out. Furthermore, an Employment Tribunal System Taskforce has been established to advise on how the system "can be made more efficient, cost-effective and user-focussed against a background of rising caseloads". Some of these proposals appear in the Employment Bill 2000–02. Proposals in the consultation paper for charging were, however, not pursued in the light of opposition at the consultation stage.

The system is clearly under enormous pressure. While claims have trebled since 1990, it has also been estimated that the number of justiciable disputes is in the range of 500,000 to 900,000 per annum, with only about 15–20 per cent of those disputes going through the employment tribunals.[44]

Appeals lie on a point of law[45] in most cases to the Employment Appeal Tribunal,[46] and in the others[47] to the Queen's Bench Division.

3. THE EMPLOYMENT APPEAL TRIBUNAL

The Employment Appeal Tribunal[48] was established by the Employment Protection Act 1975[49] as the successor of the politically controversial National Industrial Relations Court, inheriting the latter's appellate functions. Its membership comprises judges of the High Court or Court of Appeal[50] nominated by the Lord Chancellor, at least one judge of the Court of Session nominated by the Lord President of that court, and lay members appointed by the Queen on the recommendation of the Lord Chancellor and the Secretary of State, being persons who "appear ... to have special knowledge or experience of industrial relations, either as representatives of employers or as representatives of workers".[51] One of the judges is appointed President. Each appeal is normally heard by a judge

2–033

---

[44] *Dispute Resolution in Britain – A background paper* (2001) based in part on H. Genn, *Paths to Justice* (1999). This paper was published at the start of the review.

[45] Fact or law where the question is whether a person has been unreasonably excluded or expelled from membership of a trade union in a closed shop situation.

[46] See below.

[47] *e.g.* industrial training levy assessments, appeals against an improvement or prohibition notice.

[48] A superior court of record. See Phillips J., "Some notes on the Employment Appeal Tribunal" (1978) 7 I.L.J. 137; Browne-Wilkinson J., "The role of the EAT in the 1980s" (1982) 11 I.L.J. 69; Sir John Waite, "Lawyers and Laymen as Judges in Industry" (1986) 15 I.L.J. 32; Sir John Wood, (1990) 19 I.L.J. 133; and below, para. 4-033.

[49] See now the Employment Tribunals Act 1996, ss.20–28.

[50] Only the former have so far been nominated. In 2000 there were eight High Court judges (including the President) and one judge of the Court of Session nominated to the EAT. There were also nine current judges and seven QCs nominated to be judicial members.

[51] The lay members do not in practice act in a partisan manner.

sitting with two or, more unusually, four lay members.[52] Decisions can be by
a majority, and the judge can be outvoted, even on a point of law, by the lay
members. The EAT hears appeals from industrial tribunals[53] and from the
Certification Officer, who performs various functions in respect of trade
unions, mostly on points of law. The Court of Appeal has expressed the
view that the EAT has taken too wide a view of what constitutes an error of
law and has thus interfered too readily with the decisions of industrial
tribunals.[54] It suggested that the EAT should be less ready to lay down
"guidelines" for industrial tribunals. For example, whether a dismissal is
"fair" should essentially be regarded as a question of fact. The consequent
advantage of greater flexibility for industrial tribunals has to be balanced
against the consequent inconsistency amongst them.[55]

Appeals lie on a point of law from the EAT to the Court of Appeal,[56] with
the leave of either court.

4. Social Security Tribunals[57]

2–034   A variety of cash benefits and tax credits are available under the Social
Security Contributions and Benefits Act 1992 and the Tax Credits Act 1999.
These include contributory benefits (e.g. incapacity benefit, maternity
allowance, widow's benefit, bereavement benefits, retirement pension);
non-contributory benefits (e.g. attendance allowance, severe disablement
allowance, invalid care allowance, disability living allowance, guardian's
allowance); disablement benefit; job seeker's allowance; and income-related
benefits (income support, working families' tax credit, disabled person's tax
credit, housing benefit and council tax benefit).[58] Child benefit is payable
under the Child Benefit Act 1975. Several tribunals have been established to

---

[52] Normally, there should be equal numbers of members whose knowledge, etc., is as
representative of employers or of workers; however, an appeal may be heard by a judge and
one or three members with the consent of the parties, and certain appeals may be heard by a
judge alone or (in cases of national security), the President alone: Trade Union Reforms and
Employment Rights Act 1993, s.37; see now the Employment Tribunals Act 1996, s.28.

[53] Including in breach of contract cases: Employment Tribunals Act 1996, s.21(l)(g), inserted
by the Employment Rights (Dispute Resolution) Act 1998, Sched. 1, para. 17(2), correcting,
with retrospective effect (para. 17(3)), an oversight in the original drafting of the 1996 Act
which led to the EAT dealing with such cases for a period where technically it had no
jurisdiction to do so: see *Pendragon plc. v. Jackson* [1998] I.R.L.R. 17, EAT.

[54] See *Retarded Children's Aid Society v. Day* [1978] I.C.R 437; *Methven v. Cow Industrial
Polymers Ltd* [1980] I.C.R. 463; *Pedersen v. Camden London B.C.* [1981] I.C.R. 674; *Woods
v. W. M. Car Services (Peterborough) Ltd* [1982] I.C.R. 693; and the articles cited in n.48
above. See also *O'Kelly v. Trusthouse Forte plc* [1983] I.C.R. 728.

[55] See Browne-Wilkinson J., *op. cit.* n.48, p. 72: " ... there are signs that ... Industrial
Tribunals are beginning to demonstrate a lack of uniformity in their approach to what
constitutes fair industrial practice". His Lordship suggested that it would be desirable to aim
for a middle way between the early practice of the EAT and the restrictive approach of the
Court of Appeal.

[56] In Scotland, appeals lie to the Court of Session.

[57] See generally N. J. Wikeley, *Ogus, Barendt and Wikeley's, The Law of Social Security* (4th
ed., 1995), Chap. 17; D. Bonner, ed., *Social Security Tribunals Legislation 2000*, Vol. III,
Administration. Adjudication and the European Dimension (Commentary by R.C.A. White
and M. Rowland) (2000).

[58] 1992 Act, ss. 20, 63, 94, 123.

determine questions arising in the administration of these benefits.

Two discernible trends in the development of the structure of social security tribunals have been, first, the amalgamation of different tribunal jurisdictions and, secondly, the integration of tribunals within the court system. There has at the same time been a tendency for the government to restrict rights of appeal to an independent tribunal against decisions concerning benefits, although this has to an extent been checked with the implementation of the Human Rights Act 1998.

(a) The position to 1984

Prior to 1984, a distinction was drawn between the schemes based on the **2–035** insurance principle, where entitlement to benefit depended on the claimant having made appropriate contributions and otherwise falling within the rules of the scheme, and the provision of means-tested benefits involving the exercise of discretion. As regards the former, claims and questions arising under the Social Security Act 1975 and the Child Benefit Act 1975 were determined initially by an insurance officer appointed by the Secretary of State for Social Services or, for unemployment benefit, by the Secretary of State for Employment. An appeal lay to a National Insurance Local Tribunal,[59] comprising a legally qualified chairman,[60] the member from a panel representing employers and self-employed earners and one from a panel representing employed earners.[61] As regards the latter, tribunals were first set up in the 1930s and subsequently evolved into Supplementary Benefit Appeal Tribunals. These comprised a chairman appointed by the Secretary of State from a panel drawn up by the Lord Chancellor, one "ordinary member" from a panel appointed by the Secretary of State from people "appearing to have knowledge or experience of conditions in the area to which the panel relates and of the problems of people living on low incomes" and one from a panel "appearing ... to represent work people".[62] The procedures and decision-making of SBATs were contrasted unfavourably with those of NILTs.[63]

(b) Social Security Appeal Tribunals

In 1980 the supplementary benefit scheme was reformed, with detailed rules **2–036** of entitlement replacing discretions, thereby bringing it closer in form to the national insurance scheme.[64] The Health and Social Services and Social Security Adjudications Act 1983[65] provided for the merger of the two adjudication systems. Most claims were now submitted to an "adjudication officer" appointed by the Secretary of State for Social Security (including

[59] This term did not appear in the legislation, but was the title commonly used. Another label sometimes found was "Social Security Local Tribunal".
[60] This was not a legal requirement but was the almost invariable practice: see below, para. 4-016.
[61] Social Security Act 1975, s.97(2): see below, para. 4-016.
[62] Supplementary Benefits Act 1976, Sched. 4.
[63] See the first edition of this book, pp. 55–57.
[64] Social Security Act 1980, Sched. 2.
[65] Sched. 8: in force from April 23, 1984. See J. Mesher, (1983) 10 J.L.S. 135; M. Partington, "The Restructuring of SSATs: a Personal View" in C. Harlow (ed.), *Public Law and Politics* (1986), Chap. 9.

some officers of the Department of Employment to deal with unemployment benefit).[66] There was a Chief Adjudication Officer, who was required to advise adjudication officers and keep their work under review, and to report annually to the Secretary of State on standards of adjudication.[67]

Appeals lay to a Social Security Appeal Tribunal,[68] which now exercised the jurisdictions formerly exercised by NILTs and SBATs. Social Security Appeal Tribunals were organised in six regions, each headed by a Regional Chairman, and the whole system was headed by the President of Social Security Appeal Tribunals, Medical Appeal Tribunals and Disability Appeal Tribunals (subsequently generally known as the President of the Independent Tribunal Service).[69] The Lord Chancellor appointed chairmen, who had to be legally qualified.[70] There was a single panel of members constituted by the President for the whole of Great Britain. Each tribunal comprised a chairman, nominated by the President, and two members.

(c) Other adjudicating bodies

2–037   Certain questions, including whether a person was an "earner", whether he or she was "employed" or "self-employed" and whether he or she complied with "contribution conditions" necessary for receipt of contributory benefits, were determined by the Secretary of State: in practice by a member of the DSS Solicitors' Office.[71] The Secretary of State could refer a point of law, and a dissatisfied claimant could appeal on such a point, to the High Court.

Certain questions concerning disablement benefit were determined by "Medical Boards" of two medical practitioners, which also heard certain appeals on medical questions from the decisions of a medical practitioner, or adjudication officers. There was a right of appeal to a Medical Appeal Tribunal, comprising a legally qualified chairman and two doctors of consultant status.[72]

Claims to disability living allowance, disability working allowance and attendance allowance were determined by adjudication officers, with advice on medical questions from doctors employed by the Benefits Agency Medical Service.[73] There was then a right to apply for a review[74], and then to appeal on medical issues ("disability questions") to a Disability Appeal Tribunal[75] or on other matters to a SSAT.[76] A DAT comprised a legally

---

[66] Social Security Administration Act 1992, ss.20, 21, 38.

[67] ibid. s.39. See R. Sainsbury, "The Social Security Chief Adjudication Officer: The First Four Years" [1989] P. L. 323.

[68] ibid. ss.22, 40, 41, Sched. 2.

[69] The first President was Judge H. J. Byrt, who held the office from 1984: see J. Fulbrook, (1989) 18 I.L.J. 177; Interview, Legal Action, September 1989, p. 7; he was succeeded by Judge Derek Holden (1989–1992), Judge Anthony Thorne (1992–1994) and Judge Keith Bassingthwaighte (1994–1998).

[70] By virtue of the Courts and Legal Services Act 1990, Sched. 10, para. 37, the qualifications in England became, respectively, a 10-year (President) and five-year (Chairmen) general qualification under s.71 of the Act, i.e. a right of audience in any part of the Supreme Court or in all proceedings in county courts or magistrates' courts.

[71] Social Security Administration Act 1992, ss.17, 18.

[72] ibid. s.50, Sched. 2.

[73] ibid. ss.21(3).

[74] ibid. ss.30–32.

[75] See N. Wikeley, (1992) 11 CJQ 227.

[76] 1992 Act., s.33.

qualified chairman appointed by the Lord Chancellor,[77] and two members appointed by the President, one from a panel of medical practitioners and the other from a panel of persons (not medical practitioners) who were experienced in dealing with the needs of disabled persons in a professional or voluntary capacity or were themselves disabled.[78] The President nominated the members of particular tribunals.[79]

Appeals in connection with decisions concerning the maintenance of children went before the Child Support Appeal Tribunals, whose composition was the same as for SSATs.[80] The structure mirrored that of the social security tribunals, with the President of SSATs, MATs and DATs also appointed as President of the Child Support Appeal Tribunals,[81] and provision for the appointment of a Chief Child Support Commissioner and other Child Support Commissioners.[82] These tribunals were distinctive in that they handled disputes (possibly acrimonious ones) between private individuals.

(d) Reform: The Social Security Act 1998

The Social Security Act 1998[83] introduced fundamental reforms to arrangements for decision-making and appeals under legislation relating to social security, child support, vaccine damage payments and war pensions. First, the functions of the first-tier decision-makers (adjudication officers, social fund officers and child support officers) were transferred to the Secretary of State,[84] who is now the decision-maker.[85] Accordingly, they no longer enjoy formal legal independence and the Office of the Chief Adjudication Officer has been abolished.[86] Decisions may be made or issued by an officer acting under the Secretary of State's authority or by a computer for whose operation such an officer is responsible.[87]

Secondly, the functions of social security appeal tribunals, disability appeal tribunals, medical appeal tribunals, child support appeal tribunals and vaccine damage tribunals were transferred to "unified appeal

---

[77] With the same rules for eligibility as chairman of SSATs and MATs.

[78] 1992 Act, s.42.

[79] ibid. s.43.

[80] Child Support Act 1991, ss.20, 21.

[81] ibid. Sched. 3, para. 1.

[82] ibid. s.22, Sched. 4.

[83] See DSS, Improving decision making and appeals in Social Security (Cm. 3328, 1996); N.J. Wikeley, Current Law Statutes Annotated 1998, (1998) 5 J.S.S.L. 104 and (1999) 6 J.S.S.L. 155; R. Sainsbury in M. Harris and M. Partington (eds), Administrative Justice in the 21st Century (1999), Chap. 22 (arguing that the changes seemed designed to save expenditure rather than improve the lot of the average claimant).

[84] 1998 Act, s.1.

[85] ibid. s.8. (Tax credit decisions are, however, made by officers of the Inland Revenue.) Decisions may be revised (s.9) or superseded (s.10).

[86] Instead, the Secretary of State must report periodically on the standards of decision-making: 1998 Act, s.81; the President of appeal tribunals must report annually on the quality of decisions which go to appeal: Sched. 1, para. 10. Nevertheless, "there are obvious dangers in over-reliance on agencies being responsible for monitoring their own standards of adjudication": Wikeley (1998), p. 14–7.

[87] ibid. s.2.

tribunals".[88] The Lord Chancellor may appoint a lawyer of 10 years' standing to be President of appeal tribunals.[89] The President must ensure that appropriate steps are taken to secure the confidentiality of prescribed material, arrange for the training of tribunal members, and report to the Secretary of State.[90] He heads a non-departmental public body which is one of two distinct bodies within the Appeals Service, the other being an executive agency of the Department of Work and Pensions responsible for providing administrative support.

Thirdly, the Lord Chancellor must constitute a panel of persons to act as members of appeal tribunals.[91] The panel must include persons possessing prescribed qualifications. These are lawyers, registered medical practitioners, accountants and "persons, other than registered medical practitioners, who are experienced in dealing with the needs of disabled persons – (a) in a professional or voluntary capacity; or (b) because they are themselves disabled".[92] Accordingly, other lay people are no longer eligible to be tribunal members. This change was controversial.[93] It has been argued persuasively that a minority of cases[94] are particularly suitable for determination by a tribunal including persons with knowledge or experience of conditions in the area who are representative of persons living or working in the area, and that the law should be modified accordingly.[95]

Each tribunal must comprise one, two or three members drawn by the President from the panel[96] in accordance with regulations. The member, or at least one member must be a lawyer[97] and the President must nominate the chairman, who has a casting vote.[98] The tribunal may call upon expert assistance.[99] The regulations provide that a tribunal shall comprise a legally qualified panel member, except where:

---

[88] *ibid.* s.4. The legislation does not confer a specific title on these tribunals, beyond "appeal tribunals constituted under Chapter I of Part I of the Social Security Act 1998" (see ss.1(2) and 39(1)). The side note refers to "unified appeal tribunals". The Council on Tribunals refers to them under the generic heading "The Appeals Service." They may also be referred to as Appeals Service appeal tribunals or Appeals Service tribunals.

[89] *ibid.* s.5, Sched. 1. The qualification is a 10 year general qualification under s.71 of the Courts and Legal Services Act 1990 or an advocate or solicitor in Scotland of at least 10 years' standing. The first holder of the office is Judge Michael Harris.

[90] *ibid.* Sched. 1, paras 7–10.

[91] *ibid.* s.6.

[92] Social Security and Child Support (Decisions and Appeals) Regulations 1999 (S.I. 1999 No. 991), Sched. 3. In the case of medical practitioners, the Chief Medical Officer must be consulted: s.6(2).

[93] The Council on Tribunals expressed its concern at this change, given the valuable contribution of lay members previously: Annual Report for 1998–99, p. 56. A majority of chairmen, however, were broadly content with the changes: N.J. Wikeley, (2000) 7 J.S.S.L. 88.

[94] Cases raising cohabitation, misconduct or voluntary leaving, or overpayments issues.

[95] N. J. Wikeley, (2000) 7 J.S.S.L. 88.

[96] 1998 Act, s.7(1).

[97] *ibid.* s.7(2): *i.e.* have a general qualification under s.71 of the Courts and Legal Services Act 1990 or be an advocate or solicitor in Scotland. The government retreated from the position that would have other members sitting alone in some cases: Wikeley (1998), p. 14-13. Opponents recalled criticisms in the past of the quality of decision making of tribunals (such as SBATs) without a lawyer.

[98] *ibid.* s.7(3). The lawyer is invariably nominated in practice, although other possibilities are not ruled out: Wikeley (1998), p. 14-13–14-14.

[99] *ibid.* s.7(4): the expert must be a panel member: s.7(5).

(a) the case raises issues concerning industrial injuries benefit, severe disablement allowance or a vaccine damage payment, in which case there must be, in addition to the lawyer, either one medical practitioner, two medical practitioners, or one medical practitioner and another panel member appointed for the purpose of training or the monitoring of standards[1];

(b) the case concerns child support or a relevant benefit[2] and raises difficult issues relating to the balance sheet of an enterprise or trust fund, in which case there must be a lawyer and an accountant; or

(c) the case concerns attendance allowance, disability living allowance or disability working allowance, in which case the lawyer must sit with a medical practitioner and a person with a disability qualification.[3]

Appeals to a tribunal lie in cases involving a relevant benefit (unless excluded by Schedule 2 to the 1998 Act), other decisions (specified in Schedule 3)[4] or specified cases arising under other legislation.[5] In deciding an appeal, an appeal tribunal need not consider any issue not raised by the appeal, and must not take into account any circumstances not obtaining at the time when the decision appealed against was made.[6] It has been argued that the former is not to be construed as removing the inquisitorial function of tribunals and that the latter "introduces an unwelcome element of technicality into appeals to tribunals that were once supposed to be user-friendly".[7]

An appeal lies to a Commissioner on a point of law, with the leave of the chairman or other prescribed person, or a Commissioner.[8] Where an application for leave is made to a chairman or other prescribed person, and he or she considers that the decision is erroneous in law, he or she may set it aside and refer it for redetermination by the tribunal or determination by a differently constituted tribunal; if each of the principal parties expresses the view that the decision is erroneous in law, he or she must set it aside and refer the case for determination by a differently constituted tribunal.[9]

The Secretary of State must assign a clerk to service each appeal tribunal.[10]

The functions of the Secretary of State concerning social security contributions, as exercised through the Contributions Agency, have been

---

[1] In some cases it is specified that the lawyer sits with one medical practitioner.

[2] *i.e.* a benefit under Parts II to V of the Social Security (Contributions and Benefits) Act 1992, jobseeker's allowance, income support, working families' tax credit, disabled person's tax credit, a social fund payment, child benefit, and any other prescribed benefit: 1998 Act, s.8(3).

[3] S.I. 1999 No. 991, reg. 36, as amended by S.I. 1999 No. 1466, reg. 2.

[4] 1998 Act, s.12; S.I. 1999 No. 991, Parts IV, V.

[5] *e.g.* Social Security (Recovery of Benefits) Act 1997, ss. 11, 12, as amended. Amendments to the child support and vaccine damage payments legislation were effected by the 1999 Acts, ss. 40–47, and further amendments on child support by the Child Support, Pensions and Social Security Act 2000, ss. 10, 11.

[6] 1998 Act, s.12(8).

[7] White and Rowland (2000), pp. 156, 157.

[8] 1998 Act, s.14.

[9] *ibid.* s.13. This is so, however unreasonable the parties' collective view is: see White and Rowland (2000), p. 160, describing subs. (3) as "a bizarre provision".

[10] S.I. 1999 No. 991, reg. 37.

transferred to the Treasury (policy) and the Inland Revenue (operational functions), with effect from April 1, 1999.[11] Furthermore, appeals in cases concerning housing benefit or council tax benefit now lie to appeal tribunals and then the Social Security Commissioners,[12] rather than to housing review boards, whose independence was doubtful[13] and whose establishment had been the establishment of much academic criticism.[14]

(e) Social Security Commissioners[15]

2–038   The National Insurance Commissioners heard appeals from NILTs, and appeals on a point of law from Medical Appeal Tribunals and the Attendance Allowance Board. In 1980, a right of appeal on a point of law was created from SBATs to the Commissioner,[16] who were renamed Social Security Commissioners.[17] From April 23, 1984, they have heard appeals from SSATs and from 1987 these have been restricted to points of law in all cases.[18] At present there is a Chief Social Security Commissioner and 20 Commissioners.[19] In practice three sit in Edinburgh, the others in London, although they may travel to Cardiff or Liverpool to hear cases. The Chief Commissioner may convene a Tribunal of three Commissioners to hear an appeal involving a point of law of special difficulty. He is also responsible for selecting the decisions that are to be reported. Until 1980, the only

[11] Social Security Contributions (Transfer of Functions, etc.) Act 1999.

[12] Child Support, Pensions and Social Security Act 2000, Sched. 7; Housing Benefit and Council Tax Benefit (Decisions and Appeals) Regulations 2001 (S.I. 2001 No. 1002). The change was warmly welcomed by the Council on Tribunals: Annual Report for 1999–2000, para. 6. One advantage of the change is that the appeal tribunals will not be influenced (as HBRBs were) by the fact that in some cases benefit payments are not fully covered by a central government subsidy: see S. Rahilly, (2001) 8 J.S.S.L. 57.

[13] Confirmed in *R. (on the application of Bewry) v. Norwich City Council* [2001] EWHC Admin 657 (councillor membership of Board determining issue involving credibility; breach of common law requirement equivalent to that comprised in Article 6(1), ECHR; distinguished in *R. (on the application of Bibi) v. Housing Benefit Review Board of Rochdale Metropolitan Borough Council* [2001] EWHC Admin 967 (councillor membership of Board meant that it could not be independent or expert but judicial review was a sufficient remedy given that most of the facts were not substantially in issue and that the councillors had no personal interest in their finding that a tenancy was not on a commercial basis and so did not enable a claim to be made for housing benefit).

[14] See N. Wikeley, (1986) 5 C.J.Q. 18; R. Sainsbury and T. Eardley, [1992] P.L. 551 (noting the very limited training of councillors); S. Rahilly in N. Harris (ed.), *Social Security Law in Context* (2000), pp. 424–425.

[15] See Fourth Report of the Select Committee on Social Security (1999–2000) H.C. 263; R. Micklethwait, *The National Insurance Commissioners* (1976); N. Harris, (1993) 22 I.L.J. 222; D. Bonner, *et al.* (2001) 8 J.S.S.L. 9. Under the 1946 legislation there was a National Insurance Commissioner and an Industrial Injuries Commissioner, each with several deputies. The same man commonly held appointments under both schemes. In 1966, these posts were merged, the National Insurance Commissioner was retitled the Chief National Insurance Commissioner, and the deputies became full Commissioners.

[16] Supplementary Benefits Act 1976, s.15A, inserted by the Social Security Act 1979, s.6. This replaced an appeal from SBATs to the High Court that had been created in 1978.

[17] Social Security Act 1980, s.14.

[18] Social Security Act 1998, s.14, re-enacting with modifications the Social Security Administration Act 1992, s.23. See also the Social Security Commissioners (Procedure) Regulations 1999 (S.I. 1999 No. 1495).

[19] The same qualifications are specified as for appointment as President of appeal tribunals above: 1998 Act, Sched. 4, para. 1. The current chief commissioner is Judge Michael Harris (2001–) His predecessor was Judge K. A. Machtin (1990–2001).

further possibility of review was an application for judicial review. There is now a right of appeal on a point of law to the Court of Appeal, with the leave of the Commissioner or the court.[20] From 1985, they have been administered by the Lord Chancellor's Department. The Social Security Commissioners have also been appointed as Child Support Commissioners under the Child Support Act 1991.[21] The Child Poverty Action Group in evidence to the social security select committee has commended the commissioners' performance.[22]

(f) Limitation of rights of appeal

Reforms to the social security system under Part III of the Social Security Act 1986 included the replacement of lump sum "single payments" and "urgent need payments" under the supplementary benefit legislation by payments from the, cash-limited, Social Fund. In one sense this involved a return to a system of discretionary payments. The payments, most in the form of loans, are made by social fund officers appointed by the Secretary of State. In practice, however, the detailed directions given to the officers by the Secretary of State operate very much in the manner of regulations.[23] Controversially, the government decided that there should be no rights of appeal within the tribunals system.[24] The legislation provides instead for internal review by social fund inspectors, who are officials appointed as inspectors by the Social Fund Commissioner. The Commissioner is in turn appointed by the Secretary of State. The inspectors are subject to the guidance and directions issued to the social fund officers.[25]

2-039

5. COUNTY COURTS

(a) Establishment

The present county courts were originally established by the County Courts Act 1846. This Act followed a lengthy campaign, which aroused hostility in several quarters, including the Bar and certain large London solicitors'

2-040

---

[20] See *Cooke v. Secretary of State* [2001] EWCA Civ. 734 where the Court of Appeal gave guidance as to the criteria for the grant of leave by that court.

[21] See the Child Support Commissioners Procedure Regulations 1999 (S.I. 1999 No. 1305).

[22] Fourth Report, 1999–2000 H.C. 263, *Minutes of Evidence*, cited in D. Bonner *et al*, (2001) 8 J.S.S.L. 9 at 28.

[23] See *R. v. Secretary of State for Social Services, ex p. Stitt, The Times*, July 5, 1990.

[24] See H. Bolderson, (1988) 15 J.L.S. 279. The Council on Tribunals registered their objections in a Special Report, *Social Security – Abolition of independent appeals under the proposed Social Fund* (Cmnd. 9722, 1986). See generally R. Drabble and T. Lynes, [1989] P.L. 297; Ogus, Barendt and Wikeley (1995), pp. 684–685; J. Scampion, "The Use of Review in the Administrative Justice System: The Experience of Social Fund Reviews" summarised in M.Harris and M.Partington (eds), *Administrative Justice in the 21st Century* (1999), pp. 156–160 (defending the arrangements as suitable for this context, where fair, quick and clear decision-making was needed and where the system enabled inspectors' decisions to be effectively and comprehensively monitored).

[25] Social Security Act 1998, ss. 36–38; Social Funding (Application for Review) Regulations 1988 (S.I. 1988 No. 34), as amended; T. Buck, *The Social Fund — Law and Practice* (2nd ed., 2000).

firms.[26] The hostility was based essentially on fears of loss of business to provincial attornies and solicitors. In the case of the Bar there was also resistance to the development of provincial Bars, which were seen to be the only effective way of competing for county court business.[27] The aim of the Act was to set up an effective local court for minor cases, and, in particular, the recovery of small debts: proceedings in the superior courts were prohibitively expensive and civil proceedings at the assizes were prone to delay. It is ironic that similar criticisms of ordinary county court proceedings in recent times have led to the development of new, more informal, procedures for small claims, and arguments that a further tier of small claims courts should be established.[28] Indeed, right from the outset the new courts were much more heavily used by shopkeepers, traders, and other creditors than by ordinary people, their establishment leading to "an infinite expansion of credit".[29]

(b) Organisation

2–041   England and Wales is divided into districts and at least one court is held in each district.[30] The districts and locations are specified by the Lord Chancellor.[31] In 2000 there were about 220 county courts; 172 had divorce jurisdiction, and 131 bankruptcy jurisdiction.[32] In 1995, about 80 offered trial facilities under which one or more judges were available on a continuous basis to hear trials.[33] Lord Woolf recommended that arrangements should be streamlined. Outside London, there should be three or four designated civil trial centres on each Circuit, each with a series of satellite courts, and each with a Senior Civil Judge appointed for each centre.[34] This has been taken forward, subject to constraints arising from the nature of available court buildings, and with the appointment of "Designated Civil Judges" to 32 centres.[35] In London, the Central London Civil Trial Centre has been established at Park Crescent in the West End. It has two business lists and hears more complex cases sent from the other London county courts.[36]

---

[26] See B. Abel-Smith and R. Stevens, *Lawyers and the Courts* (1967), pp. 32–37; P. Polden, *The County Court 1846–1971* (1999).

[27] See R. Cocks, *Foundations of the Modern Bar* (1983), pp. 25–26, 56–57.

[28] See below, para. 12-022.

[29] Lord Westbury L.C., quoted by Abel-Smith and Stevens (1967), p. 35.

[30] County Courts Act 1984, s.l; Civil Courts Order 1983 (S.I. 1983 No. 713), as amended. The county court for the City of London is known as the Mayor's and City of London Court: the name is that of a court of similar jurisdiction abolished by the Courts Act 1971, on whose history see Polden (1999), Appendix. The court is maintained by the City of London.

[31] County Courts Act 1984, s.2.

[32] *Judicial Statistics 2000*, p. 37; Court Service website (*www.courtservice.gov.uk*). Admiralty jurisdiction was removed from over 40 courts by the Civil Court (Amendment) (No. 2) Order 1999 (S.I. 1999 No. 1011).

[33] Lord Woolf's *Interim Report on Access to Justice* (1995), p. 79. This followed a recommendation of the *Civil Justice Review* (Cm. 393, 1988), para. 176.

[34] *ibid.*

[35] *Final Report on Access to Justice* (1996), Chap. 8; LCD website (judges and QCs.).

[36] S. Webster (1994) 138 S.J. 515. A nominated Circuit judge may issue freezing injunctions (formerly known as *Mareva* injunctions) in relation to proceedings in the List: County Court Remedies (Amendment) Regulations 1995 (S.I. 1995 No.206). The Patents County Court (below, para. 2-046.) has moved to the centre from Wood Green.

A number of centres, co-located in Northampton, have been established to handle work in bulk: the Claims Production Centre, processes claims received on magnetic media from major plaintiffs[37]; the County Court Bulk Centre, attached to Northampton County Court, processes large volumes of debt recovery cases[38]; the Parking Enforcement Centre, also attached to Northampton County Court since 1997, handles the enforcement of unpaid parking charges for London and other local authorities)[39]: and a Centralised Attachment of Earnings Payments System (CAPS) deals with payment processing and monitoring and, for example, enables large employers to send one payment to cover orders made in, and previously payable to, a variety of county courts.[40]

(c) Judges

Under the original arrangements the districts were grouped into 60 county court circuits, each with its own judge appointed by the Lord Chancellor from barristers of at least seven years' standing. On the re-organisation of the criminal courts under the Courts Act 1971[41] the existing county court judges became Circuit judges.[42] Every Circuit judge is by virtue of his or her office capable of sitting as a judge for any county court district and at least one is assigned to each district by the Lord Chancellor.[43] The regular sittings are normally taken by the assigned judges. In addition, a District judge is appointed for each county court district by the Lord Chancellor, and deputy district judges may also be appointed.[44] A full-time District judge is barred from legal practice.[45] District judges were formerly called registrars; the change of title reflected the fact that their functions are now judicial. They are responsible for procedural steps in court proceedings, this responsibility being analogous to those of Masters and Registrars of the High Court, and they hear most small claims. As the small claims limit has progressively been raised, the role of District judges in hearing claims has increased accordingly. Their administrative functions have been transferred to the chief clerk or some other administrative officer, in accordance with the Lord Chancellor's directions.[46] County courts are administered by the Court Service.[47] There are substantial staffs of clerks and bailiffs.

2–042

---

[37] In 2000 it issued 52% of the total default claims issued; it is deemed to be part of the court in whose name the claim is issued.

[38] *Judicial Statistics 2000*, p. 46.

[39] *LCD Court Service Annual Report 1994–95* (1994–95 H.C. 579), p. 52 and *Annual Report 1997–98* (1997–98 H.C. 837)

[40] *LCD Court Service Annual Report 1996–97* (1996–97 H.C. 73), p. 29.

[41] See below, para. 2-051.

[42] See below, para. 4-020.

[43] County Courts Act 1984, s.5. A judge of the Court of Appeal or the High Court or a recorder may also sit as a county court judge: *ibid.*

[44] County Courts Act 1984, ss.6–9; Courts and Legal Service Act 1990, s.74 and Sched. 10 para. 57. A deputy District judge is appointed as a temporary measure. The eligibility requirement is now possession of a seven year general qualification (*i.e.* right of audience in any part of the Supreme Court or in all proceedings in county courts or magistrates courts); it was formerly being a solicitor of at least seven years' standing.

[45] Courts and Legal Services Act 1990, s.75 and Sched. 11.

[46] County Court Rules 1981, Ord. 1, r. 3. See now C.P.R. rr.2.5 which provides generally that any act of a formal or administrative character under the CPR may be performed by a court officer.

[47] See below, para. 2-055.

(d) Jurisdiction

2–043   A county court has jurisdiction in almost the whole range of civil proceedings. In some matters the jurisdiction is exclusive, in others it is exercised concurrently with the High Court. In the latter event there is in some cases a monetary limit to the county court's jurisdiction, the "county court limit," specified by Order in Council.[48] However, the High Court and County Courts Jurisdiction Order 1991,[49] following recommendations in the Civil Justice Review,[50] removed the limits for contract, tort and land law actions.

A county court may hear and determine the following matters—

(i) Contract and tort

An action founded on contract or tort.[51] This head of jurisdiction covers the bulk of cases brought in the county court.

(ii) Actions in respect of land

An action for the recovery of land or in respect of title to any hereditament.[52]

(iii) Equity proceedings

2–044   A variety of equity proceedings where the value of the property concerned is not more than £30,000[53]: these include proceedings for the administration of the estate of a deceased person, in respect of trusts for foreclosure or redemption of a mortgage, for the specific performance of an agreement for the sale of property, for the maintenance or advancement of an infant and for the dissolution of a partnership. These correspond to matters that would be dealt with in the Chancery Division of the High Court.

(iv) Admiralty proceedings

A variety of Admiralty matters,[54] such as claims for damage done by or to a ship, for loss or damage to goods carried in a ship, or for salvage, towage or pilotage. The jurisdictional limit is £5,000, except for salvage claims, where it

---

[48]   Section 145 of the County Courts Act 1984 confers power to raise monetary limits. The current limits are set by the County Court Jurisdiction Order 1981 (S.I. 1981 No. 1123, as amended by the High Court and County Courts Juridisction Order 1991 (S.I. 1991 No. 724) and s.147 of the 1984 Act.

[49]   S.I. 1991 No.724. See below, para. 2-048.

[50]   Below, para. 12-001.

[51]   County Courts Act 1984, s.15, as amended by S.I. 1991 No.724. This head does not apply to any action where title to any toll, fair, market or franchise is in question or any action for libel or slander: *ibid.* There is a similar jurisdiction in respect of money recoverable under a statute: *ibid.* s.16.

[52]   *ibid.* s.21, as amended by S.I. 1991 No. 724.

[53]   *ibid.* s.23. In addition, many specific powers under the Trustee Act 1925 and the Law of Property Act 1925 are conferred by the 1984 Act, Sched. 2.

[54]   County Courts Act 1984, ss.26, 27, as amended.

is £15,000. However, no county courts are currently designated the Lord Chancellor to take Admiralty proceedings, most of which are on or near the coast and such proceedings have to be commenced in the High Court.[55]

(v) Probate proceedings

Contentious matters arising in respect of the grant or revocation of probate or administration of estates where the value of the estate is not more than £30,000.[56]

(vi) Jurisdiction by agreement

Matters outside the monetary limits where the parties confer jurisdiction on a county court by agreement.[57]

(vii) Family matters

Any county court which has been designated by the Lord Chancellor as a **2–045** "divorce county court" has jurisdiction to hear and determine any matrimonial cause,[58] although it only has jurisdiction to try the cause if it is also designated as a court of trial.[59] A divorce county court also has jurisdiction to make orders in relation to financial relief and custody of children ancillary to proceedings for divorce, nullity or separation,[60] and, if designated by the Lord Chancellor, to make orders for financial relief where a marriage has been terminated abroad.[61] The jurisdiction of divorce county courts, so far as is exercisable by judges of such courts, is to be exercised by such Circuit judges as the Lord Chancellor may direct.[62] Every matrimonial cause must be commenced in a divorce county court,[63] and will be heard there unless it is transferred to the High Court.[64] There is also provision for the transfer of family proceedings from the High Court to the county court.[65] Principles governing the distribution and transfer of business between the High Court and county courts are set out in Directions given by

---

[55] See above, para. 2-041 and below, para. 2-061.
[56] County Courts Act 1984, s.32, substituted by the Administration of Justice Act 1985, s.51(1).
[57] ibid, ss.18 (Queen's Bench Division matters), 24 (many equity proceedings), 27(6) (most Admiralty proceedings).
[58] i.e. an action for divorce, nullity of marriage or judicial separation: Matrimonial and Family Proceedings Act 1984, s.32, as amended by the Family Law Act 1986, Sched. 1, para. 27.
[59] 1984 Act, s.33(1); Civil Courts Order 1983 (S.I. 1983 No. 713), as amended. In London, the Divorce Registry of the Family Division is deemed to be a county court for this purpose; see the 1984 Act, s.42, as amended by the Courts and Legal Services Act 1990, s.74(7).
[60] Under Parts II and III of the Matrimonial Causes Act 1973: 1984 Act, s.34(1)(a).
[61] Under Part III of the 1984 Act: ibid. ss.33(4), 34(1)(b).
[62] 1984 Act, s.36.
[63] ibid. s.33(3).
[64] Under ibid. s.39 (which applies to any family proceedings), or section 41 of the County Courts Act 1984. Prior to April 26, 1986, all defended causes had to be transferred to the High Court.
[65] Matrimonial and Family Proceedings Act 1984, s.38.

the President of the Family Division.[66] Other family matters may be dealt
with by divorce county courts, or, in some cases, any county court. Part IV
of the Family Law Act 1996[67] introduced a more coherent domestic violence
jurisdiction, with powers to grant occupation orders (which can define or
regulate right of occupation of the home) and non-molestation orders
conferred in the High Court, county courts and magistrates' courts.[68] This is
subject to the power of the Lord Chancellor to provide that certain types of
proceedings be commenced in, or transferred to, a specified level of court.[69]

The jurisdiction of the county courts concerning children was remodelled
on implementation of the Children Act 1989 in October 1991. There is a
concurrent jurisdiction across the family proceedings courts,[70] county courts
and the High Court.[71] In the county courts, the business is concentrated on
particular centres and particular judges, who receive special "guidance".
There are four levels of court centre. Ordinary county courts have no family
jurisdiction; divorce county courts can issue all private law proceedings,[72]
but contested matters are transferred to "family hearing centres" for trial;
family hearing centres can issue and hear all private law family proceedings
whether or not they are contested; "care centres" have full jurisdiction in
private and public law[73] matters.[74] As to the judiciary, "designated family
judges" have full jurisdiction in public and private law, are based at care
centres and chair local Family Court Business Committees and Family
Court Forums; "nominated care judges" similarly have full public and
private law jurisdiction; "circuit family judges" have full private law
jurisdiction[75]; district judges can hear private law family work but have a
limited jurisdiction; "nominated care district judges" have increased

---

[66] *ibid.* s.37. See *Practice Direction (Family Division: Distribution of Business)* [1992] 1 W.L.R.
586 replacing an earlier direction. A defect in the transitional arrangements led to thousands
of divorces being technically invalid: see *Nissim v. Nissim* (1987) 137 N.L.J. Rep. 1207; N.
Wikeley, (1988) 7 C.J.Q. 97. They were retrospectively validated by the Matrimonial
Proceedings (Transfers) Act 1988.

[67] Following recommendations in the Law Commission Report on *Domestic Violence and
Occupation of the Family Home* (Law Com. No. 207).

[68] ss.33–42.

[69] s.57. See the Family Law Act 1996 (Part IV) (Allocation of Proceedings) Order 1997 (S.I.
1997 No. 1896): proceedings are normally commenced in a family proceedings court or
county court (*i.e.* divorce county court, family hearing centre or care centre); provision is
made for the transfer of cases.

[70] Above, para. 2-025.

[71] Below, para. 2-065.

[72] Above.

[73] *i.e.* cases usually brought by local authorities or the NSPCC, including care, supervision and
emergency protection orders.

[74] *Judicial Statistics 2000*, p. 50; Children (Allocation of Proceedings) Order 1991 (S.I. 1991
No. 1677), as amended, Scheds 1, 2. The Principal Registry of the Family Division is treated
as if it were a divorce county court, a family hearing centre and a care centre. The original
plan was for 51 combined care and family hearing centres and 51 additional family hearing
centres: *LCD Court Service Annual Report 1990–91* (1990–91 H.C. 568), pp. 57–60. A further
seven FHCs and two CCs were established from the beginning of 1995: *LCD Court Service
Annual Report 1994–95* (1994–95 H.C. 579), p. 55. The 1991 Order also provides for the
transfer of cases.

[75] Deputy Circuit judges and recorders are only nominated for private family law proceedings,
except that a recorder can be requested to act as a judge of the Family Division of the High
Court and may hear public law family proceedings if nominated for them.

jurisdiction and can hear uncontested public law cases.[76] The detailed allocation of work is the subject of a Practice Direction.[77] Family Court Business Committees deal with administrative issues, such as the operation of the criteria for the transfer of cases; the Family Court Forums enable the professions involved in the protection and welfare of children to "discuss issues and air concerns".[78]

(viii) Other proceedings

Jurisdiction in a large number of other matters is conferred by specific statutory provisions, including hire-purchase, consumer credit, the Rent Acts, landlord and tenant, housing and sex discrimination.[79] Designated county courts have jurisdiction in bankruptcy matters,[80] race relations,[81] and patents.[82] Appeals also lie to the county court in a number of administrative matters.[83]

2–046

(ix) Jurisdiction of the District judge

Any act of a county court under the CPR may, except where an enactment, rule or practice direction provides otherwise, be performed by any judge or District judge. The general jurisdiction of District judges is now set out in a Practice Direction.[84] The main features are as follows. A District judge may not

2–047

(1) make an injunction, except where (a) the District judge otherwise has jurisdiction, (b) the injunction is sought in a money claim not yet allocated to a track where the amount claimed does not exceed the fast track financial limit, or (c) in terms agreed by the parties or ancillary to certain other orders;

---

[76] *Judicial Statistics 2000*, pp. 50–51.
[77] *Practice Direction: Family Proceedings (Allocation to Judiciary) Direction* 1997 [1997] 2 F.L.R. 780, [1997] Fam. Law 691.
[78] *LCD Court Service Annual Report 1991–92* (1991–92 H.C.102), p. 40. The local committees bring matters of national policy significance to the attention of the Children Act Sub-Committee of the Lord Chancellor's Advisory Board on Family Law. This succeeded the Children's Act Advisory Committee (see (1995) Litigation 245) which advised ministers and the President of the Family Division on detailed operational issues. The Advisory Board itself ceases its work in 2002 but new structures are to enable the work of the Sub-Committee to continue: *ABFA Annual Report 2001*, Foreword (LCD website).
[79] High Court and County Courts Jurisdiction Order 1991 (S.I. 1991 No. 734), Art. 2.
[80] Civil Courts Order 1983 (S.I. 1983 No. 713), as amended.
[81] *ibid.*
[82] A Patents County Court has been established in London under the Copyright, Designs and Patents Act 1988, ss.287–292, "to handle smaller, shorter, less complex, less important, lower value actions" than the Patents Court (below, para. 2-060.): *per* Sir Thomas Bingham M.R. in *Chaplin Patents Holdings Co. plc v. Group Lotus plc, The Times*, January 12, 1994, where the Court of Appeal upheld a decision not to transfer proceedings to the High Court.
[83] D. Price, *Appeals* (1982), pp. 46–49 lists 29 situations.
[84] *Practice Direction 2b: Allocation of Cases to Levels of Judiciary.* The limitations were formerly found in the County Court Rules 1981, Ord. 21, r. 5, as amended.

(2) make an order committing a person to prison except where authorised by an enactment;

(3) hear appeals under section 204 of the Housing Act 1996;

(4) try a case involving an allegation of unlawful indirect discrimination against a public authority.

On the other hand, a District judge has jurisdiction to hear any claim allocated to the small claims track or fast track or which is treated as allocated to the multi-track under CPR, r.8.9,[85] except claims under specified Acts of Parliament; proceedings for the recovery of land; the assessment of damages or other sum due to a party under a judgment without any financial limit; and, with the consent of the parties and the permission of the Designated Civil Judge[86] in respect of that case, any other proceedings. A case allocated to the small claims track may only be assigned to a Circuit judge with his or her consent. Where both the Circuit judge and District judge have jurisdiction in any proceedings, the exercise of jurisdiction by the District judge is subject to any arrangements made by the Designated Civil Judge for the proper distribution of business between Circuit judges and District judges.

District judges accordingly have a major role to play in hearing small claims. The court "may adopt any method of proceeding" that it "considers to be fair" and hearings are informal.[87] Prior to the Woolf reforms, District judges tried or arbitrated most small claims. Research on the handing of such cases was favourable:

> "In approach and manner, district judges are decidedly down-to-earth. When dealing with litigants in person, there is no room for standing on ceremony, for airs and graces, or for pomposity ... [S]mall claims hearings are in the main characterized by good humour and robust common sense, seasoned with large doses of legal and judicial pragmatism."[88]

(e) The boundary between High Court and County Court

2–048   The relationship between the jurisdictions of the county court and the High Court was significantly altered by the Courts and Legal Services Act 1990, implementing recommendations of the Civil Justice Review.[89] The aim was to switch an increasing proportion of civil business from the High Court to county courts; a significant number of High Court civil cases was in any event being heard by Circuit judges sitting as judges of the High Court or by deputy High Court judges. Section 1 of the 1990 Act enables the Lord Chancellor to make provision by order for the allocation of business between the High Court and county courts; jurisdiction to hear applications

---

[85] As to these, see below, para. 12-005.
[86] See above, para. 2-041.
[87] CPR r. 27.8. See generally CPR, Part 27 and *Practice Direction 27 — Small Claims Track.*
[88] J. Baldwin, *Small Claims in the County Court in England and Wales* (1997), p. 154.
[89] Below, para. 12-001.

for judicial review may not, however, be conferred on the county court. The High Court and County Courts Order 1991[90] provides that where both courts have jurisdiction, proceedings may be commenced in either, except that[91] (1) a claim for money may only be commenced in the High Court if the financial value of the claim[92] is more than £15,000; and (2) personal injuries claims[93] may only be commenced in the High Court if the financial value of the claim is £50,000 or more.[94] In cases of concurrent jurisdiction, either court may hear the case. The allocation of a case to the appropriate track (small claims track, fast track, multi-track) and the appropriate court (including arrangements for transfer) is now dealt with in the Civil Procedure Rules.[95] However each court has power to transfer a case to the other.[96] Indeed, if proceedings are required to be started in the other, it must order a transfer or, if satisfied that the person bringing them knew or ought to have known of the requirement, order that they be struck out.[97] Orders may be made on the court's own motion or on the application of any party. The discretion to transfer must be exercised with regard to—

(a) the financial value of the claim and the amount in dispute, if different;

(b) whether it would be more convenient or fair for hearings (including the trial) to be held in some other court;

(c) the availability of a judge specialising in the type of claim in question;

(d) whether the facts, legal issues, remedies or procedures involved are simple or complex;

(e) the importance of the outcome of the claim to the public in general;

(f) the facilities available at the court where the claim is being dealt with and whether they may be inadequate because of any disabilities of a party or potential witness[98];

---

[90] S.I. 1991 No.734, as amended by S.I. 1993 No. 1407, S.I. 1995 No. 205, S.I. 1996 No. 3141 and S.I. 1999 No. 1014. This order does not apply to family proceedings: Art. 12. See I.R. Scott (1991) 10 C.J.Q. 282.

[91] Other exceptions are that applications or appeals under the Local Government Finance Act 1992, ss.19, 20 must be commenced in the High Court, and applications under the Access to Neighbouring Land Act 1992 must be commenced in the county court.

[92] Financial values are calculated in accordance with CPR r. 16.3(6): Art. 9, substituted by S.I. 1999 No. 1014, Art. 9.

[93] Other than negligence claims arising out of the provision of clinical or medical services (including dental or nursing services), which are accordingly subject to the £15,000 limit.

[94] arts 4, 4A, 5 (Art. 4(A) inserted and Art. 5 amended by S.I. 1999 No. 1014, arts 4–6).

[95] Parts 26–30. See below, para. 12-005.

[96] Transfers to a county court must be to such court as the High Court considers appropriate, having regard to the convenience of the parties and other affected persons and the state of business of the courts concerned.

[97] County Courts Act 1984, ss.40,42, substituted by the Courts and Legal Services Act 1990, s.2(l), (3). There is also power for the High Court at any stage to order the transfer of proceedings commenced in (or transferred to) the county court to (or back to) the High Court: s.41, as amended by the 1990 Act, s.2(2). The court is not obliged to strike out an action if satisfied that the applicant "knew or ought to have known of the requirement"; it may instead order transfer: *Restick v. Crickmore* [1994] 1 W.L.R. 420. There is also provision for the transfer of cases between county courts and between the Royal Courts of Justice and district registries: CPR r.30.2(1), r.30.2(4).

[98] CPR r.30.3.

(g) whether the making of a declaration of incompatibility under section 4 of the Human Rights Act 1998 has arisen or may arise.[98]

A review of the 1991 changes completed in 1993 "indicated that, broadly speaking, the changes had met their objectives". In 1993–94, the number of trials in the Queen's Bench general list which resulted in an award of £25,000 or less fell to 346 (compared with 1,828 in 1990–91); the percentage of trials heard by High Court judges involving an award of £5,000 or less fell to 3.8 per cent (71 per cent in 1990–91).[99] It is also the case that the number of writs issued in the Queen's Bench Division has declined sharply, from over 100,000 in 1991–92 to 35,000 in 1994–95.[1] There were further annual reductions to 1998–99 and then, following the introduction of the Civil Procedure Rules in April 1999, a 69 per cent reduction in the number of claims issued to 6,596 in 1999–2000 and a further 19 per cent to 5,541 in 2000–01.[2]

In his *Interim Report on Access to Justice*, Lord Woolf recommended that while the High Court and county courts should be retained as separate courts and the separate status of High Court judge preserved, the two levels of court should generally have the same jurisdiction and outside London should be administered together. Proceedings could be commenced in either and then transferred by the court to the appropriate level. There would be a combined set of procedural rules. The county court should have an increased small claims jurisdiction and deal with "fast track" cases.[3] Reponses to the interim review were "overwhelmingly favourable" and its recommendations were taken forward into Lord Woolf's *Final Report on Access to Justice*[4] and the government's White Paper, *Modernising Justice*.[5] A subsequent LCD consultation paper, *Modernising the Civil Courts*[6] noted that the current geographical spread of civil courts was based on the premise that the citizen would communicate with the court by attending in person or in writing. "Revolutionary changes in society and technology" make this no longer appropriate. The paper proposed the clear separation of "back office" administration and hearing centres; the Royal Courts of Justice would be the "flagship hearing centre for civil justice" and there would be a series of primary hearing centres for the management of defended cases, and a network of supplementary civil justice venues involving the best use of technology to enable remote access and joint working with Crown and magistrates' courts, tribunals, council chambers and other agencies. Streamlined, regionally based business centres would be established for administrative work, providing customers service by telephone and email.

---

[99] *LCD Court Service Annual Report 1993–94* (1993–94 H.C. 568), p. 49.

[1] *LCD Court Service Annual Report 1994–95* (1994–95 H.C. 579), p. 37.

[2] *LCD Court Service Annual Reports 1999–2000*, p. 30, and *2000–01*, p. 26.

[3] Report (1995), pp. 73–75, 79–81. Proposals for integration were previously considered and rejected by the Gorell Committee on County Court Procedure (1908–09 H.C. 71), the Beeching Commission on Assizes and Quarter Sessions (Cmnd. 4153, 1969), p. 73, and the Civil Justice Review (Cm.394), Chap. 3. See Sir Jack Jacob, *The Reform of Civil Procedural Law* (1982), pp. 7–13.

[4] HMSO, 1996.

[5] Cm. 4155, 1998, Chap. 4. This followed a *Review of Civil Justice and Legal Aid* by Sir Peter Middleton (1997). See further, Chap. 12.

[6] January 2001, LCD website.

This would be complemented by new ways of interacting with customers and supporting the judiciary using IT.

(f) Procedural Rules and Practice Directions

Procedure in the county court was formerly governed by County Court **2–049** Rules made by a committee appointed by the Lord Chancellor. They were subject to the approval of the Lord Chancellor, either as submitted or after amendment by him.[7] The rules were substantially revised in 1981 and were to be found in editions of the *County Court Practice* (the "Green Book").[8] By virtue of the Civil Procedure Act 1997, unified "Civil Procedure Rules" govern the practice and procedure of the Court of Appeal (Civil Division), the High Court and county courts.[9] They are made by the Civil Procedure Rule Committee, which comprises the Master of the Rolls, the Vice-Chancellor, one judge of the Supreme Court, one Circuit judge, one District judge, a Master of the Supreme Court, three person with a Supreme Court qualification, three persons with the right to conduct litigation in relation to all proceedings in the Supreme Court, one person with experience in and knowledge of consumer affairs and one with experience in and knowledge of the lay advice sector.[10] The power to make rules must be exercised "with a view to securing that the civil justice system is accessible, fair and efficient" and the Committee must "try to make rules which are both simple and simply expressed".[11] The rules are published on the internet,[12] and in the White Book[13] and other publications.[14] The Lord Chancellor also now has statutory power to make practice directions, and any such directions made by any other person require his approval.[15]

(g) Register of judgments

A register recording all county court judgments and other specified orders is **2–050** maintained by a private company, Registry Trust Ltd, by agreement with the Lord Chancellor.[16] It was formerly maintained by the County Courts Branch of the Lord Chancellor's Department.

---

[7] County Courts Act 1984, s.75, as amended by the Courts and Legal Services Act 1990, s.16, Sched. 18, para. 47.

[8] County Court Rules 1981 (S.I. 1981 No. 1687). See R.C.L. Gregory Q.C., "The Genesis of the County Court Rules" (1983) 2 C.J.Q. 1.

[9] Civil Procedure Act 1997, s. 1; Civil Procedure Rules 1998 (S.I. 1998 No. 3132), as amended ("CPR").

[10] *ibid.* s.2. Proposed rules may be allowed or disallowed by the Lord Chancellor.

[11] *ibid.* ss. 1(3), 2(7).

[12] LCD website; *www.greenbook.co.uk.*

[13] *Civil Procedure The White Book 2002* (Sweet & Maxwell).

[14] *e.g. Civil Court Practice 2002* (the "Green Book") (Butterworths).

[15] County Courts Act 1984, s.74A, inserted by the Civil Procedure Act 1997, s.5(2).

[16] County Courts Act 1984 ss.73, as amended, and 73A, inserted by the Administration of Justice Act 1985, s.54; Register of County Court Judgments Regulations 1985 (S.I. 1985 No. 1807), as amended by S.I. 1986 No. 2001, S.I. 1993 Nos 710, 2173, S.I. 1996 No. 1177, S.I. 1999 No. 1845. It extends to liability orders under the Child Support Act 1991.

(h) Appeals[17]

Appeals normally lie from a District judge to the Circuit judge of the county court, and from a Circuit judge to a High Court judge of the Family Division (family proceedings), a High Court judge (final decisions in the small claims track or the fast track) or the Court of Appeal (final decisions in the multi-track, decisions on a claim under CPR, Part 8). Bankruptcy appeals lie to the Divisional Court of the Chancery Division. A second appeal to the Court of Appeal is only available if that Court considers that the appeal would raise an important point of principle or practice or that there is some other compelling reason for the Court of Appeal to hear it. Permission is normally required.[18]

6. THE CROWN COURT[19]

(a) The Beeching Royal Commission

2–051   In 1966 the Royal Commission on Assizes and Quarter Sessions was appointed, under the chairmanship of Lord Beeching, to inquire into the arrangements for the administration of justice at assizes and quarter sessions outside London, and to report what reforms should be made for the more convenient, economic and efficient disposal of the civil and criminal business dealt with by those courts. The *assize courts* were presided over by High Court judges sent out "on circuit", a system that could be traced back to the twelfth century and which had changed comparatively little since medieval times.[20] There were seven circuits of assize towns. Assizes had jurisdiction over all indictable criminal offences and exclusive jurisdiction over some, including homicide, serious crimes of violence and rape. In addition, assize courts had the same civil jurisdiction as the High Court sitting in London, although priority was given to criminal cases. There were *courts of quarter sessions* for each of the 58 counties and for 93 boroughs; there were five such courts in Greater London and one for the City of London. The borough quarter sessions were presided over by a part-time Recorder, sitting alone. The county quarter sessions comprised a bench of magistrates normally with a legally qualified Chairman or Deputy Chairman, some of whom were whole-time appointments. These courts had jurisdiction to try many indictable offences with a jury, and to hear appeals from magistrates' courts and from a variety of administrative orders. In London, the *Central Criminal Court* at the Old Bailey was in effect the assize court for criminal cases. It had a number of full-time judges, including the Recorder of London and the Common Serjeant; in addition some cases would be taken by High Court judges. In 1956, new courts known as *Crown Courts* were

---

[17] See generally, Chap. 18.
[18] CPR, Part 52; *Practice Direction 52 — Appeals*; Access to Justice Act 1999, ss. 54–57.
[19] See I.R. Scott, *The Crown Court* (1971); *The Crown Court. A guide to good practice* (four separate guides published under this or a similar title by the LCD, the CPS, the Bar Council and the Law Society).
[20] See above, para. 2-004. Additional "Commissioners of Assize", usually senior Q.C.s, could be appointed ad hoc.

established for Liverpool and Manchester to deal with both quarter sessions and assize work. A full time Recorder was appointed for each court. Responsibility for providing judges, court staff and court buildings was "as fragmented as the system itself".[21]

The Beeching Report identified many defects of assizes and quarter sessions and recommended a fundamental reorganisation. A number of features which a good court system should provide were identified[22]:

	(a)	Ease of physical access.
	(b)	An early hearing.
Convenience	(c)	The assurance of trial on a date of which reasonable notice has been given.
	(d)	Suitable accommodation.
Quality	(e)	Judicial expertise.
	(f)	Adequate and dependable legal representation.
Economy	(g)	Efficient use of all manpower.
	(h)	Optimum use of buildings.

The restricting factors were cost and the capacity of the Bar. The report's proposals were designed to[23]:

(a) simplify the structure of the courts;

(b) deploy judge power as flexibly as possible;

(c) relate court locations to travelling facilities for the public;

(d) secure the efficient administration of all court services;

(e) ensure that courts are built and maintained as economically and efficiently as possible."

The proposals, which involved the creation of a new superior court of criminal jurisdiction, to be called the Crown Court, were largely accepted. They were enacted in the Courts Act 1971, substantial parts of which were re-enacted in the Supreme Court Act 1981.

(b) The constitution of the Crown Court

The Crown Court is part of the Supreme Court of England and Wales.[24] It **2–052**
is a single court, but sittings may be conducted at any place in England and Wales, in accordance with directions given by the Lord Chancellor.[25] There are at present around 90 permanent centres.[26] The name "Central Criminal Court" has been retained for the Crown Court sitting in the City of London at the Old Bailey. There are three kinds of Crown Court centre: "first-tier" centres are visited by High Court judges, Circuit judges and recorders for the complete range of Crown Court business, and by High Court judges for

---

[21] Beeching Report, p. 31.
[22] *ibid.* p. 48.
[23] *ibid.* p. 64.
[24] Supreme Court Act 1981, s.l. Procedural rules can be prescribed by the Crown Court Rule Committee: *ibid.* s.86, as amended by the Courts and Legal Services Act 1990, Sched. 18, para. 36(2).
[25] *ibid.* s.78.
[26] See *Shaw's Directory of Courts in the United Kingdom.*

High Court civil work; "second-tier" centres are the same as first-tier except that no civil business is done; "third-tier" centres are normally visited only by Circuit judges and recorders. The centres are grouped into six circuits: Midland and Oxford, North Eastern, Northern, South Eastern, Wales and Chester, and Western.[27]

The jurisdiction of the Crown Court is exerciseable by any judge of the High Court, Circuit judge or recorder.[28] In some cases one of these may sit with not more than four justices of the peace[29]: a court must normally be so comprised when hearing an appeal[30] and may be so comprised for other proceedings, but not cases listed for pleas of not guilty.[31]

(c) Jurisdiction

2–053 The Crown Court has exclusive jurisdiction with respect to criminal trials on indictment.[32] It also has an extensive appellate jurisdiction inherited from quarter sessions, including appeals from magistrates' courts in criminal cases and appeals in a wide variety of administrative matters, such as betting, gaming and liquor licensing. Magistrates' courts may also commit convicted persons to the Crown Court for sentence.

(d) Distribution of business

2–054 The classes of cases in the Crown Court suitable for allocation respectively to a High Court judge, Circuit judge or recorder, and to a court including justices, are prescribed in directions given by the Lord Chief Justice, with the concurrence of the Lord Chancellor.[33] For the purposes of trial in the Crown Court, offences are grouped in four classes.

Class 1

These offences are to be tried by a High Court judge and include misprision of treason and treason felony, murder, genocide, torture, hostage-taking and offences under the War Crimes Act 1991, and offences under the Official Secrets Acts. A case of murder may be released by authority of a presiding judge, for trial by a deputy High Court judge, Circuit judge or deputy Circuit judge approved for the purpose by the Lord Chief Justice.

---

[27] See H.L. Deb. Vol. 314, col. 948, January 26, 1971; H.L. Deb. Vol. 321, col. 572, July 1, 1971; H.L. Deb. Vol. 343, col. 968, June 14, 1973.
[28] Supreme Court Act 1981, s.8. See below para. 4-020.
[29] *ibid.* and see below, para. 4-012.
[30] Supreme Court Act 1981, s.74, as amended by the Access to Justice Act 1999, s.79 and Sched. 15 (deleting a reference to committals for sentence); Crown Court Rules 1982 (S.I. 1982 No. 1109), as amended, rr.3–5.
[31] See below, para. 2-054.
[32] Supreme Court Act 1981, s.46.
[33] Supreme Court Act 1981, s.75: *Practice Direction (Crown Court: Business)* [2001] 1.W.L.R. 1996.

Class 2

These offences are to be tried by a High Court judge unless a particular case is released by or on the authority of a presiding judge for trial by a deputy High Court judge, Circuit judge or deputy Circuit judge, and include manslaughter, infanticide, abortion, rape, sexual intercourse or incest with a girl under 13, sedition, mutiny and piracy. A case of rape, or a serious sexual offence, may be released by a presiding judge for trial only by a Circuit judge, deputy Circuit judge or recorder approved for that purpose by the senior presiding judge with the concurrence of the Lord Chief Justice.

Class 3

These offences may be listed for trial by a High Court judge, or, in accordance with general or particular directions given by a presiding judge, by a Circuit judge, a deputy Circuit judge or a recorder who has attended a Judicial Studies Board continuation seminar and has been duly authorised by a presiding judge. They comprise all offences triable only on indictment other than those in classes, 1, 2 and 4.

Class 4

These may be tried by a High Court judge, a deputy High Court judge, a Circuit judge, a deputy Circuit judge or a recorder. They may not be listed for trial by a High Court judge except with his or her consent or that of a presiding judge, and include all offences triable either way and a number of specific offences including wounding or causing grievous bodily harm with intent and robbery.

Presiding judges, with the approval of the senior presiding judge, must issue directions as to the need where appropriate to reserve a case for trial by a High Court judge, the allocation of work between Circuit judges, deputy Circuit judges and recorders and, where necessary, the devolved responsibility of resident or designated judges for such allocation.[34] Specific provision must be made in these directions for cases in 15 specified categories, including, for example, cases involving death or serious risk to life or the use of loaded firearms, arson or criminal damage with intent to endanger life, a number of offences involving serious violence, cases where the trial may last more than 10 days or involve more than five defendants and cases involving difficult issues of law.

Most other Crown Court proceedings are normally listed for hearing by a court presided over by a Circuit judge or a recorder. Any proceedings listed for hearing by a Circuit judge or recorder, except pleas of not guilty, are stated to be suitable for allocation to a court comprising justices of the peace.

Appeals from decisions of magistrates are to be heard by (i) a resident or

---

[34] These are Circuit judges appointed by the presiding judges to have responsibility, at one or more centres, for seeing to the efficient and orderly running of the lists: *Civil Justice Review* (Cm. 394, 1988), para. 307.

designated judge; (ii) a Circuit judge, nominated by the resident or designated judge, who regularly sits at the Crown Court centre; (iii) an experienced recorder specifically approved by the presiding judges for the purpose; or, otherwise, (iv) a Circuit judge or recorder selected by the resident or designated judge for a specific case or cases.

The same Practice Direction prescribes the general principles for the distribution of business among the different court centres geographically. Generally, the magistrates committing, transferring or sending a person for trial should select the "most convenient location" of the appropriate tier of Crown Court centre, having regard to the convenience of defence, prosecution and witnesses and the expediting of the trial,[35] and to the location or locations designated by the presiding judge as the normal ones for committals from their petty sessions area. It is possible for the location to be changed.[36] In addition, the "catchment areas" are varied if the work-load at a particular Crown Court centre requires cases to be directed to a less busy centre. Arrangements can be made for a case to be transferred from one circuit to another.[37] Thirty-six centres have been designated for the trial of serious and complex fraud trials,[38] and over 60 have been equipped with live television link facilities.[39]

(e) Administration

2–055 Another important feature of the Beeching Report and the Courts Act 1971 was the establishment of a "unified court service" under the direction of the Lord Chancellor, providing administrative support to the Supreme Court, including the Crown Court and county courts.[40] The service has from 1995 been an executive agency of the Lord Chancellor's Department, and is organised on a circuit basis. The administration in each circuit is headed by a Circuit Administrator, a civil servant of Under Secretary rank responsible to the Lord Chancellor. Each of these has a small headquarters staff and three or four Group Managers working under him or her, each responsible for a particular area.[41] The Circuit Administrators work closely with the presiding judges and deal with such matters as personnel management, finance and accommodation. The Group Manager has responsibility for planning the courts' sittings and ensuring the smooth disposal of business between courts, and is a point of contact for the various parties concerned with the running of the courts.

Two High Court judges are assigned to each circuit by the Lord Chief Justice to act as presiding judges: at least one should be present in the circuit

---

[35] Magistrates' Courts Act 1980, s.7; Crime and Disorder Act 1998, s.51(10).

[36] Supreme Court Act 1981, s.76: *Practice Direction (Crown Court: Business)* [2001] 1 W.L.R. 1996, paras 12–14.

[37] *ibid.* para 9.

[38] *Practice Direction (Crown Court: Fraud Trials (No. 3))* [1993] 1 W.L.R. 158.

[39] *Practice Direction (Crown Courts: TV Links)* [1992] 1 W.L.R. 838; *LCD Court Service Annual Report 1995–96*, p.29.

[40] Courts Act 1971, s.27. See I. R. Scott, *The Crown Court* (1971), Chap. IV; E. C. Friesen and I. R. Scott, *English Criminal Justice* (1977), pp. 121–5; and I. R. Scott, *Court Administration: The Case for a Judicial Council* (1979).

[41] There is a Courts Administrator responsible for the Central Criminal Court.

at any given time. Presiding judges have certain functions in relation to the allocation of cases.[42]

Their position has been summarised as follows[43]:

"The presiding judges are the judicial authority for the circuit paralleling the administrative authority of the Circuit Administrators. ... Where they perform properly (and there is some unevenness) the presiding judges make a substantial effort to control judicial performance on their circuits. They know the capabilities of the Circuit judges and in consultation with the Circuit Administrators they see that these judges are properly assigned and utilised according to skill and expertise."

However, it was noted in the early years that the presiding judges frequently lacked confidence when dealing with their more senior colleagues, that some did not capture the respect of Circuit judges in their circuit, that there was too much doubt as to their proper role, that uncertainty was created by the fact that so much depended on the respective personalities of presiding judge and Circuit Administrator and that the judge's position was weakened by the fact that appointments are only for short periods.[44]

A Lord Justice of Appeal has been appointed as a senior presiding judge who is available for consultation by the presiding judges and relieves the Lord Chief Justice of certain administrative responsibilities.[45] The offices of presiding judge and senior presiding judge now have statutory recognition.[46]

(f) Workload

The workload of the Crown Court has increased very significantly since it was established: **2–056**

"It is undoubtedly true to say that in the light of the inexorable increase in caseloads chaos would have ensued but for the implementation of the Beeching Reforms. The number of persons working in the court service is now about 10,000 and the range of quasi-judicial and administrative tasks undertaken by this bureaucracy is far greater much more sophisticated than those attempted under the pre-1971 arrangements."[47]

Between 1979 and 1989 committals for trial received by the Crown Court more than doubled, with an average annual growth rate of over seven per

---

[42] See above.
[43] Friesen and Scott (1977), p.124.
[44] Scott (1979), p.16. An account of Judge James Pickles' relations with presiding judges on his circuit and the Lord Chief Justice is given in his book, *Straight from the Bench* (1987), Chap.1.
[45] (1983) 133 N.L.J. 732.
[46] Courts and Legal Services Act 1990, s.72.
[47] Scott (1979), p.5.

cent.[48] Since 1989, the number peaked in 1991 (104,754) but has since fallen (to 71,022 in 2000).[49]

Other important factors have been the establishment of the circuit bench and the increase in the number of High Court judges, and the court-building programme. Nevertheless, the increase in workload meant that waiting times increased dramatically.[50]

(g) Appeals[51]

2–057   Appeals in relation to trials on indictment and in cases where a defendant has been committed for sentence to the Crown Court lie to the Court of Appeal (Criminal Division).[52] Appeals from an exercise of the Crown Court's appellate jurisdiction lie to the High Court on the same basis as appeals there from the magistrates' court.

(h) The Auld Report

2–058   Lord Justice Auld's Report on his *Review of the Criminal Courts of England and Wales*[53] recommended that the Crown Court and magistrates' courts should be replaced by a unified criminal court with three divisions.[54] The Crown Division, with the same constitution as the Crown Court, would deal with all indictable only offences and the more serious either-way offences allocated to it. The District Division would be constituted by a judge, normally a District judge or recorder, sitting with at least two magistrates, and exercise jurisdiction in respect of a mid-range of either-way matters of sufficient seriousness to merit up to two years custody. These are cases that "do not warrant the cumbersome and expensive fact-finding exercise of trial by judge and jury, but which are sufficiently serious or difficult, or their outcome is of such consequence to the public or the defendants, to merit a combination of professional and lay judges, but working together in a simpler way".[55] The Magistrates' Division would be constituted by District judges or by magistrates as magistrates' courts are today. Either-way cases would be allocated by the Magistrates' Division according to the seriousness

---

[48] *Judicial Statistics 1989* (Cm. 1154), p.67.

[49] *Judicial Statistics 2000*, p.64 The highest total ever was in 1988 (106,524) before reclassification of certain offences as summary only.

[50] In 1973, of the 13,925 defendants disposed of on indictment and who had awaited trial in custody, 74% were dealt with within eight weeks of committal and 96% within 20 weeks. In 1980 the figures were 16,088, 54% and 87% respectively. See generally, I. R. Scott, "Crown Court Productivity" [1980] Crim. L.R. 193, noting the growing proportion of not guilty pleas and the lengthening of hearing times in contested cases. By 1987 of 31,443 defendants in custody, 58%. waited less than eight weeks and 85% less than 16 weeks. Between 1980 and 1983 the average waiting time for all defendants committed for trial fell from 17.3 weeks to 14.2 weeks. It stayed at roughly that figure until 1987 (12.3 weeks), 1988 (12.2 weeks)), the lowest annual average level since 1976, and 1989 (12.4 weeks). The figure rose sharply after 1991 to 16.1 in 1995: *Judicial Statistics 1995*, Tables 6.15 to 6.20 but then fell to 13.1 (1996), 13.2 (1998) and 14.2 (2000): *Judicial Statistics 1996, 1988* and *2000*. See further, para. 14-066.

[51] See generally, Chap. 18, below.

[52] See below, para. 2-070.

[53] HMSO, October 2001.

[54] Chapter 7. See further, para. 14-048.

[55] p.277, para. 26.

of the alleged offence and the defendant's circumstances, looking at the possible outcome of the case at its worst and bearing in mind the jurisdiction of each Division. A dispute as to venue would be determined by the District judge after hearing representations. The defendant would have no right of election; if the current system were to continue, the current right of election should be removed.

As regards the administration of the courts, the present Court Service and magistrates' courts committees should be replaced by a single centrally funded executive agency with responsibility for all courts, civil criminal and family (apart from the Appellate Committee of the House of Lords). There should also be greater flexibility in the allocation of cases to the judiciary, with a significant shift in heavy work from High Court judges to the Circuit bench.[56]

The proposal for establishment of an additional, middle tier of the unified criminal court has been criticised by Michael Zander[57] on the basis that, assuming abolition of the right of election, the existence of two forms by trial (by magistrates' court or Crown Court) was sufficient. It was not explained by the Auld Report how trial by a District judge sitting with magistrates would provide a more appropriate mode of trial for this class of case, although it would be cheaper.

7. THE HIGH COURT

(a) Constitution

The High Court of Justice is a court of unlimited civil jurisdiction and also has an important appellate jurisdiction in both civil and criminal matters. It is part of the Supreme Court of England and Wales,[58] and was created as part of the reorganisation of the superior courts under the Supreme Court of Judicature Acts 1873–75. It sits at the Royal Courts of Justice in the Strand[59] and at 27 first-tier Crown Court centres outside London.[60] There are three divisions: the Chancery Division, Queen's Bench Division and Family Division,[61] headed, respectively, by the Vice-Chancellor,[62] the Lord Chief Justice and the President of the Family Division.[63] Each High Court judge[64] is attached to one of the divisions, but they may be transferred to one of the others with their consent, and they may act as an additional judge

2–059

---

[56] Chapter 6.

[57] Comment on the Auld Review, LCD website and *www.lse.ac.uk/Depts/law*.

[58] The Supreme Court was thus re-titled by the Supreme Court Act 1981.

[59] The Supreme Court moved here from Westminster Hall in 1883. See F. W. Maitland, (1942) 8 C.L.J. 2; J. Kinnard in P. Ferriday (ed.), *Victorian Architecture* (1963); M. H. Port, "The New Law Courts Competition, 1866–67" (1968) *Architectural History* 75–93.

[60] See above.

[61] Supreme Court Act 1981, s.5(1). The number of divisions can be altered by Order in Council: *ibid.* s.7.

[62] Technically, the Lord Chancellor is the president and the Vice-Chancellor the vice-president of the Chancery Division, but the latter is the effective head.

[63] See below.

[64] See below.

of one of them at the request of the Lord Chancellor.[65] Different classes of business are allocated for administrative convenience to each division by rules of court,[66] although technically all the jurisdiction of the High Court belongs to all the divisions alike.[67] There have been two major reorganisations. In 1881 the Exchequer and Common Pleas Divisions were merged into the Queen's Bench Division,[68] and in 1971 the Probate, Divorce and Admiralty Division was re-named the Family Division, with Admiralty business assigned to the Queen's Bench Division, probate business other than non-contentious or common form matters assigned to the Chancery Division, and wardship, guardianship and adoption jurisdiction transferred from Chancery Division to Family Division.[69]

A joint committee of High Court judges and civil servants recommended abolition of the three separate divisions of the High Court,[70] but this recommendation was not implemented. A joint committee of the Bar and the Law Society chaired by Hilary Heilbron Q.C.[71] recommended the merger of the Chancery and Queen's Bench Divisions to form a Civil Division, presided over by the Lord Chief Justice. However, Lord Woolf, in his *Interim Report on Access to Justice*, concluded that merger was not desirable, noting among other factors the distinctive nature of the specialist jurisdictions that fall under the Chancery umbrella, the team spirit among Chancery judges and their special relationship with the Chancery Bar, and the relatively small number of Chancery judges. However, judges should be assigned to lists according to their expertise, irrespective of the division to which the list belongs.[72] A further development recommended by Lord Woolf was the appointment of a senior judge as Head of Civil Justice responsible, *inter alia*, to provide leadership for the civil justice system. Civil work should be made the express responsibility of one of the two presiding judges on each circuit, and there should be a senior civil judge appointed for each trial centre.[73] In the event, a Head of Civil Justice has been appointed,[74] and a Designated Civil Judge appointed for each trial centre,[75] but it has been left to the presiding judges to arrange for the discharge of responsibility for civil work, given that only one is usually on circuit at any time.[76]

---

[65] Supreme Court Act 1981, s.5(2), (3).
[66] Supreme Court Act 1981, s.61.
[67] *ibid.* s.5(5). Any Division to which a cause or matter is assigned has jurisdiction to grant any remedy or relief sought notwithstanding that proceedings for such remedy or relief are assigned to another Division: *Practice Direction (High Court: Divisions)* [1973] 1 W.L.R. 627. Cases may be transferred between Divisions: see J. Jacob, (1988) 7 C.J.Q. 94; *Barclays Bank v. Bemister* and *Pryke v. Gibbs Hartley Cooper Ltd* [1989] 1 All E.R. 10, CA.
[68] This was done by an Order in Council which was made on December 16, 1880 and which came into force on February 26, 1881.
[69] Administration of Justice Act 1970, with effect from August 2, 1971.
[70] Committee on the Deployment of the High Court: *Legal Action*, June 1988, p.5; (1988) L. S. Gaz. May 25, p.3.
[71] *Civil Justice on Trial—The Case for Change* (1993). See I. R. Scott, (1994) 13 C.J.Q. 9.
[72] Report, pp. 76–78.
[73] *ibid.*, pp. 58–62.
[74] The first was Sir Richard Scott V.-C. Lord Phillips M.R. became Head in 2000.
[75] See above, para. 2-048.
[76] Lord Woolf, *Access to Justice — Final Report*, pp. 92–94.

Most High Court work is taken by a single judge sitting alone.[77] This should be in open court, except where under rules of court or in accordance with the practice of the court it is dealt with in chambers.[78] A proportion of the appellate and supervisory work of the High Court is dealt with by "divisional courts", which comprise two or more judges.[79]

The business is mainly conducted by the heads of division and the puisne[80] judges of the High Court. In addition, High Court work may be taken by a deputy High Court judge, a Circuit judge, a recorder, a judge of the Court of Appeal or a former judge of the High Court or the Court of Appeal.[81]

(b) The Chancery Division

The division deals with property, trusts, the administration of estates, **2–060** corporate and personal insolvency partnership, companies, revenue cases, probate business other than non-contentious common form business, and other matters specifically assigned.[82] The Patents Court established in 1977[83] is part of this division. In addition the judges of the division have been assigned to deal with the management of the property and affairs of mental patients under the Mental Health Act 1983. This work is the responsibility of the "Court of Protection" which is in fact an office of the Supreme Court rather than a court.

The business is at present handled by the Vice-Chancellor and 17 puisne judges, two of whom are nominated to the Patents Court although they are available to help with the other work of the Division. One judge (Blackburne J.) holds the appointment of Vice-Chancellor of the Duchy of Lancaster.[84] The judges are assisted by six Chancery masters and five registrars in bankruptcy.[85] The work is done in London and at eight centres

---

[77] There is provision for a judge to sit with assessors who are specially qualified in relation to the proceedings in question: 1981 Act, s.70. They are mainly used in Admiralty proceedings. See CPR, r.35.15 and para. 20(1) of *Practice Direction 61 — Admiralty*. below, para. 2-062.

[78] Supreme Court Act 1981, s.67.1 Under CPR, r.39.2, the "general rule is that a hearing is to be in public"; this is subject to exceptions specified in r.39.3. This satisfies the requirements of Articles 6 and 10, ECHR: *R. (on the application of Pelling) v. Bow County Court* (unreported, October 19, 2000). A hearing whether in court or in chambers may be in public or private according to the requirements of r.39.2 and r.39.3.

[79] *ibid.* s.66.

[80] See below, para. 4-021.

[81] *ibid.* s.9. There have been complaints that too many High Court cases have been heard by Circuit judges and recorders sitting as deputy High Court judges. The Civil Justice Review Body thought it excessive that 30% of High Court sittings were by persons who were not High Court judges: their proposals for the transfer of business to the county court (see pp.) should mean that deputy judges would only be appointed to give them experience or to cover peaks of work or temporary shortages of judge power (Cm. 394, para. 192).

[82] *ibid.* Sched. 1. The judges who deal with bankruptcy are referred to as the "High Court of Justice in Bankruptcy" and those who deal with company matters as the "Companies Court", but these are not formally constituted as courts under the 1981 Act. On the latter, see A. Boyle and P. Marshall, *The Practice and Procedure of the Companies Court* (1997).

[83] Patents Act 1977. The judge may sit with scientific advisers: Supreme Court Act 1981, s.70; RSEC Ord. 104, r.11.

[84] This office, to which the appointment is made by the Chancellor of the Duchy, was formerly held by a Circuit judge: see para. 4-020.

[85] See R. E. Ball, "The Chancery Master" (1961) 77 L.Q.R. 331. See generally, E. Heward, *Chancery Practice* (2nd ed., 1990).

in the provinces.[86] In the latter the work is done by the Vice-Chancellor of the Duchy of Lancaster, by a High Court judge sitting at Birmingham, Bristol and Cardiff and by Circuit judges who specialise in Chancery work and who sit for this purpose as judges of the High Court.[87] The Vice-Chancellor of the Duchy and another judge effectively act as presiding judges in relation to Chancery work outside London.[88] Steps have also been taken to transfer less onerous cases to the county court,[89] Chancery expertise for this purpose being concentrated at the Central London County Court.[90]

The administrative arrangements for the Chancery Division were substantially revised in 1982[91] following the Report of the Review Body on the Chancery Division of the High Court.[92] Amongst other matters the changes were designed to produce greater flexibility in the deployment of judges and a new approach to the drafting of orders "which should eliminate their present sesquipedalian pedantry".[93] As from October 1, 1982, orders became simpler in form and drawn by clerks (known as associates) rather than professionally qualified officers, thus bringing practice more into line with the other divisions. Further changes have been effected as part of the Woolf reforms, including the introduction of case management by the court.[94]

(c) The Queen's Bench Division

2–061 This division deals mainly with claims in contract and tort, and also exercises supervisory and appellate jurisdiction over inferior courts and tribunals. The supervisory jurisdiction includes most applications for habeas corpus and all applications for judicial review.[95] The appellate jurisdiction includes appeals by case stated on a point of law from magistrates' courts and the Crown Court. Also part of this division are the Admiralty Court and the Commercial Court.[96] The work is at present handled by the Lord Chief Justice[97] and 73 puisne judges (as at December 2001). The business is done in London and at the 27 first-tier Crown Court centres in the provinces.

---

[86] Leeds, Liverpool, Manchester, Newcastle-upon-Tyne, Preston, and, as from October 10, 1982, Birmingham, Bristol and Cardiff. See *Chancery Guide* (2000), para. 12.1.

[87] *Chancery Guide* (2000), para. 12.4–12.6. They may also take equity work in county courts.

[88] Lord Woolf's *Interim Report on Access to Justice* (1995), p. 61; *Chancery Guide* (2000), para. 12.3.

[89] Under s.40 of the County Courts Act 1984.

[90] *Practice Direction (Chancery: Transfer of Business)* [1988] 1 W.L.R. 741; *Chancery Guide* (2000), para. 13.

[91] See RSC (Amendment No. 2) 1982 (S.I. 1982 No. 1111); *Practice Direction (Chancery Chambers)* [1982] 1 W.L.R. 1189.

[92] Cmnd. 8205, 1981: report by Oliver L.J. and J.M. Woolf Esq.: see R. Blackford, (1981) 78 L.S. Gaz. 590.

[93] Blackford *op. cit.* p. 590.

[94] See generally the *Chancery Guide* (2000) (Court Service website).

[95] Supreme Court Act 1981, s.61 and Sched. 1. See below, Chap. 18.

[96] Supreme Court Act 1981, s.6.

[97] The Lord Chief Justice's time in court is wholly spent on appellate work. He no longer takes applications for judicial review at first instance.

In London, the judges are assisted by 13[98] masters of the Queen's Bench Division.[99] Any act under the Civil Procedure Rules in relation to proceedings in the High Court may be performed by a master, except where an enactment, rule or practice direction provides otherwise.[1] Much of their work concerns matters arising before the hearing of a claim, including the case management of cases proceeding in London. A master may try a case treated as being allocated to the multi-track and proceeding under CPR, Part 8, and (with the consent of the parties) cases allocated to the multi-track under CPR, Part 26, and may assess damages.[2] One master sits each day as the Practice Master, to deal with procedural and practice problems arising in the Central Office and generally to supervise the work of the office. The right of audience before a master is not limited to barristers; solicitors and their clerks may appear, including unadmitted clerks. The work is normally done in chambers, which lead off from an antechamber generally known as "the Bear Garden".

(i) The Admiralty Court

This court has jurisdiction in a wide variety of matters concerning ships and aircraft, including claims arising out of collisions, claims for damage to cargo, for goods supplied and for repairs.[3] When necessary, it also exercises the jurisdiction of the High Court as a prize court.[4] From 1993, the practice of the Admiralty has been harmonised with that of the Commercial Court.[5]   **2–062**

(ii) The Commercial Court[6]

There were a number of attempts in the nineteenth century to establish some form of specialised commercial court.[7] A Commercial List was established in the Queen's Bench Division in 1895, partly as the result of dissatisfaction with the handling of a commercial case by Lawrance J.[8] This did not,   **2–063**

---

[98] This figure includes the Master of the Crown Office, who is also Registrar of the Criminal Appeal Office. These offices were combined by the Courts and Legal Services Act 1990, s.78.

[99] See A. S. Diamond, "The Queen's Bench Master" (1960) 76 L.Q.R. 504; Sir Jack Jacob, "The Masters of the Queen's Bench Division" (1971) reprinted in *The Reform of Civil Procedural Law* (1982).

[1] CPR, r.2.4. Thus, for example, a master may not make a freezing order on an order authorising a person to enter land to recover, inspect or sample property, or an injunction (subject to exceptions, as where the terms are agreed by the parties).

[2] *Practice Direction 2b — Allocation of cases to Levels of Judiciary*, paras 4.1., 4.2. See para. 12-005.

[3] Supreme Court Act 1981, ss. 20–24.

[4] *ibid.* ss. 27, 62.

[5] *Practice Direction (Admiralty Court: Practice)* [1993] 1 W.L.R. 960; *Practice Direction (Admiralty Court: Practice)* [1996] 1 W.L.R. 127. See now CPR, Parts 49 and 61 and *Practice Direction 61 — Admiralty. The Guide to Commercial Court Practice* (below) applies, with some exceptions.

[6] Sir Anthony Colman, V. Lyon and P. Hopkins, *The Practice and Procedure of the Commercial Court* (5th ed., 2000); *Civil Justice Review* (Cm. 394, 1988), Chap. 11.

[7] Colman, Lyon and Hopkins (2000), Chap. 1.

[8] See below, para. 4-024. (1895–96) 1 Com. Cas. pp. i-x; MacKihnon L.J., (1944) 60 L.Q.R. 324–325; V. V. Veeder, (1994) 110 L.Q.R. 282; Lord Parker C.J., *History and Development of Commercial Arbitration* (1959).

however, end the drift to arbitration.[9] The list was transformed into a court in 1970.[10] Particular features of the Commercial Court are that, in principle and court resources permitting, a hearing should take place at the earliest date for which the parties can be ready; pre-trial matters are dealt with by a judge rather than a master; and that the court "expects a high level of co-operation and realism" from the parties' legal representatives.[11] Statements of case must be "as brief and concise as possible".[12] The procedural rules have been revised to take account of the Woolf reforms.[13] A judge of the Commercial Court may be appointed as an arbitrator, provided the Lord Chief Justice agrees that he or she can be made available.[14] Separate lists were established in the district registries in Liverpool and Manchester in 1991, in Birmingham in 1993 and in Bristol in 1994. Cases set down in them are tried by designated circuit commercial judges sitting as High Court judges.[15] These are now termed "merchantile courts".[16]

A Commercial Court Committee was established in 1977 to consider and keep under review the working of the Court and the appeal procedures in arbitration proceedings, and to report to the Lord Chancellor.[17] A report of this committee[18] led to the enactment of the Arbitration Act 1979, which was designed to limit rights of appeal to the courts from the decisions of arbitrators, and thereby to halt a decline in the standing of London as a leading centre of international commercial arbitration.[19]

In recent years the caseload of the Commercial Court has increased significantly,[20] although it is still small in relation to the number of arbitrations. Waiting times for trial increased dramatically.[21] Three features

---

[9] See G. Wilson, *Cases and Materials on the English Legal System* (1973), pp. 31–43; R. B. Ferguson, "The Adjudication of commercial disputes and the legal system in modern England" (1980) 7 B.J.L.S. 141.

[10] Administration of Justice Act 1970, s.3(1).

[11] *Practice Direction and Commercial Court*, para. 2.2; *Commercial Court Guide* (5th ed.), para.A4.

[12] *Commercial Court Guide*, Appendix 4.

[13] See CPR, Parts 49 and 58.

[14] Arbitration Act 1996, s.93. Such appointments are rare.

[15] *Practice Direction (Commercial Lists: Manchester and Liverpool)* [1990] 1 W.L.R. 331, see G. Wingate-Saul, (1990) 140 N.L.J. 539; *Practice Direction (Mercantile List: Birmingham)* [1993] 1 W.L.R. 1401; *Practice Direction (Mercantile Court: Bristol)* [1994] 1 W.L.R.1522; see L. Curry, 9(12) *The Lawyer*, p.15, March 21, 1995; F.Meisel (1994) 13 C.J.Q. 9; I.Garrard, *The Times*, July 26, 1994, p. 35, noting that these courts were cheaper and quicker to use than the Commercial Court in London.

[16] See CPR, Parts 49 and 59, *Practice Direction 59—Merchantile Courts and Business Lists*, and the *Merchantile Courts Guide* (Court Service website).

[17] See its Annual Report for 1980 (1981) 78 L.S. Gaz. 100; Colman, Lyon and Hopkins, Chap. 2.

[18] Commercial Court Committee, *Report on Arbitration* (Cmnd. 7284, 1978).

[19] See Ferguson (1980), pp. 151–154; Kerr J., "The Arbitration Act 1979" (1980) 43 M.L.R. 45.

[20] The number of cases heard and disposed of increased from an average of 20 a year between 1946 and 1959 (*Report of the Commercial Court Users' Conference* (Cmnd. 1616, 1962) Appendix G) to a high point of 157 in 1981, declining to 108 in 1986 (*Civil Justice Review*, para. 789); the figures in recent years have been: 79 (1993), 98 (1994), 85 (1995), 104 (1996), 179 (1997), 80 (1998) and 50 (1999) (Colman, Lyon, and Hawkins (2000), p. 22.

[21] From eight months in 1980 to 24 months in 1984 for a trial due to last longer than three days. In January 1987, trials estimated to last between two and four weeks were being given fixed dates for hearing in October 1990; those estimated at over four weeks were listed for February 1991; *Civil Justice Review*, paras 791, 792. A number of applications for transfer to another division were rejected if the sole ground was to obtain an earlier trial: see J. Jacob, (1988) 7 C.J.Q. 5.

of its work are that in many cases either one or both litigants are foreigners, that a significant part of the court's work comes from London arbitrations, and that it is commonplace for cases to involve millions of pounds.[22]

Concern over waiting times led to the establishment of a working party of practitioner members of the Commercial Court Committee to examine possible reforms.[23] Its report was adopted by the Committee and its recommendations as to improved practice, particularly as to documentation and the conduct of the hearing, commended to court users in a *Guide to Commercial Court Practice*.[24] A new combined Admiralty and Commercial Court Registry was established.[25] The operation of the court was also scrutinised by the Civil Justice Review Body,[26] which made a number of recommendations, including the introduction of a minimum jurisdictional limit of £50,000 (with special exceptions for complex or difficult cases), the provision of extra judge power on a temporary basis, and dealing with formal or uncontested business by consent or by applications on paper. The Commercial Court Committee, however, expressed strong opposition to the introduction of a lower financial limit as this would deter overseas users from litigating in London and would exclude complex cases raising important issues of commercial law which ought to be determined by the Commercial Court.[27]

A crisis in the early 1990s caused by the pressure of business was relieved by the appointment of additional judges: there are now 12 Commercial Court judges, six of whom sit at any one time.[28] The recognition that the court is a "very substantial earner indeed of foreign exchange in the form of invisible earnings"[29] no doubt helped the case for additional appointments. In consequence of the Woolf reforms, a specialised procedural regime for the Commercial Court has been created within the framework of the CPR.[30] This still "differs markedly from that in the non-specialist Queen's Bench Division",[31] including different arrangements for case management.

---

[22] Goff. J., "The Commercial Court—How it Works" (1980) 77 L.S. Gaz. 1035. See generally on the working of the court, Colman and Lyon, *op. cit.*

[23] See F. Meisel, "Commercial Court Reform" (1986) 5 C.J.Q. 196.

[24] See now the *Commercial Court Guide.*

[25] RSC (Amendment) 1987 (S.I. 1987 No. 1423); *Practice Direction (QBD) (New Admiralty and Commercial Court Registry)* [1987] 1 W.L.R. 1459.

[26] Report, Cm. 394, 1988, Chap. 11 . The Review Body commissioned a Factual Study by Coopers & Lybrand, which did not endorse all the assumptions that had been made by the earlier working party: see F. Meisel, "Commercial Court Reform—The Lord Chancellor's Consultation Paper" (1987) 6 C.J.Q. 95.

[27] Colman, Lyon and Hawkins (2000), pp. 14–17, 27.

[28] M. Heaney, 9(12) *The Lawyer*, March 21, 1995, p. 14.

[29] Lord Mackay of Clashfern L.C., quoted by Heaney, *op. cit.*

[30] CPR, Parts 49 and 58, *Practice Direction 58—Commercial Court, Commercial Court Guide.*

[31] Colman, Lyon and Hawkins (2000), p. 27.

(iii) The Technology and Construction Court

2–064 There are seven full-time Circuit judges nominated by the Lord Chancellor to deal with Technology and Construction Court claims (to October 8, 1998 known as "Official Referees' business").[32] Since 1998, a High Court judge has been appointed to take charge of the TCC specialist list.[33] Examples of TCC claims include building or other construction disputes; engineering disputes; claims by and against engineers, architects, surveyors, accountants and other specialist advisers; claims by and against local authorities relating to their statutory duties concerning the development of land or the construction of buildings; claims concerning computers, software and networks; claims relating to the quality of goods sold or hired, and work done, materials supplied or services rendered; claims between landlord and tenant for breach of a repairing covenant; claims between neighbours, owners and occupiers of land in trespass, nuisance, etc.; claims relating to the environment or fires; the taking of complicated accounts; and challenges to the decision of arbitrators in construction and engineering disputes.[34] However, to be a TCC claim it must also involve issues or questions which are technically complex or where trial by a TCC judge is desirable.[35] A TCC claim may be issued in the High Court or a specified county court,[36] and is treated as if it were allocated to the multi-track. The claim is assigned to a particular TCC judge. There is provision for a case management conference and a pre-trial review.[37] While things have not had to change as much in the TCC as elsewhere in the civil justice system, there have been some changes, "with the TCC judges apparently taking a considered and incremental approach to the development of procedure".[38] There is a Technology and Construction Court Users Committee, a Technology and Construction Bar Association (TECBAR), and a Technology and Construction Solicitors' Association (TeCSA).[39]

(d) The Family Division

2–065 This division exercises the matrimonial and domestic jurisdiction of the High Court, which includes defended divorce cases, proceedings under the

---

[32] Supreme Court Act 1981, s.68, as amended by the Civil Procedure Act 1997, Sched. 2, para. 1. See E. Fay, *Official Referees' Business* (3rd ed., 1997); F. Meisel (1984) 3 C.J.Q. 97, (1986) 83 L.S. Gaz. 1294; S. Knafler, *Legal Action*, November 1989, p. 12; J. Newey, (1994) 10 Constr. L.J. 20; A. Thornton, (1998) 14 Constr. L.J. 1. The office of Official Referee, first established by the Supreme Court of Judicature Act 1873, was abolished by the Courts Act 1971. Existing holders, became Circuit judges: 1971 Act, Sched. 2. On each circuit other than the South Eastern Circuit judges have been appointed to conduct this business, although most is taken in London: see T. Heald, "Official Referee's Business in the Provinces" (1983) Constr. L.J. 91. There are further designated judges at Birmingham, Manchester and Liverpool.

[33] The first was Dyson J. The current assigned judge is Forbes J.

[34] *Practice Direction 60 — Technology and Construction Court Claims*, para. 2.1.

[35] CPR, r. 60.1(3).

[36] *Practice Direction*, paras 3.1, 3.4: Birmingham, Bristol, Cardiff, Central London, Chester, Exeter, Leeds, Liverpool, Newcastle, Nottingham and Salford.

[37] *ibid.* paras 6–10.

[38] A. Burr and R. Honey, "The Post-Woolf TCC: Any Change?" (2001) 17 Const.L.J. 378 at 394.

[39] Court Service website (Technology and Construction Court).

Children Act 1989 and matters relating to the wardship or adoption of children,[40] and deals with non-contentious or common form probate business. It also hears appeals from magistrates' courts in family proceedings.[41] The work is at present handled by the President, 17 puisne judges, and 19 District judges of the principal registry of the Family Division in London and at first-tier Crown Court centres.[42]

Many important aspects of High Court family work are dealt with by the District judges of the principal registry and District judges of the High Court, including decisions on ancillary matters (*e.g.* maintenance, adjustment of property rights and the arrangements for contact with children).

A number of proposals have been made for the establishment of "family courts"[43]. Under the present system, there has been jurisdictional confusion as between magistrates' courts, county courts and the High Court,[44] and there are also discrepancies in the substantive law applied and doubts as to whether a system of accusatorial hearings is appropriate for family matters. The Finer Committee on One Parent Families[45] recommended the establishment of family courts to take over all family matters dealt with in magistrates' courts, county courts and the High Court. The family courts would be organised in tiers, on the analogy of the Crown Court. The lowest tier would comprise Circuit judges and magistrates and sit in county courts: magistrates' court buildings would not be used. There would be facilities for conciliation and support by a professional welfare service. The government was, however, unwilling to provide extra court buildings or add to the workload of the Circuit bench. Many of the significant differences between the law applicable by the High Court and county courts on the one hand and by magistrates' courts on the other were removed,[46] moves were made to keep the domestic jurisdiction of magistrates' courts separate from criminal proceedings,[47] and steps were taken to widen the jurisdiction of the county court and improve the distribution of business between the High Court and county courts.[48]

The Lord Chancellor's Department began to take a greater interest in the

---

[40] See above, para. 2-045.

[41] Supreme Court Act 1981, Sched. 1. See above, para. 2-025.

[42] Family Proceedings Rules 1991 (S.I. 1991 No. 1247), as amended, r.2.32. The cases here may be dealt with by High Court judges or Circuit judges sitting as High Court judges.

[43] See B. M. Hoggett and D. S. Pearl, *The Family, Law and Society* (2nd ed., 1987), pp. 628–636; Lord McGregor, (1987) 6 C.J.Q.44; B. M. Hoggett, (1986) 6 L.S.I; D. Allen (ed.), *Family Justice—a Structure for the Family Court* (1986).

[44] See *The Overlapping Family Jurisdiction of Magistrates' Courts and County Courts*, Research Report of the Socio-Legal Centre for Family Studies, University of Bristol, June 1987, summarised by J. Graham Hall and D. F. Martin, (1987) 151 J.P.N. 659.

[45] Cmnd. 5629, 1974.

[46] Domestic Proceedings and Magistrates' Courts Act 1978.

[47] See the Justices' Clerks' Society, *Resolving Family Conflict in the 1980s* (1982); "Making the Domestic Proceedings Act Work: A joint declaration by the Magistrates' Association and the Justices' Clerks' Society" (1982) 146 J.P.N. 756–758; C. Latham, "Magistrates' Courts and the Family Jurisdiction: A Re-assessment of the Finer Concept of Family Court" (1983) 147 J.P.N. 233–236, 246–247.

[48] See para. 2-045.

question, issuing consultation documents in 1983[49] and 1986.[50] The Family Courts Campaign, a consortium of major organisations and individuals, began action in 1984. They showed, *inter alia*, that the net costs of reform were not as great as have been thought.[51] Lord Havers and Lord Mackay, who in turn succeeded Lord Hailsham as Lord Chancellor in 1987, showed markedly more enthusiasm for change than their predecessor. The 1986 Review identified three options: (a) to retain the existing structure but with a revised distribution of jurisdiction to eliminate duplication and overlap; (b) to create a unified court within the existing High Court and county court structure; (c) to create a wholly new court with its own structure and judiciary. In the event, however, it was a form of option (a) which was reflected in arrangements under the Children Act 1989.[52]

(f) Administration

2–066   Administrative support for the High Court is provided by the Supreme Court Group of the Court Service.[53] Apart from the masters and registrars appointed under the Supreme Court Act 1981, the officials are civil servants who are members of the Lord Chancellor's Department.[54] In London, the principal offices are the Central Office of the Supreme Court, Chancery Chambers, the Principal Registry of the Family Division,[55] the Admiralty and Commercial Court Registry and the Accounting Department.

Outside London there are district registries of the High Court in about 130 locations.[56] A District judge[57] is appointed by the Lord Chancellor as District judge of the High Court for each registry,[58] and there is provision for the appointment of deputy and assistant District judges.[59] Claims in the Queen's Bench Division may be issued in any district registry; claims in most Chancery actions may be issued out of eight Chancery district registries[60] and in certain specified cases out of any district registry.[61] The other interlocutory steps are also taken here. Matrimonial causes and most other

---

[49]   Lord Chancellor's Department, *Family Jurisdiction of the High Court and County Courts, A Consultative Paper* (1983). See J. Levin, *L. A. G. Bull.*, March 1983, pp. 5–6.

[50]   Lord Chancellor's Department, *Interdepartmental Review of Family and Domestic Jurisdiction*. For responses, see, *e.g.* (1987) 17 *Family Law* 33–34, 64–66 (Family Courts Campaign), 75–76 (Magistrates' Association); J. S. W. Black, (1986) 150 J.P.N. 422; J. Graham Hall and D. F. Martin, *ibid.* p. 436; N. Wikely, (1986) 5 C.J.Q. 288; C. Yates, (1987) J.S.W.L. 300.

[51]   J. Stringer and P. M. Smith, *Family Courts—The Price is Right*, summarised by J. Graham Hall and D. F. Martin, "Family Courts—Analysing the Cost" (1988) 152 J.P.N. 517. See also Graham Hall and Martin, "Towards a Unified Family Court—the Cost Factor" (1983) 4 C.J.Q. 223.

[52]   See above, para. 2-045.

[53]   The Review Body on the Chancery Division found that the establishment of the service had had little impact on the Division, and were highly critical of the Division's administrative arrangements.

[54]   Appointed under the Courts Act 1971, s.27.

[55]   Referred to as Principal Probate Registry or the Divorce Registry depending on which branch of the Division's work is concerned.

[56]   Supreme Court Act 1981, s.99; Civil Courts Order 1983 (S.I. 1983 No. 713), as amended.

[57]   See above, para. 2-042.

[58]   Supreme Court Act 1981, s.100.

[59]   *ibid.* ss.102, 103. Formerly they were entitled district registrars.

[60]   *i.e.* the district registries for the eight centres mentioned above, para. 2-060, n.86.

[61]   See R. Blackford and C. Jacque, *Chancery Practice Handbook* (1983), pp. 78–80, 100–101.

proceedings in the Family Division may be dealt with at those district registries that have a divorce county court within its district,[62] although they can only be tried at the Royal Courts or designated trial centre.[63] There are district probate registries in 11 places and sub-registries in 18 others.[64] District probate registrars are appointed by the Lord Chancellor.[65]

(g) Procedural rules

Rules for the purpose of regulating and prescribing the practice and procedure to be followed in the High Court and Court of Appeal were formerly made by the Supreme Court Rule Committee.[66] Most cases were regulated by the Rules of the Supreme Court.[67] These first appeared in 1885 and the most recent major revision was in 1965. The rules could not alter any matter of substantive law.[68] In 1982, a Supreme Court Procedure Committee was established by the Lord Chief Justice and the other heads of the divisions, in conjunction with the Presidents of the Senate and the Law Society, to consider and recommend reforms in practice and procedure for saving time and costs. Their recommendations were placed before the Rule Committee.[69] From 1999, practice and procedure in the High Court and Court of Appeal have been regulated by the Civil Procedure Rules 1998 as part of the Woolf Reforms.[70]

2–067

(h) Appeals[71]

Appeals lie either to the Court of Appeal (Civil Division)[72] or direct to the House of Lords.[73] The appeal lies direct to the House of Lords where the case has reached the High Court on appeal from a magistrates' court or the Crown Court in a criminal matter, or, otherwise, under the "leap frog" procedure.

2–068

---

[62] See the Family Proceedings Rules 1991 (S.I. 1991 No. 247), r.2 (definition of "district registry" for the purpose of the rules), r.2.32.

[63] Above, para. 2-045.

[64] Supreme Court Act 1981, s.104; District Probate Registries Order 1982 (S.I. 1982 No. 379).

[65] Supreme Court Act 1981, s.89, Sched. 2.

[66] Supreme Court Act 1981, ss.84, 85, as amended by the Courts and Legal Services Act 1990, Sched. 18, para. 36(1). See Sir Jack Jacob, "The Machinery of the Rule Committee of the Supreme Court" (1971) reprinted in *The Reform of Civil Procedural Law* (1982).

[67] The Rules were divided into Orders, rules and paragraphs, and were referred to in abbreviated form as (*e.g.*) RSC, Ord. 1, r.1. For a transitional period, some have been retained in a Schedule to the CPR pending their replacement by new Parts of the CPR.

[68] *e.g.* doubts as to whether certain aspects of the "New Order 53", which introduced the "application for judicial review", were *ultra vires* were settled by the enactment of section 31 of the Supreme Court Act 1981 (see below, para. 18-053).

[69] (1982) 79 L.S.Gaz. 711; Annual Reports of the committee.

[70] See above, para. 2-049.

[71] See generally Chap. 18.

[72] see below, para. 2-071.

[73] see below, para. 2-072.

8. THE LANDS TRIBUNAL

2–069   The Lands Tribunal was set up in 1949[74] to take over the jurisdiction of official arbitrators to determine disputes concerning the assessment of compensation for the compulsory acquisition of land. It consists of a President, who must be a person who has held judicial office or a lawyer of at least seven years' standing, a number of members (currently four) who are lawyers of seven years' standing, and a number who are persons with experience in land valuation (*i.e.* qualified surveyors).[75] All are appointed by the Lord Chancellor, the valuation experts after consultation with the president of the Royal Institution of Chartered Surveyors. The Tribunal's jurisdiction may be exercised by any one or more of its members, as selected by the President, and the selection depends on the nature of the matters at issue. The Tribunal's permanent office and secretariat are in London, although it may sit in the provinces if appropriate, for example to facilitate the inspection of the relevant land and buildings. In addition to the jurisdiction in respect of compensation, it has the power to determine disputes as to the valuation of land for taxation, it hears appeals from valuation tribunals, in matters concerning disputed assessments of land and buildings for rating and disputes concerning the cornial tax, and from leasehold valuation tribunals, and it has a discretionary power to vary, modify or discharge restrictive covenants under section 84 of the Law of Property Act 1925. An appeal lies to the Court of Appeal on a point of law,[76] with the permission of that court. The Lands Tribunal is regarded as having a high status in the court structure, notwithstanding that, unlike the Transport Tribunal and the Employment Appeal Tribunal, it is not constituted under the 1949 Act as a court of record.[77] Its proceedings are conducted fairly formally.

9. THE COURT OF APPEAL (CRIMINAL DIVISION)

2–070   The Court of Appeal (Criminal Division) hears appeals from trials on indictment or sentences passed by the Crown Court,[78] and references by the

---

[74] Lands Tribunal Act 1949. For its rules of procedure see the Lands Tribunal Rules 1996 (S.I. 1996 No. 1022), as amended by S.I. 1997 No. 1965, S.I., 1998 No. 22. See *www.courtservice.gov.uk/tribunals/lands*. The Tribunal is guided by the overriding objective in the CPR in exercising its powers under the Rules, although the CPR do not formally apply: *ibid.*

[75] 1949 Act, s.2(2), as amended by the Courts and Legal Services Act, 1990, Sched. 10, para. 7. To be eligible, a lawyer must possess a seven year general qualification under s.71 of the 1990 Act, *i.e.* a right of audience in any part of the Supreme Court or all proceedings in county courts or magistrates' courts.

[76] The appeal may, but need not be, by case stated; formerly, the case stated procedure applied in all cases: see 1949 Act, s.3(4), as amended by the Civil Procedure (Modification of Enactment) Order 2000 (S.I. 2000 No. 941).

[77] See *Att.-Gen. v. British Broadcasting Corporation* [1981] A.C. 303 at 338 (Viscount Dilhorne) *Cf.* the Annual Report of the Council on Tribunals, 1980–81 (1981–82 H.C. 89), p. 8: "The Lands Tribunal is generally regarded as of High Court standing . . . ."

[78] Criminal Appeal Act 1968, Parts I and II, as amended by the Criminal Appeal Act 1995.

Attorney-General under the Criminal Justice Acts 1972 and 1988.[79] It replaced the Court of Criminal Appeal[80] with effect from October 1, 1966.[81] The Lord Chief Justice is the president of the division, and the Lord Chancellor may appoint a vice-president.[82] The work is done by the Lord Chief Justice, Lords Justices and High Court judges.[83] Circuit judges approved by the Lord Chancellor may also sit at the request of the Lord Chief Justice.[84] For the following purposes, a court of the division must comprise an uneven number of judges not less than three[85]:

(i)   determining appeals against conviction;

(ii) determining appeals against a verdict of not guilty by reason of insanity;

(iii) determining appeals against a finding of unfitness to be tried because of a disability;

(iv) determining applications for leave to appeal to the House of Lords;

(v)   refusing leave to appeal in situations (i), (ii), (iii) above except where the application has already been refused by a single judge;

(vi) determining reviews of sentencing.

Otherwise, matters may be determined by a court comprising two judges.[86] A single judge may grant leave to appeal, grant bail and perform certain other functions.[87] Any number of courts may sit at the same time. The court gives a single judgment unless the judge presiding states that in his or her opinion the question is one of law on which it is convenient that separate judgments should be pronounced by the members of the court.[88] Procedural

[79]   See below, Chap. 18.
[80]   Established by the Criminal Appeal Act 1907. This Act for the first time established a right of appeal for the *accused*, as distinct from the discretion of the *judge* to refer a point to his fellow judges (see above, para. 1-010.).
[81]   Criminal Appeal Act 1966. This followed the Report of the Committee on the Court of Criminal Appeal (Chairman: Lord Donovan; Cmnd. 2755, 1965).
[82]   Supreme Court Act 1981, s.3.
[83]   On occasion, one or more of the Law Lords (see below, para. 4-021) may sit: *e.g. R. v. Husseyn* (Note) (1977) 67 Cr.App.R. 131, "explained" in *Attorney-General's References* (Nos. 1 and 2 of 1979) [1980] Q.B. 180, see below para. 18-019.
[84]   Supreme Court Act 1981, s.9, as amended by the Criminal Justice and Public Order Act 1994, s.52 (implementing a recommendation of the Royal Commission on Criminal Justice (Cm. 2263, para. 10.82). Not more than one Circuit judge may sit on an appeal; a Circuit judge may not act as the single judge; and a court including such a judge may not hear an appeal in a case tried by a High Court judge: 1981 Act, ss. 55(6), 9(6A), 56A, inserted by the 1994 Act, s.52.
[85]   Supreme Court Act 1981, s.55, as amended by the Criminal Justice Act 1988, Sched. 15, para. 80.
[86]   *ibid., e.g.* appeals against sentence. If the court is equally divided the case must be re-argued before an uneven number of judges not less than three: *ibid.* s.55(5).
[87]   Criminal Appeal Act 1968, s.31.
[88]   Supreme Court Act 1981, s.59. See *R. v. Head* [1958] 1 Q.B. 132 at 137; *R. v. Harz* [1967] 1 A.C. 760 at 765.

rules may be made by the Crown Court Rule Committee.[89] The administration of criminal appeals is handled by the Criminal Appeal Office, headed by the Registrar of Criminal Appeals.[90]

Appeals lie to the House of Lords, with the leave of the House or the Court of Appeal, where the Court of Appeal has certified that a point of law of general public importance is involved.[91]

10. THE COURT OF APPEAL (CIVIL DIVISION)[92]

2–071 The Court of Appeal was established as part of the Supreme Court by the Supreme Court of Judicature Acts 1873 and 1875. It was reconstituted with Civil and Criminal Divisions in 1966.[93] The jurisdiction of the Civil Division includes appeals from the High Court and county courts in civil matters, and from certain other courts and tribunals.[94] The Master of the Rolls[95] is president of the division, and the Lord Chancellor may appoint a vice-president.[96] The work is mainly done by the Master of the Rolls and the Lords Justices,[97] with regular assistance from the Lord Chief Justice, the President of the Family Division and the Vice-Chancellor,[98] and occasional assistance from Law Lords, High Court judges and former judges of the Court of Appeal or High Court. A court is duly constituted if it consists of one or more judges, subject to the directions of the Master of the Rolls about the minimum number of judges for specified descriptions of proceedings, and to the determination of the Master of the Rolls or a designated Lord Justice of Appeal as to the number of judges for any particular proceedings.[99] Sittings are normally held at the Royal Court of

---

[89] *ibid.* s.86, as amended by the Courts and Legal Services Act 1990, Sched. 18, para. 36(2). This comprises the Lord Chancellor and any four of: the Lord Chief Justice, two other judges of the Supreme Court, two Circuit judges, the Registrar of Criminal Appeals, a J.P., two lawyers with a Supreme Court qualification under s.71 of the 1990 Act and two lawyers with the right to conduct litigation in the High Court. See the Criminal Appeal Rules 1968 (S.I. 1968 No. 1262), as amended; *A Guide to Proceedings in the Court of Appeal Criminal Division* (revised ed., 1997) (Court Service website); D. Thompson and H. W. Wollaston, *Court of Appeal—Criminal Division* (1969); M. Knight, *Criminal Appeals* (1970); I. McLean, *Criminal Appeals* (2nd ed., 1986); Taylor, *Appeals.*

[90] This office is held in combination with that of Master of the Crown Office. See above, para. 2-061, n.98.

[91] See below, para. 2-072 and Chap. 18.

[92] For accounts of the working of the Court of Appeal see Lord Asquith, (1947-51) 1 J.S.P.T.L. (N.S.) 350, reproduced in L. Blom-Cooper, *The Language of the Law* (1965); Sir R. Evershed, *The Court of Appeal in England* (1950); D. Karlen, *Appellate Courts in the United States and England* (1963), Chap. 6; Sir John Donaldson M.R., *The Problems of a Master of the Rolls* (Holdsworth Club Presidential Address, 1985) and "The Court of Appeal" (1985) 53 Medico-Legal Jo. 148.

[93] Criminal Appeal Act 1966.

[94] See below, Chap. 18.

[95] See below, para. 4-021.

[96] Supreme Court Act 1981, s.3: for the whole court or for the Division.

[97] See below, para. 4-021.

[98] Approximately four weeks a term each for the LCJ and President; approximately half the time of the Vice-Chancellor: *Court of Appeal Civil Division Review of the Legal Year 2000–2001*, p. 15.

[99] Supreme Court Act 1981, s. 54(2)–(4A), substituted by the Access to Justice Act 1999, s. 59. Formerly, the section provided for courts to comprise an uneven number of three or more judges other than in specified classes of proceedings.

Justice, but there is a developing programme of regional sittings, which have taken place so far in Cardiff, Manchester and Exeter.

The work of the division is administered by the Civil Appeals Office. Between 1982 and 2000, this was headed by the Registrar of Civil Appeals, an office created by the Supreme Court Act 1981,[1] following the report of a Working Party headed by Lord Scarman.[2] The Scarman Committee had identified four main sources of wasted time in the Court of Appeal: (1) failure of parties to an appeal to provide the necessary documentation in a suitable form; (2) the requirement that at least two Lords Justices hear procedural applications; (3) the absence of a flexible and co-ordinated listing system; (4) the length of oral hearings. The Registrar's functions included ensuring that the proper documentation is prepared, advising those unfamiliar with the procedure and practice of the court and the establishment of a co-ordinated listing system. The Scarman Committee considered and rejected a change to the system of written briefs and limitations on the time allowed for oral argument which is the practice, for example, in the Supreme Court of the United States. This system was regarded as alien to the British tradition of oral presentation and argument, and not necessarily less expensive because of the time devoted to preparing highly complex briefs. Instead, arrangements were made for the pre-reading of documents before the oral hearing begins, and for the submission of "skeleton arguments" (i.e. an abbreviated note of arguments and other matters which would otherwise be dictated to the court at the oral hearing).[3]

Decisions as to the composition of the courts and the allocation of the cases are made by the Head of the Civil Appeals Office acting in consultation with the Master of the Rolls. In general, the constitutions of the Court of Appeal are changed about every three weeks. Civil courts are "multi-disciplinary" rather than "specialised" (e.g. all former Chancery judges sitting on a Chancery appeal) although, where possible, no appeal on a specialist topic is listed before a court none of whose members are familiar with that speciality.[4] A small team of "in-house" lawyers has been appointed, each taking charge of the case management of a group of applications and appeals, defined by reference to subject matter. They will give procedural advice to litigants in person and, where necessary, provide summaries of the issues raised for the use of judges.[5] The introduction of greater efficiency in the administration of the Court of Appeal proved insufficient to reduce the backlog of appeals; indeed the number of cases outstanding at the end of the year steadily increased.[6] In response,

---

[1] s.89 and Sched. 2. The office of Registrar was abolished by the Access to Justice Act 1999, s.70, as no longer necessary following the changes to the rules concerning the composition of the Court of Appeal (Civil Division). There is now a Head of the Civil Appeals Office and Master, and a number of deputy masters, who may determine certain incidental and straightforward matters: CPR, r.52.16.

[2] Practice Note (Court of Appeal: New Procedure) [1982] 1 W.L.R. 1312 (Sir John Donaldson M.R.).

[3] Practice Note (Court of Appeal: Skeleton Arguments) [1983] 2 All E.R. 34; Practice Direction (Court of Appeal: Presentation of Argument) [1989] 1 W.L.R. 281; Practice Direction (Court of Appeal: Skeleton Argument Time Limits) [1990] 1 W.L.R. 794.

[4] Sir John Donaldson M.R., The Problems of A Master of the Rolls (Holdsworth Club Presidential Address, 1985), pp. 9–10.

[5] Annual Review by the Master of the Rolls, 1988–89, The Times, October 13, 1989. See Practice Statement (Civil Appeals: Setting Down) [1990] 1 W.L.R. 1436.

[6] Annual Review, 1992–93, p. 2.

additional judges were appointed,[7] the requirements as to documentation were revised, skeleton arguments were to be produced earlier and exchanged, and time limits were set for oral argument in support of applications for leave to appeal and renewed applications for leave to apply for judicial review.[8] This last step moved the court further towards the American approach.[9] Significant further changes were introduced as a corollary to the Woolf reforms,[10] following a report by Sir Jeffery Bowman.[11] Appeals now lie from final decisions of a Circuit judge in a case in the small claims or fast track to a High Court judge instead of the Court of Appeal. The Court of Appeal accordingly hears appeals against the decisions of the Circuit and High Court judges in family proceedings, final decisions in cases assigned to the multi-track, and second appeals. Second appeals where cases have been decided by the county court or High Court can only lie where the Court of Appeal considers that the appeal could raise an important point of principle or practice or there is some other compelling reason.[12] Where in any proceedings in a county court or the High Court a person appeals, or seeks permission to appeal, to a court other than the Court of Appeal, the Master of the Rolls, or the court from which or to which the appeal is made, or from which permission to appeal is sought, may direct that the appeal shall be heard instead by the Court of Appeal.[13] Permission to appeal is normally required. A Court of Appeal Users' Committee has been established, and young lawyers have been recruited for fixed terms as Judicial Assistants. The jurisdictional changes have led (recently) to a small reduction in the number of applications for permission to appeal, and there has been a steady decline in the number of appeals filed, disposals, cases outstanding and disposal times.[14]

Appeals lie to the House of Lords, with the leave of the court or the House, on questions of law or fact.[15]

11. THE HOUSE OF LORDS[16]

2–072   The House of Lords hears appeals (1) from the Court of Appeal; (2) in

---

[7] *LCD Court Service Annual Report 1994–95* (1994-95 H.C. 579), pp. 31–32. Three additional judges were authorised in 1994 and three more in 1996.

[8] *Practice Statement (Court of Appeal: Procedural Changes)* [1995] 1 W.L.R. 1188; *Practice Direction (Court of Appeal: Procedure)* [1995] 1 W.L.R. 1191, superseding, *inter alia*, the practice directions mentioned above, n.3.

[9] See Leggatt L.J., "The Future of the Oral Tradition in the Court of Appeal" (1995) 14 C.J.Q. 11, noting ominously that "it is comparatively uncommon for members of the court to change their minds about whether to dismiss or allow an appeal, once they have read the skeleton arguments" (p. 15).

[10] See the Access to Justice Act 1999, ss.54–57; CPR, Part 52; *Practice Direction 52 — Appeals*.

[11] *Review of the Court of Appeal (Civil Division)* (LCD, 1997) (summary on the LCD website).

[12] 1999 Act, s.55.

[13] *ibid.* s.57.

[14] *Court of Appeal (Civil Division) Review of the Legal Year 2000–2001*, pp. 18–24.

[15] See below, and Chap. 18.

[16] See L. Blom-Cooper and Gavin Drewry, *Final Appeal* (1972); R. Stevens, *Law and Politics* (1978); A. Paterson, *The Law Lords* (1982); M. Barrett, The *Law Lords* (2001); Lord Fraser of Tullybelton, 1986 S.L.T. 33. Brief accounts of the work of the Judicial Office in supporting the Law Lords are found in the *House of Lords Annual Reports and Accounts* published by HMSO (*e.g.* 1993–94 H.L. 86), and on the House of Lords website.

certain circumstances, direct from the High Court; (3) from the Court of Session (the highest civil court in Scotland)[17]; (4) from the Court of Appeal in Northern Ireland; (5) in certain circumstances, direct from the High Court of Justice in Northern Ireland and (6) from the Courts-Martial Appeal Court.[18]

An appeal may not be heard or determined unless at least three from the following list are present: (1) the Lord Chancellor[19]; (2) the Lords of Appeal in Ordinary[20]; (3) any peer who has held one of the high judicial offices of Lord Chancellor, member of the Judicial Committee of the Privy Council, Lord of Appeal in Ordinary, judge of the Supreme Court of England and Wales or Northern Ireland or judge of the Court of Session.[21] Technically, it seems that all members of the House of Lords have the right to vote on appeals, but the practice has fallen into disuse. In the early nineteenth century lay peers were used to make up the necessary quorum but by the 1830s there were sufficient Law Lords[22] for a "professional" court to be possible.[23] In 1844 the convention that lay peers did not vote was established in *O'Connell v. R.*[24] Daniel O'Connell appealed against a conviction for conspiracy. Three Law Lords were in favour of allowing the appeal, two were against it. Several lay peers purported to vote with the minority, but were persuaded to withdraw on the ground that in reality the "Court of Law" in the House was constituted by the Law Lords and interference by lay peers would greatly lessen the authority of the House. The last occasion when a lay peer attempted to vote was in *Bradlaugh v. Clarke*[25] when Lord Denman[26] attended throughout the proceedings and purported to vote with Lord Blackburn against the majority of the Law Lords. His attempt was ignored by the Lord Chancellor and the Law Reports, but was noted by *The Times*.[27] In response to a question in the House of Commons, the Home Secretary stated that as the Appellate Jurisdiction Act 1876 had not excluded lay peers, it had been competent for Lord Denman to sit: had his

---

[17] There is no right of appeal from the highest Scottish criminal court, the High Court of Justiciary: *Mackintosh v. Lord Advocate* (1876) 3 R. (H.L.) 34; Criminal Procedure (Scotland) Act 1887, s.72. See A. J. Maclean, "The House of Lords and Appeals from the High Court of Justiciary 1707–1887" 1985 J. R. 192.

[18] Appeals in English cases are considered in detail below, Chap. 18.

[19] Above, para. 1-018, 4-021.

[20] Below, para. 4-021.

[21] Appellate Jurisdiction Act 1876, ss.5, 25; Appellate Jurisdiction Act 1887, s.5. For a current list, see the LCD website. In 1996, the internationally distinguished New Zealand judge Sir Robin Cooke was made a peer and between then and 2001 he sat on English and Scottish appeals to the House of Lords as a peer who had held high judicial office as a member of the Judicial Committee of the Privy Council; see also P. Spiller (1996) 17 N.Z. Univ. L.R. 1.

[22] The term then covered the Lord Chancellor, the Lord Chancellor of Ireland, former Lord Chancellors, ennobled judges, and occasionally a peer who had held a minor judicial office.

[23] Stevens (1978), p. 29.

[24] (1844) 11 Cl. & F. 155 at 421–426.

[25] (1883) 8 App. Cas 354. See R. E. Megarry, (1949) 65 L.Q.R. 22–24.

[26] This was the second Lord Denman, son of the Lord Chief Justice and brother of Denman J., a High Court judge, 1872–1892. "Lord Denman was aged seventy-eight at the time of his fling, and he had been a peer for nearly thirty years and a barrister for fifty, so that his was no mere indiscretion of youth and inexperience" (Megarry (1949), p. 24). He "won notoriety rather from his eccentricities than any eminent qualifications" (D.N.B.).

[27] April 10, 1883, p. 4.

opinion affected the result, he would have been asked to withdraw his vote on the precedent of *O'Connell's* case.[28]

Under the original arrangements for reorganisation incorporated in the Supreme Court of Judicature Act 1873 the appellate role of the House of Lords was to be abolished. The Court of Appeal was to be the final appeal court for England, and ultimately for Scotland, Ireland and the colonies. However, before the arrangements came into effect opposition developed in several quarters, the appeal to the House was retained and provision was made for the appointment of salaried Law Lords.[29]

2-073   Up to 1948, appeals to the House of Lords were heard in the Chamber of the House. In that year, the process of repairing the Palace of Westminister caused the House to commit the hearing of appeals to an Appellate Committee meeting in a committee room and this practice has been maintained ever since. The committee hears appeals and reports its conclusions to the House, where judgment is delivered at a judicial sitting.[30] The House, or the Appellate Committee, as the case may be, is presided over by the Lord Chancellor or, as is more usually the case, the senior Lord of Appeal in Ordinary present.[31] The Appellate Committee must be distinguished from the "Appeal Committee" which sits to consider and report on petitions for leave to appeal and other incidental matters and which normally comprises three Law Lords.

Selection of Law Lords to sit on Appeal Committees is done by the Principal Clerk to the Judicial Office; selection of Appellate Committees, although theoretically in the hands of the Lord Chancellor, has been delegated to his Permanent Secretary, who consulted the Lord Chancellor in cases of difficulty.[32] Normally, the most convenient panel available is chosen; occasionally, special considerations may apply, such as the exclusion of judges with a political background from adjudicating in a case

---

[28] Sir William Harcourt, H.C. Deb. Vol. 278, col. 68, April 12, 1883.

[29] See Stevens (1979), Chap. 2 and R. Stevens, "The Final Appeal: Reform of the House of Lords and Privy Council, 1867–1876" (1964) 80 L.Q.R. 343.

[30] A morning sitting in the Chamber of the House. Some appeals may be heard in the Chamber, *e.g.* during parliamentary recesses. In 1998, the televised hearing of the first decision of the House of Lords in the Pinochet case (*R. v. Bow Street Metropolitan Stipendiary Magistrate, ex p. Pinochet Ugarte* [1998] 4 All E.R. 897) generated interest across the world: see Barnett (2001), pp. 3–6.

[31] Seniority formerly depended on the date of first appointment to the office: Blom-Cooper and Drewry (1972), p. 179. From 1984, the first and second senior Law Lords have been specifically appointed as such by the Queen: H.L. Deb. Vol. 453, cols. 914–919, June 27, 1984: see L. Blom-Cooper, [1984] P.L. 376; A.A. Paterson, 1988 J.R. 235 at 251, n. 59. The presiding judge may exert significant influence over the course of proceedings: Paterson (1982), pp. 66–72. The most recent senior Lords of Appeal have been Lord Simonds (1954–1962); Lord Reid (1962–1975); Lord Wilberforce (1975–1982); Lord Diplock (1982–1984); Lord Fraser of Tullybelton (1984–1985); Lord Scarman (1985-1986); Lord Keith of Kinkel (1986–1996); Lord Goff of Chieveley (1996–1998); Lord Browne-Wilkinson (1998–2000); Lord Bingham (previously Master of the Rolls and then Lord Chief Justice immediately before his appointment as Senior Law Lord (2000–).

[32] See Paterson (1982), pp. 87–89. The selections have to be co-ordinated with those for the Judicial Committee of the Privy Council. There is evidence of attempts by successive Lord Chancellors, in the early years of the twentieth century, to influence the outcome of cases by their selection of panels: D. Woodhouse, *The Office of Lord Chancellor* (2000), pp. 120–122.

with party-political implications,[33] the strong desirability of one or both of the Scottish Law Lords sitting on an appeal from Scotland and the desirability of the presence of a Chancery judge in a Chancery appeal. The room for manoeuvre is in practice limited. The choice of panel is now left to the Senior Law Lord, although the Lord Chancellor determines whether he sits on a particular case.[34]

Procedure on appeals to the House of Lords is regulated by Directions and Standing Orders of the House.[35] Each side must submit a "case", drawn up by counsel, which is a "succinct statement of [their] argument in the Appeal", although in practice the oral submissions of counsel and the interchange between them and the Law Lords are of greater significance.[36] The Law Lords are generally expected to confine their propositions of law to matters covered by the argument of counsel, although this view is held today less strongly than formerly.[37] Moreover, they will not normally consider a point not raised in the courts below,[38]

"But if [the Law Lords] think it is something that really goes to the root of the thing, if they think the whole thing would be rather a mess if they did not allow it to be argued, then they would probably allow it on terms as to costs."[39]

Informal discussions among the Law Lords take place during the hearing of an appeal.[40] Judgment is invariably reserved. At the conclusion of the hearing there is a conference at which provisional opinions are expressed, and a general discussion follows. If there appears to be general agreement, it may also be agreed that a particular Law Lord should write the major opinion. Occasionally, a second conference may be convened.

Each Law Lord is entitled to write his own opinion,[41] although they attempt to avoid the unnecessary multiplication of opinions. Views differ on the desirability of multiple opinions.[42] Paterson found that of those studied:

"although in non-criminal common law cases only two active Law Lords generally favoured a single judgment in criminal appeals on a

---

[33] This was done for *Heaton's Transport Co. v. T.G.W.U.* [1973] A.C. 15. See A. Paterson, (1979) 1 B.J.L.S. 118, 126.

[34] Woodhouse (2000), p.122 (interview with Lord Irvine L.C.). The latter point may give rise to difficulty should the Lord Chancellor express a wish to sit on a case where that might not be suitable.

[35] See *Practice Directions and Standing Orders Applicable to Civil Appeals* (June 1001); *Practice Directions and Standing Orders Applicable to Criminal Appeals* (June 2001) (House of Lords website).

[36] See A. Paterson, *The Law Lords* (1982), Chaps 3 and 4.

[37] *ibid.* pp. 38–45.

[38] *ibid.* pp. 45–49.

[39] Lord Cross, cited by Paterson (1982), p. 47.

[40] The interaction among the Law Lords is discussed by Paterson (1982), Chap. 5, and Barrett (2001).

[41] Occasionally the presiding judge may press for a single opinion: see *D.P.P. v. Smith* [1961] A.C. 290 and *Heaton's Transport Ltd v. T.G.W.U.* [1973] A.C. 15: *cf.* the position in the Judicial Committee of the Privy Council, below.

[42] See Blom-Cooper and Drewry (1972), Chap. V; R. Cross, (1977) 93 L.Q.R. 378; Paterson (1982), pp. 96–109 and 183–187.

point of statutory construction, probably a majority of the active Law Lords favoured that approach".[43]

The main problem with multiple assenting judgments is that the differences in language may make it difficult to discern the *ratio decidendi*[44]; conversely, the same feature may leave subsequent judges greater scope for developing the law. The main problem with single opinions is that they may reflect an uneasy compromise. Recently, the proportion of cases with a single opinion has increased.[45]

2–074　　The House of Lords has a limited original, as distinct from appellate, jurisdiction, which includes the power to determine peerage claims and the power to conduct impeachment proceedings.[46] The right of a peer to be tried by his peers in cases of treason, felony or misprision of felony was abolished in 1948.[47]

The establishment of a Supreme Court outside Parliament has recently attracted support.[47a]

12. THE JUDICIAL COMMITTEE OF THE PRIVY COUNCIL

The Judicial Committee of the Privy Council was established in 1833,[48] largely as the result of the efforts of Lord Brougham.[49] Previously, appeals to the Crown from the colonies, which arose out of the prerogative right of the Sovereign as the fountainhead of all justice, were dealt with by a committee of the Privy Council which did not have a regular judicial composition. The 1833 Act limited the membership almost exclusively to senior judges. The present position is that the Committee comprises the Lord President of the Council, the Lord Chancellor, the Lords of Appeal in Ordinary and other members of the Privy Council who hold "high judicial office",[50] and former holders of these offices.[51] In addition, privy councillors

---

[43]　*op. cit.* p. 185.

[44]　See, *e.g. Boys v. Chaplin* [1971] A.C. 356; *British Railways Board v. Herrington* [1972] A.C. 877: below, pp. 420–421.

[45]　See P. V. Baker, (1983) 99 L.Q.R. 371; Lord Diplock *In re Prestige Group plc* [1984] 1 W.L.R. 335 at 338, referring to this as "a frequent practice in this House when dealing with questions of statutory construction"; A. Bradney, "The Changing Face of the House of Lords" 1985 J.R. 178 (statistical analysis of judgments between January 30, 1974 and March 1, 1984).

[46]　The last such cases were those of Warren Hastings (1788–1795: see P. J. Marshall, *The Impeachment of Warren Hastings* (1965)) and Viscount Melville (1806); *cf.* below, para. 4-027.

[47]　Criminal Justice Act 1948, s.30. The last trial was that of Lord de Clifford. See, W. T. West, *The Trial of Lord de Clifford* 1935 (1984), and, generally P. Marsden, *In Peril Before Parliament* (1965).

[47a]　See para. 4-032.

[48]　Judicial Committee Act 1833.

[49]　See P. A. Howell, *The Judicial Committee of the Privy Council* 1833–1876 (1979), Chap. 12; D. B. Swinfen, "Henry Brougham and the Judicial Committee of the Privy Council" (1975) 90 L.Q.R. 396; L. P. Beth, [1975] P. L. 219. See generally D. B. Swinfen, *Imperial Appeal* (1987); M. Barrett, *The Law Lords* (2001), Chap. 5.

[50]　As defined by the Appellate Jurisdiction Acts 1876, ss.5, 25 and 1877, s.5. This extends the membership of the Committee to the Lords Justices of Appeal, although they rarely sit in practice.

[51]　Judicial Committee Act 1833, s.l; Appellate Jurisdiction Act 1876, s.6; Appellate Jurisdiction Act 1887, s.3. ,

who hold or have held one of a number of judicial offices in New Zealand and other Commonwealth countries may also be members.[52] The composition of the Committee in a particular case is determined by the Senior Law Lord.[53]

The Judicial Committee hears appeals from certain Commonwealth countries, from the Channel Islands, in certain admiralty and ecclesiastical matters and from the General Medical Council[54] and other professional bodies.[55] It also has jurisdiction to determine "devolution issues".

The Commonwealth appellate jurisdiction was formerly regarded as an important unifying influence: it has now dwindled significantly as an increasing number of Commonwealth countries have abandoned the appeal.[56] For example, Canada and India abolished appeals in 1949, Sri Lanka in 1971, Malaysia in 1985. Australia (effectively) in 1986[57] and Singapore in 1994. The New Zealand National Party government proposed their abolition,[58] and appeals from Hong Kong ended with the territory's reversion to China in 1997.[59] The Committee's decision takes the form of advice to the Queen, to which effect is given by an Order in Council.[60] It is binding on the relevant Commonwealth courts.[61] A proportion of the cases heard by the Privy Council raise questions of constitutional interpretation. The handling of these cases has been analysed for guidance as to how the House of Lords might deal with matters arising under a written constitution with a Bill of Rights for the United Kingdom. There appeared to be a consensus that the judges seemed not to have been particularly well suited to

---

[52] Judicial Committee Amendment Act 1895, s.l, Sched.; Appellate Jurisdiction Act 1908, s.3. In 2001, there were six from New Zealand and one each from the Bahamas, Eastern Caribbean and Jamaica: Barrett (2001), p. 159. For an account of the experience of the Chief Justice of New Zealand in sitting on the Privy Council, see Interview with Sir Thomas Eichelbaum, [1994] N.Z.L.J. 86.

[53] H.C.Deb., February 4, 2000, col. 545w.

[54] Medical Act 1983, s.40.

[55] e.g. dentists, vets, chiropodists and remedial gymnasts: Dentists Act 1984, s.29; Veterinary Surgeons Act 1966, s.17; Professions Supplementary to Medicine Act 1960, ss.l, 9. See, e.g. Libman v. General Medical Council [1972] A.C. 217; McEniffv. General Dental Council [1980] 1 W.L.R. 328 (dentist struck off for allowing an assistant and a receptionist to fill teeth after he had completed the drilling); Le Scroog v. General Optical Council [1982] 1 W.L.R. 1238 (optician struck off for advertising).

[56] Dominions were given the power to do this by the Statute of Westminster 1931, ss.2, 3.

[57] Australia Act 1986, s.11.

[58] See B. Brown, [1995] N.Z.L.J. 82; P. J. Downey, [1995] N.Z.L.J. 205; [1995] N.Z.L.J.208–218; P. Pol, [1996] N.Z.L J. 94. See more generally on the role of the Privy Council in New Zealand law, P. Spiller, J. Finn and R Boast, A New Zealand Legal History (1995), pp. 228–234. The proposal then was generally opposed by the New Zealand legal profession, and was not implemented. The Labour Party was then opposed to the change, but, in government, now favours it: Reshaping New Zealand's Appeal Structure (Attorney-General's Discussion Paper, December 2000).

[59] See P. Wesley-Smith, (1992) 2 H.K.L.J. 118.

[60] For the republics (The Gambia, Singapore, Trinidad and Tobago) the Committee itself is the decision-making authority.

[61] At least while that country retains the appeal to the Privy Council. For example, in Viro v. R. (1978) 18 A.L.R. 257, the High Court of Australia held that it was no longer bound by decisions of the Privy Council: see R. S. Geddis, (1978) 9 Fed. L. R. 427.

handling such issues,[62] although the performance recently had been more impressive.[63]

The Judicial Committee of the Privy Council has jurisdiction to determine questions relating to the competences and functions of the legislative and executive authorities established in Scotland and Northern Ireland and of the National Assembly for Wales.[64] This includes power to determine as a court of first instance whether provisions of a Bill would be within the competence of the Scottish Parliament or Northern Ireland Assembly.[65] Otherwise, these "devolution issues" may reach the Judicial Committee on appeal or on a reference from a superior court[66] or on a reference from a law officer[67] where such an issue is not the subject of proceedings. In these cases the Judicial Committee must comprise members of the Judicial Committee who hold or have held the office of Lord of Appeal, or high judicial office in the United Kingdom. Decisions of the Judicial Committee on devolution issues must be stated in open court and are binding in all legal proceedings (other than proceedings before the Committee).[68]

As of February 2002, the Judicial Committee had determined nine cases raising devolution issues. All were from Scotland and raised issues concerning the application of the ECHR; eight of the nine[69] were criminal

---

[62] P. Wallington and J. McBride, *Civil Liberties and a Bill of Rights* (1976), pp. 32–33 "We come away with a rather neutral impression of the talents available"; G. J. Zellick, "Fundamental Rights in the Privy Council" [1982] P.L. 344 (criticising the decision in a case concerning the death penalty, *Riley v. Attorney General of Jamaica* [1983] 1 A.C. 719); B. de Smith, "The Judicial Committee as a Constitutional Court" [1984] P.L. 557; N. S. Price, "Constitutional Adjudication in the Privy Council and Reflections on the Bill of Rights debate" (1986) 35 I.C.L.Q. 946, criticising *Robinson v. R.* [1985] A.C. 956; *cf.* M. Zander, *A Bill of Rights*? (3rd ed., 1985), pp. 62–64, who takes a more favourable view. On the role of the Privy Council in developing the common law, see J. W. Harris, (1990) 106 L.Q.R. 574.

[63] See, *e.g. Pratt and Morgan v. Attorney-General of Jamaica* [1994] 2 A.C. 1; M. Grieve, "Life after Death Row," *Counsel*, July/August 1994, p. 16.

[64] Scotland Act 1998, s.103 and Sched. 6; Northern Ireland Act 1998, s.82 and Sched. 10; Government of Wales Act 1998, Sched. 8.

[65] Scotland Act 1998, s.33; Northern Ireland Act 1998, s.11.

[66] In specified circumstances, the Court of Session, the High Court of Justiciary, the Court of Appeal in Northern Ireland, the High Court and the Court of Appeal. A reference may be required by, *inter alia*, a law officer. The House of Lords may refer a devolution issue arising in judicial proceedings to the Judicial Committee unless the House considers it more appropriate, having regard to all the circumstances, that it should determine the issue.

[67] Or the Northern Ireland First Minister and deputy First Minister acting jointly in a case arising under the Northern Ireland Act 1998; or the National Assembly in a case arising under the Government of Wales Act 1998; or the Lord Advocate in a case arising under the Scotland Act 1998.

[68] Scotland Act 1998, s. 103(1); Northern Ireland Act 1998, s. 82(1); Government of Wales Act 1998, Sched. 8, para. 32. It is submitted that it is the decision as resolving the devolution issue that is binding and that, for example, a view of the scope of a particular ECHR provision, even if necessary for resolution of the devolution issue, would not be binding in a case where this did not arise as a devolution issue.

[69] See *e.g. Montgomery and Coulter v. H.M. Advocate and the Advocate General for Scotland* (DRA Nos 1 and 2 of 2000) [2001] 2 W.L.R. 779 (issues concerning the definition of "devolution issue" and the right to a fair trial under Article 6, ECHR in the context of pre-trial publicity); *Brown v. Stott* (DRA No. 3 of 2000) [2001] H.R.L.R. 9, 2001 P.C. 43 (adduction in evidence of admission by B that she was the driver at the time of an alleged offence, required by the Road Traffic Act 1988, s. 172(2)(a), not contrary to the implied right not to incriminate oneself in Article 6, ECHR); *Millar v. Procurator Fiscal Elgin* (DRA No. 5 of 2000) [2001] UKPC D4 (hearing of criminal proceedings by temporary sheriffs appointed by the Lord Advocate contrary to Article 6, ECHR); *Procurator Fiscal, Linlithgow v. Watson*

cases and one[70] concurred the compatibility with the ECHR of provisions of the legislation providing for the detention of mental patients. The composition of the Committee is effectively the same as that of the House of Lords, with, in the cases so far heard, at least two Scottish judges. Each judge gives a separate judgment. Decisions are obviously of considerable importance for the jurisdiction from which a case originates. Where not binding, they will have the same standing as a persuasive authority as a decision of the House of Lords.

The Committee sits in London. The recording of dissenting opinions has only been permitted since 1966.[71] Other than in devolution cases, there is either one unanimous opinion, or one for the majority and one for the minority. Lord Reid thought that the single opinion rule had led to Privy Council judgments being much inferior to speeches in the House of Lords:

> They are perfectly adequate to decide the particular case but not often of wider importance. Yet the same Law Lords have sat and they have taken just as much trouble. The reason is that a single judgment must get the agreement of at least all in the majority so it tends to be no more than the highest common factor of all the views."[72]

Apart from the appellate jurisdiction, the Judicial Committee may entertain an application for a declaration that a person purporting to be a member of the House of Commons is disqualified by the House of Commons Disqualification Act 1975.[73] Finally, Her Majesty may refer any matter to the Judicial Committee for hearing or consideration.[74]

13. THE COURT OF JUSTICE OF THE EUROPEAN COMMUNITIES[75]

(a) Establishment

This Court is one of the four major institutions created by the Treaties establishing the European Communities. There was originally a Court of Justice for the European Coal and Steel Community, but when the treaties

2–075

---

and Burrows. *H.M. Advocate v. JK* (DRA Nos 1 and 2 of 2000) [2001] UKPC D1 (right to hearing within a reasonable time).

[70] *Anderson. Reid and Doherty v. The Scottish Ministers* (DRA Nos 9, 10 and 11 of 2000) [2001] UKPC D5 (continued detention of restricted patients in hospital on grounds of public safety not dependent on their condition being capable of treatment).

[71] Judicial Committee (Dissenting Opinion) Order 1966. See D. B. Swinfen, "Single Judgment in the Privy Council 1833–1966" 1975 20 J.R. 153.

[72] "The Judge as Law Maker" (1972) XII J.S.P.T.L. (N.S.) 22 at 29.

[73] See s.7.

[74] Judicial Committee Act 1833, s.4. See D. B. Swinfen, "Politics and the Privy Council: Special Reference to the Judicial Committee" 1978 23 J.R. 126.

[75] S. Weatherill and P. Beaumont, *EU Law* (3rd ed., 1999), Chap. 6; T. C. Hartley, *The Foundations of European Community Law* (4th ed., 1998); L. Neville Brown and T. Kennedy, *The Court of Justice of the European Communities* (5th ed., 2000); J. Usher, *European Court Practice* (1983); K. P. E. Lasok, *The European Court of Justice: Practice and Procedure* (2nd ed., 1994); Office for Official Publications of the European Communities, *The Court of Justice of the European Community* (1995); H. Rasmussen, *On Law and Policy in the European Court of Justice* (1986).

establishing the European Economic Community and Euratom were concluded it was agreed that there should be one court for the three communities. The Single European Act of 1986 made provision for the establishment of a Court of First Instance to ease the Court's workload.[76]

(b) Composition

2–076   The Court consists of 15 judges,[77] assisted by eight advocates general.[78] It may sit either in "plenary session" (*i.e.* with all the judges entitled to be present) or, where permitted by the Rules of Procedure, in "chambers" of three, five or seven judges. It must sit in plenary session when a Member State or a Community Institution that is a party to the proceedings so requests.[79] Otherwise, the Court may assign any case to a chamber where the difficulty or importance of the case or the circumstances are not such as to require a decision of the court in plenary session.[80] Only one judgment is delivered by the Chamber or Court and it is not revealed whether the decision was unanimous or reached by a majority.

The function of the advocate general is:

"acting with complete impartiality and independence, to make, in open court, reasoned submissions on cases brought before the Court of Justice, in order to assist the Court ... ".[81]

This office has no exact equivalent in any national legal system although it is loosely based on that of *commissaire du gouvernement* in proceedings before French administrative courts, especially the Conseil d'Etat. One advocate general is assigned to each case. He or she sits on the bench, next to the judges, and may put questions to the parties. His or her opinion on the case is normally expressed about three weeks after the submissions of counsel have been heard, and, unlike such submissions on behalf of a client, "the Advocate General speaks for no-one but himself".[82] The opinion sets out the facts and relevant legal provisions, analyses the issues in the light of the case law of the court and suggests the appropriate decision for the court to adopt. It tends to be longer, more informative and less bland in style than the judgments of the court. The advocate general does not attend the deliberations of the judges. It is thought that his or her opinion is followed in about 70 per cent of cases, but this may be an overestimate.[83]

The judges and advocates general are chosen by agreement among the

---

[76] See section (f), below.
[77] Art. 221 E.C. (ex Art. 165/E.C., as amended).
[78] Art. 222 E.C. (ex Art. 166/E.C., as amended). There were nine between January 1, 1995 and October 6, 2000.
[79] Art. 221E.C. (ex Art. 165/E.C., as amended by Art.G(49)TEU). Prior to the amendment by the Maastricht Treaty, Art. 165/E.C. required plenary sessions for cases brought by a Member State or Community institution, and (unless the Court's Rules of Procedure provided otherwise) preliminary rulings.
[80] Rules of Procedure of the Court of Justice, Article 95(1).
[81] Art. 222 E.C. (ex Art. 166/E.C.). See A. A. Dashwood, "The Advocate General in the Court of Justice of the European Communities" (1982) 2 L.S. 202; K. Borgsmidt, "The Advocate General at the European Court of Justice: A Comparative Study" (1988) 13 E.L.Rev. 106; T. Tridimas, (1997) 34 C.M.L. Rev. 1349.
[82] Dashwood, *op. cit.*, p. 207.
[83] *ibid.* p. 212.

governments of the Member States. They have to be:

"chosen from persons whose independence is beyond doubt and who possess the qualifications required for appointment to the highest judicial offices in their respective countries or who are jurisconsults of recognised competence",[84]

and are appointed for a term of six years. A proportion[85] of the judges and advocates general are replaced every three years. The incumbents are eligible for re-appointment. The judges elect one of their number to be President for a (renewable) three-year term. The President's functions are to direct the judicial business and the administration of the court and to preside at hearings. One of the advocates general is designated as first advocate general, and performs certain administrative functions, including the distribution of cases among his or her colleagues.

There is one judge of each of the 15 nationalities.[86] There is one advocate general from each of the five largest states[87] and the remainder from the smaller states by rotation.

When the Treaty of Nice is in force, there will be one judge for each Member State. There will be eight advocates-general, but the Council may at the Court's request increase the number. They will act in cases which, in accordance with the Statute of the Court of Justice, require their involvement. A new Statute of the Court of Justice will provide for chambers of three and five judges; for a Grand Chamber presided over by the President of the Court, which will comprise 11 judges and will sit when a Member State or an institution of the Communities that is party to the proceedings so requests; and for the full court to sit for cases under Articles 195(2), 213(2), 216, 247(7)E.C., and other cases of exceptional importance. Decisions of the Court will only be valid where there is an uneven number of judges; and there are at least three judges (chambers), nine judges (Grand Chamber) or 11 judges (full court).[88]

(c) Jurisdiction

The jurisdiction of the Court of Justice under the E.C. Treaty[89] can be classified under four main heads: (i) applications for preliminary rulings under Article 234E.C. (ex Article 177/E.C.) in the course of proceedings in a national court or tribunal; (ii) direct actions against Member States or Community institutions; (iii) staff cases; (iv) opinions.

2–077

---

[84] Art. 223 E.C.(ex Art. 167/E.C.). See also the Protocol on the Statute of the Court of Justice.

[85] Seven or eight judges; four advocates general.

[86] These are not legal requirements but are the consequences in practice of the need for the agreement of all the Member States. The U.K. judges have been Lord Mackenzie Stuart; formerly a judge of the Court of Session (1973–1988, President 1984–1988); Sir Gordon Slynn; formerly a High Court judge and then an Advocate General (1988–1992); David Edward; a Scottish Q.C. and Professor of European Institutions at the University of Edinburgh, and then judge of the Court of First Instance, 1989–1992 (1992–).

[87] France, Germany, Italy, Spain and the United Kingdom. Those from the U.K. have been J.-P. Warner (1973–1981); Sir Gordon Slynn (1981–1988); Prof. F. Jacobs Q.C. (1988–).

[88] Treaty of Nice, Arts 27–29, substituting Arts 221–223 E.C.

[89] There are analogous procedures under the other Treaties, with some differences in point of detail between the ECSC and the others.

When the Treaty of Nice is in force, the Council will have power to confer jurisdiction on the Court in disputes relating to the application of acts adopted on the basis of the Treaty that create Community industrial property rights, and to recommend the provisions to Member States for adoption in accordance with their constitutional requirements.[90]

(i) Applications for preliminary rulings

These are considered in Chapter 18.

(ii) Direct actions

2–078 (1) *Actions against Member States.*[91] Under Article 226 E.C. (ex Article 169/ E.C.), if the Commission considers that a Member State has failed to fulfil an obligation imposed by the Treaty or secondary Community legislation, it must deliver a reasoned opinion on the matter, after giving the State concerned the opportunity to submit its observations.[92] If the State does not comply with the opinion within the period laid down by the Commission, the Commission may bring the matter before the Court of Justice.[93] Under (Article 227 E.C. (ex Article 170/E.C.) a Member State may bring similar proceedings against another Member State, after bringing the matter to the Commission's attention. If a breach is established the Court will make a declaratory order to that effect.[94] The Member State is required by (Article 228 E.C. (ex Article 171/E.C.) to take the necessary measures to comply.[95] A large majority of cases are settled before they reach the Court.

Prior to amendments effected by the Maastricht Treaty, the sanctions were political rather than legal, and there was non-compliance in a significant number of cases. The position now is that, in such cases, the Commission after giving the Member State concerned the opportunity to submit observations, may issue a reasoned opinion specifying the points on which there has been non-compliance. If the Member State fails to take the necessary measures to comply with the original judgment within the time limit laid down by the Commission, the latter may bring the matter before

---

[90] Treaty of Nice, Art. 33, inserting Art. 229a E.C.

[91] Hartley (1998), Chap. 10; Weatherill and Beaumont (1999), Chap 7: H. A. H. Audretsch, *Supervision in European Community Law* (2nd ed., 1986); A. Dashwood and R. White, (1989) 14 E.L.Rev. 388.

[92] A reasonable time must be allowed: Case 293/85, *Commission v. Belgium* [1989] 2 C.M.L.R. 527. See A. Arnull, (1988) 13 E.L.Rev. 260.

[93] See, *e.g.* Case 232/78 *Commission v. France* [1979] E.C.R. 2729: French ban on the import of mutton and lamb from the U.K. held to be an infringement of the Treaty; the dispute was eventually compromised. .

[94] Only one case under Art. 227E.C. has proceeded to judgment: Case 141/78, *France v. United Kingdom* [1979] E.C.R. 2923. *Cf.* the procedure under Art. 88 E.C. (ex Art. 93/E.C.) whereby the Commission may require a State to abolish or alter a state aid that distorts or threatens to distort competition: if the State does not comply the matter may be referred to the Court.

[95] Although Art. 228E.C. does not specify a time limit within which a judgment must be complied with, implementation must start immediately and be completed as soon as possible: Case 131/84, *Commission v. Italian Republic* [1985] E.C.R. 3531 (unreasonable delay in implementing judgment in Case 91/81, [1982] E.C.R. 2133). Implementation must be by national provisions of a binding nature, not merely by administrative circulars or practices: Case 168/85, *Commission v. Italy* [1986] E.C.R. 2945.

the Court and the Court may impose a lump sum or penalty payment on the Member State.[96] This is an "important new power, which greatly enhances the armoury of the Court of Justice".[97]

(2) *Actions against community institutions.* These include (1) actions under Article 230E.C. (ex Article 173/E.C.) for the annulment of acts of the Council and Commission[98]; (2) actions under Article 232E.C. (ex Article 175/E.C.) against the Council, the Commission or the Parliament where it has, contrary to the requirements of the Treaty, failed to act[99]; (3) actions under Article 229E.C. (ex Article 172/E.C.) to review penalties or fines imposed by the Commission; (4) actions under Article 235E.C. (ex Article 178/E.C.) for damages based on the non-contractual (including tortious) liability of the Communities.[1]

(iii) Staff cases

The court has jurisdiction under Article 236E.C. (ex Article 179/E.C.) in any dispute between the Community and its servants within the limits and under the conditions laid down in the Staff Regulations or the Conditions of Employment.

(iv) Opinions

The court may under Article 300 E.C. (ex Article 228/E.C.) give an opinion as to whether an inter-national agreement that the Community proposes to enter is compatible with the Treaty.

(d) Some aspects of procedure

Proceedings before the court are governed by the Rules of Procedure[2] drawn up by the court with the approval of the Council. There are four stages—   **2–079**

(1) Written proceedings. Proceedings are commenced by filing an application specifying the subject matter of the dispute, the form of order sought, the pleas in law on which the application is based and certain other matters. A defence must be filed within one month, and a reply and rejoinder may follow.

(2) Investigation or preliminary inquiry. The case will have been assigned by the President to one of the six chambers. He will also nominate one of the judges in that chamber to act as rapporteur. After the close of pleadings the judge-rapporteur makes a preliminary report which

---

[96] Art. 228 E.C. (ex Art. 171/E.C., as amended by Art. G(51)/TEU).
[97] Weatherill and Beaumont 1999, pp. 236–237.
[98] See below, para. 5-057 Community legislation is considered below at paras 5-033–5-060 and its interpretation at paras 6-049–6-060.
[99] See below, para. 5-059.
[1] Art. 288 E.C. (ex Art. 215/E.C.) provides that "the Community shall, in accordance with the general provisions common to the laws of the Member States, make good any damage caused by its institutions or by its servants in the performance of their duties".
[2] A codified version of the 1991 rules as amended is published on the Court of Justice website.

enables the court to decide whether the submission of any evidence is required, such as the oral testimony of witnesses, an expert's report or the personal appearance of the parties. These matters are dealt with at this stage. The judge-rapporteur then prepares a report summarising facts and arguments.

(3) Oral proceedings. The procedure includes an oral part, unless the Court determines otherwise (in cases where none of the parties gives reasons why it should be heard orally). At this stage the parties' lawyers address the court.[3] Interchange between court and advocate is a comparatively recent development. The final step of this stage is the delivery of the advocate general's opinion, which takes place in open court, normally a few weeks later.

(4) Judgment. Proceedings may be conducted in Danish, Dutch, English, Finnish, French, German, Greek, Irish, Italian, Portuguese, Spanish or Swedish. The language is chosen by the applicant, except where an application is made against a Member State or a natural or legal person having the nationality of a Member State, where the state's language is used, where use of another language is permitted at the joint request of the parties, and in applications for preliminary rulings, which are conducted in the language of the referring court or tribunal. In practice, the working language is normally French.

There are no court fees. Costs are normally awarded to the successful party against his or her opponent. The court may grant legal aid: aid for an application for a preliminary ruling is, however, regarded as an aspect of the national proceedings, and aid will only be granted by the court if it is not available in those proceedings.

(e) Administration

2–080   This is the responsibility of the Registrar and his staff. There is a Registry, translation, library and documentation and interpretation services and an information office. In addition, three legal secretaries are attached to each judge and advocate general.

(f) The Court of First Instance[4]

2–081   From 1974, the European Court pressed for the establishment of a separate administrative tribunal to deal with staff cases and thereby relieve the pressure on the Court. For over 20 years, nothing came of this although changes were made in the Court's procedures, including the greater use of

---

[3] Any lawyer entitled to practice before a court of a Member State may appear. Thus, either a barrister or solicitor from the U.K. may appear. A litigant may not normally appear in person. *Cf.* below, para. 3-016.

[4] The background is fully considered by T. Kennedy, "The Essential Minimum: The Establishment of the Court of First Instance" (1989) 14 E.L.Rev. 7. See also H. G. Schermers, (1988) 25 C.M.L.Rev. 541; Select Committee on the European Communities, Fifth Report 1987–88 (1987–88 H.L. 20); O. Due, (1988) 4 Y.E.L. 1; T. Kennedy, (1990) 15 E.L.Rev. 54; A. G. Toth in R. White and B. Smythe (eds), *Current Issues In European and International Law* (1990), Chap. 2; Brown and Kennedy (2000), Chap. 5.

chambers, and the number of judges and advocates general were periodically increased. Eventually, the Single European Act amended the main Treaties[5] to enable the Council, by a Decision, to establish a Court of First Instance of the European Communities, and amend the Rules of Procedure accordingly. The necessary Decision was made in 1988,[6] and provided for a court of 12 (now 15) members "attached to the Court of Justice of the European Communities"[7] and with its seat at the Court. It normally sits in chambers of three or five judges, but may exceptionally sit in plenary session, in accordance with its Rules of Procedure.[8] The members are appointed by common accord of the governments of the Member States for (renewable) six-year terms, and with the membership partly renewed every three years.[9] They must be "chosen from persons whose independence is beyond doubt and who possess the ability required for appointment to judicial office".[10] No separate advocates general are appointed, but the judges "may be called upon to perform the task of an advocate general",[11] again in accordance with the Rules of Procedure. A President is elected by the judges for a (renewable) three-year term.[12] The Court also appoints a Registrar.

The Court initially exercised the jurisdiction of the European Court in (1) staff cases[13]; (2) competition cases[14]; and (3) coal and steel case arising from the application of the ECSC Treaty.[15] Its jurisdiction has since been significantly expanded to include all other actions by natural or legal persons under Articles 173(2), 175(3) and 178/E.C. and actions under Article 181 (where the court may give judgments under an arbitration clause in a contract concluded by or on behalf of the Community).[16] Notwithstanding these developments, the backlog of cases is increasing in both the Court of First Instance and the Court itself.[17]

The Court of First Instance has established its own Rules of Procedure, in

---

[5] Art. 168a/E.C.; Art. 32D/ECSC; Art. 140a/Euratom. The Maastricht Treaty amended Art.168a to provide directly for the establishment of the CFI, specifically excluding only Art. 177 references from the classes of action or proceeding that may be conferred on it by the Council; the original version also excluded actions brought by Member States or Community institutions.

[6] Dec. 88/591/ECSC, E.C., Euratom, October 24, 1988, [1988] O.J. L 319/1 (November 25, 1988), [1989] 1 C.M.L.R. 323, as amended.

[7] *ibid.* Art. 1.

[8] When the Treaty of Nice comes into force, the Protocol on the Statute of the Court of Justice will provide for the Rules of Procedure to specify cases where the CFI may sit as a full court or be constituted by a single judge.

[9] Art. 225(3) (ex Art. 168a(3)/E.C.). The first judge from the U.K. was David Edward Q.C. (1989–1992). He was succeeded Mphcpd by Christopher Bellamy Q.C. (1992–1999) and Nicholar Forwood Q.C. (1999–).

[10] *ibid.*

[11] Dec. 88/591, Art. 2(3).

[12] *ibid.*, Art. 2(2). The first President was appointed as such by the Member States: Art. 11.

[13] Disputes between the Communities and their servants under Art. 179/E.C. and Art. 152/Euratom.

[14] Actions against Community institutions under Arts 173(2) and 175(3)/E.C. relating to the implementation of the competition rules applicable to undertakings.

[15] Actions against the Commission under Arts 33(2) and 35/ECSC by undertakings or associations of undertakings concerning individual acts relating to the implication of Arts 50, 57–66/ECSC. .

[16] Dec. 93/350, amending Dec. 88/591. See now Arts 230(2), 232(3), 235 and 238 E.C.

[17] Weatherill and Beaumont (1999), pp. 207–209.

agreement with the European Court and with the unanimous approval of the Council.[18]

An appeal lies to the European Court[19] against final decisions of the Court of First Instance, and decisions disposing of the substantive issues in part only or disposing of a procedural issue concerning a plea of lack of competence or inadmissibility. An appeal may be brought by (1) any unsuccessful party (except that interveners other than Member States or Community institutions may only appeal where the Court's decision directly affects them); and (2) (except in staff cases) any non-intervening Member State or Community institution. The appeal is limited to points of law, including lack of competence of the Court of First Instance, and a breach of procedure which adversely affects the appellant's interests. If the appeal is well founded, the European Court is to quash the decision and either itself give final judgment or remit the case to the Court of First Instance. In the latter event, the European Court's decision on points of law is binding.

When the Treaty of Nice comes into force, a number of changes will be made. The Court of First Instance will comprise at least one judge per Member State, the number being specified in the statute. The statute may provide for advocates general. The Court will have jurisdiction to hear and determine at first instance proceedings under Articles 230, 232, 235, 236 and 238 E.C. unless they are assigned to a "judicial panel" or reserved by the Statute for the Court of Justice. The Statute may confer jurisdiction in other matters, including preliminary rulings in specified areas. Judicial panels may be created by the Council to hear and determine at first instance certain classes of action or proceedings brought in specific areas. The Court of First Instance will have jurisdiction to determine actions or proceedings against decisions of judicial panels. First instance determination by the Court of First Instance will be subject to an appeal on a point of law to the Court of Justice, under conditions specified by the Statute. Other decisions will be subject to review by the Court of Justice, as provided for by the Statute, where there is a serious risk of the unity or consistency of Community law being affected.[20]

14. THE EUROPEAN COURT OF HUMAN RIGHTS[21]

2–082 Decisions of the European Court of Human Rights have become of increasing significance for the English legal system in recent years, and particularly since implementation of the Human Rights Acts 1998. The Convention for the Protection of Human Rights and Fundamental Freedoms of November 4, 1950, generally known as the European

---

[18] Art. 168a(4)/E.C.; O.J. 1991 L136/5.

[19] Arts 49–54 of the Protocol on the Statute of the Court of Justice, inserted by Dec. 88/591/ECSC/EEC/Euratom.

[20] Treaty of Nice, Arts 30–32, inserting new Arts 224, 225, 225a E.C.; revised Protocol on the Statute of the Court of Justice.

[21] See R. Beddard, *Human Rights and Europe* (3rd ed., 1993); J. E. S. Fawcett, *The Application of the European Convention on Human Rights* (2nd ed., 1987); D. J. Harris, M. O'Boyle and C. Warbrick, *The Law of the European Convention on Human Rights*; A.R. Mowbray, *Cases and Materials on the European Convention on Human Rights* (2001); C. Geraty, "The European Court of Human Rights and Civil Liberties: an Overview" [1993] C.L.J. 89. See also *www.echr.coe.int.*

Convention on Human Rights, was one of the first achievements of the Council of Europe, an association now of 43 states. It came into force in 1953 and there are now over 40 states which are parties to the Convention.[22] Article 1 provides that these parties "shall secure to everyone within their jurisdiction" the rights and freedoms defined in Articles 2 to 18. These are mostly civil and political rights,[23] including the right to life (Art. 2), the right not to be subjected to torture or to inhuman or degrading treatment or punishment (Art. 3), the right to liberty and security of person (Art. 5), the right to a fair trial in both civil and criminal cases (Art. 6), the right to respect for private and family life, home and correspondence (Art. 8), the right to freedom of thought, conscience and religion (Art. 9), the right to freedom of expression (Art. 10) and the right to freedom of peaceful assembly and to freedom of association with others (Art. 11). Further rights are specified in the First, Fourth, Sixth and Seventh Protocols to the Convention.[24] Article 13 requires that persons whose guaranteed rights are violated "have an effective remedy before a national authority".

For the purposes of enforcement the Convention established the European Commission of Human Rights and the European Court of Human Rights, each with one member in respect of each party. The Eleventh Protocol, adopted in 1994, provides for the merger of the Commission and the Court into a new European Court of Human Rights.[25] It still comprises one judge elected by the Parliamentary Assembly with respect to each party, with each sitting in an individual capacity and not as a representative of his or her country. Judges must be of high moral character and either possess the qualifications required for appointment to high judicial office or be jurisconsults of recognised competence.[26] They are elected for six-year terms, can be re-elected, but retire at 70.[27]

The Court can sit in committees of three judges, in Chambers of seven and in a Grand Chamber of 17.[28] Cases can be declared inadmissible or struck out by a committee where such a decision can be taken without further examination; otherwise, cases are determined by a Chamber unless released to the Grand Chamber, as may happen where a case raises serious questions of interpretation of the ECHR or its resolution before the Chamber might have a result inconsistent with an earlier judgment of the Court. Where a Chamber has delivered a judgment, any party may within

---

[22] The United Kingdom was the first state to ratify the Convention in 1951. Forty-one states had ratified as at March 19, 2001. Recent additions include Russia (1998) and Georgia (1999). Armenia and Azerbaijan signed in January 2001.

[23] Economic, social and cultural rights are protected under the European Social Charter 1961: see D. J. Harris, *The European Social Charter* (1984); A. Ph. C. M. Jaspers and L. Betten (eds), *25 years: European Social Charter* (1988).

[24] The First Protocol came into force in 1954; all Member States except Andorra, Georgia and Switzerland were parties to it as at March 19, 2001. The U.K. has ratified the Sixth (abolition of the death penalty; May 20, 1999) but not the Fourth and Seventh. Twenty-two states, not including the U.K., are parties to the Fourth Protocol.

[25] See A.R. Mowbray, [1994] P.L. 54; D. Harris, M. O'Boyle and C. Warbrick (1995), Chap. 26.

[26] Arts 21, 22.

[27] Art. 23.

[28] The judge elected in respect of the state party concerned is an *ex officio* member and if there is none or he is unable to sit, a person of the state's choice sits in the capacity of judge; the Grand Chamber includes the President of the Court, the Vice-Presidents, the President of the Chambers and other judges chosen in accordance with the rules of the Court.

three months request that the case by referred to the Grand Chamber, and a panel of five judges must accept the request if the case raises a serious question affecting the interpretation or application of the ECHR or a serious case of general importance.[29]

Alleged breaches of the Convention may be raised either by a state party[30] or by any person, non-governmental organisation or group of individuals claiming to be the victim of a violation by one of the parties of rights under the ECHR.[31] The Court may only deal with the matter if all domestic remedies have been exhausted and within six months from the date when the final decision was taken. It must not deal with an anonymous application or one substantially the same as one already examined by the Court or already submitted to another procedure of international investigation or settlement. It must declare inadmissible any individual application which it considers incompatible with the provisions of the Convention, manifestly ill-founded, or an abuse of the right of application.[32] It may strike out an application if it concludes that the applicant does not intend to pursue the application, or the matter has been resolved, or it is otherwise no longer justified to continue the examination of the application.[33] If the Court declares an application admissible it must examine the case with the parties' representatives, if necessary undertake an investigation and seek to secure a friendly settlement; in which case the application is struck out.[34] Hearings are normally held in public and documents are normally accessible to the public.[35] In most cases, a declaratory judgment is given. If the Court finds there has been a violation, and if the internal law of the state concerned allows only partial reparation to be made, the Court "shall, if necessary, afford just satisfaction to the injured party".[36] In a number of cases monetary compensation has been awarded as "just satisfaction" covering costs and expenses, pecuniary losses and non-pecuniary loss.

The Court has adopted Rules of Court.[37] As from January 1, 1983, an individual applicant may be represented by an advocate authorised to practise in any of the party states or any other person approved by the President of the Chamber, or may be given leave to present his or her own case.[38]

Legal aid may be awarded in respect of proceedings before the Commission and the Court.[39] The official languages are English and

---

[29] Art. 43.

[30] Art. 33. Few such applications have been made. One example is *Ireland v. United Kingdom* Series A, No. 25, Judgment of January 18, 1978.

[31] Art. 34. The right of individual petition is now compulsory; formerly, the state had to accept the right of individual petition (the U.K. first did so on January 14, 1966, with subsequent renewals).

[32] Art. 35.

[33] Art. 37.

[34] Arts 38, 39.

[35] Art. 40.

[36] Art. 41.

[37] ECtHR Rules of Court (as in force on November 1, 1998) (ECtHR website).

[38] *ibid.* r.86. See P. J. Duffy, [1983] P.L. 32–33. Previously, the applicant technically had no independent right to appear although in practice his or her lawyer was permitted to address the Court as part of the Commission's case.

[39] rr. 91–96.

French.[40] There is provision for the submission of written documents and an oral hearing.[41] The Court deliberates and votes on its decision in private. A judgment of the Court is prepared: each judge is entitled to annex a separate opinion, whether concurring or dissenting, or a bare statement of dissent.[42] The workload of the Court has risen dramatically in recent years. By the end of 2001 it had registered 77,768 individual applications, 13,858 of which had been received in 2001; of these, 51,894 had been declared inadmissible and judgments had been delivered in 2,789 cases, of which 889 had been delivered in 2001.[43]

As of January 2002, the Court has considered on the merits 155 cases[44] involving the United Kingdom. In 86 the Court found there to be violations of one or more Articles. Either as a consequence, or in anticipation of these findings,[45] English law has been changed in a number of significant respects.[46] For example, the law of contempt of court was amended following the *Sunday Times* case[47]; the law relating to the correspondence of persons in prisons has been radically altered[48]; the law in Northern Ireland concerning homosexual acts has been brought into line with the rest of the United Kingdom[49]; Isle of Man courts have been advised that birching is contrary to the European Convention[50]; phone tapping has been regulated

---

[40] Revised Rules of Court, r.88a, rr. 91–96. Another language may be used with the leave of the President of the Chamber.

[41] Revised Rules of Court, rr. 38, 40, 63–70.

[42] *ibid.* r. 74.

[43] *Information Note on the Court's Statistics* and Press Release 032, January 21, 2002, ECtHR website.

[44] *i.e.* excluding cases struck out and separate applications under Art. 50 where the merits have already been determined.

[45] There are also some changes that can be traced to friendly settlements or Commission decisions.

[46] See P. J. Duffy, (1980) 29 I.C.L.Q. 585–618; A. Drzemczewski, *European Human Rights Convention in Domestic Law* (1983), pp. 314–322; M. P. Furmston, *et al.*, (eds), *The Effect on English Domestic Law of Membership of the European Communities and of Ratifications of the European Convention on Human Rights* (1983); F. J. Hampson, "The United Kingdom Before the European Court of Human Rights" (1989) 9 Y.E.L. 121; R. R. Churchill and J. R. Young, (1991) 62 B.Y.I.L. 183; D. Kinley, *The European Convention on Human Rights: Compliance without Incorporation* (1993) (arguing the case for pre-legislative scrutiny in the U.K. to promote compliance)); J. P. Gardiner (ed.), *Aspects of the Incorporation of the European Convention on Human Rights into Domestic Law* (1993).

[47] See *Sunday Times Case*, Series A, No. 30, Judgment of April 26, 1979: violation of Art. 10; Contempt of Court Act 1981; S. H. Bailey, (1982) 45 M.L.R. 301. It is not certain that the Act went far enough.

[48] See the *Golder Case*, Series A, No. 18, Judgment of February 21, 1975; *Case of Silver and Others*: Series A, No. 61, Judgment of March 25, 1983: violations of Arts 6 \S 1 and 3; *Case of Campbell and Fell*, Series A, No. 80, Judgment of June 28, 1984; *Case of Boyle and Rice*, Series A, No. 131, Judgment of April 27, 1988; G. J. Zellick, [1981] P.L. 435–438, [1983] P.L. 167–169.

[49] *Dudgeon Case*, Series A, No. 45, Judgment of October 22, 1981: violation of Art. 8; Homosexual Offences (Northern Ireland) Order 1982.

[50] *Tyrer Case*, Series A, No. 26, Judgment of April 25, 1978; G. J. Zellick, [1982] P.L. 4–5. The United Kingdom does not now accept the rights of individual petition in respect of the Isle of Man.

by statute[51]; the legal regime governing courts martial has been radically revised[52]; the policy excluding homosexuals from the armed forces dropped[53]; the admission of evidence obtained under compulsion curtailed[54]; and overbroad, blanket rules excluding liability in negligence have been replaced by an approach that requires more specific attention to the policy arguments for and against liability in particular classes of case.[55] The Convention has also had some influence in statutory interpretation,[56] although judges emphasised on a number of occasions that it was not part of English law.[57] A significant measure of incorporation has now been secured by the enactment of the Human Rights 1998, which is considered in Chapter 8.

---

[51] *Malone Case*, Series A, No. 82, Judgment of August 2, 1984; Interception of Communications Act 1985 (see annotations in *Current Law Statutes 1985* by D. Foulkes). The Convention has also influenced the law affecting mental patients, children in secure accommodation, immigration, and the right of parents to forbid the imposition by a school of corporal punishment on their children.

[52] *Findlay v. U.K.* (1997) 24 E.H.R.R. 221: violation of Art. 6(1); Armed Forces Act 1996.

[53] *Smith and Grady v. U.K.* (1999) 29 E.H.R.R. 493; *Lustig-Prean and Beckett v. U.K.* (1999) 29 E.H.R.R. 548: violation of Art. 8; Mowbray (2001), pp. 335–356.

[54] *Saunders v. U.K.* (1996) 23 E.H.R.R. 313; *IJL. GMR and AKP v. U.K.*, Judgment of September 19, 2000: violation of Art. 6(1); Youth Justice and Criminal Evidence Act 1999, Sched. 3.

[55] *Osman v. U.K.* (1998) 29 E.H.R.R. 245: violation of Art. 6(1), *cf. Z. v. U.K.*, Judgment of May 10, 2001.

[56] See below, para. 6-035. A. Drzemczewski, *European Human Rights Convention in Domestic Law* (1983), pp. 166–187; M. Addo, (1995) 46 N.I.L.Q. 1.

[57] *ibid.* pp. 314–322. See, *e.g. Malone v. Metropolitan Police Commissioner* [1979] Ch. 344; *Att.-Gen. v. B.B.C.* [1981] A.C. 303 (Lord Scarman); *R. v. Secretary of State for the Home Department, ex p. Brind* [1991] 1 A.C. 696.

CHAPTER 3

LAWYERS

A. INTRODUCTION: THE "LEGAL PROFESSION"

The title "lawyer" is reserved for those who have achieved the special status   **3–001**
of membership of the "legal profession."[1] It is not a straightforward matter,
since many people perform legal tasks even though they are not lawyers. For
example, accountants may specialise in revenue law, trade union officials
may appear regularly before employment tribunals on behalf of their
members,[2] and solicitors may delegate work to legal executives and other
para-legals.[3] Conversely, many of the tasks performed by lawyers are not
strictly "legal."[4] Membership of the legal profession in England and Wales
involves qualification as either a barrister or a solicitor. It is usual to speak
of two branches of the profession, although historically it is more accurate
to speak of two professions.

It is significant that it is accepted that lawyers are members of a
"profession." Much has been written about the supposedly distinctive
attributes of professions, and how and why occupational groups seek such
status.[5] Medicine and law have been regarded as classic models, although
there are important differences between them. A particularly significant
difference is that, in medicine, discipline and representation of the profession
lie with very different bodies, whereas the Bar Council, for barristers, and
the Law Society, for solicitors, exercise both functions increasingly
uneasily.[6] The Office of Fair Trading has recently considered what is a
profession and some of the consequences which may flow from professional
recognition in a challenging statement:

"The professions are entrusted with the delivery of services of

---

[1] Academic lawyers are not necessarily qualified, but are lawyers. See M. Partington,
"Academic lawyers and legal practice in Britain: a preliminary reappraisal" (1988) 15 J.L.S.
374.
[2] See below, para. 10-011.
[3] See below, para. 3-054.
[4] See below, para. 3-004.
[5] See, *e.g.*, T.J. Johnson, *Professions and Power* (1972), pp. 21–38; R. Dingwall & P. Lewis
(eds.), *The Sociology of the Professions* (1983); R.L. Abel, *The Legal Profession in England
and Wales* (1988), esp. Chap. 1; A. Boon & J. Levin, *The Ethics and Conduct of Lawyers in
England and Wales* (1999), Chaps. 1–3; R. O'Dair, *Legal Ethics: Text and Materials* (2001),
Chap. 3.
[6] See, *e.g.*, M. Seneviratne, *The Legal Profession: Regulation and the Consumer* (1999), Chap.
7.

considerable public importance. They work within a framework of law, but within that framework their governing bodies have important degrees of freedom to control rights to enter and practise the relevant profession. The exercise of these powers can have a significant impact on the economy, on the interests of consumers, and on society generally, especially where the professions concerned have exclusive rights to supply certain services. Restrictions on supply in the case of professional services, just as with other goods and services, will tend to drive up costs and prices, limit access and choice and cause customers to receive poorer value for money than they would under properly competitive conditions. Such restrictions will tend also to inhibit innovation in the supply of services, again to the ultimate detriment of the public.

Restrictions may be justified under competition law if they are in the public interest, if they serve economic progress, if the benefits are shared with consumers and if the restrictions do not go further than is necessary or eliminate competition. However, where they go beyond those boundaries, it is important that the competition authorities should be able to take action to free the forces of competition."[7]

The Royal Commission on Legal Services had recognised five main features of a profession:[8] (a) central organisation: a governing body with powers of control and discipline; (b) the primary function of giving advice in a specialised field of knowledge; (c) the restriction of admission to those with the required standard of education and training; (d) a measure of self-regulation by the profession; and (e) the paramountcy of the duty owed to the client, only subject to responsibility to the court. Increasingly, as will be seen in this chapter, the legal profession will not satisfy these elements as not all solicitors have to be members of the Law Society, and there is an increasing reduction in the areas of work that only solicitors and/or barristers can do. Further, certain aspects are under significant challenge, not least the fact, noted above, that both branches of the profession have organising bodies which exercise both disciplinary and representative functions.

3–002   Some commentators take the view that the service is offered to the public subject to self-regulation in return for considerable autonomy from external control and it is possible to see this arrangement as a form of occupational control rather than an expression of the inherent nature of particular organisations.[9] It was the view of the Royal Commission, however, that the identified features promoted the public interest, subject to points of detail, and proposed no fundamental changes. However, as the OFT report indicates, this is no longer the position.

Some are deeply concerned about the process of professionalisation. So, Larson has described professionalisation as:

"the process by which producers of special services sought to constitute *and control* a market for their expertise ... a collective assertion of

[7] Office of Fair Trading, *Competition in professions* (2001), paras. 1 & 2.
[8] Royal Commission on Legal Services, *Report, Vol. I* (1979), pp. 28, 30.
[9] Johnson (1972), p. 45.

special social status (and) a collective process of upward social mobility."[10]

As the OFT has identified, arguments for maintaining standards tend to coincide with arguments for monopolies, restrictions on practice and high rewards.[11] Another consequence of professionalism that has historically not been addressed is the extent to which it may impede the expansion of legal services.[12] So, the issue is the extent to which the professionals control what they are prepared to supply rather than whether they endeavour to meet a need. The aspects of professionalism that may inhibit such development are that problems tend to be defined in the professional's terms and other definitions are irrelevant; outsiders may be ignored on the grounds that they are not competent to assess or criticise; "specialised knowledge" may be guarded by such means as "the creation of special forms of jargonised discourse and the fostering of an air of impenetrable mystery;"[13] the emphasis on the individual lawyer-client relationship may inhibit the development of group representation and test-case strategies;[14] and the proper advertising of services may be prevented.[15] However, it is also important to recognise that, whilst still thinking of themselves as professionals, the organisation of solicitors into firms, and larger and larger firms at that, is increasingly forcing them to act as businesses and business people. This drives them to consider how to maximise their existing markets, by, *e.g.*, advertising their existing services, and to examine the potential of alternative markets. Of course, not all solicitors are motivated by business needs, but the vast majority of firms are. It is interesting to note that increasingly it is the case that private client work is not undertaken by large City of London firms and that is particularly true of social welfare areas of work that tends to be undertaken, when undertaken by lawyers at all, by Law Centres and by private solicitors with a serious social conscience and mission.[16]

Many of the problematic features of professionalism have come under attack in recent years. The OFT produced its report on *Competition in professions* in March 2001, which is seen by some as an exemplar of such attacks. The status quo, preferred by the Royal Commission on Legal Services in 1979, has not prevailed as the pressures to modernise, reform and provide a more societally acceptable service has brought pressure to change on both barristers and solicitors.

[10] M.S. Larson, *The Rise of Professionalism* (1977), p. xvi.

[11] See below, paras 3-011–3-018.

[12] R. Cotterell, "Legal Services and Professional Ideology" (1980) Conference paper, and P. Fennell, "Solicitors, their markets and their ignorant public: the crisis of the professional ideas" in Z. Bankowski & G. Mungham (eds.), *Essays in Law and Society* (1980), p. 1.

[13] Cotterell (1980), p. 10.

[14] See below, para. 11-016.

[15] See also Chap. 8.

[16] Even if a solicitor in a large firm has such a conscience and mission it is not necessarily appropriate to fulfil the firm's pro bono mission by doing some types of work because all work requires expertise and working in company/commercial areas provides little if any background for working with private clients in social welfare areas of law.

B. THE LEGAL PROFESSION TODAY

1. ORGANISATION

3–003   The legal profession is divided into two branches: barristers and solicitors. Both are held in high regard.[17] This is in part because of the control that they exercise over admission to the profession which ensures high quality education. The Bar has developed from the work of advocates since medieval times being based, primarily, in the fours Inns of Court which still exist to-day: Gray's Inn, Inner Temple, Lincoln's Inn, and Middle Temple. Solicitors have developed a line of work originally in meeting the needs of clients unable to process litigation for themselves. The Bar has been largely untouched by government, though this is changing, and has run itself through the Inns of Court, which have been dominated by senior barristers and judges as benchers of the Inns, and also through the judicial control of practice in the courts. Solicitors have been regulated by government in one way or another since a statute of 1605 subjected solicitors[18] to a measure of control to prevent overcharging and to cut their numbers: only "skillfull" and "honest" men were allowed to practice. In 1728 an Act was passed for the better regulation of solicitors, and it introduced a roll of solicitors. In 1831 the Society of Attorneys Solicitors and Proctors and others not being barristers practising in the Courts of Law and Equity in the United Kingdom received a Royal Charter, and changed its name, in 1833, to the Incorporated Law Society of the United Kingdom. The Solicitors Act 1843 provided that the Society was to be the Registrar of Attorneys and Solicitors.[19]The governing body of the Bar is the General Council of the Bar of England and Wales.[20]

> "It fulfils the function of what might be called a 'trade union', pursuing the interests of the bar and expanding the market for the Bar's services and is also a watchdog regulating its practices and activities."[21]

It co-operates with the Inns of Court through the Council of the Inns of Court, which comprises representatives from the four Inns, the Bar Council and the Council of Legal Education. The independence of the Inns has been reduced as the Bar Council's policy is to be adopted if there is a disagreement with the Council of the Inns provided it has the support of

---

[17] See below, para. 9-009.

[18] The regulation was also concerned with attorneys, who performed similar functions to those of solicitors, although were more engaged in litigation. Attorneys no longer exist as separate from barristers and solicitors.

[19] For a fuller introduction to the development of the profession, see 1st edn. of this book, pp. 107–113; and see R. Cocks, *Foundations of the Modern Bar* (1983) and W.R. Prest, *The Rise of the Barristers – A Social History of the English Bar 1590–1640* (1986).

[20] It has 119 members: 3 officers, 14 ex-officio (the Attorney-General, the Solicitor-General, the D.P.P., leaders of the 6 circuits, chairmen of 5 specialist associations); 12 representatives of the Inns; 12 circuit representatives; 14 association representatives; 48 practising barristers; 12 employed and non-practising barristers; 4 co-opted: The General Council of the Bar, *Annual Report 2000*, p. 27.

[21] General Council of the Bar, *A Career at the Bar* (1988), p. 7.

two thirds of the profession.

The powers and duties of the Law Society are now derived from the Solicitors Act 1974, as amended. Membership of the Society is, perhaps surprisingly, not compulsory, even though it is the governing body for the profession as a whole. The Master of the Rolls may only admit as a solicitor a person certified by the Society to have complied with its training regulations and to be suitable for admission.[22] The Society also issues the "practising certificate" which every solicitor intending to practise as such must have.[23] Many of the Law Society's statutory functions relate to the maintenance of standards for the protection of the public. However, it is also the main professional association, *i.e.* representative body, for solicitors.

The General Council of the Bar and the Law Society are no longer entirely free to arrange their own affairs.[24] Competition law may, in the future, force even further changes.[25]

2. LAWYERS AND THEIR WORK

(a) Introduction

In their study of the legal profession in the United States and England, Johnstone and Hopson identified nineteen different "work tasks" performed by lawyers in the United States: giving advice, both legal and non-legal; negotiations; drafting letters and legal documents; litigation, including the preparation of cases and advocacy; investigation of facts; legal research and analysis; lobbying legislators and administrators; acting as broker; public relations; filing submissions to government and other organisations; adjudication; financing; property management; referral to clients of other sources of assistance; supervision of others' emotional support to clients; immoral and unpleasant tasks (taking care of disagreeable matters for clients which the client could do themselves but prefer to have someone else to do); acting as scapegoat; and getting business.[26] Even if this was or remains an accurate list of tasks, it is not to say that every lawyer ever or always performs all of them.[27] Some, such as advising and negotiation, are more generally significant than others. It is important to note that many, if not all, could be done by laymen. One of the challenges to the legal profession is, indeed, the competition from others for services that a lawyer provides. Can the lawyer be better, more efficient and provide value for money are critical questions for the lawyer to address.

3–004

---

[22] Solicitors Act 1974, s. 3.
[23] *Ibid.*, ss. 1 & 9–18.
[24] The first change was made by the Courts and Legal Services Act 1990 and now the Legal Services Consultative Panel has those powers by virtue of the Access to Justice Act 1999.
[25] Office of Fair Trading, *op. cit.*
[26] Q. Johnstone and D. Hopson, *Lawyers and their Work* (1967), Chap. 3.
[27] The variety of combinations in an individual lawyer was almost endless: *ibid.*, p. 77.

(b) Fusion[28]

3–005   The English pattern of legal work is complicated by the division of the profession into barristers and solicitors. One person cannot be qualified as both at the same time, though it is possible to change from one to another. Traditionally, barristers have had an exclusive right of audience in the superior courts and have been instructed only by a solicitor client and not a lay client. However, there is no *kind* of work that is done by a barrister that is not done by a solicitor. Advocacy in the lower courts has always been shared, indeed shared with non-lawyers in tribunals as well. Both barristers and solicitors do drafting work; and both give legal advice (solicitors directly to the client; barristers through an oral or written opinion to a solicitor[29]).

The different emphases on the type of work done has led to marked differences in the geographical distribution of barristers and solicitors. Barristers have to be near the superior courts and so over 35 per cent of barristers work from chambers in central London.[30] The rest are spread through over 30 provincial centres.[31] Solicitors' offices are found throughout the country.[32] There are significant organisational differences. Barristers must be self-employed to carry out the full range of their activities. They cannot share fees nor can they employ fee-earners. To gain the advantages of working together, they congregate in chambers. Solicitors may enter partnerships and, now, limited liability partnerships.[33] The usual form of organisation for solicitors is to work in partnerships. There is an increasing number of very large partnerships where it is increasingly difficult to understand that partnership remains a meaningful method of organisation.

Over the years there have been many advocates for fusion of the two branches. The profession was not always divided as it is today. The legal professions of other countries, including those originally developed from the English profession, are not normally formally divided. What does happen is that individual lawyers select to operate in particular areas of work or skill in which they have expertise and experience, so individuals may focus on advocacy, but not as a result of a choice made at the training stage as happens in England and Wales with the choice of training to be a barrister rather than a solicitor.

3–006   In 1977, the Royal Commission on Legal Services received submissions that the necessity of employing a solicitor and a barrister caused inefficiency (failures in communication, delay and the return of briefs by barristers who are double-booked or whose previous cases(s) overrun), harms the confidence of clients (barristers being regarded by some clients as too

---

[28] Royal Commission on Legal Services, *Report, Vol. 1* (1979), pp. 187–202; G. Gardiner, "Two Layers or One" (1970) 23 C.L.P. 1; M. Zander, *Lawyers and the Public Interest* (1968), pp. 271–332, (1976) 73 L.S. Gaz. 882, *Legal Services for the Community* (1978), pp. 170–174; F.A. Mann, "Fusion of the Legal Professions?" (1977) 93 L.Q.R. 367; P. Reeves, *Are Two Professions Necessary?* (1986).

[29] The reason may be the peculiar expertise of the barrister, or it may be that the opinion of a barrister will carry more weight in the particular circumstances, or it may be that the solicitor is too busy and/or that the barrister's opinion is more cost effective.

[30] BDO Stoy Hayward, *Report of the 2001 Survey of Barristers' Chambers* (2001), para. 3.5

[31] See below, para. 3-023.

[32] See below, para. 3-009.

[33] See below, para. 3-008.

remote or insufficiently prepared) and is more expensive for clients obliged to pay for two lawyers rather than one. The Law Society and the Bar opposed fusion. In particular, it was feared that fusion would lead to a serious fall in the quality of advocacy; barristers might join solicitors firms and become less accessible, particularly because smaller solicitors' firms that could not employ barristers might find it increasingly difficult to access high quality barristers; the drift from small to larger firms might continue and reduce the number of firms in smaller towns and rural areas; smaller firms might be reluctant to refer a client on to a larger firm for fear of losing business in the longer term; and there might be a reduction in the number of specialist advocates thereby reducing standards of advocacy and also reducing the pool of persons suitable to become judges. Other arguments against fusion have centred on the English form of court procedure.[34] In 1977, Mann outlined this argument as being, first, the heavy reliance on oral rather than written presentation of evidence and argument; secondly, hearings are single and continuous, so designed to make best use of judicial time at the cost of inconvenience to practitioners and clients and barristers meet this need better than solicitors; thirdly, there is the principle of judicial unpreparedness which requires the judiciary to have confidence in the advocates appearing before them. It was not surprising, therefore, that the Royal Commission unanimously recommended against fusion, notwithstanding the speculative nature of some of the arguments.

The fusion argument still goes on in the background to many of the reforms of the legal profession and of civil and criminal procedure and practice. There is an interest in the issue from the perspective of competition law and practice. In its recent report, the Office of Fair Trading has noted that "the dual structure of the profession itself ... may add unnecessarily to costs." But the view was taken that "rather than pressing now for restructuring to end the dual structure of the legal profession, the best approach is to address its remaining adverse effects through further liberalisation of professional rules ... "[35] What this accurately reveals is that much has changed since 1977 to reduce the impact of the separate professions. The government began to turn its attention to the legal profession from 1989 onwards. The objective was to open the market for legal services, thereby having an effect on the separateness of the two professions. The main targets were the restrictions preventing unqualified persons undertaking conveyancing or litigation work for reward (especially the solicitors' conveyancing monopoly); the prohibition on solicitors entering multi-disciplinary partnerships; and the Bar's exclusive rights of audience in the higher courts. A set of government consultation papers[36] led to the Courts and Legal Services Act 1990 which, amongst other significant changes, provided for the extension of rights of audience in all courts and rights to conduct litigation and undertake probate work to suitably qualified persons, whether or not barristers or solicitors; the removal of the restriction preventing banks and building societies offering conveyancing services to borrowers subject to safeguards, including a Conveyancing Ombudsman

---

[34] See Mann (1977).

[35] Office of Fair Trading, *Competition in professions* (2001), para. 49.

[36] *The Work and Organisation of the Legal Profession* (Cm. 570, 1989), *Contingency Fees* (Cm. 571, 1989), and *Conveyancing by Authorised Practitioners* (Cm. 572, 1989).

scheme; the ending of legal restrictions on multi-disciplinary and multi-national partnerships; changes to the rule of eligibility for judicial appointments to reflect enjoyment of advocacy rights rather than status as a barrister or solicitor. The Act also made changes to the schemes for dealing with complaints against solicitors. In consequence, the recent past has seen the increasing advocacy role of solicitors,[37] the increasingly frequent appointment of solicitors to the judiciary, the increasingly frequent employment of barristers by solicitors' firms and government agencies leading to arguments for changes to the rules on the work that they can do,[38] and the change to the rule that a barrister only works to a solicitor or other professional client.[39] Indeed, with other changes that are likely to occur over the future, the professions if not formally fused will in effect be fused. Transfers between the professions will become even more frequent, whether someone commences practice as one or the other will matter less since each will increasingly do the work of the other. Indeed, whilst training might not become joint, it will move closer together.[40] However, it may be the case that formal fusion does not occur because, e.g., some lawyers will wish for the attractions of self-employment at the bar as compared to organisation in firms as a solicitor (and increasingly it is becoming difficult to operate as a sole practitioner or in very small firms). Of course, should not sufficient progress be made and the disadvantages of a split profession are thought to demand it, competition law may require change.[41]

(c) Solicitors' practices and their work

(i) Numbers

3–007   As at July 31, 2000, there were 104,538 solicitors on the roll, of these 82,769 had current practising certificates. Of the solicitors with practising certificates, 30,018 were women (36 per cent). 5,009 were from ethnic minority groups (6.1 per cent). Over a half were aged 40 or less (55 per cent), with the average age being 40.5 years. Eighty per cent or 66,555 worked in private practice. Roughly a third worked in small firms (1–4 partners; 32 per cent), and in middle sized firms (5–25 partners; 32 per cent), whereas just over a third (36 per cent) worked in large firms (26+ partners). Half of all solicitors are either partners or sole practitioners. 16,324 (20 per cent) do not work in private practice, with 33 per cent of that number working in commerce and industry and 28 per cent working in local and central government. Over the previous thirty years, the total number of solicitors with practising certificates has trebled. Even more starkly, between 1990 and 2000, the number increased from 54,734 to 82,769. Whilst there has been evidence of the impact of previous recessions in legal recruitment, the profession nevertheless seems to recover with even larger numbers.

In addition to the increasing size of the profession, important trends

---

[37] See below, para. 3-016.
[38] See below.
[39] See below, para. 3-030.
[40] P. Knott, "Training the Next Millennium's Lawyers: Is there a Case for Joint Professional Legal Education?" (1999) 33 L.T. 50.
[41] This is clearly the message from the OFT. As to the powers of the OFT in relation to this issue, see OFT (2001), paras 33–42.

include the recruitment of women to the profession. In recent times, women have formed the majority of new entrants, and in 1999/2000, they formed 53 per cent of admissions to the roll. In 2000, they formed 36 per cent of the profession as compared with 23 per cent in 1990. Fewer solicitors are working in private practice, though still the vast majority do so: in 2000, 20 per cent worked outside private practice from 15 per cent in 1990. An increasingly lower proportion of solicitors are becoming partners or sole practitioners: in 2000 50 per cent were principals from 64 per cent in 1990.

(ii) Solicitors' firms: private practice

Solicitors are most likely to organise as sole practitioners or partnerships or **3-008** limited liability partnerships. Since the Administration of Justice Act 1985, it has been possible for them to incorporate, provided there is compliance with the Solicitors' Incorporated Practice Rules. As at July 31, 2000, there were 8,319 firms earning over £15,000 per year. All these firms were partnerships.

There are many kinds of solicitors' practice. There is no such thing as the typical firm. The range[42] includes firms which work almost exclusively in company and commercial work. These firms are often very large and are situated either in the City of London or other large conurbations where there are businesses for them to serve.[43] Some of these firms will be in "The Magic Circle" which consists of the top 10 firms in London.[44] Some of these firms are not based in London, but are very large national firms (and often will undertake a very wide range of work).[45] Niche firms specialise in particular areas of work such as shipping law[46] and media and entertainment law,[47] and have become increasingly popular as the necessity to specialise has grown. Some firms specialise in working as part of the

---

[42] One typology indicates that there are six kinds of firm: classical (follows the traditional image), managerial (strong managerial culture), political (organised around person commitment to particular types of client), routine (routine work done and little to distinguish one firm from another), large (the very big firms seeing a concentration of legal resources within them) and boutique (specialised firms operating in a narrow area of work): Boon and Levin (1999), pp. 73–78, and which builds upon M. McConville, J. Hodgson, L. Bridges and A. Pavlovic, *Standing Accused: The Organisation and Practices of Criminal Defence Lawyers in Britain* (1994).

[43] These large firms will have a continuing and significant impact on the organisation and regulation of the profession. As Boon and Levin point out some of the effects are negative because they attract corporate commercial work away from smaller firms which become less viable; they present a particular image of the profession to the public and policy makers; only they tend to attract the most able entrants to the profession; and they can effectively influence the professional bodies in particular directions. But their influence can be positive, *e.g.* they offer a democratic and meritocratic environment for employees: Boon and Levin (1999), pp. 77–78.

[44] Clifford Chance, Linklaters, Allen and Overy, Freshfields Bruckhaus Deringer, Herbert Smith, Lovells, CMS Cameron McKenna, Norton Rose, Slaughter and May, Denton Wilde Sapte: *Chambers Guide to the Legal Profession 2001–2002*, pp. 15–16.

[45] The big nationwide firms are: Eversheds, DLA, Hammond Suddards Edge, Beachcroft Wansboroughs, Pinsent Curtis Biddle, Masons: *Chambers Guide 2001–2002*, pp. 13–14.

[46] For the firms specialising in shipping law, see *ibid.*, pp. 757–765. Of course not all the firms covered here are niche firms.

[47] For the firms specialising in media & entertainment law, see *ibid.*, pp. 594–602. Again, not all these firms are niche firms.

Community Legal Service or the Criminal Defence Service (previously legal aid work). Some firms offer a generalist service. In size, they range from sole practitioners to very large firms. In 2000, there were 3,468 sole practitioner firms (41.7 per cent of all firms); 3,454 firms of 2–4 principals (41.5 per cent); 950 firms of 5–10 principals (11.4 per cent); 320 firms of 11–25 principals (3.8 per cent); and 127 firms of 26 or more principals (1.5 per cent).[48] The growth of firms has been in sole practitioner and very large firms, with the numbers of other firms reducing since 1990. Between them, these firms employ 194,823 people of whom 52 per cent were administrative and support staff, 16 per cent were trainees and paralegals and 33 per cent were qualified solicitors. Of the solicitors, 32,273 were principals and 31,282 were assistant solicitors. In addition, there were 30,284 other fee earners (i.e. non-solicitors, such as employed barristers, paralegals and fellows of the institute of legal executives).[49]

(iii) Solicitors' work

3–009   There has been a continuing trend for some types of work to necessitate large firms, and this is particularly true of those firms that undertake primarily company/commercial work, where the expansion has not only been domestic but also global. The clients of the large firms are often large, frequently multinational or international business, organisations that demand attention and support whenever it is needed and demand specialised expertise and experience so as to receive value for money. Whilst commercial property work and business/commercial affairs work forms 38 per cent of the work of 313 firms involved in a Law Society survey, it forms 56 per cent of the work of the largest firms. The following table provides further information.[50]

Type of work   **Size of firm**

	Sole practitioner	2–4 partners	5–10 partners	11–25 ptnrs	26–80 ptnrs	All panel firms
	Mean %	Mean %	Mean %	Mean %	Mean %	Mean %
Commercial property	8	15	9	14	18	13
Business/ commercial affairs	2	5	30	31	48	25
Personal injury, accident & medical negligence	6	10	9	17	12	11
Residential conveyancing	42	20	14	9	2	15

---

[48] Law Society, *Annual Statistical Report 2000* (2001), Table 3.10.
[49] Law Society, *Annual Statistical Report 2000* (2001), Table 4.1.
[50] Law Society, *The Solicitors Profession in England and Wales* (2000), p. 49.

Probate, wills & trusts	8	12	8	7	3	8
Family law	8	13	11	6	2	8
Crime	16	14	9	2	1	8
Housing law	2	2	1	2	1	2
Welfare benefits	*	*	1	*	–	*
Personal bankruptcy, insolvency & debt	1	*	1	1	1	1
Employment law	2	2	2	3	4	3
Consumer problems	1	1	1	1	*	1
Personal financial management	*	*	1	2	3	1
Other matters	5	6	5	7	6	6
No. of firms	*69*	*75*	*63*	*70*	*36*	*313*

This table confirms the importance of private litigants to the smaller firms and the location of social welfare work and legal aid work in smaller firms. The large firms do very little private client work. This can also be seen from the following table that forms the results of a Law Society survey of 318 firms.[51]

Type of client   **Size of firm**

	Sole pract	2–4 ptnrs	5–10 ptnrs	11–25 ptnrs	26–80 ptnrs	All panel firms
	Mean %	Mean %	Mean %	Mean %	Mean %	Mean %
Private individuals (not legally aided)	79	50	38	28	14	38
Private individuals (legally aided)	14	37	19	7	3	16
Private sector firms	5	10	22	46	64	32
Public sector bodies	*	1	1	6	4	3
Other British clients	1	1	2	3	5	3
Overseas clients	*	2	18	10	10	9
No of firms	*69*	*76*	*65*	*72*	*36*	*318*

[51] Law Society, *The Solicitors Profession in England and Wales* (2000), p. 50.

Geographically, the spread of firms is uneven,[52] as is clear from the following table.[53]

	Size of	firm by	no of	principals		
Standard region	**1**	**2–4**	**5–10**	**11–25**	**26 +**	**Total**
City of London	74	87	33	41	53	288
Rest of London	891	704	137	62	21	1,815
Rest of South East	838	734	207	52	10	1,841
South West	311	285	90	29	11	726
Wales	183	238	49	6	3	479
West Midlands	281	316	69	30	3	699
East Midlands	160	180	53	16	5	414
East Anglia	123	79	40	15	3	260
North West	298	404	137	34	10	883
Yorkshire & Humberside	183	254	89	26	6	558
North	126	173	46	9	2	356
England and Wales	**3,468**	**3,454**	**950**	**320**	**127**	**8,319**

3–010   Concentration of solicitors in conurbations and, indeed, in capital cities is hardly surprising given the nature of those cities and the business done within and from them. Firms need to be where the business is, whatever the nature of the business that the firm wishes to attract.[54] So, if a firm wishes to attract work from multinational companies, it is likely to need to be situated where they are; if a firm wishes to attract business from individuals making wills and buying and selling houses, it needs to be where they live and/or work; if a firm wishes to attract criminal business, it needs to be near the courts.[55]

Solicitors are generally much less dependent upon legal aid than barristers. Some firms, however, have specialised in legal aid work and now are members of either or both of the Community Legal Service and the Criminal Defence Service as established by the Legal Services Commission. Whilst such firms have been under pressure as the profitability of the work has declined, the move to contracting for services provides a real opportunity for such firms because each firm has to be committed to the work to get a contract, thus excluding the work being spread too thinly, and the nature of a contract means that the firms can organise themselves to make best use of the resources provided. Such work has also been

---

[52] See C. Harding and J. Williams (eds.), *Legal Provision in the Rural Environment* (1994).
[53] Law Society, *Annual Statistical Report 2000* (2001), Table 3.13.
[54] For the geographical accessibility of legal advice to individuals, see below, para. 9-010.
[55] When the law courts moved in Nottingham, this produced a substantial process of re-location for firms wishing to attract business from defendants.

traditionally viewed as low status,[56] but it is possible that the recent reforms will counteract this view. How effective this will be for the firms remains to be seen. Certainly firms have had to become much more business minded. This is also true for those firms that traditionally relied upon conveyancing. Whilst it is still a major form of business for some firms, the profit margins are significantly reduced. Competition or potential competition from non-lawyers also means that lawyers need to review what they do and, more importantly, how they do it, so as to ensure the provision of a quality service that delivers value for money such that clients continue to wish to use the service. Other drivers of the solicitors' business include the general nature of the economy, since the more buoyant it is the more work needs to be done by solicitors in supporting the makers of goods and the providers of services;[57], developments in litigation as driven by the government;[58] and the developments of work overseas.[59]

(iv) Solicitors' remuneration

In 2000, the Law Society produced the following table which gives some **3–011** information as to the rates of remuneration of solicitors.[60]

		Women	Men
		£ per annum	£ per annum
Partner (equity & salaried)	lower quartile	21,792	23,917
	median	25,833	30,917
	upper quartile	34,250	44,147
No.		132	132
Assistant/associate	lower quartile	24,833	31,500
	median	35,000	45,000
	upper quartile	49,167	79,167
No.		39	143

A somewhat different picture is given by looking at the range of salaries in the *Chambers Guide to the Legal Profession 2001–2002*, which produced the following table on the remuneration of newly qualified and assistant solicitors.[61]

[56] Goriely has concluded that there is a four-stage process in relation to such work: denial of the need; lack of legal profession response; response by advice agencies; legal professional invasion of the territory: T. Goriely, "Law for the Poor: The Relationship Between Advice Agencies and Solicitors in the Development of Poverty Law" (1996) 3 I.J.L.Profession 215 as discussed in Boon and Levin (1999), p. 58.

[57] When times are hard, lawyers still have work to do, such as insolvency work, but it is less than when times are good.

[58] See below, Chap. 11.

[59] Increasingly English law firms either have arrangements with firms in other jurisdictions or are buying such firms.

[60] Law Society, *The Solicitors Profession in England and Wales* (2000), p. 66.

[61] *Chambers Guide 2001–2002*, p. 12. See also the survey of the recruitment agency Michael Page International: *www.michaelpage.co.uk*.

	Newly Qualified	5 Years Post Qualification Experience (PQE)
London–Magic Circle	£48–54,000	£72–95,000
London–2nd Tier	£38–50,000	£52–88,000
London–3rd Tier	£37–45,000	£52–80,000
South	£18–35,000	£30–45,000
Midlands	£20–34,000	£35–60,000
North	£18–30,000	£30–55,000
Scotland	£18–28,000	£25–50,000
US Firms (London offices)	£55–80,000	£100–130,000

(v) Specialisation

3–012 There has been an increasing tendency for solicitors to specialise in certain areas of law. As the amount of new law and the areas of work have expanded, the corollary is that it is difficult to do anything but specialise. This is, of course, a serious challenge for sole practitioners, who usually need to retain focus on a relatively limited range of work, and so also specialise. It has become common for league tables to be devised to compare the reputation and workload of the leading firms in different areas of practice.[62] Specialisation has also had the consequence that the division of work between solicitors and barristers has been less clear, in particular it has meant that the role of barristers as the expert advisers is less true the more solicitors, especially in large firms, specialise.[63] Further, increasing specialisation has potential serious consequences for the profession as it may induce not just diversity but also a lack of professional coherence. Thus lawyers in the corporate sphere may have different approaches to other lawyers; their firms may approach similar problems in different ways; the divide between private practitioners and employed solicitors[64] may become a gulf and thus the professional bodies may have difficulty in speaking for and regulating the professions.[65]

The Law Society has also been behind specialisation.[66] Specialist panels of solicitors were set up to help clients identify solicitors with particular competence in the relevant area. Solicitors not on the panel could still undertake the relevant work, but increasingly it is only undertaken by panel members, and this is emphasised by the operation of the Community Legal Service. The panels, with their date of creation, are: mental health review tribunals (1983), children (1984), planning (1991), personal injury (1993),

---

[62] *e.g. Chambers Guide 2001–2002* which contains listings of the best firms in certain fields and lists the "leaders" in each such field.

[63] Boon and Levin (1999), pp. 81–82.

[64] See below, para. 3-013.

[65] See Boon and Levin (1999), pp. 89–94. Of course, as they point out, one factor in all this is growth in size which produces less professional coherence in any case. It does not necessarily follow that professional coherence is always desirable.

[66] See also Boon and Levin (1999), p. 83.

medical negligence (1995), family law (1998) and immigration law (1999). As at July 31, 2000, these panels had the following membership.[67]

Panel	No.
Mental health review tribunal	498
Children	2,080
Planning	195
Personal injury	3,181
Medical negligence	222
Family law	3,250
Immigration law	53

In addition to panel membership, certain externally validated qualifications can be obtained which provides an accreditation to a solicitor:[68]

Number	Qualification with	date of introduction		
	Local government diploma (1985)	Licensed insolvency practitioner (1986)	Rights of audience in higher courts (1994)	Qualified to conduct discrete investment business (1994)
Total awards	396	258	1,075	154

(vi) Employed solicitors

By "employed solicitors", we mean solicitors who are employees of non-solicitors.[69] The types of organisation employing solicitors outside private practice are demonstrated by the following table.[70]   **3–013**

Type of business	Offices in England and Wales	Offices elsewhere
Commerce and Industry	2,436	405
Government department	106	71
Local government	508	3
Court	282	4
Government funded services	137	21
Crown Prosecution Service	96	0
Advice service	174	2
Educational establishment	179	21
Other	260	20
Total	**4,178**	**547**

[67] Law Society, *Annual Statistical Report 2000* (2001), at Table 11.4.
[68] *ibid.*, Table 11.5.
[69] Solicitors' Practice Rules 1990, r. 4(1).
[70] Law Society, *Annual Statistical Report 2000* (2001), Table 3.3.

The numbers and importance of lawyers in industry, *i.e.* in-house lawyers, have grown substantially in recent times. They are likely to be concerned with property and planning, contracts, financial services, mergers and acquisitions, company law, debt recovery, employment law, intellectual property rights, pensions law, and EU law.[71] Lawyers in local government are likely to have to work over a very wide range in any given year.[72] Their primary areas of work fall into two categories. The first concerns areas of local authority responsibility, including housing, land use planning, highways and transportation, general local government work,[73] and social services.[74] The second concerns general legal work, in particular conveyancing, local planning inquiries, contracts, debt collection, criminal, and child care.[75] The government legal service makes extensive use of outside legal services.[76] The rules on the kind of work which may be undertaken by employed solicitors were relaxed by the Solicitors' Practice Rules 1990. Rule 4 now provides that employed solicitors can not, in any way that breaches the Employed Solicitors' Code, (a) choose an advocate; (b) exercise any extended right of audience; (c) as part of their employment do solicitors' work other than for their employer.

(vi) Monopolies

3–014   Solicitors for a long time enjoyed certain statutory monopolies. Section 20 of the Solicitors' Act 1974 made it an offence for an unqualified person to act as a solicitor and as such to commence or conduct litigation on behalf of another.[77] An unqualified person may not pretend to be a solicitor.[78]

It is also an offence for an unqualified person[79] to prepare (directly or indirectly) any instrument "relating to real or personal estate, or any legal

---

[71] R. Woolfson, J. Plotnikoff and D. Wilson, *Solicitors in the Employed Sector* (Law Society Research Study No. 13, 1994), Table 4.3, which indicates that other work includes: consumer and advertising, building law, personal injury, taxation, natural resources, and criminal law.

[72] *ibid.*, p. 23 & Table 4.2.

[73] *i.e.* all Local Government Act, constitutional and corporate matters not falling under other headings.

[74] *ibid.*, Table 4.4(a), which also indicates that the other areas of work are: environmental health, parks, recreation and tourism, economic development, environmental protection, licensing, waste collection, agriculture, arts, libraries and museums, consumer protection, education, fire and rescue, and police. Not every level of council deals with all these issues.

[75] *ibid.*, Table 4.4(b) which also indicates that other areas of work are: employment (including pensions), third party claims, and judicial review.

[76] *ibid.*, Chap. 4.

[77] This section does not apply to any act done in consequence of a right of audience: Courts and Legal Services Act 1990, s. 27(10). Of course, an individual may run their own litigation form themselves, and many do: Interim Report of the Judges' Council Working Party, *Litigants in Person in the Royal Courts of Justice London* (1995, Chair: Otton L.J.).

[78] Solicitors Act 1974, s. 21. See, *e.g. Carter v. Butcher* [1966] 1 Q.B. 526.

[79] Here the term covers a person who is not a solicitor, barrister or notary public, and there are some other exclusions: Solicitors Act 1974, ss. 22(2), 23(2). For some purposes, Scottish solicitors, licensed conveyancers, trade mark agents, patent agents and certain public officers are exempt.

proceedings",[80] to take instructions for a grant of probate or letters of administration, or to prepare papers on which to found or oppose such a grant,[81] unless he or she proves that it was not done for or in the expectation of any fee, gain or reward. An offence is committed even where the unqualified person does not personally receive the fee.[82] No person may bring proceedings to recover costs in respect of anything done by an unqualified person acting as a solicitor.[83] The Royal Commission on Legal Services found these restrictions to be in the public interest.[84] However, even in the field of conducting litigation, the view that solicitors should have a monopoly has been challenged, and the Courts and Legal Services Act 1990 allowed for an extension of their right to conduct litigation. There have also been significant challenges to the solicitors' monopolies in non-contentious areas.

(1) Conveyancing

One of the major controversies in the recent past was the abolition of the monopoly that solicitors used to enjoy in relation to conveyancing.[85] It was particularly controversial as many solicitors were economically dependent on this type of work, but there were criticisms of the low quality of such work and relatively high charges for it.[86] A majority of the Royal Commission accepted the argument that the monopoly or closed shop was in the public interest in view of the complexity of land law and of conveyancing and the need to protect clients from dishonesty, incompetence and overcharging.[87] All were agreed that a free-for-all would not be in the public interest. A system of licensed conveyancers was proposed. A system of licensed conveyancers was introduced by the Administration of Justice Act 1985, Part II.[88] The Council of Licensed Conveyancers was created. It was given the responsibility of controlling the discipline, admissions, training and professional standards of the new profession. It was required,

3–015

---

[80] Solicitors Act 1974, s. 22. "Instrument" includes a contract for the sale of land, but does not include a will, an agreement not under seal, a letter of power of attorney, or a "transfer of stock containing no trust or limitation thereof": s. 22(3). This restriction does not apply in the context of an exercise of a right of audience: Courts and Legal Services Act 1990, s. 27(10).

[81] Solicitors Act 1973, s. 23(1).

[82] *Reynolds v. Hoyle* [1976] 1 W.L.R. 207; *cf. Green v. Hoyle* [1976] 1 W.L.R. 575.

[83] Solicitors Act 1974, s. 25. This restriction does not apply in the context of an exercise of a right of audience: Courts and Legal Services Act 1990, s. 27(10).

[84] Royal Commission on Legal Services, *Report, Vol. 1* (1979), pp. 225–231.

[85] It had been sought by the Society of Gentlemen Practisers and was finally granted by William Pitt in 1804 as a *quid pro quo* for an increase in the tax on practising certificates and articles in the Stamp Act 1804: see R. Abel-Smith & R. Stevens, *Lawyers and the Courts* (1967), pp. 22–23, Kirk (1976), Chap. 7. It was moved from fiscal legislation to a Solicitors Act in 1932. The changes appear to have been agreed because of the need to collect tax rather than in the public interest.

[86] M. Joseph, *Conveyancing Fraud* (1989); Royal Commission on Legal Services, *Report, Vol. 1* (1979), pp. 243–282.

[87] For the minority view, see *ibid.*, pp. 808, 809–812, 813–816.

[88] See P. Kenny, "Administration of Justice Act 1985, Part II" in *Current Law Statutes Annotated 1985*; A. Kenny, (1986) 277 E.G. 262, 394.

inter alia, to make training rules, rules for regulating professional practice conduct and discipline, rules requiring compulsory indemnity insurance against civil liability and for setting up a compensation fund for the benefit of victims of negligence, fraud or other dishonesty by licensed conveyancers and rules for keeping accounts. This is very similar to the system for solicitors. The first licenses were granted on May 1, 1987, and solicitors have been directed to proceed in their dealings with licensed conveyancers on the same basis as with solicitors.[89] Conveyancing, nevertheless, remains an important element of the work of many solicitors[90] and it remains a relatively profitable element of their work.[91] In 1998, the average conveyancing fee, which had fallen slightly, was £294, with 61 per cent of buyers paying less than £300.[92]

For the future, perhaps the greatest challenge for conveyancers will be the impact of e-conveyancing, the introduction of which is made possible by the Land Registration Act 2002, s.95.[92a]

(2) Rights of audience

3–016   An analogous area is that of rights of audience.[93] Prior to the Courts and Legal Services Act 1990, these were limited by the practice of the courts and tribunals concerned rather than by rules of law. Litigants in person have a right of audience through the legal system.[94] At one time, barristers enjoyed a virtual monopoly of advocacy before the House of Lords, Court of Appeal and High Court.[95] They also had exclusive rights of audience in nearly all Crown Court cases.[96] Barristers and solicitors had rights of audience in the county courts and magistrates' courts. Also lay people might appear, *e.g.* police officers, local government officials and civil servants. In most tribunals there were no restrictions. Any person might attend a trial as a

---

[89] *The Guide to the Professional Conduct of Solicitors* (8th ed., 1999), Principle 25.06.

[90] In 1998, there were around 15,500 solicitors doing residential conveyancing and 17% of all solicitors in private practice spent more than 25% of their time on it: J. Jenkins, *The Conveyancing Market* (1999), at para. 2.9.

[91] In November 1998, 56% of firms doing conveyancing said that it was profitable, 32% that it broke even and 12% that it made a loss: *ibid.*, para. 2.5. The predictions for the future involved advising solicitors that they should plan "on the basis of a middle of the road prediction, with some contingency plans for a collapse. If the market booms, conveyancing fees could be increased:" *ibid.*, para. 6.15.

[92] *ibid.*, para. 2.3.

[92a] See, L. Chamberlain, "The Land Registration Act 2002: a Conveyancing Revolution — Pt I" (2002) 152 N.L.J. 1093.

[93] See, Royal Commission on Legal Services, *Report, Vol. 1* (1979), pp. 203–221.

[94] See Judges' Council Working Party, *Interim Report: Litigants in Person in the Royal Courts of Justice London* (Chair, Otton L. J.). Prosecutions in the Crown Court must be conducted by a barrister.

[95] Solicitors could appear before a single judge of the Court of Appeal (Criminal Division) sitting in chambers, in certain High Court bankruptcy applications and in any High Court proceedings heard in chambers.

[96] A solicitor might appear (a) in appeals to the Crown Court from a magistrates' court in civil or criminal proceedings or on committal for sentence, if the solicitor or anyone in the firm appeared in the court below: *Practice Direction* [1972] 1 W.L.R. 307; (b) in a wider class of cases in certain remote areas: *Practice Direction* [1972] 1 W.L.R. 5 (the areas were Caernarvon, Barnstaple, Bodmin, Doncaster and Lincoln).

friend of a party to take notes and give advice but he or she would not be accorded a right of audience.[97]

The Royal Commission on Legal Services had come down in favour of the status quo. Indeed, the Commission's enthusiasm for solicitor-advocates was markedly lukewarm:

"Many solicitors make competent advocates in magistrates' courts and some are very good. Some could achieve the same standard in the Crown Court if they could so arrange their professional lives as to enable them to concentrate on the work there."[98]

In addition to concerns about the competence of solicitors, there were concerns about the impact on the bar, fearing a "serious and disproportionate impact on the income and capacity of barristers to continue in practice."[99]

Times have moved on and attitudes have changed. Of course, competition law has had its impact, but it is not the only motivator behind change. The Law Society raised questions about the right of audience in 1984,[1] and the libel action against Cyril Smith M.P. was a forum for raising the matter in a very public way.[2] Subsequently, the judges of the Supreme Court, acting as a collegiate body, changed the rule and a Practice Direction was issued permitting solicitors to appear in the Supreme Court in formal or unopposed proceedings, and when judgment is delivered in open court following a hearing in Chambers at which that solicitor conducted the case for the client.[3] The Marre Committee subsequently supported, by a majority, the extension of rights of audience in the Crown Court to solicitors approved by a Rights of Audience Advisory Board.[4] The government's 1989 proposals were more radical still.

The Courts and Legal Services Act 1990, section 27, puts rights of audience in courts and in certain tribunals and inquiries[5] on a statutory footing. A person has a right of audience before a court **3–017**

(a) where he or she has a right of audience granted by the appropriate

---

[97] *McKenzie v. McKenzie* [1971] P. 33; *Merry v. Persons Unknown* [1974] C.L.Y. 3003. There is no right to a McKenzie adviser.

[98] Royal Commission on Legal Services, *Report, Vol. 1* (1979), p. 212.

[99] *ibid.*, p. 216.

[1] *Annual Statement 1983–84*, pp. 48–49.

[2] Mr Smith wished to have the terms of a settlement of a libel action brought against him and Radio Trent by 25 other M.P.s read to the High Court by his solicitor. There were no advocacy skills required, and it would have been unnecessarily expensive to have briefed counsel. Leonard J. held that he had no authority to allow a solicitor to appear and this was affirmed by the Court of Appeal on the ground that the public interest required that the High Court's general practices and procedures be known and not changed or departed from in piecemeal fashion: *Abse v. Smith* [1986] Q.B. 536.

[3] *Practice Direction (Solicitors: Rights of Audience)* [1986] 1 W.L.R. 545.

[4] Report of the Marre Committee, pp. 149–157. See J. Hodgson, (1988) 138 N.L.J. 615.

[5] The term "court" includes (a) any tribunal under the jurisdiction of the Council on Tribunals (b) any court-martial and (c) a statutory inquiry within the meaning of the Tribunals and Inquiries Act 1971: 1990 Act, s. 119.

authorised body,[6] and that body's qualification regulations and rules of conduct have been approved;

(b) where (a) does not apply but he or she has a statutory right of audience;

(c) where (a) does not apply but he or she has a right of audience granted by the court in question;

(d) where he or she is a party to the proceedings and would have had a right of audience as a party if the Act had not been passed;

(e) where he or she is employed or otherwise engaged to assist in the conduct of litigation and is doing so under instructions by a qualified litigation and the proceedings are being heard in chambers in the High Court or a county court and are not reserved family proceedings.

A right of audience can, however, be denied to a person for reasons which apply to him or her as an individual.

Similar rules are to apply to rights to conduct litigation, exception that the General Council of the Bar is not specified as an "authorised body.[7]

Section 27 came into force on January 1, 1991. It preserved any rights of audience, or to conduct litigation, that had been acquired before December 7, 1989.[8] This meant that the General Council of the Bar and the Law Society could continue to grant the relevant rights.

The procedure whereby other professional bodies may become "authorised bodies", and their qualification regulations and rules of conduct approved for the purpose of section 27 is set out in the Courts and Legal Services Act 1990, Schedule 4, Part I.

One of the concerns about extending rights of audience has been whether the same regulations will and can apply to all litigators. It is noticeable that the Courts and Legal Services Act 1990, section 27(2A) provides that everyone "who exercises before any court a right of audience granted by an authorised body has (a) a duty to the court to act with independence in the interests of justice; and (b) a duty to comply with the rules of conduct of the body relating to the right and approved for the purposes of this section; and those duties shall override any obligation which the person may have (otherwise than under the criminal law) if it is inconsistent with them.[9]

(3) Probate

3–018 Section 54 of the Courts and Legal Services Act 1990 contained the potential to extend the right to perform probate work for reward to banks, building societies, insurance companies and their subsidiaries, provided that they operate a complaints scheme which complied with requirements prescribed by regulations, and to other bodies approved under section 55 and Schedule

---

[6] *i.e.* the General Council of the Bar, the Law Society, and a professional body designated by Order in Council (which may include the Council for Licensed Conveyancers: s. 53). The procedures for securing and revoking designation are set out in ss. 29 & 30 and Sched. 4.

[7] Courts and Legal Services Act 1990, s. 28.

[8] *ibid.*, ss. 31–33.

[9] This provision was added by the Access to Justice Act 1999.

9.[10] Possible candidates for inclusion include legal executives, licensed conveyancers,[11] authorised conveyancing practitioners and accountants. The profession was well aware of the potential consequences for its business.[12] In fact, the business is relatively buoyant, though the major competitor for a solicitor's services is people writing their own wills rather than any will-making agency.[13]

(vii) Restrictions on practice

(1) Multi-disciplinary practices   **3–019**

Whether there should be multi-disciplinary practices is a matter for the profession.[14] A solicitor may not form a partnership with a member of another profession.[15] The reasons for not allowing such partnerships have been summarised by the Law Society as follows.[16] (a) An independent legal profession has an important democratic function to defend individual liberties; (b) MDPs might reduce consumer choice, because they would gather all the best solicitors into large firms, reducing the extent of the network of firms; (c) clients have the right to be represented by an independent lawyer; (d) MDPs represent a surrender of independence by solicitors; (e) There is evidence that MDPs would not take off; (f) MDPs might lead to an increased risk of conflicts of interest and of duties; (g) practice in an MDP could create problems with confidentiality, legal professional privilege, protection of clients' funds, and professional indemnity; (h) the conduct of non-solicitor members of an MDP could not be regulated in the same way; (i) there may be confusion as to the nature of the MDP and the qualifications of the individuals in it. The same Law Society document summarised the arguments for MDPs as follows. (a) Solicitors' independence will not automatically be lost through MDPs, but safeguards should be developed; (b) MDPs could allow clients access to a range of specialists and experts under one roof; (c) the ban on MDPs prevents solicitors competing with other professions which provide 'one-stop shopping', for which there is a demand; (d) lawyers must survive commercially; (e) clients will have a choice whether to go to a MDP or a traditional practice; (f) no major adverse consequences have occurred where

---

[10] See the *Green Paper: The Work and Organisation of the Legal Profession* (Cm. 570, 1989), Chap. 14 and the *White Paper* (C, 740,1989), Chap. 6.

[11] Courts and Legal Services Act 1990, s. 53.

[12] *Law Society Annual Statistical Report 1994*, p. 45.

[13] J. Jenkins, *Wills and Probate* (Law Society Research Paper No. 6, 1998). At para. 2.6, it is clear that, of those in 1994 who had made a will, 74% had the help of a solicitor, 15% had made their own, a bank advised 5% and a will-making agency wrote it in 1% of cases. The number of personal applications for probate has increased by 46% between 1991 and 1996, in which time the number of solicitor applications fell by 3%: *ibid.*, para. 2.7.

[14] The legislative prohibition, Solicitors Act 1974, s. 39, was repealed by the Courts and Legal Services Act 1990, s. 66.

[15] Solicitors' Practice Rules 1990, r. 7. Solicitors may form partnerships with a solicitor, a registered foreign lawyer or a recognised body (that is an incorporated practice).

[16] The Law Society, *Multi-Disciplinary Practice: Consultation* (1998), section D, at *www.lawsociety.org.uk*. See also Boon and Levin (1999), pp. 84–85.

MDPs are permitted (*e.g.* Germany and New South Wales); (g) De facto MDPs already exist; (h) we should not lag behind others considering MDPs; (i) solicitors should be entitled to choose the kind of business through which they practise; (j) the conduct rules would remain the same for solicitors in MDPs thus removing the risks of conflicts of interest, etc, identified; (k) if conflicting duties are owed, rules can prohibit an MDP undertaking both activities; (l) MDPs would enable solicitors to give appropriate status to and so retain non-lawyer staff; (m) solutions to regulatory problems should be sought; (n) there is no reason to believe that other professions' standards of client care are lower; (o) transparency to clients will avoid many of the problems; (p) it is preferable to extend the influence of solicitors into other professions.

Substantial developments towards MDPs have been made with the introduction of incorporated practices;[17] the sharing of fees with non-solicitor employees;[18] and the introduction of the rule that a solicitor who instructs an estate agent as a subagent for the sale of a property can remunerate the estate agent on the basis of a proportion of the solicitor's professional fee.[19]

Having given careful consideration to the debate, the Law Society's Council affirmed its objectives in December 1999 as "(a) the ultimate goal should be to allow solicitors who wish to do so to provide any legal service through any medium to anyone, provided that it is possible to achieve the necessary public protections; (b) the short term goal should be to investigate the ways in which it might be possible to relax the rule on fee sharing . . . ."[20] In response to this, the Law Society has made its first steps towards MDPs by adopting an approach called "Legal Practice Plus".[21] "Legal Practice Plus is a model for MDPs which would allow non-solicitors to become partners in a solicitors' practice ... ." It goes on to provide that the regulatory structure which would underpin Legal Practice Plus would comprise: (a) a contract between the registered non-solicitor partner [NSP] and the Society; (b) special Multi-Disciplinary Practice Rules and amended practice/accounts rules; and (c) guidance on legal professional privilege. Solicitors would be in ultimate control of the partnership. They would have to form a numerical majority in any partnership. The Law Society would have the power to exercise control over the NSPs through establishing a contractual, as opposed to a statutory, register. The key features of this contract would tie the NSP to similar regulatory provisions as a solicitor. Solicitors would have extra duties imposed upon them. The practice could supply services only of a kind which are normally provided by solicitors practising as solicitors.

From this what seems abundantly evident is that MDPs will eventually appear. The Law Society is hoping to be able to continue to ensure that solicitors take the lead and that their Rules will not be inappropriately diluted. Whether it should and whether solicitors are that good is something

---

[17] Administration of Justice Act 1985, s. 9.
[18] Solicitors' Practice Rules 1990, r. 7(l), provided it is not a cloak for a partnership.
[19] Solicitors' Practice Rules 1990, r. 7(2).
[20] Law Society, *Multi-Disciplinary Practice: Progress Report* (1999), at *www.lawsociety.org.uk*.
[21] Law Society, *Legal Practice Plus — First Step Towards MDPs* (2000) Report of the Working Party, at *www.lawsociety.org.uk*. See also earlier contributions at the same site.

that a more considered view can be taken upon once this chapter has been read through.

However, the European Court of Justice has ruled that, although a regulation restricting MDPs would have effects restrictive of competition, the bar council making it could have reasonably considered that it was necessary for the proper practice of the legal profession in a particular member state, and so it does not breach the competition provisions of European Union law.[22]

(2) Multi-national practices and globalisation   **3–020**

Prohibitions used to apply to multinational practices, that is solicitors engaged in practices with one or more registered foreign lawyer.[23] The pressures for change came from the developing European Union, the development of the Single Market, and the development of mutual recognition of professional qualifications. Further, solicitors practices have pushed business development into foreign markets. The changes were introduced after the Courts and Legal Services Act 1990, s. 66. Thus, solicitors may practise in England and Wales in partnership and in incorporated practices with registered foreign lawyers and to create multi-national partnerships.[24] RFLs are registered by the Law Society under the Courts and Legal Services Act 1990, s. 89. To be registered, the foreign lawyer must be a member of a legal profession which is regulated outside England and Wales as to make it appropriate for solicitors to enter multi-national partnerships with members of it; the foreign rules must not prohibit partnerships with solicitors; the applicants must be in good standing with his or her home body; and there must be no other circumstances making it undesirable to register the applicant.[25] RFLs are subject to the same rules as solicitors, and MNPs are "broadly subject to the same regulation as solicitors' practices."[26] As at July 31, 2000, there were 179 MNPs with their head offices in England and Wales.[27]

Solicitors firms are entering into arrangements with firms in the rest of the European Union and in traditional markets where law akin to English law has applied (*e.g.* Malaysia, Singapore, Hong Kong, Canada, Australia, New Zealand and the U.S.A.) and in new markets (particularly China). In many of these cases, the English firm is the dominant partner, if it does not actually take over the other company and bring it fully within the firm's ethos, approach and organisation. All the large English firms either own firms in other jurisdictions or have significant practice arrangements. This is seen to be advantageous in business terms both because the firms believe they can do the local business better and because English law has an application in many jurisdictions, not least as the normal law chosen to

---

[22] *Wouters v. Algemene Raad van de Nederlandse Orde van Advocaten (Case C-309/99)* [2002] All E.R. (D.) 233.

[23] As defined in the Courts and Legal Services Act 1990, s. 89(9).

[24] Solicitors' Practice Rules 1990, r. 7(l)b), (6).

[25] The Law Society, *The Guide to the Professional Conduct of Solicitors* (1999), p. 173.

[26] *The Guide*, Principle 8.02. For a summary of the differences, see pp. 174–5.

[27] Law Society, *Annual Statistical Report 2000* (2001), Table 3.3.

control international trade agreements (whether or not the parties to the agreement have any connection with England and Wales).

3–021   *(3) Advertising*

Advertising by solicitors used to be prohibited.[28] "Touting" was regarded as unprofessional and associated with "trade".[29] Collective advertising by the profession was acceptable. The introduction of advertising by individuals and firms was recommended both by the Monopolies Commission[30] and the Royal Commission on Legal Services.[31] The primary purpose of these recommendations was to provide information to the public rather than to drum up business.

The old restrictions on advertising have been swept away. The basic relevant principle governing a solicitor's practice is "that a solicitor should be able to give impartial and frank advice to the client, free from any external or adverse pressures or interests which would destroy or weaken the solicitor's professional independence, the fiduciary relationship with the client or the client's freedom of choice."[32] Rule 1 of the Solicitor's Practice Rules states that a solicitor must not do anything in the course of practice or permit another to do anything on his or her behalf to compromise or impair:

a.   the solicitor's independence or integrity;

b.   a person's freedom to instruct a solicitor of his or her choice;

c.   the solicitor's duty to act in the best interests of the client;

d.   the good repute of the solicitor or of the solicitors' profession;

e.   the solicitor's proper standard of work;

f.   the solicitor's duty to the Court.

Rule 2 states that solicitors "may at their discretion publicise their practices, or permit others to do so, or publicise the businesses or activities of other persons, provided there is no breach of [the Practice Rules] and provided there is compliance with a Solicitors' Publicity Code .... ." Rule 3 states that solicitors "may accept introductions and referrals of business from other persons and may make introductions and refer business to other persons, provided there is no breach of [the Practice Rules] and provided there is compliance with a Solicitors' Introduction and Referral Code .... ."

3–022   The Solicitors' Publicity Code 1990 permits advertising provided that it complies with the Practice Rules, and it cannot reasonably be regarded as

---

[28] Solicitors' Practice Rules, 1936–72, r. 1; see P. Fennell in P.A. Thomas (ed.), *Law in the Balance* (1982), Chap. 6.

[29] "[P]rofessional ideology is not exclusively anti-entrepreneurial, but ... incorporates elements of the value systems of both the 'pre-industrial gentleman' and the tradesman:" *ibid.*, p. 144.

[30] *Report on the supply of services of Solicitors in England and Wales in relation to restrictions on advertising* (1975–76, H.C. 557).

[31] Royal Commission on Legal Services, *Report, Vol. I* (1979), pp. 367–373.

[32] *The Guide to the Professional Conduct of Solicitors* (1999), Principle 11.01.

being in bad taste, is not accurate or misleading in any way, and complies with any legal requirements. Further crucial provisions of the Code are that solicitors must take responsibility for any publicity about them or their practice. Every advert must bear the solicitor's name or the firm's name, a claim can be made that a solicitor is a specialist or an expert in a particular field provided it can be justified, it may not refer to a solicitor's success rate, it may not make direct comparison with or criticism of the charges or quality of service of other solicitors, it may not contain the Law Society's armorial bearings, and it may use the CLS logo. Solicitors cannot make unsolicited visits or telephone calls except to a current or former client (to whom only visits may be made), or to another solicitor or to another potential professional connection, or in advertising properties for sale or let. Solicitors may name clients, with their written consent and in a manner not likely to prejudice the client's interests. One of the crucial pieces of information in an advert is likely to be cost, and the Code provides that publicity about charges or a basis of charging must be clearly expressed, must state what will be provided for it, when it may be increased, and whether it includes disbursements and VAT. A fee being from or upwards of a certain figure is not permitted.[33] A serious breach of the Code should be reported to the Office for the Supervision of Solicitors.[34]

Some concerns were raised about solicitor advertising by the National Association of Citizens Advice Bureaux.[35] For example, it had received a significant number of reports from CABx about solicitors who advertise services, in particular benefit advice, and then provide inadequate or wrong advice.[36]

Rule 3 permits arrangements for the introduction of business, provided there is compliance with the Solicitors' Introduction and Referral Code 1990. The basic principles are that solicitors must retain their professional independence and their ability to advise clients fearlessly and objectively. The requirements of an introducer should never undermine this independence.[37] Solicitors may not enter into arrangements with claims assessors for the introduction of personal injury clients,[38] and there are particular limits in the field of investment business.[39] Otherwise, solicitors may make arrangements with introducers, subject to restrictions designed to preserve a solicitor's independence, which include: solicitors should not become so reliant upon a limited number of sources of referrals that the interests of the introducers affect the advice given by the solicitor to clients; solicitors should be particularly conscious of the need to advise impartially and independently clients from introducers; each firm should conduct six-monthly reviews; solicitors should not pay introducers commission; and where more than 20 per cent of the firm's income derives from a single

---

[33] For the further rules, see the Code, para. 5. The Code also has provisions on descriptions of a multinational practice, naming and describing partners and staff, directory headings, flag advertising, professional stationery and international aspects of publicity.

[34] *The Guide* (1999), p. 237. Less serious breaches should be brought to the attention of solicitors by local law societies.

[35] N.A.C.A.B., *Barriers to Justice* (1995), paras. 3.49–3.56.

[36] *ibid.*, para. 3.50.

[37] Solicitors' Introduction and Referral Code 1990, s. 1(1).

[38] Solicitors' Practice Rules 1990, r. 9.

[39] *ibid.*, r. 12.

source, the firm should consider whether steps need to be taken to reduce that proportion.[40]

(d) Barristers and their work

(i) Numbers

3–023   At October 1, 2000, there were 10,132 barristers (including 1072 Q.C's) in independent practice in 604 sets of chambers. 311 of the sets of chambers were in London, the rest in the provinces. 6,591 of the barristers were in London and 3,541 were in the provinces.[41] In general, the size of the Bar has continuously increased since the early 1960s, although the rate of growth has varied. The Bar doubled in size between 1963 and 1979, and increased by almost a half between 1979 and 1989.[42] There were 6,645 barristers in 1990 and, in the last 10 years, that number has grown by 66 per cent to the position in 2000. However, the rate of increase may be reducing: from 1986 to 1998 it was 4.9 per cent annually, but has now dropped to 2.0 per cent.[43] The proportion of the profession of 10 years' call and under has shown a marked increase: in 1966 there were 769 (34 per cent of the practising Bar), and in 1983, 2,367 (46 per cent).[44] In 2000, 1,405 people were called to the Bar, of whom 757 were men and 648 were women.[45]

(ii) Work

3–024   There is an increasing tendency for barristers to specialise, but many still have a general common law practice (contract, crime, tort (especially personal injury cases), landlord and tenant, family matters). If specialising, a barrister may do so in one of the common law areas, in Chancery work (trusts, land law, conveyancing, wills, company law, revenue matters) or in one of the other specialist areas, some of which are specialisms of a more general practice. *Chambers Guide to the Legal Profession 2001–2002* lists the following: administrative and public law, agriculture, alternative dispute resolution, arbitration (international), aviation, banking, chancery, charities, church, civil liberties and human rights, clinical (including medical) negligence, commercial (litigation), company, competition and anti-trust, construction, consumer law, crime, defamation, employment, energy and natural resources, environment, EU/Competition, family and matrimonial, financial services, fraud, health & safety, immigration, information technology, insolvency and corporate recovery, insurance, local government, intellectual property, licensing, media and entertainment, partnership, pensions, personal injury, planning and local government, product liability,

---

[40]   Solicitors' Introduction and Referral Code 1990, s. 2.
[41]   The General Council of the Bar, *Annual Report 2000* (2001), at p. 27.
[42]   Royal Commission on Legal Services, *Report Vol. 1* (1979), p. 54; *Annual Report of the Bar Council 1990*, pp. 20–21. See Abel (1988), pp. 65–72.
[43]   BDO Stoy Hayward, *Report on the 2001 Survey of Barristers' Chambers* (2001), at p. 8.
[44]   *Annual Statement 1983–84*, p. 19. In 1988, about half of barristers in independent practice were 12 years or less since call: *Quality of Justice* (1989), p. 53.
[45]   The General Council of the Bar, *Annual Report 2000* (2001), at p. 27.

professional negligence, property litigation, shipping, sport, and tax.[46] In London, common law chambers are concentrated in the Temple; Chancery chambers are concentrated in Lincoln's Inn. There is no rule requiring chambers to be in one of the inns of court. Concentrations have occurred in the inns, because until fairly recently they have charged barristers only a proportion of the market rent, for the convenience of access to the courts and because of long tradition.[47] Many sets of chambers have now opened in London, but outside the Inns.[48]

A "rough guide" to the specialist work done by barristers was given in the Bar's Response to the 1989 Green Papers.[49]

Analysis of Barristers' Practices

0%–10%	10%–20%	20%–30%	30%–40%	40%–50%	50%–60%	60%–70%	70%–80%	80%–90%	90%–	100	Total
Admiralty	71	3	1	18	6	2	15	0	0	0	116
Commercial	544	204	124	72	89	38	45	45	42	62	126
											5
Criminal	512	275	268	324	344	268	310	408	431	102	416
										5	6
Defamation	144	15	3	5	4	2	3	5	4	9	194
Employment	880	121	30	16	13	8	4	2	3	2	107
											9
Family	113	524	367	212	152	79	58	66	47	65	270
	1										1
Immigration	188	24	15	5	5	3	1	7	2	2	252
Insolvency	429	63	22	10	11	4	1	2	2	2	546
International	85	19	13	8	8	2	0	0	1	12	148
Official Referees	541	97	50	31	42	16	10	9	1	2	799
Parliamentary	274	53	19	21	12	12	10	14	17	59	491
Patents	192	15	11	3	3	2	3	6	10	31	276
Restrictive Practices and Monopolies	28	4	7	3	1	3	0	1	1	0	48
Revenue	127	21	13	5	10	1	4	4	7	45	237
Chancery	649	136	73	48	43	43	36	67	57	86	123
											8
Common	134	810	554	435	288	138	122	102	75	84	395
Law	9										7
Other	258	54	40	26	29	12	13	10	13	109	564

[46] At p. 3.
[47] Royal Commission on Legal Services, *Report Vol. I* (1979), pp. 449–450.
[48] *e.g.*, the various sets of chambers on Bedford Row are just outside the inns, as are those on the Strand, Leadenhall Street, Fleet Street, etc.
[49] *Quality of Justice: The Bar's Response (1989)*, pp. 43 and 44, Fig. 5.2.

The percentages of gross earnings by area of law for barristers, at the same time, were crime 30 per cent, general civil (common law) 17 per cent, commercial general 13 per cent, tax 3 per cent and 12 per cent other specialisations.[50]

3–025   The work of barristers is, of necessity, changing. The availability of work at the criminal bar has declined, particularly as more such advocacy work is undertaken by solicitors; in general barristers no longer have a monopoly over rights of audience;[51] whilst reliance on publicly-funded work has traditionally been high, the low rates of fee increases have forced barristers to look to other areas of work; and increasing specialisation has lead to some new areas of work as have other pressures. With regard to the latter, the most noticeable is the advent of the Human Rights Act 1998 providing impetus to the work of barristers with specialisms not only in administrative and public law and in civil liberties and human rights, but also in any area where the European Convention on Human Rights does, or may, have an impact.

The BDO Stoy Hayward survey of barristers for chambers for 2001 reveals the following about the nature of practice.[52]

Type of work	2001	2000
General civil:		
Common law (Other)	3.1%	3.7%
Technology and construction court	3.3%	3.4%
Landlord and tenant (non-residential)	1.8%	1.9%
Landlord and tenant (residential)	1.6%	1.8%
Planning	1.8%	2.5%
Parliamentary and local government	2.9%	2.4%
Insolvency	2.6%	2.2%
Financial services	0.8%	1.1%
European	1.2%	0.8%
Licensing	0.3%	0.5%
Immigration	0.5%	0.5%
Personal injury	8.4%	8.0%
Professional negligence	4.6%	4.8%
Other work	2.1%	2.3%
Total General Civil	35.0%	35.7%
Criminal	23.3%	24.7%
Commercial:		

---

[50] *ibid.*, p. 45, Fig. 5.3.
[51] See above, para. 3-016.
[52] BDO Stoy Hayward (2001), at Table 9.

Commercial	12.2%	11.2%
Admiralty	0.5%	0.9%
International law	0.3%	0.3%
Restrictive practices	0.2%	0.5%
Total Commercial	13.2%	12.9%
Family:		
Children	6.6%	6.9%
Other	5.1%	4.6%
Total Family	11.7%	11.5%
Chancery:		
Contentious	4.7%	4.0%
Non-contentious	2.1%	1.9%
Total Chancery	6.8%	5.9%
Employment	3.0%	3.5%
Other specialist:		
Revenue	1.7%	1.9%
Intellectual property	2.5%	2.0%
Arbitrator or Umpire	1.2%	1.3%
Defamation	1.6%	0.6%
Total Other Specialist	7.0%	5.8%
Total	100.0%	100.0%

(iii) Remuneration

As to remuneration, the Royal Commission on Legal Services concluded **3–026** that the earnings of barristers were not out of line with those in comparable occupations, except that the earnings of barristers in the early years of practice were low.[53] A report by Coopers and Lybrand in 1985 claimed that fees for junior barristers at the criminal bar fell well below what was required to meet the principle of "fair and reasonable reward for work reasonably done."[54] The Lord Chancellor rejected the claim for a significant increase in fees, but ultimately had to raise the initial offer. However, there remain concerns about the level of fee for those barristers undertaking such publicly-funded work. According to the *Chambers Guide to the Legal Profession 2001–2002*, barrister's charges on an hourly basis were:[55]

---

[53] Royal Commission on Legal Services. *Report Vol. 1* (1979), pp. 507–542 & *Vol. 2*, pp. 579–626.
[54] Annual Statement of the Senate 1985–86, p. 76.
[55] See first table at p. 1247. These figures had shown little change from the previous year.

Seniority	Commercial	Tax	Chancery	Common Law	Criminal
QC	£250–£850	£300–£1000	£175–£600	£150–£400	£125–£400
10 yrs call	£100–£300	£200–£500	£100–£200	£100–£200	£75–£300
4–9 yrs call	£60–£200	£175–£350	£75–£175	£50–£150	£50–£150
1–3 yrs call	£25–£150	£75–£150	£30–£100	£40–£100	£25–£75

As regards barrister's remuneration, the *Chambers Guide to the Legal Profession 2001–2002* provides the following information:[56]

Seniority	Commercial	Tax	Chancery law	Common	Criminal
QC	£150,000–£1 million	£300,000–£2 million	£150,000–£1.7 million	£150,000–£425,000	£125,000–£550,000
10 yrs call	£100,000–£750,000	£200,000–£500,000	£100,000–£350,000	£75,000–£300,000	£40,000–£400,000
4–9 yrs call	£60,000–£350,000	£175,000–£350,000	£75,000–£300,000	£30,000–£200,000	£30,000–£165,000
1–3 yrs call	£25,000–£125,000	£75,000–£150,000	£25,000–£125,000	£20,000–£100,000	£10,000–£75,000

The BDO Stoy Hayward survey reveals that the range of receipts for barristers is as follows.[57]

Years' call	Receipts
0–5	£14,800–£34,300
5–10	£38,800–£78,900
Over 10	£59,300–£119,200
Q.C.s	£143,900–£278,00

Before assuming that this is a barrister's salary, some 20 per cent should be deducted for chambers expenses and a further 20 per cent on average going on personal expenses.[58] Nevertheless, it can be noticed that some barristers

[56] See second table at p. 1247.
[57] BDO Stoy Hayward (2001), Table 36 and p. 35.
[58] *Chambers Guide to the Legal Profession 2001–2002*, p. 1247. The Guide states that personal expenses includes "insurance, pensions, travel, hotels, accountancy fees, IT and legal publications." The BDO Stoy Hayward survey reveals the following information:

	%
Gross receipts	100.0
Chambers overheads	−17.4
Personal overheads	−10.8
Net income	71.8
Pension contributions	−14.4
Tax and National Insurance	−18.3
Net income after pension contributions, tax and NI	39.1

make very large sums of money indeed[59] but that some have a relatively small income. Thus, as with solicitors, there is a very wide income range.

One problem that barristers face is getting the fees paid within a reasonable time of having done the work. As *Chambers Guide to the Legal Profession 2001–2002* states, "the period between work done and fees received can be anywhere between three months and a year."[60] This problem has been a serious cause of friction. A new procedure was introduced, short of a contractual procedure,[61] and, from 2001, it has been possible for barristers and solicitors to engage in a contract.[62]

(iv) Employed barristers

There are just under 3,000 barristers who are employed in commerce, industry and central and local government.[63] Increasingly, barristers are being employed by solicitors firms and are not becoming solicitors. There have been many limits upon the work that an employed barrister[64] may do as imposed by the *Code of Conduct*. There is considerable similarity in the work done by employed solicitors and barristers such that the view was expressed as long ago as 1976 that there was effective fusion between these two parts of the profession.[65] The rules on what an employed barrister may do are constantly changing and are under further pressure to change. Now, an employed barrister "in the course of his employment may supply legal services to his employer" including other employees in relation to that person's employment and other members of a trade association where that is the employer.[66] Where the barrister is employed by a public authority (including the Government Legal Service), such services may also be supplied to another public authority with which the employer has an arrangement to supply legal services.[67] A Government Legal Service employed barrister may advise any Minister or Officer of the Crown.[68] A barrister employed as a justices' clerk may advise the justices.[69] Whilst acting in the course of employment, a barrister employed in a solicitors' firm may supply legal services to a client; a barrister employed by the Legal Services Commission may supply them to a member of the public; and a barrister employed at a Legal Advice Centre may supply services to its

3–027

---

[59] The so-called million-a-year club is, in fact, a very small proportion of the bar as a whole. *Chambers Guide 2001–2002*, p. 1247, states that it comprises some 29 Q.C.s.

[60] At p. 1247. In consequence, some, particularly young, barristers leave the profession as they do not receive enough money quickly enough to sustain their ability to practice.

[61] "The Terms of Work on which barristers offer their services to solicitors and the withdrawal of credit scheme 1988" in *Code of Conduct*, Annex G1.

[62] "The Contractual Terms of Work on which barristers offer their services to solicitors 2001" in *ibid.*, Annex G2.

[63] Bar Council, *Survey of Employed Barristers* (2001), at p. 3. For areas of work, see ibid., p. 15; for breakdown by ethnic minority and gender, see *ibid.*, pp. 12–14.

[64] An employed barrister includes not only someone employed under an employment of contract, but also someone employed as an independent contractor to supply legal services provided certain conditions are satisfied: *Code of Conduct*, para. 503.

[65] Chairman of the Solicitor's Commerce and Industry Group at (1976) 73 L.S. Gaz. 369.

[66] *Code of Conduct*, para. 501.

[67] *ibid.*, para. 501(b)(i).

[68] *ibid.*, para. 501(b)(ii).

[69] *ibid.*, para. 501(c).

clients.[70] Any employed barrister may supply legal services to any person free of charge.[71] One significant area of change is with regard to the rights to conduct litigation which an employed barrister may do provided they comply with the Employed Barristers (Conduct of Litigation) Rules.[72] There is still a reluctance to allow independent barristers to conduct litigation because of the restriction on conducting a client's affairs,[73] which are designed to ensure employed barrister may obtain full rights of audience in the higher courts.[74] There is pressure for change, not least under competition law.[75]

There is also a category of "non-practising barrister" who may advise, for free, members of the public, but is unable to appear as counsel in any court.[76]

(v) Practice guidance

3–028　The professional conduct of barristers is regulated by the profession itself, subject to the oversight of the Legal Services Ombudsman and of the law. It is the duty of every barrister to comply with the *Code of Conduct*.[77]

The general purpose of the Code "is to provide the requirements for practice as a barrister and the rules and standards of conduct applicable to barristers which are appropriate in the interests of justice ... "[78] With regard to barristers in independent practice, their purpose in particular is "to provide common and enforceable rules and standards which require them: (i) to be completely independent in conduct and in professional standing as sole practitioners;[79] (ii) to act only as consultants instructed by solicitors and other approved persons; (iii) to acknowledge a public obligation based on the paramount need for access to justice to act for any client in cases within their field of practice ... "[80] These obligations are moulded to the particular position of employed barristers.[81] Of the three key obligations for barristers in private practice, the second was under particular pressure from the Office of Fair Trading under competition law. In 2002, the Kerridge Committee recommend to the Bar Council that "the Bar should remove the general prohibition on direct access and allow barristers in independent practice to accept instructions directly from clients, subject to appropriate safeguards."[82] The process of modernisation has also attacked many of the

---

[70] *ibid.*, para. 502, (a)–(c).
[71] *ibid.*, para. 502(d).
[72] *ibid.*, para. 504. The rules are at Appendix I of the *Code of Conduct*.
[73] *ibid.*, paras. 401(b) & 307(g).
[74] Over one third of those responding had such rights: *Employed Barristers Survey* (2001), p. 5.
[75] See LECG Ltd., *Restrictions on Competition in the Provision of Professional Services: A Report for the Office of Fair Trading* (2000), paras. 258–261, found as part of Office of Fair Trading, *Competition in Profession* (2001).
[76] *Code of Conduct*, "Non-practising barristers offering legal services".
[77] *Code of Conduct*, para. 105.
[78] *ibid.*, para. 104.
[79] The Kerridge Committee has recommended that the rules against partnerships should be retained: Committee on Competition in Professions, *Report to the Bar Council* (chair S. Kerridge Q.C., 2002).
[80] *Code of Conduct*, para. 104(a).
[81] *ibid.*, para. 104(b).
[82] Kerridge Report (2002).

fundamental principles of the Bar, and whether the desire to maintain operation as sole practitioners can survive such pressures is open to serious doubt.[83]

All barristers must not engage in conduct which is "dishonest or otherwise discreditable to a barrister" or "prejudicial to the administration of justice" or "likely to diminish public confidence in the legal profession or the administration of justice or otherwise bring the legal profession into disrepute".[84]

All practising barristers have "an overriding duty to the Court to act with independence in the interests of justice". They must "assist the Court in the administration of justice and must not deceive or knowingly or recklessly mislead the Court."[85] Further, they "must promote and protect fearlessly and by all proper and lawful means the lay client's best interests and do so without regard to his own interests or to any consequences to himself or to any other person".[86] They owe their "primary duty as between a lay client and any professional client or other intermediary to the lay client and must not permit the intermediary to limit [their] discretion as to how the interests of the law client can best be served".[87] No barrister may "discriminate directly or indirectly or victimise because of race, colour, ethnic or national origin, nationality, citizenship, sex, sexual orientation, marital status, disability, religion or political persuasion."[88] Barristers are "individually and personally responsible for [their] own conduct and for [their] professional work" and they "must exercise [their] own personal judgment in all [their] professional activities."[89] The rules emphasise further the importance of the ability to be able to practice independently of interference and inappropriate pressures.[90]

In order to comply with their commitment to the administration of justice, any barrister who supplies advocacy services must not withhold such services because the nature of the case is objectionably or the client's opinions or beliefs are unacceptable or because of the source of the client's funding.[91] Further, any barrister in independent practice must comply with the "Cab-rank rule". That is they "must in any field in which [they profess] to practise in relation to work appropriate to [their] experience and seniority and irrespective of whether [their] client is paying privately or is publicly funded: (a) accept any brief to appear before a Court in which [they profess]

3–029

---

[83] See P. Kunzlik, "Rebuilding the Cathedral? – The partnership question and the effect of "modernisation" on the professionalism and ethics of the English bar" (2001).

[84] *Code of Conduct*, para. 301 (a). In addition, a barrister must not engage directly or indirectly in any occupation that may adversely affect the Bar's reputation or prejudice the practising barrister's ability to attend properly to his or her practice: *ibid.*, para. 301 (b).

[85] *ibid.*, para. 302.

[86] *ibid.*, para. 303(a)

[87] *ibid.*, para. 303(b). Their primary duty is also owed to the lay client when funded by either the Community Legal Service or the Criminal Defence Service: *ibid.*, para. 303(c). When providing such funded services, the barrister will have to comply with any duty imposed by or under the Access to Justice Act 1999 or related provisions and with the duties in Annex E to the Code: *ibid.*, para. 304.

[88] *ibid.*, para. 305.1. Where there is an allegation of indirect discrimination, there is no breach provided the barrister "proves that [it] was committed without any intention of treating the claimant unfavourably on any ground in [para 305.1]:" *ibid.*, para. 305.2.

[89] *ibid.*, para. 306.

[90] *ibid.*, para. 307.

[91] *ibid.*, para. 601

to practise; (b) accept any instructions; (c) act for any person on whose behalf [they are] instructed; and do so irrespective of (I) the party on whose behalf [they are] instructed (ii) the nature of the case and (iii) any belief or opinion which [they] may have formed as to the character reputation cause conduct guilt or innocence of that person."[92] There are a number of exceptions to the rule, so a barrister must not accept any brief or instructions that would cause them to be "professionally embarrassed", which might arise, *e.g.* as a result of insufficient experience or competence, other professional commitments, or where there is a conflict of interest.[93] Further, a barrister in independent practice is not obliged to accept a brief or instructions, *e.g.* requiring them to work outside their ordinary working year, other than at a proper fee, or where it is funded by a conditional fee agreement.[94] Queen's Counsel are not obliged to accept instructions to settle alone any document of a kind generally settled only by or in conjunction with a junior or to act without a junior if they consider that the interests of the lay client require a junior.[95] Since 1991, the Code has required the barrister to consider whether "consistently with the proper and efficient administration of justice and having regard to" the case, their practice, ability, experience and relationship with the client "the best interests of the client would be served by using" them and to advise the client if not.[96] Further, the advent of conditional fee arrangements as a means of funding litigation[97] has meant the abandonment of the cab-rank rule in this area of work.[98]

It has been said that this rule "secures for the public a right of representation in the court which is a pillar of British liberty."[99] In many ways, this is true. Barristers do indeed take cases where they may have concerns about the case. However, the greater pressure to do so may be the need to keep in business rather than this rule, especially when it is noted that it is possible to avoid taking cases by being too busy or unavailable. "In real life a barrister has a clerk whose enthusiasm for the unwanted brief may not be great, and he is free to raise the fee within limits. It is not likely that the rule often obliges barristers to undertake work which they would not otherwise accept."[1]

(vi) Restrictions on practice

3–030   (1) *Instructions and direct professional access.* Independent barristers may supply legal services only when they are instructed by a professional or BarDIRECT[2] client or is appointed by the Court.[3] The traditional version

[92] *ibid.*, para. 602.
[93] *ibid.*, para. 603.
[94] *ibid.*, para. 604.
[95] *ibid.*, para. 605.
[96] *ibid.*, para. 606.1
[97] See below, para. 11-007.
[98] P. Kunzlik, "Conditional Fees: The Ethical and Organisational Impact on the Bar" (1999) 62 M.L.R. 850. The cab-rank rule also does not apply to BarDIRECT clients.
[99] Royal Commission on Legal Services, *Report, Vol. 1* (1979), p. 31.
[1] *Per* Lord Steyn in *Arthur Hall v. Simons* [2000] 3 All E.R. 673, at p. 680.
[2] See *Code of Conduct*, Annex F.
[3] *ibid.*, para. 401(a).

of this restriction was that instructions could only be received from a solicitor. That old rule was only settled as regards contentious work in 1888 and non-contentious work in 1973.[4] They have been subsequently relaxed, *e.g.* by the Overseas Practice Rules. A major change was made when it was accepted that instructions could be received from a range of professional clients. Professional client means a solicitor, authorised litigator, Parliamentary agent, patent agent, trade mark agent, Notary, registered European lawyer, licensed conveyancer,[5] employed barrister,[6] and the representative of any body providing legal advice for free.[7] The Bar has endeavoured to oppose further change, but, facing pressure on the basis of competition law, is likely to make significant changes to the rule.[8] LECG Ltd, working for the Office of Fair Trading, identified arguments in favour of the rule being the addition of regulatory costs if direct access were enabled, plus the need for a compensation fund, accounting rules and procedures for client care and complaints, which could be regarded as an unfair burden. The arguments for reform were that barristers will be at a competitive disadvantage if they could not offer services directly to lay clients and the requirement of the rule demands that clients employ two lawyers where that is often unnecessary.[9]

(2) *Advertising and publicity.* There were old and traditional restrictions on barristers advertising. These have been swept away. Now a "barrister may engage in any advertising or promotion in connection with [their] practice which conforms to the British Codes of Advertising and Sales Promotion ... "[10] It may include photographs and illustrations of the barrister, statements of rates and methods of charging and about the nature and extent of their services, and information about previous cases.[11] Until the direct access rules change, such advertising is often limited to advertising and publicity that primarily raises profile before professional clients.

3–031

(3) *Partnerships and chambers.* The key principle for barristers in private practice is their independence, as has been clearly demonstrated so far. This is also one of the major rationales behind the rules on the manner in which a barrister may practice. Such a barrister may not enter into a partnership with another practising barrister and may not practise from the office of an unincorporated association.[12] The obligations upon the barrister demand that they "take all reasonable steps to ensure that: (i) [their] practice is efficiently and properly administered having regard to the nature of their practice; (ii) proper records are kept; [they comply] with the Terms of Work

3–032

---

[4] Annual Statement of the Bar Council 1973–74, pp. 33–34.

[5] Only in a matter in which the licensed conveyancer is providing conveyancing services.

[6] And also other practising barristers and registered European lawyers acting on their own behalf or a foreign lawyer in a matter other than advocacy.

[7] *Code of Conduct*, Definition of "professional client".

[8] Kerridge Report (2002).

[9] LECG Ltd., *Restrictions on Competition in the Provision of Professional Services: A Report for the Office of Fair Trading* (2000), paras. 262–265, found as part of Office of Fair Trading, *Competition in professions* (2001).

[10] *Code of Conduct*, para. 710.1.

[11] *ibid.* And see Kerridge Report (2002), which recommends that the rule against advertising success rates should be maintained, but the advertising of fee comparisons should not be prohibited.

[12] *Code of Conduct*, para. 403(a). In combination with the restrictions upon employed barristers, this emphasises the importance of independence. The Kerridge Report (2002) recommends the retention of the rule against partnerships.

on which Barristers Offer their Services to Solicitors ... " They must also
have "ready access to library facilities which are adequate having regard to
the nature of [their] practice." And they must have regard to any Bar
Council guidance relevant to the administration of their practice.[13] This
principle is open to challenge, though the Kerridge Report recommends
retention of the rule against partnerships.[14] However, the changing face of
civil litigation is applying significant pressure on maintaining this position.[15]

Most barristers operate from a set of chambers involving more than one
barrister. They are not in partnership and are not sharing fees. Each
barrister contributes towards rent and towards collective expenses. Whilst
some work comes into a named barrister, some may come into chambers
and be distributed to an appropriate barrister. Some work to a named
barrister may be passed on to a colleague in chambers. A proper library can
only readily be achieved by joint contributions, although any successful
barrister will have their own directly relevant materials. There are
obligations imposed upon how chambers should operate by way of
imposing obligations on the Head of Chambers.[16] One significant challenge
for the organisation of the Bar will be the developing approach of the Law
Society in relation to multi-disciplinary partnerships.[17] As these come on
stream, there will be increasing pressure from solicitors and from barristers
who perceive their advantages for barristers to work as barristers in such
arrangements.

3–033   *Queen's Counsel and junior barristers.* Another distinctive feature of
practice is the division of the bar into two ranks: Queen's Counsel[18] and
"junior" barristers. Appointment as a Q.C. is made by the Queen on the
advice of the Lord Chancellor, following an extensive process of
consultation amongst the judiciary and the legal professions. Today it is a
mark of eminence in the profession. It is also a mark of quality.[19] The main
difference as regards work done is that Q.C.s are the skilled and experienced
advocates and the expert and specialist advisers on points of law. They do
not normally do the paperwork associated with litigation unless they are
acting on their own. Ordinarily, a person "taking silk" can anticipate that
their earnings will improve, but the change can be something of a gamble,
although the risks are not as great as they were once thought to be. Most
High Court judges are appointed from amongst the Q.C.s[20] and there are
many other judicial appointments available.

At one time, there were rules of etiquette which prevented a Q.C. from

---

[13] *Code of Conduct*, para. 403.

[14] Kerridge Report(2002), recommendation (1).

[15] P. Kunzlik, "Rebuilding the Cathedral? — The partnership question and the effect of
"modernisation" on the professionalism and ethics of the English Bar" (2001), which notes a
number of the pressures pushing for partnership, notably the Woolf reforms of civil
litigation, the realisation that size matters as witnessed by the number of recent mergers and
other means of increasing the size of individual sets of chambers, the increasing difficulty, as
they grow, of working in chambers in the same way as traditionally has been the case, and
the increasing need for barristers to specialise so as to succed.

[16] *ibid.*, para. 404.2.

[17] See above, para. 3-019.

[18] "One of our Counsel learned in the Law." Q.C.s become K.C.s when there are Kings on the
throne of the United Kingdom.

[19] S. Kentridge, *Competition in the Professions: Report to the Bar Council* (2002), para. 7.7.

[20] See below, paras 4-020 and 4-023.

appearing in court without a junior (the two-counsel rule) and which entitled the junior to a fee equivalent to two-thirds of that of her or his leader. This latter rule was abolished in 1966 and replaced by an entitlement to a "proper fee".[21] The two-counsel rule was then under pressure under competition law[22] and was abrogated in 1977. Now, a Q.C. is not obliged to accept instructions (a) to settle alone a document of a kind generally settled with or by a junior, or (b) to act without a junior if he considers that the interests of the lay client require one.[23] Whether competition law will require, at some stage, further change remains to be seen, but, whilst the OFT considers that there may be a need, it is not clear what is the basis for the argument.[24] The Kerridge Report recommends that the Q.C. system is of value, as it should be retained.[25]

3. QUALITY OF SERVICE

Lawyers have always prided themselves on the quality of services that they provide. " ... Most advocates are honest conscientious people who need no other incentive to comply with the ethics of their profession." And "there is the wish to enjoy a good reputation among one's peers and the judiciary."[26] This is not mere assertion of a self-satisfied profession, but reveals an important business-based truth. If barristers, who are self-employed and reliant upon the reputation and quality of their work, have a poor reputation, fewer briefs will be sent to them and so they will be under personal financial pressure to perform better. Whilst an increasingly diverse profession reduces reliance upon accepted ethical principles,[27] it is the case that, broadly-speaking lawyers tend to adopt high standards for themselves. However, this is no protection of quality or against bad practice. Because of increasing client consumerism, making them more likely to question the quality of work done, and increasing competition for many of the services that lawyers offer, it is becoming necessary to be able to assess the quality of service and assure others of it. Simple membership of a profession is no longer a sufficient mark and guarantee of quality.[28] It is not surprising that many lawyers find it difficult to accept that anyone should question their work. Times have changed. Also, there are many more members of the profession and so the likelihood of poor quality work becomes greater. It is, though, important to recognise that most legal work is transacted well and efficiently and that most clients are satisfied with the work of their lawyers.[29] Further, lawyers tend to be held in fairly high regard by the public, though not always and not for all purposes.[30]

3–034

---

21 Annual Statement of the Bar Council 1971–72, p. 20.
22 Monopolies Commission, *Barrister Services: A report on the supply by Her Majesty's Counsel alone of their services* (1975–6 H.C. 512).
23 *Code of Conduct*, para. 605.
24 Kentridge (2002), para. 7.2.
25 Kerridge Report (2002), recommendation (5).
26 *Per* Lord Hoffmann in *Arthur Hall v. Simons* [2000] 3 All E.R. 673, at p. 693.
27 See Boon and Levin (1999), at p. 118.
28 See above, para. 3-001–3-002 and see Boon and Levin (1999).
29 See below, para. 9-009.
30 See below, para. 9-009.

Clearly, one measure of quality is the perception of the client.[31] But that is not the only possible measure, as clients may have criteria inconsistent with those acceptable criteria by which the profession operates. One of the difficulties is how to measure quality. In the context of moving towards the Community Legal Service, franchising was introduced and a part of this process was to endeavour to measure the quality of provision by measuring what was done against "transaction criteria". Lessons learned from that approach now form part of the recognition of an organisation as being a part of the Community Legal Service through the initial acceptance and on-going audit procedures.[32]

One major source of quality assurance is by way of the admission of appropriate, qualified personnel who are provided with good training.[33] Quality may also be assured, to some extent, by the professional practice rules[34] and the complaints systems for clients.[35] Another significant contribution to quality is the relatively new requirement for continuing professional development, which now applies to all solicitors and barristers.[36] This means that they have to demonstrate means whereby they have been undertaking activity that counts as continuing professional development and this ought to assist in the maintenance of the currency of practice in all its senses. Further, there is some work that can only be done if certain procedures are satisfied[37] or there are panels giving indications of expertise thereby providing some guarantee of quality.[38] Under the Community Legal Service, one means of assessing quality that may be introduced is a variant on 'mystery shopping', that is comparing advice actually given by a solicitor with that expected, by experts, to have been given.[39] When the activity is advocacy, quality assurance is supported by the role of the judges in considering a barrister's work. Judicial comments can be beneficial or detrimental to a barrister's career; judicial comments may assist the barrister in developing advocacy and trial skills. There is also the possibility of judges being involved in the disciplining of barristers on the basis of their performance in court, but it appears that judges are not particularly keen to engage in this process.[40]

4. REGULATION OF AND COMPLAINTS AGAINST LAWYERS

A major debate about the regulation of the legal professions has been commenced by the Legal Services Ombudsman in her annual report for

---

[31] See below, para. 9-009.
[32] The transaction criteria were developed by the work of Professors Sherr and Paterson and Richard Moorhead. As to the Community Legal Service, see below, paras 9-005, 9-013 and Chap. 10.
[33] See below, paras 3-051 and 3-052, and see Boon and Levin (1999), Chap. 6.
[34] See above, paras 3-013–3-022 and 3-028–3-033.
[35] See below, paras 3-035 and 3-043.
[36] The Bar Council introduced a requirement for new practitioners (i.e. in the first three years of independent practice) in October 1997 and a scheme for established practitioners was introduced as from January 1, 2001.
[37] For example, limitations upon work in financial services as imposed by the Financial Services Act 1986.
[38] See above, para. 3-012.
[39] See below, para. 10-013.
[40] Bar Council, *Blueprint for the Bar* (1994), paras. 121–126.

2001–02. So concerned is she about the ability of the Law Society and solicitors to deal with complaints that she opines the view that "the time may have come for a more radical approach to the regulation of legal services."[41] Indeed, the major theme of the report is the regulatory maze in relation to the legal professions such that the current scheme "cannot be seen to be operating in the public interest."[42] "There are too many different agencies with their own approaches and priorities, and too few co-ordinating influences, for the regulation of legal services to be seen to be operating in the public interest. Partly this is due to the fragmented nature of the professions ... Partly it is a consequence of the problematic inter-relationship of the numerous agencies which, to a greater or lesser degree, currently have responsibility for regulating the legal system and the provisions of legal services."[43] She, therefore, calls for "a regulatory body which can provide the overarching strategy that is so clearly needed."[44] Most people looking at the means of regulation would be confused and there is a crying need to review the means of regulation. No doubt the debate will be vigorous, interesting and challenging.

Much of the evidence for the above comes from the Legal Services Ombudsmen's deep concern about the way complaints are handled by lawyers. A major feature of the way complaints against lawyers are handled is the extent to which good client care is taken seriously and the preparedness of the professions to accept and welcome lay involvement. In reflecting on the 10 years of existence of the Legal Services Ombudsman,[45] the current office-holder (Ms A. Abraham), took the interesting view that

3–035

> "all the professional bodies now accept and welcome the involvement of law members in their complaint-handling activities. Leaders of the profession regularly issue public statements on the importance of good client care and effective complaint handling. In ten years, by many standards, the profession has come a long way. Yet ... the expectations of consumers of legal services, government and the public at large have moved faster still; with the result that lawyers have consistently struggled to match up to those expectations ... Why is it that lawyers have such difficulty in adapting themselves — in the words of Professor Mary Seneviratne of Nottingham Trent University ... — to a 'system of professionalism which is consumer-orientated, credible and thus appropriate for the twenty-first century'?"[46]

---

[41] Legal Services Ombudsman, *Annual Report 2001–2002* (2002), at p. 4.

[42] Legal Services Ombudsman, *Annual Report 2001–2002* (2002), at p. 6.

[43] Legal Services Ombudsman, *Annual Report 2001–2002* (2002), at p. 11. The range of areas that she includes (and which are dealt with in different parts of this book) include: "entry to professional practice; training; planning; competition; the cost and quality of, and access to, services; and complaints." The regulators include, quoting some work done by Professor John Baldwin: "the Lord Chancellor's Department, Parliament, the Master of the Rolls and the Attorney-General; other agencies of government such as the National Audit Office and the Office of Fair Trading; the courts; the Legal Aid Board; insurers; international bodies; universities and vocational organisations; the Legal Services Ombudsman; and pressure groups and voluntary organisations." Now added to the list are "the Immigration Services Commissioner, the Community Legal Service and the Legal Services Consultative Panel;" *ibid.*

[44] Legal Services Ombudsman, *Annual Report 2001–2002* (2002), at p. 6.

[45] See below, para. 3-043

[46] Office of the Legal Services Ombudsman *Annual Report 2001* (2002), p. 5.

The 2002 Annual Report indicates that huge strides still need to be made.[46a]
This section examines what is the current position.

(a) Solicitors

3–036   The primary approach for preventing problems is the ethical norms that are
adopted by solicitors. In effect, it has been the case that solicitors have
accepted a general structure to their ethical commitments and this has been
reflected in the way that they have regulated themselves.[47] One of the
traditional means to achieve this has been control over entry to the
profession and the authority to practise.[48] However, increasingly this is
under pressure, not least because of the increasing size of the profession.[49]
Now, the solicitors' profession has accepted a number of means to securing
proper approaches to legal work.

When things go wrong, there is a number of avenues open to the client
affected, although there may be considerable practical difficulties in
following them through. The first step is to raise the matter with the firm.
Since 1991, Practice Rule 15 on Client Care has obliged all principals in
private practice to have a complaints handling procedure that complies with
the Solicitors' Information and Client Care Code.[50] "The main object of the
code is to make sure that clients are given the information they need to
understand what is happening generally and in particular on (i) the cost of
legal services both at the outset and as a matter of progress; and (ii)
responsibility for clients' matters."[51] The Code, at some length, details the
costs information that must be supplied to clients, as this is likely to be a
major bone of contention and is a serious concern for most people accessing
the services of a solicitor.[52] As regards client care and complaint handling,
the Code provides standards with regard to information for clients and
complaints handling. As regards the former, the obligations are to ensure
that the client is given a clear explanation of the issues raised in a matter and
is kept properly informed about its progress; is given the name and status of
the person handling the matter and the name of the principal responsible for
its overall supervision; is told whom to contact about any service problems;
and is given details of any changes to the above. As regards complaints
handling, the obligations are imposed on principals in private practice who
must: ensure the client is told the name of the person in the firm to contact
about any problem with the service provided; have a written complaints
procedure and ensure that complaints are handled in accordance with it; and
ensure that the client is given a copy of the complaints procedure on request.

[46a] Legal Services Ombudsman, *Annual Report 2002* (2002) pp. 4–15.

[47] See Boon and Levin (1999), pp. 102–104 and 106–108.

[48] See Boon and Levin (1999), pp. 124–125. All solicitors wishing to practise must have a
current practising certificate.

[49] See above, para. 3-007 and 3-023 and Boon & Levin (1999), pp. 93 & 103–4.

[50] The Client Care Code was introduced in 1999 to provide fuller and clearer guidance as to
what was required in complaint handling. And see Boon and Levin (1999), pp. 125–128.

[51] Client Care Code, at para. 1(b).

[52] See below, paras 9-010 and 9-011.

A serious breach of the Code is a breach of Rule 15 and may be evidence of inadequate professional services.[53]

(b) Regulating solicitor's practice

The Law Society's power to make rules regulating the professional practice, **3–037** conduct and discipline of solicitors is subject to the concurrence of the Master of the Rolls.[54] After the Courts and Legal Services Act 1990, the Lord Chancellor's Advisory Committee on Legal Education and Conduct also had a role, but that Committee was abolished by the Access to Justice Act 1999. It has been replaced by Legal Services Consultative Panel, which carries out ACLEC's functions. The regulatory work of the Law Society is delegated to the Office for the Supervision of Solicitors.[55]

The standards, rules and principles[56] for solicitors are set out and amplified in *The Guide to the Professional Conduct of Solicitors*.[57] Solicitors are expected to comply with the rules.[58] Some of the basic rules have already been set out, especially those in relation to a solicitor's general duties, publicity, introductions and referrals, complaints, employed solicitors, multi-disciplinary partnerships, and multi-national practices.[59] The rules also prevent practising solicitors from providing certain legal services other than as a solicitor and provide safeguards to distinguish between a solicitor's practice and his or her other business.[60] The work that may be provided only through a solicitor's practice are the following services: work in relation to litigation (whether or not proceedings are commenced); court, tribunal or inquiry advocacy; instructing counsel; acting as an executor, trustee or nominee in England and Wales; will or trust deed drafting; giving legal advice, worked reserved to solicitors; and any legal document drafting.[61] There is also a requirement that a solicitor must not act for a client where his or her own interests conflict with the clients and a solicitor must not act where a conflict of interests arises between two or more clients. The first is an absolute prohibition;[62] the second is not. The general principle, though, in the second case is that "a solicitor or a firm of solicitors should not accept instructions to act for two or more clients where there is a

---

[53] *The Guide* (1999), at p. 27. Indeed any breach of the Code can be evidence of inadequate professional services even if it is not a breach of Rule 15: *ibid.* As to inadequate professional services, see below, para. 3-038.

[54] Solicitors Act 1974, s. 31(1).

[55] See below, paras 3-038 and 3-039.

[56] The standards usually describe important character traits such as honesty and competence; the rules prescribe particular things that must be done or not done; and the principles deal with other matters often at a fairly generalised level: see Boon and Levin (1999), p. 104.

[57] The last published edition is that from 1999. Up-dates and amendments are published on the Law Society's website: *www.lawsociety.org.uk.*

[58] The Rules are made under the Solicitors Act 1974, s. 31. It is possible for a rule to be waived in a given case: Solicitors' Practice Rules 1990, r. 17. For solicitors in private practice no general waivers are in force.

[59] See above, paras 3-013 to 3-022.

[60] Solicitors' Practice Rules 1990, r. 5 and the Solicitors' Separate Business Code 1994.

[61] Solicitors' Separate Business Code 1994, section 3.

conflict or a significant risk of a conflict between the interests of those clients."[63] Clearly, there has been some difficulty for many solicitors in identifying when a conflict of interests may arise.[64] There are some conveyancing circumstances where a solicitor can act for more than one client in an apparent conflict of interest.[65] Solicitors must ensure that every office where they or their firms practise is and can reasonably be seen to be properly supervised in accordance with certain minimum standards.[66]

The practice rules require solicitors to account to their clients where they receive more than £20 as commission, unless the client agrees that the solicitor may retain it.[67] In addition, solicitors must comply with detailed rules about the holding of client's money and the maintenance of adequate book-keeping and recording systems.[68] Whether money is held by a solicitor in a separate designated client account or a general client account, he or she must account to the client for all interest earned. All interest earned in the former must be credited to the account but, in the latter, sums in lieu will be paid in except where it is very small and the solicitor may retain any interest earned over and above that required to be paid under the Accounts Rules.[69] In many other jurisdictions sums of money not to be for the client would be required to be invested in legal education. Such a step in England and Wales would meet some of the financial problems associated for institutions and individuals with the costs of high quality legal education.

One form of client protection lies in the assurance that any losses or damages caused by the solicitor can be recovered or gained by the client. This demands that the solicitor is either sufficiently wealthy or carries sufficient insurance cover to meet such demands. In the past this has been achieved by the Solicitors' Indemnity Fund established by the Law Society on behalf of solicitors. However, such were the problems with the Fund, not least the cost to solicitors, that now the approach is the imposition of an obligation on all practising solicitors to carry adequate professional indemnity insurance under the Solicitors' Indemnity Insurance Rules 2001.

One of the most contentious issues for clients is the question of costs. Many problems would be solved were there greater compliance with the written professional standard about providing information and keeping the client informed.[70]

---

[62] *The Guide to the Professional Conduct of Solicitors* (1999), Principle 15.04.

[63] *ibid.*, Principle 15.01. See also, *e.g.* Principle 15.03 which states that "a solicitor or firm of solicitors must not continue to act for two or more clients where a conflict of interests arises between those clients."

[64] This is identified in *The Guide* itself at pp. 313–314.

[65] Solicitors' Practice Rules 1990, r. 6 (avoiding conflicts of interests in conveyancing, property selling and mortgage related services) and r. 6A (seller's solicitor dealing with more than one prospective buyer).

[66] Solicitors' Practice Rules 1990, r. 13. The minimum standards are stated in r. 13(1). See also *The Guide to the Professional Conduct of Solicitors* (1999), Principles 3.08–3.10.

[67] Solicitors' Practice Rules, r. 10.

[68] See *The Guide to the Professional Conduct of Solicitors* (1999), Part VI on Financial Regulations, which contains the Solicitors' Account Rules 1998 and other relevant rules and principles. Such rules were first made in 1935 because of a number of frauds by solicitors causing public concern: Abel-Smith & Stevens (1967), pp. 190–192.

[69] Solicitors' Account Rules, rr. 24 & 25, and coverage on them in *The Guide to the Professional Conduct of Solicitors* (1999), pp. 709–713.

[70] See above, para. 3-034 and below, para. 11-004

Solicitors: Professional misconduct and inadequate professional services[71]

The Law Society has the power to deal with both professional misconduct **3-038** and inadequate professional services. Its powers were formerly delegated to the Solicitors' Complaints Bureau and are now delegated to the Office for the Supervision of Solicitors (O.S.S.).[72] In serious cases of indiscipline the matter may go to the Solicitors' Disciplinary Tribunal which deals with allegations of unbefitting conduct or breaches of the rules of professional conduct.[73] "Professional misconduct" is undefined. The O.S.S. indicates that it includes a solicitor not keeping a client's business confidential, failing to pay money over to the client or to prepare proper accounts, to have acted in a conflict of interest, not to have handed over a client's papers and files, and stolen money or used it without the client's permission.[74] It may be, therefore, that it is conduct that other members of the profession would regard as "'dishonourable' or 'deplorable'"[75-76] It is unlikely that any breach of a practice rule is necessarily misconduct. Although the Law Society has always had the power to deal with misconduct, it has only had the power to deal with inadequate professional services since the Administration of Justice Act 1985.[77] "Inadequate professional services" is defined as "the provision by solicitors of services which are not of the quality which it is reasonable to expect of them.[78] Inadequate professional services to a client will cover problems with a solicitor such as the failure to follow the client's instructions, unreasonable delays, the provision of inaccurate or incomplete information, the failure to reply to telephone calls and letters, the failure to provide sufficient information about costs, and the failure to keep the client informed.[79] What the Law Society through the O.S.S. cannot investigate is allegations of negligence by a solicitor. Negligence is conduct of a solicitor falling below a standard which may reasonably be expected of them and entitling the complainant to damages for any loss caused.[80] The dividing line between negligence and inadequate professional services is extremely difficult to draw and, in effect, the O.S.S. deals with small negligence claims as inadequate professional services. If the O.S.S. cannot so deal with the case, it may refer the complainant to a member of the Law Society's negligence panel.

---

[71] See *The Guide*, Part VII on Complaints and Discipline.

[72] The powers are delegated from the Council of the Law Society under the Solicitors Act 1974, s. 79 to the Compliance and Supervision Committee of the Law Society and the senior staff of the O.S.S. And see Boon and Levin (1999), pp. 128–129.

[73] See below, para. 3-040. The O.S.S. refers to the S.D.T. all serious or persistent cases of misconduct and, in particular, suspected dishonesty, a criminal conviction of a mishandling of a client's money.

[74] *www.lawsociety/org.uk.*

[75-76] National Consumer Council, *The Solicitors' Complaints Bureau: A consumer view* (1994), p. 31.

[77] See now the Solicitors Act 1974, s. 37A and Sched. 1A as replaced by the Courts and Legal Services Act 1990, s. 93.

[78] Solicitors Act 1974, s. 37A.

[79] These are examples provided by the O.S.S. on its website at *www.lawsociety.org.uk.* and originally appeared in an earlier edition of *The Guide, see The Guide to the Professional Conduct of Solicitors* (6th ed., 1993), para. 30.11.

[80] See M. Mildred, "Solicitors" in R. Hodgin (ed.), *Professional Liability: Law and Insurance* (2nd ed., 1999).

In the first place all complaints should be dealt with by the solicitor concerned and then the senior partner.[81] Only then should a complaint be directed to the O.S.S. As with all organisations, the O.S.S. has targets for its work that it endeavours to meet. These have a particular current importance as the possibility of the Law Society retaining its disciplinary function alongside its representational function is under severe scrutiny. If, therefore, complaints against solicitors are handled badly or inefficiently, this will be part of the argument in favour of an independent approach to solicitors' discipline and complaints. The O.S.S. has targets agreed with the Lord Chancellor and targets agreed with the Law Society. In November 2001, it reported that it was achieving most of its targets and that the Legal Services Ombudsman was satisfied with most of the cases on which she reported.[82] However, by 2002, the LSO had to report that the OSS was not in a position to say with any accuracy whether such targets are being met. The LSO was of the view that they were not being met in any satisfactory way.[82a] The O.S.S. announces its targets to clients as follows:

- "If you make a complaint of poor service or professional misconduct (poor behaviour) to us, we will aim to deal with 50 per cent of our investigations within three months, 80 per cent within six months, 90 per cent within twelve months and the other 10 per cent within 18 months.

- If you apply for a grant from the Compensation Fund, we will aim to complete 50 per cent of applications within six months, 60 per cent within 12 months, 80 per cent within eighteen months and 98 per cent within twenty-four months.

- If you challenge your bill using the remuneration certificate procedure we will aim to complete 85 per cent of remuneration certificate applications within three months, 95 per cent within six months and the other 5% within twelve months.[83]

The LSO is deeply concerned about the ability of the Law Society to deal with complaints properly. In the foreword to her 2002 annual report, she states:

"The profession has been on the back foot again in the past year. The Law Society have marred their achievement in clearing a substantial backlog of cases by taking their eye off the ball and allowing the caseload to rise again — from 4,113 on 1 January 2001 to 5,430 at the end of March 2002, an increase of 32% in 15 months; whilst the quality of OSS' decision making remains stubbornly low. The necessary sustained and continuing improvement in the Law Society's complaint-handling activities has not yet been forthcoming and increased

---

[81] See above, para. 3-036.
[82] O.S.S., *Monthly Digest of Performance Measures and Statistics November 2001*, p. 2, at *www.lawsociety.org.uk*.
[82a] Legal Services Ombudsman, *Annual Report 2002* (2002), p. 7.
[83] *www.lawsociety.org.uk*.

oversight of the work of the OSS by my Office will be necessary in the coming year."[84]

Further, the LSO was satisfied with the way in which the OSS handled complaints in only 58 per cent of the 1,629 cases she investigated in 2001/2002.[85] Clearly major challenges lie ahead for the Law Society[86] and the oversight of the LSO, as indicated above, will no doubt prove to be awkward, though critical, for all concerned.

When a valid complaint is received by the O.S.S., it will endeavour to resolve the matter by conciliation. The National Consumers Council was highly critical of this approach in the mid-1990s because complainants were not given a choice about whether to use conciliation, complaints were not formally investigated unless the possibilities of conciliation had been exhausted and the conciliator could, effectively, impose a settlement or dismiss the complaint.[87] However, the general approach to handling complaints does involve raising the issue first with the complained against (*i.e.* the solicitor) and then endeavouring to resolve a complaint by conciliation or some other form of non-investigative process.

If conciliation does not resolve the matter, there will be an investigation by the O.S.S. Complaints are usually investigated through correspondence.[88] If there is a finding against a solicitor, the powers of the O.S.S. vary according to the nature of the complaint. If there is a finding of inadequate professional services, the OSS can: disallow all or part of the solicitor's costs; direct the solicitor to rectify an error at his or her expense; direct the solicitor to pay compensation to the client up to a limit of £1,000; or direct the solicitor to take at his or her expense such other action in the interests of the client as the OSS may specify.[89] If there is a finding of professional misconduct, the powers include[90] reprimanding the solicitor, requiring the solicitor to pay interest on a client account,[91] refusing a practice certificate or issuing a conditional certificate,[92] imposing conditions on a solicitor's current practising certificate,[93] suspending, withdrawing or imposing conditions on an investment business certificate,[94] ordering an inspection of the accounts,[95] disqualifying an accountant from giving an accountant's report on the accounts,[96] intervening in a solicitor's practice,[97] or instituting disciplinary proceedings before the Solicitors Disciplinary Tribunal.[98] Where there is a finding of undue delay, the OSS may recover money and

3–039

---

[84] Legal Services Ombudsman, *Annual Report 2001–2002* (2002), at p. 4.
[85] Legal Services Ombudsman, *Annual Report 2001–2002* (2002), at p. 7.
[86] As to the general debate on regulation, see above at para. 3-035.
[87] N.C.C. (1994), p. 57.
[88] *The Guide*, at p. 843.
[89] Solicitors Act 1974, s. 37A and Sched. 1A.
[90] See *The Guide*, p. 845.
[91] Solicitors' Account Rules 1998, r. 24.
[92] Solicitors Act 1974, s. 12.
[93] Solicitors Act 1974, s. 13A.
[94] Solicitors' Investment Business Rules 1995, r. 5.
[95] Solicitors' Account Rules, r. 34; Solicitors' Overseas Practice Rules 1990, r. 15.
[96] Solicitors' Account Rules 1998, r. 37(3).
[97] Solicitors Act 1974, Sched. 1, and see *The Guide*, p. 846.
[98] See below, para. 3-040.

papers for the client or a new solicitor.[99] Where there is a finding of dishonesty against a solicitor and the client has suffered a financial loss, a payment may be made from the Solicitors' Compensation Fund.[1] Payments from this fund are rare, because it is a "discretionary fund of the last resort"[2] and because the more likely source of compensation is from the solicitor.[3]

There is a serious debate about the regulatory role of the Law Society and, in particular, whether the Law Society can satisfy that function as well as, at the same time, being the representative body for solicitors. The Law Society has identified three matters to protect as the purpose of regulation: the public interest; the consumer interest; and a particular provider's brand.[4] As the Law Society points out, the solicitors' profession is self-regulated and this approach has been confirmed by statute.[5] But, as we have indicated, there are pressures for change. The Law Society has identified two sets of pressures:[6] one is external; the other internal. The external pressures are identified as being: significant and rapid changes in the market place; the rise of consumerism; changing client expectations; the impact of globalisation; the impact of new technology; concerns about the failings of self-regulation; the need for fair competition; government ambiguity over self-regulation; reports querying the basis of self-regulation;[7] the criticisms of the Legal Service Ombudsman about complaint handling; and the old Legal Aid Board imposing quality standards for the letting of contracts. The internal pressures are identified as being: the increasing diversity of the profession but it being handled by the same regulatory approach; some large firms see Law Society regulation as irrelevant to them partly because of their obligations to meet other regulatory requirements; the regulatory burden is unhelpful for smaller firms; the potential new challenges arising from multi-disciplinary practices; and the relevance of this form of regulation to solicitors not in private practice. The debate has been given impetus by the LSO's 2002 annual report.[7a]

(d) Disciplinary proceedings: solicitors[8]

3–040   The most serious cases are dealt with by the Solicitors Disciplinary Tribunal,[9] which is independent of the Law Society. A case may become

---

[99]   Solicitors Act 1974, Sched. 1, para. 3.
[1]   Solicitors Act 1974, s. 36 (as amended), and see *The Guide*, pp. 847–848.
[2]   E. Skordaki, et al., *Default by Solicitors* (1991), as quoted by Boon and Levin (1999), p. 133.
[3]   There used to be a Solicitors' Indemnity Fund (see Boon and Levin (1999), p. 132), but now all solicitors must carry indemnity insurance, see above, para. 3-038.
[4]   The Law Society, *Regulation of Solicitors — A Strategic Discussion Paper* (1999), at *www.lawsocietv.org.uk*.
[5]   Solicitors Act 1974.
[6]   The Law society; *Regulation of Solicitors — A Strategic Discussion Paper* (1999), at *www.lawsociety.org.uk*.
[7]   Specific reference is made of: Consumers' Association, *Leave it to the Professionals* and Fabian Society, *The Rule of Lawyers*.
[7a]   See above, para. 3-035
[8]   As Boon & Levin point out, "disciplinary mechanisms [are] often a focus of criticism:" Boon and Levin (1999), p. 105.
[9]   It was established by the Solicitors Act 1974, s. 46. See Boon and Levin (1999), pp. 129–132 and B. Swift, *Proceedings Before the Solicitors' Disciplinary Tribunal* (1996).

before the SDT either through the O.S.S. or directly.[10] Its principal function is to hear and determine allegations of unbefitting conduct or breaches of the rules of professional conduct.[11] It is for the Tribunal to determine whether there is a prima facie case.[12] Hearings are normally in public. If an allegation is proved, the Tribunal may: strike the solicitor off the roll;[13] suspend the solicitor indefinitely or for a specified period; fine the solicitor (not more than £5,000 per allegation); reprimand or censure the solicitor; exclude the solicitor from legal aid work (permanently or for a specified period); prohibit the restoration of the solicitor to the roll; or order the payment of costs.[14] The Tribunal may inform the Council of the Law Society that it is of the view that "steps" in respect of inadequate professional services should be taken.[15] In 1996, there were 249 cases before the Tribunal. The actions taken by the Tribunal were:[16]

Struck off the roll	76
Suspended from practice	26
Fined	80
Reprimanded	11
Censured	1
No order made (though allegation substantiated)	2
Order for costs only	1
Allegation not substantiated	1
Application for restoration to the roll	2
Other matters[17]	73

An appeal lies to the Divisional Court of Queens' Bench Division of the High Court[18] and then, on a point of law, to the Court of Appeal and the House of Lords. The High Court, the Crown Court and the Court of Appeal may also exercise jurisdiction over solicitors as officers of the supreme court.[19]

---

[10] *The Guide*, para. 31.02.

[11] *The Guide*, para. 31.01.1.

[12] *The Guide*, para. 31.02.2.

[13] The Court of Appeal expects that a solicitor who is found guilty of dishonesty will be struck off: *Bolton v. The Law Society* (1996) *The Times*, December 8th, but not all have been either struck off or suspended: Boon & Levin (1999), p. 131.

[14] Solicitors Act 1974, ss. 37A, 47 and Sched. 1A and *The Guide*, para. 31.05. Reports of the proceedings of the Solicitors Disciplinary Tribunal appear in the *Law Society's Gazette*.

[15] Solicitors Act 1974, Sched. 1A, para. 8.

[16] Boon & Levin (1999), p. 131.

[17] *i.e.* cases involving s. 43 orders relating to solicitors' clerks (55 cases); prohibition orders (former solicitors who have not been struck off but who cannot practise as solicitors) (6 cases); applications to end indefinite suspensions (2 cases); S.C.B. referrals (now would be O.S.S. referrals) made where the solicitor does not comply with an order or direction (9 cases); and one application was withdrawn.

[18] Solicitors Act 1974, s. 49. In some cases, i.e. applications for restoration to the roll, the appeal lies to the Master of the Rolls (ss. 43(4), 47(1)(b)) who makes a final decision.

[19] Solicitors Act 1974, ss. 50–53.

(e) Barristers

3–041   The Bar's Code of Conduct[20] is more recent than that for solicitors. It was
first published in 1981.[21] The powers were not statutory, but predicated
upon self-regulation.[22] Barrister's self-regulate, as do solicitors, entry to the
profession and the authority to practise.[23] All barristers must be called to
one of the four Inns of Court (Gray's Inn, Inner Temple, Lincoln's Inn and
Middle Temple). After pupillage,[24] the barrister is free to practise, but needs
no practising certificate akin to that required of a solicitor.

Until 1996, there were few avenues available to a lay client[25] when things
went wrong.[26] Some chambers were able to deal with complaints, and the
client could seek the instigation of disciplinary proceedings or go to law. A
judge can be involved in discussing a barrister's practice[27] and a wasted
costs order can be made against a barrister where poor service caused loss.
However, there was no practice rule demanding a complaints handling
system in chambers, nor a system at the level of the professional body, the
Bar Council. A complaints system was introduced in 1996.[28]

Complaints about a barrister's professional work[29] sent to the Bar
Council[30] are now initially considered by the Complaints Commissioner.[31-32]
A complaint may be about either professional misconduct or inadequate
professional service. The Bar Council defines professional misconduct as "a
serious error or misbehaviour by a barrister which may well involve some
element of dishonesty or serious incompetence. It might include: misleading
the court; failure to keep a client's affairs confidential; leaving a case without
good reasons at short notice; acting against a client's instructions or best
interests." The *Code of Conduct* states that "any failure by a barrister to
comply with [the] Code shall constitute professional misconduct."[33] It
defines inadequate professional service as "service towards the client falling

---

[20] See above, para. 3-028.
[21] Boon and Levin (1999), p. 134. The Bar Council's existence was statutorily recognised in the
Courts and Legal Services Act 1990, s. 31.
[22] *ibid.*
[23] As to educational requirements, see below, para. 3-051.
[24] *ibid.*
[25] As to the clients of a barrister, see above, para. 3-030.
[26] Until the Courts and Legal Services Act 1990, s. 61, a barrister could not enter a contract for
his or her services and so could not be contractually bound to deliver a service and could not
sure for fees. However, the Bar Council has, as the section allows, made a rule prohibiting a
barrister from entering into contracts, see the Bar Code, Annex D, paras. 25 and 26, and see
Boon and Levin (1999), p. 136.
[27] See above, para. 3-040.
[28] Complaints System Working Party, *Report* (1995), paras. 2–29.
[29] Complaints about a barrister's private life or non-professional work are, therefore, not taken
unless they involve an allegation of criminal or similar misbehaviour. Further, debt actions
against a barrister must be pursued through the courts. Where the barrister is employed, the
complaint should first be taken up with the employer and then with the Bar Council.
[30] Normally a complaint must be made within six months of the complaint arising. The time
limit may be extended were the matter is particularly serious or there is good reason for the
delay.
[31-32] The first Complaints Commissioner, appointed by the Bar Council, is Major General
Michael Scott.
[33] *Code of Conduct*, para. 901. However, in the Bar Council's Complaints System Working
Party, *Report* (1995), at para. 34 it was reported that not every breach in professional
misconduct, which is a more realistic approach.

significantly below that which would normally be expected of a barrister. It is not as serious as misconduct but may well have caused significant concern or inconvenience to a client such as: delay in dealing with papers; poor or inadequate work on a case; serious rudeness to the client.[34] Complaints of negligence cannot be taken through this procedure, and the Bar Council's advice is for such a complainant to seek advice from another lawyer.[35]

The Commissioner determines, after an investigation if appropriate, whether there is a *prima facie* case, and may dismiss cases where this is lacking.[36] The Commissioner may ask the barrister for their comments on a complaint, which will be sent to the complainant. If the Commissioner determines that a complaint may be justified, it is referred to the Professional Conduct and Complaints Committee (PCCC) of the Bar Council for consideration. The number of complaints received by the Complaints Commissioner in 2000 was 569, which is roughly the same as the previous year.[37] The Commissioner dismissed 52 per cent of the complaints.[38] The Commissioner is keen to keep any delay to a minimum and has set himself a standard period for complaints with which he deals of 20 weeks. This has been achieved, since the average time for a decision (whether his or that of the PCCC) was 12 weeks.[39] The Bar continues to do fairly well in its complaints handling (at least compard to the Law Society), according to the Legal Services Ombudsman, who, in her annual report for 2001–02, states:

" ... the Bar Council have maintained their high standard of complaint handling and continued to demonstrate their commitment to continuous improvement in their complaint-handling systems and activities."[40]

The PCCC consists of barristers and a panel of lay representatives.[41] The PCCC may dismiss the complaint, but only if the lay representatives agree. If the PCCC agrees that the complaint may be justified and it is a case involving inadequate professional service, it is referred to an Adjudication Panel. An Adjudication Panel is chaired by the Complaints Commissioner and consists of two barristers and one member of the panel of lay representatives. It decides whether the complaint is established and, if so,

---

[34] *ibid.*

[35] This may result in action being taken for negligence, see below, paras 3-044–3-046. Barristers have professional indemnity insurance through the Barristers' Mutual Insurance Fund.

[36] The Commissioner also dismisses the case if it is trivial or lacks validity.

[37] Complaints Commissioner, *Annual Report 2000* (2001), at para. 4. The number of complaints from lay clients fell by 4% to 450. The rise in the number of complaints initiated by the Bar Council "reflects a continuing drive against non insurance payers and those barristers who are alleged to have overcharged for their services in criminal legal aid cases:" *ibid.*

[38] This was a reduction from the previous year: *ibid.*, at para. 5.

[39] *ibid.*, at para 12. Delays that do occur are rarely owing to the Commissioner: *ibid.*, para. 14.

[40] Legal Services Ombudsman, *Annual Report 2001–2002* (2002), at p. 4. The LSO feels, however, that the Bar's response to the OFT's report on *Competition in professions* (2001) (see above, para. 3-001) has placed it on the backfoot: Legal Services Ombudsman, *Annual Report 2001–2002* (2002), at p. 4.

[41] Owing to increased work, the Complaints Commissioner has had to recruit additional personnel to the panel of lay representatives, and brought the panel up to 20 in 2000. The process of appointment was by way of national advertisement and an interview process: ibid., at paras. 20–22.

what the penalty should be. The possible penalties are to require the barrister: to apologise; to repay fees; or to pay compensation to the complainant of up to £5,000. The barrister has a right of appeal.

(f) Professional misconduct: barristers

3-042 If the Professional Conduct and Complaints Committee (PCCC) receives a reference from the Complaints Commissioner and agrees that the complaint may be justified and is a case involving professional misconduct, the case is referred to one of three different bodies. It may be referred to an informal hearing; a summary procedure panel; or a disciplinary tribunal.[42] An informal hearing consists of three barristers and one member of the panel of lay representatives. If it decides that the complaint is upheld, it may advise the barrister as to his or her future conduct; or admonish him or her; or impose one of the penalties for inadequate professional service.

A summary procedure panel also consists of three barristers and one member of the panel of lay representatives. On upholding a complaint, it may do what an informal hearing may do, and, further, it can fine a barrister or suspend him or her for up to three months.

A disciplinary tribunal is chaired by a judge with two barristers and two members of the panel of lay representatives. It deals with the most serious cases, usually sits in public and can, in addition to the penalties that the other procedures can impose, disbar a barrister or suspend him or her for an unlimited period.[43] A barrister may appeal from a summary procedure panel or a Disciplinary Tribunal to the Visitors, who are the High Court Judges. The complainant has no right of appeal, although a complainant dissatisfied with the way the Bar Council has handled a complaint may refer the matter to the Legal Services Ombudsman.[44]

In the year 2000, an additional procedure, of interim suspension, was introduced to enable the Bar Council to suspend a barrister more swiftly where the barrister was convicted of or charged with a serious criminal offence or where for reasons of illness the barrister was clearly unfit to practise.[45] No Panels sat to consider criminal cases, but there were two Fitness to Practice Panels to decide upon a barrister's fitness to practice.[46] The normal procedures would then follow.

(g) The Legal Services Ombudsman[47]

3-043 The office of the Legal Services Ombudsman (L.S.O.) was created by section 21 of the Courts and Legal Services Act 1990 "to reinforce the existing

[42] In 2000, the PCCC remanded 12% of cases for a summary hearing or disciplinary tribunal: *ibid.*, at para. 5.
[43] The Bar Council publishes the most serious decisions of the Tribunal once the timescale for appeal against sentence has passed.
[44] See below, para. 3-043.
[45] Complaints Commissioner, *Annual Report 2000* (2001), at para. 28.
[46] *ibid.*, at paras. 29 and 30.
[47] See R. James and M. Seneviratne, "The Legal Services Ombudsman: Form versus Function?" (1995) 58 M.L.R. 187 and M. Seneviratne, *The Legal Profession: Regulation and the Consumer* (1999), Chap. 6.

system with more effective measures for dealing with complaints."[48] The L.S.O. may investigate[49] the way in which certain professional bodies (currently the Law Society, the General Council of the Bar, the Council of Licensed Conveyancers,[50] the Institute of Legal Executives,[51] and the Chartered Institute of Patent Agents[52]) have handled complaints to them about members of their profession.[53] Secondly, where an allegation is investigated, the substance of the complaint to the professional body may also be investigated.[54] The second power is rarely exercised, which is not surprising in view of the oversight function ascribed to the L.S.O.[55]

The L.S.O. cannot (1) investigate any allegation while it is being investigated by the professional body concerned unless the allegation is that that body has acted unreasonably in not starting an investigation or has failed to complete an investigation within a reasonable time or the L.S.O. believes that an investigation is justified despite the investigation by the professional body,[56] (2) investigate any complaint which has been dealt with by a court, the Solicitors Disciplinary Tribunal or the Disciplinary Tribunal of the Council of the Inns of Court, since the procedures in such tribunals satisfy the need for public accountability.[57]

Between 1991 and 2001, the L.S.O. undertook 10,531 investigations.[58] In 2002, the L.S.O. completed 1,789 investigations.[59] Where the L.S.O. investigates,[60] upon completion of the investigation, a written report of the conclusions must be sent to the person making the allegation, any person in respect of whom the complaint was made, and the professional body concerned.[61] In the report, which must be reasoned, the L.S.O. may make one or more of the following recommendations:[62]

---

[48] Lord Chancellor's Department, *Legal Services: Framework for the Future* (Cm. 740, 1989), para. 10.13.

[49] The L.S.O. may at any time discontinue an investigation: s. 22(3). In conducting an investigation, the L.S.O. may require any person to furnish relevant information and produce relevant documents (s. 25(1)). The L.S.O. has the same powers as the High Court with regard to the attendance and examination of witnesses and in respect of the production of documents (s. 25(2)). Any person in contempt of the L.S.O. may be referred to the High Court (s. 25(4)–(7)).

[50] These three bodies were part of the L.S.O. original remit.

[51] This body was added to the L.S.O. remit in 1998.

[52] This body was added to the L.S.O. remit in 1999.

[53] Courts and Legal Services Act 1990, s. 22(1).

[54] Courts and Legal Services Act 1990, s. 22(2).

[55] See James and Seneviratne (1995), p. 189.

[56] Courts and Legal Services Act 1990, s. 22(5) & (6).

[57] Court and Legal Services Act 1990, s. 22(7).

[58] Office of the Legal Services Ombudsman, *Annual Report 2001* (2002), p. 4. Of those investigations, 9,456 concerned complaints about solicitors, 1,036 complaints about barristers and 39 complaints about licensed conveyancers. Some 60% of firms and 8% of barristers have been the subject of a complaint.

[59] Office of the Legal Services Ombudsman, *Annual Report 2002* (2002), p. 16. Some 1,233 inquiries did not proceed to an investigation for a variety of reasons: *ibid.*, p. 49.

[60] In some straightforward cases, there is a fast track method: James & Seneviratne (1995), p. 202.

[61] Courts and Legal Services Act 1990, s. 23(1). The same people must be informed if the L.S.O. does not investigate: s. 22(4).

[62] In 2001–2002, the L.S.O. made formal recommendations in 499 or 31% of investigations, which was a substantial increase over the previous year: *Annual Report 2002*, at p. 53.

(1) that the complaint be reconsidered by the professional body;[63]

(2) that the professional body (or any other relevant disciplinary body) should consider its powers in relation to the person about whom the complaint was made and any person who at the time was connected[64] with him or her;

(3) that the person about whom the complaint was made or any person who at the time was connected with him or her should pay compensation, as specified by the L.S.O., to the complainant for loss suffered or inconvenience or distress caused as a result of the matter about which there was a complaint;[65]

(4) that the professional body concerned should pay such compensation;[66]

(5) that a separate payment be made to the complainant in respect of costs related to the making of an allegation.[67]

These are recommendations only, but they are backed by the requirement that a person to whom a report is sent must "have regard to the conclusions and recommendations set out in the report, so far as they concern that person."[68] Further, the person or body to whom such a recommendation is made must, within three months of the date on which the report was sent, notify the L.S.O. of the action taken or proposed to be taken to comply with the recommendation.[69] Finally, any person or body failing to comply with a recommendation must publicise that failure and the reasons for it in such manner as the L.S.O. specifies.[70] If a person or body fails so to publicise, the L.S.O. may take such steps as considered reasonable to publicise the failure.[71]

The L.S.O. has a further critical role. This is in acting as the monitor of the complaints procedures of the professional bodies. To this end, the L.S.O. may make formal recommendations as to how the professional body deals with complaints,[72] have informal meetings with the professional bodies, and make formal comments in the Annual Report.[73] In 2000–2001,

---

[63] In 2001–2002, the L.S.O. made such a recommendation in 277 cases: *Annual Report 2002*, at p. 53

[64] See Courts and Legal Services Act 1990, s. 23(11).

[65] In 2001–2002, the L.S.O. made no such recommendations: *Annual Report 2002*, at p. 53.

[66] In 2001–2002, the L.S.O. made such a recommendation in 284 cases: *Annual Report 2001*, at p. 53. The sums ranged widely. The lowest award of the 354 made against the Office for the Supervision of Solicitors was £50, the average was £243.06 and the highest award was £2,000: *ibid.*, p. 54.

[67] Courts and Legal Services Act 1990, s. 23(2), (3) & (4).

[68] Courts and Legal Services Act 1990, s. 23(6).

[69] Courts and Legal Services Act 1990, s. 23(7).

[70] Courts and Legal Services Act 1990, s. 23(8).

[71] Courts and Legal Services Act 1990, s. 23(9). Any reasonable expenses incurred by the L.S.O. may be recovered as a civil debt from the person whose failure has been publicised: *ibid.*, s. 23(10).

[72] Courts and Legal Services Act 1990, s. 24(1). This is a rarely exercised power, see James & Seneviratne, at pp. 199–200, but it was exercised in 2002, see *Annual Report 2002*, p. 7.

[73] *ibid.*, p. 199. For comments on the various professional bodies performance, see *Annual Report 2002*. In 61% of investigations, the L.S.O. felt that a satisfactory outcome had been reached by the professional body: *ibid.*, at p. 52. But for the OSS and solicitors, it was as low as 58%: *ibid.*

the L.S.O. had made criticisms of the professional bodies in 107 or 6 per cent of cases but in 2001–2002 this rose to 11%.[74]

James and Seneviratne, in 1995, concluded that, with minor reservations, the office met the four criteria essential to the work of ombudsmen, that is "independence of the ombudsman from those whom he has power to investigate; effectiveness; fairness; and public accountability."[75] Their major concern was whether the L.S.O. should not be more regularly, if not always, investigating the complaint at the heart of the allegation.[76] Overall, Seneviratne's conclusion is that the "office is performing an excellent role, on a limited budget."[77]

(h) Legal proceedings against lawyers

(i) Negligence

A lawyer's misconduct or incompetence may give rise to a cause of action   **3–044**
against him or her. For example, a client may be able to sue for breach of contract,[78] breach of trust[79] or the tort of negligence.[80] The scope of negligence liability has been wider since the decision of the House of Lords in 1963 in *Hedley, Byrne & Co. Ltd. v. Heller & Partners Ltd.*[81] where it was established that a special relationship could give rise to a duty of care in the giving of information or advice, and that there would be liability in damages in such cases in respect of losses that were purely economic. In *Midland Bank Trust Co. Ltd. v. Hett. Stubbs & Kemp*[82] Oliver J. stated that the case of a layman consulting a solicitor seemed:

> "to be as typical a case as one could find of the sort of relationship in which the duty of care described in the *Hedley Byrne* case exists."[83]

His Lordship held that the authorities which indicated that the existence of a contract between a solicitor and a client precluded any action in tort[84] were inconsistent with *Hedley Byrne* and should not be followed.[85] In *Ross v. Counters*,[86] Sir Robert Megarry V.-C. took matters a step further. Solicitors failed to warn a client that his will should not be witnesses by a spouse of a beneficiary and failed to notice that this had happened. They were held liable to the disappointed beneficiary whose bequest failed. This decision

---

[74] *Annual Report 2002*, at p. 9.
[75] James and Seneviratne (1995)., p. 188.
[76] *ibid.*, p. 206 and Seneviratne (1999), at p. 209.
[77] Seneviratne (1999), at p. 209.
[78] Whilst the Courts and Legal Services Act 1990, s. 61(1) allows for barristers to enter intro contracts for their services, the Act, in s. 61(2), allows a professional rule of conduct to prevent them entering contracts. Such a rule exists: *Code of Conduct*, para. 210.
[79] *e.g., Re Bell's Indenture* [1980] 1 W.L.R. 1217.
[80] See Mildred (2000).
[81] [1964] A.C. 465, and J.L. Powell & R. Stewart (eds.), *Jackson and Powell on Professional Negligence* (5th ed., 2002), at Chaps. 10 & 11 and M.A. Jones, *Textbook on Tort* (7th ed, 2002), pp. 48–59, 65–70 & 94–131.
[82] [1979] Ch. 384, approved in *Henderson v. Merrett Syndicates Ltd.* [1994] 3 All E.R. 506.
[83] [1979] Ch. 384, at p. 417.
[84] *Groom v. Crocker* [1939] 1 K.B. 194; *Clark v. Kirby-Smith* [1964] Ch. 506.
[85] Oliver J. held that the claim in contract succeeded as well as the claim in tort.
[86] [1980] Ch. 297.

was upheld in *White v. Jones*[87] by the House of Lords by a narrow majority. Actions for negligence against solicitors and barristers have subsequently been an area of significant legal development.[88]

The position of victims of incompetence is further secured by the compulsory indemnity insurance requirements for both solicitors and barristers.[89] There are, however, a number of problems facing clients who wish to consider suing their lawyers. First, legal assistance is advisable, but someone, whose dealings with a lawyer have been unsatisfactory, probably protracted, and a source of frustration and annoyance, is unlikely to relish the prospect of involvement with yet more lawyers. In order to alleviate any possible problem of finding a lawyer prepared to take on such a case, the Law Society has established a panel of solicitors prepared to act in such cases (the "Negligence Panel").[90] A greater problem used to exist. It was that there was a special immunity for negligence in respect of acts or omissions in the conduct of litigation. The authorities concerned barristers, but the immunity was regarded as extending to a solicitor acting as an advocate.[91] The House of Lords in *Rondel v. Worsley*[92] held that a barrister was immune from action in respect of his or her conduct at trial.[93] The immunity was justified by public policy:

> "mainly upon the ground that a barrister owes a duty to the court as well as to his client and should not be inhibited through fear of an action by his client, from performing it; partly on the undesirability of relitigation as between barrister and client of what was litigated between the client and his opponent."[94]

3–045   This immunity appeared to be accepted in the period immediately after, but was limited, by the House of Lords in *Saif Ali v. Sydney Mitchell & Co.*,[95] which meant that the immunity extended only to pre-trial work[96] which was:

> "so intimately connected with the conduct of the cause in Court that it can fairly be said to be a preliminary decision affecting the way that cause is to be conducted when it comes to a hearing."[97]

Some people have reacted with surprise to the existence of the immunity.

---

[87] [1995] 1 All E.R. 691, and see C. Kessel, "Solicitor's professional negligence" (1995) N.L.J. 499 and 537.

[88] See Jackson and Powell (2002) and Jones (2001).

[89] See above, paras 3-037 and 3-041.

[90] See above, para. 3-038.

[91] *Saif Ali v. Sydney Mitchell & Co.* [1980] A.C. 198, at pp. 215, 224 and 227. The matter was put beyond doubt by the Courts and Legal Services Act 1990, s. 62 which states that anyone who was not a barrister but lawfully provided any legal services had the same immunity as a barrister.

[92] [1969] 1 A.C. 191.

[93] For a history of the immunity, see M. Seneviratne, "The rise and fall of advocates' immunity" (2001) 21 L.S. 644, at pp. 645–646.

[94] *per* Lord Wilberforce in *Saif Alt v. Sydney Mitchell & Co.* [1980] A.C. 198, at p. 212.

[95] [1980] A.C. 198.

[96] For the scope of the immunity, see Seneviratne (2001), at pp. 646–649.

[97] *Per* McCarthy P. in *Rees v. Sinclair* [1974] 1 N.Z.L.R. 180, at p. 187, endorsed by Lords Wilberforce, Diplock and Salmon. Lord Russell and Lord Keith favoured a wider test under which immunity would be extended to all work in connection with litigation.

For example, the Complaints Commissioner for the Bar Council:

> "It must have puzzled laymen (it certainly did me) why a barrister could not be sued for negligence for work he did in Court. In my early days, I had it explained to me and understood the reason for it but, nevertheless, I had a feeling of unease. This was echoed by a number of lay organisations and individuals."[98]

This "highly controversial" immunity has been abolished by the House of Lords in *J S Hall & Co. (A Firm) v. Simons; Woolf Seddon (A Firm) v. Barrett; Roberts & Hill (A Firm) v. Harris (conjoined appeals)*.[99] The public policy arguments that had been said to have been in favour of the immunity were all dismissed by the House of Lords. The arguments in favour were (1) that the barrister owes a duty to the court that transcends any duty to the client and that the necessary confidence between barristers and judges would be undermined by barristers' fear of suits; (2) that there should be a general immunity from legal action for all participants in a trial because of the adverse effects on the administration of justice if the situation were otherwise; (3) that the "cab rank rule" would be difficult to enforce if barristers had to take on clients who could then pursue actions against them, and (4) that relitigation of cases is undesirable and the correct method of challenge is via an appeal and not by collateral means.[1] For the majority of the House of Lords,[2] none of these reasons were sufficient to warrant the retention of the immunity, though for the minority,[3] there was a public interest in maintaining the immunity for barristers involved in criminal cases.

The most significant argument in favour of the immunity, and the point at which the members of the court divided in relation to criminal procedure, was the collateral attack argument. This argument was inadequate because, whilst there was a risk of cases of collateral attack, there are other more appropriate means whereby it can be handled through the abuse of court procedure relevant to both civil and criminal cases,[4] and where a case is brought against an advocate, poor cases could also be struck out through the summary procedure, and they would be less likely to attract funding support since negligence cases are not supported through the Community Legal Service.[5] In any case, where there is a wrong there ought to be a

---

[98] Bar Council Complaints Commissioner, *Annual Report 2000* (2001), at para. 7.
[99] [2000] 3 All E.R. 673. Hereafter: *Arthur Hall v. Simons*. For significant criticism of the old rule, see P. Cane, *Tort Law and Economic Interests* (2nd ed., 1996), pp. 233–238 and J. Hill, "Litigation and Negligence: A Comparative Study" (1986) 6 O.J.L.S. 183.
[1] See C.G. Veljanowski and C.J. Whelan, "Professional Negligence and the Quality of Legal Services — An Economic Perspective" (1983) 46 M.L.R. 700, at pp. 711–712 and Seneviratne (2001), at pp. 651–657.
[2] Lords Steyn, Browne-Wilkinson, Hoffmann and Millett.
[3] Lords Hope, Hutton and Hobhouse.
[4] The applicability of this procedure in relation to criminal cases under the House of Lords decision in *Hunter v. Chief Constable of West Midlands* [1982] A.C. 529 was particularly important for the majority, but was not sufficient for the minority, which was why they would have retained the immunity in criminal cases. There is also the wasted costs jurisdiction, see below, para. 3-047.
[5] *Arthur Hall v. Simons*, at pp. 680–681, *per* Lord Steyn, and pp. 699–704 *per* Lord Hoffmann. For the differences on criminal cases, see pp. 717–723, *per* Lord Hope, pp. 726–733, *per* Lord Hutton, and pp. 738–742 and 743–749 *per* Lord Hobhouse.

remedy and there has to be very good reason for not providing a remedy which the majority thought was not present.[6]

3–046   The duty to the court argument (otherwise known as the divided loyalty argument) was dismissed because, *e.g.* where there was a conflict of duty between that owed to the client and that owed to the court, the duty to the court would prevail; the existence of two such interests that might compete was an insufficient reason for an immunity as many professionals, particularly doctors, have to handle such competing interests; there was no evidence[7] that the fears of vexatious clients were likely to eventuate often or have an impact upon an advocate's practice. Further, it cannot be negligent to act in accordance with the duty to the court, so there could not be a successful action for negligence in any such case.[8]

The remaining two arguments were dismissed readily by all the judges as not being at all strong in support of any immunity. The witness analogy argument was predicated on the need to encourage freedom of speech in court, which has nothing to do with an advocate's immunity, so the argument "has on analysis no or virtually no weight at all".[9] As regards the cab rank rule argument, it could not support any solicitor immunity and "its impact on the administration of justice in England is not great."[10]

(ii) Wasted costs order

3–047   A wasted costs order may be made against a barrister or a solicitor.[11] Such a jurisdiction as applied to solicitors has been available since 1939.[12] The Courts and Legal Services Act 1990 extended the order to barristers and other representatives.[13] "Wasted costs" are those incurred by a litigant "as a result of any improper,[14] unreasonable[15] or negligent act or omission" by any legal or other representative, and the court must consider that it is unreasonable to expect the litigant to pay them.[16] General guidance in civil

---

[6]   *ibid.*, p. 683 *per* Lord Steyn & pp. 689–690 *per* Lord Hoffmann.
[7]   The wasted costs order had presented no such problems and, in Canada, there was no adverse consequence from the lack of an immunity: *Arthur Hall v. Simons*, at pp. 681–684, *per* Lord Steyn, and pp. 690–697, *per* Lord Hoffmann.
[8]   *ibid.*, at p. 687, *per* Lord Steyn, and Seneviratne (2001), at p. 652.
[9]   *Arthur Hall v. Simons*, p. 680 *per* Lord Steyn & pp. 697–699 *per* Lord Hoffmann.
[10]   *ibid.*, p. 680 *per* Lord Steyn. See also pp. 687–688 & 697 *per* Lord Hoffmann and p. 714 *per* Lord Hope.
[11]   The procedure for a wasted costs order in civil proceedings is found in the Civil Procedure Rules, r. 48.7.
[12]   *Myers v. Elman* [1940] A.C. 282.
[13]   Supreme Court Act 1981, s. 51, as amended by the Courts and Legal Services Act 1990, s. 4. See S. Fennell, "Wasted costs after the Courts and Legal Services Act 1990" (1993) 9 P.N. 25.
[14]   This includes conduct which would be regarded as a serious breach of professional conduct and also conduct which "according to the consensus of professional (including judicial) opinion can be fairly stigmatised [as improper]:" *Ridehalgh v. Horsefield* [1994] 3 All E.R. 848, at p. 861 .
[15]   It includes conduct which is vexatious or designed to harass the other side, and the motive for such action is irrelevant. Conduct is not unreasonable simply because it leads to the "wrong result". "The acid test is whether the conduct permits of a reasonable explanation:" *Ridehalgh v. Horsefield*, at pp. 861–862.
[16]   Supreme Court Act 1981, s. 51(7).

cases has been provided by the Court of Appeal in *Ridehalgh v. Horsefield*,[17] which also apply in criminal cases.[18] The court exercises a discretion at two stages: first in determining whether to provide the legal representative with the opportunity to show cause why an order should not be made and further proceedings will not always follow; secondly, even if the criteria are satisfied, the court is not bound to make an order, but would have to give sustainable reasons for not doing so.[19] One major issue[20] was in relation to negligence. The Court decided that negligence is to be understood "in an untechnical way to denote failure to act with the competence reasonably to be expected of ordinary members of the profession."[21] It is only appropriate to make an order "when, with all allowances made, an advocate's conduct of court proceedings is quite plainly unjustifiable."[22]

5. Social Background, Entry and Training

(a) Social background

Lawyers are an "elite professional group with high status, substantial earning potential and a key role in applying and administering the law."[23] Lawyers predominantly come from middle class homes.[24] The same is true of law students. The Law Student Survey shows that only a minority of

3–048

---

[17] [1994] 3 All E.R. 848.

[18] *ibid.*, p. 868.

[19] *ibid.*, pp. 867–868.

[20] Other issues, both substantive and procedural, include the following. (1) A legal representative is not to beheld to have acted improperly, unreasonably or negligently simply by acting for a party who pursues a hopeless case, because advocates are obliged to follow a client's instructions after advising against pursuing such a case. However, if the advocate crosses that line and lends assistance to proceedings which are an abuse of the court, that is another matter: *ibid.*, p. 863. (2) Courts must bear in mind the peculiar responsibility of a lawyer acting for people assisted by the legal aid scheme: *ibid.*, p. 864. (3) Whilst the representatives of the applicant for an order may anticipate that he or she will relieve the lawyers from their obligations of confidentiality in relation to privileged communications, account must be taken of the fact that this may not be the case for the other side's lawyers, and the other side is not obliged to release the obligation, which would, in effect, before the case for the applicant: *ibid.*, p. 866. (4) There must be a causal link between the conduct of the legal representative and the wasted costs: *ibid.*, p. 866. (5) Simple reliance on the advice of counsel will not avoid the jurisdiction, although it will be more reasonable to do so in the more specialist cases: *ibid.*, p. 866. (6) Threats to apply for an order must not be used as intimidation in litigation, but notice of a view that the other side's conduct could lead to such an order is acceptable: *ibid.*, pp. 866–867. (7) In general no application should be made until after the end of the trial: *ibid.*, p. 867. (8) Whilst normally the applicant will be one of the parties to litigation, the court may initiate the inquiry itself. Guidance is given as to the nature of the inquiry and then the procedure to be adopted: *ibid.*, p. 867.

[21] *Ibid.*, p. 862. Thus it is not necessary to establish all the criteria under the tort of negligence.

[22] *Ibid.*, pp. 864–865.

[23] M. Shiner, "Young, gifted and blocked! Entry to the solicitors' profession" in P. Thomas (ed.), *Discriminating Lawyers* (2000), at p. 87, who actually made the point only about solicitors, but it applies also to barristers.

[24] See Abel (1988), pp. 74–76 and 170–172 and Table 2.21: Royal Commission on Legal Services, *Report, Volume 2* (1979), pp. 57–61; S. Vignaendra, *Social Class and Entry into the Solicitors' Profession* (Law Society Research Study No. 41, 2001).

students' parents were engaged in working class occupations and that a much greater proportion of them had parents who had been to university than was the case in the general population.[25] There is clear evidence that the system of admissions to law degrees perpetuates the class structure of the legal profession.[26] Most lawyers are graduates[27] and so the social imbalance seen at the academic stage of qualification maintains the social imbalance at the professional stage. Universities are meeting the challenge to broaden the basis upon which students are admitted to law schools.[28] Universities also endeavour to widen the range of students participating in education. Since 1988, there have been more women entering law schools than men.[29] Whilst there is no suggestion of illegal discrimination in the allocation of places on law degrees, the financial demands of qualification make it easier for someone from a relatively secure financial background to succeed.[30]

We turn now to consider gender and race issues in the legal profession. We do this because, as Shiner states, it matters for fairness reasons and also for the provision of legal services:

"Laws are not created or administered in a cultural vacuum and it may be argued that the legal profession should broadly reflect the composition of the society that it serves. Opponents of such a view may reject it on the grounds that it is idealistic or even naïve. It is, however, important to distinguish between a situation in which the skewed composition of the profession reflects broad social forces (for example, those pertaining to access to higher education) and that in which biases from within the profession create, or reinforce, inequality. If certain communities face discrimination in the process by which the legal profession recruits its members, then how legitimate are any claims that the profession may make in terms of representing these communities? Equally, in such circumstances, what confidence can these communities have in the broader services provided by the legal profession."[31]

3–049   Both the Law Society and the Bar Council take equal opportunities[32] with increasing seriousness. The passage of the Sex Disqualification (Removal) Act 1919 made it possible for women to become solicitors, and the theoretical possibility of women becoming barristers became a reality. However, women

---

[25] D. Halpern, *Entry into the Legal Professions* (Law Society Research Study No. 15, 1994), pp. 21–24; E. Duff, M. Shiner, A. Boon with A. Whyte, *Entry into the Legal Professions.* (Law Society Research Study No. 39, 2000); Vignaendra (2001). See also M. King, M. Israel and S. Goulbourne, *Ethnic Minorities and Recruitment to the Solicitors ' Profession* (1990), pp. 32–34.

[26] See Abel (1988) Chap 18, esp. pp. 271–275; Vignaendra (2001); and King, Israel & Goulbourne (1990), pp. 32–34 and 37–52. See also P. McDonald, (1982) 9 J.L.S. 267 and R.G. Lee, (1984) 18 L.T. 165.

[27] Law Society, *Annual Statistical Report 2000* (2001), Chaps. 6 and 7, particularly Table 10.7.

[28] All law schools are happy to consider applicants with non-traditional qualifications, but see C. McGlynn, *The Woman Lawyer: Making the difference* (1998), at pp. 10–12.

[29] Law Society, *Annual Statistical Report 2000* (2001), para. 10.5; and C. McGlynn, *The Woman Lawyer: Making the difference* (1998), at p. 7.

[30] See below, paras 3-051–3-053.

[31] Shiner (2000) at p. 87.

[32] Their equal opportunities policies are not concerned solely with discrimination on the grounds of gender and race, but also, *e.g.* with sexual orientation and disability.

did not enter the profession in significant numbers until about 30 years ago. Now, a higher proportion of entrants are women.[33] Therefore, the proportion of women in the profession is growing.[34] However, the evidence indicates that women are less well paid than men.[35] Women have not been well represented at the upper echelons of both branches[36] nor even in academic law.[37] Women are, for example, more likely to remain as assistant solicitors than men.[38] Partnership is, on average, achieved within 10–19 years' experience. With that experience, 84 per cent of men make partner, but only 58 per cent of women.[39] The following table reflects the position of women solicitors as at July 31, 2000 and demonstrates the conclusion that women are still finding it more difficult to make progress through the profession:[40]

---

[33] In 1999–2000, 53.1% of all admissions to the solicitors' roll were women: Law Society, *Annual Statistical Report 2000* (2001), Table 10.5. In 1996–97, 47% of the traineeships registered with the Law Society were held by men and 53% were held by women: McGlynn (1998), Table 3.1. Also in that year, 52% of the people admitted to the profession were women: *ibid.*, Table 4.1. In 1996–97, 42% of the people taking the BVC were women, an increase on previous years: *ibid.*, Table 5.1.

[34] In 2001, 28% of barristers were women, and in 2000 that figure was 26%: BDO Stoy Hayward (2001), at p. 9. The rate of increase in the proportion of women solicitors is faster than that of women barristers: *ibid.*, Table 6.

[35] McGlynn (1998), at p. 83 reporting research by the Trainee Solicitors Group that revealed that women on average were paid £779 per annum less than men.

[36] In 1997, women accounted for only 16% of partners in solicitors' firms: McGlynn (1998), p. 95. A 1997 survey revealed that 27% of new partners in the largest solicitors firms were women: *ibid.*, p. 96. There are very few senior women at the Law Society: *ibid.*, pp. 97–98, and there has never been a woman president of the Society. In 1998, only 17% of silks were women, though 22% of women applicants for silk were successful as compared with 11% of men applicants: *ibid.*, Table 6.2. The Bar Council comprises 119 members of whom 28 were women (of whom 9 were representing barristers of less than 7 years' call): The General Council of the Bar, *Annual Report 2000* (2001), at pp. 26–27. There has never been a woman judge in the House of Lords. In 2001, the Lord Chancellor, all the House of Lords judges, the Lord Chief Justice, the Master of the Rolls, and the Vice-Chancellor were men. The President of the Family Division was a woman (Butler-Sloss P., the first woman ever to hold such a senior judicial position). Of the 35 Court of Appeal judges, 2 were women (Hale L.J. and Arden L.J.). Of the 17 judges in the Chancery Division, all were men. Of the 73 judges in the Queen's Bench Division, 5 were women. Of the 17 judges in the Family Division, 3 were women. So, of the 159 most senior judges, 11 were women: [2001] 3 All E.R., at pp. Iv–vi. In 1999, women represented 4% of circuit judges, 5% of recorders, 5% of assistant recorders, 4% of district judges and 135 of stipendiary magistrates: McGlynn (1998), Table 7.1.

[37] The number of women professors continues to rise, but there are still many law schools with few, if any, senior women. McGlynn's research reveals the following picture about the number of academics in the law schools she surveyed at October 1, 1997: McGlynn (1998), at Table 2.1.

	Men	Women	Total	% women
Professors	258	43	301	14
Senior staff	585	394	979	40
Lecturers	489	409	898	46
Total staff	1,332	846	2,178	39

[38] Law Society, *Annual Statistical Report 2000* (2001), paras. 2.9–2.10 and Tables 2.9 & 2.10.

[39] Law Society, *The Solicitor's Profession in England and Wales* (2001), p. 65.

[40] Law Society, *Annual Statistical Report 2000* (2001), Table 2.9.

	Men		Women		Total	
Position in firm	No.	%	No.	%	No.	%
Partners	23,108	52.8	5,418	23.9	28.526	42.9
Sole practitioners	3,582	8.2	912	4.0	4,494	6.8
Associate solicitors	1,993	4.6	1,816	8.0	3,809	5.7
Assistant solicitors	12,352	28.2	13,769	60.8	16,121	39.3
Consultants	2,487	5.7	375	1.7	2,862	4.3
Other private practice	260	0.6	373	1.6	633	1.0
All positions	43,782	100.0	22,663	100.0	66,445	100.0

Whilst the picture is constantly improving, it is not a matter about which anyone can afford complacency and some would argue that there is clear evidence of gender-based discrimination that must be tackled.[41] The idea that there is "trickle up"[42] which will solve the problem is neither sufficient nor convincing,[43] although no-one would argue for people being promoted to senior positions when not skilled sufficiently to perform the relevant tasks.

It is not only in terms of recruitment and promotion that women have faced significant problems. Work practices and ethics adopted by the professions have added to the problems. Considerable attention is now being paid to endeavouring to keep women in the profession,[44] not only because it is right so to do, but also because it is economically efficient so to do.[45] A variety of approaches have, therefore been adopted to endeavour to facilitate women staying in the profession and returning should they leave temporarily.[46] However, it must also be recognised that there is the danger that any work pattern other than the full time, over- worked position for many solicitors may result in barriers on progression appearing.[47] These barriers need to be considered carefully. The range of problems will be somewhat different for barristers, in part because they are self-employed.

---

[41] McGlynn (1998). For a view that the matter, in relation to law schools, is much more complicated, see F. Cownie, "Women in the Law School — Shoals of Fish, Starfish or Fish Out of Water?" in P. Thomas (ed.), *Discriminating Lawyers* (2000).

[42] This refers to the length of time that it takes for people to be eligible for senior positions in the law.

[43] McGlynn (1998), p. 96.

[44] More women than men leave the profession: P. Marks, *Solicitors' Career Structure Survey* (1988), p. 1 and McGlynn (1998).

[45] This reflects the costs of training solicitors, in particular, and firms not wishing to have 'wasted' their investment by seeing too many people leave the profession temporarily or permanently too early.

[46] McGlyyn (1998), pp. 100–112; Law Society, *Equal in the Law* (1988), pp. 20–21.

[47] Consider the discussion of promotion to partnership in the large City firms in R. G. Lee, "Up or Out — means or ends? Staff retention in large firms" in P. Thomas (ed.), *Discriminating Lawyers* (2000).

However, chambers can do much to put forward or hold back any individual barrister. Therefore, the equal opportunities codes for both solicitors and barristers are crucially important in achieving a proper and freely chosen representation of women and men.

There are few formal complaints of sex discrimination, but there is **3–050** evidence that fear of discrimination has, at least in the past, put off some women and ethnic minorities.[48] The Law Society has a principle of professional conduct outlawing discrimination and in 1995 the Anti-Discrimination Rules came into effect. They require every firm to have an anti-discrimination policy, with the Law Society's Model Anti-Discrimination Policy applying in lieu.[49] The Code of Conduct for the Bar contains provisions to prevent sex discrimination by a practising barrister both generally and in particular in relation to pupillage.[50] Further, the Sex Discrimination Act 1975 applies to employment in the solicitors' profession and to the offer of pupillage and tenancy at the bar.[51]

As regards opportunities for people from ethnic minorities,[52] the Royal Commission on Legal Services concluded that the position was unsatisfactory and that trends were unfavourable.[53] As with issues related to gender, there are concerns about entry to university and subsequent entry to the profession. In 1999, the percentage of ethnic minority students with a place

---

[48] M Shiner & T. Newburn, *Entry into the profession* (1995).
[49] Law Society, *The Guide to the Professional Conduct of Solicitors* (1999), Chap. 7.
[50] *Code of Conduct*, paras. 204, 303, 305.1. Barristers in independent practice are obliged to have regard to it: para. 303. The Equality Code is concerned with discrimination on a wide range of grounds and provides guidance to stop or prevent unlawful and prohibited discrimination and guidance on harassment. It also has detailed provisions in relation to selection procedures for pupils and tenants so that all applications are considered on an equal and non-discriminatory basis. A chambers selection procedure must be followed and it is recommended that chambers join the Bar Council's pupillage admissions and clearing house scheme (PACH) and the online pupillage application system (OLPAS). The code is also concerned to ensure that there can be equality of opportunity in chambers, so, *e.g.* roles and duties of pupils are to be identified and there must be fair methods for distributing briefs and work amongst pupils. Fairness must also apply to the recruitment of tenants. There is also a requirement for monitoring to ensure compliance and a scheme for complaints, with the ultimate sanction being a reference to the Professional Conduct Committee (see above, paras 3-041 and 3-042).
[51] The 1975 legislation was amended to achieve this by the Courts and Legal Services Act 1990, s. 64.
[52] For revealing and challenging research on the perspective of Black and Asian solicitors, see S. Vignaendra, M Williams and J. Garvey, "Hearing Black and Asian voices — An exploration of identity" in P. Thomas (ed.), *Discriminating Lawyers* (2000).
[53] Royal Commission on Legal Services, *Report, Vol. 1* (1979), pp. 501–504.

on a law degree was relatively high.[54] However, as there is a bias in favour of graduates from pre-1992 Universities (and in particular Oxford and Cambridge), if many of these students are in post-1992 Universities (as has certainly been the case), there is still likely to be a problem of access to the profession.

A 1989 survey showed that 5 per cent of all lawyers were from an ethnic minority.[55] In 2001, 7.3 per cent of barristers were from an ethnic minority, which comprises 3.7 per cent Asian, 2.6 per cent Blacks and 1.0 per cent other ethnic minority. As compared with solicitors, there are proportionately more Black barristers, but fewer Asian or other barristers than solicitors.[56] Ethnic minorities barristers continue to be poorly represented in the upper echelons of the profession. The 1989 survey showed that only 1 per cent of Q.C.s were from an ethnic minority.[57] The Thorpe Report discovered that, of the 1,028 benchers of the Inns of Court[58] in 1999, only 8 (0.8%) were from an ethnic minority.[59] The Report also shows that, while 35.8 per cent of male barristers of 20 years call were benchers in April 2000, only 6.7 of similarly qualified ethnic minority barristers were benchers. In 2000, there were 5,009 solicitors with practising certificates from ethnic

[54] Law Society, *Annual Statistical Report 2000* (2001), Table 7.4.

Ethnic group	Acceptances of	students from	U.K.
	Male	Female	Total
Black Carribbean	30	127	157
Black African	130	156	286
Black other	32	62	94
Indian	210	460	670
Pakistani	196	275	471
Bangladeshi	58	70	128
Chinese	26	60	86
Other Asian	55	107	162
All U.K. based ethnic minority acceptances	737	1,317	2,054
All U.K.-based acceptances	3,668	5,996	9,664
% from ethnic minorities	20.4	22.7	21.8

[55] General Council of the Bar, *Quality of Justice: The Bar's Response* (1989), pp. 267–268.
[56] BDO Stoy Hayward (2001), at p. 10.
[57] *Quality of Justice* (1989), p. 267.
[58] Benchers are the senior members of each Inn of Court.
[59] *The Times March* 4, 2002, p. 10.

minorities, which was 6.1 per cent of all solicitors and 7.0 per cent of all solicitors where there was information about ethnicity.[60]

If the cause of the poor picture is discrimination and it is hard to avoid the conclusion that there must be at least some discrimination, some action has been taken, but clearly far more needs to be done. The Thorpe Report was of the view that "The Inns [of Court] . . . have made little effort to redress the balance despite its equality code introduced in 1997."[61] Whether the 50 recommendations made by the Thorpe Report make a difference remains to be seen, but the extent of influence and control that the Inns have over entering the profession demands that change occurs, and soon. The Solicitors' Professional Conduct Rules and the Bar's Equality Code both prohibit race discrimination.[62] The option of dealing with discrimination by affirmative action has been rejected,[63] but a desire to improve the position must be present so that the currently poor position does improve and soon.

(b) Entry and training

Entry to both branches of the profession is typically through a qualifying law degree or passage of Common Professional Examination (C.P.E.) for a non-law graduate,[64] followed by a vocational educational stage and a period of on-the-job training. The Law Society and the Bar Council jointly establish, with the academic legal profession, what is to be recognised as a qualifying law degree. Although there are serious tensions between the demands of the professional bodies and what Universities, as educators, wish to provide, agreement is reached on relatively broad parameters. The current *Joint Announcement on Qualifying Law Degrees* requires that a degree, to comply with the Academic Stage and be a qualifying law degree, must ensure that its graduates achieve "an appropriate level of academic ability, [and have] a basic body of knowledge and understanding of English

3–051

---

[60] Law Society, *Annual Statistical Report 2000* (2001), at Table 1.5. The following figures, in relation to solicitors with practising certificates, are taken from the Annual Statistical Reports for 1990, 1995 and 2000.

Ethnic origin	Number		
	1990	1995	2000
White/European	37,403	52,817	66,604
Afro-Caribbean	74	202	510
Asian	477	1,250	2,788
Chinese	98	270	586
African	20	93	387
Other ethnic origin	40	355	822
Unanswered/refused	4,969	4,878	–
Unknown	11,653	3,763	11,156

[61] *The Times*, 4 March, 2002, at p. 10.
[62] See above.
[63] R.L. Abel, *The Legal Profession in England and Wales* (1988), p. 78 and see *Quality of Justice* (1989), p. 267.
[64] For an institution to offer such a course, it must have the approval, by way of a validation, of the CPE Board.

Law." This is achieved through the degree covering the "seven foundations of legal knowledge". They are: Obligations I (Contract Law); Obligations II (Law of Torts); Criminal Law; Property Law (Land Law); Public Law (Constitutional and Administrative Law); Equity & the Law of Trusts; and The Law of the European Union (which has only been a compulsory element since 1995). In addition, students must have expertise in Legal Research. To maintain the currency of knowledge and to provide some safeguard for the public, there are also time limits within which a degree may be completed.[65] Law is not taken only as the initial stage for a professional qualification. It is an academic subject in its own right and, therefore, is taught and studied for its own sake. It is a very popular subject,[66] because it is interesting, challenging and its graduates are employable (whether in the legal profession or elsewhere).

Entry to the Bar is restricted, as students, to graduates and mature students[67] and, in other cases, to the transfer of qualified legal practitioners.[68] A student entrant must join one of the Inns of Court and complete the vocational stage.[69] The academic stage, qualifying someone to be admitted as a student, is satisfied by either a qualifying law degree or a C.P.E. pass. The vocational stage comprises the Bar Vocational Course[70] at an institution approved by the Bar Council.[71] At one time the only place at which the course, and its precursors, could be taken was the Inns of Court School of Law. Students who complete these two stages and comply with the keeping of terms requirements[72] are "called to the Bar."[73] They are entitled to call themselves barristers, but are not entitled to practise unless they complete 12 month's pupillage with a barrister of at least five years' standing,[74] and may not accept instructions until the second six months of pupillage.[75] The costs of entry to the Bar are high. They include tuition fees

[65] Of course what none of this handles is the propriety or suitability of the content of law degrees or the approaches taken in teaching. For some concerns about the curriculum and other law school issues and their effects on women in the law, see C. McGlynn, *The Woman Lawyer: Making the difference* (1998), pp. 12–18.

[66] In 1999, there were 9,090 law graduates: Law Society, *Annual Statistical Report 2000* (2001), Table 7.5. This figure refers only to those students graduating with a single honours qualifying law degree: *ibid.*, para. 7.6.

[67] The Consolidated Regulations of the Honourable Societies of Lincoln's Inn, Inner Temple, Middle Temple and Gray's Inn, reg. 2(a) and Sched. 2.

[68] *ibid.*, Part IV.

[69] *ibid.*, reg.2(c).

[70] This course was introduced in 1989–90. The crucial change from the old Bar Finals Examination is the introduction and enhancement of skills training and practical exercises in addition to knowledge-based subjects.

[71] BPP Law School, Cardiff Law School, College of Law, Inns of Court School of Law, Manchester Metropolitan University, University of Northumbria Law School, Nottingham Law School and University of West of England Law School.

[72] Consolidated Regulations, reg. 9, which requires attendance at 12 qualifying sessions, that is an event of an educational and collegiate nature arranged by or on behalf of an Inn of Court.

[73] Consolidated Regulations, reg. 22, which requires that a student in not eligible for call (a) when under 21; (b) before satisfying the obligations re keeping of terms, passing the BVC or the other eligibility requirements for transfers; (c) before completing and signing the call declaration and paying the relevant fee; (d) until their name and description has been screened within their Inn. In order to have been admitted as a student, certificates of good character are also required: *ibid.*, reg. 3.

[74] *ibid.*, Part V.

[75] *ibid.*, reg. 41.2.

for the B.V.C., which are around £8,000,[76] maintenance during that year, possibly funding during pupillage, keeping term fees and the purchase of special clothes. Barristers may not earn enough to live on for a number of years,[77] and, when paid work is done, payment may come in some considerable time later.[78] In 2001, there were 783 pupils, but the number of pupils as compared with the number of barristers has been falling since 1999.[79] So concerned is the bar about the cost of qualifying that, from the end of 2002, a requirement for chambers to pay pupils at least £10,000 per year plus travel expenses was introduced.[80]

Entry to the solicitors' profession consists, first, of an academic stage, by way of completion of either a qualifying law degree or a C.P.E. pass or by way of a transfer from another profession. In 1999–2000, 73.5 per cent of admissions to the roll were direct entrants through their initial degree routes. This comprises 51.7 per cent or 3,129 of entrants with a qualifying law degree, and 21.8 per cent or 1,321 with a C.P.E. pass.[81] 20.5 per cent entered as transfers: overseas lawyers (14.9 per cent), barristers (3.3 per cent), FILEX (1.8 per cent), and justices clerks (0.6 per cent).[82] Secondly, all candidates, who must be student members of the Law Society, must take and pass a Legal Practice Course at one of the institutions validated by the Legal Practice Course Board of the Law Society.[83] In 2000–01, there were 7,376 full time places and 1,500 part time places.[84] As with qualifying as a barrister, one of the main hurdles is finance. Tuition fees range from over £5,000 to just over £7,000, and in addition, maintenance has to be added. Whilst there is a range of possible sources of finances, the most likely are the student (or their family) or their future employer. Qualification as a solicitor

3–052

---

[76] It reflects the very high cost of a programme that demands considerable high level skills training.

[77] For barristers' earnings, see above, para. 3-026.

[78] See above, *ibid.*

[79] BDO Stoy Hayward (2001), p. 11: in 2001 there was 1 pupil per 14 barristers, whereas in 1999 there was 1 pupil per 13 barristers.

[80] *The Times*, March 11 2002, p. 8.

[81] Law Society, *Annual Statistical Report 2000* (2001), Table 10.5.

[82] *Ibid.* The route was unknown in 6.0% of cases.

[83] Anglia Polytechnic University, University of Central England., Bournemouth University, BPP Law School, Cardiff Law School, College of Law (Birmingham, Chester, Guildford, London, and York), De Montfort University, Exeter University, Glamorgan University, Hertfordshire University, Huddersfield University, Inns of Court School of Law, University of Central Lancashire, Leeds Metropolitan University, Liverpool John Moores University, London Guildhall University, Manchester Metropolitan University, Northumbria University, Nottingham Law School, Oxford Institute of Legal Practice, Sheffield University, South Bank University/North London University, Thames Valley University, University of the West of England, Westminster University, Wolverhampton University.

[84] Law Society, *Annual Statistical Report 2000* (2001), Table 9.3.

is completed by a two year training contract,[85] during which a professional skills course must be taken and passed.[86]

The financial demands involved in qualification to be either a barrister or a solicitor may have a significant impact on the composition of the profession. Whilst there are means of ameliorating this through the professions funding pupillage and training contracts, there are real concerns felt by students and being expressed by various observers. Whether funding is provided may be determined quite late in a student's degree or even whilst they are on their BVC or LPC. Thus, there is the possibility that a student may have to face the prospect of at least in the short term a significant debt. It is entirely possible that students from poorer backgrounds will face this prospect with more fear than others. At present, there is a sufficiency of LPC and BVC places. Whilst there is an argument that not all successful students can go on into the profession and so there should be fewer places, in fact the better argument is that there should be a larger number of places that students can take up if they wish and provide themselves with the chance of entering the profession as opposed to the decision being taken by others. The over supply of places can only be justified in this way. The idea that they are transferable qualifications is an extremely poor argument, since they are specifically tailored to the needs of the specific professions. Indeed, the old Lord Chancellor's Advisory Committee on Legal Education and Conduct concluded that there should be no restrictions on the numbers seeking to enter the profession through limiting the number of validated places or controlling the number of training contracts or pupillages. The downside of limiting the range of persons entering the profession would be an unacceptable consequence. Rather, realistic information should be provided to students about the opportunities in the professions; law schools should review their admissions policies and make greater use of non-normal admission criteria; funding provision should be made for students on conversion courses and the professional courses; there should be a review of professional sponsorship of legal education; and there should be a fundamental reassessment of the funding of law teaching in Universities.[87] In so far as any of these may be good ideas, they largely remain aspirations. One downside of increased sponsorship by law firms of the vocational stage of training is their increasing endeavour to control it, despite often having little understanding of the educational or maturation process for the students entering those programmes.

There is a significant public interest in admissions to the profession both in terms of the composition of the profession[88] and the need for quality assurance and the safety of the public by suitable and appropriate education and training. This was a reason why, after the Courts and Legal Services Act 1990 and until the Access to Justice Act 1999, the Lord Chancellor had a

---

[85] In 1999–2000, there were 5,285 traineeships registered with the Law Society, of which 56.9% were held by women and 15.8% by people from a known ethnic minority: Law Society, *Annual Statistical Report 2000* (2001), Tables 9.7 and 9.8. A significant number of these traineeships are in the large firms, which is why they dominate the training agenda: *ibid.*, Table 9.11.

[86] This course involves: advocacy and communications skills; finance and business skills; and client care and professional standards.

[87] *First Report on Legal Education and Training* (1986), Chap. 3.

[88] See above, paras 3-048–3-050.

committee (ACLEC) that advised on education and training matters.[89] That committee engaged in a major review of legal education. That review identified the need to ensure that lawyers must be capable of being flexible and diverse in knowledge and skills, and able to compete in domestic and global markets. At the same time, lawyers must continue to contribute to fundamental democratic values, including the protection of human rights and the provision of legal services for disadvantaged sections of society. There was also an idea that the vocational stage should be joint for intending barristers and solicitors. Little happened in consequence of this review, though it provided much food for thought at least for the degree providers, where it had recognised the value of a law as an academic subject worthy of study in its own right, taught for its own sake, and, therefore, not merely a feeder for the subsequent stages of legal training. Much has happened in law degrees, but these have been more a product of the general review of appropriate approaches to learning and teaching in higher education with, *e.g.* the adoption of a benchmark for law that attempts to indicate what a graduate should have acquired upon completion of a degree programme. The major current debates are between what the profession wishes to see its trainees doing on employment and how much of that can be achieved at one or other of the education and training stages. Now the Lord Chancellor is advised by the Legal Services Consultative Panel established by the Access to Justice Act 1999, which has taken over the function, in relation to education, of ACLEC. The Panel's work programme for 2001–02 includes informing itself of developments in the field of legal education.

6. Para-Legals

Most solicitors' firms employ people who are not solicitors but do **3–054** professional work similar to that of many solicitors: they are employed as para-legals. In 2000, of the 93,839 fee-earners employed by solicitors' firms, 30,284 were not solicitors.[90] Of course, not all were para-legals: some were consultants, some were barristers. Some para-legals will be legal executives, that is Fellows of the Institute of Legal Executives (ILEX). Whilst a formal qualification is not required to work as a paralegal, the best career route is likely to lie with seeking ILEX qualification. A student[91] takes Parts I and II of the ILEX examinations[92] and, on successful completion, becomes a Member. He or she will become a Fellow provided her or she is 25 years of age and has had at least five years' experience in a legal office, including two years after passing all the examinations. A Fellow, therefore, has a general spread of knowledge and expertise in a more limited area of work than a solicitor. The contribution which a Fellow can make is highly significant:

---

[89] *i.e.* the Advisory Committee on Legal Education and Conduct. As its title indicates, it also had a significant role in professional conduct issues.

[90] Law Society, *Annual Statistical Report 2000*, Table 4.1.

[91] Somebody may qualify as a student by way of educational attainment, being a mature student, or attaining the Preliminary Certificate in Legal Studies.

[92] Part I involves study of a syllabus introducing the student to most areas of law and legal practice which are encountered in the legal profession. Part II is satisfied by studying for and passing examinations in four specialist papers: three in law and one in related legal practice.

many Fellows will be as well versed as the majority of solicitors in their particular area of work. Fellows are bound by a Code of Professional Conduct. Someone may stay as a Fellow or it may be used as a route to qualifying as a solicitor.[93] The professional standing of Fellows has been enhanced considerably.[94] FILEX can secure rights of audience in the higher courts. Complaints about the way a complaint against a Fellow has been handled by ILEX are within the jurisdiction of the Legal Services Ombudsman.[95] Alternative routes to becoming a para-legal are by achieving an alternative qualification, such as an A level or a National Vocational Qualification in the subject.

Barristers' clerks have the rather different role in chambers of acting as office administrator/manager and accountant, and as business manager and agent for each individual barrister. The title "clerk" is, therefore, very misleading. Increasingly, they are being called practice managers or executive offices, as these titles more accurately reflect the work that they do. There is no professional obligation to employ a clerk. The obligation on barristers is to ensure that their practice is administered efficiently.[96-97] The clerk manipulates the flow of work in chambers by virtue of the functions of negotiating fees and arranging each barrister's timetable, and his or her relationships, built up over many years, with solicitors' firms. Increasingly, clerks are employed on formal contracts and are paid on salaries, rather than receiving a proportion of the barristers' fees.

7. CONCLUSION

No doubt the pace of change in the legal profession will continue. Increasingly, other professions are wishing to provide many of the services traditionally associated with lawyers. This means that lawyers look for other areas of work as well as endeavouring to ensure that they maintain their lead in terms of quality and efficacy of service over other service providers. Specialism will continue apace, though increasing size has its significant disadvantages for the control and running of firms of solicitors and sets of chambers, whether partnerships or groupings of like-minded individuals. The large firms will not only wish to specialise even further, but also to expand their international influence as far and as wide as possible, but it will no doubt be in expanding in Europe that such firms primarily concentrate upon. The impact of information technology will continue to make a significant impact on practice and not just as a means of acquiring up-to-date legal knowledge and of advertising services, but also of performing

---

[93] A Fellow may thereby gain admission to a C.P.E. programme, with some exemptions, and then must take the L.P.C. No training contract is required as that has, in effect, already been completed.

[94] This is despite failing to convince the Royal Commission on Legal Services to adopt its proposals for profit-sharing, enhanced pay for executives with ILEX qualifications, compulsory arrangements for day release and payment for courses: Royal Commission on Legal Services, *Report, Vol. I* (1979), pp. 406–417. See also R.L. Abel, *The Legal Profession in England and Wales* (1988), pp. 207–210.

[95] See above, para. 3-043.

[96-97] *Code of Conduct*, para. 403.

legal tasks.[98] So business principles and business practices will become of increasing importance. The professions will, appropriately be more diverse in make up. The profession will also grow in size. All this will have a significant challenge for the ethics of the profession. Ethics will no doubt be a subject of increasing interest to practitioners and academics alike. It is likely that there will be pressure to see its inclusion in all law degree programmes.

---

[98] The Carriage of Goods by Sea Act 1992, s.1(5) facilitates IT approaches to such documentation and their transaction as bills of lading and the Land Registration Act 2002, s.95 provides for the introduction of e-conveyancing.

CHAPTER 4

JUDGES

4–001 IN this chapter we consider the men and women who are appointed to adjudicate upon such disputes as are referred to a court or tribunal for determination. The term "judge" is used in the title of this chapter in its wide sense to cover all such persons. More commonly, however, the term is used in a narrower sense to cover those who are appointed to adjudicate in the House of Lords, the Supreme Court of England and Wales (*i.e.* the Court of Appeal, the High Court and the Crown Court) and county courts. In addition, some judicial functions are performed by officers known as "masters" and "registrars". "Magistrates" or "justices of the peace" sit in the magistrates' courts (and in some cases in the Crown Court[1]). Those persons who sit on tribunals are normally simply referred to as tribunal "chairmen" or "members," although there are some with special designations, such as the Social Security Commissioners,[2] the Special and General Commissioners of Income Tax, Immigration Adjudicators and the Commons Commissioners.

A. MAGISTRATES[3]

1. NUMBERS AND FUNCTIONS

4–002 On April 1, 2001 there were 28,735 active part-time lay magistrates or "justices of the peace".[4] There was also provision for the appointment of an unlimited number of District Judges (Magistrates' Courts) and deputies

---

[1] When they are known as "judges of the Crown Court": Supreme Court Act 1981, s.8(l).
[2] See above, pp.
[3] Major studies are Sir Thomas Skyrme, *The Changing Image of the Magistracy* (2nd ed., 1983); E. Burney, *J.P: Magistrate, Court and Community* (1979); M. King and C. May, *Black Magistrates* (1985); and R. Morgan and N. Russell, *The judiciary in the magistrates' courts* (HO, LCD, 2000) (LCD website). See also P. Darbyshire, "An Essay on the Importance and Neglect of the Magistracy" [1997] Crim. L.R. 627 (arguing that the magistrates' court has supplanted jury trial as the central criminal forum but that law makers and lawyers develop the common law and statute and academics shape their research and teaching around jury trial); and "For the New Lord Chancellor — Some Causes for Concern About Magistrates" [1997] Crim. L.R. 861.
[4] *Justicial Statistics 2000* p. 94.

(formerly stipendiary magistrates).[5] Each such judge is by virtue of his or her office a justice of the peace for every commission area.[6] In the City of London, the Lord Mayor and Aldermen used to be justices *ex officio*, but by virtue of the Access to Justice Act 1999 they are only justices if appointed by the Lord Chancellor in accordance with the Justices of the Peace Act 1997.[7] Magistrates sit in the magistrates' courts[8] and in the Crown Court,[9] perform certain administrative tasks such as the granting of liquor licences, issue arrest and search warrants and sign various forms for members of the public.

2. HISTORICAL ORIGINS OF JUSTICES OF THE PEACE[10]

The history of the justice of the peace as a judicial officer can be traced to the Justices of the Peace Act 1361, which provided:

"First, That in every County of *England* shall be assigned for the keeping of the Peace, one Lord, and with him three or four of the most worthy in the County, with some learned in the Law, and they shall have Power to restrain the Offenders, Rioters, and all other Barators, and to pursue, arrest, take, and chastise them according to their Trespass or Offence; and to cause them to be imprisoned and duly punished according to the Law and Customs of the Realm, and according to that which to them shall seem best to do by their Discretions and good Advisement; and also to inform them, and to enquire of all those that have been Pillors and Robbers in the Parts beyond the Sea, and be now come again, and go wandering, and will not labour as they were wont in Times past, and to take and arrest all those that they may find by Indictment, or by Suspicion, and to put them in Prison; and to take of all them that be not of good Fame, where they shall be found, sufficient Surety and Mainprise of their good behaviour towards the King and his People, and the other duly to punish, to the Intent that the People be not by such Rioters or Rebels troubled nor endamaged, nor the Peace blemished, nor Merchants nor other passing by the Highways of the Realm disturbed, nor put in the Peril which may happen of such Offenders ... [11]

The Crown had previously appointed keepers or conservators of the peace

---

[5] Justices of the Peace Act 1977, ss. 10A, 10B, substituted by the Access to Justice Act 1999, s. 78. See below, para. 4-013.
[6] *ibid.*, s. 10C(1).
[7] 1997 Act, s.21, repealed by the 1999 Act Sched. 15; 1999 Act, s.76(1). The Lord Mayor and Aldermen in office on September 27, 1999, were treated as having been appointed under s.5: 1999 Act, Sched. 14, para 21.
[8] Above, paras 2-020–2-030.
[9] Above paras 2-051–2-058, below, para. 4-012.
[10] On the historical development of the office see E. Moir, *The Justice of the Peace* (1969); J. H. Gleason, *The Justices of the Peace in England* (1969); L. J. K. Glassey, *Politics and the appointment of Justices of the Peace* (1979); N. Landau, *The Justices of the Peace 1679–1760* (1984); Sir Thomas Skyrme, *History of Justices of the Peace* (1994).
[11] This is still in force, apart from the words "and also to inform ... in Times past."

(*Custodes Pacis*) with powers to arrest suspects and initiate criminal proceedings: the Act of 1361 gave in addition the power to determine proceedings. In 1362 the justices were required to hold formal meetings four times a year: these became known as quarter sessions. Over the ensuing centuries, more and more administrative duties were imposed by statute on the justices, including such matters as the construction and maintenance of fortifications, highways, bridges and gaols, the fixing of prices and the recruitment of soldiers. The list of provisions to be implemented or enforced became lengthy and burdensome.[12] Indeed, until the nineteenth century, the business of local government was largely entrusted to the justices. Different functions were committed to one, two or three justices or to quarter sessions. The informal meetings of two or more justices out of quarter sessions came to be known as "petty sessions," the forerunner of magistrates' courts.

The persons appointed in the counties were generally from the "gentry". In the eighteenth century, the justices came into growing disrepute. The corruption of the Middlesex Justices, described by Edmund Burke as "generally the scum of the earth", was such that they were replaced for most purposes by metropolitan stipendiary magistrates. Elsewhere, their administration of the Poor Law and the Game Laws attracted much criticism. In the nineteenth century they lost most of their administrative functions to central government departments and the new, elected, local authorities, the process of transfer culminating in the Local Government Act 1888. At the same time, their judicial functions were extended, with more offences becoming triable at petty sessions, and with the establishment and development of their matrimonial jurisdiction.[13]

3. Appointment

4–003 The Commission of the Peace is a document issued by the Crown setting out in very general terms the functions of the justices.[14] The Commission areas are specified by the Lord Chancellor by statutory instrument.[15] Justices of the peace for any commission area are appointed in the name of the Queen by the Lord Chancellor,[16] or, in Greater Manchester, Merseyside and Lancashire, by the Chancellor of the Duchy of Lancaster.[17]

---

[12] In 1485 Lambard asked, "How many Justices, think you, may now suffice, without breaking their backs, to bear so many, not loads, but stacks of statutes?": 1 *Eirenarchia* (1581), Chap. 7. F. Milton (*The English Magistracy* (1967)) gives many examples of statutory provisions, including one forbidding a man who was not a Lord to wear a cloak that did not "cover his privy member and Buttocks (he being upright)" (p. 9).

[13] From the Matrimonial Causes Act 1878 onwards.

[14] Justices of the Peace Act 1997 s. 3; The Crown Office (Forms and Proclamations) Rules 1992 (S.I. 1992 No. 1730), as amended by S.I. 1996 No. 276, art. 2, and S.I. 2000 No. 3064.

[15] Justices of the Peace Act 1997, s. 1, substituted by the Access to Justice Act 1999, s. 74. See above, para. 2-020.

[16] *ibid.* s.5(1). The appointment of magistrates is dealt with by a Division of the Judicial Group within the Lord Chancellor's Department. The post of Secretary of Commissions is held by the Director-General of the Judicial Group within the LCD.

[17] *ibid.* s.26. The policy of the two offices is almost invariably identical: Skyrme (1983), p. 240. The Chancellor of the Duchy has concurrent powers with the Lord Chancellor on the appointment, removal and residence of justices, entry on or removal from the Supplemental List and records. On other matters the Lord Chancellor has exclusive powers.

The only formal qualification for appointment laid down by statute is that the person resides in or within 15 miles of the commission area for which he or she is appointed.[18] The LCD document, *How to become a Magistrate*[19] states that the Lord Chancellor will consider a candidate's personal suitability "regardless of ethnic origin, gender, marital status, sexual orientation, political affiliation, religion or, subject to the physical requirements of the office, disability." The six key qualities sought are good character; understanding and communication; social awareness; maturity and sound temperament; sound judgement; and commitment and reliability. Candidates should have a reasonable degree of knowledge of the area for which they wish to be appointed and are generally expected to have lived there for at least 12 months. They should have satisfactory health in order that they can carry out the duties of a magistrate; those with a disability are considered on their merits.[20] People under 27 or over 65 will not generally be appointed.[21] British nationality is not a requirement, but all candidates must be willing to take the oath of allegiance. The Lord Chancellor "will not appoint—

- a serving or recently retired police officer or a civilian employee of a police force or their spouse or partner

- a member of the Special Constabulary or their spouse or partner

- a traffic warden or their spouse or partner

- anyone who has a close relative (father, mother, son, daughter, brother or sister or in-law and some other relationships) who is employed as a police officer, special constable, a civilian employee in a police force or a traffic warden in the Petty Sessional Division (court area) to which they might be appointed

- a full time member of HM forces

- anyone, in addition to those above, whose work or community activities or, those of their spouse or partner, are such as to be clearly incompatible with the duties of a magistrate e.g. employees of the Crown Prosecution Service, Prison Service, Probation Service or Magistrates' Courts Service

- an undischarged bankrupt[22]

- anyone who, or whose spouse or partner, has been convicted of a serious offence or a number of minor offences[23]

- anyone who is a member of Parliament or has been adopted as a prospective candidate for election to Parliament or paid as a full time

---

[18] *ibid.* s.6. The Lord Chancellor can direct that this restriction shall not apply: s.6(2).
[19] LCD website.
[20] After a pilot study, a number of blind magistrates have been appointed. See LCD Press Notice 224/01.
[21] In 1997, the upper age limit was raised from 55: see LCD Press Notices 143/97 and 268/98.
[22] Such a person is disqualified for being appointed or acting as a JP; the disqualification ceases on discharge or annulment of the bankruptcy order: Justices of the Peace Act 1997, s. 65.
[23] All convictions of the applicant, include fixed penalty charges, and police cautions must be disclosed in the application form.

party political agent if part of their constituency is covered by the Petty Sessional Division to which they might be appointed."

Candidates must answer a "key" question on the application form:

"is there anything in your private or working life, or in your past, or to your knowledge in that of your family or close friends, which, if it became generally known, might bring you or the Magistracy into disrepute, or call into question your integrity, authority or standing as a magistrate?"

Sexual orientation need not be disclosed. Candidates are also asked to provide a self assessment against the six key qualities. There is no property qualification[24] and women became eligible in 1919.[25]

Justices are appointed on the advice of Advisory Committees. These were first established following recommendations of the Royal Commission on the Selection of Justices of the Peace of 1910[26] in response to complaints that the Benches were dominated by Conservatives.

There are over 100 committees with overall about 2,000 members,[27] generally one for each non-metropolitan county and metropolitan district, the City of London, some of the larger urban areas and each London commission area. Most of the county committees have sub-committees or area panels. County committees are normally chaired by the Lord Lieutenant; others now select their own chairmen. Most committees have eight to 10 members, and sub-committees about six to eight. The term of office is normally nine years. Appointments to a committee are made by the Lord Chancellor, on the recommendation of an appointments committee of the advisory committee which comprises the chairman (or a nominee) and two other members, one of whom must be a non-magistrate.[28] A majority of committee members are magistrates but non-magistrates form at least a third of committee membership, names being sought from the Cabinet Office public appointments unit, local businesses, employment and social groups and (usually) by local press advertisement. Committee members are given training. Bench chairmen may not be members of advisory committees or sub-committees or play any part in the selection process.[29] It has, indeed, been argued that magistrates generally should be excluded from member-ship: "Magistrates have no more business than Circuit judges to be appointing ... their colleagues."[30] Each committee and sub-committee must have at least one supporter of each of the main political parties and at least one who is politically uncommitted; beyond that the political balance should

---

[24] This was abolished by the Liberal government in 1906: Justices of the Peace Act 1906, s.l.

[25] Sex Disqualification (Removal) Act 1919. Appointments do not, however, appear to fall within the scope of the Sex Discrimination Act 1975: see Skyrme (1983), p. 51. The proportion of women to men has increased steadily—from 1:3.5 in 1947 to 1:1.1 in 1996, and 1:1.04 in 2001.

[26] Cd. 5250.

[27] 92 in England and Wales advising the Lord Chancellor; 17 advising the Chancellor of the Duchy of Lancaster: S. Humphreys, (2000) 56 *The Magistrate* 47. In 2000 there were also about 120 sub-committees.

[28] *ibid.*

[29] *ibid.*

[30] P. Darbyshire, [1997] Crim. L.R. 861, 866.

broadly reflect its area.[31] It is the practice to check with the party headquarters that they are known supporters. Until 1988, the names of the committee members were normally kept secret in order to keep them free from pressure and lobbying,[32] although the name and address of the secretary was published. In that year, the Lord Chancellor, Lord Mackay, announced that he had asked the committees to take steps to make themselves known. About half would have done so by the end of 1988, and it would be a requirement for all by 1992.[33]

A candidate can be recommended to a committee by any person or organisation, or can put himself or herself forward. In turn, the recommendations of the committee can be rejected by the Lord Chancellor.[34] All candidates are subject to a two stage interview process, the first to determine personal suitability, the second to test judicial aptitude by discussion of at least two case studies. Once personally suitable candidates have been identified, the Advisory Committee must then have regard to the number of vacancies and the need to ensure that the composition of the bench broadly reflects the community which it serves in terms of gender, ethnicity, geographical spread, occupation and political affiliation (currently used as a proxy for social balance).[35] The process is governed by the Lord Chancellor's *Directions to Advisory Committees*, which were substantially revised in 1998 to take account of recommendations of the Home Affairs Select Committee.[36] They have since been reviewed by an LCD Equality Working Group[37] but there has been no in-depth empirical study of the current arrangements.[38]

The main areas of difficulty have been those of politics and social and ethnic background.[39] The problems here are linked. The official position as to politics is stated in the Lord Chancellor's documents, *How to become a Magistrate*:[40]

Your political views are neither a qualification nor a disqualification for appointment. This information is required only to avoid the appointment of a disproportionate number of magistrates supporting any political party."

The Lord Chancellor requires, in the interests of balance, that the voting

---

[31] Lord Chancellor's *Directions to Advisory Committees*.
[32] The Inner London Advisory Committee was an exception; membership of the Nottingham Committee was revealed in 1966.
[33] Vol. 499, H.L.Deb., July 20, 1988, cols. 1311–1313. Lists may, for example, be available in local libraries; only a few are published on the Internet (*e.g.* Lancashire).
[34] In recent years he has rarely rejected a recommendation on the grounds of personal unsuitability, it being unlikely that he would have information about candidates other than that gathered by the Advisory Committee; recommendations have, however, been rejected on grounds of occupational and political balance: King and May (1985), pp. 29–30.
[35] LCD, *Judicial Appointments Annual Report 2000–2001*, paras. 5.6, 5.7.
[36] 1995–96 H.C. 52, *Judicial Appointments Procedures*.
[37] See below, para. 4-005.
[38] For earlier critical studies of the work of Advisory Committees, see Burney (1979), Chaps. 4 and 5; King and May (1985): see para. 4-005; P. Darbyshire [1997] Crim. L.R. 861,866–868.
[39] See R. Vogler. "Magistrates' Courts and the struggle for local democracy" in C. Sumner (ed.), *Censure, Politics and Criminal Justice* (1990), Chap. 4.
[40] LCD website.

pattern for the area as evidenced by the last two general elections should be broadly reflected in the composition of the bench.[41]

4–004   As regards politics, there have been a number of separate strands of thought. Firstly, some people have been recommended for appointment as a reward for political services rather than because of their fitness for the office. This was condemned by the Royal Commissions of both 1910 and 1946–48.[42] The latter noted that there were still "political appointments" in this sense, although their extent could not be stated with precision.[43]

Secondly, the 1910 Royal Commission stated unequivocally that "it is not in the public interest that there should be an undue preponderance of Justices drawn from one political party."[44] It is not clear whether this was intended to refer to the position nationally or the composition of particular benches, but the latter view seems to be emphasised today. It was certainly the contemporary preponderance of Conservatives on the bench that led to the appointment of both the Royal Commissions of 1910 and 1946–48, by, respectively, a Liberal and a Labour government. However, overall statistics kept of political affiliation are largely based on the declared position of each justice at the time of appointment and are thus of limited reliability.[45] The Home Affairs Select Committee has noted significant discrepancies, usually where areas with a significant Labour general election majority had "a majority of magistrates whose inclinations were towards the Conservative party", and concluded that the aim of balancing the bench to take account, *inter alia*, of political leanings, had not as yet been achieved.[46] Nevertheless, it is not at all unusual for the Lord Chancellor to refuse to accept recommendations because a certain party is under-represented.[47]

Thirdly, the attention may be focused on the political affiliation of *new appointees*. This was emphasised by the 1946–48 Royal Commission, which stated that if after preliminary selection on merit:

> "it is found that a considerable majority of the proposed new justices are of one political faith, the list should be revised with a view to seeing whether equally good, or better, nominations can be made from among members of political parties. If the answer is that they cannot, then the original list should stand."[48]

---

[41] Lord Chancellor's *Directions to Advisory Committees*.

[42] Note, above; *Royal Commission on Justices of the Peace* (Cmd. 7463, 1948).

[43] *ibid.*, para. 20.

[44] Cd. 5250, Summary of Conclusions: quoted in the 1946–48 Report (Cmd. 7463, p. 4).

[45] A full breakdown for each Bench in 1994/95 was given in a LCD Memorandum to the Home Affairs Select Committee: 3rd Report 1995–96 H.C. 52, *Judicial Appointments Procedures*, vol. II, pp. 174–183. They are now included in the *Judicial Appointments Annual Report*: see Report for 2000–2001, Annex G. As at April 1, 2001 (outside the Duchy of Lancaster), the figures were 36.2% Conservative; 25.5% Labour; 13.8% Liberal Democrat; 0.5% Plaid Cymru; 24% Other and Uncommitted.

[46] *ibid.* Vol. I, p. 1x.

[47] Skyrme (1983), p. 59. It can prove difficult to find suitable candidates with a Labour background. A survey by the Labour Campaign for Criminal Justice showed that in one in three of 140 constituencies studied, people were unwilling to put their names forward because two in three Labour party nominees were not appointed. Of 1,500 J.P.s appointed a year there were 100 Labour party nominees, although that did not take account of Labour voters who were not members: *The Observer*, February 2, 1983.

[48] Cmd. 7463, para. 84.

Fourthly, some have argued that political opinions should be ignored entirely.[49] This has, however, been regarded as impractical by successive Lord Chancellors. In 1998, Lord Irvine sought views as to whether it was still relevant to attempt to achieve a political balance on benches and Advisory Committees and sub-committees; it was essential to continue to secure a social balance, but it was not clear that political balance could now be considered an adequate proxy given the social changes in society, the diminishing importance of class based voting and the rise of other values and identities.[50] The Lord Chancellor ultimately concluded reluctantly that for the time being it remained the most practical measure of social background. While 45 per cent of consultation respondents supported removal of political affiliation as a balancing mechanism, only 13 per cent favoured adoption of a geo-demographic system in its place; such systems were, indeed, difficult to apply, explain and understand and expensive and cumbersome to operate.[51] Nevertheless, he remains committed to finding an alternative to political balance as a measure of social background.[52]

Both Royal Commissions recommended that justices be drawn from different social backgrounds. The 1946–48 Report stated that:

"Care must be taken to see that there are persons in the commission representative of various sections of the community. It is an advantage that a justice should have knowledge of the way of life of other classes than the class to which he belongs, and it is essential that there should be many among the justices who know enough of the lives of the poorest people to understand their outlook and then "difficulties.""[53]

Such surveys as there have been consistently show a preponderance of professional and intermediate occupations and the under-representation of manual workers.[54] A high proportion are retired.[55]

Efforts have been made to increase the proportion of wage earners. In 1968, loss-of-earnings allowances were introduced.[56] The Employment Right Act 1996[57] provides that an employer must give an employee magistrate reasonable time off.[58] However, as Lord Hailsham pointed out,[59]

---

[49] See the dissent by Lord Merthyr and two other members of the 1946–48 Royal Commission: Cmd. 7463, pp. 92–95.

[50] *Political Balance in the Lay Magistracy: A LCD Consultation Paper* (1998) (LCD website).

[51] LCD Press Notice 329/99, October 25, 1999.

[52] S. Humphreys, (2000) 56 *The Magistrate* 111.

[53] Para. 84.

[54] See Minutes of Evidence to the Royal Commission, Appendix 4; R. Hood, *Sentencing the Motoring Offender* (1972), Chap. 3; J. Baldwin, (1976) 16 Brit. Jo. Criminol. 171; Skyrme (1983), p. 64 (showing that in 1977 8.2 percent of the magistrates were manual workers); R. Henham, *Sentencing Principles and Magistrates' Behaviour* (1990), Chap. 5; Morgan and Russell (2000), para. 2.2.4.

[55] Morgan and Russell (2000), para. 2.2.4: 26% of magistrates across eight benches surveyed; 40% according to questionnaire returns.

[56] Justices of the Peace Act 1968. See now the 1997 Act, s.10.

[57] s.50(1) See A. Samuels, (1986) 42 *The Magistrate* 58. A refusal to pay the person for the time off may constitute a failure to comply with the duty: see *Corner v. Buckinghamshire County Council* [1978] I.C.R. 836.

[58] Magistrates who are public employees are customarily given 18 days' extra paid leave to enable them to sit. Many large private firms have made similar arrangements.

[59] (1981) 37 *The Magistrate* 166.

the legislation does not oblige an employer to give a magistrate a job, or to promote him or her if he or she has one. It provides no immunity from redundancy. Lord Mackay indicated that he was prepared to appoint people who were over 60 in order to complement the categories of people on the bench:

"For example, these days it is very difficult to find people who are in levels of manufacturing industry to go on the bench during their working lives. It is important however that people with that kind of background should be on the bench.[60]

These have been proper developments, but they seem to have had relatively little effect.

4–005 It is only comparatively recently that the ethnic background of magistrates has begun to be properly investigated. King and May's Cobden Trust report,[61] based on research conducted with the co-operation of the Lord Chancellor's Department, was in many respects critical. They found evidence of racial prejudice among some members of advisory committees and sub-committees, in the form of negative racial stereotyping. There was some evidence of direct racial discrimination, and considerable evidence of indirect discrimination in the procedure adopted and the criteria applied by selectors. There were no Afro-Caribbean and few Asians among the members of advisory committees. The procedures were inefficient and amateurish, with too much emphasis placed on interview performance, and the selection criteria of "suitability" and "balance" unacceptably vague. While in some areas there had been a significant increase in the number of black magistrates appointed, the proportion on the bench in many areas still fell far short of the proportion of black people in the local community. The number of black people coming forward as candidates was small. In the event, there was no discernible official reaction to the report.

The Lord Chancellor's Department conducted a national survey of the ethnic composition of the magistracy, based on the figures on January 1, 1987.[62] At that date there were 455 (1.92%) black magistrates out of 23,730 active magistrates. The estimated proportions of black people in the general population and in the 35–54 age range (within which magistrates are normally appointed) were, respectively, 4.69% and 3.92%. The proportional rate of appointment of blacks had increased steadily from 1.77% in 1980 to 4.57% in 1986. The report also argued that

"the available pool in the black population from which magistrates can be drawn has been, and almost certainly still is, much smaller than the pool in the general population."

This was based on the points that in 1986 less than half of the black population were born in this country; that the first priority of many immigrants would have been "to establish themselves and their families

---

[60] Vol. 503, H.L.Deb., January 19, 1989, col. 330.
[61] *Black Magistrates: A Study of Selection and Appointment* (1985), reviewed by R. Pearson, (1986) 13 J.L.S. 152.
[62] Published in (1988) 44 *The Magistrate* 77–78.

before being ready to take part in public life"; and that "cultural differences, such as those affecting the position of women in some groups, will have prevented many blacks from seeing themselves as candidates for the magistracy." The report "illustrated the progress being made in the appointment of black magistrates."

The absence in the survey of any local breakdown of the statistics was however, a significant omission.[63] The Home Affairs Select Committee noted that it had not received evidence claiming that there was an acute problem with the under-representation of ethnic minorities in the magistracy.[64] The proportion of ethnic minority appointments has been steadily increasing.[65] Figures for each Bench are now published in the *Judicial Appointments Annual Report*.[66] While, overall, the composition nationally is approaching ethnic representativeness, the lay magistracy remains disproportionately white in areas with very large ethnic minorities.[67] The appointment procedures have been revised substantially since King and May's critical report in the 1980s. They were reviewed in 2000 by an Equality Working Group, established as part of the LCD's response to the report of the Stephen Lawrence Inquiry to assess the extent to which they provide equality of opportunity and supported diversity. The Group found the procedures not to be fundamentally flawed and, indeed, had many good points, but that there was room for improvement in some areas. Most Advisory Committees make concerted efforts to attract applications from people from a wide range of backgrounds. Further steps could be taken to raise the profile of the magistracy among under-represented groups and particular revisions made to the *Directions to Advisory Committees*.[68] A shadowing scheme has been launched in co-operation with Operation Black Vote, a non-party political campaign supported by a broad coalition of Black organisations.[69] The Auld Report recommended that steps should be continue to be taken with a view to providing benches that reflect more broadly than at present the communities they serve.[70]

That a political and social balance is desirable has generally been assumed or asserted rather than explained. It is possible to detect three considerations: the interests of potential appointees; the need to maintain general public confidence in magistrates' courts; and the interests of defendants. The first factor lay behind the appointment of the Royal Commissions of 1910 and 1946–48, although the Reports played down what was clearly not a respectable consideration and placed more emphasis on the second factor.

[63] See N. Dholakia, (1988) 44 *The Magistrate* 119, arguing in favour of regular ethnic monitoring, a proposal which had previously been rejected by Lord Hailsham.
[64] 1995–96 H.C. 52. *Judicial Appointments Procedures*, Vol. I. p. 1x.
[65] From 5% to 9.3% between 1994 and 2000/2001: *Judicial Appointments Annual Report 2000–2001*, para. 5.10.
[66] See Report from 2000–2001, Annex G. The overall statistics outside the Duchy of Lancaster were 89.7% white; 2% Black; 2.4% Asian; 0.8% Other; 5% Not known, (cf. 1991 Census figures for England and Wales: 94% White; 2% Black; 3% Asian; 1% Other).
[67] Morgan and Russell (2000), para. 2.2.3.
[68] *Report of the Equality Working Group* (LCD, August 2000); Progress Chart (LCD, December 2000) (LCD website). The Group's recommendations were accepted.
[69] *Judicial Appointments Annual Report 2000–2001*. para. 5.21.
[70] Chap. 4, paras 59–68. Cf. M. Zander, *Response to the Auld Review* arguing that significant improvement in the balance of the magistracy was desirable but unlikely to happen*(www. lse.ac.uk/Depts/law)*.

For example, Lord Loreburn L.C. said in evidence to the 1910 Royal Commission:

> "I regard it as an indignity and an injustice that any section of opinion should be, in practice, excluded from a legitimate ambition, and I think that it is contrary to the public interest that the authority of the bench of justices should be weakened by any widespread suspicion that the members of it are not fairly selected."[71]

The subsequent Report[72] simply took up the second strand of this reasoning. The interests of actual defendants came a poor third. It will of course be a matter of "pot luck" whether a working class defendant enjoys the supposed benefit of a court with one or more justices thought to be better able than the others to understand his or her outlook and difficulties. The respective social backgrounds of juries and justices do not seem to figure significantly among the considerations that affect the defendant's choice between summary trial and trial on indictment.[73] Lord Mackay welcomed the increasing proportion of black magistrates on the basis that

> "In addition to the special knowledge and understanding of sections of the community which black magistrates can bring to the bench, their presence in a judicial capacity can be an important factor in reassuring black defendants, witnesses and others connected with legal proceedings that they will be treated impartially by the courts."[74]

A study[75] of 160 newly appointed magistrates in three English counties suggested that there were no significant differences according to social class in attitudes concerning penal philosophy, sentencing practice, the causes of crime, court procedure, and the role of the magistrate. It was noted, however, that there may have been a tendency to appoint magistrates with particular views, whatever the social class. There were differences in attitude related to different political background, with Conservatives tending particularly to be more punitive in their penal philosophy. The authors concluded that "although the relationship between attitudes and behaviour is a problematic one, there is nevertheless a good prima facie case for arguing that differences in viewpoint expressed here are also likely to be expressed in some way in procedural and sentencing policies."[76] An earlier

---

[71] Minutes of Evidence. Lord Loreburn was caught between the pressure imposed by Liberal politicians and his own feelings that appointments should be made on merit without reference to politics: R.F.V. Heuston, *Lives of the Lord Chancellors* (1964), pp. 153–158.

[72] Report, p. 8.

[73] A. E. Bottoms and J. D. McClean, *Defendants in the Criminal Process* (1976), Chap. 4. The research did show that defendants in general had a higher opinion of the Crown Court than the magistrates, for a variety of reasons.

[74] (1988) 44 *The Magistrate* 218, 219.

[75] R. A. Bond and N. F. Lemon, "Changes in Magistrates' Attitudes During the First Year on the Bench" in D. P. Farrington *et al.* (eds.), *Psychology, Law and Legal Processes* (1979), Chap. 8.

[76] *ibid.* p. 141. *Cf.* J. Hogarth, *Sentencing as a Human Process* (1971) (survey of magistrates in Ontario); A. K. Bottomley, *Decisions in the Penal Process* (1973), Chap. 4. By contrast, a study based upon simulated sentencing exercises found that differences of sentence could not be explained by the group composition of "benches" in terms of age, political affiliation, education, sex or length of experience: A. Kapardis, (1981) 145 J.P.N. 289–291.

English study had not, however, found there to be such a correlation.[77] Indeed, the most significant factor seemed to be the general attitudes of the bench to which a particular magistrate belonged. Accordingly, it may well be that social and political background may neither be perceived to be of significance by defendants, nor actually of significance in affecting the way they are dealt with, although the evidence on the latter point is not entirely clear.

4. Undertakings on Appointment

A person selected to be a justice must give certain undertakings before being appointed. These are to complete the required training, to carry out a fair share of magisterial duties (normally to sit for at least 26 half days a year[78]) and to resign if he or she fails to honour these undertakings or becomes unable to perform the duties of a justice through changes of residence, infirmity or any other cause, to inform the justices' (clerk if he or she is summoned for or charged with a criminal offence or becomes a party to civil proceedings, and to inform the Secretary of Commissions of any conviction or court order against him or her.

4–006

5. Training

Since 1953 it has been the duty of every magistrates' courts committee to provide courses of instruction for justices in their area, in accordance with arrangements approved by the Lord Chancellor.[79] All justices appointed since January 1, 1966[80] have been required to attend a course of basic training. Compulsory refresher training was introduced in 1980. From January 1, 1996, no magistrate may take the chair unless he or she has taken a fully recognised Chairmanship Course based on the Judicial Studies Board

4–007

---

[77] R. Hood, *Sentencing the Motoring Offender* (1972); *Cf.* Hood, *Sentencing in Magistrates' Courts* (1962), where the author's findings suggested that the social composition of a bench, in combination with particular community conditions, might affect the prison rate (pp. 76–78, 119–120).

[78] In practice, J.P.s are expected to sit more frequently: the Lord Chancellor expects an average annual attendance of between 35 and 45 half-days, the average to be determined by the Advisory Committee in consultation with the MCC and Bench Chairman: Circular from Deputy Secretary of Commissioners, July 20, 1999. (Magistrates Association website).

[79] See now the Justice of the Peace Act 1997, s. 64.

[80] See *The Training of Justices of the Peace in England and Wales* (Cmnd. 2856, 1967) (White Paper). The Lord Chancellor was assisted from 1974 by an Advisory Committee on Training, chaired by Boreham J. This replaced a National Advisory Council which had been set up to consider the introduction of compulsory training. The Committee was absorbed into the Judicial Studies Board (see below, pp.) with effect from 1985. The Board's functions with respect to magisterial training are discharged by its Magisterial Committee (see the *Judicial Studies Board Annual Reports*); its function in this context is to supervise the training, not (except in the case of District Judges (Magistrates' Courts)) to perform it.

syllabus within the previous six years.[81] In the late 1990s, training was remodelled by virtue of the Magistrates' New Training Initiative. Training requirements are now centred on the acquisition of competences and not a specified number of hours of training as with the previous arrangements. Training is linked to mentoring and appraisal, through which individual training needs can be identified. An evaluation in November 2000 found the basic concept and principle of MNTI to be acceptable, workable and sound and that, in the majority of the Magistrates' Courts Committees studied, implementation was going well; however, overall, there was too much variation in implementation. It made a variety of recommendations to assist further progress.[82] However, the Magistrates' Association has argued in particular that the competences need simplification and revision.

The Judicial Studies Board Magisterial Committee is responsible for monitoring training; it has undertaken to provide assurance to the Lord Chancellor that the training provided by Magistrates' Courts Committees satisfies the requirement of section 64 of the Justice of the Peace Act 1997. In 2000–01, it visited 57 MCCs to monitor training on the Human Rights Act 1998 and found it to be satisfactory in a few and good to excellent in the majority of MCCs. It has compiled a database of training materials, provided training courses for new Bench chairmen and induction and continuation seminars for District Judges (Magistrates' Courts).[83] The Auld Report[84] found that MNTI was an improvement on what had gone before but was much criticised for its complexity; for example, there were 104 competences even for those sitting as a wing member in the adult courts. There was a lack of consistency in magistrates' training from one MCC area to another. The Report recommended that ultimate responsibility for devising and securing training should be transferred from MCCs to a strengthened Judicial Studies Board; training should in the main be provided by justices' clerks and/or legal advisers after appropriate training for the purpose; District Judges (Magistrates' Courts) should also be involved; and the MNTI scheme should be refined. The last of these points has been taken up by the Judicial Studies Board and new draft competences were published for consultation in early 2002.

6. CONDUCT AND REMOVAL

4–008 A justice of the peace may be removed by the Lord Chancellor.[85] No grounds are specified in the Act. The Lord Chancellor also has power to direct that a justice be transferred to the "supplemental list" if he is satisfied either:

---

[81] (1991) *The Magistrate* 139–142; (1992) *The Magistrate* 86; E. Ralphs and G. Norman, (1995) *The Magistrate* 58. See *R. v. Brent JJ., ex p. Richards, The Times*, December 3, 1992, where a decision that the applicant had failed chairmanship training sessions and would not be allowed to take the chair in court was held to be invalid as being unfair and perverse on the facts.

[82] *Magistrates' New Training Initiative (MNTI) Evaluation of Implementation: Final Report November 2000* (JSB website).

[83] *Judical Studies Board Annual Report 2000–2001*, Chap. 6.

[84] pp.131–134.

[85] Justices of the Peace Act 1997, s. 5.

"(a) that by reason of the justice's age or infirmity or other like cause it is expedient that he should cease to exercise judicial functions as a justice for that area, or

(b) that the justice declines or neglects to take a proper part in the exercise of those functions."[86]

Justices are also automatically transferred to the supplemental list on reaching the age of 70, or, in the case of a justice who holds or who has held high judicial office, 75.[87] A justice who is on the list may not act as a justice except to authenticate a signature or written declaration, or to give a certificate of facts within his or her knowledge or of his or her opinion as to any matter.[88] He or she may, however, be authorised by the Lord Chancellor to sit in the Crown Court up to the age of 72.

In practice, a justice would only be removed for good cause. Most who leave office have to do so because they are unable to fulfil their share of the work or because they move outside the area.[89] The Lord Chancellor has stated that he has a "firm expectation that all magistrates will conduct themselves in such a way as to command the confidence of the community ... they serve." Misconduct is defined as "conduct which in the eyes of the community as a whole, reasonably calls into question a person's suitability to sit as a magistrate;" lack of competence as a "serious and demonstrable diminution of any of the six key qualities" or failure to reach required standards in relation to training programmes. It is recognised that the independence of the judiciary must be recognised and respected; the disciplinary procedure cannot be used to question judicial decisions taken by a magistrate.[90] Justices have been removed if they or a spouse have been convicted of an offence, although a conviction for a minor motoring offence will lead to a reprimand rather than suspension or removal. Convictions for drunken driving have in recent years led to suspension during the period of disqualification rather than removal. Justices have also been removed for refusing to apply a law he or she has found distasteful,[91] and for demonstrating outside her own courthouse in support of a defendant on trial inside.[92] Allegations of incapacity or misbehaviour are normally referred to the local Advisory Committee for investigation: if they conclude that the justice should be removed, that is reported to the Lord Chancellor.

---

[86] *ibid.* s.7(4).

[87] *ibid.* s.7(2).

[88] *ibid.* s. 9.

[89] Each year, about 1 per cent of all justices on the active list are required to resign for the first reason, and 1 per cent for the second: Skyrme (1983), p. 153.

[90] S. Humphreys, (2000) 56 *The Magistrate* 74, referring to the Lord Chancellor's *Directions to Advisory Committees.*

[91] Colonel Delmer Davies-Evans, who disapproved of certain regulations governing the use of petrol, was removed in 1947 (see Skyrme (1983), pp. 156–7). A Welsh justice who stated that she was not prepared to impose penalties on people who, non-violently, broke laws which she considered unjust to the Welsh language, resigned in 1972: R. Pearson in Z. Bankowski and G. Mungham (eds), *Essays in Law and Society* (1980), pp. 89–90; see also Lord Hailsham, (1972) 28 *The Magistrate* 132–134: in a similar case, Lord Gardiner required a Welsh magistrate to resign. A number of magistrates resigned rather than enforce the community charge.

[92] Her application for judicial review of the decision was rejected: *The Times*, September 25, 1985; (1985) 135 N.L.J. 976; Lord Hailsham, (1985) 41 *The Magistrate* 149.

If the justice does not accept the committee's finding he or she is invited to make further representations to the Deputy Secretary of Commissions, who advises the Lord Chancellor. A case in 1983 showed, however, that the Committee might not permit the justice to appear before them in person and might act on allegations of which he or she is not fully informed.[93] The current directions provide for a complaints investigation hearing by a panel of Advisory Committee members at the core of the procedures; and recognise that natural justice must be observed. The justice may attend the hearing and be accompanied by a colleague or legal representative, but the latter may only give advice and observe proceedings. Where the issue is lack of competence, the justices' clerk reports to the Advisory Committee; if it is satisfied that the decision about competency has been reached in the proper way and any review procedures have been exhausted, it makes a recommendation to the Lord Chancellor.[94]

7. DISQUALIFICATION

4-009   Justices are subject to the same common law rules as to disqualification for interest or bias as other judicial officers.[95] In addition, they are expressly disqualified from acting in a case involving a local authority if they are a member of that authority.[96] A celebrated case where a magistrate was sufficiently incautious as to admit actual bias was *R. v. Bingham JJ., ex p. Jowitt*.[97] The chairman of a bench hearing a speeding case, where the only evidence was that of the motorist and a police constable, said:

> "Quite the most unpleasant cases that we have to decide are those where the evidence is a direct conflict between a police officer and a

[93] *L. A. G. Bull.*, April 1983, pp. 9–12 (two magistrates removed on account of an "adulterous association", "conducted indiscreetly in a manner likely to give rise to scandal").

[94] S. Humphreys, (2000) 56 *The Magistrate* 74.

[95] Below, para. 4-036. For cases concerning justices see *R. v. Altrincham JJ., ex p. Pennington* [1975] Q.B. 549; *R. v. Smethwick JJ., ex p. Hands, The Times*, December 4, 1980 (decision on allegation of statutory nuisance against local authority quashed because one of the justices was the wife of the former chairman of the housing committee); *R. v. Liverpool City JJ, ex. p. Topping* [1983] 1 W.L.R. 119; *R. v. Weston-super-Mare JJ., ex p. Shaw* [1987] Q.B. 640 (magistrates' knowledge of other outstanding charges against the defendant: see R. Stevens, (1986) 150 J.P.N. 788; (1986) 150 J.P.N. 805); *R. v. Metropolitan Stipendiary Magistrate, ex p. Gallagher* (1972) 136 J.P. 80; *R. v. Birmingham Magistrates' Court, ex p. Robinson* (1986) 150 J.P. 1 (see J. N. Spencer, (1986) 150 J.P.N. 307); *R. v. Downham Market Magistrates' Court, ex p. Nudd* (1988) 152 J.P. 511 (see N. A. McKittrick, (1988) 152 J.P.N. 643) (magistrates' knowledge of defendant's previous record); *R. v. Cambridge JJ., ex p. Yardline Ltd and Bird* [1990] Crim.L.R.733 (member of Bench employed as consulting surveyor by local authority conducting prosecution for demolition of listed building); *R. v. Romsey JJ., ex p. Gale* (1992) 156 J.P. 567 (notes of concluding remarks prepared before all evidence heard); *R. v. Marylebone Magistrates' Court, ex p. Perry* (1992) 156 J.P. 696 (magistrate signed warrants while listening to evidence); *R. v. Eley JJ., ex p. Burgess*, (1993) 157 J.P. 484; *R. v. Marylebone Magistrates Court, ex p. Joseph, The Times*, May 7, 1993; *R. v. South Worcestershire JJ., ex p. Daniels* (1996) 161 J.P. 121 (justice consulted sentencing guidelines during cross-examination of the defendant). See generally M. Beloff, (2001) 165 J.P.N. 436.

[96] Justices of the Peace Act 1997, s. 66. For the rules relating to disqualification of licensing justices see the Licensing Act 1964, s.193 and *R. v. Barnsley Justices* [1960] 2 Q.B. 167.

[97] *The Times*, July 3. 1974.

member of the public. My principle in such cases has always been to believe the evidence of the police officer, and therefore we find the case proved."

The conviction was quashed.

8. Legal Liability

A justice of the peace (or a justices' clerk or assistant clerk exercising the functions of a single justice) enjoys a statutory immunity from any action for damages where he or she has acted in the execution of his or her duty and within jurisdiction. Where a justice (or clerk) has acted outside jurisdiction, but in the purported execution of his or her duty, an action will only lie if he or she has acted in bad faith.[98] The position is now similar to that of judges of superior courts.[99] A court may not order any justice, or justices' clerk or assistant clerk exercising the function of a single justice, to pay costs in any proceedings in respect of any act or omission of his or hers in the execution (or purported execution) of his or her duty; this does not, however, apply in relation to any proceedings where he or she is being tried for an offence or appealing against conviction, or in which it is proved that he or she acted in bad faith in respect of the matters giving rise to the proceedings.[1] If this provision prevents a court making a costs order, the court may instead order the Lord Chancellor to make a payment in respect of costs, in accordance with regulations.[2] In specified circumstances a justice or clerk may be (or is entitled to be) indemnified out of local funds in respect of costs reasonably incurred in or in connection with proceedings[3] in respect

4–010

---

[98] Justices of the Peace Act 1997, ss. 51, 52, as amended by the Access to Justice Act 1999, s. 100 (extending the immunity to assistant clerks); these replaced the 1979 Act, ss. 44, 45, as substituted by the Courts and Legal Services Act 1990, s.108. On the pre-1990 Act provisions see L. A. Sheridan, (1951) 14 M.L.R. 267; D. Thompson, (1958) 21 M.L.R. 517; "Suing the Beaks" (1990) 154 J.P.N. 212.

[99] See below, para. 4-035. The Court of Appeal had stated the law of justices' immunity in similar broad terms in *Sirros v. Moore* [1975] Q.B. 118, but that was disapproved by the House of Lords in *In re McC (A Minor)* [1985] A.C. 528, holding that malice and lack of cause did not have to be established where an act was done outside jurisdiction. Following the award of damages against justices in a series of cases where they had acted outside jurisdiction (*In re McC (A Minor); R. v. Waltham Forest JJ., ex p. Solanke* [1986] Q.B. 983; *R. v. Manchester City Magistrates' Court, ex p. Davies* (No. 2) [1989] Q.B. 631), the Lord Chancellor acceded to pressure from the Magistrates' Association in favour of broadening the immunity.

[1] Justices of the Peace Act 1997, s. 53A(1), (2), (6), inserted by the Access to Justice Act 1999, s.98(1).

[2] 1997 Act, s. 53A(3)–(6), inserted by *ibid.*; Justices and Justices' Clerks (Costs) Regulations 2001 (S.I. 2001 No. 1296). No order can be made in favour of a public authority or official acting on behalf of a public authority; the court must determine an amount sufficient reasonably to compensate the receiving party for costs properly incurred in the proceedings.

[3] The requirement that the proceedings be "against him" was removed by the Access to Justice Act 1999, s. 99(a), allowing for an indemnity in respect of judicial review and appeals by case stated. See *Liability of Judicial Officers and Others for Costs in Court Proceedings: A Consultation Paper* (LCD, 1996). The Magistrates' Association had expressed concern following the award of costs against justices in *R. v. Newcastle-under-Lyme JJ., ex p. Massey* [1994] 1 W.L.R. 1684 and *R. Lincoln JJ., ex p. Count* (1996) 8 Admin. L.R. 233 (where the justices had acted on the (erroneous) advice of their clerk).

of any act or omission in the execution (or purported execution) of his or her duty or in taking steps to dispute any claim which might arise in such proceedings; any damages or costs ordered to be paid by him or her; and any sums payable in connection with a reasonable settlement of proceedings. There must be an indemnity in respect of criminal matters unless it is proved that the justice or clerk acted in bad faith. For other matters, the justice *may* be indemnified unless it is proved that he or she acted in bad faith; and *must* be indemnified if he or she acted reasonably and in good faith.[4] The decision is taken by the Magistrates' Courts Committee and an appeal lies to a person appointed by the Lord Chancellor.

9. JUSTICES' CHIEF EXECUTIVES AND JUSTICES' CLERKS[5]

4–011   Traditionally, the justices' clerk was both in charge of the administration of the magistrates' court and its chief legal advisor. Originally the clerks were the personal clerks to individual justices or benches; subsequently, they came to be appointed by the magistrates' courts committees subject to the approval of the Lord Chancellor. In 1989 there were 285 clerkships in England and Wales. Of the 277 members of the Justices' Clerks' Society, 150 were solicitors, 119 barristers and eight qualified by experience.[6]

Significant changes to the administration of magistrates' courts were effected by the Police and Magistrates' Courts Act 1994,[7] which introduced the office of justices' chief executive distinct from the justices' clerk. Further changes made by the Access to Justice Act 1999 enhanced the former's role, centralising responsibility for administrative functions on him or her. Each Magistrates' Courts Committee must appoint a justices' chief executive from a short list of one or more persons approved by the Lord Chancellor.[8] The chief executive must make arrangements for the efficient and effective administration of the magistrates' courts for the area to which the committee relates. The administration of the courts includes the exercise of the function of acting as clerk to the committee and of all the functions conferred or imposed on chief executives by or under any other enactment. The chief executive must allocate responsibilities among justices' clerks and the committee's staff, determine the administrative procedures to be followed by them, and organise discussions relative to matters of law

---

[4]   1997 Act, s. 54, as amended by the 1999 Act, s.99(b). There is no longer a discretion to grant an indemnity where there is bad faith.

[5]   K. C. Clarke, [1964] Crim. L.R. 620, 697; P. Darbyshire, (1980) 144 J.P.N., 186, 201, 219, 233; P. Darbyshire, *The Magistrates' Clerk* (1984); Justices' Clerks' Society, *Administering Magistrates' Courts: The Role of the Justices Clerk* (1989); H. McLaughlin, (1990) 30 Brit. J. Criminol. 358.

[6]   (1989) 45 *The Magistrate* 34.

[7]   See above, para. 2-028.

[8]   Justices of the Peace Act 1997, s.40, as amended by the Access to Justice Act 1999, ss.87 and 88(3) and Sched. 12, para. 11. See the Justices' Chief Executives and Justices' Clerks (Appointment) Regulations 1999 (S.I. 1999 No. 2397). The 1999 Act removed a requirement that the chief executive be a person eligible to be appointed as a justices' clerk. A person may not be appointed both as a justices' chief executive and justices' clerk for a petty sessions area unless the Lord Chancellor agrees; a person so appointed may only exercise the latter's functions if authorised by the committee: s.40(6), (7).

(including practice and procedure) among the justices' clerks appointed by the committee, in particular with a view to securing consistency. He or she is subject to the committee's directions, and with one important qualification, may give directions to justices' clerks and the staff of the committee as to the carrying out of their responsibilities (including the performance of statutory functions).[9] The qualification is an express guarantee of "judicial independence." Accordingly, when exercising any legal function,[10] a justices' clerk is not subject to the direction of the justices' chief executive or any other person or body, and a member of staff of the committee is not subject to the direction of any person or body other than a justices' clerk.[11] This guarantee has been criticised as too narrow, having no application to such matters as "the training of justices, to bench meetings or even remarks made when justices assemble for a day's duties."[12]

The committee also appoints justices' clerks from a short list of one or more persons approved by the Lord Chancellor. More than one may be appointed for any petty sessions area, but any decision to increase the number or have more than one for a new petty sessions area requires the Lord Chancellor's approval. Justices' clerks may be removed by the committee, subject to the approval of the Lord Chancellor in any case where the magistrates for the petty sessions area do not consent. The committee must consult the magistrates for a petty sessions area on the appointment or removal of a justices' clerk for the area.[13] No one may be appointed as a justices' clerk unless at the time of appointment he or she has a five year magistrates' courts qualification,[14] or is a barrister or solicitor and has served for not less than five years as assistant to a justices' clerk, or is or has previously been a justices' clerk.[15] Justices' chief executives and justices' clerks are employed under contracts of service, and other staff may be employed on such terms as the committee thinks fit.[16] The approval of the Lord Chancellor is required for any determination by a committee reducing the salary of a justices' chief executive or justices clerk, without his or her consent.[17]

A large number of administrative functions previously conferred on justices' clerks have been transferred to justices' chief executives,[18] and the

---

[9] 1997 Act, s.41, substituted by the 1999 Act, s.88. Formerly, the committee had power to give directions as to the division of responsibilities among the chief executive, justices' clerks and staff and to give procedural directions.

[10] *i.e.* any function exercisable by one or more justices of the peace, or the functions of a justices' clerk in giving advice to the justices about matters of law (including practice or procedure): 1997 Act, s.48(2), as amended by the 1999 Act, s.89(2).

[11] 1997 Act, s.48(1), substituted by the 1999 Act, s.89(1).

[12] See S. Baker and J. English, *A Guide to the Police and Magistrates' Courts Act 1994* (1994), p. 115. For earlier criticism on this point, see M.J. Friel, (1993) 157 J.P.N. 712.

[13] 1997 Act, s. 42. See S.I. 1999 No. 2397.

[14] *i.e.* a right of audience in all magistrates courts for five years: Courts and Legal Services Act 1990, s. 71.

[15] 1997 Act, s.43.

[16] 1997 Act, s.44(1), (2).

[17] *ibid.*, s.44(1A), inserted by the 1999 Act, Sched. 12, para. 12.

[18] 1999 Act, s.90 and Sched. 3. See the Local Government (Magistrates' Courts etc) (Amendment) Order 2001 (S.I. 2001 No. 612) (amending S.I. 1995 No. 1383); the Magistrates' Courts (Transfer of Justices' Clerks Functions) (Miscellaneous Amendments) Rules 2001 (S.I. 2001 No. 615); the Access to Justice Act 1999 (Transfer of Justices' Clerks Functions) Order 2001 (S.I. 2001 No. 618).

justices' chief executives have become collecting officers for receiving the payments of fines, periodical payments and other sums, and remitting fines and other sums to the Lord Chancellor.[19] A "strategic steer" has been given that a justices' clerk should be the professional legal adviser to justices, leaving the details of the extent to which he or she remains responsible for daily administrative/managerial duties to individual Magistrates' Courts Committees.[20]

The justices' chief executive is the head of what may be a large staff. This will include one or more justices' clerk and a number of assistants. The functions of a justices' clerk include giving advice to justices on matters of law (including practice or procedure); furthermore, rules may be made enabling things authorised to be done by, to or before a J.P. to be done instead by a justices' clerk or an assistant.[21] Categories of staff include court clerks, general administrative and clerical staff, staff employed on accounts and financial matters and ushers. As from October 1, 1980, a person may not act as a court clerk unless he or she possesses one of a series of prescribed qualifications.[22] These have in the past included, as an alternative to being a barrister or solicitor, possessing a certificate of competence or a training certificate of competence or a training certificate or holding a Diploma in Magisterial Law. From January 1, 1999, a justices' clerks' assistant may only be appointed as a court clerk if he or she is a barrister or solicitor or has passed all the necessary examinations to become a barrister or solicitor. An assistant not so qualified may act as court clerk if he or she holds a valid training certificate granted by a Magistrates' Courts Committee before January 1, 1999 (to enable training to be completed), or a training contract registered by the Law Society. A person employed as a court clerk before January 1, 1999 may, however, accept further contracts of employment as such.[23]

The justices' clerk may grant but not refuse legal aid. Under the Justices Clerks Rules 1999[24] a justices' clerk may perform a large number of functions otherwise exercisable by a single justice, such as the issuing of a summons, adjourning a hearing with the consent of the parties, asking the accused whether he or she pleads guilty or not guilty, fixing or setting aside a date, time and place for the trial of an information, giving directions for the conduct of a criminal trial and exercising powers at an early administrative

---

[19] 1997 Act, s. 41A, inserted by the 1999 Act, s.91. See the Justices Chief Executives (Accounts) Regulations 2001 (S.I. 2001 No. 463).

[20] See *The Future Role of the Justices' Clerk* (LCD, September 1998); *The Future Role of the Justices' Clerk: A Strategic Steer* (LCD, January 2000).

[21] 1997 Act, s.45, as amended by the 1999 Act, s.89(2).

[22] Power to prescribe qualifications is conferred by the 1997 Act, s.44(3). See the Justices' Clerks (Qualification of Assistants) Rules 1979 (S.I. 1979 No. 570), as amended by S.I. 1980 No. 1897, S.I. 1992 No. 1834, S.I. 1998 No. 3107, S.I. 1999 No. 2814 and S.I. 2001 No. 2269. For comment on the 1998 changes, see (1998) 162 J.P.N. 253.

[23] The Government had previously rejected, apparently on financial grounds, a proposal that only those with a professional qualification be permitted to advise in court: (1985) 149 J.P.N. 721; (1987) 151 J.P.N. 1; J.C.S., *Administering Magistrates' Courts* (1989), Chap. 12. In 1998 about a third of court clerks were not legally qualified (LCD Press Notice 256/98). A requirement that all existing court clerks be legally qualified by 2008 was subsequently modified.

[24] S.I. 1999 No. 2784.

hearing. Similarly, an information may be laid before a justice or a justices' clerk. A justices' clerk may delegate most of these matters to an assistants.[25]

One of the issues that has caused problems since the 1940s has been the role of the court clerk in magistrates' court proceedings.[26] The clerk's function is to advise on law and procedure, but not to participate in the decision on the facts. In *R. v. East Kerrier JJ., ex p. Mundy*[27] Lord Goddard C.J. stated that the clerk should not retire with the justices as a matter of course but should wait to be sent for should advice on a point of law be needed. Otherwise, observers might conclude that the clerk was influencing the justices on questions of fact, and this would constitute a breach of the principle that justice must be seen to be done. This apparently caused "alarm and despondency" in some quarters,[28] somewhat to Lord Goddard's surprise, and this led to some further "clarification,"[29] or back-pedalling (depending on one's point of view). At the same time Lord Goddard C.J. threatened that justices who knowingly disobeyed the Divisional Court's directions would be reported to the Lord Chancellor.[30] The trend thereafter was for emphasis to be placed increasingly on the point that lay justices must be given proper professional advice, and less on the need to avoid the appearance that the clerk might have given an opinion on the facts.[31]

A Practice Direction was issued in 2000 by Lord Woolf C.J. with the concurrence of the President of the Family Divison.[32] The main points are as follows:

1. A justices' clerk is responsible for: (a) the legal advice tendered to the justices within the area; (b) the performance of any of the functions set out below by any member of his/her staff acting as legal adviser; (c) ensuring that competent advice is available to justices when the justices'

---

[25] *Ibid.*, r. 3, Prior to 1993 (S.I 1993 No. 1183) judical functions could not be delegated: *R. v. Gateshead JJ., ex p. Tesco Stores Ltd* [1981] Q. B. 470; *R. v. Manchester Stipendiary Magistrate, ex p. Hill* [1983] 1 A.C. 328. See (1992) 156 J.P.N. 435.

[26] The court clerk has been described as the "key worker in setting the tone of the courtroom atmosphere": H. Parker, M. Casburn and D. Turnbull, *Receiving Juvenile Justice* (1981), p. 48.

[27] [1952] 2 Q.B. 719.

[28] (1953) 10 *The Magistrate* 65.

[29] *R. v. Welshpool JJ., ex p. Holley* [1953] 2 Q.B. 403 (justices can invite the clerk to join them as they retire to advise on a point of law; the fact that he remains while the facts are discussed not sufficient to invalidate their decision); *Practice Note (Justices' Clerks)* [1953] 1 W.L.R. 1416.

[30] *R. v. Barry JJ., ex p. Nagi Kasim* [1953] 1 W.L.R. 1320, 1322.

[31] N. Crampton, (1979) 129 N.L.J. 208; *R. v. Uxbridge Magistrates' Court, ex p. Smith* (1985) 149 J.P. 620 (no objection where the clerk left court to advise the justices, who had retired, that certain legal submissions had been erroneous; criticised by A. Heaton-Armstrong, (1986) 150 J.P.N. 340, 357); *cf. R. v. Bingham JJ., ex p. Bell*, Unreported, discussed by Heaton-Armstrong, *op. cit.* and *R. v. Eccles JJ., ex p. Fitzpatrick* (1989) 89 Cr.App.R. 324 (certiorari granted where there was a reasonable suspicion of improper influence by the clerk. For the clerk's view, see A. Turner, (1992) 156 J.P.N. 723). See also the joint statement by the Magistrates' Association and the Justices' Clerks' Society: (1975) 31 *The Magistrate* 4.

[32] *Practice Direction (Justices: Clerk to Court)* [2000] 1 W.L.R. 1886 (see A. Murdie, (2001) 145 S.J. 257; J. Guess, (2001) 165 J.P.N. 582). This revoked *Practice Direction (Justices: Clerk to Courts)* [1981] 1 W.L.R. 1163 (on which see B. Harris, (1981) 145 J.P.N. 403). *Practice Note (Justices' Clerks)* [1954] 1 W.L.R. 213, concerning the role of the clerk in domestic proceedings, remains in force. Some of these points as to the functions of a justices' clerk are also made in the Justices of the Peace Act 1997, s. 45(4), (5); it is stated that this subsection is not exhaustive (subs. (7)).

clerk is not personally present in court; and (d) the effective delivery of case management and the reduction of unnecessary delay.

2. Where a person other than the justices' clerk (a 'legal adviser'), who is authorised to do so, performs any of the functions referred to in this direction he/she will have the same responsibilities as the justices' clerk. The legal adviser may consult the justices' clerk or other person authorised by the justices' clerk for that purpose before tendering advice to the bench. If the justices' clerk or that person gives advice directly to the bench, he/she should give the parties or their advocates an opportunity of repeating any relevant submissions prior to the advice being given.[33]

3. It shall be the responsibility of the legal adviser to provide the justices with any advice they require properly to perform their functions whether or not the justices have requested that advice, on: (i) questions of law (including European Court of Human Rights jurisprudence and those matters set out in s.2(1) of the Human Rights Act 1998); (ii) questions of mixed law and fact;[34] (iii) matters of practice and procedure; (iv) the range of penalties available; (v) any relevant decisions of the superior courts or other guidelines; (vi) other issues relevant to the matter before the court;[35] and (vii) the appropriate decision making structure to be applied in any given case. In addition to advising the justices it shall be the legal adviser's responsibility to assist the court, where appropriate, as to the formulation of reasons and the recording of those reasons.

4. A justices' clerk or legal adviser must not play any part in making findings of fact but may assist the bench by reminding them of the evidence, using any notes of the proceedings for this purpose.

5. A justices' clerk or legal adviser may ask questions of witnesses and the parties in order to clarify the evidence and any issues in the case.[36]

6. A legal adviser has a duty to ensure that every case is conducted fairly.

7. When advising the justices the justices' clerk or legal adviser, whether or not previously in court, should: (i) ensure that he/she is aware of the relevant facts; and (ii) provide the parties with the information necessary to enable the parties to make any representations they wish as to the advice before it is given.

8. At any time, justices are entitled to receive advice to assist them in discharging their responsibilities. If they are in any doubt as to the evidence which has been given, they should seek the aid of their legal

---

[33] Such submissions should be heard in open court and not in some corridor or private place: *R. v. Chichester JJ., ex p. D.P.P.* (1993) 157 J.P. 1042.

[34] See, *e.g. R. v. Consett JJ., ex p. Postal Bingo Ltd* [1967] 2 Q.B. 9.

[35] This is regarded as referring to issues of fact and evidence, and not isues of law or mixed law and fact: *R. v. Uxbridge Magistrates' Court, ex p. Smith* (1985) 149 J.P. 620 (in relation to the 1981 Statement).

[36] This proposition did not appear in the 1981 Direction. Cf. *R. v. Consett JJ. ex p. Postal Bingo Ltd.* [1967] 2 Q.B. 9 (clerk may ask questions in court in order to clear up ambiguities, so long as it is at the express or implied request of the bench).

adviser, referring to his/her notes as appropriate.[37] This should ordinarily be done in open court. Where the justices request their adviser to join them in the retiring room, this request should be made in the presence of the parties in court. Any legal advice given to the justices other than in open court should be clearly stated to be provisional and the adviser should subsequently repeat the substance of the advice in open court and give the parties an opportunity to make any representations they wish on that provisional advice. The legal adviser should then state in open court whether the provisional advice is confirmed or if it is varied the nature of the variation ...

10. The legal adviser is under a duty to assist unrepresented parties to present their case, but must do so without appearing to become an advocate for the party concerned.[38]"

This statement, which is both lengthier and clearer than its predecessors, states that advice should ordinarily be given in open court and introduces the requirement that advice given first in private be repeated in open court. This will ensure compliance with the requirements of a fair and public hearing under Article 6(1), ECHR.[39] It would seem that by virtue of the 2000 Practice Direction, specific reasons will be needed to justify departure from the general position that advice is given in open court; any generalised invocation of the confidential nature of the relationship between the justices and their professional adviser, invoked in the past by defenders of the previous arrangements,[40] will not suffice.

If justices summon the clerk when only issues of fact are involved and the clerk has made no note of evidence, a conviction may well be quashed.[41]

It has been held that it is proper for the clerk, in the absence of the justices and in conjunction with the prosecutor, to explain to an unrepresented defendant that if he or she attacks a prosecution witness his or her previous convictions can be revealed to the court.[42] However, it is not appropriate to warn the defendant and a defence witness of the consequences of giving perjured evidence where such a warning has not been given to prosecution witnesses.[43]

---

[37] Similar words in the 1981 statement impliedly overruled the statements of Donaldson L.J. in R. v. Guildford JJ., ex p. Harding (1981) 145 J.P. 174.

[38] Cf. Simms v. Moore [1970] 2 Q.B. 327.

[39] Although in Clark v. Kelly 2001 J.C. 16, the High Court of Justiciary held that the giving of advice in private did not breach the public hearing requirement, following Delcourt v. Belgium (1970) 1 E.H.R.R. 355, provided that any matter on which the parties might reasonably wish to make material comment was raised in open court. See P. Plowden, (2000) 164 J.P.N. 872 noting that, depending on the way Kelly was interpreted and applied, the difference from the English Practice Direction could effectively be negligible.

[40] (1986) 42 The Magistrate 40–41; cf. A. Heaton-Armstrong, (1986) 150 J.P.N. 340, 357, arguing that advice on the law should always be given in open court.

[41] R. v. Worley JJ., ex p. Nash [1982] C.L. 1932: see the comment at (1983) 147 J.P.N. 209. Cf. R. v. Eccles JJ., ex p. Fitzpatrick (1989) 89 Cr.App.R. 324 (appearance of improper influence of decision to commit for trial) and R. v. Eccles JJ., ex p. Farelly (1992) 157 J.P. 77 (clerk spoke to justices after they had returned from their deliberations, and then went with them when they left the court again to reconsider, without any explanation).

[42] R. v. Weston-super-Mare JJ., ex p. Townsend [1968] 3 All E.R. 225.

[43] R. v. Richmond & Gilling West Magistrates, ex p. Steel [1993] Crim. L.R. 711.

In some areas, clerks rule on questions of the admissibility of evidence in the absence of the justices. This is generally accepted to be irregular as the clerk has no legal authority to rule on such matters. On the other hand it is also accepted that it is undesirable for the justices who are to determine guilt to determine disputed questions of admissibility, which may well involve hearing evidence which subsequently has to be disregarded as inadmissible. There is in fact no reason why the parties should not by agreement submit the issue to the clerk and, once a ruling is made, voluntarily abide by it: the real limitation is that the ruling will not technically be binding. It is likely to be in the defendant's interests for this to be done in the absence of the justices: it is unlikely that the justices could be persuaded to differ from the clerk's view on such a question.

It is also a well established practice for lawyers to refer doubtful points of law to the clerk in advance of the hearing in order to obtain what in practice, although again not in theory, amounts to a ruling.[44]

In the case of fine default proceedings and other proceedings for the enforcement of financial orders, the court clerk may ask questions to elicit information the justice will need to make an adjudication, for example to facilitate his or her explanation for the default; however, the adviser must not act in ad adversarial or partisan manner and should not seek to establish wilful refusal or neglect to pay, the duty of impartiality taking precedence over any role as collecting officer. It is for the justices' chief executive to decide whether another officer should be appointed to "prosecute."[45]

Where a justices clerk becomes aware during the course of proceedings that a court clerk has given erroneous legal advice to the justices, he or she may be entitled to give fresh advice to the justices, although the general principle is that decisions once made should not be reversed; the matter should normally be brought to the attention of the justices' clerk by one party with notice to the other.[46]

From time to time, suggestions are made for changing the status of justices' clerks.[47] One possibility would be to appoint them to the bench, so that they, would become, in those courts where they presided, a legally qualified chairman.[48] Another possibility would be to give them the formal power to rule on points of law, while leaving the determination of the facts, as at present, to the lay justices.[49] This is virtually the present position. There is a persistent minority of cases in which lay justices exert their power to determine a point of law contrary to the clerk's advice. Lord Widgery C.J., however, warned that if justices fly in the face of their clerk's advice

---

[44] See P. Darbyshire, (1980) 144 J.P.N. 201.

[45] *Practice Direction*, para. 11, reflecting the decision of the Divisional Court in *R. v. Corby JJ., ex p. Mort* (1998) 38 R.V.R. 383 that such arrangements did not give rise to a real danger of bias (the test for bias then applicable).

[46] *R. v. Sittingbourne JJ., ex p. Stickings, The Times*, May 9, 1996 (justices' decision to reverse ruling that prosecution evidence was inadmissible following fresh advice from justices' clerk held to be unfair as it followed a telephone call by branch Crown Prosecutor direct to the justices' clerk).

[47] Here the suggestions are usually confined to the justices' clerk personally and do not extend to his or her assistants.

[48] Conversely, it has been proposed that District Judges (Magistrates' Courts) should normally sit without a legal adviser: Auld Report, Chap 4, para. 53.

[49] See, *e.g.*, (1992) 156 J.P.N. 433.

and are subsequently reversed on appeal, costs might be awarded against them.[50]

10. MAGISTRATES IN THE CROWN COURT

The Beeching Committee[51] recommended that magistrates should sit as **4–012** assessors with Circuit judges in the Crown Court. Before reorganization, justices had participated in quarter sessions in the counties, but not in the assizes or borough quarter sessions. The Courts Act 1971[52] provided that justices may sit with a Circuit judge or recorder when conducting a trial on indictment and must do so when the Crown Court is hearing an appeal or dealing with a person committed there for sentence. Moreover, it provided that the justices would act as judges of the Crown Court and not merely as assessors. Lord Gardiner L.C. and Lord Hailsham L.C. were advised to adopt this course by Sir Thomas Skyrme,[53] who argued, *inter alia*, that the experience would be of benefit to the justices; that justices could play a valuable part in sentencing, especially where the judge had no local knowledge; and that they could exercise a useful restriction on any idiosyncrasy of a judge or recorder. However, Skyrme subsequently acknowledged that the differences between the Crown Court and quarter sessions turned out to be greater than expected. Long trials that formerly would have been dealt with at assizes were now conducted by a court including justices at the Crown Court. The Crown Court was in continuous session. Trials might be conducted by judges with no experience of sitting with lay justices. Cases commonly ran over a day and this would cause problems for many lay justices. In some areas only those who could sit for several days were summoned: courts were accordingly composed dispro-portionately of women and the elderly. On the other hand, Circuit judges had been appointed as "liaison judges", and in some areas they were able to improve relationships.[54]

Dissatisfaction with the role of justices in the Crown Court continued in many places.[55] Eventually, the Lord Chancellor directed that justices no longer sit in contested Crown Court trials.[56] More recently, the requirement

---

[50] *Jones v. Nicks* [1977] R.T.R. 72, 76. The advice concerned what might constitute a "special reason" for not imposing an endorsement following a speeding conviction. This step could now only be taken if the justices had acted in bad faith. See para. 4-010.

[51] *Royal Commission on Assizes and Quarter Sessions* (Cmnd. 4153, 1969).

[52] ss. 4, 5. See now the Supreme Court Act 1981, ss.8, 74, 75; the Crown Court Rules 1982, rr.3–5, as amended.

[53] Skyrme (1983), pp. 125–130.

[54] Suggestions that liaison judges hold annual conferences of bench chairmen, sentencing conferences and meetings with justices' clerks have, however, been criticised as going beyond their proper role: see Judge Dyer, (1987) 43 *The Magistrate* 223, and for responses: D. H. Kidner, (1988) 44 *The Magistrate* 51, and (1988) 152 J.P.N. 97.

[55] Skyrme (1983), pp. 125–130. See also G. Hawker, *Magistrates in the Crown Court* (1974): Survey by the Institute of Judicial Administration, University of Birmingham.

[56] *Practice Direction (Crime: Crown Court Business) (No. 2)* [1986] 1 W.L.R. 1041 (see now above para. 2-054.). The change was made with the agreement of the Magistrates' Association: (1987) 43 *The Magistrate* 81, 119 (the suggestion had previously been resisted: see Skyrme (1983), pp. 129–130).

that justices sit on committals for sentence has also been removed.[57]

The Lord Chancellor has directed that no justice should sit in the Crown Court unless he or she has demonstrated the range of competencies required by the Magistrates' New Training Initiative and has the support of the Bench chairman and Justices' Clerk that they have the relevant experience and competencies.[58] The justices may outvote the judge, although in the case of a tie the latter has a second and casting vote.[59] This is most likely to happen on a question of sentence, but may occur on other matters, such as the discretion to exclude evidence.[60]

11. District Judges (Magistrates' Courts)

4-013 Prior to the Access to Justice Act 1999, the Queen had power to appoint up to 60 "metropolitan stipendiary magistrates" for the inner London area,[61] and up to 56 "stipendiary magistrates" elsewhere.[62] The former could trace their existence back to 1792, when they took over criminal jurisdiction from the largely corrupt lay justices.[63] The Metropolitan Police Courts Act 1839 provided that only barristers were to be eligible for appointment. From 1964, they shared their duties with lay justices, who, with the passage of time, have been restored to respectability.

In the provinces, stipendiaries were appointed in places where there were not enough justices to cope with the work, and where, at the same time, there was a resistance to the appointment of men who had acquired wealth through industry or trade. Boroughs might petition the Home Secretary to appoint a stipendiary; alternatively, a local Act of Parliament might provide for an appointment. The role of provincial stipendiaries was to supplement rather than to replace the lay justices. The 1948 Royal Commission noted that the determining factor behind whether a particular area had a stipendiary was "not a rational assessment of the present need but the course of past history."[64] The rationalisation of commission areas, which was a by-product of local government reorganisation, provided the opportunity for the right to take the initiative in the making of new appointments to be transferred from local authorities to the Lord Chancellor.[65] The requirements of each area were assessed by the Lord

---

[57] Access to Justice Act 1999, s. 79, amending the Supreme Court Act 1981, s. 74(1). For the background, see *Magistrates Sitting as Judges in the Crown Court: A Consultation Paper* (LCD, August 1998).

[58] Deputy Secretary of Commissions Circular, July 28, 2000 (Magistrates' Association website), removing a requirement for three years' experience in view of the difficulty in securing sufficient magistrates to undertake this work.

[59] Supreme Court Act 1981, s.73.

[60] *R. v. Smith (Benjamin Walker)* [1978] Crim.L.R. 296.

[61] Justices of the Peace Act 1997, s. 16.

[62] 1997 Act, s.11, as amended by the Maximum Number of Stipendiary Magistrates Order 1999 (S. I. 1999 No. 3319).

[63] See generally F. Milton, *The English Magistracy* (1967), Chap. 2. Some of the existing justices managed to secure stipendiary appointments, but ministers in the early nineteenth century took greater care over appointments. See also, R. Bartle, (1986) 54 Medico-Legal Jo. 236.

[64] Cmd. 7463, p. 57.

[65] Administration of Justice Act 1973, s.2.

Chancellor's office.[66] Further appointments were made from time to time.[67] Where a bench was temporarily over-burdened, an acting stipendiary magistrate could be assigned to assist.[68]

The Access to Justice Act 1999[69] provided for the unification and renaming of the stipendiary bench. Accordingly, the Queen may, on the recommendation of the Lord Chancellor, appoint a person with a seven year general qualification[70] to be a District Judge (Magistrates' Courts).[71] The Lord Chancellor must designate one to be the Senior District Judge (Chief Magistrate) and may designate another as his or her deputy. A District Judge (Magistrates' Courts) may not be removed from office except by the Lord Chancellor on the ground of incapacity or misbehaviour.[72] A Deputy District Judge (Magistrates' Courts) may be appointed by the Lord Chancellor for such a period as he considers appropriate, subject to his power to remove him or her from office on the ground of incapacity or misbehaviour.[73] Significantly, there is now no limit on numbers and, while based at a particular court, such a judge is by virtue of his or her office a justice of the peace for every commission area,[74] facilitating flexibility in appointment and deployment. He or she may sit alone to deal with business that would otherwise require the sitting of two or more lay justices.[75] Existing stipendiaries became District Judges (Magistrates' Courts) or Deputies.[76] The Senior District Judge (Chief Magistrate), in part the successor to the Chief Metropolitan Magistrate, is responsible for the deployment of District Judges (Magistrates' Courts) to the courts in England and Wales where they are needed.[77]

The retiring age is 70, although the Lord Chancellor may authorise a District Judge (Magistrates' Courts) to continue in office up to the age of

---

[66] Skyrme (1983), Chap. 13.

[67] See *The Size of Benches* (H.O., L.C.D.); (1986) 42 *The Magistrate* 118; (1988) 44 *The Magistrate* 219.

[68] Popularly (or unpopularly) known as "flying stipes": they were, for example, employed in some areas during the miners' strike ((1984) 148 J.P.N. 578).

[69] s. 78, inserting ss. 10A-10E in the Justices of the Peace Act 1997.

[70] The appointment of solicitors had become possible under the Justices of the Peace Act 1949. The first was appointed in 1957. By 1983 20 solicitors had been appointed, 15 in London and five elsewhere; Skyrme (1983), p. 187.

[71] Candidates should normally be between 40 and 55 and have sat as a Deputy for at least two years or have completed 30 sittings in that capacity: *Judicial Appointments Annual Report 2000–2001*, para. 3.89; age limits have subsequently been withdrawn: LCD Press Notice 143/02.

[72] 1997 Act, s. 10A. As at March 1, 2002, there were 95 District Judges (Magistrates' Courts) (LCD website).

[73] *ibid.*, s. 10B. Candidates must normally be 35–55 and are expected to sit part-time for between 15 and 30 days each year. As at March 1, 2002, there were 162 Deputies (LCD website).

[74] *ibid.*, s. 10C.

[75] *ibid.*, ss. 10D, 10E. This now includes the Youth Court: Children and Young Persons Act 1933, Sched. 2, para. 2A, inserted by the 1999 Act, Sched. 11, para. 12(4).

[76] 1999 Act. Sched. 14, paras. 22, 23.

[77] *Judicial Appointments Annual Report, 2000–2001*, para. 3.88. The first holder of the office is Penelope Hewitt, a former provincial stipendiary magistrate; a former metropolitan stipendiary was appointed as Deputy Senior District Judge.

75.[78] The current salary is £86,176,[79] being grouped with, *inter alia*, masters and registrars of the Supreme Court and chairman of Employments Tribunals.

Traditionally, appointment to judicial office has been on the understanding that the appointee will remain in that office. Today there is a growing trend for judicial officers to be "promoted". District Judges (Magistrates' Courts) may be invited to sit as recorders. Some have been appointed to the Circuit Bench.

The English system is unique in providing for the co-existence of both professional judges and lay justices with the same jurisdiction. Proposals have from time to time been made for a magistrates court normally to comprise a professional judge sitting with lay justices; for lay justices to be replaced by stipendiary magistrates; and for additional stipendiaries to be appointed.[80] The whole question of the role of professional judges at this level has been revisited by the government, leading to the 1999 Act reform, and by the Auld Report, following major studies[81] and a working party report.[82] The growth of the professional magistracy has generated some concerns that this may constitute a threat to the lay magistracy, with fears that the professionals may be seen as "government placemen," might act in the best interests of legal professionals rather than the public interest and might inspire less confidence as power is centralised and local autonomy lost. There seems neither any real justification for such concerns nor any political wish to disband the lay magistracy.[83] The Auld Report recommended that District Judges and magistrates continue to exercise summary jurisdiction, rejecting a proposed model[84] that would have seen all minor contested cases dealt with by a mixed panel of two lay magistrates and one professional judge. Such an arrangement was, however, endorsed for the trial of less serious either-way cases.[85]

---

[78] Judicial Pensions and Retirement Act 1993, s.26 and Sched. 5, as amended by the Access to Justice Act 1999, Sched II, para 41.

[79] As from April 1, 2003. In London, these is an additional salary lead of £2,000 and a London allowance of £2,000.

[80] The number of provincial and acting stipendiary magistrates increased significantly through the 1990s: see P. Seago, C. Walker, D. Wall, [2000] Crim. L.R. 631, 636 (18 to 47 and 66 to 148 respectively between 1991 and 2000).

[81] P. Seago, C. Walker, D. Wall, *The Role and Appointment of Stipendiary Magistrates* (Centre for Criminal Justice Studies, University of Leeds, 1995) and "The Development of the Professional Magistracy in England and Wales" [2000] Crim. L.R. 631; R. Morgan and N. Russell, *The judiciary in the magistrates' courts* (HO, LCD, 2000). The evidence of the latter study was that District Judges were significantly faster and otherwise more efficient than magistrates, more interventionist and likely to sentence more heavily; most court users had confidence in both, but more in District Judges; the public generally regarded magistrates as more representative of the community.

[82] *The Role of the Stipendiary Magistracy* (the Venne Report) (LCD, February 1996); *Creation of a Unified Stipendiary Bench* (LCD Consultation Paper, 1998).

[83] See generally Seago et al, [2000] Crim. L.R. 631.

[84] A. Sanders, *Community Justice* (IPPR, 2001).

[85] Auld Report, Chap. 4 ; see above, para. 2-058.

B. TRIBUNAL CHAIRMEN AND MEMBERS

There are several patterns on which the composition of a tribunal may be **4–014** organised.[86] The variations reflect partly the differences in the kind of work undertaken by different tribunals and partly their diverse historical origins. Full-time appointments are commonly of similar status to one or other of the ranks of the judiciary. The Presidents of the Lands Tribunal, the Appeals Service and of Employment Tribunals and the Chief Social Security Commissioner receive a higher salary than a Circuit judge; regional chairmen of employment tribunals, vice-presidents of the Immigration Appeal Tribunal and Social Security Commissioners receive the same as a Circuit judge; chairmen of employment and appeals service tribunals and immigration adjudicators receive the same as District judges.[87] Most appointments are part-time.[88]

It is not possible to consider here the details of appointment and tenure for all tribunals.[89] Some general observations can, however, be made.

1. WHO APPOINTS?

The Franks Committee on Administrative Tribunals and Enquiries[90] **4–015** reported that appointments to tribunals were usually made by the minister responsible for the legislation under which they operated. They had received no significant evidence that any influence was in fact exerted on tribunal members by government departments, but recommended, nevertheless, that chairmen, whether legally qualified or not, should be appointed by the Lord Chancellor and members by the Council on Tribunals.[91] The position today is that the Lord Chancellor is involved in the appointment of a majority of chairmen. He either appoints the chairman directly[92] or appoints a panel from which a selection is made by the relevant department or President of tribunals.[93] The appointment of members has, however, not been transferred to the Council on Tribunals, and it is not seriously argued that it should be. Most tribunal members are appointed by the relevant government department: some are appointed by the Crown or the Lord

---

[86] See above Chap. 2.

[87] Judicial Salaries 2002–2003 (LCD website).

[88] Full statistics, including breakdowns by gender and ethnic origin are given in the *Judicial Appointments Annual Reports*.

[89] R. E. Wraith and P. G. Hutchesson, *Administrative Tribunals* (1973), Chap. 4; L.C.D. Memorandum on Judicial Appointments Procedures (1995), pp. 42–50; *Judicial Appointments: The Lord Chancellor's Policies and Procedures* (LCD website).

[90] Cmnd. 218, 1957.

[91] Cmnd. 218 pp. 11–12.

[92] *e.g.* the President (and members) of the Lands Tribunal: Lands Tribunal Act 1949, s.2; chairman (and members) of Mental Health Review Tribunals: Mental Health Act 1983, s.65(2), Sched. 2. Some are Crown appointments: for example, the provisions governing the appointment and tenure of Social Security Commissioners (Social Security Administration Act 1992, s.52 and Sched. 2) are very similar to those governing Circuit judges (see below, para. 4-020.).

[93] See the Tribunals and Inquiries Act 1992, s.6: examples include the chairmen of employment tribunals and Appeals Service tribunals (see above, paras 2-031, 2-037.).

Chancellor, and some by the relevant President of tribunals. The Leggatt Review of Tribunals recommended that in view of the requirement of independence and impartiality under the ECHR, the same system should be responsible for making both judicial and tribunal appointments; the Lord Chancellor should assume responsibility for all appointments to tribunals which would otherwise be made by Westminster ministers, in consultation as necessary with other members of the U.K. government or members of the devolved administrations. It was recognised that this would add significantly to the LCD's responsibilities.[94] All appointments should be for renewable terms of five or seven years, subject to specified grounds for removal for incapacity or misbehaviour.[95] Specified members of the Judicial Appointments Commission should have overall responsibility for supervising the appointment of, respectively, lawyers and non-lawyers.[96]

2. QUALIFICATIONS FOR APPOINTMENT

4-016   The Franks Committee recommended that *chairmen* of tribunals:

"should ordinarily have legal qualifications but that the appointment of persons without legal qualifications should not be ruled out when they are particularly suitable."[97]

There should be no such requirement for members. The possession of a legal qualification is thought to be desirable not so much for the expertise in handling legal rules as for the qualities necessary for good chairmanship. "Objectivity in the treatment of cases and the proper sifting of facts are most often best secured by having a legally qualified chairman...."[98] Many criticisms of Supplementary Benefit Appeal Tribunals were related to the general lack of legally qualified chairmen. They were regularly contrasted unfavourably with National Insurance Local Tribunals where a legal qualification was in practice required.[99] Not all commentators favoured a change to lawyer-chairmen, but the government indicated in 1977 that there would be a "gradual, but significant move to appoint more legally-qualified chairmen of S.B.A.T.s."[1] Between 1977 and 1980 the overall proportion of lawyer chairmen increased from 12 per cent to 26.4 per cent.[2]

In an increasing number of cases, a legal qualification or legal experience

---

[94] Report (see para. 2-010), para. 2.32.
[95] *ibid.*, para. 7.7.
[96] *ibid.*, para. 7.12.
[97] Cmnd. 218, p. 12.
[98] *ibid.*
[99] See, *e.g.* Kathleen Bell *et al.*, "National Insurance Local Tribunals: A Research Study" (1974) 3 *Journal of Social Policy* 289 and (1975) 4 *Journal of Social Policy* 1; Kathleen Bell, *Research Study on Supplementary Benefit Appeal Tribunals–Review of Main Findings: Conclusions: Recommendations* (1975); J. Fulbrook, *Administrative Justice and the Unemployed* (1978), pp. 209–220.
[1] Annual Report of the Council on Tribunals, 1976–77 (1977–78 H.C. 108), p. 26.
[2] N. Harris, "The Appointment of Legally Qualified Chairmen for S.B.A.T.s" (1982) 132 N.L.J. 495. There were some reports of consequential improvements in the conduct of proceedings.

is required by statute[3]: in others it is normally required as a matter of practice.[4] Even here, however, there may be criticism that appointees may not have sufficient (or any) experience in the relevant area.[5] It has also been noted that it has become more common for people to hold part-time appointments to more than one tribunal,[6] or for a full-time chairman to sit in addition as a recorder in the Crown Court.[7] A period in office as a part-time chairman is expected before appointment to a full time position. The tenure of part-time chairmen and members has been strengthened to ensure compliance with Article 6(1), ECHR.[8]

The background of *members* will obviously be related to the nature of the tribunal's work. An obvious example is that doctors sit on Appeals Service tribunals concerning medical questions.[9] A pattern that has been commonly adopted is that of the "representative panel". For example, in Employment Tribunals, one "wing" member is taken from a panel representing employers and the other from a panel representing employed persons.[10] Similar arrangement were made for National Insurance Local Tribunals and Supplementary Benefit Appeal Tribunals.[11] However, the use of lay members in appeals service tribunals has, amid some controversy, been reduced.[12] The Leggatt Review noted widespread support for the use of lay members, but recommended that all tribunal members should be appointed "on the basis of the particular contribution which they have to make to its work." In some cases this would involve possession of a professional qualification, for example as a medical practitioner or valuer; in others, the

---

[3] *e.g.* Presidents of Appeals Service tribunals and Social Security Commissioners (lawyer of 10 years' standing), chairmen of appeals service tribunals (from April 23, 1989: lawyer of five years' standing), Lands Tribunal members (either lawyer or qualified surveyor) President and chairmen of Employment Tribunals (lawyers of seven years' standing), chairmen of Mental Health Review Tribunals (persons of suitable legal experience). References to standing here mean the possession of a general qualification (*i.e.* right of audience in any part of the Supreme Court or in all proceedings in county courts or magistrates' courts) for the appropriate number of years: Courts and Legal Services Act 1990, s.71 and Sched. 10, paras.7, 27, 36, 37, 46. Age limits applied in practice have now been withdrawn: LCD Press Notice 143/02.

[4] *e.g.* Immigration Adjudicators.

[5] The JUSTICE Report on *Industrial Tribunals* (1987) notes (p. 47) that most appointees as chairman have little or no previous knowledge and experience of employment law and almost invariably lack industrial experience: it recommends that preference be given to candidates with previous experience in employment law, industrial relations and tribunal work; and that there should be closer links with the Circuit bench. The LCD paper, *Judicial Appointments: The Lord Chancellor's Policies and Procedures* (LCD website), states in relation to Appeals Service tribunals that prior experience of social security law is "desirable, but not essential"; however, the Lord Chancellor seeks to appoint as chairmen of employment tribunals "individuals who can demonstrate a good knowledge of employment law and who have experience of civil litigation."

[6] Wraith and Hutchesson (1973), pp. 114–115; Fulbrook (1978), p. 212.

[7] JUSTICE, *Industrial Tribunals* (1987), p. 45.

[8] See below, para. 4-020 and LCD Press Notice 284/00 announcing new arrangements for further part-time tribunal appointments, including those made by the Secretary of State for Trade and Industry to Employment Tribunals.

[9] See above.

[10] Industrial Tribunals (Constitution and Rules of Procedure) Regulations 1993 (S.I. 1993 No.2687), regs.3, 7. One panel is appointed by the Secretary of State after consultation with *e.g.* the T.U.C., the other after consultation with *e.g.* the C.B.I: see JUSTICE, *Industrial Tribunals*, p. 49.

[11] See the first edition of this book, pp. 151–152.

[12] See above, para. 2-037.

possession of specific knowledge or experience. The criteria should be
expressed in statute. It would be for Presidents and regional or district
chairmen to decide whether non-lawyer members should sit on particular
classes of case (or individual cases) and what is the function they are to
fulfil.[13]

Comparatively little has been written about the social and political
background of tribunal chairmen and members,[14] although, as with the
judiciary, women and members of ethnic minorities are seriously under-
represented.[15]

3. DISMISSAL

4–017 No power of a minister to terminate a person's membership of a tribunal is
exercisable except with the consent of the Lord Chancellor.[16]

4. TRAINING

4–018 The Council on Tribunals has noted the benefits derived from regular
meetings of tribunal chairmen, at which difficulties can be discussed and
opinions ventilated,[17] and has stressed the importance of training for both
chairmen and members.[18] In various contexts, shortcomings in the quality
of decision-making have been related to the absence of adequate training.[19]
There have also been developments in the training of tribunal chairmen,
although these have lagged behind developments in the training of

---

[13] Report (see para. 2-010), paras. 7.19–7.26.

[14] See W. E. Cavanagh and G. N. Hawker, "Laymen on Administrative Tribunals" (1974) 52
Public Administration 215 (Rent Assessment Panels and S.B.A.T.s) and the study of
N.I.L.T.s by Kathleen Bell and others: *op.cit.* n. 80 above, pp. 310–315; L. Dickens *et al.*,
Dismissed (1985), pp. 52–59 (Industrial Tribunals) and JUSTICE, *Industrial Tribunals*
(1987), pp. 45–50; J. Baldwin and S. Hill, (1987) 6 C.J.Q. 130 (Local Valuation Panels); J.
Baldwin, *et al., Judging Social Security* (1992), pp. 132–140 (S.S.A.T.s).

[15] See JUSTICE, *Industrial Tribunals* (1987), pp. 46, 47–48, 49–50. JUSTICE proposed positive
action to promote their recruitment, involving a more open, accessible and democractic
appointments process for members. The processes for the appointment of General
Commissioners of Income Tax have attracted strong criticism: *Report of the Equality
Working Group: The Lay Magistrates and the General Commissioners of Income Tax* (June
2000, LCD website).

[16] Tribunals and Inquiries Act 1992, s.7. The tribunals to which this applies are specified in
Sched. 1.

[17] Annual Report for 1976–77, pp. 19–20. In 1987, the Council organised the first conference of
Presidents and Chairmen of major tribunals falling under its jurisdiction: Annual Report for
1986–87 (1987–88 H.C. 234), pp. 6–7.

[18] *e.g.* Annual Report for 1984–85 (1985–86 H.C. 54), p. 11; for 1986–87 (1987–88 H.C. 234), p.
18; for 1987–88 (1988–89 H.C. 102), pp. 31–32; for 1988–89 (1989–90 H.C. 114), pp. 26–
27;for 1996–97 (1997–98 H.C. 376), pp. 8–11 (survey of current arrangements found a
marked scarcity of tribunal training in around a quarter of the systems surveyed).

[19] *e.g.* in respect of General Commissioners of Income Tax (Annual Report for 1987–88, p. 6);
education appeal committees (*ibid.*, p. 13); industrial tribunals, especially in sex
discrimination and equal pay cases (A. Leonard, *Judging Inequality* (1987), pp. 71–72;
JUSTICE, *Industrial Tribunals* (1987), pp. 35–38, 48, 50).

magistrates.[20] There has been little provision of training for tribunal members. The President of the Appeals Service tribunals is under an express duty to arrange for such training for chairmen and members of tribunals as he thinks appropriate.[21]

A Tribunals Committee has been established as part of the enlarged Judicial Studies Board.[22] Its role is seen as complementary to the Council on Tribunals, and to be that of promoting, encouraging and advising.[23] It has run induction courses for newly qualified chairmen, developing into a series of broader training development seminars,[24] has appointed a Tribunals' Training Co-ordinator and publishes a journal, *Tribunals*.[25] A Tribunals training needs analysis was completed in 2000.

The Leggatt Review of Tribunals found that there was a particular need for improved training in the interpersonal skills peculiar to tribunals and that national co-ordination of training was essential. The Judicial Studies Board should be given responsibility for the organisation and delivery of training for tribunal chairmen and members, for establishing national standards and monitoring the structure and content of training across all tribunals.[26]

5. Clerks to Tribunals[27]

The Franks Committee noted that the practice   4–019

"whereby the majority of clerks of tribunals are provided by the Government Departments concerned from their local and regional staffs seems partly to be responsible for the feeling in the minds of some people that tribunals are dependent upon and influenced by those Departments."[28]

They considered the possibility of establishing under the Lord Chancellor's Department a central corps of clerks for all tribunals, but rejected it on the grounds that it was difficult to see how reasonable career prospects could be held out, that it would be difficult to arrange sittings to ensure that the clerks were fully occupied and that it was in any event desirable for the civil

---

[20] For example, there was a system for training S.B.A.T. chairmen (see Annual Report of the Council on Tribunals for 1977–78 (1978–79 H.C. 74), pp. 16–17), and some training courses were held for chairmen of Local Valuation Courts (Report for 1978–79 (1979–80 H.C. 359), p. 18).

[21] Social Security Act 1998, Sched. 1, para. 8. The Regional chairmen assist in this task.

[22] See below.

[23] *Judicial Studies Board Report for 1987–1991* (HMSO, 1992), p. 57; *Report for 1991–1995* (1995), Chap. 6; *Annual Reports*.

[24] In 2000–01, the Committee ran courses on the effective use of small groups in training, training the trainers, and (for new chairs in tribunals that do not as yet have their own training programmes) tribunal skills development: *Judicial Studies Board Annual Report 2000–2001*, paras. 7.14–7.23.

[25] *ibid.*

[26] Report (see para. 2-010), paras. 7.29–7.35.

[27] See Wraith and Hutchesson (1973), Chap. 5, and pp. 300–306.

[28] Cmnd. 218, p. 13.

servants in social service departments to spend a period as tribunal clerk.[29]
To ensure that clerks did not exert a departmental influence, the Committee
stated that their duties and conduct should be regulated on the advice of the
Council on Tribunals. The duties of a clerk should generally be confined to
secretarial work, taking notes of evidence and tendering advice, when
requested, on points connected with the tribunal's functions. He or she
should not retire with the tribunal unless sent for to advise on a specific
point.

Clerks to what are now Appeals Service Tribunals were from April 1984
appointed by the President, and worked from the regional offices of his
organisation,[30] thus marking their independence from the Department of
Social Security. The current position is that officers and staff for the
President and for appeal tribunals are appointed by the Secretary of State
and clerks are also assigned to tribunals by the Secretary of State,[31] being a
function exercised by the Appeals Service. The role of the clerk does not
appear to be problematic.[32] A particularly important task is that of
explaining the nature of proceedings to appellants; a recent study found that
"tribunal clerks on the whole did a good job in difficult circumstances."[33]
The Leggatt Review of Tribunals confirmed that clerks made a vital
contribution to tribunal work and was critical of tribunals, particularly
MHRTs, that had sought to save money by reducing the availability of
clerks.[34]

C. THE CIRCUIT BENCH

4–020   The Circuit Bench was created by the Courts Act 1971 as part of the
reorganisation of the criminal courts following the Beeching Commission.[35]
The Queen may appoint Circuit judges and recorders on the recommendation of the Lord Chancellor.[36] Circuit judges are appointed to serve full-time
in the Crown Court and county courts, and recorders to serve as part-time

---

[29] *ibid.*, pp. 13–14.
[30] Social Security Administration Act 1992, Sched. 2, paras.3, 4. The organisation was
originally known as "OPSSAT" for short: see Judge Byrt (the first President),
"Administering Appeals," *Adviser*, Oct.–Nov. 1987, p. 6.
[31] Social Security Act 1998, Sched. 1, paras 6 and 11. See the Social Security and Child Support
(Decisions and Appeals) Regulations 1999 (S.I. 1999 No. 991), reg. 37.
[32] Difficulties with clerks to S.B.A.Ts were not experienced with S.S.A.Ts. see Fulbrook (1978),
pp. 229–236.
[33] J. Baldwin, *et al., Judging Social Security* (1992), pp. 168–169.
[34] Report (see para. 2-010), paras. 4.45, 4.46; cf; similar criticisms of MHRTs in the Annual
Report of the Council on Tribunals 2000–2001, Chap. 5, paras. 13–16.
[35] Royal Commission on Assizes and Quarter Sessions (Cmnd. 4153, 1969).
[36] Courts Act 1971, ss.16, 21. On January 1, 2002 there were 605 Circuit judges (including 56
women) and 1403 recorders (including 173 women); 148 of the recorders were solicitors:
Judicial Appointments (LCD website). The Lord Chancellor may appoint a former judge of
the Court of Appeal or the High Court or a former Circuit judge as a deputy Circuit judge:
Courts Act 1971, s. 24, substituted by the Supreme Court Act 1981, s. 146.

judges in the Crown Court.[37] Under the 1971 Act, only a barrister or solicitor of 10 years' standing could be appointed as a recorder. A barrister of 10 years' standing or a recorder who had held office for at least three years could be appointed as a Circuit judge. A solicitor might accordingly reach the position of Circuit judge after time as a recorder. Following changes made by the Courts and Legal Services Act 1990,[38] the qualification for the appointment of a practitioner as a Circuit judge or recorder became the enjoyment of general rights of audience in the Crown Court or the county courts for 10 years. Any person who has been a District judge, or equivalent judicial officer,[39] for at least three years, or who is a recorder, is eligible for appointment as a Circuit judge. The requirement that a solicitor serve three years as a recorder before becoming eligible for a Circuit judgeship was removed. In 2000, it was decided that the post of assistant recorder should no longer be used and appointments are now made direct to recorderships.

On reorganisation under the 1971 Act, a number of middle-rank judges automatically became Circuit judges, including the Vice-Chancellor of the County Palatine of Lancaster, the Recorder of London, the Common Serjeant, the Recorders of Liverpool and Manchester, Official Referees, the Additional Judges of the Central Criminal Court, county court judges and the whole-time chairmen or deputy chairmen of quarter sessions.[40] Most of these offices were abolished, but some were retained. The Vice-Chancellor of the County Palatine of Lancaster conducts High Court Chancery business in the North.[41] The Common Serjeant and the Recorder of London[42] sit at the Central Criminal Court. Those appointed to these offices become Circuit judges *ex officio*. In addition, the senior Circuit judges at certain large court complexes (*e.g.*, the Recorders of Liverpool and Manchester[43] and other Senior Circuit judges, the Circuit judges at the Old Bailey, the judges of the Technology and Construction Court (formerly known as Official Referees), and the specialist Circuit judges (Chancery, Merchantile and Patents judges)

---

[37] And to carry out such other judicial functions as may be conferred on them by statute. A Circuit judge or recorder may be requested to act as a judge of the High Court and (where approved by the Lord Chancellor) the Court of Appeal (Criminal Division): Supreme Court Act 1981, s.9 as amended by the Administration of Justice Act 1982, s.58 and the Criminal Justice and Public Order Act 1994, s.52(1),(2). They are addressed as "Your Honour," unless sitting as a judge of the High Court or at the Central Criminal Court when they are addressed as "My Lord" or "My Lady". Circuit judges are referred to as His (or Her) Honour Judge X and recorders as Mr (or Mrs but not Miss) recorder B: *Practice Direction (Judges: Mode of Address)* [1982] 1 W.L.R. 101.

[38] s.71 and Sched. 10, paras. 31, 32.

[39] *e.g.* Social Security Commissioner, President of Tribunals, High Court masters, District judges: see Part IA of Sched. 2 to the Courts Act 1971, inserted by the 1990 Act, Sched. 10, para. 31(2), and amended by the Access to Justice Act 1999, Sched. 11, para. 19.

[40] Courts Act 1971, Sched. 2, Part I.

[41] He is appointed by the Chancellor of the Duchy of Lancaster. From 1987, the post has been held by a High Court judge, rather than a Circuit judge: see above, para. 2-060.

[42] The Recorder is elected by the City, but appointed by the Crown to exercise judicial functions. The Common Serjeant is appointed by the Crown. They are paid by the City of London authorities.

[43] These are honorary recorderships under the Courts Act 1971, s.54. The holders are addressed as "My Lord".

are regarded as holding appointments more burdensome than that of the ordinary Circuit judge, and are paid higher salaries.[44]

The Lord Chancellor may, if he thinks fit, remove a Circuit judge from office on the ground of incapacity or misbehaviour.[45] In 1983, Judge Bruce Campbell was removed from office following his conviction for smuggling whisky and cigarettes.[46] The retiring age is 70, although the Lord Chancellor may authorise a judge to continue in office up to the age of 75.[47]

The appointment of a person as a recorder specifies the term for which he or she is appointed and the frequency and duration of the occasions when he or she will be required to sit. The term may not last beyond the year in which he or she attains 70 (subject to continuance in office to 75 authorised by the Lord Chancellor). The Lord Chancellor may terminate the appointment on the grounds of incapacity, misbehaviour or a failure to comply with the conditions of the appointment.[48] The general terms and conditions for appointment were set out in a statement by the Lord Chancellor's office.[49] Appointments are now normally for five years at a time.[50] They are expected to sit for not less than four working weeks (20 days) a year. A daily fee, travelling expenses and subsistence allowances are payable.

The tenure in office of a recorder was to an extent precarious. Appointments were not renewed where the Lord Chancellor was not satisfied as to their continuing fitness or suitability, but the process by which

---

[44] £111, 210, as compared with £102, 999, as from April 1, 2002. There have in a number of years been difficulties in recruiting Circuit judges, with in 1987–88 three refusals for every one acceptance: salary was said to be a very important factor, especially for Q.C.s, and other factors included a perceived relative lack of status: *Review Body on Top Salaries*, Report No. 28 (Cm. 581, 1989), pp. 4–5. An additional 10 per cent increase was recommended by the Board in 1990 (Cm. 938, 1990), Chap. 5. By 1995, there were "no appreciable difficulties": Review Body on Senior Salaries, Report No. 35 (Cm. 2764, 1995), p. 20.

[45] Courts Act 1971, s.17(4).

[46] *The Times*, December 6, 1983. The fact that he was removed (as distinct from resigning) enabled him to keep his pension: Rozenberg (1994), pp. 111–112. Dismissal was threatened in the case of Judge James Pickles, but not effected: *ibid.*, pp. 112–114 and below, para. 4-028. In 1999, the Lord Chancellor accepted the resignation of Judge Richard Gee following his prosecution for conspiracy to commit offences under the Theft Act 1968 (while in practice as a solicitor) in which the jury failed to reach a verdict; he had been suspended on full pay since 1995: LCD Press Notice 389/99. Removal from office would have involved application of the civil standard of proof: *ibid.* In Scotland, Sheriff Thomson was removed in 1977 because of his political activities, and Sheriff Stewart in 1992 because of "inability to perform his judicial function": (1994) 144 N.L.J. 1651, noting the dismissal of the latter's application for judicial review.

[47] 1971 Act, s. 17(1), as amended by the Judicial Pensions and Retirement Act 1993, Sch. 9, para. 1.

[48] Courts Act 1971, s.21, as amended by the Judicial Pensions and Retirement Act 1993, Sch. 6, para. 9(1).

[49] (1971) 68 L. S. Gaz. 303.

[50] Before 2000, appointments were normally for periods of three years at a time. The change was made as part of a package designed to demonstrate the independence from the executive of the part-time judiciary: *Judicial Appointments Annual Report 1999–2000* (Cm. 4783, 2000), pp. 21–22.

this was done was not always satisfactory.[51] However, the tenure of part-time judges came under scrutiny following the decision the High Court of Justiciary[52] that Scottish temporary sheriffs, appointed by the Lord Advocate, now a member of the Scottish Executive, were insufficiently independent of the executive for compliance with the requirements of Article 6 of the ECHR. The Lord Chancellor reviewed the terms of service of part-time judges in England and Wales and on April 12, 2000, he announced revised terms of service for all part-time judicial appointments.[53] Accordingly, part-time appointments are for a period of not less than five years, subject to the relevant age limit; where appointments are renewable this will normally be done automatically, except on limited and specified grounds; removal from office will likewise only be on limited and specific grounds; whenever it is administratively possible, the offer of a minimum number of sitting days will be guaranteed. Subject to statutory provision, the specified grounds for non-renewal will generally be: (a) misbehaviour; (b) incapacity; (c) persistent failure to comply with sitting requirements (without good reason); (d) failure to comply with training requirements; (e) sustained failure to observe the standards reasonably expected from a holder of such office; (f) part of a reduction in numbers because of changes in operational requirements; and (g) part of a structural change to enable recruitment of new appointees. The grounds for removal will generally be as at (a) to (e) and decisions not to renew or to remove will be taken by the Lord Chancellor only with the concurrence of the Lord Chief Justice[54] and following an investigation conducted by a judge nominated by him. Decisions under (f) and (g) will be on a "first in first out" principle and again made by the Lord Chancellor with the concurrence of the Lord Chief Justice. While part-time judges already "in real terms" enjoyed significant security of tenure, the new arrangements "put beyond reasonable doubt the safeguards guaranteeing their independence."[55] The transfer of all powers of appointment and removal to a Judicial Appointments Commission independent of government would of course place these matters beyond

---

[51] "Where possible, the recorder is warned in advance of any cause for concern, so as to give him a chance to improve. However, this cannot always be done": L.C.D., *Judicial Appointments* (1986), p. 13. It was not effectively done in the case of Manus Nunan, whose appointment was not renewed in 1985: see *The Guardian*, 13, 14 and 16 June, and December 2 1986; R Brazier, *Constitutional Practice* (2nd ed., 1994), p. 291; Judge James Pickles, *Straight from the Bench* (1987), pp. 29–41, including notes of the interview between Nunan and Lord Hailsham L.C. The words in question were omitted from the 2nd ed. of the LCD booklet.

[52] *Starrs v. Procurator Fiscal. Linlithgow* [2000] H.R.L.R. 191. Cf. *Millar v. Procurator Fiscal, Elgin* [2001] UKPC D4 (*Starrs* applied; no effective waiver); *Clancy v. Caird (No. 1)* 2000 S.C. 441 [2000] H.R.L.R. 557 (temporary judge sufficiently independent and impartial as security of tenure was to be implied). See A. O'Neill, (2000) 63 M.L.R. 429.

[53] *i.e.* deputy High Court judges, deputy Circuit judges, recorders, deputy District judges, deputy masters and registrars of the Supreme Court, deputy District Judges (Magistrates' Courts) and retired Lords of Appeal, Lords Justices of Appeal and High Court judges, and the part-time judiciary who sit on tribunals or as adjudicators.

[54] As the statutory power is expressly that of the Lord Chancellor, this could be argued to be an unlawful fetter on discretion unless the Lord Chancellor could show that he exercised an individual judgment in each case.

[55] *Judicial Appointments Annual Report 1999–2000*, paras. 2.14–2.18. Age limits have subsequently been removed: LCD Press Notice 143/02.

any argument.[56] The Lord Chancellor may appoint any person with a seven year general qualification[57] to the position of District judge or deputy District judge. The latter is a part-time appointment.

Judicial appointments are handled by the Judicial Group within the LCD and the procedures for appointment summarised in *Judical Appointments: The Lord Chancellor's Policies and Procedures.*[58] The fundamental guiding principles underpinning the Lord Chancellor's policies in selecting candidates for judicial appointment are (a) appointment is strictly on merit; (b) part-time service is normally a pre-requisite of appointment to full-time office; and (c) significant weight is attached to the independent views of members of the professional community (and others) as to suitability for judicial appointment. Candidates for appointment as Circuit judges are expected to have proved themselves first by sitting as recorders (or as holders of one of the other specified judicial offices), and recorders are not given a full appointment unless they have proved themselves after a period in training. A District judgeship is normally a full-time appointment although some permanent, part-time appointments have now been made. Some deputy District judges are on track for such an appointment; others continue to sit for renewable terms as part-timers.[59]

In 1994, the Lord Chancellor, following consultation,[60] introduced new procedures for appointments to Circuit and District judgeships.[61] These involve annual open competitions for vacancies, with advertisements in the national and legal press; the preparation and publication of job descriptions and statements of eligibility and selection criteria[62]; the adoption of application forms designed to seek information enabling applicants to be judged against the published criteria; and an interview with a panel comprising a senior member of the LCD Judicial Group, a serving judge and a lay person. The lay interviewers have been chosen from among those involved in interviewing for the magistracy.[63] These arrangements were extended to all assistant recorders appointed from April 1997. This general

---

[56] See further, below, para. 4-025.

[57] *i.e.* a right of audience in relation to any class of proceedings in any part of the Supreme Court or all proceedings in county courts or magistrates' courts (Courts and Legal Services Act 1990, s. 71): County Courts Act 1984, s. 9, as amended by the Courts and Legal Services Act 1990, Sched. 10, para. 57. District judges may sit in the county court or the High Court (see above, paras 2-042, 2-066).

[58] Revised edition, 1999, LCD website. See below, para. 4-025.

[59] *ibid.* Minimum age limits normally applied in practice were 35 (recorders and deputy District judges), 40 (District judges) and 45 (Circuit judges): *ibid.*; but these have been removed: LCD Press Notice 143/02. Newly appointed recorders and deputy District judges must attend an induction course run by the Judicial Studies Board, have a period of sitting-in with an experienced judge and a period of supervised sitting: *Judicial Appointments Annual Report 2000–2001*, para. 1.50.

[60] See LCD Consultation Paper, *Developments in Judicial Appointments Procedures* (May 1994). See D. Wheatley Q.C., (1994) 144 N.L.J. 784, arguing that the changes were of form rather than substance, although a small step in the right direction.

[61] LCD Memorandum on Judicial Appointments Procedures (1995), pp. 51–60.

[62] The selection criteria cover legal knowledge and experience; intellectual and analytical ability; sound judgment; decisiveness; communication and listening skills; and authority and case management skills; and personal qualities (integrity and independence, fairness and impartiality, understanding of people and society, maturity and sound temperament, courtesy, and commitment, conscientiousness and diligence).

[63] *Judicial Appointments Annual Report 1999–2000*, para. 1.23; from 2000, it is intended to consider appointing lay interviewers from other backgrounds.

approach has subsequently been adopted for all appointments except as deputy High Court judges and to the Court of Appeal and above where appointment is on promotion. The introduction of greater objectivity into the system is intended encourage more applications from women and members of ethnic minorities.[64] The Law Society has maintained that there is still excessive reliance on the views of serving judges, that the requirement of prior part-time service before a full-time appointment is unnecessary and disproportionately difficult for solicitors to comply with.[65]

In 1999, Sir Leonard Peach was commissioned by the Lord Chancellor to report on the operation of the appointments process in relation to judicial appointments and the appointment of QCs and in particular to advise on the appropriateness and effectiveness of the criteria and the procedures for selecting the best candidates, the extent to which candidates are assessed objectively against the criteria and the existence of safeguards in the procedures against race and sex discrimination. His report[66] concentrated on how appointments were made rather than by whom, and generally endorsed the arrangements as appropriate and effective. Key recommendations were that the established procedures should be extended to deputy High Court judges; there should be more formalisation of the process for succession planning for appointments to the High Court and above;[67] candidates should be asked to provide a self assessment against the selection criteria and nominate three to six "nominated consultees"; the consultation form should be redesigned to ensure that the comments invited are allied to the requirements of the post and that information sources are identified; there should be a pilot scheme for a one-day assessment centre (with interviews, group exercises, discussions and presentations designed to test the skills required for successful candidates); psychometric and competencies tests available on the market should be assessed for relevance to judicial appointments; a Commission for Judicial Appointments should be established to audit the judicial/QC appointment procedures and to investigate complaints about the way they have been applied; an experimental appraisal scheme for deputy District judges in the Wales and Chester circuit should be extended to all other deputy District judges with a view to extension to all part-time judicial post holders; annual self appraisal should be introduced for all part-time judges. The recommendations were broadly welcomed and most have been implemented.[68] Sir Colin Campbell, Vice-Chancellor of the University of Nottingham (an academic legal philosopher) was appointed as First Commissioner of Judicial Appointments in March 2001, and seven further Commissioners (all non lawyers) were appointed in December 2001.[69] All serve part-time. Sir Leonard rejected the Law Society's argument that the consultation with the

---

[64] See below.

[65] Evidence to the Home Affairs Committee: (1995) 145 N.L.J. 878.

[66] *An Independent Scrutiny of the Appointment Process of Judges and Queen's Counsel in England and Wales* (December 1999, LCD website).

[67] This involves formal meetings between the Lord Chancellor, senior judges and the First Commissioner for Judicial Appointments (see below, para. 4-024).

[68] *Implementation Progress of the Recommendations in Sir Leonard Peach's Report* (June 2001, LCD website).

[69] *LCD Press Notice 433/01.* Appointments were made by the Queen on the recommendation of the Lord Chancellor.

professional community should be scrapped. Having observed the process in action and subject to some recommended modifications, "to abandon the consultation process would be a neglect of a valuable input into the assessment," it being only one part of the process. The Law Society itself continues to boycott the consultation process.

A separate Joint Working Party[70] reported in September 1999 on *Equal Opportunities in Judicial Appointments and Silk*.[71] Many of its recommendations were supported by Sir Leonard Peach and were accepted. Those that were not were (1) that consideration should be given to whether in fact the requirement for part-time service was essential; (2) that income/earnings should be removed from the list of relevant considerations; and (3) that consideration should be given to establishing a (very much more) swift procedure for assessing the merits of individual applications. On the first point, Sir Leonard Peach argued persuasively that given that full-time appointments were to a higher retiring age than other professions and that the qualities of a good judge overlap but are different from those of an advocate or solicitor, "an assessed part-time period before achievement of full-office is beneficial for the individual and the general public."[72] Steps have, however, been taken to introduce part-time sittings in blocks of one or two days rather than several weeks at a time and some permanent part-time District judge appointments have been made.[73] Recommendations accepted include the provision of practical assistance to candidates from under-represented groups who have the requisite ability, the conducting of research on the factors that inhibit applications from female and ethnic minority lawyers,[74] the introduction of detailed statistical monitoring,[75] improved careers information, and other particular matters taken up by Sir Leonard Peach.

Overall, the position is improving, but it is difficult to demonstrate cause and effect. It is anticipated that the proportions of women and ethnic minority lawyers appointed will increase as the proportions of such lawyers with the requisite experience increase. In 2000/2001, 28.4 per cent of judicial appointments were women and nearly 7 per cent were of ethnic minority origin.[76] Arguments have persisted that for there to be both significant progress in appointing the best judges from a wide variety of backgrounds (including an increased number of appointments of solicitors to the higher levels) and improvement in public confidence, responsibility for judicial appointments should be transferred to an independent commission.[77] For

---

[70] With representatives of the Bar Council, the Law Society, the African, Caribbean and Asian Lawyers' Group, the Society of Asian Lawyers, the Society of Black Lawyers, the Association of Women Barristers and the Association of Women Solicitors, and secretariat provided by the LCD Judicial Group.

[71] *Judicial Appointments Annual Report 1999–2000*, Annex D (Summary of recommendations).

[72] Report, LCD website.

[73] *Judicial Appointments Annual Report 2000–2001*, paras. 1.6,1.7. The former is available to those who have had a career break; the Working Party recommended wider availability. The latter possibility is to be extended to future competitions for certain other judicial posts: Rosie Winterton M.P., Parliamentary Secretary LCD, H.C. Deb., December 19, 2001, col. *394W*.

[74] K. Malleson, and F. Banda, *Factors affecting the decision to apply for silk and judicial office* (LCD, 2000).

[75] See *Judicial Appointments Annual Reports*.

[76] *Judicial Appointments Annual Report 2000–2001*, para. 1.9.

[77] See below, para. 4-025.

example, the Law Society acknowledges that recent developments have much improved on the transparency and effectiveness of arrangements, but maintains that this further step remains necessary.[78]

D. JUDGES OF THE SUPERIOR COURTS[79]

1. THE CLASSES OF JUDICIAL OFFICE

Appointments to the High Court Bench are to the office of *puisne*[80] judge or **4–021**
Justice of the High Court.[81] A High Court judge is almost invariably knighted or made a Dame Commander of the British Empire upon appointment, but is referred to as, for example, "Mr[82] Justice Swallow".[83] Promotion to the Court of Appeal involves elevation to the position of *Lord Justice of Appeal*, which is normally associated with an appointment to membership of the Privy Council. "Swallow J." becomes "Lord Justice Swallow".[84] The next step is membership of the House of Lords as a *Lord of Appeal in Ordinary*,[85] one of the "Law Lords". Although he or she will have been addressed in court as "My Lord" from the time of his appointment as a High Court judge, it is only at this stage (in the normal course of events) that he actually acquires a life peerage, as, say, "Lord Swallow of Somerset".[86]

In addition, there are several specific judicial offices. The *Lord Chancellor*[87] has long been regarded as the head of the judiciary in England

---

[78] Law Society, *Judicial Appointments* (October 2000) (*www.lawsociety.org.uk*).
[79] See generally, J. A. G. Griffith, *The Politics of the Judiciary* (5th ed., 1997) and *Judicial Politics since 1920* (1993); Lord Mackay, *The Adminstration of Justice* (1994) Chap. 1; D. Pannick, *Judges* (1987); J. Rozenberg, *The Search for Justice* (1994), Chaps.1, 2.; K. Malleson, *The New Judiciary* (1999) R. Brazier, "The appointment and removal of the lower judiciary" (1986) 15 Anglo-Am. L. R. 173 and *Constitutional Practice* (2nd ed., 1994), Chap. 12. On the appointment, control and extra-judicial activities of the judges between 1945 and the mid-1950s, see R. B. Stevens. "The Independence of the judicary: the view from the Lord Chancellor's Office" (1988) 8 O.J.L.S. 222.
[80] Pronounced as if it were "puny". The two words are related, a puisne judge being a "junior" judge in the superior courts of common law.
[81] See the Supreme Court Act 1981, s.4(2).
[82] Or Mrs. There has not yet been a Miss and may never be a Ms. It has been suggested that an unmarried lady would be referred to as "Mrs Justice": A. Samuels, (1982) 79 L. S. Gaz. 509.
[83] Written as Swallow J. If there are two Swallows on the bench, Christian names are also used.
[84] Written as Swallow L.J. The first woman appointed to this office was Dame Elizabeth Butler-Sloss in 1988: until 1994 she was referred to as "Lord Justice", this being the designation in the Supreme Court Act 1981, s.2(3); the usage was then changed to "Lady Justice" in anticipation of a change to the Act: *Practice Note: Mode of Address: Dame Elizabeth Butler-Sloss* [1994] 1 F.L.R. 866.
[85] "The word 'Ordinary' is a technical term used in law to describe a judge who has jurisdiction to hear cases by virtue of his office. In contrast to other persons who have jurisdiction only by being peers": Lord Denning, *The Family Story* (1981), p. 184.
[86] Lord Jenkins of Ashley Gardens apparently had wished to be styled Lord Jenkins of 24 Ashley Gardens, but was thwarted by the College of Arms.
[87] *i.e.* the Lord High Chancellor of Great Britain. Written as Lord Mackay of Clashfern L.C. Incumbents since 1945 have been Lord Jowitt (1945–1951); Lord Simonds (1951–1954); Lord Kilmuir (1954–1962); Lord Dilhorne (1962–1964); Lord Gardiner (1964–1970); Lord Hailsham (1970–1974, 1979–1987); Lord Elwyn-Jones (1974–1979); Lord Havers (1987); Lord Mackay (1987–1997); Lord Irvine (1997–). See generally R. F. V. Heuston, *Lives of the Lord Chancellors, 1985–1940* (1964) and *1940–1970* (1987); I. S. Dickinson. "Aspects of appointments to the office of Lord Chancellor" 1988 S.L.T. 41 (which lists those appointed between 1830 and 1987); D Woodhouse, *The Office of Lord Chancellor* (2000).

and Wales (although not Scotland and Northern Ireland), and has now received formal recognition as "president of the Supreme Court".[88] He is an *ex officio* member of the Court of Appeal,[89] and is the president of the Chancery Division[90] although the effective head of that Division is the Vice-Chancellor. If he sits as a judge at all it is in the House of Lords or the Privy Council, and only Lord Hailsham of St Marylebone and Lord Mackay of Clashfern (previously a Lord of Appeal) of the recent Lord Chancellors have sat at all regularly.[91] It has been argued that the Lord Chancellor should no longer be head of the judiciary and sit as a judge; this arrangement is inconsistent with the principle of the separation of powers, brings little advantage, and carries the disadvantage that the Lord Chancellor appears to speak on behalf of the judges when he is in fact bound by collective cabinet responsibility, including in matters concerning the administration of justice.[92] Lord Irvine has indicated that he will not sit "in any appeal where the government might reasonably appear to have a stake in a particular outcome."[93] The line can be difficult to draw. Lord Mackay L.C. was criticised for participating in *Pepper v. Hart*,[94] which concerned the admissibility of statements made by ministers in presenting Bills to Parliament; Lord Mackay indeed dissented, referring to the increase of the costs of litigation, a matter of particular concern given his responsibility for legal aid. He defended his participation, arguing that the case concerned the independent Board of the Inland Revenue rather than a government department.[95]

The requirements of Article 6(1), ECHR, taking effect through the Human Rights Act 1998, make it even more difficult for the Lord Chancellor to sit judicially. Particularly problematic is his lack of security of tenure and the fact his position as a government minister undermines the appearance of independence. Lord Irvine has, however, refused to adopt any more restrictive rule to govern when he should sit.[96]

---

[88] Supreme Court Act 1981, s.1. He is paid £2,500 more than the Lord Chief Justice: Ministerial and other Pensions and Salaries Act 1991, s.3; Ministerial and Other Salaries Order 1996 (S.I. 1996 No. 1913), para. 4.

[89] *ibid.* s.2.

[90] *ibid.* s.5(a).

[91] See G. Drewry, "Lord Chancellor as Judge" (1972) 122 N.L.J. 855. Until the Second World War the legislative sittings of the House of Lords commenced at 4.15 p.m., enabling the Lord Chancellor to sit regularly on appeals during the standard hours of 10.30 a.m. to 4.00 p.m. However, wartime difficulties caused the start of legislative sittings to be advanced to 2.30 p.m. and the Lord Chancellor was compelled to choose between the two kinds of work: R.F.V. Heuston, *Lives of the Lord Chancellors, 1885–1940* (1964), p. xviii. See also A. Bradney, "The Judicial Activity of the Lord Chancellor 1946–1987" (1989) 16 J.L.S. 360: this sets out statistics of the judicial activity of Lord Chancellors and former Lord Chancellors in this period.

[92] Lord Steyn, "The Weakest and Least Dangerous Department of Government" [1997] P.L. 84, 89–91. For a contrary view, see Lord Woolf, (1998) 114 L.Q.R. 579, 582.

[93] H.L. Deb., February 17, 1999, col. 735.

[94] Below, para. 6-036.

[95] See Woodhouse (2001), pp. 124–126.

[96] *ibid.*, pp. 126–130, noting that the Lord Chancellor's position "appears considerably more vulnerable" that of the Bailiff of Guernsey, who is President of both the island's legislature and its Court of Appeal, and whose dual involvement in a matter concerning planning regulations was held to infringe Article 6(1), ECHR, in *McGonnell v. UK* (2000) 30 EHRR 289. Lord Irvine regards *McGonnell* as confined to the special position of the Bailiff and his role in the particular case (*ibid.*, pp. 129–130). See generally R. Corness, [2000] P.L. 166.

The Lord Chancellor has many administrative functions to perform as head of the judiciary. For example, he has the effective say in most judicial appointments and assignments, and various powers to give directions affecting the business of the courts. He also has general responsibility for the Court Service,[97] the Law Commissions, publicly funded legal services,[98] the Land Registry and the Public Records Office. He is normally a Cabinet minister, and is the Speaker of the House of Lords.[99] Lord Gardiner stated that his paperwork was about half political and half judicial administration.[1] Lord Irvine has been more active politically than most of his recent predecessors. He is appointed by the Queen on the advice of the Prime Minister, and, as a political appointment, holds office "during pleasure". He goes out of office with the government of which he is a member, and is, indeed, as subject to dismissal by the Prime Minister as any other minister.[2] There are no formal qualifications for appointment, but all have been barristers. Lord Mackay was the first who has not been a member of the English Bar.[3]

The *Lord Chief Justice of England*[4] takes precedence over all judges other than the Lord Chancellor. He is the president of the Court of Appeal (Criminal Division) and the Queen's Bench Division of the High Court. The office was created as part of the reorganisation of the superior courts under the Supreme Court of Judicature Acts 1873–75. Before then each of the superior common law courts had its own chief: the Chief Justices of the Queen's Bench and the Common Pleas, and the Chief Baron of the Exchequer. The first Lord Chief Justice of England appointed as such was, accordingly, Lord Coleridge,[5] Chief Justice of the Common Pleas from 1873, who took the office in 1880 following the deaths of Sir Alexander Cockbum C.J. of the Queen's Bench Division and Chief Baron Kelly.[6] From that date new incumbents have been ennobled if not already peers. The holder is referred to as Lord Woolf, Chief Justice or Lord Woolf Lord Chief Justice.[7]

---

[97] Courts Act 1971, s.27(1).

[98] See below, Chaps 10 and 11, paras 14-085–14-089.

[99] See generally on the functions of the Lord Chancellor: *Halsbury's Laws of England* (4th ed.) Vol. 8, paras. 1171–191; the accounts cited in Heuston (1964), p. xv, n. 1 and (1987), p. 1, n. 1; the addresses by Lord Gardiner (1968) and Lord Hailsham (1972) to the Holdsworth Club (published in B. W. Harvey (ed.) *The Lawyer and Justice* (1978); and Lord Hailsham, *The Door Wherein I Went* (1975), pp. 244–258 and (1989) 8 C.J.Q. 308.

[1] Harvey (ed.) (1978), p. 216.

[2] Viscount Kilmuir was dismissed by Harold Macmillan on the "night of the long knives" in July 1962.

[3] He had previously been Lord Advocate, a judge of the Court of Session and a Lord of Appeal.

[4] See F. Bresler, *Lord Goddard* (1977), Chap. 9.

[5] Lord Parker, (1961) 35 A.L.J. 97. Some Chief Justices of the King's Bench had styled themselves, or had been referred to informally as Lord Chief Justice of England, although this was technically incorrect. A notable example of the former was Sir Edward Coke, whose action was said to have displeased the King and to have been one of the causes of his dismissal.

[6] The opportunity was also taken to amalgamate the three common law divisions. The following have held the office: Lord Coleridge 1880–94; Lord Russell of Killowen 1894–1900; Lord Alver-stone 1900–1914; Lord Reading 1914–1921; Lord Trevethin 1921–1922; Lord Hewart 1922–1940; Viscount Caldecote 1940–1946; Lord Goddard 1946–1958; Lord Parker 1958–1971; Lord Widgery 1971–1980; Lord Lane 1980–1992; Lord Taylor 1992–1996; Lord Bingham 1996–2000; Lord Woolf 2000–.

[7] Written as Lord Woolf C.J. or Lord Woolf L.C.J.

The office of *Master of the Rolls*[8] dates from at least the thirteenth century. He was originally the keeper of the rolls or records of the Chancery, but with the passage of time he became recognised as a judge in the Court of Chancery: until 1813 he was the only judge in that court other than the Chancellor. After the reorganisation of the courts under the Judicature Acts 1873–75 he continued as a judge of first instance, but the man appointed in 1873, Sir George Jessel, was such an able lawyer that it was thought appropriate for the Master of the Rolls to become a judge of the Court of Appeal.[9] He is now the president of the Court of Appeal (Civil Division).[10] In view of the large number of important civil cases determined in that court and the power of the Master of the Rolls over the allocation of cases, the holder of that office may exert considerable influence over the development of the civil law. It was for this reason that Lord Denning, then a Lord of Appeal in Ordinary, welcomed the appointment as Master of the Rolls.[11] The holder is referred to as Lord Phillips of Worth Matravers, Master of the Rolls.[12]

The *President of the Family Division* and the *Vice-Chancellor* head, respectively, the Family and Chancery Divisions of the High Court, and are *ex officio* members of the Court of Appeal. The former office was created in 1970, with the transition from the Probate, Divorce and Admiralty Division.[13] The holder is referred to as Dame Elizabeth Butler Sloss, President.[14] The latter office was created in 1970, the holder to be nominated by the Lord Chancellor.[15] It was made a royal appointment analogous to the other heads of division in 1982.[16] The holder is technically the vice-president of the Chancery Division,[17] but is effectively the head. He is referred to as Sir Andrew Morritt, Vice-Chancellor.[18] The title "Vice

---

[8] See Lord Denning, *The Family Story* (1981), pp. 201–204; Sir John Donaldson, M.R., (1984) 17 Bracton L.J. 19 and *The Problems of A Master of the Rolls* (Holdsworth Club, 1985).

[9] Sir Robert Megarry, (1982) 98 L.Q.R. 370, 395.

[10] Supreme Court Act 1981, s.3(2).

[11] Lord Denning, *The Family Story* (1981), pp. 172, 197; "the Master of the Rolls is still one of the most coveted posts in the land": *ibid*. p. 204. Lord Denning also found himself "too often in a minority" in the House of Lords: *The Discipline of Law* (1979), p. 287.

[12] Written as Lord Phillips M.R. It is common for the holder of the office to be ennobled, although not necessarily on appointment. Recent holders have been Lord Wright 1935–1949; Lord Evershed 1949–1962; Lord Denning 1962–1982; Sir John Donaldson (Lord Donaldson from 1988) 1982–1992; Sir Thomas Bingham 1992–1996; Lord Woolf 1996–2000; Lord Phillips 2000–.

[13] See above, p. The old division was also headed by a President. The incumbents have been Sir Jocelyn Simon 1962–1971; Sir George Baker 1971–1979; Sir John Arnold 1979–1988; Sir Stephen Brown 1988–1999; Dame Elizabeth Butler-Sloss 1999   –.

[14] Written as Dame Elizabeth Butler-Sloss P. Sir Stephen was the first who was previously a Lord Justice of Appeal; Dame Elizabeth was previously a Lady Justice of Appeal.

[15] Administration of Justice Act 1970, s.5.

[16] Supreme Court Act 1981, s.lO(l). See generally Sir Robert Megarry, (1982) 98 L.Q.R. 370.

[17] 1981 Act, s.5(l)(a).

[18] Written as Sir Andrew Morritt V.C. Sir Andrew is the seventh of the modern Vice-Chancellors; the others were Sir John Pennycuick 1970–1974, Sir John Plowman 1974–1976, Sir Robert Megarry, 1974–1985, Sir Nicolas Browne-Wilkinson 1985–1991, Sir Donald Nicholls 1991–1994 and Sir Richard Scott 1994–2000. The last four holders of the office were previously Lords Justices of Appeal.

Chancellor of England" was used in the nineteenth century for the judges appointed to assist the Lord Chancellor in the Court of Chancery.[19]

One of the Lords Justices of Appeal is appointed as Senior Presiding Judge by the Lord Chief Justice, with the agreement of the Lord Chancellor.[20] There is also provision for the appointment of a vice-president of both Divisions of the Court of Appeal or a vice-president for each Division[21] and of a vice-president for the Queen's Bench Division.[22]

2. Masters and Registrars

There are a number of officers of the Supreme Court below the ranks of the 4–022 judges, who perform both administrative and judicial tasks, the latter in particular in interlocutory matters arising in the course of litigation. There are, for example,[23] a number of Masters of the Queen's Bench and Chancery Divisions, District Judges of the principal registry of the Family Division, Taxing Masters (cost judges) and Registrars in Bankruptcy. One of each of these groups is appointed as a "senior" or "chief".[24] A particularly important office is that of the Master of the Crown Office and Registrar of Criminal Appeals.[25]

3. Eligibility for Appointment and Numbers

Prior to tne Courts and Legal Services Act 1990, appointments as a judge of 4–023 the Supreme Court were confined to members of the Bar. The position now is as follows:[26]

---

[19] 53 Geo III c. 24, 1813. In 1841 two additional Vice-Chancellors were appointed. With the death of the last Vice Chancellor of England (Sir Lancelot Shadwell) in 1850 the words "of England" were dropped. The Vice-Chancellors were transferred to the Chancery Division under the Judicature Act 1873. On their death or retirement their successors were styled as High Court justices. See A. B. Schofield, (1966) L. S. Gaz. 298; Megarry, *op. cit.*

[20] Courts and Legal Services Act 1990, s.72.

[21] Supreme Court Act 1981, s. 3(3). Rose L.J. was appointed vice-president of the Criminal Division in 1997, and re-appointed in 2001. Nourse L.J. was appointed vice-president of the Civil Division from June 6, 2000, and acted as Master of the Rolls until Lord Phillips took up his appointment on October 1, 2000: LCD Press Notice 135/00.

[22] Access to Justice Act 1999, s. 69. May L.J. was appointed in 2001, in succession to Kennedy L.J.

[23] Schedule 2 to the Supreme Court Act 1981, as substituted by the Courts and Legal Services Act 1990, Sched. 10, para. 49, lists offices. See also s.89, as amended by the 1990 Act, Sched. 18, paras.37, 38. On the work of the Queen's Bench Masters see A. S. Diamond, (1960) 76 L.Q.R. 504 and Sir Jack Jacob, *The Reform of Civil Procedural Law* (1982), p. 349; on Chancery Masters see R. E. Ball, (1961) 77 L.Q.R. 331.

[24] Supreme Court Act 1981, s.89(3).

[25] These were formerly separate posts, the first carrying responsibility for civil work and appeals in the Queen's Bench Division, the second for appeals to the Court of Appeal (Criminal Division). They were amalgamated by the 1990 Act, s.78. The office of Registrar of Civil Appeals has been abolished: see above, para. 2-071.

[26] Supreme Court Act 1981, s.l0(3), as amended by the Courts and Legal Services Act 1990, s.71.

Position	Max. Number	Qualification
Puisne judges	106[27]	10 years' High Court qualification[28] or two years standing as Circuit judge[29]
Lords Justices of Appeal	35[30]	10 years' High Court qualification or High Court judge.
Lord Chief Justice Master of the Rolls President of the Family Division Vice-Chancellor }		10 years' High Court qualification or High Court judge or judge of the Court of Appeal

In order to be qualified for appointment as a Lord of Appeal in Ordinary a person has to have (1) been for 15 years a person who has a Supreme Court qualification in England,[31] an advocate in Scotland or a solicitor entitled to appear in the Court of Session and the High Court of Justiciary, or a practising barrister in Northern Ireland; or (2) have held for two years one or more of the "high judicial offices" of Lord Chancellor, or judge of the High Court, Court of Appeal, Court of Session or Supreme Court of Judicature of Northern Ireland.[32] There is a maximum number of 12.[33] By convention, two of the Lords of Appeal are Scots lawyers.[34] Most of the offices below the rank of puisne judge can be held by a person with a seven or 10-year general qualification.[35] These are much in the way of minimum requirements: for example, a lawyer can expect to wait much longer than 10 years before becoming a serious candidate for appointment to the High Court.

[27] *ibid.* s.4(1)(e). See n. 30 below.

[28] *i.e.*, a person who has a right of audience in relation to all proceedings in the High Court: 1990 Act, s.71 (3); see further, above, para. 3-017.

[29] A person of this standing is eligible for appointment as a deputy High Court judge: *ibid.* s.9(4).

[30] *ibid.* s.2(1). The number of puisne judges and Lords Justices may be increased by Order in Council: ss.4(4) and 2(4). The maximum number of puisne judges was increased from 85 to 98 by the Maximum Number of Judges (No.2) Order 1993 (S.I. 1993 No. 1255): see H. L. Deb. vol. 545, May 10 1993, col. 1048; and from 98 to 106 (anticipating implementation of the Human Rights Act 1998) by the Maximum Number of Judges Order 1999 (S.I. 1999 No. 3138). The number of Lords Justices was raised from 28 to 29 in 1993; from 29 to 32 in 1994 (Maximum Number of Judges Order 1994 (S.I. 1994 No. 3217): see H.L. Deb., Vol. 559, November 30 1994, col. 686); and from 32 to 35 in 1996 (Maximum Number of Judges Order 1996 (S.I. 1996 No. 1142)). See also below, para. 4-033.

[31] *i.e.* a person with a right of audience in relation to all proceedings in the Supreme Court: 1990 Act, s.71(3)(a); see above, para. 3-017.

[32] Appellate Jurisdiction Act 1876, ss.6, 25, as amended by the Courts and Legal Services Act 1990, Sched. 10, para. 1.

[33] Administration of Justice Act 1968, s.1. This number may be increased by Order in Council: *ibid.* It was raised from 11 by the Maximum Number of Judges Order 1994, n. 30 above.

[34] This was observed notwithstanding the appointment of a Scots lawyer as Lord Chancellor: Lord Mackay was succeeded as Lord of Appeal by Lord Jauncey of Tullichettle.

[35] Supreme Court Act 1981, Sched. 2, as substituted by the 1990 Act, Sched.10, para. 49. A "general qualification" is a right of audience in relation to any class of proceedings in any part of the Supreme Court, or all proceedings in county courts or magistrates' courts: 1990 Act, s.71(3)(c); see above, para. 3-017.

Prior to the reforms effected by the Courts and Legal Services Act 1990, solicitors were not eligible for appointment to the High Court bench and above.[36] The government argued in resisting change on this point that experience as an advocate in the Supreme Court was necessary for appointment to the bench there.[37] With the extension of rights of audience in the higher courts to appropriately qualified solicitors, the change in eligibility for judicial appointment was irresistable. However, the government also at long last accepted the case that Circuit judges should be eligible for appointment to the High Court. Such judges may be solicitors who have never had a right of audience in the higher courts; nevertheless, a successful period as a Circuit judge would seem, as a matter of common sense, to be a better demonstration of one's judicial qualities than experience as an advocate.[38] In 2000, the first appointment of a solicitor direct to the High Court was made.[39]

The expansion of eligibility for the highest judicial offices was widely welcomed during consultation on the Green Papers on Reform of the Legal Profession.[40] One concern expressed in the course of it was that if members of the Crown Prosecution Service were to be given extended rights of audience they would thereby become eligible for a judicial appointment: it was, it was argued, wrong in principle for a person to be appointed as a judge whose experience was exclusively as a prosecutor. The White Paper[41] pointed out that it was the Lord Chancellor's current practice not to appoint serving civil servants to any paid judicial office which would involve hearing criminal cases. As appointment to a full-time judicial office had in practice to be preceded by part-time judicial experience, a member of any part of the government legal service could not become a judge without first returning to private practice for a substantial period. The Glidewell Report on the Crown Prosecution Service recommended that this policy should be reconsidered, to improve the career possibilities for CPS lawyers.[42] There has been no movement on this issue.[43]

Academic lawyers are not appointed directly to the Bench in the United Kingdom, even if they are lawyers of the requisite standing.[44] Moreover, it seems to have become progressively less common for academic lawyers to be a member of either branch of the profession. It is generally agreed that it would not be appropriate to appoint academic lawyers as trial judges, in view of their lack of experience with the process of ascertaining the facts of cases. It is, however, arguable that academics should be eligible for

---

[36] See JUSTICE Sub-Committee Report on the Judiciary (1972), pp. 9–20.

[37] See (1981) 131 N.L.J. 273; (1981) 79 L. S. Gaz. 193.

[38] The first solicitor Circuit judge to be promoted was Sachs J. in 1993.

[39] Lawrence Collins J., previously a partner in Herbert Smith, who was assigned to the Chancery Division.

[40] See above, para. 3-006.

[41] *Legal Services: A Framework for the Future* (Cm. 740, 1989), pp. 42, 43.

[42] Cm. 3960, 1998, p. 179.

[43] *Recorder 2002/03 Competition: Guide for Applicants* (LCD website), noting that there must be a 12 month break after service in the GLS or CPS before applying for a recordership.

[44] The only reference to "practising" barristers related to eligibility for appointment as a Law Lord. The word "practising" does not appear in the qualification substituted by the 1990 Act. Professor Brenda Hoggett Q.C. was appointed to the Bench as Hale J. after moving from an academic post to a spell of almost 10 years as a Law Commissioner; in 1999 she was promoted to the Court of Appeal.

appointment to the Court of Appeal or the House of Lords.[45] It could not be disputed that there would be candidates with the appropriate qualities of intellect and scholarship; it would also be one method of widening the background, political and otherwise, of members of the judiciary, should that be thought to be desirable.[46]

4. METHOD OF APPOINTMENT[47]

4–024 Appointment to the positions of Lord Chief Justice, Master of the Rolls, President of the Family Division, Vice-Chancellor, Lord of Appeal in Ordinary and Lord Justice of Appeal are made by the Queen,[48] acting by convention on the advice of the Prime Minister, who, in turn, will have consulted the Lord Chancellor. The effective voice in all appointments is normally that of the Lord Chancellor,[49] following consultations with members of the judiciary and leading members of the legal profession.[50] Occasionally, the Prime Minister may override the Lord Chancellor's view

---

[45] The JUSTICE Sub-Committee on The Judiciary favoured this proposal: Report (1972), pp. 21–24.

[46] A number of academics have been appointed as tribunal chairmen, recorders or deputy High Court judges; furthermore, Professor David Pearl has become a Circuit judge and John Mesher a Social Security Commissioner.

[47] See LCD, *Judicial Appointments: The Lord Chancellor's Policies and Procedures* (above, para. 4-020); Shetreet (1976),. pp. 46–84; Lord Hailsham, *The Door Wherein I Went* (1975), pp. 254–258; Malleson (1999), Chap. 4; D. Woodhouse, *The Office of Lord Chancellor* (2001), Chap. 6; A. Paterson, "Becoming a Judge" in R. Dingwall and P. Lewis (eds.) *The Sociology of the Professions* (1983), Chap. 12; A. Samuels, "Appointing the Judges" (1984) 134 N.L.J. 85, 107; Sir Robert Megarry, "The anatomy of judicial appointment: change but not decay" (1985) 19 U.B.C. Law Rev. 113; Judge T. Lawrence, (1993) 33 Med. Sci. Law 279; Sir Thomas Legg, [2001] P.L. 62.

[48] Supreme Court Act 1981, s.10(1)(2).

[49] The Lord Chancellor deals personally with judicial appointments and relations with individual judges; these matters are not dealt with by Parliamentary Secretaries: LCD website. The Lord Advocate's influence in the appointment of Scots Law Lords has increased in the post-war period: see A. A. Paterson, "Scottish Lords of Appeal, 1876–1988" 1988 J.R. 235. "In the last 20 years, however, it is generally felt that, with promotion from the Bar being out of fashion and neither Lord President evincing any desire to move south, in the case of most appointments the candidates have almost selected themselves": *ibid.*, p. 241.

[50] The extent and method of consultation depends on the level of the appointment: LCD, *Judicial Appointments: The Lord Chancellor's Policies and Procedures* (revised ed., 1999); LCD Memorandum on Judicial Appointments Procedures (1995), pp. 18, 22, 24, 34 (Home Affairs Committee, Third Report 1995–96 H.C. 52–II). For example, Circuit judges, presiding judges, leaders of the relevant Circuit Bar and members of the Council of the Law Society are consulted on recordership appointments (the first rung of the ladder); the Lord Chancellor personally consults the four Heads of Division and the Senior Presiding Judge on High Court appointments, Heads of Division on appointments to the Court of Appeal and the Law Lords, the Lord Chief Justice and the Master of the Rolls on appointments to the House of Lords; and the views of a wider range of members of the judiciary are also sought. Their views are not necessarily endorsed by the Lord Chancellor: see J. Rozenberg, *Trial of Strength* (1997), pp. 13–15 (commenting on the appointment in 1996 of Sir Thomas Bingham M.R. rather than Rose L.J. as Lord Chief Justice). Lord Halsbury was exceptional in not consulting the Lord Chief Justice: R. F. V. Heuston, *Lives of the Lord Chancellors, 1885–1940* (1964), pp. 47–18.

in relation to senior appointments.[51] Records on potential candidates are maintained by the staff of the Lord Chancellor's Department Judicial Group, and candidates are interviewed. Increasing light was shed on the appointments process by the publication by the Lord Chancellor's Department of a booklet on *Judicial Appointments*[52] and in the Department's Memorandum of Evidence to the Home Affairs Select Committee.[53] There have been a number of developments in the procedures, although most have to date been in respect of appointments below the level of the High Court.[54]

Appointments to the High Court Bench are normally made from the ranks of Queen's Counsel who have been in practice for 20 to 30 years.[55] Junior barristers may be appointed direct but the only persons normally so appointed are the Junior Counsel to the Treasury, who, indeed, are normally elevated to the bench after their period in that position. From time to time there have been promotions from the positions of Official Referee,[56] county court judge,[57] Recorder of Liverpool or Manchester, Circuit judge[58] and Registrar of the Family Division,[59] but these constitute a fairly small minority.[60] One person has been appointed to the High Court Bench and one to the House of Lords after being an advocate general of the Court of Justice of the European Communities.[61]

Appointments are "on merit".[62] The Lord Chancellor's Department publications[63] in fact say very little on what is looked for particularly in respect of High Court appointments.[64] The qualities looked for would seem to be good character, success as a lawyer (usually as an advocate) and in a part-time or lower judicial office, the rather mystical quality known as "common sense," and good health. Those appointed are usually in their

---

[51] *e.g.* the appointment of Sir Ernest Pollock rather than Bankes L.J. as Master of the Rolls in 1923: Heuston, *Lives*, p. 428. *Cf.* Samuels (1984) 134 N.L.J. 85, 86. It was Lord Mackay's practice to submit more than one name, with comments; it seems that his first choices were not necessarily accepted by the Prime Minister: J. Rozenberg, *Trial of Strength* (1997), pp. 16–17.

[52] 3rd ed., 1995; revised ed., 1999 (LCD website).

[53] LCD, *Judicial Appointments Procedures in England and Wales*, Memorandum of Evidence to the House of Commons Select Committee on Home Affairs (1995).

[54] See above, para. 4-020.

[55] LCD, *Judicial Appointments: The Lord Chancellor's Policies and Procedures* (1999), Senior Judicial Appointments.

[56] Sir Edward Ridley (1897). The fact that he held office was regarded as counting against him rather than for him. He was the brother of the Home Secretary, and was subsequently thought to be a poor judge: See Heuston, *Lives*, pp. 49–52.

[57] The first was Sir Edward Acton (1920), the Nottingham county court judge. Ten more were elevated between 1945 and 1971.

[58] 26 were elevated between 1973 and 2000.

[59] Butler Sloss J. (1979).

[60] 26 out of 195 appointments between 1970 and 1994.

[61] Warner J. (1981); Lord Slynn (1992).

[62] See above, para. 4-020.

[63] Above, n. 50.

[64] "Practitioners who are appointed to the High Court Bench will normally have had a substantial and successful practice, often having developed areas of specialisation, and to be held in high regard by the profession": LCD, *Judicial Appointments: The Lord Chancellor's Policies and Procedures* (1999), Senior Judicial Appointments.

fifties, although some are appointed in their forties.[65] Brilliance as a technical lawyer is not regarded as a necessary precondition, although greater weight is placed on legal ability when appointments to the Chancery Division or to the appellate courts are considered. Formal offers of a position on the High Court bench are not usually declined, but there has been anecdotal evidence of an increasing number of members of the Bar who when approached informally indicate that they do not wish to be considered either at all or at that time.[66] A survey of deputy High Court judges revealed that 28 per cent of the respondents were unlikely to accept appointments, citing the High Court salary, the need to go on circuit, the loss of autonomy over working life and adverse impact on personal freedoms and family life as disincentives.[67]

From 2000, applications have been invited annually from suitably qualified practitioners and Circuit judges for appointment to the High Court, although the Lord Chancellor reserves the right to appoint those who have not made an application.[68]

Several observers have noted an improvement in the quality of judges.[69] "On the whole, I have no doubt that judges are much better educated, more polite and more patient than they used to be."[70]

Political service was formerly a significant factor in many judicial appointments.[71] Of the 139 judges appointed between 1832 and 1906, 80 were M.P.s at the time of their nomination; 11 others had been candidates for Parliament. Of those 80, 63 were appointed by their own party while in office.[72] Lord Halsbury, Unionist Lord Chancellor for three periods,[73] was criticised for making bad appointments of Tory M.P.s.[74] Lord Salisbury, the Prime Minister for most of Halsbury's time as Lord Chancellor, "would never apologise for the practice of making [legal promotions] a reward for political 'right thinking,'"[75] although he expressed the need for caution following public criticism of some of the early appointments.[76] There was contemporary criticism of the appointments of Grantham, J. C. Lawrance, Bruce, Darling, Ridley and Kekewich, all of whom turned out to be poor

---

[65] The youngest in the last 50 years were Lords Hodson and Devlin who were 42 when appointed High Court judges in 1937 and 1948 respectively.

[66] This has given the Senior Salaries Review Body "grounds for concern" although there were "no major problems at present in recruiting judges of the required calibre at all levels": Report No. 51, Cm. 5389–I, 2002, para. 4.33; the Review Body also recommended an additional 5.4 per cent increase relative to the Civil Service. See further on remuneration, para. 4-031.

[67] Report No. 41, Cm. 4245, 1999, pp. 17–19. The remuneration factor was the one most often mentioned.

[68] Of the 19 High Court judges appointed in 2000–01, seven were applicants through the High Court competition and twelve were invited to accept appointment: Judicial Appointments Annual Report 2000–2001, para. 3.11.

[69] C. P. Harvey Q.C., The Advocate's Devil (1958), pp. 33–34, comparing the fifties with the twenties, Lord Devlin, The Judge (1979), p. 24; D. Pannick, Judges (1987), p. 15.

[70] Lord Hailsham, The Door Wherein I Went (1975), p. 257.

[71] See A. Paterson, (1974) 1 B.J.L.S. 118. Party politics continued to play a larger role in the appointment of judges in Scotland. This gave rise to adverse criticism: I. D. Willock, 1969 J.R. 193; C. M. Campbell, 1973 J.R. 254.

[72] H. Laski, (1926) 24 Michigan L. R. 529.

[73] 1885–86; 1886–92; 1895–1905.

[74] See Heuston, Lives, pp. 36–66.

[75] G. Cecil (Lord Salisbury's daughter and biographer) cited by Heuston, Lives p. 36.

[76] ibid. p. 57.

judges,[77] although each had his defenders. The first four were Conservative M.P.s at the time of their appointment. Ridley had briefly been a Conservative M.P. nearly 20 years before, although that did not seem to have influenced the choice, and Kekewich had been a Conservative candidate. Heuston argues that the last two appointments were unlucky and that "four dubious appointments out of 30 during a tenure of the woolsack lasting 17 years should not weigh too heavily in the scales when making a final judgment."[78]

Lord Haldane, when Lord Chancellor between 1912 and 1915, introduced a policy of appointing "only on the footing of high legal and professional qualifications",[79] and this position, as regards puisne judgeships, has more or less been maintained since. The only political tradition that took significantly longer to die was the idea that the Attorney-General and Solicitor-General had a special claim should one of the higher judicial offices fall vacant.[80] The Attorney's claim on the position of Lord Chief Justice was supposed to be particularly strong.[81]

Between 1873 and 1945 only four of the 23 holders of the office of Attorney-General did not go on to hold one of the higher judicial offices.[82] All those appointed Lord Chief Justice, with one exception,[83] were former Attorneys. Nine of the 17 men who were Solicitor-General without becoming Attorney-General also progressed to one of the higher judicial offices.[84]

However, much controversy surrounded the appointment of Sir Gordon Hewert as Lord Chief Justice.[85] In 1921 it was arranged that Lord Reading C.J. was to become Viceroy of India. Hewart, as Attorney-General, pressed his claim to the position of Lord Chief Justice but could not be spared from

---

[77] Grantham J. attracted severe criticism in Parliament for his partisan trial of two election petitions in 1906: see H. Cecil, *Tipping the Scales* (1965), pp. 194–208; Darling J. was described by C. P. Harvey as a "real shocker" (*The Advocate's Devil* (1958), pp. 32–33) and renowned for his "jokes"; MacKinnon L. J. wrote that J. C. Lawrance J. was "a stupid man, a very ill-equipped lawyer and a bad judge. He was not the worst judge I have appeared before: that distinction I would assign to Mr Justice Ridley. Ridley had much better brains than Lawrance, but he had a perverse instinct for unfairness that Lawrance could never approach" (1944) 60 L.Q.R. 324).

[78] *Lives*, p. 66.

[79] R. B. Haldane, *An Autobiography* (1929), p. 253.

[80] J. Ll. J. Edwards, *The Law Officers of the Crown* (1964), pp. 309–334.

[81] Eighteen of the 42 Chief Justices of the Common Pleas between 1600 and 1873 were ex-Attorneys, 16 appointed directly. Between 1725 and 1873 all but two of the Chief Justices of the King's Bench were ex-Attorneys, four appointed directly: Edwards (1964), pp. 320–21.

[82] Lord Chancellor (8), L.C.J. (5), M.R. (2), Lord of Appeal (4), L.J. (4): four held two of these offices. The exceptions were Karslake (1874) who suffered a complete physical break-down in 1875, Walton (1905–8) who died in office and Patrick Hastings (1924), Attorney-General in the first Labour Government, who apparently "had no wish to be made a judge" (Lord Birkett, *Six Great Advocates* (1961), p. 37). Sir Henry James (1880–85) was given a peerage and often sat in the House of Lords.

[83] Lord Trevethin (1921).

[84] Lord Chancellor (4); L.J. (3); President of the P.D.A. (2); Lord of Appeal (1: Lord Davey, promoted from Lord Justice). Of the other eight, four held other ministerial offices (Harcourt (1873–74), Gorst (1885–86), Cripps (1930–31) and Monckton (1945)), three died in office or shortly after leaving it (Lockwood (1894–95), Melville (1929–30) and O'Connor (1936–40)), and the other, Clarke (1886–92), refused the position of Master of the Rolls in 1897.

[85] See R. Jackson, *The Chief* (1959), Chap. 9; J. Campbell, *F. E. Smith, First Earl of Birkenhead* (1983), pp. 479–481.

the Commons. Lloyd George appointed a 77-year-old Queen's Bench judge, A. T. Lawrence J., on the understanding that he would retire when called upon, although neither Lord Birkenhead L.C. nor Hewart approved of the plan. Nevertheless, in 1922 Lord Trevethin (as Lawrence became) read of his own resignation in *The Times*, and Hewart duly succeeded him. To add injury to insult, Hewart proved to be "perhaps the worst Lord Chief Justice of England since the seventeenth century. Although no imputation of corruption or dishonesty could be brought against him, as against Scroggs and Jeffreys, on the bench he rivalled them in arbitrary and unjudicial behaviour."[86]

Since 1945 the position has changed significantly. In 1946, Viscount Calde-cote C.J. was succeeded by a Lord of Appeal, Lord Goddard, after the post had been declined by Sir Hartley Shawcross, the Attorney-General.[87] Lord Goddard and his successors have not had political careers.[88] Lord Goddard was followed by Lord Parker,[89] who subsequently commented that the non-political nature of the appointment, made clear by the appointments of Lord Goddard, himself and Lord Widgery, was of "vital importance for the administration of justice in this country."[90] The only Law Officers subsequently appointed to the bench have been Lynn Ungoed-Thomas[91] and Sir Jocelyn Simon,[92] and only three of the others have become Lord Chancellor.[93] The appointment of Lord Chief Justices from amongst the ranks of the judiciary has been generally welcomed.

It has become progressively more difficult to combine membership of the Commons with a successful practice at the Bar. Lord Hailsham regretted that he was unable to appoint a single High Court judge from among M.P.s.[94] There is something of a vicious circle in that the lack of a reasonable prospect of elevation to the Bench may discourage the ablest lawyers from seeking a political career. Political experience has been regarded by some as an asset for an appointee. Lord Simon has argued that:

"although no one would wish to see a predominantly political Bench, a seasoning of judges with experience of politics and administration is far from disadvantageous; constituency duties, for example, are calculated to develop a social awareness which ordinary forensic work is not apt to inculcate."[95]

---

[86] Heuston, *Lives*, pp. 603–604; Cf. C. P. Harvey, *The Advocate's Devil* (1958), p. 32.

[87] See F. Bresler, *Lord Goddard* (1977), pp. 112–115. Shawcross had opposed the idea that there was a "right" of succession, and preferred a political career.

[88] Goddard had stood unsuccessfully as an Independent Conservative in the 1929 General Election, a brief and "ill-starred political venture": Bresler (1977), pp. 60–62.

[89] The then Attorney-General, Sir Reginald Manningham-Buller, did not actively seek the post, but would apparently have liked to have been asked: Bresler (1977), pp. 295–298.

[90] Bresler (1977), p. 297.

[91] Labour M. P. 1945–62; Solicitor General 1951; High Court judge 1962–72.

[92] Conservative M. P. 1951–62; Solicitor-General 1959–62; President of the Probate, Divorce and Admiralty Division 1962–71; Lord of Appeal 1971–77. Two previous Presidents had formerly been Solicitor-General: Sir Samuel Evans (1910–1919) and Sir Frank (later Lord) Merriman (1934–1962).

[93] Viscount Dilhorne (formerly, Sir Reginald Manningham-Buller), Lord Elwyn-Jones and Lord Havers. Lord Mackay had previously served as Lord Advocate. Between 1945 and 1990 there were 18 holders of one or both of the Law Offices.

[94] *The Door Wherein I Went* (1975), p. 256.

[95] (1965) 81 L.Q.R. 289, 295.

The social and educational background of the judges has been examined **4–025** in a number of surveys.[96] These show that the judges are overwhelmingly upper or upper middle class in origin, with over three-quarters having attended public school, and a similar proportion either Oxford or Cambridge University. Only 13 women have reached the High Court bench, and no members of the ethnic minorities.[97] A report commissioned by the Bar Council and the LCD[98] concluded that "gender discrimination appears to be institutionally present within the Bar and the judiciary" and identified a series of factors that discouraged women from applying for a judicial appointment, including the lack of role models and the reliance on informed soundings from a majority male group. Appointments are formally made "on merit" and "regardless of gender, ethnic origin, marital status, sexual orientation, political affiliation, religion or disability, except where the disability prevents the fulfilment of the physical requirements of the office".[99] The Lord Chancellor "encourages greater numbers of women and ethnic minority practitioners to apply" but is against positive discrimination or a fast-track appointment procedure for such candidates.[1] Increases in the numbers appointed to the lower judicial offices should in time affect the numbers given senior appointments.[2]

The process of socialisation at the Bar tends to mean that those from other backgrounds do not seem markedly different, if different at all, from the majority.[3] The extent to which judicial attitudes can be related to the social background of the judges is a large and debatable question.[4] Given the continuance for the foreseeable future of the policy of appointing senior judges largely from the Bar, it is unlikely that there will be any significant change in the background of the people appointed. What is more plausible is that the attitudes of successive generations may gradually change.[5]

Other countries have adopted different methods of appointment. In civil

---

[96] *The Economist*, December 15, 1956, pp. 946–947; K. Goldstein-Jackson, *New Society*, May 14, 1970; H. Cecil, *The English Judge* (revised ed., 1972), Chap. 1; J. Brock (M. Phil, dissertation, quoted in the JUSTICE Sub-Committee Report on the Judiciary (1972)); F. L. Morrison, *Courts and the Political Process in England* (1973), Chap. 3. The background of the Lords of Appeal appointed between 1876 and 1969 is examined in L. Blom-Cooper and G. Drewry, *Final Appeal* (1972), pp. 158–169. The results of these surveys are summarised by J. A. G. Griffith, *The Politics of the Judiciary* (5th ed., 1997), pp. 18–22.

[97] Elizabeth Lane J., Booth J., Butler-Sloss J. (now P.) Bracewell J., Ebsworth J., Smith J., Arden J (now L.J.), Steel J., Hale J (now L.J.) Hogg J. Hallett J., Black J., Rafferty J., Ebsworth J. was the first appointed to the Queen's Bench Division (followed by Smith and Steel JJ.); Arden J. the first appointed to the Chancery Division. As at January 1, 2002, the numbers of judges known or believed to be of ethnic minority origin were: six Circuit judges (1%), 39 recorders (3%), 0 recorders in training, 11 District judges (2.6%), 13 deputy District judges (1.7%), 3 District judges (Magistrates' Courts) (3.2%) and 8 deputy District Judges (Magistrates' Courts) 4.9%): *Judicial Appointments: Ethnic Minority Appointments* (LCD website).

[98] *Without Prejudice? – Sex Equality at the Bar and in the Judiciary*, TMS Management Consultants (1992), cited in Rozenberg (1994), pp. 84–86.

[99] LCD, *Judicial Appointments: The Lord Chancellor's Policies and Producers* (1999).

[1] *ibid.*

[2] See above, para. 4-020. The arguments for more women judges, based on equal opportunities principles and the democratic legitimacy of the judiciary collectively, are powerfully made by Dame Brenda Hale, [2001] P.L. 489.

[3] As to the social background of barristers, see above, paras 3-048–3-050.

[4] See below, para. 4-040.

[5] See P. McAuslan, (1983) 46 M.L.R. 1, 19.

law systems there is normally a career judiciary, which is part of the general civil service and separate from the legal profession. In the United States there are two basic methods of selection, *appointment* and *election*, although a compromise between the two methods is commonly applied.[6] All federal judges are appointed by the President, subject to confirmation by the Senate.[7] An appointment can in practice be vetoed by one of the candidate's home state Senators and candidates are also evaluated by the American Bar Association's influential Committee on Federal Judiciary, which makes its views known to the President and the Senate. In 1970, 82 per cent of state and local judges were elected, although real contests were rare; in 1995, only six states did not have any type of elections for judges at any level.[8] In a number of states elections are used to confirm in office judges who have been in office for a limited period following appointment by the governor, a separate Commission, or the two together.[9] It is highly unlikely that any of these methods will be introduced here,[10] although many have favoured the formal establishment of a Judicial Commission to evaluate and advise on appointments.[11] A Judicial Appointments Commission has been established to monitor the appointments process and consider complaints arising out of it.[12] The Lord Chancellor has said that he has an open mind on the question

[6] See H. Abraham, *The Judicial Process* (7th ed., 1998), Chap. 2 and *Justices and Presidents* (3rd ed., 1992).

[7] The most recent example of a presidential nominee for the Supreme Court failing to obtain confirmation is Judge Robert Bork: see R. Hodder-Williams, (1988) xxxvi *Political Studies*, 613–637; Essays on the Supreme Court Appointment Process (symposium) 101 Harv. L.R. 1146–1229 (1988).

[8] Abraham (1998), p. 36. In recent years a number of state judges (including Chief Justice Rose Bird and two associate justices of the California Supreme Court) have failed to obtain re-election following sustained political campaigns by opponents: see R. Reidinger, "The politics of judging" A.B.A. Journal, April 1 1987, p. 52.

[9] The "Missouri plan" is favoured by the A.B.A. A non-partisan Commission selects three candidates, one of whom the governor must then appoint. After one year in office he or she must be approved by the electorate, running unopposed in a separate, non-partisan judicial ballot: Abraham (1998), pp. 38–42.

[10] An argument that the Law Lords, the Lord Chief Justice and the Master of the Rolls, but not the other judges, should be elected, under a plan similar to the "Missouri Plan" is presented by D. Pannick, (1981) 131 N.L.J. 1064.

[11] Report of JUSTICE Sub-Committee on *The Judiciary* (1972), pp. 30–31, 61; JUSTICE Report on *The Judiciary in England and Wales* (1992), Chap. 6; G. Bindman, (1992) 142 N.L.J. 1035. This Commission would also deal with complaints. The conferral of the power of *appointment* on a Judicial Service Commission is advocated by C. Harlow, in Harlow (ed.), *Public Law and Politics* (1986), Chap. 10, and R. Brazier, "Government and the Law" [1989] P.L. 64, 88–91; Brazier also advocates the establishment of Circuit Judicial Committees to advise on the appointment of the lower judiciary. A Law Society discussion document has made similar proposals: (1991) 88 L. S. Gaz., February 20, pp. 6–7 taken forward in Law Society paper, *Judicial Appointments* (October 2000). See also C. Thomas, *Judicial Appointments in Continental Europe* (LCD) and K. Malleson, *The Use of Judicial Appointments Commissions* (LCD) and Malleson (1999), pp. 125–151. For a defence of reliance on the individual personal responsibility of the Lord Chancellor, see Lord Mackay, *The Administration of Justice*, (1994), Chap. 1. For a comparative discussion, see B. Harris, (1993) 15 Adelaide L. R. 191.

[12] Above, para. 4-020.

whether greater powers should be conferred on such a body.[13] The transfer of responsibility for appointing judges to such a Commission is supported by the Liberal Democrats.[14] Interestingly, the Justice (Northern Ireland) Bill 2002 proposes the establishment of a Northern Ireland Judicial Appointments Commission to select candidates for appointment or recommendation for appointment to listed judicial offices, including judges of the High Court; the First Minister and Deputy First Minister could only recommend candidates to the Queen, for appointment as a High Court judge, who had been selected by the Commission. The Commission would be required to be "representative of the community in Northern Ireland." Similarly, judges of the High Court and above could only be removed on an address by Parliament if that step had been recommended by an independent tribunal.[15] It is not obvious that the circumstances of Northern Ireland are so different that these would not be suitable models for England and Wales.

5. Promotion

The traditional view was that there was no system of "promotion" of judges. The fear was that holders of judicial office might allow their promotion prospects to affect their decision-making; care might be taken to avoid offending the senior judges or the politicians responsible for making or influencing judicial appointments. Nevertheless, the trend seems to be for judges to be elevated from the Circuit Bench more regularly, and for appointments to the House of Lords and Court of Appeal to be made from the court below. Appointments are not now made direct from the Bar to the Court of Appeal[16] or the House of Lords,[17] or direct from the High Court to the House of Lords.[18] Three Lord Chancellors, Maugham, Simonds and Dilhorne, have been appointed Lords of Appeal, but the first two of these were simply reverting to an office previously held. At first, elevation to the Court of Appeal from the High Court carried no increase in salary, although membership of the Privy Council was always conferred. The salary of a

4–026

---

[13] *Judicial Appointments Annual Report 2000–2001*, para. 2.7: following publication of the first Annual Report of the First Commissioner, the Lord Chancellor "will then decide whether it is time to go out to consultation on the possibility of an independent judicial appointments commission with a more than supervisory role." The Home Affairs Committee did not favour the idea: Third Report, 1995–96 H.C. 52–1.

[14] Lord Goodhart, H.L. Deb., 21 June 2001, col. 54.

[15] See Select Committee on the Constitution, Fifth Report 2001–2002, *Justice (Northern Ireland) Bill*.

[16] The only examples have been Slesser L.J. (1929), Scott L.J. (1935) and Somervell L.J. (1946) (all Law Officers), Duke L.J. (1918; Chief Secretary for Ireland 1916–18) and Greene L.J. (1935: leader of the Chancery bar, and subsequently Master of the Rolls). Lord Denning has written that experience as a trial judge is valuable for an appeal judge: *The Family Story* (1981), pp. 169–170.

[17] Eleven examples: five Scots, two English, two Irish. The only two since 1930 have been Lord Reid (1948) and Lord Radcliffe (1949) each of whom was an outstanding judge.

[18] Seven examples: Lords Parker (1913), Tomlin (1929), Wright (1932), Porter (1938), Simonds (1944), Uthwatt (1946) and Wilberforce (1964). Lord Slynn was appointed to the House of Lords (1992) after a period as an Advocate General of the European Community; he had previously been a High Court judge.

Lord Justice is now roughly halfway between that of a High Court judge and a Lord of Appeal, although the differentials are small.[19] Apart from the prestige of a higher judicial office, promotion means that there is no longer the disadvantage of having to spend time away from home on circuit. There is, however, no evidence that judges are affected by "promotion sickness".

6. TENURE[20]

4–027   Every judge of the Supreme Court, other than the Lord Chancellor, who holds office "during the pleasure" of (in effect) the Prime Minister:

> "shall hold that office during good behaviour, subject to a power of removal by Her Majesty on an address presented to Her by both Houses of Parliament."[21]

Similarly:

> "Every Lord of Appeal in Ordinary shall hold his office during good behaviour but he may be removed from such office on the address of both Houses of Parliament."[22]

These arrangements date from the Act of Settlement 1700.[23] Before then judicial tenure was not regulated by statute. The King appointed on his own terms, which were usually, although not invariably, "during pleasure".[24]

The Stuarts removed or suspended a number of judges who did not conform to their expectations, James II being particularly enthusiastic in this regard.[25] From 1688, William III's appointments were made during good behaviour: the Act of Settlement took away the monarch's right to choose otherwise, although it seems that William was reluctant to see the legal position changed.[26]

It is generally accepted that under these provisions a judge may be removed from office either (1) for breach of the requirement of good behaviour or (2) by the Crown on an address by both Houses of Parliament, irrespective of whether he or she has been of good behaviour. The "address" procedure is, theoretically, neither the exclusive procedure for removal, nor restricted to cases of misbehaviour. In cases of misbehaviour, there are

---

[19] See below, para. 4-031. The introduction of a differential was recommended by the Top Salaries Review Body, "in recognition of the promotion which is involved in appointment to the Court of Appeal from the High Court Bench:" Report No. 6, Cmnd. 5846, 1974, p. 31.

[20] See Shetreet (1976), pp. 1–12, 85–159; Sir Kenneth Roberts-Wray, *Commonwealth and Colonial Law* (1966), pp. 484–491; W. Finnie, 1993 S.L.T. 213.

[21] Supreme Court Act 1981, s.11(3).

[22] Appellate Jurisdiction Act 1876, s.6, as amended.

[23] Section 3. This section was to take effect should the arrangements for ensuring the Protestant succession become operative: accordingly, the section came into operation in 1714 with the accession of George I.

[24] See C. H. McIlwain, *Constitutionalism and the Changing World* (1939), pp. 294–307.

[25] See J. H. Baker, *Introduction to Legal History* (3rd ed., 1990), pp. 189–193; A. Havighurst, (1950) 66 L.Q.R. 62, 229; (1953) 69 L.Q.R. 522.

[26] D. Rubini, (1967) 83 L.Q.R. 343.

indeed a number of alternative procedures for removing a judge, which do not seem to be excluded by the Supreme Court Act 1981 or any of its antecedents:

(1) Proceedings in the Queen's Bench Division commenced by the writ of *scire facias* for the repeal of the letters patent by which the office was granted.

(2) Proceedings in the Queen's Bench Division for an injunction to restrain the judge from continuing to act in an office to which he or she is no longer entitled.[27]

(3) Conviction for a criminal offence.

In these cases the "misbehaviour" must either be connected with the performance or non-performance of official duties, or, if not so connected, must involve the commission of a criminal offence of moral turpitude. Furthermore, a judge can be removed on any ground by an Act of Parliament, or for "high crimes and misdemeanours" by impeachment.[28] Neither would be used in preference to an address: the latter, in addition, is regarded as obsolete in the United Kingdom.[29]

Today, it is likely that the address procedure would be used in any case where a judge was to be removed, and, further, that this would only be done in a case of misbehaviour,[30] although a rather wider view might be taken of "misbehaviour" for this purpose, in particular to include private immoral conduct.[31] There have been many statements to the effect that this would be the "proper" way to proceed, notwithstanding the other possibilities.[32]

Conviction for a criminal offence does not inevitably lead to resignation or removal from office. Nine judges[33] have been convicted of driving with excess alcohol, but have continued in office.

The other methods by which a judge may leave office are:

(1) resignation[34];

---

[27] S. A. de Smith and R. Brazier, *Constitutional and Administrative Law* (8th ed., 1998), p. 381.

[28] A trial by the House of Lords at the instigation of the Commons. This procedure has not been used since the trials of Warren Hastings (1788) and Lord Melville (1805). Among judges who were impeached were two Lord Chancellors, Bacon (1620) and Macclesfield (1725): see H. Cecil, *Tipping the Scales* (1964), pp. 99–126.

[29] The procedure is not obsolete in the U.S.A.: President Nixon resigned rather than face impeachment; President Clinton was tried but acquitted

[30] It seems that the address procedure can be used in cases of incapacity: see Shetreet (1976), p. 274. However, resignation would be secured by informal pressure or a judge would be removed by the Lord Chancellor: see below, n.

[31] *Kenrick's case* (1826): Cecil (1964), pp. 165–170.

[32] See Shetreet (1976), pp. 96–103.

[33] A Lord Justice in 1969, a Circuit judge in 1973, a High Court judge in 1975, two Circuit judges in 1985, a High Court Registrar in 1989 (see R. Light (1989) 139 N.L.J. 783), a District judge in 1993 (see Rozenberg (1994), p. 117, and a Circuit judge in 1999. A number were severely reprimanded by the Lord Chancellor: *The Times*, June 17, 1989; Rozenberg, *op. cit.*; LCD Press Notice 209/99.

[34] Supreme Court Act 1981, s.11(7); Appellate Jurisdiction Act 1876, s.6.

(2) reaching the retiring age of 70[35];

(3) under the procedure whereby the Lord Chancellor may remove a judge
     who is disabled by permanent infirmity from the performance of his or
     her duties and is incapacitated from resigning his or her office.[36]

A retired judge may be asked to sit as a member of the Judicial Committee
of the Privy Council or the House of Lords, or as a deputy judge, on an ad
hoc basis. However, this is no longer possible once he or she has reached
75.[37]

   If a judge were, for example, to bury a meat cleaver in someone's head the
address procedure for removal from office would work swiftly and surely.
Judges, however, do not indulge in acts of misbehaviour that are clearly
inconsistent with their remaining in office. Where matters are not clear cut,
the address procedure is complex, and uncertain in some matters of detail.
Charges have been presented on a number of occasions, but only one judge
has been removed as a consequence. Sir Jonah Barrington, a judge of the
High Court of Admiralty in Ireland, was removed in 1830 for the
embezzlement of sums of money paid into court.

7. DISCIPLINE AND CRITICISM

4–028   The mechanisms for disciplining judges who misbehave are more significant
in practice than the procedures for removal. Judges may be criticised hi
Parliament. An extreme case is that of Lord Westbury L.C., who resigned in
1865 following votes of censure passed in both Houses concerning certain
appointments he had made.
   Judges are often criticised in the press. "Scurrilous abuse" of a judge may,
however, be punished as contempt for "scandalising the court."[38] This head
of contempt must be distinguished from that concerned with publications
likely to interfere with the administration of justice in particular

---

[35] Supreme Court Act 1981, s.11(2), as amended by the Judicial Pensions and Retirement Act
      1993, Sched. 6, para. 4. A retirement age (of 75) was first introduced by the Judicial Pensions
      Act 1959, but did not apply to those in office on December 19, 1959. (One of those to escape
      was Lord Denning M.R., who retired in 1982 aged 83). The 1993 Act applies both
      retropsectively and prospectively. Judges other than High Court judges and above may be
      asked to continue (in annual steps) to 75: 1993 Act, s.26. A judge may retire on full pension
      (normally half the salary in the last 12 months of service, index-linked), (1) after 20 years'
      service (raised from 15 by the 1993 Act to bring it into line with the public and private
      sectors generally); and (2) after attaining the age of 65, or (3) if he or she is disabled by
      permanent infirmity; otherwise, pensions are paid pro rata. See, generally, annotations by J.
      Mesher in *Current Law Statutes Annotated 1993*; W. Finnie, "Judicial Tenure and Judicial
      Pensions" 1993 S.L.T. 213.
[36] Supreme Court Act 1981, s.11(8)(9). See A. Paterson, "The Infirm Judge" (1974) 1 B.J.L.S.
      83.
[37] Judicial Pensions and Retirement Act 1993, s.26(7). Lord Bridge seemed displeased by his
      forced "second retirement": see *Ruxley Electronics and Constructions Ltd v. Forsyth* [1995] 3
      W.L.R. 118, 121 (his last case).
[38] See S.H. Bailey, D.J. Harris and D.C. Ormerod, *Bailey, Harris and Jones, Civil Liberties:
      Cases and Materials* (5th ed., 2001). pp. 779–786; N. V. Lowe, *Borrie and Lowe's Law of
      Contempt*, (ed.,), pp. 226–247; C. J. Miller, *Contempt of Court* (3rd ed., 2000), Chap. 12; C.
      Walker, "Scandalising in the Eighties" (1985) 101 L.Q.R. 359.

proceedings, by, for example, influencing juries. The former head was thought to be obsolete in 1899.[39] However, proceedings were taken against the editor of the *Birmingham Daily Argus* for a spirited attack on Darling J. (an "impudent little man in horsehair, a microcosm of conceit and empty headedness").[40] He apologised, and was fined £100, with £25 costs. According to Abel-Smith and Stevens[41] "within a decade the criticism of judicial behaviour which had been so outspoken was replaced in the press by almost unbroken sycophantic praise for the judges." Similar proceedings were taken on a number of occasions in the 1920s and 1930s. Since then, press criticism of the judiciary has become more commonplace, without matching the personal insults expressed by Mr Gray. Proceedings against Quintin Hogg (as he then was), arising out of criticisms of the Court of Appeal published in *Punch*, were dismissed.[42] Salmon L.J. said.[43]

"The authority and reputation of our courts are not so frail that their judgments need to be shielded from criticism, even from the criticism of Mr Quintin Hogg. ... [N]o criticism of a judgment, however vigorous, can amount to contempt of court, provided it keeps within the limits of reasonable courtesy and good faith."

Judges are from time to time rebuked in appellate courts. Censure may be coupled with the setting aside of a conviction or the reversal of a judgment. Thus, judges have been censured for excessive interruptions,[44] threatening a jury,[45] improper behaviour on the Bench,[46] falling asleep,[47] incompetence,[48] lengthy delay (20 months) in giving judgment[49] and disloyalty to the decisions of superior courts.[50] Lord Hailsham has written that there are judges who become subject to "judge's disease, that is to say a condition of

---

[39] *McLeod v. St Aubyn* [1899] A.C. 549,561 (a colonial judge was accused of "reducing the judicial character to the level of a clown," and "being narrow, bigoted, vain, vindictive and unscrupulous." The Privy Council held that this did not require committal for contempt).

[40] *R. v. Gray* [1900] 2 Q.B. 36. The full passage is printed in 82 L.T. 534. *Cf.* above, para. 4-024, n. 77. Darling was apparently "rather amused by the vigour of its expression": D. Walker-Smith, *The Life of Lord Darling* (1938), p. 122.

[41] *Lawyers and the Courts* (1967), pp. 126–7.

[42] *R. v. Metropolitan Police Commissioner, ex p. Blackburn (No. 2)* [1968] 2 Q.B. 150.

[43] *ibid.* p. 155. Mr Hogg subsequently became Lord Chancellor as Lord Hailsham of St Marylebone.

[44] *e.g. Yuill v. Yuill* [1945] P. 15; *Jones v. N.C.B.* [1957] 2 Q.B. 55. The judge in the latter case was Hallett J., who was seen by the Lord Chancellor and resigned shortly afterwards: Lord Denning, *The Due Process of Law* (1980), pp. 58–62 ("The judge who talked too much"). See generally, A. Samuels, "Judicial Misconduct in the Criminal Trial" [1982] Crim.L.R. 221.

[45] *R. v. McKenna* [1960] 1 Q.B. 411 (Stable J. at Nottingham Assizes threatened a jury that if they did not return a verdict within 10 minutes they would be locked up all night. They returned in six minutes with verdicts of guilty, which were quashed on appeal).

[46] *R. v. Hircock* [1970] 1 Q.B. 67. The judge in a criminal trial made gestures of impatience, sighed, and several times "observed in a loud voice, 'Oh God,' and then laid his head across his arm and made groaning noises" (p. 71). The court did not condone this conduct but declined to quash the conviction as being unsafe and unsatisfactory.

[47] If the judge thereby misses something of importance: *R. v. Edworthy* [1961] Crim.L.R. 325; *R. v. Langham* [1972] Crim.L.R. 457.

[48] *Taylor v. Taylor* [1970] 2 All E.R. 609.

[49] *Goose v. Wilson Sandford & Co., The Times,* February 19, 1998. The trial judge, Harman J., resigned: LCD Press Notice 40/98.

[50] *Cassell & Co. Ltd v. Broome* [1972] A.C. 1027, below, para. 7-015.

which the symptoms may be pomposity, irritability, talkativeness, proneness to *obiter dicta*, a tendency to take short cuts."[51]

There may be complaints from barristers, solicitors or litigants, either expressed in court or in private to the judge personally, or made in some other quarter. Complaints may be made to the Lord Chief Justice or the Lord Chancellor.[52] They may be channelled through a head of chambers, the Chairman of the Bar Council, the Attorney-General, the Law Society,[53] an M.P., or some other intermediary. There is generally a preference for taking action privately. Confrontations in court between counsel and judge may be to the client's disadvantage; it is impossible to assess the extent to which they may also be, or be feared to be, to the barrister's future disadvantage. The upshot may be correspondence or an interview between the Lord Chancellor and the judge,[54] or even, on occasion, a public rebuke.[55] In 1998, the Lord Chancellor set up a Judicial Correspondence Unit with responsibility for handling complaints concerning the personal conduct of judges. He "takes a close personal interest in the handling of complaints, particularly those alleging racial or sexual discrimination" and sees all serious complaints and cases where there is a record of similar complaints from different sources about the same judge. He replies personally to complainants and to those received from peers, MPs and members of devolved legislatures."[56]

It has been doubted whether the informal pressures on judges are sufficient. Over the years there have been a few judges whose conduct has often been criticised, but who have nevertheless remained on the Bench. On the other hand, this small minority seems to have dwindled. The JUSTICE Sub-Committee[57] argued that some form of complaints machinery should be established, probably in the form of a complaints tribunal or judicial commission. Such a reform is unlikely to occur in the foreseeable future,

---

[51] *The Door Wherein I Went* (1975), p. 255.

[52] Court users are invited to send complaints "about the way the judges/registrar behaved toward you (not in the way they handled the case) or that the decision went against you" to write to the LCD's Departmental Correspondence unit: Court Service Leaflet Ex 343, *I want to complain: What do I do?*

[53] It seems that the Bar and the Law Society will only act in cases of misconduct towards barristers and solicitors, respectively: JUSTICE, Sub-Committee Report on *The Judiciary*, pp. 49–50.

[54] Or an interview with the Lord Chief Justice: one such is described by Judge James Pickles in *Straight from the Bench* (1987), p. 53–57, arising out of his publication of newspaper articles.

[55] *e.g.* the rebuke administered to Judge Pickles by Lord Mackay L.C. for holding a press conference in a pub, and referring to the then Lord Chief Justice as a "dinosaur"; and the rebuke administered to a Circuit judge for his use of the expression "people ... who work like niggers": LCD Press Notice 63/97. *Cf. R. v. Earnshaw* [1990] Crim.L.R. 53.

[56] *Judicial Appointments Annual Report 2000–2001* (Cm. 5248, 2001), pp. 74–75. In 2000–01, 2,332 complaints were received; 463 related to personal conduct; further action was taken in eight of 341 completed cases (a letter or a meeting between the judge and the relevant presiding judge); in one case a deputy District judge was not reappointed for a final possible year: *ibid.*

[57] *op. cit.*, pp. 45–61. The case for a Judicial Performance Commission is also made by D. Pannick, *Judges* (1987), pp. 96–104. A Judicial Commission with responsibilities covering the monitoring of sentences, training and complaints has been established in New South Wales by the Judicial Officers Act 1986, criticised by S. Shetreet, (1987) 10 Univ. of N.S.W. L.J. 4.

and, on the present evidence, the case for it is not made out.[58] Finally, it must be remembered that criticisms of judges in the popular press are commonly marred by such weaknesses as a failure to report accurately the full facts, a failure to understand basic principles of the conduct of trials and a failure to distinguish defects of the law from the defects of the judge.

8. TRAINING[59]

In the late 1970s certain tentative steps were taken to introduce a measure of compulsory training for newly appointed judges. From 1963 onwards a series of conferences and judicial seminars on sentencing were organised by the Lord Chief Justice and the Lord Chancellor's Office. Attendance at these was voluntary. However a Judicial Studies Board was established in 1979 following the report of a Working Party chaired by Bridge L.J.[60] **4–029**

From October 1985 the Board was re-established, with enlarged responsibilities beyond the criminal jurisdiction, namely the provision of training in the civil and family jurisdictions and the supervision of training for magistrates[61] and tribunal chairmen and members.[62] A Director of Studies has been appointed (the position held by a Circuit judge on secondment for two years). Executive functions are delegated to a Criminal Committee, chaired by a Lord Justice of Appeal, and Civil, Family, Magisterial and Tribunals committees, chaired by High Court judges.[63] An Equal Treatment Advisory Committee advises on equal treatment issues, and has issued an Equal Treatment Bench Book; its members ensure that equal treatment issues are included in all core seminar aims and objectives and incorporated into the training.[64]

---

[58] It was not endorsed by the JUSTICE Committee on *The Administration of the Courts* (1986), Chap. 4.

[59] See M. Partington, "Training the Judiciary in England and Wales" (1994) 13 C.J.Q. 319; A. Ashworth, *Sentencing and Criminal Justice* (1993), pp. 49–50, 53; Judicial Studies Board: report for 1979–82 (HMSO, 1983), report for 1983–87 (HMSO, 1988) report for 1987–91 (HMSO, 1992), report for 1991–95 (1995) and subsequent annual reports; Glidewell L.J., "The Judicial Studies Board" in C. Munro and M. Wasik, *Sentencing, Judicial Discretion and Training* (1992) ; Judge Pitchers, *JSB Journal 1997*, Issue 3, pp. 18–19; Henry L.J., *JSB Journal 1999*, Issue 8, pp. 22–23; A. Rutherford, (1999) 149 N.L.J. 1120 (interview with Waller L.J.); Malleson (1999), Chap. 5.

[60] *Judicial Studies and Information* (HMSO, 1978). The Working Party had received "widely felt and strongly voiced objection" to the use in their working paper of the term "judicial training," on the grounds that "training" might represent a threat to judicial independence, that appointees might resent the implication that they need to be "trained" and that the "public image of the judge" would be impaired. The Working Party accordingly adopted the term "judicial studies" and emphasised that their proposals would not involve "indoctrination" or "conditioning" (*ibid.* pp. 2 and 3). Lord Devlin was caustic in his condemnation of the working paper: *The Judge* (1979), pp. 18–53; *cf.* book review by E. J. Griew, [1980] Crim.L.R. 812.

[61] See above, para. 4-007.

[62] See above, para. 4-018.

[63] See *Judicial Studies Board: Annual Report 2000–2001* (JSB website).

[64] *ibid.* See Brooke. J., (1992–93) *The Magistrate* 194 on the work of its predecessor, the Ethnic Minorities Advisory Committee, and Dyson J., *JSB Journal 1998*, Issue 4, p. 19.

Since 1981 it has been essential for a recorder or assistant recorder[65], before first sitting in a criminal case, to have attended a residential induction course (now normally lasting four days) organised by the Board. The main feature is a mock trial; there are tutor group discussions of sentencing, summing up and other practical issues and some talks.[66] There is then provision for a one day seminar for newly appointed recorders and four day residential continuation seminars for Circuit judges, recorders and newly appointed High Court judges. Additional refresher seminars are organised on a Circuit basis and specialist seminars are held on such matters as serious sexual offences (a requirement for judges authorised to hear such cases) and serious fraud.[67] Also before sitting on their own they must sit for at least a week in court with an experienced Circuit judge and there is a meeting with representatives from the Probation Service and a prison visit. The Civil and Family Committees have established training arrangements on similar lines as for the criminal jurisdiction, the main recurrent activities being induction courses for new deputy District judges and for new recorders who intend to sit in civil as well as criminal cases and for Circuit judges and recorders authorised to hear family proceedings, continuation seminars for established judges, an annual seminar for District judges and an annual President's conference for family judges. Bench Books have been distributed for the different categories of judge (for example, Crown Court, Family), *Guidelines for the Assessment of Damages in Personal Injury Cases.*[68] and specimen directions to juries in the Crown Court.[69] The Board publishes the *JSB Journal* three times a year. Substantial training exercises were held in relation to implementation of the Children Act 1989, the Criminal Justice Act 1991, the Human Rights Act 1998, the *Access to Justice* reforms and pension-sharing.

There has undoubtedly been a welcome increase in the scope and effectiveness of judicial training. However, as the Board itself makes clear, extra resources in money, manpower and judge time will be required if its activities are to be developed further. The Royal Commission on Criminal Justice stated that "substantially more resources need to be allocated to judicial training than at present," with reductions in the intervals between refresher training.[70] The Board is formally independent of the LCD; its secretary is not formally appointed as accounting officer but is treated as having an analogous status.[71] Lord Bingham regards it as essential for judicial independence that control of the content and form of judicial

---

[65] From April 12, 2000, no appointments as assistant recorder have been made; recorders designate must satisfactorily complete their training programme before being authorised to sit as a recorder: *Judicial Studies Board: Annual Report 2000–2001*, para. 3.5.

[66] *ibid.*, para. 3.6.

[67] *ibid.*, paras. 3.19, 3.25.

[68] (2nd ed., 1994): see *Report for 1991–1995*, Chap. 3 and p. 38.

[69] See *www.jsboard.co.uk*.

[70] Cm. 2263, p. 140. See also the discussion by M. Partington (1994) 13 C.J.Q. 319, 328–336.

[71] See *Memorandum of Understanding for JSB* (1999) (*www.jsboard.co.uk*). The Board's independence in assessing the need for, and providing judicial training, including the content and nature of that training is expressly acknowledged. However, resources are allocated in the light both of the JSB's plan and of the overall resources available to the LCD.

education (as it should now be called) "should rest squarely in the hands of the judges themselves, and such agencies as they may employ."[72]

9. INDEPENDENCE[73]

Much importance is attached to the independence of the judiciary.[74] By that   **4–030**
is meant independence from improper pressure by the executive, by litigants
or by particular pressure groups. Reasons given in support of judicial
independence are "(1) that independence is a condition of impartiality and
therefore also of fair trials, and (2) that it makes for a separation of powers
which enables the courts to check the activities of the other branches of
government."[75] As to the first, it has been emphasised that judges must not
only be impartial but appear to be impartial. Public confidence is only
bolstered by "ostentatious impartiality."[76] As to the second, it has been
noted with concern that the public today seem less satisfied that the judges
are completely independent of the government in power.[77] An illustration of
the dangers that arise when judges are dismissed where their decisions incur
the displeasure of the executive is provided by the crisis in Malaysia in
1988.[78]

The extent to which judicial independence is (and should be) respected has
come under increased scrutiny since the 1980s. It is generally accepted that
the various factors about to be discussed are effective in securing that
particular judges in deciding individual cases are protected from improper
pressures. However, the relationship between the judiciary collectively and
the executive has been problematic over a range of contentious issues.[79] The

---

[72] Tom Bingham, *The Business of Judging* (2000), p. 67.

[73] See W. Lederman (1956) 36 Can. Bar Rev. 769; G. Borrie (1970) 18 Am.J.Comp.Law 697;
Sir Anthony Mason (1990) 13. U.N.S.W.L.J. 173; Justice M. D. Kirby, *ibid.*, 187; R.
Stevens. *The Independence of the Judiciary: The view from the Lord Chancellor's Office*
(1993), 'Judges, Politics, Politicians and the Confusing Role of the Judiciary' in K. Hawkins
(ed.), *The Human Face of Law* (1997), Chap. 11, 'A Loss of Innocence?': Judicial
Independence and the Separation of Powers' (1999) 19 OJLS 365; T. Bingham, *The Business
of Judging* (2000), pp. 55–68; Mr. Justice R. D. Nicholson, "Judicial independence and
accountability: can they co-exist" (1993) 67 A.L.J. 404; K. Marks (1994) 68 A.L.J. 173; P.
Polden, (1996) 25 Anglo-Am.L.R.; Malleson (1999), Chap. 3 and for comparative and
international perspectives, S. Shetreet and J. Deschênes, *Judicial Independence: The
Contemporary Debate* (1985).

[74] Article 6(1), E.C.H.R. provides that "[i]n the determination of his civil rights and obligations
or of any criminal charge against him, everyone is entitled to a fair and public hearing within
a reasonable time by an independent and impartial tribunal established by law." See also
Art. 14(1), I.C.C.P.R., which is in similar, but not identical terms: see S. H. Bailey, in D. J.
Harris and S. Joseph (eds.), *The ICCPR and UK Law* (1995), pp. 210–219.

[75] See T. Eckhoff, (1965) 9 *Scandinavian Studies in Law*, pp. 11–48.

[76] *ibid.* p. 12. It has been argued that this feature has been lacking in the appointment of
Scottish judges: see C. M. Campbell, 1973 J.R. 254.

[77] See D. Oliver, "The Independence of the Judiciary" (1986) 39 C.L.P. 237 and "Politicians
and the Courts" (1988) 41 *Parliamentary Affairs* 13.

[78] See [1988] N.Z.L.J. 217; F. Narinan, [1988] N.Z.L.J. 266; R. H. Hickling, [1989] P.L. 20; F.
A. Trindade, (1990) 106 L.Q.R. 51.

[79] Indeed one commentator has described the proposition that there is independence of the
judiciary (as distinct from individual judges) as a "constitutional myth": R. Stevens, (1994)
144 N.L.J. 1620, 1621.

theme that links these is the tension between the constitutional position of
the judges (particularly but not exclusively as perceived by themselves) and
the "new managerialism" in the provision of public services that has become
increasingly prominent in the administration of justice. We return to this
below.[80] First, we consider the factors that are relevant to maintaining
judicial independence; it will be noted that several are by no means clear-cut.
The appointment and the tenure of judges have already been dealt with.
Party political considerations seem to have been eliminated, although this
does not mean that the decisions of judges are not "political" in a wider
sense:[81]

> "Judges are part of the machinery of authority within the State and as
> such cannot avoid the making of political decisions."[82]

This point takes on an increased significance with the increased activism
of the higher judiciary. "Activism" here means in particular the enhanced
powers of judges under the Human Rights Act 1998 to adopt interpretations
of legislative provisions that vary from a literal meaning.[83] It leads to
arguments that while independence and impartiality in the deciding of
individual cases must vigorously be maintained, "the cloak of judicial
independence can no longer be spread so widely as to inhibit the
development of legitimate mechanisms of accountability." These should
include further developments in the appointment process (to ensure greater
representativeness), training, appraisal and the handling of complaints,
leading overall to increased public confidence. A number of the desirable
changes have, indeed, already been put into effect in respect of the lower
ranks of the judiciary.[84] At the same time, there have also been arguments in
varying forms in favour of a greater formal recognition of the separation
powers, with support for such developments as the establishment of an
independent Judicial Appointments Commission, the redefinition of the role
of the Lord Chancellor[85] and the enhancement of the role of the judiciary in
the administration of the courts.[86]

Other relevant factors include the following:

---

[80] See below, para. 4-033.

[81] A. Paterson, "Judges: A Political Élite" (1974) 1 B.J.L.S. 118. "Whoever can persuade the
members of a society that law is inevitable or to take 'law as a given', and that the legal
interpretation of a particular social situation is the only possible one, controls an important
if not vital source of power in that society. In my contention British Judges are in precisely
this position and that is why it is legitimate to characterize them as involved in the realm of
politics": *ibid.* p. 129. See also R. J. Wilson, "British Judges as Political Actors" (1973) 1 Int.
Journal of Criminology and Penology 197.

[82] J. A. G. Griffith, *The Politics of the Judiciary* (5th ed. 1997), pp. 292–293.

[83] Cf. Sir Stephen Sedley's characterisation of judicial activism in the United States as "the
deployment of principle and policy to enhance or defeat enacted legislation where no liberal
application of the constitution is possible": Forword to Malleson (1999), p. viii.

[84] Malleson (1999), *passim.*

[85] See Stevens (1997) and (1999) 19 OJLS 365; above, paras 4-020, 4-021, 4-025.

[86] See below, para. 4-033.

(a) Remuneration

Judges are paid substantial salaries,[87] which are a charge on the **4–031**
Consolidated Fund and so not subject to an annual vote in Parliament.
The current salaries are as follows: Lord Chief Justice: £185, 145; Master of
the Rolls and Senior Lord of Appeal in Ordinary: £176,327; Lords of
Appeal, President of the Family Division and Vice-Chancellor: £170,370;
Lords Justices: £161,941; High Court judges: £143,258.[88] They can be
increased, but not reduced, by the Lord Chancellor, with the consent of the
Prime Minister as Minister for the Civil Service.[89] From the time salaries
became a charge on the Consolidated Fund,[90] they could only be changed
by statute, or, between 1965 and 1973, by ministerial order.[91] Under the
National Economy Act 1931, the salaries of "persons in His Majesty's
service," which term was taken to include the judges, were reduced by 20 per
cent. The need to secure the independence of the judiciary was placed at the
forefront of their arguments both that the Act did not apply to them as a
matter of interpretation, and that it should not apply in principle.[92] The
government restored the cuts in 1934. This argument has, however, not
figured so prominently in the recent reports of the Senior (formerly Top)
Salaries Review Board on judicial salaries, in which more important
considerations seem to have been the need to attract lawyers with the right
qualities and experience and the need to maintain the judges' status in the
community. Thus the Board has taken into account both barristers' earnings
and the salaries payable to Permanent Secretaries and senior military
officers as "cross-checks" although there are no formal links with either.[93]
The Board conducted fundamental reviews in 1995–97 and 2000–02.[94] The
first recommended that pay should be based on the whole job, irrespective of
the mix between judicial and administrative responsibilities; the 2000 Report
recommended the upgrading of the posts of the Heads of Division;[95] the
2002 Report found the existing structure to be sound, that the post of Senior
Law Lord should be equated to that of Master of the Rolls, and that there

---

[87] Certainly by the standards of Professors of Law, and many University Vice Chancellors, but
not by those of leading lawyers in private practice; in 1999 the Senior Salaries Review Board
reported that the drop in the average remuneration of those recently appointed to the High
Court remains at around 60 per cent, but had stabilised over recent years: Report No. 41,
Cm. 4245, 1999, p. iv.

[88] Salaries as at April 1, 2003 arising from staged implementation of Senior Salaries Review
Body: Report No. 51, Cm. 5389-I, 2002; see H.C. Deb., col. 1443w, February 28, 2002; LCD
website, Judicial Salaries 2002–03. As to pensions, see para. 4-027, n. 35.

[89] Supreme Court Act 1981, s.12.

[90] Judges appointed after 1786. There was no change between 1851 and 1954 (Judges'
Remuneration Act 1954).

[91] Judges' Remuneration Act 1965.

[92] See Heuston, *Lives*, pp. 513–519; W. Holdsworth, (1932) 48 L.Q.R. 25 and 173 L.T. 336; E.
C. S. Wade, (1932) 173 L.T. 246, 267; Stevens (1993), pp. 50–62. The judges were "in a
mutinous mood" Lord Sankey L.C., quoted by Heuston, *op. cit.*, p. 514. However, this
"squalid incident ... had not reflected well on the judges. They had appeared selfish and out
of touch with reality ... [W]hat is striking is the amateur level of argument on both sides"
Stevens (1993), p. 63.

[93] The Senior Salaries Review Body is of the view that there should be a "broad linkage" across
the three groups notwithstanding that this operates to limit judicial salaries by comparison
with private practice: Report No. 41, Cm 4245, 1999, p. 21.

[94] See Report No. 39, Vol. II, Cm 3541, 1997; Report No. 51, Vol II, Cm. 5389-II, 2002.

[95] Report No. 45, Cm. 4567, 2000, p. 17.

should be a 5.4 per cent salary increase to take account of the need to ensure the ability to attract suitably able candidates from private practice to the High Court bench, additional job weight since the last fundamental review and an appropriate relationship with the pay of the senior civil service; and a further 2.5 per cent as the general increase for senior salaries. The Board's recommendations are normally accepted.[96] There have been no serious allegations of corruption against English judges for some centuries,[97] and it is not plausible that it is the level of salary alone that is responsible. Even attempts to bribe judges appear to be rare.

It is an accepted convention that judges may not hold paid appointments such as directorships, or carry on any profession or business. Indeed, the holders of full-time judicial appointments are now expressly barred from legal practice.[98] Even the few cases of judges taking business appointments on leaving the bench have attracted criticism.[99]

(b) Judges and the legislature

4–032   Judges of the Supreme Court and Circuit judges are disqualified from member-ship of the House of Commons.[1] The judges that are members of the House of Lords may contribute to its debates, but by a convention established comparatively recently do not take part in political controversy.[2] They tend to confine their contributions to technical questions of a legal nature. However, serving judges have not felt constrained from speaking on controversial matters where they have concerned the legal system itself. This was starkly illustrated by the criticisms, sometimes expressed in intemperate language, of Lord Mackay's Green Papers on reform of the legal profession.[3] Retired Law Lords are even less inhibited. The position in the twenties was less clear cut. In 1922 Lord Carson attacked the proposals for the establishment of the Irish Free State. He was rebuked for doing so by

---

[96]   The average 21 per cent increase recommended by the Review Body in 1992 (Report No. 33, Cm. 2015) was, however, paid in stages that was not completed until 1999: see Report No.35, Appendix E; the 8 per cent increase recommended in 2002 was paid in two stages: above n. xx.

[97]   In November 1993, it was announced by the D.P.P. that a police investigation had revealed no evidence to support corruption allegations made against Tucker J., the judge appointed to preside at the trial of Asil Nadir: see Ralph Gibson L.J. in *R. v. Central Criminal Court, ex p. Guney* [1994] 1 W.L.R. 438, 444.

[98]   Courts and Legal Services Act 1990, s.75 and Sched. 11.

[99]   In 1970, Fisher J. resigned at the age of 52 after two and a half years on the Bench in order to join a merchant bank. This provoked some criticism: see (1970) 114 S.J. 593. On the other hand, it was pointed out that a reluctant judge was unlikely to be a good one. The position of Lord Chancellor is arguably different, given the precariousness of office. Both Lord Birkenhead and Lord Kilmuir were criticised for taking business appointments, although the latter declined to draw the pension to which he was entitled. Lord Birkenhead defended his rights to take the pension, but assigned it to the benefit of certain hospitals (see Heuston, *Lives*, pp. 396–8; J. Campbell, *F. E. Smith, First Earl of Birkenhead* (1983), pp. 812–814). For discussion of this issue in New Zealand, see [1994] N.Z.L.J. 311–312.

[1]   House of Commons Disqualification Act 1975, s.l and Sched. 1. There is no disqualification applicable to recorders. In 1994 there were 9 recorder/M.P.s.

[2]   See generally L. Blom-Cooper and G. Drewry, *Final Appeal* (1972), pp. 196–215.

[3]   See above, para. 3-006; G. Drewry, (1992) 45(2) C.L.P. 187, 193–194. An example is Lord Lane's comment that "oppression does not stand on the doorstep with a toothbrush moustache and a swastika armband": H. L. Deb. Vol. 505, April 7 1989, col. 1331.

his former supporter, Lord Birkenhead L.C., but was defended by others.[4] The continued membership of the House of Lords of serving judges for the time being has been endorsed as part of the reform of the composition of the House of Lords.[5] However, it is increasingly regarded as undesirable that judges should participate in the passing of legislation that they themselves may subsequently be called upon to interpret and apply. The proposal that the final court of appeal should be a Supreme Court outside Parliament has the support so far of the Lord Chief Justice[6] and the Liberal Democrats.[7] The Select Committee on Public Administration in 2002 recommended that the Law Lords should leave the second chamber at the next general election but one.[8] In the mean time, they have, responding to a recommendation by the Royal Commission, stated that

> "they consider themselves bound by two general principles when deciding whether to participate in a particular matter, or to vote: first, the Lords of Appeal in Ordinary do not think it appropriate to engage in matters where there is a strong element of party political controversy; and secondly the Lords of Appeal in Ordinary bear in mind that they may render themselves ineligible to sit judicially if they were to express an opinion on a matter which might later be relevant to an appeal to the House.

> "The Lords of Appeal in Ordinary will continue to be guided by these broad principles. They stress that it is impossible to frame rules which cover every eventuality. In the end it must be for the judgment of each individual Lord of Appeal to decide how to conduct himself in any particular situation."[9]

(c) Judges and the executive

It is generally accepted that judges other than the Lord Chancellor should not hold ministerial office or sit in the Cabinet. Both Lord Mansfield and Lord Ellenborough served in the Cabinet while Chief Justice of the King's Bench, but both cases attracted much criticism. Lord Reading C.J. performed various executive tasks for the government during the First World War, but that can be regarded as an anomalous exception to a well-established principle, which has indeed been strengthened by the recent practice of making non-political appointments to the position of Lord Chief Justice. This leaves that anomalous position of the Lord Chancellor, which

4–033

---

[4] H. L. Debs. Vol. 49, cols.686–698, March 21, 1922; 715–727, March 22, 1922 and cols.931–974 March 29, 1922.

[5] White Paper, *The House of Lords: Completing the Reform* (Cm. 5291, 2001), paras. 81, 82; judicial members should continue to be members of the House until 75 whether or not they sit judicially. The Royal Commission on Reform of the House of Lords (Cm. 4534, 2000), Chap. 9 recommended that the Law Lords should continue to sit but that the possibility of establishing a separate supreme court be examined.

[6] JUSTICE Annual Law Lecture, October 4, 2001. Also supported by a JUSTICE Working Group chaired by Lord Alexander of Weedon.

[7] Lord Goodhart, H.L. Deb., June 21, 2001 , cols. 54–55.

[8] Fifth Report, 2001–02 HC 494, paras. 150–153.

[9] H.L. Deb., June 22, 2000, col. 419.

has attracted close attention in recent years given a combination of the higher political profile of Lord Irvine by comparison with his predecessors and the effect of Article 6 of the ECHR following implementation of the Human Rights Act 1998.[10] The official position is that

"By taking part in all three branches of government the Lord Chancellor appears to challenge the concept of the separation of powers. However, his effective purpose is actually to *maintain* the separation of powers."[11]

This is, however, asserted rather than explained. It has been argued that the presence of the Lord Chancellor in government enables government decisions, where appropriate, to be better informed by a judicial perspective and facilitates the maintenance of an appropriate relationship between the judiciary and the executive.

"The value of a Lord Chancellor is that he upholds judicial independence and can mediate between the executive and judiciary when need be. The office of the Lord Chancellor is the guarantor of judicial independence in our constitution. It holds the different parts together and withstands the pressure from all sides."[12]

One matter that has caused some controversy is the common practice of using judges as chairmen or members of Royal Commissions, Departmental Committees and Tribunals of Inquiry.[13] Indeed, judges are prominent in the ranks of "the Good and the Great". This is both expected and unexceptionable where "lawyers' law" and legal procedures are concerned. However, the subject matter of an inquiry may well be politically controversial. The judge concerned may be called upon to explain or justify the report, and indeed to argue in public the case for or against reform. The topics covered include public disorders (Red Lion Square,[14] Brixton[15]); security matters (security procedures in the public service,[16] the Vassall

---

[10] See above, para. 4-021.

[11] LCD website.

[12] Lord Williams of Mostyn (Lord Privy Seal; previously Attorney-General), H.L. Deb., July 24, 2001, col. WA211. Also, the position of the Lord Chancellor is "useful, because through it the judiciary has a representative in the Cabinet and the Cabinet have a representative in the judiciary": Michael Wills M.P., Parliamentary Secretary LCD, H.C. Deb., December 4, 2001, col. 155.

[13] See D. G. T. Williams, *Not in the Public Interest* (1965), pp. 188–191 and; [2000] P.L. 45, 53–55; P. Hillyard, (1971) 6 I.J. (N.S.) 93; G. Zellick, [1972] P.L. 1; T. J. Cartwright, *Royal Commissions and Departmental in Committees in Britain* (1975); G. Rhodes, *Committees of Inquiry* (1975); Griffith (1991), Chap. 2. Note the chairing of reviews of civil procedure, the criminal courts and tribunals by, respectively, Lord Woolf, Sir Robin Auld and Sir Andrew Leggatt (above, para. 1-032).

[14] Cmnd. 5919, 1975: Lord Scarman.

[15] Cmnd. 8427, 1981: Lord Scarman (Inquiry under the Police Act 1964).

[16] Cmnd. 1681, 1962: Lord Radcliffe (Departmental Committee). The Security Commission is also headed by a judge; the function of this standing commission, first set up in 1964, is to investigate at the Prime Minister's request, breaches of security in the public service, and to report and advise generally on security arrangements. See I. Leigh and L. Lustgarten, [1991] P.L. 215, and Lustgarten and Leigh, *In from the Cold!* (1994), pp. 476–491.

case,[17] the Profumo affair,[18] the D Notice affair[19]; mismanagement in the public service (the collapse of the Vehicle and General Insurance Company,[20] the Crown Agents[21]); events in Northern Ireland (disturbances in 1969,[22] interrogation methods,[23] legal procedures for dealing with terrorists,[24] the "Bloody Sunday" deaths in Londonderry,[25] the working of anti-terrorist legislation,[26] and police interrogation procedures[27]); the interception of communications[28]; industrial disputes (electricity supply,[29] miners,[30] and Grunwick[31]); prisons;[32] and standards in public life.[33] Sir Richard Scott, now a Lord of Appeal, presided over a lengthy and highly contentious inquiry into the Matrix-Churchill affair where the conduct of ministers and civil servants came under close scrutiny.[34] The (Saville) Bloody Sunday Inquiry has generated procedural litigation while in progress, in which rulings have been challenged successfully.[35]

The appointment of a committee is often thought to be a political delaying tactic or a mechanism for shuffling off responsibility for a controversial decision: whether or not either of these criticisms is in fact true, in a particular case it may be unfortunate for a judge to be associated with them. Moreover, the judge may find himself or herself in the midst of political controversy. He or she may be criticised for producing what is perceived by certain sections of the community, rightly or wrongly, to be a "whitewashing report",[36] or by the government for not producing such a

---

[17] Cmnd. 2009, 1963: Lord Radcliffe (Tribunal of Inquiry).
[18] Cmnd. 2152, 1963: Lord Denning. See Lord Denning, *The Due Process of Law* (1980), pp. 67–73; "It was a best-seller": *ibid.* p. 68.
[19] Cmnd. 3309, 1967: Lord Radcliffe (Committee of Privy Counsellors).
[20] 1971–72 H.C. 133: James J. (Tribunal of Inquiry).
[21] 1981–82 H.C. 364: Croom-Johnson J. (Tribunal of Inquiry).
[22] Cmnd. 566 (N.I.), 1972: Scarman J. (Tribunal of Inquiry).
[23] Cmnd. 4801, 1972: Lord Parker (Committee of Privy Counsellors).
[24] Cmnd. 5185, 1972: Lord Diplock (Departmental Committee).
[25] 1971–72 H.C. 220: Lord Widgery C.J. (Tribunal of Inquiry); and a further inquiry, which commenced in 1998 and is still in progress, chaired by Lord Saville of Newdigate.
[26] Cmnd. 5847, 1975: Lord Gardiner (Departmental Committee).
[27] Cmnd. 7497, 1979: Judge Bennett (Departmental Committee).
[28] Cmnd. 283, 1957: Birkett L.J. (Committee of Privy Counsellors).
[29] Cmnd. 4594, 1971: Lord Wilberforce (Court of Inquiry under the Industrial Courts Act 1919).
[30] Cmnd. 4903, 1972: Lord Wilberforce (Court of Inquiry).
[31] Cmnd. 6922, 1977: Scarman L.J. (Court of Inquiry).
[32] Cm.1456, 1991, Woolf L.J. (Inquiry)
[33] Cm.2850, 1995, Lord Nolan (standing body).
[34] See I. Leigh, "Matrix Churchill, Supergun and the Scott Inquiry" [1993] P.L. 630; R. Norton-Taylor, *Truth is a Difficult Concept* (1995); Sir Richard Scott, (1995) 111 L.Q.R. 596; [1996] P.L. Autumn Issue; D. Woodhouse, (1995) 48 *Parliamentary Affairs* 24; A. Tomkins, *The Constitution after Scott* (1998); B.K. Wintrobe, [1997] P.L. 18. While in progress the inquiry's working methods were the subject of political criticism led by Lord Howe: see Sir Louis Blom-Cooper, [1994] P.L. 1.
[35] See *R. v. Lord Saville of Newdigate. ex p. B (No. 1)*, The Times, April 15, 1999; *R. v. Lord Saville of Newdigate. ex p. B* [2000] 1 W.L.R. 1855; *R. (on the application of A) v. Lord Saville of Newdigate*, The Times, December 21, 2001 (evidence of soldier witnesses should not be taken in Londonderry). See B. Hadfield, [1999] P.L. 663.
[36] *e.g.* the adverse reaction to Lord Widgery's report on the Londonderry shootings: K. Boyle, T. Hadden and P. Hillyard, *Law and State* (1975), pp. 126–129.

report.[37] It is arguable that a judge is a suitable person to preside over a process for ascertaining the facts of particular incidents such as the Aberfan disaster and the Summerland fire disaster on the Isle of Man, the fire at Bradford City Football Club and the Hillsborough disaster, where there are no political overtones. Even here, however, there can be problems.[38] One way of minimising such problems is to use a retired High Court judge, although this may make little difference to public perceptions.[39] It is accepted, by contrast, that a judge should not become associated with party political research committees.[40]

A stricter view of the permissible range of extra-judicial activities is taken in the United States of America, where the separation of powers is formally entrenched as a constitutional principle. Even the exceptional cases such as the appointment of Justice Murphy as prosecutor at the Nuremberg trials and Chief Justice Warren to investigate the assassination of President Kennedy were controversial.[41]

Analogous problems have arisen in respect of the appointment of judges as members of the Restrictive Practices Court and the short-lived National Industrial Relations Court (NIRC). The former court determines whether restrictive agreements are contrary to the public interest.[42] Such determinations involve considerations that are political and economic rather than legal. The functions of the NIRC were more obviously judicial, but the context was that of industrial relations, where it was, and is, highly controversial whether orthodox legal mechanisms are appropriate in principle and workable. Its successor, the Employment Appeal Tribunal, inherited its less controversial functions.

Finally, a matter of growing controversy has been the relationship between the judiciary and the executive in the administration of the courts.

---

[37] *e.g.* the report of the Nyasaland Commission of Enquiry led by Devlin J. (H. Macmillan, *Riding the Storm* (1971), pp. 736–8); and the refusal of Harold Wilson to accept the Radcliffe Report on the D Notice Affair: see the White Paper on the D Notice System (Cmnd. 3312, 1967).

[38] In New Zealand, Mahon J. was appointed as sole member of a Royal Commission to inquire into the Mt. Erebus aircraft disaster. Certain statements in the report were held by the Supreme Court to have been made in excess of jurisdiction, and an order for costs against the airline was quashed: *Re Erebus Royal Commission* (No. 2) [1981] 1 N.Z.L.R. 618. Mahon J. resigned see [1982] N./Z.L.J. 37. An appeal to the Privy Council was dismissed: *Re Erebus Royal Commission* [1984] A.C. 808; see K. Keith, [1984] N.Z.L.J. 35; D. Currie, [1984] N.Z.L.J. 43; A Beck, "Trial of a High Court Judge for Defamation" (1987) 103 L.Q.R. 461.

[39] An example of the use of a retired judge to chair a highly sensitive inquiry is the *Stephen Lawrence Inquiry* chaired by Sir William Macpherson of Cluny (Cm. 4262, 1999); see L. Bridges, (1999) 26 J.L.S. 298; S.H. Bailey, D.J. Harris, D.C. Ormerod, *Bailey, Harris and Jones, Civil Liberties: Cases and Materials* (5th ed., 2001), pp. 144–147.

[40] Lord Avonside, a judge of the Court of Session, resigned from a Conservative Committee on the constitutional position in Scotland following public criticism, *e.g.* by the Lord Advocate: see *The Times*, July 30, 1968, August 8, 1968; R. J. Wilson, "British Judges as Political Actors" (1973) 1 Int. Journal of Criminology and Penology, 197, 199–200. "A judge must expect to forgo any kind of political activity . . . ": LCD *Guidance on Outside Activities and Interests* (June 2000, LCD website).

[41] See A. T. Mason, (1953) 67 Harv. L.R. 193; (1970) 35 *Law and Contemporary Problems* (Symposium).

[42] See R. B. Stevens and B. S. Yamey, *The Restrictive Practices Court* (1965).

Sir Nicolas Browne-Wilkinson in a public lecture[43] expressed concern that the executive, through the mechanisms for controlling public expenditure, was increasingly taking decisions that affected the conduct of cases in court, without consulting the judges. Indeed there was no formal machinery for the resolution of disputes between the judges and court administrators, below the level of the Lord Chancellor. As a result, the criterion of value for money was not properly balanced against the interests of justice.[44] Since this opening shot, there have been a number of skirmishes, with fire most commonly directed at the Lord Chancellor, Lord Mackay.[45] The publication of the 1989 Green Papers on reform of the legal profession led to judicial criticism both of their content (in particular the perceived threat to the independence of the legal profession and thereby of the judiciary) and of the lack of prior consultation with the judges.[46] The introduction of the requirement that changes to rules concerning qualification and conduct required the assent of four senior judges went some way to assuaging the fears expressed.[47] A second issue has been the number of High Court judges. Arguments from successive Lord Chief Justices and others that more High Court judges should be appointed to handle an increasing workload, so as to reduce delays and excessive reliance on Circuit judges and Q.C.s hearing civil cases as deputies, became increasingly public and pointed.[48] Steps were eventually taken in 1993 to increase the maximum number of judges by 13 and to proceed to make 10 new appointments,[49] but this did not affect the number of deputies used, particularly in the Queen's Bench Division.[50] The hand of the Treasury was seen in the delay; the "energetic support of the Lord Chancellor's Department was really needed to uphold the integrity and standing of the judiciary, support which only too frequently appeared to be lacking."[51]

A further *cause célèbre* was provided by exchanges between Lord Mackay and Sir John Wood, the then President of the Employment Appeal Tribunal. These concerned the extent to which preliminary hearings could and should be held in appeals to the Employment Appeal Tribunal in England and Wales, and were the subject of press coverage leading to a

---

[43] "The Independence of the Judiciary in the 1980s" [1988] P.L. 44. See also I. R. Scott, (1988) 7 C.J.Q. 103. Similar concerns have been expressed by Sir John Donaldson: *The Times*, April 13, 1987.

[44] One possible solution was the establishment of a collegiate body of judges responsible for the management of certain functions of court administration.

[45] See Sir Francis Purchas, "The constitution in the market place", The Third Joseph Jackson Memorial Lecture (1993) 143 N.L.J. 1604; "Lord Mackay and the Judiciary" (1994) 144 N.L.J. 527 and "What is happening to judicial independence" (1994) 144 N.L.J. 1306; rejoinder by R. Stevens, "On being nicer to James and the children" (1994) 144 N.L.J. 1620; D. Oliver, [1994] P.L. 157; Lord Ackner, (1996) 146 N.L.J. 1789.

[46] See above, para. 4-032.

[47] Sir Francis Purchas, (1993) 143 N.L.J. 1604, 1607–1608; (1994) 144 N.L.J. 1306, 1308–1309.

[48] Maximum Number of Judges (No.2) Order 1993 (S.I. 1993 No. 1255). See H.L. Deb., Vol. 545, May 10 1993, col. 1048.

[49] Purchas, (1994) 144 N.L.J. 1306, 1308–1309.

[50] *ibid.*, p. 1309. Not only has the quality of many deputies been criticised (see *ibid.*), it is seen as the ultimate objective of civil servants to concentrate work in the hands of Circuit judges "who would be under the control of the Executive and could be dismissed without reference to Parliament": Purchas, (1993) 143 N.L.J. 1603, 1605.

[51] H.L. Deb. Vol. 554, April 27 1994, cols.750–804; see also Vol. 553, March 21 1994, cols.497–500 (question).

discussion in the House of Lords, where most contributors were critical of the position taken by Lord Mackay.[52] According to the critics,[53] it appeared that Lord Mackay, in view of the growing backlog of work in the EAT, had attempted to pressurise Sir John Wood into dropping the use of preliminary oral hearings in cases where it was unclear on the face of the notice of appeal whether a point of law was raised. In one letter, Lord Mackay invited him to "consider his position". Such a change in approach would particularly prejudice unassisted litigants and was resisted by Sir John Wood. Lord Mackay's explanation was that he was simply looking for an assurance that preliminary oral hearings would not be used in *hopeless* cases, and that the Registrar's power under the EAT's statutory rules of procedure in such cases to inform the appellant that the appeal cannot proceed would in fact be used. The reference to "considering his position" was not expressed or intended to be a threat of dismissal (in any event, not a matter for the Lord Chancellor), a threat to use his power to move him from the Presidency of the EAT), or an invitation to resign. On this footing, matters were considerably less sinister than the critics suggested. Nevertheless the basis of Lord Mackay's intervention was not made clear in the correspondence (was it as the senior judge or as a member of the executive?). Lord Mackay's subsequent argument that it was as the rule-making authority responsible for the EAT's procedural rules is constitutionally novel.[54]

Other issues that have given rise to judicial criticism have been changes to judicial pensions,[55] cuts to eligibility limits for legal aid[56] and changes in the administration of the magistrates' court service that were perceived as a threat to judicial independence.[57] The particular vulnerability of Circuit judges has been noted.[58]

Most of these matters are ultimately resource-related. There must be a full and ongoing debate on whether the limits on resources made available by the state lead to an unacceptable dilution in the quality of justice; there is also an issue as to the extent to which the judges should be responsible for (as distinct from consulted about) the administration of the legal system.[59] Lord Bingham has indeed publicly acknowledged[60] that no public service, whether defence, education, health or the administration of justice, has any overriding right to demand all the resources deemed by them to be necessary or desirable. The rhetoric of judicial independence may obscure rather than illuminate these issues, particularly if it is seen simply as an argument to

---

[52] See *The Observer*, April 3, 1994; Sir Francis Purchas, (1994) 144 N.L.J. 527, 530: "the approach adopted demonstrated all the unattractive attributes of a Treasury driven policy to achieve savings at any cost."

[53] H.L. Deb., Vol. 554, April 23, 1994, cols.791–804.

[54] See Sir Francis Purchas, (1994) 144 N.L.J. 1306, 1310: "Once a law has been enacted ... the law-making process is *functus*."

[55] Judicial Pensions and Retirement Act 1993, above, para. 4-027, n. 35.

[56] Below, para. 10-021.

[57] Above, para. 2-029.

[58] Judge Harold Wilson, (1994) 144 N.L.J. 1453, noting, *inter alia*, the offence caused by the sending to all judges by recorded delivery of copies of a letter by the Lord Chancellor setting out examples of misbehaviour that would be incompatible with continuing to sit on the Bench. The power to dismiss a Circuit judge has very rarely been exercised, the most recent example being clearly a case where the Act of Settlement procedure would have been available had the person been a High Court judge (Bingham, *op. cit.*, p. 59): see para. 4-020.

[59] Above, para. 1-033.

[60] T. Bingham, *The Business of Judging* (2000), p. 57.

reinforce judicial status or to resist any change.[61] More recently, relationships seem to have improved.[62]

(d) Public statements by and about judges

Judges are expected to refrain from making party political statements; it is **4–034** sometimes said that they should refrain from criticising the policy of Acts of Parliament, but that is too restrictive. Reasoned, responsible criticism is acceptable: disparaging remarks are not. Thus, in 1978, Melford Stevenson J. was reprimanded by the Lord Chancellor, Lord Elwyn-Jones, for referring to the Sexual Offences Act 1967 as a "buggers' charter".[63] Judges were formerly inhibited by the so-called "Kilmuir rules"[64] from broadcasting on radio or television (except on special occasions, such as charitable appeals). However, these "rules" were relaxed by Lord Mackay on assuming office, judges being left to make their own decisions, after such consultation as they may think necessary.[65] Judges are now much more prepared to speak in public about their own role.[66] It is also now more common for judges, both inside and outside Parliament, to advocate changes in government policy in the legal sphere.[67]

Members of the executive are similarly expected to refrain from attacking judges, unless provoked. It is a rule of parliamentary practice that reflections must not be cast upon a judge's character or motives except on a substantive motion specifically criticising him or her or leading to an address for his or her removal, although reasoned arguments that a judge has made a mistake or was wrong are acceptable.[68] Furthermore, matters *sub judice* must not normally be discussed: subject to the discretion of the chair, and to the right of each House to legislate on any matter or to discuss any delegated

---

[61] See R. Stevens, (1994) 144 N.L.J. 1620 and works about at para. 4-030, n. 73; G. Drewry, "Judicial independence in Britain: challenges real and threats imagined" in R. Blackburn (ed.), *Constitutional Studies* (1992), Chap. 10.

[62] See Lord Woolf, (1998) 114 L.Q.R. 579, 583–586. But Lord Woolf has subsequently raised concerns about the lack of resources from the Treasury to support civil and criminal justice reforms: *The Times*, May 17, 2002, p.1.

[63] *The Times*, July 6, 1978.

[64] A letter from the then Lord Chancellor, Lord Kilmuir, to the Director-General of the B.B.C. in 1955, set out at [1986] P.L. 384–386. The Lord Chancellor disclaimed any disciplinary jurisdiction over judges, but stated that it was generally undesirable for judges to broadcast (it would, for example, "be inappropriate for the Judiciary to be associated with any series of talks or anything which could fairly be interpreted as entertainment ... ").

[65] See A. W. Bradley, [1988] P.L. at p. 166.

[66] See Rozenberg (1994), pp. 96–103, noting, *inter alia*, the willingness of Lord Taylor C.J. and others to give press conferences.

[67] See, *e.g.*, the growing judicial support for incorporation of the European Convention on Human Rights into English law (*e.g.* Sir Thomas Bingham, (1993) 109 L.Q.R. 390; Lord Taylor C.J. "The Judiciary in the Nineties", Richard Dimbleby Lecture 1992; and continued opposition to the mandatory life sentence for murder (*e.g.* by Lord Lane, Vol. 527 H.L.Deb., April 18, 1991, cols.1562–1564, and in his chairmanship of a Committee on the Penalty for Homicide set up by the Prison Reform Trust: see Lord Windlesham, [1993] Crim. L.R. 644, 656–657).

[68] *Erskine May's Parliamentary Practice* (21st ed., 1989), pp. 379–380; H.C. Deb. Vol. 865, cols.1092, 1144, 1200. December 4, 1973 (criticisms of Sir John Donaldson as President of the National Industrial Relations Court; H.C. Deb. Vol. 935, cols. 1381–4, July 19, 1977; H.C. Deb. Vol 34. cols.123–6, 285–6, December 14, 15, 1982 (description by Mrs Thatcher of a 12 month sentence for the rape of a six-year-old girl as "incomprehensible" ruled to be in order).

legislation, cases in which proceedings are active in United Kingdom courts must not be referred to in any motion, debate or question, except where a ministerial decision is in question, or in the chair's opinion a case concerns issues of national importance.[69]

(e) Judicial immunity from suit[70]

4-035   At common law, every judge of a superior or inferior court is immune from liability in damages for any act that is either (1) within jurisdiction or (2) honestly believed to be within jurisdiction[71]. The protection in (1) is available even where the judge is malicious.[72] He or she is also protected by absolute privilege in the law of defamation. Every judge:

> "should be able to do his work in complete independence and free from fear. He should not have to turn the pages of his books with trembling fingers, asking himself: 'If I do this, shall I be liable in damages?' "[73]

The rules also prevent the relitigation of the issues determined by the court.[74]

Deliberate misconduct such as corruption could lead to prosecution for a criminal offence[75] and removal from office.

(f) Disqualification for interest or bias

4-036   A judge is disqualified from hearing a case in which he or she has a direct pecuniary or proprietary interest, or in circumstances where there is a real possibility of bias on his or her part.[76] This rule applies to judges of the superior courts as much as it does to magistrates and tribunal members.

---

[69] Resolution of the House of Commons, H.C. Deb., November 15, 2001, cols. 1012–1018, replacing resolutions of July 23, 1963 and June 28, 1972 following a Report of the Joint Committee on Parliamentary Privilege, 1998–99 HC. 214, paras. 189–202. The new rules are similar to the previous ones, except that the exception is broader in applying in any case where a ministerial decision is under challenge and the rules expressly apply to proceedings of committees. Similar rules apply in the House of Lords. The previous rule was used to prevent debate on the Pinochet case while proceedings were in progress. See further, P.M. Leopold, "The *Sub Judice* Rule in the House of Lords" in B. Dickson and P. Carmichael, *The House of Lords: Its Parliamentary and Judicial Roles* (1999), Chap. 5.

[70] See A. Olowofoyeku, *Suing Judges* (1993); M. Brazier, [1976] P.L. 397.

[71] *Sirros v. Moore* [1975] Q.B. 118, Lord Denning M.R. and Ormrod L.J. Buckley L.J. held that if an act were outside jurisdiction a judge would only be immune if he or she had so acted as a result of a reasonable mistake of fact. See also *Rajski v. Powell* (1987) 11 N.S.W.L.R. 522. (The attempt of majority of the court in *Sirros v. Moore* to equate the position of judges of inferior and superior courts was subsequently disapproved: see above, para. 4-010)

[72] *Anderson v. Gorrie* [1895] 1 Q.B. 668.

[73] *per* Lord Denning M.R., in *Sirros v. Moore*, n. 71 above, at p. 136.

[74] *cf.* the immunity of advocates, above, paras. 3-044–3-046.

[75] *cf. R. v. Llewellyn-Jones* [1967] 3 All E.R. 225 (misbehaviour in a public office: misuse of funds by a county court registrar).

[76] See *R. v. Gough (Robert)* [1993] A.C. 646 (setting out a "real danger of bias" test); *Porter v. Magill* [2002] 1 All E.R. 465 (preferring the "real possibility of bias" formulation): see further below: Sir William Wade and C. F. Forsyth, *Administrative Law* (8th ed., 2000), Chap. 14.

Indeed, the leading case on disqualifying interests[77] concerned decrees made by Lord Cottenham L.C. in favour of a canal company in which he held shares. The House of Lords set aside these decrees. Lord Campbell emphasised that:

> "No one can suppose that Lord Cottenham could be in the remotest degree influenced by the interest ... but ... it is of the last importance that the maxim that no man is to be a judge in his own cause should be held sacred."[78]

The matters that may give rise to a possibility of bias include personal hostility, friendship, family relationship or acquaintance with a party or with a witness. The parties may waive the objection. The parameters of the disqualification rules have come under scrutiny in a number of recent high profile cases which take account of the impact of Article 6(1) of the ECHR. There have been two major issues. First, the division in earlier case law between support for a test that emphasised appearances ("reasonable suspicion of bias") and one that took greater account of the actual risks ("real likelihood of bias") was settled in favour of the latter by the House of Lords in *R. v. Gough*.[79] with a preference for the formulation "is there in the view of the court a real danger of bias?" This approach was, however, not followed in Commonwealth cases where a test was applied whether the events in question gave rise to a reasonable apprehension or suspicion on the part of a fair-minded and informed member of the public that the judge was not impartial.[80]

The *Gough* test in its application to judges was considered by the Court of Appeal prior to implementation of the Human Rights Act 1998 in *Locabail (UK) Ltd. v. Bayfield Properties Ltd.* and other cases.[81] While bound by *Gough*, the court thought is possible to apply the *Gough* test in such a way as to secure Article 6(1) compliance. First, it would often be appropriate to inquire whether the judge knew of the matter relied on as appearing to undermine his or her impartiality; if it was shown that it was not the appearance of possible bias would be dispelled. The judge might provide a written statement on the point; this would often, but not invariably, be accepted. There would, however, be no question of cross-examining or seeking disclosure from the judge. The court would disregard any statement by the judge concerning the impact of any knowledge on his or her mind or

[77] *Dimes v. Grand Junction Canal Proprietors* (1852) 3 H.L. Cas.759.

[78] *ibid.* p. 793. Dimes was a "crazy attorney" who had "embarked upon interminable litigation" against the Canal company. Cottenham died before judgment was given in the House of Lords: "it was a common belief that Dimes had killed Lord Cottenham": J. B. Atlay, *The Victorian Chancellors* (1906), Vol. 1, p. 415. *Cf. R. v. Mulvihill* [1990] 1 W.L.R. 438, where the Court of Appeal held that a Circuit judge was not disqualified from presiding over a trial concerning seven robberies of banks and building societies where he held 1,650 shares in one of the banks (the NatWest); there was no direct pecuniary interest and no reasonable suspicion of bias (*a fortiori*, there would be no real danger of bias under the *Gough* test, n. 76 above).

[79] Above.

[80] *e.g. Webb v.R.* (1994) 181 C.L.R. 41, High Court of Australia.

[81] [2000] Q.B. 451. The other cases were *Locabail (UK) Ltd, v. Waldorf Investment Corporation; Timmins v. Gormley; Williams v. H.M. Inspector of Taxes; R. v. Bristol Betting and Gaming Licensing Committee, ex p. O'Callaghan.*

decision. Barristers sitting as judges would know of any past or continuing personal association which might be thought to affect their impartiality; solicitors should, before sitting in a particular case, conduct a careful conflict search within their firm. In cases giving rise to automatic disqualification or where, for solid reasons, he or she feels personally embarrassed, the judge should recuse him- or herself before any objection is raised. If he or she is or becomes aware of any matter which could arguably be said to give rise to a real danger of bias, it should be disclosed to the parties. If objection is made, judgment should be exercised on it; he or she should neither yield to a tenuous or frivolous objection nor ignore an objection of substance. The court emphasised that it could not conceive of circumstances where an objection could be soundly based on the religion, ethnic or national origin, gender, age, class, means or sexual orientation of the judge. Nor, at least ordinarily, could an objection be soundly based on his or her social or educational or service or employment background or history, nor that of any member of his or her family, or previous political associations, or membership of social, or sporting or charitable bodies; or Masonic associations; or previous judicial decisions; or extra-curricular utterances; or previous receipt of instructions to act for or against any party, solicitor or advocate engaged in a case before him or her. On the other hand, a real possibility of bias might arise from personal friendship or animosity between the judge and any member of the public involved in the case; or close acquaintance with a member of the public involved in the case, particularly where the latter's credibility was in issue; or where the judge had previously rejected the evidence of an individual whose credibility was in issue in such outspoken terms as to throw doubt on the former's ability to approach the individual's evidence with an open mind; or if the judge had previously expressed views on a question at issue in such extreme and unbalanced terms as to throw doubt on his ability to try the issue with an objective judicial mind; or if, for any other reason, there were real grounds for doubting the judge's ability to ignore extraneous considerations, prejudices and predilections. If in any case there was real ground for doubt, that doubt should be resolved in favour of recusal.[82] Applying these principles, the court held[83] that there had been neither a direct pecuniary interest nor a real danger of bias where Lawrence Collins QC, sitting as a deputy High Court judge, had heard a case in circumstances that, unknown to him, his firm, Herbert Smith, had acted for parties to other proceedings against the applicant's husband. On the other hand, there was such a danger where a personal injuries case where insurers were the real defendants was

---

[82] paras. [18]–[26].

[83] The *Locabail* cases. *Cf. Williams v. H.M. Inspector of Taxes* (no real danger of bias where chairman of employment tribunal hearing complaint of sexual harassment and race discrimination at a Tax Office had worked for the Inland Revenue between 1958 and 1961 in a junior position); *R. v. Bristol Betting and Gaming Licensing Committee, ex p. O'Callaghan* (no direct pecuniary interest and no real danger of bias where it emerged that Dyson J., who had heard judicial review proceedings concerning a £5000 cost order arising out of objections by O'C to the renewal of a bookmaker's permit to Corals, was a non-executive director of a family company that rented premises to Corals elsewhere in the country; the judge was unaware that Corals were a tenant of the company).

heard by a recorder who had published articles that expressed "pronounced pro-claimant anti-insurer views."[84]

Subsequently, the Court of Appeal in *Re Medicaments and Related Classes of Goods (No. 2)*[85] held that the principles laid down in *Gough* did indeed require modification in the light of the jurisprudence of the European Court of Human Rights.[86] The difference was that when that court considers whether the material circumstances give rise to a reasonable apprehension of bias, it applies an objective test to the circumstances and does not pass judgment on the likelihood that the particular tribunal under reviewed was biased. Accordingly, an English court

"must first ascertain all the circumstances which have a bearing on the suggestion that the judge was biased. It must then ask whether those circumstances would lead a fair-minded and informed observer to conclude that there was a real possibility, or a real danger, the two being the same, that the tribunal was biased."

The material circumstances include an explanation given by the judge. If that explanation is accepted by the applicant for review it can be treated as accurate; if it is not, it becomes one further matter to be considered from the view point of the fair-minded observer. The court does not have to rule on whether it should be accepted or rejected.[87] The court held that there was a real danger of bias where a lay member of the Restrictive Practices Court, after the commencement of proceedings, applied for a post at a firm one of whose directors was a key expert witness for one of the parties. The House of Lords subsequently endorsed this approach, with the further modification that the "real possibility of bias" formulation should be used, and not "real danger."[88] It is generally accepted that these differences in formulation are unlikely to lead to differences in outcome in many cases. Indeed, it is arguable that the margin for differences of view as to the outcome when either version is actually applied to a concrete set of facts is broader than the difference between the two formulations.

The second issue has seen the extension of the category of automatic disqualification by the House of Lords in *R. v. Bow Street Metropolitan Stipendiary Magistrate, ex p. Pinochet Ugarte.*[89] Here, the House of Lords in earlier proceedings[90] had decided by three to two[91] that a warrant for the extradition of the applicant to Chile, where he had formerly been head of

---

[84] *Timmins v. Gormley. Cf. Hoekstra v. H.M. Advocate (No. 3)* 2000 J.C. 391 (held that appeal court was not an impartial tribunal where one of the judges wrote a newspaper article, shortly after an appeal raising ECHR issues was rejected, strongly critical of incorporation of the ECHR).

[85] [2000] 1 W.L.R. 700.

[86] *Delcourt v. Belgium* (1970) 1 E.H.R.R. 355; *Piersack v. Belgium* (1982) 5 E.H.R.R. 169; *De Cubber v. Belgium* (1984) 7 E.H.R.R. 236; *Borgers v. Belgium* (1993) 15 E.H.R.R. 92; *Gregory v. UK* (1997) 25 E.H.R.R. 577.

[87] paras [83]–[86].

[88] *Porter v. Magill* [2002] 1 All E.R. 465, *per* Lord Hope at paras [95]–[105].

[89] [2000] 1 A.C. 119. For analysis, see D. Woodhouse (ed) *The Pinochet Case* (2000), Chaps. 2 (D. Robertson), 3 (E. Grant), 4 (P. Catley and L Claydon); Sir David Williams, [2000] P.L.45; K. Malleson, (2000) 63 M.L.R. 119.

[90] [1998] 4 All E.R. 897.

[91] Lords Nicholls, Steyn and Hoffmann, Lords Slynn and Lloyd dissenting.

state, was valid. Amnesty International had been given leave to intervene in the proceedings, and had supported the validity of the warrant. It subsequently emerged that one of the minority, Lord Hoffmann, was a director and chair of Amnesty International Charity Ltd, which had been incorporated to carry out AI's charitable purposes. The House unanimously set aside its earlier decision. It was not suggested that Lord Hoffmann was actually biased. The House did not reach the question whether there was a real danger or possibility of bias, but held that automatic disqualification followed where the judge's decision would lead to the promotion of a cause in which the judge was involved together with one of the parties. Here, he or she would be "a judge in his own cause," even if he or she were not technically a party.[92] It is submitted that while the outcome was right, it would have been preferable to apply the real possibility of bias test rather than by introducing an extension to the automatic disqualification rule that is uncertain in scope. Following this decision, the Lord Chancellor, as head of the judiciary, wrote to the senior law lord that "we must make every effort to ensure that such a state of affairs could not occur again." In future, the chair of a committee should ensure that its proposed members should consider together whether any of their number might appear to be subject to a conflict of interest and to require any law lord to disclose any such circumstances to the parties, and not sit if any party objects and the Committee so determines."[93]

Where a judge is not technically disqualified, he or she may well refuse to act in a case where one of the parties raises an objection. Objections, however, are not commonly made. Lord Denning M.R. withdrew from a case concerning the Church of Scientology of California as the Church felt that "there was an unconscious influence operating adversely to it" in Lord Denning's previous judgments.[94] The Church had been before Lord Denning's court on eight previous occasions, and noted that his Lordship had doubted whether it was right to call scientology a "religion" and whether the Church was entitled to call itself a church. Shaw L.J. said that it was ahnost impossible to resist the application for the appeal to be transferred "even though the grounds were not merely slight but non-existent." Conversely, no objection was taken to Lord Denning's acting in a case concerning the Church Commissioners, he being one of the Commissioners,[95] or to the fact that all the members of the Court of

---

[92] Lord Hoffmann was not to be treated as a party as his links were to AICL and not AI itself (an unincorporated association); see Lord Browne-Wilkinson at p. 134.

[93] LCD Press Notice 382/98.

[94] *ex p. Church of Scientology of California, The Times*, February 21, 1978. Lord Lane C.J. stood down in *Moss v. McLachlan* [1985] 149 J.P. 167: Pannick (1987), p. 41. *Cf. Arab Monetary Fund v. Hashim (No. 8), The Independent*, April 30, 1993 (counsel should be satisfied that there is material on which an application for removal of a judge can properly be made).

[95] *Hanson v. Church Commissioners* [1978] Q.B. 823, 831. The actual management of the estate of the Church Commissioners was vested in a separate board of governors. Various "dignitaries" including the Lord Chief Justice, the Master of the Rolls and the Lord Mayor of London, were "merely titular commissioners".

Appeal hearing the appeal in the London Transport "fares" case were both users of public transport in London and London ratepayers.[96] *Guidance on Outside Activities and Interests* has been given to the judiciary by the LCD.[97]

10. THE JUDICIAL FUNCTION

In the course of legal proceedings, judges may be called upon to perform one or more of the following tasks: presiding over a trial (e.g. controlling the course of proceedings; keeping order; ruling on questions of the admissibility of evidence; deciding when to adjourn for lunch); presiding over an appeal[98]; determining a disputed question of fact; determining a disputed question of law; directing a jury on the evidence and the law; deciding what remedy to award or punishment to impose; and giving reasons for such decisions as are theirs. With the marked decline in the use of the jury in civil cases over the last 60 years, the judicial task of determining disputed questions of fact has correspondingly grown in significance. When considering the "nature of the judicial function," however, it is usual to concentrate on the ways in which judges approach the determination of disputed questions of law. Furthermore, attention is directed in particular to the appeal courts,[99] as a higher proportion of time is spent on such questions, as the arguments are more likely to be evenly balanced, and because the decisions of courts at the top of the hierarchy carry most weight. In Chapters 6, 7 and 8 we consider the principles that are applicable to the interpretation of statutes and the handling of precedent cases and the application of the Human Rights Act 1998. We shall see that there is considerable room for flexibility. Moreover, even where there is no directly relevant precedent and no applicable legislation the judge must still give an answer to any legal questions that arise.

4–037

The extent to which a judge is prepared to innovate depends upon the respective weight attached to a number of factors[1]: the need for stability and certainty in law (which suggests consistency with established principles and precedents); the wish to do justice as between the parties; the need not to usurp the role of Parliament; the need to justify a decision by reasoned argument and not merely compromise between the parties; and the need to base a decision on at least one of the issues raised by the parties. Differences in approach reflect different weight attached to these factors—in particular the first two.

Debates as to the nature of the judicial function have taken place in two

---

[96] *Bromley London Borough Council v. Greater London Council* [1983] 1 A.C. 768, 77–777.

[97] LCD website. In cases of doubt, the Lord Chancellor is willing to give advice.

[98] The president of an appellate court can have a significant influence on the course of proceedings, although his or her role is more muted than that of a trial judge sitting alone: see above, para. 2-073, n. 31.

[99] There have been a number of studies of the House of Lords: L. Blom-Cooper and G. Drewry, *Final Appeal* (1972); R. Stevens, *Law and Politics* (1979); A. Paterson, *The Law Lords* (1982) ; D. Robertson, *Judicial Discretion in the House of Lords* (1998); P. Carmichael and B. Dickson, *The House of Lords: Its Parliamentary and Judicial Roles* (1999); M. Barrett, *The Law Lords* (2001). The nature of the judicial function is analysed in J. Bell, *Policy Arguments in Judicial Decisions* (1983).

[1] See Paterson (1982), pp. 122–127.

different, but related fields: legal theory and socio-legal studies. Important contributions to the theoretical debate have come from some of our leading judges, speaking both extra-judicially and in decided cases. The judges' own perceptions of the proper judicial role are equally of importance as one of the important influences on judicial decision-making identified in empirical studies.

Historically, the theory that held sway for the longest time was the "declaratory theory" expounded by William Blackstone and others. Blackstone wrote[2] that:

> "it is an established rule to abide by former precedents, where the same points come again in litigation ... [the judge] being sworn to determine, not according to his private sentiments: he being sworn to determine, not according to his own private judgment, but according to the known laws and customs of the land: not delegated to pronounce a new law, but to maintain and expound the old one. Yet this rule admits of exception, where the former determination is most evidently contrary to reason; much more if it be clearly contrary to divine law. But even in such cases the subsequent judges do not pretend to make a new law, but to vindicate the old one from misrepresentation. For if it be found that the former decision is manifestly absurd or unjust, it is declared not that such a sentence was *bad law*, but that it was *not law*, that is, not the established custom of the realm, as has been erroneously determined."

Thus the role of the judge is to declare what the law is, not to make it. This theory was not easy to square with the unconcealed law-making activities of particular judges such as Lord Mansfield,[3] and was abused by writers such as Bentham.[4] Nevertheless, judges in the nineteenth and early twentieth centuries generally maintained (with increasing enthusiasm) the position that their function was not to make law and, indeed, that they were not concerned with the policy implications of their rulings.[5] However, this view was held less strongly in the House of Lords than in the lower courts, some of the Law Lords, with equity or Scottish backgrounds, being more concerned with principles than precedent and more likely to advert to the likely consequences of their decisions.

After 1912, the Law Lords, who tended now to be chosen from the professional judiciary, with less regard for political affiliation:

---

[2] *Commentaries*, Vol. 1, pp. 69–70.

[3] Chief Justice the King's Bench, 1756–1788. See C. H. S. Fifoot, *Lord Mansfield* (1936).

[4] *A Comment on the Commentaries* (eds. J. H. Burns and H. L. A. Hart, 1977), pp. 192–206. Bentham's objections were based in part on his opposition to theories of "natural law". Moreover, he disapproved of law-making by judges, taking the view that this was a matter for Parliament.

[5] See, *e.g.* Parke B. in *Egerton v. Brownlow* (1853) 4 H.L.C. 1, 124: "It is the province of the statesman, and not the lawyer, to discuss, and of the legislature to determine, what is the best for the public good, and to provide for it by proper enactments. It is the province of the judge to expound the law only; the written from the statutes: the unwritten or common law from the decisions of our predecessors and of our existing courts, from text-writers of acknowledged authority, and upon the principles to be clearly deduced from them by sound reason and just inference; not to speculate upon what is the best, in his opinion, for the advantage of the community."

"exhibited an increasing tendency to articulate a declaratory theory of law and to insist that the judicial function, even in the final appeal court, was primarily the formalistic or mechanical one of restating existing doctrines."[6]

At the same time there were still some judges, such as Lord Atkin and Lord Wright, who were prepared to develop private law doctrines significantly while maintaining the facade of the declaratory theory. However, there followed what Stevens terms the "era of substantive formalism" in the House of Lords:

"For the 1940s and for much of the 1950s there were no obvious signs that the Law Lords had developed rules out of broader principles of the common law or the liberal state. Indeed, there was virtually no acceptance of an element of discretion, let alone a utilitarian balancing of interests. The process, at best fell into Karl Llewellyn's category of judicial formalism, with opinions written 'in deductive form with an air of expression of single-line inevitability.'[7] At worst, the process was a restatement of the declaratory theory in such extreme form that it denied any purpose for a second appeal court. Legal rationality became an end in itself. The literal meaning of words was to be the only criterion of statutory interpretation."[8]

Deference to the executive in public law cases was to be expected in wartime: strong judicial challenges to the Labour government elected in 1945 with a large majority would obviously have been unwise. This approach was associated particularly with Lord Jowitt, the Labour Lord Chancellor, and Lord Simonds, a Law Lord between 1944 and 1962, apart from his period as Lord Chancellor from 1951 to 1954. A few judges stood out against this approach, notably Lord Denning,[9] but to little avail. The only developments could come with the application of established principles to novel factual situations.

Since the mid-1950s the position has changed. It has become generally accepted by the Law Lords that they may properly exercise a limited law-making function.[10] Lord Radcliffe argued that it was best if judges went about this task "on the quiet."[11]

"Would anyone now deny that judicial decisions are a creative, not merely an expository, contribution to the law? There are no means by which they can be otherwise, so rare is the occasion upon which a decision does not involve choice between two admissible alternatives. . . . We cannot run the risk of finding the archetypal image of the judge

---

[6] Stevens (1979), p. 196.
[7] Karl Llewellyn, *The Common Law Tradition* (1960), p. 38.
[8] Stevens (1979), pp. 319–320.
[9] See below.
[10] See generally A. Paterson, *The Law Lords* (1982).
[11] See Lord Radcliffe, *Not in Feather Beds* (1968), pp. 265–277. Professor Atiyah has argued that most of the judges "would prefer to shelter behind the declaratory theory in public, and to confine discussion of the nature and use of the creative judicial function amongst the *cognoscenti*" (1980) 15 Israel L.R. 346, 360.

confused in men's minds with the very different image of the legislator. ... [T]he image of the judge, objective, impartial, erudite and experienced declarer of the law that is, lies deeper in the consciousness of civilisation than the image of the lawmaker, propounding what are avowedly new rules of human conduct. ... Personally, I think that judges will serve the public interest better if they keep quiet about their legislative function. No doubt they will discreetly contribute to changes in the law, because ... they cannot do otherwise, even if they would. The judge who shows his hand, who advertises what he is about, may indeed show that he is a strong spirit, unfettered by the past; but I doubt very much whether he is not doing more harm to general confidence in the law as a constant, safe in the hands of the judges than he is doing to the law's credit as a set of rules nicely attuned to the sentiments of the day."[12]

The dominant influence in the House of Lords in this period was Lord Reid. In his well-known address entitled "The Judge as Law Maker" he swiftly disposed of the declaratory theory:

"We do not believe in fairy tales any more. So we must accept the fact that for better or worse judges do make law, and tackle the question how do they approach their task and how they should approach it."[13]

Where public opinion was sharply divided, whether or not on party lines, no judge should lean to one side or the other if it can be avoided; if it cannot:

" ... we must play safe [and] decide the case on the preponderance of existing authority. Parliament is the right place to settle issues which the ordinary man regards as controversial."[14]

4-038   It was so improper for judges to disregard or innovate on settled law in areas where people rely on the certainty of the law in settling their affairs, in particular in making contracts or settlements. A problem might be too complex for it to be appropriate for the judges to change some aspect of it: the only proper way forward would be for there to be legislation following a wide survey of the whole field.[15] Nevertheless, there was considerable scope for judges to mould the development of the common law, which should be done having regard to "common sense, legal principle and public policy in that order."[16] The judges did not have so free a hand when Interpreting statutes as when dealing with the common law.

In the late 1950s and early 1960s there were some indications that the House of Lords was taking a freer attitude to precedents. These led to the Practice Statement in 1966 in which the Law Lords announced that they

---

[12] Radcliffe (1968), pp. 271–272, 273.

[13] (1972) 12 J.S.P.T.L. 22. For other important contributions to the debate see Diplock L.J., "The Courts as Legislators," in B. W. Harvey (ed.), *The Lawyer and Justice* (1978), p. 263; Lord Edmund-Davies "Judicial Activism" (1975) 28 C.L.P. 1; Lord Devlin, *The Judge* (1981), Chap. 1.

[14] (1972) 12 J.S.P.T.L. 22, 23.

[15] See *Myers v. D.P.P.* [1965] A.C. 1001, 1022.

[16] (1972) 12 J.S.P.T.L. 22, 25.

would no longer regard themselves as bound by their own previous decisions.[17] Since then, the criteria for exercising the power to overrule have been analysed in some detail. Lord Reid's views have been especially influential,[18] as they have on the wider issues concerning judicial law-making. Similarly, in the field of statutory interpretation the judges have shown a greater inclination to look at the context of the words in a statute and the statute's purpose, rather than to adopt a narrow literal approach.

Paterson shows that of the 19 Law Lords who were active between 1967 and 1973 at least 12 considered that the Law Lords had an obligation to develop the common law to meet changing social conditions. An even greater proportion of the sample of barristers interviewed by him shared this view, as did at least three of the six Law Lords appointed between 1973 and 1979.[19] Ten of 1 1 Law Lords interviewed accepted that they ought to be concerned with the possible social and legal consequences of their decisions, at least within the acknowledged limitations of the information available to them.[20] A majority of the Law Lords considered that there were cases coming to the Lords to which there was no single correct solution on the basis of existing legal rules and principles, and in which they had a measure of choice.[21]

In the same period, the Court of Appeal was dominated by Lord Denning M.R., who showed a greater preference for innovation than the Law Lords, albeit coupled with varying success in persuading colleagues in the Court of Appeal to agree with him.[22]

The approach of appellate judges varies according to the context. For example, continued importance has been attached by the House of Lords to the "certainty" factor in commercial and property cases, and, to a lesser extent, in criminal law cases. Here, the willingness of the House of Lords to set aside the common law rule that a man cannot be guilty of raping his wife[23] may be compared with their refusal to abolish the presumption that a

---

[17] See A. Paterson, *The Law Lords* (1982), pp. 143–153, and below, paras 7-026–7-027.

[18] See Paterson (1982), pp. 153–169.

[19] Paterson (1982), pp. 173–174. But note the view expressed by Lord Scarman in *McLoughlin v. O'Brian* [1983] 1 AC. 410, that where "principle" requires a decision which entails a degree of "policy risk", the court's function is to adjudicate according to "principle," leaving "policy curtailment" to Parliament. The policy issue as to where to draw the line in "nervous shock" cases is "not justiciable. The problem is one of social, economic and financial policy. The considerations relevant to a decision are not such as to be capable of being handled within the limits of the forensic process": pp. 430–431. See, *contra*, Lord Edmund-Davies, pp. 427–428.

[20] Paterson (1982), pp. 177–178.

[21] *ibid.* pp. 192–195. This runs counter to the theory developed by R. M. Dworkin that there is a right answer in all hard cases and that the judges have no discretion to make law: *Taking Rights Seriously* (1977); "No Right Answer" in P. Hacker and J. Raz (eds.), *Law, Morality and Society* (1977); J. W. Harris, *Legal Philosophies* (1980), Chap. 14; Bell (1983), Chap. VIII.

[22] See Stevens (1979), pp. 488–505; Lord Denning *The Discipline of Law* (1979), Parts 1 and 7.

[23] *R. v. R. (Rape: Marital Exemption)* [1992] 1 A.C. 599. See M. Giles, [1992] Crim.L.R. 407. This decision was challenged before the European Court of Human Rights on the ground that the law was changed retrospectively, contrary to Art. 7, ECHR. However, the court ruled that there was no violation as it was reasonable foreseeable by the applicant that a court might embark on the legitimate adaptation of the ingredients of the crime: *CR and SW v. U. K.* (1995) 21 E.H.R.R. 363.

child between 10 and 14 is *doli incapax*,[24] or to develop an additional
qualified defence to murder to cover the case of the use of excessive force in
self-defence or to prevent crime or effect an arrest, reducing the offence to
one of manslaughter.[25] The former was seen as the removal of an
anachronistic common law fiction, the status of women having changed
out of all recognition since the rule was enunciated by Hale in the eighteenth
century.[26] The latter points were much more controversial, the government
having stated its intention to maintain the *doli incapax* presumption as
recently as 1990.[27] and having consistently resisted proposals to change the
scope of the law of murder or the mandatory life sentence for that offence.[28]
By contrast, there was in the 1970s and early 1980s a marked extension of
liability in such aspects of the tort of negligence as negligent misstatement,[29] omissions,[30] nervous shock,[31] economic loss,[32] and injury to
trespassers,[33] although in some of these areas, most notably economic loss,
the extension of liability has been followed by retrenchment.[34] The House of
Lords has now expressed a preference for developments in the scope of the
tort of negligence to be incremental, by analogy with existing cases, rather
than by reference to broadly-expressed principles.[35] Similarly, in *Cambridge
Water Co. Ltd. v. Eastern Counties Leather plc*[36] the House declined to
develop a general principle of strict liability for extra-hazardous activities,
preferring instead to modify the elements of the *Rylands v. Fletcher*[37] tort.[38]
In public law, there has been a whole series of cases in which the courts have
analysed, refined and sometimes extended the grounds upon which
administrative and judicial decisions of government institutions can be
challenged under the *ultra vires* doctrine.[39] In many of these, the challenges

---

[24] *C. (A minor) v. D.P.P.* [1995] 2 W.L.R. 383. The presumption prevents a child being
     convicted of a criminal offence in the absence of clear positive evidence that the child knew
     that his or her act was seriously wrong, evidence of the acts amounting to the offences alone
     being insufficient.
[25] *R. v. Clegg* [1995] 1 A.C. 482.
[26] [1992] 1 A.C. 599, 616, *per* Lord Keith.
[27] White Paper, *Crime, Justice and Protecting the Public* (Cm. 965, 1990), para. 8.4.
[28] See, *e.g.*, H.L. Select Committee Report on Murder and Life Imprisonment (1988–89 H.L.
     78); Lord Windlesham, [1993] Crim. L.R. 644. See also A. T. H. Smith, "Judicial law-
     making in the criminal law" (1984) 100 L.Q.R. 46 on the supposed distinction between
     creating new offences (which is clearly objectionable) and extending existing offences to
     cover new situations.
[29] *Hedley Byrne & Co. v. Heller & Partners* [1964] A.C. 465.
[30] *Home Office v. Dorset Yacht Co.* [1970] A.C. 1004; *Anns v. London Borough of Merton* [1978]
     A.C. 728.
[31] *McLoughlin v. O'Brian* [1983] 1 A.C. 410.
[32] *Junior Books Ltd v. Veitchi Co. Ltd* [1983] 1 A.C. 520.
[33] *British Railways Board v. Herrington* [1972] A.C. 877.
[34] See, e. g. *Leigh and Sillavan Ltd v. Aliakmon Shipping Co. Ltd* [1986] A.C. 785; *Yuen Kun Yeu
     v. Att.-Gen. of Hong Kong* [1988] A.C. 175; *D. & F. Estates Ltd v. Church Commissioners for
     England* [1989] A.C. 177; *Murphy v. Brentwood District Council* [1991] 1 A.C. 398 (over-
     ruling *Anns*).
[35] *e.g.* Lord Bridge in *Caparo Industries plc v. Dickman* [1990] 2 A.C. 605, 617–618.
[36] [1994] 2 A.C. 264.
[37] (1868) L.R. 3 H.L. 330.
[38] Adding the requirement that the damage be foreseeable; making it easier for the plaintiff to
     establish that the defendant's user of land was "non-natural".
[39] For general surveys, see A. Lester Q.C., "English judges as law makers" [1993] P.L. 269 and
     Lord Woolf, "Droit Public – English Style" [1995] P.L. 57.

have been successful.[40] Recent high profile cases have seen the House of Lords hold that ministers of the Crown are subject to the law of contempt of court.[41] and that the government's revised criminal injuries compensation scheme was unlawful.[42] The Divisional Court found that the government allocation of aid to the Pergau Dam project in Malaysia was also unlawful.[43] In others, the judges have shown restraint in circumstances where it was not obvious why restraint was any more appropriate.[44]

It is also interesting to contrast the willingness of Sir Robert Megarry V.-C. to extend the field of liability in negligence for economic loss[45] with his unwillingness to create an "altogether new right" in a case where it was claimed that there was a right to hold a telephone conversation in the privacy of one's home without molestation[46]:

> "No new right in the law, fully-fledged with all the appropriate safeguards, can spring from the head of a judge deciding a particular case: only Parliament can create such a right ... The wider and more indefinite the right claimed, the greater the undesirability of holding that such a right exists."[47]

There are some apparently formidable arguments in favour of judicial restraint in law-making. The making of new law through the legislative process[48] rather than judicially is often said to be more in accordance with democratic theory[49] and is more likely to be based on a proper examination of all the relevant information. English civil procedure generally prevents anyone but the parties to litigation giving evidence[50] and enables the parties to choose what evidence to present. Moreover, there are difficulties in

4–039

---

[40] *e.g. Ridge v. Baldwin* [1964] A.C. 40 (dismissal of a chief constable held void for breach of natural justice); *Anisminic Ltd v. Foreign Compensation Commission* [1969] 2 A.C. 147 (decision of the Commission struck down for misinterpretation of the relevant legislation notwithstanding a statutory clause purporting to exclude judicial review); *Padfield v. Minister of Agriculture* [1968] A.C. 997 and *Laker Airways v. Department of Trade* [1977] Q.B. 643 (ministerial decisions held to be abuses of discretion); *Bromley London Borough Council v. Greater London Council* [1983] 1 A.C. 768 (substantial cuts in fares held to be *ultra vires*).

[41] *M. v. Home Office* [1994] 1 A.C. 377.

[42] *R. v. Secretary of State for the Home Department, ex p. The Fire Brigades Union* [1995] 2 A.C. 513.

[43] *R. v. Secretary of State for Foreign and Commonwealth Affairs, ex p. World Development Movement Ltd* [1995] 1 W.L.R. 386.

[44] *R. v. Secretary of State for the Department, ex p. Zamir* [1980] A.C. 930 (but *cf. R. v. Secretary of State for the Home Department, ex p. Khawaja* [1984] A.C. 74); *Bushell v. Secretary of State for the Environment* [1981] A.C. 75; *R. v. Secretary of State for the Home Department, ex p. Brind* [1991] A.C. 696 (declining to hold that the doctrine of proportionality constituted an independent ground of challenge in English administrative law).

[45] *Ross v. Caunters* [1980] Ch. 297.

[46] *Malone v. Metropolitan Police Commissioner (No. 2)* [1979] Ch. 344.

[47] *ibid.* pp. 372, 373. Compare also the extension of police powers of seizure by the Court of Appeal in *Chic Fashions Ltd v. Jones* [1968] 2 Q.B. 299 and *Ghani v. Jones* [1970] 1 Q.B. 693 with the refusal of the court to create a new common law power of search: *McLorie v. Oxford* [1982] Q.B. 1290.

[48] See Chap. 5.

[49] But see Atiyah, (1980) 15 Israel L. R. 362–365.

[50] The rules could, of course, be changed. By contrast, in the United States interest groups are much more able to institute litigation, or to present arguments in cases involving other parties.

presenting *evidence* as distinct from *argument* about the possible social and economic implications of decisions. Conspicuous creativity in judicial law making is difficult to square with the "ostentatious impartiality" that is also regarded as desirable.[51] The judges have no written constitution to look to as a source of power.[52]

A more pragmatic reason sometimes advanced in favour of restraint is that:

> "if people and Parliament come to think that the judicial power is to be confined by nothing other than the judge's sense of what is right (or, as Selden put it, by the length of the Chancellor's foot), confidence in the judicial system will be replaced by fear of it becoming uncertain and arbitrary in its application. Society will then be ready for Parliament to cut the power of the judges. Their power to do justice will become more restricted by law than it need be, or is today."[53]

4-040   Nevertheless, restraint is not the same as complete withdrawal from the field. "Law reform" does not rank high in the list of priorities in the struggle for a place in the legislative timetable: if one always waited for Parliament, one would often wait in vain.

In his book, *The Politics of the Judiciary*[54] Professor Griffith argues that the discussion about how creative judges should be:

> "has been and is a somewhat unreal discussion. ... What is lacking ... is any clear and consistent relationship between the general pronounce-

---

[51] See above, para. 4-030.

[52] Although here it should be noted that the power of judicial review exercised by the Supreme Court in the United States is not expressly created by the Constitution, but is itself judge-made: see *Marbury v. Madison* (1803) 1 Cranch 137. Furthermore, a number of judges have expressed the view extra-judicially that in certain circumstances the courts might decline to give effect to statutes that violate fundamental constitutional principles: Lord Woolf, "*Droit Public* – English style" [1995] P.L. 57 (legislation removing or substantially impairing the High Court's powers of judicial review); Sedley J., "Human Rights: a Twenty-first century Agenda" [1995] P.L. 386, 391 ("obligation of the courts to articulate and uphold the ground rules of ethical social existence which we dignify as fundamental human rights"); Laws J. "Law and Democracy" [1995] P.L. 72 (protection of fundamental freedoms). These suggestions have been criticised as contrary to principle by Lord Irvine of Lairg Q.C., "Judges and decision-makers: the theory and practice of *Wednesbury* review" [1996] P.L. 59 and by J.A.G. Griffith, 'Judges and the Constitution' in R. Rawlings (ed.), *Law, Society and Economy* (1997), Chap. 13 ("I believe this kind of language lifts our feet off the ground and endangers more than our sense of balance": p. 308) and (2000) 63 M.L.R. 159. The extent to which the judges' powers of judicial review in England and Wales are a self standing common law creation has been the subject of extended academic debate: see C. Forsyth (ed.), *Judicial Review and the Constitution* (2000); M. Elliott, *The Constitutional Foundations of Judicial Review* (2001); A. Halpin, *Reasoning with Law* (2001), Chap. 4.

[53] *Per* Lord Scarman in *Duport Steels Ltd v Sirs* [1980] 1 All E.R. 529, 551. When Roger Parker Q.C. made a similar prediction in his submissions to the Court of Appeal in *Congreve v. Home Office* [1976] Q.B. 629, Lord Denning M.R. stated "We trust that this was not said seriously, but only as a piece of advocate's licence." Mr Parker subsequently apologised if anything he said had sounded like a threat. (See *The Times*, December 6 and 9, 1975.)

[54] (5th ed., 1997). For similar studies of particular areas see J. I. Reynolds, "Statutory Covenant of Fitness and Repair" (1974) 37 M.L.R. 377 (and the rejoinder by M. J. Robinson, (1976) 39 M.L.R. 43); J. Hackney, "The Politics of the Chancery" (1981) 34 C.L.P. 113.

ments of judges on this matter of creativity and the way they conduct themselves in court.[55]

Moreover, the appellate judges:

"have by their education and training and the pursuit of their profession as barristers, acquired a strikingly homogeneous collection of attitudes, beliefs and principles, which to them represents the public interest. ... The judicial conception of the public interest ... is three-fold. It concerns firstly, the interests of the State; secondly, the preservation of law and order broadly interpreted; and, thirdly, the judges' views on social and political issues of the day."[56]

They are thus concerned to preserve and protect the existing order, to serve the prevailing political and economic forces, this being generally true of all societies today, whether capitalistic or communist. This is not regarded by Griffith as a matter for recrimination: his main concern is simply to dispel the myth that the judges are "neutral."

In relation to Griffith's view that the appellate judges have acquired a homogenous collection of attitudes, Lord Devlin commented[57]:

"Since he is writing of men in their sixties and seventies whose working life has given them a common outlook on many questions, by no means all political, I have very little doubt that he is right. I have very little doubt either that the same might be written of most English institutions, certainly of all those which like the law are not of a nature to attract the crusading or rebellious spirit."

However, he suggested that whether one agrees that the application of the law has been distorted depended on whether one:

"looks at them from right or from the left. ... To my mind none of the evidence, general or specific adds much to the inherent probability that men and women of a certain age will be inclined to favour the *status quo*."[58]

He, and others, have, for instance, pointed out that in many of the cases discussed by Griffith there has been a division of opinion both between the Court of Appeal and the House of Lords, and within each court.[59]

Griffith does not suggest that anything can be done to change judicial

---

[55] pp. 283, 284. Paterson, *The Law Lords* (1982), pp. 187–189, argues that the Law Lords have been more consistent than Griffith suggests.

[56] *ibid.* pp. 295, 297. Previous editions included a reference to "the protection of property rights," and the third aspect of the public interest as "the promotion of certain political views normally associated with the Conservative party." The change in wording seems to reflect in part the disapproval by the judges of a number of policies of the Conservative government: see Griffith (1997) pp. 328–329. By 2002, it might also reflect the uncertainty as to what the views of the Conservative party are, and the extent to which they are different from those of the Labour government.

[57] (1978) 41 M.L.R. 501, 505–506.

[58] *ibid.* pp. 507, 509.

[59] B. Roshier and H. Teff, *Law in Society* (1980), p. 67.

attitudes. Lord Devlin notes that for a known bias allowance can be made:

> "[W]here novel measures are imposed by a minister or by parliament, they must be expressed in language which is emphatic enough and clear enough to penetrate the bias against them of those who are set in their ways: it is no use praying for the rejuvenation of the elderly."[60]

What these contributions to the debate do seem to suggest is that caution should be used in contemplating any dramatic extension of the powers of the judiciary, such as by the creation of a Bill of Rights on the American pattern with entrenched guarantees of civil liberties, expressed in general language, which override both legislation and administrative action. Moreover, one can be a little sceptical about claims such as those of Lord Denning[61]:

> "May not the Judges themselves sometimes abuse or misuse their power? It is their duty to administer and apply the law of the land. If they should divert it or depart from it—and do so knowingly—they themselves would be guilty of a misuse of power. So we come up against Juvenal's question, '*Sed quis custodiet ipsos custodes*?' (But who is to guard the guards themselves?). ... Suppose a future Prime Minister should seek to pack the Bench with judges of his own extreme political colour. Would they be tools in his hand? To that I answer 'No.' Every judge on his appointment discards all politics and all prejudices. You need have no fear. The Judges of England have always in the past—and always will be vigilant in guarding our freedoms. Someone must be trusted. Let it be the Judges."

On the other hand, the adoption of a "strongly liberal viewpoint" has been identified in recent public law cases in the House of Lords and the Privy Council,[62] which does provide some corroboration for Lord Denning's view. Furthermore, both the development of a common law principle of legality[63] and the new decision-making powers and duties arising from implementation of the Human Rights Act 1998[64] are explicitly founded on the furtherance of fundamental principles that underlie liberal democracies. These developments, coupled with the powers of the judges derived from the European Communities Act 1972,[65] have undoubtedly constituted a step change in the role of the judiciary in England and Wales. Correspondingly, interest in and concern about their decision-making has never been greater.

---

[60] (1978)41 M.L.R. 501, 511.

[61] *Misuse of Power (The Richard Dimbleby Lecture 1980)*, pp. 18–19. Reprinted in *What Next in the Law?* (1982).

[62] R. Gordon, "The awakened conscience of the nation," *Counsel*, March/April 1994, p. 8, citing the decisions in *Pepper v. Hart* (below, paras 6-036–6-038); *R. v. Secretary of State for the Home Department, ex p. Doody* [1994] 1 A.C. 531 (developing the obligations of public law decision-makers to give reasons for their decisions); *M. v. Home Office* [1994] 1 A.C.377 (holding that ministers may be subject to injunctions and the law of contempt); *Pratt and Morgan v. Attorney-General of Jamaica* [1994] 2 A.C. 1 (holding that delay in carrying out an execution could amount to a breach of constitutional rights); and *R. v. Secretary of State for Employment, ex p. Equal Opportunities Commission* (below, para. 5-053).

[63] See below, para. 6-039.

[64] See Chap. 8.

[65] See Chaps 5, 6.

CHAPTER 5

LEGISLATION

A. INTRODUCTION[1]

IN medieval England there was no clear distinction between legislation and   **5–001**
other forms of governmental action, and there was no settled procedure for
enactment that had to be followed. The terminology was confusing: well-
known early statutes include the "Constitutions" of Clarendon 1164, the
"Great Charter" 1215, the "Statute" of Merton 1235 and the "Provisions"
of Oxford 1258:

"A statute in the region of Edward I simply means something
established by royal authority; whether it is established by the King
in Council, or in a Parliament of nobles, or in a Parliament of nobles
and commons as well is completely immaterial."[2]

By the fifteenth century the consent of the Commons to a statute was
regarded as necessary and in early Tudor times the procedure for enactment
took on something like its modern form:

"Legislation . . . was no longer the Government's vague reply to vaguely
worded complaints, but rather the deliberate adoption of specific
proposals embodied in specific texts emanating from the Crown or its
officers."[3]

In the seventeenth century, Coke wrote that "There is no Act of Parliament
but must have the consent of the Lords, the Commons and the Royal assent
of the King."[4] The constitutional struggles of that century saw the end of
serious attempts by the Crown to assert a legislative competence rivalling
that of Parliament.[5] In the *Case of Proclamations*[6] the judges resolved that

---

[1] See generally on legislation, D. R. Miers and A. C. Page, *Legislation* (2nd ed., 1990); F. A.
   R. Bennion, *Statute Law* (3rd ed., 1990); and C. Pick, *Passing Legislation in Britain* (Foreign
   & Commonwealth Office, 1992). On the history of legislation see J. H. Baker, *Introduction to
   Legal History* (3rd ed., 1990), pp. 234–243; C. K. Alien, *Law in the Making* (7th ed., 1964),
   pp. 435–469.
[2] T. F. T. Plucknett, *Concise History of the Common Law* (5th ed., 1956), p. 322.
[3] Plucknett, (1944) 60 L.Q.R. 242, 248.
[4] 4 Coke's *Institutes of the Laws of England*, p. 25.
[5] See S. A. de Smith and R. Brazier, *Constitutional and Administrative Law* (8th ed., 1998), pp.
   73–75.
[6] (1611) 12 Co. Rep. 74.

"the King by his proclamation cannot create any offence which was not an offence before" and "that the King hath no prerogative, but that which the law of the land allows him." However, the courts subsequently upheld the Crown's claim to a power to impose taxation incidentally to the exercise of prerogative powers such as those to conduct foreign affairs, regulate trade and take emergency measures for the defence of the realm,[7] and a power to "dispense" with the operation of a statute for the benefit of an individual.[8] James II also claimed the power to "suspend" the general operation of statutes, his target being statutes that discriminated against Dissenters and Roman Catholics. The reassertion of such claims to prerogative power after the Civil War and the Restoration led to the "Glorious Revolution" of 1688 and the Bill of Rights. The latter measure, declared to be a statute by the Crown and Parliament Recognition Act 1689, provided (inter alia).

"That the pretended power of suspending of laws or the execution of laws by regall authority without consent of Parlyament is illegal ...
    That the pretended power of dispensing with laws or the execution of laws by regall authorities as it hath been assumed and exercised of late is illegal ...
    That levying money for or to the use of the Crowne by pretence of prerogative without grant of Parlyament for longer time or in other manner than the same is or shall be granted is illegal."

The prerogative powers of the Crown were in general restricted, and not abolished, but it was now clear that they could be modified or extinguished according to Parliament's wishes. Other possible rivals have also been unable to maintain any challenge to the dominance of Parliament. The Reformation Parliament established legislative supremacy over the Church.[9] In more recent times, the courts have refused to accept that a resolution of the House of Commons may alter the law of the land.[10]

Certain periods of our history have been noted for increases in legislative activity, and complaints of the difficulty of keeping abreast of the changes. Parliament passed 677 statutes in the reign of Henry VIII and these occupied almost as much space as the whole statute book had done in 1509.[11] Between 1711 and 1811 the annual number of Acts passed increased from 74 to 423. The bulk of the increase was in the number of local and private Acts. The 1811 figures included one for change of name, two for divorce, six for the settlement of private estates, 33 for inclosure and about 150 concerning local matters such as turnpike roads, canals and bridges.[12] The most dramatic increase in legislative activity has, however, been the product of the vast expansion of the activities of the state during the nineteenth and twentieth centuries, and associated factors such as the extensive reforms in

[7] Case of Impositions: Bate's Case (1606) 2 St.Tr.371; Case of Ship Money: R. v. Hampden (1637) 3 St.Tr.825.
[8] Thomas v. Sorell (1674) Vaughan 330; Godden v. Hales (1686) 11 St.Tr.1165.
[9] J. H. Baker, The Reports of Sir John Spelman Vol. II, Introduction (1978), pp. 64–70.
[10] See Stockdale v. Hansard (1839) 9 A. & E. 1, where the Court of Queen's Bench held that the scope of Parliamentary privilege could not be extended by a resolution; Bowles v. Bank of England [1913] 1 Ch. 57.
[11] See Baker, op. cit. n. 9, at pp. 43–46.
[12] S. Lambert, Bills and Acts (1971), p. 52.

the civil service and the administrative machinery, the increasingly representative nature of Parliament, the development of political parties and the strengthening of the role of the Cabinet. The balance as regards Acts of Parliament has also shifted from private legislation to public general legislation.[13]

Having established its legislative supremacy, Parliament was reluctant to delegate its powers.[14] In the eighteenth century, public general Acts tended "to be either overloaded with detail or to be directed to specific instances rather than to general rules."[15] However, some law-making powers had from the time of Henry VIII been entrusted to institutions such as the Commissioners of Sewers and the Justices of the Peace, and new powers were from time to time delegated by Parliament. In the eighteenth century, for example, extensive powers were granted to the Commissioners of Customs and Excise, and the Crown was given almost exclusive disciplinary powers over the Army. The following century saw a significant increase of social legislation, and a related extension of powers delegated to local and central government, but the real explosion of delegated legislation has been in the twentieth century.[16] In addition the accession of the United Kingdom to the European Communities has meant that a large body of Community legislation has become applicable in this country. A more recent development has been the introduction, in different forms, of devolution for Scotland and Wales, with the establishment of the Scottish Parliament and the National Assembly for Wales. The former institution has had significant legislative powers conferred upon it. We consider in turn the various forms of legislation: Acts of Parliament, subordinate or delegated legislation and European legislation.

B. ACTS OF PARLIAMENT

1. PARLIAMENTARY SOVEREIGNTY

One of the distinctive features of the constitution of the United Kingdom is   **5–002**
the doctrine of Parliamentary sovereignty.[17] A measure which has received the assent of the Queen, Lords and Commons, that assent being given separately and in the two Houses of Parliament by simple majorities, is accepted to have the force of law as an Act of Parliament. Its validity cannot be questioned in the courts and any earlier inconsistent legislation is repealed. Parliament (strictly the "Queen in Parliament") may pass any kind

---

[13] See below, para. 5-003.

[14] C. K. Allen, *Law and Orders* (3rd ed., 1965), Chap. 2.

[15] *ibid.* p. 28.

[16] In 2000 there were 45 Public General Statutes (3841 pages: 1 General Synod measures 8 local Acts. In 1999 there were 3114 statutory instruments (8556 pages of those printed).

[17] See S. A. de Smith and R. Brazier *Constitutional and Administrative Law* (8th ed., 1998), Chap. 4; A.W. Bradley and K.D. Ewing, *Constitutional and Administrative Law* (12th ed., 1997), Chap. 4; Sir William Wade, *Constitutional Fundamentals* (2nd ed., 1989), Chap. 3; C. R. Munro, *Studies in Constitutional Law* (2nd ed., 1999), Chap. 5.

of law without restriction, except that an attempt to bind its successors either as to the content of legislation or the manner and form of its enactment cannot succeed. Acts of Parliament, thus defined, are the supreme form of law; the rule of judicial obedience to them is the "ultimate *political* fact upon which the whole system of legislation hangs."[18] The definition of "Parliament" can be altered, but the process by which that can be achieved is political rather than legal. For example, there is no reason why the British people should not be able to adopt a written constitution, perhaps incorporating a Bill of Rights, which limits the powers of both government and legislature. What is unclear is how this would be done. The people of the United States did so in 1787–88 by means of a Constitutional Convention whose proposals were ratified by specially elected state conventions; the American "Bill of Rights" was added subsequently as a series of constitutional amendments. The judges would have to be satisfied that such a change was generally accepted; a constituent assembly might provide sufficient evidence. They would look to the realities of the situation, as they did at the commencement and conclusion of the Interregnum in the seventeenth century, when they adjusted first to the absence and then to the restoration of the monarchy.

The foregoing represents the orthodox view of Parliamentary sovereignty. It has of course been argued that the definition of "Parliament" is a matter of law rather than politics, and that as such it can be altered by the existing legislative process. Parliament as at present defined could then bind its successors as to the manner and form of legislation by redefining itself either generally or for specific purposes.[19] This view, however, has had more academic support than judicial. The constitutional adviser to the House of Lords Select Committee on a Bill of Rights clearly preferred the orthodox view,[20] and this seemed to be accepted by the Committee. Moreover, the "new view" suffers from the weakness that it would enable a redefinition of "Parliament" to be effected too easily; in effect by a small partisan majority in the House of Commons.[21] For the present, Coke's definition of an Act of Parliament holds good.

This remains so notwithstanding the enactment and implementation of the Human Rights Act 1998 incorporating the European Convention of Human Rights into English law. In the case of primary legislation incompatible with Convention rights, or incompatible secondary legislation where (disregarding the possibility of revocation) primary legislation prevents removal of the incompatibility, the superior courts have powers only to make a declaration of incompatibility, and the continuing validity of the provision in question is unaffected.[22] One important qualification is, however, that at least while the European Communities Act 1972 is on the statute book the judges are prepared to recognise the primacy of European Community law over inconsistent statutes. The status of an Act of Parliament passed with the intention of overriding Community law but

---

[18] H. W. R. Wade, [1955] C.L.J. 172, 188.
[19] See R. F. V. Heuston, *Essays in Constitutional Law* (2nd ed., 1964), Chap. 1.
[20] Evidence, 1977–78 H.L. 276, pp. 1–10 (D. Rippengal); Report: 1977–78 H.L. 176.
[21] Given that the House of Lords can be by-passed and that the royal assent by convention cannot be withheld (see below para. 5-009).
[22] See below, Chap. 8.

without repealing the 1972 Act has not, however, been tested.[23] This point has been developed and broadened by the Divisional Court in *Hunt v. London Borough of Hackney* and other cases[24] in the course of holding that regulations made under section 2(2) of the European Communities Act 1972[25] could lawfully amend the Weights and Measures Act 1985 so as to secure a compulsory system of metric weights and measures. One point was whether the 1985 Act had impliedly repealed or restricted the scope of section 2(2). The court held that it had not. It rejected an argument[26] that the principle of EU law that EU law prevails over inconsistent laws of member states[27] had been incorporated into English law by virtue of sections 2(1), (4) and 3(1) of the 1972 Act,[28] and that accordingly Parliament could no longer legislate contrary to EU law without withdrawing from the EU by express repeal of the 1972 Act. This argument was false as it failed to take account of the "constitutional place in our law of the rule that Parliament cannot bind its successors."[29] This rule was inconsistent with any assumption that the incorporation of EU law by the 1972 Act extended beyond laws on substantive matters to include any rule of EU law "which purports to touch the constitutional preconditions upon which the sovereign legislative power belonging to a member state may be exercised."[30] The traditional view of sovereignty was strongly affirmed:

"Parliament cannot bind its successors by stipulating against repeal, wholly or partly, of the European Communities Act 1972. It cannot stipulate against implied repeal any more than it can stipulate against express repeal. ... The British Parliament has not the authority to authorise any such thing. Being sovereign, it cannot abandon its sovereignty."[31]

However, the court went on to hold that what Parliament could not do, the common law both could do and had done:

"The common law has in recent years allowed, or rather created, exceptions to the doctrine of implied repeal: a doctrine which was always the common law's own creation. There are now classes or types of legislative provision which cannot be repealed by mere implication. These instances are given and can only be given, by our own courts, to which the scope and nature of Parliamentary sovereignty are ultimately confided."[32]

Accordingly, it was necessary to recognise a hierarchy of Acts of Parliament, "ordinary" and "constitutional", the latter being immune from implied repeal:

---

[23] See para. 5-050.
[24] [2002] EWHC 195 (Admin).
[25] Below, paras 5-050–5-055.
[26] For others, see below, para. 5-018.
[27] Below, para. 5-050.
[28] Below, *ibid.*
[29] [2002] EWHC 195 (Admin), per Laws L.J. at para. [58].
[30] *ibid.*
[31] *ibid.*
[32] *ibid.*, para. [60].

"In my opinion a constitutional statute is one which (a) conditions the legal relationship between citizen and State in some general overarching manner, or (b) "enlarges or diminishes the scope of what we would now regard as fundamental constitutional rights."[33]

Examples would be Magna Carta, the Bill of Rights 1689, the Acts of Union, the Reform Acts which distributed and enlarged the franchise, the Human Rights Act 1998, the Scotland Act 1998 and the Government of Wales Act 1998. Another was the European Communities Act 1972 which is "by force of the common law, a constitutional statute."[34] Repeal of such provisions could only be effected where it was clear that was the legislature's *actual* intention, and that would need "express words in the later statute" or "words so specific that the inference of an actual determination to effect the result contended for was irresistible." Repeal by implication, or by general words supplemented by a *Pepper v. Hart* statement[35] would not be enough.[36] It remains to be seen whether this approach will be endorsed by the Court of Appeal and House of Lords. The case for it is very persuasively presented by Laws L.J. as providing an appropriate balance between the proper supremacy of EU law and the proper supremacy of the United Kingdom Parliament. It echoes Wade's "ultimate political fact" analysis by recognising an underpinning rule of the common law whose scope lies beyond the reach of Parliament and is purely to be determined by the judges. Respect for the democratic principle is preserved by the ability of the Parliament of today to legislate (by express words) as it wishes; such respect does not require, and is indeed inimical to, any possibility that the wishes of a Parliament of yesterday might have an overriding effect.

It should be noted that while the concept of "Parliamentary sovereignty" is a doctrine of great technical legal significance it should not be taken as a guide to the reality of the legislative process. First, there have always been external influences which have imposed practical restraints on the kinds of legislation which can be passed. Second, the legislative process is today dominated by the government and not by members of Parliament acting independently. Legislation is initiated and formulated outside Parliament, the functions of Parliament are limited to those of scrutiny and legitimisation, and governments normally enjoy a secure party majority. Third, within "Parliament" the House of Commons is the dominant element.[37] Finally it must not be thought that legislation is the only method by which the government can secure its aims; much is achieved by, for example, exhortation, bargaining and the exercise of its economic power.[38]

2. PUBLIC AND PRIVATE ACTS

5–003   A distinction is drawn between public and private Acts. The former are those measures that are intended to alter the general law or deal with the

---

[33] *ibid.*, para. [62]. Cf. the principle of legality, below, para. 6-039.
[34] *ibid.*
[35] Below, paras 6-036–6-039.
[36] *ibid.*, para. [63].
[37] See below, paras 5-008–5-010.
[38] See J. J. Richardson and A. G. Jordan, *Governing under Pressure* (1979), Chap. 6.

public revenue or the administration of justice.[39] The latter are of local[40] or personal[41] concern. The procedure for enactment differs in some respects[42]; a person who wishes to rely on a private Act in court must produce a Queen's Printer's copy or an examined or certified copy of the original whereas judicial notice is taken of public Acts[43]; and a private Act may be construed strictly against the interest of the promoter, although this approach is not always followed today.[44]

An important class of private legislation is that promoted by local authorities. Section 262 of the Local Government Act 1972 provided that all local legislation (with some exceptions, including protective provisions for the benefit of any person and provisions relating to a statutory under-taking), in force immediately before April 1974, would cease to have effect at the end of 1979 in metropolitan counties and at the end of 1984 elsewhere.[45] These dates were subsequently postponed by, respectively, one year and two years.[46] Local authorities wishing to preserve particular provisions were required to promote Bills to that end. Many authorities did so,[47] although the rationalisation process proved to be less straightforward and more

---

[39] *Halsbury's Laws of England* (4th ed.) Vol. 34, para. 729. For a useful analysis of the kinds of public Bills according to their content see I. Burton and G. Drewry, *Legislation and Public Policy* (1981), pp. 32–45. The authors draw a broad distinction between innovatory "policy" Bills and non-innovatory "administration" Bills to remedy anomalies, with further sub-categories of "minor policy" Bills dealing with restricted issues within an area of public policy not otherwise intended to be changed, and "administrative reform" Bills which reorganise administrative support for an existing policy. Session-by-session surveys of legislation by Burton and Drewry have appeared in the journal *Parliamentary Affairs*. Details of the progress of Bills are set out with annual *House of Commons Sessional Information Digests* published by HMSO and on Parliament's website (*www.parliament.uk*.)

[40] Bills dealing with the constitution or election of local governing bodies must be introduced as public Bills: *Halsbury, ibid.*; below, para. 5-011. See *e.g.* the London Government Act 1963; the Charlwood and Horley Act 1974.

[41] *i.e.* a "private bill relating to the estate, property, status or style, or otherwise relating to the personal affairs of an individual" (H.L. Standing Orders 151–174). These include Bills affecting estates, and Bills to authorise a marriage between persons within the prohibited degrees of affinity: in the case of the latter, the details are now considered by a Select Committee of the House of Lords, and not on the floor of the House: 2nd Report from the Select Committee on Procedure, 1985–86 H.L. 152, approved by the House (H.L. Deb. Vol. 475, cols.709–711, June 3, 1986). Some of the prohibitions were relaxed by the Marriage (Prohibited Degrees of Relationship) Act 1986.

[42] See below, paras 5-008–5-011.

[43] The line between "public" and "private" Acts is drawn rather differently in this context: see *Halsbury's Laws of England* (4th ed.) Vol. 17, para. 150. For this purpose an Act passed after 1850 is deemed to be a public Act and "to be judicially noticed as such unless the contrary is expressly provided by the Act": Interpretation Act 1978, s.3 and Sched. 2, para. 2. For the definition of "judicial notice" see above para. 1-011, n. 32.

[44] *Maxwell on Interpretation of Statutes* (12th ed., 1969), pp. 262–3. See, *e.g. Allen v. Gulf Oil Refining Ltd* [1981] A.C. 1001, H.L.

[45] See D. Foulkes, [1976] P.L. 272; E. D. Graham, (1979) XLVII *The Table* 109; R. J. B. Morris, [1987] Stat.L.R. 2.

[46] S.I. 1979 No. 969; S.I. 1983 No. 619.

[47] An alternative approach, permitted in a few cases, was for the Secretary of State for the Environment to exercise the power conferred by s.262(9)(a) to exempt particular provisions from the general cesser: see S.I. 1986 No. 1133; Morris, *op. cit.* pp. 26–27.

expensive than had been anticipated.[48] Relatively few authorities now promote local Acts.[49]

Further work on the rationalisation of local legislation is continuing under the auspices of Law Commission, leading to provisions in the series of Statute Law (Repeals) Acts.[50] Express repeal brings greater certainty than the generalised repeal effected by the Local Government Act 1972.

The scope and procedures for enactment of private legislation were considered by the Joint Committee on Private Bill Procedure in 1987–88.[51] The committee's recommendations were designed to reduce the range of private legislation by diverting matters that could be pursued by other, non-Parliamentary procedures and included recommendations on matters of detail and procedure. The outcome was the introduction by the Transport and Works Act 1992 of a new procedure for the Secretary of State to make orders in respect of such matters as rail, light rail and light rapid transit proposals and inland waterways and broadening the scope of orders in respect of harbours.[52] Orders in relation to proposals which in the Secretary of State's opinion are of national importance require the approval of both Houses of Parliament. Orders under the 1992 Act are delegated legislation and open to challenge in the courts.[53] In addition, there were some detailed changes to private Bill procedure, including the introduction of requirements as to environmental impact assessment.[54]

Public Bills which are found to affect private interests in a manner different from the way in which they affect other private interests in the same category are known as "hybrid" Bills and are subject to an amalgam of the procedural rules applicable to public and private Bills.[55]

3. GOVERNMENT BILLS AND PRIVATE MEMBERS' BILLS

5–004   A separate distinction, within the class of public general statutes, is drawn

---

[48] Foulkes, *op. cit.*; Morris, *op. cit.*
[49] R.J.B. Morris, [1999] J.L.G.L. 122 (proposing that there should be annual Local Government (Local Provisions) Bills to enable councils to obtain legislative provisions without the need for individual local promotions).
[50] See 29th Annual Report of the Law Commission 1994 (1994–95 H.C. 244), p. 51; C. S. Phipps, (1991) 22 *The Law Librarian* 60; (1992) 23 *The Law Librarian* 35.
[51] 1987–88 H.L. 97, H.C. 625.; *Private Bills and New Procedures—A Consultation Document—The Government's Response to the Report of the Joint Committee on Private Bill Procedure*, Cm. 1110, 1990.
[52] See J. Durkin, P. Lane and M. Pete, *Blackstone's Guide to the Transport and Works Act 1992* (1992).
[53] 1992 Act, s.22 (a statutory *ultra vires* clause: see below, para. 18-043).
[54] See Vol. 187 H. C. Deb., March 13, 1991, cols.923–925; Vol. 191 H. C. Deb., May 20, 1991, cols. 721–739.
[55] P. Norton, *The Commons in Perspective* (1981), p. 104. In 1976 problems were caused for the government when the Speaker ruled that the Aircraft and Shipbuilding Industries Bill, which had completed its Committee stage, was prima facie hybrid: I. Burton and G. Drewry, (1978) 31 *Parliamentary Affairs* pp. 151–6. Recent examples include the Cardiff Bay Barrage Act 1993 and the Channel Tunnel Rail Link Act 1996.

between government and "Private Members" Bills.[56] Most of the Bills that are successful are introduced by the government of the day,[57] but Bills may also be introduced by individual M.P.s or "Private Peers". In the House of Commons certain days are set aside for Private Members' Bills and a ballot is held each session to determine which M.P.s may take priority on these days. A list of 20 names is drawn up; those near the top have some chance of success, although in practice a Bill will not get through without the support, or at least the benevolent neutrality, of the government.[58] There are other methods by which a private member may introduce a Bill,[59] but such Bills rarely proceed because of lack of time.[60] Some important measures have commenced life as Private Members' Bills, including the Public Bodies (Admission to Meetings) Act 1960 (sponsored by Margaret Thatcher M.P.), the Abortion Act 1967 (David Steel M.P.) and the Indecent Displays (Control) Act 1981 (Timothy Sainsbury M.P.). Governments tend to prefer to leave matters of conscience to Private Members' legislation: the risks generally outweigh any possible political advantages. One result is that such legislation, once in place, can become difficult to repeal or reform, as shown by the many unsuccessful attempts over the years by anti-abortionists to secure the amendment of the Abortion Act 1967.[61] A Private Members' Bill that fails may, however, provide the impetus for subsequent public

---

[56] On Private Members' Bills see P. G. Richards in S. A. Walkland (ed.) *The House of Commons in the Twentieth Century* (1979), Chap. VI; P. Norton, *The Commons in Perspective* (1981), pp. 99–102; P. G. Richards, *Parliament and Conscience* (1970); D. Marsh and Read, *Private Members' Bills* (1988); J. Gray, [1978] P. L. 242 (case study of the Unsolicited Goods and Services Acts 1971 and 1975); S. M. Cretney, "The Forfeiture Acts 1982—the Private Member's Bill as an Instrument of Law Reform" (1990) 10 O.J.L.S. 289; Sir Henry de Waal, [1990] Stat. L.R. 18. A full list of Private Members Bills passed since 1945 is contained in House of Commons Factsheet L3 (previously 67), on the Parliamentary website.

[57] The number per session has varied between 21 and 52 in the period 1985 to 2001, depending in part on the number of sitting days in the session: see the House of Commons *Sessional Information Digests*.

[58] This point is well known to members, who should be "realistic about the prospects of success": Select Committee on Procedure (5th Report, 1994–95 H.C. 38, *Private Members' Bills*, p. xxxvii). However, the adoption by the government of procedural tactics to block the Civil Rights (Disabled Persons) Bill 1993–94 (and other Bills) where it had failed to make clear its opposition generated considerable controversy.

[59] (1) After Question Time, on notice given under S.O. No. 57, or (2) under the "ten minute rule", which allows time for brief speeches for and against a Bill. Examples of the former that were ultimately successful include the Protection of Birds (Amendment) Bill 1976 (which went through all its Commons stages in 67 seconds) and the Prohibition of Female Circumcision Bill 1985 (which had been presented and had made some progress in previous sessions: see E. A. Sochart, (1988) 41 *Parliamentary Affairs* 508). Examples of the latter include the Bail (Amendment) Act 1993 and the Local Government (Amendment) Act 1993.

[60] For example, in 1999–2000, the numbers of Bills presented (and the number successful) were: government Bills 40(39); ballot Bills 20(5); S.O. No. 57 20(0); 10-minute rule Bills 57(0); Lords' Private Members Bills 7(1). (House of Commons *Sessional Information Digest* 1999–2000). The statistics for 1950–85 are given in Marsh and Read (1988), pp. 22–23. In 1995, the Select Committee on Procedure (5th Report on *Private Members' Bills*), 1994–95 H.C. 38) noted that they had not received any conclusive evidence that the balance between government and backbench members had shifted over the last 25 years, and did not recommend any changes in procedure.

[61] See D. Marsh and J. Chambers, *Abortion Politics* (1981); Marsh and Read (1988), Chap. 6.

legislation.[62] The special features of "private Acts" mentioned above do not apply to those "public general statutes" that happen to start their life as Private Members' Bills.

4. CONSOLIDATION, TAX SIMPLIFICATION AND STATUTE LAW REVISION ACTS[63]

5–005   On occasion, the law in a particular area is *codified*; the relevant rules as derived from both case-law and existing statutory provisions are set out afresh in one statute. The leading examples are the Bills of Exchange Act 1882, the Sale of Goods Act 1893 (now consolidated in the Sale of Goods Act 1979) and the Theft Act 1968. The Law Commission's objects include that of the codification of areas of English law, but it found that this kind of work could pose great problems and could require the allocation of resources on a scale which was regarded as impossible.[64] Greater progress has, however, been made in respect of the codification of criminal law.[65]

The *consolidation* of statutory provisions on a particular topic is a process that is more modest in aim, and much more commonly achieved.[66] Here, the relevant provisions are re-enacted in one or more consolidating statutes. There are four kinds of consolidation Bill. First, there are straight consolidation Bills that simply re-enact the existing texts. Second, Bills presented under the Consolidation of Enactments (Procedure) Act 1949 may include "corrections and minor improvements",[67] which must be approved by a Joint Committee of both Houses on Consolidation Bills. Third, improvements designed to facilitate the satisfactory consolidation, but beyond the scope of the 1949 Act may be proposed by the Law Commission; these are also considered by the Joint Committee.[68] Fourth, consolidation with substantial amendments may be prepared by an *ad hoc* expert

---

[62] *e.g.* the Home Buyers' Bill sponsored by Austin Mitchell in 1983–84 (see the third edition of this book, p. 120, para. 6-032 and Mitchell, (1986) 39 *Parliamentary Affairs* 1).

[63] See Lord Simon of Glaisdale and J. V. D. Webb, [1975] P.L. 285; I. Burton and G. Drewry, *Legislation and Public Policy* (1981), pp. 205–213; Lord Simon of Glaisdale, [1985] Stat. L.R. 352. On the interpretation of consolidation legislation see below.

[64] Law Commissions Act 1965, s.3(l); Law Commission's 13th Annual Report 1977–78 (Law Com. 92), para. 2.34 (codification of the law of landlord and tenant); *cf.* 15th Annual Report 1979–80 (Law Com. 107), para. 1.4 (codification of general principles of liability in criminal law). See above, para. 1-028.

[65] See above, para. 1-028.

[66] *Report of a Committee appointed by the Lord President of the Council on the Preparation of Legislation*(The Renton Report: Cmnd. 6053, 1975), pp. 17–18 and Chap. XTV; F. A. R. Bennion, *Statute Law* (3rd ed., 1990), Chap. 6.

[67] *i.e.* "amendments of which the effect is confined to resolving ambiguities, removing doubts, bringing obsolete provisions into conformity with modern practice, or removing unnecessary provisions or anomalies which are not of substantial importance, and amendments designed to facilitate improvements in the form or manner in which the law is stated ... ": 1949 Act, s.2.

[68] The Law Commission report will also cover any necessary "corrections and minor improvements." Law Commission consolidations are separate from their general law reform proposals. The Hansard Society Commission (below, para. 5-007) recommended that the pace of consolidation should continue to increase and that if necessary the drafting resources of the Law Commission be strengthened to make this possible: Report, pp. 110–111.

committee, or as an ordinary departmental Bill.[69] Where the consolidation
process requires some amendments of substance these may be included in an
ordinary Bill (normally in a Schedule)[70]; once these "pre-consolidation
amendments" have been passed one of the first three kinds of consolidation
measure can be brought forward.[71] Recent large scale consolidations include
those of the Housing legislation and the Companies legislation in 1985, the
Income and Corporation Taxes Act 1988,[72] the Planning legislation in 1990,
Water legislation in 1991, Social Security legislation in 1992 and Education
legislation in 1996.

A substantial project to rewrite primary direct tax legislation commenced
in 1995. The purpose is to make the legislation easier to understand by a
new, more logical structure; using plain language wherever possible;
rationalising the use of definitions; omitting unnecessary and obsolete
material; and using better signpostings and layout. The Tax Law Rewrite
project has a steering committee, chaired by Lord Howe, a consultative
committee and multidisciplinary drafting team. The first Act in a projected
series of seven was the Capital Allowances Act 2001. "Exposure drafts" with
a commentary were published for comment. Work is proceeding on income
tax, but less extensive and formal consultation methods are to be used. The
work is not simply consolidation as different language is to be employed.
Some minor changes in law or approach are included, for example to correct
small errors or enact on extra statutory concession.[73] A proposal to use
three part numbering was rejected by the House of Lords Procedure
Committee.[74] Following recommendations from the House of Commons
Procedure Committee,[75] the Bill was introduced in the Commons and
referred on Second Reading to a Joint Committee, with a Commons
majority and chairman.

Various Statute Law Revision Acts have been passed at intervals from
1856 for the repeal of statutory provisions that are "obsolete, spent,
unnecessary or superseded." Since 1969 the Law Commissions have
prepared Statute Law (Repeals) Bills for the repeal of enactments that in
their opinion are "no longer of practical utility." These are wider in scope.
One was passed each year between 1973 and 1978 (inclusive) and further

---

[69] For an example of the former see the *Report of the Committee on Consolidation of Highway Law* (Cmnd. 630) which led to the Highways Act 1959; (the Highways Act 1980 followed the Law Commission procedure.) For an example of the latter, see the Local Government Act 1972.

[70] Section 116 of the Companies Act 1981 enabled amendments, desirable to enable a satisfactory consolidation to be produced, to be made by Order in Council on the recommendation of the Law Commission and the Scottish Law Commission: see 19th Annual Report of the Law Commission 1983–84 (1984–85 H.C. 214), p. 34. This device was used as part of the massive consolidation of companies legislation in 1985.

[71] See, *e.g.* the Limitation Amendment Act 1980 and the subsequent consolidation measure, the Limitation Act 1980, and the Mental Health (Amendment) Act 1982 and the Mental Health Act 1983.

[72] The longest consolidation produced by the Law Commission and the longest Bill ever introduced.

[73] *Inland Revenue: Tax Law Rewrite (www.inlandrevenue.gov.uk/rewrite/index.htm)*; S. Hardy, (1988) 29 *The Law Librarian* 74; D. Salter, (1998) 19 Stat. L.R. 65.

[74] A decision rightly criticised by J.F. Avery Jones, [2001] B.T.R. 161.

[75] Second Report, 1996–97 H.C. 126, *Legislative Procedure for Tax Simplification Bills*; HC Standing Order 60.

ones in 1981, 1986, 1989, 1993, 1995 and 1998.[76] Statute Law Revision Acts are no longer promoted except in relation to Northern Ireland legislation. Both kinds of Bills are considered by the Joint Committee, and make an important contribution to the tidying up of the statute book.

The main advantage of the kinds of measures considered in this section, other than Bills for consolidation with substantial amendments, is that the Parliamentary stages, apart from consideration by the Joint Committee, are taken without debate on matters of substance.

5. PROVISIONAL ORDERS AND SPECIAL PROCEDURE ORDERS[77]

5–006   In the nineteenth century, the Provisional Order procedure was introduced as a short cut to local legislation. Many statutes provided that a Minister could make a Provisional Order granting certain powers to a local authority or statutory body, following the completion of certain prescribed formalities. Where there were objections there would normally be a local inquiry. One or more such Orders would then be placed before Parliament to be ratified by a Confirmation Act. Petitions against a Confirmation Bill could be submitted and they would be dealt with in the same manner as objections to a private Bill.[78] There are still some examples of Provisional Order powers on the statute book,[79] but the device has largely been superseded by the use of Orders subject to "special parliamentary procedure" under the Statutory Orders (Special Procedure) Act 1945.[80] This procedure also involves an opportunity for objections to be the subject of a local inquiry, and for petitions either against an Order generally or for amendment to be submitted to Parliament.[81] However, an Order against which no petitions are received comes into effect without a Confirmation Act; an Act is only required when a joint committee of both Houses amends the Order in a way unacceptable to the Minister or reports against the Order as a whole.[82]

---

[76] Provisions identified by the Law Commission as redundant may alternatively be repealed by ordinary legislation: see the 20th Annual Report of the Law Commission 1984–85 (1985–86 H.C. 247), pp. 15–16; 25th Annual Report, 1990 (1990–91 H.C. 249), p. 12.

[77] C. K. Alien, *Law and Orders* (3rd ed., 1965), pp. 76–81.

[78] See below, para. 5-011.

[79] See, *e.g.* Local Government Act 1972, ss.240, 254(8), 262(10).

[80] As amended by the Statutory Orders (Special Procedure) Act 1965, and see S.I. 1949 No. 2393; S.I. 1962 Nos.409 and 2791. The operation of the procedure was considered by the Joint Committee on Private Bill Procedure (Report, (1987–88) H.L. 9, H.C. 625), pp. 10, 50–51.

[81] For an example of a case where a minister wrongfully refused to accept a memorial from a local authority objector requiring an order to be subjected to special Parliamentary procedure, see *R. v. Ministry of Agriculture, Fisheries and Food, ex p. Wear Valley D.C.* (1988) 152 L.G. Rev. 849 (the minister held erroneously that the authority was not "adversely affected" by the order).

[82] This has been done twice: the Mid-Northamptonshire Water Board Order Confirmation (Special Procedure) Act 1949 and the Okehampton Bypass (Confirmation of Orders) Act 1985. The latter was especially controversial as the Joint Committee had reported against the Orders: see the Report of the Joint Committee on Private Bill Procedure, *loc. cit.* n. 80 above; H.C. Deb. Vol. 87, cols, 140–224, November 19, 1985, and H.L. Deb. Vol. 468, cols.1412ff, December 5, 1985.

6. General Synod Measures[83]

The General Synod of the Church of England may pass legislative proposals ("Measures") concerning the Church. A Measure is considered by the Ecclesiastical Committee,[84] which comprises 15 members of each House nominated, respectively, by the Lord Chancellor and the Speaker. The Committee reports to Parliament. A Measure approved by each House[85] is then submitted for royal assent, and when this is signified the Measure has the force and effect of an Act of Parliament.

7. Preparation and Drafting

The process by which proposals for legislation are converted into a form suitable for enactment is complex.[86] A government Bill originates from the relevant ministry or department, although the ideas may be put forward from many sources including party election manifestos, civil servants, reports of official committees and outside interest groups, whether established to defend some sectional interest or promote some cause. Occasionally, a pre-legislative Select Committee may be appointed by one or both of the Houses to examine a subject with a view to legislation. These are, however, uncommon and have not been particularly successful.[87] There is normally a considerable measure of consultation. The government may issue a "Green Paper"[88] which sets out tentative proposals, and may suggest alternatives. Legislative proposals are occasionally considered by the

5–007

---

[83] Church of England Assembly (Powers) Act 1919; Synodical Government Measure 1969. See *Hasbury's Laws of England* (4th ed.) Vol. 14, paras. 399–411.

[84] Established by the 1919 Act, s.2.

[85] Parliament must either accept or reject a Measure: it has no power to amend: *ibid.* s.4. In 1927 and 1928 Parliament rejected proposed Measures for the revision of the Prayer Book: other rejected Measures have been the Incumbents (Vacation of Benefices) Measures 1975 and the Appointment of Bishops Measure 1984 (see H. C. Deb. Vol. 64, cols.126–144, July 16 1984).

[86] See Cabinet Office, *Guide to Legislative Procedures* (1996) (an internal document); S. A. Walkland, *The Legislative Process in Great Britain* (1968); M. Zander, *The Law Making Process* (5th ed., 1999), Chap. 1; and *A Matter of Justice* (1988), pp. 236–252; D. Johnstone, [1980] Stat.L.R. 67 and *A Tax Shall Be Charged* (HMSO, 1975) (preparation of VAT legislation); Miers and Page (1990), Chaps. 2–4; E. A. Dreidger, *The Composition of Legislation* (2nd ed., 1976); G. C. Thornton, *Legislative Drafting* (3rd ed., 1987); A. Graham, [1988] StatL.R. 4. See also B. W. Hogwood, *From Crisis to Complacency?* (1987), Chap. 5 (setting the legislative process within the wider context of the shaping of public policy in Britain).

[87] See P. Norton, *The Commons in Perspective* (1981), p. 85; *First Report of the Select Committee on Procedure*, 1977–78 H.C. 588, Vol. 1, p. xiii; Miers and Page (1990), pp. 43–46. The Hansard Society Commission (below, para. 5-007) stated that such committees might occasionally be useful where a fuller inquiry is needed and legislation is not required in a hurry: Report, pp. 80–81.

[88] On white paper with green covers.

relevant departmental select committee[89] but the Select Committee on Procedure concluded that these committees should not be used principally for that purpose.[90] Following the Labour victory at the 1997 General Election, a Select Committee on Modernisation of the House of Commons was appointed to recommend improvements to the procedure for examining legislative proposals. One of the four themes in its reports has been improvements in pre-legislative scrutiny.[91] The government had declared its intention to publish more Bills in draft and the Queen's Speech now may include announcements of draft Bills. The Committee's view was that there were significant benefits in the consideration of draft Bills by committees or joint committees, the kind of committee appropriate varying according to the circumstances. Since then draft Bills on pension-splitting on divorce and on limited liability partnerships have been considered by departmental select committees; on Freedom of Information by the Select Committee on Public Administration; on food standards by an ad hoc Select Committee; and on financial services and on local government organisation by ad hoc joint committees. The impact of the scrutiny has naturally varied.[92]

Once the appropriate committee of the Cabinet[93] has approved proposals in principle, and provisionally allotted a place in the legislative programme, "Instructions" to draft are prepared by the departmental lawyers[94] and sent to the Parliamentary draftsmen: the "Parliamentary Counsel to the Treasury." The Parliamentary Counsel's office was established in 1869; there are at present 40 counsel, with chambers in Whitehall.[95] Parliamentary counsel are either barristers or solicitors. They normally work in pairs, each

---

[89] *e.g.* Abolition of the "sus" law (power under the Vagrancy Act 1824, ss.4, 6 to arrest a "suspected person or reputed thief" loitering in a public place with intent to commit an arrestable offence) following Reports of the Home Affairs Committee, 1979–80 H.C. 559, 744. See S. H. Bailey, D. J. Harris and B. L. Jones, *Civil liberties: Cases and Materials* (2nd ed., 1985), p. 55. The Hansard Society Commission (below, para. 5-007) believed that more use should be made of departmentally related select committees to examine White and Green papers and other consultative documents: Report, p. 80.

[90] First Report, 1977–78 H.C. 588, p. xiii; Second Report, 1984–85 H.C. 49, p. vi.

[91] First Report, 1997–97 H.C. 190, *The Legislative Process*, paras 19–30.

[92] The publication of draft Bills has been widely welcomed, and scrutiny has led to some improvements in drafting, but the passage of such a Bill has not necessarily been easier: H.C. Deb., April 18, 2000, col. 825. See also G. Power, *Parliamentary Scrutiny of Draft Legislation 1997–1999* (Constitution Unit, 2000) examining the costs and benefits in the light of experience and recommending steps to clarify, co-ordinate and properly resource pre-legislative scrutiny.

[93] Currently the Ministerial Committee on the Legislative Programme (LP); see also Miers and Page (1990), pp. 30–38. This Committee currently includes the President of the Council and Leader of the House of Commons (chair), Deputy Prime Minister, Lord Chancellor, Secretaries of State for Northern Ireland, Wales and Scotland, Chief Secretary, Treasury, Leader of the House of Lords, Chief Whip, Minister without Portfolio, Captain of the Gentlemen-At-Arms, Attorney General, Advocate General and Minister for the Cabinet Office, Parliamentary Secretary to the Leader of the House of Commons: *Cabinet Committee Structure* (Cabinet Office website: *www.cabinet-office.gov.uk*).

[94] Instructions for legislation concerning the Inland Revenue ae drafted by an Assistant Secretary.

[95] Of these, four are at the Law Commission, six at the Inland Revenue Tax Law Rewrite Project and one on loan to the DTI Company Law Review (see *www.parliamentary-counsel.gov.uk*: H.C. Deb., March 9, 2000, cols *784W–786W*). Some appointments are part-time. On drafting in the nineteenth century see F. Bowers, "Victorian Reforms in Legislative Drafting" (1980) 48 *Revue D'Histoire Du Droit* 329–348. The working of the office in the 1930s and 1940s is described in Sir Harold Kent, *In on the Act* (1979).

Bill being allocated to one of the Senior Counsel working with a Junior Counsel. As well as the drafts of a Bill, the counsel prepare government amendments and relevant motions, give advice on Parliamentary procedure, and attend conferences with ministers as well as sittings of both Houses and their committees. They may also assist with the drafting of Private Members' Bills supported by the government or otherwise likely to become law.[96] "The hours are unpredictable and the work arduous, but correspondingly rewarding."[97] A Bill may well go through a whole series of drafts before it is presented to Parliament, clauses being revised in the light of consultation between the draftsmen and the department. Other departments including the Treasury and outside groups may also be consulted at this stage. Firm proposals may be incorporated in a government "White Paper", and this may be debated in Parliament. The actual drafts of legislation are not, however, normally circulated outside the Whitehall machine before they have been presented to Parliament.

F. A. R. Bennion, formerly one of the Parliamentary counsel, has identified a number of "drafting parameters" which the draftsman must bear in mind, and which affect the form of Bills.[98] Some of these considerations relate to the process of enactment; others to the operation of the law once it has been enacted. The "preparational" parameters include compliance with the pre-Parliamentary and Parliamentary requirements as to the form of Bills and the stages through which they must pass (*procedural legitimacy*); strict conformity with the government's timetable for legislation and other time pressures such as those imposed by emergency legislation (*timeliness*); *comprehensibility* to members of Parliament; the need to structure a Bill in such a way that the main points of policy can be debated in a rational order (*debatability*)[99]; the choice of language that will minimise objections from those involved in the legislative process (*acceptability*)[1]; and *brevity*. The "operational parameters" include the need for the text of the Bill to carry out the government's intentions (*legal effectiveness*); the desirability that the text be open to one construction only (certainty)[2]; *comprehensibility* to the users of the statute, who will normally be practising lawyers (judge, barrister or solicitor), public officials or non-legal professional advisers[3]; and legal compatibility with the rest of the statute book, so that inconsistent provisions are specifically repealed and that the same words mean the same thing even though they appear in different statutes.[4]

---

[96] Private Bills are generally drafted by Parliamentary Agents. Scottish Bills are drafted by members of the Lord Advocate's Department: see Lord Mackay of Clashfern, [1983] Stat.L.R. 68. In 1995, four private sector contracts were awarded to draft parts of the 1996 Finance Bill; the successful applicants were two city solicitor firms, a set of tax chambers and a former member of the Parliamentary Counsel's office working as a freelance: Treasury Press Release 109/95.

[97] Civil Service Commission, Lawyers: *Civil Service Careers* (1980), p. 27.

[98] *Statute Law* (3rd ed., 1990), pp. 28–40. See also G. Engle, [1983] Stat.L.R. 7.

[99] The government may, however, wish a Bill to be drawn in such a way as to restrict opportunities for debate or amendment, for example by drawing the long title narrowly.

[1] "The red-blooded terms of political controversy are toned down. The prose style is flat." (Bennion (1990), p. 34).

[2] The government may, however, intend a provision to be ambiguous.

[3] Bennion (1990), pp. 37–38.

[4] "Contrary to most people's belief, however, there are no books of precedents in the Parliamentary Counsel's Office." (*ibid.*, p. 39).

These parameters frequently conflict. The most important are procedural legitimacy, timeliness and legal effectiveness, and these may well take priority over comprehensibility and legal compatibility. "The task of making legislative proposals understood by non-lawyer politicians while securing their legal effectiveness is one of the most formidable faced by the Parliamentary draftsmen."[5]

The report of the Renton Committee on the Preparation of Legislation[6] recognised that draftsmen had to work under pressures and constraints that made it very difficult to produce simple and clear legislation. Many statutes were well drafted, but there was cause for concern that difficulty was being encountered by statute-users. They had received complaints about the use of obscure and complex language, over-elaboration of detail in the quest for "certainty", the illogical structure of some statutes and problems created by the arrangement of the statute book in a chronological series of separate Acts. There was also criticism of the use of the "non-textual" method of amendment, whereby the amending Act set out the substance of the change proposed to be made without altering the text of the Act being amended. The Renton Committee endorsed the recent change in practice whereby statutes were amended "textually" by adding words to or deleting words from the original provision whenever convenience permitted.[7] The "non-textual" method eases the task of members of Parliament when examining an amending Bill, by enabling them to comprehend its meaning without having to "look beyond the four corners of the Bill."[8] Nevertheless, the Renton Committee thought that the needs of the user should be given priority over those of the legislator, particularly now that there was an official "loose-booklet" publication in which statutes are printed as amended (Statutes in Force). It seems that it is now settled practice to make the maximum possible use of textual amendment.[9]

The Renton Committee made a number of other proposals for reform. For example, all available methods should be used to recruit and train more draftsmen as a matter of high priority; the use of statements of principle should be encouraged, with additional guidance given where necessary in Schedules; more use could be made of examples showing how a Bill is intended to work in particular situations; statements of purpose should be used where they are the most convenient method of clarifying the scope and effect of legislation; long un-paragraphed sentences should be avoided; a statute should be arranged to suit the convenience of its ultimate users; the typographical production should be improved, and there should be more consolidation. They rejected suggestions that there should be a "crash" programme of consolidation and that it should be on a "one Act, one subject basis".[10] Under the latter proposal, each subject would have a principal Act and future legislation on the subject would be effected by textual amendment to that Act. In 1978, Sir David Renton, in an address to the Statute Law Society entitled "Failure to implement the Renton

---

[5] *ibid.*, p. 33.
[6] Cmnd. 6053, 1975.
[7] *ibid.* Chap. XIII: Statute Law Society, *Statute Law: the Key to Clarity* (1972), pp. 7–18 and *Renton and the Need for Reform* (1979), pp. 27–40.
[8] Lord Thring, *Practical Legislation* (2nd ed., 1902), p. 8, cited in Bennion (1990), p. 32.
[9] D. Johnstone, [1980] Stat.L.R. 112.
[10] Renton Report, Chap. XIV.

Report",[11] noted that there had been a small increase in the number of draftsmen and increased momentum in the consolidation process, but that Parliament had continued to pass enormous quantities of legislation, with no diminution in the amount of detail and scarcely any use of statements of purpose. The government's response to the Report had been guarded.[12] The Lord President of the Council (Michael Foot) stated in 1977 that the government regarded the recommendations concerning drafting practice:

"as a comprehensive and valuable summary of the best drafting practice, and they are being taken into account in the drafting of all current Government legislation. It is considered essential, however, that parliamentary draftsmen should retain discretion to apply the recommendations in accordance with the requirements of particular legislation."[13]

Subsequent governments have not shown any greater enthusiasm for further reforms based on the Renton Report.[14]

In the early 1990s, the whole subject was the subject of a comprehensive review by a Commission appointed by the Hansard Society for Parliamentary Government.[15] Although not an official body, the Commission consulted very widely and generated a considerable body of information from official and other sources. The Commission concluded that "the legislative process in this country has been unsatisfactory for a long time and Ministers have not, up till now, shown a willingness to change it."[16] There was an "overwhelming impression" from the evidence that "many of those most directly affected are deeply dissatisfied with the extent, nature, timing and conduct of consultation on bills as at present practised."[17] The government should "make every effort to get bills in a form fit for enactment, without major alteration, before they are presented to Parliament."[18] Consultation practice should be improved and enshrined in government guidelines, including the more frequent use of independent inquiries, and more consultation on draft texts.[19] As to drafting,[20] the Cabinet's Legislation Committee should assume the wider and longer-term role of ensuring that Bills conform with the best constitutional principles and, where appropriate, have been prepared after full and genuine consultation. Ministerial responsibility for the Parliamentary Counsel, including oversight of the drafting methods and scrutiny of the drafting of government Bills, should be assigned to the Attorney-General. The

---

[11] Statute Law Society, *Renton and the Need for Reform* (1979), pp. 2–8.
[12] *ibid.*, pp. 97–98.
[13] H.C. Deb. Vol. 941, col. 329 written answer, December 15, 1977.
[14] Lord Simon of Glaisdale, "The Renton Report—Ten Years On" [1985] StatL.R. 133; H.L. Deb. Vol. 489, cols.1417–1449, summarised at [1988] Stat.L.R. 1.
[15] *Making the Law: The Report of the Hansard Society Commission on the Legislative Process*, November 1992 (1993) (Chairman: Lord Rippon). See M. Rush, (1993) 14 Stat-L.R. 75. See also the Report of the (Conservative Party- appointed) Norton Commission to Strengthen Parliament (2000) which echoes some of the Hansard Commission recommendations.
[16] *ibid.*, p. 138.
[17] *ibid.*, p. 139.
[18] *ibid.*
[19] Chap. 3 and pp. 139–140.
[20] Chap. 4 and pp. 141–142.

number of draftsmen required should be reviewed. The drafting style adopted should be appropriate for the main users of the legislation; draftsmen should always seek for clarity, simplicity and brevity but with certainty paramount, and note the continued criticisms made by those most directly affected of the style of drafting of statute law. Ministers, civil servants and draftsmen should do all they can to eliminate unnecessary detail; some means should be found of informing the citizens, lawyers and the courts of the intention underlying the words of a statute; notes on sections should be published. The Committee also make recommendations on the Parliamentary process, access to the statute book, the programming and time-tabling of legislation and the impact of EC legislation.[21] The government's response[22] pointed to the recruitment of four additional draftsmen and an increase in the number of clauses of draft Bills published in advance for consultation.

The work of the Hansard Society Commission was built on by the Select Committee on Modernisation of the House of Commons which began its work in 1997. In view of the Commission's report, it decided not to take oral evidence. It accepted the general thrust of the criticisms set out in previous reports. The key elements of its recommendations have been[23]: (1) improved pre-legislative scrutiny;[24](2) improved explanatory material;[25](3) greater use of Special Standing Committees; (4) new arrangements for the programming of Bills; (5) the carry-over, by agreement, of some Bills from one session to the next; (6) the establishment of a parallel chamber, sitting in the Grand Committee Room in Westminster Hall, and referred to as "Westminster Hall". Some progress has been made but some of the changes (particularly carry-over and the parallel chamber) are still experimental and programming has been highly controversial.[26]

There is a recurrent debate on the issue whether there should be a move from the British style of "common-law" drafting to the "continental" or "civil law" method of drafting. The latter is said to be more lucid and succinct, with more emphasis on basic principles and purposes and less on detail. Proponents of such a move include Sir William Dale[27] and J. A. Clarence Smith[28]; opponents include F. A. R. Bennion[29] and Geoffrey

---

[21] See pp. 268, 277–278.

[22] Viscount Cranborne, Leader of the House, contributing to a debate on the Commission's report, Vol. 559 H.L. Deb., December 14, 1994, cols.1291ff., at cols.1321–1326. He stated that he was "aware of the drum beat of dissatisfaction in your Lordship's House and elsewhere over the legislative process" (col. 1321) and did state that the government wished "to make a positive contribution towards improving the quality of our legislation" (col. 1326).

[23] First Report, 1997–98 H.C. 190, *The Legislative Process*, approved by the House, November 13, 1997; Second Report, 1997–98 H.C. 389ii, *Explanatory Material for Bills*; Third Report, 1997–98 HC 543, *Carry-over of Public Bills*; Second Report, 1998–99 H.C. 194, *Sittings of the House in Westminster Hall*; First Special Report, 1998–99 H.C. 865, *Second Progress Report*; Second Report, 1999–2000 H.C. 589, *Programming of Legislation and Timing of Votes*; First Report, 2000–01 H.C. 382, *Programming of Legislation*.

[24] See above.

[25] See below, para. 5-008.

[26] *ibid.*

[27] *Legislative Drafting: A New Approach* (1977); (1981) 30 I.C.L.Q. 141; [1988] Stat.L.R. 15.

[28] Proceedings of the Ninth International Symposium on Comparative Law (1972), pp. 155–178; [1980] Stat.L.R. 14.

[29] *Statute Law* (1990), pp. 23–26; [1980] Stat.L.R. 61.

Kolts.[30] It is claimed that civilian texts are shorter, better arranged and more easily understood by laymen; common law drafting may by contrast be "a writhing torrent of convoluted indigestion."[31] Others have argued that "civilian" texts produce a considerable degree of uncertainty, which then has to be resolved by the judges; in effect legislative power is delegated to non-elected judges and officials. "Civilian" texts can be as lengthy and complex as British statutes, and can be badly drafted.[32] Of course, the ability of each side to point to examples where the other's preferred method has gone astray proves little; generalisations as to virtues and vices are easy to make but difficult to support. It is, however, unlikely in the present climate of opinion that many English judges would wish to deal with legislative provisions that were significantly more open-textured than at present, and equally unlikely that they would be regarded by many in the community as well suited to undertake that role.[33]

8. PARLIAMENTARY PROCEDURE[34]

(a) Public Bills

The legislative timetable of Parliament is managed by the government. **5–008** Detailed government Bills are examined and placed in the timetable by the Cabinet's Legislative Programme Committee, and may be considered by the full Cabinet or the appropriate policy committee. A Bill may generally be introduced in either the House of Commons or the House of Lords, although money Bills must be introduced in the Commons, and politically controversial Bills are normally introduced there.

A government Bill introduced in the Commons is presented by a minister. It receives a formal *first reading*, when only the title is actually read out, and is ordered to be printed. A day is fixed for the *second reading*. A Bill as

---

[30] Second Parliamentary Counsel, Canberra, Australia, [1980] Stat.L.R. 144.

[31] J. A. C. Smith, *op. cit.* n. 28, at pp. 158–9.

[32] See, *e.g.* the criticisms of a proposed directive of the European Commission on commercial agents expressed by the Law Commission in 1977 (Law Com. No. 84). The text was described as badly drafted, unclear, ambiguous and internally inconsistent. *Cf.* the criticisms of M. Cults "Clearer Timeshare Act 1993" by the draftsman of the Timeshare Act 1992: E. Sutherland, "Clearer Drafting and the Timeshare Act 1992" (1993) 14 Stat.L.R. 163.

[33] See above, paras 4-037–4-040.

[34] S. A. de Smith and R. Brazier, *Constitutional and Administrative Law* (8th ed., 1998), pp. 272–282; S. A. Walkland (ed.), *The House of Commons in the Twentieth Century* (1979), Chap. V; P. Norton, *The Commons in Perspective* (1981), Chap. 5; I. Burton and G. Drewry, *Legislation and Public Policy* (1981); D. Englefield, *Whitehall and Westminster* (1985), Chap. 7; P. Silk and R. Walters, *How Parliament Works* (4th ed., 1998), Chap. 6, the following Reports from the Select Committee on Procedure: Second Report, 1970–71 H.C. 538, *The Process of Legislation*; First Report, 1977–78 H.C. 588; Second Report, 1984–85 H.C. 49, *Public Bill Procedure*; Second Report, 1985–86 H.C. 324, *Allocation of Time to Government Bills in Standing Committee*; Second Report, 1986–87 H.C. 350, *The Use of Time on the Floor of the House*; Second Report, 1988–89 H.C. 330, *Private Members' Time*; Report of the Select Committee on *Sittings of the House* (the Jopling Committee), 1991–92 H.C. 20 and the reports of the Select Committee on Modernisation of the House of Commons (above, para. 5-007, n. 23); G. Drewry, (1972) 35 M.L.R. 289, (1979) 42 M.L.R. 80 and [1995] P.L. 203; T. St. J. Bates [1987] Stat. L.R. 44; D. R. Miers, [1989] Stat. L.R. 26. and (1998) 29 *The Law Librarian* 87.

printed is accompanied by "Explanatory Notes." These were introduced from the start of the 1998–99 session and replaced both the brief "Explanatory Memorandum" and, where finance was involved, "Financial Memorandum" previously issued with each Bill and the "Notes on Clauses" previously issued to MPs and peers. They are prepared by departmental officials in consultation with Parliamentary Counsel, and seek to summarise in "clear and simple English" that is "neutral in political tone rather than argumentative" the background and provisions of the Bill. They are revised when the Bill moves to the other House and after Royal Assent. They are not approved by Parliament and are not "authoritative."[35] They are published by HMSO and on the Internet[36] and are more helpful than the old Explanatory and Financial memoranda. Their legal status is regarded by the government as a matter for the courts.[37]

At the second reading stage the principles of the Bill are debated on the floor of the House.[38] If the Bill entails public expenditure or taxation this must be authorised by a *financial resolution* moved by a minister.[39] After receiving a second reading[40] the Bill proceeds to the *committee stage*,[41] either at a Standing Committee of between 15 and 60 M.P.s that reflects the party composition of the House, or in Committee of the Whole House. The latter step is taken for Bills that are either straightforward or urgent, or, at the other extreme, politically contentious or of major constitutional significance. Greater use is made of the possibility of splitting consideration of a Bill between a Committee of the Whole House and a Standing Committee.[42] The committee examines the Bill clause by clause, first considering amendments Mid then the motion that the clause, as amended, "stand part of the Bill". Amendments may be proposed by the minister in charge, backbenchers or the opposition; those to be taken are selected by the

---

[35] Sir Christopher Jenkins, (1999) 149 N.L.J. 798. Their introduction was announced by Lord McIntosh, HL Deb, January 21, 1998, col 1600.

[36] *www.parliament.uk* (Bills); *www.legislation.hmso.gov.uk* (Acts).

[37] Lord Sainsbury of Turville, H.L. Deb., November 4, 1999, cols *WA99* and *WA100*; Lord Falconer of Thoroton, H.L. Deb February 28, 2000, cols *WA43* and *WA44*.

[38] Non-controversial Bills may be referred to a Second Reading Committee of between 16 and 50 M.P.s and Scottish Bills to the Scottish Grand Committee (members for Scottish constituencies). Subsequent stages may also be taken by standing committees. Law Commission Bills are referred automatically to Second Reading Committees unless otherwise ordered by the House: HC Standing Order 59. Apart from Law Commission Bills, very little use has been made of Second Reading Committees; rare examples were the Birds (Registration Charges) Bill and the Police and Firemen's Pensions Bill in 1997 and the Royal Parks (Trading) Bill 1999–2000.

[39] In the case of some Bills, such as Finance Bills, Ways and Means resolutions are passed before the Bill is introduced. Private Members' Bills rarely include provisions involving public expenditure.

[40] Only three government Bills have failed at second reading since 1905, although it is more than a mere formality and ministers do not always approach debates with closed minds: Norton (1981), pp. 86–87. The bills were the Rent Restrictions Bill in 1924, the Reduction of Redundancy Rebates Bill in 1977 (during the period of the minority Labour government) and the Shops Bill in 1986 (following a rebellion by 72 government backbenchers: see P. Regan (1988) 41(2) *Parliamentary Affairs* 218).

[41] The committee stage for consolidation Bills may be dispensed with on a government motion, and the question on third reading put forthwith: H. C. Standing Order No. 58(4).

[42] *e.g.* Finance Bills, the Greater London Authority Bill 1998–99, the Sexual Offences (Amendment) Bill 1998–99.

chairman. Proposed new clauses are then taken, followed by the Schedules, proposed new Schedules the preamble (if any) and the long title.[43]

An innovation in the early 1980s was to send some Bills to a "Special Standing Committee" with the power to question witnesses and request the submission of evidence.[44] This procedure has been used on only a few occasions,[45] but virtually all the evidence received by the Select Committee on Procedure on its operation was enthusiastic[46] and it was enshrined permanently in Standing Orders from 1986.[47] Notwithstanding the encouragement of the Select Committee on Procedure,[48] they were not used again until the Immigration and Asylum Bill in 1998–99. "One likely reason" for their non-use was "that business managers regard the 28 day provision for Select Committee type meetings as a hindrance to the speedy process of legislation."[49]

Greater use of the procedure has again been encouraged by the modernisation committee.[50] Next, the House considers the Bill again at the *report stage*.[51] Any aspect of the Bill can be raised and new clauses and further amendments can be proposed. Debate is, however, confined to the contents of the Bill. Normally, the *third reading* immediately follows the conclusion of the report stage. Only minor verbal amendments can be made; if material amendments are necessary the, Bill has to be considered again in committee. Third reading debates are usually short.

The Bill then proceeds to the House of Lords where the stages are repeated, with some minor procedural differences. Any amendment proposed may be moved; there is no selection. The committee stage, if not dispensed with, is normally taken by a Committee of the Whole House, although a Public Bills Committee is sometimes used.[52] An important

---

[43] See below, para. 5-013.

[44] First Report from the Select Committee on Procedure, 1977–78 H.C. 588, pp. xviii–xix; H.C. Deb. Vol. 991, cols.716–834, October 30, 1980.

[45] Proceedings in the 1980–81 session on the Criminal Attempts Bill, the Education Bill and the Deep Sea Mining (Temporary Provisions) Bill; in the 1981–82 session on the Mental Health (Amendment) Bill; and in the 1983–84 session on the Matrimonial and Family Proceedings Bill. See H. J. Beynon, [1982] P.L. 193; A. Samuels, [1989] Stat.L.R. 208.

[46] *e.g.* memorandum from Sir Patrick Mayhew, the Attorney-General (Second Report from the Select Committee on Procedure, 1984–85 H.C. 49–II Appendix 2); and see generally the Report, 1984–85 H.C. 49–1, pp. viii–x.

[47] See H.C. Deb. Vol. 92, February 27 1986, cols.1083–1136. See Standing Order 91.

[48] 2nd report, 1989–90,H.C. 19, *The working of the Select Committee System*, para. 315. The Hansard Society Commission thought these should be the norm: below, para. 5-009.

[49] Modernisation Committee, First Report, 1997–98 H.C. 190, para. 44.

[50] See above.

[51] There is no report stage if a public Bill considered in Committee of the Whole House is unamended.

[52] An experiment with a Public Bill Committee on the Pilotage Bill in 1986–87 did not lead to a significant saving of time: *Report by the Group on the Working of the House*, 1987–88 H.L. 9, pp. 9–10. The use of such a committee on the Chanties Bill in 1991–92 was deemed more successful and the House of Lords Select Committee on Procedure of the House recommended continued experimentation with them (Report on *The Committee Work of the House*, 1991–92 H.C. 35–1, p. 40). The Group on Sittings of the House also recommended experimentation with informal committees convened by the minister in charge of a Bill, in which civil servants and other advisers might participate; and committees of the whole House off the floor: *Report to the Leader of the House*, 1993–94 H.L. 83, pp. 4–6; First Report of the Select Committee on *Procedure of the House*, 1994–95 H.L. 9; no such experimentation has taken place. Bills may be referred to a Grand Committee, which sits in parallel to the House, where amendments can be moved but no decision taken.

development has been the introduction by the House of Lords of special standing committees (subsequently renamed special public bill committees) to hear oral and written evidence on and then consider clause-by-clause, Bills, based on Law Commission reports, that are "largely devoid of party-political controversy".[53] The position as to implementation of Law Commission Bills has been markedly (although not sufficiently) trans-formed.[54] If amendments are made, the Bill is returned to the Commons for them to be agreed. The Commons respond with a message to the Lords which either signifies their agreement, gives reasons for disagreement or proposes other amendments.[55] Further messages may be exchanged until either final agreement is reached, the Bill lapses at the end of a session[56] or the Commons resorts to the Parliament Acts procedure.[57] Provision has now been made for the carry-over of public Bills by agreement.[58]

5–009   In recent years, significant features of the work of the House of Lords have included longer hours, a higher regular attendance, an increase in the proportions of the House's time devoted to legislative business and an increase in the self confidence of peers.[59] Claims that they have demonstrated a new independence and a new professionalism[60] have, however, been challenged.[61] The culture is likely to change with the staged removal from membership of the House of hereditary peers. Defeats of the government on important questions are still comparatively unusual.

A Bill passed in its entirety by both Houses is presented for the *royal assent*.[62] The monarch is expected by convention to give that assent; the last occasion on which it was refused was in 1707 when Queen Anne refused her assent to a Militia Bill. Assent may be signified (1) by the monarch in person (this was last done in 1854); (2) by Lords Commissioners in the presence of

---

[53] See Report from the Select Committee on *The Committee Work of the House* (1991–92 H.L.35-I), pp. 19–22, 40–41; Select Committee on the Procedure of the House, First Report 1992–93 H.L.11, para. 6; Third Report 1993–94 H.L.81 ("the procedure has already proved a valuable addition to the scrutiny function of the House." The procedure is not technically restricted to Law Commission Bills.

[54] See above, para. 1-028. The Law of Property (Miscellaneous Provisions) Bill was considered by a special standing committee (Report 1993–94 H.L.62); the Private International Law (Miscellaneous Provisions) Bill and the Family Homes and Domestic Violence Bill by special public bill committees (Reports, 1994–95 H.L. 36 and 55 respectively). Evidence was taken, inter alia, from the chairman of the Law Commission and other present and former Commissioners. See 29th Annual Report of the Law Commission 1994 (1994–95 H.C. 244), pp. 61–69. The Hansard Society Commission (above, para. 5-007) supported these moves: Report, pp. 118–119.

[55] The complexities of this process were considered by the Select Committee on Procedure, 2nd Report, 1990–91, H.C. 157.

[56] Public Bills that have not been passed normally lapse at the end of the session: private and hybrid Bills (see below) may be carried forward.

[57] See below.

[58] Modernisation Committee: First Report, 1997–98 H.C.190, paras 67–70, Third Report 1997–98 H.C. 543; H.C. Deb. Vol. 300, November 13, 1997, cols 1061–1129; House of Lords Select Committee on Procedure of the House, Report May 19, 1998. The Financial Services and Markets Bill was carried over at the committee stage at the end of the 1998–99 session.

[59] N. Baldwin in P. Norton (ed.), *Parliament in the 1980s* (1985), Chap. 5; A. Adonis, "The House of Lords in the 1980s" (1988) 41 *Parliamentary Affairs* 380; *Report by the Group on the Working of the House* (1987–88 H.L. 9).

[60] Baldwin, *op. cit.*

[61] Adonis, *op. cit.*

[62] See F. A. R. Bennion, [1981] Stat.L.R. 133.

both Houses[63]; or (3) as is normally the case today, by separate notification to each House in accordance with the Royal Assent Act 1967. The third method, unlike the others, does not involve the interruption of proceedings in the Commons. The second method is only used where royal assent coincides with prorogation.

The Parliament Acts 1911–1949 lay down special procedures whereby a Bill may be presented for royal assent when it has been passed only by the Commons.[64] A money Bill may be so presented where the Lords have failed to pass it without amendment after it has been before them for one month; a non-money Bill may be presented where it has been passed by the Commons in two consecutive sessions and the Lords have failed to pass it in each of those sessions; one year has elapsed between the Commons second reading in the first session and third reading in the second session; the Bill has been sent to the Lords at least one month before the end of each session and the Speaker certifies that the requirements of the Parliament Acts have been complied with. The certificate is conclusive for all purposes and may not be questioned in a court of law. These procedures may not be employed in respect of Bills to prolong the maximum duration of a Parliament beyond five years, to Provisional Order Confirmation Bills or private Bills. Objections by the House of Lords are normally dropped without the necessity of recourse to the Parliament Acts; the procedure has only been used three times.[65]

For the draftsman, the first publication of the Bill after first reading is an important deadline as changes thereafter have to be made by formal amendments. Indeed most of the amendments that are made are government amendments, and these tend to reflect second thoughts by the civil servants rather than the persuasive arguments of members. Amendments of substance proposed by backbenchers or opposition and actually agreed are few in number, and are more likely to be accepted in the Lords.[66] More amendments than usual were carried against the government during the passage of the Scotland and Wales Bills in 1977–78. These were controversial constitutional measures, and the Labour government was then

---

[63] Under the Royal Assent by Commission Act 1541; this was originally part of the Bill of Attainder against Catherine Howard, which did not receive the King's assent in person to spare his hearing once more the "wicked facts of the case." The Bill actually received the assent on February 11, 1542. The Reading Clerk reads out the title of the Bill; the Commissioners raise their hats; and the Clerk of the Parliaments pronounces "La Reyne le Veult." In the case of money Bills the expression is "La Reyne remercie ses bons sujets, accepte lew benevolence, et ainsi le veult"; for personal private Acts, "Soil fait comme il est désiré." If assent were refused the expression would be "La Reyne s'avisera."

[64] S. A. de Smith and R. Brazier, *Constitutional and Administrative Law* (8th ed., 1998, pp. 304–308).

[65] Welsh Church Act 1914 (disestablishment); Government of Ireland Act 1914 (Home Rule: the Act was not implemented); Parliament Act 1949; War Crimes Act 1991 (see G. Ganz, (1992) 55 M.L.R. 87). It has been argued that the Parliament Act 1949, which was passed under the 1911 Act process in order to reduce the period of delay, is itself *ultra vires* on the ground that a delegate cannot use its delegated power to enlarge the authority delegated to it; this argument has not been tested in court and is discussed by S. McMurtrie, (1997) 18 Stat. L.R. 46.

[66] See J. A. G. Griffith, *Parliamentary Scrutiny of Government Bills* (1974); P. Norton, (1976) 57 *The Parliamentarian* 17. Where the government accepts or is unsuccessful in resisting an amendment, the version proposed in debate is usually replaced at a later stage by one drafted by a parliamentary draftsman: T. Millett, [1988] Stat.L.R. 70.

in a minority in the Commons.[67] "Parliament's exposure of the successive
Bills' inherent defects and illogicalities was impressive."[68] However, "the
debates were poorly attended and the debating was done by a few stalwarts,
with most M.P.s (though a smaller proportion than usual) content to live up
to their image as lobby fodder."

The pressure on the Parliamentary timetable is such that where legislation
is particularly contentious governments may secure the placing of limits on
the time available for debate (timetable or "guillotine" motions); this may
mean that, as in the case of the Scotland and Wales Bills, important clauses
are not scrutinised by the Commons, although they will normally be
considered by the Lords.[69] The House of Commons Select Committee on
Procedure reported in 1978 that:

> "the balance of advantage between Parliament and Government in the
> day to day working of the Constitution is now weighted in favour of the
> Government to a degree which arouses widespread anxiety and is
> inimical to the proper working of our parliamentary democracy."[70]

The Select Committee on Procedure made proposals, that were not
implemented, for the earlier timetabling of controversial Bills in Standing
Committee by a Legislative Business Committee[71] or by a business
subcommittee of the relevant Standing Committee.[72] Timetabling proposals
have also made by other bodies[73] but the government and opposition front
benches have generally not been persuaded that they are workable.[74]
However, arrangements for what is now called the "programming" of
specified Bills by the House of Commons on the recommendation of a
Programming Sub-Committee of the relevant Standing Committee (for
proceedings in Standing Committee) were introduced in November 2000,
and revised in June 2001. They have proved controversial, with every
programme motion in 2000–01 being opposed and acceptance that the aim
that all clauses of Bills should properly be considered has not been
achieved.[75] The nadir was reached with the Criminal Justice and Police Bill
2000–01 where the government secured passage of a motion that it should be

---

[67] I. Burton and G. Drewry, "Public Legislation: A Survey of the Sessions 1977/8 and 1978/9"
   (1980) 33 *Parliamentary Affairs* 173, 174–186. These sessions provided "significant evidence
   for the power that still belongs to backbenchers in the House of Commons," although "only
   in a minority Parliament may the fate of Government Bills be in serious doubt. Even then,
   most legislation, being inevitable whatever the Government in power, is secure, protected by
   the close rapport between the two front benches" (p. 199).

[68] *ibid.* p. 186.

[69] See G. Ganz, "Recent developments in the use of guillotine motions" [1990] P.L. 496.

[70] First Report, 1977–78 H.C. 588, Vol. 1, p. viii.

[71] Second Report, 1984–85 H.C. 49, Part III: this proposal was defeated in the House of
   Commons (Vol. 92 H.C. Deb., February 27, 1986, cols.1083–1136; Minutes of Evidence of
   the Select Committee on Procedure (1985–86 H.C. 324-i)).

[72] Second Report from the Select Committee on Procedure, 1985–86 H.C. 324.

[73] The Hansard Society Commission (above, para. 5-007), Report pp. 121–123; Select
   Committee on Sittings of the House (1991–92 H.C. 22) (The Jopling Committee).

[74] See Vol.251 H.C.Deb., December 19, 1994, cols. 1459–1460 (Tony Newton M.P., Leader of
   the House): "the most sensible approach ... is to rely on voluntary agreements reached
   through the usual channels."

[75] See Modernisation Committee: First Report, 1997–98 H.C. 190, paras. 57–66, Second
   Report, 1999–2000 H.C. 589, First Report, 2000–01 H.C. 382.

deemed to have been reported to the House as if the clauses whose
consideration had not been completed by the Standing Committee had been
ordered to stand part of the Bill, subject to the government amendments
that had been tabled but not considered. The view has been expressed
forcefully and persuasively that the new arrangements have simply shifted
the balance in favour of the government and against the Opposition and
backbenchers.[76] The case in principle for agreed programming is strong;
however, agreement seems not to be forthcoming.

Another major change proposed by the Hansard Society Commission[77]
was the reference of most Bills to a select committee (a "first reading
committee") immediately after presentation for a preliminary examination
of the Bill's purpose, meaning and intended application. At this
"preliminary briefing stage", evidence could be taken from interested
parties and civil servants and improvements could be recommended. This
process would leave the House better informed and might reduce the need
for long second reading debates.[78] As regards the subsequent stages, after
second reading Bills should normally be committed to a special standing
committee (able to take direct evidence); Ministers should hold precommit-
tee informal factual briefings on technical or complex Bills (as was the case
with the Fisheries Bill 1992); if there are many detailed points to be further
debated at report stage, Bills should be re-committed to the special standing
committee; minimum intervals between stages should be increased to avoid
legislation being unduly rushed.[79] Finally, the Commission has suggested
the adoption of a two-year rather than one-year legislative programme.[80]

The apparent limitations on the effectiveness of Parliamentary scrutiny   **5–010**
have led to suggestions for the scrutiny of legislation by other bodies
particularly from the technical standpoint. Sir William Dale has proposed[81]
the establishment of a "Law Council" to advise the government on draft
Bills. "Its duty would be to examine them from the point of view of coherent
and orderly presentation, clarity, conciseness, soundness of legal principle,
and suitability for attaining the Government's objective," a function
performed in France by the Conseil d'Etat. It would not concern itself
with matters of policy, and its advice could be rejected by the government.
Its membership would include judges, lawyers (practising and academic) and
laymen. The Renton Committee, however, rejected proposals for formal
machinery for the scrutiny of the drafting of Bills, either before or after their
formal introduction in Parliament.[82] Before introduction, it was for
government departments to decide what advice they should obtain as to
the drafting of their Bills; after introduction, a new scrutiny stage would
"impose undue strain on a Parliamentary machine which is already under

---

[76] Memorandum by Angela Browning MP and Richard Shepherd MP to the Modernisation
Committee, 2000–01 H.C. 382, Appendix; see H.C. Deb, June 28, 2001, cols 812–890.
[77] Above, para. 5-007.
[78] This was endorsed as a possibility for some Bills by the Modernisation Committee (1997–98
H.C. 190, paras. 32, 33) but has not been approved by the House.
[79] Report, pp. 81–89.
[80] ibid., pp. 114–118.
[81] Legislative Drafting: A New Approach (1977), pp. 336–337. The case for the introduction of
pre-legislative scrutiny to promote compliance with the European Convention on Human
Rights is argued by D. Kinley, The European Convention on Human Rights: Compliance
without Incorporation (1993).
[82] Cmnd. 6053, pp. 129–133.

great pressure, and ... add to the labour of the draftsmen who have more
than enough to do as it is to keep pace with the legislative programme."

The Renton Committee did recommend new Parliamentary procedures
(1) for incorporating improvements (including the correction of obvious
inaccuracies) certified by the Speaker and the Lord Chancellor to be of a
drafting nature, after the passage of a Bill by both houses and before royal
assent[83]; and (2) for the re-enactment of statutes, in whole or in part, with
drafting improvements.[84] In addition they suggested that the Statute Law
Committee[85] should keep the structure and language of statutes under
continuous review, monitor the implementation of the Renton Committee's
recommendations and publish reports. None of these proposals has been
accepted, the third being rejected by the Cabinet apparently on the grounds
that the Committee was not an "appropriate body" to discharge these
functions and that the proposal to keep the statute book under continuous
review was not "likely to lead to any worthwhile improvements in the
drafting of legislation."[86]

(b) Private Bills[87]

5–011   Standing Orders of each House lay down a complicated series of procedural
requirements that must be observed before a private Bill is introduced,
including the giving of public notice. In practice, a promoter needs the
professional assistance of a Parliamentary Agent,[88] who drafts the Bill and
acts on behalf of the promoter thereafter. Petitions for private Bills must

---

[83] This was endorsed in principle by the House of Commons Select Committee on Procedure,
1977–78 H.C. 588, Vol. I, p. xxvii. A proposed procedure for the correction of errors *after*
royal assent did not find favour with the House of Lords (Acts of Parliament (Correction of
Mistakes) Bill [Lords], session 1976–77, withdrawn) and was not supported by the Select
Committee (*ibid.*). See A. Samuels, "Errors in Bills and Acts" [1982] Stat.L.R. 94. This is to
be distinguished from the correction of printing errors in HMSO copies of statutes: see
below, para. 5-019, n. 58.

[84] This would be modelled on the present procedure for consolidation Bills.

[85] A committee appointed by the Lord Chancellor and first established in 1868. Its membership
included M.P.s, draftsmen, judges, Permanent Secretaries, the Treasury Solicitor and the
Chairmen of the Law Commissions. It met once a year and supervised the Statutory
Publications Office, the form of Acts and the production of *Statutes in Force*. Most of its
functions in the field of consolidation and statute law revision passed to the Law
Commissions in 1965. In 1991 it was replaced by the Advisory Committee on Statute Law,
to advise the Lord Chancellor on all matters relating to the publication of the statute book.
Its membership now includes the Permanent Secretary to the LCD, the Clerk of the
Parliaments, the Clerk of the House of Commons, the Chairmen of the Law Commissions,
First Parliamentary Counsel (and his counterparts for Scotland and Northern Ireland) the
Treasury Solicitor, the Solicitor to the Scottish Office, and representatives of HMSO and the
LCD: Vol. 529 H.L.Deb., June 13, 1991, WA 65–66.

[86] *Renton and the Need for Reform*, pp. 7–8; H.L. Deb. col. 776, March 7, 1978. The Select
Committee supported the third proposal, and urged the government to reconsider its
attitude: 1977–78 H.C. 588, Vol. 1, pp. xxvii–xxviii.

[87] F. Clifford, *History of Private Bill Legislation* (1887); O. C. Williams, *Historical Development*
of Private Bill Procedure (1948); The Study of Parliament Group, "Private Bill Procedure; A
Case for Reform" [1981] P.L. 206; Joint Committee on Private Bill Procedure, 1987–88 H.L.
97, H.C. 625.

[88] See D. L. Rydz, *The Parliamentary Agents: A History* (1979) R. Owen and J. Bracken, (1998)
29 *The Law Librarian* 79.

normally be deposited by November 27 each session.[89] A local authority that wishes to promote a Bill must resolve to do so by a majority of the whole number of council members at a meeting of which 30 days' notice has been given in the local press; a second meeting must confirm the decision after the deposit of the Bill in Parliament.[90] The promoters must prove to the two "examiners", one appointed by each of the Houses, that the formalities have been observed, and this may be challenged by opponents of the Bill.

Private Bills normally proceed first in the House of Lords. The first reading is a formality; the second reading is normally so, but may be opposed. A Bill that passes the second reading is regarded as having received the conditional approval of the House. If the Bill passes the second reading opposed clauses are then referred to a Select Committee of five Lords. The House may agree to an Instruction to the Committee to the effect that the Committee should have regard to or be satisfied of certain matters before passing a particular provision. Procedure here is largely modelled on judicial proceedings: the case for and against the clause is put by counsel for the promoters and for the objectors; witnesses may be called and examined on oath; government departments may make representations and previous decisions of the Committee may be cited. Unopposed clauses are normally considered by the "Committee on Unopposed Bills", an informal meeting conducted by the Lord Chairman of Committees or his Counsel. The promoters, usually represented here by a Parliamentary Agent rather than counsel, must prove a need for the clauses. Unopposed clauses in local Bills promoted as a consequence of the Local Government Act 1972[91] were referred instead to more formal Select Committees. These applied the principles (1) that the promoters had to prove a current need in their area that could only be met by legislation; (2) that the legislation would deal effectively with the problem; and (3) that provisions to meet a need common to all or a great number of authorities should not be included in a private Bill where the government had given a firm undertaking to introduce general legislation to meet that need.[92]

After the committee stage, the report stage is usually a formality although the Bill may be amended. The Bill is given a third reading and sent to the other House where the various stages are repeated, with some differences in detail.[93]

These procedures have been described as "cumbersome and expensive"; proceedings of private Bill committees "can be casual and their decisions unpredictable" and opposed Bill committees "tend to be legalistic and time-

---

[89] Personal Bills can be deposited at any time, are customarily presented first to the House of Lords and are considered by the Personal Bills Committee of the Lords before first reading. The other stages are similar to those for other private Bills.

[90] Local Government Act 1972, s.239. A Bill may not be promoted to change a local government area, its status or electoral arrangements: *ibid.* s.70.

[91] See above, para. 5-003.

[92] See *e.g.* Special Report from the Select Committee on the County of South Glamorgan Bill, 1974–75 H.L. 347, Vol. 366 H.L. Deb., cols. 864–930, and Second Report of the Select Committee, 1975–76 H.L. 132.

[93] There are, for example, separate committees for opposed and unopposed *Bills* rather than *clauses.*

consuming".[94] Generally, private members take little interest in private legislation; when they do take an interest, however, their influence may be greater than in relation to public legislation as the whips are rarely applied and normally the government simply offers advice.[95]

9. Arrangement of Acts of Parliament[96]

The elements of a public general statute are normally arranged in the following order. A revised format for official versions of Bills and Acts was adopted as from the start of 2000–01 session.[97]

(a) Short title

5–012 This is the title by which the statute is generally known (*e.g.* the "Interpretation Act 1978"). The practice of including a section providing for the citation of an Act by a short title developed in the nineteenth century; the Short Titles Act 1896[98] conferred short titles on many statutes passed before this practice became established.

(b) Year and chapter number

5–013 A statute passed today is cited by reference either to its short title or to the calendar year in which it is passed and its "chapter number" within that year. Statutes are numbered in the order in which royal assent is given. Until 1963[99] statutes were regarded as chapters of the legislation passed in the relevant *session* rather than *calendar year*, and were numbered accordingly.[1] Thus the Interpretation Act 1889 can be cited as "52 & 53 Vict. c. 63" (chapter 63 of the session that fell in the fifty-second and fifty-third years of the reign of Queen Victoria) and its replacement, the Interpretation Act 1978 as "1978 c. 30" (Chapter 30 of 1978).

(c) Long title

This describes the scope of the Act; if a Bill is amended so as to go beyond the long title as printed in the Bill the long title must be amended as well.

---

[94] The Study of Parliament Group [1981] P.L. 206, 221. For reform proposals see *ibid.* pp. 218–227; Report of the Joint Committee on Private Bill Procedure, 1987–88 H.L. 97, H.C. 628, debated at H.C. Deb. Vol. 151, cols.474–648, April 20 1989; Government response, Cm. 1110, 1990.

[95] P. Norton, (1977) 30 *Parliamentary Affairs* 356.

[96] See F. A. R. Bennion, *Statute Law* (3rd ed., 1990), Chap. 3.

[97] See Second Report from the Select Committee on Procedure of the House, 1998–99 H.L. 52. The main changes were: a new format for clauses, with bold clause titles instead of side notes; Schedules in the same type size as clauses; more informative headers at the top of each page; some left alignment of internal headings; a new format for Repeal Schedules.

[98] Replacing the Short Titles Act 1892. See also the Statute Law Revision Act 1948, Sched 2.

[99] The practice was changed by the Acts of Parliament Numbering and Citation Act 1962.

[1] See G. Chowdharay-Best, "The Citation of Acts of Parliament" (2000) 21 Stat. L.R. 126 for a full analysis.

(d) Date

The date, given in square brackets, is that on which royal assent was signified.

(e) Preamble

Public Acts formerly[2] included a preamble, which could be lengthy, **5–014** explaining why the Act was passed. They are still necessary for private Acts, and begin with the word "Whereas." For example the Parliament Act 1911 includes the following:

"Whereas it is expedient that provision should be made for regulating the relations between the two Houses of Parliament:
And whereas it is intended to substitute for the House of Lords as it at present exists a Second Chamber constituted on a popular instead of hereditary basis, but such substitution cannot be immediately brought into operation:
And whereas provision will require hereafter to be made by Parliament in a measure effecting such substitution for limiting and defining the powers of the new Second Chamber, but it is expedient to make such provision as in this Act appears for restricting the existing powers of the House of Lords:"

(f) Enacting formula

This normally runs:

"Be it enacted by the Queen's most Excellent Majesty, by and with the advice and consent of the Lords Spiritual and Temporal, and Commons, in this present Parliament assembled, and by the authority of the same, as follows:—"

The formula is slightly different for money Bills and Bills passed under the Parliament Acts procedures.

(g) Sections and Schedules

The body of an Act is divided into *sections* (equivalent to the *clauses* of the **5–015** Bill) and *subsections*, a practice introduced by Lord Brougham's Act of 1850.[3] Each section is printed with *a marginal note* (from 2000–01, a *clause title*) indicating its content. Occasionally, errors may creep in. For example in the Married Women (Maintenance in Case of Desertion) Act 1886, a subsection (section 1(1)), which provided that a wife who had committed adultery could not claim alimony where her husband had deserted her, was

---

[2] Preambles are occasionally found in modern public Acts, particularly those which implement international conventions (*e.g.* the Oil in Navigable Waters Act 1963), public Acts of a local nature (*e.g.* the Towyn Trewan Common Act 1963) or legislation of a formal or ceremonial character (*e.g.* the John F. Kennedy Memorial Act 1964). Another example is the Canada Act 1982, which provided for the patriation of the Canadian Constitution.
[3] Interpretation of Acts Act 1850, 13 & 14 Vict. c. 21, s.2.

printed with the marginal note "custody of children". A long Act may be divided into *Chapters* or *Parts*. Sections dealing with related subject matter may be grouped under *headings*. Matters of details are commonly included in *Schedules* at the end of the Act. Each schedule is linked to one of the preceding sections and may be divided into *Parts, paragraphs* and *sub-paragraphs*. There may also be *marginal notes* (now *paragraph titles*) and *cross-headings*. A *Schedule* may be used to set out the provisions of an earlier Act as amended.[4]

The body of the Act may include the following kinds of provisions: "definitions, principal provisions, administrative provisions, miscellaneous clauses, penal clauses, clauses dealing with the making of rules or byelaws, saving clauses, temporary and transitory clauses, repeals and savings, date of coming into operation (if specified)" and the duration of the Act if it is limited.[5] "Common-form" clauses, those dealing with geographical extent, commencements, short title, citation and interpretation, are normally found at the end of the statute.

(h) Extent[6]

5–016   There is a presumption that an Act applies throughout the United Kingdom[7] and not beyond.[8] "Extent clauses" are used to negative that presumption,[9] Acts which apply only to Scotland or Northern Ireland usually include the country in brackets in the short title.[10] Statutes may expressly be made to apply to transactions abroad. For example, the English courts may exercise jurisdiction in respect of murders committed by British subjects abroad[11] and some Acts extend to the territorial waters adjacent to the United Kingdom.[12]

(i) Commencement[13]

Until 1793 each Act of Parliament was deemed to come into operation from the first day of the session in which it was passed, unless a commencement

---

[4]   Known as a "Keeling schedule". Examples include the Cinematograph Films Act 1948, Sched. 2 and the Criminal Evidence (Amendment) Act 1997, Sched. 2 (See A. Samuels, (1997) 18 Stat. L.R. 250). *cf.* Education Act 1980, Sched. 5.

[5]   Statute Law Society, *Statute Law Deficiencies* (1972), p. 6. (based on Sir Alison Russell's analysis of the general frame of a Bill.).

[6]   See F. A. R. Bennion, *Statutory Interpretation* (3rd ed., 1997), Part V.

[7]   *i.e.* England, Scotland, Wales and Northern Ireland but not the Channel Islands or the Isle of Man.

[8]   See *R. v. Jameson* [1896] 2 Q.B. 425, 430; *Draper & Son Ltd v. Edward Turner & Son Ltd* [1965] 1 Q.B. 424; *Air-India v. Wiggins* [1980] 1 W.L.R. 815.

[9]   Extent clauses normally indicate expressly that an Act applies to Northern Ireland even though this is not strictly necessary.

[10] The Renton Committee recommended that where an Act affects only England and Wales this too should be indicated in the short title: Cmnd. 6053, p. 124. This has not been implemented.

[11] Offences against the Person Act 1861, s.9

[12] *e.g.* Wireless Telegraphy Act 1949, ss.l, 6; Marine, etc., Broadcasting (Offences) Act 1967, s.1; *Post Office v. Estuary Radio Ltd* [1968] 2 Q.B. 740. See generally the Law Commission's *Report on the Territorial and Extraterritorial Extent of the Criminal Law* (Law Com. No. 91, 1978) and *Jurisdiction over Offences of Fraud and Dishonesty with a Foreign Element* (Law Com. No. 180, 1989).

[13] See Bennion (1997), pp. 201–210.

date was specified. The element of retrospectivity was seen to be unjust and the rule was changed.[14]; an Act now conies into effect at the beginning of the day on which royal assent is given, unless some other commencement date is specified.[15] Today, it is commonly provided that the Act shall come into effect on a specified date, or on a day to be appointed, and, in the latter event, that different days may be appointed for different provisions, different purposes or different areas. The advantages of delayed commencement are that it gives those affected time to prepare, and gives ministers and departments time to draw up the necessary regulations and orders after due consultation with interested parties. The main disadvantage is that it may be difficult for users to establish whether a particular provision is in force.[16] There may be many commencement orders in respect of one statute,[17] and some provisions may never be implemented, for reasons such as a lack of resources[18] and governmental second thoughts about the desirability of particular provisions.[19] Complaints have been voiced about the present position and various improvements proposed.[20] Governments have been exhorted to refrain from promoting legislation unless its implementation within a reasonable time can be foreseen.

In 1982 the Management and Personnel Office (the successor to the Civil Service Department) issued new guidance on the commencement of legislation.[21] Acts which do not provide for a commencement date to be appointed by order should provide for commencement not less than two months after royal assent (three months for consolidation Acts). Commencement provisions should be grouped at the end of any Bill in which that is practicable, if appropriate in a separate clause or Schedule; alternatively, a full list of commencement provisions should be published with the Act or in a press notice. Commencement dates should be specified in the Act where possible and appropriate; otherwise, every effort should be made to minimise the number of commencement orders and to rationalise their issue and the dates of commencement.

In interpreting statutes there is a presumption that statutes do not operate retrospectively so as to affect an existing right or obligation, except as regards matters of procedure.[22] Parliament may, however, use words in a

---

[14] Acts of Parliament (Commencement) Act 1793.

[15] Interpretation Act 1978, s.4.

[16] A most useful publication with this information is *Is it in force?*, an annual cumulative publication published in conjunction with the 4th edition of *Halsbury's Statutes of England*.

[17] See, *e.g.* the Consumer Credit Act 1974 and the Control of Pollution Act 1974.

[18] Examples include various provisions concerning legal advice and law centres (see below, para. 10-015).

[19] Examples include the Easter Act 1928, provisions of the Children and Young Persons Act 1969, the Health and Safety at Work etc. Act 1974, s.71 (see J. R. Spencer, (1981) 131 N.L.J. 644) and the Criminal Justice Act 1988 (ss.108–117: a statutory scheme for criminal injuries compensation; see below).

[20] A. Samuels, (1979) *The Magistrate* pp. 173–4; Statute Law Society Working Party on the Commencement of Acts of Parliament, [1980] Stat.L.R. 40.

[21] (1982) 79 L.S.Gaz. 968.

[22] *Re Athlumney* [1898] 2 Q.B. 547, 551–2 *per* R. S. Wright J.; *Att.-Gen. v. Vernazza* [1960] A.C. 965. See below, para. 6-045.

statute which clearly show an intention that it should so operate.[23]

It was commonly assumed that statutory provisions that were not brought into force had no legal status or effect. However, this assumption was challenged in *R. v. Secretary of State for the Home Department, ex p. Fire Brigades Union*.[24] Here, the Criminal Justice Act 1988[25] provided for a statutory criminal injuries compensation scheme to replace the scheme introduced by virtue of the royal prerogative. These provisions were, however, not brought into force. In 1993 the government announced that they would not be implemented and would be repealed in due course;[26] furthermore, the existing scheme would be replaced by a (less expensive) flat rate tariff scheme under the royal prerogative. On an application for judicial review, the House of Lords held (1) (unanimously) that the Home Secretary was under no legally enforceable duty to bring the 1988 Act provisions into force at any particular time;[27] but (2) (by three to two)[28] that while these provisions remained unrepealed it was under a duty to keep the question of implementation under review and it was an abuse or excess of power for him to exercise the prerogative power in a manner inconsistent with that duty. Of these two points, the first has the greater long-term significance, given that reliance on the royal prerogative for such programmes is highly exceptional.

(j) Definitions

5–017   Modern statutes commonly include "definition sections" in which the meaning of words and phrases found in the statute are explained, either comprehensively (X "means" ABC) or partially (X "includes" ABC). The qualification "unless the contrary intention appears" is usually added. The Interpretation Act 1978 gives definitions of a large number of words and expressions. These are applicable where the words are found "in any Act, unless the contrary intention appears."[29] For example, "Secretary of State" means "one of Her Majesty's Principal Secretaries of State".[30] The 1978 Act also provides generally that:

"In any Act, unless the contrary intention appears—

---

[23] *e.g.* the War Damage Act 1965, which reversed the decision of the House of Lords in *Burmah Oil Co. v. Lord Advocate* [1965] A.C. 75; the Northern Ireland Act 1972, which retrospectively removed limitations on the power of the Parliament of Northern Ireland to legislate for the armed forces: see S. H. Bailey, D. J. Harris and B. L. Jones, *Civil Liberties: Cases and Materials* (4th ed. 1995), pp. 291–292.

[24] [1995] 2 W.L.R. 464.

[25] ss.108–117 and Scheds.6 and 7.

[26] Lord Browne-Wilkinson was rightly critical of this statement, noting that "It is for Parliament, not the executive, to repeal legislation" (p. 474).

[27] This was "a decision of a political and administrative character quite unsuitable to be the subject of review by a court of law" (*per* Lord Keith at p. 466).

[28] Lords Browne-Wilkinson, Lloyd and Nicholls, Lords Keith and Mustill dissenting.

[29] Interpretation Act 1978, s.5 and Sched. 1. They may also apply to subordinate legislation: see *ibid.* s.23.

[30] Many statutory functions are entrusted to "the Secretary of State". This device enables these functions to be switched between departments without the need for the statute to be amended. Where amendment is necessary, as where a function is given to a particular minister, it is usually effected by a statutory instrument under the Ministers of the Crown (Transfer of Functions) Act 1946. The "Secretary of State" device makes it more difficult to discover where responsibility for a particular function commonly lies.

(a) words importing the masculine gender include the feminine;

(b) words importing the feminine gender include the masculine;

(c) words in the singular include the plural and words in the plural include the singular."[31]

There are also general provisions covering such matters as references to service by post, distance, time of day and the Sovereign, and the construction of subordinate legislation.[32]

(k) Amendments and repeals

Statutes commonly amend or repeal earlier enactments. Repeals are normally set out in a Schedule, although important changes may be included in the body of the Act. A power may be conferred by statute to repeal or modify Acts of Parliament by statutory instrument:

5–018

> "A provision by which it does so is known as a 'Henry VIII' clause, as it has been said 'in disrespectful commemoration of that monarch's tendency to absolution (sic)'. I doubt whether this is a just memorial to his late Majesty, who reigned 100 years before the Civil War and longer yet before the establishment of parliamentary legislative supremacy in our constitutional law. But the label is old and convenient."[33]

Such powers are controversial because they involve the transfer of power to change primary legislation to the executive, and they receive special scrutiny.[34] They are nevertheless an established feature of the statute book. A particularly important example is provided by section 2(2) and (4) of the European Communities Act 1972.[35] In *Hunt v. London Borough of Hackney and other cases*[36] the Divisional Court firmly rejected the argument that a Henry VIII power, such as section 2(2) and (4) of the 1972 Act, can only lawfully be exercised in relation to Acts already on the statute book at the time when the Henry VIII power is created. Accordingly, regulations made under section 2(2) could lawfully amend the Weights and Measures Act 1985 so as to introduce a compulsory system of metric weights and measures. The court held that the 1985 Act could not be taken impliedly to have repealed or restricted the scope of section 2(2) as there was no *inconsistency* between the two measures. Furthermore, the 1985 Act was itself a consolidation of

---

[31] Section 6. See, *e.g. Annicola Investments v. Minister of Housing and Local Government* [1968] 1 Q.B. 631, where the word "houses" was held to include a single house. Examples of cases where the "contrary intention" has appeared are those where the terms "every man" or "any person" have been held not to include women: *e.g. Chorlton v. Lings* (1868) L.R. 4 C.P. 374; *Bebb v. The Law Society* [1914] 1 Ch. 286.

[32] 1978 Act, ss.7–11.

[33] *per* Laws L. J. in *Hunt v. London Borough of Hackney* and other cases [2002] EWHC 195 (Admin.), at para. [13].

[34] Below, para. 5–025.

[35] Below, para. 5–050.

[36] Above.

pre-1972 legislation and section 2(2) could clearly have amended that.[37] There is also no rule of law that Henry VIII powers can only be used to effect minor or modest changes in primary legislation,[38] although any doubts about the scope of such a power should be resolved by a restrictive approach.[39]

An earlier statute may also be amended or repealed by implication where the provisions of a later Act are so inconsistent that the two cannot stand together, although the courts seek to reconcile apparently inconsistent provisions where possible.[40] The Divisional Court has, however, held that the doctrine of implied repeal cannot apply in respect of "constitutional" statutes.[41]

At common law a repealed Act was treated as if it had never existed, except in relation to transactions past and closed, but this rule was changed in 1889.[42] For example, where an offence is committed against an existing statutory provision, criminal proceedings may now be instituted even after that provision is repealed, unless the repealing enactment provides otherwise.[43] There was also a common law rule that where statute A was repealed by statute B and statute B was subsequently repealed by statute C, statute A was regarded as reviving unless the contrary intention appeared. This rule was abolished in 1850: repealed statutes stay repealed unless expressly revived.[44] Unlike the Scots, the English have never had a rule that

---

[37] "I cannot think that the law of our constitution is botched by such random consequences": *per* Laws L.J. at para. [52]. Laws L.J. also thought it "likely to be correct" that no implied repeal can be effected by a consolidation Act since it is presumed not to change the law: *ibid.*

[38] *ibid.*, at para. [73]. Similarly, there was no reason to construe section 2(2) as limited to effecting minor changes by reference to statements in Parliament; these statements fell outside the *Pepper v. Hart* parameters and, apart from *Pepper v. Hart*, an enforceable legitimate expectation could not be based on a statement in Parliament: para. [76].

[39] *R. (on the application of Orange Personal Communications Ltd.) v. Secretary of State for Trade and Industry* [2001] Eu.L.R. 165,177, *per* Sullivan J.

[40] *Vauxhall Estates Ltd. v. Liverpool Corporation* [1932] 1 K.B. 733; *Ellen Street Estates Ltd, v. Minister of Health* [1934] 1 K.B. 590. There is a presumption against implied repeal; *R. v. Governor of Holloway Prison, ex p. Jennings* [1982] 1W.L.R. 949; *Henry Boot Construction (UK) Ltd. v. Malmaison Hotel (Manchester) Ltd* [2001] Q.B. 388; *Nwogbe v. Nwogbe* [2000] 2 F.L.R. 744 (presumption applied even though a provision was left unenforceable); *cf. O'Byrne v. Secretary of State for the Environment, Transport and the Regions* [2001] EWCA Civ 499 (provisions in the Green Belt (London and the Home Counties Act 1938 preventing the sale of land in the London green belt without ministerial consent held to be impliedly repealed by the right-to-buy provisions of the Housing Act 1985). Furthermore, provisions in an Act cannot be impliedly repealed by general words in subsequent subordinate legislation: see *Hyde Park Residence Ltd. v. Secretary of State for the Environment and the Regions* (2000) 80 P.&C.R. 419.

[41] Above, para. 5-002.

[42] Interpretation Act 1889, s.38(2); see now the Interpretation Act 1978, s.16.

[43] See *Bennett v. Tatton* (1918) 88 L.J.K.B. 313; *Postlethwaite v. Katz* (1943) 59 T.L.R. 248; *R. v. West London Stipendiary Magistrate, ex p. Simeon* [1983] 1 A.C. 234 (repeal of the "sus" law held not to affect a prosecution for an offence committed before the repeal came into effect). *Cf. Aitken v. South Hams District Council* [1995] 1 A.C. 262 (notice to abate a noise nuisance under s.58 of the Control of Pollution Act 1974 continues to be effective notwithstanding repeal of s.58 by the Environment Protection Act 1990, by virtue of s.16 of the 1978 Act).

[44] See now the Interpretation Act 1978, s.15. Similarly, the repeal of an Act does not revive anything not in force or existing at the time of the repeal: *ibid.* s.16(l)(a). Hence, if statute B modifies statute A by partial repeal or substitution of words, statute A continues in effect subject to the modification notwithstanding the repeal of statute B.

a statute can be disregarded on the ground that it is obsolete[45]; such provisions have to be repealed by a subsequent statute.[46]

10. ENROLLMENT AND PUBLICATION[47]

In medieval tunes a systematic official record of parliamentary statutes was not kept. An incomplete statute roll was started in the Chancery for internal purposes in 1299 and continued to the middle of the fifteenth century. *Rotuli Parliamentorum* ("Rolls of Parliament") were kept between 1290 and 1503; they contained a general record of parliamentary proceedings, but only included some of the Acts. From 1483 "Inrollments of Acts" (records of each Act "engrossed" on parchment) were certified by the Clerk of the Parliaments and delivered to the Chancery; the officers of the Chancery commonly termed them the "Parliament Rolls" although they are distinct from the *Rotuli Parliamentorum*. From the middle of the nineteenth century two copies of each Act have been printed on vellum; one copy is kept in the House of Lords, the other in the Public Records Office.[48]

5–019

Lawyers at first relied on private manuscript collections of statutes. These formed the basis of unofficial printed collections that began to appear from 1481 onwards. From 1483 *Sessional Volumes of Statutes* were printed and published; these came to be issued by the King's or Queen's Printer but were not technically an official series published by royal or parliamentary authority. Useful collections of *Statutes at Large* appeared in the late eighteenth century, with various editors (*e.g.* Pickering (1762), Ruffhead and Runnington (1786) and Tomlins and Raithby (1811)). These covered statutes from Magna Carta to date; continuation volumes, sometimes covering several sessions, and based on the King's Printer's copies, were produced in the eighteenth and nineteenth centuries under the titles of *Statutes of the United Kingdom or Public General Statutes*. The Controller of Her Majesty's Stationery Office was appointed as the Queen's Printer in 1886. From 1940 the King's or Queen's Printer's copies of statutes have been published on an annual rather than a sessional basis, with *Public General Acts and Measures*[49] issued separately from *Local and Personal Acts*; each Act is also published individually by HMSO. From 1996, all statutes have been published on the Internet as well as on paper.[50]

---

[45] Under the doctrine of desuetude, Acts of the Scottish Parliament may become obsolete and repealed by a long period of contrary practice by the community: *M'Ara v. Magistrates of Edinburgh* 1931 S.C. 1059; *Brown v. Magistrates of Edinburgh* 1913 S.L.T. 456, 458; *Earl of Antrim's Petition* [1967] A.C. 691.

[46] See above, para. 5-002.

[47] F. A. R. Bennion, *Statutory Interpretation* (3rd ed., 1997), pp. 158–163.

[48] See. S. A. de Smith and R. Brazier, *Constitutional and Administrative Law* 8th ed., 1998), p. 90. For an analysis of the speech acts involved in the enactment process, see B.S. Jackson, "Who enacts statutes?" (1997) 18 Stat. L. R. 177, noting that the production of neither the printed nor vellum copy is necessary for the Act to come into force. A third print is made of Measures of the General Synod.

[49] These also appear in the *Law Reports Statutes* series.

[50] www.hmso.gov.uk/acts.htm. On the role of HMSO in the legislative process, see C. Tullo and A. Pawsey, (1998) 29 *The Law Librarian* 148. The trading functions of HMSO were privatised in 1996, passing to The Stationery Office (TSO).

The first official collection of statutes was the edition of *Statutes of the Realm* prepared by the Record Commissioners and published in nine volumes between 1810 and 1828. This gave texts and translations of statutes between 1235 and 1713, excluding the Commonwealth period,[51] and while a considerable improvement on what was otherwise available, was in various respects incomplete and inaccurate.[52] Later in the century, the Statute Law Committee[53] supervised the publication of the first edition of *Statutes Revised*, which comprised the public Acts in force at the end of 1878, as amended, given in chronological order. Two further editions were produced between 1888 and 1929 and in 1950. This series was superseded by *Statutes in Force*, which was published in loose booklet form rather than in bound volumes to facilitate the substitution of revised copies of statutes that are heavily amended; there are also supplements. The volumes are arranged in 124 groups (131 were originally planned) according to subject-matter.[54] These official collections are supplemented by the *Index to the Statutes and the Chronological Table of the Statutes*.[55] As a matter of citation, references to another Act in a statute passed after 1889 are, unless the contrary intention appears, to be read as referring to (a) any revised edition of the statutes printed by authority, (b) if it is not printed there, to the *Statutes of the Realm*; or (c) in other cases, to the Queen's Printer's copy.[56] Occasionally it may be necessary to go behind the published version and check its authenticity against the original source.[57] Where through a printing error a statute as printed by HMSO does not reflect the version of the vellum print, the Clerk of the Parliament authorises the issue of a correction slip. This is sometimes done where the vellum print does not reflect the version assented to by Parliament.[58]

There are various departmental compilations of statutes and regulations published by HMSO and regularly revised, such as *The Taxes Acts* (for the Inland Revenue) and several works on the law of social security (for the Department of Work and Pensions). The most important current commercial collections are *Halsbury's Statutes of England* (4th ed.: a revised edition arranged by subject matter) and *Current Law Statutes Annotated* (arranged in chronological order). There are also many collections on

---

[51] As to which see C. H. Firth and R. S. Rait, *Acts and Ordinances of the Interregnum* (1911).

[52] See T. F. T. Plucknett, *Statutes and their Interpretation in the Fourteenth Century* (1922), Chap. II.

[53] See above, para. 5-010.

[54] The published materials are, however, significantly out of date (P. Clinch, [1994] Stat. L. R. 64) and work on revised material (as distinct from newly enacted Acts) and other tables and indexes was suspended in order to concentrate on the development of a new statute law database: Lord Mackay of Clashfern L.C., Vol. 546 H.L. Deb., June 9, 1993, WA 55.

[55] This covers public and general legislation; editions since 1974 have also recorded the effect of local and personal legislation enacted since then. A *Chronological Table for Local Legislation 1797–1994* (Law Com. No; Scot Law Com. No. 155) was published by HMSO in 1996, the culmination of twenty years work by the Law Commission; an *Index to the Local and Personal Acts 1850–1995* was published simultaneously: see 31st Annual Report of the Law Commission 1996, pp. 48–50. A *Chronological Table of Private and Personal Acts 1539–1997* (Law Com. No. 256; Scot Law Com. No. 170) was published in 1998.

[56] Interpretation Act 1978, s.19.

[57] See, *e.g. R. v. Casement* [1917] 1 K.B. 98, 134, in relation to the Treason Act 1351, where the *Rotuli Parliamentorum* and the Statute Rolls were consulted.

[58] F. A. R. Bennion, *Statutory Interpretation* (3rd ed., 1997), pp. 158–160; J. J. Rankin, [1987] Stat.L.R. 53.

particular topics published in loose-leaf encyclopedias. An important advantage of these commercial publications is that the statutes are given in annotated form. Statutes and statutory instruments are also included in a range of databases including *Lexis, Westlaw* and *Lawtel,* and work is in hand for the development of an official statute law database.

11. VALIDITY

Subject to the position that arise in consequence of the European Communities Act 1972, the validity of an Act of Parliament may not be questioned in an English court; there is no Bill of Rights or other constitutional limitation to which legislation must conform as there is, for example, in the United States of America.[59] This point has arisen in cases where it has been claimed that a private Act is invalid on the ground that parliamentary standing orders have not been observed[60] or that Parliament has been misled by fraudulent misrepresentations[61]: such claims have failed. In 1982, a taxpayer argued that the change in the status of M.P.s from self-employed meant that they had become employees of the Crown and so disqualified from membership. As a result, the Social Security Act 1975, which imposed on him certain obligations to pay national insurance contributions, was invalid. His argument was emphatically and summarily rejected by Nourse J.: "the court can only look at the Parliamentary roll."[62] Of much more importance was the claim of a group of Canadian Indian Chiefs that the Canada Act 1982 was *ultra vires* on the ground that the consent of the "Dominion" of Canada had not been obtained as required by section 4 of the Statute of Westminster 1931, merely the consent of the Senate and House of Commons of Canada. Sir Robert Megarry V.-C. held[63] that he owed "full and dutiful obedience" to every Act of Parliament, and that the Canada Act 1982 was such an Act. The Court of Appeal held[64] that even on the assumption that Parliament could bind its successors by a provision such as section 4, the application failed as there had been compliance with that section. Attempts to impugn statutes on the ground that they are contrary to international law have also failed.[65]

There were in the seventeenth century dicta that Acts of Parliament "against common right and reason, or repugnant, or impossible to be performed,"[66] or contrary to natural justice by making a man judge in his

5–020

---

[59] See above, para. 5-002. The question of possible conflict with European legislation is considered below, paras 5-050–5-055. As to whether a court may exercise a jurisdiction to determine whether an *ostensibly* authentic Act of Parliament is *in fact* authentic see S. A. de Smith and R. Brazier, *Constitutional and Administrative Law* (8th ed., 1998), pp. 89–93.

[60] *Edinburgh and Dalkeith Rly. v. Wauchope* (1842) 7 Cl. & F. 710.

[61] *Lee v. Bude and Torrington Junction Railway* (1871) L.R. 6 C.P. 576; *Pickin v. British Railways Board* [1974] A.C. 765.

[62] *Martin v. O'Sullivan* [1982] S.T.C. 416, 419, affirmed [1984] S.T.C. 258.

[63] [1983] Ch. 77.

[64] *ibid.*

[65] *Mortensen v. Peters* 1906 S.L.T. 227; *Cheney v. Conn* [1968] 1 W.L.R. 242.

[66] *Dr Bonham's Case* (1610) 8 Co. Rep. 114, 118, *per* Coke C.J.; Coke subsequently expressed a different view extrajudicially: 4 *Coke's Institutes* 37, 41.

own cause[67] could be held by the judges to be void. However, these dicta were controversial even at that time, were not acted upon, and are not accepted today: "since the supremacy of Parliament was finally demonstrated by the Revolution of 1688 any such idea has become obsolete."[68] This position was reaffirmed by Lord Scarman in *Duport Steels Ltd v. Sirs*[69]:

" ... [I]n the field of statute law the judge must be obedient to the will of Parliament as expressed in its enactments. In this field Parliament makes and unmakes the law: the judge's duty is to interpret and to apply the law, not to change it to meet the judge's idea of what justice requires. Interpretation does, of course, imply in the interpreter a power of choice where differing constructions are possible. But our law requires the judge to choose the construction which in his best judgment meets the legislative purposes of the enactment. If the result be unjust but inevitable, the judge may say so and invite Parliament to reconsider its provision. But he must not deny the statute. ... Only if a just result can be achieved without violating the legislative purpose of the statute may the judge select the construction which best suits his idea of what justice requires."

This position is not challenged by the enactment of the Human Rights Act 1998.[70]

C. SUBORDINATE LEGISLATION[71]

1. DELEGATION

5–021   Each year the output of subordinate[72] legislation vastly exceeds that of Acts of Parliament. Law-making powers have been delegated by Parliament to a wide variety of public authorities, including the Crown, ministers, local authorities and public corporations. Procedural rules may be made for the

---

[67] *Day v. Savadge* (1614) Hob. 85, 87 *per* Hobart C.J.; *cf.* Holt C.J. in *City of London v. Wood* (1701) 12 Mod. 669, 686–8.

[68] *Pickin v. British Railways Board* [1974] A.C. 765, 782 *per* Lord Reid. Cf., however, the extrajudicial statements by a number of judges that particular statutory provisions might not be immune from judicial scrutiny: see above, para. 4-039.

[69] [1980] I.C.R. 161, 189–190.

[70] See below, Chap. 8.

[71] See C. K. Allen, *Law and Orders* (3rd ed., 1965); Sir William Wade and C. F. Forsyth, *Administrative Law* (8th ed., 2000), Chap. 23; S. A. de Smith and R. Brazier, *Constitutional and Administrative Law* (8th ed., 1998), Chap. 17; K. Puttick, *Challenging Delegated Legislation* (1988); Cabinet Office (Management and Personnel Office), *Statutory Instrument Practice* (2nd ed., 1987); R. Baldwin, *Rules and Government* (1995), Chap. 4; E. C. Page, *Governing by Numbers* (2001).

[72] Strictly, the term "subordinate" legislation covers "all legislation, permitted as well as authorised, that is inferior to statute law"; "delegated" legislation is that "authorised by Act of Parliament": HMSO, *Access to Subordinate Legislation* (House of Commons Library Document No. 5).

courts by Rule Committees consisting of judges and lawyers.[73] In addition, the Crown retains certain powers to legislate by virtue of the royal prerogative. There have been examples of the delegation of rule-making powers by Parliament for as long as Parliament has been acknowledged as the supreme law-making body. However, the nineteenth and twentieth centuries have seen an enormous increase, albeit "wayward and unsystematic",[74] in the extent of delegation, matching the extension of the powers and functions of government. Each of the World Wars saw the creation of a complex system of statutory powers, mostly contained in delegated legislation made, respectively, under the Defence of the Realm Acts 1914–15 and the Emergency Powers (Defence) Acts 1939–40; every aspect of national life was closely regulated.

The developments were at first welcomed on the ground that Parliament was thereby able to deal with the issues of importance while the details could be settled departmentally. Certain judges and academic commentators were less enthusiastic. The most extreme of the criticism was expressed by the then Lord Chief Justice, Lord Hewart, in a book entitled "The New Despotism" (1929). The maui objections articulated were that wide powers were given to the executive, and that the safeguards against abuse, particularly Parliamentary safeguards, were inadequate. Some people held the view that the delegation of legislative power was unwise and might be dispensed with altogether. However, it was difficult to disentangle general objections to the extension of state power from objections to the particular form that the extension took. Delegated legislation was one of the issues considered by the Committee on Ministers' Powers, which reported in 1932.[75] The Committee expressed the view that "whether good or bad" the practice of delegation was inevitable[76]:

> "the system of delegated legislation is both legitimate and constitutionally desirable for certain purposes, within certain limits, and under certain safeguards."[77]

It pointed to the pressure on parliamentary time, the technicality of the subject matter of modern legislation, the difficulty of working out administrative machinery in time to insert all the required provisions in the Bill, the flexibility of a system which allowed for adaptation to unknown future conditions without the necessity of an amending Act, and for the opportunity for experiment, and the need on occasion for emergency action. The Committee made a number of suggestions for improving the terminology, publication and scrutiny of delegated legislation. One of the members of the Committee, Ellen Wilkinson M.P., thought that certain passages gave:

> "the impression that the delegating of legislation is a necessary evil, inevitable in the present state of pressure on parliamentary time, but

---

[73] Civil Procedure Rules; Crown Court Rules.
[74] Allen (1965), p. 32.
[75] Cmd. 4060. The first chairman was the Earl of Donoughmore; he was succeeded as chairman by Sir Leslie Scott.
[76] ibid., p. 5.
[77] ibid., p. 51.

nevertheless a tendency to be watched with misgiving and carefully safeguarded."[78]

Nevertheless, since then the constitutional propriety of delegation has not seriously been questioned, although concern has been expressed at the growing tendency in recent years for statutory instruments to deal "no longer ... with means but with principles."[79]

2. THE FORMS OF SUBORDINATE LEGISLATION

5–022   The nomenclature of nineteenth century subordinate legislation was varied and confusing. Different procedures were followed for making and issuing the different kinds of rules. Some kind of regularity was created by the Rules Publication Act 1893, and the position was further improved by its replacement, the Statutory Instruments Act 1946. Today, most subordinate legislation takes the form of *statutory instruments* made under the procedure laid down by the 1946 Act or *byelaws* made under the Local Government Act 1972,[80] although other forms are possible. Different names are still used for different kinds of statutory instruments; these names merely indicate the general nature of the instrument and no longer reflect any difference as to the procedure whereby they are made and promulgated. The selection of a particular title is a matter of departmental practice.

     The following are the main kinds of subordinate legislation. *Orders in Council* are made by the Queen with the advice of the Privy Council (the "Queen in Council"). They may be made under the royal prerogative[81]; more commonly they are made under a statutory power, in which case they are normally statutory instruments. *Proclamations* are notices given by the Queen to her subjects; again, they may be made under the royal prerogative[82] or statute[83] and are published in the *London Gazette*. *Royal Warrants* are made under the royal prerogative and normally concern the pay and pensions of members of the armed forces. *Regulations, Rules, Orders, Schemes* and *Warrants* are usually statutory instruments. The usage of these terms is imprecise although "Rules" are usually[84] the procedural rules of a court or tribunal, and the term "Warrant" is used to describe some

---

[78]   *ibid.* p. 137. She felt that in the conditions of the modern state the practice "instead of being grudgingly conceded ought to be widely extended, and new ways devised to facilitate the process."

[79]   Andrew Bennett, M.P., Chairman of the Joint Committee on Statutory Instruments, in evidence to the Select Committee on Procedure: Second Report, 1986–87 H.C. 350, *The Use of Time on the Floor of the House*, pp. vii, 6. The Committee noted this view "with concern." Examples of recent legislation where the statute merely creates a framework for regulations include the Legal Aid Act 1988 and the Local Government Finance Act 1988 (on the latter, see the notes by M. Grant in *Current Law Statutes Annotated 1988*, pp. 41–12—41–13). See also K. Puttick, *Challenging Delegated Legislation* (1988), Chap. 3.

[80]   See below, para. 5-026.

[81]   *e.g.* an Order altering the constitution of a colony. An Order in Council under the prerogative may not alter the common law or statute law: *The Zamora* [1916] 2 A.C. 77, 90.

[82]   *e.g.* coinage proclamations.

[83]   *e.g.* proclamations of a state of emergency under the Emergency Powers Act 1920.

[84]   Not invariably: see the Immigration Rules.

Treasury instruments which confer an authority or an entitlement to money. *Directions* may occasionally have to be promulgated as statutory instruments.

3. Preparation of Subordinate Legislation

Subordinate legislation is generally drafted by lawyers in the government department concerned, in the Treasury Solicitor's office where the department has no legal branch, or, in cases of exceptional importance or difficulty, by one of the Parliamentary draftsmen.[85] The "division of labour" between the Parliamentary counsel responsible for statutory drafting and departmental lawyers has been described as "a basic weakness of the system",[86] although any significant change would obviously require a large increase in the number of counsel. The "preparational parameters" mentioned above[87] in relation to statutes are not applicable to nearly the same extent, although the draftsman has to take care to ensure that the instrument is *intra vires*[88]; the "operational parameters" are, however, equally important.[89] Prior consultation between the department and advisory bodies and interest groups is a well established practice[90]; consultation requirements may be imposed in the parent Act.[91] Local authority byelaws are prepared by the authority concerned but must normally conform to the models issued by government departments to stand much chance of being confirmed. Important statutory instruments may be examined by the Cabinet's Legislative Programme Committee.

5–023

4. Procedures for Making Subordinate Legislation

(a) Statutory instruments

The "statutory instrument" procedure applies to delegated legislation (1) made, confirmed or approved under a power conferred on the Crown after 1947 by statute[92] and expressed to be exercisable "by Order in Council"[93];

5–024

---

[85] E.C. Page, *Governing by Numbers* (2001), Chap. 6, discussing the relative contribution of lawyers and administrators, who are commonly relatively junior.

[86] F. A. R. Bennion, *Statute Law* (3rd ed., 1990), p. 57.

[87] At para. 5-007.

[88] See below, para. 5-028.

[89] Bennion (1990), pp. 57–58.

[90] See J. F. Garner, [1964] P.L. 105; A. D. Jergesen, [1978] P.L. 290; Page (2001), Chap. 7, noting that the process is dominated by the executive but that interest groups do have an impact, particularly where "their case can be made in a form that fits the conception of what government officials want to achieve" (p. 154).

[91] A statutory duty to consult is regarded as mandatory (see below para. 5-028). However, a court will not imply an obligation to consult if there is no express provision: *Bates v. Lord Hailsham* [1972] 1 W.L.R. 1373.

[92] Sub-delegated legislation made under a power conferred by statutory instrument is thus not normally within the scope of the 1946 Act.

[93] Statutory Instruments Act 1946, s.1(1).

(2) made, confirmed or approved under a power conferred on a minister after 1947 by statute[94] and expressed to be exercisable "by statutory instrument"[95]; (3) made under a power contained in a statute passed before 1948 to make "statutory rules"[96] within the meaning of the Rules Publication Act 1893,[97] or (4) confirmed or approved under certain powers contained in pre-1948 statutes.[98]

The procedural requirements for statutory instruments are prescribed partly by the parent Acts and partly by the 1946 Act. The parent Act may require that the instrument[99] be laid[1] before Parliament.[2] If it does it has to be laid "before it comes into operation," unless it is essential that it comes into operation sooner, in which case the Lord Chancellor and the Speaker must be informed of the reason.[3] This process merely brings the instrument to the attention of Parliament. An instrument may have to be laid in draft[4] or after it has been made. In addition, the instrument may be made subject to the "affirmative resolution" or the "negative resolution" procedure. Under the former, the instrument can only come into effect if a resolution approving it is passed, within the period (if any) specified in the parent Act, by each House (or the Commons alone if it deals with financial matters).[5] Under the latter, which is a much more common requirement,[6] but which is

---

[94]   See n. 92 above.

[95]   Statutory Instruments Act 1946, s.l(1).

[96]   Provided, in most cases, that the rule is of a "legislative" and not an "executive" character: Statutory Instruments Regulations 1947 (S.I. 1948 No. 1), reg. 2(1).

[97]   Statutory Instruments Act 1946, s.l(2). There are certain exceptions: see S.I. 1948 No. 1, reg. 2(3) and Schedule.

[98]   Statutory Instruments Act 1946, s.9(1); S.I. 1948 No. 1, reg. 2(2); Statutory Instruments (Confirmatory Powers) Order 1947 (S.I. 1948 No. 2). The rule has to be legislative rather than executive in character and subject to the requirement that it be laid before Parliament.

[99]   *i.e.* "any document by which" a power to make orders etc. is "exercised": Statutory Instruments Act 1946, s.l(1). A document referred to in regulations need not be laid provided that it is not part and parcel of the regulations: *R. v. Secretary of State for Social Services, ex p. Camden London Borough Council* [1987] 1 W.L.R. 819; and see A. I. L. Campbell, [1987] P.L. 328.

[1]   As to the meaning of "laying", see the Laying of Documents before Parliament (Interpretation) Act 1948. It normally involves delivery of copies to the Votes and Proceedings Office of the Commons and the Office of the Clerk of the Parliaments, Subordinate legislation other than statutory instruments may also have to be laid before Parliament, *e.g.* under the Immigration Act 1971; see *R. v. Immigration Appeals Tribunal, ex p. Joyles* [1972] 1 W.L.R. 1390.

[2]   Sometimes just the House of Commons: *e.g.* orders prescribing maximum rates under the Rates Act 1984: *R. v. Secretary of State for the Environment, ex p. Greenwich London Borough Council, The Times,* December 19, 1985; *R. v. Secretary of State for the Environment, ex p. Leicester City Council* (1985) 25 R.V.R. 31 (references in section 4(1) to "Parliament" to be read in context as to a reference to the House of Commons only).

[3]   Statutory Instruments Act 1946, s.4(1).

[4]   See *ibid.* s.6(1). The instrument may not be made within 40 days, and either House may resolve that it shall not be made.

[5]   An example of a draft not approved (here, by the House of Lords) was the draft Greater London Authority (Election Expenses) Order 2000; the right not to approve/to annul was last exercised in 1968.

[6]   In 1976–77 there were 127 instruments subject to affirmative procedure, 669 subject to negative procedure, 37 general instruments only required to be laid, and 197 general instruments not so required: First Report from the Select Committee on Procedure, 1977–78 H.C. 588 Vol. 1, p.. xxxi; an increasing proportion of instruments have been made subject to the first two procedures. In 1998–99, 178 affirmative instruments were laid before the Commons (150 considered in committee, 21 on the Floor and seven withdrawn) and 1,266 negative instruments so laid (28 considered in committee, one on the Floor).

less efficacious in ensuring Parliamentary scrutiny, either House may within 40 days of its being laid resolve that the instrument should be annulled.[7] Since 1973 it has been possible for proceedings on statutory instruments to be taken in Commons Standing Committees on Delegated Legislation[8] rather than on the floor of the House. Indeed, from 1994, all affirmative statutory instruments are automatically referred to a standing committee, unless de-referred on a government motion, and debates on the floor of the House are limited to one and a half hours. Nevertheless, Parliamentary scrutiny of the merits of instruments under these procedures is not particularly effective in either forum.[9]

An instrument may also be scrutinised by the Joint Committee on Statutory Instruments. This committee was first appointed in 1973, and replaced the separate committees of each House that had formerly undertaken this work.[10] The Chairman is an Opposition M.P. The Committee examines instruments laid before either House and subject to either form of resolution procedure, other instruments of a general character and special procedure orders. It may draw the attention of Parliament to a particular instrument on any of a number of specified grounds, or on any other grounds not impinging on the merits of or policy behind the instrument. The specified grounds are that:

(i) it imposes a charge on the public revenues;

(ii) it is made under an enactment excluding it from challenge in the courts;

(iii) it purports to have retrospective effect where the parent Act does not so provide;

(iv) it has been unjustifiably delayed in publication or being laid before Parliament;

(v) it has not been notified in proper time to the Lord Chancellor and the Speaker where it comes into effect before being presented to Parliament;

(vi) it may be *ultra vires*;

(vii) it appears to make an unusual or unexpected use of the powers conferred by the parent Act;

(viii) it requires elucidation as to its form or purport; or

(ix) it is defective in drafting.

---

[7] Statutory Instruments Act, 1946 s.5(l). This takes the form of an address to Her Majesty praying that the instrument be annulled, and is commonly termed a "prayer". A rare example of annulment by the House of Lords took place in respect of the Greater London Authority Elections Rules 2000 (S.I. 2000 No. 208).

[8] Prior to 1995–96, known as Standing Committees on Statutory Instruments.

[9] See First Report from the Select Committee on Procedure, 1977–78 H.C. 588, Vol. 1, pp. xxix-xxxix; J. Beatson, (1979) 12 Cornell Int. L.J. 199; P. Norton, *The Commons in Perspective* (1981) pp. 95–99; P. Byrne, (1976) 29 *Parliamentary Affairs* 366; A. Beith M.P. (1981) 34 *Parliamentary Affairs* 165.

[10] See the Report from the Joint Committee on Delegated Legislation, 1971–72 H.C. 45, H.L. 184.

Instruments subject to House of Commons proceedings only are examined
by the Commons members of the Joint Committee acting as a Commons
Select Committee on Statutory Instruments. No formal steps have to be
taken in either House following an adverse report by one of these
committees, although such reports may be referred to in other Parliamentary proceedings concerning the instruments, and the work of these
committees and their predecessors seem to have played a part in reducing
delays and improving drafting.[11] A survey published in 1988 concluded that
the technical process of scrutiny now appears to work as effectively as a
parliamentary committee can be expected to function.[12] Nevertheless, the
increasing use of delegated legislation for major policy implementation, the
lack of parliamentary time for debate, the increase in decisions taken before
the Committee's report is published and the emphasis on political rather
than legal points in debates on the merits have led to "the reality that
parliamentary scrutiny of delegated legislation is not effective democratic
control."[13] The Hansard Society Commission[14] considered the "whole
approach of Parliament to delegated legislation to be highly unsatisfactory.
The House of Commons in particular should give its procedure for the
scrutiny of statutory instruments a thorough review."[15]

The Commons Select Committee on Procedure has subsequently made
some recommendations for reform, that have yet to be implemented.[16]
These include proposals that (1) a sifting committee be established to
recommend which negative instruments merited debate and which
affirmative instruments did not; (2) "praying time" should be extending
from 40 to 60 days; (3) motions in the DL Committee should be substantive
and amendable; (4) proposals for certain very complex draft orders ("super-
affirmatives") should be laid for pre-legislative scrutiny by the relevant
departmental select committee; (5) no decision on a S.I. should be made
until it has been considered by the Joint Committee on Statutory
Instruments (matching the position in the House of Lords). These proposals
were endorsed by the Royal Commission on the Reform of the House of
Lords,[17] and are eminently sensible.

5–025   A development of some significance that was in the course of being
introduced when the Commission reported was the establishment by the

[11] See S. A. de Smith and R. Brazier, *Constitutional and Administrative Law* (8th ed., 1998), pp.
349–351.

[12] A view confirmed by E.C. Page, *Governing by Numbers* (2001), Chap. 8.

[13] J. D. Hayhurst and P. Wallington, "The Parliamentary Scrutiny of Delegated Legislation"
[1988] P.L. 547, 573–576. The conclusions are Professor Wallington's. For proposals for
minor procedural changes, see Hayhurst and Wallington, pp. 575–576; Second Report from
the Select Committee on Procedure, 1986–87 H.C. 350, *The Use of Time on the Floor of the
House*, pp. vi–xi. See also T. St. J. Bates, [1986] Stat.L.R. 114.

[14] Above, para. 5–007.

[15] Report, pp. 89–90. Particular changes proposed include review of S.I.s by departmentally
related select committees; the use of special standing committees on longer or more
complicated S.I.s; more meaningful motions for debate on an S.I. in standing committee,
including the possibility of suggesting (although not making) amendments (pp. 90–94).

[16] Fourth Report, 1995–96 H.C. 152, *Delegated Legislation*; First Report, 1999–2000 H.C. 48,
Delegated Legislation.

[17] *A House for the Future*, Cm. 4534, Chap. 7. It suggested that the sifting committee could be a
Joint Committee (except in respect of financial matters). It also proposed that the House be
given formal power to delay secondary legislation by up to three months, in place of current
power of absolute veto.

House of Lords of a Select Committee on the Scrutiny of Delegated Powers.[18] Its terms of reference are:

"to report whether the provisions of any bill[19] inappropriately delegate legislative power; or whether they subject the exercise of legislative power to an inappropriate degree of Parliamentary scrutiny."

It receives memoranda from the relevant government department and has generally been able to report to the House before the Committee stage. It has been particularly concerned with so-called "Henry VIII clauses", which enable primary legislation to be amended or repealed by subordinate legislation; the appropriate level of scrutiny (*i.e.*, affirmative or negative procedure or no parliamentary control) has been recommended according to the circumstances.[20] It has suggested that matters that should not be left to delegation include: provisions designed to ensure compatibility with the ECHR; substantial changes to electoral law; the power to increase the severity of a sentencing power; and the establishment of quasi-judicial institutions.[21] The Committee has made a useful contribution, its reports appearing on time and commanding respect and its intervention having led to changes in the legislation proposed on a number of occasions.

Special arrangements for scrutiny were introduced in respect of "deregulation orders" made under Part I of the Deregulation and Contracting Out Act 1994.[22] These orders, made by the Secretary of State, amended or repealed statutory provisions passed before the end of the 1993–94 session, in order to remove or reduce burdens on business. The procedure was thought by the government to be necessary because of the difficulty of finding time for primary legislation on such matters; however, the switch to secondary legislation aroused controversy because of the perceived inadequacy of the scrutiny arrangements. Accordingly, after a consultation stage, proposals for deregulation orders were examined by a special Deregulation Committee of the House of Commons and by the House of Lords Select Committee On Delegated Powers and Deregulation (as the Delegated Powers Scrutiny Committee became), which reported to their respective Houses. Apart from substantive scrutiny, these committees also performed the functions of the Joint Committee on Statutory Instruments in relation to proposed orders. The committees did not have the power to veto

[18] Its establishment was proposed by the (Jellicoe) Select Committee on the *Committee Work of the House* (1991–92 H.L. 35-I). It first conducted a general inquiry into the principles of its work (First Report, 1992–93 H.L. 57) and conducted a review of its work in 1994 (12th Report, 1993–94 H.L. 90). See C.M.G.Himsworth, [1995] P.L.34; P. Tudor (2000) 21 Stat. L. R. 149.

[19] It does not, however, consider Consolidation or Supply Bills.

[20] See 1993–94 H.L. 90, pp. 3–4.

[21] 37th Report, 1999–2000 H.L. 130, *Special Report for 1999–2000 — The Committee's Work*, para. 36.

[22] ss.1–6. See A. Page, *Current Law Statutes Annotated 1994*; M. Royle, (1994) 15 Stat.L.R.170. The procedures have been the subject of consideration by a number of reports of Select Committees of the House of Commons and House of Lords: see Page, *op.cit.*, p. 40–11. See also Fourth Report from the Select Committee on the Scrutiny of Delegated Powers, *Special Report on Deregulation Orders* (1994–95 H.C.48) and Vol.250 H. C. Deb., November 24, 1994. cols.764–789. The Delegated Powers and Deregulation Committee produces annual reports on its work (see *e.g.* 26th Report, 2000–02, *Special Report for Session 2000–01 — The Committee's Work*).

draft orders, but adverse reports were treated with the "utmost serious-ness".[23] Sixty days (excluding recesses) were allowed for "Parliamentary consideration" from the day that the proposed order was laid. Orders were subject to an affirmative resolution by each House. The procedure was relatively little used in the 1997–2001 Parliament. It was suggested that this procedure could form the basis for improved scrutiny of other legislation.[24]

A similar procedure has indeed been established in respect of remedial orders under the Human Rights Act 1998.[25] The Regulatory Reform Act 2001 replaced the 1994 Act powers by new arrangements that are broader in scope[26] and the Commons Committee became the Deregulation and Regulatory Reform Committee.[27] The Orders under the 1994 Act could only be used to remove or reduce burdens. The new regulatory reform orders must have that effect, but in addition can re-enact a provision that imposes a burden provided it is proportionate to the benefit expected to result from the re-enactment; make a new provision that imposes a burden that affects any person in the carrying on of the activity provided it is proportionate to the benefit expected to result from its creation; and remove inconsistencies and anomalies. An order may be made in respect of any provision of an Act passed at least two years earlier, a deregulation order under the 1994 Act or a regulatory reform order. A similar procedure applies as in the case of deregulation orders. The Minister must be of the opinion that the order does not remove any necessary protection or prevent any person from continuing to exercise any right or freedom which he or she might reasonably expect to continue to exercise. Where a burden is imposed, the Minister must be of the opinion that the order as a whole strikes a fair balance between the public interest and the interests of the persons affected by the burden; and that the extent to which the order removes or reduces burdens or has other beneficial effects for persons affected by the existing burdens makes it desirable for the order to be made. The government has undertaken to continue the practice applied to deregulation orders whereby any orders criticised by the scrutiny committees will be re-drafted or withdrawn.[28] Furthermore, it has stated that while the procedure may be used to implement important policy changes, it will not be used for measures that are both large and controversial.[29]

Once a statutory instrument is made it must be sent to the Queen's Printer and copies must as soon as possible be printed and sold by or under the

---

[23] Government response (1993–94 H.C. 404) to the *Fourth Report of the Select Committee on Procedure* (1993–94 H.C. 238), p.viii. "In normal circumstances the Government would expect to submit a revised proposal or to withdraw the proposal altogether": *ibid.*

[24] See M. Ryle, "The Deregulation and Contracting Out Bill 1994—A Blueprint for the Reform of the Legislative Process?" (1994) 15 Stat.L.R.170.

[25] See below, Chap. 8.

[26] See C. Andrews, *Current Law Statutes Annotated 2001.*

[27] See Deregulation Committee, First Special Report, 2000–01 H.C. 328, *The Handling of Regulatory Reform Orders.*

[28] C. Andrews, *op. cit.*, p. 6–3.

[29] Government Response on Regulatory Reform Order-Making: Deregulation Committee's 4th Report 2000–01 (Appendix to Deregulation and Regulatory Reform Committee, First Special Report, 2001–02 H.C. 389).

authority of the Queen's Printer.[30] The requirements as to printing and sale do not apply to instruments classified as "local"[31]; to general instruments otherwise regularly printed and published; to temporary instruments; to schedules whose printing and sale "is unnecessary or undesirable having regard to the nature or bulk of the document" and to any other steps taken to publicize them; and to confidential instruments not yet in operation.[32] The requirements may, however, be imposed by the Statutory Instruments Reference Committee appointed by the Lord Chancellor and the Speaker.[33] The Queen's Printer allocates statutory instruments received to the series for the calendar year in which they are made, and numbers them consecutively as near as may be in the order in which they are received.[34] They are cited by their number and year.[35] Since 1997, the full text of statutory instruments has been published on the Internet as well as on paper,[36] an arrangement that has instantly transformed their accessibility.

HMSO also publishes (1) periodical lists of the titles of instruments issued; (2) an Annual Edition with full texts of instruments issued, an appendix of prerogative legislation and relevant lists, tables and indices; (3) the annual *Table of Government Orders*, a chronological list showing which instruments are still in force, amended or revoked; and (4) the *Index to Government Orders*, issued every two years, which lists existing powers to make delegated legislation and current exercises of those powers according to subject matter. Butterworths publish *Halsbury's Statutory Instruments*, which lists and summarises delegated legislation in force according to subject matter, gives the annotated text of the "more important orders, rules and regulations, selected on the basis of the likely requirements of subscriber",[37] and includes a regular updating service. Regulations are available on such databases as *Westlaw* and *Lexis* and also normally included in encyclopedias on particular topics.

Rules and Orders made before 1949 are included in the series *Statutory Rules and Orders and Statutory Instruments Revised to Dec. 31st 1948*, which is arranged according to subject matter.[38]

The position as to the commencement of subordinate legislation is unclear. The subordinate legislation in question may expressly provide for

---

[30] Statutory Instruments Act 1946, s.2(1), as amended with retrospective effect by the Statutory Instruments (Production and Sale) Act 1996 (the addition of the words "or under the authority of" regularised the position that the Queen's Printer had contracted out the printing of SIs since at least 1965).

[31] See generally on local statutory instruments, R. J. B. Morris, [1990] Stat.L.R. 28.

[32] Statutory Instruments Regulations 1947 (S.I. 1948 No. 1), regs.3–8. These matters have to be "certified" by the responsible authority (*i.e.* minister) in each case. This must be done in proper form: *Simmonds v. Newell* [1953] 1 W.L.R. 826.

[33] S.I. 1948 No. 1, reg. 11. The Committee has power to determine certain other questions which may arise as to numbering, publication, classification, etc. It consists of the Lord Chairman of Committees (Lords), the Chairman of Ways and Means (Commons) and six senior officers of both Houses: *Erskine May's Parliamentary Practice* (22nd ed., 1997), p. 577.

[34] S.I. 1948 No. 1, reg. 3.

[35] Statutory Instruments Act 1946, s.2(2).

[36] See *www.hmso.gov.uk/stat.htm*.

[37] *Halsbury's Statutory Instruments: A User's Guide*, p. 5.

[38] Earlier editions were published in 1896 and 1904. Up to and including 1960 the Annual Editions were also arranged by subject-matter rather than chronologically.

its own commencement.[39] If it does not, there is some authority that an order can only come into effect when it is *made known*.[40] In a later case,[41] however, Streatfeild J. directed a jury as follows:

> "I do not think that it can be said that to make a valid statutory instrument it is required that all of these stages should be gone through; namely, the making, the laying before Parliament, the printing and the certification of that part of it which it might be unnecessary to have printed. In my judgment the making of an instrument is complete when it is first of all made by the Minister concerned and after it has been laid before Parliament."[42]

The defendant was prosecuted for breach of a schedule to a statutory instrument that had not been printed as required by the Act. Streatfeild J. held that it was not invalid for lack of publication.

Section 3(1) of the Statutory Instruments Act 1946 provides that regulations should be made for the publication by HMSO of lists snowing the dates of issue of instruments printed and sold by the Queen's Printer; in any legal proceedings, "an entry therein shall be conclusive evidence of the date on which any statutory instrument was first issued" by HMSO.

Section 3(2) provides that in criminal proceedings for a contravention of "any such statutory instrument" it is:

> "a defence to prove that the instrument had not been issued by Her Majesty's Stationery Office at the date of the alleged contravention unless it is proved that at that date reasonable steps had been taken for the purpose of bringing the purport of the instrument to the notice of the public, or of persons likely to be affected by it, or of the person charged."[43]

It is not, however, clear whether this defence is available (1) in respect of any instrument which has not been issued, including those exempted from publication requirements; or (2) in respect of an instrument which has not been issued in breach of a publication requirement; or (3) in respect only of the period between the making of an instrument and its issue in

---

[39] From 1947 all statutory instruments required to be laid before Parliament after being made must show the dates on which they come into operation; this does not, however, cover the whole field as not all instruments must be laid. Where a day is specified, the instrument comes into effect at the beginning of that day: Interpretation Act 1978, ss.4(a), 23.

[40] Bailhache J. in *Johnson v. Sargant* [1918] 1 K.B. 101. *Cf. Jones v. Robson* [1901] 1 Q.B. 673 where a requirement to give *notice* of certain orders was held to be directory (but in this case the order had been published, and the defendant knew of it).

[41] *R. v. Sheer Metalcraft Ltd* [1954] 1 Q.B. 586.

[42] *ibid.* p. 590. (There may of course be no "laying" requirement.)

[43] It has been suggested that a similar defence should be created in respect of Acts of Parliament: Statute Law Society Working Party on Commencement of Acts of Parliament, [1980] Stat L.R. 40, 51–52. The defence failed on the facts in *R. v. Sheer Metalcraft Ltd, loc. cit.* n. 41 above.

circumstances where such issue does subsequently take place.[44] Moreover, the statutory defence does not apply to subordinate legislation other than statutory instruments. There is much to be said for the principle of *Johnson v. Sargant*:[45] "To bind a citizen by a law, the terms of which he has no means of knowing,[46] is the very essence of tyranny."[47]

(b) Local authority byelaws[48]

District and London borough councils have a general power to make byelaws for the "good rule and government" of the area "and for the prevention and suppression of nuisances" therein;[49] in addition there are numerous specific byelaw making powers.[50] The procedure for making byelaws, to be followed in all cases unless specific provision is otherwise made, is laid down by section 236 of the Local Government Act 1972 Byelaws cannot take effect until they are confirmed by the appropriate minister. Public notice must be given at least one month before application is made for confirmation, and a copy must be available for inspection. The confirming authority may fix the date on which a byelaw is to come into effect; if no date is so fixed, it comes into effect one month after it is confirmed. When confirmed, a copy must be printed and deposited at the authority's offices; it must be open to public inspection without payment at all reasonable hours, and copies supplied on payment of such sum, not exceeding 20p per copy, as the authority may determine.[51]

5–026

5. ARRANGEMENT OF STATUTORY INSTRUMENTS

A statutory instrument is normally arranged in the following order:[52]

5–027

(i) Year and number of the instrument,

(ii) An indication of the subject matter; this corresponds to the categories in the lists published periodically by HMSO.

(iii) Title.

---

[44] The difficulty is created by the word "such": see D. Lanham, (1974) 37 M.L.R. 510, 521–523. The *Sheer Metalcraft* case (1) is not inconsistent with the first interpretation, but the point as to whether the defence can apply in respect of *exempted* instruments did not arise as the minister had not certified that the instrument should be exempt; (2) is inconsistent with the second interpretation; and (3) is inconsistent with the third, as there was no suggestion that the schedule was ever published.

[45] [1918] 1 K.B. 101. Lanham (*ibid.*) argues that even where a date of commencement is specified, an instrument can only come into effect when published.; *contra*: A.I.L. Campbell, [1982] P.L. 569; response by Lanham, [1983] P.L. 395.

[46] Ignorance of a published instrument would probably not be regarded as a defence: ignorance of the law is not excuse.

[47] *per* Barwick C.J. in *Watson v. Lee* (1980) 54 A.L.J.R. 1, 3.

[48] Sometimes spelt "by-laws."

[49] Local Government Act 1972, s.235(1).

[50] See *Encyclopedia of Local Government Law*, Appendix 6.

[51] Local authorities do not always seem to be aware of these obligations.

[52] See Bennion (1990), pp. 55–57.

(iv) The dates when the instrument was made, laid before Parliament and is due to come into operation.

(v) A recital naming the person making the instrument and the relevant enabling powers.

(vi) The main provisions of the instrument. These are termed *articles* (in an Order), *regulations* or *rules* as the case may be. Subdivisions are called *paragraphs*. The instrument may be divided into *Parts* and may include a *Schedule*. Common form provisions as to title, definitions and commencement are placed at the beginning.

(vii) An indication of the minister by whom the instrument was signed.

(viii) An "Explanatory Note" stated to be "not part of" the instrument.

6. VALIDITY OF SUBORDINATE LEGISLATION[53]

5–028 All delegated legislation must conform to the limits laid down expressly or impliedly in the enabling Act; if those limits are exceeded the validity of the instrument[54] may be challenged in the courts.[55] Challenges may be made directly, for example by a claim in the High Court for a declaration that the legislation is *ultra vires*; or indirectly, for example by raising the argument that an instrument is *ultra vires* as a defence to enforcement proceedings, such as a prosecution for contravening the instrument.[56] An instrument may be *ultra vires* if there has been a failure to comply with a "mandatory" procedural requirement. Some requirements are merely "directory"; the authorities are "directed" to complywith them, but compliance is not a pre-condition to the validity of the instrument. It is not easy to predict whether a court will hold a particular requirement to be mandatory or directory. In this context the duty to consult affected parties has been held to be mandatory,[57] but requirements as to publication[58] and laying[59] have been

---

[53] See generally Sir William Wade and C. F. Forsyth, *Administrative Law* (8th ed., 2000), pp. 854–870; K. Puttick, *Challenging Delegated Legislation* (1988) T. St J. N Bates, (1998) 19 Stat. L.R. 155. Successful challenges to the *vires* of statutory instruments between 1914 and 1986 are summarised by J. D. Hayhurst and P. Wallington, [1988] P.L. 547, 566–573.

[54] Or other form of delegated legislation.

[55] The courts may also ensure that prerogative legislation falls within the scope of an existing prerogative power.

[56] Resort to this latter mode of proceeding is well established and in *R. v. Reading Crown Court, ex p. Hutchinson* [1988] Q.B. 384, D.C. (pet. dis. [1988] 1 W.L.R. 308, H.L.) the Divisional Court affirmed that its availability had not been affected by the principle of *O'Reilly v. Mackman* [1983] 2 A.C. 237 that matters of *vires* should normally be raised directly on an application for judicial review. The availability of collateral challenge was confirmed by the House of Lords in *Boddington v. British Transport Police* [1999] 2 A.C. 143, overruling *Bugg v. Director of Public Prosecutions* [1993] Q.B. 473, where the Divisional Court held that collateral challenge could only be based on a claim that the instrument was substantively as distinct from procedurally invalid.

[57] *Agricultural etc. Training Board v. Aylesbury Mushrooms Ltd* [1972] 1 W.L.R. 190.

[58] *R. v. Sheer Metalcraft Ltd* [1954] 1 Q.B. 586; see above, para. 5-025.

[59] See *Bailey v. Williamson* (1873) L.R. 8 Q.B. 118; *Starey v. Graham* [1899] 1 Q.B. 406, 412; *Springer v. Doorly* (1950) L.R.B.G. 10 (W. Indian Court of Appeal); A.I.L. Campbell, [1983] P.L. 43; but see de Smith, Woolf and Jowell, *Judicial Review of Administrative Action* (5th ed., 1995), p. 275, for the argument that laying requirements should be regarded as

held to be directory. The scope of a consultation requirement was described as follows by Webster J. in *R. v. Secretary of State for Social Services, ex p. Association of Metropolitan Authorities.*[60]

" ... in any context the essence of consultation is the communication of a genuine invitation to give advice and a genuine receipt of that advice. In my view it must go without saying that to achieve consultation sufficient information must be supplied by the consulting to the consulted party to enable it to tender helpful advice. Sufficient time must be given by the consulting to the consulted party to enable it to do that, and sufficient time must be available for such advice to be considered by the consulting party. Sufficient, in that context, does not mean ample, but at least enough to enable the relevant purpose to be fulfilled. By helpful advice, in this context, I mean sufficiently informed and considered information or advice about aspects of the form or substance of the proposals, or their implications for the consulted party, being aspects material to the implementation of the proposal as to which the Secretary of State might not be fully informed or advised and as to which the party consulted might have relevant information or advice to offer."

An instrument may also be quashed if there is unfairness in the consultation process.[61]

An instrument may be *ultra vires* if its subject matter lies beyond the scope of the enabling power. For example, in *Hotel and Catering Industry Training Board v. Automobile Proprietary Ltd*[62] the House of Lords held that a power to make an order establishing a Training Board for persons employed "in any activities of industry or commerce" did not enable an order to be made in respect of members' clubs. Clear words are needed to authorise the

---

mandatory; *cf. Bain v. Thorne* (1916) 12 Tas.L.R. 57 (Sup.Ct. of Tasmania). In 1981 Ronald Biggs escaped extradition from Barbados to the U.K. because the Barbados High Court held that regulations designating the U.K. as a country to which a fugitive could be extradited should have been laid before the Barbados Parliament: *The Times*, April 24, 1981: *Biggs v. Commissioner of Police* [1982 May] W.I.L.J. 121. Note, however, that the decision turned on a provision of the Interpretation Act of Barbados to the effect that the term "shall" [*i.e.* in "shall ... be laid] was "to be construed as imperative" (*ibid.*). In *R. v. Secretary of State for Social Services, ex p. Camden London Borough Council* (unreported, February 26, 1986) Macpherson J. held that a requirement that supplementary benefit regulations "shall not be made" unless a draft had been laid before Parliament and approved by each House imposed a mandatory requirement. On appeal, the Court of Appeal assumed this to be so without deciding the point ([1987] 1 W.L.R. 819).

[60] [1986] 1 W.L.R. 1, 4–5.

[61] *R. v. Secretary of State for Health, ex p. U.S. Tobacco International Inc.* [1992] 1 Q.B.353 (ban on oral snuff quashed where the sole importers were not given the details of the scientific advice on which the ban was based).

[62] [1969] 1 W.L.R. 697. See also *R. v. Customs and Excise Commissioners, ex p. Hedges and Butler Ltd* [1986] 2 All E.R. 164 (power to demand production of the whole of the records of a business (including records concerning non-dutiable goods) held not to be "incidental" or "supplementary" to powers concerning the regulation of excise warehouses and dealings in dutiable goods); *R. v. Secretary of State for Social Services, ex p. Cotton, The Times,* December 14, 1985; *R. v. Inland Revenue Commissioners, ex p. Woolwich Equitable Building Society* [1987] S.T.C. 654 *R. v. Secretary of State for Trade and Industry, ex p. Thomson Holidays, The Times,* January 12, 2000 (order required to be founded on facts found in Monopolies Commission report and not wider in its scope)

making of subordinate legislation that interferes with fundamental rights[63] or rights conferred by other primary legislation,[64] or that amends primary legislation.[65] Subordinate legislation must be read and given effect, so far as possible, in a way that is compatible with Convention rights,[66] and public authorities will act unlawfully if they make subordinate legislation that is incompatible with such rights.[67] Subordinate legislation may also be *ultra vires* if it conflicts with directly effective Community law.[68]

The established grounds upon which byelaws may be struck down are usually said to be those of *ultra vires*, uncertainty, unreasonableness and repugnancy to the general law,[69] although the last three grounds may also be regarded as facets of the ultra vires doctrine. For example, in *Staden v. Tarjanyi*[70] a district council made a byelaw in respect of a pleasure ground which provided:

> "A person shall not in the pleasure ground ... take off, fly or land any glider, manned or unmanned, weighing in total more than four kilogrammes. ... "

The respondent flew a hang glider over the pleasure ground and was prosecuted under the byelaw. It was conceded that "in" meant "in or over". The Divisional Court held that the byelaw was invalid for uncertainty:

> " ... anyone engaged upon the otherwise lawful pursuit of hang gliding must know with reasonable certainty when he is breaking the law and

---

[63] In accordance with the principle of legality recognised by Lord Steyn in *R. v. Secretary of State for the Home Departments, ex p. Pierson* [1997] 3 All E.R. 577, 603–607 (see below, para. 6-039); see *e.g. R. v. Lord Chancellor, ex p. Witham* [1998] Q.B. 575 (Lord Chancellor's general power to fix court fees cannot be used to set such high levels that would effectively bar the poor from access to the courts), distinguished in *R. v. Lord Chancellor, ex p. Lightfoot* [2000] 2 W.L.R. 318 (deposit of £250 to be paid by debtor wishing to petition for bankruptcy did not interfere with the right of access to the court) and *R. v. Legal Aid Board, ex p. Duncan & Mackintosh, The Independent*, February 23, 2000 (right to choose one's legal representative not inherent in right of access to the court).

[64] *R. v. Secretary of State for Social Security, ex p. Joint Council for the Welfare of Immigrants* [1997] 1 W.L.R. 275 (regulations excluding from social security benefits asylum seekers who did not claim asylum on arrival held ultra vires as this was a serious impediment to the exercise of their rights under the Asylum and Immigration Appeals Act 1993; primary legislation with retrospective effect was passed to secure this: Asylum and Immigration Act 1996, s. 11).

[65] *McKiernon v. Chief Adjudication Officer, The Times*, November 1, 1989; *Britnell v. Secretary of State for Social Security* [1991] 1 W.L.R. 198; *R. v. Secretary of State for Trade and Industry, ex p. Orange Personal Communications Ltd.* (unreported, October 25, 2000); cf. *R. v. Secretary of State for the Environment, Transport and the Regions ex p. Spath Holme Ltd* [2001] 1 All E.R. 195, 202–203, *per* Lord Bingham.

[66] Human Rights Act 1998, s. 3(1), below, para. 8-006.

[67] *ibid.*, s. 6(1), below, para. 8-009.

[68] *e.g.* regulations as well as primary legislation were disapplied in *R. v. Secretary of State for Transport, ex p. Factortame (No. 2)* [1990] 1 A.C. 603; cf. *Bourgoin. SA v. Ministry of Agriculture, Fisheries and Food* [1986] Q.B. 716 (revocation of licence ultra vires); Case C–173/99, *R. (on the application of BECTU v. Secretary of State for Trade and Industry* [2001] All E.R. (EC) 647 (Working Time Regulations failed to implement directive correctly); *Secretary of State for Social Security v. Walter* [2001] EWCA Civ. 1913 (regulations held not to be directly discriminatory on the ground of sex).

[69] See *Cross on Local Government Law* (9th ed., 1996) paras. 6–06–6–10.

[70] (1980) 78 L.G.R. 614.

when he is not breaking the law. . . . [T]o be valid the byelaw must set some lower level below which the glider must not fly."[71]

The leading authority on the meaning of "unreasonableness" in the **5–029** context of byelaws is *Kruse v. Johnson*[72] where Lord Russell of Killowen C. J. stated[73] that local authority byelaws ought to be supported if possible and "benevolently" interpreted, but might be struck down if unreasonable:

"But unreasonable in what sense? If, for instance, they were found to be partial and unequal in their operation as between different classes; if they were manifestly unjust; if they disclosed bad faith; if they involved such oppressive or gratuitous interference with the rights of those subject to them as could find no justification in the minds of reasonable men, the Court might well say, 'Parliament never intended to give authority to make such rules; they are unreasonable and ultra vires'. . . . A by-law is not unreasonable merely because particular judges may think that it goes further than is prudent or necessary or convenient, or because it is not accompanied by a qualification or an exception which some judges may think ought to be there."

Successful challenges, on this ground are rare. It has been unclear whether a statutory instrument, as distinct from a byelaw, can be challenged for unreasonableness. In *Maynard v. Osmond*[74] regulations which did not allow police officers to be legally represented in disciplinary proceedings were challenged on this ground[75]; the members of the Court of Appeal did not express any doubt as to the court's jurisdiction to entertain such a challenge, but dismissed the application on the merits.

In. *R. v. Secretary of State for the Environment, ex p. Nottinghamshire County Council*,[76] the council challenged the 1985–86 guidance on expenditure limits given by the Secretary of State to local authorities, under section 59 of the Local Government, Planning and Land Act 1980, *inter alia* on the ground of unreasonableness. The guidance was required to be laid before, and approved by resolution of, the House of Commons. Lord Scarman in the House of Lords said[77]

" . . . I cannot accept that it is constitutionally appropriate, save in very exceptional circumstances, for the courts to intervene on the ground of 'unreasonableness' to quash guidance framed by the Secretary of State and by necessary implication approved by the House of Commons. . . . "

---

[71] *ibid.* p. 623. As to the test for uncertainty, see *Percy v. Hall* [1997] Q.B. 924 discussed in *Cross*, para. 6–08.

[72] [1898] 2 Q.B. 91.

[73] At pp. 99–100.

[74] [1977] Q.B. 240.

[75] The Police (Discipline) Regulations 1965 (S.I. 1965 No. 543); the regulations applicable to Deputy Chief Constables, Assistant Chief Constables and Chief Constables did permit legal representation (S.I. 1965 No. 544). The court did not accept that this constituted "unfair discrimination".

[76] [1986] A.C. 240. *Cf. City of Edinburgh District Council v. Secretary of State for Scotland* 1985 S.L.T. 551

[77] [1986] A.C. 240, 287.

The challenge failed on the merits. It is to be noted that the possibility of a challenge for unreasonableness was not completely ruled out. Indeed, the suggestion that Parliamentary approval would properly restrict the permissible scope of such a challenge has been doubted.[78] It is clearly the case that Parliamentary approval, other than in an Act of Parliament, does not render delegated legislation immune from challenges based on other aspects of the *ultra vires* doctrine.[79] In *R. v. Secretary of State for the Environment, ex p. Hammersmith and Fulham London Borough Council*[80] the House of Lords unanimously approved Lord Seaman's view, although the list of grounds of challenge said to be permissible is so lengthy[81] that it is difficult to see what kind of challenge is ruled out.[82]

The Court of Appeal has held subsequently that the true position is that delegated legislation, whether or not approved by either or both Houses of Parliament, is indeed subject to challenge on the ground of irrationality, but that in some contexts, such as that of local government finance,

"there is a heavy evidential onus on a claimant for judicial review to establish the irrationality of a decision which may owe much to political, social and economic considerations in the underlying enabling legislation."[83]

Even where there are grounds for holding delegated legislation *ultra vires*, a remedy may still be refused in the exercise of the court's discretion.[84] The

[78] Sir William Wade and C. F. Forsyth, *Administrative Law* (8th ed., 2000), pp. 26, 376–377, 854; C. M. G. Himsworth, 1985 S.L.T. 369; A.I.L. Campbell, 1986 S.L.T. 101; C. T. Reid, [1986] C.L.J. 169. A provision in the Immigration Rules was held to be unreasonable in *R. v. Immigration Appeal Tribunal ex p. Manshoora Begum* [1986] Imm. A. R. 385. The Rules "have repeatedly been held to be rules of administrative practice merely, not rules of law and not delegated legislation" but "undoubtedly have statutory force to some extent" instructions from the Home Secretary to immigration officers and statements of policy and practice (Wade and Forsyth (2000), p. 850). They are subject to Parliamentary disapproval but are not published as statutory instruments.

[79] *R. v. H. M. Treasury ex p. Smedley* [1985] Q.B. 657, 666–669 (*per* Sir John Donaldson M.R. in relation to an Order in Council); *R. v. Secretary of State for the Environment, ex p. Greater London Council* (Unreported, April 3, 1985): discussed in the articles cited in n. 78 above, and in M. Grant, *Ratecapping and the Law* (2nd ed., 1986), pp. 12–13; *R. v. Secretary of State for the Environment, ex p. Nottinghamshire County Council* [1986] A. C. 240, 247–251 (*per* Lord Scarman).

[80] [1991] 1 A. C. 521, 594–597.

[81] That the exercise of discretion frustrates the policy of the statute, that legally relevant considerations have been ignored or irrelevant considerations taken into account, that there is bad faith, improper motive, or manifest absurdity: see Lord Bridge at pp. 596–579. *Cf.* below, para. 18-050.

[82] A challenge to the merits of an exercise of discretion cannot in any event be based on the *ultra vires* doctrine.

[83] *per* Auld L.J. in *O'Connor v. Chief Adjudicating Officer and Secretary of State for Social Security* [1999] E.L.R. 209, 221, approved by the Court of Appeal in *R. (Asif Javed) v. Secretary of State for the Home Department* [2001] 3 W.L.R. 323 (Secretary of State's inclusion of Pakistan in an Order applying an expedited appeals procedure, as a country in which it appeared to him "that there is in general no serious risk of persecution" was irrational and therefore invalid); cf. *R. (on the appolication of Tucker) v. Secretary of State for Social Security* [2001] EWHC Admin 260 (housing benefit regulation held not to be irrational). See to similar effect Mustill L.J. in *R. v. Secretary of State for the Environment, ex p. the GLC and ILEA* (unreported, April 3, 1985).

[84] e.g. *R. v. Secretary of State for Social Services, ex p. Association of Metropolitan Authorities* [1986] 1 W.L.R. 1.

court may be able to hold that an invalid part of an order can be "severed," leaving the remaining part intact.[85] Finally, the court may in an appropriate case hold that an order is invalid only in so far as it affects a particular applicant.[86]

7. QUASI-LEGISLATION[87]

In recent years, greater attention has been paid to "administrative quasi-legislation"[88]: administrative rules that do not have direct legal force. There has been: **5–030**

> "an exponential growth of statutory and extra-statutory rules in a plethora of forms. Codes of practice, guidance, guidance notes, guidelines, circulars, White Papers, development control policy notes, development briefs, practice statements, tax concessions, Health Service Notices, Family Practitioner Notices, codes of conduct, codes of ethics and conventions are just some of the guises in which the rules appear.[89]"

(a) Statutory rules

There are many variables in the structure and operation of such rules: the overall picture is arguably more confused than the arrangements for delegated legislation were before the Statutory Instruments Act 1946. These variables include the following: **5–031**

— By whom they are made: a minister; a non-governmental statutory agency; a non-statutory body.

— To whom they are directed: officials; local authorities; courts and tribunals; private organisations and citizens.

— Whether they are subject to Parliamentary scrutiny: there may be a requirement for a code to be laid before Parliament (in draft or in a final version), subject to affirmative or negative procedures.

---

[85] *Dunkley v. Evans* [1981] 3 All E.R. 285 *D.P.P. v. Hutchinson* [1990] 2 A.C. 783; *cf. R. v. Secretary of State for Transport, ex p. Greater London Council* [1985] 3 All E.R. 300.

[86] *e.g. Agricultural etc. Training Board v. Aylesbury Mushrooms Ltd* [1972] 1 W.L.R. 190 (where an order was only held to be invalid in respect of a particular organisation that had not been consulted).

[87] G. Ganz, *Quasi-Legislation: Recent Developments in Secondary Legislation* (1987); R. E. Megarry, (1944) 60 L.Q.R. 125; Lord Campbell, "Codes of Practice as an Alternative to Legislation" [1985] Stat.L.R. 127; A. Samuels, "Codes of Practice and Legislation" [1986] Stat.L.R. 29; T. St. J. Bates, [1986] Stat.L.R. 114, 120–123; Vol. 469 H. L. Deb., cols.1075–1104, January 15, 1986 (debate on codes of practice); R. Baldwin and J. Houghton, "Circular arguments: The Status and Legitimacy of Administrative Rules" [1986] P.L. 239; R. B. Ferguson, "The Legal Status of Non-Statutory Codes of Practice" [1988] J.B.L. 12; R. Baldwin, *Rules and Government* (1995), Chap. 4.

[88] A term coined by Megarry, *op. cit.*

[89] Ganz (1987), pp. 1–2.

— How they are published: by HMSO, by a government department or otherwise.

— Their legal effect: there are several forms. In the case of some codes, no effect is stated, although it does not follow that they are entirely devoid of legal effect. There may be a requirement that provisions of the code be taken into account, if relevant, by a local authority, tribunal or court. It may be provided that breach of a code may be relied upon as tending to establish civil or criminal liability, and compliance as tending to negative such liability: indeed in one case as establishing liability unless the contrary is proved.

— The content: McCrudden[90] distinguishes four types of codes, although any one code may contain elements of them all:

> "Codes may include provisions (i) to codify existing non-legal practice; (ii) to codify the already existing law of the courts and/ or the previous legal interpretations on a particular issue of the body making the code; (iii) to set out recommended good industrial practice; and (iv) to interpret independently those statutory provisions for which the body making the code has some responsibility."

An alternative typology is suggested by Baldwin and Houghton,[91] who distinguish: (i) procedural rules; (ii) interpretative guides; (iii) instructions to officials; (iv) prescriptive/evidential rules; (v) commendatory rules; (vi) voluntary codes; (vii) rules of practice, management or operation; and (viii) consultative devices and administrative pronouncements.

Examples include the Immigration Rules,[92] the PACE Codes of Practice,[93] the Code of Guidance concerning Homelessness,[94] the Highway Code,[95] the Sex Discrimination Code of Practice,[96] the Code of Practice on Picketing,[97] and the Approved Documents giving guidance with respect to

---

[90] (1988) 51 M.L.R., 409, 531.

[91] [1986] P.L. 239, 240–245.

[92] Immigration Act 1971, ss.3(2), 19 (s.19 to be repealed by the Immigration and Asylum Act 1999, Sched. 6); 1999 Act, Sched. 4, para. 21: made by the Secretary of State, issued as a House of Commons paper, subject to annulment by Parliament and binding on adjudicators and the Immigration Appeal Tribunal, no consultation requirements.

[93] See below, para. 14-003.

[94] Housing Act 1996, s.182: made by the Secretary of State, published as a Circular, authorities to have regard to guidance, no laying or consultation requirements.

[95] Road Traffic Act 1988, s.38: made by the Secretary of State, who must consult such representative organisations as he thinks fit, issued via HMSO, subject to annulment by Parliament, may be relied on in legal proceedings as tending to establish or negative liability.

[96] Sex Discrimination Act 1975, s.56A: made by the Equal Opportunities Commission (with the approval of the Secretary of State), which must publish a draft and consider any representations made about it consult appropriate organisations, issued via HMSO, draft subject to annulment by Parliament, to be taken into account by Employment Tribunal if appears relevant.

[97] Trade Union and Labour Relations (Consolidation) Act 1992, ss.203–208: made by the Secretary of State, who must consult ACAS, draft to be approved by Parliament, to be taken into account by Employment Tribunal if appears relevant.

the requirements of building regulation.[98]

The position as to Parliamentary scrutiny is different in a number of respects from that for statutory instruments. On the one hand, particular codes have been examined by the appropriate departmental select committee, which does not normally happen with other forms of legislation. On the other, the Joint Committee on Statutory Instruments only has jurisdiction to examine documents, other than statutory instruments, that require Parliamentary approval; there is no provision for the merits to be debated in Standing Committee; and the likelihood of a merits debate in the Chamber is low.[99]

The perceived advantages of codes of practice and the like include the use of informal, non-technical, language; flexibility; and the promotion of uniformity of practice, particularly in the public sector.[1] Their "fundamental rationale" is the adoption of a voluntary approach rather than compulsion.[2]

While there is much to be said for this where codes are based on widespread consultation and consensus, there are nevertheless difficulties.[3] Sometimes they are introduced as an unhappy compromise between statutory regulation and inaction. In some areas the voluntary approach has broken down and compulsion has replaced persuasion. There has been criticism of the use of codes with controversial provisions that go beyond existing legislation,[4] particularly given the limited effectiveness of Parliamentary scrutiny. The haphazard variety of forms and procedures is indefensible. Proposals have been made for the strengthening of Parliamentary scrutiny, a "code of practice regulating codes of practice" and the establishment of a body "to advise on the creation of quasi-legal or voluntary rules instead of legal rules and evolve criteria for their use."[5] In December 1987, the government issued Guidance on Codes of Practice and Legislation, primarily for the use of parliamentary draftsmen, and those framing legislative proposals.[6]

---

[98] Building Act 1984, ss.6, 7: made by Secretary of State or designated body, issued via HMSO, no laying or consultation requirement, breach tends to establish and compliance to negative liability in legal proceedings.

[99] Baldwin and Houghton, [1986] P.L. 239, at pp. 26–32.

[1] In the public sector, codes of practice and other forms of guidance may be used to provide a framework for the exercise of discretionary powers, so as to promote uniformity in decision-making. However, power to give guidance will not normally authorise the issue of binding directions (*Laker Airways Ltd v. Department of Trade* [1977] Q. B. 643) and the recipient of such guidance must not fetter its discretion by regarding it as binding (*R. v. Police Complaints Board, ex p. Madden* [1983] 1 W. L. R 447). Conversely, such guidance is likely to be a legally relevant consideration and must at least be taken into account.

[2] Ganz (1987), pp. 96–98.

[3] *ibid.*, pp. 98–108.

[4] Highlighted by the decision of Scott J. in *Thomas v. National Union of Mineworkers* [1986] Ch. 20 to limit by injunction the number of pickets outside particular premises to six, in line with a provision of the Code of Practice on Picketing then made under section 3 of the Employment Act 1980.

[5] Ganz (1987), Chap. 6; A. Samuels, [1986] Stat. L. R. 29.

[6] [1989] Stat. L. R. 214.

(b) Voluntary guidance[7]

5–032   There are many examples of codes of practice, guidance and the like without
any statutory backing. In the public sector, for example, guidance may be
given by central government departments to local authorities in circulars
and other forms of communication, and instructions are commonly given to
officials within departments.[8] The effect varies widely: the legal effect may be
indirect, but the practical implications of great significance.[9] In the private
sector such codes have in some circumstances been adduced as evidence, for
example of proper professional or technical standards, and may be
incorporated into a contract.[10] They may also be recognised as appropriate
by government, even without express legislative endorsement.[11] Difficulties
as to their accessibility and uncertainties as to legal effect are even more
pronounced here.

D. COMMUNITY LEGISLATION

1. INTRODUCTION

5–033   The accession of the United Kingdom to membership of the European
Communities (the European Economic Community, the European Coal and
Steel Community and the European Atomic Energy Community) meant
that the vast and ever-increasing body of Community law became applicable
in this country.[12] The system of Community law is founded on the
provisions of the various Treaties whereby the Member States agreed to
establish the Communities, new members joined ("Accession Treaties") and
aspects of the original Treaties have been changed and augmented, most

---

[7] Ganz (1987), pp. 59–65, 75–95; Ferguson, [1988] J.B.L. 12.

[8] *e.g.* the government's policy to reduce the number of school places in the light of falling
school rolls; the use of circulars in town and country planning to state planning policy; extra-
statutory tax concessions; standing orders and circular instructions governing the management of prisons.

[9] It has been held that even non-statutory guidance, if erroneous in law, can be challenged on
an application for judicial review: *Royal College of Nursing* v. *Department of Health and
Social Security* [1981] A.C. 800; *Gillick* v. *West Norfolk Area Health Authority* [1986] A.C.
112.

[10] R. B. Ferguson, [1988] J.B.L. 12.

[11] *e.g.* the codes of practice for residential care homes (Centre for Policy on Ageing, *Home Life*
(1984 and *Better Home Life* (1996)) and nursing homes (National Association of Health
Authorities, *Registration and Inspection Nursing Homes: A Handbook for Health Authorities*
(1985)). The Secretaries of State for Social Services and for Wales asked local authorities to
regard *Home Life* "in the same light" as guidance issued under section 7 of the Local
Authority Social Services Act 1970 (which suggests that it is not technically guidance under
the Act). The codes are in practice taken into account by local authorities, inspectors and
registered homes tribunals: see D. Carson, [1985] J.S.W.L. 67, 69–70; R. Brooke Ross, [1985]
J.S.W.L. 85; R. M. Jones (ed.), *Encyclopedia of Social Services and Child Care Law* (1993),
para. D1-303.

[12] See L. Collins, *European Community Law in the United Kingdom* (4th ed., 1990), Chaps.1 and
2; J. Usher, *European Community Law and National Law, The Irreversible Transfer?* (1981);
T. C. Hartley, *The Foundations of European Community Law* (4th ed., 1998).

notably by the Single European Act of 1986,[13] the (Maastricht) Treaty on European Union of 1992,[14] the Treaty of Amsterdam (1999) and the Treaty of Nice (2001). The Maastricht Treaty introduced changes to the structure and nomenclature of the arrangements for European co-operation. The twelve Member States established among themselves a "European Union", making a new stage in the process of creating an ever closer union among the peoples of Europe in which decisions are taken as closely as possible to the citizen."[15] Its task was "to organize, in a manner demonstrating consistency and solidarity, relations between the Member States and between their peoples." The Union was founded on the European Communities, supplemented by the "implementation of a common foreign and security policy" and the development of "close cooperation on justice and home affairs."[16]

The "European Communities" thus formed one part of a broader Union; it was, however, only the Communities that possessed legislative powers affecting Member States and citizens. One final complication was that while the term "European Community" had popularly been used to cover the three communities, the ECSC and Euratom no longer having independent roles, the Maastricht Treaty substituted "European Community" for "European Economic Community" throughout the Treaty of Rome.[17]

Austria, Finland and Sweden became Member States from January 1, 1995. This structure was modified by the Treaty of Amsterdam (in effect from 1999). The EU remains with three "pillars" but the two non-EC pillars were substantially revised, with some matters moved to the EC pillar and the Justice and Home Affairs pillar re-titled as "Provisions on Police and Judicial Co-operation in Criminal Matters."[18] It also renumbered the provisions of both the Treaty on European Union and the Treaty establishing the European Community.[19] The Treaty of Nice (signed in 2001 but not at the time of writing in force) introduces further changes to take account of the substantial planned enlargement of the EU.

The Treaty provisions are sometimes termed the *primary* legislation of the Communities. The Treaties give various powers to the Council and the Commission to make laws by *regulation, directive* or *decision*, the resulting body of law being termed *secondary* legislation. Secondary legislation must conform to the express or implied limits set by the relevant treaty provisions.

---

[13] This had the objectives of "unblocking the Community's decision making process, thereby hastening the completion of a genuine common market," enhancing the role of the Parliament in the legislative process, and establishing a formal basis for European Political co-operation: A. Arnull, (1986) 11 E.L. Rev. 358; see also H.-J. Glaesner, (1986) 6 Y.E.L. 283; Symposium, (1986) 23 C.M.L. Rev. 743–840; M. A. McElhenny, (1988) 39(1) N.I.L.Q. 54.

[14] This introduced further major changes, including the establishment of a timetable for progress towards economic and monetary union with a single currency and monetary policy; further changes to legislative procedures; new fields of activity, such as culture, public health and consumer protection; and citizenship of the European Union. See D. O'Keefe and P. Twomey (eds.), *Legal Issues of the Maastricht Treaty* (1994); Harmsen, (1994) 45 N.I.L.Q. 109; D. Curtin, (1993) 30 C.M.L.Rev.17.

[15] Treaty on European Union, Title I, Article A.

[16] *ibid.*, Article B. See below, para. 5-037.

[17] *ibid.*, Title II, Article G. The ECSC Treaty expired on July 23, 2002.

[18] See D. O'Keefe and P. Twomey, *Legal Issues of the Amsterdam Treaty* (1999).

[19] Note the method of citation adopted by the Court of Justice and the Court of First Instance: see the Court of Justice website, *http://curia.eu.int/en/jurisp/renum.htm.*

Under Community law, a further distinction is drawn between laws (both primary and secondary) that have *direct application* or *effect* without any act of implementation by Member States and laws that require such implementation.

Under United Kingdom law, rules of international law such as treaty provisions can only take effect within our domestic legal system if expressly implemented by Act of Parliament. Accordingly, the government secured the passage of the European Communities Act 1972 to enable Community law to take effect within the United Kingdom.

In this section we consider, first, the main Community institutions, second, the different kinds of Community legislation and the extent to which it may be directly applicable or effective, third, the question of the supremacy of Community law, fourth, the implementation of Community law in the United Kingdom, and fifth, the methods by which the validity of Community legislation may be challenged.

2. THE COMMUNITY INSTITUTIONS[20]

5-034   The four main institutions of the European Community, established by the EC Treaty are the Commission, the Council and the European Parliament (the political institutions) and the Court of Justice. The political institutions will be considered here.[21]

(a) The Commission[22]

The Commission comprises 20 members, who must be nationals of Member States, with either one or two members from each Member State. In practice, the five largest countries (France, Germany, Italy, Spain and the United Kingdom) have two each, the rest one each.[23] Each Commissioner is in effect nominated by his or her national state, but must be acceptable to all the Member States, and is not a "representative" of his or her own country. The procedure for appointment from 1995 has been for the governments first to nominate by common accord the President of the Commission, subject to the approval of the European Parliament, and then, in consultation with him or her, to nominate the other Commissioners; they are then subject as a body to a vote of approval by the Parliament.[24] After

---

[20] See Hartley (1998) Chap. 1; S. Weatherill and P. Beaumont, *EU Law* (3rd ed., 1999), Chaps.2–4.

[21] The Court of Justice is considered above, para. 2-075.

[22] Arts 211–219 EC The Merger Treaty (1965), Arts.9–19, had previously provided for the merger of the separate High Authority (ECSC) and Commissions (EEC, Euratom) for the three communities. See G. Edwards and D. Spence (eds.), *The European Commission* (1994); E. Noel, *Working Together* (1993); M. Westlake, *The Commission and the Parliament* (1994).

[23] The United Kingdom has adopted the practice of nominating one with a Conservative and one with a Labour political background. The U.K. Commissioners have been Sir Christopher Soames and George Thomson (1973–77); Roy Jenkins (1977–81); Christopher Tugendhat (1977–85); Ivor Richard (1981–85); Lord Cockfield and Stanley Clinton Davis (1985–89); Sir Leon Brittan (1989–); Bruce Millan (1989–95); and Neil Kinnock (1995–).

[24] In 1995, although not a formal part of the procedure, the Parliament held individual hearings for each nominee.

approval, they are all appointed by common accord of the governments of the Member States.[25] Article 213(2) provides:

"The members of the Commission shall, in the general interest of the Community, be completely independent in the performance of their duties.

In the performance of these duties, they shall neither seek nor take instructions from any Government or from any other body. They shall refrain from any action incompatible with their duties. Each Member State undertakes to respect this principle and not to seek to influence the members of the Commission in the performance of their tasks. .... "

The term of office is five years (increased from four years from 1995), and may be renewed. All the Commissioners retire together. The Commission may appoint one or two Vice-Presidents.[26] Individual Commissioners can be compulsorily retired by the Court of Justice, on the application of the Council or Commission, if they are guilty of serious misconduct or no longer fulfil the conditions required for performance of their duties. Otherwise, individual Commissioners cannot be dismissed, although the whole Commission must resign if a motion of censure is passed by the Parliament. Each Commissioner is allocated special responsibility for one or more subjects.[27] The Commissioners are supported by over 15,000 staff, organised into a number of Directorates General, with a number of specialised services, including a Legal Service.

The main activities of the Commission are:

"formulating proposals for new Community policies, mediating between the Member States to secure the adoption of these proposals, co-ordinating national policies and overseeing the execution of existing Community policies."[28]

Under the EC Treaty, its task is "to ensure the proper functioning and development of the common market."[29] The Commission meets in private[30] and makes decisions by a simple majority vote. Its commitment to the furtherance of Community interests provides a balance to the Council of Ministers, which tends to reflect national interests.

[25] By virtue of the Treaty of Nice, Art. 2(22), substituting a new Art. 214(2)EC, the Council acting by qualified majority is to nominate the President, subject to approval by the Parliament. Acting by a qualified majority and by common accord with the nominee, it is to adopt the list of other persons whom it intends to nominate as Commissioners, drawn up in accordance with the proposals of each Member State. They are then all to be subject as a body to Parliament's approval; after approval they are then to be appointed by the Council by qualified majority.

[26] Art. 217EC.

[27] Under Art. 217 EC as substituted by the Treaty of Nice, Art. 2(24) it is for the President to decide on the Commission's internal organisation and the allocation of responsibilities, and (after obtaining the approval of the College *i.e.* the Commissioners) appoint Vice-Presidents. A Commissioner will have to resign if the President so requests, after obtaining the approval of the College.

[28] Hartley (1998) p. 11.

[29] Art. 211EC; *cf.* the broader objectives of the Council: below, para. 5-035.

[30] A general right of access to documents, subject to exceptions, is conferred by Commission Decision 94/90, to be replaced by rules under Reg. (EC) No. 1049/2001 of the Parliament and the Council: see below, para. 5-035, n. 34.

(b) The Council[31]

5–035 The Council of the European Union[32] comprises representatives of the Member States, each state sending a minister authorised to commit the government of that state. The Presidency is held by each Member State[33] in turn for a term of six months.

The Council is attended by different ministers according to the business to be dealt with. General matters are normally considered by foreign ministers; agriculture matters by agriculture ministers, financial matters by finance ministers and so on. The Council meets periodically, and normally in private.[34] It is supported by a General Secretariat, which is organised on similar lines to the Commission, but is much smaller. The Council's business is prepared by the Committee of Permanent Representatives (COREPER), which itself meets at two levels: COREPER II, comprising the heads of permanent delegations (ambassadors), which deals with matters of political importance, and COREPER I, comprising deputies, which deals with day-to-day business and technical matters. In turn there are many committees and expert working groups. The Council

> "takes the final decision on most EC legislation (sometimes acting jointly with the Parliament), concludes agreements with foreign countries and, together with the Parliament, decides on the Community budget."[35]

Under the EC Treaty, its task is "to ensure that the objectives set out in this Treaty are attained," and to that end "ensure co-ordination of the general economic policies of the Member States" and "have power to take

---

[31] Arts. 202EC–210EC. The Merger Treaty (1965), Arts.1–8 previously provided for the merger of separate Councils for each Community.

[32] The Council adopted this title in 1993: Council Decision 93/591 of November 8, 1993.

[33] The order is decided by the Council acting unanimously

[34] From 1993, it has held some public debates and voting outcomes have been made public, as part of a number of moves to improve the transparency of the institutions' business: *Intergovernmental Conference 1996: Commission Report for the Reflection Group* (1995), p. 39. See also Council Decision 93/731/EC on public access to Council Documents, as amended by Council Decisions 96/705 and 2000/527, giving a general right of access to documents subject to a range of exceptions; access must be refused where disclosure could undermine the protection of the "public interest," of "the individual and of privacy," of "commercial and industrial secrecy," of "the Community financial interests," of confidentiality as requested by the supplier of the information (article 4(1)) and it may be refused to protect "the confidentiality of the Council's proceedings" (article 4(2)). Decisions under article 4(1) must be made on a case by case basis; and under article 4(2) a genuine balance must be maintained between the interest of the citizen in obtaining access and the interest of the Council in preserving confidentiality; the exceptions must be construed narrowly and particular reasons for refusal required: Case T-174/95, *Svenska Journal-istforbundet v. Council* [1998] E.C.R. 11-2289. See also Article 255EC, conferring a general right of access subject to principles to be defined by the institutions; which principles were set out in Reg. (EC) No. 1049/2001 of the Parliament and Council. Under this, access is extended to documents from third parties, a document protected by an exception (other than the public interest or the protection of private life) will nevertheless be divulged if the public interest demands it, a document register will be made available to the public and the time limits for replies will be reduced to 15 working days.

[35] Hartley (1998), p. 17.

decisions."[36] The more important decisions are reserved to the Council rather than the Commission.[37]

The Treaties specify different voting arrangements for different kinds of Council decision. Some acts must be unanimous. Most require a "qualified majority."[38] Here the votes of Member States are weighted:

France, Germany, Italy, United Kingdom	: 10 votes each
Spain	: 8 votes
Belgium, Greece, Netherlands, Portugal	: 5 votes each
Sweden, Austria	: 4 votes each
Denmark, Ireland, Finland	: 3 votes each
Luxembourg	: 2 votes

A "qualified majority" is 62 of these 87 votes, where the act is based on a Commission proposal; 62 votes with 10 Member States in favour, otherwise. The arrangements mean that the five largest countries cannot outvote the smaller states.[39] A common position as to the weighting of votes in the Council has been reached to be adopted at the accession conferences arising through the process of enlargement.[40]

In many important areas the original requirement specified in the Treaties was for unanimity, the qualified majority regime only coming into effect from January 1, 1966. Even then, a convention developed whereby unanimity would be required as a matter of practice (albeit no longer as a matter of law) where "very important interests" of one or more Member States were at stake.[41] In the 1980s, this convention was applied with less force, and matters are now decided by majority votes. The Single European Act amended various Treaty provisions by substituting a qualified majority procedure for a requirement of unanimity. This process has been continued by the Maastricht and Amsterdam Treaties.

---

[36] Article 202EC.

[37] See further below, para. 5-039.

[38] Article 205EC.

[39] Following the accession of Austria, Finland and Sweden, the "blocking minority" of votes was raised from 23 to 26; however, by virtue of the so-called "Ioannina Compromise", where there are 23 to 25 against a proposal, the Council "will do all in its power to reach ... a satisfactory solution that could be adopted by at least 65 votes": see Weatherill and Beaumont (1999), pp. 87–88. The compromise has been extended up to enlargement.

[40] Declarations adopted by the Nice Intergovernmental Conference, para. 20. The weighted votes for the 27 states are to be : 29 (Germany, U.K., France, Italy), 27 (Spain, Poland), 14 (Romania), 13 (Netherlands), 12 (Greece, Czech Republic, Belgium, Hungary, Portugal), 10 (Sweden, Bulgaria, Austria), 7 (Slovakia, Denmark, Finland, Ireland, Lithuania), 4 (Latvia, Slovenia, Estonia, Cyprus, Luxembourg) and 3 Malta (total 345). For adoption of an act, 258 votes in favour, cast by a majority of members, where a proposal from the Commission is required; in other cases 258 votes cast by at least 2/3 of members. Any member can also require verification that the qualified majority represent 62% of the EU's total population. These new weightings take effect on January 2001 and the numbers will be modified according to the rate of accessions. The blocking minority when all candidate countries have acceded will be raised to 91 votes.

[41] This was reflected in the so-called "Luxembourg Accords" of January 1966: a press release enshrining the part agreement/part truce that ended a dispute between France and the, then five, other Member States.

(c) The European Parliament[42]

5–036   The Parliament consists of "representatives of the peoples" of the Member States. In 1999, the members were directedly elected, in the following proportions[43]

Germany	99
France, Italy and the United Kingdom	87 each
Spain	64
Netherlands	31
Belgium, Greece and Portugal	25 each
Sweden	22
Austria	21
Denmark, Finland	16 each
Ireland	15
Luxembourg	6
	626

This does not reflect populations: in those terms the smaller states are over-represented. Members sit in political groupings rather than by country. Much of the work is done by committees.

The Parliament exercises the powers conferred by the Treaties.[44] These have become more extensive over time.

It puts Questions to the Council and the Commission, and is involved in at least a consultative capacity in the legislative process, its role here having been strengthened by the Single European Act and the Maastricht Treaty.[45] It now has a veto over the admission of new Member States, the conclusion of association agreements with other states and certain legislative proposals.[46] It has had a progressively greater say in the determination of the Community's Budget.[47] Provisions added by the Maastricht Treaty enable the Parliament to request proposals from the Commission on matters on which it considers that a Community act is required to implement the Treaty and to set up temporary committees of inquiry; require it to appoint an Ombudsman; and entitle EU citizens, and other natural or legal persons resident or with a registered office in a Member State to address petitions to it on Community matters which affect him, her or it directly.[48]

(d) Other institutions

5–037   Other organs of the Community include the Economic and Social

---

[42] Arts 189EC to 201EC. The Parliament was referred to as Assembly in the Treaties. It resolved to call itself the "European Parliament" in 1962, and that title was recognised in the Single European Act. See F. Jacobs, *et al., The European Parliament* (1992); M. Westake, *The Commission and the Parliament* (1994).

[43] Art. 190(2)EC.

[44] Art. 189EC. These are no longer described as "advisory and supervisory powers".

[45] See below, paras 5-047, 5-048.

[46] Art. 49 E U; Art. 300(3) EC; Art. 7 EU (determination of the existence of a serious and persistent breach by a Member State of the principles mentioned in Art. 6(1) EU) (see below, paras 5-047, 5-048).

[47] Hartley (1998) pp. 44–48.

[48] Arts 192EC–195 EC.

Committee,[49] with members from each Member State representing employers, workers and others (*e.g.* farmers, the professions and the general public), which advises both Council and Commission; the Court of Auditors,[50] which carries out the audit and assists the Council and the Parliament in exercising their powers of control over implementation of the budget; the Committee of the Regions which represents regional and local bodies within the EC; and the European Investment Bank.

Finally, the arrangements for a common foreign and security policy and on police and judicial cooperation in criminal matters are found, respectively, in Title V (Articles 11 EU to 28 EU) and Title VI (Articles 29 EU to 42 EU). The EU is to "define and implement a common foreign and security policy covering all areas of foreign and security policy." Its objectives include safeguarding the common values, fundamental interests; independence and integrity of the E.U.; strengthening the security of the EU; preserving peace and strengthening international security; promoting international cooperation and developing and consolidating democracy and the rule of law and respect for human rights and fundamental freedoms. Member States are to "support the Union's external and security policy actively and unreservedly in a spirit of loyalty and mutual solidarity."[51] The EU is represented by the Presidency in matters within the CFSP, and the Presidency in association with the Commission is responsible for the implementation of decisions.[52] The general principles of and general guidelines for the CFSP are defined by the European Council;[53] decisions necessary for defining and implementing the policy are taken by the Council.[54]

Under Title VI, the EU's objective is to provide citizens with a high level of safety within an area of freedom, security and justice by developing common action among Member States in the fields of police and judicial cooperation in criminal matters and by preventing and combating racism and xenophobia. This is to be achieved by preventing and combating crime, in particular terrorism, trafficking in persons and offences against children, illicit trafficking in drugs and arms, corruption and fraud. Cooperation is to include operational cooperation and is to be promoted through Europol. Common action is to include the facilitation of extradition. The Council may adopt joint positions on action and may draw up conventions recommended to Member States for adoption.[55] Member States may accept a new jurisdiction of the Court of Justice to give preliminary rulings in relation to certain matters arising Title VI and to review the legality of framework discussions and decisions in actions.[56]

At the apex of these structures is the European Council—regular conferences of the Heads of State or of Government and the foreign ministers of the Member States. These were informal meetings, attended by

---

[49] Arts 257EC–262EC.
[50] Arts 246EC–248EC, arts. 247EC and 248EC to be amended by the Treaty of Nice, art. 2 (36), (37).
[51] Art. 11EU.
[52] Art. 18EU.
[53] See below.
[54] Art. 13EU.
[55] Arts 29EC, 30EC.
[56] Art. 35EC.

representatives of the Commission, but a regular constitution for them was provided by Article 2 of the Single European Act and now by Article 4EU, under which the European Council is to "provide the Union with the necessary impetus for its development" and "define the general political guidelines thereof." When discussing Community matters, the European Council acts as the Council of Ministers, but the two are technically distinct.

3. THE KINDS OF COMMUNITY LEGISLATION

(a) Treaty provisions concerning Community legislation

5-038   The different kinds of Community acts are described in Article 249EC (formerly) Article 189 of the EC Treaty[57]:

> "In order to carry out their task and in accordance with the provisions of this Treaty, the European Parliament acting jointly with the Council, the Council and the Commission shall make regulations and issue directives, take decisions, make recommendations or deliver opinions.
>
> A regulation shall have general application. It shall be binding in its entirety and directly applicable in all Member States.
>
> A directive shall be binding, as to the result to be achieved, upon each Member State to which it is addressed. but shall leave to the national authorities the choice of form and methods.
>
> A decision shall be binding in its entirety upon those to whom it is addressed.
>
> Recommendations and opinions shall have no binding force."

Recommendations and opinions cannot be regarded as legislative as they do not have binding effect; it has also been suggested that decisions directed to individuals, as distinct from Member States, are administrative rather than legislative in character.[58]

The Treaties require that regulations, directives and decisions state the reasons on which they are based and refer to any proposals or opinions that were required to be obtained pursuant to other Treaty provisions.[59] Regulations, directives and decisions adopted by the Parliament and the Council jointly, regulations of the Council and the Commission, and

---

[57] As amended by Art. 6 (60)/TEU. See also Art. 14/ECSC and Art. 161/Euratom. The terminology of ECSC acts is different:

EEC Euratom	ECSC
Regulations Decisions	Decisions
Directives	Recommendations
Recommendations Opinions	Opinions

The following discussion is generally confined to EC legislation.

[58] Case 19/77, *Miller v. Commission* [1978] E.C.R. 131, 161 *per* A. G. Warner.

[59] Art. 253EC.

directives of those institutions addressed to all Member States, must be published in the Official Journal. They enter into force on the date specified in them, or, if no date is specified, on the twentieth day following their publication. Other directives and decisions must be notified to those to whom they are addressed and take effect upon such notification.[60]

(b) Legislative powers[61]

Under the EC and Euratom Treaties, the major policy decisions and legislative powers are reserved to the Council; the Commission being involved with (in most cases) the formulation of legislative proposals and with the implementation of decisions. However, the Commission does have some legislative powers conferred upon it by the EC Treaty.[62] Furthermore, its position has been strengthened in two ways.   **5–039**

First, procedures have been developed for the delegation of functions from the Council to the Commission. A distinction is drawn between the laying down of general principles and detailed implementation. Only the latter process may be delegated, but that may involve rule-making by the Commission. Such arrangements were held to be lawful by the Court of Justice.[63] Express authority was provided for them by Article 10 of the Single European Act, amending Article 145 of the EC Treaty (see now Art. 202EC). Acts adopted by the Council must confer power for the implementation of the rules laid down therein by the Commission, unless ("in specific cases") the Council reserves the right to exercise directly implementing powers itself. The Council may impose certain requirements in respect of the exercise of these delegated powers, in conformity with procedures prescribed by a Council Decision. The "Commitology" Decision was adopted in 1987,[64] and corresponded for the most part to the previous informal arrangements. It was replaced by a new Council Decision in 1999.[65] Other than in the "specific cases" mentioned above, the Council may select one of a series of procedures set out in the Decision.[66]

Each procedure requires the Commission to consult a committee comprising representatives of the Member States, and chaired by a representative of the Commission. The committee must deliver its opinion within a time limit laid down by the Chairman according to the urgency of the matter.

The "advisory procedure" involves an "advisory committee". As the name suggests, the Commission must "take the utmost account of the

---

[60] Art. 254EC.

[61] See Hartley (1998), pp. 37–44, 102–129; R. Baldwin, *Rules and Government* (1995), Chap. 8.

[62] See T. C. Hartley, (1988) 13 E.L. Rev. 122–123; Cases 88–90/80, *France, Italy and the United Kingdom v. Commission* [1982] E.C.R. 2545.

[63] Case 25/70, *Einfuhr – und Vorratsstelle v. Köster* [1970] E.C.R. 1161; Case 41/69, *Chemiefarma v. Commission* [1970] E.C.R. 661; Case 23/75, *Rey Soda v. Cassa Conguaglio Zuchero* [1975] E.C.R. 1279; *cf.* Case 264/86, *France v. Commission* [1988] E.C.R. 973.

[64] Dec. 87/373, O.J. 1987, L 197/33. See K. St. C. Bradley, "Commitology and the law; through a glass, darkly" (1992) 29 C.M.L. Rev. 693.

[65] Council Dec. 1999/468 of June 28, 1999 laying down the procedures for the exercise of implementing powers conferred on the Commission: O.J. [1999] L184/23. It is reproduced in N. Foster, *Blackstone's EC Legislation 2001–2002* (12th edn, 2001), pp. 257–263.

[66] The Decision also prescribes a procedure that may be applied where the Council confers on the Commission the power to decide on "safeguard measures": Art. 6.

opinion delivered by the committee" but is not bound by it. The "management procedure" involves a "management committee", which forms an opinion acting by a qualified majority. The Commission must adopt measures which shall apply immediately, but where they are not in accordance with the committee's opinion, the Council must be informed. In that event the Commission may defer application of the measures for a period (not exceeding three months) to be laid down in each basic instrument. The Council, acting by a qualified majority, may within that period take a different decision. The "regulatory procedure" involves a "regulatory committee", again acting by a qualified majority. The Commission must adopt the measures forthwith if they are in accordance with the opinion of the committee. If they are not, or if no opinion is delivered, the Commission has to submit to the Council a proposal relating to the measures to be taken and inform the Parliament. If the Parliament considers that the proposal exceeds the implementing powers provided for in the underlying basic instrument it must inform the Council of its position. The Council may, in view of any such position, act by qualified majority on the proposal, within a period (not exceeding three months from the date of referral to the Council) laid down in the basic instrument. If it indicates opposition, the Commission must re-examine the proposal. It may submit an amended proposal, resubmit its proposal or present a legislative proposal based on the Treaty. If on the expiry of the specified period the Council has neither adopted nor opposed the proposal, the proposed implementing act must be adopted by the Commission. There is also a general provision whereby if the Parliament indicates in a resolution that any draft implementing measure would exceed the implementing powers provided for in the basic instrument, it must be re-examined by the Commission. The Commission may submit new draft measures, continue with the procedure or submit a proposal to the Parliament or the Council on the basis of the Treaty. The Commission must inform the Parliament and the Committee of the action it intends to take.

The Commission expressed reservations concerning the original version of the procedures, and complained that the Council only infrequently adopted the advisory committee procedure, preferring to use "delegation procedures which allow the national authorities to block legislation."[67] The Parliament sought to have the 1987 Decision annulled under Article 173, but the European Court held that it did not have capacity to bring such an action.[68] Subject to a reservation concerning Variant III of the original procedure (under which a simple Council majority could block a decision under the regulatory procedure), the Commission (in 1995) believed that these procedures operated satisfactorily, noting that of several thousand committee opinions adopted over the previous three years, six decisions were referred back to the Council and there were no cases where no decision was taken.[69] The 1999 Decision introduced criteria for the adoption of the appropriate procedure.[70] Thus management measures, such as those relating

---

[67] See Commission, 21st General Report on the Activities of the European Communities, 1987, point 4; 22nd General Report, 1988, point 9.
[68] Case 302/87, *European Parliament v. Council* [1988] E.C.R. 5615 (see further, below, para. 5-057).
[69] *Commission Report for the Reflection Group* (1995), p. 31.
[70] Art. 2.

to the common agricultural and fisheries policies or the implementation of programmes with substantial budgetary implications, should use the management procedure. Measures of general scope designed to apply essential provisions of basic instruments (including health and safety measures) should use the regulatory procedure. Without prejudice to these guidelines, the advisory committee procedure must be used in any case where it is considered to be the most appropriate.

The second means by which the Commission's powers have been strengthened is by the recognition by the European Court that it enjoys certain *implied* legislative powers. In *Germany v. Commission*[71] the European Court held that:

> "where an Article of the EEC Treaty—in this case Article 118—confers a specific task on the Commission it must be accepted, if that provision is not to be rendered wholly ineffective, that it confers on the Commission necessarily and *per se* the powers which are indispensable in order to carry out that task."[72]

It then proceeded to hold that the Commission enjoyed all "necessary" powers (rather than "indispensible") and took a generous view of what was "necessary".[73] It has been noted that:

> "Since the EC Treaty confers many tasks on the Commission, including such wide-ranging functions as that of ensuring that the provisions of the Treaty are applied,[74] this judgment is potentially significant though so far it has not been widely applied."[75]

(c) Direct applicability and direct effect

A distinction is sometimes drawn between the terms *direct applicability* and *direct effect*.[76] Article 249 EC provides that regulations are "directly applicable" in all Member States; they come into force without any act of implementation by Member States. No other form of Community law is expressly stated in the treaties to be directly *applicable*, and it was at first thought that those other forms of law could only take *effect* within Member States if there was an act of implementation. However, the Court of Justice

5–040

---

[71] Cases 281, 283–285, 287/85, [1987] E.C.R. 3203.
[72] *ibid.*, p. 3253.
[73] T. C. Hartley, (1988) 13 E.L. Rev. 122.
[74] Art. 211EC.
[75] Hartley (1998), p. 103. See also the "supplementary means of action" available to the Council under Art. 308 EC: *ibid.*, pp. 103–111.
[76] See J. A. Winter, (1972) 9 C.M.L.R. 425; J.-P. Warner, (1977) 93 L.Q.R. 349; A. Dashwood, (1977–78) 16 J. of Common Market Studies 229; J. Steiner, (1982) 98 L.Q.R. 229, (1990) 106 L.Q.R. 144 and (1993) 18 E.L. Rev. 3; P. Pescatore, (1983) 8 E.L. Rev 155; N. Green, (1984) 9 E.L. Rev. 295; D. Curtin, (1990) 15 E.L. Rev. 195 and (1990) 27 C.M.L. Rev. 709; P. Craig, (1992) 12 O.J.L.S. 453; G. de Búrca, (1992) 55 M.L.R. 215; N. Maltby, (1993) 109 L.Q.R. 301-Plaza Martin, (1994) 43 I.C.L.Q. 26, R. Caranta, (1995) 32 C.M.L. Rev. 703; B. De Witte in P.P. Craig and G. de Búrca (eds), *The Evolution of EC Law* (1999); C. Hilson and T. Downes, (1999) 24 E.L. Rev. 121; R. Mastroianni, (1999) 5 E.P.L. 417; C. Timmermans, (1997) 17 Y.E.L. 1.

developed the view that treaty provisions could in principle confer rights
and impose obligations directly upon individuals irrespective of any act of
implementation. In the *Van Gend en Loos* case[77] the plaintiff claimed before
a Dutch tribunal that there had been an increase in import duties which was
rendered illegal by Article 12[78] of the EC Treaty. The Court of Justice, on a
reference from the tribunal, held that Article 12 was indeed directly effective,
and could be relied upon by the plaintiff in this case. The court stated[79]:

"To ascertain whether the provisions of an international treaty extend
so far in their effects it is necessary to consider the spirit, the general
scheme and the wording of those provisions.

   The objective of the EEC Treaty, which is to establish a Common
Market, the functioning of which is of direct concern to interested
parties in the Community, implies that this Treaty is more than an
agreement which merely creates mutual obligations between the
contracting states. This view is confirmed by the preamble to the
Treaty which refers not only to governments but to peoples. It is also
confirmed more specifically by the establishment of institutions
endowed with sovereign rights, the exercise of which affects Member
States and also their citizens. Furthermore, it must be noted that the
nationals of the states brought together in the Community are called
upon to cooperate in the functioning of this Community through the
intermediary of the European Parliament and the Economic and Social
Committee.

   In addition the task assigned to the Court of Justice under Article
177, the object of which is to secure uniform interpretation of the
Treaty by national courts and tribunals, confirms that the states have
acknowledged that Community law has an authority which can be
invoked by their nationals before those courts and tribunals.

   The conclusion to be drawn from this is that the Community
constitutes a new legal order of international law for the benefit of
which the states have limited their sovereign rights, albeit within limited
fields, and the subjects of which comprise not only Member States but
also their nationals. Independently of the legislation of Member States,
Community law therefore not only imposes obligations on individuals
but is also intended to confer upon them rights which become part of
their legal heritage. These rights arise not only where they are expressly
granted by the Treaty, but also by reason of obligations which the
Treaty imposes in a clearly defined way upon individuals as well as
upon the Member States and upon the institutions of the Community."

Article 12 imposed a clear and unconditional negative prohibition, "ideally
adapted to produce direct effects in the legal relationship between Member

---

[77] Case 26/62, *Van Gend en Loos v. Nederlandse Administratie Der Belastingen* [1963] E.C.R. 1.
[78] "Member States shall refrain from introducing between themselves any new customs duties
on imports or exports or any charges having equivalent effect, and from increasing those
which they already apply in their trade with each other." Now, after amendment, Article
25EC: "Customs duties on imports and exports and charges having equivalent effects shall
be prohibited between Member States. This prohibition shall also apply to customs duties of
a fiscal nature."
[79] pp. 12–13.

States and their subjects."

In this and subsequent cases the Court of Justice has elaborated the criteria by which those *treaty provisions* that are regarded as directly effective are to be distinguished from those that are not. As more provisions have come before the court for consideration, the overall picture has become clearer.[80] The criteria[81] are:

"—the provision must impose a clear and precise obligation on Member States;

—it must be unconditional, in other words subject to no limitation; if, however, a provision is subject to certain limitations, their nature and extent must be exactly defined;

—finally, the implementation of a Community rule must not be subject to the adoption of any subsequent rules or regulations on the part either of the Community institutions or of the Member States, so that, in particular, Member States must not be left any real discretion with regard to the application of the rule in question."

A provision may, exceptionally, be held to have direct effect prospectively only.[82]

The Court of Justice has subsequently invoked these criteria to hold that **5–041** *decisions* addressed to Member States,[83] *directives*,[84] and agreements between the Community and non-Member States[85] can be directly effective. *Van Duyn v. Home Office* concerned Article 48 of the EC Treaty (now, after amendment, Article 39EC), which provided for the "freedom of movement" of workers, including the right to enter and stay in any Member State "subject to limitations justified on grounds of public policy, public security

---

[80] A useful table is given in Collins (1990), pp. 122–126.

[81] As formulated by A. G. Mayras in Case 41/74, *Van Duyn v. Home Office* [1974] E.C.R. 1337, 1354. See *e.g. Application des Gaz v. Folks Veritas* [1974] Ch. 381 (Articles 85 and 86 of the EC Treaty (now Articles 81EC and 82EC) *Rio Tinto Zinc Corporation v. Westinghouse Electric Corporation* [1978] A.C. 547 (Article 85).

[82] Case 43/75, *Defrenne v. Sabena* (No. 2) [1976] E.C.R. 455. This case concerned the direct effect of Art. 119/EEC (equal pay for men and women). The court stated: "As the general level at which pay would have been fixed cannot be known, important considerations of legal certainty affecting all the interests involved, both public and private, make it impossible in principle to reopen the question as regards the past" (p. 481). See T. Koopmans, [1980] C.LJ. 287; M. Waelbroeck, [1981] 1 Y.E.L. 115. This principle was applied in Case 309/85, *Barra v. Belgium* [1988] E.C.R. 355; Case 24/86, *Blaizot v. University of Liege* [1988] E.C.R. 379; Case C-262/88, *Barber v. Guardian Royal Exchange Assurance Group* [1990] E.C.R. I-1889; Case C-437/97, *Evangelischer Krankenhausverein Wien* [2000] E.C.R. I-1157; A. Arnull, (1988) 13 E.L. Rev. 260.

[83] See Case 9/70, *Grad v. Finanzamt Traunstein* [1970] E.C.R. 325: this concerned a decision which prohibited member states from applying specific taxes concurrently with the common turnover tax (VAT) system due to be implemented by directive.

[84] See Case 41/74, *Van Duyn v. Home Office* [1974] E.C.R. 1337; Case 148/78, *Pubblico Ministero v. Ratti* [1979] E.C.R. 162; Case 102/79, *Commission v. Belgium* [1980] E.C.R. 1473; Case 8/81, *Becker v. Finanzamt Münster-Innenstadt* [1982] E.C.R. 53. In Case 131/79, *R. v. Secretary of State for the Home Department, ex p. Santillo* [1980] E.C.R. 1585, 1610–11, A. G. Warner argued that the conditions for the direct effectiveness of Treaty provisions were subject to some qualification when applied to directives. In particular, there will nearly always be some element of discretion which will not, however, prevent a directive being held to be directly effective. See generally, D. Curtin, (1990) 15 E.L. Rev. 195.

[85] Case 104/81, *Kupferberg* [1982] E.C.R. 3641.

or public health." The scope of these limitations was further regulated by Council Directive 64/221 which provided in Art. 3(1) that, "Measures taken on grounds of public policy or of public security shall be based exclusively on the personal conduct of the individual concerned." Miss Yvonne Van Duyn, a Dutch national, was refused leave to enter the United Kingdom on the ground that she was intending to work for the Church of Scientology. The government regarded scientology as socially harmful, and although it had no power to prohibit its practice it had decided to take steps, within its powers, to curb its growth. Accordingly it decided that foreign nationals such as Miss Van Duyn should be refused entry. She claimed that the refusal was not based on her "personal conduct" and challenged its validity in the High Court. Several questions were referred to the European Court, which held (1) that Article 48 was directly effective; (2) that the relevant provision of directive 64/221 was also directly effective; but (3) that a Member State was entitled to take into account as a matter of personal conduct that the individual was associated with an organisation whose activities were considered by the state to be socially harmful.

There are, however, limitations:

"the European Court has held that directives can only confer rights on individuals (against the State); they cannot impose obligations on individuals (in favour of the State or other individuals). This means that directives are capable of only 'vertical' direct effect; unlike regulations and Treaty provisions, they are not capable of 'horizontal' direct effect."[86]

The leading case here is *Marshall v Southampton and South West Hampshire Area Health Authority (Teaching)*.[87] Miss Marshall was dismissed by the Authority from her post as a dietician when she was 62, although she wished to continue to 65. It was the Authority's policy that the normal retiring age for its employees was the age at which state retirement pensions became payable. For women, this was 60. (The Authority had waived its policy for two years in respect of Miss Marshall.) The Court held that Article 5(1) of Council Directive 76/207 (the "Equal Treatment Directive") was to be interpreted as meaning that a general policy involving the dismissal of a woman solely because she had attained or passed the qualifying age for state pension, which age was different under national legislation for men and for women, constituted discrimination on the ground of sex, contrary to that

---

[86] Hartley (1998), p. 206.

[87] Case 152/84, [1986] Q.B. 401, [1986] E.C.R. 723 (*Marshall I*). See A. Arnull, (1986) 35 I.C.L.Q. 939 and [1987] P.L. 383; T. Millett, (1987) 36 I.C.L.Q. 616; N. Foster, (1987) 12 E.L. Rev. 222. In subsequent proceedings, the European Court held that Art.6 of the Equal Treatment directive, which required Member States to introduce measures enabling the victims of unlawful discrimination to "pursue their claims by judicial process", was directly effective, and precluded the imposition of limits to the amount of compensation recoverable or the exclusion of an element for interest: Case C-271/91, *Marshall v. Southampton and South West Hampshire Area Health Authority (No. 2)* [1994] Q.B. 126. Accordingly, the statutory limit to compensation for sex discrimination (Sex Discrimination Act 1975, s.65(2)) was not applicable to claims based on Community Law: see the House of Lords decision in *Marshall (No.2)*, restoring the award of the industrial tribunal: [1994] 1 A.C. 530. Section 65(2) was subsequently repealed and provision made for the award of interest by the Sex Discrimination and Equal Pay (Remedies) Regulations 1993 (S.I. 1993 No. 2798).

directive. It could be relied upon against a state authority acting in its capacity as employer: the principle was not confined to governmental acts. It was for the national court to determine whether the Health Authority was a "state authority" for this purpose, although the Court noted that in the order for reference the Court of Appeal had referred to it as a "public authority." The Court stated that as Art. 189 of the EC Treaty (now Article 249EC) provided that a directive was binding "upon each Member State to which it is addressed", it followed

> "that a directive may not of itself impose obligations on an individual and that a provision of a directive may not be relied upon as such against such a person."[88]

Accordingly, the Court of Justice has held that a Member State cannot base criminal proceedings against an individual on the provisions of an unimplemented directive.[89]

The ruling against "horizontal direct effect" has been criticised as having **5–042** "serious consequences for the rights of the individual."[90] It has been suggested that it can be seen as a compromise between, on the one hand, the desire to give maximum effectiveness to directives and, on the other, the argument based on the wording of Article 189 (now Article 249EC) and doubts expressed by courts in France (the *Conseil d'Etat*) and Germany (the *Bundesfinanzhof*) to the effect that directives should not be regarded as having any direct effect.[91] In any event, the ruling has been reaffirmed by the Court of Justice in *Paola Faccini Dori v. Recreb SrL*,[92] where a consumer in proceedings with a trader sought to rely on the provisions of a directive on consumer protection.[93] The relevant events[94] took place in 1989 and the directive was only implemented in Italy in 1992. The Court held that the relevant provisions were unconditional and sufficiently precise in terms of the direct effect doctrine; however, to extend that doctrine to relations between individuals

> "would be to recognise a power in the Community to enact obligations for individuals with immediate effect, whereas it has competence to do so only where it is empowered to adopt regulations."[95]

---

[88] [1986] Q.B. 401, 422.
[89] Case 14/86, *Pretore di Salo v. Persons Unknown* [1987] E.C.R. 2545, 2569–2570: A. Arnull, (1988) 13 E.L. Rev. 40; Case 80/86, *Kolpinghuis* [1987] E.C.R. 3969: A. Arnull, (1988) 13 E.L. Rev. 42.
[90] Arnull, (1986) 35 I.C.L.Q. 939, 943.
[91] Hartley (1998), pp. 206–208.
[92] Case C-91/92, [1994] E.C.R. 1-3325. See W. Robinson, (1995) 32 C.M.L. Rev. 629; J. Coppel, (1994) 57 M.L.R. 859; D. Kinley, [1995] I E.P.L. 79. The same view was expressed in Case C-192/94, *El Corte Inglés v. Cristina Blasquez Rivero* [1996] E.C.R. I-1281 and Case C-97/96, *Verband Deutscher Daihatsu Händler eV v. Daihatsu Deutschland GmbH* [1997] E.C.R. I-6843.
[93] Dir.85/577/EEC, concerning protection of the consumer in respect of contracts negotiated away from business premises.
[94] Ms Faccini Dori sought to rely on the directive in claiming the right to cancel a contract for an English language correspondence course concluded at Milan Central Railway Station.
[95] p. I-3356, para. 24.

Instead, private individuals had to rely on the principles of the *Marleasing* and *Francovich* cases.[96] In reaching this conclusion the Court declined to follow the opinion of Advocate General Lenz,[97] who argued that directives should be accorded horizontal direct effect, albeit only for the future, in the interests of the effective, uniform application of Community law.

A further limitation is that once a directive has been transposed into domestic law, individuals can no longer rely on the direct effect doctrine unless the national implementing measures are incorrect or inadequate.[98]

Four further points should be noted. First, it has become necessary to determine what amounts to a "state authority". The English courts initially took a narrow view, holding that directives could give rise to legal rights

> "in employees of the State itself and of any organ or emanation of the State, an emanation of the State being understood to include an independent public authority charged by the State with the performance of any of the classic duties of the State, such as the defence of the realm or the maintenance of law and order within the realm."[99]

This did not cover the British Gas Corporation,[1] and Rolls-Royce plc[2] in the period before privatisation. Conversely, a woman police officer who was a member of the Royal Ulster Constabulary Reserve was entitled to rely on the Equal Treatment Directive (76/207) against the Chief Constable,[3] and a regulatory agency acting on behalf of local authorities was held to be an emanation of the state.[4] The Court of Justice, however, took a broader view. In *Foster v. British Gas plc*[5] it held that the Court had jurisdiction in a preliminary ruling to determine the categories of person against whom the provisions of a directive may be relied on, and that it was for national courts to determine whether a party before them fell into one of the categories so defined. The categories include "a body, whatever its legal form, which has been made responsible, pursuant to a measure adopted by the state, for providing a public service under the control of the State and has for that purpose special powers beyond those which result from the normal rules applicable in relations between individuals".[6] In the light of this ruling, the House of Lords held that British Gas, when a nationalised industry, was an emanation of the state.[7] Conversely, the Court of Appeal confirmed that

---

[96] See below, paras 5-043, 5-044.

[97] [1994] E.C.R. I-3338–I-3345.

[98] Cases C-253/96 — C-258/96, *Kampelmann v. Lanshaftsverband Westfalen-Lippe* [1997] E.C.R. I-2771; *Marks & Spencer plc v. Commissioners of Customs & Excise* [2000] S.T.C. 16 (*Becker* conditions not fulfilled where directive had been correctly transposed by legislation but the legislation had been misconstrued by the Commissioners).

[99] *per* Lord Donaldson in *Foster v. British Gas plc* [1988] I.R.L.R. 354, 356.

[1] *Foster v. British Gas plc*, above.

[2] *Rolls-Royce plc v. Doughty* [1988] 1 C.M.L.R. 569, E.A.T.

[3] Case 222/84, *Johnston v. Chief Constable of the Royal Ulster Constabulary* [1986] E.C.R. 1651, [1987] Q.B. 129; A. Arnull, (1987) 12 E.L. Rev. 56;

[4] *R. v. London Boroughs Transport Committee, ex p. Freight Transport Association Ltd* [1990] C.M.L.R. 229.

[5] Case C-188/89 [1990] E.C.R. I-3330.

[6] Paras.20, 22 and the ruling. Para. 18, by contrast, refers to "organisations or bodies which were subject to the authority of the state *or* had special powers beyond those which result from the normal rules applicable to relations between individuals" (emphasis added).

[7] *Foster v. British Gas plc* [1991] 2 A.C. 306.

Rolls-Royce plc was not,[8] concluding that the fact of state ownership of a company was not sufficient where the company was not providing a public service and had no special powers.[9] The Court of Appeal reversing the Employment Appeal Tribunal, has held that the governing body of a voluntary-aided school was an emanation of the state; they voluntarily accepted financial aid from the state and provided a public service on its behalf.[10]

Secondly, the Court of Justice has held that Community law precludes Member States in proceedings against them in national courts based on unimplemented but directly effective directive provisions from relying on national procedural rules relating to time limits.[11] However, this does not prevent Member States from setting a time limit to retrospective claims for arrears of benefit based on such provisions, provided that the same time limit applies to claims to benefit arrears under national law and that the rule is not framed so as to render virtually impossible the exercise of rights conferred by Community law.[12]

Thirdly, it was of course still necessary notwithstanding *Marshall* for the United Kingdom to take legislative steps to implement the directive in question so as to extend its benefits to all employees. This was done by the Sex Discrimination Act 1986,[13] which took effect from November 7, 1987.

Fourthly, the courts have considered whether the unamended U.K. legislation[14] could be interpreted in accordance with the Equal Treatment Directive so as to render differential retirement ages for men and women unlawful. The House of Lords in *Duke v. Reliance Systems Ltd*[15] held that it could not. This point is taken up in the following section.

Overall, Member States have tended to present arguments to the Court of Justice against direct effectiveness; Community institutions have tended, not surprisingly, to argue in favour, given that it strengthens their position at the expense of individual Member States, and helps ensure that Community law applies uniformly throughout the Member States. It enables individuals to take action to enforce the requirements of Community law without having to rely on Community institutions to act. It has also been stressed that it is inappropriate for a Member State that has failed to implement a directive or decision addressed to it to rely, in proceedings between itself and an individual, on its own failure to comply with that directive or decision on the basis that it is not directly effective.[16]

It has been argued that the

---

[8] *Doughty v. Rolls-Royce* [1992] I.C.R. 538.

[9] Relying on the terms of the ruling of the Court of Justice in *Foster* rather than para. 18, and on the subsequent approach of the House of Lords in the same case: [1991] 2 A.C. 306.

[10] *National Union of Teachers v. Governing Body of St Mary's Church of England (Aided) Junior School* [1997] I.C.R. 334.

[11] Case C-208/90, *Emmott v. Minister for Social Welfare* [1991] E.C.R. 1-3723, in respect of the three-month time limit for applications for judicial review in Ireland.

[12] Case C-338/91, *Steenhorst-Neerings v. Bestuur van de Bedrijfsvereniging voor Detailhandel, Ambachten en Huisvrouwen* [1993] E.C.R. 1-5475; Case C-410/92, *Johnson v. Chief Adjudication Officer* (No. 2) [1995] All E.R. (E.C.) 258.

[13] ss.2, 3. See B. Fitzpatrick, (1987) 50 M.L.R. 934.

[14] Sex Discrimination Act 1975, ss.l, 6.

[15] [1988] A.C. 618. See below, paras 5-053, 5-054.

[16] Case 148/78, *Pubblico Ministero v. Ratti* [1979] E.C.R. 1624, 1650: A. G. Reischl; *Marshall* [1986] Q.B. 401, 421–422.

"granting of direct effect to directives has probably done more than any other initiative by the European Court to enhance the effectiveness of Community law."[17]

Although a regulation is "directly applicable" by virtue of Article 189 of the EC Treaty (now Article 249 EC), it will not necessarily create rights and obligations which may be enforced in national courts. This depends on the wording of the regulation in question[18]: it has been argued that regulations only have "direct effect" if the criteria applicable to treaty provisions and other kinds of Community secondary legislation are fulfilled.[19] In *Consorzio Del Prosciutto Di Parma v. Asda Stores Ltd.*[20] Lord Hoffmann said[21] that

"One would normally assume ... that unless the Regulation contemplated that it would have to be fleshed out by domestic or Community legislation, it was intended to be effective to create rights or duties or both and not to be what Lord Simonds once called a 'pious aspiration.'"[22]

Finally, it should be noted that in these and other cases in this area the Court of Justice has not been consistent in its use of the *terms* "directly applicable"and "direct effect," but has tended to use them interchangeably.[23]

(d) Indirect effect

5–043   The limitations on the direct effect doctrine in the context of directives have attention on the extent to which unimplemented directives may have "indirect effect". An issue has arisen as to the extent to which national courts should have regard to an unimplemented directive in *interpreting* national legislation. Furthermore, the Court of Justice has held that the failure of a Member State to implement a directive may give rise to a liability in damages.

The Court of Justice has developed its view on the first issue over a series of cases. In *Von Colson and Kamann v. Land Nordrhein-Westfalen,*[24] it stated that even where a directive does not have direct effects,

"in applying the national law and in particular the provisions of a national law specifically introduced in order to implement Directive 76/207, national courts are required to interpret their national law in the

---

[17] Hartley (1998), p. 204.
[18] Usher (1981) *op. cit.* para. 5-033, n. 12, pp. 18–19.
[19] A. G. Warner in Case 31/74, *Galli* [1975] E.C.R. 47 and Case 74/76, *Iannelli v. Meroni; Steinike and Weinlig v. Germany* [1977] E.C.R. 557, 583; A. G. Reischl in *Ratti,* n. 16, above.
[20] [2001] UKHL 7. The House referred a question to the Court of Justice whether a regulation that referred to a specification concerning Parma ham enshrined in Italian law was sufficiently accessible to give rise to a Community right.
[21] At para. [21].
[22] *Cutler v. Wandsworth Stadium Ltd.* [1949] A.C. 398, 407.
[23] But see A. G. Warner in *Iannelli v. Merioni* [1977] E.C.R. 557 at 583 and A. G. Slynn in Case 8/81, *Becker* [1982] 1 C.M.L.R. 499, 504–5; in *Ratti,* above, A. G. Reischl argued that the term "direct applicability" should only be used in respect of *regulations.*
[24] Case 14/83, [1984] E.C.R. 1891, 1909.

light of the wording and purpose of the directive in order to achieve the result referred to in the third paragraph of Article 189."[25]

This is so whether or not the time for implementing the directive has expired.[26] It was suggested by A. G. Slynn in *Marshall v. Southampton and South West Hampshire Area Health Authority (Teaching)*[27] that this principle did not apply to require a national court to interpret legislation so that it accords with a *later* directive, "unless it is clear that the legislation was adopted with a proposed directive in mind."[28] This was criticised as too restrictive an approach,[29] but it was adopted by the House of Lords in *Duke v. Reliance Systems Ltd.*[30] However, in *Marleasing SA v. La Comercial Internacional de Alimentación SA*[31] the Court of Justice adopted a broader view. Marleasing sought an order in the Spanish courts for the annulment of a company (La Comercial) under provisions of the Spanish Civil Code that contracts lacking cause or whose cause is unlawful have no legal effect. It was alleged that La Comercial had been established as part of a scheme to defraud the creditors of another company. However, a subsequent EC directive[32] set out an exclusive list of the cases in which the nullity of a company may be declared, and lack of (lawful) cause was not on the list. The Court of Justice stated[33] that:

"the Member States' obligations arising from a directive to achieve the result envisaged by the directive and a duty under Article 5 of the Treaty to take all appropriate measures, whether general or particular, to ensure the fulfilment of that obligation, is binding on all the authorities of Member States including, for matters within their jurisdiction, the courts. It follows that, in applying national law, whether the provisions in the decision were adopted before or after the directive, the national court called upon to interpret it is required to do so, as far as possible, in the light of the wording and the purpose of the directive in order to achieve the result pursued by the latter and thereby comply with the third paragraph of Article 189 of the Treaty."

Accordingly, a national court having a case within the scope of the directive was

[25] This passage appears in the Court's reasoning: the operative part of the judgment refers only to legislation adopted for the implementation of the directive. The principle was invoked in the narrower context in Case 262/84, *Beets-Proper v. Van Lanschot Bankiers N.V.* [1986] E.C.R. 782; A. Arnull (1987) 12 E.L. Rev. 229. However, the Court repeated the wider formulation in Case 80/86, *Kolpinghuis Nijmegen B.V.* [1987] E.C.R. 3969; A. Arnull, (1988) 13 E.L. Rev. 42.

[26] *Kolpinghuis*, above.

[27] [1986] Q.B. 401.

[28] *ibid.*, p. 411.

[29] A. Arnull, [1988] P.L. 313, 317.

[30] [1988] A.C. 618, above, criticised by Arnull, *op. cit.* See also *Organon Laboratories Ltd v. D.H.S.S.* [1990] 2 C.M.L.R. 49.

[31] Case C-106/89, [1990] I-E.C.R.4135. See G. de Búrca, (1992) 55 M.L.R. 215; Prechal, (1990) 27 C.M.L. Rev. 451; P. Mead, (1991) 16 E.L. Rev. 490; N. Maltby, (1993) 109 L.Q.R. 301.

[32] First Council Directive 68/151/EEC, March 9, 1968, Art. 11.

[33] At p. 1-4159, para. 8.

"required to interpret its national law in the light of the wording and the purpose of that directive in order to preclude a declaration of nullity of a public limited company on a ground other than those listed in Article 11 of the directive."[34]

While this is a strong statement, its limits should be noted. It must be remembered that it only arises where there is an issue of *interpretation* of national law. It cannot mean that the directive must be applied irrespective of the wording of national law, for that would be to apply the direct effect doctrine between individuals, a step that the court has consistently refused to take, as in the *Marleasing* case itself.[35] This point is confirmed by the inclusion of the words "as far as possible" in paragraph 8 of the judgment.[36] The *Marleasing* approach has, subject to this understanding, been accepted by the English courts.[37]

5–044   Of potentially greater significance was the decision of the Court of Justice in *Andrea Francovich and others v. Italian Republic*.[38] A 1980 EC directive[39] provided, *inter alia*, for specific guarantees of the payment of unpaid wage claims in the event of an employer's insolvency. The deadline for implementation was October 23, 1983; Italy failed to fulfil its implementation obligation.[40] A number of workers unable to recover unpaid wages from their employers brought proceedings against the state, claiming fulfilment of the guarantees by the state or, in the alternative, compensation. The Court of Justice held (1) that the provisions of the directive were not directly effective[41]; but (2) that in order to promote the full effectiveness of Community rules, "it is a principle of Community law that the Member States are obliged to make good loss and damages caused to individuals by breaches of Community law for which they can be held responsible."[42] A further basis for this obligation was Article 5 of the EC Treaty (now Article 10EC), under which Member States are required to take all appropriate measures to ensure fulfilment of their obligations under Community law; among these is the obligation to nullify the unlawful consequences of a breach of Community law. The conditions for state liability depended on the nature of the breach of Community law. In the case of failure to implement directives they were:

(1)   the result prescribed by the directive should entail the grant of rights to individuals;

---

[34]   At p. 1-4160, para. 13.

[35]   At p. 1-4158, para. 6.

[36]   See N. Maltby, (1993) 109 L.Q.R. 301, "It does not oblige the national court to interpret national law ... *contra legem*": A.G. Van Gerven in Case C-271/91, *Marshall v. Southampton and South West Hampshire Area Health Authority (No. 2)* [1993] 4 All E.R. 586, 605.

[37]   *Webb v. EMO Air Cargo Ltd* [1993] 1 W.L.R. 49, below, para. 5-055.

[38]   Cases C-6/90 and C-9/90, [1991] 1-5357. See G. Bebr, (1992) 29 C.M.L.R. 557; P. Duffy, [1992] 17 E.L. Rev. 133; R. Caranta, [1993] C.L.J. 272; P. P. Craig, (1993) 109 L.Q.R. 595; J. Steiner, [1993] 18 E.L. Rev. 3; C. Lewis and S. Moore, [1993] P.L. 151; M. Ross, (1993) 56 M.L.R. 55.

[39]   Dir.80/887/EEC.

[40]   Confirmed in Case 22/87, *Commission v. Italy* [1989] E.C.R. 143.

[41]   They were sufficiently precise and unconditional as regards the persons entitled to and the content of the guarantee, but not as to the identity of the person liable to provide it.

[42]   [1991] E.C.R. 1-5357, 1-5415, para. 37.

(2) it should be possible to identify the content of those rights on the basis of the provisions of the directive;

(3) a causal link must exist between the breach of the state's obligation and the loss and damage suffered by the injured parties.

These conditions gave rise to "a right on the part of individuals to obtain reparation, a right founded directly on Community law."[43] It was on the basis of the rules of national law on liability that the state was to make a reparation and for national law to designate the competent courts and procedures, although the substantive and procedural conditions must not be less favourable than for similar domestic claims. Applying these principles, the national court was required to uphold the rights of the employee to obtain reparation for the state's failure to implement the directive, the state being obliged to make good the loss and damage.

The parameters of the *Francovich* doctrine were explored in the joined cases of *Brasserie du Pêcheur SA v. Federal Republic of Germany* and *R. v. Secretary of State for Transport ex p. Factortame Ltd and others (Factortame III)*.[44] In Brassierie du Pêcheur, a French company claimed compensation for damage caused by German laws that prohibited marketing under the designation "bier" (beer) beers lawfully manufactured by different methods in other Member States and that prohibited the import of beers containing additives. These laws were held to be incompatible with Article 30 of the EC Treaty (now, after amendment, Article 28EC). In *Factortame III* Spanish fishermen claimed compensation in respect of losses caused by Part II of the Merchant Shipping Act 1988.[45] Various questions were referred to the Court of Justice by the respective national courts.

Among the points made by the Court of Justice were:

(1) that the *Francovich* doctrine is applicable where the national legislature is responsible for the breach;[46]

(2) that where the legislature was acting is a field in which it had wide discretion to make legislative choices, individuals suffering loss or injury thereby are entitled to reparation where

   (i) the Community law rule breached is intended to confer rights upon them;

   (ii) the breach is sufficiently serious; and

   (iii) there is a direct causal link between the breach and the damage suffered;[47]

(3) that, subject to this, the state must make good the consequences of the

---

[43] p. 5415, paras.38–41.

[44] Cases C-46/93 and C-48/93, [1996] E.C.R. I-1029. See W. Van Gerven, (1996) 45 I.C.L.Q. 507; C. Harlow, (1996) 2 E.L.J. 1999; Downes, (1997) 17 L.S. 286; P.P. Craig, (1997) 113 L.Q.R. 67; J. Convery, (1997) 34 C.M.L. Rev. 603; R. Crawfurd Smith in P.P. Craig and G. de Búrca (eds), *The Evolution of EU Law* (1999); J. Steiner, (1998) 4 E.P.L. 69.

[45] Below, para. 5-053.

[46] *i.e.* where there is national legislation inconsistent with directly effective Community law, and not just where there is a failure to implement a directive that is not itself directly effective (as in *Francovich*).

[47] These principles are analogous to those established in respect of the non-contractual liability of Community institutions under Article 215 of the EC Treaty (now Article 288EC).

loss or damage caused by the breach of Community law in accordance
with its national law on liability, although the conditions laid down by
the national law must not be less favourable than those laid down for
similar domestic claims or framed in such a way as to make it
execessively difficult to obtain reparation;[48]

(4) that reparation cannot be made conditional upon fault (intentional or
negligent) on the part of the state organ responsible for the breach,
going beyond that of a sufficiently serious breach of Community law;

(5) that reparation must be commensurate with the loss or damage
sustained and cannot exclude a claim for loss of profits; specific
damages such as exemplary damages must be available if they might be
awarded pursuant to similar claims founded on domestic law;[49] and

(6) the obligation to make good loss or damage cannot be limited to
damage sustained after delivery of a judgment of the court finding the
infringement of Community law.

Applied to the facts of the cases involved here, the laws infringed (Articles
30 and 52 of the EC Treaty (now Article 28 EC and, after amendment,
Article 43 EC) were plainly intended to confer rights on individuals. The test
for whether the breach of Community law was sufficiently serious was
whether the Member State concerned "manifestly and gravely disregarded
the limits on its powers." Relevant factors here included the clarity and
precision of the rule breached; the measure of discretion[50] left by that rule to
the national authorities; whether the infringement and the damage caused
was intentional or involuntary; whether any error of law was excusable or
inexcusable; the fact that the position taken by a Community institution
may have contributed towards the omission; and the adoption or retention
of national measures contrary to Community law. A breach would clearly
be sufficiently serious if it had persisted despite a judgment establishing the
infringement or a clear preliminary ruling or settled case-law on the point.
These matters were for the national courts to determine, although the Court
did indicate that it would be difficult to regard the (*Brasserie du Pêcheur*)
breach of Art. 30 of the EC Treaty by the marketing prohibition as
excusable error given the settled case-law of the Court, and that the
nationality condition in *Factortame* was "direct discrimination manifestly
contrary to Community law."[51] The way was thereby opened for substantial

---

[48] *e.g.* by the conditions required to establish the English tort of misfeasance in a public office.
[49] This may include a claim for interest: Cases C–397/98 and C–410/98, *Metallgesellschaft Ltd,
v. Inland Revenue Commissioners* [2001] All E.R. (EC) 496.
[50] Under Community, not national, law: Case C–424/97, *Haim v. KVN* [2000] E.C.R. I–5123.
[51] *cf.* Case C-392/93, *R. v. H.M. Treasury, ex p. British Telecommunications plc* [1996] E.C.R. I-
1631, where the Court held that the U.K. was not to be held liable damages where it
incorrectly implemented a directive, given that the provision in question was imprecisely
worded, and the U.K. had acted in good faith and adopted an interpretation that the
provision was reasonably capable of bearing; this was not, accordingly, a "sufficiently
serious breach of Community law" of the kind contemplated by *Basserie du Pêcheur and
Factortame*. Subsequent cases include Cases C-5/94, *R. v. Ministry of Agriculture, ex p.
Hedley Lomas* [1996] E.C.R. 2553 (concerning a ban on the export to Spain of animals for
slaughter) and Cases C-178, 179, 188–190/94, *Dillenkofer v. Germany* [1996] E.C.R. 1-4845
(failure to implement directive by the deadline), where the Court indicated that there should
be liability; Case C-283/94, *Denkavit Internationaal BV v. Bundesamt für Finanzen* [1996]

awards of damages in these cases.[52] Accordingly, there is now a general principle of state liability for loss and damage caused to individuals as a result of breaches of Community law for which the State can be held responsible.[53] In subsequent cases the Court has held that it has all the necessary information to be able to assess whether the facts must be held to constitute a sufficiently serious breach of Community law.[54] Provided that the Community law rights of individuals are effectively protected, it is sufficient that reparation is provided by the responsible public law body; Community law neither requires the Member State to be liable as well nor precludes both being held liable.[55]

(e) Treaty provisions

The main treaties concerning the Communities are: **5–045**

(1) the Treaty establishing the European Coal and Steel Community (Paris, 1951);

(2) the Treaties establishing the European Economic Community and the European Atomic Energy Community (Rome, 1957);

(3) the Treaty establishing a Single Council and a Single Commission of the European Communities (Brussels 1965; the "Merger Treaty");

(4) the Treaties amending certain Budgetary Provisions of the Treaties (Luxembourg, 1970 and Brussels, 1975);

(5) the Accession Treaties (Brussels, 1972: Denmark, Ireland, Norway,[56] and the United Kingdom (with effect from January 1, 1973); Athens, 1979: Greece (with effect from January 1, 1981); Madrid and Lisbon, 1985: Spain and Portugal (with effect from January 1, 1986); Corfu, 1994: Norway,[57] Austria, Finland and Sweden (with effect from January 1, 1995);

E.C.R. I.-5063 (breach not sufficiently serious in absence of relevant case law of the Court); and Case C-66-95, *R. v. Secretary of State for Social Security, ex p. Sutton* [1997] E.C.R. I-2163, where no opinion was expressed.

[52] See *R. v. Secretary of State for Transport, ex p. Factortame (No. 5)* [2001] 1 A.C. 524 (where the House of Lords held that the U.K.'s breach had indeed been "sufficiently serious" to give rise to a claim for compensatory damages (a claim for exemplary damages was not pursued before the House); the fact that the government had acted on legal advice was not conclusive in its favour and it had in any event chosen to ignore clear contrary advice from the Commission); *R. v. Secretary of State for Transport, ex p. Factortame (No. 7)* [2001] 1 W.L.R. 942 (claim amounts to an action for breach of statutory duty; damages for distress not recoverable); and *Brasserie du Pêcheur* [1997] 1 C.M.L.R. 971.

[53] See the summary in Case C–127/95, *Norbrook Laboratories Ltd, v. Ministry of Agriculture, Fisheries and Food* [1998] E.C.R. 1–1531 paras 105–112. The three conditions (rule of law infringed must have been intended to confer rights on individuals; sufficiently serious breach; direct causal link) apply equally in cases involving non-implementation (*e.g. Francovich*) and inconsistent national legislation or administrative action (*e.g. Factortame*).

[54] *e.g.* Case C–118/00, *Larsy v. INASTI* [2000] E.C.R. I–5063.

[55] Case C–302/97, *Konle v. Austria* [1999] E.C.R. I–3099, paras 62–64; Case C–424/97, *Haim v. KVN* [2000] E.C.R. 1–5123, paras 25–34.

[56] Norway subsequently did not ratify the Treaty.

[57] Norway again failed to ratify the Treaty.

(6)   the Treaty providing for the withdrawal of Greenland[58] (Brussels, 1984 (with effect from February 1, 1985));

(7)   the Single European Act (Luxembourg and The Hague, 1986 (with effect from July 1, 1987));

(8)   The Treaty on European Union (Maastricht, 1992) (with effect from November 1, 1993);

(9)   the Agreement on the European Economic Area (Oporto, 1992; Brussels, 1993);

(10) the Treaty of Amsterdam (signed in 1997, in effect from May 1, 1999)

(11) the Treaty of Nice amending the Treaty on European Union, the Treaties establishing the European Communities and certain related acts (signed in 2000, not yet in effect).

Several of the treaties have extensive Annexes and Protocols. The treaties are published by the EC and HMSO.[59] and in various unofficial collections. There is also a series of treaties entered by the Community with non-Member States.

(f) Regulations, Directives and Decisions

5–046   Regulations are the most important form of Community secondary legislation. Under Article 189 of the EC Treaty (now Article 249EC) they are directly applicable without any act of implementation by Member States. Indeed, such acts of implementation are normally prohibited, in case they have the effect of altering the scope of the regulation in question. Member States may not, for example, enact measures which purport to interpret provisions contained in a regulation[60]; such interpretations might vary from state to state, and the regulation would no longer be uniform in application. This prohibition also ensures that provision of a regulation can clearly be perceived to be of Community origin and so subject to the judicial remedies available under Community law, and avoids any ambiguity as to the date of entry into force.[61] Domestic legislation may, however, make supplementary provision, for example by imposing a sanction for breach of a regulation[62] or by prescribing a limitation period for claims based on Community law.[63] Exceptionally, a regulation may itself expressly require Member States to introduce implementing measures.[64]

---

[58] Greenland had not been a Member State, but had been part of the Community through its association with Denmark: see F. Weiss, (1985) 10 E.L. Rev. 173.

[59] *e.g.* Cm. 455, 1988 (Consolidated text of EC Treaties); Cm. 2484, 1994 (TEU).

[60] Case 40/69, *Hauptzollamt Hamburg v. Bollman* [1970] E.C.R. 69; classification of products (turkey rumps) under an agricultural regulation; Case 34/73, *Variola v. Italian Minister of Finance* [1973] E.C.R. 981.

[61] Usher (1981), p. 17. Member States may not adopt "any measure which would conceal the Community nature and effects of any legal provision from the persons to whom it applies": Case 50/76, *Amsterdam Bulb v. Produktschap Voor Siergewassen* [1977] E.C.R. 137, 151.

[62] *Amsterdam Bulb* case, above.

[63] Case 33/76, *Rewe v. Landwirtschaftkammer Saarland* [1976] E.C.R. 1989. The periods must be reasonable and non-discriminatory.

[64] See Hartley (1998), pp. 196–199; Case 128/78, *Commission v. United Kingdom* [1979] E.C.R. 419.

Directives are used where the approximation or harmonisation of national laws is sought rather than strict uniformity. They may only be addressed to Member States. Choice of method is left to the Member States, although a time limit for implementation is commonly set.

Decisions may be addressed to Member States, to corporations or to individuals. The European Court has held that:

"a decision must appear as an act originating from the competent organisation intended to produce judicial effects, constituting the ultimate end of the internal procedure of this organisation and according to which such organisation makes its final ruling in a form allowing its nature to be identified.[65]

(g) Preparation of Community secondary legislation[66]

The treaties do not lay down a uniform legislative process to be adopted in all cases. Community legislation may occasionally be made by the Commission, but is usually made by the Council or (in accordance with a new procedure introduced by the Maastricht Treaty) by the Parliament and Council acting jointly. Under the basic "consultative procedure" the Commission first formulates a proposal after consulting national officials, experts and representatives of interest groups (the *avant-projet* stage). The draft proposal is then sent to the Council; Member States may at this stage refer it to their national parliaments. A copy is sent to the European Parliament so that a preliminary unofficial study can be commenced hi committee. The Council may, and in some cases must[67] consult the European Parliament and the European Economic and Social Committee (a consultative body representing the various categories of economic and social activity, including industry, workers and consumers). The European Parliament debates the report of its committee in plenary session. The opinions of the Parliament and the ESC are transmitted to the Council. The Council may consider the proposal in three stages: (1) in a Working Group of national experts convened by the Council secretariat; (2) in the Committee of Permanent Representatives (COREPER); and (3) in the Council itself. The Commission proposal can be amended only if the Council is unanimous.[68] Reconsultation with the Parliament is necessary

5-047

---

[65] Case 54/65, *Compagnie des Forges de Châtillon Commentry et Neuves Maison v. High Authority* [1966] C.M.L.R. 525, 538.

[66] T. St. J. N. Bates, "The Drafting of European Community Legislation" [1983] Stat.L.R. 24; Hartley (1998), pp. 37–44; Weatherill and Beaumont (1999), pp. 58–67, 117–143. Chap. 5; A. Dashwood (1994) 19 E.L.Rev. 343 S. Weatherill, *Law and Integration in the European Union* (1995), Chap. 3.

[67] A requirement to consult will be regarded as an essential procedural requirement: Case 138/79, *Roquette v. Council* [1980] E.C.R. 3333; Case 139/79, *Maizena v. Council* [1980] E.C.R. 3393: see T. C. Hartley, (1981) 6 E.L. Rev. 181. It is not sufficient that the opinion of the European Parliament is sought; an opinion must be received, unless the need for the legislation is urgent and the Parliament fails to respond to a request for an urgent opinion: Case C-65/93, *European Parliament v. Council* [1995] E.C.R. I-643. A preliminary as opposed to definitive decision may be taken by the Council before obtaining the Parliament's opinion: Case 417/93, *European Parliament v. Council* [1995] E.C.R. I–1185; See S. Boyson, (1996) 21 E.L.Rev. 145.

[68] Art 250EC.

where the text finally adopted differs in essence from that on which it has been consulted, except where the amendments essentially correspond to its wishes.[69]

The Single European Act[70] introduced a new "co-operation procedure"[71] which was applicable to some of the instances in which the EC Treaty required the Parliament to be consulted.[72] This procedure commences at the final stage of the standard legislative process. Instead of adopting the proposal forthwith, the Council adopts a "common position", acting by a qualified majority.[73] The proposal is sent to the Parliament for a second time (the "second reading"), and the Parliament (acting within three months[74]) can approve or reject it, or propose amendments.[75] If the proposal is approved, or no action is taken within three months,[76] the act will be adopted by the Council. If it is rejected, the Council (acting within three months[77]) can only adopt it by unanimity. Proposed amendments are considered by the Commission (acting within one month) and then returned to the Council. If they are approved by the Commission, the Council (acting within three months[78]) can adopt them by a qualified majority. Amendments not approved by the Commission, and any Council amendments, can only be adopted by unanimity. These arrangements constituted "a real, though small," increase in the power of the Parliament, in so far as it could, in alliance with a Member State, block a measure; as regards amendments, the arrangement in essence enshrined existing practice in legal form.[79]

The Maastricht Treaty[80] introduced a further legislative procedure, the "co-decision" or "conciliation and veto" procedure. The role of the Parliament is here enhanced still further, the procedure providing for the adoption of legislation by the Parliament and Council jointly. It applies to specified legislative powers, including some formerly subject to the co-

---

[69]   Case C-65/90 *European Parliament v. Council* [1992] E.C.R. I-4593 (*Cabotage-I*); Cases C-388/92, *European Parliament v. Council* [1994] E.C.R. I-2067 (*Cabotage-II*), Case C-280/93, *Germany v. Commission* [1994] E.C.R. I-4973.

[70]   Arts.6 and 7. See J. Fitzmaurice, (1988) 26 J. of Common Market Studies 389.

[71]   Substituted Art. 149(2) (subsequently Art. 189c) of the EC Treaty. See R. Bieber, (1988) 25 C.M.L. Rev. 711. The procedure is now governed by Art. 252 EC.

[72]   *e.g.* in respect of rules designed to prohibit discrimination on the ground of nationality (Art. 6 of the EC Treaty); common rules applicable to international transport, the operation of transport services by non-resident carriers and measures to improve transport safety (Art.75 of the EC Treaty, as amended by Art.6(16)/TEU); sea and air transport (Art. 84 of the EC Treaty); health and safety of workers (Art. 118 of the EC Treaty, as amended by Art.G(33)/TEU): Community environmental policy (Art.130s EC of the Treaty inserted by Art.G(38)/TEU). Following the Treaty of Amsterdam, these were all brought within the scope of the co-decision procedure (below): see now Articles 12EC (discrimination); 71EC (transport); 80EC (sea and air transport); 137EC (health and safety); 175EC (environmental policy).

[73]   No time limit is specified for this, unlike for the later stages.

[74]   The period may be extended by up to one month, by common accord between the Council and the Parliament: Art. 252(g) EC.

[75]   The Parliament can only reject or propose amendments by an absolute majority of its members: Art. 252(c)EC.

[76]   See n. 69 above.

[77]   *ibid.*

[78]   *ibid.*

[79]   Hartley (1998), p. 40. The evidence "shows that a significant proportion of Parliament's amendments are adopted by the Commission and ultimately by the Council: Weatherill and Beaumont (1999), p. 131. Rejection of the common position is a weapon that has been "used sparingly"; four were rejected by 1992, two in 1994 and one in 1996: *ibid.*, p. 132.

[80]   Art.G(61)/TEU.

operation procedure.[81] It was modified by the Treaty of Amsterdam. Under the co-decision procedure the Commission submits a proposal to the Parliament and the Council. The Council, by a qualified majority and after obtaining the Parliament's opinion, either (1) if it approves all of Parliament's amendments, may adopt the proposed act thus amended; or (2) if Parliament does not propose any amendments, may adopt the proposed act; or (3), otherwise, must adopt a common position. This common position is communicated to the Parliament, together with a full statement of reasons; the Commisson must also inform the Parliament fully of its position.

The Parliament (acting within three months[82]) can approve the common position, propose amendments or reject it.[83] If the common position is approved, or no action is taken within three months, the act is deemed to have been adopted. If the common position is rejected (by an absolute majority of its members) the proposed act is deemed not to have been adopted. Where amendments are proposed the amended text is sent to the Council and the Commission, and the Commission is to deliver an opinion on them. If the Commission's opinion is favourable, the Council may approve all Parliament's amendments by a qualified majority; if it is unfavourable, they may be approved unanimously; if the Council does not approve all the amendments a Conciliation Committee must within six weeks be convened by the President of the Council, in agreement with the President of the Parliament.

The Conciliation Committee comprises the members of the Council or **5–048** their representatives and an equal number of representatives of the Parliament. Their task is to reach agreement on a joint text, by a qualified majority on the Council side[84] and a majority on the Parliament side. The Commission is to take part in the proceedings and must take all the necessary initiatives with a view to reconciling the positions of Parliament and Council.[85] In fulfilling their task, the Conciliation Committee must address the common position on the basis of the amendments proposed by the Parliament. If within six weeks[86] of being convened, the Committee approves a joint text, the Parliament, acting by an absolute majority of the votes cast, and the Council, acting by a qualified majority,[87] have a further six weeks[88] in which to adopt the proposal; if either of the two fails to do so,

---

[81] e.g. legislation in respect of free movement of workers (Art. 40EC); freedom of establishment (Art.44 EC); exceptions to the right of establishment on grounds of public policy, public security or public health (Art. 46EC); mutual recognition of diplomas etc. (Art.47(1)EC): establishment of self-employed persons (Art.47(2)EC); freedom of services (Art.55 EC); consumer protection (Art. 153EC); and general environmental action programmes (Art. 175(3)EC).

[82] The period can be extended by up to one month by common accord between the Council and the Parliament: Art.251(7)EC.

[83] The proposal of amendments and rejection (but not approval) must be by an absolute majority of the Parliament's members.

[84] The normal requirement that the Council must be unanimous in amending a Commission proposal does not apply: Art. 250(1)EC.

[85] The Commission may alter its proposal at any time during the procedure, as long as the Council has not acted: Art. 250(2) EC.

[86] The period can be extended by a maximum of two weeks by common accord of the Parliament and the Council: Art. 251(7)EC.

[87] See n. 84 above.

[88] See n. 86 above.

it is deemed not to have been adopted. If the Committee does not approve a joint text, the proposal is also deemed not to have been adopted.

The significance of this procedure is that the Parliament, acting by an absolute majority, has the power of veto. The initial view of the Commission was that the procedure had worked well.[89]

The other major legislative procedure, the "assent procedure" was extended to legislation outside the budgetary process by the Maastricht Treaty.[90] Here, the assent of the Parliament is required, usually to a proposal adopted unanimously by the Council.[91] The Commission notes that this procedure is "ill-adapted to the legislative field" as Parliament may only accept or reject the instrument as laid before it.[92]

These are the main procedures. Overall, the position is excessively complex, the EC Treaty alone prior to the Treaty of Amsterdam having 22 identifiable decision-making procedures, although not all are strictly legislative.[93] The Commission identified three major weaknesses: the continued divergence between legislative procedures and the budget procedure; the complexity of the system; and the lack of logic in the choice of the various procedures and the different fields of activity where they apply. The legislative processes "need to be radically simplified, with reference to the concept of a hierarchy of acts."[94] The Treaty of Amsterdam introduced some simplification, with, for example, the virtual abandonment of use of the co-operation procedure and the expansion of the reach of the co-decision procedure.

In 1992, the report of a group appointed by the Commission under the Chairmanship of a former Commissioner, Peter Sutherland, made (inter alia) a number of recommendations to improve the quality of EC legislation.[95] The Commission's response was favourable.[96] Recommendations accepted included the adoption of more restrictive criteria for legislative intervention (the "subsidiarity" principle); better co-ordination between different departments and committees of the Commission; earlier and wider consultation; greater use of consolidated texts; consideration of the use of (directly applicable) regulations rather than directives so that a single text (albeit in different languages) is applicable throughout the Member States; and regular monitoring of the effectiveness of legislation.

---

[89] *Commission Report for the Reflection Group* (1995), p. 29. By then, two measures had failed to progress: one, on voice telephony, was rejected by the Parliament following a failure to agree at the conciliation stage, because of its provisions on implementing procedures; the other, on biotechnology, was rejected by the Parliament notwithstanding agreement at the conciliation stage.

[90] This applies, for example, to the conferral of specific tasks on the European Central Bank in stage three of economic and monetary union (Art. 105(6)EC); and proposals on a uniform procedure for elections to the Parliament (Art.190(4)EC).

[91] The assent of the Parliament is also required to other, non-legislative proposals, such as accession treaties and international agreements that (*inter alia*) have important budgetary implications or entail amendment of an act adopted under Art. 251EC Art. 300(3)EC.

[92] *Commission Report for the Reflection Group* (1995), p. 30.

[93] *Commission Report for the Reflection Group* (1995), Annex 8 (pp. 80–83).

[94] *ibid.*, pp. 31–33.

[95] *The Internal Market After 1992: Meeting the Challenge: Report to the EEC Commission by the High Level Group on the Operation of Internal Market* (1992). See R. Wainwright, (1994) 15 Stat.L.R.98.

[96] Follow-up to the Sutherland Report (SEC(92)2277 of December 2, 1992).

The subsidiarity principle is now enshrined in Article 5EC,[97] which provides:

"The Community shall act within the limits of the powers conferred upon it by this Treaty and of the objectives assigned to it therein.

In areas which do not fall within its exclusive competence, the Community shall take action, in accordance with the principle of subsidarity, only if and in so far as the objectives of the proposed action cannot be sufficiently achieved by the Member States and can therefore, by reason of the scale or effects of the proposed action, be better achieved by the Community.

Any action by the Community shall not go beyond what is necessary to achieve the objectives of this Treaty."

The principle is now applied both in the formulation of the Commission's legislative programme and in the review of the existing legislative provisions; it has led to the withdrawal of some proposals and the amendment of others.[98] Each institution must ensure compliance with the principle in exercising its own powers and reasons must be given in proposing Community legislation that demonstrate compliance. The form of Community action should be as simple as possible; other things being equal, directives should be preferred to regulations and framework directives to detailed measures. Community measures should leave as much scope for national decision as possible, consistent with securing the aim of the measure and observing Treaty requirements. The Commission must consult widely before proposing legislation, except in particular case of urgency or confidentiality.[99] The principle is useful in providing a framework for debates as to the relative effectiveness of different forms of legislation in particular contexts; it is, however, unlikely to provide a basis for direct legal challenge to the substance of legislation, as distinct from the sufficiency of the reasons given for proposing it.[1]

In order to improve transparency in the institution's business, the Commission now publishes its legislative programme on an annual basis, issues more Green and White Papers, and has promoted measures to recast, simplify and consolidate Community legislation.[2] The Parliament, Council and Commission have reached an Interinstitutional Agreement on common

---

[97] Originally inserted as Article 36 of the EC Treaty by Art.G(5)/TEU.

[98] See *Commission Report for the Reflection Group* (1995), pp. 37–38; Weatherill and Beaumont (1999), pp. 27–32; the 1993 Inter-Institutional Agreement on Procedures for Implementing the Principle of Subsidiarity reproduced in Westlake (1994), pp. 145–146; the Protocol on the Application of the Principles of Subsidiarity and Proportionality annexed to the EC Treaty by the Treaty of Amsterdam (1999), reproduced in N. Foster, *Blackstone's EC Legislation 2001–2002* (12th edn, 2001), pp. 146–148.

[99] Protocol on the application of the principles of subsidiarity and proportionality (1999). The Commission makes an annual report to the Council under the title *Better Lawmaking* on the application of these principles.

[1] Weatherill and Beaumont (1999), pp. 27–32.

[2] *Commission Report for the Reflection Group* (1995), pp. 39–40. The Parliament, Council and Commission have established accelerated procedures for consolidation proposals: O.J. C43, February 2, 1995, pp. 41–43.

guidelines for the quality of drafting of Community Legislation[3] which states that "Community legislative acts shall be drafted clearly, simply and precisely." Provisions "should be concise" and "overly long articles and sentences, unnecessarily convoluted wording and excessive use of abbreviations should be avoided." Amendments to existing legislation should be textual. Under this agreement, the institutions' legal services have produced a joint practical guide for persons involved in the drafting of legislation.[4]

(h) Publication of Community secondary legislation

5–049   Regulations, directives and decisions are published in the *Official Journal of the European Communities* ("L Series").[5] An English edition has been published from January 1973; English texts of pre-1972 secondary legislation were published in Special Editions of the *Official Journal* covering the pre-accession period, and by HMSO in a 42-volume work entitled *Secondary Legislation of the European Communities: Subject Edition* (1973). HMSO supplemented this series with an annual Subject List and Table of Effects up to the end of 1979. Users must now rely on the monthly and annual indices and lists published as supplements to the *Official Journal*. The European Community also publishes periodically a *Directory of Community Legislation In Force*.[6]

(i) Arrangement and citation of Community secondary legislation

5–050   The heading of a regulation indicates the authority by which it is made, the Treaty under which it is made and its number.[7] The date on which it is made is given, followed by an indication of the subject matter, (*e.g.* "Council Regulation (EEC) No. 2194/81 of July 27, 1981 laying down the general rules for the system of production aid for dried figs and dried grapes.")

A *preamble* including an explanation of the purposes of the regulation precedes its main provisions. These comprise numbered *articles*, which may be subdivided into *paragraphs*, and grouped under *Titles*. An *annex* may be attached. Directives and decisions are similar to regulations in form.[8] There is a Manual of Precedents.[9]

---

[3]   The Agreement was made on December 22, 1998, and published in 1999, O.J.C73, March 17, 1999.
[4]   Commission Report, *Better Lawmaking 2000*, p. 12.
[5]   Since 1968 the *Official Journal* has appeared in two series, one publishing secondary legislation (the "L Series") and the other giving general information, including drafts of proposed legislation the "C series"). It is to be renamed the Official Journal of the European Union.
[6]   Volume I: Analytical Register; Volume II: Chronological Index; Alphabetical Index. See also Sweet & Maxwell's *Encyclopedia of European Union Law* and the C.C.H. *Common Market Law Reporter*.
[7]   From 1958 to 1967 there were separate series of regulations for the EEC and Euratom; from 1968 there has been a single series. Regulations were numbered in a continuous sequence until 1963; from that time a new sequence has been started each calendar year.
[8]   From 1968 they have been numbered in a single series with recommendations, opinions and financial regulations.
[9]   *Manual of Precedents drawn up by the Legal/Linguistic Experts of the Council of the European Communities* (2nd ed., 1983).

The correct forms of citation have changed several times.[10] At present they are as follows: Council Regulation (EC) No. 2580/200; Directive 2001/105/EC of the European Parliament and of the Council; Council Decision 2001/824/EC, Euratom.

4. SUPREMACY OF COMMUNITY LAW[11]

It is well established in terms of Community law that on a matter regulated by binding Community law, that law takes precedence over the municipal law of a Member State.[12] It is immaterial whether the municipal law is enacted before or after the relevant Community law,[13] and whether it forms part of that state's fundamental or constitutional law.[14] Thus in the *Van Gend en Loos* case[15] the Court of Justice spoke of the creation of a "new legal order ... for the benefit of which the states have limited their sovereign rights."

Costa v. ENEL[16] concerned the nationalisation of Italian electricity undertakings. Costa, a shareholder in one of the undertakings (Edison Volta) refused to pay an invoice for electricity sent by ENEL, and claimed that the nationalisation was contrary to prior Community law (various articles of the EEC Treaty). The European Court, on a reference from the Italian magistrate (the Guidice Conciliatore of Milan), dealt firmly with the submission of the Italian government that a national court was obliged to apply the domestic law in preference to Community law[17]:

"By creating a Community of unlimited duration, having its own institutions, its own personality, its own legal capacity and capacity of representation on the international plane and, more particularly, real powers stemming from a limitation of sovereignty or a transfer of powers from the States to the Community, the Member States have limited their sovereign rights, albeit within limited fields, and have thus created a body of law which binds both their nationals and themselves.

The integration into the laws of each Member State of provisions which derive from the Community, and more generally, the terms and the spirit of the Treaty, make it impossible for the States, as a corollary, to accord precedence to a unilateral and subsequent measure over a legal system accepted by them on a basis of reciprocity. Such a measure

---

[10] *Secondary legislation of the European Communities: Subject Edition* (HMSO, 1973) Vol. 42, pp. vii–viii.

[11] See Hartley (1998), Chaps.7, 8; Weatherill and Beaumont (1999), Chap. 12; C. Munro, *Studies in Constitutional Law* (2nd edn); J. W. Bridge, "Abstract Law and Political Reality in the Post-European-Accession British Constitution" [1987] Denning L.J. 23.

[12] Case 26/62, *Van Gend en Loos v. Nederlandse Administrate der Belastingen* [1963] E.C.R. 1.

[13] Case 6/64, *Costa v. ENEL* [1964] E.C.R. 585.

[14] Case 11/70, *Internationale Handelsgesellschaft v. Einfuhr-und Vorratsstelle für Getreide* [1970] E.C.R. 1125; Case 106/77, *Amministrazione delle Finanze dello Stato v. Simmenthal* [1978] E.C.R. 629.

[15] Above, para. 5-040.

[16] Ente Nazionale Energia Elettrica (National Electricity Board), formerly the Edison Volta undertaking.

[17] pp. 593–594.

cannot therefore be inconsistent with that legal system. The executive force of Community law cannot vary from one State to another in deference to subsequent domestic laws, without jeopardizing the attainment of the objectives of the Treaty set out in Article 5(2)[18] and giving rise to the discrimination prohibited by Article 7[19] . . .

The precedence of Community law is confirmed by Article 189[20], whereby a regulation 'shall be binding' and 'directly applicable in all Member States.' This provision, which is subject to no reservation, would be quite meaningless if a State could unilaterally nullify its effects by means of a legislative measure which could prevail over Community law.

It follows from all these observations that the law stemming from the Treaty, an independent source of law, could not, because of its special and original nature, be overridden by domestic legal provisions, however framed, without being deprived of its character as Community law and without the legal basis of the Community itself being called into question.

The transfer by the States from their domestic legal system to the Community legal system of the rights and obligations arising under the Treaty carries with it a permanent limitation of their sovereign rights, against which a subsequent unilateral act incompatible with the concept of the Community cannot prevail. Consequently Article 177[21] is to be applied regardless of any domestic law, whenever questions relating to the interpretation of the Treaty arise."

In the *Simmenthal* case[22] an Italian judge was faced with a conflict between a Council regulation and Italian laws, some of which were enacted after the regulation. Under Italian law domestic legislation contrary to Community law was unconstitutional. However, only the Constitutional Court had jurisdiction to make such a ruling; the ordinary courts could not. The Court of Justice, on a reference by the judge, held that:

"every national court must in a case within its jurisdiction apply Community law in its entirety and protect rights which the latter confers on individuals and must accordingly set aside any provision of national law which may conflict with it, whether prior of subsequent to the Community rule. . . . [I]t is not necessary for the court to request for or await the prior setting aside of such provisions by legislative or other constitutional means."[23]

The position from the point of view of Community law is thus clear; we now consider it from the standpoint of United Kingdom law. The key provisions of the European Communities Act 1972 are contained in sections 2 and 3:

---

[18] Now Article 10(2)EC.
[19] Repealed by the Treaty of Amsterdam.
[20] Now Article 249EC.
[21] Now Article 234EC.
[22] [1978] E.C.R. 629.
[23] *ibid.* pp. 644, 645–646.

"2.—

(1) All such rights, powers, liabilities, obligations and restrictions from time to time created or arising by or under the Treaties, and all such remedies and procedures from time to time provided for by or under the Treaties, as in accordance with the Treaties are without further enactment to be given legal effect or used in the United Kingdom shall be recognised and available in law, and be enforced, allowed and followed accordingly; and the expression "enforceable Community right' and similar expressions shall be read as referring to one to which this subsection applies.

(2) Subject to Schedule 2 to this Act, at any time after its passing Her Majesty may by Order in Council, and any designated Minister or department may by regulations, make provision—

    (a) for the purpose of implementing any Community obligation of the United Kingdom, or enabling any such obligation to be implemented, or of enabling any rights enjoyed or to be enjoyed by the United Kingdom under or by virtue of the Treaties to be exercised; or

    (b) for the purpose of dealing with matters arising out of or related to any such obligation or rights or the coming into force, or the operation from time to time, of subsection (1) above;

and in the exercise of any statutory power or duty, including any power to give directions or to legislate by means of orders, rules, regulations or other subordinate instrument, the person entrusted with the power or duty may have regard to the objects of the Communities and to any such obligation or rights as aforesaid.

In this subsection "designated Minister or department" means such Minister of the Crown or government department as may from time to time be designated by Order in Council in relation to any matter or for any purpose, but subject to such restrictions or conditions (if any) as may be specified by the Order in Council ....

(4) The provision that may be made under subsection (2) above includes, subject to Schedule 2 to this Act, any such provision (of any such extent) as might be made by Act of Parliament, and any enactment passed or to be passed, other than one contained in this Part of this Act, shall be construed and have effect subject to the foregoing provisions of this section; but, except as may be provided by any Act passed after this Act, Schedule 2 shall have effect in connection with the powers conferred by this and the following sections of this Act to make Orders in Council and regulations.

3.—

(1) For the purposes of all legal proceedings any question as to the meaning or effect of any of the Treaties, or as to the validity, meaning or effect of any Community instrument, shall be treated as a question of law (and, if not referred to the European Court, be for determination as such in accordance with the principles laid down by and any relevant [decision of the European Court or any

court attached thereto)].[24]

(2) Judicial notice shall be taken of the Treaties, of the Official Journal of the Communities and of any decision of, or expression of opinion by, the European Court [or any court attached, thereto][25] on any such question as aforesaid; and the Official Journal shall be admissible as evidence of any instrument or other act thereby communicated of any of the Communities or of any Community institution."[26]

5–051   Thus, directly applicable and directly effective Community laws are given effect in the United Kingdom under section 2(1); other matters are to be dealt with by statute, or by statutory instruments under section 2(2); any question as to the meaning or effect of the treaties is to be determined in accordance with Community law of which judicial notice is to be taken (section 3). There is, however, no attempt to entrench the European Communities Act itself against repeal. It is unlikely that a court would accept that the "ultimate political fact"[27] has been redefined so as to deny effect to a statute deliberately enacted by Parliament as at present constituted which conflicts with existing Community law. It is even more unlikely that the courts would decline to recognise the express repeal of the 1972 Act.[28] Where a provision of a United Kingdom statute is followed by an inconsistent provision of Community law that is directly applicable or effective, the latter is given precedence by section 2 of the European Communities Act 1972. The position is less clear where the chronology is reversed and the U.K. statute is enacted after the inconsistent provision of Community law. If both laws were made before the 1972 Act, Community law is again given precedence by section 2. If the United Kingdom law is more recent, there are a number of possible situations and the position appears to be as follows:

(1) The United Kingdom legislation may be unclear, in which case an English court will endeavour to interpret it so as to comply with Community law, given the established presumption that Parliament does not intend the United Kingdom to be in breach of its international obligations (the "interpretation" issue).[29] In *Garland v. British Rail Engineering Ltd*,[30] Lord Diplock said.[31]

"My Lords, even if the obligation to observe the provisions of article

---

[24] Words in square brackets substituted by the European Communities (Amendment) Act 1986, s.2(a).

[25] Words added by *ibid*, s.2(b).

[26] Section 2(3) authorises the necessary expenditure; section 2(5) concerns Northern Ireland; section 2(6) concerns the Channel Islands, the Isle of Man and Gibraltar. Section 3(3)–(5) makes further provision for proof of community instruments.

[27] See above, para. 5-002.

[28] For the contrary argument that there has been a binding transfer of powers see Usher (1981), pp. 30–38; J. D. B. Mitchell, (1967–68) 5 C. M. L. Rev. 112, (1971) *Europarecht* 97, (1979) 56 *International Affairs* 33. A withdrawal from the Community would, however, be negotiated; the arrangement would be enshrined in a treaty which could be construed as a transfer back from the Community of those powers: Usher (1981), p. 38.

[29] See below, paras 5-053–5-055, 6-035, 6-049–6-060.

[30] [1983] 2 A. C. 751.

[31] At p. 771.

119 were an obligation assumed by the United Kingdom under an ordinary international treaty or convention and there were no question of the treaty obligation being directly applicable as part of the law to be applied by the courts in this country without need for any further enactment, it is a principle of construction of United Kingdom statutes, now too well established to call for citation of authority, that the words of a statute passed after the Treaty has been signed and dealing with the subject matter of the international obligation of the United Kingdom, are to be construed, if they are reasonably capable of bearing such a meaning, as intended to carry out the obligation, and not to be inconsistent with it. A fortiori is this the case where the Treaty obligation arises under one of the Community treaties to which section 2 of the European Communities Act 1972 applies."

(2) If the United Kingdom legislation is clear and unambiguously conflicts with prior Community law, an English court will then determine whether that conflict was intended by Parliament. In the case of inadvertent conflict, the Community legislation will be given priority. Where conflict is intentional, the courts will give effect to the United Kingdom legislation, and the United Kingdom will be in breach of its Treaty obligations (the "sovereignty" issue).

There have been several judicial statements, some preceding accession, which support the primacy of subsequent inconsistent Acts of Parliament, without drawing a distinction between inadvertent and intentional conflicts.[32] Both the "interpretation" and "sovereignty" issues were subsequently raised in *Macarthys Ltd v. Smith*[33] A man was paid £60 a week for managing a stockroom. Four and a half months after he left a woman was appointed in his place at £50 a week. She claimed that she was entitled to equal pay under provisions of the Equal Pay Act 1970 that had been inserted by the Sex Discrimination Act 1975. The Court of Appeal majority[34] held that Equal Pay Act provisions were confined to cases where a man and a woman were in the same employment at the same time. The words had to be given their natural and ordinary meaning and were clear; the terms of Article 119 of the EEC Treaty[35] could therefore not be used as an aid to construction. The question whether Article 119 was so confined was referred to the Court of Justice.

Lord Denning took a different view of the proper approach to construction of the English statute and then considered the sovereignty issue[36]:   **5–052**

---

[32] *e.g.* Salmon L.J. in *Blackburn v. Attorney-General* [1971] 1 W.L.R. 1037, 1041. Lord Denning M.R. left the point open; *Felixstowe Dock and Railway Co. v. British Transport Docks Board* [1976] 2 C.M.L.R. 655, per Lord Denning M.R. at pp. 664–665.

[33] [1979] I.C.R. 785, [1981] Q.B. 180; P. Schofield, (1980) 9 I.L.J. 173; T. R. S. Allan, (1983) 3 O.J.L.S. 22. See also *Shields v. E. Coomes (Holdings) Ltd* [1978] 1 W.L.R. 1408.

[34] Lawton and Cumming-Bruce L.JJ., Lord Denning M.R. dissenting on this point.

[35] "Each Member State shall during the first stage ensure and subsequently maintain the application of the principle that men and women should receive equal pay for equal work...." This was amplified by article 1 of a Council directive (Dir.75/117/EEC). Now Article 141 EC: "East Member State shall ensure that the principle of equal pay for male and female workers for equal work or work of equal value is applied."

[36] [1979] I.C.R. 785, at p. 789.

"Under section 2(1) and (4) of the European Communities Act 1972 the principles laid down in the Treaty are 'without further enactment' to be given legal effect in the United Kingdom: and have priority over 'any enactment passed or to be passed' by our Parliament. So we are entitled—and think bound—to look at article 119 of the Treaty because it is directly applicable here: and also any directive which is directly applicable here: see *Van Duyn v. Home Office* [1975] Ch. 358. We should, I think, look to see what those provisions require about equal pay for men and women. Then we should look at our own legislation on the point—giving it, of course, full faith and credit—assuming that it does fully comply with the obligations under the Treaty. In construing our statute, we are entitled to look to the Treaty as an aid to its construction: and even more, not only as an aid but as an overriding force. If on close investigation it should appear that our legislation is deficient—or is inconsistent with Community law—by some oversight of our draftsmen—then it is our bounden duty to give priority to Community law. Such is the result of section 2(1) and (4) of the European Communities Act 1972.

I pause here, however, to make one observation on a constitutional point. Thus far I have assumed that our Parliament, whenever it passes legislation, intends to fulfil its obligations under the Treaty. If the time should come when our Parliament deliberately passes an Act—with the intention of repudiating the Treaty or any provision in it—or intentionally of acting inconsistently with it—and says so in express terms—then I should have thought that it would be the duty of our courts to follow the statute of our Parliament. I do not however envisage any such situation. As I said in *Blackburn v. Attorney-General* [1971] 1 W.L.R 1037, 1040: "But, if Parliament should do so, then I say we will consider that event when it happens.' Unless there is such an intentional and express repudiation of the Treaty, it is our duty to give priority to the Treaty."

On the sovereignty issue Lawton LJ. said[37]:

"I can see nothing in this case which infringes the sovereignty of Parliament. If I thought there were, I should not presume to take any judicial step which it would be more appropriate for the House of Lords, as part of Parliament, to take. Parliament by its own Act in the exercise of its sovereign powers has enacted that European Community law shall 'be enforced, allowed and followed' in the United Kingdom of Great Britain and Northern Ireland: see section 2(1) of the European Communities Act 1972, and that 'any enactment passed or to be passed ... shall be construed and have effect subject to' section 2: see section 2(4) of that Act. Parliament's recognition of European Community law and of the jurisdiction of the European Court of Justice by one enactment can be withdrawn by another. There is nothing in the Equal Pay Act 1970, as amended, to indicate that Parliament intended to amend the European Communities Act 1972, or to limit its application."

[37]   At p. 796.

Cumming-Bruce L.J. indicated that if

"the terms of the Treaty are adjudged in Luxembourg to be inconsistent with the provisions of the Equal Pay Act 1970, European law will prevail over that municipal legislation. But such a judgment in Luxembourg cannot affect the meaning of the English statute."[38]

The Court of Justice subsequently held that Article 119 was not restricted to cases of contemporaneous employment,[39] and the plaintiff's claim was duly conceded in the English proceedings. The matter came before the Court of Appeal again on the question of costs.[40] Lord Denning M.R. said[41]:

"the provisions of Article 119 of the EEC Treaty take priority over anything in our English statute on equal pay which is inconsistent with Article 119. That priority is given by our own law. It is given by the European Communities Act 1972 itself. Community law is now part of our law; and, whenever there is any inconsistency, Community law has priority. It is not supplanting English law. It is part of our law which overrides any other part which is inconsistent with it."

The other members of the court agreed that the Community legislation prevailed.[42] Cumming Bruce L.J. emphasised that his comment at the earlier stage[43] had to be read in the context of his view (shared by Lawton L.J.) that the English statute was unambiguous. Had he been of the view that it was ambiguous, it would have been "appropriate to look at Article 119 in order to assist in resolving the ambiguity."[44]

Accordingly, it appears that both Lord Denning M.R. and Lawton L.J. distinguish between cases of inadvertent and intentional conflict: it would seem that there is no room in the case of inadvertent conflict for the application of an "implied repeal rule" as there is between two inconsistent statutes, and in the case of intentional conflicts the English statute will prevail. Furthermore, even in the case of intentional conflicts it may be that effect would only be given to the English statute if it amended or repealed the European Communities Act 1972: it would not be sufficient merely that the substantive law prescribed by statute was different from that prescribed by Community law. Lawton L.J., but not Lord Denning M.R., appears to support this view.[45] The view that the European Communities Act 1972, as a

---

[38] At p. 798.

[39] Case 129/79, [1981] Q.B. 180, E.C.J.

[40] [1981] Q.B. 199, C.A. *Cf. Re an Absence in Ireland* [1977] 1 C.M.L.R. 5, where a national insurance commissioner allowed a claimant's appeal on two grounds, one of which involved the application of Council Regulation (EEC) No. 1408/71 in preference to the provisions of the Social Security Act 1975. See also *Re Medical Expenses Incurred in France* [1977] 2 C.M.L.R. 317.

[41] At p. 200.

[42] Professor Hood Phillips suggested that even in cases of inadvertent conflict, an English court should give effect to a subsequent, unambiguous United Kingdom Act of Parliament: (1980) 96 L.Q.R. 31; *cf.* O. Hood Phillips and P. Jackson, *O. Hood Phillips' Constitutional and Administrative Law* (7th ed., 1987), pp. 74–79.

[43] Set out above.

[44] [1981] Q.B. 180, 201.

[45] This view is endorsed in *Halsbury's Laws of England*, 4th ed., Vol. 51, para. 3.14.

"constitutional" statute, is not subject to implied repeal, has now been expressed by the Divisional Court in *Hunt v. London Borough of Hackney* and other cases.[46]

5–053   As to the issues raised in *Macarthys Ltd v. Smith*,[47] it is arguable that although the Court of Appeal approached them as if there was a *conflict* between the Equal Pay Act 1970 and Article 119, the better view is that there was simply a difference between them.

> "Article 119 is directly effective, and Community law applies in the industrial tribunals; to the extent that it gave rights to Mrs Smith more extensive than the Equal Pay Act 1970 (as amended by the Sex Discrimination Act 1975), there was nothing in the 1970 Act forbidding the court from giving effect to those rights. It should follow that Mrs Smith would be entitled to rely on whichever legal rule, art. 119 or the 1970 Act, gave her more extensive rights."[48]

This approach was echoed by the Court of Appeal in *Pickstone v. Freemans plc*,[49] where it was held that while the relevant provision of the Equal Pay Act 1970[50] was unambiguous and could not be construed in conformity with the requirements of Community law, a claim to equal pay (for work of equal value) could instead be based directly on Article 119.[51] Similarly, the House of Lords in *R. v. Secretary of State for Transport, ex p. Factortame Ltd (No. 2)*,[52] following a reference to the Court of Justice,[53] accepted that Community law imposes an obligation on national courts to provide an effective interlocutory remedy to protect rights having direct effect under Community law. Accordingly, interlocutory orders should be granted against the Crown disapplying Part II of the Merchant Shipping Act 1988[54] and restraining the Secretary of State from enforcing it and related regulations against the applicants, pending the final determination by the European Court of questions concerning the compatability of these provisions with Community law. This was so notwithstanding that, as a matter of domestic law, interlocutory injunctions could not be granted

---

[46] [2002] EWHC 195 (Admin), above paras 5-002, 5-018.
[47] Above.
[48] L. Collins, *European Community law in the United Kingdom* (4th ed., 1990), p. 32.
[49] [1989] A.C. 66.
[50] Section 1(2)(c).
[51] The House of Lords took a different approach: see below. See also *Mediguard Services Ltd v. Thame* [1994] I.C.R. 751, E.A.T.
[52] [1991] 1 A.C. 603, H.L.
[53] Case C—213/89, *R. v. Secretary of State for Transport, ex p. Factortame Ltd* [1990] E.C.R. 1-2433 (known as *Factortame I* by European lawyers but titled (*No. 2*) by the Law Reports ([1991] 1 A.C. 603).
[54] The 1988 Act and associated regulations (Merchant Shipping (Registration of Fishing Vessels) Regulations 1988 (S.I. 1988 No. 1926) were designed to narrow the conditions under which fishing vessels can be registered as British (and thus entitled to fish against the U.K. quotas): vessels would have to have "a genuine and substantial" connection with the U.K. (1988 Act, s.l 4(3)). The applicants were Spanish nationals, who controlled companies that owned ships registered as British, and which would lose that registration under the new rules.

against the Crown.[55] The European Court subsequently ruled that conditions of the kind imposed by the 1988 Act were indeed contrary to Community law.[56]

The possibility of direct challenge to U.K. legislation was recognised and acted upon by the House of Lords in *R. v. Secretary of State for Employment, ex p. Equal Opportunities Commission*,[57] in granting declarations on the application of the E.O.C. that the differing threshold provisions for full-time and part-time workers' entitlement to unfair dismissal and redundancy payments were incompatible with Community law. The less favourable treatment of part-time workers, the great majority of whom were women, constituted indirect sex discrimination for which no objective justification could be established. The *Factortame* decision provided a precedent acknowledging jurisdiction to grant such a declaration.[58] The House did, however, refuse to make a declaration in terms that the Secretary of State was in breach of the provisions of the Equal Treatment Directive which require Member States to introduce measures to abolish any laws contrary to the principle of equal treatment. This was designed to facilitate actions against the United Kingdom by individuals under the *Francovich* principle,[59] but such proceedings were said to raise different issues.[60] The relevant legislation was subsequently amended to comply with Community law.[61]

Cases since *Macarthys Ltd v. Smith*[62] have for the most part raised the "interpretation issue" rather than the "sovereignty issue." The dictum of Lord Diplock in *Garland v. British Rail Engineering Ltd*[63] cited above[64] has been regarded as endorsing Lord Denning's approach in *Macarthys Ltd v.*

---

[55] *R. v. Secretary of State for Transport, ex p. Factortame Ltd* [1990] 2 A.C. 85, H.L. *per* Lord Bridge at pp. 143–150. See N. P. Gravells, [1989] P.L. 568. The House of Lords in *M. v. Home Office* [1994] 1 A.C. 377 subsequently held that, notwithstanding the views of Lord Bridge in *Factortame (No.1)* the High Court did have jurisdiction to grant injunctions against officers of the Crown.

[56] Case C-221/89, *R. v. Secretary of State for Transport, ex p. Factortame Ltd.* [1991] E.C.R. 1-3905 known as *Factortame II* by European lawyers but titled (No. 3) in the Law Reports [1992] Q.B. 680). Part II of the Merchant Shipping Act 1988 was amended by the Merchant Shipping Act 1988 (Amendment) Order 1989 (S.I. 1989 No. 2006) to comply with an interim order in Art.169 proceedings against the U.K. (Case C-246/89R, *Commission v. U.K.* [1989] E.C.R. 1-3125; Case C-246/89, *Commission v. U.K.* [1991] E.C.R. 1-4585). Part II of the 1988 Act was subsequently repealed and replaced by the Merchant Shipping (Registration, etc.) Act 1993. Questions arising out of a claim for damages by the Spanish fishermen were referred by the Divisional Court to the Court of Justice as Case C-48/93, *R. v., Secretary of State for Transport, ex p. Factortame Ltd.*: see below, para. 5-055.

[57] [1995] 1 A.C. 1.

[58] "Although the final result is not reported [following the E.C.J. decision in *Factortame II*], no doubt the Divisional Court in due course granted a declaration accordingly": *per* Lord Keith of Kinkel *cf.* above, para. 5-044.

[59] See above, para. 5-044.

[60] *per* Lord Keith of Kinkel.

[61] See the Employment Protection (Part-Time Employees) Regulations 1995 (S.I. 1995 No.31).

[62] Above.

[63] [1983] 2 A.C. 751, 771. This approach applies as much to the interpretation of delegated as to primary legislation: *Ken Lane Transport Ltd. v. North Yorkshire County Council* [1995] 1 W.L.R. 1416, D.C.

[64] At para. 5-051.

Smith[65] rather than that of the majority.[66] Lord Diplock's approach was purportedly followed in two, contrasting, decisions of the House of Lords.

In *Duke v. Reliance Systems Ltd,*[67] Mrs Duke was dismissed by her private sector employers shortly after attaining 60, in accordance with their policy that men should retire at 65 but women at 60. She claimed that this constituted discriminatory treatment under the Sex Discrimination Act 1975, s.6(2), but her claim was dismissed on the ground that section 6(4) preserved the right of the employer to operate discriminatory retirement ages. This said that section 6(2) did not apply to "provision in relation to death or retirement". It was clear that the later Council Directive Dir.76/207/EEC (the Equal Treatment Directive) did outlaw discriminatory retirement ages,[68] but (1) this did not have "horizonal direct effect" between individuals,[69] and (2) the U.K. legislation implementing the directive, the Sex Discrimination Act 1986, did not apply retrospectively so as to apply to Mrs Duke's claim. She argued, therefore, that the expression "provision in relation to ... retirement" should be interpreted as "provision consequent upon retirement," and therefore not applying to protect discriminatory retirement ages. This would enable English law to conform with the Equal Treatment Directive. The argument was rejected.[70] Lord Templeman, with whom the other members of the House of Lords agreed, said:

> "Of course a British court will always be willing and anxious to conclude that United Kingdom law is consistent with Community law. Where an Act is passed for the purpose of giving effect to an obligation imposed by a decision or other instrument a British court will seldom encounter difficulty inconcluding that the language of the Act is effective for the intended purpose. But the construction of a British Act of Parliament is a matter of judgment to be determined by British courts and to be derived from the language of the legislation considered in the light of the circumstances prevailing at the date of enactment."[71]

However, the 1975 Act was not passed in order to give effect to the (later) Equal Treatment Directive, and the words of section 6(4)

> "are not reasonably capable of being limited to the meaning ascribed to them by the appellant. Section 2(4) of the European Communities Act 1972 does not in my opinion enable or constrain a British court to distort the meaning of a British statute in order to enforce against an individual a Community directive which has no direct effect between individuals. Section 2(4) applies and only applies where Community

---

[65] Above.

[66] A. W. Bradley, in J. Jowell and D. Oliver, *The Changing Constitution* (2nd ed., 1989), p. 41 (a point omitted from the 3rd ed., 1994).

[67] [1988] A.C. 618. Applied by the House of Lords in *Finnegan v. Clowney Youth Training Programme Ltd* [1990] 2 A.C. 418.

[68] Case 151/84, *Roberts v. Tate & Lyle Industries Ltd* [1986] E.C.R. 703, [1986] I.C.R. 371; Case 152/84, *Marshall v. Southampton and South-West Hampshire Area Health Authority (Teaching)* [1986] E.C.R. 723, [1986] Q.B. 401.

[69] *Marshall*, above and see para. 5-041.

[70] It had previously been rejected by the Employment Tribunal and the Court of Appeal in *Roberts v. Cleveland Area Health Authority* [1978] I.C.R. 370, [1979] 1 W.L.R. 754.

[71] [1988] A.C. 618, 638.

provisions are directly applicable."[72]

It is clearly the case that the 1975 Act was intended at the time to preserve differential retirement ages. Indeed the United Kingdom's position was that the Equal Treatment Directive did not prohibit discriminatory retirement ages, an argument ultimately rejected by the European Court in *Marshall I*.[73]

The reasoning in *Duke* has been cogently criticised by commentators on a variety of grounds.[74] First, it is not obvious that the narrow reading of "in relation to" was a "distortion": it was certainly a less natural reading, but one that was arguably supportable given the requirements of the directive, and the obligation under Community law (via sections 2(4) and 3(1) of the European Communities Act 1972) to interpret national legislation where possible to conform with relevant directives. Secondly, it was incorrect to say that section 2(4) only applied to Community provisions that were "directly applicable."[75] Third, it gave insufficient weight to the presumed continuing intention of the United Kingdom to comply with the requirements of Community law: it is not clear that this was properly subordinated to the contemporary intention in 1975 to preserve discriminatory retirement ages. It is important, however, to see the *Duke* decision in its context. Had Mrs Duke's argument prevailed, the position would have been as if the Sex Discrimination Act 1986 had retrospective effect, and this would undoubtedly have caused severe practical difficulties. It is to be hoped that the rather doubtful reasoning employed to secure that result is not used in subsequent cases so as to undermine proper implementation by the United Kingdom of the requirements of Community law.

5–054

The decision of the House of Lords in *Pickstone v. Freemans plc*[76] is accordingly to be welcomed. Here, the House placed renewed emphasis on the need to interpret English law, where possible, so as to comply with Community law. The context of the case was significantly different from that in *Duke*. Here, the question concerned the interpretation of amendments to the Equal Pay Act 1970 specifically designed to bring English law into conformity with Community law. Prior to amendment, the Act took effect where the woman was employed (a) "on like work" or (b) on work "rated as equivalent" on a job evaluation study, with a man in the same employment.[77] The European Court held that this was inadequate to comply with Article 119 of the EC Treaty (now Article 141EC) and Council Directive Dir.75/117/EEC (the equal pay directive), which imposed a requirement of equal pay for the same work or *work of equal value*. The latter element was not fully implemented by (b), which depended on the employer having

---

[72] *ibid.*, pp. 639–640.

[73] n. 68 above.

[74] E. Ellis, (1988) 104, L.Q.R. 379; A. Arnull, [1988] P.L. 313; N. Foster, (1988) 51 M.L.R 775 and (1988) 25 C.M.L. Rev. 629; B. Fitzpatrick, (1989) 9 O.J.L.S. 336.

[75] The European Court in Case 262/84, *Beets-Proper v. Van Lanschot Bankiers N.V.* [1986] E.C.R. 782 held that national legislation, designed to implement a directive that was *not* directly effective, should be interpreted so as to conform to it: See above, para. 5-043: This obligation would apply to U.K. courts via ss.2(4) and 3(1) of the 1972 Act.

[76] [1989] A.C. 66. See A. W. Bradley, [1988] P. L. 485. *Cf. J. Rothschild Holdings v. Commissioners of Inland Revenue* [1989] 2 C.M.L.R. 612.

[77] Section 1(2)(a), (b).

consented to a job evaluation[78] study. Accordingly, the Equal Pay
(Amendment) Regulations 1983[79] introduced a new para. (c), which allowed
an "equal value" claim to be made "where a woman is employed on work,
not being work in relation to which paragraph (a) or (b) above applies. ... "
Mrs Pickstone, a "warehouse operative", made a claim under para. (c),
claiming her work was of equal value to that of a man employed as a
"checker warehouse operative". There happened to be one man also
employed as a "warehouse operative".[80] The industrial tribunal and the
Employment Appeal Tribunal accepted the employer's argument that para.
(a) applied to Mrs Pickstone's work, and that the words "not being work . . . ."
accordingly barred her claim under para. (c). The Court of Appeal[81] held
that this was indeed the position under the Equal Pay Act 1970, but that
Mrs Pickstone could base her claim directly on Article 119 of the EC Treaty.
The House of Lords interpreted the 1970 Act in such a way as to allow her
claim to proceed under it: the exclusionary words in para, (c) were intended
to have effect only where the particular man with whom she sought
comparison was employed on the same work. Here, her comparator was
employed on different work.

> "The opposite result would leave a large gap in the equal work
> provision, enabling an employer to evade it by employing one token
> man on the same work as a group of potential women claimants who
> were deliberately paid less than a group of men employed on work of
> equal value with that of the women. This would mean that the United
> Kingdom had failed yet again fully to implement its obligations under
> Article 119 of the Treaty and the Equal Pay Directive, and had not
> given full effect to the decision of the European Court in *Commission v.
> U.K.*[82] It is plain that Parliament cannot possibly have intended such a
> failure."[83]

A purposive, rather than a literal construction was necessary.[84] There is
room for argument how far this result involves a "distortion" of the
statutory language.

5–055   The proper approach of the English courts to the interpretation of
directives in the light of the decision of the European Court in *Marleasing*[85]
has been stated as follows by Lord Keith of Kinkel in *Webb v. EMO Air
Cargo (U.K.) Ltd*:[86]

> "It is for a United Kingdom Court to construe domestic legislation in
> any field covered by a Community directive so as to accord with the
> interpretation of the directive as laid down by the European Court, if

---

[78] Case 61/81, *Commission v United Kingdom* [1982] E.C.R. 2601, [1982] I.C.R. 578; S. Atkins,
      [1983] P.L. 19 and (1983) 8 E.L. Rev. 48.
[79] S.I. 1983 No. 1794.
[80] [1986] I.C.R. 886.
[81] [1989] A.C. 66. See A. W. Bradley, [1988] P.L. 485, 489–491.
[82] n. 78 above.
[83] *per* Lord Keith of Kinkel at pp. 111–112.
[84] See below, para. 6-009.
[85] Above, para. 5-043.
[86] [1992] 4 All E.R. 929, 939, 940. The other members of the House agreed with Lord Keith.
      See also *Porter v. Cannon Hygiene Ltd* [1993] I.R.L.R. 329, C.A. (N.I.).

that can be done without distorting the meaning of the domestic legislation: see *Duke v. GEC Reliance Ltd.*[87] This is so whether the domestic legislation came after or, as in this case, preceded the directive, see *Marleasing SA v. La Comercial Internacional de Alimentación SA* ... .[88]

As the European Court has said, a national court must construe a domestic law to accord with the terms of a directive in the same field only if it is possible to do so. This means that the domestic law must be open to an interpretation consistent with the directive whether or not it is also open to an interpretation inconsistent with it."

This statement has been cited on a number of occasions.[89] In *Webb* itself, the House proceeded to make a reference to the Court of Justice. In the light of the Court's ruling, the House of Lords was able to interpret the Sex Discrimination Act 1975 to accord with Community law.

The facts were that W was engaged to replace a woman on maternity leave (but employed on an indefinite rather than a short-term contract). She was dismissed when it was discovered that she too was pregnant. Section 1(1) of the 1975 Act provides that

"a person discriminates against a woman in any circumstances relevant for the purposes of any provision of this Act if—(a) on the ground of her sex he treats her less favourably than he treats or would treat a man."

Section 5(3) provides that

"a comparison of the cases of persons of different sex ... must be such that the relevant circumstances in the one case are the same, or not materially different, in the other."

The House of Lords held initially[90] that the dismissal here was on the basis of W's unavailability for work at the time when she had been particularly required, and that the reason for that unavailability (pregnancy) was not a relevant circumstance. However, the Court of Justice ruled[91] that Community law[92] precluded dismissal of an employee recruited for an unlimited term, with a view initially to replacing another employee, on the ground of pregnancy. Accordingly, the House of Lords[93] reinterpreted the 1975 Act to clarify the reason for unavailability in such a case (pregnancy) as a "relevant circumstance", pregnancy being a circumstance that could not be present in the case of the hypothetical man. While not the preferred reading, this was properly not regarded as "distortion" of the Act.

Finally, in the *Factortame* litigation[94] it was accepted by both the parties

---

[87] [1988] A.C. 618, 639–640 *per* Lord Templeman.
[88] Case C-106/89, [1990] E.C.R. I-4135.
[89] See, *e.g.*, *R. v. Secretary of State for the Environment, ex p. Greenpeace Ltd* [1994] 4 All E.R. 352.
[90] n. 86 above.
[91] Case C-32/93, *Webb v. Emo Air Cargo Ltd* [1994] Q.B. 718, [1994] E.C.R. I-3567.
[92] Arts. 2,5 of Dir.76/207/EEC (the equal treatment directive).
[93] [1995] 1 W.L.R. 1454.
[94] See para. 5-053.

and the courts that if the Court of Justice were to rule finally that the relevant provisions of the Merchant Shipping Act 1988 were incompatible with Community law, English courts would have to give effect to the latter, whether as a matter of interpretation of the 1988 Act[95] or by disapplying it as invalid.[96] The Divisional Court "made an order designed to give effect to [the] Court's judgment in *Factortame II* and, to give detailed particulars of their claim for damages."[97] This led to another reference to the Court of Justice and the ruling in *Factortame III*.[98]

5. IMPLEMENTATION OF COMMUNITY LAW IN THE UNITED KINGDOM

5–056   As has been seen, Community law that is directly applicable or effective takes effect in the United Kingdom under section 2(1) of the European Communities Act 1972.[99] In appropriate cases,[1] such law may give rise to defences that can be relied on in English litigation.[2] Alternatively, it may form the basis of an award of damages, (*e.g.* for breach of statutory duty[3] or

---

[95] *per* Lord Bridge in *R. v. Secretary of State for Transport, ex p. Factortame Ltd* [1990] 2 A.C. 85, 140, referring to s.2(1) and (4) of the 1972 Act: "This has precisely the same effect as if a section were incorporated in Part II of the Act of 1988 which in terms enacted that the provisions with respect to registration of British fishing vessels were to be without prejudice to the directly enforceable Community rights of nationals of any member state of the E.E.C." Although this can be labelled as an approach based on interpretation, this would seem to be "interpretation" of a kind more radical than adopted hitherto; the words read into the statute have a very substantial modifying effect.

[96] The Court of Appeal in *Factortame*: [1989] 2 C.M.L.R. 353, 396 (Lord Donaldson M.R.), 403–404 (Bingham L.J.), 408 (Mann L.J.).

[97] Case 48/93, *R. v. Secretary of State for Transport, ex p. Factortame Ltd. and others* [1998] E.C.R. I-1029. para. 12.

[98] Above, para. 5-044.

[99] Above, para. 5-050.

[1] See generally J. Steiner, "How to make the action suit the case: domestic remedies for breach of EEC law" (1987) 12 E.L. Rev. 102; P. Oliver, "Enforcing Community rights in the English courts" (1987) 50 M.L.R. 881; N. Green and A. Barav, "Damages in the national courts for breach of Community law" [1986] 6 Y.E.L. 55, 83–114; J. S. Davidson, (1985) 34 I.C.L.Q. 178.

[2] *e.g.* a defence to criminal proceedings: Case 63/83, *R. v. Kirk* [1985] 1 All E.R. 453; Case 121/85, *Conegate v. Commissioners of Customs and Excise* [1987] Q.B. 254; or "Euro-defences" based on EC competition law arising in civil actions: *cf. Lansing Bagnall Ltd v. Buccaneer Lift Parts Ltd* [1984] 1 C.M.L.R. 224; *Ransburg-Gema AC v. Electrostatic Plant Systems Ltd* [1989] 2 C.M.L.R. 712.

[3] *e.g.* for a breach of Art. 86/EC (abuse of a dominant position): *per* Lord Diplock in *Garden Foods Ltd v. Milk Marketing Board* [1984] A.C. 130, 141: see K. Banks, (1984) 21 C.M.L. Rev. 669; F. G. Jacobs, (1983) 8 E.L. Rev. 353; M. Friend and J. Shaw, (1984) 100 L.Q.R. 188; but not a breach of Art. 30 (prohibition of quantitative restrictions on imports and measures having equivalent effect): *Bourgoin SA. v. Ministry of Agriculture, Fisheries and Food* [1985] Q.B. 716, C.A.; or a breach of Art. 10 of Council Reg. 1422/78: *An Bord Bainne v. Milk Marketing Board* [1988] 1 C.M.L.R. 605, C.A.

the tort of misfeasance in a public office[4]), a claim in restitution[5] or the grant of an injunction,[6] as a matter of private law, or the grant of public law remedies against the Crown or other public authority.[7]

Primary legislation has been enacted to give effect to major changes, such as those consequent on the accession of new Member States,[8] major budgetary matters,[9] the Single European Act,[10] the Maastricht Treaty,[11] and the Treaty of Amsterdam.[12] Specific Community obligations may also be implemented by Act of Parliament.[13] Section 2(2) of the 1972 Act[14] authorises the making of subordinate legislation (1) to implement other Community laws that are not directly applicable or effective; or (2) to deal with matters related to Community laws that take effect under section 2(1).[15] Subordinate legislation may not, however, (1) provide for the imposition or increase of taxation; (2) be retrospective; (3) confer the power to enact sub-delegated legislation; or (4) create any new criminal offence punishable with more than two years imprisonment, or three months on summary conviction, or a fine of more than £1,000, or £100 a day.[16] It is subject to the negative resolution procedure.[17] The power under section 2(2), taken in conjunction with subs.(4), may be exercised in respect of post-1972

---

[4] An action that lies where loss is caused by *ultra vires* acts committed maliciously (*i.e.* with intent to injure the plaintiff) or with knowledge of its illegality: *Bourgoin*, n. 3 above: the parties settled for £3.5 m. (Vol. 102 H. C. Deb. July 23, 1986, col. 116, written answer). This head of liability must now be seen as subject to the ruling of the Court of Justice in *Factortame III*, above, para. 5-044.

[5] Cases C–397/98 and C–410/98, *Metallgesellschaft Ltd, v. Inland Revenue Commissioners* [2001] E.C.R. I–1027 (claim arising out of discriminatory tax provision that prevented subsidiaries of non-U.K. resident companies delaying the date of tax payment).

[6] *Garden Cottage Foods*, n. 3 above; *Cutsforth v. Mansfield Inns Ltd* [1986] 1 C.M.L.R. 1.

[7] *e.g. Van Duyn v. Home Office* [1974] 1 W.L.R. 1107, Ch.D., and Case 41/74, [1985] Ch. 358 E.C.J. (action for a declaration); *R. v. Attorney-General, ex p. I.C.I.* [1987] 1 C.M.L.R. 72 and *R. v. Intervention Board for Agricultural Produce, ex p. The Fish Producers' Organisation Ltd* [1988] 2 C.M.L.R. 661 (applications for judicial review).

[8] European Communities (Greek Accession) Act 1979; European Communities (Spanish and Portuguese Accession) Act 1985; European Union (Accessions) Act 1994 (in respect of Austria, Finland and Sweden, and Norway (who subsequently did not join)).

[9] European Communities (Finance) Acts 1985 and 2001.

[10] European Communities (Amendment) Act 1986.

[11] European Communities (Amendment) Act 1993. The process of enacting this Act was particularly fraught for the government: see discussion by P. Beaumont and G. Moir, *Current Law Statutes Annotated* (1993). A challenge to the legality of ratification of the Treaty by the government was rejected: *R. v. Secretary of State for Foreign and Commonwealth Affairs, ex p. Rees-Mogg* [1994] 2 W.L.R. 115; R. Rawlings, [1994] P.L. 254, 367.

[12] European Communities (Amendment) Act 1998.

[13] *e.g.* the Companies Acts 1980 and 1981, which implemented directives on the harmonisation of company law; the Importation of Milk Act 1983, passed in response to a judgment of the European Court which held that U.K. restrictions on the importation of UHT milk were contrary to Community rules on the free movement of goods (Case 124/81, *Commission v. United Kingdom* [1983] E.C.R. 203); the Sex Discrimination Act 1986.

[14] Sections 5 and 6 of the 1972 Act confer powers to make subordinate legislation concerning customs matters and the common agricultural policy. Statutory instruments implementing Community obligations have been made under other statutes.

[15] Note, however, the limits on such legislation in respect of Community regulations: above, para. 5-046.

[16] European Communities Act 1972, Sched. 2, as amended by the Criminal Law Act 1977, s.32 and the Criminal Justice Act 1982, ss.37, 40, 46.

[17] *ibid.* See above para. 5-024.

as well as pre-1972 statutes.[18]

Arrangements have been made for the scrutiny of Community legislation by the Select Committee of the House of Lords on the European Union (between 1974 and 1999, the Select Committee on the European Communities) and the House of Commons European Scrutiny Committee (between 1974 and 1998, the Select Committee on European Legislation).[19] These committees consider draft Community legislation and other documents prepared by the Commission for submission to the Council of Ministers proposals under the second and third pillars, any other document published by one EU institution for submission to any other and any other document relating to EU matters deposited by a minister.[20] Detailed explanatory memoranda are prepared by the government. The Commons committee concentrates on the legal and political importance of each document, reporting also on the reasons for its opinion and on any matters of principle, policy or law which may be affected; the Lords deal more with technical legal and administrative implications.[21] The Lords committee has a number of sub-committees, including one customarily chaired by one of the Law Lords on law and institutions,[22] and each of the rest considering Community proposals within a particular subject area. The committees decide, *inter alia*, whether a particular proposal should be considered further by the respective Houses. In the Commons, a debate may be held on the floor of the House or in a standing committee. In 1990, two European Standing Committees were established in order to shift debates away from the floor of the House.[23] The Procedure Committee concluded that these committees functioned very well, making a useful contribution to effective

---

[18] *Hunt v. London Borough of Hackney* and other cases [2002] EWHC 195 (Admin), above para. 5-002.
[19] Established in 1974. See 1972–73 H.C. 143 and 463-I ("Foster Committee": Commons); 1972–73 H.L. 194 ("Maybray-King Committee": Lords). See also the First Report from the Select Committee on Procedure, 1977–78 H.C. 588 Vol. I, pp. xl–xlvi; First Special Report from the Select Committee on European Legislation 1983–84 (1983–84 H.C. 527): Government response, Vol. 65 H.C. Deb., October 29, 1984, cols.800–802, written answer); Second Special Report 1985–86 (1985–86 H.C. 400): Government observations, Cm. 123, 1987; Fourth Report from the Select Committee on Procedure (1988–89 H.C. 622): Government response, Cm. 1081, 1990; First Special Report from the Select Committee on European Legislation 1993–94 (1993–94 H.C. 99), *Scrutiny after Maastricht* 27th Report of the European Legislation Committee (1995–96 H.C. 51-xxvii); Third Report of the Procedure Committee (1996–97 H.C. 77); Seventh Report of the Select Committee on Modernisation of the House of Commons (1997–98 H.C. 791, *The Scrutiny of European Business*); E. Denza, "Parliamentary Scrutiny of European Legislation" [1993] Stat.L.R. 56 A.J. Cygan, *The United Kingdom Parliament and European Union Legislation* (1998) and "European legislation before the House of Commons — the work of the European Scrutiny Committee" in M. Adenas and A. Türk, *Delegated Legislation and the Role of Committees in the EC* (2000), Chap. 9.
[20] The range of documents eligible for scrutiny has been extended over the lifetime of the committee following extensions in the range of EU activities.
[21] Joint meetings are occasionally held.
[22] The "legal eagles committee": E. Denza, [1993] Stat. L.R. 56, 59.
[23] See 1988–89 H.C. 622 and Cm. 1081, n. 19 above; First Special Report from the Select Committee on European Legislation 1989–90 (1989–90 H.C. 512) and Vol. 178 H. C. Deb., October 24, 1990, cols.375–401.

scrutiny.[24] A third Committee was established in 1998. The government has undertaken that it will normally[25] provide time for such consideration where recommended by the Select Committee prior to a proposal being discussed by the Council of Ministers (the "scrutiny reserve"). However, the scrutiny of European secondary legislation is indirect in effect, given that Parliament can at best influence only one of the members of the Council, especially now that more Council decisions are reached by qualified majorities and that the legislative process is likely to be quicker.[26] Moreover, it can be difficult to keep abreast of changes in draft proposals as they progress through the Community legislative process.

6. VALIDITY OF EUROPEAN SECONDARY LEGISLATION

(a) Article 230EC; the action for annulment

The validity of acts of Community institutions that are binding in law, and whether legislative or not, may be challenged directly by an *action for annulment* brought in the European Court of Justice[27] under Article 230 EC[28]:   **5–057**

> "The Court of Justice shall review the legality of acts adopted jointly by the European Parliament and the Council, of acts of the Council, of the Commission and the ECB, other than recommendations and opinions,[29] and of acts of the European Parliament intended to

---

[24] First Report from the Select Committee on Procedure 1991–92 (1991–92 H.C. 31), *Review of European Standing Committees*; Third Report 1991–92 (1991–92, H.C. 331), *Government Response*. Debates "have been of a much more highly focused and objective quality": E. Denza, [1993] Stat L.R 56, 58.

[25] The first formal resolution was made on October 30, 1980 (H.C. Deb. Vol. 991. col. 844); it was replaced by one on October 24, 1990 (H.C. Deb. Vol. 178, col. 400) and by the current resolution on November 17, 1998 (H.C. Deb. Vol. 319, cols 803–804). It provides that no minister should give agreement to any legislative proposal or any agreement under the second or third pillar which is still subject to scrutiny or awaiting consideration by the House; "agreement" includes agreement to a programme, plan or recommendation for EC legislation, political agreement, agreement to a common position under the co-decision or co-operation procedures and agreement to a joint text or confirmation of a common position under the co-decision procedure.

[26] See the reports on the Single European Act and Parlimentary Scrutiny: First Special Report from the Select Committee on European Legislation 1985–86 H.C. 533); Twelfth Report from the Select Committee on the European Communities 1985–86 (1985–86 H.L. 149).

[27] See above, paras 2-075–2-081: national courts may not rule acts of Community institutions invalid (Case 314/85, *Foto-Frost v. Hauptzollamt Lübeck-Ost* [1987] E.C.R. 4199). The approach adopted by the Eurpean Court to the interpretation of Community law is considered below, para. 6-049–6-060.

[28] Formerly Article 173 of the EC Treaty, as amended by Art. G(53)/TEU.

[29] This covers any act intended to have legal effect, and not merely regulations, directives and decisions: Case 22/70, *Commission v. Council (ERTA)* [1971] E.C.R. 263 (action for annulment of a Council resolution concerning negotiations leading to an international agreement between the Member States and third countries); Case C-325/91, *France v. Commission*, June 16, 1993 ("communication" intended to have legal effects annulled; commission should have adopted a directive or a decision).

produce legal effects *vis-à-vis* third parties.[30]

It shall for this purpose have jurisdiction in actions brought by a Member State, the Council or the Commission on grounds of lack of competence, infringement of an essential procedural requirement, infringement of this Treaty or of any rule of law relating to its application, or misuse of powers.

The Court shall have jurisdiction under the same conditions in actions brought by the European Parliament, by the Court of Auditors and by the ECB for the purpose of protecting their prerogatives.[31]

Any natural or legal person[32] may, under the same conditions, institute proceedings against a decision addressed to that person or against a decision which, although in the form of a regulation or a decision addressed to another person, is of direct and individual concern to the former.

The proceedings provided for in this Article shall be instituted within two months of the publication of the measure, or of its notification to the plaintiff, or, in the absence thereof, of the day on which it came to the knowledge of the latter, as the case may be."

Thus the range of acts that can be challenged by an individual is narrower than those that can be reviewed under the first three paragraphs of Article 230EC. First, the act must be a "decision" in that it must have legal effect[33] and must not be a regulation, in the sense of an act which applies to objectively determined situations and has legal effects on classes of persons defined in a general and abstract manner.[34] Second, the act must be of "direct and individual concern" to the applicant.[35] If the action is successful,

---

[30] The express reference to the Parliament was added by the Maastricht Treaty; acts of the Parliament had in any event previously been held to be subject to Art. 173 of the EC Treaty (now Article 230 EC): Case 294/83, *Parti Ecologiste "Les Verts" v. European Parliament* [1986] E.C.R. 1339.

[31] Prior to the changes effected by the Maastricht Treaty, the Court had held, initially, that the Parliament had no standing under Art. 173 (Case 302/87, *European Parliament v. Council* [1988] E.C.R. 5615) and then that it had standing to bring proceedings to safeguard its prerogatives (Case C-70/88, *European Parliament v. Council* [1990] E.C.R. 1–2041); the ruling in the latter case is now enshrined in Art. 230 EC.

[32] This term includes a Member State: Case 25/62 *Plaumann v. Commission* [1963] E.C.R. 95.

[33] Cases 8–11/66, *Cimenteries v. Commission* (the *Noordwijks Cement Accoord* case) [1967] E.C.R. 75: a notification by the Commission that certain agreements were prohibited under Art. 85 of the EC Treaty which had the effect of removing a temporary immunity from fines, was held to be reviewable even though such fines could only be imposed if further steps were taken by the Commission.

[34] Collins *op. cit.* para. 5-033, n. 44, pp. 232–234, 236–240. The Court looks to the substance and not the form; the fact that the act has been promulgated as a regulation is not conclusive. See, *e.g.* Cases 113, 118–121/77, *Japanese Ball Bearings Cases* [1979] E.C.R. 1185 where four Japanese ball-bearing manufacturers were held to be entitled to challenge a regulation imposing an import duty in general terms, but which on the facts was aimed at them. Individuals also do not have standing to challenge a directive (unless, presumably, it is a "disguised decision"): Cases T–172/98 and T–175–177/98, *Salamandar v. Parliament* [2000] E.C.R. II–2487.

[35] There are a number of cases on this point, which are not always easy to reconcile: Collins, pp. 234–256; Hartley (1998), Chap. 12; R. Greaves, (1988) 11 E.L. Rev. 119. See *e.g.* Case C–321/95P, *Greenpeace International v. Commission* [1998] All E.R. (EC) 620 (Greenpeace held not to have standing to challenge a decision authorising expenditure on a project to build power stations alleged to affect environmental rights).

the act challenged is declared by the Court to be void,[36] and the matter is remitted to the institution concerned.

Preliminary decisions can only be challenged if they affect the applicant's rights independently of the final decision: otherwise, the applicant must await the final decision and challenge that.[37]

The grounds for challenge are set out in Article 230 EC.[38] Although they are based upon the grounds for review in continental, particularly French, administrative law, arguments may be based on principles of administrative law derived from the legal systems of any Member State. The grounds may overlap in the sense that a particular set of facts may involve infringements under more than one heading.

Lack of competence corresponds to the English concept of substantive *ultra vires*[39] and the French concept of *excès de pouvoir* or *incompétence*. It may not be easily distinguishable from an allegation of *infringement of the Treaties or any rules of law relating to their application*. An example is *Meroni v. High Authority*[40] where certain decisions under the Coal and Steel Treaty were held to be improperly delegated to certain subordinate bodies. Issues of competence also arise where subordinate legislation is challenged on the ground that the Treaty article(s) relied on as authority for the measure in fact do not provide an appropriate legal basis for it. The choice of legal basis must be based on objective factors which are amenable to judicial review, which include in particular the aim and content of the measure.[41] For example, in *Germany v. Parliament and Council; R. v. Secretary of State for Health, ex p. Imperial Tobacco Ltd.*[42] the Court annulled a directive[43] that prohibited tobacco advertising and sponsorship except at the point of sale. It had been adopted on the basis of Treaty provisions on the approximation of laws of member states which had as their object the establishment and functioning of the internal market and the protection of the freedom to provide goods and services.[44] The Court held that these articles did not confer a general power to regulate the internal market; and that the directive did not actively contribute to eliminating obstacles to the free movement of goods and services or removing appreciable distortions of competition. The Court noted that the harmonization of legislation of the Member States designed to protect and improve human health, which the applicants alleged was the "centre of

---

[36] Art. 231 EC. In the case of a regulation declared void, the Court can state which of its effects shall be considered as definitive; this enables the Court, for example, to declare that a regulation remains effective until replaced by one adopted on a proper legal basis: see eg. Cases C–164/97 and C–165/97, *Parliament v. Council* [1999] E.C.R. I–1139.

[37] Compare Case 60/81, *I.B.M. v. Commission* [1981] E.C.R. 2639 (decision to institute proceedings for abuse of a dominant position not separately challengeable) *with Case 53/85, A.K.Z.O. Chemie v. Commission* [1986] E.C.R. 1965 (decision to show documents, claimed by the applicant to contain confidential information, to the complainant, challengeable).

[38] Hartley (1998), Chap. 15.

[39] On the English *ultra vires* doctrine see below, Chap. 18.

[40] Case 9/56, [1957–8] E.C.R. 133; see also Case 48/69. *I.C.J. v. Commission (the Dyestuffs case)* [1972] E.C.R. 619.

[41] Case C–300/89, *Commission v. Council* [1991] E.C.R. I–2867; Case C–271/94, *Parliament v. Council* [1996] E.C.R. I–1689, para. 14; Case 22/96, *Parliament v. Council* [1998] E.C.R I–3231, para 23.

[42] Cases C–376/98 and C–74/99, [2000] E.C.R. I–8419.

[43] EP and Council Directive (EC) 98/43.

[44] Articles 57(2), 66 and 100a of the EC Treaty (now Articles 47(2), 55 and 95EC).

gravity" of the direction, was expressly excluded by Article 129(4) of the EC Treaty (now Article 152(4)EC).

Infringement of an essential procedural requirement corresponds to the English doctrine of procedural *ultra vires* and the French concept of *vice de forme*. Only requirements of substantial importance are mandatory: for example, requirements to hold a hearing,[45] to consult the European Parliament,[46] to give reasons,[47] to state the provision under which the measure is adopted[48] and for a Commission decision to be properly authenticated.[49] Minor irregularities are ignored; for example, notification of a decision to a subsidiary rather than to the applicants where the latter had full knowledge of the decision in time to institute proceedings,[50] and the reporting of a decision in the *Official Journal* under an inaccurate title.[51]

Misuse of powers broadly corresponds to the abuse of discretion aspect of the *ultra vires* doctrine and the French concept of *détournement de pouvoir*. It covers, for example, the use of a power for an improper purpose.

(b) Article 241EC: the plea of illegality[52]

5–058 Article 241EC[53] provides that:

> Notwithstanding the expiry of the period laid down in the fifth paragraph of Article 230, any party[54] may, in proceedings in which a regulation adopted jointly by the European Parliament and the Council, or a regulation[55] of the Council, of the Commission, or of the ECB is at issue, plead the grounds specified in the second paragraph of Article 230, in order to invoke before the Court of Justice the inapplicability of that regulation."

An individual may not challenge a *regulation* under Article 230EC (above);

---

[45] Case 41/69, *ACF Chemiefarma v. Commission* [1970] E.C.R. 661; the challenge failed on the merits: see also the *Dyestuffs* case above. A hearing may be necessary even though it is not expressly required by Community legislation: Case 17/74, *Transocean Marine Paint Association v. Commission* [1974] E.C.R. 1063.

[46] See above, para. 5-047.

[47] See Art. 253EC above, para. 5-038; Case 24/62, *Germany v. Commission* [1963] E.C.R. 63. The reasons must be adequate: the act must "set out, in a concise, but clear and relevant manner, the principal issues of law and of fact upon which it is based and which are necessary in order that the reasoning which has led the Commission to its Decision may be understood" (*ibid.* p. 69). See also Case 166/78, *Italy v. Council* [1979] E.C.R. 2575. A Council directive was annulled where the statement of reasons was altered by the Council's secretariat, in a way that went beyond simple corrections of spelling and grammar: Case 131/86, *United Kingdom v. Council* [1988] E.C.R. 905.

[48] Case 45/86, *Commission v. Council* [1987] E.C.R. 1493; A. Arnull, (1987) 12 E.L. Rev. 448. These cases may also raise questions of competence: see generally K. St. C. Bradley, "The European Court and the Legal Basis of Community Legislation" (1988) 13 E.L. Rev. 379.

[49] Case C–286/95P, *Commission v. ICI plc.* [2000] All E.R. (EC) 439.

[50] *Dyestuffs* case, *loc. cit.* n. 40 above.

[51] Case 6/72, *Europemballage & Continental Can v. Commission* [1973] E.C.R. 215.

[52] Hartley (1998), Chap. 14.

[53] Formerly Article 184 of the EC Treaty as substituted by Art. G(58)/TEU.

[54] This includes Member States: Case 32/65, *Italy v. Council and Commission* [1966] E.C.R. 389.

[55] But not a *decision*: Case 156/77, *Commission v. Belgium* [1978] E.C.R. 1881. The court again looks to substance rather than form: Case 92/78, *Simmenthal v. Commission* [1979] E.C.R. 77.

if, however, he or she happens to be a party to proceedings before the Court of Justice he or she (and any other party) may do so under Article 241EC. Article 241EC may be invoked where proceedings are brought under some other provision of the Treaty which concern the party making the plea of illegality; it does not give that party an independent cause of action.[56]

(c) Article 232EC: remedy against inaction[57]

Article 232EC[58] provides that:

5–059

"Should the European Parliament, the Council or the Commission, in infringement of this Treaty, fail to act, the Member States and the other institutions of the Community[59] may bring an action before the Court of Justice to have the infringement established.

The action shall be admissible only if the institution concerned has first been called upon to act. If, within two months of being so called upon, the institution concerned has not defined its position, the action may be brought within a further period of two months.

Any natural or legal person may, under the conditions laid down in the preceding paragraphs, complain to the Court of Justice that an institution of the Community has failed to address to that person any act other than a recommendation or an opinion.

The Court of Justice shall have jurisdiction, under the same conditions, in actions or proceedings brought by the ECB in the areas falling within the latter's field of competence and in actions or proceedings brought against the latter."

The Court of Justice has built in some limitations to actions under this article. An action can only be brought where the institution in question has failed to define its position within two months. In *Lütticke v. Commission*[60] the Commission had declined to take action against France on the ground that it had in fact complied with the Treaty, and stated as much within the two months period; the court held that an action could therefore not be brought. An individual may not use Article 232EC to circumvent the restrictions that prevent him bringing an action directly against a Member State for breach of a Treaty provision,[61] or an action outside the limits of Article 230EC,[62] by attempting to bring an action against the Commission (respectively) (1) for failing to take action against the Member State or (2) failing to revoke a decision not in fact open to challenge under Article 230EC.

---

[56] Case 31/62, *Wohrmann v. Commission* [1962] E.C.R. 501.
[57] Hartley (1998), Chap. 13.
[58] Formerly Article 175 of the EC Treaty, as substituted by Art. G(54)/TEU.
[59] This includes the Council, the Commission and the Parliament: Case 13/83, *European Parliament v. Council* [1985] E.C.R. 1513: See P. Fennell, (1985) 10 E.L. Rev. 264.
[60] Case 48/65, [1966] E.C.R. 19.
[61] Under Articles 226EC and 227EC such actions can only be brought by a Member State or the Commission: See the *Lütticke* case, n. 60 above.
[62] See above, para. 5-057; Cases 10 and 18/68, *Eridania v. Commission* [1969] E.C.R. 459.

(d) Articles 234EC and 288EC

5–060   The validity of Community legislation may also be considered by the
European Court of Justice on a reference under Article 234EC,[63] or on an
action for damages under Article 288EC.[64] In such cases the restrictions
built in to Article 230EC do not necessarily apply.

---

[63] See below, Chap. 18.
[64] See above, para. 2-078, n. 1.

CHAPTER 6

STATUTORY INTERPRETATION

A. INTRODUCTION

WHILE the enactment of a statute is the culmination of Parliament's **6–001**
legislative process, it is merely the starting point for what may be many
years of existence, in some cases posing problems for generations of users. If
it is to have its proper effect it must be read and understood, although there
are many other factors which govern the extent to which a particular
measure is successful. There are various kinds of statute-user and many
matters which may cause them difficulty.[1] It cannot realistically be assumed
that all statutes are directed at the general public and are therefore designed
to be understood by them. It is argued that statutes are complicated:

" ... because life is complicated. The bulk of the legislation enacted
   nowadays is social, economic or financial; the laws they [*i.e.* statutes]
   must express and the life situations they must regulate are in themselves
   complicated, and these laws cannot in any language or in any style be
   reduced to kindergarten level, any more than can the theory of
   relativity."[2]

The user tends to be the public official charged with the duty of
implementation, the lawyer or the non-legal professional adviser, and
statutes tend to be drafted accordingly: by experts for experts. Lay people[3]
who wish to use statutes thus have to become acquainted with statute-
handling techniques, or rely on explanatory material, such as textbooks or
government leaflets, written by experts, or consult an expert personally. This
is seen by some as a vicious circle: they doubt whether statutes need to be as
complicated as experts who earn a living by explaining them to the rest of us
would have us believe.

Some of the problems of the user, even the professional user, relate to the
discovery of the relevant provisions and the establishment of an authentic,
up-to-date text. The provisions may be spread among a number of statutes
and statutory instruments which have to be read together. The uninstructed

---

[1] See F. A. R. Bennion, *Statute Law* (3rd ed., 1990), Part II (pp. 83–205) and *Understanding
   Common Law Legislation* (2001); *cf.* W. Twining and D. Miers, *How To Do Things With
   Rules* (4th ed., 1999), Chaps. 7, 8.
[2] E. A. Dreidger, cited in Bennion (1990), pp. 209–210.
[3] Or, indeed, lawyers and other professionals in matters outside their expertise.

lay person may well not accomplish even this stage. Once established, the text also has to be understood or "interpreted".[4] The task of interpretation may vary in difficulty. Some provisions can be understood automatically, without the conscious perception of any "problem" of interpretation: some problems may be easy to solve after a moment's thought. At the other extreme, a problem may be highly complex, enough to make the reader weep. Printing or drafting errors can turn a provision into gibberish.

F. A. R. Bennion[5] has identified a number of factors that may cause doubt. Some of these doubt-factors are inevitable and even desirable: others are avoidable. First, there is what he terms the technique of *ellipsis*. Here, the draftsman refrains from using certain words that he or she regards as necessarily implied: the problem is that the users may not realise that this is the case. The unexpressed words may normally be implied in statutes of a particular kind unless Parliament expressly provides to the contrary: many of the principles of judicial review of administrative action rest on this basis,[6] as do certain principles of criminal liability.[7] Alternatively the implication may arise from the words that actually are used. The judges on occasion exercise a limited power (in practice but not in theory) to rewrite statutes, although it can be difficult to predict in any particular case whether a judge will be prepared to act in that way.[8]

Second, the draftsman may use a *broad term* ("a word or phrase of wide meaning") and leave it to the user to judge what situations fall within it. Most words can be said to have a core of certain meaning surrounded by a penumbra of uncertainty. A standard example is the term "vehicle". This clearly covers motor cars, buses and motor cycles, but it is less clear whether it covers an invalid carriage, a child's tricycle, a donkey-cart or a pair of roller-skates.[9] Examples from decided cases include whether the routine oiling and maintenance of points apparatus on the railway fell within the term "relaying or repairing" the permanent way[10]; whether an accident arose "out of and in the course of [the victim's] ... employment"[11]; and whether a car from which the engine had been stolen and a car which could not move under its own power as parts were missing or rusted were "mechanically propelled vehicles" for which a licence was required.[12] Sir Rupert Cross described this sort of case as "part of the daily bread of judges

---

[4] The O.E.D. definitions of this term include both "to expound the meaning of" and "to make out the meaning of, explain to oneself."

[5] *op. cit.* n. 1 above, Chaps 15–19.

[6] *e.g.* breach of natural justice, abuse of discretionary powers: see below, Chap. 18.

[7] See below, pp.

[7] *e.g.* the effect of mistake and insanity on criminal liability. A major defect of the drafting of many statutes creating offences is that they do not make it clear whether *mens rea* is a necessary ingredient: see, *e.g. R. v. Warner* [1969] 2 A.C. 256. Another common defect is that statutes imposing duties do not indicate whether breach of a duty can give rise to a civil action: see, *e.g., Lonrho Ltd v. Shell Petroleum Co. Ltd (No. 2)* [1982] A.C. 173.

[8] See below, pp.

[9] Twining and Miers (1999), pp. 194–200, *cf.* H. L. A. Hart, (1958) 4 J.S.P.T.L. (N.S.) 144–145.

[10] *London and North-Eastern Railway v. Berriman* [1946] A.C. 278.

[11] See, *e.g. R. v. Industrial Injuries Commissioner, ex p. A.E.U. (No. 2)* [1966] 2 Q.B. 31. (accident befalling an employee overstaying a tea-break). There have been many cases on this expression: see N. J. Wikeley, *Ogus, Barendt and Wikely's, The Law of Social Security* (4th ed., 1995), pp. 306–323.

[12] *Newberry v. Simmonds* [1961] 2 Q.B. 345; *Smart v. Allan* [1963] 1 Q.B. 291: the answers were, respectively, yes and no, the main difference being that in the latter case there was no reasonable prospect of the vehicle ever being made mobile again.

and practitioners."[13] One difficulty here may be that the meaning of a statutory expression may change with the passage of time.[14] A further technical point that may arise when it has to be decided whether a set of facts conforms to a statutory description is whether that decision is one of fact or one of law. This governs whether it should be decided by the jury (if there is one) or the judge, and the extent to which the decision can be upset by an appellate court.[15]

Third, there may be *politic uncertainty*: ambiguous words may be used deliberately, for example where a provision is politically contentious, or where departments wish to minimise the risk of legal challenge.[16]

Fourth, there may be *unforeseeable developments*. These the draftsman cannot be expected to cover, although he or she may use language that is capable of extension. A well-known example of such extension is *Attorney-General v. Edison Telephone Co.*[17] where the Telegraph Act 1869, passed before the telephone was invented, was held to confer on the Postmaster General certain powers concerning telephone messages. However, extension may not be possible, and fresh legislation may be necessary. For example, new provisions of revenue law are regularly passed to meet novel tax avoidance schemes developed by smart lawyers and accountants precisely to exploit unforeseen loopholes.

Fifth, there are many ways in which the wording may be inadequate. **6–002** There may be a printing error.[18] There may be a drafting error such as the use of a word with two or more distinct meanings without a sufficient indication from the context or by a definition of which is meant, or grammatical or syntactic ambiguity. Examples of the latter include "ambiguous modification", where it is unclear which words are limited,

---

[13] J. Bell and Sir George Engle, *Cross, Statutory Interpretation* (3rd ed., 1995), pp. 75–76. Another good illustration is provided by the refusal of Parliament to define "disposal" and "disposition" for the purposes of capital gains tax: see J. Tiley, *Revenue Law* (4th ed., 2000), para 35.1.

[14] See, for example, the "public good" defence in section 4 of the Obscene Publications Act 1959: *R. v. Jordan* [1977] A.C. 699, 718, *per* Lord Wilberforce: "[the phrase 'other objects of general concern'] is no doubt a mobile phrase; it may, and should, change in content as society changes." *Cf. Dyson Holdings Ltd v. Fox* [1976] Q.B. 503 on whether the term "family" includes a "common law" spouse, criticised by D. J. Hurst, (1983) 3 L.S. 21; and *Fitzpatrick v. Sterling Housing Association Ltd.* [2001] 1 A.C. 27, where the House of Lords held that a partner in a stable and permanent homosexual relationship could be described as "a member of [the partner's] family" for the purposes of the Rent Act 1977, Schd. 1, para. 2(2). See also *R.v. Ireland*, below, para. 6-028.

[15] See above, paras 1-011–1-013, and below, Chap 18.

[16] Bennion (1990), Chap. 17; A. S. Miller, "Statutory language and the purposive use of ambiguity" 42 Va.L.Rev. 23 (1956); V. Sacks, "Towards Discovering Parliamentary Intent" [1982] Stat.L.R. 143, 157 (research on the background to a number of cases of interpretative difficulty showed that "unintelligible legislation was being added to the statute book because the Government either lacked clear objectives, or, had deliberately intended to obfuscate in order to avoid controversy").

[17] (1880) 6 Q.B.D. 244. *Cf. Royal College of Nursing v. DHSS* [1981] A.C. 800.

[18] *e.g.* the presence of the word "upon" at the end of section 6 of the Statute of Frauds Amendment Act 1828: *Lyde v. Barnard* (1836) 1 M. & W. 101; Local Government Act 1972, s.262(12) (reference to subsection (10) rather than subsection (9) in the Queen's Printer's copy, corrected in *Statutes in Force*); the presence of the word "convenient" in the Prescription Act 1832, s.8, apparently a misprint for "easement": C. Harpun, *Megarry and Wade, The Law Of Real Property* (6th ed., 2000), p. 1134.

restricted or described by a "modifier",[19] and the faulty reference of pronouns.[20] There may be an erroneous reference to another statute.[21] The draftsman may be mistaken about the law that is being altered[22] or the factual situation with which he or she is dealing. The statutory provision may be narrower[23] or wider[24] than the object of the legislation. The provision may fail to indicate an important element, such as the time at which conditions of eligibility for some benefit are to be judged.[25] There may be the type of error described as "defective deeming, or asifism gone wrong."[26] There may be conflict within a statute or between different statutes. There may simply be a slip by the draftsman.[27] Overall, Bennion states that "it is extremely common for draftsmen to produce a text which raises doubt unnecessarily."[28]

As mentioned already, various people may have to interpret statutes for their own purposes. Some may take action based on their own view of a statutory provision. For example, in *R. v. Adams*[29] police officers decided that they could rely on a search warrant in respect of certain premises which had already been used once. The statute did not deal expressly with the question whether a warrant could be used more than once: the court held that it could not. Tax assessments may well be based on the Inland Revenue's interpretation of a doubtful provision of tax law: it will be for the Commissioners of Taxes or the courts to rule on the matter if the Revenue view is challenged. The courts stand in a rather different position from other statute users in that they have the power to resolve authoritatively disputes concerning the meaning of statutory provisions: their decisions are binding on the parties and may constitute binding precedents for the future.

It is notable that the general methods of statutory interpretation are not themselves regulated by Parliament, but have been developed by the judges.

---

[19] G. C. Thornton, *Legislative Drafting* (3rd ed., 1987), pp. 23–29. *e.g.* "public hospital or school" (does "public" modify "school" as well as "hospital"?). A statute of Charles II disqualified those who lacked certain property qualifications "other than the son and heir apparent of an esquire, or other person of higher degree." In *Jones v. Smart* (1784) 1 Term Rep. 44 the court held that the words "son and heir apparent of" governed "person of higher degree" as well as "esquire."

[20] Thornton, pp. 29–32. *e.g.* "and when they arose early in the morning, behold, they were all dead corpses": 2 Kings XIX 35.

[21] *e.g.* War Damage Act 1943, s.66(2)(b), corrected by the Universities and Colleges Estates Act 1964, s.4(1), Sched. 3.

[22] *e.g. Inland Revenue Commissioners v. Ayshire Employers' Mutual Insurance Association* [1946] 1 All E.R. 537.

[23] *e.g. Adler v. George* [1964] 2 Q.B. 7: the Official Secrets Act 1920, s.3 prohibited obstruction "in the vicinity of" a prohibited place; the Divisional Court held that this was to be read as "in or in the vicinity of."

[24] *e.g.* the Criminal Law Act 1977, ss.1 and 5, which on a literal interpretation preserved a much wider range of common law conspiracies than was obviously intended; in *R. v. Duncalf* [1979] 1 W.L.R. 918 the Court of Appeal declined to give a literal reading "when the effect of so doing would be so largely to destroy the obvious purpose of this Act" (*per* Roskill L.J. at p. 923). *R. v. Duncalf* was approved by the House of Lords in *R. v. Ayres* [1984] A.C. 447. See now the Criminal Justice Act 1987, s.12.

[25] *Jackson v. Hall* [1980] A.C. 854, concerning the Agriculture (Miscellaneous Provisions) Act 1976.

[26] Bennion (1990), pp. 274–275; R. E. Megarry, *Miscellany-at-law* (1955), pp. 361–362 ("there is too be much of this damned deeming": *per* (A. P. Herbert's) Lord Mildew).

[27] *cf. R. v. Moore* (1994) 159 J.P. 101, below, para. 6-037, n. 55.

[28] *ibid.* p. 279.

[29] [1980] Q.B. 575.

The Interpretation Act 1978, which from its title might seem to fulfil such a function, has the comparatively unambitious aim of providing certain standard definitions of common provisions,[30] and thereby enables statutes to be drafted more briefly than otherwise would be the case. Where Parliament or, more realistically, the executive has been dissatisfied with judicial interpretation of particular provisions the response has been to pay close attention to the future drafting of specific provisions in that area rather than to attempt to introduce legislation giving general directions to the judiciary. In the remainder of this chapter we consider the general approaches taken by judges to the interpretation of statutes, various internal and external aids to interpretation, the main presumptions which may be invoked and proposals for reform.

B. GENERAL APPROACHES TO STATUTORY INTERPRETATION

Judicial attitudes to legislation have changed with the passage of time. One of the important factors has been the part played by statutes in the general scheme of the law: a related factor has been the conception held by judges as to the proper scope of the judicial function. Three so-called "rules" of statutory interpretation have been identified: the "mischief rule," the "golden rule" and the "literal rule," each originating at different stages of legal history. To call them "rules" is misleading: it is better to think of them as general approaches. They were analysed by Professor John Willis in his influential article "Statute Interpretation in a Nutshell".[31] He suggested that:

"a court invokes whichever of the rules produces a result that satisfies its sense of justice in the case before it. Although the literal rule is the one most frequently referred to in express terms, the courts treat all three as valid and refer to them as occasion demands, but, naturally enough, do not assign any reasons for choosing one rather than another."[32]

Thus, on some occasions the "literal rule" would be preferred to the "mischief rule": on others the reverse would be the case. It was impossible to predict with certainty which approach would be adopted in a particular case.[33] More recently, Sir Rupert Cross suggested that the English approach involves not so much a choice between alternative "rules" as a progressive analysis in which the judge first considers the ordinary meaning of the words in the general context of the statute, a broad view being taken of what constitutes the "context", and then moves on to consider other possibilities

---

[30] See above, para. 5-017.

[31] (1938) 16 Can. Bar Rev. 1.

[32] *ibid.* p. 16.

[33] This situation can be unkindly described as the "today's a day for the golden rule" approach. The tone of Professor Willis' article was one of scepticism.

where the ordinary meaning leads to an absurd result.[34] This unified "contextual" approach is supported by dicta in decisions of the House of Lords where general principles of statutory interpretation have been discussed. However, generalisations as to what judges actually do are difficult to substantiate: Sir Rupert Cross made it clear that his propositions were stated "with all the diffidence, hesitancy and reservation that the subject demands."[35]

It is important to appreciate that this analysis of the approach of judges to statutory interpretation operates at a high level of generality. It provides a framework for the solution of interpretative problems, but is not and cannot itself provide the solution. Where a problem of statutory interpretation comes before a court, counsel for each side will advance detailed arguments based on such matters as the nuances of language, the purpose of the statute, the particular aids and presumptions discussed below, and previously decided cases in the area. Different readings of the text will be examined to see which fits best into the statutory scheme. The practical consequences of the different possible interpretations will be compared. Indeed, the discussions in the House of Lords of general approaches to interpretation, on which Sir Rupert Cross's propositions were based, are not commonly cited in argument in decided cases.

6–003   The most recent major work on the subject is F. A. R. Bennion's *Statutory Interpretation*.[36] In his introduction, the author writes:

> "The natural and reasonable desire that statutes should be easily understood is doomed to disappointment. Thwarted, it shifts to an equally natural and reasonable desire for efficient tools of interpretation. If statutes must be obscure, let us at least have simple devices to elucidate them. A golden rule would be best, to unlock all mysteries. Alas, there is no golden rule. Nor is there a mischief rule, or a literal rule, or any other cure-all rule of thumb. Instead there are a thousand and one interpretative *criteria*. Fortunately, not all of these present themselves in any one case; but those that do yield factors that the interpreter must figuratively weigh and balance."[37]

The book comprises a Code, with a critical Commentary, in which various detailed interpretative criteria are enumerated, illustrated, and criticised. It is a valuable source of the many kinds of detailed arguments that might be advanced before a court, and relies to a much greater extent than the established practitioners' manuals[38] on recent case law. This is particularly important "given the changes in judicial attitudes to statutory interpretation that have occurred in the past two-to-three decades ... ."[39] There is a greater

---

[34] The current editors of his book refer instead to "a result which is contrary to the purpose of the statute": see below, para. 6-007.

[35] J. Bell and Sir George Engle, *Cross, Statutory Interpretation* (3rd ed., 1995), p. 48.

[36] (3rd ed., 1997, Supplement, 1999). For full reviews of the first edition, see D. R. Miers, [1986] P.L. 160; J. Bell, (1986) 6 O.J.L.S. 288.

[37] *ibid.*, p. 2.

[38] P. St. J. Langan, *Maxwell on the Interpretation of Statutes* (12th ed., 1969); S. G. G. Edgar, *Craies on Statute Law* (7th ed., 1971). These works have been regularly cited in court; Bennion (1997) is now cited with increasing frequency, usually in preference to the older works.

[39] D. R. Miers, [1986] P.L. 160, 162.

willingness to attempt to identify and to consider the purpose of the provision in question, and much less of (if ever there was) an inclination to adhere strictly to the supposed literal meaning of words irrespective of the context and the consequences of such a reading.[40] This point is strongly reinforced by the landmark decision of the House of Lords in *Pepper (Inspector of Taxes) v. Hart*[41] that the courts are permitted in defined circumstances to consider Parliamentary material, including statements in debate, as an aid to statutory construction. One of the arguments in favour of relaxing the previous rule that excluded reference to such material was expressed as follows by Lord Griffiths[42]:

"The days have long passed when the courts adopted a strict constructionist view of interpretation which required them to adopt the literal meaning of the language. The courts now adopt a purposive approach which seeks to give effect to the true purpose of legislation and are prepared to look at much extraneous material that bears upon the background against which the legislation was enacted. Why then cut ourselves off from the one source in which may be found an authoritative statement of the intention with which the legislation is placed before Parliament?"

It is often stated, as by Lord Griffiths in the passage just quoted, that the task of the judge is to discover the "intention of Parliament". This may be as to either the meaning or the scope of a particular word or phrase, or the general purpose that was to be achieved by the statute.[43] This concept causes difficulty for a number of reasons.[44] It cannot mean the intention of "all the members of both Houses" as some may not have been aware of the measure, and others may have opposed it. If it is taken to mean "all the members of both Houses who voted for it" there may be problems in that the majority "will almost certainly have been constituted by different persons at the different stages of the passage of the Bill,"[45] and might have had different views as to its meaning or purpose. A vote in favour of a Bill may reflect loyalty to the party whip rather than an understanding or even half-hearted approval of the measure. Even assuming that there is a "collective intention" it is difficult to see how it could be ascertained. Would it be by reference to the debates or by canvassing the opinions of the legislators individually, possibly years after the event? The former would limit the "sample" to the minority who happened to speak: the latter would be a research task which might just produce usable results in respect of a provision requiring interpretation soon after enactment, but with the passage of time it would rapidly become hopeless. In any event it is

[40] Below, para. 6-005.
[41] [1993] A.C. 593; below, paras 6-036–6-038.
[42] [1993] A.C. 593, 617. *Cf.* Lord Browne-Wilkinson's reference to "the purposive approach to construction now adopted by the courts in order to give effect to the true intentions of the legislature" (p. 635).
[43] Termed respectively "particular legislative intent" and "general legislative intent" by G. C. MacCallum Jr., (1966) 75 Yale LJ. 754.
[44] See Cross (1995), pp. 23–31; M. Radin, (1930) 43 Harv. L.R. 863, 869–872; J. M. Landis, *ibid.* pp. 886–893; D. Payne, (1956) 9 C.L.P. 96; R. Dworkin, "How to read the Civil Rights Act", *New York Review of Books*, December 20, 1979, pp. 37–43.
[45] Cross (1995), p. 24.

questionable whether even if it is possible it would be appropriate for the
meaning of a particular provision to be determined by an opinion poll of the
original legislators. Given these difficulties, and the rule that prohibited
reference to Parliamentary material,[46] it was stated that the best if not the
only evidence of the "intention of Parliament" was the wording of the
statute:

> "We often say that we are looking for the intention of Parliament, but
> that is not quite accurate. We are seeking the meaning of the words
> which Parliament used. We are seeking not what Parliament meant but
> the true meaning of what they said."[47]

The same point has been made by Lord Steyn in considering the view that
"out of considerations of piety we frequently refer to the actual intentions of
the draftsmen." In fact,

> "the subjective intention of the draftsmen is immaterial. The only
> relevant inquiry is as to the sense of the words in the content in which
> they are used."[48]

The meaning of the "intention of Parliament" must now be seen in the light
of the decision in *Pepper (Inspector of Taxes) v. Hart*.[49] Reference may now
be made in specified circumstances to Parliamentary material that

> "clearly discloses the mischief aimed at or the legislative intention lying
> behind the ambiguous or obscure words."

In the case of statements made to Parliament,

> "as at present advised I cannot foresee that any statement other than
> the statement of the Minister or other promoter of the Bill is likely to
> meet these criteria."[50]

Thus, "an authoritative statement of the intention with which the legislation
is placed before Parliament"[51] is taken to show which interpretation was
"intended by Parliament."[52] The theory on which this inference is based is
that:

> "If a Minister clearly states the effect of a provision and there is no
> subsequent relevant amendment to the Bill or withdrawal of the
> statement it is reasonable to assume that Parliament passed the Bill on
> the basis that the provision would have the effect stated."[53]

---

[46] See below, paras 6-036–6-038.
[47] *Per* Lord Reid in *Black-Clawson International Ltd v. Papierwerke Waldhof-Aschaffenburg A.
G.* [1975] A.C. 591, 613.
[48] *R. v. Ireland* [1998] A.C. 147, 158. See also J. Steyn, (2001) 21 O.J.L.S. 59.
[49] [1993] A.C. 593; below, paras 6-036–6-038.
[50] *Ibid.*, p. 634, *per* Lord Browne-Wilkinson (with whom five of the other six members of the
House agreed).
[51] *ibid.*, p. 617G, *per* Lord Griffiths.
[52] *ibid.*, p. 617A, *per* Lord Bridge.
[53] *ibid.*, p. 633, *per* Lord Browne-Wilkinson, summarising the submissions of Anthony Lester
Q.C. which he subsequently stated that he accepted (p. 634).

This, together with the rejection of the possibility of "dredging through conflicting statements of intention" in order to establish "the true intention of Parliament",[54] confirms that the "intention of Parliament" is a notional device rather than something that actually exists. The House of Lords in *Pepper (Inspector of Taxes) v. Hart*[55] was at pains to confirm the orthodox position as to the separation of powers whereby Parliament legislates and the judiciary interpret; the courts would still be interpreting the words of the Act, albeit with the assistance of a wider range of material.[56]

1. THE "MISCHIEF RULE"

The classic statement of the "mischief rule" is contained in the resolutions of the Barons of the Exchequer in *Heydon's Case*:[57]   **6–004**

> "that for the sure and true interpretation of all statutes in general (be they penal or beneficial, restrictive or enlarging of the common law,) four things are to be discerned and considered:—
> 1st. What was the common law before the making of the Act.
> 2nd. What was the mischief and defect for which the common law did not provide.
> 3rd. What remedy the Parliament hath resolved and appointed to cure the disease of the commonwealth.
> And, 4th. The true reason of the remedy; and then the office of all the Judges is always to make such construction as shall suppress the mischief, and advance the remedy, and to suppress subtle inventions and evasions for continuance of the mischief, and *pro privato commodo*, and to add force and life to the cure and remedy, according to the true intent of the makers of the Act, *pro bono publico*."

These resolutions were the product of a time when statutes were a minor source of law by comparison with the common law, when drafting was by no means as exact a process as it is today[58] and before the supremacy of Parliament was firmly established. The "mischief" could often be discerned from the lengthy preamble normally included.[59]

The "mischief rule" was regarded by the Law Commissions, which reported on statutory interpretation in 1969,[60] as a "rather more satisfactory approach" than the other two established "rules". This was so even though the formulation in *Heydon's Case* was archaic in language, reflected a very different constitutional balance between the executive, Parliament and the people than would now be acceptable, failed to make clear the extent to

---

[54] *ibid.*, p. 631, *per* Lord Browne-Wilkinson, referring to another of Mr Lester's arguments.
[55] *ibid.*, p. 639–640, *per* Lord Browne-Wilkinson.
[56] This important constitutional point was emphasised by Lord Scarman in *Duport Steels Ltd v. Sirs* [1980] I.C.R. 161, 189–190, above, para. 5-020.
[57] (1584) 3 Co.Rep. 7a, 7b.
[58] Some statutes were well drafted, such as the Statute of Uses 1535.
[59] *Black-Clawson International Ltd v. Papierwerke Waldhof-Aschaffenburg A.G.* [1975] A.C. 591 *per* Lord Diplock at pp. 637–638. See below, para. 6-019.
[60] Law Com. No. 21; Scot. Law Com. No. 11.

which the judge should consider the actual language of the statute, assumed that statutes were subsidiary or supplemental to the common law and predated rules which prevented judges considering certain material which might throw light on the "mischief" and the "true reason of the remedy".[61] Seemingly, therefore, it was the best of a bad lot.

It came to be accepted that the "mischief rule" should only be applied where the words were ambiguous[62]; one of the improvements of the "contextual approach" discussed below is that the purpose of the statute should be considered as part of the context of the statutory words, and not merely as a last resort where the words are ambiguous.

2. The "Literal Rule"

6–005   The eighteenth and nineteenth centuries saw a trend towards a more literal approach. Courts took an increasingly strict view of the words of a statute: if the case before them was not precisely covered they were not prepared to countenance any alteration of the statutory language. For example, in *R. v. Harris*[63] a statute[64] which made it an offence for someone "unlawfully and maliciously" to "stab, cut, or wound any person" was held not to apply where the defendant bit off the end of the victim's nose; the words indicated that for an offence to be committed some form of instrument had to be used.[65]

One of the leading statements of the "literal rule" was made by Tindal C. J. in advising the House of Lords in the *Sussex Peerage* case[66]:

> "My Lords, the only rule for the construction of Acts of Parliament is, that they should be construed according to the intent of the Parliament which passed the Act. If the words of the statute are in themselves precise and unambiguous, then no more can be necessary than to expound those words in their natural and ordinary sense. The words themselves alone do, in such case, best declare the intention of the lawgiver. But if any doubt arises from the terms employed by the Legislature, it has always been held a safe means of collecting the intention, to call in aid the ground and cause of making the statute, and to have recourse to the preamble, which, according to Chief Justice Dyer (*Stowel v. Lord Zouch*, Plowden, 369) is 'a key to open the minds of the makers of the Act, and the mischiefs which they intended to redress.'"

This was taken to mean that the "mischief rule" was only applicable where the words were ambiguous.

The literal rule was favoured on a variety of grounds. It encouraged

---

[61] *ibid.* pp. 19–20. See below, paras 6-036–6-038.

[62] See the *Sussex Peerage Case*, below, para. 6-005.

[63] (1836) 7 C. & P. 446.

[64] 9 Geo. IV c. 31 s.12.

[65] The judge indicated that the defendant would be indicted for aggravated assault and thus "would not escape punishment if she was guilty." *Cf. Jones v. Smart*, above, para. 6-002, n. 19.

[66] (1844) 11 Cl. & Fin. 85, 143.

precision in drafting. Should any alternative approach be adopted, an alteration of the statutory language could be seen as a usurpation by non-elected judges of the legislative function of Parliament,[67] and other statute users would have the difficult task of predicting how doubtful provisions might be "rewritten" by the judges. On the other hand judges were criticised on the ground that:

"they have tended excessively to emphasise the literal meaning of statutory provisions without giving due weight to their meaning in wider contexts ... ."[68]

"To place undue emphasis on the literal meaning of the words of a provision is to assume an unattainable perfection in draftsmanship; ... [and] ignores the limitations of language, which is not infrequently demonstrated even at the level of the House of Lords when Law Lords differ as to the so-called 'plain meaning' of words."[69]

Moreover, the literal approach is not helpful where the court is resolving a doubt as to the applicability of a "broad term".

Much has been made of a few post-war cases where literalism has perhaps been taken too far. For example, in *Bourne v. Norwich Crematorium*[70] the question was whether a capital allowance could be claimed in respect of expenditure on a new furnace chamber and chimney tower of a crematorium, as expenditure on "buildings and structures" in use "for the purpose of a trade which consists of the manufacture of goods or materials or the subjection of goods or materials to any process." Stamp J. held that it could not: it would be "a distortion of the English language to describe the living or the dead as goods or materials."[71] However, it is unlikely that either the draftsman or Parliament thought specifically of cremation in connection with capital allowances and the policy of the provisions on capital allowances would seem to cover the "trade" of cremation.[72]

The "contextual approach" discussed below is based on the literal approach, but requires greater attention to be paid to the context in which the words appear.

3. THE "GOLDEN RULE"

Some judges have suggested that a court may depart from the ordinary meaning where that would lead to absurdity. In *Grey v. Pearson*[73] Lord

6–006

---

[67] Conversely, it might be argued that a judge could conceal that his or her role was not as impersonal and objective as he or she would like it to appear by paying lip-service to the literal rule.

[68] Law Com. No. 21; Scot. Law Com. No. 11, p. 5.

[69] *ibid.* p. 17. For example, in *London and North Eastern Railway v. Berriman* [1946] A.C. 278 (below p.) members of the House of Lords who came to opposite conclusions on the meaning of "repairing" nevertheless each claimed to be applying the "fair and ordinary" (Lord Macmillan at p. 295) or the "natural and ordinary" meaning (Lord Wright at p. 301).

[70] [1967] 1 W.L.R. 691. See also *L.N.E.R. v. Berriman*, below, para. 6–011.

[71] *ibid.* p. 695.

[72] See Law Com. No. 21, pp. 5–6; Cross (1995), p. 70. The decision has not, however, been reversed by statute.

[73] (1857) 6 H. L. Cas. 61, 106 (a case concerning the construction of a will). *Cf.* the same judge when he was Parke B. in *Becke v. Smith* (1836) 2 M. & W. 191, 195.

Wensleydale said:

> "I have been long and deeply impressed with the wisdom of the rule,
> now, I believe, universally adopted, at least in the Courts of Law in
> Westminster Hall, that in construing wills and indeed statutes, and all
> written instruments, the grammatical and ordinary sense of the words is
> to be adhered to, unless that would lead to some absurdity, or some
> repugnance or inconsistency with the rest of the instrument, in which
> case the grammatical and ordinary sense of the words may be modified,
> so as to avoid that absurdity and inconsistency, but no farther."

This became known as "Lord Wensleydale's golden rule" following a
dictum of Lord Blackburn in *River Wear Commissioners v. Adamson*[74]:

> "I believe that it is not disputed that what Lord Wensleydale used to
> call the golden rule is right, *viz.*, that we are to take the whole statute
> together and construe it all together, giving the words their ordinary
> signification, unless when so applied they produce an inconsistency, or
> an absurdity or inconvenience so great as to convince the Court that the
> intention could not have been to use them in their ordinary
> signification, and to justify the Court in putting on them some other
> signification, which, though less proper, is one which the Court thinks
> the words will bear."

One controversial aspect of this "rule" was whether it could only apply
where the words were ambiguous, or whether it could also be used where the
ordinary meaning was clear but "absurd". In so far as it was confined to the
former situation it was a statement of the blindingly obvious: that where
statutory words are ambiguous an interpretation that is not absurd is to be
preferred to one that is. In so far as the "rule" could be applied in the latter
situation it was clear that it should be used sparingly.[75] Some judges argued
it could not be used in such a case at all. Lord Esher said.[76]

> "If the words of an Act are clear, you must follow them, even though
> they lead to a manifest absurdity. The Court has nothing to do with the
> question whether the legislature has committed an absurdity."

Another point of doubt was whether the concept of "absurdity" was
confined to cases where a provision was "absurd" because it was
"repugnant" to or "inconsistent" with other provisions of the statute, or
whether it extended to "absurdity" for any reason. The Law Commissions
noted that the "rule" provided no clear means to test the existence of the
characteristics of absurdity, inconsistency or inconvenience, or to measure
their quality or extent.[77] As it seemed that "absurdity" was in practice
judged by reference to whether a particular interpretation was irreconcilable

---

[74] (1877) 2 App. Cas. 743, 764–765.
[75] Lord Mersey in *Thompson v. Goold & Co.* [1910] A.C. 409, 420; Lord Loreburn in *Vickers Sons, and Maxim Ltd v. Evans* [1910] A.C. 444, 445.
[76] *R. v. Judge of the City of London Court* [1892] 1 Q.B. 273, 290. *Cf.* Lord Atkinson in *Vacher & Sons Ltd v. London Society of Compositors* [1913] A.C. 107, 121–122.
[77] Law Com. No. 21; Scot. Law Com. No. 11, p. 19.

with the general policy of the legislature "the golden rule turns out to be a less explicit form of the mischief rule.[78] The ideas behind the "golden rule" are reflected in the second and third aspects of the contextual approach discussed below.

4. THE UNIFIED "CONTEXTUAL" APPROACH

Sir Rupert Cross set out a unified approach to statutory interpretation as follows[79]:

6-007

"1. The judge must give effect to the [grammatical and][80] ordinary or, where appropriate, the technical meaning of words in the general context of the statute; he must also determine the extent of general words with reference to that context.

2. If the judge considers that the application of the words in their [grammatical and][81] ordinary sense would produce [a result which is contrary to the purpose of the statute],[82] he may apply them in any secondary meaning which they are capable of bearing.

3. The judge may read in words which he considers to be necessarily implied by words which are already in the statute and he has a limited power to add to, alter or ignore statutory words in order to prevent a provision from being unintelligible or absurd or totally unreasonable, unworkable, or totally irreconcilable with the rest of the statute.

4. In applying the above rules the judge may resort to [certain] aids to construction and presumptions . . . ."

(a) Rule 1

(i) Context

Under this approach a broader view is taken of the context than under previous approaches. The importance of context was discussed in *Attorney-General v. Prince Ernest Augustus of Hanover*.[83] A statute of Queen Anne's reign[84] provided that Princess Sophia of Hanover "and the Issue of Her

6-008

---

[78] *ibid.* Sir Rupert Cross regarded the "golden rule" as a "gloss upon the literal rule": Cross *Statutory Interpretation* (1976), p. 170. *Cf.* E. A. Dreidger, (1981) 59 Can. Bar Rev. 781.

[79] Cross (1976), p. 43; third edition by J. Bell and Sir George Engle (1995), p. 49. The label "contextual" was not attached by Cross, but is used here for convenience of reference. Rules 1 and 2 were expounded by Lord Simon in *Maunsell v. Olins* [1975] A.C. 373, 391; rule 3 by Lord Reid in *Federal Steam Navigation Co. Ltd v. Department of Trade and Industry* [1974] 1 W.L.R. 505, 508–509. The "aids" and "presumptions" are discussed in Chapters 5 to 7 of Cross's book.

[80] These words were added by the editors of the second and third editions of *Cross.*

[81] *ibid.*

[82] These words replace "an absurd result which cannot reasonably be supposed to have been the intention of the legislature" from the first edition. See pp. 89–92 of the third edition for discussion of the change.

[83] [1957] A.C. 436. See A. Lyon, (1999) 20 Stat. L.R. 174.

[84] 4 & 5 Anne c. 16.

Body and all Persons lineally descending from Her born or hereafter to be
born be and shall be ... deemed ... natural born Subjects of this Kingdom."
The preamble recited that in order that they might be encouraged to become
acquainted with the laws and constitutions of this realm "it is just and
highly reasonable that they in Your Majesties Lifetime" be naturalised.[85]
The respondent, who was born in 1914 and was a lineal descendant of
Sophia, was granted a declaration that he was a British subject. The
enacting words were clear and could not be restricted by the words in the
preamble. Viscount Simonds said[86]:

> "[W]ords, and particularly general words, cannot be read in isolation;
> their colour and content are derived from their context. So it is that I
> conceive it to be my right and duty to examine every word of a statute
> in its context, and I use context in its widest sense which I have already
> indicated as including not only other enacting provisions of the same
> statute, but its preamble, the existing state of the law, other statutes *in
> pari materia*, and the mischief which I can, by those and other
> legitimate means, discern the statute was intended to remedy ....
>
> "[N]o one should profess to understand any part of a statute or of
> any other document before he has read the whole of it. Until he has
> done so, he is not entitled to say that it, or any part of it, is clear and
> unambiguous."

Lord Normand said[87]:

> "In order to discover the intention of Parliament it is proper that the
> court should read the whole Act, inform itself of the legal context of the
> Act, including Acts so related to it that they may throw light on its
> meaning, and of the factual context, such as the mischief to be
> remedied. .... It is the merest commonplace to say that words abstracted
> from context may be meaningless or misleading."

Even after the context had been considered it could not be said that the
enacting words were unclear; the preamble itself was ambiguous; three of
their Lordships also held that there was no inherent absurdity, judged at the
time when the statute was passed, in the fact that all lineal descendants
would be naturalised.[88]

(ii) Purposive interpretation

6–009   That the object of the statute is to be considered as part of the context was

---

[85] On the death of Queen Anne without issue the Crown of England would descend on Sophia
and her heirs: Sophia's son became King George I.

[86] At pp. 461, 463. Lord Tucker expressed his "complete agreement" with Viscount Simonds'
opinion (p. 472).

[87] At p. 465. See also Lord Somervell at pp. 473–474.

[88] Most of the royal heads of Europe in the early twentieth century, including the German
Kaiser, were lineal descendants of Sophia.

emphasised in *Maunsell v. Olins*.[89] The plaintiff owned the freehold of a
farm. The farm's tenant had sublet a cottage to the Olins. If the cottage
formed "part of premises which had been let as a whole on a superior
letting" the Olins were entitled to the continued protection of the Rent Acts
after the tenant's death. The House held by three to two[90] that the word
"premises" was to be limited to dwelling-houses[91] and as the Olins were not
the subtenants of part of premises in that limited sense they were not
protected. Lord Wilberforce expressly endorsed Viscount Simonds' dictum
in the *Hanover* case.[92] Lord Simon, with whom Lord Diplock entirely
agreed, held that the term "premises" was to be construed more widely as in
ordinary legal parlance "the subject-matter of a letting" or, more
technically, as "the subject-matter of the habendum clause of the relevant
lease." He did, however, make certain general observations as to
interpretation, which were not controverted in the speeches of the
majority[93]:

"The rule in *Heydon's Case*, 3, Co.Rep. 7a itself is sometimes stated as a
primary canon of construction, sometimes as secondary (*i.e.* available
in the case of an ambiguity): *cf. Maxwell on the Interpretation of
Statutes* (12th ed., 1969), pp. 40, 96, with *Craies on Statute Law*, 7th ed.
(1971) pp. 94, 96. We think that the explanation of this is that the rule is
available at two stages. The first task of a court of construction is to put
itself in the shoes of the draftsman—to consider what knowledge he
had and, importantly, what statutory objective he had—if only as a
guide to the linguistic register. Here is the first consideration of the
'mischief.' Being thus placed in the shoes of the draftsman, the court
proceeds to ascertain the meaning of the statutory language. In this
task 'the first and most elementary rule of construction' is to consider
the plain and primary meaning, in their appropriate register, of the
words used. If there is no such plain meaning (*i.e.*, if there is an
ambiguity), a number of secondary canons are available to resolve it.
Of these one of the most important is the rule in *Heydon's Case*. Here,
then, may be a second consideration of the 'mischief'."

In 1980, Lord Scarman said in a lecture in Australia that, "In London, no
one would now dare to choose the literal rather than a purposive
construction of a statute: and 'legalism' is currently a term of abuse."[94]
Similar statements were made in *Pepper (Inspector of Taxes) v. Hart*.[95]

---

[89] [1975] A.C. 373. See also *Stock v. Frank Jones (Tipton) Ltd* [1978] 1 W.L.R. 231, 236, and
Powdrill v. Watson [1995] 2 All E.R. 65, 79 (Lord Browne-Wilkinson).
[90] Lord Reid, Lord Wilberforce and Viscount Dilhorne; Lord Simon and Lord Diplock
dissented.
[91] Viscount Dilhorne thought the term might mean "buildings".
[92] Above.
[93] p. 395. Other examples of interpretation in the light of the mischief include *Marshall v.
British Broadcasting Corporation* [1979] 1 W.L.R. 1071; *Maidstone B.C. v. Mortimer* [1980] 3
All E.R. 552 and *Royal College of Nursing of the United Kingdom v. DHSS* [1981] A.C. 800.
[94] (1981) 55 A.L.J. 175. *Cf.* Glanville Williams, "The Meaning of Literal Interpretation" (1981)
131 N.LJ. 1128, 1149, who argues that the primary question should be "What was the
statute trying to do?" followed by "Will a particular proposed interpretation effectuate that
object" and lastly, "Is the interpretation ruled out by the language?"
[95] [1993] A.C. 593; above, para. 6-004; below, paras 6-036–6-038.

Reference is now frequently made by judges to the concept of "purposive"[96] statutory construction. Sometimes the term is used broadly to describe the general approach to the construction of statutes. As such, it is misleading as the legislative purpose is but one of the factors that should be considered as part of the context.[97] More commonly, it is used in a narrower sense, in the course of comparing readings based on the literal or grammatical meaning of words with readings based on a purposive approach. It may be used even more narrowly to denote a construction that involves straining the words of the statute in order to fulfil the legislative purpose.[98] The increased frequency in the use of the term by judges coincides with a discernible change in emphasis,[99] but the magnitude of the change should not be exaggerated.

First, it should not be assumed that a purposive approach will lead to a different result than a literal approach. Indeed, the opposite is normally the case:

> "This correspondence is not surprising; indeed it is what we would expect. Parliament, having a certain purpose, naturally seeks to express this in the words used. If it did otherwise to any great extent, the legislature would be using an inefficient method."[1]

Accordingly, in a number of cases a purposive approach to construction has been adopted alongside a literal approach, each being regarded as leading to the same result.[2] The choice between different possible readings of the provision in question will commonly be influenced by a consideration of which reading best fulfils the legislative purpose.[3] On occasion, a purposive approach has been adopted where a literal approach would have led to absurdity or would have clearly defeated the purposes of the Act.[4] However, a purposive interpretation may only be adopted if judges "can find in the statute read as a whole or in material to which they are permitted by law to refer as aids to interpretation an expression of Parliament's purpose or

---

[96] *i.e.* one that will "promote the general legislative purpose underlying the provisions": *per* Lord Denning M.R. in *Nothman v. London Borough of Barnet* [1978] 1 W.L.R. 220, 228, based on the Law Commissions' Report: see below, para. 6-048.

[97] See above, para. 6-008.

[98] Bennion (1997), p.740 suggests that the term "purposive construction" is usually intended by judges to bear this meaning. *Sed quaere.*

[99] Lord Diplock in *Carter v. Bradbeer* [1975] 1 W.L.R. 1204, 1206–1207; Laws L.J. in *Ashworth Ltd. v. Ballard Ltd.* [1999] 2 All E.R. 791, 805 ("the difference between purposive and literal construction is in truth one of degree only").

[1] Bennion (1997), p. 737.

[2] *Suffolk County Council v. Mason* [1979] A.C. 705 (by both majority and minority judges): effect of designation of a footpath on a definitive map prepared under the National Parks and Access to the Countryside Act 1949; *Gardner v. Moore* [1984] A.C. 548: Motor Insurers Bureau liable to compensate victim of international criminal act; *Leverton v. Clwyd County Council* [1989] A.C. 706: woman and man employed at different establishments under the same collective agreement held to be employed under "common terms and conditions of employment."

[3] See, *e.g. Bank of Scotland v. Grimes* [1985] Q.B. 1179; *In re Smalley* [1985] A.C. 622; *Greater London Council v. Holmes* [1986] Q.B. 989; *Ferguson v. Welsh* [1987] 1 W.L.R. 1553: see below.

[4] *R. v. Ayres* [1984] A.C. 447, modified in *R. v. Cooke* [1986] A.C. 909; *cf.* Lord Diplock in *Jones v. Wrotham Park Settled Estates* [1980] A.C. 74, 105: *cf.* "rule 2" below.

policy."[5] Prior to *Pepper (Inspector of Taxes) v. Hart*[6] there were cases where the judges found it impossible to discern the legislative purpose.[7] Recourse to parliamentary material may now help to establish the purpose of a particular provision,[8] but it must be recognised that usually it does not.[9] Furthermore, there are limits to the extent to which the courts are prepared to distort the statutory language in order to fulfil the legislative purpose.[10] This point may explain why statements are still made that while "purposive construction to resolve ambiguities of statutory language is often appropriate and necessary", the courts' "traditional approach to construction" gives "primacy to the ordinary, grammatical meaning of statutory language", it remaining the "golden rule of construction that a statute means exactly what it says and does not mean what it does not say."[11] It is also illustrated by the modern approach to the interpretation of taxing statutes. The House of Lords has confirmed that a purposive approach is to be adopted:

"in determining the natural meaning of particular expressions in their context, weight is to be given to the purpose and spirit of the legislation."[12]

The previous approach whereby

"the taxpayer was entitled to stand on a literal interpretation of the words used regardless of the purpose of the statute"

and

"tax law was by and large left behind as some island of literal interpretation"

was no longer acceptable.[13]

---

[5] *per* Lord Scarman in *R. v. Barnet London Borough-Council, ex p. Nilish Shah* [1983] 2 A.C. 309, 348 (the test was not satisfied here).

[6] [1993] A.C. 593: above, para. 6-004, below, paras 6-036–6-038.

[7] Harman J. in *Re Potters Oil Ltd* [1985] BCLC 203, 207–208; Lloyd L.J. in *Hemens (Valuation Officer) v. Whitsbury Farm and Stud Ltd.* [1987] Q.B. 390, 401 (the House of Lords did not advert to this point on appeal, [1988] A.C. 601); Lloyd L.J. in *I.R.C. v. Mobil North Sea Ltd* [1987] 1 W.L.R. 389, 398, dissapproved on appeal by Lord Templeman [1987] 1 W.L.R. 1065, 1071; Mann J. in *Hadley v. Texas Homecare Ltd* and other cases (1987) 86 L.G.R. 577, 582 (list of items that may be sold on Sunday).

[8] See, *e.g.*, *Pepper (Inspector of Taxes) v. Hart* itself.

[9] See below, paras 6-036–6-038.

[10] *per* Lord Diplock in *Jones v. Wrotham Park Settled Estates*, n. 4 above; cf. "rule 3" below.

[11] *per* Lord Bridge of Harwich in *Associated Newspapers Ltd v. Wilson* [1995] 2 A.C. 454, where a majority of the House of Lords held that giving a pay rise only to those employees who agreed to switch from collective bargaining to individual contracts was not "action ... taken against" the others preventing or deterring them from being union members (contrary to the Employment Protection (Consolidation) Act 1978, s.23(l)); to extend the relevant provisions to cover omissions as well as action would require substantial recasting. See also his Lordship's remarks in *Holden & Co. v.C.P.S. (No. 2)* [1994] 1 A.C. 22, 33.

[12] *IRC v. McGuckian* [1997] 1 W.L.R. 991, 1005, *per* Lord Cooke of Thorndon. Endorsed by the House of Lords in *MacNiven v. Westmoreland Investments* [2001] 1 All E.R. 865. (See J.T., [2001] B.T.R. 153.)

[13] *ibid.*, at p. 1000, per Lord Steyn.

In *MacNiven v. Westmoreland Investments*[14] Lord Hoffmann referred to the "valuable insights" of Lords Cooke and Steyn in *McGuckian*, but also stated that

"There is ultimately only one principle of construction, namely to ascertain what Parliament meant by using the language of the statute."

Accordingly, notwithstanding the fears of some, it is clear that the courts cannot ignore the statutory language in the course of furthering any supposed general statutory purpose that taxing statutes are designed to raise money from the taxpayer; and the extent to which statutory language will be strained to have that result is limited.[15]

(iii) Application of statutory words to facts

6–010   In a number of cases the task of the court is to determine whether a particular expression, often of some generality, applies to certain facts.[16] The decision may be reached as a matter of common sense, often with the assistance of dictionaries,[17] but here, as. elsewhere, consideration of the legislative purpose may be helpful. Examples include decisions that discrimination on the ground of nationality was not prohibited as being discrimination on the ground of "national origins",[18] that painting was "construction or maintenance work",[19] that a newspaper competition card was a "literary work",[20] that demolition work falls within the expression "work of construction" for the purposes of the Occupiers' Liability Act 1957,[21] that the provision of a daily continental breakfast constitutes "board" under the Rent Act 1977,[22] that a ship of any size provided by an employer for the purposes of his business constituted "equipment" under the Employer's Liability (Defective Equipment) Act 1969,[23] that a miscellaneous variety of items (including ceramic tiles, creosote, curtain railing, roofing felt and wallpaper) were not "motor accessories,"[24] that the definition of "gypsies" as "persons of nomadic habit of life" included the

---

[14] [2001] 1 All E.R. 865, 874, 882. Lords, Nicholls, Hope, Hutton and Hobhouse agreed with Lord Hoffmann. See also to similar effect *Frankland v. IRC* [1997] STC 1450, criticised at [1998] B.T.R. 262.

[15] See Editorial, "Interpreting Tax Statutes" (1997) 18 Stat. L.R. v. (comment on *McGuckian*); N. Lee, "A purposive approach to tax statutes" (1999) 20 Stat. L.R. 124.

[16] See above, paras 1-011–1-013, 6-002.

[17] Below, para. 6-029.

[18] *Ealing London Borough Council v. Race Relations Board* [1972] A.C. 342.

[19] *Wilkinson v. Doncaster Metropolitan Borough Council* (1985) 84 L.G.R. 257.

[20] *Express Newspapers v. Liverpool Daily Post and Echo* [1985] 1 W.L.R. 1089.

[21] *Ferguson v. Welsh* [1987] 1 W.L.R. 1553, 1560.

[22] *Otter v. Norman* [1989] A.C. 129.

[23] *Coltman v. Bibby Tankers Ltd* [1988] A.C. 276. This was so, notwithstanding a statutory definition of "equipment" to the effect that it "includes any plant and machinery, vehicle, aircraft and clothing" (1969 Act, s.l(3)): this was held to be "for the purpose of clarity" and not to cut down the general meaning of "equipment". The House of Lords could not think of any rational explanation for the exclusion of "ship" from the definition section (although this was probably deliberate: Sir Denis Dobson, [1988] Stat. L.R. 126).

[24] *Hadley v. Texas Homecare Ltd* and other cases (1987) 96 L.G.R. 577.

requirement that there must be some recognisable connection between the travelling from place to place and the persons' livelihood[25] and that a "crane" is a machine that lifts objects, whether or not using the traditional means of a rope and pulley.[26]

(iv) Choice between ordinary meanings

Cases where a court has had to choose between different "ordinary meanings" include *London and North Eastern Railway Co. v. Berriman*,[27] where the issue was whether a railwayman was "relaying or repairing" the permanent way while oiling and cleaning points apparatus. He had been knocked down and killed by a train. If he had been so engaged, his window was entitled to damages and the company's failure to provide an adequate warning system would be a criminal offence. By three to two the House of Lords held that "relaying or repairing" involved putting right something that was wrong and not merely maintenance work of the kind the railwayman had been doing. The object of the statute seemed to cover workmen in this situation, but there was also a presumption that penal statutes should be strictly construed.[28]

6–011

Similarly, a narrow interpretation of the provision that a decision of the Crown Court on a matter "relating to trial on indictment" cannot be questioned by an appeal by case stated or on an application for judicial review[29] was preferred to a broad interpretation in *Re Smalley*.[30] It was not possible to discern any legislative purpose which would be served by giving the words any wider operation than in respect of decisions "affecting the conduct of"[31] the trial. An order estreating the recognisance of a surely for a defendant who failed to surrender to his bail at the Crown Court when committed for trial was not such a decision, and so could be challenged by judicial review. By contrast, in *Greater London Council v. Holmes*,[32] a purposive approach to the interpretation of the right to a home loss payment, following compulsory acquisition of land, was held to be better served by a broad rather than a narrow interpretation. It should be noted

---

[25] *R. v. South Hams District Council, ex. p. Gibb* [1995] Q.B. 158. The duties towards gypsies in Part II of the Caravan Sites Act 1968 could not have been intended to apply to those "whose moves are actuated not by need, but by caprice" (*per* Leggatt L.J. at p. 173).

[26] *Nationwide Access Ltd v. Commissioners of Customs and Excise, The Times,* March 22, 2000.

[27] [1946] A.C. 278.

[28] See further, below, para. 6-044 *cf. Ealing London Borough v. Race Relations Board* [1972] A.C. 342, where the House of Lords held by four to one that discrimination on the ground of *nationality* was not prohibited as being discrimination on the ground of "national origins".

[29] Supreme Court Act 1981, ss.28(2), 29(3).

[30] [1985] A.C. 622: see below, para. 18-059. See also *Cooper v. Motor Insurers Bureau* [1985] Q.B. 575. Contrast the statement by May L.J. in *R. v. Broadcasting Complaints Commission, ex p. Owen* [1985] Q.B. 1153, 1174.

[31] *per* Lord Bridge at pp. 642–645.

[32] [1986] Q.B. 989. See Oliver L.J. at p. 995 *Cf. Att.- Gen's Reference (No. 2 of 1994)* [1995] 1 W.L.R. 1579 (requirement that notice be give "on taking" a sample read as "on the occasion" of taking it); *R. v. Lynsey* [1995] 3 All E.R.654 ("common assault" in the Criminal Justice Act 1988, s.40, construed in broad sense to include battery).

that it has become increasingly common for judges to duck interpretative difficulties by classifying words as "ordinary English words."[33]

(v) Technical words

6–012   Examples of words used in a statute in a technical rather than an ordinary sense include "fettling" (trimming up of metal castings as they come from the foundry rather than "to put into good fettle" generally[34]); "crawling boards" (special boards with battens rather than simply boards for crawling on[35]); "offer for sale" (held not to cover the placing of a flick-knife in a shop window as this was in the law of contract merely an invitation to treat[36]); and "acceptance" (held to be used in its technical, commercial meaning, derived from the Bills of Exchange Act 1882, and not in its ordinary colloquial meaning).[37] Conversely, the majority in *Maunsell v. Olins*[38] preferred what they regarded to be the popular meaning of "premises" to the technical legal meaning.

(vi) An updating construction

In determining the ordinary meaning of statutory words, the courts will normally find a meaning that accords with modern social conditions.[39] However, "this does not mean that one can construe the language of an old statute to mean something conceptually different from what the contemporary evidence shows that Parliament must have intended."[40]

(b) Rule 2

6–013   A court may choose a "secondary meaning" where the primary meaning is

---

[33] See above, para. 1-012.

[34] *Prophet v. Plan Brothers & Co. Ltd* [1961] 1 W.L.R. 1130: See Harman LJ. at p. 1133. The word "fettle" has other meanings, as in "Tom offered to ... fettle him over the head with a brick" quoted in O.E.D.

[35] *Jenner v. Allen West and Co. Ltd* [1959] 1 W.L.R. 554.

[36] *Fisher v. Bell* [1961] 1 Q.B. 394; *cf. Partridge v. Crittenden* [1968] 1 W.L.R. 1204, *British Car Auctions v. Wright* [1972] 1 W.L.R. 1519.

[37] *R. v. Nanayakkara* [1987] 1 W.L.R. 265.

[38] See above, para. 6-009.

[39] According to Bennion (*Statutory Interpretation* (3rd ed., 1997), pp. 686–705), there is a presumption that Parliament intends to apply an "updating construction," treating the statute as "always speaking." See further, above, para. 6-001, below, para. 6-028; *R. v. Ireland* [1998] A.C. 147; *R. v. Westminster City Council, ex p. A* (1997) 9 Admin. L.R. 504; *Cutter v. Eagle Star Insurance Co. Ltd.* [1997] 2 All E.R. 311; *Victor Chandler International v. Commissioners of Customs and Excise* [2000] 1 W.L.R. 1296; *R. (on the application of Smeaton) v. Schering Healthcare Ltd.* [2002] EWHC 610 (Admin) (term "miscarriage" in 1861 statute to be construed in accordance with modern usage to mean the termination of an established pregnancy, whatever the word was understood to mean in 1861).

[40] *per* Lord Hoffmann in *Birmingham City Council v. Oakley* [2001] 1 A.C. 617, 396 (where the House of Lords held by 3-2 that the layout of premises could not of itself give rise to a statutory nuisance); *cf. Goodes v. East Sussex County Council* [2000] 1 W.L.R. 1356 (statutory duty to "maintain" highway does not entail duty to remove ice and snow).

productive of injustice, absurdity, anomaly or contradiction or a result contrary to the purpose of the statute.[41] Thus, provisions giving a power of arrest in respect of an "offender" or "a person found committing an offence" have been held to cover *apparent* offenders[42]: police officers had to act on the facts as they appeared at the time and were not to be exposed to the risk of actions for damages merely because the suspect was subsequently acquitted. A provision of the Factories Act 1937 requiring the fencing of dangerous parts of a machine while the parts were "in motion" was held not to apply where a workman turned the machine by hand in order to repair it. The machine could not have been repaired while it was fenced.[43]

A court was held entitled to grant relief to a mortgagor under an endowment mortgage, notwithstanding that the words did not strictly apply to that form of mortgage.[44] The legislative purpose of providing relief to mortgagors in temporary financial difficulties applied whatever the kind of mortgage. The notion of "absurdity" here seems not to be confined to cases where a provision is repugnant to or inconsistent with the rest of the statute.[45]

(c) Rule 3

A judge may read in words necessarily implied by the words actually used.[46] **6–014**
The line between cases of "necessary implication" and cases where the statutory language is modified to prevent an anomaly arising is, however, a fine one. It is clear that such modification should be a rare event. In *Stock v. Frank Jones (Tipton) Ltd.*[47] Lord Scarman said[48]:

"If the words used by Parliament are plain, there is no room for the 'anomalies' test, unless the consequences are so absurd that, without going outside the statute, one can see that Parliament must have made a drafting mistake. If words 'have been inadvertently used,' it is legitimate for the court to substitute what is apt to avoid the intention

[41] *cf.* the "golden rule," above, para. 6-006; *Stock v. Frank Jones (Tipton) Ltd* [1978] 1 W.L.R. 231; *R. v. Pigg* [1983] 1 W.L.R. 6, below para. 17-093; *R. v. Secretary of State for Health, ex p. Hammersmith and Fulham London Borough Council* (1998) 31 H.L.R. 475 (noting that there has been some relaxation in the degree of absurdity or inconvenience required to justify departure from the ordinary meaning; "the more absurd or inconvenient the result, or the more obvious the failure of the Act to achieve its purpose ... the clearer the language must be if it is to prevail": *per* Sir Christopher Staughton at p. 480).

[42] *Barnard v. Gorman* [1941] A.C. 378; *Wiltshire v. Barrett* [1966] 1 Q.B. 312; *Wills v. Bowley* [1983] 1 A.C. 57 (but note the strong dissenting speeches of Lord Elwyn-Jones and Lord Lowry, who took the view that it was not proper to depart from the literal interpretation of a statute where that would prejudice the liberty of the subject).

[43] *Richard Thomas and Baldwin's Ltd v. Cummings* [1955] A.C. 321.

[44] *Bank of Scotland v. Grimes* [1985] Q.B. 1179. See also *Paterson v. Aggio* (1987) 19 H.L.R. 551.

[45] See Cross (1995), pp. 93–105.

[46] *Federal Steam Navigation Co. v. Department of Trade and Industry* [1974] 1 W.L.R. 505, 508–9. *Cf.* the concept of "ellipsis": above, para. 6-001; *Adler v. George*, above, para. 6-002, n. 23. *Wiltshire v. Barrett, Barnard v. Gorman*, and *Wills v. Bowley*, n. 42 above. Contrast *R. v. Brent London Borough Council, ex p. Awua* [1995] 3 W.L.R. 215, where the House of Lords held that the term "accommodation" for the purposes of the homelessness legislation should never have been read as meaning "settled" or "permanent" accommodation.

[47] [1978] 1 W.L.R. 231.

[48] At p. 239.

of the legislature being defeated: *per* MacKinnon L.J. in *Sutherland Publishing Co. Ltd v. Caxton Publishing Co. Ltd.*[49] This is an acceptable exception to the general rule that plain language excludes a consideration of anomalies, *i.e.* mischievous or absurd consequences. If a study of the statute as a whole leads inexorably to the conclusion that Parliament had erred in its choice of words, *e.g.* used 'and' when 'or' was clearly intended, the courts can, and must, eliminate the error by interpretation. But mere 'manifest absurdity' is not enough; it must be an error (of commission or omission) which in its context defeats the intention of the Act."

In the same case Lord Simon said that:

"a court would only be justified in departing from the plain words of the statute were it satisfied that: (1) there is clear and gross balance of anomaly; (2) Parliament, the legislative promoters and the draftsman could not have envisaged such anomaly, could not have been prepared to accept it in the interest of a supervening legislative objective; (3) the anomaly can be obviated without detriment to such legislative objective; (4) the language of the statute is susceptible of the modification required to obviate the anomaly."[50]

There are a number of cases where the word "and" has been substituted for "or", and (? or) "or" for "and". *Federal Steam Navigation Co. Ltd v. Department of Trade and Industry*[51] concerned section 1(1) of the Oil in Navigable Waters Act 1955, which provided that where oil was discharged from a British ship in a prohibited sea area "the owner or master of the ship shall be guilty of an offence." The House of Lords held that where the owner and the master were separate persons both could be convicted, the provision being treated as if it read "the owner and/or the master". In *R. v. Oakes*[52] the Divisional Court treated section 7 of the Official Secrets Act 1920, which made it an offence where a person "aids or abets and does any act preparatory to the commission of an offence" under the Official Secrets Act as if it read "aids or abets *or* does any act preparatory." If read literally the result would have been "unintelligible".[53]

---

[49] [1938] Ch. 174, 201.

[50] [1978] 1 W.L.R. 231, p. 237. See also the similar remarks of Lord Diplock in *Jones v. Wrotham Park Settled Estates* [1980] A.C. 74, 105, applied in *I.R.C. v. Trustees of Sir John Aird's Settlement* [1984] Ch. 382 and *Inco Europe Ltd. v. First Choice Distribution (A Firm)* [2000] 1 W.L.R. 586, and note the cautious remarks of Sir John Donaldson M.R. in *Carrington v. Therm-A-Stor Ltd* [1983] 1 W.L.R. 138.

[51] [1974] 1 W.L.R. 505. *Cf. R. F. Brown & Co. Ltd v. T. & J. Harrison* (1927) 43 T.L.R. 394, 633, where the Court of Appeal suggested that "or" could sometimes be construed conjunctively; *cf.* MacKinnon L.J. at first instance and in *Sutherland Publishing Co. Ltd v. Caxton Publishing Co. Ltd* [1938] Ch.174, 201: "That is a cowardly evasion. In truth one word is substituted for another. For 'or' can never mean 'and'". See generally Sir Robert Megarry, "Andorandororand" in B. Rider (ed.), *Law at the Centre* (1999), Chap. 6.

[52] [1959] 2 Q.B. 350.

[53] *per* Lord Parker C.J. at p. 354. See also *R. v. Corby Juvenile Court, ex p. M* [1987] 1 W.L.R. 55, where Waite J. indicated *obiter* that he would have been prepared in effect to rectify a drafting error, in the light of the legislation's manifest purpose; and *Gateshead Metropolitan Borough Council v. L.* [1996] 3 All E.R. 264 (omission of word "ordinarily" before "reside" held to be a parliamentary slip).

In *Re Lockwood*[54] Harman J. ignored certain words of a provision[55] which would have had the effect on an intestacy of preferring more distant relations to nephews and nieces. Conversely, in *Re DWS, Deceased*[56] the Court of Appeal[57] held that words should be read in that enabled relatives to inherit on an intestacy rather than the estate devolving to the Crown as *bona vacantia*.

In *R. v. Central Criminal Court, ex p. Francis & Francis (A firm)*,[58] the House of Lords held that files of conveyancing documents in the possession of solicitors were "items held with the intention of furthering a criminal purpose" and therefore not "items subject to legal privilege"[59] protected from production to the police.[60] The solicitors had no such intention, but the majority of the House of Lords[61] held that it was sufficient that the documents were intended by a third party to be used to further the criminal purpose of laundering the proceeds of illegal drug-trafficking. This interpretation accorded with the purpose of the legislation. However, in the view of the minority[62] this could not be the grammatical meaning of the words, and such a widening of the ambit of the subsection could not be justified by any legitimate process of implication of terms.[63]

> "It is one thing to abstain from giving to the language of a statute the full effect of its ordinary grammatical meaning in order to avoid some positively harmful or manifestly unjust consequence. This I would describe as a legitimate process of construction to avoid a positive absurdity. But it is quite another thing to read into a statute a meaning which the language used will not bear in order to remedy a supposed defect or shortcoming which, if not made good, will make the statutory machinery less effective than the court believes it ought to be in order to achieve its proper purpose. Even if the lacuna appears to the court as absurd, this is what I describe, inelegantly but in order to point the contrast, as a negative absurdity. I know of no legitimate principle of construction which permits such a negative absurdity to be remedied by implying words which the court thinks necessary to enhance the operation of the statutory machinery."[64]

Lord Oliver regarded the words as clear, concise, unequivocal and unambiguous: "there is no difficulty about giving the subsection a perfectly sensible operation." It might be said to be "anomalous and incomplete" but was not necessarily "absurd".[65] By contrast, Lord Griffiths regarded an interpretation that confined the application of the exception to cases where the solicitors were party to the requisite intention as "such an extraordinary

---

[54] [1958] Ch. 231.
[55] Administration of Estates Act 1925, s.47(5), as amended.
[56] [2001] Ch. 568.
[57] Aldous and Simon Brown L.JJ., Sedley L.J. dissenting.
[58] [1989] A.C. 346.
[59] Police and Criminal Evidence Act 1984, ss. (10)(1), (2).
[60] Under the Drug Trafficking Offences Act 1986, s.27.
[61] Lords Brandon, Griffiths and Goff.
[62] Lords Bridge of Harwick and Oliver of Alymerbon.
[63] *per* Lord Bridge at pp. 371, 374.
[64] *ibid.*, p. 375.
[65] *ibid.*, p. 389.

result that I would only adopt such a construction if driven to it."[66]

6–015   In some cases, however, defective statutory provisions are regarded as beyond judicial redemption. For example, in *Inland Revenue Commissioners v. Hinchy*[67] section 55(3) of the Income Tax Act 1952 provided that a person who failed to submit an accurate tax return should forfeit £20 plus "treble the tax which he ought to be charged under this Act." Hinchy failed to declare some interest upon which the tax due would have been £14 5s. The Commissioners claimed £438 14s.6d. (three times Hinchy's total tax bill for the year plus £20). The House of Lords upheld their claim; their Lordships recognised that the result was absurd, but the words actually used were not capable of a more limited interpretation. In *Canterbury City Council v. Colley*[68] the House of Lords gave effect to a provision[69] that had the effect of requiring the compensation for revocation of a planning permission to rebuild a house to be calculated on the assumption that planning permission would be granted to rebuild the house. While this undoubtedly caused hardship to the owners, the words were "clear and express".[70] Assuming this was an anomaly, it could only be dealt with by "substantially rewriting the section".[71] This would involve "more than a mere purposive construction" and fell outside the parameters laid down by Lord Simon of Glaisdale in *Stock v. Frank Jones (Tipton) Ltd.*[72]

It may be that judges are less inhibited in reading statutory provisions as if the language were modified where they are contained in subordinate legislation. In *R. v. Stratford-on-Avon District Council, ex p. Jackson*,[73] the Court of Appeal held that the words "an application for judicial review shall be made promptly" in R.S.C. Order 53, s.4(l) were to read as if they referred to the application for leave to apply for judicial review. This was the "only sensible construction"[74] which could be given to the rule, and the construction that had been adopted in practice.[75] Similarly, in *Pickstone v. Freemans plc*[76] the House of Lords held that regulations amending the Equal Pay Act 1970 so as to enable the United Kingdom to comply with European Community law should be interpreted so as to achieve that result.

> "It may be that, in order to ... [do so], some necessary implication falls to be made into their literal meaning. The precise terms of that implication do not seem to me to matter. It is sufficient to say that the words must be construed purposively in order to give effect to the

---

[66] *ibid.*, p. 383. For other examples of "rectification", see *Deria v. General Council of British Shipping* [1986] I.C.R. 172; *McMonagle v. Westminster City Council* [1990] 2 A.C. 716 (words regarded as surplusage to avoid absurd result). *X. v. Morgan Grampian Ltd* [1991] 1 A.C. 1, 55; and *Powdrill v. Watson* [1995] 2 All E.R. 65, 85–86.

[67] [1960] A.C. 748. See also *Inland Revenue Commissioners v. Ayrshire Employers' Mutual Insurance Association Ltd* [1946] 1 All E.R. 637.

[68] [1993] A.C. 401.

[69] Town and Country Planning Act 1971, s.164(4).

[70] *per* Lord Oliver of Aylmerton at p. 409.

[71] *per* Lord Oliver at p. 406.

[72] *ibid.*, and see para. 6-014.

[73] [1985] 1 W.L.R. 1319. See also *R. v. Chief Adjudication Officer, ex p. B.* [1999] 1 W.L.R. 1695.

[74] *ibid.*, p. 1322.

[75] The drafting error was subsequently corrected by S.I. 1987 No. 1423, r. 63, Schedule.

[76] [1989] A.C. 66.

manifest broad intention of the maker of the regulations and of Parliament."[77]

Lord Oliver agreed:

" ... a construction which permits the section to operate as a proper fulfilment of the United Kingdom's obligation under the Treaty involves not so much doing violence to the language of the section as filling a gap by an implication which arises, not from the words used, but from the manifest purpose of the Act and the mischief it was intended to remedy."[78]

Finally, in *Porter v. Honey*[79] the House of Lords held that the deemed consent conferred by regulations[80] for the display of one estate agent's sale board extended by necessary implication to cover the first board displayed notwithstanding the unlawful display of subsequent boards by other agents. The result suggested by the grammatical construction of the regulation was that the first agent would be guilty of an offence where another agent, without the former's knowledge or consent, placed a second board upon the same property. Such a result would be "unjust and absurd."[81]

"We are dealing here with delegated legislation which does not receive the scrutiny of primary legislation and if in the interests of administrative convenience such an apparently unjust rule is to be introduced it should be in the clearest possible language so that the purport of the legislation can be readily recognised and the need for such a measure can be carefully considered before it is approved."[82]

C. THE CONTEXT: INTERNAL AIDS TO INTERPRETATION

There is a wide range of material that may be considered by a judge both (1) **6–016** in determining the primary meaning of the statutory words and (2) where there is ambiguity, in pointing the way to the interpretation that is to be preferred. Some of these aids may be found within the statute in question, or in certain "rules of language" commonly applied to statutory texts: others are external to the statute. We deal first with "internal aids".

It is commonly observed that statutes must be read as a whole.[83] It may perhaps be doubted whether every word of a long and complicated statute

---

[77] *per* Lord Keith of Kinkel at p. 112.
[78] *ibid.*, p. 125. *Cf.* Lord Oliver's remarks in the *Francis & Francis* case, n. 58 above. In the *Pickstone* case, his Lordship regarded the words as "reasonably capable of bearing" the secondary meaning contended for [1989] A.C. at p. 128; in *Francis & Francis*, he did not.
[79] [1988] 1 W.L.R. 1420.
[80] The Town and Country Planning (Control of Advertisements) Regulations 1984 (S.I. 1984 No. 421).
[81] *per* Lord Griffiths at p. 1422.
[82] *ibid.*, pp. 1426–1427.
[83] See, *e.g.* para. 6-008 above.

will be examined with care, but a judge may well be presented with arguments based on (1) a comparison with enacting words elsewhere in the statute or (2) one of the non-enacting parts of the statute listed in the previous chapter.[84] There is an important distinction between these two kinds of aid. Non-enacting words of a statute may be consulted as a guide to the meaning of the provision in question; however, if the words of the provision, considered in their context, are regarded as clear, any conflict between them and any of the non-enacting parts must be disregarded. Where a conflict between enacting words cannot be resolved by interpretation, the later provision takes precedence.

1. OTHER ENACTING WORDS

6–017   An examination of the whole of a statute, or at least those Parts which deal with the subject matter of the provision to be interpreted, should give some indication of the overall purpose of the legislation. It may show that a particular interpretation of that provision will lead to absurdity when taken with another section.[85] Moreover, there is at least a weak presumption that a word or phrase is to be accorded the same meaning wherever it appears in the statute. For example, in *Gibson v. Ryan*[86] the court had to decide whether an inflatable rubber dinghy and a fish basket came within the term "instrument" in section 7(1) of the Salmon and Freshwater Fisheries (Protection) (Scotland) Act 1951. It held that they did not in the light of section 10, which drew a distinction "between instruments on the one hand, boats on the other hand and baskets on, if there is such a thing, the third hand."[87] A court may, however, be satisfied that different meanings are intended.[88] There may, of course, be a definition section.[89]

2. LONG TITLE

6–018   It became established in the nineteenth century that the long title could be considered as an aid to interpretation,[90] once it was accepted that it could be amended as a Bill passed through Parliament. The long title should be read, as part of the context, "as the plainest of all the guides to the general objectives of a statute"[91] although "it will not always help as to particular

---

⁸⁴ See above, paras 5-012–5-015.
⁸⁵ See, *e.g.* cases establishing that a court could not order the forfeiture of real property used in relation to the commission of criminal offences: *R. v. Beard (Graham)* [1974] 1 W.L.R. 1549 and *R. v. Khan (Sultan Ashraf)* [1982] 1 W.L.R. 1405.
⁸⁶ [1968] 1 Q.B. 250.
⁸⁷ Diplock L.J. at p. 255.
⁸⁸ *e.g.* "whosoever being married, shall marry" in section 57 of the Offences Against the Person Act 1861, considered in *R. v. Allen* (1872) L.R. 1 C.C.R. 367: "being married" meant "being validly married" whereas "shall marry" meant "go through a marriage ceremony".
⁸⁹ Above, para. 5-017.
⁹⁰ *Fielding v. Morley Corporation* [1899] 1 Ch. 1, 34.
⁹¹ Not all long titles are as helpful in this regard as Lord Simon's words suggest.

provisions."[92] In *Fisher v. Raven*[93] the House of Lords held that the term "obtained credit" in section 13 of the Debtors Act 1869 (which made it an offence to obtain credit under false pretences) was limited to the obtaining of credit in respect of the payment or repayment of money only and did not extend to cover the receipt of money on a promise to render services or deliver goods in the future. The Act's long title:

"An Act for the Abolition of Imprisonment for Debt, for the Punishment of Fraudulent Debtors, and for other purposes"

was regarded as supporting the view that the Act concerned debtors in the ordinary sense of the word. However, in *Ward v. Holman*[94] the Divisional Court held that section 5 of the Public Order Act 1936, which made it an offence to use in any public place or meeting, *inter alia*, insulting behaviour likely to cause a breach of the peace, was not restricted to conduct at public meetings, processions and the like, notwithstanding the Act's long title. The relevant part of the long title read:

"An Act to ... make ... provision for the preservation of public order on the occasion of public processions and meetings and in public places"

but the court regarded the enacted words as wide and "completely unambiguous"[95] and, accordingly, applicable to disputes between neighbours. The position appears to be that:

"once their full context is considered in the light of the purposes of the Act, it is the unambiguous words of a section which will prevail over the long title."[96]

3. PREAMBLE

The use of preambles[97] was considered in *Attorney-General v. Ernest* **6–019** *Augustus of Hanover*.[98] The position was summarised by Lord Normand[99]:

"When there is a preamble it is generally in its recitals that the mischief to be remedied and the scope of the Act are described. It is therefore clearly permissible to have recourse to it as an aid to construing the enacting provisions. The preamble is not, however, of the same weight

---

[92] *per* Lord Simon in *Black-Clawson International Ltd v. Papierwerke Waldhof Aschaffenburg A.G.* [1975] A.C. 591, 647.

[93] [1964] A.C. 210. See also *Watkinson v. Hollington* [1944] K.B. 16; *R. v. Wheatley* [1979] 1 W.L.R. 144.

[94] [1964] 2 Q.B. 580.

[95] *per* Lord Parker C.J. at p. 587.

[96] Cross (1995), p. 128; *R. v. Bates* [1952] 2 All E.R. 842, 844, *per* Donovan J.; *R. v. Galvin* [1987] Q.B. 862.

[97] The long title is on occasion referred to erroneously as the preamble.

[98] [1957] A.C. 436, see above, para. 6-008.

[99] At p. 467. See also Viscount Simonds at pp. 462–464, and see *The Norwhale* [1975] Q.B. 589.

as an aid to construction of a section of the Act as are other relevant
enacting words to be found elsewhere in the Act or even in related Acts.
There may be no exact correspondence between preamble and
enactment, and the enactment may go beyond, or it may fall short of
the indications that may be gathered from the preamble. Again, the
preamble cannot be of much or any assistance in construing provisions
which embody qualifications or exceptions from the operation of the
general purpose of the Act. It is only when it conveys a clear and
definite meaning in comparison with relatively obscure or indefinite
enacting words that the preamble may legitimately prevail."

The preamble cannot prevail over clear enacting words.

4. Short Title

6–020   It seems that the short title should not be used to resolve a doubt as it is
given "solely for the purpose of facility of reference" or as a "statutory
nickname".[1] Some judges, however, have questioned whether it should
always be ignored.[2]

5. Headings

6–021   Unlike the previous three parts of a statute, headings, side-notes and
punctuation are not voted on in Parliament. They may nevertheless be
considered as part of the context. In *Director of Public Prosecutions v.
Schildkamp*[3] Lord Reid said:

"The question which has arisen in this case is whether and to what
extent it is permissible to give weight to punctuation, cross-headings
and side-notes to sections in the Act. Taking a strict view, one can say
that these should be disregarded because they are not the product of
anything done in Parliament . . . .
   But it may be more realistic to accept the Act as printed as being the
product of the whole legislative process, and to give due weight to
everything found in the printed Act. I say more realistic because in very
many cases the provision before the court was never even mentioned in

[1] Lord Moulton in *Vacher & Sons Ltd v. London Society of Compositors* [1913] A.C. 107, 128.
Section 4(1) of the Trade Disputes Act 1906 was held to confer upon trade unions immunity
from tort actions generally and not just in trade dispute cases. See also *R. v. Crisp and
Homewood* (1919) 83 J.P. 121, where Avory J. held that the broad enacting words of s.2 of
the Official Secrets Act 1911 were not to be altered or limited by reference to the short title
(*Cf. R. v. Galvin* [1987] Q.B. 862).
[2] Scrutton L.J. in *Re Boaler* [1915] 1 K.B. 21 40; but *cf.* Buckley L.J. at p. 27. In *British
Amusement Catering Trades Association v. Westminster City Council* [1990] 1 A.C. 147, Lord
Griffiths stated (at p. 157) that he had "given weight to the title of the [Cinematograph]
Acts" in holding that a video game was not a "cinematograph exhibition". Many other
considerations pointed to the same conclusion (see below, para. 6-033).
[3] [1971] A.C. 1, 10.

debate in either House, and it may be that its wording was never closely scrutinised by any member of either House. In such a case it is not very meaningful to say that the words of the Act represent the intention of Parliament but that punctuation, cross-headings and side-notes do not.

So, if the authorities are equivocal and one is free to deal with the whole matter, I would not object to taking all these matters into account, provided that we realise that they cannot have equal weight with the words of the Act. Punctuation can be of some assistance in construction. A cross-heading ought to indicate the scope of the sections which follow it but there is always a possibility that the scope of one of these sections may have been widened by amendment. But a side-note is a poor guide to the scope of a section, for it can do no more than indicate the main subject with which the section deals."

This case concerned section 332(3) of the Companies' Act 1948, which makes it an offence knowingly to be a party to the carrying on of a business with intent to defraud creditors or for a fraudulent purpose. However, it appeared among a group of sections grouped under the cross-heading "Offences Antecedent to and in course of Winding-Up", and section 332(1), a parallel provision making the officers of a company personally responsible for its debts in similar circumstances, included the words "in the course of the winding-up." The House of Lords held by a majority that an offence under section 332(3) could only be committed after a winding-up order had been made.[4]

It also seems that reference may be made to a heading to resolve a doubt where the enacted words are ambiguous. However, it may not be used to change the meaning of enacted words where they are regarded as clear. Thus, a woman was convicted of an indecent assault upon a boy notwithstanding that the relevant section appeared under the heading of "Unnatural Offences".[5] The words "any indecent assault" were not regarded as ambiguous so as to justify consideration of the heading.

6. SIDE-NOTES

There is no sensible reason why side-notes (now clause titles) should be ignored, as Lord Reid noted in *Director of Public Prosecutions v. Schildkamp.*[6] However, the same judge had stated in an earlier case, *Chandler v. Director of Public Prosecutions,*[7] that "side-notes cannot be used as an aid to construction" as they were inserted by the draftsman, altered if necessary during the passage of a Bill by an officer of the House, and were

6–022

[4] The effect of this decision was reversed by the Companies Act 1981, s.96 (now the Companies Act 1985, s.458): see *R. v. Kemp* [1988] Q.B. 645.

[5] Offences Against the Person Act 1861, s.62; *R. v. Hare* [1934] 1 K.B. 354. See also *R. v. Surrey (North-Eastern Area) Assessment Committee* [1948] 1 K.B. 28, 32–33.

[6] [1971] A.C. 1, 10: above, para. 6-021. See also *Stephens v. Cuckfield R.D.C.* [1960] 2 Q.B. 372; *Tudor Grange Holdings v. Citibank NA* [1992] Ch. 53 (permissible to have regard to side-note in considering what is the general purpose of the section and the mischief at which it is aimed).

[7] [1964] A.C. 763.

not considered by Parliament.[8] In *Chandler* the defendants were charged under section 1(1) of the Official Secrets Act 1911, which makes it an offence to approach a prohibited place for a purpose prejudicial to the safety of the state, in respect of a demonstration at a military airfield in favour of nuclear disarmament. The marginal note read "Penalties for spying" and it was accepted that the defendants had not engaged in "spying". Nevertheless, the House of Lords held that the defendants were rightly convicted. In so far as this case indicates that a side-note cannot change the meaning of clear enacted words it is consistent with other cases; in so far as it would prohibit any consideration of a side-note it is inconsistent.

7. PUNCTUATION

6–023   Punctuation in statutes was considered by Lord Reid in *Inland Revenue Commissioners v. Hinchy*[9]:

> "[B]efore 1850 there was no punctuation in the manuscript copy of an Act which received the Royal Assent, and it does not appear that the printers had any statutory authority to insert punctuation thereafter. So even if punctuation in more modern Acts can be looked at (which is very doubtful), I do not think that one can have any regard to punctuation in older Acts."

In modern statutes, it does now seem that punctuation will be considered to the same extent as non-enacting words, although it may be altered or ignored where necessary to give effect to the purpose of the statute.[10] In *Hanlon v. The Law Society*[11] Lord Lowry said:

> "I consider that not to take account of punctuation disregards the reality that literate people, such as Parliamentary draftsmen, punctuate what they write, if not identically, at least in accordance with grammatical principles. Why should not literate people, such as judges, look at the punctuation in order to interpret the meaning of the legislation as accepted by Parliament."

D. THE CONTEXT: RULES OF LANGUAGE

6–024   There are a number of so-called "rules of language" commonly referred to in the context of statutory interpretation by Latin tags. They are not legal rules, but "simply refer to the way in which people speak in certain

---

[8] *ibid.* p. 789.
[9] [1960] A.C. 748, 765.
[10] *Alexander v. Mackenzie* 1947 J.C. 155, 166; *R. v. Brixton Prison Governor, ex p. Naranjansingh* [1962] 1 Q.B. 211; *Luby v. Newcastle upon Tyne Corporation* [1965] 1 Q.B. 214.
[11] [1981] A.C. 124, 198. *Cf.* Lord Reid in *D.P.P. v. Schildkamp* above, para. 6-021.

contexts."[12] Moreover, they are not as precise in their operation as would be expected from their label as "rules".

1. EJUSDEM GENERIS

General words following particular ones normally apply only to such **6–025** persons or things as are *ejusdem generis* (of the same *genus* or class) as the particular ones. For example, the Sunday Observance Act 1677 provided that "no tradesman, artificer, workman, labourer or other person whatsoever, shall do or exercise any worldly labour, business, or work of their ordinary callings upon the Lord's Day." In a series of cases the prohibition was held to be restricted to "other persons" following callings of a similar kind to those specified.[13] There must normally, and perhaps invariably, be more than one species mentioned to constitute a "genus",[14] and it must be possible to construct a "genus" out of the list of specific words. In *Allen v. Emmerson*[15] it was held that the phrase "theatres and other places of entertainment" in section 33 of the Barrow-in-Furness Corporation Act 1872 did not constitute a genus. Accordingly, a fun fair required a licence under the section even though no charge was made for admission. There must be some "general words" if the principle is to apply.[16]

The *ejusdem generis* rule may be displaced where the general words should be interpreted widely to accord with the object of the statute. *Skinner v. Shew*[17] concerned a provision which enabled a person to obtain an injunction against someone claiming to be the patentee of an invention who threatened him or her with any legal proceedings or liability "by circular advertisement or otherwise", unless he or she instituted those proceedings promptly. The Court of Appeal held that the desire of Parliament was "that threats of patent actions shall not hang over a man's head" and that it would be wrong to read the section as not applying to threats sent by private letter. In *Flack v. Baldry*[18] the Divisional Court held that electricity, discharged[19] from an electric stun gun, fell within the description "any noxious liquid, gas or other thing" in the Firearms Act 1968.[20] Such a weapon as an electric stun gun came within the mischief of the Act.

---

[12] Cross, (1995), p. 134.

[13] Not, therefore, a coach proprietor (*Sandeman v. Beach* (1827) 5 L.J. (o.s.) K.B. 298), farmer (*R. v. Cleworth* (1864) 4 B. & S. 927) or barber (*Palmer v. Snow* [1900] 1 Q.B. 725).

[14] *Alexander v. Tredegar Iron and Coal Co. Ltd* [1944] K.B. 390; *Quazi v. Quazi* [1980] A.C. 744, 807–808 (*per* Lord Diplock): the term "other" in the expression "judicial or other proceedings" was held not to be confined to quasi-judicial proceedings.

[15] [1944] K.B. 362.

[16] *Attorney General's Reference (No. 2 of 1995)* [1996] 3 All E.R. 860 (offence to exercise "control, direction or influence" over a prostitute's movements, which words were to be read disjunctively, with persuasion or compulsion not necessary to establish "influence").

[17] [1893] 1 Ch. 413. *Cf.* Lord Scarman in *Quazi v. Quazi*, above, at p. 824.

[18] [1988] 1 W.L.R. 214.

[19] The House of Lords held, overruling the Divisional Court on this point, that the electricity was "discharged": [1988] 1 W.L.R. 393.

[20] s.5(1)(b).

2. Noscitur a Sociis

6-026   This tag refers to the fact that words "derive colour from those which surround them".[21] For example, the word "floors" in the expression "floors, steps, stairs, passages and gangways", which were required to be kept free from obstruction, was held not to apply to part of a factory floor used for storage rather than passage.[22] The wider context may, however, negative any such "colouration". The "*ejusdem generis* rule" can be regarded as an application of this wider principle.

3. Expressio Unius est Exclusio Alterius

6-027   "Mention of one or more things of a particular class may be regarded as silently excluding all other members of the class. . . . Further, where a statute uses two words or expressions, one of which generally includes the other, the more general term is taken in a sense excluding the less general one: otherwise there would have been little point in using the latter as well as the former."[23]

For example, a provision that imposed a poor rate on the occupiers of "lands", houses, tithes and "coal mines" was held not to apply to mines other than coal mines, although the word "lands" would normally cover all kinds of mine.[24] However, a court may be satisfied that the "exclusio" was accidental, particularly where an application of the maxim would lead to absurdity.[25]

E. THE CONTEXT: EXTERNAL AIDS TO INTERPRETATION

1. Historical Setting

6-028   A judge may consider the historical setting of the provision that is being inter-preted. In *Chandler v. Director of Public Prosecutions*[26] the defendants sought to argue that disarmament" would be beneficial to the State, and that their purpose was thus not "prejudicial to the safety or interests of the State". Lord Reid said[27]:

---

[21] *per* Stamp J. in *Bourne v. Norwich Crematorium Ltd* [1967] 1 W.L.R. 691.
[22] Factories Act 1961, s.28(l): *Pengelley v. Bell Punch Co. Ltd* [1964] 1 W.L.R. 1055.
[23] *Maxwell on Interpretation of Statutes* (12th ed., 1969), p. 293. See J. M. Keyes, (1989) 10 Stat.L.R. 1.
[24] Poor Relief Act 1601, s.1: *R v. Inhabitants of Sedgley* (1831) 2 B. & Ad. 65.
[25] *Colquhoun v. Brooks* (1888) 21 Q.B.D. 52, 65; *Dean v. Wiesengrund* [1955] 2 Q.B. 120.
[26] [1964] A.C. 763: see above, para. 6-022.
[27] At p. 791.

"Even in recent times there have been occasions when quite large numbers of people have been bitterly opposed to the use made of the armed forces in peace or in war. The 1911 Act was passed at a time of grave misgiving about the German menace, and it would be surprising and hardly credible that the Parliament of that date intended that a person who deliberately interfered with vital dispositions of the armed forces should be entitled to submit to a jury that Government policy was wrong and that what he did was really in the best interests of the country, and then perhaps to escape conviction because a unanimous verdict on that question could not be obtained."

The Victorian attitude of sympathy towards insurgents against continental governments has been considered as part of the background of the Extradition Act 1870.[28] In some cases a statute is passed to deal with a particular grievance or problem, and should be historically interpreted; normally, however, it should be "deemed to be always speaking," with the courts "free to apply the current meaning of the statute to present day conditions."[29]

2. DICTIONARIES AND OTHER LITERARY SOURCES

Dictionaries are commonly consulted as a guide to the meaning of statutory words.[30] As words are to be read in their context, as already discussed, this should only be a starting point: **6–029**

"Sentences are not mere collections of words to be taken out of the sentence, defined separately by reference to the dictionary or decided cases, and then put back into the sentence with the meaning which one has assigned to them as separate words so as to give the sentence or phrase a meaning which as a sentence or phrase it cannot bear without distortion of the English language."[31]

Textbooks may also be consulted.[32]

---

[28] *Schtraks v. Government of Israel* [1964] A.C. 556, 582, 583: *R. v. Governor of Pentonville Prison, ex p. Cheng* [1973] A.C. 931. See now the Extradition Act 1989.

[29] *per* Lord Steyn in *R. v. Ireland* [1997] 4 All E.R. 225, 233 (accordingly, "bodily harm" in the Offences against the Person Act 1861 should be read to include psychiatric illness, notwithstanding that "psychiatry was in its infancy in 1861." See also above, para. 6-020, n. 39).

[30] See, *e.g. R. v. Peters* (1886) 16 Q.B.D. 636 (definitions of "credit" in Dr Johnson's and Webster's dictionaries); *Re Ripon (Highfield) Confirmation Order 1938, White and Collins v. Minister of Health* [1939] 2 K.B. 838 (definition of "park" in O.E.D.); *Eglen (Inspector of Taxes) v. Butcher* [1988] S.T.C. 782 (definitions of "infirmity" in O.E.D.: third definition, with connotations of illness or congenital defect, preferred to first, "a weakness or want of strength", with the result that a dependent relative allowance could not be claimed under income tax legislation in respect of a healthy infant).

[31] *per* Stamp J. in *Bourne v. Norwich Crematorium Ltd* [1967] 1 W.L.R. 691, 696.

[32] *e.g. Re Castioni* [1891] 1 Q.B. 149 where Stephen J. referred to his own *History of the Criminal Law* on the meaning of "political crime"; a work by John Stuart Mill was also consulted.

3. PRACTICE

6–030   The Practice followed in the past may be a guide to interpretation. For example, the "uniform opinion and practice of eminent conveyancers has always had great regard paid to it by all courts of justice."[33] This is the case where the technical meaning of a word or phrase used in conveyancing is in issue.[34] Commercial usage may also be considered. In *United Dominions Trust Ltd v. Kirkwood*[35] the Court of Appeal had to apply the phrase "any person bona fide carrying on the business of banking."[36] Lord Denning M.R. said[37]:

> "In such a matter as this, when Parliament has given no guidance, we cannot do better than look at the reputation of the concern amongst intelligent men of commerce."

In these cases the usage or practice precedes the enactment of related technical legislation. The *subsequent* practice of those who are involved in the implementation of a statute is not generally regarded as a permissible aid.[38] A different view may be taken in respect of old statutes:

> "It is said that the best exposition of a statute ... is that which it has received from contemporary authority. ... *Contemporanea expositio est fortissima in lege*. Where this has been given by enactment or judicial decision, it is of course to be accepted as conclusive. But, further, the meaning publicly given by contemporary or long professional usage is presumed to be the true one, even where the language has etymologically or popularly a different meaning."[39]

This principle cannot be applied to modern statutes.[40]

---

[33]   *per* Lord Hardwicke L.C. in *Bassett v. Bassett* (1744) 3 Atk. 203, 208.

[34]   See *Jenkins v. Inland Revenue Commissioners* [1944] 2 All E.R. 491; *cf. Pilkington v. Inland Revenue Commissioners* [1964] A.C. 612, 634.

[35]   [1966] 2 Q.B. 431.

[36]   Moneylenders Act 1900, s.6(d).

[37]   At pp. 454, 455.

[38]   *e.g.* practice notes provided by the Central Land Board for the guidance of its staff in the administration of the Town and Country Planning Act 1947: *London County Council v. Central Land Board* [1958] 1 W.L.R. 1296. Statements in a government circular may be "simply wrong": *R. v. Wandsworth London Borough Council, ex p. Beckwith* [1996] 1 W.L.R. 60, 65, *per* Lord Hoffmann.

[39]   *Maxwell on Interpretation of Statutes* (12th ed., 1969), p. 264 cited in *R. v. Casement* [1917] 1 K.B. 98, where the court declined to take the Statute of Treasons 1351 "and read it as though we had seen it for the first time." See D. J. Hurst, "The problem of the elderly statute" (1983) 3 L.S. 21, 23–30, who notes that the term *contemporanea exposito* should (1) be confined to exposition by commentators at or near the time of enactment, and (2) be distinguished from continuous usage and custom.

[40]   *Campbell College, Belfast (Governors) v. Commissioners of Valuation for Northern Ireland* [1964] 1 W.L.R. 912 (strictly, a case concerning usage rather than *contemporanea expositio*: Hurst, *op. cit.*); *per* Lord Clyde in *Fitzpatrick v. Sterling Housing Association Ltd.* [1999] 4 All E.R. 705, 726.

4. Other Statutes In Pari Materia

Related statutes dealing with the same subject matter as the provision in question may be considered both as part of the context and to resolve ambiguities.[41] A statute may indeed provide expressly that it should be read as one with an earlier statute or series of statutes. *Later* statutes *in pari materia* cannot be regarded as part of the context of the enactment but may be considered where a provision is ambiguous, "to see the meaning which Parliament puts on the self-same phrase in a similar context, in case it throws any light on the matter."[42] **6–031**

Occasionally an argument may be based on a comparison with a statute not *in pari materia*, although such a statute will not be considered as part of the context.[43]

Where a later Act amends an earlier Act the position as to interpretation is not clear. In *Lewisham London Borough Council v. Lewisham Juvenile Court JJ.*[44] Viscount Dilhorne stated[45] that it was wrong to construe an unamended section of the earlier Act in the light of amendments made by the later Act, unless there was an ambiguity. Lord Salmon, however, said[46] that:

"the whole Act as amended should be taken into consideration when construing any section in the Act. A section of an Act, whether or not it is amended, must in my view be construed in the context of the whole Act as it stands."

The other judges did not express their views unequivocally on this point, although Lord Keith seemed to incline to Viscount Dilhorne's position and Lord Scarman to Lord Salmon's.[47] Lord Salmon's view may create difficulties for the draftsman of subsequent amendments if he or she is to be required to judge the effect of the amendments on the interpretation of unamended provisions.

Where a later Act inserts a new provision in an earlier Act, it may be held that this provision is to be interpreted by reference to the later Act.[48]

---

[41] See Viscount Simonds in the *Hanover* case, above, p.

[42] *per* Lord Denning M.R. in *Payne v. Bradley* [1962] A.C. 343, 357; *cf. Re MacManaway* [1951] A.C. 161; *Lewisham London Borough Council v. Lewisham Juvenile Court JJ.* [1980] A.C. 273, 281–2, 291; *Mendip District Council v. Glastonbury Festivals Ltd* (1993) 91 L.G.R. 447, 453.

[43] See, *e.g. R. v. Westminster Betting Licensing Committee, ex p. Peabody Donation Fund* [1963] 2 Q.B. 750; ; *cf. Brown v. Bennett (No. 2)* [2002] 1 W.L.R. 713, 726, where it was held that it was in the circumstances illegitimate to found an argument on a comparison with a statute not in *pari materia*.

[44] [1980] A.C. 273.

[45] At pp. 281–2.

[46] At p. 291.

[47] See pp. 302 and 310.

[48] *R. v. Secretary of State for the Home Department, ex p. Margueritte* [1983] Q.B. 180; see A. Samuels, [1983] Stat. L.R. 111.

5. LEGISLATIVE ANTECEDENTS

6–032 A slightly different situation from those considered in the previous section arises when the provision in question has been re-enacted in the same or similar form in a succession of statutes. For example, the origins of section 56 of the Law of Property Act 1925[49] were considered in *Beswick v. Beswick*,[50] where the House of Lords held that the term "other property" did not apply to personalty. However, the legislative antecedents should not be considered as part of the context of a consolidation measure; reference to them should only be made if the words are unclear,[51] this concept being broader than cases of "overt ambiguity".[52] In interpreting consolidation Acts there is a presumption that Parliament does not intend to alter the existing law.[53] As with all presumptions it may be rebutted by clear language.[54]

Where other statutes are considered, arguments may be based on similarities or dissimilarities in the statutory language itself, or on judicial decisions concerning provisions subsequently re-enacted. It is sometimes suggested that Parliament, or more realistically, the draftsman, must have had such decisions in mind during the preparation of consolidation legislation,[55] that there is at least a rebuttable presumption that re-enactment without alteration amounts to the Parliamentary endorsement of the decisions and that, for example, a decision of a High Court judge thus "endorsed" would have to be applied by the Court of Appeal and the House

---

[49] "A person may take an immediate or other interest in land or other property, or the benefit of any condition, right of entry, covenant or agreement over or respecting land or other property, although he may not be named as a party to the conveyance or other instrument."

[50] [1968] A.C. 58. See also *Pierce v. Bemis* [1986] Q.B. 384.

[51] *Farrell v. Alexander* [1977] A.C. 59: Lord Wilberforce at pp. 72–73, Lord Simon at pp. 82–85 and Lord Edmund-Davies at p. 97; *R. v. West Yorkshire Coroner, ex p. Smith* [1983] Q.B. 335; *R. v. Heron* [1982] 1 W.L.R. 451; *Champion v. Maughan* [1984] 1 W.L.R. 469; *Prior (Valuation Officer) v. Sovereign Chickens Ltd* [1984] 1 W.L.R. 921; *Di Palma v. Victoria Square Property Co. Ltd* [1986] Ch. 150; *Morton v. The Chief Adjudication Officer* [1988] I.R.L.R. 444 (construction of consolidating regulations); *Sheldon v. R.H.M. Outhwaite (Underwriting Agencies) Ltd* [1995] 2 W.L.R. 570 (no ambiguity or difficulty); *Associated Newspapers Ltd v. Wilson* [1995] 2 A.C. 454 (majority and minority in the House of Lords differed on whether there was a "difficulty" justifying recourse to legislative history and differed on the interpretation of that history); *R. v. Secretary of State for the Environment, Transport and the Regions, ex p. Spath Holme Ltd.* [2001] 1 All E.R. 195; *British Waterways Board v. Severn Trent Water Ltd.* [2001] 3 All E.R. 373. Indeed, "it is particularly useful to have recourse to the legislative history if a real difficulty arises," whatever the form of the consolidation measure (see above, para. 5-005) (*per* Lord Scarman in *R. v. Heron* [1982] 1 W.L.R. 451, 459, 460; *cf.* Lord Simon at p. 455 who stressed the point that the statute in issue here was not (unlike that in *Farrell v. Alexander*), a "modern consolidation Act", but was a "pure" consolidation, with verbatim reproduction of the existing enactment "with all its blemishes and imperfections"; accordingly, it was more likely to be necessary to look at the legislative history). See generally, A. F. Newhouse, "Constructing and Consolidating" [1980] B.T.R. 102; R. Bramwell, [1992] B.T.R. 69.

[52] *per* Lord Bingham in *R. v. Secretary of State for the Environment, Transport and the Regions, ex p. Spath Holme Ltd* [2001] 1 All E.R. 195, 208.

[53] *R. v. Governor of Brixton Prison, ex p. De Demko* [1959] 1 Q.B. 268, affirmed [1959] A.C. 654.

[54] *e.g. Re A Solicitor* [1961] Ch. 491.

[55] See Lord Evershed in *Ex p. De Demko* [1959] 1 Q.B. 268, 281.

of Lords.[56] The theory of "Parliamentary endorsement" was doubted by Lord Wilberforce and Lord Simon in *Farrell v. Alexander*.[57] Moreover, in *R. v. Chard*[58] the House of Lords held that while there might be such a presumption where the judicial interpretation is well settled and well recognised, it would yield to the fundamental rule that the ordinary sense of statutory words should be adhered to unless it led to some absurdity. In any event, the theory cannot apply when the authority supposedly "endorsed" is itself subsequently overruled by the House of Lords.[59] The re-enactment of words in a consolidation Act subject to one of the special parliamentary procedures precluding debate on the merits would not have an effect on the construction of those words.[60]

In the case of *codifying* statutes,[61] "the proper course is in the first instance to examine the language of the statute and to ask what is its natural meaning, uninfluenced by any considerations derived from the previous state of law."[62] The application of any presumption that the law is unaltered would destroy the utility of codification. However, the previous state of the law may be considered where a technical expression is used or a provision of the code is ambiguous.

6. STATUTORY INSTRUMENTS

The extent to which a regulation may be used in interpreting a provision in the Act under which it was made was considered in *Hanlon v. The Law Society*[63] where Lord Lowry formulated the following propositions[64]:   **6–033**

"(1) Subordinate legislation may be used in order to construe the parent Act, but only where power is given to amend the Act by regulations or where the meaning of the Act is ambiguous.

(2) Regulations made under the Act provide a Parliamentary or administrative *contemporanea expositio* of the Act but do not decide or control its meaning: to allow this would be to substitute the rule-making authority for the judges as interpreter and would disregard the possibility that the regulation relied on was misconceived or *ultra vires*.

---

[56] *Re Cathcart, ex p. Campbell* (1869) 5 Ch. App. 603, 706 (James L.J.); *Barras v. Aberdeen Fishing and Steam Trawling Co. Ltd* [1933] A.C. 402, 411–412 (Lord Buckmaster); *E.W.P. Ltd v. Moore* [1992] Q.B. 460; *Lowsley v. Forbes* [1998] 3 All E.R. 897, 906.

[57] [1977] A.C. 59, 74, 90–91. See also Denning L.J. in *Royal Crown Derby Porcelain Ltd v. Raymond Russell* [1949] 2 K.B. 417, 429; *R. v. Bow Road JJ. (Domestic Proceedings Court), ex p. Adedigba* [1968] 2 Q.B. 572, 583; E. A. Marshall, (1974) 90 L.Q.R. 170; C. J. F. Kidd, (1977) 51 A.L.J. 256.

[58] [1984] A.C. 279.

[59] *Southwark London Borough Council v. Whillier* [2001] I.C.R. 142, EAT.

[60] See also *Stubbing v. Webb* [1993] A.C. 498, 506–507 (amendment of Limitation Act 1939 in 1975 and consolidation in 1980 no endorsement of Court of Appeal decision in *Letang v. Cooper* [1965] 1 Q.B. 232.)

[61] See above, para. 5-005.

[62] *Bank of England v. Vagliano Brothers* [1891] A.C. 107, 144, 145 (Lord Herschell); applied in *R. v. Fulling* [1987] Q.B. 426 and *R. v. Smurthwaite* [1994] 1 All E.R. 898, in respect of the Police and Criminal Evidence Act 1984.

[63] [1981] A.C. 124.

[64] At pp. 193–4.

(3) Regulations which are consistent with a certain interpretation of the Act tend to confirm that interpretation.

(4) Where the Act provides a framework built on by contemporaneously prepared regulations, the latter may be a reliable guide to the meaning of the former.

(5) The regulations are a clear guide, and may be decisive, where they are made in pursuance of a power to modify the Act, particularly if they come into operation on the same day as the Act which they modify.

(6) Clear guidance may also be obtained from regulations which are to have effect as if enacted in the parent Act."

Propositions (3) and (4) were cited by Lord Griffiths in *British Amusement Catering Trades Association v. Westminster City Council*,[65] in the course of holding that a video game was not a "cinematograph exhibition," and that, accordingly, an amusement arcade did not have to be licensed under the Cinematograph Act 1909, s.1. His Lordship noted that relevant safety regulations[66] only made sense

"if the 'cinematograph exhibitions' referred to in the regulations are understood in the sense of a show to an audience; for example, there are frequent references to the auditorium ... ."[67]

7. OFFICIAL REPORTS

6–034 Legislation may be preceded by a report of a Royal Commission, the Law Commissions or some other official advisory committee. This kind of material may be considered as evidence of the pre-existing state of the law and the "mischief" with which the legislation was intended to deal. However, it has been held that the recommendations contained therein may not be regarded as evidence of Parliamentary intention as Parliament may

---

[65] [1989] A.C. 147, 158.

[66] The Cinematography (Safety) Regulations 1955 (S.I. 1955 No. 1129). In *Deposit Protection Board v. Dalia* [1994] 2 A.C. 367, 397, Lord Browne-Wilkinson stated that regulations can only be used as an aid to construction if "roughly contemporaneous with the Act being construed." This is inconsistent with the *British Amusement* case, which was not cited.

[67] [1989] A.C. 147, 158. Cf. the unwillingness of Wood J. in *R. v. Bolton Metropolitan Borough Council, ex p. B* (1985) 84 L.G.R. 78 to use the Code of Practice made under S.12G of the Child Care Act 1980 as a guide to the meaning of SS.12A to 12G; and Potts J. in *R. v. Secretary of State, ex p. Greenpeace Ltd* [1994] 4 All E.R. 352, 365: "Primary legislation is not to be construed by reference to general policy statements or departmental guidance."

not have accepted the recommendations and acted upon them.[68] The first of these propositions is generally accepted: the second proposition only survived in the *Black-Clawson* case by three to two. The question was whether a judgment in a German court dismissing the plaintiff's claim for money due, on the ground that it was brought out of time, barred such a claim in an English court. It did not have this effect at common law,[69] and the House of Lords held by four to one that this had not been altered by section 8 of the Foreign Judgments (Reciprocal Enforcement) Act 1933. Section 8 had been enacted in a form identical to clause 8 of a draft Bill attached to the report of a departmental committee of "eminent lawyers", and the report indicated that the draft Bill was not thought to change the common law. Of the majority, Lords Reid and Wilberforce held that the report could not be considered as a guide to Parliament's intention. Lord Reid thought that the rule against the citation of expressions of intention in Parliament excluded *a fortiori* such expressions in pre-Parliamentary reports. Lord Wilberforce stated that if reports were admissible as evidence of the meaning of the enacted words there would simply be two documents to construe instead of one, that it was the function of the courts to declare the meaning of enacted words, and that "it would be a degradation of that process if the courts were to be merely a reflecting mirror of what some other interpretation agency might say."[70] Viscount Dilhorne and Lord Simon of Glaisdale thought, however, that reports should be admissible as a guide to Parliament's intention; at least in a case such as this where a draft Bill had been enacted without material alteration.[71] To forbid this "would be to draw a very artificial line which serves no useful purpose."[72] "Why read the crystal when you can read the book? Here the book is already open; it is merely a matter of reading on."[73] Lord Diplock dissented as to the meaning of section 8 but agreed with Lords Reid and Wilberforce on the use of official reports. The *Black-Clawson* case must now be read in light of the decision in *Pepper (Inspector of Taxes) v. Hart*[74] permitting recourse to Parliamentary materials. Reference to *Hansard* may now make it clear whether a report has been relied upon. The House of Lords has held subsequently, without referring to either the *Black-Clawson* case or *Pepper*

---

[68] *Eastman Photographic Materials Co. Ltd v. Comptroller General of Patents* [1898] A.C. 571; *Assam Railways and Trading Co. Ltd v. Inland Revenue Commissioners* [1935] A.C. 445; *Black-Clawson International Ltd v. Papierwerke Waldhof-Aschaffenburg A. G.* [1975] A.C. 591; *R. v. Allen* [1985] A.C. 1029; *Arnold v. Central Electricity Generating Board* [1988] A.C. 288; *Hampshire County Council v. Milburn* [1991] 1 A.C. 325 (Royal Commission); *R. v. Horseferry Road Magistrates' Court, ex p. Siadatan* [1991] 1 Q.B. 280 (Law Commission Report); *D.P.P. v. Bull* [1995] Q.B. 88 (Wolfenden Report on *Homosexual Offences and Prostitution*). Cf. *R. v. Gomez* [1993] A.C. 442 where the refusal of the majority of the House to refer to the 8th Report of the Criminal Law Revision Committee led to a decision on the law of theft that "flatly contradicted the intention of Parliament", which had enacted legislation in all material respects identical to the CLRC's draft Bill: Commentary by Sir John Smith, [1993] Crim.L.R. 305. See also *R. v. Anderson* [1986] A.C. 27 (Commentary by J. C. Smith, [1985] Crim.L.R. 651). On examination, the mischief identified in a report may turn out to be narrower than that dealt with by Parliament: *R. v. Kemp* [1988] Q.B. 645.

[69] *Harris v. Quine* (1869) L.R. 4 Q.B. 653.

[70] p. 629.

[71] pp. 621–623 and 651–652 respectively.

[72] Viscount Dilhorne at p. 622.

[73] Lord Simon at p. 652.

[74] Below, paras 6-036–6-038.

v. Hart, that where a provision was enacted to give effect to a Law Commission recommendation, it was "permissible, and indeed desirable, for the courts to have regard to the view of the Law Commission" on the issue in question.[75] This straightforward approach is to be welcomed.

In *J. H. Rayner Ltd v. Department of Trade*,[76] Staughton J. held that Cabinet and department documents from the 1950s, obtained from the Public Record Office under the 30-year rule,[77] were not admissible as an aid to the interpretation of Order in Council concerning the International Tin Council.

> "It would be quite extraordinary to construe either parliamentary or delegated legislation by reference to the secret deliberations of departmental officials or of the Cabinet. One cannot, after all, even look at the deliberations in Parliament recorded by Hansard, which ought at least in theory to be a more immediate guide to the meaning of legislation than the intentions of ministers and their officials."[78]

8. TREATIES AND INTERNATIONAL CONVENTIONS[79]

6-035   Problems of statutory interpretation relating to treaties (or international conventions) may arise in four main ways. In the background are two principles: first, that a treaty cannot have effect in English law unless incorporated by statute; and second, that there is a presumption that Parliament does not legislate in such a way that the United Kingdom would be in breach of its international obligations.

(1) An Act of Parliament may implement a treaty and expressly enact that it shall be part of English law. The text will normally be given in a schedule. Here, a broad purposive construction should be adopted rather than a literal one.[80] This does not, however, mean that the broadest possible interpretation is always the right one.[81] Textbooks,

---

[75] *I. v. D.P.P.* [2001] 2 All E.R. 583, *per* Lord Hutton at paras. [22] – [24] (scope of the statutory offence of affray).

[76] [1987] BCLC 667.

[77] Public Records Act 1958, s.5.

[78] [1988] BCLC 667, 689, *per* Staughton J. The relaxation of the rule against citing Parliamentary material in *Pepper (Inspector of Taxes) v. Hart* (below, paras 6-036–6-038.) does not extend to departmental documents.

[79] See F. A. Mann, *Foreign Affairs in English Courts* (1986), Chap. 5; R. Higgins in F. G. Jacobs and S. Roberts (eds.), *The Effect of Treaties in Domestic Law* (1987), Chap. 7; L. Collins (ed.) *Dicey and Morris on the Conflict of Laws* (13th ed., 2000), pp. 9–16; D. L. Mendis, (1992) 13 Stat.L.R. 216; R. Gardiner, (1995) 44 I.C.L.Q. 620, criticising the lack of use by English judges of the rules for interpretation of treaties in the Vienna Convention on the Law of Treaties 1969.

[80] *Stag Line Ltd v. Foscolo Mango & Co. Ltd* [1932] A.C. 328, 350; *James Buchanan & Co. Ltd v. Babco Forwarding and Shipping (U.K.) Ltd* [1978] A.C. 141; *cf.* below, para. 6-060, n. 21 and R. J. C. Munday, (1978) 27 I.C.L.Q. 450; *Fothergill v. Monarch Airlines Ltd* [1981] A.C. 251; *Rothmans Ltd v. Saudi Airlines* [1981] Q.B. 368; *The Hollandia* [1983] 1 A.C. 565: see F. A. Mann, "Uniform Statutes in English Law" (1983) 99 L.Q.R. 376, who argued that the purposive approach had been carried too far.

[81] *Morris v. KLM Royal Dutch Airlines* [2001] 3 All E.R. 126 ("bodily injury" in Art. 17 of the Warsaw Convention 1929 held not to extend to mental injury or distress given that in 1929 claims for such injury or distress were not known in any of the jurisdictions of the parties to the Convention in 1929 and not mentioned in the *travaux preparatoires*).

dictionaries, expert opinion and the judgments of foreign courts may be consulted[82]; *travaux prparatoires*, such as the proceedings of the conferences at which the treaty was prepared, may also be used, albeit with caution.[83]

(2) An Act of Parliament may implement a treaty by enacting substantive provisions of English law but without expressly incorporating the text of the treaty as part of English law. Three questions may arise concerning the use of the treaty as an aid to the interpretation of the statute.

(i) Can the treaty only be considered if it is expressly referred to in the Act? The intention to implement the treaty may, for example, be mentioned in the preamble or long title.[84] In *Salomon v. Commissioners of Customs and Excise*[85] the Court of Appeal held that a relevant treaty could be consulted even if not expressly referred to in the statute. *Per* Diplock L.J.:

"If from extrinsic evidence it is plain that the enactment was intended to fulfil Her Majesty's Government's obligations under a particular convention, it matters not that there is no express reference to the convention in the statute. One must not presume that Parliament intends to break an international convention merely because it does not say expressly that it is intending to observe it."[86]

(ii) Can the treaty only be considered if the words of the statute are on their face ambiguous, or is the treaty to be read as part of the context of the statute *before* it is determined whether the words are ambiguous? The first, more restrictive, approach is supported by authority.[87] However, the courts have not been astute to hold

---

[82] See, *e.g.*. *Swiss Bank Corporation v. Brink's MA.T. Ltd* [1986] Q.B. 853.

[83] See the *Fothergill* case, n. 80 above; *Gatoil International Inc. v. Arkwright-Boston Manufacturers Mutual Insurance Co.* [1985] A.C. 255, 263–265. The material must be "public and accessible" and "clearly and indisputably point to a definite legislative intention" (*ibid.*). Reference to *travaux preparatoires* may not prove helpful: *Hiscox v. Outhwaite (No.1)* [1992] 1 A.C. 562, 593; see R. Gardiner, (1995) 44 I.C.L.Q. 620, 624–626.

[84] See, *e.g.*, Recognition of Divorces and Legal Separations Act 1971; Arbitration Act 1975; State Immunity Act 1978.

[85] [1967] 2 Q.B. 116.

[86] *ibid.*, p. 144. *Cf.* Lord Denning M.R. (in more general terms) at p. 141; Russell LJ. at p. 152. *Re Westinghouse Uranium Contract* [1978] A.C. 547; *Re State of Norway's Application* [1987] Q.B. 433. The decision of the House of Lords in *Ellerman Lines Ltd v. Murray* [1931] A.C. 126 had been thought to support a requirement of express reference, but Diplock LJ. in *Salomon* expressed the view that it was not authority for that proposition: [1967] 2 Q.B. 116, 144.

[87] Diplock L.J. in *Salomon v. Commissioners of Customs and Excise* [1967] 2 Q.B. 116, 145. References to having recourse to the terms of a treaty as aids to the construction of provisions that are "ambiguous or vague" are frequent: *e.g. Quazi v. Quazi* [1980] A.C. 744, 808 (Lord Diplock); *Fothergill v. Monarch Airlines Ltd* [1984] A.C. 251, 299 (Lord Roskill); *Minister of Public Works v. Sir Frederick Snow* [1984] A.C. 426, 435 (Lord Brandon). The principle has been formulated by Lord Diplock without *express* reference to "ambiguities" or "vagueness" but it is unlikely that he intended a different result: *The Eschersheim* [1976] 1 W.L.R. 430, 436; *Garland v. British Rail Engineering Ltd* [1983] 2 A.C. 751, 771.

statutory words to be clear, without consideration of the treaty,[88] and, in any event, the better view is that the treaty should be considered as part of the context of the enacting words.[89] This would be in conformity with the modern trend towards a broader view of "context" in statutory interpretation.[90]

(iii) If the enacted words are unambiguous, can they be read as if they were modified, by reference to the treaty? The answer here is clearly no. If the enacted words are unclear, but are reasonably capable of more than one meaning, a meaning that is consonant with treaty obligations is to be preferred to one that is not, in accordance with the presumptions mentioned above.[91] However,

"If the terms of the legislation are clear and unambiguous, they must be given effect to, whether or not they carry out Her Majesty's treaty obligations, for the sovereign power of the Queen in Parliament extends to breaking treaties (see *Ellerman Lines Ltd v. Murray*[92]), and any remedy for such a breach of an international obligation lies in a forum other than Her Majesty's own courts."[93]

Statutory words cannot be interpreted in order to produce conformity with a treaty if the words are not reasonably capable of bearing that meaning.[94]

(3) It may be argued that a statute should be interpreted in the light of an international convention such as the European Convention on Human Rights. In *Birdi v. Secretary of State for Home Affairs*[95] Lord Denning M.R. said that if an Act of Parliament contradicted the Convention "I might be inclined to hold it invalid." However, he retracted this in *Ex p. Bhajan Singh*.[96] In *R. v. Chief Immigration Officer, ex p. Salamat Bibi*[97] it was said that a court could look to the Convention "if there is any

[88] Brandon J. in *The Annie Hay* [1968] P. 341; Lane J. in *The Banco* [1971] P. 137; Warner J. in *National Smokeless Fuels Ltd v. I.R.C.* [1986] S.T.C. 300 (emphasising that a broad view is to be taken in this context of what constitutes an "ambiguity").

[89] I. Brownlie, *Principles of Public International Law* (5th ed., 1998, p.48); Bennion (1997) p. 523. Lord Denning M.R. appeared to support this position in *Salomon v. Commissioners of Customs and Excise* [1967] 2 Q.B. 116, 141.

[90] Above, paras 6-007–6-012.

[91] *per* Diplock LJ. in *Salomon's* case, [1967] 2 Q.B. 116, 143; *Post Office v. Estuary Radio Ltd* [1968] 2 Q.B. 740, 757.

[92] [1931] A.C. 126. It was not "proper to resort to the draft convention for the purpose of giving to the section a meaning other than that which ... is its natural meaning" (*per* Lord Tomlin at p. 147).

[93] *per* Diplock L.J. in *Salomon's* case, [1967] 2 Q.B. 116, 143.

[94] *cf.* Lord Diplock in *The Eschersheim* [1976] 1 W.L.R. 430, 436. However, it is not obvious that the courts should not be able in this context to employ their limited power to read statutes as if modified: above, para. 6-014.

[95] Unreported, referred to in *R. v. Secretary of State for the Home Department, ex p. Bhajan Singh* [1976] Q.B. 198.

[96] *ibid.*

[97] [1976] 1 W.L.R. 979.

ambiguity in our statutes, or uncertainty in our law."[98] It clearly cannot prevail over clear words in a statute.[99] However, it was also held (prior to implementation of the Human Rights Act 1998) that the Secretary of State was not under any legal obligation to take the Convention into account when exercising statutory discretionary powers,[1] and the fact that a right was protected by the Convention did not itself mean that it would be a "legitimate expectation" protected by principles of English administrative law.[2] It was difficult to square this restrictive approach with more positive dicta elsewhere.[3] The broader approach is now firmly reflected in the "principle of legality" recognised by the House of Lords as part of the common Iaw[4] and interpretation so as to produce conformity with Convention rights is now required by section 3 of the Human Rights Act 1998.[5] Futhermore, the Court of Appeal has held more generally that a court is entitled to take account of tne provisions of a treaty in interpreting a statute, even where the statute was not passed to *implement* any particular treaty obligation:

> "The principle ... requires that domestic legislation should be construed so as to be in conformity with an international obligation of this country if it is clear that the legislation was intended by Parliament to be in conformity with that obligation and if such a construction is one which is and was properly applicable to the terms of the legislation when first enacted. International obligations cannot alter the clear meaning of statutes. They may, however, be permitted to make clear which of more than one reasonable meaning was intended by Parliament."[6]

(4) The special case of the interpretation of Community legislation is considered below.[7]

---

[98] *ibid.* p. 984 *per* Lord Denning M.R. See, to similar effect, Lord Fraser in *Attorney-General v. B.B.C.* [1981] A.C. 303, 352; Sir Robert Megarry V.-C. in *Trawnik v. Lennox* [1985] 1 W.L.R. 532, 541; Lord Goff in *Attorney-General v. Guardian Newspapers (No. 2)* [1990] 1 A.C. 109, 283: " ... I conceive it to be my duty, when I am free to do so, to interpret the law in accordance with the obligations of the Crown under this treaty"; *Waddington v. Miah* [1974] 1 W.L.R. 683 and *R. v. Deery* [1977] Crim. L. R. 550, where the presumption against retrospective legislation was reinforced by prohibitions against the retrospective application of criminal penalties contained in the European Convention and the International Covenant on Civil and Political Rights.

[99] *R. v. Greater London Council, ex p. Burgess* [1978] I.C.R. 991; *Kynaston v. Secretary of State for Home Affairs* (1981) 73 Cr. App. R. 281.

[1] *Fernandes v. Secretary of State for the Home Department* [1981] Imm. A.R. 1 *Cf.* the powerful argument that standards derived, *inter alia*, from the Convention should be used to structure the inherently vague concept of *Wednesbury* unreasonableness: J. Jowell and A. Lester, [1987] P.L. 368.

[2] *R. v. Immigration Appeal Tribunal, ex p. Chundawadra* [1988] Imm. A. R. 161.

[3] See the cases cited in n. 98 above.

[4] Below, para. 6-039.

[5] Below, para. 8-006.

[6] *per* Ralph Gibson L.J. in *J. H. Rayner Ltd v. Department of Trade* [1989] Ch. 72, 230–231; see to similar effect, Kerr L.J. at pp. 164–166; with whom Nourse L.J. agreed on this point: p. 222. The court approved a dictum of Scarman L. J. in *Pan-American World Airways Inc. v. Department of Trade* [1976] 1 Lloyd's Rep. 257, 261.

[7] paras 6-049–6-060.

4. PARLIAMENTARY MATERIALS

6–036   It was reaffirmed by the House of Lords in *Davis v. Johnson*[8] that a court may not refer to Parliamentary materials for any purpose whatsoever connected with the interpretation of statutes. The prohibition covered such materials as reports of debates in the House and in committee, the explanatory memoranda attached to Bills and successive drafts of Bills. A number of judges openly disagreed with the rule.[9] References were occasionally made to *Hansard* in the course of particular cases, apparently without objection from other parties and without reference to the prohibition.[10] Some judges admitted to consulting *Hansard* informally.[11] Relaxation of the prohibition was opposed by the Law Commissions in view of doubts as to the reliability and availability of legislative material.[12]

By contrast legislative materials were (and are) used in many foreign jurisdictions, including the United States of America and many European countries, where they tend to be more accessible and concise. There have, however, been criticisms that the practice of referring to legislative history has been abused.[13]

In *Pickstone v. Freemans plc*[14] the House of Lords held that it is permissible to cite the terms in which delegated legislation is presented to Parliament by ministers as a guide to the intention of Parliament in approving the legislation in question, and thus as an aid to the interpretation of the legislation. The regulations in question,[15] as is almost universally the case,[16] were not subject to the Parliamentary process of consideration and amendment in Committee as a Bill would have been. Then, in *Pepper (Inspector of Taxes) v. Hart*[17] the House of Lords significantly relaxed the general prohibition as it related to Acts of Parliament. At issue was the interpretation of the Finance Act 1976, which

---

[8]   [1979] A.C. 264; *Hadmor Productions v. Hamilton* [1983] 1 A.C. 191, 232–233.

[9]   *e.g.* Lord Denning M.R. in the Court of Appeal *Davis v. Johnson* [1979] A.C. 264, 276–277.

[10] *e.g. McVeigh v. Beattie* [1988] Fam. 69, 84.

[11] *e.g.* Lord Denning M.R. in *Davies v. Johnson* (n. 9 above).

[12] Law Com. No. 21, Scots Law Com. No. 11 (1969), pp. 31–37.

[13] *ibid.*, pp. 32–34. The rules against reliance on lesgislative materials have been relaxed in Australia (by statute: Acts Interpretation Act (Cwlth), s.15AB, added in 1984) and New Zealand (by the judges: see J. F. Burrows, [1989] N.Z.L.J. 94). See also G. Bale, (1995) 74 Can. Bar Rev. 1, 23–25; Bryson J, [1992] Stat.L.R. 187.

[14] [1989] A.C. 66, H.L. See A. I. L.Campbell, 1989 S.L.T.137. See also *Conerney v. Jacklin* [1985] Crim.L.R.234, where *Hansard* was cited as a guide to the purpose of regulations, as distinct from their interpretation.

[15] The Equal Pay (Amendment) Regulations 1983 (S.I. 1983 No. 1794), amending section 1(2)(c) of the Equal Pay Act 1976, so as to comply with requirements of Community law.

[16] See above, para. 6-003 on Parliamentary scrutiny.

[17] [1993] A.C. 593. See above, paras 5-024, 5-025. Following argument before five Law Lords, a special Appellate Committee of seven Law Lords was convened under the chairmanship of the Lord Chancellor to hear argument on the exclusionary rule. The decision has spawned a vast literature: see, *e.g.*, S. D. Girvin, (1993) 22 Anglo-Am.L.R. 475; D. Miers, (1993) 56 M.L.R. 695; D. Oliveril [1993] P.L. 5; D. Davies, [1993] B.T.R. 172; T.St.J.Bates, (1993) J.L.S.S. 251, (1993) 14 Stat.L.R. 46 and [1995] C.L.J. 127; B.J. Davenport, (1993) 109 L.Q.R. 149; F.A.R.Bennion (1993) 14 Stat.L.R. 149; J. H. Baker, [1993] C.L.J. 353; S. C. Styles, (1993) 14 J.L.S. 151; Sir Nicholas Lyell Q.C. (1994) 15 Stat.L.R. 1; Lord Lester, *ibid.* p. 10; J. C. Jenkins, *ibid.*, p. 23; G. Bale, (1995) 74 Can.Bar Rev.1; J. Steyn, (2001) 21 O.J.L.S. 59.

stated that where a benefit was provided by an employer to higher-paid employees (or their families) the employees would have to pay income tax on the "cash equivalent" of that benefit.[18] The "cash equivalent" was the "cost of the benefit" less so much (if any) as was made good to those providing the benefit; the "cost of the benefit" was "the amount of any expense incurred in or in connection with its provision, and ... includes a proper proportion of any expense relating partly to the benefit and partly to other matters."[19] The appellants were members of staff of a fee-paying school, Malvern College, whose sons were educated at the school under a concessionary scheme whereby they paid one-fifth of the standard fee charged for other parents. They were assessed on income tax on the basis that the "cost of the benefit" was the relevant proportion of the overall expenditure incurred in providing facilities to all the pupils (the "average cost" basis). The taxpayers claimed that the cost should be the *additional* expenditure incurred in respect of their sons (the "marginal cost" basis). As they were filling spare places at the school, this would come to a small amount in respect of equipment and food, itself more than covered by the concessionary fee paid.

The House of Lords held (1) that without recourse to Parliamentary material, the proper interpretation of section 63 would have supported the "average cost" approach adopted by the Revenue[20]; but (2), the prohibition against reliance on Parliamentary material should be relaxed[21]; and (3) in the light of statements made by Robert Sheldon M.P., the Financial Secretary to the Treasury, at the Committee stage, it was clear that the Bill had been passed on the basis that its effect was to assess such benefits on the marginal cost to the employer, and section 63 should be construed accordingly.[22] The leading speech was given by Lord Browne-Wilkinson,[23] who stated[24] that "the exclusionary rule should be relaxed so as to permit reference to Parliamentary materials where (a) legislation is ambiguous or obscure, or leads to an absurdity; (b) the material relied upon consists of one or more statements by a Minister or other promoter of the Bill together if necessary with such other Parliamentary material as is necessary to understand such statements and their effect; (c) the statements relied upon are clear.[25] Further than this, I would not at present go."

This step was desirable:

---

[18] s.61.

[19] s.63.

[20] Lords Browne-Wilkinson, Keith of Kinkel, Bridge of Harwich, Ackner and Oliver of Aylmerton. Lords Mackay of Clashfern and Griffiths disagreed on this point.

[21] All the members of the House of Lords except Lord Mackay of Clashfern L.C.

[22] Some commentators argue that the statement made late at night to a standing committee ("comprising some eleven future cabinet ministers": Sir Nicholas Lyell, (1993) 14 Stat.L.R.1, 5) were "really describing the effects of pre-existing legislation as interpreted in practice by the Revenue rather than setting out the Government's express policy intentions with regard to new wording" (*ibid.* p. 2); and see Bennion (1997), pp. 472–487.

[23] With whom all but Lord Mackay of Clashfern L.C. expressly agreed.

[24] p. 640.

[25] *i.e.* "clearly discloses the mischief aimed at or the legislative intention lying behind the ambiguous or obscure words": *per* Lord Browne-Wilkinson at p. 634. The statement should be "directed to the very point in question in the litigation": *per* Lord Browne-Wilkinson in *Melluish (Inspector of Taxes) v. BMI (No. 3) Ltd.* [1996] A.C. 454, 481.

"The courts should not deny themselves the light which Parliamentary materials may shed on the meaning of the words Parliament has used and thereby risk subjecting the individual to a law which Parliament never intended to enact."[26]

It would facilitate the modern purposive approach to statutory construction.[27] It was also logically indistinguishable from the position taken in *Pickstone v. Freemans plc.*[28] There, the court was authorised to look at ministerial statements made in introducing regulations which *could not* be amended by Parliament; here the same would be permitted for statements "made in introducing a statutory provision which, though capable of amendment, was not in fact amended."[29] His Lordship rejected a series of arguments against the change. There was nothing constitutionally improper in relaxing the rule: the courts would still be interpreting Parliament's[30] words and would not be "questioning" the "freedom of speech and debates or proceedings" in Parliament contrary to Article 9 of the Bill of Rights.[31] Although the "practical reasons for the rule (difficulty of getting access to Parliamentary materials and the cost and delay in researching it)" were "not without substance", they could be "greatly exaggerated".[32] Experience in Commonwealth countries where the rule had been abandoned did not suggest that the drawbacks were substantial,

"provided that the court keeps a tight control on the circumstances in which references to Parliamentary material are allowed."[33]

6–037   Lord Mackay of Clashfern L.C. was alone in dissent on this point. He had no objection in principle to the change but was concerned at the "possibility at least of an immense increase in the cost of litigation."[34] The evidence from other jurisdictions did not justify the view that there had been no substantial increase in the cost of litigation there, and the Parliamentary processes involved were materially different from those in the United Kingdom.[35]

Much of the comment on *Pepper v. Hart* has been critical.[36] There have

---

[26] Lord Browne-Wilkinson at p. 638.
[27] See above, para. 6-009.
[28] Above.
[29] Lord Browne-Wilkinson at p.635.
[30] *Cf.* above, para. 6-003.
[31] See also *Prebble v. Television New Zealand Ltd* [1995] 1 A.C. 321, P.C.
[32] Lord Browne-Wilkinson at p. 633.
[33] *ibid.*
[34] p. 615.
[35] *ibid.*
[36] See, *e.g.*, Bates, (1993) 14 Stat.L.R. 46 (welcoming the relaxation in principle but noting ambiguities in Lord Browne-Wilkinson's formulation and criticising the failure to relate it to other aids to interpretation); Miers (1993) 56 M.L.R. 695 discussing, *inter alia*, the implications for parliamentary debate and the relationship between the legislature and the judiciary ("there is a real danger of the courts becoming too close to the executive's intentions" (p. 708)) ; G. Marshall in D. Oliver and G. Drewry (eds), *The Law and Parliament* (1998), Chap. IX (arguing that the exclusory rule should have been maintained on the grounds that "citizens are governed by laws and not by the wishes of legislators" and constitutionalism and the separation of powers should not permit "members of the executive and legislative branches to interpret the law as well as make it"); R. Summers in D. Butler et al. (eds), *The Law. Politics and the Constitution* (1999), Chap. 12.

been fears that the decision will, as predicted by Lord Mackay, generate a significant increase in ultimately unnecessary cost. Access to Parliamentary materials can be difficult,[37] as can identifying who are the relevant ministers or promoters and following clauses through changes in numbering in successive prints of a Bill. Lord Browne-Wilkinson himself accepted that in many, if not most cases, there would be no "crock of gold".[38] On the other hand, tables of debates on Bills have been published,[39] published annotations to Acts now commonly include relevant extracts from *Hansard*, and *Hansard* for recent sessions has become available on the internet and on CD-Rom.

Experience of the application of *Pepper v. Hart* in subsequent cases has been mixed. In very few does reference to Parliamentary material appear to have been decisive in solving an interpretative difficulty. A rare example is *Sunderland Polytechnic v. Evans*,[40] where the Employment Appeal Tribunal declined to follow one of its own previous decisions[41] on the interpretation of a provision of the Wages Act 1986, in the light of a reference to two ministerial statements in debate. Reference to *Hansard* may make clear the general purpose of a particular provision, while throwing little light on the meaning of particular words within it.[42] Help may also be gained from considering the context into which words have been added as an amendment,[43] or the absence from ministerial statements of support for a construction contended for by a party.[44]

More frequently, a reference to *Hansard* merely confirms the view of a question of construction that the judge or court would reach independently,[45] although this confirmation may make a matter that is otherwise

---

[37] Only very few law libraries (including the Houses of Parliament and the Universities of Nottingham and London) hold complete series of Standing Committee debates: see G. Holborn, (1993) 24 *Law Librarian* 141.

[38] [1993] A.C. 593 at pp. 634–635, 637. If, however, a clear statement in Parliament is found, that should obviate the need for further litigation.

[39] *Current Law Statutes Service*, Table of Parliamentary Debates (1950–2001).

[40] [1993] I.C.R. 392. Others are *R. v. Northumbrian Water Ltd., ex p. Newcastle & North Tyneside Health Authority* [1999] J.P.L. 704; *A.E. Beckett & Sons (Lyndons) Ltd. v. Midland Electricity plc* [2001] 1 W.L.R. 281.

[41] *Home Office v. Ayres* [1992] I.C.R. 175.

[42] *Building Societies Commission v. Halifax Building Society* [1995] 3 All E.R. 193, 209–210.

[43] *Grovedeck Ltd. v. Capital Demolition Ltd.* [2000] Build. L.R. 181.

[44] *Re Blackspur Group plc., The Times*, July 5, 2001.

[45] e.g. *R. v. Warwickshire County Council, ex p. Johnson* [1993] A.C. 583, H.L. (misleading price indication by Dixons electrical goods store manager not given "in the course of a business of his" within the Consumer Protection Act 1987, s.20); *Chief Adjudication Officer v. Foster* [1993] A.C. 754, H.L. (power to make regulations specifying circumstances in which persons were to be treated as being or not being severely disabled not confined to defining the degree of disability); *R. v. Secretary of State for the Home Department, ex p. Mehari* [1994] Q.B. 474 (ministerial statement pointed to a particular construction which in any case was supported by other considerations); *Elf Enterprise Caledonia Ltd v. I.R.C.* [1994] S.T.C. 785, 798; *Botross v. London Borough of Hammersmith and Fulham* (1994) 27 H.L.R. 179; *Thomas Witter Ltd v. TBP Industries Ltd* [1996] 2 All E.R. 573; *I.R.C. v. Laird Group plc* [2001] S.T.C. 689; *Re Blackspur Group plc, The Times*, July 5, 2001. Curiously, reference to Parliamentary material to confirm an interpretation was initially proposed by counsel for the appellants in *Pepper v. Hart* as one of the permitted grounds, but this was abandoned during argument: Lord Lester, (1994) 15 Stat.L.R. 10, 21. It rapidly crept into practice.

debatable "clear beyond peradventure."[46] Conversely, the statements made in Parliament may not be helpful,[47] or sufficiently clear to require any different meaning to be given to the words.[48] There are also cases where reference to *Hansard* has not been regarded as justified, on the ground that there is no ambiguity, obscurity or absurdity,[49] which may be because the point is covered by binding precedent,[50] or where a judicial invitation to counsel to undertake a *Pepper v. Hart* search has been resisted in view of the consequent delay.[51]

The conditions laid down by Lord Browne-Wilkinson have naturally been the subject of further consideration. Thus, ambiguity has been identified where the meaning of a particular phrase is uncertain in its application,[52] or where various judges or courts have differed over a point of interpretation.[53] The rules apply to ambiguity in legislation affecting criminal proceedings, and not just civil proceedings.[54] The concept of ambiguity should also apply to the position that arises where there is an inconsistency between two statutory provisions, although a different view appeared to have been taken in *R. v. Moore*.[55] While most of the statements in Parliament referred to have been those of ministers, reference has also been made to statements by the successful mover of an amendment[56] and a Parliamentary Agent before

---

[46] *Stubbings v. Webb* [1993] A.C. 498, H.L.; *per* Lord Griffiths at p. 508 (three-year limitation for period from date of requisite knowledge for personal injury actions *inter alia* for "breach of duty" not applicable to trespass to the person; reference to *Hansard* made it clear that Parliament intended to implement a Committee report. Oral argument in this and the *Johnson* and *Foster* cases (n. 45 above) had been completed before the decision in *Pepper v. Hart* was announced.

[47] There are many examples, including *Massmould Holdings Ltd v. Payne* [1993] S.T.C. 62; *Sheppard v. I.R.C* (No. 2) [1993] S.T.C. 240, 255; *Re Bishopsgate Investment Management Ltd* [1993] Ch. 481, 490, (also no ambiguity, obscurity or absurdity); *Welby v. Casswell* [1994] 2 E.G.L.R. 4; *R. v. Registered Designs Appeal Tribunal, ex p. Ford Motor Co.Ltd* [1995] 1 W.L.R. 18; *Denby v. Yeldon* [1995] 3 All E.R. 624.

[48] *Macdougall v. Wrexham Maelor Borough Council* (1993) 69 P.& C.R. 109, 122.

[49] *Islwyn Borough Council v. Newport Borough Council, The Times*, June 28, 1993, C.A.; *R. v. Secretary of State for Foreign and Commonwealth Affairs, ex p. Rees-Mogg* [1994] Q.B. 552, 556–557; *Busby v. Co-operative Insurance Society* [1994] 1 E.G.L.R. 136; *R. v. Secretary of State for the Home Department, ex p.Okello* [1994] Imm.A.R. 261; *D.P.P. v. Bull* [1995] Q.B. 88 (term "common prostitute" confined to women, as would have been confirmed by a reference to *Hansard*); *Petch v. Gurney (Inspector of Taxes)* [1994] 3 All E.R. 731; *R. v. Singleton* [1995] Crim.L.R. 236; *R. v. Director General of Fair Trading, ex p. Benham Ltd.* [2001] 1 E.G.L.R. 21; *R. v. Richmond London Borough Council, ex p. Watson* [2001] Q.B. 370.

[50] *Sheppard v. I.R.C. (No. 2)* [1993] S.T.C. 240, Aldous J.; *Dawkins v. Department of the Environment* [1993] I.C.R. 517, C.A.; *National Rivers Authority v. Alfred McAlpine Homes East Ltd* [1994] 4 All E.R. 286, 296–297, D.C.

[51] *R. v. Dorset County Council, ex p. Rolls* (1994) 26 H.L.R. 381.

[52] *Sheppard v. I.R.C. (No. 2)* [1993] S.T.C. 624, referring to Lord Diplock in *I.R.C. v. Joiner* [1975] 1 W.L.R. 1701, 1710; *I.R.C. v. Laird Group plc* [2001] S.T.C. 689. But note the limitation introduced by the *Spath Holme* decision: below, para. 6-038.

[53] *Doncaster Borough Council v. Secretary of State for the Environment* (1992) 91 L.G.R. 459, 476–477; *Chief Adjudication Officer v. Foster* [1993] A.C. 754, 772.

[54] *Botross v. London Borough of Hammersmith and Fulham* (1994) 27 H.L.R. 179, 186.

[55] (1994) 159 J.P.101, where the Court of Appeal (Criminal Division) solved a problem caused by defective drafting by refusing to apply the literal meaning of a provision as to do so would "frustrate the plain legislative intent", and reading the words "following provisions" as if they were "preceding provisions". It is difficult in any event to see that there was not "absurdity".

[56] *Chief Adjudication Officer v. Foster* [1993] A.C. 754; *Botross v. London Borough of Hammersmith and Fulham* (1994) 27 H.L.R. 179, 187 (amendment accepted by government minister).

a House of Commons Committee at the committee stage of a Private Bill.[57] The fact that a statement is made on the advice of a law officer is no reason for it to be excluded.[58] However, reference may not be made to a press release, which is a departmental and not a Parliamentary document.[59] Ministerial statements may cease to be of value where words are re-enacted following court decisions on their interpretation.[60] Reference may not be made to ministerial statements on *other* provisions.[61] The requirement that a statement be "clear" has not received separate attention, although statements cited may not be regarded as helpful.[62]

The decision in *Pepper v. Hart* has led to changes in practice. Any party **6–038** intending to refer to *Hansard* must, unless the judge otherwise directs, serve upon all other parties and the court copies of the extracts in question, with a brief summary of the argument intended to be based thereon.[63] It seems that extracts from *Hansard* will be cited in argument and decisions on whether the court is able and willing to rely on them are taken later.

As regards Parliamentary proceedings,

"If it proves necessary to correct any inadvertent ambiguity or error in a ministerial statement made during the passage of a Bill, the aim is to do this as promptly as possible at an appropriate point during the further consideration of the Bill. The best means of doing so and reading such a correction into the official record will depend on a number of factors, including the stage which the Bill has reached and the nature of the proceedings at that point."[64]

Corrections are no longer left to correspondence with Members.

The first nine years of the operation of *Pepper v. Hart* has largely borne out the fears expressed by Lord Mackay of Clashfern. Issues concerning the cost of litigation have been raised with the legal profession.[65] The possibility of reference being made to Parliamentary material has been raised in over 360 cases to date.[66] In each of these, research will have been done at the client's expense; in very few indeed does a "crock of gold" appear to have made a difference to the outcome. What cannot be estimated is the extent to which awareness of that material has influenced the supposed "independent" approach of the judges to questions of interpretation. The House of Lords considered *Pepper v. Hart* at some length in *R. v. Secretary of State*

---

[57] *London Regional Transport Pension Fund Trust Co.Ltd v. Hatt, The Times,* May 20, 1993. The statement was of no help to the court.

[58] *R. v. Secretary of State for Foreign and Commonwealth Affairs, ex p. Rees-Mogg* [1994] Q.B. 552, 566, *per* Lloyd L.J.

[59] *Elf Enterprise Caledonia Ltd v. I.R.C.* [1994] S.T.C. 785, 798. A press release was, however, mentioned by Lord Browne-Wilkinson in *Pepper v. Hart* [1993] A.C.593, 628 although the case turned on ministerial statements.

[60] *I.R.C. v. Willoughby* [1995] S.T.C. 143, 174 *per* Morritt L.J.: "In these circumstances it must be assumed that the original intention, whatever it was, was superseded by acceptance of the decisions of the courts."

[61] *Melluish v. B.M.I. (No. 3) Ltd.* [1996] A.C. 454, 481 *per* Lord Browne-Wilkinson.

[62] See above, n. 47.

[63] *Practice Direction (Hansard: Citation)* [1995] 1 W.L.R. 192.

[64] Vol.239, H.C.Deb., March 14, 1994, written answer by the Parliamentary Secretary, Lord Chancellor's Department, John M. Taylor M.P.

[65] Vol.239, H.C.Deb., March 7, 1994, col.70, written answer by Mr Taylor.

[66] *Lexis* search.

for the Environment, Transport and the Regions, ex p. Spath Holme Ltd.[67]
The question was whether a general power to make regulations restricting or
preventing increase of rent for dwellings was itself restricted to countering
general inflation in the economy. The House held unanimously that it was
not. All the members seemed concerned to a greater or lesser extent with the
costs of frequent citation of Hansard, and agreed that it was exceptional for
such citation to be helpful. Lords Bingham, Hope and Hutton were agreed
that the conditions laid down in *Pepper v. Hart* should be "strictly insisted
upon."[68] Furthermore, a distinction was to be drawn between issues as to
(1) the meaning of a statutory expression and (2) the scope of a statutory
power. The *Pepper v. Hart* exception was available in respect of the former,
but, as regards the latter, according to Lord Bingham, only

> "if a minister were, improbably, to give a categorical assurance to
> Parliament that a power would not be used in a given situation, such
> that Parliament could be taken to have legislated on that basis ... ."[69]

For Lord Hope,

> "it would be contrary to fundamental considerations of constitutional
> principle to allow it to be used to enable reliance to be placed on
> statements made in debate about matters of policy which have not been
> reproduced in the enactment."[70]

Furthermore, the *Pepper v. Hart* exception was only ever available to
prevent the executive seeking to place a meaning on words different from
that which ministers attributed to those words when promoting the
legislation in Parliament.[71] Lords Nicholls and Cooke did not accept this
distinction and argued, persuasively, that (2) is really an example of (1).[72] All
the members of the House were agreed that the particular *Hansard*
statements relied on by *Spath Holme* did not provide clear and unequivocal
support to the narrower interpretation of the power which they in fact
rejected; Lord Cooke alone regarded them as helpful in confirming that
adoption of a broader view would not thwart Parliament's intention. It is
submitted that the doubtful distinction adopted by the majority in *Spath
Holme* will have little impact in reducing the level of costs wasted in fruitless
Hansard searches. A more fundamental reconsideration is required. Lord
Steyn, writing extra-judicially,[73] has mounted a powerful attack on the
decision:

> "It remains my view that *Pepper v. Hart* has substantially increased the

---

[67] [2001] 1 All E.R. 195.

[68] *ibid.*, pp. 212, 227, 233.

[69] *per* Lord Bingham at p. 212; Lord Hutton did not comment on this qualification; Lord Hope
regarded it as a qualification applicable to both (1) and (2): see below.

[70] *ibid.*, p. 227. Lord Bingham's reservations centred more on the unlikelihood of a minister
seeking to define the legal effect of the draftman's language (p. 212).

[71] *ibid.*; repeated *orbiter* in *R. v. A.* [2001] UKHL 25, [2001] 3 All E.R. 1, 27–28.

[72] Lord Nicholls at p. 218.

[73] (2001) 21 O.J.L.S. 59. Lord Millett regards *Petter v. Hart* as a "regrettable decision": (1999)
20 Stat. L.R. 107,110.

cost of litigation to very little advantage. Many appellate judges share this view."[74]

Furthermore, it was wrong in principle to treat ministerial policy statements as a source of law. There was a case for confining *Pepper v. Hart* to "the admission against the executive of categorical assurances given by ministers to Parliament."[75] These views are echoed in *Spath Holme*, although Lord Steyn's proposed restriction on the scope of *Pepper v. Hart* would be much more radical and was only taken up by Lord Hope.[76]

It has been held that reference may be made, notwithstanding the *Pepper v. Hart* restrictions, to Parliamentary material designed to throw light on whether the purpose and object of a statute was to enact an EC directive or introduce the provisions of an international convention, as distinct from any question of the construction of a particular statutory provision.[77] Furthermore, references have continued to be made without apparent objection in other situations that do not appear to fall within the restrictions.[78] It is submitted that the former, which builds on the position taken in *Pickstone v. Freemans plc*,[79] is right and should be regarded as surviving *Spath Holme*; the latter cannot survive. Furthermore, where there is ambiguity, reference be made to the explanatory notes,[80] certainly where the *Pepper v. Hart* conditions are satisfied,[81] but without any need to rely on *Pepper v. Hart*.[82]

A final thought is that the rarity of cases in which reference to *Hansard* solves the problem is itself disappointing, providing examples of situations where it would appear that those involved in the legislative process have not fully understood what they were doing.

F. PRESUMPTIONS

1. Presumptions of General Application; the Principle of Legality

There are various presumptions that may be applied in doubtful cases. **6–039** These are to be distinguished from the "presumptions of general

---

[74] *ibid.*, p. 64.

[75] *ibid.*, p. 67.

[76] Above.

[77] *Three Rivers District Council v. Bank of England (No. 2)* [1996] 2 All E.R. 363; *U v. W. (HM Attorney General, Intervener)* (unreported, November 27, 1996); such a point would probably now be made clear by reference to the explanatory note.

[78] See Bennion (1997), p. 521–523. Whether this is sufficient to constitute a "residual right" of the court to refer (*ibid.*) is, however, highly doubtful given the absence of discussion of the propriety of the reference and the strictures expressed in *Spath Holme*.

[79] Above, para. 6-036.

[80] Above, para. 5-008.

[81] *Callery v. Gray (No. 2)* [2001] EWCA Civ 1246, [2001] 4 All E.R. 1, at paras. [51]–[54].

[82] *per* Lord Hope in *R. v. A.* [2001] 3 All E.R. 1, para. [82], applying a principle previously enunciated in respect to the explanatory note attached to a statutory instrument in *Coventry and Solihull Waste Disposal Co. Ltd. v. Russell (Valuation Officer)* [1999] 1 W.L.R. 2093, 2103.

application" whereby certain basic legal principles are presumed to apply unless excluded by express words or necessary implication.[83] These principles modify even unambiguous provisions. Examples include aspects of the *ultra vires* doctrine, such as natural justice and abuse of discretion, general principles of criminal liability, and the principle that no-one shall be allowed to gain an advantage from his or her own wrong. Striking illustrations of this last principle include *Re Sigsworth*,[84] where Clawson J. held that apparently unambiguous provisions as to the distribution of the residuary estate on an intestacy were not to be applied so as to enable a murderer to benefit from the victim's estate, and *R. v. Secretary of State for the Home Department, ex p. Puttick*,[85] where Astrid Proll, who had achieved a marriage with a citizen of the United Kingdom and Colonies by the crimes of fraud, forgery and perjury, was held not to be entitled to registration as a United Kingdom citizen, notwithstanding the absolute terms of section 6(2) of the British Nationality Act 1948. She had entered the country under a false identity, and she had committed these crimes in satisfying the Registrar General that in her assumed identity she had been divorced and there was no impediment to the marriage, and in obtaining a marriage licence.

In recent cases, many decided in the period running up to implementation of the Human Rights Act 1998, members of the House of Lords have sought to articulate a more general principle that explains and justifies this approach to the relationship between common law and statute. In *R. v. Secretary of State for the Home Department, ex p. Pierson*[86] the House of Lords by a majority,[87] and on a variety of grounds, held that the Secretary of State had acted unlawfully in increasing the tariff element of a mandatory life sentence with retrospective effect. Lord Steyn noted that the Home Secretary's powers were wide and general; there was no ambiguity in the statutory language so as to engage the presumption against the invasion of common law rights.[88] However, a

> "broader principle applies. Parliament does not legislate in a vacuum. Parliament legislates for a European liberal democracy founded on the principles and traditions of the common law. And the courts may approach legislation on this initial assumption. But this assumption only has prima facie force. It can be displaced by a clear and specific provision to the contrary."[89]

This is the "principle of legality" and protects both procedural safeguards

---

[83] See above, para. 6-001.

[84] [1935] Ch. 89.

[85] [1981] Q.B. 767. See also *R. v. Chief National Insurance Commissioners, ex p. Connor* [1981] Q.B. 758 and the Forfeiture Act 1982. *Cf. R. v. Registrar-General, ex p. Smith* [1991] 2 Q.B. 393, C.A. (similar principle applied where enforcement of an apparently clear statutory duty would facilitate crime resulting in danger to life); see A.P. Le Sueur, [1991] P.L. 326, noting that the decision ran counter to views expressed in standing committee on the provision in question.

[86] [1997] 3 All E.R. 577.

[87] Lords Steyn, Hope and Goff, Lords Browne-Wilkinson and Lloyd dissenting.

[88] See below, para. 6-041.

[89] [1997] 3 All E.R. 577, 603, citing Cross (1995), pp. 142–143. See also Lord Browne-Wilkinson at pp. 590–591, relying on the presumption that Parliament does not intend to change the common law without clearly expressing that intention: below, p. 000.

provided in the common law (such as natural justice) and substantive basic or fundamental rights (such as the right of access to the court;[90] the principle that a sentence may not retrospectively be increased;[91] the presumption that a statutory offence requires a mental element;[92] the right to family life[92a] and the principle of equality[93]). "Unless there is the clearest provision to the contrary Parliament must be presumed not to legislate contrary to the rule of law."[94] Lord Steyn reiterated this approach in the context of subordinate legislation in *R. v. Secretary of State for the Home Department, ex p. Simms,*[95] this time with the express concurrence of Lords Browne-Wilkinson and Hoffmann. The House held unanimously that a general ban on interviews between prisoners and journalists who refused to undertake not to publish any part of the interviews was unlawful. The principle of legality required an express indication to justify this interference with the fundamental and basic right asserted by the prisoners, here the right to seek through oral interviews to persuade a journalist to investigate the safety of the conviction and to publicise his or her findings in an effort to gain justice for the prisoner. There was no such indication.[96] Lord Hoffmann put it this way:[97]

> "Parliamentary sovereignty means Parliament can, if it chooses, legislate contrary to fundamental principles of human rights. The Human Rights Act 1998 will not detract from this power. The constraints upon its exercise by Parliament are ultimately political, not legal. But the principle of legality means that Parliament must squarely confront what it is doing and accept the political cost. Fundamental rights cannot be overridden by general or ambiguous words. This is because there is too great a risk that the full implication of their unqualified meaning may have passed unnoticed in the democratic process. In the absence of express language or necessary implication to the contrary, the courts therefore presume that even the most general words were intended to be subject to the basic rights of the individual."

This principle is now regularly cited[98] and provides the approach to be adopted apart from reliance on the provisions of the Human Rights Act 1998,[99] although the view has also been expressed that it does not add much, if anything, to an individual's Convention rights.[1] It remains of particular

---

[90] *Raymond v. Honey* [1983] 1 A.C. 1.
[91] *Pierson.*
[92] *B. (a minor) v. DPP* [2000] 2 A.C. 428, 460 (*per* Lord Nicholls); *R. v. K* [2001] 3 All E.R. 897.
[92a] *R. v. Secretary of State for the Home Department, ex p. Montana* [2001] 1 W.L.R. 552.
[93] *Matadeen v. Pointu* [1999] 1 A.C. 98, P.C.; *Hall & Co. v. Simons* [2000] 3 W.L.R. 543.
[94] [1997] 3 All E.R. 577, 607.
[95] [2000] 2 A.C. 115.
[96] *ibid.,* p. 130.
[97] *ibid.,* p. 131.
[98] See eg. *B. (a minor) v. DPP* [2000] 2 A.C. 428; *McNally v. Secretary of State for Education* [2001] EWCA Civ 332 (express right of education officer to attend disciplinary hearing to be regarded as subject to overriding requirements of natural justice: *per* Dyson L.J.); *R. v. Special Commissioner, ex p. Morgan Grenfell Ltd.* [2001] S.T.C. 497 (right to legal professional privilege a fundamental right but overridden by necessary implication).
[99] Below, Chap. 8.
[1] *R. v. Secretary of State for the Home Department, ex p. Montana* [2001] 1 W.L.R. 522 at para. [15]. Lord Hoffmann in *ex p. Simms* regarded s.3 of the 1998 Act as the express enactment as a rule of construction of the principle of legality: [2000] 2 A.C. 115,132.

significance, however, in so far as fundamental rights can be identified beyond those expressly dealt with in the European Convention. The concepts of "fundamental rights" and "Convention rights" are not coterminous.[2]

2. Presumptions for Use in Doubtful Cases

6-040 These have been termed "policies of clear statement"[3]; or "in effect announcements by the courts to the legislature that certain meanings will not be assumed unless stated with special clarity."[4] The courts have created a measure of protection for certain values by establishing a requirement that Parliament use clear words if they are to be compromised or overridden. There are many difficulties. The Law Commissions pointed out that there was no established order or precedence in the case of conflict between different presumptions; that the individual presumptions were often of doubtful status or imprecise in scope; that reference to a presumption was unnecessary where a court decided that the words are clear; and that there was no accepted test for resolving a conflict between a presumption, such as the presumption that penal statutes should be construed restrictively, and giving effect to the purpose of a statute, for example the purpose of factory legislation to secure safe working conditions.[5]

It is impossible to produce a definitive list of presumptions which may be applied. As the Law Commissions noted, particular presumptions may be "modified or even abandoned with the passage of time, and with the modification of the social values which they embody."[6] There is room for debate as to why certain values and not others are selected for protection, and differences of view among the judges as to the strength of the protection that ought to be accorded. For example, the presumptions concerned with protecting the existing property or money of individuals have been contrasted with the absence of any presumptions in favour of individuals claiming state benefits.[7] While there are authorities stressing in general terms the importance of protecting individual liberty,[8] and particular freedoms such as freedom of speech,[9] freedom of assembly[10] and freedom from

---

[2] This point works both ways: a Convention right may not have a common law analogue: *R. v. Worcester County Council ex p. SW* [2000] H.R.L.R. 702 (no common law right to private life).

[3] H. M. Hart and A. M. Sacks, cited in Law Com. No. 21, p. 21.

[4] Law Com. No. 21, p. 21.

[5] *ibid.* p. 22.

[6] *ibid.* p. 21. *Cf.* section (d) below.

[7] Cross (1995), p. 194; *Presho v. Department of Health and Social Security* [1984] A.C. 310; *Chief Adjudication Officer v. Brunt* [1988] A.C. 711; *Riley v. Chief Adjudication Officer (Note)* [1988] A.C. 746, C.A.

[8] "Parliament is presumed not to enact legislation which interferes with the liberty of the subject without making it clear that this was its intention": *per* McCullough J. in *R. v. Hallstrom, ex p. W.* [1986] Q.B. 1090, 1104 (in the context of detention for treatment under the Mental Health Act 1983: see M. J. Gunn, [1986] J.S.W.L. 290)).

[9] *e.g.* Lord Reid in *Cozens v. Brutus* [1973] A.C. 854, 862; Scarman L.J. in *Re F. (orse. A.) (A Minor) (Publication of Information)* [1977] Fam. 58, 99.

[10] *Cf. Beatty v. Gillbanks* (1892) 9 Q.B.D. 308; Lord Denning M. R. (dissenting) in *Hubbard v. Pitt* [1976] Q.B. 142, 178–179; *Hirst v. Chief Constable of West Yorkshire* (1986) 85 Cr.App.R. 143.

physical restraint,[11] there have been comparatively few cases outsidee last of these categories where full effect has been given to these factors.[12]

However, such cases would now be dealt with in accordance with the broader-based "principle of legality"[13] and the Human Rights Act 1998.[14] Some of the principles of interpretation that have already been mentioned are sometimes put in the form of a presumption, for example presumptions against "intending what is inconvenient or unreasonable" or "intending injustice or absurdity."[15] On the other hand, it has been suggested that now that there is a greater willingness to adopt a purposive approach to interpretation and that a wider view is taken of the context of particular provisions, "the role of presumptions in interpretation is necessarily less important than in the days of more literal interpretation."[16] Furthermore, the articulation in recent cases of an underlying principle of legality, applicable in all cases and not just cases of ambiguity, would seem to occupy much (although not all) of the ground occupied by the specific presumptions set out in this section.[17]

(a) Presumptions against changes in the common law

This is one of the more controversial presumptions, given that modern legislation may often be intended to change the common law or may deal with matters with which the common law was unconcerned, such as the "welfare state." Lord Reid formulated the presumption as follows in *Black-Clawson International Ltd v. Papierwerke Waldhof-Aschaffenburg A.G.*:[18]

6–041

> "In addition to reading the Act you look at the facts presumed to be known to Parliament when the Bill which became the Act in question was before it, and you consider whether there is disclosed some unsatisfactory state of affairs which Parliament can properly be supposed to have intended to remedy by the Act. There is a presumption which can be stated in various ways. One is that in the absence of any clear indication to the contrary, Parliament can be presumed not to have altered the common law further than was necessary to remedy the 'mischief.' Of course it may and quite often does go further. But the principle is that if the enactment is ambiguous, that meaning which relates the scope of the Act to the mischief should be taken rather than a different or wider meaning which the contemporary situation did not call for."

In *Leach v. R.*[19] a provision that a spouse of a defendant "may" be called

---

[11] *e.g. R. v. Hallstrom, ex. p. W.*, n. 8 above; *Collins v. Wilcock* [1984] 1 W.L.R. 1172.
[12] Compare the above cases with, *e.g., Duncan v. Jones* [1936] K.B. 218; *Thomas v. Sawkins* [1935] 2 K.B, 249; *Liversidge v. Anderson* [1942] A.C. 206.
[13] Above, para. 6-039.
[14] Below, Chap. 8.
[15] See *Maxwell on Interpretation of Statutes* (12th ed., 1969), pp. 199–212.
[16] Cross (1995), p. 190.
[17] Particularly, for example, the presumption against interference with access to the courts or vested rights and against the retrospective operation of legislation.
[18] [1975] A.C. 591, 614.
[19] [1912] A.C. 305; Criminal Evidence Act 1898, s.4(1). See now the Police and Criminal Evidence Act 1984, s.80.

as a witness was held not to overturn the common law rule that a wife was not *compellable*; it merely made her a *competent* witness. In *Beswick v. Beswick*[20] the House of Lords refused to interpret section 56 of the Law of Property Act 1925 in such a way as to overturn the doctrine of privity of contract. A more doubtful use of the presumption was made in *Chertsey Urban District Council v. Mixnam's Properties Ltd*[21] where the House held that a power for a local authority to attach "such conditions as ... [it] may think it necessary or desirable to impose" to a caravan site licence could only be used to impose conditions relating to the use of the land: conditions by which the authority sought to protect the interests of tenants were held to be *ultra vires*.

(b) Presumption against ousting the jurisdiction of the courts

6–042   The courts have generally looked with disfavour upon Parliament's attempts to oust their jurisdiction. Such attempts have been particularly common in the administrative law context,[22] where "exclusion clauses" have been construed narrowly[23] or evaded.[24] It is notable that where the courts have given effect to an "exclusion clause" the clause has only purported to oust their jurisdiction after a six-week period.[25]

(c) Presumption against interference with vested rights

6–043   If there is any ambiguity it is presumed that, "the legislature does not intend to limit vested rights further than clearly appears from the enactment."[26] There is an associated presumption that proprietary rights are not to be taken away without compensation.[27] It has been suggested that where the words are ambiguous, they should be construed in such a way as will cause less interference with existing rights notwithstanding that it appears that Parliament intended a more "stringent" meaning.[28]

However,

---

[20] [1968] A.C. 58, See above, para. 6-032.

[21] [1965] A.C. 745.

[22] See de Smith, Woolf and Jowell, *Judicial Review of Administrative Action* (5th ed., 1995), pp. 231–249; Sir William Wade and C. F. Forsyth, *Administrative Law* (8th ed., 2000), pp. 700–714

[23] *e.g.* where a statute provides that a decision shall be "final", that is read as meaning only that there is no right of *appeal*: the remedy of certiorari is not excluded: *R. v. Medical Appeal Tribunal, ex p. Gilmore* [1957] 1 Q.B. 574; *cf. Ex p. Waldron* [1986] Q.B. 824.

[24] *e.g.* a provision that a "determination by the Commission ... shall not be called in question in any court of law" was held not to exclude proceedings for judicial review where the "determination" was *ultra vires* and a nullity, and thus not a "determination" at all: *Anisminic Ltd v. Foreign Compensation Commission* [1969] 2 A.C. 147 (Foreign Compensation Act 1950, s.4(4)); *cf. Att.-Gen. v. Ryan* [1980] A.C. 718.

[25] *Smith v. East Elloe Rural District Council* [1956] A.C. 585; *R. v. Secretary of State for the Environment, ex p. Ostler* [1977] Q.B. 122; Wade and Forsyth (2000), pp. 714–726. Rather inconsistently, effect in excluding judicial review has been accorded to a "conclusive evidence" provision: *R. v. Registrar of Companies, ex p. Central Bank of India* [1986] Q.B. 1114.

[26] *Per* Ungoed-Thomas J. in *Re Metropolitan Film Studios Application* [1962] 1 W.L.R. 1315, 1323.

[27] *Belfast Corporation v. O.D. Cars Ltd* [1960] A.C. 490; *cf. Westminster Bank Ltd v. Beverley Borough Council* [1971] A.C. 509.

[28] *per* Winn L.J. *obiter* in *Allen v. Thorn Electrical Industries Ltd* [1968] 1 Q.B. 487.

"judges are bound to administer the law as it is, not as they would like it to be. If Parliament, in its wisdom, chooses to legislate in a way which clearly does infringe individual rights, the court is bound to give effect, however unwillingly, to such legislation."[29]

In *Secretary of State for Defence v. Guardian Newspapers Ltd*[30] the House of Lords unanimously rejected the narrow interpretation of section 10 of the Contempt of Court Act 1981[31] adopted by Scott J., who had held that the section had no application to a case where the order being sought was to enforce a property right. Lord Scarman stated that this was not

"an appropriate guide to the true interpretation of a section which has constitutional significance in that its purpose is to support for the benefit of the public the existence of 'a truly effective press.' Specifically, it is my view that, since it is 'in the interests of all of us that we should have a truly effective press,'[32] rights of property have to yield pride of place to the national interest which Parliament must have had in mind when enacting the section. I would, however, add that there certainly remains a place in the law for the principle of construction which the judge applied, namely, that the courts must be slow to impute to Parliament an intention to override property rights in the absence of plain words to that effect. But the principle is not an overriding rule of law: it is an aid, amongst many others, developed by the judges in their never ending task of interpreting statutes in such a way as to give effect to their true purpose."[33]

(d) Strict construction of penal laws in favour of the citizen

Laws which impose criminal or other penalties are strictly construed, so that **6–044** if the words are ambiguous and there are two reasonable interpretations, the more lenient one will be given.[34] Thus, the provision that "all lotteries are

---

[29] *per* Sir Nicolas Browne-Wilkinson in *E.M.I. Records Ltd v. Spillane* [1986] 1 W.L.R. 967, 973, in the course of holding that the Customs and Excise Commissioners had wide powers under the V.A.T. legislation to require the production of documents, which powers were "distasteful to those trained in the law" (*ibid*).

[30] [1985] A.C. 339.

[31] "No court may require a person to disclose ... the source of information contained in a publication for which he is responsible, unless it be established to the satisfaction of the court that disclosure is necessary in the interests of justice or national security or for the prevention of disorder or crime."

[32] *per* Griffiths L.J., [1984] Ch. 156, 167.

[33] [1985] A.C. 339, 362–363. The House of Lords (by three to two) dismissed an appeal against an order that the *Guardian* return a leaked document to the Secretary of State, in the interests of national security. The identity of the "leaker", Sarah Tisdall, was thereby discovered.

[34] *per* Lord Esher in *Tuck & Sons v. Priester* (1887) 19 Q.B.D. 629, 638; *R. v. Allen* [1985] A.C. 1029, 1034; *R. v. Clarke* [1985] A.C. 1037, 1048, 1053; but *cf. R. v. Caldwell* [1982] A.C. 341 where the House of Lords majority held that the word "reckless" was to be construed as an "ordinary English word" notwithstanding that this was contrary to: (1) the interests of the defendant; (2) the views of the Law Commission and (3) established decisions of lower courts, and that it would cause great complexity in the law: see J. C. Smith, [1981] Crim. L. R. 393.

unlawful" was not interpreted as creating a criminal offence.[35] A provision penalising the personation at an election of "any person entitled to vote" was held not to apply to a person who personated a deceased voter.[36] Other examples are *R. v. Harris*[37] and *London and North Eastern Railway Co. v. Berriman.*[38] It has, however, been suggested that while the courts still pay lip service to this principle, it is rarely applied in practice if there are social reasons for convicting.[39] In *Anderton v. Ryan*[40] the House of Lords adopted a restrictive, and purportedly "purposive," reading of section 1 of the Criminal Attempts Act 1981, so that it would not apply to some forms of impossible attempts. In so doing they took insufficient account of the Law Commission Report that led to the 1981 Act,[41] and introduced "confusion and uncertainty".[42] Their Lordships regarded some results of a broad reading of the section as absurd, and Lord Bridge found it surprising that Parliament, if intending to do so, "should have done so by anything less than the clearest express language."[43] Following devastating academic criticism,[44] the House of Lords overruled *Anderton v. Ryan* in *R. v. Shivpuri.*[45]

Statutes giving the police a power of arrest are not regarded as "penal laws" for this purpose[46]:

"no one doubts that a prime factor in the process of construction [of statutes conferring arrest powers] is a strong presumption in favour of the liberty of the innocent subject. But it is clear from the authorities at least that a statute may be held to have rebutted the presumption by something falling short of clear express language."[47]

(e) Presumption against retrospective operation

6-045   "Perhaps no rule of construction is more firmly established than this—that a retrospective operation is not to be given to a statute so as to impair an existing right or obligation, otherwise than as regards matter of procedure, unless that effect cannot be avoided without doing violence to the language of the enactment. If the enactment is expressed in language which is fairly

---

[35] Betting and Lotteries Act 1934: *Sales-Matic Ltd v. Hinchcliffe* [1959] 1 W.L.R. 1005.

[36] Poor Law Amendment Act 1851, s.3: *Whiteley v. Chappell* (1868) L.R. 4 Q.B. 147.

[37] Above, para. 6-005.

[38] Above, para. 6-011.

[39] Glanville Williams, *Textbook of Criminal Law* (2nd ed., 1983), pp. 12–18; *cf. Fisher v. Bell* (para. 6-011 above); *R. v. Ottewell* [1970] A.C. 642, 649; *R. v. Bloxham* [1983] 1 A.C. 109, 114; *Attorney-General's Reference (No. 1 of 1988)* [1989] A.C. 971, 991.

[40] [1985] A.C. 560.

[41] Law Com. No. 102.

[42] J. C. Smith, [1985] Crim. L. R. 504.

[43] [1985] A.C. 560, 583.

[44] Most notably by Glanville Williams, "The Lords and Impossible Attempts or *Quis Custodiet Ipsos Custodes?*" [1986] C.L.J. 33, acknowledged by Lord Bridge in *R. v. Shivpuri* [1987] A.C. 1, 23. See below, para. 7-027.

[45] [1987] A.C. 1: see J. R. Spencer, [1986] C.L.J. 361; P. R. Glazebrook, [1986] C.L.J. 363 (noting that the decision in *Shivpuri* involved modification of the statutory language).

[46] See above, para. 6-013.

[47] *per* Lord Bridge in *Wills v. Bowley* [1983] 1 A.C. 57, 101. It is difficult to see how such a presumption can be regarded as either "strong" or even much of a "presumption."

capable of either interpretation, it ought to be construed as prospective only."[48]

Furthermore,

> "it seems to me entirely proper, in a case where some retrospective operation was clearly intended, equally to presume that the retrospective operation of the statute extends no further than is necessary to give effect either to its clear language or to its manifest purpose."[49]

In *L' Office Cherifien des Phosphates v. Yamashita-Shinnihon Steamship Co. Ltd*,[50] the House of Lords emphasised, however, that the basis of the rule was "simple fairness". The question to what degree, if any, a particular provision has retrospective effect was to be determined not by reference to "generalised presumptions or maxims" but considering

> "whether the consequences of reading the statute with the suggested degree of retrospectivity is so unfair that the words used by Parliament cannot have been intended to mean what they might appear to say."[51]

This question in turn was to be answered by weighing a series of factors, including the degree of retrospectivity suggested; the value and nature of the rights affected on which the retrospective legislation will impinge; the clarity of the language; and the circumstances in which the legislation was enacted. The distinction between substantive and procedural rights was misleading,

> "since it leaves out of the account the fact that some procedural rights are more valuable than some substantive rights."[52]

Moreover, it was doubtful whether it was "possible to assign rights such as the present unequivocally to one category rather than another." On this

---

[48] R. S. Wright J. in *Re Athlumney* [1898] 2 Q.B. 547, 551–2. See above, para. 5-016.

[49] *per* Lord Bridge in *Arnold v. Central Electricity Generating Board* [1988] A.C. 228, 275, in the course of holding that while the Limitation Act 1975 modified retrospectively the position as to limitation in respect of actions governed by the Law Reform (Limitation of Actions, etc.) Act 1954, as amended, it did not apply so as to defeat a right to plead a time bar that had accrued under the Limitation Act 1939. See also *Pearce v. Secretary of State for Defence* [1988] A.C. 755.

[50] [1994] 1 A.C. 486, H.L.

[51] *per* Lord Mustill at pp. 524–525. The other members of the House agreed with Lord Mustill's speech.

[52] *per* Lord Mustill at p. 528. See also *Yew Bon Tew v. Kenderaan Bas Maria* [1983] 1 A.C. 553, where the Privy Council noted that an apparently "procedural" alteration, such as a change in limitation period, could affect existing rights and obligations; retrospective effect was denied to an extension in limitation period so as to affect an accrued right to plead a time bar. For other examples of cases where retrospective effect has been denied, see *Bonning v. Dodsley* [1982] 1 W.L.R. 279; *Lewis v. Lewis* [1986] A.C. 828; *Plewa v. Chief Adjudication Officer* [1995] 1 A.C. 249. Retrospective effect was given to procedural changes in *Thompson v. Thompson* [1986] Fam. 38 and *R. v. Makanjuola* [1995] 1 W.L.R. 1348, and, in view of clear words in the statute, to restrictions on right of appeal against a deportation order in *R. v. Secretary of State for the Home Department, ex p. Mundowa* [1992] 3 All E.R. 606.

approach,[53] section 13A of the Arbitration Act 1950,[54] which conferred a new power on an arbitrator to dismiss a claim for want of prosecution where there had been "inordinate and inexcusable delay", was to be interpreted as enabling an arbitrator to take account of delays before the section came into force.

In *Waddington v. Miah*[55] the House of Lords held that certain offences created by the Immigration Act 1971 were not intended to operate retrospectively. Lord Reid stated[56] that in view of the prohibitions contained in the Universal Declaration of Human Rights and the European Convention on Human Rights, "it is hardly credible that any government department would promote or that Parliament would pass retrospective criminal legislation."

On the other hand, in *Chebaro v. Chebaro*[57] the Court of Appeal held that the right conferred by the Matrimonial and Family Proceedings Act 1984, section 12(1), to apply for financial relief where a marriage "has been dissolved" by proceedings overseas, applied to a decree pronounced before the commencement of the Act. The meaning of the words used, importing a retrospective effect, was "plain and unequivocal".[58]

(f) Presumption that statutes do not affect the Crown

6–046   It is presumed that the Crown is not bound by a statute unless reference is made to it expressly or by necessary implication:

"Since laws are made by rulers for subjects a general expression in a statute such as 'any person,' descriptive of those upon whom the statute imposes obligations or restraints is not to be read as including the ruler himself."[59]

Questions may arise as to whether a particular institution is a servant or agent of the Crown and so within the "shield of the Crown".[60]

---

[53] Applied in *Antonelli v. Secretary of State for Trade and Industry* [1998] Q.B. 948 (new power under Estate Agents Act 1979 to prohibit persons from acting as estate agents if they have a conviction for fraud, dishonesty or violence, exercisable in respect of pre-commencement convictions); and *Westminster City Council v. Haywood (No. 2)* [2000] 2 All E.R. 634.

[54] Inserted by the Courts and Legal Services Act 1990, s.102; in force from January 1, 1992.

[55] [1974] 1 W.L.R. 683.

[56] At p. 694.

[57] [1987] Fam. 127.

[58] *per* Balcombe L.J. at p. 131. See also *Williams v. Williams* [1971] P. 271; *Powys v. Powys* [1971] P. 340; *Hewitt v. Lewis* [1986] 1 W.L.R. 444; *Hager v. Osborne* [1992] Fam. 94.

[59] *per* Diplock L.J. in *B.B.C. v. Johns* [1965] Ch. 32, 78; *cf.* Wrottesley J. in *Att.-Gen v. Hancock* [1940] 1 All E.R. 32, 34. *Lord Advocate v. Dumbarton District Council* [1990] 2 A.C. 580 (noted by J. Wolffe, [1990] P.L. 14); O. Hood Phillips and P. Jackson, *Constitutional and Administrative Law* (8th ed., 2001), pp. 318–320. The Crown may rely on any statutory defence that would be available to a private party: Crown Proceedings Act 1947, s.31(1). See generally, P. W. Hogg, *Liability of the Crown* (2nd ed., 1990); P. Jackson, [1990] Denning L.J. 45.

[60] See, *e.g. Tamlin v. Hannaford* [1950] 1 K.B. 18; *Town Investments Ltd v. Department of the Environment* [1978] A.C. 359; *British Medical Association v. Greater Glasgow Health Board* [1989] A.C. 1211.

(g) Others

Other presumptions that may be invoked include the presumption that   **6–047**
Parliament does not intend to violate international law,[61] and that a statute
does not apply to acts committed abroad.[62]

G. REFORM

As mentioned above,[63] Parliament has refrained from intervening to give   **6–048**
general directions to the judges as to methods of statutory interpretation.
The Law Commissions saw their report on *The Interpretation of Statutes*[64]
as a contribution to the process of educating judges and practitioners, and
only proposed a limited degree of statutory intervention. They appended
draft clauses, of which these were the first two[65]:

"1.—
(1) In ascertaining the meaning of any provision of an Act, the
    matters which may be considered shall, in addition to those which
    may be considered for that purpose apart from this section,
    include the following, that is to say—
    (a) all indications provided by the Act as printed by authority,
        including punctuation and side-notes, and the short title of
        the Act;
    (b) any relevant report of a Royal Commission, Committee or
        other body which had been presented or made to or laid
        before Parliament or either House before the time when the
        Act was passed;
    (c) any relevant treaty or other international agreement which is
        referred to in the Act or of which copies had been presented
        to Parliament by command of Her Majesty before that time,
        whether or not the United Kingdom were bound by it at that
        time;
    (d) any other document bearing upon the subject-matter of the
        legislation which had been presented to Parliament by
        command of Her Majesty before that time;
    (e) any document (whether falling within the foregoing para-
        graphs or not) which is declared by the Act to be a relevant
        document for the purposes of this section.
(2) The weight to be given for the purposes of this section to any such
    matter as is mentioned in subsection (1) shall be no more than is
    appropriate in the circumstances.

---

[61] See above, para. 6-035.
[62] See above, para. 5-016.
[63] para. 6-002.
[64] Law Com. No. 21; Scot. Law Com. No. 11 (1969).
[65] Clause 3 provided for the application of the first two clauses to subordinate legislation;
Clause 4 provided for a presumption that breach of a statutory duty should be actionable at
the suit of any person who sustains damage.

(3)   Nothing in this section shall be construed as authorising the consideration of reports of proceedings in Parliament for any purpose for which they could not be considered apart from this section.

2.—The following shall be included among the principles to be applied in the interpretation of Acts, namely—
   (a)   that a construction which would promote the general legislative purpose underlying the provision in question is to be preferred to a construction which would not; and
   (b)   that a construction which is consistent with the international obligations of Her Majesty's Government in the United Kingdom is to be preferred to a construction which is not."

Clause 1 would clarify, and in some respects relax the strictness of the rules which excluded altogether, or excluded when the meaning was otherwise unambiguous, certain internal and external aids from consideration by a court. Clause 1(1)(e) would also encourage the preparation in selected cases of explanatory material for use by the courts, which might "elucidate the contextual assumptions on which legislation has been passed."[66] Clause 2 emphasised the importance in interpretation of a provision of the general legislative purpose underlying it (clause 2)(a)) and the fulfilment of international obligations (clause 2(b)).[67]

The Renton Committee[68] approved the whole of clauses 1 and 2 except paragraphs (b) and (d) of clause 1: unrestricted admission of such materials would place too great a burden on litigants, their advisers and the courts, would do nothing to make statutes more immediately intelligible to the lay public and might greatly lengthen court proceedings. They doubted the value of clause 1(e) as it was already open to Parliament to do this.[69] Clause 2 was regarded as reflecting current practice. No opinion was expressed on the other two clauses. The Committee proposed in addition the enactment of a provision that "In the absence of any express indication to the contrary, a construction that would exclude retrospective effect is to be preferred to one that would not." It should also be made clear that a court in interpreting legislation intended to give effect to a provision of a Community treaty or instrument should take the relevant provisions of Community law into account.

Lord Scarman, who had been chairman of the Law Commission at the time of the 1969 report, introduced the Commissions' proposals as a draft Bill in 1980. The following year he introduced a Bill based on those proposals modified largely to take account of the Renton Committee's suggestions. The first Bill failed on second reading in the Lords; the second passed the Lords but was the subject of objections on the motion for second

---

[66]   See above, para. 6-036.
[67]   Law Com. No. 21; Scot. Law Com. No. 11, pp. 49–50.
[68]   Cmnd. 6053, 1975 pp. 139–148. See above, para. 5-007.
[69]   Clauses in the Matrimonial Proceedings and Properties Bill 1970 and the Animals Bill 1970, which provided that regard could be had to relevant, specified Law Commission reports, were successfully opposed in the House of Commons.

reading in the Commons, and as a Private Peer's Bill without government support did not proceed further.[70]

In so far as the proposed provisions reflect current practice they seem superfluous; the few that go beyond it, such as the use of official reports and White Papers, have been controversial, but have been overtaken by the relaxation in the prohibition against reference to Parliamentary materials achieved by the judges.[71] Clause 1(c)[72] would have the effect of disapproving the restrictive approach adopted in *Ellerman Lines v. Murray*,[73] and as such would be useful, but that decision has been largely outflanked, and might well be reconsidered by the House of Lords if the occasion were to rise. Overall, the enactment of these proposals would make little difference in practice.

The Renton Committee's recommendation that the preparation of a new Interpretation Act should be put in hand eventually led to the Interpretation Act 1978, a consolidation measure with minor changes incorporating Law Commission proposals. This is an aid to drafting rather than interpretation.[74] "At the level of general principles ... the subject does not lend itself to legislation."[75]

H. THE INTERPRETATION OF COMMUNITY LEGISLATION

I. METHODS OF INTERPRETATION

Close attention has been paid to the methods of interpretation of Community legislation adopted by the Court of Justice of the European Communities.[76] A number of different techniques have been identified, to which commentators have attached a variety of labels. The Court has consistently shown that it is more likely to be influenced by the *context*[77] and *purposes*[78] of a legislative provision than its exact *wording*[79] or the subjective intentions of those who promulgated the legislation.[80] The extent to which

6–049

---

[70] Interpretation of Legislation Bill (1979–80 H.L. Bill 141); Interpretation of Legislation Bill (1980–81)-HC. Bill 120); F.A.R. Bennion, (1981) 131 N.L.J. 840; Miers and Page (2nd ed., 1990), pp. 176–180.

[71] See above, paras 6-036–6-038.

[72] Clause 1(b) of the 1980–81 Bill.

[73] [1931] A.C. 126; above, para. 6-035, n. 86.

[74] Above, para. 5-017.

[75] Cross (1995), p. 191. Courts of Commonwealth countries where declarations of general principles of interpretation have been enacted seem rarely to refer to them in practice: W. A. Leitch, [1980] Stat.L.R. 5, 8.

[76] See the *Reports of the Judicial and Academic Conference*, Court of Justice of the European Communities, September 27–28, 1976; A. Bredimas, *Methods of Interpretation and Community Law* (1978); L. N. Brown and T. Kennedy, *The Court of Justice of the European Communities* (5th ed., 2000), Chap 14; R. Plender, "The Interpretation of Community Acts by Reference to the Intentions of the Authors" [1982] 2 Y.E.L. 57; T. Millett, [1989] Stat.L.R. 163 S. Weatherill and P. Beaumont, *EU Law* (3rd ed., 1999), pp. 184–201.

[77] "Contextual" or "Schematic" interpretation.

[78] "Purposive" or "teleological" interpretation.

[79] "Literal" interpretation.

[80] "Historical" or "subjective" interpretation.

the Court's overall approach differs from the so-called "common law" approach of English judges is debatable. It has also probably been exaggerated.[81] Certainly the ideas underlying the various techniques of interpretation adopted by the Court are more familiar than some of the labels. It should also be noted that the techniques tend to be employed cumulatively rather than as alternatives.[82]

The process of interpretation must obviously commence with an analysis of the text. However, literal interpretation, in so far as that implies an exclusive or predominant concern with wording and grammar, is not favoured. The Court has shown little inclination to hold that words carry one "plain," "ordinary" or "clear" meaning so that considerations of context and purpose are rendered irrelevant. There are several reasons for this.

(a) The method of drafting

6–050   Many of the key provisions of the EC and Euratom Treaties are drafted in general terms, and with no "definition sections". For example, Article 23 EC (ex Article 9) refers to the prohibition between member states of customs duties and "all charges having equivalent effect." Article 82 EC (ex Article 86) prohibits the "abuse by one or more undertakings of a dominant position within the common market or in a substantial part of it." It gives four examples of an "abuse" but no indication of what is meant by "dominant position". These concepts are left to be developed by the Community institutions, including the Court. The ECSC Treaty and Community secondary legislation are in general more tightly drafted, but they still, inevitably, employ broad terms.

(b) Languages

6–051   The texts of the EC and Euratom Treaties and all Community secondary legislation are published in several languages, each of which is equally authentic.[83] Arguments based on the exact wording of any one version are accordingly less compelling; it can never have been intended that Community law applies differently in different Member States. In cases of doubt it may be necessary to consider all the versions, in the light, as ever of context and purposes. For example, in *Stauder v. City of Ulm*[84] the Court considered a decision of the Commission on the sale of butter at reduced prices to persons in receipt of welfare benefits. The German and Dutch versions provided that the butter had to be exchanged for a "coupon indicating [the recipients'] names." A German citizen argued that this was an infringement of fundamental rights. The Court found that the French and Italian versions referred to a "coupon referring to the person concerned", and preferred this more liberal wording. The objective of the decision could be achieved by methods of identification other than names.

[81] P. Dagtoglou, "The English Judges and European Community Law" [1978] C.L.J. 76.
[82] There is, for example, no place for a "today's the day for the teleological rule" approach.
[83] The only authentic text of the ECSC Treaty is French. The other two basic Treaties and the Single European Act are authentic in Danish, Dutch, English, Finnish, French, German, Greek, Irish, Italian, Portuguese, Spanish and Swedish and the secondary legislation in all these except Irish.
[84] Case 29/69, [1969] E.C.R. 419.

(c) The status of the Court

The Court is in a stronger position in relation to the other Community **6–052** institutions than a national court in relation to its national parliament. Legislation is not promulgated by an elected body alone, but by the nominated Commission and Council or by the Commission and European Parliament acting jointly. The Court is expressly enjoined to "ensure that in the interpretation and application of this Treaty the law is observed"[85] and is expressly empowered to review the legality of acts of the Council and Commission.[86] It is placed on an equal footing with the other institutions in Article 7 EC (ex Article 4) Moreover, it has proved more difficult than expected for the Council to agree upon legislative proposals placed before it by the Commission. The resultant "legislative short-fall" has compelled the Court to determine questions of interpretation, and to fill gaps, in the light of the general aims of the Community and general principles of law. To an extent it has been forced to adopt a legislative role, and has not felt the need to disguise it.[87]

The Court's position in relation to the Member States is more problematic. There is an inevitable tension between the Community's harmonisation aims and the perceived interests of individual Member States. The Court could have adopted a position of neutrality; instead it has chosen to take a "partisan" line in favour of the achievement of the aims of the Community, as a kind of counterweight to the Council of Ministers, which has tended more to reflect state interests. Member States are indeed expressly required by Article 10 EC (ex Article 5) to take all appropriate measures to fulfil obligations arising out of the Treaty or acts of Community institutions, to facilitate the achievement of the Community's tasks and to abstain from any measure that could jeopardise the attainment of the objectives of the Treaty.

(d) Community purposes

The freedom of the Court to adopt a purposive approach is naturally **6–053** facilitated by the express statement of the Community's aims and objectives included in the Treaties (including their preambles). Articles 2 and 3 EC (ex Article 2 and 3)[88] provide:

"ARTICLE 2

The Community shall have as its task, by establishing a common market **6–054** and an economic and monetary union and by implementing common policies or activities referred to in Articles 3 and 4 to promote throughout the Community a harmonious, balanced and sustainable development of

---

[85] Art. 220 EC (ex Article 164).

[86] Art. 230 EC (ex Article 173) Above, para. 5-057.

[87] Note, for example, the enunciation of a rule with *prospective* effect only in the second *Defrenne* case: Case 43/75, [1976] E.C.R. 455.

[88] As substituted by Art. G (2), (3)/TEU and amended by the Treaty of Amsterdam. Art. 4 provides for economic and monetary union.

economic activities, a high level of employment and of social protection, equality between men and women, sustainable and non-inflationary growth, a high degree of competitiveness and convergence of economic performance, a high level of protection and improvement of the quality of the environment, the raising of the standard of living and quality of life, and economic and social cohesion and solidarity among Member States.

ARTICLE 3

6–055 (1) For the purposes set out in Article 2, the activities of the Community shall include, as provided in this Treaty and in accordance with the timetable set out therein:

    (a) the prohibition, as between Member States, of customs duties and quantitative restrictions on the import and export of goods, and of all other measures having equivalent effect;

    (b) a common commercial policy;

    (c) an internal market characterized by the abolition, as between Member States, of obstacles to the free movement of goods, persons, services and capital;

    (d) measures concerning the entry and movement of persons as provided for in Title IV;

    (e) a common policy in the sphere of agriculture and fisheries;

    (f) a common policy in the sphere of transport;

    (g) a system ensuring that competition in the internal market is not distorted;

    (h) the approximation of the laws of Member States to the extent required for the functioning of the common market;

    (i) the promotion of co-ordination between employment policies of the Member States with a view to enhancing their effectiveness by developing a co-ordinated strategy for employment;

    (j) a policy in the social sphere comprising a European Social Fund;

    (k) the strengthening of economic and social cohesion;

    (l) a policy in the sphere of the environment;

    (m) the strengthening of the competitiveness of Community industry;

    (n) the promotion of research and technological development;

    (o) encouragement for the establishment and development of trans-European networks;

    (p) a contribution to the attainment of a high level of health protection;

    (q) a contribution to education and training of quality and to the flowering of the cultures of the Member States;

    (r) a policy in the sphere of development cooperation;

    (s) the association of the overseas countries and territories in order to increase trade and promote jointly economic and social development;

    (t) a contribution to the strengthening of consumer protection;

    (u) measures in the spheres of energy, civil protection and tourism:

(2) In all the activities referred to in this Article, the Community shall aim

to eliminate inequalities, and to promote equality, between men and women."

Moreover, the reasons on which regulations, directives and decisions are based are stated in a preamble. The Court has attached much more importance to these express statements of purpose than to attempts to discern from other sources the subjective intentions of the authors of Community legislation.[89] Indeed, the details of the negotiations leading up to the Treaties and of debates within the Council and Commission concerning secondary legislation have not been published.[90] There have been occasional references by Advocates General to a statement made by the government of a Member State to the national parliament in the course of a ratification debate, but not to the exclusion of other considerations.[91]

In relation to purposive interpretation reference has been made to the so-called "rule of effectiveness" (régle de l'effet utile), a concept borrowed from international law. This means that, "preference should be given to the construction which gives the rule its fullest effect and maximum practical value."[92] This concept has been used as a justification for holding that the Community or one of its institutions has certain "implied powers", such as the power to require the repayment of a state aid granted in breach of the Treaty.[93] Similarly, in the E.R.T.A. Case[94] it was held that the Community had the implied power to establish treaty relations with non-Member States. The Court argued that it was the "necessary effect" or "consequence" of the making of a regulation on the harmonisation of provisions in the road transport field that the Community assume the exclusive right to conclude international agreements relating to the same subject matter.

(e) Context

References by the Court to the purposes of the Community are commonly closely associated with arguments that seek to place the provision to be interpreted in the context of relevant rules of Community law. The Court may refer to the "general scheme of the Treaty", or to other treaty provisions in the relevant Part or to general principles of Community law. In the case of secondary legislation reference will be made to the enabling provisions in the Treaty.

6–056

---

[89] In Case 136/79, *National Panasonic (U.K.) Ltd v. Commission* [1980] E.C.R. 2033, A. G. Warner argued that statements by individual members of the Council, the European Parliament, the Commission or the Commission's staff could not be relied upon for guidance as to the meaning of a Council Regulation (pp. 2066–7). See generally Plender (1982), op. cit. n. 76 above.

[90] In Case C-292/89, *R. v. Immigration Appeal Tribunal, ex p. Antonissen* [1991] E.C.R. I-745, the Court held that a declaration made by the Council at the time of adoption of certain secondary legislation, and disclosed by the Council for the purposes of litigation, could not be used for the purposes of interpretation as the content of the declaration was not referred to in the wording of the legislation.

[91] See *e.g.*. Case 6/60, *Humblet v. Belgium* [1960] E.C.R. 559.

[92] H. Kutcher, *Conference Reports* (see n. 76 above), I–41.

[93] e.g. Case 70/72, *Commission v. Germany* [1973] E.C.R. 829.

[94] Case 22/70, *Commission v. Council* (E.R.T.A.) [1971] E.C.R. 263.

(f) Examples

6–057   Striking examples of the Court's dynamic approach to interpretation are
provided by its decisions already discussed on the direct effectiveness of
treaty provisions and secondary legislation, and the supremacy of
Community law.[95] Another good example is the *Continental Can* case[96] A
New York company (Continental Can) held, through a German subsidiary
(SLW), what the Commission determined to be a dominant position over a
substantial part of the common market in meat tins, fish tins and metal
closures for glass jars. Subsequently, acting through a Belgian subsidiary
(Europemballage), Continental Can acquired a Dutch firm (TDV) which
specialised in similar products. The Commission decided that the merger
amounted to an abuse of the dominant position mentioned above, as the
effect was practically to eliminate competition in the relevant products. The
ECSC treaty expressly provided for merger control (Article 66); the EEC
Treaty did not. Nevertheless, the Court held that a merger could in principle
amount to an abuse of a dominant position contrary to Article 86 of the EC
Treaty (now Article 82 EC), although it did not do so on the facts of the
case. In so deciding the Court stated that it was necessary "to go back to the
spirit, general scheme and wording of Article 86, as well as to the system and
objectives of the Treaty."[97] It referred to the original version of Articles 2
and 3(f)[98], and to Article 85 of the EC Treaty (now Article 81 EC), which
prohibited:

> "all agreements between undertakings, decisions by associations of
> undertakings and concerted practices which may affect trade between
> Member States and which have as their object or effect the prevention,
> restriction or distortion of competition within the common market ...."

The Court observed:[99]

> "[I]f Article 3(f) provides for the institution of a system ensuring that
> competition in the common market is not distorted, then it requires a
> *fortiori* that a competition must not be eliminated. This requirement is
> so essential that without it numerous provisions of the Treaty would be
> pointless. Moreover, it corresponds to the precept of Article 2 of the
> Treaty ....
>   ... Articles 85 and 86 seek to achieve the same aim on different
> levels, that is, the maintenance of effective competition within the
> common market. The restraint of competition which is prohibited if it
> is the result of behaviour falling under Article 85, cannot become
> permissible by the fact that such behaviour succeeds under the influence
> of a dominant undertaking and results in the merger of the undertaking
> concerned."

---

[95] The *van Gend en Loos* case, above, para. 5-040 *Costa v. E.N.E.L.*, above, para. 5-050.
[96] Case 6/12, *Europemballage Corporation and Continental Can Co. Inc. v. Commission* [1973]
E.C.R. 215.
[97] *ibid.* p. 243.
[98] Art. 3(f) is now 3(g): above, para. 6-055.
[99] p. 244.

In other words, the prohibition of certain acts when done in concert by separate undertakings was not to be evaded by merger of those undertakings.

It is a matter of debate whether the Court has gone too far in its willingness to "fill gaps".[1] It is clearly obliged to make policy decisions given the points already made as to the broad terms of many key Treaty provisions and secondary legislation. It is not so clear that decisions that recognise an inherent jurisdiction in the Court outside the express heads of jurisdiction set out in the EC Treaty[2] that are reached "despite textual indications to the contrary"[3] are justifiable.[4] That there are limits is illustrated by the decisions confirming that directives are not directly effective between private individuals.[5]

(g) Restrictive interpretation

Interpretation in the light of purposes and context does not necessarily mean   **6–058** that such interpretation is "broad" or "liberal." Exceptions to general Community rules and derogations to Treaty obligations are restrictively interpreted. For example, the principle of the free movement of workers is subject to "limitations justified on grounds of public policy, public security or public health."[6] These limitations are strictly construed.[7] Restrictions may not be imposed unless the person's presence or conduct "constitutes a genuine and sufficiently serious threat to public policy",[8] and the requirements of public policy must affect "one of the fundamental interests of society",[9] although it is for the national authorities to determine whether the facts of a particular case fall within these principles.

2. GENERAL PRINCIPLES OF LAW[10]

The Court often refers to "general principles of law" derived from the   **6–059**

---

[1] See, *e.g.*, Weatherill and Beaumont (1999), pp. 193–201; H. Rasmussen, *On Law and Policy in the European Court of Justice* (1986) and (1988) 13 E.L.Rev.28.

[2] Case C-2/88 Imm., *Zvartveld and Others* [1990] E.C.R. I-3367 and I-4405 (order to Commission to send reports to a national court).

[3] *e.g.* Case 294/83, *Les Verts v. European Parliament* [1986] E.C.R.1339 (action under Art. 173 of the EC Treaty (now Article 230 EC) to review legality of act of Parliament admissible notwithstanding the absence of any reference to Parliament in Art. 173 in its original form; Case C-70/88, *European Parliament v. Council* [1990] E.C.R. I-2041, above, para. 5-057.

[4] Weatherill and Beaumont, pp. 197–201.

[5] Above, paras 5-041, 5-042.

[6] Art 39(3) EC (ex Article 48(3); Directive 64/221/EEC.

[7] Case 41/74, *Van Duyn v. Home Office* [1974] E.C.R. 1337, above, para. 5-041; Case 67/74, *Bonsignore v. Oberstadtdirektor Cologne* [1975] E.C.R. 297; Case 36/75, *Rutili v. French Minister of the Interior* [1975] E.C.R. 1219; Case 30/77, *R. v. Bouchereau* [1977] E.C.R. 1999.

[8] Case 36/75, *Rutili* [1975] E.C.R. 1219, 1231.

[9] Case 30/77, *R. v. Bouchereau* [1977] E.C.R. 1999, 2014.

[10] L. N. Brown and T. Kennedy, *The Court of Justice of the European Communities* (5th ed., 2000), Chap. 15; A. Arnull et. al., *Wyatt and Dashwood's European Union Law* (4th ed., 2000), pp. 131–150. T.C. Hartley, *The Foundations of European Community Law* (4th ed., 1998), Chap. 5.

national laws of Member States.[11] These are regarded as part of "the law" of which the Court is to ensure observance.[12] They can be employed in the interpretation of Treaty provisions but cannot override them. In relation to secondary legislation and other acts of the institutions they are not so confined: a challenge to the legality of a measure may be based on breach of one of these principles.[13]

Examples include:

— the principle of *proportionality*, which requires that:
    "the individual should not have his freedom of action limited beyond the degree necessary for the public interest";[14]

— the *audi alteram partem* principle of natural justice, which requires that persons affected by an adverse decision be given an opportunity to make representations[15];

— the principle of *equality*:
    "whereby comparable situations must not be treated differently and different situations must not be treated in the same way, unless such treatment is objectively justified"[16];

— the related principles of *legal certainty* and *legitimate expectation*, which require, respectively, that:
    "those subject to the law should not be placed in a situation of uncertaintyas to their rights and obligations" and "those who act in good faith on the basis of the law as it is or seems to be should not be frustrated in their expectations."[17]

These "general principles" include respect for "fundamental rights",[18] derived from national constitutions or from international conventions concerning human rights, such as the European Convention on Human

---

[11] They may also be derived from Treaty provisions.

[12] Article 220 EC (ex Article 164) above, para. 6-052. See also Article 230 EC (ex Article 173), above, para. 5-057, which provides expressly that a Community act may be annulled for infringement of "any rule of law relating to its application." *Cf.* Article 288(2) EC (ex Article 215(2).

[13] See above, para. 5-057.

[14] A. G. de Lamothe in Case 11/70, *Internationale Handelsgesellschaft v. EVSt.* [1970] E.C.R. 1125, 1147; *cf.* the *Rutili* case, above (requirement of a *genuine and sufficiently serious* threat to public policy to justify interference with freedom of movement). The proportionality doctrine has not generally been part of English domestic law (*R. v. Secretary of State for the Home Department, ex p. Brind* [1991] 1 A.C. 696), but this is now subject to the important qualifications that it is applicable within the spheres of EC law and the Human Rights Act 1998.

[15] Case 11/74, *Transocean Marine Paint Association v. Commission* [1974] E.C.R. 1063; *cf.* Case 136/79, *National Panasonic Ltd v. Commission* [1980] E.C.R. 2033 (no need to give prior warning of an investigation by Commission inspectors).

[16] Wyatt and Dashwood (2000), p. 142. See Case 20/71, *Sabbatini v. European Parliament* [1972] E.C.R. 345 (Council Regulation concerning expatriation allowances for employees of the Parliament held invalid on the ground of sex discrimination.)

[17] Wyatt and Dashwood (2000), p.137.

[18] T. C. Hartley, (1975–76) 1 E.L.Rev. 54; M. Dauses, (1985) 10 E.L.Rev. 398; S. O'Leary, (1995) 32 C.M.L.Rev. 519; J. Weiler, (1995) 32 C.M.L.Rev. 579; the *International Handels* case (n. 14, above).

Rights.[19] This does not mean that the Convention is part of Community law and so directly enforceable under the European Communities Act 1972: "the European Court does not deal with fundamental rights in the abstract; it only deals with them if they arise under Treaties and have a bearing on Community law questions."[20]

3. INTERPRETATION BY ENGLISH COURTS

The approach that should be taken by English judges was considered by Lord Denning M. R. in *Bulmer v. Bollinger*[21]:   **6–060**

"Beyond doubt the English courts must follow the same principles as the European court. Otherwise there would be differences between the countries of the nine. . . . It is enjoined on the English courts by section 3 of the European Community Act 1972 . . . .

No longer must they examine the words in meticulous detail. No longer must they argue about the precise grammatical sense. They must look to the purpose or intent. To quote the words of the European court in the *Da Costa* case[22], they must deduce 'from the wording and the spirit of the Treaty the meaning of the community rules.' They must not confine themselves to the English text. They must consider, if need be, all the authentic texts. . . . They must divine the spirit of the Treaty and gain inspiration from it. If they find a gap, they must fill it as best they can. They must do what the framers of the instrument would have done if they had thought about it. So we must do the same. Those are the principles, as I understand it, on which the European court acts."

The dangers of applying a strict literal interpretation to provisions of Community law are illustrated by *R. v. Henn*.[23] Article 28 EC (ex Article 30)

---

[19] Case 4/73, *Nold v. Commission* [1974] E.C.R. 491; the *Rutili* Case (n. 8 above); Case 118/75 *Watson and Belmann* [1976] E.C.R. 1185; Case 136/79, *National Panasonic (U.K.) Ltd v. Commission* [1980] E.C.R. 2033 (no infringement of the right of privacy guaranteed by article 8(1) of the European Convention: an investigation of a company's books without prior warning was held to be justified as "necessary in a democratic society in the interests of . . . the economic well-being of the country," within the one of the exceptions specified in article 8(2)); Case 63/83, *Kirk* [1984] E.C.R. 2689 (application of the principle that penal provisions may not have retrospective effect): see N. Foster, (1985) 10 E.L.Rev. 276 ; Case C–185/95P, *Baustahlgewebe GmbH v. Commission* [1998] E.C.R. I–8417 (right to legal process within a reasonable period (cf. Article 6(1), ECHR) applicable to proceedings by the Commission and before the Court of First Instance concerning the imposition of fines by the Commission on an undertaking for infringement of Community law).

[20] *Kaur v. Lord Advocate* 1980 S.C. 319, 333 (Lord Ross, Court of Session (Outer House)).

[21] [1974] Ch. 401, 425–426. See also the similar views expressed by Lord Denning M. R. in *Buchanan & Co. Ltd v. Babco Forwarding & Shipping (U.K.) Ltd* [1977] Q.B. 208, 213–214. His Lordship's attempt to apply the "European Method" of "filling gaps" to the interpretation of an international convention on the carriage of goods by road was resisted by the House of Lords: [1978] A.C. 141, 153 (Lord Wilberforce), 156 (Viscount Dilhorne) and 160 (Lord Salmon); cf. above, para. 6-035. See also the doubts as to the propriety of "gap-filling" expressed by Nolan J. in *Yoga for Health Foundation v. Customs and Excise Commissioners* [1984] S.T.C. 630.

[22] [1963] C.M.L.R. 224, 237.

[23] [1978] 1 W.L.R. 1031, C.A.; [1981] A.C. 850, E.C.J., H.L.; Case 34/79 [1979] E.C.R. 3795.

prohibits the imposition of "quantitative restrictions on imports and all measures having equivalent effect." The Court of Appeal (Criminal Division) held that the ban on the importation of indecent or obscene material imposed by section 42 of the Customs Consolidation Act 1876 did not fall within Article 30 as it imposed a total prohibition rather than a mere restriction "measured by quantity". This view was, not, however, relied upon by counsel on appeal to the House of Lords, or in argument before the Court of Justice, as it was clearly contrary to a number of earlier decisions of the Court of Justice, and inconsistent with the purposes of the Community. As a matter of common sense, a complete prohibition on the free movement of goods is likely to be more questionable under Community law than a partial restriction. Lord Diplock said that this showed "the danger of an English court applying English canons of statutory construction."[24] It is submitted that the Court of Appeal's interpretation was excessively "literalist" even by English standards.

---

[24] [1981] A.C. at p. 914. See also *R. v. Licensing Authority, ex p. Smith, Kline & French Laboratories Ltd* [1990] 1 A.C. 64, 75 (Dillon L.J.), 84 (Balcombe L.J.) and 87 (Staughton L.J.) (need to adopt a purposive and not a semantic approach to the interpretation of EC directives). An appeal to the House of Lords was dismissed, the matter being determined by reference to English law: [1990] 1 A.C. 64, 90. See to the same effect the House of Lords in *Litster v. Forth Dry Dock & Engineering Co. Ltd* [1990] 1 A.C. 546 and *Shanning International Ltd. (In Liquidation) v. Rasheed Bank* [2001] UKHL 31 [2001] 1 W.L.R. 1462.

Chapter 7

JUDICIAL PRECEDENT

A. INTRODUCTION[1]

ONE of the hallmarks of any good decision-making process is consistency: **7–001** like cases should be treated alike. Consistency is not, however, always appropriate, as, for example, where a case is seen with the passage of time and changes of circumstance no longer to offer a just solution to a recurring problem. Moreover, there are always difficulties in determining whether two cases are truly "like". Nevertheless, unjustifiable inconsistency may lead to a sense of grievance on the part of those affected and to a reasonable suspicion that the people making the decisions do not know what they are about. One of the main functions of the superior courts of law is the authoritative determination of disputed questions of law. A court's decision is expected to be consistent with decisions in previous cases and to provide certainty for the future so that the parties and others may arrange their affairs in reliance on the court's opinion. These considerations are reflected in the English system of judicial precedent.

The decisions of judges must be reasoned, and the reasons will include propositions of law. A judge in a later case is bound to consider the relevant case law and will normally accept the propositions stated as correct unless there is good reason to disagree; in some circumstances he or she is required to accept them even if they are in his or her view obviously wrong. So all relevant precedents are to a greater or lesser extent "persuasive", and some of them may be "binding" under what is termed the doctrine of *stare decisis*.[2] The characteristic that an individual precedent may be binding is distinctive of common law systems. In continental systems based upon codes that are theoretically complete, judicial decisions are not, technically, sources of legal rules. They may, however, carry great persuasive weight, particularly where there is a trend of cases to the same effect, and they have

---

[1] See generally Sir Rupert Cross and J. W. Harris, *Precedent in English Law* (4th ed., 1991); L. Goldstein (ed.), *Precedent in Law* (1987) (note the bibliography at pp. 249–273).

[2] "Keep to what has been decided previously:" Cross and Harris (1991), p. 3. The term is most commonly used to refer to the common law notion of *binding* precedent (Cross and Harris (1991), p. 100: "the general orthodox interpretation of *stare decisis* ... is *stare rationibus decidendis* ('keep to the *rationes decidendi* of past cases').") Alternative possible usages are (1) broader: referring to the general desirability of conformity with past precedents (*cf.* Cross (1977), p. 4), and (2) narrower: referring to the obligation to follow the *decision* (*i.e.* order of the court) in a past case that is not reasonably distinguishable, as distinct from the principle of law on which the decision was based (Cross and Harris (1991), pp. 100–101).

been of great importance in the development of certain areas of the law.[3]

Under the English system, a proposition stated in or derived from case. A is binding in case B if (1) it is a proposition of law; (2) it forms part of the *ratio decidendi* of case A (the reason or ground upon which the decision is based); (3) case A was decided in a court whose decisions are binding on the court that is deciding case B; and (4) there is no relevant difference between cases A and B which renders case A "distinguishable". A precedent which is not binding may nevertheless be persuasive. These points are developed below. As we shall see, judges faced with a precedent that they do not like have a number of possible escape routes to explore, and there is for the litigant who can afford it the possibility of recourse to a higher court for a bad precedent to be overruled. The system seeks to balance the general benefits of consistency and certainty against the requirement of justice in individual cases.

On one view judges are seen as picking their way through dusty old volumes of law reports and loyally following the precedents without too much regard for the justice of the case. On another they are seen as paying lip service to the system, and "loyally" following all the precedents that they agree with; those that they do not agree with are distinguished on spurious grounds, or just ignored. These views lie at the extremes and contain elements of caricature as well as truth. It is not possible to make a useful generalisation about judicial behaviour in practice; there are variations in approach from judge to judge, and the same judge may even vary his or her position according to the nature of the case to be decided.[4]

The notion that judges ought generally to abide by relevant precedents developed over several centuries.[5] Blackstone wrote in the eighteenth century that it was "an established rule to abide by former precedents, where the same points come again in litigation ... unless flatly absurd or unjust",[6] and Parke J. said in 1833[7]:

> "Our common-law system consists in the applying to new combinations of circumstances those rules of law which we derive from legal principles and judicial precedent; and for the sake of attaining uniformity, consistency and certainty, we must apply those rules, where they are not plainly unreasonable and inconvenient, to all cases which arise; and we are not at liberty to reject them, and to abandon all analogy to them, in those to which they have not yet been judicially applied, because we think that the rules are not as convenient and reasonable as we ourselves could have devised."

The practice of relying on precedents in equity was also established by the

---

[3]   *ibid.* pp. 10–15. R. David and J. Brierley, *Major Legal Systems in the World Today* (3rd ed., 1985), pp. 133–149; R. David, *English Law and French Law* (1980), pp. 21–26.

[4]   See further above, paras 4-37–4-40

[5]   See C. K. Alien, *Law in the Making* (7th ed., 1964), pp. 187–235, 380–382; T. Ellis Lewis, (1930) 46 L.Q.R. 207, 341, (1931) 47 L.Q.R. 411, (1932) 48 L.Q.R. 230; W. H. D. Winder, (1941) 57 L.Q.R. 245 (precedent in equity); G. J. Postema," Some roots of our notion of precedent" and J. Evans, "Changes in the doctrine of precedent during the nineteenth century" in Goldstein (1987), Chaps.1, 2.

[6]   *Blackstone's Commentaries* 69, 70.

[7]   *Mirehouse v. Rennell* (1833) 1 Cl. & F. 527, 546.

eighteenth century. The modern strict rules whereby a single precedent can be binding, and precedents can be binding even if "unreasonable and inconvenient", developed in the nineteenth and twentieth centuries. Important factors were the regularisation of and improvements in law reporting following the establishment of the Incorporated Council of Law Reporting[8] and the reorganisation of the courts with a clear hierarchical structure in the latter part of the nineteenth century.[9] The rule that appellate courts are normally bound by their own previous decisions was clearly established for the House of Lords in 1898[10] and for the Court of Appeal in 1944.[11]

B. PROPOSITION OF "LAW"

Decisions on questions of fact may not be cited as precedents.[12] The line between "law" and "fact" may, however, be difficult to draw. An issue is one of fact where it turns on the reliability or credibility of direct evidence, or on inferences from circumstantial evidence. For example, the fact that someone was driving at a high speed may be established by the testimony of a witness, or by inference from such evidence as tyre marks. More difficult are cases which raise an issue whether the facts found conform to a legal description. Such issues are sometimes classified as issues of fact. For example, whether conduct is "unreasonable," and so a breach of the duty of care for the purposes of the tort of negligence, is a question of fact. In *Baker v. E. Longhurst & Sons Ltd*[13] Scrutton L.J. stated[14] that "if a person rides in the dark he must ride at such a pace that he can pull up within the limit of his vision. ... " This was treated as a proposition of law until the Court of Appeal ruled that it was not.[15] In *Qualcast (Wolverhampton) Ltd v. Haynes*[16] the House of Lords held that a county court judge could not be bound by precedent to hold that an employer who failed to give instructions to an employee as to the use of protective clothing had been negligent.

Where a legal description contained in a statute is "an ordinary word of the English language" its application to the facts found is a question of fact, and it may not be the subject of judicial definition or interpretation.[17] The judges are particularly inclined to classify questions as questions of fact

7–002

---

[8] See below, para. 7-038.

[9] See above, para. 2-003.

[10] See below, para. 7-026. It was changed in 1966.

[11] See below, paras 7-015–7-024.

[12] *Qualcast (Wolverhampton) Ltd v. Haynes* [1959] A.C. 743. Otherwise, "the precedent system will die from a surfeit of authorities" (per Lord Somervell at p. 758), or the judges might be "crushed under the weight of our own reports" (*per* Lord Denning at p. 761).

[13] [1933] 2 K.B. 461.

[14] At p. 468.

[15] *Tidy v. Battman* [1934] 1 K.B. 319; *Morris v. Luton Corporation* [1946] 1 K.B. 114; Lord Greene hoped that this "suggested principle" would "rest peacefully in the grave" (p. 116). *Cf. Worsfold v. Howe* [1980] 1 W.L.R. 1175.

[16] [1959] A.C. 743.

[17] See above, para. 1-011.

where they wish to avoid the proliferation of authorities.[18] However, where words are used in an unusual sense, or a statute has to be "construed" or "interpreted" before it can be applied, a question of law is raised.[19] The construction of particular words in a contract similarly does not give rise to a binding decision on a point of law.[20]

C. DETERMINING THE RATIO DECIDENDI

1. RATIO AND DICTUM

7–003   A proposition of law can only be binding if it forms part of the *ratio decidendi*[21] (commonly shortened to *ratio*) of the case.

Sir Rupert Cross and J. W. Harris, in the leading English monograph on precedent, gives this description[22]:

> "The *ratio decidendi* of a case is any rule of law expressly or impliedly treated by the judge as a necessary step in reaching his conclusion, having regard to the line of reasoning adopted by him, or a necessary part of his direction to the jury."[23]

They also point out that a judge may adopt more than one line of reasoning leading to the same result, in which case there may be more than one *ratio*. A proposition of law stated by a judge that is not necessary for his or her conclusion is termed an *obiter dictum* or *dictum*.[24] It may, for

---

[18] *e.g. R. v. Industrial Injuries Commissioner, ex p. A.E.U. (No. 2)* [1966] 2 Q.B. 31, 45, 48–49, *per* Lord Denning M.R., in relation to the expression "arising out of and in the course of his employment."

[19] Denning L.J. in *British Launderers' Association v. Borough of Hendon Rating Authority* [1949]. 1 K.B. 462, 411–472; Lord Reid in *Cozens v. Brutus*, above, para. 1-011.

[20] *per* May L.J. in *Ashville Investments Ltd v. Elmer Contractors Ltd* [1989] Q.B. 488, 495 (construction of an arbitration clause); *Clarke v. Newland* (unreported, December 21, 1988) (interpretation of restrictive covenant in a partnership agreement). In *Customs and Excise Commissioners v. Le Rififi Ltd* [1995] S.T.C. 103, the Court of Appeal held that the same principle applied to the construction of a VAT assessment form.

[21] Usually pronounced "rayshio", although variants may be encountered in practice.

[22] *Precedent in English Law* (4th ed., 1991), p. 72. This formulation was expressly endorsed by the Court of Appeal in *R. (Kadhim) v. Brent London Borough Council Housing Benefit Review Board* [2001] 2 W.L.R. 674.

[23] *cf.* the narrower definition proposed by N. MacCormick (in L. Goldstein (ed.), *Judicial Precedent* (1987), Chap. 6, p. 170): "A *ratio decidendi* is a ruling expressly or impliedly given by a judge which is sufficient to settle a point of law put in issue by the parties' arguments in a case, being a point on which a ruling was necessary to his justification (or one of his alternative justifications) of the decision in the case." It is narrower in that it refers to a "ruling" by the judge (so as to cover the interpretation of a statute rather than the statute itself where one is involved), and a requirement that it be necessary for the *justification* for the decision, rather than the decision itself.

[24] Not "an *obiter*". The plural is *obiter dicta*. For examples of cases where it has been held that a particular proposition was not necessary for the decision, see *Penn-Texas Corporation v. Murat Anstalt (No. 2)* [1964] 2 Q.B. 647, 661 (Lord Denning M.R.); *Re State of Norway's Application (No. 2)* [1988] 3 W.L.R. 603, 618–620 (May L.J.), 629–631 (Balcombe L.J.), 646–649 (Woolf L.J.); *Rickless v. United Artists Corp.* [1988] Q.B. 40.

example, be a proposition wider than is necessary for the facts of the case, or a proposition concerning some matter not raised in the case. Statements of law on points which are fully argued by counsel and considered by the judge, but which do not technically play any part in determining the result, are sometimes termed "judicial *dicta*".[25]

Conversely, where a court *assumes* a proposition of law to be correct without addressing its mind to it, the decision of that court is not binding authority for that proposition.[26] However, this rule "must only be applied in the most obvious of cases and limited with great care."[27] It will normally only apply where the point has not been expressly raised before the court and there has been no argument on it; it may, however, be the case that a point has not been argued but "scrutiny of the judgment indicates that the court's acceptance of the point went beyond mere assumption. Very little is likely to be required to draw that latter conclusion; because a later court will start from the position, encouraged by judicial comity, that its predecessor did indeed address all the matters essential for the decision".[28]

2. The Principle Enunciated by the Judge

The task of determining the *ratio* of a case can be complicated, and writers on the subject are not agreed as to how that task is approached by the judges in practice, or how, in theory, it should be approached.[29] It is impossible to assert with confidence that there is any one method of approach which is invariably adopted by the judges. The obvious starting point is the wording of the judgment in question. A judge in giving the reasons for his or her decision will normally indicate the proposition[30] of law upon which he or she regards the decision as based. He or she will explain why he or she thinks this proposition is correct, usually by referring to earlier authorities and showing that it makes good sense. These "explanations" or "justifications" must be distinguished from the proposition of law which they support, as

7–004

---

[25] Megarry J. in *Brunner v. Greenslade* [1971] Ch. 993, 1002–3.

[26] *per* Warner J. in *Barrs v. Bethell* [1982] Ch. 294, 308, relying on Lord Diplock in *Baker v. The Queen* [1975] A.C. 774, 788 and Russell L. J. in *National Enterprises Ltd v. Racal Communications Ltd* [1975] Ch. 397. 406; *Pritchard v. J. H. Cobden Ltd* [1988] Fam. 22, 38, 49; *re Hetherington* [1990] Ch. 1. These authorities were approved by the Court of Appeal in *R. (Kadhim) v. Brent London Borough Council Housing Benefit Review Board* [2001] 2 W.L.R. 674. This principle., however, has not always been observed, e.g. in respect of the *Havana case*: see below, para. 7-021.

[27] *per* Buxton L.J. in *Kadhim* at para. [40].

[28] *ibid.* It had previously been suggested that the matter turns on whether the court in the earlier case had "turned its mind to the point" and not on whether the point has been argued: *R. v. Charles* (1975) 63 Cr.App. R. 252, 259 (Bridge L.J.); *Meer v. London Borough of Tower Hamlets* [1988] I.R.L.R. 399, 402 (Balcombe L.J.).

[29] See, *e.g.* Cross and Harris (1991) Chap. 2; A. L. Goodhart, "Determining the *Ratio Decidendi* of a Case" in *Essays in Jurisprudence and the Common Law* (1931), pp. 1–26; the somewhat acerbic dispute between J. L. Montrose and A. W. B. Simpson: (1957) 20 M.L.R. 124, 413, 587, (1958) 21 M.L.R. 155; A. L. Goodhart, (1959) 22 M.L.R. 117; Simpson, in A. G. Guest (ed.) *Oxford Essays in Jurisprudence* (1961), Chap. VI; N. H. Andrews, (1985) 5 L.S. 205, 209–222; N. MacCormick in L. Goldstein (ed.), *Judicial Precedent* (1987), Chap. 6.

[30] There may be more than one relevant proposition; the singular is used here for convenience.

only the latter can be part of the *ratio*.[31] The proposition as enunciated by the judge has a good claim to be regarded as the *ratio*. For example, the editor of a published law report who endeavours to state the *ratio* in the headnote to the case, will frequently use actual sentences from the judgment. A judge in a later case will commonly summarise the effect of a case by citing a passage from the judgment, and saying that a particular sentence or passage sets out "the *ratio*." In many cases, the judge will be content to leave the matter there. However, it may be necessary for the judgment in the earlier case to be subjected to careful analysis (by academic commentators, by counsel, and ultimately by the judge) for the *ratio* to be determined.

In some cases, the rulings are "so embedded in the reasoning as to require minor grammatical reconstruction in order to obtain more explicitly stated forms of them."[32] There may be differing views as to whether a particular ruling was "necessary for the decision".[33] It may be unclear, where a number of different reasons are given for a decision, whether each is to be regarded as a *ratio*.[34] Further difficulties may arise from the differing levels of generality of language that may be used in the formulation of propositions of law: the *ratio* may subsequently be restated in wider or narrower form.[35]

Then, in "extreme cases, judges may do no more than indicate that it is because the facts of the case are certain facts viewed under certain fact-descriptions that the decision ought to be as it is."[36] Here, the method for determining the *ratio* suggested by A. L. Goodhart[37] can be employed: that is, by taking account of (a) the facts treated expressly or impliedly by the judge as material, and (b) the decision as based on them. Other features of Goodhart's theory were (1) that the *ratio* was not found in the reasons given on the rule of law set forth in the opinion (although the opinion might furnish a guide for determining which facts the judge considered material and which immaterial); (2) the inclusion of a series of rules for finding which facts were and were not material; (3) that the judge's view on this question had to be accepted by subsequent courts. The theory was offered as being of general application, and, indeed, as "a guide to the method which I believe most English courts follow."[38] Both claims are doubtful, the first because of

---

[31] *cf.* Goodhart (1931), pp. 3–4: "A bad reason may often make good law."

[32] MacCormick (1987), p. 180.

[33] A good example here is provided by a proposition stated by Lord Bridge in *R. v. Secretary of State for the Home Department, ex p. Khawaja* [1984] A.C. 74, 117, to the effect that the Home Secretary could not base a "conducive to the public good" deportation order (Immigration Act 1971, s.3(5)(b)) on a ground arising from the circumstances of the original entry of the person concerned. Divergent views were subsequently expressed on (1) what Lord Bridge meant; (2) whether it was necessary for the ultimate decision in *Khawaja*; (3) whether it should anyway be followed even if *obiter*: compare *In re Owusu-Sekyere* [1987] Imm. A.R. 425, C.A., with *R. v. Immigration Appeal Tribunal, ex p. Patel* [1988] Imm. A.R. 35, C.A. The matter was ultimately resolved by the House of Lords (through Lord Bridge) holding that the proposition was "simply mistaken": *Ex p. Patel* [1988] A.C. 910, 922.

[34] See below, para. 7-008.

[35] See below, para. 7-005.

[36] MacCormick (1987), p. 180.

[37] Goodhart (1931), pp. 1–26.

[38] A. L. Goodhart, (1959) 22 M.L.R. 117, 124.

the downplaying of the principle as enunciated by the judge,[39] and the second simply because "there seems little or no evidence to support this."[40] Nevertheless, the method remains potentially helpful where; probably through faulty technique, the reasons given for a decision do not include an express indication of the relevant principle of law.

3. THE "INTERPRETATION" OF PRECEDENTS

The judge who is called upon to determine a disputed point of law chooses 7-005 the generality of the language in which he or she expresses a conclusion. The proposition may be very general, it may be closely tailored to the facts of the case or it may be formulated at some intermediate level. Most, although not all judges are reluctant to make general statements of law, and it is anyway well established that a judgment must be read in the light of the facts of the case in which it was given. In *Quinn v. Leathem*,[41] the Earl of Halsbury L.C. said that:

"every judgment must be read as applicable to the particular facts proved, or assumed to be proved, since the generality of the expressions which may be found there are not intended to be expositions of the whole law, but governed and qualified by the particular facts of the case in which such expressions are to be found."

This point is commonly made where the judge in case B wishes to hold that the *ratio* of case A is narrower than that apparently expounded by the judge or court in case A, and is accordingly not applicable. An example of this is given by the decision of the majority of the Privy Council in *Mutual Life and Citizens' Assurance Co. Ltd v. Evatt*,[42] which sought to restrict the scope of liability in tort for negligent misstatement to cases where the defendant was or claimed to be in the business of giving information or advice of the relevant kind. The speeches in the leading case, *Hedley Byrne & Co. Ltd v. Heller and Partners Ltd*[43] were interpreted to support the incorporation of such a condition, notwithstanding the dissent of Lord Reid and Lord Morris of Borth-y-Gest, who had taken part in the *Hedley Byrne* decision and who said that they were "unable to construe the passages from our speeches cited in the judgment of the majority in the way in which they are there construed."[44] Conversely, a proposition stated by a judge may be

---

[39] *Cf.* Cross and Harris (1991), pp. 63–71, criticising Goodhart's "scanty regard to the way in which the case was argued and pleaded, the process of reasoning adopted by the judge and the relation of the case to other decisions" (*ibid.* p. 67).

[40] Lord Lloyd and M. D. A. Freeman, *Lloyd's Introduction to Jurisprudence* (5th ed., 1985), p. 1117 (omitted from the 6th ed., 1994).

[41] [1901] A.C. 495, 506. *Cf.* Diplock L. J. in *Miller-Mead v. Minister of Housing and Local Government* [1963] 2 Q.B. 196, 235–236.

[42] [1971] A.C. 793. On the Privy Council and precedent, see below, paras 7-022, 7-028.

[43] [1964] A.C. 465.

[44] [1971] A.C. 793, 813. The minority position has been preferred by several English judges: see *Esso Petroleum Co. Ltd v. Mardon* [1975] Q.B. 819, 830 (Lawson J.) and [1976] Q.B. 801, 827 (Ormrod L.J.); *Howard Marine and Dredging Co. Ltd v. Ogden & Sons Ltd* [1978] Q.B. 574, 591 (Lord Denning M.R.), 600 (Shaw L.J.).

regarded as too restrictive. A well known example is *Barwick v. The English Joint Stock Bank*,[45] where Willes J. said:

"The general rule is, that the master is answerable for every such wrong of the servant or agent as is committed in the course of the service and for the master's benefit, though no express command or privity of the master be proved."[46]

It had previously been doubted whether a master was vicariously liable in respect of the fraud, as distinct from the non-deliberate wrongdoing, of a servant. On the facts of the case the master had benefited, albeit unwittingly, from the fraud. Subsequently, in *Lloyd v. Grace, Smith & Co.*[47] the House of Lords held that an employer could be vicariously liable for the fraud of an employee committed in the course of employment, notwithstanding that the employer received no benefit. The reference to the "master's benefit" was not to be regarded as part of the *ratio* of *Barwick's* case in the light of Willes J.'s judgment when read as a whole and of judgments in other cases both before and after *Barwick*. These are examples of the *ratio* of a case being reformulated *by a court not bound by it*. It has indeed been doubted whether courts "exercise any power of correcting statements of law drawn from binding decisions."[48]

4. CASES WHERE NO REASONS ARE GIVEN

7-006   The report of an old case may simply contain a statement of the facts, the arguments of counsel and an order of the court based on those facts. Here, the *ratio* has, if possible, to be inferred, but its authority is understandably very weak.[49] It would be most unusual for such a case to be decisive in modern litigation.

5. JUDGMENTS WITH MORE THAN ONE RATIO

7-008   A number of distinct points of law may be at issue in a case, each of which taken separately would be sufficient to determine the case in favour of one side (say the plaintiff). The judge may be content to take one point only, give judgment for the plaintiff, and decline to comment on the other points. Instead, he or she may express an opinion on these points, while making it clear that the decision is to rest on the first point and that the other remarks are *dicta*. Yet again, he or she may state a conclusion on each point without any distinction, resolving them all in favour of the plaintiff. In the third

---

[45] (1866) L.R. 2 Ex. 259.
[46] *ibid.* p. 265.
[47] [1912] A.C. 716.
[48] See A. W. B. Simpson, (1959) 22 M.L.R. 453, 455–457.
[49] Cross and Harris (1991), p. 47.

situation, each conclusion is a separate *ratio*, and in principle, each *ratio* is binding.[50]

6. The Ratio Decidendi of Appellate Courts[51]

Determining the *ratio* of the decision of an appellate court where separate **7–009** judgments are given can be a difficult task. Some principles are reasonably clear. Where all the members of the court are agreed as to the result of the case, any *ratio* that commands the support of a majority is binding.[52] For example, in a three-member court where two judges support ground A and the third ground B, ground A is the *ratio*. If three judges support ground A and two ground B, there are two *rationes*. Where a judge dissents as to the result, his or her views must technically be disregarded for the purpose of ascertaining the *ratio* on the ground that his or her reasons cannot be "necessary" for a decision he or she opposes. Dissenting judgments may, however, carry persuasive weight. Where there is no majority in favour of any particular *ratio*, a later court may hold that the case has no discernible *ratio* which has to be followed, although it may not adopt any reasoning which would show the decision itself to be wrong.[53] In some cases there may be much time and effort spent in the search for a *ratio* which is as elusive as the holy grail.[54]

A further complication arises where the Court of Appeal bases a decision on point A, but the case proceeds to the House of Lords, which (1) dismisses the appeal, but (2) bases its decision on point B, (3) holds that on a proper analysis point A does not arise and (4) expresses no view on the soundness of point A. In *R. v. Secretary of State for the Home Department, ex p. Al-Mehdawi*[55] the Court of Appeal held that the previous decision of the Court of Appeal[56] is no longer binding authority for point A, although it remains

---

[50] *Jacobs v. London County Council* [1950] A.C. 361, 369 (Lord Simonds); *Behrens v. Bertram Mills Circus Ltd* [1957] 2 Q.B. 1, 24–25 (Devlin J.); *Miliangos v. George Frank (Textiles) Ltd* [1975] Q.B. 487, 502–503 (Lord Denning M.R.); R. E. Megarry, (1958) 74 L.Q.R. 350; *City of Westminster v. Clarke* (1991) 23 H.L.R. 506, *per* Dillon L.J. at p. 515 and Balcombe L.J. at p. 516 (the decision of the Court of Appeal was subsequently reversed by the House of Lords: [1992] 2 A.C. 288). On other occasions Lord Denning argued that the Court of Appeal is not necessarily bound by both or all the *rationes* of an earlier *Court of Appeal* decision: *Hanning v. Maitland (No. 2)* [1970] 1 Q.B. 580; *Ministry of Defence v. Jeremiah* [1980] 1 Q.B. 87. On this he stood alone: see Hazel Carty, (1981) 1 L.S. 68, 71–72.

[51] Cross and Harris (1991), pp. 84–96; G. Paton and G. Sawer, (1947) 63 L.Q.R. 461; A. M. Honore, (1955) 71 L.Q.R. 196.

[52] *e.g. Amalgamated Society of Railway Servants v. Osborne* [1910] A.C. 87. A statement "I agree" may simply indicate concurrence with the order proposed in the leading judgment and not necessarily all the reasoning: Lord Russell of Killowen (then Russell L.J.), Address to the Holdsworth Club of the University of Birmingham 1968–69, reprinted in B. W. Harvey (ed.), *The Lawyer and Justice* (1978).

[53] See the analysis of the decision of the House of Lords in *Central Asbestos Ltd v. Dodd* [1973] A.C. 518 by the Court of Appeal in *Re Harper v. National Coal Board (Intended Action)* [1974] Q.B. 614.

[54] See, for example, the decision of the House of Lords in *Chaplin v. Boys* [1971] A.C. 356. First-year law students are not recommended to read this case; it should, however, be one of the party pieces of students of conflict of laws.

[55] [1990] 1 A.C. 876.

[56] Here, *R. v. Diggines, ex p. Rahmani* [1985] Q.B. 1109, C.A., on appeal: [1986] A.C. 475.

of "powerful persuasive influence".[57] Counsel for the Secretary of State had argued that this was so either (1) because point A had been replaced by point B as the *ratio* of the decision, or (2) as an additional exception to the rule in *Young v. Bristol Aeroplane Co. Ltd.*[58] The Court of Appeal seemed to accept the first of these arguments, but did not expressly reject the second.

D. THE HIERARCHY OF THE COURTS AND THE RULES OF BINDING PRECEDENT

7–010 Broadly speaking, a court is only *obliged* to follow the decisions of courts at a higher or the same level in the court structure, and there are a number of exceptions even to that requirement. For the purposes of the following discussion it must be assumed that all the other factors mentioned in Section A above are present which combine to make a precedent binding in a particular case.

1. MAGISTRATES COURTS AND COUNTY COURTS

7–011 Decisions of these courts are rarely reported outside the pages of local newspapers, but even if they were properly reported they would not constitute precedents binding on anyone. They do not bind themselves, although it is to be expected that an individual magistrate or county court judge will attempt to be consistent in his or her own decision-making. A magistrates' court may also be reminded by the clerk of the practice of the local bench, and other benches in the area. The matter upon which a "local view" may develop will rarely be a point of law; more commonly it will relate to a procedural requirement or the exercise of discretion, as in sentencing or the granting of bail.[59] Magistrates' courts and county courts are bound by decisions of the High Court, Court of Appeal and House of Lords.

2. THE CROWN COURT

7–012 Decisions of judges in the Crown Court are reported rather more frequently than' those of magistrates' and county courts. This is partly because the judge may be a High Court judge whose pronouncements are inevitably more authoritative, and partly because reports of cases on points of criminal

---

[57] *per* Taylor L.J., [1990] 1 A.C. 876, 883. Taylor LJ. had, indeed, been a party to the Court of Appeal decision in *ex p. Rahmani*, and ultimately, here, remained of the same opinion. The decision on the point in question was, however, ultimately reversed by the House of Lords: *ibid.*

[58] [1944] K.B. 718. See below, paras 7–016–7–024.

[59] See, e.g. *R. v. Nottingham JJ., ex p. Davies* [1981] 1 Q.B. 38 where the practice of the City of Nottingham bench of refusing to hear full argument on a third or subsequent application for bail, unless there were "new circumstances", was endorsed by the Divisional Court.

law, even at this level, find an outlet in the pages of publications such as the Criminal Law Review and the Criminal Appeal Reports. However, there is no regular reporting, and it has been suggested that Crown Court decisions are merely persuasive authorities whatever the status of the judge.[60] The Crown Court is bound by decisions of the Court of Appeal and the House of Lords. It has been asserted that it is not bound by decisions of the Divisional Court,[61] but this is hard to square with the rule that Divisional Courts are normally bound by their own previous decisions.[62]

3. THE HIGH COURT

The decision of a High Court judge is binding on inferior courts, but not technically on another High Court judge, and certainly not on a Divisional Court (*i.e.* a court of two or more judges). High Court judges are reluctant to depart from the decisions of other High Court judges,[63] Chancery judges being particularly loath to disagree with their colleagues for fear of upsetting transactions affecting property rights and the like.[64] There are, however, examples of judicial disagreement, one of the most notable being on the question whether failure to wear a seat-belt in a car can amount to contributory negligence. This had to be settled by the Court of Appeal.[65] It has been suggested that a decision should be followed unless the later judge is convinced that it was wrong; and that a decision of a High Court judge should more readily be followed by a deputy High Court judge on the ground that the former possesses a higher status.[66] However, it has been stated that where there are conflicting decisions of judges of co-ordinate jurisdiction, the later decision should thereafter be preferred, provided that it was reached after full consideration of the first decision: the only, rare, exception would be where the third judge was convinced that the second judge was wrong in not following the first, for example where some binding or persuasive authority had not been cited in either of the first two cases.[67] This view has been cited with approval on a number

7–013

---

[60] A. Ashworth, "The Binding Effect of Crown Court Decisions" [1980] Crim.L.R. 402–403; *cf.* Cross and Harris (1991), pp. 6, 123. Some cases are reported in the regular law reports: see, *e.g. R. v. Bourne* [1939] 1 K.B. 687, where the summing up of Macnaghten J. on the pre-Abortion Act 1967 law of procuring an abortion was generally accepted as authoritative (*cf.* [1938] 3 All E.R. 615).

[61] *R. v. Colyer* [1974] Crim.L.R. 243 (Judge Stinson).

[62] See below, para. 7-014.

[63] See *Police Authority for Huddersfield v. Watson* [1947] K.B. 842, 848, where it is explained by Lord Goddard C.J. to be a matter of "judicial comity". A similar approach is adopted by the Employment Appeal Tribunal in respect of its own previous decisions; "An EAT will normally treat an earlier decision as authoritative unless it is convinced that the decision is wrong": *per* Peter Gibson L.J. in *London Borough of Lambeth v. Tunde Apelogun-Gabriels* [2001] EWCA Civ.1852.

[64] There are also many fewer Chancery judges than Queen's Bench judges and so they are more likely to meet each other; whether this boosts "judicial comity" is a matter for speculation.

[65] *Froom v. Butcher* [1976] Q.B. 286 answered the question in the affirmative.

[66] *per* Sir Louis Blom-Cooper Q.C. in *R. v. Hertsmere Borough Council, ex p. Woolgar* (1996) 27 H.L.R. 703; applied by Stephen Richards Q.C. in *R. v. London Borough of Southwark ex p. Bediako* (1997) 30 H.L.R. 22.

[67] *Colchester Estates (Cardiff) v. Carlton Industries plc* [1986] Ch. 80.

of occasions,[68] although it has been emphasised that the matter remains one of judicial comity: there is no new head of binding precedent.[69] Indeed, Lindsay J. in *In Re Saunders (A Bankrupt)*[70] pointed out that

"At my request I had my attention drawn to cases on the subject of judges of coordinate jurisdiction following each other. As none is strictly binding on me I am, entertainingly, not bound by the decisions as to how far I should regard myself as bound."

4. DIVISIONAL COURTS

7–014   A Divisional Court is bound by decisions of the Court of Appeal and the House of Lords. In *Huddersfield Police Authority v. Watson*[71] and *Younghusband v. Luftig*,[72] Divisional Courts of the King's Bench Division, in each case presided over by Lord Goddard C.J., held that they were bound by previous Divisional Court decisions to the same extent that the Court of Appeal was bound by its own previous decisions.[73]

The matter was reconsidered by the Divisional Court in *R. v. Greater Manchester Coroner, ex p. Tal*.[74] It was held that the position was different where a Divisional Court was exercising the supervisory jurisdiction of the High Court on an application for judicial review,[75] and was faced by a previous decision of the Divisional Court acting in the same capacity. Its position was analogous to that of a judge at first instance faced with a previous decision of another judge of first instance: here, the judge in the later case would follow the earlier decision

"unless he is convinced that that judgment is wrong, as a matter of

---

[68] *Taylor Woodrow Property Co. Ltd v. Lonrho Textiles Ltd* [1985] 2 EGLR 120, B. Hytner Q. C., sitting as a deputy High Court judge (in respect of two conflicting decisions of the Court of Appeal); *Elite Investments Ltd v. T. 1. Bainbridge Silencers Ltd.* [1986] 2 EGLR 43, Judge Paul Baker Q.C., sitting as a judge of the High Court; *Glofield Properties Ltd, v. Morley* [1988] 1 EGLR 113, Hutchison J; *Re A. E. Fair Ltd* [1992] B.C.L. 333, where Ferris J. on this basis followed a decision of Vinelott J. in preference to an earlier decision of his own (thus taking judicial comity long way); this course of action was subsequently commended by Dillon L.J. in *Bishopsgate Investment Ltd v. Maxwell* [1993] Ch.l, 14; the Court of Appeal in that case upholding Vinelott J.'s approach; *Chancery pic v. Ketteringham, The Times*, November 23, 1993, David Neuberger Q.C. sitting as a deputy High Court judge. The later decision that is preferred may be one of the Court of Session: *Minister of Pensions v. Highman* [1948] 2 K.B. 153; *Banks v. Kokkinos* [1999] 3 E.G.L.R. 133.

[69] *Forsikringsaktieselskapet Vesta v. Butcher* [1986] 2 All E.R. 488, Hobhouse J.

[70] [1997] Ch. 60, 79. Here, the judge declined to follow two High Court decisions where there had not been full argument on the relevant point.

[71] [1947] K.B. 842: on an appeal from quarter sessions in a civil case concerning police pensions.

[72] [1949] 2 K.B. 354: on an appeal by case stated from justices in a criminal case.

[73] Under *Young v. Bristol Aeroplane Co. Ltd*, below, paras 7-016–7-024. The possibility of the Divisional Court applying one of the *Young v. Bristol Aeroplane* exceptions was acknowledged by Lord Goddard in the latter case: [1949] 2 K.B. 354, 361.

[74] [1985] Q.B. 67. See P. Jackson, (1985) 101 L.Q.R. 157.

[75] See below, paras 18-046–18-059.

judicial comity; but he is not bound to follow a judge of equal jurisdiction."[76]

The same principle of *stare decisis* was applicable where two Divisional Court decisions were involved:

"We have no doubt that it will be only in rare cases that a divisional court will think it fit to depart from a decision of another divisional court exercising this jurisdiction."[77]

Ex p. Tal was one of these "rare cases",[78] the Divisional Court holding that any error of law made by an inferior court or tribunal caused it to act outside its jurisdiction.[79] It declined to follow *R. v. Surrey Coroner, ex p. Campbell*,[80] where it had been held that this principle applied only to *tribunals*, and not *courts*, such as a coroner's court.[81] The court in *Ex. p. Tal*[82] also expressed doubts, *obiter*, as to whether the strict approach to precedent in cases where the Divisional Court was acting in an appellate capacity was still appropriate. Robert Goff L.J. noted that at the time of *Younghusband v. Luftig*,[83] the Divisional Court was the final court of appeal in criminal cases tried summarily,[84] and the House of Lords, in most cases the final court of appeal, regarded itself as bound by its own previous decisions (subject to narrow exceptions).[85] Neither of these points remained true in 1984. In criminal cases at least, his Lordship[86] could see no reason why the Divisional Court should not adopt the more flexible approach of the Criminal Division of the Court of Appeal,[87] in preference to the narrower approach of the Civil Division based on *Young v. Bristol Aeroplane Co Ltd*.[88]

In subsequent cases, the approach to precedent of the Divisional Court in *Ex p. Tal*[89] has been cited with approval on numerous occasions,[90] although

---

[76] *ibid.*, at p. 81, *per* Robert Goff L.J., citing *Huddersfield Police Authority v. Watson* [1947] K.B. 842, 848, *per* Lord Goddard C.J.

[77] [1985] Q.B. 67, 81, *per* Robert Goff L.J.

[78] Others are *R. v. Chief Metropolitan Stipendiary Magistrate, ex p. Secretary of State for the Home Department* [1988] 1 W.L.R. 1204; *R. v. Governor of Brockhill Prision, ex p. Evans* [1997] Q.B. 443

[79] Under the principle of *Anisminic Ltd v. Foreign Compensation Commission* [1969] 2 A.C. 147.

[80] [1982] Q.B. 661.

[81] In accordance with dicta of Lord Diplock in *Re Racal Communications Ltd* [1981] A.C. 374.

[82] n. 74 above.

[83] n. 72 above.

[84] See below. It had also been the final court of appeal under the police pensions legislation in *Huddersfield Police Authority v. Watson*, n. 71 above.

[85] See below.

[86] [1985] Q.B. 67, 78, 79.

[87] See below, para. 7-025. A more flexible approach had also been adopted in two nineteenth century Divisional Court cases, both concerning criminal appeals: *Fortescue v. Vestry of St Matthew, Bethnal Green* [1891] 2 Q.B. 170; *Kruse v. Johnson* [1898] 2 Q.B. 91. These cases were not cited in *Huddersfield Police Authority v. Watson* and *Younghusband v. Luftig*.

[88] Below, paras 7-016–7-024.

[89] n. 74 above.

[90] *Hornigold v. Chief Constable of Lancashire* [1986] Crim. L. R. 792 (appeal in a criminal case); *R. v. Chief Metropolitan Stipendiary Magistrate, ex p. Secretary of State for the Home Department* [1988] 1 W.L.R. 1204 (application for judicial review); *R. v. Metropolitan Stipendiary Magistrate, ex p. London Waste Regulation Authority* [1993] 3 All E.R. 113

some judges seem happier to disregard a previous Divisional Court decision if this can be done by reference to a "*Young v. Bristol Aeroplane Co. exception*".[91] It has also been emphasised that *Ex p. Tal*

"was not intended to provide freedom to parties to re-argue points simply on the ground that they might persuade the Court to reach a different conclusion. Before a point may be re-argued, the party must be able to indicate, at the outset of the argument, specific material on the basis of which it might properly be submitted that the Court may be convinced that the previous decision was plainly wrong."[92]

Divisional Court decisions are binding on High Court judges sitting alone[93] and inferior courts, but not the Employment Appeal Tribunal.[94]

5. THE COURT OF APPEAL (CIVIL DIVISION)

(a) The general position

7–015   Decisions of the Court of Appeal are binding on the Divisional Court, the Employment Appeal Tribunal, High Court judges[95] and inferior courts. The Court of Appeal is bound to follow decisions of the House of Lords. On occasion, the House has felt it necessary to remind the Court of Appeal of this. In 1970, Captain Jack Broome R.N. (retd.) brought a libel action against David Irving and Cassell & Co. Ltd., respectively author and publisher of a book entitled *The Destruction of Convoy P.Q.17*. The case was heard over 17 days by Lawton J. and a jury.[96] The jury awarded £15,000 "compensatory damages" and £25,000 "exemplary damages." The situations in which exemplary damages could be awarded had been listed by

---

[91] *R. v. Plymouth JJ, ex p. Driver* [1986] Q.B. 95, 123–124 (*per incuriam*); *R.v. Plymouth JJ., ex p. Hart* [1986] Q.B. 950 (conflicting decisions); *R.v. Weston-super-Mare JJ., ex p. Shaw* [1987] Q.B. 640, 648 (conflicting decisions): all applications for judicial review; *Shaw v. D.P.P.* [1993] 1 All E.R. 918 (*per incuriam*).

[92] *Hornigold v. Chief Constable of Lancashire* [1986] Crim. L.R. 792.

[93] *Huddersfield Police Authority v. Watson* [1947] K.B. 842, 848; *Ettenfield v. Ettenfield* [1939] P. 377, 380; *contra: Elderton v. United Kingdom Totalisator Co. Ltd* (1945) 61 T.L.R. 529 where a judge of the Chancery Division declined to follow the decision of a Divisional Court of the Queen's Bench Division.

[94] *Portec (U.K.) Ltd v. Mogensen* [1976] I.C.R. 396, 400; *Breach v. Epsylon Industries Ltd* [1976] I.C.R. 316, 320.

[95] Even an *ex parte* decision of the Court of Appeal: *The Alexandras P.* [1986] Q.B. 464. In *Lane v. Willis* [1972] 1 W.L.R. 326, 332, Davies LJ. rebuked Lawson J. for expressing the opinion, though accepting he was bound by it, that a Court of Appeal decision was wrong.

[96] It survived an interruption by Welsh language demonstrators: *Morris v. Crown Office* [1970] 2 Q.B. 114.

Lord Devlin in *Rookes v. Barnard*[97], a decision of the House of Lords, and the principles subsequently applied by the Court of Appeal to the tort of defamation.[98] Not surprisingly, Lawton J. had directed the jury accordingly in the *P.Q.17* case. Both author and publisher appealed against the award of exemplary damages. The Court of Appeal, after a nine-day hearing, rejected the appeal.[99] The case fell within one of the situations in which Lord Devlin had held that exemplary damages could be awarded,[1] the judge's direction had been adequate and the jury's award was not perversely large. The Court of Appeal was not, however, content with that. The members of the court (Lord Denning M.R., Salmon and Phillimore L.JJ.) took the view that the law on exemplary damages as expounded by Lord Devlin was "unworkable." Lord Denning M.R. said that the common law on exemplary damages had been well settled before 1964, that there were two House of Lords cases[2] which had approved that settled doctrine and which Lord Devlin must have "overlooked" or "misunderstood," that *Rookes v. Barnard* had not been followed in Commonwealth courts, and that the new doctrine was "hopelessly illogical and inconsistent." He concluded:

"I think the difficulties presented by *Rookes v. Barnard* are so great that the judges should direct the juries in accordance with the law as it was understood before *Rookes v. Barnard*. Any attempt to follow *Rookes v. Barnard* is bound to lead to confusion."[3]

Surprisingly, there was no discussion of the question whether Lord Devlin's statement formed part of the *ratio decidendi* of *Rookes v. Barnard*.

Cassells appealed to the House of Lords; a 13-day hearing was held before seven Law Lords. The Court of Appeal's decision to uphold the jury's verdict was affirmed by a majority.[4] Lord Devlin's approach to exemplary damages was endorsed, with varying enthusiasm, by a majority. The approach of the Court of Appeal to *Rookes v. Barnard* was roundly condemned. Lord Hailsham L.C.:

"[I]t is not open to the Court of Appeal to give gratuitous advice to judges of first instance to ignore decisions of the House of Lords in this way and, if it were open to the Court of Appeal to do so, it would be highly undesirable. ...

"The fact is, and I hope it will never be necessary to say so again, that, in the hierarchical system of courts which exists in this country, it is necessary for each lower tier, including the Court of Appeal, to accept loyally the decisions of the higher tiers. Where decisions

---

[97] [1964] A.C. 1129. The other members of the House expressly concurred with Lord Devlin's statement on exemplary damages.

[98] *McCarey v. Associated Newspapers Ltd* [1965] 2 Q.B. 86; *Broadway Approvals Ltd v. Odhams Press Ltd* [1965] 1 W.L.R. 805.

[99] *Broome v. Cassell & Co. Ltd* [1971] 2 Q.B. 354.

[1] See W. V. H. Rogers, *Winfield and Jolowicz on Tort* (15th ed., 1998), pp. 774–750. See now *Kuddus v. Chief Constable of Leicestershire* [2001] 2 W.L.R. 1789.

[2] *E. Hulton & Co. v. Jones* [1910] A.C. 20 and *Ley v. Hamilton* (1935) 153 L.T. 384.

[3] [1971] 2 Q.B. 354, 381, 384.

[4] *Cassell & Co. Ltd v. Broome* [1972] A.C. 1027. It has been described as "what may well be the most hostile *affirmation* of a Court of Appeal decision in our history": Julius Stone, "On the Liberation of Appellate Judges — How not to do it!" (1972) 35 M.L.R. 449.

manifestly conflict, the decision in *Young v. Bristol Aeroplane Co. Ltd* offers guidance to each tier in matters affecting its own decisions. It does not entitle it to question considered decisions in the upper tiers with the same freedom."[5]

Other members of the House of Lords added their voices to the chorus of disapproval.[6] They pointed out that the parties had been put to much expense in litigating broad legal issues unnecessary for the disposal of their dispute.[7] Lord Devlin had not overlooked the two House of Lords cases (*Ley v. Hamilton* was discussed at length in his speech) and, on proper analysis, they were not binding authorities on the award of exemplary damages.[8]

The House of Lords similarly found it necessary to assert its authority over the Court of Appeal in *Miliangos v. George Frank (Textiles) Ltd.*[9]

Since the retirement of Lord Denning M.R., the loyalty of the Court of Appeal to decisions of the House of Lords has not been in question.

(b) Young v. Bristol Aeroplane Co. Ltd

7–016   In *Young v. Bristol Aeroplane Co. Ltd*[10] the Court of Appeal[11] held that it was bound by its own previous decisions, and by decisions of courts of co-ordinate jurisdiction such as the Courts of Exchequer Chamber. Three exceptions were identified. First a decision of the Court of Appeal given *per incuriam* need not be followed. Secondly, where the court is faced by previous conflicting decisions of the Court of Appeal or a court of co-ordinate jurisdiction, it may choose which to follow. Thirdly, where a previous decision of the Court of Appeal, although not expressly overruled, cannot stand with a subsequent decision of the House of Lords, the decision of the House must be followed. Since *Young's* case further light has been thrown on the scope of these three exceptions and suggestions have been made for additional ones. Lord Denning M.R. fought, almost single-handed, against the notion that the Court of Appeal should be bound by its own previous decisions at all. In addition, it has been unclear whether the grounds upon which the Court of Appeal may question one of its own decisions may be employed by a court lower in the hierarchy in respect of a decision of a higher court. These matters are considered in turn.

---

[5] [1972] A.C. 1027, 1054.

[6] See Lord Reid at pp. 1084, 1091–3; Lord Wilberforce at pp. 1112–1113; Lord Diplock at pp. 1131–1132; Lord Kilbrandon at pp. 1132, 1135.

[7] *cf.* below, para. 18-038, n. 4.

[8] Viscount Dilhorne dissented on this last point: [1972] A.C. at pp. 1109–11.

[9] [1976] A.C. 443, discussed below, para. 7-021.

[10] [1944] K.B. 718.

[11] A "full court" consisting of Lord Greene M.R., Scott, MacKinnon, Luxmoore, Goddard and du Parcq L.JJ. Note that it was held in this case a "full court" is bound by previous Court of Appeal decisions to the same extent as a court ordinarily constituted. See further below para. 7-025. It has been suggested, obiter, by Beldam L. J. that the *Young* principles should be applied by the Employment Appeal Tribunal in respect of its own previous decisions: *Tracey v. Crosville Wales Ltd* [1996] I.C.R. 237, 257–258. The point was left open by Waite and Otton L. JJ; a different view was taken in *London Borough of Lambeth v. Tunde Apelogun-Gabriels* [2001] EWCA Civ. 1853: above, para. 7-013, n. 63.

(c) Accepted exceptions to Young v. Bristol Aeroplane Co. Ltd

(i) Decisions given per incuriam

If interpreted and applied literally the *per incuriam* doctrine could be used to   **7–017**
evade the effect of any decision thought to have been reached "through want
of care." However, the term in this context is interpreted narrowly. A
decision will not be regarded as *per incuriam* merely on the ground that
another court thinks it wrongly decided, that it has been inadequately
argued[12] or that the decision contains points which are not derived from the
arguments of counsel.[13] In *Morelle v. Wakeling*, Sir Raymond Evershed
M.R. said that as a general rule the *per incuriam* doctrine could only apply
to:

> "decisions given in ignorance or forgetfulness of some inconsistent
> statutory provision or of some authority binding on the court
> concerned: so that in such cases some part of the decision or some
> step in the reasoning on which it is based is found, on that account to be
> demonstrably wrong."[14]

In *Dixon v. British Broadcasting Corporation*[15] a decision on the construction of a statutory provision was regarded as *per incuriam* on the ground
that other relevant provisions which threw light on the words in question
had not been brought to the attention of the court. A clearer example is
Bonulami v. Home Secretary.[16] An order was obtained under the Bankers'
Books Evidence Act 1879 for the inspection of bank accounts to obtain
evidence in criminal proceedings. The Court of Appeal (Civil Division) held
that it had no jurisdiction to entertain an appeal as this was a "criminal
cause or matter",[17] notwithstanding that in an earlier[18] case it had heard
such an appeal: The point as to jurisdiction had not been taken or
considered by counsel or any member of the court:

> "Failure to consider a statutory provision is one of the clearest cases in
> which, on the principles laid down in *Young v. Bristol Aeroplane Co.
> Ltd.*, this court is not bound to follow its own decisions."[19]

---

[12] *Morelle v. Wakeling* [1955] 2 Q.B. 379, 406; *Miliangos v. George Frank (Textiles) Ltd* [1975]
Q.B. 487, 503 (Lord Denning M.R.); *cf. Chief Adjudication Officer v. Brunt* [1988] A.C. 711,
724, 726, C.A.

[13] per Lord Diplock in *Cassell & Co. Ltd v. Broome* [1972] A.C. 1027, 1131.

[14] [1955] 2 Q.B. 379, 406. See generally, P. Wesley-Smith, (1980) 15 J.S.P.T.L. (N.S.) 58. In
Industrial Properties Ltd v. A.E.I. [1977] Q.B. 580 dicta in a Court of Appeal decision were
held to have been made *per incuriam* on the ground that the court had misunderstood a
decision of the Court of Exchequer Chamber; they had only been referred to an inadequate
report of that decision.

[15] [1979] Q.B. 546.

[16] [1985] Q.B. 675. See also *White v. Chief Adjudication Officer* [1986] 2 All E.R. 905; *Pearce v
Secretary of State for Defence* [1988] A.C. 755, 785, C.A.; *Rakhit v. Carty* [1990] 2 Q.B. 315;
R. v. Fennell (Peter) [2000] 1 W.L.R. 2011 (decision *per incuriam* where relevant provisions,
including the Interpretation Act 1978, had not been cited).

[17] Supreme Court Act 1981, s.18(1)(a): see below, para. 18-022.

[18] *R. v. Grossman* (1981) 73 Cr. App. R. 302.

[19] *per* Stephenson L. J. at [1985] Q.B. 675, 682.

The exact scope of the *per incuriam* doctrine has been thrown into some doubt by three judgments of Sir John (subsequently Lord) Donaldson M.R. In *Duke v. Reliance Systems Ltd*[20] he put it in narrow terms, as applying where the court *must* (not *might*) have reached a different conclusion had a statute or binding precedent been drawn to its attention. In *Williams v. Fawcett*,[21] the Court of Appeal disapproved one of the grounds of a number of decisions[22] in which it had been held that a notice to show cause why the respondent should not be committed to prison for breach of a non-molestation order had to be signed by the "proper officer" of the county court. There was no warrant for this requirement in the statute or procedural rules. Sir John Donaldson M.R. recognised the dangers of treating a decision as given *per incuriam* simply on the ground that it could be demonstrated to be wrong, but argued that this was an "exceptional" case for various reasons: (1) the clearness with which the growth of the error could be detected if the decisions were read consecutively; (2) the cases were concerned with the liberty of the subject[23]; (3) they were by no means unusual; and (4) they were "most unlikely to reach the House of Lords, which, if we do not act is alone able to correct the error which has crept into the law."[24]

Subsequently, in *Rickards v. Rickards*[25] the Court of Appeal declined to follow its own previous decision in *Podbery v. Peak*,[26] in which it had been held that the Court of Appeal had no jurisdiction to entertain an appeal against the refusal of a judge to grant leave to appeal out of time. The court in *Rickards*, which included Lord Donaldson M.R., was satisfied that the decision in *Podbery v. Peak* was wrong, but noted that in practice it was unlikely that litigants would incur the cost of appealing to the House of Lords on this point.[27] Further considerations that justified treating *Podbery v. Peak* as a decision given *per incuriam* were (1) that it related to a procedural rule rather than substantive law (erroneous decisions as to procedural rules affecting only the parties engaged in the relevant litigation); and (2) that it involved the jurisdiction of the court, errors on matters of jurisdiction being "particularly objectionable".[28] It was stated that this

---

[20] [1988] Q.B. 108. See above, para. 5-053.
[21] [1988] Q.B. 604. See also *M v. P (contempt: committal); Butler v. Butler* [1993] Fam. 167 and *Nicholls v. Nicholls* [1997] 1 W.L.R. 314, confirming the breadth of the court's discretion to rectify technical defects in committal orders.
[22] *Lee v. Walker* [1988] Q.B. 1191 and several unreported decisions.
[23] Although it was noted that the present decision would not be beneficial to the contemnors, who would be deprived of a technical ground of challenge to their imprisonment; *Williams v. Fawcett* is therefore not to be equated with the "special exception" recognised in the Criminal Division of the Court of Appeal: see below, para. 7-025.
[24] [1988] Q.B. 604, 616–617.
[25] [1990] Fam. 194.
[26] [1981] Ch. 344.
[27] Leave was granted in *Bokhari v. Mahmood* (unreported, 1988) for the point to be taken to the House of Lords, but the appeal was not pursued.
[28] "Either because it will involve an abuse of power if the true view is that the court has no jurisdiction or a breach of the court's statutory duty if the true view is that the court is wrongly declining jurisdiction": per Lord Donaldson M.R. at p. 203.

extended approach to the *per incuriam* doctrine should only be adopted in "rare and exceptional" cases.[29]

In more recent cases, the narrowness of the scope of this extension to the *per incuriam* doctrine has been emphasised. In *Re Probe Data Systems (No.3)*[30] the Court of Appeal regarded these authorities as establishing that

> "in order to come within this category, it must be shown not only that the decision involved some 'manifest slip or error', but also that to leave the decision standing would be likely to produce serious inconvenience in the administration of justice, or significant injustice to citizens, or some equally serious consequences."[31]

However, in other cases, an apparently broader approach has been adopted. Thus, in *R. v. Parole Board, ex p. Wilson*[32] the Court of Appeal departed from the decision in *R. v. Secretary of State for the Home Department, ex p. Gunnell*[33] in holding that a discretionary life sentence prisoner was entitled to disclosure of the reasons, report or facts adverse to his request for release. This was justified, as "the liberty of the subject was in issue"[34] and he would in any event be entitled to see the information once section 34 of the Criminal Justice Act 1991 was brought into force.

Finally, it should be noted that in some cases the *per incuriam* doctrine has been regarded as confined to the narrow formulation of *Morelle v. Wakeling*.[35] However, as *Williams v. Fawcett*[36] and cases following it were not cited they are presumably *per incuriam* on this point.

(ii) Conflicting decisions

Decisions in the Court of Appeal may conflict. The decision in case A may not be cited to the court in case B, whereas both cases A and B are cited in case C[37]; case A may not have been reported,[38] or may simply have been

---

[29] Lord Donaldson M.R. at p. 203 Balcombe L.J. at p. 206; Nicholls L.J. at p.210; *cf.* Lord Donald-son M.R. in *Langley v. North West Water Authority* [1991] 1 W.L.R. 697, confirming that "any departure from previous decisions of this court is in principle undesirable and should only be considered if the previous decision is manifestly wrong. Even then it will be necessary to take account of whether the decision purports to be of general application and whether there is any other way of remedying the error, for example, by encouraging an appeal to the House of Lords." This proposition was endorsed by the Court of Appeal in *Limb v. Union Jack Removals Ltd.* [1998] 1 W.L.R. 1354 at paras. 34, 35. However, the court confusingly seemed not to regard it as an aspect of the *per incuriam* doctrine itself. See further below, para. 7-020.

[30] [1992] BCLC 405.

[31] *per* Scott L.J. at p. 414.

[32] [1991] 1 Q.B. 740. See also *Jones v. Vans Colina* [1996] 1 W.L.R. 1580, where it was asserted that a decision regarded as incorrect was *per incuriam*, without further analysis.

[33] *The Times*, November 7 1984.

[34] Lord Taylor CJ. at p. 755 citing only this factor from the many mentioned by Lord Donaldson M.R. in *Williams v. Fawcett* [1986] Q.B. 604, 615 and 616.

[35] See above. See *e.g. ACE Insurance SA-NV v. Zurich Insurance Company* [2001] EWCA Civ. 173.

[36] See above.

[37] See the cases discussed in *Fisher v. Ruislip-Northwood Urban District Council* [1945] K.B. 584. The decision in case B may be regarded as given *per incuriam*: see *W. A. Sherratt Ltd v. John Bromley Church Stratton Ltd* [1985] Q.B. 1038.

[38] *e.g. Cathrineholm A/S v. Norequipment Trading Ltd* [1972] 2 Q.B. 314.

overlooked. Cases A and B may be decided by different divisions of the Court of Appeal at roughly the same time. Case A may be cited in case B but, in the view of the court in case C, erroneously interpreted. The resulting confusion may be settled by the Court of Appeal choosing which case or line of cases to follow and overruling any cases that conflict.[39] It has been argued that the court should be bound by the earlier case, case A (as the court in case B was not entitled to depart from it[40]) and, alternatively, that it should follow case B (as the later case[41]) but neither argument has prevailed.

(iii) Decisions impliedly overruled by the House of Lords

7–019   In *Young v. Bristol Aeroplane Co. Ltd.*[42] Lord Greene M.R. stated that the Court of Appeal was not bound by a previous decision which "although not expressly overruled, cannot stand with a subsequent decision of the House of Lords."[43] This principle was relied upon by Oliver J. in *Midland Bank Trust Co. Ltd v. Hett, Stubbs & Kemp*[44] where he declined to follow the decision of the Court of Appeal in *Groom v. Crocker*[45] on the ground that it was inconsistent with the subsequent decision of the House of Lords in *Hedley Byrne & Co. Ltd v. Heller & Partners Ltd.*[46]

(iv) Decisions on interlocutory appeals and applications for permission to appeal

7–020   In *Boys v. Chaplin*[47] the Court of Appeal held that it was not bound by a previous decision of the Court of Appeal where that court comprised two Lords Justices hearing an interlocutory appeal. It is the nature of the appeal that is crucial, not the number of members of the court. In *Langley v. North Western Water Authority*[48] the Court of Appeal affirmed, *obiter*,[49] that "the

[39] *ibid.; Ross-Smith v. Ross-Smith* [1961] P. 39; *Ashburn Anstalt v. Arnold* [1989] Ch. 1; *cf. Midland Bank Trust Co. Ltd v. Hett, Stubbs & Kemp.* [1979] Ch. 384; *Esselte AB v. Pearl Assurance plc* [1997] 1 W.L.R. 891.

[40] A.L. Goodhart, (1947) 9 C.L.J. 349. This point was expressly left open by the Court of Appeal in *Dairy International Ltd v. Tazzyman* [1997] 1W.L.R. 1256.

[41] R. N. Gooderson, (1950) 10 C.L.J. 432. This was given as one reason for choosing between conflicting decisions in *Circuit Systems Ltd v. Zuken-Redac (UK) Ltd* [1997] 1 W.L.R. 721. Conversely, it was expressly rejected as an argument in *Starmark Enterprises Ltd v. CPL Distribution Ltd* [2001] EWCA Civ. 1252, the Court of Appeal holding that the later of two conflicting decisions had erroneously distinguished the earlier, and that the earlier should be followed.

[42] [1944] K.B. 718.

[43] *ibid.* p. 722.

[44] [1979] Ch. 384. The case concerned the liability of a solicitor for negligence: see above, para. 3-044.

[45] [1939] 1 K.B. 194. Authorities following *Groom v. Crocker* and decided after *Hedley Byrne* were regarded as inconsistent with the decision of the Court of Appeal in *Esso Petroleum Co. Ltd v. Mardon* [1976] Q.B. 801.

[46] [1964] A.C. 465.

[47] [1968] 2 Q.B. 1. Applied in *Welsh Development Agency v. Redpath Dorman Long Ltd* [1994] 1 W.L.R. 1409, although the court there did not have its attention drawn to *Langley v. North West Water Authority* [1991] 1 W.L.R. 697.

[48] [1991] 1 W.L.R. 697.

[49] *per* Lord Donaldson M.R. at p. 710.

authority of a two judge court should today be regarded as being the same as that of a three judge court." It was not clear whether this was intended to cast doubt on the reasoning of *Boys v. Chaplin*.[50] Lord Donaldson M.R. noted that, in that case, Lord Denning M.R. and Diplock L.J.[51] relied on "the summary nature of the argument under the then existing practice in the case of interlocutory appeals heard by two judge courts"; he contrasted this with the "present practice", where the division of work between two and three-judge courts was not determined by whether there will be no need for other than brief argument or the point is of minimal importance other than to the immediate parties."[52] Since *Langley*, the distinction between interlocutory and final appeals has been abolished, and it is difficult to see what remains of the *Boys v. Chaplin* exception. In *Cave v. Robinson Jarvis and Rolfe*[53] Potter L.J. stated:[54]

"In a broad sense, the modern equivalent of the *Boys v. Chaplin* paradigm of a decision reached under time constraints and on the basis of brief argument is the decision of a Lord Justice or Lords Justices upon an oral application for leave to appeal."

Such decisions are not binding on later substantive appeals or applications for leave.[55] In *Cave*, the Court of Appeal followed a previous decision[56] of a two judge court on an interlocutory appeal, which though *ex tempore* had been carefully considered. Sedley L.J. suggested[57] that the decision not followed in *Boys v. Chaplin* would today be overset

"not because it was an interlocutory decision of a two-judge court, but either because this court was satisfied that it was outdated, unjust and incontestably wrong or because, this court having had to leave it standing, the House of Lords overruled it."

The Court of Appeal decision in *Cave* was overturned by the House of Lords, but the House did not express a view on whether the lower court had been right to follow *Brocklesby*.

(d) Possible exceptions to Young v. Bristol Aeroplane Co. Ltd

(i) Inconsistency with an earlier House of Lords decision

Lord Greene M.R.'s summary of conclusions in the *Young's* case and the head notes of most of the reports indicate that a Court of Appeal decision which is inconsistent with *any* House of Lords case, whether prior or subsequent, does not bind the Court of Appeal. The relevant passage from

7–021

---

[50] [1968] 2 Q.B. 1.
[51] At pp. 23 and 35 respectively.
[52] [1991] 1 W.L.R. at p. 710.
[53] [2001] EWCA Civ 245 [2002] 1 W.L.R. 581.
[54] para. [24].
[55] *ibid*; *Clarke v. University of Lincolnshire and Humberside* [2000] 3 All E.R. 752, 761–762.
[56] *Brocklesby v. Armitage & Guest (Note)* [2002] 1 W.L.R. 598.
[57] para. [31].

the main body of Lord Greene's judgment,[58] however, includes the word "subsequent." Moreover, in *Williams v. Glasbrook Bros.*[59] Lord Greene expressly asserted that the exception was so limited; if the Court of Appeal misinterprets an earlier House of Lords decision "nobody but the House of Lords can put that mistake right."[60] This position has been supported by Lord Denning M.R.[61] and Lord Simon,[62] and is to be preferred "in the interests of certainty."[63] Against these authorities, and in favour of a more widely drawn exception to *Young's* case, are the decision of the Court of Appeal in *Fitzsimons v. The Ford Motor Co.*[64] and the opinion of Lord Cross in *Miliangos v. George Frank (Textiles) Ltd.*[65]

The *Miliangos* case illustrates some of the difficulties that can arise. In 1960 the House of Lords in the *Havana* case[66] made a decision which was based on the unchallenged assumption that a judgment in an English court could only be given in sterling. The actual point in issue was the date at which a debt payable in U.S. dollars had to be converted to the equivalent in sterling for the purposes of proceedings in England to enforce payment. In *Schorsch Meier G.m.b.H. v. Hennin*[67] the Court of Appeal[68] held (1) that the operation of the *Havana* case had been limited by Article 106 of the EEC Treaty (since repealed), which was regarded as enabling EEC nationals to obtain judgments in a foreign currency and (2) (Lawton L.J. dissenting) that in any event the *Havana* rule could be disregarded as the fact that sterling was no longer a stable currency meant that the rationale behind the rule no longer stood. On the latter point, the majority founded themselves on the maxim *cessante ratione legis cessat ipsa lex* (if the reason for a law ceases to be valid the law itself ceases). In *Miliangos v. George Franks (Textiles) Ltd* a plaintiff who was not an EEC national sought to take advantage of the second *ratio* of *Schorsch Meier*. Bristow J.[69] held that he was obliged to follow the House of Lords decision in *Havana* in preference to that of the Court of Appeal in *Schorsch Meier*, notwithstanding the fact that it had been cited to the court in *Schorsch Meier*. The *Havana* rule could only be altered by statute or another decision of the House. On appeal, the Court of Appeal[70] then held that *Schorsch Meier* was binding (1) on courts beneath the Court of Appeal in the hierarchy and (2) on the Court of Appeal itself, the relevant exception to *Young v. Bristol Aeroplane Co. Ltd* being confined to inconsistent *subsequent* House of Lords decisions. The House of Lords held (1) that the Court of Appeal had acted incorrectly in *Schorsch Meier* in failing to follow *Havana*; but (2) (Lord Simon dissenting) that the *Havana*

---

[58] Above, para. 7-017.

[59] [1947] 2 All E.R. 884.

[60] *ibid.* p. 885. If the House of Lords decision had not been cited, the Court of Appeal decision would be *per incuriam*: see above.

[61] *Miliangos v. George Frank (Textiles) Ltd* [1975] Q.B. 416, 502.

[62] *ibid.* [1976] A.C. 443, 478–479.

[63] Sir Rupert Cross, *Precedent in English Law* (3rd ed., 1977), p. 143, a statement omitted from the fourth edition.

[64] [1946] 1 All E.R. 429. This was not cited in *Williams v. Glasbrook Bros.*

[65] [1976] A.C. 443, 496.

[66] *United Railways of Havana and Regla Warehouses Ltd* [1961] A.C. 1007.

[67] [1975] Q.B. 416.

[68] Lord Denning M.R., Lawton L.J. and Foster J.

[69] [1975] Q.B. 487, 491.

[70] [1975] Q.B. 487, 499.

case should be overruled. As to the dilemma facing the trial judge and the Court of Appeal in *Miliangos*, Lord Cross[71] took the view that *Schorsch Meier* should not have been followed (endorsing Bristow J.'s approach), Lord Simon[72] thought that the Court of Appeal in *Miliangos* had acted correctly, and the other members of the House of Lords expressed no definite opinion.[73] The position taken by Bristow J. and Lord Cross assumes that:

> "the *Schorsch Meier* majority decision was not law in any proper sense, since it was reached in total disregard of the proper law as it then existed in a rule of the House of Lords, and which ... bound the Court of Appeal to reach a decision contrary to that actually reached."[74]

However, the analogous argument is not accepted in cases of "horizontal conflict" between decisions in the same court. Thus, where Court of Appeal decisions conflict, the Court of Appeal in a subsequent case may choose which to follow.[75]

More recently, in *Holden & Co. v. Crown Prosecution Service*[76] the Court of Appeal asserted a preference for the broader view, relying on a dictum of Lord Wright in *Noble v. Southern Railway Co.*[77] However, none of the other relevant authorities on the point were cited (except *Young v. Bristol Aeroplane Co. Ltd*[78] itself) and the decision on this point might therefore be open to challenge as reached *per incuriam*.

(ii) Inconsistency with a Privy Council decision

In *Worcester Works Finance Ltd v. Cooden Engineering Co. Ltd*[79] Lord Denning M.R. said:[80]   **7–022**

> "Although decisions of the Privy Council are not binding on this Court, nevertheless when the Privy Council disapproves of a previous decision of this Court or casts doubt on it, we are at liberty to depart from the previous decision."

This statement can be seen as part of Lord Denning's battle against the rule that the Court of Appeal is bound by its own previous decisions, and it is not clear whether it is still authoritative in the light of the strictures of the House of Lords in *Davis v. Johnson*.[81]

---

[71] [1976] A.C. 443, 496.
[72] [1976] A.C. 443, 470.
[73] Professor Cross thought the desirability of contradictory statements on this point to be "highly questionable" and that there was "something to be said for the discreet silence" of the other three members of the House: P. M. S. Hacker and J. Raz (eds.), *Law, Morality and Society* (1977), p. 153.
[74] C. E. F. Rickett, (1980) 43 M.L.R. 136, 141.
[75] See above, para. 7-018.
[76] [1990] 2 Q.B. 261, *per* Lord Lane C. J. at p. 272.
[77] [1940] A.C. 583, 598.
[78] [1944] K.B. 718.
[79] [1972] 1 Q.B. 210.
[80] At p. 217.
[81] Below. On the Privy Council and precedent see further below, paras 7-028, 7-032.

(iii) Other possibilities[82]

7–023   In *B. v. B.*[83] the Court of Appeal held that section 1(1) of the Domestic
Violence and Matrimonial Proceedings Act 1976 did not give a county court
jurisdiction to grant an injunction excluding a spouse[84] from the from the
"matrimonial home" where that spouse had a proprietary interest in the
home. A few days later this decision was followed by the Court of Appeal in
Cantliff v. Jenkins.[85] These cases caused some consternation, as the plain
words of the statute seemed to give the county court that jurisdiction. The
point was raised again in *Davis v. Johnson,* and a five-member Court of
Appeal was assembled.[86] Only Cumming-Bruce L.J. held that the earlier
cases were correctly decided. Goff L.J. held that they were binding even
though they were wrong. The other three members of the court held that
they were wrong, and, on a variety of grounds, not binding. Lord Denning
said that:

> "while the court should regard itself as normally bound by a previous
> decision of the court, nevertheless it should be at liberty to depart from
> it if it is convinced that the previous decision was wrong."[87]

Either the Court of Appeal should take for itself guidelines similar to those
taken by the House of Lords,[88] or this should be regarded as an additional
exception to *Young v. Bristol Aeroplane Co. Ltd.*[89] Lord Denning had long
argued for such a change,[90] but had been unable to convince either his
colleagues or the House of Lords.

Sir George Baker P. was prepared to distinguish *B. v. B.* on the ground
that the welfare of a child was not involved as it was in *Davis v. Johnson.* If
that distinction were not acceptable,[91] a new exception to *Young v. Bristol
Aeroplane Co. Ltd* should be created:

> "The Court is not bound to follow a previous decision of its own if
> satisfied that that decision was clearly wrong and cannot stand in the
> face of the will and intention of Parliament expressed in simple
> language in a recent statute passed to remedy a serious mischief or
> abuse, and further adherence to the previous decision must lead to

---

[82] See also *R. v. Secretary of State for the Home Department, ex p. Al-Mehdawi* [1990] 1 A.C.
876, above, para. 7-009.

[83] [1978] Fam. 26, decided on October 13, 1977 by Bridge, Waller and Megaw L.JJ.

[84] Whether real, or for want of a better expression, "common law".

[85] [1978] Fam. 47, decided on October 20, 1977 by Stamp, Orr and Ormrod L.JJ. The couple
were joint tenants.

[86] [1979] A.C. 264. Lord Denning M.R., Sir George Baker P., Goff, Shaw and Cumming-Bruce
L.JJ.: described by Lord Denning as "a court of all the talents" [1979] A.C. 264, 271.

[87] [1979] A.C. 264, 278–282.

[88] See below, paras 7-026, 7-027.

[89] [1944] K.B. 718.

[90] *The Discipline of Law* (1979), pp. 297–300; *Gallie v. Lee* [1969] 2 Ch. 17, 37; *Hanning v.
Maitland (No. 2)* [1970] 1 Q.B. 580, 587; *Barrington v. Lee* [1972] 1 Q.B. 326, 338. He
temporarily conceded defeat in *Tiverton Estates Ltd v. Wearwell Ltd* [1975] Ch. 146, 160–
161, but raised the point again in *Davis v. Johnson* and suffered a "crushing rebuff" (*The
Discipline of Law* (1979), p. 299).

[91] That this distinction was not acceptable was subsequently conceded in the House of Lords.

injustice in the particular case and unduly restrict proper development of the law with injustice to others."[92]

Shaw L.J. suggested a new exception to *Young's* case that was even narrower:

"in some such terms as that the principle of *stare decisis* should be relaxed where its application would have the effect of depriving actual and potential victims of violence of a vital protection which an Act of Parliament was plainly designed to afford to them, especially where, as in the context of domestic violence, that deprivation must inevitably give rise to an irremediable detriment to such victims and create in regard to them an injustice irreversible by a later decision of the House of Lords."[93]

The House of Lords unanimously dismissed an appeal; *B. v. B.* and *Cantliff v. Jenkins* were overruled.[94] However, the House strongly reafffirmed the rule that the Court of Appeal was bound by its own previous decisions, subject to clearly defined exceptions which did not include those advanced in the Court of Appeal. The argument in favour of *Young's* case was summarised by Lord Diplock[95]:

"In an appellate court of last resort a balance must be struck between the need on the one hand for the legal certainty resulting from the binding effect of previous decisions, and, on the other side the avoidance of undue restriction on the proper development of the law. In the case of an intermediate appellate court, however, the second desideratum can be taken care of by appeal to a superior appellate court, if reasonable means of access to it are available; while the risk to the first desideratum, legal certainty if the court is not bound by its own previous decisions grows even greater with increasing membership and the number of three-judge divisions in which it sits ... ."

The argument against is that "the House of Lords may never have an opportunity to correct [an] error; and thus it may be perpetuated indefinitely, perhaps for ever."[96] Litigants may be unable to finance a further appeal; the case may be settled; an insurance company or big employer who wins in the Court of Appeal may " buy off an appeal to the House of Lords by paying ample compensation to the appellant."[97] Lord

---

[92] [1979] A.C. 264, 290.
[93] [1979] A.C. 264, 308.
[94] Lord Diplock alone thought that *B. v. B.* had been correctly decided, making the overall division of appellate judicial opinion eight all: [1979] A.C. 264,323. That case had concerned the situation where the man was sole tenant. However, his Lordship held that an injunction could be awarded where both parties were joint tenants: as the facts of *Davis v. Johnson* fell into that category he was in favour of dismissing the appeal.
[95] [1979] A.C. 264, 326. Viscount Dilhorne, Lord Kilbrandon, and Lord Scarman expressly agreed with Lord Diplock's views on precedent: [1979] A.C. 264, 336, 340, 349. See also Scarman LJ. in *Tiverton Estates Ltd v. Wearwell Ltd* [1975] Ch. 146, 172–173 and in *Farrell v. Alexander* [1976] Q.B. 345, 371.
[96] *per* Lord Denning M.R. in *Davis v. Johnson* [1979] A.C. 264, 278.
[97] *ibid.* p. 278.

Diplock responded by pointing out that in view of *Cantliff v. Jenkins* there had been no need for anything but the briefest of hearings in the Court of Appeal, and an appeal to the House could have been heard and decided quickly. The argument of delay and expense could also be used to justify any High Court or county court judge in refusing to follow a decision of the Court of Appeal that he thought was wrong. There is also the possibility of using the "leap-frog" procedure under the Administration of Justice Act 1969.[98]

Lord Salmon expressed some sympathy for Lord Denning's views, but said that "until such time, if ever, as all his colleagues in the Court of Appeal agree with those views, *stare decisis* must still hold the field."[99] In view of the large number of Lord Justices, keeping to *stare decisis* might be "no bad thing". He suggested that where the Court of Appeal gave leave to appeal from a decision it felt bound to make by authority and with which it disagreed, it should have the statutory power to order that the costs of the appeal be paid from public funds. This would be a very rare occurrence, and the cost minimal.

According to the Court of Appeal *stare decisis* does not prevent an English court giving effect to a change in a rule of international law notwithstanding the existence of English precedents based on the old rule.[1] It also seems that the Court of Appeal is not bound by its own previous decisions where it is the court of last resort, with no possible appeal to the House of Lords.[2]

(e) Can lower tiers rely on the exceptions to Young v. Bristol Aeroplane Co. Ltd?

7–024   This question was answered in the negative by Lord Hailsham L.C. in *Cassell & Co. Ltd v. Broome*,[3] but there have been cases where the Divisional Court or a trial judge has declined to follow a decision of the Court of Appeal on the ground that it was inconsistent with a House of Lords decision,[4] and the point cannot be regarded as settled. It is difficult, for

---

[98]   See below, para. 18-038. Lord Diplock [1979] A.C. 264, 324–325.

[99]   [1979] A.C. 264, 344.

[1]   *Trendtex Trading Corporation v. Central Bank of Nigeria* [1977] Q.B. 529, 554 (Lord Denning M.R.), 579 (Shaw L.J.) (a case on the scope of the doctrine of state immunity). Stephenson L.J. dissented on this point. The Court of Appeal's decision was followed by Robert Goff J. and the Court of Appeal in *I Congreso del Partido* [1978] Q.B. 500 and [1981] 1 All E.R. 1092, and Lloyd J. in *Planmount Ltd v. Republic of Zaire* [1981] 1 All E.R. 1110; but not by Donaldson J. in *Uganda Co. (Holdings) Ltd v. Government of Uganda* [1979] 1 Lloyd's Rep. 481. The House of Lords in *I Congreso del Partido* endorsed the general approach of the Court of Appeal in *Trendtex* but did not advert to the "precedent" aspect: [1983] 1 A.C. 244.

[2]   Lord Denning M.R. in *Davis v. Johnson* [1979] A.C. 264, 282.

[3]   [1972] A.C. 1027, 1054; above, para. 7-015. In *Baker v. The Queen* [1975] A.C. 774, 788, Lord Diplock stated that a lower court could not rely on the *per incuriam* rule in relation to the decision of a higher court, but could choose between conflicting decisions.

[4]   *R. v. Northumberland Compensation Appeal Tribunal, ex p. Shaw* [1951] 1 K.B. 711, where the Divisional Court declined to follow the decision of the Court of Appeal in *Racecourse Betting Control Board v. Secretary for Air* [1944] Ch. 114 on the ground that it was inconsistent with the views expressed by the House of Lords in *Walsall Overseers v. L.N.W. Ry. Co.* (1878) 4 App.Cas.30 and the Privy Council in *R. v. Nat. Bell Liquors Ltd* [1922] 2 A.C. 128, which cases had not been cited. The *Shaw* case was not cited in *Cassell & Co. Ltd v. Broome*. See also *Midland Bank v. Hen, Stubbs & Kemp*, above, para. 7-019; *The Alexandros P.* [1986] Q.B. 464; *Hughes v. Kingston upon Hull City Council* [1999] Q.B. 1193.

example, to see that a trial judge should follow a decision of a higher court given in ignorance of a binding statutory provision. According to Lord Denning M.R., where decisions of the same court conflict, lower courts should follow the later case[5]; Donaldson J. disagreed.[6]

6. THE COURT OF APPEAL (CRIMINAL DIVISION)[7]

This court is obviously bound by decisions of the House of Lords. It is also generally bound by its own previous decisions and those of its forerunners, the Court of Criminal Appeal and the Court for Crown Cases Reserved. However, as the liberty of the subject is involved, *stare decisis* is not applied with the same rigidity as in the Civil Division. A decision may not be followed if it falls within one of the established exceptions to *Young v. Bristol Aeroplane Co. Ltd.*[8] An example is *R. v. Gould*[9] where the Court of, Appeal (Criminal Division) followed a decision of the Court of Crown Cases Reserved in 1889[10] in preference to a later conflicting decision of the Court of Criminal Appeal in 1921,[11] on the question whether *mens rea* was an essential ingredient of the offence of bigamy. In addition, Diplock L.J. stated in *Gould* that:

7–025

"if upon due consideration we were to be of opinion that the law had been either misapplied or misunderstood in an earlier decision of this court or its predecessor, the Court of Criminal Appeal, we should be entitled to depart from the view as to the law expressed in the earlier decision notwithstanding that the case could not be brought within any of the exceptions laid down in *Young v. Bristol Aeroplane Co. Ltd.*"[12]

It has been uncertain whether this power is available wherever the court is convinced that the earlier decision is wrong, as this *dictum* suggests, or only where overruling is in the interests of the defendant. The preponderance of authority supports the latter, narrower view. A clear statement was made by the court in *R. v. Spencer*[13]:

---

[5] *Davis v. Johnson* [1979] A.C. 264, 279. See to the same effect *Taylor Woodrow Property Co. Ltd v. Lonrho Textiles Ltd* [1985] 2 EGLR 120, B. Hytner Q.C. (sitting as a deputy High Court judge); Warner J. in *Re Smith (a bankrupt)* [1988] Ch. 457.

[6] *Uganda Co. (Holdings) Ltd v. Government of Uganda* [1979] 1 Lloyd's Rep. 481, 485: a trial judge should "seek to anticipate how the Court of Appeal itself would ... resolve the conflict."

[7] See G. Zellick, [1974] Crim.L.R. 222; R. Pattenden, [1984] Crim.L.R. 592.

[8] [1944] K.B. 718. See above, paras 7–016–7–023. For an example of an application of the *per incuriam* doctrine, see *R. v. Ewing* [1983] Q.B. 1039, disapproving *R. v. Angeli* [1979] 1 W.L.R. 26 on the ground that it could not stand with the decision of the House of Lords in *Blyth v. Blyth* [1966] A.C. 643; and *R. v. El-Gazzar* (1986) 8 Cr.App.(S) 182.

[9] [1968] 2 Q.B. 65. Other examples are *R. v. Preece, R. v. Howells* (1976) 63 Cr.App.R. 28; *R. v. Maginnis* [1986] Q.B. 618.

[10] *R. v. Tolson* (1889) 23 Q.B.D. 168.

[11] *R. v. Wheat* [1921] 2 K.B. 119.

[12] [1968] 2 Q.B. 65, 69.

[13] [1985] Q.B. 771. Followed in *R. v. Pope (Alan)* [2001] EWCA Crim 972 where no exception to *Young* was available.

"As a matter of principle we respectfully find it difficult to see why there should in general be any difference in the application of the principle of *stare decisis* between the Civil and Criminal Divisions of the Court, save that we must remember that in the latter we may be dealing with the liberty of the subject[14] and if a departure from authority is necessary in the interests of justice to an appellant, then this court should not shrink from so acting."[15]

This restriction does not apply to decisions on matters of sentencing. In *R. v. Newsome, R. v. Browne*[16] the Court of Appeal (Criminal Division) overruled two earlier decisions of the court[17] to the effect that a judge could not increase a sentence of imprisonment once passed to ensure that it would not be suspended even if this were to be done immediately. Widgery L.J. said[18] that if a court of five members is constituted:

"to consider an issue of discretion and the principles upon which discretion should be exercised, that court ought to have the right to depart from an earlier view expressed by a court of three, especially where it was a matter in which the court did not have the opportunity of hearing argument on both sides."

The view that a "full court"[19] has greater power to overrule than an ordinarily constituted court was also held by the Court of Criminal Appeal,[20] although it has been rejected by the Divisional Court[21] and the Court of Appeal.[22] It seems in practice that a full court is not necessary where one of the exceptions to *Young v. Bristol Aeroplane Co. Ltd* is applied, but is thought appropriate where overruling is contemplated on wider grounds.[23] In *Newsome* Widgery L.J. stressed that the court would be more reluctant to depart from an earlier decision where guilt or innocence was

---

[14] The defendant's "liberty" appears not to be at stake where he or she has been fined but not imprisoned: *R. v. Burke* [1988] Crim.L.R. 839, C.A.

[15] *ibid.*, p. 779, *per* May L.J. See, to the same effect, Lord Goddard C.J. in *R. v. Taylor* [1950] 2 K.B. 368, 371 (Court of Criminal Appeal), referring to the "bounden duty" of the court to reconsider an erroneous decision, on the strength of which "an accused person has been sentenced and imprisoned"; Lord Diplock, *obiter*, in *D.P.P. v. Merriman* [1973] A.C. 584, 605: the liberty of the court "to depart from a precedent which it is convinced was erroneous is restricted to cases where the departure is in favour of the accused": this *dictum* was applied by the court in *R. v. Jenkins* (1983) 76 Cr.App.R. 313, 318 (the better view here is that the consideration was irrelevant as the court was choosing between conflicting decisions and not overruling a single decision: J. C. Smith, [1983] Crim.L.R. at pp. 388–389), and in *R. v. Howe* [1986] Q.B. 626, 642.

[16] [1970] 2 Q.B. 711, decided in July 1970.

[17] *R. v. Corr, The Times*, January 16, 1970 and *R. v. Maylam* (unreported) decided on February, 26 1970. In *Newsome and Browne*, the actual sentences were suspended as it was "the only fair thing to do" (a form of prospective overruling: see below, para. 7-027).

[18] At p. 717.

[19] A term which usually denotes a court of more than the usual number of judges (*e.g.* five or seven for the Divisional Court, five for the Court of Appeal and seven in the House of Lords) and not a court of all the judges eligible to sit.

[20] *R. v. Taylor* [1950] 2 K.B. 368.

[21] *Younghusband v. Luftig* [1949] 2 K.B. 354: curiously, a criminal case.

[22] In the exercise of its civil jurisdiction: *Young v. Bristol Aeroplane Co. Ltd* [1944] K.B. 718, 725.

[23] *Gould* was decided by a three-member court: see Zellick [1974] Crim.L.R. 222, 231–232.

involved as distinct from the exercise of the court's discretion. In practice, the court seems reluctant to depart from its own previous decisions, even where it regards them as doubtful, and overruling would be in the accused's interests. Instead, the matter is left for the House of Lords.[24]

It is uncertain whether the Court of Appeal (Criminal Division) is bound by decisions of the Court of Appeal (Civil Division), and *vice versa*. Before reorganisation the Court of Appeal and Court of Criminal Appeal seemed not to be bound by each other's decisions.[25]

A decision of the court is treated as a binding authority notwithstanding that the appellant who has won the argument on the point of law has had his or her appeal dismissed under the proviso to section 2 of the Criminal Appeal Act 1968.[26]

7. THE HOUSE OF LORDS

Decisions of the House of Lords are[27] binding on courts lower in the hierarchy, including, if not especially, the Court of Appeal. In *London Tramways v. London County Council*[28] the House of Lords held that it was bound by its own previous decisions in the interests of finality and certainty in the law. It was accepted that a decision could be questioned where it conflicted with another decision of the House or was made *per incuriam*.[29] Other exceptions were suggested. However, ever, as the House was the final court of appeal the correction of error was normally dependent on the vagaries of the legislative process. In 1966 Lord Gardiner L.C. made the

7–026

---

[24] See the cases discussed by R. Pattenden, [1984] Crim.L.R. 592, 599–602. Pattenden's argument that the "special exception" in criminal cases no longer survives predates the reaffirmation of its existence in *R. v. Spencer*, n. 13 above.

[25] See *Hardie & Lane v. Chilton* [1928] 2 K.B. 306, C.A. versus *R. v. Denyer* [1926] 2 K.B. 258, C.C.A. and the statement of Lord Hewart C.J. in the Court of Criminal Appeal at 20 Cr. App. Rep. 185.

[26] As originally enacted; see below, para. 18-013. Here the distinction between *ratio* and *dictum* is "meaningless in practice": Cross and Harris (1991), p. 80; above, paras 7-003–7-009.

[27] The dismissal by the House of Lords of a petition for leave to appeal against a decision of a lower court does not constitute implied approval of that decision by the House: *Re Wilson* [1985] A.C. 750, 756.

[28] [1898] A.C. 375: not "London Street Tramways" see the list of errata at the start of the [1898] A.C. volume (Cross and Harris (1991), p. 102, n. 22). See D. Pugsley, (1996) 17 Legal History 172.

[29] See above, para. 7-017. For an example of a choice by the House of Lords between two conflicting decisions of its own, see *Moodie v. Inland Revenue Commissioners* [1993] 1 W.L.R. 266 (following *Ramsay (W.T.) Ltd v. I.R.C.* in preference to *I.R.C. v. Plummer* [1980] A.C. 896). See J. Tiley, [1991] B.T.R. 402; D. Sandler, [1993] C.LJ. 399. Lord Templeman stated (at p. 273): "Faced with conflicting decisions, the courts are entitled and bound to follow *Ramsay's* case because in *Plummer's* case this House was never asked to consider the effect of a self-cancelling scheme and because the principle of *Ramsay's* case restores justice between individual taxpayers and the general body of taxpayers." It is submitted that these are substantive reasons for preferring *Ramsay*, rather than a rule that the later of two conflicting decisions must always be followed.

following statement on behalf of himself and the Lords of Appeal in Ordinary[30]:

> "Their Lordships regard the use of precedent as an indispensable foundation upon which to decide what is the law and its application to individual cases. It provides at least some degree of certainty upon which individuals can rely on the conduct of their affairs, as well as a basis for orderly development of legal rules.
>
> Their Lordships nevertheless recognise that too rigid adherence to precedent may lead to injustice in a particular case and also unduly restrict the proper development of the law. They propose, therefore, to modify their present practice and, while treating former decisions of this House as normally binding, to depart from a previous decision when it appears right to do so.
>
> In this connection they will bear in mind the danger of disturbing retrospectively the basis on which contracts, settlements of property and fiscal arrangements have been entered into and also the especial need for certainty as to the criminal law.
>
> This announcement is not intended to affect the use of precedent elsewhere than in this House."

A press notice issued at the same time[31] indicated that the statement was of great importance although it should not be supposed that it would frequently be applied. An example of a case where it might be used would be where an earlier decision was "influenced by the existence of conditions which no longer prevail, and that in modern conditions the law ought to be different." The change would also enable the House to pay greater attention to Commonwealth decisions critical of the House. As predicted the power has been used sparingly. Members of the House seem reluctant to state expressly that an earlier decision is "overruled" even where that appears to be the case.

The decision in *The Aello*[32] on a point of shipping law[33] was overruled in the *Johanna Oldendorff*.[34] As we have seen, the *Havana* case,[35] or at least the assumption upon which it was based, was overruled in *Miliangos v. George Frank (Textiles) Ltd.*[36] The decision in *Congreve v. Inland Revenue*

---

[30] *Practice Statement (Judicial Precedent)* [1966] 1 W.L.R. 1234. Lord Denning M.R. and Lord Parker CJ. were also present. See R. W. M. Dias, [1966] C.L.J. 153; R. Stone, [1968] C.L.J. 35; J. Stone, (1969) 69 Columbia L. R. 1162. The circumstances surrounding the introduction of the Statement and the way in which it has been used are examined by A. Paterson in *The Law Lords* (1982), Chap. 6 and pp. 154–169 and G. Maher, [1981] Stat.L.R. 85. See also below, para. 7-031.

[31] See M. Zander, *The Law-Making Process* (4th ed., 1994), pp. 192–193.

[32] [1961] A.C. 135.

[33] The test for determining when a ship has "arrived" in port. The expense of delay in discharging cargo from an "arrived" ship caused, for example, by congestion at the berths, normally falls on the charterer and not on the owners of the vessel.

[34] *E. L. Oldendorff v. Tradax Export* [1974] A.C. 479. This was the first occasion when the statement was clearly used. It has been argued that it had already been used in *Conway v. Rimmer* [1968] A.C. 910 and *British Railways Board v. Herrington* [1972] A.C. 879: see Paterson (1982), p. 164. On *Conway v. Rimmer*, see J. Stone, *op. cit.* n. 30 above.

[35] [1961] A.C. 1007: see above, para. 7-021.

[36] [1976] A.C. 443. In the same year the Statement was used in the Scottish case of *Dick v. Burgh of Falkirk* 1976 S.L.T. 21.

Commissioners[37] was overruled in *Vestey v. Inland Revenue Commissioners (Nos.1 and 2)*[38] on the ground that the earlier decision, on a point of construction of a Finance Act, had led to unforeseen results that were "arbitrary, potentially unjust and fundamentally unconstitutional."[39] The law as to the liability of the occupiers of land towards trespassers was restated by the House, with some differences of formulation among their Lordships, in *British Railways Board v. Herrington*.[40] The law as expounded, more restrictively, by the House in *Robert Addie & Sons (Collieries) Ltd v. Dumbreck*[41] was, according to the headnote in the Law Reports, "reconsidered".[42] Then, the House in *R. v. Secretary of State for the Home Department, ex p. Khawaja*[43] overruled the decision in *R. v. Secretary of State for the Home Department, ex p. Zamir*[44] holding that a person could only be removed as an "illegal immigrant" if the *court* was satisfied that the entry was illegal: it would no longer be sufficient that the *immigration officer* was satisfied and had some evidence for that belief. The issue concerned the liberty of the subject and did not fall into any of the categories in which the *Practice Statement* indicated the need for special caution.

Most spectacularly, the House of Lords in *R. v. Shivpuri*[45] overruled its earlier decision in *Anderton v. Ryan*[46] which had misinterpreted the Criminal Attempts Act 1981 in holding that a defence of impossibility in the criminal law had to an extent survived the Act. *Anderton v. Ryan* had been adversely criticised by almost all the academic commentators, most notably by Professor Glanville Williams in an article in the Cambridge Law Journal.[47] Among the grounds for Professor Williams' criticism were that the House disregarded (1) the bulk of the relevant academic literature, (2) the Law Commission report that led to the 1981 Act[48] and (3) the plain words of the Act. Lord Bridge, who had been a party to the decision in *Anderton v. Ryan*, delivered the main speech in *R. v. Shivpuri*. He acknowledged that the earlier decision was wrong, that there was no valid ground on which it could be distinguished, and that it should be overruled, notwithstanding the "especial need for certainty in the criminal law".[49] He was undeterred by the consideration that *Anderton v. Ryan* was recent: "If serious error is embodied in a decision of this house has distorted the law, the sooner it is

7–027

---

[37] [1948] 1 All E.R. 948.
[38] [1980] A.C. 1148.
[39] *per* Lord Wilberforce at p. 1176.
[40] [1972] A.C. 879.
[41] [1929] A.C. 358.
[42] Lord Reid's word at p. 879. Lord Reid (p. 898) and Lord Morris did, however, say that *Addie's* case was "wrongly decided." Lord Pearson regarded the *Addie* formulation as an "anomaly" which "should be discarded" (p. 930). Lord Diplock rejected it "as amounting to an exclusive or comprehensive statement" of the duty owed to a trespasser (p. 941). Lord Wilberforce spoke of "developing" the law in *Addie's* case (p. 921). See now the Occupiers' Liability Act 1984.
[43] [1984] A.C. 74.
[44] [1980] A.C. 930.
[45] [1987] A.C. 1.
[46] [1985] A.C. 560.
[47] "The Lords and Impossible Attempts, or *Quis Custodiet Ipsos Custodes?*" [1986] C.LJ. 33.
[48] *Attempt, and Impossibility in relation to Attempt, Conspiracy and Incitement* (Law Com. No. 102, 1980).
[49] A reference to the 1966 *Practice Statement*, above para. 7-026.

corrected the better."[50] He could not see how anyone could have acted in reliance on *Anderton v. Ryan* in the belief that he or she was acting innocently, and now find that, after all, he or she was to be held to have committed a criminal offence. A decision to follow *Anderton v. Ryan* would "be tantamount to a declaration that the Act of 1981 left the law of criminal attempts unchanged following the decision in *R. v. Smith (Roger)*."[51] He concluded by referring to Professor Williams' article:

"The language in which he criticises the decision in *Anderton v. Ryan* is not conspicuous for its moderation, but it would be foolish, on that account, not to recognise the force of the criticism and churlish not to acknowledge the assistance I have derived from it."[52]

Nine months later, in *R. v. Howe*[53] the House of Lords again departed from an earlier decision in a criminal law case, overruling *D.P.P. for Northern Ireland v. Lynch*.[54] In *Howe*, it was held that duress can never be a defence to murder: in *Lynch* it had been held that it could be raised as a defence by a principal in the second degree, albeit not the actual killer. Here, the arguments in favour of overruling were significantly weaker than in *R. v. Shivpuri*.[55] Finally, in *Murphy v. Brentwood District Council*,[56] the House overruled its decision in *Anns v. Merton London Borough Council*,[57] and held that a local authority owes no duty of care in tort to protect the purchaser of a house from economic losses caused by defects in the house. *Anns* was contrary to established principle, and overruling would restore certainty to the law.

Other invitations to the House to overrule a past decision have not been accepted. A remarkable example is *Jones v. Secretary of State for Social Services*[58] where four out of seven members of the House held that the earlier decision of the House in *Re Dowling*[59] on a point of national insurance law[60] was incorrect, but only three thought that *Re Dowling*

---

[50] [1987] A.C. 1, 23.

[51] [1975] A.C. 476, also known as *Haughton v. Smith* [1973] 3 All E.R. 1109, H.L. Criticism of this decision had led to the 1981 Act.

[52] [1987] A.C. 1, 23. Professor Williams' campaign on this issue stretched over decades: see P. S. Atiyah, *Pragmatism and Theory in English Law* (1987), pp. 180–183. On *Shivpuri*, see J. R. Spencer, [1986] C.L.J. 361; P. R. Glazebrook, [1986] C.L.J. 363; [1986] Crim.L.R. 536, commentary by J. C. Smith; E. M. Clare Canton, (1987) 137 N.L.J. 491, also commenting on *Howe*, below.

[53] [1987] A.C. 417.

[54] [1975] A.C. 653.

[55] See [1987] Crim.L.R. 480, commentary by J. C. Smith; C. Gearty, [1987] C.L.J. 203; H. P. Milgate, "Duress and the Criminal Law: Another about turn by the House of Lords" [1988] C.L.J. 61; L. Walters, "Murder under duress and judicial decision-making in the House of Lords" (1988) 8 L.S. 61.

[56] [1991] 1 A.C. 398. See J. W. Harris, (1991) 11 O.J.L.S. 416.

[57] [1978] A.C. 728.

[58] [1972] A.C. 944. Alternatively entitled *R. v. National Insurance Commissioners, ex p. Hudson*. See J. Stone, (1972) 35 M.L.R. 449, 469–477.

[59] *R. v. Deputy Industrial Injuries Commissioner, ex p. Amalgamated Engineering Union, re Dowling* [1967] 1 A.C. 725.

[60] Whether a decision by a National Insurance Commissioner (adjudicating a claim for industrial injuries benefit) that injuries were caused by an industrial accident, was binding on a Medical Appeal Tribunal (adjudicating a subsequent claim for industrial disablement benefit).

should be overruled. The main "defector" was Lord Simon of Glaisdale, who stated[61] that the 1966 declaration should be used most sparingly; that a variation of view on a matter of statutory construction would rarely provide a suitable occasion for its use unless it could be convincingly shown that a previous, erroneous, construction was causing administrative difficulties or individual injustice; that the House should be reluctant to encourage litigants to reopen arguments once concluded; that there was much to be said for each side of this case; and that *Re Dowling* was not unworkable and could in any event be altered more appropriately by Parliament.[62] In *Fitzleet Estates Ltd v. Cherry*[63] the House refused to review a 1965 majority decision on a point of tax law, in the absence of any new argument, any change of circumstances or any suggestion that it was productive of injustice. In *Hesperides Hotels Ltd v. Muftizade*[64] the House declined to modify the long established rule that the High Court has no jurisdiction to entertain an action for damages for trespass to land situated abroad.[65] The rule was accepted in other jurisdictions, a change might involve conflict with foreign jurisdictions and there had been no change of circumstances. In *President of India v. La Pintada Compania Navigacion S. A.*[66] the House declined to depart from an earlier decision[67] that the common law does not award general damages for delay in payment of a debt. Much of the injustice caused by this decision had been removed by a combination of legislative and judicial intervention; Parliament had declined to accept a recommendation from the Law Commission[68] that would have covered the case here, while accepting other recommendations in the area; and reversal of the common law rule would have the effect of overriding restrictions in the statutory provisions that had been enacted. Perhaps the most remarkable recent decision of this kind has been that in *R. v. Kansal (No.2)*[69] where it

---

[61] At pp. 1024–1025. Lord Wilberforce would not have favoured overruling *Re Dowling* if its *ratio* had been narrowly interpreted (see pp. 995–996). Lord Diplock was in favour of overruling but recognised he was in the minority and so he reluctantly agreed that the appeal should be allowed (p. 1015). *Cf.* Lord Reid in *R. v. Knuller* [1973] A.C. 435, 455–456, where he expressed the view that the House should not overrule *Shaw v. D.P.P.* [1962] A.C. 220, notwithstanding that he had dissented in *Shaw* and still thought that it had been wrongly decided *cf.* Lord Hailsham and Lord Edmund-Davies in *R. v. Cunningham* [1982] A.C. 566, 581, 582. See R. Brazier, [1973] Crim.L.R. 98.

[62] It was so altered: see N. J. Wikeley and others, *Ogus, Barendt and Wikeley's The Law of Social Security* (4th ed., 1995), p. 331.

[63] [1977] 1 W.L.R. 1345. Similarly, in *Paal Wilson & Co. v. Partenreederei Hannah Blumenthal* [1983] 1 A. C. 854 the House declined to overrule the recent decision in *Bremer Vulkan v. South India Shipping Corp.* [1981] A. C. 909, which had "provoked serious disquiet among the whole commercial community" (per Lord Goff in *Food Corporation of India v. Antclizo Shipping Corporation (The Antclizo)* [1988] 1 W.L.R. 603,606). One point was "the special need for certainty, consistency and continuity in the field of commercial law" (*per* Lord Brandon at p. 913). See B. J. Davenport, (1988) 104 L. Q. R. 493. The House called for the matter to be considered by Parliament and this led to the Courts and Legal Services Act 1990, s.102.

[64] [1979] A. C. 508.

[65] *British South Africa Co. v. Companhia de Moçambique* [1893] A. C. 602.

[66] [1985] A. C. 104. See P.M.N., [1984] 3 LMCLQ 365.

[67] *London, Chatham and Dover Railway Co. v. South Eastern Railway Co.* [1893] A. C. 429.

[68] Law Com. 88 (Cmnd. 7229, 1978) Report on Interest: see the Administration of Justice Act 1982, Sched. 1. The relevant recommendation had indeed been rejected by the government: see P.M.N., *op. cit.*, p. 366.

[69] [2002] 1 All E.R. 257.

was held[70] that the House should not depart from its previous decision in *R. v. Lambert*[71], notwithstanding that a majority[72] regarded it as erroneous. *Lambert* was a recent decision, it represented a possible view that had not been shown to be unworkable and it related only to a point of transitional concern.[73]

In other cases, the House may simply be convinced that the earlier decision was correct.[74]

Harris[75] suggests that an analysis of the case law reveals certain underlying considerations. First, the House must be convinced that it is in a position to substitute a ruling which will make a "net improvement in the law"[76] secondly, the House will normally decline to overrule a decision where there are no new arguments not considered in the earlier case and no material change in circumstances; thirdly, it is a reason not to overrule a decision that people have regulated their affairs in reliance on it; fourthly, importance may be attached to the fact that legislation appears to have been enacted on the assumption that the impugned decision represents the law; fifthly, there is some support for the view that the House should not overrule an earlier decision where the issue is moot, the ruling on it making no difference to the outcome of the present case.

In *Jones v. Secretary of State for Social Services*,[77] Lord Simon of Glaisdale suggested that consideration should be given to the introduction, preferably by statute, of a power for the House of Lords to overrule a decision "prospectively" (*i.e.* for future cases only). Such a power is exercised by the United States Supreme Court[78] and in several states in the U.S.A. This involves the express recognition that the notion that judges do not make law is a fiction, but avoids the undesirable consequences of retrospectively upsetting established arrangements.[79] There are difficulties in choosing the date of transition: for example, should the litigant who has successfully argued that a case should be overruled be entitled to the retrospective effect of that decision, notwithstanding the general determination that the rule should be changed prospectively? If the answer is no, litigants will have little incentive to mount the necessary arguments. Lord Devlin has opposed the general idea of prospective overruling on the ground that it "turns judges into undisguised legislators."[80] The House of Lords

---

[70] Lords Slynn, Lloyd, Steyn and Hutton, Lord Hope dissenting.

[71] [2001] UKHL 37, [2001] 3 W.L.R. 206.

[72] Lords Lloyd, Steyn and Hope.

[73] For further discussion, see below, para. 8-015.

[74] See, *e.g., Smoker v. London Fire and Civil Defence Authority* [1991] 2 A. C. 502 (*Parry v. Cleaver* [1970] A.C. 1), *R. v. Reid* [1992] 1 W.L.R. 793 (*R. v. Laurence* [1982] A. C. 510).

[75] Cross and Harris (1991), pp. 135–143, "Towards principles of overruling—when should a final Court of Appeal second guess?" (1990) 10 O.J.L.S. 135 and (1991) 11 O.J.L.S. See also A. Paterson, *The Law Lords* (1982), pp. 156–167, identifying criteria that reflected the dominant consensus of the Law Lords in the mid-1970s.

[76] Cross and Harris (1991), p. 138.

[77] [1972] A.C. 944, 1026–7. See also his Lordship's statement in *Miliangos v. George Frank (Textiles) Ltd* [1976] A.C. 443, 490, and Lord Diplock, [1972] A.C. 944, 1015.

[78] See, *e.g. Mapp v. Ohio* 367 U.S. 643 (1961); *Linkletter v. Walker* 381 U.S. 618 (1965); *Miranda v. Arizona* 384 U.S. 436 (1966).

[79] See generally W. Friedmann, (1966) 29 M.L.R. 593; M. D. A. Freeman, (1973) 26 C.L.P. 166; A. Nichol, (1976) 39 M.L.R. 542; Cross and Harris (1991), pp. 228–232.

[80] Lord Devlin, "Judges and Lawmakers" (1976) 39 M.L.R. 11, 20: reprinted in *The Judge* (1979), p. 12.

changed a rule of *practice* (as distinct from a rule of *law*) prospectively in *Connelly v. D.P.P.*[81]

In practice a decision of the House of Lords on an appeal from Scotland or Northern Ireland will be regarded as binding on English courts lower in the hierarchy on points where the law of the two countries is the same.[82]

8. The Privy Council

Decisions of the Judicial Committee of the Privy Council are not technically   **7–028**
binding on English courts except in respect of matters where an appeal lies from such a court to the Privy Council.[83] Furthermore, decisions of the Judicial Committee on devolution issues and issues of legislative competence are expressly made binding in all legal proceedings (other than proceedings before the Committee).[84] Apart from this, Privy Council decisions may still be highly persuasive.[85] The Privy Council will normally follow its own previous decisions, but is not bound to do so.[86] It is not bound to follow decisions of the House of Lords on common law issues, although the latter have great persuasive authority: the common law may develop differently in different parts of the Commonwealth.[87] A House of Lords decision on the interpretation of recent legislation common to England and another part of the Commonwealth will however, be treated as binding.[88]

9. The Court of Justice of the European Communities

The decisions of this court on matters of Community law are binding on   **7–029**
English courts up to and including the House of Lords.[89] It tends to follow

---

[81] [1964] A.C. 1254.
[82] Cross and Harris (1991), p. 22, *Heyman v. Darwins Ltd* [1942] A.C. 356, 401 (Lord Porter); *Glasgow Corporation v. Central Land Board* 1956 S.C. (H.L.) 1: where the law of "crown privilege" was held to be different in the two countries; *Re Tuck's Settlement Trusts, Public Trustee v. Tuck* [1978] Ch. 49, 61 (Lord Denning M.R.).
[83] *e.g.* in ecclesiastical and prize matters: *Combe v. Edwards* (1877) 2 P.D. 354. In *Port Line Ltd v. Ben Line Steamers Ltd* [1958] 2 Q.B. 146, Diplock J. declined to follow a Privy Council decision that was in his view wrongly decided.
[84] *e.g.* Scotland Act 1998, s. 103(1); see further para. 2-074.
[85] See, *e.g.* above, para. 7-022, below, para. 7-032.
[86] *Gideon Nkambule v. R.* [1950] A.C. 379; *Fatuma Binti Mohamed Bin Salim v. Mohamed Bin Salim* [1952] A.C. 1; *Baker v. The Queen* [1975] A.C. 774, 787–788; *Lewis v. Attorney General of Jamaica* [2001] 2 A.C. 50 (prerogative of mercy in death penalty case to be exercised by procedures that were fair and amenable to judicial review)
[87] *e.g.* on the right to punitive damages in tort: the Privy Council in *Australian Consolidated Press Ltd v. Uren* [1969] 1 A.C. 590 did not follow the House of Lords decision in *Rookes v. Barnard* [1964] A.C. 1129; and on the liability of a local authority in respect of the inspection of buildings in the course of construction the Privy Council in *Invercargill City Council v. Hamlin* [1996] 2 W.L.R. 367 did not follow the decision of the House of Lords in *Murphy v. Brentwood District Council* [1991] 1 A.C. 398 (above, para. 7-027).
[88] *de Lasala v. de Lasala* [1980] A.C. 546.
[89] See above, paras 5-050–5-055; European Communities Act 1972, s.3(1).

its own previous decisions, although it is not bound to do so.[90] The Court of First Instance is expressly bound by decisions of the Court of Justice on points of law in cases referred back to the Court of First Instance.[91] Otherwise, it will regard itself as bound by decisions of the Court of Justice and will not lightly depart from its own previous decisions.[92]

10. TRIBUNALS

7–030 Where there is a hierarchy of tribunals, the decisions of the appellate tribunals will bind lower tribunals. For example, social security appeal tribunals (now Appeals Service tribunals) must follow decisions of the social security commissioners (formerly known as the national insurance commissioners).[93] Tribunals are not permitted to lay down precedents binding on themselves,[94] the emphasis, in theory at least, being on deciding each case on its own facts. However, the case law of some tribunals is systematically reported[95] and general principles tend to become established,[96] and the "essential differences in practice from, say, the House of Lords or the Court of Appeal ... are not as marked as one might think."[97] In the context of social security appeals, a Tribunal of Commissioners has held[98] that in determining whether to be bound by a decision of a previous Tribunal, it should adopt and adapt the principles laid down in the 1966 *Practice Statement*[99] concerning the House of Lords, and not the principles laid down in *Young v. Bristol Aeroplane Co. Ltd.*[1]

---

[90] Cases 2, 8, 29, 30/62, *Da Costa en Schaake NV v. Nederlandse Belasting-administratie* [1963] E.C.R. 31; L. N. Brown and T. Kennedy, *The Court of Justice of the European Communities* (5th ed., 2000), Chap. 16; T. Koopmans in D. O'Keefe and H. G. Schermers (eds.), *Essays in European Law and Integration* (1982); A. G. Toth, "The authority of judgments of the European Court of Justice: binding force and legal effect" (1984) 4 Y.E.L. 1.

[91] Statute of the Court of Justice, art. 54, second para, (as amended to take account of the establishment of the Court of First Instance).

[92] Brown and Kennedy (2000), pp. 375–377.

[93] *R.(I) 12/75* (Tribunal of Commissioners); N. J. Wikeley, *Ogus, Barendt and Wikely's The Law of Social Security* (4th ed., 1995), pp. 680–681. A single Commissioner should follow a decision of a Tribunal of Commissioners on a point of legal principle unless there are compelling reasons why he should not: *ibid.; R.(U) 4/88(T)*; it has been held that tribunals and Commissioners are bound by decisions of the High Court and above: *ibid.*; but this is now subject to the qualification that the Commissioners now regard decisions of the High Court on substantive points of social security law made on judicial review as those of a court of co-ordinate jurisdiction, and so to be followed unless the Commissioner is convinced that they are wrong: *R(IS) 15/99*.

[94] *Merchandise Transport Ltd v. British Transport Commission* [1962] 2 Q.B. 173, C.A., in relation to the Transport Tribunal.

[95] In the context of social security, the Commissioners have emphasised that adjudicating officers and tribunals are bound by unreported Commissioners' decisions as well as reported: *R.(I) 12/75; R. (SB) 22/86*.

[96] J. A. Farmer, *Tribunals and Government* (1974), Chap. 3, pp. 171–180.

[97] *ibid.* p. 175.

[98] *R.(U) 4/88*.

[99] Above, para. 7-026.

[1] Above, paras 7-016–7-024.

11. THE NATURE OF RULES OF BINDING PRECEDENT

Apart from the 1966 *Practice Statement*, propositions as to the binding **7–031**
effects of previous decisions have been contained in the judgments of
decided cases. It has been pointed out that such propositions cannot form
part of the *ratio* of a case as they are "necessarily irrelevant to the issues of
law and fact that have to be decided by the court."[2] Professor Cross[3] argued
that this only seems applicable to statements of higher courts about the way
in which lower courts should behave,[4] but that in any event statements
about the rules of precedent are statements about the courts' own practice
which fall outside the *ratio-obiter* distinction. The 1966 *Practice Statement*
owed its validity "to the inherent power of any court to regulate its own
practice."[5] The possibility that the Court of Appeal might change the rule
that it is bound by its own previous decisions by a similar practice statement
has been mooted.[6] However, Lord Simon of Glaisdale asserted that any
change would require legislation,[7] Cumming-Bruce L.J. accepted loyally
that the constitutional functions of the House of Lords include that of
declaring with authority the extent to which the Court of Appeal is bound
by its previous decisions,[8] and Lord Denning in any event failed to persuade
his colleagues that a change would be desirable.[9]

E. PERSUASIVE AUTHORITIES[10]

Precedents that are not technically binding may be cited as persuasive **7–032**
authorities. The extent to which a precedent will be persuasive may depend
on a variety of factors including the status of the court, the country in which
it was located, the reputation of the judge, whether the relevant proposition
formed part of the *ratio*, whether the judgment was considered or *ex*

---

[2] Glanville Williams, (1954) 70 L.Q.R. 469, 471; *cf.* Diplock L.J. in *Boys v. Chaplin* [1968] 2 K.B. 1,35.
[3] "The House of Lords and the Rules of Precedent" in P. M. S. Hacker and J. Raz (eds.), *Law, Morality and Society* (1977), pp. 144–160. For the contrary argument that pronouncements on precedent do indeed establish rules of law, see P. J. Evans, [1982] C.L.J. 162, criticised by L. Goldstein, [1984] C.L.J. 88, with a reply by Evans, *ibid.* p. 108. For the argument that they establish rules of *customary* law, see P. Aldridge, (1984) 47 M.L.R. 187. For the argument that the 1966 *Practice Statement* established, or modified, a constitutional convention, see Lord Simon of Glaisdale in *R. v. Knuller* [1973] A.C. 435, at p. 485 and A. R. Blackshield, in L. Goldstein (ed.), *Judicial Precedent* (1987), Chap. 5.
[4] *ibid.* p. 154.
[5] *ibid.* p. 157; Salmon L.J. in *Gallic v. Lee* [1969] 2 Ch. 17, 49; Lord Denning M.R. in *Davis v. Johnson* [1979] A.C. 264, 281; Lord Salmon in *Davis v. Johnson* (above para. 7-023).
[6] *ibid.*
[7] *Miliangos v. George Frank (Textiles) Ltd* [1976] A.C. 443, 470.
[8] *Davis v. Johnson* [1979] A.C. 264, 311.
[9] See above, para. 7-023.
[10] See R. Bronaugh, "Persuasive precedent" in L. Goldstein (ed.), *Judicial Precedent* (1987), Chap. 8.

tempore[11] and whether the judge in the later case agrees with it. Thus the attention of the court may be drawn to the *ratio* of a decision of an English court lower in the hierarchy, to *obiter dicta*, to a dissenting judgment, to a decision of the Privy Council or to a court abroad. A good example of a consideration of the advantages and disadvantages of the overruling by the House of Lords of an established line of authorities at the level of the Court of Appeal is provided by *Mannai Investment Co. Ltd. v. Eagle Star Life Assurance Co. Ltd.*[12] Here the House by 3 to 2[13] held that a notice to determine a lease that contained a minor misdescription would be effective provided that, construed against its contextual setting, it would unambiguously inform a reasonable recipient how and when it was to operate. The House overruled a Court of Appeal decision of some 50 years standing[14] that had prescribed a stricter approach. The majority were satisfied that this contextual approach to the interpretation of notices was consistent with the modern approach to the construction of contracts and would not generate uncertainty or interfere with legitimate expectations, the stricter approach being one which allowed "one party to take unmeritorious advantage of another's verbal error."[15] The minority took the view that the existing law should not be disturbed as it was clear and well settled and disputes were rare.

Great weight will be attached to considered statements by the House of Lords whatever their technical standing. For example, in *Hedley Byrne & Co. Ltd v. Heller and Partners Ltd,*[16] the House of Lords held that the existence of a special relationship could give rise to a duty to take care in giving information or advice; breach of the duty could in turn lead to an action for damages in respect of purely economic losses. The Court of Appeal had held that such a duty could not arise, following its earlier decision in *Candler v. Crane, Christmas & Co.*[17] The House overruled the *Candler* decision and endorsed the dissenting judgment in that case by Denning L.J. Having found that a duty of care *did* arise as the plaintiffs claimed, the House nonetheless found for the *defendants* on the ground that they had effectively disclaimed responsibility for the statements in question. There was much debate on the issue whether the observations concerning the duty of care were *obiter*.[18] Cairns J. in *W. B. Anderson and Sons Ltd v. Rhodes*[19] regarded such a suggestion as "unrealistic":

> "When five members of the House of Lords have all said, after close examination of the authorities, that a certain type of tort exists, I think that a judge of first instance should proceed on the basis that it does

---

[11] Lord Russell of Killowen has suggested that unreserved judgments should be approached with "great caution:" *op. cit.* p. 420, n. 50; *cf.* Lord Reid in *Haley v. London Electricity Board* [1965] A.C. 778, 792.

[12] [1997] A.C. 749. See P.V. Baker, (1998) 114 L.Q.R. 55. For another example, see *Sudbrook Trading Estate Ltd v. Eggleton* [1983] 1 A.C. 444.

[13] Lords Steyn, Hoffmann and Clyde, Lords Goff and Jauncey dissenting.

[14] *Hankey v. Clavering* [1942] 2 K.B. 326.

[15] *per* Lord Hoffmann at p. 780.

[16] [1964] A.C. 465.

[17] [1951] 2 K.B. 164.

[18] See W. V. H. Rogers, *Winfield and Jolowicz on Tort* (13th ed., 1989), p. 274, n. 97.

[19] [1967] 2 All E.R. 850.

exist without pausing to embark on an investigation whether what was said was necessary to the ultimate decision."[20]

Similarly, it became accepted that solicitors acting as advocates were entitled to the same immunity from legal action as barristers, notwithstanding that the view had been expressed in decisions of the House of Lords concerning barristers.[21]

The "neighbour principle" expounded by Lord Atkin in *Donoghue v. Stevenson*[22] can be regarded as part of the *ratio* of his speech, but not as part of the *ratio* of the House of Lords as a whole.[23] Nevertheless the principle was influential in subsequent decisions which extended the scope of the tort of negligence,[24] although the most recent decisions in the area have emphasised that it should be used, cautiously and is not the sole determinant of the existence of a duty of care.[25] By contrast, dicta of Lord Diplock[26] setting out a broader approach to the jurisdiction of a criminal court in respect of offences where elements take place abroad were adopted by the Privy Council (in respect of Hong Kong)[27] and the Supreme Court of Canada[28] but the Court of Appeal subsequently held that they could not be regarded sufficient to displace earlier, binding Court of Appeal authority to the contrary.[29]

Decisions of the Privy Council may be strongly persuasive, particularly now that membership of the Judicial Committee is mainly drawn from Lords of Appeal.[30] The Privy Council decision in *The Wagon Mound (No. 1)*[31] is accepted to be the leading authority on remoteness of damage in the tort of negligence, and has been applied in preference to the decision of the Court of Appeal in *Re Polemis*.[32]

The desirability of uniformity between Scottish and English courts on points common to both systems has often been stressed, particularly on the

---

[20] *ibid.* p. 857.
[21] For the present position, see above, para. 3-044.
[22] [1932] A.C. 562, 580.
[23] Two of the five members dissented and the other two did not expressly concur with Lord Atkin's formulation: see R. F. V. Heuston, (1957) 20 M.L.R. 1, 5–9.
[24] See, *e.g. Hedley Byrne & Co. Ltd v. Heller and Partners Ltd* [1964] A.C. 465.
[25] See, *e.g. Murphy v. Brentwood District Council* [1991] 1 A.C. 398.
[26] *Treacy v. DPP* [1971] A.C. 537.
[27] *Liangsiriprasert v. US Government* [1991] 1 A.C. 225.
[28] *Libman v. R.* (1985) 21 D.L.R. (4th) 174.
[29] *R. v. Manning* [1999] Q.B. 980. The issues have from June 1, 1999 been dealt with by Part 1 of the Criminal Justice Act 1993.
[30] Similarly, decisions of the House of Lords and Court of Appeal are of high persuasive authority in the courts of the Isle of Man, given that the Privy Council is the final court of appeal from a Manx court: *Frankland v. The Queen* [1987] A.C. 576, P.C.
[31] *Overseas Tankship (U.K.) Ltd v. Morts Dock Engineering Co. Ltd* [1961] A.C. 388.
[32] *Re Polemis and Furness, Withy & Co. Ltd* [1921] 2 K.B. 560: see *Doughty v. Turner Manufacturing Co. Ltd* [1964] 1 Q.B. 518, C.A.; *Smith v. Leech Brain & Co. Ltd* [1962] 2 Q.B. 405, 415, where Lord Parker C.J. indicated *obiter* that the *Wagon Mound* case enabled a trial judge to follow other decisions of the Court of Appeal prior to *Polemis*. The test for remoteness is now whether the kind of damage was reasonably foreseeable: the former test was whether the damage was the direct consequence of the defendant's conduct. *Cf.* Robert Goff J. in *I Congreso del Partido* [1978] Q.B. 500, 517–519.

construction of statutes and revenue and taxation matters.[33] The citation of overseas authorities seems to be increasingly common.[34] Lord Denning would not, however, in practice have followed a decision of the deputy magistrate of East Tonga in preference to six decisions of the House of Lords.[35] There have been complaints that counsel, particularly in busy appellate courts, cite too many authorities both English and foreign[36]; at the same time, counsel owes a duty to the court to cite all relevant authorities whether for or against him.

Textbooks may be cited as authorities although they can never be binding.[37] Some treatises have long been accepted as authoritative guides to the law in previous centuries, including the Abridgments of the Year Books[38] compiled by Fitzherbert and Brooke, the treatise known as "Glanvill" dating from the late twelfth century, Bracton's *De Legibus et Consuetudinibus Angliae* from the thirteenth, Littleton's *Tenures* from the fourteenth, Fitzherbert's *Nature Brevium*, Coke's *Institutes of the Laws of England* first published in 1628, eighteenth century works on criminal law by Hale, Hawkins and Foster[39] and Blackstone's *Commentaries on the Laws of England* first published in 1765–69. These works are not cited often today, the ones on criminal law perhaps being referred to most commonly.[40] It used to be convention that living authors could not be cited as authorities, although their words could be adopted by counsel as part of his or her argument,[41] on the doubtful ground that while alive the author might change his or her mind.[42] This convention is no longer observed,[43] and books and articles by authors both living and dead are commonly cited.[44] In appropriate cases reference may also be made to principles of Roman law, and especially, in that regard, Justinian's *Digest*.[45]

---

[33] See, *e.g. Abbott v. Philbin (Inspector of Taxes)* [1960] Ch. 27, rvsd. [1961] A.C. 352; *Westward Television Ltd v. Hart (Inspector of Taxes)* [1969] 1 Ch. 201, 212; *Secretary of State for Employment and Productivity v. Clarke, Chapman & Co. Ltd* [1971] 1 W.L.R. 1094, 1102.

[34] See R. J. C. Munday, (1978) 14 J.S.P.T.L. (N.S.) 201, 203–207.

[35] See the (regrettably) fictional report of *Grenouille v. National Union of Seamen* reproduced in Denning, *The Family Story* (1981), pp. 219–220.

[36] See, to *e.g.* Lawton L.J., (1980) 14 L.T. 163, 166.

[37] *Cordell v. Second Clanfield Properties Ltd* [1969] 2 Ch. 9, 16: Megarry J. in relation to Sir Robert Megarry and H. W. R. Wade, *The Law of Real Property*.

[38] See below, para. 7-038.

[39] Sir Matthew Hale, *The History of the Pleas of the Crown*, published posthumously in 1736 but written in the previous century; William Hawkins, *Pleas of the Crown* (1716); Sir Michael Foster, *Crown Cases and Crown Law* (1762).

[40] See, *e.g. Button v. D.P.P.* [1966] A.C. 591; *R. v. Merriman* [1973] A.C. 584 (*Hale* and *Hawkins*).

[41] See, *e.g.* Vaughan Williams L.J. in *Greenlands Ltd v. Wilmshurst* (1913) 29 T.L.R. 685, 687.

[42] Lord Reid, (1972) 12 J.S.P.T.L. (N.S.) 22. This convention was the basis of somewhat leaden jokes to the effect that certain celebrated works were "fortunately" not works of authority.

[43] See *Halsbury's Laws of England* (4th ed.) Vol. 26, para. 587.

[44] For example, in criminal law cases references to books by Glanville Williams and Sir John Smith and B. Hogan are frequent; in administrative law, Sir William Wade and C. F. Forsyth, *Administrative Law*, (8th ed., 2000) and de Smith, Woolf and Jowell, *Judicial Review of Administrative Action* (5th ed., 1995) are similarly authoritative. See the splendid story by A. Arden, [1980] Conv. 454, 458 (review of the 4th ed. of *de Smith*).

[45] See, *e.g. Coggs v. Bernard* (1703) 2 Ld. Raym. 909 and *Dalton v. Angus* (1881) 6 App. Cas.740.

F. DISTINGUISHING

A precedent, whether persuasive or binding, need not be applied or followed **7–033**
if it can be "distinguished:" *i.e.* there is a material distinction between the
facts of the precedent case and the case in question. What counts as a
"material" distinction is obviously crucial. The judge in the later case is
expected to explain why the distinction is such as to justify the application of
a different rule. If the distinction is spurious, the judge may be criticised or
reversed or, if the case distinguished is generally regarded as a bad
precedent, applauded for his or her boldness. There is no test or set of tests
for whether a distinction is legally relevant; it all depends upon the
circumstances of the case.

An example is provided by *R. v. Secretary of State for the Environment, ex
p. Ostler*.[46] In 1956, the House of Lords in *Smith v. East Elloe R.D.C.*[47]
ruled that a provision[48] that the validity of a compulsory purchase order
should not be questioned in any legal proceedings, other than a statutory
application to quash made within six weeks, meant what it said: an action to
impugn an order on the ground of fraud could not be brought some six
years later. However, in *Anisminic Ltd v. The Foreign Compensation
Commission*[49] the House held that section 4 of the Foreign Compensation
Act 1950, which provided that a determination by the Commission "shall
not be called in question in any court of law", was not effective to render
immune from judicial review a purported determination that was in truth a
nullity and thus not a "determination" at all. The decision in *Smith v. East
Elloe R.D.C.* was adversely criticised but not overruled. In *Ostler* the Court
of Appeal was faced with an ouster clause of the kind at issue in *Smith v.
East Elloe R.D.C.*, and it followed *Smith* in preference to *Anisminic*, which
was distinguished on a variety of grounds. For example, the point was taken
that section 4 of the 1950 Act purported to exclude judicial review altogether
whereas the provision in *Ostler* was more akin to a limitation period in that
it excluded review only after a six-week period. It was said that *Anisminic*
concerned a "judicial" decision and *Ostler* an "administrative" one. Their
Lordships were not, however, unanimous as to their reasons, and Lord
Denning M.R. subsequently indicated extra-judicially that he no longer
regarded most of his own as sound.[50]

G. PRECEDENT AND STATUTORY INTERPRETATION

A decision on a question of the construction of a statute is binding to the **7–034**
same extent as a decision on other kinds of question.[51] Thus it is applicable

---

[46] [1977] Q.B. 122.
[47] [1956] A.C. 736.
[48] Acquisition of Land (Authorisation Procedure) Act 1946, Sched. 1, Part IV, paras.15, 16.
[49] [1969] 2 A.C. 147.
[50] *The Discipline of Law* (1979), pp. 108–109.
[51] Per Lord Reid in *Goodrich v. Paisner* [1957] A.C. 65, 88 and *London Transport Executive v. Betts* [1959] A.C. 211, 232.

in cases concerning the same words in the same Act and "in all cases which do not provide substantial relevant differences."[52] The same words appearing in a different statute may be interpreted differently, although a decision on the construction of a particular set of words may be used as a guide when other statutes dealing with the same or a similar subject-matter are considered.[53] If words which have been the subject of construction by a court are re-enacted by Parliament without alteration, a court will be very slow to overrule that decision but not always unwilling to do so.[54] Moreover Lord Wilberforce has stated that[55]:

> "Self-contained statutes, whether consolidating previous law, or so doing with the amendments, should be interpreted, if reasonably possible, without recourse to antecedents,[56] and that recourse should only be had when there is a real and substantial difficulty or ambiguity which classical methods of construction cannot resolve."

H. RATIO DECIDENDI AND RES JUDICATA

7–035   In its wider meaning the term "judgment" is used to cover the whole of the judge's pronouncement after the arguments of each side have been heard (*e.g.* as in "I will deliver my judgment after lunch"). In its narrower meaning it is used to cover the order of the court as distinct from the reasons for it (*e.g.* "There will be judgment for the plaintiff for £500"). Assuming the order lies within the judge's jurisdiction it is binding on the parties (*res judicata*). They may not reopen the issue that has just been determined, unless a statute has provided for an appeal.[57] Thus the court's *order* is binding on the *parties* under the *res judicata* doctrine; the *ratio decidendi* is binding on other *courts* in accordance with the principles outlined above under the doctrine of binding precedent. A startling illustration of the distinction was provided by the following series of cases. A testator, John Arkle Waring, left annuities to Mr Howard and Mrs Louie Burton-Butler "free of income tax". In 1942 the Court of Appeal in *Re Waring, Westminster Bank Ltd v. Awdry*,[58] on an appeal in which Howard was a party, held that income tax had to be deducted. Louie was not a party as she was in an enemy occupied country. Leave to appeal to the House of Lords

---

[52] *Goodrich v. Paisner, ibid.*
[53] *ibid.*; Lord Upjohn in *Ogden Industries Pty Ltd v. Lucas* [1970] A.C. 113, 127; *R. v. Freeman* [1970] 1 W.L.R. 788 (meaning of "firearm" in successive Firearms Acts).
[54] *Royal Crown Derby Porcelain Ltd v. Raymond Russell* [1949] 2 K.B. 417, 429, *per* Denning L. J.; *cf. R. v. Bow Road JJ., ex p. Adedigba* [1968] 2 Q.B. 572.
[55] *Farrell v. Alexander* [1977] A.C. 59, 73. Lord Simon and Lord Edmund-Davies agreed with this approach *cf.* above, para. 6-032.
[56] *i.e.* the history of the provisions and the cases decided on them.
[57] See Chap. 18. In the case of courts and tribunals with a jurisdiction limited by statute there is also the possibility of judicial review under the *ultra vires* doctrine where the jurisdiction has been exceeded or abused.
[58] [1942] Ch. 426.

was refused. Four years later the House of Lords in *Berkeley v. Berkeley*[59] overruled the *Awdry* case. Subsequently, Jenkins J. held that the *Awdry* case was *res judicata* so far as Howard was concerned notwithstanding that its *ratio* had been overruled in *Berkeley v. Berkeley* and that Louie's annuity would be dealt with in accordance with the latter case.[60]

I. LAW REPORTS[61]

(a) Introduction

Any legal system that is based to any significant extent upon judicial precedent requires an effective system whereby those precedents are reported and indexed. In theory, a case may be cited as a precedent even it if has not been reported. In practice, comparatively few cases are referred to in textbooks or cited in court unless they have been reported in one of the series of published law reports, although such references are becoming more common.[62] Occasionally a judge has referred to an unreported case with which he was concerned as counsel or judge.[63] Indexed transcripts of all unreported cases in the Court of Appeal (Civil Division) are kept in the Supreme Court Library[64] and some are listed in *Current Law* and copies of unreported House of Lords decisions are kept in the House of Lords Records Office. Transcripts of many decisions of the High Court, most of the Court of Appeal and all of the House of Lords and Privy Council are now available on the Internet.[65] Thousands of unreported cases decided since January 1, 1980, including all decisions of the House of Lords and Court of Appeal (Civil Division), are included on *Lexis*.

7–036

(b) A modern law report

A full law report today commonly includes the following information: The names of the parties[66]; the court in which the case was decided; the name of

7–037

---

[59] [1946] A.C. 555.

[60] *Re Waring, Westminster Bank v. Burton-Butler* [1948] Ch. 221.

[61] See generally Sweet & Maxwell's *Guide to Law Reports and Statutes* (4th ed., 1962); P.A. Thomas, *Dare and Thomas, How to use a law library* (4th ed., 2001), Chap. 2; W. W. S. Breem, in E. M. Moys (ed.), *Manual of Law Librarianship* (2nd ed., 1987), Chap. 4: "Primary sources: law reports"; P. Clinch, *Using a Law Library* (2nd ed., 2001); G. Holborn, *Butterworths Legal Research Guide* (2nd ed., 2001).

[62] R. J. C. Munday, (1978) 14 J.S.P.T.L. (N.S.) 201, 207–216.

[63] *e.g. Wilkinson v. Downton* [1897] 2 Q.B. 57, 61; *Harling v. Eddy* [1951] 2 K.B. 739, 746 (Denning L.J.).

[64] From 1951, an official note has been made of all Court of Appeal (Civil Division) decisions (see (1951) 95 S.J. 266). A microfiche edition of the transcripts 1951–1980 is available from HMSO (see V. Tunkel, (1986) 136 N.L.J., 1045). Transcripts of decisions of the Court of Appeal (Criminal Division) from 1960 are held by the Criminal Appeal Office in the Royal Courts of Justice (Breem, in Moys (1987), p. 143). The arrangements for transcribing cases are considered by Breem, *op. cit.*, pp. 144–146, and S. Cole, (1988) 19 *The Law Librarian* 89.

[65] See further, below para. 7-038.

[66] Appeals to the House of Lords since 1974 carried the same title as in the court of first instance: *Procedure Direction* [1974] 1 W.L.R. 305. Previously, the name of the appellant appeared first.

the judge or judges; the date or dates of the hearing; the headnote (a summary of the decision prepared by the reporter)[67]; lists of the cases discussed and cited; the previous history of the litigation, including a summary of the claims made and the result of proceedings in lower courts; the facts[68]; the names of counsel; the arguments of counsel[69]; an indication of whether judgment is reserved by the inclusion of the expression *Cur. adv. vult*[70]; the judgment or judgments[71]; the order of the court and an indication of whether leave to appeal is granted or refused; the names of the solicitors; the name of the barrister who reports the case.

(c) Law reporting[72]

7–038   The earliest law reports were contained in the "Year Books" compiled annually between the thirteenth and sixteenth centuries. These reports concentrated upon points of procedure and pleading rather than the final decisions of the courts, and were written first in Norman French and later in "law French" (an amalgam of English, French and Latin).[73] These are today mainly of interest to legal historians. Between the sixteenth and nineteenth centuries a large number of "private" or "nominate" reports appeared. Most were named after the reporter. They varied widely in their style and content, their accuracy and their reputation.[74] Some, such as those of Coke, Plowden and Saunders were of high authority. Others were regarded as of little value.[75] Some were in law French; most were in English. The focus of attention switched from the pleadings to the Court's decision and the best reports included the full reasons. The first to be published in more or less the form we have today, although not verbatim reports, were Burrow's reports of the eighteenth century. The first that regularly published reports of newly decided cases were Durnford and East's "Term Reports". The private reports are cited by the name, usually abbreviated, of the reporter or the reports, the volume and the page.[76] The year is not technically part of the reference but is normally included.[77] Most of the cases in the private reports were reprinted in *The English Reports* published in 176 volumes between 1900 and 1930. There was also a series entitled *The*

---

[67] The headnote may be inaccurate (see, *e.g. Young v. Bristol Aeroplane Co. Ltd*, above, para. 7-021) although modern headnotes are generally reliable. It may include a summary of the facts or simply be the reporter's version of the *ratio decidendi.*

[68] The facts stated in the judgments may be left unedited or the reporter may set out the facts separately.

[69] These are only regularly printed in a few sets of reports such as The Law Reports and Lloyds' Law Reports. Interjections from the bench may also be included. The original transcripts commonly record the post – judgment submissions of counsel (and rulings) on such matter as costs.

[70] *Curia advisari vult*: "the court wishes to consider the matter."

[71] In full reports these are printed verbatim, in some, such as in the Criminal Law Review and the Solicitors' Journal, only summaries are given.

[72] See J. H. Baker, *An Introduction to English Legal History* (3rd ed., 1990), pp. 204–214; L. W. Abbott, *Law Reporting in England 1485–1585* (1973), reviewed by Baker, [1974] C.L.J. 156; P. Reeves, (1989) 86 L. S. Gaz. July 26; R. Munday, (2001) 165 J.P.N. 162.

[73] See J. H. Baker, *Manual of Law French* (1979).

[74] C. K. Allen, *Law in the Making* (7th ed., 1964), pp. 221–232.

[75] *e.g.* Barnardiston: see R. G. Logan, (1987) 18 *The Law Librarian* 87.

[76] *e.g. Coggs v. Bernard* (1703) 2 Ld. Raym. 909 (Lord Raymond).

[77] In round brackets. Where the year is part of a reference it is given in square brackets.

Revised Reports edited by Sir Frederick Pollock and included such cases reported between 1785 and 1865 as were "still of practical utility".[78]

The patchwork coverage of private enterprise law reports was seen to be unsatisfactory.[79] In 1865 a council consisting of the Attorney-General, the Solicitor-General, two barristers from each of the inns of court, two sergeants and two solicitors was formed; in 1870 it was incorporated as "The Incorporated Council of Law Reporting for England and Wales" with as its primary object:

> "the preparation and publication in a convenient form, at a moderate price, and under gratuitous professional control of Reports of Judicial Decisions of the Superior and Appellate Courts of England."

The Council is not funded by the state and is non-profit-making.[80] Its reports are semi-official in that judgments appearing in the Law Reports are revised by the judges, and that this series should be cited in preference to any alternative.[81] It is increasingly common for them to be referred to by the judiciary as "official" even through technically they are not.[82] The corrections may make the report conform to what was actually said; on occasion a report is changed to conform to what the judge meant to say, which is rather more controversial.[83] There have been three series of the Law Reports: the first from 1865 to 1875,[84] the second from 1875 to 1890[85] and the third from 1891 to date.[86] The Incorporated Council also publishes the (unrevised) "Weekly Law Reports" and the "Industrial Cases Reports". There are a number of series of specialist official reports including the "Reports of Tax Cases" published under the direction of the Inland Revenue, the "Reports of Patent, Design and Trade Mark Cases" published by the Patent Office and the "Immigration Appeal Reports" published by HMSO. There are also a number of series associated more obviously with private enterprise, of which the "All England Law Reports" is a general

---

[78] See R. G. Logan, (1982) 13 *The Law Librarian* 23.

[79] See W. T. S. Daniel, *The History and Origin of "The Law Reports"* [1884].

[80] *Incorporated Council of Law Reporting v. Att.-Gen.* [1972] Ch. 73. The Court of Appeal held that the Council's purposes were charitable.

[81] *Westminster Bank Executors and Trustee Co. (Channel Islands) Ltd v. National Bank of Greece S.A. (Practice Note)* [1970] 1 W.L.R. 1400; *Bray v. Best* [1989] 1 W.L.R. 167, 169; *Practice Direction (Law reports: Citation)* [1991] 1 W.L.R. 1; *Practice Direction (CCA: Citation of Authority)* [1995] 1 W.L.R. 1096; *Practice Direction (CA: Citation of Authorities)* [2001] 1 W.L.R. 1001.

[82] R. Munday, (2001) 165 J.P.N. 162.

[83] See, *e.g. Ghani v. Jones* [1970] 1 Q.B. 693; R. M. Jackson, [1970] C.L.J. 1, 3; (1969) 119 N.L.J. 1011; (1970) 120 N.L.J. 423. See further R, Munday, (2001) 165 J.P.N. 162, 342.

[84] *e.g. Osgood v. Nelson* (1872) L.R. 5 H.L. 636. A reference to this series normally includes the year of the decision (in round brackets as it is not technically part of the reference); the letters "L.R."; the volume number of the relevant series; the abbreviation for that series (there were 11 in all, running concurrently); and the page number.

[85] *e.g. Huth v. Clarke* (1890) 25 Q.B.D. 391. A reference no longer includes the letters "L.R." and there are six series: one for Appeal Cases and one for each of the five divisions of the High Court (reduced to three in 1888).

[86] *e.g. Ridge v. Baldwin* [1964] A.C. 40. A reference includes the year of the *report*, not the decision, in square brackets; the series (A.C.; Q.B.; Ch.; Fam.) and the page number.

series rivalling the Weekly Law Reports.[87] The trend is for an increasing number of cases to be reported and for new series of reports to be started,[88] with concomitant problems of expense for law libraries and practitioners, duplication[89] and pressure on research time. Brief law reports also appear in an increasing number of daily newspapers.[90] These are usually printed shortly after judgment has been given, and are compiled by barristers and are so citable in court.[91]

The system of law reporting was examined by a committee which reported in 1940.[92] The committee did not favour any radical change, such as giving the Incorporated Council a monopoly of reporting or the licensing of reporters. The majority rejected the proposals of A. L. Goodhart, who wrote a dissenting report, that a shorthand writer should take down the text of every judgment, that a transcript be sent to the judge for correction and that the corrected report be filed in the court records and made available to any reporter or member of the public for a small fee. The reasons put forward were the cost, the extra burden on the judges and the fact that almost every decision of importance was already reported: "What remains is less likely to be a treasure house than a rubbish heap in which a jewel will rarely, if ever, be discovered."[93] This position has, however, been reached by the widespread availability of databases of transcripts of cases,[94] coupled with the adoption, for ease of reference, of a neutral citation system for the House of Lords, both divisions of the Court of Appeal and the Administrative Court.[95] From January 11, 2001,[96] all judgments in the House of Lords, Court of Appeal and High Court have been issued with paragraph numbers in square brackets; and judgments in the House of Lords, Court of Appeal and Administrative Court have been numbered consecutively through the year.[97] From 2002, neutral citation numbering has been extended to all judgments given by the High Court in London, and, at the request of someone wishing to include it in a report, High Court

---

[87] The criteria for the selection of cases for reporting in the Law Reports and the All England Law Reports are considered by N. H. Andrews, "Reporting Case Law" (1985) 5 L.S. 205, 225–231, based on information supplied by the editors of these series. See also, F. D. Cumbrae-Stewart, "The aim and form of law reports" (1985) 59 A.L.J. 616.

[88] R. J. C. Munday, (1978) 14 J.S.P.T.L. (N.S.) 201–203. See also D. Milman, (1987) 8 Co. Law. 242, noting several new series of company law reports. The trend continued through the 1990s; see R. Munday, (2002) 166 J.P.N. 6, 29.

[89] A glance at Sweet & Maxwell's *Current Law Citator* will confirm this.

[90] The *Times* has printed law reports for over 100 years. It has been joined by the *Financial Times, Guardian, Independent and Daily Telegraph*: see M. Findlay, *The Law Magazine*, March 18, 1989, p. 31. These reports are indexed in the *Daily Law Reports Index* published by Legal Information Resources Ltd, which commenced publication in 1988 (with fortnightly, quarterly and annual cumulations).

[91] They must be distinguished from summaries of cases in the "news" pages of *The Sun* (etc.).

[92] Report of the Law Reporting Committee (HMSO, 1940).

[93] *ibid.* p. 20.

[94] See below.

[95] See *Practice Direction (Sup Ct: Form of Judgments, Paragraph Marking and Neutral Citation* [2001] 1 W.L.R. 194. See R. Munday, (2001) 165 J.P.N. 342. On the introduction of such a system in Canada, see M. Felsky, (1998) 29 *The Law Librarian* 159.

[96] From the first judgment in 2001 in the case of the House of Lords.

[97] *i.e.* [2001] EWHL 1, 2, 3 etc; [2001] EWCA Civ 1, 2, 3 etc; [2001] EWCA Crim 1, 2, 3 etc.; [2001] EWHC Admin 1, 2, 3 etc.

judgments delivered outside London.[98] Once a case is reported, its neutral citation is to appear in front of the citation from the law report series.

Decisions of the Court of Justice of the European Communities are reported in the *European Court Reports,* an official series, and in the *Common Market Law Reports,* a private enterprise series, which includes in addition reports of the decisions of national courts on Community law matters.

The most significant developments in recent years have been in the field of the computerisation of statutes, statutory instruments and law reports. Butterworths offer the American *Lexis* system, which includes English, Scottish and American materials; and European and Commonwealth materials. A vast amount of material is now available on the Internet. It is now normal practice for there to be a fully searchable database of all judgments for each of the leading appellate courts in the United States and the Commonwealth, and international courts such as the Court of Justice of the European Communities and the European Court of Human Rights.[99] There are databases of decisions of the House of Lords and the Privy Council[1] and the SmithBernal database gives access to transcripts of decisions of the High Court and Court of Appeal.[2]

(d) The citation of precedents

Until recently, the only condition for admission of a report has been that it has been vouched for by a barrister present during the whole time when the judgment was given.[3] However, in *Roberts Petroleum Ltd v. Kenny Ltd,*[4] the House of Lords stated that in future it would decline to allow transcripts of unreported judgments of the Court of Appeal (Civil Division) to be cited in the House without leave; such leave would only be granted on counsel giving an assurance that the transcript contained some relevant principle of law that was binding on the Court of Appeal and of which the substance, as distinct from the mere choice of phraseology, was not to be found in any judgment of that court that appeared in one of the generalised or specialised series of reports. The Court of Appeal broadly followed suit.[5] In practice, the judges seem reluctant to prevent the citation of unreported cases.[6]

7–039

---

[98] *Practice Direction (HC: Neutral Citations)* [2002] 1 W.L.R. 346. The form is now [2002] EWHC 1, 2, 3 etc. followed by (Ch), (Pat), (QB), (Admin), (Comm), (Admlty), (TCC) or (Fam) as the case may be.

[99] *http://europa.eu.int/cj/en/index.htm; www.echr.coe.int*

[1] *www.publications.parliament.uk/pa/ld/ldjudinf.htm; www.privy-council.org.uk/judicial-committee.*

[2] *www.casetrack.com.*

[3] See *Parkinson v. Parkinson* [1939] P. 346, 348, 351–352; *Birtwistle v. Tweedale* [1954] 1 W.L.R. 190n: *Estates Gazette* report not admitted. *Cf. Baker v. Sims* [1959] 1 Q.B. 114 and *Smith v. Wyles* [1959] 1 Q.B. 164. A report by a person who is a solicitor or has a Supreme Court qualification (*i.e.* a right of audience in relation to all proceedings in the Supreme Court) has the same authority as if it had been by a barrister: Courts and Legal Services Act 1990, s.115.

[4] [1983] 2 A.C. 192. See R. J. C. Munday, (1983) 80 L. S. Gaz 1337; N. H. Andrews, (1985) 5 L.S. 205. Note the critical response of F. A. R. Bennion (*ibid.* p. 1635) and N. Harrison (Managing Director of the company which markets *Lexis*), (1984) 81 L. S. Gaz. 257.

[5] *Practice Statement (Court of Appeal: Authorities)* [1996] 1 W.L.R. 854.

[6] R. Munday, (2002) 166 J.P.N. 6, 9.

The expansion of the number of law reports and the revolution in the means of access to transcripts adds to the cost of preparing and arguing cases as the number of at least possibly relevant authorities that can be identified increases. This naturally conflicts with the policy of seeking to increase the efficiency of litigation. In an attempt to curb the citation of authorities, Lord Woolf C.J. issued a Practice Direction[7] providing that a judgment in specified categories may not in future be cited before any court unless it clearly indicates[8] that it purports to establish a new principle or to extend the present law. The specified categories are: applications attending by one party only; applications for permission to appeal; decisions on applications that only decide that the application is arguable; and (subject to exceptions) county court cases. As regards other categories of judgment (including those of the Court of Justice of the European Communities and the European Court of Human Rights), the courts will in future pay particular attention to any indication given by the court delivering the judgment that it was seen as only applying decided law to the facts or otherwise not extending or adding to existing law. Advocates seeking to cite a judgment containing such indications will be required to justify their decision. Furthermore, advocates will be required to state (in any skeleton argument and appellant's or respondent's notices) in respect of each authority they wish to cite the proposition of law that it demonstrates and the parts of the judgment that support that proposition. Reasons must be given for citing more than one authority in favour of a given proposition. Authorities from other jurisdictions must not be cited without proper consideration of whether it does indeed add to the existing body of law. Where they are cited, the advocate must indicate what it adds that is not to be found in authority in this jurisdiction or the justification for adding to domestic authority. It remains to be seen how this will affect practice. There is always the risk that the time taken in the substantive citation of a case will simply be replaced by time arguing about whether it should be cited.

Both the High Court and Court of Appeal require that where a case has been reported in official law reports published by the Incorporated Council of Law Reporting for England and Wales it must be cited from that source. It is now permissible to cite a copy of a reproduction of a judgment in electronic form provided it is easily legible (12-point font preferred, 10 or 11 point acceptable), and the advocate presenting the report is satisfied that it has not been reproduced in a garbled form.[9]

---

[7] *Practice Direction (CA : Citation of Authorities)* [2001] 1 W.L.R. 1001. See R. Munday, (2002) 166 J.P.N. 6, 32.

[8] By an express statement to that effect in respect of judgments after April 8, 2001; by an indication from the language used in earlier judgments. An example is the decision of the Court of Appeal in *London Borough of Lambeth v. Tunde Apelogun-Gabriels* [2001] EWCA Civ 1853.

[9] *Practice Direction,* n. 95 above.

CHAPTER 8

THE HUMAN RIGHTS ACT 1998

A. INTRODUCTION[1]

The United Kingdom has been subject to the European Convention on **8–001** Human Rights since it came into force in 1953. Individuals have been able since 1966 to bring cases against the UK through the ECHR machinery, and the European Court of Human Rights has found violations in a series of cases.[2] There has also been an extensive ongoing debate as to whether the European Convention should be incorporated into English law, so as to enable individuals who would otherwise have to pursue, usually over a number of years, a claim before the European Court of Human Rights, to have the issues addressed by an English court. Various models have been proposed, including simple incorporation of the ECHR as it stands and the enactment of a Bill of Rights with a text drawn as appropriate from a range of International treaties, including the ECHR, by which the UK is bound.[3] Further variants would see a Bill of Rights set in the context of a written constitution, with the fundamental elements of both entrenched as a higher form of law, which could not be amended by ordinary legislation, but only through some special process of constitutional amendment.[4] These variants would require modifications (to say the least) of the traditional doctrine of Parliamentary sovereignty.[5] Among the main political parties, the Liberal Democrats have tended to favour developments of this kind and the Conservatives have tended to oppose them. Traditionally, the Labour party has been opposed to moves that would enhance the powers of the (unelected and supposedly conservative) judiciary. However, the policy of the Labour party changed in the 1990s[6] and a measure of incorporation of the European Convention on Human Rights became one of a series of constitutional

---

[1] See generally on the Human Rights Act 1998, C. Baker (ed.), *Human Rights Act 1998: A Practitioner's Guide* (1998); M. Hunt, *Practitioner's Guide to the Human Rights Act 1998* (1998); R. Clayton and H. Tomlinson, *The Law of Human Rights* (2000); S. Grosz, J. Beatson and P. Duffy, *Human Rights: The 1998 Act and the European Convention* (2000); Lord Lester and D. Pannick, *Human Rights Law and Practice* (1999); J. Wadham and H. Mountfield, *The Human Rights Act 1998* (2nd ed., 2000).
[2] See above, para. 2-082.
[3] *E.g.* IPPR, *A Written Constitution for the United Kingdom* (2nd ed., 1993).
[4] See S.H. Bailey, D.J. Harris and B.L. Jones, *Civil Liberties: Cases and Materials* (4th ed., 1995), pp. 14–26; M. Zander, *A Bill of Rights?* (4th ed., 1996).
[5] See above, para. 5-002.
[6] *A New Agenda for Democracy*, adopted by the Labour Party Conference in 1993.

measures[7] secured by the Labour government elected in 1997 early in its term of office. The White Paper, *Rights Brought Home: The Human Rights Bill*[8] placed the practical effect of non-compliance at the centre of its case:

"It takes on average five years to get an action into the European Court of Human Rights once all domestic remedies have been exhausted; and it costs an average of £30,000. Bringing these rights home will mean that the British people will be able to argue for their rights in the British courts — without this inordinate delay and cost. It will also mean that the rights will be brought much more fully into the jurisprudence of the courts throughout the United Kingdom, and their interpretation will thus be far more subtly and powerfully woven into our law."[9]

The situation adopted respects the traditional doctrine of Parliamentary sovereignty in that the judges are not accorded power to strike down primary legislation that is incompatible with a Convention right; instead they may make a declaration of incompatibility (section 4) which in turn may pave the way for a special form of amending legislation (a remedial order). Beyond that there is a new rule for the interpretation of legislation (section 3) and a new rule that it is unlawful for a public authority to act in a way incompatible with a Convention right (section 6). The provisions of the Human Rights Act can affect both the interpretation and application of legislation and the development of the common law, and can reach into most areas regulated or affected by law. One controversial matter is, however, the extent to which its provisions may regulate the relationship between two parties neither of whom is a public authority.[10]

The basic purpose of the Act is stated to be "to give further effect to rights and freedoms guaranteed under the European Convention on Human Rights."[11]

B. KEY CONCEPTS AND PROVISIONS

1. CONVENTION RIGHTS

8–002   "Convention rights" are the rights and fundamental freedoms set out in Article 2 to 12 and 14 of the Convention, Articles 1 to 3 of the First Protocol and Articles 1 and 2 of the Sixth Protocol, as read with Articles 16 to 18 of

---

[7] Others were the devolution measures: the Scotland Act 1998 and the Government of Wales Act 1998.
[8] Cm. 3782, 1997.
[9] Para. 1.14.
[10] Below.para. 8-013.
[11] *Human Rights Act* 1998, Long Title. For the purpose of the Act, " 'the Convention' means the Convention for the Protection of Human Rights and Fundamental Freedoms, agreed by the Council of Europe at Rome on November 4, 1950 as it has effect for the time being in relation to the United Kingdom": section 21(1).

the Convention, but subject to any derogation or reservation.[12] They are set out in Schedule 1 to the Act and cover, respectively, the right to life (Article 2), the prohibition of torture (Article 3), the prohibition of slavery and forced labour (Article 4), the right to liberty and security (Article 5), the right to a fair trial (Article 6), no punishment without law (Article 7), the right to respect for private and family life (Article 8), freedom of thought, conscience and religion (Article 9), freedom of expression (Article 10), freedom of assembly and association (Article 11), the right to marry (Article 12), the prohibition of discrimination affecting the enjoyment of Convention rights and freedoms (Article 14), the protection of property (First Protocol, Article 1), the right to education (First Protocol, Article 2),[13] the right to free elections (First Protocol, Article 3), abolition of the death penalty (Sixth Protocol, Article 1) and provision for the death penalty in time of war (Sixth Protocol, Article 2).

Nothing in Articles 10, 11 and 14 is to be regarded as preventing the imposition of restrictions on the political activity of aliens; nothing in the Convention may be interpreted as implying any right to engage in any activity or perform any act aimed at the destruction of Convention rights or their limitation to a greater extent than provided for in the Convention; and restrictions permitted under the Convention are not to be applied for any purpose other than those for which they have been prescribed.[14]

Some Convention rights are absolute. For example, Article 2 provides that:

"No one shall be subjected to torture or to inhuman or degrading treatment or punishment."

Others are drafted with closely defined qualifications, exclusions or exceptions. For example, Article 5 provides that:

"Everyone has the right to liberty and security of person. No one shall be deprived of his liberty save in the following cases and in accordance with a procedure prescribed by law."

It proceeds to list six situations of lawful arrest or detention, including lawful detention after conviction by a competent court, lawful arrest and

---

[12] Section 1(1), (2). As to derogations and reservations, see sections 14–17. The text of the 1998 Act included the existing reservation (to First Protocol, Article 2), and derogation (to Article 5(3)), in respect of extended detention under the Prevention of Terrorism legislation. The derogation was withdrawn from February 26, 2001 (Human Rights Act (Amendment) Order 2001 (S.I. 2001 No. 1216) but a fresh derogation was made in 2001 in respect of provision in the Anti-Terrorism, Crime and Security Act 2001 for an extended power to arrest and detain a foreign national with a view to deportation on national security grounds (Human Rights Act 1998 (Amendment No. 2) Order 2001 (S.I. 2001 No. 4032)). See A. Tomkins, [2002] P.L. 205.

[13] The UK has entered a reservation to the second sentence of Article 2 ("In the exercise of any function which it assumes in relation to education and to teaching, the State shall respect the right of parents to ensure such education and teaching in conformity with their own religious and philosophical convictions.'" This was accepted "only so far as it is compatible with the provision of efficient education and training, and the avoidance of unreasonable public expenditure": see 1998 Act, Sched. 3, Part III.

[14] Articles 16 to 18.

detention effected for the purpose of bringing the person before the competent legal authority on reasonable suspicion of having committed an offence, detention of a minor by lawful order for the purpose of educational supervision and the lawful detention of persons for the purpose of the spreading of infectious diseases, of persons of unsound mind, alcoholics or drug addicts or vagrants.

Article 6(1) provides that:

> "In the determination of his civil rights and obligations or of any criminal charge against him, everyone is entitled to a fair and public hearing within a reasonable time by an independent and impartial tribunal established by law. ... "

Judgment must be pronounced publicly but the press and public may be excluded from all or part of the trial in prescribed circumstances. The rest of Article 6 sets out specific rules applicable to those charged with criminal offences.

Yet other articles are drafted subject to broadly drawn exceptions. One example is Article 8, concerning respect for private and family life.[15]

Articles 9, 10 and 11 provide, respectively, for the right to freedom of thought, conscience and religion, the right to freedom of expression and the "right to freedom of peaceful assembly and to freedom of association with others" subject to similarly worded exceptions.

Some of these articles are considered further in more detail below.[16]

2. The Authority of European Court of Human Rights Jurisprudence

8–003   Any court or tribunal determining a question which has arisen under the Act in connection with a Convention right must take into account, so far as it is of the opinion that it is relevant, any judgment, decision or advisory opinion of the European Court of Human Rights; certain opinions and decisions of the European Commission or Human Rights;[17] and decisions of the Committee of Ministers taken under Article 46.[18]

In *R. (on the application of Holding and Barnes plc) v. Secretary of State for the Environment, Transport and the Regions*[19] Lord Slynn said:[20]

> "Your Lordships have been referred to many decisions of the European Court of Human Rights on Article 6 of the Convention. Although the Human Rights Act 1998 does not provide that a national court is

---

[15] See below, para. 8-022.

[16] See below, paras 8-016–8-025.

[17] *i.e.* opinions in a report under Article 31 of the Convention as to whether the facts found constitute a breach of the Convention; decisions by the Commission under Article 26 in connection with the exhaustion of domestic remedies and the requirement that it deal with a matter within six months from the date on which the final decision was taken; and decisions by the Commission under Article 27(2) that a petition is inadmissible as incompatible with the provisions of the Convention, manifestly ill-founded, or an abuse of the right of petition.

[18] 1998 Act, s. 21(1).

[19] [2001] UKHL 23, [2001] 2 W.L.R. 1389.

[20] Para. [26].

bound by these decisions it is obliged to take account of them so far as they are relevant. In the absence of some special circumstances it seems to be that the court should follow any clear and constant jurisprudence of the European Court of Human Rights. If it does not do so there is at least a possibility that the case will go to that court which is likely in the ordinary case to follow its own constant jurisprudence."

Lord Hoffmann said[21] that had the decisions of the Court "compelled a conclusion so fundamentally at odds with the distribution of powers under the British Constitution, I would have considerable doubts as to whether they should be followed." The other members of the House did not comment expressly on this point. All were agreed that there was no inconsistency between English law and the ECHR.[22]

Lord Slynn's approach has been echoed by the Court of Appeal in *R. (on the application of Anderson and Taylor) v. Secretary of State for the Home Department.*[23] Here, the court held that while it was of the view that the fixing of the tariff element of a mandatory life sentence by the Home Secretary should conform to the requirements of Article 6(1), ECHR, and did not do so, it should defer to the contrary view of the European Court of Human Rights, which was in any event about to reconsider the principles applicable in this area. The court took account of the other court's particular expertise as an international court in the interpretation of the ECHR and considerations of comity.

3. THE MARGIN OF APPRECIATION AND PROPORTIONALITY

The jurisprudence of the European Court of Human Rights recognises that **8–004** in considering whether there has been compliance with the ECHR member states are in some contexts accorded a "margin of appreciation." This takes account of the fact that the ECHR machinery is subsidiary to the national systems safeguarding human rights, leaving to those national systems in the first place the task of securing the Convention rights and freedoms.[24] Furthermore, some of the concepts enshrined in ECHR articles do not have a uniform European content.[25] Accordingly,

"by reason of their direct and continuous contact with the vital forces of their countries, State authorities are in principle in a better position than the international judges to give an opinion on the exact content of these requirements as well as on the 'necessity' of a 'restriction' or 'penalty' intended to meet them ... [I]t is for the national authorities to

---

[21] Para. [76].

[22] See further, para. 8-021.

[23] [2001] EWCA Civ 1698. Lord Slynn's dictum was relied on in argument by counsel for the Secretary of State but only referred to by one member of the court.

[24] *Handyside v. UK* (1996) 1 EHRR 737, para. 48.

[25] *ibid.*, giving as an example the absence of a "European conception of morals" for the purposes of consideration of one of the justifications for interferences with freedom of expression ("the protection of ... morals") set out in Article 10(2).

make the initial assessment of the reality of the pressing social need implied by the notion of 'necessity' in this context.

Consequently, Article 10(2) leaves to the Contracting States a margin of appreciation."[26]

However, the power of appreciation is not unlimited, and the decisions of member states are subject to "supervision" by the European Court, which must decide whether the reasons given by national authorities to justify measures of "interference" are relevant and sufficient, applying a test of proportionality.[27] The scope of the power of appreciation does, however, vary according to context. For example the concept of "maintaining the authority ... of the judiciary," another justification found for interference with freedom of expression found in Article 10(2), has a "far more objective notion" than the protection of "morals", the domestic law and practice of member states revealing "a fairly substantial measure of common ground." Here, "a more extensive European supervision corresponds to a less discretionary power of appreciation."[28] Contexts in which a margin of appreciation has been recognised include the establishment of justifications for interference with protected rights and freedoms under paragraph 2 of Articles 8 to 11;[29] areas where the article in question contains vague expressions;[30] and where the Court has to determine whether a state has failed to comply with a positive obligation to protect a Convention right.[31]

The "margin of appreciation" doctrine does not as such apply where an English court is reviewing decisions and acts of public authorities by virtue of the Human Rights Act 1998.[32] That doctrine itself comprises separate elements: first, the appropriate measure of deference by a court to a public authority and secondly, the deference of an international court to state authorities. Only the former could itself be relevant at the domestic level.[33] Nevertheless, in some contexts it will be appropriate for a reviewing court to recognise a 'discretionary area of judgment'. This point has been made by Lord Hope of Craighead:[34]

"[I]n the hands of the national courts also the Convention should be seen as an expression of fundamental principles rather than as a set of mere rules. The questions which the courts will have to decide in the application of these principles will involve questions of balance between competing interests and issues of proportionality.

In this area difficult choices may have to be made by the executive or

---

[26] *ibid.*

[27] *ibid.*, paras 49, 50.

[28] *Sunday Times v. UK* (1979) 2 E.H.R.R. 245, para. 59.

[29] Above.

[30] *E.g.* determination by a member state that the "life of the nation" is threatened by a "public emergency" so as to justify a derogation under Article 15: *Lawless v. Ireland (No. 3)* (1961) 1 E.H.R.R. 15, para. 207.

[31] *E.g. X. Y and Z v. UK* (1997) 24 E.H.R.R. 143 and *TP and KM v. UK.*, Judgment of May 10, 2001, below, para. 8-018.

[32] *per* Lord Hope of Craighead in *R. v. DPP. ex p. Kebilene* [2000] 2 A.C. 326, 375; *R. (on the application of ProLife Alliance) v. BBC* [2002] 2 All E.R. 756, para. [31].

[33] M. Fordham and T. de la Mare, "Identifying the Principles of Proportionality" in J. Jowell and J. Cooper, *Understanding Human Rights Principles* (2001), pp. 54–55.

[34] *ibid.*

the legislature between the rights of the individual and the needs of society. In some circumstances it will be appropriate for the court to recognise that there is an area of judgment within which the judiciary will defer, on democratic grounds, to the considered opinion of the elected body or person whose act or decision is said to be incompatible with the Convention. The point is well made at page 74, paragraph 3.21 of Lester and Pannick (eds) *Human Rights Law and Practice* (1999), where the area in which these choices may arise is conveniently and appropriately described as the 'discretionary area of judgment.' It will be easier for such an area of judgment to be recognised where the Convention itself requires a balance to be struck, much less so where the right is stated in terms which are unqualified. It will be easier for it to be recognised where the issues involve questions of social and economic policy, much less so where the rights are of high constitutional importance or are of a kind where the courts are especially well placed to assess the need for protection."

Examples of contexts in which an area of discretionary judgment has been recognised include: the decision of the Secretary of State that the purposes behind a deportation order justified the consequential interference with family life;[35] decisions of planning inspectors on the balance between interference with private and family life (Article 8(1)) on the one hand and furtherance of the legitimate aims of the planning system on the other;[36] the decision of Ashworth Hospital Authority to adopt a policy that no condoms should be issued to detained patients at Ashworth Special Hospital;[37] decisions of the Prison Service as to policies in the management of prisons;[38] the decision of the Secretary of State to exclude an alien in the light of risks of public disorder notwithstanding consequent interference with freedom of expression;[39] decisions of the Press Complaints Commission in rejecting complaints of infringement of privacy in breach of its Code of Practice;[40] the decision of the legislature to impose a reversed onus of proof in respect of defences to the offence of having a bladed article in a public place;[41] the legislature's decisions as to the arrangements for termination of shorthold

---

[35] *R. (on the application of Samaroo) v. Secretary of State for the Home Department* 1 [2001] EWCA Civ 1139; *R. (on the application of Mahmood) v. Secretary of State for the Home Department* [2001] 1 W.L.R. 840; *R. v. Secretary of State for the Home Department ex p. Isiko* [2001] H.R.L.R. 295.

[36] *Buckland v. Secretary of State for the Environment, Transport and the Regions* [2001] EWHC Admin 524; *Clarke v. Secretary of State for the Environment. Transport and the Regions* [2001] EWHC Admin 800 (citing the ECtHR decision in *Chapman v. UK* (2001) 10 B.H.R.C. 48, para. 92 and *Buckley v. UK* (1997) 23 E.H.R.R. 101, para. 75, referring to the wide margin of appreciation enjoyed by national authorities in planning cases).

[37] *R. (on the application of H) v. Ashworth Hospital* [2001] EWHC Admin 872, [2002] 1 F.C.R. 206. See also *R. (on the application of N) v. Ashworth Special Hospital Authority* [2001] H.R.L.R. 1010 (policy of random monitoring of telephone calls upheld).

[38] *R. (on the application of P, Q and QB), v. Secretary of State for the Home Departments* [2001] EWCA Civ 1151, [2001] 1 W.L.R. 2002.

[39] *Farrakhan v. Secretary of State for the Home Department* [2001] EWHC Admin 781; reversed on the facts by the Court of Appeal: [2002] EWCA Civ 606 (held appropriate "to accord a particularly wide margin of discretion to the Secretary of State": para. [71]).

[40] *R. (on the application of Ford) v. Press Complaints Commission* [2001] EWHC Admin 683.

[41] *Lynch v. DPP* [2001] EWHC Admin 882.

and introductory tenancies[42] and the distribution of state benefits;[43] decisions of local authorities concerning children who might be at risk.[44] However, the extent of that area may vary considerably according to the circumstances; for example, while a very high degree of respect might be accorded to the views of broadcasters in regulating the content of broadcast entertainment, less would be according in respect of the regulation of day-to-day news reporting, and very little in the regulation of the content of party-political broadcasts as the time of a general election. The courts are "ultimately the trustees of our democracy's framework."[45]

8–005   The approach to be adopted by the courts in reviewing decisions where the decision-maker is required to comply with the Convention as a matter of law[46] was summarised as follows by Lord Phillips of Worth Matravers M.R. in *R. (on the application of Mahmood) v. Secretary of State for the Home Department.*[47] First, even where human rights are at stake, the role of the court is supervisory; it does not substitute its own decision for that of the executive and must bear in mind that there will often be an area of discretion permitted to the executive before a response can be demonstrated to infringe the Convention. Secondly, in conducting a review of a decision affecting human rights, the court must subject it to "the most anxious scrutiny." Thirdly, instead of merely applying the tests of *Wednesbury* unreasonableness, as modified as regards decisions affecting human rights,[48] the court must:

> "ask the question, applying an objective test, whether the decision-maker could reasonably have concluded that the interference was necessary to achieve one or more of the legitimate aims recognised by the Convention."

The third of these propositions was subject to modification by the House of Lords in *R. (on the application of Daly) v. Secretary of State for the Home Department.*[49] Here, the House of Lords held that a blanket rule requiring that on a cell search a prisoner was not to be present when prison officers examined his legally privileged correspondence was unlawful. Lord Steyn stated[50] that Lord Phillips M.R.'s third proposition needed "clarification" as it did not make sufficiently clear the distinction between even heightened

---

[42] *Donoghue v. Poplar Housing and Regeneration Community Association Ltd* [2001] EWCA Civ 595; *McLellan v. Bracknell Forest Borough Council* [2001] EWCA Civ 1510, [2002] 1 All E.R. 899.

[43] *Waite v. London Borough of Hammersmith and Fulham* [2002] EWCA Civ 482; *R. (on the application of Carson) v. Secretary of State for Work and Pensions* [2002] EWHC 978 (Admin).

[44] *R. (on the application of S). v. Swindon Borough Council* [2001] EWHC Admin 334.

[45] *R. (on the application of ProLife Alliance) v. BBC* [2002] 2 All E.R. 756, para. [36].

[46] This will normally arise in proceedings under s.7, in respect of an act made unlawful by s.6: see below, para. 8–009.

[47] [2001] 1 W.L.R. 840 at paras [37]–[40].

[48] See *R. v. Ministry of Defence, ex p. Smith* [1996] Q.B. 517, 554, below, para. 18–050. The extent to which the proportionality principle differs from the recent flexible approach to *Wednesbury* review has been much discussed: see *e.g.* M. Fordham and T. de la Mare, "Identifying the principles of proportionality" in J. Jowell and J. Cooper (eds), *Understanding Human Rights Principles* (2001), pp. 27–89; I. Leigh, [2002] P.L. 265.

[49] [2001] UKHL 26, [2001] H.R.L.R. 1103, [2001] 2 W.L.R. 1622.

[50] Paras [25]–[28]. The other members of the House expressly agreed with Lord Steyn.

scrutiny *Wednesbury* review and the test of proportionality required for the purposes of the ECHR and the Human Rights Act 1998. The proper approach in applying the proportionality test was set out by the Privy Council in *de Freitas v. Permanent Secretary of Ministry of Agriculture, Fisheries, Lands and Housing.*[51] In determining whether a limitation (by an act, rule or decision) is arbitrary or excessive the court should ask itself:

"whether: (i) the legislative objective is sufficiently important to justify limiting a fundamental right; (ii) the measures designed to meet the legislative objective are rationally connected to it; and (iii) the means used to impair the right or freedom are no more than is necessary to accomplish the objective."

Most cases would be decided in the same way under the *Wednesbury* and proportionality approaches,[52] but, "the intensity of review is somewhat greater under the proportionality approach." Three concrete differences were, first, that:

"the doctrine of proportionality may require the reviewing court to assess the balance which the decision maker has struck, not merely whether it is within the range of rational or reasonable decisions."

Secondly,

"the proportionality test may go further than the traditional grounds of review in as much as it may require attention to be directed to the relative weight accorded to interests and considerations."

Thirdly, even the heightened scrutiny test developed in *ex p. Smith* is not necessarily appropriate to the protection of human rights in view of the fact that the European Court of Human Rights in the same case found the approach to be inadequate given that it effectively excluded any consideration by domestic courts of the question whether the interference with the applicants' rights answered a pressing social need or was proportionate to the national security and public order aims pursued.[53] All this does not however mean that there had been a "shift to merits review."

In *R. (on the application of Samaroo) v. Secretary of State for the Home Department*[54] the Court of Appeal held that in deciding what proportionality requires in any particular case the issue will normally have to be considered in two stages. The first question is "can the objective of the measure be achieved by means which are less interfering of an individual's rights?" At the second stage, it is assumed that the means employed are necessary in the sense that they are "the least intrusive of Convention rights that can be devised in order to achieve the aim." The question here is "does the measure have an excessive or disproportionate effect on the interests of

---

[51] [1999] 1 A.C. 69, *per* Lord Clyde at p. 80.
[52] The *Daly* case was itself an example of this as the policy was unlawful applying both common law (see Lord Bingham's speech) and Convention principles.
[53] *Smith and Grady v. UK* (1999) 29 E.H.R.R 493, at para. 138.
[54] [2001] EWCA Civ 1139, *per* Dyson L.J. at paras [14]–[23].

affected persons?" The *Daly* case illustrated the application of the first question: the blanket policy was unlawful as the legitimate aim of maintaining security in prison would be met by a rule that entitled prison officers to examine privileged correspondence of an individual prisoner who was attempting to intimidate or disrupt a search, or whose past conduct had shown that he was likely to do so. The *Samaroo* case illustrated the application of the second question. It was clear that in general terms the objective of preventing crime and disorder was sufficiently important to justify limiting a fundamental right (here the right to family life) and that the deportation of those convicted of serious criminal offences (especially, as here, drug trafficking offences) was a measure rationally connected to that objective. The only issue here was whether a deportation had a disproportionate effect on the applicant's rights under Article 8(1). The task of the Secretary of State was within his discretionary area of judgment to "strike a fair balance" between the legitimate aim and the affected person's Convention rights. The task of the court in reviewing his decision was supervisory of that discretionary area of judgment. It had to decide:

"whether the Secretary of State has struck the balance fairly between the conflicting interests of [the applicant's] right to respect for his family life on the one hand and the prevention of crime and disorder on the other. In reaching its decision, the court must recognise and allow to the Secretary of State a discretionary area of judgment."[55]

Factors relevant in determining to what extent (if at all) there should be deference to the decision-maker, include[56] (a) the nature of the Convention right; is it absolute or does it require a balance to be struck? The court is less likely to defer to the decision maker in the former case; (b) the extent to which the issues require consideration of social, economic or political factors; the court will usually accord considerable deference in such cases because it is not expert in the realm of policy making, nor should it be because it is not democratically elected or accountable; (c) the extent to which the court has special expertise, for example in relation to criminal matters; (d) where the rights claimed are of especial importance (*e.g.* freedom of expression and access to the courts) a "high degree of constitutional protection" will be appropriate. In the present case, a "significant margin of discretion" to the decision of the Secretary of State was appropriate. The Convention right was not absolute and the court did not have expertise in judging how effective the deportation policy was as a deterrent. It was for the Secretary of State to show that he had struck a fair balance.[57] How much weight he gave to each factor would be the subject of

---

[55] *ibid.*, para. [35].

[56] Based on Lester and Pannick (eds), *Human Rights Law and Practice* (1999), para. 3.26.

[57] In *R. (on the application of H) v. Ashworth Hospital* [2001] EWHC Admin 872, [2002] 1 F.C.R. 206 Sir Christopher Bellamy Q.C. held (para. [113]) that where the applicant complained of a failure by a public authority to protect his rights, it was for him to persuade the court that there was some further step which the decision maker could not reasonably have omitted to take. (It is submitted that it is not obvious that that should be so; where the authority has been requested and refused to take a particular step, it should in principle be required to justify that position).

careful scrutiny by the court and the court would interfere with the weight accorded by the decision-maker

"if, despite an allowance for the appropriate margin of discretion, it concludes that the weight accorded was unfair and unreasonable."[58]

On the facts, the Secretary of State was entitled to regard Class A drug trafficking offences as very serious; to attach importance to his general policy of deporting those convicted of importation of Class A drugs to protect UK residents and to deter others; and to attach particular weight to the applicant's role as a "crucial part of the organisation." He recognised the serious interference with the applicant's right to family life under Article 8(1). Overall, the Secretary of State conclusion was a "fair and reasonable conclusion that he was entitled to reach."[59]

Cases where the public authority has failed to establish a justification for the interference with the applicant's rights and freedoms under the proportionality approach are relatively unusual. Illustrations include: *Daly*;[60] *R. (on the application of Farrakhan) v. Secretary of State for the Home Department*[61] (at first instance but reversed on appeal[62]); *Aston Cantlow and Wilmcote with Billesley Parochial Church Council v. Wallbank*[63] and *R. (on the application of Hirst) v. Secretary of State for the Home Department*.[64]

Finally, it should be noted that there are, exceptionally, some situations where it is *for the court itself* to determine whether the interference with the claimant's Convention rights is proportionate. Examples include an exercise of discretion by the High Court to grant injunctive relief to enforce planning legislation.[65]

---

[58] para. [39].
[59] para. [41]. *cf. Buckland v. Secretary of State for the Environment. Transport and the Regions* and other cases [2001] EWHC Admin 524, para. [56] where Sullivan J. in respect of an appeal in a planning case against an inspector's decision rejected the submission that it was for the court to "satisfy itself that the right balance has been struck by the inspector that would be to embark on a merits review."
[60] Above.
[61] [2001] EWHC Admin 781. Held to be insufficient evidence that there was more than a nominal risk that community relations would be endangered if the ban on the applicant's entry to the UK for the limited purpose and duration sought were lifted.
[62] [2002] EWCA Civ 606. Held that the Secretary of State had provided a sufficient explanation for a decision that turned on his personal, informed, assessment of risk to demonstrate that his decision was not disproportionate, although the merits of the appeal were "finely balanced."
[63] Liability of particular owners of former glebe land to contribute to chancel repairs held to be arbitrary in its incidence (contrary to the First Protocol, Article 1) and unjustifiably discriminatory (contrary to Article 14) as it was not a proportionate means of maintaining historic buildings, and so lacked a reasonable and objective justification.
[64] [2002] EWHC 602 (Admin) (policy imposing blanket ban on prisoner having telephone contact with the media held unlawful by Elias J.).
[65] *South Buckinghamshire District Council v. Porter* and other cases [2001] EWCA Civ 1549, [2002] 1 All E.R. 425.

3. INTERPRETATION OF LEGISLATION AND DECLARATIONS OF INCOMPARTIBILITY

(a) The boundary between interpretation and amendment

8–006   Section 3(1) of the 1998 Act provides that:

> "So far as it is possible to do so, primary legislation[66] and subordinate legislation[67] must be read and given effect in a way which is compatible with Convention rights."

This provision applies to primary and subordinate legislation whenever enacted[68], but does not affect the validity, continuing operation or enforcement of (1) any incompatible primary legislation and (2) any incompatible secondary legislation if (disregarding any possibility of revocation) primary legislation prevents removal of the incompatibility.[69] In these cases a court,[70] in any proceedings where it determines whether a provision is compatible with a Convention right, may make a *declaration of incompatibility*. Such a declaration does not affect the validity, continuing operation or enforcement of the provision and is not binding on the parties to the proceedings in which it is made.[71] Where a court is considering the possibility of a declaration of incompatibility, the Crown is entitled to notice in accordance with rules of court and a minister of the Crown (or his nominee), a member of the Scottish Executive, and a Northern Ireland minister on department is entitled, on giving notice in accordance with rules of court, to be joined as a party to the proceedings.[72] Following a declaration of incompatibility or a finding by the European Court of Human Rights in proceedings against the UK that a provision is incompatible with an obligation of the UK arising from the Convention, a minister of the Crown may make a remedial order, subject to the approval

---

[66] i.e. any public general, local and personal or private Act of Parliament, any measure of the Church Assembly or the General Synod of the Church of England; certain Orders in Council; and certain orders made under primary legislation bringing one or more provisions of that legislation into force or amending any primary legislation: s.21(1).

[67] i.e. any Order in Council that does not qualify as primary legislation; any Act of the Scottish Parliament, the Parliament of Northern Ireland or the Northern Ireland Assembly; and any order, rules, regulations scheme, warrant, by-law or other instrument made under primary legislation, under an Act of any of the bodies just mentioned or an Order in Council applying only to Northern Ireland, or by a member of the Scottish Executive, a Northern Ireland minister or department in the exercise of prerogative or other executive functions on behalf of Her Majesty.

[68] Section 3(2)(a).

[69] Section 3(2)(b), (c). For the argument that section 3(2)(b) operates as a limit to the broad duty arising under section 3(1), so that section 3(1) may not be invoked to support a proposed reading that "would have the effect of so impairing the operation and/or effectiveness of the clause under scrutiny so as to render it for all practical purposes a dead letter, or close to a dead letter" see C. Gearty, (2002) 118 L.Q.R. 248, 250–258.

[70] i.e. the House of Lords, the Judicial Committee of the Privy Council, the Courts-Martial Appeal Court, the High Court of Justiciary sitting otherwise as a trial court, the Court of Session, the High Court and the Court of Appeal in England and Wales and in Northern Ireland: section 4(5).

[71] Section 4(1)–(4), (6).

[72] Section 5.

of each House of Parliament, amending primary legislation or amending or revoking subordinate legislation.[73] It is of course also possible for other processes for amendment to be adopted, including fresh primary legislation. The fast-track order procedure is indeed only available if the minister considers there are "compelling reasons" for proceeding under section 10.

The obligation imposed by section 3(1) is not confined to any particular institution or person. Accordingly, as well as applying to courts and tribunals it will apply to government departments and local authorities and will govern their approach to the interpretation of legislation conferring functions upon them. Legislation is to be interpreted in such a way to be compatible "so far as it is possible to do so." The modern approach for statutory interpretation expects statutory provisions to be interpreted in their context, with the notion of "context" construed widely. It is accepted that judges may read in words necessarily implied and have a limited power to add to, alter or ignore statutory words in order to prevent a provision from being unintelligible or absurd or totally unreasonable, unworkable or totally irreconcilable with the rest of the statute.[74]

This approach includes the power to read statutory provisions as qualified by broad principles that reflect fundamental values of the common law and which Parliament is presumed to intend to be applicable unless the contrary is expressly stated, such as the substantive principles of judicial review,[75] the general principles of criminal liability such as the presumption in favour of a requirement of *mens rea* for criminal offences[76] the principle that no person should be allowed to benefit from his own wrong,[77] and respect for legal professional privilege.[78]

Courts and tribunals required to determine an issue of compatibility will clearly be expected to use all legitimate techniques of statutory interpretation to read and give effect to a provision so as to be compatible with Convention rights. The same is presumably true of other persons and bodies to whom the obligation under section 3(1) applies, although it may well in practice prove difficult to criticise them should they decline to adopt an approach based on one of the more sophisticated judicial techniques of statutory interpretation (such as the power in limited circumstances to treat statutory language as modified). In any event, there will come a point where the words of a provision are so unequivocal that effect has to be given to them notwithstanding incompatibility. So much is assumed in the existence of the power of certain courts to grant a declaration of incompatibility.[79]

Nevertheless, it has been made clear that the enactment of section 3(1) does involve the addition of an extra dimension to the ordinary methods of

[73] Section 10 and Sched. 2. A remedial order has been made following the decision in *R. (on the application of H) v. Mental Health Review Tribunal*, below, para. 8-008: see the Mental Health Act 1983 (Remedial Order 2001) (S.I. 2001 No. 3712).

[74] Above, para. 6-014.

[75] See Chap. 18.

[76] See J.C. Smith, *Smith & Hogan Criminal Law* (8th edn, 1996), Chaps 6 (crimes of strict liability) and 10 (general defences); *Sweet v. Parsley* [1970] A.C. 132.

[77] See *e.g. R. v. Secretary of State for the Home Department, ex p. Puttick* [1981] Q.B. 767; *R. v. Registrar-General, ex p. Smith* [1991] 2 Q.B. 393.

[78] *R. v. Special Commissioners of Income Tax, ex p. Morgan Grenfell & Co. Ltd* [2002] UKHL 21, [2001] 3 All E.R. 1.

[79] Lord Hope in *R. v. Lambert* [2001] 3 W.L.R. 206, 233–235, paras [70]–[81]; Lord Nicholls in *In re S(FC)* [2002] UKHL 10, [2002] 2 All E.R. 192, para. [38].

interpretation. In *R. v. A.*[80] the House of Lords considered the ambit of the statutory prohibition on the introduction at a trial for a sexual offence evidence of the complainant's sexual behaviour unless one of a number of narrowly drawn exceptions applied. One of these was that there was an issue of consent and the behaviour was alleged to be so similar to any such behaviour which took place as part of the event in question or at or about the same time as that event that the similarity could not reasonably be explained as a coincidence.[81] The House held that this was to be interpreted as giving rise to a test for admissibility of whether the evidence was so relevant to the issue of consent that to exclude it would endanger the fairness of the trial under Article 6. Lord Steyn recognised that the "ordinary methods of purposive construction" of s.41(3)(c) could not cure the excessive breadth of section 41 so far as it related to previous sexual experience between a complainant and the accused. "Whilst the statute pursued desirable goals, the methods adopted amount to legislative overkill." However,

> "the interpretative obligation under section 3 of the 1998 Act is a strong one. It applies even if there is no ambiguity in the language in the sense of the language being capable of two different meanings. It is an emphatic adjuration by the legislature.... Section 3 ... places a duty on the court to strive to find a possible interpretation compatible with convention rights. Under ordinary methods of interpretation a court may depart from the language of the statute to avoid absurd consequences: section 3 goes much further. Undoubtedly, a court must always look for a contextual and purposive interpretation: section 3 is more radical in its effect. ... In accordance with the will of Parliament as reflected in section 3 it will sometimes be necessary to adopt an interpretation which linguistically may appear strange. The techniques to be used will not only involve the reading down of express language in a statute but also the implication of provisions. A declaration of incompatibility is a measure of last resort."[82]

8–007 Accordingly, section 41 was to be read as subject to the implied provision that evidence or questioning required to ensure a fair trial under Article 6 should not be treated as inadmissible. It would seem that this extra dimension is closely analogous to the power to read statutory provisions as qualified by broad common law principles set out above.

---

[80] [2001] UKHL 25, [2002] 2 A.C. 45. Other examples include *R. v. Lambert* [2001] 3 W.L.R. 206 (defence available to defendant charged with possession of drugs to prove that they neither believed nor suspected nor had reason to suspect that substance in their possession was a controlled drug interpreted as imposing evidential burden not a legal burden as otherwise there would be a violation of the presumption of innocence in Article 6(2)); *Cachia v. Faluyi* [2001] EWCA Civ 998, [2001] 1 W.L.R. 1966 (word "action" in the Fatal Accidents Act 1976, s. 2(3) ("Not more than one action shall lie for and in respect of the same subject matter of complaint") to be interpreted as "served process" to protect claimant's right of access to the court).

[81] Youth Justice and Criminal Evidence Act 1999, s.41(3).

[82] Paras [43]–[45]. See to similar effect, Lord Slynn at paras [11]–[13], [15]; Lord Clyde at paras [136], [140]; Lord Hutton at paras [160]–[163]. Lord Hope of Craighead (paras [109]–[110]) took a narrower view holding that section 3 could not be used to imply a general provision of this nature but only to "read down" the actual words of section 41.

In *Donoghue v. Poplar Housing and Regeneration Community Association Ltd.*[83] the Court of Appeal indicated *obiter* that the court should always first ascertain whether, absent section 3, there would be any breach of the convention as, otherwise, section 3 could be ignored; if it had to rely on section 3 it should limit the extent of the modified meaning to that which is necessary to achieve compatibility; section 3 did not entitle the court to *legislate*, its task was one of *interpretation*; the views of the parties and of the Crown as to whether a "constructive" interpretation should be adopted could not modify the task of the court, which was under a duty to adopt section 3 where it applied; where a compatible result could not be reached through interpretation, the court retained a discretion whether to grant a declaration of incompatibility, which would presumably be influenced by the usual considerations which apply to the grant of declarations.[84]

The boundary between interpretation and (impermissible) amendment was held by the House of Lords in *In re S(FC)*[85] to have been crossed in that case by the Court of Appeal.[86] The Court of Appeal had held that provisions of the Children Act 1989 concerning care orders should be subject to modifications that enhanced the role of the court. The House disapproved one of these, namely that the guardian *ad litem* or local authority had the right to apply to the trial court if starred milestones in the care plan were not achieved within a reasonable time of the date set at trial. This would depart from a "cardinal principle" of the Act "that the courts are not empowered to intervene in the way local authorities discharge their parental responsibilities under final care orders."[87] In ascribing a meaning by virtue of section 3(1), it was important for a court to identify clearly the particular statutory provision(s) whose interpretation led to that result; here, the Court of Appeal had not identified any such provision of the 1989 Act, and indeed there was none. The introduction of the starring system would have far reaching practical effects on the workload of local authorities and their allocation of scarce financial and other resources; "these are matters for decision by Parliament not the courts." [88] Furthermore, the starring system went much further than provide a judicial remedy to victims of actual or proposed conduct that would be unlawful under Articles 6 and 8.

Two points emerge. First, it would seem that the practical effects of a particular modification of statutory language by virtue of section 3(1) interpretation may properly be relevant in determining whether the boundary has been crossed. Nevertheless, it is submitted that it would be wrong to confine section 3(1) in all cases to the making of small changes. Secondly, it is also submitted that it would be wrong for section 3(1) to be confined to securing what would be effectively textual modifications to specified provisions. Such an approach would fail to take account of the powers of the courts to read statutes as modified (in the absence of clear words to the contrary) by fundamental, albeit broadly stated, principles.[89]

---

[83] [2001] EWCA Civ 595.
[84] *per* Lord Woolf C.J. at para. [75].
[85] [2002] UKHL 10, [2002] 2 All E.R. 192.
[86] *Re W & B (children); Re W (children)* [2001] EWCA Civ 757, [2001] H.R.L.R. 1120.
[87] Para. [42].
[88] Paras [43], [44].
[89] See above.

The strength of the interpretative obligation under section 3(1) is confirmed by the point that it may require a court below the level of the House of Lords to disregard a decision of the House.[90] It does not, however, enable a court to change substantive law with effect retrospectively prior to commencement of the HRA.[91]

Finally, in any case where a declaration of incompatibility is made, it will *ex hypothesi* have proved impossible to secure compatibility via section 3(1).[92]

(b) Declarations of incompatibility

8–008   Declarations of incompatibility have been made in a small number of cases, as follows. In *Wilson v. First County Trust (No. 2)*[93] the Court of Appeal held that section 123(3) of the Consumer Credit Act 1974, in so far as it prevented a court from making an enforcement order unless a document containing *all* the prescribed terms had been signed by the debtor or hirer, was incompatible with Article 6(1) and the First Protocol, Article 1. In *R. (on the application of H) v. Mental Health Review Tribunal*[94] the Court of Appeal found that the reversed burden of proof, in respect of matters justifying the detention of a mental patient, in section 73 of the Mental Health Act 1983 was incompatible with Article 5. In *R. (on the application of International Transport Roth GmbH) v. Secretary of State for the Home Department*[95] the Court of Appeal held that the penalty regime applicable to lorry drivers and haulage companies as persons responsible for clandestine entrants was incompatible with Article 6 and the First Protocol, Article 1. The penalty imposed under the scheme was disproportionate to its goal. In two cases,[96] Moses J. granted declarations that provisions governing particular benefits payable to "widows" constituted unjustifiable gender discrimination contrary to Article 14, taken with Article 8 or First Protocol, Article 1. A declaration of incompatibility granted by the Divisional Court in *Alconbury* was, however, set aside on appeal to the House of Lords,[97] and one granted by Keith J. in *Matthews v. Ministry of Defence* set aside by the Court of Appeal.[98]

The limits to the power to grant a declaration of incompatibility were

---

[90] *R. (on the application of IH) v. Secretary of State for the Home Department* [2002] EWCA Civ 646; *R. (on the application of C) v. Secretary of State for the Home Department* [2002] EWCA Civ 647 (powers of Mental Health Review Tribunal following order for conditional discharge of patient broader than held in *Campbell v. Secretary of State for the Home Department* [1988] 1 A.C. 120).

[91] *Wainwright v. Home Office* [2001] EWCA Civ 2081.

[92] See below. For example, it has been held that the term "widow" cannot be interpreted to include "widower": *Hooper and others v. Secretary of State for Work and Pensions* [2002] EWHC 191 (Admin).

[93] [2001] 3 W.L.R. 42.

[94] [2001] 3 W.L.R. 512. A remedial order has been made: see above, para. 8-006, n. 73.

[95] [2002] EWCA Civ 158. Simon Brown and Jonathan Parker L.JJ., Laws L.J. dissenting.

[96] *Hooper and others v. Secretary of State for Work and Pensions* [2002] EWHC 191 (Admin); *R. (on the application of Wilkinson) v. Inland Revenue* [2002] EWHC 182 (Admin).

[97] See para. 8-020.

[98] [2002] EWHC 13 (QB); [2002] EWCA Civ 773 (Crown Proceedings Act 1947, s.10, preventing claims in tort by servicemen against the Crown where death or injury is certified as attributable to service for the purposes of entitlement to a war pension, not incompatible with Article 6).

explored by the House of Lords in *In re S(FC)*.[99] The House held that the Children Act 1989 provisions regulating care orders were not incompatible with Articles 8 and 6(1). If a local authority performed its duties in accordance with the legislation then in the ordinary course of events there should not be any infringement of the Article 8 rights of the child or the parent. The fact that the Act entrusted responsibility to the local authority was not itself such an infringement given that it was an experienced and responsible public authority. Neither did the fact that the court did not retain an ongoing supervisory role. If an authority failed to discharge its responsibilities under the Act, leading to an infringement of Article 8, a remedy would be available under sections 7 and 8 of the Human Rights Act 1998. Furthermore, the absence of an express remedial procedure from the Children Act 1989 could not *itself* constitute a breach of Article 8, or indeed of any Convention right (given that Article 13, ECHR, which provided that everyone whose Convention rights are violated "shall have an effective remedy" was not reproduced in the 1998 Act).[1] As regards the argument that the 1989 Act was inconsistent with Article 6(1), the House held that there were indeed some conceivable child care decisions where English law might not satisfy the requirements of Article 6(1). These included decisions affecting children with no parent or guardian able and willing to become involved in questioning a care decision by a local authority. However, the absence of provision for access to a court as guaranteed by Article 6 from a particular statute:

> "does not, in itself, mean that the statute is incompatible with Article 6(1). Rather, this signifies at most the existence of a lacuna in the statute."[2]

A statutory lacuna is not statutory incompatibility. However, there were also some child care decisions made while a care order was in force where Article 6(1) might require access to a court, but where such access would be inconsistent with the underlying basic principle of the Children Act 1989, as distinct from any express provisions of that Act. The House left open the question which incompatibility of this kind was sufficient for the purpose of section 4.[3]

Finally, it should be noted that the fact that existing incompatible legislation may, in the interests of legal certainty, be applied to a claimant pending necessary reform does not necessarily itself constitute a breach of the Convention.[4]

---

[99] [2002] UKHL 10, [2002] 2 All E.R. 192.
[1] *per* Lord Nicholls at paras [52]–[64].
[2] *ibid.* paras [65]–[86].
[3] *ibid.*, paras [87], [88].
[4] *Hooper and others v. Secretary of State for Work and Pensions* [2002] EWHC 191 (Admin), paras [120]–[129].

5. Unlawful Action

(a) The scope of section 6

8–009   Section 6(1) provides that:

> "It is unlawful for a public authority to act[5] in a way which is incompatible with a Convention right."

This does not apply to an act if as the result of one or more provisions of primary legislation the authority could not have acted differently,[6] or in the case of one or more provisions of, or made under, primary legislation which cannot be read or given effect in a way compatible with Convention rights, the authority was acting so as to give effect to or enforce those provisions.[7]

The application of the exceptions set out in subsection (2) have been considered in a number of cases. In *R. (on the application of Holdings and Barnes plc) v. Secretary of State for the Environment, Transport and the Regions and other cases*[8] the Divisional Court held that subsection (2)(a) applied in respect of legislation that required the Secretary of State himself to take decisions under the Transport and Works Act 1992, the Highways Act 1980 and the Acquisition of Land Act 1981. Furthermore, the court held that the power to call-in planning applications under section 77 of the Town and Country Planning Act 1990 could not be given effect in a way that was compatible with Article 6(1), either by concluding that some call-ins might not be incompatible (as were the local authority (which did not have Convention rights under the Act) was the relevant applicant for permission or by reading section 77 in such a way as to preclude all call-ins). On the first point, in practice there were unlikely to be any cases in which the civil rights and obligations of persons eligible to take proceedings under section 7 of the Human Rights Act 1998 were not affected; and the fact that a local authority could not proceed under section 7 did not mean that it had no Article 6(1) rights. Accordingly, subsection (2)(b) applied to section 77. In the case of "recovered appeals," the Secretary of State had a choice between delegating to the inspector and recovering the appeal. However, the term "one or more provisions" was not to be read as referring to the whole statutory scheme (under which the Secretary of State could always act compatibly by delegating the appeal). It was to be taken as referring to the specific provision[9] that enabled the Secretary of State to recover an appeal. Accordingly, subsection (2)(b) applied to that provision. The House of Lords allowed an appeal[10] on other grounds and did not need to address these issues.

It has subsequently been held that section 6(2)(b) does indeed apply in any case where the *exercise* of a power conferred by legislation would necessarily

---

[5] This includes a failure to act, but not a failure to introduce in or lay before Parliament a proposal for legislation or make any primary legislation or remedial order: section 6(6).
[6] Section 6(2)(a).
[7] Section 6(2)(b).
[8] [2001] H.R.L.R. 10.
[9] 1990 Act, Sched. 6, para. 3.
[10] See para. 8-020.

involve incompatibility with a Convention right. It is no answer that compatibility could simply be achieved by refraining from exercising the power in question.[11] The same position arises (and section 6(2)(b) applies) where a power which could be exercised so as to secure conformity would need to be exercised in every case and so turned into a duty; the power as such would be extinguished.[12] On the other hand, section 6(2)(b) does not apply where regulations are incompatible with Convention requirements, unless the legislation requires the regulations to be made in that form; in the former circumstances the regulations can (and presumably should) be quashed.[13]

(b) "Public authority"

"Public authority" includes (a) a court or tribunal and (b) any person **8–010** certain of whose functions are functions of a public nature,[14] but not either House of Parliament[15] or a person exercising functions in connection with proceedings in Parliament.[16] A government department or local authority would, for example, appear to be an obvious "public authority" without reference to (a) or (b) and so all of its acts would appear to be subject to section 6(1).

The Court of Appeal has stated that the definition of who is a "public authority" and what is a "public function" should be given a "generous interpretation."[17] The court held that the role of a housing association which was a registered social landlord in providing accommodation for the defendant and then seeking possession was so closely assimilated to that of the local authority that it was performing public functions. Among the points made was that the mere fact that a body performed an activity which otherwise a public body would be under a duty to perform did not mean

---

[11] *R. v. Kansal (No. 2)* [2001] UKHL 62, [2002] 1 All E.R. 257, *per* Lord Hope at para. [88]. *Cf.* cases where the power can legitimately be read down, but not extinguished, so as to secure conformity: *Friends Provident Life Office v. Secretary of State for the Environment. Transport and the Regions* [2001] EWHC (Admin) 820 (not every exercise of power to *refuse* to call-in a planning application would necessarily be incompatible with Article 6).

[12] *Hooper and others v. Secretary of State for Work and Pensions* [2002] EWHC 191 (Admin) (existence of extra-statutory power to make payment to widower analogous to benefit payable to widow held not a bar to grant of declarations of incompatibility).

[13] *R. (on the application of Bono) v. Harlow District Council* [2002] EWHC 423 (Admin).

[14] In relation to a particular act, a person is not a public authority by virtue only of (b) if the nature of the act is private: section 6(5). The purpose of this provision was said by Stanley Burnton J. in *R. (on the application of Heather) v. Leonard Cheshire Foundation* [2001] EWHC Admin 429, para. [91] to be "to exclude from the obligation of a hybrid authority to comply with Convention rights both its private functions and its acts of a private nature (such as the purchase of stationery) carried out in connection with the exercise of its public functions."

[15] Apart from the House of Lords in its judicial capacity: section 6(4).

[16] Section 6(3).

[17] *Donoghue v. Poplar Housing and Regeneration Community Association* [2001] EWCA Civ 595, [2001] 2 F.L.R. 284, para. [58], *per* Lord Woolf C.J. Other examples of bodies exercising a public function include a voluntary adoption agency exercising powers under the Adoption Act 1976 and regulations (*R. (on the application of Gunn-Russo) v. Nugent Care Society* [2001] EWHC Admin. 566). Bodies held not to be public authorities include Lloyd's (*Doll-Steinberg v. The Society of Lloyd's* [2002] EWHC 419 (Admin)).

that such performance was necessarily a public function.[18] What can make an act, which would otherwise be private, public:

> "is a feature or a combination of features which impose a public character or stamp on the act. Statutory authority for what is done can at least help to mark the act as being public; so can the extent of control over the function exercised by another body which is a public authority. The more closely the acts that could be of a private nature are enmeshed in the activities of a public body, the more likely they are to be public. However, the fact that the acts are supervised by a public regulatory body does not necessarily indicate that they are of a public nature. ... "[19]

Also of particular importance was the closeness of the relationship between the council (Tower Hamlets London Borough Council) and Poplar. Poplar had been created by Tower Hamlets to take a transfer of local authority housing stock; five of its board members were also Tower Hamlets councillors; Poplar was subject to the guidance of Tower Hamlets as to the manner in which it acted towards tenants. The defendant at the time of transfer was a sitting tenant of Tower Hamlets and it was intended that she would be treated no better and no worse than if she remained a tenant of Tower Hamlets. In a borderline case, such as this, it was very much a question of fact and degree.[20]

In *R. (on the application of Heather) v. Leonard Cheshire Foundation*[21] Stanley Burnton J. held that the expression "public function" was to be accorded the same meaning as under C.P.R. Part 54.[22] This could not involve a "purely functional" test as it would then apply, for example, to the provision of education by private schools and of residential care to fee-paying patients. The adjective "public" in section 6 was used "in the sense of governmental."[23] Here, the judge held, distinguishing *Donoghue*, that a charitable foundation which ran a care home, the majority of whose residents were funded by their local authority or health authority, was not exercising a public function. The foundation was established by private individuals, not the local authority; no purchasing authority was able to require the foundation to accept a particular person as a service user or resident; the statutory regulation was less extensive; there was no relationship with a statutory authority as integrated as that as that between Poplar and Tower Hamlets.[24] The Court of Appeal dismissed an appeal,[25] holding

---

[18] *ibid.*, giving as an example the provision by a small hotel of bed and breakfast accommodation as a temporary measure.

[19] *ibid.*, para. [65].

[20] *ibid.*, paras [65], [66]. See also *Aston Cantlow and Wilmcote with Billesley Parochial Church Council v. Wallbank* [2001] EWCA Civ 713, [2001] 3 W.L.R. 1323 (PCC held to be either a public authority or a person exercising a public function (in respect of a notice to repair a chancel which had statutory force).

[21] [2001] EWHC Admin. 429.

[22] See para. 18-054.

[23] Para. [86].

[24] The position was accordingly the same as pre-commencement, where it had been held that such a body was not subject to judicial review: *R. v. Servite Housing Association, ex p. Goldsmith and Chatting* [2001] L.G.R. 55.

[25] [2002] EWCA Civ 366, [2002] 2 All E.R. 936.

that the degree of public funding of the activities of an otherwise private body was relevant but not determinative; the Foundation was neither standing in the shoes of the local authorities nor exercising statutory powers.

(c) Proceedings under section 7

A person who claims that a public authority has acted (or proposes to act) in a way made unlawful by section 6(1) may, if he or she is (or would be) a "victim of the unlawful act", bring proceedings (including a counterclaim) against the authority under the Act in the appropriate court or tribunal (as determined in accordance with rules)[26] or rely on the Convention right(s) concerned in any legal proceedings.[27] If the proceedings are brought on an application for judicial review, the applicant is to be taken to have a sufficient interest in relation to the unlawful act only if he is, or would be, the victim of that act.[28] The concept of a "victim" is intended to reflect the approach of the European Court of Human Rights[29] and is narrower than the concept of "sufficient interest" which, as currently applied, accords standing to public interest groups as well as affected individuals.[30] Proceedings must be brought before the end of (a) one year beginning with the date on which the act complained of took place; or (b) such longer period as the court or tribunal considers equitable having regard to all the circumstances, subject to any rule imposing a stricter time limit in relation to the procedure in question.[31]

8–011

(d) Judicial remedies

Where the court or tribunal finds that an act (or proposed act) of a public authority is (or would be) unlawful under section 6(1), it may grant such relief or remedy, or make such order, within its powers as it considers just and appropriate. However, damages may be awarded only by a court which has power to award damages, or to order the payment of compensation, in civil proceedings. No award of damages is to be made unless, taking account of all the circumstances of the case, including any other relief or remedy granted or order made in relation to the act in question by that or any other court, and the consequences of any decision (of that or any other court) in respect of that act, the court is satisfied that the award is necessary to afford "just satisfaction" to the person in whose favour it is made. In determining whether to award damages or the amount of an award, the court must take into account the principles applied by the European Court of Human Rights in relation to the award of compensation under Article 41 of the

8–012

---

[26] See section 7(9)–(12). In England and Wales rules are made by the Lord Chancellor or the Secretary of State or are rules of court.
[27] 7(1), (2) "Legal proceedings" includes (a) proceedings brought by or at the instigation of a public authority; and (b) an appeal against the decision of a court or tribunal: section 7(6).
[28] Section 7(3)
[29] Section 7(7). See Baker (*op cit.* n.1), pp. 40–44.
[30] See para. 18-054.
[31] Section 7(5).

Convention.[32] A public authority against which damages are awarded is to be treated for the purposes of the Civil Liability (Contribution) Act 1978, as liable in respect of damage suffered by the person to whom the award is made.[33] Proceedings under section 7(1)(a) in respect of the judicial act of a court (including an act done on the instructions or on behalf of a judge) may be brought only by exercising a right of appeal, on an application for judicial review (unless the court is not amenable to judicial review) or in such other forum as may be prescribed by rules.[34]

(e) The effect of the Act on private relations

8–013   The extent to which the Human Rights Act 1998 can have effect between parties neither of which is a public authority has generated considerable academic discussion. Much of the debate has been couched in terms of a question whether the Act has "horizontal effect" between private parties in addition to "vertical effect" between a private party and the state, language used in respect of the extent to which EU law has direct effect.[35] It has, However, been cogently argued that this terminology is unhelpful and misleading in that it assumes as valid a sharp distinction between the spheres of public and private law which is itself controversial.[36] There is "no such firm distinction, because the very presence of law introduces a public element: private relations are in part constituted by both statute and common law, and the State lurks behind both."[37] The real issue is the extent or degree to which the 1998 Act affects the law governing wholly private relations.

The first point to note is that the Act creates a new right to bring a direct claim for breach of Convention rights only against a public authority.[38] While the term "public authority" is to be interpreted autonomously and may extend to include bodies or persons who would not be so regarded for other purposes[39] it remains the case that there is a significant "private sector" not subject to such claims. However, it is also significant that it is expressly made unlawful for a public authority to act in a way which is

---

[32]   The Court under Article 41 may only award pecuniary compensation; this covers pecuniary and non pecuniary loss and costs and expenses, but not aggravated or exemplary damages: see Baker (op cit) n.1. pp. 45–56. For discussion, see D. Fairgrieve, [2001] P.L. 695. For an example, see *Marcic v. Thames Water Utilities Ltd (No. 1)* [2001] 3 All E.R. 698 and *(No. 2)* [2001] 4 All E.R. 326, where the judge awarded damages in respect of a sewerage undertaker's failure to remedy flooding that constituted a breach of the claimant's rights under Article 8(2); on appeal, the Court of Appeal held that this was right but that damages were also available at common law: [2002] 2 All E.R. 1.

[33]   Section 8.

[34]   Section 9(1),(2). In proceedings in respect of a judicial act done in good faith, damages may not be awarded beyond the extent required by Article 5(5) of the Convention; the award is made against the Crown, and no award can be made unless the responsible minister (or his nominee) is joined as a party: s.9(3)–(5).

[35]   See paras 5–041, 5–042.

[36]   Sir Stephen Sedley, *Freedom, Law and Justice* (1999); M. Hunt, "The 'Horizontal Effect' of the Human Rights Act: Moving Beyond the Public-Private Distinction" in J. Jowell and J. Cooper (eds), *Understanding Human Rights Principles* (2001), pp. 161–178.

[37]   Hunt, *op. cit.*, p. 173.

[38]   Sections 6, 7: above, para. 8–009–8–011.

[39]   Above, para. 8–010.

incompatible with a Convention right.[40] A court is a "public authority". It is accordingly argued that in considering the application of the law (whether legislation or common law) in the determination of disputes between private parties, the court is *obliged* to produce a solution that conforms to Convention rights. Such rights therefore become enforceable between private parties.[41] This position has been resisted on two main grounds. First, there are a number of indications in both the terms and structure of the 1998 Act[42] and in debates on the passage of the Human Rights Bill through Parliament[43] that this was not the intention. Secondly, the "Convention rights" referred to in the 1998 Act are themselves under ECHR jurisprudence rights against the state and not against private individuals.[44] The latter point might not be decisive to the extent that a Convention right against the state might itself require the state (through the court) to create a private law right enforceable between private parties in order to dispose of the litigation in a way compatible with that Convention right. The fact that there was not a blanket intention automatically to achieve this result in the case of all Convention rights does not mean that such a result might not properly be reached in relation to some of them.

The opposite position would have been for the 1998 Act to have *no effect whatsoever* on legal relations between private parties. This was not the intention either. The point was explored in the context of the consideration of an amendment proposed by Lord Wakeham that would have provided specifically that a court had no duty to act compatibly with the Convention in a case where neither party before it was a public authority. The amendment was intended to make it clear that the Act did not itself cerate a private law right of privacy. Lord Irvine L.C., in resisting the amendment, said:

> "We ... believe that it is right as a matter of principle for the courts to have the duty of acting compatibly with the Convention not only in cases involving other public authorities but also in developing the common law in decided cases between individuals. Why should they not? In preparing this Bill, we have taken the view that it is the other course, that of excluding Convention considerations altogether from cases between individuals, which would have to be justified. We do not

---

[40] 1998 Act, s. 6.

[41] Sir William Wade in J. Beatson et al. (eds), *Constitutional Reform in the United Kingdom: Principles and Practices* (1998), p. 61, [1998] E.H.R.L.R. 520 and "Horizons of Horizontally" (2000) 116 L.Q.R. 217.

[42] In particular, the enactment of provisions dealing expressly with direct claims against public authorities.

[43] Lord Irvine L.C.: (in discussing section 6(1)) "We decided first of all that a provision of this kind should apply only to public authorities ... and not to private individuals. ... The Convention had its origins in a desire to protect people from the misuse of power by the state, rather than from the actions of private individuals" (H.L. Deb. Vol 582, col. 1232, 3 November 1997) and Jack Straw M.P., H.C. Deb. Vol 314, col 406, 17 June 1998, cited by G. Phillipson, (1999) 62 M.L.R. 824, 826–827.

[44] Sir Richard Buxton, "The Human Rights Act and Private Law" (2000) 116 L.Q.R. 48. *Cf.* Wade, (2000) 116 L.Q.R. 217, arguing in response that the process of translation into domestic law has broadened their scope.

think that that would be justifiable; nor, indeed, do we think that it would be practicable."[45]

This passage is itself ambiguous. It has naturally been cited by Wade in support of his position,[46] in that the development of the common law by the courts is said to flow from the duty to act compatibly.[47] In any event, it certainly does provide powerful confirmation that the Act was intended to have a significant measure of indirect effect on laws affecting private parties, and this is endorsed in varying terms by most commentators.[48] For example, Hunt's view is that the courts are under an obligation to act compatibly with the Convention in determining the outcomes of private law litigation by developing the common law,

> "but subject to the ultimate constraint that it must not create entirely new causes of action where nothing analogous previously existed."[49]

The courts have not fully resolved these arguments. In *Douglas and others v. Hello! Ltd*[50] the Court of Appeal discharged an interim injunction granted to restrain the publication by *Hello!* magazine of photographs of the wedding of Michael Douglas and Catherine Zeta-Jones. Exclusive publication rights had been granted to the third claimant, the proprietors of *OK!* magazine. One issue was the effect of the Human Rights Act 1998 on the possible development of a right of privacy. Sedley L.J. concluded that this was not the place, at least without much fuller argument, to resolve the question

> "does [the 1998 Act] simply require the courts' procedures to be Convention-compliant, or does it require the law applied by the courts, save where primary legislation plainly says otherwise, to give effect to the Convention principles?"

However, if the step from the existing law of confidentiality to privacy

> "is not simply a modern restatement of the scope of a known protection

---

[45] H.L. Deb., Vol. 583, col 783, 24 November 1997; a passage that "is rapidly becoming the best-known paragraph of the whole of *Hansard*" (Buxton, (2000) 116 L.Q.R.48,58).

[46] (2000) 116 L.Q.R. 217, 222–223.

[47] A proposition inconsistent with earlier statements by Lord Irvine. Note Wade's comment that "it may be fair to assume that the Government, being alerted by Lord Wakeham's amendment to the prospect of horizontality, had decided to accept it" ((2000) 116 L.Q.R. 217, 223). It is submitted that the existence of such a crucial change of mind cannot be left to inference; given that Lord Irvine was arguing against a position under which Convention considerations would be *irrelevant*, it is equally, if not more plausible, to conclude that he merely sought to make it clear that Convention considerations were *relevant* in developing the common law, a proposition that most support.

[48] See M. Hunt, "The 'Horizontal Effect' of the Human Rights Act" [1998] P.L. 423 and *op. cit.* n. 36 above; Lester and Pannick, *Human Rights: Law and Practice* (1999), pp. 31–32; S. Grosz, J. Beatson and P. Duffy, *Human Rights: the 1998 Act and the European Convention* (2000), pp. 89–93; G. Phillipson, (1999) 62 M.L.R. 824 (Convention rights in this context "figure only as principles to which the courts must have regard" (p. 848)); I. Leigh, (1999) 48 I.C.L.Q. 57.

[49] *op. cit.*, n. 36, pp. 177–178.

[50] [2001] H.R.L.R. 512, [2001] Q.B. 967. See A. Young, [2002] P.L. 232.

but a legal innovation ... then I would accept [counsel's] submission ... that this is precisely the kind of incremental change for which the Act is designed: one which without underpinning the measure of certainty which is necessary to all law gives substance and effect to section 6. ... "[51]

This point was reinforced by reference to section 12 of the 1998 Act, which provides that if a court is considering whether to grant any relief (which includes any remedy or order other than in criminal proceedings and therefore extends to litigation between private parties) which, if granted, might affect the exercise of the Convention right to free expression, it must, *inter alia*, have particular regard to the importance of that right. Where the material in question is claimed or appears to be journalistic, literary or artistic material, the court must also have regard to the extent to which the material has, or is about to, become available to the public, or it is, or would be, in the public interest for the material to be published, and to any relevant privacy code. These requirements make clear,

"the direct applicability of at least one article of the Convention as between one private party to litigation and another."[52]

Sedley L.J. concluded that

"we have reached a point at which it can be said with confidence that the law recognises and will appropriately protect a right of personal privacy."[53]

Brooke L.J. noted this dilemma:

"On the one hand, Article 8(1) ... appears to create a right, exercisable against all the world, to respect for private and family life. On the other hand, Article 8(2) ..., section 8 of the Act, and the general philosophy of both the Convention and the Act (namely that these rights are enforceable only against public authorities), all appear to water down the value of the right created by Article 8(1)."[54]

Nevertheless, his Lordship appeared to accept the position that

"it is the judges who must develop the law so that it gives appropriate recognition to Article 8(1) rights."

Whether this would be by an extension of the law of confidence or by recognising the existence of new relationships which give rise to enforceable legal rights was not for the court on this occasion to predict.[55] Keene L.J. similarly held that the duty of the courts under section 6(1) of the 1998 Act

---

[51] *ibid.*, paras [128], [129].
[52] *ibid.*, paras [131]–[133].
[53] *ibid.*, para. [110]. Note, however, that the Court of Appeal subsequently held that there was no tort of invasion of privacy at common law prior to implementation of the HRA and that it was for Parliament to create such a tort, in so far as it went beyond the legitimate extension of the law of confidence: *Wainwright v. Home Office* [2001] EWCA Civ 2081.
[54] *ibid.*, para. [82].
[55] *ibid.*, para. [88].

"arguably includes their activity in interpreting and developing the common law, even where no public authority is a party to the litigation."

Whether this extended to creating a new cause of action was controversial, but did not fall to be determined as reliance here was placed on the law of confidence; the boundaries of that law were not immutable and the current state of English law was likely to protect the privacy of a purely private wedding.[56]

Subsequently, in *Venables v. News Group Newspapers Ltd*[57] Dame Elizabeth Butler-Sloss in the Family Division stated expressly that the section 6(1) obligation,

"does not seem to me to encompass the creation of a free-standing cause of action based directly upon the articles of the convention"

but does require the court,

"to act compatibly with Convention rights in adjudicating upon existing common law causes of action, and that includes a positive as well as a negative obligation. ... "[58]

This endorses the middle position. At the time of writing (April 2002), the House of Lords has yet to pronounce directly on these matters.

Finally, it is not disputed that the interpretative obligation under section 3 may apply to legislation that regulates the relations of private parties, although not with retrospective effect.[59]

6. OTHER MATTERS

8–014 A person's reliance on a Convention right does not restrict any other right or freedom conferred on him by or under any law having effect in any part of the UK, or his right to make any claim or bring any proceedings which he could make apart from sections 7 to 9.[60] Special provisions apply where a court is considering granting any relief which might affect the exercise of the Convention right to freedom of expression or the exercise by a religious organisation of the Convention right to freedom of thought, conscience and religion.[61] A minister in charge of a Bill in either House of Parliament must, before the second reading, make a statement in writing either that in his view the provisions of the Bill are compatible with the Convention rights, or that, although he is unable to make such a statement, the government wishes the House to proceed with the Bill.[62]

---

[56] *ibid.*, para. [1661].
[57] [2001] Fam. 430.
[58] para. [27].
[59] *Wainwright v. Home Office* [2001] EWCA Civ. 2081.
[60] Section 11.
[61] Section 12, 13
[62] Section 19.

7. COMMENCEMENT

The 1998 Act was brought fully into force on October 2, 2000.[63] Section **8–015**
22(4) provides:

> "Paragraph (b) of subsection (1) of section 7 applies to proceedings
> brought by or at the instigation of a public authority whenever the act
> in question took place; but otherwise that subsection does not apply to
> an act taking place before the coming into force of that section."

Section 7(1)(b) is the provision that enables a victim of an unlawful act (by
virtue of section 6(1)) to "rely on the Convention right or rights concerned
in any legal proceedings." The meaning of these provisions have been
considered in two decisions of the House of Lords. In *R. v. Lambert*[64] the
House of Lords held by a majority[65] that section 22(4) prevents a person
convicted at a criminal trial held before commencement from relying at an
appeal brought after commencement on an argument that there was a
breach of his Convention rights at the trial (here, that the imposition by the
Misuse of Drugs Act 1971 of a reverse burden of proof violated the
presumption of innocence enshrined in Article 6(2)). The majority held that
the reference in section 22(4) to "proceedings brought by or at the
instigation of a public authority" was intended to reflect the distinction
drawn in section 7(6), which provides:

> "In subsection (1)(b) 'legal proceedings' includes—
>
> (a) proceedings brought by or at the instigation of public authority;
>   and
> (b) an appeal against the decision of a court or tribunal."

Accordingly, an appeal by an unsuccessful defendant was not to be treated
as a proceeding brought by or at the instigation of a public authority.
Considerable confusion and uncertainty would be produced if the
examination of pre-commencement trials could be opened up on post-
commencement appeals. Given that this was the proper interpretation of
sections 22(4) and 7(1)(b), it was not possible for the appellant to rely on
sections 6[66] or 3(1), which had no express retroactive effect, as producing a
different result.[67] A further point was that the wording of section 7(1)(a) by
virtue of section 9 covered the bringing of an appeal and section 7(1)(a)
clearly did not apply to any act taking place before commencement.[68] Lord

---

[63] Section 22(3); Human Rights Act 1998 (Commencement No. 2) Order 2000 (S.I. 2000 No. 1
      85 1). Sections 18 (effect of appointment of judge to ECtHR), 20 (supplemental power to
      make orders) and 21(5) (abolishing the death penalty under the Army Act 1955, the Air
      Force Act 1955 or the Naval Discipline Act 1957) came into effect on the passing of the Act.

[64] [2001] 3 W.L.R. 206. See G. Dingwall, (2002) 65 M.L.R. 450.

[65] Lords Slynn of Hadley, Hope of Craighead, Clyde and Hutton, Lord Steyn dissenting.

[66] *i.e.* the argument that the Court of Appeal as a "public authority" would act unlawfully now
      if it acted in a way incompatible with a Convention right.

[67] *per* Lord Slynn at paras [7]–[14]. Lord Clyde adopted the same approach at paras [140]–[142]
      and Lord Hutton at paras [169]–[176].

[68] *per* Lord Clyde at para. [139].

Hope of Craighead held that the retrospective use of section 7(1)(b) was permitted at the stage of any appeal against the decision of a court in proceedings brought by or at the instigation of a public authority; however, an accused whose trial took place before commencement was only entitled to rely on an appeal after commencement on an alleged breach of Convention rights *by the prosecuting authority*. It did not enable him to challenge a ruling by the court itself.[69] Lord Steyn dissented, holding that the House of Lords was not entitled to act unlawfully now by upholding a conviction obtained in breach of a Convention right.[70]

The issues were reconsidered five months later by the House of Lords in *R. v. Kansal (No. 2)*.[71] Here, the issue was whether the defendant in a post-commencement appeal could argue that his Conviction rights had been breached by the prosecution in deciding to adduce evidence of answers obtained under compulsion in bankruptcy proceedings. The House comprised the same Law Lords with the substitution of Lord Lloyd for Lord Clyde. The House held that its previous decision in *Lambert*, reached after a full argument, should be followed. Lord Slynn was not persuaded that the decision in *Lambert* was wrong, and did not accept that a valid distinction could be drawn between acts of the judiciary and acts of the prosecution.[72] Lord Hutton considered the *Lambert* decision to be correct.[73] Lord Lloyd thought that the decision in *Lambert* was plainly erroneous but should be followed.[74] Lord Steyn reaffirmed his view that the majority in *Lambert* was mistaken; this view was reinforced by the considerations (1) that the word "proceedings" covers both trials and appeals; (2) that the words "proceedings brought by or at the instigation of a public authority" in section 22(4) were "singled out for special treatment in recognition of the United Kingdom's international obligations" under the ECHR from the date of ratification by the UK in 1951 or the date of conferment of the right of petition in 1966; and (3) that the discretion of the Courts of Appeal to refuse to extend time for leave to appeal provided an effective filter in respect of old convictions. However, it would be wrong now to depart from the ratio of *Lambert*.[75] Lord Hope agreed that *Lambert* was wrongly decided and was the only member of the House to argue that it should now depart from it.[76] He identified a number of anomalies that arose if the majority were right. First, an appeal by the prosecution by way of case stated following an acquittal at trial held prior to commencement would be proceedings brought by a public authority. Secondly, a reference by the Attorney General to the Court of Appeal under section 36 of the Criminal Justice Act 1988 for review of a sentence pronounced prior to commencement which he considered unduly lenient would also be a separate proceeding by a public authority. Thirdly, where a conviction was quashed on other grounds, the defendant would be able to rely on Convention rights at any retrial. Fourthly, the interpretation of section 22(4) as excluding

---

[69] Paras [101]–[107].
[70] Paras [27]–[31].
[71] [2001] UKHL 62, [2002] 1 All E.R. 257.
[72] Paras [8]–[10].
[73] Paras [101]–[109].
[74] Paras [17]–[24].
[75] Paras [25]–[27].
[76] Paras [50]–[72].

appeals would apply in civil cases, and even where the decision at first instance was in the defendant's favour and an appeal was taken after commencement by the public authority.[77]

It is unfortunate that the matter was not made clearer in the 1998 Act and that the interpretation which a majority of the House in *Kansal (No. 2)* thought to be wrong remains the law. Defendants in pre-commencement trials will of course be able to take Convention points to the European Court of Human Rights. The Court of Appeal has accepted that in consequence of the view of the majority in *Kansal (No. 2)* that *Lambert* was wrongly decided, *Lambert* should not be applied beyond its strict ratio.[78] *Lambert* has, however, been applied in civil cases.[79]

For the purpose of section 22(4), judicial review proceedings are to be regarded as proceedings brought by the applicant and not by the Crown (a public authority) as the Crown's involvement is nominal only.[80]

Section 3(1) of the Act[81] cannot be used to change substantive law with retrospective effect.[82]

C. SPECIFIC CONVENTION RIGHTS

This section considers the major provisions of the ECHR applicable in the context of the administration of justice, as interpreted and applied by both the European Court on Human Right[83] and English courts, the latter in

8–016

---

[77] Paras [73]–[74].

[78] *R. v. Lyons and others* [2001] EWCA Crim 2860, para. [45] (the court, however, rejected arguments (1) that where a conviction at a pre-commencement trial was found by the ECtHR to be in breach of Article 6 of the Convention, the Court of Appeal was bound to quash the conviction; and (2) that contemporary standards of fairness required the convictions to be quashed where evidence had been admitted of answers given under compulsion. The admission of such evidence had been expressly authorised by Parliament and there was no ground prior to commencement for regarding the legislation as impliedly repealed).

[79] *R. (on the application of Anufrijeva) v. Secretary of State for the Home Department* [2001] EWHC Admin 895; *R. (on the application of Langton) v. Department for the Environment, Food and Rural Affairs* [2001] EWHC Admin 1047; *Pearce v. Governing Body of Mayfield Secondary School* [2001] I.R.L.R. 669; *Wainwright v. Home Office* [2001] EWCA Civ 2081; *Hooper and others v. Secretary of State for Work and Pensions* [2002] EWHC 191 (Admin). A similar result was reached in a planning case decided before *Lambert*: *Masbey v. Secretary of State for the Environment* (unreported, December 13, 2000). In *Aston Cantlow and Wilmcote with Billesley Parochial Church Council v. Wallbank* [2001] EWCA Civ 713, [2001] 3 W.L.R. 1323 it was conceded that a person served with a Chancel repairs notice pre-commencement could raise an argument based on breach of Convention rights on an appeal on a preliminary issue heard post-commencement; this seems difficult to square with *Lambert* but can be reconciled on the basis that there had been no final determination of liability pre-commencement.

[80] *R. (on the application of Ben-Abdelazziz) v. Haringey London Borough Council* [2001] EWCA Civ 803.

[81] See above, paras 8-006, 8-007.

[82] *Wainwright v. Home Office* [2001] EWCA Civ 2081 (HRA cannot be relied upon for the creation of a common law tort of privacy prior to implementation).

[83] See generally D.J. Harris, M. O'Boyle and C. Warbrick, *The European Convention on Human Rights* (1995); A. Mowbray, *Cases and Materials on the European Convention on Human Rights* (2001); J. Simor and B. Emerson, *Human Rights Practice* (2001). See above, para. 2-082.

particular in the period that has followed implementation of the Human Rights Act 1998.

(a) Article 2

8–017 This provides generally that "everyone's right to life shall be protected by law." More specifically, "no one shall be deprived of his life intentionally" save in the execution of a sentence of a court following his conviction of a crime for which this penalty is provided by law."[84] Furthermore, deprivation of life is not to be regarded as a contravention of Article 2,

> "when it results from the use of force which is no more than absolutely necessary
>
> a   in defence of any person from unlawful violence;
> b   in order to effect a lawful arrest or to prevent the escape of a person lawfully detained;
> c   in action lawfully taken for the purpose of quelling a riot or insurrection."[85]

This "ranks as one of the most fundamental provisions in the Convention" and is non-derogable in peacetime. Its provisions must be "strictly construed."[86] In particular, the test of "absolute necessity" in Article 2(2) involves "a stricter and more compelling test of necessity" than that normally applicable when determining whether state action is "necessary" under other articles of the Convention. "The force used (which may extend to non-intentional killings) must be strictly proportionate to the achievement of the aims" set out in subparas. a, b and c. The Court must subject deprivation of life to "the most careful scrutiny," taking account not only the actions of state agents who actually administer the force but also the surrounding circumstances, including the planning and control of the actions in question.[87] Accordingly, attention may be focussed under Article 2 on the structure of the law regulating the use of force in (for example) the prevention of crime; the planning of operations that may involve the use of force by state agents; and the acts that involve the use of force.[88] An operation must be "planned and conducted in such a way as to avoid or minimise, to the greatest extent possible," any risk of the lives of innocent bystanders.[89] The general obligation under Article 2(1) requires each state not only to have appropriate provisions of substantive criminal law, but also

---

[84] Article 2(1).
[85] Article 2(2).
[86] *McCann v. UK* (1995) 21 EHRR 97, at para. 147.
[87] *ibid.*, paras 149, 150.
[88] See *e.g. McCann v. UK*, above which arose out of the killing of three unarmed suspected IRA terrorists in Gibraltar by SAS soldiers. The ECtHR held that the applicable legal standard in the law of Gibraltar (use of force must be reasonably justified) was sufficient as applied in practice to comply with Article 2; that there was no premeditated plot to kill the suspects; that the actions of the soldiers did not violate Article 2(2) as they honestly (although mistakenly) believed them to be necessary to prevent detonation of a car bomb; but (by 10 votes to nine) that there was a violation arising out of a lack of appropriate care in the control and organisation of the arrest operation.
[89] *Ergi v. Turkey*, Judgment of July 28, 1998. para. 79.

in appropriate circumstances, to take positive operational measures lo protect individuals at risk.[90]

A further requirement implied into Article 2 is that states must undertake effective investigations into all killings (whether or not by stage agents), involving "some form of independence and public scrutiny capable of leading to a determination of whether the force used was or was not justified."[91]

(b) Article 3

This provides that "no one shall be subjected to torture or to inhuman or degrading treatment or punishment." It is the subject of no exceptions and cannot be the subject of a derogation. "Inhuman treatment" has been held to include such matters as the adoption of a practice of violence by police officers leading to intense suffering and physical injury[92] and the causing of severe mental distress and anguish;[93] "degrading treatment" to include actions "such as to arouse in their victims feelings of fear, anguish and inferiority capable of humiliating and debasing them and possibly breaking their physical or moral resistance"[94]; and "degrading punishment" to include judicial corporal punishment.[95] Apart from liability based on the actions of state officials themselves, the state is obliged by Article 3 to undertake an effective official investigation where an individual raises an arguable claim that he or she has been seriously ill-treated by state officials in breach of that article.[96] Furthermore, the state must take positive steps,

8–018

---

[90] *Osman v. UK* (1998) 29 EHRR 245 (no violation of Article 2(1) on the facts where police failed to arrest person who subsequently murdered Mr Osman and seriously injured his son; it must be established "that the authorities knew or ought to have known at the time of the existence of a real and immediate risk to the life of an identified individual or individuals from the criminal act of a third party and that they failed to take measures within the scope of their powers which, judged reasonably, might have been expected to avoid the risk" (para. 120). *Cf. Kaya v. Turkey.* Judgment of March 28, 2000 (violation established).

[91] *Kava v. Turkey* (1998) 28 EHRR 1 . The UK has been found to have violated this requirement in a series of cases arising out of killings in Northern Ireland: eg. *Jordan v. UK*, Judgment of May 4 2001.

[92] *Ireland v. UK* (1978) 2 EHRR 25, para. 174 (interrogation techniques used in Northern Ireland in 1971); *Tomasi v. France* (1992) 15 EHRR 1 (large number of blows inflicted on terrorist suspect).

[93] *Kurt v. Turkey* (1998) 27 EHRR 91.

[94] *Ireland v. UK,* above, para. 167.

[95] *Tyrer v. UK* (1978) 2 EHRR 1; *cf. Campbell and Cosans v. UK* (1982) 4 EHRR 293 (no breach of Article 3 arising from risk of corporal punishment in state school); *Costello-Roberts v. UK* (1993) 19 EHRR 112 (no breach of Article 3 arising from case of corporal punishment in non-state funded school).

[96] *Assenov v. Bulgaria* (1998) 28 E.H.R.R. 652; *Salman v. Turkey,* Judgment of June 27, 2000 (inadequate investigation of death in police custody; obligation to investigate not confined to cases where it is apparent that the killing was caused by an agent of the state); *Jordan v. UK,* Judgment of May 4, 2001 (lack of effective investigation into death of person shot by police officer); *R. v. DPP. ex p. Manning* [2001] Q.B. 330 (coroner's inquest held to be full and effective inquiry into death of prison inmate); *R. (on the application of Wright) v. Secretary of State for the Home Department* [2001] EWHC Admin 520 (inquest into death of prison inmate from asthma attack held not to be an effective official investigation as a key witness was not called although he was available and willing to attend, shortcomings in medical treatment were not explored and the claimants were not represented); *R. (on the application of Green) v. Police Complaints Authority* [2002] EWCA Civ 389 (no requirement based on Articles 2 and 3 for PCA to disclose witness statements to victim prior to conclusion of any

including the enactment of appropriate criminal offences, to protect persons from being subject to Article 3 mistreatment by other private persons,[97] although there is a wide margin of appreciation.[98]

In *Z v. UK*[99] the Court held that the failure of a local authority to take steps to protect four children in its area from severe neglect, deprivation and abuse at the hands of their parents constituted a breach of Article 3; the authorities had been aware of the serious ill-treatment and neglect suffered by the children for over four years. The government did not contest the Commission's findings of a breach of Article 3. On the other hand, the refusal by the Director of Public Prosecutions of proleptic immunity from prosecution to a husband whose wife was suffering from a progressive degenerative illness and who wished to assist her suicide has been held not to fall within Article 3. It did not constitute proscribed "treatment" and the state was not under a positive obligation to ensure that a competent, terminally ill person who wished but was unable to take her own life should be entitled to seek assistance of another without that person being exposed to the risk of prosecution.[1]

(c) Article 5

8–019   Articles 5 to 7 contain a series of provision of importance for the administration of justice. Article 5 provides as follows:

> **"Article 5 — Right to liberty and security**
>
> 1   Everyone has the right to liberty and security of person. No one shall be deprived of his liberty save in the following cases and in accordance with a procedure prescribed by law:
>
> a   the lawful detention of a person after conviction by a competent court;
>
> b   the lawful arrest or detention of a person for non-compliance with the lawful order of a court or in order to secure the fulfilment of any obligation prescribed by law;
>
> c   the lawful arrest or detention of a person effected for the purpose of bringing him before the competent legal authority on reasonable suspicion of having committed an offence or when it is reasonably considered necessary to prevent his committing an offence or fleeing after having done so;

---

[97]   *A v. UK* (1998) 27 EHRR 611 (caning of child by stepfather sufficiently serious to engage Article 3; criminal law that provided defence of reasonable chastisement to be disproved beyond reasonable doubt held to be inadequate protection).

[98]   *cf. Osman v. UK* (1998) 29 EHRR 245, para. 115–116 (Article 2); *Rees v. UK* (1986) 9 EHRR 56, para. 37 (Article 8), cited by Lord Bingham in *R. (on the application of Pretty) v. Director of Public Prosecutions* [2001] UKHL 61, para. [15].

[99]   Judgment of May 10, 2001. *Cf. V v. UK* (1999) 30 EHRR 121, where the Court held that the trial and sentence of two 11-year old boys for the murder of a two-year old (when they were 10) did not violate Article 3.

[1]   *R. (on the application of Pretty) v. Director of Public Prosecutions* [2001] UKHL 61.

d   the detention of a minor by lawful order for the purpose of educational supervision or his lawful detention for the purpose of bringing him before the competent legal authority;

e   the lawful detention of persons for the prevention of the spreading of infectious diseases, of persons of unsound mind, alcoholics or drug addicts or vagrants;

f   the lawful arrest or detention of a person to prevent his effecting an unauthorised entry into the country or of a person against whom action is being taken with a view to deportation or extradition.

2   Everyone who is arrested shall be informed promptly, in a language which he understands, of the reasons for his arrest and of any charge against him.

3   Everyone arrested or detained in accordance with the provisions of paragraph 1.c of this article shall be brought promptly before a judge or other officer authorised by law to exercise judicial power and shall be entitled to trial within a reasonable time or to release pending trial. Release may be conditional by guarantees to appear for trial.

4   Everyone who is deprive of his liberty by arrest or detention shall be entitled to take proceedings by which the lawfulness of his detention shall be decided speedily by a court and his release ordered if the detention is not lawful.

5   Everyone who has been the victim of arrest or detention in contravention of the provisions of this article shall have an enforceable right to compensation."

Article 5 provides safeguards against arbitrary detention. For it to apply there must be a "deprivation" of physical liberty, and not merely a restriction on freedom of movement. The distinction is one of degree, and turns on such matters as the type, duration, effects and manner of implementation of the measure in question.[2] To be lawful, the deprivation must fall within one or more of the prescribed situations, which are to be narrowly interpreted, and be in accordance with a procedure prescribed by law. There are implied obligations that when the state detains a person, the authorities must "account for his or her whereabouts," and that the authorities "must take effective measures to safeguard against the risk of disappearance and to conduct a prompt effective investigation into an arguable claim that a person has been taken into custody and has not been seen since."[3]

For lawful detention after conviction under Article 5(1)(a) there has to be a sufficient connection between the order of the court following conviction and the detention in question.[4] This has been held to cover the exercise by the Home Secretary of power to recall a life sentence prisoner who

---

[2] *Enel v. Netherlands* (1976) 1 E.H.R.R. 647 (detention of soldier in locked cell fell within Article 5; confinement during off duty hours in an unlocked building in barracks did not); *Guzzardi v. Italy* (1980) 3 E.H.R.R.333 (confinement of Mafia suspect to small hamlet on island fell within Article 5). Restrictions on freedom of movement are covered by the Fourth Protocol, Article 2 (which has not been ratified by the UK).

[3] *Kurt v. Turkey* (1998) 27 E.H.R.R. 91, para. 124.

[4] *Van Droogenbroek v. Belgium* (1982) 4 E.H.R.R. 443, para. 39.

committed further offences after his release.[5] Article 5(1)(b), *inter alia*, authorises detention in accordance with a court order, and is not violated merely because the order is set aside on appeal.[6] Article 5(1)(c) authorises the lawful exercise of police powers of arrest[7] provided there is on the facts "reasonable suspicion" or arrest or detention is "reasonably considered necessary" as the case may be. Where challenged, the government must "furnish at least some facts or information capable of satisfying the Court that the arrested person was reasonably suspected of having committee the alleged offence.[8]

For a person to be detained as a person of "unsound mind" under Article 5(1)(e), he or she must be "reliably shown to be of 'unsound mind'," the mental disorder "must be of a kind or degree warranting compulsory confinement" and the "validity of continued confinement depends upon the persistence of such a disorder."[9] Such a person must be detained in a hospital, clinic or other appropriate institution.[10]

Detention for the purposes of deportation or extradition under Article 5(1)(f) will not be justified where it exceeds a reasonable time[11] or where, in the absence of a power to extradite, a person is deported in circumstances that amount to disguised extradition.[12]

By virtue of Article 5(2)

"any person arrested must be told, in simple, non technical language that he can understand, the essential legal and factual grounds for his arrest, so as to be able, if he sees fit, to apply to a court to challenge its lawfulness in accordance with paragraph 4. ... "[13]

The information must be conveyed promptly, although not necessarily at the very moment of arrest. This echoes the requirement of the common law as to the exercise of arrest powers.[14]

Those arrested under Article 5(1)(c) must be brought before a judicial officer promptly (Article 5(3)). Review by a public prosecutor is likely to be insufficient.[15] Exercises of power to keep terrorist suspects in custody for up to five days without review by a judge have been held to violate this

---

[5] *Weeks v. UK* (1987) 10 E.H.R.R. 293.

[6] *Bentham v. UK* (1996) 22 E.H.R.R. 293.

[7] See below, paras 14-006–14-013 on police arrest powers in England and Wales.

[8] *Fox. Campbell and Hartley v. UK* (1980) 13 E.H.R.R. 157, para. 34; the fact that F and C had previous convictions for terrorist acts connected with the IRA was insufficient on its own to constitute reasonable suspicion of the commission of terrorist offences seven years later. Cf. *Margaret Murray v. UK* (1994) 19 E.H.R.R. 193.

[9] *Winterwerp v. Netherlands* (1979) 2 E.H.R.R. 387, para. 39; *Johnson v. UK* (1997) 27 E.H.R.R. 296 (authorities entitled to a measure of discretion in deciding whether to order the immediate and absolute discharge of a person no longer suffering from the mental disorder which led to the confinement).

[10] *Aerts v. Belgium* (1998) 29 E.H.R.R. 50.

[11] *Quinn v. France* (1995) 21 E.H.R.R. 529; *cf. Chahal v. UK* (1996) 23 E.H.R.R. 413 (C had been detained for a considerable time but the authorities had acted with due diligence).

[12] *Bozano v. France* (1986) 9 E.H.R.R. 297.

[13] *Fox. Campbell and Hartley v. UK* (1990) 13 E.H.R.R. 157, para. 40.

[14] See below, para. 14-012.

[15] *Huber v. Switzerland*, Judgment of October 23, 1990: *Assenov v. Bulgaria* (1998) 28 E.H.R.R. 652.

requirement.[16] Where persons arrested under Article 5(1)(c) are to be tried, they are also entitled to trial within a reasonable time or to release pending trial, the time requirement here being less onerous than the requirement of "promptness" as regards the review of detention. Neither the proceedings themselves nor the provisional detention of accused persons may be prolonged beyond a reasonable time, the former covering the whole period to the end of the trial.[17] What is reasonable naturally depends on the circumstances.[18] A provision automatically denying bail in specified circumstances is likely to be held to violate this requirement.[19]

Where a person is detained by a person or body which is not itself a "court", such as the police, the lawfulness of the detention must be decided speedily by a court (Article 5(4)). To be a court, a body must be independent of the executive and the parties, be able to consider all aspects of the justification for detention and able to make a binding decision.[20] Where a person is detained indefinitely, reviews must normally be available at reasonable intervals.[21]

(c) Article 6

Article 6 provides: **8–020**

Article 6 — Right to a fair trial

1   In the determination of his civil rights and obligations or of any
     criminal charge against him, everyone is entitled to a fair and
     public hearing within a reasonable time by an independent and
     impartial tribunal established by law. Judgment shall be pro-

---

[16] *Broan v. UK* (1988) 11 E.H.R.R. 117. The government subsequently derogated from the requirements of Article 5(3), and then withdrew the derogation following the introduction of revised arrangements under the Terrorism Act 2000: See Bailey, Harris and Jones (2001), pp. 586–587.

[17] *Wemhoff v. Federal Republic of Germany* (1968) 1 E.H.R.R. 55, paras 4–9.

[18] *Wemhoff*, paras 10–17 (W's detention between 1961 and his conviction in 1965 in exceptionally complicated fraud case held to be reasonable); *W v. Switzerland* (1993) 17 E.H.R.R. 60.

[19] *Caballero v UK* (2000) 30 E.H.R.R. 643.

[20] *De Wilde, Ooms and Versyp v. Belgium (the 'vagrancy' cases)* (1971) 1 E.H.R.R. 373; *Chahal v. UK* (1996) 23 E.H.R.R. 413 (judicial review and advisory panel ("Three Advisers") system insufficient for compliance in respect of detention in the context of deportation on national security grounds).

[21] *Winterwerp*, para. 55; *X v. UK* (1981) 4 E.H.R.R. 188 (review by habeas corpus proceedings of detention under Mental Health Act 1959, following recall, insufficient for compliance with Article 5(4) as habeas corpus proceedings dealt only with the lawfulness of detention under domestic law; reviews by Mental Health Review Tribunals were also insufficient as their functions were advisory only, the position on this point subsequently being changed to secure compliance by the Mental Health Act 1983); *Weeks v. UK* (1987) 10 E.H.R.R. 293 (role of Parole Board and judicial review in considering recall of discretionary life sentence prisoner and periodic examination of detention insufficient for compliance with Article 5(4)); *Thynne, Wilson and Gunnell v. UK* (1990) 13 E.H.R.R. 666 (arrangements for review of continued detention of discretionary life sentence prisoner by the Parole Board and judicial review following completion of the "tariff" period (ie the indication by the trial judge of the period considered necessary to meet the requirements of retribution and deterrence) held to violate Article 5(4)); *Cf. Wynne v. UK* (1994) 19 E.H.R.R. 333 (no requirement for a continuing remedy in respect of mandatory life sentence prisoners); *Hussain v. UK* (1996) 22 E.H.R.R. 1 (continuing remedy required after expiration of tariff period in respect of juvenile detained during Her Majesty's Pleasure); *T. v. UK, V v. UK* (1999) 30 E.H.R.R. 121 (continuing remedy required during tariff period where tariff set by Home Secretary).

nounced publicly but the press and public may be excluded from all or part of the trial in the interests of morals, public order or national security in a democratic society, where the interests of juveniles or the protection of the private life of the parties so require, or to the extent strictly necessary in the opinion of the court in special circumstances where publicity would prejudice the interests of justice.

2   Everyone charged with a criminal offence shall be presumed innocent until proved guilty according to law.

3   Everyone charged with a criminal offence has the following minimum rights:

   a   to be informed promptly, in a language which he understands and in detail, of the nature and cause of the accusation against him:

   b   to have adequate time and facilities for the preparation of his defence;

   c   to defend himself in person or through legal assistance of his own choosing or, if he has not sufficient means to pay for legal assistance, to be given it free when the interests of justice so require;

   d   to examine or have examined witnesses against him and to obtain the attendance and examination of witnesses on his behalf under the same conditions as witnesses against him;

   e   to have the free assistance of an interpreter if he cannot understand or speak the language used in court."

Key concepts that may give rise to issues under Article 6(1) include whether there is (a) a "determination of civil rights and obligations"; (b) a "criminal charge"; (c) a "fair and public hearing"; (d) "within a reasonable time; (e) "by an independent and impartial tribunal." The applicable principles are as follows:

"*Determination of civil rights and obligations*" Here, a broad view has been adopted. For this provision to apply to a case (or "contestation"[22]) it is not necessary that both parties be private persons. Furthermore, the character of the governing legislation, for example, as civil, commercial or administrative law, and whether the matter falls within the jurisdiction of an ordinary court or a specialist administrative body are of little consequence.[23] It must be shown that there is a genuine and serious dispute[24] and that its resolution has a direct effect (is "directly decisive for") a civil right or obligation.[25] In *Ringeisen v. Austria*[26] it was held that Article

---

[22] The words "contestation sur" appear in the French text of Article 6 (rather than "determination of") and thus has no direct counterpart in the English text. It should be given a substantive rather than a formal meaning: *Le Compte. Van Leuven and De Meyere v. Belgium* (1981) 4 EHRR 1, para. 45

[23] *Ringeisen v. Austria* (1971) 1 EHRR 455, para. 94.

[24] *Benthem v. The Netherlands* (1985) 8 EHRR 1, para. 32

[25] *Le Compte, Van Leuven and De Meyere*, above, para. 47.

[26] Above. See also *König v. Germany* (1978) 2 EHRR 170 (Article 6 applicable to decisions of administrative court to revoke authorisations to run clinic and to practise medicine; concept of "civil rights and obligations" must be interpreted autonomously and not solely by reference to the domestic law of the respondent state and is not confined to private law disputes in the traditional sense).

6 applied to the decision of an administrative Commission, applying administrative law principles, whether to approve a contract for sale of agricultural land for building as being in the public interest.

"Civil rights" may include entitlements to social insurance and welfare benefits provided by the state,[27] and issues concerning contributions to social insurance schemes,[28] but not situations where benefits may be provided by the state as a matter of discretion.[29]

In *R. (on the application of Holding and Barnes plc) v. Secretary of State for the Environment, Transport and the Regions.*[30] the House of Lords considered the application of these principles to the planning system, in particular the power of the Secretary of State to determine directly whether planning permission should be granted, where a particular planning application was called-in or an appeal "recovered" from final determination by a planning inspector, or the Secretary of State was the statutory decision-maker. Lords Slynn, Hoffmann, Clyde and Hutton[31] rejected an argument, raised on an intervention by Scottish ministers, that these planning decisions did not involve the *determination* of civil rights and obligations but were simply the exercise of legal powers which affected, perhaps changed, such rights and obligations; a decision on judicial review whether a planning decision was lawful would, however, constitute the determination of a civil right to a lawful decision. A "dispute" or "contestation" arose at least from the time when a power was exercised and objection was taken to that exercise.[32] The members of the House were agreed that, in the light of the European Court's jurisprudence,[33] Article 6(1) clearly applied in this context.

Similarly, a decision to grant planning permission to X in respect of Y's land[34] and a decision to grant planning permission to X in respect of X's land for a development that will detrimentally affect both the enjoyment by Y of his home and its monetary value,[35] are determinations that affect Y's civil rights.

These cases may be compared with the decision in *R. (on the application of Vetterlein) v. Hampshire County Council.*[36] Here, the council granted

---

[27] *Feldbrugge v. Netherlands* (1986) 8 EHRR 425 and *Deumeland v. Germany* (1986) 8 EHRR 448 (social insurance); *Salesi v. Italy* (1993) 26 EHRR 187 (welfare benefits); the ECtHR found in *Feldbrugge* that the private law features of the arrangements (effect on claimant in her personal, economic capacity; close connection with the contract of employment; affinities with insurance under the ordinary law) outweighed the public law features (relevant rules enshrined in legislation; compulsory nature of the insurance; assumption by the state of responsibility for social protection).

[28] *Schouten and Meldrum v. Netherlands* (1994) 19 EHRR 432.

[29] *Machatova v. Slovak Republic* (1997) 24 EHRR CD44 (payment of a hardship allowance).

[30] [12001] UKHL 23, [2001] 2 W.L.R. 1389.

[31] paras [27–]38, [131]–[135], [145]–[157], [181]–[184].

[32] *per* Lord Clyde at para. [147].

[33] Including *Bryan v. UK* (1995) 21 EHRR 342; *Chapman v. UK,* Judgment of January 18,2001.

[34] *British Telecommunications plc v. Gloucester City Council* [2001] EWHC Admin 1001.

[35] *R. (on the application of Katho) v. Rhondda Cynon Taff County Borough Council* [2001] EWHC Admin 527; *Friends Provident Life Office v. Secretary of State for Transport, Local Government and the Regions* [2001] EWHC Admin 820 (civil rights of owner of shopping centre held to be directly affected by proposed new large retail development); *R. (on the application of Adlard) v. Secretary of State for the Environment. Transport and the Regions* [2002] EWHC 7 (Admin).

[36] [2001] EWHC Admin 560. See also *R. (on the application of Cummins) v. London Borough of Camden* [2001] EWHC Admin 1116 (effect of proposed development on view from claimant's flat and on playground associated with the block of flats too remote).

planning permission for an incinerator notwithstanding objections on environmental grounds from the claimants, who lived, respectively, 1.63, 1.79 and 2.14 miles from the centre of the application site. Sullivan J. held that Article 6(1) did not apply. Even if it could be assumed that close proximity to and/or likelihood of significant impact from a proposed development "may bring an objector's civil rights into play" there was no "genuine and serious" dispute here:

> "The grant of permission was not 'directly decisive' of such rights as the claimants may have. The claimants connection with the decision to grant planning permission is tenuous at best, and the environmental consequences for them ... are remote in the extreme."[37]

Further examples of situations involving the determination of civil rights and obligations include a decision of the Crown Court hearing an appeal from licensing justices[38] the decision of a professional disciplinary tribunal that a person was not fit to practise;[39] the determination under regulations whether a person was to be treated as possessing capital of which he had deprived himself for the purpose of decreasing the amount that he might be liable to pay for his residential care;[40] the decision of a review panel in respect of the termination of an introductory tenancy;[41] and a decision of the Secretary of State to withdraw support provided under Part VI of the Immigration and Asylum Act 1999 from a destitute asylum-seekers.[42]

A person's right to express a preference to which school his child should attend is not a "civil right."[43] Similarly, there is no private right for a person to receive education suitable to his needs, which would be engaged, for example, by a decision concerning exclusion of that person from a school.[44] Furthermore, the decision of an Independent Appeal Panel whether to reinstate an excluded pupil does not engage Article 6(1) by virtue of its effect on the civil right to enjoy a fair reputation; the proceedings are not directly decisive of reputation and the potentiality for damage is recognised through the requirement that natural justice be observed in those proceedings.[45]

"Criminal charge" This too must be given an autonomous interpretation and a matter may be classified as "criminal" for the purposes of Article 6 that would not be so classified in domestic law.[46] Relevant factors include the type of national law embodying the offence (and how such conduct is

---

[37] paras [66], [67]. See further below, para. 8-022, concerning rejection of a claim under Article 8.

[38] *R. (on the application of Smith), v. Lincoln Crown Court* [20011 EWHC Admin 928.

[39] *R. (on the application of Fleurose) v. Securities & Futures Authority* [2001] EWCA Civ 2015.

[40] *R. (on the application of Beeson) v. Dorset County Council* [2001] EWHC Admin 986.

[41] *McLellan v. Bracknell Forest Borough Council* [2001] EWCA Civ 1510.

[42] *R. (on the application of Husain) v. Asylum Support Adjudicator* [2001] EWHC Admin 832.

[43] *Re JC* (unreported, July 31, 2000); *cf. Simpson v. UK* (1989) 64 DR 188.

[44] *R. (on the application of B) v. Head Teacher of Alperton Community School* and other cases [2001] EWHC Admin 229, where it was held that the right to sue in negligence recognised in *Phelps v. Hillingdon London Borough Council* [2000] 3 W.L.R. 776 did not constitute such a private right.

[45] *ibid.*, considering *Golder v. UK* (1975) 1 EHRR 524, *Helmers v. Sweden* (1993) 15 EHRR 285 and *Fayed v. UK* (1994) 18 EHRR 393; followed in *R. (on the application of S) v. Head Teacher of Claremont High School* [2001] EWHC Admin 513.

[46] *Engel v. The Netherlands* (1976) 1 EHRR 647; *Attorney General's Reference (No. 2 of 2001)* [2001] 1 W.L.R. 1869 (in general the term "charge" corresponds to the sense used in English criminal procedure, and does not in the ordinary way extend to interrogation or interview).

dealt with in other jurisdictions), the nature of the conduct prohibited and the severity of the punishment.[47] Disciplinary proceedings may or may not fall within Article 6 according to the circumstances.[48] For example, Article 6(1) does not apply to proceedings of an Independent Appeal Panel appointed under the School Standards and Framework Act 1998 concerning exclusion of a pupil from a state school on disciplinary grounds notwithstanding that the misconduct alleged constituted a criminal offence. Although expulsion was significant it did not lead to a denial of access to the educational system or constitute the determination of a criminal charge. The relevant provisions were not part of the general law applicable to persons generally; the sanction was not criminal and not disproportionate to the disciplinarian objective it existed to achieve.[49] Similarly, it does not apply to internal disciplinary mechanisms whereby an employer decides whether or not to trust an employee and whether he has been guilty of a fundamental breach of contract.[50]

"*Fair and public hearing*" This may include a right of effective access to a court.[51] "equality of arms" including adequate disclosure of relevant evidence[52] and the right of a defendant to participate effectively in his or her criminal trial.[53] Courts must give reasons for their judgments, although the extent of this obligation depends on the circumstances and a detailed answer to every argument is not necessarily required.[54]

The right of access may be held to have been denied where there is a broad blanket rule excluding civil liability where competing public policy arguments cannot be evaluated,[55] but not merely where domestic law after

---

[47] *ibid.* para. 82.

[48] *ibid.*: military disciplinary offences leading to liability only to light punishment not within Article 6; other, more serious, disciplinary offences were. Cf. *Campbell and Fell v. UK* (1984) 7 EHRR 165 (prison disciplinary proceedings attracting serious loss of remission subject to Article 6); *R. v. Secretary of State for the Home Department ex p. Carroll, Al-Hasan and Greenfield* [2001] EWCA Civ 1224 (proceedings for prison disciplinary offence where maximum penalty was 42 additional days not criminal); *R. (on the application of Fleurose) v. Securities and Futures Authority* [20011 ECWA Civ 2015 (proceedings before the disciplinary appeal tribunal of the Securities and Futures Authority not criminal); *Han & Yau v. Commissioners of Customs and Excise* [2001] EWCA Civ 1048, [2001] S.T.C. 1188; *Official Receiver v. Stern* [2001] 1 W.L.R. 2230.

[49] *R. (on the application of B) v. Head Teacher of Alperton Community School* and other cases [2001] EWHC Admin 229.

[50] *R. (on the application of H) v. Hertfordshire County Council* [2002] EWCA Civ 146.

[51] *Golden v. UK* (1975) 1 EHRR 524 (rights of access to a court by prisoner for determination of civil claim); *Airey v. Ireland* (1979) 2 EHRR 305 (rights of access must be practical and effective).

[52] *Rowe and Davis v. UK* (2000) 30 EHRR 1. Cf. the common law of natural justice, below, p. 000.

[53] *Stanford v. UK.* Judgment of February 23, 1994 (implicit right to hear and follow proceedings not violated by use of glass screens in front of the dock which caused a minimal loss of sound); *V v. UK* (1999) 30 E.H.R.R. 121 (violation of Article 6(1) where 11-year old defendant was tried for murder in adult court (with modifications); the fact the was represented by skilled counsel was not sufficient given his immaturity and disturbed emotional state).

[54] *Hiro Balani v. Spain* (1995) 19 E.H.R.R. 566; *Garcia Ruig v. Spain* (2001) 31 E.H.R.R. 222. This does not require magistrates to give reasons for rejecting submissions of no case: *Moran v. DPP* [2002] EWHC 89 (Admin); professional judges must, however, give reasons: *Flannery v. Halifax Estate Agencies Ltd* [2000] 1 W.L.R. 377 (pre HRA); *English v. Emery Reimbold & Strick Ltd* [2002] EWCA Civ 605.

[55] *Osman v. UK* (1999) 1 L.G.L.R. 431.

the proper and fair examination of the claim determines that no remedy is available in a given situation.[56] The right of access may require the Civil Procedure Rules to be interpreted in such a way (via section 3(1) of the 1998 Act) as to remove an unjustifiable hindrance to a litigant's right to proceed.[57] The right to a public hearing is subject to exceptions where exclusion "from all or part of the trial" is "in the interests of morals, public order or national security in a democratic society, where the interests of juveniles or the protection of the private life of the parties so require, or to the extent strictly necessary in the opinion of the court in special circumstances where publicity would prejudice the interests of justice."[58]

"Within a reasonable time" Each case must be assessed according to its circumstances, including the complexity of the case, the applicant's conduct and the manner in which the matter was dealt with by the administrative and judicial authorities.[59] The reasonable time may begin to run before the formal launch of proceedings.[60]

"Independent and impartial tribunal" This requirement echoes the common law *nemo judex* principle.[61] "Independent" and "impartial" are separate, but closely related requirements. As to the former, regard must be had to the manner of the appointment of the tribunal members, their terms of office, the existence of guarantees against outside pressure and the question whether the tribunal presents an appearance of independence.[62] There are two aspects to the question of "impartiality": first, "the tribunal must be subjectively free of personal prejudice or bias"; secondly, "it must also be impartial from an objective viewpoint, that is, it must offer sufficient guarantees to exclude any legitimate doubt in this respect. ... "[63] These

---

[56] *Z. v. UK*, Judgment of May 10, 2001; *T.P. and K.M. v. UK*, Judgment of May 10, 2001. There may, however, be a breach of Article 13 (absence of effective remedy, see para. 8-024). See also *Matthews v. Ministry of Defence* [2002] EWCA Civ 773 (bar to tort claim by servicemen held to be a substantive not procedural limitation and so not in violation of Article 6(1)).

[57] *Goode v. Martin* [2001] EWCA Civ 1899, [2002] 1 All E.R. 620.

[58] Article 6(1)

[59] *König v. Germany* (1978) 2 EHRR 170, para. 99 (delays of over 10 years in administrative proceedings that were still not concluded and a delay of over 5 years in separate proceedings each held to breach Article 6(1)).

[60] *ibid.*, para. 98. On the application of these principles to the domestic criminal process see *Attorney General's Reference (No. 2 of 2001)* [2001] 1 W.L.R. 1869 (unreasonable delay in breach of Article 6(1) does not necessarily render a conviction unsafe, but may in appropriate circumstances be remedied by being taken into account in sentencing; *R. v. James (David John)* [2002] EWCA Crim 1119 (no violation of Article 6(1) following five year delay in complex fraud case).

[61] See paras 4-036, 18-051.

[62] *Findlay v. UK* (1997) 24 EHRR 221, para. 73. It is not necessary that the "guarantees" "must as a matter of law be formal, in some way cast in stone" (*per* Laws L.J. in *R. v. Spear* [2001] 2 W.L.R. 1692, para. [35]); the question is whether a reasonable man apprised of the relevant facts available to the "persistent, even dogged inquirer as a member of the public" would conclude that there was a real doubt as to the tribunal's impartiality or independence (*Scanfuture UK Ltd, v. Secretary of State for Trade and Industry* [2001] I.R.L.R. 416, EAT; *R. (on the application of Husain) v. Asylum Support Adjudicator* [2001] EWHC Admin 832).

[63] *ibid.* See *McGonnell v. UK* (2000) 30 EHRR 289 (sufficient doubt for breach of Article 6(1) as to Guernsey judge's impartiality when participating in planning appeal arose from his previous act in presiding over Guernsey's parliament when it considered the detailed development plan for the land in question); *V v. UK* (1999) 30 EHRR 121 (breach of Article 6(1) in role of Home Secretary in determining tariff for juvenile murderers; independent means, inter alia, "independent ... of the executive").

requirements have led to the reintroduction of a more subjective approach in applying the *nemo judex* principle.[64]

The absence of an independent and impartial tribunal may, however, be cured if the proceedings before it are subject to "subsequent control by a judicial body that has full jurisdiction and does provide the guarantees of Article 6(1)."[65] It has been accepted that this does not require a full appeal on the merits of every administrative decision taken by the executive that affects private rights.[66] the extent to which judicial review or a statutory application to quash provides "full jurisdiction" has been considered in a number of cases by the European Court and Commission.[67] In *Bryan v. UK*[68] the Court held that because the appointment of an inspector to hear an appeal against an enforcement notice could be revoked by the executive where the executive's own policies might be in issue, the inspector's appointment did not satisfy Article 6(1) requirements as to the appearance of independence. However, the High Court's powers of review were sufficient for compliance with Article 6(1) overall. The Court stated that in making this assessment, it was necessary to have regard to matters such as the subject matter of the decision appealed against, the manner in which it was arrived at and the content of the dispute, including the desired and actual grounds of appeal. Here, the court noted the quasi-judicial character of the proceedings before the inspector, the inspector's duty to exercise independent judgment, the requirement that inspectors must not be subject to any improper influence, and the stated mission of the inspectorate to uphold the principle of openness, fairness and impartiality. Any short-comings in these respects could have been reviewed by the High Court. The High Court was able to deal with most of the points in fact raised by the appellant. As to the facts and planning merits, the High Court did not have jurisdiction to substitute its view for that of the inspector, but could intervene if the inspector had taken into account irrelevant factors or had omitted to take account of relevant factors or if the evidence was not capable of supporting a finding of fact or if the decision was perverse or irrational. Such an approach by an appeal tribunal on questions of fact could reasonably be expected in specialised areas of the law such as this, particularly where the facts had already been established in the course of a quasi-judicial procedure governed by many of the Article 6(1) safeguards.[69]

Bryan v. UK has been applied in respect of the decision of an inspector to **8–021** dismiss an appeal against a discontinuance notice[70] and in determining a

---

[64] Above, para. 4-036.

[65] *Albert and Le Compte v. Belgium* (1983) 5 EHRR 533, para. 29.

[66] European Commission of Human Rights in *Kaplan v. UK* (1980) 4 EHRR 64, para. 161.

[67] *ISKCON v. UK*; App. No. 20490/92, March 8, 1994 (Commission) (no violation of Article 6(1) in determination by inspector of appeal against enforcement notice); *Bryan v. UK* (1995) 21 EHRR 342; *Chapman v. UK.* (2001) 10 B.H.R.C. 48 (no violation of Article 6(1) in determination by inspector of appeal against enforcement notice); *Howard v. UK.* App. No. 10825/84, July 16, 1987 (Commission); *Varey v. UK*, App. No. 26662/95, October 27,1999 (Commission) (no violation of Article 6(1) in determination of Secretary of State to dismiss appeals against refusal of planning permission, contrary to inspectors' recommendations).

[68] Above.

[69] Paras 40–47.

[70] *O'Brien v. Department of the Environment. Transport and the Regions* (unreported, January 28, 2001).

planning appeal.[71] However, in *R. (on the application of Holding and Barnes plc) v. Secretary of the State for the Environment, Transport and the Regions*[72] the Divisional Court granted a declaration that provisions enabling the Secretary of State to call-in planning applications, to direct that a planning appeal should be determined by himself rather than his inspector (a "recovered appeal") and to approve compulsory purchase and highway orders were incompatible with Article 6(1). This was on the ground that the Secretary of State was not independent and impartial and that the processes in question were not saved by the possibility of challenge before the High Court by a statutory application to quash. The court held that *Bryan v. UK* was distinguishable and that it was impossible to read the relevant provisions in such a way (for example by enlarging the permissible grounds of appeal) as to comply with Article 6(1).

The House of Lords unanimously allowed an appeal[73] on the ground that, while the Secretary of State could not be seen objectively as independent and impartial (and this was accepted by him), the powers of the High Court were in fact sufficient.[74] Furthermore, this overall conclusion applied even to decisions where the financial interests of other government departments were engaged, although particular points might arise in subsequent proceedings. It was noted that decisions were taken by ministers who so far as possible had no connection with the area from which the case came, assisted by a decision officer who worked separately from other civil servants involved in casework. There would also have been an inquiry conducted by an inspector, who would report to the Secretary of State. The situation whereby, in practice in rare and controversial cases, decisions on planning policy could be made by a democratically accountable member of the executive was well entrenched in UK constitutional practice and the House expressed itself satisfied that this conformed to Article 6(1):

> "To substitute for the Secretary of State an independent and impartial body with no central electoral accountability would not only be a recipe for chaos: it would be profoundly undemocratic."[75]

Lord Hoffmann noted[76] that a distinction was to be drawn between matters of fact and matters of planning policy or expediency. It was only in relation to the former that the additional safeguards identified in *Bryan v. UK* in respect of the inspector's involvement were needed to justify the limited review of findings of fact by the High Court. It was separately accepted by the European Court of Human Rights in *Zumtobel v. Austria* that:

> "respect must be accorded to decisions taken by administrative authorities on grounds of expediency"[77]

---

[71] *Bhamjee v. Secretary of State for the Environment. Transport and the Regions* (unreported, January 23, 2001).

[72] [2001] H.R.L.R. 10. See to the same effect the decision of the Court of Session in *County Properties Ltd v. The Scottish Ministers* [2000] H.R.L.R. 677.

[73] [2001] UKHL 23.

[74] Applying *Bryan v. UK* and *Zumtobel v. Austria* (1993) 17 EHRR 116.

[75] *per* Lord Nolan at para. [60].

[76] Paras [98]–[117].

[77] (1993) 17 EHRR 110, para. [32].

and as regards these matters

"there has never been a single voice in the Commission or the European Court to suggest that our provisions for judicial review are inadequate to satisfy Article 6."[78]

For Lord Slynn, the powers of the High Court were already sufficient; however, the express recognition of proportionality and review for mistakes of fact as permissible grounds of challenge would be desirable and make the position even clearer.[79] This was left open by other members of the House.[80]

The distinction between matters of policy and matters of fact has been applied in subsequent cases, with, where the decision-maker is not independent and impartial, judicial review being recognised as an adequate remedy in respect of the former but not the latter.[81] The Court of Appeal has held that, notwithstanding the dicta of Lord Slynn in *Alconbury*, mentioned above, it was not a legitimate process of interpretation to enlarge the powers of a court with jurisdiction to consider appeal on points of law so as to enable it to redetermine questions of (non-jurisdictional) fact on the ground that this was necessary to secure compliance with Article 6(1).[82]

Non-compliance overall with the requirement of access to an independent

---

[78] Para. [122].

[79] Paras [51]–]54].

[80] Lord Nolan at para. [62], Lord Clyde at para. [169] (expressing some scepticism).

[81] *R. (on the application of Vetterlein) v. Hampshire County Council* [2001] EWHC Admin 560 (opportunity for objectors to a grant of planning permission to make detailed representations during the public consultation process and to address the committee where the issues were question of professional judgment sufficient to constitute a fair hearing (although the right to a fair hearing did not in fact arise on the facts)); *British Telecommunications plc v. Gloucester City Council* [2001] EWHC 1001 (judicial review sufficient in respect of policy matters); *R. (on the application of Katho) v. Rhondda Cynon Taff County Borough Council* [2001] EWHC Admin 527 (council not independent and impartial as regards grant of planning permission in respect of its own land, but judicial review adequate remedy as the primary facts and inferences from those facts were not in dispute); *Friends Provident Life Office v. Secretary of State for Transport. Local Government and the Regions* [2001] EWHC 820 (assessment of likely impact of proposed development to be regarded for this purpose as planning judgment rather than "an issue of fact and the evaluation of fact"); *McLellan v. Bracknell Forest Borough Council* [2001] EWCA Civ 1510, [2002] 1 All E.R. 899 (review panel independent and impartial as regards decision to proceed with termination of introductory tenancy but judicial review adequate remedy where issue was reasonableness of termination decision); *cf. Adan v. London Borough of Newham* [2001] EWCA Civ 1916, [2002] H.R.L.R. 470 (dicta that review officer not independent and impartial as regards review of homelessness application but appeal on point of law would be an adequate remedy unless there was a material dispute as to the primary facts; in such cases it would be necessary for an independent and impartial review officer to be appointed through use of statutory contracting out powers); *Begum v. London Borough of Tower Hamlets* [2002] EWCA Civ 239, [2002] 2 All E.R. 668 (disapproving dicta in *Adan* that appeal on point of law (equivalent to judicial review) would not constitute an adequate remedy in all cases). There is no residual requirement in a case concerning judgment and discretion rather than fact finding for there to be an oral hearing at first instance: *R. (on the application of Adlard) v. Secretary of State for the Environment. Transport and the Regions* [2002] EWCA Civ 735.

[82] *Adan v. London Borough of Newham* [2001] EWCA Civ 1916 (Brooke LJ. and David Steel J., Hale L.J. dissenting on this point). The views of the Court of Appeal in *Adan* on Article 6 were *obiter*, and were disapproved by the Court of Appeal in *Begum v. London Borough of Tower Hamlets* [2002] EWCA Civ 239, [2002] 2 All E.R. 668. The court in *Begum* did not need to express a view on this point.

and impartial tribunal has been found in respect of housing benefit review boards;[83] part-time sheriffs in Scotland appointed by the Lord Advocate with a limited term of office[84] the Crown Court when constituted (in accordance with the rules) to hear an appeal from licensing justices so as to include other members of the licensing committee to which those justices belonged;[85] and a panel including councillors appointed to determine question arising under regulations made under the National Assistance Act 1948.[86]

Article 6(2) and (3) impose particular requirements, including the presumption of innocence, in respect of persons "charged with a criminal offence." These are also applicable to disciplinary proceedings that fall within Article 6(1),[87] but do not apply in respect of anti-social behaviour orders made under the Crime and Disorder Act 1998.[88]

(e) Article 8

8–022   This provides:

> "**Article 8 — Right to respect for private and family life**
>
> 1.   Everyone has the right to respect for his private and family life, his home and his correspondence.
> 2.   There shall be no interference by a public authority with the exercise of this right except such as is in accordance with the law and is necessary in a democratic society in the interests of national security, public safety, or the economic well-being of the country, for the prevention of disorder or crime, for the protection of health or morals, or for the protection of the rights and freedoms of others."

"Private life" is a concept that is not confined to "an 'inner circle' in which the individual may live his own personal life as he chooses and to exclude therefrom entirely the outside world" but extends to cover, to a degree, the right to establish and develop relationships with other human beings, and

---

[83]   R. (on the application of Bewry) v. Norwich City Council [2001] EWHC Admin 657, [2002] H.R.L.R. 21 (councillor membership of Board determining issue involving credibility; breach of common law requirement equivalent to that comprised in Article 6); distinguished in R. (on the application of Bibi) v. Housing Benefit Review Board of Rochdale Metropolitan Borough Council [2001] EWHC Admin 967 (councillor membership of Board meant that it could not be independent or expert in the Alconbury sense, but judicial review was a sufficient remedy given that most of the facts were not substantially in issue and that the councillors had no personal interest in their finding that a tenancy was not on a commercial basis and so did not enable a claim to be made for housing benefit).

[84]   Starrs v. Ruxton 2000 J.C. 208.

[85]   R. (on the application of Smith) v. Lincoln Crown Court [2001] EWHC Admin 928 (judicial review of the Crown Court held to be an inadequate remedy).

[86]   R. (on the application of Beeson) v. Dorset Council [2001] EWHC Admin 986 (the panel had to comprise "at least" one independent member and so a fully independent panel could actually be appointed; the key issue was one of credibility and so judicial review was an inadequate remedy).

[87]   Albert and Le Compte v. Belgium (1983) 5 E.H.R.R. 533, para. 39.

[88]   R. (on the application of M (a child)) v. Manchester Crown Court [2001] EWCA Civ 281, [2001] H.R.L.R. 763.

activities of a professional or business nature[89] but without extending the notion of "private" to the whole of an individual's business or professional life.[90] Article 8 will apply where the dividing line between an individual's business and professional life and his private life is not clearly distinguishable, as where the activities in question occur at a place where access to the public is excluded and some domestic authority is exercised.[91] However, it appears that it does not apply to, for example, the establishment by the Department of Health of a Consultancy Service Index listing the names and former employers of individuals (inter alia) prosecuted for an offence concerning children or disciplined for placing a child at risk. Reference to the Index would only be made following an application by the individual for employment related to children and the information that would be accessed from previous employers would concern conduct in the course of employment and thus in the public domain.[92]

Article 8 covers "the physical and moral integrity of the person, including his or her sexual life."[93] It applies (inter alia) to the collection of secret information concerning individuals[94] and the disclosure of medical records and information concerning patients[95] and the sale of the electoral register to commercial concerns, including the claimant's name and address, which he was compelled to provide to the electoral registration officer.[96] It does not, however, apply to confer a right to die,[97] or to the mere communication to a person by a public authority of its decision to take a step that is a precursor to enforcement action.[98]

The notion of "family life" is not confined solely to families based on marriage and may encompass other de facto relationships; when deciding whether a relationship can be said to amount to "family life" relevant factors may include whether the couple live together, the length of their relationship and whether they have demonstrated their commitment to each other by having children together or by other means.[99] Article 8 has been held to be applicable in a range of cases concerning the decision making of

---

[89] *Niemietz v Germany* (1992) 16 EHRR 97, para. 29 (search of applicant's office covered by Article 8); *Amann v. Switzerland*, Judgment of February 16, 2000 (interception of a private telephone call concerning a business matter covered by Article 8).

[90] *R. v. Worcester County Council, ex p. SW* [2000] H.R.L.R. 702, 717–718.

[91] *ibid.*

[92] This view was expressed *obiter* by Newman J. in *ibid.*, the case preceding implementation of the Human Rights Act 1998.

[93] *X and Y v. Netherlands* (1985) 8 EHRR 235, para. 22. Cf. *Smith and Grady v. UK* (1999) 29 EHRR 493; *Lustig-Prean and Beckett v. UK* (1999) 29 EHRR 548 (breaches of Article 8 in respect of investigations into and administrative discharges of homosexual members of the armed forces).

[94] *Leander v. Sweden* (1987) 9 EHRR 433.

[95] *Z v. Finland* (1995) 25 EHRR 371.

[96] *R. (on the application of Robertson) v. City of Wakefield Metropolitan Council* [2001] EWHC Admin 915.

[97] *R. (on the application of Pretty) v. Director of Public Prosecutions* [2001] UKHL 61.

[98] *R. (on the application of Denson) v. Child Support Agency* [2002] EWHC 154 (Admin) (Article 8(1) might be engaged if the person was in a vulnerable category).

[99] *X, Y and Z v. UK* (1997) 24 EHRR 143 (de facto family ties held to link a (female to male) transsexual and a woman (who had lived together for over 10 years) and their child (by AID)).

local authorities concerning children in care[1] and adoption,[2] and the policy of the Prison Service with respect to the length of time babies would be permitted to live with their mothers in prison.[3] It also applies to the payment of benefits to a surviving spouse, given that availability of pecuniary support "does have a significant effect on the relationship of a family prior to the death of a spouse".[4]

The right to respect for private and family life has been held to give rise to an obligation for the State to facilitate access to information about an individual's past[5] and hazardous activities that have exposed the applicants to health risks.[6]

The term "home" is to be construed broadly; it is not confined to a residence legally established in accordance with national law but extends to long-term residence on land in caravans albeit contrary to planning law.[7] Enforcement action under planning law may accordingly infringe Article 8,[8] as may eviction from a council house.[9] However, Article 8(1) does not impose a general obligation on local authorities to remedy problems caused by a design defect.[10] Similarly, causing, or allowing others to create, severe environmental pollution[11] and failing to warn of environmental risks[12] may constitute breaches. States are, however, accorded a wide margin of appreciation, particularly in respect of arguments that they should take

[1] See TP and KM v. UK, Judgment of May 10, 2001; Re W. & B. (children): Re W. (children) [2001] EWCA Civ 757, [2001] H.R.L.R. 1120.

[2] In re B (a minor) [2001] UKHL 70, where the House of Lords held that the balancing exercise required by Article 8 does not differ in substance from the balancing exercise undertaken by a court when deciding under English law whether adoption would be in the best interests of the child.

[3] R. (on the application of P. Q and QB) v. Secretary of State for the Home Department [2001] EWCA Civ 1 151 (it was held that the policy that children should leave at 18 months should be applied more flexibly).

[4] Hooper and others v. Secretary of State for Work and Pensions [2002] EWHC 191 (Admin), paras [14] — [35] (violation of Article 14 in conjunction with Article 8).

[5] Gaskin v. UK (1989) 12 EHRR 36.

[6] McGinley and Egan v. UK (1998) 27 EHRR 1 (no infringement found).

[7] Buckley v. UK (1996) 23 EHRR 101. See also R. v. North and East Devon Health Authority, ex p. Coughlan [2000] 2 W.L.R. 622.

[8] Buckley v. UK, above (no infringement found); Donoghue v. Poplar Housing and Regeneration Community Association Ltd [2001] EWCA Civ 595, [2001] 3 W.L.R. 183 (shorthold tenancy); London Borough of Harrow v. Qazi [2001] EWCA Civ 1834 (eviction of person by local authority following termination of joint tenancy by spouse held to engage Article 8); Sheffield City Council v. Smart [2002] EWCA Civ 04 (Article 8 applied to termination of non-secure tenancy granted to homeless person). Occupation of a plot as a trespasser by a traveller for a fortnight was insufficient to make it a "home"; eviction nevertheless engaged Article 8 as the result of the effect on private and family life: Ward v. Hillingdon London Borough Council [2001] EWHC Admin 91, [2001] H.R.L.R. 825.

[9] McLellan v. Bracknell Forest Borough Council [2001] EWCA Civ 1510 (introductory tenancy); London Borough of Lambeth v. Howard (2001) 33 H.L.R. 636: Donoghue v. Poplar Housing and Regeneration Community Association Ltd. [2001] EWCA Civ 595, [2001] 3 W.L.R. 183.

[10] Lee v. Leeds City Council; Ratcliffe v. Sandwell Metropolitan Borough Council [2002] EWCA Civ 06 (a violation of Article 8(1) may, however, arise on the facts of a particular case).

[11] Lopez Ostra v. Spain (1994) 20 EHRR 277; cf. Powell and Rayner v. UK (1980) 12 EHRR 355 (no infringement found); R. (on the application of Vetterlein) v. Hampshire County Council [2001] EWHC Admin 560 (applicants' "generalised environmental concerns" in respect of proposed incinerator held too remote to engage Article 8).

[12] Guerra v. Italy (1998) 26 EHRR 357.

positive steps in support of the rights protected by Article 8(1).[13]

For an interference with rights protected by Article 8(1) to be justified by reference to Article 8(2), it must be (a) "in accordance with the law;" (b) "necessary in a democratic society"; and (c) for a legitimate aim. To be "in accordance with the law", the interference must have some basis in domestic law (such as primary and delegated legislation but not internal instructions); the law must be "adequately accessible: the citizen must be able to have an indication that is adequate, in the circumstances, of the legal rules applicable to a given case"; and a norm to be regarded as "law" must be "formulated with sufficient precision to enable the citizen to regulate his conduct: he must be able — if need be with appropriate advice — to foresee, to a degree that is reasonable in the circumstances, the consequences which a given action may entail."[14] As regards what is "necessary in a democratic society," it has been stated that:

"(a) the adjective 'necessary' is not synonymous with 'indispensable', neither has it the flexibility of such expressions as 'admissible', 'ordinary', 'useful', 'reasonable or desirable'. ...

(b) the Contracting States enjoy a certain but not unlimited margin of appreciation in the matter of the imposition of restrictions, but it is for the Court to give the final ruling on whether they are compatible with the Convention.

(c) The phrase 'necessary' in a democratic society means that, to be compatible with the Convention, the interference must, inter alia, correspond to a 'pressing social need' and be 'proportionate to the legitimate aim pursued.'

(d) Those paragraphs of Articles of the Convention which provide for an exception to a right guaranteed are to be narrowly interpreted. ... "[15]

Accordingly, enforcement action under planning law has been held to be necessary for the well-being of the economy and for public safety.[16]

The application of these principles by the European Court is illustrated by the decision in *TP and KM v. UK*.[17] Here, it was not disputed that the removal of KM into care by the local authority until she was returned a year later constituted an interference with the right to respect for the family life of both KM and her mother, TP. The removal was based on a wrongful assessment of the need for an emergency measure based, inter alia, on the misinterpretation of statements made by KM when interviewed to mean

---

[13] See e.g. *X, Y and Z v. UK* (1997) 24 EHRR 143 (no obligation for UK to recognise parental rights for transsexual who was not the biological father, in absence of generally shared approach among the contracting states); *Rees v. UK* (1986) 9 EHRR 56 (no obligation to amend birth registration sysem to alter recorded sex of post-operative transsexual); *Sheffield and Horsham v. UK* (1998) 27 EHRR 163.

[14] *Silver v. UK* (1983) 5 EHRR 347, paras 85–88, applying the principles developed in respect of Article 10 by the Court in *Sunday Times v. UK* (1979) 2 EHRR 245.

[15] *ibid.*, para. [97].

[16] *Buckley v. UK* (1996) 23 EHRR 101.

[17] Judgment of May 10, 2001. Cf. *R. (on the application of S) v. City of Plymouth* [2002] EWCA Civ 388 (Court of Appeal ordered disclosure of information by local social services authority to claimant about her adult son C who was in the authority's guardianship under the Mental Health Act 1983).

that KM had been abused by TP's boyfriend. The Court held that the removal, based on a court order, was in accordance with the law and pursued legitimate aims (protecting the health or morals and the rights and freedoms of the child). As to whether the removal was "necessary in a democratic society" the Court noted the state's wide margin of appreciation, particularly when assessing the necessity of taking a child into care. However, stricter scrutiny was called for in respect of any further limitations, such as restrictions on parental rights of access or other legal safeguards designed to secure effective protection of respect for family life. Furthermore, the decision-making process had to be fair. Here, the removal of KM into care was supported by relevant and sufficient reasons, notwithstanding the mistake as to the identity of the alleged abuser, and was a proportionate measure necessary in a democratic society for protecting KM's health and rights. However, while KM was in care, TP's access was severely restricted. The UK had a positive obligation to protect the interests of the family by considering disclosing the material on which the removal had been based (including the video of the interview with KM and transcript) to TP, even in the absence of a request for it by her. The material should have been disclosed or the matter referred to a court promptly to allow TP an effective opportunity to deal with the allegations that KM could not be returned safely to her care. The failure to do so deprived TP of an adequate involvement in the decision-making process concerning the care of her daughter and so there was a failure to respect TP and KM's family life.

The Court of Appeal has held that where otherwise there may be a breach of Articles 6(1) and 8, the provisions of the Children Act 1989 concerning care orders should be read as subject to modifications that enhance the role of the court.[18] On appeal only one of these modifications was upheld.[19] In other contexts it has been held that although the phraseology is different there is no difference in substance between the approach of English law and the requirements of Article 8.[20]

In the case of some decisions that interfere with the right to respect for the claimant's home, it will be necessary for the court itself to be satisfied, when the decision is challenged, that the decision on the particular facts is necessary and proportionate to the aim to be achieved.[21] In the case of others, where the claimant's interest in the land is more limited, the balance is drawn by the legislation and the role of the court will simply be to ensure

---

[18] *Re W. & B. (children); Re W. (children)* [2001] EWCA Civ 757, [2001] H.R.L.R. 1120. The modifications were that a trial judge should have a wider discretion to make an interim care order, and that either the guardian *ad litem* or the local authority had the right to apply to the trial court for further directions if starred milestones in the care plan were not achieved within a reasonable time of the date set at trial.

[19] *In re S(FC)* [2002] UKHL 10. See above, para. 8-007.

[20] *In re B (a minor)* [2001] UKHL 70 (confirmation of adoption orders); *R. (on the application of S) v. Swindon Borough Council* [2001] EWHC Admin 334 (decisions concerning children who may be at risk).

[21] *e.g. Chapman v. UK* (2001) 10 B.H.R.C. 48 (enforcement notice requiring removal of mobile home); *Lambeth London Borough Council v. Howard* (2001) 33 H.L.R. 636 (termination of secure tenancy).

compliance with the procedures and to review the decision on *Wednesbury* principles.[22]

(f) Article 10

This provides: **8–023**

"Article 10 — Freedom of expression

1   Everyone has the right to freedom of expression. This right shall include freedom to hold opinions and to receive and impart information and ideas without interference by public authority and regardless of frontiers. This article shall not prevent States from requiring the licensing of broadcasting, television or cinema enterprises.

2   The exercise of these freedoms, since it carries with it duties and responsibilities, may be subject to such formalities, conditions, restrictions or penalties as are prescribed by law and are necessary in a democratic society, in the interests of national security, territorial integrity or public safety, for the prevention of disorder or crime, for the protection of health or morals, for the protection of the reputation or rights of others, for preventing the disclosure of information received in confidence, or for maintaining the authority and impartiality of the judiciary."

The structure of Article 10, conferring a right to freedom of expression, is similar to that of Article 8. It brings into play a wide range of laws that impinge on that freedom, including those, for example, that protect the reputation of individuals (defamation), protect the administration of justice from prejudicial press comment (contempt of court), and prohibit the publication of indecent or obscene material. Most of the cases turn on the question whether the restriction can be justified under Article 10(2). For example, in *Handyside v. UK*[23] was held that the conviction of the publisher of the Little Red Schoolbook under the Obscene Publications Act 1959 and associated seizures of copies did not breach Article 10. The interferences with expression were prescribed by law and had an aim that was legitimate under Article 10(2) ("the protection of morals in a democratic society"); the national authorities had been entitled to conclude, within their margin of appreciation, that the interferences were necessary for that purpose, in that they were a necessary response to a pressing social need. This decision may be compared with that in *Sunday Times v. UK*[24] where the Court held that an injunction granted to restrain publication of an article setting out evidence and argument relevant to civil actions against the distributors of thalidomide, a drug which caused babies to be born with deformities, violated Article 10. The interference with free expression was prescribed by

---

[22]   *e.g. McLellan v. Bracknall Forest Borough Council* [2001] EWCA Civ 1510 (introductory tenancy); *Sheffield City Council v. Smart* [2002] EWCA Civ 04 (non-secure tenancy granted to homeless person).

[23]   (1976) 1 E.H.R.R. 737.

[24]   (1979) 2 E.H.R.R. 245.

law (the common law of contempt of court), had a legitimate aim (maintaining the authority of the judiciary), but was not a proportionate response to a social need sufficiently pressing to outweigh the public interest in freedom of expression. The main problem was that the common rule applied constituted an absolute prohibition on the prejudgment of issues in pending cases. The exceptions in Article 10(2) are to be interpreted narrowly.

(g) Article 13

8–024   This article, which does not appear in the Human Rights Act 1998, provides:

> **"Article 13 — Right to an effective remedy**
> Everyone whose rights and freedoms as set forth in this Convention are violated shall have an effective remedy before a national authority notwithstanding that the violation has been committed by persons acting in an official capacity."

Accordingly, where an individual has an arguable claim to be the victim of a violation of ECHR rights, he or she should have a remedy before a national authority (not necessarily judicial) to have the claim decided and, if appropriate to obtain redress; the aggregate of remedies under domestic law may be sufficient.[25] The requirements of Article 13 are less onerous than those of Article 6(1) (which is applicable in a narrower range of circumstances).[26] The police complaints system does not provide an effective remedy in respect of alleged abuses of authority contrary to the ECHR by police officers.[27] In *Z v. UK*,[28] the European Court of Human Rights held that child victims of ill treatment and abuse by their parents did not have an effective remedy for the damage they had suffered as a result of the failure of the local authority to protect them (contrary to Article 3). The government accepted that the availability of compensation from the Criminal Injuries Compensation Board (which covered only criminal acts), the possibility of complaining to the Local Government Ombudsman (whose recommendations were not legally enforceable) and the complaints procedure under the Children Act 1989 was insufficient alone or cumulatively to satisfy the requirements of Article 13. The Court noted that the decision of the House of Lords in *X (Minors) v. Bedfordshire County Council*[29] barred proceedings in negligence, and the government's submission that in the future under the Human Rights Act 1998 victims of human rights breaches would be able to bring proceedings in courts empowered to award damages. It did not consider it appropriate

> "to make any findings as to whether only adversarial court proceedings could have finished effective redress, though judicial remedies indeed furnish strong guarantees of independence, access for the victim and

---

[25] *Silver v. UK* (1983) 5 EHRR 347.
[26] *ibid.*, para. [109].
[27] *Khan v. UK* (2000) 8 B.H.R.C. 310, paras [45]–[47].
[28] Judgment of May 10, 2001.
[29] [1995] 2 A.C. 633.

family and enforceability of awards in compliance with the requirements of Article 13,"[30]

A breach of Article 13 was found on a similar basis in *TP and KM v. UK*.[31]
An English court should "strive to avoid" a risk that the UK be in breach of
Article 13.[32]

(h) Article 14

This article provides: **8–025**

> **"Article 14 — Prohibition of discrimination**
>   The enjoyment of the rights and freedoms set forth in this
> Convention shall be secured without discrimination on any ground
> such as sex, race, colour, language, religion, political or other opinion,
> national or social origin, association with a national minority,
> property, birth or other status."

This does not constitute a free standing prohibition of discrimination on the
stated grounds (which are themselves given as examples);[33] complaints must
be concerned with one of the substantive protected rights and freedoms
taken in conjunction with Article 14.[34] Furthermore, it does not prohibit
every difference in treatment, but only those differences where "other
persons in an analogous or relevantly similar situation enjoy preferential
treatment" and "there is no objective and reasonable justification."[35]
    The existence of such a justification must be "assessed in relation to the
aims and effects of the measure under consideration, regard being had to the
principles which normally prevail in democratic societies." A difference in
treatment must pursue a "legitimate aim" and there must be a "reasonable
relationship of proportionality between the means employed and the aim
sought to be realised."[36] Accordingly, different legislative provision may be
made for the different countries of the U.K. "to take account of regional
differences and characteristics of an objective and reasonable nature."[37]
    The fact that objectively different statutory regimes have different
arrangements as to access to an independent appeal tribunal does not
involve discrimination based on the claimant's personal characteristics, and

---

[30] paras [105]–[111].

[31] Judgment of May 10, 2001, paras [104]–[110] (in respect of breach of Article 8). This arose
      out of *M. v. Newham London Borough Council*, heard with *X (Minors) v. Bedfordshire
      County Council*, above.

[32] *R. v. Canterbury Crown Court, ex p. Regentford Ltd* [2001] H.R.L.R. 362, para. 19, *per*
      Waller L.J.

[33] This matter is addressed in Protocol 12, which will come into force when ratified by ten
      states in respect of those states and any subsequent states to ratify.

[34] *Belgian Linguistic case (No. 2)* (1968) 1 E.H.R.R. 252, para. 9. It is not necessary to
      establish breach of the substantive right of freedom in question: *Abdulaziz. Cabales and
      Balkandali v. UK* (1985) 7 E.H.R.R. 471, para. 71; it is sufficient that "a personal group is
      treated, without proper justification, less favourably than another, even though the more
      favourable treatment is not called for by the Convention:" *ibid.*, para. 82.

[35] *Beleian Linguistic case (No. 2)*, para. 10; *Stubbings v. UK* (1996) 23 E.H.R.R. 213, para. 70.

[36] *ibid.*, para. 10.

[37] *Magee v. UK*, Judgment of June 6, 2000.

so does not engage Article 14.[38] An illustration of an objective and reasonable justification for a difference based on national origin is provided by *R. (on the application of Mitchell) v. Coventry University*[39] where regulations that classified a British citizen born and brought up in Hong Kong as an "overseas" student for the purpose of liability to pay university fees, while classifying former British dependent territory citizens resident in Hong Kong, within three years before September 1, 2000, and who emigrated to the UK, as "home" students, were upheld. Classification as a home student primarily depended on three years' ordinary residence in the UK subject to exceptions for recent immigrants; these exceptions had been withdrawn other than for former BDT citizens in Hong Kong for a transitional period following the change of status of Hong Kong. There was not a "relevant similarity" as the claimant had never fallen within the exceptions in the regulations; the suggested comparators had always done so, in both their broad and narrow form.[40]

D. PRACTICAL IMPLEMENTATION OF THE ACT

8–026   Distinctive features of the implementation process have been an extensive training exercise for the judiciary, superintended by the Judicial Studies Board[41] and a full programme for guidance and training for government departments and other public bodies and the general public, overseen by a Human Rights Unit formerly located in the Home Office but now transferred to the Lord Chancellor's Department.[42] Parliament has established a Joint Committee on Human Rights to scrutinise Bills and report on other matters related to human rights.[43]

E. IMPACT OF THE ACT

8–027   A number of features can be identified from the first 18 months in which the

---

[38] *R. (on the application of Beeson) v. Dorset County Council* [2001] EWHC Admin 986; cf. *St. Brice v. London Borough of Southwark* [2001] EWCA 1138 (Article 14 not engaged by differences between county court and High Court in rules governing litigation).

[39] [2001] EWHC Admin 167. See also *Hooper and others v. Secretary of State for Work and Pensions* [2002] EWHC 191 (Admin) (objective justification for government's timetable for introducing changes to regime for widow's pension so as to secure equality); *R. (on the application of Carson) v. Secretary of State for Work and Pensions* [2002] EWHC 978 (Admin) (objective justification for decision that pensioners resident outside the UK should not be included in annual uprating of state retirement pensions).

[40] The court assumed for the purposes of argument but did not decide that Article 2 of Protocol 1 extended to govern access to higher education.

[41] See above, para. 4-029

[42] See LCD website.

[43] See *e.g.* Sixth Report, 2001–02 H.L. 57, *The Mental Health Act 1983 (Remedial) Order* 2001; Seventh Report, 2001–02 H.L. 58, *Making of Remedial Orders*; D.J. Feldman, "Parliamentary Scrutiny of Legislation and Human Rights" [2002] P.L. 323.

Human Rights Act 1998 has been in operation.[44] The Act has certainly been cited and discussed in a large number of decided cases, although the caseload has not been as great as anticipated.[45] In some, a bad HRA point is taken as the last resort of the desperate. In many, points require extended analysis as the jurisprudence of the Act settles down and the undoubted difficulties of interpretation and application are addressed.

The House of Lords and Court of Appeal have decided landmark cases that provide guidance on important issues such as the proper approach to interpretation under section 3(1), the proportionality test, the discretionary area of judgment to be accorded to decision-makers and the extent to which the Act operates retrospectively. The extent to which the Act has made a difference to the *outcomes* of decided cases is in fact relatively limited. The principles applied under the Act commonly lead to the same result as the common law and the ordinary processes of statutory interpretation and judicial review, particularly with the development of the principle of legality and the more flexible approach to *Wednesbury* review. There have been few cases where there has been a declaration of incompatibility, the use of section 3(1) to provide a reading for a statutory provision that could not have been achieved through other processes of statutory interpretation, or a finding that legislation or a decision is not a proportionate response to a legitimate objective. A number of such cases have, indeed, been overturned on appeal. Nevertheless, there are a number of areas where a significant impact can be discerned, including aspects of the criminal process, prisoners' rights, issues arising from the requirement of independence and impartiality for those who determine civil rights and obligations and developments in the area of privacy.

---

[44] See generally, P. Craig, "The Courts, the Human Rights Act and Judicial Review" (2001) 117 L.Q.R. 589; F. Klug and K. Starmer, [2001] P.L. 654; A. Ashworth, [2001] Crim. L.R. 855.

[45] See statistics provided by the Human Rights Unit (LCD website).

PART II

SOLVING LEGAL PROBLEMS

CHAPTER 9

PROBLEMS ABOUT PROBLEMS

We encounter a difficulty at the beginning of this part of the book by **9–001** directing our attention to the solution of "legal" problems. How should such problems be defined? Are there distinctions to be drawn between legal problems and social problems? How effective are lawyers in solving legal problems? What is a problem?

These are issues which have been the subject of research and discussion in the last few decades reflecting the growing awareness of the existence of an unmet need for legal assistance with problems and the development of law centres and other agencies to meet it. They are central to the debate over the provision of legal services and the response to these issues will affect the formulation of policy.

This chapter explores some of these issues and Chapter 10 assesses the strengths and weaknesses of the major agencies currently involved in giving advice and solving problems. Throughout both chapters we shall be particularly concerned with the role of lawyers.

A great deal of emphasis is placed on the role of courts in settling disputes. The law student learns much of his or her law from decided cases.[1] Public attention is inevitably focused upon the adversarial context, civil and criminal procedure is lengthy and complex, books on the English legal system (including ours) usually devote a considerable amount of space to litigation, and English procedure tends to individualise grievances and tailor them to the adversarial model.[2] Yet it remains true that only a tiny fraction of legal matters end up in court.[3] If it were otherwise the court system would simply collapse under the strain.

This is partly explained by the lawyer's ability to advise on and negotiate settlements to the mutual satisfaction of the parties to a dispute.[4] In addition, parties to disputes are increasingly looking to alternative methods of resolving disputes and government policy encourages or requires the use of means of resolution other than litigation in many areas.[5] Alternative dispute resolution is both acceptable and essential. Further, some matters

---

[1] Through the doctrine of *stare decisis*, see Chap. 7, above.
[2] Whilst the individual action has been the only source of litigation in the past, there is an increasing recognition of the importance of group actions, see below, para. 11-016.
[3] See para. 11-025, below.
[4] See paras 11-025–11-031, below.
[5] See below, paras 11-032–11-040.

are non-contentious and rarely result in litigation.[6] Other matters are resolved on the receipt of information or advice about the law.

However, many legal matters do not emerge for legal assistance, let alone litigation, because they are never identified as legal problems by the sufferers or never reach lawyers, or, having reached lawyers, are not recognised as problems within the lawyer's or the law's purview.[7] This situation is unacceptable and any scheme to provide public legal services must be judged on its ability to bridge the gap by involving lawyers or appropriate advisers in the resolution of all matters that require their assistance.[8]

A. WHAT IS A PROBLEM?

9–002 This may appear to be an odd question to pose, but it has a bearing on our approach to the provision of legal services and the involvement of lawyers. Does a situation only become a problem when a sufferer identifies it as something about which he or she can do something? If the mood is one of resigned acceptance, that the situation represents one of life's difficulties, that there is no help to be obtained in dealing with the matter,[9] should we consider that such a person has a problem?

This is not confined to legal problems (although in many situations there may be an unrecognised legal problem) but has its effects in other areas as well. The failure on the part of the sufferer to appreciate that solutions might exist may be the result of a combination of factors including ignorance,[10] apathy,[11] complexity of the situation,[12] generality of the problem and the extent of financial or physical resources to rectify matters.[13] When the need for assistance is not even recognised, there is

---

[6] This is generally true of conveyancing, wills and probate and agreeing contractual relationships, all of which often, though not always or necessarily, involve a lawyer. The amount of litigation that these areas, and others, produce may seem large but it is very small when compared with the number of transactions.

[7] This general difficulty has been termed "unmet legal need". See, *e.g.*, R. Abel-Smith, M. Zander and R. Brooke, *Legal Problems and the Citizen* (1973); P. Morris, R. White and P. Lewis, *Social Needs and Legal Action* (1973); A. Byles and P. Morris, *Unmet need: the case of the neighbourhood law centre* (1977); H. Genn, *Meeting Legal Needs?* (1982); D. Harris *et al.*, *Compensation and Support for Illness and Injury* (1984); The Committee on the Future of the Legal Profession, *A Time for Change* (1988), Chair: Lady Marre, Chap. 7 [hereafter, the Marre Committee]; P. Robertshaw, *Rethinking Legal Need: The Case of Criminal Justice* (1991); Legal Action Group, *A Strategy for Justice* (1992); R. Smith (ed.), *Shaping the Future* (1995); Lord Chancellor's Department, *Legal Aid — Targeting Need* (Cm. 2854, 1995); H. Genn, *Paths to Justice* (1999).

[8] For the Government's approach to this problem as a matter of social exclusion, see below, para. 10-001.

[9] Genn, in her recent study, identified these people as "lumpers", see below, para. 9-008.

[10] See para. 9-008, below.

[11] *Ibid.*

[12] H. Genn, "Who Claims Compensation: Factors Associated with Claiming and Obtaining Damages" in Harris *et al.* (1984), esp. pp. 70–76; and Genn (1999).

[13] The sufferer may recognise a problem but see no realistic opportunity of solving it, see Genn (1984), esp. pp. 73–76. See also the Marre Committee (1988), para. 7.15 & Genn (1999).

considerable difficulty for any advice agency in providing assistance. The role of the lawyer or adviser in taking the initiative in identifying problems with which help can be provided becomes important and it is in this type of work that the law centres have been particularly successful. The identification of the problem then is made by the adviser rather than the sufferer and the relationship between the *need* for legal services and the *demands* actually made by clients is exposed.[14]

If the provision of legal services were to be limited to those matters in which the sufferer realises there is a problem for which a lawyer may be of assistance, the provision would be relatively limited. However, law centres and the Citizens Advice Bureaux have long existed to meet a greater need. And it is for this reason that a part of the newly focussed legal aid provision, the Community Legal Service, has information provision and signposting by agencies as essential elements of its provision.

B. WHEN IS A PROBLEM "LEGAL"?

The attribution of a particular "legal" character to certain problems   **9–003**
underlies the research which has been done into "unmet legal need", for it is by no means every problem which requires a lawyer's assistance in its resolution. Equally, not every problem with which a lawyer is asked to deal is a legal one. Traditionally, lawyers have been proud of their reputation as advisers on general financial and property matters.[15] In any event, it would be pointless to define as legal problems only those which are *actually* dealt with by lawyers, for that would exclude all those problems which never reach them, but which should.

Would it be realistic to define legal problems as those with which private practitioners normally deal? There are two factors to this definition: the selection of appropriate problems by potential clients and the lawyer's acceptance of them as appropriate for him or her to handle. The consequence is a range of problems with which solicitors normally deal, and a possible definition of legal problems. However, this is a very restrictive definition. If a client does not identify the landlord's failure to repair a rented house as a legal problem or if a solicitor viewed it as outside her or his field, it would not be a legal problem. This cannot be right.[16]

There is often, therefore, a narrow perception of the circumstances in

---

[14] For an early analysis of this particular problem, see Adamsdown Community Trust, *Community Need and Law Centre Practice* (1978), pp. 36–37.

[15] Their traditional role is affected by regulation in certain areas, introduced for the benefit of clients, *e.g.*, with regard to the giving of financial advice, the changes introduced by the Financial Services Act 1986, and by the increasing difficulty of being able to justify non-fee-paying activity, such as counselling.

[16] Acceptance of this approach would, by definition, mean that there was no unmet legal need.

which it is appropriate to approach a solicitor.[17] There have been criticisms of the narrow nature of the work of most solicitors and it is true that the legal advice and assistance scheme (now legal help) was introduced in 1973 to extend the range of work of solicitors. Building on this approach, the Community Legal Service is likely to herald further development in certain areas of work as the contracting approach encourages firms to specialise and to undertake the work.[18] Business needs will always drive solicitors to expand their areas of work. This is true for the contracting approach of the CLS and is true for the work of, *e.g.* firms specialising in corporate/ commercial work who need to respond to the increasing demands of their clients.

Another approach is objectively to define a problem as legal against categories of types of problem. This emphasises the problems with which a solicitor *could* deal. It was this approach which was adopted by Abel-Smith, Zander and Brooke in their research into unmet legal need, published as *Legal Problems and the Citizen* in 1973. They chose 17 specific and common situations as the basis of a questionnaire.[19]

An objective definition is open to criticism on the grounds of particular exclusions from, or inclusions in, the categories and the extent of the categories themselves. A more fundamental objection is that it may be exclusive rather than *inclusive*, in the sense that our thinking may be confined to those matters which fall within accepted categories rather than accepting that all situations to which the law pertains can give rise to legal problems despite the fact that there is no immediately available legal framework for their solution. In particular, the categories are set by legal specialists rather than the potential clients and so represent a normative ascription of what is a legal problem from the supply side. What the approach fails to achieve is an assessment of what are legal problems from the point of view of a potential client, from the demand side, which has been identified as felt and expressed need. Indeed it is suggested that this is the failing of most approaches to legal need.[20]

---

[17] See, *e.g.* Genn (1999) below; R. Craig, M. Rigg, R. Briscoe and P. Smith, *Client's Experiences of Using a Solicitor for Personal Matters* (Law Society Research Study No. 40, 2001); J. Jenkins and V. Lewis, *Client Perceptions: Existing and Potential Clients; Experiences and Perceptions of Using a Solicitor for Personal Matters* (1995), Chap. 2; J. Jenkins, E. Skordaki and C.F. Willis, *Public Use and Perception of Solicitors* (1989), Chap. 5; Abel-Smith, Zander and Brooke (1973), pp. 156–160; Research Surveys of Great Britain, *Report on Awareness, Usage and Attitudes towards the Professional Services and Advice Provided by Solicitors* (1986); G. Chambers and S. Harwood, *Solicitors in England and Wales: Practice, Organisation and Perceptions — First Report: The Work of Solicitors in Private Practice* (1990); and G. Chambers & S. Harwood, *Solicitors in England and Wales: Practice, Organisation and Perceptions — Second Report: The Private Practice Firm* (1991).

[18] See below, paras 10-001–10-008.

[19] The situations were: taking a lease, repairs undone, attempted eviction of the client (a tenant), attempted eviction by the client (a landlord), buying a house, defective goods, instalment arrears, unpaid debt owed, taken to court for debt, death in the family, making a will, accidents, social security benefits, employment problems, matrimonial problems, court proceedings, and juvenile court proceedings: Abel-Smith, Zander and Brooke (1973), Chap. 8.

[20] This is the taxonomy developed by J.S. Bradshaw in *Problems and Progress in Medical Care* (1972) and discussed in P. Robertshaw, *Rethinking Legal Need: The Case of Criminal Justice* (1991). Felt need is limited because it is what the client may want without any idea of what may be available, whereas expressed need is " 'felt' need translated into action, or economic demand."

A definition of a legal problem as "an unresolved difficulty to which the **9–004** law is relevant" may appear to be too vague and begging too many questions.[21] However, it may form the basis of a new approach to problems to which lawyers and advisers will not seek to establish the legal nature of the problem and then find the relevant law, but will rather seek to establish the nature of the problems and then contemplate whether any part of the law might be relevant.[22] The adoption of such an approach demands an open mind on the part of the lawyers to listen to and offer an acceptable approach to the problem identified by the potential client.

The advantages of this approach are: first, there is less of a risk of inappropriately distinguishing legal and, say, social problems.[23] It follows that social welfare law issues become as much a matter for private practitioners as for law centres and advice agencies. Secondly, there is an encouragement to clients to make use of legal services, because they can identify lawyers as one of the "correct" agencies to approach. This, then, can assist in overcoming the narrow perception of what lawyers can do. The need for business development, in fact, produces a powerful incentive for lawyers to develop new areas of work. Thirdly, a new remedy or novel application of the law may result from the approach, because of the need for imagination on the part of the lawyer, thus again potentially creating greater business.

In Genn's major study,[24] she undertook an initial screening survey (with a sample size of 4,125 adults) which estimated the incidence of justiciable problems. She took the same approach to what is a legal problem as indicated here and the types of problems were selected after focus group meetings with advice agencies, members of the public and solicitors. This produced the following list: "employment problems; problems relating to owning residential property; problems with renting out rooms or property; problems to do with living in rented accommodation; problems with faulty goods and services; problems to do with money; problems to do with relationships and other family matters; problems connected with having children aged less than 18; injuries and health problems arising from accidents or poor working conditions requiring medical treatment; problems with discrimination in relation to sex/race/disability; problems with unfair treatment by the police; problems with immigration or nationality issues; problems with receiving negligent/wrong medical or dental treatment."[25] Some of the respondents, who had had a non-trivial justiciable problem, were followed up by the main survey (face-to-face interviews with 1,134 adults). Before engaging in the interviews, the problem types were reviewed as a result of the evidence from the screening survey, and this produced the following list[25a]:

---

[21] See Royal Commission on Legal Services, *Report, Vol. 1* (1978), para. 2.2 and the Marre Committee (1988), para. 7.3.

[22] Categorisation is essential for initial teaching, but is not determinative of what the law can do.

[23] For an early criticism of this dichotomy, see P. Morris, R. Cooper & A. Byles, "Public Attitudes to Problem Definition and Problem Solving: A Pilot Study" (1973–74) 3 Brit. J. Social Work 301.

[24] Genn (1999).

[25] *ibid.*, pp. 21–22.

[25a] *ibid.*, p. 56.

Problems with neighbours	[including those owning and those renting property].
Divorce and separation	[including divorce proceedings, problems with ex-partners, problems about residence and contact, problems about payment or maintenance, violent or abusive relationships with a partner, or ex-partner].
Employment problems	
Consumer problems	[including goods and services].
Accidental injury and work-related ill health	
Problems over money	[including money owed, insurance companies rejecting claims, incorrect bills, unfair tax demands, incorrect advice about insurance, pensions, etc., mismanagement of pension fund, unfair refusal of credit, harassment from creditors].
Freehold problems	[alterations to property, planning permission, buying or selling property, communal repairs or maintenance, repossession of the home, squatters].
Problems with landlords	[poor/unsafe living conditions, getting deposit back, getting landlord to do repairs, agreeing terms of lease, harassment by landlord, eviction or threats of eviction].
Tribunal matters	[DSS benefits and education problems].

We have indicated what we consider to be the best working definition of a legal problem, but the discussion will be without practical significance unless an effective means of ensuring that those who have legal problems, however defined, secure legal assistance. It is this problem that we go on to address and which the Government anticipates will be met by the introduction of the Community Legal Service.

C. THE COMMUNITY LEGAL SERVICE AND THE MEETING OF NEED

9–005   One reason for the introduction of the Community Legal Service is to endeavour to ensure that there is a meeting of legal need. One of the functions of the Regional Legal Services Committees is to identify need and to ensure that that need is met. The RLSC must undertake a needs assessment and that feeds into the contracts that will be let by the Legal Services Commission for government funded legal work. One way of achieving these objectives is through Community Legal Service Partnerships.[26] These "bring together organisations offering legal advice and

---

[26] There were CLSPs covering 85% of the population of England and Wales by March 31, 2001: Legal Services Commission, *Annual Report 2000/01* (HC Paper 97, 2001), para. 2.43.

services — such as solicitors in private practice, Citizens' Advice Bureaux, law centres, and local authority in-house services among others. They include representatives of the Commission, local authorities, and other funders, providers and users of legal and advice services. Partners act together to co-ordinate and improve access to, and delivery of, legal services. ... Each CLSP works to agree and implement a strategy for the funding and development of legal services able to meet the needs of the community."[27]

D. LEGAL PROBLEMS AND THE USE OF LAWYERS

The best people to assist with legal problems are not always lawyers. So, **9–006** for example, trading standards departments in local authorities have always been highly skilled in handling consumer problems and Citizens Advice Bureaux have been and continue to be a major source of advice on a wide range of problems.[28] The reasons for this view include the need for speed, flexibility and informality, and concerns about the experience and knowledge base of lawyers in certain areas of work, particularly social welfare law. One aim of the CLS is to make further inroads into this issue and there are likely to be more niche firms offering a service that includes social welfare law advice and help.

1. WHO USES SOLICITORS?

A person may use a solicitor for a variety of purposes. Large corporations **9–007** have the ability either to employ their own lawyers and/or to set criteria for the engagement of independent firms of lawyers to deliver the services that they require. In these cases, the client can be the powerful player in the lawyer/client relationship. However, where it is individuals or small or medium sized enterprises who are the clients, then the position may be and often is very different. Thus, individuals may use solicitors for a relatively narrow range of work and, as we shall see, may be wary of using them for a variety of reasons including ignorance of their value and concerns over cost and accessibility.

The 1994 survey of client perceptions of solicitors services[29] largely confirmed the results of earlier surveys[30] which have shown the narrowness of the matters on which solicitors are consulted by individuals. Solicitors are

---

[27] Legal Services Commission, *Annual Report 2000/01* (HC Paper 97, 2001), paras. 2.42 and 2.45.

[28] See below, para. 10-008. In Genn's study, 31% of those surveyed and who had received advice stated that their first source of advice was a CAB: Genn (1999), Figure 3.2.

[29] J. Jenkins and V. Lewis, *Client Perceptions — Existing and Potential Clients: Experience and Perceptions of Using a Solicitor for Personal Matters* (1995).

[30] M. Zander, (1969) 66 L.S. Gaz. 174; Morris, Cooper and Byles, (1973–74); Adamsdown Community Trust, (1978); R.C.L.S., Vol. 2, s. 8, pp. 173–198; Research Surveys of Great Britain (1986); Jenkins, Skordaki and Willis (1989), Chap. 5.

likely to be used for buying and selling a home (40 per cent), making a will (13 per cent), divorce and matrimonial problems (9 per cent), dealing with someone's estate (8 per cent), compensation for injury (6 per cent), and motoring (4 per cent) and other offences (3 per cent).[31] Spontaneous answers to questions indicated that the public are most of solicitors' services in relation to conveyancing and property matters (70 per cent), wills, trusts and settlements (48 per cent), divorce (41 per cent), and law and order and criminal convictions (33 per cent).[32]

The 2000 survey of client's experience of using a solicitor for personal matters largely confirms this picture.[33] Sixteen per cent of adults had consulted a solicitor within the previous 12 months. The most common reason for consulting a solicitor was conveyancing or other issues related to buying and selling a home (28 per cent), with divorce, matrimonial and child care matters, will-making, compensation for personal injury or medical accident, and probate being the next most common.[34] This survey also reveals that the clients who used a solicitor "were more likely to be male, aged 25–54 and in social grades ABC1 (professional, managerial and non-manual workers), compared with the general population. Conveyancing clients tended to be aged 25–44, while clients seeking help with wills and probate were typically at the older end of the age range."[35] This is not surprising given the ages at which people are likely to be seeking their own accommodation and at which they consider their own mortality or become the potential beneficiaries of a deceased relative. Clients from social grade E (dependent on state benefits) were a relatively large proportion of those seeking advice in relation to divorce.[36] "Injury compensation clients were typically in the youngest age groups and were the only group skewed towards social grade C2 (skilled manual workers)."[37] The provision of legal advice on such matters by trade unions may be part of the explanation for this fact.[38] Indeed, some of the explanations may well lie in the awareness of legal advice of certain groups of the community.

In Genn's study, about 40 per cent of those in the screening survey had experience of "one or more justiciable problem during the previous five years."[39] "The type of problems most frequently experienced were those relating to faulty goods and services (11 per cent); money problems (9 per cent); injuries/health problems resulting from accidents or poor working conditions (8 per cent); owning residential property (8 per cent); living in rented accommodation (7 per cent); employment problems (6 per cent); relationships and family matters (6 per cent). ... The problems least frequently experienced by the sample were those relating to: negligent medical or dental treatment (2 per cent); discrimination as a result of race, sex or disability (1 per cent); unfair treatment by the police (1 per cent);

---

[31] Jenkins and Lewis (1995), Table 4.
[32] *ibid.*, para. 2.14 and Table 5.
[33] R. Craig, M. Rigg, R. Briscoe & P. Smith, *Client's Experiences of Using a Solicitor for Personal Matters* (Law Society Research Study No. 40, 2001).
[34] *ibid.*, para. 1.2.
[35] *ibid.*
[36] *ibid.*
[37] *ibid.*
[38] See below, para. 10-011.
[39] Genn (1999), p. 23.

immigration or nationality issues (> 1 per cent)."[40] Having ruled out trivial problems, the following table reveals what action, if any, was taken.[41]

Problem	Talked/ wrote other side	Sought advice	Threatened legal action	Did nothing	Went to court	Ombudsman	Mediation Concliat'n	Took other action
Faulty goods and services	76%	30%	18%	13%	3%	2%		9%
Money	71%	35%	10%	10%	6%	3%	1%	10%
Emp'mt	52%	56%	14%	16%				
Owning residential property	66%	56%	14%	12%				
Living in rented	69%	37%	5%	11%	2%	0%	0%	
Relationship and family	49%	57%	18%	14%	25%		5%	11%
Children	68%	55%	21%	5%	26%	1%	8%	25%
Injuries/ health	28%	39%	14%	37%	8%	1%	1%	12%
Other	42%	27%	5%	35%	11%	2%	1%	12%

Where someone did not take action, the following reasons were given.[42]

Problem	Nothing could be done	Not very important	No dispute	Cost too much	Too much time	Damage relation- ship	Scared	Other side taking action	Other
Faulty goods and services	22%	20%	8%	6%	6%	4%	1%		33%
Money	15%	26%		7%	4%				33%
Employment	33%	13%	27%	25%	4%	2%	5%		14%
Owning residential property	22%	17%	15%	7%	5%	20%	2%	8%	5%
Living in rented	27%	38%	2%	16%		2%	2%		13%
Relationships and family	23%	3%	23%			17%	6%		28%
Injuries & health	10%	17%	56%	1%	3%	1%	1%	2%	11%
Other	31%	20%	10%	6%	6%	8%	6%		12%

---

[40] *ibid.*, pp.23–24.
[41] This table is compiled from information in *ibid.*, Chap. 2.
[42] This table is compiled from information in *ibid.*, Chap. 2.

Where someone did seek advice (usually after attempting to resolve the matter themselves), their first sources of such advice are shown by the following table.[43]

Source of advice	Percentage
Solicitor	24
CAB	31
Local council	9
Police	7
Trade Union/staff association	5
Employer	4
Insurance company	3
MP/Local councillor	3
Consumer advice/trading standards	2
Social worker/social services	2
Other advice agency	2
Trade association	2
Health and Safety office	1
Ombudsman	1
Welfare rights	1
Housing association	1
Barrister	0.4
Law centre	0.4
Other legal consultant	0.3
Court staff	0.2
Other adviser	10

2. IGNORANCE AND APATHY

9–008   Genn discovered in some of her early work that ignorance of the law did dissuade some potential claimants from seeking legal advice in relation to personal injuries, and legal advice was often only sought after other sources of advice, which often was ill-informed, had been accessed.[44] The Marre Committee was subsequently convinced that ignorance was a major cause of people not seeking legal advice even when it was appropriate.[45] Further, some people take the view that "it's not worth pursuing it" or "let's just forget about it" or "it's just one of those things." The Oxford Study shows

---

[43] *ibid.*, Figure 3.2.
[44] H. Genn, "Who Claims Compensation: Factors Associated with Claiming and Obtaining Damages" in D. Harris *et al, Compensation and Support for Illness and Injury* (1984), esp. pp. 75–76, 65–67.
[45] The Committee on the Future of the Legal profession, *A Time for Change* (1988), Chair: Lady Marre [hereafter, the Marre Committee], paras. 7.17–7.39.

that this type of apathy is a major reason in explaining why people do not seek legal advice.[46] This has been recently confirmed by subsequent work undertaken by Professor Genn.[47] The information provided above from her study reveals that considerable numbers of people do nothing about a non-trivial justiciable problem. Most initially endeavour to deal with it themselves. Many who decide to do so, do eventually obtain advice, but "about [only] five per cent of all those interviewed said that they had unsuccessfully tried to contact one of the advice organisations. ... "[48] "There was also evidence that a substantial minority of respondents (about one in five) ... had considered seeking advice, but in the event failed to take any steps to do so. The most common sources of advice *considered* but not contacted ... were solicitors (about 6 per cent) and CABx (about 5 per cent). The most common reasons for not making contact ... was a belief that nothing could be done about the problem (21%). Other common reasons ... were that it would involve too much trouble, or that it would be too expensive."[49] These, and other factors, will be identified below.

Whilst ignorance may sometimes be a problem,[50] Genn's study raises serious doubts since she discovered that " ... while some people were unsure about where to go for advice, most respondents were aware of the existence of the Citizens Advice Bureaux. Indeed, just over half of all respondents to the main survey (57%) said that they had actually obtained advice from a CAB at some time in the past." So the picture is not a clear cut one, as Genn points out, "despite this general knowledge about the existence of CABx and other local advice centres, if they existed, it was also clear that the public often experienced problems in finding out about opening times, managing to get through on the telephone, and being force to take time off work in order to visit a CAB because they were only open during working hours. All of these matters created barriers to advice-seeking, even among those who were relatively knowledgeable about sources of advice and might have used advisers in the past."[51]

Apathy or something akin to it was a particular issue identified in Genn's study. Something like one in twenty took no action at all. This group was termed by her, the "Lumpers". Certain characteristics were identified. First, they "were most likely to have experienced problems relating to money, accidental injury or work-related ill health, employment, clinical negligence, or unfair action by the police. They were significantly less likely to have obtained outside advice about any problem in the past. ... Over half of those who failed to take action to resolve their problem had an annual income of less than £10,000 (52 per cent compared with 35 per cent of self-helpers and 31 per cent of those taking action with advice), and were more likely to be living in rented accommodation than those who took action. Those who took no action were more likely to have no educational qualifications and much less likely to be educated to degree level than those who took action (14 per cent of those taking no action had degree level

---

[46] Genn (1984).
[47] *Paths to Justice* (1999).
[48] *ibid.*, p. 76.
[49] *ibid.*, p. 75.
[50] Genn's research also revealed "a depth of ignorance about the legal system and a widespread inability to distinguish between criminal and civil courts:" *ibid.*, p. 247.
[51] *ibid.*, p. 76.

qualifications as compared with about one third of those who took action)."[52] "The main reasons given by respondents for failing to take any action to resolve their problem were that the problem was over and done with (about one in four cases), or that there was nothing that could be done about the problem (about one in five cases). Those who said that there was nothing that could be done about the problem were, of course, making this judgement without the benefit of any advice."[53] It is particularly interesting to note that the lumpers had thought about their strategy. Their reasons "convey, on the whole, a rather negative and powerless quality."[54]

The Marre Committee identified four potential solutions.[55] First, the teaching of legal and rights awareness in schools.[56] Secondly, the use of public relations, that is encouraging good public relations exercises about legal advice. Thirdly, media advertising by solicitors.[57] Finally, the provision of information from the professional bodies directed to specific areas rather than generalised campaigns. What Genn identifies is that no simple strategy is possible, but it seems likely that the direction of the CLS could have some success. This is because the direction that the government is taking in driving the CLS partly as a response to social exclusion is predicated on her work.[58]

3. THE PUBLIC IMAGE

9–009   The image of an advice-giving agency is crucial because it is at the stage of the identification of an appropriate agency that most people are obstructed on the way to solving their problem.[59] For a repeat player, their impression of the first contact with a solicitor will be telling. Where the client is a first time player, identifying an agency with a strong image will assist. In the 2000 survey of client's experiences of using a solicitor for personal matters, it was reported that most clients used smaller firms of solicitors. Forty per cent used firms with 2–4 partners and approximately 33 per cent used firms with 5–10 partners, whereas only 10 per cent used a large firm (which is hardly surprising since many large firms increasingly offer little to private clients and may well be intimidating to access off the street) and 5 per cent used a sole practitioner.[60] Further, it was reported that the most important reason for choosing a law firm was a recommendation from someone else, followed

---

[52] *ibid.*, p. 69.
[53] *ibid.*, pp. 69–70. Other reasons were: "expressions of powerlessness, fear of becoming involved in acrimony, concern about the cost of taking formal action [and] there was some evidence that negative experiences of the legal system of negative beliefs about legal processes gleaned from media stories contributed to decisions to take no steps . . . :" *ibid.*, p. 71.
[54] *ibid.*, p.70.
[55] The Marre Committee (1988), paras. 7.20–7.39.
[56] See also R. Smith (ed.), *Shaping the Future* (1995), Part III and Genn (1999) p. 255.
[57] See above, paras 3-021–3-022.
[58] See below, para. 10-001.
[59] The Marre Committee (1988), paras. 7.48–7.93.
[60] R. Craig, M. Rigg, R. Briscoe and P. Smith, *Client's Experiences of Using a Solicitor for Personal Masters* (Law Society Research Study No. 40, 2001), para. 1.2.

by previous experience of the firm, the good reputation of the firm and convenient offices.[61]

The 2000 Client's Experiences survey reported that "more than half of all those seeking legal advice in the last 12 months felt that their law firm had been very good overall, and well over three-quarters felt that it had been good or very good. At the other end of the scale, one in ten rated the firm as poor or very poor, and a similar proportion rated it fair. Clients involved in wills or probate cases were the most likely to give positive ratings, whereas for conveyancing and particularly divorce or injury cases, views were slightly less favourable. They key reasons given for a positive rating were that the people handling their case had been very experienced and professional, that they did everything the client wanted, were efficient and provided a good service. Poor ratings were most often put down to generally poor service, with further mentions of inefficiency, things taking longer than necessary, not showing an interest in the client and not keeping the client informed. ... 83 per cent of clients rated their solicitor[62] good or very good overall, the majority saying that he/she was very good (60 per cent). Only 7 per cent of clients rated their solicitor poor; divorce clients were the most likely to do this."[63] This presents a similar picture to that from the 1994 Client Perceptions survey which discovered that "the public continue to hold an image of solicitors that is generally good but not exceptional. Of the six professions evaluated, solicitors fall approximately in the middle range while NHS doctors were regarded most highly on all criteria. Estate agents, on the other hand, were the profession held in the least regard. Over a third of respondents held solicitors to be well respected (34 per cent) with doctors being the only profession to have more people attribute them with this characteristic (74 per cent). Bank managers and dentists were equally well respected with associations of 27 per cent and 26 per cent respectively. Only 4 per cent of respondents considered estate agents to be well respected."[64]

The Marre Committee indicated that there are two particular problems with the image of lawyers. First, there is a fear of lawyers. They are unapproachable because of the inaccessibility of their premises and their unwelcoming nature, their work methods do not tie in with client needs and a poor response to the needs of linguistic minorities. The Committee recommended greater use of shop premises, innovative work practices, the need for interpreters and the need for professional bodies to support and encourage people from cultural and ethnic minorities to enter the legal profession.[65] Secondly, there is dissatisfaction with lawyers.[66] It seems fairly clear that the Law Society's initiatives in client care are having some impact[67] and other work may be making a difference.[68] Traditionally Law

---

[61] *ibid.*

[62] As opposed to the firm.

[63] R. Craig, M. Rigg, R. Briscoe and P. Smith, *Client's Experiences of Using a Solicitor for Personal Matters* (Law Society Research Study No. 40, 2001), paras. 1.4 and 1.7.

[64] J. Jenkins and V. Lewis, *Client Perceptions — Existing and Potential Clients: Experience and Perceptions of Using a Solicitor for Personal Matters* (1995), para. 3.2.

[65] The Marre Committee (1988), paras 7.40–7.47. As to the recruitment of lawyers from ethnic minorities, see above, para. 3-051.

[66] *ibid.*, paras. 7.48–7.93.

[67] See above, para. 3-034, but note the comments of the Legal Services Ombudsman, at para. 3-035.

[68] See above, Chap. 3

Centres have not suffered from the problems associated with solicitors firms, but they have a different attitude and agenda.

4. COST AND ACCESSIBILITY

9–010   Genn in her study identified cost as a noticeable barriers to accessing legal advice. The cost of legal advice will continue to be a problem, because professional services are expensive. However, advice is available through the Community Legal Service which will often be free for those eligible to receive it, the CLS will ensure a range of advice and representation services and there continues to be a commitment to consider a range of means of paying for legal services (particularly representation through the so-called 'no win, no fee' system)[69] and a commitment to driving the costs of the various aspects of the legal system down wherever possible. Of course, perception of cost as well as actual cost may be a problem. Genn's research revealed that, in the main survey, "about three out of four respondents disagreed or strongly disagreed with the suggestion that lawyers' charges were reasonable for the work that they do (72 per cent)."[70] When advice had been received, there was some increase in the feeling that the charges were reasonable.[71] It is also important to note that Genn's research revealed a view that "the legal system works better for the rich than the poor."[72] Further, there was some evidence that there was a perception that legal aid was gradually being withdrawn,[73] which would raise concerns about costs.

Changes to legal aid provision and the introduction of the Community Legal Service and the Criminal Defence Service have certainly lead to a new approach to endeavouring to ensure that those in need of legal advice are aware of sources of that advice. So the commitment to Information Points and the obligation for anyone involved in the CLS to "signpost" people to a more appropriate service should, increasingly, overcome problems of ignorance of the scheme and the availability of the advice. What will be crucial is the range of Information Points that appear over the next few years.[74] Genn certainly identified that how someone identified an adviser is an important issue to address. This can be seen in a number of different ways. Usually, the idea of contacting an adviser came from the individual themselves "or that it seemed obvious (41 per cent); that it had been suggested by a friend/relative/work colleague (21 per cent; or because the respondent had had experience of a similar situation (11 per cent Respondents' accounts of how they found their adviser varied depending on who the adviser was. Where CABx were concerned, respondents mostly

---

[69] This is the contingency fee system, see below, para. 11-007.
[70] Genn (1999), p. 236.
[71] "About 18% agreed or strongly agreed that lawyers' charges were reasonable for the work that they do as compared with only eleven percent of those who had obtained non-legal advice about their problem and 14% of those who had handled their problem without advice:" *ibid.*, p. 238.
[72] "Almost three-quarters of respondents agreed or strongly agreed with [that] proposition:" *ibid.*, p. 234.
[73] *ibid.*, p. 235.
[74] See below, para. 10-007.

seemed to know where they were located, although there was difficulty in establishing opening times and getting appointments. In the case of solicitors, respondents asked among friends and work colleagues, walked into the nearest office to where they lived or worked, or used the Yellow pages."[75] "Another useful pathway to advice was by using friends and relatives whose job was the provision of advice."[76] Signposting from the first source of advice will also be a vital part of the CLS, as Genn's research demonstrates. "Those who sought advice first from a CAB were referred on to a variety of second advisers. In about half the cases where CABx made a referral this was to a solicitor (49 per cent). In a little under one in five cases, referral by the CAB was to the local authority (17 per cent) and in 10 per cent of referrals to a consumer advice centre. ... First advisers other than the CAB or solicitors were also quite likely to refer respondents on to other organisations."[77]

As regards the geographical aspect of accessibility, Genn discovered that "travelling did not appear to be a problem. About one quarter [of those seeking advice] said that they did not have to travel any distance to see their first adviser. Among those who did have to travel, most had a journey of *less* than five miles, although a small minority travelled considerable distances (about two percent ... had to travel more than 50 miles). This suggests that ... geographical accessibility of advisers was not a problem.[78]

5. BARRIERS

Of the above problems that may be faced by clients, it would seem that **9–011** the most obvious differential obstruction (so dependent upon the financial wherewithal of the potential client) is cost. Some studies show that those in the higher socio-economic groups use lawyers more often than those in the lower groups.[79] Poverty appears to be a primary cause for failure to seek legal advice. There are also problems of lack of influence, energy and awareness.[80] On the other hand, the Oxford Study revealed that people from the higher socio-economic groups are *less* likely to make a claim for damages consequent upon personal injury being suffered.[81] The most important factor in determining whether an accident victim obtained damages was found to be access to advice, both pre-legal and legal, which may be offered without it even being sought. The most frequent suppliers of pre-legal advice were trade unions,[82] medical personnel, employers, the police, the potential defendant, the AA/RAC,[83] own insurance company, workmates and fellow patients, friends and relatives.[84] All the factors so far

---

[75] Genn (1999), p. 91.
[76] *ibid.*, p. 93.
[77] *ibid.*, p. 96.
[78] Genn (1999), p. 90.
[79] See above, para. 9-007.
[80] J. Carlin and J. Howard, "Legal Representation and Class Justice" (1965) 12 *U.C.L.A. Law Review* 381.
[81] Genn (1984), esp. pp. 51–56, Table 2.6.
[82] See below, para. 10-011.
[83] See below, para. 10-012.
[84] Genn (1984), pp. 65–67, 76 & Table 2.11. See also Jenkins, Skordaki & Willis (1989), p. 19.

identified must be relevant. Their impact will, however, vary. So *e.g.*, the poorer a person may be, the less likely they will be to access legal advice, unless they are aware of the free or cheap schemes. If someone is in an active trade union and suffers a work or non-work accident, they are quite likely to be encouraged to take advantage of the trade union scheme to seek legal advice and contemplate litigation for damages.

The 1994 Client Perception survey revealed that there was little difference between men and women in the frequency of their use of solicitors, but that the elderly used solicitors more rarely than others.[85] Further, it revealed that "ethnic minority respondents had a lower awareness of the services provided by solicitors than the total population."[86] The 2000 Client Perceptions survey revealed similarly that solicitors were not regularly accessed by the elderly or, indeed the very young, but clients were more likely to be male.[87]

Lawyers have increasingly been seeking clients for business reasons.[88] It is necessary for all fee earners to hit financial targets which are achieved by having clients. Thus, there is an imperative to seek new business. One way of seeking new business is to develop new areas of expertise. The increasing specialisation of lawyers and the law is one way in which this has been achieved.[89] The developments in law have been so huge that it has been necessary for lawyers to specialise and increasingly clients wish to have expert help on such specialised problems. Not only has this occurred as lawyers respond as business persons to the demands of large companies, but business and social awareness interests also have allowed certain lawyers to expand their work in social welfare fields. One noticeable area has been in the expansion of the numbers of lawyers involved in mental health law and in the specialisation that that areas has undergone to the benefit of clients. Prior to the extension, in December 1982, of legal advice and representation to work before Mental Health Review Tribunals (MHRT) the number of lawyers working in the field was very small. However, since that extension and an increasing interest in the field, the expansion has been particularly noticeable. Now the areas of work are not limited to detained patients seeking discharge from hospital by a MHRT but, as is *e.g.*, demonstrated by increasing numbers of cases, extend to how people are detained in hospital, how people not detained are received into hospital, what community care provision there is, how people are to be identified as making decisions for themselves, etc. Indeed, there are now firms of solicitors that specialise almost exclusively in this type of work.

E. UNMET LEGAL NEED

9–012   If any problem with a legal element or aspect to it is a legal problem requiring legal assistance, this is a very wide approach. However, it seems to

---

[85] J. Jenkins and V. Lewis, *Client Perceptions — Existing and Potential Clients: Experience and Perceptions of Using a Solicitor for Personal Matters* (1995), Table 2.

[86] *ibid.*, para. 7.5.

[87] See above, para. 9-007.

[88] This varies from the frowned upon ambulance-chaser to the solicitor advertising his or her services as widely and accessibly as possible.

[89] See above, Chap. 3.

be the only possible starting point in endeavouring to determine what legal need there is and how to respond to it. For some, especially large companies and wealthy individuals, it is relatively easy to identify legal need and to ensure that it is satisfied. This is because the problems of ignorance and apathy and the barriers of cost and accessibility are likely to be minimal problems, if problems at all. However, when attention is turned upon either an individual, who is not wealthy, or a small or medium sized enterprise, then these problems become fully worthy of recognition and resolution, especially the poorer and less aware the potential clients may be.

Abel-Smith, Zander and Brooke undertook a pioneering study.[90] Their solution to how to identify legal need was to assess, in respect of each category of problems identified,[91] what would constitute " ... a risk of substantial loss or disadvantage which would be important for the individual concerned."[92] This was a valid approach for research, but identifying the proposition has not proved particularly valuable to subsequent researchers.[93] However, Robertshaw drew attention to the need to contemplate legal need from the perspective of the potential client, who may find it difficult to identify anything other than a feelings that some sort of assistance is required, rather than merely to see it from the perspective of the suppliers of advice who may have a vested interest in which is identified as work that lawyers do but are not providing it.[94]

Other background work to the present position was undertaken by the Royal Commission on Legal Services which appeared to accept that legal need can be identified by reference to the existence of a legal problem on which an individual wishes to be advised, since it recommended that solicitors should offer free initial half-hour interviews.[95] In the context of the old legal aid system, individual need was tested by a combination of the means, merits and reasonableness tests, which relied upon factors such as whether a solicitor would advise a private client to pursue the claim, whether there is sufficient benefit in pursuing the matter and whether the defendant could satisfy a claim. However, this approach can be stultifying because it fails to recognise the need to go outside the normal boxes and challenge existing decisions and approaches and be prepared to work in areas not traditionally thought to be relevant to lawyers. Indeed, the Government commented in the 1995 Consultation Paper on Legal Aid that the "existing scheme tends to channel clients and money to solicitors. It encourages a system of lawyer led services, and delivers what lawyers are best able to supply."[96]

---

[90] R. Abel-Smith, M. Zander & R. Brooke, *Legal Problems and the Citizen* (1973).
[91] *i.e.* taking a lease, repairs undone, attempted eviction of the client (a tenant), attempted eviction by the client (a landlord), buying a house, defective goods, instalment arrears, unpaid debt owed, taken to court for debt, death in the family, making a will, accidents, social security benefits, employment problems, matrimonial problems, court proceedings, and juvenile court proceedings: *ibid.*, Chap. 8.
[92] *ibid.*, p. 12.
[93] *ibid.*, p. 280 and see, *e.g.* The Marre Committee (1988), para. 7.10.
[94] P. Robertshaw, *Rethinking Legal Need: The Case of Criminal Justice* (1991).
[95] R.C.L.S., Vol. I, pp. 134–135.
[96] *Legal Aid — Targeting Need* (1995), para. 3.8.

F. MEETING UNMET NEED

9–013   Legal aid was the traditional means whereby the problem of unmet need would be met. The Labour Government has taken the view that unmet need is a problem of social exclusion and so has put the requirement to meet the need high on its list of priorities. "Social exclusion is what happens when people or areas suffer from a combination of linked problems such as lack of access to services, unemployment, poor skills, low incomes, poor housing, crime, poor health and family breakdowns.[97] The Government takes the view that "lack of access to reliable legal advice can be a contributing factor in creating and maintaining social exclusion. Poor access to advice has meant that many people have suffered because they have been unable to enforce their legal rights effectively, or have even been unaware of their rights and responsibilities in the first place. They are unable to get justice."[98] Thus, the Government is committed to the CLS as a means of addressing social exclusion. It intends to ensure that needs are identified not only through the work of Community Legal Service Partnerships,[99] but also by building upon Professor Genn's work[1] and thus commissioning a "long-term research project to measure and characterise levels of legal need in England and Wales in the social welfare and family categories of law,"[2] which are the highest priorities for addressing social exclusion. The Government has identified two other areas for further action through the CLS. One is the "formation of a working group to help develop measurements to be used to value the contribution of the CLS." The other is for the Lord Chancellor's Department "and other government departments to work to ensure that CLS Partnerships form strong links with Local Strategic Partnerships and other initiatives such as Job Centre Plus[3] and Connexions,[4] so that legal and advice services are involved in local plans."[5] In so doing, the Government intends to meet the LCD target of "increasing the number of people who receive suitable assistance in priority areas of law, involving fundamental rights or social exclusion, by 5 per cent by 2004.[6] Whether the need will be met depends upon the success of the Community

---

[97] Lord Chancellor's Department, *Social Exclusion* (2001), *www.lcd.gov.uk.* using the Social Exclusion Unit's definition from July 2000.

[98] *Ibid.*

[99] See below, para. 10-023.

[1] *Paths to Justice* (1999).

[2] *Social Exclusion* (2001). The first elements commences in 2002 and is being undertaken by the Legal Services Research Centre, see *www.lsrc.org.uk.*

[3] "Jobcentre Plus is a modern service for people of working age who are looking for work or claiming benefits. It will give people the help and support they need to find work and become independent. Jobcentre Plus will provide a high quality service to employers, helping them find the right people to fill their jobs, quickly and successfully. Jobcentre Plus brings together the best of the Employment Service, which runs Jobcentres, and those parts of the Benefits Agency for people of working age:"*www.jobcentreplus.gov.uk*

[4] "Connexions offers a range of guidance and support for 13 to 19 year olds, to help make the transition to adult life a smooth one:" *www.connexions.gov.uk.*

[5] *Social Exclusion* (2001).

[6] *ibid.*

Legal Service, especially in its support of Law Centres,[7] which is considered in Chapter 9.

What Genn proposes as means to resolve some of the problems that she identifies is to be set within the results of the study revealing that there are many non-trivial justiciable problems which most people endeavour to resolve for themselves by contacting the other side. Such people are motivated to see a resolution of their problem.[8] Levels of success in resolving problems by self-help vary with the type of problem. So *e.g.*, "self-helpers who took on the other side in consumer matters were comparatively successful ... by comparison with, say, those who tried to deal with employment problems alone."[9] Indeed success depends not only on the nature of the problem, but also "the competence of the person dealing with the problem and the intransigence of the opposition."[10] Thus, it tends to be the more serious and intractable problems that are taken to advice, and these tend to be those "concerning divorce and separation, neighbours, ownership of property, employment, and accidental injury."[11] Taking advice does not, of course, guarantee success. Where the advisor was a solicitor, about one third were resolved by agreement, one third by going to court or tribunal and one third were left unresolved. Where the advisor was an advice agency, about one third were resolved by agreement, about 10 per cent went to court or tribunal and just over half were unresolved.[12] Some types of problems are particularly hard to resolve (*e.g.*, employment, neighbour and landlord problems), but legal advice raises the prospect of resolution.[13] As Genn stresses, the matter is more complex than indicated here, but she makes a very important point which is that "the importance of problem-type as well as person-type in influencing the approach taken to the resolution of justiciable problems means that policy aimed at providing more effective access to successful dispute resolution must have regard not only to the *number* of justiciable problems confronted by the public, but to the *types* of problems experienced, and the ease or difficulty with which those problems can be resolved."[14] In looking further at what people want and need, Genn concludes that "there is little evidence of any 'rush' to law. On the contrary for most types of problem ... involvement in legal proceedings is a rare exception."[15] This does not indicate a low desire to resolve problems, but "there is a widespread perception that legal proceedings involve uncertainty, expense and potential long-term disturbance and that only the most serious matters could justify enduring those conditions."[16] One clear message from Genn is "the profound need for knowledge and advice about obligations, rights, remedies, and procedures for resolving justiciable problems. This is a need that exists to varying

---

[7] It is clear that the Government anticipates a growth in the number and work of Law Centres since most of the examples of successful addressing social exclusion in legal advice are provided by the work of Law Centres, *see Social Exclusion* (2001).

[8] "The primary concern for most people is simply to solve the problem:" Genn (1999), p. 211.

[9] *ibid.*, p. 251.

[10] *ibid.*

[11] *ibid.* Indeed some of the more serious problems are taken directly to solicitors.

[12] *ibid.*, p. 251.

[13] *ibid.*, p. 252.

[14] *ibid.*, p. 253.

[15] *ibid.*, p. 254.

[16] *ibid.*, p. 254.

degrees across all social, educational, and cultural boundaries and for all types of justiciable problem. It is a trite observation that citizenship requires knowledge. ... [17] Genn expects levels of individual competence to rise, but nevertheless "there are challenges here for the Community Legal Service, for the courts, for schools, and, indeed, for the judiciary in considering how a co-ordinated programme of public education could be mounted to provide a better understanding of matters that are fundamental to citizenship."[18] The other challenges are to ensure that the advice givers are high in quality and approachable to clients, that information about their availability and service is widely available and that the provision of advice is inter-linked. These are clearly intended to be addressed by the CLS. A further implication is the need to ensure that sufficient knowledge about legal need is obtained to ensure the planning and funding of appropriate forms of advice and where and how it should operate; this the government is committed to undertaking. Finally, Genn's conclusions have potential impact for procedural change, alternative dispute resolution, public funding of legal services, and the substantive law.[19] But she concludes with a consideration of "the access to justice dilemma" which is "whether the objective of legal policy should be to enhance access to legal forums for the resolution of disputes, or whether it should be aimed at preventing problems and disputes from arising, equipping as many members of the public as possible to solve problems when they do arise without recourse to legal action, and diverting cases away from the courts into private dispute resolution forums. It is no an answer to say that they should be twin objectives of policy, because they logically conflict."[20]

---

[17] ibid., p. 255.
[18] ibid., p. 258.
[19] ibid., pp. 258–263.
[20] ibid., p. 263.

CHAPTER 10

INFORMATION AND ADVICE SERVICES

By discussing in the preceding chapter the ways in which the public may **10–001** perceive a problem as a "legal" problem and the steps which the profession might take to assist in the identification of problems which require legal advice for their solution we have already indicated that we are concerned, in the main, with the provision of information and advice by lawyers. However, legal advice has not been provided solely by lawyers and the Community Legal Service is not established on the basis that lawyers will be the only source of legal advice and information. Further, the focus is on individuals accessing legal information and advice. When it is companies, particularly large companies, different factors apply. Here there are fewer problems associated with ignorance or concerns over cost. Many companies require law firms to bid for business and in so doing must convince the companies that they will provide quality and value for money. It is only when we turn back to individuals that we see the problems arising. Indeed, the Government elected in May 1997 sees access to legal services as one strand in its desire to tackle social exclusion.[1]

The Community Legal Service (CLS) is the Government's means of replacing the old legal aid scheme. One of its objectives is to provide a more far reaching service that draws together the relatively disparate elements of information advice and help, so that all people, "regardless of their personal circumstances, will be able to get the right help for their problems."[2] The CLS "aims to be

- accessible. Everyone is eligible for help from a member of the Community Legal Service. But different providers use different criteria to decide which clients they can help. They base this on issues such as the area of law concerned, the strength of your case and whether you can get financial aid. Each CLS provider will be able to tell you whether you are eligible for help form them.

- positive. Whatever type of legal advice you need, the CLS will help you to identify where you stand. We'll help you find the best course of positive and practical action to tackle problems quickly.

- transparent. There should be no hidden charges with a CLS provider. You should be told at the start if you have to pay anything and, if so,

---

[1] Lord Chancellor's Department, *Social Exclusion* (2001), www.lcd.gov.uk.
[2] Lord Chancellor's Department, Press Release 107/00, April 3, 2000 announcing the launching of the Community Legal Service.

how much. You should not incur costs without knowing about them.

- reliable. You will be sure of getting information or help from trained staff when you approach any member of the CLS. If the first person you see cannot help with your particular issue, they are required to help you find someone who can.

- impartial. CLS members are required to treat everybody fairly and responsibly. Practical information and help is available to everyone, whatever your background."[3]

These are to be achieved by the Service establishing different levels of service that are interlinked, so ensuring that providers are aware of the local environment in which they operate and are able to signpost clients to more appropriate providers of the service of which they stand in need. Each member of the CLS is to be able to satisfy a relevant quality mark for the level of service that they provide so as to provide minimum guarantees to their clients. Not all advice and information or legal assistance provision will be provided by organisations or people that are members of the CLS. However, where government funding is required by the organisation or the client, membership of the CLS is likely to prove to be essential (especially for the poorer client). It seems likely that the CLS will grow and may challenge the independence of certain advice providing organisations.

The best means of approaching the organisation of the CLS is to look to the quality marks since these vary according the service provided by the organisation in question. The quality marks available are:

"Self-help information

10–002 This level is for services that rely on the public accessing information themselves. The service will have the CLS Directory and provide leaflets, directories, websites or other computer-based systems, or other published materials where there is little or not interaction with the public. Examples would be information stands or websites in public areas, doctors' surgeries and libraries.

Assisted Information

10–003 This is for organisations that have a dedicated information service, although this does not have to be the sole purpose of the organisation. There should be staff that are able to help clients access information, to identify where a client needs further information or advice and help clients select an appropriate service where they will be able to receive this. The service will not provide advice.

---

[3] As stated on the CLS website: *www.justask.org.uk.*

General Help

The Quality Mark defines General Help as services that provide the   **10–004**
following

- Diagnosing clients' problems.

- Giving information and explaining options.

- Identifying further action the client can take.

- Giving basic assistance, e.g. filling in basic forms, contacting third parties to seek information.

This will generally be done in one interview although there may be some follow-up work. The client then retains responsibilities for further action.

General Help with Casework

The service may also be providing a casework service, *i.e.* taking action on   **10–005**
behalf of clients in order to move the case on. This may include negotiation and advocacy on the client's behalf to third parties of the telephone, by letter or face-to-face. By definition, most cases will involve follow-up work with the service provider retaining responsibility for this.
The current Casework categories are as follows:

1. Welfare Benefits

2. Housing

3. Consumer/General Contract

4. Debt

5. Employment

6. Immigration/Nationality

7. Health an Community Care

8. Disability Casework

9. Casework for Young People

10. Casework for Asylum Seekers and Refugees

11. Race Equality Casework

Specialist Help'[4]

Currently there is no new Quality Mark for the provision of specialist help   **10–006**
because there is reliance on an enhanced version of the existing Legal Aid

---

[4] Community Legal Service, *Quality Mark Standard* (2000), at pp. 4–5, and available on the
CLS website: www.justask.org.uk.

Franchise Quality Assurance Standard. Specialist help basically refers to the provision of legal advice and representation provided by legally qualified persons.

A. THE SPECIAL FEATURES OF INFORMATION AND ADVICE PROVISION

10–007   As part of the CLS, there will be organisations that provide information. Not all such organisations will have to be part of the CLS, but the Quality Mark that the CLS demands provides clients accessing organisations with minimum guarantees. Where what is being provided is a self-help information service, the service will involve "members of the public using directories, published materials or websites to find the information they need". The provider will have little or not interaction with clients. "Providers must ensure that the information, including the CLS Directory ... and information leaflets or other material, is up to date and accessible. The organisation also needs to have a mechanism to find out if the service is meeting the needs of clients. If there is interaction with the public, staff will be signposting people to other providers as necessary."[5]

The CLS anticipates that there will be Quality-Marked provision of legal information in such places as libraries and doctors' surgeries. It is not anticipated that this will be interactive, but it will provide answers to basic questions and provide information about how to obtain further advice. The Legal Services Commission was pleased to report that in June 2001 there were "847 CLS Information Points at either the Self Help or Assisted Information Level."[6] The range of organisations interested or providing such a service includes a national chain of supermarkets, the Prison Service, the Benefits Agency, the Court Service and an NHS Trust. In addition, the Association of Chief Police Officers has recommended that police stations should seek to become Information Points at the Self Help level. The Commission anticipates that the next few years will see a significant increase in the availability of this type of information.[7]

Further, there is a considerable and increasing amount of information available. With the development of various media, legal information has been much more readily available to those who access the various types of media. For example, television has found that consumer programmes have been a valuable source of audience figures. These programmes often deal with the provision of legal advice, especially when something has gone wrong with a purchase. With the growth of the Internet, there has been an explosion in the availability of such information. Many law firms feel that it is obligatory not only to advertise their services on their own website, but also to provide a service for readers free of charge. The latter may be regarded as a more sophisticated form of marketing by encouraging clients to approach the firm for further information, advice and representation as required.

---

[5] *Quality Mark Standard*, at p. 19.
[6] Legal Services Commission, *Annual Report 2000/01* (HC Paper 96, 2001), para. 2.38.
[7] *ibid.*

B. AGENCIES OFFERING LEGAL ADVICE

1. CITIZENS' ADVICE BUREAUX[8]

The CAB Service owes its existence to wartime necessity, having its origins **10–008** in the combined operation by the Ministry of Health, the National Council for Social Service and the Family Welfare Association in 1938 to provide advice and information in the war emergency. Government assistance terminated with the war's end and local Bureaux were left to scrape along on what they could glean from local authorities and other sources. The service was revived at the beginning of the 1960's by the injection of government funding and was stimulated by mention in two major inquiries (the Molony Committee on Consumer Protection in 1962 and the Royal Commission on Legal Services in 1980). When the central body, the National Association of Citizens' Advice Bureaux (NACAB), was reviewed in 1984, the CAB service was described as " ... an invaluable national asset."[9]

"The CAB Service aims

- to ensure that individuals do not suffer through lack of knowledge of their rights and responsibilities or of the services available to them, or through an inability to express their needs effectively

and equally:

- to exercise a responsible influence on the development of social policies and services, both locally and nationally.

The CAB Service is independent and provides free, confidential and impartial advice to everybody regardless of race, sex, disability or sexuality."[10]

As the NACAB Annual Report for 2000/2001 states "Citizens Advice Bureaux help clients solve millions of problems every year through the provision of quality advice, from general advice on everyday issues to specialist advice, negotiation and representation."[11] The main categories of problems with which CABx help are: benefits (1,723,205 queries in 2000/ 2001); consumer and utilities (1,174,764); employment (631,768); housing (600,198); legal (479,189); relationships (387,726); tax (153,944); and other (707,473).[12] An indication of the developing nature of the provision of advice is that not only do CABx see people in person and answer telephone queries, but also 360,000 people accessed the website *www.adviceguide.org.uk* which provides the CAB information on-line.[13] Clearly the CAB service

---

[8] J. Citron, *Citizens Advice Bureaux: For the Community, by the Community* (1989); J. Richards, *Inform, Advise and Support: 50 Years of the Citizens Advice Bureau* (1989).

[9] *Review of the National Association of Citizens' Advice Bureaux* (the Lovelock Report: Cmnd. 9139, 1984).

[10] NACAB Annual Report 2000/2001 (see *www.nacab.org.uk*) at introduction.

[11] *ibid.*, at p. 6.

[12] *ibid.*

[13] *ibid.*

meets a real need. Much of the CAB information and advice is provided by trained volunteers. In 2000/2001 there were 21,581 volunteers, of whom 11,913 worked as advisers, 6,615 as management committee members, and 3,053 as volunteer administrators. At the same time, there were only 4,487 paid staff in the CAB service. NCAB, however, has had to state that the CAB service is finding it "increasingly difficult to recruit new volunteers."[14]

Different strategies will be adopted according to the nature of the queries and the resources available to any individual CAB. Advisers are at least trained to provide information and advice. They will be at least able to provide appropriate information and sign-posting, where appropriate, to a more suitable service. In some cases, a particular CAB may be able to provide a more specialised service. For example, some CABx can provide significant support in preparing for legal cases, such as Employment Tribunal hearings.[15]

Even though very significant costs are saved through the support of volunteers, the service is still expensive, not least because of the provision, by NACAB, of an essential information system. In 2000/2001 NACAB cost £21.7 million. This cost was largely covered by a grant from the Department of Trade and Industry of £20.2 million. In addition to the cost of the central organisation, the Bureaux funding largely came from local authorities (£53.3 million or 59 per cent)) and the remaining £38 million from the private sector (1 per cent), the National Lottery (8 per cent), charitable trusts (3 per cent), Community legal services (15 per cent), Health Authorities (4 per cent), Single regeneration funding (1 per cent) and other sources, including the Coalfields Regeneration Trust, NACAB Partnership Grants, European Funding and the Probation Service (8 per cent).[16]

2. OTHER AGENCIES

10–009   There is a wide range of other agencies. Many of them are members of the Federation of Information and Advice Centres (FIAC). For example, in the Nottingham area, the following agencies are members of the Federation: Bestwood Advice Centre; Carers' Council Allies in Adult Mental Health; Clifton Welfare Rights Advice Centre; Forest Fields Advice Centre; Hucknall & District Voluntary Advice Centre; Keyworth Advice Centre; Meadows Advice Group; Nottingham Repetitive Strain Injury Support Group; Nottingham Trent University Union of Students Advice Centre; Nottingham University UNU Student Advice Centre; Nottinghamshire Outworkers Support Group; Scargill Walk Centre; Shelter Nottinghamshire Housing Advice Centre; Sherwood Advice Centre; St Ann's Welfare Rights Advice Group; Stapleford Advice Bureau; West Bridgford Advice Centre.[17] The mission of FIAC and, therefore, of its members is "to ensure access to good quality information and advice services in order that people can fully

---

[14]   ibid.
[15]   A case in the NACAB Annual Report 2000/2001 details the work done by Littlehampton CAB in preparing evidence and representation at four Employment Tribunals on behalf of a group of dinner ladies who had lost their jobs: ibid., p. 3.
[16]   ibid., p. 9.
[17]   Information available through the FIAC website: www.fiac.org.uk.

achieve, protect and exercise their rights."[18] FIAC was established in 1979, it became a registered charity in 1988 and by the mid 1990's its membership had increased to nearly 1,000 centres. It is the largest UK network of advice-providing organisations; some centres provide general advice; some serve a particular community and some provide specialist advice.[19] To be a member, "all ... centres must be non profit-making, be providing advice which is fee at the point of delivery and be independent of central or local government control. They must also meet basic membership criteria relating to issues such as accountability and equal opportunities."[20] Clients may "expect that [an] enquiry is dealt with in complete confidence, without bias, prejudice and judgement, that no actions are taken without [their] authority, that the advice is accurate and complete and that the service is free."[21]

There are some Consumer advice Centres through which local council Trading Standards Departments provide advisory services.[22] These centres provide both pre-shopping advice on quality, fitness and value for money and a complaints service for disgruntled consumers. Housing advice is also often provided through centres, many of which have been council run. Councils also often provide a welfare rights service. Some charities provide sources information and help, including DIAL UK (Disability Information and Advice Lines); Shelter, the housing charity; the Child Action Poverty Group; and Gingerbread, a charity concerned to support one parent families.

C. SPECIALIST AGENCIES OFFERING LEGAL ADVICE TO MEMBERS

One of the benefits of membership of some organisations is that legal advice may be made available. The advice may be connected to the main business of the organisation. Legal advice may be made available either through the employment of lawyers within the organisation[23] or by the engagement of lawyers in private practice at the expense of the organisation.   **10–010**

1. TRADE UNIONS[24]

Legal services provided through a trade union have been, and remain, a   **10–011**
significant factor in the recruitment and retention of members. It appears

---

[18] *ibid.*
[19] *ibid.*
[20] *ibid.*
[21] *ibid.*
[22] Under the Local Government Act 1972, ss. 137 & 142.
[23] But account must be taken of the limits on practice of employed solicitors, see above, para. 3-013.
[24] See G. Latta and R. Lewis, "Trade Union Legal Services" (1974) XII *British Journal of Industrial Relations* 561; R. Lewis and G. Latta, "Union Legal Services" (1973) 123 N.L.J. 386; M. Zander, *Legal Services for the Community* (1978), pp. 305–308; R. Lewis, "Legal Services in the Trade Union" in *Advice Services in Welfare Rights* (ed. Brooke), Fabian research series 329 (1976).

that most, if not all, trade unions offer some form of legal advice service to members. The offering may be limited to employment related matters,[25] it may be extensive[26] or it may provide an employment plus service.[27] The latter appears increasingly to be the norm. An employment plus service is likely not only to provide free legal advice on employment law issues, but also a service to deal with injuries as a result of accidents and to provide a wills and conveyancing service.[28]

2. MOTORING ORGANISATIONS

10–012   The original motoring organisations, the Automobile Association and the Royal Automobile Club, provide a variety of benefits to their members, including legal advice. Understandably, their legal services are limited to matters relating to motoring (but *e.g.*, the RAC includes legal expenses insurance in its insurance services[29]) covering primarily advice on general motoring law, disputes with garages, and claims arising out of accidents.[30]

3. THE CONSUMERS' ASSOCIATION

10–013   The Consumers Association (CA) began in 1957 as a small group publishing a magazine with the results of the comparative testing of aspirins and kettles and has since become a multi-million pound organisation with influence over manufacturers and retailers as well as those responsible for the formulation of consumer policy.[31]

The information function is performed through the magazine *Which?* available to subscribers, but having a general impact because of its availability in libraries and the extent to which it is referred to and talked about in the media. Unfavourable mention in *Which?* is regarded as a major problem for manufacturers. Solicitors services were considered in the October 1995 edition. The researchers sought advice from a number of lawyers and compared that advice with the ideal answer. Provided the comparator is correct, this approach (mystery shopping) provides an informative assessment of the quality of a solicitor's work, and is being considered as a quality measure under the CLS.[32] Unsurprisingly, this was criticised by a number of solicitors. More validly, concerns were expressed

---

[25] *e.g.*, the GMB provides a legal service limited to employment rights, but including non-employment accidents: *www.gmb.org.uk*. See also CWU: *www.cwu.org* and UNIFI: *www.unifi.org.uk*.

[26] *e.g.*, BECTU's legal services include employment law, accidents, wills, conveyancing and free initial legal advice by telephone on all non-employment issues: *www.bectu.org.uk*. See also NASUWT: *www.teachersunion.org.uk* and UNISON: *www.unison.org.uk*.

[27] *e.g.* NATFHE: *www.natfhe.org.uk*: TGWU: *www.tgwu.org.uk*; UCATT: *www.ucatt.org.uk*.

[28] See the various trade union websites accessible through the website of the Trades Union Congress: *www.tuc.org.uk*.

[29] This is an increasingly important means of funding litigation, see below, para. 11-006.

[30] For the AA, see *www.theaa.com*; for the RAC, see *www.rac.co.uk*.

[31] As exemplified by its critical report on the Metro in July 1981, see *The Times*, June 29, 1981.

[32] See para. 10-023, below.

about the accuracy of the comparator and of the assessment of how good in comparison was the advice given. Law often does not allow for merely one answer or approach. A retraction with regard to one firm had to be published in the November 1995 edition.

On the legal advice side, the CA operates a legal service for individual members on payment of a separate subscription. Legal advice, in the form of answers to reader's questions, is also contained in the magazines, and there are statements of law in other CA publications.[33]

D. LAW CENTRES[34]

One of the most significant developments in the provision of legal help in the last part of the 20th century was the emergence of law centres. Drawing some inspiration from the American system of neighbourhood law firms but adapting themselves to local conditions and the rules of the legal profession in this country, law centres provide a local base for the dissemination of legal services outside the legal profession.

10–014

1. THE BEGINNINGS[35]

Some provision was made for the giving of legal advice by salaried solicitors outside the ambit of private practice in the Legal Aid and Advice Act 1949, but the part of the Act (section 7) which would have established full-time paid solicitors located at Legal Aid Area Headquarters and travelling to smaller places was never brought into force. An alternative scheme for the provision of advice was proposed and adopted after 10 years of pressure had failed to get the original scheme implemented.

10–015

The real origins of the law centre movement are usually attributed to the publication of pamphlets by the lawyers of the Conservative and Labour parties and the individual initiative of pioneers who became impatient at the slowness of official bodies in responding to the pressure for change. *Justice for All*[36] analysed the unmet need for professional legal services and proposed the establishment of local legal centres in places of deprivation, to be staffed by salaried lawyers and to exist with and be supplemental to the private profession. It was suggested that the type of work undertaken by the centres should be restricted but that they should be free of those rules of professional etiquette that then existed (*e.g.* advertising and touting for

---

[33] E.g., *The Good Food Guide* attempts to set out the law about eating in a restaurant.

[34] For a comprehensive survey of the origins and development of the law centre movement, see M. Zander, *Legal Services for the Community* (1978), Chaps. 2 & 3; Royal Commission on Legal Services, *Report, Vol. 1* (1979), Chap. 8; Law Centres Federation, *The Case for Law Centres* (1989); R. Widdison, (1988) L.S. Gaz. March 16, pp. 35–37; JUSTICE, *Law Centres* (1995); the Law Centres Federation website: *www.lawcentres.org.uk.*

[35] See also "Significant Dates in the Development of Law Centres and the Law Centre Federation" at *www.lawcentres.org.uk.*

[36] A report of the Society of Labour Lawyers in the Fabian research series, no. 273 (1968).

business) which would inhibit their work.[37] It is not, perhaps, surprising that the solution of the Conservative lawyers in their pamphlet, *Rough Justice*,[38] to the same problem was the introduction of subsidies for practitioners operating privately in deprived areas and an extension of the assistance given by lawyers to voluntary advice agencies. However, they were prepared to countenance the appointment of salaried lawyers as a last resort.

The Law Society moved from implacable opposition to the salaried lawyers proposal in the 1949 Act and *Justice for All* to acceptance of salaried solicitors as part of its own proposals for an Advisory Liaison Service.[39] This Service would provide legal help to CABx and other agencies; would establish close liaison between the local profession and CABx and other relevant services; would provide oral advice for the public in cases that could be readily disposed of; would maintain permanent advisory centres where necessary, offering advice and assistance short of proceedings or representation in court; and would set up permanent local centres offering representation in magistrates' courts and county courts and the conduct of litigation where this could not be undertaken by solicitors' firms.

Part II of the Legal Advice and Assistance Act 1972 appeared to be designed to give the Law Society the power to carry out these proposals. But it was then frustrated by the failure of successive Governments to bring Part II into force.

2. Development

10–016   Impatient of the slow progress being made officially, local lawyers and community workers set up a law centre in North Kensington in 1970.[40] A variety of other centres emerged in 1973–1974; by October 1982 there were 38 centres around the country,[41] by 1987–1988 there were 61,[42] by 1995 there were 55,[43] and in 2001 there were 52.[44] In order to be a Law Centre, properly so called, the organisation must be a member of the Law Centres Federation.

The struggle for most of the centres has always been for funds.[45] Traditionally, the sources of funds has been grant-aid from public or charitable funds, with major sponsors being the local council. Funding sources "emerged and [grew] in ... unco-ordinated, sporadic fashion in response to local initiatives."[46] The introduction of block contracting for legal aid raised the prospect of more secure funding for law centres, and this is confirmed by the funding approach under the Community Legal

---

[37] *ibid.*, pp. 61–62.
[38] Society of Conservative Lawyers, *Rough Justice* (1968).
[39] *Legal Advice and Assistance*, Memorandum of the Council of the Law Society (1969).
[40] C. Robinson *et al.*, *Coming of Age: North Kensington Law Centre 1970–88*.
[41] 31st *Legal Aid Annual Reports* (1980–81), pp. 128–129. And see M. Zander and P. Russell, "Law Centres Survey" (1976) L.S. Gaz. 208 and the Royal Commission on Legal Services, Vol. 2, Part. B, Section 3.
[42] 38th *Legal Aid Annual Reports* (1987–88), pp. 102–103.
[43] JUSTICE, *Law Centres* (1995), p. 4 and Appendix 2.
[44] www.lawcentres.org.uk.
[45] It is this which explains the fluctuation in membership of the Law Centres Federation.
[46] JUSTICE, *Law Centres* (1995), p. 17.

Service,[47] but that does not contain a guarantee of funding for law centres. Law centres will qualify for funding if they go through the same procedures as private practitioners, which requires the obtaining of a contract for the provision of certain legal work and the maintenance of standards of operation and provision of legal advice and assistance.[48]

A further initial problem was the necessity to obtain an exemption (a "waiver") from the Law Society's rules in relation to advertising and touting for business. Ultimately, an agreement was reached, in 1977, about the conditions under which the Law Society would grant waivers to law centres and it was thereafter no longer a problem.[49]

3. WORK

"Law Centres provide a free and independent professional legal service to people who live or work in their catchment areas. ... Law Centres are managed democratically by individuals and organisations from their local areas. They work closely with their communities and provide the kind of services that are most suitable for that area. This accountability means that they complement the services of other community groups and advice agencies in the areas, ensuring that there is no duplication of work and providing the local groups with back-up legal advice when needed."[50] In consequence, they prioritise their areas of work and specialise in "welfare rights, immigration and nationality, housing and homelessness, employment rights, and sex and race discrimination."[51] They do work in other areas, dependent upon local need and these other areas may include "mental health, disability rights, education rights, juvenile crime and children's rights."[52]

10–017

Law Centres work by employing "solicitors, barristers, legal advisers and community workers."[53] In consequence of their mission to provide "a more efficient and comprehensive service for their users", they not only support individual case work but also work with groups, provide training and information, pro-actively identify legal issues in their area, comment on proposed legal changes and provide legal support for community and other local organisations.[54]

To become a law centre and a member of the Law Centres Federation, an organisation must meet minimum requirements for membership:

independence ...
control by consumers of law centre services ...
six staff, including two lawyers ...
a defined catchment area ...

[47] See below.
[48] See below, at paras 10-021–10-025.
[49] M. Zander, "Waivers — the end of a long story?" (1977) 127 N.L.J. 1236.
[50] "What do Law Centres do?" at *www.lawcentres.org.uk*.
[51] "What areas of law do they deal with?" at *www.lawcentres.org.uk*.
[52] *ibid.*
[53] *ibid.*
[54] *ibid.*

a non-profit-making structure
capacity to represent clients in court
a commitment to equal opportunities."[55]

4. THE FUTURE

10–018   Client satisfaction with law centres has always been high. For example, it
was reported in 1992 that law centre workers are approachable and
accessible.[56] Many organisations, including political parties, are supportive
of the work of law centres.[57] The Labour Government of 2001 sees the law
centres as contributing to the amelioration of social exclusion.[58] Law
Centres have played a significant part in the provision of legal advice.
Whether their future is any more certain than it has been in writing previous
editions of this book still remains to be seen. It is dependent upon the
continuing willingness of funders to provide the necessary resources.
Assuming that law centres have the operational and strategic facilities to
do so, which seems likely considering the detailed criteria for membership,
the availability of contracts as part of the Community Legal Service may
secure their future especially as Community Legal Service Partnerships
develop so that there is greater cooperation and negotiation in the provision
of legal advice and assistance in any given locality. It is very important to
note that the Legal Services Commission has made an encouraging start in
this area. It is helping to fund a number of law centres and is examining a
revised system for making grants.[59]

E. SOLICITORS IN PRIVATE PRACTICE

10–019   Whilst there are many different sources of legal advice and many of these
will form part of the Community Legal Service, it is still lawyers that are the
major purveyors of legal advice.[60] This is true, even if we discount the role of
the lawyer and big business. In providing legal advice, even to big business,
two questions arise, and they are in relation to cost and availability. As
regards legal advice to big business, the lawyer has to be available as the
client requires and cost will have been a factor in determining whether the
lawyer's firm gets the client's business.
      Evidence that the cost of a solicitor's advice, or fear of that cost, and the
relative inaccessibility of many offices had led to the original speculation

---

[55] JUSTICE (1995), p. 4 taking the information from the guidelines for membership of the
   LCF. See also "How can you start a Law Centre?" at *www.lawcentres.org.uk*.
[56] L. Hiscock and G. Cole, "Law centre client perceptions of the service they received at the
   Centres they visited" (1992).
[57] JUSTICE (1995), p. 13.
[58] Lord Chancellor's Department, *Social Exclusion* (2001), at *www.lcd.gov.uk*.
[59] Legal Services Commission, *Annual Report 2000/01* (HC Paper 97, 2001), at para. 2.27.
[60] See also above, Chap. 8

about the degree of unmet legal need.[61] In consequence, there was a substantial growth in alternative provision of legal advice, not least through the expansion of the CABx and the creation of Law Centres. Lawyers, therefore, have responded to the problems as they are a part of the CAB and Law Centre movement, but also lawyers in private firms have responded. Some of that response has been by the motivation of the lawyers, which motivation may be to meet client needs or to develop the business, and some as a product of the changes in the legal aid scheme, leading to the recent creation of the Community Legal Service. Thus, more legal advice is available, more readily and there is more information available about it and its cost.[62]

If clients are able to pay the bill, they can get advice from a solicitor of their choice as often as they desire and on whatever topic they choose. If they cannot pay the bill, they must rely on the services provided voluntarily by solicitors and barristers; or a law centre; or come within the Community Legal Service; or use another agency or service; or do without.[63] Within the context of the objectives of the Community Legal Service, doing without is unacceptable and the Government sees access to legal advice as one means of addressing social exclusion.[64]

1. Voluntary Schemes

Many lawyers have been involved in the provision of free legal advice, being **10–020** generous with their time and talents. Many are accustomed to rendering assistance to those who are genuinely unable to afford professional fees. Recently, there has been a concerted effort to encourage pro bono work by both barristers and solicitors.[65] This has built upon a number of initiatives, not least the poor persons' procedure in litigation[66] and other initiatives as identified by the Rushcliffe Committee in 1944 (such as clients not charged by their solicitor; advice-giving by stipendiary magistrates, magistrates clerks and county court registrars; a Poor Mans' Lawyer Service in London and the provinces staffed by volunteers; trade union legal advice; and CABx).[67]

A typical means whereby lawyers offer their services free is through the

---

[61] See above, para. 9-012.

[62] Information comes not only from the Community Legal Service and its commitment to information provision and sign-posting, but also from the advertising of services by lawyers (see Chap. 3).

[63] As Genn discovered, there is a large proportion of the population who will indeed 'lump it' and take no action when presented with a problem to which there might be a legal solution, see above, para. 9-008.

[64] Social Exclusion (2001), and see above, para. 10-006.

[65] See above, Chap. 3.

[66] A formal procedure was instituted in 1914 and was described as " ... the first regular scheme for legal aid in the Supreme Court": H. Kirk, Portrait of a Profession (1976), p. 164. It was put under the control of the Law Society in 1923 as a result of the proposals of the Lawrence Committee, The Report of the Poor Persons' Rules Committee (Cmd. 2358, 1925). It could not cope with the increasing pressure of work in the 1930s and ultimately was overtaken by the Legal Aid Scheme in 1949.

[67] Report of the Committee on Legal Aid and Advice (Cmd. 6641, 1945), pp. 17–21.

CAB service. A CAB will establish a system of advisory sessions by local solicitors, operating on a rota basis, giving free legal advice to clients on an appointments basis. The purpose might be either to resolve a problem at that interview or to provide initial advice that will lead to further advice either through that or another solicitor's firm.[68] These schemes have the encouragement of the Law Society and the support of many members of the profession.

The importance of such a scheme should not be underestimated. It ensures that the solicitor only sees those clients who have been identified by a volunteer worker as being in need of professional advice; it provides a free initial interview to encourage those who may be worried about cost; and it permits the solicitor to take on those clients who may need more extensive legal assistance. The drawback is that everything is dependent upon the existence of a CAB in the locality, its willingness to establish and run a scheme and the preparedness of the local solicitors to give freely of their time and expertise.[69]

The more frequent scheme involves lawyers providing some of their advice to some of their clients without recouping the full or any of the cost. The free initial interview, either through a CAB or under the Community Legal Service, is not merely a service but often makes good business sense as it may encourage clients who would not otherwise use a solicitor to do so.

2. THE COMMUNITY LEGAL SERVICE

(a) Background

10–021　The Community Legal Service has taken over all aspects of the original Legal Aid service. One aspect of the old scheme was to do with the provision of legal advice and information. It was known as the Green Form Scheme. It had come into existence as a consequence of the Legal Advice and Assistance Act 1972. The object of that scheme was to make readily available a cheap and effective source of legal advice for those who would otherwise be unable to afford it. So, a solicitor could give oral or written advice on the application of English law to any particular circumstances in relation to the person seeking advice, and on any steps which he or she might appropriately take.[70] The client could also be given "assistance" in taking those steps.[71] Whilst the subject range covered by the scheme was very wide, the solicitor was limited to the provision of advice and assistance and could not provide representation. There were limits on the amount of assistance that could be provided and financial limits controlled eligibility for the scheme. Whilst there were extensions, notably the advice by way of representation scheme that enabled representation at some tribunals, and

---

[68] At one time there was a practice rule presenting a problem with this (and which required a waiver), but all that is now required is compliance with the Solicitors' Introduction and Referral Code 1990.

[69] These schemes are highly valued in the CABx, see, *e.g.* NACAB, *Annual Report 1981–1982*, p. 8.

[70] Legal Aid Act 1988, s. 2(2).

[71] *ibid.*, s. 2(3).

duty solicitor schemes at courts and police stations, the scheme, as with the entire Legal Aid service, was under severe pressure and Government determined that reform was necessitated. The major criticisms of the scheme appear to have been fivefold. First, that it was administered by solicitors and so what support it provided depended on the work that solicitors were prepared to do. There was a view that solicitors were not expanding sufficiently into social welfare law areas, and so not providing as extensive a service as the funders, the Government, expected. Secondly, that the initial limit on the amount of work that a solicitor could do was too low.[72] This would mean that either the solicitor would stop the work or have to work on without an extension, thus risking not being paid or would have to wait for an extension to be authorised which "is time-consuming, causes delay and raises difficulties with clients."[73] Thirdly, that the financial criteria were too strict. The limits for eligibility were much lower than for civil legal aid and the limit for disposable weekly income was extremely low and had become harsher as time progressed. Further, the scheme had originally had a form whereby the client made a contribution, but this was removed. Therefore, the scheme was only available to a very small number of people. The consequence was that either people were not getting necessary advice or were placing too heavy a burden upon the other agencies, such as CABx.[74] Fourthly, that the scheme was not sufficiently well known to attract those who needed it. Raising the level of public awareness was a constant source of concern. There were frequent schemes to endeavour to raise awareness. But advertising campaigns were sporadic and their effect was very difficult to assess. Fifthly, that the system was open to abuse by solicitors. Baldwin and Hill had discovered that official in area legal aid offices "tended to view members of the legal profession with considerable suspicion," but more on the basis that solicitors might make full or excessive use of the scheme than that there was malpractice or dishonesty. Indeed, "evidence of serious abuse of the green form scheme has always proved elusive."[75]

Notwithstanding the deficiencies, the Scheme was well regarded, so that Baldwin and Hill concluded,

" ... we have found ourselves at the end of the research thoroughly persuaded of its merits. Notwithstanding the serious criticisms we have made in the report about certain aspects of the scheme, the results, taken as a whole, demonstrate that the green form scheme represents an invaluable social service and provides a source of immediate legal advice to those who need it .... [Many] more people are assisted under the ... scheme than are assisted under all other forms of legal aid put together. This is remarkable given that the ... scheme makes up only about a fifth of the total legal aid budget."[76]

---

[72] J. Baldwin and S. Hill, *The Operation of the Green Form Scheme in England and Wales* (1988), p. 62, Table 14.
[73] *ibid.*, pp. 54–64.
[74] NACAB, *Barriers to Justice* (1995).
[75] Baldwin and Hill (1988), Chap. 4, esp. pp. 67 and 79.
[76] *ibid.*, pp. 128, 129. For a more sceptical view, see A. Sanders and L. Bridges (1990) 140 N.L.J. 85, and response, S. Hill (1990) 140 N.L.J. 323 and reply by Sanders and Bridges (1990) 140 N.L.J. 496.

When examining the Community Legal Service as it replaces the Green Form Scheme, it can be seen that many of its aspects are clearly intended to meet some of the criticisms of the existing scheme without losing its strengths. Thus, not all solicitor firms can participate. They must have a contract with the CLS which demands certain quality standards be met. Information and sign-posting are both critical aspects of the CLS. The intention is that there is a wider range of information provision and that all elements of the CLS are able to ensure that a client who cannot be helped by them can be sign posted to a service that can help.

(b) Solicitors and the CLS

10–022   The involvement of solicitors is with the specialist help aspect of CLS provision, as well as the provision of advice and information. So, the elements of the CLS to which solicitors will contribute lie primarily in the following parts of the Service as established by the Access to Justice Act 1999: "the provision of help by the giving of advice as to how the law applies in particular circumstances," "the provision of help in preventing, or settling or otherwise resolving, disputes about legal rights and duties," "the provision of help in enforcing decisions by which disputes are resolved, and" "the provision of help in relation to legal proceedings not relating to disputes."[77] In providing such services, the provider is obliged, in so far as is reasonably practicable, to

(a) "promote improvements in the range and quality of services provided as part of the Community Legal Service and in the ways in which they are made accessible to those who need them,

(b) secure that the services provided in relation to any matter are appropriate having regard to its nature and importance, and

(c) achieve the swift and fair resolution of disputes without unnecessary or unduly protracted proceedings in court."[78]

In order to be a provider of relevant services, a solicitors firm must obtain a contract with the Community Legal Service and then it will receive funding from the Community Legal Service Fund. In order to obtain a contract, the provider must meet certain quality standards. These standards vary according to the level of service that the provider seeks to offer. In the initial stages, the CLS has been able to establish the necessary quality standards for the lower levels of service, but is adopting the existing quality standards that applied to solicitors firms, with minor adaptions. These standards had arisen from the move to franchising services under the Legal Aid Board which had meant the introduction of contracts for the provision of services provided certain standards were met and then funding would follow, so the scheme was the same in outline to that under the CLS. Thus, the quality standards could easily be used in the transitional phase. Consultation on new quality standards is on going.

The obtaining of a quality mark is a crucial element of the CLS for

---

[77] Access to Justice Act 1999, s. 4(2)(b),(c),(d) and (e).
[78] *ibid.*, s. 4(4).

whatever involvement the organisation requires. "The Quality Mark is the quality standard for legal information, advice and specialist legal services. It comprises a set of standards designed to ensure that a service is well run and has its own quality control mechanisms that relate to the quality of the information or advice the service provides. ... The standards cover seven key quality areas, known as the Quality Framework:

Access to Service:	This covers planning the service, making others aware of the service and non-discrimination
Seamless Service:	This covers active signposting and referral to other agencies and awareness of any appropriate CLA partnership arrangements.
Running the Organisation:	This covers the roles and responsibilities of key staff and financial management.
People Management:	This covers equal opportunities for staff, training and development, supervisors and supervision and casework criteria.
Running the Service:	This covers client information and case management, independent review of files and feedback to advisers.
Meeting Clients'Needs:	This covers information to clients, confidentiality, privacy and fair treatment and maintaining quality where someone else delivers part of the service.
Commitment to Quality:	This covers complaints, other user feedback and maintaining quality procedures."[79]

The above produces a basic Quality Framework:[80]

A. ACCESS TO SERVICE	The aim of the CLS is to improve access to legal services and to base the delivery of services on local needs and priorities.
	Members of the CLS should be aware of the environment in which they operate and develop their services to meet the needs of their community.
B. SEAMLESS SERVICE	Where a member of the CLS cannot provide the particular service needed by the client, they must inform the client and direct them to an alternative service provider, where available.
C. RUNNING THE ORGANISATION	Members of the CLS must have structures and procedures that ensure effective management of the organisation and its resources.
D. PEOPLE MANAGEMENT	Members of the CLS must ensure that staff possess or acquire the skills and knowledge required for meeting the clients' needs.

[79] Community Legal Service, *Quality Mark*, at p. 3.
[80] *ibid.*, p. 18.

E. RUNNING THE SERVICE	Members of the CLS must have processes and procedures that ensure an effective and efficient service to their clients.
F. MEETING CLIENTS' NEEDS	Clients using a CLS provider are entitled to receive advice and information relevant to their needs.
G. COMMITMENT TO QUALITY	All members of the CLS are committed to improving the quality of their service

10–023 In meeting the above, new detailed standards have had to be set for all levels of service, except the specialist standard. The specialist standard is initially the Legal Aid Franchise Quality Assurance Standard (LAFQAS). The two areas that needed immediate amendment were referral, to comply with the general sign-posting commitment, and client satisfaction. As the CLS states, "Active signposting is where an adviser identifies an appropriate provider with the client. ... This is the minimum level of assistance that we would expect an organisation working at the specialist help standard to achieve. Referral is that process by which the adviser makes contact with the selected provider to arrange an appointment and provides the selected provider with appropriate records and information. ... We expect organisations to conform to the requirements as quickly as possible and give a positive statement to that effect as referral is a key foundation of the CLS."[81] There is some concern amongst the legal profession about the amount of work that this may require, since it demands that each firm have a very clear picture of what legal advice and assistance is available. There are two responses to this concern. The first is that it is impossible for anyone to provide legal advice in a vacuum and it seems reasonable to expect firms to be aware of what is available. Secondly, the fact that the CLS should be delivered through local CLS Partnerships should ensure that the necessary information is readily available either formally through the Partnership or informally through the networks that will inevitably swiftly develop. The CLS is examining ways by which client satisfaction can be measured. The existing Transaction Criteria[82] were developed as a proxy to direct assessment of quality because

---

[81] *ibid.*, p. 61.

[82] They have been used since 1994 by the Legal Aid Board. The CLS describes them, at *ibid.*, p. 15, as "a well-established means of assessing that the basic issues essential to the provision of a competent casework service have been addressed." They will be used in the audit process and a "random sample of closed casefiles will be selected and audited against the transaction criteria to determine a level of compliance rating. Transaction criteria are based on best practice. In order to demonstrate success against the transaction criteria it will be necessary for the auditor to find objective evidence on the casefile. Evidence may be found in a number of sources *e.g.* case sheets, attendance notes, letters to the client or other parties, etc. Factual information may be obtained from such sources as official documents, reports and documents supplied by the client. Transaction criteria seek objective evidence of:
- Information obtained from the client and other sources.
- Advice given based on that information.
- Practical steps taken following that advice.
... The transaction criteria scoring system is such that a single omission will not in itself indicate a major reduction in the rating. ... Transaction criteria audits will be conducted using a random sample of the organisation's closed casefiles. It is envisaged that the audit will consist of a minimum of 10 casefiles per category. ... [I]t is envisaged that the scoring structure may be similar to the example detailed below:

they enable a detailed file review to determine, from an objective audit, what was done by the solicitor in a given client's case. Whilst there will be on going work on seeking some acceptable means of direct assessment, other aspects of client satisfaction can be measured more immediately. What is proposed is that "a client questionnaire, used by individual organisations to ascertain the opinions of their clients on the service they were given, would be a valuable addition to the quality measures already in place."[83] What these will be able to measure include "helpfulness and approachability of the organisations staff, timely response to telephone calls, understandable information, good explanations, listening behaviour, etc." What the CLS wishes to move towards, therefore, is more direct measures of the quality of the advice "*i.e.*, was the information, advice and recommendations made to a client the most accurate and most suitable from a legal standpoint" and "peer review is certainly part of the solution together with mystery shopping."[84]

A part of assuring the quality of information provision is in the means whereby the Quality Mark is obtained. This is achieved by the application process and the ongoing audit of standards. There are eight stages to this process which the CLS anticipates will ensure minimum levels of quality in the provision of legal information and advice.

1. Making an application.

2. Acceptance of application.

3. Desk-top review.[85]

4. Preliminary audit (excludes Self-help and Assisted Information).

5. Pre-Quality Mark audit (excludes Self-help and Assisted Information)[86] and Transaction Criteria assessment.

- The transaction criteria booklet will be divided into two sections. The first will deal with case management requirements and the second with category specific requirements e.g. advice and action issues.
- For an individual casefile to achieve a 'pass mark' it will be required to achieve a minimum score in both sections of the booklet. Certain questions may be 'weighted' according to the importance of the issue addressed.
- For the subject category to pass the transaction criteria audit, at least three-quarters of the casefiles audited must achieve a 'pass' result. It follows that in a sample size of 12 files, at least 8 must achieve the required score.

Success at the transaction criteria will be a mandatory requirement for all organisations undertaking a pre or post Quality Mark audit:" *ibid.*, pp.16–17.

[83] *ibid.*, p. 62.
[84] *ibid.*, pp. 61 and 62.
[85] "This is the process whereby the auditor make a systematic comparison between the requirements of the standard and the evidence provided by the applicant:" *ibid.*, p. 11.
[86] The following audits occur: *ibid.*, p. 14.

Application Level	Audit Type
Self-help Information	Random audit (after the award has been made)
Assisted Information	Random audit (after the award has been made)
General help	Preliminary audit

6.   Decision and recommendation.

7.   Certification.

8.   Post Award audits.[87,88]

(c) Funding of legal advice — Legal Help

10–024   The Legal Services Commission will only fund the following services as part of the CLS: (1) Legal Help; (2); Help at Court; (3) Approved Family Help; (4) Legal Representation; (5) Support Funding; (6); Family Mediation; (7) other services approved by the Lord Chancellor.[89] The funded help in connection with litigation is dealt with in Chapter 11. It is important to be aware that separate funding is available in connection with family law litigation, although we do not, in general, examine it further.

Legal Help "provides initial advice and assistance with any legal problem. ... [A Lawyer] can give general advice, write letters, negotiate, get a barrister's opinion and prepare a written case if [the client] has to go before a court or a tribunal."[90] In order to be a provider of Legal Help, any organisation must have a contract with the Legal Services Commission under which it provides CLS work under either a General Civil or Criminal Contract. The contract holder can, then, provide Legal Help, where the client satisfied the necessary criteria, without the need to seek approval. It is, therefore, called "Controlled Work."[91]

The lawyer can provide Legal Help until his or her charges reach a total of £500.To continue the work, he or she must have the authority of a Regional Director of the Legal Services Commission.[92]

Legal Help may only be provided "where there is sufficient benefit to the client, having regard to the circumstances of the matter, including the personal circumstances of the client, to justify work or further work being carried out."[93] That "Help may only be provided if it is reasonable for the matter to be funded out of the Community Legal Service Fund, having

	Pre-Quality Mark audit which may include transaction criteria
General help with casework	Preliminary audit
	Pre-Quality Mark audit including transaction criteria
Specialist Help	Preliminary audit
	Pre-Quality Mark audit including transaction criteria

---

[87]   For General and Specialist Help standards, there will be an annual audit visit: *ibid.*, p. 15.
[88]   *ibid.*, p. 9.
[89]   Legal Services Commission, *The Funding Code* (2000), at para. 1.1.
[90]   Legal Services Commission, *A Practical Guide to Community Legal Service Funding* (2001), paras. 1.2 and 2.1
[91]   Legal Services Commission, *The Funding Code Procedures* (2000), at para. A2.
[92]   Legal Services Commission, *A Practical Guide to Community Legal Service Funding* (2001), para. 2.1.
[93]   Legal Services Commission, *The Funding Code* (2000), at para. 5.2.1.

regard to any other potential sources of funding."[94] The funding in connection with litigation, other than from the CLS, that is or may be available is dealt with in Chapter 11. The detailed provisions on the funding of Legal Help are to be found in the Legal Services Commission's *Funding Code Procedures* (2000).

A client must be assessed as financially eligible and the lawyer must have satisfactory evidence from the client as to their means before he or she assesses their financial eligibility.[95] There is an upper financial limit for the costs of Legal Help.[96] The client's disposable capital must not exceed £3000. As regards disposable income, if the client is on income support or income-based jobseeker's allowance, he or she will be eligible. Otherwise, the client's gross income must be less than £2,000 per month. If it is more, the client is not eligible. If it is less, the lawyer must then calculate the client's disposable monthly income. If it is less than £601 per month, the client is eligible. Where the client is eligible, no contribution to costs will subsequently have to be paid out of either capital or income, but any money recovered through Legal Help or Help at Court must be used to pay the lawyer's bill. This is the statutory charge. The first charge on any money recovered, therefore, is the statutory charge. It only comes from money or property gained from the dispute. It will not apply where you recover all your costs from the other side, because costs have thereby been paid. There are also circumstances in family litigation where the charge does not apply. If Legal Help is refused, the lawyer is obliged to give reasons.[97]

Legal Help is not available where a client has received Legal Help for the same matter in the previous six months, except where special circumstances apply that justify such funding.[98]

(d) Funding of advice — Help at Court

Help at Court involves help and advocacy for a client in relation to a particular hearing, without formally acting as legal representative in the proceedings. An example given by the Legal Services Commission is in an application to suspend a warrant for possession in a housing case.[99] The same criteria for eligibility apply as for Legal Help, plus the requirements that (a) Help at Court may only be provided if the nature of the proceedings and the circumstances of the hearing and the client are such that advocacy is appropriate and will be of real benefit to the client; and (b) Help at Court may not be provided if the contested nature of the proceedings or the nature of the hearing is such that, if any help is to be provided, it is more appropriate that it should be given through Legal Representation.[1] Help at Court, like Legal Help, is controlled work, so it is for the lawyer to

10–025

---

[94] *ibid.*, para. 5.2.2.
[95] Legal Services Commission, *The Funding Code Procedures* (2000), at para. A2.5. The information from the client must be kept on file and so is available, *e.g.* to the auditing process.
[96] This can only be exceeded by application to a Regional Director of the Legal Services Commission.
[97] *ibid.*, para. A2.7.
[98] Legal Services Commission, *The Funding Code Procedures* (2000), at para. A3.3.
[99] Legal Services Commission, *A Practical Guide to Community Legal Service Funding* (2001), para. 2.1.
[1] *ibid.*, para. A5.3.

determine eligibility, within the constraints of the contract with the Legal Services Commission. In essence, the same further provisions on eligibility apply as for Legal Help, indeed Legal Help can be continued into Help at Court.[2]

(e) Duty solicitor schemes

10–026 For many years, there have been duty solicitor schemes, whereby a person may receive legal advice from a solicitor either at a police station or at a court. These schemes now fall under the new Criminal Defence Service which came in to operation on April 2, 2001. The two duty solicitor schemes now operate under the Criminal Defence Service: Duty Solicitor Arrangements 2001.[3] The Legal Services Commission (LSC) is obliged to establish local schemes in each identified region[4] (the regions being: London South, London East, London West, South Eastern, Southern A, Southern B, South Western A, South Western B, South Wales, North Wales, West Midlands A, West Midlands B, East Midlands A, East Midlands B, Eastern A, Eastern B, North Western A, North Western B, North Eastern A, North Eastern B, Yorkshire & Humberside A, Yorkshire and Humberside B, and Merseyside).[5] The LSC is "responsible for ensuring that all members of Local Schemes are competent to undertake Duty Solicitor work."[6]

The first such scheme was initiated by the Bristol Law Society in 1972 to provide legal advice to defendants appearing at the local magistrates' court.[7] Those involved were satisfied with the results and the scheme provided the model for others which followed. It was up to local initiative to follow up on this start, and so development was patchy and unco-ordinated over the country. By mid-1975 there were 29 duty solicitor schemes operating[8] and the Law Society felt it necessary to prepare and publish a guide for the assistance of local law societies.[9] The Royal Commission on Legal Services, in 1979, described these schemes as " ... indispensable in a number of ways: they provide pre-trial advice to defendants who are often confused or ignorant and who have not previously obtained it, they encourage the adequate preparation of bail applications and help to reduce the number of ill-advised pleas, whether of guilt or innocence, and the number of remands required."[10]

The consequential move to a uniform scheme commenced with section 1 of the Legal Aid Act 1982 which enabled the Law Society to act under the scheme-making powers that had appeared in section 15 of the Legal Aid Act 1974. The first statutory scheme was the Legal Aid (Duty Solicitor) Scheme 1983.[11] It is this scheme, and its successors, which has been taken over by the Criminal Defence Service (CDS). Firms of solicitors can opt to participate in

---

[2] *ibid.*, para. B4.
[3] Available on the Legal Services Commission website: *www.legalservices.gov.uk*.
[4] Criminal Defence Service: Duty Solicitor Arrangements 2001, para. 3.2.
[5] *ibid.*, Schedule 1.
[6] *ibid.*, para. 4.3.
[7] (1972) L.S. Gaz.819.
[8] *25th Legal Aid Annual Reports* [1974–75], pp. 6–7.
[9] (1975) 72 L.S. Gaz. 577–579.
[10] Royal Commission on Legal Services, *Report Vol. 1* (1979), p. 93.
[11] *34th Legal Aid Annual Reports* [1983–84], pp. 185–197 & 37–43.

the service and to be allowed to do so must gain a General Criminal Contract with the Legal Services Commission, which, as with civil work, includes an audit process to ensure that certain quality assurance standards are met. An important innovation of the CDS is that the Legal Services Commission has employed lawyers to act as Public Defenders who can provide the same service as that delivered by lawyers in private practice.

There are two duty solicitor schemes. One is that available to provide free legal advice and assistance at a police station to anyone questioned about an offence, whether arrested or not. There is no means test for this advice and no payment has to be made. In some serious circumstances the police can delay a person's access to legal advice under section 58 of the Police and Criminal Evidence Act 1984.[12] The scheme means that a duty solicitor is available 24 hours a day. Of course, any given person being questioned could, alternatively, either ask to see a list of local solicitors or contact their own solicitor. The duty solicitor scheme has to be staffed. This is achieved by the adoption of one of three models: rota, panel or a combination of both. The other scheme provides free legal advice and assistance at a magistrates' court. As the public advice recommends, it is better to have sorted out representation before arriving at court,[13] but this scheme ensures that it is possible to avoid defendants being unrepresented. All courts have a duty solicitor scheme[14] at which advice and assistance, including advocacy assistance, are provided free of charge and without a means test. The advice that the duty solicitor can provide is that about bail, whether to plead guilty or not guilty, how to get a solicitor and to apply for a representation order, the type of sentence that might be imposed, representation at the first appearance before a magistrate, and on fines and other court orders where there is a risk of imprisonment.[15] This duty solicitor scheme is staffed by the scheme being either an attendance or Call In scheme (the latter may be by way of a rota or a list) or a combination of both.[16]

The proportion of suspects who receive legal advice at the police station has increased, but that proportion is still relatively low. The request rate in 1988 was 25 per cent, increasing to 32 per cent in 1991 and 40 per cent in 1995–6; and the consultation rate in 1988 was 19 per cent, increasing to 25 per cent in 1991 and 34 per cent in 1995–6.[17] It does seem rather difficult to understand why, in the 21st century, these figures are so low. Some suspects

---

[12] See below, para. 14-022.

[13] Legal Services Commission, *Criminal Defence Services at the police station and in court* (2001), p. 4.

[14] Legal Aid Board, *Annual Report 1999–2000* (HC 664, 2000), para. 4.3.

[15] Legal Services Commission, *Criminal Defence Services at the police station and in court* (2001), p. 5.

[16] Legal Services Commission, *Criminal Defence Service: Duty Solicitor Arrangements 2001*, para.6.2(a).

[17] A. Sanders and R. Young, *Criminal Justice* (2nd ed., 2000), p. 221, using figures derived from T. Bucke and D. Brown, *In Police Custody: Police Powers and Suspects' Rights Under the Revised Pace Codes of Practice* (Home Office Research Study no. 174, 1997). As Sanders and Young go on to point out, advice is more often sought for serious than for minor offences, indeed "advice is sought and received in over half of all cases involving offences tried in the Crown Court." This is, as they point out, understandable, but what is not understandable is, "the great variations which persist between different police stations." The evidence for the latter comes from Bucke and Brown (1997) and from D. Brow, T. Ellis and K. Larcombe, *Changing the Code: Police Detention under the Revised PACE Codes of Practice* (Home Office Research Study no. 129, 1992).

have a predisposition to seek advice which others lack, some perceive that advice would be of little benefit (which is bound to be true in many minor offences), some are confident that they can do as well without advice as with it, some believe that nothing can help, some trust the police to act fairly, some wish to get out of the station as quickly as possible and believe that advice will delay the process, some have a low opinion of the quality of advice that they are likely to receive and of the scheme itself.[18] (Some of the problems for suspects accessing legal advice are the product of police practices,[19] but some are the product of the practices of solicitors. Some suspects have previous experience of the scheme which was poor.[20] Sanders and Young discovered that, at least in the early stages of duty solicitor schemes, problems created by solicitors included the following:[21]

(1) The unavailability of solicitors, even when the request is to have the advice of someone from the duty solicitor scheme. The problems were identified as either being that the schemes did not require someone always to be on duty; or that the scheme was simply over stretched by demand.

(2) Often legal advice was provided not by a solicitor but by a paralegal, who was not always trained properly for the task. One study identified the possible problems of using non-qualified and untrained staff as being: lack of legal expertise; lack of confidence; role conflict; and over-identification with the police.[22]

(3) Often advice would be given over the telephone rather than in person, which, except in very clear cases, can lead to poor, inaccurate or detrimental advice.[23]

(4) Often there are doubts about the quality of the advice and assistance. In origin this centred on some confusion as to the role of the legal adviser. Some did very little, being both passive and compliant. The failure of legal advisers to act is most starkly seen in the case of the "Cardiff Three", where the Court of Appeal commented that "the solicitor appears to have been gravely at fault for sitting passively through this travesty of an interview" which clearly contravened the rules against oppression.[24] Whilst there are difficulties associated with the role, a more interventionist or adversarial stance is necessitated and is increasingly the case.

Many of these criticisms were taken seriously. The Royal Commission on

---

[18] Sanders and Young (2000), pp. 221–222.

[19] *ibid.*, pp. 223–228.

[20] "Duty solicitors are crap anyway, they work for the fucking police and the courts" *ibid.*, p. 222, quoting Choongh (1993).

[21] Sanders and Young (2000), pp. 229–237.

[22] M. McConville and J. Hodgson, *Custodial Legal Advice and the Right to Silence* (Royal Commission on Criminal Justice Research Study no. 16, 1993), pp. 30–34.

[23] Whilst there was improvement in consequence of changes in the obligations of duty solicitors in the mid 1990s, a subsequent study still discovered that about 20 per cent of suspects secured advice by telephone: Sanders and Young (2000), pp. 232–233 reporting from L. Bridges, E. Cape, A. Abubaker and C. Bennett, *Quality in Criminal Defence Services* (2000).

[24] *R v. Paris, Abdullahi and Miller* (1993) 97 Cr. App. R., at p. 104, and see Commentary by D. Birch at [1994] Crim. L.R. 362.

Criminal Justice recommended that steps be taken to improve the quality of the legal advice made available:

(1) The guidance to solicitors (the Law Society's *Advising Clients at the Police Station*) on their roles should be made more widely known, be better understood, and more consistently acted upon. Specifically, it was recommended that the Law Society actively progress their production of a training video.[25]

(2) Steps should be taken to ensure that the client's own solicitor and their representatives should meet the same standards as duty solicitors. This should be the case even where the solicitor is not working under the legal aid scheme.[26]

(3) The training education, supervision and monitoring of all legal advisers who operate at police stations should be reviewed.[27]

Important steps have been taken to address many of the concerns.

(1) Tightening the appointment process for duty solicitors and their representatives. Thus improvements were made in the quality and commitment of the persons appointed to duty solicitor schemes.[28] The current criteria determining appoint to a duty solicitor scheme require the Legal Services Commission to appoint only those solicitors who are "competent to undertake Duty Solicitor work"[29] and normally someone is appointed to both a police station and a magistrates' court scheme.[30] So the applicant must provide evidence of that competence, either through membership of a previous scheme or by accreditation.[31] Applicants must have "comprehensive experience of criminal defence work, including the provision of advice in the Police Station and advocacy in the Crown Court or magistrates' court throughout the 12 months prior to the application...."[32] A member of a scheme must hold a current practising certificate, not be a special constable, not be suspended or excluded from membership of another scheme, not be

---

[25] Royal Commission on Criminal Justice, *Report* (Cm. 2263, 1993), p. 38.
[26] *ibid.*
[27] *ibid.*
[28] The person to be appointed would have to hold a current practising certificate, be willing to act personally and to undertake the majority of the rota duties allocated, have a regular criminal practice, have comprehensive experience of defence work, and adequate experience of providing advice to persons arrested and held in custody, and to act in a non-discriminatory way. S/he must have attended an advocacy training course, unless sufficiently experienced, and a police station advice course, unless substantially experienced. The applicant must agree not to provide money or other gifts to suspects, except food, drink and smoking material for immediate consumption. The applicant then went through a rigorous selection process, including an interview. The appointment would last for five years, during which time certain aspects would be monitored: Duty Solicitor Arrangements 1994, paras. 32–48.
[29] *Criminal Defence Service: Duty Solicitor Arrangements 2001*, para. 4.3.
[30] *ibid.*, para. 4.19.
[31] *ibid.*, paras. 4.4 and 4.6. On accreditation, see also Legal Aid Board, *Annual Report for 1999–2000* (HC Papers 664, 2000), paras. 4.9–4.11.
[32] *Criminal Defence Service: Duty Solicitor Arrangements 2001*, para. 4.5. Certain periods are disregarded, *e.g.* maternity leave and sickness: para. 4.5(b).

facing a criminal charge or have been convicted of a non-rehabilitated criminal offence, and not be the subject of an adverse finding through the professional misconduct bodies.[33]

(2) Tightening the requirements for continued membership of a scheme.[34] A duty solicitor must:[35] undertake "at least two hours of continuing professional development annually on issues relevant to the law, practice and procedure in the Police Station or magistrates' courts;"[36] undertake personally a set minimum number of rota turns in magistrates' courts and rota cases at the police station;[37] and continue to do evidenced general criminal defence work and police station work.[38]

(3) Clarifying the obligations upon duty solicitors.[39] Thus the suspect was more likely to receive at least advice.[40] The current clarification of the obligations is backed by the possibility of suspension from the scheme.[41] Suspension may occur where a duty solicitor: unreasonably failed to attend a police station; sent a representative when he or she should have attended personally; failed to accept a reasonable number of calls; failed to accept rota cases; unreasonably failed to carry out duties or comply with requirements of the scheme; is under criminal investigation or has been convicted of a crime or is being investigated by the Office for the Supervision of Solicitors; does not demonstrate the necessary level of competence; no longer complies with the location rules; is no longer a fee earner within a firm that is a Criminal Defence Service supplier with a contract; or some other good reason.[42]

(4) The gradual move towards a rota scheme means that it is highly likely that a duty solicitor will be available unless the scheme is swamped with business at a particular time. This is also contributed to by the contracting scheme imposing clearer burdens upon the solicitors gaining a General Criminal Contract.

---

[33] *ibid.*, para. 4.18. As to refusal of membership and appeals, see paras. 4.21–4.23. See also Legal Aid Board, *Annual Report for 1999–2000* (HC Papers 664, 2000), paras. 4.12 4.14.

[34] Where a member's circumstances change, s/he is under an obligation to notify the Legal Services Commission: *Criminal Defence Service: Duty Solicitor Arrangements 2000*, para. 5.10.

[35] Failure to comply with these requirements may lead to suspension from the scheme: *ibid.*, paras. 5.2 and 5.3.

[36] *ibid.*, para. 5.1(a).

[37] *ibid.*, para. 5.1(b).

[38] *ibid.*, para. 5.1(c). The evidence is that the solicitor must have accepted at least 12 police station cases annually involving attendance at the police station, or all cases where fewer were offered.

[39] See the Legal Aid Board Duty Solicitor Arrangements 1994 and the Legal Aid Board Legal Advice and Assistance at Police Stations Register Arrangements 1994 in the *Legal Aid Handbook 1995*, pp. 457–486.

[40] The duty solicitor was under an obligation to accept the case and to provide initial advice on the telephone: Duty Solicitor Arrangements 1994, para. 53. Also s/he was under an obligation to attend the police station where the crime was an arrestable offence and where the suspect was to be interviewed, go through an identification process or complained of serious maltreatment by the police: *ibid.*, para. 54.

[41] *ibid.*, para. 5.4.

[42] *ibid.*, para. 5.4. As to the period of suspension, appeals, etc, see paras. 5.5–5.9 and 7.13–7.22. Local instructions on the operation of the scheme may be issued under paras. 6.13–6.15.

(5) Improving quality assurance, which does not necessarily mean that the advice and assistance must be provided by a solicitor, as many paralegals are as well qualified and skilled in this particular area. What has been achieved is a clearer position as to who can be a non-solicitor providing advice and assistance.

(6) It is for the Legal Services Commission to decide what scheme to adopt.[43] The difficulty with this is that if a rota scheme is not adopted, there is less of a guarantee of availability of a duty solicitor. However, it would seem that there is a preference for rota schemes.[44]

(7) Being aware of a scheme makes it more likely that a suspect will request advice and assistance, and the Legal Services Commission is required to "take steps to ensure that potential clients are made aware of the availability of the Duty Solicitor at Police Stations and magistrates' court."[45]

(8) Improving contact between the police station and the duty solicitors through the use of the Duty Solicitor Call Centre Service. In 1999/2000 it answered 95 per cent of its calls from police stations and duty solicitors within 20 seconds. It deployed 93 per cent of rota cases and 87 per cent of panel cases within 30 minutes.[46]

It is possible that there will still be some problems with the schemes. Whilst, **10–027** considerable effort has been made to address many of the problems, and they have clearly had their impact, the cause of some of the problems may not be addressed at least fully by these changes. Sanders and Young have suggested three reasons why the scheme, and the Police and Criminal Evidence Act 1984, have been ineffective and which may not be addressed by such changes:

(1) Enforcement is in the hands of those same officers and solicitors who may not have a vested interest in adhering to the rules. As regards solicitors, this is compounded by the poor rate of pay and the frequently unsociable hours.

(2) Police stations are police territory, but the main suspects for breach of the rules (the police) are also the gatekeepers.

(3) The rules themselves have allowed for bending.

The last figures under the old scheme revealing work done under the Duty Solicitor Schemes are to be found in the Legal Aid Board Annual Report for 1999–2000,[47] which, of course, pre-dates the introduction of the Criminal Defence Service. This reveals that in 1999–2000, there were duty solicitor schemes covering all police stations and courts in England and Wales.[48] There was a 0.2 per cent increase in demand for police station duty

---

[43] *ibid.*, para. 6.2.
[44] *ibid.*, paras. 6.1–6.8.
[45] *ibid.*, para. 6.12.
[46] Legal Aid Board, *Annual Report for 1999–2000* (HC Papers 664, 2000), para. 4.4.
[47] Legal Aid Board, *Annual Report for 1999–2000* (HC Papers 664, 2000).
[48] *ibid.*, para. 4.3.

solicitors, whereas the position as regards court schemes was more complex.[49] The number of duty solicitors as members of schemes has increased from 5,257 in January 1993 to 6,154 in January 2000.[50] As regards a measure of quality, performance against targets for police station schemes was as follows:[51]

Police Station Duty Solicitor Targets	Percentage of schemes meeting target in the 6 month period to:	
	April 1999	April 2000
95 per cent of all cases should result in a duty solicitor being available	98%	99%
80 per cent of rota cases to be passed by the call centre service within 30 minutes	100%	99%
75 per cent of panel cases to be passed by the call centre service within 30 minutes	92%	91%

The first set of figures for the work of the Criminal Defence Services are to be found in its Annual Report for 2000/2001.[52] These figures reveal the number and type of defendant assisted by the magistrates' courts duty solicitor scheme:[53]

Category	1990/91	1995/96	1996/97	1997/98	1998/99	1999/2000	2000/01
No of defendants assisted	224,772	260,939	276,875	301,668	266,727	240,081	415,743
Defendants assisted							
Adults	95.8%	92.5%	92.1%	92.2%	92.6%	91.8%	88.7%
Juveniles	4.2%	7.5%	7.9%	7.8%	7.4%	8.2%	11.3%
Defendant's circumstances							
In custody	40.8%	34.8%	34.4%	35.2%	32.3%	24.0%	19.4%
On bail	59.2%	65.1%	65.6%	64.8%	67.7%	76.0%	80.6%
Assistance given							
Advice only	17.7%	16.6%	15.9%	15.6%	14.4%	9.2%	4.2%
Representation	82.3%	83.3%	84.0%	84.3%	85.6%	90.8%	95.8%

[49] ibid., para. 4.2. The implementation of reforms to the Criminal Justice System, the Early First Hearings and Early Administrative Hearings lead to an increase in the number of standby only claims by duty solicitors and a reduction in the number of defendants actually using a duty solicitor in court.

[50] ibid., para. 4.7.

[51] ibid., para. 4.8.

[52] Legal Services Commission, Annual Report 2000/01 (HC Paper 97, 2001).

[53] ibid., Table Criminal 6. Other years' figures appear in these statistics, that is for each year between 1990/91 and 1995/96.

Similar information is not recorded for Police Station schemes, but for both schemes payments made are recorded.[54]

Magistrates courts duty solicitor schemes–payments made

Year	No of claims	% with defendants	Defendants assisted	Amount paid £'000s	Cost per £	Defendant Annual growth	Cost per defendant at 1990/91 prices
1990/91	63,092	94.2	229,144	7,084	£30.91	7.0%	£30.91
1995/96	80,606	94.5	264,126	13,005	£49.24	5.7%	£42.27
1996/97	80,750	95.1	273,181	13,943	£51.04	3.7%	£42.91
1997/98	83,363	95.8	297,046	15,215	£51.22	0.4%	£41.57
1998/99	85,957	96.6	304,902	16,177	£53.06	3.6%	£41.73
1999/00	155,499	91.7	258,588	25,385	£98.17	85.0%	£76.37
2000/01	337,660	98.5	465,260	48,784	£104.85	6.8%	£78.96

Legal advice at police stations — payments made

Year	No of stand-by claims paid	% with suspects (all claims)	No of suspects assisted	Amount paid £'000s	Cost per £	Suspect assisted Annual growth	Cost per suspect at 1990/1991 prices
1990/91	99,811	47.0	397,479	37,056	£93.23	3.8%	£93.23
1995/96	104,125	66.2	706,732	81,975	£115.99	12.5%	£99.59
1996/97	104,448	67.3	720,094	89,951	£124.92	7.7%	£105.02
1997/98	107,221	69.9	765,975	99,995	£130.55	4.5%	£105.96
1998/99	106,053	70.6	764,870	105,112	£137.42	5.3%	£108.08
1999/00	110,342	70.6	749,571	109,069	£145.51	5.9%	£113.20
2000/01	104,262	69.9	760,495	117,336	£154.29	60%	£116.19

(f) Legal Help and Green Form usage

Although the replacement of the Legal Aid Board by the Legal Services Commission and the replacement of Green Form scheme advice and assistance by Legal Help make exact comparisons between the schemes difficult, in fact the close identity of the two schemes means that the figures on usage of the old scheme are still relevant. The green form scheme was, historically, the most widely used part of the old legal aid scheme. It is possible to look at the last year of the old scheme (1999/2000) and the first year of the new scheme (2000/2001). In 2000, the green form scheme accounted for 20 per cent of all Legal Aid Fund expenditure and for 48.1 per

10–028

[54] *ibid.*, Tables Criminal 5 and Criminal 7.

cent of all acts of assistance.[55] The overall pattern of usage in the 1990's shows a fairly stable take up of the scheme, but it then began to grow, reaching a peak of 1.6 million acts of assistance in 1993–4. The old Legal Aid Board revealed that this increase was "principally fuelled by increased demand for advice on social and economic matters, such as housing, debt and welfare benefits. ..." After changes to eligibility in 1993, the demand reduced for a period, but since 1996 the demand again grew. "The most rapidly growing categories of advice overall were immigration & nationality and welfare benefits." The figures reveal a down turn in late 1999, but this is more due to the fact that, under a contracting system, the figures are only revealed as holders of franchises, and now contracts, report on usage rather than having to make individual green form claims at about the time of the advice and assistance.[56] As regards cost, the Legal Aid Board has shown that the average cost of the old green form scheme increased by 36.3% in real terms between 1989 and 2000. The explanation given was an increase in the "implied time" spent on each act of assistance (this was worked out by the LAB on the basis of the claim figures presented).[57] Further, the disbursements (expenses) claimed by solicitors is a significant element in cost, but varies between different types of work, amounting to 1.2 per cent in debt cases and 23.2 per cent in divorce and judicial separation work.[58] To give a reflection of the sort of work under taken under a legal advice and assistance scheme, the following table reflects the number of bills paid by the Legal Aid Board to solicitors for 1999–2000:[59]

Type of advice given	Number of bills paid	Average profit costs	Bills paid with disbursements	% with disbursements	Average disbursements paid	Average total cost	Total paid £'000
Divorce and judicial separation—petitioners	116,293	£155.83	22,286	19.2	£17.84	£159.24	**18,519**
Divorce & judicial separation—respondents	12,985	£221.89	3,008	23.2	£30.39	£228.93	**2,973**
Other family matters	225,087	£98.24	6,637	2.9	£22.70	£98.91	**22,263**
Crime	371,021	£72.29	5,125	1.4	£47.30	£72.94	**27,062**
Landlord and tenant, housing	106,187	£109.44	10,619	10.0	£154.51	£124.90	**13,262**
Hire purchase and debt	72,066	£88.53	859	1.2	£30.31	£88.89	**6,406**

[55] It had amounted to 49.8% of all acts of assistance in 1993–4 (its peak) and for 45.2% in 1998–9: Legal Aid Board, *Annual Report 1999–2000* (HC Paper 664, 2000), at Appendix, Section 3, para. 3.1.
[56] *ibid.*, paras. 3.2–3.5.
[57] *ibid.*, para. 3.6.
[58] *ibid.*, para. 3.7.
[59] *ibid.*, Table Advice 4.

Employment	17,034	£112.06	351	2.1	£77.25	£113.65	**1,936**
Accidents and injuries	58,099	£105.06	5,225	9.0	£52.84	£109.81	**6,380**
Welfare benefits	147,338	£94.74	10,742	7.3	£87.90	£101.15	**14,903**
Immigration and nationality	106,849	£356.58	58,167	54.4	£138.68	£432.07	**46,167**
Consumer problems	26,748	£93.10	532	2.0	£52.38	£94.14	**2,518**
Other matters	106,328	£83.70	6,529	6.1	£38.87	£86.09	**9,154**
Totals	**1,366,035**	**£116.69**	**130,080**	**9.5**	**£93.36**	**£125.58**	**171,542**

Thus, criminal work accounted for 27.2 per cent of the work and 15.8 per cent of the cost of the green form scheme; all family matters accounted for 25.9 per cent of the work and 25.5 per cent of the cost; assistance on welfare benefits accounted for 10.8 per cent of the work and 8.7 per cent of the cost; immigration & nationality work accounted for 7.8 per cent of the work and 26.9 per cent of the cost; and landlord & tenant and housing work accounted for 7.8 per cent of the work and 7.7 per cent of the cost. As a comparison, in 1994–5, the proportion of crime cases was just over 25 per cent, family cases just over 15 per cent, matrimonial cases just over 12 per cent, welfare benefits at 9.5 per cent, landlord and tenant and housing at nearly 8 per cent, hire purchase and debt at just over 6 per cent, accidents and injuries at nearly 5 per cent, immigration and nationality at over 3 per cent consumer and employment each at just over 1.5 per cent, and the rest at about 12.5 per cent.[60] Other than the significant change in the amount of immigration & nationality work, there is a remarkable consistency in the type and relative proportion of work that is undertaken and it confirms many of the lessons learned from Chapter 8, above.

In 2000/2001 Legal Help work started, completed and billed has been recorded by the Legal Services Commission as follows:[61]

	New matters started	*Completed matters reported*
Family	**318,496**	**297,125**
Non-family		
Actions against the police etc	5,574	6,221
Clinical negligence	4,550	4,874
Community care	2,070	1,660
Consumer	12,194	14,491
Debt	52,193	50,145
Education	3,131	3,184
Employment	12,362	12,706

---

[60] *Legal Aid Board Annual Report 1994–95* (H.C. 526, 1995), Tables Advice 1 and Advice 2.
[61] Legal Services Commission, *Annual Report 2000/01* (HC Paper 97, 2001); Table at p. 17.

Housing	90,456	86,727
Immigration	138,841	108,600
Mental health	23,706	23,886
Personal injury	10,587	23,152
Public law	1,477	1,290
Welfare benefits	35,771	127,495
Total non-family	**485,332**	**464,458**
Total	**803,828**	**761,583**

3. CONCLUSION

10–029   As the Legal Services Commission itself point out.[62] the above figures reflect the importance of family work and the shifting priority, as stated by the Government, towards social welfare work. To what extent these changes will improve the provision of legal advice and assistance to those most in need and thus assist in meeting social exclusion remains to be seen, but the research evidence should be available both from the work of the Community Legal Service and of the Criminal Defence Service and also from the on-going research on legal need[63] promised to follow on from Professor Genn's research.[64] There is, therefore, some evidence that there is a move towards a more integrated approach to the provision of legal services, at least to the most needy. Of course, there is still much reliance on the non-government controlled, market dependent provision of legal service, but no doubt that will meet expressed needs and the CLS/CDS will respond to properly identified needs and the two will, in combination, be more successful than any approach that has preceded it.

---

[62]   *ibid.*, para. 2.60.
[63]   See above, para. 9-013.
[64]   See above, Chap. 9.

PART III

PRE-TRIAL PROCEDURE

CHAPTER 11

FEATURES OF LITIGATION AND OTHER METHODS OF DISPUTE RESOLUTION

In Part II we looked at advice and information. Now we begin a Part called **11–001** Pre-trial Procedure and it may appear that we are progressing inexorably towards the courtroom. Yet between the recognition of a dispute which may end in a trial and its actual arrival before the judge lies a lengthy period of negotiation before or during the operation of the formal pre-trial procedure. An understanding of the significance of these negotiations, which may sometimes more accurately be described as bargaining, and the resulting settlements is fundamental to civil litigation. We concentrate on civil matters, even though in the criminal context there is the analogous feature of "plea bargaining".[1] The other two topics we consider in this chapter, costs and delay, have significance in both civil and criminal litigation, and are interrelated with pre-trial negotiations. Finally, in the civil context, we consider the increasingly important topic of resolving disputes by methods other than litigation.

Influencing both civil and criminal procedure before and at trial, the English adversarial approach permits the parties to dictate the issues to be resolved and — to a limited extent — to settle the pace of the action. In the previous edition of this book the following statement appeared at this point:

> "In civil cases, the court has had no role in directing the course of the proceedings except on the application of one or other party. It has always been able to impose penalties on parties who break the rules without permission, by the award of costs against them, but it has not been able to enforce the rules of its own volition."

It is indicative of the extent of the so-called "Woolf reforms" (more accurately: the Civil Procedure Rules 1998[2] ("the C.P.R.") — completely

---

[1] "Plea bargaining" is dealt with in Chapter 17 on the Criminal Trial. On the point of comparison between criminal and civil matters, see H. Genn, *Hard Bargaining* (1987), esp. at Chap. 2.

[2] S.I. 1998/3132. Subsequent amendments to the date of writing (the end of January 2002) appear in the Civil Procedure (Amendment) Rules 1999 (S.I. 1999/1008); Civil Procedure (Amendment) Rules 2000 (S.I. 2000/221); Civil Procedure (Amendment No. 2) Rules 2000 (S.I. 2000/94); Civil Procedure (Amendment) Rules 2001 (S.I. 2001/256); Civil Procedure (Amendment No. 2) Rules 2001 (S.I. 2001/1388); Civil Procedure (Amendment No. 3) Rules 2001 (S.I. 2001/1769); Civil Procedure (Amendment No. 4) Rules 2001 (S.I. 2001/2792); Civil Procedure (Amendment No. 5) Rules 2001 (S.I. 2001/4015) and Civil Procedure (Amendment No. 6) Rules 2001 (S.I. 2001/4016).

changing the face of civil procedure in England and Wales from April 26, 1999 — that that simple statement must now be wholly revised. In addition, since, although the rules themselves are a statutory instrument, the accompanying forms and "practice directions" ("PDs") which must be read alongside the rules are not, not all amendments require a statutory instrument. For an up to date set of rules and practice directions, the reader is best advised to use the Lord Chancellor's Department's website[3] and for forms, the website of the Court Service.[4] This chapter is believed to be up to date to the 26th update to the Civil Procedure Rules, most of whose amendments became effective on March 25, 2002.

In civil cases after April 26, 1999, the court is responsible for the "active management" of cases.[5] Except where positively prohibited from so doing, it may exercise its powers on an application or on its own initiative.[6] In order to ensure that rules are followed, the court has a whole range of sanctions, which may be imposed in advance, up to and including the striking out of one or both parties' cases.

The parties select the issue or issues on which to fight — although the court may narrow them — and the evidence — although the court may limit the types and extent of evidence — with which to support their case. Whilst it might be thought to be in the interests of the parties to conceal what they know so that negotiation, in the form of bargaining, can proceed more effectively through a process of bluff and ambush, the court will, in pursuit of its objective of dealing with cases justly,[7] demand that as much as possible be disclosed in the early stages so that the matters really in dispute can be identified and the strength of the evidence assessed. As we will see in Chapter 11, the parties have positive obligations to assist in that process.[8]

A. COSTS

1. CIVIL CASES[9]

11–002   The costs involved in civil litigation are of the utmost importance to the parties — they may prevent an action ever being brought, they may render a victory in court Pyrrhic when damages are swallowed up in costs, they may prevent a meritorious appeal, and they will always be a factor in the risk of litigation.

---

[3] *http://www.lcd.gov.uk*
[4] *http://www.courtservice.gov.uk*
[5] CPR Part 1.
[6] CPR r. 3.3.
[7] CPR Part 1.
[8] See CPR r 1.3 and Courts and Legal Services Act 1990 ss. 27 and 28, inserted by Access to Justice Act 1999, s. 42.
[9] This topic is dealt with more fully in J O'Hare and K Browne, *O 'Hare and Hill, Civil Litigation* (10th ed.) (2001), Chap. 38. See also *Civil Procedure* (Spring, 2002, Sweet and Maxwell: hereafter "*The White Book,*"), Vol. 1, pp. 860–1061: *The Civil Court Practice* (2002, Butterworths: hereafter "*The Green Book 2001*"), Vol. 1, pp. 684–832; *Blackstone's Civil Practice* 2001 at Chaps 63, 66 and 68.

Clearly civil litigation is often very expensive. Lawyers are familiar with the concept that the costs in a case can easily be greater than the amount actually in dispute between the litigants. In some circumstances, litigation should be avoided and there is ever increasing encouragement for parties to a dispute to look to alternative methods of resolution.[10] For many people the costs of litigation are difficult, impossible, or off-putting. When litigation is necessary, it is important, if a system of civil justice is to be fair, that litigants must "have an equal opportunity, regardless of their resources, to assert or defend their legal rights."[11]

In his Interim Report, Lord Woolf concluded that the then level of costs was not an inevitable or necessary feature of litigation and that the then current attitudes to litigation were a major factor in creating high costs and costs uncertainty. Clearly costs could not have been the only concern. Lord Woolf identified certain basic principles which must be met by a civil justice system: it must be just in the result it delivers; it must be fair and seen to be so, its procedures must be proportionate to the nature of the issues involved, cases should be processed with reasonable speed; it must be understandable to those who use it, it must be responsive to its users' needs, it should provide such certainty as the disputes allow, and it should be effective in delivering on those principles.

In parallel with Lord Woolf's investigations, however, was a political initiative that the Court Service should be self- funding.[12] This had already resulted in a vast increase in court fees over a short period: for example, it cost £55 to issue a writ in 1993, but £500 to issue the same claim in 1998.[13] This, of itself, acted as a disincentive to the issue of court proceedings, particularly in the small claims track where a further fee of £80 payable by the claimant on allocation was particularly contentious and later withdrawn

---

[10] The court process itself now requires the parties to consider whether they should seek resolution by another means: CPR r. 1.4(2)(e) "encouraging the parties to use an alternative dispute resolution procedure if the court considers that appropriate and facilitating the use of such procedure."

[11] This is one of the basic principles which should be met as identified by Lord Woolf: Interim Report, p. 3.

[12] In 2000/2001 the overall percentage of the costs of running the civil courts recovered through court fees was 92%: *The Court Service Annual Report and Accounts 2000–2001*, (November 2001, The Stationery Office), p. 13.

[13] Fees are scaled in accordance with the value of the case — these are maxima. Fees in High Court cases are prescribed by the Supreme Court Fees Order 1999 (S.I. 1999/687) as amended by the Non-Contentious Probate Fees Order 1999 (S.I. 1999/688); Family Proceedings Fees (Amendment) Order 1999 (S.I. 1999/2549); Supreme Court Fees (Amendment) Order 1999 (S.I. 1999/2569); Supreme Court Fees (Amendment) Order 2000 (S.I. 2000/641); Supreme Court Fees (Amendment No. 2) Order 2000 (S.I. 2000/937); Supreme Court Fees (Amendment No. 3) Order 2000 (S.I. 2000/1544) and Supreme Court Fees (Amendment No. 4) Order 2000 (S.I. 2000/2382).

The equivalent, generally slightly lower fees in the county court are governed by the County Court Fees Order 1999 (S.I. 1999/689), amended by the Distress for Rent (Amendment Rules 1999) (S.I. 1999/2360); County Court Fees (Amendment) Order 1999 (S.I. 1999/2548); County Court Fees (Amendment) Order 2000 (S.I. 2000/639); County Court Fees (Amendment No. 2)) Order 2000 (S.I. 2000/939); County Court Fees (Amendment No. 3) Order 2000 (S.I. 2000/1546); County Court Fees (Amendment No. 4) Order 2000 (S.I. 2000/2310) and County Court Fees (Amendment) Order 2001 (S.I. 2001/1385).

in such cases.[14] The Woolf reforms have been in operation for 2½ years at the time of writing and research on whether or not they have achieved Lord Woolf s objectives is limited.[15] The extent to which they can be said to have been successful in the field of costs as elsewhere is considered in Chapter 11.

Costs have to be looked at in two respects, first the costs which may be ordered to be paid by one of the parties to the other in litigation, and, secondly, the costs which a client is obliged to pay the solicitor. It is not necessarily the case that the successful party will receive costs from the losing party which will cover the whole of the solicitor's bill.

(a) Costs payable in litigation

11–003   In deciding whether to begin or continue litigation, one major factor is whether a party will have to pay the costs or be able to recover them from the other party.

The principles in relation to the assessment of costs after a trial (known, prior to April 1999, as "taxation of costs") do not prevent the parties reaching their own agreement about costs where a settlement is effected before trial.[16] Indeed, in the majority of cases, costs are agreed between the parties. Nevertheless, the assessment rules[17] remain significant in providing the framework within which the parties can negotiate.

The steps are, first, that the judge must decide who should pay costs and on what basis.[18] The judge may award costs of different issues to different parties. Secondly, a costs judge (previously a "taxing officer") must determine exactly what costs are to be paid (this is now known as "detailed assessment of costs"). If the trial lasts one day or less, the trial judge will probably do this him or herself on the basis of schedules of costs submitted by the parties in advance of the trial. This procedure, which may also be adopted in relation to the costs of any short pre-trial hearing, is known as "summary assessment of costs".[19]

---

[14]   The question of court fees remains contentious. In February 2001, solicitors responding to the *Law Society's Third Woolf Questionnaire*, 41% of whom thought that court fees were causing hardship for litigants, identified the following fees in particular: issue fees (fixed on a scale from £27 for a county court claim valued at under £200 to £500 for a claim worth more than £50,000); allocation fees (£80); listing questionnaire fees (payable on requesting a trial date and fixed at £200, £300 or £400 depending on court or track). The full response to the questionnaire is available on the website of the Law Society of England and Wales: *http://www.lawsociety.org.uk/home.asp.*

[15]   See, however, the Lord Chancellor's Department paper, *Emerging Findings* (March 2001).

[16]   Where the parties have compromised on all issues except for the amount of costs payable, this can be determined by the court under CPR r. 44.12A.

[17]   CPR rr. 43.4,44.7; Part 47; PD 43–48 paras 3, 28–49.

[18]   Note that Lord Woolf's proposal that in the fast track there would be an overall cap on costs recoverable (Final Report, chapter 4) has been implemented — to date at least — only to the extent that there is a cap on the costs of the trial day itself, CPR Part 46.

[19]   CPR r. 43.3, 44.7; PD 43–48 paras. 3, 13 and 14. *A Guide to Summary Assessment* can be found on the Court Service website. The effectiveness or otherwise of summary assessment, as a pragmatic method of assessing and awarding costs is one of the more contentious areas of the reforms: Alien, "Inconsistent Judges plague Woolf Reforms", 2001 98(13) L.S.G. In a Law Society survey of February 2001, 62% of respondents said that the "judicial approach to summary assessment is not working." (*Response to Third Woolf Questionnaire, op. cit.*). Problems identified in that survey included the complexity and time involved in producing the documents required to allow summary assessment to take place; "arbitrary" or unreasoned deductions made by the assessing judge and a perceived inexperience in dealing

Lord Woolf, in his Interim Report, expressed some concerns about the damage produced by the adversarial approach and considered the argument that the rule that costs normally follow the result (the "costs indemnity" rule) can induce a "win at all costs mentality [which] is supported by some research which indicates that the existing rule has the tendency to increase expenditure on cases when compared with a system where each party bears its own costs."[20] However, the rule tends only to support meritorious cases where there are greater expectations of success. The arguments for the rule were identified in the Interim Report: 1) "it is fairer that a party who has succeeded in litigation should at least be able to recover the major proportion of his [or her] own costs from his [or her] unsuccessful opponent." 2) "the rule deters unmeritorious litigation and encourages earlier settlement." It also identified the arguments against the rule. 1) "It may deter meritorious as well as unmeritorious claims." 2) "It favours the wealthy litigant over the less wealthy." 3) "It can so increase the costs at stake that parties feel impelled to go on, thus making it impossible to reach a settlement."[21] The fear of the nuisance action should have been reduced if not removed by the increased powers under the C.P.R. for the court to remove unmeritorious claims, if necessary, of its own volition.[22] No person bringing litigation should be immune from the financial risk factor, because of the burdens imposed on society and the courts of taking such a step, and so Lord Woolf concluded that the rule should stay, but recommended that the rule be made more effective, particularly to encourage co-operative and discourage unco-operative conduct by the parties.

Lord Woolf ultimately proposed that the recoverable costs in fast track cases should be limited[23] to a maximum of £2,500 according to a regime that banded cases in relation to the amount claimed and provided for a percentage of the fixed costs[24] to be recoverable if the case settled prior to trial. This however, has yet to be incorporated into the C.P.R. and, more than two years into the new regime, it seems uncertain that it ever will be. It is, however, the case that the recoverable costs of the *trial* in the fast track[25] are limited by C.P.R. Part 46 and that in any case the court may predetermine the amount of a jointly-appointed expert's fees that will be recoverable from the losing party.[26]

Nevertheless, the basic rule remains that "costs follow the event", that is to say the successful party can expect the judge to order the loser to pay

with costs by judges principally recruited from the Bar (thought to be unfamiliar with the tasks normally undertaken by solicitors in preparation for trial or other hearings).

[20] Interim Report, p. 201. See A. A. S. Zuckerman, "Reform in the Shadow of Lawyers' Interests" in Zuckerman and Cranston (eds.) *Reforming Civil Procedure* (1995).

[21] Interim Report, pp. 202–203.

[22] See, for example, the power to strike out a claim or defence under CPR r 3.4.

[23] Final Report, chapter 4. See also Sir Peter Middleton's *Review of Civil Justice and Legal Aid* ("the Middleton Report", September 1997); the Lord Chancellor's Department research paper *Solicitors' fixed costs in civil claims* (1998) and Goriely, Butt and Sherr, *Costing Fast Track Procedures Through Hypothetical Studies*, (Lord Chancellor's Department research paper, 1998).

[24] Disbursements (*i.e.* expenses over and above the solicitors' fees) were to be recoverable separately.

[25] The usual way of dealing with claims worth between £5,000 and £15,000. See para. 12-005 *et seq.*

[26] CPR r 35.8(4). See further below, para. 15-005 *et seq.*

some or all of his or her solicitor's bill.[27] It was stated in *AEI Rediffusion Music Limited v. Phonographic Performance Limited (Costs)*[28] by Lord Woolf M.R. (as he then was) that:

"I draw attention to the new Rules because, while they make clear that the general rule remains, that the successful party will normally be entitled to costs, they at the same time indicate the wide range of considerations which will result in the court making different orders as to costs. From April 26, 1999 the "follow the event principle" will still play a significant role, but it will be a starting point from which a court can readily depart. ... The most significant change of emphasis of the new Rules is to require courts to be more ready to make separate orders which reflect the outcome of different issues."

Other factors to be considered[29] are:

a. The conduct of the parties, including:
  a. Conduct before and during proceedings including the extent of compliance with any pre-action protocol;[30]
  b. Whether or not it was reasonable for a party to pursue or contest a particular issue within the case;
  c. The manner in which a party has conducted the case;[31]
  d. Whether a successful claimant has exaggerated the claim.
b. Partial success;
c. Any offer to settle drawn to the court's attention (this will normally have been made under C.P.R. Part 36[32]).

The court has a great deal of flexibility in the order it makes and can, for example, order a party to pay:

a. A proportion of the opponent's costs (*e.g.* 50%);
b. A stated amount (*e.g.* £5,000) towards the opponent's costs;
c. The opponent's costs from or until a certain date;
d. The opponent's costs incurred prior to the issue of proceedings;
e. The opponent's costs relating to particular steps in proceedings;
f. The opponent's costs of a distinct part of the proceedings (*e.g.* liability);
g. Interest on the opponent's costs.[33]

---

[27] See CPR r 44.3(2): "If the court decides to make an order about costs — (a) the general rule is that the unsuccessful party will be ordered to pay the costs of the successful party; but (b) the court may make a different order."

[28] [1999] 1 W.L.R. 1507; [1999] 2 All E.R. 299; *The Times*, March 3, 1999; *The Independent*, February 24, 1999, C.A. For some other early expressions of intent as to the "loser pays" principle, see *Liverpool C.C. v. Rosemary Chavasse Ltd and another (Costs)* [2000] C.P. Rep. 8, Ch D.; *Scholes Windows Ltd v. Magnet Ltd (No. 2)* [2000] E.C.D.R. 266, Ch D.

[29] CPR rr 44.3 (4) and (5).

[30] A stage of procedure acting as a precursor to the formal issuing of court proceedings. See Chap. 12.

[31] For an application of this rule where one party had instructed a comparatively small regional firm of solicitors whilst the other had instructed a very large City firm, see *Mars UK Ltd. v. Teknowledge (No. 2)*, [1999] 2 Costs L.R. 44; *The Times*, July 8, 1999, Ch D.

[32] See para. 12-028.

[33] Other conventional types of order frequently used in interim hearings (*i.e.* hearings prior to the trial) are set out in PD 43–48 para. 8.5.

However, if the form of the order, whether it relates to the whole costs of the winning party or not, is expressed as anything other than an order for payment of a stated amount, the next stage is to calculate the amount payable. At a short hearing, where summary assessment is appropriate, the court will carry out this evaluation immediately by way of "summary assessment". Alternatively, a judge may order that costs are to be subjected to detailed assessment. In either case, assessment will be on one of two bases:

(a)   The standard basis,[34] where the court will:
    i)   Only allow costs which are "proportionate to the matters in issue"; and
    ii)   "Resolve any doubt which it may have as to whether costs were reasonably incurred or reasonable and proportionate in amount in favour of the paying party."
(b)   The indemnity basis,[35] where the court will "resolve any doubt which it may have as to whether costs were reasonably incurred or were reasonable in amount in favour of the receiving party."

Thus it is only in cases of debate about the reasonableness of costs incurred that the different bases of assessment themselves produce any difference in the actual costs received. From the point of view of the receiving party, the indemnity basis is the preferred basis, since then the burden of establishing that the expenditure was unreasonable lies upon the other party. Aside from the specific power to award indemnity costs where a claimant's Part 36 offer has been rejected[36] it was thought that costs would be awarded on an indemnity basis only in exceptional cases, for example cases in which "the conduct of the litigation was deserving of moral condemnation".[37] There is, however, recent authority that under the C.P.R. the award of indemnity costs is not so limited, but that the court will simply consider what is appropriate under C.P.R. rr. 44.3 and 44.3.[38]

The subsequent procedure is for the solicitor for the receiving party — generally within a time limit of three months from the making of the costs order[39] — to compile a "notice of commencement" and a bill of costs[40] and

---

[34] CPRr 44.2(2)

[35] CPR r 44.2(3)

[36] CPR r 36.21. As to Part 36 offers and payments generally see below, para. 12-028.

[37] *The White Book, Autumn 2001* Vol 1, p 803 (but see *Reid Minty v. Taylor*, n. 38 below). Indemnity costs can be awarded as a sanction for failure to comply with rules, practice directions or court orders: *Biguzzi v. Rank Leisure Plc*, [1999] 1 W.L.R. 1926, C.A.; *Petrotrade Inc. v. Texaco Ltd.* [2001] C.P. Rep. 29, C.A including, apparently, a refusal by the parties to adopt the court's suggestion that "alternative dispute resolution" ("ADR") be attempted: *Dyson and another v. Leeds City Council (No. 1)*, [2000] C.P. Rep. 42, C.A. General guidance on the circumstances in which indemnity costs might be ordered in the past was contained in *Cepheus Shipping Corp. v. Guardian Royal Exchange Assurance* [1995] 1 Ll. Rep. 647; *Munchenbeck & Marshall v. McAlpine* [1995] 44 Con. L.R.; *Morgan Grenfell & Co Limited v. SACE* [2001] EWCA Civ 1932. However, for a much more recent expression of the principles in the explicit context of the CPR, see also *Reid Minty v. Taylor*, n. 38 below.

[38] Bacon, "Costs Update", (2001) 145 Sol. J. 1183, summarising the October 2001 then unreported case of *Reid Minty v. Taylor* [2001] EWCA Civ 1723, 2001 WL 1171953, C.A.

[39] CPR r 47.7. See also *The White Book, Spring 2002*, p. 887.

[40] The content of which is prescribed by PD 43–48 para. 4. See generally on detailed assessment, O'Hare and Browne, *O'Hare and Hill, Civil Litigation, op. cit.*, p 676.

send it to the paying party together with any supporting documents.[41] If the parties are unable to agree the amount of costs, the receiving party will then request a "detailed assessment hearing".[42] The preparation of a bill of costs for detailed assessment is a very skilled and detailed task. Specialists ("costs draftsmen") exist who undertake the drafting of the bill, usually for a commission calculated on the total amount of the bill or for a salary if employed by a large firm of solicitors. This payment is allowable on assessment[43] and so may be recoverable from the losing party.

The costs judge hears the parties and decides any issues in dispute, either allowing the item in the bill to stand or disallowing or reducing it. The total arrived at by this process is the total of "assessed costs" and is the amount which the loser is required to pay. In making these decisions, the costs judge may make reference to standard hourly rates figures agreed by liaison between the courts and local law societies.[44] The costs awarded are, however, if awarded on the standard basis, unlikely to cover all the work the solicitor has undertaken on behalf of the client but a proportion closer to 60 or 70 per cent.

There are some circumstances, other than those set out in C.P.R. r 44.5, in which costs are not awarded to the successful party. One is inherent in the operation of C.P.R. Part 36.[45] Another is that in the various stages of pre-trial procedure the party who is ultimately successful may have failed in an application (for example, to have his or her opponent's case struck out as having "no real prospect of success" under C.P.R. Part 24) and to have been penalised at that time by the award of costs against him or her in respect of that pre-trial hearing. Costs of such hearings will normally be summarily assessed at the time of the hearing and must be paid within 14 days of the hearing.[46] Further, in order to ensure that the client, who often will not have attended the hearing, is aware of the way in which the action is being conducted on his or her behalf, the solicitor must inform the client in writing of the adverse costs order within 7 days of its having been made.[47]

Three other related matters should be mentioned. First, where the successful party is a party to a conditional fee agreement with his or her solicitors (and counsel) the success fee and insurance premium are *prima facie* recoverable from the losing party at the conclusion of the proceed-

---

[41] CPR r 47.6, PD 43–48 para. 32.3. Where the receiving party has the benefit of a conditional fee agreement (see below, para. 11-007), these details will include details of the success fee and insurance premium.

[42] CPR r 47.14, PD 43–48 para. 40.

[43] PD 43–48 para. 45.

[44] Senior Costs Judge Hurst produced a report in November 2001 on "*Benchmark costs*" which is at the date of writing under consideration, setting out proposed bands of allowable costs for different regions of the country by seniority of the lawyer involved. So, for example, the range of rates for solicitors in Nottingham would be £80 p/h to £140 p/h whilst that for the City of London would be £110 p/h to £325 p/h. For a summary see The Litigation Letter, December 2001, Vol 20, No 10 (LLP Professional Publishing).

[45] See below, para. 12-028.

[46] CPR r 44.8

[47] CPR r 44.2, PD 43–48 para. 7.

ings.[48] Secondly, the successful unassisted party in an action where the opponent has Legal Services Commission funding (previously known as "legal aid") may be awarded costs against the Commission where certain statutory conditions are met.[49] Finally, people who conduct their own litigation are entitled to costs in respect of their own time and effort spent preparing and presenting the case.[50]

(b) Costs payable to solicitor (private funding)

The successful party will often receive money in payment of costs from the losing party. However, this will not necessarily cover the costs that the successful party must pay to his or her solicitor. If the matter, as is usual, does not end up in court, the agreed costs may also not cover all expenditure.

11–004

The solicitor is obliged to present a bill within a reasonable time of concluding the work.[51] The client's contractual obligation is to pay the bill presented by the solicitor. Ultimately the solicitor[52] is entitled to sue the client for "proper costs". What costs are proper may ultimately be determined independently by detailed assessment,[53] but this is a highly unusual step for a solicitor to take; the better approach would be a simple debt action, or, in appropriate circumstances, insolvency proceedings against the client.

The concern for the client is whether the solicitor is overcharging. It is difficult for the client to assess whether the costs are appropriate for the service received.[54] A solicitor is obliged to provide information as to costs as soon as instructed by the client under Practice Rule 15[55] and the Solicitors' Costs Information and Client Care Code 1999.[56] The main object of the code is "to make sure that clients are given the information they need to understand what is happening generally and in particular on i) the cost of legal services both at the outset and as the matter progresses; and ii) responsibility for clients' matters".[57] This provides that at the outset the solicitor should give "the best information possible about the likely overall

---

[48] CPR r 44.3A, 44.3B, PD 43–48 para. 9, 10, 14, 19. See also *Callery v. Gray (No. 1)* [2001] E.W.C.A. Civ 1117; [2001] 1 W.L.R. 2112, C.A; *Callery v. Gray (No. 2)* [2001] E.W.C.A. Civ 1246; [2001] 4 All E.R. 1, C.A. and *Sarwar v. Alam* [2001] E.W.C.A. Civ 1401; [2000] 4 All E.R. 541, C.A. However, as we will see, below, para. 11-013, if the unsuccessful party is in receipt of public funding, it is unlikely that any costs will be recoverable from him or her.

[49] Community Legal Service (Cost Protection) Regulations 2000 (S.I. 2000/824p — as amended by Community Legal Service (Cost Protection) (Amendment) Regulations 2001 (S.I. 2001/823) and Community Legal Service (Cost Protection) (Amendment No. 2) Regulations 2001 (S.I. 2000/3812) — reg. 5.

[50] CPR r 48.6, PD 43–48 para. 52

[51] *The Guide to the Professional Conduct of Solicitors*, (1999, 8th ed., Law Society, hereafter *Professional Conduct*), Principle 14.06.

[52] But not normally until the bill has been outstanding for at least a month, *ibid*, Principle 14.09

[53] This procedure is also available to determine a reasonable amount of costs payable by a client to his or her own solicitor as well as between opposing parties. See for example, CPR r 48.8, PD 43–48 para. 54.

[54] This is true for commercial as well as for private clients.

[55] Solicitors Practice Rules 1990, *Professional Conduct, op. cit.*, p 9.

[56] *ibid.*, Chapter 13.

[57] *ibid.*, 13.02, para. 1.

costs, including a breakdown between fees, VAT and disbursements,"[58] "explain clearly ... the time likely to be spent in dealing with a matter, if time spent is a factor in the calculation of the fees",[59] how the fees are calculated,[60] discuss how charges may be met and consider whether insurance might cover costs as well as "whether the likely outcome ... will justify the expense or risk involved, including, if relevant, the risk of having to bear an opponent's costs."[61] When confirming the client's instructions and at intervals during the pre-trial process, the solicitor should confirm in writing "all information required to be given by the code including all decisions relating to costs and the arrangement for updating costs information."[62] Where the client is paying privately, the solicitor should explain that the client may set an upper limit on the firm's costs, either provide a realistic estimate[63] or range of possible costs or explain why it is not possible to give a realistic forecast, and tell the client how much the costs are at regular intervals (at least every six months). If the privately paying client is receiving advice in a contentious matter, the solicitor must also explain to that client that he or she will be responsible for the solicitor's costs whatever the outcome of the litigation may be, that he or she may well have to pay the other side' costs if he or she loses, that if he or she wins, the costs from the loser may well not cover all his or her costs, and that if the opponent is publicly funded[64] costs may not be recoverable even if he or she wins.[65] Where the client is publicly funded he or she must be informed of the effect of the statutory charge; that if he or she loses there may still be a contribution to the winner's costs despite the public funding; that if he or she wins he or she may not get an order for full costs (and in any case the costs may not be paid) and of their obligation to pay any assessed contribution.

11–005   Although many firms will have standard letters and internal systems intended to ensure that the code is followed, it is a fact that the Code was reissued in 1999 in a more precise and directive format than its predecessor in an attempt to reduce problems with clients. If solicitors always complied with the Code, many of the problems with clients would disappear. Prior to the introduction of the 1999 code, the Legal Services Ombudsman stated that "full compliance with the written professional standard is ... an absolutely essential safeguard for clients, and very much in the interests of

---

[58] *ibid.*, 13.02, para. 4(a).

[59] *ibid.*, 13.02, para. 4(b).

[60] The options include a fixed fee for the job, an hourly rate plus mark up, a percentage of the value of the transaction and a conditional fee agreement with or without success fee.

[61] *ibid.*, 13.02, para. 4(k).

[62] *ibid.*, 13.02, para. l(d) (i).

[63] The proliferation of computerised case management and budgeting programs mean that, at least in straightforward cases, reasoned estimates can be given.

[64] Expressed as "legally aided" but now replaced by the Community Legal Service Fund, see below, para. 11–008 *et seq.*.

[65] Access to Justice Act 1999, s 11(1) "Except in prescribed circumstances, costs ordered against an individual in relation to any proceedings or part of proceedings funded for him shall not exceed the amount (if any) which is a reasonable one for him to pay having regard to all the circumstances ... " See also Community Legal Service (Cost Protection) Regulations 2000 (S.I. 2000/824), as amended by Community Legal Service (Cost Protection) (Amendment) Regulations 2001 (S.I. 2001/823) and Community Legal Service (Cost Protection) (Amendment No. 2) Regulations 2001 (S.I. 2001/3812).

solicitors themselves if they are to avoid complaints about costs."[66] The National Association of Citizens' Advice Bureaux had noted in 1995 that complaints about costs were a major area of CAB work and that there was poor compliance with the previous standard.[67] Research sponsored by the National Consumer Council then concluded that "a significant minority [of clients] do not always receive the kind of information on costs required by the ... standards."[68]

Has the 1999 Code made any difference? In 1998, 11 per cent of cases referred to the Legal Services Ombudsman involved a failure to inform about costs.[69] In 1999/2000, 4 per cent of cases involved "excessive costs" and 3% inadequate costs information.[70] The 2000/2001 percentages were identical to those of the previous year[71] although the number of investigations by the Ombudsman against solicitors was rising.[72] In August 2001, however, the Consumers' Association, in a survey of 340 clients who

---

[66] *Fourth Annual Report of the Legal Services Ombudsman* 1994 (H.C. 459, 1995) para. 3.12
[67] NACAB, *Barriers to Justice* (1995), paras 3.6–3.15. See also J. Jenkins and V. Lewis, *Client perceptions — Existing and potential clients: experiences and perceptions of using a solicitor for personal matters* (1995).
[68] N. Harris, *Solicitors and Client Care* (1994), p. 22.
[69] *"Modernising Justice" ... Modernising regulation?* (1998/1999) Annual Report of the Legal Services Ombudsman, p. 29.
[70] *Demanding Progress*, (1999/2000) Annual Report of the Legal Services Ombudsman, p. 36.
[71] *Reflecting Progress*, (2000/2001) Annual Report of the Legal Services Ombudsman, p. 37.
[72] The Legal Services Ombudsman's reports over the three years show investigations against solicitors as follows:

1998/99	1999/2000	2000/2001
1466	1337	1507

This should, however, be compared with the number of complaints to the Law Society or Office for the Supervision of Solicitors over the same periods:

1998/99	1999/2000	2000/2001
30,988	17,177	16,085

A further feature of the Ombudsman's concerns over this period, reflected in the titles of the reports, was the degree of failure and backlog in the complaints-handling bodies of the various professions: the OSS, in particular. Government concern was indicated by the provision in Access to Justice Act 1999, ss.5 1 and 52 giving the Lord Chancellor power to appoint a Legal Services Complaints Commissioner who would regulate and if necessary, fine, the professional bodies, see "LCD poised to act on complaints régime", (1999) 96(12) L.S.G., 1.

In any event, a Legal Services Consultation Panel, a body with a majority of lay members, was established on January 1, 2000 to advise the Lord Chancellor on issues arising from regulation of the legal sector. The Law Society's current proposals for improvement of its self-regulation appear in its document *Blueprint for Change* published on March 23, 2001 and to be found on the Law Society's website. For further discussion of complaints against the legal profession and the activities of the Office for the Supervision of Solicitors, see The Customer Management Consultancy Ltd, *Satisfaction in a Super-Escalated Complaint Environment*, (report to the Legal Services Ombudsman); Abraham, "Care for Clients", (1999) 96(38) L.S.G. 24; Davies, "Can the Office for the Supervision of Solicitors expect a happy birthday? — short review of the first three years", (1999) 15(3) P.N. 173–184; Allen and Clarke, "Keeping the Client Happy", (2000) 97(16) L.S.G. 26–28, 30–33; Seneviratne, "Consumer Complaints and the legal profession: making self regulation work?", (2000) 7(1) I.J.L.P.,39–58.

had felt dissatisfied with the service provided by their solicitors found that the majority still complained of inadequate information about costs.[73]

Solicitors "must not take unfair advantage of the client by overcharging for work done or to be done".[74] So, if a solicitor deliberately overcharges, disciplinary action would follow.[75] If a client believes that he or she has been overcharged, the matter can be dealt with by the Office for the Supervision of Solicitors ("OSS"), which will investigate, allowing both solicitor and client to comment, using the following criteria (which are applicable to any complaints submitted to the OSS whether or not about overcharging):

> The correct standard of proof to apply is the flexible civil standard taking account of the gravity of the allegations, the potential consequences and the context of the particular case. Serious allegations against solicitors involving elements such as alleged dishonesty, or deceit, or matters of a similar nature must be proved to a level which admits no reasonable doubt, whilst less serious allegations need to be proved on the balance of probabilities ... ."[76]

The disciplinary action to follow depends on the outcome of the OSS' decision.[77]

Assessing the propriety of costs will depend on whether they relate to a contentious matter, which term applies only once a claim has begun.[78] If a client objects to the bill submitted by the solicitor in such a matter an application may be made to the High Court for detailed assessment of the bill.[79] If granted,[80] assessment is carried out on the "indemnity basis" but it is presumed that the costs a) have been reasonably incurred, if they were incurred with the express or implied approval of the client; b) have been reasonable in amount, if their amount was expressly or impliedly approved by the client; c) have been unreasonably incurred, if they are of an unusual nature or amount and the solicitor failed to inform the client that, as a result, they might be irrecoverable from the opponent.[81] It should be noted that, unless the order for assessment was made on the application of the solicitor and the client failed to attend or a court order provided otherwise, then, if the bill is reduced by one-fifth or more on assessment, the solicitor

---

[73] J. Farrar, "Arrogant, incompetent, negligent and unprofessional ... "Which?, August 2001, p. 8. For the Law Society's position on these issues, see *Law Society Addresses ... "*, *Which?* "*Concerns*, Law Society Press Release August 2, 2001 and the more wide-ranging *Blueprint for Change* published on March 23, 2001. Both documents can be found on the Law Society's website.

[74] *Professional Conduct, op. cit.*, Principle 14.12.

[75] See S. Fennell, "The quality of solicitors' services" (1992) 8 P.N. 115 at p. 121. See also more recent comment listed at n. 72 above.

[76] Law Society Gazette, March 18, 1998, quoted in *Professional Conduct, op cit.*, at 30.02.

[77] As to disciplinary action against solicitors, see above para. 3-038

[78] The definition is to be found in the Solicitors' Act 1974, s. 87 and see O'Hare and Browne, *O'Hare and Hill, Civil Litigation* (10th ed. Sweet and Maxwell), p. 24.

[79] Solicitors' Act 1974, s.70. The application will be brought using the CPR Part 8 procedure under CPR rr. 48.8 and 48.9 and PD 43–48, sections 55 (where there is a conditional fee agreement) and 56 (generally).

[80] An order must be granted if the request is made within one calendar month of delivery of the bill, otherwise the court has a discretion: Solicitors' Act 1974, s. 70, and see O'Hare and Browne, *O'Hare and Hill, Civil Litigation, op. cit.*, p. 697 *et seq.*

[81] CPR 4. 48.8 and see O'Hare and Browne, *O'Hare and Hill, Civil Litigation, op. cit*, p. 697.

will pay the costs of the assessment, otherwise the client will do so.[82]

As we have seen, where the business is contentious, the client is assisted in paying what is owed to the solicitor if he or she wins, since costs are then likely to be obtained from the losing party.

In non-contentious civil matters, the client may have the fees reviewed by the Law Society, a jurisdiction delegated to the Office for the Supervision of Solicitors, by seeking a remuneration certificate provided the bill does not exceed £50,000.[83] Normally, the client must pay the disbursements, VAT and 50 per cent of the costs sought by the solicitor prior to seeking the certificate.[84] The client may then be charged such sum as is fair and reasonable "to both solicitor and entitled person" having regard to all the circumstances of the case and, *inter alia*, its complexity, the skill and responsibility involved, the time spent, number and importance of documents prepared or perused, the place where the business was conducted (*e.g.* abroad or at unconventional times), the property involved, the importance of the matter to the client and any express prior approval by the client to the undertaking of the work or the amount of the costs.[85] Fennell has identified the advantages of this system as being that it is free and the client is not personally involved. The disadvantages are that the client may be unaware of the system because the solicitor is only obliged to inform the client of a right to a certificate before bringing proceedings to recover fees or before charging interest, and not when the bill is delivered;[86] (although in practice many solicitors' firms have this information pre-printed on their invoices in any event); the OSS may not be perceived as sufficiently impartial;[87] and the courts have been prepared to uphold a compromise on a bill prior to the client being advised of his or her rights and so the client loses the right to a certificate, whereupon the client would have to challenge the compromise in court.[88] If still unsatisfied, the client has the right to apply to the High Court for an order to have the bill assessed.[89] If granted, the costs judge assesses the costs on the same basis contentious case. Fennell points out that this process will involve the client paying the costs of assessment unless the bill is reduced by at least one-fifth;[90] it is a formal, litigious procedure; and the client may not have been informed of this right on delivery of the bill but only prior to the solicitor suing for fees.

---

[82] Solicitors' Act 1974, ss. 7(9) and (10).
[83] Solicitors' Remuneration Order 1994 (S.I. 1994/2616), art. 4(1). A client may not seek a remuneration certificate after the expiry of one month from the date on which the client was given information under Art. 8, see below, after a bill has been delivered and paid, or after a court order for assessment of costs, *ibid.*, Art.9. See also *Professional Conduct, op. cit.*, Principle 14.08 and Chap. 30.
[84] *ibid.*, Art. 11(1).
[85] *ibid.*, Art. 3.
[86] *ibid.*, Art. 3(2).
[87] Fennell was writing about the Law Society but the perception of impartiality point was still valid according to the National Consumer Council, when the jurisdiction was transferred to the Solicitors' Complaints Bureau, *The Solicitors' Complaints Bureau* (1994). The Solicitors' Complaints Bureau has, in turn, been replaced by the Office for the Supervision of Solicitors.
[88] Fennell (1992), p. 122.
[89] Solicitors Act 1974, s.70.
[90] Solicitors' (Non-Contentious Business) Remuneration Order 1994, art. 5(1): if the costs judge allows less than half of the sum originally charged to the client, this will be reported to the Law Society.

(c) Costs payable to solicitor (insurance)

11–006   It is possible that a litigant may have legal expenses insurance which is "payment of an annual premium to carry cover, in given categories of cases, for a claimant's[91] legal costs (including any costs awarded against him [*sic*]) up to a limit of indemnity."[92] A policy is either personal or commercial and is either a "stand-alone" policy or an "add-on policy" (that is added on to household or motor insurance).[93] Its take-up is comparatively small in the stand-alone format, "[a]lthough free-standing policies have not proved successful, legal expenses insurance, in the form of cheap but limited add-on policies to car or house insurance is probably more widespread in this country than generally believed."[94] Very many individuals, however, remain simply unaware that they have such cover in its "add-on" format.[95]

A second form of insurance is "after the event insurance", whereby a party to litigation or potential litigation may buy the insurance *after* the cause of action has arisen. The risk covered is, therefore, not, as in legal expenses insurance, the risk of litigation occurring, but the risk of losing litigation that it is known is likely to occur or that has already been instigated. Whilst it is by no means confined to this area, the most common usage of after-the-event policies is in conjunction with conditional fee agreements.[96] The premium paid for an after the event policy, as opposed to that for a before the event policy, is potentially recoverable from a losing opponent in litigation.[97]

(d) Costs payable to solicitor (conditional fee agreements)[98]

11–007   The conditional fee agreement ("CFA"), often, and somewhat misleadingly

---

[91]   Here used in the technical sense of a person claiming under a policy: potential defendants may have and use legal expenses insurance.

[92]   Lord Chancellor's Department, "Review of the Financial Conditions for Legal Aid: Eligibility for Civil Legal Aid; A Consultation Paper" (1991) quoted in N. Rickman and A. Gray, "The Role of Legal Expenses Insurance in Securing Access to the Market for Legal Services" in Zuckerman and Cranston (1995), *op. cit.*, p. 305

[93]   V. Prais, "Legal Expenses Insurance" in Zuckerman and Cranston (1995), p. 434. See also Prais, "A question of insurance", (1999) 149 N.L.J. p. 1372; Greer, "Legal Expenses Insurance — have they really got you covered?", (1999) 149 N.L.J. p 781, Samuels, "Legal Expenses or Litigation Insurance", (1998) 17 C.J.Q., 16.

[94]   Middleton Report, *op. cit.*, para. 5.51.further quoting an expenditure on premiums in 1995 in the region of £25 million.

[95]   For an indication of the extent to which the advising solicitor must ask the client to search for previously unsuspected insurance cover, see *Sarwar v. Alam* [2001] E.W.C.A. Civ 1401; [2000] 4 All E.R. 541, C.A., where the claimant, a car passenger, was, unknown to him, covered by the insurance policy of the *defendant* driver. See also, Allen, "After-the event insurance failure highlighted", (2000) 97(30), L.S.G. 4 and Marshall, "Making a Good Recovery", (2001) 151 N.L.J. 1856. The government has shown a desire to encourage the development of this form of insurance, perhaps through employment packages: *Legal Aid — Targeting Need* (Cm. 2854, 1995), paras 3.36–3.37.

[96]   For comment on this type of insurance, see Harrison, "After the event insurance: a dose of reality", (2001) 151 N.L.J. 1373.

[97]   Access to Justice Act 1999, s. 29; CPR rr. 43.2(ii) and (m); PD 43–48 para. 11.10.

[98]   For some background and evaluative information, see KPMG, *Conditional Fees — a Business Case* (1998, report to the Lord Chancellor's Department); *Access to Justice with Conditional Fees*, (1998, Lord Chancellor's Department consultation paper); *Conditional Fees — Sharing the risk of Litigation* (September 1999, Lord Chancellor's Department consultation paper); NACABx, *Conditional Fees — Sharing the risk of Litigation: A response by the CAB service* (2001).

called a "no win: no fee" agreement, was developed in the context of a proposed reduction in public funding for civil litigation.[99]

The common law indemnity principle prescribed that a losing party could not be asked to pay to the successful party any *more* than the successful party was obliged to pay to his or her own solicitor. In a "no win: no fee agreement" the client and solicitor have, in effect agreed that, the client having been successful, the amount the client will pay to the solicitor in respect of the solicitor's work on the case is nought. Consequently, it was thought, the losing party could not be compelled to pay any of the successful party's costs at all.[1] At one time, such agreements amounted to the common law offence of champerty,[2] but from the time of the Criminal Law Act 1967, s.13 until 1995, such agreements were not an offence but were unenforceable contracts and were contrary to the professional rules of conduct.[3]

Consequently, the CFA is a creature of statute: Courts and Legal Services Act 1990, s. 58. Initially, the availability of conditional fee agreements was confined to personal injury, insolvency and human rights cases.[4] Subsequently virtually all civil proceedings were brought into the ambit of the scheme.[5]

The detail of the CFA is a complex subject beyond the scope of this book.[6] Put at its simplest, the solicitor[7] and client agree that if the client loses the case — and in a complex case they may have to define in advance what "win" or "lose" actually mean — the client will not pay any costs to

---

[99] See below, para. 11-008 See also the Middleton Report, *op. cit.*

[1] The position was further complicated by a number of cases in which unconventional charging arrangements that apparently contravened the indemnity principle and/or were void for champerty (see n. 2 below) were considered and sometimes permitted: *Hodgson v. Imperial Tobacco Ltd (No. 1)*, [1998] 1 W.L.R. 1056, C.A.; *Thai Trading Co. v. Taylor* [1998] Q.B. 781, C.A.; *Bevan Ashford v. Geoff Yeandle (Contractors) Ltd* [1999] Ch. 239, Ch. D.; *Hughes v. Kingston-upon-Hull City Council*, [1999] Q.B. 1193, Q.B.D.; *Awwad v. Geraghty & Co.*, [2001] Q.B. 570, C.A. The effect of *Thai Trading* (where a solicitor acting in litigation for his wife agreed to restrict his own charges to anything recovered from the opponent) in particular can now be achieved by a "conditional fee agreement without a success fee" under statute. For a historical review, see Peysner, "A revolution by degrees: from costs to financing and the end of the indemnity principle", [2001] Web J.C.L.I., 1.

[2] See J.W.C. Turner, *Kenny's Outlines of Criminal Law* (18th ed., 1962), para. 475.

[3] See, for example, Solicitors' Practice Rules 1990, r. 8 (as amended in 1999): "A solicitor who is retained or employed to prosecute or defend any action, suit or other contentious proceeding shall not enter into any arrangement to receive a contingency fee in respect of that proceeding, save one permitted under statute or by common law."

[4] The Conditional Fee Agreements Regulations 1995, (S. I. 1995/1675).

[5] The exceptions being family proceedings and criminal proceedings other than claims under Environmental Protection Act 1990, s. 82. The development can be seen in the Conditional Fee Agreements Order (S. I. 1998/1860) and The Conditional Fee Agreements Order 2000 (S. I. 2000/823) which replaced it. For more general guidance on the procedure to be adopted when entering into a conditional fee agreement, see The Conditional Fee Agreements Regulations 2000 (S.I. 2000/692); The Collective Conditional Fee Agreements Regulations 2000 (S.I. 2000/2988); *Professional Conduct, op. cit.*, Chap. 14; Bar Council: Conditional Fee Guidance reproduced in the White Book, *op. cit.*, Vol. 2, P. 1565; CPR rr 44.3B, 44.15,44.16.

[6] For a detailed discussion of the operation of the conditional fee agreement, see Underwood, *No Win, No Fee, No Worries* (2001, EMIS Professional Publishing) and *Conditional Fees* (ed. Bawdon, Napier and Wignall) (2001, Law Society).

[7] If a barrister is also engaged in the case, he or she may enter into a separate CFA (sometimes called a "conditional retainer agreement" or "CRA") with the client in respect of his or her fees.

the solicitor.[8] As we have seen from the time of the Criminal Law Act 1967, s. 13, until 1995, such agreements were not an offence but were unenforceable contracts and were contrary to the professional rules of conduct.[9]

The arguments in favour of a conditional fee system include: it allows litigation which would not otherwise be brought; the lawyers involved act more conscientiously on behalf of their client and it is a simpler method of payment.[10] The arguments against such systems include: it is an open invitation to unprofessional conduct;[11] lawyers will refuse to take on weaker cases; there is increased pressure to win and so accept an early settlement (when costs are relatively low) rather than run the risk, at heavier cost, of going to trial.[12]

It is important to note, however that disbursements such as court fees, expert's fees and counsel's fees may still be payable by the client to his or her own solicitor if the client loses, depending on the terms of the CFA.[13] In addition, as a losing party, the client will normally expect to have to pay the opponent's costs, but this risk is frequently — and invariably in personal injury cases — provided for by an after the event insurance policy taken out

---

[8] The conditional fee agreement should not be confused with the "contingency fee", common in the USA but (at present) illegal in litigation in England: Solicitors Practice Rules 1990, rule 8. In a contingency fee, a successful lawyer becomes entitled to a percentage of the client's damages awarded at trial, irrespective of the amount of work done by the lawyer on the case. In principle, this is less likely to result in under-compensation of the client as the damages in the USA are likely to be awarded by a jury and often therefore are considerably larger than equivalent awards in England (although frequently reduced on appeal). For an idea of the likely difference in the amount of damages considered appropriate by a jury and the amount considered appropriate by a judge sitting alone, one might compare English personal injury awards with English libel awards.

An extreme and dramatic example of the effect of a contingency fee on U.S. lawyers undertaking a large case (bearing the costs of investigation and the pre-trial procedures themselves in anticipation of a substantial award of damages) is provided in J. Harr, *A Civil Action*, (1995), Arrow Books Limited and the Paramount Pictures feature film of the same title.

For further discussion of the distinction, see Peysner, "What's wrong with contingency fees?" (2001) 10(1) Nott. L.J. 22 and Walters, "Contingency fee arrangements at common law", (2000) 116 L.Q.R. 2000, 371. Note, however, that contingency fees are not illegal where no court proceedings are brought — they are frequently used as a means of funding by claims management companies and claims assessors who seek to negotiate a settlement without recourse to the courts. See further the report of the Blackwell Committee, *The investigation of non-legally qualified claims assessors and employment advisers who act for reward* (February 2000), p. 105.

[9] As strict contingency fees remain in the context of litigation: Solicitors' Practice Rules 1990 (as amended), rule 8.

[10] R.C.L.S. Report, p. 176.

[11] This is most graphically illustrated by the "ambulance-chasing" lawyers, see Zander (1989), pp. 55–56. There is already concern that the CFA system may not always be operated by lawyers for the benefit of clients: Rozenberg, "Clients are Losers in 'no win, no fee' cases", *Daily Telegraph*, January 29, 2001, p. 8; Verkaik, "Solicitors 'using legal reforms to overcharge'", *The Independent*, May 21, 2001, p. 5.; Bawdon, "Conditional Fee Agreements", (2001) 151 N.L.J. 156

[12] For discussion prior to Courts and Legal Services Act 1990, s. 58, see R.C.L.S. Report, at p. 77; the majority in *Wallersteiner v. Moir (No. 2)* [1975] Q.B. 373 (Lord Denning M.R., in the minority, put in a strong plea for the contingency fee in a particular type of company law action brought by a shareholder); M. Zander, *Legal Services for the Community* (1978), p. 218; R. White, "Contingent Fee: A Supplement to Legal Aid?" (1978) 41 M.I.R. 286; *Civil Justice Review* (1989), para.389.

[13] In some cases, whilst these sums remain strictly payable, the firm of solicitors may elect to write them off.

at the same time as the CFA.

In the absence of such a policy, the client will have to pay the opponent's costs out of his or her own funds: the principal reason why "no win: no fee" is a misnomer.

If the client wins the case, however, the client agrees to pay not only the solicitor's normal rate, but normally also a "success fee" calculated as a percentage of those normal fees,[14] Originally this success fee was deducted from damages, potentially causing under-compensation of the client. It also made the CFA less attractive to defendants who, in the absence of a counterclaim, did not expect to receive damages and would have to pay any success fee out of their own funds. Consequently, Access to Justice Act 1999, s. 29 amended Courts and Legal Services Act 1990, s. 58 to allow both the success fee[15] and the insurance premium to be recoverable from the losing party.[16] That this amendment was not *ultra vires* was confirmed by the Court of Appeal in *Callery v. Gray (No. 1)*.[17]

The agreement, which must be in writing,[18] signed by client and lawyer,[19] must state the particular proceedings or parts of them to which it relates; the circumstances in which the lawyer's fees and expenses or part of them are payable; what payment, if any, is due upon partial failure of those circumstances to occur, irrespective of those circumstances occurring, and upon termination of the agreement; the amounts payable and whether the amounts are limited by reference to the damages recovered on behalf of the client; where there is a success fee, the reason for setting it at a particular

---

[14] The main distinction in concept, therefore, between a conditional fee agreement with a success fee and a U.S-style contingency fee, is that the amount paid by the winning client under a CFA remains calculated on a basis related to the amount of work done by the lawyer on the case. The percentage cannot exceed 100%: Courts and Legal Services Act 1990, s. 58(4)(c); Conditional Fee Agreements Order 2000 (S.I. 2000/823), para. 4. A further restriction that in no circumstances should the success fee amount to more than 25% of the damages was originally imposed voluntarily) and, in the House of Lords, [2002] UKHL 28, [2002] 1 W.L.R. 2000 by the Law Society. It is envisaged that the amount of the success fee represents the risk of losing — a strong case should have a lower success fee than a weak case. As a guide, an appropriate percentage for a claimant in a straightforward road accident case is apparently 20% *Callery v. Gray (No. 1)* [2001] E.W.C.A. Civ 1117; [2001] 1 W.L.R. 2112 C.A. The firm of solicitors, as a whole, should of course seek to ensure that the number of cases lost is no greater than the number of cases won to ensure that the firm continues to operate at a profit. Barristers can also enter into CFAs with their clients but will have different considerations in doing so, see Wignall, "CFAs and the Bar", (2001) 151 N.LJ. 355.

[15] Or at least that part it representing the risk of losing the case as opposed to recompensing the solicitor for delayed payment: CPR r 44.3B (l)(a)

[16] CPR rr 43. 2, 44.3A, 44.3B. The existence of the CFA (but not the amount of the success fee) is notified to the opponent as early as possible in the proceedings and ideally as part of the pre-action protocol: CPR r 44.15. The court can reduce the success fee recoverable on assessment of costs if its amount is unreasonable: PD 43–48 para. 11.8.

[17] See also *Callery v. Gray (No. 2)* [2001] E.W.C.A. Civ. 1246; [2001] 4 All E.R. 1, C.A. approved by the House of Lords, [2002] UKHL 28, [2002] 1 W.L.R. 2000 dealing specifically with the recoverability of an after the event insurance premium of £350. The criteria on the basis of which the court will decide whether the premium is recoverable are set out in PD 43–48 para. 11.10.

[18] See, for example, the Law Society model conditional fee agreement for personal injury cases reproduced in the *White Book, op. cit.*, Vol 2, p. 1658 and the Chancery Bar Association's Terms of Engagement for use where counsel is to be retained on a conditional fee basis, *ibid.*, p 1568.

[19] Conditional Fee Agreements Regulations 2000 (S.I. 2000/692, as amended by the Collective Conditional Fee Agreement Regulations 2000, S.I. 2000/2988), Art. 5.

percentage; and that certain matters have been drawn to the client's attention (whether the client might be entitled to public funding, the circumstances in which the client will have to pay the solicitor's fees and expenses, when the client might be liable to pay the other side's costs and when assessment of the lawyer's fees and expenses might be sought).[20]

Now that the insurance premium and success fee are potentially recoverable from a losing opponent, it is essential that the opponent is aware of the additional risk, especially as the maximum success fee is a 100 per cent uplift on the solicitor's normal fees. Consequently, specified information about the CFA must be notified to the opponent[21] although this does not include the amount of the success fee or how it is to be calculated?[22]

(e) Costs payable to solicitor (public funding)

(i) Development of the current regime of public funding of civil litigation

11–008   The modern Legal Services Commission scheme for civil cases — the Community Legal Service Fund — which still provides financial assistance (subject to eligibility) in connection with some types of proceedings in most of our civil courts, has come a long way since 1495 when statute provided for poor people, at the discretion of the Lord Chancellor, to sue without payment to the Crown, and to have lawyers assigned to them without fee.[23] more formal Poor Persons Procedure was established in 1914[24] and was put under the control of the Law Society in 1925.[25] The Law Society provided the necessary administrative structure. Further, its involvement made more likely the necessary free provision by solicitors of their services. Government money was only made available to meet the costs of the administrative work involved.

The Poor Persons Procedure, dependent upon the charity of the legal profession,[26] could not cope with the increasing pressure of work in the 1930s and was supplemented in 1942 by a Services Divorce Department. This department, consisting of salaried solicitors employed by the Law Society with government funds, dealt with the matrimonial problems occasioned by the Second World War. It must have been in the minds of the

---

[20]   *ibid.*, arts 2 and 3 and Law Society Guidance on conditional fee agreements, *Professional Conduct, op. cit.*, p 303.

[21]   CPR r. 44.15; PD 43–48, section 19. Where the CFA is entered into prior to the issue of proceedings, this notification should take place during the "pre-action protocol" period: PD Protocols, para. 4A.

[22]   Some drawbacks to the scheme were pointed out at the outset in J. Rozenberg, *The Search for Justice* (1994), p. 187.

[23]   An Act to admit such persons as are poor to sue *in forma pauperis*.

[24]   Described as " ... the first regular scheme for legal aid in the Supreme Court": H. Kirk, *Portrait of a Profession* (1976), p. 164.

[25]   After it had fallen into complete chaos and on the recommendation of a committee under Mr Justice P.O. Lawrence (The Poor Persons' Rules Committee (Cmd.2358, 1925).

[26]   Given the modern restrictions in the availability of public funding, one might compare the current popularity of pro bono work amongst solicitors: many high street firms will offer at least a "first free interview" and an increasing number of larger and City firms have specific *pro bono* programmes. For further information see, for example, the following websites: Free Representation Unit, *http://www.fru.org.uk*; the Bar Pro Bono Unit, *http://www.barprobono.org.uk*: the Solicitors' Pro Bono Group, *http://www.probonogroup.org.uk*

members of the Rushcliffe Committee as they took evidence. The Committee was set up, with Lord Rushcliffe in the chair, in 1944, to review the provision of professional help for those who were unable to afford it, in both civil and criminal matters. The Committee's report[27] provided the basis upon which the Law Society was invited by the Lord Chancellor to undertake the task of organising a legal aid scheme, which resulted in the Legal Aid and Advice Act 1949 and the regulations made thereunder. The legislation, later amended by the Legal Aid Act 1974, relied heavily upon the decisions of the Rushcliffe Committee. Subsequently, the first major concern perceived with the system of legal aid was that confusions and inefficiency were created by too many people having the ability to decide whether or not to grant help.[28] Consequently, the administration of the scheme was removed from the Law Society and placed in the hands of the Legal Aid Board by the Legal Aid Act 1988.

So matters remained until the 1990s when both Conservative and Labour administrations had proposals to reduce the Legal Aid budget. In parallel with the Woolf Inquiry, Sir Peter Middleton reviewed both public funding.[29] The reduction in availability of public funding eventually apparent in the Access to Justice Act 1999, implemented for civil cases in April 2000 was consciously effected in parallel with the development and expansion of the conditional fee agreement. So, for example, whilst personal injury cases are, in the main, now exempt from public funding, they are precisely the type of case in which the conditional fee agreement was initially developed and has proved most popular.

The Legal Services Commission ("LSC"),[30] created by Access to Justice Act 1999, ss. 1–3 oversees both the Community Legal Service ("CLS"),[31] respect of civil proceedings and the Criminal Defence Service ("CDS") in respect of criminal proceedings. Opinions appear to differ as to the precise terminology that should replace "legal aid" and "legally aided" but we will adopt the terminology used in the C.P.R. — "LSC funding".[32]

Whilst, from April 2001, only "suppliers" with a specific contract with the LSC are permitted to deal with publicly funded disputes,[33] it should be

---

[27] *Report of the Committee on Legal Aid and Advice* (Cmd. 6641, 1945). This report also contains a good review of the then existing facilities for legal aid and advice.

[28] See *Legal Aid Efficiency Scrutiny* (Lord Chancellor's Department, 1986), followed by the White Paper, *Legal Aid in England and Wales: A New Framework* (Cm. 118, 1987).

[29] *Review of Civil Justice and Legal Aid* (the Middleton Report), September 1997. For other material demonstrating policy in the context of civil public funding, see the Lord Chancellor's Department May 1999 consultation paper *The Community Legal Service* and its 2001 report *Social Exclusion*.

[30] Much information about the LSC can be obtained from its website: *http://www.legalservices.gov.uk*. The Commission itself is a twelve-person committee. Below the Commission itself is a head office in London and regional offices throughout England and Wales, liaison being provided by Regional Legal Services Committees in each region.

[31] The CLS has its own website "Just Ask!", specifically designed for the lay enquirer: *http://www.justask.org.uk*. Leaflets designed to assist the public are also available on the LSC website.

[32] CPR r. 43.2(l)(i). The LSC itself appears to prefer the term "CLS funding" in the specific context of civil proceedings.

[33] Access to Justice Act 1999, s. 6(3) and Community Legal Service (Funding) Order 2000 (S. I. 2000/627), as amended by the Community Legal Service (Funding) (Amendment) Order 2000 (S. I. 2000/1541), the Community Legal Service (Funding) (Amendment) Order 2001 (S. I. 2001/831) and the Community Legal Service (Funding) (Amendment No. 2) Order 2001 (S. I. 2000/2996). This extends the earlier system of Legal Aid franchising under which

borne in mind that the modern system of funding is not intended to be confined to solicitors and barristers. The CLS is, by statute, committed to "promoting the availability of and "securing (within the resources made available, and priorities set ...) ... that individuals have access to services that effectively meet their needs."[34] These services are defined[35] to include "general information about the law" and "advice". Consequently the intention is to develop "Community Legal Service Partnerships" incorporating both lawyers and such advice providers as CABx and Law Centres.[36]

Contracts to "suppliers" may, therefore, be limited to 1) "information" in respect of websites or non-specific information centres[37]; 2) "general help" for more specialist advice and support organisations which may conduct a certain amount of casework such as housing or immigration advice centres or 3) "specialist help" which will include solicitors dealing with the kind of matter that fell within the remit of the old Legal Aid Board. Organisations successfully obtaining contracts will, it is intended, be identifiable by a CLS "Quality Mark".[38]

(ii) The scope of the scheme in respect of civil litigation

11–009   Public funding for the conduct of litigation (*i.e.* "specialist help") is not available[39] in the following categories of case: negligence cases involving death or personal injury[40] (other than clinical negligence cases) or involving damage to property; boundary disputes, trusts, defamation and malicious falsehood; matters of company or partnership law or matters arising out of a business carried on by the applicant.[41] In addition, public funding is not

firms which satisfied the Legal Aid Board's quality assurance criteria had certain powers of the Legal Aid Board devolved to them. The "General Civil Contract" can be found on the LSC website. The scope and type of work permitted by a contract is divided into a number of different categories so that, for example a firm may only have a contract to deal with housing and immigration but not family or clinical negligence work. For a review of the testing of the new procedures, see Moorhead, *Pioneers in Practice, The Community Legal Service Pioneer Project Research Report* (2000).

[34] Access to Justice Act 1999, s. 4(1).
[35] *ibid.*, s. 4(2)
[36] These groupings are supported by a Partnership Support Fund of £900, 000 in 2001/02: *Legal Services Commission Annual Report 2000/01*, para. 2.43.
[37] According to the *Legal Services Commission Annual Report 2000/01*, para. 2.38 there were, in June 2001, 847 information points in existence under this scheme and organisations that had shown interest in participating included a chain of supermarkets.
[38] By April 2001, over 10,000 organisations had obtained or were in the process of obtaining a Quality Mark (*Legal Services Commission Annual Report 2000/01*).
[39] Subject to certain exceptions contained in *Lord Chancellor's Direction: Scope of the Community Legal Service Fund, Exceptions to the Exclusions*, (Apriil 2, 2001), available on the Lord Chancellor's Department website.
[40] Some very high value (where costs are likely to exceed £25,000) personal injury claims may, as an exception, still be eligible for funding. In 2000/2001 153 investigative help certificates and 2,040 full representation certificates were issued in personal injury cases (*Legal Services Commission Annual Report 2000/01*, p. 21). The general public remains, apparently, largely unaware that public funding has been removed in principle from personal injury claims: Eagelsham, "Confusion over legal aid for injury claims", *Financial Times* August 11, 2001, 4.
[41] Access to Justice Act 1999, s.6(6) and Sched. 2, as amended by the Community Legal Service (Scope) Regulations 2000 (S.I. 2000/822). Funding is not normally available in cases involving foreign law, including that of Scotland and Northern Ireland; Access to Justice Act 1999, s. 19.

available for conveyancing or will-making.[42] The Lord Chancellor has, however, a general discretion under Access to Justice Act, s. 6.8(b) to fund individual cases that would otherwise be excluded.[43]

Where funding is available for litigation, it is only available to those who fall within certain financial limits and whose cases satisfy the merits test[44] and other requirements of the CLS Funding Code issued initially in October 1999 under section 8 of the Access to Justice Act 1999.

However, in the kinds of civil dispute where funding is available, a number of different levels of funding are available in mainstream (*i.e.* non-family) cases:

Legal help — This is equivalent to what used to be known as the "green form" or "Claim 10" scheme. The solicitor is allowed to conduct preliminary work only (such as an initial interview or compliance with a pre-action protocol) up to a value of £500[45] where the client is in receipt of some specific benefits (such as income support, income-based job seekers' allowance, *etc.*) or has a monthly disposable income not exceeding £601 and disposable capital not exceeding £3000.[46] As at June 14 2001, 803, 828 new matters were started under this scheme, of which 318,496 were family cases.[47]

Help at court — This is equivalent to what used to be known as "ABWOR" (assistance by way of representation). A solicitor who is present in the court building at the relevant time is allowed to represent a litigant at a particular hearing even though he or she is not more formally instructed by the litigant, up to a value of £500.[48]

Legal representation — this is available in the following courts and tribunals in non-family cases: House of Lords, Court of Appeal, High Court, county court, Employment Appeal Tribunal, Mental Health Review Tribunal,[49] Immigration Adjudicator and Immigration Appeal Tribunal and in some instances in certain tax tribunals.

It may be "full representation" in which case it will cover the full conduct of litigation for a client, including advocacy and settlement negotiations. Alternatively "investigative help" may be provided. This will normally provide support only in investigation of the strength of a claim. In 2000/

---

[42] Subject to certain exceptions authorised by Access to Justice Act 1999, s. 6(8) and currently contained in *Lord Chancellor's Direction: Scope of the Community Legal Service Fund, Exceptions to the Exclusions, op. cit.*

[43] This discretion is apparently frequently used to permit representation at inquests, in particular those concerning deaths in police custody (*Legal Services Commission Annual Report 2000/01*, para. 2.82).

[44] Advice or assistance provided by an advice centre with an LSC contract may, of course, be free and non-means tested: Community Legal Service (Financial) Regulations 2000 (S.I. 2000/516), reg. 3.

[45] Extensions of this limit are possible.

[46] The Community Legal Service (Financial) (Amendment No. 3) Regulations 2001 (S. I. 2001/ 3663) relaxed the eligibility criteria, allowing, according to the Lord Chancellor's Department estimate (press release November 30, 2001) an additional 5 million people to qualify for public funding of their cases from December 3, 2001.

[47] *Legal Services Commission Annual Report 2000/01*, para. 2.59. This excludes a further 58,122 claims under the old "green form" scheme in the transitional period. The system can now be operated electronically as well as by submission of paper forms (*ibid.*, para. 4.45)

[48] Again, extensions are possible.

[49] Representation in this tribunal is, exceptionally, not subject to a means test.

2001 174,017 legal representation certificates were granted, of which 129,366 were in family cases.[50]

Support funding — This is intended to be an adjunct to a conditional fee agreement.[51] "Investigative support" provides support only in investigation of the strength of a claim with a view to a conditional fee agreement. "Litigation support" is partial funding of high cost litigation otherwise being funded by a conditional fee agreement

The cost of assistance, except in cases subject to Support Funding,[52] is met by the Legal Services Commission, although a contribution may be required from the funded party in cases other than Legal Help and Help at Court.[53]

(iii) Making an application

11–010   Applications for Legal Help and Help at Court[54] are processed immediately by the solicitor in possession of the appropriate CLS contract by completion of a form. If the applicant is eligible for assistance no contribution is payable.

In applications for Legal Representation, Investigative Help and Full Representation, the applicant will need to complete a detailed form CLS APP1 (requiring, in the case of applications for Full Representation, an indication in percentage terms of the likely prospects of success in the case) and also a financial application form CLSMEANS1 unless in receipt of Income Support or income-based Jobseeker's Allowance.[55]

The assessment of the applicant's resources, which determines financial eligibility for representation, and of the merits of the case is in most cases undertaken by an "assessment officer" in the appropriate LSC regional office.

As with Legal Help and Help at Court, the two significant financial assessments in Full Representation are of the applicant's *disposable income and disposable capital.* These are calculated by reference to the regulations[56] and allowance is made from income for certain items, including dependent children, income tax, national insurance, maintenance payments, housing costs and certain welfare benefits. Capital includes the value, after making allowance for any mortgage, of the applicant's home insofar as it exceeds £100,000. Additional capital allowances are available to pensioners. In immigration cases the financial criteria are identical to those set out above in respect of Legal Help. In other non-family and non-immigration cases,

---

[50] *Legal Services Commission Annual Report 2000/01*, para. 2.59.
[51] See above, para. 11-007.
[52] The support is provided by way of interim payments to the solicitors acting.
[53] Access to Justice Act 1999, s. 10 and Community Legal Service (Costs) Regulations 2000 (S.I. 2000/441) amended by the Community Legal Service (Costs) (Amendment) Regulations 2001 (S.I. 2001/822).
[54] And for certain immigration and family assistance.
[55] Community Legal Service (Financial) Regulations 2000 (S.I. 2000/516), reg 4.
[56] Access to Justice Act 1999, s. 7 and Community Legal Service (Financial) Regulations 2000 (S.I. 2000/516) as amended by the Community Legal Service (Financial) (Amendment) Regulations 2001 (S.I. 2001/950); Community Legal Service (Financial) (Amendment No. 2) Regulations 2001 (S.I. 2001/2997) and, as from December 3, 2001, Community Legal Service (Financial) (Amendment No. 3) Regulations 2001 (S.I. 2001/3663).

other than those under Support Funding, the levels of eligibility as from December 3, 2001[57] are:

Income
Gross monthly income exceeding £2,000 a month: ineligible
Disposable income of £683 or less a month: eligible subject to contribution as below:
Disposable income of £506 to £683 a month: eligible subject to monthly contribution of £72.91 plus ½ of any income in excess of £505.
Disposable income of £381 to £505 a month: eligible subject to monthly contribution of £31.25 plus 1/3 of any income in excess of £380.
Disposable income of £260 to £380 a month: eligible subject to monthly contribution of ¼ any income in excess of £255.
Disposable income of £259 or less a month: eligible without contribution

Capital
Disposable capital exceeding £8,000: ineligible unless the case is likely to be of particularly high cost.
Disposable capital of £8,000 or less: eligible subject to contribution payable as an immediate lump sum of all disposable capital in excess of £3,000.
Disposable capital of £3,000 or less/income support/income-based jobseekers' allowance: eligible without contribution.

If the applicant is potentially eligible on financial grounds, the assessment officer will go on to consider whether the merits test is made out. The assessment of the merits of the case, as defined by the Funding Code, is complex. Initial considerations are that funding will be refused if alternative funding is available,[58] alternative means of dispute resolution have yet to be tried and exhausted[59] or if the case will be allocated to the small claims track.[60] In the absence of such bars to public funding, then, using Full Representation as an example:

Full Representation is not available if:

1. Prospects of success are unclear, or

2. Prospects of success are "borderline" (*i.e.* it is not possible to say that they exceed 50% and there are no additional factors of "significant wider public interest" or "overwhelming importance to the client"; or

3. Prospects of success do not exceed 50%; or

4. Prospects of success exceed 50% but the relevant additional criterion cannot be satisfied:

---

[57] Community Legal Service (Financial) (Amendment No. 3) Regulations 2001 (S.I. 2001/3663).
[58] Funding Code, paras 5.4.2 and 5.7.1.
[59] *ibid.*, para. 5.4.3
[60] *ibid.*, para. 5.4.6. For the small claims track, see Chap. 15, para. 12-005.

> (a) Prospects of success exceed 80% and likely damages exceed likely costs; or
>
> (b) Prospects of success are 60–80% and likely damages exceed likely costs by 2:1; or
>
> (c) Prospects of success are 50–60% and likely damages exceed likely costs by 4:1; or
>
> (d) The claim is not for damages but "the likely benefits to be gained from the proceedings justify the likely costs".[61]

(iv) The Funding Certificate and the Applicant's Contribution

11–011   If the application is approved by the regional director,[62] a certificate is issued, subject to the acceptance by the applicant of any conditions attached to it.[63] The certificate will set out the level of service to be provided[64] and may be limited to the taking of particular steps in the action. So for example, in the first instance the certificate may be limited to the taking of counsel's opinion and another application may have to be made to the regional director to amend the certificate for further action if counsel's opinion appears to warrant it. All certificates will set out the maximum amount of costs that may be incurred.[65]

If the application is successful and no contribution is payable, the regional director issues a certificate to the applicant's solicitor, and a copy is sent to the client,[66] If the applicant is successful but there is a contribution to pay, an offer of a certificate, with a requirement to make arrangements to pay the contribution, is made. The applicant has 14 days in which to signify acceptance and to pay any contribution or, if permitted to do so, to provide an undertaking to pay.[67] Contributions from income, it should be noted, are payable every month during the period of LSC funding.

The contributions payable are significant financial burdens, particularly for an applicant towards the top end of the financial eligibility range. Given that the eligibility for free public funding is so low, it is interesting to note that in 2000–2001 84.8 per cent of the certificates issued had contributions assessed at nil.[68] This figure appears to suggest that the requirement of a contribution continues to act as a serious deterrent to people applying for public funding. The analysis of maximum contributions determined during 2000–2001 in the Legal Services Commission Annual Report contains the following figures:

---

[61] *ibid.*, para. 5.7.
[62] If actual or likely costs exceed £25,000 or, if the case proceeds to trial, £75,000, the application will be referred to the Special Cases Unit: *ibid.*, para., C23.
[63] *ibid.*, paras C14 and C15.
[64] Investigative Help, Full Representation, Investigative Support, Litigation Support, etc.
[65] *Funding Code, op. cit.*, para. C33.3
[66] *ibid.*, paras C14 and C16.1
[67] *ibid.*, para. C15.
[68] *Legal Services Commission Annual Report 2000/01*, para. 2.72.

Annual contribution required	Number	%
Nil	147,577	84.8%
Under £150	1,956	1.1%
£150-£299	3,394	2.0%
£300-£499	4,056	2.3%
£500 and over	17,032	9.8%
Total	174,015	100%

Once a certificate has been issued there are wide powers vested in the regional director to amend it.[69] The regional director also has power to discharge or revoke it upon the happening of specified events, including failure by the client to provide information, abuse or misrepresentation by the client, or where the applicant's financial position improves so that he or she is able to fund legal action.[70] In the case of refusal to grant a certificate or upon discharge or revocation of a certificate there are various rights of review by the regional director and by a separate Funding Review Body.[71]

Obviously there may be circumstances in which the normal procedure of application and issue cannot be followed because of the urgency of the matter and a procedure exists for obtaining an emergency certificate in such cases.[72]

(v) The liabilities of the LSC funded client

When the provision of legal services for those who could not afford the normal fees was dependent upon the charity of the profession, the relationship between client and lawyer must have been somewhat awkward. The object of the legal aid and now of the Community Legal Service scheme is to ensure that the relationship between solicitor and funded client is on exactly the same basis as that between solicitor and private client.[73] To that end, a client's financial obligations are to the Community Legal Service Fund and the solicitor receives payment out of the Fund.[74]

11–012

The full financial obligations of a funded client will, inevitably, depend upon the outcome of the case. As will be seen below, the funded client is usually under no obligation to pay any costs to the solicitor whatever the result; but may be under a liability to pay costs to a successful opponent.

If the funded client is *successful*, costs may be payable by the opponent in the normal way.[75] These costs are paid into the Community Legal Service

---

[69] Funding Code, para. C36. Alternatively, a solicitor authorised by a contract with the Legal Services Commission to do so may amend the certificate, *ibid.*, para. C37.

[70] *ibid.*, section 15.

[71] *ibid.*, paras C57, C58 and section 16.

[72] *ibid.*, section 3.

[73] Access to Justice Act, s. 22.

[74] Access to Justice Act 1999, s. 5. The rates of payment to suppliers of legal services are governed by the Community Legal Service (Funding) Order 2000 (S.I. 2000/627), as amended by Community Legal Service (Funding) (Amendment) Order 2000 (S.I. 2000/1541); Community Legal Service (Funding) (Amendment) Order 2001 (S.I. 2001/831) and Community Legal Service (Funding) (Amendment No. 2) Order 2001 (S.I. 2001/2996).

[75] For an explanation of costs, see para. 11-003.

Fund and go to defray the actual costs of the claim in the accounts rendered to the Fund by solicitors and counsel acting for the funded client. If the costs recovered are *not* sufficient to cover the costs to the Fund, the difference is recouped from the contribution made by the funded client. Any balance remaining from the contribution is returned.[76]

However, where the contribution, if any, is not sufficient to make up the difference, the Legal Services Commission has a first charge on any property, including money, recovered or preserved by the funded client in the proceedings.[77] This is the "statutory charge". The charge means that the Commission is entitled to recover the shortfall on expenditure from the Community Legal Service Fund out of the property that has been recovered or preserved by the funded client in the proceedings. Consequently, the funded client will not receive the full amount of a money award, the Legal Services Commission retaining sufficient to cover the shortfall, or other property will come subject to a charge which may be enforced by the Commission. However, the charges on both money and other property may be postponed or other property substituted, especially where the money or property is required to provide somewhere for the funded client to live.[78] It is, therefore, very important to establish whether the property was recovered or preserved in the proceedings, since only then does the statutory charge apply. The Legal Services Commission will be concerned to resist any attempt to defeat the charge.[79] Further, there are certain exceptions to the charge, including, in normal circumstances, the client's clothes, furniture or tools of his or her trade.[80]

The charge helps to reduce the cost to the Exchequer of public funding.[81] Indeed, the statutory charge, along with costs recovery, may be more significant, for funding purposes, than contributions.[82] The statutory charge can be harsh in its impact on a claimant who sees a large proportion of his or her damages disappear into repayment of the costs of obtaining those damages in the first place.[83]

If the funded client is *unsuccessful*, his or her liability to the Legal Services Commission, is limited to the amount of his or her contribution and, in that

[76] Access to Justice Act 1999, s. 10(5). Community Legal Service (Financial) Regulations 2000, reg. 40(1).
[77] Access to Justice Act, s. 10(7) and Community Legal Service (Financial) Regulations 2000 (S.I. 2000/516) as amended, regs. 42 to 50.
[78] Community Legal Service (Financial) Regulations 2000 (S.I. 2000/516) as amended, reg. 52.
[79] As to whether property has been recovered or preserved, see *Hanlon v. Law Society* [1981] A.C. 124 (property is recovered or preserved if it was in issue in the proceedings, recovered by the claimant if the subject of a successful claim, preserved by the respondent if the claim fails); *Curling v. Law Society* [1985] 1 W.L.R. 470 (property recovered where possession of property obtained through proceedings); see also *Van Hoorn v. Law Society* [1985] Q.B. 106. As to the castigation by the court of any attempts to defeat the charge, see *Manley v, Law Society* [1981] 1 W.L. R. 335. In limited circumstances, however, the statutory charge may be waived: Community Legal Service (Financial) Regulations 2000 (S.I. 2000/516) as amended, regs. 46–47.
[80] Community Legal Service (Financial) Regulations 2000 (S.I. 2000/516) as amended, reg. 44.
[81] Net payments from the Fund in 2000/2001 were £231.7m in respect of Legal Help and £560.2 for civil representation: *Legal Services Commission Annual Report 2000/01*, para. 2.61. The sum which the Lord Chancellor has decided to pay into the Community Legal Service Fund for 2001–2002 is £732m: *Lord Chancellor's Direction: Community Legal Service Fund Specific Budgets 2001–2002* (April 2, 2001).
[82] Lord Chancellor's Department, *Legal Aid — Targeting Need* (Cm. 2854, 1995), para.12.4.
[83] See, *e.g.* National Consumer Council, *Ordinary Justice* (1989), pp. 92–94.

respect, the Commission bears the financial risk of litigation. However, it is possible for the court to order a funded client to pay the opponent's costs in the action. The court must first consider, whether, on normal grounds, an award for costs should be so made.[84] If an award should be made it can only order the funded client to pay an amount in respect of the opponent's costs "which shall not exceed the amount (if any) which is a reasonable one for him to pay having regard to all the circumstances including a) the financial resources of all parties to the proceedings, and b) their conduct in connection with the dispute to which the proceedings relate".[85] This is not likely to be an especially serious problem for the funded party since if no contribution has been expected, he or she is not likely to be able to pay much in the way of costs to the opponent. This leaves successful unassisted parties in a rather unfortunate position.

(vi) The costs of successful unassisted parties

It is only since 1964 that a successful party not in receipt of public funding has been able to obtain costs from the body responsible for public funding at all. It is not easy to obtain such an award. Section 11(4)(d) of the Access to Justice Act 1999 and regs 5 to 7 of the Community Legal Service Regulations s. 2000 (as amended)[86] permit a court, on the application of a successful party not in receipt of public funding; to award costs to be paid by the Legal Services Commission if, under reg. 5:   **11–013**

(i) the unsuccessful funded party has the benefit of costs protection;[87]

(ii) the proceedings are finally determined in favour of the non-funded party;

(iii) the court has ordered the party in receipt of funding to pay costs but these do not cover the full costs;

(iv) the non- funded party has applied to the Commission within 3 months of the costs order;

(v) it is just and equitable that the costs should be paid out of public funds;

(vi) as respects the costs incurred in a court of first instance, the funded client instituted the proceedings and the non-funded party will suffer [severe] financial hardship unless an order is made.[88]

After December 3, 2001, where the non-funded party is an individual, the hardship need not be "severe". This does to some extent mitigate, at least in

[84] See above, para. 11-003.;

[85] Access to justice Act 1999, s. 11(1). This costs protection does not apply to the extent that the LSC funding is Help at Court, Litigation Support, Investigative Help and, in most cases, Legal Help: Community Legal Service (Cost Protection) Regulations 2000 (S.I. 2000/824), as amended, reg. 3.

[86] *Op. cit.*

[87] See para. 11-003, n. 49, above.

[88] Community Legal Service (Cost Protection) (Amendment No. 2) Regulations 2001 (S.I. 2001/3812), reg. 4(2).

respect of successful non-funded individuals, the approach of the courts in respect of the precursor to this rule in the Legal Aid Act 1988 and its predecessors, which required "severe" financial hardship in all cases. The initial approach of the courts was to adopt a highly restrictive interpretation, meaning that trifling sums were awarded in costs.[89] The courts have subsequently, however, accepted that in principle it is possible for private and public companies to suffer severe financial hardship.[90] The courts will, it is suggested, look at the effect that costs will have on the party's financial position and decided on the facts whether "financial hardship" in the case of an individual or "severe financial hardship" in the case of a corporate body, will be suffered.

However, it remains perilous to be sued by a person in receipt of public funding as the risk of failing to recover the costs of defending must be weighed against the merits of the defence and the amount of damages sought from the defendant. Lawyers representing commercial concerns may often be forgiven, therefore, for advising on an entirely pragmatic basis that it is not worth defending a claim brought by a publicly- funded individual.

(v) Critique

11–014 There is little, if any, current support for litigation to be financed from public funds irrespective of the means of the parties. Whilst there are obvious objections on the grounds of overall cost and whether it is fair that public moneys should be used to support people who can readily afford litigation, it is the case that there is some litigation which is unavoidable, but involves the parties in costs and which should be supported. Whether and, if so, to what extent, the new system achieves a suitable balance between the rationing of available resources and avoiding the stifling of unmeritorious claims remains to be seen. What one should remember, however, is that the current system was consciously developed in the context of the availability of the conditional fee arrangement as another alternative means of funding.

The costs of litigation thrown away as a result of the death or illness of a judge in the course of a trial can be covered by public funds if the Lord Chancellor thinks it fit to do so.[91]

(f) Costs payable to solicitor (organisational support)

11–015 Some clients may be able to obtain financial support for litigation through

---

[89] See *Nowotnik v. Nowotnik* [1967] P. 83, C.A. The fact that the husband had not had to restrict his activities on account of his solicitor's bill led the court to conclude that there was no severe financial hardship. The costs awarded were, according to the court in *Hanning v. Maitland (No. 2)* [1970] Q.B. 580, C.A., at p. 587: 1964–5, £74; 1965–6, £838; 1966–7, £243; 1967–8, £251; 1969–9, £239. It was in *Hanning v. Maitland* at p. 588 that Lord Denning M.R. said that the "severe financial hardship" condition, applying to courts of first instance only, should not be construed so as "to exclude people of modest income or modest capital who find it hard to bear their own costs."

[90] *Kelly v. London Transport Executive* [1982] 1 W.L.R. 1055; *Thew (R. & T.) Ltd v. Reeves* [1982] Q.B. 1283.

[91] Administration of Justice Act 1985, s. 53 brought into force on October 1, 1988 by Administration of Justice Act 1985 (Commencement No 5) Order 1988 (S.I. 1988/1341). Alternatively, it is possible to obtain insurance to cover the risk of such an eventuality.

the support of an organisation. The typical organisations which provide such support are trades unions, which often provide general legal support,[92] and pressure groups which usually provide support for a particular issue and will support litigation where it furthers the objectives of the group. In appropriate cases, organisations such as the Equal Opportunities Commission[93] or the Commission for Racial Equality[94] will support litigation.

(g) Costs payable to solicitor (multi-party actions)

Multi party actions may receive public funding.[95] These claims, which may be subjected to a group Litigation order under C.P.R. rr. 19.10 to 19.15, generally fall into two categories, that is, claims arising out of a specific event, such as a disaster, and claims based on a common cause, such as a harmful drug.[96]   **11–016**

(h) Costs payable to solicitor (other proposed methods)

Two further methods of funding have been suggested in the past but are yet to be adopted. The first is a fixed costs scheme, proposed by the Law Society in 1987.[97] Zander describes this scheme; as meaning that solicitors would pay a premium to an insurance company and the client would pay a fixed amount to cover the costs in the event of the case being lost.[98]   **11–017**

An alternative is the suggestion that a contingency legal aid fund might be established.[99] The fund would be financed by contributions from successful litigants. It would pay lawyers on a normal basis but recoup costs on a contingency basis. The lawyer, therefore, would be paid whatever the outcome of the case.[1] Zander, whilst seeing some merit in the proposal, indicated that the major problem would be the initial funding, particularly if the Fund were to be established on a voluntary basis.[2] The idea remained a possibility in the Middleton Report: " ... it might be particularly appropriate for very expensive cases where it was not practicable for even a large firm to bear the amount of risk involved"[3] conducting such a case under a conditional fee agreement. In the event, this lacuna has been filled by "Support Funding" through the Community Legal Service.[4]

---

[92] See A. Boon, "Ethics and Strategy in Personal Injury Litigation" (1995) 22 J.L.S. 353.
[93] http://www.eoc.org.uk.
[94] http:/www.cre.gov.uk/legaladv/assist_cre.html.
[95] Funding Code, Part D and Legal Services Commission Multi-Party Action Arrangements 2000.
[96] See also Woolf Issue Paper, *Multi-party actions* (1996) and Final Report, Chap. 17.
[97] Law Society's Contentious Business Committee, *Improving Access to Justice* (1987), see M. Zander, *Matter of Justice* (1989), pp. 56–57.
[98] ibid., p. 57.
[99] *Legal Aid — Targeting Need* (Cm. 2854, 1995), para.3.34. See also the Middleton Report, *op. cit.*
[1] Such a fund was proposed by JUSTICE in *Trial of Motor Accident Cases* (1966), criticised by R.C.L.S., Report, pp. 177–178. JUSTICE reiterated the call in its *Memoranda on the Green Papers issued by the Lord Chancellor's Department: Contingency Fees* (1989). See also N.C.C., *Ordinary Justice* (1990), pp. 191–193. The Law Society's Contentious Business Committee put forward a similar proposal: *Improving Access to Justice* (1987).
[2] Zander (1989), p. 56.
[3] *Op. cit.*, para. 5.56.
[4] See above, para. 11-009.

(i) Costs and settlement

11–018   The doubts as to whether costs will be available to a party and the possibility that what costs are payable by the other party will not cover the full costs of seeking legal assistance may have been assuaged to some extent by the CFA but otherwise will be powerful factors in decisions as to whether and when to settle.

Another procedure, contained in CPR Part 36, which may place either party in further difficulties is that of a formal offer of settlement, which can be made by either party and can be made prior to the issue of proceedings. The defendant may make a payment into court in purported satisfaction of the claimant's claim. Alternatively, or in addition, the claimant may make an offer to accept a certain sum in satisfaction of his or her claim. On notification of the payment or offer, the offeree may accept the payment or offer or may continue the action. Offers may be made under Part 36 in respect of non-monetary issues, such as the percentage of liability.

If the claimant does not do "better" than the defendant's payment in or other offer, the claimant will normally be made liable for the defendant's assessed costs from the time the payment or offer could have been accepted, even though he or she has "won" the case.[5] If the defendant does not do better than an offer made by the claimant, then he or she will normally be made liable, not only to pay the damages, interest and costs that are a normal consequence of a defendant losing a claim, but also to pay those costs on an indemnity basis from the time the offer could have been accepted, together with additional interest at a maximum of 10 per cent above base rate on both damages and costs.[6] The judge in making an award of damages will know neither that such a payment or offer has been made nor its amount[7] and so cannot set the damages or result to ensure that the payment or offer is or is not beaten. The rule is open to criticism as being a "blunt instrument" to achieve its objective and as operating unfairly on the defendant, the provision for additional interest, in particular, being suggested to place an unfair pressure on the defendant to capitulate without trial rather than to run the risk of paying substantial sums in increased interest.[8] Part 36 adds considerably to the risk element in litigation.

2. CRIMINAL CASES

11–019   To what extent can the "loser pays costs" rule apply in criminal matters? This rule is of lesser significance because of the existence of public funding

---

[5] CPR r. 36.20.
[6] CPR r. 36.21.
[7] CPR r 36.19(2)
[8] Prior to April 1999 the availability of the "payment in" procedure was limited to defendants and so could be described, as it was in the previous edition of this book, as potentially operating unfairly on the claimant. Arguably CPR Part 36 operates unfairly on the defendant who has to judge whether or not to accept a claimant's offer against the risk of paying the substantial sum represented by additional interest at 10% above base rate on the whole amount in dispute and on the claimant's costs over a period representing much of the pre-trial life of the case.

through the Criminal Defence Service[9-10] and because prosecutions brought by the Crown Prosecution Service are funded by government.[11] Further, the defendant does not have the option of minimising costs by deciding not to go ahead with the case! The defendant does, though, have the right to plead guilty and/or to bargain about charge and plea,[12] either of which might reduce the costs involved in a trial. Criminal courts, though, have powers to make orders about costs in various circumstances.

A defendant's costs order may be made in favour of an acquitted defendant by the Crown Court or a magistrates' court.[13] These costs are awarded out of central funds. The award covers what the court considers is reasonably sufficient to compensate the party for expenses properly[14] incurred in the proceedings and directly related to them.[15] In both the magistrates' court and the Crown Court, an order should normally be made whether or not an *inter partes* order is made, unless there are positive reasons for not making an order. The example given of such a reason is where the defendant's own conduct brought suspicion on himself or herself and so misled the prosecution into thinking that the case was stronger than it was.[16] A defendant's costs order may be made by a) a magistrates' court where an information has been laid but not proceeded with, or where the court decides not to commit the accused for trial, or where, on summary trial, the court dismisses the information;[17] b) the Crown Court where a person is not tried for an offence for which he or she was indicted, or has been acquitted. It may exercise its discretion where a person is convicted on some counts but not others (in which case only part of the costs may be ordered to be paid), and it may also make an order in favour of a successful appellant.[18] There are also circumstances in which the Divisional Court and the Court of Appeal may make defendant's costs orders: by the Divisional Court on determining proceedings in a criminal cause or matter; and by the Court of Appeal (exercising its discretion on the same principles as the Crown Court) when it allows an appeal against conviction or sentence, on appeal against a preparatory hearing order or ruling, to cover the costs of representation where there is an Attorney-General's reference on law or sentence, and on determining an application for leave to appeal to the House of Lords.[19]

[9-10] See below, para. 10-026.
[11] See below, para. 14-033.
[12] See below, para. 14-045.
[13] Prosecution of Offences Act 1985, s.16(1), (2) and *Practice Note (Criminal Law Costs)* [1991] 2 All E.R. 924, as amended by *Practice Note* [1999] 4 All E.R. 436. The *Consolidated Criminal Practice Direction* of 8th July 2002 does not include provide about costs but indicates that practice directions relating to criminal costs are "likely to be revised in the near future".
[14] A requirement of the Prosecution of Offences Act 1985, s. 16(6). Costs not properly incurred include those in respect of work unreasonably done, or costs wasted by failure to conduct proceedings with reasonable competence and expedition (note that in such cases a wasted costs order may be made, see *ibid.*, s. 19A and above, para. 3-047): *Practice Note (Criminal Law Costs)* [1991] 2 All E.R. 924 at para. 5.1.
[15] Prosecution of Offences Act s. 16(6) and *Practice Note (Criminal Law Costs)* [1991] 2 All E.R. 924 at para. 1.5 and see paras. 1.6-1.8.
[16] *Practice Note (Criminal Law Costs)* [1991] 2 All E.R. 924 para. 2.2, substituted by *Practice Note* [1999] 4 All E.R. 436. The provision is applied to magistrates' courts by para. 2.1.
[17] *ibid.*, para 2.1.
[18] *ibid.*, paras. 2.2-2.4.
[19] *ibid.*, paras 2.5-2.8.

Costs may be awarded to a successful *private prosecutor*[20] out of central funds[21] in relation to proceedings for an indictable offence and before the Divisional Court in respect of a summary offence.[22] Costs are not awardable in summary trials. Costs are awarded, except where there is good reason for not doing so, which would be, for example, where a prosecution was instituted without good cause.[23] The costs awardable are those which are just and reasonable.[24]

An award of costs may be made against a convicted defendant.[25] The costs awarded will be those that the court considers just and reasonable.[26] The judge has a discretion to exercise in determining whether to make such an order, taking account of whether the defendant chose to contest a strong case against him or her and whether the defendant must have known the real truth of the matter.

3. TRIBUNALS

11–020   We shall repeat elsewhere that it is difficult to generalise about tribunals. Broadly the parties to a dispute which is settled by a tribunal will bear their own costs, subject to any specific rules applicable to a particular tribunal. We can merely give a number of examples.

In the unified Appeal Service tribunals created by the Social Security Act 1998, the claimant will receive only compensation for loss of earnings (if any) and travelling expenses. These are payable whatever the outcome of the hearing. No costs can be awarded against the claimant.

In Employment Tribunals, s.13(1) of the Employment Tribunals Act 1996[27] permits the award of costs or expenses in principle. The tribunal will not normally, however, make an award of costs as, under the Employment Tribunal (Constitution and Rules of Procedure) Regulations 2001[28] an award will be made only where the party or a party's representative has acted vexatiously, abusively, disruptively or unreasonably, or the bringing or conducting of the proceedings by a party was misconceived. This may be a fixed sum not exceeding £10,000 award by the tribunal, a fixed sum agreed by the parties or for costs to be subject to detailed assessment.

In the Lands Tribunal, costs are within the discretion of the tribunal[29] and

---

[20] *i.e.* not a public authority or a person acting on behalf of a public authority: Prosecution of Offences Act 1985, s.17(2).
[21] Prosecution of Offences Act 1985, s.17.
[22] *Practice Note (Criminal Law Costs)* [1991] 2 All E.R. 924, at para.3.1.
[23] *ibid.*, at para. 3.1.
[24] Prosecution of Offences Act 1985, s. 17(2).
[25] *ibid.*, s.18.
[26] *ibid.*, s.18(2) and see also *Practice Note (Criminal Law Costs)* [1991] 2 All E.R. 924, at para. 6.1.
[27] As amended by the Employment Rights (Dispute Resolution) Act 1998.
[28] S.I. 2001/1171.
[29] Lands Tribunal Rules 1996 (S.I. 1996 No. 1022).

it is interesting to note that of the seven Lands Tribunals bills taxed in 2000, the average amount allowed on taxation was £115,193.[30]

The last example is highly unusual. Legal Services Commission funding is not generally available for tribunals, (the exceptions are the Employment Appeal Tribunal, Mental Health Review Tribunal, Immigration Adjudicator and Immigration Appeal Tribunal and in some instances certain tax tribunals), they are intended to be cheap and both sides are clearly expected to bear their own costs.[31]

4. CIVIL PROCEEDINGS — WHAT DO THEY ACTUALLY COST

It was one of the earliest conclusions of Lord Woolf's inquiry[32] into the civil litigation system that "excessive cost deters people from making or defending claims" and that the "problem of disproportionate cost occurs throughout the system. It is most acute in smaller cases where the costs of litigation, for one side alone, frequently equal or exceed the value of what is at issue."[33] Initially, the Woolf Inquiry requested research by the Supreme Court Taxing Office with the assistance of Professor Hazel Genn, which gave information about average costs, confirmed the view that disproportionate cost is a significant problem and provided fascinating information as to the components of the costs in a sample of 673 cases.[34] Further research was carried out by the Supreme Court Taxing Office on a sample of 2,184 cases ranging in value from £5 to £660m, for the purposes of the Final Report.[35]

In this latter research, there was a difference in average costs allowed by the taxing office between different types of case: medical negligence cases had a mean average of costs allowed at £29,380; personal injury cases at £19,382; professional negligence at £32,866 and official referees' cases[36] at £35,844. Costs as a percentage of claim value could be shown as follows:[37]

11–021

---

[30] *Judicial Statistics 2000* table 10.1 p. 99. A further 93 bills were taxed in the Queen's Bench Division from other tribunals, the average amount allowed being £10,876. The figure is quite startling in comparison with the much lower figure for claims in the Queen's Bench Division.

[31] There are some examples of money being made available to agencies providing a representation and advice service for those using tribunals, *e.g.* government grants are made to specialist advice services, by virtue of Immigration Act 1971, s.23. The Royal Commission on Legal Services advocated that this approach should be adopted more widely.

[32] Interim Report.

[33] *ibid.*, p. 9

[34] *ibid.*, pp. 252 *et seq.*

[35] Final Report, Annex II gives a summary of the main findings of this subsequent research.

[36] Now the Technology and Construction Court, see, from March 2002, CPR Part 60.

[37] Graph based on information contained in Final Report, Annex III, table 4.

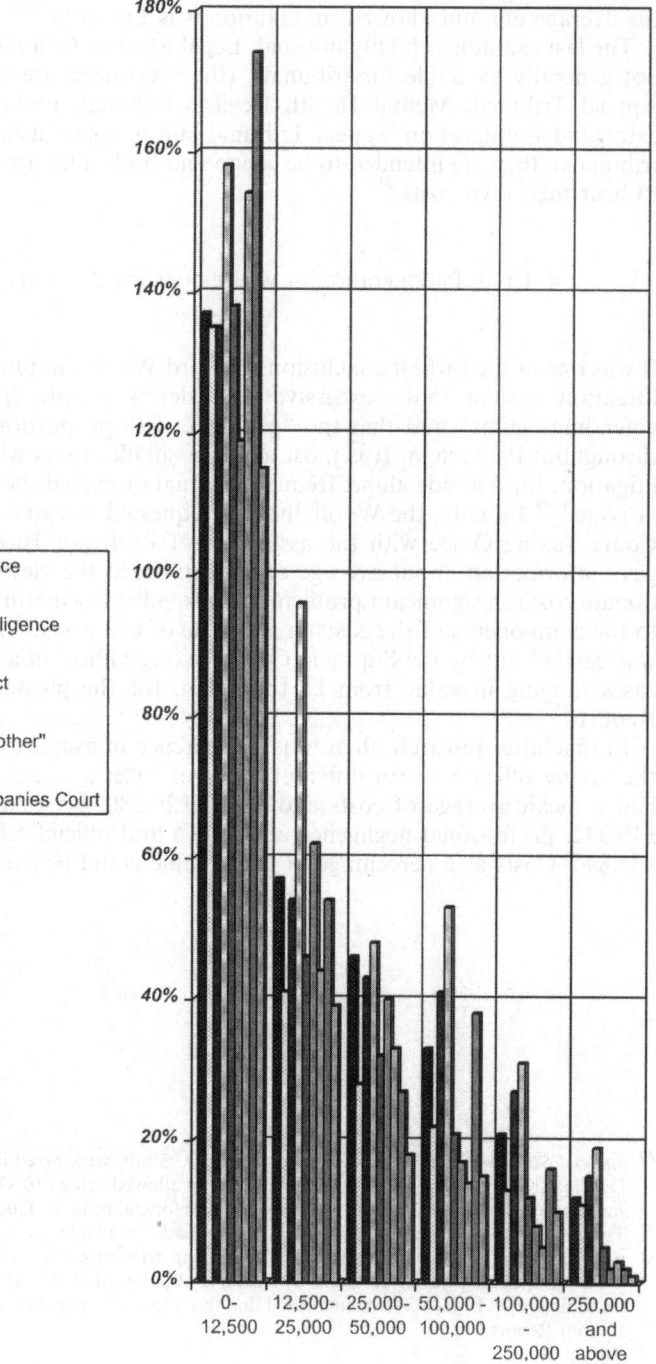

"There is a lack of proportionality between costs and claim value at the lower end of the claim value scale. ... in 40 per cent of the lowest value claims,[38] the costs on one side alone were close to, or exceeded, the total value of the claim. By way of contrast, in 60 per cent of claims over £250,000, costs represented less than 20 per cent of the value of the claim."[39]

Following the implementation of the Woolf reforms, it is more difficult to see whether Lord Woolf's desire to make the cost of litigation "more affordable, more predictable and more proportionate to the value and complexity of individual cases" has been achieved, or if so, to what extent. In March 2001 , the Lord Chancellor's Department, in its paper *Emerging Findings*, considered it "too early to provide a definitive view on costs"[40] but had convened a Costs Working Group and commissioned a report on the possible benchmarking of costs in civil cases.[41] It is, however the case that the Judicial Statistics for 2000, whilst they will necessarily involve a majority of cases commenced under the old regime, show an average amount at which bills were allowed after assessment in the Queen's Bench Division in the High Court of £21,560.[42]

There is some support for the contention that, the CPR demanding that a great deal of the preparatory work is done prior to the issuing of court proceedings, there is in fact an *increase* in costs overall: more costs being incurred in the early stages of the case prior to any possible settlement.[43]

Of the three surveys quoted in *Emerging Findings*, one, by the firm Wragge & Co., found that just over 40 per cent of respondents thought costs had decreased, just over 30 per cent thought there had been no change and 20 per cent thought there had been an increase. Conversely, a survey by CEDR of lawyers in private practice found that just under 20 per cent of respondents thought costs had decreased, 30 per cent thought there had been no change and over 40 per cent thought costs had increased!

B. DELAY

Delay causes problems in both civil and criminal matters despite the existence of time-limits which are intended to expedite cases. The reasons for delay differ in civil and criminal procedure, not least because of the temptation in civil matters — arguably frustrated by the effect of the Woolf reforms — for the parties to agree through their lawyers to delays in proceedings.

11–022

---

[38] Less than £12,500.
[39] Final Report, Annex III, para. 16.
[40] *Emerging Findings, op. cit.*, para. 7.1.
[41] Following a recommendation in Final Report, Chapter 7.
[42] *Judicial Statistics 2000*, table 10.1
[43] *Emerging Findings, op. cit.*, para. 7.7. See also the Law Society *Response to the Third Woolf Questionnaire* (February 2001) in which 45% of respondents identified this "frontloading" of cases as being a problem.

1. Civil Matters

11–023   "There are four areas in which delay or a lengthy timescale is a matter
for concern:

— the time taken to progress a case from the initial claim to a final
hearing;
— the time taken to reach settlement;
— delay in obtaining a hearing date; and
— the time taken by the hearing itself."[44]

The reasons for the slow progress of actions at these stages were diverse.
At the outset, then as now, the plaintiff (now claimant) might be slow to
contact a solicitor;[45] later, negotiations for a settlement might drag on;[46]
where relevant, the extent of the plaintiffs (now claimant's) injuries might

---

[44] Interim Report, p. 13. The earlier *Civil Justice Review* (1989), para. 49, identified delay
occurring "at three main stages, namely: (i) before proceedings are commenced; (ii) between
the commencement of proceedings and the point where the case is either settled or is ready
for trial; and (iii) between readiness for trial and the trial itself." One study prior to the
Woolf reforms showed that in cases where writs or summons (now claim forms) were issued,
the major component of elapsed time was the period between issue of writ or summons and
the settlement or trial: Incubon (1986), para.4.2. That study also revealed that in personal
injury litigation at that time the three principal causes of delay were: (i) the medical
circumstances of the case; (ii) the long wait for trials in the Royal Courts of Justice; and (iii)
a lack of clear or prompt response from the other side: *ibid.*, para. 4.8.1. Further analysis of
delay appears in Final Report, Annex III and is a factor considered in the Middleton
Report.

[45] The time taken for an incident causing personal injury to advice first being sought was found
in the Incubon Study to be, expressed as medians (that is half the cases took more than the
time and half took less), 3.4 months for cases ultimately at the Royal Courts of Justice, 1.6
months for cases ultimately at District Registries (for provincial High Court cases) and 1.9
months for county court cases: Incubon (1986), Appendix 1. The figures only relate to those
cases where proceedings were actually issued. The reasons why people may take so long to
see a solicitor are, in part, explored in Chap. 8 above. It is, however, thought that the period
of delay in seeking legal advice is, generally, decreasing: Final Report, Annex III, para. 36.

[46] The Incubon Study showed that the median period from incident to settlement, where
proceedings were issued, for the various types of case, were 43.7 months (Royal Courts of
Justice), 37.5 months (District Registry cases), 22 months (county court cases): Incubon
(1986), Appendix 1. In his Interim Report, Lord Woolf noted that settlement often occurred
at a very late stage of the proceedings, involving the parties in substantial additional costs.
At that time, personal injury cases often took 4–6 years to settle: Interim Report, p. 13.
Additional research carried out on a sample of 2,184 cases for the Final Report showed that
medical negligence cases were the longest (an average of 65 months from first instruction of
solicitor to resolution); followed by personal injury cases (56 months) and professional
negligence claims at (41 months). Unsurprisingly, cases without such a high investigative and
evidential element, such as Companies Court cases, took much less time (approximately 13
months): Final Report, Annex III, para. 21.
The CPR allow (r. 26.4 and PD 26 para. 3) for a formal stay (a pause) to be granted in
ongoing proceedings so that the building- up of solicitors' costs can be halted whilst the
parties attempt settlement. Further modern indications are that the imposition of pre-action
protocols prior to the issue of proceedings with their concomitant obligations to exchange
information and, in some cases (as for example in the Professional Negligence pre-action
protocol) explicit reference to settlement negotiations are causing many more cases to settle
at a much earlier stage. See for example, *Judicial Statistics 2000* and the Lord Chancellor's
Department paper *Emerging Findings* (March 2001).

not become clear until the end of a lengthy period of treatment;[47] investigations might have to be carried out to ascertain the evidence;[48] expert opinions may have to be obtained; communication and action by both sides might be slow; the advice of counsel might be taken; the length of time spent waiting for the trial to begin could, prior to the Woolf reforms, be substantial;[49] ierrors may be made by the professionals involved;[50] the developing litigation ethos might, historically, have necessitated the lengthening of the process before trial for tactical reasons.[51]

Delay created by these reasons, both human and procedural, could prove to be extremely frustrating to the parties, particularly to the plaintiff (now the claimant) who might feel that delay amounted to a denial of justice.[52]

The complexities of the law itself can add to the amount of time taken to resolve a case. *Saif Ali v. Sydney Mitchell and Co.*[53] provides an example of a remarkably prolonged action under the pre-CPR regime, complicated by the

---

[47] This was often said to be a good reason for delay, but, as Lord Woolf pointed out in the Interim Report, "even in such cases it should be possible to dispose of issues of liability, and to award interim damages": Interim Report, p. 13. The award of an interim payment (*i.e.* a sum on account of damages) was available prior to the Woolf reforms and is now to be found in CPR rr. 25.6 to 25.9 and PD 25b.

[48] The modern régime, however, assumes that such investigations are carried out prior to issue of proceedings in the pre-action protocol stage. The effect seems to be that early investigation and exchange of information may make early settlement more likely. However, where the case does go to court, an enforced period in the region of three or four months before proceedings can be issued adds to the delay and to the expense of the trial. For further discussion of the effect of pre-action protocols, see Chap. 14 and *Emerging Findings, op. cit.* The effect of weight and complexity on delayed issue of proceedings was, however, apparent even at the time of the Final Report: Annex III, paras 31–33.

[49] Lord Woolf noted that, in part because of late settlement of cases, and thus late withdrawal, there was overlisting at the courts in order to ensure full use of the judges' time; this of necessity produced wastage. The Winn Committee on Personal Injuries Litigation had drawn attention to this problem as early as 1968 (Cmnd. 3691) and regarded it as deplorable. In 1986 the Incubon Study found that the mean waiting periods from setting down (the stage at which the parties indicated that they had completed the pre-trial procedure and were ready for trial) until trial were 10.2 months for Royal Courts of Justice cases, 5.1 months for District Registry cases and 1.9 months for county court cases: Incubon, (1986), Appendix 1. By way of comparison the 2000 *Judicial Statistics*, tables 3.9 and 4.17 give the average time between setting down and start of trial in the Queen's Bench Division (combining Royal Courts of Justice and District Registries) in 2000 as 31 weeks (approximately 7.5 months) and in the county court — whose workload has been vastly increased since the period of the Incubon Study — 26 weeks (approximately 6.5 months).

[50] See J. Hern, "Court v. solicitor errors" (1990) Law Society Gazette, May 2, p. 32.

[51] Historically, at least, delay could easily be compounded by high usage of interim procedures which could be of doubtful appropriateness, such as applications for wide disclosure of documents, for interim injunctions or the pursuing of unmeritorious appeals from interim orders, see the Interim Report, pp. 14 and 150–179 and R. Cranston " 'The Rational Study of the Law': Social Research and Access" in Zuckerman and Cranston (1995). The impact of CPR Part 1, the overriding objective which places the management of cases to trial in the hands of the judge, as well as the reduction in the scope of civil appeals in CPR Part 52, is intended to frustrate such tactics, particularly when, as was often the case, they were employed by the wealthier of the parties (who could afford the costs of making such unnecessary applications) to the case to place pressure on the less wealthy.

[52] Because the onus was firmly on the plaintiff to keep the action moving, it was he or she who was most likely to become frustrated by delay. This factor is not entirely absent from the CPR Various writers have referred to a recognisable medical condition, "litigation neurosis", which can afflict those enmeshed in an unfinished action; see below, para. 11-031, n. 36

[53] [1978] Q.B. 95, C.A.; [1980] A.C. 198, H.L.

expiry of the limitation period.[54] It is clearly an unusual case, but there was still a considerable lapse of time whilst what were then the normal procedures were being followed. The timetable was as follows:[55]

March 26, 1966	Mr. Saif Ali, a passenger in a car driven by his friend Mr. Akram, was injured in a collision with a car driven by Mrs. Sugden.
October 16, 1966	Mrs. Sugden was convicted of driving without due care and attention.
1967	Mr. Ali and Mr. Akram consulted a solicitor with a view to making a claim. The solicitor took counsel's opinion.
October 1968	The solicitor instructed the barrister to draft the pleadings[56] and advise.
November 14, 1968	A writ[57] and statement of claim[58] was issued claiming damages against Mr. Sugden only, alleging that his wife was driving as his agent at the time of the accident. Mr. Sugden was the owner of the car and he had insured it.[59]
Later	A meeting was held between Mr. Ali's solicitor and the insurance company at which the company indicated that the agency question might be disputed and that contributory negligence might be alleged against Mr. Akram.
March 26, 1969	The limitation period expired[60] without any amendment to the writ, and without Mr. Ali issuing proceedings against either Mr. Akram or Mrs. Sugden, the actual drivers in the collision.[61]
August 29, 1969	The writ was served on Mr. Sugden.[62]

---

[54] Jacob states that the Limitation Acts have "operated in a sort of blind, mathematical way without regard to the merits of the claim or the circumstances of the parties or any other consideration": Jacob (1987), p. 268. He makes certain recommendations for reform: *ibid.*, pp. 269–270. In April 2001 the Law Commission also recommended simplification, particularly in the context of the Human Rights Act 1998: *Limitation of Actions* (Report No. 270).

[55] The timetable is culled from the judgments in both the Court of Appeal and the House of Lords. There are, unfortunately, some discrepancies in the dates given in the two courts — naturally, the House of Lords' version has been accepted!

[56] Now "statement of case"

[57] Now "claim form".

[58] Now "particulars of claim".

[59] Under the CPR, however, a further delay of several months would have occurred here prior to the issue of the claim, whist the parties complied with the Personal Injury Pre-Action Protocol. Whilst this procedure lengthens the delay at this stage, it might well have resulted in settlement or at least in information becoming available to both parties that would reduce the delay at later stages in the action.

[60] In a personal injury action such as this, proceedings must be issued within three years of the cause of action arising.

[61] There would appear to have been good cases against both the actual drivers — presumably Mr. Ali was advised to proceed against Mr. Sugden because he was the insured person, and was reluctant to proceed against Mr. Akram who was his friend.

[62] At this time, a writ remained valid for a year after its issue. Under the new regime a claim form normally remains valid only for four months after issue: CPR r. 7.5.

October 16, 1969	Mr. Sugden entered a defence denying his wife's agency.[63]
November 1969	The barrister advised that Mr. Ali should be separately represented.[64]
June 24, 1971	Mr. Sugden amended his defence and admitted that his wife *was* acting as his agent.
January 21, 1972	Mr. Sugden applied to the court for leave[65] to withdraw his admission of agency with consent of the plaintiff's solicitors. Leave was granted.
May 9, 1972	The House of Lords decision in *Launchbury v. Morgans*[66] led Mr. Ali's advisers to believe that it was impossible to continue the action.
April 22, 1974	The action against Mr. Sugden was discontinued and Mr. Ali's impregnable claim had disappeared.
September 19, 1974	Freshly advised, Mr. Ali issued a writ against the solicitors who had represented him until November 1969 alleging negligence.[67]
May 29, 1975	The defendant solicitors issued a third party notice against the barrister whose advice they had taken,[68] asking that he should indemnify them on the grounds that they had acted on his advice.
July 26, 1976	The barrister successfully applied to have the third party notice struck out on the grounds that it disclosed no cause of action.
February 24, 1977	The solicitors successfully appealed to Kerr J. and the third party notice was restored. The barrister successfully appealed to the Court of Appeal and the third party notice was again struck out.[69]

---

[63] Under the new regime it is at this stage that the court becomes actively involved in the management of the case to trial. It is highly unlikely that a modern court would have permitted the subsequent four-year delay in the personal injury action.

[64] It was perceived too late that Mr. Ali's interests and Mr. Akram's interests were not identical!

[65] Now "permission".

[66] [1973] A.C. 127: a case in which the House of Lords held that a husband who had borrowed his wife's car to go on a "pub-crawl" was not her agent for the purpose of fixing her with liability for his negligent driving.

[67] Under the new rgime, this would have had to have been preceded by a full exchange of information over weeks or months under what is now the Professional Negligence Pre-Action Protocol.

[68] Now a "Part 20 claim", *i.e.* a document joining the barrister in Mr. Ali's action.

[69] [1978] Q.B. 95. The court relied heavily on *Rondel v. Worsley* [1969] A.C. 191. Under the current, limited, appeal system it is unlikely this appeal would have proceeded this far, let alone to the House of Lords: see CPR Part 52 and P.D. 52.

November 2, 1978   The solicitors successfully appealed to the House
                         of Lords and the third party notice was restored.[70]
                         N.B. The third party action between the solicitors
                         and the barrister did not decide that he *was*
                         negligent, merely that *if* he had been negligent, he
                         would be liable to the solicitors. The question
                         whether he was negligent remained for trial if
                         disputed by the barrister.

Prior to Lord Woolf's investigations, two official committees[71] had
considered the incidence and causes of delay with particular reference to
personal injuries litigation and the Civil Justice review had considered the
general problem of delay in the civil justice system.[72] In 1988 a High Court
judge was given charge of the general list cases of the Queen's Bench. Cases
which had been settled or withdrawn were removed from the list and
sanctions for non-compliance were introduced. Non personal injury cases
involving claims below £20,000 were identified for transfer to the county
court and three extra Circuit judges sat in the High Court for three months
to take Queen's Bench cases[73] It appeared that in relation to non-jury-trial
cases, these steps had some initial success.[74] As a consequence of the Civil
Justice Review the relationship between the High Court and the county
court was re-examined, increasing the number of cases heard in the county
court.[75]

Lord Woolf's approach to dealing with delay was to increase the role of
the courts in the management of litigation, and this lay at the heart of his
proposals in the Interim Report (1995). This was refined in the Final Report,
which contains in Appendix III a detailed analysis of the cost and delay
before trial in a sample of over 2000 cases selected by the Supreme Court
Taxing Office:

> "It is unreasonable in my view to expect clients to wait on average two
> to three years for the resolution of a dispute ... The way to achieve
> [reduction in that delay] is for the court to determine an appropriate
> timetable to bring cases to final disposition."[76]

As we have indicated in the footnotes to this section, it is unlikely that
such a degree of delay as demonstrated in *Saif Ali* would be permitted under
the current regime, although one must nevertheless realise that the pre-trial
stages are by no means instantaneous. The pre action protocol procedure
which we will examine in Chapter 15, whilst encouraging settlement, can, if
no settlement is reached by means of the protocol, add several months
before formal court proceedings can be issued. In 2000, the average time

---

[70] [1980] A.C. 198.
[71] *Report of the Committee on Personal Injuries Litigation* (Cmnd. 3691, 1968), Chair, Winn
L.J.; *Report of the Personal Injuries Litigation Working Party* (Cmnd. 7476, 1979), Chair
Cantley J. For a brief consideration of their proposals, see the first edition of this book, pp.
376–387.
[72] *Civil justice Review, Report of the Review Body on Civil Justice* (Cm. 394, 1989).
[73] So summarised in the *Civil Justice Review* (1989) para. 55
[74] *Judicial Statistics 1995*, pp. 25 and 35.
[75] For the jurisdiction points, see above, Chapter 2.
[76] Final Report, Chapter 2, para. 31.

between issue of proceedings (following completion of any pre-action protocol) and requesting a trial date was, in the Queen's Bench Division, 133 weeks.[77] A further 31 weeks elapsed, on average, before the start of the trial.[78]

2. CRIMINAL MATTERS

Although the delay in criminal cases is of a different order of magnitude, it still gives rise to concern. The concern is expressed on behalf of defendants in custody because they may ultimately be acquitted or given non-custodial sentences, and on behalf of defendants on bail because of the uncertainty and unpleasantness of a pending criminal trial. In addition there are difficulties associated with trials relating to incidents that happened in times long gone by. Witnesses forget.   **11–024**

There is, in theory, an eight-week time limit between committal and trial on indictment,[79] but that rule may be dispensed with by the Crown Court and the following figures idicate the present position. In England and Wales in 2000, of the 89,252 defendants committed for trial, 43.2 per cent were dealt with in less than eight weeks;[80] of the 46,448 who pleaded guilty, 60 per cent were dealt with in less than eight weeks; and of the 29,439 who pleaded not guilty, only 17.2 per cent were dealt with in less than eight weeks. Indeed, of this latter group ("not-guilty pleas"), since 51 per cent overall were dealt with in less than 16 weeks, one concludes that 49 per cent had to wait longer than 16 weeks for trial.[81]

Delays for defendants in trials on indictment were giving cause for concern as long ago as 1975, when the James Committee reported, but at that stage over 70 per cent of cases were disposed of within eight weeks.[82] The matter has attracted further attention[83] and continues to do so.[84] A number of steps were implemented to seek to reduce overall delay.[85]

---

[77] *Judicial Statistics*, 2000, table 3.8

[78] *ibid.*

[79] See below, para. 14-065.

[80] *Judicial Statistics 2000*, tables 6.15 and 6.16. One may compare these figures with those from *Judicial Statistics 1995*, quoted in the previous edition of this book, where 39 per cent of all defendants were dealt with in less than eight weeks. Of those pleading guilty, 50 per cent were dealt with in less than eight weeks. Of those pleading not guilty, 19 per cent were dealt with in less than eight weeks and 14 per cent of those making not guilty pleas had to wait longer than 16 weeks for trial.

[81] *ibid.*, table 6.16.

[82] *The Distribution of Criminal Business between the Crown Court and the Magistrates' Courts*, Cmnd. 6323 (1975), para. 23.

[83] For example, Narey, *Review of Delay in the Criminal Justice System* (1997), *Modernising Justice* (December 1998); the Crime and Disorder Act 1998, *Time Intervals for Criminal Procedure in the Magistrates' Courts – October 2000* (Lord Chancellor's Department Information Bulletin April 2000); the Auld review: *Criminal Justice: The Way Ahead*, Cm 5074 (February 2001).

[84] See, for example on a related issue: A. Towler, "Woolf disappointed by criminal appeal delays", Law Society Gazette 11th July 2002, p. 4.

[85] For a summary of steps taken following the Crime and Disorder Act 1998, see Ernst & Young, *Reducing Delay in the Criminal Justice System: Evaluation of the Pilot Schemes* (Home Office, August 1999). See also *Evaluation Report of the Joint Performance Management Pilot Scheme on Cracked Ineffective and Vacated Trials* (Lord Chancellor's Department, October 2001).

Nevertheless, the overall figure for 2000 shows, as we have seen, less than 45 per cent of cases being disposed of within eight weeks.

Those defendants awaiting trial in custody might seem to be the most seriously disadvantaged by delay and they do tend to take priority. In 2000, 56.5 per cent of this group waited less than eight weeks for trial, and 83.4 per cent less than 16 weeks. The figures for those defendants on bail were 38.2 per cent and 62.6 per cent respectively.[86]

The situation differs around the country and the *average* length of time between committal and trial for those pleading not guilty varies from 12.5 weeks on the Wales and Chester Circuit to 24.5 weeks on the Northern Circuit.[87] The national average for those pleading not guilty is 19.6 weeks. For those pleading guilty, the *average* length of time varies from 7.1 weeks on the Wales and Chester Circuit to 12.8 weeks on the Northern Circuit. The national average for those pleading guilty is 10.8 weeks.[88] All of these figures represent a small improvement on those quoted in the third edition of this book.

One of the problems with trial at Crown Court[89] is with producing lists of cases which are accurate enough to enable prediction of the timing of the case for the benefit of the defendant and advocate and the most efficient use of judicial and court time. The Royal Commission on Criminal Justice had "no solution to the listing problem and despite all the complaints made to us about it, no different system was suggested to us that was obviously better than the present case."[90] Since then, a number of the changes to the criminal justice system may have contributed to a streamlining and reduction in the delay. The *Criminal Statistics 2000*,[91] for example, explain that the average waiting time for trial in the Crown Court (from committal to the beginning of the trial) has fallen from 12 weeks in 1997 to 14.3 weeks in 2002 because of the plea before venue procedure resulting in omission of the "committal" stage for defendants pleading guilty in the magistrates' court.[92]

As regards delay at magistrates' courts, further reference can be made to the *Criminal Statistics 2000*. As regards indictable offences (including offences triable either way), in 2000 the average number of days from offence to completion was 100 days. This was, apparently, "the lowest it had been since 1986".[93]

---

[86] *Judicial Statistics 2000*, table 6.17.
[87] *ibid.*, table 6.18.
[88] *ibid.*
[89] The pre-trial procedure itself has the potential to produce delay for a variety of reasons; see below, Chap. 13.
[90] The Royal Commission on Criminal Justice, *Report* (Cm. 2263, 1993), para. 40. See also J. Plotnikoff and R. Woolfson, *From Committal to Trial: Delay at the Crown Court* (1993).
[91] Cm. 5312.
[92] *ibid.*, para. 1.15.
[93] *ibid.*, para. 1.13.

C. SETTLEMENT

Cost and delay are just two of the factors which persuade the great majority   **11–025**
of those involved in civil disputes to effect a compromise and settle their
differences before trial. Increasingly they do so before issuing court
proceedings at all. The then Lord Chief Justice in 1980 commented that,
"If it were not that a high proportion of cases are compromised long before
they reach court the administration of justice would soon grind to a halt; the
courts would be overwhelmed by the volume of work."[94] This sentiment is
still true and posits a fundamental dilemma in civil procedure: are
settlements fair? The courts now have the obligation to encourage them.[95]

1. WHO SETTLES WHEN?

The settlement of a dispute is achieved by an agreement between the parties   **11-26**
to abandon any further claim in respect of the subject of the dispute. It takes
the form of a legally binding contract and the normal rules of contract apply
to establish the existence, meaning and effect of the agreement.[96] In general
the parties are completely free to negotiate the terms of the settlement[97] A
settlement may be arrived at more usually before proceedings have begun —
a result encouraged by the pre-action protocols — but may also be arrived
at after proceedings have begun, including during the course of the trial.[98]
Once agreement is reached, the settlement is just as final as a judgment[99]
and, unless the agreement has been improperly procured, the issues of fact
and law raised in the original claim may not be the subject of further
litigation.[1]

There is limited official information on settlements, since until recently,
settlement would not necessarily be recorded on court files, and thus to some
extent deductions have to be made from the information available in the
judicial statistics, supported by the available research.

(a) Information from the judicial statistics

The judicial statistics inevitably provide an incomplete picture since the only   **11–27**
information available relates to matters where proceedings have been issued
and many disputes may already have been settled by then.

---

[94] In the course of the foreword to the first edition (1980) of D. Foskett, *The Law and Practice of Compromise*. The 5th edition is due to be published in 2002.
[95] CPR Part 1. See below, para. 12-002. Previously the court's role was limited to ratifying settlements involving children and patients under the Mental Health Act and this active jurisdiction is retained in CPR Part 21 and P.D. 21.
[96] D. Foskett, *The Law and Practice of Compromise* (3rd ed., 1991)
[97] There are some exceptions, *e.g.* settlements involving children and patients: see CPR Part 21 and P.D. 21.
[98] The court will require to be informed of the fact of settlement: see, for example, the rider to that effect on the allocation questionnaire. If the case is settled within 7 days of filing the listing questionnaire that makes final arrangements for trial, the relevant fee (up to £400) is refundable, presumably as an incentive.
[99] The settlement should be recorded in a "consent order" sealed by the court: CPR r. 40.6.
[1] Foskett (1985) Pt.I

The following figures are taken from the *Judicial Statistics* for 2000 and relate to the Queen's Bench Division. A total of 26, 876 claim forms and originating summonses[2] were issued in 2000. Of these, 5,599 were issued by the Royal Courts of Justice in London and 21,277 by district registries.[3] This is a 63 per cent overall reduction since 1999,[4] which reflects not only the increasing role of the county courts but also the significant deterrent effect of the C.P.R.[5] Further information is given for the Royal Courts of Justice:

CLAIMS ISSUED	5, 599
JUDGMENT GIVEN WITHOUT TRIAL	933
CASES SET DOWN FOR TRIAL	3,220
SETTLED WITH CONSENT ORDER, STRUCK OUT OR WITHDRAWN BEFORE HEARING	1,390
SETTLED DURING TRIAL	720
DETERMINED AFTER TRIAL	590

Clearly these figures are not entirely comparable because they relate to cases at different stages in the procedure. Most of the cases determined after a trial would have been begun by a writ issued in 1998 or a claim form issued in 1999. However the figures do give an indication of the proportion of cases resolved by settlement rather than trial.

It will be seen that a high proportion of cases disappear after the issue of a claim form, presumably because they are either settled or discontinued. A high proportion end in a swift judgment because the defendant is in default or because under C.P.R. Part 24 the claimant or defendant has no real case. About one case in two goes through all the pre-trial procedure and is set down for trial. Even then, about half are withdrawn, many settled, before a hearing. A surprisingly high number of cases are settled "at the door of the court" with the parties in attendance ready for trial.[6] A number of settlements require the formal approval of the court.[7] The Lord Chancellor's Department's most recent figures suggest that, on average, only 20 per cent of claims issued now reach trial,[8] What is perhaps more significant, assuming that the number of civil causes of action remains roughly the same, is the dramatic decrease in the number of claims being issued, even when the redistribution of work to the county courts is taken

---

[2] A means of commencement of proceedings at the date of writing almost completely superseded by the Part 8 claim form.

[3] *ibid.*, table 3.1

[4] For an even more dramatic comparison, the pre-Woolf 1994 figures quoted in the previous edition of this book included a total of *153, 624* writs and originating summonses issued.

[5] See para. 12-035

[6] The prospect of immediate trial concentrates the minds of the parties and their advisers wonderfully. In its paper, *Emerging Findings* (March 2001), the Lord Chancellor's Department concluded that, of cases settling prior to trial, fewer were now doing so at the door of the court (*i.e* literally on the morning of the trial or otherwise very close to the trial date) as opposed to earlier in the pre-trial procedure, in fast track cases from 50% settling early in 1998/1999 to 70% in 1999/2000 (para. 4.3) and in multi-track cases from 63% to 72%.

[7] See CPR Part 21.

[8] *Emerging Findings, op. cit.*

into account: from 153, 624 Queen's Bench Division claims in 1994[9] to 26, 876 in 2000.[10] A huge proportion of disputes, it seems, are settled without recourse to the courts at all.[11]

The statistics above relate to all actions in the Queen's Bench Division. A slightly different picture emerges if we sift out the figures relating to personal injury negligence actions alone — the category most discussed in relation to the efficacy of settlements. Again from the Judicial Statistics for 2000[12] the table now looks like this:

CLAIMS ISSUED	1,024
JUDGMENT GIVEN WITHOUT TRIAL	not specified
CASES SET DOWN FOR TRIAL	not specified
SETTLED WITH CONSENT ORDER, STRUCK OUT OR WITHDRAWN BEFORE HEARING	850
SETTLED DURING TRIAL	490
DETERMINED AFTER TRIAL	260

From these figures we can see that a high proportion of the cases disposed of in 2000 were personal injury claims (1,340 out of 2,110), hence the attention paid to this category of cases.

(b) Research information

Research on the position following the Woolf reforms is, as yet, limited.   **11–028** Earlier research[13] was, however, consistent in demonstrating that the vast majority of claims settle without recourse to trial; perhaps the most dramatic being that of the Pearson Commission that 86 per cent of cases settled without proceedings being started. In March 2001 the Lord Chancellor's Department[14] reported that "[a]necdotal evidence suggests that pre-action protocols are working well to promote settlement before issue and to reduce the number of ill-founded claims", quoting a survey by the Association of Personal Injury Lawyers to the effect that 48 per cent of their respondents believed settlement had been reached earlier and that 33 per cent of claims avoided litigation. As we have already seen, there is empirical evidence that far fewer cases are reaching the point of issue of proceedings,[15] and of those that enter the court system, late settlements at the door of the court are reducing.[16]

We should now have demonstrated to your satisfaction the enormous importance of the process of settlement. It is the normal procedure in the vast majority of cases. Is it fair?

---

[9] *Judicial Statistics 1995*, Cm. 3290, Chap. 3.

[10] *Judicial Statistics 2000*.

[11] Possibly by use of one of the many methods of alternative dispute resolution ("ADR"), see para. 11-032 below.

[12] *Judicial Statistics 2000*, tables 3.2, 3.3, 3.4, 3.5.

[13] Including that of the Winn Committee: *Report of the Committee on Personal Injuries Litigation* (Cmnd. 3691,1968); the Pearson Commission (1978, Cmnd. 7054) and the Oxford Study: D. Harris *et al.*, *Compensation and Support for Illness and Injury* (1984).

[14] *Emerging Findings, op. cit.*, para. 3.12 *et seq.*.

[15] *Judicial Statistics, 2000*. See above, para. 11-027.

[16] *Emerging Findings, op. cit.*, para. 4.1 *et seq.*

2. NEGOTIATIONS FOR A SETTLEMENT

11–029   The settlement process is very much a matter of bargaining, and it is
bargaining of a difficult and expensive character. As economists would
say, the case involves a bilateral monopoly, since the plaintiff has to
"sell" his claim to one potential buyer — the insurer — and the insurer
has to "buy" the claim from only one potential seller — the plaintiff."[17]

Having taken pains in Part II to point out that there are a number of non-
legal sources of advice and assistance, we do not now wish to give the
impression that the negotiation of settlements is exclusively the province of
lawyers. Other agencies are quite heavily involved, some in the capacity of
e.g. mediator or arbitrator,[18] others commercially[19] or representing the
interests of members in a more specialised field[20]

Settlements can be examined by considering personal injury claims, in
which they play a major role, and which have been the subject of research
and critical assessment.[21] It is clear that the analysis in the first paragraph
holds good, whoever the parties actually are. The claimant cannot shop
around for the best offer, the two parties must deal with each other and
strike an acceptable bargain through their own negotiating skill.

The defendant in a personal injury action is likely to be represented by an
insurance company, which takes complete control of and financial
responsibility for the claim. If the defendant is not insured, he or she is
not likely to be worth suing.[22] The staff in the claims department of an
insurance company will be skilful and experienced negotiators, with
adequate resources to deal with claims.[23]

The claimant in a personal injury claim is the person hurt as a result of an
accident. He or she is unlikely to have any skill or previous experience in
seeking compensation for injury and is, therefore, largely dependent on the
legal advice sought and received.[24] The routes to seeing a solicitor — for
those claimants who choose to instruct a solicitor — vary. Some accident
victims seek legal advice through an agency such as their trade union, which

---

[17] Cane (1993), p. 226. A "plaintiff" is, under the new system, now a "claimant".

[18] See below para. 11-032.

[19] Most readers will have seen television and other advertising on the part of non-lawyer claims
assessors and claims management companies. For further information about claims
assessors see the report of the Blackwell Committee: *The investigation of non-legally
qualified claims assessors and employment advisors who act for reward* (February 2000).

[20] Primarily the trades unions, but also the motoring organisations, see above para. 11-015 and
Cane (1993), p.219. Advice agencies also involve themselves on behalf of clients, from time
to time taking an active part in negotiation and settlement.

[21] See, in particular, Harris *et al.* (1984); H. Genn, *Hard Bargaining* (1987); see also Cane
(1993). We consider claims by individuals, but group actions are becoming increasingly
significant and present different issues, see Cane (1993), pp. 227–230.

[22] Unless rich, either personally or because the defendant is a large company or other
organisation (*e.g.* considerable sums of health service finance fund the defence of legal
actions brought against health authorities and their employees). In road traffic accident
cases, however, the Motor Insurers' Bureau provides a potential remedy in respect of
untraced or uninsured defendant drivers.

[23] See Genn (1988), pp. 7–8 and 50–52, 63.

[24] See H. Genn, "Who Claims Compensation: Factors associated with Claiming and Obtaining
Damages" in Harris et al. (1984), p. 76.

will place them in touch with an experienced solicitor. Other claimants will adopt the common, often haphazard methods of seeking legal advice, which may result in a claimant seeing a solicitor who is not experienced in the field. Checking whether the solicitor is on the Law Society's Personal Injury Panel should, and/or whether the firm has a Legal Services Commission contract in respect of personal injury litigation however, assist in locating a specialist.

Once the claimant has found a solicitor, the problems that may face the claimant in the initial stages of negotiation must be discussed. Two questions arise: first the liability question, *i.e.* is the defendant liable in law? Secondly the quantum question, *i.e.* if the defendant is liable, how much should the damages be?[25]

Proving liability will depend, if it is denied by the defendant, upon three factors. First, the information which the client has about the accident. It is likely that the client will see the solicitor some time after the accident, when memory may already have begun to fade. Indeed there is some evidence which shows that the longer the delay in seeing a solicitor, the less likely damages will be obtained.[26] Secondly, more may be discovered about the accident. Prior to the Woolf reforms, research indicated that it was often the case that a plaintiff's solicitor either did not have the resources to undertake investigations or was loath to seek out all available reports even though much was and is available in terms of police accident reports, health and safety reports and so on.[27] The effect of the reforms, however, is to impose on both parties an obligation to carry out investigations prior to the issue of proceedings and to communicate the results of those investigations to each other, with copies of appropriate documents under *e.g.* the Personal Injury Pre-Action Protocol.[28] The aims of the Personal Injury Pre-Action Protocol are explicitly (our italics):

(a) "more pre-action contact between the parties

(b) better and earlier exchange of information

(c) better pre-action investigation by both sides

(d) *to put the parties in a position where they may be able to settle cases fairly and early without litigation*

(e) to enable proceedings to run to the court's timetable and efficiently, if litigation does become necessary."

In its March 2001 paper, *Emerging Findings*, the Lord Chancellor's Department suggested that "[e]arly indications show that the introduction

---

[25] The separateness of these issues is reflected in the fact that it is possible for split trials to be ordered so that, *e.g.* liability can be established whilst waiting for the medical condition of the claimant to be diagnosed adequately and before the quantum issue is determined: PD 26 para.9.1; PD 29 para. 5.3(7) Whilst awaiting determination of quantum, the claimant can apply for interim payments on account of damages: CPR rr. 25.6 to 25.9, PD 25b. Indeed, some insurance companies will offer voluntary interim payments to, for example, allow the claimant to undertake medical treatment privately and therefore more quickly, recognising that the more quickly the claimant is treated, the more quickly he or she will be, for example, back at work, thus reducing the overall claim for damages for comparatively small outlay.

[26] D. Harris, "Claims for Damages: Negotiating, Settling or Abandoning" in Harris *et al.* (1984), p. 104 and Table 3.7.

[27] Genn (1987), pp. 67–69.

[28] Described further in Chap. 11. See also Final Report, Chapter 10.

of pre-action protocols has been key in encouraging a new settlement culture".[29]

11–030   Thirdly, there is the question of how good the witnesses will be when, and if, it comes to establishing a case in court. Any witnesses will need to be contacted and the quality of their evidence assessed. Overall, it is not a simple — and therefore not an inexpensive — process to discover whether there is enough evidence to pursue a claim. If a possible claim does emerge from the evidence available, an attempt will be made to put a monetary value on the injuries suffered by the claimant. At this stage negotiations are likely to begin and are encouraged by the protocols:

> "Parties and their legal representatives are encouraged to enter into discussions and/or negotiations prior to starting proceedings. The protocol does not specify when or how this might be done but parties should bear in mind that the courts increasingly take the view that litigation should be a last resort, and that claims should not be issued prematurely when a settlement is in reasonable prospect."[30]

To establish the possible quantum of damages, it is necessary to obtain as much information as possible about the injuries which the client suffered, and the future effect of such injuries, in particular upon the client's earning capacity. The client will, therefore, need a medical report.[31] Evaluating quantum is particularly difficult. In an American experiment, 20 pairs of practising lawyers negotiated on identical information about a case. The highest outcome was $95,000; the lowest $15,000; and the average was just over $47,000![32] Most solicitors will refer to the Judicial Studies Board Guidelines[33] — a publication giving "tariffs" for different kinds of injury, as well as one of the publications giving reports of recent awards.[34] Use of these resources can, however, only provide a range of appropriate awards and the parties must negotiate within that range to reach a settlement. Normally the result will be payment of one lump sum in the same way that damages consequent on a successful court action are also paid in a lump sum,[35] although interim awards[36] and awards of provisional damages[37] can be made. It is, however, possible for the injured party and the insurance company to agree on a "structured settlement". Under such a scheme sums of money are paid over periodically either for a fixed period or until the

---

[29] para. 3.15.

[30] Personal Injury Pre-action Protocol para. 2.13.

[31] Which, if proceedings are issued, must be attached to the particulars of claim: PD 16 para. 4.3.

[32] G.R. Williams, *Legal Negotiation and Settlement* (1983) referred to in Genn (1987), p. 77.

[33] Judicial Studies Board *Guidelines for the Assessment of General Damages in Personal Injury Cases* (4th ed., Blackstone).

[34] Such as *Kemp & Kemp on Quantum*. A typical report describes the injuries suffered by the claimant and the amounts awarded under the various heads of damage.

[35] See below para. 15-010.

[36] CPR rr. 25.6 to 25.9 and PD 25b.

[37] *i.e.* awards made now on the basis that a specified further medical condition (such as epilepsy or ostheoarthritis) will not develop within a specified period, the claimant having the right to apply for additional damages if the condition does develop within the period. Jurisdiction to make such an order is provided by Supreme Court Act 1981, s. 32A and County Courts Act 1984, s. 51 and currently implemented by CPR Part 41 and PD 41.

death of the injured party. These sums can then be varied over time to reflect changes consequent upon the damage caused to the injured party.[38]

The orthodox view of civil pre-trial procedure, and that which underlies Lord Woolf's thinking,[39] is that the more the two parties know about the real issues between them, the more likely it is that a "realistic" settlement can be reached.[40] A careful balance must be struck, however, between providing information in accordance with an early request or under a pre-action protocol,[41] and protecting one's client's interests. Whilst negotiations are conducted in an atmosphere of pressure, the danger of an over aggressive, adversarial approach is that it is often inimical to the interests of the parties[42] and an approach that resists revealing much information to the other side was easily identified[43] as a major reason for delay in the civil justice system.

Thus, the quality of the negotiators and their approach play a significant role in the settlement that is achieved. Insurance company representatives are almost invariably skilled, but the levels of skill and experience of the claimant's solicitor may vary considerably and the research evidence suggests that this is a highly significant factor in the settlement process.[44] Individual negotiators will differ in their approach from the combative and confrontational to the co-operative and may have differing views as to the effectiveness of such different approaches., particularly in the context of the spirit of cooperation enshrined in the CPR.[45]

Clearly there is considerable pressure on the various parties to the negotiation. Since the claimant is a prime contributor, it must be realised that it is important to utilise what advantages are possessed, consequently there is considerable pressure on him or her as well.

3. PRESSURES

The pressure to conclude a settlement is almost always on the claimant   **11–031**
who can be placed at a considerable disadvantage against the skilled

---

[38] The payments are financed by the purchase of an annuity by the liability insurer, and, by an Inland Revenue concession, are not taxable as income. See R. Lewis (1988) 15 J.L.S. 392; D.K. Allen (1988) 104 L.Q.R. 448. Procedure is provided in PD 40c.

[39] Final Report, Chapter 10.

[40] This is the especial function of the pre-action protocols, see below, para. 12-010, of statements of case, see below, para. 12-016; disclosure, see below, para. 12-026; requests for further information under CPR Part 18, see below, para. 12-017 and exchange of witness statements and experts' reports, see below para. 15-005. All these procedures except for the pre-action protocol take place well after the start of the action and all, as we have already seen, a considerable time after the accident.

[41] The requirement that some indication must be given in advance — see below, pp. # — of the method of funding may provide material for the opponent to draw inferences as to the client's financial position, even if this information is not explicitly revealed.

[42] Interim Report.

[43] See above, para. 11-029, n. 13.

[44] See Genn (1987). It is perhaps ironic in this context that skills training in negotiation (contentious and non-contentious) no longer forms part of the curriculum of the Legal Practice Course undertaken by intending solicitors.

[45] See Genn (1987), esp. pp. 46–50, 53. For an analysis of the co-operative approach, see Fisher, Ury and Patton, *Getting to Yes* (2nd ed., 1997, Arrow).

defendant.[46] Broadly, the pressures are attributable to delay, cost and the risk of litigation.

We have considered the delay that, even after the Woolf reforms, is likely to occur in a personal injury claim which goes to trial in the High Court.[47] The incentive to settle and clear the matter up quickly is significant. The claimant may be urgently in need of the money. It is he or she who will be incurring additional expenses as a result of the accident and whose earning power may have been impaired. Social security payments are unlikely to be adequate compensation for loss of earnings and injuries. Interest is payable on damages from the date of the cause of action to the date of judgment in all personal injury cases (unless there are special reasons to the contrary) and the court may order interest on that basis in other cases,[48] but the claimant may prefer to have the money in hand. An interim payment may be awarded by the court on application, but an order will only be made when it is clear that the defendant will be held liable at trial.[49]

---

[46] A claimant in a personal injury claim is, unless particularly unlucky, likely to be a first-time user of the system. An insurance company is, of course, in the business of dealing with such claims.

[47] See above para. 11-023.

[48] Supreme Court Act 1981, s. 35A; County Courts Act 1984, s. 69. Claimants in debt cases may be entitled to rely on a more advantageous rate of interest under Late Payment of Commercial Debts (Interest) Act 1998, s. 1.

[49] Supreme Court Act 1981, s. 32. An order may be made at an interim hearing if the following criteria are satisfied:

CPR r. 25.7: "(1) The court may make an order for an interim payment only if—

(a) the defendant against whom the order is sought has admitted liability to pay damages or some other sum of money to the claimant;

(b) the claimant has obtained judgment against that defendant for damages to be assessed or for a sum of money (other than costs) to be assessed;

(c) except where paragraph (3) applies, it is satisfied that, if the claim went to trial, the claimant would obtain judgment for a substantial amount of money (other than costs) against the defendant from whom he is seeking an order for an interim payment; or

(d) the following conditions are satisfied—

(i) the claimant is seeking an order for possession of land (whether or not any other order is also sought); and

(ii) the court is satisfied that, if the case went to trial, the defendant would be held liable (even if the claim for possession fails) to pay the claimant a sum of money for the defendant's occupation and use of the land while the claim for possession was pending.

(2) In addition, in claim for personal injuries the court may make an order for an interim payment of damages only if—

(a) the defendant is insured in respect of the claim;

(b) the defendant's liability will be met by—

(i) an insurer under section 151 of the Road Traffic Act 1988; or

(ii) an insurer acting under the Motor Insurers Bureau Agreement, or the Motor Insurers Bureau where it is acting itself; or

(c) the defendant is a public body.

(3) In a claim for personal injuries where there are two or more defendants, the court may make an order for the interim payment of damages against any defendant if—

(a) it is satisfied that, if the claim went to trial, the claimant would obtain judgment for substantial damages against at least one of the defendants (even if the court has not yet determined which of them is liable); and

(b) paragraph (2) is satisfied in relation to each of the defendants.

(4) The court must not order an interim payment of more than a reasonable proportion of the likely amount of the final judgment.

(5) The court must take into account—

There is some evidence that delay and associated anxiety can cause a recognisable psychological state of "litigation neurosis",[50] a complaint which disappears on the resolution of the dispute. It is almost inevitable that the circumstances associated with a legal dispute will cause worry and upset, but long delays weaken the spirit as well as the claim.[51]

The claimant has little to gain by delay. It may be that the injuries are such that their full effects will not become apparent for some time and a hasty settlement might lead to an underestimation of the damage,[52] but generally any attempts to delay — even if ultimately frustrated by the case management powers of the court — are on the side of the defendants.[53] Lord Woolf explicitly recognised the risks of delay:

"Delay before the start of proceedings is just as undesirable (and can be just as expensive) as delay in the course of litigation. There would be no point in offering a fast track timetable of 20 or 30 weeks to a claimant who has spent two or three years in fruitless negotiations before bringing the case to court at all. What is needed is a system which enables the parties to a dispute to embark on meaningful negotiation as soon as the possibility of litigation is identified, and ensures that as early as possible they have the relevant information to define their claims and make realistic offers to settle."[54]

D. ALTERNATIVE DISPUTE RESOLUTION ("ADR")

"In future, government departments will only go to court as a last resort. ... Instead, government legal disputes will be settled by mediation or arbitration whenever possible."[55]

(a) contributory negligence; and
(b) any relevant set-off or counterclaim."

[50] See the material cited by P. Cane, *Atiyah 's Accidents, Compensation and the Law* (4th edn. 1987) p. 151 and the footnotes thereto. The converse may also be true: many solicitors have encountered clients for whom the litigation forms their principal interest in life.

[51] The circumstances of the claimant are also important. An elderly, infirm person might want to receive money quickly in order to enjoy it.

[52] See above, para. 11-029, n. 12. The power to award provisional damages is unlikely to assist the *settlement* process, since it only applies to judgments. Indeed it could conceivably encourage claimants to go to court to take advantage of the power. It will not be possible to reopen settlements on this account so that the claimant will now have an additional choice to make in deciding on settlement or litigation. On the other hand, it may give the claimant greater bargaining power with the defendant, since a settlement may now be in the defendant's interests.

[53] A modern example of delay on the part of the defendant is the alleged tendency of some defendants to wait out the maximum three months for a full response to the claimant under the Personal Injury Pre-Action Protocol. See further Law Society *Response to Third Woolf Questionnaire* in which 15% of respondents said that pre-action protocols were not generally complied with, defendants, insurers and loss adjusters being identified as classes of parties that did not comply. 68% of respondents said that courts did not impose sanctions for breach of protocols.

[54] Final Report, Chapter 10, para. 4.

[55] Lord Chancellor's Department press release, March 23, 2001.

11–032   As this quotation indicates, methods of resolving disputes other than going
through a process of adjudication by the courts have become increasingly
popular.[56] Organisations designed to support this approach have become
well established in the last ten years.[57] Whilst the courts cannot, as they can
in some other jurisdictions, notably in the United States, compel the parties
to attempt an alternative method of resolution prior to engaging in
litigation,[58] number of initiatives are already in place encouraging the use of
mediation in particular[59] and judges are specifically directed to encourage
use of an alternative dispute resolution procedure "if the court considers
that appropriate and [to facilitate] the use of such procedure".[60]

Settlement by simple negotiation between the parties or their representatives can be seen as a form of ADR since it avoids the necessity of
adjudication by a court. Settlement by negotiation also indicates some of the
problems that, potentially, face all forms of ADR. Negotiation is a
contractual matter. There is often an imbalance of power between the
contracting parties, which the parties may seek to address by using expert
lawyers in the field. In the past there has been a dichotomy between those
who advocated a "litigation first" approach to negotiation and those who
advocated a more conciliatory approach designed to achieve a compro-

---

[56] A booklet produced for the general public by the Lord Chancellor's Department: *Resolving
Disputes without Going to Court* is available on the LCD website and another, *Alternatives to
Court*, can be found on the LSC website. A comparatively low-cost mediation scheme at the
Birmingham Civil Justice Centre, available in all cases except those suitable for the small
claims track, mediations taking place on the court premises after the end of the court's
working day, was introduced in December 2001: Lord Chancellor's Department press
release December 7, 2001. A similar scheme has been in place at the Central London County
Court since 1996.

[57] For example, the ADR group and CEDR.

[58] *Emerging Findings*, (March 2001), para. 4.11 suggests that there is a "clear view" in this
jurisdiction that ADR should not be made compulsory. See further R, Ingelby, "Court
Sponsored Mediation: The case against Mandatory Participation" (1993) 56 M.L.R. 441.
The practice in the Commercial Court of making "ADR orders" (Commercial Court Guide,
section G and Appendix 7) is persuasive rather than mandatory in nature: "The parties shall
take such serious steps as they may be advised to resolve their disputes by ADR
procedures ... "

[59] See for example the power to stay litigation for a month or more to allow the parties to seek
to resolve the claim otherwise than by litigation: CPR r. 26.4; the pilot mediation scheme for
small claims in the Central London County Court described in H. Genn, *The Central London
County Court Pilot Mediation Scheme* (1998) Lord Chancellor's Department research paper;
and the power of the Commercial Court, now contained in the Commercial Court Guide,
(section G and Appendix 7) to make "ADR orders". According to *Emerging Findings, op.
cit.*, para. .4.13, over 130 ADR orders were made in the first year of the CPR contrasted with
43 in the preceding year. There is also a mediation scheme in the Court of Appeal. In April
2001 the government announced the introduction of a "quality mark" for mediation: Lord
Chancellor's Department press release April 26, 2001.

[60] CPR r. 1.4. Other explicit references appear elsewhere, for example in the Pre-Action
protocol for Construction and Engineering Disputes, section 5, which prescribes a meeting
between the parties prior to the instigation of court proceedings:
The aim of the meeting is for the parties to agree what are the main issues in the case, to
identify the root cause of disagreement in respect of each issue, and *to consider (i)
whether, and if so how, the issues might be resolved without recourse to litigation*, and (ii) if
litigation is unavoidable, what steps should be taken to ensure that it is conducted in
accordance with the overriding objective as defined in Part [sic] 1.1 of the Civil Practice
Rules." (our italics).
In addition, the Legal Services Commission has an interest in ADR and will, for example,

mise.[61] The modern paradigm, however, in accordance with the dictates of the C.P.R., is to regard litigation as a last resort and only one amongst a bouquet of different methods of dispute resolution.[62] It is no accident that an increasing number of firms of solicitors no longer have a "Litigation Department" but rather a "Dispute Resolution Department."

There are various forms of ADR in addition to negotiation,[63] for example:

(a) Arbitration;

(b) Ombudsmen;

(c) Expert-determination;

(d) Mediation-arbitration ("med-arb.");

(e) Early neutral evaluation ("ENE");

(f) Conciliation;

(g) Mediation; and

(h) Online dispute resolution ("ODR")

We can only provide a brief description of each of these in this text. Those wishing to pursue the topic of ADR further are advised to consult the increasing numbers of specialist texts on the individual forms of ADR.[64]

(a) Arbitration[65]

Arbitration has a long and dignified history and is frequently used in, for example, the resolution of construction disputes. The case is evaluated by an arbitrator or panel of arbitrators, who may be experts in the relevant field

11–033

---

specifically fund mediation in family cases. Guidance in clinical negligence cases subject to public funding requires reasons for failing to pursue ADR to be recorded and, if necessary, reported to the Regional Office. Funding certificates in such cases may be limited to pursuing ADR rather than litigation (Funding Code Guidance, May 2001).

[61] For examples prior to the Woolf reforms, see A. Boon, "Ethics and Strategy in Personal Injury Litigation" (1995) 22 J.L.S. 353; C. Menkel-Meadow, "Lawyer Negotiations: Theories and Realities — What we can learn from mediation" (1993) 56 M.L.R.

[62] A CEDR survey quoted in *Emerging Findings, op. cit.*, para. 4.12 showed a 141% increase in the number of commercial mediations since the introduction of the new regime. For a discussion of ADR in this context, see further *ADR Discussion Paper* (1999) and *ADR Discussion Paper: summary of responses* (2000), both available on the Lord Chancellor's Department website. Whether this increase will continue is a matter of some debate: Lind, "ADR and mediation — boom or bust?" (2001) 151 N.L.J. 1238; Hickman, "Shake on it, pal", (2001) 98(29) L.S.G., 22; Harvey, "A case of arrested development?", Legal Week 2001, 3(25), 25.

[63] Some theorists do not include negotiation as a form of ADR. According to *ADR Discussion Paper: summary of responses, op. cit.*, para. 5, others do not include the comparatively formalistic arbitration.

[64] For example, Brown and Marriott, *ADR: Principles and Practice* (1999, 2nd ed. Sweet and Maxwell); Kendall, *Expert Determination* (3rd ed, 2001, Sweet and Maxwell); Boulle and Nesic, *Mediation, Principles, Process, Practice* (2001, Butterworths); Tweedale and Tweedale, *A Practical approach to Arbitration Law* (1999, Blackstone Press).

[65] See the consolidating Arbitration Act 1996.

rather than lawyers.[66] The decision, which is legally binding, is, however, made on the basis of the relevant substantive law. Procedure may be very similar to that used in litigation: the filing of statements of case; examination of witnesses and so on. Consequently, although arbitration may have the benefit of privacy, it may not be less expensive or less formal than litigation.

A related procedure available in construction cases is that of "adjudication", the principal feature of which is the speed by which a decision is made available: generally within 28 days of referral to the adjudicator.[67]

(b) Ombudsmen

11–034   Ombudsmen exist in a number of fields, generally in relation to public (*e.g* the Local Government Ombudsman) or quasi-public bodies (*e.g.* the Banking Ombudsman or the Legal Services Ombudsman). Their function is to deal with complaints in the relevant sector and they may have powers to award compensation or only to make recommendations to the body against whom the complaint is made out.

(c) Expert-determination

11–035   A straightforward example of this method of ADR is sometimes used in boundary disputes. The parties agree to be bound by the decision of an independent expert, in the example, a surveyor who comes to a conclusion as to the correct siting of the boundary.

(d) Mediation-arbitration ("med-arb.")

11–036   As its name suggests, this is a combination of mediation and arbitration. The parties begin by mediating, but if they fail to resolve the dispute by mediation, have agreed in advance to submit the dispute to binding arbitration.

(e) Early neutral evaluation ("ENE")

11–037   In this form of ADR, the parties consult an independent third party, often a lawyer, who provides his or view of the merits of the case on the basis of short submissions from each side. This view is not binding on the parties but, if it is, for example, a view on whether or not a clause in a contract is likely to be enforceable as a matter of law, allows the parties to seek an informed resolution of the dispute by other means, such as negotiation. The Commercial Court offers a "without prejudice, non-binding" early neutral evaluation service by a commercial judge who, following the evaluation, takes no further part in the case.[68]

---

[66] Many, are, however, members of the Chartered Institute of Arbitrators.

[67] Housing Grants, Construction and Regeneration Act 1996, s. 108; Scheme for Construction Contracts (England and Wales) Regulations 1998 (S.I. 1998/649).

[68] Commercial Court Guide, G2, p 121.

(f) Conciliation

Conciliation, often confused with mediation, is used in particular in the **11–038**
resolution of industrial disputes by the Advisory, Conciliation and
Arbitration Service ("ACAS"). It is also used by the Office for the
Supervision of Solicitors.[69] Of the two, conciliation often involves more
active work on the part of the conciliator. Andrews has identified the
advantages of conciliation as opposed to resolution by court adjudication as
the following (all of which also apply to mediation):

(1) "*secrecy*: the parties can keep their dispute and negotiation is private
    and confidential";[70]

(2) "avoidance of acrimony: a conciliated settlement can be reached
    without the bitterness associated with litigation";[71]

(3) "*flexibility*: it is possible to settle matters which lie beyond the compass
    of the law or legal judgment";[72]

(4) "*multiple parties*";

(5) "saving face: a conciliated settlement enables the parties to avoid the
    'winner takes all' aspect of most judgments";[73]

(6) "continuing associations: the consensual resolution of a dispute will be
    valuable when the parties are not merely casually connected by a single
    transaction ... ' but have a continuing relationship";

(7) "achieving a reconciliation: conciliation's greatest potential benefit is that
    it might bring about a complete reconciliation between the parties."[74]

(g) Mediation

Mediation has become the archetypal form of ADR to the extent that the **11–039**
expression "ADR" is sometimes casually assumed to *mean* mediation. It
shares many factors with conciliation, the distinguishing factor being that
the mediator is less likely to become actively involved in the resolution but is
more likely to take a "facilitative" role, possibly by using the technique of
"shuttle diplomacy", assisting the parties to find means of moving forwards
to a resolution. Mediation will normally be conducted under the aegis of one

---

[69] A process examined in Ward, More than Lip Service, (2001) 98 L.S.G. 28.

[70] Conciliation has this in common with most other forms of ADR. Privacy is of interest to
many large firms and companies and to many individuals, particularly where revelation of
the matter in dispute could be embarrassing or financially damaging. This is the particular
advantage, for example, that arbitration holds over litigation.

[71] Again, many forms of ADR, mediation in particular, seek to encourage the parties to co-
operate and focus on the future rather than to consider themselves as in intransigent
opposition.

[72] A factor common to mediation but not the case in arbitration where the decision is made
according to law as it would be in court.

[73] Again, a factor conciliation has in common with mediation but not with arbitration.

[74] Andrews (1994), pp. 407–408.

or other of the mediation organisations such as CEDR or the ADR Group[75] and its results will be binding if the parties agree in advance that that is to be the case.[76]

(h) Online Dispute Resolution ("ODR")

11–040 Methods of resolution of dispute through the internet vary[77] but can be divided into two main types:

(a) Virtual mediation. In this model, rather than sharing physical space such as a hotel or conference centre for a mediation, mediator and parties communicate via secure chat rooms provided by a specialist Internet organisation.

(b) "Blind bidding" systems. These can be used to resolve such issues as the amount of damages payable. The parties enter the figures they would be prepared to pay (or to accept) into the computer system and, as soon as the two figures are within a pre-arranged percentage, the computer notifies the parties that they have reached a settlement.

ADR has significant consequences not only for procedure, but also for the substantive law. The more disputes, and the more difficult they are, which are resolved by ADR, the less those disputes are resolved in a publicly accountable environment. Further, the disputes may be resolved without full consideration of the legal imperatives. Finally, ADR means that fewer cases are before the courts, so the courts have fewer opportunities to develop the law and provide appropriate legal solutions to the many problems which arise. So ADR is not a side-effect-free cure-all. It is important that it be used and that its development be backed by the government only for the right reasons. The saving of money alone is an insufficient reason. The objective must be the improvement of access to justice. We end this section where we began, with the Lord Chancellor's initiative advocating the use of ADR by the government in its own disputes:

---

[75] Whilst mediation organisations have their own training schemes, there are at the time of writing, calls for more centralised training and regulation of mediators: see Chadwick, "Finding its Feet", (2001) 15(36) Lawyer 2001, 33. The Law Society's Training Standards (June 2000) for civil/commercial mediation are available on its website and provide a straightforward guide to the structure and procedures of a mediation conducted under the Law Society's Code of Practice for Civil/Commercial Mediation (*Professional Conduct, op. cit.*, Chap. 22). For other debates surrounding the conduct of mediation, including whether or not the mediator need be an expert in the field of the dispute, see Shapiro, "Tough Talking", (2001) 145 Sol. J. 1036 and "Six Appeal", (2001) 3(25) Legal Week 29.

[76] For further recent discussion, see Goriely and Williams, "*Resolving Civil Disputes: Choosing between out-of-court schemes and litigation*" (1997, Lord Chancellor's Department research paper); Marsh, (2000) 2(7) Legal Week, 15; Gibb, "How litigation is losing out to mediation — disputes are solved in days instead of months, saving companies vast sums of money", *The Times*, June 26, 2001, Law 3.

[77] Examples quoted in Ross, "Online Dispute Resolution — Why Settle for less?" Internet Newsletter for Lawyers, May/June 2000, p 7, (*www.venables.co.uk/n0 105ste.pdf*) include the US-based *http://www.resolutionroom.com*, the Scottish *http://www.intersettle.co.uk* and the English organisations *http://www.WeCanSettle.com; http://www.eSettle.co.uk* and *http://www.TheClaimRoom.com*. A longer list of similar organisations appears in Consumers International, "Disputes in Cyberspace 2001" at *http://www.consumersinternational.org*

" ... there will still be cases which are not suitable for ADR such as those involving intentional wrongdoing, abuse of power, public law, human rights and vexatious litigants. There will also be disputes where a legal precedent is needed to clarify the law or where it would not be in the public interest to settle.[78]

[78] Lord Chancellor's Department press release, March 23, 2001.

CHAPTER 12

PRE-TRIAL CIVIL PROCEDURE

12–001 At this stage we move from a comparative approach, taking account of civil, tribunal and criminal procedure, and concentrate on civil procedure. The procedures which must be followed before a trial in the High Court or county court, and indeed even before initiating the court process,[1] should be used by the parties to expose the real area of difference between them and concentrate attention upon it. Issues that are not in dispute should be eliminated and the scope of the disagreement narrowed. If the parties are not able or prepared to narrow the issues in this way, increasingly the court will step in to narrow the issues of its own volition. Using the procedures, and particularly in the current regime, the pre-action protocols, in this way has the dual effect of preparing the case as precisely as possible for trial and of encouraging a settlement by revealing to the parties the exact nature of their dispute.

In any consideration of civil procedure, however, it is important to understand the major shift in approach by the courts enshrined in the Civil Procedure Rules 1998,[2] brought into force on April 26, 1999 and often colloquially referred to as "the Woolf Reforms". The Civil Procedure Rules 1998 ("CPR") are divided into "Parts", each of which contains a number of rules. Almost all Parts are accompanied by one or more practice directions ("PDs") giving more precise details of procedure. Further, at the date of writing, the CPR still had annexed to it Schedules 1 and 2, these being the remnant of the old rules[3] yet to be incorporated into the CPR A continuous process of review is gradually bringing the matters covered by the schedules within the ambit of the main rules: so, for example, October 2001 brought into force Parts 55 and 56 of the CPR, which govern many types of property litigation. The CPR themselves are updated and corrected at regular intervals. At the date of writing (January 2002) the CPR had received their

---

[1] Pre action protocols.

[2] S.I. 1998/3132 under the power conferred by Civil Procedure Act 1997, s.2. For a list of amending statutory instruments up to and including Civil Procedure (Amendment No. 6) Rules 2001, see Chap. 10, n.#

[3] Schedule 1 contains the remainder of the Rules of the Supreme Court ("R.S.C.") governing the High Court and Schedule 2 contains the equivalent remainder of the County Court Rules ("C.C.R.").

26th update and a 27th was scheduled for early March 2002.[4] This chapter is believed to be up to date to that update, most of whose amendments will become effective on March 25, 2002.

The Woolf reforms are the latest manifestation of a longstanding dissatisfaction with the process of judicial resolution of civil disputes.[5] The complexity of pre-trial procedure, particularly in the High Court, had been said to act not only as a deterrent to all but the most determined litigant but also as a weapon for the recalcitrant defendant who might manipulate it so as to place the pressure of the delay upon the plaintiff (now known as the "claimant").

Lord Woolf s review of the system comprised an interim report (the "Interim Report"), published in June 1995[6] and a final report ("the Final Report") in July 1996[7] accompanied by a set of draft civil procedure rules known at the time from the colour of their binding as "the brown book".[8] Following a period of consultation, redrafting and testing[9] the new rules, enacted as a statutory instrument in 1998 were brought into force in England and Wales on April 26, 1999.[10]

The nature of the reforms can only be summarised here. Lord Woolf's starting point was, however, perhaps best expressed in the Interim Report when he identified the adversarial culture, for which lawyers and the system were responsible, as creating an environment in which "questions of expense, delay, compromise and fairness may have only low priority. The consequence is that expense is often excessive, disproportionate and

---

[4] These updates have in the past been made on a (roughly) monthly basis. Consequently, for effective use of the CPR it is essential to consult the most up to date version available. Given the regularity of updates, this will frequently not be a textbook or even such practitioners' texts as the widely used White Book, *op. cit.*, but the Lord Chancellor's Department website: *http://www.lcd.gov.uk*. Similarly the most up to date information about fees and court forms is generally found on the Court Service website: *http://www.courtservice.gov.uk*

[5] Prior to the two Woolf Reports, for example, came the *Report of the Review Body on Civil Justice* (Cm. 394, 1989); *Civil Justice on trial — the case for change: Report by the Independent Working Party set up by the General Council of the Bar and the Law Society* (1993) (Chair H. Heilbron, Vice Chair: H. Hodge). In addition the courts had sought to move towards a more "managed" system: *Practice Direction* [1995] 1 All E.R. 385 — in introducing this practice direction the Lord Chief Justice said "The aim is to try to change the whole culture, the ethos, applying in the field of civil litigation." See also J. Rozenberg, *The Search for Justice* (1995) pp 171-182 and C. Glasser, *Solving the Litigation Crisis* (1994) quoted in the Interim Report at p 5.

[6] Lord Woolf, *Access to Justice: An Interim Report* (1995) (hereafter the Interim Report).

[7] Lord Woolf: *Final Report on Access to Justice* (1996) (hereafter the Final Report).

[8] This to distinguish them from the principal publication containing the then Rules of the Supreme Court ("the White Book", *op. cit.*) and that containing the County Court Rules ("the Green Book" *op. cit*). Following the reforms, and somewhat confusingly for the novice, both the White Book and the Green Book contain the text of the unified Civil Procedure Rules.

[9] As, for example, the following Lord Chancellor's Department research papers: Goriely, Butt and Sherr, *Costing Fast Track Procedures through Hypothetical Studies*, (1998); Peysner, Unell, Scott, McLachlan, *Report of the Fast Track Simulation Project* (1998)

[10] A sudden rise in the issue of civil proceedings in the months immediately prior to 26th April 1999 is commonly attributed to a misconceived belief amongst practitioners that claims brought before "Woolf-Day" would proceed under the familiar old rules. See the Lord Chancellor's Department paper *Emerging Findings* (March 2001) at 3.3. In fact, Part 51 of the CPR contains transitional provisions designed to bring all pending cases within the ambit of the new rules as far as possible. Cases where no action was taken by the parties during a year of grace expiring on April 26, 2000 ran the distinct risk of being struck out.

unpredictable; and delay is frequently unreasonable."[11] Further, the problems of delay, cost and complexity remained "the key problems facing civil justice to-day."[12]

During the consultation process, steps were taken to implement some of the proposals contained in the Interim Report, such as the appointment of the then Vice-Chancellor of the Chancery Division as the Head of Civil Justice.[13]

Finally, however, Lord Woolf's proposals were grouped under the following series of objectives:[14]

a.   Litigation will be avoided wherever possible;

b.   Litigation will be less adversarial and more co-operative;

c.   Litigation will be less complex;

d.   The timescale of litigation will be shorter and more certain;

e.   The cost of litigation will be more affordable; more predictable, and more proportionate to the value and complexity of individual cases;

f.   Parties of limited financial means will be able to conduct litigation on a more equal footing;

g.   There will be clear lines of judicial and administrative responsibility for the civil justice system;

h.   The structure of the courts and the deployment of judges will be designed to meet the needs of litigants;

i.   Judges will be deployed effectively so that they can manage litigation in accordance with the new rules and protocols; and

j.   The civil justice system will be more responsive to the needs of litigants.

Whether and if so to what extent the new regime as currently operating meets these objectives[15] will be considered at the end of this chapter, once we have examined the pre-trial procedure in more detail.

However, in order to set the discussion that follows in context, a number of preliminary points should be made:

---

[11] Interim Report, p. 7.

[12] *ibid.*

[13] Others listed in the Final Report, p.2 include the involvement of the Judicial Studies Board in training judges in their new role of managers of cases; the encouragement of ADR in a Lord Chancellor's Department publication *Resolving Disputes without Going to Court* and proposals for a unified rule making committee. The Civil Justice Council, an advisory body formed in response to the recommendation in the Interim Report that a body should be formed "with responsibility for overseeing and co-ordinating the implementation of [Lord Woolf's proposals" first met in 1998, having been constituted under Civil Procedure Act 1997, s.6. Summaries of its meetings and the subjects of its discussion can be found on its website at *http://www.civilijusticecouncil.gov.uk*. A white paper, *Modernising Justice*, setting out the government's objectives at this time was published in December 1998.

[14] Final Report, section 1, para.9.

[15] Much anecdotal evidence can be found in the legal press over the last two years. The Lord Chancellor's Department is, however, conducting its own evaluation, the initial findings of which are contained in its paper *Emerging Findings* (March 2001).

A. THE OVERRIDING OBJECTIVE.

A useful guide to the ethos of the new regime can be obtained from Part 1 of the CPR (otherwise known as the "overriding objective"). This is the governing principle to be employed by the courts in exercising their powers of case management.[16] Consequently, we set it out here in full:

12–002

"1.1(1) These Rules are a new procedural code with the overriding objective of enabling the court to deal with cases justly.

(2) Dealing with a case justly includes, so far as is practicable

(a) ensuring that the parties are on an equal footing;
(b) saving expense;
(c) dealing with the case in ways which are proportionate

(i) to the amount of money involved;
(ii) to the importance of the case;
(iii) to the complexity of the issues; and
(iv) to the financial position of each party;

(d) ensuring that it is dealt with expeditiously and fairly; and
(e) allotting to it an appropriate share of the court's resources, while taking into account the need to allot resources to other cases.

1.2 The court must seek to give effect to the overriding objective when it

(a) exercises any power given to it by the Rules; or
(b) interprets any rule.

1.3 The parties are required to help the court to further the overriding objective.

1.4(1) The court must further the overriding objective by actively managing cases.

(2) Active case management includes

(a) encouraging the parties to co-operate with each other in the conduct of the proceedings;
(b) identifying the issues at an early stage;
(c) deciding promptly which issues need full investigation and trial and accordingly disposing summarily of the others;
(d) deciding the order in which issues are to be resolved;
(e) encouraging the parties to use an alternative dispute resolution procedure if the court considers that appropriate and facilitating the use of such procedure;
(f) helping the parties to settle the whole or part of the case;
(g) fixing timetables or otherwise controlling the progress of the case;

---

[16] For some examples of its application, see *Maltez v. Lewis, The Times,* May 4, 1999, Ch. D; *Jenkins v. Grocott* [2001] C. P. Rep. 15, Q.B.D.; *GKR Karate UK Ltd. v. Yorkshire Post Newspapers* [2000] 1 W.L.R. 2571, [2000] 2 All E.R. 931, [2000] C.P. Rep. 47, C.A.; *Law v. St. Margarets Insurances Ltd.* [2001] EWCA Civ 30; [2001] All E.R. (D) 97, C.A. and *Holmes v. SGB Services plc.,* [2001] EWCA Civ 354, C.A.

(h) considering whether the likely benefits of taking a particular step justify the cost of taking it;

(i) dealing with as many aspects of the case as it can on the same occasion;

(j) dealing with the case without the parties needing to attend at court;

(k) making use of technology; and

(l) giving directions to ensure that the trial of a case proceeds quickly and efficiently."

The court's powers in respect of these obligations are set out in CPR Part 3 and include the following:

"3.1(2) Except where these Rules provide otherwise, the court may:

(a) extend or shorten the time for compliance with any rule, practice direction or court order (even if an application for extension is made after the time for compliance has expired);

(b) adjourn or bring forward a hearing;

(c) require a party or a party's legal representative to attend the court;

(d) hold a hearing and receive evidence by telephone or by using any other method of direct oral communication;

(e) direct that part of any proceedings (such as a counterclaim) be dealt with as separate proceedings;

(f) stay the whole or part of any proceedings or judgment either generally or until a specified date or event;

(g) consolidate proceedings;

(h) try two or more claims on the same occasion;

(i) direct a separate trial of any issue;

(j) decide the order in which issues are to be tried;

(k) exclude an issue from consideration;

(l) dismiss or give judgment on a claim after a decision on a preliminary issue;

(m) take any other step or make any other order for the purpose of managing the case and furthering the overriding objective.

3.1(3) When the court makes an order, it may:

(a) make it subject to conditions, including a condition to pay a sum of money into court; and

(b) specify the consequence of failure to comply with the order or a condition.

(4) Where the court gives directions it may take into account whether or not a party has complied with any relevant pre-action protocol.

(5) The court may order a party to pay a sum of money into court if that party has, without good reason, failed to comply with a rule, practice direction or a relevant pre-action protocol.

(6) When exercising its power under paragraph (5) the court must have regard to:

(a) the amount in dispute; and

(b) the costs which the parties have incurred or which they may incur.

3.3(1) Except where a rule or some other enactment provides otherwise, the court may exercise its powers on an application or of its own initiative.

3.4(2) The court may strike out a statement of case if it appears to the court:

(a) that the statement of case discloses no reasonable grounds for bringing or defending the claim;

(b) that the statement of case is an abuse of the court's process or is otherwise likely to obstruct the just disposal of the proceedings; or

(c) that there has been a failure to comply with a rule, practice direction or court order … "

1. RELEVANCE OF EARLIER DECISIONS

The words "a new procedural code" were inserted into CPR Part 1 at a **12–003** comparatively late stage. The intention seemed to be to create a *tablua rasa*, a blank page unsullied by the laxities of the past. The effect of this was, however, to create uncertainty in the professions, particularly where there were well-established precedents on rules that appeared in identical terminology in the new canon of rules. After two years, procedural case law specific to the new regime is now developing, but the approach to the relevance of old decisions is by no means consistent.[17] Perhaps the most significant statement of intent in this respect, however, comes from Lord Woolf sitting in *Biguzzi v. Rank Leisure plc*.[18]

"The whole purpose of making the CPR a self-contained code was to send the message[19] which now generally applies. Earlier authorities are no longer generally of any relevance once the CPR applies."

2. TERMINOLOGY

Even if the older cases on procedural matters have ceased to be relevant, the **12–004** CPR are only a "procedural code" and do not seek to supplant the whole corpus of English substantive law. Lawyers have had to become bilingual, understanding pre-1999 terminology such as "plaintiff; "writ"; "default summons" and *"ex parte"* when reading older cases, whilst using the modern equivalents in their day to day practice. For current purposes, however, the most significant changes in terminology are those replacing "plaintiff with "claimant" and "writ" or "county court (default) summons" with "claim form".

---

[17] For some examples, see *Purdy v. Cambran*, [2000] C.P. Rep. 67, C.A.; *Lombard Natwest Factors Ltd. v. Arbis, The Times* December 10, 1999, Ch. D.

[18] [1999] 1 W.L.R. 1926; [1999] 4 All E.R. 934; [2000] C.P. Rep. 6; *The Times*, October 5, 1999, C. A. Further reinforcement has come much more recently in *Reid Minty v. Taylor* [2001] EWCA Civ 1723,2001 WL 1171953, C.A.

[19] That the court is in control and that timelimits are now more important than ever.

B. TRACKS

12–005   Prior to 1999, it was essential to understand the differences in procedure between the county court (governed by the County Court Rules) and the High Court (governed by the Rules of the Supreme Court). The effect of the Woolf reforms has not been, as one might have predicted, to amalgamate the two courts as well as to merge their rules of operation. Consequently, the two levels of court, with their individual personnel and particular jurisdictions remain and are discussed in more detail at para. 12-006 below.

In order to understand the operation of the new regime it will, however, be important to understand the concept and significance of the "track" system. Whilst the detailed effects of the individual tracks will be discussed below, as a summary:

The *small claims track* occupies the territory formerly occupied by the small claims court in the county court. Its jurisdiction was raised from £1,000 to £3,000 in 1996 and (for most purposes[20]) to £5,000 in 1999 when the CPR were implemented. In 2000, 55, 836 small claims hearings were held, of which 33,490 were in debt claims.[21]

The *fast track* will occupy the majority of the remainder of defended civil cases, being the "normal track" for claims above the small claims limit but whose value does not exceed £15,000.[22] Most fast track claims will proceed in the county court.

Cases not fulfilling the criteria for the small claims track or the fast track will be allocated to the *multi track*, the "hallmarks" of which are expressed to be "(1) the ability of the court to deal with cases of widely differing values and complexity, and (2) the flexibility given to the court in the way it will manage a case in a way appropriate to its particular needs."[23]

Alongside the continuing evolution of the pre trial process contained in the CPR, the civil courts have also been required to deal with the effect of the implementation in England and Wales in October 2000 of the Human Rights Act 1998. The impact of this Act on civil procedure is largely twofold: the civil courts have become a forum for those seeking remedies against public authorities infringing their human rights and, as public authorities themselves, the courts have an obligation to uphold the human rights of individual litigants, both in their right under art 6 to a fair and

---

[20] CPR r. 26.6(1) provides that personal injury claims worth in total less than £5,000 may proceed in the small claims track only if the financial value of the element of the claim relating to personal injury (as opposed to, for example, the cost of repair of a vehicle damaged in the accident) does not exceed £1,000. Claims by residential tenants against their landlords for repairs will only proceed in the small claims track if neither the cost of repair nor any other claim exceeds £1,000.

[21] *Judicial Statistics 2000*, tables 4.8 and 4.19. In the previous year, the statistics for which will have included some claims brought under the old rules, there were 88, 389 small claims hearings: *Judicial Statistics 1999*, tables 4.7 and 4.8.

[22] Increased from the recommendation in the Final Report of £10,000. Such claims will only under CPR r. 26.6(5) proceed in the fast track procedure if the trial "is likely to last for no longer than one day" and only limited (or no) expert evidence will be required.

[23] PD. 29 para. 3.2.

public trial but also in other areas including the rights to freedom of expression and the right to privacy.[24]

Despite the stated intention of the new regime to make the procedure easier for the layperson to understand, procedural complexities remain and generally speaking continue to necessitate the services of a lawyer or other person providing the appropriate legal service in the pursuit of a claim.

In the previous edition of this book, we went on to consider the availability of legal representation under the legal aid scheme in civil proceedings on the basis that, since many people are unable to meet the costs of litigation from their own resources, the availability of representation under the legal aid scheme would often be the crucial factor in deciding whether the case went on at all. Clearly it remains the case that the average individual is unable to fund litigation, but the position of legal aid is now very different. Following concerns expressed by both Conservative and Labour administrations about the extent of legal aid expenditure public funding should be considered more as a default provision than as a primary resource for funding individuals' cases.

The different methods of funding are discussed in Chapter 11.

C. THE COUNTY COURT

The county court has a wide jurisdiction. Its jurisdiction is now synonymous with that of the High Court in many instances.[25] Most of the claims in the county court are based upon contract and tort. In 2000 1, 871, 923 claims were issued,[26] 1, 631, 966 (87 per cent) of which were "money" claims.[27] **12–006**

It is explicit from the amendment to the High Court and County Courts Jurisdiction Order 1991 that provided that claims could not normally be brought in the High Court unless valued at over £15,000 that the county courts should take cases from the High Court. During 2000, the total number of claims issued in the Queen's Bench Division of the High Court was 26, 876, a drop of 63 per cent from the 1999 figure (which itself showed a drop of 37 per cent from the 1998 figure).[28] However since the issue of county court proceedings over the same period fell, albeit by a much smaller amount, some of the reduction may reasonably be attributed to the effect of

---

[24] And in mediating between the two rights, particularly where the grant of an injunction intended to protect the complainant's privacy might have the effect of restricting the freedom of expression of, for example, a journalist wishing to publish information said to be of public interest: *Douglas and Zeta Jones v. Hello! Limited, The Times,* 16th January 2001; [2001] 2 W.L.R. 992; [2001] 2 All E.R. 289; C.A.

For a case where the court acknowledged that the result would have been different in the absence of the Human Rights Act, see *Goode v. Martin,* [2001] EWCA Civ 1899, *The Times,* January 24, 2002, C.A.

[25] As a consequence of recommendations in the *Civil Justice Review* (1989) introduced by the High Court and County Courts Jurisdiction Order 1991 (SI 1991 No 724).

[26] In the light of the expressed aim of the Woolf reforms to avoid litigation where possible, it is worth noting that this figure is, according to *Judicial Statistics 2000,* a decrease of 6% on the 1999 figures which themselves showed a decrease of 11% on the 1998 figures.

[27] *Judicial Statistics 1999* and *2000,* table 4.1.

[28] *Judicial Statistics 2000,* table 4.1.

the Woolf reforms in encouraging disputants to resolve their differences in ways other than litigation.[29]

Despite the Woolf reforms, there are still jurisdictional questions to be assessed in determining in which court to commence an action — set out conveniently in PD. 7 para. 2 — but there are wide provisions for transfer.[30] Nevertheless, sanctions may be applied against the claimant who has issued proceedings in the wrong court.[31]

Following the harmonisation of the procedural rules governing the High Court and county court it is no longer possible to say that county court procedure is of itself any easier to follow for the lay person than High Court procedure. It is, perhaps still true that the only circumstances in which a lay person finds it relatively easy to pursue litigation unaided is through the small claims process. Since almost all county court cases will be proceeding in the small claims or fast track,[32] the Court Service has a commitment to provide a trial date within 20 weeks of allocation[33] which may be quicker than in the High Court.

Whilst there are, at the date of writing, still minor differences in procedure between the two courts in (for example) the methods of enforcement available, and the fact that there may still be a feeling that a claim brought in the High Court is in some way more intimidating to a recalcitrant defendant, any perceived disadvantages of a county court action should have been reduced to the minimum.

D. THE HIGH COURT

12–007 Unless a specific enactment requires proceedings to be brought in the High Court, then, as from April 26, 1999, proceedings for claims whose value does

---

[29] Analysis on a month by month basis in *Emerging Findings, op. cit.*, indicates a substantial drop in the issue of proceedings both in the county court and in the Queen's Bench Division of the High Court immediately after the reforms — for example, in the High Court figures, from just over 12,000 claims in March 1999 down to just under 2,000 claims in May 1999. Figures subsequently rose but to nothing approaching the previous level.

[30] CPR Part 30 and PD. 30.

[31] CPR r. 30.2(2)

[32] Examples of exceptions are personal injury cases worth less than £50,000 and claims proceeding in the London county courts where by PD. 29 para. 2, claims brought in the Royal Courts of Justice (the London office of the High Court) of a value less than £50,000 "will generally" be transferred to one of the London county courts.

[33] The process of allocating a claim to a track once the statements of case of both parties have been filed. For definitions of "allocation" and "statement of case" see paras 12-016 and 12-021. Allocation should take place approximately a month to two months after issue. It should, however, be noted that the pre-action protocol may take up to three months to complete and that even once the action has been formally commenced, the statements of case stage may take another month or two. Consequently the whole period from initial letter of claim to fast track trial may still be in the region of a year. *Judicial Statistics 2000* indicates at table 4.17 that the average period between issue and trial in the county court is 74 weeks. This does, compare favourably — but only just — with the average waiting period for a county court trial described in *Judicial Statistics 1995*, Cm. 3290, p 35, of 79 weeks.

not exceed £15,000 cannot be brought in the High Court.[34] There will be some exceptions under specific enactments, as, for example, the Human Rights Act 1998 which provides at s. 4 that claims arising from judicial acts can only be brought in the High Court or above.

E. COURT PROCEDURE GENERALLY

In the previous edition of this book, we moved on to separate sections considering the procedure in the county court and in the High Court. It would be inconsistent with the harmonisation of the procedural rules governing the two courts enshrined in the CPR to continue that approach. Under the new regime, as we have seen above, the more significant distinction is between small claims track, fast track and multi-track case management models. Whilst, as we have seen, in fact, small claims and most fast track cases will be dealt with in the county court and most multi track claims in the High Court, the distinctions between the tracks are not necessarily co-extensive with the distinction between the two courts. **12–008**

1. COURT MANAGEMENT OF LITIGATION

It was a fundamental tenet of Lord Woolf s thinking[35] that the courts should wrest control of the procedure from the parties; the parties (or perhaps more correctly, their legal representatives) being perceived as in large part responsible for delay and the running up of large fees. Consequently CPR Parts 1 and 3 confer significant powers on the court to control the progress of a claim towards trial and to impose sanctions on any party impeding that progress. In particular, although it may be regarded as a sanction of last resort[36] a party's claim or defence may be struck out for failure to comply with rules or court orders. **12–009**

The guiding principle is, as we have seen, enshrined in CPR Part 1, otherwise referred to as the "overriding objective".

Further, since the incorporation of the European Convention of Human Rights into English law by virtue of the Human Rights Act 1998,[37] the court, as a "public authority" within the meaning of the Act has been subjected to sanction if it permits breaches of human rights.[38] The obvious human right with which the court will be concerned is that guaranteeing a

---

[34] High Court and County Courts Jurisdiction Order 1991; S.L 1991/724, amended by High Court and County Courts Jurisdiction (Amendment) Order 1999, S.I. 1999/1014.

[35] Earlier attempts had been made to seek to increase the efficiency of the system, such as Practice Direction [1995] 1 All ER 385. The aim of this practice direction was, according to the then Lord Chief Justice, "to try and change the whole culture, the ethos, applying in the field of civil litigation".

[36] *Biguzzi v. Rank Leisure plc*, [1999] 1 W.L.R. 1926; [1999] 4 All E.R. 934; [2000] C.P. Rep. 6; *The Times,* October 5, 1999, C. A.

[37] Which came into force in October 2000.

[38] Principally in respect of the parties to litigation before the court, but also in respect of others, such as witnesses.

fair and public trial within a reasonable time (art 6). It is as a direct result of art 6 that arrangements were made for all hearings, even short procedural pre-trial hearings, to take place in public.[39] As to the "fairness" of the trial, it was thought prior to implementation of the Act that it might become commonplace for appeals to include, automatically or by way of after-thought, an allegation that the appellant had been deprived of a fair trial. Lord Woolf, sitting in the Court of Appeal, announced the approach the courts would take to such allegations:

> "In my judgment, cases such as this, do not require any consideration of human rights issues, certainly issues under article 6. It would be highly undesirable if the consideration of those issues was made more complex by the injection into them of article 6 style arguments. I hope that judges will be robust in resisting any attempt to introduce those arguments. ... When the 1998 Act becomes law, counsel will need to show self restraint if it is not to be discredited."[40]

The court must also ensure that orders it makes do not cause breaches of human rights and this will often involve the court in seeking to strike a fair balance between two competing rights.[41] Where one of the rights involved is that of freedom of expression, s. 12 of the Human Rights Act 1998 imposes further obligations on the court.

2. Prior to Commencing an Action: the Pre-action Protocols

12–010   Although prior to April 26, 1999 it was considered good practice for the plaintiff (through his or her legal representatives) to write a "letter before action" to the proposed defendant, outlining the nature of the claim and, in a liquidated claim, inviting payment within, say, 7 days, this was regarded perhaps as a warning at most, with the added potential benefit that it might provoke payment or meaningful negotiations.

It is, of course, a tenet of the Woolf reforms that litigation should be avoided wherever possible.[42] Accordingly, Lord Woolf recommended that "pre-action protocols" should be developed to govern the pre-issue stages of litigation. It was intended that these should:

a.   Encourage the use of alternative dispute resolution ("ADR");

---

[39]   This has had a particular impact, following *Scarth v. UK* (1999) Application no. 33745/96, E.C.H.R., on small claims track hearings. These had previously been not only informal, but also by way of arbitration and held in private. The holding of hearings in public is now the invariable case at least in principle, subject to predictable exceptions (such as the need to protect a child): CPR r. 39.2. In practice the rooms normally used by district judges and masters for pre-trial hearings are not of a size to accommodate large numbers of the interested public.

[40]   *Daniels v. Walker, The Times* May 17, 2000, [2000] 1 W.L.R. 1382, C.A.

[41]   A number of recent cases involving injunctions give good examples of the way in which the courts seek to achieve this balancing act e.g., *Douglas and Zeta-Jones v. Hello! Ltd., op.cit.*

[42]   It is thought that the use of pre-action protocols is a contributing factor to the decrease in the number of civil claims being issued: *Emerging Findings op. cit.*, paras. 3.12 to 3.16 inclusive.

b. Promote "economy" in the use of expert witnesses — the parties are encouraged to make consensual arrangements for expert evidence in particular to agree to the use of a single expert witness between them rather than one each;

c. Enable parties to obtain and exchange information (such as, for example, information about the likely value of the claim);

d. Assist parties to comply with the tight timetable likely to be set by the court for the pre-trial stages once (if at all) court proceedings were issued.

At the date of writing there are six approved pre-action protocols for: personal injury claims, defamation claims, construction and engineering disputes; clinical negligence, professional negligence and judicial review cases. Others are in development.[43] Whilst each contains matters specific to the nature of the type of claim under discussion, the essential structure of a protocol is a timetable for letters setting out, in the claimant's case, the nature and details of the claim (and proposals for expert evidence) and in the defendant's case, a reasoned response setting out the extent to which the claim is disputed. There are sanctions for failure to comply with the appropriate protocol.[44]

In cases other than those to which an approved protocol applies, the parties must, however, engage in very similar behaviour,[45] subject again to sanctions for failure to do so.

---

[43] Draft pre-action protocols for disease and illness claims and housing repair claims can be found on the Law Society's website and a draft intellectual property protocol is on the Lord Chancellor's Department's website. In October 2001 the Lord Chancellor's Department issued a consultation paper including a draft pre-action protocol of general application intended to be used in any case to which no specific protocol applies.

[44] In the words of PD. Protocols, para. 2.3
"(1) an order that the party at fault pay the costs of the proceedings, or part of those costs, of the other party or parties;
(2) an order that the party at fault pay those costs on an indemnity basis;
(3) if the party at fault is a claimant in whose favour an order for the payment of damages or some specified sum is subsequently made, an order depriving that party of interest on such and in respect of such period as may be specified, and/or awarding interest at a lower rate than that at which interest would otherwise have been awarded;
(4) if the party at fault is a defendant and an order for the payment of damages or some specified sum is subsequently made in favour of the claimant, an order awarding interest on such sum and in respect of such period as may be specified at a higher rate, not exceeding 10% above base rate (c.f., CPR r.36.21(2)), than the rate at which interest would otherwise have been awarded."
The extent to which a protocol has been complied with must also be indicated to the court at the allocation stage and the extent of compliance or non-compliance will be a factor when the court is considering the award of costs: CPR r. 44.3(5).

[45] PD Protocols, para 4:
"In cases not covered by any approved protocol, the court will expect the parties, in accordance with the overriding objective and the matters referred to in CPR 1.1(2)(a), (b) and (c), to act reasonably in exchanging information and documents relevant to the claim and generally in trying to avoid the necessity for the start of proceedings."

3. Commencing an Action

12–011　To begin a claim, the claimant must file a number of documents, including a cheque for the appropriate issue fee,[46] the claim form and any notice of funding,[47] at the court office.[48] In some cases this can now be done over the internet.[49]

The particulars of claim may be filed at this stage or alternatively filed within 14 days after the claim form (once "issued" by the court) has been served on the defendant.[50] The claim form is a prescribed form requiring information to be given as to the nature of the claim and its value (to establish that the court has jurisdiction).[51] There is no specific form for the particulars of claim (although it must comply with the requirements of CPR Part 16 and of PD. 16[52]) even though the object of the particulars is to inform the defendant with sufficient particularity of the claim against him or her. The claimant must supply them.In certain types of case (such as personal injury claims) additional prescribed documents must accompany the particulars of claim.[53] There is, however, a general discretion to add to or include in the particulars of claim any or all of the following:

a.　Any point of law on which the claim is based;

b.　The name of any witness the claimant intends to call; and

c.　Any document "necessary to" the claim.[54]

The claim form, and, if separate, the particulars of claim, must contain a "statement of truth".[55] This statement is in the words "I believe/the claimant believes that the facts stated in this claim form/these particulars of claim are true". It is normally signed by the actual claimant rather than by his or her legal representative[56] and the sanction for signing without an

---

[46] It often surprises litigants to know the amount of the fee, which, depending on the value of the claim, can be up to £500. See, for the High Court, the Supreme Court Fees Order 1999 (as amended), S.I. 1999/687 and for the county court, the County Court Fees Order 1999 (as amended), S.I. 1999/689.

[47] Such as a conditional fee agreement.

[48] CPR r. 7.2 (1).

[49] A scheme, "Money Claim online" (*http://www.courtservice.gov.uk/mcol*) for claims involving fixed sums less than £100,000, is being piloted between December 17, 2001 and June 16, 2003. Payment of court fees is by credit or debit card.

[50] CPR r. 7.4.

[51] CPR r. 16.2, 16.3, PD. 16 para. 2 and PD. 7 para. 3

[52] See for example, the list of contents of the particulars of claim at CPR r. 16.4 and the further details required by PD. 16 paras. 3 to 9 inclusive.

[53] In a personal injury claim, a medical report setting out the claimant's injuries and a "schedule of past and future expenses and losses" ("special damages"): see PD. 16 para. 4. Additional requirements for fatal accident claims, recovery of land, hire purchase, Competition Act 1998 and human rights claims are also set out in PD. 16.

[54] PD. 16 para. 13.3.

[55] PD. 7 para. 7 and CPR r. 22 (l)(a).

[56] although it can be signed by the legal representative: PD. 22 para. 3.8.

honest belief in the truth of the document is a penalty for contempt of court.[57]

If legal help is sought the lawyer is likely to rely on the precedents which are published, treating with a considerable degree of caution any published prior to 1999. The claim form (with or without the particulars of claim) is then sealed by the court. This is the official commencement of the court proceedings.[58] The sealed claim form is then sent to the defendant, usually by the court but sometimes by the claimant.[59] The process of transmitting the sealed claim form to the defendant is known as "service" and may be carried out in a number of ways including facsimile transmission and in limited circumstances, e-mail.[60]

Generally, proceedings are brought under CPR Part 7. However, in cases where the claimant "seeks the court's decision on a question which is unlikely to involve a substantial question of fact",[61] such as possession proceedings or judicial review, the alternative Part 8 procedure is available. The Part 8 procedure omits most of the normal stages of exchange of evidence and proceeds to an early hearing of the merits of the dispute.

County Court/High Court which court for issue?

A claim form cannot be issued in the High Court unless the value of the claim exceeds £15,000.[62] As we will see, this is the same financial limit as for the "multi-track" case management model, the result being that for practical purposes, all High Court cases will be multi-track.[63] If the claim is for personal injuries, however, the claim cannot be started in the High Court unless its value exceeds £50,000. This does not, however, prevent claims whose value exceeds either figure being issued in the county court, perhaps for reasons of convenience. Aside from merely financial considerations, claims should be begun in the High Court if their complexity or importance in the context of public interest demand it.[64] After issue, however, claims may be transferred, not only between High Court and county court, but also to the specialist courts such as the Technology and Construction Court, the Commercial Court or the Mercantile Court

12–012

---

[57] CPR r. 32.14. See also *Malgar v. R. E. Leach (Engineering) Ltd., The Times,* 17th February 2000; [2000] C.P. Rep. 39, Ch. D), *per* Scott V.C.:

"it is important that flagrant breaches of the obligation to be responsible and truthful in verifying statements of case and in verifying witness statements should be policed and enforced if necessary by committal proceedings."

A claim form, particulars of claim or any other statement of case from which the statement of truth has been omitted altogether is not a nullity, but is vulnerable to being struck out: PD. 22 para. 4.

[58] PD. 7 para. 5.1.

[59] CPR Part 6 and PD. 6.

[60] See generally CPR Part 6 and PD. 6.

[61] CPR r. 8.1(2) and PD. 8 para. 1.1.

[62] PD. 7 para. 2.1 and High Court and County Courts Jurisdiction Order 1991(S.I. 1991/724), amended by High Court and County Courts Jurisdiction (Amendment) Order 1999 (S.I. 1999/1014). However, if the claim is issued in the Royal Courts of Justice in London, PD. 29, para. 2 provides for the transfer of cases worth less than £50,000 to a county court in the London area.

[63] There is, however, an exception where a statute provides that only a particular court has jurisdiction. See for an example PD. 7 para. 2.10 and the Human Rights Act 1998.

[64] PD. 7 para. 2.4.

Statutes and individual provisions of the CPR may, however, regulate the jurisdiction of the courts. So, for example, whilst Human Rights Act claims can be brought in either court, if the subject of the complaint is a judicial act, the claim must be commenced in the High Court.[65]

Fast track

12–013   A claim form in the (imaginary) case of *Wilkinson v. Walkertronic Super Hi-Fi-Vid Ltd.* follows, with the basic particulars of claim and the response pack. Where the claimant is a litigant in person, the style of the documentation will be less formal (although if it is not compliant with CPR Parts 7 and 16 and their accompanying practice directions, it may be vulnerable to being struck out[66]) but the information on which the claim is based must appear clearly so that the defendant knows what is the case against him or her. This claim is likely to be allocated to the fast track and has been issued in the county court.

High Court

12–014   We will also consider the (equally imaginary) case of *George and Hacker v. Reliable Nag Supply Stables (a firm)*, a claim worth in excess of £65,000. This claim will be issued in the High Court and is likely to be allocated to the multi-track.

---

[65]   PD. 7 para. 2.10. For specific jurisdictional provisions, particularly as to the jurisdiction of masters and district judges to make certain types of order, see PD. 2B Allocation of Cases to Levels of Judiciary.

[66]   CPR r. 3.4(2)(a).

 **Claim Form**

In the
NOTTINGHAM COUNTY COURT
Claim No.

Claimant

CYRIL JACK WILKINSON
24 YEW DRIVE
LENTON
NOTTINGHAM
NG7 1SS

SEAL

Defendant(s)

Walkertronic Super Hi-Fi-Vid Limited
TRADING ADDRESS:
UNIT 17
THE LAURELS SHOPPING PRECINCT
NOTTINGHAM
NG1 Y77

Brief details of claim

The Claimant's claim is for damages estimated at £6,210.00 and interest arising from the Defendant's supply, in breach of a contract of 1st February 2001 made between the Claimant and the Defendant, of a defective computer game.

Value

I expect to recover more than £5,000 but less than £10,000.

Defendant's name and address		£
Walkertronic Super Hi-Fi-Vid Limited	Amount claimed	To be determined
	Court fee	£230.00
UNIT 17	Solicitor's costs	To be determined
THE LAURELS SHOPPING PRECINCT	Total amount	£230.00
NOTTINGHAM NG1 Y77	Issue date	3rd October 2001

The court office at

is open between 10 am and 4 pm Monday to Friday. When corresponding with the court, please address forms or letters to the Court Manager and quote the claim number.

N1 Claim form (CPR Part 7)(10.00)

N1/1

	Claim No.	

Does, or will, your claim include any issues under the Human Rights Act 1998? ☐ Yes ☒ No

Particulars of Claim (attached)~~(to follow)~~

Statement of Truth

*(I believe)~~(The Claimant believes)~~ that the facts stated in these particulars of claim are true.
* I am duly authorised by the Claimant to sign this statement

Full name CYRIL JACK WILKINSON

Name of Claimant's solicitor's firm Popp, Lees and Stone

signed C J *Wilkinson*   CJ WILKINSON   position or office held

*(Claimant)~~(Litigation friend)(Claimant's solicitor)~~ (if signing on behalf of firm or company)
*delete as appropriate

Popp, Lees and Stone
Haltergate
Nottingham
NG1 6FF

DX Nottingham 1
Fax: 0115 787878
E-Mail: PLSsolicitors@service.co.uk

Claimant's or Claimant's solicitor's address to
which documents or payments should be sent if
different from overleaf including (if appropriate) details
of DX, fax or e-mail.

Response Pack

You should read the 'notes for the Defendant' attached to the claim form which will tell you when and where to send the forms.

Included in this pack are:

- either **Admission Form N9A** (if the claim is for a specified amount) or **Admission Form N9C** (if the claim is for an unspecified amount (or is not a claim for money))
- either **Defence and Counterclaim Form N9B** (if the claim is for a specified amount) or **Defence and Counterclaim Form N9D** (if the claim is for an unspecified amount or is not a claim for money)
- **Acknowledgment of service** (see below)

Complete

If you admit the claim or the amount claimed and/or you want time to pay	the admission form
If you admit part of the claim	the admission form and the defence form
If you dispute the whole claim or wish to make a claim (a counterclaim) against the Claimant	the defence form
If you need 28 days (rather than 14) from the date of service to prepare your defence, or wish to contest the court's jurisdiction	the acknowledgment of service
If you do nothing, judgment may be entered against you	

Acknowledgment of Service

Defendant's full name if different from the name given on the claim form

In the	NOTTINGHAM COUNTY COURT
Claim No.	
Claimant (including ref.)	CYRIL JACK WILKINSON
Defendant	WALKERTRONIC HI-FI-VID LIMITED

Address to which documents about this claim should be sent (including reference if appropriate)

	if applicable
fax no.	
DX no.	
Tel. no. Postcode	e-mail

Tick the appropriate box

1. I intend to defend all of this claim ☐
2. I intend to defend part of this claim ☐
3. I intend to contest jurisdiction ☐

If you file an acknowledgment of service but do not file a defence within 28 days of the date of service of the claim form, or particulars of claim if served separately, judgment may be entered against you.

If you do not file an application within 28 days of the date of service of the claim form, or particulars of claim if served separately, it will be assumed that you accept the court's jurisdiction and judgment may be entered against you.

Signed _____

(Defendant)(Defendant's Solicitor) (Litigation friend)

Position or office held (if signing on behalf of firm or company) _____

Date

The court office at

is open between 10 am and 4 pm (4.30 pm in High Court) Monday to Friday. When corresponding with the court, please address forms or letters to the Court Manager and quote the claim number.

N9 Response Pack (4.99)

Oyez 7 Spa Road, London SE16 3QQ © Crown Copyright.

N9

1999 Edition 4.99

Admission (unspecified amount, non-money and return of goods claims)

In the
NOTTINGHAM COUNTY COURT

Claim No.	
Claimant (including ref.)	CYRIL KACK WILKINSON
Defendant	WALKERTRONIC HI-FI-VID LIMITED

- Before completing this form please read the notes for guidance attached to the claim form. If necessary provide details on a separate sheet, add the claim number and attach it to this form.

- If you are not an individual, you should ensure that you provide sufficient details about the assets and liabilities of your firm, company or corporation to support any offer of payment made.

In non - money claims only

☐ I admit liability for the whole claim
(Complete section 11)

In return of goods cases only

Are the goods still in your possesion?

☐ Yes   ☐ No

Section A Response to claim *(tick one box only)*

☐ I admit liability for the whole claim but want the court to decide the amount I should pay / value of the goods

OR

☐ I admit liability for the claim and offer to pay [   ] in satisfaction of the claim
(Complete section B and sections 1-11)

Section B How are you going to pay the amount you have admitted? *(tick one box only)*

☐ I offer to pay on (date) [   ]

OR

☐ I cannot pay the amount immediately because *(state reason)*

[   ]

AND

I offer to pay by instalments of £ [   ]
per (week)(month)
starting *(date)* [   ]

1 Personal details

Surname [   ]

Forename [   ]

☐ Mr ☐ Mrs ☐ Miss ☐ Ms

☐ Married ☐ Single ☐ Other *(specify)* [   ]

Age [   ]

Address [   ]

Postcode [   ]

Tel. no. [   ]

2 Dependants *(people you look after financially)*

Number of children in each age group

under 11 [ ]   11-15 [ ]   16-17 [ ]   18 & over [ ]

Other dependants *(give details)* [   ]

3 Employment

☐ I am employed as a [   ]

My employer is [   ]

Jobs other than main job *(give details)* [   ]

☐ I am self employed as a [   ]

Annual turnover is _ _ _ £ [   ]

☐ I am not in arrears with my national insurance contributions, income tax and VAT

☐ I am in arrears and I owe _ _ £ [   ]

Give details of:
(a) contracts and other work in hand [   ]

(b) any sums due for work done [   ]

☐ I have been unemployed for [years] [months]

☐ I am a pensioner

4 Bank account and savings

☐ I have a bank account

☐ The account is in credit by _ _ _ £ [   ]

☐ The account is overdrawn by _ _ £ [   ]

☐ I have a savings or building society account

The amount in the account is _ _ _ £ [   ]

5 Residence

I live in
☐ my own property   ☐ lodgings
☐ jointly owned house ☐ rented property
☐ council accommodation

6 Income

My usual take home pay *(including overtime, commission, bonuses etc)*	£	per
Income support	£	per
Child benefit(s)	£	per
Other state benefit(s)	£	per
My pension(s)	£	per
Others living in my home give me	£	per
Other income *(give details below)*	£	per
	£	per
	£	per
Total income	**£**	**per**

8 Priority debts

(This section is for arrears only. Do not include regular expenses listed in box 7.)

Rent arrrears	£	per
Mortgage arrears	£	per
Council Tax/Community Charge arrears	£	per
Water charges arrears	£	per
Fuel debts: Gas	£	per
Electricity	£	per
Other	£	per
Maintenance arrears	£	per
Others *(give details below)*		
	£	per
	£	per
Total priority debts	**£**	**per**

7 Expenses

(Do not include any payments made by other members of the household out of their own income)

I have regular expenses as follows:

Mortgage *(including second mortgage)*	£	per
Rent	£	per
Council Tax	£	per
Gas	£	per
Electricity	£	per
Water charges	£	per
TV rental and licence	£	per
HP repayments	£	per
Mail order	£	per
Housekeeping, food, school meals	£	per
Travelling expenses	£	per
Children's clothing	£	per
Maintenance payments	£	per
Others *(not court orders or credit debts listed in boxes 9 and 10)*		
	£	per
	£	per
	£	per
Total expenses	**£**	**per**

9 Court orders

Court	Claim No.	£	per

Total court order instalments	**£**	**per**

Of the payments above, I am behind with payments to *(please list)*

10 Credit debts

Loans and credit card debts *(please list)*

	£	per
	£	per
	£	per

Of the payments above, I am behind with payments to *(please list)*

11 Declaration

I declare that the details I have given above are true to the best of my knowledge

Signed

Date

Position or office held *(if signing on behalf of firm or company)*

N9C

2000 Edition 2.2000
N9C/2

Defence Form

In the NOTTINGHAM COUNTY COURT	Claim No.
CYRIL JACK WILKINSON	Claimant
WALKERTRONIC hI-FI-VID LIMITED	Defendant(s)

I dispute the Claimant's claim because:-

Statement of Truth

*(I believe)(The Defendant(s) believe(s)) that the facts stated in this defence form (and any continuation sheets) are true.
*I am duly authorised by the Defendant(s) to sign this reply form.

Signed_____ Date_____
*(Defendant(s))(Litigation friend *(where the Defendant is a child or a patient)*)(Defendant's Solicitor)
*delete as appropriate

Full name_____

Name of Defendant's Solicitor's firm_____

position or office held_____
(if signing on behalf of firm or company)

Defendant's or Defendant's Solicitor's address to which documents should be sent.				if applicable	
		DX	Ref. no.		
			fax no.		
			DX no.	DX	
			e-mail		
	Postcode		Tel. no.		

N11 Defence Form (10.01)

Defence and Counterclaim
(unspecified amount, non-money and
return of goods claims)

In the	
NOTTINGHAM COUNTY COURT	

Claim No.	
Claimant (including ref.)	CYRIL JACK WILKINSON
Defendant	WALKERTRONIC HI-FI-VID LIMITED

- Fill in this form if you wish to dispute all or part of the claim and/or make a claim against the Claimant (a counterclaim).
- You have a limited number of days to complete and return this form to the court.
- Before completing this form, please read the notes for guidance attached to the claim form.
- Please ensure that all the boxes at the top right of this form are completed. You can obtain the correct names and number from the claim form. The court cannot trace your case without this information.

How to fill in this form

- Set out your defence in section 1. If necessary continue on a separate piece of paper making sure that the claim number is clearly shown on it. In your defence you must state which allegations in the particulars of claim you deny and your reasons for doing so. **If you fail to deny an allegation it may be taken that you admit it.**
- If you dispute only some of the allegations you must
  - specify which you admit and which you deny; and
  - give your own version of events if different from the Claimant's.

- If the claim is for money and you dispute the Claimant's statement of value, you must say why and if possible give your own statement of value.
- If you wish to make a claim against the Claimant (a counterclaim) complete section 2.
- Complete and sign section 3 before returning this form.

Where to send this form

- Send or take this form immediately to the court at the address given on the claim form.
- Keep a copy of the claim form and the defence form.

Community Legal Service Fund (CLSF)

- You may qualify for assistance from the CLSF (this used to be called 'legal aid') to meet some or all of your legal costs. Ask about the CLSF at any county court office or any information or help point which displays this logo.

1. Defence

Defence (continued)

Claim No.

2. If you wish to make a claim against the Claimant (a counterclaim)

If your claim is for a specific sum of money, how much are you claiming? £

- To start your counterclaim, you will have to pay a fee. Court staff will tell you how much you have to pay.

- You may not be able to make a counterclaim where the Claimant is the Crown (e.g. a Government Department.) Ask at your local county court office for further information.

My claim is for (please specify)

What are your reasons for making the counterclaim?
If you need to continue on a separate sheet put the claim number in the top right hand corner

3. Signed

(To be signed by you or by your solicitor or litigation friend)

*(I believe)(The Defendant believes) that the facts stated in this form are true. *I am duly authorised by the Defendant to sign this statement

* delete as appropriate

Position or office held (if signing on behalf of firm or company)

Date

Give an address to which notices about this case can be sent to you

Postcode

Tel. no.

if applicable

fax no.

DX no.

e-mail

N9D

2000 Edition 12.00
N9D/2

IN THE NOTTINGHAM COUNTY COURT   CLAIM NO NG0178943

B E T W E E N

Cyril Jack Wilkinson

Claimant

– and –

Walkertronic Super Hi-Fi-Vid Limited

Defendant

PARTICULARS OF CLAIM

---

1   By a written contract[67] made on 1st February 2001 the Claimant purchased from the Defendant for the sum of £150.00 a Magivid electronic football game ("the Game") for use in conjunction with a computer owned by the Claimant ("the Agreement").

2   The Defendant entered into the Agreement in the course of its business as a general electrical retailer.

3   Consequently it was an implied term of the Agreement that the Game should be of satisfactory quality.[68]

4   Further or alternatively, on 1st February 2001 at the Defendant's premises, the Claimant made known to Mr. Evans of the Defendant, the particular purpose for which the Game was being bought, that is, for use in conjunction with the Claimant's computer, the gist of the Claimant's words being "I'm going to use this with an Apple Mac".

5   It was therefore an implied term of the Agreement that the Game would be fit for that purpose.[69]

6   The Claimant used the Game on three occasions, but whilst in use on February 5th 2001 it exploded ("the Explosion") causing damage to the Claimant's computer and setting fire to a pair of curtains. Structural damage was caused to the door and window and decorations in the same room were damaged by smoke and scorching.

7   The Explosion was caused by the Defendant's breach of contract.

8   In breach of the terms set out in paragraphs 3 and 4 above the Game was not of satisfactory quality and/or was not fit for its purpose.

---

[67] Note that a copy of this contract must be attached to the particulars of claim: PD. 16 para. 7.3.

[68] Sale of Goods Act 1979, as amended, s. 14(2).

[69] Sale of Goods Act 1979, as amended, s. 14(3).

PARTICULARS

The Game was liable to overheat when used more than once in the same day.

The Game overheated within 10 minutes of being connected to the Claimant's computer.

9   As a result of the matters set out above the Claimant has suffered loss and damage:

PARTICULARS OF LOSS AND DAMAGE

Refund of price paid	£ 150.00
Value of the computer	£ 2,000.00
Replacement of curtains	£ 60.00
Redecoration and structural repairs	£4.000.00
TOTAL ESTIMATED LOSSES	£ 6,210.00

10   Further the Claimant claims interest under s. 69 of the County Courts Act 1984 on such damages as may be awarded to him at such rate and for such period as the Court thinks fit.

AND THE CLAIMANT CLAIMS

1   Damages

2   Interest under s. 69 of the County Courts Act 1984

                                          Popp, Lees and Stone

Statement of truth[70]

I believe that the facts stated in these Particulars of Claim are true

C J Wilkinson

Cyril Jack Wilkinson
Claimant

Dated 3rd October 2001

                                          Popp, Lees and Stone
                                                        Solicitors
                                                        Haltergate
                                                      Nottingham
                                                        NG1 6FF
                                        Solicitors for the Claimant

---

[70] See CPR Part 22 and PD. 22 for statements of truth generally.

Together with the claim form and particulars of claim,[71] the defendant receives a "response pack"[72] containing forms on which to acknowledge service of the claim, admit the claim, or to deny it, or to counterclaim. An admission, acknowledgment or defence must be returned to the court within 14 days. If the defendant merely acknowledges service (perhaps because he or she needs more time to investigate and set out a defence) then a defence must also be filed within 28 days.[73]

If the claim form is served on its own with particulars of claim to follow, the defendant need not respond until the particulars of claim arrive.[74]

Failure to submit an acknowledgement or defence on time will permit the claimant, normally on submission of the appropriate form and without a hearing, to have a judgment entered against the defendant immediately.[75] If the defendant does file a defence, the court will send out allocation questionnaires[76] which, when completed, will assist the court in allocating the claim to one of the three tracks and in setting a timetable for the pre-trial stages.

4. THE DEFENCE

A defendant to any action may wish to dispute all or part of the liability **12–015** asserted by the claimant or may disagree with the amount claimed whilst admitting liability or may wish to dispute the claim and make a counterclaim against the claimant. The forms within the response pack permit all these possibilities. It is not necessary to use the form to serve a defence and most legal representatives will draw up a separate document by way of defence, if only because the space to give details on the form is rather limited. Whichever option is used, the content of the defence must comply with CPR rr 16.5 and 16.6 and PD. 16 paras 10 to 13 inclusive.

In the defence the defendant will respond to the individual allegations set out by the claimant. The choice of responses[77] to any particular allegation is to:

(a) Admit. So, for example, Walkertronic is likely to admit paragraph 1: that there was a contract between itself and Mr. Wilkinson.

(b) Deny. If the defendant denies an allegation it must give reasons for the denial. This is a deliberate change to the old rules where it was often sufficient for the defendant to say simply "Paragraph 4 is denied" thus requiring the claimant to guess whether the reason for the denial was, for example, a dispute as to the facts or a fundamental difference as to

---

[71] If the two are served separately, the response pack accompanies the later particulars of claim.

[72] CPR r. 7.8(1).

[73] CPRr. 15.4.

[74] CPR r. 9.1(2). The position is different in the Commercial Court for which the separate Commercial Court Guide and, from 25th March 2002, CPR Part 58 and PD. 58 should be consulted.

[75] CPR Part 12.

[76] CPR r. 26.3.

[77] CPR r. 9.2.

the legal principles involved. Consequently, Walkertronic may deny the allegation of breach, giving as its "reason" that the game was operating satisfactorily when tested shortly before sale.

(c) "The defendant is unable to admit or deny and requires the claimant to prove...." This middle route (sometimes called "not admitting") allows the defendant to deal with matters to which he or she cannot respond because he or she does not have the information. So, for example, Walkertronic may take this approach towards the allegations of loss.[78]

As with the particulars of claim, PD. 16 may prescribe particular contents in particular types of case[79] and there is the option under PD. 16 para. 13.3 to include:

a. Any point of law on which the defence is based;

b. The name of any witness the defendant intends to call; and

c. Any document "necessary to" the defence.[80]

The defence must also contain a statement of truth.[81]

The court will send a copy of the defence to the claimant. Filing of the defence also triggers the court's sending out of allocation questionnaires.[82]

Statements of case (previously "pleadings")

12–016   Since the adversarial system depends upon the two parties selecting the issues for resolution and acquiring the evidence to support them, it is necessary that the parties should communicate to each other the elements of their case. The system of statements of case (we have already looked at some statements of case when we considered the claim form, the particulars of claim and the defence) amounts to a formal exchange of allegations so as to define with clarity and precision the matters which are in dispute. They also reduce, in furtherance of the overriding objective, the possibility of one party being surprised by the case of the other at trial. The format and to a large extent the content of statements of case is prescribed by the CPR, particularly Parts 7, 15, 16 and 20 and their accompanying practice directions.[83]

If the claimant has served a claim form not accompanied by the particulars of claim, the first document to be prepared and served is the particulars of claim (which will be accompanied by the response pack). In the particulars of claim the claimant's claim against the defendant must be set out, with the facts which will be relied on for support, the injury/loss that

---

[78]   PD. 16 para. 13.3.
[79]   For example, in a personal injury case, the defendant must respond specifically to the medical report and schedule of losses attached to the particulars of claim: PD. 16 para. 12.
[80]   PD. 16 paras. 4.2 and 4.3 require, *inter alia*, a medical report and a schedule of "past and future expenses and losses" to be annexed to the particulars of claim.
[81]   PD. 15 para. 2, PD. 16 para. 11; CPR r. 22.1(l)(a).
[82]   CPRr. 26.3.
[83]   These Parts do not apply to some specialist claims such as those brought under Part 8, defamation claims (Part 53), possession proceedings (Part 55) and probate claims (Part 57): PD. 16, para 1.

has been suffered and the remedy which is sought. The document should be "concise"[84] but sufficiently full to allow the defendant to ascertain the case against him or her and to prepare a defence.

The art of drafting statements of case is therefore very important. Statements of case should state facts only, although matters of law or evidence may optionally be included in accordance with PD. 16 para. 13.3. They must state only the material facts and those material facts must be set out with sufficient detail but without excessive detail. Drawing that latter balance is where the real skill lies.

Finally and fundamentally, each statement of case must be capable of having a statement of truth attached to it.

In *George and Hacker v. Reliable Nag Supply Stables (a firm)* the particulars of claim could be set out as follows:

IN THE HIGH COURT OF JUSTICE CLAIM NO.G0167234

QUEEN'S BENCH DIVISION

NOTTINGHAM DISTRICT REGISTRY

B E T W E E N

PETER GEORGE (1)

MARTIN HACKER (2)

Claimants

– and –

RELIABLE NAG SUPPLY STABLES (a firm)

Defendant

PARTICULARS OF CLAIM

---

1 The Claimants and the Defendant entered into an oral contract ("the Contract") on 25th June 2000 for the sale by the Defendant to the Claimants of a piebald gelding known as Skipper ("the Horse") for the price of £65,000, paid by the Claimants to the Defendant on 25th June 2000.

PARTICULARS[85]

At approximately 3pm on 25th June 2000, at a meeting held on the premises of the Defendant, the First Claimant said to Mrs. Wooldbridge of the Defendant words to the effect "Is Skipper still on the market? We're still looking for something for general hacking and jumping at local gymkhana level." Mrs. Wooldbridge replied that he was still available and that his price

---

[84] CPR r. 16.2.
[85] PD. 16 para. 7.4.

had been reduced to £65,000. The First Claimant replied "Then we'll take him".

2 The Defendant sold the Horse in the course of its business as horse traders.

3 Consequently it was an implied term of the Contract that the Horse would be of satisfactory quality, specifically sound and in good health.[86]

4 Further or alternatively, as set out in paragraph 1 above, the Claimants made known to the Defendant a specific purpose for which the Horse would be required, namely general hacking and for jumping at the local gymkhanas. Consequently it was an implied term of the Contract that the Horse would be fit for such purposes.[87]

5 The Claimants took delivery of the Horse from the Defendant on 26th June 2000.

6 In breach of the terms set out in paragraphs 3 and 4 above, the Horse was not of satisfactory quality and/or was not fit for its purpose.

PARTICULARS

The Horse was found to be suffering from Bastard Strangles and was therefore entirely useless and worthless to the Claimants.

7 As a result of the matters set out above the Claimants have suffered loss and damage.

PARTICULARS

Cost price of Horse	£65,000.00
Fees paid to Sutton Riding Enterprises for the care of alternative horse from 1st July to 20th August	£290.00
TOTAL ESTIMATED LOSS	£65,290.00

8 Further the Claimants claim interest under s.35A Supreme Court Act 1981 on the amount found due to them at such rate and for such period as the Court thinks fit.

AND THE CLAIMANTS CLAIM

(1) Damages

(2) Interest under statute

Popp, Lees and Stone

Statement of truth

[86] Sale of Goods Act 1979, as amended, s. 14(2).
[87] *Ibid.*, s. 14(3).

I believe that the facts stated in these Particulars of Claim are true

Peter George   *Martin Hacker*

Peter George   Martin Hacker

Claimants

Dated 10th November 2001

> Popp, Lees and Stone
> Solicitors
> Haltergate
> Nottingham
> NG1 6FF
> Solicitors for the Claimant

The defendant may consider that the information given in the particulars **12–017** of claim is defective or insufficient to allow a defence to the claim to be prepared. In an extreme case, the defendant may seek to have the claim struck out under CPR r. 3.4 on the basis that it "discloses no reasonable grounds for bringing ... the claim" or to apply for summary judgment against the claimant under CPR Part 24 on the basis that the claimant has "no real prospect of succeeding ... and there is no other compelling reason why the case ... should be disposed of at a trial". Alternatively, the defendant is entitled to request "further information" from the claimant under CPR Part 18. In the case of George and Hacker, the defendant wishes to know more:[88]

---

[88] Readers familiar with earlier editions of this text may note that the positive requirement to set out full details of an oral contract in the particulars of claim have drastically reduced the defendant's request at this stage.

IN THE HIGH COURT OF JUSTICE   CLAIM NO. NG0167234

QUEEN'S BENCH DIVISION

NOTTINGHAM DISTRICT REGISTRY

B E T W E E N

PETER GEORGE (1)

MARTIN HACKER (2)

Claimants

– and –

RELIABLE NAG SUPPLY STABLES (a firm)

Defendant

REQUEST UNDER CPR PART 18 BY THE CLAIMANT FOR FURTHER INFORMATION FROM THE DEFENDANT MADE ON 18th FEBRUARY 2001[89]

QUESTION 1

Of paragraph 6

6. In breach of the terms set out in paragraphs 3 and 4 above, the Horse was not of satisfactory quality and/or was not fit for its purpose.

PARTICULARS

The Horse was found to be suffering from Bastard Strangles and was therefore entirely useless and worthless to the Claimants.

PLEASE STATE

At which time it is alleged the Horse was discovered to be suffering from Bastard Strangles and how long it is alleged that the condition had existed.

QUESTION 2

Of paragraph 7

7 As a result of the matters set out above the Claimants have suffered loss and damage.

---

[89] See PD. 18 para. 1.6.

PARTICULARS

Cost price of Horse	£65,000.00
Fees paid to Sutton Riding Enterprises for the care of alternative horse from 1st July to 20th August	£290.00
TOTAL ESTIMATED LOSSES	£65,290.00

PLEASE STATE

Full particulars of the stabling provided for the alternative horse at Sutton Riding Enterprises and a detailed analysis of the fees charged.

The Claimant expects a response to this request by 4pm on 1st March 2001.

Martin Martinson[90]

Dated 18th November 2001

Furlong & Co
43 Bridle Lane
Nottingham
NG7 5RR
Solicitors for the Defendant.

In due course the defendant must serve a defence on the claimant. There are specified time limits for the conduct of statements of case and there are limits to the extent that these can be dispensed with by the consent of the parties[91] without the court's prior permission. The court may extend time by order but will consider the effect of any delay on the overall timetable and the imperatives of the overriding objective.

Having been given the necessary information about the claimant's case (whether in the statements of case or during the pre-action stage), the defendant must settle on his or her tactics. In defence, he or she may choose to refute the whole of the claimant's claim and the facts on which it is based, or may admit the whole claim whilst pleading an explanation which allows liability to be avoided, or may admit the whole case but object that it discloses no cause of action or may adopt a combination of these approaches or adopt them as alternatives.[92] Naturally, the wider the

---

[90] Note that it is possible to detect from the nature of the signature that the request was drafted by a barrister ("counsel"). Whilst all court documents "drafted by a legal representative" must bear the signature of that legal representative, documents drafted by solicitors will be "signed" in the name of their firm: PD. 5 para. 2.1. Documents drafted by barristers, on the other hand, are "signed" in the name of the individual barrister.

[91] For example, the period for filing a defence can be extended by the parties for a maximum of 28 days, thereafter the permission of the court will have to be sought: CPR r. 15.5.

[92] Defences in the alternative can sometimes appear extremely confusing. In relying on alternatives, one should take care to ensure that the party is still capable of signing a statement of truth in relation to the facts contained in the statement of case (i.e., the claimant cannot simultaneously believe in the truth of mutually inconsistent facts). Those relying on a multiplicity of alternative defences will also have to be prepared to meet a court determined to reduce the case to its essentials under CPR rr. 1 4(2)(b) and (c).

defence, the wider the issues that remain for resolution at the trial, the greater must be the claimant's preparations and the greater the likelihood that a pro-active judge applying CPR rr. 1.4(2)(b) and (c) — which, it should be remembered, the parties are under a duty to assist the court in furthering — will require the defendant to narrow its case before those preparations begin. This is because if the defendant is not prepared to admit any of the facts pleaded by the claimant they may all have to be proved in court with a consequent increase in the length and costs of the case. However, in addition to the powers of the judge to narrow the issues, either party may serve notice under CPR r. 32.18 requiring the admission of facts with a penalty in costs for unjustified refusal. If the defendant does make substantial admissions in the defence, it will have the effect of disclosing and narrowing the issues between the parties so that — however effective the pre-action stages have been in this respect — both parties are now aware of precisely what remains in dispute. In order that the statements of case should disclose clearly what remains in dispute, any issue of fact in a statement of case must be specifically denied or it will normally be deemed to have been admitted.[93]
For the purpose of the later case management of the claim, it should be noted that it is the filing of a defence that triggers the distribution by the court of allocation questionnaires.[94] Where a claim is not to be defended, then default judgment will normally be entered and the only issue for discussion will be the means and method of payment. Consequently there is no need for the court to become involved in any management of the claim towards a hypothetical trial of the merits.

12–018   So far we have omitted consideration of one important possibility. The defendant may wish to make a claim against the claimant in addition to defending the claimant's claim. It is not necessary to bring a separate claim. It is possible to add a *counterclaim*[95] to the defence. Set out below is the defence and counterclaim of the Reliable Nag Supply Stables.

---

[93] CPR r. 16.5(3).
[94] CPR r. 26.3.
[95] CPR r. 20.2(l)(a), 20.4 and PD. 20 para. 6.

IN THE HIGH COURT OF JUSTICE CLAIM NO. NGO167234

QUEEN'S BENCH DIVISION

NOTTINGHAM DISTRICT REGISTRY

B E T W E E N

PETER GEORGE (1)

MARTIN HACKER (2)

Claimants and Part 20 Defendants

− and −

RELIABLE NAG SUPPLY STABLES (a firm)

Defendant and Part 20 Claimant[96]

DEFENCE AND COUNTERCLAIM

DEFENCE

1 Except that it is denied that the First Claimant made any statement as to the intended purpose for which the Horse was required, Mrs. Wooldbridge having no recollection of any such statements being made, paragraph 1 of the Particulars of Claim is admitted.

2 Paragraphs 2 and 3 of the Particulars of Claim are admitted.

3 Paragraph 4 of the Particulars of Claim is denied for the reasons set out in paragraph 1 above.

4 Paragraph 5 of the Particulars of Claim is admitted.

5 Paragraph 6 of the Particulars of Claim is denied.

REASONS

The Horse underwent a veterinary inspection on 24th June 2000 and was not suffering from Bastard Strangles or from any other infection at that time.

6 The Defendant is unable to admit or deny but wishes the Claimants to prove the amount of the losses set out in paragraph 7 of the Particulars of Claim.[97]

---

[96] For the format of the heading, see PD. 20 para. 7.

[97] The award of interest being in the discretion of the court, it is not normally regarded as necessary to respond to it specifically.

7   Further or alternatively, it was an express term of the Contract that the Defendant would exchange the Horse for another if the Horse should within 14 days prove unsuitable to the Claimant.

8   By a further agreement made at or about the beginning of July 2000 ("The Second Contract") between the Defendant and the Claimants under the express term referred to in paragraph 7 above, the Claimants agreed to exchange the Horse for another and to take delivery of a suitable bay mare ("the Mare") owned by the Defendant pending their decision to retain the Horse or the Mare.

9   In breach of the Second Contract, the Claimants failed to make any decision as to which of the horses they would retain and, on or about 21st August 2000, returned the Mare to the Defendant thereby repudiating the Contract.

10   If and to the extent, if at all, which is denied for the reasons set out above, that the Defendant is liable to the Claimants, it will seek to set off the damages and sums counterclaimed below to extinguish or diminish such liability.

COUNTERCLAIM

11   It was an implied term of the Second Contract that the Claimants would take reasonable care of the Mare whilst in their custody.

12   In breach of the term set out in paragraph 11 above, the Claimants failed to take reasonable care of the Mare:

PARTICULARS

When the Claimants returned the Mare to the Defendant its ribs were protruding, its hooves were broken, its coat was dull and ungroomed, 3 shoes were missing and it was in poor health.

13   As a result of the breaches set out in paragraph 12 above, the Defendant suffered loss and damage.

PARTICULARS

1 Loss of profit on the sale of ahorse	£15,000
2 Transport costs on delivery and collection	£500
3 Veterinary costs for the Mare	£2,000
4 Farrier's fees for the Mare	£1,000
5 Loss of value of the Mare	£10.000
TOTAL ESTIMATED LOSSES	£28,500

6   Further the Defendant claims interest under s35A Supreme Court Act 1981 on the amount found to be due to the Defendant at such rate and for such period as the Court thinks fit.

AND the Defendant counterclaims

1   Damages under paragraph 13 above

2   Interest under statute

Furlong & Co

Statement of truth

I believe that the facts stated in this Defence and Counterclaim are true

Patricia Wooldbridge

Patricia Wooldbridge, Partner

Dated 21st November 2001

Furlong & Co
43 Bridle Lane
Nottingham
NG75RR
Solicitors for the Defendant and Part 20 Claimant.

Where a defence raises new facts, the claimant may wish to file a reply[98] and   **12–019**
where a counterclaim has been made it is usual for the claimant to file a
defence.[99] These should be combined into a single document[1] and will
usually be the final documents in the statements of case. Although in theory
the defendant might file a *rejoinder*, the claimant a *surrejoinder*, the
defendant a *rebutter* and the claimant a *surrebutter*, doing so requires the
express permission of the court[2] and they are rare to the point of near, if not
total, extinction.

Below, we set out a reply to defence and defence to counterclaim in
George and Hacker's case.

---

[98] CPR r. 16.7.
[99] Indeed, the claimant risks a default judgment being entered for the amount of the
counterclaim if no defence is filed: CPR Part 12, applied to counterclaims by CPR r. 20.3(3).
[1] PD. 15 para. 3.2.
[2] CPR r. 15.9.

IN THE HIGH COURT OF JUSTICE   CLAIM NO. NGO167234

QUEEN'S BENCH DIVISION

NOTTINGHAM DISTRICT REGISTRY

B E T W E E N

PETER GEORGE (1)

MARTIN HACKER (2)

<u>Claimants and Part 20 Defendants</u>

– and –

RELIABLE NAG SUPPLY STABLES (a firm)

<u>Defendant and Part 20 Claimant</u>[3]

REPLY TO DEFENCE AND DEFENCE TO COUNTERCLAIM

REPLY TO DEFENCE

1   For the reasons set out below, the Claimants join issue with the Defendant except insofar as paragraphs 2, 4 and 7 of the Defence and Counterclaim are concerned.

DEFENCE TO COUNTERCLAIM

2   It is admitted that the Second Contract described in paragraph 8 of the Defence and Counterclaim was made, but it is denied that the Defendant offered a suitable horse in exchange, the Mare being in poor condition at the time of its delivery to the Claimants.

3   The Claimants paid employees of Sutton Riding Enterprises to attend to the Mare and informed the Defendant at all times of the poor condition of the Mare.

4   Consequently, whilst it is admitted that the Claimants returned the Mare to the Defendant on or about 21st August 2000, it is denied that the Claimants repudiated the Contract as alleged in paragraph 9 of the Defence and Counterclaim or in any other way.

5   For the reasons set out above, paragraph 10 of the Defence and Counterclaim is denied.

6   Paragraph 11 of the Defence and Counterclaim is admitted.

7   Whilst it is admitted that the Mare was ill when returned to the Defendant, that illness was the direct result of the Mare's having been in poor condition at the time of its delivery to the Defendant.

---

[3] For the format of the heading, see PD. 20 para. 7.

Consequently it is denied that the Claimants are in breach of the term set out in paragraph 12 of the Defence and Counterclaim or in any other way.

8 For the reasons set out above, paragraph 13 of the Defence and Counterclaim is denied.

Popp, Lees and Stone

Statement of truth

I believe that the facts stated in this Reply to Defence and Defence to Counterclaim are true

Peter George   *Martin Hacker*

Peter George   Martin Hacker

Claimants

Dated 30th November 2001

Popp Lees and Stone
Solicitors
Haltergate
Nottingham
NG1 6FF
Solicitors for the Claimant and Part 20 Defendant

Statements of case — the consequences of failure

If the defendant fails to file an acknowledgement of service in time, or files an acknowledgement of service but then fails to file a defence in time; or if a claimant fails to file a defence to the defendant's counterclaim in time then the opponent is entitled to enter a "default" judgment against him or her.[4] If the claim is for a specified sum, then the judgment will be a final judgment for the amount claimed, interest and fixed costs. If the claim is not for a specified sum then judgment will be entered on liability only and there will then be a "disposal hearing"[5] which the parties will be able to appear and dispute the amount of damages prior to final judgment being entered.

12–020

5. ALLOCATION

As we have seen, once a defence has been filed, the court begins the process that will lead it to be in a position to manage the case. Both (or in more complex cases, all) parties are sent an allocation questionnaire by the court.[6]

12–021

---

[4] CPR Part 12. There are limited circumstances in which default judgment is not permitted and a hearing must be convened.

[5] PD. 26 para. 12.8.

[6] Procedure in some of the more specialist courts such as the Commercial Court, is different: see, for example, the Commercial Court Guide and, from March 2002, CPR Part 58 and PD. 58.

This must be completed and returned to the court within 14 days, the claimant paying a fee of £80.[7] If the questionnaires are not returned in time, the parties risk the claim being struck out.[8] From March 2002, the parties may not agree between themselves to alter the date for return of the questionnaires.[9]

A copy of the questionnaire (which should, unless the claim falls within the small claims limits — be accompanied by a fully calculated estimate of costs incurred to date and to be incurred in the future running of the claim[10]) follows:

---

[7] Following representations by such institutions as the Civil Justice Council and the National Association of CABx, the fee is not payable in what will be small claims cases under £1,000.

[8] PD. 26 para. 2.5.

[9] CPR r. 26.3 (6A).

[10] PD. 26 para. 2.1(2).

Allocation questionnaire

In the
HIGH COURT OF JUSTICE
QUEEN'S BENCH DIVISION
NOTTINGHAM DISTRICT REGISTRY

Claim No.	NG0167234

Last date for filing with court office	4PM 25TH NOVEMBER 2001

To be completed by, or on behalf of,

RELIABLE NAG SUPPLY STABLES (A FIRM)

who is [1st] [2nd] [3rd] [ ] [Claimant]
[Defendant] [Part 20 claimant] in this claim

SEAL

Please read the notes on page five before completing the questionnaire.

You should note the date by which it must be returned and the name of the court it should be returned to since this may be different from the court where proceedings were issued.

If you have settled this claim (or if you settle it on a future date) and do not need to have it heard or tried, you must let the court know immediately.

Have you sent a copy of this completed form to the other party(ies)?   [x] Yes   [ ] No

A Settlement

Do you wish there to be a one month stay to attempt to settle the claim, either by informal discussion or by alternative dispute resolution?   [ ] Yes   [x] No

B Location of trial

Is there any reason why your claim needs to be heard at a particular court?   [ ] Yes   [x] No

If Yes, say which court and why?

C Pre-action protocols

If an approved pre-action protocol applies to this claim, complete **Part 1** only. If not, complete **Part 2** only. If you answer 'No' to the question in either Part 1 or 2, please explain the reasons why on a separate sheet and attach it to this questionaire.

Part 1	The* _____ protocol applies to this claim.
*please say which protocol	Have you complied with it? [ ] Yes [ ] No

Part 2	No pre-action protocol applies to this claim.
	Have you exchanged information and/or documents (evidence) with the other party in order to assist in settling the claim? [x] Yes [ ] No

1

D   Case management information

What amount of the claim is in dispute?

£ 65,290.00

Applications

Have you made any application(s) in this claim?   ☐ Yes ☒ No

If Yes, what for?   [   ]   For hearing on [   ]
(e.g. summary judgment, add
another party)

Witnesses

So far as you know at this stage, what witnesses of fact do you intend to call at the trial
or final hearing including, if appropriate, yourself?

Witness name	Witness to which facts

Experts

Do you wish to use expert evidence at the trial or final hearing?   ☒ Yes ☐ No

Have you already copied any experts' report(s) to the other   ☐ None yet ☐ Yes ☒ No
party(ies)?   obtained

Do you consider the case suitable for a single joint expert in any field?   ☒ Yes ☐ No

Please list any single joint experts you propose to use and any other experts you
wish to rely on. Identify single joint experts with the initials 'SJ' after their name(s).

Expert's name	Field of expertise (e.g. orthopaedic surgeon, surveyor, engineer)
Marjorie Bartlett	Veterinary surgeon

Do you want your expert(s) to give evidence orally at the trial or final hearing? ☐ Yes ☒ No

If Yes, give the reasons why you think oral evidence is necessary:

continue over

Track

Which track do you consider is most suitable for your claim?
Tick one box

☐ small claims track ☐ fast track ☒ multi-track

If you have indicated a track which would not be the normal track for the claim, please give brief reasons for your choice

E Trial of final hearing

How long do you estimate the trial or final hearing will take?

2		
days	hours	minutes

Are there any days when you, an expert or an essential witness will not be able to attend court for the trial or final hearing?

☐ Yes ☒ No

If Yes, please give details

Name	Dates not available

F Proposed directions *(Parties should agree directions wherever possible)*

Have you attached a list of the directions you think appropriate for the management of the claim?

☒ Yes ☐ No

If Yes, have they been agreed with the other party(ies)?

☒ Yes ☐ No

G Costs

*Do **not** complete this section if you have suggested your case is suitable for the small claims track **or** you have suggested one of the other tracks and you do not have a solicitor acting for you.*

What is your estimate of your costs incurred to date?

£ 5, 000

What do you estimate your overall costs are likely to be?

£ 20,000

In substantial cases these questions should be answered in compliance with CPR Part 43

H Other information

Have you attached documents to this questionnaire? ☐ Yes ☒ No

Have you sent these documents to the other party(ies)? ☐ Yes ☒ No

If Yes, when did they receive them? [   ]

Do you intend to make any applications in the immediate future? ☐ Yes ☒ No

If Yes, what for? [   ]

In the space below, set out any other information you consider will help the judge to manage the claim.

Signed [   ] Date [   ]

[Counsel][Solicitor][for the][1st][2nd][3rd][   ]
[Claimant] [Defendant][Part 20 claimant]

Please enter your firm's name, reference number and full postal address including (if appropriate) details of DX, fax or e-mail

		if applicable	
		fax no.	
		DX no.	DX
Tel. no.	Postcode	e-mail	
Your reference no.			

N150

N150/4

On receipt of the completed questionnaires, the court then begins the process of allocation. Allocation is the process whereby, acting on information provided by the parties in their allocation questionnaires, the court allocates the claim to one of the three tracks.[11] The criteria for the decision are set out in CPR r. 26.8:

a. The financial value (if any) of the claim (excluding interest, costs, admitted amounts, any potential deductions for contributory negligence);

b. The nature of the remedy sought;[12]

c. The likely complexity of facts, law or evidence;

d. The number of parties;

e. The value and complexity of any Part 20 claim (such as a counterclaim);

f. The amount of oral evidence required to decide the case;

g. The importance of the case to those not directly involved with it (such as the general public or others in the process of bringing similar claims);

h. The views of the parties (expressed in their allocation questionnaires); and

i. The circumstances of the parties.

The parties are encouraged to co-operate with each other when completing their questionnaires. If the court is unable to make a decision about the appropriate track, it may convene an allocation hearing at which the parties can make representations about the appropriate track.[13]

If the court is able to make the decision, a notice of allocation will be sent to the parties.[14] The court may also be able to provide some directions to progress the case towards trial, either because it is able to sanction a list of suggested directions submitted by the parties or because the case can be managed without any further information from the parties. The court may well at this stage be able to give the parties a trial date or a trial "window". Alternatively — and this is a specific question on the allocation questionnaire — the court may halt the progress of the case towards trial, normally for up to a month, to allow the parties to try to resolve their dispute by alternative dispute resolution or negotiation.[15]

It is a significant change from the old system in that it requires the parties to be able to say at this comparatively early stage of the proceedings, for example, which witnesses they propose to call or how long they think the trial should last. The fact that failure to file the allocation questionnaire within the time limit may lead to one's case being struck out is intended to concentrate the parties' minds.[16]

---

[11] CPR r. 26.5.
[12] County court judges cannot, for example, at present make declarations of incompatibility under Human Rights Act 1998, s.4. Similarly there are restrictions on the level of judge who can grant an injunction: PD. 2B.
[13] CPR r. 26.5(4).
[14] CPR r. 26.9.
[15] CPR r. 26.4. See also Chap. 11, para. 11-025 et seq.
[16] PD. 26 para. 2.5.

The small claims track

12–022   As we have seen, the small claims track is, generally speaking, reserved for claims of £5,000 or less, with variations for personal injury claims (where the global value must not exceed £5,000 but the personal injury element must not be worth more than £1,000) and housing disrepair claims (where the cost of repairs must not exceed £1,000 and any additional claim must not exceed a further £1,000). Raising the jurisdictional limit was seen to be important to maintain access to this system and the limit has steadily risen over the years from £20 in 1846, to £1,000 as a consequence of the Civil Justice Review in 1989 and to £3,000 in 1996 as a result of Lord Woolf's Interim Report.[17] The limit was extended to its current position in 1999 on implementation of the reforms.

To summarise the scale of the court's involvement in small claims cases, in 2000, approximately 73 per cent of all claims brought in the county court were within the small claims limits and in 2000 55,836 small claims hearings were held.[18] The average length of a hearing was 66 minutes.

All small claims cases will be dealt with in the county court, courts which themselves owe their establishment to concerns about the cost and complexity of civil procedure, which persuaded the government of the day to introduce the County Courts Act 1846 against much opposition from parts of the legal profession. The court was intended to provide a cheap, accessible and simple forum for the recovery of small debts and demands. It was the criticisms of the costs and complexity in small claims, set out most convincingly by the Consumer Council in *Justice Out of Reach* which led to the procedural reforms of the early 1970s. Further published evidence and public pressure have provoked more change in recent years, including, but not limited to, the effect of the Woolf reforms.[19]

The objective of the changes over the 20 years prior to the Woolf reforms has been to make the procedure more attractive to the litigant in person and less expensive than before. If anything, the objective of the Woolf reforms was to extend these aims to all courts. One reform that has had to be jettisoned, however, was that of making arbitration the normal form of resolution[20] in order to make the process less formal. Whilst the hearing remains expressly informal,[21] the express description of it as "arbitration" has fallen foul of the right to a "trial" under art 6 of the European Convention on Human Rights now incorporated into English law in the Human Rights Act 1998.[22] The hearing must now normally take place in public[23] although since a significant degree of informality has been retained, this may be a distinction without a difference in fact.

---

[17] For background, see the following consultation papers: *Access to Justice — the small claims procedure; Small Claims Appeals — Proposed New Procedures* (2000).

[18] *Judicial Statistics 2000*, tables 4.8 and 4. 11.

[19] See, for example, the concerns expressed by the Civil Justice Council and by N.A.C.A.Bx. about the allocation fee of £80 in the context of small claims.

[20] This was achieved first by Practice Direction [1973] 1 W.L.R. 1178, and then by the County Court (Amendment) Rules 1980 (S.I. 1980/1807). Both have been superseded by the CPR

[21] CPR r. 27.8.

[22] *i.e.*, art 6 of the ECHR, which guarantees a fair and public trial within a reasonable time before an independent tribunal.

[23] PD. 27 para. 4.

The claimant must follow the common procedure outlined above up to the point of allocation, when the court will make its decision as to allocation to the small claims track in accordance with the jurisdictional limits set out above and the normal criteria in CPR r. 26.8.

Many of the more complex rales about evidence, expert and other witnesses and Part 36 offers and payments do not apply in the small claims track. Following allocation to the small claims track the court will impose directions, normally without a directions hearing, and give a date for the final hearing. A number of standard directions are set out in an appendix to PD. 27 but in summary the parties will not normally be permitted to rely on expert evidence at the hearing (whether given orally or in writing) and the parties must supply each other, not less than 14 days before the hearing, with copies of all documents on which they intend to rely at the hearing. The hearing will be informal and the strict rules of evidence will not apply. In particular, there will be limits on the amount of cross-examination that will be permitted.

Legal Services Commission funding is not normally available for representation during the hearing although both parties may have received some initial assistance or advice that is covered by the scheme. It is expected that the parties will appear in person although there is no prohibition on appearing by a lawyer or by a lay representative.[24] Normally, no costs, including a solicitor's charges and sums allowed to a litigant in person in lieu are allowed except for the costs of issuing the claim, or, in proceedings for an injunction or specific performance a sum for legal advice and assistance not exceeding £260 and any further costs awarded against a party who has behaved unreasonably.[25]

The fast track

The fast track rules (CPR Part 28 and its practice direction) envisage that the court will be able to impose directions without seeing the parties.[26] This may be optimistic, especially where one or both parties do not have legal representation. If this is the case then, prior to allocation of a potential fast track case, the court may convene an "allocation and directions hearing". In either case the directions given will seek to further the overriding objective enshrined in CPR Part 1.   **12–023**

A list of possible directions appears in the appendix to PD. 28. However, for present purposes it is sufficient to set out the "typical timetable" given by way of example in PD. 28 para. 3.12:

Disclosure	within 4 weeks from the making of the order
Exchange of statements of witnesses of fact	within 10 weeks from the making of the order
Exchange of expert's reports	within 14 weeks from the making of the order
Distribution of listing questionnaires by the court	within 20 weeks from the making of the order

---

[24] PD. 27 para. 3.
[25] CPR r. 27.14
[26] PD. 28 para. 2.2.

| Return of completed listing questionnaires | within 22 weeks from the making of the order |
| Trial (1 day) | within 30 weeks from the making of the order |

If a party wishes to vary the timetable, then the dates can be varied by consent, unless the date sought to be altered is that of the return of the listing questionnaire, the trial or trial period or a date for completion of another task, variation in which will make it necessary to alter any of those dates.[27] In any of those cases, the court's express permission must be obtained. Failure to comply with directions potentially attracts a number of sanctions, from striking out of the defaulter's claim or defence to costs.[28]

Should the dispute remain unresolved by the time all the directions have been completed, further directions for the immediate preparation of and course of events at trial will be made at listing when, again, the parties are required to file questionnaires to assist the court.

The multi-track

12–024   As in fast track, it is possible that the court might be able to give directions simply by reading the allocation questionnaires and material submitted with those questionnaires (which, as can be seen from the questionnaire, may include a list of directions agreed between the parties) and without seeing the parties. However, as multi track cases are likely to include complexities of law or evidence, there is specific provision in the multi track for one or more case management hearings described as "case management conferences" or, for those taking place close to the trial and specifically concerned with the immediate preparation for and conduct of the trial "pre-trial reviews".[29] The court has express power to convene such hearings "whenever it appears necessary or desirable to do so".[30]

The case management conference, in particular, is a significant expression of what is designed to be one of the "hallmarks" of the multi track: "the flexibility given to the court in the way it will manage a case in a way appropriate to its particular needs".[31] For that reason it is required that, where there is legal representation, a person "familiar with the case and with sufficient authority to deal with any issues that are likely to arise" should attend any case management conference or pre trial review.[32]

The format of the hearing may be less formal than other hearings, taking the form of a business meeting or discussion rather than following the

---

[27] CPR r. 28.4.

[28] *Biguzzi v. Rank Leisure plc.* [1999] 1 W.L.R. 1926; [1999] 4 All E.R. 934; [2000] C.P. Rep. 6; *The Times*, October 5, 1999, C. A.; *Jones and another .v Telford and Wrekin District Council*, *The Times*, July 29, 1999, C.A.; *Baron v. Lovell, The Times*, September 14, 1999, C.A.; *Woodward v. Finch* [1999] C.P.L.R. 699, C.A.

[29] CPR r. 29.2 and 29.4, PD. 29 para. 3.3.

[30] PD. 29 para. 3.6.

[31] PD. 29 para 37; the other "hallmark" being "the ability of the court to deal with cases of widely differing values and complexity".

[32] CPR r. 29.3(2) and PD. 29 para. 5.2. The parties should consider bringing their clients in any event: PD. 29 para. 5.6. Some courts have also exercised their powers under CPR r. 3.1(2)(c) to require the partiesto accompany their legal representatives to these hearings. See also *Matthews v. Tarmac Bricks & Tiles Ltd*, [1999] C.P.L.R. 463, *The Times*, July 1, 1999, C.A.

normal structure for interim hearings of applicant's submissions followed by respondent's submissions.

The topics of discussion at a case management conference are almost limitless (although if the court wishes to impose a single expert instructed jointly by the parties or an assessor, this must be done at a case management conference).[33] However, one of the court's principal concerns will be to narrow the areas in dispute under CPR r. 1.4(2)(b) and (c). Consequently the court might order the preparation of a case summary, or the parties might themselves decide that a case summary would be of assistance.[34] A case summary is simply a short document setting out the issues of fact that are agreed or in dispute and the evidence the parties consider will be needed to resolve those areas of dispute.

Other matters that may be considered at a case management conference include:

a. Whether the claimant's claim is clear (*i.e.* should further information be provided under CPR Part 18?);

b. Whether any statements of case require amendment;

c. Disclosure of documentary evidence;

d. Expert evidence;[35]

e. Factual evidence (*i.e.* arrangements for exchange of witness statements);

f. Clarification of expert evidence and questions to experts;

g. Whether it will be appropriate to order a split trial (*e.g.* that liability is resolved before the parties incur the additional costs of proving quantum).[36]

The distribution and submission of listing questionnaires will proceed as in the fast track. There may at this stage be a hearing to set a timetable for trial and to fix the trial date if these matters have not already been resolved at earlier hearings.[37]

If a party wishes to vary the timetable, then the dates can be varied by consent, unless the date sought to be altered is that of the case management conference or pre trial review, the return of the listing questionnaire, the trial or trial period or a date for completion of another task, variation in which will make it necessary to alter any of those dates.[38] In any of those cases, the court's express permission must be obtained. Failure to comply with directions potentially attracts the same range of sanctions, from striking out of the defaulter's claim or defence to costs as in the fast track.

---

[33] PD. 29 para. 4.13.

[34] PD. 29 para. 5.6(3), 5.7.

[35] Note PD. 29 para. 5.5: the court will expect to be able to identify the experts to be used by name (or at least by field) and to order whether or not the expert will appear at the trial to give oral evidence. If a party has pre-empted a direction about experts, that party is at risk that the costs already incurred in instructing an expert who may not be permitted by the court, will be irrecoverable even if that party is successful at trial.

[36] PD. 29 para. 5.3.

[37] CPR r. 29.7, 29.8.

[38] CPR r.29.5 PD. 29 para. 6.1. See also *Rollinson v. Kimberly Clark Ltd* [2000] C.P. Rep. 85, *The Times*, June 22, 1999, C.A.

6. OTHER PRE-TRIAL MATTERS

Summary judgment

12–025   It would obviously be an unacceptable delaying tactic for a defendant to indicate an intention to defend when there was no real defence, thus gaining time in which to pay a debt or damages which could not seriously be disputed. Consequently, even prior to the Civil Procedure Rules, there was a procedure allowing a plaintiff in these circumstances to request the court to enter judgment for him or her summarily. The court had to balance the objectives of the plaintiff in seeking not to incur the costs and delay involved in pursuing to trial a case to which there was no real answer with those of the defendant in seeking to vindicate him or herself.

In his Interim Report, Lord Woolf recommended the enlargement of this jurisdiction to allow its use by defendants against claimants as well as by claimants against defendants. The result appears in CPR Part 24 and can be used by either party (and indeed, the court can convene a Part 24 hearing against either party of its own volition).

The test is set out as follows:

> "The court may give summary judgment against a claimant or defendant on the whole of a claim or on a particular issue if:
>
> (a)   it considers that:
>
> (i) that claimant has no real prospect of succeeding on the claim or issue; or
>
> (ii) that defendant has no real prospect of successfully defending the claim or issue; and
>
> (b)   there is no other compelling reason why the case or issue should be disposed of at trial."[39]

Consequently either party may apply to the court for a hearing to decide whether judgment should be given on the whole or part of a claim if the application can be supported by evidence stating that the applicant believes that their opponent has no real prospect of succeeding on the claim or issue or defending it, as appropriate.[40] The opponent has the opportunity to adduce evidence[41] in response. At the hearing (although the court has power to deal with this or any other pretrial hearing on the telephone, by video conference or even on the papers without any oral representations)[42] the master or district judge has the task of balancing the rights of the claimant and the defendant, applying a test described by Lord Woolf in *Swain v. Hillman*[43] in the following terms:

---

[39]   CPRr. 24.2.

[40]   PD. 24 para. 2.3(b).

[41]   It is unusual to allow oral examination of the parties at this or any other pre-trial hearing. CPR r. 32.6.

[42]   CPR r. 3.1(d); PD. 23 para. 2.

[43]   [2001] 1 All E.R. 91; [2001] C.P. Rep. 16; *The Times*, November 4, 1999, C.A. See also *Three Rivers District Council and another v. Bank of England (No. 3)*, [2001] UKHL 16; *The Times*, March 23, 2001, [2001] All E.R. 513, H.L. and *Royal Brompton Hospital NHS Trust v. Hammond and other (No. 5)*, [2001] EWCA Civ 550, *The Times*, May 11, 2001, C.A.

"The words 'no real prospect of being successful or succeeding' [*sic*] do not need any amplification, they speak for themselves. The word 'real' distinguishes fanciful prospects of success ... "

There are a number of options open to the court, but, perhaps where the claim or defence has a real prospect of success, but not a strong one, the court may make a conditional order, requiring payment of a sum of money into court as a condition of that party being permitted to continue with the claim or with the defence.[44] Such conditions, which can be applied in other circumstances, particularly as a sanction for failure to comply with rules, orders or pre-action protocols,[45] may have the effect of discouraging the party with the weak case, or at least inducing careful consideration of the strength of the case. The master or district judge may, however, decide in favour of the applicant, granting judgment on the claim where the applicant is a claimant or striking out or dismissing the claim if the applicant is a defendant, thus greatly speeding up the process of litigation in accordance with the overriding objective.

Disclosure and inspection

So that each party may be aware of documents relating to issues in the case, rules requiring "disclosure"[46] of those documents place an obligation on the litigant to disclose their existence and, possibly, to disclose their content. Where there is a pre-action protocol, then, as we have seen, much disclosure should take place even before the court becomes involved in the dispute. Even where there is not a protocol, then similar behaviour should involve disclosure of many documents in advance. Further, documents may be and in some cases must be attached to the particulars of claim. To assist in this process, either party may call on the court to intervene by making an order for disclosure prior to issue of the claim form.[47]

12–026

Nevertheless, as the real areas of dispute may not become apparent until the final statement of case has been filed, there is further provision for disclosure as part of the case management directions.

The parties and ultimately the court will have to decide on matters including:

a. The scope of search — how far should the parties search in archives and obscure storage facilities for documents that might be of only tangential relevance to the case?

b. The scope of disclosure. The normal and default provision is for

---

[44] PD. 24 para. 5.

[45] CPR r. 3.1(3) and (5).

[46] Known as "discovery" prior to 1999.

[47] s. 33 Supreme Court Act 1981, s. 52 County Courts Act 1984 and CPR r. 31.16. The statutory restriction of this procedure to personal injury claims was removed on implementation of the Civil Procedure Rules by the Civil Procedure (Modification of Enactments) Order 1998. For the approach of the courts to this jurisdiction, see: *Burrell's Wharf Freeholds Ltd. v. Galliard Homes Ltd.* [2000] C.P. Rep. 4, T.C.C.; *Bermuda International Securities Ltd. v. K.P.M.G.* [2001] EWCA Civ 269; [2001] C.P. Rep. 73, *The Times*, March 4, 2001, C.A.

"standard disclosure" — that is disclosure of documents that are of direct probative value. Documents falling within standard disclosure are those:

  i. On which the disclosing party relies;
 ii. Which adversely affect the case of the disclosing party; adversely affect the case of another party; or which support the case of another party; and
iii. Those which the disclosing party is required to disclose by a relevant practice direction.[48]

The parties and or the court may, however, consider that disclosure could be limited to a smaller category of documents. What is unlikely to be permitted, however, in a normal case, is more wide-ranging disclosure.[49]

Once the extent of the search and the scope of the disclosure obligation have been defined, then each party must normally produce a list of documents in proper form within the deadline imposed by the court. The documents are divided into three categories — those which the claimant or defendant has in his or her control and is willing to produce; those which he or she has but is not willing to produce and those which he or she has had in his or her control but has no longer. Objections to the production of documents for inspection will be based on one or more of the privileges to which a litigant is entitled.[50] Note that the list must contain a "disclosure statement" equivalent to a statement of truth[51]. A copy of the list of documents in *George and Hacker v. Reliable Nag Supply Stables* is set out on the page that follows:

---

[48] CPR r.31.6.

[49] Such as that permitted, under the old regime, by the principles set out in *Compagnie Financiere et Commercials du Pacifique v. Peruvian Guano Co.* (1882) L.R. 11 Q.B.D. 55, C.A. From March 2002, however, such disclosure (of any documents that will "enable the party applying for disclosure either to advance his own case or to damage that of the party giving disclosure; or lead to a train of enquiry which has either of those consequences") will again be available, in appropriate cases, by application to the court for "specific disclosure" under CPR r. 31.12: PD. 31, para. 5.5.

[50] There are certain recognised privileges — legal professional privilege, privilege against self-incrimination; "without prejudice" documents; Crown privilege or public interest immunity. See further, O'Hare and Browne, *O'Hare and Hill, Civil Litigation* (10th ed. Sweet and Maxwell) at p. 555; the White Book, *op. cit.*, Vol. 1 pp. 629 *et seq.*; *Blackstones' Civil Practice* (2001, Blackstones), at Chap. 48. Note however CPR r. 35.10 removing privilege from instructions to an expert witness and PD. 21 para. 6.3 which requires production to the court in certain circumstances of instructions to counsel that would otherwise attract legal professional privilege (although there must presumably be some doubt whether a mere practice direction is capable of removing privilege). The section of CPR r. 48.7 containing a similar provision in relation to wasted costs orders, has been declared ultra vires: *General Mediterranean Holdings S.A. v. Patel* [2000] 1 W.L.R. 272; [1999] 3 All. E. R. 673, Q.B.D. Further, but only where the documents in question come under CPR r. 31.6(b) (*i.e.* those that adversely affect the disclosing party's case, adversely affect another party's case or support another party's case), inspection can be withheld on the ground that it would be "disproportionate" (CPR r. 3.3(2)).

[51] CPR rr. 31.10(5); 31.23 and PD. 31, para 8.

List of Documents: Standard Disclosure

In the	
	HIGH COURT OF JUSTICE QUEEN'S BENCH DIVISION NOTTINGHAM DISTRICT REGISTRY
Claim No.	NG0167234
Claimant (including ref)	PETER GEORGE (1) MARTIN HACKER (2)
Defendant (including ref)	RELIABLE NAG SUPPLY STABLES (A FIRM)
Date	16TH FEBRUARY 2002

Notes:

- The rules relating to standard disclosure are contained in Part 31 of the Civil Procedure Rules.
- Documents to be included under standard disclosure are contained in Rule 31.6
- A document has or will have been in your control if you have or have had possession, or a right of possession, of it or a right to inspect or take copies of it.

(1) Insert date.

Disclosure Statement

I state that I have carried out a reasonable and proportionate search to locate all the documents which I am required to disclose under the order made by the court on ( ) 12th February 2002

(I did not search for documents -

1. pre-dating June 2000

2. located elsewhere than at my home or that of the Second Claimant

3. in categories other than Contractual documents and care records of horses

)

I certify that I understand the duty of disclosure and to the best of my knowledge I have carried out that duty. I further certify that the list of documents set out in or attached to this form, is a complete list of all documents which are or have been in my control and which I am obliged under the order to disclose.

I understand that I must inform the court and the other parties immediately if any further document required to be disclosed by Rule 31.6 comes into my control at any time before the conclusion of the case.

(I have not permitted inspection of documents within the category or class of documents (as set out below) required to be disclosed under Rule 31(6)(b) or (c) on the grounds that to do so would be disproportionate to the issues in the case.)

Signed *Peter George*   Peter George   **Date** 16th February 2002

(Claimant)(~~Defendant~~)(~~'s litigation friend~~)

Position or office held *(if signing on behalf of firm or company).*
Please state why you are the appropriate person to make the disclosure statement.

I was personally involved in all the events giving rise to the claim.

continued overleaf

N265 List of Documents: standard disclosure (4.99)

N265/1

List and number here, in a convenient order, the documents (or bundles of documents if of the same nature, e.g. invoices) in your control, which you do not object to being inspected. Give a short description of each document or bundle so that it can be identified, and say if it is kept elsewhere i.e. with a bank or solicitor.

I have control of the documents numbered and listed here. I do not object to you inspecting them/producing copies.

1	Defendant's receipt for £65,000	25th June 2000
2	Care logbook for the Horse	Various dates
3	Account of Sutton Riding Enterprises	20th August 2000
4	Care logbook for the Mare	Varous dates
5	Letter Claimants' solicitors to Defendant	20th October 2001
6	Correspondence and copy correspondence between Claimants' solicitors and Defendant's solicitors	Various Dates
7	Claim form, statements of case, applications and orders common to the parties	Various dates

List and number here, as above, the documents in your control which you object to being inspected. (Rule 31.19).

I have control of the documents numbered and listed here, but I object to you inspecting them:

1 All notes, memoranda, drafts and witness statements not previously filed in interim applications prepared solely for the purpose of the conduct of the Claimants' case or in the contemplation thereof which fall within standard disclosure.

2 All communications of whatsoever nature passing between the Claimants and their solicitors or counsel which fall within standard disclosure.All communications of whatsoever nature passing between the Claimants, their solicitors or counsel and their expert witness or witnesses which fall within standard disclosure.

3 Instructions to, opinions of counsel and drafts produced by counsel which fall within standard disclosure.

4 All notes, proofs, reports or expert memoranda called into existence for the purpose of assisting the Claimants or their solicitors or counsel in the conduct of the action or in contemplation thereof which fall within standard disclosure.

Say what your objections are.

I object to you inspecting these documents because:

Other than the instructions to an expert witness within category 2 above, they are by their very nature privileged. I object to you inspecting any such instructions to an expert witness which may fall within standard disclosure under CPR r. 35.10(4).

N265/2

List and number here, the documents you once had in your control, but which you no longer have. For each document listed, say when it was last in your control and where it is now.

I have had the documents numbered and listed below, but they are no longer in my control.

N/A

Further information to assist in proving one's case can be obtained through the Part 18 procedure described above. In addition, a power currently contained in Supreme Court Act 1981, s. 34 and County Courts Act 1984, s. 53 allowing orders for post-commencement disclosure against non-parties to the claim (such as, for example, the claimant's employer in a personal injury case) was in 1999 extended to all cases.[52]

Exchange of witness statements

12–027   As a result of proposals in the Civil Justice Review, from 1992 it became the practice for the court to order exchange of written statements of the oral evidence which each party intends to use at trial. This provision is now contained in CPR Part 32. Those statements are required to be in a standard format (PD. 32), in the witness' own words "as far as practicable"[53] and to contain a statement of truth.[54] Generally speaking, an adjunct to the order for exchange will be that the statements stand as evidence in chief at the trial: i.e. that after the witness has confirmed that the statement is his or her own, the court will proceed straight to cross examination.

If a statement is not served in respect of a witness, then prima facie that witness cannot be called to give evidence at trial.[55] This of course causes difficulties with a useful but unco-operative witness whose attendance at trial can be compelled by use of a witness summons but to little effect if the evidence is inadmissible because of the failure to exchange a statement. To deal with this deadlock, the CPR provide for use, subject to the court's permission, of a "witness summary" to replace the unobtainable witness statement.[56] We will discuss witnesses of fact further in Chapter 15.

Expert witnesses

See Chapter 15.

---

[52] Civil Procedure (Modification of Enactments) Order 1998. The relevant rules appear in CPR r. 31.17.

[53] A cautionary tale is provided in *Alex Lawrie Factors Ltd. v. Morgan and others*, [2001] C.P. Rep. 2; *The Times*, August 18, 1999, C.A. Here, the written evidence of a party who wished to set aside a transaction on the grounds of undue influence had been drafted by her lawyers, who included such matters as technical comment on the relevant cases on the topic. Reading this document, the court was forced to conclude that the party appeared to be so knowledgeable that she could hardly have been acting under undue influence! For an example of a judge's concern at the *manner* in which the statement was obtained, see *Aquarius Financial Enterprises Jnc and another v. Certain Underwriters at Lloyd's* (2001) 151 N.L.J., Q.B.D., Commercial Court.

[54] The penalty for signing without an honest belief in the truth of the facts so verified is contempt of court. See *MBNA American Bank N.A. and another v. Freeman* [2000] All E.R. (D) 1743, Ch D.

[55] CPR r. 32.10. Conversely, if the statement is exchanged but the witness is not called, any other party may rely on the statement as hearsay: CPR r. 32.5(5) and *Society of Lloyd's v. Jaffray*, *The Times*, August 3, 2000, Q.B.D.

[56] CPR r. 32.9.

CPR Part 36

As we have seen in outline in Chap. 10, prior to 1999 it was possible for a **12–028** defendant, at any time after issue of proceedings, to pay money into court in attempted satisfaction of the plaintiffs claim. The plaintiff could then choose whether to accept the amount paid in and discontinue the action, or carry on the action in the hope of obtaining a greater sum at trial. The penalty for the plaintiff was that he or she would normally bear all the costs of the action from the date the payment in could have been accepted (normally 21 days after payment was made) unless awarded a sum in excess of the amount the defendant had paid in.

This useful procedure allowed a defendant to use it to protect himself or herself from a zealous plaintiff who wanted to have the "day in court" or to apply pressure to accept a sum in settlement rather than risk a heavy bill in costs and it has been incorporated into Part 36 of the CPR. It is important to stress two points. First that the plaintiff could not and the claimant cannot now both accept the sum and continue the action. Second, the judge is not told of the payment until the questions of liability and damages have been settled.[57]

So useful a procedure is it, indeed, that it has been extended under the CPR in a number of ways. Firstly, and most significantly, the procedure has been opened to claimants. A claimant may use the Part 36 procedure to say, for example, "I am prepared to accept £20,000 in settlement of my claim ostensibly valued at £30,000". As with the defendant's payment, if the offer is accepted, that is the end of the claim. If the defendant does not accept the offer then, as with the defendant's payment, it is kept secret from the trial judge. If the defendant does not at trial obtain a better result than the offer (*e.g.* in this case an award of damages against the defendant of less than £20,000), the defendant will be penalised. The question is, of course, how to penalise a defendant in this situation. The defendant will having lost the case, have to pay the claimant's damages and a large part if not all of the claimant's costs irrespective of the Part 36 offer. The answer imposed by CPR r. 36.21 is that the court will, unless it is unjust, require the defendant to pay additional interest of up to 10 per cent above base rate on damages and costs from the last date the defendant could have accepted the offer as well as the claimant's costs on an indemnity basis. If the offer was made very early in the proceedings, this additional interest can amount to a very large sum.[58]

---

[57] Suggestions for streamlining the system, in particular for removing the requirement for the defendant to support the offer by making an actual payment, appear in the August 2001 Lord Chancellor's Department consultation paper *Payments into court in satisfaction of claims.*

[58] For example: *All-In-One Design and Build Ltd. v. Motcomb Estates Ltd., The Times*, April 4, 2000; Q.B.D., T.C.C.; *Dew Pitchmastic plc. v. Birse Construction Ltd. (No. 2), The Times*, June 21, 2000, Q.B.D., T.C.C.; *Petrotrade Inc. v. Texaco Ltd.*, [2001] C.P. Rep. 29, *The Times*, July 10, 2000, C.A.; *Amber v. Stacey*, [2001] 2 All E.R. 88; [2001] 1 W.L.R. 1225, C.A.; *Scammell v. Dicker*, [2001] 1 W.L.R. 631, [2001] C.P. Rep. 64, *The Times*, February 14, 2001; C.A.; *McPhilemy v. Times Newspapers Ltd., The Times*, July 3, 2001, C.A. *Reid Minty v. Taylor* [2001] EWCA Civ 1723, [2002] 2 All ER 150, CA; *Quorum AS v. Schramm and others (Costs)* [2002] 2 Ll Rep 72, QBD, Commercial Court; *Kiam v. MGN Ltd (Costs)* [2002] EWCA Civ 66, [2002] 2 All ER 242, CA; *Huck v. Robson* [2002] EWCA Civ 398, [2002] 3 All ER 263, CA.

Secondly, for both claimants and defendants the procedure is extended beyond simple offers of money. So, for example, in a tort claim, the defendant might offer under Part 36 to accept 60 per cent liability, suggesting that the claimant was 40 per cent contributorily negligent.

Finally the CPR seek to allow Part 36 to be used prior to the issue of proceedings.[59]

F. PRE TRIAL REMEDIES

12–029 Pre-trial remedies are "designed to deal with the position of the parties pending the trial, to maintain as far as possible the status quo ante and to preserve, protect and where necessary enhance the rights and interests of the parties in the inevitable interval between the start of the proceedings and the trial." There are many remedies available, a non-exclusive list of which appears in CPR r. 25.1, but perhaps the three most significant are the interim injunction, the freezing injunction and the search order.

Interim injunction

12–030 The significance of the interim injunction is not only that it is a speedy and effective method of preserving the status quo ante prior to a trial, but also that the decision of the judge on the granting of an injunction is often taken by the parties as an indication of what the trial judge would do and therefore the proceedings may go no further.

An interim injunction is usually negative in form, that is to restrain the defendant from doing something, rather than mandatory, that is, requiring an act to be done. It is effective because a breach of an injunction is a contempt of court which is punishable by imprisonment, fine and sequestration of property, as appropriate. Further the injunction does not just affect the parties to the action, it also applies to anyone knowing of it and its terms. Third parties then are under an obligation to observe its terms at least so that steps amounting to a breach are not taken, under the penalty of sanctions for contempt of court.

Such an injunction can be granted in either High Court or county court proceedings. It is usually applied for on the basis of the other party being informed and thus able to challenge the granting of the injunction. However, in an emergency it may be applied for and granted without notice to to the other side.[60] In appropriate circumstances an injunction can be obtained prior to the issue of proceedings.[61]

An interim injunction will be granted if the principles laid down in *American Cyanamid Co. v. Ethicon Ltd.*[62] are satisfied. First the applicant must establish that there is a good arguable claim to the right which is to be protected. Secondly the applicant must show that there is a serious question to be tried. Thirdly, the grant depends on which way the balance of

---

[59] CPR r. 36.10. See *Huck v. Robson, op. cit.,* n. 58.
[60] CPR r.25.2(2)(b).
[61] CPR r. 25.2, 25.3
[62] [1975] A.C. 396, H.L. The principles have survived the introduction of the CPR: *Imutran Ltd. v. Uncaged Campaigns Ltd. and another* [2001] 2 All E.R. 385; [2001] C.P. Rep. 28, Ch. D. This case also investigates the impact of the Human Rights Act 1998, s. 12 on the criteria.

convenience lies. Further, and since the implementation of the Human Rights Act 1998 in October 2000, the court may have to consider whether or not the grant of the injunction infringes the respondent's human rights, particularly when the injunction, if granted, might prevent the respondent exercising his or her right of freedom of expression.[63]

Freezing injunction

The freezing injunction — known prior to 1999 as a Mareva injunction[64] — is a specialised form of interim injunction used to prevent not only a foreign defendant transferring assets abroad and thus out of the jurisdiction and defeating an action but also to prevent a defendant within the jurisdiction transferring assets abroad or concealing them in England and Wales. It is an interim remedy falling within the ambit of Part 25 of the CPR

    12–031

The injunction is effective because it is swift and secret and not only does it act against the defendant who would be in contempt of court for breach but also against innocent third parties. The main advantage of this is that it applies to banks through which transfer of assets is most likely to take place, especially in an age of the computerised transfer of funds. The third party has a right to be paid all reasonable expenses and costs, thus having a right of set-off in connection with an account which has become the subject of a freezing injunction.

Such an injunction may be granted in either the High Court or the county court. A standard form order is attached to PD. 25 and variations from this order must be brought to the specific attention of the court when the application is made.[65] A freezing injunction is usually applied for without notice to the respondent, so that the opponent cannot defeat its effect consequent upon notice of an application. The claimant must then show a good arguable case, must make full and frank disclosure of all the facts that the judge will need to know, including in particular information of the existence of assets that are desired to be the object of the injunction, and must make clear the grounds for believing that without an injunction there is a real risk of any judgment in his or her favour not being satisfied as well as demonstrating compliance with CPR r. 25.3 and, if the application is prior to the issue of proceedings, CPR r. 25.2(2(b). As with all injunctions, the claimant must normally provide an undertaking as to damages, that is the ability to cover the expenses of the defendant should the claimant's case ultimately fail. Further and as with any order the court is asked to make, the court must consider whether granting the order will further the overriding objective as well as its obligations under the Human Rights Act 1998.

Search order

The search order — known prior to 1999 as an Anton Piller order[66] — is a special form of mandatory injunction derived initially from the inherent

    12–032

---

[63] See especially Human Rights Act 1998, s.12.

[64] *Mareva Companiera Naviera v. International Bulk Carriers* [1980] 1 All E.R. 213, C.A.

[65] *Memory Corporation plc. and another v. Sidhu* [2000] 1 W.L.R. 1443, C.A.; *Interoute Communications UK Ltd. v Fashion Gossip Ltd. and others, The Times,* November 10, 1999, Ch. D.

[66] *Anton Piller A.G. v. Manufacturing Process Ltd.* [1976] 1 Ch. 55; [1976] 2 W.L.R. 162; [1976] 1 All E.R. 779, C.A.

power of the court to make an order for the detention or preservation of property which is the subject matter of a cause, and of documents and articles relating to it. It was placed on a statutory footing by Civil Procedure Act 1997, s. 7 and is an interim remedy within the ambit of CPR Part 25. The order often empowers the claimant to enter the defendant's premises and search for and seize material documents and articles ("execution of the order"), but, as it is not a search warrant, no force may be used in entering premises. A large number of caveats intended to protect the interests of the defendant — including the requirement allowing the defendant to claim legal privilege in respect of documents; allowing the defendant a period within which to take legal advice and most significantly, providing for the search to be supervised by an independent solicitor ("the supervising solicitor") who subsequently provides a written report to the court on the way in which the search was carried out — are contained in the standard order attached to PD. 25. As with the freezing injunction, any variation from the standard order must be drawn to the court's attention when the application is made.[67]

Such an order may be granted in High Court or county court proceedings. The application is without notice to the defendant, for obvious reasons, and consequently the applicant must give full disclosure of all facts the judge is likely to need to know.[68] The claimant must provide evidence describing the premises and the relevant property or documents and showing some strong evidence that serious harm or serious injustice will be done if the order is not made. As usual, the claimant must provide an undertaking as to damages and as with any order the court is asked to make, the court must consider whether granting the order will further the overriding objective as well as its obligations under the Human Rights Act 1998.[69]

Other pre-trial remedies

12–033   Other remedies include the High Court power to make interim receivership orders, the High Court and county court power to make interim orders relating to property relevant to an action, the limited power to prevent a defendant leaving the jurisdiction, and the High Court or county court power to make an order requiring an interim payment on account of any damages, debt or other sum which a defendant may be held liable to pay.[70] A remedy exclusive to defendants (including defendants to counterclaims), obliged to defend a claim brought by a claimant who may be discovered to have insufficient funds to reimburse the defendant his or her costs when he

[67] As can other relevant factors of which the judge should be made aware: *Elvee Ltd v. Taylor* [2001] EWCA Civ 1943, *The Times*, December 18, 2001, C.A.
[68] Failure to do so can lead to the discharge of the order: *Gadget Shop Ltd. v. The Bug.com and others*, [2001] C.P. Rep. 13; *The Times*, June 28, 2000, C.A and *St. Merryn Meat Ltd v. Hawkins* [2001] C P Rep 116; *Daily Telegraph*, July 10, 2001, Ch. D
[69] The order is not, intrinsically, a breach of human rights: *Chappell v. U.K.*, [1990] 12 E.H.R.R 1; *The Times*, 6th April 1989, E.C.H.R. The way in which it is obtained or executed might, however, lead to such a breach: see *St. Merryn Meat Ltd v. Hawkins, op. cit.*
[70] CPR rr 25.6 to 25.9 inclusive and PD. 25B. See also: *South West Water Services Ltd. v. International Computers Ltd.*, [2001] Lloyd's Rep. P.N. 353, Q.B.D., T.C.C.; *Parry v. North West Surrey Health Authority, The Times*, January 5, 2000, Q.B.D.; *Harmon CFEM Facades (UK) Ltd v. The Corporate Officer of the House of Commons* [2001] C.P. Rep. 20; *The Times*, November 15, 2000, Q.B.D., T.C.C.

or she is vindicated at trial, is that of security for costs:[71] an order whereby the claimant must pay into court for safekeeping an amount of money representing the defendant's costs in defending the claim.

G. HAVE THE WOOLF REFORMS ACHIEVED THEIR OBJECTIVES?

A great deal of thought and a greater amount of ink has been spilt over the last two and a half years in seeking to evaluate the real effect of the reforms on the court, the practitioner and on the client. Certain effects are immediately apparent from such empirical studies as the 1999 and 2000 Judicial Statistics,[72] showing a remarkable drop in the number of civil claims now issued. Otherwise evidence of the effect of the reforms in more anecdotal form is overwhelming and the Lord Chancellor's Department is in the process of conducting its own investigations of which the March 2001 paper *Emerging Findings* is the first product. **12–034**

a. Litigation will be avoided wherever possible;

As we have seen from examination of the judicial statistics, there has been a startling drop in the number of civil claims issued in the last two and a half years. If one assumes that the number of litigatable disputes has not decreased then, to that extent, litigation as a process has been avoided. What is yet to be explored is the real rationale for the reduction. **12–035**

A possible rationale is, of course, one of cost. A litigant in person may incur no lawyer's fees, but is generally obliged to pay the prescribed court fees of up to £500 on issue and, for claimants, a further £80 on filing the allocation questionnaire. The fees alone, then, can, especially in a small claims track case, rapidly approach the value of the claim. It is, however, fair to say that as a result of representations by such organisations as N.A.C.A.Bx. and the Civil Justice Council, the allocation fee was, in early 2000, remitted in small claims cases with a value of less than £1,000.

The initial fall in the number of issued cases was almost certainly a result of the concern of lawyers and their clients about entering an unfamiliar and untried procedure. A survey by the firm Lovells, quoted in *Emerging Findings* (March 2001), suggested that 7 per cent of that firm's clients were now consciously treating litigation as a last resort.

b. Litigation will be less adversarial and more co-operative;

Emerging Findings located evidence that claims were becoming compromised earlier in the life of the litigation rather than — literally — at the door of the court on the day of trial. They found that 70 per cent of fast track cases (during the period November 1999 to December 2000) settled prior to **12–036**

---

[71] CPR rr 25.12 to 25.15 inclusive. An alternative ground is that, as a result of the foreign residence of the claimant, an order for costs would be difficult to enforce.
[72] *Op. cit.*

the day of trial.[73] Logically, the emphasis of the CPR on earlier and earlier disclosure of evidence and identification of the issues in dispute should contribute to this effect — the earlier the real nature of the dispute and the strengths and weaknesses of the case are revealed, the earlier the parties are able to identify areas of potential compromise. The fact that much or all of this process may take place prior to the issue of proceedings will also contribute to the reduction in the number of claims issued — the impact of the pre action protocols and similar behaviour acting as an incitement to compromise the dispute instead of issuing proceedings.

An additional contributory factor towards the compromise of cases is the tactical use of CPR Part 36.[74] A CEDR Civil Justice Audit is quoted in *Emerging Findings* to the effect that 74 per cent of the lawyers surveyed felt CPR Part 36 had made settlement easier.

It is, of course, entirely possible to argue that the pragmatic settlement of cases outside the formal court system detracts from the concept of "justice" — a pragmatic result, particularly a result reached when one party is obliged to consider the risk incumbent on pursing litigation with the risk of a penalty under CPR Part 36 being imposed if he or she does not do well enough at trial, is not a "just" result.

c. Litigation will be less complex;

12–037   Clearly, the fact that the rules are now (almost entirely) unified, removes a level of complexity from civil litigation: the litigant and especially the litigant in person no longer needs to penetrate often quite subtle differences between the rules in the two courts. Set against this, however, is the proliferation of specialist guides for individual courts: the Queen's Bench Division Guide (for the Royal Courts of Justice); the Mercantile Court Guide and the Commercial Court Guide. Any person new to civil procedure who attempts to comprehend the mysteries of Parts 20 or 36 would be forgiven for a belief that the new rules are, in places at least, significantly more complex than the old. The authors of *Emerging Findings* commit themselves only to the comment that unification means that "the Civil Procedure Rules are developing to meet these criteria". It is clearly anticipated in *Emerging Findings* that the court's ability to narrow the issues and to control the evidence adduced to prove or disprove those issues, powers typically exerted at the case management conference is a "key factor" towards the simplification of litigation

d. The timescale of litigation will be shorter and more certain;

12–038   The average period between issue of proceedings and trial in the county court is now 74 weeks *i.e.* 18 and a half months.[75] In addition, it is

---

[73] A similar, but much less significant, drop in settlements close to trial was also identified in multi-track cases.

[74] See para. 12-028.

[75] *Judicial Statistics 2000*, table 4.17. This does, compare favourably — but only just — with the average waiting period for a county court trial described in *Judicial Statistics 1995*, Cm. 3290, p 35, of 79 weeks.

important to realise that the pre-action protocols may add a further 3 to 4 months prior to issue. *Emerging Findings* discovered that the waiting time for small claims hearings rose shortly after the implementation of the CPR but has settled to a generally lower figure.[76] Generally, it seems, waiting times to trial seem to be dropping, if slowly.[77] The question remains, however, whether, particularly for an individual litigant, a period approximating two years before trial and the potential of recovery, is adequate.[78] The Lord Chancellor's Department retains as one of its objectives, the reduction of the duration of civil cases by March 2002 by speeding up administration.[79]

Is the timescale more certain? The court is encouraged to fix a trial date or trial window comparatively early in the process.[80] Timetabling decisions should be worded in terms giving a date (and sometimes a time of day) by way of deadline. However, whilst a solicitor or barrister will be accustomed to, for example, a hearing starting late or being held over to a second day, as an inconvenience, any vagary in the timetable may be devastating to a litigant in person who has taken time off work.[81]

e. The cost of litigation will be more affordable; more predictable, and more proportionate to the value and complexity of individual cases;

Emerging Findings considers it too early to be definitive about costs and the Lord Chancellor's Department continues to conduct and to commission research into the subject, including the possibility of providing "benchmarks" for recoverable costs. Anecdotally, however, practitioners complain that the cost of litigation has increased as a direct result of the obligation to carry out a great deal of work at the early stages of litigation, particularly as a result of the pre-action protocols.[82]

12–039

---

[76] 522 days in 2000 as against 663 in 1997.

[77] A further indication can be found in Practice Note (Court of Appeal (Civil Division): Listing Windows and hear-by dates), *The Times*, July 25, 2001, C.A. reducing the hear-by dates in appeals from 15 months to 12 months. The Court of Appeal attributed this reduction to improvements in the court service. An additional factor might, of course, be the fact that the grounds for appeal have been significantly constricted. See further Chap. 18 and *Judicial Statistics 2000*.

[78] As we will see in Chap. 15 however, judgment in one's favour by no means guarantees recovery. It should also be noted that there are means by which the claimant can obtain payments on account of damages to ameliorate the wait: CPR rr. 25.6 to 9 and PD. 25b.

[79] *Departmental Report* (Cm. 5107, March 2001), p10.

[80] On allocation in the small claims track (CPR r. 27.4); "as soon as practicable after the date specified for filing a completed listing questionnaire" in the fast track (giving the parties at least 3 weeks notice of the actual date) (CPR r. 28.6); "as soon as practicable after" filing of the listing questionnaire, the listing hearing or pre-trial review in the multi-track (CPR r. 29.8).

[81] For a discussion of the perspective of the litigant in person, see Gibb, "When the Quest for Justice sours", *The Times*, November 28, 2000.

[82] See the various sources quoted in *Emerging Findings, op. cit.*

f. Parties of limited financial means will be able to conduct litigation on a more equal footing;

The litigant in person is perhaps the most obviously potentially disadvantaged person in the civil litigation system. *Emerging Findings* located anecdotal evidence that the new system was thought to be more friendly to litigants in person than to lawyers. In addition there is governmental support for the concept that legal advice should be more widely available, particularly in more informal, less intimidating contexts[83] — such as the court information kiosk in Telford.[84] Where lawyers are retained, *Emerging Findings* quoted a number of surveys conducted by lawyers and allied organisations such as CEDR.[85] The consensus of clients surveyed was generally in favour of the reforms. Lawyers, especially those schooled under the old regime, may have been more cautiously accepting.[86]

g. There will be clear lines of judicial and administrative responsibility for the civil justice system;

12–040   This aspect of the reforms is not covered in *Emerging Findings*. It is, however, clear that the Lord Chancellor is seeking to regularise the system and to identify specific lines of authority at least within the higher reaches of the Lord Chancellor's Department and the Court Service.[87]

---

[83] Some aspects of this approach were considered in Chap. 11 when we looked at the current regime for public funding of litigation

[84] For further plans to modernise and streamline the court infrastructure, see the Lord Chancellor's Department consultation papers *Civil Justice* (September 1998) and *Modernising the Civil Courts* (January 2001) and report *Civil Justice.2000* (June 2000). A Court Service Customer Satisfaction survey reported in February 2001 that 79 % of litigants were satisfied with the overall level of service received from court staff and 86% with the counter service and clarity of the new court forms and leaflets — Lord Chancellor's Department press release April 11, 2001.

[85] Wragge & Co had found 89% of their clients to be in favour, Eversheds 54% and CEDR 80%.

[86] For example, Alien, "Inconsistent Judges plague Woolf Reforms", 2001 98(13) L.S.G. referring to a Law Society survey of 50 firms of solicitors, 80% of which were in favour of the reforms but 62% of which referred to problems caused by inconsistency between judges, to difficulties with the process of summary assessment of costs (see para. 11-003) and generally to difficulty in recovering, even when successful, costs incurred during the substantial pre-action stages encouraged by the CPR See also Sutton and Summers "Woolf s Reforms — a curate's egg? 7 out of 10 for the new system", *The Times*, October 26, 1999; Leslie, "An End of Year Report", Counsel, June 2000 pp 32–33; Exall, "The language of Woolf, one year on", S.J. 2000 144(15) p 366–367; Eaglesham, "Lawyers favour Woolf Reforms", *Financial Times* April 26, 2000; Gibbs et al "Verdict on Woolf shake-up — it's a qualified success", *The Times*, May 2, 2000.

[87] Each civil court or group of civil courts had, for example, from a very early stage in the reforms, a designated judge responsible for overseeing implementation (Lord Chancellor's Department press release October 27, 1998). Within the more public arena, publicity was given to the individual areas of responsibility of named parliamentary secretaries within the Lord Chancellor's Department: Lord Chancellor's Department press release June 18, 2001.

h. The structure of the courts and the deployment of judges will be designed to meet the needs of litigants;

i. Judges will be deployed effectively so that they can manage litigation in accordance with the new rules and protocols; and

j. The civil justice system will be more responsive to the needs of litigants.

All of these factors are related to the infrastructure of the court system. **12–041** Serious investigation is underway into improving the technological infrastructure of the courts.[88] The litigant, particularly the litigant in person, is overwhelmed by sources of information, particularly on the internet.[89]

A number of proposals for improving and streamlining the infrastructure of the civil court system are set out in the Lord Chancellor's Department January 2001 consultation paper *Modernising the Civil Courts*:

a) more effective internal administration of courts, by largely separating the administrative activities of the courts (in, for example, issuing claim forms) from the centres in which hearings take place.

b) More imaginative methods of interacting with court users by telephone, e-mail and the internet, almost unimaginably, for those schooled under the old regime, proposing "round the clock services by telephone and internet enabling the customer to conduct business on-line or to obtain forms and leaflets at convenient times."[90]

---

[88] See above, n. 71.

[89] See for example, the court service website (*http://www.courtservice.gov.uk/*), which includes, as well as a complete set of court forms, a series of advice leaflets designed for litigants in person; Just Ask!, a website of the Legal Services Commission (*http://www.justask.org.uk/*) designed for use by lay members of the public and the Lord Chancellor's Department website (*http://www.lcd.gov.uk/*), less ostensibly designed for the lay court user but nevertheless containing a complete set of court rules; and the Civil Justice Council website (*http://www.civiljusticecouncil.gov.Uk/*). There are also more specific sources of information such as CAFCASS (*http://www.cafcass.gov.uk/*) dealing with children and family court issues.

[90] *Modernising the Civil Courts*, executive summary. Starting points in this direction include the electronic issue of proceedings by bulk court users in Northampton (Lord Chancellor's Department press release September 18, 2000); a touch-screen kiosk in a public library in Telford (Lord Chancellor's Department press release April 17, 2001) and hearings taking place by video-conference (Lord Chancellor's Department press release July 26, 2000). The Lord Chancellor's Department is apparently considering a "Court Service Call"Centre"; Departmental Report (Cm. 5107, March 2001), p25. Reference has already been made (see above, para. 12-011) to the pilot for an online method of issuing court proceedings.

Not all proposed improvements are quite so philanthropic in intention, however Modernisation of the Commercial Court was announced explicitly in terms that:

"A modernised Commercial Court will enhance the UK's position as a major international centre for legal services. ... The new Court will safeguard Britain's position in a highly competitive world market. Last year, UK legal services attracted about £800 million in invisible earnings."

Lord Chancellor's Department press release, March 26, 2001.

c)   Improving the internal management of the courts by, for example, creating electronic files accessible to court staff and to judges.[91]

How, one wonders, will the average litigant in person, pursuing the supplier of defective consumer goods in the small claims track, react to this focus on technology? Court Service surveys seem to indicate increased satisfaction with the courts generally.[92] However, sometimes it is the simplest factor that makes the greatest impression — in an article in *The Times* in 2000, one litigant in person's principal complaint was related to perceived discourtesy to her in a judge who, she said, took telephone calls during the hearing.[93]

---

[91] Funds of £17.9m were apparently allocated to the creation of electronic diaries and to a more effective system for dealing with bulk housing applications: LCD press release August 2, 2001. A further development, is a trial of e-mail applications to the Preston County Court in place of more formal hearings attended by the parties: LCD press releases, December 14, 2000 and January 15, 2001.

[92] See n. 168 above. 34 courts (including some criminal courts) now hold charter marks in respect of their "delivery of service to the public", *ibid.*, p 26 and the current target is to improve the level of service to 85% in 2001, 2002. At the end of December 2000, the figure was at 87.2%, *ibid.*, p. 10.

[93] Gibb, "When the Quest for Justice sours", *The Times*, November 28, 2000.

CHAPTER 13

PRE-HEARING: TRIBUNALS

IN the preceding chapter we used the actions in the county court and the **13–001**
Queen's Bench Division as examples of civil procedure. For this chapter
there is no standard model. Generalisation about tribunal procedure is
almost impossible in the face of divergent practice in different tribunals[1] and
there is no accepted pattern. However, there are certain common principles
and objectives in tribunal adjudication and there are common procedural
problems to be solved. This chapter sets out to a examine these objectives
and the way in which they influence procedure prior to a tribunal hearing;
the common problems which procedural rules must attempt to solve; the
amount of legal advice or help which is available; and finally, the pre-
hearing procedure adopted in two particular tribunals as illustrative of the
various solutions designed to meet the needs of individual claimants and
individual tribunals.

A. THE COMMON OBJECTIVES

The starting point of any discussion must be the Franks Report[2] and its **13–002**
assertion that tribunals should display three common characteristics:
openness, fairness and impartiality.[3] It is clear that the attainment of each
of these objectives will have implications for the procedural rules adopted.

In requiring that tribunals should be open, the Committee intended that
the proceedings should be given sufficient publicity so that they were known
to those who might need to make use of them. In addition, it was stated that
the essential reasoning underlying decisions should be made known to the
parties.[4]

Openness means more than the adoption of a rule of procedure that, save
where the personal interests of the claimant would be prejudiced, tribunal
hearings should be conducted in public. It signifies rather a notion of
availability or accessibility—that tribunal adjudication is open to all those
who might have a problem lying within the jurisdiction of a particular

---

[1] The various types of tribunal and their jurisdiction are discussed above, paras 2-007–2-016,
2-018.
[2] Report of the Committee on Administrative Tribunals and Enquiries (Cmnd. 218, 1957).
[3] *ibid.* In particular, paras. 23–25, 41–42. The characteristic of impartiality is reinforced by the
requirements of Article 6(1), ECHR (above, para. 8-020).
[4] *ibid.*, para. 98.

tribunal. In order that a tribunal is *accessible* to the public, each citizen needs to be aware of his or her right to use the tribunal where appropriate[5]; the information given in official publications and forms must be comprehensible; tribunal hearings need to be conveniently located; advice and assistance needs to be available either through the Community Legal Service or through other agencies; and the procedure to be followed both prior to and during the hearing should be sufficiently clear that the claimant can follow it and understand the implications of seeking a tribunal hearing. Establishing the right procedural rules is but one aspect of making tribunals accessible to the public.

The objectives of fairness and impartiality are closely linked, and are especially important to a system which does not have the weight and authority enjoyed by the courts in the public esteem. Naturally, the claimant must be assured dial the adjudication is even-handed or he or she will dismiss the whole proceedings as unfair but the procedure to be followed is also crucial. Every claimant will judge the fairness of the tribunal (and hence assess its credibility and reputation) by reference to the way in which the case has progressed and the extent to which he or she has been able to put his or her own side of the argument in the knowledge of the case that has to be met. Procedural fairness — the feeling induced in the claimant that he or she has had "a fair crack of the whip" — is absolutely essential and according to the Franks Committee depends upon, " . . . the adoption of a clear procedure which enables parties to know their rights to present their case fully and to know the case which they have to meet."[6]

As well as displaying these three characteristics, tribunals are also expected to offer informal, cheap and quick adjudication, providing a contrast to the procedures of the High Court.[7] The problem lies in achieving an acceptable standard of decision-making based on adequate information and argument, without rendering tribunals as formal, expensive and slow as the civil courts.

Before a tribunal case reaches a hearing it must be prepared for adjudication and the parties must be in a position to participate fully at the hearing. There are, broadly, three stages in pre-hearing procedure which might be termed, "knowing your rights", "knowing the ropes", and "knowing the case".

B. "KNOWING YOUR RIGHTS"—IDENTIFYING THE TRIBUNAL

13–003   Courts do not have to advertise. There is a general awareness that civil courts are the venue for settling disputes, (although there may be some difficulty for individuals in perceiving that they have a problem capable of legal settlement), and as to criminal courts, defendants have little choice

---

[5] This goes back to the question of ensuring that problems are recognised and identified accurately; see Chap. 9.

[6] Franks Report (1957) para. 42.

[7] For a comparison between courts and tribunals, see R. E. Wraith and P. G. Hutchesson, *Administrative Tribunals* (1973), Chap. 10. *Cf.* above, para. 2-015.

about whether they wish to avail themselves of the court's jurisdiction. In respect of tribunals, the first difficulty for the parties may lie in realising that there is a body with jurisdiction over their grievance whose assistance might be invoked. The various tribunals need to be sufficiently well publicised so as to alert people to their existence and powers.

In general, individuals may take their case to a tribunal as a result of a decision of a Government department which affects them (a citizen/state dispute), or as a result of experiencing an event or series of events which the law places within the jurisdiction of a particular tribunal (normally a citizen/citizen dispute). Into the former category would fall appeals to Appeals Service tribunals[8]; to the General Commissioners of Income Tax[9]; to Immigration Appeal Tribunal[10] and many others. Into the latter category would fall applications to an Employment Tribunal[11] or to a Rent Assessment Committee.[12] This division is significant because in citizen/state dispute the individual concerned may be notified of the existence of the tribunal and of the right of appeal at the time that the decision is notified. Thus, the claimant knows of the right of appeal and, usually, how to make application. He or she may not know what are the implications of an appeal or precisely how to go about preparing the case, but he or she is given a start.

In respect of citizen/citizen disputes it is for the applicant to realise that, if he or she is unfairly dismissed or the rent is too high, that there is an opportunity to pursue the grievance in a tribunal. Some tribunals must, therefore, give special consideration to how they can make the public aware of their jurisdiction.

1. The Availability of Legal Advice

With very limited exceptions, legal aid and now funding for legal representation under the Legal Services Commission Funding Code has not been available for *representation* at tribunal hearings.[13] The green form **13–004**

---

[8] Where the original decision is made by an officer of the Benefits Agency, see above, para. 2-037.

[9] Against an income tax assessment, the tribunal being arranged in accordance with the Taxes Management Act 1970.

[10] Against the decision of an immigration adjudicator under the Immigration and Asylum Act 1999, Part IV.

[11] See above, paras 2-031, 2-032.

[12] Rent Assessment Committees exercise jurisdiction under Part I of the Housing Act 1988 in determining rents for assured periodic tenancies', mis is to replace its jurisdiction under the Rent Act 1977 to review the decisions of rent officers as to fair rents for protected tenancies (such tenancies can only exceptionally come into existence since 1988). They have also exercised the jurisdiction formerly exercised by rent tribunals: Housing Act 1980, s.72. As Leasehold Valuation Tribunals they deal with disputes arising in the management of residential property, including the reasonableness of service charges.

[13] Legal representation is available for cases in the Employment Appeal Tribunal, Mental Health Review Tribunals, the Proscribed Organisations Appeal Commission, Immigration Adjudicators, the Immigration Appeal Tribunal, the Protection of Children Act Tribunal, and some cases concerning penalties classed as criminal in ECHR terms before the VAT and Duties Tribunal and the General and Special Commissioners of Income Tax; this is subject to financial and merits criteria (except that representation at a MHRT is available regardless of financial resources but subject to a reasonableness test). See further below, para. 16-021.

legal advice scheme, was intended to provide a source of advice for the public on matters relating to tribunals and how to use them.[14] It was however, a source of regret to the Lord Chancellor's Advisory Committee on Legal Aid that the green form scheme was not used more extensively for advice on tribunal matters.[15]

It is difficult to quantify precisely the number of tribunal cases dealt with by solicitors under the green form scheme. The study by Genn and Genn of representation at tribunals found that solicitors were consulted by 4 per cent of appellants before Social Security Appeal Tribunals, 27 per cent of appellants to Immigration Adjudicators, 36 per cent of applicants to Industrial Tribunals and over 60 per cent of patients applying to Mental Health Review Tribunals.[16] It was Social Security Appeal Tribunals that had by far the highest case load, and the contribution of solicitors here under the green form scheme or otherwise was clearly very limited.

The replacement of the legal aid and advice schemes by the Community Legal Service established by the Access to Justice Act 1999 was in part driven by a policy that increased emphasis in public funding should be given to social welfare law.[17] As at March 2001, Controlled Work contracts had been issued to solicitors' offices and not for profit organisations in a number of categories potentially relevant to tribunal work.[18] Community Legal Service Partnerships covered 85 per cent of the population of England Wales.[19] Among the high priority areas for funding were social welfare issues, such as housing, debt, employment rights and benefit advice. As regards Legal Help, the three largest numbers of completed matters reported for 2000/01 were immigration, welfare benefits and housing.[20] It is difficult to assess how far these arrangements meet needs.[21] One of the activities of Community Legal Service Partnerships has been to attempt an assessment of local needs.[22]

---

[14] In 1969, the Law Society asserted that the introduction of a legal advice scheme would encourage solicitors to operate in areas of unmet legal need and ensure that adequate legal services would be provided. See above, para. 10-021.

[15] See, *e.g. 26th Legal Aid Annual Reports* [1975–76], p. 58.

[16] H. Genn and Y. Genn, *The Effectiveness of Representation at Tribunals* (L.C.D., 1989), pp. 15, 30, 39, 56. See further on this study, below, paras 13-006, 16-018.

[17] See *Annual Report of the Legal Services Commission, 2000–01*, p. 6.

[18] Mental health 355, Employment 373, Housing 788, Welfare benefits 636, and Immigration 548: *ibid.*

[19] *ibid.*, p. 13.

[20] 108,600, 91,119 and 86,727, respectively, out of a total of 761,583; the figures for mental health and employment were respectively 23,886 and 12,706. The corresponding figures for Legal Representation final bills paid were 1,192; 185; 13,531; (which would include a large number of cases in the county court) 82 and 264: *ibid.*, p. 17.

[21] The Legal Services Commission has commissioned a research project on this (the Measurement and Evaluation of Legal Need Research Project), which is in progress: *ibid.*, p. 14.

[22] See *e.g.* Greater Nottingham CLSP, *Advice Services in Nottinghamshire An Analysis of Need and Supply* (LCD website) applying Predictive Need Models published by the LSC in March 2000.

2. OTHER SOURCES OF ADVICE

The agencies discussed in Chapter 10 (CABx, independent advice centres, **13–005** law centres, Trade Union, etc.) are available to offer help to individuals, but therr work has been supplemented by the growth of specialist groups. Some of these are attached to large, generalist agencies, some exist independently.[23] Many sources of advice and information are now avaliable the Internet.[24]

Although Citizens Advice Bureaux have been prominent in developing tribunal assistance and representation, no standard pattern of organisation has emerged. Instead, individual schemes have grown up according to the particular circumstances in different parts of the country. Inevitably, the availability of resources has had a great influence on the type of provision made and its effectiveness. In the West Midlands, a specially funded scheme set up an individual tribunal unit independent of the bureaux in the area, but offering training and support to them and their clients.[25] In Newcastle upon Tyne, a smaller unit was situated within the bureau dealing specifically with cases referred on to it through the bureau. In Chapeltown, Leeds a Tribunal Assistance Unit offered a service to claimants through the local bureau.[26] In other areas, salaried welfare rights workers have been appointed to provide expertise for a group of bureaux. The universal experience has been that contact with any form of expertise, however provided, has raised the general level of advice-giving in respect of tribunal matters by the ordinary volunteer in the bureau.[27] This, together with the greatly increased demand for assistance with social security and employment problems, has enhanced the value of the CAB service to the general public. The CAB service does not routinely collect statistics or the amount of tribunal work done by CAB. A survey in 2000-01 showed that of the 501 bureaux that responded, 475 offered representation for SSATs, 456 for Disability Tribunals, and 443 for Employment Tribunals. All reported that there was a great deal of unmet need for representation.[28]

---

[23] A survey of some of these specialist groups is contained in R. Lawrence, *Tribunal Representation, The Role of Advice and Advocacy Services* (1980).

[24] See *Welfare Rights Bulletin* 158: web works wonders.

[25] The original project was jointly funded by the National Association of Citizens Advice Bureaux and the EEC Action Against Poverty Programme. The report on the project and its significance for tribunal advice and advocacy services generally is E. Kessler, *et al.*, *Combatting Poverty: CABx, Claimants and Tribunals* (1980). The unit now acts as a specialist support unit for CABx, organises training courses and provides a national information service through a telephone hotline, *The Adviser* magazine and the Internet (Advice guide): see J. Citron, *Citizens Advice Bureaux* (1989), pp. 54–56. It acts in a consultative capacity, but occasionally offers representation.

[26] *Tribunal Assistance, the Chapeltown Experience* (NACAB Occasional Paper No. 14, 1982), describes and evaluates the scheme.

[27] See Lawrence, *op. cit.* at p. 75. *Chapeltown Citizens' Advice Bureau, Leeds, Tribunal Assistance Unit, Progress Report — First Two years* (NACAB Occasional Paper No.6. 1979), at pp. 7–8.

[28] NACAB response to the LCD consultation on the Leggatt Report (November 2001) (NACAB website).

The Free Representation Unit[29] is an independent group, now based in offices Vesulam Street, London WC1, which offers an advocacy service in cases referred to it by advice agencies. In fact, this Unit may not be involved at the pre-hearing stage and may rely heavily on the referring agency 'for the initial advice to the claimant and preparation of the case. The Unit employs two salaried case workers, one for social security cases and one for employment cases, and there is a solicitor, and an administrative assistant, the funding coming from the Bar Council, the Inns of Court individual barristers, referral agencies, who pay a small annual income, and training days.[30] These support a hundred or so volunteer representatives, many of whom are Bar students or pupil barristers, some qualified lawyers.[31] They take on around 1,000 cases a year.

Other independent groups[32] have based themselves in advice centres offering a service to clients of that centre and those referred by other statutory or voluntary agencies. Finally, there is a growing number of welfare rights and advice units provided by local authority social service departments and offering advice and advocacy services.[33]

The advice available is, therefore, dependent partly upon local initiatives and there is certainly no systematic national coverage.

3. SEEKING ADVICE

13-006 A study of tribunal representation conducted for the Lord Chancellor's Department[34] looked at the proportion of appellants before four tribunals (Social Security Appeal Tribunals, Immigration Adjudicators, Industrial Tribunals and Mental Health Review Tribunals) who sought advice before the hearing. From information drawn from case files,[35] it appeared that only

---

[29] *FRU Prospectus*, see also the FRU's Annual Reports and *www.fru.org.uk*; Westgate, *Counsel*, Vol. 2, No. 1, Michaelmas/Autumn 1986, p. 12; H. Brooke Q.C. and T. Leaver, *ibid.* p. 13; General Council of the Bar, *Quality of Justice: The Bar's Response* (1989), pp. 72–76 (indicating the Bar Council's wish for FRU services to be expanded); N. Lieven, *Counsel*. February 1991, p. 22; D. Conn, *Legal Action*, December 1993, p. 9; M. Pennycook, *Counsel*, March/April 1994, pp. 23–24. FRU work has also been developed in Birmingham.

[30] Pennycook, *op.cit.*

[31] A Bar Pro Bono Unit, "Bar in the Community" was established in 1996: *www.barprobono. org.uk*; and a Solicitors Pro Bono Group, was formed in 1997 to support and promote pro bono work across the solicitors' profession (*www.probonogroup.org.uk*). In 2000, the SPBG and the Law Centres Federation launched Law Works to co-ordinate pro bono activities and provide training.

[32] *e.g.* Birmingham Tribunal Representation Unit; Walsall Advice and Representation Project; South Wales Anti-Poverty Action Centre; the London Advice Services Alliance representation service.

[33] See *e.g.* the Harlow Welfare Rights and Advice Service, the Nottinghamshire Welfare Rights Service, Manchester Advice Welfare Rights Service.

[34] H. Genn and Y. Genn, *The Effectiveness of Representation at Tribunals* (L.C.D., 1989), discussed by R. Young (1990) 8 C.J.Q. 16 and T. Mullen (1990) 53 M.L.R. 230.

[35] Likely to understate the position.

22 per cent[36] of SSAT appellants sought advice before the hearing.[37] The corresponding figures for the other three were much higher: 80 per cent for Immigration Adjudicators,[38] 70 per cent for Industrial Tribunals,[39] and 64 per cent for MHRTs,[40] again with regional and other variations The study suggested that failure to seek advice (or representation) often stemmed from ignorance about the nature of appeals (ranging from over-confidence to bewilderment). In other cases, appellants who recognised a need for advice either did not know where to go or could not obtain or pay for representation.[41]

C. "KNOWING THE ROPES"—MAKING APPLICATION TO A TRIBUNAL

Rules of procedure begin to take effect when an applicant decides to invoke the jurisdiction of the tribunal by making an application for a hearing. Prior to that he or she may have tried to effect a settlement of the grievance in the same way as would have been done in a civil matter, but because a significant proportion of tribunal matters concern the correctness of a decision made by a government department or agency the scope for settlement may be fairly limited.[42] However, it is increasingly common for there to be express provision for seeking review of a decision by the decision-maker.[43] In other cases, particularly where an application to an Employment Tribunal may be in prospect, there are pre-hearing procedures expressly designed to secure a mutually acceptable resolution of the problem.[44]

13–007

---

[36] Of these, 31 per cent went to a CAB, 16 per cent to a solicitor, and the rest went to a wide variety of sources including trade unions, tribunal units, law centres, welfare rights centres, social workers, general advice centres, unemployment centres, pressure groups and church groups.

[37] Genn and Genn (1989), pp. 13–15. There were considerable variations according to region and type of case: *ibid.* pp. 15–18.

[38] *ibid.* pp. 29–32; the main sources were UKIAS and solicitors.

[39] *ibid.* pp. 38–43; the main sources were solicitors and trade unions (appellants), outside or in-house lawyers (respondents).

[40] *ibid.* pp. 56–57; dominated by solicitors.

[41] *ibid.* pp. 59–62, 221–222.

[42] This is dependent upon the procedures of the Department concerned. In social security matters an application to a tribunal ensures an initial review of the decision by an officer, and there is some evidence to suggest that the intervention of an advice agency can get "mistakes" straightened out without recourse to a tribunal: Chapeltown Tribunal Assistance Unit, *Progress Report—First Two Years* (see above, n. 26), at pp. 11, 12; Genn and Genn (1989), pp. 136–137; J. Baldwin, N. Wikeley and R. Young, *Judging Social Security* (1992), Chap. 3.

[43] See *e.g.* the Social Security and Child Support (Decisions and Appeals) Regulations 1999 (S.I. 1999 No. 991), Part II, Chapter I (revisions) and Chapter II (supersessions); M. Harris, "The place of formal and informal review in the administrative justice system" in M. Harris and M. Partington (eds), *Administrative Justice in the 21st Century* (1999), Chap. 2, criticising a move from formal review to informal revision arrangements.

[44] In the Employment Tribunal procedure, emphasis is placed upon conciliation and the mediating role of the Advisory Conciliation and Arbitration Service, although this usually occurs after the application has been made.

In relation to the making of an application there are three procedural aspects to be considered. What form should the application take? What information should it contain? Within what time limit, if any, should it be made? These are questions which have been considered and answered in the civil courts, and they are obviously questions which are common to all tribunals. It would be tempting to assume that a Code of Procedure could be devised to encompass all tribunals and make specific provision for these and other points. The Franks Committee[45] moved towards this position with a recommendation that a Council on Tribunals should formulate the procedural rules for each tribunal, based on principles common to all tribunals but tailored to suit the needs of the particular tribunal.[46] In the event, the Tribunals and Inquiries Act 1958 merely provided that the Council on Tribunals (established by the Act) should be consulted when procedural rules were made in respect of certain specified tribunals.[47]

What form should an application to a tribunal take? Many tribunals[48] encourage or require the completion of a printed form, a method of application which can either assist or hinder the applicant. He or she may be deterred from pursuing the case by the complexity or unintelligibility of the questions, but will at least be shown the information required and sometimes directed towards a source of help and advice.[49] Again, the nature of the dispute may have an effect on procedure in that in citizen/state disputes the jurisdiction is likely to be automatic and the applicant will not have to show the grounds which bring the matters within the tribunal's jurisdiction. In citizen/citizen disputes the applicant's first job will be to establish that the case falls within the tribunal's jurisdiction and a printed form with appropriate questions will be helpful both to tribunal and applicant.

The different procedural approaches of Appeals Service tribunals and Employment Tribunals are illustrated later in the chapter.[50] In many cases the applicant has the opportunity of including matters for the consideration of the tribunal in the application, or in a subsequent statement. Ultimately, he or she may make representations at the hearing (if one is held)[51] and it is likely to be the style and conduct of the hearing which determines how much advance information is required by the tribunal.

All tribunals find it necessary to impose time limits within which an

---

[45] Report of the Committee on Administrative Tribunals and Enquiries (Cmnd. 218, 1957).

[46] *ibid.*, paras.63–64.

[47] Now Tribunals and Inquiries Act 1992, s.8. Procedural rules are normally contained in a statutory instrument made by the Minister whose Department is responsible for the particular tribunal. The Council has published Model Rules of Procedure (Cm. 1434, 1991) for the guidance of those who draft such rules.

[48] For example, the use of Forms IT1 and IT3 for Employment Tribunals (below para. 13-011) is not mandatory; it is now proposed that an application form should become mandatory, with proper guidance on completing the form provided to applicants and respondents and ensuring that the needs of disadvantaged applicants are met: *Routes to Resolution: Improving Dispute Resolution in Britain: Government Response* (November 2001, DTI website), paras, 73, 74.

[49] *e.g.* the form of originating application to an Employment Tribunal states that a Trade Union or C.A.B, may be able to give advice, information, and help in filling the form. D.W.P. leaflets include similar advice.

[50] See below.

[51] Not all tribunals will hold an oral hearing. The Social Security Commissioner may determine an appeal without a hearing as may a Rent Assessment Committee.

application must be submitted, and some impose limits on later stages of the procedure.[52] The balance has to be struck between allowing a tribunal to make a speedy determination in a dispute (based on evidence which is not too far distant in time) and ensuring that an applicant is not unduly prejudiced by the limit. The Council on Tribunals has taken a particular interest in this matter and has welcomed the extension of time limits in some tribunals.[53] In addition it is desirable that there should be a procedural rule allowing for applications to be made out of time where there is good cause.[54]

D. "KNOWING THE CASE"—THE PRE-HEARING EXCHANGE OF INFORMATION

" ... citizens should know in good time the case which they will have to **13–008** meet, whether the issue to be heard by the tribunal is one between citizen and administration or citizen and citizen. ... We do not suggest that the procedure should be formalised to the extent of requiring documents in the nature of legal pleadings. What is needed is that the citizen should receive in good time beforehand a document setting out the main points of the opposing case. It should not be necessary ... to require the parties to adhere rigidly at the hearing to the case as previously set out, provided always that the interests of another party are not prejudiced by such flexibility.[55]

The amount of pre-hearing activity and the precision with which the parties are required to formulate and disclose their respective cases can vary very considerably from tribunal to tribunal. Before 1984, the applicant was given the greatest latitude in Social Security Appeal Tribunals. He or she was not required to produce any specific grounds of appeal or indicate what his or her argument might be. This was then changed, and an appeal to an

---

[52] An application to an Appeals Service tribunal must be made within one month of the date of notification of the decision against which the appeal is brought or, where a written statement of reasons is requested, within 14 days of the expiry of that period: S.I. 1999 No. 991, reg. 31; an application to an Employment Tribunal in respect of unfair dismissal within three months of dismissal; Employment Rights Act 1996, s. 111(2). There are no time limits on the hearings and the Council on Tribunals has regularly expressed disquiet at the long backlog of cases awaiting hearing by various tribunals.

[53] Annual Report of the Council on Tribunals, 1980–81, at p. 23.

[54] *e.g.* for Appeals Service tribunals, time can be extended for up to a year where it was not practicable because of special circumstances (such as serious illness) for an application to be made within the time limit: S.I. 1999 No. 991, reg. 32; for Employment Tribunals, the claim can be presented "within such further period as the tribunal considers reasonable in a case where it is satisfied that it was not reasonably practicable for the complaint to be presented before the end of that period of three months": Employment Rights Act 1996, s. 111(2). See, *e.g. Palmer v. Southend-on-Sea Borough Council* [1984] I.C.R. 372 (question what is reasonably practicable essentially one of fact for the tribunal); *Machine Tool Industry Research Association v. Simpson* [1988] I.C.R. 558 (not reasonably practicable to bring complaint until employee has knowledge of fundamental fact that made the dismissal unfair).

[55] Report of the Committee on Administrative Tribunals and Enquiries (Cmnd. 218, 1957), at pp. 17–18.

Appeals Service tribunal now must "contain particulars of the grounds on which it is made".[56] It is not clear how much detail is necessary.[57] The applicant will receive from the adjudication officer a full statement of facts, submissions, statutory authorities and Commissioner's decisions.[58] This document will also be sent to members of the tribunal and is likely to form the basis of the hearing. There is a power for the tribunal chairman to require the applicant to furnish such further particulars as may reasonably be required.[59]

The parties before a Rent Assessment Committee are more likely to have had a full opportunity of finding out about the case.[60] Where the issue concerns the determination of a fair rent for a protected tenancy, before the matter can come before a Rent Assessment Committee, application must be made to a rent officer. This application can be made by either landlord or tenant or both jointly, but if the application is not joint, the other party is invited to take part in consultations with the rent officer and the applicant to consider what rent should be registered.[61] Only if one party is dissatisfied with the rent which is registered can he or she appeal to the Rent Assessment Committee, who then invite both parties to make written or oral representations. By the time of the hearing, both parties will have had the opportunity to familiarise themselves with all the circumstances and the representations made by each of them. Subject to a few exceptions, no new protected tenancies can be granted after the commencement of the Housing Act 1988. The Rent Assessment Committee does, however, have jurisdiction under Part I of the Act to fix the rent of an assured tenancy or assured shorthold tenancy where the landlord proposes a rent increase.[62] Here, the tenant applies directly to the committee, and the committee then serves a notice on both parties specifying a period of not less than seven days during which either written representations or a request to make oral representations may be made by that party to the committee. The committee may make such inquiry (if any) as it thinks fit.[63] The tenant must complete an application form providing factual details about the premises,[64] but there is no requirement for the tenant to indicate why he or she objects to the proposed rent increase. Accordingly, the parties here may be less well-

---

[56] Social Security and Child Support (Decisions and Appeals) Regulations 1999 (S.I. 1999 No. 991), reg. 33. It must also include sufficient particulars to enable the decision appealed against to be identified: *ibid.*

[57] Where the Secretary of State is satisfied that the form, although not completed in accordance with the instructions, includes sufficient information to enable the appeal or application to proceed, he may treat the form as satisfying these requirements: reg. 33(4); similarly if a letter is sent rather than the approved form: reg. 33(5). If it does not the Secretary of State may request further information in writing; if this is not forthcoming, the form or letter is placed before a legally qualified panel member: reg. 33(8).

[58] See below, where an example is reproduced.

[59] 1999 Regulations, reg. 38(2).

[60] See generally R. E. Megarry, *The Rent Acts* (1988), Vol. 1, Chaps. 24 and 25, Vol. 3, Chaps. 16 and 17; J. E. Martin, *Residential Security* (2nd ed., 1995), Chaps.10 and 14.

[61] Rent Act 1977, Sched. 11, para. 3, as amended.

[62] Housing Act 1988, S.13(4)(a), 14. There are certain other matters also within its jurisdiction under Part I.

[63] Rent Assessment Committee (England and Wales) Regulations 1971 (S.I. 1971 No. 1065), reg. 2A, inserted by S.I. 1988 No. 2200, and amended by S.I. 1997 No. 3007.

[64] Prescribed by the Assured Tenancies and Agricultural Occupancies (Forms) Regulations 1997 (S.I. 1997 No. 194).

informed by the time of the hearing than in cases where the committee's function is that of reviewing the decision of a rent officer.

A third approach is adopted in the Employment Tribunal.[65] The forms by which an applicant makes the application and the respondent indicates an intention to defend the case, require a certain minimum amount of information. In particular, the applicant is required to state "the grounds, with particulars thereof, on which relief is sought."[66] This ensures at the outset that both sides will have some idea of the case to be met. Thereafter there are opportunities for both formal and informal exchange of information.

The tribunal has wide powers of case management. It may at any time, on the application of a party or of its own motion, give such directions on any matter arising in connection with the proceedings as appear to be appropriate. These may include any requirement relating to evidence (including the provision and exchange of witness statements), and the provision of further particulars or written answers to questions. There are also powers to require the attendance of witnesses and the production of documents, and to require one party to grant the other such disclosure or inspection as might be granted under CPR r.31. In cases of non compliance, a case may be struck out or a respondent debarred from defending, in whole or in part, or a costs order can be made.[67] These formal procedures reinforce informal requests for information which either party may make of the other. In addition, the tribunal has the power to order discovery of documents.[68] In race and sex discrimination cases there is a "question-and-answer procedure," analogous to interrogatories in civil procedure.[69] Standard questionnaires are available for the purposes of this procedure.[70]

A new procedure was introduced in 1980 which had the effect of disclosing information to the parties. The "pre-hearing assessment" was an attempt to reduce the number of cases going to a hearing by bringing the parties together, without witnesses, to undergo a review of the application. This operated to expose the case to both sides and although there was no power to strike out an unworthy case there was a possible penalty on costs at the hearing if the tribunal indicated, at the pre-hearing assessment, that there was no reasonable prospect of a successful application or defence.[71] These procedures owe more to the High Court and county court than to other tribunals, but overall did not prove to be a success.[72] They were

---

[65] For procedure in Employment Tribunals generally see, I. T. Smith and G. Thomas, *Smith and Wood's Industrial Law* (7th ed., 2000), Chap. 8, pp. 401–435; M. J. Goodman, *Industrial Tribunals' Practice and Procedure* (4th ed., 1987); *Employment Tribunal practice and procedure* (I.D.S. Employment Law Handbook, (3rd ed., 2002) (1994)).

[66] Rules of Procedure, r.l; The Rules of Procedure appear as Sched. 1 to the Employment Tribunals (Constitution and Rules of Procedure) Regulations 2001 (S.I. 2001 No. 1171). Strictly speaking, there is no requirement that the printed forms be used so long as the required information is given in another form, *e.g.* a letter. However, it is crucial that the grounds and particulars are given, so the form is usually regarded as helpful.

[67] Rules of Procedure, r.4(l)(a).

[68] *ibid.* r.4.

[69] Sex Discrimination Act 1975, s.74; Race Relations Act 1976, s.65.

[70] Sex Discrimination (Questions and Replies) Order 1975 (S.I. 1975 No. 2048); Race Relations (Questions and Replies) Order 1977 (S.I. 1977 No. 842).

[71] *ibid.*, r.6.

[72] See Smith and Wood, (2000), p. 426. There was a decline in their use; they could make conciliation more difficult.

replaced by "pre-hearing reviews" which include a power for the tribunal conducting the review to require a party to pay a deposit of £150 (now an amount not exceeding £500) if he or she wishes to continue the proceedings, in respect of contentions that have no reasonable prospect of success.[73] This last step was opposed by the Council on Tribunals, without success.[74] It was proposed that tribunals should be empowered to dismiss a hopeless case at a pre-hearing review, and where no notice of appearance is lodged, to dismiss a case without a hearing.[75] This was not implented, but the former has again been proposed.[76]

Informally, there may be an exchange of information because of the involvement of conciliation officers. All applications and subsequent documents are sent to ACAS[77] and a conciliation officer is under an obligation to attempt a conciliation either at the request of one of the parties, or of his or her own volition.[78] This conciliation may be rejected by the parties but it is likely to lead to some informal exchange of information unless the conciliation officer never even gets his foot in the door. Could this process usefully be adapted to assist settlements in the High Court?

These examples of pre-hearing procedure, necessarily selective, are intended to illustrate three different approaches to the objective set out by the Franks Committee. Full obligatory disclosure by one side; opportunity to disclose by both sides, but no obligation and no penalty for non-disclosure; limited obligatory disclosure by both sides, with opportunities for further disclosure supported by sanctions.

E. PRE-HEARING PROCEDURE IN TWO TRIBUNALS

13–009 We have already contrasted some of the procedural aspects of social security tribunals and industrial tribunals in making general points about procedure. Below we set out two cases which illustrate the progress of a case towards a hearing in an Appeals Service tribunal and an Employment Tribunal. It was noted at the outset that it is difficult to produce "typical" tribunals for consideration, and it is no easier to produce "typical" cases from a single tribunal. One of the alleged virtues of the tribunal system is its flexibility in dealing with differing circumstances. These examples at least demonstrate the documentation involved and indicate the normal procedure.

---

[73] Employment Act 1989, s.20, giving the Secretary of State power to make regulations for pre-hearing reviews; see now Rules of Procedure, r.7.

[74] Annual Report of the Council on Tribunals for 1987–88 (1988–89 H.C. 102), pp. 36–38; Annual Report for 1988–89 (1988–90 H.C. 114), pp. 33–34.

[75] Green Paper, *Resolving Employment Rights Disputes: Options for Reform* (Cm. 2707, 1994), pp. 37–38.

[76] *Routes to Resolution: Improving Dispute Resolution in Britain: Government Response* (November 2001, DTI website), paras 65, 66. See the Employment Bill 2002.

[77] The Advisory Conciliation and Arbitration Service.

[78] Employment Tribunals Act 1996, ss.18, 19. See Smith and Wood, (2000), pp. 434–435. L. Dickens *et.al.*, *Dismissed* (1985), Chap. 6. In 1999–2000, 71 per cent of applications notified to conciliation officers were settled or withdrawn without a hearing: ACAS Annual Report 2000–01.

1. An Appeals Service Tribunal

Facts: Mr Edward Jones made a claim for Income Support on behalf of his **13–010** aunt, Mrs Margaret Jones. Mrs Jones was incapable of managing her financial affairs and was living in a care home. A decision maker decided that she was entitled to IS from June 12, 2001. Mr Jones appealed, claiming that payment should be from the date of claim (January 25, 2001). The Schedule of Evidence (Form AT47), prepared for the hearing, included the Appeal submission, Appeal letter (entered on the form in leaflet GL24 *If you think our decision is wrong*). Form AT2, which set out the full facts and the decision maker's decision, and relevant correspondence. A set of the documents was sent to Mr Jones. This asked him to indicate whether he wished to withdraw the appeal (no); whether he wanted an oral or paper hearing (oral); who would attend (himself and a representative from Gumby Council); dates within the next three months when they would not be available to attend a hearing; and whether an interpreter or signer would be needed (no); and to provide any further evidence (none). He was warned that if he did not return the form within 14 days the Appeals Service "will assume that you do not want to continue with your appeal and it may be brought to an end without a hearing."

At the hearing, the Tribunal rejected Mr Jones' appeal. We reproduce Form AT2 and (for convenience here rather than in Chapter 16 on the Tribunal Hearing) the Record of Proceedings and the Decision Notice.

APPEAL TRIBUNAL

For hearing on

Appeal Register Number

Sheet   Line

IN CONFIDENCE

Appeal or reference to Appeal Tribunal

Benefit: Income Support   **Tribunal:**   Gumby

FULL NAMES OF PERSONS CONCERNED   National Insurance Number

	(Surname)	(Other Names)	AA010203A
Name of claimant			
Mrs	Jones	Margaret	

Address: "The Elms"
4 Wortley Street
Gumby
GY49 3AB

Section 1

Date of decision   13/7/01

Date of decision notified   13/7/01

Date of appeal   31/7/01

Section 2 — The Decision

Mrs Jones is entitled to Income Support from 12/6/01, this being the date her capital fell below the prescribed limit of £16,000.

Section 3 — The Appeal

The letter of appeal is attached to this submission as document 1.

Form AT2

4 Summary of Facts

1 Mrs Jones is a 87 year old woman, on 25/1/01 a SP1 Income Support claim form was received in the Benefits Agency. On page 1 of the form it states Mrs Jones is in the Elms Care Centre.

2 On page 9 of the form details of her savings are listed. These total £16338.73.

3 On page 28 of the form Mrs Jones states she moved to her current address on 26/1/01 and adds she has capital of between £10,000 and £16,000, therefore a weekly tariff income will apply.

4 On page 29 the weekly charge for her accommodation is stated as £328.09

5 On page 37 it is requested that Mr Edward Jones, Mrs Jones' nephew, be contacted as he is applying for receivership from the Court of Protection for Mrs Jones. The form is signed and dated by Mr Jones on 25/1/01.

6 On 9/2/01 Mr Jones replied to a request for confirmation of Mrs Jones' savings. He stated that all the details were with the Court of Protection in London, and requested the claim to be held until they are available.

7 On 22/5/01 Mr Jones submitted a copy of a letter from Smiths Solicitors to confirm that they hold the sum of £4585.52 from Mrs Jones' National Savings Account. They confirm that the sum of £10627.28 has been sent directly to the Accountant General of the Supreme Court, a statement of account was also submitted. This shows total receipts of £5997.65 and payments of £1083.50 leaving £4914.15 to be credited to the receivership account.

8 On 30/5/01 Mr Jones submitted a statement from the Court of Protection showing a balance of £11442.75 in Mrs Jones' special account.

9 On 15/6/01 Mr Jones submitted a copy of the Lloyds TSB Treasurers account, this shows the deposit of £4914.15 on 17/5/01, and on 12/6/01 a payment of £3151.49 for her nursing home fees.

10 On 13/7/01 the Decision Maker considered the claim, he decided that Mrs Jones was entitled to Income Support from 12/6/01, this being the date her capital fell below the £16000 limit. In reaching his decision the Decision Maker also had regard to the fact that Mrs Jones' claim only became valid on 30/5/01, the date all the information needed to process her claim was received in the Benefits Agency. In the letter issued to Mr Jones he was informed that the claim to Income Support could not be backdated to 25/1/01, however the wording on the letter was incorrect as the claim had been paid from 12/6/01, the date her capital fell below the limit and backdating of the claim was not an issue.

On 31/7/01 Mr Jones appealed against the decision not to allow Mrs Jones' claim to Income Support from 25/1/01, the date the claim was made. He states that there should be no reference to "backdating" as a claim had been made at the correct time, and the delay in providing the information was due to the Court of Protection.

12   Mr Jones was contacted by telephone regarding the appeal, it was
     explained that the wording on the letter was incorrect and the correct
     decision was explained. Mr Jones was advised that the appeal would
     continue but that the decision under appeal relates to Mrs Jones' capital.

13   On 11/9/01 a different Decision Maker reconsidered the claim, he was
     however satisfied that Mrs Jones' capital did exceed the limit until 12/6/
     01 and was therefore unable to revise the decision.

5 The Decision Makers Submission

The disputed decision was made in accordance with the following Acts and
Regulations

1   The law says that "No person shall be entitled to Income Support if his
     capital, or a prescribed part of it, exceeds the prescribed amount."

Section 134(1) of the Social Security Contributions and Benefits Act 1992

2   For the purposes of section 134(1) (no entitlement to Income Support if
     capital exceeds a prescribed amount), the prescribed amount is £8,000 in
     all cases except where Regulation 53(1B) applies (persons living
     permanently in either a Nursing Home, a Residential Care Home, or
     in Residential Accommodation) when the prescribed limit is £16,000.

Regulation 45 of the Income Support (General) Regulations 1987

3   (1) Subject to paragraph (2), the capital of a claimant to be taken into
         account shall be the whole of his capital calculated in accordance
         with this Part ... .
     (2) There shall be disregarded from the calculation of a claimant's
         capital under paragraph (1) any capital, where applicable, specified
         in Schedule 10.

Regulation 46 of the Income Support (General) Regulations 1987

4   I submit that the questions for determination by the tribunal are as follows:
     (A) Is Mrs Jones a permanent resident in a home?
         Mrs Jones states on claim form her stay is not temporary, she is
         therefore permanently in the home.
     (B) What is the capital limit applicable to her claim?
         The capital limit that applies to Mrs Jones claim is £16,000.
     (C) What capital did Mrs Jones have at the date of her claim?
         Mrs Jones had £11442.75 in her Court of Protection account and
         £4914.15 balance from her 2 accounts held by the solicitors, her
         total capital is therefore £16356.90.
     (D) From what date does her capital fall below the £16,000 limit?
         The payment of £3151.49 on 12/6/01 reduces her capital to below
         £16,000.

5   I submit therefore that Mrs Jones is entitled to Income Support from
     12/6/01, this being the date her capital falls below the £16,000 limit.

Appeals Service
For Social Security, Child Support and Vaccine Damage

RECORD OF PROCEEDINGS
Held on 15/11/2001

INCOME SUPPORT Appeal Tribunal	**Hearing date notified** on 26/10/2001

	(Other name)	(Surname)	Tribunal Reg:
Appellant:	Mr E	Jones	NI: AA010203A

Respondent:

Oral Hearing Requested   *Yes/~~No~~

Venue: Gumby

CONSTITUTION OF TRIBUNAL

Chairman: Mrs P. Mitchell

Member: ————————

Member: ————————

REPRESENTATIVES FOR THE:

Adjudication Authority:

Appellant: Mr F Butcher, Gumby Council

Respondent:

Others (State capacity) Mr S Johnson (AS)
                                     Miss J Brown (Social Worker)

Appellant: *Not present	Originating Office: Gumby BA
Respondent: ~~*Not present~~	

DOCUMENTS HANDED IN PRE/*AT THE HEARING AND RETAINED AFTER THE HEARING NUMBERED 1-

NB: Please remember to record in text documents considered but returned without a copy being retained at the end of the hearing.

Chairman's introduction / independence

Mr Butcher: Argued – capital not accessible to Mrs Jones because not capable. Capital not available to Mr Jones because not appointed by Court of Protection, therefore she had not capital. CIS 494/1990.

Had capital been available excess over capital limit would have been gone within one week due to fees.

Mrs Jones: August 2000 – 24/1/01. Paid previous home up to 6.12.00 then couldn't pay from 7.12.00. Losing memory couldn't remember things. Smiths consulted October 2000. Application before application for I.S. made on 25.1.01. Not aware that direction requested for the release of funds prior to the appointment of a receiver. Received money 17.5.01 from solicitor. £494.15. P. 25.

MAT only: Appellant *was/*was not medically examined.   *delete as appropriate

Chairman's signature: .... Date ....

For clerks use only. Record of proceedings issued to parties on ....
TAS/RP

Appeals Service
For Social Security, Child Support and Vaccine Damage

Appeal Tribunal   **Held at:** Gumby   **Held On:** 15/11/2001

Appellant: *Mr E Jones*   **Tribunal Reg. No:**

                                               NI No: AA010203A

Respondent: Secretary of State

Decision of the Tribunal

Appeal is Disallowed

The decision of the Secretary of State issued on 13/07/2001 is CONFIRMED

Mrs Jones is entitled to Income support from 12 June 2001 this being the date her capital fell below the prescribed limit of £16,000.

At the time of the application for Income Support Mrs Jones was incapable of managing her own affairs and an application was made to appoint Mr Jones her receiver. Mrs Jones was not capable of withdrawing her funds and Mr Jones had no authority to do so, nevertheless, these funds were still Mrs Jones' capital and have to be counted as her capital.

Although Mrs Jones had debts outstanding at the time the application for Income Support was made on the 25 January 2001, as these were not secured against capital that cannot be taken into account. Reg 49 Income Support (General Regulations) 1987.

Payment of benefit under a Tribunal award can be suspended if the Secretary of State decides to appeal to a Social Security Commissioner.

Signed Chairman:	Date: 15/11/2001

Decision Notice issued to -   Appellant on 15/11/2001

Statement requested: Yes/No   Respondent on: 15/11/2001

                                               Second Respondent on:

AS/DN/SS

Appeals Service
For Social Security, Child Support and Vaccine Damage

STATEMENT OF REASONS
FOR DECISION
This statement is to be read together with the decision notice issued by the tribunal.

Unified Appeal Tribunal. Held on 15th November 2001

	(Surname)	(Other name)	Tribunal Reg:
Appellant:	Jones	E appointee for Margaret Jones	NI: AA010203A

Respondent:

1. Mr Jones made a claim for Income Support on the 25th January 2001 on behalf of his Aunt Margaret Jones. The application is made by Mr Jones as his aunt is incapable of managing her own financial affairs and he is applying to the Court of Protection to be appointed her Receiver. Such application being dealt with by Smiths Solicitors.

2. He gave capital details of savings, which at the end of the application totalled £16338.73.

3. Mrs Jones was resident at The Elms Care Centre and at the date of the application for Income Support she had debts for accommodation charges at a previous home of £889. Her weekly accommodation charge amounted to £328.09 for The Elms and the funding not met from her retirement pension and other income was left outstanding pending the completion of the application for receivership.

4. A Receiver's Bank Account was opened by Mr Jones on the 5th May 2001 with a deposit of £1484.37 being retirement pension.

5. The Receivership application was completed and funds from Smiths Solicitors as detailed in a letter dated 10th May 2001 was credited to the Receiver's Bank Account on the 17th May 2001. Smiths Solicitors paid into Court in accordance with the order of the Court of Protection the sum of £11442.75 on the 12th May 2001.

6. Mr Jones settled the outstanding accommodation charges of £889 on the 17th May 2001 and £3151.49 on the 12th June 2001.

7. A decision maker decided on the 13th July 2001 that Mrs Jones was entitled to Income Support from 12th June 2001, this being the date her capital fell below the £16000 capital limit.

8. Mr Jones appealed against this decision on the 31st July 2001 indicating that he disagreed because there was no back payment and that payment should be from the date of claim being 25th January 2001. The delay in processing the claim has been because of legal imperatives. This should not compromise her eligibility for full payment of Income Support from the day the claim was first submitted.

9. The decision maker reconsidered the decision on the 11th September 2001 but did not change the decision.

10. It is the decision of the 13th July 2001 that is the subject of today's appeal.

11. None of the debts outstanding at the date of the claim were secured and cannot therefore be disregarded.

Appellant's Full Name: **Jones E appointee for Margaret Jones**	Tribunal Reg:
	Date of Hearing: 15th November 2001

12   The Capital balance of £16338.73 was available to Mrs Jones at the time of the application on the 25th January 2001.

13   Her capital balance fell below £16000 on the 12th June 2001 when the accommodation charge arrears were paid.

REASONS

The question before the tribunal was when Mrs Jones' capital fell below the threshold at which Income Support would be payable. The amount of the capital and of the debts outstanding were not in dispute. The question was whether the capital was available to Mrs Jones or could be disregarded.

The tribunal considered the provisions of Schedule 10 of the Income Support (General) Regulations 1987 which contains the list of capital that can be disregarded. None of Mrs Jones' capital comes within this schedule.

The tribunal considered whether any of the debts could be deducted from the capital before calculating the amount of the capital value. The only exception is secured debts under Regulation 49 or 50 and accommodation charges do not come within this exemption.

Mr Butcher on behalf of Mr Jones argued that the monies in the accounts should be treated like uncleared cheques in that Mr Jones did not have access to the monies until the Court of Protection application was completed. The situation on an uncleared cheque was considered in CSB 589/1987 where it was decided that the monies did not become part of the claimant's capital until it was cleared funds in her account. The position in Mrs Jones' case can be distinguished in that when a cheque is presented to a bank the drawing bank can refuse to fulfil the obligation to meet the cheque if there are insufficient funds in the payers account. Mrs Jones' funds are available to her if she had the mental capacity to claim them. There is no risk that such funds will not be paid to her which would be the situation should a cheque not be met.

The tribunal also considered whether the funds could be treated as funds in an account where access is denied for a period of time. I.e. an account where there would be penalties for early withdrawal. If this were the case the value of the capital may be less. (CIS 494/1990). The tribunal do not accept this is the case because although Mr Jones could not obtain direct access to the monies in the accounts until the application to the Court of Protection was settled, the solicitors instructed by him could have made an application for an interim direction when making the application for receivership. The effect of such an application is to release monies to solicitors to permit the solicitors to pay legitimate bills of the Court of Protection patient, in this case Mrs Jones. The tribunal does not accept the fact that such an application was not made helps Mrs Jones. The funds were not frozen and would not have been reduced in value by taking an early withdrawal therefore the value should be counted in full until such time as they actually reduce below the £16000 threshold.

For the above reasons the appeal did not succeed.

The above is a statement of the reasons for the Tribunal's decision under Regulation 53(4), The Social Security and Child Support (Decisions and Appeals) Regulations 1999.

Signed Chairman: Date: 15th November 2001

For clerk's use only
Decision notice issued to

Statement requested: *Yes/No

Appellant on ....
Respondent on ....…......
Second Respondent on ....…....

TAS/STATEMENT

An Employment Tribunal[79]

Facts: Mr Seamer had been employed by Convoy Carriers as a lorry driver **13–011** for 10 years. One day in May 2001 he was called into the office of the Managing Director where there were four bottles of gin on the table. The Managing Director said that they had been found in Mr Seamer's car and accused him of stealing them. In the presence of Mr Seamer he telephoned the police and reported the alleged theft. An argument ensued in which Mr Seamer protested his innocence. Both men lost their temper and abused each other. Eventually, the Managing Director told Mr Seamer that he was sacked, with immediate effect, and that he could collect a week's wages from the Accounts Department.

Mr Seamer subsequently went to the Jobcentre where he obtained an application form to send to the Employment Tribunal. He filled in the form and sent it off, having been told by a friend that his Union might help him.

Mr Seamer submitted the form to his local Employment Tribunal office. To help him he was given an explanatory leaflet and a small booklet, How to apply to an Employment Tribunal England & Wales[80]

On receipt of an application (Form IT1) the office attempts to ensure that it discloses a cause of action within the jurisdiction of the tribunal? Given that the information on the form can be very sparse this is not always an easy job. If it appears that there is no jurisdiction, the application is returned to the applicant,[81] otherwise it is sent to the respondent with Form IT2, "Notice of Originating Application", which requires the respondent to enter an appearance within 14 days. In this case the company wishes to dispute the application. It gives "notice of appearance," by completing and returning Form IT3. Forms IT1 and IT3 are reproduced below.

---

[79] The jurisdiction of the tribunal is set out above, para. 2-031. The rules of procedure governing the tribunal are to be found in the Employment Tribunals (Constitution and Rules of Procedure) Regulations 2001 (S.I. 2001 No. 1171).

[80] Revised September 2001. Prepared the Employment Tribunals Service, and available free. A copy can be downloaded from *www.employmenttribunals.gov.uk* or obtained from the Employment Tribunals Service.

[81] With a letter pointing out why it appears that the application is outside the jurisdiction. This does not prevent the applicant making a further application and, if it is accepted, the original defective application is not disclosed to the respondent.

Application to an Employment Tribunal

For office use

Received at ET

Case number

Code

Initials

♦ If you fax this form you do not need to send one in the post.
♦ This form has to be photocopied. Please use CAPITALS and black ink (if possible).
♦ Where there are tick boxes, please tick to one that applies.

1 Please give the type of complaint you want the tribunal to decide (for example, unfair dismissal, equal pay). A full list is available from the tribunal office. If you have more than one complaint list them all.

Unfair dismissal

2 Please give your details

Mr [/] Mrs [ ] Miss [ ] Ms [ ] Other _____

First names Barry

Surname Seamer

Date of birth 23.9.60

Address
23 Wood Lane
Darbyville
Notts

Postcode

Phone number

Daytime phone number

Please give an address to which we should send documents if different from above

Postcode

3 If a representative is acting for you please give details
(all correspondence will be sent to your representative)

Name

Address
Not yet but I'm going
to the Union

Postcode

Phone   Fax

Reference

4 Please give the dates of your employment

From 1/3/1990 to 1/2/2001

5 Please give the name and address of the employer, other organisation or person against whom this complaint is being brought

Name Convoy Carriers plc

Address
23 London Road
Darbyville

Notts

Postcode

Phone number

Please give the place where you worked or applied to work if different from above

Address

Postcode

6 Please say what job you did for the employer (or what job you applied for). If this does not apply, please say what your connection was with the employer

Driver (HGV)

IT1(E/W)

7 Please give the number of normal basic hours worked each week

Hours per week

45

9 If your complaint is not about dismissal, please give the date when the matter you are complaining about took place

8 Please give your earning details

Basic wage or salary

£   £14,000   per year

Average take home pay

£   :   per

Other bonuses or benefits

£ 25 night   per week
allowance

10 Unfair dismissal applicants only

Please indicate what you are seeking at this stage, if you win your case

☐ Reinstatement: to carry on working in your old job as before (an order for reinstatement normally includes an award of compensation for loss of earnings).

☐ Re-engagement: to start another job or new contract with your old employer (an order for re-engagement normally includes an award of compensation for loss of earnings).

☐ Compensation only: to get an award of money.

Please give details of your complaint

If there is not enough space for your answer, please continue on a separate sheet and attach it to this form.

My boss (Mr Hacker) told me that some bottles of gin that were missing from the depot had been found on the back seat of my car. The car was at the depot. He told me not to come back to work and gave me a week's wages. He called me a thief. I told him that I hadn't pinched the gin and that I had been fitted up, but he did not believe me. I did not pinch the gin. I have been interviewed by the Police, but they have not told me whether they will prosecute me.

12 Please sign and date this form, then send it to the appropriate address on the back cover of this booklet (see postcode list on pages 13-16).

Signed

Date

1 June 2002

IT1/E/W/

EMPLOYMENT TRIBUNALS

In the application of

Case Number
(please quote in all correspondence)

* This form has to be photocopied, if possible please use Black Ink and Capital letters
* If there is not enough space for your answer, please continue on a separate sheet and attach it to this form

1. Full name and address of the Respondent:

CONVOY CARRIERS PLC

23 LONDON ROAD
DARBYVILLE
NOTTS

Post Code:

Telephone number:

DARBYVILLE 1249

2. If you require documents and notices to be sent to a representative or any other address in the United Kingdom please give details:

POPP, LEES AND STONE

83 MAIN STREET
GUMBY
NOTTS

Post Code:

Reference:

Telephone number:

3. Do you intend to resist the application? (Tick appropriate box)

YES   NO

[/]   [ ]

4. Was the applicant dismissed? (Tick appropriate box)

YES   NO

[/]   [ ]

Please give reason below

Reason for dismissal:

5. Are the dates of employment given by the applicant correct? (Tick appropriate box)

YES   NO

[/]   [ ]

please give correct dates below

Began on	
Ended on	

6. Are the details given by the applicant about wages/salary, take home or other bonuses correct? (Tick appropriate box)

YES   NO

[/]   [ ]

Please give correct details below

Basic Wages/Salary	£	per
Average Take Home Pay	£	per
Other Bonuses/Benefits	£	per

PLEASE TURN OVER

For office use only
Date of receipt   Initials

Form IT3 E&W - 8/98

7. Give particulars of the grounds on which you intend to resist the application.

(a)   The applicant was fairly and properly dismissed on February 1, 2001 for stealing goods belonging to a client of the company.

(b)   The goods in question were found by a security officer in the back of the applicant's car.

(c)   When questioned the applicant failed to give a satisfactory answer to the Managing Director, Mr P J R Hacker.

(d)   Honesty is of the utmost importance among our staff.

(e)   The matter is in the hands of the Police.

8. Please sign and date the form.

Signed   Dated

DATA PROTECTION ACT 1984
We may put some of the information you give on this form on to a computer. This helps us to monitor progress and produce statistics. We may also give information to:
* the other party in the case
* other parts of the DTI and organisations such as ACAS (Advisory Conciliation and Arbitration Service), the Equal Opportunities Commission or the Commission for Racial Equality.
Please post or fax this form to : The Regional Secretary

* IF YOU FAX THE FORM, DO NOT POST A COPY AS WELL
* IF YOU POST THE FORM, TAKE A COPY FOR YOUR RECORDS

Form IT3 E&W 8/98

At the same time as the originating application is sent to the respondent it is also sent to a conciliation officer.[82] *He receives a copy of the notice of appearance in due course. He is obliged to assist the parties in reaching a conciliation if he is requested to do so, or if he thinks there is a reasonable prospect of success.*[83] *In this case he sees both parties individually. Mr Seamer wants his job back. Convoy Carriers will not give it to him. Mr Seamer has sought the assistance of his Union and they ask the company for more information. The company refuses but is ordered to give further particulars after an application to the Tribunal by the applicant. A standard form direction would be*:

Regional Office of the Employment Tribunals
(address)
To: Convoy Carriers PLC,
    23 London Road,
    Darbyville,
    Notts.
Case No. 12345/01 Seamer v. Convoy Carriers PLC

1. An application has been received from the Applicant for further particulars of the grounds on which you rely. This application has been referred to the Chairman of Tribunals who by virtue of the powers conferred upon him under rule 4(1) of the Rules of Procedure has granted an order as follows.

2. The particulars requested in the letter dated September 4, 2001 (copy enclosed) should be furnished to Mr D. York, National Union of Lorry-men, York Row, Darbyville by October 30, 2001 and a copy sent to this office.

3. Your attention is drawn to the fact that rule 4(8) provides that if an order "8 under rule 4(1) is not complied with, a tribunal, before or at the hearing, may, strike out the whole or part of the originating application, or, as the case may be, of the notice of appearance and, where appropriate, direct that a respondent shall be debarred from defending altogether.

A. Bowler
Dated 1, October 2001 Assistant Secretary of the Employment Tribunals
Mr York (Mr Seamer's Union representative) had asked for further particulars of the company's normal security procedures; a list of other employees dismissed on the grounds of dishonesty in the preceding five years; and reasons why the company considered it reasonable to dismiss Mr Seamer immediately without awaiting the outcome of police investigations. The necessary information was supplied. No pre-hearing review was held[84] *and the case was listed for hearing on December 10, 2001. Mr Seamer lost.*

---

[82] An employee of ACAS.
[83] The evidence points to a considerable number of cases settled without a tribunal hearing. The conciliation officer is in a position to assist in negotiations leading to any result— compensation, reinstatment or the withdrawal of the application.
[84] See above, para. 13-008.

This example demonstrates a relatively straightforward case where the issue between the parties is clear and unlikely to be resolved in advance of the hearing. Much more documentation can be generated, but this is essentially under the control of the parties and is dependent upon the amount of information that is requested. This is in contrast with the Appeal Service Tribunal where the appellant receives the full documentation whether he or she wants it or not. Again, even in this simple case, the advisability of securing skilled assistance can be appreciated.

CHAPTER 14

PRE-TRIAL CRIMINAL PROCEDURE

14–001   In this chapter we consider the stages in the process before the trial for those suspected of having committed criminal offences.[1]

There are a number of preliminary points that should be noted. First, any examination of English pre-trial criminal process is hindered by the lack of definition and codification of this increasingly complex and important area of law. There remain no generally applicable definitions of key concepts in criminal procedure; indeed, the *procedures* adopted provide the best guidance as to whether any given action is civil or criminal in nature. These factors cause immediate difficulty in exposition and examination of the law. There is little doubt that a clarification of the process by codification would be a tremendous benefit. Calls for such a Code have been made by distinguished academics[2] and most recently in the Auld Report.[3] L.J. Auld observed that there is no true criminal justice " 'system' worthy of the name, only a criminal justice process to which a number of different Government departments and agencies and others make separate and sometimes conflicting contributions".[4]

The government's objectives include: ensuring that there is a just and effective outcome to criminal investigations; dealing with cases with appropriate speed; meeting the needs of victims, witnesses, jurors; respecting the rights of defendants and to treat them fairly; and promoting confidence in the criminal justice system.[5]

The second introductory point is to acknowledge a number of the reasons why the rules of pre-trial criminal process are so frequently challenged in the courts and repeatedly amended by statute, with the resulting complexity that such volatility produces. The most obvious reason is the potential conflict behind the different objectives that the rules are designed to achieve: an efficient process, which maximises fairness and reliability for the suspect and protects his other rights. The tension between securing optimal efficiency

---

[1]   For detailed consideration of the increasingly complex procedures, see J. Sprack, *Emmins on Criminal Procedure* (8th ed., 2000); *Archbold* (2002); *Blackstone's Criminal Practice* (2002).

[2]   See J. Spencer, "The Case for a Code of Criminal Procedure" [2000] Crim.L.R. 519. Spencer argues that this would be easier to achieve than a code for substantive criminal law. The principal reasons in support of codification are identified as coherence, accessibility, simplicity, removing contradictions and inconsistency, and a desire to view criminal procedure in the round. The proposals for codification include the Scottish model (see the Criminal Procedure (Scotland) Act 1975), or European models. The choice is between consolidation and reconstruction.

[3]   *Review of the Criminal Courts* (2001), Chap.1. *www.criminal-courts-review.org*

[4]   Chapter 8, para. 1, and see Ashworth, *The Criminal Process* (1998), pp.22–24.

[5]   See Auld (2001), Chap. 2, para. 7.

and respecting fundamental rights has become particularly acute in recent years as successive governments' initiatives to combat crime have relied on changes in the rules of procedure and evidence rather than the substantive law. At the same time, the implementation of the Human Rights Act 1998 has led to a predicted increase in the number of challenges to pre-trial procedure, with Article 6 rights (*e.g.* presumption of innocence, equality of arms in pre-trial disclosure, etc.) being those most commonly in issue.[6] A further explanation for the complexity of the pre-trial procedural rules is that they are, by and large, rules made by lawyers for lawyers, and as such, there is no pressure for them to be as accessible to the layman as should the substantive law. In this respect, the pressure for codification is less, but would still greatly improve and simplify matters. A final reason for the degree of complexity of the rules is that many of these regulations can be altered with greater ease than for example substantive criminal law, because many of the rules derive from secondary legislation only. The result is that they are repeatedly amended without consolidation, adding to their inaccessibility and complexity.

It should also be noted that the precise boundaries of the criminal process are under pressure, with, for example, the concept of a formal criminal sanction becoming increasingly unclear.[7] As noted, English law has no precise definition of the term "criminal process", nor indeed of the terms "crime" or "criminal". Although there may be particular parliamentary definitions in the context of specific legislation, the terms have all escaped general definition by the courts. The implementation of the Human Rights Act 1998 has placed the courts under a greater pressure to define the concept of a "criminal charge" for the purposes of Article 6 of the ECHR. Although the expression has an autonomous Convention meaning,[8] English courts have had to consider a number of borderline cases that might be perceived by many as criminal in nature.[9] Hopefully, a code would resolve this problem.

Obviously, this call for adequate definitions of key concepts in criminal procedure is not merely to facilitate exposition or to fulfil a desire for academic purity. It will affect the quality of justice. Research into many aspects of the process has repeatedly confirmed the very strong influences the conduct of the pre-trial process has on the quality of justice delivered in the trial process. Efficiency is an important concern, not only in securing

---

[6] See A. Ashworth, "Criminal Proceedings After the Human Rights Act 1998: The First Year" [2001] Crim.L.R. 855. The E.H.R.L.R. publishes tables of cases spectifying the Articles relied on in Human Rights Act 1998 cases. There can be no doubt as to the impact of Article 6 on domestic law despite Auld L.J.'s claim that "it adds little of substance to domestic law". Chap. 2, para. 12.

[7] See, *e.g.* the discussion of anti-social behaviour orders in *McCann v. Manchester Crown Court* [2001] 1 W.L.R. 1084 and that of football banning orders in *Gough v. Chief Constable of Derbyshire* [2001] 4 All E.R. 289. See also the many cases dealing with drug confiscation orders, especially *Phillips v. U.K.* [2001] Crim.L.R. 817. See further A. von Hirsch, "Overtaking on the Right" (1995) 145 N.L.J. 1501.

[8] *Engel v. Netherlands* (1979–80) 1 E.H.R.R. 647; *Benham v. U.K.* [1996] 22 E.H.R.R. 293. See generally Emmerson and Ashworth, *Human Rights and Criminal Justice* (2001), Chap. 4; K. Starmer *et al.*, *Criminal Justice, Police Powers and Human Rights* (2001), pp. 155–156.

[9] In addition to those in n. 7 above see those involving civil penalties for non-payment of income tax (*King v. Walden* [2001] STC 822) and VAT (*Han & Yau v. Customs & Excise* [2001] STC 1188; *Georgiou v. U.K.* [2001] STC 80). See generally on some of these D. Ormerod, "Caution with Tax Investigation" [2001] B.T.R. 194.

legitimate convictions, but also in ensuring that the innocent are not convicted. However, throughout this chapter the reader should bear in mind that pre-trial criminal procedure should not be regarded as simply a means to an end. The application of the procedures affect the manner of investigation, the rights afforded to the suspect, and, most significantly, have a considerable impact on the criminal trial itself. The rules of pre-trial criminal procedure should be designed to respect human rights and due process, with the safeguards being sufficient to ensure that the deprivation of liberty and other infringements of the suspect's autonomy do not "outweigh social goals sought through invoking the criminal law".[10] A trial (whether contested or not) is a necessary pre-condition for the imposition of a formal criminal sanction,[11] but the pre-trial process has a critical impact on that trial.

> "There are few who would now propound the view that the centrepiece of the English criminal process is the trial, and that the few earlier procedures are merely designed to ensure that no one is put on trial unless there is a good case against them and that dangerous people are kept in custody before trial."[12]

The change of view described in this quotation, has resulted from research into the operation of the criminal justice system, which has developed particularly strongly from the 1970s onwards.[13] In particular, attention has been paid to the various pressures that lead to pleas of guilty and the avoidance of contested trials before a jury. "It has become commonplace that early decisions in the criminal process seem strongly associated with and determinative of later decisions. ... "[14] For example, a confession made by a suspect to the police may well be crucial, given the difficulties that will thereafter arise in challenging it or explaining it away in court.[15] Similarly, a defendant who is remanded in custody will have to overcome a host of practical problems in the organisation of a defence that do not arise if bail is granted.[16] Moreover, the whole system would break down were it not that a very high proportion of those who are prosecuted for an offence plead guilty. In 2000, there were guilty pleas in 60 per cent of cases in the Crown

---

[10] Fixed penalty charges for certain motoring offences do not technically constitute "fines". The increasing use of fixed penalty notices, *e.g.* for minor public order offences (see the Criminal Justice and Police Act 2001 hereafter CJPA) is a controversial issue that deserves closer scrutiny than it has so far been afforded. See also the recommendations in the Auld Report (2001), Chap. 9, for greater use of fixed penalty notices. Auld L.J. called for prosecutorial discretion to be exercised in favour of the fixed penalty notice. Chap. 9, para. 21. The DPP (David Calvert-Smith Q.C.) called for the decriminalisation of a number of offences to be replaced with fixed penalties: *Sunday Times*, Apri 15, 2001.

[11] A. Sanders and R. Young, *Criminal Justice* (2nd ed., 2000), p.8.

[12] A. Ashworth, "Criminal Justice and the Criminal Process" (1988) 28 Brit. J. Criminol. 111 at 112.

[13] For general surveys see especially A. Ashworth, *ibid.* and *The Criminal Process* (2nd ed. 1998); A. Sanders and R. Young, *Criminal Justice* (2nd ed., 2000); S. Uglow, *Criminal Justice* (1995); N. Padfield, *Text and Materials on the Criminal Justice Process* (2nd ed., 2000); M. Wasik, T. Gibbons and M. Redmayne, *Criminal Justice: Text and Materials* (1999).

[14] Ashworth, *op. cit.* n. 12, p. 113.

[15] See below, para. 14-025.

[16] See below, para. 14-053.

Court.[17] Accordingly the outcome of the vast majority of cases is determined by the processes considered in the present chapter, and only a minority by the trial process considered in Chapter 17. In truth this reflects only a fraction of all crime that occurs, since research has revealed that only approximately half of all offences committed are reported.[18] The rate of attrition is considerable. In 2000 there were 5.2 million notifiable offences recorded by the police,[19] the detection rate for crimes was 24 per cent (the rate has been dropping since the 1960s when it was around 45 per cent), with 1.7 million offenders ultimately found guilty or cautioned.[20]

The incredible pressures on the criminal justice system take their toll. The recognition in the 1990s that miscarriages of justice had occurred in a series of high profile cases[21] has led to a wealth of discussion of the aspects of the system that had contributed to them. Many related to the pre-trial stages, including the fabrication of evidence by the police, mistaken identification, unreliable work by forensic scientists, unreliable confessions, and non-disclosure of evidence.[22] These matters were the subject of consideration by the Royal Commission on Criminal Justice (hereafter RCCJ)[23] which was appointed in 1991. However, by the time the Commission reported in 1993 the government's central concern appeared to have reverted from the prevention of miscarriages of justice to the control of crime; and the RCCJ's Report itself, influenced as it was by the terms of reference drafted by government,[24] did not have the prevention of miscarriages as its central organising theme.[25] Its recommendations have been heavily criticised,[26] and they certainly "favoured the interests of the police and prosecution agencies more than those of suspects".[27] Nevertheless, its proposals continue to be influential in government legislation such as the Criminal Procedure and Investigation Act 1996.

[17] *Criminal Statistics for England and Wales 2000* (2001), Chap. 6. In 2000, 1.7 million offenders were found guilty or cautioned. *ibid.* para. 1.9.

[18] See, *e.g.* C. Mirrless-Black, T. Budd, S. Partdridge. and P. Mayhew, *The 1998 British Crime Survey* (1998).

[19] *Criminal Statistics for England And Wales 2000* (2001), Table 1.1.

[20] *ibid.*, para. 1.9.

[21] See "Chronology of *Causes Celebres*" C. Walker, in C. Walker and K. Starmer (eds), *Justice in Error* (1993), pp. 6–13, including references to the Guildford Four, the Maguire Seven, the Birmingham Six, Judith Ward, the Tottenham Three (Silcott, Raghip and Braithwaite), Stefan Kiszko, the Darvell bothers, and the Cardiff Three (Paris, Abdullahi and Miller), and cases arising out of the activities of the West Midlands Police Serious Crimes Squad. See also J. Rozenburg, "Miscarriages of Justice" in E. Stockdale and S. Casale (eds), *Criminal Justice Under Stress* (1992) and C. Walker and K. Starmer (eds), *Miscarriages of Justice: A Review of Justice in Error* (1999). Miscarriages continue to come to light. See recently the murder conviction of Stephen Dowling overturned after 27 years. The Criminal Cases Review Commission increases the opportunity for such cases to come to light, including those from some time ago, as, *e.g.* in *R. v. Bentley* [1999] Crim.L.R. 330. See below, Chap.18, para. 18-018.

[22] Walker, (1993) pp. 13–15. Other issues concern the conduct of the trial, the presentation of the accused in a prejudicial manner and appeal procedures (*ibid.*). See also the JUSTICE *Report on Miscarriages of Justice* (1989).

[23] (1993) Cm. 2263.

[24] See below, para. 14-091.

[25] The Commission was heavily criticised for its very limited conclusions and for its methodology — see, *e.g.* L. Bridges, "Normalizing Injustice: The RCCJ" (1994) 21 J. Law and Soc. 20.

[26] See, *e.g.* Sanders and Young (2000), pp. 19–20.

[27] *ibid.* p.19.

Throughout the 1990s and into the new millennium, criminal justice reform continues to be driven by efficiency and crime control values,[28] and increasingly by the influence of managerialism[29] and by consumerism. Even taking account of the wide range of diverse influences now brought to bear on the process, Packer's classic exposition of the two competing models of criminal justice — crime control and due process — serve a useful mechanism for evaluating the process. These and other, more sophisticated models, have been developed in an attempt to explain more effectively the interrelationships of the policies and principles at stake[30] and will be considered later in the chapter (Part K).

As noted, criminal procedure is constantly evolving and is the subject of relentless scrutiny and review. Readers should be aware that the specific provisions referred to in this chapter may well soon be superseded. The government has unveiled its plan for overhaul of the criminal justice system generally[31] and pre-trial criminal process will be significantly affected by the recommendations of the Auld *Review of the Criminal Courts*. This important Report examined the

> "practices and procedures of, and the rules of evidence applied by the criminal courts at every level, with a view to ensuring that they deliver justice fairly, by streamlining all their processes, increasing their efficiency and strengthening the effectiveness of their relationships with others across the whole of the Criminal Justice System, and having regard to the interests of all parties including victims and witnesses, thereby promoting public confidence in the role of law".

The terms of reference are indicative of the breadth of the issues examined in this chapter.[32] We will consider its recommendations throughout.

The material in this chapter is divided into three broad parts. First, we consider the process of investigation of offences (section A); secondly, the process whereby a decision is taken whether a prosecution should be instituted (sections B and C); and thirdly, the pre-trial procedures in criminal cases (sections D to J). We conclude with an attempt to evaluate some of the basic features of the system (section K). As an indication of the overall structure and complexity of the criminal process, we provide the following diagram taken from the Home Office Criminal Justice website.

---

[28] *e.g.* The Narey review on expediting justice, *Review of the Delay in the CJS* (1997), (hereafter, Narey.)

[29] See especially N. Lacey, "Government as Manager, Citizen as Consumer" (1994) 57 M.L.R. 534 on the impact of "auditing" on criminal justice; C. Jones, "Auditing Criminal Justice" (1993) 33 Brit. J. Criminol. 187; A. James and J. Raine, *The New Politics of Criminal Justice* (1998).

[30] A. Bottoms and J. McLean, *Defendants in the Criminal Process* (1976).

[31] *Criminal Justice: The Way Ahead* (2000) Cm. 5074.

[32] See for comparison the terms of reference of the Report of the Royal Commission on Criminal Justice, Cm. 2263 (1993), which refers to consideration of "effectiveness", convicting the guilty, acquitting the innocent and "efficient use of resources": p.iii.

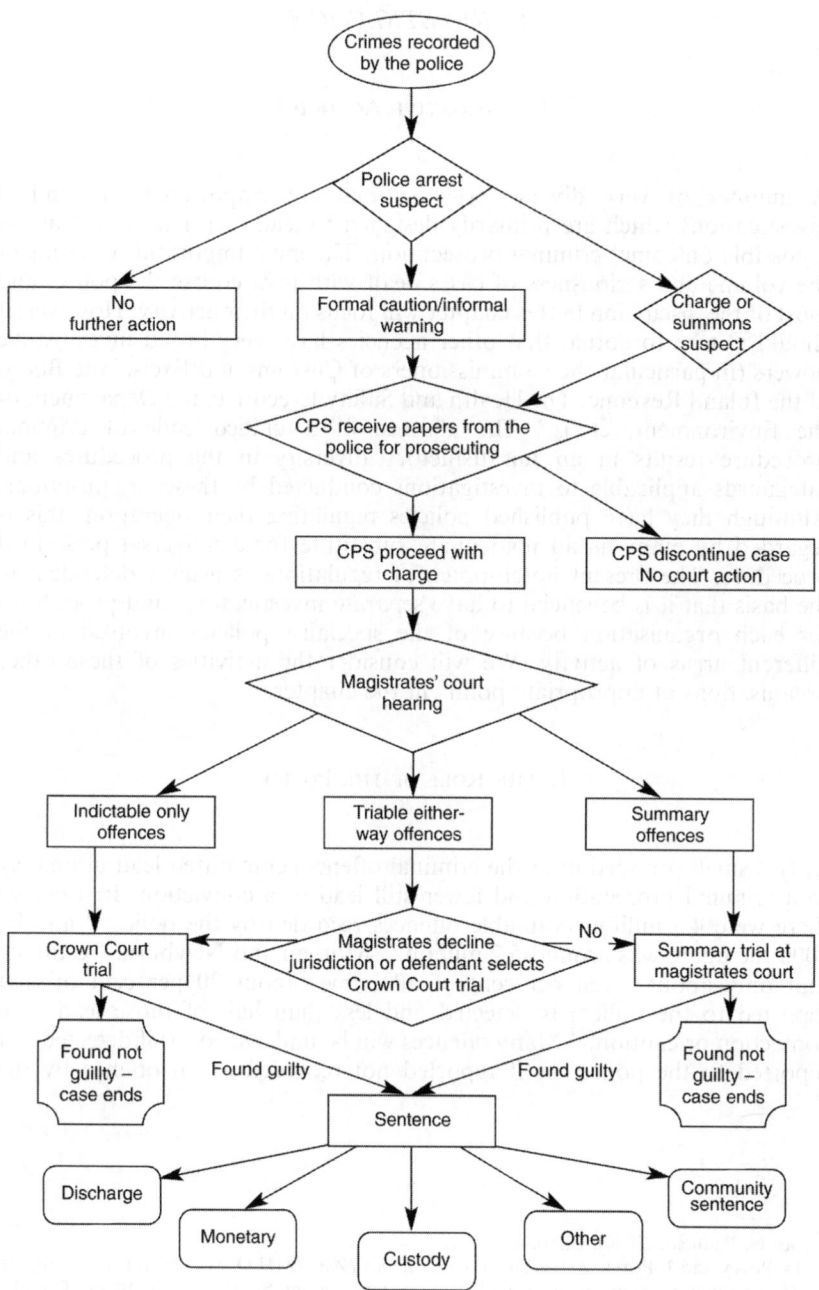

A. INVESTIGATION

INVESTIGATIVE AGENCIES

14–002   A number of very diverse organisations are empowered to conduct investigations which are primarily designed to lead to (or have at least as a possible outcome) criminal prosecution. The most important, in terms of the volume and seriousness of cases dealt with is of course the police, and most of the discussion in this chapter will focus on their activity. However, it should not be forgotten that other agencies have very broad investigative powers (in particular the Commissioners of Customs and Excise, the Board of the Inland Revenue, The Health and Safety Executive, the Department of the Environment, etc.).[33] The absence of a unified code of criminal procedure results in an unsatisfactory diversity in the procedures and safeguards applicable to investigations conducted by these organisations. Although they have published policies regulating their operation, this is regarded by many as an inadequate substitute for a universal prescribed procedure. The present hotch-potch of regulations is usually defended on the basis that it is beneficial to have separate investigations and procedures for each organisation because of the specialist policies involved in the different areas of activity. We will consider the activities of these other organisations at appropriate points in the chapter.

1. THE ROLE OF THE POLICE

14–003   Only a small proportion of the criminal offences committed lead ultimately to a criminal prosecution and fewer still lead to a conviction. In 1998–99 there were 4.5 million notifiable offences recorded by the police,[34] and by 2000 the figure was around 5.2 million.[35] Morgan and Newburn,[36] estimate that only about seven per cent of all crime (about 20 per cent of that reported to the police) is detected and less than half of those lead to a conviction or caution.[37] Many offences will be undetected, or if detected not reported to the police, or if reported not recorded as an offence by the

---

[33]   See N. Padfield, (2000), Chap. 4.

[34]   D. Povey and J. Prime, *Recorded Crime Statistics 1998–99* (H.O. Statistical Bulletin 18/99). The true figures are probably around five times this amount. See C. Mirrless-Black, T. Budd, S. Partdridge and P. Mayhew, *The 1998 British Crime Survey* (HORS III, 1998). See generally on the problem of statistics in this area M. Maguire, "Crime Statistics: Patterns and Trends" in M. Maguire, R. Morgan and R. Reiner (eds), *Oxford Handbook of Criminology* (2nd ed., 1997). See also the statistics in the *British Crime Survey* (Home Office, 2000).

[35]   See above, n. 19.

[36]   R. Morgan and T. Newburn, *The Future of Policing* (1997).

[37]   *ibid.* p.37.

police.[38] Home Office research statistics collected in *Digest 4* show that in 1997, three in 100 offences committed led to a criminal conviction or a police caution. Only one in 300 resulted in a custodial sentence.[39] Of the offences that do come to the attention of the police, it seems that the overwhelming majority are reported by members of the public and only a fraction discovered by the police themselves.[40] About a third of the "members of the public" quoted in these surveys are in fact organisations, store detectives or security firms.[41] These figures reflect the well-established fact that the police are not primarily employed in detecting crime, but in a vast range of other peace-keeping activities.[42]

Some indication of the pressures on police forces can be gleaned from the figures in the Home Office paper *Criminal Justice: The Way Ahead*,[43] which reveals that in an average day, the police receive 25,500 "999" calls, make 5,000 arrests, and conduct 2,200 stops and searches.

Once offences have come to the attention of the police,

> "the clear message that emerges from practically all recent empirical studies ... is that the police are rarely faced with the classic situation of detective fiction, that of the search for the unidentified perpetrators of known offences".[44]

In most cases the process of detection is straightforward as the offender is, for example, caught red-handed, identified by the victim or other witnesses or found by the police at or near the scene of the crime, or is one of a few people with ready access to the crime or an obvious motive, or gives himself or herself up.[45] In a significant number of cases an offence is admitted

---

[38] See generally A. K. Bottomley and K. Pease, *Crime and Punishment: Interpreting the Data* (1986), pp. 34–41. The different forces take different approaches to the recording of crime so that the figures are easily distorted and must be treated with caution: D. Farrington and E. Dowd, "Why Does Crime Decrease?" (1984) 149 J.P.N. 506.

[39] G. Barclay and C. Tavares, *Digest 4* (1997), p.29.

[40] See Ashworth, (1998), p. 142 and for earlier statistics see A. Ashworth, *The English Criminal Process: a Review of Research* (1984), p. 12, based, *inter alia*, on D. Steer, *Uncovering Crime* (RCCP Research Study No. 7, HMSO, 1980); A. K. Bottomley and C. Coleman, *Understanding Crime Rates* (1981); J. Burrows, "How Crimes Come to Police Notice" (H.O. Research Bulletin No. 13, 1982), pp. 12–15. A 1992 survey found that only 5% of recorded crimes come to notice as a result of police patrols or observations: M. Maguire and C. Norris, *The Conduct and Supervision of Criminal Investigations* (RCCJ Research Study No. 5, 1992), p. 8 above, n. 5. See also J. Shapland and J. Vagg, *Policing by the Public* (1988).

[41] Burrows, *op. cit.*

[42] See Sanders and Young, (2000), p.65; R. Morgan and T. Newburn, *op cit.* n. 3.

[43] (2001), p.9.

[44] Bottomley and Pease, (1986), p. 46, based on R. Mawby, *Policing the City* (1979) and Steer (1980). See further the articles collected in R. Reiner, *Policing I* (1996), Part II, "The Role of the Police in Practice"; R. Reiner, *The Future of Policing* (2000). For a recent illustration of the diversity see Home Office, *Diary of a Police Officer* (2001). This involved a report on a "typical shift" of a police officer in an attempt to identify ways in which to "free up" time so that officers could perform more "reassurance policing", (p.v). *www.homeoffice.gov.uk*.

[45] In Steer's study (1980) of indictable offences dealt with by the Oxford police, these accounted for 47% of a random sample and 71% of a sample of serious cases: p. 73, Table 3.4. See generally pp. 71–78, 96–116.

during an interview concerning other offences,[46] or the offender is identified as such following a search of his or her property, or of his person when taken into police custody.[47] In only a minority of cases[48] are special detection skills used (*e.g.* involving informants, fingerprint search, DNA profiles, local police knowledge, police records). Research by Phillips and Brown[49] found that of the 4,250 arrests they examined, in 71 per cent of cases the arresting officer claimed that the basis of his reasonable suspicion was from only one source of evidence. In 40 per cent of all cases the main ground for the suspicion derived from "a police observation of the offence".[50] Given the limitations on police manpower and increases in the crime rate, it is unsurprising that most effort are focused on investigations where a result is most likely, and on the more serious cases.[51] It should also be noted that the increasing use of surveillance and undercover policing as an element of intelligence-led policing strategies mean that the potential offender has often been identified by the police at an earlier stage in the criminal conduct.

The arrangements for the supervision of police investigations were one of the matters specified in the RCCJ's terms of reference.[52] The RCCJ were "less satisfied" with arrangements for supervising routine police inquiries than those in major investigations; indeed research found that supervision as such scarcely applied in most of the cases studied.[53] A "new approach to supervision" was recommended throughout the police service, with improved training in supervision at all levels, detective training and training in investigation to be overhauled. Part IV of the Criminal Justice and Police Act 2001 has now created a Central Police Training and Development Authority as a non-departmental public body to oversee such matters.

The RCCJ also recommended that police performance should be assessed on the basis of other factors besides arrest and conviction rates.[54] New guidelines already introduced for the supervision of serious crime squads were welcomed, particularly in the light of the activities of the West Midlands Police Serious Crime Squad.[55] As regards major inquiries, the RCCJ endorsed moves to introduce external case reviews conducted by

---

[46] Many offences thereby come to the attention of the police for the first time. Such admissions may be made with a view to the other offences being "taken into consideration" "TIC" during sentencing. See below, para. 17-078. Since PACE, TICs have declined considerably in number, with increasing use being made of interviews in prison: M. Maguire and C. Norris, (1992), p. 9.

[47] Steer, *op cit.*, 41% and 20% respectively: *ibid.*

[48] Steer, *op cit.*, 13% and 11% respectively: *ibid.*

[49] *Entry into the Criminal Justice System: A Survey of Arrests and their Outcomes* (HORS No. 49, 1998); see also Sanders and Young, (2000), p.72.

[50] *ibid.* p. 41.

[51] *ibid.* pp. 71–72.

[52] See below, para. 14-091; Cm. 2263, pp. 18–23.

[53] J. Baldwin and T. Moloney, *The Supervision of Police Investigations in Serious Criminal Cases* (RCCJ Research Study No.4, HMSO, 1992); M. Maguire and C. Norris, *The Conduct and Supervision of Criminal Investigations* (RCCJ Research Study No.5, HMSO, 1992); B. Irving and C. Dunningham, *Human Factors in the Quality Control of CID Investigations* (RCCJ Research Study No.21, HMSO, 1993).

[54] The RCCJ welcomed the developments in appraisal that should lead to officers being assessed on the basis of their skills, abilities and attitudes: H.O. Circular 104/1991.

[55] Civil Liberties Trust, *Unsafe and Unsatisfactory* (1991); Police Complaints Authority, *Report on the Investigation in the West Midlands Police Serious Crime Squad* (1991).

H.M. Inspectorate of Constabulary,[56] the opening of police files for all major inquiries and debriefing following major investigations. The government accepted all the recommendations except that for case reviews (on which there would be further discussion).[57]

One fundamental point emphasised by the RCCJ was that:

"the police should see it as their duty when conducting investigations to gather and consider all the relevant evidence, including any which may exonerate the suspect. ... A greater emphasis, such as the police service now advocates, on thorough investigation will not only help to ensure that innocent people are not convicted of crimes which they did not commit but also that fewer guilty people are acquitted because the evidence against them fails when tested in court."[58]

The adoption, once the view is taken that a particular suspect is guilty, of a blinkered approach that concentrates on the construction of a case against him or her and which downplays (or conceals) evidence that points to a different conclusion, has been a recurrent criticism of the police approach to investigations.[59]

Part II of the Criminal Procedure and Investigation Act 1996 provides statutory definitions of the duties of police investigators in relation to the collection, storage and disclosure of information and other material in an investigation.[60] An important feature of the 1996 Act is that, in the course of defining the duties and responsibilities of the police in respect of disclosure, it provides a definition of criminal investigation, and makes it clear that the police are under a duty to investigate the crime not the individual suspect, so that all lines of inquiry must be pursued. The Strasbourgh Court has also recognised the duty to carry out effective investigation into crime.[61] Despite recent reforms, many commentators claim that the police, by the nature of their profession, continue to structure cases against individual suspects.[62]

To facilitate the process of investigation, the law provides the police with a series of powers to interfere with the legal rights of members of the public: powers of arrest and detention, powers to enter and search land and buildings and to search persons, and powers to seize property and conduct surveillance. The law also establishes a framework for controlling the exercise of such powers by setting conditions as to who may exercise the power and the circumstances in which they may be exercised, and by providing for supervision or periodic reviews. It also provides remedies for a breach of legal requirements. Given that most police powers authorise the commission of what would otherwise be torts or crimes (*e.g.* assault, false imprisonment, trespass to land, trespass to goods), exceeding the limits of a

---

[56] HMIC has produced a number of important Thematic Reports on policing, and continues to produce annual reports on each force, *www.hmic.gov.uk/hmic/*.

[57] RCCJ Interim Government Response, LCD, Home Office, Law Officers' Department, Feb. 1994, p. 7.

[58] Cm. 2263, p. 10.

[59] See below, para. 14-068; M. McConville, *et al., The Case for the Prosecution* (1991).

[60] The statute is supplemented by a Code of Practice issued by the Home Secretary under powers in s.23.

[61] See especially *Osman v. U.K.* (1998) 29 E.H.R.R. 245; *Aydin v. Turkey* (1997) 25 E.H.R.R. 251.

[62] See Sanders and Young (2000) Chap. 5.

particular power may well expose the officers concerned (and the Chief Constable, who is vicariously responsible in tort)[63] to an action for damages or a criminal prosecution. This is a reflection of the fundamental guarantee that the police are subject to the rule of law and must justify contraventions of the law by reference to a statutory or common law power.[64] In addition to breaches of the law, officers are also subject to disciplinary regulations which may be contravened even where no tort or crime is committed.[65] The internal accountability of the police remains controversial, and is currently under review, with plans for an independent police complaints commission.[66] It is hoped that the introduction of this body, coupled with the increasingly close scrutiny of operations and thematic reviews by Her Majesty's Inspectorate of Constabulary will assuage the public fears that the police operate without adequate checks.[67] The police powers are not usually subject to a requirement of prior independent judicial supervision, and some leave considerable discretion in the hands of the individual officer.

The key statute regulating police powers over the citizen is the Police and Criminal Evidence Act 1984, (PACE)[68] although this has been supplemented by many others including the Criminal Justice and Public Order Act 1994, the Crime and Disorder Act 1998, the Regulation of Investigatory Powers Act 2000 and the Criminal Justice and Police Act 2001.

PACE extended the formal powers of the police in certain significant respects but narrowed them in others. It also strengthened the controls over the exercise of police powers in general and clarified and strengthened the rights of defendants in custody. Many of these controls are, however, found not in the Act itself but in Codes of Practice made by the Secretary of State.[69] As the foreword to the original Code noted, these were intended to provide clear and workable guidelines for the police, balanced by safeguards for the public. The sanctions for breach of a Code tend to be more indirect

---

[63] See generally, S.J. Bailey, D.J. Harris and Jones, D.C. Ormerod *Civil Liberties, Cases and Materials* (5th ed., 2001), pp. 2; Feldman, *Civil Liberties and Human Rights in England and Wales* (2nd ed., 2002).

[64] See T. Jones, T. Newburn and D. Smith, "Policing and the Idea of Democracy" (1996) 36 B.J. Criminal 182.

[65] See Bailey, Harris and Jones (2001), pp. 120–141.

[66] See the Police Reform Bill 2002. Also J. Harrison and M. Cunneen, *An Independent Police Complaints Commission* (2000) Liberty.

[67] In 2000–01, there were 18,911 complaints received by the police, 34% of which were informally resolved and 34% withdrawn or dispensed with. 9,842 required investigation, with 903 complaints substantiated. Disciplinary charges were proved against 1,202 officers resulting in 125 officers being dismissed or required to resign, 291 officers were fined/reprimanded/cautioned, and 760 officers received written warnings. See D. Povey and J. Cotton, *Police Complaints and Discipline* (Home Office Statistical Bulletin 21/01, 2001).

[68] This followed the Report of the Royal Commission on Criminal Procedure, Cmnd. 8092 (1981) but differed in some important matters from its recommendations. See below, para. 14-092.

[69] Under ss.66, 67. There are at present five Codes: Code A on Powers of Stop and Search; Code B on Search and Seizure; Code C on the Detention, Treatment and Questioning of Persons; Code D on the Identification of Persons; and Code E on Tape Recording. Codes A to D were issued in 1985, and revised with effect from April 1, 1991; Code E was issued in 1988; revised versions of all five codes were issued with effect from April 10, 1995. New revisions to Code A have been made in 1997 and 1999, and to Code C in 1999 and D in 2002. Five new Codes are due to be issued in 2002. A new code — code F — has been introduced to deal with video-recorded statements: *www.homeoffice.gov.uk/pcrg/* see also PACE 1984 (Codes of Practice) (Visual Recordings of Interviews) Order 2002 (S.I. 2002 No. 1266).

than for breach of the substantive law.[70] The intention was to strike a satisfactory balance between police powers and the rights of subjects, but it remains doubtful whether that has been achieved.[71] However, Brown, reviewing 10 years of research into PACE, concluded that it had "introduced a greater element of fairness into pre-trial procedures" with suspects being more aware of their rights, and that there were benefits for the police in terms of clearer and more certain powers.[72]

There is not the space here for more than a brief survey of the police powers.[73] One important general point to note throughout is that the structure of police powers is such that the police officer at the lowest level of the organisation, *i.e.*, those dealing with suspects, have the greatest amount of discretion. This is not typical of an organisational structure; usually the level of discretion increases further up the hierarchy. This breadth of discretion renders it all the more important that the powers are carefully prescribed by the statutes and narrowly interpreted by the courts.

2. POLICE POWERS

It is necessary to provide a brief explanation of a number of recurring **14–004** expressions found in police powers. Many of the police powers depend on the presence of reasonable "suspicion", "cause" or "belief" in the existence of a state of affairs. There is a spectrum with reasonable suspicion at the lower end.[74] It "arises at or near the starting point of an investigation of which the obtaining of prima facie proof is the end ... Prima facie proof consists of admissible evidence. Suspicion can take into account matters that could not be put in evidence at all."[75] It does not presuppose that the police should have obtained sufficient evidence to bring charges. The Strasbourgh Court has confirmed that "reasonable suspicion presupposes the existence of facts or information which would satisfy an objective observer that the person concerned may have committed a criminal offence. What may be

---

[70] Other persons who investigate offences must have regard to any relevant provision (See *R. v. Twaites and Brown* (1990) 92 Cr.App.R. 106 (Ladbrokes investigators); *R. v. Bayliss* (1993) 98 Cr.App.R. 235 (store detective), but not for example teachers investigating pupils offences (*G. v. DPP* [1989] Crim.L.R. 150), and the Codes are admissible in evidence and if relevant to civil or criminal proceedings, are to be taken into account by the court or tribunal. However, breach of a Code by a person does not of itself render him or her liable to any civil or criminal proceedings (ss.67(8)-(11)). Breach of a Code may give rise to exclusion of evidence: see below, para. 14-025.

[71] For a sceptical view, see A. Sanders, "Rights, Remedies and the Police and Criminal Evidence Act" [1988] Crim.L.R. 802.

[72] D. Brown, *PACE Ten Years On: A Review of the Research* (HORS 155).

[73] For fuller treatment see Feldman, (2002), Part II, Chap. 6. Bailey, Harris and Jones, (2001) Chap. 3; V. Bevan and K. Lidstone, *Investigation of Crime: A Guide to Police Powers* (2nd ed., 1996); E. Cape and J. Luqmani, *Defending Suspects at Police Stations: The Practitioners Guide to Advice and Representation* (3rd ed., 1999); M. Zander, *The Police and Criminal Evidence Act 1984* (3rd ed., 1995); D. Feldman, *The Law of Entry, Search and Seizure* (1986); R. T. H. Stone, *Entry, Search and Seizure* (2nd ed., 1989); H. Levenson and F. Fairweather, *Police Powers: a Practitioner's Guide* (3rd ed., 1996); Symposia, [1985] P.L. 388 *et seq.*, [1985] Crim.L.R.535 *et seq.* and [1990] Crim.L.R.452 *et seq.*

[74] On definitions of reasonable suspicion see *Shaaban Bin Hussein v. Hong Fook Kam* [1970] A.C. 942.

[75] *ibid., per* Lord Devlin at 948.

regarded as 'reasonable' will however depend on all the circumstances."[76] The English courts have adopted a compatible definition,[77] and officers rely on the specific guidance provided in the Code of Practice A. Despite efforts in the Codes of Practice, accompanying PACE, to guard against the abuse of powers based on such a low threshold, Home Office research has recently confirmed that officers' suspicions (at least as regards stop and search) are aroused as a result of appearance, (including youth; type of vehicle; incongruence; "in some cases" ethnicity); being known to the police; and fitting the suspect description.[78]

A further general threshold test worth noting is the statutory power for a constable to use reasonable force wherever it is necessary in the exercise of any power under PACE.[79]

A final important concept throughout the PACE regime is that of "serious arrestable offences". This is defined in section 116 of the 1984 Act, and is employed in respect of several of the powers in the Act. It covers (1) a group of arrestable offences that are always "serious", and (2) any other arrestable offences that have led or are intended or likely to lead to specified consequences.[80] Unfortunately, it lacks the specificity in definition that is desirable given the important consequences that flow from its application.

(a) Stop and search

14–005 Prior to the 1984 Act, the powers to stop and search people were haphazard and unsatisfactory. PACE extended the general powers of the police to stop and search persons and vehicles. They are used extensively. In 2000–01 there were 714,100 recorded stops of people/vehicles.[81]

Under section 1 of PACE a constable may stop and search a person or vehicle in a public place if he or she has reasonable grounds to suspect he or

---

[76] *Fox, Campbell and Hartley v. U.K.* (1990) 13 E.H.R.R. 157; *Guzzardi v. Italy* (1980) 3 E.H.R.R. 333; *Brogan v. U.K.* (1988) 11 E.H.R.R. 117.

[77] See *O'Hara v. Chief Constable of the RUC* [1997] A.C. 286 and *Castorina v. Chief Constable of Surrey* (1988) N.L.J.R. 180.

[78] See, *inter alia*, P. Quinton, N. Bland and J. Miller, *Police Stops, Decision-making and Practice* (HORS Paper No. 130, 2000). This and a series of related research papers is examined in Bailey, Harris and Ormerod, Chap. 3.

[79] 1984 Act, s.117. The use of handcuffs does not breach safeguards in Art. 3 of the ECHR: *Rainien v. Finland* (1997) 26 E.H.R.R. 543.

[80] 1984 Act, s.116(6), (7). Serious harm to the security of the State or public order; serious interference with the administration of justice or the investigation of offences; death; serious injury; substantial financial gain or serious financial loss to any person (loss being serious if "having regard to all the circumstances, it is serious for the person who suffers it"). See *R. v. McIvor* [1987] Crim.L.R. 409 (Sheffield Crown Court) (theft of 28 beagles worth £880, collectively owned by a hunt, held not to involve serious financial loss); *R. v. Eric Smith* [1987] Crim.L.R. 579 (Stafford Crown Court) (robbery of two video recorders and £116 cash held not to be a serious arrestable offence). See *Archbold* (2002), para. 15-17.

[81] See M. Ayres *et al., Arrests for Notifiable Offences* (H.O. RSD 19/01, 2001) which found that the proportion of adults stopped by the police while on foot (3%) has remained constant throughout the 1990s. Men aged 16–29 are most likely to be stopped by the police. In the 2000 British Crime Survey 25% of adults said they had been stopped while in a vehicle and 15% while on foot. Young black males were much more likely to be stopped while in a vehicle (39%) than either Asian (29%) or young white males (25%). Even among those aged over 30, black males were more likely to be stopped. See L. Sims and A. Mayhill, *Policing and the Future: Findings From the 2000 BCS* (H.O. RSD 136/01, 2001).

she will find stolen goods; an offensive weapon (made or adadpted for causing injury or intended by the person having it with him for such use), articles adapted for use in burglary, theft, obtaining by deception or taking a vehicle without authority, or a knife or other bladed or sharply pointed article.[82] There are similar powers under other statutes authorising searches, for example, for drugs, for firearms and for intoxicating liquor on those at, or travelling to, sporting events.[83] All these powers are now subject to the safeguards set out in section 2 of the 1984 Act, which, *inter alia*, require the constable, before commencing a search, to give his or her name and that of his or her police station, the object of the proposed search, the grounds for the search, and, if out of uniform, documentary evidence that he or she is a constable. A failure to comply with these requirements will render the search unlawful and the officer will not be acting in the execution of his duty.[84] The search, if conducted, is to be proportionate to what the person is suspected of having done/possessing, and the length of time for detention must not extend beyond the time taken for the search and must in all the circumstances be reasonable.[85] The courts are however unlikely to exclude evidence obtained by an illegal search.[86]

The person searched may not be required to remove any clothing in public other than an outer coat, jacket or gloves, and only a constable in uniform may stop a vehicle. A record must be made of the search (stating the object of the search, the grounds for it, and the time, place and result) unless it is not practicable to do so.[87] The imposition of these statutory requirements may cause officers to attempt to conduct as many searches as possible by consent, so that the safeguards do not apply. Research suggests that the stop and search powers are now used increasingly as an intelligence gathering exercise, rather than with a view to arrest for an offence. Quinton and Bland[88] found that some forces used the power to stop the same individuals repeatedly as a means of monitoring the whereabouts of "known criminals". This was considered to be an effective use of the power, with improved targeting of searches increasing arrest rates.[89] Miller, Bland and Quinton,[90] found substantial variation between forces in the extent to which searches are used,[91] but that searches appear to have a "minor role" in detecting offenders for the range of all crimes involved, and a "relatively small role" in detecting offenders.[92]

---

[82] Police and Criminal Evidence Act 1984, s.1, as amended by the Criminal Justice Act 1988, s.140.

[83] See the list in Annex A to the *Code of Practice for the Exercise by Police Offices of Statutory Powers of Stop and Search* (HMSO, 1995) (Code A). Note also the recent additional powers under the Terrorism Act 2000, ss. 44–47.

[84] *Osman v. DPP* (1999) 163 J.P. 725.

[85] Code A, para. 3.3.

[86] See *R. v. McCarthy* [1996] Crim.L.R. 818; *cf. R.v. Fennelly* [1989] Crim.L.R. 142.

[87] 1984 Act, s.3.

[88] *Modernising the Tactic* (Police Research Series Paper No. 128 ??, 1999).

[89] See the further research on information gathering, P. Quinton, N. Bland, and J. Miller, *Police Stops, Decision making and Practice* (Police Research Series Paper No. 130, 2000).

[90] *The Impact of Stops and Searches on Crime and the Community* (Police Research Series Paper No 127, 2000).

[91] *ibid.* p. 12.

[92] *ibid.* p. 27.

The Criminal Justice and Public Order Act 1994, as subsequently amended by the Knives Act 1997 and Crime and Disorder Act 1998 has extended stop and search powers quite significantly. Section 60 of the Criminal Justice and Public Order Act 1994 introduced a new power to "stop and search *in anticipation* of violence". Where a police inspector[93] reasonably believes that incidents involving serious violence may take place and that it is expedient to do so to prevent their occurrence, he or she may authorise that the section 60 powers shall be exercisable "at any place within the locality for a period not exceeding twenty four hours".[94] These powers enable a uniformed constable to stop any pedestrian or vehicle and search for offensive weapons or dangerous instruments.[95] What is significant here is that the constable need not reasonably suspect that the pedestrian or vehicle is carrying such an item. The power is intended to allow the police to stop and search "*before* they have a reasonable suspicion against a person".[96]

The Crime and Disorder Act, as now amended by the Anti-Terrorism, Crime and Security Act 2001, extends the powers of the officer conducting a stop and search yet further by introducing powers to remove and seize disguises worn to conceal the wearer's identity.[97] In *DPP v. Avery*,[98] the court held that the officer exercising these powers (at that time under the Crime and Disorder Act) was not required to give his name, station or reasons for his action. Because of fears of insensitivity in relation to religious dress, a new Note for Guidance was included in the revised and latest version of Code A. Recent Home Office research into the stop and search powers found that these broader powers in section 60 (and others that were not triggered by specific need for reasonable suspicion) were much less effective, and it was recommended that they be reviewed in light of their inefficiency and the negative impact they have on public confidence.[99]

The police also have a power to carry out general road checks on the written authority of a police superintendent.[1] The aim must be to find a person who has committed or is intending to commit an offence, a witness to an offence or a person unlawfully at large.[2] In each case the offence must be a "serious arrestable offence".

Article 5 of the ECHR does not expressly authorise stops and searches, it merely provides that deprivation of liberty must be in accordance with law and exercised for specified purposes. Deprivation of liberty on reasonable suspicion is legitimate provided, under Article 5(1)(c), that the detention relates to the commission of an offence *and* is with the purpose of bringing the suspect to court. It has been questioned whether the current stop and

---

[93] Formerly the requirement was a superintendent (or above).
[94] This may be extended for a further 24 hours by a superintendent.
[95] *i.e.* instruments which have a blade or are sharply pointed.
[96] M. O'Brien, Under Secretary of State for the Home Office, Commons Standing Committee B, June 9, 1998, col. 788.
[97] Section 4A. See *Archbold* (2002), para. 15–66.
[98] [2001] EWCA Admin 748.
[99] J. Miller, N. Bland and P. Quintan, *The Impact of Stops And Searches on Crime and the Community* (Police Research Series Paper No. 127, 2000), p. 59.
[1] 1984 Act, s.4.
[2] These are specified in Sched. 5 and include, *inter alia*, treason, murder, manslaughter, rape, kidnapping, certain sexual offences, certain firearms offences and causing death by dangerous driving. They also include drug trafficking offences: see the Drug Trafficking Act 1994, ss. 1(3)(a) to (f), as amended.

search powers are compatible with this requirement. The purpose of an arrest must be to bring the suspect before a competent judicial authority[3] but in *Brogan v. United Kingdom*[4] the European Court recognised that the fact that arrest did not lead to a charge did not render it contrary to Article 5, and by analogy stop and search would seem to be compatible.

The exercise of stop and search powers remains very controversial. One of the most recurring concerns is the fact that black people are more likely to be stopped and searched than white.[5] Code of Practice A under the 1984 Act emphasises, *inter alia*, that a person's colour, dress or hairstyle can never itself be a reasonable ground for suspicion,[6] but it is still doubted whether the reasonable ground standard is generally met.[7] Quinton, Bland, and Miller[8] in their review of the concept of reasonable suspicion and its application concluded that there needs to be further clarification of the concept, since generalisations are still used by police officers in practice. Stone and Pettigrew[9] concluded that a disproportionate number of searches could be due to: ethnic bias in officers; a larger proportion of ethnic groups in the population available to be stopped and searched; and a higher concentration of minority groups in the areas targeted.

Prompted by the Stephen Lawrence Inquiry, the Home Office has recently conducted a wholesale review of the exercise of the powers. The *Macpherson Report*[10] recommended that the powers of the police should be retained, but that records be made of all "stops" and "stops and searches" and "voluntary" stops. The records should include the reasons for the stop, the outcome, and the self-defined ethnic identity of the person stopped, and that a copy of the record be provided to the person stopped. This would allow for effective monitoring of the powers. Pilot studies have found, however, that recording ethnicity is extremely provocative in these circumstances.

Stone and Pettigrew[11] also explored public experiences of stop and search, reporting that "there was a very strong perception that the way in which stops and searches are currently handled causes more distrust, antagonism, and resentment than any of the positive effects they can have". However, despite this, all ethnic groups felt that stops and searches should remain if fundamental changes were made in the ways the powers are used (especially as regards the police attitude and the provision of reasons for the search).

---

[3] *Lawless v. Ireland* (1961) 1 E.H.R.R. 1; *McVeigh, O'Neill & Evans v. U.K.* (1981) 5 E.H.R.R. 71.

[4] (1989) 11 E.H.R.R. 117. See Q. Whitaker, in K. Starmer *et al.*, (2001), Chap. 10; Emmerson and Ashworth, (2001), Chap. 5.

[5] C. F. Willis, *The Use, Effectiveness and Impact of Police Stop and Search Powers* (H. O. Research and Planning Unit Paper 15, 1983); M. McConville, [1983] Crim.L.R. 605; T. Bucke, *Ethnicity and Contacts with the Police: Latest Findings from the British Crime Survey* (HORS No. 59, 1997). See more generally, *Crime, Policing and Justice: the experience of Ethnic Minorities — Findings from the 2000 British Crime Survey* (2001) HMSO.

[6] 1984 Act, s.66; Code A paras 1.6–1.7A. Discrimination in the exercise of these powers may give rise to an Article 14 claim. J.Wadham and H. Mountfield, *Blackstones Guide to the Human Rights Act 1998* (1999), p. 113.

[7] D. Dixon *et al.*, "Reality and Rules in the Construction and Regulation of Police Suspicion" (1989) Int. Jo. Sociology of Law 185.

[8] *Police Stops, Decision-making and Practice* (Police Research Series Paper No. 130, 2000).

[9] *op. cit.*

[10] *The Views of the Public on Stops and Searches* (Police Research Paper No. 129, 2000), p. 68.

[11] *op cit.*

Miller[12] also examined the ethnicity of those stopped and searched and explored the complexity behind these oft-cited statistics on racial bias. The findings of the research did not suggest a general pattern of bias against those from minority ethnic backgrounds.[13]

The figures for stops and searches have steadily increased, in part due to more comprehensive recording. The proportion leading to an arrest has, at the same time, declined.[14] There is a danger in relying too heavily on these statistics since stops will not be recorded unless accompanied by a search, and there are hundreds of thousands of consensual stops and searches that will not be recorded at all.[15]

PACE Code of Practice A governing stop and search powers confirms that the Act and Code do not "affect the ability of an officer to speak to or question a person in the ordinary course of his duties (and in the absence of reasonable suspicion) without detaining him or exercising any element of compulsion".[16]

The Home Office has issued a new Draft Code of Practice Code A for consultation.[17] The Draft reflects the responses to the *Macpherson Report* and seeks to improve the monitoring of stops and searches and, in particular, guaranteeing that all stops as well as stops and searches will be recorded.[18]

(b) Arrest[19]

14–006 An arrest amounts to a deprivation of liberty and as such must comply with Article 5 of the ECHR, by being in accordance with law, and fulfilling one of the specified purposes listed — the most pertinent being that in Article 5(1)(c) of bringing a person before the competent legal authority on reasonable suspicion of having committed an offence.[20] As Lord Hope observed in *R. v. HMP Brockhill, ex p. Evans (No. 2)*[21] any detention that is unlawful in domestic law will automatically be contrary to Article 5 of the ECHR.

Powers of arrest in English law can be grouped in to five categories.

---

[12] *Profiling Populations Available for Stops and Searches* (Police Research Series Paper No. 131, 2000).

[13] *ibid.* p.84.

[14] See the figures in the Home Office, *Operation of Certain Police Powers under PACE*, published annually.

[15] On the particular danger of using stop and search statistics as performance indicators of effective policing, see B. Loveday, "The Impact of Performance culture on criminal Justice Agencies in England and Wales" (1999) 27 J. Soc. of Law 351. The Home Office has now produced a consultation document on the *Recording of Police/Public Encounters* (2002).

[16] para. 1, n. 1B.

[17] March 2002.

[18] paras 4.11–4.18

[19] See generally, *Archbold*, (2002), pp. 15–152 *et seq*; Sanders and Young (2000), Chap. 3; Bailey, Harris and Ormerod (2001), pp.275–297; Feldman (2002), Part II, Chap. 6; Emmerson and Ashworth (2001), Chap. 5.

[20] See *Brogan v. U.K.* (1988) 11 E.H.R.R. 117; *Fox, Campbell and Hartley v. U.K.* (1990) 13 E.H.R.R. 157.

[21] [2000] 3 W.L.R. 843.

(i) Arrest with a warrant[22]

In some cases an arrest is authorised by a warrant issued by a justice of the **14–007** peace under section 1 of the Magistrates' Courts Act 1980, as an alternative to the issue of a summons.[23] The issue of an arrest warrant or a summons follows the laying of an information on oath to the effect that the person named has, or is suspected of having, committed an offence. A warrant should not be issued where a summons would be equally effectual, but may, for example, be employed where the defendant fails to answer to a summons.[24] Using a summons as a way of initiating the prosecution process is preferable to the more intrusive alternative of arrest. The trend in English law is however to move towards a wider use of the arrest powers, and increasingly to use powers of arrest without a warrant, and consequently, over which there is no prior judicial supervision.

(ii) Arrest without a warrant for "arrestable offences"

Section 24 of the Police and Criminal Evidence Act 1984 gives the police and **14–008** members of the public general powers to arrest without a warrant in respect of the more serious offences classified as "arrestable offences".[25] These are:

— offences for which the sentence is fixed by law (*e.g.* murder, treason);

— offences for which a person of 21[26] or over (not previously convicted) may be sentenced to five years' imprisonment (*e.g.* theft, criminal damage, assault occasioning actual bodily harm);

— other offences specified in section 24(2) that would not otherwise be arrestable offences (*e.g.* some offences under the Customs and Excise Acts, offences under the Official Secrets Act 1989, taking a motor vehicle without authority) and related offences (conspiracy, attempt, aiding and abetting, etc.). The list of the offences in section 24 grows longer each year (recent additions include posting prostitutes' cards in phone boxes and kerb crawling), and now includes a diverse range of offences.[27] It must be questioned to what extent these are all cases in which a power of arrest is necessary.

The "arrestable" offences may be in the present, the past or the future. Thus, any person may arrest anyone who *is* in the act of committing an

---

[22] The other warrants to arrest including, for example, those for extradition, are not examined here.

[23] See below, para. 14-052.

[24] See below.

[25] This replaced similar provisions in the Criminal Law Act 1967, s.2, which in turn had replaced common law powers of arrest for felonies.

[26] From a day to be appointed this will become 18: see Criminal Justice and Courts Services Act 2000, s.77.

[27] The latest additions being under the Anti-Terrorism, Crime and Security Act 2001, s. 94(3), rendering, *e.g.* unauthorised presence in a restricted zone or on an aircraft arrestable offences. See generally, C. Walker, *The Anti-Terrorism Legislation* (2002).

arrestable offence or whom he or she has reasonable grounds for suspecting to be committing such an offence. Where an arrestable offence has *been* committed, any person may arrest anyone who is guilty of it, or whom he or she has reasonable grounds for suspecting to be guilty. (Here, the offence must have been committed by someone.)[28] Where a constable has reasonable grounds for suspecting that an arrestable offence has been committed, he or she may arrest anyone whom he or she has reasonable grounds for suspecting to be guilty of it. A constable may arrest anyone who is about to commit an arrestable offence or whom he or she has reasonable grounds for suspecting to be about to commit such an offence.[29] It will be seen that the powers of the police here are wider than those of private citizens. The powers of citizens to effect arrests were, historically, no different from police, but now it is clearly much more limited. The increasing trend towards private security (in shopping centres and other public places), will mean that the "citizens' arrest" powers come under closer scrutiny in the future. The Home Office is currently reviewing proposals to impose greater obligations on private individuals and companies to make arrests and pursue private prosecutions of offenders for, *e.g.* shoplifting.

There is some question as to the ECHR compatibility of some of the powers of arrest under section 24. The availability of a power of arrest without the proof of reasonable suspicion of the commission of an offence does seem to conflict with Article 5(1)(c). This matter has not been directly addressed by the English courts.[30]

(iii) Arrest without a warrant by virtue of "general arrest conditions"

14–009   A novel feature of the 1984 Act was the introduction in section 25 of general arrest powers exercisable by the police in respect of all offences other than arrestable offences. These are available where for some reason or another an arrest is necessary notwithstanding that the offence in question is comparatively trivial. Where a constable has reasonable grounds for suspecting such an offence has been or is being committed or attempted, he or she may arrest the relevant person "if it appears to him [or her] that service of a summons is impracticable or inappropriate because any of the general arrest conditions are satisfied". The "general arrest conditions" are:

(a) that the name of the relevant person is unknown to, and cannot readily be ascertained by, the constable;

(b) that the constable has reasonable grounds for doubting whether a name furnished is the real name;

---

[28] See *Walters v. W. H. Smith & Son Ltd* [1914] K.B. 595 (common law); *R. v. Self* [1992] 3 All E.R. 476 (section 24(5)). Later cases have interpreted *Self* restrictively. *Stanley v. Benning* (1998) 14 July, C.A. (Civ. D.) held that as "a matter of principle" no one in civil law can be debarred from alleging that an acquittal was incorrect. It is therefore always open to the defendant to challenge a claimant's acquittal in civil cases involving torts for wrongful arrest under section 24(5).

[29] On the difficulties created by this being too premature for even a charge of attempt, see *R. v. Geddes* [1996] Crim.L.R. 894.

[30] See generally Emmerson and Ashworth, (2001), Chap. 5, especially pp. 181–182; and see *Guzzardi v. Italy* (1980) 3 E.H.R.R. 333, and *Ireland v. U.K.* (1978) 2 E.H.R.R. 25.

(c) that the relevant person has failed to furnish a satisfactory address for service, or the constable has reasonable grounds for doubting whether an address furnished is a satisfactory one;

(d) that the constable has reasonable grounds for believing that an arrest is necessary;

(e) to prevent the relevant person causing physical injury to himself or herself or any other person; suffering physical injury; causing loss of or damage to property; committing an offence against public decency; or causing an unlawful obstruction of the highway; or

(f) to protect a child or other vulnerable person from the relevant person.

In *Edwards v. DPP*[31] the Divisional Court confirmed that, where it is sought to justify an arrest by reference to section 25, there must be evidence that this power was in the officer's mind at the time of the arrest. Subsequently, the Court of Appeal has held that an officer conducting an arrest under section 25 should explain both the offence which the arrestee was suspected of committing and also the relevant arrest condition relied upon under section 25, *e.g.* to ascertain a name and address. It is not enough simply to say that the failure to provide a name and address was the cause of the arrest.[32] This power is an extremely broad one and is open to potential abuse by officers. It is nevertheless probably compatible with the ECHR.[33]

(iv) Arrest without warrant under specific statutory powers

The 1984 Act repealed many specific statutory powers of arrest available to **14–010** the police, while preserving powers under numerous Acts listed in Schedule 2. These include powers under the Immigration Act 1971 and the Mental Health Act 1983. Section 26 of PACE removes many of the former statutory powers, but has been held not to remove, *e.g.* the power of arrest under the Vagrancy Act 1824, section 6. because it applies to all citizens.[34] Similarly, it has been held that the powers of arrest for being drunk and disorderly in public were held not to have been repealed by section 26 of PACE.[35]

Other specific powers of arrest have been created since PACE.[36] There is, in particular, a very broad power of arrest under the Terrorism Act 2000, section 41. The failure to provide a comprehensive code of arrest powers

---

[31] (1993) 94 Cr.App.R. 301.
[32] *Ghafar v. Chief Constable of West Midlands Police*, May 21, 2000, CA (Civ. Div.), unreported.
[33] See Q. Whitaker in K. Starmer *et al.*, (2001) Chap. 10, p. 99.
[34] *Gapper v. Chief Constable of Avon and Somerset* [1999] 2 W.L.R. 928.
[35] *DPP v. Kitching* (1990) 154 J.P. 293, DC.
[36] *e.g.* Sporting Events (Control of Alcohol, etc.) Act 1985, s.7(2); Public Order Act 1986, s.3(6) (affray), s.4(4) (fear or provocation of violence), s.5(4) (harassment, alarm or distress) (see in particular on these very extensively used powers the research paper by D. Brown and T. Ellis, *Policing Low Level Disorder: the Use of section 5 of the Public Order Act 1986* (HORS, 1994 No. 135), ss. 12(7), 13(10) and 14(7) of the Public Order Act 1986 (processions and assemblies); Criminal Justice and Public Order Act 1994, s.61 (power to remove trespassers from land), s.63 (raves) and s.68 (aggravated trespass).

diminishes the protection afforded to individuals in safeguarding their liberty.

(v) Arrest at common law

14–011   At common law, there is a power to arrest for breach of the peace where a breach of the peace is taking place or reasonably anticipated.[37] This power is not confined to constables and was not modified by the 1984 Act. Recent case law prompted by the pressure to ensure compatibility with Article 5 of the ECHR has clarified the scope of the arrest powers for breach of the peace.[38]

(vi) Common requirements

14–012   There are a number of conditions that must be fulfilled for an arrest to be valid, apart from the existence of a relevant power of arrest. Some are derived from the common law and some from statute. Very commonly, the arrestor is required to have "reasonable grounds" to believe or suspect the arrested person to be guilty of an offence. If the validity of the arrest is challenged in legal proceedings the onus lies on the arrestor to establish to the satisfaction of the court that objectively reasonable grounds existed: it is insufficient that the arrestor honestly believed that he or she had such grounds.[39] The concept of reasonable suspicion lies between that of suspicion without any proof and that of prima facie proof based on admissible evidence (i.e. evidence that if not controverted would be sufficient for a conviction).[40] Whether it exists in a particular case is a question of fact not law, and it is unusual for an arrest to be held unlawful for lack of reasonable grounds.[41] This is a low threshold test and there is a danger that it will be abused by officers.

       If the arresting officer has made a reasonable but erroneous interpretation

---

[37]   *Bibby v. Chief Constable of Essex* (2000) 164 J.P. 297; *McGrogan v. Chief Constable of Cleveland* [2001] EWCA Civ 86. See also D. Nicholson and K. Reid, "Arrest for Breach of the Peace and the ECHR" [1996] Crim.L.R. 764; *R. v. Howell (Erroll)* [1982] Q.B. 416, DC; *Albert v. Lavin* [1982] A.C. 546. The court in *Howell* stated that "there is a breach of the peace whenever harm is actually done or is likely to be done to a person or in his presence to his property or a person is in fear of being so harmed through an assault, an affray, a riot, unlawful assembly or other disturbance" (*per* Watkins L.J. at 427).

[38]   See *Foulkes v. Chief Constable of Merseyside* [1998] 3 All E.R.705; *Bibby v. Chief Constable of Essex* (2000) 164 J.P. 297; on the ECHR interpretation of breach of the peace see *Steel v. U.K.* (1999) 28 R.H.R.R. 603.

[39]   See above, *R. v. Inland Revenue Commissions, ex p. Rossminster Ltd* [1980] A.C. 952 at 1011, *per* Lord Diplock.

[40]   *Dumbell v. Roberts* [1944] 1 All E.R. 326; *Hussein v. Chong Foot Kam* [1970] A.C. 942.

[41]   See generally S. H. Bailey and D. J. Birch, [1982] Crim.L.R. 475. An arrest may be based on hearsay evidence: *Erskine v. Holland* [1971] R.T.R. 199; *R. v. Evans* [1974] R.T.R. 232. See also the *Code of Practice for the Exercise by Police Officers of Statutory Powers of Stop and Search* (HMSO, 1995) (Code A), paras 1.6–1.7A. See also *Doorson v. Netherlands* (1996) 22 E.H.R.R. 330. The ECtHR adopts a similar view to the U.K. courts on the requirements for a lawful arrest.

of the law, he will not have a reasonable suspicion and the arrest will be unlawful.[42] The reasonableness of the officer's decision is to be based on the information available to him at that time.[43] The courts have accepted that reasonable suspicion can be founded on the basis of information provided and does not require the police to believe a suspect to be guilty.[44] In *O'Hara v. Chief Constable of the RUC*, the House of Lords confirmed that reasonable suspicion could be founded on information from senior officers, but not merely on an instruction to arrest.[45] The ECtHR has emphasised that it is necessary for the officer to have formed a suspicion based on objective grounds.[46] As well as possessing the requisite reasonable grounds, the arrestor must in fact suspect the particular arrestee.[47]

The arrestor, or another officer,[48] must make it clear that the arrestee is under compulsion either by physical means, such as taking him or her by the arm, or by using words of compulsion to which the arrestee accedes.[49] The use of reasonable force is sanctioned by PACE: section 117.[50] The arrestee must be informed that he or she is under arrest, and of the ground for arrest, at the time of the arrest or as soon as practicable thereafter.[51]

An arrest is unlawful if the person arrested is not told the ground of arrest in compliance with section 28(3); however, the arrest becomes lawful once the ground is given.[52] The degree of information that it is necessary for the officer to provide has been the subject of dispute. It has been held, for example, that when arresting a suspect for drug dealing, it is not necessary to specify the class of drugs involved. To do so would be to require undue technicality.[53] The Court of Appeal has held that the trial judge should direct the jury whether the words of the officer are capable in law of amounting to a sufficient basis to inform the defendant of the arrest, but leave to the jury the decision as to whether they were spoken.[54] This requirement of adequate information was an important common law requirement, and it is also found in Article 5(2) of the ECHR — a suspect must be informed properly in a language he understands of the reason for

---

[42] *Todd v. DPP* [1996] Crim.L.R. 344.

[43] *Redmond-Bate v. DPP* (1999) 163 JP 744.

[44] *Castorina v. Chief Constable of Surrey* [1988] N.J.L.R. 180; this can be from a police national computer check: *Hough v. Chief Constable of Staffordshire, The Times*, February 14, 2001. See also *Murray v. U.K.* (1994) 19 E.H.R.R. 193; *Brogan v. U.K.* (1988) 11 E.H.R.R. 117.

[45] [1997] A.C. 286.

[46] *O'Hara v. U.K.* [2002] Crim.L.R. 493, acknowledging the difficulty in being able to prove this when the investigation involved reliance on informers.

[47] *Castorina v. Chief Constable of Surrey* (1988) 138 N.L.J. 180; *Chapman v. DPP* (1988) 153 J.P.

[48] See *Dhesi v. Chief Constable of West Midlands*, (*The Times*, May 9, 2000.

[49] *Alderson v. Booth* [1969] 2 Q.B. 216.

[50] See also the Criminal Law Act 1967, s.3.

[51] See *Nicholas v. Parsonage* [1987] R.T.R. 199 (arrest under section 25); *DPP v. Hawkins* [1988] 1 W.L.R. 1166 (arrest not retrospectively unlawful if the ground is not given when it first becomes practicable); *Abbassy v. Commissioner of Police of the Metropolis* [1990] 1 W.L.R. 385 (no need to specify a particular crime or give a technical definition of the offence; sufficient to use commonplace language). See *Fox, Campbell and Hartley v. U.K.* (1990) 13 E.H.R.R. 157. There is no need for the reasons to be provided in writing: *X v. Netherlands* (1966) 9 Y.B. 474.

[52] *Lewis v. Chief Constable of the South Wales Constabulary* [1991] 1 All E.R. 206.

[53] *Clarke v. Chief Constable of North Wales, The Independent*, May 22, 2000, CA (Civ. Div.), per Brooke L.J., with whom Sir Christopher Staughton agreed; Sedley L.J. dissented.

[54] *R. v. Green* October 15, 1996, CA (Crim. Div.).

his arrest.[55] The need to explain the grounds for the arrest are not necessary where the arrestor is a private citizen and the fact or ground of arrest is obvious. There is a further, general exception where it is not reasonably practicable to impart the information before the arrestee escapes from arrest.[56]

More controversially, in *R. v. Chalkley and Jeffries*[57] the court confirmed that it is acceptable for the police to inform the suspect of one reason for the arrest that would be technically applicable even if they are in fact investigating him or her for another more serious offence that is not disclosed. The danger with this concession to the police for the use of holding charges is that the suspect will not perceive the seriousness of his or her situation and will, for example, decline legal assistance.

The arrestor must regard his or her action of arrest in the sense of a possible first step in the criminal process: if, for example, he or she simply detains someone for questioning with no thought of arrest it cannot be a valid arrest.[58] In addition, to ensure compliance with Article 5 the arrest must be "for the purpose of securing [the] fulfilment [of an obligation prescribed by law] and not, for instance, punitive in character".[59]

Finally, as the power of arrest is a statutory discretion exercisable (normally) by a public official, a particular exercise may be challenged as an *ultra vires* abuse of discretion.[60] In practice, the police officer may well exercise the discretion not to arrest but to turn a blind eye, particularly given the bureaucracy involved his or her processing an arrestee. This has recently been estimated at an average three and a half hours spent per arrestee.[61]

(vii) The effects of PACE

14–013   The potential benefits of the PACE arrest regime are that it provides a relatively comprehensive code and does incorporate safeguards such as the requirement of reasonable suspicion in most cases and that the suspect must be cautioned after arrest. On the negative side, the threshold of reasonable suspicion is very low, and in some cases the powers can be exercised even without reasonable suspicion. In addition, the powers represent a move away from judicially supervised arrest with practically any offence becoming arrestable for perhaps trivial reasons triggered under section 25.

Statistics on arrest are maintained separately by police forces and collated by H.M. Chief Inspector of Constabulary. Research on the immediate effects of PACE suggested that the level of initial evidence on which arrests

---

[55] *Murray v. U.K.* (1994) 19 E.H.R.R. 193.

[56] PACE 1984, s.28. The requirements as to giving the ground of arrest were based on the common law: *Christie v. Leachinsky* [1947] A.C. 573. See also *Gelberg v. Miller* [1961] 1 W.L.R. 153; *R. v. Telfer* [1976] Crim.L.R. 562.

[57] [1998] 2 Cr.App.R. 79.

[58] *Kenlin v. Gardiner* [1967] 2 Q.B. 510; *R. v. Brown* (1976) 64 Cr.App.R. 231.

[59] *McVeigh v. U.K.* (1981) 25 D.R. 15, Euro Comm.

[60] *Holgate-Mohammed v. Duke* [1984] A.C. 437 (where the challenge failed on the merits); *Plange v. Chief Constable of South Humberside Police, The Times*, March 23, 1992 (arrest where officer knew that there was no possibility of a charge would be unlawful as the officer had acted on an irrelevant consideration or for an improper purpose): *cf.* below, ???.

[61] See the *Diary of a Police Officer* (2001), p.vi. *www.homeoffice.gov.uk.*

were based had become stronger, with a greater emphasis on independent evidence, although there was still a proportion of suspects who were arrested on limited evidence.[62]

More recent research has been conducted reviewing the impact of PACE.[63] In one extensive survey, Phillips and Brown found that 87 per cent of people arrested had been arrested on the basis of suspicion of committing an offence.[64] They reviewed the procedures following arrest and provided a comprehensive socio-demographic breakdown of arrests and the circumstances leading to arrest.[65] As with stop and search, there are concerns that arrests are not founded on reasonable suspicion, and that there are disproportionate arrest rates of members of ethnic groups.[66]

The broader concerns with the arrest powers in England are that there is a greater move towards depriving individuals of their liberty earlier in the investigative process based on a low threshold of suspicion, and without judicial supervision.[67]

(c) Entry, search and seizure

The police[68] have a wide variety of powers to enter and search premises, and seize property, either with or without a warrant. A large number of statutes enable a judge or magistrate to issue a warrant authorising the entry to and   **14–014**

---

[62] B. L. Irving and I.K. McKenzie, *Police Interrogation: the Effect of the Police and Criminal Evidence Act 1984* (1989), pp. 64–66, 145–147, 193. Here, Irving's 1979 study of practice in Brighton (RCCP Research Study No. 2, 1980) was replicated in 1986 and again in 1987. *cf.* K. Bottomley, *et al., The Impact of PACE: Policing in a Northern Force* (1991), Chap. 4, where research in the period 1987–88 suggested that the changes in arrest powers had comparatively little effect on day-to-day policing on the streets, although the view of most police officers was that there had been a significant reduction in the previous practice of arresting suspects "on a hunch".

[63] *E.g.* D. Brown, *PACE Ten Years On: A Review of the Research* (1997), above.

[64] *Entry into the Criminal Justice System: A Survey of Police Arrests and their Outcomes* Home Office Research and Statistics Paper 185, 1998, p. 27.

[65] 85% of arrestees were male; 15% were juveniles (under 17); 54% were unemployed, 27% employed; and 14% pupils or students; 78% were white, 13% black and 7% Asian (96% of whom were male); over 60% of those arrested had previous convictions; 10% were known to be subject to a court order at the time of arrest. Further statistics on arrest are available annually from the Home Office in its Statistical Bulletins on "The Operation of Certain Police Powers in England and Wales". See those referred to above in respect of stop and search. Philip's and Brown's study "was not designed to explore the links between unemployment and crime, but it does provide striking evidence of the high level of unemployment among criminal suspects" (p. 18). The reason for disproportionate numbers is described as "complex" (p.13). Whether suspects had a criminal history varied considerably according to the offence for which they had been arrested. Figures were higher for those arrested for prostitution, burglary, vehicle related crime and public order, but lower for shoplifting, criminal damage, other theft, and offences of sex and violence(p.20). See also H.O., *Findings from the 2000 BCS* (2001).

[66] See especially the H.O. research of M. Fitzgerald and R. Sibbitt, *Ethnic Monitoring in Police Forces* HORS 173, 1997; Philips and Brown, (1998); S. Holdaway, *The Racialisation of British Policing* (1996) pp. 84–104; D. Smith "Ethnic Origins, Crime and Criminal Justice" in M. Maguire, R. Morgan and R. Reiner (eds), *The Oxford Handbook of Criminology* (2nd ed., 1997).

[67] See P. Hillyard and D. Gordon, "Arresting Statistics and the Drift to Informal Justice in England and Wales" (1999) 26 J.L.S. 502.

[68] We do not consider here the powers of the security services nor the specific statutory powers of various regulatory bodies.

search of specified premises. For example, warrants may be granted to search for stolen goods, obscene publications, drugs and a host of other items.[69]

Prior to PACE, the powers of entry, search and seizure were incoherent and there were some very broad common law powers. If the police were lawfully on premises, whether by consent or in the execution of a warrant or a power to enter premises without a warrant, the decision in *Ghani v. Jones*[70] authorised the seizure of a wide range of material, the ambit of the power to seize being wider than the powers of entry and search. Doubt was cast on whether this broad common law power has survived PACE and the Human Rights Act 1998, but the House of Lords has affirmed its status.[71]

Article 8 of the ECHR protects against infringements of privacy, in the home or workplace, unless prescribed by law and necessary and proportionate to a legitimate aim. The most pertinent legitimate aim here is that of the prevention and detection of crime. The European Court has emphasised repeatedly the importance of adequate safeguards against abuse, notwithstanding the margin of appreciation,[72] especially if the search is conducted otherwise than with judicial supervision.[73]

The 1984 Act introduced a new general power for justices of the peace to issue warrants authorising entry and search for evidence relating to a serious arrestable offence,[74] other than "items subject to legal privilege",[75]

---

[69] Theft Act 1968, s.26; Obscene Publications Act 1959, s.3; Misuse of Drugs Act 1971, s.23; for a full account, see R. T. H. Stone, *Entry, Search and Seizure* (3rd ed., 1997), Chap. 4. The powers are sometimes extremely broad, for example, that under section 26 of the Theft Act is not limited to searching and seizing goods to return them to their rightful owner; it includes a general power to search and seize stolen goods whether identified in the warrant or not: *R. v. Chief Constable of Kent, ex p. Cruikshank*, February 19, 2001, CA (Civ. Div.). See also the wide powers in the Terrorism Act 2000, Sched. 5, para. 3.

[70] [1970] 1 Q.B. 693, CA.

[71] See *R. v. MPC, ex p. Rottman* [2002] 2 W.L.R. 1315, reversing *Rottman v. MPC* [2002] Crim.L.R. (May), DC.

[72] See *Niemitz v. Germany* (1992) 16 E.H.R.R. 97; *Funke v. France* (1993) 16 E.H.R.R. 297.

[73] See *Camenzind v. Switzerland* (1999) 28 E.H.R.R. 458, para. 45.

[74] 1984 Act, s.8. On the endorsement of warrants between U.K. jurisdictions see *R. v. Manchester Stipendiary Magistrates, ex p. Granada* [2000] 1 W.L.R. 1. See generally, C. Walker, [1997] C.L.J. 114.

[75] *ibid.* s.10: generally, communications involving legal advice between professional legal adviser and client, communications concerning legal proceedings, and items enclosed with or referred to in such communications. Documents relating to the date, time and duration of a lawyer client meetings are not privileged: *R. v. Manchester Crown Court, ex p. Roger* [1999] 2 Cr.App.R. 267, DC. See also *R. v. R* [1995] 1 Cr.App.R. 183 (blood sample ordered by solicitor falls within section 10). An expert's report ordered by a solicitor is privileged: *R. v. Davies*, March 4, 2002. Items held with the intention of furthering a criminal purpose are not covered (s.10(2)), regardless of whether the intention is that of the holder or another person: *R. v. Central Criminal Court, ex p. Francis & Francis* [1989] A.C. 346; although such items are likely to be special procedure material: *R. v. Guildhall Magistrates' Courts, ex p. Primlaks Ltd* [1990] 1 Q.B. 261. This definition of the exception may be too broad to be compatible with the ECHR. No legal privilege attaches to a defendant's written statement to his solicitor, voluntarily handed over to the prosecution: *R. v. Cotrill* [1997] Crim.L.R. 56, CA. For comprehensive analysis see J. Auburn, *Legal Professional Privilege: Law and Theory* (2000), Chap. 8. See also *Archbold* (2002), para. 15–103.

"excluded material"[76] or "special procedure material".[77] The magistrate must be satisfied that it is not practicable to communicate with a person who could consent to entry; or although a person could permit entry, it is not practicable to communicate with a person who could permit access to the evidence; or entry to the premises will be denied unless a warrant is produced; or the purposes of the search might be frustrated or seriously prejudiced unless entry could be gained immediately under warrant. Existing powers to grant search warrants were thereafter also subject to the restriction that they could not authorise searches for such material.[78] Instead, an order granting access to excluded material or special procedure material may be granted by a Circuit judge, in limited circumstances. The first set of conditions is that there are reasonable grounds for belief that a serious arrestable offence has been committed, special procedure material which is likely to be relevant evidence and of substantial value to the investigation will be present, alternative methods of securing the evidence have failed or would be futile, and that it is in the public interest to permit access to the material. The second set of conditions are that there are reasonable grounds for believing that excluded material or special procedure material is on the premises and otherwise a search would be permissible within an existing search warrant power.[79] In *R. v. Central Criminal Court, ex p. Bright*,[80] the Divisional Court stressed that the judge had to be satisfied that the statutory requirements for such an order had been established. The judge was not simply asking himself whether the decisions of the constable making the applications were reasonable. If the judge was satisfied that the access conditions existed, he or she was not bound to make the order, but had a discretion to refuse. The judge could take account of factors such as the impact on third parties, the antiquity of matters, the potentially nominal sentence that might be passed, the potential stifling of public debate and the risk of requiring a person to incriminate himself.

---

[76] *ibid.* s.11. This covers confidential personal records, human tissue or tissue fluid taken for medical purposes and confidential journalistic material ("personal records" and "journalistic material" being further defined in ss.12 and 13). Excluded material can, however, be disclosed voluntarily by the holder: *R. v. Singleton* [1995] 1 Cr. App. R. 431 (dental records). Hospital records of patients' admission to and discharge from a mental hospital are "personal records" within PACE, s. 12, as they are records "relating to" their mental health: *R. v. Crown Court at Cardiff, ex p. Kellam* (1993) 16 .B.M.L.R. 76, DC.

[77] *ibid.* s.14. This covers confidential and journalistic material falling outside the definition of "excluded material".

[78] *ibid.* s.9(2).

[79] *ibid.* s.9(1) and Sched. 1. Excluded material is more sensitive than special procedure material and only accessible under (2): see *R. v. Central Criminal Court, ex p. Brown, The Times,* September 7, 1992. Non-compliance with an order is a contempt of court. The application is made *inter partes*, prior notice being given to the person holding the material. The material in question must be specified, either in the notice of application or otherwise: *R. v. Central Criminal Court, ex p. Adegbesan* [1986] 1 W.L.R. 1292; *R. v. Manchester Crown Court, ex. p. Taylor* [1988] 1 W.L.R. 705; but the evidence on which the application is based need not: *R. v. Inner London Crown Court, ex p. Baines & Baines* [1988] Q.B. 579. The suspect need not be notified if he or she is not the holder of the material: *R. v. Leicester Crown Court, ex p. DPP* [1987] 1 W.L.R. 1371. The judge may hold the hearing in open court or in chambers: *R. v. Central Criminal Court, ex p. DPP, The Times,* April 1, 1988. See generally R.T. Stone, [1988] Crim.L.R. 498 and A. A. S. Zuckerman, [1990] Crim.L.R. 472.

[80] [2001] 2 All E.R. 244, DC.

In the last resort, a Circuit judge may issue a warrant authorising a constable to enter and search for such material.[81]

In a series of cases it was acknowledged that PACE presented practical difficulties when large volumes of disputed material were stored on premises.[82] Section 15(5) of PACE, authorises only one entry in pursuit of a warrant, so that it was impossible to complete a search of a large volume of material with a single warrant. The Criminal Justice and Police Act 2001 remedies this problem by providing the power to remove material to be examined elsewhere, and by allowing for the removal of intrinsically linked material (*e.g.* on a computer hard disk). The extended powers allow for seizure even where it may be legally privileged.[83] Specific protection is, however, provided to legally privileged material which can be seized.[84] The 2001 Act requires that notice is given to the occupier specifying what has been seized and the grounds on which it has been seized. The information must include the notification of a right to apply to a judge for the return of seized material and an explanation of how to apply to be present at any examination of the material seized.[85] The occupier or some other person with an interest in the property has an opportunity to be present at the examination.[86] There is a right to apply to the appropriate judicial authority to challenge the use of the powers. The court, on a successful application can order the return of material or, *inter alia*, order that it be examined by an independent third party. There is a duty to secure the material seized pending the hearing of such applications. The Criminal Justice and Police Act 2001[87] also amended PACE so that search warrants and production orders in respect of special procedure material can be endorsed for execution in Scotland.[88]

The 1984 Act clarified and strengthened the safeguards governing the issue and execution of *all* search warrants.[89] For example, entry and search must be within one month of the date of the warrant; it must be at a reasonable hour and the officer in charge must first attempt to communicate with the occupier, unless it appears that would frustrate the object of the

---

[81]   *ibid.* Sched. 1, paras 12–14. This is available, *e.g.* where use of the order procedure might seriously prejudice the investigation.

[82]   *R. v. Chesterfield Justices, ex p. Bramley*, [2001] 1 All E.R 411, DC; *R. v. H.M. Customs and Excise, ex p. Popely* [2000] Crim.L.R. 388, DC; *R. v. Inland Revenue Commissioners, ex p. Tamosius Partners (a firm)* [2000] Crim.L.R. 390, DC.

[83]   See ss. 50–70.

[84]   Section 54. Section 55 provides protections similar to those in PACE for special procedure material but does not apply where the underlying power of seizure is found in legislation where such protection is not afforded.

[85]   Section 52.

[86]   Section 53(4).

[87]   See generally M.Wasik, "Legislating in the Shadow of the HRA: The CJPA 2001" [2001] Crim.L.R. 931.

[88]   See also HO Circular 31/2001. Part X of the Criminal Justice and Public Order Act 1994 deals with the enforcement of arrest warrants across U.K. jurisdictions. Section 86 of the 2001 Act amends PACE so that section 4 of the Summary Jurisdiction (Process) Act 1881 applies to orders and warrants for special procedure and excluded material.

[89]   Sections 15,16. See also the *Code of Practice for the Searching of Premises by Police Officers and the Seizure of Property found by Police Officers on Persons or Premises* (HMSO, 1995) (Code B). See *Archbold* (2002), paras 15-104 and 15-151, Feldman, *Entry, Search and Seizure*, Chap. 6.

search; before the search commences,[90] the officer must identify him or herself and state the purpose of the search and the grounds for undertaking it; the warrant must be shown and a copy of the warrant must be given to the occupier or left at the premises.[91] Searches are only to be conducted to the extent necessary to achieve the object of the search.[92] Breach of these last requirements renders the search and seizure unlawful.[93] Compliance with these requirements is also vital to ensure ECHR compatibility. Courts have been strict in requiring that relevant documentation must be completed, but generous in interpreting when the documents should be made available to the accused. A full record must be kept of searches[94] and a search register must be maintained at each sub-divisional police station with copies of all records required by Code B.[95] The courts have accepted that it is not always necessary for there to be precise details of the materials sought specified on the face of the warrant.[96]

The apparent safeguard of judicial supervision for many PACE searches by the requirement of a warrant being obtained under section 8 may in practice be illusory. In a survey of two city forces, it was found that section 8 had been rarely used.[97] The example of 860 searches of premises disclosed that 12 per cent were conducted under a judicial warrant and 87 per cent under post-arrest powers (75 per cent under section 18, two per cent under section 32, and six per cent following and entry to arrest under section 17).[98] In addition, it has been argued that the judiciary have failed to provide adequate protection for material, when issuing warrants.[99]

There appears to be a steady decline in the use of warrants in favour of the police use of powers to search without prior judicial authorisation. In particular there has been reliance on section 18:[1] in the case of arrestable offences, a constable may be authorised by an officer of the rank of inspector or above to enter and search any premises occupied or controlled by a person under arrest if the constable has reasonable grounds to suspect that there is evidence relating to the offence in question or a similar or related arrestable offence.[2] Requirements for officers to notify occupants of the reasons for searches are applicable when entry is being effected under

---

[90] Not before entry: *R. v. Longman* (1988) 88 Cr.App.R. 148
[91] The occupier may ask a friend or third party to be present unless it would seriously hinder the investigation: para. 5.11.
[92] Section 16(8), Code B.5.9. Premises must be left secure: B.5.12.
[93] *R. v. Chief Constable of Lancashire, ex p. Parker* [1993] Q.B. 577.
[94] Code B.7.
[95] Code B.5.8.
[96] *R. (on the application of Paul Da Costa) v. Thames Magistrates Court* [2002] S.T.C. 267. The case also acknowledged that, the use of questionnaires distributed to those present at the premises being searched may breach section 16(8) of PACE.
[97] Lidstone, (1996), p.334.
[98] *ibid.* p.355, n. 67.
[99] *e.g.* for journalists material: R. Costigan, "Fleet Street Blues; Police Seizure of Journalists Material" [1996] Crim.L.R. 231.
[1] *Lidstone*, p. 362, n. 87.
[2] *ibid.* s.18. This power, unlike s.32, is not limited to cases where the person was there at the time of or immediately before arrest. The authorisation must be contained in an independent document (a record of oral authority included in a notebook is insufficient): *R. v. Badham* [1987] Crim.L.R. 202 (Wood Green Crown Court).

section 18.[3] It remains possible for the police to conduct searches by consent, provided this is given in writing.[4]

The 1984 Act also provides a series of powers for the police to enter premises without a warrant; to execute an arrest warrant; to arrest for an arrestable offence or certain other specified offences which list is regularly added to; including to pursue[5] and recapture a person unlawfully at large; to save life or limb or prevent serious damage to property.[6] The constable must have reasonable grounds for believing that the person sought is there. The constable exercising this power must, unless it is impracticable or undesirable give the occupier a legitimate reason for doing so (not merely that he wants to speak to the occupier).[7] All common law powers of entry were abolished, save that of entry to deal with or prevent a breach of the peace.[8]

Powers of seizure under section 19 are very wide, with a requirement that the officer lawfully on premises reasonably believes that the item was obtained in connection with the commission of an offence or as a consequence of a commission of an offence, that it is not legally privileged, and that it is necessary to seize the item to avoid concealment, loss or destruction.[9] Powers of seizure have been interpreted broadly, and it has been held that the police even have powers under sections 18 and 19 to seize the premises themselves where they are mobile.[10]

For entry to premises to be justified by reference to section 17(1)(b) to arrest a person for an arrestable offence, the police officer entering must have reasonable grounds to suspect the person sought to be guilty of the offence in question; the provision cannot justify entry to effect an unlawful arrest.[11] There is no statutory power of entry for search without a warrant in an extradition context: "arrestable offences" are to be construed as limited to offences so defined in English law.[12]

Where a person is arrested by a constable away from a police station, that person may be searched on arrest if the constable has reasonable grounds to

---

[3] *e.g.* in *Linehan v. DPP*, [2000] Crim.L.R. 685 where officers refused to slide a warrant under the door and the occupier refused to view the warrant pressed to the window. The officers failed to explain the reason for the search. Disappointingly, however, the courts have imposed less stringent requirements of record keeping under s. 18 in some situations. *Krohn v. DPP* [1997] C.O.D. 345, DC, decided under section 18(7). *Cf.* the requirement in section 18(4), which is mandatory. See also *Odewale v. DPP* [2001] 2 Arch. News 2.

[4] Consent by a purported victim of crime does not render inadmissible evidence discovered when the "victim" is prosecuted relying on evidence discovered: *R. v. Sanghera* [2001] 1 Cr.App.R. 299.

[5] Pursuit must be almost contemporaneous with entry: *D'Souza v. DPP* [1992] 4 All E.R. 545.

[6] Section 17. See the court's stay of proceedings when the police had entered, without statutory authority, the premises of an unconscious person to check for the identity of relatives and had discovered quantities of drugs: *R. v. Veneroso* [2002] Crim.L.R. 306 (April).

[7] See *O'Loughlin v. Chief Constable of Essex* [1998] 1 W.L.R. 374 on appeal to the HL; see also *Linehan v. DPP* [2000] Crim.L.R. 685.

[8] As to which see *Thomas v. Sawkins* [1935] 2 K.B. 249; *McLeod v. Metropolitan Police Commissioner* [1994] 4 All E.R. 553; *McLeod v. U.K.* (1999) 27 E.H.R.R. 493. See Feldman, (2002), pp. 601–614.

[9] Section 19(2).

[10] *Cowan v. Metropolitan Police Comr* [2000] 1 W.L.R. 254, CA (Civ. Div.).

[11] *Kynaston v. DPP* (1987) 87 Cr.App.R. 200, DC.

[12] *R. v. Metropolitan Police Comr, ex p. Rottman* [2002] Crim.L.R. 50 (DC); [2002] 2 W.L.R. 1315 (HL).

believe that he or she may present a danger to self or others, or has something which might be used to assist an escape, or which might be evidence relating to an offence. In addition, the constable may enter and search any premises in which the person was at the time of or immediately before the arrest, for evidence relating to the offence in question, if he or she has reasonable grounds to believe that such evidence is there.[13]

Although PACE provides a comprehensive code of search powers, adequate protection against an unjustifiable invasion of privacy is only secured by the strict interpretation adopted by the courts.[14]

(d) Police/state surveillance[15]

Policing has become increasingly reliant on forms of surveillance of suspects that fall short of arrest and do not involve overt entry and seizure from the premises of the individual. Initially such activities were pursued only by the intelligence agencies, but they now form a significant part of everyday policing. Until recently the only detailed regulation of intrusive surveillance was of telephone tapping under the Interception of Communications Act 1985, and the internal Home Office guidelines which regulated other surveillance techniques. The last decade has seen a number of legislative reforms, prompted by the United Kingdom's repeated failure to comply with the ECHR, which have usually been narrowly-tailored direct responses to European Court rulings.[16] The absence of adequate domestic safeguards and regulation was also heavily criticised by domestic courts, notably by the House of Lords in *R. v. Khan*[17] where listening devices were covertly fitted to a suspect's house without, "astonishingly", any statutory regulation of the police action.[18]

Under Article 8 of the ECHR, secret surveillance must be prescribed by law, as well as being necessary and proportionate to achieve a legitimate aim identified in Article 8(2).[19] As the European Court has forcefully explained, state surveillance "can undermine or even destroy democracy on the ground of defending it".[20] There is no doubt that state surveillance is an interference with the private life of the citizen,[21] and that Article 8 will be applicable to police surveillance; the main question will be as to whether the interference

14–015

---

[13] 1984 Act, s.32.

[14] See especially *R. v. Chief Constable of Warwickshire, ex p. Fitzpatrick* [1999] 1 W.L.R. 564.

[15] See Emmerson and Ashworth, (2001), Chap. 6; K. Starmer *et al.*, *Criminal Justice, Police Powers and Human Rights* (2001), Chaps 5, 6, 7, 8 and 9. ; Bailey, Harris and Ormerod (2001), pp.256–274; *Archbold* (2002), para. 15–252 *et seq.*

[16] See *Malone v. U.K.* (1984) 7 E.H.R.R. 14 leading to the Interception of Communications Act 1985; *R. v. Khan* [1997] A.C. 558 leading to the Police Act 1997.

[17] [1997] A.C. 558.

[18] See *Khan v. U.K.* [2000] Crim.L.R. 684; (2001) 31 E.H.R.R. 45.

[19] *Kopp v. Switzerland* (1998) 27 E.H.R.R. 91; *Klass v. Germany* (1978) 2 E.H.R.R. 24. The ECHR and covert surveillance are reviewed by S. Uglow in The Human Rights Act 1998: Part 4: Covert Surveillance and the European Convention on Human Rights [1999] Crim.L.R. 287.

[20] *Klass v. Germany* (1979–80) 2 E.H.R.R. 214.

[21] *Kopp v. Switzerland* (1998) 27 E.H.R.R. 91; *Valenzuela v. Spain* (1999) 28 E.H.R.R. 483; *Khan v. U.K.* [2000] Crim.L.R. 684. See also the recent decision in *Amann v. Switzerland* (2000) 30 E.H.R.R. 843, which seems to adopt a strict approach in interpreting Article 8.

is in accordance with law,[22] is necessary and proportionate to a legitimate aim,[23] and is sufficiently accessible and precise to prevent arbitrary application. A breach of domestic law regarding surveillance will lead to an automatic breach of Article 8.[24]

There is little doubt that the reliance on undercover policing will increase as technology develops to permit this as criminal activity diversifies in more sophisticated ways, and as policing becomes more intelligence led and targeted.[25] It is necessary for the law to have clear regulation, on the process of the authorisation for operation of, and remedies against, such intrusive policing activities.

Interception of public communications was first regulated by the Interception of Communication Act 1985,[26] which proved to be an unduly narrow and very unsatisfactory piece of legislation, some provisions of which necessitated repeated scrutiny by the House of Lords.[27] The protection under the Act was very limited in its application, and is now replaced by the more comprehensive scheme in Part III of the Police Act 1997. The Act provides further limited regulation of surveillance involving entry on/interference with property, and establishes a Commission to regulate such matters. The 1997 Act does not provide a comprehensive Code, nor establish an independent body to supervise such activity.[28] The Act provides immunity from civil and criminal liability for those acting under its terms.[29] The Act does not affect the interception of post or public telecommunications which are now regulated by the Regulation of Investigatory Powers Act 2000.

Under the 1997 Act, in cases of non-sensitive surveillance (*i.e.* not relating to a dwelling, office, hotel bedroom or likely to involve confidential material), the "authorising officer"[30] (or if that is not reasonably practicable a "designated deputy") may issue an authorisation. The authorising officer must believe: that the investigation concerns serious crime as defined in the Act; that the action proposed is necessary because it is likely to be of substantial value in the prevention or detection of serious crime; and that the action sought to be achieved cannot reasonably be achieved by other

---

[22] See *Valenzuala v. Spain* (1999) 28 E.H.R.R. 483.

[23] See generally Emmerson and Ashworth, (2001), Chap. 6 and Q. Whitaker, "Surveillance: General Principles and the Police Act 1997" in K. Starmer *et al.*, (2001).

[24] It is questionable whether English law provides an adequate remedy for such breaches, given the courts' resistance to excluding evidence obtained (*R. v. Khan* [1997] A.C. 558; *R. v. P* [2000] W.L.R. 463).

[25] See generally HMIC, *Policing with Intelligence* (1997); Justice, *Under Surveillance* (1998); S. Davies, *Big Brother: Britain's Web of Surveillance and the New Technological Order* (1996).

[26] See also the Security Services Act 1989 and the Intelligence Services Act 1994.

[27] See *R. v. Preston* [1994] 2 A.C. 130; *R. v. Effik* [1995] 1 A.C. 309; *Morgans v. DPP* [2000] 2 W.L.R. 386; *R. v. Sargent* [2001] 3 W.L.R. 992.

[28] As the Bill passed through Parliament, there were many calls for an independent judicial body to authorise all covert surveillance. The resulting provisions represent a compromise whereby all authorisations are reviewed by an independent commission, but some of those reviews are conducted *after* the authorisation has been given by senior police officers.

[29] Section 92. See generally ss. 91–108. Part III came into force in full on February 22, 1999, as did the Code of Practice issued under section 101: Police Act 1997 (Commencement No. 6) Order 1999 (S.I. 1999 No. 151); Police Act 1997 (Authorisation of Action in Respect of Property) (Code of Practice) Order 1998 (S.I. 1998 No. 3240).

[30] *i.e.* Chief Constable, Metropolitan Police Commissioner or Assistant Metropolitan Police Commissioner, Director Generals of NCIS and NCS, etc.

means.[31] In deciding whether to grant authorisation, the degree of intrusion into the privacy of those affected must be balanced against the gravity of the offence.[32] Once the authorisation has been given, it must be reported to the Commissioners for scrutiny.

Cases of sensitivity must receive *prior* approval of the Commissioner.[33] This must occur in cases where:

> "any of the property specified in the authorisation: is used wholly or mainly as a dwelling or as a bedroom in a hotel; or constitutes office premises; or the action authorised is likely to result in any person acquiring knowledge of: matters subject to legal privilege; confidential personal information; or confidential journalistic material".[34]

The Commissioner must scrutinise the applications and authorisations given by officers "as soon as is reasonably practicable". The Commissioner notifies the authorising officer if valid or notifies the applicant whether the authorisation is given accordingly. Applications for authorisation should specify the "identity or identities of those to be targeted (where known); the property which the intrusive surveillance will affect; the identity of individuals and/or categories of people, where known, who are likely to be affected by collateral surveillance; details of the offence planned or committed; and of the intrusive surveillance involved; how the authorisation criteria have been met; and of any action which may be necessary to retrieve any equipment used in the surveillance. In case of a renewal of an authorisation, the results obtained so far, or a full explanation of the failure to obtain any results. Subsequently it should be recorded whether authority was given or refused, by whom and the relevant time and date.[35] In cases of

---

[31] 'Serious crime' is very broadly defined as conduct which constitutes one or more offences if, and only if: it involves the use of violence, results in substantial financial gain or is conducted by a large number of persons in pursuit of a common purpose, or the offence or one of the offences is an offence for which a person who has attained the age of 21 and has no previous convictions could reasonably be expected to be sentenced to imprisonment for a term of three years or more. Note that serious crime is therefore defined in broader terms than an "arrestable offence".

[32] Special care should be taken where religious ministers, medical or professional counsellors or therapists are involved. Similarly, regard should be had to collateral intrusion into the privacy of persons not suspected.

[33] s.97(2).

[34] See s.98. Legal privilege is broadly defined as in PACE, s.10. For definitions of confidential personal information see s.99. The Code defines it as "information held in confidence concerning an individual (whether living or dead) who can be identified from it, and relating: (a) to his/her physical or mental health; or (b) to spiritual counselling or other assistance given or to be given; and which a person has acquired or created in the course of any trade, business, profession or other occupation, or for the purposes of any paid or unpaid office. It includes both oral and written information and also communications as a result of which personal information is acquired or created." Information is held in confidence if: it is held subject to an express or implied undertaking to hold it in confidence; or it is subject to a restriction on disclosure or an obligation of secrecy contained in existing or future legislation: Code of Practice (2000), paras 1.10, 2.10. Confidential journalistic material includes "material acquired or created for the purposes of journalism and held subject to an undertaking to hold it in confidence, as well as communications resulting in information being acquired for the purposes of journalism and held subject to such an undertaking". In exceptional cases of urgency, an authorisation which should require prior approval can be given by the authorisating officer, but the Commissioner's approval must then be sought.

[35] Code of Practice, para. 2.15.

urgency, these authorisation procedures need not be complied with.[36] There are provisions governing the recording and reporting of authorisations, and regulating the renewal and cancellation of authorisations.[37] In general terms, it is not clear that the distinction between the categories of place protected by the legislation are appropriate to guarantee the privacy to be expected therein. The Act was merely a response to the United Kingdom's failings in ECHR terms rather than a principled and structured solution to the problem of undercover surveillance.

More recently, controversial legislation has been introduced which aims to provide a more comprehensive code of policing and surveillance, including surveillance of internet data. The Regulation of Investigatory Powers Act 2000,[38] (RIPA) regulates surveillance of the types of communication not dealt with in the Police Act 1997: pagers, e-mails, mobile phones, etc. The growth of "cybercrime", coupled with the fact that ordinary forms of criminal activity can be facilitated by internet use (especially fraud, counterfeiting, etc.)[39] rendered a regulatory scheme desirable, and the enactment of the Human Rights Act 1998 served as a catalyst for immediate legislation.

RIPA 2000 extends the powers in relation to postal and telecommunications surveillance by replacing the Interception of Communications Act 1985 (which is repealed). All forms of covert surveillance other than those involving covert entry upon or interference with property or wireless telegraphy are now regulated by RIPA.[40]

The Act aims to ensure compliance with the Human Rights Act 1998, and this is apparent from its structure: each authorisation must be based on necessity and proportionality, and the list of specified aims reflect those in Article 8(2).[41] It is not clear whether the Act achieves compatibility with the Convention. In particular, there are difficulties in the absence of independent supervision of the activities (especially directed surveillance), and of the

---

[36] s.97(3).

[37] See s.95. They are normally of three months duration. The authorisation record should always record "every occasion when interference with property or wireless telegraphy has occurred; the result of periodic reviews of the authorisation; and the date of every renewal": Code of Practice (2000), para. 2.32.

[38] See also the comprehensive discussion of the provisions by Q. Whitaker, "Surveillance: General Principles and the Police Act 1997" in K. Starmer et at., Criminal Justice, Police Powers and Human Rights (2001).

[39] See D.S. Wall, [1998] Crim.L.R. (Special ed.) 79, and O. Ward, (2001) 151 N.L.J. 337 for a discussion of cybercrimes (cybertrespass, cybertheft, cyberobscenity and cyberviolence) and the current methods of regulation and policing of the internet.

[40] Regulation of Investigatory Powers Act 2000 (Commencement No. 1 and Transitional Provisions) Order 2000 (S.I. 2000 No. 2543). See also Q. Whitaker, "The Interception of Communication" in K. Starmer et al., (2001).

[41] The supervision of covert police activities is governed by Part IV of RIPA which provides powers for the appointment of interception of communications commissioners. Provision is also made for the appointment of intelligence service commissioners and chief surveillance commissioners and a tribunal to consider complaints (see s.65). This is less satisfactory than a requirement of full judicial supervision in every case, and the prior authorisation of the Commissioners is not required for every act of surveillance.

inadequate protection for material of an especially confidential status.[42] The provisions of the Act have been heavily criticised by commentators.[43]

Part I of the 2000 Act regulates surveillance over post and telecommunications.[44] The Secretary of State is responsible for authorising all intercepts (which can only be requested by senior officers).[45] The warrants are for limited duration,[46] and the authorisation is reviewed by the independent Interception Commissioner.[47] Although authorisation can be justified on very wide grounds, including the prevention and detection of crime, these provisions represent an improvement on those contained in the 1985 Act, since, for example, they extend to private telephone networks that are connected to public telecommunications systems.[48]

Part II of RIPA provides for the statutory regulation for the first time of covert human policing (undercover officers, informers, entrapment, etc.). All such policing was previously governed only by Home Office guidelines. The bodies regulated by the Act include the police, NCS, NCIS, Customs and Excise, MI5 and MI6.[49] There has been a significant growth in the use of deception[50] and undercover tactics in policing in the last decade, and although regulation is now found in the Codes of Practice of the Association of Chief Police Officers ACPO, as well as those issued under RIPA, a more comprehensive Code would be desirable.

RIPA makes a crucial (but as many have argued flawed) distinction between "directed"[51] and "intrusive" surveillance.[52] "Directed surveillance" is defined as covert surveillance that is undertaken in relation to a specific investigation or a specific operation which is likely to result in the obtaining of private information about a person. "Intrusive surveillance" is defined as covert surveillance carried out in relation to anything taking place on residential premises.[53] Greater protection is afforded for intrusive surveillance than in respect of directed surveillance; with intrusive surveillance requiring authorisation from the Home Secretary or specified senior officers.[54] The grounds for authorisation include that the surveillance is

---

[42] See further Y. Akdeniz, N. Taylor and C. Walker, "RIPA 2000 bigbrother.gov.uk: State Surveillance in the Age of Information and Rights" [2001] Crim.L.R. 73.

[43] Akdeniz, et al., (2001); P. Mirfield, "RIPA: The Evidential Aspects" [2001] Crim.L.R. 91; Q. Whitaker, "Surveillance and Covert Human Intelligence Sources Under RIPA" in K. Starmer et al., (2001).

[44] Prompted by Halford v. U.K. [1997] 24 E.H.R.R. 523. Replacing the 1985 Act with a similar scheme but which covers non-public telecommunications systems — including switchboards, etc. See also the Code of Guidance issued in April 2002.

[45] s.6(2).

[46] Usually three months: s.9(6).

[47] These changes were proposed in the Consultation Paper Interception of Communication in the U.K. Cmd. 4368, (1999).

[48] See R. v. Allan [2001] Crim.L.R. 739.

[49] See further the Draft Code of Practice issued pursuant to s.71 of the Regulation of Investigating Powers Act 2000. Section 71 of RIPA came into force on August 13, 2001 (Regulation of Investigatory Powers Act 2000 (Commencement No. 2) Order 2001 (S.I. 2001 No. 2727)).

[50] See on this A. Ashworth, "should the police be allowed to use deceptive practices?" (1998) 114 L.Q.R. 108.

[51] s.26(2).

[52] s.26(3)–(5).

[53] As defined in s.48.

[54] See RIPA 2000 (Prescription of Officers, Ranks and Positions) Order 2000 (S.I. 2000 No. 2417).

necessary and proportionate to the detection/prevention of serious crime.[55] The authorisation procedure for directed surveillance is much less rigorous, being satisfied by a designated person — in the police, a superintendent. Although the Code specifies that authorising officers should not "ideally be responsible for authorising their own activities",[56] the procedure lacks sufficient independent supervision and has been heavily criticised. The distinction between intrusive and directed surveillance will obviously affect the likelihood of the authorisation being granted and the degree of scrutiny the request receives, and yet the distinction rests on the place being investigated and not on the person affected or the degree of privacy in the individual circumstances.

Part II of the Act also provides for the regulation of "covert human intelligence sources" (informants and other undercover sources). These are defined as people who "establish or maintain a personal relationship with a person for the covert purpose of using the relationship to obtain information or provide access to information to another person or covertly disclosing information obtained by the use of such a relationship or as a consequence of the existence of such a relationship".[57] Given the increased use of such individuals in the era of intelligence-led policing, regulation is welcome, but it is noticeable that the authorisation procedure is limited to that for directed surveillance. There is no offence of failure to obtain an authorisation, but such a failure will amount to an unlawful act under the Human Rights Act 1998.[58]

One of the most controversial aspects of RIPA is the introduction in Part III of powers to compel the compulsory disclosure of encryption keys (or a plain text copy) for electronically-held material.[59] The fear that criminals would be able to exploit the internet and electronic communications systems and that their activities would not be capable of effective investigation and detection led to these far reaching provisions. Despite these powers, which were introduced in the face of considerable opposition, the Act has in fact been criticised for failing to keep pace with technology,[60] and it is inevitable that future amendment will be necessary.

(e) Detention[61]

14–016   PACE greatly improved the position of the suspect in police detention. Prior to the Act the Judges' Rules offered the only protections and these were not of statutory status, were confusing and did not offer comprehensive protection. The pre-PACE provisions[62] had merely required the police to bring detainees to court "as soon as practicable". If this was not practicable

---

[55] s.81(3).

[56] Code of Practice, para. 3.10.

[57] s.26(8).

[58] s.65. Challenges to the legitimacy of surveillance should be made through the tribunal established for this purpose.

[59] See the Home Office, *Building Confidence in Electronic Commerce: A Consultation Document* (1999).

[60] See Akdeniz *et al.*, (2001); H.C. Deb. March 6, 2000, col. 806.

[61] See generally Sanders and Young, (2000), Chap. 4; Bailey, Harris and Ormerod, (2001), pp. 297–348. D. Feldman, [1990] Crim.L.R. 452; *Archbold* (2002), paras 15–181 *et seq*.

[62] Magistrates' Courts Act 1980, s.43(4).

within 24 hours, the police had to consider whether to grant bail, and had indeed to grant bail unless the offence appeared to be "serious" (a term that was not defined). Part IV of the 1984 Act introduced for the first time detailed arrangements regulating the length of time persons may be kept in custody by the police before a court appearance. Under the new arrangements, a person arrested by a constable must be taken to a police station as soon as practicable.[63] This should normally be a "designated police station" (*i.e.* one of the stations designated by the chief officer of police as having enough accommodation for detained prisoners).[64] In some circumstances any station may be used, but no-one may be kept longer than six hours at a non-designated station.

Under section 29 of PACE an individual may be present at the police station without being arrested. The volunteer is free to leave at any time unless he is arrested.[65] The protection afforded to the volunteer is extremely unsatisfactory and requires further legislative clarification, especially as to the information that must be compulsorily provided to such a person and the remedies for breach of these protections. If a person is not arrested, but is cautioned, the officer who cautions him must also inform him that he is not under arrest, that he is not obliged to remain, but that if he does he is entitled to free legal advice.[66]

(i) The custody officer[67]

An important feature of the arrangements for protection during detention is the division of function between the "custody officer" and the officers concerned with the investigation. One or more custody officers (of at least the rank of sergeant) must be appointed for each designated police station[68] and a variety of duties are imposed directly on that officer once a person has been brought to the station. Subject to a few exceptions, the custody officer must not be involved in the investigation.[69] The custody officer is supposed to provide independent scrutiny of the suspect's position in detention. Custody officers have, however, been very heavily criticised. McConville, Sanders and Leng describe officers in their research who were "complicitous in the creation of [an] off-the-record interview by permitting the case officer to visit the suspect in the cells or by authorising his release to the   **14–017**

---

[63] 1984 Act, s.30. Any delay in taking the suspect to the station must not be used to circumvent the procedural guarantees in relation to questioning. See *R. v. Khan* [1993] Crim.L.R. 54; *R. v. Raphaie* [1996] Crim.L.R. 812.

[64] *ibid.* s.35.

[65] See on the abuse by the police of this situation J. McKenzie, R. Morgan and R. Reiner, "Helping the Police with their Inquiries" [1990] Crim.L.R. 22.

[66] Code C.3.15.

[67] See further Ashworth (1998), pp.120–121; Sanders and Young, (2000), pp. 189–201.

[68] There is a *duty* to appoint one and a *discretion* (which must be exercised reasonably) to appoint more: *Vince v. Chief Constable of the Dorset Police* [1993] 2 All E.R. 321. The custody officer is not debarred by the statute from participating with other officers in a ploy involving placing suspects in a bugged cell: *R. v. Bailey and Smith* [1993] 3 All E.R. 513 (not the original authors).

[69] *ibid.* s.36. An officer of any rank may perform the functions of a custody officer if such an officer is not readily available: s.36(4).

interviewroom without recording it".[70] However, in research for the Home Office, Brown[71] found that "custody officers show considerable independence in the way they carry out their job although practical constraints limit their examination of the evidence against a suspect when considering whether to authorise detention.[72] It is important that there is no detention without adequate justification, as Article 5(i)(c) of the ECHR requires.[73]

The range of important responsibilities falling on the custody officer includes:

- The evaluation of whether the person arrested was lawfully arrested. The custody officer is entitled to assume, in the absence of any evidence to the contrary, that the arrest is lawful.[74]

- The custody officer (CO) must determine, as soon as practicable, whether there is sufficient evidence to charge the person arrested (D).[75] It remains unclear as to how the CO is to answer that question. Cape has questioned whether the section is in conflict with the Code of Practice owing to the vagueness of the expression "sufficient evidence to charge".[76] In *R. v. McGuiness*,[77] the court held that the words "sufficient evidence to prosecute" and "sufficient evidence for a prosecution to succeed" (in Code C 16.1)[78] must involve some consideration of any explanation or lack of one from the suspect.[79]

- If in the CO's view there is not sufficient evidence,[80] D must be released (with or without bail), unless the CO has reasonable grounds for believing that D's detention without charge is necessary to secure or preserve evidence relating to an offence for which D is under arrest, or to obtain such evidence by questioning him or her.[81] In that case the CO may authorise D to be kept in police detention, and, if this is done, must open a "custody record" in respect of D, *i.e.* a written record of the various stages and incidents of the period in detention.

---

[70] *The Case for the Prosecution* (1991), p.58.

[71] *Pace Ten Years On* (1997).

[72] *ibid.* p. 2. On the ECHR requirement of independent review under detention, see Art. 5(3); *Schiesser v. Switzerland* (1979) 2 E.H.R.R. 417; Emmerson and Ashworth, (2001).

[73] *Punzelt v. Czech*, April 25, 2000; *Jecius v. Lithuania*, July 31, 2000.

[74] *Clarke v. Chief Constable of North Wales*, May 22, 2000, CA (Civ. Div.), unreported; *DPP v. L* [1999] Crim.L.R. 752.

[75] s.37.

[76] "Detention without Charge, What Does Sufficient Evidence to Charge Mean?"[1999] Crim.L.R. 874.

[77] [1999] Crim.L.R. 318, C.A.

[78] Below, pp. ??

[79] It seems that in practice this is not always the case. For example, in *Martin v. Chief Constable of Avon and Somerset*, October 29, 1997, CA (Civ. Div.) unreported, M was arrested in possession of a small quantity of cannabis, and signed the officer's pocketbook admitting possession. He was nevertheless detained for four hours. The Court of Appeal was not prepared to find that the trial judge could not conclude that s. 37 was exercised properly on the evidence available.

[80] Phillips and Brown, (1998), found that in 61% of cases the evidence on arrest was reported to be sufficient to charge p. 43.

[81] s.37(2).

- If in the CO's view there is sufficient evidence to charge, D must be (i) charged or (ii) released without charge, either with or without bail.[82] Release on police bail is governed by provisions of the Bail Act 1976, as amended by Part II of the Criminal Justice and Public Order Act 1994.[83] Philips and Brown, in research for the Home Office, found that 52 per cent of those arrested in their survey were charged, 17 per cent cautioned, and in 20 per cent of cases there was no further action. Around 17 per cent of suspects were initially bailed for further inquiries, but 44 per cent of these led to no further action.[84]

- If at any time the CO becomes aware that the grounds of detention have ceased to apply, and he or she is not aware of any other grounds on which continued detention under the Act could be justified, he or she must order D's immediate release[85] This is to be without bail unless it appears to the CO (1) that there is need for further investigation of any matter in connection with which D was detained, or (2) that proceedings may be taken against D in respect of any such matter.[86]

- Once D is charged with an offence, the CO must order his or her release (with or without bail[87]). Bail cannot be granted in certain cases[88]: unless: (1) D's name and address cannot be ascertained satisfactorily; or the CO has reasonable grounds for believing (2) that D will fail to appear in court to answer to bail; or (3) that where D is arrested for an imprisonable offence, D's detention is necessary to prevent him or her from committing an offence; or (4) that where D is arrested for a non-imprisonable offence, D's detention is necessary to prevent him or her causing physical injury to another or loss or damage to property; or (5) that D's detention is necessary to prevent him or her from interfering with the administration of justice or the investigation of offences (or an offence); or (6) that D's detention is necessary for his or her own protection. In any of these circumstances, the CO may authorise D to be kept in police detention[89]; Bucke and Brown found that 20 per cent of defendants were refused bail and that 63 per cent were granted unconditional bail.[90]

- The CO also has general responsibilities for the welfare of those in detention including ensuring that the requirements of the Act and the

---

[82] ibid. s.37.

[83] ss.25–30 and Sched 3. (See PACE, s.47, as amended by the 1994 Act, s.27 and the Access to Justice Act 1999, s.90, Sched. 13, paras 125, 127.) Section 47A (added by the Crime and Disorder Act 1998, s.119(1), Sched. 8, para. 62) provides for bringing suspects before early administrative hearings.

[84] Black and Asian suspects were more likely to be bailed than white suspects: p. 82.

[85] s.39

[86] ibid.

[87] For analysis see J. Raine and M. Willson, "Police Bail with Conditions" (1997) 37 B.J. Criminol. 593.

[88] Criminal Justice and Public Order Act 1994, s.25. See generally Sanders and Young, (2000), p.200.

[89] PACE, s.38, as amended by the 1994 Act, s.28(2). In the case of an arrested juvenile (generally persons between 10 and 17) there is a further ground; i.e. that the CO has reasonable grounds for believing that D ought to be detained in his or her own interests: s.38(1)(b).

[90] (1997), Chap. 7.

Code of Practice governing detention are observed.[91] The CO has a vital role in ensuring that D is informed of his rights from the moment of detention. Under Code C,[92] where a person arrives at a police station under arrest, or is arrested there, the CO must tell him clearly of (1) his right to have someone informed of the arrest; (2) his right to consult privately with a solicitor, and the fact that independent legal advice is available free of charge; and (3) his right to consult the Codes of Practice.[93] He must be given (1) a written notice setting out these rights, his right to a copy of the custody record, the terms of the caution (see below), and the arrangements for obtaining legal advice; and (2) an additional notice setting out his entitlements while in custody.[94] Whether the provision of the information is of effective use to the suspect in such circumstances is debateable.[95]

- The CO also has a very important role to play in ensuring that vulnerable suspects are adequately protected with the special safeguards relating to the presence of appropriate adults. Special arrangements apply where the person appears to be deaf, or there is doubt about his hearing, or is juvenile, or is mentally handicapped or suffering from a mental disorder, or is blind or seriously visually handicapped or unable to read.[96] These normally require the involvement of an independent third party such as an interpreter, an approved social worker or an "approved adult" as the case may be.

- A custody record must be opened as soon as it is practicable for each person who is brought to a police station under arrest or who is arrested at the police station having attended there voluntarily.[97] The CO is responsible for the accuracy and completeness of the custody record and for ensuring that it accompanies the detained person on any transfer to another station.[98] Where the person leaves police detention, or is taken before a court, he or she, and his/her legal representative or appropriate adult is entitled, on request, to be given a copy of the record and, on giving reasonable notice, to inspect the original.[99] The custody record will prove crucial if a challenge is made to the detention of the suspect in an attempt to have evidence excluded.[1] As elsewhere in PACE one of the main safeguards for the suspect is the provision of records of all police action.

These various responsibilities may lead a CO into conflict with an officer

---

[91] PACE, s.39. See the *Code of Practice for the Detention, Treatment and Questioning of Persons by Police Officers* (HMSO, 1995) (Code C).
[92] See above.
[93] Code C.3.1.
[94] Code C.3.2.
[95] See Sanders and Young, (2000), p. 209.
[96] Code C.3.6–C.3.14.
[97] Code C.2.1.
[98] Code C.2.3.
[99] Code C.2.4, C.2.5.
[1] In *R. v. Heslop* [1996] Crim.L.R. 730 the Court of Appeal dismissed H's appeal where his admission to murder was recorded in the officer's notebook and signed by H. H had claimed that it should also have been recorded in the custody record. The court denied any such statutory requirement.

of higher rank involved in the investigation. Such matters must be referred to an officer of the rank of superintendent or above.[2]

In view of the importance of the decision to charge a suspect, it has been suggested that it would be advantageous to have CPS legal advisers assisting custody officers with the decisions about charging. The *Narey Report*[3] recommended such a scheme, but once it had been implemented in pilot areas, researchers found it to be unhelpful.[4] The *Auld Report* has, more recently, recommended that the CPS should take over responsibility from the police for charging defendants, in all but minor cases. The aim is to reduce the number of cases in which charges need to be amended when subsequently reviewed by the CPS and to reduce delay. The alteration of charges not only adds to delay but raises false expectations for victims. The government has launched a pilot scheme to evaluate this.[5] These schemes seem to be in conflict of the Philips principle of separation between the investigative and prosecutorial functions. The perception will certainly be that the CPS are not acting as ministers of justice but in a partisan role. Arguably, the act of charging is appropriate for the CPS to perform as an initial step in the prosecution process.

(ii) Periodic reviews

Provision is made for there to be periodic reviews of a person's continued detention in custody. Thus a "review officer" (the CO if D has been arrested and charged, otherwise an inspector or above not directly involved in the investigation) must carry out a review not later than six hours after the detention was first authorised, and then at intervals not longer than nine hours, although these can in some circumstances be postponed.[6] If D has not been charged by the time of the review, the review officer considers again the matters considered by the CO when initially processing D. If D has been charged by then, the CO performs the functions of the review officer. Before authorising D's continued detention the review officer must give D (unless asleep), or any solicitor representing D who is available, an opportunity to make representations about the detention.[7]

14–018

Compliance with these time limit requirements can be important in subsequent false imprisonment actions. For example, in *Roberts v. Chief Constable of Cheshire Constabulary*,[8] R was arrested on suspicion of burglary at 10.50 p.m. and taken to a police station where detention was authorised at 11.25 p.m. At 1 a.m. he was transferred to another station and continued detention was authorised at 1.45 a.m. The first review was conducted at 7.45 a.m., and thereafter at 4.20 p.m. before R was released without charge at 6.55 p.m. R claimed that the first review should have occurred earlier. The Court of Appeal held that the police failure to comply

[2] *ibid.* s.39(6).
[3] 1997.
[4] J. Baldwin and A. Hunt, "Prosecutors Advising in the Police Station" [1998] Crim.L.R. 521.
[5] LCD, Press Release, March 5, 2002.
[6] s.40(4).
[7] *ibid.* s.40.
[8] [1999] 2 All E.R. 326, CA (Civ. Div.).

with mandatory provisions in section 34 rendered the detention unlawful and that it was irrelevant that the detention would have been lawfully continued had the review in fact taken place when it should have. The review should have occurred at 5.25 a.m. and the continued detention after that time was a false imprisonment (even though R was unaware of that at the time).

There were concerns that the requirement for reviews to be conducted by officers in person led to inefficiency, and attempts were made in some forces to conduct video and telephone reviews. In *R. v. Chief Constable of Kent, ex p. Kent Police Federation*[9] it was held that the review under section 40 could not occur by video-link. The Divisional Court also cast doubt on the legality of the telephone review as prescribed in Code C. The Criminal Justice and Police Act 2001[10] immediately reversed the decision, allowing for reviews to be conducted by telephone or by video-link where necessary. In addition, it provides the opportunity to make custody decisions regarding charging, detention and bail by video-link where the custody officer is at a different station. It is questionable whether a video-link will provide an adequate guarantee of the welfare of the detainee, but there is no doubt it will improve efficiency, particularly in forces with remote police stations.

(iii) Time limits for detention without charge[11]

14–019   As to the periods of detention, a person cannot be kept in police detention for more than 24 hours without being charged. The "detention clock" normally starts (the "relevant time") when D arrives at the first police station to which he or she is taken after arrest, or, if D is arrested at a police station after attending voluntarily, at the time of arrest. There are special provisions governing persons brought from another police area or outside England and Wales. After the 24-hour period, a person who is not charged must be released, either with or without bail.[12] Exceptionally, however, a longer period of detention without charge may be authorised. This requires the authority of an officer of the rank of superintendent or above, who must have reasonable grounds of believing that D's continued detention is necessary to secure or preserve evidence relating to the offence for which D is under arrest, or to obtain such evidence by questioning him or her; that the offence in question is a serious arrestable offence; and that the investigation is being conducted diligently and expeditiously.[13] The period of detention can be extended by a further 12 hours beyond the initial 24. Authorisation cannot be given by the superintendent after the expiry of the

---

[9] [2000] Crim.L.R. 854.
[10] s.73 inserting ss.40A and 45A.
[11] Special provisions made under the Terrorism Act 2000, with longer periods of detention possible (seven days maximum) with supervision by a Senior District Judge. These special provisions are not dealt with here, see generally, C. Walker, *The Anti-Terrorism Legislation* (2002).
[12] PACE, s.41.
[13] *ibid.* s.42.

24-hour period or before the second review.[14] In 1999–2000, 570 people were detained for more than 24 hours before being released without charge.[15]

Detention can only be extended beyond the 36-hour period on the authority of a warrant of further detention granted by a magistrates' court.[16] The criteria for the grant of a warrant are the same as for authorisation of continued detention by a superintendent. D must be brought before the court and is entitled to legal representation. The application must be made within the 36-hour period, or, if it is not practicable for a court to sit at the expiry of 36 hours, within six hours thereafter.[17] The warrant may extend the detention for such period as the court thinks fit, up to a maximum of 36 hours.[18] Fresh applications may be made to the court, on the same basis, for the warrant to be extended for further periods not exceeding 36 hours, up to a maximum of 96 hours.[19] The application must be in writing and explain the progress of the investigation and the reason that an extension is sought. If an application for a warrant or an extension is refused, and in any event at the expiry of the 96 hour period, D must be charged or released, with or without bail. Release may, however, be postponed until the expiry of any period of detention that has already been authorised.[20] Full details of the various steps involved in extending periods of detention must be entered in the custody record. Home Office statistics reveal that warrants for detention are rarely refused: in 1999–2000, 224 were made and none of the applications was refused.[21]

Statistics on detention times and the influences drawn from them have been controversial since the original studies conducted for the RCCP. The RCCP found that about 75 per cent of suspects were dealt with within six hours and about 95 per cent within 24 hours. A survey conducted by the Metropolitan Police for three months in 1979 showed that only 0.4 per cent of 48,343 persons had been held for over 72 hours without charge or release.[22] Brown[23] in a review of 10 forces found considerable variations from station to station in the length of detention without charge, this being strongly linked with the seriousness of the crime in question, but also perhaps with differences in the custody officer's approach to PACE. The RCCJ did not think any changes in detention limits was necessary although recommended that further national statistics should be maintained.[24]

---

[14] PACE.

[15] Taken from G. Wilkins and P. Hayward, *Operation of Certain Police Powers Under PACE 1999–2000* (Home Office Research Bulletin 03/01, 2001).

[16] *i.e.* a court of two or more justices sitting otherwise than in open court: section 45(1).

[17] If an application is made after the 36-hour period, the court will dismiss it if it appears that it would have been reasonable for the police to make it within that period: s.43(7); see *R. v. Slough Magistrates' Court, ex p. Stirling* (1987) 151 J.P. 603.

[18] PACE, s.43.

[19] *ibid.* s.44.

[20] For example, by a superintendent where a warrant of further detention is refused (see s.43(15), (16)), or by a warrant if an extension is refused (see s.44(7)(8)).

[21] G. Wilkins and P. Hayward *Operation of Certain Police Powers Under PACE 1999–2000* (Home Office Research Bulletin 3/01, 2001).

[22] RCCP Report, para. 3.96.

[23] D. Brown, *Detention at the Police Station under the Police and Criminal Evidence Act 1984* (H.O. Research Study 104, 1989).

[24] Cm. 2263 (1993), p. 30.

(iv) Detention after charge

14–020   Article 6(3) of the ECHR requires that, on being charged, D must be informed, "in a language which he understands and in detail, of the nature and cause of the accusation against him".[25]

Where D is kept in detention after charge, he or she must be brought before a magistrates' court as soon as is practicable. If this is to be a local court this must be on the day D is charged or the following day; if this is to be a court in a different petty sessions area, D must be removed to that area as soon as practicable and brought before the court on the day of his or her arrival in the area or the following day. If necessary, the clerk to the justices must make special arrangements for a court to sit.[26] A magistrates' court having power to remand a person in custody may, if the remand is for a period not exceeding three clear days, commit him to police detention for the purposes of inquiries into other offences.[27]

(v) The effects of PACE

14–021   Commentators noted dramatic falls in the levels of complaints about treatment by the police in the charge room or cells[28] and improvements in arrangements for the welfare of suspects.[29] However, there are specific problems with the scheme PACE protection for detainees revealed by researchers. The initial authorisation of detention by the custody officer has been found to be, in practice, a formality.[30] Phillips and Brown found it to be exceptional for the custody officer to refuse detention. Of the 4,250 cases examined, only one case was refused.[31]

Furthermore, it has been claimed that the review process (at least at six and 15 hours) tends to become routinised, with little heed paid to any representations.[32] Phillips and Brown in their research for the Home Office found that the average time spent without charge was six hours 40 minutes. The average time for those who sought legal advice was just over nine hours; while for those who did not it was five and a half hours.

---

[25] Art. 6(3). See *Brozick v. Italy* (1989) 12 E.H.R.R. 37 and *Pelissier v. France* (1999) 30 E.H.R.R. 715. Code C, para. 16 requires D to be given a written notice of the offences charged.

[26] PACE, s.46. The clerk has a discretion to arrange for a local court or for a court in another division, in accordance with the wishes of the local justices: *R. v. Avon Magistrates' Courts Committee, ex p. Brooms* [1988] 1 W.L.R. 1246.

[27] Magistrates' Court Act 1980, s. 128(7), (8), as inserted by the 1984 Act, s. 48. In the case of children and young persons, 24 hours: Children and Young Persons Act 1969, s.23(14). There is no power (in s.128(7)) to remand to any other magistrates' court: *R. v. Penrith Justices, ex p. Morley* (1991) 155 J.P.N. 92, 155 J.P. 137.

[28] M. Maguire, (1988) 28 Brit. J. Criminol. 19, 41.

[29] *ibid.* B. L. Irving and I. K. McKenzie, *Police Interrogation: the effects of the Police and Criminal Evidence Act 1984* (1989), pp. 196–198 (replicating the RCCP Research Study No. 2, 1980).

[30] I. McKenzie, R. Morgan and R. Reiner, [1990] Crim.L.R. 22 at 22–27.

[31] (1998), p. 49.

[32] Bottomley, *et al.*, (1991), pp. 91–92. No doubt this will be exacerbated by video review.

The RCCJ[33] noted that the police were "not entirely comfortable with the custody officer role" and that "performance of it, though improving, still leaves something to be desired". They recognised that it might also be unrealistic to expect a custody officer to take an independent view of a case investigated by colleagues.[34] Nevertheless, the role was recommended to remain with the police rather than be handed to the CPS or an independent body. The RCCJ recommended that steps should be taken to develop and strengthen performance of the role, including the delegation of clerical and administrative tasks to civilians under the custody officer's control; refresher-training; the centralisation of custody officer functions within forces wherever practicable and their provision as a separate specialist service; the introduction of computerisation of the custody record process to a national standard; and continuous video-recording (including sound-track) of all the activities in the custody office, the passages and stairways leading to the cells and, if feasible, the cell passage and doors of individual cells.

Improvements in custody suite safeguards have also been prompted by a desire to reduce the number of deaths in custody.[35] The improvements have included: in-cell CCTV; life signs monitors; keeping cell hatches closed but ensuring adequate ventilation in cells; evaluation using nurses and community psychiatric nurses in cell suites; introducing the Association of Police Surgeons' medical forms; and recommending that forces consider establishing "custody users groups".[36]

(e) Treatment of persons in custody

Part V. of the 1984 Act and the Code of Practice on Detention (Code C) give **14–022** the police certain powers to obtain evidence from persons in custody but, more importantly, make detailed provisions as to the conditions in which such persons are kept. It is important to note that the suspect in police custody, is, at that stage of the proceedings, only held on the basis of — at the minimum — a reasonable suspicion; no charges have been laid.

The ECHR is significant in offering protection under Article 5 and Article 3 also protects against torture or inhumane or degrading treatment or punishment. There are occasions on which excessive force used by police officers in the course of detention will amount to a breach of Article 3.[37] If the suspect enters police custody without injury and later suffers such, it is

---

[33] Cm. 2263, pp. 30–34.

[34] Researchers have, however, observed instances of conflict between custody and investigating officers over detention before charge and other matters: Bottomley *et al.*, (1991), Chap. V.

[35] See Home Office, *Deaths in Police Custody Statistics for England and Wales, April 1998 to March 1999*, confirm that in 1998–99, 67 people died in police custody or otherwise in the hands of the police. See the Butler Report, *Inquiry into CPS Decision-Making in Relation to Deaths in Custody and Related Matters* (1998).

[36] *PCA Annual Report 1998–99*. For a medical review of the problems, see Sir Montague Levine, (1998) Medico-Legal Journal 97. See also Home Office, *Drunks and Disorder: Processing Intoxicated Arrestees in Two City Centre Custody Suites* (2002).

[37] See *Rubitsch v. Austria* (1995) 21 E.H.R.R. 573; *Assenov v. Bulgaria* (1998) 28 E.H.R.R. 65; *Selmouni v. France* (1999) 29 E.H.R.R. 403. See also *R. v. DPP, ex p. Treadaway* (1994) (1997) July 31, D.C.

incumbent on the State to provide an explanation for the injury.[38] In extreme cases Article 2's protection of a right to life might also have a role to play, particularly as regards deaths in custody.[39]

As a further safeguard against maltreatment, the custody suite of every police station is subject to an inspection, without warning, from the Independent Custody Visitors (formerly Lay Visitors). These are people selected from the local community who have the right to enter the custody suite to check on the well-being of its occupants.[40]

As noted, one of the main safeguards in the PACE system is the custody officer who has the many responsibilities for the welfare of the suspect as outlined above.[41] The CO must make a record of everything the person detained (D) has with him or her and if necessary D may be searched to enable this to be done.[42] A more intrusive *"strip search"* — a search involving the removal of more than outer clothing — may be necessary to achieve this. Strip searches are conducted in around three per cent of detentions.[43]

An officer of the rank of inspector[44] or above may authorise an *intimate search* if he or she has reasonable grounds for believing D may have concealed on him or her anything which he or she could use to cause physical injury, or a Class A drug (possessed with criminal intent).[45] In 1999–2000 there were 170 intimate searches, 135 of which were for drugs, with 25 leading to the discovery of Class A drugs. In 1999–2000 of the 170 searches, four were carried out by a police officer, 12 in the presence of a suitably qualified person, and 138 by a suitably qualified person.[46]

An inspector[47] may also authorise D's *fingerprints*[48] to be taken without consent if he or she has reasonable grounds for suspecting D's involvement in a criminal offence and that the fingerprints will tend to prove or disprove

---

[38] See *Aksoy v. Turkey* (1996) 23 E.H.R.R. 553.

[39] The latest recommendations to reduce deaths in custody are contained in a PCA publication *One Year On, Deaths in Police Custody: the Risks Reduced* (1999). On deaths in custody, see A. Leigh, G. Johnson and A. Ingram, *Deaths in Police Custody: Learning the Lessons* (1998) P.R.S. No. 26. The PCA report notes that Art. 2 of the ECHR provides a right to life protected by law. Under the Human Rights Act 1998, "any force failing to provide adequate training for officers, systems and medical care for the preservation of life of incapacitated prisoners may be exposed to legal action". See also PCA, *Policing Acute Disturbance* (2001).

[40] For operation of the scheme see H.O. Circular 15/2001.

[41] Note also the special responsibilities as regards the child or young person detained in the station (see s.37 as amended) and the responsibilities regarding those with handicaps and disabilities.

[42] PACE s.55, as amended by the Criminal Justice Act 1988, Sched. 15, para. 99. Items may be seized on the same grounds as those set out in s.54(4): s.55(12).

[43] T. Bucke and D. Brown, *In Police Custody: Police Powers and Suspects' Rights under the Revised PACE Codes of Practice* (1997), p. 48.

[44] Formerly the requirement was for a superintendent: see s.78, CJPA 2001.

[45] *ibid.* s.55, as amended by the 1988 Act, Sched. 15, para. 99. Items may be seized on the same grounds as those set out in s.54(4): s.55(12).

[46] M. Ayres *et al.*, *Arrests for Notifiable Offences and the Operation of Certain Police Powers Under PACE*, (Home Office Statistical Bulletin 19/01, 2001).

[47] Formerly the requirement was a superintendent or above, see s.79, CJPA 2001.

[48] s.78(8) of the CJPA 2001 extends the definition of fingerprints to "a record of the skin pattern and other physical characteristics or features of the fingers or palms", and s.78(7) allows for electronic fingerprinting. Note that the National Automated Fingerprints Identification System gives all forces access to a full national database of convicted criminals' fingerprints on their use at trial. See also *R. v. Buckley* (1999) 163 J.P. 561.

that involvement.[49] Section 78 of the CJPA 2001 also authorises fingerprints to be retaken from a person convicted or charged with any recordable offence if the quality was poor or the originals are unusable, and allows for compulsory fingerprinting in cases where the suspect has been cautioned or reprimanded for a recordable offence.

The inspector[50] has a similar power to authorise a "*non-intimate sample*"[51] to be taken without consent.[52] Before it is taken the suspect must be warned of its potential use in speculative searches and told of the reasons why the sample is being taken. Non-intimate samples are taken in around seven per cent of cases across a wide range of offences, but most often in cases of rape and other sexual offences.[53] Approximately five per cent of these samples are taken consensually. In most cases, non-intimate samples are taken after charge,[54] rather than as a part of the investigation itself.[55] There is currently no PACE guidance on taking other samples (*e.g.* voice samples).[56]

An "*intimate sample*"[57] may only be taken if there is *both* authorisation by an inspector[58] *and* written consent.[59] Authorisation need not precede consent.[60] Under PACE, the authorising officer had to have reasonable

---

[49] *ibid.* s.61. No such authorisation is necessary if D has been charged with, informed that he or she will be reported for, or convicted of, a "recordable offence" (*i.e.* an offence specified in the National Police Records (Recordable Offences) Regulations 1985 (S. I. 1985 No. 1941)); all imprisonable offences and a few others). Fingerprinting may be taken at any time with consent. Broadly similar provisions govern the photographing of persons arrested: Code D.4. Over 40% of suspects have their photographs taken, with around 10% having them taken without consent. T. Bucke and D. Brown, (1997), p. 49. The amendment to PACE by the Anti-Terrorism, Crime and Security Act 2001 allows for the photographing of suspects and retention of their images (subject to their being charged, prosecuted for a recordable offence, cautioned or warned for a recordable offence or their having consented).

[50] Formerly the requirement was a superintendent: CJPA 2001, s.80.

[51] *i.e.* sample of hair other than pubic hair; a sample taken from or from under a nail; a swab taken from any part of the body including the mouth but not any other body orifice; saliva; or a footprint or similar impression of any part of the body other than a part of the hand: s.65, definitions substituted by the Criminal Justice and Public Order Act, ss.58, 59(1). The definition of non-intimate sample is amended by the CJPA 2001, s.81 so that "skin impressions'" may be taken (previously footprints were the only listed non-intimate sample of this nature). The 1994 Act reclassified samples from mouth swabs as non-intimate, in accordance with a recommendation by the RCCJ (Cm. 2263, pp. 14–15). This assists DNA profiling: see B. Steventon, (1995) 59 J. Crim. Law 411.

[52] PACE, s.63, as amended by the 1994 Act, s.55: prior to the 1994 Act this power was confined to suspected serious arrestable offences; the RCCJ (Cm. 2263, pp. 14–15) merely recommended extension of sampling powers to assault and burglary.

[53] T. Bucke and D. Brown, (1997), p. 43. See the extension of the powers under the Criminal Evidence (Amendment) Act 1997 in relation to the taking and storage of such samples.

[54] The Criminal Evidence (Amendment) Act 1997 allows for non-intimate samples to be taken from a person to whom the Act applies (*inter alia*: those imprisoned for sexual, violent and other specified offences).

[55] Bucke and Brown (1997), p. 45.

[56] See on voice identification D. Ormerod, "Sounds Familiar: Voice Identification Evidence" [2001] Crim.L.R. 595; and see *P.G. v. U.K.* [2002] Crim. L. R. 595.

[57] *i.e.* a sample of blood, semen or any other tissue fluid, urine or pubic hair, a dental impression, or a swab taken from a person's body orifice other than the mouth: s.65, definitions substituted by the 1994 Act, s.58. The reference to dental impressions was added on the recommendation of the RCCJ (Cm. 2263, p. 15).

[58] Formerly the requirement was of a superintendent.

[59] PACE, s.62, as amended by the 1994 Act, s.54. A court or jury may draw such inferences as appear proper from a refusal without good cause, and a refusal may constitute corroboration: s.62(10).

[60] *R. v. Butt* [1999] Crim.L.R. 414.

grounds to suspect involvement in a serious arrestable offence; this was broadened significantly to *any* recordable offence by the Criminal Justice and Public Order Act 1994.[61] The definition of an "intimate sample" was extended by the 1994 Act,[62] with dental impressions now included, but mouth swabs relegated to the non-intimate category.[63] Suspects should be cautioned in accordance with Code D Note for Guidance A before a sample is taken. Home office researchers found that intimate samples are taken "very rarely",[64] with blood being the most common form of sample.

The protections in the PACE scheme for taking samples have been eroded by successive statutes. Formerly, an intimate sample other than a sample of urine could only be taken by a registered medical practitioner (or registered dentist in the case of dental impressions).[65] Under the CJPA 2001, the taking of an intimate sample can now be taken by a registered nurse. Section 62(1A) of PACE allows for intimate samples to be taken when a person is not in police detention, if the persons's previous two non-intimate samples have been taken in the course of the investigation and they have proved insufficient.[66]

As a further development, section 57 of the Criminal Justice and Courts Services Act 2000[67] provides new powers for police to take non-intimate samples, including urine, to test for specified Class A drugs. These powers apply to people who have been *charged* with an offence. This provision followed widespread concern at the number of arrestees who tested positive for Class A drugs in a pilot study: some areas had rates as high as 78 per cent.[68] The power is subject to a number of conditions: (1) that the detainee is charged with a "trigger offence" (essentially those related to Class A drugs and acquisitive offences), or another offence and an inspector or above has reasonable grounds to suspect that Class A drug misuse caused or contributed to the offence charged; (2) that the detainee is over 18; (3) that the officer has requested a sample; (4) that the officer informs the detainee of the grounds for authorisation (if appropriate) and warns that a failure to provide a sample without good cause may render the person liable to prosecution.[69] The results can be used in sentencing, and in making decisions relating to bail and detention.[70] There is no prohibition on using the results in evidence.

Recent amendments to PACE enable samples to be checked against records (which is particularly significant in the case of DNA samples), and

---

[61] s.54 amending s.62.

[62] s.58.

[63] The latter change was effected in Northern Ireland by the Criminal Justice Act 1988, Sched. 14; for criticism see M. Gelowitz, [1989] Crim.L.R. 198 and C. Walker and I. Cram, [1990] Crim.L.R. 479.

[64] Bucke and Brown, (1997), p. 46.

[65] PACE, s.62(9), as amended by the 1994 Act, s.54(5).

[66] An inspector must authorise such a sample and the suspect must consent.

[67] Inserts a new s.63B into PACE.

[68] See T. Bennett, *Drug Testing of Arrestees Research Programme* (1999). See recently A. Sondhi, J. O'Shea and T. Williams, *Statistics from the Arrest Referral Monitoring Programme for October 2000–March 2001* (HORS, 2001).

[69] Subsection (8) provides an offence with maximum imprisonment of three months for failing to provide a sample. Samples are taken by persons as prescribed in regulations made by the Secretary of State.

[70] s.57(7).

for a constable to require a charged or convicted person to attend a police station to have a sample taken.[71] Provision was made for the destruction of fingerprints or samples unless the person concerned was convicted.[72] Use of DNA from destroyed samples to create a database for statistical use is permissible.[73] The House of Lords also held[74] that although DNA samples should have been destroyed under PACE, this did not prevent the admissibility of evidence derived from samples gained from an investigation based on those illegally held samples.[75] Section 82 of the CJPA 2001 now removes the obligation to destroy samples and prints where the suspect was cleared of an earlier offence.[76] The retention of samples and private data is subject to the safeguards in Article 8 of the ECHR.[77] The English courts have held that the retention of DNA samples and fingerprint evidence after a suspect has been cleared of the offence is not incompatible with Article 8.[78]

The use of intimate samples at trial will not constitute a breach of the privilege against self-incrimination. As the ECtHR noted in *Saunders v. U.K.*,[79] the right not to incriminate oneself does not extend to the use in criminal proceedings of material "which may be obtained from the accused through the use of compulsory powers but which has an existence independent of the will of the suspect such as, *inter alia*, documents acquired pursuant to a warrant, breath, blood and urine samples, and bodily tissues for the purpose of DNA testing".[80] Article 8 privacy issues could arise however.

Other important rights provided for the suspect by PACE include the right to have someone informed[81] when arrested and to have access on

---

[71] PACE, s.63A, inserted by the 1994 Act, s.56.

[72] This applied to DNA profiles. PACE, s. 64, as amended by the 1994 Act, s. 57, to enable samples that would otherwise have to be destroyed to be retained for statistical purposes only. *R. v. Nathaniel* [1995] 2 Cr.App.R. 565, CA.

[73] *R. v. Willoughby* [1997] 1 Arch. News 2.

[74] *Attorney-General's Reference No. 3 of 1999* [2001] 2 A.C. 91; and see [2000] Crim.L.R. 995 and commentary.

[75] For an application of the House of Lords decision, see *R. v. Langley* [2001] EWCA Crim 732, CA (Crim. Div.).

[76] This puts the decision of the House of Lords in *Attorney-General's Reference No. 3 of 1999* on a statutory footing. A new s.64(3AA) is substituted for the old s.3(A) and (B) and also allows for samples from volunteer mass screenings to be retained if the person is convicted or has given consent (which cannot be withdrawn).

[77] See *Murray v. U.K.* (1994) 19 E.H.R.R. 193; *X. v. Germany* (1976) 3 D.R. 1024. See further, Q. Whitaker, "General Surveillance and the Collection and Retention of Personal Data" in K. Starmer *et al.*, (2001).

[78] See *R. v. Chief Constable of South Yorkshire, ex p. Marper*, March 22, 2002.

[79] (1997) 23 E.H.R.R. 313; see Emmerson and Ashworth, (2001), para. 15–27.

[80] para. 69.

[81] PACE, s.56. This replaced the Criminal Law Act 1977, s.62. In addition, the person responsible for the welfare of an arrested child or young person must, if practicable be informed: Children and Young Persons Act 1933, s.34(2)–(11), substituted by the 1988 Act, s.57.

request to legal advice.[82] Currently, around one-fifth of suspects exercise the right to have a person contacted to inform them of the detention.[83] This right is recognised by the ECHR[84] and is regarded as particularly important for contact with the family of detainees.[85] Under PACE Code C, if the third party chosen cannot be contacted, D may choose up to two alternatives; attempts beyond these may be allowed as a matter of discretion.[86] D must be informed that any letter, call or "message (other than to a solicitor) may be read or listened to as appropriate and may be given in evidence; a telephone call may be terminated if abused; the costs can be at public expense at the discretion of the custody officer.[87] D may receive visits at the custody officer's discretion.[88] If a friend, etc., makes inquiries about D's where-abouts, the information must be given if D agrees, provided there has been no decision to delay D's right to communicate.[89] D's communication with others may be denied or delayed by an officer of the rank of inspector or above if he considers that they may result in either of the conditions in section 56(5)(a) or (b) (in the case of a person detained for an arrestable or serious arrestable offence).[90]

Even more important is the right to consult a solicitor[91] privately[92] at any time. The right of access to a solicitor vests in the detainee alone, so that a solicitor has no right of access to a client in the custody area.[93] Code C provides that all people in police detention must be informed that they may

---

[82] *ibid.* s.58. This express legal right replaced the much weaker statement in the Preamble to the Judges Rules that a person under investigation should be able to consult a solicitor privately, even if he or she was in custody, provided no unreasonable delay or hindrance was caused to the investigation or the administration of justice. This was not a legal requirement: in practice few suspects asked to see a solicitor and many requests were refused: see below, see text below. In *R. v. Chief Constable of South Wales, ex p. Merrick* [1994] 1 W.L.R. 663, DC, the court recognised a common law right of access to a lawyer of a person on remand in custody at a magistrates' court (s.58 of PACE was not applicable).

[83] D. Brown, *PACE Ten Years On* (1997), p. 3.

[84] See *McVeigh, O'Neill, and Evans v. U.K.* (1981) 5 E.H.R.R. 71.

[85] See *Cicek v. Turkey* February 27, 2001.

[86] Code C.5.1.

[87] Code C.5.7.

[88] Code C.5.4.

[89] Code C.5.5.

[90] The officer must have reasonable grounds for believing that exercise of the right will lead to interference with evidence connected with a serious arrestable offence; interference with or injury to other persons; or the alerting of others suspected of such an offence but not yet arrested; or will hinder the recovery of any property obtained as the result of such an offence, or the value of the suspect's proceeds of drug trafficking.

[91] This extends to cover a trainee solicitor, a duty solicitor representative or an accredited representative on a register maintained by the Legal Aid Board (now Legal Services Commission); other representatives are to be admitted unless an officer of the rank of inspector or above considers that such a visit will hinder the investigation of crime: Code C.6.12. See *R. v. Chief Constable of the Avon and Somerset Constabulary, ex p. Robinson* [1989] 1 W.L.R. 793. There can be no blanket ban on a particular solicitor's representative: *R (Thompson) v. C.C. of Northumbria* [2001] EWCA Civ 321.

[92] See Emmerson and Ashworth (2001), Chap. 5, part L. See *S. v. Switzerland* (1992) 14 E.H.R.R. 670 and Article 6(3)(c); *R. (M). v. M.P.C.* [2002] Crim.L.R. 215, holding that failure to provide the accused with a room for private consultation did not breach Art. 6(3) is probably wrongly decided see *PG and JH v. U.K.* [2002] Crim.L.R. 308, finding a breach of Art. 8 where police cells were bugged. The Terrorism Act 2000, Sched. 8, para. 9 provides that an Assistant Chief Constable can, in specified circumstances, direct that consultation will be in the sight and hearing of an independent officer.

[93] *Rixon v. Chief Constable of Kent, The Times,* April 11, 2000, CA (Civ. Div.).

at any time consult and communicate privately, whether in person, in writing or on the telephone, with a solicitor and that independent legal advice is available free of charge from the duty solicitor.[94] A poster advertising the right to legal advice must be prominently displayed in the charging area of every police station.[95] No police officer must at any time do or say anything with the intention of dissuading a person in detention from obtaining legal advice.[96] D is reminded of the right to legal advice at the beginning of each interview.[97]

The right of access to a solicitor is backed by a statutory 24-hour duty solicitor scheme. Research on the operation of the PACE arrangements indicated that initially there was a significant increase in the number of suspects seeking legal advice, although they still only constituted a minority; that a variety of ploys were used by the police to discourage exercise of the right; that only a small proportion of suspects had a lawyer with them during police interrogation; and that there might have been a rise in the number of suspects who refused to make admissions.[98] Phillips and Brown confirmed early research findings that those who might benefit most from legal advice "often did not request it because they were anxious not to delay their time in custody or because they were told that they probably would not be charged".[99] Their research also revealed that requests for legal advice varied significantly depending on the offence, and the station at which the suspect was held. In addition, "significant predictors of demand for legal advice [included] ethnic[ity], employment status; previous convictions; condition on arrival at the station; and whether answering police bail".[1]

The improper denial of the right to legal advice is likely to lead to exclusion under section 78 of PACE of any confession.[2] Denial of the right to legal advice might also constitute a breach of Article 6 of the ECHR. The ECtHR has repeatedly emphasised the importance of "prompt" access to legal advice.[3] The right is recognised as important under the Convention; it is not absolute but it is of "paramount importance" when inferences from silence are in issue.[4]

Delay in the exercise of these rights can only be authorised by an officer of the rank of superintendent or above in respect of a person in custody for a serious arrestable offence: the officer must have reasonable grounds for

---

[94] Code C.6.1. On ECHR guarantees of free legal representation, see Art. 6 and *Pakelli v. FRG* (1984) 6 EHRR 1.

[95] Code C.6.3.

[96] Code C.6.4.

[97] Code C.11.2.

[98] See Sanders and Young (2000), pp. 491–492; D. Brown, *Detention at the Police Station under the Police and Criminal Evidence Act 1984* (HORS No. 104, 1989), Chap. 3 and HORPU Bulletin 26; A. Sanders *et al., Advice and Assistance at Police Stations and the 24 Hour Duty Solicitor Scheme* (LCD, 1989) and A. Sanders and L. Bridges, [1990] Crim.L.R. 494; B.L. Irving and I. K. McKenzie, *Police Interrogation* (1989), pp. 53–59, 113–115,157–164,199–200; A. Sanders and L. Bridges in C. Walker and R. Starmer (1999).

[99] (1998), p. 59.

[1] *ibid.* p. 62.

[2] See *R. v. Samuel* [1998] Q.B. 615.

[3] *Imbroscia v. Switzerland* (1993) 17 E.H.R.R. 444; *Murray v. United Kingdom* (1996) 22 E.H.R.R. 29; *Condron v. United Kingdom* (2001) 31 E.H.R.R. 1; [2000] Crim.L.R. 679. *Magee v. U.K.* [2000] Crim.L.R. 681; *Averill v. United Kingdom* [2000] Crim.L.R. 682. See also the U.N. *Basic Principles on the Role of Lawyers* (1990) principles 5 and 8.

[4] See below para. 14-024. See also Youth Justice and Criminal Evidence Act 1999, s. 58.

believing that exercise of the right will lead to interference with evidence connected with a serious arrestable offence; interference with or injury to other persons; or the alerting of others suspected of such an offence but not yet arrested; or will hinder the recovery of any property obtained as the result of such an offence, or the value of the suspect's proceeds of drug trafficking.[5] In any event, D must be allowed to exercise these rights within 36 hours of the "relevant time".[6] Phillips and Brown[7] found no instance of delay in their survey of 4,250 cases. In one research study, there was no such finding in a sample of 12,500 cases, and previous research has found the percentage of cases to be less than one per cent.[8]

Where a person is permitted to consult a solicitor, who is available when the interview begins or is in progress, the solicitor must be allowed to be present at the interview.[9] The solicitor may only be required to leave if his conduct is such that the investigating officer is unable properly to put questions, and on the authority of an officer not below the rank of superintendent.[10]

The quality of legal advice remains controversial. A report by Sanders *et al.*[11] was critical of the quality of service provided by duty solicitors, with a high proportion relying on telephoned advice rather than attendance in person. Phillips and Brown's research confirms that telephone advice is still much more likely from a duty solicitor than a suspect's own.[12] In the last few years there has been a rise in the number of face-to-face consultations, with a decline in telephone advice.[13] Moreover, the length of the consultation lasted, on average, 15 minutes, which represents a considerable increase than that revealed in earlier research.[14] The Legal Aid Board changed the rules to require attendance in person other than in exceptional cases where the suspect is to be questioned about an arrestable offence or an identity parade is to be held, or the suspect complains of serious maltreatment by the police.[15] The use of unqualified legal advisers presents concern: 35 per cent of cases where the suspect had requested his own solicitor involved unqualified advisers (prior to the Law Society's accreditation scheme).

---

[5] "Will" not "might": *R. v. Samuel* [1988] Q.B. 615: on the ECHR dimension, see *Bonzi v. Switzerland* (1978) D.R. 185; Emmerson and Ashworth (2001), para. 5–38.

[6] 1984 Act, ss.56(2)–(9), 58(5)–(11), as amended by the Drug Trafficking Offences Act 1986, s.32; Code C, Annex B(A). Access may not be delayed on the ground that the solicitor might advise the person not to answer any questions: *ibid.* Part (A)3. Access may only be delayed by reference to the specific circumstances of the case: general fears that solicitors will unwittingly carry out messages, etc., will not be sufficient: *R. v. Samuel*, above; *cf. R. v. Alladice* (1988) 87 Cr.App.R. 380; *R. v. Davison* [1988] Crim.L.R. 442.

[7] (1998), p. 281.

[8] T. Bucke and D. Brown (1997), p. 23.

[9] Code C.6.8.

[10] If readily available, and otherwise an officer not below the rank of inspector who is not connected with the investigation: Code C.6.9, C.6.10.

[11] Sanders, *op. cit.* n. 98.

[12] *op. cit.* p. 66.

[13] T. Bucke and D. Brown (1997), p.24.

[14] *ibid.* (1998), p.28.

[15] See E. Cape, *Legal Action*, March 1991, p. 21.

Research was critical of the quality of legal advice made available.[16] The RCCJ found the evidence on the quality of legal advice to be "disturbing" but, rather weakly, thought the answer lay in improved training, supervision and monitoring.[17] Brown's review, in *PACE Ten Years On*, found that around 38 per cent of suspects now request legal advice and that the figure is rising. By 1997, Bucke and Brown reported that the figure was 40 per cent.[18] Of those who request legal advice, around 80 per cent receive it.[19] Custody officers were successful in contacting advisers in 88 per cent of cases in Phillips and Brown's study. Nevertheless commentators claim that: "whether by accident or design, many officers discourage recourse to legal advice much of the time".[20]

Ironically it is the behaviour of defence lawyers that has recently prompted the Metropolitan Police Commissioner to attack the legal profession for its role in escalating crime rates and the hinderance of the police.[21] At the same time, Sanders and Young write that suspects are "nearly as much at risk from legal representatives as from the police themselves".[22]

PACE Code C sets out in some detail many other requirements as to the physical conditions in which detainees are kept[23]; the handling of any complaints[24] about treatment in custody and medical treatment,[25] the welfare of detainees being the basic responsibility of the custody officer. Concerns about the care and welfare of the suspect in detention have increased in recent years. Phillips and Brown found that four per cent of arrestees were too drunk to be dealt with on arrival, one per cent were violent and one per cent were totally unco-operative with the custody officer.[26] There have been suggestions to "divert" these people from the police custody suite into other facilities, *e.g.* "detoxification facilities".[27]

Soon after PACE came into force, Maguire reported that the levels of

---

[16] See J. Baldwin, *The Role of Legal Representation at the Police station* (RCCJ Research Study No. 3, HMSO, 1992); M. McConville and J. Hodgson, *Custodial Legal Advice and the Right to Silence* (RCCJ Research Study No. 16, HMSO, 1993).

[17] pp. 37–39.

[18] On the legal profession's attitude to duty solicitor schemes see Sanders and Young (2000), pp. 228–230, and see the discussion of the impact of the new Criminal Defence Service.

[19] D. Brown, *PACE Ten Years On* (1997), p. 2.

[20] Sanders and Young (2000), p.227. On the poor quality of legal advice see L. Bridges and S. Choongh, *Improving Police Station Legal Advice* (1998) and L. Bridges, E. Cape, A. Abubaker and C. Bennett, *Quality in the Criminal Defence Service* (2000).

[21] Sir John Stevens, *The Sunday Times* March 10, 2002. See, *e.g.* B. Houlden, (2002) 152 N.L.J. 381, commenting on Sir John Stevens' statements.

[22] p. 228. See also E. Cape, "Incompetent Police Station Advide and the Exclusion of Evidence" [2002] Crim.L.R. 471.

[23] Code C.5, covering, *e.g.* visits, provision of writing materials, and giving an additional right to make one telephone call; C.8., covering, *e.g.* the heating, cleanliness and ventilation of cells, bedding, toilet facilities, clothing, meals, exercise and hourly visits.

[24] Code C.9.1. Complaints must be dealt with by an officer of at least the rank of inspector not connected with the investigation.

[25] Code C.9.2–9.6. Special provision is also made for the treatment in custody of the mentally ill, the handicapped, and overseas nationals: C.1.4, 1.6, 3.6–3.14.

[26] *op. cit.* p. 51. See also HORS Paper No. 183, *Drugs and Crime: The Results of Research on Drug Testing and Interviewing Arrestees.* (2001) HORS No. 183. See also A. Sondhi *et al., Statistics from the Arrest Referral Monitoring Programme* ((Home Office, 2001).

[27] See further *Deaths in Custody, Statistics for England and Wales Apr 1999–Mar 2000* (Home Office, 2000).

complaints about treatment by the police in the charge room or cells had fallen dramatically in three of the four areas studied, and that conditions in charge rooms and cells, although not fully satisfactory, had clearly improved. He was surprised by the relaxed and even polite manner in which the procedures were often carried out.[28] Irving and McKenzie noted that the custody officer role and the record-keeping requirements "have, in Brighton at least, eliminated casual infringement of suspects' welfare rights". Moreover, "the system is now so constituted that if a serious breach of the rules governing the welfare of prisoners does occur, a serious conspiracy would now be necessary to avoid its detection".[29] Despite these early indications the safeguards in PACE do not always protect the suspect adequately against police impropriety, and yet, in successive amendments to the Act the protections have been eroded by Parliament.

(f) Questioning

14–023   Detailed provision is made in PACE Code C governing the questioning of persons in custody. This replaced the non-statutory Judges' Rules and Administrative Directions to the Police, which had previously provided guidance as to the proper conduct of interrogations.[30] As noted at the beginning of the chapter, the pre-trial process has an enormous impact on the trial process. The significance of the interview in securing confessions and incriminating evidence cannot be underestimated. We offer an outline of the most important aspects of the regulation of questioning.[31]

When introduced, the PACE scheme of regulating questioning represented a clear improvement on the previous procedures. Since then, its effectiveness in protecting the suspect has been undermined in a number of ways: successive parliamentary amendments to PACE have diluted the protections on offer, and, particularly in the case of the right to silence, have undermined the policy behind the scheme. In addition, the protection that PACE offered has been recognised to be defective, for example, in its failure to offer adequate remedies for the breaches of the protections and because some of the key protections are contained only in the Codes of Practice and not in the statute itself. Since PACE, there has however also been an increased awareness of the dangers of false confessions from all suspects in custody not just those in specific categories of vulnerability. The RCCJ did not make any substantial recommendations to improve the position, and although the Human Rights Act 1998 has in some areas led to strengthening of protections, the scheme still has the potential to allow miscarriages of justice. The implementation of a Code of Criminal Procedure, as recommended by Auld,[32] would provide an opportunity to strengthen the protections.

---

[28] (1988) 28 Brit. J. Criminol. 19 at 41.
[29] B. L. Irving and I. K. McKenzie, *Police Interrogation: the Effects of the Police and Criminal Evidence Act 1994* (1989), pp. 196–198.
[30] The Judges' Rules originated in 1906, with revised versions issued in 1964 and 1978 together with related Administrative Directions from the Home Office. Compliance with the Rules would tend to ensure that a confession was admissible. Breach of a particular Rule or Direction might, but in practice normally did not, render the confession inadmissible.
[31] See Sanders and Young, (2000), Chaps 4 and 5 and *Ashworth* (1998), Chap. 4 for excellent reviews.
[32] Chapter 1.

(i) The right to silence

A central feature of the position of a person under interrogation (at least in **14-024** theory) has until recently been the so-called "right to remain silent" or "right of silence".

In general, the police may ask any person such questions as they think appropriate.[33] However, the person asked is normally under no duty to answer.[34] A mere refusal to answer cannot constitute the offence of obstructing a police officer in the exercise of his or her duty.[35] The position at common law was that the jury at trial could not normally be expressly invited to draw any adverse inferences from the silence of the accused before the trial (although they could not be stopped from doing so in the privacy of the jury room).[36] Code C required a suspect normally to be cautioned before questioning and on arrest in the terms: "You do not have to say anything unless you wish to do so, but what you say may be given in evidence", or other words to the same effect.[37] In practice, only a minority of suspects

---

[33] For the contrary historical position see *Sanders and Young* (2000), Chap. 5.

[34] There are some exceptions where a refusal to give information is itself an offence: *e.g.* the Companies Act 1985, ss. 434–436 (investigation of the affairs of a company); and see the non-exhaustive list in Sched. 3 of the Youth Justice and Criminal Evidence Act 1999. The ECtHR has found convictions based on evidence secured by these compulsory powers to be contrary to Art. 6 of the ECHR: *Saunders v. U.K.* (1997) 23 EHRR 313. Following *Saunders*, the Attorney-General published guidelines preventing the use of answers obtained in such circumstances being used at trial unless the defendant himself introduced the answers or the prosecution was for an offence of refusing to answer etc. These guidelines have now been put on a statutory footing in the Youth Justice and Criminal Evidence Act 1999 s.59. See also *R. v. Faryab* [2000] Crim.L.R. 180. Several problems remain. First, the Youth Justice and Criminal Evidence Act 1999 does not apply to all statutory compulsory questioning powers. Sched. 3 provides a list of the most obvious examples of commercial concern. Second, even in those cases in which the Act applies, there is the question of whether it is legitimate to rely on the material that derives from or is discovered as a result of the compulsory questioning. See *Attorney-General's Reference (No.7 of 2000)* [2001] Crim.L.R. 736. The European Court has restricted the scope of the protection of the privilege against self-incrimination to cases where the inquiry is a criminal one by a prosecutorial body. This has already been influential in the House of Lords' consideration of cases arising under the Human Rights Act 1998. In *R. v. Hertfordshire County Council, ex p. Green Environmental Industries Ltd* [2000] 2 W.L.R 373 it was held that a notice to supply information under the Environmental Protection Act 1990, s.71(2) was not a breach of Art. 6. This was an "extra-judicial" inquiry, and s. 78 of PACE gave a discretion to exclude evidence obtained which would therefore have ensured a fair trial. A similarly narrow view was taken in relation to compulsory questions relating to road traffic offences where the Privy Council held that the public interest in road safety outweighed the limited sanction that would arise from a failure to answer questions: *Brown v. Stott* [2001] 2 All E.R. 97. In the recent case of *I.J.L., G.M.R. A.K.P. v. U.K.*, [2000] 9 B.H.R.C. 222, [2001] Crim.L.R. 133 the European Court refused to accept the argument that "a legal requirement for an individual to give information demanded by an administrative body necessarily infringes Article 6 of the Convention". The ECHR and domestic jurisprudence on this issue continues to develop: see *J.B. v. Switzerland* [2001] Crim.L.R. 748 and commentary. Note that a suspect's refusal to give a name and address may lead to an arrest under the general arrest conditions or detention in custody.

[35] If the refusal is combined with positive acts that obstruct the police, such as abuse, threats or misleading answers the position may be different: *e.g. Ricketts v. Cox* (1981) 74 Cr.App.R. 298 (abuse: although the case is doubtful on its facts: see Bailey, Harris and Ormerod (2001), p. 159).

[36] See J. A. Andrews and M. Hirst, *Criminal Evidence* (1987), paras 8.10–8.12, 19.86–19.95.

[37] C.10 (1991 ed.).

questioned by the police relied on their right of silence.[38] Indeed, commentators noted the considerable psychological pressures on suspects:

> "To remain silent in a police interview room in the face of determined questioning by an officer with legitimate authority to carry on this activity requires an abnormal exercise of will."[39]

It was a matter of some debate how important confessions or admissions were in establishing the prosecution case. The police certainly regarded interrogation as a central feature of their work, a very high proportion of suspects who made confessions subsequently pleaded guilty, with, *inter alia*, a consequent saving of police time, and only a very small proportion of those who confessed were ultimately acquitted.[40] On the other hand, the research concerning Crown Court cases conducted by Baldwin and McConville for the RCCP indicated that the prosecution's case would only have been fatally weakened had the accused's statement not been adduced in about 20 per cent of cases.[41] Furthermore, false confessions and police misconduct, usually in the form of the inventing of confessions, were identified by JUSTICE as two of the five common threads through most of the allegations of miscarriages of justice made over the years.[42]

In various ways, the arrangements under the 1984 Act were designed to encourage exercise of the right of silence and to improve the reliability of confessions. Thus, a person who asks for legal advice may not be interviewed[43] until he or she has received it unless:

(1) exercise of the right of access to such advice can properly be delayed[44]; or

---

[38] This was confirmed in the Report of the Royal Commission on Criminal Procedure, Cmnd. 8092 (1981), pp. 83–84, based on research it had commissioned: see P. Softley, Research Study No. 4 (confession or admission made by 61% of the 187 suspects in the study); B. Irving, Research Study No. 2 (admissions made by 65% of the 60 suspects observed). See also J. Baldwin and M. McConville, Research Study No. 5 (*Confessions in Crown Court Trials*) and *Courts, Prosecution and Conviction* (1981), Chap. 6; J. Vennard, Research Study No. 6. (*Contested Trials in Magistrates' Courts*) and H.O. Research Study No. 71 (1982); M. Zander, [1979] Crim.L.R. 203; B. Mitchell, [1983] Crim.L.R. 5.

[39] Irving, *op. cit.* p. 153. On the psychology of the interrogation process, see B. Irving and L. Hilgendorf, Research Study No. 1 (*Police Interrogation: The Psychological Approach*); B. Irving and I. K. McKenzie, *Police Interrogation: the Effect of the Police and Criminal Evidence Act 1984* (1989), pp. 17–25, 235–240; G. H. Gudjonsson, *The Psychology of Interrogations, Confessions and Testimony* (1992).

[40] M. McConville and J. Baldwin, *Courts, Prosecutions, and Convictions* (1981), Chap. 5, esp. pp. 106–114.

[41] *ibid.* Chap. 6. Evaluations of case papers were made by independent assessors. Research concerning contested magistrates' court cases suggested that confession evidence was most influential in cases based on circumstantial rather than direct evidence: Vennard (1980) and (1982).

[42] JUSTICE, *Miscarriages of Justice* (1989), p. 4. The point is reinforced by the presence of unreliable confessions at the heart of many of the high profile miscarriage of justice cases: Walker in C. Walker and K. Starmer (eds), *Justice in Error* (1993), p. 14, citing the Guildford Four, the Birmingham Six, Judith Ward, the Tottenham Three and Cardiff Three cases. See also K. Starmer and M. Woolf in C. Walker and K. Starmer, (1999).

[43] The definition of "interview" has caused particular difficulty (see H. Fenwick, [1993] Crim.L.R. 174; S. Field, (1993) 13 L.S. 254). The current definition is "the questioning of a person regarding his involvement in a criminal offence or offences which ... is required to be carried out under caution" (Code C.11.1A).

[44] Above, para. 14-022.

(2) an officer of the rank of superintendent or above has reasonable grounds for believing that

(3) delay will involve an immediate risk of harm to persons or serious loss of or damage to property,[45] or awaiting the arrival of the solicitor would cause unreasonable delay to the process of investigation; or

(4) the solicitor nominated cannot be contacted or refuses to attend (and D declines to ask for a duty solicitor or the duty solicitor is unavailable); or

(5) D agrees in writing or on tape that the interview may be started at once.[46]

In situations (3) and (4), an officer of the rank of inspector or above must agree for the interview to proceed.

As noted, if D is allowed to consult a solicitor, and the solicitor is available, D must be allowed to have him or her present during the interview. The solicitor may only be required to leave the interview if his or her conduct is such that the investigating officer is unable properly to put questions to the suspect, and then only on the authority of an officer of the rank of superintendent or above.[47] Research suggests that the legal representative is rarely likely to be anything like so interventionist as to present this problem.

Ten years after PACE had been enacted, the government took the view that the safeguards it had introduced were sufficient to justify inroads on the "right of silence" to the extent of permitting the jury or magistrates in certain circumstances to draw adverse inferences from a suspect's silence. This was despite the fact that one year before the changes were introduced, a majority of the RCCJ had concluded that no change should be made to the right to silence in the police station.[48] They believed that:

"the possibility of an increase in the convictions of the guilty is outweighed by the risk that the extra pressure on suspects to talk in the police station and the adverse inferences invited if they do not may result in more convictions of the innocent."

---

[45] It is only on this ground that a person heavily under the influence of drink or drugs can be interviewed at all or an arrested juvenile or a person who is mentally ill or mentally handicapped, a person who has difficulty in understanding English or a hearing disability can be interviewed in a police station in the absence, respectively, of an appropriate adult or of an interpreter: Code C.11.14, 12.3, 13.2, 13.5, and Annex C. Interviews outside the police station are permitted in limited circumstances: Code C.11.1. See *DPP v. Blake* [1989] 1 W.L.R. 432 (estranged father of juvenile not an "appropriate adult": see Note for Guidance 1C). On the role of the "appropriate adult" in investigations, see: B. Littlechild, "Reassessing the Role of the Appropriate Adult". [1995] Crim.L.R. 540; J. Hodgson, "Vulnerable Suspects and Appropriate Adults" [1997] Crim.L.R. 785; C. Palmer, "Still Vulnerable After All These Years" [1996] Crim.L.R. 633.

[46] Code C.6.6.

[47] Code C.6.8–6.11. The Notes for Guidance (6D) state that a solicitor may challenge an improper question or the manner in which it is put or advise the client not to reply to particular questions; *cf. ibid.* Annex B(A)3, above.

[48] *ibid.* pp. 50–55, endorsing the position of the RCCP on this point (see Cmnd. 8092, para. 4.50).

They recognised the frustration of the police caused by exercise of the right to silence, but thought that experienced professional criminals who wished to remain silent were likely to continue to do so and to justify their position by stating at trial that their solicitors had advised them to say nothing until the allegations against them had been fully disclosed. Research evidence[49] suggested that between six per cent and 10 per cent of suspects outside the Metropolitan police district and between 14 per cent and 16 per cent inside exercised their right of silence to some extent[50]; that the right was exercised more often by suspects detained for serious crimes; and that most who were silent in the police station either plead guilty later or were subsequently found guilty. The majority did, however, accept that the position should be changed as regards defence disclosure after disclosure by the prosecution.[51]

Two members of the RCCJ disagreed and thought that it should be possible at trial for adverse inferences to be drawn from silence in the police station; the right to silence offered little or no protection to the vulnerable and safeguards could be strengthened in other ways. The government, noting the disagreement within the RCCJ, rejected the majority's view and introduced legislation to permit adverse inferences to be drawn at trial from silence in specified circumstances. Changes along these lines had previously been recommended by the Criminal Law Revision Committee[52] and, indeed, adopted as government policy,[53] but then, respectively, dropped in consequence of the storm of opposition aroused[54] and postponed, probably in view of the concern generated by certain widely publicised miscarriages of justice.[55] They had however, already been introduced in Northern Ireland.[56]

---

[49] Summarised by the RCCJ at pp. 53–54.

[50] D. Brown, *The Incidence of Right to Silence in Police Interviews: The Research Evidence Reviewed* (HORPU, unpublished).

[51] See below, para. 17-???.

[52] 11th Report, *Evidence (General)*, Cmnd. 4991 (1972). See generally D. J. Galligan, (1988) 41 C.L.P. 69.

[53] H.C. Deb., Vol. 133, May 18, 1988, col. 466 (announcement by the Home Secretary). How the changes were to be effected was the subject of the *Report of the Working Group on the Right of Silence* (Home Office, 1989).

[54] See M. Zander, (1974) 71 L. S. Gaz. 954 and "The Right of Silence in the Police Station and the Caution" in P. Glazebrook (ed.), *Reshaping the Criminal Law* (1978), pp. 344–363.

[55] The issue was included in the terms of reference of the RCCJ. There was also considerable opposition to the Working Group's proposals: see A. A. S. Zuckerman, "Trial by Unfair Means" [1989] Crim.L.R. 855; J. Wood and A. Crawford, *The Right to Silence: The Case for Retention* (1989); S. Greer, (1990) 53 M.L.R. 709; B. Irving and I. McKenzie, (1990) 1 Jo. of Forensic Psychiatry 167. For arguments in favour of change, see G. Williams, [1988] Crim.L.R. 97. For further contributions to the general debate see S. Greer and R. Morgan (eds), *The Right of Silence Debate* (1990); S. M. Easton, *The Case For The Right to Silence* (1998); R. Leng, *The Right to Silence in Police Interrogation: A Study of Some of the Issues Underlying the Debate* (RCCJ Research Study No. 10, HMSO, 1993); D. Morgan and G. Stephenson, *Suspicion and Silence* (1994).

[56] Criminal Evidence (Northern Ireland) Order 1988 (S.I. 1988 No. 987). See J. D. Jackson, (1989) 40 N.I.L.Q. 105, [1991] Crim.L.R. 404, (1993) 44 N.I.L.Q. 103 and [1995] Crim.L.R. 587. See JUSTICE, *The Right of Silence Debate: The Northern Ireland Experience* (1994). The details of the Northern Ireland provisions have been amended to bring them into line with sections 34 to 38 of the 1994 Act.

The Criminal Justice and Public Order Act 1994 provides that "such inferences as appear proper" may be drawn at various stages of the trial process by a court or jury (and in some circumstances, a judge) in four situations.[57] First, inferences may be drawn from silence at trial: section 35[58] (these are discussed in Chapter 17 below). As regards the pre-trial process, there are three situations to consider.

Section 34(1), provides:

"where, in any proceedings against a person for an offence, evidence is given that the accused—

(a) at any time before he was charged with the offence, on being questioned under caution by a constable trying to discover whether or by whom the offence had been committed, failed to mention any fact relied on in his defence in those proceedings; or

(b) on being charged with the offence or officially informed that he might be prosecuted for it, failed to mention any such fact, being a fact which in the circumstances existing at the time the accused could reasonably have been expected to mention when so questioned, charged or informed ... ."

In consequence of the introduction of section 34, the caution has been changed to the following[59]:

"You do not have to say anything. But it may harm your defence if you do not mention when questioned something which you later rely on in court. Anything you do say may be given in evidence."

It will be noted that while this caution has to be administered (*inter alia*) on arrest,[60] the questioning of a suspect should normally only take place in a police station, where the safeguards of access to legal advice and recording requirements apply.[61]

The second provision affecting the pre-trial process and incrimination is section 36 under which adverse inferences can be drawn from the failure of an accused to account for objects, substances or marks found on arrest on him or her or his or her clothing or footwear[62] or in his possession or in any place in which he or she is at the time of arrest. The arresting or investigating officer must reasonably believe that the object, etc., may be attributed to the suspect's participation in the commission of an offence specified by the officer, who must inform the suspect that he or she so believes. The constable must also inform the suspect in ordinary language of the effect of the section should he or she fail to comply with the constable's request. Similar provisions apply to an accused's failure to account for his or her presence at a place at or about the time the offence for which he or she

---

[57] See I. Dennis, [1995] Crim.L.R. 4, 9–18; R. Pattenden, [1995] Crim.L.R. 602; P. Mirfield, [1995] Crim.L.R. 612.

[58] See below.

[59] PACE, Code C.10.4.

[60] Code C. 10.3.

[61] See para. 14-025.

[62] Or the condition of the clothing or footwear.

was arrested is alleged to have been committed (section 37). The special warnings that must be given to the suspect under Code C: 10.5A–C explain the offence that is being investigated, what the suspect is to account for, the officer's belief that the fact may be due to the suspect's involvement in the offence, that a court may draw an inference from a refusal to account for the fact and that a record of the interview will be available as evidence. Research reveals that the warning is given in 39 per cent of cases in which a suspect has remained silent,[63] but that the warning is often not understood by the suspect.[64]

The European Court of Human Rights' jurisprudence has proved to be extremely important in restricting the impact of these abrogations of the right to silence in domestic law. Although there is no express right to silence on the face of Article 6, the court found such a right to be embodied in the Article 6 right to a fair trial.[65] In construing the Northern Irish legislation on which the current English provisions were constructed, the ECHR held in *Murray v. United Kingdom*[66] that drawing inferences from silence:

> "is a matter to be determined in the light of all the circumstances of the case, having particular regard to the situations where inferences may be drawn, the weight to be attached to them by the national courts and their assessment of the evidence and the degree of compulsion inherent".[67]

The provisions in sections. 34–37 have recently been amended in to ensure compliance with this ruling from the ECtHR. Under section 34(2A) no adverse inferences can be drawn from silence or a failure to explain substances, etc., unless the accused has been allowed an opportunity to consult a solicitor prior to being questioned, charged, or informed as mentioned.[68]

In another extremely important decision, *Saunders v. United Kingdom*[69] the European Court examined the use of compulsory questions — those backed by a sanction for a failure to answer *per se* . The majority decision is important for the right to silence generally:

> "the right not to incriminate oneself, in particular, presupposes that the prosecution in a criminal case seek to prove their case against the accused without resort to evidence obtained through means of coercion or oppression in defiance of the will of the accused. In this sense the right is closely linked to the presumption of innocence contained in article 6(2)".

---

[63] T. Bucke *et al.*, (2000), p. 39.
[64] *ibid.* pp. 39–40.
[65] In *John Murray v. U.K.* (1996) 22 E.H.R.R. 29 the court accepted that the right to remain silent under police questioning and the privilege against self-incrimination were generally recognised international standards which lay at the heart of the notion of a fair procedure under Art. 6. However, the drawing of adverse inferences from the defendant's refusal, at arrest, during police questioning and at trial to explain his presence at a house where an IRA informer had been held captive was held not to infringe Art. 6; these were reasonable inferences to draw in all circumstances of the case.
[66] [1996] 22 E.H.R.R. 29.
[67] para. 61.
[68] As inserted by the Youth Justice and Criminal Evidence Act 1999, ss.58(1), (4).
[69] (1997) 23 E.H.R.R.313.

This also led to English legislation being amended to ensure compliance.[70]

In the other significant United Kingdom case to go before the ECtHR, *Condron v. United Kingdom*,[71] the Court held that the jury must be properly directed to consider the suspect's reasons for silence and that adverse references could not form the sole or main basis for conviction. The Court also held that where a suspect is advised to remain silent by his lawyer appropriate weight must be given to that fact by the domestic court in considering whether an adverse inference should be drawn. This decision has also directly affected the domestic law, with juries now being instructed that no adverse inference can be drawn against defendant's pre-trial silence unless the failure to answer the question is because they have no answer that will stand up to scrutiny.[72]

The English courts' approach to the sections has been to interpret them relatively restrictively. Lord Bingham observed in *R. v. Bowden*[73] that as the "sections restrict rights preserved at common law as appropriate to protect defendants against the risk of injustice, they should not be construed more widely than the statutory language requires". In *R. v. Argent*[74] Lord Bingham laid down the criteria to be met at trial before the jury may draw an inference under section 34. The six conditions are that: there must be proceedings against a person for an offence; the alleged failure to mention facts must occur before charge; the alleged failure must occur during questioning under caution by a constable; the questioning must be directed to trying to discover whether or by whom the alleged offence had been committed; the alleged failure must be to mention any fact relied on in his defence; the failure to mention a fact which in the circumstances existing at the time was a fact the accused could reasonably have been expected to mention when so questioned.[75]

Adverse inferences cannot be drawn under section 34 unless the accused relies on a fact at trial that he could have been expected to mention; merely putting the prosecution to proof is not sufficient to trigger the inferences,[76] nor will providing a written defence statement,[77] nor will a defendant's admission of an element of the prosecution case be sufficient.[78] In any case in which the section does not apply, the jury must be warned that they should not draw any adverse inferences.[79] Where the jury are invited to draw adverse inferences they must be provided with clear judicial guidance on the task.[80] No adverse inferences are to be drawn if the accused has

---

[70] See Youth Justice and Criminal Evidence Act 1999, s.59.

[71] (2001) 31 E.H.R.R. 1.

[72] See further on its impact A. Jennings, A. Ashworth and B. Emmerson "Silence And Safety: The Impact Of Human Rights Law" [2000] Crim.L.R. 879.

[73] [1997] 2 Cr.App.R. 176 at 181.

[74] [1997] 2 Cr.App.R. 27.

[75] His lordship emphasised that the time referred to is the time of questioning, and account must be taken of all the relevant circumstances existing at that time. Matters to be taken into account include the time of day, the defendant's age, experience, mental capacity, state of health, sobriety, tiredness, knowledge, personality and legal advice.

[76] *R. v. Moshaid* [1998] Crim.L.R. 420.

[77] See *R. v. Ali* [2001] 6 Arch. News 2.

[78] *R. v. Belts and Hall* [2001] 2 Cr.App.R. 257.

[79] *R. v. McGarry* [1998] 3 All E.R. 805.

[80] See *R. v. Birchall* [1999] Crim.L.R. 311; *R. v. Gill* [2001] 1 Cr.App.R. 61. See also *Condron v. U.K.* [2001] 31 E.H.R.R. 1.

remained silent in response to interviews conducted beyond the point at which it has been established that there is sufficient evidence to charge.[81] No adverse inferences will be drawn unless there exists a prima facie case against the accused without relying on such evidence.[82] Silence cannot form the sole or main element of evidence against the accused.[83]

However, adverse inferences that can be drawn are not limited to the fact that the defendant must have lied in fabricating the new line of defence, but can also include that the defendant refused to reveal his defence earlier because his explanation would not stand up to scrutiny.[84] Most importantly, the provision of legal advice to remain silent cannot in itself prevent the adverse inferences being drawn.[85] This creates significant problems for lawyers faced with advising a client, aware that there may be a waiver of privilege at trial,[86] and scrutiny of the advice.[87]

Although section 34 does not require the police to disclose the whole of their case to the suspect,[88] one clear impact of the provisions has been to encourage legal advisers to ask for more information at the time of the interviews.[89] This leads to greater pressure on the investigator — the reverse of the intended impact of the provisions. However, this has also made the legal advisers task more difficult, since "wrong" advice on silence could lead to serious consequences at trial.

Suggestions for further modification of the scheme have included a recommendation to include an obligation on the police to apply to the court to have a legal adviser appointed if a suspect declines to instruct one.[90] There is no doubt that the rules will require further refinement before the appropriate balance between crime control values and due process is struck. This is unlikely to occur when the political pressures for stronger crime control are so great. As Jackson has noted recently, the provisions have invested the police interview with "such evidential significance that it can truly be said to have assumed a formal status akin to that of a court hearing".[91]

The inroads into the so called right to silence remain controversial[92] especially given the continuing concern over the effectiveness of safeguards

[81] *R. v. McGuiness* [1999] Crim.L.R. 318; *R. v. Pointer* [1997] Crim.L.R. 676; *R. v. Gayle* [1999] Crim.L.R. 502; *R. v. Ioannou* [1999] Crim.L.R. 586.

[82] See *R. v. Hart* [1998] 6 Arch News 1; *R. v. Gill* [2001] 1 Cr.App.R. 61.

[83] s.38(3); *Condron* (above).

[84] *R. v. Daniel* [1998] 2 Cr.App.R. 373; *Beckles and Montague* [1999] Crim.L.R. 148; *R. v. Taylor* [1999] Crim.L.R. 77.

[85] *R. v. Condron* [1997] 1 Cr.App.R. 185; *Condron v. U.K.* [2001] 31 E.H.R.R. 1.

[86] See *R. v. Bowden* [1999] 2 Cr.App.R. 176. See also E. Cape, "Sidelining Defence Lawyers Police Station Advice After Condron" (1997) 4 E. & P. 386.

[87] See *R. v. Roble* [1997] Crim.L.R. 449; *Condron v. U.K. op. cit..* Bucke *et al.*, p. 51.

[88] *R. v. Imran* [1997] Crim.L.R. 754.

[89] Bucke *et al.*, p.23.

[90] See Jackson, (2001) E. & P. 145 at 171.

[91] J. D Jackson, "Silence and Proof: Extending the Boundaries of Criminal Proceedings in the U.K." (2001) E. & P. 145 at 147.

[92] See S. Easton, "Legal Advice, Common Sense and the Right to Silence" (1998) 2 E. & P. 109; S. Seabrooke, "More Caution Needed on Section 34 of the Criminal Justice and Public Order Act 1994" (1999) 3 E. & P. 209; R. Pattenden, "Silence: Lord Taylor's Legacy" (1998) 2 E. & P. 141; see generally, I.H. Dennis, *The Law of Evidence* (1999), pp.119–137. See also the excellent review by Dennis: "Silence in the Police Station: the Marginalisation of Section 34" [2002] Crim.L.R. 25.

for suspects at the police station[93] and the lack of research data to support police claims that the exercise of the right to silence in a significant number of cases seriously impedes the investigation of offences. The effectiveness of the 1994 provisions is also contentious. Recent Home Office research has concluded that "[t]here are strong grounds for arguing that the provisions have led to greater efficiency in the investigative and prosecution process".[94] In particular, the legal adviser is better able to advise his client because the police will have been compelled to disclose more of their case at an earlier stage. This leads to a more efficient decision-making process regarding charging. A benefit to the suspect also lies in the police being compelled to investigate the story provided by the suspect, thereby weeding out weaker cases. This also encourages investigation of all lines of inquiry relating to the crime rather than the suspect *per se*. In addition, the provisions lead to greater certainty of conviction in cases where the evidence is already strong.[95] Bucke *et al.* conclude that: "whatever philosophical standpoint is adopted, it seems clear that the change in the law has not led to undue practical disadvantages to the defendant".[96] However, academic commentators have argued that the sections produce undue complexity at trial and are too costly in terms of the number of collateral issues and appeals that they generate.[97]

Bucke *et al.* found that, since the 1994 Act, there has been no significant rise in the proportion of suspects requesting legal advice. The figure remained stable at around 40 per cent.[98] The percentage of suspects exercising their right to silence has not altered dramatically since the Act. Those who obtained legal advice were "far more likely to refuse" all questions than those who had not.[99] More serious allegations were more likely to lead to silence as was a suspect having a previous record (13 per cent as opposed to five per cent). Bucke *et al.*[1] also assert that there is no reported "miscarriage of justice" resulting from a vulnerable suspect losing his right to silence.

---

[93] See below.

[94] T. Bucke *et al.*, *The Right to Silence – The Impact of the CJPOA (1994)* (2000), p. 70.

[95] See T. Bucke *et al.*, (2000), pp. 70–73.

[96] T. Bucke *et al.*, (2000), p. 73.

[97] See D. Birch, "Suffering in Silence: A Cost-Benefit Analysis" [1999] Crim.L.R. 769.

[98] "Before the Act, 10% of suspects refused to answer all questions, 13% refused to answer some, and 77% answered all. Under the Act, 6% refused to answer all questions, 10% refused to answer some, and 84% answered all." T. Bucke *et al.*, p. 31.

[99] *ibid.* p. 78.

[1] Of those who received legal advice before the Act, 20% refused to answer all questions, 19% refused to answer some, and 61% answered all. After the Act those figures are 13%, 9% and 78%. For those who did not receive legal advice, the figures before the 1994 Act were: 3% refused to answer all: 9% refused to answer some; and 88% answered all questions. After the Act, the figures are 2%, 6%, and 92%. The Act seems to have had the greatest impact on black suspects far fewer of whom now refuse to answer questions. See Sanders and Young, (2000), pp. 257; Ashworth, (1998), p.106–108. *ibid.* Jackson, M. Wolfe and K. Quinn, *Legislating Against Silence: The Northern Ireland Experience* (2000) after reviewing NI provisions concluded was that "whereas terrorism suspects had not greatly changed their approach to interviews, they were more likely to testify after the 1988 Order" — 54% in 1991 compared with 6% in 1987. *ibid.*, p. 33.

(ii) Interviewing[2]

14–025   Code C prescribes that an accurate record must be made of each interview
with a suspect.[3] Interviews must normally take place at a police station[4]and
the record must normally be made during the course of the interview, which
implies either tape recording the interview or making contemporaneous
notes. These were regarded as essential safeguards for the suspect if false
confessions were to be avoided and yet were not incorporated as specific
statutory criteria with appropriate remedies.

Defining the time at which an interview occurs has proved problematic.
The constant conflict is between on the one hand treating any dialogue
between the police and the suspect as an interview so that the caution is
issued and the PACE safeguards are triggered, and on the other, seeking to
allow the police to engage in limited initial exchanges which may serve to
dispel suspicion and thus avoid escalating the confrontation with the
individual.[5] The correct time to caution is when there are grounds for
suspicion (objectively assessed) but insufficient evidence to support a prima
facie case of guilt.[6] Similarly, it is important that the definition of interview
extends to those conversations occurring after charges have been laid, or
should have been laid, so that the suspect is not denied the PACE
protections.[7] In recent research for the Home Office, Brown[8] found that
"little supervision or monitoring of interviews occurs ... [and] some
unregulated interviewing continues to occur outside the interview room".

In addition to regulating the interviews, PACE governs the general
welfare and environment of the suspect throughout his time in the police
station, and this is important because of the potential impact on interview
vulnerability. Eight hours must normally be allowed in any period of 24

---

[2] See Sanders and Young, (2000), Chap. 5 and Ashworth, (1998), Chap. 4.

[3] Code C. 11. The Code (since the 1991 revision) makes it clear that a written record must be
kept of all interviews and other comments by suspects, and, unless impracticable, shown to
the suspect.

[4] Following a decision to arrest, the suspect may not be interviewed about the relevant offence
except at a police station unless the consequent delay would be likely to lead to interference
with or harm to evidence or other people or lead to the alerting of other suspects not yet
arrested; here, interviewing must cease once the relevant risk has been averted or the
necessary questions put: Code C.11.1. Research studies for the RCCJ showed that
questioning outside the police station still occurred in a significant proportion of cases (10%
in one study, 8% in another); it was, however, impossible to estimate the frequency of pre-
interview "discussions" between police and suspect, possibly with the use of inducements or
threats: Cm.2263, pp. 26–27. On the recommendation of the RCCJ any "significant"
statement or silence which occurred before arrival at the station must be put to the suspect at
the start of any interview there: Code C.11.2A.

[5] See, *e.g.* conversations with the business partner of the deceased: *R. v. James* [1996]
Crim.L.R. 650; conversations regarding luggage, etc., by Customs and Excise: *R. v. Nelson
and Rose* [1998] 2 Cr.App.R. 399. On continuing problems of the definition of interview see
D. Wolchover and A. Heaton Armstrong, [1995] Crim.L.R. 356 who consider the issue of
C.11.14 applying to non-suspects and the problems of vulnerable suspects. See also *R. v.
Kirk* [1999] 4 All E.R. 698, CA (questioning on holding charges).

[6] *R. v. Nelson and Rose*; [1998] 2 Cr.App.R. 399, CA (Crim. Div.). A second caution may be
necessary on arrival at the station if conversations with the suspect then occur: *R. v. Miller*
[1998] Crim.L.R. 209, CA.

[7] See *R. v. Pointer* [1997] Crim.L.R. 676.

[8] *PACE Ten Years On* (1997), p. 30.

hours free from questioning, travel or other interruptions, if possible at night. Interview rooms must be adequately heated, lit or ventilated. Breaks must normally be made at recognised meal times and at two-hour intervals. Full details must be recorded of the periods and of incidents of the interrogation. Written statements under caution must be taken in accordance with Annex D to the Code.

All interviews by police officers at police stations with a person suspected of an indictable offence[9] must be tape-recorded in accordance with the *Code of Practice on Tape Recording* (PACE, Code E).[10] The RCCJ "unreservedly welcome[d] this advance".[11] The main practical difficulties have concerned the preparation by the police of written summaries.[12] This has proved very time-consuming for the police; on the other hand, research found that in less than a third of the cases examined could the summaries be said to provide an accurate and succinct record of the interview.[13] The latest version of Code E merely requires that a written record be made in accordance with national guidelines approved by the Secretary of State.[14] The RCCJ noted Baldwin's finding that there were additional benefits to video over audio-taping in some 20 per cent of the cases studied, although showing such recordings to jurors and magistrates might have some prejudicial effect, for example, symptoms of nervousness might be mistaken for symptoms of guilt; a powerful visual impact might distract from what was said. The RCCJ majority recommended further research.[15] The Criminal Justice and Police Act 2001 now makes provision for the video-taping of interviews,[16] and provides for a further Code to be drafted.[17] No doubt this will offer better protection of the suspect, but it must be remembered that the video can only record what occurs in the police interview room and only when it is switched on. There are also proposals to video-record all witness statements.

Question marks over the effectiveness of the PACE regime in protecting the interests of suspects under interrogation, and in minimising the risk of false confessions[18] remain. The formal position of the suspect is now considerably enhanced by comparison with the pre-PACE position. However, effectiveness of the formal structure is undermined by such

---

[9] Other than espionage and terrorism – but see now Sched. 8 of the Terrorism Act 2000.

[10] Police and Criminal Evidence Act 1984 (Tape-recording of Interviews) (No. 1) Order 1991 (S.I. 1991 No. 2687) and (No.2) Order 1992 (S.I. 1992 No. 2803). On the protracted process by which this was achieved, see P. Mirfield, *Confessions* (1985), pp. 19–40 and J. Baldwin, [1985] Crim.L.R. 695.

[11] Cm. 2263, p. 39.

[12] Originally required by Code E.5.3.

[13] J. Baldwin, *Preparing the Record of Taped Interview* (RCCJ Study No.2, HMSO, 1992). In the view of the Home Office, improvements followed the issue of further guidance in H.O. Circular 21/1992, Cm. 2263, p. 39. See also the disucssion in *R. v. Miller* [1998] Crim.L.R. 209.

[14] Note for Guidance 5A.

[15] See further A. Leonard, (1991) 141 N.L.J. 1512; M. McConville, [1992] Crim.L.R. 532 and (1992) 142 N.L.J. 960 and 1120; J. Baldwin, (1991) 141 N.L.J. 1512 and (1992) 142 N.L.J. 1095. See RCCJ, Cm. 2263, pp. 39–40. See also on the risks of video evidence at trial: D.W. Elliott, "Video-Tape Evidence and the Risk of Overpersuasion" [1998] Crim.L.R. 159.

[16] s.76, inserting s.60A into PACE.

[17] See now the PACE 1984 (Codes of Practice)(Visual Recording of Interviews) Order 2002 (S.I. 2002 No. 1266).

[18] See Sanders and Young (2000), pp. 304–316.

factors as the poor quality of much legal advice in the police station.[19] Furthermore, access to taped records of interviews has demonstrated the very poor quality of much of the interviewing conducted by police officers.[20] In response, "the police service, on an official level at least, has been stressing of late that questioning a suspect is only part of the process of investigation — and a decreasingly important part".[21]

A Home Office Circular[22] laid down principles of investigative interviewing, emphasising, *inter alia*, the points that the role of interviewing should be to obtain accurate and reliable information in order to discover the truth about matters under police investigation, that interviewing should be approached with an open mind, that when questioning anyone a police officer must act fairly and that vulnerable people must be treated with particular consideration at all times. These developments were welcomed by the RCCJ.[23] The RCCJ (by a majority) rejected proposals that a conviction should never be based solely on an uncorroborated confession, and (unanimously) rejected proposals that no confession should be admissible unless made or confirmed in the presence of a solicitor. However, they did recommend (unanimously) that the judge at trial should warn the jury that great care is needed before convicting on the basis of a confession alone.[24] The recommendation was ignored.

In addition to these changes to the regime of police interrogation, there has been an important change in the law governing the admissibility of confessions and admissions in evidence.[25] At common law, the test was whether a confession was "voluntary, in the sense that it has not been obtained from the suspect by fear of prejudice or hope of advantage, exercised or held out by a person in authority, or by oppression".[26] The case law was directed more to the technicalities of this definition than the realities

---

[19] Above, para. 14-022.

[20] J. Baldwin, "Police Interview Techniques" (1993) 33 Brit J. Criminol. 325, *Cf.* the observations of the Court of Appeal in *R. v. Paris, Abdullahi and Miller* (1993) 97 Cr.App.R. 99.

[21] *ibid.* pp. 325–326.

[22] 22/1992. H.O. Circular 7/1993 announced a new national training package for basic interviewing skills. See Sanders and Young, (2000), pp.293–295.

[23] Cm. 2263, pp. 11–14. T. Williamson, "Reflections on Current Police Practice" in D. Morgan and G. M. Stephenson, *Suspicion and Silence* (1994), Chap. 7, noting (at p. 111) that the principles of investigative interviewing were not yet widely understood. See also T. Newton, "The Place of Ethics in Investigative Interviewing by Police Officers" (1998) Howard Jnl. 52. See also, E. Shepherd and R. Milne, "Full and Faithful: Ensuring Quality Practice and Integrity of Outcome in WitnessInterviews" in A. Heaton-Armstrong, E. Shepherd and D. Wolchover, (eds), *Analysing Witness Testimony* (1999) and see B. Clifford and A. Memon, "Obtaining Detailed Testimony: The Cognitive Interview" *ibid.*

[24] Cm. 2263, pp. 57–68. On corroboration and confessions see R. Pattenden, "Should Confessions be Corroborated" (1991) 107 L.Q.R. 319; Sanders and Young, (2000), pp. 310–313.

[25] See generally: M. Hirst, *Andrews and Hirst on Criminal Evidence* (4th ed., 2001), Chap. 19; D. Wolchover and A. Heaton Armstrong, *Wolchover and Heaton-Armstrong on Confession Evidence* (1996); P. Misfield, *Silence and Improperly Obtained Evidence* (1997); I.H. Dennis, *The Law of Evidence* (1st ed., 1999); A. Keane, *The Modern Law of Evidence* (5th ed., 2000), Chap. 13; D. J. Birch, "The Pace Hots Up: Confessions and Confusions under the 1984 Act" [1989] Crim.L.R. 95.

[26] Paragraph (e) of the preamble to the Judges' Rules, based on *Ibrahim v. R.* [1914] A.C. 599 at 609 (basic test for "voluntariness") and see *R. v. Prager* [1972] 1 W.L.R. 260 and *R. v. Hudson* (1980) 72 Cr.App.R. 163 (oppression).

of the reliability of confessions.[27] The key provisions are now section 76 of PACE, which relates to confessions, and section 78, which concerns the exclusion of all kinds of evidence. The basic test is found in section 76(2):

"(2) If, in any proceedings where the prosecution proposes to give in evidence a confession[28] made by an accused person, it is represented to the court that the confession was or may have been obtained

(a) by oppression[29] of the person who made it; or
(b) in consequence of anything said or done which was likely, in the circumstances existing at the time, to render unreliable any confession which might be made by him in consequence thereof, the court shall not allow the confession to be given in evidence against him[30] except in so far as the prosecution proves to the court beyond reasonable doubt that the confession (notwithstanding that it may be true) was not obtained as aforesaid."[31]

Section 78(1) provides:

"In any proceedings the court may refuse to allow evidence on which the prosecution proposes to rely to be given if it appears to the court that, having regard to all the circumstances including the circumstances in which the evidence was obtained, the admission of the evidence would have such an adverse effect on the fairness of the proceedings that the court ought not to admit it."

This is applicable to confessions as well as other kinds of evidence.[32]

---

[27] See, generally, RCCP Report (1981), pp. 91–95.

[28] This "includes any statement wholly or partly adverse to the person who made it, whether made to a person in authority or not and whether made in words or otherwise" (s.82(l)); it therefore covers any admission, not just a full confession. However, it seems not to apply to statements which are intended to be exculpatory, but which become damaging at the trial, *e.g.* by then being shown to be evasive or false or inconsistent with the maker's evidence at the trial: *R. v. Sat-Bhambra* (1988) 88 Cr.App.R. 55; *R. v. Park* (1994) 99 Cr.App.R. 270; *R. v. Western* [1997] 1 Cr.App.R. 474. See generally, A. Vahit Bicak, (2001) J.Crim.Law 85. On mixed statements – those with an inculpatory and exculpatory effect – see *R. v. Aziz* [1996] A.C. 41.

[29] This "includes torture, inhuman or degrading treatment, and the use or threat of violence (whether or not amounting to torture)": s.76(8). Note that torture is a criminal offence under s.134 of the Criminal Justice Act 1988. Note also the protections in Art. 3 of the ECHR as outined above. For further information on their interpretation and application see D.J. Harris, M. O,'Boyle and C. Warbrick, *The Law of the EHCR* (1995), Chap. 3; J. G. Merills, Human Rights in Europe: "A Study of the European Convention on Human Rights" (4th ed., 2001).

[30] If a confession is put before the jury and the judge subsequently has doubts about oppression or reliability, it is too late for exclusion under s.76, although the judge could discharge the jury or direct the jury to disregard the statement under the common law: *R. v. Sat-Bhambra*, above.

[31] The court may require this to be proved of its own motion: s.76(3).

[32] *R. v. Mason* [1988] 1 W.L.R. 139. The court's common law powers to exclude evidence were preserved by s.82(3). The ambit of these powers was uncertain, although they clearly included power to exclude evidence whose probative value was outweighed by its prejudicial effect: *R. v. Sang* [1980] A.C. 402. In *Matto v. Wolverhampton Crown Court* [1987] R.T.R. 337, Woolf L.J.(as he then was) indicated that s.78 was if anything wider than the common law (p. 346).

The courts have employed these sections to exclude confession evidence rather more vigorously than had been anticipated. The first hurdle is that of "oppression", to which the Court of Appeal in *R. v. Fulling*[33] accorded its dictionary meaning as the "exercise of authority or power in a burdensome, harsh or wrongful manner; unjust or cruel treatment of subjects, inferiors etc., the imposition of unreasonable or unjust burdens".

The court noted, with apparent approval, a quotation in the dictionary under this definition: "There is not a word in our language which expresses more detestable wickedness than oppression", and continued: "We find it hard to envisage any circumstances in which such oppression would not entail some impropriety on the part of the interrogator."[34] This definition is narrower than the concept of "oppression" at common law,[35] but wider than that suggested by the definition section in the Act.[36] There have been few cases in which a confession has been excluded on this ground.[37] In *R. v. Fulling*[38] itself, D confessed while (so she claimed) in distress following the revelation by the interrogator that her boyfriend had for some three years been having an affair with the woman currently held in the next cell: this was held not to constitute oppression. The most notorious case where oppression has been found is *R. v. Paris, Abdullahi and Miller*[39] (the "Cardiff Three"), where the Court of Appeal (Criminal Division) quashed the convictions of the three appellants for murder. Miller had been interviewed for some 13 hours. Having denied involvement over 300 times, he was finally persuaded to make admissions. Lord Taylor C.J. stated that each member of the court had been "horrified" by what they heard in the tape recording of one interview:

> "Miller was bullied and hectored. The officers ... were not questioning him so much as shouting at him what they wanted him to say. Short of physical violence, it is hard to conceive of a more hostile and intimidating approach by officers to a suspect."[40]

Moreover, Miller's solicitor

---

[33] [1987] Q.B. 426. The decision is criticised for its ambiguity in Sanders and Young, (2000), p.284.

[34] *ibid.*, p. 432. See also *R. v. Hughes* [1988] Crim.L.R. 545, CA (no police misconduct, so not oppression where, through a misunderstanding, D did not see the Duty Solicitor).

[35] "something which tends to sap, and has sapped, that free will which must exist before a confession is voluntary" (*per* Sachs L.J. in *R. v. Priestly* (1967) 51 Cr.App.R. 1); *cf.* Edmund Davies L.J. in *R. v. Prager* [1972] W.L.R. 260 at 266.

[36] The term "includes" in the definition suggests that it was not intended to be exhaustive.

[37] To date there are very few decisions: *R. v. Davison* [1988] Crim.L.R. 442 (Central Criminal Court) and commentary, *R. v. Ismail* [1990] Crim.L.R. 109; *R. v. Beales* [1991] Crim.L.R. 118 (Norwich Crown Court) (officer deliberately misstated evidence in order to pressurise suspect).

[38] See [1987] Q.B. 426.

[39] (1992) 97 Cr.App.R. 99. *Cf. R. v. Emmerson* (1990) 92 Cr.App.R. 284; *R. v. Heaton* [1993] Crim.L.R. 593; *R. v. L.* [1994] Crim.L.R. 839, where pressure applied (*e.g.* raised voice) did not amount to oppression. Moreover, officers are "not required to give up after the first denial or even after a number of denials": *per* Lord Taylor C.J. in *Paris* at 104.

[40] p. 103.

"appears to have been gravely at fault for sitting passively through this travesty of an interview".[41]

Attempts have subsequently been made to address the defects of interviewing techniques illustrated by cases such as this.[42] To date, there are very few decisions in which a confession has been excluded on this ground. Breaches of the law or codes will not necessarily constitute oppression, nor[43] will a failure to allow D to see a duty solicitor owing to a misunderstanding,[44] nor will the use by a police officer of a raised voice and bad language, expressing impatience and irritation, for a short time during an otherwise low-key interview, amount to oppression.[45] Counsel for the defendant in *R. v. Samuel*[46] felt unable to argue that "the conduct of the police in delaying access to a legal representative amounted to oppression. The distinction between oppressive and non-oppressive conduct is a matter of degree. Interviews that were constructed in a tendentious, persistent, aggressive and prurient manner would be excluded,[47] and oppression in one interview may taint subsequent interviews and lead to their exclusion.[48]

Section 76(2)(a), in requiring the prosecution to prove the absence of oppression may in fact be of greater symbolic rather than practical significance. Any confession excluded under this head could also be excluded under the category of unreliability (below – section 76(2)(b)), or under section 78. It could be argued, in light of the interpretation in *Fulling*, that the section is used by the courts to exclude evidence of confessions as a means of disciplining the police. The courts deny that they have such a disciplinary function, but despite the explicit statements to this effect,[49] some cases suggest otherwise.[50]

The second hurdle to the admissibility of a confession under PACE is that of "unreliability" and this has been invoked more frequently. Under section 76(2)(b) the prosecution have to prove that the confession was not unreliable. The word "unreliable" ... means "cannot be relied upon as being the truth".[51] Moreover, the question is whether *any* confession which the accused might make in consequence of anything said or done was likely to be rendered unreliable, not whether the confession made was unreliable.[52] The question is as to the reliability of "any" confession made in "such" circumstances as those alleged.[53]

Section 76(2)(b) has been invoked in a diverse range of circumstances,

---

[41] p. 104.
[42] Above para. 14-025.
[43] *R. v. Parker* [1995] Crim.L.R. 233.
[44] *R. v. Hughes* [1988] Crim.L.R. 545.
[45] *R. v. Emmerson* (1990) 92 Cr.App.R. 284.
[46] [1988] Q.B. 615.
[47] *R. v. Ridley*, December 17, 1999, unreported, CA (Crim. Div.).
[48] *Burut v. Public Prosecutor* [1995] 2 A.C. 579, PC (manacled and hooded suspects being interrogated suffered oppression).
[49] See, *e.g. R. v. Chalkley and Jeffries* [1998] 2 Cr.App.R. 78.
[50] See, *e.g. R. v. Mason* [1988] 1 W.L.R. 139.
[51] *per* Stuart-Smith L.J. in *R. v. Crampton* (1990) 92 Cr.App.R. 369 at 372; R. v. Cox [1991] Crim.L.R. 276.
[52] *ibid.*
[53] *R. v. Bow Street Magistrates, ex p. Proulx* [2001] 1 All E.R. 57; [2000] Crim.L.R. 997 and commentary.

including, for example, where a child has been interviewed in the absence of an "appropriate adult"[54]; where there have been doubts about the reliability of a confession by a person of low intelligence[55]; where proper records of the confession have not been kept[56]; where there has been an improper inducement[57]; where there has been denial of access to a solicitor[58]; where, in one case, a drug addict was held in custody for 18 hours without being allowed the prescribed rest periods[59]; and even because of the solicitor's interventions.[60]

In principle, this hurdle is not limited to breaches of the law or of the Codes, but as most of the requirements are designed to promote reliability, breaches of them are a common factor to many of the cases. One controversial limitation is that the unreliability must arise from something "said or done", and this has been held not to include anything said or done by D himself,[61] although this has been seriously doubted.[62]

As with the claim of oppression under section 76(2)(a) if an interview is improperly conducted this may lead to the exclusion of subsequent interviews even though they are conducted according to the rules.[63] This is a question of fact and degree. The extent to which the factors which led to

---

[54] *DPP v. Blake* [1989] 1 W.L.R. 432, CA.

[55] *R. v. Harvey* [1988] Crim.L.R. 241 (Central Criminal Court): (psychopathic woman of low intelligence may have confessed after hearing her lover confess in order to protect her); *R. v. Everett* [1988] Crim.L.R. 826, CA (man of 42 with mental age of eight: judge had taken no account of his mental condition); *R. v. Delaney* (1988) 88 Cr.App.R. 338, CA (D educationally subnormal and proper records not kept); *R. v. Raghip, The Times*, December 9, 1991 (psychological evidence of mental condition admissible and court not bound by whether D's IQ was above an arbitrary figure for the mentally defective); *R. v. Kenny* [1994] Crim.L.R. 284. In a number of cases, the confessions of mentally handicapped suspects have been quashed by the Court of Appeal as unsafe and unsatisfactory, irrespective of any question as to their admissibility: see *R. v. Moss* (1990) 91 Cr.App.R. 371; *R. v. Mackenzie* (1992) 96 Cr.App.R. 98; *R. v. Brine* [1992] Crim.L.R. 122; *R. v. Wood* [1994] Crim.L.R. 222. If the accuseds' mental state is in issue, expert evidence should be called: *R. v. O'Brien* [2000] Crim.L.R. 676.

[56] *R v. Doolan* [1988] Crim.L.R. 747; *R v. Waters* [1989] Crim.L.R. 62 (W was also wrongly questioned after charge); *R. v. Chung* (1990) 92 Cr.App.R. 314, CA; *R. v. Joseph* [1993] Crim.L.R. 205, C.A. In the absence of a proper record, the prosecution may be unable to discharge its onus of proving reliability beyond reasonable doubt: *R. v. Delaney* [1989] Crim.L.R. 139 and commentary.

[57] *R. v. Phillips* (1987) 86 Cr.App.R. 18, CA (statement that if D confessed, offences could be taken into consideration rather than prosecuted); *R. v. Howden-Simpson* [1991] Crim.L.R. 49 (threat to pursue more than two charges); *R. v. M.P.C., ex p. Thompson* [1997] Crim.L.R. 211 (formal offer of caution for confession); *R. v. Barry* (1991) 95 Cr.App.R. 384, CA (prosecution unable to prove beyond reasonable doubt that statement was not made in response to offer of assistance in obtaining bail). The particular problem of the coercion that officers are able to exert by threats and offers in relation to bail are discussed in Sanders and Young, (2000), p. 287.

[58] *R. v. Gerald* [1999] Crim.L.R. 315.

[59] *R. v. Trussler* [1988] Crim.L.R. 446 (Reading Crown Court).

[60] *R. v. M* [2000] Arch News 2.

[61] *R. v. Goldenberg* (1988) 88 Cr.App.R. 285, (D's argument that his confession was unreliable as his motive was to obtain bail, or credit for helping the police, held not to fall within s.76(2)).

[62] *R. v. Crampton* (1990) 92 Cr.App.R. 369 (doubtful whether merely holding an interview with a suspect undergoing withdrawal symptoms is "something done" within the meaning of s.76(2)); *R. v. Walker* [1998] Crim.L.R. 211.

[63] *R. v. Ismail*; [1990] Crim.L.R. 109, CA; *R. v. McGovern* (1990) 92 Cr.App.R. 228; *R. v. Glaves* [1993] Crim.L.R. 685; *R. v. Neil* [1994] Crim.L.R. 441. See generally, P. Mirfield, "Successive Confessions and the Poisonous Tree" [1996] Crim.L.R. 554.

the exclusion of the first interview impact on the others will be crucial, as will the extent to which the suspect had an opportunity to exercise informed and independent choice regarding the subsequent interview.[64] The opportunity to seek legal advice before the subsequent interview is also very important.[65]

Section 76 is drafted in terms of its application only to prosecution evidence, and the House of Lords has so far declined to decide whether it applies to defence evidence where co-accuseds' confessions relied on by an accused even though the confessions were obtained in breach of Codes.[66]

Section 76(4)(a) of PACE allows for the admissibility of material discovered as a result of inadmissible confessions – e.g. where a confession has been excluded on grounds of oppression, but the confession revealed the whereabouts of the weapon involved in the crime, the weapon can be admitted but no reference can be made by the prosecution as to the inadmissible confession. This follows the common law.[67] Section 76(4)(b) also follows the common law by allowing the prosecution to adduce evidence of the manner in which a suspect expresses himself even if the confession in which that is revealed is inadmissible.[68] If a confession is excluded under section 78, there is no comparable statutory mechanism for admitting material discovered or expressions of the suspect. The common law should apply, in which case both should be admissible.

Confessions are also liable to be excluded under the very broad discretion in section 78 of PACE.[69] The court in exercising that discretion is to have regard to the manner in which the evidence was obtained. Examples of the diverse range of cases in which evidence has been excluded include: where the police have denied access to a solicitor in breach of section 58[70]; where a suspect is not told that a solicitor has come to the police station at another person's request[71]; where D has not been advised of the right to legal

---

[64] *R. v. Nelson and Rose* [1998] 2 Cr.App.R. 399.

[65] See *Prouse v. DPP* (1999) All E.R. (D) 748.

[66] *R. v. Myers* [1998] A.C. 124. See further Andrews and Hirst, (2001), Chap. 19, and M. Hirst, "Confessions as Proof of Innocence" [1998] C.L.J. 146. The Law Commission has recommended amendment to PACE to deal with co-accuseds' confessions: Report No. 245, *Hearsay and Related Topics* (1997), para. 8.95.

[67] *R. v. Warwickshall* (1783) 1 Leach 263.

[68] *e.g.* suspect's unusual spelling ('Blady Belgiam') identical to that used by the offender: *R. v. Voisin* [1918] 1 K.B. 531.

[69] For cogent analysis of way in which the section has been utilised in excluding unfairly obtained evidence, see A. Choo and S. Nash, "What's the Matter with Section 78?" [1999] Crim.L.R. 929. See also K. Grevling, "Fairness and the Exclusion of Evidence" (1997) 113 L.Q.R. 606 on the imprecision of the section.

[70] *R. v. Samuel* (1988) 87 Cr.App.R. 232; *R. v. Parris* (1988) 89. Cr.App.R. 68 (superintendent's order that D to be kept incommunicado under s. 56 wrongly assumed to exclude access to a solicitor under s.58); *R. v. Walsh* (1989) 91 Cr.App.R. 161. Exclusion is not, however, automatic, and may not follow where D is aware of his rights: *R. v. Alladice* (1988) 87 Cr.App.R. 380 (D admitted he was well able to cope with the interviews, that he understood the caution and was aware of his rights); *R. v. Dunford* (1990) 91 Cr.App.R. 150 (D had a record and was aware of his right not to answer questions); *R. v. Oliphant* [1992] Crim.L.R. 40 (presence of a solicitor would have added nothing to what O knew of his legal rights; *R. v. Anderson* [1993] Crim.L.R. 447 (even if a solicitor had been present and advised silence, A would not have acted on such advice).

[71] Contrary to Code C, Annex B, para. 3: *R. v. Franklin, The Times*, June 16, 1994 (proviso applied).

advice[72]; where a proper record of the interview was not made[73]; where there was a breach of Code C. 11.3 relating to inducements[74]; where there is a breach of a requirement to caution.[75]

Where the allegation is that there has been a breach of the Code of Practice, the courts will not necessarily exclude the evidence, even if there is a "significant or substantial" breach.[76] The court will consider the nature rather than the number of breaches,[77] and the court will be influenced by whether the police acted in bad faith.[78] The courts will also be especially vigilant where the suspect is a vulnerable person.[79] Unlike section 76, section 78 is a very open ended discretion,[80] but there is no clear guidance as to which party must establish the potential unfairness.[81]

There is also the opportunity for the courts to exclude evidence under any

[72] *R. v. Absolam* (1988) 88 Cr.App.R. 332 (no caution before questioning; no proper record); *R. v. Beycan* [1990] Crim.L.R. 185.

[73] *R. v. Keenan* [1990] 2 Q.B. 54 (officers unaware of Code C); *R. v. Canale* [1990] 2 All E.R. 187 (where the breaches were described as "flagrant", "deliberate", and "cynical"); *R. v. Bryce* [1992] 4 All E.R. 567 (interview after tape recorder switched off at B's request; no fresh caution and no contemporaneous record); *R. v. Cox* (1992) 96 Cr.App.R. 464 (questioning before arrival at police station held to be "interview" to which Code C.11 requirements applied). In *R. v. Keenan*. Hodgson J. emphasised the importance of these provisions as safeguards against "verballing" by the police (*i.e.* "the police inaccurately recording or inventing the words used in questioning a detained person"). *Cf. R. v. Matthews, Dennison, Voss* (1989) 91 Cr.App.R. 43 where the Court of Appeal declined to interfere with the trial judge's exercise of discretion to admit a confession notwithstanding breach of the recording requirements (the confession included correct details as to where the victim's clothes were found); and *R. v. Dunn*, (1990) 91 Cr.App.R. 237 where there were breaches of the recording requirements but a confession was held to be admissible as D's solicitor's clerk was present at the interview and so able to protect his interests.

[74] *R. v. Howden-Simpson* [1991] Crim.L.R. 49 (the police indicated they would proceed on only two of a series of charges if D admitted one).

[75] *R. v. Absolam* (1988) 88 Cr.App.R. 332; *R. v. Hunt* [1992] Crim.L.R. 582 (H seen by a police officer to have a flick knife and asked what it was for; it was held that there was ample evidence to suspect commission of an offence and he should have been cautioned); *R. v. Okafor* [1994] 3 All E.R. 741; *cf. R. v. Shah* [1994] Crim.L.R. 125. See also *R. v. James* [1996] Crim.L.R. 650 (questioning suspects' business partner regarding inconsistencies without caution); *R. v. Kirk* [1999] 4 All E.R. 698 (unfair to caution in relation to lesser offence when sufficient to caution on much more serious offence at that time).

[76] "The task of the court is not merely to consider whether there would be an adverse effect on the fairness of the proceedings, but such an adverse effect that justice requires the evidence to be excluded. *per* Saville J., in *R. v. Walsh* (1989) 91 Cr.App.R. 161 at 163.

[77] *R. v. Stewart* [1995] Crim.L.R. 500.

[78] *per* Lord Lane C.J. in *R. v. Alladice* (1988) 87 Cr.App.R. 380 at 386. As I. Dennis points out in his article "Reconstructing the Law of Criminal Evidence" [1989] C.L.P. 21 at 34, if the courts are . protecting rights and not disciplining the police, the question of good faith or bad is immaterial.

[79] In *R. v. Aspinall* [1999] 2 Cr.App.R. 115, there had been a clear breach of the Code when a schizophrenic had been interviewed without an appropriate adult or solicitor. The trial judge had been wrong to deny the need for an appropriate adult, and should have asked whether the fairness of the trial was affected by the police interview, bearing in mind that the suspect might appear normal to a layperson. The court also acknowledged that there had been a breach of Art. 6 because the denial of access to a legal adviser was particularly important in a vulnerable suspect case.

[80] As to whether there is in truth any discretion once a court has determined that the reception of the evidence would have an adverse effect on the fairness of the proceedings, see *R. v. Chalkely and Jeffries* [1998] 2 Cr. App.R. 79

[81] See *R. v. Anderson* [1993] Crim.L.R. 447. In *R. (on the application of Saifi) v. Governor of Brixton Prison* [2001] 4 All E.R. 168 the Court of Appeal doubted whether there was truly a "burden of proof issue".

common law power, since section 82(3) of PACE expressly preserves these powers.

One problem that has presented a particular difficulty for the courts is that which arises when the police practice deliberate deceptions on the suspect in order to secure evidence.[82] The courts have been most troubled by those cases in which the deception has involved not only lies made to the suspect, but also where his legal representative has been duped. For example, in *R. v. Mason (Carl)*,[83] D confessed to arson after the interrogators falsely told him, and his solicitor, that they had found at the scene a fragment of a bottle which had contained inflammable liquid and that D's fingerprint was on the fragment. This was described as "reprehensible":

"We hope never again to hear of deceit such as this being practised on an accused person, and more particularly possibly on a solicitor whose duty it is to advise him, unfettered by false information from the police."[84]

A more recent example is the decision to stay the prosecutions for murder of five defendants who had been illicitly tape-recorded in their private conversations with their legal advisers.[85]

There are, however, tricks and stratagems that the police may legitimately use in securing evidence where they suspect that the crime has been committed. Thus, in *R. v. Christou and Wright*[86] the Court of Appeal declined to exclude evidence of transactions concerning stolen property conducted at a "shady" jeweller's shop ("Stardust Jewellers") run for three months by undercover police officers. The transactions were recorded by cameras and sound recording equipment. The court noted that "the trick was not applied to the appellants; they voluntarily applied themselves to the trick",[87] and held that admission of the evidence was not unfair. Furthermore, the requirements of Code C did not apply as the appellants were not being questioned by police officers acting as such. While the undercover officers had asked questions about the areas to be avoided in selling the goods, this was at least partly to maintain their cover. However, where it is established that undercover officers have used their pose in order

---

[82] A. Ashworth offers a thorough examination of the many arguments that can be advanced for and against deceptive police practices, (1998) 114 LQR 108. These include arguments that: criminals deserve reduced rights only, so no harm is done to them by police deception; the criminal relies on deception, so it is not unfair for him to be treated in similar fashion; entrapment and deception might be wrong in general, but in the specific context they will benefit the community. On the other hand, by deceiving suspects, the police infringe the integrity principle, they abuse the power of the state, and reduce confidence in the criminal justice system.

[83] [1988] 1 W.L.R. 139.

[84] *ibid.* p. 144.

[85] *R. v. Gray and Others, The Times*, January 30, 2002 (Nottingham Crown Court, Newman J.).

[86] [1992] Q.B. 979. *Cf. R v. Smurthwaite, R. v. Gill* [1994] 1 All E.R. 898 where the Court of Appeal declined to exclude the evidence of recordings of conversations in which the defendants solicited police officers posing as contract killers to kill their respective spouses.

[87] *per* Lord Taylor C.J. at 989.

to circumvent the requirements of the Code, the evidence will be excluded.[88] The line is not necessarily easy to draw.[89] The courts' willingness to exclude confessions for breaches of the Act or the Codes does much to make their requirements effective.[90]

These and many other issues regarding the exclusion of confession evidence obtained improperly remain difficult to interpret because there appear to be so many possible (often conflicting) principles upon which the decisions are based.[91]

(g) Entrapment evidence

14–026   As the pressure to combat crime, and particularly those types of crime in which detection is very difficult – drug dealing being a prime example – the police use of entrapment techniques to reveal the suspect's willingness to engage in crime has increased in recent years. These cases are readily distinguishable from those in which evidence is obtained after the commission of the offence. There are an increasing number of entrapment type cases being brought before the appellate courts because of the increase in proactive policing, and particularly at present, because of an increased awareness of the ECHR which has had a considerable impact. The leading decision of the European Court of Human Rights is that in *Teixiera de Castro v. Portugal*,[92] in which there was found to be a breach of Article 6 where two undercover officers incited the accused to commit a drugs offence which he would not otherwise have committed. The European Court of Human Rights distinguished the earlier case of *Ludi v. Switzerland*,[93] where the suspect had already been actively involved in buying drugs. The

---

[88]   *R. v. Bryce* [1992] 4 All E.R. 567 (court excluded answers to questions that were not necessary to maintain cover and were not contemporaneously recorded). See also *R. v. MacLean and Koosten* [1993] Crim.L.R. 687; *R. v. Cadette* [1995] Crim.L.R. 229; *R. v. Edwards* [1997] Crim.L.R. 348.

[89]   See discussion by G. Robertson Q.C., "Entrapment Evidence" [1994] Crim.L.R. 805. Covertly-recorded conversations to which police officers are not party, but in situations set up by them, have been admitted in a number of cases: see *R. v. Jelen, R. v. Katz* (1989) 90 Cr.App.R. 456; *R. v. Ali (Shaukat), The Times*, February 19, 1991; *R. v. Bailey and Smith* [1993] 3 All E.R. 513 (conversation between B and S placed together in a police cell, with connivance of custody officer, after charge and remand by magistrates). A case that goes even further is *R. v. Roberts* [1997] 1 Cr.App.R. 217 where R and a fellow suspect, C, were charged with robbery. C then asked to be placed in a cell with R in the hope that R would admit the offence and exculpate C. R made incriminating remarks, which were recorded in this bugged cell. The Court of Appeal upheld the trial judge's decision to admit the recordings since proper authorisation had been obtained to bug the cell and the trial judge had found that there had been no deception by the police, because C was a suspect and not a police informer. See generally, G. Morgan, (2002) 152 N.L.J. 453..

[90]   See, *e.g.* a general instruction issued by the deputy chief constable of Avon, in part responding to case law, set out in *R. v. Chief Constable of the Avon and Somerset Constabulary, ex p. Robinson* [1989] 2 All E.R. 15, CA.

[91]   See especially P. Mirfield, *Silence and Improperly Obtained Evidence* (1997). The relevant principles themselves have been helpfully analysed by commentators, and include, apart from reliability and fairness, the protection of rights and the deterrence of police misconduct. See also A. Ashworth, "Excluding Evidence as Protecting Rights" [1977] Crim.L.R. 723; I.H. Dennis, (1989).

[92]   (1998) 28 E.H.R.R. 101.

[93]   (1993) 15 E.H.R.R. 173.

European approach focuses on whether the suspect is "predisposed" to commit the crime.

The English courts have struggled to find the correct response to these policing techniques.[94] Recently, the House has confirmed that English law is not in conflict with the ECtHR approach in *Teixeira*.[95] The Lords held that the officers had not overstepped the boundaries of legitimate policing when they had made one approach to a person who was suspected of drug dealing and they had been successful in buying drugs at the market rate and with no other inducement on their first request. In contrast, in the *Attorney-General's Reference (No. 3 of 2000)*,[96] the Lords held that the officers had overstepped the mark when they had pressurised the suspect over a period of time (15 calls) and offered inducements (cheap cigarettes). It was held that it would be unfair (and should lead to a stay of proceedings for abuse of process) for an undercover officer to incite or instigate an offence that the suspect would not otherwise have committed. If the officer merely provides an unexceptional opportunity for the suspect to take advantage there would be no unfairness in admitting the evidence at trial and no stay of proceedings. The House of Lords also emphasised that the previous record of the accused is not determinative, but that a reasonable suspicion of offending or willingness to offend is important.[97]

A number of important issues remain to be resolved in this area, including, the use of entrapment techniques by non-police agencies,[98] the development of a Code of Practice for undercover policing, and the use of the more extreme "manna from heaven" random virtue-testing tactics employed by the police with no identifiable target individual under suspicion.[99]

(h) Identification evidence[1]

Identification evidence is recognised as one of the kinds of evidence that   **14–027** must be treated with especial caution:

> "Identification, whether by sight or hearing, is evidence which can seem

---

[94] This is an area on which there is a wealth of literature and a mass of case law, and we cannot offer more than an outline here. See generally from the literature: Ashworth [2002] Crim.L.R. April, (2000) M.L.R. 633; D. Ormerod and A. Roberts (2002) 6 E. & P. 38; S. Bronnitt and D. Roche, (2000) E. & P. 77; M. Maguire and T. John, (1996) 4 European Jnl of Crime, Criminal Law, and Criminal Justice 316; A. Roberts, (2000) 73 Police Journal 263. From the cases, see especially, *R. v. Smurthwaite and Gill* (1994) 98 Cr.App.R. 437; *Amin v. Nottingham City Council* [2001] 1. W.L.R. 1071.

[95] *R. v. Loosely* [2001] UKHL 53.

[96] [2001] UKHL 53.

[97] The House of Lords emphasised that in *Teixeira* the officers had been acting without judicial supervision and had no reasonable grounds to suspect T of drug dealing. The decision is a welcome one, but there are issues of entrapment that still need to be resolved and also the ACPO and Customs and Excise Code Of Practice (1999), Part 5, "Undercover Operations".

[98] See especially *R. v. Shannon* [2001] 1 W.L.R. 51; *R. v. Hardwicke* [2001] Crim.L.R. 220 (newspaper journalists disguised as Arab Sheikhs to induce drug purchase).

[99] See *DPP v. Williams* (1994) 98 Cr.App.R. 209 (officers leaving cargo of cigarettes in unlocked van).

[1] See further Hirst (2001), Chap. 10; Cross and Tapper, (1999), XVII, Section 2; *Archbold* (2002), Chap. 14; Emmins, (2000), pp.47–50.

immensely convincing and compelling to a jury but can also, notoriously, be mistaken."[2]

There are, accordingly, special arrangements governing the gathering of such evidence[3] and how it is dealt with at the trial.[4]

The former is now governed by the *Code of Practice for the Identification of Persons by Police Officers* (Code D) made under PACE. This area of law is in a volatile state, with major changes to the Code of Practice being temporarily introduced following a controversial decision of the House of Lords, pending a complete revision of the Code.[5] In *R. v. Forbes*,[6] the House of Lords resolved an important dispute over the interpretation of the Code as to whether it was necessary to hold an identification procedure even where, *e.g.* the suspect was known to the witness. They held that, following the form of words in the Code of Practice, there *must* be a formal procedure, save in exceptional circumstances.[7]

The modifications to the Code make a fundamental alteration to the hierarchy of visual identification procedures in all cases of disputed identification. The modifications also allow the identification officer to delegate arrangements for or conduct of identification procedures to approved persons.[8]

It is important to note that the methods of testing the identification only apply where the suspect is "known", *i.e.* that there is sufficient evidence in relation to an individual to arrest him or her. It is not sufficient that the person matches a description circulated to officers.[9] The methods for establishing identifications (in the new order of preference), are:

(a) Formal identification parades where the suspect is seen by the witness with (usually seven) others of similar appearance[10] *or*, (at the investigating officer's preference), particularly if it can be completed sooner, a video film identification, where the suspect is filmed with others of similar appearance.[11] This is a clear shift to making the

---

[2] JUSTICE Report on *Miscarriages of Justice* (1989), p. 10. Well-known cases of miscarriages of justice based on identification evidence include those of Laslo Virag and Luke Dougherty, which led to the Devlin Committee on *Evidence of Identification in Criminal Case* (1975–76 H.C. 338). Earlier miscarriages of justice had included the conviction of Alfred Beck which led to the Court of Criminal Appeal being established in 1907. See also R. Nobles and D. Schiff, *Understanding Miscarriages of Justice: Law, the Media, and the Inevitability of Crisis* (2000); R. Pattenden, *English Criminal Appeals 1844–1994: Appeals Against Conviction and Sentence* (1996).

[3] In all cases, it is extremely important that accurate records are made of descriptions that are provided by witnesses *R. v. El Hanachi* [1998] 2 Cr.App.R. 226.

[4] On the latter, see text below.

[5] Police and Criminal Evidence Act 1984 (Codes of Practice) (Temporary Modifications to Code D) Order 2002 (S.I. 2002 No. 615). The new provisions substitute new para. 2 into the Code, and add new Annexes A (video), B (identification parades), C (group identifications), D (confrontation) and E (photographs).

[6] [2001] UKHL 40. See A. Roberts, (2002) J.Crim.Law 250.

[7] See now the new Code D, para. 2.14.

[8] Copies are available from *http://Rwww.legislation.hmso.gov.uk/si/si2002/20020615.htm*.

[9] *Coulman v. DPP* [1997] C.O.D. 91.

[10] The foils on parade can be adorned with make up to resemble the accused if necessary: *R. v. Marrin* February 4, 2002, unreported.

[11] A significant problem with the procedures is that the foils are selected to resemble the suspect rather than the description of the suspect that the witness first provided.

procedure more efficient for the officers. A parade/video identification must be held whenever a suspect disputes an identification and consents to a parade, unless the circumstances justify a group identification. A video/parade may also be held if the investigating officer considers that it would be useful and the suspect consents. No parade needs to be held where the witness is clear that he or she would be unable to identify the suspect (*e.g.* having seen only clothing).[12] Code D, para 2.15 (as inserted) provides that an identification procedure need not be held, if, "in all the circumstances, it would serve no useful purpose in proving or disproving whether the suspect was involved in committing the offence."

(b) Group identifications involve the suspect being viewed in an informal group of people, commonly in a public place. These may be offered initially if the identification officer considers that it will be more satisfactory and easier to arrange than a parade or video.[13] The group identification will also be offered where the video or parade are considered impracticable. Group identifications may take place with the suspect's consent, or covertly where he or she refuses to co-operate with a parade or group identification or has failed to attend. A group identification may also be arranged if the investigating officer considers, whether because of the witness's fear or otherwise, that that would be more satisfactory than a parade.

(c) Covert video identification or group identification are permitted.[14] An officer may obtain images of the suspect for use in a video identification procedure before the suspect is given information and written advice about the proposed identification procedure.

(d) Confrontations occur where the suspect alone is confronted by the witness. Confrontations do not require the suspect's consent but may only take place if a parade or group or video identification is impracticable, for example as a result of the suspect's non-co-operation.[15] The suspect has no statutory right to a confrontation.

The procedures are arranged by an "identification officer", who is not involved in the investigation, and is of the rank of at least inspector who need not be in uniform. (The new modifications to the Code allow for the delegation of responsibilities to civilian staff.) As a further safeguard, a

---

[12] See *R. v. Nicholson* [2000] 1 Cr.App.R. 182; *R. v. Gayle* [1999] 2 Cr.App.R. 130.

[13] Code D, para. 2.18.

[14] para. 2.24.

[15] Code D2 and Annexes A (parades and group identifications), B (video identifications) and C (confrontations). Identification from photographs, photofits, etc., is confined where possible to the process of investigation: see Annex D. JUSTICE (above) were informed that formal parades are usually held in about 80 per cent, of cases where such evidence was possible (p. 10). Code D.4.1, 4.2 deal with taking photographs of suspects, and D.4.3 makes clear that force may not be used to obtain such. There is no power to use reasonable force in securing compliance with the identification procedures: *R. v. Jones and Nelson, The Times* April 21, 1999.

video or colour photograph must be taken of each parade or group identification.[16]

As noted, the House of Lords in *R. v. Forbes* held that save in exceptional cases an identification procedure must be conducted. The new version of the Code makes some unsatisfactory attempts to regulate the difficult question of when circumstances are so exceptional that no procedure is needed. In paragraph 2.15, the Code provides that no procedure needs to be held if "it would serve no useful purpose", including, for example, where "the suspect is already well known to the witness, or where there is no reasonable possibility that a witness would be able to make an identification". The provision offers little guidance as to when a procedure might be safely avoided, and it could provide a means of avoiding all identification procedures where the witness knows the suspect.

At trial, the courts seem willing to exclude identification evidence under section 78 of PACE where the identification officer has concluded too readily that a procedure is impracticable[17] or where there have been other breaches of Code D.[18] Section 78 could have a significant role to play in excluding identification evidence following the House of Lords decision in *Forbes*[19] which will lead to more identification parades being conducted even where the suspect is known to the witness. If there is a breach of the Code and the trial judge decides that the evidence should nevertheless be admitted, the jury can assess the impact of the breach.[20]

There has been an increasing awareness of the subtleties of the dangers of eyewitness identification and of memory-based evidence in general, which is in part as a result of the growing literature in psychology and law,[21] and

---

[16] This requirement was introduced into the 1995 version of Code D on the recommendation of the RCCJ (Cm. 2263, p. 11). Other changes introduced in line with RCCJ recommendations were that a record must be made of the description of the suspect as first given by a potential witness, before the witness takes part in a parade, etc., and a copy given to the suspect's solicitor before any parade, etc. (Code D.2.0). The RCCJ also encouraged that the establishment of purpose-built suites be extended to all major urban areas.

[17] *R. v. Gaynor* [1988] Crim.L.R. 242 (Liverpool Crown Court); *R. v. Brittain and Richards* [1989] Crim.L.R. 144 (Leeds Crown Court); *R. v. Nagah* (1990) 92 Cr.App.R. 344, CA (street identification inadmissible as parade was practicable); *R. v. Gayle* [1999] 2 Cr.App.R. 130 (the officer will be obliged to explain a failure to hold a parade).

[18] *R. v. Gall* (1989) 90 Cr.App.R. 64 (investigating officer took part in the conduct of a parade); *R. v. Conway* (1990) 91 Cr.App.R. 143, (parade not held although requested: no good reason); *Powell v. DPP* [1992] R.T.R. 270; *R. v. Finley* [1993] Crim.L.R. 50; *R. v. Hope, Limburn and Bleasdale* [1994] Crim.L.R. 118; *R. v. Alien* [1995] Crim.L.R. 643; *cf. R. v. Quinn* [1990] Crim.L.R. 581 (evidence of identification of Q while on trial in a Dublin court admitted); *R. v. Grannell* (1989) 90 Cr.App.R. 149 (breach of Code D, but no unfairness); *R. v. Hutton* [1999] Crim.L.R. 74 (masked parade members). See also *R. v. Hawksley* (2002) QBD, March 27, holding that the failure of a police officer to record the identification he made was not fatal to the admissibility of the evidence.

[19] [2001] 2 W.L.R. 1.

[20] *R. v. Quinn* [1995] 1 Cr.App.R. 480, approved in *R. v. Forbes*, [2001] 2 W.L.R. 1 at 14.

[21] On eyewitness and memory see especially M. Kebbell and G. Wagstaff, *Face Value Evaluating the Accuracy of Eyewitness Identification* (1999), p.2. Cutler and Penrod, *The Eyewitness, Psychology and the Law* (1995). On memory and its evidential implications see generally New Zealand Law Commission Evidence Miscellaneous Paper No. 13, *Total Recall – The Reliability of Witness Testimony* (1999), Chap. 2; A. Kapardis, *Psychology and Law: a Critical Introduction* (1997); A Memon, A. Vrij and R. Bull, *Psychology and Law: Truthfulness, Accuracy and Credibility* (1998); R. Roesch, S. Hart and J. Ogloff, *Pscyhology and Law: the State of the Discipline* (1998); A. Heaton-Armstrong, E. Shepherd and D. Wolchover, *Analysing Witness Testimony* (1999).

there is no doubt that the Codes of Practice will need to be refined in the light of this learning. Other forms of identification evidence are becoming increasingly common. These have included, facial mapping evidence,[22] video superimposition evidence, and voice identification evidence.[23] Further regulation and prescription of the correct procedures to ensure the reliability of evidence in each of these methods would be welcome. With the greater number of CCTV cameras in public places, there is an increasing availability of footage of suspects for the police to rely upon. Future Codes of Practice may have to incorporate guidelines on the legitimate uses of such footage and impose safeguards against the use of poor quality material.[24]

(i) Forensic evidence

As a reflection on society's ever-increasing reliance on technology and science, in a significant number of cases,[25] the police seek the assistance of forensic scientists.[26-27] Their work may give rise to a wide range of admissible prosecution evidence, of which DNA profiling, the analysis of blood specimens and drugs, and tests for the presence of explosives are merely some of the best-known illustrations. Police forces tend to rely on the laboratories of the Forensic Science Service (established as a "Next Steps" executive agency of the Home Office in 1991), what was formerly the Metropolitan Police Forensic Science Laboratory, the Laboratory of the Government Chemist (an executive agency of the Department of Trade and Industry, whose forensic science work mainly involves illicit drugs and documents suspected of being forged) and the Defence Research Agency (an executive agency of the Ministry of Defence which covers forensic investigation for the illegal use of explosives). The FSS and MPFSL merged in 1996. Also in 1996, ACPO and the FSS drew up guidelines to assist the

14–028

---

[22] See *R. v. Stockwell* (1993) 97 Cr.App.R. 260; *R. v. Clarke* (1995) 2 Cr.App.R. 425; *R. v. Hookway* [1999] Crim.L.R. 750 (facial mapping evidence alone sufficient to found a conviction).

[23] See generally, *R. v. Hersey* [1998] Crim.L.R. 818; R. Bull and B. Clifford, "Earwitness Testimony" in A. Heaton-Armstrong, E. Shepherd and D. Wolchover, *Analysing Witness Testimony* (1999).

[24] Where the police video-taped the defendant at court and adduced the evidence of a facial mapping expert, comparing it to that of CCTV footage from the crime scene, the Court of Appeal upheld the conviction for robbery despite the breaches of the Codes of Practice and Art. 8 of the ECHR: *R. v. Loveridge and Lee* [2001] EWCA Crim. 1034. See also D. W. Elliott, "VideoTape Evidence and the Risk of Over Persuasion" [1998] Crim.L.R. 659.

[25] About one third of all contested Crown Court cases involve the use of scientific evidence of which about 25% are truly forensic: see Ashworth, (1998), p.132; Sanders and Young, (2000), pp. 339–343.

[26-27] See, especially, M. Redmayne, *Expert Evidence and Criminal Justice* (2000), Chap. 2. See also, *e.g.* C. Jones, *Expert Witnesses* (1994); C. Walker and R. Stockdale, in C. Walker and K. Starmer, *Miscarriages of Justice: Review of Justice in Error* (1999); A. Gallop, (2002) 152 N.L.J. 1112. P. Roberts, "Science in the Criminal Process" (1994) 14 O.J.L.S. 469, "Forensic Science Evidence after Runciman" [1994] Crim.L.R. 780 and "What Price a Free Market in Forensic Science Services" (1996) 36 Brit. J. Criminol. 37; RCCJ (Cm. 2263), Chap. 9 and RCCJ Research Studies No. 6 (G. Robertson, *The Role of Police Surgeons*), No. 9 (B. Steventon, *The Ability to Challenge DNA Evidence*), No. 11 (P. Roberts and C. Willmore, *The Role of Forensic Science Evidence in Criminal Proceedings*); C. Walker and R. Stockdale, "Forensic Evidence and Terrorist Trials in the U.K." [1995] C.L.J. 69; M. Pereira, "The FSS – Past Present and Future" (1988) Medico-Legal Journal 74.

police in making better use of forensic science in their investigations. The guidelines sought to ensure that police use of forensic science was fully integrated into investigations. Police authorities may also run their own in-house laboratories for more routine work and employ Scenes of Crime Officers or (civilian) Examiners (SOCOs) who examine scenes of crime for traces that can be sent for forensic examination.

Defence lawyers tend to use experts in private practice, who normally act as "defence examiners". They:

> "advise defence lawyers about the strength of prosecution evidence, suggest alternative avenues for scientific investigation or alternative interpretations of prosecution data and results, and assist generally in the development of case management strategies".[28]

The defence increasingly have access to the services of the FSS and other public sector laboratories.

Errors in the performance and evaluation of forensic tests and non-disclosure of forensic evidence were a feature of a number of the high profile miscarriage of justice cases.[29] This has led to a reconsideration of the arrangements for quality control within the FSS and the larger public sector laboratories[30] and the extension of disclosure requirements.[31] Furthermore, the RCCJ recommended that a Forensic Science Advisory Council should be set up to report to the Home Secretary on the performance of both public sector and private sector laboratories and experts.[32] Its responsibilities would include continuing review of the effectiveness of the organisation of the public sector laboratories, the devising of arrangements for external inspection and assessment of both public and private sector laboratories and oversight of the developments of a code of practice. The RCCJ endorsed developments already under way for the public sector laboratories to introduce charges on a commercial basis, but relied on the proposed Council to "ensure that undue competitiveness does not lead to a diminution in standards."[33] Finally, the RCCJ proposed that there should be a pre-trial discussion between the two sides in all cases in which scientific evidence is being lead; the defence should give advance notice of any grounds on which they intend to dispute prosecution expert evidence; prosecution and defence expert witnesses should produce a written account of what is agreed and what is in dispute, with a preparatory hearing held in cases of substantial disagreement.[34] Some of these points are subsumed in the general proposals for defence disclosure and preparatory hearings.[35]

The *Auld Report* recommended that the prosecution and defence should

---

[28] P. Roberts, (1994) 14 O.J.L.S. 469 at 489.
[29] See C. Jones, *Expert Witnesses* (1994), Chap. 10 and Walker and Stockdale, *op. cit*. n. 26; the cases of the Birmingham Six, Judith Ward and the Maguire Seven.
[30] P. Roberts (1996) 36 Brit. J. Criminol. 37 at 52.
[31] RCCJ (Cm. 2263), pp. 149–150.
[32] *ibid*. pp. 150–151.
[33] *ibid*. p. 148. On the growth of non-FSS suppliers see Redmayne, (2000), pp. 26–27. For a powerful argument that a market approach to forensic science services is flawed in principle, see P. Roberts, (1996) 36 Brit. J. Criminol. 37. Note that in 1998 the FSS was converted by the government to trading fund status.
[34] For discussion, see P. Roberts, [1994] Crim.L.R. 780 at 785–788.
[35] See below, Parts H and I.

normally arrange for their experts to discuss the case before the trial and to try to identify common areas of agreement and dispute.[36] It was also recommended that the court could also order such a discussion to occur. This may prove to be a significant improvement, particularly if the discussion is one conducted by documented report so that the precise claims of the forensic experts are subject to validation and challenge by the opposing experts before trial.

The methods for obtaining samples and gathering evidence that may be subject to forensic examination are discussed above, and the manner of its uses at trial are considered below in Chapter 17.

It is inevitable that reliance will be placed on forensic evidence which is perceived, at least by the general public, to be compelling, if not conclusive. It is vital that the defendant is able to challenge the reliability and validity of such evidence and that adequate safeguards exist to ensure the quality of evidence in these categories. Moreover, the courts must ensure that juries are alert to the dangers of over reliance on forensic evidence, and are appraised of its limitations.[37]

In addition to the difficulties regarding the manner in which forensic evidence is gathered and evaluated, there are growing concerns over the storage and recording of so much confidential information. Originally, provision was made for the destruction of fingerprints or samples when the suspect was acquitted, but this requirement has now been removed.[38] Coupled with the retention of the material for use in statistical databases, and the alleged stock of illegally held material, there will be many millions of samples held, affecting a large proportion of the community, and the significant civil liberties concerns ought to be addressed more fully by Parliament.[39] In August 2001, it was reported that the National DNA Database, managed by the FSS had reached 1.5 million profiles (half its overall target).[40] There has been considerable government investment of £187 million to expand the database so that upwards of three million profiles will be held by April 2004.

It is important to maintain tight controls on the quality of the service provided by the FSS. Admittedly, the FSS can only work with the material with which they are presented from the investigation into the crime, but

---

[36] Recommendation No. 271, Chap. 11.

[37] The courts have been alert to the dangers of over-reliance on DNA. For example, in *R. v. Walters* [2001] EWCA Crim 1261, evidence of DNA from cigarette ends found at the scene of a series of burglaries was felt, on appeal, to be too weak to sustain conviction, particularly since there was a possibility that the defendant's brother had committed the crime. The method by which DNA profiling is conducted is described in an accessible manner by Lord Taylor C.J. in *R. v. Gordon* [1995] 1 Cr.App.R. 290. See below Chap. 17.

[38] Section 82 of the Criminal Justice and Police Act 2001, s.82.

[39] *R. v. Willoughby* [1997] 1 Arch. News 2. See also the substantial expansion of the databases and holding of material introduced by the Criminal Evidence (Amendment) Act 1997 which allows for non-intimate samples to be taken from a person to whom the Act applies (*inter alia*: those imprisoned for sexual, violent and other specified offences). Home Office research reports that "the vast majority of samples were taken in order to build up the DNA database and, while the proportion of suspects sampled appears relatively small, it should be noted that approximately 1.5 million people enter police custody every year. Selective sampling therefore is likely to add a substantial number of people to the database over the forthcoming years." Bucke and Brown, (1997), p. 72.

[40] Every week approximately 1,600 DNA matches are made either connecting a suspect to a crime scene or linking crime scenes together.

internal auditing is vital.[41] In 2001, the Auld Report recommended that consideration be given to the establishment of a single self-governing body with the role of "setting or overseeing the setting, of standards and of conduct for forensic scientists of all disciplines, the maintenance of a register of accreditation for them and the regulation of their compliance with it".[42] A Council for the Regulation of Forensic Practitioners is also recommended, as one amendment to the improvement of the scheme for the admissibility of expert evidence.

B. THE RESPONSIBILITY FOR INSTITUTING PROSECUTIONS[43]

14–029   The historical development of the English prosecution process placed emphasis upon the role of the private individual as prosecutor. As the police forces grew so they began to assume the responsibility for bringing prosecutions (but only exercising individual rather than statutory rights); and practice diverged from that in Scotland where a public prosecutor (the procurator fiscal) became established and the right of private prosecution diminished.[44] In fact, for many years the theory of the private prosecution in England no longer matched the reality of the situation, not only because of the powers of the Director of Public Prosecutions,[45] but also because of restrictions placed by statute upon private prosecutions for many offences.[46] In practice, the majority of prosecutions were brought by the police and almost all the balance by other public agencies. Truly private prosecutions were highly unusual.[47] Furthermore, from 1986 the conduct of most classes of criminal proceedings has been taken over by the Crown Prosecution Service established by the Prosecution of Offences Act 1985. The fiction that the prosecution is acting in a private capacity is not maintained. This has taken on a special significance in the human rights era, since there have been attempts to argue that the CPS acts directly on behalf of the victim. The House of Lords has rejected this argument: the CPS should not be seen as the representative of the victim in the criminal trial.[48] The English courts have also recently confirmed that although there are many diverse bodies that might wish to represent the interests of the victims in a case they should

---

[41] Annual reports and accounts are published: see the most recent *FSS Annual Report and Accounts 2000/01*, H.C. Paper No.13 (Session 2001/02).

[42] Recommendation No. 262.

[43] See generally, Sanders and Young, (2000), Chap. 6; Emmins, (2000), Chap. 3; Ashworth, (1998), Chap. 6; I. Sigler, "Public Prosecution in England and Wales" [1974] Crim.L.R. 642; *The Royal Commission on Criminal Procedure* (Cmnd. 8092, 1980); JUSTICE, *The Prosecution Process in England and Wales* (1970); P. Devlin, *The Criminal Prosecution in England* (1960); M. McConville, "Prosecuting Criminal Cases in England and Wales: Reflections of an Inquisitorial Adversary" (1984) VI(1) Liverpool L.R. 15; K. de Gama, "Police Powers and Public Prosecutions: Winning by Appearing To Lose?" (1988) 6 Int. J. Sociology of Law 339.

[44] For favourable comment on which see the Auld Report (2001), Chap.10, para. 12.

[45] Below, para. 14-036.

[46] By requiring the consent of the DPP, the Attorney-General, a High Court judge or some other authority, to the proposed prosecution.

[47] See further below, para. 14-041.

[48] See *R. v. Weir* [2001] Crim.L.R. 653.

only be allowed to intervene in a trial on behalf of the victim in an exceptional case and on overwhelming grounds.[49]

The CPS is of course a public body and as such is bound to act in accordance with the ECHR,[50] although, in fact, the ECHR has not provided a very clear obligation on the prosecuting authorities to prosecute, rather there is an obligation to act fairly and to provide an adequate *process* for the prosecution.[51]

1. PROSECUTION ARRANGEMENTS BEFORE THE PROSECUTION OF OFFENCES ACT 1985[52]

(a) Police prosecutions

Prior to the establishment of the Crown Prosecution Service, the responsibility of deciding whether or not to prosecute suspects and the conduct of proceedings for less serious offences were regarded as two of the main functions of the police, as aspects of their general duty to enforce the law.[53] **14–030**

The procedure adopted varied according to the practice of the force concerned but the initial steps were normally taken in the name of the officer who had decided on the prosecution. Sometimes in the name of the Chief Constable, more often in the name of the head of the appropriate division or subdivision. If there was any legal difficulty, for example in deciding the appropriate charge or assessing the weight of the evidence on a particular charge, the police were able to take advice either from a prosecuting solicitors' department established by the police authority or from a private firm employed for that purpose. The growth of prosecuting solicitors' departments had a significant effect on police prosecutions, but that effect was haphazard since the constitution, size and operation of such departments was entirely a matter for local discretion and varied from force to force.

By the 1980s, 31 of the 43 police forces in England and Wales were able to draw on the expertise of their own prosecuting solicitors' department for legal advice and for representation in court.[54] It was clear that a prosecuting solicitor acted on instructions from the police and was merely an adviser in a solicitor/client relationship, but the line of authority, the budgetary controls,

---

[49] See *Re Pinochet Ugarte* (No. 2) [1999] 2 W.L.R. 272, HL.

[50] Human Rights Act, s.6. See further Emmerson and Ashworth, (2001), para. 18–53.

[51] See *R. v. DPP, ex p. Manning* [2000] 3 W.L.R. 463; *R.(Amin) v. Home Secretary* [2002] EWCA Crim 390.

[52] See S. Uglow, *Criminal Justice* (1995), Chap.4; Sanders and Young, (2000), Chap.6, pp. 317–319.

[53] *Final Report of the Royal Commission on the Police* (Cmnd. 1782, 1962), para. 59.

[54] The Metropolitan Police and the City of London force had their own special arrangements, leaving 10 forces to rely on private practitioners to provide the necessary service. See *Royal Commission on Criminal Procedure, The Investigation and Prosecution of Criminal Offences in England and Wales: The Law and Procedure* (hereafter RCCP I) (Cmnd. 8092–1, 1980), Appendix 22.

the amount of advocacy undertaken and the degree of "independence" enjoyed varied greatly from force to force.[55]

If the police *did* decide on a prosecution it was quite possible for a police officer to present the case in the magistrates' court. The Royal Commission on the Police suggested that it was undesirable for police officers to act as prosecutors save in minor cases.[56] In practice, the police could not conduct cases in the Crown Court and only prosecuted in the magistrates' court in straightforward cases.[57] In some areas, *all* prosecutions were undertaken by prosecuting solicitors. In serious cases, a measure of control was exerted by the Director of Public Prosecutions and the Law Officers.

(b) The Director of Public Prosecutions and the Law Officers[58]

14–031   The basic functions of the DPP have always included those of undertaking prosecutions of particular importance or difficulty and advising chief officers of police. Indeed, prior to the establishment of the CPS and the DPP's new role as head of the service, these were his main functions. Regulations 6 and 7 of the Prosecution of Offences Regulations 1978 (since revoked) required cases in a number of classes to be referred to the DPP. These gave the DPP an important co-ordinating function in these cases, which cases tended to be of a serious or sensitive nature. In addition, two further devices strengthened his position.

First, many statutes provided (and many still do) that prosecutions could only be brought in respect of certain offences with the consent of the DPP. This had become a popular provision where the offence was controversial, or the statutory provision slightly ambiguous, or public policy considerations were involved, or mitigating factors might be present or where vexatious or trivial private prosecutions might be brought.[59]

The second power strengthening the DPP's position was a general power vested in the DPP by sections 2 and 4 of the 1979 Act to take over criminal proceedings and then to deal with them as he wished, including the offering of no evidence if he so chose. This power was equally applicable to private prosecutions and was used, for example, to discontinue a private prosecution brought against a person to whom the DPP had given a promise of immunity from proceedings in return for giving evidence for the prosecution at another trial.[60] In that case it was held that the court had no power to interfere with the Director's exercise of discretion in how he conducted proceedings taken over by him or her.

All these powers taken together gave the DPP a significant amount of control over prosecution policy in relation to serious criminal offences.

---

[55] An analysis of the system is to be found in *The Prosecution System, Survey of Prosecuting Solicitors, Departments*, RCCP Research Study No. 11 (HMSO, 1980).
[56] Cmnd. 1782, para. 381.
[57] RCCP I, paras 144–145.
[58] For a general description see below, para. 14–036.
[59] See the evidence of the DPP to the RCCP, part of which is reproduced at RCCP I, para. 159.
[60] *Turner v. DPP* (1978) 68 Cr.App.R. 70. See also statements about the circumstances in which it is proper to grant such immunity in *R. v. Turner* (1975) 61 Cr.App.R. 67 (no relation). The matter was further considered in *Raymond v. Att.-Gen.* [1982] Q.B. 839, where the Court of Appeal confirmed that the power to "conduct" proceedings under s.4 included the power to discontinue them, pointing out that control was exercised over the DPP by the Attorney-General who was, in turn, accountable to Parliament.

The two important provisions relating to the Attorney-General[61] were his power to enter a *nolle prosequi* in proceedings on indictment[62] and the requirement of his consent to the prosecution of certain offences.[63] These remain after the Prosecution of Offences Act 1985. A notable example is the Law Reform (Year and a Day) Act 1996 under which the Attorney-General's consent is required for a prosecution for homicide offences if the victim dies three years or more after the event causing death, and the defendant has already been convicted in respect of his or her conduct.

The grant of a *nolle prosequi* by the Attorney-General stops proceedings on indictment immediately and is entered on the court record. It does not actually amount to an acquittal, so the accused may be indicted again on the same charge,[64] but another *nolle prosequi* may then be granted. A request for such a grant may be made by any person and the exercise of the power is equivalent to the DPP taking over proceedings and offering no evidence or a prosecutor offering no evidence, except that in both the latter cases the effect would formally be an acquittal.

The requirement of consent by the Attorney-General to prosecution was to be found in 39[65] statutes at the time of the Royal Commission on Criminal Procedure and included in that category were offences under the Public Order Act 1936,[66] the Hijacking Act 1971 and the Suppression of Terrorism Act 1978. These indicated that the primary responsibility of the Attorney-General in deciding whether to give consent was to weigh factors of national and public significance, conscious that he was the Minister answerable in Parliament for all matters connected with the conduct of criminal proceedings. However, it was clearly established that the Attorney-General's decision should be made on quasi-judicial and not on political grounds.[67]

---

[61] On the work of the Attorney-General see Lord Steyn, "The Weakest and Least Dangerous Department of Government" [1997] P.L. 84.

[62] This is a common iaw power not subject to any control by the courts: *R. v. Comptroller of Patents* [1899] 1 Q.B. 909.

[63] *cf.* the powers of the DPP referred to earlier. The manner in which the Att.-Gen.'s consent is to be provided and the degree of detail necessary are considered in *R. v. Cain* [1976] Q.B. 496.

[64] *Archbold* (2002), para. 1–251 relying on *Goddard v. Smith* (1704) 3 Salk. 245. See also *Ridpath* (1713) 10 Mod 152.

[65] DPP's evidence to the RCCP, Appendix 11. See Appendix A to the Law Commission Consultation Paper No. 149, *Consents to Prosecution* (1997). The list had grown to 67 offences by 1997.

[66] Including that created by the Race Relations Act 1976 of incitement to racial hatred, then s.5A of the 1936 Act.

[67] Statement by the Prime Minister to the House of Commons, February 16, 1959 (H.C. Deb., Vol. 600, col. 31), part of which is cited in RCCP I, para. 164. Questions can be asked in the House and, in one celebrated case, led to the downfall of the first Labour Government following the withdrawal of a prosecution for incitement to mutiny against J.R. Campbell, editor of a Communist publication, *Workers Weekly*: see J.LI. I. Edwards, *The Law Officers of the Crown* (1964), Chap. 11 and *The Attorney-General, Politics and the Public Interest* (1984), pp. 310–318; F. H. Newark, (1969) 20 N.I.L.Q. 19; N. D. Siederer, (1974) 9 Jo. of Contemporary History 143; J. F. Naylor, *A Man and an Institution* (1984), pp. 140–149, 156–157 (biography of Sir Maurice Hankey); K. D. Ewing and C.A. Gearty, *The Struggle for Civil Liberties* (2000). The independent role of the Attorney-General is fully considered in the two works by Edwards.

(c) Criticisms

14–032   These arrangements were subjected to close scrutiny, first by JUSTICE in 1970, and then by the Royal Commission on Criminal Procedure in 1981. JUSTICE[68] argued that the responsibility for prosecutions in all but trivial cases should be taken out of the hands of the police and given to a national prosecuting authority. In support of this recommendation it was said that:

(a) a police officer might convince himself of the guilt of a suspect and become psychologically committed to a prosecution;

(b) public policy and the circumstances of the individual were relevant considerations in the decision to prosecute;

(c) the English system was unique in Europe in allowing the whole process from interrogation to prosecution to be effectively under the control of the police in the majority of cases;

(d) investigators found it difficult to achieve the necessary detachment in taking what is essentially a "judicial-type" decision whether or not to prosecute;

(e) police involvement might influence the conduct of the prosecution in deciding appropriate charges or otherwise "bargaining" with a suspect, or in putting pressure on counsel at trial to take a particular line;

(f) police officers were not trained as lawyers or advocates and those tasks involving the expertise of lawyers or advocates should not be undertaken by the police.

The RCCP's approach was to analyse and establish the standards for judging the adequacy of a prosecution system; to measure the existing system by those standards; and then to recommend any changes necessary to achieve the standards. Put briefly, the RCCP decided that the system should be judged on fairness, openness and accountability, and efficiency.

"Is the system fair; first in the sense that it brings to trial only those against whom there is an adequate and properly prepared case and who it is in the public interest should be prosecuted (that is, tried by a court) rather than dealt with in another way (by cautioning, for example), and secondly in that it does not display arbitrary and inexplicable differences in the way that individual cases or classes of case are treated locally or nationally? Is it open and accountable in the sense that those who make the decisions to prosecute or not can be called publicly to explain and justify their policies and actions as far as that is consistent with protecting the interests of suspects and accused? Is it efficient in the sense that it achieves the objectives that are set for it with the minimum use of resources and the minimum delay? Each of these

---

[68] *The Prosecution Process in England and Wales* (1970). See also J. Sigler, [1974] Crim.L.R. 642; A. S. Bowley, [1975] Crim.L.R. 442.

standards makes its own contribution to what we see as being the single overriding test of a successful system. Is it of a kind to have and does it in fact have the confidence of the public it serves?"[69]

In considering the question of *fairness* in then existing arrangements the Commission concentrated on the issues of whether the "right" people were brought to trial, and in a way which demonstrated "consistency" in policy and practice in the various police forces.

On the former issue, the RCCP discussed the extent to which it was possible or desirable to separate the role of the investigator from that of lawyer in the prosecution process. In an analysis of the respective functions of the United States District Attorney, the Scottish Procurator Fiscal and the Canadian Crown Counsel, the RCCP considered that the two roles there had not been entirely separated.[70] The District Attorney used his staff in an investigative capacity both to improve the quality of cases presented by the police and to deal with major fraud, corruption and "white-collar" crime.[71] The Procurator Fiscal was directly involved in the investigation of violent deaths and in the most serious cases would see and take statements from police and witnesses before deciding whether to prosecute.[72] By contrast, in the provinces of British Columbia and Ontario, Crown Counsel were responsible entirely for the conduct of prosecutions *once the police had decided to bring a person to trial.* Crown Counsel had no investigative function, but the police retained a part of the lawyer's function in the initial decision to prosecute. The RCCP concluded that if any of these systems were more effective in putting the "right" people on trial it was not because they had succeeded in separating the functions of investigator and prosecutor. On the same issue the RCCP considered the evidence of acquittal statistics which indicated that a high proportion of acquittals ordered and directed by the judge at the Crown Court were the result of insufficient prosecution evidence.[73] The failure of prosecution witnesses at trial accounted for many of these cases, but there were clearly some cases where it should have been foreseen that the evidence would be inadequate. The lack of fairness demonstrated by such cases was only mitigated by their relative infrequency.[74]

Statistics contained in the Report showed that there was, indeed, a degree of inconsistency in prosecution policy and practice,[75] and that there was no

---

[69] RCCP Report, para. 6.8.

[70] *ibid.* paras 6.30–6.39.

[71] See further, J. Sigler, *An Introduction to the Legal System* (1968), pp. 79 *et seq.*; H. Mueller, "The Position of the Criminal Defendant in the U.S.A." in J. A. Coutts (ed.), *The Accused* (1966), pp. 102–104

[72] The role and powers of the Procurator Fiscal are described in *Criminal Procedure in Scotland and France* (HMSO Edinburgh, 1975), and by Lord Kilbrandon, "Scotland: Pre-Trial Procedure," in *The Accused, op. cit.* See also S. R. Moody and J. Tombs, *Prosecution in the Public Interest* (1982).

[73] RCCP Report, para. 6.19. See also M. McConville and J. Baldwin, *Courts Prosecution and Conviction* (1981).

[74] The RCCP Report suggested that one-fifth of directed acquittals might fall into this category. However, directed acquittals only formed 7%, of all cases disposed of by the Crown Court and the Crown Court only dealt with approximately 15% of all indictable offences. See RCCP Report, para. 6.22.

[75] *ibid.* para. 6.40. Inconsistency was primarily evident in the statistics relating to the use of the caution for both adults and juveniles.

effective machinery for achieving conformity.[76] Although this created unfairness, the RCCP concluded that it was not the main focus of public concern and that the solution, the strengthening of central control or a national prosecution service, could find better justification on the ground of openness and accountability than on the ground of improved fairness.

The question of *accountability* was complicated because of the implications for the defendant of any public scrutiny of the exercise of the discretion to prosecute. Questioning the decision of the prosecutor after an acquittal might amount to a "retrial" if the prosecutor attempted to defend the decision. If the prosecutor was required to defend a decision not to institute proceedings, unwarranted doubts might be cast on the suspect without the suspect having an opportunity to defend him- or herself.

However, the RCCP considered that those problems could be overcome by generalising the issue involved, and that accountability in the "explanatory and co-operative mode" to a local supervisory authority was desirable.[77] Additionally, a prosecution agency would clearly be accountable to the body providing it with funds for its economic efficiency and organisation. There was an obligation on the Attorney-General to answer in Parliament questions on the exercise of discretion, and the courts had some limited degree of control, but there was no real local supervision.[78]

The *efficiency* of a prosecuting system was not to be judged solely in terms of the efficient use of resources. Delays in preparation causing adjournments and inadequate preparation causing the collapse of cases certainly cost money, but could also cause injustice, inconvenience and frustration to all those concerned in the process.

At the same time, the concept of efficiency was notoriously difficult to use in relation to the criminal justice system; objectives were hard to define in precise terms and it was accordingly difficult to measure whether they had been achieved. The best the RCCP could propose was uniformity in prosecution arrangements, which would make possible the detection of inefficiencies in the system, and assist in achieving nationally such consistency in the application of general prosecution policies as was thought desirable.[79]

The RCCP concluded that " ... there is a case for some change. Indeed, not a single witness who has addressed this part of our terms of reference in detail has argued that there should be absolutely no change made. The areas of debate are on the direction and extent of change".[80]

Obviously impressed with the Canadian experience, the RCCP recommended that the police should retain sole responsibility for the investigation of offences and the initial decision whether to prosecute, and that thereafter the prosecutor should take over the conduct of the case and decide whether

---

[76] See above, para. 14-030.
[77] The Commission adopted terminology coined by G. Marshall, "Police Accountability Revisited" in Butler and Halsay (eds), *Policy and Politics* (1978). The "explanatory and co-operative model" is described as a type of accountability in which the supervisory authority has no power to bind or to reverse executive decisions, but where a means is provided for challenge, for the requirement of reasoned explanation and the communication of advice and recommendation. RCCP Rep., para. 6.50.
[78] See para. 14-030 for the controls then in place.
[79] RCCP Report, para. 6.64.
[80] *ibid.* para. 6.65.

to proceed as charged, or modify or withdraw the charges.[81] The major advantage of this proposal appeared to be that it indicated a reasonably clear demarcation of function, but it also would serve to maintain the primary responsibility of the police for investigation whilst enhancing the independent status of the prosecutor. This has become known as the "Philips Principle", denoting that it was one of the most significant of the RCCP recommendations.

The RCCP proposed that the prosecutor should be designated "Crown prosecutor" and that the organisation should be locally based drawing heavily upon the existing prosecuting solicitors' departments. Obviously, every police force would need to have such a department (which would then also offer an advice service to the police) and, consistent with the RCCP'S declared standards, a local supervisory authority would need to be designated for the purposes of accountability. After examining various possibilities,[82] a majority of the RCCP favoured the development of existing police authorities into police and prosecutions authorities with additional powers to supervise the functioning of the prosecution service. Central involvement in the prosecution process should continue in the form of the DPP; Ministerial responsibility for the new prosecution service should rest either with the Home Secretary or the Attorney-General, and the Minister should be empowered to set national standards for staffing and performance.[83]

These proposals had a mixed reception,[84] but were broadly accepted by the government, with the exception that the new prosecution service was to be nationally and not locally based.[85] Accountability of a prosecutor to a local body would not be "a proper or efficient arrangement". In matters of prosecution policy the service should be required to conform to guidance from the Attorney-General and not from local authorities; and "to give local authorities responsibility for finance and manpower alone would be to divorce control over policy from control over resources, which would not be conducive to sensible and efficient management of the new service".[86]

---

[81] *ibid.* paras 7.5. *et seq.*
[82] *ibid.* paras 7.21 *et seq.*
[83] RCCP Report, para. 7.60.
[84] See generally, A. F. Wilcox, [1981] Crim.L.R. 482.
[85] *An Independent Prosecution Service for England and Wales* (Cmnd. 9074, 1983). The White Paper included, as an Annex, the report of an inter-departmental Working Party on Prosecution Arrangements.
[86] Cmnd. 9074, p. 9.

2. Prosecution Arrangements under the Prosecution of Offences Act 1985[87]

(a) The Crown Prosecution Service[88]

14-033   The 1985 Act established the Crown Prosecution Service. It is headed by the DPP, who is now appointed by the Attorney-General and not the Home Secretary.[89] The DPP and the headquarters staff continue to be based in London. England and Wales are divided by the DPP into 42 Areas (and London) based on police areas.[90] Staff are appointed by the DPP. Any member of the CPS who has a "general qualification" may be designated by him or her as a Crown Prosecutor. The DPP must designate a Chief Crown Prosecutor for each Area, who is responsible to him or her for supervising the operation of the Service in that Area.[91] The Glidewell Report[92] recommended that the Chief Crown Prosecutors should be selected with a view to their being respected people of stature within the community on a par with local judges or the Chief Constable.[93]

The CPS employs around 6,000 people including barristers and solicitors, and these members of the service are accorded the limited rights of audience enjoyed by solicitors holding practising certificates.[94] The Lord Chancellor had introduced the opportunity for Higher Court Advocates to conduct Crown Court trials, and, following recommendations of the Narey

---

[87]   See the symposium in [1986] Crim.L.R. 3–44; K. W. Lidstone, (1987) 11 Crim. L.J. 296. For comparative material on public prosecutors see J. Fionda, *Public Prosecutors and Discretion: A Comparative Study* (1993); Special Issue of (2000) European Journal of Crime, Criminal Law and Criminal Justice; S. Uglow, *Criminal Justice* (1995), Chap. 4.

[88]   See generally *www.cps.gov.uk*. See also for a review of statistics, the National Audit Office Report, *The Crown Prosecution Service* (1997).

[89]   1985 Act, s.2. The DPP must possess a 10 year general qualification under the Courts and Legal Services Act 1990, s.71 (*i.e.* a right of audience in any part of the Supreme Court or all proceedings in county courts or magistrates' courts).

[90]   There were originally 31 Areas, grouped in four Regions (Northern, Midland, London and South East, South and West): see *Crown Prosecution Service Annual Report for 1987–88* (1987–88 H.C. 563), p. 45. These were reduced to 13 in 1993, including a new unified London area. The aim was to enhance the role and responsibilities of Chief Crown Prosecutors and to provide a shorter and more direct means of communication and accountability: *Annual Report of the CPS for 1993–94* (1993–94 H.C. 444), Chap. 2. This proved to be an unsatisfactory arrangement which led to an over-centralised and over-bureaucratised service. In 1997 the CPS was reorganised into 42 areas coterminous with the police areas: see Attorney-General's Written Answer H.C., Vol. 294, cols 73–74, May 21, 1997. This was a move that was approved by the Glidewell Report, Cm. 3960 (1998), *The Review of the CPS*. Many of that Report's recommendations were designed to rationalise the management of the CPS, with the introduction of a Chief Executive at H.Q. and attempts to decentralise the structure. The Report estimated that the top 400 lawyers in the CPS spent less than one-third of their time on casework and advocacy, illustrating the over bureaucratisation of the service.

[91]   1985 Act, s.1, as amended by the 1990 Act, Sched. 10, para. 61(1).

[92]   *The Review of the CPS* Cm 3960 (1998).

[93]   See Glidewell Report, Chap. 10; see also N. Addison, (1997) 147 N.L.J. 787.

[94]   *ibid.* s.4(i). See above, pp. 133–138. The Lord Chancellor was given power to give additional rights of audience to Crown Prosecutors: s.4(3). Sir Robert Andrew in his *Review of Government Legal Services* (HMSO, 1989) recommended that this power should be exercised in respect of suitably qualified members of the CPS (pp. 51–53). See now the Access to Justice Act 1999, s.106.

Report,[95] section 36 of the Access to Justice Act 1999 puts on a statutory footing the higher court rights of audience for employed lawyers.[96] Concerns have, however, been raised about the desirability of the CPS lawyers prosecuting cases in the Crown Court without the intervention of an independent barrister in private practice. By 2001, there were 277 Higher Court Advocates employed by the CPS.[97]

Under the Courts and Legal Services Act 1990, arrangements could be made for proceedings to be conducted on behalf of the CPS by any person with a "general qualification", appointed by the DPP who would then have all the powers of a Crown Prosecutor, but could exercise them subject to any instructions given by a Crown Prosecutor.[98] The Narey Report[99] recommended that the CPS should attempt to free up resources by allowing the DPP to confer on non-qualified staff the power to review files and to conduct less contentious cases in the magistrates' court.[1] Following these recommendations section 7A of the Prosecution of Offenders Act 1985[2] provides that CPS designated caseworkers may undertake certain work (bail applications and conduct other than trials) by appearing in the magistrates' court. They are also to have the powers of a Crown Prosecutor in relation to conduct of criminal proceedings other than presenting cases. Designated caseworkers[3] may deal with summary only offences in the magistrates' court where the trial is that of an adult, there are no challenges to bail and there are no significant factual disputes.[4] This is likely to occur in a substantial number of cases. In 2000–01, for example, there were 774,453 guilty pleas dealt with in the magistrates' court.

The designated caseworker cannot review (or present) a case which is indictable; where there is likely to be a contested trial; where the accused has elected jury trial or the magistrates' court has declined jurisdiction; the case

---

[95] M. Narey, *Review of Delay in the Criminal Justice System* (1997).
[96] Employed CPS lawyers, can become Higher Court Advocates. For details of this in operation see Appendix C to the *CPS Annual Report 2000–2001* (2001).
[97] By the end of March 2001, Higher Court Advocates had undertaken around 4,070 sessions, against a target of 2,900, during which they dealt with over 11,000 Crown Court hearings, and a number contested trials at the Crown Court for the first time: *CPS Annual Report 2000–2001*, (2001), p.20.
[98] *ibid.* s.5, as amended by the Courts and Legal Services Act 1990, Sched. 10, para. 61(2).
[99] Narey (1997).
[1] The use of unqualified staff within the CPS to review certain categories of cases (most summary offences) to decide whether a prosecution should proceed had been controversial. A case would only be passed to a Crown Prosecutor where the "case screener's" view was that there was insufficient evidence or a prosecution would be against the public interest, or if he or she considered that that would be helpful. The Divisional Court held that this arrangement was *ultra vires*, there being no express or implied power to delegate such decisions to persons other than Crown Prosecutors and qualified agents: *R. v. Director of Public Prosecutions, ex p. Association of First Division Civil Servants* (1988) 138 N.L.J. 158. An appeal was taken to the Court of Appeal but the case was settled by agreement. Under that agreement, case examiners vetted a more limited range of cases, and a decision whether or not to proceed would always be taken by a lawyer. Law clerks were also used to respond to bail applications in the Crown Court and High Court, but this practice was stopped in the light of legal advice that it was unlawful in the absence of express authority in the Prosecution of Offences Act 1985: *Annual Report of the Crown Prosecution Service for 1988–89* (1988–89 H.C. 411), pp. 17–18.
[2] As inserted by s.53 of the Crime and Disorder Act 1998, s.53.
[3] Who must have been through probation and have three years or more as a caseworker or be legally qualified and have undergone specialist training.
[4] Where the accused admits the offence or the witness to the offence is a police officer.

is to be dealt with under transfer procedures; the offence requires the consent of the DPP or Attorney-General; the case is considered to be a sensitive one (*e.g.* a fatal accident); the facts are disputed leading to the possibility of a 'Newton' hearing; or the offence is one which carries obligatory disqualification and that issue will be in dispute.[5] It is likely that, despite reservations, the remit of caseworkers will be extended in the future.[6]

Evaluations of the pilots of the present scheme identified a tension between the quality and expedition of the work.[7] In particular, in 7.1 per cent of cases examined there was inadequate information on the file reviewed by the caseworker to warrant his or her decision to prosecute, and there was concern that the caseworkers were reviewing cases outside their remit. However, at most pilot sites in the review the conclusion was that there was inadequate use made of the lay presenters to enable effective and efficient use of CPS resources.[8] The DPP is obliged, in the *Annual Report of the CPS* to report on the selection and functioning of caseworkers.[9] There were, by 2001, 222 designated caseworkers.[10]

Serious concerns have been raised about the use of administrators to make decisions affecting prosecution, even in these limited circumstances.[11] The decision is one that is crucial to the defendant, the victim and also has the potential to affect relations with the police.

(b) Functions of the Crown Prosecution Service

14–034   The Crown Prosecution Service's declared aim is "to contribute to the reduction both of crime and the fear of crime and to increase public confidence in the criminal justice system by fair and independent review of cases and by firm, fair, and effective prosecution at court".[12] The CPS's stated objectives are:

> "to deal with prosecution cases in a timely and efficient manner in partnership with other agencies; to ensure that the charges proceeded with are appropriate to the evidence and to the seriousness of the offending by the consistent, fair and independent review of cases in accordance with the Code for Crown Prosecutors; to enable the courts to reach just decisions by fairly, thoroughly and firmly presenting prosecution cases; rigorously testing defence cases and scrupulously complying with the duties of disclosure; to meet the needs of victims and witnesses in the criminal justice system, in cooperation with other criminal justice agencies".[13]

---

[5] See *CPS Annual Report, 2000–2001* (2001), Annex C.
[6] See *Criminal Justice: The Way Ahead* (2001), para. 3.14.
[7] See CPS Inspectorate, *Thematic Report 2/99 on the Evaluation of Lay Review and Lay Presentation* (1999) See the reservations expressed in the Glidewell Report (1998), paras 18 and 19.
[8] *ibid.* para. 9.13.
[9] s.7A(7).
[10] See *CPS Annual Report, 2000–2001* (2001), p.21.
[11] On lay representation see also the CPS Inspectorate Report: *The CPS Inspectorate's Report on the Evaluation of Lay Review and Lay Presentation* (1999).
[12] *CPS Annual Report, 2000–2001* (2001).
[13] *ibid.*

More specific legal requirements on the functioning of the CPS are imposed by the 1985 Act. In truth this Act is phrased in terms of a set of functions conferred on the DPP, acting under the superintendence of the Attorney-General, however, it is also provided that every Crown Prosecutor shall have all the powers of the DPP as to the initiation and conduct of proceedings, acting under his or her direction.[14] Section 3(2) of the 1985 Act provides that it is the duty of the DPP:

"(a) to take over the conduct of all criminal proceedings, other than specified proceedings, instituted on behalf of a police force (whether by a member of that force or by any other person);

[(aa) to take over the conduct of any criminal proceedings instituted by an immigration officer (as defined for the purposes of the Immigration Act 1971) acting in his capacity as such an officer;][15]

(b) to institute and have the conduct of criminal proceedings in any case where it appears to him that—

    (i) the importance or difficulty of the case makes it appropriate that proceedings should be instituted by him; or

    (ii) it is otherwise appropriate for proceedings to be instituted by him;

(c) to take over the conduct of all binding over proceedings instituted on behalf of a police force (whether by a member of that force or by any other person);

(d) to take over the conduct of all proceedings begun by summons issued under section 3 of the Obscene Publications Act 1959 (forfeiture of obscene articles);

(e) to give, to such extent as he considers appropriate, advice to police forces on all matters relating to criminal offences;

(f) to appear for the prosecution, when directed by the court to do so, on any appeal under—

    (i) section 1 of the Administration of Justice Act 1960 (appeal from the High Court in criminal cases);

    (ii) Part I or Part II of the Criminal Appeal Act 1968 (appeals from the Crown Court to the criminal division of the Court of Appeal and thence to the House of Lords); or

    (iii) section 108 of the Magistrates' Courts Act 1980 (right of appeal to Crown Court) as it applies, by virtue of subsection (5) of section 12 of the Contempt of Court Act 1981, to orders made under section 12 (contempt of magistrates' courts); and

(g) to discharge such other functions as may from time to time be assigned to him by the Attorney-General in pursuance of this paragraph."

---

[14] 1985 Act, s.1(6). Similarly, where the consent of the DPP is required by statute, that consent can be expressed by a Crown Prosecutor: s.l(7). It need not be in writing: *R. v. Jackson* [1997] Crim.L.R. 755.

[15] As inserted by the Immigration and Asylum Act 1999, s.164.

The key provision governing the relationship between the CPS and the police is section 3(2)(a). The usual task of the CPS is to take over proceedings instituted by the police. Proceedings are "instituted" for these purposes when information is laid before a justice of the peace before the issue of a summons or arrest warrant, or when a person charged with an offence after being taken into custody without a warrant is informed of the particulars of the charge, or when a voluntary bill of indictment is preferred before the court.[16] In these cases, the question for the CPS is whether proceedings should be continued or discontinued.[17] Express provision for the discontinuance of proceedings is made by section 23.[18] This has proved to be a controversial provision and is discussed below.

The Auld Report recommends that these procedures be streamlined, so that there would be a common form of commencement of all *public* prosecutions, (with the voluntary bill on indictment being abolished).[19]

In the case of a person taken into custody without a warrant and charged, but where no magistrates' court has been informed of the charge, the prosecutor may discontinue proceedings by giving notice to the person concerned. Where proceedings have otherwise been instituted, but are still in their "preliminary stages" (*i.e.* before the court commences to hear evidence at a summary trial, or before committal or being sent to the Crown Court), the prosecutor may discontinue them by giving notice, with reasons, to the clerk of the court. The accused must also be informed, but need not be given reasons, and has the right to require the proceedings to continue (within 35 days). The discontinuance of proceedings under section 23 does not prevent the institution of fresh proceedings in respect of the same offence.[20] If the prosecutor wishes to discontinue at a later stage, the court's consent may be necessary.[21]

There is a limited range of offences which can still be prosecuted to conclusion by the police. These are the "specified proceedings" mentioned in section 3(2)(a), and comprise a number of less serious road traffic offences,[22] some commonly dealt with by the fixed penalty procedures. They remain "specified" provided that there is a written plea of guilty. If the case is contested, it must then be dealt with by the CPS. Apart from these offences,

---

[16] s.15(2). If more than one of these is applicable, the earliest time is taken.

[17] s.15(3) provides that reference as to the conduct of any proceedings include references to their being discontinued.

[18] As amended by the Criminal Justice and Public Order Act 1994, Sched. 4, Pt. II, para. 62.

[19] See Chap. 10, para. 57.

[20] Section 23(9).

[21] At the Crown Court, the approval of the judge is necessary: *R. v. Broad* (1979) 68 Cr.App.R. 281, but at committal proceedings, the consent of the justices is *not* required: *R. v. Canterbury and St Augustine's JJ., ex p. Klisiak* [1982] 1 Q.B. 398. The RCCJ recommended (Cm. 2263, p. 77) that the CPS should be given power to discontinue proceedings up to the beginning of the trial in both the magistrates' court and the Crown Court. The Auld Report (2001) recommended that the CPS should have the power to discontinue any case up to and including the time of pre-trial assessment without requiring the consent of the defendant or the approval of the court. This would allow for a case to be reinstated if appropriate. Any discontinuance at a later stage would result in an acquittal except in special circumstances following an application to the court: Chap. 9, para. 67. This reflects the Runciman proposal that was not adopted.

[22] Prosecution of Offences Act 1985 (Specified Proceedings) Order 1999 (S.I. 1999 No. 904); see the discussion of the previous versions by J. N. Spencer, (1988) 152 J.P.N. 691. See also (1989) 139 N.L.J. 1739.

all proceedings instituted by the police must be taken over by the CPS. Where the only involvement of the police[23] is that they charge the suspect, the proceedings are not "instituted"[24] by the police. Section 3(2)(b) preserves the right of the CPS to institute proceedings in serious or difficult cases.

The 1985 Act also preserves the right of private prosecution by providing that nothing in Part I shall preclude any person from instituting any criminal proceedings, or conducting any proceedings which the DPP is not under a duty to take over.[25] The DPP does, however, still have power to take over private prosecutions at any stage.[26] The CPS will take over and discontinue a prosecution where, on the evidence, there is no case to answer, which involves a different test from that applied when deciding whether to initiate a prosecution. If a prosecution is taken over, the prosecutor may of course exercise the power to discontinue under section 23.

Crown Prosecutors are given guidance as to the exercise of their powers by the Code for Crown Prosecutors issued by the DPP under section 10.[27]

(c) Relationship between the Crown Prosecution Service and the police[28]

As has been mentioned, the crucial feature of this relationship is that in most cases it is still a matter for the police to determine whether proceedings should be *instituted*. They may obtain the advice of the CPS before so deciding, but this is only done in a minority of cases.[29] As a result, the CPS normally has no involvement in cases where the police decide not to prosecute, including the cases where the caution procedure is adopted. This makes it more difficult for a rational prosecution policy to be developed[30]

14–035

---

[23] Including the NCS: see the Police Act 1997, Sched. 9, para. 48. See also the Prosecution of Offences Act 1985 (Specified Police Forces) Order 1985 (S.I. 1985 No. 1956).

[24] *R. (Hunt) v. C.C.R.C.* [2001] Q.B. 1108, [2001] Crim.L.R. 324; Woolf L.C.J. declined to follow his own interpretation of the word "instituted" from *R. v. Ealing JJ., ex p. Dixon* [1990] 2 Q.B. 91, favouring the narrower view of Watkins L.J. in *R. v. Stafford Justices, ex p. Customs and Excise* [1991] 2 Q.B. 339. Proceedings are only "instituted" on behalf of the police where the police have investigated and arrested the suspect in question. This interpretation restricts the circumstances in which the DPP must take over the case, and, with a diverse range of potential prosecutors involved, inhibits consistency. See also *R. v. Croydon JJ., ex p. Holmberg* (1993) 12 Tr. L.R. 10 (local authority entitled to act as prosecutor in proceedings under the Trade Marks Act 1985); Auld Report (2001), Chap. 10, para. 53.

[25] Thus a private prosecution may be brought where the DPP has decided not to exercise the power under s.3(2)(b) of the 1985 Act (text above) *Bow Street Stipendiary Magistrate, ex p. South Coast Shipping* [1993] Q.B. 645 (private prosecution for manslaughter arising out of the collision (between the *Bowbelle* and the *Marchioness* on the River Thames in 1989).

[26] 1985 Act, s.6. On when it is appropriate for the DPP to take over proceedings see *R. v. DPP, ex p. Duckenfield* [2000] 1 W.L.R. 55.

[27] See below. Exceptional circumstances of non-compliance may lead to a conviction being quashed: *R. v. Liverpool City Justices and the CPS, ex p. Price* (1998) 162 J.P. 766.

[28] See Glidewell Report (1998), Chap. 7.

[29] The research by Baldwin and Hunt, [1998] Crim.L.R. 52 suggests that the police are not inclined to seek advice even when it is from a CPS lawyer in the station for that purpose. Similarly, earlier research of a survey of 13 branches in the last quarter of 1991 found that advice was sought in, on average, 4.3% of cases finalised (ranging from 0.7% to 13.9% for particular branches: D. Crisp and D. Moxon, *Case Screening by the Crown Prosecution Service: How and Why Cases are Terminated* (H.O. Research Study No. 137,1994), p. 7.

[30] *cf.* M. McConville, (1984) VI(1) Liverpool L.R. 15 at 28. This is exacerbated by the fixed penalty schemes.

although it might be thought unlikely that the police will drop a case that the CPS would have been prepared to prosecute. There is the danger that cases dealt with by the police without CPS scrutiny provide an opportunity for the police to hide badly investigated cases.

Furthermore, doubts have been expressed as to the effectiveness in principle of a system in which the CPS review occurs after the initial decision to prosecute has been taken. It has been argued that there is a natural tendency for the police, once satisfied as to who is responsible, to consider as mistaken any material that points in another direction,[31] this tendency being present in a number of notorious miscarriages of justice.[32] The prosecutor would be constrained by the information provided by the police, and

> "it would be irrational and indefensible in most cases if the prosecutor did *not* endorse police action, because the file is constructed in order to leave this as the only proper option".[33]

A further related danger identified by Sanders and Young is that the test applied by the CPS in deciding whether to discontinue a case focuses on the question of likely conviction rather than on guilt. This encourages police officers to strengthen weak cases.[34] The question to discontinue a case is a pivotal one in the prosecution process, and it is particularly important for the CPS since the number of non-jury acquittals of cases is often used as a measure of the CPS's success. This increases pressure to drop cases that are only marginally likely to succeed, but that action is a major source of conflict with the police.

The underlying tension between the CPS and police persists as for example with the dependence on the provision of files from the police.[35] It is reported that in only 43 per cent of cases are the files delivered on time and of the appropriate quality for the CPS to proceed.[36]

Suggestions were made in the RCCP that prosecutors might be given some powers of direction over investigations and the decision to prosecute might be removed altogether from the police.[37] This was not implemented, but the separation between police and CPS became an important feature of the RCCP proposals and of the subsequent legislation. Recent reforms have, however, made inroads into the independence built into the structure. Narey,[38] recommended increasing CPS involvement in policing by locating

---

[31] McConville, *op. cit.* pp. 28–32; A. Sanders, "Constructing the Case for the Prosecution" (1987) 14 J.I. S. 229.

[32] The Evans, Virag and Dougherty and Confait cases: see L. Kennedy, *Ten Rillington Place* (1961); Devlin Report on the *Evidence of Identification in Criminal Cases* (HMSO, 1976); Fisher Report on the Confait Case (HMSO, 1977). See also the case of Bruce Lee.

[33] McConville, *op. cit.* p. 30. *Cf.* A. Sanders, [1986] Crim.L.R. 16 at 27, who argues that the structure gives the prosecutors power to drop cases but little incentive to do so; and K. W. Lidstone, (1987) 11 Crim. L.J. 296 at 310–312.

[34] (2000), p. 332.

[35] The *CPS Annual Report 200–2001* (2001).

[36] "Results published quarterly by Her Majesty's Inspector of Constabulary (HMIC) show that in 2000–2001, 94% of expedited files met the quality standard, while police performance on both the timeliness and quality of full files has remained broadly constant: 71% met the timeliness target; 55% were fully satisfactory in terms of quality; and 43% met both the timeliness and quality targets." *CPS Annual Report 2000–2001* (2001), p. 12.

[37] See McConville, Sanders and Lidstone, *op. cit.*.

[38] *Review of Delay in the Criminal Justice System* (1997), Chap. 3.

prosecutors in police stations. This would allow the CPS to play a role in reviewing the charges laid at the earliest availability and thereby reduce the number of charges that needed to be altered. To ensure that CPS could respond promptly to police enquiries so that the scheme would operate at all times, it was also recommended that the CPS should provide on-call advice in evenings and weekends advising officers on charges. In the pilot scheme, it was found however that the police only sought advice out of hours on 12 occasions.[39] A related aim of these recommendations of the early involvement was for the CPS to be able to identify those cases in which an "abbreviated file" would suffice (with only five documents) which would facilitate hearing and conviction within 24 hours, with a duty solicitor being responsible for the defence. The Glidewell Report also recommended that the CPS take responsibility for the prosecution process as soon as the defendant has been charged, arrange initial magistrates' hearings and take responsibility for the availability and care of witnesses. Criminal Justice Units (CJUs) were created to implement this and to deal with fast track cases.[40]

Baldwin and Hunt considered very early pilot schemes of the CPS lawyers being present in the police station, and raised obvious concern that this could undermine the already fragile appearance of the independence between the police and CPS. The research[41] found that the CPS were asked for advise in 1.8 per cent of cases, but statistics on charging accuracy indicates that advice should be sought far more often. Baldwin and Hunt took the view that the benefits of a lawyer in a police station scheme did not outweigh the resource implications and that the schemes would always depend on the ability of the investigating officer to identify a point of law. Further problems included the fact that officers often felt that they did not require assistance, and that it was not always practical to seek that assistance. Baldwin and Hunt felt that advice should have been sought in 48 of the 600 cases sampled. Nevertheless, the Auld Report also recommended that the CPS should take control of the prosecution at an earlier stage, with a more proactive role in the case.[42] This was seen as a way of reducing the problem created by the police overcharging and the consequent effects of having to amend the changes (with the anguish for victims) and of a greater risk of late amendments to the indictment or plea bargains for lesser charges being struck.[43] The recommendations have been cogently criticised by Zander[44] as being based on nothing more than opinion. As Zander points out, it is impossible to say why it has been necessary to amend an indictment

---

[39] Ernst & Young, *Reducing Delay in the Criminal Justice System: Evaluation of the Pilot Schemes* (1999).
[40] See Chap. 8. See also the CPS press release February 20, 2001, and CPS, *An Early Assessment of Allocated CJUs* (2001). These are to be increased in number. See the latest government proposals in *Criminal Justice: The Way Ahead* (2001), Chap. 1. By March 31, 2001, there were 17 co-located Criminal Justice Units in police premises, and three in CPS premises. A further 56 Criminal Justice Units are planned by March 31, 2002: *CPS Annual Report 2000–2001* (2001), p. 10.
[41] [1998] 521 Crim.L.R.
[42] Chap. 10, para.12.
[43] Chap. 10, para. 35.
[44] *www.lse.ac.uk/Depts/law.*

and to what extent the amendment is a factor in delay.[45] It is certainly easier to overcharge and reduce the charges later than to attempt to introduce more serious ones.[46] At present it is difficult to identify the precise scope and causes of overcharging, although it is disturbing to note that the CPS Annual Report 1999–2000 reveals that 22 per cent of police charges for assault, public order and road traffic cases were incorrect.[47]

The need for closer working practices on the laying of appropriate charges is made even more important by the abolition of the committal proceedings for indictable offences.[48] The Auld Report recommended that in "all but minor, routine cases, or where there is a need for a holding charge, [the CPS] should determine the charge and initiate the prosecution. The precise offences that could be left to the police without advance intervention by the Service could be provided by national guidelines contained within the Criminal Procedure Code." This should develop a "better understanding by the police of the evidential test governing decisions to prosecute; a general increase in the speed with which cases proceed to trial; and greater confidence of victims, witnesses and the general public in the process as a result of fewer cases being discontinued after charge or continuing on reduced charges".[49] Pilots of the scheme have been initiated.[50]

Arguably, the decision to prosecute is a trial-related matter (and quasi judicial) rather than an investigative matter. As such, it could be seen to be more appropriate for the CPS to take the principal responsibility. In addition, the earlier involvement of the CPS could lead to the collection of better quality evidence that is more focused on the needs of the trial. However, this must be offset against the practical difficulties and the drawbacks that flow from the public perception that the CPS and police are not independent.[51]

(d) Role of the Attorney-General and the DPP under the new arrangements

14–036   Mention has been made earlier in this chapter[52] of the various powers and duties of the DPP and Law Officers that provided a measure of central co-ordination and control under the old arrangements, including requirements for cases to be reported to the DPP, consents to prosecution,[53] the DPP's general power to take over prosecutions, and the Attorney-General's power

---

[45] A recommendation that the CPS take responsibility for charging was unanimously rejected by the RCCJ, para. 21. This was largely on practical grounds. It should be noted that it would also lead to a deterioration in CPS police relations.

[46] Although the false expectations of the victim are important, these cannot be as strong as those of the accused.

[47] Cited in Auld Report (2001), Chap.10, para. 37.

[48] See Crime and Disorder Act 1998, s.51, below, para. 14-043.

[49] Chap. 10, paras 44 and 45.

[50] See CPS Press Release, March 5, 2002.

[51] The position is under review. See CPS, *Review of the Role and Practices of the CPS* (2002).

[52] See above.

[53] Some of the consent requirements mentioned above para. 14-031 have been re-enacted: see now, *e.g.* Public Order Act 1986, s.27(1) (incitement to racial hatred offences); Aviation Security Act 1982, s.8(1) (offences against safety of aircraft); Official Secrets Act 1989, s.9 (most offences under the Act).

to issue a *nolle prosequi*. Note that any function of the Attorney-General may be exercised by the Solicitor-General.[54]

These all still exist, but are obviously no longer the main vehicle for exerting central control or influence over prosecutions. They may, however, still be of importance in respect of prosecutions brought other than by the police. Requirements that proceedings may only be instituted by or with the consent of the Attorney-General or the DPP do not prevent an arrest or the remand in custody or on bail of a person charged with an offence.[55] Accordingly a prosecution may get to the stage of a charge by the police and an initial court appearance without reference to the Attorney-General or the DPP. However, a summons should not be issued by a justice of the peace, clerk to the justices or authorised delegate unless he or she is satisfied, *inter alia*, that any necessary authority to prosecute has been obtained.[56] This is the only procedure open to non-police prosecutors, unless the police are prepared to charge on their behalf.[57]

When the consent of the DPP to the prosecution is required, that may now be expressed by a Crown Prosecutor.[58] There are internal arrangements within the CPS governing which cases are to be referred to headquarters.[59] The courts have approved of the Crown Prosecution Service acting within the general authority of the DPP and exercising his powers without express instruction to do so.[60]

The Law Commission[61] recently reviewed the scheme of consents in light of other measures for controlling prosecutions (the Attorney-General's power to enter a *nolle prosequi*, the power to prevent vexatious litigants from commencing proceedings, and the powers of the DPP to take over and discontinue proceedings under section 23 of the Prosecution of Offences Act 1985). The Commission concluded that some of the consent restrictions had been "arbitrarily imposed", and that there are "anomalies and even absurdities" amongst the list. In terms of principle, the wide range of statutes containing consent requirements has made "substantial inroads into the much-acclaimed principle of the ordinary individual's right to set the criminal law in motion".[62] The Law Commission proposed abolition of the existing consent requirements and replacement with three categories of offences only requiring a consent provision: (i) where it is very likely that a defendant will reasonably contend that prosecution for a particular offence would violate his or her ECHR rights; (ii) those involving national security

---

[54] Law Officers Act 1997, s.1. Nothing in that section requires anything done by the Solicitor-General to be done in the name of the Solicitor-General instead of the name of the Attorney-General: *ibid.*, s.1(4)(b).

[55] Prosecution of Offences Act 1985, s.25, re-enacting s.6 of the 1979 Act: see *R. v. Elliott* (1985) 81 Cr. App. R. 115 (the Attorney-General's consent to a prosecution under the Explosive Substances Act 1883 was given eight weeks after charge: it was held that, in view of s.6 of the 1979 Act, the proceedings were instituted at the defendant's first court appearance); *cf. R. v. Whale and Lockton* [1991] Crim.L.R. 692.

[56] *R. v. Gateshead JJ., ex p. Tesco Stores Ltd* [1981] Q.B. 470 at 478.

[57] See below.

[58] Prosecution of Offences Act 1985, s.1(7).

[59] See *Annual Report of the CPS 1986–87* (1987–88 H.C. 14), Chap. 8 and *www.cps.gov.uk*.

[60] *R. v. Liverpool Crown Court, ex p. Bray* [1987] Crim.L.R. 51. (prosecutor seeking voluntary bill of indictment).

[61] *Consents to Prosecution, Consultation Paper No. 149* (1997); Report No. 255 (1998).

[62] The Consultation Paper provides a comprehensive account of the history and process and catalogues all of the statutory obligations to obtain such consent.

or with an international element (*i.e.* related to the international obligations of the State (which would be exercised by the Attorney-General)), to combat international terrorism or involve responses to international conflict or have a bearing on international relations; (iii) offences which create a high risk that private prosecution might be abused *and* where such proceedings will cause the defendant irreparable harm. As a restriction on the exercise of the powers of consent, the recommendation was that the powers could only be delegable to the Head of Central Casework and not to any CPS lawyer. The Law Commission also recommended automatic notification of private prosecutions to the CPS except where the DPP has licensed an organisation or person to bring criminal proceedings without such notification.[63] The Auld Report supports the recommendations made by the Law Commission.[64]

The DPP does not have the power to guarantee not to prosecute and to offer immunity to an offender in advance of a possible crime.[65]

(e) CPS operations[66]

14–037   The workload of the CPS is substantial. In 2000–2001, the CPS dealt with 115,732 Crown Court cases and 1,354,713 magistrates' cases.[67] There is no question but that the organisation operates under incredible pressure.

It is generally agreed that the CPS got off to a bad start, many of its problems stemming from a lack of resources.[68] Its official complement for staff was inadequate for the work it had to do and it was unable to recruit up to its complement. Private practice lawyers were employed as agents in a higher proportion of cases than planned or thought desirable, and this added to the expense of the operation as a whole. A recurrent theme in the criticism of the service was the inadequate preparation of cases, particularly less important cases being handled by inexperienced staff, leading to the late service of papers, delays and the unnecessary discontinuance of cases. Relations between the CPS and the police were too often strained, the former criticising the quality and late delivery of files, the latter complaining that cases were discontinued unnecessarily and that the CPS demanded a higher standard of file preparation than had been the norm. Others drew attention to instances both of the dropping of winnable cases and of the continuation of cases doomed to failure.

Throughout the 1990s steps were taken in response to these difficulties. A combination of higher salaries, major recruitment initiatives and the

---

[63] This would alert the CPS which could choose to take over the proceedings under s.6.

[64] Chap.10, para. 51–52.

[65] See *Pretty v. DPP* [2001] UKHL 61.

[66] See A. Ashworth, "Developments in the Public Prosecutor's Office in England" (2000) Euro Journal of Crime, Criminal Law and Criminal Justice for an accessible review of CPS. See generally on the CPS, Ashworth, Chaps 5 and 6; Sanders and Young, (2000), Chap. 5; A. Sanders, "From Suspect to Trial" in M. Maguire, R. Morgan and R. Reiner (eds), *Oxford Handbook of Criminology* (2nd ed. 1997).

[67] *CPS Annual Report 2000–2001* (2001), pp. 26–30.

[68] See the Glidewell Report (1998), Chaps 8, 10; National Audit Office, *Review of the Crown Prosecution Service* (1988–89 H.C. 345); Second Report of the Committee of Public Accounts, *Review of the Crown Prosecution Service* (1989–90 H.C.164); Fourth Report of the Home Affairs Committee (1989–90 H.C. 118). The story of the establishment of the CPS is told from the point of view of its first head in Sir Thomas Hetherington, *Prosecution and the Public Interest* (1989); *cf.* J. Rozenberg, *The Case for the Crown* (1987), Chap. 4.

recession enabled the CPS to recruit substantially to its complement and reduce reliance on agents. A number of initiatives supported and improved liaison at national and local levels.[69] Internal administrative arrangements were repeatedly reorganised, the most significant change being the ill-fated reduction in the number of CPS areas.[70]

The RCCJ endorsed "the unambiguous separation of the roles of investigator and prosecutor".[71] They were encouraged by what they saw as the "improving performance of the CPS, although noting that it may still remain patchy in some areas".[72] They did not recommend that the CPS should supervise police investigations: CPS staff did not possess the appropriate skills and experience and there would be a serious confusion of roles.[73] However, the police were encouraged to seek the advice of the CPS in appropriate cases in accordance with agreed guidelines. Furthermore, it would not be practicable to give the CPS responsibility for framing the initial charge (CPS staff could not be posted to all police stations.)[74] The RCCJ thought the police should undertake to meet all reasonable requests from the CPS to make further inquiries, but fell short of recommending that the DPP be given power to require this to be done.[75]

During the 1990s the criticism continued to be heaped upon the CPS and the Labour Government, newly elected in 1997, recognised that a wholesale review of the CPS was necessary.[76] The Glidewell Review[77] was established to "examine the organisation and structure of the CPS together with the CPS policies and procedures and to consider whether and if so what changes are necessary in order to provide for the more effective and efficient prosecution of crime through local public prosecutors". It made 75 recommendations and was generally well-received, although it did draw criticism for its focus on management and administration rather than legal issues.[78]

The Glidewell Report concluded that the 1993 reorganisation had been a mistake and had led to overcentralisation and unnecessary bureaucracy.[79] As an example of the overadministration and inefficiency in the Service, the Report estimated that the top 400 lawyers in the CPS spent less than one-third of their time on casework and advocacy. The Report was critical of the

---

[69] Including trilateral meetings with the LCD and the Home Office, participation in the work of the Working Group on Pre-Trial Issues and the Standing Commission on Efficiency (*Annual Report of the CPS, 1990–91*, pp. 17, 19–20). On the proposed restructuring of the Criminal Justice Agencies, see Auld Report (2001), Chap. 8.

[70] Above, para. 14-033.

[71] Cm. 2263, p. 69.

[72] *ibid.* p. 70.

[73] *ibid.* pp. 22–23, 71–72.

[74] *ibid.* p. 72–73. Notwithstanding this, pilot schemes for CPS lawyers to work in police stations and police administrative support units were established in a number of areas (CPS Press Notice, January 26, 1996). See now the CJUs discussed above.

[75] *ibid.* pp. 73–74.

[76] On poor morale in the CPS see F. Bawdon, (1998) N.L.J. 491, and see F. Davies, (1997) 161 J.P.N. 207 for a description of media attacks at the time.

[77] *The Review of the CPS* Cm 3960, (1998).

[78] See, *e.g.* comments at (1998) N.L.J. 824 at 861.

[79] paras 12–13.

way in which the CPS had been managed,[80] and proposed a different structure for operation and accountability.[81]

As far as the success of the CPS in conducting trials and performing its legal functions, Glidewell expressed concern at the number of non-jury acquittals in Crown Court cases.[82] In an attempt to optimise the use of the lawyers' skills within the CPS, it was recommended that there should be a shift in gravity from the magistrates court to the Crown Court with lawyers present (especially for PDHs), and that the Central Casework section be strengthened to become a centre of excellence,[83] with better training and staffing to equip it to deal with the most complex cases.[84]

Although one of the triggers for the Report was the drop in conviction rates in the 1990s,[85] in terms of evaluating performance of the CPS, Glidewell has been criticised for failing to grasp this nettle, stating instead that it was impossible to draw conclusions from the conflicting statistics available.[86]

The Report recommended establishing an independent inspectorate, and this was implemented by the Crown Prosecution Service Inspectorate Act 2000.[87] The inspections will occur on a two-year cycle (rather than a four-year cycle as originally envisaged). During 2000–2001, the Inspectorate published reports of its inspections on 17 CPS Areas, identifying examples of good practice, and also areas for improvement. The Inspectorate also undertook "thematic reviews" on various important issues.[88]

In addition to the major structural changes in the short life span of the CPS, there have been numerous operational changes. Under the auspices of the Working Group on Pre-Trial Issues, a manual of guidance for the preparation and presentation of prosecution files to the CPS by the police was produced jointly in 1992.[89] The manual of guidance has been updated in 2000 with a view to further streamlining with two file categories: expedited files for those cases in which no trial will occur in the magistrates' court and the full file for trials in the magistrates' court and Crown Court cases.

---

[80] Leading to Dame Barbara Mills, the then DPP, retiring early — see (1998) N.L.J. 773.

[81] Chap. 10.

[82] Chap. 4, para. 58. In 2001, 20% of cases in the Crown Court led to judge-directed acquittals; 12% of cases resulted in jury acquittals and 72% in convictions. *CPS Annual Report 2000–2001* (2001), p.28.

[83] para. 18.

[84] See Chap. 9.

[85] See (1998) J.P.N. 22.

[86] *e.g.* chap.4, para. 11.

[87] See Chap. 4, paras 37–38. The CPS internal inspectorate produced a number of important thematic reviews. See, *e.g. Adverse Cases* (2000), *Disclosure* (2000). There are also specialist reports such as the *Racist Incident Monitoring Scheme* annual reports. In 2001, the Report showed a 50% increase in racist crimes over the previous year. Of the 2,417, 24% were dropped, 36% of which was owing to a failure on the part of a witness.

[88] Including disclosure, and on performance indicator compliance and case outcomes; and joint inspections with other criminal justice system inspectorates; the implementation of section 1 of the Magistrates' Courts' Procedures Act 1998; and progress made in reducing delay in the Youth Justice system *CPS Annual Report 2000–2001*, (2001), p.7.

[89] See Efficiency Scrutiny, *Administrative Burdens on the Police in the Context of the Criminal Justice System* (June 1995), Chap. 3.

(f) The future

The Glidewell Report made the recommendation that the CPS be given an **14-038** appropriate opportunity to effect the changes proposed before any further reorganisation was contemplated. The Report expressed the hope that the CPS could become a "lively, successful and esteemed part of the criminal justice system", but felt that this description did not currently apply.[90]

The CPS is still the target for heavy criticism. In 2001 for example, the Denman Report on Racial Discrimination in the CPS found that there was "institutional" racism in the Service.[91] The ease with which criticism can be levelled at the CPS is increased by the availability of targets and performance indicators which are continually being imposed.[92] These include aims of: meeting time guidelines in committals in 78 per cent of cases; meeting time guidelines in briefs to counsel in 82 per cent of cases; reducing the cases of no submission acceded to in the magistrates' court to 7.5 per cent per 100,000; reducing non-jury acquittals to six per 1,000. Such targets and performance indicators illustrate the impact of managerialism on the CPS,[93] but do at least allow for effective monitoring of some aspects of its functions.

The CPS is currently committed to a substantial recruitment campaign,[94] and the government has made a 23 per cent increase in funding for 2001–02.[95] The government has also announced plans to establish a "prosecution college" to improve the training and skills of CPS employees, and to further develop joint police initiatives.[96] The programme of continual reform of the CPS continues unabated.[97]

3. THE SERIOUS FRAUD OFFICE

The Serious Fraud Office (SFO)[98] was established by the Criminal Justice **14-039** Act 1987, following the Report of the Roskill Committee on Fraud Trial.[99]

---

[90] See Executive Summary, para. 26.

[91] para. 3.2.1. See also B. Mhalanga, *Race and the CPS* (1997). The Inquiry's principal findings, were that: "for a large public employer, the CPS responded slowly to modern equal opportunities legislation and practices; although ethnic minority staff are well represented overall, they are seriously under-represented in both the higher administrative grades and the higher lawyer grades. This pattern cannot simply be attributed to historical factors." (para. 3.2.1).

[92] For example in its *Business Plan 2001–02* (2001).

[93] See also the *CPS Strategic Plan 2000–2004* (2001), and the *Departmental Investment Strategy* (2001) available from the CPS website, which specify targets such as improving by 5% the satisfaction of victims and witnesses by 2004.

[94] See (2001) S.J. 3.

[95] See *Criminal Justice: The Way Ahead* (2001), p.5.

[96] *Criminal Justice: The Way Ahead* (2001), p.54.

[97] See the recent consultation paper on deaths in custody, etc., *Review of the Role and Practices of the CPS* (2002).

[98] J. Wood, "The Serious Fraud Office" [1989] Crim.L.R. 175; Criminal Justice Act 1987 (*Current Law Statutes 1987*: Annotations by I. Leigh); P. Carey, (1989) 139 N.L.J. 1629 (comments on some of the SFO's early cases; above pp. 21–22. See also A. Arlidge, J. Parry and I. Gatt, *Arlidge and Parry on Fraud* (2nd ed., 1996), Chap. 14, 15, 16; D. Kirk and A.J. Woodcock, *The Investigation of Serious Fraud* (2nd ed., 1997).

[99] HMSO, 1986.

Its jurisdiction covers England, Wales and Northern Ireland. The Director of the Serious Fraud Office is appointed by the Attorney-General, and acts under his or her superintendence.[1] Staff are appointed by the Director.[2] The Director may (i) investigate any suspected offence which appears to him or her on reasonable grounds to involve serious or complex fraud; (ii) institute and have the conduct of any prosecutions which appear to him or her to relate to such fraud; and (iii) take over the conduct of any such proceedings at any stage. He or she may designate any member of the office who is a barrister or solicitor to exercise the Director's powers for the purposes of (ii) and (iii), and such persons have the same rights of audience as Crown Prosecutors.[3] Where the Director has the conduct of a case, the DPP's responsibilities cease.[4] The main distinctive feature of the Office's work is that it extends to the investigation as well as the prosecution of offences, and it has wide powers to require the person under investigation and any other person whom the Director has reason to believe has relevant information to answer questions or otherwise furnish information, and to require the production of documents.[5] These inquisitorial powers and their potential to infringe the privilege against self-incrimination have given rise to particular problems under the ECHR.[6]

The SFO concentrates on a comparatively small number of the most serious cases: the prosecution of other serious fraud cases continues to be handled by the Fraud Investigation Group within CPS headquarters.[7] The Glidewell Report recommended that all fraud work in the CPS be handled by Special Casework Units, with a specialist Unit in London.[8]

4. OTHER AGENCIES[9]

14–040 There is little doubt that police have greatest impact on the number of criminal prosecutions (even when road traffic cases are taken out of the equation). Despite this, and the greater symbolic significance of police role in investigation of crime, nevertheless, the non-police agencies play an important role in investigating a wide range of (sometimes very serious) criminal offences. Government departments, local authorities, nationalised industries and other public bodies may all have cause to institute prosecutions within their particular field. A survey was undertaken on behalf of the Royal Commission on Criminal Procedure[10] which concen-

---

[1] Criminal Justice Act 1987, s.1
[2] 1987 Act, Sched. 1, para. 2.
[3] *ibid.* s.1, as amended by the Access to Justice Act 1999.
[4] *ibid.* Sched. 1, para. 5. Statutory requirements for the consent of the DPP to a prosecution are not, to prohibit the taking of any step by the Director: *ibid.* para. 4
[5] *ibid.* s.2.
[6] See *Saunders v. U.K.* (1996) 23 E.H.R.R. 313.
[7] In 1999–2000 the SFO worked on 95 cases. It had 81 continuing cases at the end of the year with an aggregate value of alleged sums at risk of £1.38bn. Eight trials were concluded with 12 defendants, 11 convicted, one acquitted. See the *SFO Annual Report 1999–2000* (2000), p.21.
[8] Chap.9, para. 40–41.
[9] see Sanders and Young, (2000), pp. 364–377 and Ashworth, (1998), Chap. 5.
[10] *Prosecutions by Private Individuals and Non-Police Agencies*, RCCP Research Study No. 10 (HMSO, 1980). See also A. Samuels, [1986] Crim.L.R. 33.

trated on particular courts and identified the Post Office, the British Transport Police, the Department of the Environment and local authorities[11] as contributing almost 70 per cent of the non-police prosecutions in those courts.[12]

5. PRIVATE PROSECUTIONS

"This historical right which goes right back to the earliest days of our legal system, though rarely exercised in relation to indictable offences, and though ultimately liable to be controlled by the Attorney-General (by taking over the prosecution and, if he thinks fit, entering a *nolle prosequi*) remains a valuable constitutional safeguard against inertia or partiality on the part of authority."[13]

14–041

Lord Wilberforce thus stated the traditional view of the private prosecution.

In fact, the growing practice of requiring the consent of the DPP or Attorney-General to prosecution, the establishment of the CPS and the considerable cost of mounting a private prosecution now combine to minimise the significance of this historical right. We have already noted the requirement of consent[14] but cost is an even more discouraging factor. Legal aid is not available to a private prosecutor who must meet the cost of investigation, preparation and representation[15] out of his or her own pocket. A court may award costs to a successful private prosecutor[16] but he or she also runs the risk of having them awarded against him or her if he or she is not successful. In addition, if the prosecution was vindictive, the prosecutor risks the possibility of an action in malicious prosecution.[17] A private prosecutor has no right of access to documents, such as police statements, reports and photographs, held by the CPS.[18]

---

[11] Local authorities are empowered by s.222 of the Local Government Act 1972 to bring prosecutions. These are usually in relation to public nuisances. In *Middlesborough BC v. Safeer* [2001] Crim.L.R. 923 the power to use s.222 of the Local Government Act 1972 was held not to be so restricted that the Council could not bring a prosecution against a taxi driver for driving without insurance.

[12] *op. cit.* n.2., Table 2.3 at p. 15.

[13] *Gouriet v. Union of Post Office Workers* [1978] A.C. 435 at 477.

[14] At para. 14-031 above.

[15] The Crown Court can allow a private prosecution to be conducted in person: *R. v. Southwark Crown Court, ex p. Tawfick* (1995) 7 Admin. L.R. 410 (by virtue of the Courts and Legal Services Act 1990, s.27(2)(c)).

[16] Prosecution of Offences Act 1985, s.17: costs can only be awarded in respect of proceedings for an indictable offence, and proceedings in the Divisional Court or the House of Lords in respect of a summary offence. They cannot cover investigation expenses. See further pp. 538–539.

[17] "See W.V.H. Rogers, *Winfield and Jolowicz on Tort* (15th ed.), pp. 678–687; see also *R. v. Belmarsh Magistrates' Court, ex p. Watts* [1999] 2 Cr.App.R. 188.

[18] *R. v. Director of Public Prosecutions, ex p. Hallas* (1987) 87 Cr.App.R. 340. Material provided to the CPS is confidential and the providers do not expect it to be publicly accessible: *Taylor v. Director SFO* [1999] 2 A.C. 177. The CPS has to be extremely careful not to infringe the privacy of those who have provided information. For a discussion of the problems it faces see *Review of the Role and Practices of the CPS* (2002); see also *R. (Green) v. PCA, Secretary of State for the Home Department and others* [2002] EWHC 389.

There have, of course, been some notable private prosecutions,[19] but in general, they are confined to offences of shoplifting and common assault.[20] There is also the possibility of a civil claim against the person who has allegedly committed the wrong.[21] In some areas supermarkets and other large concerns are encouraged by the police to conduct their own prosecutions for shoplifting. Section 42 of the Offences Against the Person Act 1861 dictated a private prosecution in the majority of cases where common assault occurred,[22] but this section was repealed by the Criminal Justice Act 1988.[23] A greater use may be made of private prosecutions, particularly in light of recent government suggestions that private companies might take a greater responsibility for being required to bring prosecutions, as for example with stores and supermarkets bringing prosecutions for shoplifting,[24] and pilot schemes of civilian investigations for such offences are ongoing.[25]

The Auld Report was not prepared to recommend abolition of the right of private prosecution, but recommended that any court in which a private prosecution is commenced should have a duty to alert the DPP. The DPP should then apply the evidential and public interest tests in deciding whether to discontinue any case taken over.[26]

C. THE EXERCISE OF DISCRETION IN PROSECUTIONS

14-042   Not every criminal offence is prosecuted. The courts could not possibly cope with the workload and, in any event, prosecution may not always be the

---

[19] A recent example in England is the prosecution of young men accused of the murder of Stephen Lawrence mounted by the victim's family following the dropping of charges by the CPS: see E. Saunders, (1995) 145 N.L.J. 1423, noting the successful outcome of committal proceedings, and rehearsing the difficulties of such prosecutions. The prosecution ultimately failed. See also the case involving the officers on duty at Hillsborough: *R. v. DPP, ex p. Duckenfield* and see *R. v. DPP, ex p. Camelot* (1998) 10 Admin. L.R. 93 (private prosecution rather than judicial review appropriate means of challenge). Two cases brought by Mrs Mary Whitehouse aroused interest: *R. v. Lemon* [1979] A.C. 617, where the accused was convicted of blasphemous libel and the Crown subsequently took over the case on appeal; and *Whitehouse v. Bogdanov*, where the accused was acquitted on a charge of procuring an act of gross indecency between males contrary to section 13 of the Sexual Offences Act 1956 which resulted from his producing a play (*The Romans in Britain*), containing a scene of intercourse between males (one non-consenting). The prosecution was discontinued after the judge had ruled that there was a case to answer and the Attorney-General eventually entered a *nolle prosequi*. See [1982] P.L. 165.

[20] RCCP Research Study No. 10 (see above, n. 10), Chap. 5.

[21] *e.g. Francisco v. Diedrick, The Times*, April 3, 1998, in which the CPS did successfully take up a murder prosecution when new evidence came to light.

[22] The section specified that in cases of common assault the prosecution should be brought "by or on a behalf of the party aggrieved".

[23] Common assault and battery were made summary offences by s.39 of the 1988 Act.

[24] See the Home Office, *Diary of a Police Officer* (2001). For the limitations on corporations and unincorporated associations laying an information see *Rubin v. DPP* [1990] 2 Q.B. 80 at 89; *R. v. Ealing Justices, ex p. Dixon* [1990] 2 Q.B. 91. For statistics on retail crime see G. Barclay and C. Tavares *Digest 4* (1998), Chap. 1; *Crimes Against Retail Premises* (HORF No. 26).

[25] See *Criminal Justice: The Way Ahead* (2001), p.87.

[26] Para. 47–49.

most effective means of dealing with a violation of the criminal law. If some offenders are to be "let off" whilst others are brought before the courts it is important to know when such a decision may be made, by whom and on what principles. The exercise of this particular discretion has attracted considerable attention.[27]

1. The Police

A choice exists as soon as a police officer discovers that a criminal offence **14-043** may have been committed. Should an investigation be started if the situation is unclear? If the facts are already clear should action be taken to ensure that the offence is formally considered for prosecution? This problem is faced by every police officer present at an incident and it must be resolved on individual initiative and or in accordance with instructions received from a superior officer. Although it may be the officer's inclination to warn a motorist driving without lights not to repeat the offence, the Chief Constable may have decided, as a matter of policy, to prosecute all such offenders and issued instructions accordingly. The discretion exercised in this way by the officer concerned is otherwise generally uncontrolled, except where failure to take action may itself amount to a criminal offence or neglect of duty.[28] As noted earlier, the police is unusual in organisational terms, in that those lower in the hierarchy have a great deal of discretion.

The courts have examined the exercise of discretion at a senior level which would affect the way that the officer on the spot carries out his or her duties.[29] In *R. v. Metropolitan Police Commissioner, ex p. Blackburn (No. 1)*,[30] Mr Raymond Blackburn applied for an order of mandamus directed to the Commissioner requiring him to enforce the provisions of the Betting, Gaming and Lotteries Act 1963 in London gaming clubs. It appeared that the Commissioner had sanctioned a force order which effectively stopped observation in gaming clubs by the police and prevented any attempt to enforce the Act.[31] The Court of Appeal held that, whilst the police had a discretion not to prosecute, it was not proper to take a policy decision that certain offences would *never* be prosecuted since that was to negate the exercise of discretion and would amount to a failure in their duty to enforce the law. However, the courts will not interfere in cases where it is alleged

---

[27] See C. Harding and G. Dingwall, *Diversion in the Criminal Process* (1998). On diversion techniques which take the offender out of the prosecution process see also A. Sanders, "Diverting Offenders from Prosecution: Can we Learn from Other Countries" (1986) 150 J.P. 614; A. F. Wilcox, *The Decision to Prosecute* (1972); N. Osborough, "Police Discretion not to Prosecute Juveniles" (1965) 28 M.L.R. 179; D. Steer, *Police Cautions: A Study in the Exercise of Police Discretion* (1970); D. G. T. Williams, "Prosecution, Discretion and the Accountability of the Police"; in R. Hood (ed.) *Crime, Criminology and Public Policy* (1974); and the works cited in n. 6 and below.

[28] *R. v. Dytham* [1979] Q.B. 722 (criminal offence of wilful neglect of duty).

[29] See Sanders and Young (2000), pp. 319–321.

[30] [1968] 2 Q.B. 118. As to judicial review of CPS decisions not to discontinue proceedings, see below, para. 14-041.

[31] The terms of the relevant instructions are set out in the judgment of Lord Denning M.R. at 134–135. In the event, the instructions in question were withdrawn before the appellate hearing and the Commissioner, through counsel, gave an undertaking to that effect.

that the police are not paying *enough* attention to particular offences or prosecuting in sufficient numbers. Mr. Blackburn again sought an order of mandamus in *R. v. Metropolitan Police Commissioner, ex p. Blackburn (No. 3)*[32] this time in respect of the Obscene Publications Act 1959, but the court would not grant it. Whereas in the first case the police had deliberately decided not to prosecute, in this case they were hampered by lack of resources and the uncertainty of the law. "It is no part of the duty of this court to presume to tell the (Commissioner) how to conduct the affairs of the Metropolitan Police, nor how to deploy his all too limited resources."[33] The courts have also acknowledged that the *efficient* use of resources is a proper matter for the police to consider when deploying its officers,[34] and this could have a clear impact on the manner in which policies are created and implemented and how individual officers respond to given circumstances.

Given that an individual officer may be under instructions about how to deal with particular offences and will also have received training for this task, what considerations are likely to be taken into account in the exercise of discretion? Naturally, the gravity of the offence is likely to be uppermost but the officer may also think about the evidence likely to be available in a prosecution; the degree of certainty that the offence has been committed; the attitude of the victim; the personal circumstances of the offender and the efficacy of a prosecution compared with other ways of dealing with the problem. These are, on a local level, not dissimilar to the considerations appropriate to the decisions of the CPS on whether to continue a prosecution.[35] In this case, however, the decision will need to be taken quickly and often without the help and advice of colleagues. If the officer decides not to arrest or report for prosecution he or she might issue a warning to the offender, attempt a conciliation between offender and victim, or even take the offender into preventive arrest.[36]

Assuming that an officer has arrested an offender or reported him or her for prosecution the decision will pass to a more senior officer. At this stage the police may decide to prosecute, to caution, to administer an informal warning or to take no further action (nfa).[37] They may have the benefit of advice from the CPS (see above). If the decision is to prosecute, there is also an exercise of discretion in selecting the particular charge.

The practice differs according to the method of procedure adopted: arrest and charge, or summons. Under the former, the person is arrested (either outside or at the police station) and charged at the police station. After charge the suspect will either be kept in custody and brought by the police before a magistrates' court, in accordance with the requirements of section 46 of the Police and Criminal Evidence Act 1984[38] or, as is more usual,

---

[32] [1973] Q.B. 241. For a further instalment in the drama see *R. v. Metropolitan Police Commissioner, ex p. Blackburn, The Times*, March 6, 1980. Mr Blackburn referred to the Master of Rolls in the course of that case as, "the greatest living Englishman" Lord Denning is reported to have replied, "Tell that to the House of Lords."

[33] *per* Roskill L.J. at p. 262.

[34] *R. v. Chief Constable of Sussex, ex p. Independent Traders Ferry Ltd.* [1998] 3 W.L.R. 1260, HL.

[35] See below, para. 14-031.

[36] Discussed by Wilcox, *op. cit.* p. 106.

[37] Philips and Brown (1998) found that one-fifth of all arrests ended in no further action, p.83.

[38] Above, para. 14-020.

released on bail subject to a duty to attend a magistrates' court on a specified date. Here a decision to charge is made initially by the investigating officer, but must be approved by the CO, who must be satisfied that there is sufficient evidence.[39] COs play a pivotal role. The CPS initiatives following Narey and Glidewell to introduce the opportunity for earlier CPS involvement in the review of the charges were in part designed to assist the CO in this difficult task, however, the pilot studies on these initiatives reveal that COs very rarely sought advice on charging from lawyers.[40]

Where a person is reported for summons, the investigating officer prepares a file and passes it to a more senior officer, who decides whether a prosecution should be instituted. Where a decision not to prosecute is contemplated, the case must be passed up the hierarchy, usually to a Detective Superintendent; a decision to prosecute can be taken at the level of Detective Inspector or Detective Chief Inspector.[41] Overall, the arrest and charge procedure is the normal method used in respect of indictable offences, and the summons procedure the normal method for summary offence,[42] but police forces vary considerably in the respective proportions in which they are used.[43] There is clearly scope for these schemes to be included in a statutory scheme to improve consistency and transparency.[44] This would also involve the public scrutiny of the success of the schemes, which appear to have significant benefits of speed and avoidance of the expensive court process.

The caution, a formal warning issued by the police in circumstances where they are satisfied that the offence is capable of proof but do not intend to prosecute, has only rarely received statutory mention[45] and its use has developed by practice rather than by law. Until 1994 it was government policy, enshrined in a series of Home Office Circulars,[46] to encourage the increasing use of cautions, diverting offenders from the prosecution process. Cautioning was much more frequently used in respect of juveniles than adults; indeed, there was a presumption that a first-time juvenile offender would be cautioned. Sections 65 and 66 of the Crime and Disorder Act 1998 now provide a special procedure for the reprimand and warning of young

---

[39] See above, para. 14-016; 1984 Act, s.37(1)(7); *Code of Practice on Detention, etc.*, Code C.16.1. The equivalent step prior to PACE was the decision of the charge sergeant whether to accept a charge on the basis of an oral report from the investigating officer. In practice refusals were rare; "charge sergeants (uniformed officers) do not see CID work as their business, so accepting a CID charge is often a mere formality": A. Sanders, "The Prosecution Process" in D. Moxon (ed.), *Managing Criminal Justice* (1985), pp. 72–73.

[40] Above, para. 14-016. For criticism of the CO in this role see Sanders and Young (2000), pp. 329 and 331.

[41] Sanders, *op. cit.* pp. 70–72.

[42] See *Criminal Statistics for England and Wales* (2001).

[43] See R. Gemmill and R. F. Morgan-Giles, *Arrest, Charge and Summons* (RCCP Research Study No. 9, HMSO, 1986), based on figures for 1976 and 1978; R. Tarling, P. Jones and A. Sanders, "Police Bail" (1986) 21 H.O.R.B. 52 at 54–55, based on figures for 1980.

[44] See Ashworth (1998) pp.152–156.

[45] The Street Offences Act 1959, s.2; the Children and Young Persons Act 1969, s.5(2) (not in force: repealed by the Criminal Justice Act 1991, s.72).

[46] H. O. Circulars 70/1978, 14/1985 and 59/1990. The 1985 Circular encouraged the wider use of cautioning for adults.

offenders.[47] The reprimands and warnings must be given at a police station, in the presence of an appropriate adult where the offender is under 17.[48]

In 1994, revised National Standards for cautioning were issued.[49] The main features remain the same. Thus, there must be evidence of guilt sufficient to give a realistic prospect of conviction; the offender must admit the offence[50]; and the offender must understand the significance of a caution and give informed consent to being cautioned.[51] Consideration should be given to whether a caution is in the public interest, taking account of the public interest principles set out in the *Code for Crown Prosecutors*.[52] The Circular makes clear that cautions should never be used for the most serious indictable-only offences such as murder or rape,[53] and multiple cautioning should only be used where the subsequent offence is trivial or there has been a sufficient lapse of time since the first caution to suggest that it had some effect.[54] The views of the victim should be sought but should not be regarded as conclusive. Evidence on which the belief in the offender's guilt is based must not have been improperly obtained.[55] A failure to follow the guidelines on cautioning may lead to it being quashed.[56]

The numbers of offenders cautioned grew dramatically from 190,000 in 1984 to 321,000 in 1992, but has since declined significantly. In 1997 there were only four per cent of recorded offences cleared up by caution[57] with a total of 282,000 (189,000 indictable; 93,000 summary) in 1997. The rate had fallen yet further by 2000, with 239,000 cautions.[58] Of these, 150,900 were for indictable offences.[59] The success of the caution appears to be limited.

---

[47] No cautioning is now permitted of a young offender. If an officer has sufficient evidence for him to believe that there is a reasonable prospect of conviction and the young person admits the offence, and the officer is satisfied that it would not be in the public interest for there to be a prosecution, and the young person has not previously been convicted, the officer may reprimand any young offender who has not previously been reprimanded or warned, or may warn the person in more serious cases.

[48] This action will trigger the Youth Offending Team to arrange a rehabilitation programme. On the conflict this system creates for the appropriate adult, see J. Williams, [2000] Crim.L.R. 911. There is no need for the juvenile to consent. Statistics reveal that in 2000 there were 68,000 juvenile reprimands and warnings (only the last seven months being national figures, the earlier period being from seven pilot areas): see *Criminal Statistics for England and Wales 2000*, (2001), para. 5.21, Tables 5A, 5B. See further C. Flood-Page, S. Campbell, V. Harrington and J. Miller, *Youth Crime: Findings from the 1998/99 Youth Lifestyles Survey* (HORS No 209, 2000); J. Dignan, [1999] Crim.L.R. 48; and A. Morris, L. Gelsthorpe, [2000] Crim.L.R. 18 on the 1998 Act requirements.

[49] H. O. Circular 18/1994. See R. Evans, "Cautioning: Counting the Cost of Retrenchment" [1994] Crim.L.R. 566.

[50] *R. v. Metropolitan Police Commissioner, ex p. P* [1995] T.L.R. 305.

[51] A caution costs a defendant his good character in a subsequent trial: see *R. v. Martin* [2000] Crim.L.R. 615; see further and R. May, "The Legal Effect of a Police Caution" [1997] Crim.L.R. 491.

[52] See below, para. 14-044.

[53] Cautions in such cases were previously "discouraged", but were nevertheless used. Note that a caution in such cases will result in the individual being subject to a Sex Offender's Order: see K. Soothill, B. Francis, and D. Sanderson, [1997] Crim.L.R. 482.

[54] Multiple cautioning was said by politicians to have brought the system into disrepute: see R. Evans, [1994] Crim.L.R. 566 at 567.

[55] *R. v. Chief Constable of the Lancashire Constabulary, ex p. Atkinson* (1998) 162 J.P. 275; *Commissioner of Police of the Metropolis, ex p. Thompson* [1997] 1 W.L.R. 1519.

[56] *R. v. M.P.C., ex p. P* (1995) 160 J.P. 367.

[57] *Digest 4* (1998), p.31.

[58] See *Criminal Statistics for England and Wales 2000* (2001), Table 5.1, para. 5.23.

[59] para. 5.19, Table 5.1.

There is a marked decline in its effectiveness with an individual after the first caution.[60] Concern has also been voiced over the wide variations in the cautioning rates in different police areas.[61]

Other informal warnings must be carefully distinguished from a formal caution and cannot be referred to in subsequent proceedings. Motoring offences are dealt with differently by the administration of a written caution which is not dependent upon an admission by the offender and may not be referred to in subsequent proceedings for another offence.[62]

The caution has serious consequences for individuals and it is important not only that the policies for its use are monitored at force and national level, but that individual decisions are capable of being reviewed.[63]

There is no mechanism in England and Wales which allows a prosecutor to impose a fine or to order a caution. The Auld Report recommended that there should be a system of conditional cautioning where the prosecutor, with the agreement of the offender, administers a caution and imposes a fine. This would be achieved by providing a discretionary power for the CPS not to prosecute or to withdraw a prosecution on condition that the offender submitted to some penalty or supervision. A later breach of the condition would reactivate the prosecution.[64]

2. THE CODE FOR CROWN PROSECUTORS

Prior to the establishment of the CPS, as we have seen, the decision to **14–044** prosecute would in most cases be taken by the police, in some cases with the advice of a prosecuting solicitor, or by a member of the DPP's office. It was clear that the police did not adopt a blanket policy of prosecutions, and did take other factors into account, but there was comparatively little formal evidence of what those factors were.[65] More was known of the approach of the DPP, particularly through his evidence to the Royal Commission on Criminal Procedure.[66] In February 1983, the Attorney-General issued

---

[60] Table 5C and 5D. See also Home Office Research Findings No. 52,*Police Cautioning in the 1990s.* (2000) HORF No. 52.

[61] H.O. Circular 18/1994. See R. Evans (1997), p. 4; R. Evans and R. Ellis, *Cautioning in the 1990s* (HORF No. 52, 1997); D. Crisp and D. Moxon, *Case Screening by the CPS: How and Why Cases are Terminated* (HORS 137, 1995), Chap. 4; G. Hughes, A. Pilkington, and R.Leistein, "Diversion in the Culture of the Severity" (1998) 37 Howard J.C.J. 16; G. Laycock and R Tarling, "Police Force Cautioning: Policy and Practice" in Moxon (ed.) (1985), Chap. 6; H. Giller and N. Tutt, [1987] Crim.L.R. 367 and 587; C. Wilkinson and R. Evans, [1990] Crim.L.R. 165 and (1990) 29 Howard Journal 155; R. Evans, [1993] Crim.L.R. 572; C. Harding and G. Dingwall, *Diversion in the Criminal Process* (1998), Chap. 7.

[62] RCCPI, para. 153.

[63] See R. Evans, "Challenging a Police Caution Using Judicial Review" [1996] Crim. L.R 104, arguing that the availability of judicial review is an important safeguard.

[64] Chap. 9, paras 43-48.

[65] See, however, the account by a former chief constable: A. F. Wilcox, *The Decision to Prosecute* (1972), and the research project conducted by A Sanders between 1980 and 1983: Sanders, [1985] Crim.L.R. 4, and "The Prosecution Process" in D. Moxon (ed.), *Managing Criminal Justice* (1985), Chap. 7.

[66] A useful extract from the evidence submitted is to be found at RCCP I, Appendix 25. See generally G. Mansfield and J Peay, *The Director of Public Prosecutions* (1987), the report of a research project on the operation of the DPP's Office prior to the Prosecution of Offences Act 1985: the case samples studied dated from 1982 and 1983.

Criteria for Prosecution,[67] setting out the approach of the Attorney-General and the DPP to the institution of prosecutions in cases for which they were responsible. The intention was, however, that they be taken into account by all those responsible for prosecutions. The *Criteria* subsequently formed the basis of the *Code for Crown Prosecutors* issued by the DPP.[68] There have been four versions of the Code, the latest one being in 2000, following, for the first time, public consultation on the revisions to the previous 1994 Code. Research into the effectiveness of the 1994 Code included assessments of the application of the key "evidential" and "public interest" tests.[69] The research revealed that although the 1994 revised Code was more accessible and intelligible to the public, it did little to improve the consistent interpretation and application by the CPS. Prosecutors were found to rely more regularly on policy documents from CPS headquarters and the internal (confidential) CPS manual. The conclusion was that the new Code was a "signpost rather than a map" – it gave a general indication rather than a detailed route.[70]

David Calvert Smith Q.C., the DPP, introduced the new 2000 Code, explaining that it reflected the greater need for openness and incorporated changes as a result of the Narey, Glidewell and Macpherson Reports and the changes made to the disclosure rules and by the Human Rights Act 1998. It also aimed to improve "joined up justice", *i.e.* greater inter-agency co-operation.[71]

The Code is to be applied by the CPS "so that it can make fair and consistent decisions about prosecutions"[72] reflecting the duty of the CPS "to make sure that the right person is prosecuted for the right offence and that all relevant facts are given to the court". Crown Prosecutors must be "fair, independent and objective". Their key task is to review cases sent by the police to make sure they meet the tests set out in the Code. This is a "continuing process" so that prosecutors can take account of any change of circumstances.[73] The CPS is a public authority for the purposes of the Human Rights Act 1998, and Crown Prosecutors must apply the ECHR principles in accordance with the Act.[74] The decision to prosecute is approached in two stages: (1) the *evidential test* and (2) the *public interest*

---

[67] (1983) 147 J.P.N. 223; Home Office Circular 26/1983. See A. Sanders, "Prosecution Decisions and the Attorney-General's Guidelines" [1985] Crim.L.R. 4: he doubted that the *Criteria* would generally have much effect in reducing "inconsistency, weak cases and shady practice", but noted that they had led to changes in at least two forces (*ibid.* pp. 17, 18).

[68] The Code, as amended, is published in *Archbold* (2002). It is available on the CPS website.

[69] See A. Hoyano, L. Hoyano, G. Davis and S. Goldie, "A Study of the Impact of the Revised Code for Crown Prosecutors" [1997] Crim.L.R. 556.

[70] A. Hoyano, L. Hoyano, G. Davis and S. Goldie, "A Study of the Impact of the Revised Code for Crown Prosecutors" [1997] Crim.L.R. 556. On the previous version, issued in 1994, see *Annual Report of the Crown Prosecution Service 1994–95* (1994–95 H.C. 472), p. 6, see "The New Code for Crown Prosecutors": (1) A. Ashworth and J. Fionda, "Prosecution, Accountability and the Public Interest" [1994] Crim.L.R. 894; (2) Response by R. K. Daw *ibid.*p. 904. On previous versions of the Code, see A. Ashworth, "The 'Public Interest' Element in Prosecutions" [1987] Crim.L.R. 595; R. K. Daw, (1989) Jo. Crim. Law 485. See generally C. Harding and G. Dingwall (1998), Chap. 8.

[71] See (2000) N.L.J. 1494. For criticism of joined up justice in the criminal justice setting, see Auld (2001), Chap. 8.

[72] Code, para. 1.1.

[73] Code, para. 3.

[74] para. 2.5.

test.[75] As to the first stage, Crown Prosecutors "must be satisfied that there is enough evidence to provide a 'realistic prospect of conviction' against each defendant on each charge", taking account of what the defence case may be. This is difficult test to apply at such an early stage of proceedings. There is a "realistic prospect of conviction" where a properly directed jury or bench of magistrates is more likely than not to convict.[76] Crown Prosecutors must consider whether the evidence can be used and is reliable. Relevant considerations are whether any evidence may be excluded by the court, for example, because of the way it was gathered; whether it is likely that a confession is unreliable, for example, because of the defendant's age, intelligence or lack of understanding; what explanation the defendant has given and the weight a court is likely to attach to it; whether a witness's background is likely to weaken the prosecution case, as where he or she has a dubious motive or relevant previous conviction; and whether evidence of identification is strong enough (if identity is in issue). Crown Prosecutors should not ignore evidence because they are not sure on these points; they should, however, "look closely at it when deciding if there is a realistic prospect of conviction".[77] In conducting the assessment of the evidence, the CPS will probably incorporate, implicitly, an element of the public interest test.[78]

There have been calls for a lowering of the standard of the evidential test and by others for a raising of the standard. Applying a lower standard would increase the number of cases going to trial. This would have a number of consequences, including: a greater number of cases where there is a directed acquittal (with the consequent disappointment for the victim whose hopes have been raised); a greater number of guilty people being convicted; and, more disturbingly, a greater number of innocent people being convicted. One other consequence would be that criticism arising from the number of acquittals would be directed at the courts rather than the CPS for discontinuance. There would be increased cost from the number of trials and these would also impact on the delay in court listings.

If the evidential test is passed, Crown Prosecutors must then consider if a prosecution is needed in the public interest.[79] A prosecution[80] will usually take place unless there are public interest factors tending against prosecution which clearly outweigh those tending in favour.[81] These must be balanced "carefully and fairly" and those that can affect the decision to

---

[75] Code, paras 5 and 6. See Ashworth (1998) pp.180–181.

[76] The test is objective: Crown Prosecutors should not take into account any perceived local views of juries or magistrates: Code, para. 5.2. See also Ashworth (1998), p.182.

[77] para. 5.

[78] See J. Baldwin, [1997] Crim.L.R. 586.

[79] The DPP, and now the CPS, are guided by a statement made by a former Attorney-General, Lord Shawcross, in the course of a House of Commons debate. "It has never been the rule in this country. I hope it never will be that suspected criminal offences must automatically be the subject of prosecution": H. C. Deb., Vol. 483, col. 681, January 29, 1951 (para. 6.1).

[80] The 1994 Code referred to a limiting factor "in cases of any seriousness". The Narey Report recommended that the CPS should no longer be allowed to discontinue cases on public interest grounds because they consider the offence is not serious. The Glidewell Report did not support this recommendation (Chap. 4, para. 40).

[81] In previous versions of the Code, prosecutors had to consider "whether the public interest requires a prosecution". This *could* be interpreted as suggesting a presumption *against* prosecution. The revised version makes it clear that there is a presumption *in favour* of prosecution.

prosecute "usually depend on the seriousness of the offence or the circumstances of the offender". The Code provides non-exhaustive lists of common public interest factors for and against prosecution.[82] As regards factors in favour, it is noted that "the more serious the offence, the more likely it is that a prosecution will be needed in the public interest". A prosecution is likely to be needed if:

(a) a conviction is likely to result in a significant sentence;

(b) a weapon was used or violence was threatened during the commission of the offence;

(c) the offence was committed against a person serving the public (for example, a police or prison officer or a nurse);

(d) the defendant was in a position of authority or trust;

(e) the evidence shows that the defendant was a ringleader or an organiser of the offence;

(f) there is evidence that the offence was premeditated;

(g) there is evidence that the offence was carried out by a group;

(h) the victim of the offence was vulnerable, has been put in considerable fear, or suffered personal attack, damage or disturbance;

(i) the offence was motivated by any form of discrimination against the victim's ethnic or national origin, sex, religious beliefs, political views or sexual orientation, or the suspect demonstrated hostility towards the victim based on any of those characteristics;

(j) there is a marked difference between the actual or mental ages of the defendant and the victim, or if there is any element of corruption;

(k) the defendant's previous convictions or cautions are relevant to the present offence;

(l) the defendant is alleged to have committed the offence whilst under an order of the court;

(m) there are grounds for believing that the offence is likely to be continued or repeated, for example, by a history of recurring conduct; or

(n) the offence, although not serious in itself, is widespread in the area where it was committed.[83]

A prosecution is less likely to be needed if:

(a) the court is likely to impose a nominal penalty;

(b) the defendant has already been made the subject of a sentence and any further conviction would be unlikely to result in the imposition of an additional sentence or order, unless the nature of the particular offence requires a prosecution;

---

[82] The *absence* of a factor is not to be taken as a factor tending in the opposite direction: *Explanatory Memorandum*, para. 4.26.
[83] para. 6.4.

(c) the offence was committed as a result of a genuine mistake or misunderstanding (these factors must be balanced against the seriousness of the offence);

(d) the loss or harm can be described as minor and was the result of a single incident, particularly if it was caused by a misjudgement;

(e) there has been a long delay between the offence taking place and the date of the trial, unless:

- the offence is serious;
- the delay has been caused in part by the defendant;
- the offence has only recently come to light; or
- the complexity of the offence has meant that there has been a long investigation;

(f) a prosecution is likely to have a bad effect on the victim's physical or mental health, always bearing in mind the seriousness of the offence;

(g) the defendant is elderly or is, or was at the time of the offence, suffering from significant mental or physical ill health, unless the offence is serious or there is a real possibility that it may be repeated. The Crown Prosecution Service, where necessary, applies Home Office guidelines about how to deal with mentally disordered offenders. Crown Prosecutors must balance the desirability of diverting a defendant who is suffering from significant mental or physical ill health with the need to safeguard the general public[84];

(h) the defendant has put right the loss or harm that was caused (but defendants must not avoid prosecution solely because they can pay compensation); or

(i) details may be made public that could harm sources of information, international relations or national security.[85]

While the Code lists these competing factors, it is also made clear that prosecutors must not simply add up the number of factors on each side: they "must decide how important each factor is in the circumstances of each case and go on to make an overall assessment".[86]

They must also always take account of the consequences for the victim of the decision whether to prosecute. "It is important that a victim is told about a decision which makes a significant difference to the case in which he is involved." It is difficult for the CPS to strike a balance between meeting the victim's needs and not being placed under inappropriate pressure in individual cases to pursue a case which is not in the public interest because of the victim's circumstances.[87] At the same time the CPS must be careful to respect the confidentiality of material when disclosing reasons to the victims.

Where the defendant is a youth, prosecutors must also consider his or her

---

[84] The CPS has access to material that might influence the decision about a particular defendant. This is accessed via Public Interest Case Assessment schemes. See D. Crisp , C. Whitaker and J. Harris, *Public Interest Case Assessment Schemes* (HORS 138, 1995).

[85] para. 6.5.

[86] para. 6.6.

[87] On this see A. Sanders and R. Young (2001) 151 N.L.J. 44.

interests; the stigma of a conviction can cause very severe harm to his or her prospects and young offenders can sometimes be dealt with without going to court. However, prosecutors "should not avoid prosecuting simply because of the defendant's age. The seriousness of the offence or the youth's past behaviour may make prosecutions necessary."[88]

Finally, where necessary, Crown Prosecutors should apply the Home Office guidelines on cautioning and tell the police it they think a caution would be more suitable than a prosecution.[89]

As to charges,[90] Crown Prosecutors should select charges which (a) reflect the seriousness of the offending; (b) give the court adequate sentencing powers; and (c) enable the case to be presented in a clear and simple way. Thus they may not always continue with the most serious charge and should not continue with more charges than are necessary. Indeed, they should never go ahead with more charges than are necessary, or a more serious charge, in order to encourage a defendant to plead guilty to some, or a less serious charge. They should not change the charge simply because of the venue in which the case will be heard.

As to mode of trial,[91] Crown Prosecutors must apply the national guidelines.[92] Speed must never be the only reason for asking for summary trial, but prosecutors should consider the effect of any likely delay if a case is sent to the Crown Court and any possible stress on victims and witnesses if the case is delayed.

Crown Prosecutors should only accept a guilty plea if they think the court is able to pass a sentence that matches the seriousness of the offending, and never just because it is convenient. Care must be taken when considering pleas that would enable the accused to avoid the mandatory minimum sentence.[93]

If the CPS tells a suspect or defendant that there will not be a prosecution or that the prosecution has been stopped, that is normally the end of the matter. However, a prosecution may be re-started (a) in rare cases where the original decision was clearly wrong; (b) where the prosecution has been stopped so that more evidence which is likely to become available in the fairly near future can be collected (here, the prosecution will tell the defendant that the prosecution may well start again); or (c) in other cases where more significant evidence is discovered later.[94]

The Code also makes clear that "police officers should take account of the Code when they are deciding whether to charge a person with an offence".[95]

---

[88] This is much weaker than the provisions in the 2nd Code that "the youth of the offender" was a public interest factor against prosecution and that juveniles should not be prosecuted unless exceptional circumstances dictated otherwise.

[89] para. 6.11.

[90] Code, para. 7.

[91] Code, para. 8.

[92] Below, para. 17-027.

[93] Code, para. 9.

[94] *ibid.* para. 10. On stays of proceedings for abuse of process where the prosecution have reneged on promises see below, para. 17-027.

[95] *ibid.*, para. 1.2

In many respects the Code seems eminently reasonable, albeit at a high level of generality: what is important is how it is applied in practice. One aspect that has been controversial is the "realistic prospects of conviction" test.[96] It has been argued that this weighs too heavily against prosecution.[97] Statements on prosecution policy for particular offences or situations were published from time to time. There are now published charging standards which have been introduced to enhance consistency. The charging standards relate to offences against the person, driving offences and public order.[98] These increase the transparency of the decision-making process and could be usefully expanded to a wider range of offences.

Quality of decision

The RCCJ gave some consideration to the quality of decision-making by the **14–045** CPS, noting criticisms of decisions to prosecute cases that might have been discontinued on public interest or evidential grounds.[99]

Research into the reasons for discontinuance[1] found that 58 per cent of non-motoring and 47 per cent of motoring cases were discontinued on evidential grounds; and 35 per cent and 24 per cent respectively on public interest grounds; and the remainder on grounds including the impossibility of tracing the defendant (five per cent and 24 per cent respectively) or refusal of an adjournment by a court (three per cent). As is to be expected, the CPS is less likely to drop serious cases on public interest grounds. Only five per cent of terminated cases were dropped before the first court appearance and in 37 per cent of cases the defendant had no advance notification. This research was available to the RCCJ. They regarded the fact that only five 5 per cent of cases were discontinued before the first court appearance as "disappointingly small". However, they found that this research also

---

[96] This test originally appeared as a "reasonable prospect of conviction" test in the Attorney-General's *Criteria for Prosecution* (above, p. 713), and became a "realistic prospect" in the first *Code for Crown Prosecutors*. The latter does not appear to import a higher standard (A. Ashworth, *The Criminal Process* (1994), p. 163). However, it is more stringent than the "prima facie" standard previously applied by the police; under this test, there had to be "enough admissible evidence to prove all the necessary elements of the offence and evidence that does not appear so manifestly unreliable that no reasonable tribunal could safely convict upon it": RCCP, paras 6–10. It was reformulated following criticism by G. Mansfield and J. Peay, *The Director of Public Prosecutions* (1987), pp. 52–54, 217–225.

[97] G. Williams, "Letting off the Guilty and Prosecuting the Innocent" [1985] Crim.L.R. 115, criticised by P. Worboys, [1985] Crim.L.R. 764. Prof. Williams proposed that the prosecutor should consider (1) whether he or she believes the suspect to be guilty; (2) whether a prosecution would have a fair chance of success; (3) whether considerations of humanity or public policy stand in the way of proceedings; and (4) whether he or she has the resources to justify bringing a charge.

[98] *Archbold* (2002), Supplement E 13. See A. Ashworth and J. Fionda, [1994] Crim.L.R. 894 at 902 citing *A Statement of Prosecution Policy: Domestic Violence* (CPS, 1993), annexed to the Government Reply (Cm. 2269) to the Third Report from the Home Affairs Committee (1992–93, H.C. 245), *Domestic Violence*; and *Charging Standards: Offences against the Person* (CPS, 1994) (see [1994] Crim.L.R. 777; this is the first in a series).

[99] Cm. 2263, pp. 74–78.

[1] D. Crisp and D. Moxon, *Case Screening by the Crown Prosecution Service* (H.O. Research Study No. 137, HMSO, 1994), based on a sample of cases in 1991. See also the CPS's own surveys, *e.g. Annual Report of the CPS, 1994–95*, pp. 7–8.

indicated that the public interest criteria were being appropriately applied.[2] Other research, on ordered and directed acquittals[3] found that of 100 case files studied, 45 acquittals were unforeseeable (over half because the victim or key witness disappeared or refused to testify); 27 were foreseeable and 28 possibly foreseeable; in 25 of the cases, the evidential weakness was present and foreseeable before, at or just after committal; at a minimum, 15 should have been discontinued or manifest deficiencies in the evidence rectified. There were instances of inadequate advice from prosecuting counsel. The RCCJ's response was to recommend that counsel's advice should be sought and given in good time.[4]

The problem persists. In 2000, the CPS discontinued 166 000 cases.[5] A growing concern is that managerial and economic influences will begin to make an impact on the way that prosecutors make their decision whether to discontinue, with an increasing pressure to meet targets of success, particularly those measured in terms of the proportion of discontinued cases. The Glidewell Report called for more effective research into the reasons for the discontinuance and for better statistical information.

One safeguard against this willingness to discontinue cases is that the victim of the offence will be dissatisfied with such an outcome. The ability of the victim to act as a monitor on inappropriate dropping of cases is enhanced by the increasing pressure on the CPS to keep the victim informed of progress of his or her case. The Glidewell Report[6] and the Macpherson Report have been the major catalysts for a growing commitment to meeting the needs of the witness in the criminal trial.[7] There is no doubt that the CPS regards the harm or loss suffered by the victim as an important consideration in the decision whether to prosecute, and the CPS has further self-imposed obligations regarding the treatment of the victim and witness in the criminal trial. These include: to ask the courts to set dates that are not inconvenient to the witness; to explain to the witness what will happen in court; to arrange assistance for and look after the witness at trial; to explain the results of the decisions, cases and appeals; and to remind courts of the possibility of compensation awards. In relation to cases in which there has

---

[2] Cm. 2263, pp. 76–77. Trials with Public Interest Case Assessment Schemes in which probation officers prepare reports on defendants in selected cases for prosecutors have been generally welcomed by those involved, have led to increases in the proportion of public interest discontinuances, but have not generated savings sufficient to cover their costs: D. Crisp *et al., Public Interest Case Assessment Schemes* (H.O. Research Study No. 138, HMSO, 1995).

[3] B. Block, C. Corbett and J. Perry, *Ordered and Directed Acquittals in the Crown Court* (RCCJ Research Study No. 15, HMSO, 1993) and [1993] Crim.L.R. 95.

[4] Cm. 2263, pp. 77–78. The RCCJ also welcomed the introduction of team working (above, p. 706).

[5] See *CPS Annual Report 2000–2001* (2001), pp.26–29.

[6] para. 55.

[7] See the material at *www.cps.gov.uk/cps d/victims.htm.* Original pilot schemes of meeting victims in cases where prosecutions were dropped were suspended following fears for the safety of CPS officials: Minutes of Evidence, Home Affairs Committee, May 9, 2000, H.C. Paper 476–I (Session 1999/2000).

been a death, the CPS will meet with the bereaved relatives to discuss the case.[8]

This need to respect the victim's needs will place an increasing pressure on the working practices of the CPS, but it cannot be allowed to obscure the fact that the CPS is not a representative of the victim.[9] If detailed reasons for the discontinuation of cases are to be a formal requirement, there will have to be considerable guidance to ensure consistency in the approach, and that confidentiality is maintained.[10]

3. PROSECUTIONS BY OTHER AGENCIES[11]

The CPS prosecutes 95 per cent of Crown Court and 25 per cent of magistrates' court cases. Most of the prosecutions brought by non-police agencies arise out of the enforcement of regulatory legislation in the context of business, including legislation concerning protection of the health and safety of employees,[12] trading standards[13] and protection of the environment.[14] Those who enforce this kind of legislation tend to prefer other methods of securing compliance, such as advice, negotiation and warning, with prosecution as a last resort. The internal decision-making arrangements tend to make prosecution more difficult than non-prosecution.[15] It has been noted that the potential defendants tend to be middle class (companies, managers, self-employed) rather than working class (who comprise the majority of those dealt with by the police).[16] However, it has been argued that the class bias exhibited by the prosecution patterns arises not from deliberate bias on the part of the law enforcers, but reflects more fundamental economic and social differences between different types of "crime" and "criminal".[17]

14–046

A similar contrast can be drawn between the rarity of prosecutions for tax evasion and the much more common use of prosecutions for social security

---

[8] This is extended to a wider range of offences in a pilot scheme: see CPS Press Release January 7, 2002. On victims being adequately informed see the discussion in the Auld Report (2001), Chap. 10, particularly at para. 252 where it is recommended that the CPS should inform the victim of the substitution of lesser charges, the acceptance of a plea to lesser charges or the dropping of the case as a whole. See also the statements in *R. v. DPP, ex p. C*, March 10, 2000, unreported.

[9] The extent to which the CPS should respond to the victim's needs is considered in the *Review of the Role and Practices of the CPS* (2002), Chap. 5. See also *R. v. DPP, ex p. Stacey* October 20, 1999, unreported.

[10] See the Review (2002), *op. cit.* Chap. 5, pp. 35–37.

[11] See Auld Report (2001) Chap. 9, paras 49–52.

[12] See W. G. Carson, "White Collar Crime and the Enforcement of Factory Legislation" (1970) 10 Brit. J. Criminol. 383, and *The Other Price of Britain's Oil* (1982); D. Kloss, [1978] Crim.L.R. 280.

[13] R. Cranston, *Regulating Business* (1979) (enforcement of trading standards); B. Hutter, *The Reasonable Arm of the Law* (1988) (environmental health officers); H. Croall, (1988) 15 J.L.S. 293 and (1989) 29 Brit. J. Criminol. 157.

[14] See G. Richardson, A. Ogus and P. Burroughs, *Policing Pollution* (1982); K. Hawkins, *Environment and Enforcement* (1984); M. Weatt, (1989) 29 Brit. J. Criminol. 57.

[15] See A. Sanders, "Class Bias in Prosecution" (1985) 24 Howard Journal 176, comparing the "institutional propensity to prosecute" of the police with the "propensity not to prosecute" of the Factory Inspectorate.

[16] Sanders, *op. cit.*

[17] *ibid.* pp. 194–197.

frauds.[18] Other agencies to compare include the Commissioners for Customs and Excise,[19] the Board of the Inland Revenue,[20] the Health and Safety Executive,[21] the DSS.[22]

The powers of such organisations give rise to two distinct problems. First, there is the question to what extent they should be permitted to conduct both investigative and prosecutorial functions, given the importance of the separation of these functions in relation to the mainstream criminal process. Secondly, there is the question of maintaining consistent standards in the prosecution policies themselves. Commentators have drawn attention to the fact that the regulatory authorities are often more compliance orientated in their outlook.[23] With such a diverse range of authorities, each protecting their own interests, it is inevitable that different prosecution policies evolve. This is unobjectionable provided certain minimum criteria are met: the prosecution policy must not be capricious or arbitrary or discriminatory; it must be published and accessible to the public; and the courts must exercise the power of review of its execution and application. The Codes should strive to match the level of protection that is afforded to the criminal suspect investigated by the police and prosecuted by the CPS. Occasionally, prosecution policies have clashed.[24] There is a Whitehall Prosecutors Group which meets to ensure that policies are consistent in all agencies.[25]

One argument that is commonly relied upon to justify the right of the organisations to conduct prosecutions is that there is no restriction placed on the individual bringing a purely private prosecution (see above). It is not clear that the right of a private prosecution necessarily justifies other

[18] See the Grabiner Report Into the Informal Economy (1999). See M. Levi, [1982] B.T.R. 36; Report of the Keith Committee on the *Enforcement Powers of the Revenue Departments* (Cmnd. 8822, 1983); S. Uglow, "Defrauding the Public Purse" [1984] Crim.L.R. 128; R. Smith, "Who's Fiddling? Fraud and Abuse" in S. Ward (ed.), *DHSS in Crisis* (1985); D. Cook, *Rich Law, Poor Law* (1989). D. Cook, *Poverty, Crime and Punishment* (1997). The approach of both the police and other agencies to the investigation and prosecution of fraud is considered by M. Levi, *Regulating Fraud* (1987).

[19] For criticism of Customs and Excise prosecutions see G. McFarlane (1999) 149 N.L.J. 1123. See also Customs and Excise, the Gower-Hammond Report (2001) on prosecution and investigation policies.

[20] The overwhelming acceptance of the IRC's power to prosecute was accepted by the Court of Appeal, despite there being no express statutory power: *R. (or the appn of Hunt) v. C.C.R.C.* [2001] Crim.L.R. 324; *R. v. W.* [1998] S.T.C. 550. Its policy of selective enforcement was accepted in *R. v. IRC, ex p. Mead and Cook* [1992] S.T.C. 482; *R. v. IRC ex p. Alien* [1997] S.T.C. 1141. See J. Roording, [1996] Crim.L.R. 240.

[21] On the HSE see the protocol with the CPS for work-related deaths (1998) 148 N.L.J. 911. See D. Bergman, (1999) 149 N.L.I. 1656 questioning the HSE failure to prosecute in thousands of cases.

[22] See recently on the new DSS powers, G. McKeeva, "Detecting, Prosecuting and Punishing Benefit Fraud: The Social Security Administration (Fraud) Act 1997, (1999) 62 M.L.R. 261.

[23] On other agencies see A. Reiss "Styles of Regulatory Justice" in K. Hawkins and J. Thomas (eds), *Enforcing Regulation* (1984); on prosecutions of regulatory offences see S. Antrobus and I. Cooper, (2001) S.I. June 8, pp.520, 553, 574. See also G. Richardson, *Strict Liability for Regulating Crime: the Empirical Research* [1987] C.L.R. 295. The different policies of prosecution have also been highlighted by, *e.g.* the Grabiner Report into the Informal Economy (1999).

[24] See, *e.g. R. v. W.* [1998] (CPS and Inland Revenue policies on tax evasion). But, see the written answer of the Attorney-General in *Hansard* April 8, 1998, col. 231, on the strengthened arrangements for liaison between the prosecuting authorities of the inland Revenue and the CPS. See S. Lewis and R. Clutterbuck, [1998] Crim.L.R. 139.

[25] See *CPS Annual Report 2000–2001* (2001), p.13.

agencies activities. A distinction could be drawn between truly private prosecutions and those brought on behalf of the "State" (perhaps any central government departments). It might be considered advantageous if *all* prosecutions other than those taken by private individuals were taken over by the CPS. There would be greater consistency, and separation from the investigation, which might be desirable provided that the prosecuting authority acknowledged the necessary differences of policy between departments.[26]

4. JUDICIAL REVIEW AND THE DECISION TO PROSECUTE[27]

Decisions of the police or another enforcement agency to prosecute and of the CPS not to discontinue a prosecution are open to challenge on an application for judicial review.[28] The possibility of judicial review of police decisions was recognised (as regards a decision not to prosecute) in *R. v. Metropolitan Police Commissioner, ex p. Blackburn (No.1)*[29] and (as regards a decision to prosecute and not caution a juvenile) in *R. v. Chief Constable of the Kent County Constabulary, ex p. L.*[30] The House of Lords has however subsequently held that in the absence of dishonesty, *mala fides* or some exceptional circumstance, a decision to prosecute cannot be challenged by way of judicial review.[31] A decision not to prosecute remains reviewable because no other remedy is available.[32]

    14–047

In recent years there have been a number of successful actions,[33] and in *R. v. DPP, ex p. Manning* it was emphasised that the standard of review cannot be set too high. Nevertheless, many applications, particularly earlier ones, failed. In *ex p. L*[34] the Divisional Court upheld a decision to prosecute L (aged 16) for breaking another boy's nose and kicking him in the head, where all the criteria for cautioning were satisfied apart from the question of

---

[26] Obviously there would have to be a clarification of what was a private as opposed to a state prosecution, and drawing this distinction could be difficult in some cases.

[27] M. Burton, [2001] Crim.L.R. 374; C. Hilson, [1993] Crim.L.R. 739. See also Y. Dotan, "Should Prosecutorial Discretion Enjoy Special Treatment in Judicial Review" [1997] P.L. 513 (on Anglo-Israeli comparisons), and R. Jones (1997) 161 J.P. 422 on accountability in the French system.

[28] *R. v. General Council of the Bar, ex p. Percival* [1991] 1 Q.B. 212 (disciplinary proceedings against a barrister); *R. v. Inland Revenue Commissioners, ex p. Mead* [1993] 1 All E.R. 772 (Inland Revenue decision to prosecute for tax evasion. Stuart-Smith L.J. held that judicial review was available in principle but Popplewell J. disagreed; both judges agreed that the application failed on the merits); *R. v. DPP, ex p. C* [1995] 1 Cr.App.R. 136 (CPS decision to discontinue proceedings); *cf. R. v. DPP, ex p. B* [1993] 1 All E.R. 756 (heard with *ex.p. L*, above) (CPS decision not to discontinue proceedings against a juvenile). *Hayter v. L* [1998] 1 W.L.R. 854 (victim seeks judicial review of magistrates' stay for abuse for D who has been cautioned.).

[29] See above.

[30] [1993] 1 All E.R. 756.

[31] *R. v. DPP, ex p. Kebilene* [2000] 2 A.C. 326.

[32] *ibid.*

[33] *R. v. DPP, ex p. Jones* [2000] Crim.L.R. 858; *R. v. DPP, ex p. Treadaway* October 31, 1997; *R. (Joseph) v. DPP* [2001] Crim.L.R. 489; *R. v. DPP, ex p. Manning* [2001] Q.B. 330.

[34] n. 30 above.

seriousness of the offence. In *ex p. B*,[35] the same court upheld a decision to prosecute B (aged 12) for theft of a bag. Here, there was no question of a caution as B denied the offence. The court held that allegations that the investigation into, *inter alia*, B's home and social circumstances had been inadequate were not made out on the facts. Such cases will now be extremely rare.

In contrast there will be a likely increase in the number of challenges of the decision not to prosecute. In *R. v. DPP, ex p. C*,[36] the Divisional Court quashed a decision of the CPS to *discontinue* a prosecution of a man for buggery of his wife. The prosecutor reasoned that although consent was no defence to buggery of a woman, there was insufficient evidence that (as she claimed) she did not in fact consent. Considering it as a case of consensual buggery, the public interest did not require a prosecution, the matter being more appropriately dealt with in a matrimonial court. The Divisional Court held, however, that the prosecutor had failed "to bring his mind fully to bear on whether the evidential sufficiency criteria were satisfied in relation to non-consensual buggery." In particular, he had assumed too readily that the husband's "line of defence" would have been consent and not a denial that he had buggered her. There was ample medical corroboration on the latter point. Accordingly, he had failed to "have regard to any lines of defence which are plainly open to ... the accused" as required by paragraph 4 of the Code.[37] The matter was remitted to the CPS for reconsideration.

The possible grounds for a successful challenge were summarised in *R. v. DPP, ex p. C*[38] as being where a decision was reached,

"(1) because of some unlawful policy (such as the hypothetical decision in *Blackburn* not to prosecute where the value of goods stolen was below £100); or

(2) because the DPP failed to act in accordance with her own policy as set out in the Code; or

(3) because the decision was perverse. It was a decision at which no reasonable prosecutor could have arrived."

The removal of detailed provisions in the current version of the Code[39] makes a successful application for judicial review even more unlikely. Similarly, the courts in *ex.p. L* and *ex.p. B*[40] recognised that it would be very difficult in practice to establish that the authorities had made a decision "regardless of or clearly contrary to" a settled policy of the DPP, such as the policy of cautioning juveniles[41] or the (more general) policy of giving special consideration to the interests of juveniles in determining whether the public interest required a prosecution.

---

[35] n. 28 above. In *ex p. Mead*, n. 28 above, the court upheld the selective prosecution policy of the Inland Revenue.

[36] n. 28 above.

[37] The equivalent in the current draft of the Code is that the prosecution "must consider what the defence case may be": para. 5.1.

[38] [1995] 1 Cr.App.R. 136 at 141. The court left open the argument that the CPS had adopted an unlawful policy. G. Dingwall, "Judicial Review and the DPP" [1995] C.L.J. 265.

[39] Above, p.

[40] n. above

[41] Now see the Crime and Disorder Act 1998, ss. 65 and 66.

Amongst the most controversial issues regarding the decision to prosecute and the question of judicial review of the decision are those involving deaths in custody.[42] These cases raise a prior problem. It is only possible to seek judicial review and to challenge the decision not to prosecute if the reasons for the decision are made available. Although there is no general duty, even in the more victim-friendly CPS Code, the courts have held that this may be necessary. Where a suspect has died in custody and an inquest jury has returned a verdict of unlawful killing, implicating an officer against whom there was prima facie evidence, any failure to prosecute must at least be explained.[43]

Decisions of the Attorney-General not to prosecute are, not open to judicial review, because of his or her "unique constitutional position".[44] Furthermore it should be noted that the CPS does not owe a duty of care in negligence in the conduct of its prosecution of a defendant.[45]

D. THE CLASSIFICATION OF OFFENCES[46]

If a decision is taken to prosecute an offender, the Crown Prosecutor, or relevant prosecuting agency, must decide on the appropriate charge.[47] The selection of the charge is important because it may determine the court in which the case will be tried and, hence, the mode of trial. We have already recorded that both the magistrates' court and the Crown Court have original criminal jurisdiction and the work is divided between them according to the seriousness of the charge. In the Crown Court, the trial is "on indictment" with a judge and jury, and in the magistrates' court the trial is summary and conducted by the magistrates. Criminal offences are classified according to the way in which they are to be tried and the number of categories was reduced to three by the Criminal Law Act 1977,[48] which

14–048

---

[42] Following a number of high profile cases in the 1990s which did not result in a prosecution, an independent Inquiry was established to ascertain how the CPS should make the decision: the Butler Report, *Inquiry into the CPS Decision-Making in relation to Deaths in Custody and Related Matters* (1999). See G. Smith, (1997) N.L.J. 1180. The CPS procedures now require that the independent advice of Treasury Counsel be taken and that if the DPP disagrees with the advice, the Attorney-General and Solicitor-General are to be consulted. See CPS Press Release, July 31, 1997.

[43] *R. v. DPP, ex p. Manning* [2001] Q.B. 330. See further the Butler Report recommendations about the way in which CPS decisions regarding prosecution in such cases was to be handled. M. Burton, "Reviewing CPS decisions not to prosecute" [2001] Crim.L.R. 374; see CPS Press Release on the case, January 25, 2002. See also *R. v. CPS, ex p. Hutchins* June 13, 1997, unreported, Brooke J.

[44] *R. v. Att.-Gen., ex p. Taylor, The Independent*, August 3, 1995 (application by T and her sister for judicial review of the Attorney-General's decision not to prosecute certain newspapers for contempt of court in respect of prejudicial coverage of their murder trial, following the quashing of their convictions). See also *The Review of the Role and Practices of the CPS* (2002).

[45] *Elguzouli-Daf v. Commissioner of Police of the Metropolis; McBrearty v. Ministry of Defence* [1995] Q.B. 335, CA; see S. O'Doherty (1997) 161 J.P.N. 718.

[46] See Emmins (2000), Chap. 7; *Archbold* (2002), para. 1-11-1-73.

[47] He or she can, of course, substitute a different charge for that originally preferred by the police, and can add further charges.

[48] The pertinent parts of this Act were re-enacted in the Magistrates' Courts Act 1980.

was based upon the report of the James Committee on the *Distribution of Criminal Business between the Crown Court and the Magistrates' Courts.*[49]

Section 14 of the 1977 Act provided that there should be offences triable only on indictment; offences triable only summarily; and offences triable either way.[50] A fourth category has been added by section 40 of the Criminal Justice Act 1988, which provides that, in certain circumstances, a summary offence may be added to an indictment tried at the Crown Court.[51]

There have been a number of significant changes to the way that these classifications apply, and the process is extremely complex; we can offer only an overview of the procedure and problems. As Ashworth observes, mode of trial decisions have implications for a wide range of issues: "length of delay before trial, probability and duration of remand in custody, degree of support for witnesses, the degree of anxiety for defendants, the probability of acquittal, the severity of sentence if convicted, the cost to the public".[52]

1. OFFENCES TRIABLE ONLY ON INDICTMENT

14–049   All offences at common law were triable on indictment. The other two categories are creatures of statute and, therefore, in the absence of any specific provision an offence will be triable on indictment. In practice, this category is reserved for the most serious offences including murder, manslaughter, rape, robbery, causing grievous bodily harm with intent, blackmail and riot. Some offences were "downgraded" by the Criminal Law Act 1977, Schedule 2[53] so as to be triable either way, in recognition of the fact that, *inter alia*, appearing to be the keeper of a bawdy house[54]; not providing apprentices or servants with food[55], assaulting a clergyman at a place of worship[56] and bigamy[57] were no longer regarded as the gravest of offences. The trend has been to reserve indictable offences for the most serious circumstances and most new offences are triable either way or summarily.

---

[49] (Cmnd. 6323, 1975). The Committee was chaired by James L.J.

[50] Section 14 was repealed by the Magistrates' Courts Act 1980, s.154 and *not* re-enacted but it is a convenient statement of the three categories. Sections 17–25 of the 1980 Act adopted the same tripatrite system. The Interpretation Act 1978, Sched. 1 defines each of the three categories. The procedures hereafter stated apply to adults. In the case of juveniles, summary trial is almost always the mode of trial, even for indictable offences: see Magistrates' Courts Act 1980, s.24. In the exceptional cases in which juveniles are tried in the Crown Court, English law has adopted a special procedure in light of the ECHR ruling in *T. v. U.K.* (2000) 30 E.H.R.R. 121, see *Practice Direction (Crown Court: Young Defendants)*[2000] 1 W.L.R. 659. This chapter does not deal with the very specialist regulation of youth trial process. In general, 10–17 year old are tried in the Youth Courts, which are akin to the magistrates' courts. See generally, C. Ball, K. McCormac and N. Stone, *Young Offenders* (1995), *Blackstone's Criminal Practice 2002*, D. 22.

[51] See below.

[52] (1998), p.242. The victim will also be affected by the decision in terms of the delay and anxiety about the proceedings. Research also shows that they are less likely to receive compensation in the Crown Court. See Ashworth (1998), p.263.

[53] Now to be found in Magistrates' Courts Act 1980, Sched. 1.

[54] Disorderly Houses Act 1751, s.8.

[55] Offences Against the Person Act 1861, s.26.

[56] *ibid.* s.36.

[57] *ibid.* s.57.

Section 51 of the Crime and Disorder Act 1998 removes the requirement for committal proceedings for offences triable *only* on indictment.[58] Offenders charged with such offences must be "sent" to the Crown Court for trial without committal.[59]

These "indictable only procedures" were implemented following the Narey Report on delay, and are clearly designed to speed up the process of such cases. The Narey Report found that indictable-only cases spent, on average, 87 days in the magistrates' court before committal. The legislative solution adopted was to remove the requirement for committal. Under the new procedure, the first appearance in the Crown Court has to occur within eight days of the magistrates' court hearing in a case where the defendant is in custody, and in 28 days where the defendant is on bail. The time limits are designed to be short, with time running from receipt of the notice in the Crown Court, which must occur within four days of the magistrates' hearing.[60] These are much stricter time limits than those that could be demanded under the ECHR requirement for prompt trials.[61]

Another saving introduced by this new procedure is that the first hearing in the Crown Court may be conducted by a CPS Designated Caseworker rather than by counsel.[62]

Section 51 and Schedule 3 of the 1998 Act result in the following rather complex procedures[63]:

The court *shall* send the following to the Crown Court:

(a) D, charged with an indictable only offence to be tried for that offence.[64]

(b) D, charged[65] with an indictable only offence and any either way[66] or summary offence (which carries a sentence of imprisonment/driving

---

[58] See generally, R. Leng, R. Taylor and M. Wasik, *Blackstone's Guide to the Crime and Disorder Act 1998* (1998), Chap. 5.

[59] On the implementation, see Crime and Disorder Act 1998 (Commencement No. 3) Order 1998 (S.I. No. 3263). Detailed procedures are set out in s.52(6) of the 1998 Act.

[60] This has prompted fears that defence solicitors will not have adequate time to review material.

[61] See recently on the impact of Article 6(1) of the ECHR *R. v. James* [2002] EWCA Crim 1119.

[62] The first hearing allows for a plea to be taken and for scheduling of the case.

[63] The procedure allows for a challenge by the defence to the Crown Court for the charge to be dismissed. The judge is to dismiss charges if it appears to him that the evidence would not be sufficient for a jury to properly convict him (Sched. 3, para. 2). Similar safeguards exist relating to reporting restrictions (Sched. 3, para. 3). See for the procedure on dismissal of charges under s.51 the Crime and Disorder Act 1998, (Dismissal of Charges Sentencing) Rules 1998 (S.I. 1998 No. 3048), and for procedure see Indictments (Procedure) (Modification) Rules 1998 (S.I. 1998 No. 3045); Magistrates' Courts (Modification) Rules 1998 (S.I. 1998 Nos. 3046 and 3047), and Crime and Disorder Act 1998 (Service of Prosecution Evidence) Regulations 1998 (S.I. 1998 No. 3115).

[64] s.51(1).

[65] This extends beyond "charged" in a police station. It includes an allegation of a criminal offence that would result in criminal proceedings. A charge of an indictable only offence arising out of the same facts as an earlier indictable only charge or either way offence is covered by the s.51 procedure. The date of the first appearance is the significant one if challenges arise from the commencement date: *R. v. Bow Street Magistrates' Court, ex p. Salubi et al* [2002] EWHC 919 Admin. The court also noted that the magistrates' power to stay proceedings as an abuse of process remained unaffected by s.51, but that it would be exercised rarely.

[66] Magistrates' Courts Act 1980, s.38A(6).

disqualification) where that offence is related[67] to the indictable only offence.[68]

(c) E, jointly charged on a related either way offence with D who faces an indictable only offence (or related either way or other relevant offence) and D is, *at this hearing*, sent to the Crown Court on that indictable only charge.

(d) E, who has been sent to the Crown Court to face an either way offence (with which he or she is jointly charged with D) must also be sent to the Crown Court on any related either way or summary offences with which he or she is charged.

(e) F, a child or young person who is jointly charged in an indictable only offence with D, an adult, must be sent to the Crown Court if the court considers it necessary in the interests of justice to do so.

Magistrates *may* send the following:

(a) D, who has already been sent to the Crown Court for an indictable only offence and who now appears charged with any either way or summary offence (which carries a sentence of imprisonment/driving disqualification) where that offence is related to the indictable only offence.

(b) E, jointly charged on a related either way offence with D who faces an indictable only offence where D has already been sent to the Crown Court on that indictable only charge.

(c) F, a child or young person jointly charged with an adult charged with an indictable only offence where F faces a related either way or summary offence (for which the penalty is imprisonment or disqualification), may be sent whether D has been previously sent for trial or is being sent for trial at this hearing.

Related either way offences[69] are included in the indictment and tried in the Crown Court in the normal way. If by the time of the Crown Court trial the indictable only offence has been dropped, the Crown Court applies the plea before venue procedure outlined below and conducts a mode of trial hearing (both discussed below). The prosecution is obliged within specified time periods to provide copies of the documents containing the evidence on which the charges sent under section 51 are based.[70]

If a summary offence is sent to the Crown Court the summary offence is not included in the indictment and is only put to the accused only if he or she is convicted of the indictable offence. In the event that he or she pleads not guilty to the summary offence, the Crown Court's only response can be to send the case back to the magistrates,[71] unless the summary offence falls

---

[67] By s.50(12)(c) and (d), an offence is related to an indictable-only offence if it "arises out of circumstances which are the same as or connected with those giving rise to the indictable-only offence".

[68] s.50(11).

[69] s.51(12)(c).

[70] See The Crime and Disorder Act 1998 (Service of Prosecution Evidence) Regulations 2000 (S.I. 2000 No. 3305).

[71] See section 41 of the 1988 Act. Para. 6 of Sched. 3 of the 1998 Act reflects this procedure.

within section 40 of the 1988 Act in which case the Crown Court could hear it.[72] The pilots of the indictable only initiative introduced under section 51 were evaluated by Ernst and Young[73] who concluded that it significantly reduced the time from charge to completion for all indictable only cases with a reduction in annual costs of £15.7 million.[74] Magistrates' courts were reported to have welcomed the removal of these indictable cases from their committal workload,[75] and the CPS had welcomed the opportunity to become more involved in Crown Court proceedings. The Report acknowledged that there would be an impact on administrative costs including the additional burden of earlier preparation of papers by police and FSS, placing these institutions which are already under pressure under yet greater time constraints. There was also be an increase in Crown Court workload, with extra CPS costs, higher legal aid costs to Counsel and solicitors and some "brought forward" costs arising from the earlier conclusion of cases — including an impact on prisons. The evaluation nevertheless concluded that the indictable only initiative improves the overall quality of justice for defendants, victims and witnesses.[76-77] There was no finding that it had any impact on the plea rates.

2. Offences Triable only Summarily

Magistrates actually deal with the vast majority of trials in this country (around 97 per cent) and they have exclusive jurisdiction in summary trial. Summary offences must be created by statute and the designation of an offence as summary prevents a jury trial. It was the proposed reclassification of certain offences as triable only summarily which caused much heated criticism of the James Report.[78] (The recent proposals to remove the right of election for mode of trial have generated much the same concerns.)   **14–050**

The Criminal Law Act 1977 made provision for the "down-grading" of certain offences which might previously have come before a jury,[79] and no strenuous objection was taken to allocating a number of road traffic offences (including driving with a blood-alcohol concentration above the prescribed limit[80]), assaulting a police constable,[81] threatening behaviour in public

---

[72] Sched. 3, para. 6(8) and see further below.

[73] *Reducing Delay in the criminal Justice System: Evaluation of the Indictable only Initiative* (Home Office, 2000). Bridges is critical of the research by Ernst and Young: see (1999) Legal Act., Oct. p.7.

[74] *ibid.* The average time between charge and completion for a bail case was reduced from 228 to 194 days and from 172 to 141 for custody cases. The number of hearings saved in the magistrates' far outweighed those added in the Crown Court (average of only one extra).

[75] *ibid.* In addition, it was recommended that amendment be made to the procedure so that a single justice should have the ability to send a case to the Crown Court.

[76-77] The Report also recommended that advance information packages should be available before the first hearing in the magistrates' court, and, further, that all CPS lawyers should be allowed to appear in the Crown Court to present cases prior to the PDH.

[78] *The Distribution of Criminal Business between the Crown Court and Magistrates' Courts* (Cmnd. 6323,1975).

[79] 1977 Act, s.15 and Sched. 1.

[80] Now the Road Traffic Act 1988, s.5 (as amended).

[81] Now the Police Act 1996, s.89. Concern was expressed about these changes: see E. J. Griew, *Current Law Statutes Annotated 1977*, General Note to ss.15–17.

places[82] "and other offences to the magistrates alone. The major controversy was caused by a proposal about theft.

The James Report took the view that

"small thefts should not be triable on indictment. ... In the last analysis society has to choose between two conflicting aims. On the one hand is the existing right of the citizen to be tried by a judge and jury on any charge of theft or criminal damage, however small the amount involved. On the other is the right, especially important to anyone defending a serious charge, to be tried as soon as possible. ... At present, defendants on serious charges are suffering the injustice of long-delayed trial, while the time of the Crown Court is partly occupied with minor cases of low monetary value."[83]

The Committee went on to recommend that where a person was charged with theft or a related offence, where the value of the property involved did not exceed £20, that offence should be triable only summarily.[84] That was included in the Criminal Law Bill.

This raised squarely the question of what sorts of offence should entitle a defendant to trial by jury and the reactions to the proposal were emotional.[85] The Bill was introduced into the House of Lords and by the time it reached the House of Commons the clause which would have enacted the proposal had been withdrawn by the government. It is interesting to note that a similar proposal relating to criminal damage where the value of the property damaged was less than £200 was accepted and such an offence is now triable only summarily.[86] The crucial difference was said to be the element of dishonesty inherent in the offence of theft: " ... people lose a lifetime's reputation for probity by a single action of dishonesty of a material triviality. ... [Small thefts] remain offences which are serious in the eyes of all honest men."[87]

The offences of taking a motor vehicle without consent and driving while disqualified[88] were changed from triable either way to summary offences by

---

[82] Public Order Act 1936, s.5, as substituted by Race Relations Act 1965, s.7: see now the Public Order Act 1986, ss.4, 4A, 5 (and now the racially aggravated versions of these offences under the Crime and Disorder Act 1998).

[83] James Committee Report (see n. 78 above), para. 87.

[84] *ibid.*, para. 100.

[85] See the speeches of members of the House of Lords during the debate on the second reading of the Criminal Law Bill, H. L. Deb., Vol. 378, cols. 801–873, December 14, 1976.

[86] Magistrates' Courts Act 1980, s.22, as amended, and Sched. 2. The limit was subsequently raised to £400 then to £2,000 and most recently to £5,000 by the Criminal Justice and Public Order Act 1994, s.46; s.22 of the 1980 Act which sets out a special procedure to be adopted in these cases, on which see *R. v. Salisbury Magistrates' Court, ex p. Mastin* (1986) 84 Cr.App.R. 248; *R. v. Braden* (1987) 152 J.P. 92; *R. v. Fennell* [2000] 1 W.L.R. 201. On the difficulty in valuing property in such cases see *R. v. Colchester Justices, ex p. Abbott* (2001) 165 J.P. 386, (GM crop damage); *R. v. Bristol Magistrates Court, ex p. E* [1998] 3 All. E.R. 798. The value is as to the damage to the property, not any consequential loss; *R. v. Colchester Magistrates' Court, ex p. Abbott* (2001) 165. J.P. 386; *R. v. Alden* (2002) 166 J.P.N. 294.

[87] *per* Lord Edmund-Davies in the debate referred to in n. 85, above.

[88] Theft Act 1968, s.12; Road Traffic Act 1972, s.99 (now re-enacted in the Road Traffic Act 1988, s.103).

the Criminal Justice Act 1988.[89] Common assault and battery were also made summary offences.[90] The pressure to reclassify other offences, such as small thefts, as summary only has continued.[91]

Aside from the higher rates of conviction in the magistrates' court, one significant disadvantage to an accused facing a summary offence is that there is a much reduced requirement of advance information or disclosure as compared with that for indictable offences. Doubt was cast on whether this conflicts with Article 6 by denying the accused the chance to know the case against him and by infringing the equality of arms principle.[92] The European Court has recognised the need for the defendant to have adequate access to the prosecution file irrespective of the venue of the trial.[93] The Attorney General's Guidelines on *Disclosure of Information in Criminal Proceedings* now impose clear obligations of disclosure in the magistrates' court. As has been noted, the Guidelines serve to ensure that the accused has primary disclosure of material on which the prosecution proposes to rely.[94] It is anticipated that this will increase yet further the number of defendants prepared to elect for trial in the magistrates' court.

3. OFFENCES TRIABLE EITHER WAY[95]

This category is now comprised of (1) those offences specifically mentioned in the First Schedule to the Magistrates' Courts Act 1980[96]; (2) all other offences which prior to the 1977 Act were triable either on indictment or summarily and which were not redesignated[97]; and (3) all offences **14–051**

---

[89] Section 37. Penalties greater than the maximum applicable in the magistrates' court had been imposed in only a small number of cases: *Consultative Paper on the Distribution of Business between the Crown Court and the Magistrates' Court* (Home Office, 1986), paras 17–20.

[90] Criminal Justice Act 1988, s.39. This reduced the work of the Crown Court by 6%: see *Criminal Statistics for England and Wales 1989*, para. 6.12. Formerly these were triable either way, unless, anomalously, the prosecution was brought by or on behalf of the victim, in which case these were triable summarily or on indictment *at the discretion of the justices*: see *R. v. Harrow JJ., ex p. Osaseri* [1986] Q.B. 589; E.J. Griew, [1983] Crim.L.R. 710.

[91] See *e.g.* D. Wolchover, "The Right to Jury Trial" (1986) 136 N.L.J. 530 at 576 (critical of the proposal); N. A. McKittrick, "Curbing the Right to Jury Trial" (1988) 152 J.P.N. 515. In 1989, an internal LCD study found that 11–12% of the Crown Court caseload would be saved if theft and handling offences in respect of goods below £100 in value and similar offences were made summary only: RCCJ Report, p. 88. The Home Office sought views on the reclassification of minor thefts, possession of an offensive weapon, and some other offences as summary only (Home Office, *Mode of Trial: A Consultation Document* (Cm. 2908, 1995), pp. 2–4); the government was, however, aware of the objections to these changes.

[92] But see the controversial statements in *R. v. Stratford Justices, ex p. Imbert* [1999] 2 Cr.App.R. 276, DC. *Obiter* this was not a breach of Art. 6, nor would the position alter after the Human Rights Act 1998. See Emmerson and Ashworth (2001), pp. 14–108.

[93] *Foucher v. France* (1998) 25 E.H.R.R. 234.

[94] para. 43. See also T. Owen, "Disclosure" in K. Starmer *et al.*, *Criminal Justice, Police Powers and Human Rights* (2001), pp.143–144.

[95] For a good historical account of the problem with either way offences, see Auld Report (2001), Chap. 10, para. 123–127, and for a review of the present procedure, see paras 128–132.

[96] Re-enacting Sched. 3 to the Criminal Law Act 1977.

[97] Magistrates' Courts Act 1980, s.17. For the difficult relationship between s.17 and the plea before venue procedure see (1997) J.P.N. 1011 but see *R. v. Kelly* [2001] R.T.R.5: the determination of mode of trial of small value offences is addressed before plea before venue.

established since 1977 as triable either way. Amongst the important offences triable either way are all indictable offences under the Theft Acts 1968 and 1978 (save for robbery, blackmail, assault with intent to rob and some burglaries); most of the offences under the Criminal Damage Act 1971, including arson; and certain offences under the Perjury Act 1911, the Sexual Offences Act 1956, the Forgery and Counterfeiting Act 1981 and the Public Order Act 1986.[98–99]

In respect of offences triable either way it is, of course, necessary to provide a procedure for determining the mode of trial. Save where the prosecution is being carried on by the Attorney-General, the Solicitor-General or the DPP, and trial on indictment is required by him,[1] the accused may opt for summary trial or trial on indictment. The court may impose trial on indictment, but may (at present) not insist on summary trial if the defendant[2] objects. The procedure for determining mode of trial has been the subject of repeated amendment. In 1995 the government issued a consultation document[3] seeking views on the possible reclassification of certain offences as summary only,[4] and, substantial changes were enacted as a result. These oblige the defendant to enter a plea *before* the mode of trial decision is made.

The Criminal Procedure and Investigations Act 1996 introduced this preliminary procedure "plea before venue", which was designed to maximise the opportunity to keep the greatest number of cases possible in the magistrates' court.[5] The present procedure (in outline) is as follows.[6]

(i) The charge is written down and read to the accused.[7]

(ii) It is explained to the accused that if he or she indicates a guilty plea, the trial will be dealt with summarily, but that the case may be

---

[98–99] See *Archbold* (2002), para. 1.25.

[1] *ibid.* s.19(4). The DPP must obtain the consent of the Attorney-General: *ibid.* s.19(5), inserted by the Prosecution of Offences Act 1985, s. 31(5), Sched. 1, Pt 1, para. 2.

[2] In the case of adult joint defendants, if one consents to summary trial and the other elects for jury trial, the justices are not obliged to commit both for trial: *R. v. Brentwood JJ., ex p. Nicholls* [1992] 1 A.C. 1 and see *R. v. Wigan JJ, ex p. Layland.* See the plea for this decision to be overturned: A. Samuels, [1999] Crim.L.R. 726.

[3] Home Office, *Mode of Trial: A Consultation Document* (Cm. 2908, 1995).

[4] See above, para. 14-044.

[5] See A. Edwards, [1997] Crim.L.R. 321; R. Leng and R. Taylor, *The Blackstone's Guide to the CPIA 1996* (1996); S. Enright, (1997) 147 N.L.J. 1691. The hearing can occur before a lone magistrate: s.18(5).

[6] Magistrates' Courts Act 1980, ss.19–21 as heavily amended by the Criminal Procedure and Investigations Act 1996, ss.49 and the Powers of Criminal Courts (Sentencing) Act 2000, s.165. Magistrates are obliged to follow the procedure strictly otherwise their decision will be liable to be quashed as *ultra vires.*

[7] Who should be present unless: it impracticable owing to his or her disorderly behaviour; or, provided there is legal representation, the accused consents to being absent and there is a good reason for the absence; or, where there is a live link from a remand facility: see Crime and Disorder Act 1998, s.57. See further on live links the Learmont Report, *Review of Prison Service Security and Escape from Parkhurst Prison on Tuesday 3rd January 1995*, Cm. 3020 (1996).

committed for sentence in the Crown Court if the magistrates are of the opinion that their sentencing powers are inadequate.[8]

(iii) Following the explanation, the accused is asked to indicate a plea.[9]

(iv) If the indication is guilty, the court proceeds as if this was a guilty plea received at a summary trial.[10] If the magistrates wish to keep open the option of committing to the Crown Court for sentencing they should make that explicit to the accused to prevent any misunderstanding and any legitimate expectation arising.[11]

(v) If the indication is one of not guilty, the court listens to any representations from the prosecutor and the accused about the most suitable mode of trial.[12]

(vi) The court proceeds to decide on the more suitable mode of trial, taking into account the nature of the case, whether the circumstances make the offence one of a serious character, whether the limited powers of punishment of a magistrates' court would be adequate,[13] and any other relevant circumstances.[14]

(vii) If the court considers summary trial more appropriate, that should be explained to the accused, as should the fact that he or she need not consent to summary trial but can opt for trial by jury, and that after a summary trial the magistrates have power to send him or her to the Crown Court for sentence.[15]

(viii) If the accused consents to summary trial, the case proceeds.

---

[8] See Powers of Criminal Courts (Sentencing) Act 2000, ss.3, 17A, and see the Home Office Circular 45/1997 which provides a suitable form of words explaining the process, which is particularly important with unrepresented defendants. Extracts appear in *Blackstone's Criminal Practice (2002)*, p. 1081.

[9] The Magistrates' Courts Act 1980, s.17A(5).

[10] If the court adjourns for sentencing reports having indicated an intention to deal with the case without committing the case to the Crown Court for sentencing, then in the absence of further information affecting the gravity of the case, a decision to commit for sentence will be subject to judicial review: *R. v. Norwich Magistrates Court, ex p. Elliott* [2000] 1 Cr.App.R. (S) 152. Note that if D pleads guilty to a scheduled offence (*e.g.* criminal damage) s.22 prevails so that the case is dealt with summarily: *R. v. Kelly* [2001] R.T.R. 5. See on the difficulty created when this is committed to the Crown Court with an indictable only offence: *R. v. Alden* (2002) 166 J.P. 294.

[11] *R. v. Wirral Magistrates Court, ex p. Jermyn* [2001] Crim.L.R. 45 (can commit without new information but dangers of false expectation of D cannot be ignored); see also *R. v. Feltham Justices, ex p. Rees* [2001] Crim.L.R. 47.

[12] Magistrates' Courts Act 1980, s.19(2)(b).

[13] On the significance of considering this see *R. v. Flax Burton Magistrates Court, ex p. Commissioners of Customs and Excise* (1996)160 J.P. 481.

[14] This is a very broad remit and could include for example that an insanity plea is better dealt with in the Crown Court: see *R. v. Horseferry Road Magistrates Court, ex p. K* [1997] Q.B. 23. A controversial question is whether the court should take account of the accused's antecedents at that stage see S. White, "The Antecedents of the Mode of Trial Guidelines" [1996] Crim.L.R. 471 and *R. v. Warley Justices, ex p. DPP* [1999] 1 W.L.R. 216. The express ban on taking account of the antecedents in the 1990 guidelines was removed in the 1995 version.

[15] Under the Powers of Criminal Courts (Sentencing) Act 2000, s.3.

(ix) If the accused elects trial on indictment, the magistrates proceed with committal proceedings.[16]

(x) If the court considers that trial on indictment is more appropriate it will proceed with committal proceedings and the accused effectively has no choice in the matter.[17]

The advantages of the plea before venue system are that it reduces delay and relieves the congestion in the Crown Court, reduces the number of cracked trials (those in which a guilty plea is made at the last minute), and saves money.[18] The obvious effect is that fewer cases will be committed to the Crown Court for trial, but the indications are that this has led to a considerable increase in the number of early guilty pleas, which has led to an increase in numbers of committals for sentence.[19] There were 1,693 such cases between April and June 1997; as compared with 5,878 cases in April to June 1998 once the plea before venue was implemented.[20] This increase in the number of guilty pleas made at the plea before venue stage is inevitable because this will give the accused the opportunity to maximise any sentencing discount[21]; but this carries with it the danger that innocent people will indicate a guilty plea earlier to secure a lesser sentence rather than risk defending the accusation with a potentially higher sentence if convicted. The accused can use the system tactically to maximise sentencing discount and the time spent as a remand prisoner as well as increasing his chances of being sentenced only by the magistrates. There is also the danger that a greater number of equivocal pleas will be made, and of the problems of dealing with the summary equivalents of pleas in bar (*i.e.* challenges on the basis of double jeopardy, etc.).

The plea before venue scheme has led to not only an increase in the number but also the seriousness of cases committed for sentence.[22] The L.C.D. Consultation Paper on the plea before venue operation pointed to the problem of the composition of the Crown Court when hearing sentencing cases from the magistrates' court. This is an acute problem where the magistrates are hearing a case of such seriousness that they would never entertain hearing it alone in the magistrates' court, and would have no experience of dealing with the issues involved.

---

[16] See below, para. 14-063.

[17] The Magistrates Courts Act 1980, s.21.

[18] See for comment G. Bavidge and K. Kerrigan, "Plea Before Venue" (1998) 148 N.L.J. 62; P. Tain, "Plea Before Venue" (1998) S.J. 156.

[19] Powers of Criminal Courts (Sentencing) Act 2000, s.3; formerly the Magistrates Courts Act 1980, s.38.

[20] See LCD, *Magistrates Sitting as Judges in the Crown Court* (1998), a consultation paper in which proposals to remove justices sitting in the Crown Court on sentencing are discussed. See also S. Sisson *et al.*, *Cautions, Court Proceedings and Sentencing, England and Wales 1998* (1999), reporting a 160% increase in the number of committals for sentence, and a reduction in the number of guilty pleas at the Crown Court.

[21] *R. v. Rafferty* [1999] 2 Cr.App.R. (S) 449; *R. v. Barber* [2001] EWCA 2267. See N. Padfield, "Plea Before Venue" (1997) 147 N.L.J. 1396, who argues that the system will not necessarily save money or improve consistency in sentencing as many hardened criminals will seize the chance to reduce further their sentence. See also L. Bridges, (1999) Legal Action, Oct., p.6.

[22] LCD Paper *op. cit.*, para. 25.

Other problems generated by the plea before venue system include those in relation to disclosure.[23] The plea before venue would place the accused in an extremely difficult position unless there was adequate disclosure of the case against him before his or her plea indication is required. The courts have recently held that the prosecution cannot withhold all advance disclosure until the accused has indicated a plea.[24]

(a) Mode of trial

Where the examining justices are faced with the decision on mode of trial, they must give proper consideration to all relevant factors and should not be persuaded by the accused (or prosecutor) to allow a summary trial where the offence ought really to be tried on indictment. There are a number of examples of magistrates' courts being severely criticised for allowing serious cases to be tried summarily.[25] The justices are aided somewhat by a provision that they may, during a trial[26] (before the conclusion of the prosecution evidence[27]), decide to discontinue the summary trial and proceed as examining justices if the prosecution case reveals the offence to be more serious than might at first have appeared.[28] The reverse change is possible, from committal proceedings to summary trial, subject, in this case, to the consent of the accused.[29] **14–052**

The defendant should be permitted to change his or her election if he or she has not properly understood the nature and significance of the choice of

---

[23] See also Bavidge and Kerrigan (1998), p.134.

[24] See *R. v. Calderdale Magistrates Court, ex p. Donaghue and Cutler* [2001] Crim.L.R. 141 and commentary. See generally, Ashworth (1998), p.250.

[25] See, *e.g. R. v. Coe* [1968] 1 W.L.R. 1950; *R. v. Northamptonshire Magistrates' Court, ex p. Customs and Excise Commissioners, The Independent*, February 23, 1994 (decision to try £200,000 VAT fraud summarily quashed); *R. v. Horseferry Road Magistrates Court, ex p. DPP* [1997] C.O.D. 89, (possession of 114 ecstasy tablets); *cf. R. v. Derby JJ., ex p. DPP, The Times*, August 17, 1999 (banging victims head on wall — not using a weapon).

[26] But not on the basis of pleading only: see *R. v. St Helens Magistrates Court, ex p. Critchley* [1988] Crim.L.R. 311; *cf. R. v. Newham Juvenile Court, ex p. F (A Minor)* (1984) 84 Cr.App.R. 81.

[27] Not after a plea of guilty has been accepted: *R. v. Dudley JJ., ex p. Gillard* [1986] A.C. 442, HL; *R. v. Telford JJ., ex p. Darlington* (1987) 87 Cr.App.R. 194; *R. v. Bradford Justices, ex p. Grant* (1999) 163 J.P. 717; and not prior to the commencement of summary trial: *R. v. Southend Magistrates' Court, ex p. Wood* (1986) 152 J.P. 97; *R. v. St. Helens Magistrates' Court, ex p. Critchley* (1987) 152 J.P. 102. See R. Stevens, (1987) 151 J.P.N. 848. This includes hearing submissions on a preliminary point: *R. v. Horseferry Road Magistrates Court, ex p. K* [1997] Q.B. 23. See *Archbold* (2002), para. 1–65.

[28] Magistrates' Courts Act 1980, s.25(2), as amended by the Criminal Procedure and Investigation Act 1996, s.47. But, not merely because co-accused have been committed for trial: *R. v. Charley Magistrates' Court, ex p. Darbyshire* [1994] C.L.Y. 997; *R. v. Wigan Magistrates' Court, ex p. Layland* (1995) 160 J.P. 223.

[29] *ibid.* s.25(3), (3A), (4), as amended by the Prosecution of Offences Act 1985, s.31(5)(6), Scheds. 1, 2. See *R. v. Liverpool JJ., ex p. CPS* (1989) 90 Cr.App.R. 261. No power exists

the mode of trial.[30] Similarly, if he or she has made a decision on the wrong view of the facts.[31] To minimise the risk of misinformed pleas, the prosecution is obliged, on the defence requesting it, to provide a summary of the case and/or copies of the written statements prior to the mode of trial decision,[32] and prior to the plea before venue. Unless the court is satisfied that no injustice will result, there should be an adjournment to allow for consideration of the material.[33] The court should not exercise the power to alter the mode of trial because it disagrees with the original determination of the mode of trial made by a different bench.[34]

In the absence of bad faith on the part of the prosecutor or of unfairness or prejudice to the accused, the prosecutor may substitute a summary offence for an either way offence even if the purpose is to deprive the accused of the "right" to jury trial[35]; in effect denying an opportunity to a greater chance of acquittal. The prosecution can in many cases dictate the venue by charging summary only offences or an either way offence and a summary only in the alternative. If the accused elects trial at the Crown Court, the CPS could drop the either way charge leaving the summary trial.[36] In the converse situation the court must be careful not to allow the prosecutor to add an indictable only charge as a way of overruling the magistrates' earlier decision to try the defendant summarily.[37] If the prosecutor disagrees with the magistrates' decision to try the accused summarily, judicial review may be sought. These situations raise difficult questions about the ethics of prosecuting on which English law has yet to provide adequate guidance.[38]

In the 1980s there was a steady increase in the number and proportion of triable either way cases committed for trial in the Crown Court.[39] This led to higher costs and greater numbers being imprisoned. Home Office research indicated that a high proportion, over 60 per cent, were committed at the discretion of the magistrates rather than at the insistence of the defendant, and that there were considerable variations in practice among the courts

other than under the statute: *R. v. Herefordshire JJ., ex p. J.*.

[30] *R. v. Birmingham JJ., ex p. Hodgson* [1985] Q.B. 1131, DC (unrepresented defendants had been under the misapprehension that they had no defence; earlier authorities considered); see B. Gibson, (1985) 149 J.P.N. 67. See also *R. v. Forest Magistrates' Court, ex p. Spicer* (1988) 153 J.P. 81; *R. v. Bourne JJ., ex p. Cope* (1988) 153 J.P. 161. The magistrates have a broad discretion in this application: *R. v. Southampton Justices, ex p. Briggs* [1972] 1 W.L.R. 277.

[31] See *R. v. Isleworth Crown Court and Uxbridge Magistrates Court, ex p. Buda* [2000] 1 Cr.App.R. (S) 538.

[32] See Magistrates' Court (Advance Information) Rules 1985 (S.I. 1985 No. 601).

[33] *R. v. Calderdale Justices, ex p. Donaghue and Cutler* [2001] Crim.L.R. 141.

[34] *R. v. Birmingham Stipendiary Magistrate, ex p. Webb* (1995) 95 Cr.App.R. 75.

[35] *R. v. City of Liverpool Stipendiary Magistrate, ex p. Ellison* (1988) 153 J.P. 433; *Cooke v. DPP* (1992) 156 J.P. 497.

[36] On the CPS Code and the charging standards and whether they legitimate these practices see above, para. 14-044.

[37] *R. v. Redbridge Justices, ex p. Whitehouse* (1992) 94 Cr.App.R. 332.

[38] For discussion, see Ashworth (1998), p.254.

[39] From 55,000 to 93,500 between 1979 and 1987, an increase from 15% to 21% of all defendants proceeded against for either-way offences: *Criminal Statistics 1979*, Table 4.5; *1989*, Table 6.4.

surveyed.[40] Guidelines were formulated in some areas to enhance consistency[41] and magistrates were encouraged to retain more cases within their jurisdiction.[42] National guidelines were published in October 1990.[43] They were updated in 1995 and were recently re-examined[44] in light of the changes introduced by plea before venue, which has, obviously, reduced the pressure on magistrates.

The National Guidelines set out some general considerations,[45] based on the case law, but concluding with the proposition that in general, either way offences should be tried summarily unless the court considers that one or more of the features specified in the guidelines for particular offences is present and that its sentencing powers are insufficient. Examples of these (aggravating) features are, for burglary in a dwelling: entry in the daytime when someone is present or at night when the house is normally occupied; the alleged offence is one of a series of similar offences; soiling, ransacking, damage or vandalism occurs; the offence has professional hallmarks; or the unrecovered property is of high value (£10,000 or more). For theft and fraud, the features include breach of trust by a person of substantial authority; offences committed or disguised in a sophisticated manner; or by an organised gang; or where the victim is particularly vulnerable (*e.g.* the elderly or infirm); or where the unrecovered property is of high value. The guidelines also state directly that some offences should generally be committed for trial: these include violent disorder and supply or possession with intent to supply of a Class A drug.[46] Where cases involve complex questions of fact or difficult questions of law, the court should consider committal for trial.

---

[40] C. Hedderman and D. Moxon, *Magistrates' Court or Crown Court? Mode of Trial Decisions and Sentencing* (H.O. Research Study No. 125, HMSO, 1992). See also studies by A. E. Bottoms and J. D. McClean, *Defendants in the Criminal Process* (1976), Chap. 4; C. R. Searle, (1989) 153 J.P.N. 526; and D. Riley and J. Vennard, *Triable Either Way Cases: Crown Court or Magistrates' Court?* (H.O. Research Study No. 98, 1988); J. Gregory, *Crown Court or Magistrates' Court* (1976).

[41] N. A. McKittrick, "Considerations in Determining Mode of Trial" (1987) 151 J.P.N. 468, setting out guidelines formulated by the liaison judges in the East Midlands. A revised version is set out at (1989) 153 J.P.N. 314. *Cf.* the study by Searle, *op. cit.*, of cases in Nottingham.

[42] *cf.* letter from the Home Office to the Magistrates' Association summarising the research and suggesting that it was unlikely that the increase in committal rates was accounted for by an increase in the level of the seriousness of offences: (1989) 45 The Magistrate 65. Note that the cost of proceedings in the magistrates' court is around £500 compared with around £8,600 in the Crown Court (*Digest 4* (1998) *op.cit.*); Sanders and Young (2000), p.487 suggest that a fairer comparison of prices is of guilty pleas in each court: magistrates' courts cost around £210, Crown Court, £1,400.

[43] *Practice Note (Mode of Trial: Guidelines)* [1990] 1 W.L.R. 1439. The guidelines have been revised and reissued with the endorsement of the Lord Chief Justice. See *Archbold* (2002), para. 1-40a for the current versions and generally S. White, [1996] Crim.L.R. 471.

[44] *R. v. Warley Magistrates Court, ex p. DPP and others* [1998] 2 Cr.App.R. 307.

[45] It has been emphasised that the guidelines are only that: *R. v. Derby Justices, ex p. DPP, The Times*, August 17, 1999.

[46] Section 3 of the Crime (Sentences) Act 1997 s.3 introduced a further problem for charges of Class A drug trafficking, because automatic sentences flow from a defendant having two previous convictions for drugs offences. See comment at (1998) 162 J.P.N. 238.

(b) Committal for sentence

14–053   On the question of committal for sentence, the Divisional Court has
emphasised that each offence charged is to be considered separately, and
that magistrates must take account of discount for early guilty plea in
deciding whether a case needs to be committed for sentence.[47] Although the
statute does not expressly provide for the prosecution to address the court
on the questions of venue for sentence, the Divisional Court has accepted
that both parties could be heard if they desired.[48] It was also emphasised
that great care must be taken not to give an accused the belief that
committal for sentence has been ruled out,[49] and that all aspects "of
character and antecedents" are to be taken into account in deciding whether
to commit for sentence.[50] If necessary there should be an adjournment.[51] If
there are disputes about the facts, it may be necessary to conduct a *Newton*
hearing to decide whether to commit for sentence.[52]

Following the introduction of the plea before venue system, there has
been a marked increase in the number of committals for sentence to the
Crown Court. However, research has shown that the magistrates often
commit cases for sentence which result in sentences well within the
magistrates' own powers, with 62 per cent of all those committed for
sentence receiving a penalty that could have been imposed by the
magistrates.[53] It has been argued that the figure is rather misleading since
it includes all cases committed, including those in which the Crown Court
and magistrates sentencing powers are identical.[54] Other research has
demonstrated that if only cases under section 38 (*i.e.* straightforward
committals) are compared, 60 per cent of those committed for sentence were
sentenced to terms that lay *outside* the magistrates powers.[55] The Auld
Report estimates that 55 per cent of defendants convicted by the Crown
Court after committal for trial receive sentences which lie within the
magistrates' power.[56]

The problem of whether to commit for sentence is exacerbated by the plea
before venue scheme because the magistrates are acting on less information
when committing for sentence, and are much less likely to have access to all
mitigating information. Freeman's research showed that when magistrates
committed for sentence after receiving more information the subsequent

---

[47] *R. v. Warley Magistrates Court, ex p. DPP* [1998] 2 Cr.App.R. 307
[48] *ibid.*
[49] See S. Forster, (2002) 166 J.P.N. 100. See also *R. v. Nottingham Magistrates' Court, ex p.
    Davidson* [2000] 1 Cr.App.R. (S) 167; *R. v. Horseferry Road Magistrates' Court, ex p. Rugless*
    (2000) 164 J.P. 311.
[50] *R. v. Warley Magistrates Court, ex p. DPP and others* [1998] 2 C.A.R. 307 at 316.
[51] This in itself is not enough to give rise to a legitimate expectation: *R. v. Norwich Magistrates'
    Court, ex p. Elliott* [2000] 1 Cr.App.R. (S) 152.
[52] On committal for sentence on a summary trial of offence triable either way see *Practice
    Direction* [2001] 4 All E.R. 63.
[53] See C. Flood-Page and A Mackie, *Sentencing Practice: an Examination of Decisions in
    Magistrates' Courts and the Crown Court in the Mid-1990s* (HORS No. 180, 1998).
[54] See J. Freeman, "Committal for Sentence from Magistrates' Courts to the Crown Court"
    (1999) 163 J.P.N. 284.
[55] *ibid.*
[56] (2001), Chap. 10, para. 150.

Crown Court sentence is more likely to be a heavier one than if the Crown Court initiates the pre-sentence report.[57]

(c) Mode of trial decisions and reform

Before the plea before venue scheme was introduced, research into **14–054** defendants' reasons for choosing between summary trial and trial by jury (where a choice is permitted) suggested that the major factor was the intended plea: defendants intending to contest the case commonly regarded trial by jury in the Crown Court as offering a fairer hearing and a better chance of acquittal, in comparison with the magistrates' courts which were said to be biased in favour of the prosecution.[58] A significant number of defendants intending to plead guilty also wished to be dealt with in the Crown Court, notwithstanding larger sentencing powers, given their confidence in sentencing by a judge rather than by magistrates.[59] "Some defendants want a better chance of acquittal rather than a lesser penalty if convicted."[60] Reasons cited most frequently for those choosing summary trial were to get the case to court quickly, the chance of a lighter sentence, to avoid lengthy court proceedings and the triviality of the case.[61] In addition, defendants elect Crown Court trial for tactical reasons including taking the opportunity to maximise their time on remand. There is also the heavy influence of legal advice on election to be borne in mind.[62]

Research in the early 1990s highlighted the apparent oddities in the exercise of choice by both defendants and magistrates.[63] As noted, magistrates' sentencing powers would have been sufficient to deal with the majority of cases where they had declined jurisdiction; most defendants who elected Crown Court trial were influenced by the prospects of acquittal, but 82 per cent ended up pleading guilty to all charges on which they were convicted; while more than half of those who elected jury trial said that the possibility of a lighter sentence influenced their decision, in fact the Crown Court made far more use of custody than the magistrates, court irrespective of area.[64]

It should be noted that further exhortations to magistrates drawing

---

[57] Freeman (1999) concludes that cynicism about lenient Crown Court sentencing is misplaced.

[58] But see P. Darbyshire, [1997] Crim.L.R. 861 at 869.

[59] Another factor was to elect for trial in the Crown Court in order to gain access to the prosecution case against the defendant. This incentive was removed by the Magistrates' Court (Advance Information) Rules 1985 (S.I. No. 1985, 601), requiring the prosecution, on request, to provide the accused with either copies of the prosecution witness statements or with a summary of the facts (r.4). There remains disquiet as to the disparity of compliance in different CPS areas.

[60] Ashworth (1998), p.259. See below for a discussion of the quality of justice in the magistrates' courts.

[61] Hedderman and Moxon (1992) and Riley and Vennard (1988), confirming earlier surveys by Bottoms and McClean (1976) and J. Gregory, *Crown Court or Magistrates' Court?* (HMSO, 1976).

[62] See Ashworth (1998), pp. 246–249 for comment.

[63] Hedderman and Moxon (1992).

[64] On the additional danger of racially discriminatory elements in the mode of trial procedures see I. Brown and R. Hullin, "A Study of Sentencing in the Leeds Magistrates Court: The Treatment of Ethnic Minority and White Offenders" (1992) 32 Brit. J. Criminol. 41.

attention to the research findings appear to have had some effect. In 1998, 72 per cent of either way cases in the Crown Court were at the magistrates' decision not the defendant's election, this had grown from a figure of 62 per cent in 1992.[65] In 2000, of the 82,598 committals for trial, 38,914 were at the magistrates' direction, 16,351 at the defendants' election and 27,333 were for indictable only offences.[66]

The RCCJ recommended that in the light of the early research, changes should be made to introduce a more rational division of either way cases between magistrates' courts and the Crown Court. If prosecution and defence were agreed on venue, that would be decisive; otherwise, the matter would be determined by the magistrates, the defence no longer having the right to insist on jury trial. This would be likely to lead to fewer cases being sent to the Crown Court. The Commission noted that "trial in a magistrates' court is many times cheaper". Beliefs that trial in the Crown Court would be fairer or offer a better chance of acquittal were not relevant. As to the first point, magistrates' courts "conduct over 93 per cent of all criminal cases and should be trusted to try cases fairly".[67] The RCCJ appeared undisturbed by the absence of research on the quality of criminal justice in the magistrates' court.

In 1999 and again in 2000 the government unsuccessfully introduced Criminal Justice (Mode of Trial) Bills into Parliament. There was tremendous opposition from many quarters. The proposals were based on the RCCJ recommendations, despite these having been the subject of very cogent criticism.[68]

Prior to the first Bill being laid before Parliament, the Home Office issued a Consultation Paper,[69] which sought to justify these controversial proposals to remove the accused's right to elect in favour of the magistrates' decision as to trial venue.

Consideration of the original options proposed provides a clear indication of most of the arguments at stake. The options were:

1. Retaining the status quo. This would allow each defendant to elect mode of trial. It reflects the common belief that Crown Court trial is fairer. It would also allow defendants' to insist on a jury trial in a case where they felt their reputation was at stake. However, the system adds to delay, and few defendants actually insist on the Crown Court trial to protect their reputation.[70] The election for Crown Court trial is arguably a tactic to create further delay, therefore putting pressure on the CPS to accept lower charges, on the prosecution witnesses to drop the case, and generally to avoid the "evil day" of trial. Further

---

[65] Sanders and Young (2000), p.542.

[66] *CPS Annual Report 2000–2001*, (2001), Table 7. See also *Criminal Statistics for England and Wales 2000* (2001), p.232.

[67] Cm. 2263, pp. 85–89.

[68] See A. Ashworth, [1993] Crim.L.R. 830; L. Bridges, (1993) 143 N.L.J. 1542; L. Bridges, (2000) Legal Action, July 6, p.8.

[69] *Determining Mode of Trial in Either Way Cases* (1998). Mode of trial options were also discussed in Chap.6 of Narey (1997). For criticism see Sanders and Young (2000), pp.540–548 and L. Bridges, S. Choongh, and M. McConville, *Ethnic Minority Defendants and the Right to Elect Jury Trial* (CRE, 2000).

[70] Only one in ten such defendants has a "good reputation" with no previous convictions (*ibid.*).

arguments against the system are that the majority of defendants who elected Crown Court appearances then went on to plead guilty anyway.[71]

2. Reclassification of some offences as triable summarily only (*e.g.* theft under £90). It was estimated that this would take around 2,000 cases per year out of Crown Court. However, this option lacks the desired flexibility to respond to the circumstances of each case.

3. Abolition of election for trial. This rests on the simple question – what logical reason is there for allowing the accused to choose trial venue rather than the magistrates making that decision. The Paper sought to rebut arguments based on a "fundamental" or "constitutional" rights to a jury. It was pointed out that the right of election was a relatively modern phenomenon.[72] The Home Office also pointed to the low level of election for Crown Court trial by the accused (28 per cent),[73] and emphasised that the proportion of those defendants who plead not guilty in the Crown Court is the same whether they elected or were committed. It also pointed to chances of an acquittal in the Crown Court as being around 40 per cent compared to 25 per cent in the magistrates' court,[74] suggesting that the quality of justice was equal and that defendant's had nothing to fear if they were committed to the Crown Court against their wishes.[75] This option is supported by arguments of efficiency — around 15,000 committals for trial each year would be saved.[76] One problem in evaluating these issues in the absence of conclusive data. The Auld Report was also critical of the "lack of current, comprehensive or well based data bearing on the issue", but concluded that either way offences are around 25 per cent of the total workload of the criminal courts and that 11 per cent are committed to the Crown Court.[77]

4. A compromise position. Removal of the defendant's right to elect in

---

[71] 60% of these who elected pleaded guilty before trial. 15% of those who elected were aquitted by jury.

[72] Rejecting the popular misconception of Magna Carta giving such a right. P. Derbyshire, "An Essay on the Importance and Neglect of the Magistracy" [1997] Crim.L.R. 627 argues that the "symbolic function of the jury far outweighs its practical significance ... It is no longer the central fact-finding forum." (p.627).

[73] But this was still around 22,000 people in 1997.

[74] M. Zander reported on these statistics as misleading — (1999) S.J. 967.

[75] Ashworth (1998) provides a thorough analysis of the so called "right" to a jury trial, see p.256. The fairness of the procedure in the Crown Court as qualitatively better than in magistrates' courts is borne out by research. The claims of a greater chance of acquittal in the Crown Court do not necessarily demonstrate better rectitude in decision-making. The Judicial Studies Board has been evaluating the Magistrates' New Training Initiative which was introduced in 1998 to improve training and mentoring of magistrates. The Judicial Studies Board evaluation which is in general a positive report is available at *www.jsboard.co.uk*.

[76] The Home Office, *Criminal Justice (Mode of Trial) Bill Briefing Note* explains that the resource savings from the Bill are over £100 million, most from prison savings. The accuracy of the proposed savings in cost are doubted by N. Ley, "Inferior Justice" (1999) N.L.J. 1316.

[77] Chap. 4, para. 150. But note the Auld Report's recommendation that changes should be made to improve the magistrates' system, not to avoid it: "No system of justice should be structured or operated on the basis that part of it is not working properly; it should be made to work properly at all levels": Auld (2001), p.269.

certain case—*e.g.* where earlier similar convictions were recorded against the defendant.

The subsequent Criminal Justice (Mode of Trial) Bill No. 1 would have removed the need for the accused's consent to be tried summarily when charged with an either way offence, but provided an interlocutory appeal in the Crown Court against the magistrates' decision. In the Bill[78] one of the major concerns of the opponents to the reform was specifically addressed by the requirement that magistrates should take into account the reputation of the accused in deciding whether to retain jurisdiction or commit for a Crown Court trial.[79] The Bill was opposed by many legal practitioners (including the Bar Council, Law Society, Legal Action Group) and by JUSTICE and Liberty, In the explanatory notes to the Bill, it was estimated that there would be a net saving of £105m per annum. The £105 million savings included, it was later revealed, estimates on prison savings because the magistrates would sentence fewer people to custody.[80] The Bill failed to be enacted.

The second Bill—the Criminal Justice (Mode of Trial) (No. 2) Bill 2000 contained some important and less palatable differences. There was no requirement for the magistrates to consider the defendant's livelihood and reputation.[81] The second Bill also did not explicitly refer to the magistrates having an obligation to consider the seriousness of the offence. As an important safeguard, the Bill did require magistrates to give reasons for their decision. It was estimated that under the proposal 14,000 fewer cases would be heard in the Crown Court, with new estimates of £128 million being saved (£84 million on savings from prisons). It differed substantially from the RCCJ recmmendations[82] and was subject to more vehement opposition.[83]

We can offer only an outline of the many different arguments relied upon

---

[78] For some of the mass of comment on the Mode of Trial Bill see: B. Block, (1997) 161 J.P. 274; Editorial (1999) N.L.J. 881; Editorial (1999) N.L.J. 549; Editorial (1999) 149 N.L.J. 1581; N. Ley, (1999) 149 N.L.J. 1316; D. Wolchover and A. Heaton Armstrong, (1998) 148 N.L.J. 1613; (2000) 150 N.L.J. 158. See A. Watson, (1998) 163 J.P.N. 636. See S. Choongh, (1998) 162 J.P.N. 936.

[79] The Bill derived support from the Police Federation, ACPO, the LCJ, Lord Bingham, the Magistrates' Association, and Sir Iain Glidewell the author of the Report on the CPS.

[80] See Auld (2001), Chap. 5, para. 144.

[81] This did appease those who claimed that the first Bill gave rise to two-tier justice with jury trials for the wealthy only.

[82] S. Enright, "A Silly and Dangerous Bill" (2000) 150 N.L.J. 12 pointing out the Home Secretary's change of attitude to his proposal from when it was put forward by Michael Howard the Home Secretary in 1997.

[83] Jack Straw denounced lawyers' opposition to the Bill as "Hampstead Liberalism" see (2000) S.J. 2. J. Straw explained the Bill in an interview at (2000) 150 N.L.J. 670; see reply by S. Enright (2000) 150 N.L.J. 724; see also J. Gibbons, (1999) 149 N.L.J. 1108; A Rutherford (2000) 150 N.L.J. 1442; M. Zander, (2000)150 N.L.J. 366 explaining his change of attitude from that to the first Bill.

in opposition to the proposals, which included: the "right" to a jury trial,[84] the preferences for Crown Court trial and the implicit criticism of the quality of justice in the magistrates' court,[85] and those relating to efficiency gains in the criminal process.[86] Sanders and Young regard these arguments in favour as "theoretically weak and empirically duff".[87] Many regard the proposal as another example of the continual erosion of "due process rights" in the name of efficiency. The proposals would clearly reduce defendant's bargaining power in the trial process, whilst placing the magistrates' court in a failsafe position: they can elect to retain jurisdiction and always commit the defendant to the Crown Court for sentence if the case proves suitable.

A specific concern was raised in relation to the racially discriminatory impact of the proposed provisions, as Ashworth explains, "the probability that more Afro-Caribbeans choose the Crown Court suggests that abolition of the defendant's right of election might amount to indirect discrimination, and would certainly be so perceived".[88] The Home Office Briefing Note, however, points to research demonstrating the racial neutrality of the Bill, with higher rates of conviction for whites in magistrates' courts and no difference in sentencing of the races in either Crown Courts or magistrates' courts.[89]

The Auld's Report describes the debate over the mode of trial as "mired" by a number of features including "over-emotive and legally and historically mistaken arguments exaggerating the status" of the defendants' right to trial by jury.[90] It is also describes the debate as "arid".[91] The government's claims regarding savings are treated as "highly speculative" and it is

---

[84] See recently B. Houlder, "The Importance of Preserving the Jury System and the Right of Election for Trial" [1997] Crim.L.R. 875 and P. Darbyshire, [1997] Crim.L.R. 911. The Narey Report was critical of the defendants right to elect and doubted the weight of the historical and constitutional basis for this "right". See also (1999) 62 Law and Contemporary Problems (Special Issue on the Common Law Jury); P. Duff, "The Defendant's Right to Trial by Jury: A Neighbour's View" [2000] Crim.L.R. 85, comparing the Scots system and concluding that removal of the right to elect trial by jury is not so objectionable as many critics claim. But note the correspondence with L. Bridges at [2000] Crim.L.R. 512, and the recognition that the systems are substantially different. The Auld Report (2001) also dismisses analogy with the Scottish system (Chap. 5, para. 122). On the ECHR dimension to the jury system coming under attack from Art 6. of the ECHR see L. Blom-Cooper, "Article 6 and Modes of Criminal Trial" [2001] E.H.R.L.R. 1 arguing that the quality of justice need not necessarily be diminished in the absence of the jury. The description of a "right" to a jury trial is described as "distinctly misleading".

[85] The advantage of a Crown Court trial with adequate disclosure, trained judges, and a jury would be available only in most serious cases. For defence of the magistracy see P. Darbyshire, "For the New Lord Chancellor—Some Causes for Concern About Magistrates" [1997] Crim.L.R. 861.

[86] The assumptions about savings are not all borne out by research. For example, the Bill is criticised by Sanders and Young (2000) at pp.544–45, questioning the research. In particular they point out that Hederman and Moxon's study on the committal rates was of convicted defendants only and underestimates numbers of not-guilty pleas.

[87] p.546.

[88] (1998), p.264. see also C. Griffiths, (1999) Counsel April.

[89] See Annex A.

[90] Chap. 5, para. 158.

[91] Chap. 5, para. 172.

suggested that they "lacked principle".[92] The Report regards the government reliance on arguments that magistrates sentence less heavily than Crown Courts as "fundamentally flawed",[93] because its premise is that one trial forum is not working properly. The government, instead of evaluating the concerns and attempting to remove any disparity, are accused of having opted for the cheaper version.[94]

The Auld Report's extensive review of the magistrates' courts' work and of the merits of the jury[95] leads to a number of important recommendations, including that the magistrates should decide where the defendant is to be tried. The arguments for a "constitutional right" to jury trial are rejected as mistaken,[96] with the ultimate issue being regarded as one of policy over how resources should be used in the criminal justice system. The conclusion is that if defendants perceive the magistrates' courts as less fair, it is not appropriate to allow them to avoid that court; the law should strive to improve magistrates' courts.[97] Although the right to elect would be removed, and the magistrates would make that decision, in the event of any dispute, Auld recommends that a District Judge would make the decision.[98] There would be an appeal possible from either side, to the Crown Court to be dealt with speedily.

The recommendations do, however, include the very important requirement that the power of the magistrates to commit for sentence should be abolished. This is an improvement on previous mode of trial proposals because it does not leave the accused doubly exposed. In other respects it is unclear precisely which model of mode of trial is being proposed by Auld.

Despite the lack of detail, as Jackson[99] comments, Auld raised the level of debate on the issue of mode of trial. He notes that the Report adopts a pragmatic approach of seeing what works, which has the attraction of flexibility, but marks a decisive shift away from jury trial.[1] These proposals are certainly among the most controversial in the Auld Report. The government initially intended to include a third Mode of Trial Bill in its legislative programme and if necessary to force the legislation through using the Parliament Act 1911. It now appears that the government is reconsidering the proposals along with the Auld recommendations.

The number of summary only cases will be substantially reduced if the Auld Report's recommendations on decriminalisation are accepted. In particular, the proposals in relation to television licence evasion,[2] and the increased use of Fixed Penalty Notices will have a significant impact on the volume of magistrates' hearings.[3]

The Auld Report recommendations would also cause a radical change in the way in which mode of trial decisions are made if the Unified Criminal Court structure was adopted. In particular, all indictable offences would be

[92] Chap. 5, para. 159.
[93] Chap. 5, para. 163.
[94] Chap. 5, para. 163.
[95] Chaps 3, 4, 5.
[96] Chap. 5, para. 166.
[97] Chap. 5, para. 169; see also Darbyshire, [1997] Crim.L.R. 861–869.
[98] Chap. 5, para. 171.
[99] [2002] Crim.L.R. 249.
[1] p. 256.
[2] pp. 369–371.
[3] See generally Chap. 10.

dealt with by the "Crown Division", the summary only matters would be dealt with by the "Magistrates' Division" and the new "District Division" would deal with either way matters which were not allocated to one of the other two courts.[4] The legal rulings, case management and sentencing would be dealt with by the professional judge. The whole tribunal would make findings of fact.[5] The either way cases to be heard by the District Division could be limited to those with a maximum sentence in the given circumstances of the case (viewed at its worst) of "say two years" or a "substantial financial or other punishment".[6] The District Division would consist of a judge (usually a District Judge) and two experienced magistrates, or, at the defendant's election, a judge sitting alone.[7] Every case would begin in the Magistrates' Division with an allocation hearing for pleas to be taken. All indictable only cases would be sent to the Crown Division and all summary only cases would remain in the Magistrates' Division. The either way cases would be allocated on the basis of their seriousness "looking at the case at its worst from the point of view of the defendant".[8] In the event of linked charges, the allocation would be to the Division with jurisdiction to hear the most serious of the charges.[9] There would be a right of appeal (on paper only) to a Circuit judge.[10] A District Judge would resolve issues of uncertainty.[11] This scheme of restructuring is designed to reflect Auld's key principles including that the use of different tribunals, practices and procedures should not detract from the fairness of the hearing or the justice in the outcome and the nature of the "tribunal to which a case is allocated and its procedures should be proportionate in form, time and cost to the seriousness and/or complexity of the alleged offence and the severity of the potential sentence".[12] Zander estimates that the total number of cases that would be allocated to the new District Division would be approximately 16,000 per annum.[13] R. Amlot Q.C. estimates that the "right' to a jury would be lost in approximately 90 per cent of cases.[14] Jackson notes that the lack of evidence about the operation of such a hybrid court is a "fatal weakness" in the proposal.[15]

---

[4] The middle tier of jurisdiction "combines the advantages of the legal knowledge and experience of the professional judge with community representation in the form of lay magistrates" (Chap. 7, para. 23).

[5] Chap. 7, para. 31–32.

[6] Chap. 26, para. 26. "If there is a real possibility that the appropriate sentence on conviction would exceed six months custody, but not, say two years, the matter should be allocated to the District Division" (Chap. 7, para. 37).

[7] Chap.7, para. 30.

[8] Chap. 7, para. 38.

[9] Chap. 7, para. 39.

[10] Chap. 7, para. 40.

[11] Chap. 7, para. 38.

[12] ibid. p. 269.

[13] Op cit., www.lse.ac.uk/Depts/law.

[14] (2001) 151 N.L.J. 1461

[15] [2002], p. 261.

(d) Electing jury waiver

14–055 There have also been less contentious proposals for the defendant to be given the choice to elect a trial by Crown Court judge sitting *without a jury*.[16] This method of trial has been adopted in a number of other jurisdictions: Canada, New Zealand and several Australian States. The arguments against such a scheme include its potential to undermine the institution of the jury trial; that it runs contrary to the jury trial culture; and the possible judicial unwillingness to perform the task. The Auld Report recommended that defendants should be able to opt for trial by judge alone provided the court consents after hearing representations from both parties.[17] Auld relied on the example of the Northern Ireland Diplock Courts and extensive research conducted into their workings.[18] The popularity of the system was felt to lie in the "provision of a simpler, speedier and cheaper process than trial by jury", and, in part, by the opportunity for reasons for decisions to be provided.[19] Where the offence is serious and factually or legally complex or where the defence is technical, or where the offence charged carries great social opprobrium, where there has been considerable adverse pre-trial publicity, where the evidence relied on is particularly hazardous in the hands of lay decision makers, the option for jury waiver should be available.[20] Auld left for further consideration whether the jury waiver should be available for all indictable offences, and how the procedure would be developed to avoid "judge shopping" and to deal with the complexities of multiple defendants.

(e) Special courts

14–056 There have also been calls for a more radical division of cases into separate categories of offence with specialist courts. These suggestions have been based on the U.S. experience of specialist drug courts, which offer a more efficient process for drug crimes, and have more focused and appropriate disposal regimes.[21] The most developed English programme was that piloted in Wakefield, Yorkshire, where cases of adults charged with offences relating to drug use were heard by magistrates who had received specialist training in the social context of drug users. The Wakefield courts also established a

---

[16] See S. Doran and J. Jackson, "The Case for Jury Waiver" [1997] Crim.L.R. 155.

[17] See Chap. 5, paras 110–118.

[18] See J. Jackson and S. Doran, *Judge without Jury: Diplock Trials in the Adversary System* (1995).

[19] Chap. 5, para. 110.

[20] As Jackson (2002) notes, if the Review adopts the position that a defendant has the right to waive jury trial, why should he not have a right to elect one? *Op. cit.* p.263.

[21] There is a substantial literature on these types of courts. See in particular S. Behenko, "Research on Drug Courts: A Critical Review" (1998) 1 National Drug Court Institute, 1; General Accounting Office, *Drug Courts: An Overview of Growth, Characteristics and Results* (1997); U.S. Dept of Justice, *Defining Drug Courts: The Key Components* (1997). The English literature is developing, but see: P. Bean, (1997) 161 J.P.N. 180.

specialist domestic violence court.[22] Further developments in this manner seems inevitable.

4. SUMMARY OFFENCES IN THE CROWN COURT[23]

The present pre-trial process is further complicated by sections 40 and 41 of **14–057** the Criminal Justice Act 1988.[24] Under section 41 where a magistrates' court commits a person to the Crown Court for trial of an either way offence, it may also commit him or her for trial of any summary offence which is (a) punishable with imprisonment or disqualification from driving, and (b) arises out of circumstances which appear to be the same as or connected with those giving rise to the either way offence. If the summary offence relates to an indictable only offence it must be sent to the Crown Court under the indictable only initiative discussed above. A decision to exercise the committal for sentence power cannot be questioned on appeal or on an application for judicial review. If the defendant is convicted on the indictment,[25] and then pleads guilty to the summary offence, the Crown Court can deal with it then and there, although it can only exercise the sentencing powers that the magistrates' court would have had. If the defendant pleads not guilty, the matter has to be remitted for trial in the magistrates' court, unless the prosecution state that they would not wish to offer evidence in which case the Crown Court must dismiss the charge. If the Court of Appeal allows an appeal against conviction for the associated either way offence, it must set aside the conviction for the summary offence, and it may direct that no further proceedings be taken in relation to it.

Following the implementation of the indictable only initiative under section 51 of the Crime and Disorder Act 1998, it may be that a summary offence related to an indictable only offence is heard by the Crown Court. If before arraignment in the Crown Court the indictable only offence has been dropped, the Crown Court must apply the same plea before venue procedure that the magistrates' court would have applied in these circumstances.

Section 40[26] applies to a narrower range of summary offences, but enables them to be added to the indictment and actually tried in the Crown Court (not just added with a view to their being sentenced there). The offences are those which were made summary only by sections 37 to 39 of the 1988 Act,[27] and any other offence punishable by imprisonment or a driving disqualifica-

---

[22] The Courts are discussed in detail by C. Walsh, (2001) Howard Jnl 26; see also T. Thomas, (1999) 149 N.L.J. 1015.

[23] See Emmins (2000), pp.193–195. Section 40 and 41 of the Magistrates' Courts Act 1980 are described by Auld as "a muddle" Chap. 7, para. 39.

[24] See D. Tucker, (1989) L.S. Gaz., 15 March, p. 23; *Archbold* (2002), paras 1–13, 1–25.

[25] See *R. v. Bird* [1995] Crim.L.R. 745.

[26] As amended by the Criminal Procedure and Investigations Act 1996, and the Crime and Disorder Act 1998.

[27] Common assault (including battery (*R. v. Lynsey* [1995] 2 Cr.App.R. 667), taking a motor vehicle without authority, driving while disqualified, criminal damage not exceeding £5,000. Assaulting a prison custody officer (Criminal Justice Act 1991, s.90(1)) or a secure training centre custody officer (Criminal Justice and Public Order Act 1994, s.13(1)) were added by the 1994 Act, Sched. 9, para. 35.

tion and specified by the Secretary of State.[28] A summary offence in one of these categories can be added to the indictment if it is (a) founded on the same facts or evidence as a count charging an indictable offence, or (b) part of a series of offences of the same or similar character as an indictable offence which is also charged.[29] In either case, the relevant facts or evidence must be disclosed in the committal papers or in material disclosed in the process of the accused being sent for trial in the Crown Court under section 51. The offence is tried as if it were an indictable offence, but if the person is convicted, the Crown Court (as under section 41) may only exercise the sentencing powers that the magistrates' courts would have had.[30] Where a person is committed for trial for a summary offence under section 41, and the offence falls in one of the section 40 categories, it may be dealt with at the Crown Court under that section rather than under section 41. The count may only be included if it falls within section 40(1)(2) or where the accused is sent for trial under section 51.[31] Under section 41, summary offences which are related to an indictable only offence must be sent to the Crown Court if they carry a sentence of imprisonment or disqualification from driving. If the summary charges are brought before the indictable one, the magistrates have a discretion whether to send them to the Crown Court.

The sections provide a more convenient procedure for dealing with cases involving both summary and indictable offences but at the cost of adding significantly to the complexity of the law.

E. GETTING THE ACCUSED INTO COURT[32]

14–058 If an accused is to be prosecuted for an offence, he or she must actually be brought before a court to have the charge tried or at least to have it determined how and when the trial process should begin. As we have already seen there are two basic methods by which this can be done: by

---

[28] s.40(4)(5).

[29] *cf.* the Indictment Rules 1971, r.9: below, para. 17-019. It is insufficient that a summary offence is linked to another summary offence on the indictment by virtue of s.40: *R. v. Callaghan* [1992] Crim.L.R. 191. Misjoinder of a summary offence does not render the whole indictment invalid: *ibid.; R. v. Simon* [1992] Crim.L.R. 444 (*obiter*); *R. v. Smith (B.P.)* [1997] 1 Cr.App.R. 390. In *R. v. Lewis* (1991) 95 Cr.App.R. 131, a count alleging common assault on a police officer at the police station after L's arrest for threatening to kill his former girlfriend and another man was held not to be founded on the same facts on evidence or to be part of a similar series of offences as counts based on the threats. The decision of the court in *Lewis* that misjoinder rendered the whole indictment a nullity was inconsistent with the decision in *Callaghan* (above), which was not cited, and disapproved, *obiter*, in *Simon* (above). See also *R. v. Cox* [2001] 5 Archbold News 2, where the Court of Appeal interpreted the section as requiring sufficient factual or evidential overlap to make it just and convenient for the relevant offences to be tried together. See *Archbold* (2002), para.1–19. In *R. v. Smith* [1997] 1 Cr.App.R. 390, driving a conveyance — taken without consent — and driving without a licence were both committed on the same day but not treated as part of a series of offences, of some or similar character, as an offence of dangerous driving committed six weeks later.

[30] s.40(2).

[31] It is not legitimate to include a count where there has been a transfer of trial under s.53 of the 1991 Act: *R. v. T and K* [2001] 1 Cr.App.R. 446; *R. v. Wrench* [1996] 1 Cr.App.R. 340.

[32] See Emmins (2000), pp.17–27.

arrest (without warrant) and charge, or by summons.[33] A variant of the second method involves issue of a warrant for the arrest of the accused rather than a summons.[34] The police may also be willing to charge a person on behalf of a private prosecutor.[35]

An information is merely a statement of the suspected offence and offender, either written or verbal, in terms specified by the Magistrates' Courts Rules 1981,[36] which is placed before a magistrate or the justices' clerk[37] so that a summons or warrant may be issued. If a warrant is required the information must be in writing and on oath,[38] so requiring the attention of a magistrate since a clerk may not act where the information is on oath.[39] The examination of such documents is extremely limited given the volume of cases to be dealt with.

There have been concerns over delay in summons procedures, with research showing that between 1985 and 1995 the "average time taken by the police to charge or summons a defendant (from the date of offence) deteriorated from 38 to 45 days; the average time between charge or summons and the first listing of the case at magistrates' courts deteriorated from 18–28 days; and the average time between the first listing and completion of the case at magistrates' courts deteriorated from 41–60 days".[40]

A typical information would be set out as follows.[41]

NOTTINGHAM MAGISTRATES' COURT

DATE: March 28th 2002

ACCUSED: Henry Frederick Smailey

ADDRESS: Woodland Hall Grove, Cripston, Nottingham

ALLEGED OFFENCE: Henry Smailey on February 14th, at the School of Law, University Park, Nottingham, dishonestly stole the property of N. P. Gravells, Esq., contrary to section 1 of the Theft Act 1968.

THE INFORMATION OF: Gavin Edmunds, Police Constable 1234

ADDRESS: Cripston Police Station, Jug Road, Cripston, Nottingham.

TELEPHONE: 9999999

---

[33] See above, para. 14-020.. Not all persons originally arrested without warrant and subsequently proceeded against are charged: a proportion are reported for summons instead. Powers of arrest without a warrant are considered above, para. 14-008.

[34] These both depend upon the decision of a magistrate after the laying of an information by a named person. Not, *e.g.* in the name of a police force: *Rubin v. DPP* [1990] 2 Q.B. 80 (although the information here was not held invalid as the identity of the relevant constable could easily have been ascertained and the defendant had suffered no injustice).

[35] *R. v. Stafford JJ., ex p. Commissioners of Customs and Excise* [1991] 2 Q.B. 339.

[36] S.I. 1981 No. 552, and the accompanying Magistrates' Courts Forms Rules 1981 (S.I. 1981 No. 553).

[37] Justices of the Peace Act 1979, s.28(1).

[38] Magistrates' Courts Act 1980, s.1(3).

[39] Justices' Clerks Rules 1970 (S.I. 1970 No. 321), r.3.

[40] Narey (1997), Chap.2, para. I.

[41] Magistrates' Courts (Forms) Rules 1981, Form. 1.

WHO UPON OATH STATES THAT THE ACCUSED COMMITTED
THE OFFENCE OF WHICH PARTICULARS ARE GIVEN ABOVE

TAKEN AND SWORN BEFORE ME

Cordelia Lear
JUSTICE OF THE PEACE
JUSTICES' CLERK

The information procedure does not seem to be commonly used to
procure a warrant[42] (the conditions for the grant of which are, in any event,
carefully prescribed[43]). On the grant of a summons, which is a judicial
matter, the magistrate, the clerk or the clerk's delegate[44] should satisfy him-
or herself that the offence is known to the law; that it is not out of time; that
the court has jurisdiction and that the informant has the requisite authority
to prosecute.[45] Furthermore, he or she should consider all the relevant
circumstances, which may include information beyond that supplied by the
informant.[46] There is no obligation to make inquiries provided the issuing
party does not close his eyes to the information available.[47]

A warrant should only be issued if it appears that a summons will be
ineffective.[48] The summons, if issued, will not look very different from the
information.[49]

NOTTINGHAM MAGISTRATES' COURT

DATE: March 28th 2002

TO THE ACCUSED: Henry Frederick Smailey

OF: 32 Woodland Hall Grove, Cripston, Nottingham

YOU ARE HEREBY SUMMONED TO APPEAR ON May 20th 2002,
AT 10.30 a.m. BEFORE THE MAGISTRATES' COURT at the

---

[42] RCCPI, para. 179.

[43] By the Magistrates' Courts Act 1980, ss.l(4), 13(2), as substituted by the Criminal Procedure
and Investigations Act 1996, s.48. Broadly speaking, the alleged offence must be indictable
or punishable with imprisonment, or the accused must have failed to respond to a summons,
or his or her address is not sufficiently known for a summons to be served.

[44] See above, para. 4-011.

[45] R. v. Metropolitan Stipendiary Magistrate, ex p. Klahn [1979] 1 W.L.R. 933.

[46] R. v. Tower Bridge Metropolitan Stipendiary Magistrate, ex p. Chaudhry [1993] 3 W.L.R.
1154 (magistrate entitled to refuse to issue summons alleging causing death by reckless
driving arising out of incident in respect of which the CPS had already laid informations
alleging driving without due care and attention and other minor offences); cf. R. v. Bingley
Magistrates' Court, ex p. Morrow, The Times, April 28, 1994 (magistrates entitled to refuse
summons for murder against a doctor for removing life support from a patient where a civil
court had granted a declaration that this could be done without incurring civil or criminal
liability).

[47] R. v. Clerk to the Bradford Justices, ex p. Sykes (1999) 163 J.P. 224 (previous repeated
vexatious informations to be taken into account).

[48] O'Brien v. Brabner (1885) 49 J.P.N. 227.

[49] Magistrates' Courts (Forms) Rules 1981, Form 2. See generally, the Magistrates' Court
Rules 1981, r.98.

Magistrates' Court Centre, Nottingham to ANSWER TO THE FOLLOW-
ING INFORMATION

ALLEGED OFFENCE: You on February 14th 2002 at the School of Law,
University Park, Nottingham dishonestly stole £5, the property of N. P.
Gravells, Esq., contrary to section 1 of the Theft Act 1968.

PROSECUTOR: Trevor Gun, Chief Inspector of Police

ADDRESS: Cripston Police Station, Jug Road, Cripston, Nottingham

Cordelia Lear
JUSTICE OF THE PEACE

The accused should then respond to the summons and attendance at court
on a specified day has therefore been secured. The process can be continued
on that day. If he or she fails to respond, a warrant may then be
appropriate.

In general, magistrates cannot try a summary offence unless the
information was laid within six months from the time when the offence
was committed.[50] The information is regarded as laid when it is received at
the office of the clerk to the justices in the relevant area. For this purpose it
is not necessary for it to be considered personally by a justice or justices'
clerk; such consideration is only a necessary pre-condition for the issue of a
summons or warrant on the basis of the information.[51] The laying of an
information before a decision to prosecute has been taken, in order to
comply with the time limit, may constitute an abuse of the process of the
court, causing the court to decline jurisdiction,[52] as may excessive delay
before issuing a summons.[53]

If the accused has been arrested by warrant or without warrant it is the
duty of the police then to procure his or her attendance at court. He or she
will have been given bail by the police or by the warrant to appear on an
appointed day or will have been brought to court in custody. If the accused
is in custody after arrest without a warrant he or she must be brought before
a magistrates' court in accordance with the requirements of the Police and
Criminal Evidence Act 1984.[54]

The Crime and Disorder Act 1998, implementing proposals from Narey,
also introduced early first hearings. These impose an obligation on the
custody officer who grants bail to an accused, subject to his appearance
before the magistrates' court, to appoint a date for that appearance not later
than the first sitting of that court or if necessary, on the advice of the clerk,
at a later date.[55] The early first hearing is used to deal with summary or

---

[50] Magistrates' Courts Act 1980, s.127.
[51] *R. v. Manchester Stipendiary Magistrate, ex p. Hill* [1983] 1 A.C. 328 at 342–343,
disapproving dicta in *R. v. Gateshead JJ., ex p. Tesco Stores Ltd* [1981] Q.B. 470.
Information fed into a computer system within the time limit, although printed out after it,
were held to be properly laid in *R. v. Pontypridd Juvenile Court, ex p. B.* (1988) 153 J.P. 213.
[52] *R. v. Brentford JJ., ex p. Wong* [1981] Q.B. 445.
[53] *R. v. Fairford JJ., ex p. Brewster* [1976] Q.B. 600.
[54] See above, para. 14-020.
[55] Crime and Disorder Act 1998, s.45.

either way offences where it is expected that the defendant will plead guilty. The case can be presented, in adult courts, by a non-qualified CPS worker.[56]

Technically, when an accused is arrested without warrant and charged at the police station an information is laid when the charge sheet is remitted by the police to the justices' clerk for inclusion on the court list,[57] but this is in reality a fiction and offenders who are brought to court in this way will never have the facts initially scrutinised by a magistrate.

The RCCP concluded that the summons and warrant procedure was a virtual dead letter since the consideration given to the decision to prosecute by the justices' clerk or magistrate was minimal. It was proposed that there should, in future, be a single procedure for getting an accused to court, the making of a formal "accusation" by the police fixing the date and time of the first court appearance.[58] This recommendation was not accepted.

Where an accused is arrested the question will arise at what stage, if at all, he or she should be released before trial. Clearly, it will be rare for a case with any degree of complexity to be resolved immediately, and the question will arise as to whether the court should order the accused's detention in the period of the adjournment.

A magistrates' court, on adjourning a case and determining to remand the accused, may remand him in custody or on bail.[59] Section 128(1), of the Magistrates Court Act 1980 states that, whenever a magistrates' court has power to remand a person, it may either remand him in custody or remand him on bail in accordance with the Bail Act 1976.

The Auld Report recommended a common form of procedure for the commencement of public prosecutions. This would involve a charge which would be administered orally, with a later manual service by way of written copy, or by postal service of a written charge. There would in addition be a statutory requirement to attend court on a specified date, backed by a power of arrest for failure to attend. The court would be provided with a written copy of the charge at the same time as the accused. The same system would be applicable to private prosecutions, but the private prosecutor would be required to obtain permission from the court before making a charge. Existing provisions for court listings would also be standardised.[60]

---

[56] On the Narey reforms see L. Bridges, (1999) Legal Action October p.8, identifying a range of circumstances in which the early first hearings will be potentially disadvantageous to the defendant, because the denial of time in the pre-trial process also denies an opportunity for review. See also (1999) Legal Action, Jan., p.6.

[57] The process is described and commented on in RCCPI, para. 182.

[58] RCCP Report, para. B.4.

[59] Magistrates' Courts Act 1980, ss. 5(1), 10(1) and 18(4).

[60] Chap.10, para. 57.

F. BAIL OR CUSTODY?[61]

Introduction

To deprive an accused[62] of liberty pending trial may be to keep in custody **14–059** an innocent person or one who, though convicted, ultimately receives a non-custodial sentence. The presumption of liberty is a strong one and is endorsed by the ECHR, Article 5,[63] and recognised as fundamental in key constitutional statutes in English law including the Habeas Corpus Act 1679 and the Bill of Rights 1688.[64] However, to allow an accused liberty pending trial may be to permit him or her to disappear, commit further offences, or interfere with witnesses and obstruct the course of justice. The refusal or grant of bail is a difficult decision, raising "some of the most acute conflicts in the whole criminal process"[65] calling for the very clearest safeguards to be in place before a defendant who has not yet faced trial is detained.[66]

Ensuring compliance with the ECHR is a major concern in English law at present.[67] The European Court emphasised the importance of the guarantee under Article 5(3) for trial within a reasonable time as well as the right to be

---

[61] See generally, Ashworth (1998), Chap. 7; Emmins (2000), Chap. 6; Law Commission, *Bail and the Human Rights Act*, Report No.269 (2000); M. Strange, "Bail" in K. Starmer *et al., Criminal Justice, Police Powers and Human Rights* (2001), Chap. 11; E. Cape, *Legal Action*, October 1989, p. 11 and November 1989, p. 21; N. Corre and D. Wolchaker, *Bail in Criminal Proceedings* (1999); R. Morgan and S. Jones, "Bail or Jail?" in E. Stockdale and S. Casale, *Criminal Justice under Stress* (1992), Chap. 2; P. Cavadino and B. Gibson, *Bail: The Law, Best Practice and the Debate* (1993); M. King, *Bail or Custody* (Cobden Trust, 1971); A. K. Bottomley, *Decisions in the Penal Process* (1973), pp. 93–105, and "The Granting of Bail: Principles and Practice" (1968) 31 M.L.R. 40; M. Zander, "Bail: A Reappraisal" [1967] Crim.L.R. 25 at 100, 128; M. Winfield, *Lacking Conviction* (1984); C. Chatterton, *Bail: Law and Practice* (1986);

[62] We use the term "accused" throughout this section to include those arrested, those on trial, and those convicted. The following discussion considers only the approach in relation to adult offenders.

[63] Under Article 5(3) every person detained should be brought promptly before a judge or other officer authorised by law to exercise judicial power and by Article 5(4) he or she is entitled to take proceedings by which the lawfulness of his detention shall be decided speedily by a court and his release ordered if the detention is not lawful. On the impact of the Human Rights Act 1998 on bail see J. Burrow, (2000) 150 N.L.J. 677 at 736; see also M. Strange, "Bail" in K. Starmer *et al.* (2001). See also Lord Bingham's comments on the fundamental presumption of liberty in *R. v. Manchester Crown Court, ex p. McDonald and others* [1999] 1 All E.R. 805.

[64] Failure to bail a bailable person is an offence at common law. See *Archbold* (2002), Chap. 3. See also the U.N. International Covenant on Civil and Political Rights, Article 9(3).

[65] Ashworth (1998), p.207.

[66] *ibid.*, p.209. See also U. Raifeartaigh, "Reconciling Bail Law with the Presumption of Innocence" (1997) 17 O.J.L.S. 1.

[67] M. Strange, in K. Starmer *et al.* (2001) suggests that a number of changes may be necessary to ensure that the English approach to bail complies with the ECHR. She notes that there is a danger of complacency because of the similarity of the ECHR and Bail Act 1976 (p. 106). In particular it will be necessary for the courts to provide fuller reasons, look more deeply at grounds for refusing bail, and to provide greater notice to the defence. See also Emmerson and Ashworth (2001), Chap. 13. The specific guarantees of Article 5 must be complied with, and the presumption of innocence in Article 6(2) is also important. Article 5 is of course also concerned to guarantee against arbitrariness in the decision: *Winterwerp v. Netherlands* (1979) 2 E.H.R.R. 387. See also K. Starmer, *European Human Rights Law* (1999), Chap. 7.

released pending trial.[68] The Law Commission has recently considered the domestic position and provided a comprehensive examination of the ECHR and English bail in its Report No. 269.[69]

The issue of bail is raised as soon as a person is taken into custody and remains live until trial and, indeed, between conviction and appeal. The procedure by which the accused is released subject to a requirement to surrender to custody again at a specified time and place is termed the "granting" of bail. Bail may be granted by the police, the magistrates' court, the Crown Court, the High Court and the Court of Appeal under a variety of extremely complex statutory provisions and common law decisions,[70] but the granting of bail in all criminal proceedings must be in accordance with the principles set out in the Bail Act 1976. Bail may be granted unconditionally, subject to conditions, subject to a surety or be denied and the accused remanded in custody.

The Bail Act which came into force in the Spring of 1978, was a response to the widespread disquiet about the operation of the system of bail and resulted from the Report of a Home Office Working Party[71] which had been established in 1971 "to review practice and procedure in magistrates' courts relating to the grant or refusal of bail and to make recommendations".[72] Before considering the general principles it is helpful to define two important terms.

A *surety* is a person who is willing to undertake to secure the surrender of the accused to custody. The grant of bail may be made conditional upon the accused finding a suitable surety or sureties.[73] Whoever is willing to be a surety must enter into a *recognisance*, which is a formal acknowledgement that he or she will owe the Crown a specified sum of money if the accused fails to surrender to custody. No money is payable by the surety unless the accused actually absconds.[74] The surety is in general not responsible for the

---

[68] *Wemhoff v. Germany* (1979) 1 E.H.R.R. 55.

[69] *Bail and the Human Rights Act 1998*, Report No. 269 (2000).

[70] See text below.

[71] *Bail Procedures in Magistrates' Courts*, Report of the Home Office Working Party (1974).

[72] Although the terms of reference of the Working Party referred specifically to magistrates' courts the provisions of the Bail Act 1976 actually went somewhat wider.

[73] Bail Act 1976, s.3(4). Personation of bail is an offence under the Forgery Act 1861, s.34. On the procedures for taking sureties and ensuring that the surety is suitable, see Bail Act 1976, s.8

[74] The recognisance may not be forfeited if the surety has made every effort to secure the appearance of the accused and acted with all due diligence, but the obligation is upon the surety to satisfy the court that all or part of the sum should not be forfeited. A surety who acts on legal/professional advice should not be penalised merely because the court disagrees with that advice: *R. v. Bristol JJ., ex p. Nisar Ahmed* [1997] C.O.D. 12 (where surety became aware of D's absconding and on legal advice did not notify the court). The court reviewed the principles of forfeiture in *R. v. Maidstone Crown Court, ex p. Lever and Connell* [1996] 1 Cr.App.R. 524, and emphasised that any reductions in the sum payable by the surety would be exceptional. In general, only in exceptional cases will the court order that the recognisance should not be forfeited: Magistrates' Courts Act 1980, s.120 (as amended); *R. v. Southampton JJ., ex p. Green* [1976] Q.B. 11; *R. v. Waltham Forest JJ., ex p. Palfrey* (1980) 2 Cr.App.R.(S.) 208; *R. v. Knightsbridge Crown Court, ex p. Newton* [1980] Crim.L.R. 715; *R. v. Ipswich Crown Court, ex p. Reddington* [1981] Crim.L.R. 618; *R. v. Wells Street Magistrates' Court, ex p. Albanese* [1982] Q.B. 333; *R. v. Uxbridge JJ., ex p. Heward-Mills* [1983] 1 W.L.R. 56; *R. v. Inner London Crown Court, ex p. Springall* (1986) 85 Cr.App.R. 214; *R. v. York Crown Court, ex p. Coleman and How* (1987) 86 Cr.App.R. 151; *R. v. Reading Crown Court, ex p. Bello* [1992] 3 All E.R. 353. In *R. v. Leicestershire Stipendiary Magistrate,*

accused's compliance with any condition other than attendance at court.[75] The amount of the recognisance is a matter for the police officer or court granting bail. The Crime and Disorder Act 1998 now provides that where a defendant fails to answer bail to the Crown Court, the court is required to declare the automatic forfeiture of any recognisance, and is empowered to issue a summons to the surety and determine whether all or part of it shall be estreated.[76] The use of sureties has been accepted by the European Court as compatible with the Article 5.[77]

The imposition of sureties has been found to operate in practice in a discriminatory fashion against the poor, effectively excluding their chances of bail.[78] Statutory criteria are now fixed for determining the suitability of persons who may offer to be sureties where the grant of bail is conditional upon finding sureties.[79] In considering the suitability of a proposed surety, regard may be had, *inter alia*, to financial resources, character and any previous convictions, and "proximity" to the accused.[80] It is irresponsible (and possibly deserving of professional discipline) for a lawyer to tender someone as a surety unless confident on reasonable grounds that the surety would be met.[81] If a court or police officer considers a proposed surety to be unsuitable there is provision for appeal.[82]

Prior to the Bail Act it was quite common for the accused to be required to enter into a personal recognisance, but this provision has now been abolished.[83] The accused may be required to provide "security" for his surrender on bail.[84]

1. General Principles Relating to the Grant of Bail

The Bail Act introduced a general right to bail for accused persons and certain others subject to exceptions specified in a Schedule to the Act. In fact, the exceptions are substantial and this has led commentators to speak

14–060

---

ex p. Kaur (2000) 164 J.P. 127, the Magistrates' Court was wrong in failing to take into account the impact of the sale of the matrimonial home (put up by K as surety on her sons' case of VAT fraud) and the impact it would have on others who had contributed to the purchase price.

[75] However, parents standing surety for a juvenile may be required to ensure compliance with orders if consenting: sea s.3(7).

[76] Amending s.120 of the Magistrates' Courts Act 1980.

[77] *Schertentleib v. Switzerland* (1980) D.R. 137.

[78] See Cavadino and Gisbson, pp.40–46. On the potentially discriminatory impact of bail decisions on racial groups and between sexes, see Ashworth (1998), pp.232–234.

[79] Bail Act 1976, s.8(2). See generally J. Morton, "Sureties" (1985) 135 N.L.J. 981.

[80] "Proximity" to the accused includes consideration of kinship, place of residence or other matters.

[81] *R. v. Birmingham Crown Court, ex p. Ali* [1999] Crim.L.R. 504. On Surety see K. Parsons, "Duties of a surety: A Summary of the Current Law" (1998) 142 S.J. 154.

[82] Bail Act 1976, s.8(5).

[83] *ibid.* s.3(2).

[84] *ibid.* Section 3(5) of the Bail Act 1976 was replaced by the Crime and Disorder Act 1998, s.54(l)(2). The amendment stemmed from the Narey Report (1997) recommendation that the accused might, in many cases have difficulty in finding a readily available surety. See *R. v. Truro Magistrates Court, ex p. Stevens, The Times* July 27, 2001, although security is not defined, cash or kind would usually be expected. The court has power to take security from a third party on the accused's behalf, but the court should identify with clarity the asset being used as security and avoid loose expressions (*e.g.* "title deeds").

of a "presumption in favour of bail" rather than a "right to bail". In addition, the Act focused attention upon the need for information about the accused to be available to the court so that the bail decision could be an informed one, and required reasons to be given to the accused where bail was not granted so that he or she might more effectively conduct an appeal against the decision.

Section 4 of the Bail Act 1976 creates the *right to bail*:

"(1) A person to whom this section applies shall be granted bail except as provided in Schedule 1 to this Act.

(2) This section applies to a person who is accused of an offence when

(a)   he appears or is brought before a magistrates' court or the Crown Court in the course of or in connection with proceedings for the offence, or

(b)   he applies to a court for bail [or for a variation of the conditions of bail] in connection with the proceedings."

This does not create a right to bail for those convicted who are seeking bail pending appeal. There are additional categories brought within the entitlement and some that are excepted.[85] Where the accused gives an indication at the plea before venue that he will plead guilty, and is committed to the Crown Court, it will be usual not to alter his bail status.[86] By virtue of section 25 of the Criminal Justice and Public Order Act 1994 (as amended[87]), bail will not be granted where a person is charged with murder, attempted murder or manslaughter or rape or attempted rape after having previously been convicted of such an offence or culpable homicide (and, in the case of manslaughter or culpable homicide only, been sentenced to imprisonment or long-term detention)[88] unless there are exceptional circumstances to justify the grant of bail. The original form of section 25 was to *prohibit* bail in such cases, and the European Court confirmed that this breached Article 5.[89] It is important to note that section 4 applies to the

---

[85]   Within the entitlement — a person remanded for reports after conviction (Bail Act 1976, s.4(4)); a person brought before the court for breach of community orders (s.4(3)). Excluded from entitlement — a person convicted of the offence charged (unless remanded for reports) (s.4(2)); a fugitive offender (s.4(2)); a person who the court is satisfied should be kept in custody for his or her own protection or (if a child or young person) his or her own welfare (Sched. 1, Part I, para. 3; Part II, para. 3) (this is compatible with the ECHR: *IA v. France*, September 23, 1998; a person charged with treason (s.4(7)); a person arrested for absconding or breach of bail granted (Sched. 1, Part I, para. 6; Part II, para. 5).

[86]   *R. v. Rafferty* [1998] 2 Cr.App.R.(S.) 449. When a person who had been on bail pleaded guilty at the plea before venue, the usual practice is to continue bail, even if a custodial sentence is anticipated at the Crown Court.

[87]   By the Crime and Disorder Act 1998 and the Powers of Criminal Courts (Sentencing) Act 2000, s.165(1). On the changes made by the Crime and Disorder Act 1998 see A. Edwards, "Improving Criminal Procedure" [1998] Crim.L.R. 29.

[88]   s.25(3). On the policing of granting bail to defendants charged with murder, see E. Tennant, (1999) 163 J.P.N. 730. This has given rise to concern large numbers of mentally ill defendants are remanded in custody. See M. Kennedy, C. Truman, S. Keyes, and A. Cameron, "Supported Bail for Mentally Vulnerable Defendants" (1997) 36 Howard Jnl. 158.

[89]   *Carballero v. U.K.* [2000] Crim.L.R. 587; *S.B.C. v. U.K.* (2002) 34 E.H.R.R. 619, and see *Ilijokov v. Bulgaria* [2001] 7 Archbold News 7. See also the Law Commission in its Report No. 269 on *Bail and the Human Rights Act 1998* where it concluded that exceptional circumstances must be construed so that it encompasses a defendant who would not pose a

grant of bail by courts only. The grant of bail by the police, considered below, is not subject to this provision.

Schedule 1 of the Act creates the *exceptions to the right to bail*, and distinguishes between defendants accused or convicted of offences punishable with imprisonment[90] and those not punishable with imprisonment.[91] In respect of the imprisonable offences the accused need not be granted bail if the court is satisfied that there are substantial grounds for believing[92] that the accused would, if released on bail:

(a) fail to surrender to custody,[93] or

(b) commit an offence while on bail,[94] or

(c) interfere with witnesses or otherwise obstruct the course of justice,[95] whether in relation to himself or any other person.

(The Law Commission has recommended that the Bail Act should be amended to make it clear that the court must be satisfied that there are substantial grounds for believing that the defendant, if released on bail, *would* commit further offences, fail to surrender to bail, interfere with witnesses or otherwise obstruct the course of justice.[96])
The accused also need not be granted bail if:

(a) He or she is already serving a custodial sentence or has been bailed and arrested for absconding, or,

(b) the offence is indictable or triable either way; and

(c) it appears to the court that he was on bail in criminal proceedings on the date of the offence.[97]

---

real risk of committing a serious offence if released on bail para. 8-46. On the conflict of s.25 with the ECHR see P. Leach, "Automatic Denial of Bail and the European Convention" [1999] Crim.L.R. 300 doubting whether s.56 of the Crime And Disorder Act 1998 remedies this problem. See also, M. Strange, (2001), p. 121.

[90] Sched. 1, Part I.
[91] Sched. 1, Part II.
[92] See *R. v. Mansfield JJ., ex p. Sharkey* [1985] Q.B. 613.
[93] On the fear of absconding and the ECHR see *Lettellier v. France* (1991) 14 E.H.R.R. 83; *Clooth v. Belgium* (1991) 14 E.H.R.R. 717. See Law Commission, Part V.
[94] The fear of offending on bail is recognised as a relevant factor in granting bail in ECHR case law: *Toth v. Belgium* (1991) 14 E.H.R.R. 551; see also M. Strange, (2001) p.1 12. For criticism of this as a legitimate ground for consideration see Ashworth (1998), Chap. 7. There ought to be a requirement of proportionality so that remand would occur only if custody was likely on a conviction at trial. See further the discussion of the Law Commission in its Report No. 269. Parts II and III The conclusion of the Commission was that this criterion is compatible with the ECHR provided that the decision to withhold bail is necessary and proportionate to a real risk that the defendant would commit an offence if released, (para. 3.11). See also U. ni Raifeartaigh, "Reconciling Bail Law with the Presumption of Innocence" (1997) 17 O.J.L.S. 1, questioning why granting bail should be a significant problem given the realisation that there are many convicted criminals released from prison who may pose a threat.
[95] Sched. 1, Part I, para. 2.
[96] Report, para.7.35.
[97] 1976 Act, para. 2A, inserted by the Criminal Justice and Public Order Act 1994, s.26. The addition of this ground was justified by reference to the large number of crimes said to be committed by persons on bail (estimated to be c. 10%–12% of those remanded on bail, c.

The European Court has emphasised that the decision as to bail should include a consideration of the individual's circumstances.[98]

The Law Commission concluded that paragraph 2A was incompatible with the ECHR, Article 5: the mere fact that the accused was on bail at the time of the offence should not be the sole basis for refusing bail, although it might be a legitimate basis for denying bail on the belief that the accused might commit future offences whilst on bail.

The accused who has been convicted need not be granted bail if it appears to the court that it would be impracticable to complete inquiries or make a report without keeping him or her in custody.[99] The accused need not be granted bail where the court is satisfied that it has not been practicable for want of time, to obtain sufficient information since the proceedings were instituted to make a proper decision on bail.[1] This last point emphasises that the court must have access to information about the defendant[2] because it is required to have regard to specified matters (as far as they appear relevant) including (and these are not exhaustive):

(a) the nature and seriousness of the offence (and the probable method of dealing with it);

(b) the character, antecedents, associations and community ties of the defendant;

(c) the defendant's record in respect of any previous grants of bail;

(d) the strength of the evidence against him or her,[3] except in the case of an accused whose case is adjourned for inquiries or a report.

50,000 in 1991: see P. M. Morgan, *Offending While on Bail: a Survey of Recent Studies* (HORPU Paper. No. 65, 1992). The overall number had increased from c. 35,000 in five years; however, the *proportion* of those on bail committing offences appears to have remained constant, the increase arising from an increase in the total number remanded on bail: Morgan and Jones (*op cit.* n. 61, above), pp. 41–45. D. Brown, *Offending on Bail and Police Use of Conditional Bail* (HORS No. 72, 1998), found that the figures for those committing offences on court bail were 15% and on police bail were 12%. Four per cent of all those on bail committed three or more offences. The problem is most acute with young offenders. Those most likely to offend are bailed in relation to acquisitive crime, especially theft from vehicles.

[98] *W. v. Switzerland* (1994) 17 E.H.R.R. 60; *Mansor v. Turkey* (1995) 20 E.H.R.R. 535.

[99] para. 7, Sched. 1, part I.

[1] *ibid.* para. 5. This has potential to delay bail which should be available. It should be read restrictively. The Law Commission Report No. 269 concludes that this is compatible with the ECHR provided that detention is for a short time as needed to find relevant information and there is no lack of diligence in the prosecution (para. 6-13–6-17). The remand under para. 5 does not amount to a denial for the purposes of para.2 of Part IIA.

[2] Bail information schemes where a probation officer deals speedily with practical issues of fact finding on the day of the bail hearing have been tested. Morgan and Henderson, *Remand Decisions and Offending on Bail: Evaluation of the Bail Process Project* (HORS No. 184, 1998) found that there was a lack of ready availability to the police, prosecutors and magistrates of the defendant's criminal record and other relevant information. For discussion of bail information schemes, see C. Lloyd, *Bail Information Schemes: Practice and Effect* (HORPU No. 69, 1992). and G. Mair and C. Lloyd, in F. Paterson (ed.), *Understanding Bail in Britain* (1996).

[3] Sched I, para. 9. The European Court has confirmed that the prosecution are obliged to disclose to the defence material on which it proposes to rely in bail hearings: *Nikolova v. Bulgaria*, March 25, 1999; see on requirements in English law *R. v. DPP, ex p. Lee* [1999] 2 All E.R. 237.

In respect of non-imprisonable offences the defendant may only be denied bail if it appears to the court that he or she has previously failed to surrender to bail and that the court believes that, if released, he or she would again fail to surrender to custody.[4]

The court, if it is to refuse bail, must be "satisfied that there are substantial grounds for believing" that one of the specified situations exists. This formulation of the standard of proof is a compromise reached after much debate both in the House of Commons and the House of Lords. The original draft was "satisfied that it is probable"; an amendment in the Lords substituted, "satisfied that there is an unacceptable risk"[5] and the eventual compromise was thought to pitch the standard of proof somewhere between the two.[6]

The extent to which the formal rules of evidence apply in bail hearings is a controversial issue. In *DPP v. Havering Magistrates' Court*[7] the Divisional Court rejected the need for compliance with all formal procedures and recommended that the court when considering bail could be satisfied on the quality of the material provided. The accused has a right to cross-examine witnesses if oral-evidence is called.[8]

The Auld Report, questions the quality of bail decisions currently being made, particularly since 24 per cent of a sample of 1,283 alleged offenders granted bail were subsequently convicted or cautioned for an offence whilst on bail.[9] The average length of a bail hearing in London Magistrates' Court was also found to be a mere six minutes.[10] The Auld Report also commented on the inconsistency of bail decision-making, particularly in the magistrates,[11] and recommended that: listing practices allow more time for bail applications; better information be provided for all interested parties; better training of magistrates takes place with regard to Article 5 and risk assessment; efficient bail information schemes are provided; bail notices and orders are issued with clarity; and that there is diligent recording of bail decisions.[12] The Law Commission in its Report No. 269 also proposed

---

[4] Sched. 1, Part II, para. 2, or that he or she is kept in custody for his own protection, that he is already serving a custodial sentence, or that he has been arrested under s.7. See Law Comm., para. 5.10. For criticism of the way that bail applications are made and the informal nature of the decision-making see A. Hucklesby, [1997] Crim.L.R. 269. The speed at which applications are processed is also criticised, and the Auld Report (2001) recommended that all those who were considering bail applications should take more time to consider these matters. See also the Law Commission criticism, *op. cit.*, paras 4.20–4.23.

[5] See the speech of Lord Hailsham, H.L. Deb., April 6, 1976, Vol. 369, col. 1544 *et seq.*

[6] H.C. Deb., November 2, 1976, Vol. 918, col. 1323–4, Mr Brynmor John, then Minister of State, Home Office. See also Law Commission, No. 269, Part X.

[7] [2001] 1 W.L.R. 805. On the applicability of Article 6 guarantees in the bail application see *De Wilde, Ooms and Versyp v. Belgium* (1971) 1 E.H.R.R. 373 and *Lamy v. Belgium* (1989) 11 E.H.R.R. 529 It is arguable that the present practice of hearing bail applications in the absence of the accused may be subject to challenge under Article 6. See Strange, p. 116, relying on *TW v. Malta* (1999) 29 E.H.R.R. 185.

[8] See further the extensive examination of this case by the Law Commission, Report No. 269, Part IX.

[9] Chap. 10, para. 76.

[10] Auld Report, (2001), Chap. 10, para. 78.

[11] Chap. 10, para. 79–80. ACPO have criticised the CPS for failing to take bail hearings seriously (Auld Report (2001), Chap. 10, para. 81). See the Law Commission's *Guide for Bail Decision Takers* (2001).

[12] (2001), p. 430.

appropriate training and guidance on the bail decision making process for magistrates and judges.[13]

Bail conditions

14-061   If bail is refused by the court or conditions are imposed on the grant of bail in respect of anyone to whom section 4 of the Act applies, the court must make a record and give reasons for withholding bail or imposing the conditions with a view to enabling the accused to make application to another court.[14] The court has a duty to inform an unrepresented accused of his right to challenge make further application to other courts.[15] This is a logical requirement, given that the courts are now directed towards examining specific considerations in the refusal of bail. The accused is entitled to know in what respect he or she is considered unsuitable for bail. Furthermore, reasons must now be given where the court grants bail to an accused when the prosecution opposed it.[16] The court having heard a full argument on bail must issue a certificate confirming this.[17]

The court may attach conditions to bail[18] necessary to secure that the accused:

(a) surrenders to custody;

(b) does not commit an offence while on bail;

(c) does not interfere with witnesses or otherwise obstruct the course of justice;

(d) makes him- or herself available for the purposes of enabling inquiries, or a report to be made to assist the court in dealing with him or her for the offence.[19]

---

[13] *op. cit.*, n. 8, Part IV. See also its *Guidance for Bail Decision Takers and their Advisers (2001)*.

[14] Bail Act 1976, s.5(3), as amended by the Criminal Justice and Police Act 2001 s. 129(1) inserting a new (2A) and (2B) in s.5. The European Court has explained the need for reasons to be provided: *Tomasi v. France* (1992) 15 E.H.R.R. 1; *Neumeister v. Austria* (1968) 1 E.H.R.R. 91; *Sabita v. Italy*, April 6, 2000. For critical comment on English law's failure to meet these requirements see M. Strange (2001), p.115; Law Commission part IXA.

[15] s. 5(6).

[16] Bail Act 1976, Sched. 1, Part I, para. 9A, inserted by the Criminal Justice Act 1988. This provision was passed in view of public concern about bail being too readily granted in cases of serious alleged violence. The ECHR requires that reasons be provided for bail or its denial: *Tomasi v. France* (1992) 15 E.H.R.R. 1; *Neumeister v. Austria* (1968) 1 E.H.R.R. 91; see also M. Strange in Starmer et al. (2001), p.115.

[17] Bail Act 1976, ss.5(6A)–(6C).

[18] The European Court has accepted the application of conditions in such cases: *Stogmuller v. Germany* (1985) 44 D.R. 195. The Law Commission, Report No. 269, recommended an additional power to make bail conditions where necessary for the defendant's own protection (para. 9A27).

[19] Bail Act 1976, s.3(6), Sched. 1, para. 8(1). The power to attach conditions extends to both imprisonable and non-imprisonable offences (see *R. v. Bournemouth Magistrates' Court, ex p. Cross* (1988) 89 Cr.App.R. 90). For the argument that a surety of good behaviour might be imposed as a condition of bail under the court's binding-over powers, see N. Corre, [1986] Crim.L.R.162. See also B. P. Block, (1990) 154 J. P. N. 83; P. W. H. Lydiate, *ibid.*, p. 132.

(e) before the time appointed for him or her to surrender to custody, he or she attends an interview with an authorised advocate or authorised litigator.[20]

In this context, it is not necessary that the court has "substantial grounds" for its conditions: it is sufficient that it perceives "a real and not fanciful risk" of, for example, an offence being committed.[21] In the case of a person accused of murder, the court *must*, unless it considers that satisfactory reports of his or her medical condition have already been obtained, impose bail conditions requiring that he or she undergo examination by two medical practitioners to enable such reports to be prepared.[22] Similarly, the magistrates' court must require that the accused is examined by a medical practitioner when the court has adjourned[23] following a finding that the accused committed the criminal act and requires information on his or her mental state.

The imposition of conditions on the grant of bail can be a very serious matter.[24] It is not uncommon for the magistrates to require the accused to report regularly to a police station as a condition of bail, or to observe a curfew, or to reside[25] in or keep away from particular places. The most common condition imposed was found in recent research to be residence at specified address (78 per cent) and a prohibition on contacting a specified individual was a condition in 46 per cent of cases, and a requirement to report to a police station was imposed in 18 per cent of cases. In serious matters the accused may be required to surrender his or her passport.[26] It is arguable that the conditions attached ought to relate primarily to securing the attendance of the accused in court but they can also be used to curtail potentially criminal activities pending the trial of the alleged offence.[27]

---

[20] As defined in section 119(1) of Courts and Legal Services Act 1990. Inserted by Crime and Disorder Act 1998, s.54(2). This is to deal with defendants who are obstructive in proceedings and is designed to reduce the number of wasted hearings. See H.O. Circular 34/98.

[21] *R. v. Mansfield JJ., ex p. Sharkey* [1985] Q. B. 613.

[22] Bail Act 1976, s.3(6A), (6B), inserted by the Mental Health (Amendment) Act 1982, s.34. The grant of bail without complying with this requirement is a nullity: *R. v. Central Criminal Court, ex p. Porter* [1992] Crim.L.R. 121.

[23] Under Powers of Criminal Courts (Sentencing) Act 2000, s.11(1).

[24] See J. Raine and M. Willson "The Imposition of Conditions in Bail Decisions" (1996) 35 Howard Jnl. 256. Conditions might be suggested by the defence in the hope of securing bail.

[25] On the legitimacy of curfews on bail conditions see A. Gillespie, "Curfew and Bail" (2001) 151 N.L.J. 465, questioning whether a breach of Article 8 might arise with "doorstep conditions" where an officer checks that a curfew is being kept, but concluding they are legitimate if necessary and proportionate. See also Law Commission, Parts IXA and IXB.

[26] Rainer and Willson (1996) Guidance was given by the Home Office in Circular 206/1977 of November 18, 1977. Courts were, *e.g.* requested to be especially selective in requiring regular reporting to a police station as this can be burdensome for the police and also raise identification problems.

[27] During the 1984–85 miners' strike, striking miners charged with criminal offences were frequently granted bail subject to conditions prohibiting picketing at premises other than the defendant's own place of work: the practice was controversial (see S. McCabe and P. Wallington, *The Police, Public Order, and Civil Liberties* (1988), pp. 97–98), but held to be lawful by the Divisional Court (*R. v. Mansfield JJ., ex p. Sharkey* [1985] Q. B. 613). See also *R. v. Bournemouth Magistrates' Court, ex p. Cross* (1988) 89 Cr.App.R. 90 (bail conditions prohibiting defendants charged with disturbing a fox hunting meet from attending another hunt meeting held valid). See Ashworth (1998), pp. 233 for criticism.

Under the Criminal Justice and Police Act 2001, conditions of electronic monitoring may be imposed on young offenders in limited circumstances; there are suggestions for this scheme to be extended to adults.[28] The Auld Report, recognising the impact of conditions, recommends a limited right of appeal against conditions imposed in bail if the condition relates to residence away from home and/or to the provision of a surety or giving of a security.[29]

2. APPLICATION OF THE PRINCIPLES

14–062   The Bail Act resolved many of the ambiguities of the earlier law, but did not affect the court's practices. There were two periods of significant reduction in the number of prisoners on remand.[30] The number of remand prisoners continues to grow even though the proportion of remands is relatively low.[31] Home Office statistics indicate however, that there are significant variations in the use of custodial remands among different petty sessional divisions.[32] There was no significant impact on the number and or quality of remand applications when the CPS took responsibility for prosecutions in 1985.[33]

An issue which initially concerned the courts was the procedure to be adopted on successive applications for bail. The magistrates' court is given power, prior to the commencement of the hearing, to remand an accused person in custody for a period not exceeding eight clear days [34]and this may be appropriate where the prosecution are not yet ready to proceed with the case. In complex cases this meant a court appearance occurring every eight

---

[28]   A new section 3AA is inserted. See *Archbold* (2002), 3–11a. See on the privacy issues, Ashworth (1998), p.235. On the conditions in relation to bail hostels, see also s.3(6ZA).

[29]   (2001) p.433

[30]   One after the Home Office Circular 155/1975 which urged the courts to take a more liberal view on bail, and the other after the Bail Act 1976.

[31]   See Ashworth (1998), pp.218–219. M. Zander, "The Operation of the Bail Act in London Magistrates' Courts" (1979) 129 N.L.J. 108. See also, R. Vogler, "The Changing Nature of Bail," *LAG, Bulletin*, February 1983, p. 11; R. East and M. Doherty, "The Practical Operation of Bail," *LAG Bulletin*, March 1984, p. 12; R. Morgan, "Remands in Custody" [1989] Crim.L.R. 481.

[32]   P. Jones, "Remand Decisions in Magistrates' Courts" in D. Moxon (ed.) Managing Criminal Justice (1985) Chap. 10. Home Office Statistical Bulletin 7/87, discussed by B. Gibson, (1987) 151 J.P.N. 520 and B. Rowland, (1987) 151 J.P.N. 651. The Home Office has emphasised the need for consistency: Home Office Circular 25/1988: (1988) 44 *The Magistrate* 173. On variations in the use of bail in the magistrates' court and the responsibilities of the CPS and defence for the perpetration of such variations see A. Hucklesby, "Court Culture: An Explanation of Variations in the Use of Bail by Magistrates' Courts" (1997) Howard J.C.J. 129. The regular appearances by the same individuals in the courts led them to anticipate and perpetuate certain attitudes of the courts.

[33]   See C. Stone, *Bail Information for the CPS* (1988); A. Hucklesby, (1997) *op. cit.*

[34]   Magistrates' Courts Act 1980, s.128(6), subject to ss.128A and 129. Section 129 empowers the court to make further remand in the accused's absence in specified circumstances (illness, etc.). Where an accused has been bailed from a police station following charge, the court has power to appoint a later date for appearance: s.43(l).

days for a considerable length of time.[35] At every appearance the accused was entitled to request bail and would normally appear before differently constituted courts each time.[36] In Nottingham, the City justices adopted a policy under which after a second application[37] for bail they would not consider on subsequent applications matters previously before the court unless there had been a change in circumstances.[38] In effect, remand in custody became automatic. A group of Nottingham solicitors organised an application for mandamus by Clive Edgar Davies, charged with various offences of criminal damage and rape, directing the justices to hear the full facts supporting an application for bail made on April 10, 1980[39] and determine it accordingly. In *R. v. Nottingham JJ., ex p. Davies*[40] the Divisional Court refused the application.

It was argued on behalf of Davies that he had a right to bail which was only defensible on the specified grounds; that the court has a duty to consider the grant of bail on every occasion on which the accused appears; and that the fact of a previous remand could not, of itself, satisfy the justices that one of the specified grounds still existed. The court did not accede to the argument and Donaldson L.J. based his judgment primarily upon a notion of *res judicata*.[41] The finding of the original court that Schedule 1 circumstances existed,

" ... is to be treated like every other finding of the court. It is res judicata or analogous thereto ... It follows that on the next occasion when bail is considered the court should treat, as an essential fact, that at the time when the matter of bail was last considered, Schedule 1 circumstances did indeed exist. Strictly speaking, they can and should only investigate whether that situation has changed since then."[42]

The court also indicated that the position of the accused is safeguarded by the provision for an application to a High Court judge for bail.[43]

---

[35] This can clearly be oppressive since the accused is being held in custody without trial, but it is well established that an unreasonable delay on the part of the prosecution will be a good reason for granting bail: *R. v. Nottingham Justices, ex p. Davies* [1981] Q.B. 38 at 44.

[36] At the time of Davies' application (see note above) the Nottingham bench consisted of 320 justices, with up to 25 courts sitting each day. The chance of getting the same justices two weeks running was negligible. On the proportion of defendants who did not seek bail on their first appearance see B. Brink and C. Stone, "Defendants Who Do Not Ask for Bail" [1999] Crim.L.R. 152.

[37] After the *second* application, because the first is usually made by a duty solicitor (see above, para. 14-054) who may not be fully briefed so as to make a proper application. On the second application the accused will normally be legally aided and represented by his or her own solicitor who should then be in a position to place all relevant matters before the court.

[38] A policy apparently inspired by certain remarks made by Ackner J. to a meeting of justices' clerks and reported in (1980) 36 *The Magistrate* 34, 97. The actual wording of the Nottingham policy is contained in the report of *Davies* [1981] Q.B. 38 at 41.

[39] The date was significant because that was Davies' third application for bail.

[40] [1981] Q.B. 38.

[41] A final judgment already decided by a competent court on the same question.

[42] [1981] Q.B. 38 at p. 44.

[43] See below, para. 14-060.

This decision excited both favourable[44] and unfavourable[45] comment, and was in certain respects in need of retirement.[46] It has now been codified by section 154 of the Criminal Justice Act 1988.[47] This provides:

"(1) If the court decides not to grant the defendant bail, it is the court's duty to consider, at each subsequent hearing while the defendant ... remains in custody, whether he ought to be granted bail.

(2) At the first hearing[48] after that at which the court decided not to grant the defendant bail[49] he may support an application for bail with any argument as to fact or law that he desires (whether or not he has advanced that argument previously).

(3) At subsequent hearings the court need not hear arguments as to fact or law which it has heard previously."[50]

This makes it clear that while the court is not obliged to hear repeated arguments, it has a discretion to do so; the position is, accordingly, a little more flexible than that suggested by Donaldson L.J. in *ex p. Davies*. The Law Commission concluded that this was compatible with the ECHR but recommended that the passage of time might be a sufficient reason in a given case to require a full argument to be heard by the court.[51]

The position has also been affected to some extent by the provisions of section 59 and Schedule 9 of the Criminal Justice Act 1982.[52] This enables the court to remand an accused in his or her absence for up to three successive remand hearings provided that he or she consents and is legally

---

[44] Anon., "Bail Applications" (1980) 144 J.P.N. 319; editorials in (1980) 36 *The Magistrate* 97 at 135; K. Polak, "Applications for Bail" (1980) 144 J.P.N. 525.

[45] M. Hayes, "Where Now the Right to Bail" [1981] Crim.L.R.20. In "Bail — a Suitable Case for Treatment" (1982) 132 N.L.J. 409, J. Burrow analyses other less predictable effects of the decision.

[46] See S. Holdham, (1985) 135 N.L.J. 471; P. W. H. Lydiate, "Bail Procedure in Magistrates' Courts: Basic Procedures" (1987) 151 J.P.N. 164, 181. See also *R. v. Reading Crown Court, ex p. Malik* [1981] Q.B. 451 and *R. v. Slough JJ., ex p. Duncan and Embling* (1982) 75 Cr.App.R. 384 (different views expressed on whether as a general rule reaching the stage of committal for trial would constitute a change in circumstances: Donaldson L.J. in the *Reading* case indicated *obiter* that it would; Ormrod L.J. in the *Slough* case that it would not necessarily do so).

[47] Inserting a new Part IIA in Sched. 1 to the Bail Act 1976.

[48] Occasions when a person is remanded in his or her absence (see below) are not "hearings": *R. v. Dover and East Kent JJ., ex p. Dean* (1991) 156 J.P. 357.

[49] A decision that it has not been practicable to obtain sufficient information to decide to grant bail is not a "decision not to grant bail" for these purposes: *R. v. Calder JJ., ex p. Kennedy* (1992) 156 J.P. 716.

[50] This is a different formula to that adopted by Donaldson L.J. This could be read as restricting the accused to two applications only, and that they must be the first two hearings (see *Archbold* (2002), para. 3-18a). Moreover, it is unclear whether the whole of the bail issue or the new arguments only need to be heard. In *R. v. Blyth Juvenile Court, ex p. G* [1991] Crim.L.R. 693, fresh arguments were accepted without there having to have been a major change in circumstances.

[51] Report No. 269, para. 12.9 and para. 12.23. See also *Bezicheri v. Italy* (1989) 12 E.H.R.R. 210.

[52] Inserting s.128(1A)–(1C), (3A)–(3E) of the Magistrates' Courts Act 1980, as amended by the Criminal Procedure and Investigations Act 1996. See C. May, *Remands in the Absence of the Accused*(1985), (HORPU Paper No. 34, 1985), estimating a saving of 2% on total escort costs. On the power to make sureties continuous see s.128(4), and *R. v. Wells Street Magistrates' Court, ex p. Albanese* [1982] Q.B. 333.

represented. This alleviates the problem of constant weekly journeys for the accused who does not wish to contest the remand, but *ex p. Davies* still applies to prevent the non-consenting accused from seeking bail on every remand appearance. Section 155 of the Criminal Justice Act 1988[53] authorised the introduction of a new power for the court to remand in custody for a period up to 28 days without the accused's consent. This is exercisable where the accused has previously been remanded in custody for the same offence and the court has set a date for the next stage in the proceedings.[54]

3. POLICE BAIL[55]

The Police and Criminal Evidence Act 1984 establishes a number of **14–063** situations in which a person in police custody may be released on bail. The decision in most cases is taken by the custody officer. Where the custody officer orders a person's release under section 34, this must be without bail unless it appears to the custody officer (1) that there is need for further investigation of any matter in connection with which he or she was detained, or (2) that proceedings may be taken against him or her in respect of any such matter[56]: if it does so appear, the person must be released on bail. In other situations, there is a discretion to release with or without bail, where a person is released before charge (section 37); after charge (section 38); after 24 hours detention (section 41); after 36 hours detention (section 42); or where a warrant for further detention is refused or expires (sections 43, 44).[57] In each case a release on bail "shall be a release on bail granted in accordance with sections 3, 3A, 5 and 5A of the Bail Act 1976 as they apply to bail granted by a constable"[58] and shall be subject to a duty to appear before a magistrates' court on the date of the next available court sitting[59] or to return to the police station as directed by the custody officer, who must specify the time and place.[60] The option of requiring the accused to return to the police station can be employed to give the police time to continue their inquiries, and to decide whether they wish to prosecute and if so on what charges.

---

[53] Inserting s. 128A of the Magistrates' Courts Act 1980.

[54] Magistrates Courts Act 1980, s.128A(2). The provision was first introduced experimentally in specified areas, but now extends to all petty sessions areas: Magistrates' Courts (Remands in Custody) Order 1991 (S.I. 1991 No. 2667). This followed a Home Office report which concluded that there was "little evidence" to support the concerns expressed during the passage of the 1988 Act that this "would cause an increase in the time spent in custody": P. F. Henderson and P. Morgan, *Remands in Custody for up to 28 days: the Experiments* (HORPU Paper No. 62, 1991). The Prison Reform Trust was, however, critical of this conclusion: see Cavadino and Gibson (1993), Chap. 11.

[55] See R. Tarling, P. Jones and A. Sanders, "Police Bail" (1986) 21 H.O. Research Bulletin 52; J. Wadham, "Bail from Police Stations", *Legal Action*, December 1988, pp. 24–25.

[56] Or in case of juvenile that he or she reprimanded or warned under section 65 of the Crime and Disorder Act 1998.

[57] See ss.37(2), (7)(b), 38(1); 41(7); 42(10); 43(15)(18); 44(7).

[58] PACE, s.47(l), as amended by the Criminal Justice and Public Order Act 1994, s.27(1)(a). These sections comprise general provisions (s.3), conditions of police bail (s.3A) and supplementary provisions (ss.5, 5A).

[59] PACE, s.47(3A).

[60] PACE, s.47(3).

Where an accused is released on police bail after being charged, the custody officer has the power to attach conditions (other than a condition requiring residence in a bail hostel or that the accused makes himself available for enabling inquiries or a report to be made).[61] Where the custody officer has granted police bail, he or she or another custody officer at the same police station may vary the conditions at the request of the person on bail, and may impose conditions or more onerous conditions.[62] Conditions may only be imposed (or varied) if it appears to the officer necessary to do so for the purpose of preventing that person from failing to surrender to custody, committing an offence while on bail or interfering with witnesses or otherwise obstructing the course of justice.[63] The custody officer must give reasons for imposing or varying conditions, and these must be included in the custody record.[64] Where a custody officer grants bail and imposes conditions, or varies conditions, a magistrates' court on the application by or on behalf of the person on bail may grant bail or vary the conditions.[65] The police now have an express power of arrest for failure to answer to police bail.[66] As Raine and Willson observe, the police are really exercising a judicial function in imposing such conditions. The new power to attach conditions was felt "not to have delivered the efficiency advantages that its advocates had anticipated".[67] Hardly any change in the working pattern of the courts was recorded to have resulted.[68]

In the case of indictable or either way offences, the prosecution may apply to the appropriate magistrates' court for the grant of police bail to be reconsidered, and the court may vary or impose conditions or withhold bail. An application must be based on information not available to the custody officer when the decision was taken.[69] This applies only to offences triable on indictment or either way.

If the accused is in police custody as the result of a warrant issued by a magistrate or the Crown Court, then the warrant itself will dictate the granting of bail and the previous provisions will not apply. Either the warrant will be "endorsed for bail"[70] in terms which must be observed by the police, or it will require the police to bring the accused before the court

---

[61] Police and Criminal Evidence Act 1984, s.47(lA), inserted by the Criminal Justice and Public Order Act 1994, s.27(l)(b); Bail Act 1976, ss.3(6), 3A, as amended and inserted by *ibid.* s.27(2)(3). The introduction of this power was recommended by the RCCJ, Report, para. 5.22. Section 3A applies s.3 with modifications to conditions in the case of police bail. Research suggests that these are being used when previously unconditional bail would have been granted: J. Raine and M. Willson, "Police Bail with Conditions" (1997) 37 Brit. J. of Criminol. 593.

[62] Bail Act 1976, s.3A(4), applying s.3(8) in different terms to cases of police bail.

[63] *ibid.* s.3(A)(5); *cf.* s.3(6), n. 23, above.

[64] *ibid.* s.5A(2), (3), inserted by the 1994 Act, Sched. 3, para. 2, applying s.5(3),(4), in different terms to cases of police bail.

[65] Magistrates' Courts Act 1980, s.43B, inserted by the 1994 Act, Sched. 3, para. 3.

[66] Police and Criminal Evidence Act 1984, s.46A, inserted by the 1994 Act, s.29.

[67] n. 62, p.602.

[68] See also R. Raine and J. Willson, (1996) Howard J.C.J. 256; (1995) J.L.S. 22.

[69] Bail Act 1976, s.5B, inserted by the 1994 Act, s.30. if the court grants bail in the face of prosecution opposition it must give reasons: ss. 8A–C as inserted by the Criminal Justice and Police Act 2001, s.129.

[70] Magistrates' Court Act 1980, s.117. The magistrate issuing the warrant will state on the warrant that the person arrested is to be released subject to a duty to appear at a specified court and time: s.117(2)(a).

immediately.[71] In this case, of course, the grant of bail is, strictly speaking, made by the court and not the police.

The use of police bail is substantial. In general, the more serious the type of offence, the higher the proportion of those arrested who are held in custody. Research in the 1980s found that the highest proportion was in respect of robbery (57 per cent); and burglary, sexual offences and criminal damage all exceeded the average.[72]

4. Bail from the Magistrates' Court

If the accused has been arrested without warrant, and has not been bailed by the police, or arrested with a warrant which is not endorsed for bail, he or she must be brought before a magistrates' court and will then have an opportunity to request bail. Indeed, the court is under an obligation to consider the question of bail even if no application is made.[73] Only comparatively minor cases can be disposed of at one appearance in the magistrates' court. The court accordingly has express power to adjourn:

14–064

(1) an inquiry as examining justices, either before or during the inquiry[74];

(2) a summary trial, either before or during the trial[75];

(3) proceedings to determine mode of trial in the case of offences triable either way[76]; and

the hearing, where the court has begun to try an offence triable either way, but decides to discontinue summary trial and proceed to inquire as examining justices, it has a duty to adjourn the hearing.[77]

On these occasions, the court may, and sometimes must, remand the accused, which simply means a direction that he or she should be held in custody for a specified period, or that he or she should be released on bail with an obligation to appear again before the court on a specified date.[78] The court must remand in situation (1); in situations (2) and (3) where the offence is triable either way and either the accused initially attends the court

---

[71] See the form of warrant set out as Form 4, the Magistrates' Courts (Forms) Rules 1981 (S.I. 1981 No. 553).

[72] See R. Tarling, P. Jones and A. Sanders, "Police Bail" (1986) 21 H.O.R.B. 52, Table 2, based on 1980 figures.

[73] Because of the provision in the Bail Act 1976, s.4(l) that a person to whom the Act applies *shall* be given bail except where Schedule 1 applies. See J. N. Spencer, (1986) 150 J.P.N. 724; P. H. W. Lydiate, (1987) 151 J.P.N. 25.

[74] Magistrates' Courts Act 1980, s. 5(1).

[75] *ibid.* s.10(1). This power may be exercised after conviction and before sentence, to enable inquiries to be made: s.10(3). There is also a power to adjourn a trial to enable a medical examination and report to be made; this power is available where the offence is punishable with imprisonment and the court is satisfied that the accused did the act or made the omission charged: s.30.

[76] *ibid.* s.18(4).

[77] *ibid.* s.25(2), as amended by the Criminal Procedure and Investigations Act 1996, Sched. 1, imposing a duty to adjourn.

[78] *ibid.* s.128(1).

in custody or has at any time been remanded[79]; and where it commits the accused for trial[80] or sentence[81] in the Crown Court. Otherwise the court may either remand the accused or simply adjourn the hearing without remanding, although the latter step is normally only taken in minor cases, usually road traffic matters.[82] Under section 5B of the Bail Act 1976[83] the prosecutor may apply to the magistrates' court for a grant of bail by it to be reconsidered on the same basis as a grant of police bail may be reconsidered.[84] In deciding whether to remand on bail or in custody the magistrates must have regard to the provisions of the Bail Act but may take advantage of section 154 of the Criminal Justice Act 1988[85] to lessen the burden of continuing applications. The position is further eased by the provision for extended remands in custody.[86] The most significant factors influencing remand decisions in the magistrates' courts are whether the police have granted bail,[87] the seriousness of the offence and court policy. In 2000, 29 per cent of those bailed by magistrates and 20 per cent of those remanded in custody were acquitted. Nine per cent of those bailed and 29 per cent of those remanded in custody were committed to the Crown Court.[88]

Although magistrates make the formal remand decisions, it has been argued that there are various professional decision-makers involved in the remand process and that many decisions are taken prior to the formal hearing.[89] In her research, Hucklesby discovered that that in 85 per cent of cases the CPS did not request a remand, and in only nine per cent of *all* cases was there a contested remand hearing in court. The major influences on the remand decision were the police, CPS, defence lawyers (who sometimes withhold the right to make effective bail applications from clients). In only 12 per cent of all cases did the CPS actually provide a rationale to the court

---

[79] *ibid.* ss.10(4), 18(4).

[80] *ibid.* s. 6(3).

[81] *ibid.* s.38. Or adjourns for medical reports under, s.30. See Powers of Criminal Courts (Sentencing) Act 2000, s.3.

[82] Emmins (2000), p. 82.

[83] Inserted by the Criminal Justice and Public Order Act 1994, s.30.

[84] See above, para. 14-057.

[85] Above, para. 14-056.

[86] Above, para. 14-056. Adjournments under ss.10(3) and 30 (see n. 76 above) may be for not more than four weeks at a time (if the accused is on bail) or three weeks at a time (if he or she is in custody); or three weeks for a medical examination where the court is satisfied that the accused performed the act or omission and requires medical reports on his or her mental or physical condition (Powers of Criminal Courts (Sentencing) Act 2000, s.11) and the accused may be remanded for the period of the adjournment: s.128(6)(b). Remands on bail may be for longer than eight days if the accused and the other party consent: s.128(6)(a). The accused may be further remanded if he or she is unable to appear by reason of illness or accident: 129(1): see *R. v. Liverpool City JJ., ex p. Grogan* (1990) 155 J.P. 450 (magistrates must have solid grounds for finding this to be established). See recently, A. Hucklesby, "Court Culture: An Explanation of the Variations in the Use of Bail by Magistrates" (1997) 36 Howard Jnl. 129; P. Jones, "Remand Decisions in Magistrates' Courts" in D. Moxon (ed.), *Managing Criminal Justice* (1985), Chap. 10. See also P. M. Morgan and R. Pearce, *Remand Decisions in Brighton and Bournemouth* (1989) (HORPU Paper 53); P. M. Morgan, (1990) 29 H. O. R. B. 18.

[87] See A. Hucklesby, "Remand Decision-Makers" [1997] Crim.L.R. 269, who found that in almost half of the cases where the CPS opposed bail, the defence did not contest it.

[88] *Criminal Statistics for England and Wales 2000*, (2001), Table 8.5.

[89] A. Hucklesby, [1997] Crim.L.R. 269.

for its request for remand/conditional bail. The Law Commission emphasised the need for accurate recording of the applications made and reasons given.

5. BAIL FROM THE CROWN COURT

The Crown Court may grant bail to an accused who is in custody pending a **14–065** hearing in the Crown Court (after committal for trial or sentence); or being "sent" to the Crown Court under section 51 of the Crime and Disorder Act; or pending an appeal against conviction or sentence by the magistrates; or pending the completion of the hearing in the Crown Court; or pending the statement of a case for the High Court or the outcome of an application for judicial review; or pending an appeal to the Court of Appeal where the Crown Court has given a certificate under the Criminal Appeal Act 1968[90]; or following an adjournment for medical reports.[91]

If, in any of those cases, the accused is actually before the court then application is made orally to the judge, otherwise the application is in writing in a specified form and the accused is not entitled to be present at the hearing.[92] The jurisdiction of the court is quite separate from that of the justices and the High Court, and prior applications to either of those courts will not diminish the obligation of the Crown Court judge[93] to consider the application on its merits and exercise discretion.[94] However, the accused may not make repeated applications to the Crown Court unless there is a change in circumstances.[95]

An important addition to the powers of the Crown Court is the power to grant bail on an application by a person who has been refused bail by a magistrates' court.[96] The application may only be made where the magistrates have heard full argument before refusal.[97] Legal aid is available for the application.[98] This reform was a response to criticism that there was

---

[90] Supreme Court Act 1981, s.81, as amended, *inter alia*, by Criminal Justice Act 1982, s.29 and the Criminal Justice and Public Order Act 1994, Sched. 9, para. 19, Sched. 10, para. 48. See also, *Practice Direction* [1983] 1 W.L.R. 1292. There is also inherent jurisdiction to grant bail during a trial on indictment and for the period of adjournment for reports following conviction. See *Practice Note* [1974] 1 W.L.R. 770. On the Court of Appeals powers of bail pending appeal and quashed convictions pending a retrial, see Criminal Appeal Act 1968, ss. 19 and *Archbold* (2002), para. 7–262.

[91] Under the Powers of Criminal Courts (Sentencing) Act 2000, s.11.

[92] Crown Court Rules 1982, r.19.

[93] Ideally the one who will try the case: see *Practice Direction (Crown Court Business: Classification)* [1987] 1 W.L.R. 1671, para. 6 and *R. v. Isleworth Crown Court, ex p. Clarke* [1998] 1 Cr App. R. 257.

[94] *R. v. Reading Crown Court, ex p. Malik* [1981] 1 Q.B. 451.

[95] There is no specific provision in the Crown Court Rules to this effect, but the Divisional Court in the *Reading* case (above) indicated that simultaneous or immediately consecutive applications to more than one Crown Court judge will not be permitted.

[96] Criminal Justice Act 1982, s.60, amending the Supreme Court Act 1981, s.81. See also, *Practice Direction* (1983) 77 Cr.App.R. 69.

[97] For the certification procedure to be adopted see Criminal Justice Act 1982, s.60(3), inserting new subsections 5(6A), (6B), (6C) in the Bail Act 1976 (s.5(6A), as amended by the Criminal Justice and Public Order Act 1994, Sched. 4, Pt II, para. 23(b)).

[98] For consideration of routine tape-recording, see Law Commission, No. 269, Part X. Access to Justice Act 1999, Sched. 3, para. 2(2). See further *Archbold* (2002), para. 6–147.

no effective appeal against refusal of bail by the magistrates other than an expensive and difficult application to the High Court.

Furthermore, by virtue of the Bail (Amendment) Act 1993, the prosecution now has the right to appeal to the Crown Court against a decision by a magistrates' court to grant bail. This only arises where (1) the accused is charged with or convicted of an offence punishable by five years' imprisonment or more; (2) the prosecution is conducted by the CPS[99]; and (3) the prosecution made representations against bail before it was granted. The matter is reheard and the Crown Court judge may remand the accused in custody [1]or grant bail with or without conditions. If the accused has not yet been committed to the Crown Court, the judge should stipulate a date, within the statutory limits, for remand. The prosecution should make a specific request for this.[2] The CPS must give oral notice of the appeal at the conclusion of the proceedings[3] and the notice must be confirmed in writing, and Crown Court hearing must occur within 48 hours.[4]

CPS guidance states that the number of appeals under these provisions should be small and should only be instituted in cases of grave concern; relevant factors include risk to victims, the lack of established identity or any community ties and a strong indication that the accused may abscond.[5]

6. Bail from the High Court

14–066   A judge of the High Court may exercise both the inherent jurisdiction to grant bail and the statutory powers vested in the High Court by the Criminal Justice Act 1967.[6] The application for a writ of habeas corpus has now largely been superseded by a bail application. The ability of the accused to make an application to the High Court was specifically mentioned in the *Davies* case[7] as a check on the accuracy of magistrates' decisions, and an additional safeguard is provided by the application to the Crown Court set out above. Application to the High Court was always a difficult operation

---

[99] Or a person prescribed by order: the Bail (Amendment) Act 1993 (Prescription of Prosecuting Authorities) Order 1994 (S.I. 1994 No. 1438) lists the SFO, the DTI, Customs and Excise, the DSS, a universal service provider within the meaning of the Postal Services Act 2000, and the Inland Revenue. See for the procedure the Magistrates' Courts Rules 1981, r.93A.

[1] The judge should indicate that the period of remand in custody should not exceed eight days from the date when the applicant last appeared before the magistrates: *Re Bone* [1995] C.O.D. 94.

[2] *Re Szakal* [2000] 1 Cr.App.R. 248.

[3] Which is satisfied if five minutes late: *R. v. Isleworth Crown Court, ex p. Clarke* [1998] 1 Cr.App.R. 257

[4] *i.e.* the prosecution must commence the appeal within that time: *R. v. Middlesex Guildhall, ex p. Okoli* [2001] 1 Cr.App.R. 1.

[5] Emmins (2000), p. 442.

[6] s.22, as amended by the Bail Act 1976. The court also has jurisdiction under the Criminal Justice Act 1948, s.37, to grant bail where the accused is applying for certiorari to quash a decision of a magistrates' court or the Crown Court, or appealing by case stated from the Crown Court. See also *R. v. Croydon Crown Court, ex p. Cox* [1997] 1 Cr.App.R. 20 holding that judicial review is not an appropriate remedy. The court also has jurisdiction to grant bail to any person to whom magistrates refused bail: s.22. The power extends to modifying the terms of magistrates' bail.

[7] *R. v. Nottingham JJ., ex p. Davies* [1981] Q.B. 38, see above, para. 14-056.

because legal aid was rarely granted, forcing applicants to rely on the Official Solicitor.[8]

The accused must apply to a judge in chambers either through his or her own solicitor by summons and affidavit, or by giving written notice to the judge that he or she wants bail.[9] In the latter case, the judge will then appoint the Official Solicitor to act on the accused's behalf. The Official Solicitor will not actually represent the applicant at a hearing in chambers (as his or her own lawyer would) but merely prepares a set of papers for the judge to consider, along with the police submissions. This is widely regarded as an unsatisfactory form of procedure and research demonstrates that the success rate in bail applications made by the Official Solicitor is much lower than in applications made by a lawyer instructed by the applicant.[10] The legally-aided right of appeal referred to above ought to obviate this problem.

The Auld Report recommends that there is no longer any need for the jurisdiction of the High Court to hear afresh an application for grant of bail following consideration by the magistrates or Crown Court.[11] There would under the proposal made remain a right of appeal on a point of law.

7. BREACH OF BAIL

An estimated 11 per cent of those bailed at the magistrates' court or Crown Court fail to appear. In 1997, 44,000 offenders were found guilty of failing to surrender to bail.[12] Twenty four per cent of those given bail committed one or more offences while on bail.[13] In 2000, 13 per cent of those bailed at magistrates' courts, nine per cent of those bailed at the Crown Court and 12 per cent of those bailed at all courts failed to appear at court.[14] That year, 41,800 persons were proceeded against for failing to surrender to bail,[15] with 3,700 bench warrants issued.[16]

14–067

The Bail Act 1976 replaced the defendant's personal recognisance with a new criminal offence of failing to surrender to custody without reasonable cause.[17] If a defendant has reasonable cause for failure to surrender to custody at the appointed time and place, he or she must surrender as soon as

---

[8] See the Law Society's criticisms of the Official Solicitor procedure in a paper, *Report on Legal Aid for Bail Applications* (January 1972), and comment in *LAG Bulletin*, January 1980, p. 28.

[9] RSC, Ord. 79, r.9(4), (5). CPR 1998 (S.I. 1998 No. 3132), Sched 1.

[10] N. Bases and M. Smith, "A Study of Bail Applications through the Official Solicitor to the Judge in Chambers" [1976] Crim.L.R. 541.

[11] para. 86–88.

[12] G. Barclay and C. Tavares, *Digest* 4 (1998), p.34.

[13] *ibid.* p.34.

[14] *Criminal Statistics for England and Wales 2000 (2001)*, Table 8.9.

[15] *ibid.* Table 8.5.

[16] *ibid.* Table 8.9.

[17] Bail Act 1976, s.6(1). Appearance at the arraignment necessarily involves surrendering to custody: *R. v. Central Criminal Court, ex p. Guney* [1996] 2 W.L.R. 675, HL (in respect of the departure to Northern Cyprus of Asil Nadir). *Cf. DPP v. Richards* [1988] Q.B. 701 (compliance with court's procedure requiring D to report to inquiry counter sufficient to surrender to bail); *R. (Hart) v. Bow Street Magistrates' Court*, *The Times*, January 17, 2002.

reasonably practicable thereafter, or be guilty of an offence.[18] The burden of showing reasonable cause is on the defendant.[19] Powers of arrest are attached to the offence.[20] The accused may be fined or imprisoned on summary conviction, or by the Crown Court, where the offence is dealt with as if it were a criminal contempt of court.[21] Where the accused has failed to surrender to bail granted by a magistrates' court, proceedings are initiated by the court by its own motion, following an invitation by the prosecutor, the proceedings then being conducted by the prosecutor.[22] Where the accused has failed to surrender to police bail, proceedings should be commenced by charge or the laying of an information.[23]

In the event of failure to surrender, any personal security given by the accused[24] may be forfeited, as may the sums of money promised by the sureties – "estreating a surety's recognizance". Normally those sums would be forfeited in full, but the court must exercise a proper discretion as to whether any part of the sum should be remitted on account of the sureties' behaviour, responsibility or means.[25] Legal Aid is not available for a surety in forfeiture proceedings.[26]

There are also controversial powers of arrest for anticipated breach of bail, which may be exercised whenever an officer has reasonable grounds for believing that the accused is *not likely* to surrender or that bail is *about to be broken or has been broken*.[27] The accused must be taken before a court within 24 hours.[28] The court is empowered to remand the person in custody

---

[18] *ibid.* s.6(2). Bail granted by the magistrates ceases when the accused surrenders to the Crown Court even if not arraigned: *R. v. Kent Crown Court, ex p. Jodka* (1997) 161 J.P. 638; *R. v. CCC, ex p. Guney* [1996] A.C. 616.

[19] s.6(3). Errors of legal representatives may be a reasonable cause: see *DPP v. Speede* [1998] 2 Cr.App.R. 108.

[20] *ibid.* s.7.

[21] The maximum penalties are three months' imprisonment or a fine not exceeding level 5 on the standard scale; 12 months imprisonment or a fine at the Crown Court (the offence does not constitute a contempt of court (although treated as such), and so the two years' maximum penalty under the Contempt of Court Act 1981 is inapplicable: *R. v. Reader* (1986) 84 Cr.App.R. 294; *R. v. Lubega* (1999) 163 J.P. 221.) Bail Act offences should be dealt with separately from the other substantive matters and put clearly to the defendant: *R. v. Boyle* [1993] Crim.L.R. 40; *R. v. How* [1993] Crim.L.R. 201. An appeal lies as of right: Administration of Justice Act 1960, s.13(1)(2)(b) but judicial review does not: *R. v. Manchester Crown Court, ex p. Massey* [2000] 2 Archbold News 1.

[22] *Practice Direction (Bail: Failure to Surrender)* [1987] 1 W.L.R. 79. This "clarified" the decision of the Divisional Court in *Schiavo v. Anderton* [1987] Q.B. 20, which had raised the possibility of the proceedings being conducted by the justices' clerk rather than the prosecutor (see B. Gibson, (1986) 150 J.P.N. 212; G. J. Bennett and B. Hogan, All E.R. Rev. 1986, p. 112, and note the criticisms expressed in *Murphy v. DPP* [1990] 1 W.L.R. 601). As the proceedings are not commenced by laying an information, the six-month time limit in the Magistrates' Court Act 1980, s.127 does not apply: this is helpful where the accused absconds abroad and remains there for some years, as in *Schiavo v. Anderton*, above. See also *R. v. Teeside Magistrates Court, ex p. Bujnowski* (1997) 161 J.P. 302.

[23] Failure to surrender here is not tantamount to defiance of a court order.

[24] *i.e.* any security taken where it appears likely that the accused will leave Great Britain: Bail Act 1976, s.3(5).

[25] See above, para. 14-053.

[26] See *R. v. the Chief Clerk Maidstone Crown Court, ex p. Clarke* [1995] 2 Cr.App.R. 617.

[27] Or that a surety has given written notice to the police that the bailed person is unlikely to surrender to custody and that the surety wishes to be relieved of the obligation. See section 7(3).

[28] Section 7(4)(a); see also *R. v. Governor of Glen Parva Young Offenders Institution, ex p. G (A Minor)* [1998] 2 Cr.App.R. 349.

or to alter the conditions of bail, or re-impose existing conditions.[29] The Law Commission in its Consultation Paper (above) doubted whether the power to arrest on such a belief alone and the potential for this to operate against an accused charged with a non-custodial offence would withstand scrutiny under the ECHR. An officer has the power to arrest even where the arrestee is not charged with an imprisonable offence.[30] In its Report No. 269 the Commission recommended that the power be read restrictively to ensure compliance with the ECHR. Bail should be granted to those arrested under section 7(3) unless the section 7(5) criteria are met and detention is otherwise necessary for a permitted purpose.[31a]

The frequency of offending while on bail was examined recently by Hucklesby and Marshall,[31] who found that the provisions of section 26 of the Criminal Justice And Public Order Act 1994 had had little effect on the numbers who committed offences on bail. The main impact was the shift to imposing conditional bail (finding a 17 per cent increase in use since 1994 Act).

Absconding by defendants has created considerable difficulties. There is a specific offence of failing to appear (see above). The House of Lords has recently held that a trial judge may decide, after considering the position with extreme caution, to conduct the trial in the absence of the accused.[32]

8. NUMBERS OF REMAND PRISONERS

The *Criminal Statistics for England and Wales 2000*[33] report that 4,000 **14–068** people were remanded in custody by magistrates in 2000, this represented 14 per cent of all those remanded.[34] Twenty-six per cent of those committed for trial at the Crown Court in 2000 were remanded.[35] Sixty-two per cent of those committed on bail to the Crown Court for trial and 77 per cent of those committed in custody eventually pleaded guilty.[36] Seventy-six per cent of those pleading guilty, after having been committed in custody to the Crown Court for trial and 41 per cent of those pleading guilty after having been so committed on bail were sentenced to immediate custody.[37] Forty-four per cent of those remanded in custody before trial at magistrates' courts or the Crown Court were sentenced to custody.[38]

---

[29] See *R. v. Liverpool JJ., ex p. DPP* [1993] Q.B. 233.
[30] See further B. Hargreaves, (2000) 164 J.P. 917.
[31a] See para. 7.22 and *ex p. Havering* [2001] 1 W.L.R. 805, para. 38.
[31] "Tackling Offending on Bail" (2000) Howard J.C.J. 150.
[32] See *R. v. Haywood* [2002] UKHL.
[33] (2001).
[34] Table 8.4.
[35] Table 8.6.
[36] Table 8.7. See also R. Pearce, *Waiting for Crown Court Trial: the Remand Population*, HORPU Paper No. 40 (1987), based on 1980–84 data.
[37] Table 8.7.
[38] Table 8.8. The *Criminal Statistics* recognise that the number of remands is probably under-recorded (para. 30, Appendix 2).

The increase in the number of remand prisoners has caused severe problems of overcrowding, sometimes involving detention in police, rather than prison, custody.[39]

All remand prisons have been required to provide a bail information scheme and a bail information officer to assemble information for the courts. Each prison should also have a Legal Service Officer for the purpose of ensuring that prisoners have access to legal advice.[40]

Apart from the Bail Act change to a presumption in favour of bail, other contributions to reducing the pressure have been the establishment of more bail hostels[41] and schemes for the collection of information about the accused that would justify release on bail.[42] New schemes are subject to approval by a Bail Practice Committee of the Association of Chief Officers of Probation. A National Steering Group, chaired by the Home Office, advises on strategic and policy considerations.[43] The schemes have the support of all the agencies concerned (probation service, CPS, police, Home Office) and monitoring over a six-month period showed an overall trend in favour of bail of 13 per cent where bail information sheets are presented to the CPS compared with cases where they are not.[44] Consideration is being given to the involvement of the private sector.[45] There have also been experiments with electronic monitoring ("tagging") schemes, in which the defendants are remanded on bail subject to conditions prescribing periods of curfew (as now for juveniles), their continued presence at home during these periods being monitored by means of an electronic device.[46]

---

[39] Authorised for periods not exceeding three clear days by the Magistrates' Courts Act 1980, s. 128(7), (8). See (1987) 151 J.P.N. 433.

[40] See Prison Service Orders 6100, 6101, 2605: Auld Report (2001), Chap.10, para.71.

[41] Under the Criminal Justice Act 1982, s.53. See H. Lewis and G. Mair, *Bail and Probation Work II: the Use of London Probation Bail Hostels for Bailees* (1988). HORPU Paper No. 50 (1988); Cavadino and Gibson (1993), Chap. 7. National Standards were issued by the Home Office in 1992. Bail support schemes, mostly for juveniles, have been introduced in some areas with Home Office funding: *ibid.* p. 116.

[42] (1987) 151 J.P.N. 433 at 523; G. Mair, *Bail and Probation Work: the ILPS Bail Action Project* (HORPU Paper No. 46, 1988). Cavadino and Gibson (1993), pp. 94.

[43] *Bail Information*: Report of the Bail Practice Committee on the expansion of Bail Information Schemes in 1988–89 (1990). On specialist bail schemes see M. Kennedy, C. Truman, S. Keyes and A. Cameron, "Supported Bail for Mentally Vulnerable Defendants" (1997) Howard J.C.J. 158, examining psychiatric bail provision and the need for such a facility in London, finding around 20% of all mental health cases in London magistrates courts who might benefit.

[44] *ibid.* (1990) 46 *The Magistrate* 35. See also C. Fiddes and C. Lloyd, (1990) 29 H.O.R.B. 23. See also C. Lloyd, *Bail Information Schemes: Practice and Effect* (HORPU Paper No. 69, 1992) (confirming that bail information "succeeds in influencing remand decisions, and thereby diverting defendants from remands in custody" (p.iii)). Other surveys are summarised by Cavadino and Gibson (1993), Chap. 6.

[45] *Private Sector Involvement in the Remand System* (Green Paper, Cm. 434, 1988).

[46] G. Mair and C. Nee, *Electronic Monitoring: The Trials and Their Results* (H.O. Research Study 120, 1990). The results were not encouraging (the scheme was expensive and over half the 50 people monitored offended or broke conditions while on bail). Nevertheless, provision for electronic monitoring in support of curfew orders imposed after conviction was introduced by the Criminal Justice Act 1991, s.12. See also P. Morgan and P. Henderson, *Remand Decisions and Offending on Bail* (HORS No. 184, 1998).

G. COMMITTAL PROCEEDINGS

The position in relation to committal proceedings has become increasingly   **14–069**
complex, but the principle underpinning the scheme is straightforward:
before an accused can be tried on indictment there should normally be a
preliminary inquiry into the case conducted in the magistrates' court.[47] The
magistrates, referred to in this context as "examining justices",[48] are
required to decide whether to commit the accused for trial at the Crown
Court, or whether to call a halt to the proceedings at that point if there is
not "sufficient evidence to put the accused on trial for any indictable
offence".[49] There has been a considerable reduction in the circumstances in
which committal proceedings are held. Section 51 of the Crime and Disorder
Act 1998 (discussed above) requires that cases involving offences triable on
indictment only are sent to the Crown Court without committal. A number
of alternatives to committal exist, notably in cases of serious or complex
fraud cases,[50] cases concerning child abuse,[51] and if the prosecution seek a
voluntary bill of indictment which permits the case to be taken straight to
the Crown Court. This procedure is discussed further later in this section.

(a) Historical background

Until 1968 there was only one form of committal proceedings. This   **14–070**
procedure was termed a "full", "conventional", "long" or "old-style"
committal to contrast it with the alternative form introduced by section 1 of
the Criminal Justice Act 1967, termed a "paper" or "new-style" committal.

Full committal proceedings consisted of the oral presentation of evidence
for the consideration of the court. The prosecution had to call sufficient of
its witnesses to establish a prima facie[52] case against the defendant (although
there was no obligation to call every potential prosecution witness) and they
were subject to cross-examination and re-examination, with the whole of
their evidence written down, read back to them and authenticated
("depositions"). At the close of the prosecution case, the defence could
submit that the evidence given disclosed no prima facie case. If the court
acceded to the submission it discharged the defendant; if it did not, the
defence chose whether to offer any evidence. If it did, which was unusual,
the witnesses were called and their evidence was treated in exactly the same
way as for the prosecution. The court made its decision on all the evidence.
If the defence did not offer evidence, the magistrates committed for trial

---

[47] Although not necessarily the one in which the magistrates' court has jurisdiction to try the
case.
[48] Note that one magistrate may sit as an examining bench: Magistrates' Courts Act 1980, s.4.
[49] Magistrates' Courts Act 1980, s. 6(1), as substituted by the Criminal Procedure and
Investigations Act 1996, s.47. The requirement to hold committals stems from section 2 of
the Administration of Justice (Miscellaneous Provisions) Act 1933.
[50] See the Criminal Justice Act 1987 introducing a new notice of transfer system.
[51] See the Criminal Justice Act 1991 extending the notice of transfer system. For full discussion
see Emmins (2000), p.190.
[52] *i.e.* evidence on which a reasonable jury could convict the accused.

immediately. In 1992, there were around 8,000 full committals.[53]

The full oral procedure was varied somewhat by provisions which permitted the court to accept written evidence subject to specified conditions.[54] This led to a marginally shorter hearing, but old-style committals tended to take a long time and were regarded as wasteful of resources. The Criminal Justice Act 1967 provided an alternative procedure — a paper committal — which was less cumbersome and was a welcome improvement.

The *paper committal* allowed the magistrates to commit a case for trial at the Crown Court without giving any consideration to the prosecution (or defence) evidence provided that all the evidence was in the form of written statements.[55]

Between 1975 and 1989 no fewer than nine official reports recommended reform or abolition of the scheme of committal proceedings.[56] The dual system was particularly heavily criticised and was recognised to be very inefficient.[57] The RCCJ recommended the abolition of committal proceedings, noting that only seven per cent of committals were old style and that they did not act as an effective filter.[58] The Criminal Justice and Public Order Act 1994 [59]provided for the introduction of new arrangements for the transfer of cases from the magistrates' court to the Crown Court, modelled on the provisions applicable in serious and complex fraud cases and child abuse cases.[60] The transfer for trial system intended to be implemented and contained in the 1994 Act would have produced automatic transfer of proceedings to the Crown Court performed without (in most cases) any hearing. However, following consultation, it emerged that these arrangements would prove expensive and unworkable.[61] Accordingly, the Criminal Procedure and Investigations Act 1996 provided for the repeal of the transfer provisions of the 1994 Act before they had even been implemented![62] It also made the major change of abolishing the option of old-style committal proceedings.[63]

---

[53] RCCJ, Chap. 6, para. 23.

[54] Criminal Justice Act 1967, s.2. Now Magistrates' Courts Act 1980, s.102. The conditions are that the statement is signed; that it contains a declaration that it is true to the best of the maker's knowledge; that a copy is given to the other party; that no party objects.

[55] See now the Magistrates' Courts Act 1980, s.6(2), as amended. "Legally represented" means merely that the accused has a legal representative acting for him or her, not necessarily present in court. Tendered to the court in accordance with section 102 of the Magistrates' Courts Act 1980. The court may commit for trial without considering the contents of the statements unless the accused is not legally represented or the defence submits that the statements disclose insufficient evidence.

[56] I. Brownlee and C. Furniss, "Committed to Committals?" [1997] Crim.L.R. 3,4 reviewed the reform proposals and questioned whether they have been effective in producing just results or merely efficient systems.

[57] See the second edition of this book. Abolition was, for example, recommended by the RCCP (Cmnd. 8092, para. 8.30).

[58] Report, para. 6.26.

[59] s.44 and Sched. 4.

[60] Below, para. 14-082.

[61] See *Hansard*, H.L., February 5, 1996, col. 76; *Hansard*, H.C., Standing Committee B, April 30, 1996, col. 8.

[62] See generally R. Leng and R. Taylor, *Blackstones' Guide to the Criminal Procedure and Investigations Act 1996* (1996).

[63] Inserting new ss. 5A–5C and substitutes a new s.6(1), (2) in the Magistrates' Courts Act 1980.

(b) Current law

The procedure is now that there are two types of committal. Under section **14–071**
6(1) of the Magistrates' Courts Act 1980, the examining magistrates
consider the documentary evidence to decide whether an accused should be
sent to the Crown Court. Under section 6(2) of the 1980 Act, there can be a
committal without consideration of the evidence.[64]

Section 6(1) committals (with consideration of the evidence) apply to all
unrepresented defendants and in those cases in which the legal representative requests it. Obviously, the hearings will only be necessary where the
accused has pleaded not guilty to an offence which is triable either way.
Indictable only offences are sent to the Crown Court immediately under
section 51 of the Crime and Disorder Act 1998 and summary offences and
guilty pleas are dealt with in the magistrates' court or committed for
sentence.[65]

The magistrates hear an outline of the case from the prosecutor who
adduces the prosecution evidence (all in documentary form). The types of
evidence that can be adduced by the prosecution are carefully prescribed in
the Criminal Procedure and Investigations Act 1996. These are limited to
documents and exhibits, and the conditions for each type of statement are
found in 5A–5E of the 1996 Act.[66] Significantly, under the 1996 Act[67] a
statement under the Magistrates' Courts Act 1980, s. 5B, adduced at
committal "may without further proof be read as evidence on the trial of the
accused", but if the accused objects to the statement it cannot be read.[68]
Despite such an objection, the court "may order that the objection shall
have no effect if the court considers it to be in the interests of justice so to
order".[69]

The magistrates' court is then under a duty to forward various documents
to the Crown Court.[70]

The defence do not have an opportunity to adduce evidence, but can
make a submission of no case to answer.[71] Note that sections 76 and 78 of
PACE have no application in committal proceedings, and so there is no

---

[64] See ss. 6(1) and 6(2) as substituted by the Criminal Procedure and Investigations Act 1996,
s.47, Sched. 1, para. 4.
[65] Note the exceptional powers in ss. 40 and 41 of the Criminal Justice Act 1988 discussed
above.
[66] s.5B deals with written signed declarations provided to the defence before committal; s.5C
with depositions by the prosecution witness in advance of committal where reluctant to give
a statement; s.5D with hearsay which could be admissible at trial under ss.23, 24 of the
Criminal Justice Act 1988; s.5E with self proving/otherwise admissible formal documents,
e.g. driving licences; and s.5F allows copies of documents. See further, Leng and Taylor
(1996), pp. 78–80. The provisions replace the old deposition scheme under s.3(3) of the
Criminal Justice Act 1925. A deposition may be taken under the Magistrates' Courts Act
1980, s. 97A where a person "is likely to be able to make on behalf of the prosecutor a
written statement containing material evidence" and "the person will not voluntarily make
the statement". A summons and, ultimately, a warrant, can be issued to secure that person's
attendance.
[67] Sched. 2, para. 1(2).
[68] *ibid.* para. 1(3)(c).
[69] *ibid.* para. 1(4).
[70] r.11 of the Magistrates' Courts Rules 1981.
[71] See *R. v. Barking Justices, ex p. DPP* (1995) 159 J.P. 353.

opportunity for objection to evidence in an attempt to exclude it.[72] The prosecutor responds to any defence submission. The standard of proof required is very low for the court to be satisfied—there needs only to be a prima facie case.[73] Cases will be rejected where no evidence is available to prove an essential element of the offence and where prosecution evidence is so manifestly unreliable that no reasonable tribunal could convict on it.[74] If the submission of no case is rejected the bench has the charges read to the accused and formally announces the decision to commit to a specified Crown Court.

If the accused is discharged by the magistrates at the end of the committal proceedings this is not the equivalent of an acquittal at trial. He or she may be charged again with the same offence, and be required to undergo committal proceedings again, whereas an acquittal at trial effectively prevents any further proceedings for the same offence.[75]

Committals without Consideration of the Evidence occur under section 6(2). The examining justices can commit without considering any evidence against the accused if he or she is represented and consents to this procedure. Defence representatives should seek a 6(1) committal if the evidence served does not disclose a prima facie case.[76] As Sprack notes "committals without consideration of the evidence are a pure formality, and may take 5 minutes or less to accomplish".[77] The prosecution simply presents a bundle of papers to be transmitted to the Crown Court.[78] If the magistrates are satisfied that the evidence tendered by the prosecution falls within section 5A(3) of the Act they may commit the accused for trial for the offence without consideration of the evidence.[79]

Since Article 6 of the ECHR applies fair trial guarantees to the proceedings as a whole, it is essential that committal proceedings respect those guarantees. There must be some doubt whether this is always the case with the most perfunctory examination in many cases. The defendant is usually present at committal but if the conditions of the statute are met, committal can occur in his absence.[80]

---

[72] Magistrates' Courts Rules 1981, r.70(5) provides for parts of documents to be treated as inadmissible. See also *R. v. Highbury Magistrates Court, ex p. Boyce* (1984) 79 Cr.App.R. 132.

[73] This was explained in the *Practice Direction (Submission of No Case)* [1962] 1 W.L.R. 227.

[74] On the difficulty in applying the case to answer test see Brownlee and Furniss, [1997] Crim.L.R. 3; Magistrates' Courts Rules 1981, r.7.

[75] If he or she is discharged after committal proceedings the plea of *autrefois acquit* (below, para. 17-024) is not available because there has been no trial for the offence. The prosecutor will have to choose whether to abandon the prosecution, or seek further evidence with a view to beginning proceedings again, or invoke the voluntary bill procedure, repeated use of committal proceedings may in an appropriate case be restrained as vexatious or an abuse of process: *R. v. Manchester City Stipendiary Magistrate, ex p. Snelson* [1977] 1 W.L.R. 911.

[76] On the uses of adverse inferences from silence as evidence in committal, see G. Branston, "The Drawing of an Adverse Committal from Silence" [1998] Crim.L.R. 189.

[77] Emmins (2000), p. 185 and see his example of the typical dialogue of a proceeding.

[78] The procedure is governed by Magistrates' Courts Rules 1981, r.6. A committal under s. 6(2) is valid if the court is satisfied that the evidence tendered falls within s.5A(3). The absence of a statement which is crucial to support the prosecution case does not render the committal defective: *R. v. Harding (deceased)* [1998] Crim.L.R. 877.

[79] See further Magistrates' Courts Rules 1981, r.6.

[80] Under s.6(1) or (2). See *R. v. Liverpool City Magistrates Court, ex p. Quantrell* [1999] 2 Cr.App.R. 24; *R. v. Bow Street Magistrates, ex p. Government of Germany* [1998] Q.B. 556, and see P.D. Brunning, "Committal for Trial in Absence" (1999) 163 J.P.N. 564 discussing

If in the course of a summary trial the case appears to be more suitable for Crown Court, the magistrates shall adjourn the hearing and recommence committal proceedings.[81] On committing a person for trial in the Crown Court, the magistrates' court must specify the place at which he is to be tried.[82] In selecting the place of trial the court must have regard to (a) the convenience of the defence, the prosecution and the witnesses; (b) the expediting of the trial; and (c) any direction given by or on behalf of the Lord Chief Justice on the allocation of business.[83]

The place of the trial is determined mainly by the nature of the charge on which the accused is committed. Criminal offences triable on indictment are divided into classes according to their seriousness[84] and the classes are distinguished by stipulations about the seniority of the judge required to try the case. In the light of these, the magistrates must specify the most convenient location of the Crown Court. In practice, each magistrates' court is informed by the presiding judge for the circuit of the location to which proceedings should normally be transferred.[85]

An accused or the prosecutor may make an application to a High Court judge to substitute another place of trial [86]and such applications are usually made in cases where it is feared that local prejudice and hostility will endanger the prospects of a fair trial.[87]

Reporting restrictions apply to committal proceedings.[88] After considerable controversy, the Criminal Justice Act 1967 placed a ban on the full reporting of proceedings where the accused is committed for trial, so as to minimise the risk of publicity prejudicial to the accused (especially important since only the prosecution case is presented).[89] However, the accused (or any of the accused if there is more than one) may apply for the restrictions to be lifted.[90] The court must accede to the application, subject to the requirement where one of two or more accused objects to the lifting of restrictions that it is in the interests of justice to do so.[91] In all cases, certain basic items of information are exempt from the restrictions, including the

---

both cases which although reaching a sensible and welcome result, do so with very little authority in support.

[81] Magistrates' Courts Act 1980, s.25.

[82] Magistrates' Courts Act 1980, s.7. As to powers to remand in custody or on bail, see above, para. 14-058.

[83] See the *Practice Direction (Crown Court: Allocation of Business)* [1995] 1 W.L.R. 1083.

[84] *ibid.*

[85] See the most recent guidance in *Practice Direction (Crown Court: Allocation of Business)* [2001] 1 W.L.R. 1996.

[86] Supreme Court Act 1981, s.76, as substituted by the Criminal Justice And Public Order Act 1994, s.168(1).

[87] For example, the trial of Brady and Hindley, the Moors Murderers, was held in Chester rather than the more likely location in Manchester, and the trial of those convicted of the Birmingham pub bombings was held in Lancaster. Prejudice is not the only ground for altering the venue, see *Halsbury's Laws of England* (4th ed.), Vol. 1 1(2), para. 938.

[88] Magistrates' Courts Act 1980, s.8.

[89] See the 2nd edition of this book, pp. 663–664. Full reporting can occur in some cases: see s.8.

[90] 1980 Act, s.8(2).

[91] 1980 Act, s.8(2A); this was added by the Criminal Justice (Amendment) Act 1981, s.1, changing the position that any one defendant could have restrictions raised contrary to the wishes of co-defendants. The magistrates must weigh the balance of interest between defendants who disagree over the reporting of proceedings: *R. v. Leeds JJ., ex p. Sykes* [1983] 1 W.L.R. 132. All the co-defendants must have the chance to make representations: *R. v. Wirral District Magistrates' Court, ex p. Meikle* (1990) 154 J.P. 1035.

identity of the court and the names of the justices; the names, and occupations of the parties and witnesses and the ages of the accused and witnesses; the charges (or a summary); the court's decision; the names of legal representatives; the date and place to which proceedings are adjourned; arrangements as to bail and legal aid. Breach of the restrictions is a summary offence. These restrictions are in addition to any other restrictions imposed by an enactment.[92]

The Crown Court Rules provide that the trial should not normally begin before the expiration of 14 days or after the expiration of eight weeks from transfer.[93] Home Office statistics reveal that the average time taken in 2000 from committal to a start of the hearing in the Crown Court was 14.3 weeks (rising slightly as a result of the introduction of the plea before venue procedure).[94]

(c) Custody time limits

14–072   A much more complex scheme of time limits for the "preliminary stages" of proceedings for an offence is established by regulations made under section 22 of the Prosecution of Offences Act 1985.[95] "Custody time limits" may be imposed to govern the period for which a defendant may be kept in custody before the start of summary trial; and, in cases of trial on indictment, for specified "preliminary stages" before arraignment in the Crown Court. "Overall time limits" may be set for the same stages. These rules have been the subject of a considerable amount of case law and have been repeatedly amended. The principles applicable in custody time limit extension cases were reviewed by the Lord Chief Justice in *R.v. Manchester Crown Court, ex p. Macdonald*[96] in which the presumption of liberty and the significance of Article 5 of the ECHR were emphasised.[97] The overriding purpose of custody time limits is to ensure that periods in custody for unconvicted defendants are as short as practically possible; to oblige the prosecution to

---

[92] 1980 Act, s.8(7). It is possible for magistrates to lift reporting restrictions but forbid publication of particular matters under s.4(2) of the Contempt of Court Act 1981: *R. v. Horsliam JJ., ex p. Farquaharson* [1982] Q.B. 762. However, it has been held that magistrates should be slow to impose restrictions under s.4(2) *in addition* to those applicable to committal proceedings: *R. v. Beaconsfield JJ., ex p. Westminster Press Ltd, The Times*, June 28, 1994.

[93] Supreme Court Act 1981, s.77; Crown Court Rules 1982, r.24. This requirement is, however, directory and not mandatory: in an appropriate case the Crown Court may grant an extension of time, even after the eight-week period has expired: *R. v. Governor of Spring Hill Prison, ex p. Sohi and Dhillon* (1987) 86 Cr.App.R. 382

[94] *Criminal Statistics for England and Wales 2000* (2001), para. 1.15. *Digest 4*, Chap. 4 reveals that the average time between the date of committal at magistrates' courts and the start of the hearing at the Crown Court was 13.2 weeks in 1998 compared with 16.7 weeks in 1994.

[95] See Corbett and Korn, "Custody Time Limits in Serious and Complex Cases: Will they Work in Practice" [1987] Crim.L.R. 737.

[96] [1999] 1 Cr.App.R. 409. For a summary of the decisions under the custody time limit regime see A. Samuels, "Custody Time Limits" [1997] Crim.L.R. 260 concluding that the "system seems to be working reasonably well", and yet "that the rules should be repealed" (p.268).

[97] See in particular the European Court's decisions in *Wemhoff v. Germany* (1968) 1 E.H.R.R. 55; *Stögmuller v. Austria* (1969) 1 E.H.R.R. 155; *Zimmerman v. Switzerland* [1983] 6 E.H.R.R. 17.

prepare diligently for trial,[98] and to give the courts power to control extensions.

Many of the difficulties that have arisen in the cases could be avoided with better preparation, if the plea and directions hearing was held early and trial dates are set well within the time limit period.[99]

The effect of expiry of a custody time limit is release on bail[1]; and of an overall time limit that the proceedings are stayed.[2] However, the court may extend a time limit[3] if it is satisfied that the need for the extension is due to (i) the illness or absence of the accused, a necessary witness, a judge or a magistrate; (ii) a postponement which is occasioned by the ordering of the court of separate trials in the case of two or more accused; or, (iii) some other good and sufficient cause for doing so[4]; *and,* the prosecution has acted

---

[98] "The prosecution need not show that every stage of preparation of the case has been accomplished as quickly and efficiently as humanly possible. ... What is required is such diligence and expedition as would be shown by a competent prosecutor conscious of his duty to bring the case to trial as quickly as reasonably and fairly possible." The specified period is a maximum not a target.

[99] See *R. v. Worcester Crown Court, ex p. Norman* [2000] 2 Cr.App.R. 1. Judicial review of the decision in respect of custody time limit extensions is possible (s.22(13)). Trials should not be fixed for hearing on dates outside the custody time limits without rigorous examination and attempts to find earlier trial dates: *R. v. Preston Crown Court, ex p. Barraclough* [1999] Crim.L.R. 973; *R .v. Bradford Crown Court, ex p. Leadbetter* [2000] 4 Archbold News 1.

[1] A court order for release is necessary and a defendant may have to make an application: see *Olotu v. Home Office* [1997] 1 W.L.R. 328 (no private law right against the CPS arises). See also *R. v. Sheffield JJ., ex p. Turner* [1991] 2 Q.B. 472 (magistrates bound to release on bail on expiry of limit notwithstanding that application for extension had been deferred by consent; however, expiry of limit between first appearance and committal does not prevent the accused lawfully being detained in custody for up to the specified period between committal and trial); see now s.76 of the Criminal Procedure and Investigations Act 1996 amending the Prosecution of Offenders Act 1985, s.22. Custody periods begin at the close of the day during which D was first remanded and expire at the relevant midnight thereafter: *R. v. Governor of Canterbury Prison, ex p. Craig* [1991] 2 Q.B. 195.

[2] See *R. v. Croydon Youth Court, ex p. DPP* (2000) 165 J.P. 181.

[3] The Crown Court, if the defendant has been committed for trial or indicted; otherwise the magistrates' court. A decision of a magistrates' court to grant or refuse an extension may be taken on appeal to the Crown Court (s.22(7)(8)); such a decision of the Crown Court may be the subject of an application for judicial review (see s.22(13)). The matter cannot be raised on any appeal against conviction (s.22(10)). An extension order must be announced in clear terms and not left to be inferred: *In re Ward, Ward and Bond* (1990) 155 J.P. 181. On the obligations of parties in custody time limit applications see *Practice Direction (Application to extend custody time limits),* December 18, 1988, unreported; *Archbold* (2002), para. 1-272. A reapplication may be made in exceptional circumstances where the judge has acted on a fundamental error of fact: *R. v. Bradford Crown Court, ex p. Crossling* [2000] 1 Cr.App.R. 463.

[4] Which may include the defence's need for time: *McKay White v. DPP* [1989] Crim.L.R. 375; a desire for specific counsel: *McDonald* (above); or the lack of a court or a trial judge: *R. v. Norwich Crown Court, ex p. Cox* (1992) 97 Cr.App.R. 145; *cf. R. v. Norwich Crown Court, ex p. Stiller* (1992) 156 J.P. 624; such cases are to be approached with great caution: *R. v. C.C.C., ex p. Abu-Wardeh* [1997] 1 W.L.R. 1083; *R. v. Birmingham C.C., ex p. Cunningham,* March 13, 2002. Neither the seriousness or complexity of the offence, nor the shortness of the period of the extension are good and sufficient reasons: *R. v. Governor of Winchester Prison, ex p. Roddie* [1991] 1 W.L.R. 303; *R. v. Leeds C.C., ex p. Briggs* [1998] 1 Cr.App.R. 413; and nor is the protection of the public: *R. v. C.C.C., ex p. Abu-Wardeh* [1997] 1 W.L.R. 1083; or the fact that the accused would be otherwise entitled to bail: *R. v. Guildford Crown Court, ex p. Fraser* [1995] C.O.D. 316; matters relevant to the granting of bail are not relevant: *R. v. Sheffield Crown Court, ex p. Headley* [2000] 2 Cr.App.R. 1. Absconding by D not in itself sufficient: *R. v. Blair,* October 7, 1998; pending extradition can be sufficient: *R. v. Woolwich Crown Court, ex p. Gilligan* [1998] 2 All E.R. The standard of proof in these

with all due diligence and expedition.[5] There is no strict evidential regime for the custody time limit hearings.[6] The Divisional Court will be reluctant to interfere with a decision on review. The court should always address its mind to the section 22 criteria and should not extend limits "on the nod". Evidence may not always be necessary depending on the complexity of the case.

The standard limits to be met are 70 days between first appearance and commencement of committal proceedings or summary trial in either way offences and 112 days between committal and trial; 70 days between first appearance and summary trial for an either way offence (56 days if the decision for summary trial taken within 56 days) 112 days between committal for trial and arraignment.[7] For indictable only offences under section 51 of the Crime and Disorder Act 1998, the time limit is 182 days including time spent in custody in the magistrates' court or 112 days — whichever is the longer.[8] For summary offences the time limit is 56 days from the accused's first appearance until the start of the summary trial.[9] The

---

matters is on the balance of probabilities: *R. v. Governor of Canterbury Prison, ex. p. Craig* [1991] 2 Q.B. 195. See A. Turner, [1993] 7 Archbold News.

[5] s.22(3), as amended. This is not a disciplinary provision: *R. v. Leeds Crown Court, ex p. Bagoutie*, *The Times*, May 31, 1999. Chronic staff shortages are reasons for a lack of "due expedition" and not the basis for a finding that the prosecution had acted with all due expedition: *ex p. Roddie*, above; see also *R. v. Central Criminal Court, ex p. Behbehani* [1994] Crim.L.R. 352 (lack of due expedition in that copies of crucial tape recordings should have been served on the defence earlier). Lack of due expedition by an independent body (FSS) is not fatal: *R. v. C.C.C., ex p. Johnson, The Independent*, January 21, 1999; delay in itself will not be fatal: *R. v. Leeds C.C., ex p. Bagoutie, The Times*, May 31, 1999. Due expedition does extend to future obligations on the prosecution: *R. v. Birmingham C.C., ex p. Bell* (1997) 2 Cr.App.R. 363; *R. v. Woolwich C.C., ex p. Gilligan* [1998] 2 All E.R. 14; dependence on foreign police investigations will not be lack of diligence: *DPP v. Blackfriars Crown Court* [2001] W.L. 98222. The court should be provided with a summarised chronology of events to evaluate claims: *R. v. Chelmsford Crown Court, ex p. Mills* (1999) 164 J.P. 1. The delay caused by the prosecution doing something it was not obliged to do is irrelevant: *R. v. Southwark Crown Court, ex p. DPP* [1999] Crim.L.R. 394; *R v. Woolwich Crown Court, ex p. Smith*, May 1, 2002, unreported. The question is whether the prosecution have done what is necessary to achieve the relevant committal in the time limit: *R. v. Leeds Crown Court, ex p. Briggs (No 2)* [1998] 2 Cr.App.R. 424. The court should require such diligence and expedition as would be shown by a competent prosecutor conscious of his duty to bring the case to trial as quickly and reasonably as possible: *R. v. Manchester Crown Court, ex p. McDonald*; see further S. O'Doherty, (1998) 162 J.P. 539, (1999) 163 J.P.N. 411; C. Wells and L. Rose, (2000) 144 S.J. 225.

[6] See *Wildman v. DPP* [2001] Crim.L.R. 565 and commentary; *R. (Rippe) v. Stafford Crown Court* [2002] Crim.L.R. (485).

[7] Prosecution of Offences (Custody Time Limits) Regulations 1987 (S.I. 1987 No. 299), as amended by S.I. 1988 No. 164, S.I. 1989 Nos. 767 and 1107, S.I. 1995 No. 555 and S.I. 2000 No. 3284. An indication by counsel at a preliminary hearing of the intended plea does not constitute the hearing of an "arraignment": *R. v. Bristol Crown Court, ex p. Commissioners of Customs and Excise* [1990] C.O.D. 11. Arraignment is not to be used as a mechanism for defeating the right to bail: *R. v, Maidstone Crown Court, ex p. Hottstein, The Times*, November 4, 1994; *R. v. Maidstone Crown Court, ex p. Clark* [1995] 1 W.L.R. 831 (arraignment quashed where D was unable to enter informed pleas in view of the service on the day of additional material by the prosecution). See s.23 of the Prosecution of Offenders Act 1985 as amended by the Crime and Disorder Act 1998, s.119.

[8] See Prosecution of Offences (Custody Time Limits) (Modification) Regulations 1998.

[9] reg. 4A of the Prosecution of Offences (Custody Time Limits) Regulations 1987, as amended. See also Prosecution of Offences (Custody Time Limits) (Amendment) Regulations 1999 (S.I. 1999, No. 2744).

trial starts when a guilty plea is taken or the prosecution present evidence.[10] Where an accused is already held in custody at the time of the imposition of the custody time limits, the same limits apply.[11] The time limits do not apply to the period between trial and retrial.[12] Under the ECHR, reasonable time guarantees in Article 6 apply from the moment of charge until the determination of a final appeal.[13] More rigorous standards of time-keeping must apply where the defendant is in custody.[14] The English time limits fall well within the periods considered to be reasonable by the ECHR when interpreting the right to trial within a reasonable period.[15]

Where a defendant is charged on different dates with more than one offence, a separate limit applies in respect of each offence, even if they arise from the same facts and could be included as alternatives.[16] The House of Lords has confirmed that there will be no new custody time limit triggered if the new offence introduced merely restates the one charged. If the prosecution introduce a new charge which amounts to an allegation of a new offence, a new time limit will be triggered,[17] and if an accused absconds the time limit may be suspended.[18]

The European Court has reiterated that the persistence of a reasonable suspicion is critical to the legality of continued pre-trial detention. The Court will examine whether domestic courts have required special diligence in the pre-trial preparations.[19]

Non statutory maximum pre-trial issue time guidelines were established in 1992 and are agreed by all criminal justice agencies. The guidelines cover each stage of the process from police bail to the arraignment in the Crown Court.[20] There is a constant pressure for greater speed and efficiency in the pre-trial process. Following recommendations in the Home Office Consultation Paper *Reducing Remand Delays*,[21] the government has introduced overall time limits for all cases. These were implemented in the Crime and Disorder Act 1998.[22] There are time limits governing the period between first appearance and the start of trial, first appearance and committal, and

---

[10] s.11B and see *R. v. Leeds C.C., ex p. Whitehead* [1998] 7 Archbold News 1.

[11] *R. v. Peterborough Crown Court, ex p. L* [2000] Crim.L.R. 470.

[12] *R. v. Leeds C.C., ex p. Whitehead* [1998] 7 Archbold News 1.

[13] *Neumeister v. Austria* (1979–80) 1 E.H.R.R. 91.

[14] *Abdoella v. Netherlands* (1992) 20 E.H.R.R. 585.

[15] See: Art. 5(3), *Wemhoff v. Germany* (1968) 1 E.H.R.R. 55, see also, *e.g.* the excessive delay in some jurisdictions: *Ferrantelli and Santangelo v. Italy* (1996) 23 E.H.R.R. 288 (16yrs!); see further M. Strange, in K. Starmer *et al.*, (2001), p.109. Relevant criteria include the seriousness of the offence, reason for delay, effect on the accused and the behaviour of the authorities.

[16] *R. v. Wirral District Magistrates' Court, ex p. Meikle* (1990) 154 J.P. 1035; *R. v. Waltham Forest Magistrates' Court, ex p. Lee* (1993) 157 J.P. 811. The preferral of new charges solely to defeat custody time limits will, however, be an abuse of process (*ibid.*; *cf. R. v. Great Yarmouth Magistrates, ex p. Thomas, Davis and Darlington* [1992] Crim.L.R. 116).

[17] *R. (Wardle) v. Crown Court at Leeds* [2001] 2 W.L.R. 865; [2001] Crim LR and commentary. The decision may well be challenged under the ECHR, Art. 5. Their lordships acknowledged that the position was unsatisfactory. The minority were of the view that new time limits should not occur if the new offence could have been included in the alternative.

[18] See s.22(b), as amended by s.43 of the Crime and Disorder Act 1998.

[19] See *Punzelt v. Czech Republic* (2001) 33 E.H.R.R. 49.

[20] See further H.O. Circular 24/1998, Annex 4.

[21] Narey (1997).

[22] s.43 of the Act amends s.22 of the Prosecutions of Offences Act 1985 so as to allow new limits to be set.

between committal to the start of the Crown Court trial.[23] Where overall time limits are exceeded, the result is not an acquittal, but that the proceedings are stayed. This allows the proceedings to be reinstituted within three months with the authorisation of the DPP.[24] If the accused is intending to rely on an alibi defence he or she must notify the prosecution of the particulars of the alibi not later than seven days after the transfer of proceedings to the Crown Court. If he or she fails to give the requisite notice the alibi defence can only be relied upon at trial with the special permission of the court.[25]

A decision to commit or refuse to commit for trial cannot be the subject of an appeal by case stated to the High Court, as it is not a "final" decision.[26] It may be challenged on an application for judicial review,[27] but such an application will only be successful where the magistrates have acted without jurisdiction.[28] Judicial review is only rarely available solely on the ground that the examining justices have acted on evidence that will or may be inadmissible at trial; however, erroneously admitting evidence may lead to the quashing of a committal where there was "a really substantial error leading to a demonstrable injustice".[29]

Examining justices have a discretion to discharge the accused on a committal if the proceedings constitute an abuse of process. This can arise as a result of delay,[30] or where the prosecution have deliberately manipulated the criminal process so as to take unfair advantage of the accused.[31] Questions of abuse should be dealt with prior to the committal

---

[23] Special limits apply in relation to Youth Crimes. See Home Office, *Tackling Delays in the Youth Justice System* (1997).

[24] s.45 of the 1998 Act introducing a new s.22B to the 1985 Act.

[25] Criminal Procedure and Investigations Act 1996 s.74. See *R. v. Fields and Adams* [1991] Crim.L.R. 38; *R. v. Johnson* [1994] Crim.L.R. 949.

[26] *Atkinson v. U.S. Government* [1971] A.C. 197 and *Cragg v. Lewes District Council* [1986] Crim.L.R. 800; *Streames v. Copping* [1985] Q.B. 920 (decision that information was not bad for duplicity).

[27] See below, n. 30.

[28] *e.g.* where the offence is summary only: *cf. R. v. Hatfield JJ., ex p. Castle* [1981] 1 W.L.R. 217, and *R. v. Horseferry Road Magistrates' Court, ex p. Doung, The Times,* March 22, 1996; *R. v. Wigan Justices, ex p. Sullivan* [1999] C.O.D. 21. It is not appropriate to use judicial review to challenge committal on the basis of insufficiency of evidence save in exceptional cases: *R .v. Whitehaven Justices, ex p. Thompson* [1999] C.O.D. 15. Quashing committals by way of judicial review does not render the proceedings void *ab initio: Re Najam* [1998] 10 Archbold News 2.

[29] *Neill v. North Antrim Magistrates' Court* [1992] 1 W.L.R. 1220, per Lord Mustill at p. 1233. In *R. v. Bedwellty JJ., ex p. Williams* [1997] A.C. 225, HL, it was held a committal could be quashed because of inadmissible evidence having been received, even though some admissible evidence was also before the justices. The House in *Bedwellty* also held that, "in a clear case", a committal could be quashed on the basis of *insufficiency of evidence.* This was so even where additional evidence to establish a prima facie case could have been adduced at the Crown Court. This was applied in *R. v. Belmarsh Magistrates' Court, ex p. Gilligan* [1998] 1 Cr. App. R. 14, DC, where the committal was quashed owing to inadmissible evidence having been received. See also *R. v. Whitehaven JJ., ex p. Thompson* [1999] C.O.D. 15 DC. Challenges to committal based on admissible evidence will usually be dealt with on a submission of no case at the close of the prosecution evidence in the Crown Court.

[30] *R. v. Grays Justices, ex p. Graham* [1982] Q.B. 1239; *R. v. Bow Street Magistrates', ex p. DPP* (1989) 91 Cr.App.R. 283.

[31] *R. v. Derby Crown Court, ex p. B* (1984) 80 Cr.App.R. 164, HL.

proceedings.[32] Discontinuance in the magistrates' court is in accordance with section 23 of the Prosecution of Offences Act 1985. Proceedings may be discontinued at any time during the preliminary stages which are defined to include: (i) in the case of a summary offence any stage after the court has begun to hear evidence for the prosecution at the trial; (ii) in the case of an indictable offence, any stage of the proceedings after the accused has been committed for trial or the court has begun to hear evidence for the prosecution at a summary trial; (iii) in any stage of the proceedings after an accused has been sent for trial under section 51 of the Crime and Disorder Act 1998.[33]

The Auld Report was highly critical of the present scheme with the six methods of a case moving from the magistrates' court to the Crown Court. "There is little over-all coherence or consistency in these procedures, which are a product of piecemeal reforms over the years. Some procedures allow the defence a challenge before the matter goes to the Crown Court and some do not. And there are slightly different procedures for each course. A simple form of procedure common to all cases should be found."[34] The Auld recommendation for a unified court would resolve the problem because all cases would start in the Magistrates' Division and either remain there or be allocated to one of the other two Divisions of Court after a first hearing.[35]

2. THE VOLUNTARY BILL PROCEDURE[36]

It is convenient to deal with the voluntary bill procedure at this point since it is a way of getting an indictable offence tried *without* committal by the magistrates. A bill of indictment must be preferred against a defendant as a preliminary to the trial. A bill may only be preferred if proceedings against the defendant have been committed for trial, or as directed by the Court of Appeal (*e.g.* where ordering a new trial) or by a High Court judge.[37]

14–073

A written application to a High Court judge for consent to the preferring of a bill of indictment must state reasons for the application, whether there have been previous applications and the application must be accompanied by the bill of indictment. If committal proceedings have been taken, the application must be accompanied by copies of the documents identifying

---

[32] *R. v. Clerkenwell Magistrates Court, ex p. Bell* [1991] Crim.L.R. 468.

[33] See further the Magistrates' Courts (Discontinuance of Proceedings) Rules 1986 (S.I. 1986 No. 367). Discontinuance in the Crown Court is governed by the Prosecution of Offences Act 1985, s.23A which allows for discontinuance before the indictment is preferred.

[34] Chap. 10, para. 220

[35] *ibid.* para. 203.

[36] See C. M. Chatterton and P. K. Brown, *Committals for Trial to the Crown Court* (1988), pp. 232–241; C. Lewis (1981) 78 L.S. Gaz. 1442; *Practice Direction (Crime: Voluntary Bills)* [1999] 1 W.L.R. 1613; *Archbold* (2002), para. 1–213.

[37] Administration of Justice (Miscellaneous Provisions) Act 1933, s.2(2), as amended by the Criminal Procedure and Investigations Act 1996, Sched. 1. The 1933 Act abolished the grand jury, which had had to find a bill of indictment to be a "true bill" before the accused could stand trial: the decision in the case of bills preferred, following committal proceedings or with the consent of a High Court judge, was a formality; the presentation of a bill by a private person was a rarity.

relevant materials.[38] The defendant has no right to a hearing, although the judge, may in the exercise of discretion, entertain written or, perhaps, in very exceptional circumstances, oral representations.[39] The decision of a judge to issue a voluntary bill is not susceptible to challenge on an application for judicial review.[40]

This procedure allows an accused to be put on trial at the discretion of a High Court judge and is rarely used, but could be effective in circumventing committal proceedings where unusual problems arose.[41] The procedure should not be used as a means of depriving the accused of an opportunity to seek dismissal of a charge under section 51 of the Crime and Disorder Act 1998.[42]

The preferment of a voluntary bill is an exceptional procedure. Consent should only be granted where good reason to depart from the normal procedure is clearly shown and only where the interests of justice, rather than considerations of administrative convenience, require it.

The Crown Court judge has the inherent jurisdiction to amend an indictment once the defendant is before the court. This power has been used to amend an indictment by adding a new count based on evidence not before the examining justices, even though the voluntary bill procedure could have been used and would have afforded the protection to the defendant of a High Court judge reviewing the merits of the additional count.[43] The fairness of the voluntary bill procedure has been called into question, particularly because it is an *ex parte* procedure, and because of the lack of clarity in the application procedure, or in the manner in which the preferment of the bill can be challenged.[44] A defendant can challenge as an abuse of process a voluntary bill procedure.[45] However, the availability of judicial review to challenge a voluntary bill remains unclear.[46]

The use of the voluntary bill procedure can be controversial. Three prison officers were put on trial for murder in this way after a stipendiary

---

[38] The Indictments (Procedure) Rules 1971 (S.I. 1971 No. 2084), rr.6–10, as amended by the Crime and Disorder Act 1998 govern the procedure. To be valid, the bill must be signed by a proper officer of the court certifying compliance with the requirements: *R. v. Morais* (1988) 87 Cr.App.R. 9; *R. v. Laming* (1989) 90 Cr.App.R. 450. The applicant (unless the DPP or a Crown Prosecutor: *R. v. Liverpool Crown Court, ex p. Bray* [1987] Crim.L.R. 51) must file an affidavit in support of the application. An indictment preferred by a voluntary bill may be amended on the same basis as an indictment resulting from committal or transfer: *R. v. Wells* (1994) 159 J.P. 243.

[39] *R. v. Raymond* [1981] Q.B. 910, criticised by G. Harrison, (1986) J. Crim. Law 383, but approved by the Privy Council in *Brooks (Lloyd) v. DPP of Jamaica* [1994] 1 A.C. 568. See *Archbold* (2002), para. 1–213.

[40] *R. v. Manchester Crown Court, ex p. Williams and Simpson* (1990) 154 J.P. 589; *contra, R. v. IRC, ex p. Dhesi, The Independent*, August 14,1995.

[41] *e.g.* where the defendant disrupted committal proceedings (*R. v. Paling* (1978) 67 Cr.App.R. 299); or to prefer an indictment against two defendants, one of whom has already been committed for trial.

[42] See *R. v. X and Y* [1999] 5 Archbold News 4. The procedure may be used where there have been deliberate attempts by the defence to frustrate the committal by a technical objection: *R. v. DPP, ex p. Moran* [1999] 3 Archbold News 3.

[43] See *R. v. Osieh* [1996] 2 Cr.App.R. 145. For criticism see J.C. Smith, [1996] Crim. L.R. 889 *cf.* the views of S. Farrell and D. Friedman [1998] Crim.L.R. 616.

[44] See Farrell and Friedman (1998), p. 620.

[45] See *Hickey et al v. H.M. Customs and Excise*, July 17, 1998, unreported. Buckley J.

[46] See *R. v. Manchester Crown Court, ex p. Williams and Simpson* [1990] Crim.L.R. 654 — no; *R. v. Commissioner for Tax, ex p. Dhesi, The Independent*, November 13, 1995 — yes.

magistrate discharged them after committal proceedings, and 15 youths charged variously with murder, affray and riotous assembly were put on trial by voluntary bill after committal proceedings had been in progress for nearly three weeks with no sign of finishing.[47] Both cases excited considerable comment. The preferment of a voluntary bill may however in some circumstances amount to an abuse of process.[48]

The Auld Report recommended the abolition of the voluntary bills procedure, seeing little point in retaining a procedure designed to provide an exceptional alternative to committal proceedings, when committal proceedings themselves have been replaced.[49] The Auld proposal is to maintain "the same form of charge throughout the case and subject it to the same procedural and drafting requirements in all Divisions of the Court".[50] The prosecution "should be required to serve on the court and all parties at the latest by the pre-trial assessment date a final trial copy of the charges on which it will rely".[51] Thereafter, further amendments would be permissible only with the leave of the trial court. There are other complex procedures governing the inclusion of other counts in an indictment and of the joinder of people or charges separately committed.[52]

H. DISCLOSURE OF EVIDENCE[53]

In a civil case, the pre-trial procedure can be operated so as to allow each party to discover the essentials of the case to be met and to discover the basic issues in dispute between the parties. In a criminal matter, despite the introduction of the plea and directions hearing and the pre-trial review mechanisms, the two sides have much less scope for selecting the ground on which they wish to fight and all issues may be intentionally left in dispute

14–074

---

[47] The three men were charged with the murder of Mr Barry Prosser, a prisoner, in Winson Green prison, Birmingham. One of the accused had been the subject of *two* unsuccessful committal proceedings on the same charge. This case provides another example of change of venue, the trial being transferred to Leicester Crown Court because of all the publicity that had been generated. The charges against the youths arose out of the death of Terence May, a motorcyclist, in Thornton Heath, South London.

[48] *Brooks (Lloyd) v. DPP of Jamaica* [1994] 1 A.C. 568. The preferment of a bill of indictment following a finding of no case to answer in committal proceedings was said to be justified only in "exceptional circumstances"; however, the court had to have regard to the "interests of the Crown acting on behalf of the community" as well as the interest of the accused (Lord Woolf at 581, citing Gibbs and Mason JJ. in *Barton v. R.* (1980) 147 C.L.R. 75, 101).

[49] Chap. 10, para. 58.

[50] *ibid.* para. 59.

[51] *ibid.* See also Chap. 10, paras 221–228.

[52] See *Archbold* (2002), paras 1-216–1-222.

[53] See, D. Corker, *Disclosure in Criminal Proceedings* (1996); J. Niblett, *Disclosure in Criminal Cases* (1997); J. Plotnikoff and R. Woolfson, *"A Fair Balance?" Evaluation of the Operational Disclosure Law* (HORDS Occasional Paper No 76, 2001); Andrews and Hirst, *Criminal Evidence* (4th ed., 2001), pp.125–135; T. Owen in K. Starmer *et al.* (2001); Emmerson and Ashworth (2001), Chap. 14, Part G. Although there is a procedure whereby formal admissions can be made under Criminal Justice Act 1967, s.10, thus eliminating the necessity for undisputed evidence to be given orally at trial.

until the trial.[54] However, it can be a considerable advantage to the prosecution, defence and to the court if by the time of the trial the two sides have some indication of the evidence to be given and the arguments to be raised. It is important to recall that non-disclosure of evidence by the police and others to the prosecutor, or the prosecutor to the defence have been recurrent themes in many of the high-profile miscarriage of justice cases.[55] The RCCJ made proposals for greater disclosure by the defence, with some restriction on the prosecution's disclosure duties. The Criminal Procedure and Investigations Act 1996 introduced these reforms but unfortunately they have since proved to be extremely unsatisfactory, with further guidelines having to be issued to render the scheme workable and to ensure compatibility with the ECHR. The Act has been extremely heavily criticised by many commentators and practitioners. The CPS Inspectorate Report, *The Thematic Review of the Disclosure of Unused Material*[56] concluded that "the Criminal Procedure and Investigations Act 1996 is not at present working as Parliament intended, nor does its present operation command the confidence of criminal practitioners".

Plotnikoff and Woolfson found that many respondents regarded the statutory scheme as so unsatisfactory that practitioners had returned to the common law principles.[57] The disclosure procedure has come under greater pressure because of the changes introduced in the Crime and Disorder Act to speed up pre-trial hearings. One of the conclusions of Plotnikoff and Woolfson's report was that: "88 per cent of barristers, 87 per cent of defence solicitors, 84 per cent of CPS respondents, 61 per cent of judges and 44 per cent of justices' clerks were dissatisfied with the way the Criminal Procedure and Investigations Act 1996 was operating".[58]

The obligation on the prosecution to disclose matters to the defence is one of the most onerous, and a failure to comply is likely to render the trial unfair. Article 6 of the ECHR has played an important part in shaping the current disclosure obligations, and should lead to further refinement of the system. There is no right to disclosure expressed in the Convention, but the European Court has recognised that it is fundamental to ensure the "equality of arms". The defendant's right to adequate time to prepare his

---

[54] Although there is a procedure whereby formal admissions can be made under the Criminal Justice Act 1967, s.10, thereby eliminating the need for undisputed evidence to be given at trial orally.

[55] See C. Walker in C. Walker and K. Starmer, *Justice in Error* (1993), p. 14, referring to, *inter alia*, the Guildford Four, the Maguire Seven, the Darvell brothers and Judith Ward in particular. Other examples include Stefan Kiszko. See also J. Niblett, *Disclosure in Criminal Cases* (1997); B. Fitzpatrick in Walker and Starmer (1999). Chaps 1, 3.

[56] (2000) For surveys and reports commenting (almost universally in negative terms) see: ACPO and the National Crime Faculty, *Disclosure and the CPIA: Implementation in Practice* (1998); *The Annual Report of the Chief Inspector of the CPS* (1998–9); Criminal Bar Association, *Disclosure Provisions Survey*; H.Hallett, (1998) *Counsel*, Dec.; LCD, *Draft Attorney-General's Guidelines on Disclosure: A Consultative Document* (2000); J. Plotnikoff and R. Woolfson, *"A Fair Balance"?: Evaluation of the Operation of Disclosure Law* (HORDS Occasional Paper No. 176, 2001).

[57] *ibid.* para. 1.6. In response to concerns from all branches of the profession and agencies involved in the criminal justice system, the Home Office established a steering group to conduct research into the effectiveness of the Criminal Procedure Investigations Act. See C. Clarke, "HO/Government Perceptions, Past and Present Proposals for Future Strategy" (2000) Med. Sci. 103.

[58] p. 121.

defence[59] and the requirement of equality of arms[60] are both important principles which place obligations on the prosecuting authority. The accused must have access to as much material as possible if the adversarial trial is to remain fair.

1. DISCLOSURE BY THE PROSECUTION

It is a fundamental principle of a fair trial that the defendant must know the case against him and have an opportunity to prepare his defence. Clearly, the prosecution are under a duty to disclose to the defence the whole of the evidence on which they propose to rely. This obligation arises at the latest when the defence are served with committal papers.[61-62] This aspect of disclosure is not generally controversial. Article 6(3)(b) of the ECHR requires the accused to have "at his disposal, for the purposes of exonerating himself, or of obtaining a reduction in his sentence, all relevant elements that have been or could be collected by the competent authorities".[63] What is more controversial is the extent to which the prosecution have to disclose to the defence any material that is not used for the prosecution case, where the unused material might undermine the prosecution case or assist the defence.[64]

14–075

(a) Background[65]

The extent to which the prosecution has to disclose information has developed rapidly over the last decade. Some requirements were clear at common law, including that of notifying the defence of, at least, the name and address of a witness who could give material evidence but would not be called by the prosecution[66]; making expert and technical evidence available;

14–076

---

[59] *Edwards v. U.K.* (1992) 15 E.H.R.R. 417.

[60] *Jespers v. Belgium* (1981) 27 D.R. 61.

[61-62] It may be necessary to have full disclosure before even this early stage so that a defendant can make an informed choice regarding his plea before venue and even earlier, so that he can make an informed choice about consenting to a caution. See J. Appozardi, [2002] Crim.L.R. 295, discussing the decision in *DPP v. Ara* [2001] 4 All E.R. 559. See also *R. v. DPP, ex p. Lee* [1997] 2 All E.R. 737, considering the possible need to disclose early to assist with bail applications or motions to stay proceedings, or other material assisting the defendant's preparation for trial.

[65] *Jespers*, para. 58.

[64] Recall that the forensic capabilities of the defence are severely limited when compared to those of the State. In addition, the prosecution are not desperately seeking a conviction, they are acting as ministers of justice and should not abuse the process. See for further discussion the speech of Lord Hope in *R. v. Brown* [1998] A.C. 367.

[65] See Corker (1996), Chap. 3.

[66] There was disagreement between Lord Denning M.R. and Diplock L.J. in *Dallison v. Caffery* [1965] 1 Q.B. 348 on the extent of the obligation. The Master of the Rolls was of the opinion that prosecuting counsel should make the witness' statements available to the defence. Diplock L.J. thought it was enough to make the witness available by notifying a name and address, (*cf. R. v. Bryant and Dickson* (1946) 31 Cr.App.R. 146; *R. v. Lawson* (1989) 90 Cr.App.R. 108). See further, Corker (1996), Chap. 3, pp.25–27.

giving the defence a copy of any statements made by a prosecution witness which conflict with the evidence given at trial[67]; making known any convictions affecting the credibility of prosecution witnesses.[68] In 1981, the Attorney-General issued guidelines setting out the additional material which must be made available to the defence, with exceptions for especially prejudicial or sensitive information.[69] The guidelines were overtaken by cases reconsidering the extent to which the common law requires disclosure.[70] The leading case was *R. v. Ward*[71] where the Court of Appeal on a reference from the Home Secretary quashed the convictions of Judith Ward for complicity in a series of bombings in the 1970s. The Court of Appeal found that the non-disclosure of a series of items of evidence[72] constituted material irregularities and that the prosecution were under a duty to disclose to the defence "material evidence"—that which tends either to weaken the prosecution case or to strengthen the defence case.[73] Some elements of the scheme adopted in *Ward* were refined in subsequent cases, in particular, in *R. v. Davies, Johnson and Rowe*,[74] and *R. v. Keane*[75] and some of these aspects of the common law are still important under the present statutory scheme for disclosure.

The common law expansion of disclosure obligations met with considerable criticism from the police, who claimed that the balance between defence access to material and preserving sensitive sources had swung too far towards the accused, and noted that vast quantities of information now had to be examined and disclosed.[76] The RCCJ [77]thought that the arrangements

---

[67] *R. v. Howes*, March 27, 1950, CCA (unreported), cited in Archbold, *Criminal Pleading, Evidence and Practice* (43rd ed.), para. 4–179.

[68] *R. v. Collister and Warhurst* (1955) 39 Cr.App.R. 100.; *R. v. Paraskeva* (1982) 76 Cr.App.R.162. The same principle applies to disciplinary findings against police officers: *R. v. Edwards* [1991] 1 W.L.R. 207, and the request by a prosecution witness for a reward: *R. v. Rasheed, The Times*, May 20, 1994. See also *R. v. Guney* [1998] 2 G. App. R. 242.

[69] *Practice Note* [1982] 1 All E.R. 734.

[70] The guidelines did not have legal force and conflicted with the case law: see *R. v. Brown (Winston)* [1994] 1 W.L.R. 1599.

[71] [1993] 1 W.L.R. 619. See also *R. v. Reilly* [1994] Crim.L.R. 279; *R. v. McCarthy* (1994) 158 J.P. 283.

[72] Including material experimental data that might have cast doubt on the evidence of forensic scientists called by the prosecution; statements made to police officers withdrawing confessions made to other officers; other statements by W which cast doubt on her reliability as a witness.

[73] The test was *materiality not admissibility: R. v. Preston* [1994] 2 A.C. 730. "Material" documents are those which are (1) relevant or possibly relevant to an issue in the case; or (2) raise or possibly raise a new issue whose existence is not apparent from the evidence the prosecution proposes to use; and (3) hold out a real (as opposed to fanciful) prospect of providing a lead on evidence which goes to (1) or (2): *R. v. Melvin* (unreported, December 20, 1993), approved by the Court of Appeal in *R. v. Keane* [1994] 1 W.L.R. 746 at 752. The term "issues in the case" was given a "broad interpretation": *R. v. Brown (Winston)* [1994] 1 W.L.R. 1599, 1606.

[74] [1993] 1 W.L.R. 613.

[75] [1994] 1 W.L.R. 746.

[76] See, *e.g.* C. Pollard, [1994] Crim.L.R.42 (Mr Pollard was Chief Constable of the Thames Valley Police).

[77] Cm. 2263, pp. 91–97. These recommendations are considered by J. Glynn, [1993] Crim.L.R. 841.

as to sensitive material were satisfactory.[78] It was recommended that such cases should be dealt with by High Court judges or nominated Circuit judges. However, they accepted that, otherwise, the burden on the prosecution had gone "beyond what is reasonable", and they made recommendations for change. The government subsequently published a consultation document[79] setting out a more detailed scheme that in its view would reduce the burdens on the prosecution to a greater extent than proposed by the RCCJ. The government claimed that the scheme would significantly reduce the volume of material that must be disclosed for no good purpose but not increase the risk of a miscarriage of justice. Critics suggested that it would merely "accept the risk of further miscarriages as the cost of achieving economy".[80]

(b) The current law

Provisions on disclosure are now contained in the Criminal Procedure and Investigations Act 1996,[81] and the *Attorney-General's Guidelines* (2000).[82] The scheme places obligations on both the prosecution and defence. The Criminal Procedure and Investigations Act 1996 applies to all criminal investigations commenced on or after the April 1, 1997.[83] It is illustrated in outline in the diagram overleaf.

14–077

---

[78] On the understanding that the procedure outlined in *Davies* did indeed extend to sensitive material falling outside the scope of public interest immunity (contrary to the subsequent decision in *Brown*, n. 71 above).

[79] *Disclosure: A Consultation Document* (Cm. 2864, 1995).

[80] R. Leng, [1995] Crim.L.R. 704 at 708. The CPS estimates that it spends £6 million per annum complying with the disclosure requirements, but that examinations by CPS lawyers of all unused material would cost £30 million extra. The cost to police forces in terms of disclosure officers' time to comply with disclosure was estimated to be £5.8 million: Plotnikoff and Woolfson (2001), pp. 109–110.

[81] Part 1. On the implementation of the new scheme for disclosure see J. Sprack, "The Criminal Procedure Investigations Act 1996: The Duty of Disclosure" [1997] Crim.L.R. 308; A. Edwards, "The Procedural Aspects" [1997] Crim.L.R. 321; Corker, (1996), Chap.5.

[82] And see the LCD, *Draft Attorney-General's Guidelines Consultation Document* (2000).

[83] The investigation could occur before the offence has been committed: *R. v. Uxbridge Magistrates' Court, ex p. Patel* [2000] Crim.L.R. 383.

Regime for Disclosure of Unused Material

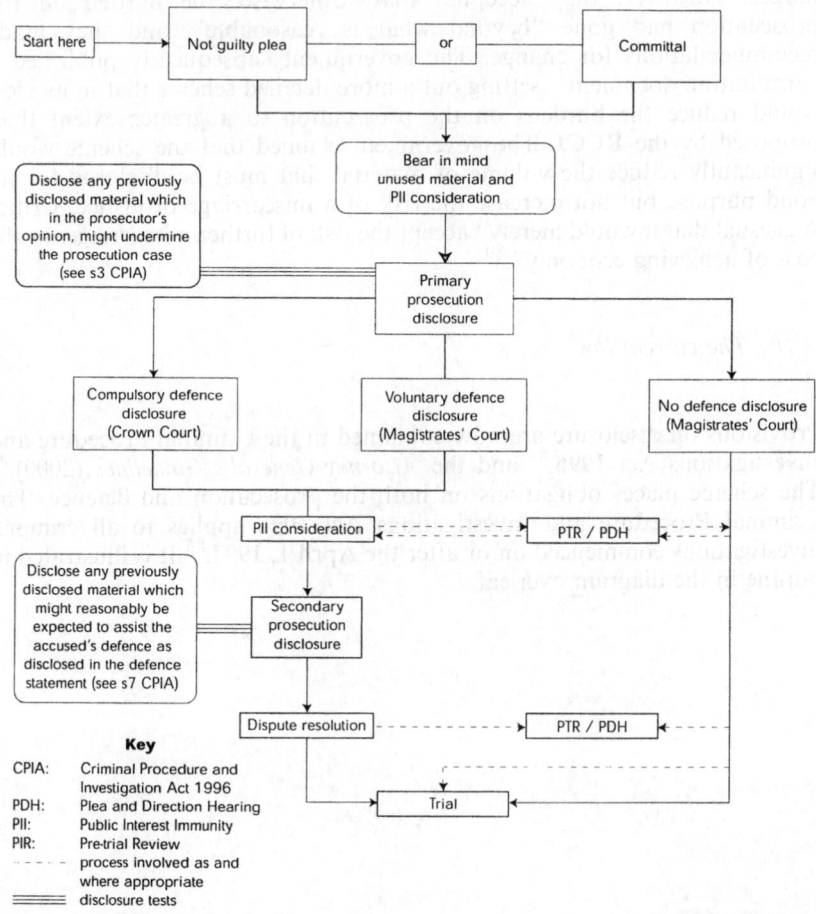

Flowchart 2

From: J. Plotnikoff and R. Woolfson *"A Fair Balance"? Evaluation of the Operation of Disclosure Law* (H.O. RDS Paper No. 76, 2001).

Recognising the significance of the need for a complete record of information to be maintained as a prerequisite to adequate disclosure, the Act places a statutory duty on those charged with investigating offences to record and retain information[84] and a Code of Practice provides further detail on the manner of the collation and recording.[85] The Code makes detailed provision for the retention[86] of crime reports, final versions of witness statements (draft versions if inconsistent), interview records and tapes and forensic and expert evidence, as well as material calling into question the veracity of a witness. The officer has to prepare a schedule of relevant material and specify on it any "sensitive material".[87] If there is a large volume of material which has not been examined because it is presumed to be irrelevant, the defence should be alerted to its existence.[88] The investigator has a duty to alert the prosecutor to material which might undermine the case.[89] Police procedures governing disclosure are also set out in the Joint Operational Instructions.[90] The police interviewed by Plotnikoff and Woolfson agreed that the disclosure officer's role was of critical importance, especially in serious crime. Many forces have plans to alter their disclosure arrangements because, in particular, it was felt by many that if the police/CPS co-location schemes were continued, disclosure issues would be dealt with more effectively.[91]

The Act clearly places a considerable burden on the investigator, and the success of the scheme turns on the bona fides and proficiency of this officer. Once the police have assembled the schedule, the obligation passes to the prosecutor.

(c) Primary disclosure

The prosecutor must review the schedule of material[92] and disclose that **14–078** which in his or her opinion might undermine the case for the prosecution

---

[84] Criminal Procedure and Investigations Act 1996, s.23.

[85] Criminal Procedure and Investigations Act 1996, s.26. Paragraph 5.1 of the Code makes the investigator responsible for ensuring that any information relevant to the investigation is recorded and retained, whether it is gathered in the course of the investigation (*e.g.*, documents seized in the course of searching premises) or generated by the investigation (*e.g.*, interview records). If there is any doubt about the relevance of material, the investigator should retain it. The *Attorney General's Guidelines* (2000) suggest that the disclosure officer should not be someone whose role is likely to result in a conflict of interest (para.7).

[86] See P. Plowden and K. Kerrigan, "Cards on the Table?" (2001) N.L.J. 735 at 820, discussing cases in which evidence that might have been valuable to the defence was inadvertently destroyed. In *R(Ebrahim) v. Feltham Magistrates Court* [2001] EWHC Admin 130, the court concluded that it was still possible for the accused to have a fair trial where the destruction of CCTV evidence did not prevent the accused putting forward his defence.

[87] *i.e.* that which it is not in the public interest to disclose (para. 6.12 provides examples). The *Attorney-General's Guidelines* (2000) emphasise that descriptions by disclosure officers in non-sensitive schedules should be detailed, clear and accurate.

[88] *Attorney-General's Guidelines* (2000), para. 9.

[89] Code, para. 7.3.

[90] See Plotnikoff and Woolfson (2001), p. 17.

[91] *ibid.*, pp. 21–23.

[92] *i.e.* material in the prosecutor's possession acquired in connection with the case or which he or she has been allowed to inspect.

against the defence.[93] The decision is one to be made by the prosecutor and cannot be abdicated to a judge.[94]

However, primary disclosure will not apply if the court upholds a public interest immunity (PII) claim or where disclosure is otherwise prohibited (*e.g.* by the RIPA 2000, s.17).[95] The prosecutor must also at this stage serve on the defence a document indicating the nature of other prosecution material prescribed by the Code of Practice and which has not been disclosed, other than material covered by PII. In relation to the material that is primary disclosure material, the prosecutor alerts the defence to the existence of the material and allows them access to it or copies of it depending on what is most suitable and practicable. The duty of disclosure arises as soon as is reasonably practicable.[96] The prosecutor has a duty to review disclosure schedules to ensure that they are accurate and complete. If the prosecutor considers that because of an omission or because certain material cannot be disclosed, it would be impossible for a fair trial to occur, he or she should discontinue the case.[97]

The key element of this procedure is the prosecutor's decision as to what might "undermine" the case. The use of this expression was designed to narrow the scope of disclosure from that imposed at common law.[98] In the course of the debates on the Criminal Procedure Investigations Act 1996, the Home Office Minister, Mr David McLean, explained that the word undermine "is not confined to material raising a fundamental question about the prosecution ... the disclosure scheme is aimed at undisclosed material that might help the accused notwithstanding the fact that there is enough evidence to provide a realistic prospect of conviction".[99] The *Attorney-General's Guidelines* (2000) which were introduced to clarify some of the problems with the 1996 Act provide further guidance. The explanation of the key terms "undermine" and "potentially undermine" which are central to the decision that the prosecutor must make, are explained as "anything that tends to show a fact inconsistent with the

---

[93]   Criminal Procedure Investigations Act 1996, s.3. If the investigator comes into possession of any new material after complying with the duties described above, then this must be treated in the same way (para. 9.1).

[94]   *R. v. B.* [2000] Crim.L.R. 50.

[95]   Special limitations also apply to protected material under the Sexual Offences Act 1997 to prevent the proliferation of gaol pornography.

[96]   Criminal Procedure and Investigations Act 1996, s.13. Plotnikoff and Woolfson (2001), p. 71, found that primary disclosure was served at, or just, after committal in most cases (90% according to the CPS; 60% according to the defence). Many respondents from all areas of the criminal justice system felt that non-sensitive unused material was often withheld from the accused (including 15% of judges being of this opinion).

[97]   *Attorney-General's Guidelines* (2000), para. 21.

[98]   See *R. v. Keane* [1994] 1 W.L.R. 746 where the court held that the correct test was whether it was evidence that was relevant or which might raise a new issue or hold out a real prospect of providing a lead on such evidence. Note that a wide interpretation of "undermine" is supported by the decision of the European Court in *Rowe and Davis v. U.K.* (2000) 30 E.H.R.R. 1. The European Court emphasised that the right to a fair trial means that the prosecution authorities should disclose to the defence all material evidence in their possession for and against the accused to ensure the "equality of arms". This suggests that the current obligations of primary disclosure may be too narrow, and that *all* evidence which is material to the case ought to be disclosed, not merely that which *might* tend to undermine the prosecution case: B. Emmerson, "Prosecution Disclosure in Criminal Cases: The ECHR and the Human Rights Act 1998" (2000) Med. Sci. Law 125.

[99]   H.C. Standing Committee B, May 14, 1996, col. 34.

elements of the case ... ".[1] Material which could lead to the exclusion of evidence, stay for abuse, or which may affect the reliability of the accused's confession should be disclosed.[2]

One controversial issue is the obligation to disclose prosecution witnesses' records. Although there is no explicit statutory provision dealing with previous convictions of prosecution witnesses, there seems little doubt that these should be disclosed as potentially undermining the prosecution case.[3] Following the common law position explained in *R. v. Mills*,[4] the prosecution are probably obliged to supply the defence with copies of *any* witness statements from unreliable witnesses that the prosecution do *not* propose to call. The converse does not apply: the fact that the accused is an informer need not be disclosed by the defence to the prosecution.[5]

A number of problems with primary disclosure remain. First, it presumes that the schedule of material will have been accurately recorded by the police,[6] and that it will have been accurately and comprehensively disclosed to the prosecutor for him or her to make a decision on disclosure. Plotnikoff and Woolfson found that primary disclosure decisions are rarely included in the brief to the prosecuting barrister, with 75 per cent of barristers suggesting that their instructions rarely contain an adequate account of the reasons for primary disclosure. The danger is not just that the police will deliberately withhold material from the prosecutor, but that this will occur despite the police officer's best efforts.[7] The respondents to Plotnikoff and Woolfson's survey emphasise that the drawing up of the schedules of material is an onerous task.[8] The CPS and other legal advisers found that unused material was commonly omitted from schedules/wrongly listed, especially in high volume crimes such as burglary, but also in serious drugs and sexual offence cases.[9] The C.P.S described the quality of descriptions by

---

[1] paras 36–38.

[2] *Attorney-General's Guidelines* (2000), para. 38.

[3] See *R. v. Vasilou* [2000] Crim. L. R. 845 and commentary; *cf. R. v. Ecclestone*, July 10, 2001, CA; *R. v. Jamil* [2002] Crim. L. R. Information adverse to a police witness should be disclosed: *R v. Guney* [1998] 2 Cr.App.R. 242. Plotnikoff and Woolfson's research (p. 46) revealed that only one of 39 CPS areas in the survey kept a record of the adverse judicial comments relating to police officers, as required by *R. v. Guney* (1998) 2 Cr.App.R. 242. See also on the disclosure of adverse information on the prosecution witness Plotnikoff and Woolfson (2001), Chap. 5. Similarly, where reliance is placed on a witness turning Queen's evidence it is necessary for the prosecution to offer to disclose the witness's convictions to the jury unless the defence request otherwise: *R. v. Taylor*; *R. v. Goodman* [1999] Crim.L.R. 407. Evidence of the accused's own record must be disclosed to the defence within 21 days of committal. See *Practice Direction (Crime: Antecedents) (No. 2)* [1997] 1 W.L.R. 1482. In their research Plotnikoff and Woolfson (2001), Chap. 3, found that the procedures for checking on adverse information on prosecution witness was poor, with checks not always performed, and entries recorded in only 24% of relevant cases. The results on criminal record checks on prosecution witnesses were revealed to the defence as primary disclosure in only 4% of all cases.

[4] [1998] 2 A.C. 382.

[5] *R. v. Denton*, February 15, 2002.

[6] For an example of a case in which the police failed to record the details of an alleged offence see *R. v. Abbassi* discussed at (2000) 150 N.L.J. 1666.

[7] On the continued dependence on the police in the disclosure regime see *R. v. Jackson* [2000] Crim.L.R. 377.

[8] Plotnikoff and Woolfson (2001), Chap. 4.

[9] *ibid.* Fig. 4, p.27.

disclosure officers as poor in a large number of cases.[10] In a long and complex investigation the volume of material produced will run to tens of thousands' of pages of material.[11] Plotnikoff and Woolfson found that 72 per cent of defence barristers, but only 45 per cent of prosecution barristers often discussed disclosure matters when instructed.[12] There was considerable disparity between the CPS claims about their processing of unused material and the less positive experience of the barristers instructed by them. Second, there is the problem of the inevitable delay in disclosing material to the defence, particularly where there is a large volume of material.[13] Thirdly, there is the problem inherent in the "undermining" test being applied because it depends on the subjective perceptions of the prosecutor. This is, as Ashworth observes, a far cry from the "equality of arms" required by the fair trial guarantees of Article 6.[14]

(d) Public interest immunity (PII)

14–079 Material which would be subject to primary disclosure but which is believed to be protected by PII is subject to special procedures which have proved very controversial in a number of cases. The investigator will produce, in the course of the investigation, a schedule of sensitive material (*e.g.* relating to informers and covert human intelligence sources).[15] This information is passed to the prosecutor who must apply to the court for PII if he or she thinks that it is necessary to do so.[16] At common law the Court of Appeal in *Ward* held that the prosecution should disclose the material to the court for its decision as to whether the public interest was against the defence having access to the material. The Court of Appeal refined these requirements in *R. v. Davis, Johnson and Rowe*[17] and the Criminal Procedure Investigations Act 1996 preserves these common law rules in relation to PII.[18]

The procedure for a PII application has undergone some significant

---

[10] Over 60% in some categories, *ibid.* Fig. 5. p. 29. On routine revelation to the CPS see Plotnikoff and Woolfson (2001), Chap. 7.

[11] Plotnikoff and Woolfson found that the average size of the file of unused material studied by the CPS in a serious case was 54.6 inches deep: Table 12, p. 35.

[12] p. 52.

[13] See the discussion by R. Toney, "Disclosure of Evidence and Legal Assistance at Custodial Interrogation: What does the ECHR Require" (2001) 5 E. & P. 39, considering the potential breaches of the Convention under existing English law; see also Emmerson and Ashworth (2001), para. 14–114.

[14] (1998), p.134.

[15] D. Corker, "The Criminal Procedure Investigations Act 1996 Disclosure Regime; PII and Third Party Disclosure, The Defence Perspective" (2000) Med. Sci. Law 116, noting that the effectiveness of the Act is again dependant on the conscientiousness of the investigator.

[16] Prosecution counsel should also be meticulous in ensuring that all potential PII material has been reviewed: *R. v. Menga* [1998] Crim. L. R. 58.

[17] (1993) 97 Cr.App.R. 110.

[18] s.21(2). *Rowe and Davis v. U.K.* [2000] 30 E.H.R.R. 1; [2000] Crim.L.R. 584 confirms that the pre-*Ward* disclosure rules in England were in breach of Article 6 because they allowed prosecutors to withhold evidence (even from the judge if it related to PII) which might have undermined their case. The decision also casts doubt on the compatibility of the 1996 procedure for secondary disclosure being delayed until after the defence disclosure. See further the commentary by A. Ashworth, [2000] Crim.L.R. 584; and C. Walker and G. Robertson in Walker and Starmer, (1999).

developments following the implementation of the Human Rights Act 1998. The European Court has repeatedly emphasised the significance in the adversarial trial of the concept of equality of arms whereby the State has an obligation to "gather evidence against and for the accused and to allow access to all relevant material before trial".[19]

In *R. v. Davis, Johnson and Rowe*, the Court of Appeal[20] adopted a tripartite model for PII applications. In most cases there would be a hearing for PII with the defence being notified of the hearing, the type of material involved, and the defence having an opportunity to make representations. In exceptional cases where even to reveal the application to the defence could be contrary to the public interest, the prosecution would not be obliged to disclose the category of material held and there would be an *ex parte* hearing. In the most extreme cases, the prosecution need not even alert the defence to the proposed *ex parte* hearing.[21]

In determining PII, the judge is not restricted to considering only admissible evidence.[22] The court has an obligation to review whether the level of secrecy from the defence remains necessary.[23] The court is also under a duty throughout the trial to keep under review the decisions made as to PII.[24] The obligations on trial judges with a PII application can be onerous; in one case it was reported that the judge spent 11 days reading material before being able to rule on disclosure.[25]

This tripartite PII scheme was examined by the ECtHR in *Rowe and Davis v. United Kingdom*[26] where the European Court held there was a legitimate need in some cases for public interest immunity certificates to attach to certain prosecution material, but that this category should be narrowly construed. The procedure must involve the judicial decision as to whether the material was strictly necessary as PII, and it is for the court of first instance, not the appeal court to deal with PII applications.[27] In *Jasper v.*

---

[19] *Jespers v. Belgium* (1981) 27 D.R. 61; *Edwards v. U.K.* (1993) 15 E.H.R.R. 417; *Benendoun v. France* (1994) 18 E.H.R.R. 54. On *Edwards v. U.K.* in the ECtHR see the comment by S. Field and J. Young, "Disclosure, Appeals, and Procedural Traditions: *Edwards v. U.K.*" [1994] Crim.L.R. 264.

[20] [1993] 1 W.L.R. 613.

[21] There is no need for an *ex parte* application where there was nothing to be said which could not be said in the presence of defence counsel: *R. v. Smith* [1998] 2 Cr.App.R. 1 (adequate records must always be kept of such *ex parte* application hearings).

[22] *R. v. Law, The Times*, August 15, 1996.

[23] The procedure was incorporated in the Crown Court (Criminal Procedure Investigations Act 1996) (Disclosure) Rules 1997 (S.I.1997, No. 698).

[24] s.15. On PII see Plotnikoff and Woolfson (2001), Chap. 10 recognising that it is difficult to monitor PII work but that in general it was felt by practitioners that the number of applications for PII had risen since 1996. Approximately 36% of PII applications in the cases examined were successful.

[25] *R. v. W.* [1997] 1 Cr.App.R. 166 at 168. In *R. v. W.* the judge had relied on counsel to sift the disputed material and discard the irrelevant before the judge ruled on it. This practice was endorsed by the Court of Appeal.

[26] (2000) 30 E.H.R.R. 1, [2000] Crim.L.R. 584. In *Rowe and Davis v. U.K.*, the European Court did not address the fairness of the *ex parte* procedure under the Criminal Procedure and Investigations Act 1996 and Crown Court (Criminal Procedure and Investigation Act 1996) (Disclosure) Rules 1997. See the subsequent decisions of the English Court of Appeal: *R. v. Davis, Rowe and Johnson (No.2), The Times*, April 24, 2000; *(No. 3)* [2001] 1 Cr.App.R. 8.

[27] See *Atlan v. U.K.* [2001] Crim. LR. 819.

United Kingdom,[28] the ECtHR held, by a bare majority, that the exceptional procedure whereby an *ex parte* PII application can be made without notification to the defence of the category of material was compatible with Article 6,[29] in spite of the claims that judicial bias or error would go undetected.[30] The ECtHR distinguished the situation in *R. v. Davis, Johnson and Rowe* where the pre-Criminal Procedure Investigations Act 1996 procedure meant that the trial judge was unaware of the materials. The slender majority in *Jasper* means the issue is likely to be challenged in the future.[31] There is also scope for challenge to the most extreme procedure where the defence would not even be aware of the PII application. Serious misgivings remain about how a defendant can have a fair trial in the absence of knowledge of material, which might undermine the prosecution case. The ECtHR has rejected a "special counsel" approach under which an independent barrister would conduct the defence presentation at PII applications. The Auld Report however recommended that there should be a new scheme whereby special independent counsel would represent the defendant in PII applications.[32]

(e) Defence disclosure[33]

14–080   Prior to the 1996 Act the defence was able to avoid revealing its case (apart from in alibi and in certain other exceptional situations). The RCCJ[34] felt that there were "powerful reasons for extending the obligations on the defence to provide advance disclosure". This would encourage earlier and better preparation of cases, and might result in the prosecution being dropped in the light of defence disclosure, an earlier resolution through a plea of guilty, or an earlier trial date. The length of the trial could be more readily estimated, leading to a better use of time both of the court and of those involved in the trial. Cases where the defendant withholds the defence to the last possible moment "in the hope of confusing the jury and evading investigation of a fabricated defence" ("ambush defences"[35]) would be kept

---

[28]   (2000) 30 E.H.R.R. 441; [2001] Crim.L.R. 586. An *ex parte* application may not be made by the defence: *R. v. Turner* [1995] 1 W.L.R. 264 at 267. In *Jasper v. U.K.* and *Fitt v. U.K.* [2000] Crim.L.R. 586, the European Court accepted that where the trial judge had reviewed the PII application and the defence were notified, there was no breach of Art. 6.

[29]   The decision was by a bare majority of 9:8. See further the commentary on this case by A. Ashworth, [2001] Crim.L.R.586.

[30]   The *Attorney General's Guidelines* (2000) provide further guidance for the PII application in paras 41 and 42.

[31]   But see *PG and JH v. U.K.* [2002] Crim.L.R. 308. For a detailed analysis of the ECHR and disclosure, see T. Owen, "Disclosure" in K. Starmer *et al.*, (2001). See also on PII obligations, *Report on the Inquiry into the Export of Defence Equipment and Dual Use of Goods in Iraq and Related Prosecutions*, Section K.

[32]   Chap. 10, paras 191–197, *cf.* discussion by Owen (2001), p. 148 and see *Chahal v. U.K.* (1997) 23 E.H.R.R. 413.

[33]   See Corker (1996), Chap. 2.

[34]   pp. 97–100.

[35]   The Crown Court Study (RCCJ Research Study No. 19 by M.Zander and P. Henderson) showed that "ambush defences" were considered by prosecution counsel to have occurred in 7% of contested cases, by the CPS in 10% and by the police in 26%. They were considered by the CPS to have caused "serious problems" in 3% of contested cases and by the police in

to a minimum. Michael Zander dissented from these recommendations[36] on the ground that it was "contrary to principle for the defendant to be made to respond to the prosecution's case until it has been presented at the trial". Given that the burden of proof lies throughout on the prosecution, "it is not the job of the defendant to be helpful either to the prosecution or to the system. His task, if he chooses to put the prosecution to the proof, is simply to defend himself." Furthermore, ambush defences were in fact rare and when they occur "usually do not pose much of a problem".[37] The majority's proposals would in fact "cause extra delay, cost and general inefficiency in the system – to little, if any, purpose", given the general nature of the defence disclosure requirement.

The government subsequently accepted the majority's diagnosis of the "problem", but its provisional proposals[38] involved less onerous "primary prosecution disclosure"[39] and more onerous defence disclosure, requiring the defence to "provide sufficient particulars of its case to identify the issues in dispute between the defence and the prosecution before the commencement of the trial".[40]

The Criminal Procedure and Investigations Act 1996, as finally enacted, only provided for the defence to be required in the case of indictable offences tried at the Crown Court to give a "defence statement" to the prosecution. This sets out "in general terms the nature of the accused's defence",[41] and indicates "the matters on which he takes issue with the prosecution" and the reasons for doing so.[42] The disclosure must occur within 14 days of the prosecution's primary disclosure.[43] Defence statements may be given

---

8%. See also R. Leng, [1995] Crim.L.R. 704 at 706–707. The RCCJ asserted that the consequences in the minority of cases (said without supporting evidence, to be "often the most serious") were unacceptable (p. 98).

[36] Cm. 2263, pp. 221–223.

[37] See above, n. 36.

[38] *Disclosure: A Consultation Document* (Cm. 2864, 1995), pp. 15–16.

[39] Above, para. 14-072.

[40] These included the names and addresses of defence witnesses, written expert evidence and any evidence which might support a defence. Such disclosure "is in the interest of justice and should assist the better management of trials". Disputes as to whether there has been compliance would be settled at a preliminary hearing. The sanction for non-compliance would be the possible drawing of adverse inferences by the court. Professor Zander's objections applied with even greater force to these proposals. Furthermore the Consultation Document did not suggest that the police should be inhibited from interviewing the defence witnesses: this is particularly objectionable given the opportunity it provides for the police to "deconstruct or tamper with the defence case".

[41] See the reassurances as to the generality in H.C. Deb., Committee B, May 1, 1996, cols 66–69. The Solicitor-General in the parliamentary debates issued reassurances as to the obligations on defendants, and specifically that there would be no requirement to provide details of the evidence: "the fear that this might require the defence to set out its oral cross-examination is not well founded. That is not intended at all" (*Hansard*, H.C. Committee, May 16, 1996, cols 66–69). See D. Calvert-Smith, "The Prosecuting Attorney's Role Making The Criminal Procedure Investigations Act 1996 Work to Facilitate Fair Trials and Just Verdicts" (2000) Med. Sci. Law. 110, making clear that the CPS will not use the defence statement as part of its case.

[42] s.5(6).

[43] Criminal Procedure Investigations Act 1996 (Defence Disclosure Time Limits) Regulations 1997 (S.I. 1997 No. 684), reg. 2. The defence may apply for an extension, specifying their belief on reasonable grounds that it is not possible to meet the deadline, but that application must be made before the deadline expires (reg. 3). Defence statements were found by Plotnikoff and Woolfson to be rarely served within 14 days ((2001), p.71).

voluntarily in other cases. There are well established duties of disclosure in relation to alibi evidence, and the defence must disclose details including the names and addresses of witnesses.[44] In Plotnikoff and Woolfson's research, defence disclosure was found to be a bare denial of guilt in 54 per cent of all cases surveyed. However, the prosecution only sought further information in eight per cent of cases. There was little advice sought or offered by barristers on the compliance of the defence statement (65 per cent not offered, 90 per cent not sought). The survey also revealed that advocates are rarely briefed to raise defence disclosure failures when prosecuting.

Comments may be made at trial and inferences may be drawn by the tribunal of fact if the defence does not serve a statement (at all or in time) or sets out inconsistent defences.[45] There can be no conviction on an adverse inference alone.[46] Tactically, defence statements are likely to be kept very vague, with only sufficient information to avoid adverse inferences being drawn, leaving some flexibility to amend the version of events without also triggering the adverse inferences.[47] Where an adverse inference is allowed, the judge must warn the jury of the appropriate uses they can make of the evidence.[48]

The most significant objection to the defence disclosure provisions is that they pose a threat to the presumption of innocence,[49] although there has been no direct challenge under Article 6(2) of the ECHR. However, the prosecution will not rely on defence statements as part of the case against the accused.[50] The English courts have acknowledged that there is a need for extreme caution before allowing any adverse inferences to be drawn, particularly where the allegation is that there is an inconsistency between the defence at trial and that made in an advance statement.[51] One problem is that the earlier statement may not be that of the accused but of the defence solicitors. The Court of Appeal has recommended that defendants sign such statements.[52] Further difficulties arise with the privilege against self-incrimination and the waiver of legal privilege if the document is that of the solicitor, these have not been addressed directly.

One further problem with this scheme arises where there are multiple defendants in a single case. If Dl provides information to the prosecution, it is arguable that the prosecution then comes under a duty to disclose that

---

[44] Criminal Procedure Investigations Act 1996, s.74, abolishing s.11 of the Criminal Justice Act 1967 and see now Criminal Procedure Investigations Act 1996, s.5(7).

[45] s.11. On inferences, Plotnikoff and Woolfson found that 43% of judges would initiate legal argument on adverse inferences ((2001), p.72).

[46] s.11.

[47] On the potential uses for the defence statement of disclosure, see S. Thompson, "Defence Statements — Weighting the Scales or Tipping the Balance on a Submission of No Case" [1998] Crim.L.R. 802.

[48] See also *R. v. Burge and Pegg* [1996] 1 Cr.App.R. 163.

[49] See R. Leng, "Losing Sight of the Defendant" [1995] Crim.L.R. 704.

[50] Otherwise than under s.11 or to rebut an alibi, see *Attorney-General's Guidelines* (2000), para. 18. See C. Parry and M.I. Tregilgas-Davey, (1999) S.J. 520.

[51] *R. v. Wheeler* (2000) 164 J.P. 565.

[52] *R. v. Wheeler* (2000) 164 J.P. 565; *R. v. Tibbs* [2000] 2 Cr.App.R. 309 (inconsistent statements). It is not necessary to seek leave to cross examine on such discrepancies, but leave is required before any comment on the inconsistency is made to the jury. Defence statements were found by Plotnikoff and Woolfson to be signed by the accused in 14% of cases in which a statement was made ((2001), p.72). The compulsion to do so is doubted in *R. v. Maidstone Crown Court, ex p. Sullivan* [2002] Crim.L.R. (Aug).

information to D2, even though Dl's statement may be used by D2 against Dl.[53] There is no section 78 discretion to exclude such evidence and there is no common law discretion to exclude evidence as between co-accused.[54] The ECommHR has held that there is no duty to disclose a co-defendant's psychiatric reports not withstanding its potential to assist the co-accused.[55]

(f) Secondary prosecution disclosure

Once the prosecution is in receipt of the defence disclosure, if any, the investigator is under a duty to review the material and alert the prosecutor to any material which might in light of this, reasonably be expected to assist the defence.[56] The disclosure officer must certify that the duties under the Code have been met. The prosecutor must then disclose to the defence any material which might reasonably be expected to assist the accused's defence as disclosed in the defence statement.[57] This is a more objective test than that of "undermine" in the primary disclosure context and is supplemented by obligations under the Code of Practice.[58] If no such material exists, the prosecutor must provide the defence with a written statement to that effect. All secondary disclosure must occur as soon as reasonably practicable.[59] Limitations in respect of PII and statutorily protected material apply here as with primary disclosure.[60]

14–081

There are fewer objections to the secondary disclosure regime since it relies on the more objective assessment of the value of the material. The *Attorney General's Guidelines*[61] emphasise that prosecutors should be "open, alert and responsive" to requests.[62] Secondary disclosure extends to linked material relating to the defence such as forensic reports, identification procedures, etc.[63]

Section 8 of the Criminal Procedure Investigations Act 1996 provides a mechanism for the defence to challenge secondary prosecution disclosure. The defence application must relate to matters alleged not to be disclosed by the prosecution in secondary disclosure. The defence must show reasonable cause to believe the prosecution is withholding material and that there is reasonable cause to believe that the undisclosed material might be reasonably expected to assist the defence case as disclosed. Plotnikoff and Woolfson's survey found that 53 per cent of judges said they would grant section 8 disclosure automatically provided the material was not sensitive.[64]

Throughout the proceedings, the prosecutor has a statutory duty to

---

[53] See s. 3(2).
[54] *Lobban v. The Queen* [1995] 2 Cr.App.R. 573.
[55] See *Hardiman v. U.K.* [1996] E.H.R.L.R. 425; see also *R. v. Reid* [2002] Crim.L.R. 211.
[56] Code, para. 8.2.
[57] s.7.
[58] s.7.
[59] s.13(2).
[60] s.7(5). See also Regulation of Investigatory Powers Act 2000, s. 17.
[61] (2000), paras 39 and 40.
[62] para. 40 of the *Attorney-General's Guidelines* (2000) lists examples of types of material that ought to be disclosed.
[63] *Attorney-General's Guidelines* (2000), para. 40.
[64] p. 73.

review questions of disclosure.[65] If at any time he or she forms the view that material might undermine the prosecution case or reasonably be expected to assist the defence, it *must* be disclosed.

(g) Third party material

14-082 Where the material, which might undermine the prosecution case or assist the defence, is in the possession of a third party (*e.g.* social services or an education department) special problems arise.[66] If the material has been used by the police in the investigation, it will be held by the prosecution and the usual rules of disclosure will apply. The prosecutor is under an obligation to inform relevant agencies,[67] and to make efforts to secure the information, especially if it is likely to undermine the prosecution case or assist the defence.

If material is not within the prosecution possession but the defence is aware of its existence and seeks to obtain it, a witness summons under the Criminal Procedure Attendance of Witnesses Act 1965, ss.2–4 must be sought.[68] The witness summons procedure has been examined by the courts and in *H(L)*[69] the very limited purpose of section 2 and section 97 was noted to be to produce documents "likely to be material evidence".[70] An application must be made in writing specifying why the material is sought and why it is believed to be material evidence. There must be a supporting affidavit.[71] The court, in considering whether to compel the third party to disclose the material will balance the potential damage to confidentiality against the potential benefit to the defendant.[72] Research has found that there are few applications for disclosure of material from agencies but they can be onerous and costly.[73] Mackie and Burrows report that most requests were from social services and education departments. The CPS had little involvement in securing such material but there were many speculative defence applications and many practitioners were unaware of the Criminal Procedure and Investigations Act 1996 regulations. The defence application

---

[65] s.9.

[66] See also D.A.H. Rodwell, "Applications for Third Party Material Where PII is Likely to be Claimed" [1998] Crim.L.R. 332.

[67] See *Attorney General's Guidelines*, para. 29 and see Home Office, *Giving Evidence or Information About Suspected Crimes: Guidance for Departments and Investigations* (H.O., 1997).

[68] Magistrates' Courts Act 1980, s.97, and see Criminal Procedure Investigations Act 1996, s.66. See also the guidance in *Attorney-General's Guidelines* (2000), paras 30–33.

[69] [1997] 1 Cr.App.R. 176 (Reading Crown Court, Sedley J.).

[70] If the defence insist on calling the witness and the department/agency resists disclosure costs may be awarded against the defence.

[71] For comment on the procedural rules see D. Corker, "Third Party Disclosure" (1999) 149 N.L.J. 1006 at 1063. The article reviews tactical approaches to defence disclosure.

[72] Under para. 3.5 of the Criminal Procedure Investigations Act 1996 Code of Practice, the investigator should ask the third party to retain the material and inform the prosecutor of its existence. Material viewed by the officer even though not obtained by him or her must be recorded under para. 4.4 of the Code of Practice See CPS Inspectorate, para. 8.25; Owens, (2001), p. 141.

[73] Mackie and Burrows *A Study of Requests for Disclosure of Evidence to Third Parties in Contested Trials* (HORS 134, 2000).

for third party disclosure must not be a fishing expedition and must state why a summons is required. The obligation on third parties is much less than that on the prosecution.[74]

As elsewhere, the ECHR appears to impose broader obligations of disclosure than domestic law.[75]

(h) The Court of Appeal and disclosure

Challenges to the PII procedure and decisions not to disclose material to the defence are often raised in appeals to the Court of Appeal (Criminal Division). Its obligation is to ensure that the trial was fair and that the conviction is safe. With questions of disclosure this means that the Court of Appeal will be obliged to consider whether the trial judge would have been likely to order disclosure and whether the reasonable jury would have been likely to come to a different conclusion on the evidence disclosed.[76] The European Court has accepted that the Court of Appeal is capable, in such cases, of rectifying errors of disclosure at trial by undertaking its own review of the disputed material.[77] If no opportunity for consideration of the material at the appeal is possible, a breach of Article 6 would occur.[78]   **14–083**

(i) Summary trials[79]

The prosecution duty of primary disclosure is applicable whenever the accused pleads not guilty. Once the primary disclosure has been complied with, the accused may voluntarily provide a defence statement. If a defence statement is provided the prosecutor comes under an obligation to make secondary disclosure.[80]   **14–084**

The *Attorney-General's Guidelines*[81] make it clear that the prosecutor should, in addition to complying with the obligations under the Criminal Procedure and Investigations Act 1996, provide to the defence all evidence upon which the Crown proposes to rely in a summary trial. "Such provisions should allow the accused or their legal advisers sufficient time properly to consider the evidence before it is called. Exceptionally, statements may be withheld for the protection of witnesses or to avoid interference with the course of justice."[82]

---

[74] *R. v. Brushett* [2001] Crim.L.R. 471.
[75] See T. Owen *op. cit.* p.142; *Jespers v. Belgium* (1981) 27 D.R. 61.
[76] *R. v. Botmeh* [2002] Crim.L.R. 209.
[77] *Edwards v. U.K.* (1992) 15 E.H.R.R. 417.
[78] See *Rowe and Davis v. U.K.* (2000) 30 E.H.R.R. 1;*IJL, GMR v. U.K.* [2001] Crim.L.R. 133.
[79] See Corker (1996), Chap. 1.
[80] The statute also allows for adverse comment and inferences to be drawn as in the trial on indictment (above), see s. 11.
[81] (2000), para. 43. *cf. R. v. Stratford Justices, ex p. Imbert* [1999] 2 Cr.App.R. 276, in which the Divisional Court held that Article 6 did not require advance disclosure in the magistrates'. This must be regarded as *obiter*, and wrong. See now para. 42 of the *Attorney-General's Guidelines* (2000). See further Emmerson and Ashworth (2001), para. 14–108.
[82] para. 43.

PII applies in the magistrates' court.[83] If the court orders that the material is to be withheld the accused may apply for a review of that ruling. One practical difficulty of the PII system in the magistrates' court arises because the applications are made *ex parte* and are heard by the bench that will have to adjudicate the issues.[84]

The ECtHR has recognised the importance of disclosure in guaranteeing a fair trial even at the summary trial level.[85] Plotnikoff and Woolfson found that primary disclosure occurred in around two-thirds of summary trials, but that defence statements were very rarely served.[86] In the vast majority of cases primary disclosure was made more than two weeks before trial.[87]

The obligation to reveal the prosecution's case prior to the defendant having indicated a plea in the magistrates' court is more controversial. The Magistrates' Courts (Advance Information) Rules 1985[88] provide that, in the case of offences triable either way, the prosecution must, upon request, provide the defence either with copies of the prosecution witnesses' written statements or with a summary of the facts and matters of which the prosecutor proposes to adduce evidence. The request should be made prior to the plea before venue hearing and complied with as soon as is practicable. The court at the plea before venue hearing must satisfy itself that the accused is aware of the right to advance information. If a request is not complied with, the proceedings must be adjourned unless the court is satisfied that the conduct of the case will not be substantially prejudiced.[89] Prior to the introduction of the rules a wide variety of informal disclosure practices had developed in different areas.[90] There was optimism that such practices would lead to more guilty pleas, fewer elections for trial and other savings.[91] In practice, although improving the fairness of proceedings, the 1985 Rules were not as successful in this regard as hoped, and, indeed, were commonly regarded as increasing delays.[92] The difficulty with the advance information rules is that the defendant does not have access to full advance information before he or she is required to indicate a plea. The accused is seriously disadvantaged because he or she cannot make an informed choice

---

[83] s.14.

[84] See *R. v. South Worcester JJ., ex p. Lilley* [1995] 1 W.L.R. 1595; *R. v. Stipendiary Magistrate for Norfolk* (1997) 161 J.P. 773: R (*on the application of DPP v. Acton Youth Court* [2001] 1 W.L.R. 1828. Section 14 of the Criminal Procedure Investigations Act 1996 does not require the bench to review the PII applications; *cf.* the Crown Court procedure. See also Plotnikoff and Woolfson (2001), p. 84.

[85] *Foucher v. France* (1998) 25 E.H.R.R. 234.

[86] p. 65.

[87] *ibid.*

[88] S.I. 1985 No. 601; *R. v. Haringey JJ., ex p. DPP* [1996] Crim.L.R. 327; criticised by J. Pugh, (1985) 149 J.P.N. 327 and Anon., *ibid.*, p. 499.

[89] Failure to comply will only exceptionally amount to an abuse of process: *King v. Kucharz* (1989) 153 J.P. 336.

[90] See J. Baldwin, *Pre-Trial Justice* (1985) and (1985) 149 J.P.N. 179; F. Feeney, "Advance Disclosure of the Prosecution Case" in D. Moxon (ed.), *Managing Criminal Justice* (1985), Chap. 9 (describing two pilot schemes established by the Home Office); J. Baldwin, [1987] Crim.L.R. 315 and 805, [1987] 151 J.P.N. 409 and (1988) 152 J.P.N. 2596 (on the role of case summaries prepared by the police).

[91] *ibid.*

[92] J. N. Spencer, (1986) 150 J.P.N. 356; J. Morton, (1988) 152 J.P.N. 104.

about a guilty plea, and yet is under pressure to plead at the earliest opportunity to maximise the sentencing discount.[93]

The Divisional Court in *R. v. DPP, ex p. Lee*,[94] concluded that there should be pre-committal disclosure of: previous convictions of a complainant or deceased that could reasonably be expected to assist the defence when applying for bail; material which might allow the defence to make a pre-committal application to stay proceedings for abuse; material which might affect the outcome of the committal or the charges on which the accused was committed; material which would enable the defence to make preparation for trial which would be significantly less effective if disclosure were delayed. The responsible prosecutor must ask what immediate disclosure, justice and fairness required in the circumstances. Difficulties remain because the magistrates lack power to control early disclosure.[95]

(j) Critical review[96]

The Criminal Procedure Investigations Act 1996 has been subjected to close critical examination, and it has recently been claimed that the Act is so defective and leaves so much power in the hands of the police that it presents a real risk of future miscarriages justice.[97] There have been many calls for independent supervision. Sharpe[98] has suggested that reform requires an independent commissioner with the power to review cases and monitor the accuracy of disclosure by the police. Epp considers the possibility of an Investigation Review Department to supervise the investigative role, and a filter hearing at which compliance with the Code would have to be demonstrated. Ede[99] describes the results of national CPS surveys in which police completion of disclosure schedules was identified as inadequate, unreliable and incomplete. The pattern of failure is described as "horrifying". The profession's own ad hoc surveys found over 200 separate examples of non-disclosure. Not only is the pattern of unreliable police scheduling, but the lack of confidence in the system is startling. Seventy per cent of those surveyed reported that "the disclosure provisions of the Criminal Procedure Investigations Act 1996 are unworkable in the interests of justice".[1] The examples of non-disclosure included all varieties of material including

14–085

---

[93] See D. Sunman, "Advancing Disclosure: Can the Rules for Advance Information in the Magistrates' Court be Improved?" [1998] Crim.L.R. 798.

[94] [1999] 1 W.L.R. 1950. In *R v. DPP, ex p. Beaney and King* (1999) unrep., the DC confirmed *ex p. Lee* and emphasised that the prosecutor has a duty to ask whether it is necessary to make inquiries to seek material from the police which would be disclosed. The court also stressed that defence requests for pre-committal disclosure should not be made automatically, but should identify the material and purpose.

[95] See J. Epp, (2000) E. & P. 127.

[96] For recent criticism of the practical operation of the Criminal Procedure Investigations Act 1996 see the special issue of Med. Sci. Law (2000), Vol. 40.

[97] See C. Taylor, "Advance Disclosure: Reflections on the Criminal Procedure Investigations Act 1996" (2001) 40 Howard J.C.J. 114.

[98] (1999) J. Crim. Law 67; [1999] Crim.L.R. 273.

[99] R. Ede, "The CPIA in Practice — The Legal Profession's Experience" (2000) 40 Med. Sci. Law 97.

[1] *ibid.* at 98.

statements by complainants that directly contradicted their earlier statement. The survey also revealed that there was a lack of knowledge on the part of disclosure officers as to what type of material ought to be disclosed as listed and listed on the schedule.[2]

In short, the 1996 Act places too much power in the hands of the police officer who: is potentially biased, will be likely to construct a case against the accused, and has inadequate knowledge of what is likely to be useful for the defence if disclosed.[3] In addition, schedules are not scrutinised with sufficient care by the CPS and the defence ends up with only a partial disclosure. Miscarriages of justice are inevitable. Even the DPP is recorded as noting that there are dangers of innocent people being convicted.[4] The Criminal Cases Review Commission ranks non-disclosure as the third most common reason for referral of cases.[5]

In an empirical study of the operation of the 1996 Act, and the *Attorney General's Guidelines* (2000), Plotnikoff and Woolfson examined 193 prosecutor files and interviewed all those involved in the criminal justice agencies.

As far as the police operation was concerned, they found that the officer in charge of the investigation was very likely to be the disclosure officer with a member of the investigative team performing the task in serious cases. Disturbingly in 21 per cent of police forces, responsibility for "schedule completion" did not lie with the officer in charge nor, in many cases, with any single individual.[6] Barristers, the C.P.S, defence solicitors and justices' clerks complained of police failure to include material on an unused material schedule.[7] The authors also found that there were many instances of undated schedules (37 per cent); that descriptions of items on schedules were "poor" in 73 per cent of cases; that good reasons for sensitivity were given in only 43 per cent of cases; only 14 per cent of forces had special provisions to deal with sensitive material; separate schedules were prepared for multiple defendants cases in only nine per cent of such cases; 43 per cent of disclosure officers thought better training was needed; and 28 per cent thought better guidance on categorisation of unused material was needed.[8]

The Auld Report recommended that there should be a single set of statutory rules imposing a duty on the prosecution to provide its proposed evidence in sufficient time to enable the defence to prepare for trial.[9] The Report also recommended that the Criminal Procedure Investigations Act 1996 scheme should be retained, and that this should be consolidated in a single statute setting out the "duties and rights of all parties involved". The

---

[2] See for graphic examples of failings in disclosure the catalogue in R. Ede, (2000) pp.99–101.

[3] See C. Taylor, (2001) Howard Jnl. 114; J. Epp, (2000) E. & P. 188. Plotnikoff and Woolfson found that 82% of judges, 38% of CPS respondents, 30% of senior police officers, and 27% of disclosure officers felt that it was unrealistic to expect police officers to identify undermining material (p.121). Eighty two per cent of judges had criticised officers on their disclosure role (p. 73). Significant numbers of cases were reported as stayed for abuse of process as a result of disclosure failings. See generally Chap. 12.

[4] (2000) 40 Med. Sci. Law at 101. See, *e.g. R.v.Higgins* [2002] EWCA Crim 336 (failure to disclose inconsistent identification statements).

[5] See *Annual Report 1999–2000*, para. 2.4.

[6] Plotnikoff and Woolfson (2001), p. 20.

[7] *ibid.* p. 26.

[8] See generally Plotnikoff and Woolfson (2001), Chap. 3.

[9] pp. 445, Chap. 10, paras 117–120.

police would retain responsibility for retaining, collating and recording information, but should be subject to spot audits by the CPS or HMIC. The prosecutor would have responsibility for identifying and considering all potentially disclosable material and should have ultimate responsibility for the completeness of the material recorded. The test for disclosability would be the same for primary and secondary disclosure, with the question being whether there is "material which in the prosecutor's opinion might weaken the prosecution case or assist that of the defence". This would be supplemented by automatic disclosure of certain categories of material.

Defence disclosure would remain as at present, but more effective use of defence statements would be encouraged by professional conduct rules and training. A new statutory scheme for third party disclosure should be considered.[10]

I. A PRE-TRIAL REVIEW[11]

There were, for many years, arrangements for a hearing between committal **14–086** and trial designed to enable the judge to make orders that may be necessary to secure the proper and efficient trial of the case in the light of intended plea and other information provided by each side.[12] Rules for such a hearing were promulgated for the Central Criminal Court in 1977,[13] and provided the model for rules adopted at Crown Court centres in other circuits. One limitation on their effectiveness was that such a review did not have the force of law and nothing decided at one was enforceable at the trial.[14] Moreover, nothing said or done at the pre-trial review can be used in evidence at the trial without the consent of the party affected.[15]

The Roskill Committee on Fraud Trials noted that there had been no qualitative or quantitative research into the effects of pre-trial reviews, but had the impression that they operated sensibly and efficiently in many but not all of the cases in which they were conducted.[16] They recommended a more formal procedure for serious fraud cases.[17]

In the Crown Court there are four similar types of pre-trial hearings: plea and directions; statutory pre-trial hearings under the Criminal Procedure and Investigations Act 1996; preparatory hearings for long or complex cases; and preparatory hearings in serious fraud cases.

---

[10] Chap. 10, paras 185–190.
[11] See generally, D. N. Kirk and A.J.J. Woodcock, *Serious Fraud: Investigation and Trial* (2nd ed., 1997), Chap. 13; Archbold (2002), para. 2–102 *et. seq.*
[12] See A. Samuels, (1982) 146 J.P.N. 677 at 686.
[13] See Archbold, *Criminal Pleading, Evidence and Practice* (43rd ed.), para. 4–43. They also appear in Appendix 27 of RCCP I, together with the rules adopted on the North Eastern Circuit.
[14] *per* Watkins L.J. in *R. v. Hutchinson* (1985) 82 Cr.App.R. 51 at 56.
[15] *R. v. Hutchinson* (1985) 82 Cr.App.R. 51.
[16] *Report on Fraud Trials* (HMSO, 1986), pp. 79–86.
[17] *ibid.* pp. 87–113; below, pp. 761–762.

Plea and directions hearings in the Crown Court[18] apply to all cases (other than serious fraud). At a plea and directions hearing (PDH), pleas are taken, and in contested cases "the prosecution and defence will be expected to assist the judge in identifying the key issues, and to provide any additional information required for the proper listing of the case". The advocate briefed in the case should appear in the PDH "whenever practicable". Before the PDH, where the defendant intends to plead guilty to all or part of the indictment, the defence must notify the probation service, the prosecution and the court as soon as this is known. This will enable the defendant to be sentenced at the PDH "whenever possible".[19] In contested cases, prosecution and defence are expected to inform the court of a series of matters including the issues in the case, the number of witnesses, admitted facts, exhibits and schedules, alibis, points of law and evidence expected to arise, the estimated length of the trial, witness and advocate availability. The judge can make "such order or orders as lie within his or her power as appear to be necessary to secure the proper and efficient trial of the case". A standard questionnaire issued by the LCD, agreed if possible between prosecution and defence, should be given to the judge.[20] These hearings are typically short. A pilot study showed their introduction resulted in a reduction in both the number of cases listed and the number of "cracked" trials.[21] The hearing takes place within six weeks of committal (if the accused is on bail) and within four weeks (if in custody). The 1996 Act allows judges to make binding rulings at the PDH or any other preliminary hearing. The rulings may follow an application or be of the judge's own motion, and may relate to any question as to admissibility or any question of law arising.[22] The ruling has binding effect until the case is disposed of — by a jury verdict, or the case being dropped. The judge may discharge or vary the ruling if it is in the interests of justice to do so. Reporting restrictions apply in relation to such rulings.

The Home Office Effectiveness Review identified several problems with the current working of the PDH. These included the fact that things were often done at the last minute; committal papers were commonly served on the defence very late (41 per cent of cases less than seven days before

---

[18] *Practice Direction (Crown Court: Plea and Directions Hearings)* [1995] 1 W.L.R. 1318. This replaced Practice Rules published on October 25, 1994 and is based on Recommendation 92 of the Report of the Working Group on Pre-Trial Issues (1990). The Working Group comprised representatives of the LCD, the Law Officers' Department, the Home Office, the Justices' Clerks Society and the CPS See also the *Practice Direction (Crown Court: Business)* [2001] 1 W.L.R. 1996 on the allocation of PDHs to classes of judge.

[19] Narey (1997), found that only 21% of defence counsel and 9% of prosecutors did so (Chap. 7).

[20] See those in *Archbold* (2002) supplement. Admissions made under para. 10(f) are admissible at trial, but, material provided by the defence in the questionnaire will not normally be referred to at trial, and if the judge is considering using it at trial counsel should be allowed to make representations to the judge: *R. v. Diedrick* [1997] 1 Cr.App.R. 361.

[21] *i.e.* cases listed for trial before a jury but where, often on the day, the trial is abandoned, *e.g.* because the defendant pleads guilty or no evidence is offered. See Home Office, *Improving the Effectiveness of Pre-Trial Hearings in the Crown Court: A Consultation Document* (Cm. 2924, 1995). See also the Review of the *Effectiveness of Plea and Directions Hearings in the Crown Court* (1998), reporting that 41% of judges, 48% of defence counsel, 69% of prosecution counsel, 73% of the CPS and 68% of Court Managers favoured its retention in all cases — para. 8.8.

[22] Criminal Procedure and Investigations Act 1996, s.40.

committal)[23]; prosecution briefs were returned in 42 per cent of cases (CPS figure) and in 37 per cent (prosecution counsel's figures);[24] defence solicitors reported that the brief had been returned in 21 per cent of cases and defence barristers in 18 per cent of cases.[25] To illustrate how substantial this problem is, the review found that in 87 per cent of cases the brief was returned on the day before the PDH or on the day itself.[26] The level of early interaction is also illusory. In 96 per cent of cases there had been no contact between prosecution and defence counsel prior to the PDH.[27] CPS representatives met with counsel before the day of the PDH in only three cases out of 144.[28] In 58 per cent of cases defence counsel had not met with the defendant prior to the PDH.[29] There was also some clear indication that the parties did not comply with the obligations imposed: the defence failed to make timely supply to the court and the prosecution of a full list of the prosecution witnesses they wanted to attend at trial in 77 per cent.[30] Nor was the objective of having the same counsel at the PDH and at the trial attained: 74 per cent of prosecution and 41 per cent of defence counsel changed.[31]

One significant advantage of the PDH is the opportunity for defence lawyers to meet their clients other than in custody. The Auld Report recommends that this opportunity be available via video links.[32] Other advantages include the opportunity for the opposing counsel to confer before the trial; the opportunity for counsel to endorse advice to the instructing solicitors; and the opportunity for all parties to meet to ensure adequate preparation.

The Auld Report suggests that "there are mixed views among the judiciary and practitioners" as to the value of the PDH, with much depending "on the style and vigour of individual Resident Judges ... In the main, they are perfunctory proceedings. As many as 30 to 40 may be listed a day in some of the larger centres, taking the form of a report on progress, good or bad, and the fixing of a trial date or the judge chivvying the parties into getting on with basic matters of preparation and to resolving issues that they may or may not have discussed before then."[33]

Auld's antipathy to the PDH reflects the emphasis in the report on the lawyers taking responsibility.

"In courts at all levels the main players — the police, prosecutors and defence lawyers — should take the primary responsibility for moving the case on. They should concentrate on improving the quality of the preparation for trial rather than trying to compensate for its poor

---

[23] para. 4.3.
[24] Table, p.20.
[25] para. 5.11 173.
[26] *ibid.*
[27] para. 5.30.
[28] para. 5.6.
[29] para. 5.18.
[30] para. 5.38.
[31] para. 6.31.
[32] Chap. 10, para. 260.
[33] *ibid.* para. 209.

quality by indulging in a cumbrous and expensive system of, often unnecessary and counterproductive court hearings."[34]

Preparatory hearings[35]

14–087   The second development has been the introduction of *preparatory hearings*. Initially these were available only in serious fraud cases, but the government proposed that judges should have the power to make binding rulings in *all cases* on any question as to the admissibility of evidence and any other question of law, at any point after the committal of a case to the Crown Court. These would take place at a PDH or another preliminary hearing. At these hearings, the judge, apart from the power to make binding rules on issues of law or evidence, would have other powers to identify, simplify and narrow the issues in dispute.[36] Save in exceptional circumstances, the same judge should conduct both the preparatory hearing and the proceedings in front of the jury.

These powers were introduced by the Criminal Procedure and Investigation Act 1996.[37] The procedures follow very closely those of the fraud trial scheme on which they were based.[38] A preparatory hearing is an opportunity to resolve legal issues before a jury is sworn. An application for a preparatory hearing must be made within 28 days of committal or transfer, and may be made by either party, or the court may, of its own motion, initiate one. The trial judge may make an order for a preparatory hearing at any time prior to the jury being sworn. This type of hearing should be held where the judge believes that the indictment reveals "a case of such complexity or a case whose trial is likely to be of such length that substantial benefits are likely to accrue".[39] The pre-trial hearings under these provisions should not, however, be used in cases of complex fraud.[40] The scope for their use in other cases extends *e.g.* to the complexity of a prosecution under the Official Secrets Act 1989.[41]

The purpose of the hearing is to identify material issues for the jury,[42] assist the jury to understand, expedite proceedings, and help the judge manage the trial. The judge may order the prosecution to prepare its evidence and any explanatory material in such form as appears to the judge likely to aid comprehension by the jury. The judge may also order the prosecution to provide the defence with a case statement of principal facts,

[34] *ibid.* para. 220.
[35] *See* Kirk and Woodcock (1997), Chap. 3.
[36] Cm. 2914, 1995. The RCCJ's proposals took a different form with provision for the exchange of papers sufficient in less complex cases and the possibility of binding rulings confined to preparatory hearings that would take place in a minority of cases: Cm. 2263, pp. 101–109. Professor Zander dissented, favouring the development of PDHs: pp. 223–233.
[37] ss.28–38. See R. Leng, and R. Taylor, *Blackstone's Guide to the CPIA 1996* (1996), Chap. 3.
[38] See Criminal Procedure and Investigations Act 1996 (Preparatory Hearings) Rules 1997 (S.I. 1997 No. 1052).
[39] Criminal Procedure Investigations Act 1996, s.29(1).
[40] See the special provisions for such cases, para. 14-082 below.
[41] *R. v. Shayler*, March 21, 2002, HL.
[42] Criminal Procedure Investigations Act 1996, s.29(1).

witnesses, etc., and may order the defence to disclose the principal issues of its case. Failure to comply with the disclosure orders will result in adverse inferences being capable of being drawn, as in a case where the defence depart from the disclosure at trial. This is subject to the judge giving leave to draw such inferences.[43] The judge will make rulings on points of law and on the admissibility of evidence.[44] The pre-trial rulings made *must* be those within the purposes of the preparatory hearing — identifying material issues for the jury, assisting them to understand the issues, expediting proceedings before them, and helping the judge to manage the trial. Reporting restrictions apply to preparatory hearings.[45]

The Act also introduced the opportunity to appeal from the judge's ruling at the preparatory hearing[46] and this route to securing the opinion of the appellate courts has proved particularly useful in resolving difficult questions of law before the trial commences.[47]

In the magistrates' court the problem of pre-trial difficulties occurs before summary trial, but the number of cases in which a formal pre-trial review is beneficial may be more limited. Prior to implementation of section 48 of the Criminal Law Act 1977, the Nottingham justices' clerks instituted a scheme on their own initiative which was alleged to save money as well as reducing delay and frustration caused by the repeated adjournment of trials where the defence had been caught unprepared by the prosecution.[48] In approximately 20 cases each week, prosecution and defence met at an appointed time for "an informal but candid discussion" without a magistrate present. The benefits of such a scheme were said to include a saving of court time by inducing "realistic" pleas; early notification of points of law that may arise; a reduction in the length of contested cases; confirmation of readiness for trial; and a general tidying-up to ensure that the case can go ahead when listed. About a dozen other courts introduced similar schemes, some short-lived, and with differences in the details of the arrangements.[49] The schemes were indeed perceived to have advantages in promoting the efficient disposal of cases, but there were doubts as to the adequacy of the safeguards for the accused (who in most schemes was not permitted to be present)[50] and the Law Society emphasised that any disclosure of the defence case could only be done with the express or implied authority of the client.[51] The introduction of the requirements for advance disclosure of the prosecution case led to modifications to most although not all of the schemes that

---

[43] Criminal Procedure Investigations Act 1996, s.34(2), (3), (4).

[44] Criminal Procedure Investigations Act 1996, s.31(2).

[45] s.37, names, addresses, etc., can be published. The court may lift restrictions: s.37(3).

[46] ss.35–36. See Criminal Procedure Investigations Act 1996 (Preparatory Hearings) (Interlocutory Appeals) Rules 1997 (S.I. 1997 No. 1700).

[47] See, *e.g. R. v. Z* [2000] 2 A.C. 483; see also *R. v. R, The Independent*, April 10, 2000, where the CA accepted the possibility of considering an appeal under s.35 on questions of excluding evidence under s.78 of PACE.

[48] The scheme is glowingly described and commended in A. Debruslais, "Pre-Trial Disclosure in Magistrates' Courts: Why Wait?" (1982) 146 J.P.N. 384, and was the subject of a study by J. Baldwin: *Pre-Trial Justice* (1985). See for a brief description Auld Report (2001), Chap. 10, para. 206.

[49] See J. Baldwin and F. Feeney, "Defence Disclosure in the Magistrates' Courts" (1986) 49 M.L.R. 593.

[50] Baldwin (1985), Chap. 7.

[51] "Pre-Trial Reviews in the Magistrates' Court: Guidance for Defence Solicitors" (1983) 80 L. S. Gaz. 2330.

remained.[52] The reviews are no longer required as a vehicle for disclosure by the prosecution, and "tend to be held in fewer cases and often are confined to those cases that present particular procedural or evidential difficulties".[53] Surveys suggested that pre-trial Reviews had "much to commend them", particularly by facilitating earlier settlements of cases.[54] The Auld Report criticises the piecemeal development of the system and the absence of any clear process used consistently to deal with pre-trial reviews.[55]

Following the Narey recommendations on reducing delay, the Crime and Disorder Act 1998 introduced early administrative hearings in cases likely to be contested in the Magistrates' Court.[56] These are designed to allow the accused to have explained to him the nature of the proceedings, the implications of the charge, and the legal aid applications.[57] The Act provides for the accused to appear before a single justice or justices' clerk in cases other than those sent to the Crown Court under section 51. The hearing deals with legal aid and other administrative matters.[58]

J. SPECIAL ARRANGEMENTS FOR FRAUD AND CHILD ABUSE CASES

14–088   The pre-trial procedures of the Crown Court discussed in the previous section are generally applicable, but special arrangements exist in respect of serious and complex fraud cases under the Criminal Justice Act 1987.[59] The Act was passed following the Report of the Committee on Fraud Trials, chaired by Lord Roskill,[60] although it differs in some important respects from the Committee's recommendations.[61]

The first modification to orthodox procedures is that the normal transfer procedure can be replaced by a special notice of transfer procedure.[62] This can be put into effect where a person has been charged with an indictable offence, and, in the opinion of the "designated authority"[63] or one of its

[52] J. Baldwin, (1987) 151 J. P. N. 611. The schemes in some areas were discontinued. A survey showed that 43 of 218 magistrates' courts that responded operated a formal PTR system while a further 30 conducted them on an informal or ad hoc basis: A. Mulcahy, I. Brownlee and C. Walker, "An Evaluation of Pre-Trial Reviews in Leeds and Bradford Magistrates' Courts" (1993) 33 H.O.R.B. 10 at 11. See also Brownlee, Mulcahy and Walker, (1994) 158 I P. N. 234 at 250.

[53] J. Baldwin, op. cit. at 613.

[54] See Mulcahy et al., op. cit.

[55] Chap. 10, para. 206.

[56] s.50.

[57] See Narey (1997), Chap. 5, and R. Leng and R. Taylor, and M. Wasik (1998), Chap. 5.

[58] The clerk has no power to remand in custody nor without the parties consent, to impose any bail conditions: s.50(4).

[59] See the annotations to this Act by I. Leigh in Current Law Statutes Annotated 1987. See Archbold (2002), para. 2-89 et seq.

[60] HMSO, 1986. See M. Levi, (1986) 13 J. L. S. 117.

[61] In particular, the government rejected a recommendation that trial by jury be replaced in some cases by a fraud trials tribunal: see text below.

[62] 1987 Act, ss.4–6, as amended, and see Criminal Justice Act 1987 (Preparatory Hearings) Rules 1997 (S.I. 1997 No. 1051). See Kirk and Woodcock, (1997), Chap. 2.

[63] The DPP, the Director of the Serious Fraud Office, the Commissioners of Inland Revenue, the Commissioners of Customs and Excise or the Secretary of State.

officers, the evidence would be sufficient for proceeding for transfer and reveals a case of fraud of such seriousness and complexity that it is appropriate for its management to be taken over by the Crown Court without delay. A "notice of transfer" must be served on the magistrates' court in whose jurisdiction the offence has been charged, not later than the time at which the prosecution would be required to serve a notice of the prosecution case. The court's functions thereupon cease, except in respect of such matters as bail and legal aid.[64] The notice must specify the proposed place of trial,[65] and the charge or charges, and a copy of the notice and (copies of the documents containing the evidence including oral evidence) on which the charge or charges are based must be given to the defendant and to the Crown Court.[66]

A decision to give notice of transfer "shall not be subject to appeal or liable to be questioned in any court". The decision can be challenged by judicial review if one of the preconditions has not been complied with.[67] Furthermore, any person to whom the notice relates may apply to the Crown Court for any charge to be dismissed on the ground that the evidence disclosed would not be sufficient for a jury properly to convict him or her of it.[68] Applications may be made orally or in writing, but oral evidence may only be given with the leave of the judge, and leave is only to be granted if it appears to him or her that the interest of justice so requires.[69] A challenge to section 6 should be made by way of judicial review rather than by voluntary bill application.[70] A discharge has the same effect as a refusal by a magistrates' court to commit for trial, except that no further proceedings on a charge may be brought except by a voluntary bill of indictment.[71] There is no right of appeal at the interlocutory stage against a refusal to dismiss a charge, but judicial review may be granted in exceptional circumstances.[72]

The Criminal Justice Act 1987 also made major modification by introducing formal arrangements for "preparatory hearings" in place of the arrangements that exist for pre-trial reviews in the Crown Court.[73] The aims of such a hearing are (a) identifying issues likely to be material to the jury's verdict; (b) assisting its comprehension of such issues; (c) expediting proceedings before the jury; or (d) assisting the judge's management of the

---

[64] See The Magistrates' Courts (Notice of Transfer) Rules 1988 (S. I. 1988 No. 1701), as amended by the Magistrates' Court (Notice of Transfer) Rules 1997 (S.I. 1997 No. 708).

[65] See *Practice Direction (Crown Court) (Fraud Trials) (No.4)* [1998] 1 W.L.R. 1692.

[66] The Criminal Justice Act 1987 (Notice of Transfer) Regulations 1988 (S. I. 1988 No. 1691) and the Criminal Justice Act 1987 (Notice of Transfer) (Amendment) Regulations 1997 (S.I. 1997 No. 737), Criminal Justice Act 1987 (Notice of Transfer)(Amendment) Regulations 2001 (S.I. 2001 No. 444). On the obligations of the prosecution see *R. v. Cheung* [1999] 8 Archbold News 3.

[67] See *R. v. Salford Magistrates' Court, ex p. Gallagher* [1994] Crim.L.R. 374.

[68] 1987 Act, s.6, substituted by the Criminal Justice Act 1988, s.144; The Criminal Justice Act 1987 (Dismissal of Transferred Charges) Rules 1988 (S. I. 1988 No. 1695). This is the *Galbraith* test; *R. v. X* [1989] Crim.L.R. 726, Henry J., Southwark Crown Court.

[69] Criminal Justice Act 1987 (Dismissal of Transferred Charges) Rules 1988 (S.I. 1988 No. 1695), rr.2 and 3.

[70] *R. v. Snaresbrook Crown Court, ex p. Serious Fraud Office, The Times*, October 26, 1998, *cf. Practice Direction (Voluntary Bill)* [1999] 2 Cr.App.R. 442.

[71] Above, para. 14-067.

[72] *R. v. Central Criminal Court, ex p. Director of the Serious Fraud Office* [1993] 1 W.L.R. 946.

[73] 1987 Act, ss.7–10; Criminal Justice Act 1987 (Preparatory Hearings) Rules 1988 (S.I. 1988 No. 1699).

trial.[74] A judge of the Crown Court may order a preparatory hearing where it appears that substantial benefits are likely to accrue, on the application of prosecution or defence or of his or her own motion. They are not confined to cases which have been the subject of a notice of transfer. The judge has power to order the prosecution to prepare and serve a "case statement" setting out the principal facts, names of witnesses, exhibits and propositions of law that the prosecution will be relying upon. The prosecution should also indicate any documents or other matters that in their view should be agreed by the defendant.[75] On compliance with such an order, the judge may order the defendant to prepare and serve a written statement setting out in general terms the nature of the defence, and to indicate any objections to the case statement, any point of law which he or she wishes to take, and the extent to which documents or other matters specified by the prosecution are agreed.[76] The defendant need not, however, disclose who will give evidence[77] or serve the case statement on a co-defendant.[78] The preparatory hearing is regarded as part of the trial and not as a preliminary to it, and accordingly starts with the arraignment[79] of the defendant. The hearing is conducted by the judge who is to preside at the trial proper,[80] and counsel briefed to appear at the trial should take part in the hearing. The judge has the same powers to order disclosure as exist before the hearing,[81] and there is a general duty on each party to inform the court of any significant matter which might affect the proper and convenient trial of the case. More importantly, the judge may determine any question as to the admissibility of evidence and any other question of law relating to the case.[82] Any such order or ruling will take effect at the trial, subject to two qualifications. First, an appeal against the order or ruling can be taken forthwith to the Court of Appeal (Criminal Division), but only with the leave of the judge or the Court of Appeal.[83] The preparatory hearing can continue meanwhile, but the jury cannot be sworn until after the appeal is determined or

---

[74] As now found in the preparatory hearings (above).

[75] See *Re Case Statement made under section 9 of the Criminal Justice Act 1987* (1993) 97 Cr.App.R. 417.

[76] The judge has no power to prohibit the prosecution from re-interviewing witnesses in the light of the defence statements or to control such further interviews: *R. v. Nadir, R. v. Turner (John)* [1993] 1 W.L.R. 1322.

[77] Except in relation to an alibi or expert evidence: see para. 17-043.

[78] *Re Tariq* [1991] 1 W.L.R. 101.

[79] See para. 17-022.

[80] Other than in exceptional circumstances such as death or illness: *R. v. Southwark Crown Court, ex p. Customs and Excise Commissioners* [1993] 1 W.L.R. 764 and see *R. v. Lord Chancellor, ex p. Maxwell* [1997] 1 W.L.R. 104.

[81] Parties may depart from the case disclosed: s.10, as inserted by the Criminal Procedure Investigations Act 1996, s.72. Such a departure may, with leave, result in adverse comment by the parties and judge.

[82] But only questions that accord with the specified aims of preparatory hearings, not, *e.g.* a question whether proceedings should be dismissed as an abuse of process: *Re Gunawardena, Harbutt and Banks* [1990] 1 W.L.R. 703; *R. v. Hedworth* [19971 1 Cr.App.R. 421. This includes questions as to the construction of the indictment: *R. v. G, S and N* [2002] Crim.L.R. 59; and questions of law, not the exercise of discretion: *R. v. Smithson* [1994] 1 W.L.R. 1052. The court will not allow this procedure to be abused to invite the Court of Appeal to look at any interlocutory matter: *R. v. C* [2002] Crim L.R. 316.

[83] The Criminal Justice Act 1987 (Preparatory Hearings) (Interlocutory Appeals) Rules 1988 (S.I. 1988 No. 1700). See *Case Statements made under section 9 of the Criminal Justice Act 1987* (1993) 97 Cr.App.R.417.

abandoned. Secondly, the order or ruling can be varied or discharged by the judge at the trial.

Under section 9A, the trial judge who has ordered a preparatory hearing may make any order that could be made regarding disclosure at the hearing and may make such an order before the hearing.[84]

The imposition of a requirement that the defence disclose its case at the preparatory hearing was controversial, in that this was required before the prosecution had proved its case.[85] In the 1987 Act's final form, the defendant is only required to set out the nature of the defence in general terms, and need not disclose the names of defence witnesses. Moreover, no part of the defence case revealed at the preparatory hearing can be disclosed at the trial proper, unless either the defendant consents, or there has been a departure from the case as indicated at the hearing. Either party is at liberty to depart from the case disclosed at the hearing, but if there is such a departure, or a failure to comply with a requirement imposed at the hearing, the judge (or any other party, with the leave of the judge) may comment, and "the jury may draw such inference as appears proper".[86]

There are reporting restrictions in respect of applications for dismissal, preparatory hearings and related interlocutory appeals, analogous to those for committal proceedings.[87] It has been argued that decisions of the Court of Appeal have removed the legal argument from the preparatory hearings to informal pre-trial review, thereby rendering them less amenable to review or challenge.[88] The preparatory hearings have, in some cases, become extremely long and onerous proceedings.[89]

(a) Transfer of child cases

The Criminal Justice Act 1991[90] introduced similar arrangements for transfer in respect of offences of a violent or sexual nature where there is a child witness (who may be the victim, or someone who witnessed the commission of the offence). There is no provision for preparatory hearings. Special pre-trial arrangements should be made in relation to young defendants.[91]

14–089

---

[84] As inserted by the Criminal Procedure Investigations Act 1996, Sched 3, para. 4.

[85] I. Leigh, *op. cit.*, n. 60 above, para. 14-082.

[86] 1987 Act, s.10 (1).

[87] *ibid.*, s.11, *cf.* above, para. 14-082. A new s.11 was substituted by the 1996 Act, Sched. 2, para. 6.

[88] See A. Jones, "The Decline and Fall of the Preparatory Hearing" [1996] Crim.L.R. 460. The courts have, it is claimed, defeated one of the primary purposes of providing a route of appeal from preparatory hearings. For a consideration of many practical proposals for improvement, including mandatory meetings of the parties, more structured plea-bargaining, better definition of issues for the jury: J. Fisher, M. Raphael and G. McGregor, (2000) 150 N.L.J. 398 at 435.

[89] In the infamous *Maxwell* case there were over 60 such hearings.

[90] s.53 and Sched. 6, as amended by the Criminal Procedure and Investigations Act 1996, Sched.3, para. 5.

[91] See *Practice Direction (Crown Court: Trial of Children and Young Persons)* [2000] 1 Cr.App.R. 83.

(b) Reform

14–090 The Auld Report has made controversial recommendations to move away from plea and direction hearings and other pre-trial hearings to a system based on better co-operation between the parties with standard timetables for mutual compliance and the possibility of written directions from the court where necessary.[92] National timetables would be drawn up with appropriate lists for specific action to be taken according to the type of case. These would be issued at the early administrative hearing. The parties would have to comply with the disclosure and pre-trial assessment deadlines unless written leave was granted by the court. A critical point in the process will be the "pre-trial assessment date" by which time the parties should have completed and sent to the trial court a "check list showing progress in preparation and as to readiness for trial, and seeking, if appropriate, written directions". Pre-trial hearings would only occur if necessary for the "timely and otherwise efficient" preparation for trial. At pre-trial hearings, the defendant should, if he or she consents, participate from the place of remand if he or she is in custody, via a live-link video. The sanctions for a pre-trial hearing being necessitated without good cause would be for an order as to the payment of a publicly funded defence advocate, and/or to reprimand the advocate publicly, and/or to make costs orders against one or both parties.

This would represent a very significant shift in emphasis, with an expectation that the parties will be eager to resolve issues without judicial direction. The parallels with civil procedure reforms are obvious.[93]

The Auld Report also recommends that as an alternative to jury trial in serious and complex fraud cases, the trial judge should be able to order that the trial occurs without a jury, being heard instead by the judge alone (if the defendant wishes) or by the judge sitting with lay members.[94] Having reviewed the options for such a tribunal proposed by the Roskill Committee, Auld favours the composition of a judge and lay members.[95] The tribunal would be drawn from a panel of experts established and maintained by the Lord Chancellor's Department. The arguments for a jury trial in such cases[96] include: the fundamental institutions of a jury trial; the randomness of jury selection; the jury's ability to determine issues of dishonesty; the absence of evidence of jury incompetence in such cases; the fact of a jury causing matters to be explained more clearly; and, against the jury: the lack of experience in commercial matters; the complexity of the subject matter; the length of the trials (and the consequent unrepresentative nature of the jury); the strain on all parties; the belief that judges and experts would deal with cases more expeditiously; the provision of reasons for the decision with a judge and experts; a reduction in the cost flowing from a more expeditious process.

---

[92] See Chap. 10, paras 204–235. The Report is heavily critical of pre-trial hearings.
[93] But see M. Zander, [2000] Crim.L.R. 419 for a review of crucial differences between civil and criminal procedure.
[94] Chap. 10, para. 192.
[95] Chap. 10, para. 191. See D. Corker, [2002] Crim.L.R. 283.
[96] Chap. 10, pp. 202–203.

K. OBTAINING LEGAL ADVICE AND REPRESENTATION[97]

We stressed the importance of state funded legal assistance and advice in **14-091**
civil proceedings by dealing with it at the beginning of the Civil Procedure
chapter.[98] Its availability may determine whether the case goes ahead at all.
In criminal proceedings it is not relevant to that issue, but must be made
available as a way of ensuring that defendants have what specialist help they
need in the presentation of their defence. Different criteria are obviously
required for the grant and administration of state funded assistance in
criminal cases.[99]

Legal advice and professional assistance may be required by defendants at
two quite different stages. They will initially have to deal with the police and
face interrogation by them, the results of which are likely to have a
considerable influence on their case at trial. They may wish to be advised
how to conduct themselves to the best advantage at this stage of the
procedure, particularly in light of the significance of the answers they
provide or the silence they adopt. As has been noted above, the interview
stage of the pre-trial criminal process is taking on an increasing significance
in the outcome of cases. If charged, the accused will want assistance in the
preparation and presentation of his or her case at and before the trial. The
extent to which lawyers are involved in these two distinct situations is
different. Almost all those charged with serious offences are represented at
trial, many fewer are "represented" during interrogation at the police
station.[1]

The importance of access to effective legal representation as a human
right cannot be ignored.[2] Article 6(3)(b) of the ECHR provides that a
person charged with a criminal offence must be provided with "adequate
time and facilities for the preparation of his defence". In addition, Article
6(3)(c) provides that everyone charged with a criminal offence has the right
to "defend himself in person or through legal assistance of his own choosing
or, if he has not sufficient means to pay for legal assistance, to be given it
free when the interests of justice so require". The legal representation must
be effective, and as such the State will be obliged to intervene in the event of
the legal service provided to an accused being manifestly unsatisfactory.[3] As
Jennings points out, the State's obligation to monitor the effectiveness of
representation will increase with the implementation of the Criminal

---

[97] *Archbold* (2002), Chap. 6, II. See the excellent outline in the guide for clients: *A Practical Guide to the Criminal Defence Service* (2001), *www.legalservices.gov.uk*.
[98] See Chap. 11.
[99] It was only in 1980 that both schemes were put under the aegis of the same government department. Formerly, criminal legal aid was the responsibility of the Home Office.
[1] See the discussion above para. 14-002.
[2] See Ashworth, "Legal Aid, Human Rights and Criminal Justice" in Young and Wall (eds) (1996).
[3] See *Daud v. Portugal* (1998) 30 E.H.R.R. 400; *Artico v. Italy* (1981) 3 E.H.R.R. 1; *Kaminski v. Austria* (1991) 13 E.H.R.R. 36. See generally on the ECHR protection Emmerson and Ashworth (2001), Chap. 14; A. Jennings in K. Starmer *et al.*, (2001), pp.167–169.

Defence Service because of the greater degree of State involvement.[4] The Auld Report also emphasised recently that it was "critical" to the provision of a fair trial that there existed a scheme for just and efficient working of defence lawyers.[5]

In practical terms what the ECHR guarantees mean is that the representative must be appointed early enough to be able to deal effectively with the case.[6] In general, the accused will be able to select his own representative, but this is not an unlimited right,[7] and the State may select an appropriate counsel for him or her irrespective of his wishes, where that is relevant and there are sufficient grounds for doing so.[8] In some circumstances the defendants' right to represent himself or his desire not to be represented can be overridden and appropriate counsel appointed to act on his behalf.[9] Once selected, the lawyer does not have to supply unlimited services to the accused; it is legitimate to have regard to the budgets imposed on him or her by the state funding system.[10]

The other important aspect of the ECHR and the European Court's case law in this area is that it recognises the need for the accused to be offered *free* legal assistance if it is in the interests of justice to do so.[11] There is not an unfettered right to "legal aid", but in determining whether a case is one in which it is in the interests of justice to require assistance, the European Court has adopted a strict stance.[12]

1. Legal Advice at the Police Station

14–092 As we have seen, the Police and Criminal Evidence Act 1984 strengthens the right of those being interviewed by the police to have access to legal advice, and the courts have emphasised the importance of these rights in excluding evidence of confessions obtained in breach of them.[13]

The duty solicitor advice scheme[14] can be used for the purpose of securing the services of a solicitor at the police station.[15] The suspect can of course rely on his or her own private legal adviser. Alternatively, he or she can rely on a duty solicitor who must, under the new system, be accredited with the

---

[4] *ibid.* p. 168.
[5] Chap. 10, pp.400–404.
[6] *X and Y v. Austria* (1978) D.R. 160.
[7] See *R. v. Mills* [1997] 2 Cr.App.R. 206; *Goddi v. Italy* (1984) 6 E.H.R.R. 457.
[8] See *Croissant v. Germany* (1992) 16 E.H.R.R. 135, para. 129.
[9] See ss.34–36 of the Youth Justice and Criminal Evidence Act 1999, discussed below Chap. 17, para. 17-060 and *Croissant; Imbroscia v. Switzerland* (1994) 17 E.H.R.R. 441.
[10] See *M v. U.K.* (1984) 36 D.R. 155. See also *Procurator Fiscal, Fort William v. McLean*, August 11, 2000 cited in Emmerson and Ashworth (2001), para. 14–29. See recently *R. v. Oates*, *The Times* April 25, 2002, holding that Article 6(3) does not require legal aid to allow the appellant to renew her appeal against conviction.
[11] *Pakelli v. Germany* (1984) 6 E.H.R.R. 31, Emmerson and Ashworth (2001), para. 14–25.
[12] See Emmerson and Ashworth (2001), para. 14–28 and see *Granger v. U.K.* (1990) 21 E.H.R.R. 469; *Benham v. U.K.* (1996) 22 E.H.R.R. 293.
[13] See above, para. 14-025.
[14] As now amended by the Criminal Defence Service, see the *Defence Service Manual* available from *www.legalservices.gov.uk*. On the history of the provisions see A. Sanders, "Access to Justice in the Police Station: An Elusive Dream" in Young and Wall (eds) (1996).
[15] See above, para. 14-022. This is free of charge irrespective of the suspect's means.

Criminal Defence Service. The Public Defenders scheme which is currently being piloted in six areas will mean that the duty solicitors available may include representatives from the local office of the public salaried defenders.[16] The Criminal Defence Service has implemented "Police Station Payment Schemes" and the General Criminal Contract to regulate the provision of services by "crime suppliers"(!), i.e. solicitors.[17] If the suspect selects his own private representative, it will be permissible for advice to be provided at the station by a solicitor, or a probationary representative.[18]

In theory, the accused has the opportunity, the means and the motive to ensure that he or she is properly advised on the most advantageous way to conduct him- or herself at the police station. In practice, only a minority of accused persons receive that advice. We have already examined the detail of the provision of legal advice in the police station and its difficulties.[19]

2. ADVICE AND REPRESENTATION AFTER CHARGE

From 1988 the Legal Aid Act 1988, which had established the Legal Aid Board, had governed the provision of "legal aid".[20] These have now been abolished and replaced under the Access to Justice Act 1999, with the Legal Services Commission which manages the Community Legal Service and the Criminal Defence Service.   **14–093**

The criticisms of the Legal Aid scheme and its replacement have been examined in detail in Chapter 10 above.[21] In short, these were, in the criminal context that the means test for eligibility rendered the scheme unfair and that it was in general an inefficient scheme prone to delay and abuse.[22] The Legal Aid bill had spiralled. In 1992–93 the cost was £507 million and in 1997–98 that had grown to £733 million. In the Crown Court, spending went from £221 million in 1992–93 to £349 million in 1997–98.[23] The framework under which the fees were paid was outdated and inflexible with inappropriately financed incentives. These encouraged delay and adjournments.[24] The costs were extremely high in the Crown Court, with 94

---

[16] See above Chap. 10 for a discussion of the implementation of the scheme and the concerns about effective monitoring during the pilot as well as the anxiety about the use of publicly employed lawyers.

[17] See generally LSC, *Criminal Defence Service: Duty Solicitor Arrangements* (2001).

[18] Although a probationary representative should not advise on indictable only offences.

[19] Above Chap. 10.

[20] Access to Justice Act 1999 (Commencement No. 3, Transitional Provisions and Savings) Order 2000 (S.I. 2000 No. 774) bringing into force, Access to Justice Act 1999, s.l, on April 1, 2000. On the legal aid system see J. Parry, *Legal Aid in Criminal Proceedings* (1996); R. Young and D. Wall, (eds), *Access to Criminal Justice* (1996) in which the authors and contributors analyse the development and operation of the system in the broad criminal justice context.

[21] See also L. Bridges, " The Reform of Criminal Legal Aid" in Young and Wall (eds) (1996); F.G. Davies, (1998) 162 J.P.N. 376.

[22] See the discussion above in Chap. 10. See also T. Goriely, "The Development of Criminal Legal Aid in England and Wales" in Young and Wall (eds) (1996).

[23] See *Modernising Justice*, para. 6.6. On the statistics provided, see A. Tunkel, (1997) 147 N.L.J. 1020, see also LCD, *Striking the Balance* (1996).

[24] *Modernising Justice*, para. 6.7.

per cent of defendants making no contribution.[25] The system of means testing for contributions costs almost as much to administer as it recouped. The public had lost confidence in the system with so much being spent on some very high cost cases. The government sought to introduce a system that was better focused on quality and value for money,[26] and which would keep to a minimum delay.[27]

The primary vehicle for the provision of publicly funded legal assistance in criminal cases is the Criminal Defence Service, as established under section 12 of the Access to Justice Act 1999. In short, the essential differences from the legal aid scheme are that only those solicitors accredited with the CDS are eligible to conduct state funded work.[28]

The CDS has as its objective "to ensure that people suspected or accused of a crime have access to advice, assistance and representation, as the interests of justice require".[29] From the commencement, on April 2, 2001, solicitors must hold a "General Criminal Contract" if they are to carry out any criminal defence work funded by the Legal Services Commission.[30] The implementation of the new scheme has been extremely problematic, with considerable resentment from the legal profession. One week before the scheme was due to take effect, only around 100 of the 3,400 firms who undertook criminal legal aid work had signed up for the new scheme.[31]

The accredited firms are subject to a Code of Conduct[32] and have to meet quality standards and will be subject to monitoring to ensure that standards are maintained. The Code outlines *inter alia* duties on anti-discrimination, duties to protect clients, and duties to the court.[33] Contracts are standardised and only in very high cost cases will an individual contract be capable of being granted to the accredited solicitors so that funding for that case can occur on an individual basis specific to its needs.

The CDS scheme applies only in criminal proceedings.[34] The accused still has a right to select his own private lawyer, or to rely on the duty schemes — there is a duty solicitor scheme for the police station and one for the

---

[25] *Modernising Justice*, para. 6.8.

[26] *ibid.* para. 6.11.

[27] See also the recommendations in Narey (1997), Chap. 4, noting that 50% of adjournments were due to legal aid issues.

[28] Access to Justice Act 1999, s,12(4).

[29] See the LCD paper, *CDS: Establishing a Salaried Defence Service and Draft Code of Conduct for Salaried Defenders Employed by the Legal Services Commission* (2000) and response by the Legal Services Consultative Panel. Both are available from *www.legalservices.gov.uk*.

[30] In an effort to ensure quality all firms are audited against the contract to ensure they continue to meet quality assurance standards.

[31] See J. Morton, (2001) 151 N.L.J. 325; and comments at (2000) S.J. 986; (2001) S.J. 198.

[32] In accordance with the Access to Justice Act 1999, s.16.

[33] See *www.hmso.gov.uk/conduct.htm*.

[34] See also the Criminal Defence Service (General) (No. 2) Regulations 2001 (S.I. 2001 No. 1437), reg. 3(2). Comparison can be made with s.19(5) of the Legal Aid Act 1988 which defined "criminal proceedings" as including "proceedings for dealing with an offender for an offence or in respect of a sentence". In *R. v. Recorder of Liverpool, ex p. McCann, The Times*, May 4, 1999, DC, it was held that this covered an application for the removal of a driving disqualification, but not drug cash seizures: *R. v. Crawley JJ., ex p. Ohakwe, The Times*, May 26, 1994, DC; nor are proceedings in relation to recognisance of bail surety: *R. v. Chief Clerk of Maidstone Crown Court, ex p. Clark* [1995] 2 Cr.App.R. 617.

magistrates' court. Only Criminal Defence Service accredited firms will be able to offer services under the duty scheme.[35]

We can only offer an outline of the scheme here, but the following diagram provides an effective illustration of the new structure.

(a) Criminal Defence Service

The Choice Process

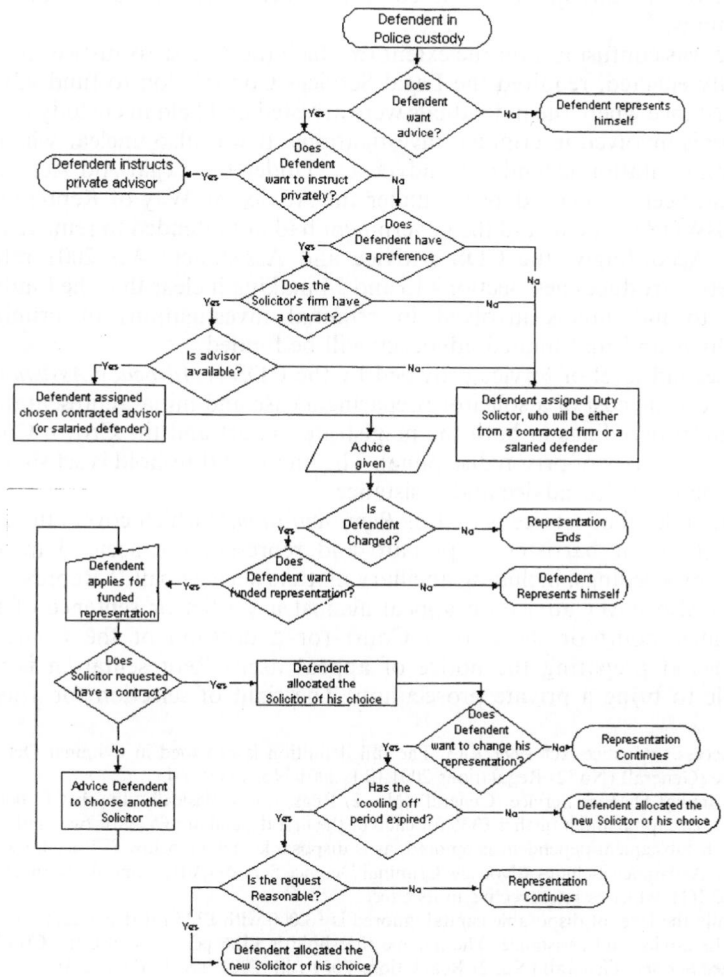

[35] See Access to Justice Act 1999, s.15 and Criminal Defence Service (General) (No. 2) Regulations 2001 (S.I. 2001 No. 1437), r. 11.

The CDS operates three levels of service. *Advice and Assistance* covers general help from a solicitor including giving general advice, writing letters, negotiating, getting a barrister's opinion and preparing a written case.[36] Financial eligibility for advice and assistance is calculated on the basis that certain individuals are automatically eligible — those on job seeker's allowance, income support, etc. — and for others the calculation turns on their income and capital.[37] The Commission funds such advice and assistance as it considers appropriate: (a) for individuals who are arrested and held in custody at a police station or other premises, and (b) in prescribed circumstances, for other individuals who are involved in investigations which may lead to criminal proceedings, or are before a court or other body in such proceedings, or have been the subject of such proceedings.[38]

There was confusion over the extent to which the Access to Justice Act, as originally enacted, required the Legal Services Commission to fund advice and assistance where the individuals were arrested and held in custody or for individuals involved in criminal investigations. It was also unclear whether legal representation extended to advocacy. Under the Legal Aid Act 1988 there had been funded advocacy under the Advice by Way of Representation (ABWOR) system, and the government had not intended to remove this facility. Accordingly, the CDS (Advice and Assistance) Act 2001 retrospectively introduces new sections 13 and 14 making it clear that the funding applies to individuals involved in criminal investigations or criminal proceedings and that limited advocacy will be funded.

The second level of service provided by the CDS is *Advocacy Assistance*. This covers the cost of a solicitor preparing a case and initial representation in certain proceedings in both the magistrates' court and the Crown Court (as well as in cases of prison discipline). The financial threshold is set slightly higher than that for advice and assistance.[39]

The final level of service is that of *Representation*,[40] which covers the cost of a solicitor or barrister to prepare and represent the accused in any criminal proceedings, including ancillary matters such as bail.[41] Representation can also cover advice on appeal against a verdict or sentence of the magistrates' court or the Crown Court (or a decision of the Court of Appeal) and preparing the notice of appeal itself. Representation is not available to bring a private prosecution. The right of selection for a legal

---

[36] See Access to Justice Act 1999, s.13. The full definition is provided in Criminal Defence Service (General) (No. 2) Regulations 2001 (S.I. 2001 No. 1437), r.4.

[37] See Criminal Defence Service (General) (No. 2) Regs, r.5(5). Basically, the first £1,000 of disposable capital and a further £335 for each of the first dependant; £535 for two, and £100 for each subsequent dependent is ignored, as is disposable income below £87 per week.

[38] s.13(1). Assistance includes advocacy: Criminal Defence Service (Advice and Assistance) Act 2001, s.1(1), which is retrospective in its effect.

[39] Basically the level of disposable capital ignored is £3,000 with £335 for dependants etc., as with the advice and assistance. The income threshold is £186 per week. See the Criminal Defence Service (General) (No. 2) Regulations 2001 (S.I. 2001 No. 1437), r. 5(3).

[40] Access to Justice Act 1999, s.14. The Criminal Defence Service (Funding)(Amendment No. 3) Order 2001 (S.I. 2001 No. 3341) and the Criminal Defence Service (Funding)(Amendment) Order 2002 (S.I. 2002 No. 714) replace the Legal Aid in Criminal Cases and Care Proceedings (Costs) Regulations 1989 and apply to representation work. For an explanation of their operation see A. Hall, [2001] Archbold News, September.

[41] See generally the Criminal Defence Service (General) (No 2) Regulations 2001 (S.I. No. 1437).

representative is not unlimited. There are certain limitations on the exercise, which prescribe the type and number of representatives that may be selected.[42]

The accused makes an application for representation (orally or in writing),[43] and a representation order is made by the court if the court feels that it is in the "interests of justice" that the accused should be represented. The test echoes that found in the ECHR cases (above). The interests of justice require the court to take into account (a) whether the accused would be at risk of losing his liberty, or livelihood or suffering serious damage to his reputation[44]; (b) whether the case will involve consideration of a substantial question of law; (c) whether the individual may be unable to understand the proceedings or to state his own case; (d) whether the case will involve tracing, interviewing, or expert cross-examination of witnesses and whether it is in the interests of another person that the accused be represented.[45]

If the representation order is refused, the applicant must receive reasons for the decision and a review of that decision may be requested.[46] If the magistrates refuse to allow representation, a further application may be made to the Crown Court. If the accused makes the application in the Crown Court this requires a statement of the accused's means. The form is returned before the PDH or preliminary hearing. If the accused fails to return the form a Recovery of Defence Costs Order (RDCO) could be made against him or her. The solicitor has a duty to report any suspicions as to the accuracy of the information the accused provides on the form.[47] Section 15(1) of the Access to Justice Act 1999 provides that an individual who has been granted a right to representation may select any representative or representatives willing to act for him; and, where he does so, the Commission is obliged to fund that representation.[48]

The degree of choice of legal representation that should be available for the accused has been a controversial issue.[49] The ECHR, as noted above, supports the right to choose, but does not give an unfettered right. The CDS scheme allows for the accused to choose from the accredited representatives, but there is a strong expectation of continued representation so that one solicitor will follow the case from start to finish. In particular, there is a

---

[42] See the Access to Justice Act 1999, s.15(2).

[43] Form A. Representation applications can be heard by a single magistrate: Criminal Defence Service (General) Regulations 2001 (S.I. 2001 No. 1437), Sched. 3, para. 2(6), and regs 8–11.

[44] See under previous law, *R. v. Liverpool City Magistrates Court, ex p. McGhee* [1993] Crim.L.R. 609 (community service order is not a deprivation of liberty); and see *R. v. Highgate JJ., ex p. Lewis* [1977] Crim.L.R. 611; *R. Chester Magistrates, ex p. Ball* (1999) 163 J.P. 757 (the court failed to take reputation into account).

[45] Access to Justice Act 1999, Sched. 3, para. 5(2). See also *R. v. Scunthorpe Justices, ex p. S, The Times*, March 5, 1998 (16-year-old not able to conduct cross-examination of police officer).

[46] See Criminal Defence Service (General) (No. 2) Regulations 2001 (S.I. 2001 No. 1437), rr.8,9 and Criminal Defence Service (Representation Order Appeals) Regs 2001 (S.I. 2001 No. 1168). See comment at (2001) 151 N.L.J. 1395 and see generally the old "Widgery criteria" *Legal Aid in Criminal Proceedings* (1966) Cmnd. 2934, para. 180.

[47] r.24.

[48] See further Criminal Defence Service (General) (No. 2) Regulations 2001 (S.I. 2001 No. 1437), regs 11–187,19–24 and dealing with the level of, and change of, representation.

[49] See the LCD Paper, *CDS: Choice of Representation* (2000) and J. Epp and D. O'Brien, (2000) 150 N.L.J. 1664.

desire to prevent the tactic of the accused dismissing his legal team on the eve of the trial thereby securing a further delay in the proceedings.[50] It is necessary to strike the balance between the defendant's right to choose and to feel confident in the legal representation he or she receives and the need to ensure efficiency in the system.[51]

(b) Recovery of defence costs orders (RDCOs)[52]

14–095 The Crown Court may order that costs are recovered from a defendant who has been granted representation. The court will assess whether it is reasonable to impose such an order having regard to all the circumstances including the defendant's means.[53] An RDCO can be made for the full amount of the costs incurred in representing the accused, but is not available if the accused has only appeared in the magistrates' court, is committed for sentence, is appealing to the Crown Court against sentence, or, other than in exceptional circumstances, has been acquitted. The RDCO is not to be regarded as part of the sentence and is not dependent on a conviction.

In addition, if the accused fails to complete the representation forms (Form B), the court will refer the matter to the Special Investigations Unit of the Legal Services Commission. The SIU reports its findings to the court. It is an offence knowingly to provide false information.[54] The judge will also request that the solicitor provides an estimate of costs.[55] On the basis of this information the judge can make an RDCO requiring the accused to pay (to the Legal Services Commission) a specific sum up to the total costs. The judge can also order that the accused's assets are frozen.[56] As an important safeguard, any information provided to the Commission cannot be disclosed except in accordance with the specific statutory criteria.[57]

(c) Very high costs cases

14–096 Those cases which are likely to exceed 25 days at trial, or where the defence

---

[50] See further the LCD Consultation Paper, *Establishing a Salaried Defence Service and Draft Code of Conduct for Salaried Defenders Employed by the LSC* (2000) and Access to Justice Act 1999, s.15(2).

[51] See the disturbing suggestion in Narey (1997), Chap. 4, that where there is a conflict, "choice must come second to speed".

[52] Defence costs are recovered under the RDCO scheme set up under section 17 of the Access to Justice Act 1999. See also the CDS (Recovery of Defence Costs Orders) Regulations Order 2001 (S.I. 2001 No. 856); and the CDS (Recovery of Defence Costs Orders) (Amendment) Regulations 2002 (S.I. 2002 No. 713).

[53] *ibid.* r.11 and 12.

[54] s.21.

[55] CDS (Recovery of Defence Costs Orders) Regulations Order 2001 (S.I. 2001 No. 856), r.10

[56] CDS (Recovery of Defence Costs Orders) Regulations Order 2001 (S.I. 2001 No. 856), r.15. Generally, no order for recovery will be made against the first £3,000 of D's capital and the first £100,000 of capital in his main dwelling is also ignored. The income of the accused is only taken into account if it exceeds gross £24,000 per annum. (CDS (Recovery of Defence Costs Orders) Regulations Order 2001 (S.I. 2001 No. 856), r.9.)

[57] Access to Justice Act 1999, s.20.

will be likely to cost in excess of £150,000 for one defendant are governed by a separate set of rules.[58] The Legal Services Commission has established a Criminal High Cost Cases Unit to manage the VHCC and arrange individual contracts.[59] If a solicitor is instructed in what he or she believes is likely to be such a case, the solicitor notifies the CHCC Unit. The Unit then assess the cases and decides whether to enter a VHCC contract on that specific case,[60] and if so, a template for the solicitor to comply with is issued and kept under review. The Unit agrees the correct band of funding and assigns a manager to the individual case.

(d) The Public Defence Service[61]

As the next phase of its reform of the legal aid system, the government has **14–097** introduced the "Public Defender". The LCD in its Consultation Paper[62] developed the idea that was introduced in the White Paper *Modernising Justice*, in which the government claimed that properly funded salaried defenders can be more cost-effective and provide a better service than lawyers in private practice.[63] It was felt that a system with Public Defenders would be cheaper, easier to monitor, more flexible and because it lacked a profit motive would be more focused on securing justice. Criticisms of the public defenders scheme are that it lacks independence from the government, and that it is perceived as such, that there will be a lack of independence of mind from the lawyers employed and that there is a greater risk of improper interference by the State. There is also the danger that it will be under-funded and overloaded with work and that it will fail to secure high quality staff. Furthermore, it could lead to less choice for the accused, by reducing access to the private sector.

The service exists alongside the private providers, reflecting the governments' aim to optimise the balance between the public and private sectors. If it is to gain acceptance, the salaried defence service — the Public Defender Service as it has become known — will have to maintain the highest standards of quality and independence in its work. Public defenders will have a separate career structure and the service will employ lawyers at

---

[58] See Criminal Defence Service (General) (No. 2) Regulations 2001 (S.I. 2001 No. 1437), r.2 and Criminal Defence Service (Choice in Very High Cost Criminal Cases) Regulations 2001 (S.I. 2001 No. 1169).

[59] The unit also has responsibility for the Serious Fraud Panel. See the CDS, *Ensuring Quality and Controlling Cost in Very High Criminal Cases* (1999).

[60] If it is a serious fraud case the solicitor must be accredited as a member of the serious fraud panel.

[61] See above Chap. 8.

[62] See further the LCD Consultation Paper, *Establishing a Salaried Defence Service and Draft Code of Conduct for Salaried Defenders Employed by the LSC* (2000); see also comment at (2000) 150 N.L.J. 923.

[63] The Government reviewed schemes in USA, Canada, Australia and concluded that a mixed scheme with public defenders and private representatives available was the most effective solution. The Canadian research quoted refers to the high quality of the work provided with no effect on the outcomes of cases and the respect and confidence of the profession and the judiciary. See C. Frazer, (2000) 150 N.L.J. 670 casting doubt on the claims about the Canadian experience. See also the response by the Legal Services Consultative Panel (2000) available from the website.

all levels so that those with higher rights of audience will be employed to conduct in-house work. They will all be subject to CDS performance standards. It is hoped to provide access to lawyers from a wide range of backgrounds.

The Public Defenders will be bound by the codes of the profession to which they belong, and also by the terms of a specific Code of Practice for the Public Defender, which will seek to emphasise their independence from government. The Code of Conduct expressly requires public defenders not to put clients under pressure to plead guilty, and in particular, not to advise a client to plead guilty unless satisfied that the prosecution can discharge the burden of proof.[64] In addition, the Code emphasises that the defender is to do his or her utmost, consistent with the lawyer's duty to the court, to promote and work for the best interests of the client. [65] It also specifies that the defender is to act independently and not to allow their independence to be compromised by clients, prosecuting authorities, courts or others.[66] As a further safeguard of independence, the Legal Services Commission will not disclose to the prosecution material in connection with the defence that will be of use to the prosecution.[67]

The first four pilot offices are in Birmingham, Liverpool, Middlesborough and Swansea. At the time of writing (March 2002) it is too early to assess the impact of the system. It is vital that the service gets off to a better start than did the CPS, with adequate funding, high calibre staff and above all, adequate mechanisms to ensure independence and maintain public confidence.

L. EVALUATIONS

14–098 As a conclusion to this chapter it is valuable to place some of the detailed analysis of the complex legal structure in a broader theoretical context.

1. THEORETICAL APPROACHES

14–099 Major official reviews in the area of criminal procedure were undertaken by the Royal Commission on Criminal Procedure[68] (RCCP), the Royal Commission on Criminal Justice[69] (RCCJ) and the Auld Review. The RCCP's term of reference were to examine whether changes were needed in

---

[64] See the concerns expressed with the original code in the *Legal Services Commission Consultative Committee Response to the LCD Consultation Paper on Salaried Defence Service* (2000), para. 1.

[65] para. 2.

[66] para. 3.2.

[67] See the LSC (Disclosure of Information) (Amendment) Regulations 2001.

[68] *The Investigation and Prosecution of Criminal Offences in England and Wales: The Law and Procedure* (Cmnd. 8092–1, 1981). Twelve Research Studies were commissioned.

[69] Report (Cm. 2263, 1993). The extensive literature on the RCCJ includes the following: M.McConville and L.Bridges (eds), *Criminal Justice in Crisis* (1994); S. Field and P. Thomas (eds), "Justice and Efficiency? The Royal Commission on Criminal Justice" (1994) 21 J.L.S. 1–164 (special issue); Symposium, [1993] Crim.L.R. 808 *et seq.*; L. Bridges and M. McConville, (1994) 57 M.L.R. 75; M. Zander, *ibid.* p. 264; reply by Bridges and McConville, *ibid.* p. 267; R. Young and A. Sanders, (1994) 14 O.J.L.S. 435.

England and Wales, in:

"(i) the powers and duties of the police in respect of the investigation of criminal offences and the right and duties of suspects and accused persons, including the means by which these are secured;
(ii) the process of and responsibility for the prosecution of criminal offences; and
(iii) such other features of criminal procedure and evidence as relate to the above".

The RCCJ's terms of reference were:

"to examine the effectiveness of the criminal justice system in England and Wales in securing the conviction of those guilty of criminal offences and the acquittal of those who are innocent, having regard to the efficient use of resources"

and in particular to consider whether changes were needed in eight specific areas.[70]

The Auld Review was established to report on the

"practices and procedures of, and the rules of evidence applied by, the criminal courts at every level, with a view to ensuring that they deliver justice fairly, by streamlining all their processes, increasing their efficiency and strengthening the effectiveness of their relationships with others across the whole of the criminal justice system, and having regard to the interests of all parties including victims and witnesses, thereby promoting public confidence in the rule of law".[71]

As we have seen, many features of pre-trial criminal procedure and practice flow from the recommendations of the RCCP and RCCJ bodies although, often significantly, modified by the government. The same can be expected from Auld. The RCCP Report led to the Police and Criminal Evidence Act 1984 and the Prosecution of Offences Act 1985. The RCCJ Report led to changes introduced by the Criminal Justice and Public Order Act 1994, the Criminal Appeal Act 1995,[72] and the Criminal Procedure and Investigations Act 1996. At the same time many changes have been introduced simply as a matter of government policy.[73] The approach of adopting reform following reviews provides the opportunity for fundamental theoretical issues to be addressed in a way that altering criminal procedure as a basic matter of government policy does not. Whether the

---

[70] (i) the conduct and supervision of police investigations; (ii) the role of the prosecutor and the disclosure of material to the defence; (iii) the role of experts; (iv) the arrangements for the defence of accused persons, access to legal advice and expert evidence; (v) the "right to silence"; (vi) the powers of the court in directing proceedings and the courts' duty in considering evidence; (vii) the role of the Court of Appeal; and (viii) arrangements for considering and investigating allegations of miscarriages of justice.

[71] Report, (2001), para. 1.

[72] See below, Chap. 18.

[73] See, e.g. changes in sentencing, below, para. 17-082, and in the organisation of the police and the courts, e.g. above, pp. 60–63 (magistrates' courts).

opportunity is seized is a separate matter.

The reform of criminal procedure is often explained in terms of striking a "balance", although this concept of balancing is used without adequate elaboration.

(a) The "fundamental balance" in the criminal process

14–100 In formulating its recommendations – in respect of the matters within its terms of reference — the RCCP was required to have regard "both to the interests of the community in bringing offenders to justice and to the rights and liberties of persons suspected of crime", and to take into account the "need for the efficient and economical use of resources".

The RCCP regarded the task of reviewing the criminal process with what it termed the "fundamental balance" between the interests of the community, and the rights and liberties of individual citizens as the "central challenge" which faced it.[74] Previous official reports on aspects of criminal justice[75] had made no, or only passing, reference to the concept, although the debate that followed the Eleventh Report of the Criminal Law Revision Committee had revealed the main schools of thought on the nature, and role of, a possible balance in pre-trial criminal procedure. The most controversial of the recommendations in the Eleventh Report involved the restriction of the suspect's right of silence when interrogated by the police. The supporters of the change took a utilitarian approach: "the law should be such as will secure as far as possible that the result of the trial is the right one".[76] The many improvements in criminal law, procedure and trial over the previous century justified the removal of safeguards that appeared to unduly favour the defence. Leading opponents took a libertarian stance, and argued that:

" ... in reality the right of silence formed a vital issue in the whole constitutional relationship in a free society between the individual and the state. ... Each step in the criminal process, ... including the right of silence, must be judged not only as a means to the goal of reaching a reliable verdict, but also, and equally important, for its coherence with a liberal understanding of how free persons, including suspects in the police station, at all stages ought to be treated."[77]

A third, distinct, approach was to regard some, although not necessarily all, of the individual's rights in pre-trial procedure as negotiable, provided that appropriate checks and safeguards were introduced. Thus a minority of the Criminal Law Revision Committee was prepared to modify the right of silence only if statutory provision was made for the use of tape recorders.[78] In general terms it was the third approach that the RCCP purported to

---

[74] RCCP Rep., p. 4.
[75] Royal Commission on Police Powers and Procedure (Cmd. 3297, 1929); Royal Commission on the Police (Cmnd. 1728, 1962); Eleventh Report of the Criminal Law Revision Committee on Evidence (General) (Cmnd. 4991, 1972).
[76] Eleventh Report, p. 15.
[77] RCCP Rep., pp. 9, 10.
[78] *ibid.* pp. 10, 11.

adopt, although not simply as a series of compromises between the other main schools of thought. Some commentators on the Report took the view that an appropriate balance had not been struck[79]; others were less sceptical.[80]

By contrast with the RCCP, the Royal Commission on Criminal Justice did not even attempt to explore theoretical issues in any depth. The approach of the RCCJ was to examine the separate elements set out in the terms of reference,[81] and make such detailed, practical recommendations as they thought appropriate. They noted that it could be argued that "there is a potential conflict between the interests of justice on the one hand and the requirement of fair and reasonable treatment for everyone involved, suspects and defendants included, on the other".[82]

They accepted that these would not be reconcilable throughout the system in the eyes of all those involved. However,

"we do believe that the fairer the treatment which all the parties receive at the hands of the system the more likely it is that the jury's verdict, or where appropriate the subsequent decision of the Court of Appeal, will be correct."[83]

This discussion is both curious and revealing. The Commission's conception of the "interests of justice" was not explained, but the contrast drawn with the fair treatment of individuals suggests that it is "the conviction of those guilty of criminal offences and the acquittal of those who are innocent" (taking words from the terms of reference). This suggests a return to utilitarianism. The possibility that an individual's right to fair treatment might itself be a fundamental value that requires respect in its own terms, irrespective of whether it promotes or diminishes the "correctness" of verdicts is not recognised or explored. Ultimately the Commission attempted to by-pass the issue with its claim that

"when taken as a whole our recommendations serve the interests of justice without diminishing the individual's right to fair and reasonable treatment".[84]

However, the cautionary "when taken as a whole" suggests that the Commission accepted that some particular recommendations might be prejudicial to individual rights.

Both the RCCJ's refusal to address theoretical issues directly, and the implicit theoretical approach that was discerned from its recommendations

---

[79] *e.g..* D. McBarnet, [1981] Crim.L.R. 445 (noting the wider powers to be given to the police, the removal of traditional safeguards, the weakness and vagueness of the safeguards proposed in their place, and that the research was heavily dependent on police sources, and even then selectively ignored); M. McConville and J. Baldwin, (1982) 10 Int. Jo. Sociology of Law 287.

[80] Albeit with particular reservations: L. H. Leigh, (1981) 44 M.L.R. 296; B. Smythe, [1981] P.L. 184 at 481.

[81] Above, para. 14-091.

[82] Cm. 2263, p. 8.

[83] *ibid.*

[84] *ibid.*

were the subject of much adverse comment.[85] Commentators criticised the RCCJ's elevation of the resources issue to "coequal status" with the traditional concerns of convicting the guilty and acquitting the innocent[86] and its

> "uncritical acceptance of the theory of criminal justice implicit in a liberal reading of its terms of reference — terms which place efficiency on all fours with justice, and which construct the conviction of the innocent as no more important than the acquittal of the guilty".[87]

In the event, its recommendations seemed mostly to be directed at improvements in the efficient management of the system at the expense of the presumption of innocence. Most had

> "no bearing whatsoever on the cultural and structural features of the system which led to miscarriages of justice, and some of those which do are likely to exacerbate those underlying causes rather than the reverse".[88]

Lord Justice Auld in his Review also recognised the need for a "balance of some sort to be struck between the community's interest in providing an efficient and economic system for administering justice, bearing in mind also its many other commitments, and the manner of fair trial that it provides for offences of different seriousness".[89]

The greater and more explicit emphasis in the Auld Review on the efficiency of the system further complicates the idea that there can be any true objectivity in the exercise of "balance" in this context. In particular, the community's interest is recognised to comprise separate interests in protection against crime and also in the swift administration of justice. Although the concept of efficiency in the process might at first appear neutral, in reality, introducing procedures designed to streamline the system and reduce delay is seldom an exercise in which the defendant's interests are promoted.

The Auld Review refrained from adopting any general theoretical model, favouring a pragmatic approach. The validity of this approach have been questioned, particularly since, in the most part, Lord Justice Auld refrained from commissioning any empirical work from which to draw these pragmatic conclusions.

Any discussion of a "balancing of interests" between two opposing factions is over simplistic. In reality there are many groups and individuals each with competing interests none of which can be assigned precise values, and some of which are so fundamental that they should not feature in any such exercise.

---

[85] See M. McConville and L. Bridges (eds), *Criminal Justice in Crisis* (1994), Part I, especially Chaps 1–5 by, respectively, L. Bridges and M McConville, N. Lacey, D. Nobles and R. Schiff and C. Wells. *Cf.* the defence of the RCCJ on this point by one of its members, M. Zander, (1993) 143 N.L.J. 1364.
[86] Bridges and McConville, *op. cit.* p. 11.
[87] Lacey, *op. cit.* n. 86.
[88] *ibid.* pp. 40–41.
[89] Chap. 2, para. 18.

(b) Theoretical models

An evaluation of the merits of a "balancing exercise" can be more effectively **14–101** achieved when viewed in the context of opposing theoretical models.

The Royal Commission on Criminal Procedure, for example, characterised the "two main opposing groups" in the right of silence debate as "those who gave paramountcy to the principles of the presumption of innocence and the burden of proof, and those who saw the purpose of the criminal justice system as being a means to the end of bringing the guilty to justice".[90] The identification by the Royal Commission of these two major schools of thought echoes the two theoretical models of the criminal process proposed by Herbert L. Packer as an aid to the evaluation of the criminal justice system in the United States, the Due Process Model and the Crime Control Models.[91] These models represented

> "an attempt to abstract two separate value systems that compete for priority in the operation of the criminal process. Neither is presented as either corresponding to reality or representing the ideal to the exclusion of the other."[92]

Moreover, they did not represent the difference between the law as it should be ("law in the books") and the law as in fact it operated ("law in action"). They were extremes, and reality lay at some point on the spectrum between them. Indeed, there was some common ground in the two models assumptions: (1) that the functions of defining conduct that may be treated as criminal is separate from, and prior to, the process of identifying and dealing with persons as criminals; (2) that when it appears that a crime has been committed and that there is a reasonable prospect of apprehending and convicting its perpetrator, criminal process ought ordinarily to be invoked; (3) that there are limits to the powers of government to investigate and apprehend persons suspected of committing crimes (*e.g.* the security and privacy of the individual may not be invaded at will); (4) that accused persons may, if they wish, force the operators of the process to demonstrate to an independent authority (the court) that they are guilty. Differences between the models lay in part in the strength and content of these assumptions, particularly the fourth.

Under the Crime Control Model, the most important function of the criminal process is the repression of criminal conduct. To fulfil this purpose, the system must operate efficiently. It must have the capacity to apprehend, try, and convict a high proportion of offenders whose offences become known, and to do so with speed and finality. This leads to an emphasis on informality and uniformity, and on minimising the occasions for challenge. Extra-judicial processes are preferred to judicial: the expertise of police and prosecutors is relied upon to screen out those who are probably innocent; those who are left in should be processed as speedily as possible, preferably with a plea of guilty at the trial stage.

---

[90] RCCP Rep., p. 11.
[91] H. L. Packer, *The Limits of the Criminal Sanction* (1969), Part II.
[92] *ibid.* p. 153.

"The image that comes to mind is an assembly-line conveyor belt down which moves an endless stream of cases, never stopping, carrying the cases to workers who stand at fixed stations and who perform on each case as it comes by the same small but essential operation that brings it one step closer to being a finished product. ... "[93]

By contrast, the Due Process Model resembles an obstacle course. "Each of its successive stages is designed to present formidable impediments to carrying the accused any further along in the process."[94] This model stresses the dangers of error in informal, non-adjudicative fact finding: people are notoriously unreliable observers of disturbing events and confessions to the police may be induced by physical or psychological coercion. Formal, adjudicative, adversary fact finding processes, in which the case is heard by an impartial tribunal and the accused has a full opportunity to challenge the case against him or her, are necessary to reduce the dangers of error. Mistakes (convicting the innocent, setting the guilty free) should be eliminated to the fullest extent possible. (Under the Crime Control Model, such mistakes are acceptable in so far as they do not interfere with the repression of crime (*e.g.* by allowing too many guilty people to escape).) Apart from the question of reliability, there is also a concern to prevent official oppression of the individual, and emphasis on the presumption of innocence and on securing compliance with the procedural rules governing the criminal process, perhaps with the exclusion of illegally obtained evidence or reversal of convictions where the rules are breached. On the assumption that the resources made available for the operation of the criminal process are limited, a preference for Due Process values over Crime Control values will lead to a reduction in the quantitative output of the system.

Writing in the late 1960s, Packer concluded that the criminal process as it actually operated in the large majority of cases in the United States probably approximated to the Crime Control Model. On the other hand, judicial decisions based on the U.S. Constitution were pushing the law nearer to the Due Process Model.[95] For McConville and Baldwin, writing in 1981, the English system too in many ways conformed to the Crime Control Model. Although the police-suspect encounter was one of the key exchanges in the criminal process, the safeguards available to suspects in custody were virtually non-existent. Similarly, there was a lack of Due Process safeguards surrounding pleas of guilty, and connected procedures such as plea bargaining; almost 90 per cent of all defendants charged with serious offences pleaded guilty, and trial by jury (the epitome of the Due Process Model) was used by only five per cent of those eligible to be so tried. The function of the jury was thus "largely symbolic — to uphold due process

---

[93] *ibid.* p. 159.

[94] *ibid.* p. 163.

[95] *ibid.* p. 239. Major cases included *Miranda v. Arizona* 384 U.S. 436 (1966) (suspects in custody must be advised of their rights, which include the right of access to a lawyer before interrogation); *Mapp v. Ohio* 367 U.S. 643 (1961) (rule excluding illegally obtained evidence applicable to state as well as federal prosecutions); *Gideon v. Wainwright* 372 U.S. 325 (1963) (state must provide counsel for defendants financially unable to provide their own). See more recently *US v. Leon* (1984) 104 S Ct. 3405.

values in the occasional show trial". [96] Another commentator, McBarnet, stressed the point that it would not be correct to regard the substance of the law as reflecting Due Process values which are then subverted "by policemen bending the rules, by lawyers negotiating adversaries out of existence, by out-of-touch judges or biased magistrates ... ". In reality "the law governing the production, preparation and presentation of evidence does not live up to its own rhetoric . ... Police and court officials need not abuse the law to subvert the principles of justice; they need only use it".[97]

Developments since then have, like the system as a whole, reflected both Due Process and Crime Control values. However, the latter have tended to predominate.[98] Thus as regards pre-trial procedure, the introduction of the PACE regime has seen the significant extension of police powers of arrest, stop-search, detention and evidence-gathering. While many of these powers are comparatively rarely used, the numbers of arrest and stop-searches have rocketed.[99] The requirement of "reasonable suspicion" does not seem to be a practical constraint,[1] supervision of police officers on the street is minimal, and powers are used disproportionately against "the young, male, working class and black".[2] Even in the wake of the Stephen Lawrence Inquiry and its indictment of the police as institutionally racist, these concerns persist.[3]

Little has been done to restrict or regulate the use of the very broad discretion in operational policing. More effective schemes of monitoring have been implemented, but these bring with them further problems, as, e.g. with the stop and search powers discussed above. Similarly, attempts to regulate the use of police powers for surveillance which have become so common in this era of intelligence-led policing have, arguably, been inadequate. In particular there is a lack of independent scrutiny of authorisations for covert police operations which have the potential to infringe the suspects most personal privacy.

Crime control values can also be clearly identified in the continual expansions to police powers (e.g. to take samples, to retain samples, to take covert video footage of suspects). At the same time, the safeguards the suspect in custody are diluted (e.g. with lower ranks of officer authorising action, and samples being retained indefinitely).[4]

In contrast, the increased regulation of the interrogation process,

---

[96] M. McConville and J. Baldwin, *Courts, Prosecution and Conviction* (1981), pp. 3–7.

[97] *ibid.*; (1981), pp. 154–157. See also D. McBarnet, "False Dichotomies in Criminal Justice Research" in J. Baldwin and A. K. Bottomley, *Criminal Justice: Selected Readings* (1978), Chap. 2. *Cf.* McConville *et al., The Case for the Prosecution* (1991), Chap. 9, criticising McBarnet's approach in so far as it would focus attention on the law (and the judicial and political elites who made it) and regard the practice of "the system's low-level officials such as the police" as relatively unimportant; and for its assumption that legal rhetoric does not form part of the law itself.

[98] See R. Sanders and A. Young, *Criminal Justice* (2nd ed., 2000).

[99] See above, para. 14-005.

[1] Indeed arrests of persons in fact guilty of an arrestable offence are lawful: see above, p. 667.

[2] A. Sanders and R. Young, "The Rule of Law, Due Process and Pre Trial Criminal Justice" (1994) C.L.P. 125 at 137. *Cf.* R. Reiner in R. Morgan and R. Reiner (eds), *The Oxford Handbook of Criminology* (1994), p. 727 (cited by Sanders and Young) referring to a study that confirmed "that the weight of adversarial policing falls disproportionately on young men in the lower socio-economic and least powerful social group". See further, A. Sanders, "From Suspect to Trial", *The Oxford Handbook of Criminology* (2nd ed., 1997).

[3] See above para. 14-005.

[4] See above, para. 14-022.

including the right of access to legal advice, and the enforcement of that regulation by judicial decisions to exclude confession evidence certainly reflects both the rhetoric and practice of Due Process. However, the limits must be noted: many suspects are interrogated without a lawyer present; the quality of much of the legal advice is poor; and there is no rule that illegally obtained evidence is inadmissible.[5] These Due Process-based developments have nevertheless been used to justify attenuation of the "right of silence", itself an embodiment of Due Process values.[6] The inherently coercive interrogation process remains in police hands and convictions may still be based solely on a confession. While interrogations in serious cases are now tape-recorded, confessions may be influenced by off-the-record deals made outside the police station, in police cells or while the tape-recorder is switched off.[7-8] The crucial need for a change in attitude so that the police approach investigations (and interviews) with an open mind is to be addressed only as a matter for police (re) training. Additionally, the quality of legal advice needs to be improved, and it may be desirable to prescribe that a legal adviser should be present at all interviews. Such reforms will be resisted, in part at least because of the pressures of economy and efficiency, as well as on the usually ill-explained basis that the "balance" in criminal procedure already weighs too heavily in the suspect's favour.

Arguably, the significance of the exchanges that occur in the police station are now so great for the defendant throughout the rest of the criminal process, that the safeguards need to be substantially increased, not reduced.

Another Due Process development, the disclosure requirements imposed by the courts, has been modified by the Criminal Procedure and Investigation Act 1996.[9] However, the government's Crime Control objective, seeking to maximise the efficiency with which cases are despatched, is clearly reflected in the legislation, with, for example, the most crucial role being performed by the police, and the obligation on the accused to issue a defence statement before secondary prosecution disclosure is forthcoming. The system has in fact proved to be tremendously inefficient and a major source of potential miscarriages of justice.

The effect of the Crown Prosecution Service as an antidote to these trends is uncertain, given its undoubted dependence on the case as presented to it by the police. While much of the criticism here is that too few cases are discontinued, the government is torn between supporting police complaints that cases are dropped unnecessarily, and imposing greater pressure on the CPS to optimise efficiency in the system by discontinuing weak cases.[10] The fragile relationship of the CPS and the police is further threatened by the pressure in recent reforms for greater CPS involvement at an earlier stage of the process.

The introduction of the CDS is unlikely to improve the protection afforded to the suspect, and has the potential to cause further problems unless it can maintain, and be perceived to maintain, its independence.

Finally, while evaluation of the criminal justice process from the

---

[5] See above, para. 14-022.
[6] Above, para. 14-024.
[7-8] Above, para. 14-025.
[9] cf. above, Part M.
[10] Above, para. 14-044.

standpoints of Due Process and Crime Control is in our view helpful, it should be noted both that the dichotomy has its critics[11] and that other models have been proposed.[12]

2. HUMAN RIGHTS

The trend towards Crime Control summarised in the preceding section has **14–102** arguably been countered in recent years by the revolution in criminal proceedings brought about by the Human Rights Act 1998. There can be no doubt that the courts will continue to struggle with difficult conflicts between domestic law processes and the often vague but fundamental guarantees of the European Convention.

The European Convention on Human Rights and the International Covenant on Civil and Political Rights have been drawn upon, particularly by Ashworth, in proposing a "general framework of ethical principles" for the criminal process.[13] Accordingly, he has identified[14] the right to be treated with humanity and without degradation[15]; the right of victims to compensation[16]; the right of innocent persons not to be convicted[17]; the right to be treated fairly and without discrimination[18]; the right to be presumed innocent[19]; the principle of legality (*i.e.* "the law should state clearly and in advance the body of rules and exceptions relating to the rights

---

[11] See A. Ashworth, *The Criminal Process* (1998), pp. 28–29, criticising (1) a lack of a clear explanation of the relationship between the two models; (2) the assumption that there was a significant relationship between the system of pre-trial justice and the crime rate; (3) the underestimation of the importance of resource management; (4) the absence of allowance for victim-related matters; and (5) internal inconsistencies (*e.g.* the emphasis on speed in only the Crime Control model). See also Sanders and Young (2000), Chap. 1, in which the authors discuss their "freedom" model. This seeks to evaluate the freedoms of potential and actual victims against harm with the due process freedoms of suspects and defendants. They argue that a human rights approach is not a sufficient answer to the problem of balancing crime control and due process. The ultimate goal of their system is to ensure the optimum protection of freedom overall.

[12] See, in addition to Ashworth (1998) and Sanders and Young (2000), A. Bottoms and J. D. McClean, *Defendants in the Criminal Process* (1976), pp. 226–232, and M. King. *The Framework of Criminal Justice* (1981), Chap. 2. Bottoms and McClean identify a third, Liberal Bureaucratic Model, based on the viewpoint of the "enlightened courts administrator": this purports to prefer Due Process values to Crime Control values, but imposes pressures (*e.g.* in support of summary trials and guilty pleas) to make the system workable, and in so doing in practice reinforces Crime Control. King analyses models, three based on the perspectives of typical participants: (i) Due Process (defence lawyers), (ii) Crime Control (police), and (iii) Medical (probation officers: emphasis on reabilitation); and three based on the work of social theorists: (iv) Bureaucratic (emphasising the management of crime and criminals), (v) Status Passage (emphasising the public degradation of the defendant) and (vi) Power (emphasising the maintenance of class domination).

[13] A. Ashworth, *The Criminal Process* (1998), Chap. 3; S. H. Bailey, "Rights in the Administration of Justice" in D. J. Harris and S. Joseph (eds), *The ICCPR and United Kingdom Law* (1995), Chap. 6.

[14] *ibid.* pp. 57–67. As to derogation, see *ibid.* p. 67–71.

[15] *cf.* Art. 3, ECHR, Art.7, ICCPR, prohibiting the use of torture or inhuman or degrading treatment or punishment. These obligations are non-derogable.

[16] See below, para. 17-083.

[17] Reflected in a number of the rights that follow.

[18] Art.14, ECHR; Arts 2(l) and 26, ICCPR.

[19] Art.6(2), ECHR; Art. 14(2), ICCPR.

and powers that may be taken over individuals during the criminal process")[20]; reasonable grounds for arrest and detention[21]; the right to be brought before a court[22]; the right to prepare a proper defence[23]; the right of the victim to respect in the criminal process[24]; the right to trial within reasonable time[25]; and the principle of equality of arms between defence and prosecution.[26]

There is no doubt that the period immediately following the enactment of the Human Rights Act 1998 has seen an enormous deluge of human rights and European Convention arguments being deployed in the courts. It is still rather early to evaluate the growing domestic human rights jurisprudence in the criminal process.[27]

The Human Rights Act 1998 has already had a significant impact on all aspects of the criminal process including: the regulation of the police conduct[28]; the circumstances in which adverse inferences from silence might be drawn at trial[29]; the amendment of pre-trial procedures such as bail;[30] and, on the preparation for trial generally, especially in relation to the disclosure of evidence.[31] The ECHR could serve as an important bulwark against the increasing pressure for reform based on Crime Control values.

There remains a constant tension between the interests identified above, but in recent years, there has been a growing recognition and exploration of other important interests influencing the criminal justice process.

3. THE ROLE OF THE VICTIM

14–103   Increased attention has been paid to the role of the victim.[32] Two paradoxes have been noted.[33] First, there is the contradiction that the victim has a crucial role to play in reporting the offence to the police and as the major agent in detecting the offender, but that little account is taken of the victim's attitudes and experiences by the professionals involved in the criminal justice system. Second, initially at least, "major projects aimed at fulfilling

---

[20] cf. the prohibition of retrospective criminal laws: Art. 7, ECHR; Art. 15, ICCPR.

[21] Art. 5(1)(c), ECHR; cf. Art. 9(1)(3), ICCPR.

[22] Art. 5(3), ECHR; Art. 9(3), ICCPR

[23] Art. 6(3), ECHR; Art. 14(3), ICCPR.

[24] Below.

[25] Art. 6(1) ECHR; Art. 14(3)(c), ICCPR.

[26] Derived from the requirement that trials be fair: Art. 6(1), ECHR; Art. 14(1), ICCPR.

[27] See Ashworth, [2001] Crim.L.R. 911.

[28] See especially the introduction of RIPA 2000 and the House of Lords decision in *R. v. Looseky* [2001] UKHL 53 on entrapment.

[29] See especially, the decisions of *Condron and Condron v. U.K.* [2001] EHRR 1 discussed above, p.000; and the amendments made by the Youth Justice and Criminal Evidence Act 1999.

[30] See above, 14-071.

[31] See above.

[32] See especially, A. Crawford and J. Goodey (eds), *Integrating a Victim Perspective within Criminal Justice* (2000); C. Pollard, [2000] Crim.L.R. 5; R. Young and B. Goold, [1999] Crim.L.R. 126; C.Hoyle, E.Cape, R. Morgan and A. Sanders, *Evaluation of the One Stop Shop and Victim Statement Pilot Projects* (1998); and R. Morgan and A. Sanders, *The Uses of Victim Statements* (1999).

[33] J. Shapland, J. Willmore and P. Duff, *Victims in the Criminal Justice System* (1985), Chap. 10. See, generally, S. Walkate, *Victimology* (1989).

victims' needs have been set up without regard to, or even investigation into, victims' expressed needs".[34] These projects include the Criminal Injuries Compensation Scheme (a state scheme for compensating the victims of violent crime),[35] schemes for compensation or reparation by offenders,[36] victim support schemes[37] and mediation or conciliation schemes,[38] forming part of a move towards restorative justice.

Initially, the police seemed to be rather more responsive to the needs of victims than have magistrates' courts.[39] The government has responded by strengthening the compensation provisions, and by issuing a Victims' Charter which sets out the "rights and entitlements" of crime victims.[40] Among its features are the duty of the police to keep victims informed of all important stages in a case; the duty of the CPS to ensure that full details of injuries or losses have been established before trial and to advise prosecutors to correct statements made in court which denigrate a victim's character; the right of the families of murder victims to be consulted about the timing of the killer's release and whether restrictions should be placed on where he or she lives and works. This all, however, falls short of giving the victim a formal role in the criminal justice process as a party to the prosecution, which some argue is necessary for the victims' rights to have any substance.[41] As society becomes increasingly litigious, attempts to launch legal challenges by victims who are unhappy by their treatment by agencies in the criminal justice process seem inevitable.

In recent years there has been a greater attempt to evaluate the victim's needs and also to examine victim preferences in the criminal process. For example, Home Office research by Mattinson and Mirrlees-Black found that overall victims' sentencing performances were more lenient than could be expected from comparing them to the general public's opinions. In particular, they found that victims were willing to accept reparation from the offender.[42]

---

[34] *ibid.* p. 178.

[35] See especially N. Lacey, "Government as Manager, Citizen as Consumer" (1994) 57 M.L.R. 534).

[36] Criminal courts' powers are examined in Chap. 17 below.

[37] Schemes whereby volunteers visit victims and offer emotional and practical support. The reactions of both victims and police are generally positive: T. Newburn, (1989) 26 H.O.R.B. 22; and see M. Maguire and C. Corbett, *The Effects of Crime and the Work of Victims Support Schemes* (1987); D. Trust, *Help for Victims of Crime and Violence* (1989); M. L. Gill and R. I. Mawby, *Volunteers in the Criminal Justice System* (1990), Chap. 5. Schemes to help victims and witnesses attending the Crown Court have also been established. See below, Chap. 17, para. 17-060.

[38] See T. F. Marshall and S. Merry, *Crime and Accountability: Victim/Offender Mediation in Practice* (HMSO, 1990); M. Wright, [1995] Crim.L.R. 187.

[39] J. Shapland and D. Cohen, "Facilities for Victims: the Role of the Police and the Courts" [1987] Crim.L.R. 28. See also T. Newman and S. Merry, *Keeping in Touch* (1990) HORS No. 116.

[40] *The Times*, February 23, 1990. The Charter is published by the Home Office. See D. Miers, (1992) 55 M.L.R. 482; H. Fenwick, [1995] Crim.L.R. 843. A new edition was published in 1996.

[41] But *cf.* Ashworth, (1998), arguing that decisions as to prosecution, bail or custody and punishment should be taken in the public interest and not according to the personal views of the victim. On the development of victim impact statements in other jurisdictions, see A. Ashworth, [1993] Crim.L.R. 498. See also A. Sanders and R. Young, (2001) 151 N.L.J. 44.

[42] *ibid.* p. 41

The greater awareness[43] of the plight of the victim and the desire to regain public confidence in the criminal justice system indicate a growing influence for the victim in pre-trial process. In addition to securing better respect for the victim in terms of information and facilities provided, the victims' influence may be a major catalyst in diverting a greater proportion of cases away from formal prosecution in the courts. This would echo the increasing interest in restorative justice.

Since October 2001, victim personal statements have been taken by the police and these statements about how the crime has affected the person's life will be used in the process of decision making throughout the criminal process, *e.g.* with bail, and by the CPS.

The Home Office has recently published a review of the Victim's Charter,[44] and the Home Office Report *Criminal Justice : The Way Ahead*[45] also proposes changes aimed to establish a new Charter of Rights setting out standards of service on how victims should be treated, and a new Ombudsman to review complaints. The specific objectives are to ensure that victims are able to chart the progress of their case online, and are kept fully informed by the relevant criminal justice agencies. In addition, all victims of sexual or violent offences will be informed of relevant release dates for offenders and of any conditions imposed.

M. FUTURE DEVELOPMENTS

14–104   The pressure for further reform of the pre-trial criminal process continues unabated. In addition to the 328 recommendations of the Auld Report, many of which have an impact on pre-trial procedures, there is the government's flagship report, *Criminal Justice: The Way Ahead*, which demonstrates a commitment to further substantial change. There are clearly identifiable themes in the future reform proposals.

Efficiency, managerialism and consumerism

14–105   Many of the most recent legislative changes have been introduced solely in an attempt to speed up the process or to save money, with little concern for the protections of the suspect.[46] When viewed in combination some of these reforms appear to have as their sole objective the securing of the earliest possible guilty plea. The frustration with the delay in the process was clear from the comments in the Auld Report that

---

[43]   See G. Barclay and C. Tavares, *Digest 4*, Chap. 2 on victims and see J. Mattinson and C. Mirrlees-Black, *Attitudes to Crime and Criminal Justice: Findings from the BCS* (2000) HORS 200.

[44]   See the Home Office *Review of the Victim's Charter* (2001).

[45]   (2001), p.69.

[46]   See the introduction of the plea before venue and transfer for trial, and also the controversial mode of trial proposals.

"there are limits to what can be expected of cooperation between the parties, particularly when the issue is as to guilt as well as sentence. Guilty defendants seeking to avoid conviction have not the same urgency as the public about the need for an efficient criminal justice system. Some innocent defendants, advised by their lawyers to keep their cards close to their chests, are equally unenthusiastic. And, as is now increasingly recognised, there are other individuals involved in the process, such as victims, witnesses and jurors whose interests need attention."[47]

Attempts to improve efficiency are clearly at the forefront of the proposals for future reform, as is demonstrated most recently by the terms of reference of the Auld Report being to "streamline" processes and "increase their efficiency".[48] One impact of the drive for efficiency should certainly be to render less unwieldy the structure for organisation and management of the criminal justice process. Lord Justice Auld commented that at present:

" there is no system worthy of the name, only a criminal justice process to which a number of different government departments and agencies and others make separate and sometimes conflicting contributions".[49]

The Auld Report proposes a new Criminal Justice Council to replace existing advisory and consultative bodies with a national criminal justice board to replace existing planning and operational bodies and local criminal justice boards to give effect to national policy.[50] This new streamlined managerial structure should reduce the degree of haphazard reform and help reduce complexity in the procedures which are implemented.

As elsewhere in the legal system, the criminal process has felt the effects of the growing importance of managerialism. In the pre-trial process this can be seen in the greater significance accorded to monitoring, protocols, and performance targets of the agencies, and of the desire to improve the "service" provided to clients in the criminal justice system. The most glaring examples discussed above include the performance targets of the CPS.

As for consumerism, there is a danger that as "crime" is such a political issue, every government will respond to popular (mis)conceptions about crime rates. This can lead to over hasty reactions to issues given an over inflated significance as a result of particular headline cases. In the long run these can seriously diminish the protection afforded to the suspect in the pre-trial process.[51] This is a particularly pernicious threat, because the trial process, and especially the paradigm of the seldom used jury trial, will remain largely unscathed as the inroads are made into fundamental safeguards arising before trial (*e.g.* the right to silence). These processes

---

[47] Chap. 10, para. 1.
[48] See also Narey (1997); Glidewell (1998)
[49] Chap. 8, para. 1.
[50] See on Auld: M. Zander, (2001) 151 N.L.J. 1461; I. Francis, (2001) 151 N.L.J. 1700; P. Tain, (2001) S.J. 1056; M. Zander, (2001) S.J. 1100; M. Zander, www.lse.ac.uk/Depts/law; J. McEwan, M. Redmayne and Y. Tynsley, (2002) 6 E & P. 163; and the special issue of Med. Sci and Law, (2002) Vol. 42.
[51] See the report by Mattinson and Mirrlees-Black (2000) *op cit.* n. 44 which found that most people thought that crime had increased throughout a period when it had dropped by 10%.

are, as we have seen, as important in protecting against miscarriages of justice as those at trial, and yet they are more readily sacrificed without public concern.

Retaining public confidence in the criminal justice system is important; but responding to public satisfaction surveys by amending the criminal process will not always serve to promote public confidence in the long term. Research has shown that those who have the poorest knowledge of the system "tend to have lower opinions of the courts and sentences".[52] This carries with it a much broader and often unrecognised danger of relying on statistics which can be manipulated as easily in this area as elsewhere.[53]

---

[52] See Mattinson and Mirrlees-Black (2000), p. 8.
[53] On changes to crime statistics methodology see Home Office, *Review of Crime Statistics: A Discussion Document* (2000). For a comparison of criminal statistics across jurisdictions, see G. Barclay, G. Tavares and A. Siding, *International Comparisons of Criminal Justice Statistics 1999*, (Home Office 6/01, 2001). See also Home Office, *Improving Public Attitudes to the Criminal Justice System: The Impact of Information* (2002) HORS No. 245.

PART IV

THE HEARING

CHAPTER 15

THE CIVIL TRIAL

From the variety of different civil proceedings we take the action in the   **15–001**
Queen's Bench Division as our example, as we did in the chapter on pre-trial
civil procedure.[1] However we shall also make reference to the county court,
both in its fast track and in its small claims jurisdictions.[2]

It is arguable that very little time should be spent considering the civil
trial, since so much effort is expended on resolving the case prior to that
stage.[3] The alternative resolution of disputes is an approach promoted by
the Woolf reforms.[4] Indeed discussion of the trial stage is almost incidental
to the Woolf reports and CPR Part 39 "Miscellaneous Provisions relating to
hearings" and its practice direction occupy a paltry 11 pages out of the three
volume Civil Procedure Rules. However, the civil trial is important not only
in being the final point for the resolution of disputes, but also as it is only at
trial in the High Court or on appeal from a trial that precedents may be set
which will clarify and develop the law.[5] Without decisions of such a nature
the law would stagnate, failing to address the many existing and future
problems which society presents.

A. ADVERSARIAL PROCEDURE

Adversarial procedure is the fundamental, characteristic feature of English   **15–002**
civil justice.[6]

"You have two adversaries in every civil dispute — someone asserting a
right, someone denying it. Someone contending for one thing, someone
contending against it."[7]

---

[1] See Chap. 11.
[2] Some multi track cases in high value personal injury cases will also take place in the county
court.
[3] See above, para. 12-035.
[4] See for example CPR r. 1.4(2)(e).
[5] Subject to the court's ability to depart from precedent in pursuit of the higher obligation to
protect human rights. See also N. Armstrong, "Making Facts", in A. A. S. Zuckerman and
R. Cranston (eds.) *Reforming Civil Procedure* (1995), pp. 99–100.
[6] Sir Jack I. H. Jacob, *The Fabric of English Civil Justice* (1987),p.5. Adversarial procedure
can be compared with the inquisitorial system, see *ibid.* pp. 5–19. See also N. Andrews,
Principles of Civil Procedure (1994), Chap. 3 and Interim Report p. 29.
[7] Sir Jack I. H. Jacob, "The Adversary System of Civil Litigation" (1983) City of London Law
Review 17, 18.

Lord Woolf, whilst not recommending the abandonment of the adversarial principle, identified it as a major cause of many of the problems associated with the civil justice system. What he sought to recommend was the retention of the best aspects of the adversarial approach combined with a more interventionist management role for the courts.[8] This has, as we have seen, most significance for the pre-trial stage,[9] but has implications also for the trial stage.

Judicial unpreparedness is not necessarily conducive to effectiveness and efficiency. The Civil Justice Review recommended that judges should read case papers before the hearing[10] and to some extent this is mirrored in the CPR where PD 28 para 8 indicates that, at least in the fast track "the judge will generally have read the papers in the trial bundle". The number of cases proceeding through the courts having decreased so dramatically since the Woolf reforms, judges should now have more time to read into the case. It is the function of the parties, normally through counsel or solicitor-advocate[11] to bring the evidence and argue the law that will win the case subject to constraints placed on them by the procedural judge during the case management process. It was excessive litigant and lawyer control of the process with which Lord Woolf was in profound disagreement: this is why he introduced judicial case management.[12]

As a result of the Woolf reforms, important changes have been introduced which have an impact on the trial stage, particularly in the fast and small claims tracks. Excessive use of documents[13] and expert witnesses[14] has been controlled, oral examination in chief has been almost entirely replaced by submission of written witness statements[15] and hearsay has ceased to be inadmissible in civil proceedings.[16] The latter reflects the reality that "the

---

[8] Lord Woolf's general approach was to propose a system that would be "*less* adversarial and more cooperative" (our italics). Specific ways in which this would be achieved are set out in the Interim Report Chap. 18 (use of ADR); and in the Final Report in Chaps. 10 (openness and co-operation, pre-action protocols) and 13 (expert witnesses). As we will see below, the use of the "joint" expert witness is a peculiarly non-adversarial procedure.

[9] See above, para. 12-002.

[10] Civil Justice Review, *Report of the Review Body on Civil Justice* (Cm.394, 1989), paras. 261–265. See also Lord Woolf's comments on judicial case management and judicial workload in Final Report, Chap. 2. As to what, as opposed to whether, the judge will have read, see *Barings plc (in liquidation) and another v. Coopers and Lybrand and others*, [2001] E.W.C.A. Civ 1163, *The Times* 19th October 2001, C.A.

[11] In the light of the increasing numbers of solicitors obtaining rights of audience in the higher courts — see, for example, "City Firms call time at the Bar?" (1999) 13(40), The Lawyer, 12 — (and indeed members of other professions, such as patent agents) the word "advocate" will be used hereafter as a generic term.

[12] See, for example, CPR Part 1.

[13] CPR r. 31.6

[14] CPRr.35.1

[15] CPR r. 32.5(2). For a discussion of the procedure by a practitioner, see Harrison, "First Principles and Witness Statements", (2001) 151 N.L.J. 649–650.

[16] Civil Justice Review (1989), paras 266–270, Law Commission, The *Hearsay Rule in Civil Proceedings* (L.C. Consultation Paper No 117, 1991) and Civil Evidence Act 1995, s.l (also CPR rr. 33.1 to 33.5 inclusive). It should, however, be remembered that the court has express authority (although presumably subject to the obligation to provide a fair trial under art 6) to "exclude evidence that would otherwise be admissible" CPR r. 32.1.

rules of evidence play an almost insignificant part in the civil trial process."[17]

The consequence of the CPR should be that the case is much better prepared for the trial than in the past.[18] The consequences of this assumption are particularly noticeable in the fast track where:

a. The trial will not last more than 4 hours (*i.e.* a single court "day");

b. There will not normally be an opening speech;

c. Written witness statements will stand as evidence in chief;[19]

d. Time allowed for presentation of evidence, for cross-examination and for closing submissions may be limited in advance;

e. Expert evidence at trial will normally be submitted in writing rather than orally;

f. The recoverable costs of the fast track trial will not exceed £350 if the claim is for a sum of up to £3,000; £500 for a claim of £3,000 to £10,000 and £750 for a claim of more than £10,000.[20]

Any or all of these approaches may be adopted in the multi-track where the case management conference[21] and pre-trial review[22] will involve the parties in clearly identifying issues for trial and those which can be resolved before trial. In addition there are moves to require the parties to cut back on citation of authorities.[23] Fixed dates or fixed "trial windows" are now the norm.

At the beginning of a multi-track trial, always assuming it is permitted by the judge, the *opening speech* is made on behalf of the claimant. The object of the opening speech is to outline the case with reference to the evidence that is to be called. The opening may be briefer — and indeed, subject to a time limit by the judge — in a civil case than in a criminal case since there will not normally be a jury and the advocate will not have to explain such matters as the burden and standard of proof to the judge. The advocate has in the past at least not been able to assume that the judge has any familiarity with the papers in the case so his or her job has been summarised as being: " ... to explain the whole case to the judge; to read the pleadings,[24] the

---

[17] Jacob (1987), p. 266. Under the CPR one might conclude that the power of the court to include or exclude evidence under CPR rr. 32.1 and 35.1 supersedes questions of technical admissibility. For an introduction to the law of evidence in civil trials see O'Hare and Browne, *O Hare and Hill Civil Litigation, op. cit.*, Chap 31.

[18] See above para. 12-002.

[19] See CPR r. 32.5(2): the "witness statement shall stand as [the witness'] evidence in chief unless the court orders otherwise."

[20] CPR Part 46. Lord Woolf in fact recommended that the total recoverable costs of a fast track case (that is, the cost of the trial and the pre-trial procedure as opposed to the costs of the trial day alone) should be restricted (Final Report, Chap .4)). This recommendation has yet to be implemented.

[21] See CPR r. 29.3 and PD. 29 para 5.

[22] CPR r. 29.3. It is not unknown for judges to set a timetable for the trial including the length of time each advocate may spend on examining each witness and in making closing submissions.

[23] Practice Direction (Citation of Authorities) [2001] 2 All E.R. 510, C.A.

[24] Now "statements of case".

letters and other documents . . ., to summarise what all the witnesses he is calling will say and how his client views the issue."[25]

15–003   Normally any agreed reports or other documentary evidence are put in evidence in the opening speech.[26] It will be entirely in accordance with the dictates of the Woolf reforms that, the judge having had the opportunity to read the relevant papers, it may be indicated to the advocate that there is no need to cover all the points in the opening speech and indeed the opening speech may be dispensed with altogether. This illustrates the advantage of trial by judge alone — the judge can move the advocates on where matters are understood or undisputed without the constraint of ensuring that the jury have grasped the issue, and, if the judge is prepared and the issues have been effectively narrowed during the pre-trial stages, considerable time and costs can be saved during the trial in line with the overriding objective. At the conclusion of the opening speech, if any, for the claimant, the first witnesses are called.

It is no accident that there are, except in the case of jointly appointed expert witnesses, witnesses for the claimant and witnesses for the defendant. The parties are, within the constraints of CPR r. 32.1,[27] which may be used to limit the number of witnesses called and/or the amount of time any individual witness spends in the witness box, free to choose the people who can give evidence to support their contentions and the witnesses line up behind the "litigant gladiators" clearly identified with one side or another.[28]

The claimant's advocate will begin by calling each claimant's witness in turn. Assuming, which is by no means certain, that the questioning of a witness by the advocate "on the same side" is permitted by the court,[29] it is termed *examination in chief*.[30] In examination in chief on behalf of the claimant a witness is questioned to extract testimony which is expected to be favourable to the claimant. The claimant's solicitor will have prepared in advance a formal witness statement of the evidence to be given by the witness, which will have been exchanged with the statements of witnesses for

---

[25] *Going to Law* (1974) a report by JUSTICE, at para. 16.

[26] e.g. medical reports or those of other experts, particularly those of jointly-instructed experts.

[27] Note that CPR r. 32.1 is the only section of CPR Part 32 to apply in the small claims track.

[28] A phrase taken from Jacob (1983). The CPR jointly-instructed expert, however, occupies the middle ground. Although such an expert witness has been instructed by both parties, if he or she appears to give oral evidence at the trial (which is by no means certain), it appears to be developing practice, endorsed by the codes of guidance for expert witnesses, that the expert can be subject to cross-examination by both parties. As we will see, cross-examination of one's own witnesses is not normally permitted. Other variations to the normal rules appear in Civil Evidence Act 1995, s.3 (implemented by CPR r. 33.3) under which a party who has tendered evidence as hearsay can be required by their opponent to produce the witness at trial for cross-examination by that opponent.

[29] Under CPR r. 32.5(2) the written witness statement will normally be used in place of questioning by way of oral examination in chief.

[30] As to the judge's role in examining witnesses for both the claimant and the defence see para. 15-009 below.

the defendant on penalty of not being permitted to call the witness at all.[31] The advocate will use the witness statement as the basis of his or her questions. The advocate must observe two rules during the examination. Leading questions[32] must not be asked and the witness' evidence given in court must not be contradicted by reference to a conflicting statement of that witness in the witness statement.[33] Neither a solicitor (including a solicitor-advocate) nor a barrister is, any longer, prohibited from merely discussing the case or the evidence to be given with a potential witness, but, as there remain stringent prohibitions against "coaching" or "rehearsing" witnesses, it is quite possible that there may be variations in testimony when the witness is under examination[34] A potentially significant difference between the barrister and the solicitor-advocate, although this will very much depend on the way in which the case has been run, is that a solicitor-advocate may be the same solicitor who has managed the case in all its detail throughout the pre-trial procedure.[35] A barrister is perhaps more likely to have been brought in, either in the final stages with a view to conducting the trial, or for specific tasks, such as the drafting of statements of case. Although the witness statement is intended to be "if practicable, ... in the

---

[31] CPR r. 32.4, 32.10

[32] A leading question is one which suggests to the witness the answer which the advocate expects. "What time did the accident occur?" is a proper question. "The accident occurred at 7.30pm did it not?" is a leading question and, therefore, prohibited. It is commonly agreed between the advocates and the judge that, if oral examination in chief is to take place at all a witness may be "led" on non-contentious issues to save time.

[33] It is, of course, open to the advocate to ask a witness to think again about an answer, but the discrepancy between the answer and the earlier statement may not be suggested. In an extreme case, the advocate might seek to have the earlier statement put in as evidence at the end of the examination in chief: Civil Evidence Act 1968, s. 2(2). As oral examination in chief is disappearing, the scope for such discrepancies arising in examination in chief are, of course, diminishing.

[34] Law Society Code for Advocacy, *Professional Conduct, op. cit.*, at Chap. 21: "Advocates must not when interviewing a witness out of court: (a) place witnesses who are being interviewed under any pressure to provide other than a truthful account of their evidence; (b) rehearse, practise or coach witnesses in relation to their evidence or the way in which they should give it." Other regulation on contact with witnesses from the solicitor's perspective appear at principles 21.10 and 19.02, *ibid. The Code of Conduct of the Bar of England and Wales* (7th ed.) adds to the two principles adopted by solicitors the further requirement at para. 705 that a barrister "except with the consent of the representative for the opposing side or of the court, communicate directly or indirectly about a case with any witness, whether or not the witness is his lay client, once that witness has begun to give evidence until the evidence of that witness has been concluded." Whilst there is no longer any bar on barristers having contact with witnesses otherwise, the Bar's *Guidance on Preparation of Witness Statements, Preparing Witness Statements for use in Civil Proceedings, Dealings with Witnesses* (2001) indicates at para. 9 that "a barrister should exercise his discretion and consider very carefully whether and to what extent such contact is appropriate, bearing in mind in particular that it is not the barrister's function ... to investigate and collect evidence."
For a trenchant criticism of the way in which a particular witness statement had been obtained, in this case by neither solicitor nor barrister, see *Aquarius Financial Enterprises Inc and another v. Certain Underwriters at Lloyd's* (2001) 151 N.L.J., Q.B.D., Commercial Court.

[35] There are, however, limitations: a solicitor may not act as advocate if, *inter alia*: he or she is likely to be called as a witness or where his or her connection with the client would mean that it was difficult for them to maintain professional independence; he or she is a company director and the company is a party to the proceedings; or, more significantly in this context, if the solicitor has been responsible for deciding on a course of action and the legality of that action is in dispute in the proceedings. Law Society's Code for Advocacy para. 4.

intended witness's own words,"[36] most are actually drafted by lawyers and it is quite possible that there may be variations in testimony when the witness is under examination, particularly as both professional codes prohibit the "coaching" of witnesses.

Lord Woolf, concerned about the satellite industry in drafting witness statements since it became the norm for them to be exchanged in 1992, said:

> "A Commercial judge expressed the position very clearly. He said: 'From the court's point of view they may save time and reduce costs, but there are downsides. First, an enormous amount of time is now spent by lawyers ironing and massaging witness statements; that is extremely expensive for clients, and the statements can bear very little relation to what a witness of fact would actually say. Second, they can produce an unfair result because a witness can be unfairly caught saying something contrary to that which a lawyer has put in his statement. It may not be dishonesty, but inexperience in checking lengthy statements, that leads to being caught, and time is taken up in the trial trying to resolve which it is. Third, the exchange also allows lawyers to spend hours preparing cross-examination and can thus lead to prolix cross-examination. That prolixity is compounded by the fact that the statement crosses every 't' in the first place and those 'ts' cannot be left unchallenged'."[37]

considered that a comparatively free reign should be permitted for witnesses to amplify their statements orally in the witness box.[38] This has not however, found a place in the final version of the CPR[39] where amplification is prima facie restricted.

If, as is increasingly the norm,[40] there is no oral examination in chief, the witness may be asked no more than to identify him or her-self and to confirm the accuracy of the witness statement that has been exchanged on his or her behalf, before being handed over to examination by the advocate for the other side. It is essential, therefore, that those who draw up witness statements do so in the knowledge that, in effect, they are producing in written form the evidence in chief[41] at the trial, it being unlikely that the witness will be permitted to amplify the statement simply to remedy omissions made by the person who took down the statement.

15–004   At the conclusion of the oral evidence in chief, if any, or once the accuracy of the statement has been confirmed and (if necessary) the court has read the statement, if there is to be no oral evidence in chief, the advocate for the defendant is given the opportunity (although again this may be subject to a predetermined limitation in time) to cross examine in an attempt to shake the testimony of the witness or to extract information useful to the defendant's case. In cross examination the advocate is at liberty to exploit

---

[36] PD. 32 para. 18.1.
[37] Interim Report, Chap. 22.
[38] Final Report Chap. 12 paras. 55 to 58 inclusive.
[39] CPR r. 32.5(3) and (4).
[40] CPR r. 32.5(2)
[41] See PD. 32 at para. 18.1 "The witness statement must, if practicable, be in the intended witness's own words . . .". See also *Aquarius Financial Enterprises Inc and another v Certain Underwriters at Lloyd's*, (2001) 151 N.L.J., Q.B.D, Commercial Court.

contradictory statements made by the witness and, in order to assist him or her in doing so, has a copy of the witness' witness statement provided to the defendant in advance.[42]

The case for the defendant is put in exactly the same way, with, subject to the permission of the court, an opening speech and the examination of witnesses (which, as we have seen, may amount only to cross-examination). After the defence evidence has been heard, the defendant's advocate may make a closing speech (again potentially subject to a pre-determined time limit) summarising his or her view of the evidence and the law to which the claimant's advocate may reply. Again, and consistently with the objectives of CPR Part 1 and art. 6, the judge has a discretion to indicate to the advocates that argument on a particular point which may already have been decided or which is considered to be irrelevant need not be recited. At any point in the proceedings the judge may decide to look at the place in which the events in issue took place. The judge would normally be accompanied at a "view" by the parties and their legal representatives but may order instead that he or she be accompanied only by, say, the parties' expert witnesses.

Ultimately the judge is required to give a reasoned judgment, stating the conclusions on the factual issues in dispute and the legal implications of those findings of fact.[43]

There are variations to the above procedure. First, the judge may sit with assessors. Secondly there are a few cases where the judge may sit with a jury. Thirdly the court may order separate trials of liability and quantum of damages.[44] Finally, preliminary questions of fact and law can be heard before the main trial.[45]

B. WITNESSES AND EXPERT EVIDENCE

Lay witnesses may well be under pressure in giving evidence. It will be for the advocate to decide who to call, taking into account, for example, of whether they will provide evidence that is convincing enough to be a valuable aid to the presentation of the case.   **15–005**

The pressures on an expert witness will be less, particularly since such a witness will have had time to reflect on the evidence to be given and may, as a "professional" witness, even have received training in his or her role.[46] In many civil trials part of the evidence is likely to be given by such witnesses, although as we have seen, particularly in the fast track, that evidence will be given by way of written report instead of oral evidence during the trial and even in a multi track case the general principle is that

---

[42] CPR r. 32.4
[43] There is an entitlement to a reasoned judgment even in the much more informal small claims track hearing: CPR r. 27.8(6).
[44] See for example, PD. 29 para. 5.3(7).
[45] An alternative method of resolving a preliminary issue of fact but perhaps more particularly of law (such as the proper construction of a document) would be to use the summary judgment procedure in CPR Part 24.
[46] This is not to suggest that the witness will have been "coached" in relation to this particular case but that those who regularly appear as expert witnesses may seek generic training in presenting themselves in court provided by an organisation such as Bond Solon Training Ltd. Such training, with the caveat that it "should never lose sight of the fundamental point that the expert's duty is to assist the court", was endorsed by Lord Woolf: Final Report, Chap. 13, para 54.

"expert evidence is to be given in a written report unless the court directs otherwise".[47] In the small claims track, the court's express permission is required to rely on expert evidence at all.[48] Expert evidence is opinion evidence and opinion evidence is admissible from an expert, though not from an ordinary witness. Experts are not limited to giving opinion evidence. They may:

"(a) assist a party to establish the facts and to assess the merits of a case and with its preparation; (b) give to the court, as evidence, their expert opinion where opinion evidence apart from that of an expert would not be strictly admissible; (c) give factual evidence on a subject, where, because of their expertise, their evidence will have greater weight than that of an unqualified witness. Evidence as to foreign law will fall into this category. So does the evidence which surveyors sometimes give, in additional to their opinion evidence, as to measurements they have made or examinations which they have carried out; (d) conduct enquiries on behalf of the court and report to the court as to their findings; and (e) sit as assessors with judges to assist the court to understand the technical evidence which the court has to consider."[49]

The right of the parties to adduce expert evidence is somewhat restricted by the Civil Evidence Act 1972[50] and to a much greater extent by the CPR both explicitly[51] and by judges in the exercise of their case management function.[52] In addition, the expert's duties, rights, obligations and even the format of his or her report are closely prescribed by CPR Part 35 and its practice direction.[53] A Draft Code of Guidance for Expert Witnesses,[54]

---

[47] CPR r. 35.5(1).
[48] CPR r. 27.5. One should note that the only provisions of CPR Part 35 that apply in the fast track are rr. 35.1, 35.3, 35.7 and 35.8
[49] Interim Report p. 181.
[50] s. 2
[51] See for example CPR rr. 35.1, 35.4 and 35.5.
[52] See, for example, *Matthews v. Tarmac Bricks & Tiles Ltd, The Times*, 1st July 1999, C.A.; *Baron v. Lovell, The Times*, September 14, 1999, C.A., *Daniels v. Walker*, [2000] 1 W.L.R. 1382, C. A.; *Cosgrove and another v. Pattison and another* [2000] C.P. Rep. 68; *The Times*, February 13, 2001, Ch. D. See also Lowenstein, "A new role for the expert witness", (2000) 164(39) J.P. 2000 757–780; Fetto, "Keeping the Woolf away from your expert", (2001) 151 N.L.J. 6985; Gayler "Changing our minds", (2001) 145(3) Sol. J. 55.
[53] See in particular from March 25, 2002, PD. 35 para 1.
[54] Its principal point of interest was to seek to regulate experts instructed by the parties to assist them without appearing in court — the so-called "advice" expert described at (a) in the quotation above — who might be instructed, for example, to provide a technical view on a potential claim in order to advise whether or not a prima facie cause of action in, say, infringement of patent or clinical negligence existed. Advice experts would include those instructed, at considerable risk that the cost of their employment would not be recoverable, to comment on the findings of a joint expert.
For the situation where a purported expert is unable or unwilling to comply with CPR Part 35, see *Stevens v. Gullis and Pile*, [2000] 1 All E.R. 527, C.A and *Pearce v. Ove Arup Partnership Ltd.* [2002] ECDR CN2, Ch. D. where it was suggested that the expert's failure to comply with his obligations under the CPR should be reported to his own professional body. The current position on the question how far the expert must be independent of the parties appears to be stated in *Liverpool Roman Catholic Archdiocesan Trustees Inc v. Goldberg (No. 3), The Times*, August 14, 2001, Ch. D where the proposed expert was a friend and colleague of the instructing party. The Academy of Experts Code, see n.56 below, suggests at para 2.2.1) " ... a useful test of 'independence' is that the expert would give the same opinion if given the same instructions by an opposing party."

originally intended to provide the basis of a further practice direction or protocol, was under discussion by a Lord Chancellor's Department Working Party for several years and was "issued" in December 2001.[55] In the interim, however, one of the professional bodies for expert witnesses, the Academy of Experts, had published its own guide[56] which had been used by its members over a long period. Both will require adjustment to keep up with amendments to the CPR, particularly those of the 26th update to the rules, coming into force on 25th March 2002.

Where expert evidence is permitted, it will be inadmissible without the court's permission unless a report containing the expert's evidence (even if the expert is to give oral evidence at the trial) is exchanged in advance of the trial.[57] A party will not be allowed to call expert evidence at trial unless both the court's prior permission has been obtained to adduce expert evidence in respect of a particular issue[58] and the disclosure procedure has been followed.[59] The object of such disclosure is to save expense, where possible by discovering whether there is a real dispute between the parties and to avoid either party being taken by surprise on a technical matter and forced to seek an adjournment. The disclosure (by simultaneous exchange if the parties each have their own expert on the same issue) of reports also allows for technical issues to be further narrowed by submitting clarificatory questions to experts[60] and/or by having the experts for the opposing parties meet to see if they can reach areas of agreement.[61]

The rationale for such close control was identified by Lord Woolf in the Interim Report:

> "The need to engage experts was a source of excessive expenses, delay, and in some cases, increased complexity, through the excessive or inappropriate use of experts. Concern was also expressed as to their failure to maintain their independence from the party by which they have been instructed."[62]

and re-addressed in his Final Report, the original proposals apparently having "provoked more opposition than any of my other recommendations." The fundamental tenets of the new regime, identified in the Final Report[63] are:

---

[55] *Code of Guidance on Expert Evidence: A Guide for Experts and Those Instructing Them For the Purpose of Court Proceedings.* It can be found on the website of the Expert Witness Institute at *http://www.ewi.org.uk/main/code_of_guidance.htm*

[56] *CPR Code of Guidance For Experts and those Instructing Them.* It can be found on the website of the Academy Of Experts at *http://www.academy-experts.org/defaultin.htm*

[57] CPR r. 35.13.

[58] CPR r. 35.4

[59] CPRr. 35.13.

[60] CPR r. 35.6. For an example of such questions, see *Mutch v. Alien* [2001] C.P.Rep. 77, C.A.

[61] CPR r. 35.12 as amended from March 25, 2002. Arrangements for such meetings are clarified by both Codes.

[62] Interim Report, p. 181.

[63] Final Report, Chap. 13. Many of these principles in fact only restated the existing law: *National Justice Compania Naveria SA v. Prudential Assurance Co. Ltd (The Ikarian Reefer) (No. 1)* [1995] 1 Lloyd's Rep. 455, C.A. From March 25, 2002, however, they are stated more explicitly than ever in PD 35 para 1.

a.   A statement that "the expert's function is to assist the court". His or her
     duty is more explicitly defined as a duty on the expert to "help the court
     impartially on matters within his expertise."[64]

b.   The court to have "complete control" over the use of expert evidence,
     including:

     i.   Ordering that no expert evidence is required at all (either in relation
          to the whole dispute or to a particular issue);[65]
     ii. Limiting the number of experts to be called by each party;
     iii. Ordering that expert evidence should be given by a jointly
          instructed expert;[66]
     iv. Receiving expert evidence in written form only;[67]

c.   Requiring experts for the parties (assuming separate experts) to meet to
     see whether they can narrow the areas of dispute.[68]

15–006   Lord Woolf had, in his Interim Report, proposed that it should be the norm
that, rather than each party instructing, for example, an expert accountant
to calculate the amount of the claimant's losses; each coming to different
results between which the court had to choose, a single expert should be
appointed jointly by the parties to make a neutral calculation. There was in
fact already a limited power to appoint a "court expert" on the application
of one or both parties in R.S.C. Ord. 40, but it was little used.

The response to this particular proposal was described by Lord Woolf in
his Final Report[69] as "particularly strong ... it is clear that the idea is
anathema to many members of the legal profession in this country who are
reluctant to give up their adversarial weapons." A particular fear at the time
was that the imposition of a joint expert on a case would increase, rather
than decrease costs,[70] as each party would then feel the need to instruct its
own "shadow" or "advice" expert to comment on the findings of the joint
expert: three experts then becoming involved in the case rather than two.[71]

---

[64]   See C.P.R, r. 35.3 which adds the rider that this obligation "overrides any obligation to the
      person from whom [the expert] has received instructions or by whom he is paid."
      Exceptionally, this rule also applies to small claims track cases.
[65]   See CPR rr. 35.1 (which also applies in the small claims track) and 35.4. Note in particular
      that expert evidence will normally be adduced in writing rather than orally in the fast track
      (CPR r. 35.5(2)) and that in the small claims track express permission must be obtained to
      rely on expert evidence at all (CPR r. 27.5).
[66]   CPR rr. 35.7 and 35.8. Exceptionally, both these rules also apply to small claims track cases.
      It should be noted that the court can limit the recoverable fees of the joint expert, thus
      requiring the parties to be economical in their choice of expert, or to bear the risk of the
      expenditure on expert witnesses: CPR r. 35.4(4).
[67]   As with witness statements, it is the invariable practice that written reports of experts are
      exchanged prior to trial. CPR r. 35.5 adds the rider that the provision of written-only expert
      evidence will be the norm in the fast track.
[68]   CPR r. 35.12.
[69]   Chap. 13.
[70]   The use of the joint expert must be proportionate to the case. For a case in which the expert
      ran into difficulties with the fee limit imposed by the court, see *Kranidiotes v. Paschali* [2001]
      EWCA Civ 357, [2001] C.P. Rep. 81.P.C.
[71]   In some quarters at least, this fear has materialised: The Lord Chancellor's Department
      paper *Emerging Findings, op. cit.*, cites findings of the large city firm Freshfields to the effect
      that parties were likely to appoint "shadow experts" to comment on the findings of the joint
      expert.

Lord Woolf's view remained: "As a general principle, I believe that single experts should be used wherever the case (or the issue) is concerned with a substantially established area of knowledge and where it is not necessary for the court directly to sample a range of opinions."[72] The Lord Chancellor's Department has estimated that in 2000, in county court cases where expert evidence was relied on at all, 41 per cent involved jointly instructed experts.[73] In February 2001 the Law Society found that 36 per cent of respondents to its survey considered use of joint experts to be "very common"; 56 per cent experienced "occasional" use of joint experts and 8 per cent had never encountered a joint expert at all.[74]

What is, apparently, clear, is that the report of the "joint expert", where the procedure is used, is only a preliminary step. So, in *Daniels v. Walker*,[75] where one of the parties objected to the findings of the joint expert and sought permission from the court to call an expert witness of his own, Lord Woolf in the Court of Appeal said:

> "In a substantial case such as this, the correct approach is to regard the instruction of an expert jointly by the parties as the first step in obtaining expert evidence on a particular issue. It is to be hoped that in the majority of cases it will not only be the first step but the last step. If, having obtained a joint expert's report, a party, for reasons which are not fanciful, wishes to obtain further information before making a decision as to whether or not there is a particular part (or indeed the whole) of the expert's report which he or she may wish to challenge, then they should, subject to the discretion of the court, be permitted to obtain that evidence."

The obligations of the expert witness are perhaps best considered by examining the prescribed content of the written report for multi track and fast track cases[76] which will frequently, especially in the fast track, be the only way in which the expert evidence is presented at trial. Note that this list of contents is stated as at March 25, 2002 and that both Codes referred to earlier suggest additional content.

a. Details of qualifications;

b. Literature and other material relied on;

---

[72] Final Report, Chap. 13, para 19.

[73] *Emerging Findings, op. cit.* para. 4.20. Neither of the two Codes permits a jointly appointed expert to meet privately with representatives of one party in the absence of representatives of the other with express prior consent of the other. For an example of attempts to meet the joint expert in the absence of the other party, see *MP v. Mid Kent Healthcare NHS Trust* [2001] EWCA Civ 1703; [2002] 1 W.L.R. 210, C.A.

[74] *Response to Third Woolf Questionnaire, op. cit.*

[75] [2000] 1 W.L.R. 1382, C.A. See also *Cosgrove and another v. Pattison and another* [2000] C.P. Rep. 68; *The Times*, February 13, 2001, Ch. D; *Alderson and another v. Stillorgan Sales Ltd* [2000] EWCA Civ 1060; 2001 WL 825127, Ch. D; and, for the European perspective on a similar issue, *Mantovanelli v. France* (1997) E.H.R.R. 370.

[76] PD. 35, para. 1.

c.   A statement "setting out the substance of all facts and instructions given to the expert which are material to the opinions expressed in the report or upon which those opinions are based";[77]

d.   Identification of facts that are within the expert's own knowledge (as opposed, for example, to those which the expert has been told of by those instructing him or her or which the expert has been asked to assume);

e.   Details of tests and experiments carried out, including whether or not they were undertaken under the expert's supervision;

f.   Where there is a range of opinion on the issue, a summary of the range of opinion and the expert's reasons for adopting his or her position;

g.   A summary of conclusions;

h.   If the expert's opinion is qualified in any way, details of the qualification;

i.   A statement that the expert understands his or her duty to the court,[78] has complied and will continue to comply with it;

j.   A statement of truth: "I confirm that insofar as the facts stated in my report are within my own knowledge I have made clear which they are and I believe them to be true, and that the opinions I have expressed represent my true and complete professional opinion";

Item c) on the list bears some explanation. Lord Woolf had expressed concern that pressure was placed on experts to adopt a particular view.[79] After consultation, in the Final Report, he remained of the view that transparency of instructions was vital.[80] Many experts will satisfy their obligations in this respect by simply attaching a copy of the letter of instruction to their reports but the nature of this obligation is also discussed in both Codes.

The expert witness may be different from an "ordinary" witness in that evidence is being given on matters within a field of knowledge, often, in multi track cases, after a prolonged examination. However, where permission is given for oral expert evidence in addition to the written report, the expert witness is examined and cross-examined in just the same way. Where the parties are permitted to have separate, individually instructed experts, those experts are just as much the "property" of one party, subject to their overriding duty "to help the court on the matters

---

[77] PD. 35, para 2.2(3). Both Codes discuss the nature of instructions both in this context and in the context of what the expert will expect to be provided with by those instructing him or her.

[78] In the Commercial Court the statements are expanded to include reference to the Commercial Court Guide.

[79] It is and always was highly unethical to require an expert to alter his or her opinion: *National Justice Compania Naviera S A v. Prudential Assurance Co. Ltd (The Ikarian Reefer) (No. 1)* [1995] 1 Lloyd's Rep. 455, C.A.

[80] Final Report Chap. 13 paras. 31 to 33 inclusive. Where a joint expert is ordered, the instructions are jointly drafted by the parties (and therefore the content is known to both) or, if the expert is sent separate instructions by each party, those instructions are copied to the opponent: CPR r. 35.8(2).

within [their] expertise."[81] The temptation for parties to indulge in a battle of experts in court, sometimes hoping to win the point by the sheer volume of evidence or by the eminence of their witness(es) may have been reduced by the familiar use of joint experts and such matters as the court's power to approve or disapprove the instruction of an expert in advance and to limit the recoverable costs of an individual expert,[82] promoting economy in their selection.

An additional power, which could be useful, is contained in the Supreme Court Act 1981, s.70 and County Courts Act 1984, s. 63 and now implemented by CPR r. 35.15 which allows the appointment of assessors or scientific advisers to assist in the hearing and disposal of the action. These are people who sit with the judge at the trial of the action and their role is considered more fully later in this chapter.

C. THE USE OF THE JURY IN CIVIL CASES

Jury trial is wholly exceptional and confined to a handful of cases. The erosion in the use of juries has been gradual. It appears to have begun with the introduction of the discretionary use of juries in all but six causes of action in 1833[83] and was continued by the temporary suspension of jury trial beginning during the First World War and ending in 1925.[84]   **15–007**

The current position, now found in section 69 of the Supreme Court Act 1981, was first established in 1933.[85] Section 69 provides, first, for a qualified right to jury trial in some cases, and, secondly, for a discretion to order jury trial in other cases.

The qualified right to jury trial applies in cases of fraud,[86] libel, slander,

---

[81] CPR r. 35.3

[82] CPR r. 35.4(4)

[83] Rules of the Supreme Court 1883, Ord. XXXVI. The causes of action in which there was a right to jury trial were: libel, slander, malicious prosecution, false imprisonment, seduction and breach of promise of marriage. These provisions formed the basis of the statutory reform in 1933. An analysis of the decline in the use of the jury, on the basis of statistics then available, is contained in R. M. Jackson, "The Incidence of Jury Trial during the Past Century" (1937) 1 M.L.R. 132. Jackson does not advance the view that the 1833 Rules were significant in reducing the number of jury trials, but the figures seem to support that contention. See also, M. G. Buckley, "Civil Trial by Jury" (1966) 19 C. L. P. 63. A good chronological account is provided by Bankes L.J. in *Ford v. Blurton* (1922) 38 T.L.R. 801 at pp. 802–803.

[84] The Juries Act 1918 provided for trial by judge alone unless the court ordered otherwise, subject to the right to jury trial in a category of cases slightly wider than that in the 1883 Rules. This provision was continued by the Administration of Justice Act 1920 but repealed by the Administration of Justice Act 1925

[85] The Administration of Justice (Miscellaneous Provisions) Act 1933, s.6. The number of jury trials declined sharply after 1933.

[86] The meaning of fraud in this context was considered by Sir Robert Megarry V.-C. in *Stafford Winfield Cook v. Winfield* [1981] 1 W. L. R. 45. For a recent example, see *Inland Revenue Commissioners v. Kingston Crown Court and another*, July 24, 2001, Lawtel C0101706, D.C.

malicious prosecution[87] and false imprisonment.[88] Jury trial is to be granted unless "the court is of the opinion that the trial requires any prolonged examination of documents or accounts or any scientific or local examination which cannot conveniently be made with a jury ... "[89] This qualified right is exercised most frequently in defamation actions (that is, libel and slander). The decision whether to permit jury trial depends upon a balance of the desire to grant trial by jury where requested and the need to take a realistic view about the material with which juries can deal in a trial and the length of time which a trial is expected to take or, put another way, the efficient administration of justice.[90] After considerable debate about the outcome of a number of celebrated libel actions,[91] the Court of Appeal now has the power either to order a new trial on the ground that damages awarded by the jury are excessive or inadequate or, without the agreement of the parties, to substitute for the sum awarded by the jury such sum as appears to the court to be proper.[92] As the jury's control over awards of damages lessens, it is possible that jury trial will become less attractive to claimants.[93]

Further, the court has a discretion to order jury trial in other cases.[94] Jury trial should be ordered only in exceptional cases[95] and it will be very difficult to persuade a judge to exercise the discretion to order trial by jury, especially in the context of CPR Part 1. The factors to be taken into account are: the need for uniformity in the award of damages in personal injury cases, the jury being ignorant of the conventional figures in comparable cases;[96] that in

---

[87] For a recent example, see *Isaac v. Chief Constable of the West Midlands Police*, [2001] E.W.C.A. Civ 1405, 2001 WL 1040303, C.A.

[88] Or any other questions or issues prescribed: Supreme Court Act 1981, s. 69(l)(c). County Courts Act 1984, s. 66 provides the equivalent for the county courts. Any application for a claim to be tried by a jury is made within 28 days of filing a defence: CPR r. 26.11. Queen's Bench Division Guide (applying to the Royal Courts of Justice in London) provides the following at para. 8.3: "Claims for libel and slander (defamation), fraud, malicious prosecution and false imprisonment will be tried by a judge and jury unless the court orders trial by a judge alone."

[89] Supreme Court Act 1981, s.69(l).

[90] *Beta Construction Ltd. v. Channel Four Television Co. Ltd.* [1990] 1 W.L.R. 1042. The national importance of the issues may render jury trial appropriate even if there is considerable documentary evidence: *Rothermere v. Times Newspapers* [1973] 1 W.L.R. 448. The case concerned an article written by Bernard Levin in *The Times*, March 19, 1971, entitled "Profit and dishonour in Fleet Street." However, due care must be taken not to overburden the jury, as may have occurred in *Orme v. Associated Newspapers Group*, March 31, 1981, (unreported) (Q.B.D.); December 20, 1982 (unreported) (C.A.), where the trial, involving alleged defamation of the Moonies, lasted more than five months and 117 witnesses were called. *McDonald's Corporation v. Steel and Morris* [1997] E.W.H.C. Q.B. 366 (the "McLibel trial") in 1996, currently the longest trial in British legal history occupying 313 hearing days, was heard without a jury. Lawyers are required to take great care in estimating the length of trial so as to avoid "hardship and inconvenience" to jurors: Queen's Bench Division Guide, para. 8.3.2.

[91] *e.g.* cases brought by Jeffrey Archer, Koo Stark, Sonia Sutcliffe and Sir Elton John.

[92] Courts and Legal Services Act 1990, s. 8; *Grobbelaar v. News Group Newspapers Ltd. and another*, [2001] E.W.C.A. Civ 33, [2001] 2 All E.R. 437, C.A.

[93] The existence of a pre-action protocol for defamation claims will add to the effect. However in the Royal Courts of Justice in 2000, 241 defamation claims were nevertheless issued: *Judicial Statistics 2000*, table 3.2.

[94] Supreme Court Act 1981, .s.69(3).

[95] *Ward v. James* [1966] 1 Q. B. 273, *per* Lord Denning MR. at p. 303. In the event this case was sent for jury trial but the court was influenced by factors peculiar to it. The point was emphasised in *Williams v. Beasley* [1973] 1 W.L.R. 1295, *per* Lord Diplock at p. 1299H.

[96] *Ward v. James* [1966] 1 Q. B. 273, *per* Lord Denning M.R. at pp. 296–300, 303.

such cases the severity[97] or unusual[98] nature of the injuries are not exceptional circumstances, but if they are unique or nearly so[99], jury trial may be appropriate; the possibility of dishonesty[1] or deliberate lying; the fact that the honour and integrity of the person applying for jury trial may be at stake;[2] the fact that trial without a jury is speedier and less expensive;[3] the proposition that, in the circumstances, trial by judge alone is "more likely to achieve a just result than trial by jury."[4] Further, Lord Diplock indicated that jury trial should not be ordered either simply because there might be a conflict of evidence, since many cases will involve issues of credibility and that is not a sufficient reason to depart from the "usual rule" of trial by judge alone[5] or simply because a party has the "mistaken belief ... that judges as a class are likely to be biased against him or in favour of his opponent" since to decide on that basis would provide such beliefs with credence, whereas the system is based upon "an impartial judiciary."[6] Additional and overriding concerns of the modern judge asked to order trial by jury will be compliance with CPR Part 1: the overriding objective.

If a jury trial does take place it, as in criminal proceedings, is controlled by the provisions of the Juries Act 1974. The qualification for service of jurors, the procedure for summoning, the compilation of panels, the ballot and swearing of jurors, and the right to challenge for cause are all exactly the same for civil and criminal trials.[7] Majority verdicts may be accepted in civil cases, although there is greater flexibility than in criminal matters since the parties to the action may proceed by agreement with an incomplete jury.[8] The discretion to exclude a juror from service which may be exercised by the appropriate officer or by the court[9] is likely to be exercised more freely in civil matters where there may be considerable hardship or inconvenience caused by a long trial.

D. SHOULD THE JURY BE RETAINED IN CIVIL CASES?

In the previous edition of this book, it was considered that, if the debates on the Supreme Court Bill 1981 were any guide, that this was already an academic question. Parliament at that time showed itself unwilling to

15–008

---

[97] *Sims v. William Howard and Son Ltd* [1964] 2 Q.B. 409.

[98] *Watts v. Manning* [1964] 1 W.L.R. 623.

[99] *Hodges v. Harland and Wolff Ltd.* [1965] 1 W.L.R. 523. In this highly unusual case the plaintiff (in the then current terminology) was injured whilst using a diesel-driven air compressor. The spindle of the machine caught in his trousers and avulsed his penis and scrotal skin. Jury trial was ordered. The observations of Davies L.J. at pp. 1087–1088 are helpful in setting out the difficulties of jury trial.

[1] *Sims v. William Howard and Son Ltd.* [1964] 2 Q.B. 409 *per Pearson* L.J. at p. 419.

[2] *Ward v. James* [1966] 1 Q. B. 273, *per* Lord Denning M.R. at p. 295; *Williams v. Beasley* [1973] 1 W.L.R. 1295, *per* Lord Diplock at p. 1298H.

[3] *Williams v. Beasley* [1973] 1 W.L.R. 1295, *per* Lord Diplock at p. 1299H.

[4] *ibid, per* Lord Diplock at p. 1299H

[5] *ibid, per* Lord Diplock at p. 1298–9.

[6] *ibid.* at p. 1299H.

[7] See below Chapter 17.

[8] Juries Act 1974, s. 17.

[9] Juries Act 1974, s. 9(2), (4).

countenance any further restriction on the right to jury trial, let alone its abolition.[10] The debate about jury trials in general, raising its head again in the context of the results of Auld L.J.'s review of the criminal courts,[11] has extended to the civil context particularly in the context of a spate of well-publicised libel trials[12] as well as the introduction of the Defamation Act 1996, implemented by Part 53 of the CPR and supplemented by a specific pre-action protocol for defamation cases.

The disadvantages of jury trial appear to be the additional time, and consequential additional expense of a jury trial, the variability of jury verdicts, the potential hardship and inconvenience suffered by individual jurors in lengthy cases, the unrealistic expectations that lay people[13] should listen to and comprehend complex and extensive evidence, the unpredictability of jury verdicts and the reluctance of the Court of Appeal to interfere with jury awards,[14] and the additional burden which may be placed on advocates and judge where complex questions of law are in issue.[15]

These reasons are sound pragmatic grounds for the proposition that jury trial is not the "best" mode of trial for all civil claims and that trial by judge alone would normally be preferable. But are any of the reasons sufficiently strong to support the view that trial by jury should not be permissible?

The Faulks Committee on Defamation[16] recommended restrictions on the use of juries in defamation actions whilst rejecting arguments for their total abolition. The Committee concluded that in defamation cases the court should have the same discretion to order jury trial as in other civil cases and that the function of the jury should be limited to deciding issues of liability,

---

[10] Jacob (1987), pp. 156–160.

[11] *A Review of the Criminal Courts of England and Wales* (September 2001), Chap. 5

[12] *Grobbelaar v. News Group Newspapers Ltd. and another, op. cit.*, thought to be the first case in more than 100 years in which a jury's award of damages was set aside as "perverse" (Scott-Bayfield, "Defamation Update", (2001) Sol. J. 145 (21), p.501); *Loutchansky v Times Newspapers Ltd. and others* [2001] E.M.L.R. 933, Q.B.D.; *McPhilemy v. Times Newspapers Ltd. and others* [2001] E.W.C.A. Civ 871, [2001] E.M.L.R. 34, C.A.; *Berezovsky and another v. Forbes Inc. and another*, [2001] E.W.C.A. Civ 1251, [2001] E.M.L.R. 45, C.A.; *Hamilton v. Al Fayed and others* [2001] 1 A.C. 395, H.L. (affirming decisions below); *Irving v. Penguin Books Ltd. and another*, [2001] EWCA Civ 1197; 2001 WL825o74.

[13] Note, however, that Auld L.J., *ibid.*, proposes removing many of the existing bars to eligibility for jury service, which would, *inter alia*, allow lawyers to sit on juries.

[14] See *Grobbelaar v. News Group Newspapers Ltd. and another, op. cit.*, where the jury's award of £85, 000 against the defendant was set aside by the Court of Appeal. See Melville-Brown, "Media Law", Law Society Gazette, April 30, 2000.

[15] These defects of the jury as a mode of trial are culled from various sources including: M.G. Buckley, "Civil Trial by Jury" (1966) 19 C.L.P. 63; W.R. Cornish, *The Jury* (1968), Chap. 8; P. Devlin, *Trial by Jury* (1956), pp. 130–135; *Hodges v. Harland and Wolff Ltd* [1965] 1 W.L.R. 523; *Ward v. James* [1966] 1 Q.B. 273; and the *Report of the Committee on Defamation* (Cmnd. 5909, 1975) (The Faulks Committee). Very recent examples of concern about costs and the use of juries in libel trials under the CPR are cited in Hickman, "The Press Gang", Law Society Gazette, June 19, 2001 and in Melville-Brown, "Media Law", (2000) 97(16) L.S.G.38 discussing *Irving v. Penguin Books Ltd. and another, op. cit.* A number of factors have conspired, however, over the last few years that should reduce the number of defamation cases coming to trial and hence to a jury: the Defamation Act 1996 and CPR Part 53 contain new defences (innocent dissemination) and a new regime allowing for summary disposal of defamation claims. In addition, the pre-action protocol for defamation claims is also intended to reduce the number of claims that come to trial.

[16] *Report of the Committee on Defamation, op.cit.*

leaving the assessment of damages to the judge.[17] The following summarises the view of the Committee:

> "We believe that much of the support for jury trials is emotional, and derives from the undoubted value of juries in serious criminal cases, where they stand between the prosecuting authority and the citizen. But the true function of the civil jury is to weigh facts impersonally and recompense the claimant for an injury that he may have sustained — tasks for which the judge is trained by many years of experience and for which jurors have no training at all.[18]

Is it right to describe the support for the jury as "emotional"? Various distinguished judges have declared the constitutional importance of the right to jury trial. For example, Atkin L.J. in *Ford v. Blurton* described jury trial as "the bulwark of liberty, the shield of the poor from the rich and the powerful."[19] Although the argument of Atkin L.J. may appear to be more suited to the jury in criminal trials, there is some truth in it in relation to civil trials. However, if judges are independent of the state and other vested interests,[20] perhaps the argument has lost much of its force. A different argument is that it is desirable to involve as many people as possible in the administration of justice[21] and that the jury stands between the judges and the person in the street to ensure that ordinary standards are applied in the doing of justice.[22]

Even if there may be criticism of the distinction between the five specified causes of action and other civil cases, trial by jury is unlikely to be abolished in civil matters, but responsibility lies with the judges for ensuring that the worst features of jury trial are not often evident.

E. THE ROLE OF THE JUDGE

In civil matters the judge normally sits alone to determine the outcome of the action. The incidence of jury trial has already been explained, but there are a number of situations in which the judge may have the assistance of others sitting with him or her. The composition of the Employment Appeal Tribunal, with lay members and High Court judges, exemplified the formal introduction of lay expertise into the judicial process, but there is a general

15–009

---

[17] *ibid.*, paras. 455–457.

[18] *ibid*, para. 496.

[19] (1922) 38 T.L.R. 801 at 805. See also, to similar effect, Bankes L.J. in the same case. The same point was made by Mr. Frank Dobson M.P. in the debates on the Supreme Court Bill when he said: "Jury service is more important to the preservation of individual liberty and the preservation of our judicial system than all the scurvy race of lawyers put together."

[20] See above, Chapter 4.

[21] See, *e.g.*, the evidence of Sir Peter Rawlinson Q. C. and Viscount Dilhorne given to the Faulks Committee (1975), para.477.

[22] On a pragmatic level, Lord Denning M.R. supported the jury for the protection of a person's honour and integrity or to discover when one party may be lying; *Ward v. James* [1966] 1 Q.B. 273, at p. 295.

power[23] to call in the aid of one or more assessors or scientific advisers in particular cases.

Assessors are used especially in certain types of admiralty proceedings in the Queen's Bench Division,[24] but there is nothing to prevent a judge, provided it is consistent with CPR Part 1 and the obligations of art 6 to do so, using an assessor in other cases. It may cause expense and inconvenience to the parties if the hearing has to be adjourned so that the judge may find and appoint an appropriate expert, but there is strong (albeit pre-Woolf) support for that course of action, in preference to obtaining assistance from an expert after the hearing has concluded and before judgment is given.[25] In modern practice, one would expect that the need for an assessor would be identified during the initial pre-trial stages, on allocation or during the clarification of issues in dispute during the course of a case management conference

Scientific advisers may be appointed in an action for the infringement of a patent and will render similar assistance to the judge. The role of both assessor and scientific adviser is to listen to the evidence and give the judge such assistance as may be required in formulating the judgment and, if an opinion is taken on the outcome, that opinion and the reasons for it may be taken into account by the Court of Appeal in the event of an appeal.

In a civil action, it may prove difficult for the judge to refrain from intervening with questions and observations. However, the judge — within the confines of art 6 — does not have to attain the standards of objectivity and neutrality that appertain in a criminal trial, since usually no jury is present. The procedure is relatively flexible in a civil trial and the absence of the jury enables the judge to take a more positive line over matters which may be considered to be irrelevant or uncontentious. However, the judge must not take such an active part in the case that it appears that the advocates are deprived of the conduct of the action. Denning L.J., long before the CPR or the Human Rights Act 1998, put the judge's role as follows:

> "The judge's part ... is to hearken to the evidence, only himself asking question of witnesses when it is necessary to clear up any point that has been overlooked or left obscure; to see that the advocates behave themselves seemly and keep to the rules laid down by law; to exclude irrelevancies and discourage repetition; to make sure by wise intervention that he follows the points that the advocates are making and can assess their work; and at the end to make up his mind where the truth lies."[26]

It is suggested that it is a legitimate inference from the positive obligations imposed on the trial judge by CPR Part 1 and to ensure a fair and

---

[23] Supreme Court Act 1981, s. 70; County Courts Act 1984, s. 63. See also CPR r. 35.15 and PD. 35 para. 6.

[24] Where the assessor is normally one or more of the Elder Brethren of Trinity House: from March 25, 2002 CPR r 61. 13.

[25] From Devlin J. in *Esso Petroleum Co Ltd. v. Southport Corporation* [1956] A. C. 218 at pp. 222–223. His view was supported by the House of Lords in the same case.

[26] *Jones v. National Coal Board* [1957] 2 Q.B. 55 at p. 64.

independent trial under art. 6 that judges will no longer be entitled to take such a passive role.[27]

If sitting alone, the judge may take time to decide where the truth lies, or, more accurately, whether the claimant has satisfied the burden of proof,[28] and give a reserved judgment at a later date, or an extempore judgment may be given at the conclusion of the hearing. If sitting with a jury, the judge must sum up the evidence and direct on the law as would be done in a trial on indictment. Ultimately judgment will be given.

F. THE JUDGMENT AND REMEDIES

A judgment is a reasoned decision in which the judge will normally set out **15–010** the facts of the case as he or she has decided, and give the conclusions on the law applicable to them. Some of the arguments put by the advocates may be rehearsed so as to set the decision in context,[29] and an opinion is likely to be given on all matters relating to the action which might be relevant if the losing party were to appeal. In particular, there may be findings of fact which are not crucial to the judgment given at first instance but which might become relevant if the Court of Appeal were to take a different view of the law. The trial judge will be attempting to avoid the expense and difficulty of a new trial if the appellate court changes a part of the judgment.[30]

The remedies available in civil proceedings are various, dependent upon the action being brought by the claimant.[31] There is an important adage worthy of repetition. It states that where there is a legal right there is, or ought to be, a legal remedy and where there is no remedy there is no right. There is an extensive range of remedies which may be added to or varied[32] by judicial decision or through the legislature. The remedies that were available varied according to whether the action was one in the High Court or the county court. However, section 3 of the Courts and Legal Services Act 1990 provides that county courts may make the same remedial orders as

---

[27] For the position where a judge has to withdraw from a case because of an inability to provide a fair trial, see, *R. v. Bow Street Magistrates, ex parte Pinochet (No. 2)* [2001] 1 A.C. 119, H.L.; *Locabail (U.K.) Ltd. v. Bayfield Properties Ltd. and others* [2000] Q.B. 451, C.A.

[28] *i.e.* whether the claimant has proved his or her case on a balance of probabilities.

[29] Because it is the responsibility of the parties — within the constraints of the judicial case management applied to the case — to advance argument on the issues which they wish to be decided it is always important to know whether a particular line of argument has been canvassed or not when assessing a judgment. In respect of appellate decisions reported in the Law Reports series, the major arguments of the advocates are normally set out as part of the report.

[30] *e.g.*, although a judge may find against a claimant on the question of the defendant's liability in negligence, the quantum of damages will be determined lest the Court of Appeal reverses on the liability point (unless it has already been arranged that there should be a split trial). If no finding had been made on quantum the issue would have to be the subject of another trial.

[31] See, generally, F. H. Lawson, *Remedies of English Law* (2nd ed.) and M. Tilbury, M. Noone and B. Ketcher, *Remedies* (1988) (this is an Australian work drawing on considerable English material).

[32] If a new remedy affects the substantive law, it can only be created by Act of Parliament.

the High Court.[33] Damages is the most likely remedy sought in an action in the Queen's Bench as considered here and in Chapter 11, but readers should be aware that other remedies are available. In particular, the claimant may be seeking the recovery or restitution of property, one of the many equitable remedies, such as an order for specific performance,[34] or an injunction,[35] or a declaration.

Damages is the common law term for an order requiring payment of money. An award of damages may be made in relation to a vast range of wrongs and indebtedness.[36] The traditional division of damages is into liquidated and unliquidated damages: liquidated where the claimant specifies a set sum of money as owed at law in the original claim (described in the CPR as "claims for a specified sum"); unliquidated ("claims for an unspecified sum") where the court must calculate the sum to be paid if liability is established, unless there is agreement on the quantum of damages between the parties. The method by which unliquidated damages are assessed is of most concern.

Damages can be claimed primarily on a contract or tort claim, and the basis for awarding damages will be slightly different dependent upon the action. The basic theory of damages for contract is that they should provide a sum that will, financially at least, fulfil the claimant's expectation under the promise made. The basic theory of tort damages is that the claimant, so far as money can, should be returned to the position before the wrong was done. However, it would appear that, despite the theoretical differences, modern law is taking a more pragmatic attitude.

High Court judges are, for example, frequently called upon to assess damages in cases where the defendant has negligently inflicted personal injuries upon the claimant.[37] There are normally two basic aspects of such an award: (i) compensation for non-pecuniary losses, and (ii) compensation for pecuniary or economic losses. Under the first head there may be damages for pain and suffering and loss of amenity[38] or, where the part of a body injured has no apparent function, the injury itself.[39] Damages for loss of amenity are awarded roughly in accordance with a tariff dependent on the seriousness of the injury or injuries.[40] Under the second head fall damages

---

[33] County courts do not have the power to order certain kinds of injunctions, declarations of incompatibility under the Human Rights Act 1998 or orders of kinds to be prescribed by the Lord Chancellor.

[34] Available to enforce contractual obligations.

[35] The prime form of injunction is prohibitory since it forces a defendant to desist from wrongful conduct or forbids wrongful conduct when it has not even started, *i.e.* the *quia timet* injunction. A mandatory injunction requires the doing of some act.

[36] Whilst this chapter concentrates on actions in contract and tort, an award of damages can be made in relation to a claim in quasi-contract, in certain equity actions, *e.g.* where recission is allowed for innocent misrepresentation, or where a trustee commits a breach of trust. Further, certain tribunals may also make awards of compensation, *e.g.*, an employment tribunal for unfair dismissal.

[37] See W.V.H.Rogers, *Winfield and Jolowicz on the Law of Tort* (16th ed.).

[38] *e.g.*, damages for the loss of a leg, which may be increased where the claimant was a keen sports player whose enjoyment of life is thus substantially impaired.

[39] *e.g.*, a spleen, *Forster v. Pugh* [1955] C.L.Y. 741.

[40] Details of damages given in personal injury cases are given in *Kemp and Kemp on the quantum of Damages* (looseleaf and CD Rom). The "tariff" is set out in the Judicial Studies Board *Guidelines for the Assessment of General Damages in Personal Injury Cases* (4th ed.) Blackstone.

for such items as lost earnings[41] and medical expenses.

For example, in *Lim Poh Choo v. Camden and Islington Area Health Authority*[42] the plaintiff (in the terminology then current), an NHS registrar, suffered serious brain damage after a minor operation. She was ultimately awarded £229, 298.64. This included £20,00 for pain and suffering and loss of amenities; £3,956 for expenses to the date of trial; £16,500 for the costs of care in Malaysia; £1,923 for travelling expenses; £4,226.64 for the costs of care in the United Kingdom to date; £14,213 for loss of earnings to the date of trial; £76,800 for the costs of future care and £92,000 for the loss of future earnings including pension rights.

At the end of the judgment, the successful party's advocate must ask formally for judgment to be entered for the client in the terms which the judge has indicated. The advocate may ask for "judgment for the claimant for £229, 298.64" or "judgment for the defendant and that the claimant's claim be dismissed". At this stage the question of any interest payable on a money judgment will be raised by the advocate, who will also ask for costs.[43] It is at this stage that the trial judge is made aware of the details of any Part 36 offer or payment[44] and can decide whether or not to impose any penalising orders on a party who has failed to do better that the opponent's payment or offer.[45]

Traditionally, money judgments were expressed in sterling, but since 1975 it has been possible for a court to give judgment in a foreign currency.[46]

Contrary to previous practice, the final responsibility no longer rests with the successful party or his or her solicitor. By CPR r. 40.3, the order containing the judgment will normally be drawn up by the court.[47] Having obtained judgement, the successful party must go on to enforce it. Contrary, perhaps, to expectations, that party's troubles may only just be beginning!

---

[41] In the most serious cases there will be the difficult task of estimating the loss of earnings in the future.

[42] [1980] A.C. 174.

[43] See para. 11-003.

[44] See para. 12-028.

[45] See CPR rr. 36.20 and 36.21.

[46] *Miliangos v. George Frank (Textiles) Ltd.* [1976] A.C. 443, not following the previous authority, Re *United Railways of Havana and Regla Warehouses Ltd.* [1961] A.C. 1007. See also PD. 40 para 10.

[47] Unless the court orders one of the parties to draw it up, one of the parties agrees to draw it up, the court dispenses with the need to draw up the order or the order is a consent order. Where the order is drawn up by one of the parties, sufficient copies of it for all the parties must be filed with the court no later than 7 days later for sealing by the court. CPR rr. 40.3 and 40.4 and PD. 40B para 1

G. ENFORCING JUDGMENT[48]

(a) INTRODUCTION

15-011   [T]he machinery of the enforcement of the judgments and orders of the court constitute the very foundation of the judicial process. It represents the coercive power of the court in the exercise of its judicial authority. It expresses the will of the state to buttress the judiciary ... and makes their judgments and orders authoritative and obligatory, binding and conclusive."[49]

If judgment is obtained, the order of the court may be declaratory or constitutive[50] and nothing more need be done. In most instances, however, the order will require the performance of some further act or acts or the abstention from acts. The law appears to lean heavily in favour of inducement rather than direct compulsion. The form of the court order will frequently demonstrate this: thus the normal order in an action for damages requires the defendant to pay the claimant the specified figure.

Many defendants obey court orders out of law-abiding motives.[51] Others will be influenced by the appreciation that practical procedures exist to secure performance or obedience. These procedures might be said to form a system of enforcement, which Jacob, however, has described as being

> "an unplanned, unsystematic, haphazard, complex system. It operates, especially in relation to money judgements, largely on a hit-or-miss basis. In relation to both money and non-money judgments, it is in part effective, but in part it is ineffective, inefficient, somewhat random and sometimes oppressive."[52]

These sentiments were shared by the Lord Chancellor's Department in 2000: "[t]he picture that emerges is of an enforcement system that is not particularly effective, difficult to understand and prone to excessive delay."[53]

---

[48] Jacob (1987), pp. 185–210; Sir Jack Jacob, "The enforcement of Judgment Debts" in *The Reform of Civil Procedural Law* (1982); O'Hare and Browne, *O'Hare and Hill Civil Litigation op.cit.*, Chaps. 40 and 41. As to the enforcement of foreign judgments and the enforcement of judgments outside England and Wales, see O'Hare and Browne, *O'Hare and Hill Civil Litigation op.cit.*, Chap. 40 although from March 2002 enforcement of judgments with E.U. countries will be governed by Council Regulation (EC) No 44/2001 of December 22, 2000 (on jurisdiction and the recognition and enforcement of judgments in civil and commercial matters). Consequential amendments have been made to the CPR

[49] Jacob (1987), pp. 185–186 and see Andrews (1994), p. 514.

[50] "Constitutive" orders are extremely various and extend across many areas of law. Examples in the civil law are adoption and legitimation orders, award of guardianship, divorces, appointment of trustees, dissolution of partnerships, liquidation of companies, adjudication in bankruptcy. Sometimes the order merely records a fact, an example being the declaration that a seeming marriage was always null and void. See Lawson (1980) Chap.17.

[51] However in the report of the *First Phase of the Enforcement Review* (July 2001) (hereafter Enforcement Review) it was suggested that at least £600 million a year was lost in unpaid judgments.

[52] Jacob (1987) p. 188.

[53] Enforcement Review, *op. cit.*

Attempts are being made, however, to rationalise a system which, at the time of writing, still operated under a "rump" of the pre-Woolf court rules, and consequently used different procedures depending whether the claim was proceeding in the High Court or the county court and in some circumstances demanded that a claim be transferred from one court to the other in order in search of the most efficient or most appropriate means of enforcement. Parts 70 to 73 inclusive were incorporated into the CPR in March 2002 in order to deal with enforcement in a consistent and coherent way. This is the end result of a process commenced in March 1998 and culminating in July 2001[54] with a report containing 40 proposals seeking to (1) make the process more straightforward and comprehensible; (2) improve recovery rates; (3) achieve fairness for both debtors (who may genuinely not have the means to pay) and creditors and finally (4) to speed up the process. In July 2001 a Green Paper[55] was issued and was intended to be followed by a White Paper containing draft legislation in early 2002. Such adjustments as can be made without primary legislation are, it appears, included in the 26th update to the CPR

At present, however, even when the new amendments are included, the procedures that exist are variously derived from the common law, equity and statute. They are primarily aimed at specific forms of judgment, but they are capable of being used for any type of judgment if they can be effective. Thus sequestration, authorising the seizure of all or any property of the defendant within the jurisdiction, imposition of a fine and committal to prison are all drastic sanctions suitable for flagrant breaches of orders such as injunctions, but in extreme circumstances they can be used to enforce other types of judgment where there has been a civil contempt of court. Imprisonment for a few civil debts may also be imposed, separately from a finding of contempt of court.

A brief description of the main execution orders available follows, together with an indication of the new amendments, but prior to seeking such an order it may be necessary to discover the debtor's means. This can be achieved by an "order to obtain information from a judgment debtor" under CPR Part 71 (previously "oral examination" of the judgment debtor) normally in the judgment debtor's local county court.[56] It is suggested in the Green Paper[57] that this procedure might be strengthened by increased court involvement and by the possibility of obtaining information from third parties such as the debtor's employer. From October 2000, of course, the

---

[54] It is worth noting that the review itself commented on the paucity of statistical information about the effectiveness of the enforcement process but that, for example, the Court Service had provided figures suggesting that only approximately 35% of county court warrants of execution (see below) result in payment. It is perhaps a function of the complexity of the procedure that, when warrants that are technically unenforceable are removed from the equation, the figure for satisfied warrants rises to 75%: Enforcement Review, para. 17. There had been a series of consultation papers: 1) *How can the enforcement of civil court judgments be made more effective?* (June 1998); 2) *Key Principles for a new system of enforcement in the civil courts* (May 1999); 3) *Attachment of Earnings orders, charging orders and garnishee orders* (October 1999); 4) *Warrants and Writs, oral examinations and judgment summonses* (January 2000). A number of interested bodies, including N.A.C.A.Bx., responded.

[55] *Towards Effective Enforcement: A Single Piece of Bailiff Law and a Regulatory Structure for Enforcement*, Lord Chancellor's Department, July 2001, (Cmd. 5096).

[56] PD. 71 para. 2.1

[57] Chap. 6.

impact of the Human Rights Act 1998 is also significant in the development of enforcement procedures.

(b) ENFORCEMENT OF MONEY JUDGMENTS

(i) Fieri Facias or warrant of execution

15-012 These forms of enforcement operate against the debtor's chattels and goods. The High Court form is the writ of *fieri facias*.[58] This writ is issued to the sheriff of the county where the defendant's goods are located and the sheriff's officers enforce the writ by seizing goods sufficient to cover in value the amount owed under the judgment, the costs of execution and expenses.

The county court form is the warrant of execution[59] which requires the court bailiff to carry out the order. The seized goods must be expected to cover only the amount owed under the judgement and the costs of execution.

Where the sum to be enforced is £5,000 or more, enforcement proceedings must be taken in the High Court, regardless of in which court the trial was heard. Where the sum is less than £600, enforcement must be through the county court. For sums in between, enforcement may be through either court.[60]

The exercise of this concurrent jurisdiction is vast. In 2000, 49, 465 writs of fieri facias were issued in the Queen's Bench Division and 470,270 warrants of execution were issued.[61] By section 15 of the Courts and Legal Services Act 1990 the list of goods that are exempt from seizure has been streamlined. The Green Paper *Towards Effective Enforcement — A single piece of bailiff law and a regulatory structure for enforcement* (July 2001) seeks views on whether a detailed list should be provided.

(ii) Third Party Debt Orders (previously "garnishee proceedings")

15-013 By these proceedings, the successful party, the judgment creditor, obtains the judgment debt by "attachment" of a debt owed to the judgment debtor by a third party, *i.e.* a debt owed to the judgment creditor by a third party is automatically paid to the judgment creditor. From March 2002 the procedure is governed by CPR Part 72 and PD. 72. In 2000, 412 garnishee orders were made absolute in the Queen's Bench Division of the High Court.[62] Using a slightly different procedure, 3, 174 garnishee summonses were issued in the county courts.[63] The Enforcement Review suggested that garnishee orders — renamed "third party debt orders — should be replaced by a simplified procedure in which the debtor's personal circumstances

---

[58] CPR Sched. 1, R.S.C. Ord. 46 and PD. R.S.C. 46
[59] C. P. R. Sched. 2 C.C.R Ord. 26 and PD. R.S.C. 46. Warrants of execution can now sometimes be obtained online. See *http://www.courtservice.gov.uk/mcol/warrant.htm*
[60] High Court and County Courts Jurisdiction Order 1991 (S.I. 1991/724) as amended.
[61] *Judicial Statistics* 2000, tables 3.11 and 4.19 respectively.
[62] *Judicial Statistics 2000*, table 3.11.
[63] *ibid.*, table 4.19.

would be a factor in whether an order was made.[64] This has now been implemented in CPR r 72.7 by allowing the judgment debtor to obtain a "hardship payment order".

(iii) Attachment of earnings

A third party debt order is not available with regard to earnings. The **15–014** Attachment of Earnings Act 1971 for the first time empowered the courts to enforce employers to make deductions from the earnings of employees to be paid into court to satisfy the employee's debts. This is primarily a jurisdiction of the county court,[65] the High Court only having power to attach for payment of maintenance orders and not judgments generally.[66] In 2000, 35,545 orders were made to secure the payment of a judgment debt.[67]

The Enforcement Review proposed a "substantial overhaul" of this procedure, suggesting amongst other proposals (1) a fixed tariff of deductions rather than individual calculations in each individual case, themselves reliant on the debtor's ability and willingness to complete the appropriate forms, (2) finding a mechanism to track debtors on change of job and (3) introducing a national register of orders.

(iv) Charging orders

Charging orders are statutory orders whereby charges are created on **15–015** property governed, from March 2002, by CPR Part 73 and PD. 73. The judgment creditor becomes in effect an equitable chargee with rights to recoup his or her debt from the income of the property or from its sale in due course. Consequently, the debtor cannot, for example, sell the property without satisfying the debt or having the order transferred to other property. The principal property so chargeable is land or any interest in land, and the charge is registrable under the Land Charges Act 1972. Government and company stocks, dividends and interest on such stock and moneys in court may also be subjected to a charging order.[68] An application for a charging order must be made in the county court unless the judgment debt exceeds £5,000 in which case the application may be made in the High Court.[69] In 2000, 446 charging orders were issued in the Queen's Bench Division of the High Court and applications were made for 16, 357 orders in the county court.[70]

(v) Equitable execution: appointment of a receiver

Where none of the other means of execution is likely to be effective, it is **15–016** possible for a receiver to be appointed to take income due to the judgment debtor and apply it towards the debt owed to the judgment creditor[71]

---

[64] Section 6.
[65] CPR Sched. 2, C.C.R. Ord. 27
[66] Attachment of Earnings Act 1971, s. 1
[67] *Judicial Statistics 2000*, table 4.20.
[68] See CPR r. 73.6.
[69] Charging Orders Act 1979, s. 1(2).
[70] *Judicial Statistics 2000*. tables 3.11 and 4.19 respectively.
[71] CPR Sched. 1, R.S.C. Ord. 30.

Because of the effectiveness of the other means of execution and since it is cumbersome, this is a rarely used means of enforcement.

(c) POSSESSION ORDERS

(i) Land

15–017   The procedure governing the procedure for mounting possession claims is found in CPR Part 55 and its practice direction.[72] The means of enforcement remains a writ of possession in the High Court[73] and a warrant for possession in the county court.[74] The bailiffs acting under the possession order clear all people from the premises, whether they were parties to the proceedings or not. This is a very important procedure, because it may well be dangerous for a successful party otherwise to attempt to occupy land which has been awarded by the court. In 2000, enforcement proceedings were issued in respect of 649 High Court possession claims and 134, 478 county court possession claims.[75]

(ii) Goods

15–018   Judgments for delivery of goods may or may not contain an option in the defendant to pay the value instead of giving up the goods. Where there is no such option, execution is by way of writ of delivery in the High Court[76] which instructs the sheriff to cause the goods to be delivered to the claimant. In the county court, a similar procedure is undertaken through the warrant of delivery.[77] In 2000, the High Court issued 66 writs for delivery and 8, 243 county court warrants for delivery of goods were issued?[78]

(d) MANDATORY AND PROHIBITORY ORDERS

(i) Specific performance

A failure by a seller to execute an instrument in response to a judgment for specific performance may be overcome by the appointment of someone else (usually a Chancery master or someone else) to execute it in the seller's stead.[79]

---

[72] Civil Procedure (Amendment) Rules 2001. The Enforcement Review suggested the unification of the existing rules for possession and its streamlining. For a description of the new procedure, see the website run by barrister Gary Webber: *http://www.propertyla-wuk.net.*
[73] CPR Sched. 1, R.S.C. Ord. 45 rule 3.
[74] CPR Sched 2. C.C.R. Ord. 26 rule 17.
[75] *Judicial Statistics 2000*, tables 3.11 and 4.19.
[76] CPR Sched. 1 R.S.C. Ord. 45 rule 4.
[77] CPR Sched. 2 C.C.R. Ord. 26 r. 16.
[78] *Judicial Statistics 2000*, tables 3.11 and 4.19.
[79] CPR Sched. 1 R.S.C. Ord. 45 rule 8.

(ii) Injunction

The injunctions that may be imposed as a means of execution are the same   **15–019**
as those that may be imposed as a remedy consequent upon the trial.[80]

(e) CONCLUSION

Such enforcement procedures form the largest component of the work of the   **15–020**
civil courts, accounting for a substantial proportion of their resources.[81]
This is reflected in the figures quoted above from the Judicial Statistics 2000.
For this reason, as we have seen, debt enforcement procedures were
examined as a part of the Civil Justice Review in 1988,[82] by the Enforcement
Review from 1998 and continue to be the subject of vigorous examination at
the date of writing.[83]

---

[80] See above, para. 15-010.
[81] Civil Justice Review (1988), para. 534(i).
[82] *ibid.*, Chap. 9. "Debt enforcement" is not limited to the enforcement of judgment debts:
ibid., para. 534.
[83] See Enforcement Review (July 2000); the Green Paper *Towards Effective Enforcement — a
single piece of bailiff law and a regulatory structure for enforcement* (July 2001). An Advisory
Group on Enforcement Service Delivery was formed in September 2001.

CHAPTER 16

THE TRIBUNAL HEARING

16–001 AT the hearing, the chairman of the tribunal has the difficult task of ensuring that a sufficient level of informality is achieved so that the parties do not feel inhibited in putting their respective cases, whilst maintaining some procedural and evidentiary safeguards so that the rights of the parties are not prejudiced in an unacceptable way.

We made the point in the previous chapter on tribunals that it is scarcely possible to choose a "typical" tribunal and the observations hereafter draw on a variety of sources. However, just as there are common problems to be solved in devising an appropriate pre-hearing procedure, so there are common problems in the conduct of hearings. What procedural rules, if any, should be followed? What evidence will be admitted? What role should the chairman play and what responsibilities does he or she have? What sort of representation, if any, should be permitted/encouraged, and how should it be funded?

A. PROCEDURE

16–002 Differing approaches to the achievements of procedural fairness may be observed, but in most tribunals much is left to the chairman in determining the form of the hearing. Three illustrations may demonstrate that the amount of guidance given by the appropriate rules is often minimal.

1. APPEALS SERVICE TRIBUNAL

Where an appeal is made to an appeal tribunal, the clerk to the tribunal must direct the appellant and any other party to notify him or her whether he or she wishes to have an oral hearing or is content for there to be a "paper hearing."[1] Otherwise the appeal may be struck out.[2] The chances of success are likely to be greater where the appellant opts for an oral hearing. The procedural regulations for Appeals Service Tribunals for provide that:

---

[1] Social Security and Child Support (Decisions and Appeals) Regulations 1999 (S.I. 1999 No. 991), reg. 39(1).

[2] Under *ibid.*, reg. 46(1)(c).

"Subject to the following provisions of this Part,[3] the procedure for an oral hearing shall be such as the chairman, or in the case of an appeal tribunal which has only one member, such as that member, shall determine."[4]

This general power is qualified in certain respects by other provisions. Fourteen days' notice of an oral hearing must be given, unless waived. Representation is permitted;[5] witnesses may be called;[6] every person who has the right to be heard shall be given an opportunity of putting questions directly to any witnesses called at the hearing and of addressing the tribunal;[7] the hearing shall be in public unless the appellant requests a private hearing or the chairman directs that the hearing shall be private on the grounds that intimate personal or financial circumstances may have to be disclosed or that national security is involved[8]; any party to the proceedings is entitled to be present and to be heard.[9]

It is the chairman who decides how these requirements should be fulfilled and it is to be expected that there will be variations in procedure from chairman to chairman. The Social Security Commissioners[10] may correct procedural irregularities on appeal, but it will be apparent that the provisions are so widely drafted that such an irregularity will have to be very serious before it will be regarded as material.[11]

A common procedure[12] is for the claimant (or his or her representative) to state the case and call witnesses[13]; the claimant and his witnesses may then be questioned by the chairman, and/or the members, and/or the presenting

---

[3] *i.e.* Chapter IV (oral hearings), V (Decisions of Appeal Tribunals and Related Matters) of Part VI (Appeal Tribunals for Social Security Contracting Out of Pensions, Vaccine Damage and Child Support).

[4] S.I. 1999 No. 991, reg. 49(1).

[5] *ibid.*, reg. 49(8).

[6] *ibid.*, reg. 49(11)

[7] *ibid.*, reg. 49(11).

[8] *ibid.*, reg. 49(6)

[9] *ibid.*, reg. 49(7). "Part to the proceedings" is defined in reg. 1(3), and in the case of appeals to an appeal tribunal mean the Secretary of State (or Board of Inland Revenue or an officer of the Board in contributions cases), and any other person who is one of the principal parties for the purpose of sections 13 and 14 of the Social Security Act 1998 (redetermination of appeals by tribunal; appeal from tribunal to Commissioner) or who has a right of appeal under other specified provisions.

[10] See above, para. 2-038 The Commissioners constitute an appeal body from the decisions of Appeals Service tribunals.

[11] In practice the most important ground of appeal is failure to state the reasons for a decision adequately: N. J. Wikeley, *Ogus, Barendt and Wikeley's The Law of Social Security* (4th ed., 1995), p. 678.

[12] Suggested in *Social Security Appeal Tribunals: a guide to procedure*, pp. 24–25. However, it is not just the order of events which is significant but the attitude and appearance of the tribunal members. One of the original authors, representing a nervous claimant at a NILT had been at pains to explain in advance the informality of the procedure and distinguish it from court procedure as seen in "Crown Court" on television. The opening remarks of the chairman of the tribunal were, "Good afternoon, I must warn you, Mrs X, that you must tell the truth in these proceedings —we are just like a court." If the claimant had been unrepresented, the niceties of procedure would have mattered little after that!

[13] This assumes that the claimant attends or is represented. The tribunal has a discretion to proceed with the hearing in the absence of the appellant: S.I. 1999 No. 991 reg. 49(4), (5); and if a claimant fails to attend without giving a reasonable explanation "it will usually be right to proceed with the hearing": *Guide to Procedure*, p. 18.

officer[14]; the presenting officer then makes a submission and is subject to questioning; the claimant is asked for any final observations. However, the Appeals Service Guidance on the Tribunal Hearing[15] states

> "The way in which the Tribunal actually hears your appeal will vary according to the benefit being considered, the number of members and the issue that the Tribunal has to decide. Each Chairman will have developed to an extent their own way of conducting a hearing .... The Chairman will ... usually explain the procedure he or she wishes to follow and seek your agreement to going ahead in that way. It may be that they will wish you to start by explaining why you think the decision is wrong."

At the conclusion of the hearing, the members of the tribunal consider their decision in private.[16]

Every decision must be recorded in summary by the chairman (or single member); this must be included in a decision notice in such written form as has been approved by the President of appeal tribunals.[17] Copies of the notice must be sent or given to every party to the proceedings as soon as may be practicable after the appeal has been decided.[18] A party may apply to the chairman (or single member) for a copy of a statement of the reasons for the tribunal's decision within one month of the sending or giving of the decision notice. If the decision is not unanimous, the notice must indicate that one member dissented and the statement of reasons must include the reasons given for the dissent.[19]

The role of the presenting officer in the procedure of an Appeal Service tribunal is interesting in that he or she is expected to put forward the view of the officer who made the decision against which the claimant is appealing, but is also expected to exercise individual judgment and assist the tribunal in reaching a proper resolution of the case.[20] This may require him or her to advance arguments on behalf of the appellant if he or she thinks that they should be brought to the attention of the tribunal, although there have been differing views expressed about the enthusiasm with which presenting

---

[14] The presenting officer is an officer of the D.W.P. specifically assigned to present cases before tribunals. Some presenting officers, therefore, become very experienced "advocates" and well known to their local tribunal.

[15] www.appeals-service.gov.uk.

[16] The clerk to the tribunal (but not the presenting officer) is permitted to remain with the members during their deliberations: S.I. 1999 No. 991, reg. 49(12).

[17] S.I. 1999 No. 991, reg. 53(1)–(3).

[18] The prescribed form includes a space where there may be written summary grounds for the decision: there are conflicting Commissioner's decisions on whether a failure to state such grounds is a breach of procedure: CIB/668/98; CIB/4497/98: see D. Bonner (ed), *Social Security Tribunals Legislation 2000* Vol. III (Commentary by R. White and M. Rowland), pp. 538–539.

[19] S.I. 1999 No. 991, reg. 53(4), (5).

[20] For a lawyer's analysis of this role, see Diplock L.J. in *R. v. Deputy Industrial Injuries Commissioner, ex p. Moore* [1965] 1 Q.B. 456 at p. 486. A claimant would not necessarily take the same view, even if he knew what was meant by *lis inter partes* and *amicus curiae*.

officers have fulfilled that function.[21] The tribunal and the claimant may be assisted insofar as it is unlikely that a presenting officer will be defending at a hearing his or her own decision on an original claim and objectivity may be easier to display in those circumstances.[22] The unusual practice of allowing decision-makers to defend their own decisions as presenting officers is likely to emphasise the adversarial nature of the proceedings at the expense of the inquisitorial.

It is legitimate to ask to what extent an inquisitorial mode is adopted in the hearing. It is true that the tribunal members are more involved in the direct questioning of both sides than a judge would be, and the informal structure of the proceedings allows particular points, once raised, to be followed through to a conclusion immediately if that appears convenient.[23] The functions of the statutory authorities (decision-maker, tribunal, Commissioner) have been described as

"investigatory or inquisitorial. A social security appeal tribunal is exercising quasi-judicial functions and forms part of the statutory machinery for investigating claims. ... Its investigatory function has as its object the ascertainment of the facts and the determination of the truth. ... "[24]

As an aspect of this

"It is open to a tribunal and indeed it is the members' duty, whenever they identify a point in favour of the claimant, notwithstanding that it has not been taken by the claimant, to consider it and to reach their decision in the light of it."[25]

[21] M. Herman, *Administrative Justice and Supplementary Benefits* (1972); K. Bell, *Research Study on Supplementary Benefit Appeal Tribunals, Review of Main Findings: Conclusions: Recommendations* (D.H.S.S. 1975). The *Decision Makers Guide* (Vol. 1, para. 06424) states that "The role of the presenting officer is that of *amicus curiae* ... and not an advocate. The presenting officer should not put questions to any appellant or witness in a hostile manner think in terms of 'winning' the case." Despite this, during observations of hearings for the study by Genn and Genn (1989) "many Presenting Officers were seen to argue their cases forcefully and to display pleasure when their decision was ultimately confirmed" (p. 161). Baldwin, Wikeley and Young (*Judging Social Security* (1992), Chap. 7), found that while most of the POs interviewed seemed to have a reasonable grasp of the *amicus curiae* concept, the role adopted most often in practice was neutral and reactive (in 20 per cent of cases, the PO appeared to adopt the full *amicus curiae* role; in 8 per cent an adversarial position was taken) (pp. 184–185)

[22] The *Decision Makers Guide* states (Vol. 1, para. 06420) that "The who made the decision under appeal can attend the hearing and present the case personally. However, the DM is usually represented by the presenting officer." Cases where there have been no PO have attracted criticism of the Social Security Commissioner: CI/1524/2000; CI/5972/1999.

[23] One of the original authors experienced a NILT in which he was interrupted in the midst of representations by comments from the claimant's husband who was attending the hearing as a "member of the public" and who was sitting at the back of the room. The chairman encouraged him to speak up and proceeded to deal with the point he raised by questioning both the claimant and the insurance officer. Having dealt with it to his satisfaction the chairman asked if the husband had any further observations ...

[24] R(S) 1/87, pp. 6–7 (Commissioner V. G. H. Hallett).

[25] R(SB) 2/83, p. 557 (Tribunal of Commissioners). This includes a duty to ensure that all relevant questions have been asked of a claimant, although not necessarily to adjourn to enable a claimant who has chosen not to appear to deal with the matter: R(IS)11/99, paras 31, 32. Furthermore, where the claimant does not appear, the matter should be mentioned in

Moreover, the presenting officer should attempt to present a balanced view. However, there are limits. A tribunal is not expected to question facts presented by a claimant just in case after further investigation they might prove to be materially different in the claimant's favour, especially where there is no suggestion that the claimant is unsure of the facts as presented.[26]

" ... [T]he primary duty for making out his case falls on the claimant,[27] and he must not expect to rely on the tribunal's own expertise. We would be slow to convict a tribunal of failure to identify an uncanvassed factual point in favour of the claimant in the absence of the most obvious and clear cut circumstances."[28]

Moreover, exhortations that an inquisitorial approach should be adopted do not necessarily reflect the actual practice.[29]

An example of a record proceedings at a particular Appeals Service Tribunal hearing, is reproduced in Chapter 13.[30]

2. THE EMPLOYMENT TRIBUNAL

16–003 The rules of procedure for a hearing at an Employment Tribunal are, in some respects, more explicit. The objectives to be attained at the hearing are included as part of the rules. In respect of the Appeals Service tribunal, we noted that the normal provision is simply for the chairman to determine the procedures, for the Employment Tribunal, the rules specify that:

"The tribunal shall, so far as it appears to it appropriate, seek to avoid formality in its proceedings and shall not be bound by any enactment or rule of law relating to the admissibility of evidence in proceedings before the courts of law. The tribunal shall make such enquiries of persons appearing before it and witnesses as it considers appropriate and shall otherwise conduct the hearing in such a manner as it considers most appropriate for the clarification of the issues before it and generally to the just handling of the proceedings."[31]

Although those may be the implicit objectives of other tribunals, it is interesting that they should be explicit for the Employment Tribunal, and consequently ironic that the Employment Tribunal is generally reckoned to

---

the full statement of reasons: *ibid*, paras 37, 38.

[26] *ibid.*, p. 558. It was contended on behalf of the claimant that the local tribunal should, of its own motion, have investigated the origin and nature of funds in a personal account in a building society, in order to determine whether they truly represented business assets and not personal monies. That contention was rejected.

[27] But see para. 16-007 on the burden of proof in Appeals Service tribunals.

[28] R(SB) 2/83, p. 558.

[29] The study by Genn and Genn (1989) found that while SSAT chairs consistently expressed the belief that proceedings were inquisitorial, this was denied by many experienced representatives, whose views were "often based on the perception that tribunals did not have the time to delve in sufficient detail into appellants' cases:" pp. 159–163.

[30] See above, para. 13-010.

[31] The Employment Tribunals (Constitution and Rules of Procedure) Regulations 2001 (S.I. 2001 No. 1171), Rules of procedure, r. 11(1).

be one of the more formal and legalistic of the tribunals. It is also now provided that the overriding objective of the procedural rules is "to enable tribunals to deal with cases justly." This includes, so far as practicable, (a) ensuring that the parties are on an equal footing; (b) saving expense; (c) dealing with the case in ways which are proportionate to the complexity of the issues; and (d) ensuring that it is dealt with expeditiously and fairly. A tribunal must seek to give effect to the overriding objective when it exercises any power under, or interprets the rules, and the parties must assist the tribunal to further the overriding objective.[32]

The hearing takes place in public unless the tribunal is of the opinion that a private hearing is appropriate on the grounds of national security or other specified grounds[33]; a party is entitled to give evidence, call witnesses, question any witness and address trie tribunal.[34] If a party has failed to attend the hearing, the tribunal must consider the originating application or notice of appearance, any written representations submitted and any written answer[35] received, but subject to that provision, the hearing may proceed or may be adjourned, or the application may be dismissed, at the discretion of the tribunal.[36]

The order of events at a hearing is likely to differ with the nature of the claim.[37] In the ordinary unfair dismissal case the burden of proof lies with the employer to show that the dismissal was not unfair and the employer will normally be called on first. If the employee alleges constructive dismissal, or the employer otherwise disputes the fact of dismissal, then it will be for the employee to begin and make out his of her case. Whoever has the first word, the procedure thereafter is, in form, similar to court procedure with the calling, examination and cross-examination of witnesses leading to final statements on both sides. The chairman and members of the tribunal may ask more questions and become more involved in the proceedings than a judge would, and the rales about the correct form of examination and cross-examination are relaxed along with the rules of evidence,[38] but an observer at a hearing would receive a strong impression of adversarial procedure and formality. It has also been emphasised that the tribunal is not "an inquisitorial body in the same sense as for example a medical or other tribunal dealing with a disablement issue as part of the statutory machinery for determining benefit claims." It has no duty "to conduct a free standing inquiry of its own" or go beyond the issues and evidence raised by the parties.[39]

---

[32] ibid., reg. 10.

[33] ibid., rr. 8(2), 10(2), (3). Breach of this requirement renders the decision unlawful: Storer v. British Gas plc [2001] 1 W.L.R. 1237 (hearing held in regional chairman's office protected by coded security lock not a hearing in public, notwithstanding that no member of the public was actually prevented from attending).

[34] ibid., r. 11(2).

[35] See above, para. 13-008.

[36] ibid., rr. 10(5), 11(3).

[37] For Employment Tribunal procedure generally, see I. T. Smith and G. Thomas, Smith and Wood's Industrial Law. (7th ed., 2000), pp. 401–435); Sir John C. Wood, Industrial Law (5th ed. 1993), pp. 309–324; Sweet & Maxwell's Encyclopedia of Employment Law, Part A7 Tribunal Practice and Procedure (I.D.S. Handbook Series 2 No. 4, 1994).

[38] See paras 16-005–16-009. below for further discussion.

[39] Rugarmer v. Sony Music Entertainment UK Ltd; McNicol v. Balfour Beatty Rail Maintenance Ltd (unreported, July 27, 2001, E.A.T.), para. 47.

3. RENT ASSESSMENT COMMITTEES

16–004   The Rent Assessment Committee[40] exercises jurisdiction of three main kinds. It receives and determines objections against the fixing and registration (or confirmation) of a fair rent by a rent officer[41]; it fixes the rent of an assured tenancy where the landlord proposes a rent increase[42]; and, when exercising the powers of a rent tribunal, it controls rent and security of tenure in respect of "restricted contracts."[43] Some potential confusion was created by the Housing Act 1980 in the abolition of the rent tribunal and the reallocation of its functions to a Rent Assessment Committee.[44] However, since the Housing Act 1988[45] no new restricted contracts can be created and there are now very few applications under the old Rent Tribunal jurisdiction.[46] A number of matters can now be referred to rent assessment committees constituted as leasehold valuation tribunals. These include jurisdiction concerning leasehold enfranchisement,[47] the determination of the reasonableness of and other matters relating to service charges,[48] the determination of questions concerning a tenant's right to buy the landlord's interest when it has been disposed to a third party,[49] the appointment of a manager for flats,[50] the determination of the terms on which a landlord's interest can be required compulsorily,[51] and the determination of questions concerning rights of collective enfranchisement and lease renewal conferred on the tenants of flats.[52]

   The RAC is unusual in that it does not need to hold a hearing. The obligation lies on the landlord and the tenant to request the opportunity to make oral representations and there are provisions for the disposal of the matter on written representations in the absence of an application for a

---

[40] See generally R. E. Megarry, *The Rent Acts* (1988), Vol. 1, Chaps.24 and 25, Vol. 3, Chaps.16 and 17; J. C. Martin, *Residential Security* (2nd ed., 1995), Chaps.10 and 14; S. Blandy, [2001] J.H.L. 43 and S.McGrath, [2001] J.H.L. 53 (LVTs).

[41] Under the provisions of the Rent Act 1977, Pt. IV.

[42] Under the Housing Act 1988, Pt. I.

[43] As defined in Rent Act 1977, ss.19–21.

[44] s.72. The provisions of the section are, at first sight, so startling that they may properly be set out in full:

    (1) Rent tribunals, as constituted for the purposes of the 1977 Act, are hereby abolished and section 76 of the 1977 Act (Constitution, etc. of rent tribunals) is hereby repealed.

    (2) As from the commencement of this section the functions which, under the 1977 Act, are conferred on rent tribunals shall be carried out by rent assessment committees.

    (3) A rent assessment committee shall, when constituted to carry out functions so conferred, be known as a rent tribunal."

The object appears to be to achieve a uniformity of appointment for the two bodies, without altering their functions.

[45] s. 36.

[46] See P. Sparkes, *A New Landlord and Tenant* (2001), pp. 164–165, 238.

[47] Leasehold Reform Act 1967, Pt. I.

[48] Landlord and Tenant Act 1985, s. 19. See also s.20C (limitation of service charges: costs of proceedings) and Sched., para. 8 (right to challenge landlord's choice of insurers).

[49] Landlord and Tenant Act 1987, ss. 11-13, substituted by the Housing Act 1996, Sched. 6, Pt. II.

[50] 1987 Act, Pt. II, ss. 24A, 24B inserted by the Housing Act 1996, s.86(l), (5).

[51] 1987 Act, s. 31.

[52] Leasehold Reform, Housing and Urban Development Act 1993, Pt. I, s. 91.

hearing.[53] It should be emphasised that the absence of a hearing does not relieve the tribunal of considering the matter, indeed it points up the inquisitorial role because the committee then have an obligation to make such inquiry as they think fit and consider any information supplied or representation made by the parties.[54] This demonstrates the necessity for procedural safeguards throughout the determination of an issue—they are not confined to a hearing. Leasehold Valuation Tribunals must hold a hearing, but may proceed in the absence of a party or any other person who has indicated an intention to appear if they are satisfied that notice has been given to that party or person.[55]

If the landlord or tenant requests the opportunity to make oral representations then the RAC will arrange a hearing. For the hearing, the procedural rules are slightly different in respect of the RAC and RAC (RT) but it is unlikely that the formal differences are reflected in the actual procedure adopted by the chairman.

The RAC rules provide that, " ... the parties shall be heard in such order, and ... the procedure shall be such as the committee shall determine" and "a party may call witnesses, give evidence on his own behalf and cross-examine any witnesses called by the other party."[56] Each party may be heard in person "or by a person authorised by him in that behalf," whether or not a solicitor or barrister.[57] The rules specify that the hearing shall be in public unless the committee decide otherwise "for special reasons."[58]

B. EVIDENCE

In civil and criminal trials there are clear rules about the sort of evidence which may be given; the location of the burden of proof; and the standard of proof. Such clear rules are not to be found in tribunal adjudication. In the adversarial procedure of the civil or criminal trial the burden of proof is normally readily identified, but where there is an inquisitorial atmosphere in tribunals it is more difficult to locate. Some of the rules which render relevant evidence inadmissible at a trial rely heavily for their justification on the inability of a jury to decide the proper weight to be given to potentially prejudicial evidence. An experienced tribunal chairman, it is said, ought to be able to attribute the correct amount of weight to almost every piece of relevant information. Further, it is always argued that the absence of "strict" rules of evidence enhances the informality of tribunal procedure and makes it more comprehensible to the lay person.

16–005

---

[53] Rent Act 1977, Sched. 11, paras.6, 7(1)(b), 9 and Rent Assessment Committee (England and Wales) Regulations 1971 (S. I. 1971 No. 1065), reg. 6 (RACs); Rent Act 1977 s.78(1), (2); Rent Assessment Committees (England and Wales) (Rent Tribunal) Regulations 1980 (S. I.1980 No. 1700), reg. 4 (RAC (RT)).

[54] 1977 Act, Sched. 11, paras.7(1)(a), 9(1) (RACs); Rent Act 1977, s.78(2) (RAC (RT)).

[55] Rent Assessment Committee (England and Wales) (Leasehold Valuation Tribunals) Regulations 1993 (S.I. 1993 No. 2408) regs. 5–7, as amended by S.I. 1997 No. 1854.

[56] S.I. 1971 No. 1065, reg. 4. Similar rules apply to LVTs: S.I. 1993 No. 2408, reg. 6(a),(c).

[57] Rent Act 1977, Sched. 11, para. 8; S.I. 1993, No. 2408 reg. 6(b).

[58] S. I. 1971 No. 1065, reg. 3(1); S.I. 1993 No. 2408, reg. 5(5).

However, a balance needs to be maintained between the requirements of informality and the interests of the parties to the tribunal. It may be assumed that some rules of evidence are specifically designed to prevent a conclusion being reached on unreliable information,[59] so that it would not be acceptable to abandon the principles of evidence altogether in tribunal adjudication. We shall hope to illustrate how tribunals cope with the problems of onus and standard of proof, relevance and admissibility.

1. GENERAL PRINCIPLES[60]

16–006   There is an important difference between courts and tribunals in that many tribunals rely on the expertise of the chairmen and members in determining questions of fact.[61] It is interesting to note that the jury, at its inception, was intended to rely upon the collective knowledge of its members, although such knowledge could now constitute a reason for excusal or challenge.[62] The justification for tribunal adjudication rests partly on the expertise of the adjudicators in the appropriate field, and there is ample authority for the proposition that they may rely on their own specialist knowledge to interpret evidence given to them by the parties or to fill in gaps where evidence has not been given.[63] Were this not the case there would be no possibility of an appeal succeeding in a social security matter where the appellant chose not to appear, was unrepresented and made no written representations. The chances of success for such an appellant are slender but they do exist.[64]

Those tribunals which are not merely administrative bodies but exercise a judicial function are bound to conform to the rules of natural justice.[65] The way in which a tribunal deals with evidence must accord with those rules which require, broadly, that the proceedings must be fair in all the circumstances. In respect of the giving of evidence it seems that every party to a hearing must be given an opportunity to put his or her case and to call relevant evidence in support.[66] That right is supported by the rules of procedure of some tribunals[67] and although there was a discretion on the

---

[59]   The exclusion of hearsay evidence is based mainly on its potential unreliability, and such evidence is treated with considerable caution in tribunal proceedings although it is admissible, see para. 16-009 below.

[60]   There is little available material about the use of evidence in tribunals, but see R. E. Wraith and P. G. Hutchesson, *Administrative Tribunals* (1973), pp. 265–273; J. Fulbrook, *Administrative Justice and the Unemployed* (1978), pp. 268–276; C. Yates, [1980] I. S. W. L. 273 (supplementary benefit appeals) and [1980] Conv. 136 (rent tribunals); J. G. Logie and P. Q. Watchman, (1989) 8C.J.Q. 109 (SSATs); P. J. Rowe, (1994) 1 J.S.S.L. 9.

[61]   Indeed, expertise is a criterion for the appointment of members in a number of tribunals, see above, para. 4-016.

[62]   See below, para. 17-089.

[63]   J. A. Smillie, "The Problem of 'Official Notice'—Reliance by Administrative Tribunals on the Personal Knowledge of their Members" [1975] P. L. 64.

[64]   There are reported instances in K. Bell *et al.*, "National Insurance Local Tribunals: A Research Study" (1975) 4 *Journal of Social Policy* 1.

[65]   See Sir William Wade and C. F. Forsyth, *Administrative Law* (8th ed., 2001), Chap. 15. All the tribunals we have so far considered have a judicial function.

[66]   *R. v. Hull Prison Board of Visitors, ex p. St Germain (No. 2)* [1979] 1 W. L. R. 1401.

[67]   See above, paras 16-002–16-004.

part of the chairman of Supplementary Benefit Appeal Tribunals to exclude evidence which was clearly irrelevant or immaterial, that discretion had to be exercised with care and with a due regard to the necessity of allowing justice to be seen to be done.[68] In the Employment Tribunal it has been suggested that there is no discretion to exclude evidence which would be admissible and probative; there is clearly a discretion to include evidence which would be inadmissible.[69] The latter discretion is often referred to as a discretion to disregard the "strict" rules of evidence.[70] Accordingly, it will be an error of law for a tribunal to refuse to admit probative evidence unless it can be shown that to admit it would be unfair or its prejudicial effect would outweigh its probative value.[71]

2. THE STANDARD OF PROOF AND THE BURDEN OF PROOF

Proof beyond reasonable doubt is the standard adopted in the trial of cri   **16–007** minal matters, and in civil cases the party bearing the burden of proof must establish the case on a balance of probabilities.[72] It is the latter standard that is adopted in tribunal proceedings,[73] although some writers suggest that in particular tribunals the chairman and members may not always identify the standard as clearly as that.[74] In determining a case on the balance of probabilities "the inherent probability or improbability of an event is itself a matter to be taken into account when weighing the probabilities." The more serious the allegation the greater its inherent improbability and, accordingly, "the stronger must be the evidence that it did occur before, on the balance of probability, its occurrence will be established."[75] The standard of proof is

---

[68] Although this proposition is taken from R(SB) 6/82 and related to Supplementary Benefit Appeal Tribunals, it is likely to have wider application as an expression of one of the requirements of natural justice. The dilemma for a tribunal chairman is that he or she may not be able to take a view about the relevance of evidence until it has been heard.

[69] *Rosedale Mouldings Ltd v. Sibley* [1980] I.C.R. 816. The first part of the proposition was doubted in *Snowball v. Gardner Merchant Ltd* [1987] I.C.R. 719, where the E.A.T. suggested that an industrial tribunal might properly "decide not to admit evidence which would be admissible under the strict rules of evidence, if, for example, it considered it to be unfair to do so or, as in the field of criminal law, its prejudicial effect outweighed its probative value" (p. 722).

[70] This is a significant phrase because it embodies the notion that some basic rules of evidence must still apply, even in tribunals. The phrase is also to be found in respect of hearings in the small claims track: CPR r.27.8(3).

[71] *Rosedale Mouldings*, above (where the wrongly excluded evidence was "highly probative": *Snowball* at p. 725); *Parks v. Lansdowne Club* (Unreported, May 14, 1996, E.A.T.) (prima facie probative tape recorded evidence wrongly excluded; no balancing exercise conducted by the tribunal).

[72] For a full consideration of the standard of proof in civil and criminal matters, see C. Tapper, *Cross and Tapper on Evidence* (9th ed., 1999), pp. 138–156.

[73] See e.g. R(I) 32/61; R (IS) 17/95 (SSAT).

[74] There was particular doubt about SBAT s.: J. Fulbrook, *Administrative Justice and the Unemployed* (1978), p. 272. There are isolated examples where a higher standard of proof has been required, *e.g. Judd v. Minister of Pensions and National Insurance* [1966] 2 Q.B. 580, where the Divisional Court held that the Minister must establish his or her case beyond reasonable doubt in certain matters before the Pensions Appeal Tribunal.

[75] *per* Lord Nicolls of Birkenhead in *Re H (Minors) Sexual Abuse: Standard of Proof* [1996] A.C. 563, 586, applied in the context of school exclusion appeals in *R. v. Governing Body of Dunraven School, ex p. B* [2000] E.L.R. 156, *per* Brooke L.J. at p. 204; *R. v. Governors of the W School, ex p. K* (unreported, October 6, 2000).

closely linked in repotted decisions of tribunals with the question of the
burden of proof and who bears it. In an early decision of a National
Insurance Commissioner the formulation of Lord Birkenhead L.C. in
Lancaster v. Blackwell Colliery Co.[76] was adopted:

> "If the facts which are proved gave rise to conflicting inferences of
> equal degrees of probability, so that the choice between them is a mere
> matter of conjecture, then of course the applicant fails to prove his case,
> because it is plain in these matters the onus is on the applicant. But
> where the known facts are not equally balancing probabilities as to
> their respective value, and where a reasonable man might hold that the
> more probable conclusion is that for which the applicant contends, then
> the arbitrator is justified in drawing an inference in his favour."

The question of which party, if any, bears the burden of proof in tribunal
proceedings really needs to be examined in respect of each individual
tribunal,[77] starting from the assumption that it will normally be the party
making the assertion who must prove it. That assumption, which derives
from the position in the civil or criminal trial,[78] may not be appropriate
where the proceedings are conducted on a truly inquisitorial basis with the
tribunal reaching an evaluation of the information presented, yet it exercises
a powerful influence.

It may not, of course, be necessary to rely on an assumption. Provision
may have been made by statute,[79] or by procedural rules,[80] or in the
decisions of particular tribunals,[81] stipulating where the burden of proof will
lie. Where the jurisdiction of the tribunal is original, rather than appellate, it
will also usually be clear where the burden lies, even if it may shift during the
hearing. In the Employment Tribunal, for example, when the applicant
alleges that he or she has been unfairly dismissed it will be for the *employer*
to prove that the dismissal was not unfair. If the employer disputes that
there has been a dismissal the onus lies with the *employee* to prove that there
has.[82]

In respect of some tribunals, no importance attaches to the question of

---

[76] (1919) 12 B.W.C.C. 400 at p. 406, cited in C I 401/50.

[77] We have already made the point that it is impossible to generalise about tribunals. The
examples which follow are from tribunals which we have described elsewhere.

[78] See C. Tapper, *Cross and Tapper on Evidence* (9th ed., 1999), pp. 115–136.

[79] Employment Rights Act 1996, ss. 210(5), 163(2), providing that on a reference to a tribunal a
person's employment during any period shall be deemed to have been continuous unless the
contrary is proved, and that a dismissal shall be presumed to have been on account of
redundancy, unless the contrary is proved. *Cf. Secretary of State for Employment v. Globe
Elastic Thread Co.* Ltd [1980] A.C. 506. See also, Jobseekers Act 1995, s.14(l), excusing from
disqualification for jobseeker's allowance those who can prove that they were not directly
interested in the relevant trade dispute, and Employment Rights Act 1996 s. 98(4), which is
interpreted as imposing no burden of proof on either party in respect of the reasonableness
of a dismissal: *Post Office (Counters) Ltd v. Heavey* [1990] I.C.R. 1.

[80] *e.g.* The Immigration and Asylum Appeals (Procedure) Rules 2000 (S.I. 2000 No. 2333),
r.39, which deals specifically with the burden of proof and locates it on the appellant or the
Secretary of State depending on the fact in issue.

[81] *e.g.* The decision of the National Insurance Commissioner that the burden of proof on the
allegation of cohabitation should lie with the insurance officer, R(G) 1/53. This decision has
been consistently followed.

[82] See above, para. 16-003.

burden of proof because the tribunal is arriving at a valuation rather than establishing a right or claim. The Rent Assessment Committee provides an example in that it is the obligation of the committee to arrive at its own judgment of a fair rent in the light of any representations made by the landlord and/or tenant.[83] Neither has the burden of proof—the committee must make its own decision which may not reflect the contentions of either party.

As regards Appeals Service tribunuls, the general position appears to be[84] that it is for the claimant to make out his or her entitlement[85]; that where there are exceptions from basic entitlements it is for those who assert that the exceptions apply to prove that they do[86]; and that once a decision has been made awarding benefit for a particular period, the onus of proving that grounds exist for reviewing the decision lies on those who assert that the existing decision is wrong.[87] However, the basic principle that it is for the claimant to establish entitlement is modified to the extent that the tribunal conforms to the rhetoric of adopting an inquisitorial rather than accusatorial approach.[88]

Thus, in *R. v. National Insurance Commissioner, ex p. Viscusi,* [89] which concerned a claim for industrial disablement benefit, Buckley L.J. had this to say:

"As regards the burden of proof, as Lord Denning M.R. has pointed out, these are not adversary proceedings: they are inquisitorial proceedings; and in such proceedings questions of burden of proof do not arise in the same way in which they would in proceedings between parties in a law suit. It is for the medical board or the medical appeal tribunal, as the case may be, to investigate the case inquisitorially and to decide whether the claimant is entitled to benefit under the Act. But, of course, the fact remains that the medical board or the medical appeal tribunal, as the case may be, must be satisfied that the claimant is entitled to benefit: and so, in a sense, and subject to such statutory assumptions as are prescribed by the Act itself, it does rest with the claimant in the end to make out his claim."

---

[83] See above, para. 16-004.

[84] See J. Mesher in A. Kiralfy (ed.), *The Burden of Proof* (1987), Chap. 11, "Social Security Law". Before amalgamation, lie position was less clear in SBATs than NJILTs: see C. Yates, [1980] J.S.W.L. 273, 274–276.

[85] *R. v. National Insurance Commissioner, ex p. Hudson and Jones* [1970] 1 Q.B. 477; *R. v. National Insurance Commissioner, ex p. Viscusi* [1974] 1 W.L.R. 646; see also, *e.g.* R(I) 32/61; R(SB) 15/81; R(SB) 2/83(T); 8/84 ("It is for the claimant to establish his title to a single payment ... " (p. 882)).

[86] *e.g.* disqualifications for unemployment benefit under: the Social Security Contributions and Benefits Act 1992, s.28: R(U) 2/60 (for the insurance officer (now adjudication officer) to prove that the claimant lost her job through misconduct); R(U) 20/64 (for the insurance officer to prove that claimant left employment voluntarily; if this is done, it is for the claimant to prove that he or she did not leave without just cause): Mesher (1987), pp. 220–222. See now the Jobseekers Act 1995, s.19. Another example is discontinuance of benefit on the ground of cohabitation: R(SB) 17/81; *Crake v. Supplementary Benefits Commission* [1982] 1 All E. R. 498.

[87] R(I) 1/71; Mesher (1987), pp. 225–227.

[88] Mesher (1987), pp. 214–218. See above, para. 16–002.

[89] [1974] 1 W.L.R. 646.

3. Relevance and Admissibility

16–008   Detailed exclusionary rules have been developed in civil and criminal matters which render certain evidence inadmissible on the grounds that it would be unduly prejudicial or unreliable. Inevitably, the operation of such rules can lead to the exclusion of evidence which is highly relevant to the facts in issue. In tribunal proceedings the test of *relevance* is given priority with the consequence that very little evidence is likely to be excluded altogether from consideration. It may be that particular sorts of evidence are treated with some circumspection by the chairman and members, but it is expected that they will be able to assess the value and reliability of the evidence given and accord it appropriate weight in their deliberations. Many of the strict exclusionary rules of evidence result from a fear that a jury will be unable to judge satisfactorily how much significance to attach to inherently unreliable or prejudicial evidence,[90] and that fear should not be present when it is tribunal members who are adjudicating. Consequently, the strict rules of evidence are normally disregarded in favour of a much wider test of admissibility:

> " ... technical rules of evidence, however, form no part of the rules of natural justice. The requirement that a person exercising quasi-judicial functions must base his decision on evidence means no more than it must be based upon material which tends logically to show the existence or non-existence of facts relevant to the issue to be determined, or to show the likelihood or unlikelihood of the occurrence of some future event the occurrence of which would be relevant. It means that he must not spin a coin or consult an astrologer, but he may take into account any material which, as a matter of reason, has some probative value in the sense mentioned above. If it is capable of having any probative value, the weight to be attached to it is a matter for the person to whom Parliament has entrusted , the task of deciding the issue."[91]

This statement of Diplock L.J. has been cited with approval on a number of occasions and applied to different adjudications. The judge was actually dealing with the decision of a deputy Industrial Injuries Commissioner on a claim for industrial injury benefit, but his words have also been held to apply to an appeal to the Minister under the Town and Country Planning Act 1962[92]; an adjudication by a prison Board of Visitors under the Prison Rules 1964[93]; and a formal investigation of a complaint of unlawful discrimination under the Race Relations Act 1976.[94] This general rule, that evidence is admissible in tribunal proceedings if it is of some "probative value", even though it would be inadmissible in court, has been embodied in procedural

---

[90] That is why the rules are stricter in criminal cases, but have been relaxed in civil cases where it is now highly unusual to have a jury, see para. 15-007. above.
[91] *R. v. Deputy Industrial Injuries Commissioner, ex p. Moore* [1965] 1 Q.B. 456 at p. 488.
[92] *T. A. Milter Ltd v. Minister of Housing and Local Government* [1968] 1 W.L.R. 992.
[93] *R. v. Hull Prison Board of Visitors, ex p. St. Germain* (No. 2) [1979] 1 W.L.R. 1401.
[94] *R. v. Commission for Racial Equality, ex p. Cottrell* [1980] 1 W.L.R. 1580.

rules[95] and adopted in tribunal decisions.[96] It would appear that probative means relevant.

This rule of admissibility has been formulated in the context of the principles of natural justice and it is still the case that there is an obligation to ensure that each party has a full and fair hearing. In the Employment Tribunal the general rule has been expressed in a slightly modified way to permit the exclusion of evidence where its admission, " ... could in some way adversely affect the reaching of a proper decision in the case."[97] In social security tribunals the general rule was followed and many reported decisions expressed the power of the tribunals to admit any relevant evidence.[98] Indeed in Case R(IS) 5/93, the Social Security Commissioner (V.G.H. Hallett) held that the tribunal had erred in law in refusing to listen to hearsay evidence simply because it could not be tested by cross-examination.

The weight that is to be attached to relevant evidence is a matter for the tribunal and it is instructive to consider the approach of various tribunals in respect of hearsay evidence—the sort of evidence which tribunals have most often been invited to exclude.

4. Hearsay

A hearsay statement is one which is made, orally or in writing, by a person **16–009** other than the witness testifying and which is offered to prove a fact asserted in the statement.[99] An officer, investigating the question of whether a person in receipt of unemployment benefit (now jobseeker's allowance) is actually working, states that he has interviewed the claimant's next door neighbours who have told him that they saw the claimant leave his house every morning with a bag of tools, and that the claimant has admitted to them that he is "making a bit on the side". The statement of the officer, when put to the tribunal by the presenting officer at the hearing of the claimant's appeal against disqualification from benefit, would constitute hearsay.

The rules restricting the admissibility of hearsay evidence in civil courts and documentary evidence in criminal courts are much less stringent than they were,[1] but the rules concerning oral hearsay statements in criminal matters remain strict and their justification is said to be that hearsay evidence cannot properly be tested in court because of the absence of the

---

[95] *e.g.* The Immigration and Asylum Appeals (Procedure) Rules 2000 (S.I. 2000 No. 2333), r. 37 (1): "The appellate authority may receive oral, documentary or other evidence of any fact which appears to that authority to be relevant to the appeal, even though that evidence would be inadmissible in a court of law."

[96] See below, n.99

[97] *Coral Squash Clubs Ltd v. Matthews* [1979] I.C.R. 607, at p. 611. The Employment Appeal Tribunal in that case held that it was " ... clear that an Industrial Tribunal is not bound by the strict rules of evidence but should exercise its good sense in weighing matters which come before it" (*ibid*).

[98] *e.g.* R(I) 36/61, R(I) 13/74, R(U) 12/56, R(U) 5/77.

[99] This is a very abbreviated definition. Interested students should consult C. Tapper, *Cross and Tapper on Evidence* (9th ed., 1999), Chap. XIII.

[1] Reforms were effected by the Civil Evidence Acts 1968 and 1995 and the Criminal Justice Act 1988.

maker of the statement; and depends upon the potentially inaccurate repetition of the statement by the witness.[2] Set against those difficulties is the undeniable fact, recognised by tribunals, that, "If tribunals were obliged to reject hearsay evidence ... many claimants would find it quite impossible to establish their claims."[3]

In the Employment Tribunal the policy merely seems to be to require the members of the tribunal to consider carefully what *weight* to attach to admitted hearsay evidence. In *Coral Squash Clubs Ltd v. Matthews*,[4] the tribunal had refused to admit hearsay evidence about alleged licensing offences by the manager of a squash club, on the grounds that where the allegation was of a criminal offence and where the witnesses could have been located and produced the strict rule of exclusion should be applied. Their decision was reversed by the Employment Appeal Tribunal who ruled the evidence to be admissible, holding that the question of criminality was not in issue before the tribunal and that the failure to produce witnesses merely went to the weight of the evidence. The E.A.T. stated that a tribunal should, " ... exercise its good sense in weighing the matters that come before it."[5]

Social security tribunals have taken much the same view. In an early decision, a Commissioner warned that the value of evidence which would be inadmissible in a court of law must be carefully considered and may be of very little weight,[6] and that phrasing has been adopted in subsequent decisions.[7] A particular type of hearsay which social security tribunals have been unwilling to accept is the statements of claimants' representatives. The Commissioner has said that such statements are not evidence and that where questions of fact are in issue on which a claimant or other qualified witness can speak they should be called to give evidence.[8] It has indeed been suggested that

"In practical terms, the result would seem to be that the use of hearsay is so severely restricted that it is virtually inadmissible. Indeed there is no reported case known to the authors in which a Commissioner has upheld the decision of an appeal tribunal which acted solely or principally on the basis of hearsay evidence."[9]

---

[2] See Law Reform Committee, 13th Report, *Hearsay Evidence in Civil Proceedings* (Cmnd. 2964, 1966); Criminal Law Revision Committee, 11th Report, *Evidence (General)* (Cmnd. 4991, 1972), pp. 132–154.

[3] R(U) 12/56.

[4] [1979] I.C.R. 607.

[5] *ibid.*, at p. 611. Examples of cases where hearsay has been held to be admissible include *Jones t/a Plas-y-Bryn Nursing Home v. Hughes* (unreported, December 4, 2001, E.A.T.) (use of results of questionnaire to staff about conduct of a colleague for limited purpose of providing a context for gauging seriousness of particular act of misconduct held not to be erroneous in law).

[6] C.I. 97/49.

[7] R(G) 1/51; R(U) 12/56; R(U) 5/77.

[8] R(I) 36/61. The same principle applies to the adjucation officer's representative: R(SB) 10/86.

[9] J. G. Logie and P. Q. Watchman, (1989) 8 CJ.Q. 109, 116.

What is lacking is a clear policy on the criteria to be applied in determining the admissibility and reliability of hearsay evidence.[10]

5. WITNESSES

The requirement of natural justice that a party should be given a fair hearing **16–010** is normally taken to comprehend the right to put his or her own case and correct or contradict statements that have been made by the other party.[11] This is likely to be achieved by the calling of witnesses. The right to call witnesses is set out in the procedural rules for the tribunals we have so far considered in detail.[12] However, the right appears to be subject to the discretion of the chairman. The chairman's obligation is to ensure a fair hearing, but he or she is not required to hear every witness that one of the parties might wish to call.

The position in social security tribunals was stated by a Commissioner in R(SB)6/82. The decision related to a SBAT, but the principles are presumably equally applicable to Appeals Service tribunals. In that decision, the chairman of a SBAT had refused to hear a witness whom the claimant wished to call. On the facts, the Commissioner concluded that there had been an error of law since the witness appeared to have relevant and material evidence to give, and the case was remitted for re-hearing. On the general point the Commissioner said:

"Tribunals are not bound to hear evidence which is clearly irrelevant or immaterial, whether it be from a witness actually giving evidence before the tribunal or from a proposed witness. The discretion to stop or curtail such evidence should, however, always be exercised with care, and in its exercise due regard should in my view always be paid to the necessity of allowing justice to be seen to be done."[13]

Employment Tribunals would, no doubt, adopt similar criteria. Other aspects of the law of evidence relating to witnesses have been held to be applicable to tribunal adjudications, including the principles that a witness's testimony can be accepted even though not corroborated,[14] and that a witness's answers to questions concerning his or her credibility must be accepted as final (to avoid undue preoccupation with side-issues).[15]

---

[10] In *Jones t/a Plas-v-Bryn Nursing Home v. Hughes*, above, the judge took account of the number of colleagues who reported inappropriate behaviour, the absence of any suggestion of collusion or prejudice, the restrained nature of most of the criticism (which carried "its own conviction"), and the fact that the appellant had the opportunity to comment on the statements.

[11] See generally Sir William Wade and C.F. Forsyth *Administrative Law* (8th ed., 2001), Chap. 15.

[12] See above, para. 16-006.

[13] R(SB) 6/82. para. 5, a decision of Mr J. S. Watson.

[14] R(I) 2/51; R(SB) 33/85; R(SB) 12/89 (social security tribunal)s; *Ojeda v. Beverley Hills Bakery & Gift Baskets* (Unreported, April 24, 1998, E.A.T.) (no corroboration required in respect of claim of sexual harassment).

[15] *Aberdeen Steak Houses Group plc v. Ibrahim* [1988] I.C.R. 550, E.A.T. (Industrial Tribunals); *cf. Snowball v. Gardner Merchant Ltd* [1987] I.C.R. 719, E.A.T.

C. THE ROLE OF THE CHAIRMAN

16–011   The references to the chairman in the last two sections of this chapter will
already have demonstrated the significance of his role. The task of any
chairman, whatever the nature of the tribunal, is to ensure that:

> " ... the proceedings are conducted with scrupulous fairness to all
> parties and that the proper balance is struck between formality and
> informality. In particular, he must make sure at the outset that the
> parties fully understand the issue, especially when they are not legally
> represented; and he must ensure that they have an opportunity to
> present their cases adequately."[16]

Different chairmen may quite properly take different views about how to
conduct tribunal hearings whilst pursuing the objectives referred to in the
preceding paragraph, and the chairman's discretion is substantial. Since so
much depends on the chairman it is important briefly to examine three
issues—the appointment and qualification of chairmen; training provision;
the adequacy of judicial and other safeguards intended to ensure procedural
fairness.

1. Appointment and Qualification

16–012   The formal position on appointment and qualification is set out in Chapter
4.[17] The involvement of the Lord Chancellor in the appointment of the
majority of tribunal chairmen is intended to demonstrate, and preserve,
their independence of the relevant government department. As to
qualification, the controversy is over the desirability of requiring that a
chairman should be legally qualified.
    The inherent difficulty in tribunal adjudication will by now have become
apparent. It is desirable to achieve a high standard of decision-making
coupled with demonstrable procedural fairness, whilst retaining the
informality, cheapness and speed which are meant to be the hallmarks of
the tribunal. Lawyer-chairmen seem to have less difficulty in achieving the
former than the latter. Two examples will suffice.
    When the Industrial Tribunal was created, the procedural rules
specifically required the chairman, in setting the procedure, to seek to
avoid formality so far as it was appropriate to do so.[18] All chairmen of
Employment Tribunals are lawyers of not less than seven years' standing[19]
and the appellate body is presided over by a High Court judge.[20] The

---

[16] *Report of the Council on Tribunals 1959*, p. 6.
[17] Above, para. 4-016.
[18] See above, para. 16-003.
[19] Above, para. 4-016, n.3.
[20] For the composition of the Employment Appeal Tribunal, see above, para. 2-033.

Employment Tribunal has become formal, with predictable procedure and a large body of case-law.[21] That can hardly be a coincidence.

The Supplementary Benefit Appeal Tribunal was accustomed to non-lawyer chairmen. There was no prohibition on the appointment of lawyers but by 1980, after 14 years of existence,[22] only one chairman in four was legally qualified.[23] Kathleen Bell's research,[24] published in 1975, was not especially complimentary to the existing chairmen:

" ... generally speaking, they did not fully comprehend the complexities of the work ... too often proceedings were unsystematic, inconsistent and over-influenced by sympathy or otherwise. Separate deliberations were frequently non-existent when the appellant was absent, and in other instances were quite often somewhat rambling and of rather poor quality. We examined a large number of official Reports of Proceedings, the majority of which did not adequately record a reasoned decision."[25]

This view was supported by other commentators.[26] Following the Bell Report there was a determined effort to appoint more lawyers as SBAT chairmen. Following the merging of SBATs and NILTs into Social Security Appeal Tribunals,[27] now Appeals Service tribunals, the chairmen are all lawyers of at least five years' standing,[28] and a regional and national structure of full-time chairmen has been created.[29]

Appeals Service tribunals are obviously more closely modelled on the NILT than the SBAT and expected to achieve the standards set by the NILT. The NILT certainly achieved a reputation as one of the best models of an informal tribunal with a qualified chairman.[30] In the view of Professor Lewis, who had some harsh criticism of SBATs, NILTs [were] " ... usually a model of balancing informal expertise with order and legality."[31]

The debate over the desirability of lawyer-chairmen involves many of the

[21] It has attracted both judicial and academic criticism on that account. The criticism reflects a particular view of the functions of an I T. See the observations of Lord Denning M.R. in *Walls Meat Co. Ltd v. Khan* [1979] 1 I.C.R. 52, at p. 56; Lawton LJ. in *Clay Cross (Quarry Services) Ltd v. Fletcher* [1979] I.C.R. 1, at p. 8; Ormrod L.J. in *National Vulcan Engineering Insurance Group Ltd v. Wade* [1978] I.C.R. 800, at p. 808; Dunn LJ. in *Methven v. Cow Industrial Ltd* [1980] I.C.R. 463, at p. 470.

[22] SBATs were created by the Ministry of Social Security Act 1966 as the successor to national assistance appeal tribunals.

[23] N. Harris, "The Appointment of Legally Qualified Chairmen for SBATs" (1982) 132 N.L.J. 495.

[24] *Research Study on Supplementary Benefit Appeal Tribunals, Review of Main Findings: Conclusions: Recommendations* (HMSO, 1975).

[25] *ibid.*, at p. 6.

[26] A. Frost and C. Howard, *Representation and Administrative Tribunals* (1977); M. Herman, *Administrative Justice and Supplementary Benefits* (1972); N. Lewis, "Supplementary Benefits Appeal Tribunals" [1973] P.L. 257.

[27] Above, p. 68. These arrangements came into effect in April 1984 and there were transitional provisions which eliminated all non-lawyer chairmen.

[28] *ibid.* The period was formerly seven years.

[29] There is a President of the Independent Tribunal Service and a number of Regional Chairmen with supervisory and training responsibilities.

[30] There appears to have been no specific requirement that chairmen of NILTs should be qualified lawyers, but it was an almost unbroken rule of practice.

[31] N. Lewis, "Supplementary Benefit Appeal Tribunals" [1973] P.L. 275.

same arguments that are deployed in respect of legal representation at tribunals.[32] The skills of the lawyer are thought to lie in order, objectivity and procedure rather than speed, informality and expertise. The Franks Committee were early advocates of the legally-qualified chairman. "Objectivity in the treatment of cases and the proper sifting of facts are most often best secured by having a legally qualified chairman."[33] The Committee also noted that there had been substantial agreement on this matter among witnesses. Later writers have advanced further arguments[34]: the ability of lawyers to uphold basic legal principles in the field of administrative adjudications[35]; the maintenance of firm control over tribunals bred out of confidence and expertise[36]; the natural inclination of lawyers to control bias and prejudice in the presentation of cases; and the grasp of legal questions which is relevant in most areas of tribunal work.[37]

These views have not gone unopposed,[38] and even the advocates of lawyer-chairmen have not usually gone so far as to suggest that chairmanship should be the exclusive province of lawyers,[39] yet the recent developments have been along that line. It is unfortunate that other very suitable people may be excluded from chairmanship. The presence of a lawyer-chairman is certainly no guarantee of good chairmanship; a survey found that in one of every six SSAT hearings observed, "the chairman's conduct of the case was in our view open to serious criticism", citing particular examples of cases where the chairman was "accusatory in approach", "too dominant" or "maintained a severe, stern tone of voice throughout."[40]

2. TRAINING

16–013   Arrangements for the training of tribunal chairman and (especially) members have long been recognised to be inadequate. In recent years steps have been taken to improve the position, but the matter is yet to receive the attention and the resources that are necessary.[41]

---

[32] See below, paras 16-016–16-022.

[33] Report of the Committee on Administrative Tribunals and Enquiries (Cmnd. 218, 1957), para. 55.

[34] They are collected and analysed by J. Fulbrook, *Administrative Justice and the Unemployed* (1978), pp. 215–219.

[35] H. W. R. Wade, *Towards Administrative Justice* (1963), p. 43.

[36] H. L. Elcock, *Administrative Justice* (1969), pp. 50–53.

[37] Especially in the Employment Tribunals, and in the determination of claims in respect of industrial injuries.

[38] R. M. Titmuss, "Welfare 'Rights', Law and Discretion" (1971) 42 *Political Quarterly*, pp. 113–132.

[39] The Franks Committee (above, n.33) recommended that," ... the appointment of persons without legal qualification should not be ruled out when they are particularly suitable." (para. 55).

[40] Baldwin, Wikeley and Young, *Judging Social Security* (1992), pp. 115–119.

[41] See above, para. 4-018.

3. Correction of Procedural Irregularities

In the major tribunals we have so far considered there is a provision for a **16–014**
right of appeal to an appellate body who have the power to correct
procedural irregularities.[42] Where there is no appellate body[43] or where the
appeal does not properly deal with the defect alleged judicial review may be
sought. That remedy is considered in Chapter 18.[44] Both the existence of the
appellate body and the ultimate oversight of the courts provide the
safeguard against the wrongful exercise of chairman's considerable
discretion.

D. THE ROLE OF THE "WING" MEMBERS

It is a distinctive feature of the tribunal system that it gives considerable **16–015**
scope for lay participation in adjudication. Some of the alleged disadvantages of lawyer-chairmen may be moderated by the presence of lay people as
members of the tribunal.

The appointment of the lay members has already been described,[45] and
there is comparatively little in the way of research work into how the laymen
approach their task and the nature of their relationship with the chairman.[46]
In relation to social security tribunals there was doubt about the extent of
their participation in the hearing and the adjudication, although it was
recognised that a lack of participation might result from the absence of
training and guidance. Indeed, a survey found that few wing members said
very much, that two-thirds of those members who remained silent were
entirely passive and that many " can be said to have given the appearance of
being seriously out of their depth." Furthermore it appeared that members
frequently failed to participate actively in the deliberations.[47] The role of lay
members in Appeals Service tribunals has now been reduced.[48]

E. REPRESENTATION BEFORE TRIBUNALS

" ... it is desirable that every applicant before any tribunal should be able to **16–016**
present his case in person or to obtain representation."[49]

---

[42] The Employment Appeal Tribunal for Employment Tribunals, and the Social Security
Commissioners for Appeals Service tribunals.
[43] *e.g.* there "may be" no appeal from the Immigration Appeal Tribunal.
[44] paras 18-046–18-059.
[45] Above, para. 4-016.
[46] See J. Fulbrook, *Administrative Justice and the Unemployed* (1978), pp. 226–229; J. Baldwin,
N. Wikeley and R. Young, (1992), pp. 143–153.
[47] Baldwin, Wikeley and Young (1992), pp. 146–147.
[48] See above, para. 2-037.
[49] R.C.L.S. Vol. 1 para. 15.11, p. 169.

In order to achieve this objective, the Royal Commission on Legal Services asserted that tribunal procedure would need to be simplified wherever possible; the existing schemes for representation by lay persons would need to be developed and funded; and legal aid would need to be made available for certain cases.[50] These findings were based on a significant amount of evidence received by the Commission[51] which was in addition to the published research already available.[52] An important study was subsequently commissioned by the Lord Chancellor's Department, covering Social Security Appeal Tribunals, Industrial Tribunals, Mental Health Review Tribunals and Immigration Adjudicators.[53] The whole question of tribunal representation is one which has continued to attract much attention, especially because of the large numbers of cases currently being determined by tribunals.[54]

In this section we consider six related issues, the first three relating to the present position and the second three to possible future provision of representation. What are the rules about representation? Who are the representatives? What do they do? Should lawyers be involved in representation less often, more often, or not at all? Should legal involvement be funded under the Legal Aid Scheme? In what way, if at all, should schemes of representation by lay persons be developed?

1. The Rules

16–017   Article 6(2) of the ECHR provides that everyone charged with a criminal offence has the right to defend himself in person or through legal assistance of his own choosing; a person who does not have sufficient means has the right to free legal assistance when the interests of justice so require. "Criminal charge" for this purpose has to be given an autonomous meaning and accordingly some cases determined by a tribunal and not by a criminal court may be covered by Article 6(2).[55] In *R. (on the application of Fleurose) v. Securities and Futures Authority Ltd.*[56] the Court of Appeal held that the determination by the SFA's Disciplinary Appeal Tribunal of an appeal under the SFA's code applicable to traders in securities did not constitute the determination of a criminal charge. The offence was restricted to a specified group rather than the public at large and the penalty, although

---

[50]   ibid.
[51]   The Commission received evidence from both lawyers and non-lawyers active in the tribunal representation field. Its own research is contained in Vol. 2. Section 4, pp. 91–101.
[52]   Notably the studies carried out by Professor Kathleen Bell, *Research Study on Supplementary Benefit Appeal Tribunals, Review of Main Findings: Conclusions: Recommendations* (D.H.S.S. 1975): "National Insurance Local Tribunals," *Journal of Social Policy,* Vols.3.4 and 4.1 (1974/5). Other studies include R. *Lawrence Tribunal Representation* (1980); E. Kessler *et al., Combatting Poverty: CA.Bx., Claimants and Tribunals* (NACAB Occasional Paper No. 11, 1980); R. Lawrence, "Solicitors and Tribunals" [1980] J.S.W.L. 13; *Tribunal Assistance, the Chapeltown experience* (NACAB Occasional Paper, No. 14, 1982).
[53]   H. Genn and Y. Genn, *The Effectiveness of Representation at Tribunals* (L.C.D., 1989), discussed by R. Young, (1990) 9 CJ.Q. 16 and T. Mullen, (1990) 53 M.L.R. 230.
[54]   See Chap. 2.
[55]   See above, para. 8-020.
[56]   [2001] E.W.C. A. Civ 2015.

serious in that it would involve loss of livelihood, could not involve loss of liberty.[57] That did not conclude the question of the right to (free) legal assistance as such a right could in appropriate circumstances be regarded as inherent in the right to a fair hearing in Article 6(1). Mr Fleurose had legal representation before the first instance Disciplinary Tribunal but not the Appeal Tribunal. The Appeal Tribunal had been presided over by a former Law Lord (Lord Bridge), who was "at pains to take points on Mr Fleurose's behalf." There was no additional point that could have been advanced at the appeal hearing for which representation by a trained lawyer was needed. There was accordingly no unfairness resulting from the lack of legal representation. The court left open the question "whether in this class of case, the Convention ever requires that free legal representation be provided."[58] The situation here may be contrasted with the position with respect to matters referred to the Financial Services and Markets Tribunals by individuals against whom the Financial Services Authority have decided to take action in respect of alleged market abuse.[59] Here the sanctions that may be applied extend to members of the general public and are not confined to particular groups such as securities traders. Accordingly, the government agreed that a special legal assistance scheme should be established on the assumption that proceedings would be classified for Convention purposes as involving the determination of a criminal charge.[60]

Apart from the ECHR, and whether or not there is an absolute right to legal representation protected by the principles of natural justice,[61] it is rare for such a right to be specifically denied by tribunal rules.[62] However, a right to legal representation is only useful if the applicant has sufficient funds to pay a lawyer[63]; can find one who is competent in the field; and if the case is one in which the skills of a lawyer will be significant. As we shall see, representation by lawyers in tribunals is not generally common.

Some tribunals place restrictions on representation by persons other than lawyers,[64] but the usual provision is for an unfettered right to representation.[65] The ability of the applicant to select an appropriate representative has resulted in the appearance before tribunals of a wide variety of representatives.

---

[57] The court applied principles set out in *Han & Yau v. Commissioners of Customs and Excise* [2001] EWCA Civ 1048 and *Official Receiver v. Stern* [2001] 1 W.L.R. 2230.

[58] para. 23. The issue appears to have centred on the right to *free* legal assistance as distinct from the right to have such assistance at all.

[59] Financial Services and Markets Act 2000, s. 127(4).

[60] *ibid.*, ss. 134, 135; Financial Services and Markets Tribunal (Legal Assistance) Regulations 2001 (S.I. 2001, No. 3632). See further, below, para. 16-021.

[61] See Sir William Wade and C. F. Forsyth, *Administrative Law* (8th ed., 2001), at p. 514

[62] The only exception seems to be Health Authority discipline committees. Before that tribunal paid representation by a lawyer is not permitted, he or she may only appear as a "friend" not address the Committee or put questions to witnesses: National Health Service (Service Committees and Tribunal) Regulations 1992 (S.I. 1992 No. 664), Sched. 4, para. 5(3), substituted by S.I. 1996 No. 703. See further below, para. 16-020.

[63] Save in exceptional circumstances, see para. 16-021 below.

[64] For example, representation by non-lawyers is only permitted at the discretion of the Performing Rights Tribunal, the Lands Tribunal and the Commons Commissioners, see R.C.L.S. Vol. 1, para. 15.3.

[65] See the procedural rules of the tribunals considered, above.

2. Who are the Representatives?

16–018   Some distinctions must be made between the different tribunals in that they
attract different representatives.

The study by Genn and Genn showed that Citizens Advice Bureaux were
the most frequent representatives at SSATs (closely followed by family or
friends); the UKIAS before Immigration Adjudicators; lawyers and trade
unions at Industrial Tribunals; and solicitors at MHRTs.[66] The proportion
of all appellants represented at the hearing varied considerably. 16 per cent
of SSAT, appellants were represented, but only 12 per cent by agencies or
individuals with experience of representation or with any special expertise.[67]
In contrast, 90 per cent of appellants at immigration hearings, 58 per cent of
applicants and 73 per cent of respondents at Industrial Tribunals, and 61 per
cent of applicants at MHRTs were represented by someone other than a
relative or friend.[68]

Although there will always be some who defy categorisation, it is possible
to discern five groupings from amongst those people who undertake
representation.

First, there are those who represent at tribunals as a result of a
professional interest in their members or clients. We are referring here
principally to trade union representatives, employers' organisation representatives and social workers who go to a tribunal with a client.
Representation has been a significant feature of the legal services supplied
by trade unions to their members,[69] and this is particularly marked in the
field of national insurance, industrial injuries and employment issues. This
has resulted in the trade unions taking a cautious view over the future
development of lay or legal representation. They have appeared not to be
anxious to have competitors providing alternative services to their
members.[70] Social workers have been involved in the work of social security
tribunals. This group of representatives should be in a position to offer
effective representation as a result of skill and experience acquired in
particular tribunals.

The second group consists of representatives provided by *voluntary
organisations* for the benefit of their members. The Benson Commission
noted the work done by the Royal British Legion in Pensions Appeal
Tribunals,[71] and the Claimants' Unions have specialised in the area of social
security tribunals.[72]

The third group consists of representatives provided by *generalist or
specialist advice agencies* for the benefit of anyone who wishes to consult the
agency and accept an offer of help. The Citizens Advice Bureaux have

---

[66] Genn and Genn (1989), pp. 19, 33, 46, 58. R.C.L.S. Vol. 2, Section 4, Tables 4.7; Bell,
Research on S.B.A.T.s, at pp. 15–16 (see n. 52, above).
[67] Genn and Genn (1989), pp. 19–22.
[68] *ibid.*, pp. 32–35, 43–53, 56–59.
[69] G. Latta and R. Lewis, "Trade Union Legal Services" (1974) *XII British Journal of
Industrial Relations* 561; R. Lewis and G. Latta, "Union Legal Services" (1973) 123 N.L.J.
386; TUC's annual *Trade Union Trends Survey, Focus on Employment Tribunals.*
[70] See G. Bindman, "Trade Unions and Legal Services" *LAG Bulletin*, March 1979, 56.
[71] R.C.L.S., Vol. 1, para. 15.16.
[72] On the role of the Claimants' Unions, see H. Rose, "Who Can de-label the Claimant," in M.
Adler and A. Bradley, *Justice, Discretion and Poverty* (1976).

provided such a service to the public,[73] and there are other examples of advice agencies becoming involved in representation as an incidental part of their general service. Specialist agencies, like the Child Poverty Action Group, provide representation in then-own field.[74] The United Kingdom Immigrants Advisory Service (UKIAS) provided an interesting example of a specialist agency set up with public funds to deal with enquiries on a particular topic. It was described by the Benson Commission as, " ... a unique counselling and advocacy service dealing with one field of tribunal work and manned by a full time salaried staff."[75] In 1992 its responsibilities were split between the Refugee Legal Centre and the Immigration Advisory Service.[76]

The fourth group consists of representatives provided by various specific *tribunal representation projects*. The C.A.B. service has been associated with major schemes in Birmingham, Leeds, Sheffield, Newcastle and Wolverhampton and has also provided the stimulus for other local initiatives.[77] The Free Representation Unit provides representation before tribunals in London.[78] The various tribunal representation schemes have come under close scrutiny, since they may provide a model for the development of lay representation. They are all organised on a different basis and attract funds from different sources but this variety may prove fruitful in the evaluation of alternative models. We consider their organisation further, at a later point in this chapter.

The fifth group consists of *lawyers*. We have already noted that lawyers do provide some representation in tribunals, but this is normally at the expense of the client. Very few tribunals have rules as to costs which would allow the recovery of legal expenses.[79] Some representation is funded publicly but it is exceptional. Funding for Legal Representation is available for a small number of tribunals; Legal Help may be available in respect of preparatory work.[80] Assistance short of representation can no doubt prove very irritating for the tribunal and it appears that solicitors may have been remunerated for assistance which has spilled over into representation.

[73] Although it is fair to point out that much has depended on the ability and willingness of volunteers in a particular bureau to undertake the task of representation, and there is considerable pressure and CABx resources. The coverage has consequently been patchy. A majority of CABx provide a representation service of some sort, although not necessarily for more than the occasional case: interview with a NACAB representative cited by J. Baldwin, (1989) 8 C.J.Q. 24, 36. By 1995, in 86 per cent of bureaux, advisers undertook representation themselves: NACAB Annual Report 1994–95, p. 21. A 2000–01 survey showed that 475 of 501 bureaux which responded offered representation at SSATs, 443 at Employment Tribunals, with smaller numbers for others: NACAB response to LCD Consultation on the Leggatt Report (*www.nacab.org.uk*).

[74] CPAG can take up a limited number of more complex cases such as appeals to the Commissioners, and then only if referred by local advisers: *National Welfare Benefits Handbook* 1995–96, p. 421.

[75] R.C.L.S. Vol. 1 para. 15.17: See further, para. 16-022.

[76] *www.refugee-legal-centre.org.uk; www.iasuk.org.uk*. They are now funded under the Immigration and Asylum Act 1999, s. 81. Other providers of immigration advice and representation (other than solicitors and barristers) are now regulated by an Immigration Services Commission and Tribunal under Part V of the 1999 Act (see *Legal Action*, April 2001, p. 9).

[77] See above, para. 13-005.

[78] *ibid.*

[79] See above, para. 11-0020.

[80] See above, para. 10-021.

There must inevitably be a composite group of "everybody else." Particularly in SBATs, the category of friends and relatives as representatives was significant. As we shall shortly demonstrate, the role of a "representative" can be very restricted, and it may be sufficient that his attendance has ensured the attendance of the applicant. That job can be done as well (possibly better) by a friend as by an advocate.

3. WHAT DO REPRESENTATIVES DO?

16–019 This may seem to be an odd question. However, we use it to demonstrate that the assistance offered by a representative may range more widely than simply putting the applicant's case at a hearing.

From the outset, the representative is likely to be involved in an advice-giving role whether he or she is an expert in the field or not.[81] It is obvious that those experienced representatives who have gained a thorough knowledge of their subject are able to evaluate the merits, and likely success, of the applicant's case and can act accordingly. This advisory role is significant because it may operate to exclude the weak and unmeritorious cases at an early stage.[82] If the effect of this screening is to allow the representative only to pursue those cases believed to be worthwhile, he or she gains an enhanced reputation with the tribunal in respect of the cases that are pursued through to a hearing. Moreover, the scarce resources of advice agencies and the like should not be used to support hopeless cases.

There are some reservations expressed about the validity of this advisory role, not least because the adviser may be constituting him- or herself as the adjudicator rather than the tribunal, and coming between the applicant and the tribunal. It is argued that applicants should be given the confidence and expertise to use the system themselves rather than experience the "interference" of another expert who would come to some tidy arrangement with the tribunal leaving the claimant as isolated as ever.[83] This is a minority view, however, and most of the representation schemes that have been established place emphasis on the provision of advice by an "expert" at an early stage.[84] There is also the reservation expressed by some about

> "doing the Government's job for them. You are telling someone to leave the country or not to ... claim a benefit. You are the soft police."[85]

A second function of a representative may be to act as a negotiator on

---

[81] Even the next-door neighbour might be asked whether or not to appeal!

[82] See Genn and Genn (1989), pp. 134–135.

[83] The Claimants' Union recognises a "right" to be represented whatever the merits of the case might appear to be. See generally, R. Lawrence, *Tribunal Representation* (1980), p. 18; H. Rose, "Who Can De-Label the Claimant?" in M. Adler and A. Bradley, *op. cit.*

[84] Some of the tribunal representation schemes operate on a "consultancy" basis whereby volunteer lay representatives themselves receive help and guidance at the early stages of a possible appeal (see, for example, the West Midlands project—*Combatting Poverty*, n.52 above). Others give a direct service to the claimant but rely heavily on the expertise of the representatives.

[85] Quotation from a Law Centre, cited by Genn and Genn (1989), pp. 134–135.

behalf of the applicant with a view to effecting a settlement of the problem.[86] We noted the importance of settlements in the civil process in Chapter 11[87]—they also have their place in the tribunal process. The intervention of a third party on behalf of an applicant may produce a change in the decision which satisfies the claimant. This might be called anti-representation since it has the effect of preventing a tribunal hearing, but it benefits both the applicant and the tribunal.[88]

A third function of representation may be simply to ensure the attendance of the applicant. This is sometimes referred to as a "hand-holding exercise."[89] The published figures demonstrate that an applicant has a higher chance of success at a tribunal if he or she attends, whether or not represented, than if he or she does not attend.[90] Claimants who receive an unfavourable decision on their claim may immediately give notice of appeal without giving thought to how to pursue the appeal.[91] On receipt of the appeal papers they decide not to go along to the hearing because the case is not arguable, or they are frightened, or ignorant of the process, or no longer interested. If they seek advice at all, they may simply need the reassurance that someone will attend the tribunal with them and help them through the procedure—not necessarily as an advocate but as a friend. Once at the hearing, with the presence of a supporter they are able to respond sufficiently to the tribunal to allow the case fully to be considered.

A fourth function is that of preparing the case for the hearing, good preparation being fundamental to the success of appeals. This includes interviewing the client, collecting documentary evidence, arranging for witnesses to attend and researching the law. Most appellants and applicants are likely to have difficulty in identifying the facts relevant to the case and securing the necessary evidence.[92]

This may seem quite a late stage to be arriving at the representative's job of representing. At the hearing, the function of the representative is to put forward the applicant's case without coming completely between the applicant and the tribunal. The representative should not forget that the tribunal will be interested to hear from the applicant directly.[93] The need to marshal the arguments for the benefit of the tribunal will be dictated partly by the complexity of the subject matter and partly by the procedure adopted.[94] The skills required are not necessarily those of the advocate—but

---

[86] *ibid.*, pp. 135–138.

[87] Above, paras. 11-025–11-031.

[88] One of the arguments advanced in favour of the extension of representation is its effect in diminishing the caseload of tribunals.

[89] Particularly by the Citizens Advice Bureaux. See the NACAB Administrative Circular (1974), cited in R. Lawrence, *Tribunal Representation* (1980), p. 59. This circular is no longer current, but the function remains the same.

[90] K. Bell, *op. cit.* (above, n.52); Genn and Genn (1989), p. 68 (S.S.A.T.S); this is not a surprising finding. Attendance at least allows the tribunal the possibility of questioning the claimant.

[91] This does not mean that a high proportion of the recipients of adverse D.S.S. decisions appeal: see Genn and Genn (1989), pp. 130–134.

[92] Genn and Genn (1989), pp. 138–147.

[93] The Social Security Commissioner has, on occasion, criticised a representative who appears to have dominated the hearing to the exclusion of the applicant. (See R(I) 36/61).

[94] In the Employment Tribunal, for example, the representative has his or her job defined by the adoption of a fairly standard, adversarial procedure. See above.

it helps the tribunal if the representative can present a logical, orderly, relevant analysis of the issues and the evidence. Statistics show that the represented claimant is better off at a tribunal.[95] This point is confirmed by the study by Genn and Genn,[96] which also indicates that specialist representatives have the greatest effect on the probability of success.[97]

Finally, the expertise gained by the representative and his or her familiarity with the system may be used for the benefit of others in the exchange of information and pressure for reform. In the informal world of tribunals the shared experience is invaluable. This sharing may be formal, through publications,[98] or informal, through word of mouth but it is undoubtedly a factor in the increasing success of lay representatives.

Much of this section has been directed towards the less formal tribunals and the experience of the Employment Tribunal is somewhat different. There, the actual representation at the hearing takes on the major significance and the other functions are consequently diminished.[99] It is not surprising that with considerable lawyer representation the emphasis has been placed upon advocacy.

Overall it was the clear conclusion of the study by Genn and Genn that representation of appellants and applicants increases the accuracy of tribunal decision-making and improves the fairness of the process by which decisions are reached.[1] Arguments that tribunals proceedings are informal and simple, and that representation is accordingly unnecessary and undesirable, are ill-founded.[2] The view of tribunals, representatives and presenting officers in the four areas studied

> "was that much of the law with which they were concerned was complex and the adjudicative function of tribunals was often a highly technical forensic process."[3]

Moreover,

> "the experience of unrepresented appellants and applicants indicates that, even in the most informal hearings, they have difficulty in expressing themselves; they do not understand the relevance of the rules and regulations that are quoted to them; and when they lose, frequently leave in a state of disappointment and frustration."[4]

It was the unanimous belief of representatives interviewed that "no matter

---

[95] Although there are some reservations about the interpretation of the evidence: R. Lawrence, *Tribunal Representation* (1980), pp. 19–20.

[96] Genn and Genn (1989), Chap. 3. Other factors independently associated with success were the type of case, number of witnesses, georgraphical location (SSATs) and the identity of the chair or the adjudicator (SSATs, ITS, Immigration hearings).

[97] Welfare rights centres, tribunal units and law centres for social security appeals, U.K.I.A.S. and lawyers for immigration hearings.

[98] For example, information is disseminated through NACAB and CPAG literature (*e.g.*, respectively, through *The Adviser and the Welfare Rights Bulletin*), and other periodicals.

[99] The negotiation function is, to some extent, undertaken by the conciliation officers of A.C.A.S., see above, para. 13-008.

[1] Genn and Genn (1989), pp. 247–248.

[2] *ibid.*

[3] *ibid.*, p. 244; and generally Chap. 4.

[4] *ibid.*, pp. 246–247; and generally Chap. 7.

how well-intentioned tribunals might be, it was impossible to compensate for lack of representation"; on the other hand, the majority of chairs of S.S.A.T.s and industrial tribunals believed that they could compensate for lack of representation. The observation of hearings for the purpose of the study tended to confirm the former view.[5]

Finally, some fears have been expressed about the extent to which an involvement with representation will inevitably result in a commitment to reform of the system, an over-identification with the position of the applicants, or an engagement in political activity.[6] How objective/disinterested can a representative remain? This anxiety has been examined and answered effectively by David Bull, whose analysis of the range of advocacy and its implications for the representatives is very convincing.[7]

4.Should Lawyers be Involved More? Less? At All?

The answer to this particular question depends upon the skills which lawyers bring to tribunal representation and the effect that the deployment of those skills is likely to have on the style and procedure of tribunals. It further depends upon the objectives which a system of tribunals seeks to achieve, and upon the complexity of the law which is being administered, the nature of the particular tribunal under consideration and upon the nature of the particular case under consideration, for there may be especial circumstances which warrant the attention of a lawyer.   **16–020**

Given all these variables it is difficult to formulate a single answer. Perhaps the convenient starting-point is to ask whether lawyers have a place in tribunal representation at all. Against the proposition that a citizen should have a right to legal representation in all forms of judicial or quasi-judicial proceedings[8] may be put the assertion that lawyers "spoil" tribunal adjudication by detracting from those qualities which tribunals are alleged to display, namely speed, informality, cheapness and expertise.[9] In particular, it has been argued that, in respect of areas in which discretion is an important element, the introduction of "legalism" is likely to hinder the operation of discretion to the disadvantage of the claimant.[10] These arguments have not prevailed[11] and there is, apparently, only one example

---

[5] *ibid.*, pp. 215–216.
[6] This has been a particular fear of NACAB who are very sensitive about allegations of political involvement and campaigning.
[7] D. Bull, "The Anti-Discretion Movement in Britain: Fact or Phantom?" [1980] J.S.W.L. 65.
[8] See above, para. 16-017.
[9] For the virtues (alleged) of tribunal adjudication, see above, para. 2-015. It is interesting to note that in the small claims track (see above, para. 12-022.) legal representation is not prohibited but it is discouraged because of the limitation of the recovery of costs.
[10] R, M. Titmuss, "Welfare 'Rights', Law and Discretion," (1971) 42 *Political Quarterly*, pp. 113–132. The subject is discussed fully in J. Fulbrook, *Administrative Justice and the Unemployed* (1978), pp. 275–293.
[11] Indeed, in the social security field benefits (first supplementary benefit, now income support) have become rule—rather than discretion-based and there is no longer a right of appeal to a tribunal in respect of the main remaining discretion-based benefit (social fund payments).

of a tribunal which positively prohibits legal representation.[12] It would certainly be difficult now to make a case for a blanket prohibition on legal representation, and it is generally accepted that lawyers have *some* part to play.

The more difficult question is the *extent* to which lawyer-representation is desirable. In practice, this question is closely linked with the possibility of providing public funds for such representation, for without funding the likelihood that an applicant will be able to pay for the services of a lawyer is slim.[13] However, until a positive case has been made for legal representation, funds will not be made available. What is the strength of the case?

There has been comparatively little evidence of the extent to which lawyers are involved in tribunal work or, incidentally, of their likely response if money were to be made available to allow them to undertake more.[14] Statistics from the research studies that have been done demonstrate the very low proportion of cases in social security tribunals which have lawyer representatives[15] and although the proportion is much higher in Employment Tribunals[16] there is little to indicate whether a few firms provide representation as a specialist service or whether most firms will undertake this type of work.[17] If the Employment Tribunal is any guide the presence of lawyer representatives is likely to formalise procedure and reinforce the adversarial style of the proceedings. This fear has been expressed also in respect of social security tribunals, not least because the criticisms levelled at such tribunals by lawyers tend to focus on the failure to follow a consistent and clear judicial process in adjudication.[18] The lawyers' response to such a failure is normally to formulate procedural rules and safeguards to be operated by lawyers.

The research conducted by Professor Bell indicated that there was no great enthusiasm amongst appellants for professional advocates; rather they were anxious to see the tribunal play a more *enabling* role thereby improving the opportunity for appellants to put their own case.[19] Few among the

---

[12] Discipline committees of Health Authorities: see the National Health Service (Service Committees and Tribunals) Regulations 1992 (S.I. 1992 No. 664), as amended by S.I. 1996 No. 703. These replaced Service Committees of Family Health Service Authorities from April 1, 1996, with a jurisdiction now confined to claims by an authority that the practitioner is in breach of his or her terms of service, and matters concerning overpayments. Since 1996 there has been a separate procedure for complaints by patients. Contrast the procedure under which a practitioner may be removed from the list of practitioners undertaking to provide family health service on grounds of efficiency, fraud or unsuitability; here, decisions are made by the Health Authority with an appeal lying to the Family Health Services Appeal Authority (superseding, from 2001, the National Health Service Tribunal); legal representation is expressly permitted before the Authority (Family Health Service Appeal Authority (Procedure) Rules 2001 (S.I. 2001 No. 3750), r.11), as was the case before the Tribunal.

[13] This is especially the case in social security tribunals where there is likely to be only a relatively small amount of money at stake. Costs are not normally awarded by tribunals, see para. 11-020 above.

[14] R. Lawrence, "Solicitors and Tribunals" [1980] J.S.W.L. 13; N. Harris, "Solicitors and Supplementary Benefit Cases" (1983) 34 N.I.L.Q. 144.

[15] K. Bell, *op. cit.* below, n.18 R.C.L.S. Vol. 2, Section 4; Genn and Genn (1989), p. 20.

[16] R.C.L.S. Vol. 2, Section 4, Tables 4.7, 4.8; Genn and Genn (1989), pp. 44–45, 50.

[17] R. Lawrence, *op. cit.* n. above, inclines to the former view.

[18] K. Bell, *Research Study on Supplementary Benefit Appeal Tribunals. Review of Main Findings: Conclusions: Recommendations*, (DHSS, 1975), at pp. 19–20.

[19] *ibid.*, p. 18.

tribunals and representatives interviewed for the study by Genn and Genn believed that lawyers were necessarily best equipped to conduct tribunal representations; the most common view was that specialisation and experience were the most important qualifications.[20]

Despite fears that lawyerly skills may frustrate some of the objectives of tribunal adjudication, the prevailing view is that legal representation is desirable in particular circumstances. This view is based mainly upon the combined arguments of legal complexity in certain fields and the importance of the issues to the individual claimant. The Royal Commission on Legal Services was content merely to state, " ... there are cases when a denial of legal aid for representation by a lawyer will put the applicant at a disadvantage. We have in mind, for example, cases before Supplementary Benefit Appeal Tribunals which involve allegations of cohabitation or dishonesty, and some of the claims before Industrial Tribunals which involve difficult problems of law and fact."[21] The study by Genn and Genn concluded that while the main development should be in the direction of increased funding to lay agencies, this would not provide the complete answer. There might be a need for skilled legal representation before the explicitly adversarial Industrial Tribunals, and to fill gaps left by the uneven geographical coverage of lay advice and representation agencies.[22]

The Benson Commission had considered much evidence on the provision of legal representation in tribunals and concluded that there are *some* cases before *all* tribunals hi which it was necessary. The identification of those cases is problematic, but some indication of the factors which might necessitate legal representation is given by the tests formulated to govern the granting of legal aid. The assumption seems to have been made that legal representation will only really be available when funding for legal representation is available[23] and we discuss in the next section the criteria which might be adopted in determining eligibility.

5. WHEN SHOULD FUNDING FOR LEGAL REPRESENTATION BE AVAILABLE FOR TRIBUNALS?

There is no serious dispute that it would be inadvisable for funding for legal **16–021** representation to be made immediately available for all cases in all tribunals. Different reasons would be given by different people. The expense; the inappropriateness; the availability of skilled lay representation; the possible lack of interest amongst the solicitors' profession[24] would all be reasons used to reject the extension of funding to all cases. There is an equal measure of agreement about the need to extend such funding to *some* tribunal cases,

---

[20] Genn and Genn (1989), p. 245; generally pp. 171–178, 193–198, 210–215.

[21] R.C.L.S. Vol. 1 para. 15.24.

[22] Genn and Genn (1989), pp. 249–250.

[23] This is why the two issues of whether lawyers should be involved, and whether they should be paid out of the Legal Aid Fund are extremely difficult to disentangle. When they are needed, they should be paid for ... See the evidence of The Law Society in *R.C.L.S. Memorandum No. 3* (1978). Evidence to the same effect was received from the Council on Tribunals, the President of Industrial Tribunals and other individuals. This view was supported by the Lord Chancellor's Advisory Committee on Legal Aid.

[24] See R. Lawrence, "Solicitors and Tribunals" [1980] J.S.W.L. 13, at pp. 19–25.

but two difficulties arise. First, it is difficult to agree the criteria which would establish eligibility; second, the advocates of the development of lay representation would not wish the extension of legal aid to be viewed as an alternative to funding better organised and more comprehensive schemes of lay representation.

The Council on Tribunals consistently advocated the extension of legal aid,[25] and its view was supported by the Lord Chancellor's Advisory Committee,[26] by the President ofIndustrial Tribunals[27] and by other groups and individuals. It was the formulation of the test of eligibility submitted by the Council on Tribunals which won the approval of the Benson Commission, subject to some additions. The Council proposed in their evidence to the Commission that an applicant for legal aid should show " . . . that in the particular circumstances of his case he reasonably requires the services of a lawyer, and the certifying committee shall in this respect have regard to the suitability and availability of any other forms of assistance." The Council instanced several situations where representation by a lawyer might be regarded as appropriate—

"(i) where a significant point of law arises,
(ii) where evidence is likely to be so complex or specialised that the average layman could reasonably wish for expert help in assembling and evaluating the evidence and in its testing or interpretation,
(iii) where a test case arises,
(iv) where deprivation of liberty or the ability of an individual to follow his occupation is at stake."[28]

To these situations the Commission added three others: where the amount at stake is significant *to the claimant*; where suitable lay representation is unavailable; where the special circumstances of the individual make legal representation desirable.[29]

These criteria, it is suggested, would be applied by the appropriate legal aid committee and used to determine whether the "merits" tests for legal aid had been satisfied. An alternative view, that legal aid should be granted or recommended by the chairman of the appropriate tribunal,[30] was not supported by the Benson Commission.

It is evident that these criteria were formulated upon the assumption that there would be an adequate lay representation service available, and the

---

[25] *e.g. Annual Reports*, 1976–77, p. 6; 1987–88, pp. 17–21; 1994–95, p. 7. The Franks Committee had made such a recommendation in 1958: *Report*, para. 89.

[26] This subject was first considered at length in the *24th Report of the Law Society on Legal Aid and Advice*, 1973/74, pp. 47–55. Thereafter it recurred in the *33rd Legal Aid Annual Reports* (1982–83), pp. 194–209; the *35th Reports* [1984–85], pp. 232–243; *38th Reports* (1987–88), pp. 103–105; *39th Reports* (1988–89), pp. 112–114.

[27] In his evidence to the Royal Commission on Legal Services, referred to in R.C.L.S. Vol. 1, at para. 15.28.

[28] *ibid.*, para. 15.28; endorsed by the Lord Chancellor's Advisory Committee on Legal Aid: *33rd Legal Aid Annual Reports* [1982–83], at p. 205. These criteria were endorsed in the Council's Annual Report for 1994–95, p. 9.

[29] *ibid.*, The Commission's additions were criticised and rejected by the Lord Chancellor's Advisory Committee: *33rd Annual Reports* [1982–83], at p. 205.

[30] See, for example, R. Micklethwait, *The National Insurance Commissioners* (1976), at p. 56.

supporters of such a service feared that these might be regarded as alternative, rather than complementary, developments. This dilemma confronts the reformer who wishes to advance the cause of tribunal representation but takes the view that the more important use of public funds is in the training and organisation of lay representatives. To oppose the extension of legal aid may appear to be siding with the forces of darkness; to support it, with limited funds available, may be reducing the possibility of more general improvement.

The Government's response to the Benson Commission was not encouraging[31]; it noted that all those involved in tribunal proceedings were already eligible, subject to means, for legal advice and assistance[32] and that assistance by way of representation was available for proceedings in mental health review tribunals. "Extensions of assistance by way of representation and legal aid are made where it is shown to be necessary and resources allow."[33]

The Lord Chancellor's Advisory Committee on Legal Aid subsequently recommended that legal aid should be extended as a matter of priority to bail applications to the immigration appellate authorities, and to the Immigration Appeal Tribunal, the Social Security Commissioners, Industrial Tribunals and the Vaccine Damage Tribunal.[34] The Government's position was to reiterate its response to the Benson Royal Commission. Indeed, it was stated that, pending the outcome of the research project on the effectiveness of representation, "the Government does not intend that there should be any general extension of publicly funded tribunal representation."[35] Given that outcome, noted at a number of points in the chapter, it is likely that any future development will be in the area of lay representation. This position was supported by the Legal Aid Efficiency Scrutiny[36] and the Legal Aid Board,[37] but their respective suggestions that the extension of representation might be funded by restricting the scope of the green form scheme were widely criticised as unrealistic and undesirable.[38]

The current position is that the Access to Justice Act 1999 provides that funding for legal representation may not be provided except in specified proceedings, and the only tribunals mentioned are the Employment Appeal Tribunal, Mental Health Review Tribunals, Immigration Adjudicators and the Immigration Appeal Tribunal and the Proscribed Organisations Appeal

---

[31] *The Government Response to the Report of The Royal Commission on Legal Services*, (Cmnd. 9077, 1983).

[32] See above, pp. 491–510.

[33] *Response*, above n. 31, p. 18.

[34] *33rd Legal Aid Annual Reports* [1982–83], pp. 194–209; *35th Annual Reports* [1984–85] pp. 236–242 (adding the Vaccine Damage Tribunal to the list). The Council on Tribunals' list of priorities was longer, and included MHRTs, Medical Appeal Tribunals and Immigration Adjudicators (see Annual Report for 1987–88 (1988–89 H.C. 102), p. 18).

[35] White Paper on *Legal Aid in England and Wales, A New Framework* (Cm. 118, 1987), para. 30.

[36] (L.C.D. 1986), Vol. 2, Part IV. See further above pp. 515–517.

[37] *Second Stage Consultation on the Future of the Green Form Scheme* (1989), para. 12.

[38] *e.g.* responses to the Legal Aid Board by the Lord Chancellor's Advisory Committee (*39th Legal Aid Annual Reports* (1988–89), p. 96), the Law Society (Response, p. 28) and NACAB (Response, p. 7).

Commission.[39] The Lord Chancellor may by direction require or authorise that funding be provided for excluded services, and he has done so in respect of Legal Help, Help at Court and Legal Representation in all proceedings before the Protection of Children Act Tribunal, in specified proceedings[40] before the General and Special Commissioners of Income Tax and VAT and Duties Tribunals. Also covered are appeals from those tribunals to the superior courts in the same circumstances. Cases are eligible even where they arise out of the running of a business.[41]

Cases may also qualify by reference to the Lord Chancellor's authority to the LSC to fund excluded services in Legal Representation (or Legal Help or Help at Court) in proceedings which have a significant wider public interest,[42] other than proceedings arising out of the carrying on of the client's business.[43] Examples of particular cases where a significant WPI has been found to exist have included representation before the Pensions Appeal Tribunal to consider whether schizophrenia could arise from military service,[44] and before the Social Security Commissioner to consider whether certain elements of jobseekers' allowance benefit were discriminatory against men.[45] He may also authorise the funding of individual cases on the request of the LSC,[46] but this will be in "extremely unusual cases."[47] The client must be financially eligible for Legal Representation; relevant Funding Code criteria must be satisfied; no alternative means of funding must be available; and there is either a significant wider public interest, or the case is of "overwhelming importance"[48] to the client, or there is

---

[39] Sched. 2, para. 2(1), as amended by the Community Legal Service (Scope) Regulations 2000 (S.I. 2000 No. 822) and the Terrorism Act 2000, Sched. 14, para. 19. Advocacy before the Lands Tribunal and the Commons Commissioner was excluded for the first time "because they do not have sufficient priority to justify public funding": *Lord Chancellor's Revised Guidance* on *Applications for Exceptional Funding* (applying from November 1, 2001), para. 5. See also *LSC Funding Code-Criteria*, Section 12 — Mental Health (no financial test but an application may be refused if it is unreasonable in the particular circumstances of the case for LR to be granted); *LSC Funding Code — Criteria*, Section 13 — Immigration (most of the normal financial and merits criteria apply; LR will be refused if the prospects of achieving a successful outcome are unclear or borderline (save where the case has a significant wider public interest, is of overwhelming importance to the client or raises significant human rights issues) or poor; save where the case has a significant wider public interest, LR will be refused unless the likely benefits justify the likely costs, such that a reasonable private paying client would be prepared to take the proceedings).

[40] *i.e.* where it is in the interests of justice for the client to be legally represented and the proceedings concern penalties declared by the courts to be criminal in ECHR terms or where an appeal reasonably seeks to argue that they are such criminal penalties.

[41] Lord Chancellor's Direction, *Tribunal Funding*, April 2, 2001 (LCD website).

[42] *i.e.* "the potential of the proceedings to produce real benefit for individuals other than the client (other than benefits to the public at large which normally flow from proceedings of the type in question)": *LSC Funding Code-Criteria*, para. 2.4.

[43] Lord Chancellor's Direction, *Scope of the Community Legal Service Fund Exceptions to the Exclusions*, April 2, 2001, para. 11.

[44] Public Interest Advisory Panel Report 01/62 (LSC, *Focus* 37. p. 13): rating "significant".

[45] PIAP/01/56 (*Focus 36*, p. 32): rating "significant;" cf. PIAP/01/66 (*ibid*, p. 34): no SWPI on the facts.

[46] Access to Justice Act 1999, s.6(8)(b); *Lord Chancellor's Revised Guidance on Applications for Exceptional Funding* (applying from November 1, 2001) (LSC, *Focus 36*, pp. 25–28).

[47] *Revised Guidance*, para. 2.

[48] *i.e.* "a case which has exceptional importance to the client, beyond the monetary value (if any) of the claim, because the case concerns life, liberty or physical safety of the client or his or her own family, or a roof over their heads": *LSC Funding Code-Criteria*, para. 2.4.

convincing evidence that there are other exceptional circumstances such that without public funding for representation it would be practically impossible for the client to bring or defend the proceedings, or the lack of public funding would lead to obvious unfairness in the proceedings. However, the Lord Chancellor has noted that the mere fact the opponent was represented does not necessarily make the proceedings unfair; "most tribunals are designed to be accessible to unrepresented clients." He will use "as a benchmark" those very exceptional cases where the ECtHR had indicated that the right of access to the court had effectively been denied because of the lack of public funding.[49] It is clear that tribunal representation through either of these routes will be rare.[50]

The ECHR also lies behind the establishment of a separate legal assistance scheme specifically for market abuse cases before the Financial Services and Markets Tribunal.[51] Applications for funding are made to the Tribunal. The Tribunal must grant assistance to an individual if satisfied that it is in the interests of justice to do so and the applicant's financial resources are such that he or she requires assistance in meeting the legal costs in relation to proceedings before the Tribunal. The Tribunal must take account of specified factors including whether an adverse decision would be likely to cause the individual to lose his or her livelihood or suffer serious damage to reputation; whether a substantial question of law might arise; whether the individual might be unable to understand the proceedings or state his or her own case; whether the proceedings might involve the tracing, interviewing or cross-examination of witnesses on behalf of the individual; and whether it is in the interests of another person that the individual be represented. A contribution may be payable in accordance with detailed rules set out in the regulations. These criteria echo a number of those recommended in the past by the Council or Tribunals and might be applied in other analogous cases. The costs of the scheme are met by a levy on the community regulated by the Financial Services Authority.[52]

The Leggatt Report[53] noted that Professor Genn's research in the 1980s showed that appellants benefited significantly from representation.[54] However, it concluded (without the support of any research evidence) that representation

"not only often adds unnecessarily to cost, formality and delay, but it

---

[49] *Revised Guidance*, paras. 8, 9,10. The guidance was revised following judicial review proceedings in *R. (on the application of Jarrett) v. LSC* [2001] EWHC Admin 389 and it incorporates the principles set out in *X. v. UK* (1984) 6 E.H.R.R. 136; see A. Lockley, *Legal Action*, August 2001. pp. 18–19.

[50] As at March 31, 2001, 14 applications for exceptional funding in individual inquiry/tribunal cases had been refused by the LSC, and 6 had been referred to the Lord Chancellor (4 granted, 2 pending): LSC Annual Report, 2000–01, p. 24.

[51] See above para. 16-017 and the Financial Services and Markets Tribunal (Legal Assistance) Regulations 2001 (S.I. 2001 No. 3632), made under the Financial Services and Markets Act 2000, ss. 134, 135.

[52] 2000 Act, s. 136.

[53] Above, para. 2-010.

[54] See above, para. 16-019. Supported by recent research on legal representation in unfair dismissal cases in employment tribunals: A. Sinclair, N. Botten and S. Cahill, "Unfair Dismissal, Representation and Compensation" [2000] 5 Web JCLI (legal representation appeared to be a significant determinant of both success and compensation).

also works against the objective of making tribunals directly and easily accessible to the full , range of potential users."

It asserted that implementation of its recommendations overall

"should radically reduce the need for representation whilst meeting human rights requirements."[55]

Where appellants were still in need of representation, the remit of the CLS should be extended, on an exceptional basis, to specific cases or classes of cases rather than to particular tribunals. Cases would have to have a reasonable prospect of success, and representation should be provided where required because the appellants' personal circumstances (such as inadequate knowledge of English or mental or physical disability) or the complexity of the case in fact or law make it unreasonable to expect the case to be presented by themselves. The LSC should set tribunal-specific criteria, under the Lord Chancellor's direction where appropriate, against which applications for public funding would be tested. There should be pilot studies in specific tribunals.[56]

This overall approach is open to criticism[57] on a variety of grounds. First, the assumption that accessibility to the unrepresented can be achieved in the vast majority of cases is unsupported by research evidence and, indeed, runs counter to the research by Professor Germ. Secondly, the failure to consider the possibility of developing lay representation services is disappointing. The approach does, however, chime in with the consistent reluctance of successive governments to extend publicly funded tribunal representation, an approach that is only really explicable on grounds of cost.

6. How Should Lay Representation be Developed?

16–022   "If agencies which provide advice and representation before tribunals are to give an adequate service, they should have enough money to provide training for staff, an up-to-date information service and proper administrative support ... we recommend that public funds should be made available to approved agencies to assist in the training of tribunal representatives."[58]

"[The recommendation is] accepted in principle subject to further consideration being given to timing and the availability of resources."[59]

If the Government were to make available resources to implement the Benson Commission recommendation, then consideration would have to be given to the most effective method of organising schemes of lay representation. There is a variety of schemes already in existence which

[55] LCD, 2001, para. 4.21.
[56] *ibid.*, paras. 4.22–4.26.
[57] M. Adler, "Self-help is no substitute" (2001) 8(2) *Tribunals* 19; *Legal Action*, October 2001, p. 3; NACAB response to the LCD consultation on the Leggatt Report.
[58] R.C.L.S. Vol. 1, paras.15.20, 15.21.
[59] *Response*, above n. 10, at p. 18.

might provide a guide for national development.

Lawrence[60] distinguished three types of scheme which could be observed amongst the 16 or so existing tribunal units. He characterised these types as *referral agencies, advice bureau based and support units.*[61]

The *referral agencies* accept tribunal cases at the hearing stage from another agency which has done all the preparatory work and got the case ready for the tribunal. The representatives attached to such agencies operate purely as advocates and will send the applicant back to the original agency if there is any follow-up work to be done after the hearing has taken place. Typical of this kind of organisation of specialist advocates is the Free Representation Unit.[62] Such a unit normally relies heavily on the initial competence of some other agency[63] to prepare the case in such a way that it is ready for a hearing.

Advice bureau based units operate from or alongside established agencies, often CABx, with particular responsibility for taking on the tribunal representation work of that agency. This is, in some ways, the easiest unit to develop since it can emerge from the expertise of workers in the bureau in response to a perceived need for the work.[64] The Newcastle Tribunal Assistance Unit[65] exemplifies that process, and the Chapeltown unit in Leeds is similarly bureau-based.[66] These units have a wider role because of the close connection with a bureau and find themselves involved in formal and informal training of bureau workers as well as advice and representation. The value of having a unit attached in this way is the effect it has of raising the general level of advice-giving in the host agency. It is clear that the tendency at first is for the agency to push all problems in the subject area of the unit onto the unit, including perfectly routine enquiries. After an initial period, however, the general competence to handle such enquiries increases and the work of the agency is consequently strengthened.[67]

Support units are those which are not intended directly to offer representation, but rather to train, inform, advise and assist other representatives in the area which is served by the unit. The NACAB/EEC Tribunal Project in the West Midlands[68] operated in this way from the outset although the staff found the need to deal with some casework in order to retain their own expertise in representation. Of course, such units depend on their ability to stimulate interest in representation amongst agencies in the area and it can be difficult to break down reluctance on the part of

---

[60] R. Lawrence, *Tribunal Representation* (1980).

[61] *ibid.,* at p. 84.

[62] Above, para. 16-018.

[63] This may be an unsatisfactory feature of such a scheme. The particularly fruitful parts of the other two types of scheme depend on the contact between representative and adviser and the building up of the general level of advice-giving,

[64] The drawback of this type of unit is that it relies heavily on the skills of few people. Holidays, illness, pressure of work can then disrupt the representation service quite significantly.

[65] Established in 1974 with the support of the Newcastle CAB. It experienced a rapid rise in workload and subsequently attracted work from a wide area.

[66] See *Chapeltown CAB, Leeds, Tribunal Assistance Unit Progress Report—First Two years Aug. 1976–Aug. 1978* (NACAB Occasional Paper No. 6,1979); *Tribunal Assistance, The Chapeltown experience* (NACAB Occasional Paper No. 14, 1982).

[67] R. Lawrence, *op. cit.,* esp. Chap. 5; Tribunal Assistance (above, n. 66), pp. 56–58.

[68] *Combatting Poverty: CABx, Claimants and Tribunals* (NACAB Occasional Paper No. 11, 1980); above, para. 16-016, n.52.

volunteers.[69] The task is less easy for support units than for bureau-based services with their constant contact with both workers and clients.

This categorisation does not take account of all the units presently in operation[70] but it may offer some guidance for future development. The Citizens Advice Bureaux network would seem to provide a good basis for bureau-based units. However, geographical coverage is still incomplete and it might prove hopelessly expensive to provide bureau-based units in rural areas where there is relatively less work to do. Support units are not directly effective and seem to take longer to stimulate a reliable service. In the longer term, however, they have a much broader effect on the area they serve.

A further kind of service, commended by Genn and Germ,[71] is the single-purpose agency, exemplified by the former United Kingdom Immigrants Advisory Service. It is, however, doubtful that it would be practicable to extend this model generally to all tribunals in which there is a representation problem.[72]

The Lord Chancellor's Advisory Committee advocated the development of a strong voluntary lay representation service, possibly based on the CABx, utilising the skills of "resource lawyers." Such a scheme would complement legal representation funded by legal aid in difficult cases and would be closest to the *support units* of the models we have discussed.[73]

7. Procedural Reform

16–023   The preceding sections have all made one important assumption: that the tribunal system will continue in much the same way, becoming, if anything, rather more legalistic. The need for improved representation is based on that assumption.

The Benson Commission recommended a review of the procedures of tribunals in order to ensure that applicants in person are able to conduct their own cases whenever possible.[74] Such a review might have an effect on the need for representation, but would raise again the fundamental principles of tribunal adjudication. In the end, the question, "What kind of representation do we need?" is linked inextricably with the question, "What kind of tribunals do we want?" As we have seen, the study by Genn and Genn strongly reinforces the view that the idea that procedures can be simplified, given the great complexity of much of the law dealt with by tribunals, is unduly optimistic.

[69] *ibid.*, pp. 47–56.
[70] R. Lawrence, *op. cit.* at p. 85.
[71] Genn and Genn (1989), pp. 193–198, 250.
[72] See T. Mullen, (1990) 53 MLR. 230, 234–235.
[73] *3rd Annual Legal Aid Reports* [1982–83], pp. 201–203; 35th Reports [1984–85], pp. 235–236.
[74] R.C.L.S., Vol. 1., paras.15.12, 15.13.

CHAPTER 17

THE CRIMINAL TRIAL

THIS chapter examines the criminal trial. It should be read taking a critical **17–001**
approach, bearing in mind the many competing values at stake, which are
described in outline by Packer's two models of criminal justice.[1] Without
necessarily agreeing with either of Packer's models, or suggesting that they
represent an accurate or exhaustive account of the criminal process,
Packer's models provide a useful mechanism for evaluating the objectives of
the trial process and the extent to which the present trial rules, principles
and policies fulfill these objectives.[2] Packer's "crime control model"
emphasises the importance of the repression of criminal behaviour in the
most efficient manner. There is a requirement for high rates of arrest and
conviction, and a major interest in promoting speed and finality in the
criminal justice system. There is, therefore, an emphasis on informal, routine
procedures, relying heavily on the work of the police to determine guilt.
Consequently, whatever procedures are used presume guilt. The "due
process model" stresses the need to protect the accused against error.
Whereas the crime control model looks like a conveyor-belt approach to
criminal justice, the due process model looks more like an obstacle course.
Every stage in the due process model assumes the innocence of the accused
and requires formidable impediments to be overcome to establish guilt.
Therefore the trial stage is, therefore, essential to the due process model.

The rhetoric of the English criminal justice process reflects the due process
model, particularly in the period immediately following the enactment of the
Human Rights Act 1998. Obvious examples include the presumption of

---

[1] See H. L. Packer, *The Limits of the Criminal Sanction* (1968). Packer's models are discussed
more fully in relation to pre-trial criminal procedure at para. 14-093 above, where also
attention is drawn to the "fundamental balance" between the interests of the community and
the rights and liberties of individual citizens considered by the Royal Commission on
Criminal Procedure. For a summary of Packer's models, see R. C. A. White, *The
Administration of Justice* (3rd ed., 1999), Chap. 7. For the enthusiastic reader, M. King, *The
Framework of Criminal Justice* (1981) provides a method of examining the criminal justice
system by building more models on to those created by Packer. See also M. Wasik, T.
Gibbons and M.Redmayne, *Criminal Justice Text and Materials* (1999).

[2] For a detailed critique of Packer's models see A. Sanders and R. Young *Criminal Justice*
(2nd ed., 2000), pp.22–33. Attempts have been made to reinterpret Packer's models as not
being in conflict, but rather, that the due process goals qualify those of the crime control
model: see A. Ashworth, *The Criminal Process* (2nd ed., 1998), pp.25–27 and Chap. 2
generally, and "Criminal Justice and the Criminal Process" (1988) 28 B.J. Crim. 111.
Ashworth's reinterpretation of Packer is criticised by Sanders and Young (2000), pp.26–27.
See also D. Smith, "Case Construction and the Goals of Criminal Process" (1998) 37 B.J.
Crim. 319; P. Duff, "Crime Control Due Process and 'the Case for the Prosecution'" (1998)
38 B.J. Crim. 611.

innocence, reflected in the prosecution bearing the burden of proof in a criminal trial, and the "fair trial" guarantees of Article 6 of the ECHR and the impact these have on the interpretation of the rules relating to the admissibility of evidence. The impact of the Human Rights Act 1998 and the ECHR is being particularly keenly felt in the criminal trial owing to the very broad guarantees in Article 6 and their expansive interpretation by the European Court. The impact on evidence and procedural law is far more marked than with the substantive law. Article 6(1) of the European Convention on Human Rights provides:

> "In the determination of . . . any criminal charge against him, everyone is entitled to a fair and public hearing within a reasonable time by an independent and impartial tribunal established by law. Judgment shall be pronounced publicly but the press and public may be excluded from all or part of the trial in the interests of morals, public order, or national security in a democratic society, where the interests of juveniles or the protection of the private life of the parties so require, or to the extent strictly necessary in the opinion of the court in special circumstances where publicity would prejudice the interests of justice."[3]

The impact of the ECHR on domestic law is so significant that it has already generated a domestic human rights jurisprudence[4] in criminal justice. Commentators have offered interesting rights-based models by which the criminal justice process can be evaluated.[5] As an example, we will consider Ashworth's critique of Packer's model on a human rights-based approach later in the chapter. Other alternatives for evaluation of the system that have recently been proposed will also be examined.[6]

Because of the impact of the Human Rights Act 1998, due process guarantees might appear, in 2002, to be more substantial than they really are. The flurry of cases in the wake of the Act has emphasised existing protections and extended the scope of some. However, it should not be forgotten that there has also been a relentless legislative drive towards improving efficiency in the criminal process. This has not always attracted the same high profile as when "human rights" arguments have triumphed in the courts. The efficiency driven initiatives in the process usually demonstrate a clear "crime control" leaning. As many commentators

---

[3] See D.J. Harris, M. O'Boyle and C. Warbrick, *Law of the European Convention on Human Rights* (1995), Chaps 6, 11 and 14; *Archbold (2002)*, Chap 16. See generally Emmerson and Ashworth, *Human Rights and Criminal Justice* (2001); K Starmer, *Blackstone's Human Rights Digest* (2000); K. Starmer *et al.*, *Criminal Justice Police Powers and Human Rights* (2001); A. Ashworth, "Criminal Proceedings After the Human Rights Act 1998: The First Year" [2001] Crim. L.R. 855. Article 6 protection applies to the whole of the criminal process, not just the trial proper; a fair trial includes the pre-trial actions and appeals. Art. 6 has potential to influence many aspects of English criminal procedure and has already made some significant impact. The Lord Chancellor's Department has published statistical updates of the impact of the HRA: *www.lcd.gov.uk/humanrights/hrimpact.htm*. The number of cases received by the Court of Appeal (Criminal Division) fell from 2,643 between October 2, 1999 and January 3, 2000 to 2,491. 277 cases contained Human Rights Act points.

[4] A. Ashworth, "Criminal Proceedings After the Human Rights Act 1998: The First Year" [2001] Crim. L.R. 855.

[5] See especially Ashworth, (1998).

[6] See, *e.g.* Sanders and Young's "freedom" model below, para. 17-102.

observe, it is inappropriate to dismiss the crime control model too quickly. Examples of practices that reflect the crime control model in the English process include the many cases being diverted from trial, the channelling of cases into the magistrates' courts, the police occasionally violating the rules governing their powers and many, perhaps too many, guilty pleas being entered.[7] The crime control model plays a greater role in the English criminal justice system than would at first appear.

It may be of some value in reading this chapter to consider the differences between processes designed to establish the truth of events and procedures adopted in the English criminal trial.[8] At the criminal trial, it is for the prosecution to establish its case against the accused to the satisfaction of the magistrates or jury beyond a reasonable doubt through an adversarial procedure. Considerable efforts are made to ensure "fairness" in the procedure, so the court cannot take account of all possible forms of evidence. The trial procedures are also firmly bedded in the oral tradition with witnesses being called to give oral testimony on oath and be subjected to cross-examination in full view of the accused and the trier of fact. Recent moves to protect vulnerable witnesses and to enhance the quality of the evidence received demonstrate an increasing willingness to move away from the strict oral tradition.[9] The Law Commission and Auld Report[10] have also recently made recommendations that would recognise that undue adherence to the orality principle does not necessarily serve to produce the best evidence for the trial nor to assist the witness to deliver their evidence with maximum effect and minimum stress.[11]

Outside the criminal trial, judgments as to the truth of a matter are likely **17–002** to be made, not by adversarial methods, but inquisitorially; not so as to be satisfied beyond reasonable doubt, but as more likely than not; not by evidence which passes the rules of legal admissibility, but on any reliable evidence.[12] It is not the objective of the criminal trial to establish the truth of what happened, although it is presumably believed that the criminal trial will produce results that closely resemble the truth of the matter. The merits of the adversarial system and the potential advantages of an inquisitorial approach[13] are frequently called into question, particularly when the current

---

[7] As to diversion from trial, see above para. 14-043 and the fixed penalty notice scheme noted briefly below at para. 17-006; the Police and Criminal Evidence Act 1984 prevents what may have been regular violations, see above Chap. 14; as to the debate concerned with "plea bargaining" see para. 17-039 below.

[8] See, further, Z. Bankowski, "The Jury and Reality" in M. Findlay and P. Duff (eds), *The Jury Under Attack* (1988) and works referred to therein.

[9] See the reforms in Part II of the Youth Justice and Criminal Evidence Act 1999. On orality, see generally J. Spencer, [1994] Crim. L.R. 628. But note *Luca v. Italy* [2001] Crim. L.R. 747.

[10] Cmnd. 5074 (2001), *www.criminal-courts-review.org.uk*.

[11] See the Auld Report recommendations to relax rules on previous consistent statements as evidence at trial and the rules relating to the witness refreshing memory from statements before trial, pp.548–556.

[12] See J. McEwan, "Adversarial and Inquisitorial Proceedings" and J. Jackson, "Evidence: Legal Perspectives" in R. Bull, and D. Carson (eds.), *Handbook of Psychology in Legal Contexts* (1995). "Trial Procedures" in C. Walker and K. Starmer, *Miscarriages of Justices: A Review of Justice in Error* (1999). On the many different systems falling within the general classification as inquisitorial see M. Damaska, "Evidential Barriers to Conviction and 2 Models of Criminal Process: A Comparative Study" (1973) 121 U. Penn. L.R. 506.

[13] Note that the Auld Report states that the criminal trial is an investigation for the truth. Chap. 1, para. 12.

criminal trial process is perceived as being under acute stress.[14] The
adversarial trial process has frequently been criticised for inhibiting "a
problem solving approach."[15] Some aspects of English criminal trial process
might be regarded as shifting towards a more inquisitorial process,[16] and
evidence of a general convergence of inquisitorial and adversarial systems
has also been suggested.[17]

Many might regard the emphasis on the full panoply of adversarial trial
processes as being of greater symbolic than practical significance bearing in
mind that so few cases reach the Crown Court, and so few of those result in
a full jury trial. Nevertheless, the jury trial still represents the paradigm of
the criminal trial in England and Wales.

It is important also to record at the outset that the criminal trial process is
constantly evolving. There is a continual pressure for change, both to
improve the procedures in principled legal terms and to improve efficiency.
This occurs not only from the natural evolution of the common law which is
particularly volatile in this area, but also from successive government reviews
and policy initiatives.[18] These all too often lead to over-hasty legislation.

In recent years the criminal trial has also come under pressure to
recognise the significance of other interests and objectives peripheral to the
determination of guilt or innocence. The most prominent influences have
included an increased recognition of the victim's role in the criminal justice
system.[19] In addition, there is a discernable trend towards consumerism in
which "users" of the criminal justice system must be satisfied by the
"service" they receive.[20] There are also the obvious signs of the impact of

---

[14] See recently, *e.g.*, C. Pollard, "Public Safety, Accountability and the Courts" [1996] Crim. L.R.
152; A. Ashworth, "Crime Community and Creeping Consequentialism" [1996] Crim. L.R. 220.

[15] C. Pollard, *op cit.* 155

[16] As for example with enhanced disclosure regimes and a diminution of the orality principles.

[17] See N. Jorg, S. Field and C. Brants in C. Hardin, P. Fennell, N. Jorg, and B. Swart, *Criminal
Justice in Europe* (1995). For comparisons with the English procedure see L.H. Leigh and L.
Zedner, *A Report of the Administration of Criminal Justice in the Pre-trial Phase in England
and Germany* (RCCJ Research Study No. 1, 1992). For a brief but accessible account of the
French system, see S. Wesley, "A Glimpse of French Criminal Justice" (1998) N.L.J. 326 at
148 669; note the proposals to reduce the scope of cases for *juges d'instruction* see R. Jones,
"Criminal Procedure in France" (1999) J.P.N. 592.

[18] On the political pressures and criminal justice 163 development see Wasik, Gibbons and
Redmayne, (1999), pp.7–35.

[19] See JUSTICE, *Victims in Criminal Justice* (1998). Some have fashioned approaches to the
criminal process which focus on the victim: see J. Dignan, and M. Caradino, "Towards a
Framework for Conceptualising and Evaluating Models of Criminal Justice from a Victim
Perspective" (1996) 4 Int. R. Victimology 153.; J. Shapland, "The Criminal Justice System
and the Victim" (1985) 10 Victimology 585. This is a concern echoed throughout the Auld
Report (2001).

[20] See the recent research finding, C. Mirrlees-Black, "Confidence in the CJS: Findings from
the 2000 BCS" (No. 137 HORSD, 2001): 69% of people are confident that the system
respects the rights of the accused and treats them fairly; 46% that it is effective in bringing
people who commit crime to justice; 34% that it deals with cases promptly and efficiently;
26% that it meets the needs of victims. (For detailed breakdown of rates of confidence
according to age, profession, education and gender, see Table 1.) The survey revealed that
men are less confident than women, and middle aged less confident than young/old, with the
more educated/professional classes being least confident in the system's effectiveness in
bringing people to justice, meeting the needs of victims, and dealing with cases efficiently and
promptly. Ethnic minorities have more confidence in many aspects of the criminal justice
system, but not regarding fair treatment of suspects and witnesses, where concern is directed
at the police (p.4).

managerialism,[21] with more monitoring, protocols, performance indicators and processes to guarantee efficiency being implemented.

As the government has recently observed in its flagship report *Criminal Justice: The Way Ahead* the criminal justice system should be "effective at preventing offending and reoffending; efficient in the way it deals with cases; responsive at every stage to the needs of the victims and the law-abiding community; and accountable for the decisions it takes".[22] It is under constant pressure to achieve these aims, and this generates an incredible internal pressure on the process because the objectives are not always in harmony. These pressures become most acute in the trial process where under close public scrutiny "results" and final determinations have to be made. The numerous Government Commissions and Reports that have affected the trial process over the last decade or so are considered in this chapter, as are the relevant recommendations of the Auld Report.[23]

The Criminal Courts Review was established to report on the

"the practices and procedures of, and the rules of evidence applied by, the criminal courts at every level, with a view to ensuring that they deliver justice fairly, by streamlining all their processes, increasing their efficiency and strengthening the effectiveness of their relationships with others across the whole of the criminal justice system, and having regard to the interests of all parties including victims and witnesses, thereby promoting public confidence in the rule of law."[24]

It will be appreciated that these were extremely broad terms of reference and that the Review was bound to generate considerable controversy.[25]

---

[21] See N. Lacey, "Government as Manager, Citizen as Consumer" (1994) 57 M.L.R. 534; Sanders and Young (2000), pp.40–44. See as an example the LCD Consultation Paper, *Transforming the Crown Court* (1999) and Ackner, (1999) 149 N.L.J. 1816. See also M. Narey, *Review of Delay in the Criminal Justice System* (1997).

[22] (2001) p. 5.

[23] (2001).

[24] Report, *www.criminal-courts-review.org.uk*. para 1.

[25] See on the Report comments at: (2001) 145 S.J. 1056, 1100; (2002) 146 S.J. 41; (2001) *Counsel* 8; Zander, (2001) 151 N.L.J. 1774; I Francis, (2001) N.L.J 1700; G. Morgan, (2002) 152 N.L.J. 41 see also the collection of articles in [2002] Crim. L.R. April.

Criminal Statistics for England and Wales 2000 (2001) Cm 5312.

Figure 1.1 *Flows through the Criminal Justice System, 2000*

The Trial process and the number of defendants involved can be illustrated by the diagram below.

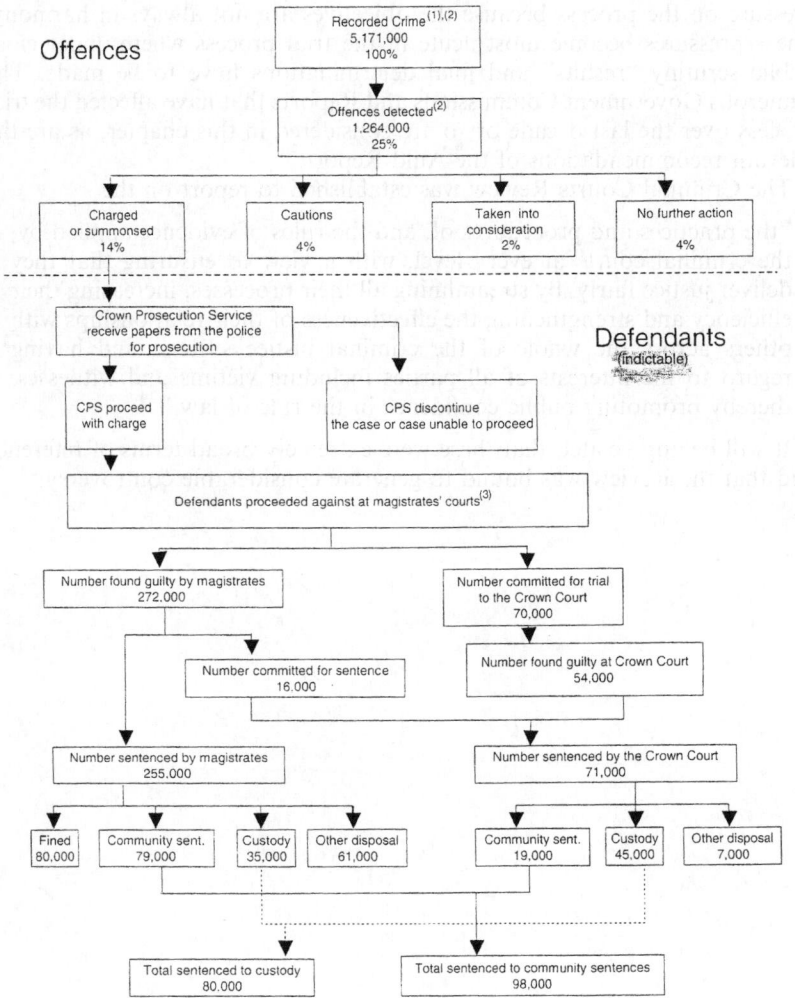

(1) Covers all indictable, including triable either way, offences plus a few closely associated summary offences.
(2) In the financial year 2000/01.
(3) See Table 6.3 for numbers of proceedings terminated early and defendants discharged at the committal proceedings stage or dismissed.

A. SUMMARY TRIAL[26]

"No country in the world relies on magistrates as we do."[27]

There are almost 500 magistrates' courts around England and Wales and the **17–003** bulk of their work concerns minor offences, their powers of sentencing are limited and their decisions create no legal precedents. Nevertheless they do deal with the vast majority of criminal cases[28] (around 97 per cent) and they constitute the tribunal most likely to be encountered by the "ordinary" person.[29–30] Despite this, there is surprisingly little public awareness of their functioning or even of the composition of the magistrates' court. In recent years the work of the magistrates has come under very close academic and government scrutiny, largely because of the attempts to maximise efficiency in the criminal justice process by channeling more cases into the cheaper and quicker magistrates' court process. This research has revealed some

---

[26] The body of literature on the summary trial is expanding. For an accessible account see J. Sprack, *Emmins on Criminal Procedure* (8th ed., 2000). The practitioners' works are *Stone's Justices Manual* and *Blackstone's Criminal Practice*, both published annually. The Auld Report also provides an excellent overview of the subject in Chap. 3. The other sources relied on Flood-Page and Mackie, *An Examination of the Decisions in Magistrates' Courts and the Crown Courts in the Mid-1990s*, (HORS 1998). E. Burney, *J.P., Magistrate, Court and Community* (1979); P. Carlen, *Magistrates' Justice* (1976); A. P. Carr, *Criminal Procedure in Magistrates' Court* (1983); P. Darbyshire, *The Magistrates' Clerk* (1984); J. Gregory, *Crown Court or Magistrates' Court?* Office of Population Censuses and Surveys (HMSO, 1976); B. Harris, *The Criminal Jurisdiction of Magistrates* (11th ed., 1988); H. Parker, M. Sumner and J. Jarvis, *Unmasking the Magistrates* (1989); J. W. Raine, *Local Justice* (1989); P. J. Rowe and S. J. Knapp, *Evidence and Procedure in Magistrates' Courts* (3rd ed., 1989); R. Tarling, *Sentencing Practice in Magistrates' Courts HORS (No. 56, 1981); J. Vennard, Contested Trials in Magistrates' Courts*, RCCP Research Study No. 6, 1980); J. Vennard, *Contested Trials in Magistrates' Courts*, HORS No. 71, 1981); C. Hedderman and B. Noxon, *Magistrates' Courts or Crown Court? Mode of Trial Decisions and Sentencing* (Home Office Research Study No. 125, 1992). For a brief summary of the work of the Home Office Research and Planning Unit, see D. Moxon, "Current Research Bearing on the Work of Magistrates' Courts" (1984) 148 J.P.N. 634;

[27] Auld Report (2001), Chap. 3, para 1. Comparison with other European systems reveal that England and Wales is the only jurisdiction in which there is such a high proportion of criminal cases, including serious cases decided by lay people, (p. xiii).

[28] In 2000 there were 1,905,800 defendants proceeded with in the magistrates' court. (*Criminal Statistics for England and Wales 2000*, Cmnd. 5312 (2001), Table 1.1). The number of proceedings for summary non-motoring offences increased by 12%. There were falls for indictable offences (of 4%) and summary motoring offences (2%) (Table 6A). The introduction of the plea before venue system in 1997 led to substantial changes in the 1998 figures for those committed for sentence (160% rise), but this fell by 15% in 2000 (para. 6.15).

[29–30] This Chapter does not deal in detail with the special rules and procedures governing the trial of juveniles and young people. The Youth Court structure is similar to that of the magistrates' court, with the magistrate presiding. The most significant differences are in the limitations on reporting and open access to the courts and in the range of disposal powers available. On reporting restrictions and juveniles see particularly the review by Bingham L.C.J in *McKerry v. Teesdale and Wear Valley JJ.* (2000) 164 J.P. 355 and *R. v. CCC, ex p. W, B and C* [2001] 1 Cr. App. R. 7. Consider also the ECHR dimension to trials of juveniles addressed in *T v. U.K. and V v. U.K.* [2000] Crim. L.R. 187, and the international obligations under the Bejing Rules as adopted by the U.N. General Assembly November 29 1985, r.8. See generally on Youth Courts, *Blackstone's Criminal Practice 2001*, para. D21, and C. Ball, K. McCormac and N. Stone, *Young Offenders: Law, Policy and Practice* (2nd ed., 2001). See *Criminal Statistics for England and Wales 2000*, Cmd. 5312 (2001), fig. 1.1.

interesting aspects of the manner of work of the magistrates as compared with the functioning of the Crown Court, and also of the differences between the lay and professional magistrates.

We have already considered the ways in which the appearance of a person accused of a summary offence or an offence triable either way can be secured in the Magistrates Court.[31] In short, this will be because the offence is one that is triable summarily only or because it is an either way offence and it has been determined that it should be tried in the magistrates' court. We have also explained the procedure adopted by the court in selecting the mode of trial of an offence triable either way.[32] If summary trial is the appropriate way of determining guilt or innocence for the offence charged, the first formal step is for the magistrates' clerk[33] to read the information to the accused or the defendant (these terms are used inter-changeably), and secure a plea to that information.

1. THE INFORMATION[34]

17–004   The information is the formal document containing the allegation(s) against the accused.[35] Unlike an indictment it does not contain a separate statement of the alleged offence and then the particulars alleged to constitute the offence.[36] It merely contains a statement that combines the essential facts and the alleged offence. Each information should allege one offence only.[37] It is sufficient if the accused is given reasonable notice of the charge to be met and the way in which it is alleged the offence was committed.[38] The use of plain, non-technical language is intended to simplify matters for the accused. This is consistent with the broader principle of a fair trial that the accused must know the case against him and be able to understand the accusations.[39] This is particularly important in summary proceedings where there is a greater chance that the accused will be unrepresented. The magistrates' court can allow for defective informations to be corrected by granting an adjournment.[40] Specimen informations[41] relating to criminal

---

[31] See above.

[32] See above.

[33] As a result of the changing nature of the magistrates' clerk's responsibilities in the proceedings, particularly in light of the Human Rights Act 1998, their responsibilities have been clarified in *Practice Direction (Justices: Clerk to the Court)* [2000] 1 W.L.R. 1886, on which see *Blackstone's Criminal Practice 2001*, para. D.19.29 *et seq.*, and above, para. 4-011. See further Auld Report (2001), pp. 114–117.

[34] See generally, *Blackstone's Criminal Practice 2001*, Chap. D18.

[35] For the full form of an information, see para. 14-052–2 above.

[36] Specimen indictments are set out at paras 17-017-17-019.

[37] For the difficulty in deciding whether the information alleges more than one information (and thereby infringes the rule against duplicity), see *Blackstone's Criminal Practice 2001*, D18.2. The question is essentially one of degree and it is possible to cure defects in the course of the trial: see Magistrates' Courts Act 1980, s.123.

[38] The rules relating to the drafting of an information are contained in the Magistrates' Courts Rules 1981 (S.I. 1981 No. 552). The most informal style permitted is to be found in r. 100. See further the comments of Watkins L.J. in *Rubin v. DPP* [1990] 2 Q.B. 80 at 86.

[39] See especially the explicit guarantee in *Pelissier v. France* (2000) 30 EHRR 715.

[40] On a lack of specificity in the information see generally *Hunter v. Coombs* [1962] 1 W.L.R. 573. For information on the frequency and length of adjournments see *Criminal Statistics* (above), Table 6.4.

[41] The prescribed full form of information is to be found in the Magistrates' Courts (Forms)

damage, theft and carrying an offensive weapon follow:

(i) Henry Frederick Smailey on the 1st day of March 2002 did without lawful excuse damage a motor vehicle, namely a Ford Focus number Y123 ABC, belonging to John Smith intending to damage the property or being reckless as to whether that property would be damaged; contrary to section 1(1) of the Criminal Damage Act 1971.

(ii) Henry Frederick Smailey on the 1st day of March 2002 stole £15 belonging to John Smith; contrary to sections 1 and 7 of the Theft Act 1968.

(iii) Henry Frederick Smailey on the 1st day of March 2002 without lawful authority or reasonable excuse had with him in a public place, namely the Victoria Shopping Centre, Nottingham, an offensive weapon, namely a bayonet; contrary to section 1(1) of the Prevention of Crime Act 1953.[42]

For a summary offence the information must be laid within six months of the time when the offence was committed.[43] Even if a previous information has been laid in time, that will be insufficient unless the one the defendant actually faces is also laid within the six-month period.[44] The time limit on laying of the information is obviously designed to ensure a speedy resolution to the prosecution.[44a] However, this absolute time limit could be seen as denying a victim the opportunity to obtain justice, particulalrly if there has been undue delay in investigating the complaint.[45] The average time from offence to completion for defendants in indictable cases in the magistrates' court in 2000 was 108 days.[46]

Rules 1981 (S.I. 1981 No. 553), Form 1. Amendments can occur outside the six-month time limit for informations provided this is in the public interest: *R. v. Scunthorpe JJ., ex p. M* (1998) 162 J.P. 635; *R. v. Newcastle upon Tyne Magistrates' Court, ex p. Poundstretcher* [1998] C.O.D. 256.

[42] Note that these are all statutory offences and as such there is a mandatory requirement to refer to the statute creating the offence: r.100(2); see *Atterton v. Browne* [1945] K.B. 122.

[43] Magistrates' Courts Act 1980, ss.127(1),(2)(a).

[44] *R. v. Network Sites Ltd, ex p. London Borough of Havering* [1997] Crim. L.R. 595.

[44a] On the discretion not to proceed in circumstances of delay see *R v. Newcastle-upon-Tyne Justices ex p. John Bryce Contractors Ltd* [1976] 1 W.L.R. 517 and *R. v. Brentford Justices ex p. Wong* [1981] O.B. 445 The accused can challenge a prosecution on grounds of unconscionable delay if there has been prosecution inefficiency which has created prejudice for the accused: *R. v. Gateshead, JJ. ex p. Smith* (1982) 75 Cr.App. R. 200. For an example see *R. v. Watford JJ. ex p. Outrim* [1983] R.T.R. 26 (22 month delay in drink driving summons).

[45] This problem might arise, for example, where the offence alleged is summary only and is a complaint against a police officer. For a proposal to require 14 days' notice of a potential case to be served and extension of time limit to three years, see Anon., "Summary Time-Limits and Police Protection" (1998) 162 J.P.N. 259.

[46] See *Criminal Statistics* (2001), para. 1.12.

Lay and professional magistrates

17–005   Lay magistrates sit in the commission area for which they are appointed. This geographical limitation is designed to enhance the local knowledge that can be brought to bear on a case.[47] District Judges have national jurisdiction.[48] The Auld Report considered the desirability of magistrates sitting otherwise than in their own appointed area and concluded that the transfer between commission areas posed no problem and could indeed be beneficial.[49] As to the allocation of work between the District Judges and lay bench, the Venne Report[50] recommended that stipendiaries (now District Judges) should be presumed to deal with cases involving complex points of law or evidence, mode of trial decisions, those cases involving inter-linked or lengthy issues, and those involving considerations of public safety, public interest immunity and extradition.[51] The Auld Report supported and fully endorsed this procedure.[52] In most cases the listing decision is one for the justices' clerk.[53] The Narey recommendations, as implemented in the Crime and Disorder Act 1998 allow some case management powers to be exercised by a single magistrate.[54] Underlying many of the recent proposals for the division of work between the branches of the profession is an assumption that each is performing the same basic function. This raises broader questions about the extent to which lay magistrates are in fact surrogate jurors and community representatives and whether District Judges, as legal professionals, should be regarded in the same light.[55]

2. PRESENCE OF THE ACCUSED

17–006   At a trial on indictment, the accused must be in court to enter a plea and is normally present through the whole trial.[56] Summary trial is different in that provision is made for guilty pleas to be made by post and also, where the accused fails to appear at the appointed time and place, for trial in the absence of the accused.[57–58] Both these procedures are designed to spare the time and expense of the participants where there is no real intention to

---

[47] This does not allow magistrates to make assumptions without hearing evidence: see *Carter v. Eastbourne BC* (2000) 164 J.P. 273. Difficulties also arise because of knowledge of local repeat offenders. This has the potential to conflict with the right to a fair trial under Art. 6. See M. Strange in K. Starmer *et al*, (2001), and *R. v. Altrincham JJ. ex, p. Pennington* [1975] Q.B. 549; *Brown v. U.K.* (1986) 8 E.H.R.R. 272.

[48] Access to Justice Act 1999, inserting s. 10C(I) of the Justice of the Peace Act 1997. See generally on the locality of justice in the magistrates court and the effect of the evolution of the District Judges, P.Seago, C. Walker and D. Wall, [2000] Crim. L.R. 631 at 648–651.

[49] p.100. Moreover, in the event of a unified court being adopted as recommended in the Auld Report, transfer of lay magistrates to adjoining areas would be expected.

[50] *The Role of the Stipendiary Magistracy* (1996).

[51] *ibid.*, p.14.

[52] Chap, 3. para. Chap. 46, ch.3. recommending that District Judges and lay magistrates do not sit together routinely or as a mixed tribunal.

[53] See Auld, p.113 on the difficulties of allocating work effectively.

[54] See the discussion in Chap 14, para. 14-043. above.

[55] See the discussion in Chap 14, para. 14-048 regarding the proposals to create a hybrid court to reflect the relative attributes of the two branches.

[56] See para. 17-037 below. Trials in *absentia* are not incompatible with the ECHR: *Colozza v. Italy* (1985) 7 E.H.R.R. 516.

[57–58] See Magistrates' Courts Act 1980, s.11(1).

defend the charge, but they are hedged with certain safeguards to ensure that injustice does not result.

Section 11 of the Magistrates' Courts Act 1980 allows for proceedings to continue in the accused's absence, but if proceedings have begun by summons, the case should not proceed unless the summons has been proved to have been served on the accused within a reasonable time of the hearing or the court is satisfied that the accused has appeared on a previous occasion to answer the information.[59] If the accused is ignorant of the proceedings, he can, under section 14 of the Magistrates' Courts Act 1980 make a statutory declaration that he was unaware of the summons/proceedings. This must be served on the justices' clerk within 21 days. The effect of this is to render all proceedings void, and a differently constituted bench must then try the information afresh.

If the prosecution does not appear for the hearing, and the accused does, the magistrates may dismiss the information. If evidence has previously been received on an earlier occasion, they may proceed in the absence of the prosecution.[60] Great care must be taken not to infringe fundamental guarantees of natural justice where there is a decision to continue in the absence of a party rather than to adjourn.[61] This is particularly important in view of the need to respect the guarantees found in Article 6 of the ECHR including an opportunity for the accused to be represented, to have witnesses against him examined and to a "fair trial" in the broadest sense. There is also the need to maintain open justice in the summary trial and to be seen to be doing so.

Written pleas of guilty made by post may be entered only if the offence is a summary offence punishable by not more than three months' imprisonment. A written plea of guilty is retractable in writing until the date of the hearing.[62] The safeguards to ensure that no injustices result from this procedure are that the accused must be served with a statement of the facts alleged by the prosecution and an explanatory note in addition to the usual summons; a wish not to be present must be made clear by the accused in writing; the statement of facts, the plea and anything which the accused has written in relation to mitigation or personal financial circumstances must be read out in court by the clerk; and no information is given to the court by the prosecution other than that contained in the documents.[63] This court procedure is very strict and any deviation will result in the proceedings being a nullity.[64] An amended version of this procedure may now also be used even when the defendant is present, provided he or she consents.[65] If the accused pleads guilty by post, there is no need for him to attend in person. If he pleads not guilty by post, the court will usually adjourn in his absence

---

[59] See also Magistrates' Courts Act 1980, s.55(3).

[60] Magistrates' Courts Act 1980, ss.15, 56.

[61] See *R. v. Swansea Justices and Davies, ex p. DPP* (1990) 154 J.P. 709.

[62] Magistrates' Courts Act 1980, s.12(6).

[63] Magistrates' Courts Act 1980, s.12; Magistrates' Courts (Procedure) Act 1998, s.1(2). The option is made available at the discretion of the prosecution: *Blackstone's Criminal Practice 2002*, paras D19.13.

[64] See *R. v. Epping and Ongar JJ., ex p. Breach* [1987] R.T.R. 233 and *Blackstone's Criminal Practice 2001*, para. D18.11.

[65] Magistrates' Courts Act 1980, s.12A (added by the Criminal Justice and Public Order Act 1994) and see *Blackstone's Criminal Practice 2002*, para. D19.13. The use of this procedure was scrutinised in the Auld Report (2001).

and fix a date for trial. If the accused does not respond or fails to appear, there will usually be a further adjournment before, finally, the prosecution occurs in his absence. The accused must be given a fair opportunity to be present, but this is not an unlimited one.[66]

A magistrates' court has a general discretion to proceed with a trial in the absence of the accused,[67] including where the right to be present has been voluntarily waived by the accused, for example, by abusing it as a consequence of indecent, outrageous or unseemly behaviour, or ceasing to claim it by deliberately jumping bail. In such cases, a plea of not guilty is entered on behalf of the accused.[68] In any case, the court must be cautious in the exercise of its discretion ensuring that the convenience of the parties does not override the interests of the administration of justice.[69] It is important that magistrates retain a discretion to require physical presence of the accused for the hearing and/or for sentencing. The Divisional Court has emphasised that convenience and expedience in the system should not outweigh the need for the presence of the accused in serious cases.[70]

The Magistrates' Courts (Procedure) Act 1998 introduced a procedure that is further designed to speed up the process of summary hearings. The accused is issued with a summons, but rather than that being a simple statement of facts of no evidential status, the summons is accompanied by a witness statement. This procedure is designed to reduce the administrative burden on the police. If the accused pleads guilty, the court clerk can summarise the witness statements[71] for the bench for sentencing. If the accused pleads not guilty, there is a normal hearing and if the defendant does not respond, a prosecution is required but reliance on the witness statements is permissible. A Magistrates' Court Service Inspectorate Study of the *Implementation of section 1 of the Magistrates' Court (Procedure) Act 1998* revealed a very disappointing picture, with only 40 per cent of police forces having introduced this scheme; and 11 per cent of police forces stating no intention to do so. There was also confusion over the use of the scheme (it being non-compulsory) and with little formal monitoring, there was doubt whether it would prove successful. Where used, it was shown to have reduced adjournments and delay.[72]

Note should also be made of the fixed penalty notice system, used not only for parking offences, but for a wide range of road traffic offences including, for example, for speeding, not wearing a seat belt or crash helmet and violating a red light. These notices have proved very productive, with

---

[66] *R. v. Ealing Magistrates' Court, ex p. Burgess* [2000] Crim. L.R. 855.

[67] Magistrates' Courts Act 1980, s.11. The accused may show, within 21 days after finding out about the proceedings, that he or she did not know of the summons or proceedings until after their commencement in which case the conviction would be set aside under the Magistrates' Courts Act 1980, s.14. See J. Sprack, *Emmins on Criminal Procedure* (8th ed., 2000), p.145.

[68] And the prosecution evidence is heard. Service of the summons must be proved. On contempt proceedings for, *inter alia*, unruly behaviour see *Practice Direction (Magistrates' Court: Contempt)* [2001] 1 W.L.R. 1254.

[69] Harris (1988), p. 242. See also H. Brayne, (2002) 152 N.L.J. 373.

[70] *R. v. Dewsbury Magistrates' Court, ex p. K, The Times,* March 16 1994. For statistics on the proof in absence cases see *Criminal Statistics* (2001) approx 12% of cases in 2000.

[71] Usually contained in a statement admissible under s. 9 of the Criminal Justice Act 1967.

[72] (2000), p.iii. H.M. MCSI produces thematic reports on its inspections of magistrates' courts procedures and service: see *www.mcsi.gov.uk/reports/thematicsindex.htm.*

around 7.5 million being issued each year for motoring and parking offences.[73] The motorist is issued a ticket giving brief particulars of the offence and the name of the clerk to whom payment of a fixed sum must be made. This system produces an end result similar to that where the full court system is used, but there are significant time and costs savings for all involved.[74] The fixed penalty notice scheme has now been adopted for a range of low-level disorder offences under the Criminal Justice and Police Act 2001, Part I.[75] Those receiving such notices from constables are offered the opportunity to pay the fixed penalty, and in doing so will incur no criminal liability and suffer no criminal record.[76] The use of these notices in relation to "real" crime rather than regulatory road traffic offences is very controversial, but in view of the cost efficiency of the system, it is likely that they will be applied in a broader range of circumstances in the future.[77] The Auld Report recommends the use of a fixed penalty notice system in relation to television licence evasion[78] and for a wider range of motoring offences than at present,[79] especially offences under the Road Traffic Offenders Act 1988 and also for "a wider range of infringements that are presently the subject of a criminal prosecution".[80] The use of such procedures presents a potential conflict with Article 6 of the ECHR unless all of the fair trial guarantees are protected. The Article 6 provisions apply to all "criminal charges" — and that expression has an autonomous Convention meaning which is only influenced but not determined by the domestic law classification.[81] Fixed penalty notices should be regarded as criminal. Further review of the merits of the fixed penalty notice scheme is called for.

3. THE PLEA[82]

The substance of the information will be explained to the accused, if present in the magistrates' court, and he or she will be asked to plead. A plea is usually only sought to the general issue, that is, the accused is asked to plead guilty or not guilty. However, preliminary points may be raised; for example, whether the court has jurisdiction to try the accused or whether the

17–007

---

[73] See G. Barclay and C. Tavares, *Information on the Criminal Justice System in England and Wales: Digest IV* (1999), Home Office.

[74] See Emmins (2000), pp.67–68.

[75] See M. Wasik, "Legislating in the Shadow of the Human Rights Act 1998: The Criminal Justice and Police Act 2001" [2001] Crim. L.R. 931.

[76] See s.2.

[77] See for support of their use P. Tain, "On the Spot Fines" (2001) S.J 145 548, describing them as "useful means of dealing promptly with some minor offenders whose offences have taken up a great deal of court time".

[78] pp. 369–371.

[79] pp. 371–375.

[80] Recommendation no.142.

[81] This will be determined by reference to the classification of the offence in domestic law, the nature of the offence and the severity of the penalty: *Engel v. Netherlands* (1979–80) 1 E.H.R.R. 647, para. 82. Art. 6 protections apply to the whole of the criminal process, not just the trial proper; a fair trial includes the pre-trial actions and extends to post-trial appeals; *Benham v. U.K.* (1996) 22 E.H.R.R. 293. See also A. Jennings in K. Starmer *et al.*, (2001), pp.155–6.

[82] See Ashworth, (1998), Chap. 9.

information charges more than one offence. If these points are successfully raised, the trial cannot continue.[83]

The magistrates have the jurisdiction to stay proceedings for an abuse of process as recognised by the House of Lords in *R. v. Horseferry Road Magistrates Court, ex p. Bennett*.[84] This power can be exercised where there has been unconscionable delay, or where the prosecution have manipulated or misused the process of the court so as to deprive the accused of the opportunity of a fair trial.[85] The power is to be exercised sparingly.[86] It is often safer for the magistrates to decline to stay proceedings and leave the matter to be dealt with by the High Court on an application for judicial review.[87]

In a summary trial where the accused is present, the magistrates' clerk reads out the information. The accused is asked to plead guilty or not guilty. The accused's plea must be freely made and unambiguous, and should normally be made personally.[88] The accused's response determines the remainder of the procedure. The court has a discretion to allow a change of plea at any time before sentence.[89]

There is, however, no specific procedure to deal with the situation where the accused does not reply to the information. The procedure available in the Crown Court to consider fitness to plead is not available to a magistrates' court.[90] The full insanity plea is, however, available in the magistrates' court.[91] In the event of a defendant appearing unfit, the possibilities are either to discontinue the proceedings, and perhaps contact the social services department; or to commit the accused for trial in the

---

[83] Special pleas may be entered as those in response to an indictment: see para. 17-022, below, although technically the pleas of *autrefois acquit* and *autrefois convict* only apply to indictments. The same effect is achieved in magistrates' courts by dealing with the matter on a plea of not guilty: see *Connelly v. DPP* [1964] A.C. 1254. See *Blackstone's Criminal Practice 2002*, para. D19.22 and Harris (1988), pp. 243–254. The prosecution can, with leave of the court, withdraw the summons, but this does not equate to a plea of guilty: the prosecution may be instituted by a fresh summons at a later date. See *R. v. Grays JJ., ex p. Low* [1990] 1 O.B. 54; *London Borough of Islington v. Michalaeides* [2001] Crim. L.R. 843. The repeat prosecution will often not be regarded as oppressive because the accused will not have been in jeopardy at the first hearing: see *N. Yorkshire Trading Standards v. Coleman* (2001) 166 J.P. 76; *Holmes v. Campbell* (1998) 162 J.P. 655.

[84] [1994] 1 A.C. 42. See generally *Archbold (2002)*, para. 4–50. On abuse where there is a loss of evidence in the magistrates' court see *R. (Ebrahim) v. Feltham Magistrates' Court and another* [2001] Crim. L.R. 741, [2001] 1 All E.R. 831; *R. v. Elliott* at [2002] May 9, CA and see S. O'Doherty, (2000) 164 J.P. 536.

[85] *R. v. Willesden JJ., ex p. Clemmings* (1987) 87 Cr. App. R. 280.

[86] *R. v. Oxford City JJ., ex p. Smith*, 75 Cr. App. R. 200 (1982) 204.

[87] *R. v. Belmarsh Magistrates', ex p. Watts* [1999] 2 Cr. App. R. 188, DC. On the difficulties of the same bench of magistrates hearing abuse claims and conducting the full hearing, see *R. v. Worcester JJ., ex p. Bell* (1993) 157 J.P. 921.

[88] *R. v. Wakefield JJ., ex p. Butterworth* [1970] 1 All E.R. 1181; *R. v. Gowerton JJ., ex p. Davies* [1974] Crim. L. R. 253; *R. v. Kingston upon Thames Magistrates' Court, ex p. Davey* (1985) 149 J.P. 744.

[89] *S (an infant) v. Manchester City Recorder* [1971] A.C. 481.

[90] *R. v. Metropolitan Stipendiary Magistrate Tower Bridge, ex p. Aniifowosi* (1985) 149 J.P. 748. As to "fitness to plead" see below para. 17-042.

[91] On any charge involving *mens rea*: see *R. v. Horseferry Road Magistrates' Court, ex p. K* [1997] Q.B. 23.

Crown Court if the offence can be tried on indictment[92]; or to enter a plea of not guilty, and then determine whether the accused did the act or made the omission charged and, if so, adjourn pending medical reports as a result of which the court may order hospitalisation without convicting the accused.[93]

Where the offence is triable either way and the accused is unfit to give consent to a summary trial, the magistrates' court has the exceptional power to proceed as if he has consented, provided that the accused is represented. This enables the court to use the power in section 37 of the Mental Health Act 1983 to hospitalise without convicting.[94] Section 11 of the Powers of Criminal Courts (Sentencing) Act 2000 allows the magistrates to adjourn for medical reports. If the court adjourns under section 11, and bails the accused, it must order a medical examination of the accused. There is no power under this procedure to impose a custodial sentence on an absent accused.

The other options open to the prosecution before the plea is made are to withdraw a summons or to offer no evidence. Magistrates have no discretion not to try an information, except in cases of an abuse of process.

4. THE GUILTY PLEA

If, as is most common, the accused enters a guilty plea,[95] the court can convict him without hearing evidence. (In the magistrates' court, the incidence of guilty pleas is very high, and often approaches 90 per cent.[96]) Alternatively, the court can proceed to hear the facts of the case from the prosecution, including any further offences that the accused wishes to have taken into consideration and any previous convictions. These facts are not usually elicited from witnesses unless there is some substantial disagreement,[97] but are presented by the prosecutor concerned. The procedure before sentence is considered below.

17–008

In certain circumstances social inquiry reports are required, for example, before community punishments can be imposed, and it is normal for a case to be adjourned if such a report is necessary or desirable.[98] The probation

---

[92] This raises separate problems regarding the accused's ability to consent to a summary trial.

[93] Mental Health Act 1983, s.37(3); Powers of Criminal Courts (Sentencing) Act 2000, s.11; see *R. v. Lincoln (Kesteven) JJ., ex p. O'Connor* [1983] 1 W.L.R. 335; M. Wasik, "Hospital Orders without Trial" (1983) 147 J.P.N. 211 and *Blackstone's Criminal Practice 2001*, paras. D19.17 and D19.23. See J. Evans and A. Tomison, "Assessment of the Perceived Need for a Psychiatric Service to a Magistrates Court" (1997) 37(1) Med. Sci. Law 161 (4.9% of cases of suspects held overnight in police custody needed psychiatric help). See also, C. Chambers and K. Rix, "A Controlled Evaluation of Assessment by Doctors and Nurses in a Magistrates Court Mental Health Assessment and Diversion Scheme (1999) 39(1) Med. Sci. Law 38 (assessments by doctors/nurses enabled magistrates to reduce remands in custody of people suspected of suffering mental illness and to grant bail in more cases). See also T. Exworthy and J. Parrott, "Evaluation of a Diversion from Custody Scheme at Magistrates' Courts" (1993) J. For Psych. 497.

[94] See *R. v. Lincoln (Kesteven) JJ., ex p. O'Connor* [1983] 1 W.L.R. 335.

[95] It is unclear whether this can come unilaterally from a legal representative: *R. v. Williams* [1978] Q.B. 373; *Blackstone's Criminal Practice 2001*, Para. D19.18.

[96] See D. Riley and J. Vennard, HORS 98, p.6. See *Criminal Statistics* (2001): 82% of defendants in summary cases pleaded guilty, (para.1.13).

[97] Magistrates' Courts Act 1980, s.9(3).

[98] Magistrates' Courts Act 1980, s.10(3).

service is responsible for compiling a report and it will be available to the bench at the adjourned hearing, when the defence will have the opportunity of seeing and commenting upon it. With or without a report, the bench will listen to anything that may be said by the defence by way of mitigation of sentence.

Where the defendant pleads guilty, there is a sentencing discount as in the Crown Court.[99] There is very strong evidence from recent research that quite explicit charge bargaining occurs in the magistrates' court whereby the prosecution offer to accept a guilty plea to a lesser charge than that originally laid, to encourage the accused to plead guilty.[1]

5. THE NOT GUILTY PLEA

17–009 A plea of not guilty normally results in an immediate adjournment to an agreed date so that the prosecution and defence can assemble their witnesses and court time can be allocated.[2] The prosecution can of course offer no evidence in which case that is the end of the matter and there can be no retrial of the same offence.[3] At the recommencement of the adjourned hearing the procedure will follow the normal adversarial lines. The prosecution is entitled to address the court through an opening speech[4a] and will then lead evidence through witnesses[4] who will be subject to examination in chief, cross-examination and, perhaps, re-examination.[5] If the case is not especially difficult, the prosecution will often start with witnesses immediately, since, with an experienced bench, there is no need to stress general points which might be necessary at a trial on indictment.[6] If the case has been adjourned after the prosecution witnesses have testified, the bench is permitted to seek a refresher of their testimony from the prosecutor, with the defence having the right to respond to it.[7] Magistrates do not have the power to dismiss a case on grounds of perceived unfairness without hearing any evidence except where there is unconscionable delay or where because of an abuse of the process the accused is unable to receive a

---

[99] See below, para. 17-039.

[1] See Ashworth, (1998), p.272, and A. Mulcahy, "The Justifications of Justice: Legal Practitioners Accounts of Negotiated Case Settlement in Magistrates Courts" (1994) 34 Brit. J. Criminal. 411. Note the CPS Code, para 11, which stipulates that convienience should not be a sufficent reason to amend charges. See Sanders and Young, (2000), p.441.

[2] See M. Wasik and A. Turner, "Sentencing Guidelines for Magistrates' Courts" [1993] Crim. L.R. 345 at 355. For a review of the use of adjournments in Scotland and calls for more proactive intervention from justices see F. Leverick and P. Duff, "Court Culture and Adjournment in Criminal Cases: A Tale of Four Courts" [2002] Crim. L.R. 39. There is no opportunity to challenge by judicial review a refusal to adjourn: *North Somerset District Council v. Richards* (2002) February 26.

[3] *R. v. Pressick* [1978] Crim. L.R. 377.

[4] On securing the presence of witnesses in the magistrates' court see Magistrates' Courts Act 1980, s.97.

[4a] Magistrates Court Rules 1981, r.13, and see *Blackstone's Criminal Practice 2002*, para D20.1 and Harris (1988), pp. 257–261.

[5] The order of proceedings is similar to that in trial on indictment, see paras 17-021–17-036 below

[6] *e.g.*, the burden and standard of proof, the need to listen carefully to the evidence, etc.

[7] *L and B v. DPP* [1998] 2 Cr.App. R. 69, DC.

fair trial and the proceedings are stayed.

At the close of the prosecution case, the defence may submit that there is no case to answer. The magistrates stop the hearing if they find that no reasonable tribunal could convict on the prosecution evidence, either because an essential element of the offence has not been proved or because the evidence has been discredited on cross-examination.[8] The magistrates must not say whether *they* would convict on the evidence so far presented, merely whether a reasonable bench *could* convict. Prosecution advocates permitted to address the bench on a submission of no case if it relates to points of law, but this creates problems by comparison with the procedure in the Crown Court since magistrates will hear the arguments about the disputed item of evidence as a question of law, and then later go on to decide the issues of fact. If the submission of no case is accepted, the accused is discharged. There is no obligation for the magistrates to provide reasons for the rejection on a submission of no case.[9] If it is rejected, the right of the defence to call witnesses and build a defence is not prejudiced. The defence then calls evidence, with the accused as the first witness.[10] The accused is not obliged to give evidence.

At the close of the defence case, the defence is entitled to make a closing speech to the bench. Exceptionally, the prosecution may be permitted to speak again and, if so, the defence will be given a second opportunity.[11] The defence is always entitled to the last word.

The clerk should take a note of the evidence throughout the hearing.[12] The summary trial is in open court reflecting the importance of the principle of open justice, but the magistrates may, under their inherent jurisdiction, hear representations in chambers during the trial.[13] All parties should be present on such occasions and the clerk should take appropriate notes of such hearings.

Concern has recently been expressed at the scope and frequency of the reporting restrictions used in magistrates' courts.[14] It has been emphasised that the "public nature of the proceedings deters inappropriate behaviour on the part of the court. It also maintains the public confidence in the

---

[8] The criteria are contained in a *Practice Note* [1962] 1 All E.R. 448 (criticised by E. C. J. McBride, (1990) 154 J.P.N. 99) and see *Blackstone's Criminal Practice 2001*, para. D19.8. Justices are warned against forming a view without hearing the whole of the evidence save in the two cases mentioned in the text. Where (a) there is no evidence to prove an essential element of the offence or (b) the prosecution evidence is so discredited by cross-examination or so manifestly unreliable that no reasonable tribunal might safely convict.

[9] See *Moran v. DPP* [2002] EWHC 89 (Admin).

[10] PACE, s. 79.

[11] Magistrates' Courts Rules 1981, r.13.

[12] *Practice Direction (Justices: Clerk to Court)* [2000] 1 W.L.R. 1886, para. 4.

[13] *R. v. Nottingham Magistrates' Court, ex p. Furnett* (1996) 160 J.P. 201. See also *R. v. Birmingham Magistrates' Court, ex p. Ahmed* [1995] Crim. L.R. 503.

[14] See M. Dodd, "Lifting the Veil of Secrecy: Reporting Restriction Orders" (2001) J.P.N. 498, discussing widespread use of orders under s.4(2) and 11 of the Contempt of Court Act 1981 to prohibit information about the defendant. The excessive use of orders might stem from misconceived privacy arguments under Article 8 of the ECHR. On open hearing generally, see also the very important statements in *R. v. Central Independent TV plc* (1994) 2 F.L.R. 151. See also *R. v. Richards* (1999) 163 J.P. 246, confirming the magistrates' power to clear the court when a witness is frightened.

administration of justice. It enables the public to know that justice is being administered impartially. It can result in evidence becoming available."[15] Undoubtedlly, public confidence in the criminal justice system is important, and public hearings do serve to promote that confidence.

The rules of evidence are very similar for summary trial as for trials on indictment. The crucial differences that do exist flow from the fact that magistrates make the decisions arising in the trial on points of law and are also the tribunal of fact. Other significant differences stem from the different disclosure regimes that operate in each court.[16] The strict division of the functions between judge and jury in the Crown Court is impossible in the magistrates' court. The problem is most acute where the defence challenges prejudicial evidence that the prosecution seek to rely on.[17] Magistrates have a discretion as to when they choose to deal with challenges to admissibility[18]; but should be alert to the dangers of the accused tactically leaving the challenge to the end of the prosecution case.[19] As a classic example of the dilemma, it is for the magistrates to decide, for example, whether a confession is admissible in accordance with the Police and Criminal Evidence Act 1984.[20] They must obviously be informed of the accused's confession. If they decide it is not admissible they must attempt to determine the guilt of the accused without taking account of the confession.[21] Such a task is extraordinarily difficult, but is nevertheless essential where the deciders of fact and law are one (or three) and the same.[22] Wasik[23] has recently examined the principled and practical difficulties of the magistrates operating as triers of law and fact and has identified a number of grounds on which risks of bias and evidential regimes in magistrates' and Crown Courts differ. In particular these arise because the evidential regime in the magistrates' court is more "relaxed" with some points of evidence not being taken and the defendant being unrepresented.[24]

---

[15] *per* Lord Woolf M.R. in *R. v. Legal Aid Board, ex p. Kaim Toder (A firm)* [1998] 3 All E.R. 541 at 549.

[16] See above paras 14-068–14-018.

[17] See Rowe and Knapp (1989), pp. 76–79 and *Blackstone's Criminal Practice 2001*, para. D19.6. There is also an increasing awareness of potential problems with identification evidence in the magistrates' court: see *Bailey v. DPP* (1998) 162 JP 126, and A. Roberts, (2001) J.P.N. 756.

[18] *R. v. Chief Constable of Kent* [1982] Crim. L.R. 682.

[19] The power to deal with challenges as preliminary issues was recently approved in *A v. DPP* (2000) 164 J.P. 317, DC (facts revealing prima facie defence of duress).

[20] In magistrates' courts the dual function of the justices as judges of both fact and law generally renders the "trial within a trial" an unnecessary sophistication, though one must be held where the admissibility of a confession is in issue: *R. v. Liverpool Juvenile Court, ex p. R.* [1988] Q.B. 1. See *Blackstone's Criminal Practice 2002*, para. D20.6 and R. Pattenden, *Judicial Discretion and Criminal Litigation* (2nd ed., 1990), pp. 313–314. As to the admissibility of confessions, see para. 14-025.

[21] It is not necessary for the bench to refer the case to another bench to conduct the hearing of the trial proper.

[22] For the situation in a trial on indictment, para. 17-067. There is no requirement that a magistrate who has led a public interest immunity hearing should be compelled to disqualify himself from hearing the case proper: *R. v. Stipendiary Magistrate for Norfolk, ex p. Taylor* [1998] Crim. L.R. 276.

[23] M. Wasik, "Magistrates: Knowledge of Previous Convictions" [1996] Crim. L.R. 851.

[24] See also P. Darbyshire, "Previous Misconduct at Magistrates' Courts — Some Tales from the Real World" [1997] Crim. L.R. 105 criticising the Law Commission Consultation Paper No. 141, *Evidence in Criminal Proceedings: Previous Misconduct of a Defendant* (1996) for

It is likely that challenges under the Human Rights Act 1998 will be mounted on various aspects of the magistrates' approach to the law of evidence.[25]

As far as public confidence in the summary trial system and the perception of bias is concerned, the problems of magistrates having prior knowledge of the regular offenders in their area in particular also produces a significant problem. Darbyshire[26] concludes, controversially, that the only "honest and safe" way of dealing with the problem is to admit all the defendant's previous convictions prior to trial.[27]

6. THE UNREPRESENTED DEFENDANT

It has so far been assumed that the accused who appears[28] at a magistrates' court is represented by either a barrister or a solicitor. The availability of legal aid[29] and the existence of duty solicitor schemes at magistrates' courts[30] means that representation is more readily available than in the past. However, many defendants in magistrates' courts are unrepresented, and this is not likely to change for the foreseeable future.[31] At least when pleading not guilty, the lack of representation is a major disadvantage.[32] There is an inherent inequality of resources in a criminal trial where "the State" brings a legal action against an individual (even against corporation). This inequality is at its most acute when the accused is unrepresented. The difficulties for an unrepresented defendant include ignorance of procedure and of legal rules of evidence and substantive criminal law; the pressure imposed by a bewildering situation; an inability to understand, or even hear, what is going on; and the difficulty of putting forward one's own case sensibly, clearly and intelligibly.[33] The principal safeguard is that the clerk is under a duty to assist an unrepresented defendant in the presentation of his or her case.[34] Other safeguards exist, including, fundamentally, that the charge must be explained to an unrepresented accused in straightforward

17–010

---

[25] For arguments on likely challenges in relation to s.78 of PACE see J. Keeley, "A Fair Trial in the Magistrates' Court: The Possible Effects of Art. 6(1)" (2000). 164 J.P.N. 182. On the independence of the magistrates, and magistrates as impartial tribunals see M. Beloff, "Fair Trials and the HRA: Magistrates in the Role Against Bias" (2001) 165 J.P.N. 436.

[26] "Some Tales from the Real World" [1997] Crim. L.R. 105 reviewing the Law Commission's

[27] ibid.

[28] For trial in the absence of the accused, see para. 17-006, above.

[29] As to the granting of legal aid, see para. 14-087, above. On the impact of the ECHR see Granger v. U.K. (1990) 12 E.H.R.R. 469.

[30] See above, para. 14-087, and Emmins (2000), pp. 35–6 and 486–7.

[31] See H. Astor, "The Unrepresented Defendant: A Consideration of the Role of the Clerk in Magistrates' Courts" (1986) 13 J.L.S. 225 at 237.

[32] One now rather dated study showed that of 111 defendants who pleaded not guilty at a magistrates' court, 30% of those unrepresented were acquitted, whereas 64% of those represented by lawyers were acquitted: M. Zander, "Unrepresented Defendants in Magistrates' Courts" (1972) 122 N.L.J. 1041 . On the other hand, a study by the Lord Chancellor's Department suggested that acquittal rates did not vary on the basis of representation: Lord Chancellor's Department, Report of a Survey of the Grant of Legal Aid in Magistrates' Courts (1983), Table 17, quoted in M. Zander, Cases and Materials on the English Legal System (8th ed., 1999), p. 334 (hereafter, Zander, Cases and Materials (1999)).

[33] See S. Dell, Silent in Court (1971) quoted in Zander, Cases and Materials (1999), pp. 337-338.

[34] Practice Direction [2000] 1 W.L.R. 1886, para. 10.

language.[35] These obligations and the other willing efforts of the clerk may ameliorate, but cannot eliminate these difficulties.[36] Any inequality of resources between prosecution and defence strikes deep at the heart of an adversarial system: when a significant imbalance exists, the system does not work fairly.[37]

7. THE VERDICT

17–011　　The magistrates normally retire to consider their decision. Where the trial is before a bench of lay magistrates, rather than a District Judge (formerly known as stipendiary magistrate), a majority[38] must be satisfied beyond reasonable doubt that the charge is proved before they can convict. As noted above, analogies between magistrates and jurors are far from precise.

The magistrates decide questions of both fact and law and they will have the benefit of advice from their clerk, which, in practice, they accept.[39] The clerk has a duty to advise on matters of law including ECHR and Human Rights Act 1998 jurisprudence, questions of mixed fact and law, practice and procedure, penalties available, relevant decisions of superior courts and other guidelines, other relevant matters and appropriate decision-making structures and by assisting the court as to the formulation of reasons.[40] The clerk is also able to offer advice on sentencing, but should be careful not to be perceived as advocating a particular disposal power. The clerk must not appear to be influencing the magistrates' decision on the facts when giving legal advice.[41] This is a very difficult line to tread.

The appellate courts have been at pains to emphasise that justice must be seen to be done in magistrates' courts. In particular, it is improper for a third party to be with the magistrates in the retiring room whilst they consider their verdict. Even the briefest of interventions may raise doubts about what has transpired between an outsider and the magistrates, and so is strictly forbidden.[42] A similar rule is imposed to preserve the inviolability of the deliberations of a jury.[43]

There is, however, a difference between a jury engaged in fact-finding and

---

[35] Magistrates' Courts Rules 1981, r.13A.

[36] Astor (1986), p. 238. See, further, Darbyshire (1984), pp. 170–181.

[37] See A. Sanders and R. Young, *Criminal Justice* (2000), p. 258 and J. Jackson, "Trial Procedures" in C. Walker and K. Starmer (eds), *Justice in Error* (1993), p. 131. See also Article 6 of the ECHR, and the discussion of the "equality of arms" principle in Emmerson and Ashworth, *Human Rights and Criminal Justice* (2001).

[38] Which is the reason why magistrates normally sit in threes, see para. 4-002 above. The chairperson has no casting vote so that if a two-person court is divided the case must be retried: *R. v. Redbridge JJ., ex p. Ram* [1992] Q.B. 384.

[39] The advice from the clerk is regulated by *Practice Direction (Justices: Clerk to Court)* [2000] 1 W.L.R. 1886. For a fuller consideration of the status and role of the clerk, see para. 4-011, above. As to the practice of accepting that advice, see *R. v. Jones-Nicks* [1977] R.T.R. 72 and see Emmins (2000), pp. 156–157 and *Blackstone's Criminal Practice 2001*, para. D18.30.

[40] *Practice Direction (Justices: Clerk to Court)*. [2000] 1 W.L.R. 1886, para. 3.

[41] *Practice Note (Justices' Clerks)* [1953] 1 W.L.R. 1416; *Practice Direction (Justices: Clerk to Court)* [2000] 1 W.L.R. 1886, para. 4; and see *Blackstone's Criminal Practice 2002*, para. D19.31.

[42] *R. v. Stratford upon Avon JJ., ex p. Edmonds* [1973] R.T.R. 356.

[43] See para. 17-091, below.

the position of magistrates. The jury have already received instruction on the law from the judge in a summing-up. The magistrates will receive advice if they ask for it from the clerk, which they may seek in the course of their deliberations. The influence a clerk has over the magistrates is a matter of conjecture. Speculation that the clerk may have played too substantial a role in the verdict can be fuelled by his or her presence in the retiring room for a substantial period. The courts will quash a conviction if the clerk visits the retiring room where there is no good reason for doing so.[44] The best approach is for legal advice, including not only advice on questions of law and practice and procedure but also refreshing the magistrates' memory as to matters of evidence and principles of sentencing, to be given in open court, when the advocates on both sides can contribute to the advice being proffered.[45] However, if it is thought that the magistrates have retired to consider their verdict having been misinformed as to the law, the clerk may inform them of the correct position.[46] Such advice given in the retirement room is provisional and should be explained in open court.[47]

On returning to court, the magistrates give their verdict of guilty or not guilty with some limited provision of reasons.[48] Although the ECHR requires that as an element of the fair trial, the court should provide reasons for its judgment, there is at present no obligation on a magistrates' court to provide reasons.[49] However, there is growing pressure for the bench, and particularly the District Judges, to give reasons. The *Practice Direction* for justices' clerks does imply that reasons must be supplied.[50] The Divisional Court has recently confirmed that the law relating to the duty to give reasons remained as enunciated by Lord Bingham in *McKerry v. Teesdale and Wear Valley Justices*.[51] The essence of the exercise is to inform the accused why he has been found quility. This can usually be achieved in a few sentences

If the verdict is guilty the procedure will follow the same course as after a plea of guilty. If not guilty, the accused will be discharged. There is no opportunity for the magistrates to use alternative verdicts as can occur in the Crown Court where the accused might be found guilty of a lesser offence under the Criminal Law Act 1967, s.3.[52]

---

[44] In *R. v. Guildford JJ., ex p. Harding* (1981) 145 J.P. 174 the conviction was quashed because the clerk had retired with the magistrates to advise them when the case was absolutely straightforward.

[45] See, *Practice Direction (Justices: Clerk to Court)* [2000] 1 W.L.R. 1886, para. 8; *Blackstone's Criminal Practice 2001*, para. D18.30. On the need for the parties to be able to comment on third party advice offered to the court in compliance with Article 6 of the ECHR see: *JJ v. Netherlands* (1999) 28 E.H.R.R. 168; *Krcmar v. Czech Republic*, May 3, 2000.

[46] See *R. v. Uxbridge JJ., ex p. Smith* [1985] Crim. L.R. 670.

[47] *Practice Direction (Justices: Clerk to Court)* [2000] 1 W.L.R. 1886, para. 8.

[48] See *McGowan v. Brent Justices* [2002] Crim. L.R. (412). See also *Helle v. Finland* (1996) E.H.R.R. Emmerson and Ashworth, (2001) para. 14–124; A. Jennings, in K. Starmer *et al.*, (2001), p. 172. Juries are however excused from explaining the basis of their decisions: see para. 17-092, below. Magistrates may be required to record their findings of fact and the principles of law upon which they reach their decision, if required by the convicted defendant to state a case for consideration by the Administrative Court: see para. 18-008, below.

[49] There is no duty on the magistrates to give reasons when committing a defendant for Crown Court sentence: *R. v. Wirral Magistrates' Court* October 20, 2000.

[50] See further, B. Emmerson and Ashworth (2001), para. 14–184.

[51] *R (McGowan) v. Brent Justices* [2001] EWHC Admin 814. *McKerry v. Teesdale and Wear Valley Justices* (2000) 164 J.P. 355, 362.

[52] There is a fear that such a power would be misused in the magistrates' court. See *R. v. Liverpool Youth Court, ex p. H* [2001] Crim. L.R. 487.

There is an important and extremely wide power in section 142 of the Magistrates' Courts Act 1980 which allows magistrates to set aside a decision where it is in the interests of justice to do so.[53] This is regarded as a "slip rule" to rectify errors and not a power to be used to order a rehearing where the right of appeal to the Crown Court has been lost (*e.g.* by pleading guilty).[54] The magistrates may order a rehearing by a differently constituted bench having made a section 142 order.

8. SENTENCING[55]

17–012 Not only is it the function of the magistrates to determine guilt, but they must also impose a sentence upon the offender. The magistrates have a power to adjourn after convicting but before sentencing in order to enable inquiry to be made about the accused.[56] The magistrates will hear reports, antecedents and mitigation before pronouncing sentence[57]. The decision as to sentence must be made by at least a majority. The magistrates are obliged under the Powers of Criminal Courts (Sentencing) Act 2000[58] to give reasons for a custodial sentence. Maximum sentences are laid down in respect of each offence. Some offences can be punished by imprisonment (with or without a fine); some by a fine, or lesser sentence, alone. Where the offence is one triable summarily only, magistrates may not at present impose a term of imprisonment greater than six months for any single offence or the maximum provided in the relevant statute whichever is the lower.[59] Special rules operate in relation to sentencing under the Criminal Damage Act 1971 depending on the value of the property damaged.

The maximum fine is laid down by reference to the standard scale of fines that was introduced in 1982. It has five levels. Currently level 1 imposes a maximum fine of £200, level 2 a maximum fine of £500, level 3 a maximum fine of £1,000, level 4 a maximum fine of £2,500 and level 5 (otherwise known as the statutory maximum) a maximum fine of £5,000. The Auld Report concluded that there was no "well-based support" for a change in the maxima, but noted that the matter might need to be reviewed in the light of the Halliday recommendation for a combined custody and community service order of up to 12 months.[60]

Where the offence is triable either way and is being tried summarily, magistrates still cannot impose a term of imprisonment more than six months, and the maximum fine they may impose is that specified in the statute and may be greater than £5,000. There is no maximum aggregate fine

---

[53] See *R. v. Gwent Magistrates' Court, ex p. Carey* (1996) 160 J.P. 613; *R. v. Ealing JJ. ex p. Sahota* (1998) 162 J.P. 3.

[54] See *R. v. Croydon Youth Court, ex p. DPP* [1997] 1 Cr. App. R. 411.

[55] For detailed consideration of sentencing in the magistrates court see *Blackstones Criminal Practice 2002* Chap. D.21.

[56] Magistrates' Courts Act 1980, s.10(3).

[57] See J. Shapland, *Between Conviction and Sentence* (1981).

[58] s.79(4).

[59] Powers of Criminal Courts (Sentencing) Act 2000, s.78(1).

[60] See Auld (2001), p.101; Halliday Report, *Making Punishments Work: A Report of a Review of the Sentencing Framework for England and Wales* (2001), para. 0.11, recommendations 15–18.

that can be imposed on conviction for a number of offences dealt with together.

Rarely would the maximum term of imprisonment or fine be imposed.[61] In 1992, five per cent of cases in the magistrates' court resulted in a custodial sentence being imposed. By 2001, the figure had risen to 12 per cent.[62]

It is not necessarily the case that imprisonment, for example, will be imposed when it is available as a sentencing option. If imposed it can run consecutively or concurrently to existing sentences or those contemporaneously imposed. Indeed a major question for the magistrates is whether to impose a custodial sentence or not. The range of non-custodial sentences available include, not only imposing a fine, but also placing someone on probation, ordering attendance at an attendance centre, suspending or partially suspending a sentence of imprisonment, ordering someone to make payment of a compensation order,[63] sentencing undertake a community punishment or granting an absolute or conditional discharge, or to as well as specific (options available for young people).[64] As an indication of the proportion of different sentences issued in the magistrates' court, in 2000 there were 1.9 million defendants proceeded against in the magistrates' court (of which 492,000 were for indictable offences). There were 1,367,000 defendants found guilty in the magistrates, of which 272,000 involved indictable offences.[65] The number proceeded against in the magistrates' courts by type of offence also revealed 626,700 summary non-motoring cases and 792,200 summary motoring cases.[66] The numbers of offenders sentenced in the magistrates' courts to the various sentences available in 2000 were: absolute discharge 15,500; conditional discharge 103,200; fine 1,010,800; probation order 49,400; supervision order 10,900; community service order 41,700; attendance centre order 7,000; combination order 16,000; curfew order 2,400; reparation order 4,000; action plan order 4,300; drug treatment and testing order 200; secure training order 100; detention and training order 3,900; young offender institution 11,400; imprisonment 44,500; suspended imprisonment 1,200; otherwise dealt with 23,300.[67]

The magistrates have the very important power to commit a case to the **17–013** Crown Court for sentencing when the offence is triable either way and the magistrates are of the opinion that the offence is so serious that the

---

[61] For a plea to raise the maximum sentence for magistrates to 12 months imprisonment, see also A. Samuels, (1999) 163 J.P. 993.

[62] *Criminal Statistics for England and Wales 2000*, Cm. 5312 (2001).

[63] Powers of Criminal Courts (Sentencing) Act 2000, s.131. Compensation for victims was ordered in 90,700 cases in magistrates' courts in 1997 (an average amount of compensation for an indictable offence was £196). In 1997, 45% of offenders convicted of an offence of violence against the person were ordered to pay compensation at magistrates' courts, 46% for robbery and 54% for criminal damage: Barclay S and Tavares, *Digest IV*. See M. Wasik, "The Compensation Order on Sentence" (1999) J.P.N. 504, calling for clearer separation between punishment and compensation to avoid confusing the objectives.

[64] As to sentencing in magistrates' courts, see Emmins (2000), pp. 193–195 (for offences triable summarily only) and pp. 246–247 (for offences triable either way). See *Blackstone's Criminal Practice 2002*, paras E3.16–3.18. For statistics see *Criminal Statistics for England and Wales 2000*, Cm.5312 (2001), the range of sentencing options is set out clearly in Appendix 1. The figures for the 1.35 million people sentenced in the magistrates' court are set out in ch.7, see especially Table 7.1.

[65] See *Criminal Statistics for England and Wales 2000*, Cm. 5312 (2001), fig. 1.1.

[66] *Criminal Statistics*, Table 6A.

[67] See *Criminal Statistics*, Table 7.1. p.168.

punishment warranted lies beyond their power, or the custodial sentence is greater than that which the magistrates can impose and is needed to protect the public where the accused is convicted of an offence of violence or sex.[68] The power to commit is used frequently, (around 91,000 cases in 1997[69] but with over half those cases sent to the Crown Court, the sentence actually imposed could have been imposed by the magistrates themselves. Flood-Page and Mackie found this to be true in 62 per cent of cases.[70] Since 1997 there has been an increase in the number of committals for sentence, and this is as a direct result of the plea before venue provisions introduced in the Criminal Procedure and Investigation Act 1996.[71] Previously an accused might have been committed for trial at the Crown Court and then pleaded guilty, now it is more common to indicate a quilty plea at the plea before venue but thereafter to be committed for sentence to the Crown Court.[72] In addition, there is an increase in the seriousness of the cases being committed for sentence, and this is felt to give rise to a problem because the lay magistrates sitting in the Crown Court can out-vote the judge at that hearing, despite their inexperience in dealing with such serious cases. Proposals have been put forward by the Lord Chancellor's Department for legislation to remove the requirement that magistrates sit as judges in the Crown Court on committals for sentence from the magistrates' court, and in cases of appeal against sentence from the magistrates' court.[73]

As noted, the important power in section 142 of the Magistrates' Courts Act 1980 allows the magistrates to alter any decisions, including those as to sentence. The section is drafted in extremely broad terms and allows the magistrates to increase the sentence if necessary.[74]

There has been considerable disquiet about the disparity in magistrates' sentencing.[75] The obstacles in the way of achieving uniformity of approach[76] were identified by Wasik and Turner as being: (a) little authority assisting magistrates in their sentencing jurisdiction; (b) the size and diversity of the magistracy militated against a consistent approach; (c) the independence of

---

[68] Powers of Criminal Courts (Sentencing) Act 2000, s.3. On the procedure for committing for sentence see *R. v. Warley JJ. ex p. DPP* [1999] 1 W.L.R. 216. If the magistrates' court finds that their powers of sentence are not sufficient for an offence triable either way, they may commit the offender to Crown Court for sentence. See Emmins (2000), pp.169 and see *Blackstone's Criminal Practice 2001*, paras D20.3–20.9. Having given assurances to retain jurisdiction the magistrates ought not to renege on those: *R. v. Horseferry Road Magistrates' Court, ex p. Rugless* [2000] 1 Cr. App. R. (S.) 484.

[69] See *Criminal Statistics 2000*, p.231, 232.

[70] p.89.

[71] The number of defendants committed for sentence in 1998 showed an increase of 11,900.

[72] *ibid.* para. 22.

[73] See *Magistrates Sitting as Judges in the Crown Court* (LCD Consultation Paper, 1998). It should be noted that this would also reduce costs: in 1997/98 the cost of justices allowances when sitting on committals for sentence and appeals was £305,000: *ibid.* p.32.

[74] See *Blackstone's Criminal Practice 2002*, para. D21.12.

[75] See M. Wasik: and A. Turner, "Sentencing Guidelines for the Magistrates' Courts" [1993] Crim. L.R. 345 at 347–348, and see Raine (1989), pp. 86–94 and 97–98 and Parker, Summer and Jarvis (1989).

[76] For anecdotal cases of discrepancies in sentencing between lay magistrates and District Judges, see A. Ostrin (2001) 165 J.P. 181. See also the Home Office research, *www.homeoffice.gov.uk/rds/pdfs/lsp2000.pdf*.

the magistracy might militate against the acceptance of guidelines.[77] This was addressed by the implementation of the principled approach of the Criminal Justice Act 1991[78] and the introduction of the Magistrates Association *Sentencing Guidelines* in 1992, (since revised in 1997) which were both a development of an earlier approach[79] and a means of fulfilling the approach of the 1991 Act. The *Guidelines* aim "to improve 'consistency of approach' and [they] identif[y] the central task of the sentencer to be 'how to assess the relative *seriousness* of each case and how to arrive at a commensurate penalty' ".[80]

More recently, specific concerns have now been raised questioning the dangers of stereotyping in sentencing in the magistrates' court.[81] In addition, the propriety of the application of the sentencing discount for early guilty pleas being applied in the magistrates' court has also been called into question.[82] The problem is more acute in the magistrates' court because of the possibility of the defendant being unrepresented and the lower level of disclosure of the prosecution case. The pressure to strike a plea bargain deal is arising earlier in the process, particularly as a result of the plea before venue regime and the introduction of Early First Hearings.[83]

Flood-Page and Mackie found that the average custodial sentence in the Magistrates' Court for those pleading guilty was 3.7 months as compared to a sentence of 3.8 months for those pleading not guilty.[84] Henham[85] found that in 90 per cent of cases sentencers indicated that they had taken account of the early plea, but concluded that the discount scheme had "done little to regulate the pragmatic" nature of decision making in sentence discounts"[86].

---

[77] Wasik and Turner (1993), pp. 345–346. The "bench effect" has been described as a significant factor in sentencing decisions, that is a particular bench of magistrates adopting a general approach; see Tarling (1981) and Raine (1989), pp. 94–100.

[78] See below, para. 17-081.

[79] The Magistrates Association began producing *Suggestions for Road Traffic Offences* in 1966 and the *Sentencing Guide for Criminal Offences (other than Road Traffic)* in 1989; see Wasik and Turner (1993), pp. 346–347.

[80] *Sentencing Guidelines* p. ii, quoted in Wasik and Turner (1993), pp. 348–349. See P.G. Hawker and F.G. Davies, "Sentencing Guidelines Revisited" (1997) 161 J.P.N. 55.

[81] See L. Gelsthorpe and N. Loucks, "The Remanding and Sentencing of Female Offenders in Magistrates' Courts" (1997) 161 J.P.N. 1132, finding that sentences exhibit general reluctance to fine women. The result is a disproportionate number of discharges and severe sentences. The evidence suggests that magistrates make stereotypical judgments on gender, which in turn suggests that more effective training is necessary. See generally, C. Hedderman and L. Gelsthorpe, *Understanding the Sentencing of Women* (HORS No 170, 1997) and A. Rutherford, "Women Sentencing and Prisons" (1997) 147 N.L.J. 424. On racial monitoring in the magistrates' court see the *Report of the Magistrates Courts Service Issues Group; Justice in Action* (2000) responding to the Macpherson Report into the death of Stephen Lawrence."

[82] See the *Magistrates' Association Sentencing Guidelines* (1997), para. 2.4: "the law requires that the court reduces the sentence for a timely guilty plea, but the provision should be used with judicial flexibility. A timely guilty plea may attract a sentencing discount of up to one third but the precise amount of discount will depend on the facts of each case and a last minute plea will attract only a nominal discount." See *R. v. Isleworth Crown Court ex p. Buda* [2000] 1 Cr. App. R. (S.) 538.

[83] See above paras 14-045.

[84] p. 34.

[85] "Reconciling Process and Policy: Sentence Discounts in the Magistrates' Court" [2000] Crim. I. R. 436.

[86] p.450. For criticism of the methodology see Sanders and Young, (2000), pp. 408–410.

9. Do Magistrates Reach The Right Result?

17–014   The answer to this question, as with the question whether juries arrive at the right result,[87] depends upon what is meant by "right result" and must inevitably be impressionistic. Care must be taken with assertions either that magistrates or that juries acquit too many people. Comparing the statistics on rates of acquittal in the magistrates' courts and Crown Courts is apt to mislead since there are a number of factors that may influence the venue of the trial and the not guilty plea in that venue. In 2000, of those pleading not guilty 67 per cent in the Crown Court were acquitted; 36 per cent were found not guilty in the magistrates' court.[88] Even so, there are many different beliefs about summary trial, including that an accused has a greater chance of acquittal before a jury, that magistrates' impose lighter sentences in circumstances where the Crown Court and magistrates have the same sentencing powers, that judges impose lighter sentences in the same circumstances, and that magistrates' courts are biased in favour of the prosecution.[89] Further, there is some evidence that the criminal fraternity lack confidence in magisterial decision-making[90]: "Defendants do not expect justice to be done in the magistrates' court."[91] It is unclear whether that is because they believe magistrates get decisions wrong, or because they get them right. As the Auld Report recently recognised,: "it is impossible for outside researchers and reviewers to evaluate the relative 'correctness of juries' verdicts and magistrates' courts' decisions"[92]. The Auld Report was clear in its message that reliance for reform of the magistrates and assessment of the effectiveness of the magistrates' work ought not to be based on public opinion.[93]

In assessing the quality of justice dispensed in the magistrates' court, what is important above all else is that magistrates' courts provide trials that are fair and in accordance with principles of due process. There must be accountability and consistency in their decision-making whatever the pressures of efficiency in the process. There have been many attempts to improve the quality of justice in summary trials. The Auld Report echoes the concerns about the success and the quality of summary justice.[94]

The debate as to the comparable quality of justice in the magistrates' and the Crown Court has persisted for decades. Vennard's early study of contested trials in the magistrates' court[95] gives some support to the view that magistrates do weigh evidence carefully and reach a verdict that is broadly in line with identifiable features of the evidence heard. The criticism

---

[87]   See para. 17-094 below.
[88]   See *Criminal Statistics* (2001), Table 6.3; para.1.14, Table 6C.
[89]   Bottoms and McLean (1976), Chap. 4; Parker, Sumner and Jarvis (1989), p. 60; and D. Riley and J. Vennard, "Triable-Either-Way Cases: Crown Court or Magistrates' Court?" (1988) 25 *Home Office Research Bulletin* 31 at 34.
[90]   Riley and Vennard (1988), p. 34. See *R.v. Highgate JJ. ex p. Riley* [1996] R.T.R. 150 (JP reprimanding D for calling police officer a liar).
[91]   Saunders and Young (2000), p. 537
[92]   Chap. 3, para. 24.
[93]   p.105.
[94]   See Chaps 3 and 4.
[95]   Vennard (1980) Vennard (1981) and J. Vennard, "Acquittal Rates in Magistrates' Courts" (1981) 11 *Home Office Research Bulletin* 21.

most frequently made of magistrates is that they place too much credibility on the evidence of police officers and are generally too "prosecution-minded".[96] This criticism emanates not only from the accused who opts for trial by jury because it is "fairer", or because magistrates are amateurs who cannot be expected to get it right, or because they estimate that there is a better chance of acquittal,[97] but also from amongst those individuals and organisations who gave evidence to the James Committee.[98]

The research study undertaken by Vennard had as its aims[99]:

(i) to appraise and itemise for contested cases the substance of the evidence presented by the prosecution and the defence, and attempt to quantify weaknesses and strengths in that evidence—such as whether or not the credibility of witnesses was impugned; and

(ii) to attempt to explain the trial outcome in contested cases in relation to the type of evidence presented by both parties and to criteria pertaining to witness credibility.

On somewhat limited evidence, Vennard concluded that her findings indicated that " ... magistrates' decisions whether to convict or acquit are strongly associated with a few quantifiable indices of the evidence adduced by the parties and the credibility of witnesses".[1] Strong associations were detected between direct evidence implicating the accused given by the prosecution witnesses whose credibility was not impugned, and conviction. Conversely there was a strong association between acquittal, the prosecution witnesses' lack of credibility, and the lack of direct evidence. These findings are not startling but they may reassure critics that magistrates are generally operating along rational lines.

For another slightly more recent view, which relies partly upon different work by Vennard on acquittal rates, one may look at King's response[2] to proposals by the Justices' Clerks Society[3] that more trials should be diverted into the magistrates' court. King was dismissive of claims that magistrates offer a better quality of justice than juries and argued vigorously against proposals to reduce the right to jury trial.[4]

Further, even more recently, Sanders and Young's review of the research evidence, leads them to conclude that the defendants perception as to the

---

[96] See, e.g., evidence to the James Committee, *The Distribution of Criminal Business Between the Crown Court and the Magistrates' Court*, Cmnd. 6323, (1975); B. Wootton, *Crime and Penal Policy* (1978).

[97] Gregory (1976).

[98] See n. 93, above.

[99] Vennard (1981), p. 4.

[1] *ibid.* p. 20.

[2] M. King, "Against Summary Trial" *L.A.G. Bulletin*, April 1982, p. 14.

[3] "A Case for Summary Trial-Proposals for a Redistribution of Criminal Business" published by the Justices' Clerks Society.

[4] It was certainly the experience of the James Committee (1975) that its proposals to remove the right to trial by jury for minor thefts brought an outraged response, not least in the House of Commons. The proposal, originally incorporated in the Criminal Law Bill 1977, disappeared during the Bill's progress through Parliament. The opposition was, it is true, based more on a commitment to jury trial than on an antipathy to magisterial justice. See para. 14-044 above.

unfairness of magistrates' court trial are accurate.[5] They identify a number
of possible explanations for the higher acquittal rates in the Crown Court
compared with magistrates' court: (a) more people have to be convinced in
the Crown Court (at least 10 out of 12 rather than two out of three)[6]; (b) the
social composition of the magistrates[7] compared with juries[8] militates more
in favour of conviction in a magistrates' court; (c) magistrates become
"case-hardened" whereas juries come fresh to the criminal justice system
(case hardening is offset, according to the Auld Report, by the infrequency
of the magistrates' sitting, their training, the changing constitution of each
panel, the presence of a clerk and their obligation to explain their
decisions[9]); d) magistrates' court procedures place defendants at a greater
disadvantage because of the lack of disclosure requirements[10]; the
magistrates are aware of inadmissible evidence (*e.g.*, confessions), and
justices' clerks have a significant impact.[11] They conclude that it "is no
exaggeration to say that magistrates' courts are crime control courts
overlaid with a thin layer of due process icing. At every twist and turn in the
process, defendants are saddled with handicaps which undermine their
willingness or ability to stand for their rights in court."[12] In consequence,
they express surprise that the RCCJ in 1993 wished to reduce the right to
jury trial, especially since no research was commissioned to examine justice
in the lower courts.[13]

There is no question that the magistrates' court offers a swifter, cheaper
criminal process (the estimates are that the uncontested magistrates hearing
is seven times cheaper than a Crown Court hearing).[14] The pressure to
channel more and more cases into the magistrates has been increasing over
the years, most recently with the government twice introducing a Bill to
remove the defendant's right to jury trial at his own election and
empowering the magistrates to make the decision as to venue. This Criminal
Justice (mode of Trial) Bill has twice been defeated (in different guises) in the
House of Lords. The Auld Report has now endorsed a similar scheme.

17–015   There is no doubt that the government is anxious to maximise the use that
can be made of the more efficient process in the magistrates' court.[15] The
Home Secretary re-iterated in a letter to *The Times*,[16] the government's view
that there was "no evidence to suggest that the quality of justice dispensed in
the magistrates court is inferior to that in the Crown Court". Academic

---

[5] Sanders and Young (2000), pp. 530-548.
[6] On the question of whether magistrates are properly regarded as surrogate jurors, see the Auld Report (2001), p.l04.
[7] See above, paras 4-003–4-004.
[8] See below, para. 17-086.
[9] p.98. See also the discussion at pp.106–107.
[10] As to disclosure in the Crown Court, see above, paras 14-068–14-076.
[11] Sanders and Young (2000), pp. 530–548.
[12] *ibid.* (2000), p. 548.
[13] *ibid.* (2000), p. 546.
[14] See Sanders and Young (2000), p.487.
[15] The government concern for efficiency in the magistrates' system is explicitly reiterated in a number of Lord Irvine's speeches to the AGM of the Magistrates' Association (October 11, 1997; October 17, 1998; October 30, 1999) and the Council of the Magistrates' Association: (July 24, 1997; March 5, 1999).
[16] January 24, 2000.

opinion is less convinced. Sanders and Young refer to magistrates as "unpaid, part-time amateurs".[17]

The questions that remain are whether the magistrates are sufficiently accountable,[18] socially representative,[19] and whether they offer a lesser form of justice or one that is merely different from that in the Crown Court. Research has shown that although the magistracy is not wholly representative, they command respect.[20] "Magistrates are not wholly reflective of the communities from which they are drawn, but nevertheless they have an important symbolic effect of law participation in the system which should not be undervalued."[21] There are many aspects to these difficult questions that cannot be addressed here. Fundamentally, it has to be questioned what the primary purpose of the magistrates' court is. Is it a diluted form of (swifter) justice? Are magistrates surrogate jurors? Are magistrates community representatives in the criminal justice system?

More recently there has been a more specific interest not just in comparing the quality of justice dispensed by the magistrates as compared with the Crown Court, but that of the lay magistrates compared with the District Judges (Magistrates' Court) the old "Stipendiary". The research demonstrates that while District Judges are capable of dealing with a greater volume of cases more quickly than the lay magistrates,[22] they are more expensive than lay magistrates (not least because they convict more people thereby adding to the prison costs!).[23] Other research conducted recently by Flood-Page and Mackie[24] found that professional magistrates are more likely than lay magistrates to impose custodial sentences. Morgan and Russell in their research found that there was nothing to suggest that any differences in decision-making patterns were attributable to the professional magistrates who tended to be dealing with more serious cases.[25] Auld recommended no significant change in the numbers of lay or professional magistrates.[26]

Morgan and Russell[27] considered the balance between lay and professional magistrates and how the system can utilise both to maximum effect. The research was conducted into the opinions of the public and opinions of magistrates and court users. The efficiency of the lay and professional

---

[17] (2000), p.486. On misconduct by particular magistrates see F. Bennion, (2000) 164 J.P. 196; and *R. v. Weston-Super-Mare Magistrates' ex p. Taylor* [1981] Crim. L.R. 179.

[18] See S. Doran and R. Glenn, *Lay Involvement in Ajudication: Review of the Criminal Justice System in Northern Ireland* (Criminal Justice Review Research Report No.11, 2000).

[19] See P. Darbyshire, [1997] Crim. L.R. 681.

[20] The Auld Report p.95, citing Morgan and Russel.

[21] The Auld Report, p.98.

[22] See also R. Morgan and N. Russell, *The Judiciary in the Magistrates' Court* R.D.S. No. 66, 2000). The Auld Report detailed criticism that is made of Morgan and Russell's costings based on their failure to allow for the various factors involved in the cases District judges hear. (p.97). See also Auld (2001), p.95.

[23] For a criticism of the costings and calculations used by in Morgan and Russell's study see Auld (2001), pp. 96–97 where the question of principle regarding different sentencing practice is examined. On the differences between the two branches see P. Seago, C. Walker and D. Wall, "The Development of the Professional Magistracy in England and Wales" [2000] Crim. L.R. 631.

[24] (1998), Chap. 7.

[25] p.49.

[26] p.102.

[27] *The Judiciary in the Magistrates Courts* (2000).

magistrates studied reveals that professional magistrates deal with more cases more swiftly[28]: estimates were that they would deal with 30 per cent more cases than lay magistrates. The professional magistrates took fewer adjournments and were more likely to inspire greater confidence in court users with greater consistency, efficiency, confidence, and by providing better reasons.[29]

Sanders[30] research has also questioned the extent to which the magistrates' court "embodies the core values which underlie serious crimes." His radical suggestion to improve the system was for three tiers of tribunal with District Judges sitting alone to hear controversial cases, a mixed court comprising lay members and District Judges to try contested cases and either way sentencing cases and the judge and jury to deal with the most serious crimes. Sanders' proposal for a District Judge to sit alone in cases in which legal issues arise and with lay magistrates when "social skills" are necessary was designed to maximise the opportunity for respective skills of the branches to be deployed and to create a closer parallel with the paradigm judge and jury.[31] The Auld Report rejects Sanders approach describing it as "depriving summary justice of the best features of professional lay judges sitting separately."[32] It was regarded as prohibitively expensive.[33]

An odd situation has developed whereby the lay magistrates fear that they are likely to be downsized in favour of District Judges who are perceived as more efficient. At the same time, District Judges are concerned that they will not be provided with the more difficult (and stimulating) cases, but that these will continue to be distributed randomly within the court.[34] Neither group wished to sit together to hear cases; lay magistrates enjoy the opportunity to chair their own cases, and District Judges feeling that they do not need help.[35] Auld rejected the idea that there was a national policy to replace lay magistrates with District Judges as a way of maximising efficiency.[36] There are merits in both lay magistrates (characterised by Auld as including participative democracy and community justice) and in the greater consistency, efficiency and legality of the District Judges.[37] The Auld Report recommended that the work between District Judges and lay magistrates should continue to be allocated as at present, with "mixed tribunals" needed only for training purposes and "local 'cultural'

---

[28] Average time per trial by lay magistrates is 34 minutes and 24 minutes by the District Judge (p.42). See Morgan and Russell, pp.34–43.

[29] Chap. 2. For detailed qualitative assessment of the magistrates' performance — including attentiveness, courtesy, avoidance of jargon—see p.45.

[30] Community Justice and Modernising the Magistracy in England and Wales (2001) and see A. Sanders, (2001) 165 J.P. n.56.

[31] See Community Justice: Modernising the Magistracy in England and Wales (2001); the Auld Report, p. 104.

[32] p. 105.

[33] The Auld recommendations for a unified criminal court, with three levels of jurisdiction: the Crown Division, the District Division and the Magistrates' Division are examined above. The District Division would involve the judge as the sole judge of law, with the magistrates as equal judges of fact with the judge. Pre-trial hearings and questions of the admissibility of evidence would be dealt with by the judge in the absence of the magistrates.

[34] See Morgan and Russell, p.31.

[35] See Auld Report, p.102.

[36] Auld Report, p. 103–4.

[37] p.98.

advantages". It was also clearly recommended that there should be no extension of the justices' clerks' case management jurisdiction.

The division of work and roles to be played in summary justice by the lay magistrates and District Judges are certain to come under even closer scrutiny in the future. It may be that there is no ideal solution, with some commentators concluding that "it is impossible to evaluate the relative justice of the decision-making of District Judges and magistrates".[38]

The recent research into the magistrates' courts has also revealed an astonishing ignorance on the part of the general public as to how summary justice is delivered. Seventy-three per cent of the public were unaware of the difference between the lay and professional magistrates.[39] Lay magistrates were felt to represent the views of the public better than professional judges and were felt to be more likely to be sympathetic to the defendant's circumstances. It was, however, felt that professional magistrates were better at assessing guilt and managing the case more efficiently. The research revealed that the public felt that summary offences of a non-serious nature could be dealt with by a single magistrate. However, these often illogical and certainly ill-informed views expressed by the public were dismissed as "valueless" and "uninformed opinion" on the relative strengths of the branches of the magistracy.[40] An important point echoed throughout the Auld Report[41] is that "[p]ublic confidence is not an end in itself; it is or should be an outcome of a fair and efficient system".[42]

Efforts to maintain and enhance public confidence have included a greater emphasis on selection and training of magistrates. Morgan and Russell found that the magistracy, whilst not representative of the community as a whole, did command confidence. However, Auld concluded that there was "scope for improvement" in the recruitment of magistrates, so as to better reflect national and local communities and to develop fairer and more efficient and consistent procedures and sentencing.[43] It was also recommended that the selection and appointment procedures for magistrates should also be improved to better reflect the community,[44] with a National Recruitment Strategy.[45] The Judicial Studies Board has taken some responsibility for evaluating the Magistrates' New Training Initiative[46] and has called for implementation of National Performance Standard.[47] The Magistrates' Court Service Inspectorate is a permanent monitoring system forming part of the LCD. Its aim is to improve the quality of service, efficiency and effectiveness in the magistrates' court service. In its report

[38] p. 103.
[39] Morgan and Russell, p.xi.
[40] Auld (2001), p. 96.
[41] p.105.
[42] p. 106.
[43] Auld (2001), p.98.
[44] pp. 126–129.
[45] On proposals for improved training in the magistrates see Auld, pp 129–131, recommending that the Judicial Studies Board take responsibility.
[46] See *Final Report on MNTI* (2000).
[47] The Judicial Studies Board evaluation which is in general a positive report is available at *www.jsboard.co.uk*.

Assessing Quality of Service in the Magistrates' Courts Service,[48] the inspectorate explains the framework of indicators and standards used. The main indicators are treatment of users, availability of information and facilities. There are numerous secondary categories of quality indicator. This is a very clear example of the impact of managerialism and consumerism on the criminal justice system with repeated emphasis on the "convenience" of facilities, "personal treatment" offered and the "amenities" available.[49] The Judicial Studies Board has been evaluating the Magistrates New Training Initiative that was introduced in 1998 to improve training and mentoring of magistrates.

B. TRIAL ON INDICTMENT[50]

17-016   A trial on indictment (that is one that takes place in the Crown Court), most commonly arises when an adult defendant has been charged with an offence that is triable only on indictment, or has been charged with an either way offence and has elected to be tried on indictment.[51] The pre-trial procedures that will be applicable before a case reaches the Crown Court have been discussed above, where the differences between the schemes and the controversial reforms are examined. In an attempt to expedite the most serious cases more efficiently, the Crime and Disorder Act 1998, s.51, introduces a scheme whereby offences triable only on indictment are not dealt with by committal proceedings but proceed directly to the Crown Court, following a preliminary ruling by the magistrates.

If proceedings are transferred from a magistrates' court for trial in the Crown Court, those proceedings are begun by the "preferment of a bill of indictment". This procedure simply involves sending the bill of indictment[52] to the appropriate officer of the Crown Court for signature.[53] Once it is signed, the accused may be brought before the court.[54] Then the accused

---

[48] *www.mcsi.gov.uk*

[49] On the public perception of the quality of service in the magistrates see Appendix G.

[50] The leading practitioner work, *Archbold* (Sweet and Maxwell) deals with all aspects of the trial on indictment: *Archbold* is published annually and updated by supplements throughout the year.

[51] Other methods by which the trial on indictment may arise include preferment of a voluntary bill, see above, para. 14–067 (on which see now *Practice Direction (Supreme Court: Voluntary Bills) (No.2)* [1999] 1 W.L.R. 1613), notice of transfer by prosecution under the Criminal Justice Act 1987, s.4 (complex frauds) or s.53 (chid witness cases); or by order of the magistrates that the accused is sent for trial on an indictable only offece under s.51 of the Crime and Disorder Act 1998. The Auld Report recommended streamlining of these procedures.

[52] Ultimate responsibility for this lies with counsel for the prosecution (*Archbold (2002)*, para. 1–111) but in most cases it is now the responsibility of the Crown Prosecution Service to draft and determine the form of an indictment: Procedural Notice issued by the Crown Prosecution Service and the Lord Chancellor's Department, (1989) 139 N.L.J. 188. See also *R. v. Newland* [1988] Q.B. 402. Once counsel has been instructed he or she becomes responsible for the propriety of the indictment: *R. v Moss* [1995] Crim. L.R. 828.

[53] The appropriate officer retains for the time being the responsibility for signing indictments. On the procedural requirements to be complied with see *R. v. Jackson* [1997] 2 Cr.App. R. 497.

[54] Where the accused has been committed for trial, the bill of indictment should, subject to

must be asked to plead to the indictment, in a process known as arraignment. Unlike summary proceedings there is no general time limit for the issue of proceedings for an indictable offence.[55] Article 6 of the ECHR provides that a trial must occur within a reasonable time.[56] The time runs from the suspect being charged with an offence (which might be at the time of arrest).[57] The Court of Appeal has confirmed that in domestic law, in determining whether a hearing has taken place within a reasonable time for the purposes of Article 6, the relevant period normally begins with the charge or summons of the accused. The time period might begin with an earlier interview if the accused was materially prejudiced by the State action prior to the charge/summons. The Court has emphasised that it is not essential that a stay of proceedings be issued as an appropriate remedy for delay, but that sentencing discount or awards of compensation might be adequate.[58] The *Criminal Statistics for England and Wales* reveal that the average waiting time for trials in the Crown Court, from committal to the start of the hearing, rose from 12 weeks in 1997 to 14.3 weeks in 2000. This is largely attributable to increased numbers of defendants at the magistrates' court pleading guilty and so being taken out of the equation.[59]

The indictment is the formal statement of the charge(s) against the accused and should contain the statement of the offence (a description of the offence), and the particulars of the offence, that is a brief statement of the essential facts that constitute the offence.[60] The statement of the offence should be precise, using the recognisable common law name,[61] the statutory

some exceptional cases, be preferred within 28 days of the date of notice of transfer, unless that period is extended: Indictment (Procedure) Rules 1971 (S.I. 1971 No. 2084), r.5, as amended. The time limit is not mandatory: *R. v. Urbanowski* (1976) 62 Cr. App. R. 229, CA; *R. v. Soffe* (1982) 75 Cr. App. R. 133, CA.

[55] Delay in bringing proceedings may be regarded as an abuse of process and thus cause criminal proceedings to be stopped, see generally A. Choo, *Abuse of Process and Judicial Stays of Criminal Proceedings* (1993). The court has an inherent jurisdiction to stay proceedings for abuse of process on grounds of delay: see *e.g. Bell v. DPP of Jamaica* [1985] A.C. 937. There have been a number of successful prosecutions where the proceedings have occurred 20 years or more after the commission of the offence, although these do give rise to concerns about the quality of evidence available: see *R. v. G (Y)* [1999] Crim. L.R. 825; *R. v. M* [1999] Crim. L.R. 922; *R. v. Jenkins* [1998] Crim. L.R. 411 ; and see J.S.B. Direction No.37.

[56] See also Article 5(3). See most recently on the ECHR and delay the Privy Council decision in *Procurator Fiscal v. Watson* [2002] UKMRR 542.

[57] See *Ewing v. U.K.* (1988) 10 E.H.R.R. 141, *X v. U.K.* (1979) 17 D.R. 122 and generally, B. Emmerson and A. Ashworth (2001), pp.350–353. The Article will not be breached if delays are due to the defendant or his legal representatives (*Konig v. FRG (No 1)* (1979) 2 E.H.R.R. 170, but will be breached where the delay is the fault of the prosecution, or due to administrative delay: *Orchin v. U.K.* (1984) 6 E.H.R.R. 391.

[58] *Attorney-Generals' Reference (No. 2 of 2001)* [2001] 1 W.L.R. 1869. See further A. Webster, "Delay and Article 6(1): An End to the Requirement of Prejudice" [2001] Crim. L.R. 786 considering the availability of a remedy of stay of proceedings for abuse where delay does not cause serious prejudice to the accused.

[59] *Criminal Statistics* (2001), para 1.15. For the Auld recommendations on time limits see pp. 504–508.

[60] See generally, *Archbold (2002)*, Chap. 1, especially para. 1–108 *et seq.*

[61] *e.g.* murder; manslaughter; blasphemy; conspiracy to corrupt public morals.

name and derivation,[62] or sufficient details of a statutory offence.[63] The particulars must give "reasonable information as to the nature of the charge",[64] so that the accused knows the details of the charge and the prosecution may not shift its ground during the trial.[65] The fair trial guarantees in Article 6 include that the accused must know the charges against him.[66] In addition, Article 7 guarantees that there should be no retrospective criminalisation (which has been interpreted to mean that the offence must be drafted with sufficient precision that the citizen is able to regulate his behaviour).[67] It is possible that a number of offences in English criminal law will face challenges for a lack of certainty in definition.[68] At a minimum, it is essential that the counts of the indictment are drafted with sufficient detail to meet the requirements of the ECHR and to ensure that the accused has sufficient information to prepare his defence and challenge the prosecution case.[69]

It is vital that the counts of an indictment are specific. If, for example, a count alleges different types of conduct it will be important for the jury to be directed so that they must be unanimous as to the type of conduct they find proved.[70]

Three specimen indictments follow: a common law offence, a precise statutory description and a statutory offence for which there is no short description. They are taken from decided cases and reflect particular difficulties of those cases. Simpler cases will produce simpler indictments.

---

[62] *e.g.* theft, contrary to s.1 of the Theft Act 1968; robbery, contrary to s.8(1) of the Theft Act 1968; arson, contrary to s.1(1) and (3) of the Criminal Damage Act 1971. See the Indictment Rules 1971 (S.I. 1971 No. 1253), r.6.

[63] *e.g.* removing an article from a place open to the public, contrary to s. 11(1) of the Theft Act 1968; sexual intercourse with a girl under 13, contrary to s.5 of the Sexual Offences Act 1956.

[64] The Crown is not obliged to prove every particular: *R. v. Hancock* [1996] 2 Cr.App. R. 554; Indictment Rules 1971 (S.I. 1971 No. 1253), r.3(1).

[65] The accused, if he or she requests, is entitled to a copy of the indictment free of charge: *ibid.* r.10(1).

[66] For a review of cases decided under the Human Rights Act see E. Martin Salgado and C. O'Brien, [2001]4, E.H.R.L.R. 376. "Criminal charge" in Article 6 has an autonomous convention meaning, and will be determined by reference to the classification of the offence in domestic law, the nature of the offence and the severity of the penalty: *Engel v. Netherlands* (1979–80) 1 E.H.R.R. 647, para. 82. English law continues to struggle in making the distinction in many diverse contexts, recently: *King v. Walden* [2001] S.T.C. 822 (income tax penalties) ; *Han and Yau v. Customs and Excise* [2001] S.T.C. 1188 (VAT penalties); *R v. FSA, The Times,* May 15, 2001 (Financial Service Authorities penalties); *McCann v. Manchester Crown Court* [2001] 1 W.L.R. 1084 (anti-social behaviour orders). See also *Phillips v. U.K.* [2001] Crim. L.R. 817; *Putz v. Austria* (2001)32 E.H.R.R. 271.

[67] The ECtHR interpretation of Article 7 is such that it protects against retroactive application of the criminal law through expansive interpretation at common law. (*X and Y v. U.K.* (1982) 28 D.R. 77). See generally *Kokkanakis v. Greece* (1994) 17 E.H.R.R. 397; and Emmerson and Ashworth (2001) Chap. 10.

[68] *e.g.* the potential challenges against offences of dishonesty and gross negligence manslaughter, both of which leave considerable discretion in defining the scope of the offence to the jury.

[69] See generally *Pelissier v. France* (2000) 30 E.H.R.R. 715. For potential difficulties in English law see, *e.g.* the difficulties with the breadth of indictment for aiders and abettors (see *R. v. Rackman* [1997] 2 Cr.App. R. 222) and the broad common law offences such as cheating the public revenue: *R. v. Litanzios* [1999] Crim. L.R. 669. On the desirability of clear and comprehensive indictments see Bowes, "The Form of Indictments" [1995] Crim. L.R. 114.

[70] *R. v. D* [2001] Crim. L.R. 160 and commentary.

(i) Shaw v. DPP[71]

Statement of offence: Conspiracy to corrupt public morals   **17–017**

Particulars of offence: Frederick Charles Shaw on diverse days between the 1st day of October 1959 and the 23rd day of July 1960 within the jurisdiction of the Central Criminal Court, conspired with certain persons who inserted advertisements in issues of a magazine entitled "Ladies' Directory" numbered 7, 7 revised, 8, 9, 10 and a supplement thereto, and with certain other persons whose names are unknown, by means of the said magazine and the said advertisements to induce readers thereof to resort to the said advertisers for the purposes of fornication and of taking part in or witnessing other disgusting and immoral acts and exhibitions, with intent thereby to debauch and corrupt the morals as well of youth as of divers other liege subjects of Our Lady the Queen and to raise and create in their minds inordinate and lustful desires.

(ii) R. v. Miller[72]

Statement of offence: Arson, contrary to section 1(1) and (3) of Criminal   **17–018**
Damage Act 1971

Particulars of offence: James Miller on a date unknown between August 13 and 16, 1980, without lawful excuse, damaged by fire a house known as No. 9, Grantham Road, Sparkbrook, intending to do damage to such property or reckless as to whether such property would be damaged.

(iii) R. v. Markus[73]

Statement of offence: Conniving at a corporation fraudulently inducing the   **17–019**
investment of money contrary to sections 13(1)(b) and 19 of the Prevention of Fraud (Investments) Act 1958

Particulars of offence: Edward Jules Markus between August 25, 1970, and January 15, 1971, within the jurisdiction of the Central Criminal Court being a director of Agricultural Investment Corporation S.A. of the First National Investment Corporation S.A. and of Agri-International S.A. and of Agri-International (U.K.) Ltd connived at the fraudulent inducement of Agricultural Investment Corporation S.A., through its agents First National Investment Corporation S.A. and Agri-International S.A. and Agri-International (U.K.) Ltd of Dr Hermann Schlick and Mrs Theodoline Schlick to take part in an arrangement to invest $1038.32 in Agri-Fund (the said investment being an arrangement with respect of property other than securities, the purpose or pretended purpose of which was to enable the said Dr Hermann Schlick and the said Mrs Theodoline Schlick to participate in the profits alleged to be likely to arise from the holding of Agri-Fund) by

---

[71] [1962] A.C. 220.
[72] [1983] 2 A.C. 161.
[73] The offence in question has since been repealed, but the indictment is a good example of the types of offence that lack clear succinct definition.

representations that Agricultural Investment Corporation S.A. was genuinely carrying on an honest business and that moneys invested in Agri-Fund
were immediately redeemable at the option of the investor which
representations both he and the said corporation knew to be misleading
false and deceptive.

These examples satisfy the requirements that an indictment should include
such information as to the time and place of the offence so as to indicate to
the accused the acts which are alleged to constitute the offence,[74] a
reasonably clear description of any property involved,[75] the identity of any
"victim" or a description reasonable so as to be identifiable, any factual
circumstances necessary to the offence,[76] and any special mental element
required by the offence which is not inherent in the statement of the offence.[77]

Indictments may contain more than one offence provided they are
founded on the same facts or for in part of a series of offences of the same or
a similar character, but the charges must be separated and are then known
as "counts".[78] Whenever the trial involves more than one count of an
offence, there are difficulties in guaranteeing that the accused knows
precisely what is alleged in each count,[79] and for the jury in being agreed in
their verdict on the same facts in each relevant count. In addition, the judge
must be clear on which facts are proved against the accused for the purposes
of determining sentence. It is important that the prosecutor does not
overload the indictment with charges such that it does not fairly and
accurately reflect the alleged criminality of the defendant.[80]

Three particular difficulties that arise in the context of the contents of the
indictment are: the danger of duplicity, the use of specimen counts, and the
joinder of indictments.

The rule against duplicity is easy to state, but can cause problems in
practice. In short, the rule is designed to guarantee that "no one count of the
indictment should charge the defendant with having committed two or more

---

[74] An allegation as to time may be made in ordinary language, and the dates between which the
offence may be quite a long way apart, as in Shaw's indictment. It is only in a few cases that
either time or place is of the essence of the offence (*e.g.* the victim's age), in which case
greater particularity is required.

[75] In Miller's indictment, No. 9, Grantham Road, Sparkbrook. The name of the owner of the
property is unnecessary in most cases.

[76] *e.g.* in an indictment for theft, the particulars must state that the property in question
belonged to another, but does not have to state who that other was.

[77] *e.g.* the particulars on an indictment for an offence under s.18 of the Offences Against the
Person Act 1861 should allege an intent to do grievous bodily harm to the victim or to resist
or prevent lawful apprehension, as appropriate. The particulars of an indictment for arson
under s.l(1) and (3) of the Criminal Damage Act 1971 must allege either an intent to destroy
or damage another's property, or recklessness as to whether such property would be
destroyed or damaged. On the specific necessity to spell out the *mens rea* of the charge in the
indictment, see *R. v. Ike* [1996] Crim. L.R. 515.

[78] On the purpose of the provision of particulars see *R. v. Hancock* [1996] 2 Cr. App. R. 554;
Archbold (2002), para. 1–117. The court must avoid the possibility that the particulars lack
sufficient specificity to inhibit the defendant preparing the case.

[79] The indictment should make clear whether the accused is charged as an accessory or the
principal offender: *R. v. Taylor, Harrison and Taylor* [1998] Crim. L.R. 582. This is especially
problematic with joint enterprises: see *R. v. Greaterex* [1999] 1 Cr. App. R. 126.

[80] See *R. v. Canavan* [1998] 1 Cr. App. R. 79.

separate offences".[81] This is particularly difficult in cases where the accused's conduct continues over a long period of time.

The use of specimen counts can also be difficult in practice. A specimen count is laid against a defendant as a typical example of the conduct alleged. In such cases it is imperative that the count is drafted with great care to ensure that the accused knows the extent of the accusation against him.[82]

The rule on joinder (i.e. when different offences with different counts can be joined together for the one trial) are governed by the Indictment Rules 1971[83] which provide that charges may be joined together if founded on the same facts, they are part of a series of offences or are of similar character.[84] The indictment may join two or more accused (rather than joining counts) either if they are both named in the same count in the indictment or in separate counts which would legitimately lie on one indictment.[85] Joining offenders and offences is a pragmatic issue which involves balancing the additional burden on the parties and the trier of fact and the broader issues of the interests of justice.[86]

Indictments may be amended provided that no risk of injustice results, and this includes the possibility of new counts being added to the indictment,[87] but indictments should not be overloaded with counts that render the trial unduly complex and place an unfair burden on the accused and/or the jury.

Auld concludes that the CPS should be given greater powers and responsibilities over charging to reduce the number of cases in which amendment is made.[88]

Certain serious offences (e.g. murder) may only be tried by judges of sufficient seniority.[89] The listing is according to class of offence. There are

[81] Indictment Rules 1971, r.4(2). See *Archbold (2002)*, para 1-135–1-146.
[82] *R. v. Rackham* [1997] 2 Cr. App. R. 222.
[83] r.9. See the leading authority *R. v. Christou* [1997] A.C. 117, [1996] Crim. L.R. 911, in which the House of Lords confirmed the discretion of the judge to order counts to be tried together. See also *R. v. Lockley and Sainsbury* [1997] Crim. L.R. 455, recognising that technical points should not prevail to nullify the whole indictment where there was a misjoinder, provided there was no possible prejudice to the accused.
[84] The trial judge has the power to sever them in the interests of justice. See r.5(3) and *R. v. Christou* [1997] A.C. 117; *Archbold (2002)*, paras 1-154-1.180. Note also the criticism in the Law Commission's Consultation Paper No. 141, *Evidence in Criminal Proceedings: Previous Misconduct of a Defendant* (1996). See Emmerson and Ashworth, (2001), p.349. For evidence that jurors are confused by joinder, see Darbyshire, Maughan and Stewart, (2001), p.973.
[85] *R. v. Assim* [1996] 2 Q.B. 249.
[86] See *Archbold (2002)*, para. 1–147; *R.v. Ruiz* [1995] Crim. L.R. 151; *R. v. Wrench* [1996] 1 Cr. App. R. 340. Once ordered to be joined, administrative errors would not alter that amendment of the indictment *R. v. Palmer* [2002] EWCA Cim. 892.
[87] See J.C. Smith, "Adding Counts to the Indictment" [1996] Crim. L.R. 889, criticising the decision in *R. v. Osieh* [1996] 2 Cr. App. R. 144 that it was permissible for a judge to add a count to the indictment which was not founded on the facts found by the examining magistrates. On the rules governing the amendment of the indictment see *Archbold (2002)*, para. 1–147. It is important that amendments to the indictment are fair to the accused by not significantly changing the nature of the prosecution case against the defendant: *R. v. O'Connor* [1997] Crim. L.R. 516. On special problems of adding and amending counts on an indictment for retrial see *R. v. Hemmings, Miller and Hoines* [2000] Crim. L.R. 56. Late amendments cause special problems: see *R. v. Piggott* [1999] 2 Cr. App. R. 320.
[88] P.399.
[89] The listing of all offences before certain levels of judge has been called into question by research suggesting that assistant recorders were more likely to pass unduly lenient sentences, see, *e.g.* Ashworth, Genders, Mansfield, Percy and Player *Sentencing in the Crown*

four classes defined in the *Practice Directions (Crown Court Business: Classification)*.[90] There are procedural and administrative guidelines as to the allocation of business within the Crown Court that are not examined here.[91]

I. HEARING IN OPEN COURT

17–020   It is regarded as essential to the administration of justice that hearings take place in open court. A public hearing protects litigants against the administration of justice occurring in secret without adequate scrutiny,[92] and reflects the importance of the interest society has in, literally, seeing that justice is fairly administered. It is endorsed by the guarantees in Article 6 and by the Strasbourg Court's jurisprudence.[93] Public trials and media reporting are essential to the administration of justice.[94] Nevertheless, there are some occasions on which either or both may be restricted,[95] and allowance for this is made in Article 6 (of the ECHR):

> "the press and public may be excluded from all or part of the trial in the interests of morals, public order, or national security in a democratic society, where the interests of juveniles or the protection of the private life of the parties so require, or to the extent strictly necessary in the opinion of the court in special circumstances where publicity would prejudice the interests of justice."[96]

Concern about the number of cases taking place out of the eye of the public became so great that a right of appeal against orders restricting or preventing reports of or restricting access to trials on indictment was introduced by section 159 of the Criminal Justice Act 1988.[97] A distinction has been recognised between the general public and the media having

---

Court (Criminoiogical Centre for Research, Oxford Occasional Paper No 10, 1984). See also Lovegrove, "The Listing of Criminal Cases in the Crown Court is an Administrative Discretion" [1984] Crim. L.R. 738.

[90] [1987] 1 W.L.R. 1671. For a criticism of the operation of the *Practice Direction* see S. Shute "Who Passes Unduly Lenient Sentences?" [1999] Crim. L.R. 603.

[91] See *Practice Direction (Crown Court: Allocation of Business)* [1995] 1 WLR 1083; *Practice Direction (Crown Court: Allocation of Business)(No. 2)* [1998] 1 W.L.R.1244; *Practice Direction (Crown Court: Allocation of Business)(No. 3)* [2001] 1 W.L.R. 203; *Practice Direction (Crown Court: Allocation of Business) (No. 4)* [2001] 1 W.L.R. 399.

[92] See *Pretto v. Italy* (1984) 6 E.H.R.R. 182, para. 21; *Riepan v. Austria*. [2001] Crim. L.R. 231.

[93] See *Werner v. Austria; Szuces v Austria* (1998) 26 E.H.R.R. 310. See generally, Emmerson and Ashworth, pp.393–403; A. Jennings in K. Starmer *et al.*, (2001), p.161. The English courts have long-accepted that criminal proceedings should occur in the presence of the accused: *R. v. Agar* (1990) 90 Cr. App.R. 318, *R. v. Preston* [1994] 2 A.C. 130.

[94] See *Attorney-General v. Leveller Magazine* [1979] A.C. 440; Art. 6(1) of the European Convention on Human Rights (emphasising the need for a "fair and public hearing" and that judgment is to "be pronounced publicly") and *Archbold (2002)*, para. 4–3, Chap. 16.

[95] On the procedure for this see Crown Court Rules 1982, r.24A. See the special measures that can be adopted in the case of vulnerable witnesses under the Youth Justice and Criminal Evidence Act 1999.

[96] See also Article 10 and Cram, "Automatic Reporting Restrictions in Criminal Proceedings and Article 10 of the ECHR" [1998] E.H.R.L.R. 742.

[97] Much of the credit for the creation of this provision is due to Tim Crook and the National Union of Journalists, see, *e.g. R. v. Central Criminal Court, ex p. Crook, The Times*, November 8, 1984. There is no right of appeal against a refusal to order a reporting restriction: *R. v. L* [2002] February 22.

unlimited access to trials. For example, it is necessary for the media to be present at an obscenity trial to report on the nature of the allegedly obscene material, but there is no such necessity for the public to be present.[98]

Both the Crown Court and the Magistrates' Courts[99] can sit *in camera* where (a) there is the possibility of disorder, (b) a witness would refuse to testify publicly, (c) the effect of a public hearing on possible future prosecutions would be too damaging.[1] In addition, there are statutory powers under the Official Secrets Act 1920 and the Children and Young Persons Act 1933 relating to the removal of the public from the courtroom.[2] As regards medial reporting, the media has a general freedom to report, subject primarily to liability for contempt of court.[3] Section 4 of the Contempt of Court Act 1981 allows for postponing reporting where that is necessary to avoid "a substantial risk of prejudice to the administration of justice". This does not extend to protecting the welfare of the accused.[4]

Three other aspects of the public nature of the criminal trial deserve attention. First, given primacy of the role of cross-examination in the English criminal trial, the courts will not allow evidence to be given from anonymous sources where that would deprive the defendant of the opportunity of examining the witness effectively.[5] There is a related problem of preserving the known witness's identity from the press and public. There exists the possibility of the witness's identity[6] being withheld from the public but not from the parties.[7] The Court of Appeal has recently confirmed a judge's power to clear the public gallery where a witness in a murder trial refused otherwise to testify.[8] Witness's addresses are not to be disclosed in

---

[98] See *Archbold (2002)*, para. 4–6.

[99] Even though s.121(4) of the Magistrates' Courts Act 1980 obliges magistrates' courts to sit in open court; see *Blackstone's Criminal Practice 2002*, paras. D2.49; D2.54; *Archbold (2002)*, para. 4–3.

[1] *Archbold (2002)*, para. 4–6.

[2] *Archbold (2002)*, paras 4.12–4.16.

[3] See *Archbold (2002)*, paras 4.17–4.28 and 28.78; C.J. Miller, *Contempt of Court* (3rd ed. 2000); S. H. Bailey, D. J. Harris and D.C. Ormerod, *Bailey Harris and Jones Civil Liberties: Cases and Materials* (5th ed., 2001), Chap. 7. Reporting is also limited by the need to comply with general rules relating to contempt of court to protect the trial from being prejudged or prejudiced and also by other statutory rules, such as s. 11 of the Contempt of Court Act 1981 on withholding of names and various provisions to protect the identity of children and victims of sexual offences. See the additional powers in the special measures under the Youth Justice and Criminal Evidence Act 1999 regarding nominated representatives of the press in certain cases (below).

[4] *R. v. Newton Abbey JJ., ex p. Belfast Telegraph Newspapers Ltd The Times*, August 27, 1197; *R. v. Sherwood ex p. The Telegraph and others* (2001) unreported, May 3, 2001.

[5] See Emmerson and Ashworth, pp.393–400; S. Enright, "The Anonymous Witness" [1996] 156 N.L.J. 1632. The procedure for permitting a witness to retain anonymity is set out in *R. v. Taylor* [1995] Crim. L.R. 253. It is essential that the defendant is not prejudiced by the anonymity. The ECHR jurisprudence is considered in *Doorson v. Netherlands* (1996) 22 E.H.R.R. 330, *Visser v. Netherlands* [2002] Crim. L.R. 495. Other examples of the need to preserve anonymity include, for example, declining to give reasons for allowing an appeal against conviction where there was an overriding public interest in protecting informants: *R. v. Doubtfire* [2001] Crim. L.R. 813.

[6] Particular difficulties might arise with pre-trial disclosure where prosecution witnesses include informers, see *R. v. Adams* [1997] Crim. L.R. 292. See further F. Davies, (1996). J.P.N. 751.

[7] See *R. v. Watford Magistrates' Court, ex p. Lenman* [1993] Crim. L.R. 388, DC, and see *R. (Al Fawaz) v. Governor of Brixton Prison* [2001] 1 W.L.R. 1234.

[8] *R. v. Richards* [1999] Crim. L.R. 764. Kitchen and R. Elliott, *Key Findings from the*

open court unless necessary for evidential reasons.[9] Secondly, the court has the power to protect the anonymity of a child or young person[10] or victims of sexual offences.[11] Thirdly, the names of judges and magistrates trying cases cannot be withheld or concealed.[12] This reflects the broader principle that the judge in a case must be seen to be impartial.

Saturation media coverage and interest in serious crimes has created significant difficulty in exceptionally high profile cases such as the killing of Jill Dando, and the retrial of Michael Stone for the murder of members of the Russell family.[13] In such cases it is difficult to ensure that the prior press coverage has not rendered a fair trial impossible.

2. THE ORDER OF PROCEEDINGS

17–021 We shall consider the proceedings at trial in some detail in this chapter and see them from the point of view of the various parties to the trial: the accused, counsel, witnesses, the judge and the jury. At the outset it is useful to set out the chronology of the trial from the first appearance of the accused until he or she leaves the court.[14]

(a) The arraignment[15]

17–022 The accused[16] is brought to the bar of the court and the indictment is read out and a plea in respect of each count is sought separately.[17] Requirements of a fair trial include an expectation that the accused will be present

---

Vulnerable Witness Survey (RDS No.147 2001) found that 11% of victims of sexual offences and intimidated witnesses had had the gallery cleared at trial; 30% more thought it would have been helpful.

[9] See the Lord Chief Justice approving the Criminal Justice Consultation Council's Trial Issues Group statement of National Standards of Witness Care in the Criminal Justice System 161 J.P.N. 353.

[10] Youth, Justice and Criminal Evidence Act 1999, s. 45 replacing CYPA 1993, s. 39. See *R v. Winchester Crown Court, ex p. B* [1999] 1 W.L.R. 788 describing the balance exercise, and see its application in *R v. St Alban's Crown Court, ex p. T* (2002), May 20, *Chief Constable of Surrey v. J.H.G.* (2002) May 20, recognising the exceptional need to take account of effects on the family.

[11] Sexual Offences (Amendment) Act 1976, Sexual Offences (Amendment) Act 1992.

[12] *R. v. Felixstowe JJ., ex p. Leigh* [1987] Q.B. 582. See also the *Resolution of the Magistrates' Association Council Relating to the Publication of Names of Justices* (1985) and *Blackstone's Criminal Practice 2001*, para. D2.55.

[13] See, *e.g. R. v. Taylor* (1994) 98 C. App. R. 361; *R. v. Stone* [2001] Crim. L.R. 465 and commentary; *R.v. Croydon Magistrates' Court, ex p. Simmons*, unreported January 26, 1996. On publicity and its effects on the jury see N. Steblay, J. Beservic, S. Fulero, B. Jiminez-Lorente, "The Effects of Pre-Trial Publicity on Jurors Verdicts: A Meta Analytical Review" (1999) 23 Law and Human Behaviour 219. The Court of Appeal in *R. v. Andrews (Tracy)* [1999] Crim. L.R. 156, sanctioned the use of questionnaires to ascertain the jury's knowledge in exceptional circumstances. See generally, D. Corker and M. Levi, "Pre-Trial Publicity and its Treatment in English Courts" [1996] Crim. L.R. 622.

[14] See also Emmins (2000), Chap. 18; D. Barnard, *The Criminal Court in Action* (4th ed., 1994).

[15] See *Archbold* (2002), para. 4–97. There are special procedures relating to serious fraud and other cases in which preparatory hearings are ordered: see the Criminal Procedure and Investigation Act 1996, s.30.

[16] For pleas by corporations see Criminal Justice Act 1925, s.33, as amended.

[17] See *R. v. C.C.C., ex p. Guney* [1996] A.C. 616

throughout the hearing unless there has been a clear and unequivocal waiver.[18] The plea may be to the "general issue", that is a plea of "guilty" or "not guilty". If a defendant fails to plead to an indictment, the court must decide whether this is due to mental or physical incapacity or whether wilful silence.[19] Alternatively, a plea of a special nature may be entered. The arraignment of an individual must occur within a reasonable time of his being committed. This is not a right recognised formally by the ECHR, but has been supported by much of the Strasbourg Court's jurisprudence on trial within a reasonable time. The present domestic scheme is regulated by the complex statutory regime in the Prosecution of Offences Act 1985.[20] The rules serve to promote the efficiency that serves both the crime control objectives, and also the due process rights of the accused who is not kept awaiting trial in custody while presumed innocent.

The arraignment is the point of the trial where issues such as double jeopardy, the jurisdiction of the court to try the accused and errors in the indictment may be raised.[21]

(i) Double jeopardy

A basic principle is that no person should be tried twice for the same offence. **17–023** Consequently "the unwarranted harassment of the accused by multiple prosecutions" is avoided.[22] The principle is established in English law[23] by the availability of the special pleas in bar: the pleas of *autrefois acquit*; of *autrefois convict*; and of pardon.[24] These pleas are rarely used in practice, because the accuracy of court records ensures that people are rarely prosecuted for the same offence twice.[25] The philosophy underlying the double jeopardy protection is encapsulated in this succinct statement:

"the State with all its resources and power should not be allowed to

---

[18] See *R. v. Hayward; R. v. Jones; R. v. Purvis* [2002] UKHL 5, where the House of Lords catalogued the relevant principles to be applied in deciding whether to try the accused in his absence. The judicial discretion to try the defendant in his absence must be exercised with great care, and fairness to the defendant was of prime importance. On the E.C.H.R. dimension to the absent defendant see *Colozza v. Italy* (1985) 7 EHRR 516 and Emmerson and Ashworth (2001), pp.400–403.

[19] See below paras 17–041–17–042.

[20] s. 22 as amended. See above para. 14-066.

[21] As will be seen in the relevant passages, these issues can also be raised at other points in the sequence of the trial. See *Archbold (2002)*, para 4–100 *et seq.*

[22] See M. L. Friedland, *Double Jeopardy* (1969), pp. 3–4.

[23] On recent developments on double jeopardy in the USA see *Hudson v. U.S.* (1997) 118 S. Ct. 488, and for detailed critique of the U.S. Supreme Court jurisprudence see A. Amar, "Double Jeopardy law made simple" (1997) 106 Yale L.J. 1807. The International Protections against Double Jeopardy are considered by Emmerson and Ashworth, (2001) Chap. 12.

[24] The possibility of similar questions arising through issue estoppel must be recognised, although such an argument is probably inapplicable to the criminal law: *DPP v. Humphrys* [1977] A.C. 1, except in habeas corpus applications: *R. v. Governor of Brixton Prison, ex p. Osman* [1991] 1 W.L.R. 281. The more likely method of raising these questions is through the inherent power of the judges to prevent oppression of an accused where there is an abuse of process. Abuse of process is a claim being considered by the courts much more frequently in recent years, see Choo, (1993), and Pattenden (1990), pp. 32–38.

[25] See Emmins (2000), pp.245–249.

make repeated attempts to convict an individual for an alleged offence thereby subjecting him to embarrassment, expense and ordeal, and compelling him to live in a continuing state of anxiety and insecurity."[26]

The significance of double jeopardy is also recognised in the ECHR, where Article 4 of Protocol 7 provides that "no one shall be liable to be tried or punished again in criminal proceedings under the jurisdiction of the same State for an offence for which he has already been finally acquitted or convicted in accordance with the law and the penal procedure of that State".[27] A derogation exists for a fundamental defect in the first trial or for new evidence coming to light.[28] As Emmerson and Ashworth observe, the root of the problem in double jeopardy is the difficulty in attaching precise weight to the "valves of accuracy and finality in the criminal justice system".[29]

The question of whether a defendant is facing a double jeopardy trial can be complex, but ultimately the question is whether the accused is "in jeopardy" of conviction for the "same offence" on more than one occasion. The concept of the "same offence" has been construed narrowly by the Court of Appeal. In *R. v. Beedie*,[30-31].

Parliament has already made inroads into the protection against double jeopardy, and there are proposals to make much more significant exceptions to the rule. The Criminal Procedure and Investigation Act 1996[32] allows for a second prosecution of an acquitted person where the accused has been convicted of an offence of witness or juror intimidation, and the court convicting the accused of that intimidation offence specifies that in its opinion there is a "real possibility" that but for such intimidation there would not have been an acquittal on the principal trial. The second prosecution for the main offence can only take place when the High Court grants an order quashing the first acquittal[33] if satisfied that it is likely that but for the interference or intimidation the accused would not have been acquitted, that it does not appear to be contrary to the interests of justice to take proceedings again, that the accused has had an opportunity to make representations to the High Court, and that the conviction for intimidation will still stand.

The Court of Appeal is empowered to order a retrial where a conviction is

---

[26] Stevens J. In the U.S. Supreme Court in *Hudson v. U.S.* (1997) 118 S.Ct. 488 at 499.

[27] See *eg. Sailer v. Austria* [2002] ECHR 382 37/97. See also Article 14 of the International Covenant on Civil and Political Rights.

[28] See *Gradringer v. Austria*, October 23, 1995, A 328-C; *Oliveira v. Switzerland* (1998–V) p.1990. See also the discussion "in Law Commission Paper No 156, *Double Jeopardy* (1999), Part III. See further Emmerson and Ashworth (2001), Chap.12.

[29] p.313.

[30-31] [1998] Q.B. 356. The Court of Appeal declined to interpret Lord Morris's statements in *Connelly*, which had been regarded as expressing the views of the majority, as requiring a broad approach to the problem. See Emmins, pp.247–248. B charged with manslaughter having been already been convicted in an earlier prosecution for a specific statutory offence brought by the Health and Safety Executive in relation to the same facts — the death of the tenant from the faulty gas fire in B's premises.

[32] ss.54–57. For consideration of their compatibility with Protocol 7 see Emmerson and Ashworth (2001), p.309.

[33] See *Archbold (2002)*, para. 4.128; *Blackstone's Criminal Practice 2002*, para. D11.41; see F. Sinclair, (1997) S.J. 538.

found to be unsafe.[34]

As regards the possibility of re-opening acquittals on new evidence, the Law Commission has recently examined the possible options for reform of the double jeopardy rule, and has finally proposed some minor amendments to the rule.[35] One significant trigger for the recent reappraisal of the rule was the Inquiry into the Murder of Stephen Lawrence.[36] The Law Commission originally proposed a number of exceptional situations in which a retrial would be allowed despite an initial acquittal: where the offence was very serious; where there was new evidence rendering the case substantially stronger that at the original trial; that it was highly probable that the jury would convict and the new evidence could not have been obtained at the time of the original trial. However, serious doubts as to the desirability of the reform on the double jeopardy rule were raised by many, including the Law Society[37] and many criminal practitioners.[38] As a result, in its Report in 2001, the Law Commission retreated from these broader original proposals and recommended only the abolition of the double jeopardy rule in relation to murder trials. This will apply retrospectively. The Law Commission recommendation is that the Court of Appeal (Criminal Division) should be empowered to quash an acquittal where reliable and compelling new evidence of the accused's guilt becomes available and a retrial would be in the interests of justice. The evidence would have to be such that the defendant was clearly guilty. The compromise position adopted by the Law Commission affecting murder only has been described as "difficult to defend either in terms of the moral culpability of the offender or in terms of the danger" which the offender poses to the public.[39]

It is important to note that the discussion in this part of the chapter has considered the position of the accused relying on his earlier acquittal to bar any future prosecution. There is, in addition, the separate issue of the prosecution use of previous *acquittals* in the criminal trial. In *R. v. Z*,[40] the House of Lords ruled that evidence of previous acquittals is admissible on behalf of the prosecution where the accused later faces charges for other conduct.[41]

---

[34] See below Chap. 17.

[35] See Law Commission Consultation Paper No. 156, *Double Jeopardy* (1999) Law Commission Report No. 267, *Double Jeopardy and Prosecution Appeals* (2001). *www.o-pen.gor.uk/lawcomm*. The original recommendation for the creation of a new statutory exception to the rule to allow a retrial where significant new evidence comes to light is reviewed by I. Dennis, "Rethinking Double Jeopardy: Justice and Finality in Criminal Process" [2000] Crim. L.R. 933.

[36] *The Stephen Lawrence Inquiry: Report of an Inquiry by Sir William Macpherson of Cluny*, Cm. 426–I (1999). See discussion by H. Kennedy Q.C. and M. Linton, *The Guardian*, July 17, 2001.

[37] Comment at (1999) 143 S.J. 201

[38] See, *e.g.* comment at (2000) 144 S.J. 201.

[39] Emmerson and Ashworth (2001), p.313.

[40] [2000] 3 W.L.R. 117, HL. On *R .v. Z* see P. Roberts, "Acquitted Misconduct Evidence" [2000] Crim. L.R. 952.

[41] *cf. Sambasivam v Public Prosecutor of Malaysia* [1950] A.C. 458.

(ii) Autrefois acquit and autrefois convict[42]

17–024   The appropriate plea, depending upon whether the accused has already been acquitted (*autrefois acquit*) or convicted (*autrefois convict*) of the same offence, or substantially the same offence, is normally made in writing before the beginning of the trial, although it may be made at any stage. There must be a valid conviction; other findings bringing proceedings to an end do not qualify. After such a plea, it is for the judge without a jury to decide whether the plea is successful.[43] The burden of proof is on the accused to establish this on the balance of probabilities.[44]

     The circumstances in which either plea will be available were explored in *Connelly v. DPP*[45] The House of Lords, mainly through the speech of Lord Morris, indicated that the pleas are not limited to circumstances where an accused has been charged with exactly the same offence arising out of the same set of circumstances. A person previously acquitted or convicted of an offence cannot be tried again for that same offence or a substantially similar offence or an offence that was a proper alternative.[46] A proper alternative offence is one of which the accused could have been found guilty at the earlier trial instead of that named in the indictment. So, for example, if Fred is acquitted of murdering Ann, he cannot later be charged with her murder, even if there is fresh evidence, nor can he be charged with her manslaughter or causing her death by reckless driving or causing her grievous bodily harm with intent. Recent decisions of the Court of Appeal have construed *Connolly* narrowly.[47] Further, if the accused has previously been acquitted of an offence that, as a matter of fact, is essential to establish guilt of the offence charged, he or she cannot be tried for that lesser offence later.[48] This can give rise to difficulties in interpreting clusters of related offences.[49]

     However, the plea of *autrefois convict* does not operate to prevent a person being tried on a charge which is more serious than the one of which he or she has originally been convicted. So, for example, if Dorothy attacks and seriously injures Michael she may be convicted of causing grievous bodily harm with intent. If Michael dies after the trial from the injuries, Dorothy may be tried for murder.[50] Note also that there is no strict rule that the Crown should not seek a third trial if the jury fails to agree on two previous occasions.[51]

---

[42] For a full treatment of the law, see *Archbold (2002)*, paras 4-116-4-163; *Blackstone's Criminal Practice 2001*, paras D11.38–48; Emmins (2000), pp. 245–49.

[43] Criminal Justice Act 1988, s.122.

[44] *R. v. Cologhan* (1976) 63 Cr. App. R. 33.

[45] [1964] A.C. 1254.

[46] The power to enter an alternative verdict is provided by the Criminal Law Act 1967, s.6, which has been widely interpreted by the House of Lords in *R. v. Wilson; R. v. Jenkins and another* [1984] A.C. 242; see *Archbold (2002)*, para. 4-455.

[47] In *R. v. Beedie* [1998] Q.B. 356, Rose L.J. quoted Lord Devlin in *Connolly* "for the doctrine to apply it must be the same offence both in fact and law".

[48] Consequently, an earlier acquittal of theft precludes a trial for robbery on the same facts, because theft is an essential element in proving robbery, see Theft Act 1968, ss.1 and 8.

[49] See, *e.g. R. v. G* [2001] Crim. L.R. 898 relating to assault and section 47 of the Offences Against the Person Act 1861.

[50] See the Law Reform (Year and A Day Rule) Act 1996.

[51] *R. v. Henworth* [2001] Crim. L.R. 505. It is not an abuse of process for a prosecution to be brought based on the same facts as those in domestic proceedings for contempt of court for a breach of an injunction: *CPS v. Tweddel* March 1, 2001 unrep.

Pardon. The plea that the accused has already been pardoned for the offence, should be entered prior to the arraignment.[52] Pardons now always follow convictions, so the plea has become obsolete.

(iii) Jurisdiction

The plea is that the court has no jurisdiction to try the accused for the relevant offence. The plea is concerned with the territorial jurisdiction of the court. The Crown Court can, as a general rule, only try crimes committed in England and Wales.[53]

17–025

(iv) Errors in the indictment

There are many technical rules about the drafting of indictments, primarily concerned with the requirements that indictments must be (a) positive and (b) not duplicitous. The rules are discussed in the works on criminal procedure.[54] Such errors as perceived by the accused may be raised for consideration through a number of avenues, but primarily by applying to the judge to quash the indictment[55] by an abuse of process claim. These are not technically pleas as such. It is also possible at this stage to challenge a criminal charge by asserting that the legislation under which the offence is charged is *ultra vires*. This need not be entered as a formal plea.[56]

17–026

It is most unlikely that the almost obsolete demurrer will be used to object to the wording of the indictment.[57]

(v) Abuse of process

Although not technically a plea in bar, it is worth considering at this stage the motion to stay proceedings for an abuse of process[58] which has the same effect if pleaded successfully. This is an area in which the law has developed rapidly in recent years. The court has an inherent jurisdiction to prevent its own process being abused.[59] The trial judge in a criminal case does not have the responsibility for instituting a prosecution, nor to prevent one being

17–027

---

[52] See *Archbold (2002)*, paras 4-16–4-163; *Blackstone's Criminal Practice 2002*, para. D10.51. For recent consideration of the prospective pardons see *Attorney-General of Trinidad and Tobago v. Phillip* [1995] 1 A.C. 396, PC. See also on the full extent of the pardon, *R. v. Secretary of State for the Home Department, ex p. Bentley* [1994] Q.B. 439, DC. See the powers of the Criminal Cases Review Commission discussed below, para. 18-018.

[53] See *Archbold (2002)*, para. 4–111; *Blackstone's Criminal Practice 2001*, para. D1.73 *et seq.*

[54] *Archbold (2002)*, paras 1–108–1–197; *Blackstone's Criminal Practice (2001)*, D10. For a recent review see S. O'Doherty, (1999) 163 J.P.N. 663.

[55] As to a motion to quash the indictment and the errors that may be raised, see *Archbold (2002)*, paras 1–236-1–241; *Blackstone's Criminal Practice 2001*, para. D10.39; *Emmins (2000)*, Chap. 6.

[56] See *Boddington v. British Transport Police* [1998] 2 All E.R. 210.

[57] *Archbold (2002)*, para. 4–99.

[58] See Choo, *Abuse of Process and Judicial Stay of Proceedings* (1993).

[59] See *Connelly v. DPP* [1964] A.C. 254; *DPP v. Humphreys* [1977] AC 1; *R. v. Horseferry Road Magistrates' Court, ex p. Bennett* [1994] 1 A.C. 42; *R. v. Derby Crown Court, ex p. B* [1996] AC 487; *R. v. Mullen* [1999] 2 Cr.App. R. 143.

brought which is in his opinion undesirable, but he has the power to stay proceedings if they constitute an abuse of process. The accused who seeks a stay must prove, on the balance of probabilities, that it is either impossible for him to receive a fair trial, or that it would be unfair to try him. The usual basis of the claim is that the prosecution has manipulated the process or misused the powers of the court,[60] reneged on a promise to the accused's detriment,[61] contributed to the commission of the offence,[62] or there has been excessive delay.[63] The power to stay for abuse is a broad power, but it is vital that the courts have that power to maintain the integrity of the criminal justice process, and ensure that the executive action is conducted within the rule of law. The discretion is to be exercised sparingly because there is a very strong public interest in people who are alleged to have committed crimes facing trial.[64] There remains scope for the development of the abuse of process doctrine.[65] Specific guidance on the procedure to be adopted in making a claim of abuse is contained in the *Practice Direction: (Crown Court: Abuse of Process)*.[66]

(b) The empanelling and swearing of the jury

17–028   If a plea of not guilty is entered, a jury of twelve people will be empanelled and, after an opportunity for challenges, sworn. The indictment will be read to the jury that will be told of its obligation to listen to the evidence and to determine guilt or innocence. The precise order in which speeches are delivered will depend on whether the accused is represented and whether he

---

[60]   See, *e.g. R. v. Dean* [1998] 2 Cr App. R. 177.

[61]   On prosecutors reneging on promises not to prosecute see also *R. v. Townsend, Dearsley and Bretscher* [1998] Crim. L.R. 126; *R. v. Thomas* [1995] Crim. L.R. 938; *R.v. Bloomfield* [1997] 1 Cr. App. R. 135; *R.v. Drury* [2001] Crim. L.R. 847.

[62]   It is for the trial judge, in the exercise of his discretion, to decide whether there had been an abuse of process which amounted to an affront to the public conscience and thereby required proceedings to be stayed: *Latif and Shahzad*, [1996] Crim. L.R. 414 HL. See also *R.v. Mullen (No.2)* [1999] 3 W.L.R. 777; *R.v. Hardwicke and Thwaites* [2001] Crim. L.R. 220.

[63]   There have been prosecutions after a delay of 33 years (*R. v. King* [1997] Crim. L.R. 298) and 56 years (*R. v. Sawoniuk* [2000] Crim. L.R. 456). For an argument that the Human Rights Act 1998 created a new right to a fair trial within a reasonable time as an independent right, see A. Webster, "Delay and Article 6(1): an End to the Requirement of Prejudice?" [2001] Crim. L.R. 786, considering whether a stay of proceedings in such cases depends on serious prejudice from the delay. A delay of five years and one month was held not to be oppressive: *R. v. James* [2002] twCA Crim. 1119. See also *Procurator Fiscal v. Watson* [2002] UK PC19.

[64]   *R. v. B* [1996] Crim. L.R. 406. (19-year delay). On the need for the trial judge to warn the jury about difficulties in cases of delay which are not see *R. v. J* [1997] Crim. L.R. 297 and *R. v. Jenkins* [1998] Crim. L.R. 411 (30 years).

[65]   One is the issue of detrimental reliance, which really involves two issues: (i) is detrimental reliance necessary, and (ii) what constitutes sufficient detriment. Practically all early cases, although involving different types of representation being made by the prosecution, have resulted in the defendant altering his position to his detriment. For example by providing the police with self-incriminating evidence (*R. v. Croydon JJ., ex p. Dean* [1993] Crim. L.R 759., and see Lord Oliver in *ex p. Bennett* [1994] A.C. 42 at 70); pleading to a lesser charge (*R. v. Thomas* [1995] Crim. L.R. 938); pleading on the basis of a sentencing indication (*Peverett* [2001] Crim. L.R. 60); pleading to some charges so that others are dropped (*Edgar v. DPP* (2000) 164 J.P. 471); and being prejudiced by disclosure to a co-accused (*Townsend, Dearnsley and Bretscher* [1997] 2 Cr. App. R. 540). The striking anomaly is *Bloomfield* (1997) 1 Cr. App. R.135 where the defendant suffered no detriment.

[66]   [2000] 1 W.L.R. 1322. Written notice is required and skeleton arguments are to contain the relevant propositions and all authorities.

chooses to testify. The order is set out clearly in the Table of Order of Speeches in *Archbold*.[67]

The Auld Report makes several recommendations that would have significant impact on the way the trial proceeds, including the introduction of a detailed speech initial judicial address to the jury and a defence advocate's opening address.[68]

(c) The opening speech[69]

Counsel for the prosecution addresses the jury. The function of the opening is to explain to the jury the basic elements of the prosecution case, the evidence that is to be called and the burden and standard of proof. Even allowing for the fact that any mistakes may ultimately be corrected by the judge in the summing-up, it is vital that prosecution counsel does not claim more than can be proved for it may eventually be difficult for the jury to remember whether allegations made in the speech were actually substantiated by the evidence.[70] Equally counsel must not refer to any evidence that is inadmissible,[71] or which defending counsel has indicated will be challenged as inadmissible. Counsel should avoid using emotive language that is likely to prejudice the jury against the accused.

17–029

(d) The prosecution case

Witnesses called by the prosecution give their evidence in turn (examination-in-chief) and may be subjected to questioning by the defence (cross-examination).[72] Counsel for the prosecution may have the final word with each witness (re-examination) but must ask questions only on matters raised in the course of cross-examination. The way in which and the sort of questions counsel asks and whether evidence is admissible are both decided upon by the judge alone.[73]

17–030

(e) Defence submission of no case to answer

At the close of the prosecution case the defence may ask the trial judge to direct the jury to acquit the accused because there is no case to answer.[74] The power is used sparingly, but a failure properly to halt a case on a

---

[67] (2001), para 4–304.

[68] pp.518–524.

[69] See *Archbold (2002)*, para. 4–268.

[70] A particular example of the dangers is to be found in the trial of James Hanratty, where a vital piece of evidence was referred to in the opening speech but never proved in evidence; see L. Blom-Cooper, *The A6 Murder*. In any event, it may be tactically more sensible to pitch the opening on a relatively low key lest the jury should later be disappointed with the prosecution witnesses.

[71] The opening of such evidence will not automatically lead to the quashing of a subsequent conviction: *R. v. Jackson* [1953] 1 W.L.R. 591. The normal course would be for the judge to discharge the jury and recommence the trial if the defendant has been seriously prejudiced.

[72] For the special rules restricting the accused's right to cross-examine witnesses in person, see below, para. 17-037.

[73] See para. 17-063 and paras 17-065–17-068.

[74] See *R. v. Galbraith* (1980) 73 Cr. App. R. 124; *R. v. Shippey* [1988] Crim. L.R. 767; *Archbold (2002)*, para. 4-295.

submission can constitute an abuse of process.[75] If this submission is accepted, the trial ends and the accused is acquitted. This submission and the judge's deliberation on the matter occur in the absence of the jury. If the submission fails the trial continues, and no reference to the submission should be made in the presence of the jury. If at the conclusion of the evidence, the trial judge is of the opinion that no reasonable jury properly directed could safely convict, he should raise the matter with counsel, even if no submission of no case to answer had been made.[76] It is possible to halt the trial on the same basis at any point after the submission.[77]

(f) Defence opening speech

17–031   Defence counsel is only entitled to make an opening speech to the jury if at least one witness (other than the accused) is to be called as to the *facts* of the case. Otherwise, counsel must simply start to call evidence.[78]

(g) The defence case

Witnesses called by the defence are examined. If the accused is called as a witness he or she should be the first defence witness so that he gives his testimony before hearing that of all the other witnesses.[79] They may be cross-examined by prosecution counsel and re-examined by defence counsel. The defence may again raise a submission of no case to answer.[80]

(h) Re-opening

17–032   In an exceptional case the prosecution will be allowed to re-open the case to rebut matters that have arisen. This should arise only where the evidence could not have been foreseen as likely to arise, or where evidence unexpectedly becomes available to the prosecution after the close of its case or the evidence is of a formal nature and has been inadvertently omitted from the prosecution case. Similarly, the defence may in an exceptional case be allowed to re-open its case if new material comes to light. It is worth noting at this point that, theoretically at least, the judge has the power to call a witness of his own accord. This is an exceedingly rarely exercised power. A witness so called may be cross-examined by both parties with leave of the judge.[81] There are cogent proposals for this power to be exercised more frequently, provided it is commensurate with the judge remaining impartial and being seen to be such.

Auld recommends that a discussions between counsel and the judge should occur at this point in the trial so as to "take stock" and ensure that the material for the summing up is clear.[82]

---

[75]   *R. v. Smith* [2000] 1 All E.R. 263.
[76]   This was more desirable than the practice of judges writing to the Court of Appeal expressing concern at the verdict of a jury: *R. v. Brown (Jamie)* [1998] Crim. L.R. 196.
[77]   See *R. v. Brown (Davina)* [2001] Crim.L.R.675.
[78]   See the Criminal Evidence Act 1898, s.2.
[79]   See PACE, s.79.
[80]   *R. v. Anderson, The Independent*, July 3, 1998.
[81]   *R. v. Roberts* (1984) 80 Cr. App. R. 89; *R.v. Aylesbury Crown Court, ex p. Lait* [1999] C.L.Y. 990.
[82]   pp. 529–531.

(i) Closing speeches

Both counsel may address the jury at the close of the evidence. The **17–033**
prosecution goes first and the defence has the last word.[83] In the closing
speech prosecution counsel may review the evidence and emphasise alleged
strengths in the prosecution case and weaknesses in the defence. The length
of the speeches is a matter for judicial discretion.[84] Neither counsel should
refer to matters that have not been adduced in evidence. The jury is likely to
be reminded once again of the burden and standard of proof.

(j) The summing-up[85]

The trial judge must sum up the evidence to the jury, directing it as to the
law and explaining its function. It is usual for the judge to discuss with
counsel, in the absence of the jury, the proposed content of his summing-up
before delivering it. The value of this exercise has become crucial in relation
to a number of offences in particular. In all cases it has the potential to
clarify the issues for the summing-up which should therefore render the
summing-up more helpful for the jury, and it should serve to prevent
unmeritorious appeals on the minutae of the summing-up.

   The summing-up must contain a direction on the burden and standard of
proof, a review of the facts and should provide adequate guidance on the
elements of the offence. The judge will adopt standard "specimen
directions" issued by the Judicial Studies Board.[86]

(k) The verdict

The jury retires to consider its verdict. The jury remain together in the **17–034**
custody of the bailiff in the court precincts. The jury is incommunicado
except for essential communications from the jury bailiff. Only very
exceptionally is evidence admitted after the retirement of the jury. A
unanimous verdict is the first objective, but a majority verdict may
eventually be acceptable. The verdict of the jury is announced by the
person known as the "foreman" in open court.

(l) Information for sentencing

Since not all the necessary information is provided during the trial to enable **17–035**
an appropriate sentence to be imposed, after conviction an information
gathering exercise is often undertaken, which includes the possibility of a
plea in mitigation being made by either defence counsel or the accused in
person.

---

[83] On the content appropriate of the defence closing see *R. v. Tuegel* [2000] 2 Cr.App. R. 361.
[84] *R. v. Haggard* [1995] Crim. L.R. 347.
[85] See the Auld Report, pp. 532–538.
[86] See *www.jsboard.org.uk*.

(m) Sentence

The judge passes sentence on the accused.

(n) Appeal

17–036   The defendant can appeal against conviction and/or sentence with the leave of the judge or of the Court of Appeal. The prosecution can, in exceptional cases, appeal against what it considers to be an unduly lenient sentence. The Law Commission has recently proposed that an appeal against a ruling by a judge which has the effect of terminating proceedings should be available for the prosecution.[87] The rulings in question include: rulings in advance of trial; a ruling made during the prosecution case; a ruling at the close of the prosecution case regarding a submission of no case to answer. The appeal will only be available if the case is one in which had the accused been convicted, the Attorney-General could have referred the sentence to the Court of Appeal as being unduly lenient. The procedures for appeals are considered below in Chapter. 18. The defendant may further pursue an unsuccessful appeal via the Criminal Cases Review Commission. Appeals from either party from decisions of the Court of Appeal or the Divisional Court lie to the House of Lords subject to leave and strict compliance with procedures.

3. THE ACCUSED

17–037   Historically, the accused laboured under a considerable disadvantage in the criminal trial. The Criminal Law Revision Committee, considering the rules of evidence in criminal cases, identified the following difficulties that had hindered the accused[88]:

(i) The "indecent haste" with which trials were conducted, in a potentially unfair manner.[89] Representation, legal aid and judicial unwillingness to curtail trials now ensure that there are few complaints of brevity. If anything now, the complaint is that trials go on too long.[90]

(ii) Legal representation was severely restricted before 1836.[91] The arrival

---

[87] See Law Commission Report No 267, *Double Jeopardy and Prosecution Appeals* (2000).

[88] Criminal Law Revision Committee, *Eleventh Report, Evidence (General)* (Cmnd. 4991, 1972), pp. 10–12. The recommendations of this comprehensive yet controversial report were implemented in part by PACE and by the Criminal Justice and Public Order Act 1994.

[89] Mr Justice Hawkins described one 1840s Old Bailey Trial which lasted two minutes 53 seconds as "a high example of expedition", and stated that trials after dinner lasted on average four minutes: Hawkins, *Memoirs*, cited in the CLRC 11th Report (1972), p. 11.

[90] The length of fraud trials is a particular concern, see Law Commission, Consultation Paper No. 155, *Fraud and Dishonesty* (1999).

[91] Prior to the Trials for Felony Act 1836, the defence counsel in felony trials was limited to arguments on points of law and giving advice to the defendant on how he or she should conduct his or her case. See on the historical aspects of counsel's obligations J. H. Langbein, *The Prosecutorial Origins of Defence Counsel in the Eighteenth Century: The Appearance of Solicitors* (1999) C.L.J. 314 tracing use of defence counsel to 1730 and earlier for treason, as

of legal aid has ensured representation in at least all serious cases, although the accused may occasionally still be unrepresented.[92]

(iii) The accused was not permitted to give evidence on oath in all cases. The Criminal Evidence Act 1898 provided the accused with this right in all cases.[93]

(vi) There was only rarely a right to appeal against conviction. A general right of appeal was provided by the Criminal Appeal Act 1907.[94] There is now also the opportunity to pursue a failed appeal via the Criminal Cases Review Commission.

Since all these obstacles to a fair trial have been removed, and, according to the CLRC, because of the improved quality of juries and magistrates, it has been suggested that the accused is in a very strong position in the criminal trial.[95] This view has not been accepted by all commentators. McBarnet,[96] on completion of a critical examination of the criminal justice system, concluded that the "process of conviction is easier than the rhetoric of justice would have us expect — and easier still the lower the status of the defendant".[97] Whilst the law appears to provide considerable protection for the accused, there are many exceptions, which reduce the protection in reality. At the time she was writing, McBarnet was able to point to the fact that the actual operation of the right to silence does not guarantee that the accused need not incriminate himself or herself; and whilst there is in many cases a formal right to jury trial, the vast majority of cases are tried without a jury.[98] Since then the right to silence has been substantially diminished, and other changes have meant that even the rhetoric of justice is viewed by many commentators as less convincing.[99]

The implementation of the Human Rights Act 1998 and the greater reliance on the ECHR jurisprudence have reinvigorated the debate about the accused's position in the English criminal trial. As noted, at the same time as the fundamental guarantees of Article 6 are being endorsed in domestic courts, parliamentary reforms of the criminal trial process continue to be driven by efficiency and by concerns about the ordeal of the witnesses in the trial. The protections for the accused in the criminal trial are rarely strengthened or endorsed in new legislation.

The first procedural question relating to the attendance of the accused concerns the attendance at the Crown Court.[1] There is a fundamental

---

a result of judicial practice/discretion, some resistance, especially where no points of law arose. This also removed any chance of inquisitorial responsibility on tribunal to investigate for itself.

[92] As to the availability of legal aid, see above, para. 14-087. See criticisms of Sanders and Young (2000), pp. 489-505.

[93] The accused could only make an unsworn statement from the dock, which would carry little credibility with the jury: see M. Cohen, "The Unsworn Statement from the Dock" [1981] Crim. L.R. 224.

[94] As to criminal appeals, see Chap. 18, below.

[95] CLRC Eleventh Report (1972), pp. 10–12.

[96] D. J. McBarnet, *Conviction: Law, the State and the Construction of Justice* (1981).

[97] *ibid.* p. 155.

[98] *ibid.* pp. 154–155.

[99] See, *e.g.* Sanders and Young (2000) Chap. 1 and below, Part C.

[1] The procedures for conducting pre-trial hearings in the absence of the accused are

requirement to a fair trial. If in custody, the accused is brought to court from prison; if on bail, the accused is informed of the time and date of the trial and told to attend. The accused *must* attend court so as to answer in person when the indictment is put, because no one else may enter a plea.[2] Whilst needing to be present at the arraignment, the accused may be absent for the trial, although that will happen only in exceptional cases, because the accused needs to be present in order to "hear the case against him and have the opportunity ... of answering it".[3] This important safeguard of requiring the physical presence of the accused is echoed in Article 6 of the ECHR, which, implies a right to be present to participate in the proceedings.[4] The defendant may waive his right by conduct or failing to attend.[5] Such cases include those where the accused is violent or disorderly,[6] is ill,[7] absconds from the trial,[8] or remains absent having informed the court of his belief that no fair trial would occur.[9]

The Court of Appeal has recently reaffirmed the principles dictating when a trial can occur in the absence of the accused.[10] A defendant has a general right to attend and be represented, but those rights can be waived wholly or in part. The decision to proceed in the absence of a defendant (or his legal representatives) falls within the discretion of the trial judge. That discretion is to be used in rare and exceptional cases, particularly if the defendant is unrepresented. In exercising the discretion the judge must consider fairness to both defence and prosecution and all the relevant circumstances, especially: whether the absence is voluntary; whether an adjournment might be appropriate or sufficient to deal with the problem; the likely length of any adjournment; whether there is an unequivocal waiver of the right to representation; whether instructions could still be proffered; the potential

considered in Chap. 13 above.

[2] *R. v. Heyes* [1951] 1 K.B. 29 and see *Archbold (2002)*, para. 3–197. In some circumstances, the failure of the accused to plead personally to the indictment results in a mistrial: *R. v. Boyle* [1954] 2 Q.B. 292; *R. v. Ellis* (1973) 57 Cr. App. R. 571. However, if the trial had proceeded as though a "not guilty" plea had been recorded no material irregularity had necessarily occurred: *R. v. Williams* [1978] Q.B. 373 and see *Archbold (2002)*, para. 4–98. As to the position in summary trials, see para. 17-006. above. The parents of child defendants will also be required to attend: see Children and Young Persons Act 1933, s. 34A.

[3] *R.v. Lee Kun* (1916) 11 Cr. App. R. 293, 300, *per* Lord Reading. See *Archbold (2002)*, para. 3–197; *R. v. Howson* (1982) 74 Cr. App. R. 172; and G. Zellick, "The Criminal Trial and the Disruptive Defendant" (1980) 43 M.L.R. 121 at 284.

[4] See *Ekbatani v. Sweden* (1991) 13 E.H.R.R. 504, para. 25. See also A. Jennings in K. Starmer *et al.*, (2001), pp. 162–165.

[5] See, *e.g. Colozza v. Italy* (1985) 7 E.H.R.R. 516.

[6] See *Archbold (2002)*, para. 3–200a. It is possible to handcuff or restrain an accused, but only if there is a danger of escape or violence, and whether such restraint is justified should be investigated in court without the jury, see *R. v. Vratsides* [1988] Crim. L.R. 251; *R. v. Rollinson* (1997) 161 J.P. 107. See also *R. v. Berry* (1897) 104 L. T. Journ. 110, where the accused performed an impromptu striptease on the clerk's table. On the use of handcuffs see *R. v. Mullen* [2000] Crim. L.R. 873 accepting that the potential prejudice to the accused of his being seen in handcuffs is ameliorated by a suitable warning to the jury from the judge.

[7] *R. v. Pearson, The Independent,* February 25, (1998); *R.v. Orton* (1873), cited in *Archbold (2002)*, para. 3–200b; *R. v. Howson* (1981) 74 Cr. App. R. 172, where it was indicated that the discretion must not be exercised if the accused's defence could be prejudiced by his or her absence.

[8] *R. v. Jones (No. 2)* [1972] 1 W.L.R. 887; *R.v. Charles and Tucker* [2001] Crim. L.R. 732 and commentary; [2001] 2 Cr. App. R. 209; *Archbold (2002)*, para. 3–199.

[9] *R. v. Donnelly* [1998] Crim. L.R. 1311, CA.

[10] See *R. v. Hayward* [2001] Q.B. 862.

disadvantage to the defendant in continuing; the seriousness of the offence charged; the risk of the jury reaching an improper conclusion from speculating about the defendant's absence; the general public interest, the interest of the victims and the witnesses; and the undesirability, in joint trials, of severing trials.

Note that the prosecution can, with the agreement of the defence, and the court,[11] offer no evidence against the accused in his absence. An accused who is likely to intimidate a witness may be removed from the presence of the witness, but not out of hearing.[12]

The problem of whether the accused has a right to "confront his accuser" remains a problem for the English courts.[13-14] The most acute difficulties have arisen in relation to vulnerable witnesses, particularly child sexual abuse victims who are in fear of seeing the alleged abuser in person. The law's response has been to prevent the accused from cross-examining the witness directly, thereby reducing the degree of confrontation, and by allowing witnesses to give evidence by live link, from behind screens and in the most serious cases by video-recorded testimony under the special measures provisions of the Youth Justice and Criminal Evidence Act 1999.[15] Whether the inability visually to confront an accuser inhibits the accused from having a fair trial in any meaningful sense is doubtful.

The second procedural question relates to the accused's response on arraignment after the indictment has been read. The accused is required to answer to every count on the indictment and each plea will be recorded. In the great majority of cases the plea will be "guilty" or "not guilty", although there are several other possibilities.[16]

It is worth noting that the prosecution does not always have to proceed to trial but could (a) offer no evidence or (b) let counts lie on the file.[17]

There are other procedural matters concerning the accused as well as his or her attendance and arraignment, particularly the extent to which character and antecedents can be referred to, the extent to which inferences can be drawn from silence and the extent to which the credibility of prosecution witnesses can be attacked. These matters are dealt with in discussing the roles of other participants in the trial.

---

[11] See the Auld Report (2001) recommendation that the prosecution should be able to drop the case without the consent of either at any stage before the end of the prosecution case. Recommendation No 171.

[12] *R. v. Smellie* (1919) 14 Cr. App. R. 128. As to the statutory extension of this power in relation to the use of live television links, especially in child abuse cases, see para. 17-060 below. See J. Spencer and Flin, *The Evidence of Children* (1993).

[13-14] *Cf.* U.S. Constitution Amdt. VI. Note Article 6 requirements that the defence have the right to examine witnesses. See A. Jennings in K. Starmer *et al* (2001), pp.168,- and M. Strange in K. Starmer *et al* (2001), p.191.

[15] ss.16–35. See L. Hoyano, "Variations on a Theme by Pigot: Special Measures Directions for Child Witnesses" [2000] Crim. L.R. 250; D. Birch, "A Better Deal for Vulnerable Witnesses" [2000] Crim. L.R. 223; L. Hoyano, "Striking a Balance Between the Rights of Defendants and Vulnerable Witnesses:Will Special Measures Contravene Guarantees of a Fair Trial" [2001] Crim. L.R. 948.

[16] See para. 17-024, above.

[17] See *Archbold (2002)*, paras 4–188–4–191; Blackstone's *Criminal Practice 2002*, paras D11.26 and D11.27.

(a) The plea of guilty[18]

17–038   The defendant's acknowledgment of guilt must be unmistakable. It must be made freely by the accused in person, who must have knowledge of the elements of the offence.[19] The accused must not be under undue pressure from counsel or the court. A plea entered under the threat of withdrawal of legal representation would, for example, vitiate the plea.[20] It is quite proper for defence counsel to advise the accused, perhaps in very forceful terms, that a plea of guilty could be advantageous in securing a lesser sentence and/ or that the evidence seems to point strongly to guilt. Counsel must also stress that a guilty plea should only be entered if the accused has actually committed the alleged offence.[21]

Plea bargaining

17–039   The importance attached to the accused's freedom to enter the plea desired is reflected in the "plea bargaining" cases where it was suspected that unfair pressure had been placed on the accused.[22] "Plea bargaining ... describes the practice whereby the accused enters a plea of guilty in return for which he will be given some consideration that results in a sentence concession."[23] There are a number of ways in which this problem arises.

The first method can be accurately described as charge bargaining: a plea arrangement made between prosecution and defence counsel whereby a plea of guilty to a lesser charge on the indictment is accepted in return for the prosecution not proceeding with the more serious charge(s).[24] The second

---

[18] The proportion of defendants pleading guilty in the Crown Court in 2000 varied from 31% for sexual offences to 73% for burglary and 91% for summary offences (*Criminal Statistics for England and Wales*, (2001), para. 6.25).

[19] *R. v. Golathan* (1915) 11 Cr. App. R. 79; *Archbold (2002)*, para. 4–104. For the dangers of pleas entered by counsel, see *R .v. Ellis* (1973) 57 Cr. App. Rep. 571.

[20] *R. v. Smith and Bleaney* [1999] 6 Arch. News, 1.

[21] See *Blackstone's Criminal Practice 2002*, para. D11.34 on involuntary pleas and see below, para. 17-052 on the obligations of defence counsel. See also the Bar Council Standards, para 12.1–12.5.3.

[22] The particular pressure that gives rise to concern is where it appears to the accused that the judge has indicated to counsel that an unsuccessful plea of not guilty will attract a heavier sentence: *R. v. Turner* [1970] 2 Q.B. 321, see para. 17-064, below.

[23] J. Baldwin and M. McConville, *Negotiated Justice* (1977), p. 19. This early research study is a prerequisite for any detailed study of the subject of plea bargaining. See also, P. Thomas, "Plea Bargaining and the *Turner* Case" [1970] Crim. L.R. 559; A. Davis, "Sentences for Sale: A New Look at Plea Bargaining in England and America" [1970] Crim. L.R. 150 and 218; R. Purves, "That Plea-Bargaining Business" [1971] Crim. L.R. 470; S. McCabe and R. Purves, *By-Passing the Jury* (1972); Bottoms and McLean (1976); J. Baldwin and M. McConville, "Plea Bargaining: Legal Carve-Up or Legal Cover-Up" (1978) 5 B.J.L.S. 228, "Plea Bargaining and the Court of Appeal" (1979) 6 B.J.L.S. 200, "The Influence of the Sentencing Discount in Inducing Guilty Pleas" in J. Baldwin and A. K. Bottomley (eds), *Criminal Justice: Selected Readings*, "Preserving the Good Face of Justice: Some Recent Plea Bargain Cases" (1978) 128 N.L.J. 872, and *Court, Prosecution and Conviction* (1981); S. Moody and J. Tombs, "Plea Negotiations and Scotland" [1983] Crim. L.R. 297; S. Moody and J. Tombs, *Prosecution in the Public Interest* (1982); Wasik, Gibbons and Redmayne (1999), pp.375–388; M.McConville, "Plea Bargaining, Ethics and Politics" (1998) 25 J. Law and Soc. 562; G. Fisher, "Plea Bargaining's Triumph" (2000) Yale L.J. 857; J. Morton, "Behind Closed Doors" (2000) 150 N.L.J. 1843; Sanders and Young (2000), p. 441 *et seq*.

[24] See para. 17-048, below. See *Archbold*, (2001), para. 4–107.

method by which the sentence concession is obtained is a plea of guilty to the offence charged. A guilty plea attracts a lighter sentence.[25] The amount of discount can be substantial.[26] In some cases the discount will operate not only to reduce the severity of a particular form of sentence but also to alter the type of sentence from, for example, custodial to non-custodial. The prosecution are not obliged to accept a plea of guilty to a lesser alternative offence. If the prosecution do reject such a plea, the prosecution can call evidence of it in the trial.[27]

The value of a guilty plea in the criminal process is that it reduces the time and money spent on achieving convictions, it obviates the need for a trial and the inherent difficulties of proof, it spares the witnesses an experience which can be both unpleasant and distressing,[28] and it is alleged to demonstrate an attitude of contrition and remorse on the part of the accused. The advantages to the prosecution of offering concessions or inducements to persuade the accused to plead guilty are the certainty and economy thereby secured. These advantages must be balanced against the need to ensure that offenders are convicted of offences only when they are actually guilty and which properly represent the seriousness of their behaviour.[29] The danger of the accused pleading guilty under pressure to obtain the maximum sentencing discount or failing to make a free informed decision about his plea should not be underestimated.

The dangers associated with the sentence discount which increase the possibility of innocent people pleading guilty are well established:

"[The sentencing discount], by encouraging defendants to convict themselves through a guilty plea, [reduces the effect of the due process] principle that the burden of proof rests on the prosecution. The prosecution of cases involving no more than vague allegations and other potential misuses of state prosecutorial power may be left unchecked. Moreover, the high guilty plea rate to which the sentence discount contributes means that there is little incentive for the prosecuting authorities to ensure that only properly prepared cases are brought to trial. ... A further problem is that the discount principle penalises those who stand on their right to put the prosecution to proof."[30]

The *Criminal Statistics for England and Wales* 2000 reveal that 76 per cent of those who pleaded not guilty were given immediate custody on conviction whereas only 64 per cent of those pleading guilty were, on conviction given immediate custody. In addition, the average sentence length for a not guilty plea resulting in conviction was 39 months compared with 24 months

---

[25] See D. A. Thomas, *Current Sentencing Practice*, and *R.v. Cain* [1976] Q.B. 496.

[26] Archbold (2000), para. 5-155, suggests that the extent of the reduction is between one fifth and one third of what would otherwise have been the sentence, and see *Blackstone's Criminal Practice 2001*, para. El.18. The discount now has statutory recognition: Powers of Criminal Courts (Sentencing) Act 2000, s.152.

[27] See *R. v. Hazeltine* [1967] 2 Q.B. 857.

[28] This may be a particularly significant factor where the charges include sexual offences: *R. v. Grice* (1977) 66 Cr. App. R. 167.

[29] See below, paras 17-047–17-050 for the obligations of prosecuting counsel. See also the Bar Council guidelines.

[30] Sanders and Young (2000), pp. 427-28.

following a guilty plea.[31]

For the truly guilty defendant and the prosecution, a plea bargain represents a mutually beneficial compromise. A guilty plea is obtained and so is a sentence concession. However, these concessions also operate (intentionally) as inducements and create enormous pressure on the accused who is at his/her most vulnerable in facing this most difficult of decisions in the criminal process. There are, significant problems both with charge-bargaining and with the sentence discount.

The Attorney-General has issued guidelines regarding the acceptance of pleas by the prosecution. These draw attention to the overriding principle that justice must be conducted in public except in exceptional circumstances. When prosecutors accept pleas or reduce charges they should be prepared to explain their reasons in open court. Full records should be kept of discussions in chambers.[32]

Although the early research of McCabe and Purves suggested that the guilty pleas obtained were justified in the light of the evidence and the benefit to the criminal justice system,[33] subsequent research has largely demonstrated that defendants' changes of plea, especially when late, are contrary to the actual wishes of the accused, being based upon the advice of the lawyers,[34] resulting in the supposed imprisonment of innocent people.[35] Having noted the inability of the judiciary to control this problem, Sanders and Young conclude that charge bargaining has the "potential to undermine adversarial due process and to increase the risk that innocent persons will plead guilty".[36] They point out that in 1993 the Royal Commission on Criminal Justice merely stated that it could "see no objection to such discussions, but the earlier they take place the better; consultation between counsel before the trial would often avoid the need for the case to be listed as a contested trial".[37] The concern of the Commission was with the wastage of resources of the "cracked trial", that is the trial which was believed to be contested, but at which the accused pleads guilty.[38]

If a guilty plea is made in error by the accused, it may be withdrawn, and the trial judge may permit, at his discretion, a change of plea at any time before sentence.[39]

---

[31] *Criminal Statistics* (2001), para. 7.23
[32] *Attorney-General's Guidelines on the Acceptance of Pleas* [2001] 1 Cr. App. R. 28.
[33] S. McCabe and R. Purves, *By-passing the Jury* (1972) and see Sanders' and Young (2000), p. 466.
[34] See below, paras 17-048 and 17-052 and as to the role of the lawyers.
[35] A. Bottoms and J. McClean, *Defendants in the Criminal Process* (1976) and J. Baldwin and M. McConville, *Negotiated Justice* (1977). However, the Crown Court Survey discovered that few innocent people were persuaded to plead guilty; see M. Zander and P. Henderson (1993), pp. 96–98.
[36] Sanders and Young (2000), p. 480.
[37] RCCJ, Report (1993), p. 114.
[38] In fact not all parties are disappointed; the CPS, whilst recognising the resources wastage, also appreciated the guilty plea, especially when the prosecution was not convinced that it would get a conviction: Zander and Henderson (1993), p. 156. These cracked trials are extremely common, with around 16,500 in 1999: Sanders and Young (2000), p.396.
[39] *S (an infant) v. Manchester Recorder* [1971] A.C. 481. Late changes of plea may well be made when the accused indicates that his or her original plea was made as a result of threats, See, *e.g. R. v. Dodd, Pack and others* (1982) 74 Cr.App.R. 50. Where the allegation of the threat was that it was made when the accused was represented by counsel, it is unlikely that the change of plea will be allowed.

The Auld Report also considered the merits of the existing practice of charge-bargaining, and recommends that the prosecution should only be able to amend the charge laid up until the time of the pre-trial assessment and thereafter only with the court's permission. The recommendations also included a greater responsibility on the CPS for accurate charging.[40] It was found that 23 per cent of all indictments had to be amended before trial.[41] In addition, the Report suggests the introduction of a new "caution plus scheme" in which the prosecutor with the consent and approval of the court would caution the offender.[42]

(b) The plea of not guilty[43]

This plea occasions little difficulty. It constitutes a denial of the prosecution's allegations and requires them to prove all the elements of their case, except those facts admitted by the defence.[44] The plea must be entered by the accused personally.[45]

17–040

A plea of not guilty may be changed during the trial with the leave of the judge.[46] There are many reasons for a change of plea, including a realisation of the effect of sentence discount with a guilty plea, and the possibility of an unwelcome outcome of the trial if the plea of not guilty is maintained.[47] It has been held that if a not guilty plea is changed to guilty, it is not necessary for the judge to require the jury formally to return a verdict since the plea is a public admission.[48] The ordinary practice is however for the jury to return a verdict whenever the accused is in their charge, even in cases of a formal change of plea to guilty.

(c) The accused not pleading

The expectation is that the accused will be able, with legal representation, to plead. However, the accused may "stand mute", that is make no reply or no intelligible reply, when the charge is put. A jury must then be empanelled[49] to determine whether the accused is "mute of malice" or "mute by visitation of God". The issue is tried like any other jury matter by the bringing of evidence, examination of witnesses, summing-up and verdict. An adjournment may be necessary to provide facilities by which the accused can communicate. If the accused is found to be mute of malice (the prosecution

17–041

---

[40] pp.408–413.

[41] See CPS Annual Report 1999–2000, Auld Report, pp.408–413.

[42] p.380.

[43] 35% of those pleading not guilty at the Crown Court in 2000 were convicted. Conviction rate generally varied from *e.g.* 82% for summary offences, 52% for drug offences, 23% for criminal damage: *Criminal Statistics for England and Wales 2000* (2001), para. 6.27.

[44] Admissions may be made at various stages of criminal proceedings in accordance with the Criminal Justice Act 1967, s.10: see Emmins (2000), p.283.

[45] For instances where a plea of not guilty is entered on behalf of the accused.

[46] The judge also has a discretion to allow an accused to alter his plea back to not guilty: *R. v. Drew* [1985] 1 W.L.R. 914. As to the procedure to be adopted on change of plea, see *R. v. Ellis* (1973) 57 Cr. App.R. 571.

[47] In *R. v. Sullivan* [1984] A.C. 156 the accused changed his plea to guilty, because when he raised the claim that he assaulted someone when in an epileptic fit it was made clear that he was raising the defence of insanity which would result in his being sent to a mental hospital.

[48] *R. v. Poole* [2002] Crim. L.R. (242).

[49] In the normal way, see para. 17-087 below.

having proved it beyond a reasonable doubt[50]) a plea of not guilty is formally entered on behalf of the accused.[51] If found to be mute by visitation of God the question arises as to whether the accused is fit to plead to the charge at all.

(d) Fitness to plead

17–042 The question of fitness to plead may arise not only where the accused has remained silent on arraignment and been found mute by visitation of God, but also where there is a defence submission of unfitness or the prosecution bring the matter to the judge's attention.[52] The question is "whether the accused is under a disability, that is to say under any disability such that ... it would constitute a bar to his being tried. ... "[53] This issue is determined by a jury[54] considering the evidence and reaching a verdict in the normal way.[55] Recent research demonstrates an increase in the number of such pleas which suggests that the Criminal Procedure (Insanity and Unfitness to Plead) Act 1991 is being used to protect vulnerable mental offenders.[56] Broader questions of the appropriateness of the mentally disordered and vulnerable offenders being dealt with through the normal criminal process have also been raised.[57]

Because it is desirable that a person charged with a criminal offence should stand trial if possible and should have the chance to show that the prosecution case is inadequate, the question of fitness to plead may be deferred until the opening of the defence case, at the discretion of the trial judge.[58] The onus of proving the question of fitness lies with the party raising it. If raised by the defence it must be proved on a balance of probabilities; if raised by the prosecution it must be proved beyond

---

[50] *R. v. Sharp* [1960] 1 Q.B. 357, CA.

[51] Criminal Law Act 1967, s.6(1). *Archbold (2002)*, para. 4–164 et seq.

[52] See *O'Donnell* [1996] Crim. L.R. 121 on the correct procedure to be adopted. See also R. Mackay and G. Kearns "An Upturn in Unfitness to Plead? Disability in Relation to the Trial under the 1991 Act" [2000] Crim. L.R. 532, assessing the impact of the 1991 Act. See generally R. D. Mackay, *Mental Condition Defences in the Criminal Law* (1995).

[53] Criminal Procedure (Insanity) Act 1964, s.4(1), as substituted by the Criminal Procedure (Insanity and Unfitness to Plead) Act 1991, s.2.

[54] If a jury has found the accused mute by visitation of God the same jury may be resworn to try the issue of fitness, or a new jury may be used.

[55] Criminal Procedure (Insanity) Act 1964, s.4(5). There must be written oral evidence of two doctors: s.4(6). For a critique of the operation of the fitness to plead procedure see R. MacKay and G. Kearns, "The Trial of the Facts and Unfitness to Plead" [1997] Crim. L.R. 644.

[56] *ibid.* See also D. Grubin, *Fitness to Plead in England and Wales* (1996) and *R. v. Antoine* [2000] 2 W.L.R. 703, HL; *Attorney-General's Reference No. 3 of 1998* [1999] 2 Cr. App. R. 214; P. Wilcock, (2002) 152 J.P.N. 439.

[57] On the success of the diversion schemes whereby mental disordered offenders are diverted from the criminal justice system, see J. Laing, "Diversion of Mentally Disordered Offenders: Victim and Offender Perspectives" [1999] Crim. L.R. 805, examining their effectiveness in meeting the needs of offenders, recognising the rights of victims and minimising the risk to their police, and see generally J. Laing, *Care, or Custody? Mentally Disordered Offenders in the Criminal Justice System* (1999). Note that fitness to plead inquiry is not a determination of a charge for the purposes of Article 6 of the ECHR: *R.v. M; R.v. Kerr; R.v. H* [2002] Crim. L.R. 57.

[58] Criminal Procedure (Insanity) Act 1964, s.4(2). The same process then applies: s.4A(5).

reasonable doubt.[59] In deciding whether the accused is unfit, the jury must determine whether or not the accused can instruct a solicitor and counsel, plead to the indictment (that is understand the charge and the significance of a plea), challenge jurors, understand the evidence, and give evidence.[60] If the jury finds the accused unfit to plead, it must then determine whether he or she "did the act or made the omission charged against him as the offence" and, if so, make such a finding.[61] The "act" in this question relates exclusively to the *actus reus* of the offence. However, regard at this stage can be had to the defence of provocation, and [62] defences of self-defence, accident or mistake may also be raised, and the jury should acquit unless the prosecution has disproved these elements.[63] If the jury is satisfied that the accused did perform the act or omission the court will make an appropriate disposal order in accordance with section 5 of the Act. If not so satisfied, the jury must acquit the accused.[64]

At one time, the mandatory consequence of a finding of unfitness was that the person had to be transferred to a mental hospital. This was the case even if the individual had no (treatable) mental disorder, which is not a requirement for the finding.[65] However, the changes introduced to the procedure by the Criminal Procedure (Insanity and Unfitness to Plead) Act 1991 alleviated some of these problems by avoiding the finding affecting someone who did not commit the act or make the admission. In addition, that Act made significant changes to the consequences that flow from a finding of unfitness. Under section 5 of the amended Criminal Procedure (Insanity) Act 1964,[66] the court may make an admission order to such hospital as the Secretary of State specifies, make a guardianship order under the Mental Health Act 1983, make a supervision and treatment order, or make an order for the accused's absolute discharge. These are not findings of guilt.[67] This procedure should avoid the criminal justice system being responsible for the detention of innocent but mentally unfit people in hospital.[68]

(e) Right to silence[69]

We consider here the problems of the defendant's silence and its effect at **17–043**

---

[59] *Quaere* where the judge raises the issue. The question of the onus and standard of proof is considered in *R. v. Podola* [1960] 1 Q.B. 325, which is of general interest on the question of fitness to plead.

[60] *R. v. Pritchard* (1836) 7 C. & P. 303; *R. v. Robertson* [1968] 1 W.L.R. 1767. See, Smith and Hogan, *Criminal Law* 10th ed., 2002, pp. 213–217

[61] Criminal Procedure (Insanity) Act 1964, s.4A(2) and (3).

[62] *R.v. Grant* [2002] Crim. L.R. 403.

[63] See *R. v. Antoine* [2000] 2 W.L.R. 703 HL; *Attorney-General's Reference No. 3 of 1998* [1999] 2 Cr. Ap. R. 214.

[64] *ibid.* s.4A(4).

[65] See C. Emmins, "Unfitness to Plead: Some Thoughts Prompted by Glenn Pearson's Case" [1986] Crim. L.R. 604.

[66] As amended by the Powers of Criminal Courts (Sentencing) Act 2000.

[67] *R. v. Southwark Crown Court, ex p. Koncar* [1998] 1 Cr.App. R. 321; *Archbold (2002)*, paras 4–175, 4–185.

[68] See *Archbold (2002)*, para. 4–166. The person might still be admitted to hospital, but through the non-criminal procedures within the Mental Health Act 1983, Part II. See generally R. D. Mackay, *Mental Condition Defences in the Criminal Law* (1995).

[69] See the major textbooks on the law of evidence and for more detailed reviews of the issues surrounding the right to silence; see K. Starmer and M. Woolf, in C. Walker and K. Starmer

trial. It was always the case that a judge had to be particularly careful in addressing the jury where the accused had made no answer to the police and/or had not disclosed a defence until trial, and when the accused had exercised the right to give evidence at trial. The so called "right to silence" was predicated on the propositions that the accused should not be required to provide any evidence which might be incriminating and is entitled to make the prosecution prove its case without answering questions before or at the trial. There was a specific obligation to disclose a notice of alibi defence, and notices in respect of expert evidence, as well as more detailed pre-trial disclosure in serious fraud cases.[70] Some comment could be made by the judge. It was safest for the judge not to comment on the accused's failure to disclose a defence until trial or to answer questions before trial, with some exceptions. Where the accused failed to testify, the accepted comment was that established by Lord Parker C.J. in *R. v. Bathurst*[71]:

" ... the accused is not bound to give evidence, he can sit back and see if the prosecution have proved their case, and that, whilst the jury have been deprived of the opportunity of hearing his story tested in cross-examination, the one thing that they must not do is to assume that he is guilty because he has not gone into the witness box."

What the judge could *not* do was to suggest to the jury that guilt could be assumed from silence. Proposals for change from this traditional position had been made, controversially, by the Criminal Law Revision Committee in 1972,[72] but only limited changes were recommended by the Royal

---

(1999) S. Greer and R. Morgan (eds), *The Right of Silence Debate* (1990); S. M. Easton, *The Right to Silence (1998)*; S. C. Greer, (1990) 53 M.J.R. 709; R. Leng, *The Right to Silence in Police Interrogation: A Study of Some of the Issues Underlying the Debate* (RCCJ Research Study No. 10, HMSO, 1993); D. Morgan and G. M. Stephenson, *Suspicion and Silence* (1994); I. Dennis, [1995] Crim L.R. 4 at 9–18. On the implementations of the silence provisions and the history see J. Wood and A. Crawford, *The Right to Silence* (1989); A., Zuckerman, [1989] Crim. L.R. 855; J. Coldrey (1991) 20 Anglo-Am. L.R.; D. Morgan and G. Stephenson (eds), *Suspicion or Silence: the Right to Silence in Criminal Investigations* (1994). For academic comment on the implementation and operation of the sections, see P. Mirfield, *Silence Confessions and Improperly Obtained Evidence* (1998). See also: I Dennis, (1995) 54 C. L.J. 342, [1995] Crim. l.R. 4; S Easton, [1998] 2 Int. J.F. & P.; J. Jackson, [1993] 44 N.I.L.O. 103; R. Pattenden, [1995] Crim. J.R. 602;. Pattenden, [1998] 2 E & P. 141; D. Birch, [1999] Crim. J.R. 769; Sir Stephen Sedley, "Wringing Out the Fault: Self Incrimination in the 21st Century" [2001] N.J.L.O. 107. For a summary of the debate preceding enactment, see the Home Office Research Study by T. Bucke, R. Street, and B. Brown, *The Right to Silence: The Impact of the Criminal Justice and Public Order Act 1994* (2000), Chap. 1. On the right to silence provisions in Northern Ireland, see the review by J. Jackson, M. Wolfe and K. Quinn, *Legislating Against Silence: The NI Experience* (2000), revealing that terrorist suspects were more likely to testify after the 1988 Order (the equivalent of the s.34 provision). Their conclusion was that the order had, generally, the contrary effect to that expected and that there had been a marked "decline in convictions in those cases which have been contested." see (p.144). On the constitutionality of the right to silence, P.J., Shwikkard, "Is it Constitutionally Permissible to Infringe the Right to Remain Silent" (2001) 5 E. & P. 32.

[70] These were statutory obligations: see Criminal Justice Act 1967, s.11 (alibi); PACE 1984, s.81 (experts); Criminal Justice Act 1987 s.2 (fraud).

[71] [1968] 1 All E.R. 1175, at p. 1178. See also *R. v. Martinez-Tobon* [1994] 1 W.L.R. 388.

[72] *Eleventh Report: Evidence (General)*, Cmnd. 4991.

Commission on Criminal Justice.[73] However, major changes were introduced by sections 34–38 of the Criminal Justice and Public Order Act 1994. The right to keep silent *is not abolished* but greater risks are now run by the accused who maintains that position, before or at trial.[74] Much has been written of the extremely controversial reforms. It remains unclear whether they have been successful in securing more convictions of defendants (particularly hardened criminals).[75]

Bucke *et al.*[76] found that since the 1994 Act, the percentage of suspects exercising their right to silence has not altered dramatically. Before the Act, 10 per cent of suspects refused to answer all questions, 13 per cent refused to answer some, and 77 per cent answered all. Under the Act, six per cent refused to answer all questions, 10 per cent refused to answer some, and 84 per cent answered all.[77] Those who obtained legal advice were "far more likely to refuse" all questions than those who had not. More serious allegations were more likely to lead to silence as was a suspect having a previous record (13 per cent as opposed to five per cent). Of those who received legal advice before the Act, 20 per cent refused to answer all questions, 19 per cent refused to answer some, and 61 per cent answered all. After the Act those figures are 13 per cent, nine per cent and 78 per cent respectively. For those who did not receive legal advice, the figures before the 1994 Act were: three per cent refused to answer all; nine per cent refused to answer some; and 88 per cent, answered all questions. After the Act, the figures are two per cent, six per cent and 92 per cent respectively.[78]

Following the enactment of the 1994 Act, the common law position relating to the right to silence still pertains when the statutory provisions are inapplicable, and in such circumstances, it is incumbent on the trial judge to direct the jury that they should not draw adverse inferences from silence.[79]

---

[73] RCCJ, Report (1993), pp. 54–55. The majority recommended that "it is when but only when the prosecution has been fully disclosed that defendants should be required to offer and answer to the charges made against them at the risk of adverse comment at trial on any new defence they then disclose or on any departure from the defence which they previously disclosed". See also the recommendations of the Home Office Working Group (1989). For powerful adverse criticism of the proposals, see A. A. S. Zuckerman, [1989] Crim. L.R. 855; J. Wood and A. Crawford, *The Right of Silence: The Case for Retention* (1989); S Greer, (1990) 53 M.L.R 709; B. Irving and I. McKenzie, (1990) 1 J. Foresenic Psychiatry 167. For arguments in favour of change, see G. Williams, "The Right of Silence" and the Mental Element' [1988] Crim. L.R. 97.

[74] It is important to note also that adverse inferences can be drawn against a defendant who fails adequately to disclose a defence later relied on at trial: Criminal Procedure and Investigation Act 1996, s.11. On the potential to draw adverse inferences from the failure to make adequate defence disclosure, see S. Thompson, "Defence Statements — Weighting the Scales or Tipping the Balance on a Submission of No Case" [1998] Crim. L.R. 802.

[75] See D.J. Birch, "Suffering in Silence; A Cost-Benefit Analysis of Section 34 of the Criminal Justice and Public Order Act 1994" [1999] Crim. L.R. 769. T. Bucke, R. Street, and B. Brown, *The Right to Silence: The Impact of the Criminal Justice and Public Order Act 1994* (2000) conclude that: "whatever philosophical standpoint is adopted, it seems clear that the change in the law has not led to undue practical disadvantages to the defendant" (p.73). See also the excellent review by I. Dennis " Silence in the Police Station: The Marginalisation of Section 34" [2002] Crim. L.R. 25.

[76] T. Bucke, R. Street, and B. Brown, *The Right to Silence: The Impact of the Criminal Justice and Public Order Act 1994* (2000).

[77] p. 31.

[78] p.33.

[79] *R.v. McGarry* [1999] 1 W.L.R. 1500.

As Lord Bingham C.J. observed in one of the leading cases (*R. v. Bowden*[80]) sections 34–38 "restrict rights recognized at common law as appropriate to protect defendants against the risk of injustice [and as such] should not be construed more widely than the statutory language requires".

This common law protection against incrimination from silence is supported by Article 6 of the ECHR which although it does not expressly provide a "right to silence" has been interpreted expansively by the European Court as implicitly providing a protection against self-incrimination and providing a "right to silence" as part of the fundamental guarantees of the fair trial.[81] In *Funke v. France*,[81a] the ECtHR recognised: "the right of anyone charged with a criminal offence, within the autonomous meaning of the expression in Article 6, to remain silent and not to contribute to incriminating himself." Particularly important are the ECHR guarantees against drawing adverse inferences where the accused has not had an opportunity to seek legal advice or from convicting a person exclusively on his silence.[82]

It is important to note that there is often confusion as to the precise ambit of the protections regarding silence, and this confusion is exacerbated by misleadingly using the expression interchangeably with the "privilege against self-incrimination". The privilege against self-incrimination is a different issue arising, *inter alia*, when the accused is questioned under powers that are backed by sanctions for failure to reply. Domestic law has been heavily influenced by the ECtHR decision in *Saunders v. U.K.*,[83] where the defendant had been convicted of offences in relation to the Guinness-Distillers take–over. His conviction rested in part on the answers he provided to questions under compulsion — *i.e.* where the failure to answer is itself an offence. The Strasbourg Court held that this constituted an infringement of the privilege against self-incrimination. The majority stated: "the right not to incriminate oneself, in particular, presupposes that the prosecution in a criminal case seek to prove their case against the accused without resort to evidence obtained through means of coercion or oppression in defiance of the will of the accused. In this sense the right is closely linked to the presumption of innocence contained in article 6(2)."[84]

---

[80] [1999] 2 Cr.App. R. 176 at 181.

[81] See *Saunders v. U.K.* (1996) 23 E.H.R.R. 313; *Murray v. U.K.* (1996) 22 E.H.R.R. 29; *Condron v. U.K.* [2000] Crim. L.R. 679.

[81a] (1993) 16 E.H.R.R. 297.

[82] See, *e.g.* *Condron v. U.K.* [2000] Crim. L.R. 679; *Heaney and McGuiness v. Ireland* [2001] Crim. L.R. 481; see further Ashworth, [2001] Crim. L.R. 855, p. 866.

[83] [1997] 23 E.H.R.R. 313.

[84] The European Court has vacillated between strong and weak approaches to this: compare *Funke v. France* (1993) 16 E.H.R.R. 297 with *J.B. v. Switzerland* [2001] Crim. L.R. 748. High profile cases on self-incrimination were some of earliest applications of the ECHR in argument in domestic criminal cases soon after implementation of the Human Rights Act 1998: *Brown v Stott* [2001] E.H.R.R. 78 (see R. Pillay, "Self-Incrimination and Article 6: The Decision of the Privy Council in *Procurator Fiscal v. Brown*" [2001] E.H.R.R. 78.) See also *R. v. Hertfordshire County Council, ex p. Green Environmental Industries Ltd* [2000] 2 W.L.R. 373; *Attorney-General's Reference No. 7 of 2000* [2001] EWCA Crim. 888.

The statutory scheme

Section 34 of the Criminal Justice and Public Order Act 1994[85] provides that   **17–044**
where an accused, before charge, when questioned under caution or after
charge, "failed to mention any fact relied on in his defence" in criminal
proceedings and that fact was one "which in the circumstances existing at
the time the accused could reasonably have been expected to mention when
so questioned, charged or informed" then the judge (or magistrates) may
"draw such inferences from the failure as appear proper."[86] There can be no
conviction on silence alone,[87] and juries must be reminded of this in any case
to which section 34 applies.[88] Section 34(2A) as inserted by section 58 of the
Youth Justice and Criminal Evidence Act 1999 was added to bring English
law into compliance with the Article 6.[89] As a result, no adverse inferences
may now be drawn from the accused's silence unless he or she had an
opportunity to consult with a legal adviser.[90]

The Court of Appeal has emphasised that there are numerous hurdles to
overcome before the jury can begin drawing inferences from silence.[91] In
addition to the requirement that proceedings have been instituted, the
alleged failure to mention facts, which must have taken place before the
defendant was charged, has to have occurred while the accused was
undergoing questioning under caution, the objective of which was to
establish whether or by whom the alleged offence was committed.
Furthermore, the alleged failure has to be to mention any fact which the
defendant relies on in his defence, and it is for the jury to decide, as a
question of fact, whether there is some fact so relied on and whether the
defendant failed to mention such fact when being questioned. Finally, the
relevant fact has to be one which, in the circumstances, the defendant could
reasonably have been expected to mention, taking account of that particular
defendant's characteristics, such as age, health and mental capacity, and
legal advice as relevant circumstances. Whilst the issue requires appropriate
jury directions, the matter should then be left for the jury to decide and it
will only rarely be the case that a judge should direct a jury that they should
or should not draw the appropriate inference.[92] The burden of proof
remains on the prosecution throughout.[93]

Section 34 only comes into play if the accused relies on a fact at trial that
it is reasonable to expect him previously to have mentioned. It is clear that if
the accused remains silent at trial and offers no evidence by way of a defence
— *i.e.* simply puts the prosecution to proof — the section has no part to

---

[85] Note also ss.36 and 37 are concerned with the failure to account for objects, substances,
marks and presence.
[86] Criminal Justice and Public Order Act 1994, s.34(1) and (2).
[87] *ibid.* s.38.
[88] *R. v. Abdullah* [1999] 3 Arch. News 2.
[89] *Murray v. U.K.* (1996) 22 E.H.R.R. 29. See R. Munday, "Inferences from Silence and
European Human Rights Law" [1996] Crim. L.R. 370, discussing the implications of
Murray, which held that M's right to a fair trial had been violated because he did not have
access to a lawyer in the first 48 hours of detention.
[90] On the need to have access to a legal adviser before adverse inferences can be drawn see also
A. Jennings, "Resounding Silence" (1996) 146 N.L.J. 725 at 746, 821.
[91] See especially *R. v. Argent* [1997] 2 Cr. App R. 27.
[92] See *R. v. Francom* [2001] Crim. L.R. 1018.
[93] *R. v. Gowland-Wynn* [2001] EWCA 2715.

play.[94] Difficulties arise if the accused puts forward a theory or proposition that is not "a fact."[95] In these cases the section should have no part to play and no adverse inferences should be drawn. "Fact" is to be construed applying a dictionary definition.[96]

Inferences can only be drawn from a failure to mention such "facts" where, if in the circumstances at the time, the accused could reasonably be expected to mention them. As such, the personal characteristics of the accused must be considered (and this should not be done in a restrictive manner[97]) including age, experience, mental capacity, health, sobriety, tiredness and personality and the extent of the accused's knowledge of the case against him. Where the accused remains silent on legal advice that does not in itself prevent adverse-inferences being drawn.[98] This may result in the accused waiving his lawyer client privilege at trial in order to explain why he was silent.[99] Jennings, Ashworth and Emmerson suggest that the correct approach involves two stages (i) that the jury should take account of the fact that D has been advised by legal representatives to remain silent and (ii) if the defendant's resulting silence was or may have been because of the reason relied on at trial no adverse inference should be drawn.[1]

Research has revealed a list of no fewer than 25 factors that lead practitioners to advise no comment in interview. The most common reason is insufficient police disclosure, followed by insufficient evidence and third, was the "physical or mental condition of the client". Other factors included a fear of incriminating other people, the implausibility of the statement, and the police already being poised to charge.[2] On the factors that led advisers to recommend that clients answer questions, the most important was the category of the defence followed by fear of adverse inferences being drawn and a belief that the police would be less likely to charge the accused if he or she had an explanation.

If there was silence at the investigative stage, and a fact is relied on at trial and it is reasonable to have expected the accused to have mentioned it the section allows inferences to be drawn. Under section 34 the prosecution have to establish a prima facie case against the accused before reliance on the silence can be made. The jury must be reminded of this obligation.[3] Many inferences *might* be drawn: that the accused is guilty, that he was

[94] *R. v. Moshaid* [1998] Crim. L.R. 420.

[95] See *R. v. Nickolson* [1999] Crim. L.R. 61; *R. v. B (MT)* [2000] Crim. L.R. 181.

[96] *R. v. Milford* [2001] Crim. L.R. 330. *cf. R. v. Belts and Hall* [2001] Crim. L.R. 755 and *R. v. Tibbs* [2001] Crim. L.R. 759 on adverse inference under the CPIA 1996, s.ll.

[97] *R. v. Argent* [1997] 2 Cr. App. R. 27.

[98] *R. v. Condron; R. v. Roble* [1997] Crim. L.R. 499. ECtHR rulings require the domestic court to give appropriate weight to this fact.

[99] *R. v. Bowden* [1999] 1 W.L.R. 923. It is not hearsay for the defendant to rely on the advice given by his solicitor for him to remain silent: *R. v. Daniel* [1998] Crim. L.R. 819. On the difficulties in calling a solicitor to testify as to why the accused did not mention a relevant fact when interviewed, see D. Wright, "The Solicitor in the Witness Box" [1998] Crim. L.R. 44.

[1] J. Williams, (1997) S.J. 566.

[2] The problem still remains where adverse inferences are drawn or her the defendant has been asked questions beyond the point at which there was sufficient evidence to charge him when with an offence, (in breach of PACE Code C C.11.4; 16.1) See *R. v. Pointer* [1997] Crim. L.R. 676; *R.v. Gayle* [1999] Crim. L.R. 502 and *Archbold (2002)*, para. 15–402 and recently *R. v. Elliott.* [2002] EWCA Crim. 931.

[3] *R. v. Milford* [2001] Crim. L.R. 330.

unwilling to expose his defence to scrutiny, that the accused is turning on his co-accused, etc.[4] The jury must be directed with great care as to what permissible uses may be made of the accused's pre-trial silence: *Condron v. U.K.*[5-6]

The silence provisions continue to provoke controversy, not only as to their efficiency, but as to the more pernicious effects they have on the criminal process.[7] Jackson has argued that the loss of the right to silence has transformed parts of what were purely investigative activities of the police into a formal part of the proceedings against the accused. The danger of this shift is that unlike other legal proceedings the safeguards for the accused at that early stage are minimal.[8]

Silence at trial

As regards the failure to testify at trial, section 35 of the Criminal Justice **17–045** and Public Order Act 1994 provides that at a trial[9] and at the conclusion of the prosecution case (the matter does not arise where there is no case to answer) if the accused does not give evidence or then answer questions (without good cause, *e.g.* physical or mental condition[10]), "it will be permissible for the court or jury to draw such inferences as appear proper from his failure to give evidence or his refusal, without good cause, to answer any question". Whilst the accused is not compelled to give evidence,[11] the risks in failing to give evidence are enhanced, since the inference that the court may draw is that the accused is guilty of the offence charged.[12] However, the accused cannot be convicted solely, or mainly,[13] on an inference drawn from silence,[14] and inferences of guilt will not be drawn

---

[4] See the particular difficulties that have been experienced with cut throat defences which are revealed at trial for the first time: *R .v. Mountford* [1999] Crim. L.R. 575.

[5-6] [2000] Crim. L.R. 679 (judges direction had allowed the jury to draw an adverse inference even if they had been satisfied that the reason for the silence was the solicitor's advice. The jury should have been directed that if they believed that the silence could not sensibly be attributed to their having no answer to the questions, or none that would stand up to cross-examination, they should not draw an adverse inference.) On *Condron v. U.K.* and other silence cases in Europe see A. Jennings, A. Ashworth and B. Emmerson, "Silence and Safety: The Impact of Human Rights Law" [2000] Crim. L.R. 879.

[7] On developments to the right to silence under the Labour Government, see D. Wolchover and A Heaton Armstrong, "Labour's Victory and the Right to Silence" (1997) 147 N.L.J. 1382, noting the impact on legal aid costs and reporting that many solicitors regard the Act as bizarre.

[8] See J. Jackson, "Silence and Proof: Extending the Boundaries of Criminal Proceedings in the U.K." [2001] E. & P. 145.

[9] If the accused's guilt is not in issue or "it appears to the court that the physical or mental condition of the accused makes it undesirable for him to give evidence", the provisions do not apply: s.35(1).

[10] *R. v. Friend* [1997] 1 W.L.R. 1433. See E. Cape, "Mentally Disordered Suspects and the Right to Silence" (1996) 146 N.L.J. 80; S. Sharpe "Vulnerable Defendants and Inferences from Silence" (1997) 147 N.L.J. 842.

[11] *R. v. Cowan* [1996] Q.B. 373; s.35(4).

[12] s.35(3). See *Murray v. D.P.P.* [1994] 1 W.L.R. 1.

[13] Following the decision of the European Court in *Murray v. U.K.* (1996) it is necessary to warn the jury that they should not convict "mainly" on silence.

[14] s.38.

where the prosecution has a weak case.[15] If the defence seek to rely on good cause for failing to testify, they must adduce evidence on the *voir dire*. On the *voir dire*, the judge may take account of expert evidence, and the conduct of the accused before and after the offence.[16]

The Court of Appeal provided clear guidance in *R. v. Cowan* as to how the judge should direct the jury. A jury must find that there was a case to answer on the prosecution evidence before drawing an adverse inference from the defendant's silence, and they must be reminded that the burden of proof remained on the presecution. They should also be told that the defendant is entitled to remain silent and an inference from failure to give evidence cannot on its own prove guilt. Judges should warn the jury that the condition for holding a defendant's silence against him is that the only sensible explanation for that silence is that he has no answer to the case or none that could stand up to cross-examination[17a]. Without these directions the jury may attach undue importance to the defendant's absence from the witness box.

The drawing of inferences may be regarded as a significant infringement in the existing rights of the accused to a fair trial, and may reflect a move towards the crime control model.[17] This is echoed by the introduction of new powers and the extension of existing ones in relation to the taking of samples and specimens from suspects considered in Chapter 14 above.[18]

4. REPRESENTATION AND THE OBLIGATIONS OF COUNSEL[19]

17–046 The availability of legal aid[20] ensures that it is very unusual to find an unrepresented accused in the Crown Court. Those who are unrepresented have normally chosen to conduct their own defence.[21] If the accused dismisses counsel, the judge must warn the defendant of the dangers in proceeding without counsel,[22] and may adjourn for new counsel to be instructed unless of the opinion that this is not in the interests of justice (*e.g.* because it is likely that the accused will dismiss him also or will be mute of malice offering no instruction[23]). Ultimately, the defendant may insist on proceeding without counsel.[24] Both prosecution and defence counsel are under obligations to behave in accordance with professional standards and in a particular manner in the course of the trial. We can offer a brief examination of some examples. So far as is reasonably practicable, a

---

[15] *Murray v. DPP* [1994] 1 W.L.R. 1; *Waugh v. The King* [1950] A.C. 203.

[16] See also *R. v. Chadwick and others* [1998] 7 Archbold News 3.

[17a] Counsel should be consulted as to be the appropriate directions: *R. v. Gough* [2002] Crim. L.R. 526.

[17] See, further, below, para. 17–105.

[18] These have been significantly expanded from those in PACE 1984.

[19] See Emmerson and Ashworth, (2001), p.338; M. Strange in K. Starmer *et al*, (2001), Chap. 12.

[20] On the Criminal Defence Service see para. 14-087 above. On the potential inadequacy of the system from an ECHR dimension, see M. Strange, p.127; *Kamasinski v. Austria* (1989) 13 E.H.R.R. 36; *F v. U.K.* (1992) 15 E.H.R.R. CD 32.

[21] If the defendant is unrepresented, the judge is under an obligation to ensure the proper conduct of the trial.

[22] *Mitchell v. R.* [1999] 1 W.L.R. 1679, PC.

[23] *Ricketts v. R.* [1998] 1 W.L.R. 1017, PC.

[24] *R. v. Mills* [1997] 2 Cr.App. R. 206.

defendant is entitled to choose his representative.[25] The overriding question is of meeting the requirements of justice for both the prosecution and the defence in the circumstances of the particular case.[26] It is also worth noting that under Article 6(3)(c) of the ECHR, everyone charged with a criminal offence has a minimum right "to defend himself through legal assistance of his own choosing or, if he has not sufficient means to pay for the legal assistance, to be given it for free when the interests of justice so require".[27] This includes the right to have adequate opportunity to organise his defence in an appropriate way and without restriction as to the possibility to put all relevant defence arguments before the trial court."[28]

The ethical dimension to the representation of the accused in a criminal trial and to the role of the prosecutor is often overlooked. Ashworth and Blake[29] in their illuminating study identified six key ethical issues for the defence: defending a person believed to be guilty, where the advocate believes that perjury has been or will be committed, where the defence lawyer knows of an error of law in the proceedings which favours the defence, where the defence lawyer knows of an error of fact in the proceedings which favours the defence, where the defence lawyer offers advice to a cheat who wishes to plead not guilty, where the defence lawyer and the defendant disagree on the conduct of the defence. Ethical difficulties for the prosecutor were described as including: where the prosecutor realises that the court or the defence has made an error which favours the prosecution, where the prosecutor realises that certain evidence may have been obtained unfairly, where the prosecutor enters into a plea negotiation despite doubts about the charges being sustainable, where the prosecutor makes representations in favour of a custodial remand, at the instigation of the police, even though the legal requirements are not strictly fulfilled.[30] Counsel must be careful to avoid appearing for the Crown against defendants whom they have previously defended,[31] and it is important that counsel avoid any conduct that might give rise to a perception of bias generally.[32]

---

[25] On the new Criminal Defence Service see D. O'Brien and J. Arnold, "Defending the Right to Choose: Legally Aided Defendants and Choice of Legal Representative" [2001] E.H.R.L.R. 409. See also the LCD Paper, *Criminal Defence Service: Choice of Representation* (1999); R. Moorhead, "Third Way Regulation: Community Legal Service Partnerships" (2001) 64 M.L.R. 543.

[26] *R. v. De Oliveira* [1997] Crim. L.R. 600.

[27] *Imbrioscia v Switzerland* (1993) 17 E.H.R.R. 441. See generally, Emmerson and Ashworth, Chap. 4. In English law, "criminal charge" remains largely undefined, and the question arises as to whether Article 6 protections such as those relating to representation apply in non-criminal commissions in which there are potential legal consequences for witness as, *e.g.* in the Scott or Lawrence inquiries. See generally, H. Grant "Commissions of Inquiry — Is There a Right to be Legally Represented" [2001] P.L. 377.

[28] *Can v. Austria* (1985) Com.Rep A/96.

[29] See M. Blake and A. Ashworth, "Some Ethical Issues in Prosecuting and Defending Criminal Cases" [1998] Crim. L.R. 16. The authors also considers the appropriate ethical limits of cross-examination. See recently L. Ellison, "The Mosaic Art?: Cross-examination and the Vulnerable Witness (2001) 21 L.S. 353.

[30] See also the interesting comparative work by Kai Ambos, "The Status, Role and Accountability of the Prosecutor of the International Criminal Court: A Comparative Overview on the Basis of 33 National Reports" (2000) Euro. Jnl Crime, Crim. Law and Crim. Justice, 89, reviewing very different roles and responsibilities of prosecuting counsels in domestic proceedings.

[31] *R. v. Dann* [1997] Crim. L.R. 46.

[32] See *e.g.* the decision in *R. v. Batt* [1996] Crim. L.R. 910 that cohabiting barristers ought not

Counsel should always act in accordance with the rules and etiquette of the Bar.[33] "A barrister has an overriding duty to the court to act with independence in the interests of justice: he must assist the court in the administration of justice and must not deceive or knowingly or recklessly mislead the court."[34] The latter principle is of the utmost importance and impinges upon the task of counsel at several points in the trial.

There can be little doubt that the increasingly consumerist attitude to criminal justice will result in a greater number of complaints and appeals against conviction being brought on the basis of alleged incompetence of counsel.[35]

(a) Prosecuting counsel

17-047 The Standards Applicable to Criminal Cases annexed to the Code of Conduct for the Bar of England and Wales state that[36]

"Prosecuting counsel should not attempt to obtain a conviction by all means at his command. He should not regard himself as appearing for a party. He should lay before the Court fairly and impartially the whole of the facts which comprise the case for the prosecution and should assist the Court on all matters of law applicable to the case."[37]

This view has found judicial expression at various times and prosecuting counsel have even been described as "ministers of justice assisting in the administration of justice".[38] A distinguished Old Bailey judge, who had been Senior Prosecuting Counsel at that court, warned a prosecutor against feeling pride or satisfaction in the mere fact of success, or boasting of the percentage of convictions secured over a period of time. It is, he said, " ... no rebuff to his prestige if he fails to convince the tribunal of the prisoner's

---

to appear against each other in the same trial.

[33] *Code of Conduct for the Bar of England and Wales* (7th ed., 2000), as amended. "The general purpose of this Code is to provide the requirements for practice as a barrister and the rules and standards of conduct applicable to barristers which are appropriate in the interests of justice in England and Wales ... ": *ibid.* para. 104 and see above, Chap. 3.

[34] *ibid.* para. 302. The full text is reproduced in *Archbold (2002)*, Supplement, Appendix C. A barrister's other duties include the obligation to act honestly and with proper regard to the public confidence in the profession, to exercise independent, professional judgment and to promote fearlessly the client's best interests: *ibid.* paras 303, 305, 306.

[35] The test to be applied is unclear. See *Boodram v. The State* [2002] Crim. L.R. 524 and commentary. See generally R. Shiels, "Blaming the Lawyer" [1997] Crim. L.R. 740. Examples might include failing to serve an alibi notice — see *R.v. Nangle* [2001] Crim. L.R. 507. Errors in the criminal trial are not always attributable to incompetence; counsel often have incredibly short periods of time in which to prepare cases.

[36] See *Archbold (2002)*, para. B.32, supplement no. 1. See also the CPS publication, *National Standards of Advocacy* which represent the basis for assessment of CPS advocates, *www.cps.gov.uk/cps a/nsa.htm*. They deal with professional ethics, advice on planning and preparation, courtroom etiquette, rules of procedure, etc.

[37] *ibid.* Annex H, para. 10.1 *et seq.* (hereinafter, *Standards in Criminal Cases*). See also the Report of Mr Justice Farquharson's Committee on the Role of Prosecuting Counsel (1986), set out in *Archbold* (1995), paras. 4–72 to 4–80. On the particular relationship of prosecuting counsel with those instructing him see the conclusion of the Farquharson Committee and the *Code of Professional Work* in the *Code of Conduct of the Bar*.

[38] *R. v. Puddick* (1865), set out in *Archbold (2002)*, para. 4–96.

guilt."[39] It is highly undesirable for prosecuting counsel to use unnecessarily emotive language that can only excite sympathy for the victim or prejudice against the accused.[40] What is required of prosecuting counsel is an element of objectivity in conducting the trial process. This will often be difficult to achieve.

Three broad areas require careful consideration and the exercise of judgment by counsel: the desirability and propriety of a plea arrangement; the nature and presentation of the prosecution case at trial; the amount of assistance which needs to be given to the defence or the judge.

(i) The plea arrangements

As noted, where there are a number of counts in the indictment or where one count contains alternative charges or where the jury might convict of a lesser charge, it is not uncommon for the defence to offer or the prosecution to seek a plea of guilty to a lesser charge in return for an agreement from the prosecution to offer no evidence on the more serious charge. This is a form of plea-bargaining. In a sense, there is a double advantage in these circumstances. Assume that the accused is charged on one indictment containing two separate counts of rape and one count of indecent assault. If, in return for an agreement to accept not guilty pleas to the counts of rape, the accused agrees to plead guilty to the other count of indecent assault he will render himself liable to a less severe sentence on the lesser charge and also receive credit for a guilty plea. Clearly, the offer of a plea arrangement creates a certain amount of pressure on the accused.[41] Sanders and Young review the arguments that barristers acting for the prosecution have a number of reasons, other than the client's best interests, for seeking to settle a case. These include that they are expected to seek bargains since that is in the interests of the administration of justice, and the comity of the Bar; and the fact that a barrister may do both prosecution and defence work which encourages agreements.[42] Note also that given the methods by which barristers are paid for a case, it is not in their interest to persuade the accused to plead guilty too early.

The advantages of a guilty plea for the prosecution are obvious: there is a saving of time and money; witnesses are spared the experience of testifying; the inevitable uncertainty of the trial is exchanged for the certainty of a plea.[43] On the other hand, "a Crown Prosecutor must never accept a guilty plea just because it is convenient".[44] Justice demands first that the offence in the indictment should be prosecuted where the evidence supports the

17–048

---

[39] C. Humphreys, "The Duties and Responsibilities of Prosecuting Counsel" [1955] Crim. L.R. 739.

[40] *Archbold (2002)*, para. 4–96. See also *R.v. Gonez* [1999] All E.R. (D) 674, emphasising that counsel was not to excite emotions or inflame the minds of the jury but to be clinical and dispassionate.

[41] For a consideration of the pressures on the accused, see para. 17-039 above.

[42] Sanders and Young (2000), Chap. 7, Part 3.

[43] See Sanders and Young, (2000), p.399.

[44] *Code for Crown Prosecutors*, para. 9.1. See also the Home Affairs Committee Fourth Report for Session 1989–90, *Crown Prosecution Service* (H.C. 118–1) paras 36–44.

charge,[45] unless there are exceptional factors suggesting otherwise, and secondly that the court should be able to pass a sentence that matches the seriousness of the offending.[46]

The award of an automatic sentencing discount for a plea of guilty is clearly driven by a desire to maximise efficiency in the system with more people pleading guilty at the earliest possible stage of the proceedings. The other saving is that a trial resulting in conviction would lead to a longer sentence than is imposed under the discount system, leading to greater costs incurred in the prison service.[47]

Flood-Page and Mackie[48] found that 64 per cent of offenders pleading guilty from the outset received a sentence of less than 18 months compared to 55 per cent of those who changed an initial not guilty plea to guilty. Where defendants were convicted following a trial, 45 per cent received sentences of less than 18 months.[49] There were still inconsistencies in the application of discounts, but the results confirmed that the earlier the plea the better the discount for custodial sentences, but that there was no significant effect on community punishments.[50] The results also suggest that a higher proportion of ethnic minority defendants plead guilty.[51]

Based on empirical research, Henham argues that sentencing discounts are objectionable from the point of view of due process because they conflict with the presumption of innocence by removing the need for the prosecution to prove its case.[52] Henham has also shown that the relationship between the plea, the discount, the timing and the type of offence is important. The guilty plea rate differs for different offences and triggers different proportions of discount percentages (for example, very few people plead guilty to a rape charge). The percentages of those pleading guilty are also geographically distinct with significantly lower rates being recorded in London. His research confirmed that the extent of discount is often not articulated even to the extent of not declaring that no sentence discount has been given. The system is flawed by this lack of transparency.

Sanders and Young offer a telling critique of the sentencing discount system,[53] highlighting a number of principled deficiencies including that the defendant who persists in putting the prosecution to proof, asserting the presumption of innocence, is penalised for doing so, and pointing out the dangers of the closed deals struck in possible contravention of the requirement of a public hearing under Article 6(1). In sum they conclude that it is impossible to increase the pressure on the guilty to plead guilty

[45] This is based upon *R. v. Soanes* (1948) 32 Cr. App. R. 136, which, in part, whilst not representing the present position, (as will be seen from the following discussion in the text) does represent a commonly held view.

[46] *Code for Crown Prosecutors* (2000), para. 9.1. The Code is available from *www.cps.gov.uk*.

[47] See R. Henham, "Bargain Justice and Justice on Demand? Sentence Discounts and the Criminal Process" (1999) 62 M.L.R. 515 reporting on empirical work into the effectiveness of what was then s.48 of the Criminal Justice Act. See also D. Thomas, "Viewpoint" (1994) 2 Sentencing News 12.

[48] *Sentencing Practice: an Examination of Decisions in the Magistrates' Courts and the Crown Court in the Mid 1990s* (HORS No. 180, 1998).

[49] p.90.

[50] Their methodology is criticised by Sanders and Young, (2000) p.412.

[51] See further Sanders and Young, (2000), p.431.

[52] For criticism of the methodology see Sanders and Young, (2000), p.413.

[53] Chap. 7, Part 3

without increasing the pressure on the innocent to do likewise, and that under the present scheme, large numbers of defendants are "getting ripped off".[54]

Ashworth is equally critical, but approaches the sentencing discount from a rights-based perspective. He argues that sentencing discounts openly conflict with human rights and the presumption of innocence.[55] They are also potentially discriminatory producing a de facto racial bias.

A significant aspect of the plea-bargaining scheme is that defence counsel will merely be negotiating for an "offer" that can be put to the client, whilst reminding the client that a plea of guilty should be entered only if he or she is actually guilty. The vigour with which defence counsel commends the arrangement that has been negotiated may be related to factors other than the strength of the evidence and the story of the client.[56]

The arrangement of pleas is a common feature of the trial on indictment and it is alleged that it can be improperly facilitated by the CPS "overcharging" the accused at the outset. If more serious charges are included on the indictment when the evidence is, at best, equivocal, prosecuting counsel has more to bargain with. The Code for Crown Prosecutors discourages a proliferation of charges and prohibits proceeding with a more serious charge "just to get a defendant to plead guilty to a less serious one".[57] The Attorney-General has issued guidelines on the procedure for the acceptance of pleas,[58] which refers to the Code for Crown Prosecutors, and considers the circumstances in which a plea is to be reduced or fewer charges are to be offered. The guidelines emphasise the need for records to be kept of any exchanges. It is also important that, if a case has been listed for trial but a plea to a lesser offence is accepted or no evidence is offered, the views of the victim (or family of the bereaved) should be taken into account, and they should be kept informed of the developments. New guidelines on the responsibilities of counsel include advise on the appropriate role in the plea bargaining exercise.[58a] The prosecution advocate may ask the defence if a plea will be forthcoming, but should not indicate that a particular plea will be acceptable before that has been offered (para. 6.1). Where the defence offers a plea, the prosecution advocate may discuss this with a view to establishing that it is acceptable, i.e. "that it reflects the defendant's criminality and provides the court with sufficient powers to sentence appropriately (para. 6.2). The plea should be put in writing and the document should be passed to the CPS (para. 6.6). The prosecution advocate is under a duty to discuss matters with the victim/ victim's family if a plea is to be accepted or no evidence is to be offered (para. 6.3). There is also an obligation to check the acceptability of the plea with the CPS (para. 6.5). There is also a duty to ensure that the accused understands the basis of the plea accepted (para. 6.6).

---

[54] p. 436.

[55] See A. Asworth (1998), pp.286–292. A. Ashworth, "The Impact on Criminal Justice" in B. Markesinis (ed.) The Impact of the Human Rights Bill on English Law (1998), p.141.

[56] Plea charging has significant implications for certain types of offence, e.g. vast number of lower charges are accepted in cases of violence, A. Cretney and G. Davis, Punishing Violence (1995) p.138, and in domestic violence cases, Hoyle, Negotiating Domestic Violence: Police, Criminal Justice and Victims (1998), p.159.

[57] Code for Crown Prosecutors, para. 7.2.

[58] Attorney-General's Guidelines on the Acceptance of Pleas [2001] 1 Cr.App. R. 425.

[58a] See the new Farquarson Committee Guidlines (2002).

There are two particular constraints on plea arrangement. First, prosecuting counsel exercise no significant formal influence over sentence.[59] Plea bargaining in England and Wales is less blatant than in the USA because English prosecutors do not seek to persuade the court as to the appropriate sentence, and the judge is unlikely to have indicated a likely sentence for a guilty plea.[60] No bargain is directly permissible about the length of sentence on particular charges, but is permissible about the charges to be proceeded with. However, if the prosecution have agreed or acquiesced in a bargain struck between defence and the judge as to sentence, they should then be estopped from referring the sentence to the Court of Appeal as unduly lenient.[61] Even if not openly seeking a longer sentence, the prosecution will influence the sentence passed by the selection of charges at the outset, and by influencing the mode of the trial. In addition, the prosecution must inform the court of the minimum sentence possible and inform the court of the accused's antecedents. Finally, If it appears to the Attorney-General that a sentence in an indictable only offence or a certain specified indictable offence is unduly lenient, he may refer the sentence to the Court of Appeal.

Secondly, consideration must be given to the role of the judge. The respective roles of prosecuting counsel and judge have not been clearly defined, but it would seem that counsel has the right to offer no evidence on the indictment as a whole or to offer no evidence on a particular count. It is also the responsibility of the prosecution to decide whether to drop a particular charge.[62] The Court of Appeal has accepted the approach propounded by the *Farquharson Committee on the Role of Prosecuting Counsel*[63] that the decision is for prosecuting counsel subject to three important qualifications:

(1) If counsel seeks the approval of the judge, in particular where it is desirable to reassure the public at large that the course proposed is a proper one, counsel must abide by the judge's decision.[64]

(2) Where the judge takes a view on the basis of the information available that counsel is taking the wrong decision, the judge may decline to proceed with the case until counsel has consulted with the Director of Public Prosecutions on whether to proceed in the light of the judge's comments. In

[59] Prosecuting counsel is limited, in effect, to rehearsing the facts about the previous record of the defendant. See G. Zellick, "The Role of Prosecuting Counsel in Sentencing" [1979] Crim. L.R. 493; M. King, "The Role of Prosecuting Counsel in Sentencing — What about Magistrates' Courts?" [1979] Crim. L.R. 775 and *Standard in Criminal Cases*, para. 11.8.

[60] See for criticism P. Darbyshire, "The Mischief of Plea Bargaining and Sentencing Rewards" [2000] Crim. L.R. 895.

[61] See *Attorney General's Reference No. 44 of 2000* [2001] 1 Cr. App. R. 416.

[62] *R. v. Grafton* (1993) 96 Cr. App. R. 156. See *Archbold (2002)*, para. 4–94.

[63] A copy of the Report is to be found in *Archbold (1995)*, paras 4–72 to 4–80, and in *Counsel* (Trinity issue). On the basis of that Report, Sir Thomas Hetherington, the previous DPP, considers the relationship between the prosecution and the courts: *Prosecution and the Public Interest* (1989), pp. 169–171. See also Crown Prosecution Service, *The Crown Court: A Guide to Good Practice for the Courts* (1990).

[64] This proposition is supported by *R. v. Broad* (1978) 68 Cr. App. R. 281. In the Yorkshire Ripper case, the judge was asked whether he would accept the agreement between the prosecution and the defence to accept a plea by Peter Sutcliffe of guilty of manslaughter by diminished responsibility when charged with murder. The judge refused to accept the agreement, presumably because the public interest demanded a trial for murder.

the final analysis, the judge has no right to prevent counsel proceeding as decided.[65]

(3) Where a decision has to be made on whether to proceed during the course of the trial, that decision is to be made by counsel. The prosecution cannot discontinue proceedings after the end of its case without the leave of the judge.

None of this guidance relates to the power of the Attorney-General to enter a *nolle prosequi* to end the proceedings, which may be done at any stage.

(ii) The presentation of the prosecution case

Apart from planning the general strategy of the prosecution case, counsel[66] **17–049** has four specific tasks in its presentation. Opening and closing speeches are made, prosecution witnesses are examined and defence witnesses are cross-examined. In each of these tasks rules of conduct as well as rules of procedure and evidence must be observed.

The *opening speech* to the jury is of the utmost importance. The greatest level of concentration and understanding is likely to be exhibited at the beginning and end of a trial. It is highly undesirable that prosecuting counsel should open the case with unnecessarily emotive language, and where the offences charged are likely to excite particular sympathy for the victim or prejudice against the accused. Counsel should warn the jury not to be influenced by such emotions in weighing the evidence.[67]

In *examination-in-chief* of prosecution witnesses, counsel must obey the golden rule of sticking to the facts in issue. Counsel should not use leading questions[68] (except on uncontentious matters and with the agreement of the

---

[65] See also the Guidelines to Prosecution Counsel given by the Bar Committee of the Senate of the Four Inns of Court and the Bar (1984), as approved in *R. v. Jenkins* (1986) 83 Cr. App. R. 152. In *R. v. Renshaw* [1989] Crim. L. R. 811, the Court of Appeal, referring to the Farquharson Report (1986), emphasised that it is important for the judge to listen to the reasons of counsel for offering no evidence, in particular since counsel may well have information not available to the judge, otherwise the judge is not in a position to decide whether to approve or disapprove counsel's proposed course of action.

[66] Counsel is not employed by the Crown Prosecution Service, whose lawyers have limited rights of audience. The relationship between the instructing lawyer from CPS and counsel was considered by the Farquharson Committee (1986) and quoted in the *Standards in Criminal Cases*. Para. 11.6 deals with some of the difficult cases:

"(a) where counsel has taken a decision on a matter of policy with which his [or her] professional client has not agreed, it would be appropriate for him [or her] to submit to the Attorney-General a written report of all the circumstances, including his [or her] reasons for disagreeing with those who instructed him [or her]; (b) when counsel has had an opportunity to prepare his [or her] brief and to confer with those instructing him [or her], but at the last moment before trial unexpectedly advises that the case should not proceed or that pleas to lesser offences should be accepted, and his [or her] professional client does not accept such advice, counsel should apply for an adjournment if instructed to do so; (c) subject to the above, it is for prosecuting counsel to decide whether to offer no evidence on a particular count or on the indictment as a whole and whether to accept pleas to a lesser count or counts."

[67] *Archbold (2002)*, para. 4–268; *Blackstone's Criminal Practice 2002*, para D.14.5 See also the Farquharson Report (1986).

[68] *i.e.* a question which by its form suggests the desired answer. "You saw the defendant take the jewellery and put it in his pocket, didn't you?"

defence[69]) and there are certain other constraints on the lines of questioning.[70] Whether a question is a leading one is a matter for the judge to decide. Prosecution evidence regarding previous misconduct of the accused is subject to strict limitation.

In *cross-examination* of defence witnesses, prosecuting counsel is entitled to test their evidence fully and fairly subject to the normal constraints on the line of questioning.[71] Counsel may ask leading questions. If prosecuting counsel does choose to question the accused, there are statutory restrictions upon the putting of questions about the criminal past and bad character of the accused.[72]

As a matter of practice, the prosecution must present all the evidence on which they intend to rely before the close of their case.[73] However, further evidence may, exceptionally, be called, at the discretion of the trial judge where it was not previously available, was omitted inadvertently, or used to rebut matters arising *ex improviso*.[74]

Counsel will also have an opportunity to make a closing speech.[75]

(iii) Assisting the other participants—the defence and the judge

17–050 Prosecuting counsel has an obligation to assist the defence by the disclosure of certain evidence. The disclosure provisions are considered more fully elsewhere,[76] but in brief the prosecution must inform the defence of the name and address of any person who has made a statement related to the prosecution but is not to be called as a witness; of the existence of statements made previously by a prosecution witness which are inconsistent with evidence given at trial by the witness; and of the previous convictions, if any, of prosecution witnesses which are known to the prosecution. These disclosures may materially assist the defence case and further assistance requested by the defence may be rendered by the prosecution at their discretion.[77]

The obligation to assist the judge is made clear in the Code of Conduct. Not only must counsel assist by arguments on point of law or procedure

---

[69] There are other exceptions to the general rule; *e.g.* when the witness called for the prosecution turns out to be hostile, *i.e.* deliberately obstructive, the Criminal Procedure Act 1865, s.3 permits the use of leading questions to cross-examine the witness to elicit the expected information: see M. Hirst, *Andrews and Hirst, Criminal Evidence* (4th ed., 2001), paras 7.50–51.

[70] *e.g.* questions about previous inconsistent statements may not generally be put (unless the witness is hostile), nor questions impugning the witness's credit. Counsel must not vilify, insult or annoy any witness: *Code of Conduct*, para. 610(e). For suggestion that counsel should adopt cognitive interviewing skills see P. Davies, "Cognitive Interviewing" (1997) N.L.J. 147 1705. This allegedly produces better accounts because the story the witness tells is his own.

[71] That is it should be directed to an issue in the case or to the credit of a witness. Questions can be put about previous inconsistent statements, see the Criminal Procedure Act 1865, ss.4 and 5.

[72] See Criminal Evidence Act 1898, s.3.(below).

[73] *Archbold (2002)*, paras 4-335–4-354; *Blackstone's Criminal Practice 2002*, para. F.6.1

[74] See recently, *Jolly v. DPP* [2000] Crim. L.R. 471 for a summary of the position.

[75] See the Criminal Evidence Act 1898, s.2.

[76] See paras 14-068–14-079 above.

[77] See *Standards in Criminal Cases*, paras. 114(c) and (d).

arising during the trial, but it is also "the duty of prosecuting counsel to assist the court at the conclusion of the summing-up by drawing attention to any apparent errors or omissions of fact or law".[78] Needless to say, this duty has to be discharged with considerable tact.

Influencing the court with regard to sentence is not part of the duties of prosecuting counsel, although the prosecution may now request that the Attorney-General seek a review by the Court of Appeal of a sentence believed to be unduly lenient.[79]

(b) Defence counsel[80]

Counsel defending a client in a criminal case may face conflict between the duty to the court and the duty to the client. It may be asked how counsel can act as advocate for someone who is "obviously guilty", or put forward a defence or a mitigation which appears to be based on the slenderest of evidence. The answer given by the Bar Council is that, consistent with counsel's duty not knowingly to deceive or mislead the court,[81] every accused person has a right to have the prosecution case tested and their own case put.[82] In a statement following the case of *R. v. McFadden*,[83] in which the trial judge had criticised counsel for wasting time, the Chairman of the Bar said[84]:

17–051

> "It is the duty of counsel when defending an accused on a criminal charge to present to the court, fearlessly and without regard to his personal interests, the defence of that accused. It is not his function to determine the truth or falsity of that defence, nor should he permit his personal opinion of that defence to influence his conduct of it. ... Counsel also has a duty to the court and to the public. This duty includes the clear presentation of the issues and the avoidance of waste of time, repetition and prolixity. In the conduct of every case counsel must be mindful of this public responsibility."[85]

The "cab-rank" principle is intended to ensure that every accused can

---

[78] *Standards in Criminal Cases*, para. 11.7.
[79] *ibid.* para. 11.8. As to the review of sentencing, see the Criminal Justice Act 1988, s.36, and para. 17-076 below.
[80] See generally *Archbold (2002)*, para. 4–307. See on the historical aspects J. H. Langbein, *The Prosecutorial Origins of Defence Counsel in the Eighteenth Century: The Appearance of Solicitors* (1999) Camb. L.J. 314 tracing use of defence counsel to 1730 and earlier for treason, as a result of judicial practice/discretion, dispite some resistance, especially where no points of law arose.
[81] *Code of Conduct*, para. 202.
[82] This is one of the fundamental principles of the Bar: see *Standards in Criminal Cases*, Responsibilities of Defence Counsel and para. 3-028, above.
[83] (1976) 62 Cr.App.R. 187.
[84] Melford Stevenson J. had taken a very dim view of the length of the trial in which the evidence had occupied over 30 days, and the closing speeches for the defence six and a half days. There were seven defendants, but the judge thought that counsel had behaved improperly and took the unusual course of inviting the taxing master to look carefully at the fees allowed counsel on legal aid taxation.
[85] (1976) 62 Cr. App R. 193. The complaints against defending counsel were investigated by the Professional Conduct Committee of the Bar, and rejected.

engage an advocate.[86] Counsel must " ... endeavour to protect his client from conviction except by a competent tribunal and upon legally admissible evidence sufficient to support a conviction for the offence charged".[87] Counsel should "ensure that the defendant is never left unrepresented at any stage of his trial".[88] Counsel's opinion of the weight of evidence and the credibility of any defence being suggested by the client will obviously be factors in the advice which defence counsel gives. Where counsel had to leave/withdraw from a case, the court has a discretion to adjourn for the accused to find representatives.[89]

(i) Advising on plea and the accused's confession

17–052 Counsel cannot leave a client unaware of the concessions to be gained from a sentence discount[90] or plea arrangements.[91] However, it must be made clear to the accused that there is complete freedom of choice of plea and that the accused has complete responsibility for it.[92] In practice the advice and attitude of defence counsel can be crucial, as the study by Baldwin and McConville[93] demonstrates. For example, 48 per cent accused people gave as their reason for changing their plea the advice that they had received from counsel. It is difficult to offer advice which will inevitably carry great weight whilst leaving the accused free to make up his or her mind. In 21 out of 121 studied cases there was evidence that the advice given was not fair or proper.[94]

Counsel may give the accused an assessment of the strength of the prosecution case and the likelihood of acquittal, the details of any plea arrangement which has been or might be negotiated, the possible range of sentence and the discount for a guilty plea, the credibility of any defence which may be advanced, and the dangers of attempting to discredit prosecution witnesses, especially the police. If the accused is misled by counsel into pleading guilty (*e.g.* where counsel assures the accused that such pleas will not affect other charges) a fair trial is jeopardised. The court always has the discretion to allow a plea to be withdrawn.[95]

Counsel must not "devise" facts for his client, *e.g.* by suggesting a defence that is more plausible than that claimed.[96] Also important is counsel's attitude and demeanour. If the accused is given the impression that counsel has no hope or confidence of an acquittal or appears indifferent to the accused's protestations of innocence, the pressure on the accused will be further increased.

The Court of Appeal, in considering defence counsel's obligations to

---

[86] See, para. 3-029 above.
[87] *Standards in Criminal Cases*, para. 12.1.
[88] *ibid.* para. 16.2.1.
[89] *R. v. Al-Zubeidi* [1999] Crim. L.R. 906.
[90] For the position in the Magistrates' Court see para. 17-008 above, and in the crown court, para. 17-048 above.
[91] See para. 17-048., above.
[92] Para. 17-038.
[93] *Negotiated Justice* (1977), Chap. 3.
[94] See also Sanders and Young, (2000), pp.446–453.
[95] *R. v. W* (AG) [1999] Crim. L.R. 87.
[96] See *Written Standards*, para. 5.8. See A. Hutchinson, "The Perjury Problem" (2001) 151 N.L.J. 160.

advise a client, has observed that if need be the advice may be in strong terms, but that counsel must emphasise that the accused should only plead guilty if actually guilty.[97] If defence counsel deprives the accused of the freedom of plea, a guilty plea would be a nullity.[98] However, such cases are rare since the advice needs to be couched in extreme terms to contravene the guidelines. If an innocent client decides to plead guilty, counsel must continue to represent the client, "but only after he has advised what the consequences will be and that what can be submitted in mitigation can only be on the basis that the client is guilty.[99]

Sanders and Young suggest that the barrister may not always be acting in the best interests of her or his client. This, they suggest, is because of the barrister's obligation to the court and the administration of justice as well as to the client[1] (although this is not as significant as prosecution counsel's responsibilities), the low standard fees for legal aid work encourage the barrister to seek late guilty pleas, barristers are under considerable pressure of work often receiving briefs shortly before seeing the client so they are often ilIll-prepared and "ill-disposed to fight on a defendant's behalf", and many criminal barristers are not of particularly high quality".[2]

Counsel may discover that the client is guilty of the offence charged. This may emerge from the client in clear terms in the form of a confession or as a result of inconsistent statements or from supposition on the part of counsel. A conflict then arises between the duty to the client and the duty to the court. If the discovery is based upon inconsistent statements or counsel's suspicions or speculations, no general guidance is provided by the Code of Conduct since it all depends on the actual circumstances of the particular case.[3] If the discovery is based upon a confession, it is made clear that counsel is not prevented from appearing in the accused's defence, nor does it release counsel from "his imperative duty to do all that he honourably can for his client".[4] However, a confession limits what counsel may do. Counsel "must not assert as true that which he knows to be false. He may not connive at, much less attempt to substantiate, a fraud.[5] Counsel may not suggest that someone else committed the crime or call any evidence known to be false. Counsel may take objections to the competency of the court, to the form of the indictment, to the admissibility of evidence and to the

---

[97] *R. v. Turner* [1970] 2 Q.B. 321 at 326. See also *Standards in Criminal Cases*, para. 12.3. The decision in Turner poses a difficult ethical dilemma for defence lawyers who believe that the accused's chances are improved by pleading guilty to a lesser charge even though the accused insists on his innocence. See A. Ashworth and M. Blake, "Some Ethical Issues in Prosecuting and Defending Criminal Cases" [1998] Crim. L.R. 16 at 25.

[98] *R. v. Peace* [1976] Crim.L.R. 119; *R. v. Inns* (1975) 60 Cr.App.R. 231.

[99] *Standards in Criminal Cases*, para. 12.5.

[1] See above, para. 17-057.

[2] Sanders and Young (2000), pp. 455–466. In the USA, questions have been raised on numerous occasions about the standard of advocacy and representation afforded to indigent defendants. See R. E. Priehs, "Appointed Counsel for Indigent Criminal Appellants: Does Compensation Influence Effort?" (1999) The Justice System Journal 73.

[3] *ibid.* para. 13.6. The *Written Standards* deal with circumstances in which counsel receive documents to which they are not entitled.

[4] *ibid.* para. 13.2. It is also important to bear in mind: "(a) that every punishable crime is a breach of common or statute law committed by a person of sound mind and understanding; (b) that the issue in a criminal trial is always whether the defendant is guilty of the offence charged, never whether he is innocent; (c) that the burden of proof rests on the prosecution."

[5] *ibid.* para. 13.1.

evidence admitted. "In other words, a barrister must not ... set up an affirmative case inconsistent with the confession made to him."[6] Further, since the issue in a criminal trial is whether or not the accused is guilty and the burden of proof lies on the prosecution, counsel may test the prosecution evidence and may argue that the case against the accused has not been established.[7]

(ii) Correcting defects

17–053   The conflict between the duty to the client and the duty to the court may also arise with regard to defence counsel's obligations in respect of procedural error, or factual or legal errors made by the court, not noticed by the prosecution.[8] One view, proceeding partly from the conception of the trial as a game in which the underdog (the accused) is entitled to the benefit of any errors, is that defence counsel is under no obligation to correct the judge. The Code of Conduct, however, requires counsel to bring all authorities, (that is all relevant statutes and cases, including those unfavourable to the defence) and any procedural irregularity to the attention of the court before the summing up has begun.[9] Points of procedural irregularity must not be reserved so as to form the basis of an appeal.[10]

(iii) The conduct of the defence

17–054   If, at the end of the prosecution presentation, defence counsel believes that a case has not been established against the accused, a submission of no case to answer may be made which, if successful, results in the acquittal of the accused. The judge must decide whether or not the prosecution have adduced evidence on which a jury, properly directed, could convict in accordance with the law.[11] Ordered acquittals occur where the judge orders an acquittal before the trial commences. Directed acquittals are those in which the judge directs the jury to acquit once the trial has formally commenced.

If the Crown Prosecution Service consider with due care whether or not to prosecute there should be relatively few successful submissions of no case unless, for example, the prosecution witnesses fail to appear or do not support the case for the prosecution.[12] However, in the years since the CPS was introduced the number of directed acquittals in the Crown Court has increased dramatically. The number of directed acquittals is at present around 55 per cent, and it is claimed that most of these (70–80 per cent) non-jury acquittals were foreseeable at an early stage.[13] This certainly calls into

---

[6]   *ibid*. para. 13.3.
[7]   *ibid*. para. 13.4.
[8]   *ibid*. para. 13.5.
[9]   If they are noticed by the prosecution, they should be raised with the judge: see para. 17-050, above. *Code of Conduct*, para. 610(c).
[10]   *ibid*.
[11]   *R. v. Galbraith* [1981] 1 W.L.R. 1039 and see Emmins (2000), p.284.
[12]   However, see above, Chap. 14.
[13]   See J. Baldwin, "Understanding Judge Ordered and Directed Acquittals" [1997] Crim. L.R. 536.

question the effectiveness of the CPS function of reviewing charges.[14] The CPS is in a difficult position with a clear obligation to consider each charge seriously, being conscious also of the potential criticism to be faced if the prosecution is rejected at trial.[15]

In his study of non-jury acquittals, Baldwin[16] discovered that 44 per cent of ordered acquittals were attributable to the failure of a witness to attend or because the witness retracted the statement; 3.2 per cent were due to witnesses proving untrustworthy prior to trial; 15.9 per cent were as a result of the judge concluding that there was no realistic prospect of conviction or that the evidence was insufficient; 14.3 per cent were attributable to the successful conviction of others in the case; 11.1 per cent due to a legal problem or questions about the conduct of the investigation. Directed acquittals occurred usually where a key witness had not come up to proof (34 per cent) or with other evidential problems (32 per cent) or insufficient evidence (12 per cent). Baldwin concluded that a lack of experience in CPS workers and their working very closely with the police were very important reasons for the CPS pursuing charges that were rejected at trial. These pressures flow in part from a lack of true independence,[17] and from internal inadequacies in CPS funding and management. Further reasons for the high proportion of directed/ ordered acquittals include the unwillingness of counsel to drop a case[18] and in many cases the very late briefing of counsel leaving no real opportunity for them to advise the CPS to discontinue a weak case.

The problem is one that is unlikely ever to be conclusively resolved since as Baldwin observed, the "task of establishing whether there is a realistic prospect of conviction is a largely subjective evaluation".[19]

Defendant's costs are payable under a defendant's costs order (Prosecution of Offences Act 1985, s.16) and are usually payable whenever a case is discontinued. Situations in which costs might be denied are where the defendant's conduct has brought suspicion on himself and has misled the prosecution into thinking the case against him is stronger than it is".[20]

The Auld Report recommended that "urgent consideration" be given to changing the structure of the public funding of defence fees in criminal cases so as properly to reward and encourage adequate and timely preparation of cases.[21]

If the case proceeds, the formal procedure for the defence will be the same as for the prosecution,[22] with an opening speech, witnesses and a closing

---

[14] See further A. Ashworth, "Developments in the Public Prosecutor's Office in England and Wales" (2000) Eur. Jnl of Crime, Criminal Law and Criminal Justice, p.257–275. See also A. Hoyano, L. Hoyano, G. Davis and S. Goldie, "A Study of the Impact of the Revised Code for Crown Prosecutors" [1997] Crim. L.R. 556.

[15] CPS inspectorate reports on acquittals are generally supportive of the prosecutor's decision to pursue the case — 78% were felt to be through no forseeable reason. See CPS Inspectorate Report, (1999), para. 2.4.

[16] J. Baldwin, "Understanding Judge Ordered and Directed Acquittals" [1997] Crim. L.R. 536.

[17] For analysis see Ashworth (1998), p.277; Sanders and Young, (2000), p.553.

[18] Baldwin exposes the lack of rigour in scrutiny of the cases in CPS, or by counsel, who avoid discontinuing a case lest they lose work from the CPS. For a response to Baldwin's article see P. Lewis, "The CPS and Acquittals by Judge: Finding the Balance" [1997] Crim. L.R. 653.

[19] p.540.

[20] Practice Direction (Crime: Costs) [1999] 1 W.L.R. 1832; Practice Direction (Crime: Costs), [1991] 1 W.L.R. 498.

[21] pp.400–404.

[22] Counsel should therefore observe rules relating to conduct as regards the limits of cross examination: Code para. 708(a).

speech.[23] Counsel is not restricted to commenting only on the evidence led, but should not ask the jury to make a recommendation of mercy.[24] Effectively putting the defence case begins before calling defence witnesses by laying an adequate foundation in probing and challenging prosecution witnesses in cross-examination. The most problematic issues are those of the tactical conduct of the case, *e.g.* counsel will have to advise the accused whether he should testify and of the consequences of not doing so.[25] A major problem will often be the extent to which prosecution witnesses can be attacked without allowing the prosecution to place in evidence details of the (bad) character of the accused, including any previous convictions.

The normal rules of evidence prevent evidence being given by prosecution witnesses about the accused's character[26] and also forbid cross-examination of the accused on that subject.[27] Such cross-examination may, however, be permitted where the defence has sought to establish the accused's good character or cast imputations upon the character of the prosecutor or prosecution witnesses or deceased victim.[28] It is this latter rule which creates the problem, for the dividing line between an emphatic denial of guilt (which does not expose the accused to attack) and an allegation of lies or misconduct by the prosecution witnesses (particularly police officers) may be a very narrow one.[29] Counsel, if instructed by the accused to allege that the whole of the prosecution case is a "put-up job", will have to advise on the consequences of running that particular defence. To assist counsel, the trial judge will usually give a warning when a line of cross-examination is being used which may expose the accused to cross-examination as to character.[30]

(iv) After the verdict

17–055   Defence counsel, after a plea or verdict of guilty, will usually make a plea in mitigation of sentence on behalf of the client. As favourable a view as possible is put on the client's circumstances and suggestions may be made as to why particular sentences would or would not be appropriate. Care must be taken in referring to third parties during mitigation, for they will have no opportunity to contest any assertions. No allegation may be made which is " ... merely scandalous, or intended or calculated to villify insult or annoy a ... person".[31]

---

[23]   *Archbold (2002)*, para. 4–310 *et seq.*
[24]   *R. v. Black* (1964) 48 Cr.App. R. 52.
[25]   Code, para. 12.4.
[26]   See below para. 17-066.
[27]   See generally, C. Tapper, *Cross and Tapper on Evidence* (9th ed., 1999)), Chaps 6 and 7.
[28]   Criminal Evidence Act 1898, ss 1-3, as amended by the Criminal Justice and Public Order Act 1994 and the Youth Justice and Criminal Evidence Act 1999.
[29]   See *R. v. Tanner* (1977) 76 Cr.App.R. 56 and the discussion in *Archbold (2002)*, paras 8–186 — 8–193. The most helpful dictum is that of Lord Hewart C.J. in *R. v. Jones* (1924) 17 Cr. App.R. 117 at 120: It is " ... one thing to deny that he had made the confession, but it is another thing to say that the whole thing was a deliberate and elaborate concoction on the part of the inspector: that seems to be an attack on the character of the witness." General guidance is to be found in a decision of the House of Lords, *Selvey v. DPP* [1970] A.C. 304. Rape trials in which the accused alleges consent are treated as a separate special category in which the shield is not lost: *R. v. Cook* [1959] 2.Q.B. 340 permissible.
[30]   *ibid.* at p. 342A; *R. v. Cook* [1959] 2 Q.B. 340 at 348. On the permissble extent of the cross-examination see *R. v. McLeod* [1995] 1 Cr. App. R. 591.
[31]   *Code of Conduct*, para. 610(e) and para. 5.10.

Save in exceptional circumstances, it is defence counsel's duty to see the client after conviction and sentence.[32] Counsel may give initial advice on appeal or the existence of grounds of appeal.[33]

5. WITNESSES

In most contested trials, witness evidence will be called by the prosecution   **17–056**
and the defence.[34] People who might be witnesses may be unwilling to appear or there may be some doubt about their capacity to give evidence.[35] Whether a witness satisfies the legal requirements to give evidence (*i.e.* is a "competent" witness) is a matter of law for the judge. Prosecuting and defence counsel exercise considerable discretion in who they will call. They must bear in mind not only the legal requirements but also the practical consideration that there is no point in calling someone who will not "come up to proof", that is, someone who will not be able to provide a convincing and consistent story in court, particularly under cross-examination. In certain cases it may be necessary to call expert witnesses. Counsel is permitted to communicate with witnesses whom he expects to call. In the case of the defendant, character and expert witnesses, counsel may interview them.[36] In the case of other witnesses the communication is limited to explaining the courts procedure and putting the witness at case.[37] Counsel must not coach any witness as to the substance of his evidence or the manner in which to testify.

(a) Competence of witnesses

The primary question for determining "competence" is whether a person   **17–057**
will be capable of giving intelligible evidence. Until recently the law regarding competence was less certain and presented problems in cases involving child witnesses or those with a learning disability or mental disorder. The law, especially as regards children, has changed significantly, largely in response to the recognition of child abuse and the need to enable children, who are often the only witnesses, to give evidence. The latest amendments were contained in the Youth Justice and Criminal Evidence Act 1999.

Under section 53(3) "all persons are (whatever their age) competent to give evidence". The crucial issue is whether the witness is able to give intelligible testimony. Issues of competence may arise, *e.g.* where the witness is a child or someone suffering from a mental disorder. Where there is some doubt, the matter should be raised before the witness begins testifying.[38]

---

[32] *Standards in Criminal Cases*, para. 17.2.
[33] As to appeais in criminal cases, See Chap. 18.
[34] Some cases, *e.g.* can be proved on scientific evidence alone.
[35] On the procedural requirements for securing witness attendance see *Archbold (2002)*, paras 8-1–8-2.
[36] *Written Standards*, para. 6.3.1.
[37] *ibid.* para. 6.1.2.
[38] See Youth Justice and Criminal Evidence Act 1999, ss.53–56 on the procedure for competence. Expert evidence may be necessary, especially where the issue is whether a mentally ill person can given intelligible testimony. See *R. v. Deakin* [1994] 4 All E.R. 769; *R. v. Barratt* [1996] Crim. L.R. 495.

The 1999 Act places the burden on a party calling a witness to satisfy the judge (on the balance of probabilities) that the witness will be able to give intelligible evidence. In determining this question, in the absence of the jury, the judge should have regard to any special measures or directions that may be available to the witness (*e.g.* live link TV; communication aids, etc.), and may receive expert evidence if necessary.[39]

"Competence" also raises potential problems whether the accused and the accused's spouse can testify. The accused has been allowed to give evidence on his or her own behalf since the Criminal Evidence Act 1898,[40] but only became generally competent for the prosecution by virtue of section 80 of the Police and Criminal Evidence Act 1984.[41]

The accused is not competent for the prosecution. A co-accused may give evidence for the prosecution if he has ceased to be on trial — *i.e.* he has pleaded guilty, or has been acquitted or a *nolle prosequi* has been entered by the Attorney-General.

(b) Compellability of witnesses

17–058 Most people can be compelled to be witnesses, with the exception of the accused and the accused's spouse. However, the accused's spouse is compellable on behalf of the accused generally,[42] and for the prosecutions[43] and co-accused in cases of assault or violent offences on the spouse witness or people under-16 and sexual offences committed against the spouse witness or someone under 16 or the inchoate versions of these offences. In such exceptional cases the policy of protecting the sanctity of marriage is outweighed by the need to obtain evidence for such serious offences to which the spouse will be likely to be the only available witness.[44] There are many other miscellaneous categories of individuals over whom special claims of incompellability may arise (*e.g* diplomats, judges). Once a witness is compellable, he or she must answer questions posed in the proceedings, and a failure to do so is a contempt of court.[45]

(c) Oaths

17–059 As a general rule, the oral testimony of every witness must be given on oath.[46] Witnesses who do not wish to testify on a religious text may affirm instead. Practical advice on which holy books are used for different religious and the way in which religions may wish to, *e.g.* wash, cover heads, remove

---

[39] s.54(5)

[40] s.1. The accused's spouse has been competent for the defence since the 1898 Act, see the Police and Criminal Evidence Act 1984, s.80, as amended by the Youth Justice and Criminal Evidence Act 1999, s.53.

[41] Police and Criminal Evidence Act 1984, s.80 as amended. He or she is not competent if a co-accused is charged in the proceedings. As to the many difficulties in interpreting the section regarding both the competence and compellability of spouses, see P. Creighton, "Spouse Competence and Compellability" [1990] Crim. L.R. 34. This applies to married couples only: *R.v. Pearce* [2002] Crim. L.R, July.

[42] PACE, s.80(2A).

[43] s.80(2A).

[44] For discussion see Andrews and Hirst, paras 8.23–8.31.

[45] See, *e.g. R. v. Bird* (1997) 161 J.P. 96; *R.v. Maguire* [1996] Crim. L.R. 833.

[46] On the form and procedure of the administration of the oath see Oaths Act 1978.

shoes is provided to the judiciary.[47] Prior to the Youth Justice and Criminal Evidence Act 1999 children could only give evidence unsworn. Under the 1999 Act, all those under 14 give unsworn evidence. Witnesses over that age may give sworn or unsworn evidence. Section 55(2) provides that a witness who has a sufficient "appreciation of the solemnity of the occasion" should give sworn evidence. There have been suggestions that the jury attaches little weight to the witness taking oath. The Auld Report has recommended that the oaths be replaced with solemn promises, better reflecting today's more secular society.[48] Some have questioned whether it would be more effective simply to remind each witness of the offence and penalty of perjury before they gave evidence.

(d) Giving evidence

A witness gives evidence initially in response to questions from counsel by whom he or she was called.[49] "Leading" questions must be avoided.[50] The witness is then available to counsel for the other side for cross-examination, where the object will be to elicit evidence favourable to the cross-examiner's case and to discredit unfavourable evidence. The judge has the power to ask questions of a witness, but should exercise caution in doing so, particularly with the defendant as a witness. Finally, counsel who called the witness is entitled to re-examine the witness, but must not raise any new issues.[51]

    17–060

    A witness appearing at trial to give their remembered account of events that may have occurred many months ago may seem like an unlikely way to get the best evidence of what happened. The significance placed on such a procedure rather than on documentary evidence illustrates the importance of the principle of orality which still underpins the English criminal trial: all evidence is best delivered orally by the person with direct knowledge of events. This pays little heed to the evidence from psychological research which reveals how fragile are witness' memories, how suggestible they are in questioning and how weak are juror's perceptions/judgments based on witness demeanour.[52] Nor does it pay adequate attention to the fact that the

---

[47] See JSB practical guide on race, *www.jsb.co.uk/etac/race + courts.htm*. See *R. v. mehrban* [2002] Crim. L.R. 439.

[48] pp. 598–600.

[49] Usually, the witness will be giving evidence in conformity with the case which counsel is putting; however, as to the position if the witness turns out to be hostile, see para. 17-049 above. As to the usual rule of the inadmissibility of out-of-court statements which are to the same effect as the in-court evidence, see *Fox v. G.M.C.* [1960] 3 All E.R. 225 and *R v. Roberts* [1942] 1 All E.R. 187; usually, a witness may not refresh memory in court but must speak from their own recollection of the events, but there is an exception in that a witness may refer to a contemporaneous note of the matters to which the testimony relates. Witnesses are encouraged to refresh their memories out of court by reference to their original witness statements, and in some cases may interrupt their testimony in order to do so, see *R. v. Da Silva* (1990) 90 Cr.App.R. 233; *R. v. Ribble JJ., ex p. Cochrane* [1996] 2 Cr. App. R. 554. Rules provide that the prosecution must tell the defence if their witnesses have seen their statements prior to giving evidence, see HO Circular 82/1969. For reform proposals see Auld Report, Chap. 11.

[50] See para. 17-049 above.

[51] *R. v. Harman* [1985] Crim.L.R. 326.

[52] See G. Millar and J. Burgoon, "Factors Affecting Assessments of Witness Credibility" in L. Kerr and R. Bray (eds), *The Psychology of the Courtroom* (1982); Jeremy A Blumenthal, "A Wipe of the Hands. A Lick of the Lips: The Validity of Demeanor Evidence in Assessing Witness Credibility" (1993) 72 Nebraska Law Review 1157; Marcus Stone, "Instant Lie Detection: Demeanour and Credibility in Criminal Trials," [1991] Crim. L.R. 821; Olin Guy

witness will be allowed to read earlier witness statements in order to refresh his/her memory before going into the witness box. The jury is surely misled if they think that the witness is really recalling details from months before. The Auld Report recommends relaxing the rule so that witnesses can use prior statements as evidence,[53] and points towards the future use of video-recording of all witness statements.

Giving evidence in court is a trying experience.[54] Consequently, counsel has to be aware of the possibility of the witness not coming up to proof *i.e.* the capacity of the witness not only to retell the story convincingly when responding to examination-in-chief, but also to be able to stick to that story when subject to cross-examination.

In the last decade, much has been done to improve the support and guidance provided to those who are to give evidence, without overstepping the boundary and offering "coaching" in how they should testify. The Witness Service provides help to all witnesses in the Crown Court ensuring that the witness has advance information and by answering non-legal questions. Introduced in 1996, the Service has been acknowledged anecdotally to play a significant role in reducing the ordeal of appearing as a witness. However, independent academic research has suggested that the Service does "little to ameliorate" the unpleasant experience of giving evidence in a Crown Court.[55] The more recent findings[56] reveal that 76 per cent of witnesses were very or fairly satisfied with their overall treatment in the criminal justice system. The witnesses' satisfaction with court officials was high. Moreover, levels of satisfaction were strongly related to provision of information to witness.[57] Almost 20 per cent of witnesses felt intimidated by the process and 25 per cent by an individual person (the figure rose to 57 per cent with child witnesses).[58] Thirty-nine per cent of witnesses said they would not be happy to be a witness again.[59]

One simple way of improving the lot of the witness is her to ensure that adequate information is provided to them prior to the trial. Shapland and Bell,[60] found that in 992 of Crown Court centres and 67 per cent of magistrates' courts familiarisation visits are offered.[60a] Rather disturbingly, the survey revealed that 79 per cent of magistrates' courts and 97 per cent of

---

Wellborn III, "Demeanor" (1991) 76 Cornell Law Review 1075.

[53] pp. 548–551.

[54] See Royal Commission on Criminal Justice, *Report* Cm. 2263 (1993), p. 128.

[55] A. Riding, "The Crown Court Witness Service: Little Help in the Witness Box" (1999) 38 Howard Jnl 411.

[56] E. Whitehead, "*Key Findings from the Witness Satisfaction Survey 2000*" (HORSD No. 133, 2001).

[57] 80% of prosecution witnesses and 72% of defence witnesses received helpful information.

[58] 42% of those reported the incident to police.

[59] 87% were satisfied with the CPS; 67% with the defence; and an impressive 95% with the judge. Most concerned were women (68%) and children (69%). Problems identified by witnesses included delay in court (17% waited four hours; 37% in magistrates' courts waited at least one hour). The separation of defence and prosecution witnesses in waiting was preferred, and treatment in cross-examination was very influential in the overall satisfaction ratings. Witness Services exist in Crown Court centres and in 1997/98 offered support to 120,550 people: *Digest IV*, p. 17.

[60] "Victims in the magistrates' courts and Crown Court" [1998] Crim. L.R. 537.

[60a] See their discussion of other facilities (authors information points, waiting areas for witnesses, refreshment facilities, child care facilities) and for witness support services in general.

Crown Courts had experienced some form of intimidation of victims and witnesses. In the most recent Home Office research, 64 per cent of vulnerable or intimidated witnesses were very or fairly satisfied with their overall treatment within the criminal justice system.[61] The *Auld Report* recommends much greater provision of information for witnesses.[62]

For some witnesses, the trauma of a court appearance will be particularly severe. This has been made graphically apparent in child sexual abuse cases. Many of these cases have not been prosecutions of the alleged abuser, but civil child-care cases where the rules of evidence are less stringent. However, if a prosecution is instituted, it will be necessary to consider whether the victim can give evidence. As has already been seen, the first hurdle is whether or not the child is competent to give evidence, although this is now much less of a problem, with the focus being on the ability of the child to give an intelligible account.[63] If competent, it has to be considered whether the child will be able to give evidence in the daunting atmosphere of the court under the gaze of the alleged abuser. The court has always had the power to screen the witness from the gaze of the accused, although the witness must be open to the view of the courts.[64] Provisions in the Criminal Justice Acts 1988 and 1991 provided for children in certain cases to give their evidence through live television link[65] and[66] by allowing for the admissibility as evidence in chief of a pre-recorded interview between an adult and a child.[67] The major deficiency in these legislative schemes was that the child witness still had to be present at the courtroom to face cross-examination live (whether in the court room or through a live link). Following further research into the ordeal of giving evidence as a child, a complainant in a sexual case, or as a vulnerable witness[68] generally,[69] the Youth Justice and Criminal Evidence Act 1999 introduced radical new reforms aimed explicitly at improving the quality of the evidence obtained from witnesses and ensuring that the trial process is not so intimidating that it deters people from reporting crime.

Part II of the Youth Justice and Criminal Evidence Act 1999 introduces special measures that may be ordered by the judge to assist witnesses. The

---

[61] S. Kitchen and R. Elliott, *Key Findings from the Vulnerable Witness Survey* (HO RDS No. 147, 2001.

[62] pp.558–590.

[63] See Youth Justice and Criminal Evidence Act 1999, s.53.

[64] *R. v. Smellie* (1919) 14 Cr.App.R. 128 and *R. v. X* (1990) 91 Cr.App.R. 36. See now the Youth Justice and Criminal Evidence Act 1999, s.2.

[65] Criminal Justice Act 1988, s.32, and see J. R. Spencer and R. Flin, *The Evidence of Children* (2nd ed., 1993).

[66] s.54 of the 1991 Act added s.32A to the Criminal Justice Act 1988.

[67] Great care has to be taken with these interviews, see the *Memorandum of Good Practice on Video Recorded Interviews with Child Witnesses for Criminal Proceedings*; G. Davies, C. Wilson, R. Mitchell and J. Milsom, *Videotaping Children's Evidence: An Evaluation* (1995) and *Blackstone's Criminal Practice 2002*, para. F16.21. See also *R. v. C* (1995) 159 J.P. 521; *R. v. Redbridge Youth Court* [2001] EWHC Admin 209.

[68] Vulnerable groups include for example those in fear and victims of domestic violence. See recently A. Cretney and G. Davies, "Prosecuting Domestic Assault: Victims Failing Courts or Courts Failing Victims?" (1997) 36 In Howard p.146.

[69] See Davies *et al.* (1995), which discovered, however, that there was much scepticism as to the value of the procedure for the interests of justice and the children themselves. The most comprehensive review was the interdepartmental report *Speaking Up for Justice* (1999). See generally on the Act D.J. Birch and R. Leng, *Blackstone's Guide to the Youth Justice and Criminal Evidence Act 1999* (2000), J. McEwan, [2000] 4 E & P.I.

Act categorises those witnesses who are eligible by reason of age (under 17) or incapacity, or fear or distress. Further special protection is afforded to child witnesses and those giving evidence in sexual and other specified cases. In those cases in which the special measures are not automatic, the judge must assess which of the special measures are to be ordered, focusing on the extent to which they might enhance the *quality* of the witnesses' evidence. The measures that can be ordered include the use of screens to shield the witness (section 23), the use of live link television (section 24) the possibility of giving evidence in a private chamber (section 25), the removal of wigs and gowns (section 26), the use of video recorded evidence in chief (section 27) and cross-examination recorded on video before the trial (section 28),[70] the use of intermediaries to communicate with witnesses or conduct the examination (section 29) and other aids to communication.[71] The aim of the Act is to maximise the opportunity for all witnesses who can give an intelligible account to give the best account possible.[72]

In the event that a witness is in fear, his or her earlier witness statement, if it exists in documentary form, may be admissible as evidence without the witness attending to give oral evidence. The trial judge must be satisfied that it is in the interests of justice to admit the document, and there are also other criteria to be met.[73]

In every case, the witness will be subjected to examination not only regarding his or her testimony relating to the facts in issue in the trial on which he or she has given evidence in chief, but also on his or her credibility. In particular, questioning as to previous convictions, bias or a general reputation for untruthfulness will be likely. In recent years concerns have arisen in a number of trials with the payments to witnesses by the media, see *R. v. West* (1996) 2 Cr. App. R.374. These matters can be explored in cross-examination, but there is a danger that the witness will be so tainted as to cause the trial to be unfair.[74].

All such questioning must comply with the Code of Conduct of the Bar, by which each barrister is bound to show courtesy and respect to witnesses. Particular difficulties arise in cross-examining police officers as regards their disciplinary record,[75] the complainant in a sexual case and the accused. The judge can also question the witnesses, but this must be done cautiously.

In relation to the cross-examination of the complainant in a sexual case,

---

[70] On admissibility of video evidence in child witness cases and the opportunity for the jury to reconsider transcripts of the interviews see *R. v. Welstead* [1996] Crim. L.R. 48 and *R. v. Rawlings* [1995] Crim. L.R. 335; *R. v. B* [1996] Crim. L.R. 499; *R. v. Morgan* [1996] Crim. L.R. 600.

[71] See Crown Court (Special Measures Directions and Directions Prohibing Cross Examination) Rules 2002, S.I. 2002/1688; Magistrates' Courts (Special Measures Directions) Rules 2002, S.I. 2002/1687. Note also the Auld recommendations to reduce the formality of language. Chap. 11, para. 188.

[72] On the increased use of IT in court rooms to facilitate the giving of eidence and its comprehension by the jury see Auld, Chap. 11.

[73] See Criminal Justice Act 1988, ss.23–28. See also the decisions in *R v. Waters* (1997) 161 J.P. 249 and *R.v. Radak* [1999] 1 Cr. App. R. 187 confirming the ECHR compatibility of such a scheme. See also the admissibility of pre-recorded video statements under this scheme: *R.v.D.* [2002] EWCA Crim. 990.

[74] See the LCD Press Release [2000] C.L.Y. 112.

[75] See *R.v. Edwards* [1991] 1 W.L.R. 207; *R. v. Edwards (Maxine)* [1996] 2 Cr. App. R. 345; J. Dein, "Police Misconduct Revisited" [2000] Crim. L.R. 801; *R.v.Guney* [1998] 2 Cr. App. R.242.

see sections 40–43 of the Youth Justice and Criminal Evidence Act 1999 represent a very significant step towards a broader and more effective "rape shield" in the criminal trial. Unfortunately, the provisions are so deficiently drafted that they are likely to be challenged in Strasbourg and will certainly benefit from reformulation. The sections have already had to be "read down" to comply with the ECHR.[76]

The aim of the sections is to restrict the scope of the questioning on previous sexual behaviour unless the evidence is relevant and falls within a designated category (because it is similar to the conduct alleged on this occasion or occurred at or about the same time) and the court is satisfied that a refusal to allow the cross-examination might result in an unsafe conviction.

One of the least controversial measures in the 1999 Act is that which prohibits the defendant who is representing himself from cross-examining the complainant in a sexual case, in cases with "protected witnesses",[77] and in any case in which the judge considers that the quality of the evidence given by the witness is likely to be diminished by such cross-examination, and that evidence would be likely to be improved by a direction prohibiting cross-examination by the defendant, and it is not contrary to the interests of justice to prohibit it.[78] Provision is made for the defendant to be legally represented in such cases, and for the court to appoint a legal representative if the defendant fails to do so. The judge must also warn the jury that no adverse inferences should be drawn from the ruling forbidding self-representation. The judge always has the power to restrain improper questioning, even from professional representatives, and the judge will be especially alert to the danger of the accused conducting inappropriate cross-examination in those circumstances in which he is allowed to perform the examination in person.[79]

The restriction on the cross-examination of the defendant as a witness is governed by the Criminal Evidence Act 1898. In general, the accused ought not to be asked questions that reveal his previous convictions or previous charges laid against him or indeed his bad character generally. This protection from such questioning will be lost when the accused leads evidence of his own good character, or attacks the character of the prosecution witness or deceased victim (even where it is necessary to do so to

---

[76] *R. v. A* [2001] UKHL 25. On which see P. Mirfield, (2002) 118 L.Q.R. 20; J. McEwan, [2001] E. & P. 257; D. Birch, [2001] Crim. L.R. 908. See also *R.v. T* [2002] Crim. L.R.73. See generally: D.W. Elliott, (2000) 150 N.L.J. 1150; N. Kibble, "The Sexual History Provisions: Charting a Course Between Inflexible Legislative Rules and Wholly Untrammelled Judicial Discretion?" [2000] Crim. L.R. 274; L. Ellison, "Cross-Examination in Rape Trials," [1998] Crim. L.R. 605; A Geddes, "The Exclusion of Evidence Relating to a Complainant's Sexual Behaviour in Sexual Offence Trials" (1999) 149 N.L.J 1084; J. Watson, "Exclusion: The Victim's Point of View" *ibid.* 1085. See *Speaking Up for Justice: Report of the Interdepartmental Working Group on the Treatment of Vulnerable or Intimidated Witnesses in the Criminal Justice System* (Home Office, June 1998), Chap. 11. See also D. Brereton, "How Different are Rape Trials? A Comparison of the Cross-Examination of Complainants in Rape and Assault Trials" (1997) 37 Br. J. Crim. 342.

[77] S. 35 defines these as including children and sexual complainants.

[78] *Ibid.*, section 36

[79] See the decision in *R. v. Brown* [1998] 2 Cr.App. R. 364, which promoted these provisions in the Youth Justice and Criminal Evidence Act 1999. On the ECHR compatibility see *Oyston v. United Kingdom* [2002] Crim. L.R 497.

make out his defence). The rules are especially harsh when they operate as between co-accused at trial.[80]

(e) Expert witnesses

17–061 The function of an expert witness in a criminal trial is to assist the jury in matters outside the jury's competence or normal knowledge.[81] For example an expert may prove, from scientific tests, that the accused has handled explosives[82] or, from DNA testing, that the accused had sexual intercourse with the victim,[83] or, from examining a vehicle, that a road traffic accident was caused by brake failure. Expert evidence will not be admitted to resolve a question on which the jury can bring their own experience to bear, for example, on a defence of provocation, the effect on an ordinary man of discovering that his girlfriend was pregnant by another man,[84] on a prosecution for publishing an obscene book, the effect it may have on an ordinary person likely to read it.[85] There is no limit to the subjects on which the courts are prepared to receive expert evidence.[86] The jury are not bound by the views of the expert.[87]

The precise definition of who constitutes an "expert" remains unclear. The traditional rule is that an expert is one proved to the satisfaction of the court to have such qualification by reason of study or experience: *R. v. Silverlock*.[88] The courts have taken an overly generous attitude to who might qualify as an expert, with "ad hoc" experts being accepted where their expertise derived from the investigation into the case, *e.g.* where a police officer had viewed a film repeatedly, he was treated as an expert witness on

---

[80] See *Murdoch v. Taylor* [1965] A.C. 574; *R. v. Corelli* [2001] Crim. L.R. 114; *R. v. Neary* [2002] EWCA Crim. 1736.

[81] See *R. v. Turner* [1975] Q.B. 834. See generally, M. Redmayne, *Expert Evidence and Criminal Justice* (2000). As to the work of such experts, see I. R. Freckleton, *The Trial of the Expert* (1987); D. J. Gee, "The Expert Witness in the Criminal Trial" [1987] Crim.L.R. 307; P. Roberts and C. Willmore, *The Role of Forensic Science Evidence in Criminal Proceedings* (RCCJ Research Study No.11 1993); RCCJ Report, Chap. 9; R. Stockdale and C. Walker, "Forensic Evidence" in C. Walker and K. Starmer (eds), *Justice in Error* (1993) and C. Walker and R. Stockdale, "Forensic Evidence" in C. Walker and K. Starmer (eds) *Miscarriages of Justice: A Review of Justice in Error* (1999).

[82] Care must, of course, be taken in what tests are used and what they establish and in presenting the evidence accurately, reliably, fairly and credibly. Failure in these respects was part of the reason for the interim report on the Maguire case concluding that their convictions for taking part in IRA explosions were unsafe, see Sir John May, *Interim Report on the Maguire Case* (1990). The Court of Appeal quashed the convictions.

[83] See K. F. Kelly, J. J. Rankin and R. C. Wink, "Method and Application of DNA Finger-printing: A Guide for the Non-Scientist" [1987] Crim.L.R. 105; R. M. White and J. J. D. Greenwood, "DNA Fingerprinting and the Law" (1988) 51 M.L.R, 145; and T. Burke *et al.* (eds). *DNA Fingerprinting: Approval and Applications* (1991). On the dangers of the use of the prosecutor's fallacy in DNA evidence see *R. v. Doheny* [1997] Crim. L.R. 669. See generally, M. Krawczak, *DNA Fingerprinting* (2nd ed., 1998).

[84] See *R. v. Turner* [1975] Q.B. 834.

[85] See *R. v. Anderson* [1972] 1 Q.B. 304. By contrast, if the question was the effect a publication would have on a child, expert evidence might be admissible, see *DPP v. A & BC Chewing Gum Ltd* [1968] 1 Q.B. 159.

[86] *R. v. Robb* (1991) Cr. App. R. 161.

[87] *R. v. Stockwell* (1993) 97 Cr. App. R. 260.

[88] [1894] 2 Q.B. 766.

the events.[89] Similarly, confusion remains over the scope of expert evidence, with a lack of precise definition of which matters fall outside the knowledge and experience of the jury. The present test tends to lead to an inquiry into whether the subject matter is abnormal or not, when a more useful test might be to question whether the evidence would be helpful to the jury irrespective of their understanding of the subject matter.[90] There are very few additional safeguards against the English courts admitting controversial novel forms of evidence (e.g. facial mapping, video-super imposition,[91] voice identification evidence etc). This is in stark contrast to most other jurisdictions where the judiciary undertake a gatekeeping function to prevent evidence of dubious relevance or reliability from being admitted. In particular, the U.S. Supreme Court has imposed an obligation that any novel scientific or technical evidence must be demonstrated to be reliable, and in answering that question the court will consider the falsifiability of the technique or science in question, whether it has been subjected to peer review and/or publication, whether the technique or science has a known potential error rate, to what extent the discipline is subject to standards and controls, and whether there is support of a body of the scientific community for the technique.[92]

Problems with forensic science and other expert evidence have been partly to blame for some of the recently identified miscarriages of justice in England and Wales. The Royal Commission on Criminal Justice reporting in 1993 made a number of recommendations to address some of the identified problems. A major problem had been that the forensic laboratory services have been available largely only to the prosecution and have become prosecution-minded, such that there can be a failure to exercise true scientific objectivity in dealing with the evidence and a failure to pass on information and interpretations of value to the defence rather than the prosecution.[93] In consequence, the Royal Commission recommended that the forensic science facilities should become available to the defence as well as the prosecution.[94] The efficacy of this scheme will depend upon legal aid being available for the purpose.[95] Quality control was also obviously a contributory factor to the errors in earlier cases, and the Royal Commission made a raft of proposals intended to address this problem.[96] At the end of the day, of course, quality control relies upon the individuals wishing and being able to act independently and honestly and not wishing to assist in "case construction" rather than case assessment.

The *Auld Report* recommends that a better system of accreditation and monitoring of scientific evidence occurs with more detailed criminal

[89] *R. v. Clare and Peach* [1995] 2 Cr.App. R. 333.
[90] See generally, M. Redmayne, *Expert Evidence and Criminal Justice* (2000).
[91] *R. v. Clark* [995] 2 Cr. App. R. 425. *Stockwell* (1993) 97 Cr. App. R. 260; *R. v. Robb* (1991) 93 Cr. App. R. 161.
[92] *Daubert v. Merrett Dow* 125 R. v. Ed. 2d. 469 (1993). For discussion see Slovenko, (1998) 2 E. & P. 190; Graham, (1998) 2 E. & P.211. And see generally, Redmayne (2000), and S.J. Odgers and J.T. Richardson "Keeping Bad Science Out Of The Courtroom – Changes In American And Australian Expert Evidence Law" (1995) U.N.S.W. Law Journal.
[93] See J. Rozenberg, "Miscarriages of Justice" in E. Stockdale and S. Casale (eds), *Criminal Justice Under Stress* (1992) and P. Roberts and C. Willmore, (1993).
[94] RCCJ Report, p. 149.
[95] See Sanders and Young (2000), p.342
[96] RCCJ Report, Chap. 9.

procedure rules and a greater opportunity for pre-trial discussion of the
materials so that the area and extent of scientific dispute is more focused by
the time of trial.

6. THE ROLE OF THE JUDGE[97]

17–062   "The Judge is not an advocate. Under the English and Welsh system of
criminal trials he is more like the umpire at a cricket match, he is certainly
not the bowler whose business it is to try to get the batsman out."[98] The
characterisation of the judge as the umpire or referee in our adversarial
system is not entirely appropriate in the context of the trial on indictment.[99]
It is true that the judge should apply the rules, allow counsel to present the
case without undue hindrance, not intervene unduly and that ultimately the
decision on matters of fact belongs to the jury. However, it is equally true
that the judge exercises a very considerable discretion in respect of many
aspects of the trial and it is reasonably clear that the way in which that
discretion is exercised may have a significant bearing on the outcome.
Indeed, in certain circumstances, the judge's ruling will determine the case.
The judge's impartiality must, of course, be beyond doubt.[1] The Human
Rights Act 1998 and the increased awareness of the ECHR[2] that it has
engendered has served to underline the significance of impartiality. The
independence of members of the judiciary was also brought sharply into
focus in the course of the *Pinochet* litigation.[3]
    In considering the extent of the judge's discretion and the possible effects
of its exercise we should bear in mind the relationship between judge and
jury.
    In simple terms, the separation of functions between the judge and the
jury is that the judge is to deal with matters of law and the jury with matters
of fact. It is the judge's function to determine certain procedural matters; to
consider any plea-bargaining; to decide upon the admissibility of evidence;
to sum up on the law and the evidence for the benefit of the jury; and to pass
sentence. It will be seen that the distinction between matters of law and
matters of fact is often blurred, and that the judge, in any case, has
considerable influence in the determination of matters of fact.
    Whilst the judge has a significant impact in some areas, in other areas, he

---

[97] See *Jones v. National Coal Board* [1957] 2 Q.B. 55, discussed by Lord Denning in *The Due
Process of Law* (1980), pp. 58–62. See P. Devlin, *The Judge* (1979) and, for a unique account
by the judge of a criminal trial, P. Devlin, *Easing the Passing* (1985). See also R. Pattenden
(1990); A. Samuels, "Judicial Misconduct and the Criminal Trial" [1982] Crim. L.R. 221; J.
Jackson, "Judicial Responsibility in Criminal Proceedings" (1997) C.L.P. 59; C. Walker in
Walker and Starmer (1999).
[98] *per* Cumming-Bruce L.J. in *R. v. Gunning*, July 7, 1980, unreported.
[99] See M.E. Frankel, "The Search for the Truth: An Umpireal View" (1975) 123 U. Penn. L. R.
1031.
[1]   The ECtHR has emphasised the importance of the impartiality of the judiciary. See *Castillo
Algar v. Spain* (2000) 30 E.H.R.R. 827.
[2]   The ECHR jurisprudence on impartiality is contained in number of cases, principal ones
being *Piersack v. Belgium* (1983) 5 E.H.R.R. 169; *Le Compte v. Belgium* 4 (1982) E.H.R.R. 1.
[3]   *R. v. Bow St. Magistrates' Court, ex p. Pinochet Ugarte (No 2)* [1999] 1 All E.R. 577 and see
Locabail v. Bayfield Properties [2000] Q.B.45. See generally above.

or she has very little influence. For example, in relation to plea-bargaining, the judge is not a key player, and yet it might be thought that greater judicial involvement would be more likely to protect the interests of the defendant, as well as paying adequate respect to the administration of justice.[4] There is clearly a dilemma in considering to what extent to involve the judge in such matters. At the same time, there is a clear desire to see jury involvement, although their role in the criminal justice system is in fact minimal.[5] There does not appear to be a public desire to see judicially controlled criminal justice, if only because of suspicions about what judges might do. Set against this is the ability of the judge to exercise independent judgment. A further dimension to this debate was added by the Human Rights Act 1998 whereby the judiciary are more specifically empowered as the guardians of human rights. Although they do not have the power to strike down legislation as incompatible with the ECHR, they are capable of reading down legislation, and in some cases this has involved such extensive reinterpretation as to amount to judicial legislating, even in relation to Acts passed after the Human Rights Act 1998.[6]

The dilemma as to the appropriate extent of pro-active judicial control of criminal cases can be considered by noting the recommendations of the Royal Commission to introduce a form of judicial management of cases. Arguably this reflects a lack of confidence in the parties ability adequately to progress a case. The Commission recommended that "wherever practicable in complex cases judges should take on responsibility for managing the progress of a case, securing its passage through the various stages of pre-trial discussion to preparatory hearing and trial and making sure that the parties have fulfilled their obligations both to each other and to the court".[7] This goes much further than the administrative responsibilities currently lying with presiding and resident judges.[8] The danger of making such changes is that the delicate balance necessitated within an adversarial approach is affected without due consideration given to whether it has had an inappropriate effect upon the rights of the defendant.

The *Auld Report* has recommended that changes be made to the system of allocation of cases (ticketing) so that judges are better matched to cases, with the shift in emphasis resulting in more work falling on circuit judges.[9]

(a) Procedural matters

From the outset, the judge has control over the progress of the trial and the administrative and procedural problems that may arise. The judge must decide questions relating to the form of the indictment and any necessary amendment to it[10]; the taking of the plea from the accused and its

17–063

---

[4] See below.
[5] See below.
[6] See, e.g. the decision of the HL in *R. v. A* [2001] UKHL 25.
[7] RCCJ Report (1993), p. 142.
[8] *ibid.*
[9] See pp. 234–239. See also the calls for better recruitment of ethnic minority and women judges, pp.254–262.
[10] As to questions relating to the form of the indictment, for example, whether the indictment discloses any offence, see *Archbold (2002)*, paras 1-108–1-198. *R. v. Nelson* (1977) 65 Cr.App.R. 119, is instructive on the obligations of defence counsel to draw irregularities to the notice of the court, *cf.* para. 17-053 above.

acceptability[11]; whether a special plea of *autrefois acquit* or *autrefois convict* has been successfully raised by the accused; whether to stay proceedings for abuse[12]; the determination of preliminary points raised by counsel; and the desirability of separate trials.[13] Whilst these may be classed as procedural questions, their importance should not be underestimated. In some cases the determination of the procedural point may settle the whole issue.

The empanelling and swearing of the jury is subject to judicial control. The judge will settle any question over challenges.[14] Once sworn, with the case proceeding, the jury may be discharged by the judge for a variety of reasons.[15] The effect of discharging the jury is not to acquit the accused—he or she may be remanded for a second trial.[16]

It is also the judge's responsibility to maintain order in court. The judge has powers of punishment for contempt where there is misbehaviour.[17] Similarly, the judge has the power to protect the proceedings from publicity that would inhibit a fair trial.[18]

Although counsel for the prosecution and the defence must conduct their respective cases in accordance with the Code of Conduct, the judge has a significant role in controlling the questioning of witnesses by counsel[19] and in restraining counsel from improper practices. Control should be discreet and the judge must resist the temptation to take over the questioning or to criticise counsel's conduct to such an extent that the jury might thereby be

---

[11] For the role of the judge in relation to prosecuting counsel's obligations in plea arrangements, see para. 17–048 above. In *R. v. Winterflood* (1978) 68 Cr.App.R. 291, the trial judge appears to have taken the initiative in suggesting the addition of a charge to the indictment to which the accused might plead guilty.

[12] See *Practice Direction (Crown Court: Abuse of Process)* [2000] 1 W.L.R. 1322.

[13] The practice is to join several charges together on one indictment where they are founded on the same facts or form part of a series of offences of the same or similar character and so have one trial: Indictment Rules 1971, r.9. See C. Yates, "How Many Counts to an Indictment?" [1976] Crim.L.R. 428.

[14] See para. 17-089 below.

[15] See para. 17-090 below.

[16] *R. v. Randall* [1960] Crim.L.R. 435. In this case the jury was discharged after returning verdicts of not guilty, which were then stated to be majority verdicts. (Majority verdicts were not at that time acceptable.) The plea of *autrefois acquit* at the second trial was rejected.

[17] There is a summary power to punish contempts "in the face of the court" which exists to maintain the dignity and authority of the judge and to ensure a fair trial and which applies in a magistrates' court: Contempt of Court Act 1981, s.12. See *Balogh v. Crown Court at St Albans* [1975] 1 Q.B. 73, discussed in Lord Denning, *The Due Process of Law* (1980), pp. 12–18. The accused was apprehended before he livened up court proceedings by introducing "laughing gas" into the ventilating system at St Albans Crown Court. See also, *Morris v. Crown Office* [1970] 2 Q.B. 114 (group of students breaking up a libel trial); *R. v. Aquarius* [1974] Crim.L.R. 373 (disruptive behaviour of defendant); *R. v. Logan* [1974] Crim.L.R. 609 (outburst by defendant after sentence); *Lecointe v. Courts Administrator of the Central Criminal Court* (1973, unreported) (distribution of leaflets at the Old Bailey inciting people to picket the court); *R. v. Powell* (1994) 98 Cr.App.R. 224 (member of public wolf-whistled at a female juror from the public gallery). See generally S. H. Bailey, D. J. Harris and D.C.Ormerod, *Bailey Harris and Jones, Civil Liberties: Cases and Materials* (5th ed., 2001), Judge Pickles sentenced a witness to five days imprisonment for her failure to give evidence against her ex-boyfriend, the Court of Appeal quashed the finding of contempt because the trial was not fair, but made clear that a person who refuses without adequate excuse to give evidence to the court may be punished, which will usually mean imprisonment *R. v. Renshaw* [1989] Crim.L.R. 811.

[18] See above para. 17-020.

[19] The line of questioning must be relevant and material and witnesses should be treated courteously.

prejudiced.[20] The judge must be, and be seen to be, scrupulously fair.[21] Judicial interruptions to cross-examination of the defence may result in an unfair trial if they deprive the accused of a chance to put his or her case and/ or otherwise give an appearance of bias.[22]

(b) Plea bargaining[23]

The judge has to be very careful in playing any role in plea arrangements, **17–064** although he or she is now obliged to state in open court that there was a reduction in sentence as required by the Powers of Criminal Courts (Sentencing) Act 2000. The extent to which it is proper for the judge to indicate in advance the nature of the sentence discount[24] that will be offered if the accused enters a guilty plea in a particular case gives rise to difficulties. Whilst the benefit to the accused is tangible when the prosecution offers an arrangement, it is not precisely quantifiable. When the judge indicates a view about sentence, the inducement is precise and the pressure to plead greatly increased. Moreover, it is not clear that the judge will always be able to make an accurate decision since the estimation at that stage will be based on far less information than would an orthodox sentencing assessment following a full trial or formal guilty plea.

The Court of Appeal considered the matters of principle involved in judicial intervention in the highly controversial case of *R. v. Turner*.[25] Turner had pleaded not guilty on a charge of theft. During an adjournment he was advised by counsel to change his plea. Turner knew that counsel had seen the judge and thought that counsel was relaying the views of the judge when he said that a guilty plea was likely to result in a non-custodial sentence, whereas a finding of guilty would bring a custodial sentence. Turner was repeatedly told that the choice of plea was his. He changed his plea to guilty and later appealed on the ground that he did not have a free choice in retracting his original plea.

The appeal was allowed on the basis that the accused may have felt that the views expressed were those of the trial judge and might, therefore, have been deprived of his freedom of plea.[26] On the general issue Lord Parker C.J. made four observations.[27]

(i) Counsel must give the best advice he or she can, in strong terms if need be, including the advice that a plea of guilty is a mitigating factor which may allow the court to pass a lesser sentence. The accused must be told not to plead guilty unless he or she has committed the offence

---

[20] *R. v. McFadden* (1976) 62 Cr.App.R. 187, and see Samuels (1982), p. 223.

[21] It is not appropriate to indicate to counsel that the accused's hope of acquittal is almost gone: *R. v. Alves* [1996] Crim. L.R. 599. See recently *Randell v. the Queen* [2002] UK PC 19.

[22] See, *e.g. R v. Frixou* [1998] Crim. L.R. 352 where the judge asked the accused 106 of the total 189 questions!

[23] As to the position of the accused, and prosecuting and defence counsel, see paras 17-039, 17-048, 17-052, above.

[24] As to the reduction in sentence in response to a guilty plea, see para. 17-039, above.

[25] [1970] 2 Q.B. 321.

[26] This is the basic question which the court will consider in all cases of this kind: "Has the plea been made freely and voluntarily?" *cf. R. v. Inns* (1975) 60 Cr.App.R. 251; *R. v. Peace* [1976] Crim.L.R. 119.

[27] [1970] 2 Q.B. 321 at 326–327.

charged.[28]

(ii) The accused must have freedom of choice of plea.[29]

(iii) There must be freedom of access between counsel and judge in order that matters that cannot be mentioned in open court may be communicated. Counsel for the defence and the prosecution should both be present as well as the defence solicitor, if he or she so wishes. Any such meetings should only take place when really necessary and the judge should only treat them as private where necessary.[30]

(iv) A judge should never indicate the sentence he or she is minded to impose, save that counsel may be told that whatever the plea, he or she is minded to impose a particular type of sentence, *e.g.* probation, or a fine, or a custodial sentence. A judge should never say that on a finding of guilt a more severe sentence would be passed, nor should it be indicated that on a guilty plea he or she would pass a particular sentence, lest it be thought that a more severe sentence would result after a finding of guilt. Any discussion on sentence should be communicated by counsel to the accused.

Those observations appear to have limited the judicial role substantially and established a clear code of procedure, but they contain one major difficulty. The judge is told never to indicate that a sentence passed after a conviction would be more severe than a sentence passed after a guilty plea. Given the acknowledged rule that guilty pleas lead to sentence discounts, how can this principle be observed? The judge is not permitted to say what everyone knows. The Court of Appeal in *R. v. Cain*[31] subsequently acknowledged this difficulty, but the authority of *R. v. Turner* was strengthened by a subsequent *Practice Direction*[32] that reaffirmed the procedure set out by Lord Parker.

The *Auld Report* recommends the introduction by way of judicial sentencing guidelines for a system of graduated discounts. There would be a formal request from the accused through his advocate for the judge to give a prior indication of sentence in the event of a guilty plea.[33] The request would occur in open court with counsel and would be recorded. There would have to exist adequate safeguards for the judge to be satisfied that the accused is not under pressure to plead falsely.

To sum up in relation to plea bargains, the present judicial role should be

---

[28] See, further, para. 17-052 above.
[29] See para. 17-038, above.
[30] The necessity to limit the discussions in the judge's room has been emphasised by the Court of Appeal in *R. v. Smith* [1990]1 W.L.R. 1311, drawing attention to the words of Mustill L.J. in *R. v. Harper-Taylor* (1988) 138 N.L.J. 80 where the requirement that justice be done in public for all to see and hear was emphasised. Thus, whilst the jury may have to be required to withdraw, rarely should meetings take place outside the courtroom. If such meetings do take place, there must be a shorthand note-taker present, as stated in *R. v. Smith*, in part to avoid the sort of unseemly dialogue between judge and counsel which took place at the end of Smith's trial. See also *R. v. Pitman* [1991] 1 All E.R. 468. Any indication given by a judge will not bind the Court of Appeal who hear an Attorney-General's Reference for an unduly lenient sentence: *Attorney-General's Reference (No. 40 of 1996)* [1997] 1 Cr.App. R. (S.) 357.
[31] [1976] Q.B. 496.
[32] [1976] Crim. L.R. 561.
[33] pp.434

limited to the consideration of arrangements negotiated between counsel, although the ultimate decision on plea arrangements lies with counsel,[34] and to the indication of the particular type of sentence whether the sentence follows a guilty plea or conviction after a not guilty plea. The trial judge is not permitted to withhold a sentencing discount which is otherwise applicable because he or she disapproves of a bargain stuck by counsel.[34a] Once the judge becomes involved in indicating alternative sentences any accused is likely to be under the same pressure as Turner and, " ... once he felt that this was an intimation emanating from the judge, it is really idle in the opinion of this court to think that he really had a free choice in the matter".[35]

(c) Admissibility of evidence

One of the functions of the trial judge is to control the input of material **17–065** upon which the jury will ultimately base its decision. This the judge does by applying the complex body of rules that make up the law of evidence.[36]

(i) Relevance and admissibility

The evidence a jury hears must be both relevant and admissible. Evidence is **17–066** relevant if it is logically probative or disprobative of some matter that requires proof, *i.e.* if it makes that matter more or less probable.[37] Thus when a person is accused of murder it is relevant to prove that he or she had a motive to kill the victim, that he or she was seen in possession of the murder weapon, and that he or she was unwilling to account for his or her movements at the time the murder was committed. None of these matters would, standing alone, be likely to establish beyond reasonable doubt that the accused committed the offence, but the proof of each tends to render guilt more probable, which is all that is required.

Not all evidence that is relevant is also admissible. Relevant evidence may have various deficiencies, the most common of which are that it may be unreliable or prejudicial to a fair trial, it may be privileged material or it may have been unfairly obtained. An array of technical rules of exclusion has therefore developed to prevent such evidence being given. Thus the hearsay rule operates to exclude statements not made in court as evidence of the truth of the facts stated, since statements which are not made while giving evidence are considered insufficiently *reliable* to be acted upon by a jury.[38]

---

[34] See paras. 17-048; 17-052, above.
[34a] *R. v. March* [2002] All E.R (D) 210.
[35] [1970] 2 Q.B. 321 at 326B, *per* Lord Parker C.J.
[36] See generally C. Tapper, *Cross and Tapper on Evidence* (9th ed., 1999); M. Hirst, *Andrews and Hirst on Evidence* (4th ed., 2001); I.H. Dennis, *The Law of Evidence* (2nd ed., 2002).
[37] *per* Lord Simon in *DPP v. Kilbourne* [1973] A.C. 729 at 756, HL
[38] "[Hearsay evidence] is not the best evidence and it is not delivered on oath. The truthfulness and accuracy of the person whose words are spoken to by another witness cannot be tested by cross-examination, and the light which his demeanour would throw on his testimony is lost": *Teper v. R.* [1952] A.C. 480 at 486, *per* Lord Normand. The principal deficiency is the inability to cross-examine the declarant. For a detailed analysis of the rule see A. Choo, (1993). For proposals to reform the law relating to hearsay, see the Law Commission, *Evidence and Criminal Proceedings: The Hearsay Rule and Related Issues* (L.C. Consultation

Thus, for example, it would be inadmissible hearsay for a police officer to give evidence that a person interviewed during the investigation told the police officer that the accused had committed the crime. It would be a different matter if the person concerned came to court and made the same statement on oath.[39] An example of a rule which operates to exclude prejudicial evidence is that which prohibits the giving of evidence of the accused's bad character, including previous convictions. If the jury heard such evidence, it is feared that it would be so incensed that it would give it undue weight in assessing the case against the accused.[40] These fears have now been substantiated by shadow jury research.[41]

The Law Commission has now proposed a controversial reform of the rules under which the previous misconduct evidence of the accused would be adduced in the course of the trial. The rules would clarify the 'central set of facts' about which any party should be free to adduce relevant evidence without constraint, and provide strict criteria for admitting evidence of bad character that falls outside these "central facts". The proposals would also restrict the use of bad character evidence against witnesses in general and should be welcomed at least in that respect. The Law Commission recommend that the jury may need to be warned about the absence of any character evidence (to avoid speculation) and the dangers of giving undue weight to bad character evidence that is admitted.[42]

The rules of exclusion of evidence of any type are seldom absolute and the judge must be familiar with the various exceptions which exist and under which evidence may be received. Exceptions are frequently made in respect of evidence that is not subject to the deficiency against which the rule of exclusion is designed to guard. This is a consequence of the evolutionary nature of the subject and the absence of any attempt to codify the general rules of criminal evidence.[43] Thus a confession made by an accused person,

---

Paper No. 138, 1995) and A. A. S. Zuckerman, "The Futility of Hearsay" [1996] Crim. L.R. 4; D. C. Ormerod, ' "The Hearsay Exceptions" [1996] Crim. L.R. 16; J. R. Spencer, "Hearsay Reform: A Bridge Not Far Enough?" [1996] Crim. L.R. 29; and the Law Commission Report, No. 245, *Evidence and Criminal Proceedings: The Hearsay Rule and Related Issues* (1997); and C. Tapper, "An Overview" [1998] Crim. L.R. 771.

[39] When evidence is presented directly to the court in this way, not only is it subject to the sanction of the oath, but also the reliability of the evidence can be tested by cross-examination, and the witness's demeanour seen by the jury. The validity of the claims that the jury are better able to detect insincerity or ambiguity or misperception when they are able to see the witness are untestable in the absence of jury research.

[40] Such evidence is not necessarily devoid of probative value: *DPP v. Kilbourne* [1973] A.C. 729 at 757, *per* Lord Simon. But a jury might think it proved more than it does: in other words, the probative value of the evidence is outweighed by its prejudicial effect, see *Boardman v. DPP* [1975] A.C. 421 at 456, *per* Lord Cross. The leading authority is *DPP v. P* [1991] A.C. 447

[41] The dangers of the jury making decisions on moral prejudice and/or from reasoning prejudice are well established. The Law Commission produced a detailed review of the "similar fact" rule in its Consultation Paper No 141, *Evidence in Criminal Proceedings: Previous Misconduct of a Defendant* (1996). On this see P. Roberts, "All the Usual Suspects" [1997] Crim. L.R. 75; J. McEwan, "Law Commission Dodges the Nettles in Consultation Paper No.141" [1997] Crim. L.R. 93; P. Darbyshire, "Previous Misconduct and Magistrates' Courts — Some Tales from the Real World" [1997] Crim. L.R. 105.

[42] See Law Commission, *Evidence of Bad Character in Criminal Proceedings* (Report No. 273, 2001). See J. McEwan, "Previous Misconduct at the Crossroads: Which Way Ahead?" [2002] Crim. L.R. 180; P. Mirfield, (2002) 6 E & P. 141; M. Redmayne, (2002) 6 E & P 71.

[43] *Cf.* the Australian position.

though hearsay, may be given in evidence, as it is a statement that goes against the interest of the person making it and so is unlikely to be unreliable.[44] Exceptions may also be made where the need to prevent the giving of certain evidence is outweighed by other factors. Thus, although there is a general rule against admissibility, evidence of the previous misconduct of the accused may be received where it is of an enhanced relevance or probative force in proving the case against him or her; for instance where a man is charged with drowning his wife in the bath and it is proved that his previous wives drowned in similarly unusual circumstances.[45]

Exceptions to the rules of exclusion are generally hedged about with conditions to prevent the admission of undesirable and/or unreliable evidence. Thus, for example, where it is proposed to rely upon a confession made by an accused person, the prosecution must, by virtue of section 76 of the Police and Criminal Evidence Act 1984, be able to prove beyond reasonable doubt that it was not obtained either:

"(a) by oppression of the person who made it; or

(b) in consequence of anything said or done which was likely, in the circumstances existing at the time, to render unreliable any confession which might be made by him in consequence thereof".[46]

(ii) Determining admissibility

Where the admissibility of an item of evidence, such as a confession, is contested, it would obviously be inadvisable for argument to take place in front of the jury, who would then hear that a confession had been made, even if it were subsequently ruled to be inadmissible. There is therefore a special procedure whereby matters relating to the admissibility of evidence may be determined in the absence of the jury,[47] and this is known as the trial within a trial or *voire dire*. Witnesses may be called in the usual way,[48] and legal argument heard, after which the judge makes his or her ruling.[49]

17–067

---

[44] Numerous other exceptions to the hearsay rule exist. Much documentary hearsay is admissible under Part II of the Criminal Justice Act 1988, for example. Oral statements made by participants in events in the heat of the moment and before they have had time to concoct anything to their advantage are admissible at common law, see *R. v. Andrews* [1987] A.C. 281. For a more complete statement of the exceptions see the Law Commission Consultation Paper n.40 above.

[45] *R. v. Smith* (1915) 11 Cr.App.R. 229.

[46] Police and Criminal Evidence Act 1984, s.76(2).

[47] For the difficulties presented to magistrates, as triers of fact and law see para. 17-009 above.

[48] Although a special oath is used, which is known as the "*voire dire*", and from which the procedure takes its name: "I swear I will true answer make to all such questions as the court shall demand of me."

[49] The trial within a trial may form a significant, and sometimes lengthy, part of the proceedings. When the "Birmingham Six" came to trial, a "trial within a trial" was held to determine the admissibility of confessions made by the accused, which lasted eight days, at the end of which the statements were admitted by the judge, Bridge J., who gave a reasoned decision covering 15 pages: *McIllkenny v. Chief Constable of West Midlands Police Force* [1980] Q.B. 283 at 314, *per* Lord Denning M.R.

(iii) Discretionary exclusion

17–068   Where the strict rules of evidence might operate unfairly, a trial judge has various discretionary powers to exclude from the jury's consideration evidence that is both relevant and otherwise admissible.[50] The best known and most frequently exercised power is to be found in section 78 of the Police and Criminal Evidence Act 1984, which provides that the judge:

> "may refuse to allow evidence on which the prosecution proposes to rely to be given if it appears to the court that, having regard to all the circumstances, including the circumstances in which the evidence was obtained, the admission of the evidence would have such an adverse effect on the fairness of the proceedings that the court ought not to admit it".

An example of the use of this power might be in respect of a confession, which, though it was not obtained in circumstances rendering it inadmissible under section 76 of the 1984 Act,[51] was nevertheless procured in breach of the rules governing interrogation in such a way that it would be unfair to admit it.[52] Other examples of the exclusion of evidence under this discretion include evidence obtained in breach of the Codes relating to identification evidence and evidence obtained in breach of other Codes of Practice relating to search and seizure. In addition to the power conferred by section 78,[53] the trial judge may exclude evidence by virtue of the discretion vested in him or her by the common law[54] and by various statutes.[55] There is also the power to stay proceedings for abuse of process which is exercised in some situations in which the evidence has been obtained unfairly such that it is unfair to try the accused or where he cannot have a fair trial.[56]

In *Latif & Shahzad*[57] Lord Steyn acknowledged a "considerable overlap" between the section 78 principles and those applicable to abuse of process. The abuse of process doctrine meant that the trial judge must:

---

[50]   See generally R. Pattenden (1990), Chap. 7.

[51]   See above.

[52]   See, *e.g. R. v. Samuel* [1988] Q.B. 615 in which the accused confessed to robbery after having been denied access to his solicitor in breach of s.58 of the Police and Criminal Evidence Act 1984. The court regarded this denial of "one of the most important and fundamental rights of a citizen" as sufficient justification for exclusion of the confession under s.78. Special provisions relating to access apply in relation to those suspected of terrorist offences: see Terrorism Act 2000, s.125(1), Sched. 15, para. 5(1).

[53]   The section is not applicable in committal proceedings: s.78(3), as inserted by the Criminal Procedure are Investigation Act 1996, s.47. Some confusion has arisen as to the applicability of the section in extradition proceedings, but it is clear that it should apply: *Re Proulx* [2000] Crim. L.R. 997 and commentary. *Cf.* the dictum of Lord Hoffmann in *R v. Governor of Brixton Prison, ex p. Levin* [1997] A.C. 714.

[54]   The judge has power at common law to exclude evidence at his or her discretion where the prejudicial effect of prosecution evidence outweighs its probative value, and (in certain cases) where evidence has been improperly obtained, see *R. v. Sang* [1980] A.C. 402.

[55]   See, *e.g.* Criminal Justice Act 1988, s.25: power to exclude admissible documentary evidence where not in the " interests of justice" to admit it. This power contains the very unusual power to exclude relevant defence evidence.

[56]   For an excellent discussion of the narrow approach to s. 78 and comparisons with the abuse of process doctrine see A. Choo and S. Nash, "What's the Matter with Section 78" [1999] Crim. L.R. 729.

[57]   [1996] 1 W.L.R. 104, p.109.

"weigh in the balance the public interest in ensuring that those that are charged with grave crimes should be tried and the competing public interest in not conveying the impression that the court will adopt the approach that the end justifies any means".

More recently still, in *R. v. P*,[58] Lord Hobhouse pointed out that a defendant is not entitled to have unlawfully obtained evidence excluded simply because it has been so obtained. Lord Hobhouse also emphasised that the English courts would not adopt a scheme of mandatory exclusion of evidence obtained in breach of a Convention right".[58a]

The ECtHR influence cannot be ignored; in certain areas it has a profound effect on domestic law. For example, in *Teixiera de Castro v. Portugal*,[59] the Court found a breach of Article 6 where undercover officers incited the offender to commit an offence which he would not otherwise have committed. The House of Lords has, as a result, been required to re-address English law on the propriety of undercover operations involving enticement. It has confirmed that English law is not in conflict with the ECHR jurisprudence, but that evidence obtained as a result of undercover entirement will be liable to be excluded form the trial.[60]

(d) Summing-up[61]

The other major matters of law which are the responsibility of the judge are those which must be explained to the jury so that it can reach a proper decision.[62] The judge will deal with these matters in the summing-up, telling the jury that it must accept his or her direction on issues of law. Summing up is of particular significance since the jury, conscious of the impending duty to decide the fate of the accused, will be particularly attentive and because of this the material they hear, as the last information before they retire, will have a greater impact.

17–069

Lord Hailsham, at the time the Lord Chancellor, emphasised the judge's obligations in summing up:

"The purpose of a direction to a jury is not best achieved by a disquisition on jurisprudence or philosophy or a universally applicable circular tour round the area of law affected by the case. The search for universally applicable definitions is often productive of more obscurity than light. A direction is seldom improved and may be considerably damaged by copious recitations from the total content of a judge's notebook. A direction to a jury should be custom-built to make the jury understand their task in relation to a particular case. Of course, it must include references to the burden of proof and the respective role of jury and judge. But it should also include a succinct but accurate summary

---

[58] [2001] 2 W.L.R. 463.
[58a] See *R. v. Khan* [1997] A.C. 587; *Khan v. UK* [2000] Crim. L.R. 508; *P.G. v. UK* [2002] Crim. L.R. 308.
[59] (1998) 28 E.H.R.R. 101.
[60] See *R. v. Looseley* [2001] 53; See also A. Ashworth [2002] U.K.H.L. Crim. L.R. 161.
[61] See *Archbold (2002)*, para. 4–368.
[62] On the dangers of juries being ill informed after summing-up see I. Francis, "Mystical Reverance for the Jury" (2001) 151 N.L.J. 63.

of the issues of fact as to which a decision is required, a correct but concise summary of the evidence and arguments on both sides and a correct statement of the inferences which the jury are entitled to draw from their particular conclusions about the primary facts."[63]

Achieving such a summing up may well be difficult, especially in the case of long and complex trials.[64] It is common and approved practice for the trial judge to discuss with counsel the precise details of the summing-up before it is delivered. It would seem proper to suggest that many of the problems might be avoided if judges were careful to ensure that the language they use is that which a jury is likely to understand[65] and that the length of time taken to deliver a summing-up is as little as possible consistent with clarity.[66] As the House of Lords pointed out: a judge should not be compelled to give meaningless or absurd directions.[67]

A summing-up usually consists of the following elements.[68]

(i) A direction as to the respective tasks of judge and jury

17–070 The jury is told that it is for the judge to decide upon matters of law and for it to decide upon matters of fact and that it should not be influenced by any judicial opinions expressed about the evidence[69]; it is for the jury to decide what facts have been proved.[70] It would be naive to think, however, that the views of the judge, if expressed, have no bearing on the jury's decision.[71]

---

[63] *R. v. Lawrence* [1982] A.C. 510. See also *R. v. McVey* [1988] Crim.L.R. 127.

[64] See para. 17-096, below for consideration of whether the jury should be involved in long complex cases, especially fraud cases.

[65] The point is made, *e.g.* by R. Harding, "Jury Performance in Complex Cases" in Findlay and Duff (1988), Chap. 5; by M. Levi, "The Role of the Jury in Complex Cases" in Findlay and Duff (1988), Chap. 6; and by E.Griew, "Summing Up the Law" [1989] Crim.L.R. 768, who supports his argument, at p. 773, with American research which suggests "that a good many vocabulary items freely used in jury instructions are incomprehensible to an alarming percentage of jurors ... " In the Crown Court Survey, it was found that most jurors perceived no difficulties with legal jargon in understanding their case: Zander and Henderson (1993), p. 212. Very few jurors had difficulty with the judge's direction on the law: *ibid.* pp. 216–217. For research which demonstrates how incompetent most jurors are when presented with complex material in the course of a fraud trial, see T. Honess, M. Levi and E. Charman, "Juror Competence in Processing Complex Information: Implications from a Simulation of the Maxwell Trial" [1998] Crim. L.R. 763. The authors conclude that with some screening and more assistance, 80% of jurors are competent to deal with complex trials.

[66] Many jurors, in the Crown Court Survey, were of the view that they could have coped without the judge summing up on the facts, although fewer took this view with the longer cases: *ibid.*, pp. 214–215. See on the virtue of brevity in summing up *R. v. Farr* (1999) 163 J.P. 193. A two-minute summing up was upheld in *R. v. Brown* [1995] Crim. L.R. 746.

[67] See *R. v. Aziz* [1996] 1 A.C. 41.

[68] Always to include all these elements is likely to be unnecessary and, sometimes, very confusing, see Griew (1989) and Pattenden (1990), pp. 177–212.

[69] See also Darbyshire *et al.* (2001), p.39 for the impact on the jury of these directions.

[70] *R. v. Bradbury* (1920) 15 Cr.App.R. 76; *R. v. Mason* (1924) 18 Cr.App.R. 131. The jury may decide upon a verdict which may appear to be "perverse" despite this statement, provided it realises it has that opportunity: see para. 17-095 below. There are also some rare circumstances in which the judge may direct a conviction, see below, para. 17-075.

[71] At its lowest, the position of the summing-up at the end of the trial must give it significance. Add to that the respect accorded to a professional's view by lay people and their natural tendency to rely on the judge's analysis and the judge's influence is clear.

(ii) A direction as to the burden and standard of proof

The judge should tell the jury about the burden and standard of proof.[72] **17–071**
Prosecuting counsel may have done so in the opening speech and it may
have been referred to during the trial. The judge tells the jury that the
burden of proving the guilt of the accused lies on the prosecution save in the
case of the common law defence of insanity[73] and subject to any statutory
exception.[74] This is echoed by Article 6 and the jurisprudence of the
Strasbourg Court.[75] Ashworth and Blake[76] examined the rise in the number
of offences which are created with a burden of proof on the accused. The
authors classified all offences in *Archbold* (1995) triable in the Crown Court
in which there is a legal burden of proof. in the operating against the
defendant, and asked whether there is anything to justify this "large-scale
derogation" from what ought to be a basic principle."

The standard that must be satisfied is proof beyond a reasonable doubt.[77]
So if, for example, Vera, a defendant, raises the issue by stating that an
apparent attack was carried out in self-defence, it is for the prosecution to
prove beyond reasonable doubt that she was not acting in self-defence,
rather than on Vera to prove on a balance of probabilities that she was so
acting. The judge directs that the jury must be satisfied so that they are sure
of the accused's guilt.[78] Until recently this has not been thought to create

---

[72] *R v. Bentley* [1999] Crim. L.R. 330; [2000] 1 Cr.App. R. 307. If a case gets to the stage of a
summing-up, Griew has doubted whether talk of the burden of proof is appropriate, since
the prosecution must by then have established a *prima facie* case, otherwise a submission of
no case to answer would have succeeded; and, in reality, the jury must rely on all the
evidence, not just that provided by the prosecution, but also that provided by the defence:
Griew (1989). If the jury ask for further guidance, the judge should use similar words to that
used in the original direction: *R. v. Milligan, The Times*, March 11, 1989. See generally, B.
Shapiro, *Reasonable Doubt and Probable Cause* (1991).

[73] As established in *M'Naghten's Case* (1843) 10 Cl. & F. 200.

[74] Such exceptions may be express, see, *e.g.* the defence of diminished responsibility in the law
of murder, Homicide Act 1957, s.3(2) and see *R. v. Lambert* [2001] 1 Cr. App. R. 205 or
implied, see *R. v. Hunt* [1986] A.C. 352, HL. The possibility that the burden may be imposed
on the accused impliedly by statute and how it can be decided that the burden is so imposed
have been vigorously criticised by P. Mirfield in "The Legacy of Hunt" [1988] Crim.L.R. 19,
but see the rejoinder by D.J. Birch in "Hunting the Snark: the Elusive Statutory Exception"
[1988] Crim.L.R. 221.

[75] *Barbara v Spain* (1989) 11 E.H.R.R. 360. For the decisions of the HL on the burden of proof
and the Human Rights Act 1998 see *R v. DPP, ex p. Kebilene* [2000] 3 W.L.R. 972; [2000]
Crim. L.R. 486. *R. v. Lambert* [2001] 1 Cr. App. R. 205, and see G. Dingwall [2002] 65
M.L.R. 450.

[76] "The Presumption of Innocence in English Criminal Law" [1996] Crim. L.R. 306.

[77] See *Archbold (2002)*, para. 4–384. If the burden lies upon the defence, the standard is the
lower one of the balance of probabilities: *R. v. Carr-Briant* (1943) 29 Cr.App.R. 76. As to the
prosecution standard, the actual formulation of the direction to the jury has varied.
"Satisfied so that you feel sure" has its supporters: *Walters v. The Queen* [1960] 2 A.C. 26; *R.
v. Summers* (1952) 36 Cr.App.R. 14. So does, "satisfied beyond all/any/a reasonable doubt":
DPP v. Woolmington [1935] A.C. 462; *R. v. Lawrence* [1982] A.C. 510. For the judge who
wishes to be doubly safe, the direction, " ... satisfied beyond reasonable doubt so that you
feel sure of the defendant's guilt" has also been approved: *Fergusan v. The Queen* [1979] 1
W.L.R. 94.

[78] The expression is lacking in clarity — and deliberately so. In *R. v. Wickramaratne* [1998]
Crim. L.R. 565 where the jury expressed concern at what weight should be given to their
"feelings", the Court of Appeal recommended that the judge should remind them of the
direction on the burden of proof and advise to put feelings aside.

many problems. Montgomery[79] recently surveyed responses by potential English jurors to the English direction on the burden and standard of proof as compared to the U.S. directions. Earlier research had shown that jurors set the "beyond reasonable doubt" formula as lying between 51 per cent–92 per cent.[80] Montgomery applied a strict U.S. test "proof precluding every reasonable hypothesis" compared with the English "satisfied so that you are sure" test. The results of the small sample (with some question marks as to methodology) was that the less defined and more subjective English test led to fewer convictions. Very few would, under either test, convict on less than 75 per cent certainty. Montgomery's conclusions are challenged by Zander,[81] who argues that on the basis of empirical research conducted for the *Review Auld Report*, 51 per cent of the general public would require themselves to be 100 per cent sure before convicting. Thrity-one per cent of magistrates would share this view. Approximately 75 per cent of both samples would need to be at least 90 per cent sure before convicting.

The summing-up and the simple direction on the burden of proof has been observed, however, to cause greatest difficulties in cases where the crime can be established on the basis of a number of different, mutually exclusive grounds. If, for example, six jurors are satisfied that the accused committed the offence according to one of the bases alleged by the prosecution, and the other six on an alternative mutually exclusive ground, how can the jury really be satisfied as to the guilt of the accused?[82] This also raises the important question whether the case has been put in such a way that the accused can be said to have had a fair opportunity to know the case against him.

The problem of inconsistent verdicts — where the jury return acquittals on some counts and guilty verdicts on others which suggests a logical inconsistency in their decision-making — is also a difficult one. The Court of Appeal must consider whether there is a rational way in which verdicts can be explained.[83] It is not sufficient that the jury have, for example, merely demonstrated by their verdicts that the victim's credibility was in doubt on some counts.[84] For a successful appeal, it is necessary to show not only that there is a logical inconsistency in the verdict, but also that it is not possible to postulate a legitimate claim of reasoning which could explain the inconsistency.[85] The courts seem to allow for a conviction where a "legitimate train of reasoning" by the jury leads to a "logical inconsistency".

---

[79] "The Criminal Standard of Proof" (1998) N.L.J. 582.

[80] R. Hastie (ed.), *Inside the Juror: The Psychology of Juror Decision-making* (1993), pp. 100–106.

[81] "The Criminal Standard of Proof — How Sure is Sure?" (2000) 150 N.L.J. 1517.

[82] See J. C. Smith, "Satisfying the Jury" [1988] Crim. L.R. 335. See also the decision in *R. v. D* [2000] 8 Arch. News 2; *R. v. Gianaetto* [1997] 1 Cr.App. R. 1; *R. v. Brown* (1983) 79 Cr.App. R. 115. On the *Brown* problem of jury inconsistentcy see P. Robertshaw, "The Conjunctive or Disjunctive Jury" (1999) J. Crim. L 231.

[83] *R v. IK* [1999] Crim. L.R. 740It.

[84] *R v. Hayward* [2000] Crim. L.R. 189.

[85] *R. v. G* [1998] Crim. L.R. 483 and commentary by JCS, and *R. v. Fielder-Beech* [1998] Crim. L.R. 503.

(iii) Alternative verdicts returned by the jury

The judge should put alternative verdicts to the jury where appropriate,[86]   **17–072**
but the judge is to ensure that the defendant has a fair trial on the evidence
presented and there is no improper prejudice to the accused, ensuring also
that the jury are not distracted from the main issue. It may be preferable to
amend the indictment rather than leave alternatives to the jury. Before
returning an alternative verdict the jury must acquit on the more serious
charge or be discharged from returning a verdict. This can render the
selection of the appropriate charge for the offence extremely important.[87]
On hearing an appeal, the Court of Appeal has the power to substitute an
alternative verdict justified by the evidence as found at trial.

*(iv) A direction as to the definition of the offence charged and the facts which
have to be proved before there can be a conviction*

The judge must explain to the jury the legal requirements of the offence   **17–073**
charged and the facts of which the jury must be convinced before it can
convict. This often is not easy. In a case of theft, for example, the judge
should say that the property stolen must have belonged to someone else and
must have been appropriated by the accused, who must have been dishonest
and intending to deprive the other person permanently of the property.[88]
Even that seemingly straightforward statement creates difficulties. What is
an appropriation? What amounts to dishonesty? What if the property has
been "borrowed", to be returned at some (distant) future date?[89] Some
difficulties may be resolved by judges relying on model directions created by
the courts[90] and specimen directions produced by the Judicial Studies Board
with the approval of the Lord Chief Justice.[91] On the other hand, it might be
questioned whether use of such directions may not introduce excess
rigidity[92] and, in particular, whether it might not confuse the jury both by
using overly complex (lawyerly) language and by introducing superfluous
elements of law.[93]
   The judge should not direct the jury on matters not raised in the case, but
may be obliged to raise alternative defences not relied on explicitly by the
accused (*e.g.* provocation as a defence to murder where the accused has
alleged that he was acting in self-defence and would not wish to undermine
the chances of that defence by also pleading provocation which, by

---

[86] *R. v. Bergman* [1996] 2 Cr. App. R. 399.
[87] On the tactics of prosecuting counsel selecting the correct charge or overcharging, see *R. v. Fernandez* [1997] 1 Cr. App. R. 123.
[88] Theft Act 1968, s.1.
[89] All these questions give rise to considerable difficulty in the law of theft as will immediately be apparent from a perusal of J. C. Smith, *The Law of Theft*, (8th ed., 1997).
[90] See, *e.g.* the model direction as to the meaning of "recklessness" in the offences under the Criminal Damage Act 1971 established by Lord Diplock in *Commissioner of Police for the Metropolis v. Caldwell* [1982] A.C. 341 at 354.
[91] *Judicial Studies Board Report for 1991–1995*, para. 4.22. Reports are available from *www.jsboard.co.uk*.
[92] See Lord Hailsham's statement in *R. v. Lawrence*, above.
[93] Griew (1989), who points out that there may be a temptation amongst trial judges to provide too much legal information in order to make their directions appeal-proof.

definition, admits that he lost his temper).[94]

A simple example of theft raises starkly the problem of the distinction between matters of law and matters of law and fact when considering what to say about words like "dishonesty". The judge must direct the jury on issues of law. The problem that arises is the tendency, increasingly exhibited by the courts, to have to regard at least with some words appearing in the definition of criminal offences as words of the ordinary English language whose meaning is not, therefore, a question of law.[95] This was the approach taken with regard to "dishonesty" by the Court of Appeal in *R. v. Feely*,[96] which was trenchantly criticised largely on the ground that it was leaving to the jury a decision which was properly that of the judge.[97] This approach is still adopted in the interpretation of some words, although judges usually provide definitions where possible.[98] Of course, the greater the number of issues of law upon which the judge gives a direction, the fewer the opportunities for the exercise of discretion or common sense by the jury and the greater is the control of the judge.[99]

As to "dishonesty", the Court of Appeal in *R. v. Ghosh*[1] has decided not to leave the matter entirely to the jury, which would mean that the jury could in effect apply its own standards.[2] Neither has the court provided a detailed legal definition, which would perhaps be impossible to achieve. Instead it has indicated that, as a matter of law, the accused will be dishonest if the jury decides: (i) that what was done was dishonest by the standards of ordinary, decent people; and (ii) that the accused must have realised that what was being done was by those standards dishonest.[3]

This failure to provide clear definitions precludes a citizen from predicting with any certainty whether his conduct will be regarded as criminal. The ECHR guarantees in Article 7 that there should not be retrospective criminalisation. If a common law offence or definition of an element of the offence is too vague or depends substantially on the jury's definition (on a case by case basis) it may conflict with Article 7.[4]

---

[94] See, *e.g. R. v. Jonshon* [1989] 1 W.L.R. 740 and S. Doran, "Alternative Defences and the Invisible Burden on the Trial Judge" [1991] Crim. L.R. 878; *Archbold (2002)*, paras 4–378–4–379.

[95] See Lord Reid in *Brutus v. Cozens* [1973] A.C. 854 (on the meaning of the word "insulting" in the Public Order Act 1936, s.5, since repealed by the Public Order Act 1986, s.40(3)); Lawton L.J. in *W v. L* [1974] Q.B. 711 (on the meaning of "mental illness" in the Mental Health Act 1959).

[96] [1973] Q.B. 530.

[97] See, *e.g.* D. W. Elliott, "Law and Fact in Theft Act Cases" [1976] Crim.L.R. 707; G. Williams, "Law and Facts" [1976] Crim.L.R. 472 at 537; E. J. Griew, *Dishonesty and the Jury* (1974); A. Briggs, "Judges, Juries and the Meaning of Words" (1985) 5 L.S. 314.

[98] No *definition* (as opposed to explanation) of the meaning of "intention" has been provided by the courts in a series of recent cases, see Smith and Hogan (10th ed., 2002), pp.70–77. The most recent decision is that of the HL in *R. v. Woolin* [1998] 4 All E.R. 103.

[99] The jury will usually follow such a direction by the judge, and thus the exercise of discretion is limited. The jury is, of course, permitted to exercise discretion outside the judge's direction, which some might describe as not legitimate or perverse, see para. 17-095, below.

[1] [1982] 2 Q.B. 1053. See commentary at [1982] Crim.L.R. 608, and D. W. Elliott, "Dishonesty in Theft: A Dispensable Concept" [1982] Crim.L.R. 395.

[2] *R. v. Feely* [1973] Q.B. 530, CA. See Smith (1997).

[3] *R. v. Ghosh* [1982] 2 Q.B. 1053 1064.

[4] See *Kokkinakis v. Greece* (1994) 17 E.H.R.R. 397; *CR v. U.K.* at (1995) 21 E.H.R.R. 363; *Mattocia v. Italy* [2001] E.H.R.L.R. 89. For an argument that because of the primacy of the dishonesty element in the offence of cheating it is incompatible with Article 7, see D.

(v) A direction as to evidential points

It may be necessary for the judge to give directions about the evidence which **17–074**
the jury has heard. The judge should remind the jury that speeches by
counsel do not form part of the evidence. The jury may have to be warned of
the legal requirements in relation to certain evidence lest it relies upon that
evidence too readily in deciding questions of fact. The judge again exercises
control over the jury.

An example is where the defence is one of mistaken identity, since
eyewitness evidence may be based on a fleeting glimpse. Rarely would, for
example, a by-passer have more than a swift glimpse of the bank robber
running out of a bank to the getaway car. In such circumstances it is
possible for witnesses genuinely and honestly to be convinced that they are
right. They may, in fact, be mistaken. The jury must be informed of the
problems which can arise. Before the summing-up, the judge may withdraw
the evidence from the jury if it is "poor" and the prosecution should inform
the defence of any material discrepancies between the description originally
given and the accused's actual appearance. In the summing-up, the judge
should warn the jury of the need for caution; the circumstances in which the
identification took place should be drawn to the attention of the jury, in
particular the length of time the observation could have lasted and the
conditions; the judge should remind the jury of any weaknesses that have
become apparent and point out to the jury that evidence of recognition of
someone known can be relied upon more satisfactorily than identification of
a stranger.[5]

Other important discussions on issues of evidence will include the uses
that can be made of a defendant's failure to disclose an item of evidence
before trial or his failure to testify. The Judicial Studies Board provides a
specimen direction for the judge to deliver when a defendant has failed to
testify.[6] Similarly, the judge will give a special warning when the defendant
has lied about issues peripheral to the main ones in the case,[7] or where
evidence of a particular witness carries a special hazard (*e.g.* a co-defendant
or someone who may be tainted by an improper motive[8]). It is also
important that the judge gives a direction as to the "good" character of the
accused (where he has one).[9] The judge ought not to refer to the defendant's
failure to call any witness, lest this confuse the jury as to the burden of
proof.[10] The judge must be careful not to make improper comments on the
defendant's testimony, which is not to say that he cannot comment in strong
terms where necessary.[11] The judge should also avoid making adverse
comment in front of the accused, even where the jury are absent.[12]

Ormerod, "Cheating the Public Revenue" [1998] Crim. L.R. *cf. R. v. Pattni* [2001] Crim.
L.R. 627; 570.

[5] *R. v. Turnbull* [1977] 2 Q.B. 224. For a comprehensive listing of the rules relating to evidence
of identification, see *Archbold (2002)* Chap. 14.

[6] See [1996] 1 Cr.App. R. 69. See also the guidance in *R. v. Cowan* [1996] 1 Cr.App. R. 1.

[7] See *R. v. Lucas* [1981] Q.B. 720; *R. v. Burge and Pegg* [1996] 1 Cr.App. R. 163.

[8] See *R. v. Spencer and Smails* [1987] A.C. 128; *R. v. Makunjuola* [1995] 2 Cr.App. R. 469.

[9] See *R. v. Vye* (1993) 97 Cr.App. R. 134. And this must not be done sarcastically: *R. v. Lloyd*
[2000] 2 Cr. App. R. 355.

[10] See *R. v. Wright* [2000] Crim. L.R. 510; *R. v. Khan* [2001] Crim. L.R. 673.

[11] *R. v. Winn-Pope* [1996] Crim. L.R. 521.

[12] *R. v. Roncali* [1998] Crim. L.R. 584.

(vi) A summary of the evidence in the case

17–075   It is for the judge to put the case before the jury by reviewing the facts and a
failure to do so is a procedural irregularity.[13] In a complex case, this will
involve a substantial amount of the evidence being rehearsed for the jury's
benefit.[14] Whether this is really an appropriate function is doubtful,
especially as it may be unnecessary, may provide the judge with too much
influence over the jury, and may make it appear as though the prosecution is
being supported by the judge.[15]

Whilst the determination of matters of fact is for the jury, the judge is
entitled to comment on matters arising out of the evidence,[16] including the
strength of the respective cases[17] the demeanour and quality of witnesses,[18]
the credibility of evidence and the quality of any argument. Comment may
be in strong terms provided that, overall, it is not unfair[19] and the jury is
reminded clearly and forcefully that they have the ultimate responsibility for
deciding issues of fact.[20] It is vital that the judge puts the defence to the
jury[21] no matter how ridiculous it seems.[22] It is not incumbent on a judge to
repeat the whole of the defendant's lengthy statements in interviews
provided he refers to the salient passages.[23]

---

[13] *R. v. Adamo-Taylor* [2000] 2 Cr.App. R. 194. This is especially important if jurors need a
warning about hazardous evidence.

[14] The judge keeps a note of the evidence– a process which has a significant effect on the speed
of the criminal trial—and will remind the jury of it in the summing-up. However, merely
reading out such notes, especially in complex cases, was criticised by the Court of Appeal in
R. v. Charles (1979) 68 Cr.App.R. 334, see Emmins (2000), p. 293. The judge must also be
careful to put the defence case fully and properly, see *R. v. Tillman* [1962] Crim.L.R. 261; *R.
v. Hamilton* [1972] Crim.L.R. 266. For a particularly abbreviated summing-up consisting
almost entirely of a low, prolonged whistle, see *Pie-powder*, by a circuit tramp (1911), p. 70,
cited in Samuels (1982). For an incisive consideration of the function of summing-up, see
Griew (1989).

[15] D. Wolchover, "Should Judges Sum Up on the Facts?" [1989] Crim.L.R. 781 and the
findings of the Crown Court Survey for the Royal Commission on Criminal Justice. (1993).

[16] See *R. v. Evans* (1990) 91 Cr.App.R. 173. For an interesting account of the summing-up in
the *Oz* case, see T. Palmer, *The Trials of Oz* (1971). There was a great deal of comment
contained in that summing-up which was later the subject of appeal: *R. v. Anderson* [1972] 1
Q.B. 304.

[17] "[I]n *O'Donnell* (1917) 12 Cr.App.R. 219 a conviction was upheld where the judge said that
the prisoner's story was a 'remarkable' one and contrary to previous statements he had
made, but in *Canny* (1945) 30 Cr.App.R. 143 repeatedly telling the jury that the defence was
'absurd' and that there was no foundation for defence allegations amounted to a direction to
find the case against the accused proved. The conviction was therefore quashed.": Emmins
(2000), p. 293.

[18] "I thought he was a jolly good witness. He wasn't prepared to whitewash all of *Oz* like some
of the other so-called experts and I can't say fairer than that": *per* Judge Argyle, quoted in
Palmer (1971), p. 252.

[19] *R. v. Middlesex Justices, ex p. DPP* [1952] 2 Q.B. 758; *R. v. O'Donnell* (1917) 12 Cr.App.R.
219; *R. v. Canny* (1945) 30 Cr.App.R. 143.

[20] *R. v. West* (1910) 4 Cr.App.R. 179; *R. v. Beeby* (1911) 6 Cr.App.R. 138; *R. v. Frampton*
(1917) 12 Cr.App.R. 202. The following is an example of such a direction: " ... if I now
express an opinion and you agree, well, that's alright. If not, you can disagree. You do not
have to do what I tell you. What I think is irrelevant. *You* have to decide": *per* Judge Argyle,
Palmer (1971), p. 239.

[21] *R. v. Curtin* [1996] Crim. L.R. 831; *R. v. Akhtar* [2000] 1 Arch. News 2.

[22] *e.g. R. v. Marr* (1989) 90 Cr.App. R. 154, where the accused claimed to have tripped and to
prevent himself from falling had grasped the female victim by the crotch to support himself.

[23] *R. v. Soames-Waring* [1999] Crim. L.R. 89.

Comments may be other than verbal[24]: gesture, tone of voice and facial expression can all speak volumes in indicating the judge's view of the merits, and such matters do not appear in the transcript.[25] The Court of Appeal appears to be unwilling to interfere with a conviction on the ground that the judge has overstepped the permissible limits of comment unless the summing-up is very defective.[26] The judge must not become or appear to become a prosecutor.[27] An informal constraint on the extent of judicial comment is the possibility that the jury will react against a very strong direction to convict and, out of perversity or sympathy for the accused or some other motivation, bring in a verdict of acquittal.

Although there have been cases which suggest that a judge may direct a conviction,[28] the current position of the Court of Appeal is that such a direction should never be given.[29]

In the event that the judge realises that he or she has given an erroneous direction in summing up, or an error has been drawn to his attention by counsel, he may recall the jury and re-direct. Both prosecution and defence counsel are obliged to seek rectification of errors of which they become aware.[30]

The Judicial Studies Board has, through the production of specimen directions,[31] reduced the number of appeallable errors made in summing up. The Judicial Studies Board was established in 1979 to provide training for the judiciary in criminal law. Its activities now cover wider aspects of judicial training. In addition to its issuing of model directions, its continuing training and induction programmes for the judiciary and its monitoring and evaluation objectives, the JSB produces other important practical guides.[32]

(e) Sentencing[33]

Once the jury have found the accused to be guilty of an offence or after the   **17–076**

---

[24] On the use of language in judicial statements see also the recent U.S. research: S. Philips, *Ideology in the Language of Judges: How Judges Practice Law, Politics and Courtroom Control* (1998).

[25] See Wolchover (1989).

[26] *cf. R. v. Anderson* [1972] 1 Q.B. 304. Such defects will occur where the judge usurps the jury's function, as in *R. v. Canny* (1945) 30 Cr.App.R. 143, see n. 19 above. This issue may also overlap with the question of whether a judge can direct a conviction, see text below.

[27] See recently the guidance given by Simon Brown L.J. in *R. v. Nelson* [1997] Crim. L.R. 234.

[28] See, *e.g. R. v. Ferguson* (1970) 54 Cr. App. R. 410; *Archbold (2002)*, para. 4–411.

[29] *R. v. Gent* (1988) 89 Cr. App. R. 247 *R. v. Gordon* (1991) 92 Cr. App.R. 50; and see *Archbold (2002)*, paras 4–411–4–412. The possibility of a judge being able to direct a jury where there is no evidence for a matter where the burden is on the defence is argued both in *Archbold (2002)*, para. 4–413 and by J. C. Smith in the Commentary to *R. v. Wright* [1992] Crim L.R. 596.

[30] *R. v. Langford, The Times*, January 12 2001.

[31] There were complaints that the Judicial Studies Board directions were not publicly available and yet were being relied upon by judges as authoritative texts: see R. Munday, "The Bench Books: Can the Judiciary Keep a Secret?" [1996] Crim. L.R. 296. The directions are now published on the website. See also the published correspondence between Kennedy L.J. and Roderick Munday at [1996] Crim. L.R. 529. See also R.Moday, (2002) J. Crim. Law 158 criticsing an unduly rigid adherence to specimen directions.

[32] *e.g. Race and the Courts* (1999) emphasising the need for judges to be colour conscious, not colour blind.

[33] See *Archbold (2002)* Chap. 5. For a brief description of the sentencing function of magistrates, see paras, 17–012–17–013 above. See D. A. Thomas, *Current Sentencing Practice*

accused has pleaded guilty, it is for the judge to pass sentence on the offender. The judge must have the necessary information available about the offence and the offender. If this is available, sentencing may occur immediately; if not, there may be an adjournment.

(i) Information for sentencing[34]

17–077 The judge must be provided with the facts of the offence. Where the accused has pleaded guilty, these facts will not as yet have been set out. They are now given by the prosecutor, unless disputed, in which case there may be a "Newton" hearing at which the prosecutor is obliged to prove them.[35] This hearing follows a normal adversarial format with strict rules of evidence applying and the judge directing himself or herself as if he or she were a jury.

The prosecutor will then provide evidence as to the offender's "antecedents", that is previous convictions, educational history, employment record, home circumstances and resources. The evidence should be produced in accordance with the Practice Direction laid down by the Lord Chief Justice.[36] The defence may challenge the evidence, in which case the prosecutor must prove it. Further information may be contained in a variety of reports,[37] in particular a social inquiry report, prepared by either a probation officer or a social worker, considering the factors leading to the offence and a recommendation as to appropriate sentence.[38]

The courts also rely on risk assessments, with a recognition that these can provide better information qualitatively and quantitatively than antecedents thereby producing a greater likelihood of the optimal disposal. This should also lead to a more effective use of the limited resources of the criminal justice system, and provide better protection for the victim and the public.[39] Other reports that will be offered to the court include medical and psychiatric reports and reports from places where a person has been held,

(looseleaf); A. Ashworth, *Sentencing and Criminal Justice* (3rd ed., 2000); M. Wasik, *Emmins on Sentencing* (3rd ed., 1998); C. Harding and L. Koffman, *Sentencing and the Penal System: Text and Materials* (2nd ed., 1995); E. Stockdale and K. Devlin, *Sentencing* (1987); N. Padfield and N. Walker, *Sentencing: Theory, Law and Practice* (2nd ed., 1996); R. Henham, *Criminal Justice and Sentencing Policy* (1996); M. Wasik and C. Munro, *Sentencing Judicial Discretion and Training* (1992); A. Ashworth and A. von Hirsch, *Principled Sentencing* (2nd ed., 1998); A. Ashworth and M. Wasik, *Fundamentals of Sentencing Theory: Essays in Honour of Andrew von Hirsch* (1998); Wasik, Gibbons and Redmayne, (1999), Chap. 5.
[34] See *Archbold (2002)*, Chap. 5.
[35] So-called after the decision of the Court of Appeal in *R. v. Newton* (1983) 77 Cr.App.R. 13. For the proliferation of cases on this see *Archbold (2002)*, para. 5–10. On what to do with disputed Newton hearings see K. Browne, "Handling an Unexploded Newton Bomb" (1998) 142 S.J. July 24, 742.
[36] *Practice Direction (Crime: Antecedents (No.2)* [1997] 1 W.L.R. 1482. On the recording, storage and access to criminal convictions see S. Uglow, "Criminal Records Under the Police Act 1997" [1998] Crim. L.R. 235.
[37] *Archbold (2002)*, para. 5–34. See the Powers of Criminal Courts (Sentencing) Act 2000, ss.156, 157, 162.
[38] R. Horn and M. Evans, "The Effect of Gender on Pre-Sentence Reports" (2000) 39 Howard Jnl 184 reveal in their empirical research that PSRs were often written by someone of the same gender as the offender and that motivations for male and female offenders were explained differently. The main motivations for women to offend were identified as money and drugs; for men, they were money, drugs and alcohol.
[39] See C. Clarkson and R. Morgan (eds), *The Politics of Sentencing Reform* (1995).

such as a remand centre or prison when on remand in custody. The court has the power to remand a person to hospital for the preparation of medical reports.[40] The court is obliged to obtain and consider a pre-sentence report in determining whether to impose a custodial sentence.[41]

The recent reforms in sentencing place a greater emphasis on the court's familiarity with a defendant's antecedents. There is therefore an ever greater requirement of vigilance on criminal practitioners to be aware of criminal records.[42] There is also a greater need for caution in the recording and transcription of records and in their being kept up to date. Counsel has a duty to inform himself or herself of the court's sentencing powers, and to correct the judge should he or she fall in to error.[43]

(ii) Plea in mitigation[44]

Once the court has received reports and material for sentencing, the defence   **17–078** may then make a plea in mitigation.[45] Some indication of the likely sentence may be given by the judge to give defence notice of what the mitigation should relate to (especially where the judge is considering imposing a longer than normal sentence).[46] Defence counsel should be restrained in the presentation of mitigation and should not impugn the character of witnesses. If the defence seek to rely on evidence in the course of the plea, they bear the burden of proving it.[47] The plea of mitigation will usually be made by the advocate, and it is important to note the protection in section 83 of the Powers of Criminal Courts (Sentencing) Act 2000 (PCC(S)A) whereby a court shall not impose a custodial sentence on an adult who has not previously been imprisoned or accused unless he or she legally represented.

Prosecution counsel should monitor defence claims and if necessary request a Newton hearing to resolve disputes.[48] The prosecution's role in sentencing is a neutral one and there is no objective of seeking a heavier sentence. The judge is entitled to seek the assistance of prosecution counsel whenever necessary.[49] Even if not openly seeking a longer sentence, the prosecution will influence the sentence passed by the selection of charges at the outset, and by influencing the mode of the trial. In addition, the prosecution must inform the court of the minimum sentence possible and inform the court of the accused's antecedents.

It is worth remembering that the prosecution can appeal unduly lenient sentences. The Court of Appeal's power has prompted questions about whether the courts will be unduly influenced by public opinion. Only cases

---

[40] See Mental Health Act 1983, s.35.
[41] Powers of Criminal Courts (Sentencing) Act 2000, s. 181.
[42] See M. Wasik, "The Vital Importance of Certain Previous Convictions" [2001] Crim. L.R. 363.
[43] *R. v. Brown* [1996] Crim. L.R. 134.
[44] *See Archbold (2002)*, para. 5–42.
[45] See also para. 17-055.
[46] *R. v. O'Brien* (1995) 16 Cr.App. R. (S.) 556.
[47] *R. v. Guppy* [1994] Crim. L.R. 614.
[48] See *Archbold (2002)*, para. 5–33.
[49] *Attorney-General's Reference No. 7 of 1997* [1998] 1 Cr.App. R. (S.) 268.

from Crown Court may be referred, apart from exceptional other cases.[50] Shute[51] in his review of power notes that sometimes sentences have been doubled in length by the Court of Appeal.[52]

Finally, as an aspects of the plea in mitigation an offender may have other cases taken into consideration.[53] This clears up outstanding offences and the offender is likely to get a substantial sentencing reduction for those offences so as to reward honesty. The offender is still only liable for the maximum sentence available for the offence to which he pleaded guilty or was convicted, not for the those offences taken into consideration as well. The scheme whereby courts take into consideration other offences raises very difficult issues regarding the presumption of innocence and the fair trial guarantees. Ashworth, for example, argues that sentencing discounts generally conflict with and the presumption of innocence.[54]

Sentencing may be deferred for up to six months to allow the court to take account of the offender's post-conviction behaviour and any other relevant circumstances.[55] The court will make clear to the offender that sentence is deferred and explain why. The court passing sentence at the end of the period of deferment should be appraised of the reasons for deferring so as to assess whether the accused has complied with any relevant obligations.[56]

(iii) Sample counts[57]

17–079   If the offending has been committed repeatedly over time, the prosecution might choose to prosecute for one specific example of this offending at an identifiable point in the period of time. If this course is adopted and the accused is convicted, he should not be sentenced for offences other than that for which he has been found guilty.[58] If the accused pleads guilty to the sample count, sentencing occurs on that understanding.[59]

(iv) What sentence is imposed?[60]

17–080   A sentence is laid down for each offence.[61] For a very limited range of

---

[50] *e.g.* indecent assault; s. 14, Offences Against the Person Act 1861.

[51] On the References see S. Shute, "Who Passes Unduly Lenient Sentences? How Were They Listed?: A Survey of Attorney-General's Reference Cases, 1989–1997" [1999] Crim. L.R. 603.

[52] See also S. Shute, "Prosecution Appeals Against Sentence: The First Five Years" (1994) 57 M.L.R. 745. Between 1989 and 1997 there were 367 reviews.

[53] See *Archbold (2002)*, para. 5–24.

[54] See A. Ashworth, "The Impact on Criminal Justice" in B. Markesinis (ed.), *The Impact of the Human Rights Bill on English Law* (1998), p.141.

[55] Powers of Criminal Courts (Sentencing) Act 2000, s. 1 . See *Archbold (2002)*, para. 5–48.

[56] See *R. v. George* [1984] 1 W.L.R. 1082.

[57] M. Chapman, "Specimen Counts and Sentencing: A principled Approach and the Proper Procedure" (1997) J. Crim. L. 315 reviewing recent English decisions and warning of the danger of infringement of a fair trial and the presumption of innocence.

[58] *R.v. Canavan* [1998] 1 Cr. App. R. 79.

[59] *R.v. Huchison* [1972] 1 W.L.R. 398; *Archbold (2002)*, para. 5–14.

[60] A number of different options are open where an offender is under 21. See *Archbold (2002)*, Chap. 5, Part IV.

[61] If the offender has been committed by the magistrates to trial on indictment for an offence

offences the penalty is fixed by law. Murder is the main example, since the judge is obliged to impose a sentence of life imprisonment.[62] If the offence is a common law offence, the sentence is a maximum of life imprisonment or a fine. If the offence is a statutory offence, the statute will lay down the punishment. Section 109 of the Powers of Criminal Courts (Sentencing) Act 2000[63] requires the Crown Court to impose a life sentence on any person convicted of a second "serious offence" unless there are exceptional circumstances. A serious offence *includes* attempted murder, manslaughter, wounding, grievous bodily harm, rape, unlawful sexual intercourse with a girl under 13, various firearms offences, robbery with a firearm.

Where an offender has a mental disorder, a hospital order may be imposed under the Mental Health Act 1983.[64]

In all cases, when imposing sentence, the judge pronounces sentence in open court and in many circumstances will provide reasons for the sentence.[65]

Article 7 of the ECHR protects against retrospective increases in penalty. This has given rise to a number of controversial challenges particularly in relation to the imposition of confiscation orders on property.[66] Other possible challenges under the Human Rights Act 1998 might be based on discrimination in sentencing (Article 14) and on the conditions of imprisonment (Article 3).

Any sentence laid down in a statute is a maximum and that maximum is rarely imposed. The judge has a wide range of possible sentences from which to choose. Broadly speaking, for people over 21,[67] these fall into the non-custodial and the custodial options. The Powers of the Criminal Courts

triable either way and also a related summary offence within s.41 of the Criminal Justice Act 1988, the Crown Court has the sentencing powers which the magistrates' court would have had on conviction at summary trial.

[62] Murder (Abolition of Death Penalty) Act 1965, s.l. Powers of Criminal Courts (sentencing) Act 2000, s.93. See further N. Padfield, [2002] Crim. L.R. 190 on the proposals regarding tarrifs in murder cases.

[63] This is a consolidation statute which repeals and replaces all earlier sentencing powers of the court. For a call for consolidation see D. Thomas, "The Case for Consolidation" [1997] Crim. L.R. 406 seeking a "simpler and more accessible" form of legislation.

[64] See *Blackstone's Criminal Practice 2002*, para. E24.3. On the proposals to deal with people with untreatable severe personality disorders see Home Office and Department of Health, *Managing People with Severe Personality Disorder: Proposals for Policy Development* (1999) and A.M. McAlinden, "Intermediate Sentences for the Severely Personality Disordered" [2001] Crim. L.R. 108.

[65] See the obligations in Powers of Criminal Courts (Sentencing) Act 2000, s.79(4) wherever a custodial sentence is imposed. See also the *Practice Direction (Custodial Sentences: Explanations)* [1998] 1 W.L.R. 278.

[66] See generally A. Ashworth, "Sentencing and the HRA" (1999) 163 J.P.N. 64. Noting that sentencing will be relatively lightly affected, noting possible challenges to excessive sentences under Art 3. These could be particularly important in relation to mentally ill offenders. Other challenges under the Human Rights Act and the ECHR have included those to discretionary life sentences, see *Weeks v. U.K.* (1987) 10 E.H.R.R. 293; and to mandatory sentences life *Wynne v. U.K.* (1994) 19 E.H.R.R. 333. Arguments could be made a that sentence is discriminatory (Art. 14). On victims rights to participate in sentence/procedure see claim under Art. 8 in *McCourt v. U.K.* (1993) 15 E.H.R.R. C.D. Delay between act and sentence could amount to a breach of Art. 6 in *Howarth v. U.K.* App. no, 38081/97. D's unduly lenient sentence was altered to two years after imposition of original and held to breach Art. 6.

[67] The sentences available where the offender is under 21 are different, see *Archbold (2002)* Chap. 5, Part IV.

(Sentencing) Act 2000 consolidates the sentencing options available to courts: absolute discharge (ss.12 and 14)[68]; conditional discharge (ss. 12–15); parental bind-overs, discharges and fines (s.150); fines (ss.126–129, 135–142)[69]; Compensation orders (ss.130–134); restitution orders (ss.148 and 149); forfeiture orders (ss.143–145); community orders (ss.46–50); probation orders (ss.41–45), now "community rehabilitation orders" under the Community Sentences Act 2000[70] combined orders (s.51)–now community rehabilitation and punishment order under the Community Sentences Act 2000[71]—curfew orders (ss.37–40); Attendance centre orders (ss.60–62); Supervision orders (ss.63–68); Action plan orders (ss.69–72); Drug treatment and testing orders (ss.52–58); suspended prison sentences (ss.118–121 and 125); mandatory life sentence for second serious offence (ss.109–112 and 115); Minimum seven-year sentence for third offence in class A drug trafficking (ss.110 and 112–115); Minimum three year sentence for third domestic burglary (ss.111–115); mandatory custody for life on murder (s.93); and various special sentencing powers for young offenders including detention and training orders (ss.100–107) and detention at Her Majesty's pleasure (ss.90–92), and long term detention (ss.91–92). Further, there are a variety of other orders, such as an order to pay costs to the prosecution or compensation to the victim,[72] which, whilst not being sentences, have much the same effect as a fine as far as the offender is concerned.

The custodial option is imprisonment, which may be suspended or partly suspended,[73] and since the Criminal Justice Act 1991 sentences are to be suspended only in exceptional circumstances.[74]

There has been an increasing awareness that community sentences are largely more appropriate than imprisonment for dealing with factors associated with persistence in re-offending and that a dramatic reduction in the rate and seriousness of offending could best be achieved by improvements to the probation practice together with opportunities to embrace new developments in sentencing.[75]

New powers of sentencing and disposal are constantly being introduced.[76] For example, reparation orders under sections 67–68 of the Crime and Disorder Act 1998 are a new power to deal with 10–17 year olds, whereby

---

[68] In 2000, the proportion of discharges fell by 1% to 16%. (*Criminal Statistics for England and Wales 2000* (2001), para.7.9, Table 7.2) with a total of 121,800.

[69] In 2000, 70% of all offenders were fined. (*Criminal Statistics for England and Wales* (2001) para.7.9, Table 7.2 Total = 1,017,100 offenders fined.

[70] Probation orders rose from 18–24% in 2000. (*Criminal Statistics for England and Wales* (2001), Table 7.24 with a total of 56,700.

[71] Community service orders rose from 30–35% in 2000 (*Criminal Statistics for England and Wales* (2001) Table 7.24) with a total of 50,200. Total community sentences reached 156,100.

[72] In 2000 102,400 offenders were ordered to pay compensation orders (*Criminal Statistics for England and Wales 2000* (2001), Table 7.20:

[73] See Powers of Criminal Courts (Sentencing) Act 2000 above.

[74] On what constitutes exceptional circumstances see M.Wasik, "The Suspended Sentence" (1998) 162 J.P.N. 176.

[75] *Effective Sentencing: Evidence from Research with Particular Reference to Community Sentences and the Work of the Probation Service* (1998) presented in a memorandum to the House of Commons Home Affairs Committee, 3rd Report (1998). For a review of community penalties see A. Rutherford 147 N.L.J. (1997) 1159. See generally *www.fairer-sentencing.co.uk*.

[76] For more radical suggestions see *e.g.* M. Bagaric, "New Criminal Sanctions: Inflicting Pain Through the Denial of Employment and Education" [2001] Crim. L.R. 184.

the offender has to make specific reparation to the victim or the community harmed up to a maximum of 24 hours' work.[77] The examples given include writing a letter of apology, repairing criminal damage, collecting litter, etc.[78] Some have viewed these as marking a major shift towards including restorative justice in mainstream English criminal justice,[79] others have viewed the reform less optimistically.[80] A related dimension to the use of restorative disposal powers is to rely on restorative cautioning. This involves victims and others affected being invited to participate in the cautioning of the offender.[81] As a further example of innovative disposal powers the government introduced "action plan orders" in the Crime and Disorder Ac 1998.[82] These are a new community sentence under which 10–17 year olds are intensively supervised in a programme of education and activities specified by the court. Further developments have been made in the Youth Justice and Criminal Evidence Act 1999.[83]

---

[77] Reparation orders as introduced by the Crime and Disorder Act 1998 are not truly 'restorative' since the professionals remain in control. The reparation order made shall be "such as in the opinion of the court are commensurate with the seriousness of the offence". s. 67(5). The order may combine with compensation order. M. Wasik, (1999), discusses the operation of these provisions, questioning whether they cast the net of potential victims too widely for practical operation of reparation to satisfy each victim. There are theoretical difficulties: "The operation of reparation orders within a desert framework is, then, bound to create significant problems of principle." This stems from desert-based theory focusing on proportionality between offenders not between offender and victim: see L. Zedner, *Reparation and Retribution: Are They Reconcilable?* [1994] 57 M.L.R. 228 (1994) 57 M.L.R. 228. For discussion as to whether these are really crime control or restorative justice see R. Evans and K. Puech, "Reprimands and Warnings: Populist Punitiveness or Restorative Justice" [2001] Crim. L.R. 794.

[78] For further information on reparation orders see the Guidance Document available at *www.homeoffice.gov.uk/cdact/repord.htm.*

[79] J. Dignan, "The Crime and Disorder Act and the Prospects of Restorative Justice" [1999] Crim. L.R. 48.

[80] A. Morris and L. Gelsthorpe, "Something Old, Something Borrowed, Something Blue, but Something New? ... " [2000] Crim. L.R. 18.

[81] For a discussion of the practical application of such a scheme see R. Young and B. Goold, "Restorative Police Cautioning in Aylesbury—From Degrading to Reintegrative Shaming Ceremonies" [1999] Crim. L.R. 126. See generally A. von Hirsch and A. Ashworth, *Principled Sentencing* (1998) Chap.7. On reparation and victims see also M. Wasik, "Reparation: Sentencing and the Victim" [1999] Crim. L.R. 740, for an excellent discussion of many of the fundamental issues involved including who constitutes as victim.

[82] ss. 69–70.

[83] On the developments in the Youth Justice and Criminal Evidence Act 1999 see C. Ball, "A Significant Move Towards Restorative Justice, or a Recipe for Unintended Consequences?". [2000] Crim. L.R. 211 who considers the new orders available to deal with youth crime, in particular the mandatory referral orders involving a "programme of behaviour" from the Youth Offending Panel. The accused, by personally taking responsibility, is forced to acknowledge the impact of his wrongdoing on lives of others and is therefore less likely to re-offend. The Act also enhances the victim's position by allowing for their participation in youth offender panels. These supplement court hearings with group meeting of offenders, parents, victims and the youth offending team. On restorative justice generally, see S. Walther, "Reparation and Criminal Justice: Can they be Integrated?" (1996) Euro. J. Crime and Criminal Law and Criminology 163; see also the Home Office Crime Reduction Research Series Paper, No. 9, *An Expoloratory Evaluation of Restorative Justice Schemes* (2001), and No. 10, *An International Review of Restorative Justice* (2001).

(iv) Imposing a particular sentence

17–081   The judge must choose an appropriate sentence. For many years, the Court of Appeal had been developing a sophisticated tariff approach to sentencing by the setting of guidelines in an endeavour to ensure consistency in sentencing.[84] Parliament has been developing a principled approach since the introduction of the Criminal Justice Act 1991.[85] The objective is to ensure that the sentence fits the seriousness of the offence, that imprisonment is only used where necessary, and that reasons are given for the sentences imposed. So, *e.g.* what is now section 79 of the PCC(S)A creates statutory criteria for the imposition of a custodial sentence and states, at: s. 79(2):

> " ... the court shall not pass a custodial sentence on the offender unless it is of the opinion—
>
> (a)   that the offence, or the combination of the offence and one or more offences associated with it, was so serious that only such a sentence can be justified for the offence; or
>
> (b)   where the offence is a violent or sexual offence, that only such a sentence would be adequate to protect the public from serious harm from him."

A more detailed account of the imposition and appropriateness of individual sentences and sentencing policy lie beyond the scope of this book. The Auld Report recommended codification of the entire law of sentencing.[86]

(v) Changes in sentencing approach

17–082   There have been a number of very controversial reforms in sentencing within the last decade. These include the Crime (Sentences) Act 1997[87] which introduced automatic life sentences on a second conviction for a serious[88] violent or sexual offence; seven-year minimum sentences on third convictions for dealing class A drugs; and three-year minimum sentences for

---

[84] On calls for a sentencing council to produce coherence and consistency in sentencing guidance, see A. Ashworth, "Sentencing and the Constitution" (1990) 1 K.C.L.J. 29. Ashworth, "Disentangling Disparity" in C. Pennington and S. Lloyd-Bostock *The Psychology of Sentencing: approaches to consistency and disparity* (1987) Chap 3. The *Auld Report* calls for codification of sentencing, Chap. 1.

[85] There were many problems with the details of the original scheme introduced, but a significant number have been resolved by subsequent statutory amendment.

[86] See Chapter 1, pp. 20–22.

[87] On the 1997 Act see the government White Paper, *Protecting the Public*, Cm. 3190 (1996).The Bill was criticised by the then Lord Chief Justice: see comments reported at (1997) 161 J.P.N. 136 who commented on its "indiscriminate scatter-gun proposals". *Cf.* the views of P. Coad, (1997) 161 J.P.N. 159, who defends the proposals. See also J.P. Cavadino, (1997). J.P.N. and Editorial, (1997) 147 N.L.J. 117.

[88] Serious offence is defined in the Act in section 2(5). The offences for which the defendant receives the automatic sentence need not be of the same kind. The Act was criticised for its numerous conflicts with existing statutory and common law approaches, particularly in relation to the concept of dangerousness.

a third conviction on domestic burglary. The courts are empowered to depart from this regime only in "exceptional cases". The obvious danger with such a scheme is that the automatic life sentence fails to protect the defendant by ignoring his particular circumstances and there is clearly an increased risk of wrongful convictions. In addition, there will be an increase in the number of trials rather than guilty parties, with all the consequences that brings, including that the victim is more likely to have to testify. Furthermore, there is the unsubstantiated belief that increased sentences will have the greater deterrent effect.[89] The Crime (Sentences) Act 1997 was described as "the most profoundly unsatisfactory piece of populist sentencing legislation for many years" beach.[90] It has been held that these automatic provisions do not Article 7 of the ECHR by retrospectively aggravating the penalty for a first serious offence committed before the Act came into force. The Court of Appeal did however acknowledge that breaches of Articles 3 and 5 of the ECHR might arise if the sentences were wholly disproportionate to the offence.[91]

Less controversially, the Sex Offenders Act 1997 established an obligation to register sex offenders.[92] Similarly, the Crime and Disorder Act 1998 provides further powers for sex offenders orders to protect the public from serious harm. Those subject to this regime are obliged to inform the police of changes in name and address.[93] In addition, the Crime and Disorder Act introduced new offences with higher sentences for racially aggravated crimes.[94]

---

[89] See generally, M. Wasik, "The Crime (Sentences) Act 1997" (1998) 162 J.P.N. 36 and 56. For calls for an extension of the scheme to other crimes see P. Coad, "Bringing Down Crime" (2000) 164 J.P.N. 639. For further information on the 1997 Act see the Home Office Circular, 54/1997 and www.homeoffice.gov.uk/circulars.

[90] See R. Henham, "Making Sense of the Crime (Sentences) Act (1997)" (1998), M.L.R. 223. See R. Hood and S. Shute, 58 "Protecting the Public: Automatic Life Sentences, Parole and High Risk Offenders" [1996] Crim. L.R. 788; R. Henham, "Anglo-American Approaches to Cumulative Sentencing and the Implications for U.K. Sentencing Policy" (1997) 36 Howard Jnl 263; C. Clarkson, "Beyond Just Deserts: Sentencing Violent and Sexual Offenders" (1997) 36 Howard Jnl. 284. (D.A. Thomas, "The Crime (Sentences) Act 1997", [1998] Crim. L.R. 83). The Act's introduction of mandatory minimum sentences met with hostility from many members of the senior judiciary speaking in the parliamentary debates. For a catalogue of cogent criticism see Thomas. The Act does not empower judges with greater sentences, it simply compels them to impose mandatory sentences. The Act prescribes custodial sentence for offenders convicted for the third time of a Class A drug dealing offence. The Act also introduced new powers to sentence offenders suffering from a psychopathic disorder to periods of imprisonment and to give a direction that the person be admitted to hospital for treatment. See on this N. Eastman and J. Peay, "Sentencing Psychopaths: Is the 'Hospital and Limitation Direction' an Ill-Considered Hybrid?" [1998] Crim L.R. 93.

[91] R. v Offen [2001] 2 W.L.R. 253. See more recently, Attorney-General's Reference (No. 124 of 2001) [2002] EWCA Crim 197. The automatic sentences have even been upheld in relation to the mentally ill: R.v. Newman [2000] 2 Cr. App. R. (S.) 227; Cf. R. v. Buckland [2000] Crim. L.R. 307.

[92] See ss. 1–6.

[93] s.6. Archbold (2002) para. 20–271 a. For concerns regarding the application of the register to the cautioning procedure see K. Soothill, B. Francis, and B. Sanderson, "A Cautionary Tale: The Sex Offenders Act 1997, the Police and Cautions" [1997] Crim. L.R. 482. Research has revealed that a large proportion of sex offenders were cautioned, especially for consensual acts. The number has declined in more recent years.

[94] On race and sentencing generally, see R. Hood, Race and Sentencing (1992) and A. von Hirsh and J.V. Roberts, "Racial Disparity in Sentencing: Reflections on the Hood Study" (1997) Howard Jnl. 227.

In an effort to improve the appropriateness of sentencing powers generally the Sentencing Advisory Panel was established under sections 80–81 of the Crime and Disorder Act 1998 as an independent non-departmental public body reporting annually to the Home Office and the Lord Chancellors Department. It provides, on its own initiative, views on appropriate sentencing guidelines to the Court of Appeal.[95] For example, the panel commissioned a survey of public attitudes to burglary. Respondents generally believed that courts were too soft on burglary, but when provided with a fact scenario there was in fact agreement with the sentence passed or even suggestions for a more lenient sentence.[96] The Panel publishes consultation papers as part of its reviewing exercise and has commissioned and conducted numerous research projects.[97] It has been extremely well received.

The ever-expanding prison population remains a major concern. The Home Office predicts that by 2007 the prison population will be 80,000.[98] Statistics suggest that women are the fastest growing sector in prison; numbers rose by 59 per cent between 1993–97.[99] In 2000, 1.42 million offenders were sentenced in courts in England and Wales.[1] The number of people given immediate custodial sentences at all courts was 106,200 in 2000. This represented a 1 per cent increase on 1999 and was the highest figure since 1928.[2] The average population in custody in 2000 was 64,600.[3] The average length of Crown Court sentences for males aged 21 and over rose from 24.1 months in 1999 to 24.2 months in 2000.[4]

Public opinion on sentencing and prisons remains ill-informed, with nearly 80 per cent of people continuing to believe that current sentences are too lenient. There is considerable public debate (academic and otherwise) as to sentencing policy generally. Ashworth and Hough,[5] identify numerous problems with taking heed of public opinion in view of the inadequate knowledge on which such opinions are based,[6] and the confusion between

---

[95] See, *e.g.* on environmental offences (1999) 163 J.P.N. 824; on offensive weapons, (1999) J.P.N. 909; racially aggravated offences, (2000) J.P.N 156; on handling stolen goods (2000) 164 J.P.N. 772; on domestic burglary, (2001) 165 J.P.N. 236. The Court of Appeal has adopted some of the panel's recommendations see *e.g. R. v. Mashaollahi* [2001] 1 Cr. App. R. (S.) 96.

[96] See P. Tain, (2001) 452.

[97] The panel consults a wide number of organisations in preparing these views. Further information on its work is available from *www.sentencing-advisory-panel.gov.uk.*

[98] *Projections and Long Term Trends in the Prison Population to 2008* (Home Office Statistical Bulletin 08/01, May 23, 2001).

[99] See the discussion by P. Rock, *Reconstructing a Women's Prison* (1996) and see A. Rutherford, "Women Sentencing and Prisons" (1997) 147 N.L.J. 424.

[1] *Criminal Statistics for England and Wales 2000 (2001),* para.7.8.

[2] *Criminal Statistics for England and Wales 2000 (2001),* para.1.19.

[3] *Criminal Statistics for England and Wales 2000 (2001),* para 1.21.

[4] *Criminal Statistics for England and Wales 2000 (2001),* para.7.15. For detailed material on the proceedings and conviction rates in the Crown Court by offence, offender and sex, see Criminal Statistics for England and Wales 2000, Chap. 6.

[5] A. Ashworth and M. Hough "Sentencing and the Climate of Opinion" [1996] Crim. L.R. 776,

[6] See generally, S. Shute, "The Place of Public Opinion in Sentencing Law" [1998] Crim. L.R. 465, concluding that there are a number of cases in which it has been made clear that judges are "at the very-least" bound to consider the relevance of public opinion, without letting it take an overriding weight. One of the problems identified by Shute is that the public's opinion on sentencing is: ill-informed so see, for example, the degree of misinformation on

general sentencing policy and sentences in particular cases.

(vi) Victims and sentencing

One of the most recent controversial issues of sentencing policy relates to the   **17–083**
increasing significance in the court's consideration of the use of victim
impact statements. The Court of Appeal has emphasised that judges should
not make unsupported assumptions about the effect of an offence on a
victim, but should take account of particularly damaging effects if known
and proved in a proper form and served on the accused. The statement of
the victim himself or herself should be approached with caution but should
be received by the court,[7] but the views of the victim or his or her relatives as
to the appropriate level of sentence should not be taken into account. In
some instances there will be a significant impact on a victim if a sentence of
imprisonment is imposed.[8]
   The victim input to the sentencing process can be defended on grounds of
proportionality and as a move towards restorative justice and can be seen as
a way of making the system more efficient by providing better information.[9]
It could also be defended on the ground that the process will benefit the
victim and act in a therapeutic fashion.[10] There is a value inherent in
participation of all parties in the legal process. The danger is that such a
system raises the expectations of the victim who perceives their input as
more significant than it really is. Some also argue that the victim input is
useful for the purposes of fulfilling the restoration/compensation of victims.
In England and Wales, there is no clear adoption of any of these
rationales.[11] There are also significant practical problems in accepting
victim statements, including: defining who constitutes a victim for these
purposes (*e.g.* does it include the relatives of the deceased victim?);
regulating the content of the statement (is it to be limited to the views of
the victim as to what happened? their views on appropriate sentence?); and

rape sentences reviewed by K. Soothill and C. Grover, "The Public Portrayal of Rape
Sentencing: What the Public Learns of Rape Sentencing from Newspapers" [1998] Crim.
L.R. 455, and M. Hough, "People Talking About Punishment" [1996] 35 Howard Journal of
Criminal Justice 191. The need for accurate portrayal of sentences by the media was
emphasised by the Home Office Research: M. Hough and J. Roberts, *Attitudes to
Punishment: Findings from the British Crime Survey* (HORS No 179, 1997).

[7] *R. v. Perks* [2001] 1 Cr. App. R. (S.) 19, *Archbold (2002)* para. 5–23.
[8] *e.g.* child neglect: *R. v. S* [1996] 2 Cr. App. R. (S.) 256.
[9] See on this extremely controversial topic I. Edwards, "Victim Participation in Sentencing:
The problem of Incoherence" (2001) Howard Jnl. 39, who looks at the justifications for the
inclusion of victim impact statements on sentencing, and examines the approaches in U.S.
and S. Australian jurisdictions where the victim has in some cases the right to read a
statement to the sentencing court.
[10] In Home Office Research conducted in 1998, R. C. Hoyle, E. Cope, R. Morgan and A.
Sanders, *Evaluation of the One Stop Shop and Victim Statement Pilot Projects*, Home Office
1998) assessed the feelings of victims about the process of completing the report.
[11] Morgan and A. Sanders, *The Uses of Victim Statements* (1999) considered the uses to which
victim statements have been put and comments on reports and experiences of criminal justice
personnel: R. C. Hoyle, E. Cope, R. Morgan and A. Sanders, *Evaluation of the One Stop
Shop and Victim Statement Pilot Projects*, Home Office 1998), finding that 60% wanted to
make a statement for expressive reasons, 55% for instrumental reasons and 43% for
procedural reasons. See further the Home Office Special Conferences Unit, *The Role of
Victims in the Criminal Justice Process* (1999).

what form the statements are to take.[12]

Victim statements are currently made in about 30 per cent of cases. Only around one third of victims claim to feel better for having done so, with 18 per cent feeling worse.[13]

The effectiveness of the victim impact statements (VIS) scheme has been scrutinised by a number of researchers. Erez's review of research in Australia and in the USA demonstrates that VIS do not generate the significant practical difficulties in operation; moreover, the claim is that VIS provides therapeutic benefits for the victim and enlightens the sentencer.[14] Other researchers conclude that VIS fail not only the victim but also the courts.[15] Sanders, Hoyle and Cape identify six common purposes of victim participation: (1) giving victims a "voice" for therapeutic purposes; (2) for enabling the interests and views of victims to be taken into account in decision-making; (3) ensuring that victims are treated with respect by criminal justice agencies; (4) reducing the stress for victims of criminal proceedings; (5) increasing victim satisfaction with the criminal justice system; (6) increasing victim co-operation, as a result of any of the above objectives being fulfilled.[16]

Ashworth has also been extremely critical of the use of the victim impact statement. He argues that the victims' procedural rights (increased involvement in the system) and substantive rights (which include being given information and treated fairly) can be achieved without relying on VIS. He suggests that it would be preferable to empower victims by use of substantive rights without the disadvantages attaching to procedural rights.[17] Ashworth[18] observes that

> "once the idea of victims' rights is closely scrutinised, however, the strength of its appeal becomes diluted. It is one thing to argue for the right of victims to compensation, support and sympathetic treatment both from law enforcement agencies and in court. It is quite another thing to argue that they should have the right to be represented in court, to submit a victim impact statement, or to be allowed to voice an opinion on sentence."[19]

---

[12] For calls for victims to be permitted to give oral presentation at sentencing see J. A. Grohovsky, "Giving Voice to Victim — Why the Criminal Justice System in England and Wales Should Allow victims to Speak up for Themselves" (1999) J. Crim L. 416 arguing that this empowers the victim and that judges would be not unduly influenced by an emotional plea. Victim Impact Statements could be limited to personal descriptions or include recommendation for sentence. On present sentencing attitudes to a victim's forgiveness see *Darvill* (1987) 9 Cr. App. R. (S.) 225.

[13–14] A. Sanders, C. Hoyle, R Morgan and E. Cape, "Victim Impact Statements: Don't Work, Can't Work" [2001] Crim. L.R. 447. p. 450

[14] E. Erez, "Who's Afraid of the Big Bad Victim? Victim Impact Statements on Victim Empowerment and Enhancement of Justice" [1999] Crim. L.R. 545. See also C. Pollard, "Victims and the Criminal Justice System: A New Vision" [2000] Crim. L.R. 5, considering victim in context of restorative justice and calling for greater social awareness in criminal justice by involving victims in disposal process. Pollard also questions the process of sentencing and its contrast with "truth finding" processes at trial. (*sic*, p. 11).

[15] Above p.454

[16] Above p.448

[17] See Ashworth, "Victim Impact Statements and Sentencing" [1993] Crim. L.R. 498.

[18] "Crime, Community and Creeping Consequentialism" [1996] Crim. L.R. 220

[19] p.224.

The potential effectiveness of the VIS schemes is also related to the desirability of systems of compensation as an aspect of sentencing. The number of cases in which compensation orders are made is significant.[20] Compensation for victims was ordered in 90,700 cases in magistrates' courts in 1997 (an average amount of compensation for an indictable offence was £196). Forty-five per cent of offenders convicted of an offence of violence against the person were ordered to pay compensation at magistrates' courts, 46 per cent for robbery and 54 per cent for criminal damage. In 1997, 6500 offenders were ordered to pay compensation to victims by the Crown Court. The average amount of compensation for an indictable offence was £998. Nineteen per cent of offenders convicted of violence at CC and 19 per cent convicted of criminal damage at the crown court paid compensation.[21]

VIS and compensation might also be regarded as aspects of a broader theory which, as noted, is currently having a significant impact in sentencing: restorative justice. The philosophy on which this theory is based can most helpfully be summarised in terms of the "three Rs" of responsibility, restoration and reintegration.[22] One of the primary aims of most restorative justice approaches is to engage with offenders to bring home the consequences of their actions and an appreciation of the impact they have had on the victim(s) of their offences. Other aims are to make reparation with the victim (if agreeable) and to seek reconciliation.[23]

The Home Office has recently introduced a "victim personal statement" scheme[24] which is designed to give victims a more formal say in how they have been affected by crime and is intended to assist all criminal justice agencies. This is an optional scheme in which victims participate. The Home Office emphasises that this is *not* a victim impact statement. Police should emphasise to victims that the statement will not be necessarily taken into account in sentencing if the victim expresses an opinion on sentence.

7. THE JURY[25]

(a) Historical background[26]

The decision of the Fourth Lateran Council in 1215 to withdraw the   **17–084**

---

[20] See M. Wasik, "The Compensation Order on Sentence" (1999) 163 J.P.N. 504, calling for clearer separation between punishment and compensation to avoid confusing the objectives.

[21] *Digest IV* (1998), p.18.

[22] See *Auld Report* (2001), pp.387–391.

[23] See J. Dignan (1999), and generally, B. Galaway and J. Hudson, *Restorative Justice: International Perspectives* (1996).

[24] Home Office Circular 35/2001.

[25] Vast amounts of material are available. That to which we shall particularly be referring in this section includes: P. Darbyshire, A. Maughan, and A. Stewart, *What Can the English Legal System Learn From Jury Research Published up to 2001?* (2001), *www.criminal-courts-review.org.uk*; W. R. Cornish, *The Jury* (1971); Lord Devlin, *Trial by Jury* (1956); N. Walker with A. Pearson (eds), *The British Jury System* (1975); J. Baldwin and M. McConville, *Jury Trials* (1979); M. McConville and J. Baldwin, *Courts, Prosecution and Conviction* (1981); M. D. A. Freeman, "The Jury on Trial" (1981) 34 C.L.P. 65; M. Findlay and P. Duff (eds), *The Jury Under Attack* (1988); S. Enright and Morton, *Taking Liberties: The Criminal Jury in the 1990s* (1990); N. Vidmar, *World Jury Systems* (2000); *Auld Report* (2001), Chap. 5.

[26] Sir Frederick Pollock and F. W. Maitland, *History of English Law* (2nd ed., 1898), Vol. II,

support of the Roman Catholic Church from the process of trial by ordeal is generally recognised as the factor which prompted the adoption of the jury system for the determination of criminal cases. That the jury was in existence before 1215 is undisputed, since it would have been almost the only means of collecting information in administrative as well as judicial matters.[27] In addition to determining issues which were relevant to the king, juries came to be used for determining issues of interest to private individuals and were available to replace trial by battle.[28] When trespass was alleged, including the allegation of a breach of the king's peace, a writ of *venire facias* went to the sheriff who summoned a group of twelve[29] men to meet and give a verdict on the allegation. On the demise of trial by ordeal the jury was used to determine the guilt of alleged criminals.[30]

In the beginning, the role of the jury was unclear.[31] Were the twelve individuals to deliberate and deliver a verdict to the judge, or was the judge to treat them as witnesses, examine them and then come to a decision? The resolution of this question shaped the future of the jury and the future of criminal procedure.[32] In the event, the collective deliberative role of the jury prevailed and the transition from knowledge to ignorance as the primary characteristic of a juror began. The landmarks are well known. By 1367 it had become established that the verdict had to be unanimous.[33] Witnesses began to give evidence and the jury were prevented from talking to any outsider until they reached a verdict.[34] In *Bushell's* case it was established that the jury had the right to give a verdict according to its conscience.[35] By the eighteenth century it was finally established that a juror should not take part in a case of which he had personal knowledge. Now a juror should be excused where he or she is personally concerned in the facts of the case or is closely connected with a party or prospective witness.[36]

(b) The role of the jury

17–085 Discussing the role of the jury in the modern trial has become controversial since it is argued by many that it is impossible to conduct any meaningful

---

pp. 618–650; W. S. Holdsworth, *History of English Law* (3rd ed., 1922), Vol. 1, pp. 312–350; J. H. Baker, *An Introduction to English Legal History* (3rd ed., 1990), Chap. 5. For an account of the function of the grand jury see A. Watson, "The Grand Jury in England's Past and America's Present" (1998) 162 J.P.N. 839.

[27] The practice of getting a group together and putting them under oath to tell the truth had been highly effective for the Normans.

[28] Under Henry II two assizes existed: the grand assize and the petty assize. It was the petty assize which evolved into the jury.

[29] Why twelve? The answer is unknown, although it is the same number as the Apostles of Christ and the ancient tribes of Israel. Psychological evidence suggests that this is not the optimal size for the decision-making. See N. Fay, S. Garrod and J. Carletta, "Group Discussions Interactive Dialogue or as Serial Monologue" (2000) 11 Psy. Science 41. See generally, Darbyshire *et al.*, (2001) p.40.

[30] C. Wells, "Instructions Given by Henry III to Itinerant Justices 1219" (1914) 30 L.Q.R. 97.

[31] Pollock and Maitland (1898), pp. 622 *et seq.*

[32] Guiding procedure into the adversarial system and away from the inquisitorial system with its emphasis on judicial involvement.

[33] Baker (1990), p. 90.

[34] *ibid.* p. 89.

[35] *R. v. Sheriffs of London, ex p. Bushell* (1670) Vaughn 135.

[36] *Practice Direction* (1988) 87 Cr.App.R. 294.

examination of the role until we are aware of the way that juries actually function. At present, there is little modern research into the working of the English jury. There is a mass of other material (largely from the USA).[37]

The jury has been described as having three functions.[38] First, it is the jury that is to decide the facts and it is on those facts which it then determines guilt. The jury is to arrive at its verdict by considering whether it is satisfied that the prosecution has proved its case solely on the evidence presented at the trial and in accordance with the direction of the judge as to the law.[39] Secondly, the jury adds certainty to the law, since it gives a general verdict. The jury merely states that the accused is either guilty or not guilty, and gives no reasons. The decision is not open to dispute. Thirdly, the jury represents the "just face" of the criminal justice system, since it can arrive at its unchallengeable decision on any basis it chooses. In particular, it is proper for the jury to arrive at an acquittal according to its conscience,[40] even if a conviction is clearly required according to the relevant law.

Whilst the jury has these functions, it is not all that should be said about its role, particularly since they could be performed by other bodies. Jury service is described as an important public duty.[41] It has been suggested that the jury satisfies the constitutional role that no-one should be tried apart from judgment by one's peers. Whilst this claim is frequently made, however, it does not follow that the phrase "judgment by one's peers" has a consistent meaning. Marshall suggests that it can mean one, or more, of the following:

"1. A claim to the judgment of one's peers, or equals or neighbours

2. A claim to the judgment of a body of fair-minded persons

3. A claim to the judgment by an independent or impartial body of persons

4. A claim to the judgment of a randomly chosen body of persons

5. A claim to the judgment of a representative body of persons."[42]

---

[37] On research generally see P. Robertshaw, "Method and Ethics in Advancing Jury Research" (1998) 38 Med. Sci. Law 328; and Darbyshire *et al.*, (2001).

[38] See P. Duff and M. Findlay, "The Jury in England: Practice and Ideology" (1982) 10 International Journal of the Sociology of Law 253. See also, M. Findlay, "The Role of the Jury in a Fair Trial" in Findlay and Duff (1988), Chap. 10. See Lord Steyn, "The Role of the Bar, The Judge and the Jury: Winds of Change" [1999] P.L. 51; "the jury is an integral and indispensable part of our constitutional arrangements". Lord Steyn refers to the Home Office Proposals in 1998 to remove the accused's right to elect a jury trial as "bad". Lord Steyn would, however, abolish the jury in fraud trials (see pp.58–59) preferring a judge to sit with two assessors. Steyn argues that judges should say less, and unnecessary legal material should be removed from directions. Lord Steyn questions whether the LSB manuals lead to too much law being explained to the jury, and calls for a reconsideration of the *Stonehouse* decision that leaves matters to the jury.

[39] As to the respective roles of judge and jury, see para. 17-062, above and as to the obligation upon the prosecution, see para. 17-049., above.

[40] As established in *Bushell's Case*. See also T. A. Green, *Verdict According to Conscience, 1200–1800* (1985) for a history of the jury in this role.

[41] *Practice Direction* (1988) 87 Cr.App.R. 294.

[42] G. Marshall, "The Judgement of One's Peers: Some Aims and Ideal of Jury Trial" in Walker with Pearson (1975), p. 5.

In fulfilling its functions and its constitutional role, there are a number of qualities which enable a jury to perform effectively. Thus a jury, it is said, should be independent, impartial and representative, and it should be randomly selected. It is not the case that these qualities are always consistent; for example, a representative jury may be partial[43] and random selection does not necessarily produce fairness in the trial.[44]

(c) Qualification for jury service and selection

17–086   To *qualify* for selection as a juror, a person must be aged between 18 and 70,[45] registered as a parliamentary or local government elector, and have been ordinarily resident in the United Kingdom for any period of at least five years since the age of 13.[46]

A person selected will not be permitted to serve as a juror if he or she falls into the categories of people disqualified or ineligible under Schedule 1 of the Juries Act 1974.

The people *disqualified* are those who (1) at any time have been sentenced in the United Kingdom to life imprisonment, custody for life, or a term of five years or more imprisonment or youth custody, or to be detained during Her Majesty's pleasure; or (2) at any time in the last ten years have in the United Kingdom served any part of a sentence of imprisonment, youth custody or detention, or had imposed a suspended sentence of imprisonment or order for detention or a community service order; or (3) at any time in the last five years has been placed on probation in the United Kingdom; or (4) are on bail in criminal proceedings.[47]

The people who are *ineligible* for jury service fall into four categories[48]: (1) the judiciary,[49] (2) others concerned, or in the last ten years concerned with the administration of justice, including barristers (and their clerks), solicitors and trainees, the staff of the Crown Prosecution Service, authorised advocates or litigators, court staff, prison officers and prison custody officers, police officers and forensic scientists, (3) the clergy,[50] and

---

[43] See M. Findlay with P. Byrne, "Introduction" in Findlay and Duff (1988).

[44] See Darbyshire *et al.* (2001); S. Lloyd-Bostock and C. Thomas, "Decline of the Little Parliament: Juries and Jury Reform in England and Wales" (1999) 62 Law and Contemporary Problems 7. This is a particular problem when faced with the issue of the racial mix of a jury; see below.

[45] People who are aged more than 65 are entitled, if they wish, to be excused from jury service: Juries Act 1974, s.9, Sched. 1, Part III, as amended by the Criminal Justice Act 1988, s.119(2). As to excusal from jury service, see p., below.

[46] Juries Act 1974, s.l, as amended by the Criminal Justice Act 1988, s.119(1). See Darbyshire *et al* (2001), pp.143–145.

[47] Juries Act 1974, Sched. 1, Part II, as amended by the Juries (Disqualification) Act 1984, further amended by the Criminal Justice and Courts Services Act 2000, s.74, Sched. 7, Pt II, para. 47(1)(3). This amending legislation significantly increased the number of people who were consequently disqualified from jury service. Category (4) was added by the Criminal Justice and Public Order Act 1994. Whether suspects should be disqualified is a matter of debate, particularly as people on bail are innocent until proved guilty.

[48] Juries Act 1974, Sched. 1, Part I, as amended, as further amended by the Criminal Justice and Courts Services Act 2000, ss. 74, 75. See *Archbold (2002)*, para. 4–122 for an exhaustive list.

[49] The "judiciary" includes not only the holders of high judicial office, but also, amongst others, Circuit judges, Recorders, Masters of the Supreme Court and J.P.s.

[50] Including vowed members of a religious order living in a religious community.

(4) mentally disordered persons.[51] Having a qualifying law degree does not render its holder ineligible. The Auld Report recommended that the categories of ineligibility be abolished.[52]

The objectives of disqualification and ineligibility are first to exclude from participation people who are or have been intimately concerned with the administration of justice, presumably on the basis either that a jury with lawyers on it will not decide according to the judge's direction but might use its own superior knowledge of the law, or that current or previous involvement in the criminal justice system will deprive the jury of its impartiality. The second objective is to exclude from participation those who are demonstrably incompetent. There is at least an implicit assumption that a basic level of intellectual ability is necessary for a person to be able to be involved in the performance by the jury of its various functions.[53]

The qualifications for jury service were revised in 1972,[54] when the requirement that a juror should be an occupier of a house with a prescribed rateable value was abolished, and the electoral register adopted as the basis of qualification. There had been growing criticism of the composition of the jury, and its unrepresentative nature.[55] Since the adoption of the new qualification, research has demonstrated[56] that the composition of juries has changed profoundly. Selection of jurors from the electoral register used to be a matter for individual summoning officers. Since February 1981, random selection by computer has been utilised.[57] A number is allotted to every person on the electoral register, and a random number programme is then run through the computer to produce the jury list. Selection is made from the register of electors, and that creates the potential for under-representation of certain groups.[58] The Auld Report has recommended that

---

[51] The Juries Act 1974, as amended by the Mental Health (Amendment) Act 1982 and the Mental Health Act 1983.

[52] pp.144–149. See also Darbyshire et al. (2001),

[53] As to the discharge of people who cannot understand a case. Such reasoning does not explain the exclusion of the clergy, but may explain the exclusion of monks and nuns who choose to live in a religious community removed from everyday life. Arguably such people are ineligible because of the moral influence they might have on other jurors and/or because their religious beliefs would inhibit their reasoning. See further the Report of the Departmental Committee on Jury Service, Chair: Lord Morris Cmnd. 2627 (1965); White (1985), p. 78.

[54] By the Criminal Justice Act 1972, which implemented some of the recommendations of the Morris Committee (1965).

[55] In Lord Devlin's oft-quoted phrase, the property qualification produced a jury which was, " ... predominantly male, middle-aged, middle-minded and middle-class": Trial by Jury, p. 20. It is reported that when Bernard Rothman and others were tried at Derby Assizes in 1932 on charges relating to a mass trespass on private land near Kinder Scout in the Peak District, the jury consisted of two brigadier-generals, three colonels, two majors, three captains and two aldermen: The Guardian, January 18, 1982.

[56] Jury Trials, pp. 94–99.

[57] Seem. Zander, A Matter of Justice (1988), p. 217; see also, R. Tarling, "The Random Selection of Jurors", Home Office Research Bulletin No. 13 (1982) and Lord Chancellor's Department, The Crown Court: A Guide to Good Practice for the Courts (1990), paras 9.1–9.2.

[58] See R. May, "Jury Selection in the USA: Are there lessons to be learned?" [1998] Crim. L.R. 270. On the jury summons and the way in which a more diverse pool can be gathered than by the use of an electoral register, see D. Schreckhise and C.H.Sheldon, "The Search for Greater Jury Diversity: The Case of the US DC System for the Eastern District of Washington" (1998) 20 The Justice System Journal 95. The sample, when gathered from a range of sources, was found to be more diverse, younger, less well-educated, more likely to

the databases from which a jury is selected should be extended to include *e.g.* driving licence information. This will improve the randomness of the selection of the jury by increasing the pool of potential jurors.

The precise representations of socio-economic groups and ethnic groups on juries is unclear. There is evidence that juries are less middle class[59] and much younger than before,[60] but there is still an under-representation of women and members of ethnic minorities.[61] The most significant challenges to the composition of the jury remains that relating to race: two-thirds of all juries are white.[62] The failure to ensure a representative jury[63] has been explained by Bohlander as being that "there exists the distinct possibility that the different lifestyle, mentality and experience arising from member-ship of an ethnic minority will not be taken sufficiently into account in trials where members of such a minority are the defendants".[64]

The Auld Report makes a very controversial recommendation to allow a judge to empanel up to three jurors from an ethnic minority in a case in which race is likely to be an important issue. This model is based on American research.[65] It has been criticized because it rests on the assumption that a randomly selected jury will not be capable of hearing a case without racial bias. Moreover, the selected jurors might well regard themselves as second-class jurors,[66] and there is no evidence that this will produce greater public confidence in the system.[67] Further research is called for to establish the necessity for and appropriateness of such a scheme.

However, the discretion does not extend to securing the establishment of a representative jury. The Court of Appeal in *R. v. Ford*[68] decided that a

---

include racial minorities and to bear a greater resemblance to the population. The problem of jurors being reluctant to serve seems to be universal; see *e.g.* in the USA. R. Seltzer, "The Vanishing Juror: Why There Are Not Enough Available Jurors" (1999) 20 Justice System Journal 203. See Darbyshire *et al.*, p.4

[59] *Jury Trials* Table 10, p. 95. See Sanders and Young (2000), p559.

[60] *ibid.* Table 11, p. 96. 27% of jurors empanelled in Birmingham in 1975 and 1976 were under 30.

[61] The Crown Court Survey discovered that more men than in the general population serve on juries (53% on juries and 48% in the general population); that most juries had a wide spread of ages; that most jurors were working full-time (69%); that there was a slight over-representation of clerical workers and under-representation of skilled manual workers; and that there were more people who left school later than in the general population: Zander and Henderson (1993), pp. 234–241. Ethnic mix is considered in the text following. See for a critical survey Darbyshire *et al.* (2001), pp.3–10.

[62] Zander and Henderson (1993), p. 241.

[63] For further consideration in the context of the abolition of the defence right of peremptory challenge, see below, para. 17-089.

[64] M. Bohlander, " 'By a jury of his peers'–The Issue of Multi-racial Juries in a Polyethnic Society" (1992) XIV(1) Liverpool L.R. 67. Sanders and Young (2000), p.567.

[65] pp. 156–159. See Darbyshire *et al* (2001), pp.16–18. The results extrapolated from research by L. Bridges, S. Choongh and M. McConville, *Ethnic Minority Defendants and the Right to Elect Jury Trial* (2000) could suggest that there are lower conviction rates in some instance where a greater proportion of the jury shares D's ethnicity.

[66] See J. Abramson, *We, The Jury*, (1994), Chap. 3.

[67] See generally N. King, "The Effects of Race Conscious Jury Selection on Public Confidence in the Fairness of Jury Proceedings: An Empirical Puzzle" (1994) 31 American Crim. L.R. 1177.

[68] [1989] 3 All E.R. 445. The court's reasons for rejecting the power were that it would interfere with random selection, that the power would have to be granted by statute and that it interferes with the responsibility of the Lord Chancellor's Department to summon jurors, *ibid.* pp. 448–449.

trial judge has no power to interfere with the composition of the jury or the jury panel in order to produce a multi-racial jury and that there is no principle that a jury should be racially balanced. Recent attempts to construct a jury (for reasons other than race) by selecting on the basis of their postcodes has been rejected.[69] The argument in favour of racially balancing the jury is to avoid partiality as, for example, in the trial of Rose, a black man accused of murder, where the judge had asked potential jurors to disqualify themselves if they had strong views against black people or supported the extreme Right or the extreme Left.[70] This would not, however, now be appropriate in the light of the appeal in R. v. Ford. The Royal Commission on Criminal Justice proposed very limited proposal for engineering a racially mixed jury, but only in cases with "unusual and special features".[71] Sanders and Young have pointed out that "cases with such features are likely to be rare".[72] Further consideration should be given to a proposal by the Commission for Racial Equality for "a special procedure to be available where the case is believed to have a racial dimension which results in a defendant from an ethnic minority community believing that he or she is unlikely to receive a fair trial from an all-white jury".[73] Such procedures might be especially important in cases charged as racially aggravated under the Crime and Disorder Act 1998. Simply relying upon random selection, and failing to address real concerns about jury composition is not likely to satisfy the deep concerns held about the criminal justice system by many people from an ethnic minority. In R. v. Rankine[74] the Court of Appeal did not comment adversely on the judge reading out to the jury a statement that the accused felt that an all white jury could not try his case fairly.

The damage done to the criminal justice system by the perception of racist juries is demonstrated by cases such as Sanders v. U.K.[75] where the ECtHR found a breach of Article 6 when the trial judge had failed to discharge a jury having discovered that they had made racist jokes.

It is not possible to challenge the summoning officer on the basis that the jury panel is not representative, because no black person is on the panel, although if bias or other impropriety could be shown then a challenge could be founded.[76] The Auld recommendation to create racial quotas on juries would remove this problem.

---

[69] See *Tarrant* [1998] Crim. L.R. 342.

[70] This, and other examples, are to be found in M. Zander, *A Matter of Justice* (1988), pp. 222–226. See also *R. v. Broderick* [1970] Crim. L.R. 155, where the Court of Appeal had said that the trial judge could go no further than ascertaining whether there was a non-white juror on the panel. This possibility is now questionable in the light of the decision in *R. v. Ford*; see also *R. v. Danvers* [1982] Crim.L.R. where the judge, Mr Recorder Cowley Q.C. at Nottingham Crown Court, rejected a challenge to the array (*i.e.* the whole panel) on the ground that it was unrepresentative, holding that it was no requirement in law that there should be a non-white member of a jury or a jury panel; approved in *R. v. Ford*. See Baldwin and McConville (1979), pp. 97–98; A. Dashwood, "Juries in a Multi-racial Society" [1972] Crim.L.R. 85; the commentary to *R. v. Danvers* by G. W. Hoon at [1982] Crim.L.R. 681; and Buxton, [1990] Crim.L.R. 225 at 234–235.

[71] RCCJ, Report (1993), pp. 133–134, as quoted in Sanders and Young (1994), p. 359.

[72] *ibid.*

[73] RCCJ, Report (1993), p. 133.

[74] [1997] Crim. L.R. 757.

[75] *Sanders v. UK* [2000] Crim. L.R. 767.

[76] *R. v. Ford* [1989] 3 All E.R. 445 at 450. As to challenge, see below para. 17-089.

(d) Summons, empanelling and vetting

17–087   The people selected for jury service receive a summons requiring them to attend at the Crown Court at a specified time.[77] Accompanying the summons are a form, which is intended to identify those ineligible or disqualified, and a set of notes,[78] which explains something of the procedure of jury service and the functions of the juror.[79] A failure to attend the Crown Court can result in a fine, as can unfitness for service through drink or drugs after attendance.[80] Again, the implicit assumption is that a person must be competent in order to act as a juror. This principle, in the circumstances, permits derogation from the requirement that the jury be randomly selected. Darbyshire *et al.,* found that up to one in six people did not attend, and that there was no sanction ever imposed on such individuals.[81] The Auld Report recommends that a failure to serve should attract a fixed penalty notice fine.[82]

Those summoned for service constitute the jury panel for that court and from that panel the jury for an individual case will be selected.[83] The panel may be divided into parts relating to different days or sittings.[84] The jury list contains the names, addresses and dates for attendance of the panel. The parties to the case and their lawyers are entitled to inspect the list before or during the trial.[85] Such information may assist counsel in deciding whether to challenge any of the jurors but, since the occupation of jurors is no longer provided, there is very little on which defence counsel may rely for a challenge for cause without further investigation into the individual's life.[86]

---

[77]   The power to summon is granted to the Lord Chancellor by the Juries Act 1974, s.2, who delegates it to such officers. See the Contracting Out (Jury Summoning Functions) Order 1999 (S.I. 1999 No. 2128) made under the Deregulation and Contracting Out Act 1994, ss.69 and 77(1)(b). See *Archbold (2002),* para. 4–209. In so summoning jurors, the officer is required to have regard to the convenience of the persons summoned and where they live, in particular to the desirability of selecting jurors within reasonable daily travelling distance of the place where they are to attend: *ibid.* s.2(2). See Lord Chancellor's Department (1990), paras 9.3–9.5.

[78]   The information that is presented to prospective jurors can be found at *www.courtservice.gov.uk/fandl/ujury.htm.* In addition, see the Court's Charter pamphlet on jurors, *www.courtservice.gov.uk/kiosk.*

[79]   The notes assist the juror in the task by dealing with the swearing-in and challenges, trial procedure, the verdict, secrecy, taking notes, etc.

[80]   Juries Act 1974, s.20, as amended by the Criminal Justice and Public Order Act 1994, Sched. 10, para. 28. The person summonsed must attend and not someone standing in for them. In response to claims of juror impersonation (see S. Enright, "Britain's Reluctant Jurors" (1989) 138 N.L.J. 538), the Lord Chancellor's Department has emphasised that it is a criminal offence for any person to impersonate a juror, and as a matter of routine court staff will check on identity: (1989) 138 N.L.J. 758. A failure to comply with security procedures to enter the court in a faliure to be available for service: *R. v. Dodds* [2002] Crim. L.R. (Aug).

[81]   On the Imposition of fines see the procedure to be adopted as outlines in *R. v. Dodds* [2002] Crim. L.R. (Aug).

[82]   p.6.

[83]   See para. 17-089 below. The Lord Chancellor's Department has set targets and introduced management controls to monitor and review the number of jurors who are summoned to attend court each day against the number who actually sit on trials: Lord Chancellor's Department (1990), para. 9.6.

[84]   Juries Act 1974, s.5.

[85]   *ibid.* s.5(2), (3).

[86]   See below, para. 17-089. In 1973 the occupation of jurors was removed from the list by the Lord Chancellor in the exercise of powers under the Courts Act 1971, s.32, now the Juries

The controversial subject of *jury vetting* surfaced in 1978 as a result of the trial of a soldier and two journalists (Aubrey, Berry and Campbell) on charges under the Official Secrets Act 1911. It became apparent during the trial that the jury panel had been investigated[87] by the prosecuting authority, and, in the ensuing public debate, the Attorney-General published the guidelines under which the vetting had been carried out.[88]

The guidelines make clear that vetting may involve the search of criminal records for the purpose of ascertaining whether or not a member of the panel is a disqualified person,[89] or the limited further investigation of members of the panel (a) in security or terrorist cases[90] with the object of revealing political beliefs which are so biased that they might interfere with the juror's fair assessment of the facts or lead a juror to exert improper pressure on fellow jurors, or (b) in security cases alone with the object of discovering whether a juror might be in danger of making improper use of evidence given *in camera*.[91] A further investigation is made, on the personal authority of the Attorney-General, using the records of Police Special Branches and, with regard to the cases in (b), the security services, and is known as an "authorised check". No checks other than with these sources and no general inquiries may be made except to the limited extent that they may be needed to confirm the identity of a juror. The information gleaned from an authorised check is sent to the Director of Public Prosecutions, who decides what information ought to be provided to prosecuting counsel. Consequently, a juror may be asked to stand by for the Crown[92] provided it is appropriate to exercise that power in the circumstances,[93] but the prosecution is under a duty to ask a juror to stand by where he or she might be biased against the defendant.[94]

The legality of the original guidelines was contested in *R. v. Sheffield Crown Court, ex p. Brownlow*, where a majority of the Court of Appeal

---

Act 1974, s.5(l), to determine the information included on the list; see H. Harman and J. Griffith, *Justice Deserted: The Subversion of the Jury* (1979).

[87] In the first trial, defence counsel made an application to have the jury discharged. One of the accused said so on television with the result that the first trial was stopped and the jury discharged. This gave the opportunity for the matter to be raised directly at the beginning of the second trial. The Attorney-General's Guidelines were first published during the course of the second trial on October 11, 1978.

[88] The current full text is to be found at (1989) 88 Cr. App. R. 124 and in *Archbold (2002)*, para. 4–214. For the original text before the 1986 amendment, see (1981) 72 Cr. App. R. 14.

[89] The Annex to the Guidelines contains the Recommendations of the Association of Chief Police Officers with regard to the carrying out of checks on the previous convictions of the jury panel to ensure that disqualified persons do not sit on a jury. For the full text, see (1989) 88 Cr.App.R. 125.

[90] These are cases described as being exceptional types of cases of public importance for which the provisions as to majority verdicts and the disqualification of jurors may not be sufficient to ensure the proper administration of justice. Jury vetting is thus a further safeguard in (a) security cases, defined as cases in which national security is involved and part of the evidence is likely to be heard in *camera*, and (b) terrorist cases, of which no definition is provided: *Attorney-General's Guidelines* (1989) 88 Cr.App.R. 124.

[91] *ibid.*

[92] See below, para. 17-089.

[93] As to the guidance on the exercise of the power of stand by as a consequence of jury vetting, see the *Attorney-General's Guidelines*, paras 9, 10, 11 and 12.

[94] The prosecution is only obliged to give a (general) indication of why a juror may be inimical to their interests: *Attorney-General's Guidelines*, para. 11.

(Civil Division) said *obiter* that they were unconstitutional.[95] The point was not strictly in issue since the court decided, in any event, that it had no jurisdiction to review an order made by a Crown Court judge, but the condemnation of the practice was clear. However, in the Criminal Division of the Court of Appeal the point was argued in *R. v. Mason*[96] and the court had no hesitation in upholding the legality of vetting, although the judgment is specifically restricted to the use of vetting for the purpose of ascertaining convictions. The Court confirmed the propriety of vetting the panel for convictions, passing the information to the prosecution, using it to exercise the right to stand by and passing the information to defence counsel if it would be fair so to do. Whether jury vetting in security and terrorist cases is acceptable remains to be argued.

The practice of jury vetting is alleged to undermine the jury as a random selection of fellow citizens assembled for the purpose of determining guilt[97] and so represent a dangerous move to grant excessive power to the State in favour of the crime control model.[98]

On the other hand, exclusion of people within the Attorney-General's Guidelines may prevent partiality on the part of the jury, and prevent the verdict of the jury being unduly swayed by the prejudices of one particular member, consequently maintaining public confidence in the general verdict.[99]

It is not known how widespread jury vetting is. As Sanders and Young point out, "the secrecy surrounding the practice is itself a denial of due process values".[1]

(e) Excusal and discretionary deferral

17–088   Any member of a jury panel may be excused service on the basis of previous service,[2] or on showing entitlement to be excused,[3] or, at the discretion of the appropriate officer, for good reason.[4]

The first two provisions are straightforward, but the discretion to excuse from service is not one which is widely known. The notes which accompany

---

[95] [1980] Q.B. 530, Lord Denning M.R, Shaw L.J. and Brandon L.J. expressed serious doubts about the practice.

[96] [1981] Q.B. 881.

[97] See Harman and Griffith (1979); A. Nicol, "Official Secrets and Jury Vetting" [1979] Crim. L.R. 284; Zander, *Cases and Materials* (1993), pp. 432–438; Freeman (1981).

[98] Sanders and Young (2000), p. 562.

[99] See, further, A. Freiberg, "Jury Selection in Trials of Commonwealth Offences" in Findlay and Duff (1988), Chap. 7 and Zander, *A Matter of Justice* (revised ed., 1989), pp. 227–228.

[1] Sanders and Young (2000), p.562.

[2] Juries Act 1974, s.8. People summoned who have served or attended to serve on a jury in the preceeding two years or been excused jury service for a period which has not finished are entitled to be excused.

[3] *ibid.* s.9(1) and Sched. 1, Part III, as amended by the Criminal Justice Act 1988, s.119(2). Those entitled to be excused include people aged more than 65, members and officers of either House of Parliament, M.E.P.s, members of the armed forces and members of the medical and other similar professions; practising members of religious orders/societies whose beliefs are incompatible with the task.

[4] *ibid.* s. 9(2). If the appropriate officer refuses to excuse a person from jury service an appeal to the court may be made: *ibid.* s.9(3). Any person who so appeals must be given an opportunity to make representations in support of the appeal: *Practice Direction* (1988) 87. Cr.App.R. 294. See *R. v. Guildford Crown Court, ex p. Siderfin* [1990] 2 Q.B. 683 and *Archbold (2002)*, para. 4–228.

the jury summons make no mention of excusal. The discretion is exercised in accordance with a *Practice Direction*[5] which makes clear that the normal presumption where a person is not entitled to be excused as of right is in favour of requiring a person to serve when summoned, because

"jury service is an important public duty which individual members of the public are chosen at random to undertake .... There will however be circumstances where a juror should be excused, for instance where he or she is personally concerned in the facts of the particular case or is closely connected with a party or prospective witness. He or she may also be excused on grounds of personal hardship or conscientious objection to jury service. Each application should be dealt with sensitively and sympathetically."[6]

A person's attendance may be deferred once if it is shown to the appropriate officer that there is good reason for it.[7]

The Home Office research in 1999 found that 38 per cent of those summoned were excused.[8]

Recent concern has also been expressed at the ease with which some people are excused jury service with little or no scrutiny of the reasons provided. The danger is that juries will come to be constituted almost exclusively of the elderly and unemployed. There are numerous reasons for the seeking excusal with medical reasons, childcare commitments, employment, holidays, etc, all playing a part.[9]

The Crown Court Study for the Runciman Commission showed the following[10]

---

[5] (1988) Cr. App. R. 294.

[6] Concern has been expressed that the frequency of the grant of excusal adversely affects the representativeness of the jury, see *The Times*, October 25, 1988. See J. Airs and A. Shaw, *Jury Excusal and Deferral* (HORS No. 102, 1999) finding that 13% of jurors were ineligible/disqualified or excused as of right; 15% failed to attend or the summons was returned undelivered; 38% were excused (of which 40% were medical, 20% because of child care); 34% were available for jury service and almost half of that group deferred (39% because of a holiday). For calls for a reduced scope to the category of ineligibility see T. Aldridge "Verdict of a Third of You" (1999) S.J. 1133.

[7] See Derbyshire *et al.* (2001), pp.3–10, and A. Shaw and J. Airs, *Jury Excusal and Deferral* (H.O. RDS No 102, 1999); H. Fukurai, "The Representative Cross-Section Requirement: Jury Representativeness and Cross-Sectional participation from the Beginning to the End of the Jury Selection Process" (1999) 23 Int. J. Comp. and Applied Crim. J. 56.

[8] *ibid.* Table 8.41, p.238.

[9] See pp. 149–152. On jurors' negative attitudes to service see Darbyshire *et al.*, p.44. The Crown Court Study carried out for the Runciman Royal Commission included jury questionnaires. Jurors were asked "How interesting have you found being on jury service?" The majority said they found it either "Very interesting" (74%), or "Fairly interesting" (22%). Only 4% were negative about the experience. Jurors were asked to rate the jury system overall. One third (33%) thought it was a "Very good system" and 47% thought it was a "Good system". 15% had no particular view. Only 3% thought it a "Poor system" and 2% a "Very poor system".

[10] R. Buxton, "Challenging and Discharging Jurors–1" [1990] Crim.L.R. 225. The judicial power to discharge jurors is considered further at para. 17-090 below. See also *Re Osman* [1999] 1 Cr.App. R. 126 in which a profoundly deaf juror was discharged.

Jurors' Occupations	Sample	General Population
Professional/managerial	29	31
Clerical/administrative Office work	22	17
Service industry	14	20
Skilled manual	19	23
Unskilled manual	7	7
Other	7	2

The Auld recommendations include a requirement that a person would have to demonstrate that there was a good cause for excusal irrespective of his or her profession.[11]

Trial judges have a discretion to discharge a juror to prevent scandal and perversion of justice, and this may permit the exclusion of someone who is, for example, completely deaf.[12] Inevitably a number of people are excluded who might make very good jurors, and exclusions mean that the jury is definitely not representative of the whole of society. In 1999, J. McWhinney, the Chief executive of the British Deaf Association (who is profoundly deaf) had a jury summons discharged because of the difficulty of having an interpreter in the jury room rather than because of any potential inability to follow proceedings.[12a] A blind juror served on a jury in 1999.[12b]

(f) Ballot, challenges and swearing in[13]

17–089 From the jury panel, the jury for a particular case is selected by ballot in open court.[14] The clerk of the court has the names of all members of the panel. The names are put on cards, the cards are shuffled and the clerk reads out the names from the pile of cards. Hence, a random selection should be achieved from a randomly-selected panel. It is legitimate to call by numbers in the event that there is a fear of jury intimidation.[15]

On entering the jury box to be sworn, each juror may be challenged by the prosecution or the defence.[16] The defence has only the right to challenge for cause. The prosecution has the right to challenge for cause or to require a juror to stand by.

Challenge for cause has been fairly unusual,[17] but the abolition of

---

[11] Juries Act 1974, s.9A, inserted by the Criminal Justice Act 1988, s. 120.

[12] Airs and Shaw (1999); Darbyshire *et al.* (2001),

[12a] See D. Silas, "Have You Heard?" (1999) Legal Action, 6. See also *Re Osman* [1996] 1 Cr. App. R. 128.

[12b] See "Diary of a Blind Juror: Vision in Court", *The Guardian*, September 29, 1999. See also S. Enright, "The Deaf Juror and the 13th Man" (1999) N.L.J. 1720, arguing that there are principled objections to the interpreter sitting with the jury and the practical objection that the deaf juror can less effectively assess the witness's demeanour. Research has shown that witness demeanour may be misleading as an indicator of credibility. See above para. 17-060.

[13] *Archbold (2002)*, paras 4–233 *et seq.*

[14] Juries Act 1974, s.11.

[15] See *R. v. Comerford* [1998] 1 Cr. App. R. 235.

[16] See the procedure outlined in *Archbold (2002)*, para. 4–235. The prosecution's power is from the Juries Act 1825, s.29) and that of the defence from the Juries Act 1974, s.12(1). See R. Buxton, "Challenging and Discharging Jurors–1" [1990] Crim. L.R. 225.

[17] In a survey of 3,165 cases the defence challenged for cause in 39 cases, *i.e.* 1% and the prosecution challenged for cause in 25 cases, *i.e.* 1%: J. Vennard and D. Riley, "The Use of Peremptory Challenge and Stand by of Jurors and their Relationship to Trial Outcome" [1988] Crim.L.R. 731.

peremptory challenge and the imposition of restrictions on the prosecution's right to stand by[18] "have given new practical importance to what had been thought to be [this] largely obsolescent institution".[19] It is possible to challenge the panel,[20] but the most likely use of challenge is to individual jurors. Challenge can be on statutory grounds, that is on the basis of ineligibility or disqualification, or common law grounds.[21] There are four possible forms of common law challenge all still properly known by their Latin titles:

 (i) *propter honoris respectum*, that is privilege of peerage;

 (ii) *propter delictum*, that is past criminal conviction;

 (iii) *propter defectum*, that is lack of requisite qualification;

 (iv) *propter affectum*, that is presumed or actual bias in the juror.

Of these grounds of challenge, the first three are relatively straightforward, since they refer back to ineligibility and disqualification.[22] Bias requires further consideration. In this context it means "whether the individual juror will be able to, and will, be loyal to his oath to give a true verdict according to the evidence".[23] Buxton classifies bias into three headings:

(a) Connection with the case[24] or with the parties,[25] and if there is a connection, bias is in effect assumed;

(b) Knowledge of the accused's character[26] and if there is knowledge, bias is also in effect assumed;

(c) General hostility,[27] in this case, bias is not assumed but must be established.

It follows from the meaning of bias that the fact that a juror is of a particular race or holds a particular religious belief cannot be the basis of a challenge for cause on the grounds of bias (or any other ground).[28]

---

[18] See below.

[19] Buxton (1990), p. 225.

[20] *ibid.* pp. 225–226.

[21] As to ineligibility for and disqualification from jury service, see para. 17-086 above. On statutory challenge, see Buxton (1990) *op. cit.*, p. 227 and on common law challenge, see *ibid.* pp. 227–234 and *Archbold (2002)*, paras 4-243–4-246.

[22] See Buxton (1990), pp. 228–229. Buxton, at p. 228, points out that, whilst not all criminal convictions can ground a challenge for cause as such, nevertheless a criminal conviction might ground a challenge on some other basis such as bias, as indicated by the Court of Appeal in *R. v. Mason* [1981] Q.B. 881.

[23] Buxton (1990), pp. 229–230.

[24] *e.g.*, that the juror is personally connected with the facts of the particular case, see *ibid.* p. 230.

[25] *e.g.* that the juror is related to one of the parties, see *ibid.*

[26] Personal knowledge is intended here, not that gained through the media, which may, though, in exceptional circumstances be sufficient, see *ibid.*, pp. 231–232.

[27] *e.g.*, the holding of political opinions. The court in *R. v. Swain* (1838) 2 M. & Rob. 112 emphasised the need to establish more than mere general hostility. In that case two jurors' active opposition to the Poor Law Act 1834 founded such a challenge, see Buxton (1990), p. 232.

[28] *R. v. Ford* [1989] 3 All E.R. 445 at 449 and see above, para. 17-086.

Jurors cannot be questioned before being challenged to ascertain whether
there is ground for bias, consequently basing a challenge on heads (iii) and
(iv) may be particularly difficult, especially since the defence only has
information as to the juror's name and address and not as to occupation.[29]
If a challenge is made, it is tried by the trial judge.[30] The burden of proof lies
on the party challenging. Witnesses may be called to support or defeat the
challenge, but a prima facie case must be made before the challenged juror
may be cross-examined, upon which fairly stringent limits are placed.[31] It is
worth noting at this point that in any issue of bias arising in a criminal trial
in England and Wales, the question of bias is assessed according to the test
recently described in *In re Medicaments and Related Classes of Goods (No
2)*.[32] The House of Lords has subsequently approved this ECHR-
compatible test of bias:[33] would a fair minded and informed observer
conclude that there was a real possibility, or real danger, the two being the
same, that there was bias.

In 1988 the defence right of peremptory challenge was abolished. This
right had meant that the defence could exclude, without reason, up to
three[34] members of the jury. Abolition of the right was proposed by the
Roskill Committee[35] in fraud trials. The call for complete abolition appears
to have followed on from the acquittal of the accused in the "Cyprus
Secrets" trial.[36] The main objection to this form of challenge was that it
interfered with the random selection of a jury and that the effect of this
unacceptable possibility would be heightened where in a trial involving more
than one accused they combine their challenges and consequently radically
alter the composition of the jury. The other objections were that the use of a
challenge would lead either to juries being more likely to acquit or to juries
being more likely to convict, and that the form of challenge brought the
criminal justice system into disrepute.

However, the evidence suggested that the peremptory challenge was not

---

[29] The restriction on questioning is imposed by *R. v. Dowling* (1845) 7 St. Tr. (N.S.) 381; *R. v.
Stewart* (1845)1 Cox C. C. 174; Buxton (1990), p. 226. See recently *R. v. Andrews* [1999]
Crim. L.R. 156 on the questioning of potential jurors to ascertain whether they had an
interest in the case (*e.g.* knowledge of adverse publicity); *Archbold (2002)*, para. 4–248.
Compare the very different position in the United States where potential jurors may be
questioned to ascertain whether they might be prejudiced. In one case it took four months to
question 1,035 people before a jury could be sworn. See Harman and Griffith (1979), pp. 26–
27 and M. George, "Jury Selection, Texas Style" (1988) 138 N.L.J. 438. Buxton (1990), p.
227, n. 15 points out that the recommendation of the Roskill Committee on Fraud Trials to
re-instate the provision of a juror's occupation has not been implemented.

[30] Juries Act 1974, s.12(l). The judge may order that the hearing of a challenge for cause be *in
camera* or in chambers: Criminal Justice Act 1988, s.118(2).

[31] See *Archbold (2002)*, para. 4–247.

[32] [2000] 1 W.L.R. 700 rather than the familiar *Gough* test ([1993] A.C. 646).

[33] *Porter v. Magill, The Times*, December 14, 2001.

[34] Until the Criminal Law Act 1977, s.43 (repealed by the Criminal Justice Act 1988, s.170) it
had been possible to challenge seven jurors.

[35] *Report of the Departmental Inquiry on Fraud Trials* (HMSO, 1986), para. 7.38.

[36] The accused pooled their peremptory challenges. Consequently they were able to alter the
composition of the jury. For a survey of the recent history to the abolition of the peremptory
challenge, see Zander (1989), pp. 217–222.

excessively used[37] and that the peremptory challenge did not have a significant effect on the rate of acquittals. Indeed conviction rates increased where challenges had been exercised! Further, it has been suggested that the composition of the jury has little effect upon verdict.[38]

This evidence only rebutted the practical use and effect of the challenge and did not address the question of principle: should such interference with random selection adversely affecting the impartiality of the jury be permitted.

The case for retaining the challenge included the argument that the peremptory challenge assisted in the obtaining of a non-biased jury by excluding people having the characteristics believed by experienced defence lawyers to predispose them to fail to decide a case in accordance with the evidence.[39] On the other hand, peremptory challenge was one of the few, admittedly limited, ways in which the accused could attempt to achieve a representative jury in terms of race[40] and sex and thus a jury which would be more likely be impartial.[41] It will be noted that both sides were able to argue that their proposal more satisfactorily provided for the impartiality of the jury.[42]

The prosecution still retains the right to stand by for the Crown, which is similar to the peremptory challenge.[43] The prosecution has the right (without providing a reason) to require someone not to sit on the jury (stand by) unless there are not enough members of the panel left from which to produce a jury.[44] Any challenges thereafter have to be for cause. Whilst this right of standing by still exists, its use has been limited through the issuing of guidelines by the Attorney-General which specifically state that the abolition of the peremptory challenge means that "the Crown should assert its right to stand by only on the basis of clearly defined and restrictive criteria".[45] These

---

[37] In a survey of 3,165 cases undertaken by Vennard and Riley the peremptory challenge was used in 704 cases, *i.e.* 22%. More detailed figures show its use in relation to the number of accused people, which suggests that "there was no evidence of the widespread pooling of challenges which is often thought to alter the balance of the jury in multidefendant cases". Vennard and Riley (1988), pp. 735, 736, 738.

[38] See Vennard and Riley (1988), p. 738, referring to the review of research by Hastie and Penrod: R. Hastie and S. Penrod, *Inside the Juror* (1983). The same conclusion is arrived at by Baldwin and McConville (1979), pp. 104–105; by Zander (1989), p. 226 and by J. J. Gobert, "The Peremptory Challenge–An Obituary" [1989] Crim.L.R. 528.

[39] Whether the views of the lawyers as to who will be biased and who will not are accurate is doubtful, but a challenge means that lawyers may give full vent to their sad experiences of jurors not deciding cases according to the evidence, see Gobert (1989).

[40] Since there is no power in the judge to achieve such a jury by exercise of the power of discharge, according to the Court of Appeal in *R. v. Ford* [1989] 3 All E.R. 445, the racial composition of a jury is a matter purely of chance; and see above, para. 17-086.

[41] See N. Blake, "The Case for the Jury" in Findlay and Duff (1988), Chap. 9; Zander (1989), pp. 217–222 and Gobert (1989).

[42] As to the arguments for and against the peremptory challenge, see Blake in Findlay and Duff (1988) and Zander (1989), pp. 217–222.

[43] *Archbold (2002)*, para. 4–250 and see the Attorney-General's Guidelines set out in *Archbold (2002)*, para. 4–251. The prosecution had a right of peremptory challenge until 1305. The constitutionality of the right to stand by was confirmed in *R. v. McCann* (1991) 92 Cr.App.R. 239.

[44] Technically, the Crown is exercising a challenge for cause but the trial of the cause is postponed until the panel is exhausted: *R. v. Parry* (1837) 7 C. & P. 836; *R. v. Casement* [1917] 1 K.B. 98. See also, J. F. McEldowney, "Stand By for the Crown: an Historical Analysis" [1979] Crim.L.R. 272.

[45] (1989) 88 Cr.App.R. 123, para. 3.

criteria do not include the right to influence the overall composition of the jury nor should the right be exercised with a view to tactical advantage,[46] but the right may be used in connection with jury vetting or where a juror is manifestly unsuitable and the defence agree with the exercise of the power.[47] The judge has a residual power to exclude a juror at his discretion, as for example where the juror is infirm and counsel has not challenged.[48]

A juror, having entered the jury box and remained unchallenged, is then sworn[49] in. The juror's oath makes no reference to the possibility of deciding according to conscience:

> "I swear by Almighty God that I will faithfully try the defendant[s] and give a true verdict[s] according to the evidence."[50]

When 12 have been sworn the accused may be "given in charge" to the jury and the trial can begin.[51] Each jury should, save in exceptional circumstances hear only once case as a group. Therefore the members are distributed back in the pool from which future jury groups will be selected.[52]

(g) Discharge[53]

17–090   The judicial power to discharge[54] the entire jury or individual jurors once the trial has begun is closely related to the challenge for cause considered above. Consequently, there is no power to discharge a jury because of its racial mix.[55] A judge's decision to discharge a jury or juror is unchallengeable, whereas if the judge decides not to discharge, that decision may be challenged on appeal against conviction by the accused on the basis that the conviction is to be regarded as unsafe because there was no discharge.[56]

If doubt arises about the capacity to act as a juror because of physical disability or insufficient understanding of English, an individual juror may be discharged. It may also be appropriate to accommodate a juror where

---

[46] *ibid.* para. 1.
[47] The power, therefore, can be used where it becomes apparent that a juror selected to try a complex case is illiterate: *ibid.* para. 5. The limitation on the right of stand by would not entirely satisfy Gobert, who argued that peremptory challenge did not need to be abolished, but that any perceived problems should have been resolved by less drastic methods, *e.g.,* a rule not to permit the aggregation of challenges, in a multi-defendant trial: Gobert (1989).
[48] See *e.g. R. v. Mason* [1981] Q.B. 881, 887.
[49] See *Practice Direction (Crime: Jury Oaths)* [1984] 1 W.L.R. 1217. Some jurors may wish to affirm, either if their faith will not permit them to swear on the New or Old Testament, or they have belief in a deity.
[50] Oaths Act 1978, ss.1, 4; *Practice Direction* [1984] 3 All E.R. 528. An alternative form is provided for jurors who wish to affirm.
[51] This is not an essential part of trial procedure. At the end of the swearing-in, the clerk may read the indictment to the jury and tell them that it is their "charge" to say whether the accused is guilty or not.
[52] See Juries Act 1974, s.11.
[53] See R. Buxton, "Challenging and Discharging Jurors–2" [1990] Crim.L.R. 84, and *Archbold (2002),* para 4-253.
[54] Juries Act 1974, s.16.
[55] *R. v. Ford* [1989] 3 All E.R. 445, and see para. 17-089 above. See H. Fukurai, E.W. Butler and R. Krooth, *Race and the Jury: Racial Disenfranchisement and the Search for Justice* (1993).
[56] Juries act 1974 s.18. See *Archbold (2002),* para 4-263 on the approach of the Court of Appeal and the decision in *R. v. Panayis* [1999] Crim. L.R. 84; Buxton, (1990–I), 284–285.

necessary by exercising the discharge power, for example, on the death of a relative.[57]

The discharge power enables the judge to deal with irregularities and improprieties before and after the retirement of the jury to consider its verdict. If something untoward might have happened the judge has the power to investigate by questioning the jurors.[58] Before retirement, the sort of matters which may lead the judge to discharge a juror are: drunkenness; inattention to the proceedings; frivolous behaviour; acquisition of information which ought not to be available to a juror, such as existing knowledge of the accused's bad character; or contact with someone outside the jury which in the circumstances is an irregularity rather than acceptable conduct and which may interfere with the course of justice.[59] In view of the nexus between challenge and discharge, an important ground for discharge is bias in a juror becoming apparent later than the time for challenge. In some cases the bias of an individual juror may lead to the discharge of the jury as a whole, since the accused's right to a fair trial has been prejudiced.[60] The trial judge ought not to make inquiry into the eligibility of a juror on the basis of a jury note or question save to ensure that adequate inquiry was made of the juror before the trial commenced.[61]

A long trial can place a considerable strain on the jury and there are provisions which allow the discharge of individual jurors in the course of a trial in the event of illness or other good reason.[62] So long as the jury does not fall below nine members, the trial can proceed.[63]

It is not always necessary for a judge to discharge a jury even where there have been attempts to influence or intimidate them.[64] The integrity of the jury is what matters and the trial judge is the master of his or her court, and is entitled to question members of the public regarding "seemingly untoward conduct" in the court. In considering discharging the jury, the cost of a retrial is not a factor for the judge to consider.[65] The trial judge retains the power to set aside the discharge of the jury where that was ordered on a

---

[57] ibid. p. 285. The power must be exercised by a High Court or Circuit judge or recorder.

[58] R.v. Appiah [1998] Crim. L.R. 134.

[59] ibid. pp. 286–287. See also Putnam (1991) 93 Cr.App. R. 281 and Thorpe [1996] 1 Cr.App. R. 269. The judge can investigate by questioning the jury or jurors to ascertain whether there has been any interference: see R. v. Appiah [1998] Crim. L.R. 134.

[60] ibid. pp. 287–288, commenting on R. v. Spencer [1987] A.C. 128 where the House of Lords decided that the failure to discharge the jury after three of them had been in discussion with a biased, discharged juror who may well have influenced them, meant that the conviction had to be quashed as being unsafe. Caution must be exercised: R.v. Doherty [1997] 1 Cr.App. R. 274.

[61] R. v. Obellim [1997] 1 Cr.App. R. 355.

[62] Juries Act 1974, s.16, provides that a juror can be discharged when incapable of continuing to act through illness or for any other reason. The power to discharge should be exercised generously. Trial by jury depends upon the willing co-operation of the public and, in any event, an aggrieved and inconvenienced juror is not likely to be a good one: R. v. Hambery [1977] Q.B. 924.

[63] Juries Act 1974, s.16(1). The number required for a majority verdict is adjusted accordingly: see para. 17-093, below.

[64] R. v. Thorpe [1996] Crim. L.R. 273 (suspicious liaison between member of public and juror (her fiancee)).

[65] R. v. Blackwell [1996] Crim. L.R. 428. See also R. v. Walker [1996] Crim. L.R. 752, the court should not take account of early aborted trial and length of present trial.

mistaken belief that they were unable to reach a verdict provided the jury had not dispersed or communicated with others.[66]

After retirement, the jury must not separate or speak to anyone.[67] If there is any such separation or communication the jury will normally be discharged.[68] A single juror may be discharged after the jury have retired if the judge exercises his discretion to do so.[69]

(h) The trial, the summing-up and the deliberations

17–091   During the course of the trial the members of the jury sit together in the jury box and listen to the evidence and the speeches of counsel. Jurors are entitled to take notes if they wish.[70] Such notes taken are subject to the same restrictions of secrecy as the jurors' deliberations. Jurors may also ask questions.[71] At an early stage of the trial, probably at the first adjournment, the jurors will be warned not to discuss the case with anyone except amongst themselves, and then only in the jury room. This instruction is designed to prevent outside influences on jurors[72] and may be reinforced by a reminder not to come to a view about the case until all the evidence and arguments have been heard.[73] Research confirms that the most important factor in the jury's decision-making is the evidence in the case.[74] There has been a growing concern about the impact of pre-trial publicity and the potential prejudice to jurors,[75] particularly in high-profile cases.

The contents of the summing up have been noted in the preceding section, as well as the significant place it has in the sequence of the trial. Prichard,[76] suggests that the judge should give the jury a *pro forma* to assist in their decision-making, but questions whether this would add to delay and intimidate the jury thereby preventing "principled acquittals". It would provide a more structured debate in the jury room and would render appeals

---

[66] *R. v. Aylott* [1996] 2 Cr.App. R. 169.

[67] As to other aspects of the secrecy of the jury room, see text below the dangers of the jury not being properly chaperoned see J. Morton, (2001) N.L.J. 394.

[68] Buxton, (1990–91), pp. 288–291. Permission may be granted under the Juries Act 1974, s.13, which, since the amendment of the Criminal Justice and Public Order Act 1994, includes the period after retirement of the jury.

[69] *R. v. Wood* [1997] Crim L.R. 229.

[70] Although some have doubted the value of this (see Cornish (1971), pp. 50–51), the Royal Commission has recommended that the judge should explain in the opening remarks that they may make notes: RCCJ, Report (1993), p. 134. This was based upon the discovery that jurors frequently found notes helpful: Zander and Henderson (1993), pp. 201–212.

[71] They rarely do so: Zander and Henderson (1993), pp. 213–214.

[72] Not necessarily sinister influences: the juror must give a verdict according to the evidence adduced in court and not on any other basis.

[73] This instruction may not always be heeded. The anonymous juror in the Thorpe trial revealed that the jury had decided on acquittal on the first day of the trial: see "Thorpe's Trial: How the Jury Saw It" *New Statesman*, July 27, 1979.

[74] See Darbyshire *et al.* (2001), p.12; but note also the reports that jurors do not follow the warnings against reasoning from propensity: V. Hans and A.N. Doob, "Section 12 of the Canadian Evidence Act and the Deliberation of Simulated Juries" (1976) 18 Crim. L.Q. 235.

[75] See D. Corker and M. Levi, "Pre-trial Publicity and its Treatment in the English Courts" [1996] Crim. L.R. 622 considering the relationship between pre-trial publicity, prejudice, and a willingness to exercise powers of contempt. On discharging the entire jury as a result of press publicity see the press reports of the abandonment of the first trial of the Leeds Footballers at Hull Crown Court in May 2001.

[76] "A Reform of the Jury Trial" (1998) 148 N.L.J. 475.

more easily processed, and could enhance respect for the jury.[77] The Auld Report[78] has recommended that juror's be provided with better information on decision-making and also encouraged more effective summings-up with questionnaires to focus the jury on the right inquiries.[79]

The initial direction on verdict will be that unanimity should be achieved, and although the jurors will know from the notes provided that a majority verdict is possible, the object of the deliberations should be unanimity.[80] The jury will be instructed to appoint a foreman when they retire. At the end of the summing up the jury retires to the jury room to consider its verdict and are kept together privately until a verdict is reached or it is discharged.[81] It will only be in an exceptional case that the trial judge asks the jury to consider the verdict without retiring to the jury room.[82] In a complex case the jury may be provided with written instructions to assist their deliberations.[83] Darbyshire et al. discovered that on average, three jurors per average jury are responsible for 50 per cent of the discussion.[84]

The judge must be careful not to put the jury under pressure to reach a verdict, in particular, he or she should avoid indicating a particular time by which they should return a verdict,[85] and must be cautious in the words chosen to encourage a jury to reach a verdict without undue pressure.[86] The judge is under a continuing duty to assist the jury.[87]

The jury bailiff must ensure that no one comes into contact with the jury except by leave of the court.[88] In particularly difficult cases it may be necessary to provide overnight hotel accommodation for the jurors under the close supervision of the court. If the jury are allowed to separate during their consideration of the verdict, the trial judge should remind them of the need to decide the case on the evidence and not to talk to anyone about the case other than in the jury room and not to allow others to talk to them about the case.[89]

If the jury requires further information from the judge to explain a point in the summing-up, or if guidance is required, the normal practice is for counsel to be consulted and the jury, if necessary, brought back into court.

---

[77] For disturbing evidence of how poor jurors' grasp of the directions is see Darbyshire et al. (2001), p.26 and on how significant the direction is for the deliberation see N. Finkel, *Commonsense Justice: Juror's Notions of the Law* (1995).

[78] pp. 532–538.

[79] On written instructions to the jury see Darbyshire et al: (2001), pp.35–36.

[80] See *R. v. Daly* [1999] Crim. L.R. 88.

[81] Circumstances are now somewhat less primitive than when juries were locked up without refreshment to encourage them to concentrate. Juries are now allowed refreshment at their own expense: Juries Act 1974, s.15.

[82] *R. v. Rankine* [1997] Crim. L.R. 757. The jury dealt with the case without retiring, but although the conviction was quashed, the Court of Appeal approved the practice on the facts of that case. For criticism see I. Khan and C. Thatcher, "Justice on a Show of Hands" (1997) N.L.L. 1182.

[83] *R. v. McKechnie* (1992) 94 Cr.App. R. 51.

[84] p.31.

[85] *R. v. Duggan* [1992] Crim. L.R. 513.

[86] See *R. v. Watson* [1988] Q.B. 690 at 700. *R. v. Baker* [1998] Crim. L.R. 351.

[87] *R. v. Naway, The Times*, June 8, 1999.

[88] Juries Act 1974, s.13. This rule is enforced very strictly and any breach of it is likely to lead to the discharge of the jury or the later quashing of any conviction: *R. v. Prime* (1973) 57 Cr.App.R. 632; *R. v. Goodson* [1975] 1 W.L.R. 549; *R. v. Davis* (1960) 44 Cr.App.R. 235.

[89] *R. v. Oliver* [1996] 2 Cr.App. R. 514. see e.g. juror making mobile phone calls; *R. v. Farooq* [1995] Crim. L.R. 169.

The judge then tries to resolve the problem and may, if appropriate, remind the jury of the evidence. The jury should not receive any further evidence once they have begun their deliberations.[90] The jury can and often do ask questions of the judge as they are entitled to do. The correct procedure is for their questions to be relayed to the judge who, except when responding to questions unconnected with the trial, should deal with the question in open court so that counsel are present.[91] This reduces the risk that the judge will be perceived as influencing the jury one way or another. It is arguable that defence counsel ought to be informed of all communications from the jury. The only exception to this policy of openness with jury communications is that the trial judge ought never to reveal jury voting figures if these have been revealed to him. Matters drawn to the judges' attention which relate to "domestic" matters of the jury and those relating to the trial are distinguishable; it is necessary always to inform counsel of jury communications relating to the trial and desirable though not essential in the first.[92] Once a verdict has been received and the court concludes that it is unambiguous it cannot investigate further.[93]

Jury communications to the judge can create considerable difficulty. In *Schot and Barclay*,[94] a juror's note to the judge explaining the absence of a verdict on the "conscious" beliefs (*sic*) of the juror had led the judge to ask for an explanation which then led him to discharge the jury. The judge initiated contempt proceedings against *Schot and Barclay* (the jurors). S claimed that she just did not understand the case, and B refused to take part. The judge found both in contempt and sentenced them to 30 days imprisonment. On appeal, the Court quashed the convictions holding that it was incorrect for the judge to investigate the circumstances, and finding that the judge should have given a majority verdict direction in those circumstances.

Jurors will not be permitted to take tools into the jury room to conduct experiments relevant to the case (*e.g.* scales for weighing drugs).[95] The jury may be provided with exhibits if requested, but in the case of tapes they should be replayed if at all in open court.[96] A jury should not be allowed, *e.g.* a knife after retiring. In the event that the jury have any materials in the retiring room, the judge must warn them as to their legitimate uses.[97] No new evidence may be received at this stage, so that if an exhibit is tampered with the trial may be unfair.[98]

The jurors will select a person known as a "foreman" to speak for the jury on all matters and, ultimately, to deliver the verdict. An important aspect of

---

[90] *R. v. Owen* [1952] 2 Q.B. 362 (oral evidence); *R. v. Davies* (1975) 62 Cr.App. R. 194 (documentary); *R.v McNamara* [1996] Crim. L.R. 750 (requesting the defendant to turn to provide a profile view).

[91] See *R. v. Gorman* [1987] 1 W.L.R. 545.

[92] *R. v. Brown and Stratton* [1998] Crim. L.R. 505; *R. v. Conroy and Glover* [1997] 2 Cr. App. R. 285. On the desirability for the judge to keep defence counsel informed of any inquiry into the jury's proceedings see *R. v. Obellim* [1996] Crim. L.R. 601.

[93] *R. v. Hart* [1998] Crim. L.R. 418; *Ramstaed v. The Queen* [1999] 2 A.C. 92.

[94] (1997) 161. J.P. 473

[95] See *Stewart* (1989) 89 Cr.App. R. 273.

[96] *R. v. Riaz* (1991) 94 Cr.App. R. 339; *R. v. Hagan* [1999] 1 Cr. App. R. 464.

[97] *R. v. Crees* [1996] Crim. L.R. 830.

[98] See *R. v. Kaul* [1998] Crim. L.R. 135; *cf. R. v. Abrar*, *The Times*, May 26, 2000, where the new evidence was revealed only by an examination of the exhibit.

the role of the foreman is to chair the jury's deliberations. Consequently, he or she has the possibility of significantly influencing the decision.[99] The method of selection is a matter for the jury.[1] In some other jurisdictions, juries select a foreman at the outset, and their judges have suggested that not to do so would be "disastrous".[2]

The deliberations of the jury are kept secret. Jurors are told that what is said in the jury room should not be disclosed to anyone even after the trial is over.[3] There have been examples of this instruction being ignored and some of what is known about the jury and the way in which it approaches its task emanates from the published experiences of individual jurors.[4] Statute makes it contempt of court to obtain, disclose or solicit any particulars of statements made, opinions expressed, arguments advanced or votes cast by members of a jury in the course of their deliberations in any legal proceedings.[5]

The sacrosanct principle of the privacy of the jury deliberations does not extend to events occurring with the jury outside the jury room. By restricting the principle in this way the Court of Appeal were able, without contravening the Contempt of Court Act 1981, to conduct an inquiry into the incidents of a jury in a hotel during their deliberations where the jury had sought to contact, via a ouija board, the victim of the alleged murder they were trying.[6]

Reasons against allowing research into the jury's deliberations include: the need to maintain finality and certainty in a case; the need to protect the jury; the need to prevent friction between jurors. The secrecy of the jury room is said to be the basis on which trial by jury continues to exist. The arguments in favour of secrecy have been stated extra-judicially by Mr Justice McHugh[7]: (l) it is necessary to ensure freedom of discussion in the jury room; (2) it protects jurors from outside influences; (3) if the public knew how juries reached decisions, the jury would lose its place in the public esteem; (4) without it citizens would be reluctant to serve as jurors; (5) it is necessary to ensure the finality of the verdict; (6) it protects the community satisfaction which flows from a unanimous verdict; (7) it enables juries to bring in unpopular verdicts; (8) it prevents unreliable disclosures by jurors and prevents verdicts being misunderstood; (9) it protects the privacy of the individual juror and prevents harassment; (10) it protects jurors from pressure to explain their reasons for a verdict; (11) it prevents vendettas

[99] J. Baldwin and M. McConville, "Juries, Foremen and Verdicts" (1980) 20 Brit.J.Criminol. 35.

[1] The question apparently often put is, "Has anybody been on a jury before?" A juror who admits to experience often becomes foreman.

[2] See the N.Z. research below, para. 17-074.

[3] As they are informed in the notes accompanying the jury summons.

[4] E. Devons, "Serving as a Juryman in Britain" (1965) 28 M.L.R. 561; D. Barber and G. Gordon (ed.), *Members of the Jury* (1976).

[5] Contempt of Court Act 1981, s.8(l). Such proceedings for contempt may only be brought by, or with the permission of, the Attorney-General, or on the motion of a competent court: s.8(3). A competent court for this purpose is one which has jurisdiction to deal with the alleged contempt. This includes attempts by the defence to investigate matters: *Mickleburgh* [1995] 1 Cr.App. R. 297; *McCluskey* (1994) 98 Cr.App. R. 216; *Schot* [1997] 2 Cr.App. R. 383.

[6] *R. v. Young* [1995] Q.B. 324. See J. Spencer, [1995] Camb. L.J. 519.

[7] "Jurors' Deliberations, Jury Secrecy, Public Policy and the Law of Contempt" in Findlay and Duff (1988), pp. 62–65.

against jurors; (12) it prevents enormous public pressures being placed on jurors.

The arguments against secrecy and in favour of disclosure have been stated by the same author[8]: (1) it will make juries more accountable; (2) it will enable injustices to be cured; (3) it could lead to inquiries into the reliability of convictions; (4) it could lead to worthwhile reforms of the legal system; (5) it may have an educational effect on the public; (6) it is necessary to ensure that jury trial can be properly examined to see if it is working;[9] (7) it is required by each juror's freedom of expression.

The current approach in banning all investigation of the jury's deliberations maybe regarded as over-simplistic. The case that takes this furthest is *R. v. Miah and Akhbar*[10] in which the Court of Appeal suggested that the ban extended to "anything said by one juror to another about the case from the moment the jury is empanelled at least provided what is said is not overheard by anyone who is not a juror". There are distinctions to be drawn between maintaining the secrecy of the jury room to prevent salacious media reporting on the deliberations, the investigation of jury deliberations as part of a serious academic research project, and the investigation of the deliberations for the purposes of an appeal against conviction. The desires sometimes competing for finality and frankness could lead to a conflict with the need for impartiality and the need for public confidence in the jury.

The over-inclusiveness of the ban as far as the appellate courts is concerned is *e.g.* demonstrated by the inability of the court to inquire into a verdict in a capital case where it was clear that the jury had misunderstood the word "unanimous" and returned a verdict of guilty on a vote of 8:4.[11] In some instances, jurors have even contacted the Court of Appeal about concerns over the way the verdict was reached.[12] There is surely a very strong case for relaxing the rules in relation to appellate courts investigating impropriety in the jury deliberations.[13] Support for this might derive from the ECHR decisions on the impropriety in the jury room such as those in *Sanders v. U.K.*, discussed above.

As far as academic research into the jury is concerned, "[t]he one recommendation of the [Royal] Commission that has received almost unequivocal support from the academic community is that s.8 of the Contempt of Court Act 1981 should be amended so as to permit proper research into jury decision-making".[14] The limited examples of research and

---

[8]   *ibid.* pp. 65–67.
[9]   Jury research is not made impossible, but is made much harder, by the secrecy requirement; see S. McCabe, "Is Jury Research Dead"? in Findlay and Duff (1988), Chap. 2, and see para. 17-094 below.
[10] [1997] 2 Cr.App.R. 12. *c.f. R. v. M* [2002] EWCA Crim.
[11] *Nanan v. State* [1986] A.C. 860.
[12] *R. v. Less* and see Zander, "The Complaining Juror" (2000) 150 N.L.J. 723.
[13] See *R.v. Miah and Akhbar* [1997] 2 Cr.App.R. 12 and *R. v. Millward* [1999] 1 Cr.App.R. 61; *R.v. Kirkham, The Times*, 26 March, 1996, *R.v. Mickleborough* [1995] 1 Cr.App.R. 297. See also J.C. Smith, "Is Ignorance Bliss? Could Jury Trials Survive Investigation?" (1998) 38 Med.Sci. Law 98.
[14] Sanders and Young (2000), p. 607. As to the evaluation of the performance of juries, see below paras 17-094–17-096.

shadow jury research have proved extremely enlightening.[15] However, the Auld Report felt confident that there existed adequate research, and that the only amendment to the rules on secrecy should be to allow the Court of Appeal to investigate alleged impropriety in the deliberations. Auld expressed "grave doubts whether intrusive research of the sort requiring amendment of the 1981 Act would be wise or that it would produce any definitive answer or one that would enable us with confidence to substitute some other system".[16]

As for the media publication of juror's accounts, the claim for a diminution of the strict rule on secrecy of the jury room is much weaker.[17]

(i) The verdict

The jury returns its verdict in open court with the foreman answering the questions posed. A verdict is given on each count, save that where the counts are in the alternative, a verdict is only taken on one, and the jury are discharged from returning a verdict on the other (this leaves the Court of Appeal open to substitute such a verdict if necessary[18]). The jury is entitled to return verdicts in relation to alternative offences[19] and the judge will have explained this to them if it is appropriate, after having warned counsel of his intention to do so. Care must be taken to ensure that the accused's right to a fair trial is not jeopardised by this course of action.[20] There are procedures to deal with the situations where the jury returns verdicts which are ambiguous or inconsistent or where the verdict returned is for an offence less than that charged in the indictment where that has been left to the jury.[21]

If the jury's verdict is misunderstood, it can be corrected immediately, provided the jury has not been discharged[22] and if performed promptly so that the jury has not had an opportunity to hear further prejudicial material against the accused or discuss the case with others.

The judge is obliged to accept the jury's verdict unless it is one on which the indictment cannot be lawfully returned, or is ambiguous, or is inconsistent.[23] The judge ought not to seek clarification of the basis for

17–092

---

[15] See, *e.g.* the Oxford Centre for Socio-Legal Studies Research into the impact on juries of knowing that the accused has a previous conviction. The findings were that recent convictions for offences similar to that now charged and convictions for child sex offences were particularly prejudicial. See Law Commission Consultation Paper No. 141 (1996); S. Lloyd-Bostock and C. Thomas, "Decline of the Little Parliament: Juries and Jury Reform in England and Wales" (1999) 62 Law and Contemporary Problems 7. See also S. Lloyd-Bostock "The Jury in the UK: Juries and Jury Research in Context" in G. Davies, S. Lloyd-Bostock, M. McMurran and C. Wilson, *Psychology, Law and Criminal Justice — International Developments in Research and Practice* (1996).

[16] p.166, para. 82.

[17] See on the publication of second hand accounts of the juror's views in the Blue Arrow trial, *Attorney-General v. Associated Newspapers* [1994] 2 W.L.R. 277.

[18] See Criminal Appeal Act 1968, s.3.

[19] See Criminal Law Act 1967, s.6(3).

[20] See *Pelissier v. France* (2000) 30 EHRR 715.

[21] See *Archbold (2002)*, paras 4–451 – 4–464.

[22] *R. v. Andrews* (1985) 82 Cr.App. R. 148. Where a jury foreman unambiguously reports a unanimous verdict the Court of Appeal is not permitted to interfere, even where the juror raised the point with the judge: *Millward* [1999] Crim. L.R. 164. If the error is recognised at once, the problem can be rectified at that time: *Maloney* [1996] C.A.R. 303.

[23] See *R. v. Robinson* [1975] Q.B. 508.

the verdict except in cases of voluntary manslaughter where the judge needs to know for sentencing purposes whether the jury are concluding that the verdict is one of killing under provocation or diminished responsibility, rather than involuntary manslaughter. In any case the jury may make a recommendation of leniency but will never be invited to do so by the judge or counsel, even if they expressly ask permission to do so.[24]

If the jury cannot agree on a verdict they are discharged and the accused may be retried. By convention, where two juries cannot return a verdict, an accused is not prosecuted a third time.[25]

There is little doubt that jurors can find the exercise a harrowing task and there have been suggestions that more debriefing and even counselling should be provided in traumatic cases.[26]

Majority verdicts[27]

17–093   The requirement that the verdict be unanimous, which had stood since the thirteenth century, was abandoned by the Criminal Justice Act 1967, which introduced the majority verdict. The governing provision is now the Juries Act 1974, s.17:

> "(1) ... the verdict of a jury in proceedings in the Crown Court or the High Court need not be unanimous if
>
> (a) in a case where there are not less then eleven jurors, ten of them agree on a verdict; and
> (b) in a case where there are ten jurors, nine of them agree on a verdict.
>
> ...
>
> (3) The Crown Court shall not accept a verdict of guilty by virtue of subsection (1) above unless the foreman of the jury has stated in open court the number of jurors who respectively agreed to and dissented from the verdict.
> (4) No court shall accept a verdict by virtue of subsection (a) ... unless it appears to the court that the jury have had such period of time for deliberation as the court thinks reasonable having regard to the nature and complexity of the case; and the Crown Court shall in any event not accept such a verdict unless it appears to the court that the jury have had at least two hours for deliberation."

At the outset the jury is directed to reach an unanimous verdict[28] and no

---

[24] *R. v. Langham* [1996] Crim. L.R. 430.
[25] On hung juries, see Chap. 13 of the N.Z. research below, para. 17–094.
[26] See Darbyshire *et al.* (2001) p.42.
[27] See generally, *Archbold (2002)*, para. 4–433. On jury unanimity and homicide charges see the special problems discussed by R. Taylor, "Jury Unanimity in Homicide" [2001] Crim. L.R. 283; D. Clark, "Jury Unanimity a Practitioner's Problem" [2001] Crim. L.R. 301. At a summary trial, there is normally a bench of three magistrates and conviction is by majority, see para. 17–011, above.
[28] See para. 17–091, above and see *R. v. Daly* [1999] Crim. L.R. 88.

mention should normally be made of the majority verdict procedure.[29] However, as has been mentioned, the jurors know of the procedure from the notes accompanying the jury summons.

A *Practice Direction*[30] sets out the procedure which ensures that the safeguards contained in the Act (a minimum period of deliberation and a statement in open court of the majority) are observed. The stages are as follows:

1. If the jury returns[31] within two hours,[32] only a unanimous verdict is acceptable. If there is no unanimity the jury is sent back for further deliberation.

2. If the jury returns after two hours ten minutes[33] have elapsed it is asked if a verdict has been reached. If it is not unanimous and the judge considers that the jury has had a reasonable time for deliberation and having regard to the nature and complexity of the case the judge will direct it that a majority verdict is acceptable, although they should still try to reach unanimity.

3. When the jury finally returns, a precise set of questions is asked:

    (i) Have at least ten (or nine as the case may be) of you agreed upon your verdict? If "Yes",
    (ii) What is your verdict? Please answer only "Guilty" or "Not Guilty".
    (iii) (a) If "Not Guilty," accept the verdict without more ado.
         (b) If "Guilty," is that the verdict of you all or by a majority?
    (iv) If "Guilty" by a majority, how many of you agreed to the verdict and how many dissented?

The foreman must state in open court the number of jurors who agreed to and dissented from the verdict before the judge can properly accept a guilty verdict, but there is no requirement that the precise words of the *Practice Direction* be used so long as it is clear to the ordinary person how the jury divided.[34] The formulation of the questions in the *Practice Direction* is

---

[29] *R. v. Thomas* [1983] Crim.L.R. 745. The fact that the judge told the jury in the summing-up that he was entitled to take a majority verdict after at least two hours was held not to be such a significant irregularity that there was the risk of a miscarriage of justice. The fear is of "inviting" the jury to disagree from the start: see also *R. v. Modeste* [1983] Crim.L.R. 746. *R v. Porter* [1996] Crim. L.R. 126.

[30] [1967] *R. v.* W.L.R. 1198, as clarified by *Practice Direction* [1970] 1 W.L.R. 916. These are directory, not mandatory in nature: *Shields* [1997] A.C. 758.

[31] "Returns" in the context of the *Practice Direction* includes being sent for by the judge who may be wondering how the deliberations are progressing.

[32] The statutory requirement that not less than two hours should be allowed for the initial deliberation is mandatory: *R. v. Barry* [1975] 1 W.L.R. 1190. The initial period may be such longer time as the judge thinks reasonable. A complicated case is an instance where a longer period is to be expected: Juries Act 1974, s.17(4); *R. v. Bateson* (1969) 54 Cr.App.R. 11; *R.v. Thornton, R. v. Stead* (1989) 89 Cr.App.R. 54.

[33] *Practice Direction* [1970] 1 W.L.R. 916. The period that has elapsed since the last member of the jury left the jury box must be stated in open court before the jury is asked for its verdict. The extra ten minutes allows for the practical necessities of electing a foreman and returning from the jury room to the court room.

[34] *R. v. Pigg* [1983] 1 W.L.R. 6.

intended to prevent anyone (other than the jurors) knowing whether a not guilty verdict was reached by a majority.[35] Even the Court of Appeal will not look behind the verdict that was read out, even in the face of a letter from the foreman stating that the wrong figures were read out.[36]

Before the introduction of the majority verdict, it was the case that if a jury failed to reach a unanimous verdict it was discharged and the accused might or might not be retried at the discretion of the prosecution. The majority verdict was introduced because fears of jury "nobbling" (*i.e.* intimidation) had been expressed and it was argued that the unanimity rule made it too easy for professional criminals to threaten or intimidate one member of a jury into holding out for a not guilty verdict.[37] However, the evidence in favour of these arguments put forward by the government to support the majority verdict was at best scanty.[38] The government relied also on the argument of efficiency that the reform would save resources in avoiding the consumption of time for the police and others involved in a second trial, although little importance was attached to this argument.[39]

Very strong arguments against the use of majority verdicts have been advanced.[40] The unanimity principle rather than the majority verdict reduces the risk of convicting the innocent, unanimous verdicts command greater community acceptance and thus the public has greater confidence in the criminal justice system, and the evidence suggests that the rate of hung juries, that is where the jury is discharged after being unable to agree, has not been much affected by the introduction of the majority verdict.[41] Further, Freeman has argued that the introduction of the majority verdict weakens the effect of the requirement that the prosecution must prove its case beyond a reasonable doubt, since if one member of a jury of twelve people is not satisfied of the guilt of the accused that is a clear indication that there is a reasonable doubt as to the prosecution's case and so the accused should be acquitted.[42] Maher has pointed out that this argument rather assumes that proof beyond a reasonable doubt is a concept which can be described in terms of probability. However,

> "it can be said that insisting on an unanimity rule is not always necessary in order to show that the principle of proof of the guilt of the accused beyond reasonable doubt is being taken seriously. For if a jury is large in size and is also representative of the community or society in general, then some relaxation of the rule may not frustrate the purpose of the principle which is to give the accused a right not to be convicted of a charge unless the case against him has been made out at a level of

---

[35] Thus avoiding a sort of second-class acquittal. See *R. v. Adams* [1969] 1 W.L.R. 106.

[36] *R. v. Millward* [1999] 1 Cr.App. R. 61. See *R.v. Tantram* [2001] Crim. L.R. 824 where the conviction was quashed after the jury sought to correct a verdict error 27 minutes after the trial.

[37] See P. Duff and M. Findlay, "The Politics of Jury Reform" in Findlay and Duff (1988), Chap. 13, pp. 212–215 and N. Blake in *ibid.*, p. 143. See also, P. Byrne, "Jury Reform and the Future" in *ibid.* Chap. 12, p. 191.

[38] See, *e.g.* Blake *op. cit.*

[39] See Duff and Findlay in Findlay and Duff (1988), p. 213.

[40] See Sanders and Young (2000), pp.567–568.

[41] D. Brown and D. Neal, "Show Trials: The Media and the Gang of Twelve" in *ibid.* Chap. 8, p. 134.

[42] Freeman (1981). See also Brown and Neal in Findlay and Duff (1988), p. 134.

practical certainty. The rule of unanimity may also be relaxed where this right receives adequate protection by other means . . . . But it can be said that if no such safeguards exist for an accused then jury verdicts must be unanimous, or be near to unanimity, if the accused's right to proof of his guilt at the level of practical certainty is to be upheld."[43]

The introduction of majority verdicts and the consequent debate can be usefully elucidated by referring back to Packer's models of criminal justice. The government appears to have been aware that most of its arguments in favour of majority verdicts were crime control model arguments, which may be why emphasis was also placed on the claim of improving fairness to the accused by preventing jury nobbling, (emphasising values of the due process model).[44] Further, Maher's argument for accepting the majority verdict is conditional upon true respect being granted to the principles of due process.

(j) Is the jury competent to make decisions?[45]

It has been asserted that the jury acquits too many people,[46] but the evidence supporting such a claim is, at best, equivocal.[47] Darbyshire et al. extrapolate from U.S. research that there are approximately 225 wrongful convictions and 4,000 wrongful acquittals per annum.[48]   **17–094**

The question of competence is unanswerable, depending as it does on a series of assumptions about the jury that cannot be tested in the absence of permission to conduct jury research. In particular, questions arise as to whether it is proper for juries to decide cases on whatever grounds it chooses, regardless of the direction on the law by the judge, and, secondly, whether the jury is capable of understanding the evidence and making decisions in complex cases.[49] These doubts may be regarded as an attack on the independence of the jury since some would argue that the very arbitrariness and prejudice of which complaint is made proves that independence.[50] There are a series of more complex questions such as whether the public expects the jury to "get the result right" or to act as a guardian of certain standards of due process.

The New Zealand Law Commission[51] conducted extensive research, led by Warren and Young at the University of Wellington, into all aspects of

---

[43] G. Maher, "The Verdict of the Jury" in *ibid.* Chap. 3, pp. 45–49, esp. p. 49.

[44] Duff and Findlay in *ibid.* pp. 212–215.

[45] As to the functions of the jury, see para. 17-085, above.

[46] See, in particular, Sir R. Mark, "Minority Verdicts" (1973), extracted in M. Zander, *Cases and Materials on the English Legal System* (6th ed., 1993), pp. 471–475 and see Sanders and Young (2000), pp.567–569 for a particularly telling critique.

[47] See the statistics referred to above, which do not distinguish between pleas of guilty and not guilty; S. Butler, "Acquittal Rates" and J. Vennard, "The Outcome of Contested Trials" in D. Moxon (ed.), *Managing Criminal Justice* (1985); Zander (1993), pp. 475–476. Sir Robert Mark's other grounds of complaint such as the professional criminal being let off too frequently, and the activities of crooked lawyers are responded to by Zander (1993), pp. 475–478. See for a vigorous critique of Mark's argument: Sanders and Young (2000), pp. 370–379.

[48] p.32.

[49] See also J. Cooper et al., "Complex Scientific Testimony: How Do Jurors Make Decisions" (1996) 20 Law and Human Behaviour 379.

[50] See, *e.g.* Brown and Neal in Findlay and Duff (1988); and Mr Justice McHugh in *ibid.*

[51] Report No 69, *Juries in Criminal Trials* (2001) available in full from *www.lawcom.govt.nz.*

jury selection, excisal, decision-making, secrecy, etc. Their conclusions were that

"in the great majority of cases, jurors are conscientious and their decisions are sound. The virtual absence of criticism of the conduct of juries in even the most controversial cases, is striking. The essentially anonymous verdict of ordinary citizens chosen at random given to the process the legitimacy of total independence; they are indeed the 'little parliament' to which community decision making is delegated."[52]

The Report also recognises one further important function of the jury as "educating the public about the workings of the criminal justice system".

(i) Do juries arrive at "perverse" verdicts?[53]

17–095   There are two aspects of the question whether juries reach "perverse" verdicts: first, whether a jury's decisions according to conscience should be permitted, and, secondly, what the function of the jury is when matters of conscience are not raised.

(1) "Perverse" verdicts and the conscience of the jury

If the value of trial by jury lies in the involvement of the public in the criminal process, thus permitting the exercise of "community conscience" and providing the "just face" of the law,[54] the jury, it can be argued, must be entitled to arrive at decisions which appear to be contrary to the law. Thus the jury's acquittal of Clive Ponting of charges under section 2 of the Official Secrets Act 1911 may be viewed as the jury exercising its constitutional role to arrive at a decision according to its conscience.[55]

Ponting had passed to Tam Dalyell M. P. documents relating to the sinking of the Argentinian battleship, the *General Belgrano*, by a British submarine during the Falklands War in 1982. These documents were clearly covered by section 2, and the judge directed the jury that, on his understanding of section 2, Ponting had no authorisation to pass them to someone such as Dalyell and there was no other lawful justification for Ponting's act. Nevertheless the jury acquitted him.

On the other hand, it can be argued that permitting juries to decide according to their conscience is completely inappropriate in "enlightened times".[56] Thus, the acquittal of Ponting may be regarded as wholly

---

[52] p.81. *cf.* the calls for abolition of jury. See A. Bell, "Twelve Good Men and True! Bah Humbug" (1997) 147 N.L.J. 1857, by a juror who was disgusted by what he found.

[53] See T.A. Green, *Verdict According to Conscience* 1200–1800, (1985).

[54] As to this function of the jury, see para. 17-085. above.

[55] C. Ponting, *The Right to Know: The Inside Story of the Belgrano Affair* (1985). See also N. MacCormick, "The Interest of the State and the Rule of Law" in P. Wallington and R. M. Merkin, *Essays in Memory of Professor F. H. Lawson* (1986). See recently the acquittal of the GM crop protestors.

[56] The phrase is that of Jeremy Bentham in *Draft of a Code for the Organisation of the Judicial*

improper. If the law is wrong, the proper means of challenge and change is through the democratic process. As Blom-Cooper has argued,"it cannot be for a single jury, unelected and chosen at random from one tiny corner of the nation, to thwart the democratic process either by disapplying the Act of Parliament or determining that a prosecution is official persecution of the accused".[57]

(2) "Perverse" verdicts and jury decision-making

Whatever view is taken as to the acceptability of the jury acting according to its conscience, there may be an argument about "perverse" verdicts in a different sense. Whether juries' verdicts may be described as "perverse" on a more general basis depends upon what the role of the jury in decision-making is perceived to be. If a narrow approach is taken, a verdict is right if it is reached by the jury after an honest, careful and reasonable attempt to apply the law (as explained by the judge in the summing-up) to the facts as it finds them, taking no other circumstances into account.[58] Then both greater certainty in the outcome of trials and greater consistency in juries' decisions is achieved.[59] A broad approach might perceive a verdict to be right where it is a verdict of acquittal, say, after a consideration of the evidence which indicated guilt or even without any consideration of the evidence at all, provided it nevertheless results from a reasonable exercise of discretion in favour of the accused reflecting the jury's sympathy, clemency or disapproval of the prosecution.

The narrow approach will view more acquittals as perverse verdicts and hence leads to the argument that reform of the jury is necessary. Jury research has been undertaken to attempt to consider whether juries do arrive at "perverse verdicts". Because of the limitations imposed upon researchers, the methods employed to analyse and explain the decision-making process and the verdicts reached in particular cases have necessarily been indirect.[60] One approach has been to compare the verdict of the jury in selected cases with the "verdict" of the professional participants in the trial; the other has been to arrange for a "mock" or "shadow" jury to listen to a case and then observe its deliberations when required to give a verdict. Both methods have their drawbacks but the results are illustrative of different features of jury decisions.

Major English research studies have been conducted which take account

Establishment in France (1790), quoted in G. Marshall, "The Judgement of One's Peers: Some Aims and Ideal of Jury Trial" in Walker with Pearson (1975), p. 1. On perverse verdicts see V. Bethell's campaign, discussed by J. Morton, "A Propos" (2001) 151 N.L.J. 142.

[57] L. Blom-Cooper, "Article 6 and Modes of Criminal Trial" [2001] E.H.R.L.R. 1 at 6.

[58] The argument is not denying the jury's function to be the decider of the facts.

[59] See, *e.g.*, on the general point about consistency, Lord Devlin, *The Judge* (1979), Chap. 5; also E.J. Griew, *Dishonesty and the Jury* (1974) and G. Williams, *The Proof of Guilt* (1963), Chap. 10.

[60] See McCabe in Findlay and Duff (1988). See also R. Eldin, "A Juror's Tale" (1988) 138 N.L.J. 37.

of the views of the professionals.[61] The first, by McCabe and Purves,[62] dealt with 475 accused tried on indictment over a two-year period, concentrating solely on the 115 who were acquitted by the jury. The second, by Baldwin and McConville,[63] dealt with 2,406 accused who appeared in the Birmingham Crown Court over an 18-month period, concentrating on the 500 accused who contested their cases. The latter study is, therefore, of wider significance since it looks at all jury verdicts and not solely acquittals. There were some differences of methodology but both studies sought to explain the relevant verdicts by reference to the views of counsel,[64] solicitors, the judge and police officers.[65]

The first study attempted to categorise the 115 acquittals[66] according to the views of the professionals. It appeared that only 15 of the 115 acquittals were based on a deliberate decision to go against the evidence. All the others were explicable on the grounds of weakness in the prosecution case, the failure of prosecution witnesses or the credibility of the accused's explanation. Many of the acquittals were regarded as correct by the professionals and the proportion of perverse verdicts was established as low in relation to acquittals[67] and very low in relation to all contested cases.[68]

In the second study, Baldwin and McConville concluded that it was not possible to determine an overall pattern in the cases where the outcome was regarded as questionable. Those cases included convictions as well as acquittals and so doubts are raised about the conventional wisdom that the accused gets the benefit of the doubt from the jury. A similar proportion of wayward verdicts occurred in this study[69] and the authors agreed that it was a tiny fraction of all cases that pass through the criminal courts, yet they pointed out the serious nature of the cases tried by the jury and concluded that trial by jury is " ... an arbitrary and unpredictable business".[70] The authors recognised that the significance of their research was limited to an assessment of the accuracy of verdicts and that the political and constitutional issues were also very important. They believed, however, that the political and constitutional debate should be informed by as much knowledge as possible about the veracity of jury verdicts.

In sum, the English evidence[71] demonstrates that there is an identifiable, if relatively small, number of cases in which juries reach perverse verdicts, although views differ on whether these deviations can be explained on any particular basis.

---

[61] Reference should also be made to M. Zander, "Are Too Many Professional Criminals Avoiding Conviction — A Study of Britain's Two Busiest Courts" (1974) 37 M.L.R. 28.

[62] S. McCabe and R. Purves, *The Jury at Work* (1972).

[63] J. Baldwin and M. McConville, *Jury Trials* (1979).

[64] The Bar did not co-operate in the Birmingham survey.

[65] The police did not co-operate in the Oxford survey.

[66] In the Oxford study there were a further 58 cases in which the accused was acquitted on the direction of the judge.

[67] One verdict in eight amongst the jury acquittals, and one verdict in eleven amongst all acquittals.

[68] One verdict in 32 amongst the accused dealt with in the period of the study.

[69] *Jury Trials* Chaps. 4 and 5.

[70] *ibid.* p. 132.

[71] There has been more extensive research in America, starting with H. Kalven and H. Zeisel, *The American Jury* (1966) (The Chicago Jury Project); see McCabe in Findlay and Duff (1988). In England, Zander's conclusions are broadly in line with the other studies.

In the course of the Oxford study,[72] McCabe and Purves also utilised the "shadow" jury technique. In 30 cases, a second "jury" was installed in the court to listen to the proceedings and then to deliberate and reach a verdict. This method has the drawback that the degree of pressure which exists when a jury is dealing with the fate of an accused is lacking in mock deliberations, but the main conclusions pointed to the care and determination of the jurors to go about their task methodically, discount their prejudices and look for evidence on which to base their verdict.[73] This would suggest that in real cases the jury is likely to display the same, or an even greater, degree of conscientiousness and application. On the other hand, some evidence suggests that jury trial is a lottery when considering the competence of jurors to follow and remember evidence and think through the issues raised logically and carefully.[74]

A growing concern since the Human Rights Act has been whether there should be an obligation on the jury to give reasons to ensure compatibility with Article 6. *Van De Hurk* v. *Netherlands*[75] obliges courts to give reasons for their decisions, but does not require detailed answer for every argument. Blom-Cooper argues that the existing composite judge and jury function satisfies the need because the trial judge directs the jury in full.[76]

The New Zealand Law Commission has undertaken valuable research in the area,[77] which if the ban on research was lifted could be replicated in England and Wales. The conclusion of the study was that to assist in decision making, jurors should receive more information in the style in which it would be presented in every day life. In particular, they should be provided with a glossary of terms, a set of detailed notes, visual aids, and decision trees and flow charts. The research also suggested that there should be more attempt for the parties to agree more of the issues and to settle common ground before the trial proper. This would enable the jury to focus more clearly on the contentious issues. The New Zealand research also found that jurors were often unprepared for the task of judging another. The research recommended that "streamlining the evidence for the jury is one valid objective of case flow management, and the focus of this should be the elimination of irrelevant or repetitive evidence, but that it must be done cautiously and with regard for the circumstances of each case".[78] Maximising the information available to the jury (*e.g.* by providing copies of the judge's notes) is not just about saving money and time but also about better equipping the jury to make their decision. The New Zealand research also concluded that the jury should be actively encouraged to ask questions during the trial. The jury should be encouraged to review evidence before they take the first vote amongst themselves.[79]

---

[72] S. McCabe and R. Purves, *The Shadow Jury At Work* (1974). See also, A. P. Sealy, "What Can Be Learned from the Analysis of Simulated Juries?" in Walker with Pearson (1975).
[73] *ibid*. p.61.
[74] See *The Times*, October 24, 1988.
[75] pp. 173–176.
[76] (1994) 18 E.H.R.R. 481, para. 61. See also *Ruiz Torifa* v. *Spain* (1995) E.H.R.R. 553. *Hiro Balain v. Spain* (1995) 19 E.H.R.R. 566; *Georgiadis v. Greece* (1997) 24 E.H.R.R. 606.
[77] See also on reasons from the jury J. Gibbons, "Explaining the Verdict" (1997) N.L.J. 1454.
[78] On the N.Z. research see I. Francis, "A Beginning a Middle and an End … but not Necessarily in that Order" (2001) 151 N.L.J. 229. See the Auld recommendations for juries to provide answers to specified questions: Chap. 11, para. 41-55.
[79] Report No. 69 (2001) para. 335.

The Auld Report recommended the enactment of a statutory provision emphasising the duty of the jury to return a verdict according to law, which could then be drawn to the jury's attention.[80]

(ii) The jury in complex cases

17–096   A similar debate about the ability of the jury to cope with the information and how it is possible to monitor their use of the information is encountered when considering the role of the jury in complex cases. The debate relies more upon the nature of the trials, such as fraud trials and trials involving scientific evidence, which, it is suggested, means that the jury cannot competently arrive at proper decisions. The inherent complexity of some cases was part of the argument that led to the abolition of the jury in most civil cases.[81] In the context of criminal cases, the Roskill Committee on Fraud Trials concluded that "we do not find trial by a random jury a satisfactory way of achieving justice in cases as long and complex as [many fraud trials]. We believe that many jurors are out of their depth."[82] Consequently, the Committee recommended that for complex fraud cases, the jury should be abolished and trial should take place before a Fraud Trials Tribunal.[83] This conclusion was reached even though the Committee stated that it was unable to obtain accurate evidence to suggest "that there has been a higher proportion of acquittals in complex fraud cases than in fraud cases or other criminal cases generally".[84] Indeed the Roskill Committee appears to have based its view, in so far as it was based on any evidence, at least in part on the conclusions of the study by Baldwin and McConville.[85] However, Baldwin and McConville had concluded that none of the questionable acquittals that they reported had been in a complex fraud case. In fact the jury had convicted in six of the eight cases which involved complex fraud issues and the two acquittals appeared to have been regarded as broadly justified.[86]

On that basis one author has suggested that the assertion of the Roskill Committee about the incompetence of the jury is really an article of faith.[87] Similar doubts about jury competence have been raised in cases involving scientific evidence.[88] The research on the decision-making of juries[89]

---

[80] *ibid.* para. 384.
[81] See above.
[82] *Fraud Trials Committee: Report*; Chair: Lord Roskill (1986), para. 8.35.
[83] *ibid.* para. 8.51.
[84] *ibid.* para. 8.35.
[85] *Jury Trials* (1979), see above.
[86] *ibid.* pp. 61–62.
[87] R. Harding, "Jury Performance in Complex Cases" in Findlay and Duff (1988), p. 77. Mr Merricks, a member of the Roskill Committee, felt that the case for change was not made out, partly because of the evidence and partly because most people making submissions were in favour of the jury. See also, M. Zander, "The Report of the Roskill Committee on Fraud Trials" [1986] Crim.L.R. 423. See D. Colrer, [2002] Crim. L.R. 283.
[88] See, *e.g.* Harding in Findlay and Duff (1988), pp. 82–90, concentrating on the Australian criticism of jury performance in such cases as the *Chamberlain* case. See also the criticisms of jury competence considered in M. Levi, "The Role of the Jury in Complex Cases" in Findlay and Duff, (1988), Chap. 6; and Lord McCluskey, *Law, Justice and Democracy* (1986) (Reith Lectures).
[89] See above.

suggests that juries are competent to make decisions, including decisions in complex cases. It has been suggested that the real fault in complex cases lies not with the jury, but rather with other participants in the criminal trial.[90]

Levi concluded that jury performance would be considerably improved if "greater care were devoted to the instruction of the jury on points of evidence and on the method to be followed when assessing it".[91] In particular there appears to be a tendency for judges to attempt to make their decisions to the jury "appeal proof" by full, undifferentiated reference to all the relevant law and any guideline judgments that exist, without taking sufficient care to emphasise simply and only those matters necessary for the decision of the jury on the facts of the particular case and in response to the actual issues raised by counsel.[92]

The Home Office/Lord Chancellor's Department Consultation Document[93] questions whether an alternative to the jury trial should be available in cases of serious and complex fraud. The paper considers the arguments for alternatives to the traditional jury trial and examines how suitable cases for an alternative trial would be identified and segregated from the mainstream. The four alternatives to the orthodox jury trial that were considered are:

(i) specialist juries in which the jury members were screened for suitability, or where selection would occur from a specially selected pool of suitable jurors;

(ii) judges sitting withoutjurors but possibly with a panel of judges;

(iii) a Roskill Committee – style tribunal of judge with a small panel of specially qualified members; and

(iv) trial by single judge with a jury assisting in making key decisions — the judge would produce a document to clarify the issues for a jury.

In addition to the principled and practical merits of each option, the paper considers the costing implications of the alternatives. The daily rates for possible members of tribunals in 1998 prices were: jury £412; circuit judge £411; High Court judge £604 and lay tribunal members £250. Rhodes[94] suggests that these proposals were objectionable on principle, pragmatism and cost. He questions why the serious fraud trial should be singled out given the difficulties that can arise in the trial of any serious offence. Identifying the jury's four purposes as: to do justice, be independent of the judiciary, protect against oppression and maintain a monitor on the police, Rhodes argues that there is no evidence that the jury is not understanding

---

[90] As pointed out by both Harding in Findlay and Duff, and Levi in *ibid.*

[91] Levi *op. cit.* p. 109. The Roskill Committee recognised this problem and, in fraud cases where there was still to be jury trial, made a number of recommendations to improve jury comprehension, including the use of visual aids and proper preparation of documentation: *Fraud Trials Committee* (1986), Chap., 9. The same point is made with regard to the judge's responsibility in summing up to the jury, see para. 17-069 above.

[92] *ibid.* pp. 109–111. The same point is made by E. Griew, "Summing Up the Law" [1989] Crim.L.R. 768.

[93] *Juries in Serious Fraud Trials* (1998).

[94] "Juries in Serious Fraud Trials" (1998) 148 N.L.J. 582.

the process in his 30 years experience. He concludes that jury is "the very touchstone of our liberties".[95]

(k) Replacing the jury?[96]

17–097   Questions have been raised about the role and efficacy of the jury. Although not frequently suggested, replacement of the jury by some other method of determining facts in criminal matters must be considered. There would appear to be four options.[97]

(i) The single judge[98]

17–098   Most civil trials are conducted by a judge alone[99] deciding both fact and law. In criminal matters the District Judge magistrate has the same function. The role of the District Judge is somewhat restricted because of the lesser degree of seriousness of the offences tried and also because any appeal against conviction is by way of rehearing, so that there would be significant differences in merely transposing to the Crown Court.

The advantages of this option include time-saving at trials[1] through not having to explain so many matters to the jury the District Judge the reduction in the likelihood of decision-making being affected by outside influences,[2] and the reduction in the likelihood of verdicts not in accordance with the law. It may also increase confidence in the system by professional users. Reviews and monitoring of the system are easier and more effective because of the obligation on the judge provide reasons. The consistency of decision-making is also enhanced by the judge applying pre-arranged professional guidelines.

The disadvantages of this option include the lack of community participation, the loss of the independence and impartiality of the jury, and the possibility that the judge would become case-hardened or prosecution-minded. Further, there would be little protection against eccentricity, and decisions on guilt being taken by one person might be too onerous a burden.[3]

---

[95] cf. the article by M. C. Davies, "After R. v. Clowes (No 2): An Act of Theft Empowered — A Jury Impoverished" (1997) 61 J.Crim. Law 99.

[96] See, W. R. Cornish, The Jury (1968), Chap. 10. See on reform I Francis, "Juries: the Worst Form of Trial, Except for all the Rest." (2001) 151 N.L.J. 582. See also I. Francis, "The Best or All Possible Worlds" (2001) 151 N.L.J. 63 on the comparisons between the way jurors and magistrates perform their functions and the support they are offered.

[97] Assuming that we are considering alternative types of tribunal rather than adjustment to the jury, such as the reduction of the number of jurors.

[98] See J. Jackson and S. Doran, Judge without Jury (1995). See also D. Corker, [2002] Crim. L.R. 283, analysing the Auld recommendation for the abduction of juries infraud and other complex trials.

[99] See above for the significance of the jury in civil trials.

[1] See the importance of the District Judge in the magistrates' court.

[2] The judge may be more immune to threats. This line of reasoning lay behind the introduction of single judge courts in certain trials in Northern Ireland in 1973 as a result of the Diplock Report (Report of the Commission to Consider Legal Procedures to Deal with Terrorist Activities in Northern Ireland, Cmnd. 5185 (1972), see now, the Northern Ireland (Emergency Provisions) Act 1978.

[3] See, e.g. S. Greer and A. White, "Restoring Jury Trial to Terrorist Offences in Northern Ireland" in Findlay and Duff (1988), Chap. 11.

The most comprehensive treatment of the issue of the single judge in recent years has been by Jackson and Doran.[4] Drawing upon experience and research into the Diplock Courts in Northern Ireland, the authors argue that the task of jury fact-finding ought not to be considered in isolation from the context of the judicial control, and that there ought to be a re-division of the tasks between judge and jury to utilise their respective strengths.

They conclude that it is not possible to compare in any meaningful sense judges and jurors since jurors have the freedom to ignore the law.[5] Judges, however: are better equipped to deal with evidence that requires intellectual exercises; are more likely to arrive at the correct conclusion (although it is acknowledged that that is a very legalistic non-holistic way of looking at the trial[6]); do more than decide questions of law, they filter the evidence heard by the jury[7]; are not case hardened, but rather "hard logicians" preferred by counsel because they will not respond emotively[8]; are trained to approach cases more atomistically. Jury absence would allow for judges to question witnesses more vigorously,[9] and allow judge to intervene in closing speeches.[10] As far as the jury is concerned, the authors conclude that juries should be left to deal with cases on credibility — that is what society wants the jury to be doing.[11] The jury is chosen to arbitrate between the individual and the state because it is impartial and independent.[12] A jury trial is to be viewed as a trial on the merits and not on only the legal considerations.[13]

(ii) The bench of judges

Some of the disadvantages of the single judge option, such as the possibility **17–099** of becoming prosecution-minded or making eccentric decisions, might be avoided by a bench of three or five judges. The disadvantages of this option include that it would be enormously expensive and recruitment might be difficult and that the nature of the judiciary would be transformed because a considerable increase in the number of judges would allegedly weaken the bench. There would be considerable implications for the legal profession if a career judiciary were necessitated.

Many of the disadvantages associated with decision-making by professionals would remain, in particular the absence of community participation in trial. The willingness of benches of judges of the Court of Appeal to permit convictions to stand where new evidence has emerged after the trial which might cause a jury to entertain reasonable doubt serves to increase the distrust of such decision-making tribunals.[14]

---

[4] "Judge and Jury: Towards a New Division of Labour in Criminal Trials" (1997) 60 M.L.R. 759.
[5] ibid., p.764.
[6] p.766.
[7] p.767.
[8] p. 764. In case of a submission of no case, the judge is more interventionist and leaves no room for the jury to do any work.
[9] p.774.
[10] p.774.
[11] p.769.
[12] p.760.
[13] p.772.
[14] A development initiated by the decision of the House of Lords in *Stafford v. DPP*, [1974] A.C. 878. It is heavily criticised in Lord Devlin, *The Judge* (1979) pp. 148–176.

(iii) The composite tribunal

17–100   On certain appeals from the magistrates' court, a Crown Court judge sits with two lay magistrates.[15] Some European jurisdictions[16] rely heavily upon the composite tribunal of lay people and judge and one observer, at least, has professed himself to be impressed by the system.[17]

The advantages would include the probability that trials would be speedier because the judge would be involved in all discussions, and that the lay people involved would be able to outvote the judge thus maintaining the overriding influence of representatives of the community.

Possible disadvantages would include whether the judge would have too significant a say in most cases and whether decision-making would still be independent and impartial so as to preserve a fair trial. Furthermore, the lay people might have to be trained which could mean that they would no longer be representatives of the community.

(iv) The special jury

17–101   The special jury is an option which seeks to satisfy the demand for community participation and independence, but to ensure competence through training. Thus a jury is still selected from non-lawyers, but the only people eligible to serve on such a jury are those who have been trained for jury service. Consequently, the objective of random selection may be defeated and trial would be in the hands of a select group of people, albeit not all lawyers.

C. EVALUATIONS

17–102   Critical analysis of all aspects of the criminal trial is essential. It may be that Packer's two-model system[18] will help readers to think through the many issues in relation to the criminal trial. For example, it might be suggested that the crime control model, emphasising the necessity to reduce criminal conduct and requiring that the system operate efficiently, helps to explain why it has been proposed that more offences be tried summarily where the accused does not need to be present, why plea bargaining is permitted, why the right to silence has been restricted and why proposals for jury reform are made, especially in relation to the alternatives to the jury, and on particular aspects such as the majority verdict, jury vetting and jury composition.[19] On the other hand, it could be suggested that the due process model helps to

---

[15] See para. above. It used to be possible for lay magistrates to sit with a judge at a trial on indictment, but that was unusual and they did not take part in the decision: Supreme Court Act 1981, s.8(l).

[16] Described in Cornish (1968).

[17] Cornish was particularly complimentary about the Scandinavian system: *ibid.* Chap. 10.

[18] For a description of these models, see above, para. 14-093.

[19] See P. Duff and M. Findlay, "The Politics of Jury Reform" in Findlay and Duff (1988), Chap. 13. See generally Sanders and Young (2000) pp. 597–607.

explain certain developments with regard to the criminal trial, for example, the developments as to the exclusion of evidence under the Police and Criminal Evidence Act 1984 and the end of the mandatory corroboration warning for several offences under the Criminal Justice and Public Order Act 1994.[20]

However, Packer's models are intended to be extremes, recognising that systems actually adopt a compromise or balance,[21] as the Royal Commission on Criminal Procedure set out to achieve in its "fundamental balance"[22] and which the Royal Commission on Criminal Justice recognised.[23] It is also necessary, therefore, to consider whether that balance is actually being achieved, or whether too much emphasis is being placed on the desire to control crime or on the desire to ensure that the accused gets a fair trial.

Packer's model might be regarded as overly simplistic with the two conflicting positions advanced. This has caused some to offer more sophisticated explanations of the process, reinterpreting Packer's model. Ashworth is critical of the ubiquitous balancing in the criminal justice system. It is described as a "pervasive notion"[24] with the danger that balancing involves an unacceptable disguise for weight being attached to incomparable factors in an exercise with apparent transparency. Ashworth is concerned to identify the principles that should serve to protect the rights of the suspect throughout the criminal process.

Five main criticisms of Packer's model are advanced. First that Packer's model does not explain the relationship between due process and crime control albeit accepting that they are not absolutely polar. Secondly, Packer assumes that the crime control model is capable of affecting crime rates. Thirdly, Packer underestimates the resource management in the process. Fourthly, the models make no allowance for the victim in the system. Finally, there are internal critiques, *e.g.* delay is bad for both crime control and due process. On this basis, it is argued that Packer's two models are no longer satisfactory for interpreting the tendencies of the criminal justice model.[25]

A further alternative approach is that advanced by Sanders and Young, who argue that the freedom of the individual to be free from injury/damage/harm is a primary purpose of the criminal law while the procedural laws of criminal process are designed to ensure freedom of suspect. The authors seek to evaluate the existing criminal process by assessing the extent to which rules/procedures maximise relative freedoms. Their aim is to protect against a net loss of freedom overall. The problem with the approach, as acknowledged by the authors, is that the model requires some sort of calculation of freedom which is not readily susceptible to objective evaluation.

---

[20] See I. H. Dennis, "The Criminal Justice and Public Order Act 1994: The Evidence Provisions" [1995] Crim.L.R. 4 at 6–9.

[21] See para. 14-093 above.

[22] See para. 14-092 above.

[23] The Royal Commission was, however, required to pay significant attention to efficiency and cost and it failed to make clear its basic approach for which it has been criticised, see, *e.g.*, Sanders and Young (2000), Chap. 1.

[24-25] (1998), p.30.

[25] pp.32.

An evaluation on the basis of these models or the fundamental balance can be undertaken on any of the topics in this chapter.

There are a number of aspects of the criminal trial that warrant very detailed critical analysis and we have selected a few with whom to conclude the discussion of the trial.

(a) Magistrates' court or Crown Court trial?[26]

17–103   In addition to the proposals to alter the way in which cases are distributed between the courts in the pre-trial process,[27] there have been suggestions to simply increase the number of offences triable only in the magistrates' courts. The arguments in favour tend to be largely based upon efficiency, since magistrates' trials will be cheaper and will be shorter, there is the possibility of written pleas of guilty, the trial may proceed in the absence of the accused and magistrates may be less likely to acquit.[28]

These appear to be arguments founded on the concept of crime control. However, that does not necessarily make them bad or wrong, provided that adequate protections for the accused are provided. It is this side of the balance which may be missing, in view of the poor levels of legal representation[29] and the need for the magistrates to decide matters of both law and fact.[30]

A move towards magistrates' court trial may, of course, be thought to be fundamentally inappropriate if, for example, there is a belief that jury trial is an essential element in a fair trial or that only jury trial represents the essential requirement of community participation.

(b) Plea bargaining[31]

17–104   In the course of this chapter two forms of plea bargaining have been considered from the perspective of the various participants in the criminal trial, not least the accused. They are the plea arrangement between counsel for the accused to plead guilty to a lesser charge, otherwise known as charge bargaining,[32] and the sentencing discount available on a plea of guilty by the

---

[26] See the discussion in Chap. 14 above.
[27] See para. 14-048.
[28] See para. 17-014.
[29] See para. 17-010 above.
[30] See para. 17-001 above.
[31] See Sanders and Young (2000). M.E. Vogel, "The Social Origins of Plea Bargaining: Conflict and the Law in Process of State Formation 1830-1860" (1999) Law and Society Rev. 161 discusses the early use of plea bargaining in the USA and demonstrates that it was used as a tool of the advocates who were politically ambitious. See also A. Alschuler, "Plea Bargaining and its History" (1979)13 Law and Society Rev. 211; J.H. Langbein, "Understanding the Short History of Plea Bargaining" (1979) 13 Law and Society Rev. 261; L.M. Mather, "Comments on the History of Plea Bargaining" (1979) 13 Law and Society Rev. 281; D.D. Guidorizzi, "Should We Really Ban Plea Bargaining? The Core Concerns of Plea Bargaining Critics" (1998) 47 Emory L.L. 753. See H. Jung, "Plea Bargaining and its Repercussions on the Theory of Criminal Procedure" (1997) Euro. J. Crime, Criminal Law and Criminology 112, discussing the victim's perspective.
[32] See para. 17-039 above.

accused.[33] Some would argue that there are really three types of bargain: the charge bargain, the fact bargain, and the plea bargain proper where the accused changes his plea to accept a low sentence and avoid trial.

Plea bargaining has much to say for it in terms of efficiency by encouraging the guilty to plead guilty, and in saving considerable resources by having fewer contested trials. However, it seems generally to be accepted that the inducements to plead guilty, if they are regarded as legitimate at all, should not be such that they create a substantial danger of the innocent pleading guilty. The pressures exerted by defence counsel giving advice to the accused "in strong terms" are long established, having been identified by Baldwin and McConville in their research study which concentrated on 121 Crown Court defendants who made late changes of plea from not guilty to guilty.[34] The criticisms made of the attitude and performance of counsel caused the publication of the research to be surrounded with controversy, but the conclusions of the study were that the sentencing discount and the rules governing the interrogation of suspects by the police were primarily responsible for any deficiencies exposed, rather than the conduct of the participants in the criminal process.[35]

Although lip-service is paid to the notion that the sentencing discount is based on the expression of remorse, the primary justification for the inducements to plead guilty is administrative expediency. In a system which places so much emphasis upon the assumed innocence of the accused and the right to require the prosecution to prove their case, the existence of strong pressures to plead guilty may appear quite contradictory. The evidence currently available allows no complacency and suggests that more attention needs to be focused on those who plead guilty and, as a result, do not participate in the elaborate procedures described in the rest of this chapter.[36]

The Runciman Commission recommended that the plea bargaining system needs to become more structured. This would have enhanced the transparency of the activity. The government response was introduced to section 48 of the Criminal Justice and Public Order Act 1994 (now section 152 of the Powers of Criminal Courts (Sentencing) Act 2000), which provides that a court should give greater sentencing discount the earlier the plea is made. However, Henham has found that the sentencers failed to comply with the requirements of the section by failing to state in open court

[33] See paras 17-008; 17-048, above. See recently R. Henham, "Truth in Plea Bargaining: Anglo American Approaches to the Use of Guilty Plea Discounts at the Sentencing Stage" (2000) Anglo American Law Review 1. Henham seeks to examine the explicit relationship between sentencing discount and pleas, and looks for greater transparency in the system. See also R. Henham, "Bargain Justice or Justice Denied?: Sentence Discounts and the Criminal Process." (1999) 62 M.L.R. 515.

[34] *Negotiated Justice* (1977). The research technique involved detailed interviews with defendants accused of serious crimes. The interviews were conducted soon after the trial had finished and it is inevitable that the particular sample might be inclined to protest innocence and exaggerate the pressures involved. Nevertheless, it would appear that the number of people wrongly convicted after a guilty plea may be underestimated.

[35] *ibid*. Chap. 6.

[36] See further, S. Dell, *Silent in Court* (1971); S. McCabe and R. Purves, *By-Passing the Jury* (1972); Bottoms and McClean (1976). See also McBarnet (1981).

what discount was being awarded. Only nine per cent of the cases examined involved a complete explanation of the reasons for the discount.[37]

There have been some very forceful criticisms of plea bargaining, including Darbyshire's[38] catalogue of the problems identified from the many research projects in this area. These include the fact that discount rewards: are racially divisive; punish those who elect trial; reward the guilty; are efficiency based rules at the cost of the defendant's rights; increase the likelihood of induced confessions; lead to the not guilty pleading guilty; encourage lazy prosecuting and defending; assume a defendant has adequate knowledge and is well informed of his rights and the options available to him; ignores the principle of open justice; and marginalise the victim. One aspect of the law regarding plea bargaining which gives rise to continuing concern is the extent to which it is permissible for counsel to communicate with the judge before the plea to ascertain what likely sentence would be imposed in the event of a plea to a particular charge. The Court of Appeal in *Turner* emphasised that judges should never indicate a likely sentence, except that if appropriate, it is permissible to indicate what the sentence will not be however the accused pleads. The decision in *Turner* poses a difficult ethical dilemma for defence lawyers who believe that the accused's chances are improved by pleading guilty to a lesser charge even though the accused insists on his innocence.[39] The Runciman Commission found that 90 per cent of barristers and two-thirds of judges wanted the rule in *Turner* relaxed to allow "full and realistic discussion between counsel and the judge about the plea and especially sentence".[40]

The Auld Report makes a controversial recommendation that the *Turner* principle be relaxed so that the judge be allowed to indicate to the accused (at his or her request) what the likely sentence on a guilty plea would be. The judge would have to be satisfied in the court in the presence of the parties and a court reported, but otherwise in private, of the voluntariness of the request and of the accused's competence to understand the consequences of the action. The judge would also be obliged to give a warning to the accused that a guilty plea should be made if he or she is in fact guilty. The judge would be provided with adequate information to make the appropriate assessment of the sentence. Once the sentencing indication is provided, the court will be bound by that. The Auld recommendations clearly reflect the views and desires of those in practice over the very cogently expressed academic opinions cited at length in the Report.[40a]

(c) "Right to silence"

17–105 The restrictions on the right to silence[41] may well be argued to be an example of the move towards the crime control model, since they make the

---

[37] *op.cit.* (2000), p.13.
[38] "The Mischief of Plea Bargaining and Sentencing Rewards" [2000] Crim. L.R. 894, See. M. McConville, "Plea Bargaining: Ethics and Politics" (1998) 25 Journal of Law and Society 562.
[39] See A. Ashworth and M. Blake, "Some Ethical Issues in Prosecuting and Defending Criminal Cases" [1998] Crim. L.R. 16 at 25.
[40] See also M. McConville and L. Bridges, (1993) 143 N.L.J. 160.
[40a] Chap.10, paras 91-114.
[41] See above, paras 17-043–17-045.

task of the prosecution slightly easier and deprive the accused of the adversarial system right to make the prosecution prove its case without assistance from the defence. When implemented it was almost impossible to find anyone, other than the government and the police, in support of the restrictions imposed on the right *prior to trial*. As Dennis[42] points out, the case for reform when examined was not strong. The arguments were: (1) that "in practice the right to silence has been relied upon mainly by groups such as suspected terrorists, professional criminals suspected of serious crimes such as armed robbery, and businessmen and others suspected of sophisticated offences of serious fraud",[43] but the evidence does not support such conclusions; (2) "that silence on the part of such suspects is evidentially significant; it is thought to be a generally reliable indicator of a consciousness of guilt"[44] but reasons for silence are not simply guilt, but also protection of others and systemic reasons; (3) "silence in the police station decreases the chance of prosecution and increases the chance of acquittal at trial if there is a prosecution",[45] but again the evidence fails to support the reason. However, Home Office research has shown that the restrictions have, since their implementation, been effective in achieving their objective.

The restrictions on the right of silence at trial have not been so universally condemned, even though they strike at the heart of the adversarial system, that the prosecution must prove its case. This is because the accused retains the right of silence, but at greater risk,[46] and, as Dennis points out,[47] "at trial the accused will usually be legally represented .... He [or she] will know the case against him [or her], and ... will have had a full opportunity to hear and test the evidence against him [or her]. The trial takes place in public before an impartial judge and jury." Is this perspective convincing?

(d) Jury reform

If crime control were the dominant motive in jury reform, arguments for abolition of the jury would be anticipated, since juries are inefficient and may acquit too many people, their decisions are unpredictable, and there is no appeal against an acquittal. In fact, proposals for the abolition of the jury are very rarely put forward, perhaps because of the popular support the jury receives through an ingrained belief that it is a constitutional protection against improper action by the State or simply that it is every person's right to be tried by one's peers.

The arguments are actually concerned with what crimes should be tried by the jury.[48] Many advocates of the jury are firmly of the view that it is under

17–106

---

[42] I. H. Dennis, "The Criminal Justice and Public Order Act 1994: The Evidence Provisions" [1995] Crim. L. R. 4 at 11–14. He draws upon research including JUSTICE, *Right of Silence Debate: The Northern Ireland Experience* (1994); R. Leng, *The Right to Silence in Police Interrogation: A Study of Some of the Issues Underlying the Debate* (RCCJ Research Study No. 10, 1993); and M. McConville and J. Hodgson, *Custodial Legal Advice and the Right to Silence* (RCCJ Research Study No. 16, 1993).

[43] Dennis (1995), p. 11.

[44] *ibid.* p. 12.

[45] *ibid.* p. 13.

[46] See above, para. 17-045.

[47] *ibid.* p. 18.

[48] See above.

attack, but that the attack is not direct or frontal against the institution of the jury itself.[49] Some advocates take the view that the attack is predicated on the basis of the crime control model. This model explains, it is argued, the move in favour of majority verdicts,[50] the change in disqualification conditions excluding a considerable number of potential jurors,[51] and the acceptance of jury vetting.[52] On the other hand, it might be suggested that the recent alterations are merely redressing the balance from a position where too many of the provisions were far too favourable to the accused.

(e) Victims[53]

17–107 Until recently victims were not regarded as important players in the full criminal justice process. The prosecution (unless a private prosecution) is not brought on behalf of any individual victim, but by the State. More recently the victim's role has come to be recognised in the criminal justice system — see, for example, the *Victim's Charter*.[54] Many might regard this move to recognise victims' rights as a move back to the position of the last century where victims occupied a central role in the criminal justice system.[55] Arguments for victims' rights are usually associated with ensuring better crime control, with the criminal justice system being seen to avoid victimising those who are already the victims of crime.[56] There are difficult issues raised above including the extent to which victims should have a say in charge bargaining and in sentencing. There needs to be great caution in ensuring that victims are given an appropriate opportunity to contribute to the process, whilst not being bound by the victim's requests.[57] There is no doubt that the English criminal process will have to clarify the appropriate

---

[49] See, *e.g.* P. Duff and M. Findlay, "The Politics of Jury Reform" in Findlay and Duff (1988), Chap. 13; Freeman (1981); Lord Devlin, *Trial by Jury* (1956); Lord Devlin, "Trial By Jury for Fraud" (1986) 6 O.J.L.S. 311.

[50] See para. 17-093, above

[51] See para. 17-086, above.

[52] See para. 17-087, above.

[53] J. Shapland, J. Wellmore and P. Duff, *Victims in the Criminal Justice System* (1985). For an analysis of the various provisions for victims in the criminal justice system and an argument that extensions and enforcement of victims 'rights must not be undertaken without great caution for impact on defendants' rights see H. Fenwick, "Procedural Rights of Victims of Crime: Public or Private Ordering of the Criminal Justice Process?" (1997) 60 M.L.R. 317. See A. Sanders and R. Young, "Discontinuances, the Rights of Victims and the Remedy of Freedom" (2001) 151 N.L.J. 44.

[54] (1996).

[55] Fenwick, (1997), p.318.

[56] The deficiencies in the present support for witnesses and victims are discussed by J. Shapland and E. Bell, "Victims in the Magistrates' Courts and Crown Court" [1998] Crim. L.R. 537, reviewing a survey conducted in 1996.

[57] Note the considerable opposition to victims rights movements, e.g. in the USA discussed by B. Pizzi: "Victims rights in the U.S." (1998) 148 N.L.J. 1805 including discussion rights to be consulted before plea bargains and to present argument in sentencing — particularly in taking account of victim statements in capital cases — see *Payne v. Tene* (1991) 501 U.S. 808.

expectations and responsibilities of the victim in the criminal process to a greater extent than at present.[58]

(f) Managerialism

Many of the changes implemented to the criminal process in the last decade **17–108** in particular have been directed towards improving efficiency in the system. This has led, inevitably, to the adoption of managerial ideas — processes, monitoring, performance standards and protocols, and to the adoption of a language that seems ill-suited to the criminal court system. For example, a Lord Chancellor's Department Consultation Paper[59] describes ".. levels of service and support to our customers [*sic*] which rival the best of any modern organisation [*sic*] whether in the public or private sector".

Leaving the jargon aside, the real concern should be to ensure that the management of the process is efficient without diminishing the quality of justice delivered. Rationalising the infrastructure of the institutions and agencies responsible for criminal process in England and Wales was clearly one of Lord Justice Auld's primary objectives, and if his recommendations are implemented should serve to improve the criminal trial process. Other aspects of managerialism might also serve to enhance the quality of justice provided that they are not in conflict with a fair trial.[60]

---

[58] The impact of the HRA on victims is considered by J. Wadham and J. Arkinstall, (2000) 150 N.L.J. 1023, particularly examining Article 2's protection of the right to life. Under the ECHR the State must protect its citizens against loss of life/privacy, inhuman treatment, by providing an adequate remedy in criminal law, as, *e.g.* in *X* and *Y v. Netherlands* (1985) 8 E.H.R.R. 235; *A v. U.K.* (1999) 27 E.H.R.R. 611; *McCann v. U.K.* (1995) 21 E.H.R.R. 97.

[59] *Transforming the Crown Court* (1999). See also the recent Audit Commission Report (2002), and M. Zander (2002) 152 N.L.J. 981

[60] See C. Pollard, "Public Safety, Accountability and the Courts" [1996] Crim. L.R. 151. In response, A. Ashworth, "Crime, Community and Creeping Consequentialism" [1996] Crim. L.R. 220, considers a rights-based focus to the question of reform, asking what "foundation" many of the so-called rights in the trial process have.

CHAPTER 18

APPEALS AND JUDICIAL REVIEW

A. INTRODUCTION

18–001   IN this chapter we consider the various mechanisms for correcting errors in, and otherwise reviewing, the decisions of courts and tribunals. There are two basic kinds of legal procedure that are available for these purposes. An *appeal* may be provided by statute: indeed it will only be available if a statute has so provided, as the common law does not recognise any rights of appeal as such. The common law has provided only for the *review* of decisions either on the ground that the body which made the decision had no jurisdiction in the matter, or on the ground that the formal record of proceedings revealed that there had been some error of law. Where the body was an inferior body of limited jurisdiction, the appropriate remedy was a writ of certiorari to remove the proceedings into the Court of King's Bench: if the decision was shown to be defective it would be quashed. If such a body was proposing to act outside the jurisdiction in the future, a writ of prohibition would lie to prevent it from so acting; if it failed to perform a duty, the appropriate remedy was a writ of mandamus. These "prerogative" remedies would be available to challenge, for example, the decisions of justices of the peace in summary criminal proceedings or in civil cases. Where, however, the decision was that of one of the superior courts, or followed a criminal trial on indictment at the assizes or quarter sessions, the remedy was a writ of error, closely analogous to certiorari.[1] There were also informal devices whereby matters could be adjourned so that the views of other judges could be obtained[2] and special procedures for the review of decisions in the Court of Chancery.[3]

In the nineteenth and early twentieth centuries, writs of error were replaced by statutory appeals. The prerogative writs continued to be available in respect of the courts of summary jurisdiction, but now in parallel to statutory appeals. They were also increasingly used to correct the decisions of local authorities, government departments and statutory tribunals. In 1938 they became prerogative "orders" rather than writs,[4] and in 1978 they came to be exclusively available on a new procedure termed an "application for judicial review".[5]

---

[1] See above, para. 2-005.
[2] *ibid.*
[3] *ibid.*
[4] Administration of Justice (Miscellaneous Provisions) Act 1938, s.7.
[5] See below, paras 18-046–18-059.

Apart from these basic options there are various other avenues for the redress of grievances, some of which are enshrined in statute (*e.g.* references by the Criminal Cases Review Commission to the Court of Appeal (Criminal Division)), some dependent on an exercise of the royal prerogative (*e.g.* the prerogative of mercy) and some informal.

There are two basic functions fulfilled by mechanisms for appeal or review. The first is that of the correction of errors of fact, substantive law or procedure made by the court or tribunal below. The second is that of the harmonious development of the law. Appellate courts commonly comprise a number of judges whereas trial courts and tribunals normally have a single judge or legally qualified chairman, sitting alone or with a jury or lay members. Appellate judges tend to be of greater experience and seniority than trial judges and their case load tends to be smaller, giving greater time for consideration; these factors become more pronounced the higher one moves up the courts hierarchy. In limited circumstances fresh evidence may be admitted before the reviewing court. Appellate courts may also correct divergences of approach among different courts of first instance.[6]

B. VARIABLE FACTORS IN APPEAL AND REVIEW MECHANISMS

There are a number of factors which must be taken into account when considering any legal procedure for redressing a grievance:　**18–002**

(1) Who can institute an appeal?[7]

(2) Can the appeal be brought as of right or only by the permission of a court or other body?

(3) What are the permissible grounds for an appeal?

(4) What is the time limit within which an appeal must be brought?

(5) To which court or tribunal does the appeal lie?

(6) What material may the appellate body consider?

(7) Who may appear as parties on the appeal?

(8) What are the powers of the appellate court?

C. APPEALS

In this section we consider appeals from courts and tribunals.[8] We　**18–003**

---

[6] *e.g.* the Court of Appeal in *Froom v. Butcher* [1976] Q.B. 286 settled the difference between judges who held that failure to wear a seat belt in a car would normally constitute contributory negligence and those who did not: the former approach was approved.

[7] For convenience this is to be taken here to include "seek review".

[8] As to the constitution and functions of appellate courts, see Chap. 2.

concentrate on appeals in basic civil and criminal cases: in addition a vast number of rights of appeal have been created in special cases which cannot be covered in detail.[9] The appeals are presented in four groups:

(1) Summary criminal proceedings and civil proceedings originating in magistrates' courts;

(2) Criminal proceedings on indictment;

(3) Civil cases originating in a county court or the High Court;

(4) Appeals in administrative law matters.

The basic principles governing rights of appeal from a court seem to be that: (1) there should be one chance to appeal on the facts or merits and a series of opportunities to take points of law up the hierarchy of the courts; (2) there should be one chance to appeal as of right, with further appeals being dependent upon obtaining leave; and (3) that an acquittal by a jury in a criminal case should be regarded as final. Appeals from tribunals or public authorities tend to be limited to points of law. The ECHR does not provide a right of appeal in Article 6, but Protocol 7, Article 2 does provide such a right in respect of both conviction and sentence. Protocol 7 has not been incorporated into domestic law by the Human Rights Act 1998. ECHR protections do nevertheless apply, because the European Court applies Article 6 guarantees to the appeal proceedings where they exist in domestic law.[10]

1. Appeals from Magistrates' Courts

18–004   A person aggrieved by a decision of a magistrates' court in a criminal case, or in certain civil cases, has the option of (1) appealing on fact or law to the Crown Court or (2) appealing on a point of law alone direct to the High Court, by way of "case stated". If the first option is chosen, an appeal lies thereafter to the High Court as in (2). In family cases, the appeal lies only to the High Court.

Once a case reaches the High Court, further appeals in criminal cases lie only to the House of Lords, and further appeals in civil cases lie on the same basis as in other civil cases determined by the High Court. In a criminal case, where the magistrates commit a convicted person to the Crown Court for sentence, the appeal thereafter lies to the Court of Appeal (Criminal Division).[11] The Auld Report (2001) comments that the present appeal system in English law is "mixed and overlapping", with "procedural impediments to its ability both to do justice in individual cases and adequately to protect the public interest". The main recommendation is to

---

[9] A list may be found in D. Price, *Appeals* (1982).
[10] See *Delcourt v. Belgium* (1969) 1 E.H.R.R. 355; *Tolstoy v. U.K.* (1995) 20 E.H.R.R. 442. See generally M. Strange, in K. Starmer *et al.*, *Criminal Justice, Police Powers and Human Rights* (2001), Chap. 19; Emmerson and Ashworth, *Criminal Justice and Human Rights* (2001), Chap.17.
[11] Criminal Appeal Act 1968, s.10: see below, para 18-016.

streamline the process so that there will be similar bases for appeal in each level of jurisdiction, to replace the existing duplication with a single procedure and to improve the matching of the tribunal to the complexity of the case.[12]

(a) Appeals from magistrates' courts to the Crown Court[13]

The defendant in a criminal case may appeal to the Crown Court, as of right, (a) if he or she pleaded guilty,[14] against sentence; or (b) if he or she did not plead guilty, against the conviction or sentence.[15] "Sentence" includes any order made on conviction other than an order for costs and certain other orders.[16] Similarly, a person may appeal against an order for contempt of a magistrates' court[17] or an order binding him or her over to keep the peace or to be of good behaviour.[18] The prosecutor or complainant may not appeal against an acquittal or a refusal to make an order.[19] This right to appeal does not preclude a challenge by way of judicial review if the complaint is of any impropriety or denial of a fair trial.[20] The Criminal Cases Review Commission can refer to the Crown Court any conviction of the magistrates' court.[21] There has been less detailed academic scrutiny of the operation of the appellate jurisdiction of the Crown Court than of the Court of Appeal.

18–005

---

[12] Chap. 12, para. 4.

[13] See *Blackstone's Criminal Practice 2002*, Part D-26; A. Keogh, *Criminal Appeals and Review Remedies for Magistrates' Court Decisions* (1999); Emmins (2000), Chap. 25.

[14] There is no opportunity to appeal against conviction from a guilty plea: *R. v. Birmingham Crown Court, ex p. Sharma* [1988] Crim. L.R. 741; see A. Keogh, (1999), Chap. 5. In 2000 there were 13,902 appeals against magistrates' courts decisions, with 5,341 against conviction, 7,691 against sentence and 870 other (*e.g.* licences): *Judicial Statistics 2000*, and see K. Malleson and S. Roberts, [2002] Crim. L.R. 274, n.9. If the plea of guilty was "equivocal" the defendant may appeal to the Crown Court to set aside the conviction and remit the case to the magistrates with a direction to enter a plea of "not guilty" and try the case summarily: the magistrates' court is obliged to comply with the direction provided that there has been a proper inquiry by the Crown Court and sufficient evidence from which it could find that the plea had been equivocal: *R. v. Plymouth JJ., ex p. Hart* [1986] Q.B. 950. A plea is equivocal where something emerges during the trial which throws doubt on it, *e.g.* in theft, "guilty, but I took it by mistake". See *R. v. Durham Quarter Sessions, ex p. Virgo* [1952] 2 Q.B. 1. The Crown Court should seek affidavit evidence from the chairman of the bench or the clerk before sending it back: *R. v. Rochdale JJ., ex p. Allwork* [1981] 3 All E.R. 433. The Crown Court may also remit a case where it subsequently transpires that a plea of guilty was made under duress: *R. v. Huntingdon Crown Court, ex p. Jordan* [1981] Q.B. 857.

[15] Magistrates' Courts Act 1980, s.108(1). The power of the magistrates' court to reopen any order made by them which has not been subsequently determined by a higher court has been extended by Criminal Appeal Act 1995, s.26, leaving a very broad discretion in the magistrates' hands. See *Collett v. Bromsgrove DC* [1997] Crim. L.R. 206.

[16] *ibid.* s.108(3). Probation orders and orders for conditional discharge were formerly excluded: see now the Powers of Criminal Courts (Sentencing) Act 2000, s.14. See further the catalogue of orders in *Archbold* (2002), paras 2–161–2–172a.

[17] Contempt of Court Act 1981, s.12(5).

[18] Magistrates' Courts (Appeals from Binding Over Orders) Act 1956, s.1; *Hughes v. Holley* (1988) 86 Cr. App. R. 130.

[19] Such a right may be expressly conferred, *e.g.* the Customs and Excise Management Act 1979, s.147: offences under the Customs and Excise Acts.

[20] See *R. v. Hereford Magistrates' Court, ex p. Prussia* [1997] 2 Cr. App. R. 340 (doubting *R. v. Peterborough JJ., ex p. Dowler* [1996] 2 Cr. App. R. 561.) See further *Archbold* (2002), para. 2–160.

[21] Criminal Appeal Act 1995, s.11.

Notice of appeal must be given within 21 days after the day on which the decision or sentence appealed against was given.[22] The notice must state the grounds for appeal. The Crown Court may extend the time for giving notice of appeal either before or after it expires.[23] There is no longer an obligation on magistrates' clerks to supply notes of evidence to the accused.[24] The appellant may abandon the appeal by giving notice in writing up to three days before the hearing of the appeal.[25]

The appeal is treated as a complete rehearing,[26] and the procedure is exactly the same as at a summary trial in the magistrates' court. Appeals are heard by a circuit judge or recorder who must normally sit with two magistrates.[27] The appeal can be heard notwithstanding the absence of the appellant,[28] even where he or she has not instructed counsel to appear on his or her behalf.[29] The relevant witnesses will attend the court and give evidence as at the original trial. The parties are not, however, confined to the evidence placed before the magistrates. The Crown Court may find the case proved on a basis other than that found by the magistrates' court.[30] Where the appeal is against sentence only, it is usual for the prosecution merely to put forward facts which had been admitted or found by the magistrates, although there is no technical reason why sworn evidence should not be given.[31] The Crown Court can pass sentence on a different factual basis than that found in the magistrates' court.[32]

The powers of the Crown Court are as follows.[33] It may correct any error or mistake in the order or judgment against which the appeal is brought, and at the end of the hearing may:

[22] Crown Court Rules 1982 (S.I. 1982 No. 1109), r.7, as amended by the Crown Court (Amendment) Rules 2001 (S.I. 2001 No. 614). See *Archbold* (2002), para. 2–180.
[23] *ibid.*
[24] Criminal Defence Service (General) (No. 2) Regs, 2001 (S.I. No. 1437 2001), which contain no provision analogous to the Legal Aid in Criminal and Case Proceedings (General) Regulations 1989 (S.I. 1989 No 344), r.42.
[25] Crown Court Rules 1982, r.11; Magistrates' Courts' Act 1980, s.109.
[26] See *Drover v. Ragman* [1951] 1 K.B. 380; *Northern Ireland Trailers v. Preston Corporation* [1972] 1 W.L.R. 203; *Hughes v. Holley* (1986) 86 Cr. App. R. 130: these cases show that the court must, however, consider the state of affairs existing at the time the order was appealed against. Appeals against binding-over orders are to be conducted as a rehearing: *Shaw v. Hamilton* [1982] 1 W.L.R. 1308.
[27] See *Practice Direction (Crown Court: Business)* [2001] 1 W.L.R. 1999.
[28] *R. v. Croydon Crown Court, ex p. Clair* [1986] 1 W.L.R. 746 (the Crown Court had refused to hear the appeal in the appellant's absence: mandamus was granted requiring them to do so). The Crown Court cannot quash a decision on the basis that the defendant was denied the opportunity to have his case heard owing to his representatives error, if the magistrates have acted correctly: *R. v. Secretary of State for Home Department, ex p. Al Medawi* [1990], 1 A.C. 876.
[29] *R. v. Crown Court at Guildford, ex p. Brewer* (1987) 87 Cr. App. R. 265 (the appellant's counsel was present, but, following refusal of an application for an adjournment, took no further part in the proceedings as he had no instructions to do so).
[30] *Hingley-Smith v. DPP* [1998] 1 Arch. News 2, DC.
[31] *Paprika Ltd v. Board of Trade* [1944] K.B. 327; *Shaw v. Hamilton* [1982] 1 W.L.R, 1308; *Williams v. R.* (1983) 77 Cr. App. R. 329; *R. v. Telford JJ., ex p. Darlington* (1987) 87 Cr. App. R. 194.
[32] *Bussey v. DPP* [1999] 1 Cr. App. R. (S.) 125 (departure from facts to be explained to accused).
[33] Supreme Court Act 1981, s.48, as amended by the Criminal Justice Act 1988, s.156. See *Archbold* (2002), para. 2–178.

(a) confirm, reverse or vary any part of the decision appealed against, including a determination not to impose a separate penalty in respect of an offence[34];

(b) remit the matter with its opinion thereon to the authority whose decision is appealed against; or

(c) make any order in the matter as it thinks just and exercise any power which that authority might have exercised.

These powers are subject to any limit or restriction imposed by any other enactment. A punishment in a criminal case may be more or less severe than that awarded by the magistrates' court, provided that it could have been imposed by that court.[35] The court must give reasons for its decision.[36] Costs may be awarded against an unsuccessful appellant[37] and may be awarded to a successful appellant out of central funds.[38]

In civil matters, appeals lie to the Crown Court in respect of a variety of licensing matters.[39] The right was exercised by 14,000 people in 2000.[40] The *Auld Report* recommends a significant change to the procedure by abolishing the defendant's right of appeal against conviction and/or sentence in the magistrates' court to the Crown Court.[41] There would be a right of appeal to the Crown Division (Crown Court) with leave of that court on the same basis as an appeal would be granted leave from the Crown Court to the Court of Appeal. The Crown Court hearing such an appeal would comprise a single judge (High Court, circuit or recorder depending on the circumstances). It was felt that this recommendation would reflect quality of summary justice.

(b) Appeals from magistrates' courts to the High Court by "case stated"

Any person who was party[42] to any proceedings before a magistrates' court or who is "aggrieved"[43] by its decision may question the decision on the ground that it is wrong in law or in excess of jurisdiction by applying to the **18–006**

---

[34] Prior to the enactment of s.156 of the 1988 Act, the subsection merely referred to a power to vary "the decision appealed against", The Divisional Court in *Dutta v. Westcott* [1987] Q.B. 291 gave the words a strained interpretation in holding that the Crown Court was empowered to vary the penalty imposed for another offence dealt with by the magistrates on the same occasion, but which was not appealed against: the amendment gave express authority for this.

[35] Supreme Court Act, s.48. See *Arthur v. Stringer* (1986) 84 Cr. App. R. 361.

[36] *R. v. Harrow Crown Court, ex p. Dave* [1994] 1 W.L.R. 98; *R. v. Inner London Crown Court, ex p. London Borough of Lambeth Council* [2000] Crim. L.R. 303; failure to do so could render the Crown Court's decision invalid: *R. v. Kingston Crown Court, ex p. Bell* (2000) 64 J.P. 633.

[37] Prosecution of Offences Act 1985, s.18(1)(b).

[38] Prosecution of Offences Act 1985, s.16(3); see also *Johnson v. RSPCA* (2000) 164 J.P. 345.

[39] See, *e.g.* Licensing Act 1964, ss.21, 5ø, 81B, 146, 154.

[40] Chap. 12, para. 16.

[41] Chap. 12, para. 35.

[42] *e.g.* defendant *or prosecutor* in a criminal case: *R. v. Newport (Salop) JJ., ex p. Wright* [1929] 2 K.B. 416.

[43] This covers a person who is not a party but whose legal rights are affected by the decision: *Drapers Company v. Holder* (1892) 57 J.P. 200, *e.g.* the owner of stolen goods who seeks a restitution order.

justices for them to state a case for the opinion of the High Court.[44] An application may not be made following committal proceedings,[45] at an interlocutory stage in a summary hearing,[46] to challenge a decision by the magistrates declining jurisdiction,[47] where there is otherwise a right of appeal to the High Court or where the decision is said by an enactment to be "final".[48] The application must be made within 21 days, and any right to appeal to the Crown Court is lost when this is done.[49] The justices may refuse to state a case if they are of opinion that the application is "frivolous",[50] but may not do so where the application is made by or under the direction of the Attorney-General. If they do exercise their power to refuse, the applicant may seek an order of mandamus from the High Court to compel them to state a case, and the High Court has a discretion whether to make an order.[51]

The procedure for stating a case is regulated by the Magistrates' Courts Rules 1981.[52] The application is made to the clerk to the justices. Unless the application is refused, a draft case must be sent to the parties, and it may be amended by the justices in the light of any representations received. The case must state the facts found and the questions of law or jurisdiction on which guidance is sought. It must specify any finding of fact which is claimed to be unsupported by evidence, but it may not otherwise contain a statement of evidence.[53] In practice it is normally prepared by the clerk. An appeal by way of case stated may be withdrawn by the appellant without leave.[54]

In criminal cases the appeal is heard by a Divisional Court of the Queen's Bench Division; otherwise, it is normally heard by a single judge. Where the appeal relates to the enforcement of a maintenance order, the appeal lies to the Family Division.[55] The appellant must lodge the case in the Crown

---

[44] Magistrates' Courts Act 1980, s.111(1).

[45] *Atkinson v. United States Government* [1971] A.C. 197; *Cragg v. Lewes District Council* [1986] Crim. L.R. 800.

[46] *Streames v. Copping* [1985] Q.B. 920 (to challenge a disputed ruling that the magistrates had jurisdiction). *Cf. Loade v. DPP* [1990] 1 Q.B. 1052 (Divisional Court has no jurisdiction in a criminal case to entertain an appeal by case stated at an interlocutory stage of an appeal to the Crown Court); there is such a jurisdiction in civil cases, but justices should exercise their power only in exceptional circumstances (*R. v. Chesterfield JJ., ex p. Kovacs* [1992] 2 All E.R. 325).

[47] *Pratt v. A. A. Sites Ltd* [1938] 2 K.B. 459: the remedy here is to apply for judicial review: see *Streames v. Copping*, at 928 (May L.J.).

[48] 1980 Act, s.111(1). See *Liverpool City Council v. Worthington, The Times*, June 16, 1998.

[49] *ibid.* s.111(4). See *P. & M. Supplies (Essex) Ltd v. Hackney London Borough Council* (1990) 154 J.P. 814. An appeal by case stated against conviction will not debar an appeal to the Crown Court against sentence, and vice versa: an appeal by case stated on both matters debars the appeal to Crown Court completely: *R. v. Winchester Crown Court, ex p. Lewington* [1982] 1 W.L.R. 1277.

[50] This term includes cases where the argument on the point of law cannot succeed, *e.g.* where the law has been authoritatively stated in a superior court. "Frivolous" has been interpreted as meaning "futile, misconceived, hopeless or academic": *R. v. Mildenhall Magistrates' Court, ex p. Forest Heath D.C.* (1997) 161 J.P. 401.

[51] On the procedure where magistrates refuse to state a case see *R. v. Blackfriars Crown Court, ex p. Sunworld* [2000] 1 W.L.R. 2102. See generally A. Keogh, (1999), Chap.11.

[52] S.I. 1981 No. 552, as amended, rr.76–81.

[53] See *Turtington v. United Cooperatives Ltd* [1993] Crim. L.R. 376.

[54] *Collett v. Bromsgrove District Council* (1996) 160 J.P. 593.

[55] R.S.C., Ord. 56, r.5, as set out in Civil Procedure Rules 1998 (S.I. 1998 No. 3/32), Sched I. An appeal is normally heard by a single judge unless the court directs that it should be heard by a Divisional Court.

Office or the Principal Registry of the Family Division within 10 days of receiving it, and must serve a copy on the respondent within four days of so lodging it. The High Court may return the case for amendment.[56]

On an appeal, the High Court may reverse, affirm or amend the decision or remit it to the justices for their reconsideration in the light of the court's opinion, or make such other order as the court thinks fit.[57] Apart from the obvious power to correct errors of law, such as the misinterpretation of a statute, the court will treat any decision unsupported by the evidence, or otherwise one which no reasonable magistrates could reach, as erroneous in law.[58] The court may take the view that in the light of its ruling on the law in a criminal case the defendant is clearly guilty or clearly innocent, in which event it will direct the magistrates to convict or acquit as the case may be. Otherwise the matter will be left to the magistrates. The Divisional Court may order the magistrates' court to make an appropriate order or otherwise to complete unfinished proceedings; or to conduct a rehearing before the same or a different bench. The rehearing should only be ordered if it will not deny the accused a fair trial.[59] Appeal against sentence should normally be directed to the Crown Court.[60] The *Auld Report* makes a radical recommendation that there should be no right of appeal to the High Court by an appeal by way of case stated, and no right to challenge the magistrates' decision by way of judicial review.[61] This is currently a rarely used avenue of appeal; in 2000 there were 125 appeals by way of case stated and 336 claims of judicial review.[62] Malleson and Roberts point out that the proposals will nevertheless reduce the efficiency of the system.[63]

There were 2,029 applications for leave to appeal against conviction, of which 430 were granted, and 5,545 applications for leave to appeal against sentence of which 1,426 were appealed. Thirty per cent of appeals against conviction and 67 per cent of sentencing appeals were successful.[64]

(c) Appeals from magistrates' courts to the High Court in family cases

In certain family matters an appeal lies to the Family Division of the High Court. These include the making or refusal of orders under the Domestic Proceedings and Magistrates' Courts Act 1978[65] and varations of maintenance orders.[66] The appeal can raise matters of fact or law and is not by case stated. A notice of motion must be served and the appeal entered within six weeks of the decision challenged.[67] The court may receive further   **18–007**

---

[56] Supreme Court Act 1981, s. 28A, inserted by the Statute Law (Repeals) Act 1993, Sched. 2, para. 9, as substituted by The Access to Justice Act 1999, s.61.

[57] *ibid.*

[58] *Bracegirdle v. Oxley* [1947] 1 K.B. 349. This is significantly narrower than the appeal on the merits to the Crown Court: see section (a) above.

[59] *Griffith v. Jenkins* [1992] 2 A.C. 76, *cf.* the Divisional Court decisions in *Maydew v. Flint* (1984) 80 Cr. App. R. 49; *Rigby v. Woodward* [1957] 1 W.L.R. 250.

[60] *R. v. Eating JJ., ex p. Scrafield* [1994] R.T.R. 195 (application for judicial review rejected).

[61] Chap. 12, para. 35.

[62] Chap. 12, para. 16.

[63] [2002] Crim. L.R. 272.

[64] *Auld Report,* 12, para. 38. Statistics between April 2000 and March 2001.

[65] Other than interim maintenance orders, against which no appeal lies. Appeals as to the *enforcement* of maintenance orders lie by case stated: see section (b), above.

[66] Maintenance Orders Act 1958, s.4(7). See *Hackshaw v. Hackshaw* [1999] 3 F.C.R. 51.

[67] Family Proceedings Rules 1991 (S.I, 1991 No. 1247, as amended), r.8.2. This appeal regime

evidence (but in practice does so only in exceptional circumstances), draw its own inferences of fact and may make any order that the magistrates might have made and any other order that the case might require, or may remit the matter with its opinion for rehearing by the magistrates.[68] Appeals from the making of or refusal to make an order under the Children Act 1989 also lie from the magistrates' court to the Family Division.[69] Notice of appeal must normally be served within 14 days. Appeals are heard by a judge of the Family Division at the nearest convenient High Court centre.[70] On an appeal the High Court may make such orders as may be necessary to give effect to its determination of the appeal.[71]

(d) Appeals from the Crown Court to the High Court

18–008   Where there has been an appeal from a magistrates' court to the Crown Court, any party to the proceedings[72] may appeal by case stated on a point of law or jurisdiction to the High Court.[73] The procedure is similar to that for such appeals from the magistrates' court direct to the High Court.[74] The same right of appeal is available in respect of any other decision of the Crown Court[75] except one relating to trial on indictment and in certain licensing matters.[76]

(e) Appeals from the High Court to the House of Lords[77]

18–009   In civil cases which have reached the High Court on appeal, further appeals lie on the same bases as in other civil matters determined by the High Court.[78] Until 1960 there was, however, no further right of appeal in a

---

is distinct from that under the Children Act 1989 (see below): *P. v. P. (Periodical Payments) [1995] 1 F.L.R. 563.*

[68]   RSC, Ord. 55, r. 7.

[69]   Children Act 1989, s.94. See Family Proceedings Rules 1991, r.4.22, (as amended). See Re O (*Family Appeals: Management*) [1998] F.L.R. 431

[70]   *Practice Direction (Appeals from Magistrates' Courts)* [1992] 1 W.L.R. 261.

[71]   1989 Act, s.94(4). The principles of *G. v. G. (Minors: Custody Appeal)* [1985] 1 W.L.R. 647 (below, para. 18-2026) broadly apply to appeals under s.94: *Re M (Section 94 appeals)* [1995] 1 F.L.R. 546, CA and see *Re W* [1999] 3 F.C.R. 337. Fresh evidence will only be received in exceptional circumstances: *Croydon London Borough Council v. A* [1992] Fam. 169; *cf. S v. Merton London Borough Council* [1994] 1 F.C.R. 186.

[72]   *i.e.* in a criminal case, either prosecutor or defendant.

[73]   Supreme Court Act 1981, s.28. Through an oversight the powers of disposal available in respect of appeals from the magistrates' court (n. 56 above) are not available in respect of appeals from the Crown Court; the Law Commissioin has recommended that they should be: Report on *Administative Law: Judicial Review and Statutory Appeals* (Law Com. No. 226, 1994), p. 105.

[74]   Crown Court Rules 1982, (S.I. 1982 No. 1109), r.26, and *cf.* above pp. For the procedure on applications see *DPP v. Coleman* [1998] 1 All E.R. 912.

[75]   *e.g.* matters such as firearms licensing where an appeal lies direct to the Crown Court: see P. J. Clarke and J. W. Ellis, *The Law Relating to Firearms* (1981), pp. 104–111; *Kavanagh v. Chief Constable of Devon and Cornwall* [1974] Q.B. 624.

[76]   Supreme Court Act 1981, s.28(2) *cf.* s.29(3), As to appeals in relation to trials on indictment, see below, para. 18-010 and on the relationship between appeals by case stated and applications for judicial review, see below para. 18-059. The Law Commission (*op. cit.* n. 175 above), has recommended that no new case stated appeals be created and that appeals on a point of law are to be preferred: p. 106.

[77]   See A. Keogh, (1999), Chap. 12.

[78]   See below, para. 18-022.

criminal case, and the Divisional Court of the Queen's Bench Division was the final authority on many matters concerning summary offences.[79] Under the Administration of Justice Act 1960[80] either the prosecutor or the defendant may appeal to the House of Lords on a point of law of public general importance. Leave must be obtained from either the Divisional Court or the House of Lords: the Divisional Court must certify that a point of law of general public importance is involved,[81] and it must appear either to that court or to the House of Lords[82] that the point ought to be considered by the House. On the appeal, the House may exercise any of the powers of the Divisional Court or may remit the case to it.

2. APPEALS FOLLOWING TRIAL ON INDICTMENT

(a) Appeals from the Crown Court to the Court of Appeal (Criminal Division)

An acquittal by a jury in a criminal case is regarded as sacrosanct: the prosecutor has no right of appeal however perverse the verdict of the jury.[83] However, persons convicted[84] of an offence on indictment may appeal to the Court of Appeal (Criminal Division).[85] The powers of the Court of Appeal were remodelled by Part I of the Criminal Appeal Act 1995, following recommendations of the Royal Commission on Criminal Justice.[86] The powers of the Court of Appeal have been the subject of considerable controversy following this reform, and as a result of the Human Rights Act

18–010

---

[79] For example, there was no right to appeal against the unsatisfactory decisions in *Thomas v. Sawkins* [1935] 2 K.B. 249 and *Duncan v. Jones* [1936] K.B. 218: see S. H. Bailey, D. J. Harris and B. L. Jones, *Civil Liberties: Cases and Materials* (4th ed., 1995), pp. 248–251, 259–264.

[80] ss.1–9.

[81] There is no right to appeal against the refusal of a certificate: *Gelberg v. Miller* [1961] 1 All E.R. 618n. HL.

[82] The application for leave is made first to the Divisional Court and only if that court refuses to the House of Lords. See *Archbold* (2002), para. 7–20.

[83] The Attorney-General may refer cases where there has been an acquittal to the Court of Appeal (Criminal Division), but not so as to affect the defendant: See below, para. 18–019. Furthermore, the High Court now has power to quash acquittals tainted by interference with or intimidation of a juror or witness: Criminal Procedure and Investigations Act 1996, ss. 54–56; see also Magistrates' Courts (Criminal Procedure and Investigations Act 1996) (Tainted Acquittals) Rules 1997. This exceptional power arises only where (a) the defendant was acquitted, (b) a person has subsequently been convicted of an offence relating to the administration of justice, (c) that offence was in connection with the proceedings leading to the acquittal, the High Court certifies that there is a real possibility that the interference was a "but for" cause of the acquittal and it is in the interests of justice to order a retrial. The Law Commission has produced very important reform proposals: (a) allowing for a retrial following an acquittal in certain circumstances, thereby eroding the "double jeopardy" safeguard (b) recommending that some "terminating" rulings by a judge should be capable of being appealed by the prosecution (see above para. 17-023). On perverse verdicts, see also Auld (2001), Chap. 5, recommending that juries be forbidden from returning such.

[84] This includes a person who pleaded guilty: *R. v. Lee (Bruce)* [1984] 1 W.L.R. 578; *R, v. Swain* [1986] Crim.L.R. 480; and where a verdict has been returned, but the judge has postponed sentence: *R. v. Drew* [1985] 1 W.L.R. 914.

[85] Criminal Appeal Act 1968; Criminal Appeal Rules 1968 (S.I. 1968 No. 1262, as amended) (hereafter "CAR,"); *Guide to Proceedings in the Court of Appeal Criminal Division* (1997); P. O'Connor, [1990] Crim.L.R. 615.

[86] Cm. 2263, 1993, Chap. 10. See Sir John Smith, [1995] Crim.L.R. 920.

1998 which has caused a re-focusing of the inquiry from safety to broader concerns of unfairness.[87]

(i) Appeals against conviction

In 2000, 56,120 defendants were convicted in the Crown Court.[88] Auld also recommends abolishing the right to challenge a decision of the Crown Court sitting in its appellate capacity.[89] No right of appeal by way of case stated or judicial review would be available, but there would be an appeal to the Court of Appeal. That court would have jurisdiction similar to the present courts when hearing appeals by way of case stated or a claim for judicial review.[90]

18–011 (1) *Grounds and procedure.* The person convicted may only appeal if either (a) a certificate from the trial judge that the case is fit for appeal or (b) leave of the Court of Appeal (Criminal Division) is obtained.[91]

The appellant must either serve the trial judge's certificate on the appropriate officer of the Crown Court with a notice of appeal, or serve notice of application for leave to appeal.[92] The notice must be served within 28 days of conviction, although the time limit may be extended by the court.[93] The grounds of the appeal or application must be stated,[94] but may be varied or amplified within such time as the court may allow.[95] The appellant may apply for bail,[96] and be present at the hearing.[97]

---

[87] See below, para. 18-014.

[88] *Judicial Statistics 2000* (2001), Tables 6.9 and 1.7.

[89] Chap. 12, para. 44.

[90] *Auld Report,* 12, para. 37.

[91] 1968 Act, s.1 (2), as substituted by the Criminal Appeal Act 1995, s.l. Prior to this change, the person convicted could appeal as of right on any ground which involved a question of law alone.

[92] *ibid.* s.18(1); CAR 1968, r.2(1). The Crown Court forwards the notice to the Criminal Appeal Office with the trial documents and any others which may be required: *Practice Direction (Crime: Notices of Appeal)* [1988] 1 W.L.R. 34; *Archbold* (2002), para. 7–40.

[93] 1968 Act, s.18(2). Leave may be granted some years later. See, *e.g. R. v. Foster* [1985] Q.B. 115, where F was convicted of rape in 1977, following a plea of guilty. Another man confessed to and was convicted of the offence in 1981. F was granted a free pardon in 1982 (see below, para. 18–012 and leave to appeal in 1984, when the conviction was quashed. The court has rejected a claim that to deny an extension of time when the basis of the appeal is a change in the law is contrary to Article 7 of the ECHR: *R. v. Jones (Beatrice)* [1999] Crim. L.R. 820. The European Court has accepted that reasonable time limits can be imposed on appeals: *Vacher v. France* (1996) 24 E.H.R.R. 482. The restrictions on appeal must not be such as to destroy the essence of the right: *Omar v. France* (1998) 29 E.H.R.R. 210.

[94] CAR 1968, r.2(2)(a). If leave is limited to only specified grounds of appeal, the Court of Appeal will not hear argument on other grounds without granting leave: *R. v. Jackson* [1999] 1 All. E.R. 572; *R. v. Cox* [1999] 2 Cr.App.R. 6.

[95] CAR 1968, r.2(2)(c). This may be after the 28-day period.

[96] Bail may be granted by the Crown Court (Supreme Court Act 1981, s.811(f) and (1A) to (1G), inserted by the Criminal Justice Act 1982, s.291) or the Court of Appeal (Criminal Division) (Criminal Appeal Act 1968, s.19, as substituted by the 1982 Act, s.29(2)(b)). See *Practice Direction (Crown Court: Bail Pending Appeal)* [1983] 1 W.L.R. 1292.

[97] *ibid.* s.22. He or she is entitled to be present except in four cases where the leave of the court is necessary: (1) the appeal is on a point of law alone; (2) for an application for leave to appeal; (3) for an ancillary application; (4) where he or she is in custody after a verdict of not

If it appears to the Registrar of Criminal Appeals that the notice of appeal or application for leave to appeal does not show any substantial ground he or she may refer the appeal or application to the court for summary determination, and the court, if it considers the appeal to be frivolous[98] or vexatious, may dismiss the appeal summarily.[99]

The defendant at the trial should be seen by his or her solicitor and counsel in the event of conviction or sentence and advised on whether there appear to be reasonable grounds for an appeal.[1] The defendant may only pursue an appeal under sections 1 and 2 of the 1968 Act once, even where he or she seeks to adduce fresh evidence on the second occasion.[2] An appeal abates on the death of the appellant.[3] If the accused has pleaded guilty he will only be able to pursue an appeal against conviction if his plea was a result of a ruling which was erroneous and left him with no legal escape from a verdict of guilty. If the ruling of the judge was such as to lead to the admission of damaging evidence against the accused, and he or she pleaded guilty recognising the case was hopeless, the plea would be treated as an acknowledgement of the truth of the facts.[4]

Applications for leave to appeal are normally dealt with by a single judge who examines the papers and may grant leave, refuse it, or refer the case to the court.[5] If leave is refused an application may be renewed to the court within 14 days.[6] The court will hold a hearing, which may be combined with

---

guilty by reason of insanity or of a finding of disability. There is no right for the appellant to be present: *Monnell and Morris v. U.K.* (1987) 10 E.H.R.R. 205.

[98] *e.g.* the ground of appeal could not possibly succeed on argument: *R. v. Taylor* [1979] Crim.L.R. 649.

[99] Criminal Appeal Act 1968, s.20, as substituted by the Criminal Justice Act 1988, s.157. The original form of s.20 made this procedure available only in respect of appeals involving a question of law alone. The Auld Report recommends that judges should be empowered, when considering applications for leave, to give procedural directions for the hearing of the appeal (Chap. 12, para. 75).

[1] *Guide to Proceedings in the Court of Appeal Criminal Division* (1997). See also M. Zander, [1972] Crim.L.R. 132, [1975] Crim.L.R. 364 and *Practice Note* [1974] 2 All E.R. 805. The RCCJ was very critical of the quality of legal advice given at this stage, and the arrangements for access to advice from prison: Cm. 2263, pp. 164–167, based on J. Plotnikoff and R. Woolfson, *Information and Advice for Prisoners about Grounds for Appeal and the Appeals Process* (RCCI Research Study No.18, 1993).

[2] *R. v. Pinfold* [1988] Q.B. 462; *R. v. Berry* [1991] 1 W.L.R. 125: there are two apparent exceptions: where the decision on the original appeal is a nullity and where, owing to some defect in procedure, the appellant on the first appeal being dismissed suffered an injustice, (*e.g.* the appellant has not been notified of the hearing of the appeal, or counsel has been unable to attend (*ibid.*.)). A case may also be referred back to the Court of Appeal by the Criminal Cases Review Commission (a power previously exercised by the Home Secretary), see below, para. 18-018.

[3] *R. v. Kearley (No.2)* [1994] 2 A.C. 414. *cf. R. v. Hawkins* [1997] Crim. L.R. 134, and commentary. The appeal may be continued with the approval of the Court of Appeal under s. 44A of the Criminal Appeal Act 1968, as inserted by s. 7(1) of the Criminal Appeal Act 1995. See, *e.g. R. v. Whelan* [1997] Crim. L.R. 659 (widow seeking to pursue deceased husband's appeal against sexual offence convictions).

[4] *R. v. Kennedy* [1998] Crim. L.R. 739, *R. v. Chalkley and Jeffries* [1998] 2 All. E.R. 155.

[5] On the difficulties in achieving this preparation see Auld Report (2001), Chap.12, paras 79–86. The average waiting time for an appeal has fallen dramatically and is now between eight and nine months: Auld, Chap.12, para. 80.

[6] See *Practice Direction* [1999] All E.R. 669 requiring section arguments to be lodged within 14 days. An extension to the initial 28-day period will readily be granted if reasonable grounds are shown; however, the time limit of 14 days for a renewal application will be enforced strictly and only extended in exceptional circumstances: *R. v. Towers* (1984) 30 Cr.App.R.

the hearing of the appeal on the merits. Legal aid may be granted for further advice and assistance and for representation before the single judge or the court.[7] The single judge and the court have power, when refusing an application for leave to appeal, to direct that part of the time during which a person has been in custody after lodging his application should not count towards sentence.[8] In both 1970 and 1980 the then Lord Chief Justice issued a reminder of the existence of this power in view of the delay caused to the hearing of meritorious appeals by the lodging of huge numbers of hopeless applications.[9] In the two years after 1970 the number of applications for leave to appeal was cut by a half, although the problem subsequently recurred. In the 1980 Direction, it was stated a direction for loss of time "will normally be made unless the grounds are not only settled and signed by counsel, but also supported by the written opinion of counsel". Counsel should only so act where he or she considers that the proposed appeal is properly arguable. Moreover, a direction will also normally be made where an application is renewed to the court after the single judge has refused it as wholly devoid of merit: here, whether or not the grounds have been settled and signed by counsel.[10] The European Court has accepted this practice.[11]

The administrative tasks in relation to appeals are performed by the Criminal Appeal Office, headed by the Registrar of Criminal Appeals. The documents in the case, including, if appropriate, a transcript, are assembled by the office.[12] As a matter of practice, skeleton arguments must be lodged with the Registrar and served on the prosecuting authority within 14 days of receipt by the advocate of leave. Similarly the skeleton argument of the prosecuting advocate must be lodged within 14 days.[13] If leave is granted, a lawyer on the staff of the office then prepares a descriptive "summary" of the facts and grounds of appeal to assist the full court. This should usually be available to counsel.[14] There is no automatic right for a convicted appellant to be present at the appeal, and no such right is expressed in the ECHR.[15] Equally, the European Court has accepted that appeals on points of law can occur in private.[16]

The Auld Report recommends that academic lawyers should be able to sit

231.

[7] See on the grant of legal aid para 14-086 above. On the obligation to comply with Article 6, see the decisions of the European Court in *Grainger v. U.K.* (1990) 12 E.H.R.R. 469; *Maxwell v. U.K.* (1994) 19 E.H.R.R. 197.

[8] Criminal Appeal Act 1968, s.291, as amended by the Criminal Justice Act 1988, Sched. 15, para. 27. Thus a direction may not be made if leave is granted, or where there is a certificate under ss.l or 11(1A) of the 1968 Act, or s.81(lB) of the Supreme Court Act 1981. Auld recommends amendment to the present composition of the Court of Appeal so that it is not always necessary for a Lord Justice of Appeal to sit, and in straightforward appeals, the court should comprise two High Court judges and one Circuit judge: Chap.12, para. 94.

[9] Lord Parker C.J., (1970) 54 Cr.App.R. 280; Lord Widgery C.J., (1980) 70 Cr.App.R. 186.

[10] *R. v. Gayle, The Times*, May 28, 1986.

[11] *Monnell and Morris v. U.K.* (1987) 10 E.H.R.R. 205.

[12] Criminal Appeal Act 1968, s.32; CAR, rr. 18–20. The Registrar may determine that only a "short transcript" is necessary, covering charges, pleas, summing-up and evidence after verdict. The appellant here may obtain a full transcript at his or her own expense. In practice, a transcript of evidence is rarely needed: *R. v. Campbell, The Times*, July 21, 1981.

[13] See *Practice Note* [1999] 1 All E.R. 669.

[14] *Practice Direction (CA) (Criminal Division) (Criminal Appeal Office Summaries), The Times*, October 7, 1992.

[15] *cf. Werner v. Austria* (1998) 26 E.H.R.R. 310; *Prinz v. Austria* February 8, 2000.

[16] *Axen v. Germany* (1983) 6 E.H.R.R. 195; *cf. Ekbatani v. Sweden* (1988) 13 E.H.R.R/ 504.

as ad hoc judges of the court or to supply written briefs to the court or points of law.[17] The Report also calls for measures to allow the Court of Appeal to "slow down" to allow more time for preparation and judgment writing.[18]

(2) *Evidence.*[19] The court, under section 23(1) and (3) of the Criminal Appeal Act 1968[20], *may* "if they think it necessary or expedient in the interests of justice": (a) order the production of any document, exhibit or other thing connected with the proceedings; (b) order the examination of any witness who would have been a compellable witness at the trial, whether or not he or she was called; and (c) receive any evidence which was not adduced in the proceedings from which the appeal lies.[21]   **18–012**

In considering whether to receive any evidence, the Court of Appeal must have regard in particular to

"(a) whether the evidence appears to the court to be capable of belief;
 (b) whether it appears to the court that the evidence may afford any ground for allowing the appeal;
 (c) whether the evidence would have been admissible in the proceedings from which the appeal lies on an issue which is the subject of the appeal[22]; and
 (d) whether there is a reasonable explanation for the failure to adduce the evidence in those proceedings".[23]

Between 1966 and 1995, section 23(2) of the 1968 Act provided for a *duty* of the court to receive evidence which was "likely to be credible", and which would have been admissible his the proceedings from which the appeal lay on an issue which was the subject of the appeal, and the court was satisfied that there was a reasonable explanation for the failure to adduce it at trial. The RCCJ thought that the "likely to be credible" test, which was interpreted as "evidence well capable of belief",[24] imposed too high a threshold.[25]

---

[17] Chap. 12, para. 89.

[18] Chap. 12, para. 95.

[19] See R. Pattenden, *Judicial Discretion and Criminal Litigation* (2nd ed., 1990), pp. 355–358.

[20] As amended by the Criminal Appeal Act 1995, s.41.

[21] The court may examine such material as it thinks fit in deciding whether to order production of documents or the attendance of witnesses at the hearing of the appeal; it is not confined to material relating to the trial and the documents placed before the court by the parties: *R. v. Callaghan* [1988] 1 W.L.R. 1, a pre-appeal review in the Birmingham pub bombers' case. The appellants sought to prevent the judges reading documents relating to other litigation and police inquiries arising out of the case, unless raised by the parties; the court held that its jurisdiction was not so confined, but acceded to the appellants' request in the exercise of its discretion. See also *Callaghan v. U.K.* (1989) 60 D.R. 296.

[22] *i.e.* the issue must have been raised first at the trial: *R. v. Melville* [1976] 1 W.L.R. 181.

[23] 1968 Act, s.23(2), as substituted by the Criminal Appeal Act 1995, s.41. Under (d) the test is whether evidence could with "reasonable diligence" have been obtained for use at the trial: *R. v. Beresford* (1971) 56 Cr.App.R. 143: B had failed to mention his presence at the "Poco a Poco Club" until he sought leave to introduce an alibi witness on the appeal. The court held that he had not used reasonable diligence and in any event disbelieved the witness. See also *R. v. Haynes* [2002] EWCA Crim. 1855.

[24] *per* Edmund Davies L.J. in *R. v. Stafford and Luvaglio* (1968) 53 Cr.App.R.1 at 3.

[25] Cm. 2263. p. 174.

In *R. v. Lattimore and others*[26] the Court of Appeal emphasised that the conditions limiting the old section 23(2) duty were not to be read as limiting the discretion under section 23(1).[27] This case arose out of the killing of Maxwell Confait, which was shortly followed by a fire at the house where he lived. Two youths were convicted of killing him (one for murder, one manslaughter) and those two and another were convicted of arson, solely on the basis of their own confessions. Three years later the Home Secretary referred the cases to the Court of Appeal (Criminal Division).[28] The court, acting under section 23(1), received the evidence of three expert witnesses who had given evidence at the trial (two fire experts and a pathologist) and two further medical witnesses who gave evidence as to the time of death. However, they refused to admit evidence of persons who sought to throw light on the killer's identity, as they doubted its credibility and admissibility and in any event did not need to rely upon it. In addition, the Crown was permitted to call a fire expert and a forensic pathologist who had given evidence at the trial. The court held that this evidence showed that the lapse of time between the killing and the fire was much greater than had originally been thought and it threw sufficient doubt on the confessions for the homicide and arson convictions to be quashed. Scarman L.J. stated that the medical evidence was presented to the Court of Appeal "in a much sharper focus than it was at the trial".[29] In other cases under the original version of section 23 fresh evidence was admitted where another person confessed to the crime for which the appellant was convicted,[30] where prosecution witnesses subsequently made statements inconsistent with their testimony[31] or had subsequently been found to have fabricated confessions attributed to suspects in other cases,[32] and where it was claimed that there was an irregularity at the trial.[33] Exceptionally, fresh evidence could be admitted following an unequivocal plea of guilty,[34] or where an arguable line of

---

[26] (1975) 62 Cr.App.R. 53.

[27] *ibid.* p. 56.

[28] See below, para. 18-018.

[29] (1975) 62 Cr. App. R. 53 at 60. The events were subsequently the subject of an Inquiry by Sir Henry Fisher: 1977–78 H.C. 90, which concluded that "on a balance of probabilities" all three were involved in the arson and that two (excluding one of the two originally convicted for it) were involved in the killing. The report made a number of recommendations concerning the interrogation process and other aspects of the case.

[30] *R. v. Ditch* (1969) 53 Cr. App. R. 627.

[31] *R. v. Conway* (1979) 70 Cr. App. R. 4.

[32] *R. v. Williams, The Times,* January 27, 1994.

[33] *R. v. Leggett and others* (1969) 53 Cr. App. R. 51: interruptions by the Chairman of Quarter Sessions (*e.g.* when it appeared that an address by counsel to the jury would be protracted "he observed in a loud voice, 'Oh, God,' and then laid his head across his arm and made groaning noises": p. 56). Appeal dismissed.

[34] *R. v. Lee (Bruce)* [1984] 1 W.L.R. 578; *R. v. Foster* [1985] Q.B. 115 (F. had received a free pardon for offences of which another had now been convicted); *R. v. Swain* [1986] Crim. L.R. 480 (evidence that there was a risk that D's mind was affected by LSD when he changed his plea to guilty).

defence was not pursued at trial.[35] As Lord Bingham C.J. emphasised recently, there is "a crucial obligation on a defendant in a criminal case to advance his whole defence and any evidence on which he relies before the jury trial. He is not entitled to hold evidence in reserve and then seek to introduce it on appeal following conviction."[36]

Under the current version of section 23, the discretion under section 23(1) is now structured by reference to the conditions set out in subsection (2) and there is no longer a *duty* to receive evidence in specified circumstances. However, it will be noted that the court ultimately retains a discretion to receive evidence even where there is no reasonable explanation for the lack of adduction at trial. The RCCJ urged "that in general the court should take a broad, rather than a narrow, approach" to their powers to receive evidence.[37] The appellant has a right to be present when issues of fact are decided by the Court of Appeal. This is supported by the European Court's interpretation of Article 6.[38]

(3) Disposition. Section 2 of the Criminal Appeal Act 1968 as originally **18–013** enacted provided that:

"2(1)—Except as provided by this Act, the Court of Appeal shall allow an appeal against conviction if they think—

(a) that the verdict of the jury should be set aside on the ground that under the circumstances of the case it is unsafe or unsatisfactory; or

(b) that the judgment of the court of trial should be set aside on the ground of a wrong decision of any question of law; or

(c) that there was a material irregularity in the course of the trial, and in any other case shall dismiss the appeal:

Provided that the Court may, notwithstanding that they are of the opinion that the point raised in the appeal might be decided in favour of the appellant, dismiss the appeal if they consider that no miscarriage of justice has actually occurred.

(2) In the case of an appeal against conviction the Court shall, if they allow the appeal, quash the conviction."

These grounds for intervention were somewhat wider than those that were open to the Court of Criminal Appeal under the Criminal Appeal Act

---

[35] *R. v. Ahluwalia* [1992] 4 All E.R. 889. The court did, however, emphasise that it required much persuasion to allow a defence to be raised for the first time on appeal if the option had been exercised at trial not to pursue it; here a contemporary report on D stated that she suffered from "endogenous depression" at the time she killed her husband: D was not consulted about the report and it was unclear why it had not been pursued as the basis of a diminished responsibility defence. The court ordered a retrial.

[36] *R. v. Jones* [1997] 1 Cr. App. R. 86 at 93; see also *R. v. Borthwick* [1998] Crim. L.R. 274.

[37] Cm. 2263, p. 174.

[38] *Ektabani v. Sweden* (1988) 13 E.H.R.R. 504; *Pelissier v. France* (2000) 30 E.H.R.R. 715. For consideration of whether English law complies see Strange (2001), p.241.

1907.[39] The RCCJ criticised the drafting of section 2 as "confusing".[40] For example, the grounds overlapped in that an error of law or an irregularity at trial might cause the court to think that the original conviction was unsafe or unsatisfactory; it was doubtful whether there was any difference between "unsafe" and "unsatisfactory"; the wording of the proviso appeared difficult to reconcile with (a) and (b). Accordingly, they recommended (by a majority) that section 2 be redrafted to provide a single broad ground of appeal, that a conviction "is or may be unsafe". If it was unsafe, the appeal would be allowed outright; if it might be, the conviction would be quashed and (normally) a retrial ordered.

Section 2 now provides that

"(1) Subject to the provisions of this Act, the Court of Appeal—

(a) shall allow an appeal against conviction if they think that the conviction is unsafe; and

(b) shall dismiss such an appeal in any other case."

Under the original version of section 2, verdicts were set aside as unsafe and unsatisfactory where, for example, there had been a misdirection as to the ingredients of the offence charged or the burden of proof, the judge had improperly withdrawn an issue from the jury or failed to put a line of defence to them, evidence was wrongfully admitted or excluded or, exceptionally, where counsel's decision not to call the defendant "was taken either in defiance of or without proper instructions, or when all the promptings of reason and good sense pointed the other way".[41] Decisions on some of these points could also amount to a wrong decision on a point of law under section 2(1)(b). The "material irregularity" ground in section 2(1)(c) was designed to cover procedural irregularities,[42] although other defects were sometimes so described. Under this head the Court of Appeal could interfere with an exercise of discretion[43] by the judge where he or she had "erred in principle or there is no material on which he could properly

---

[39] The court could allow an appeal if they thought that the verdict was unreasonable, or could not be supported by the evidence or otherwise there was an error of law or a miscarriage of justice. The wider grounds were first enacted in the Criminal Appeal Act 1966.

[40] Cm. 2263, pp. 167–169. See also R. J. Buxton, (1993) 109 L.Q.R. 66.

[41] *R. v. Clinton* [1993] 4 All E.R. 998 at 1005. The question was not the extent of counsel's ineptitude but the effect on the trial according to the (then) terms of the 1968 Act, s.2(1)(a). *Cf. R. v. Goutam* [1988] Crim. L.R. 109 and *R. v. Ensor* [1989] 1 W.L.R. 497, discussed in *Clinton*. In suggesting in *Ensor* that the court would only intervene in cases of "flagrantly incompetent advocacy", the court was only giving "general guidelines" as to the correct approach and was not intending to derogate from the wording of s.2(1)(a). There remains confusion over whether the test is based solely on the effect of counsel's errors on the fairness of the trial and the safety of the conviction, or whether it is necessary also to demonstrate "flagrant incompetence" (*R. v. Donnelly* [1998] Crim. L.R. 131) or "*Wednesbury— unreasonableness*" (*R. v. Ullah* [2000] 1 Cr. App. R. 351). See recently *Boodram v. The State* [2002] Crim. L.R. and commentary and *R. v. Nangle* [2001] Crim. L.R. 506. See also the Bar Council guidance on such appeals.

[42] *per* Lord Salmon in *DPP v. Shannon* [1975] A.C. 717 at 773.

[43] *e.g.* to sever counts in an indictment, to permit cross-examination of a defendant on his or her previous convictions or to discharge a jury.

have arrived at his decision",[44] or the court thought that the judge's ruling might have resulted in injustice to the defendant.[45]

The approach to section 2(1)(a) was described as follows by Widgery L.J. in *R. v. Cooper*[46]:

> "[I]n cases of this kind the court must in the end ask itself a subjective question, whether we are content to let the matter stand as it is, or whether there is not some lurking doubt in our minds which makes us wonder whether an injustice has been done. This is a reaction which may not be based strictly on the evidence as such; it is a reaction which can be produced by the general feel of the case as the court experiences it."

Indeed, a conviction could be quashed as unsafe and unsatisfactory where the specific grounds of appeal were rejected.[47]

The new single ground of appeal was criticised for covering only part of one of the original grounds specified in section 2[48] Parliament was assured by the Home Secretary that   **18–014**

> "in substance it restates the existing practice of the Court of Appeal and I am pleased to note that the Lord Chief Justice has already welcomed it."[49]

According to the Minister of State, the Lord Chief Justice and the senior judiciary believed that "the new test re-states the existing practice of the Court of Appeal".[50] Accordingly, the RCCJ's unanimous view that the Court of Appeal "should be readier to overturn jury verdicts that it has shown itself to be in the past"[51] does not appear to have been reflected in the new drafting of section 2,[52] although it may find its way into the court's approach in practice.[53] The change of statutory wording has generated a number of appeals, created unnecessary confusion in the law, but has,

---

[44] Devlin J. in *R. v. Cook* (1959) 43 Cr.App.R. 138 at 147.

[45] *R. v. McCann* (1991) 92 Cr.App.R. 239: the court held that the trial judge should have ordered a retrial of the three charged with conspiracy to murder Mr Tom King, following public statements made by Mr King and Lord Denning concerning the proposal to change the law on the right to silence.

[46] [1969] 1 Q.B. 267 at 271. The case was one of alleged mistaken identification and another man of similar appearance had admitted to a witness that he had committed the crime: even though all the evidence had been before the jury, the conviction was quashed. For other examples of "lurking doubts" see *R. v. Pattinson* (1973) 58 Cr.App.R. 417; *R. v. Spencer* [1987] A.C. 128.

[47] *R. v. Bracewell* (1978) 68 Cr.App.R. 44.

[48] See Sir John Smith, [1995]1 Crim. L.R. 920 at 923–925.

[49] Vol. 256, H. C. Deb. col. 24 March 6, 1995, cited by Smith, *op.cit.*

[50] Standing Committee B, March 21, 1995, col. 26, cited by Smith, *op.cit.*

[51] Cm. 2263, p. 162.

[52] The words "or may be" in the RCCJ's recommendation for s.2 were thought by some to send this signal; however, given that a conviction is "unsafe" if there is merely a "lurking doubt" (see above), it is difficult to see what of substance was added by those words: see Smith, *op.cit.* n.48 above, pp. 921–922.

[53] The RCCJ's wish to see a broader approach to incompetent advocacy, noting that a conviction may be unsafe even where incompetence is not "flagrant" (Cm. 2263, p. 174) was already to be reflected in the Court of Appeal decision in *R. v. Clinton* (above, p. para. 18-013, n.41).

finally, been accepted as producing no change to the Court of Appeal's practice.[54]

It was recognised in *R. v. Graham (H.K.)*[55] that the new section required the court to focus on the sole question of whether the conviction was "safe". There could not be a safe conviction if the defendant was not correctly convicted of the offence charged, irrespective of whether he would have been convicted of another offence.

One of the most controversial aspects of the new wording of section 2 was whether a conviction could be regarded as unsafe despite their being little doubt as to the accused's guilt. This problem arises in a number of cases, usually where there has been some procedural error or impropriety. The Court of Appeal initially took the view that there was no opportunity to quash a conviction as unsafe on the grounds of procedural irregularity.[56] Subsequently, the Court of Appeal has rejected this view, favouring a wide interpretation of section 2 so that a conviction could be regarded as unsafe on grounds unrelated to the issue of guilt.[57] This broader ground takes the position almost back to the pre-1995 law.[58]

Two further factors have complicated the controversy. First, the courts re-examined the principle that an appeal could be successful following a plea of guilty. In *R. v. Chalkley and Jeffries*,[59] the Court held that a conviction should not be treated as unsafe simply because the defendant had pleaded guilty following a ruling from the trial judge on a point of law, unless the ruling was erroneous and left the accused with no possibility of an acquittal.[60] It seems therefore that if the accused's plea of guilty is made in the face of a ruling which does not completely deny him the opportunity to deny the charge, he will be precluded from relying on the Court of Appeal to quash his conviction following a subsequent guilty plea.[61]

The second complicating factor has been the influence of the ECHR jurisprudence on Article 6, particularly following the enactment of the Human Rights Act 1998. Article 6 guarantees a fair trial in the determination of a criminal charge, and this includes appeals. After much confusion, the House of Lords has now confirmed that any conviction which involves a breach of Article 6 must also be unsafe.[62] It has been accepted, however, in line with ECHR rulings,[63] that the Court of Appeal's examination of the evidence in the case may be sufficient to cure the defect of the trial, thereby rendering the proceedings as a whole "fair".[64]

---

[54] On the difficulties of the unified ground of appeal see *Auld Report* (2001), Chap.12, para. 8–10, where it is recommended that the term should be clarified to make clear that it deals also with procedural impropriety. The tests for appeals against conviction and sentence would be the same for every level of court and would be based on the existing Court of Appeal process.

[55] [1997] 1 Cr. App. R. 302.

[56] *R. v. Chalkley and Jeffries* [1998] 2 Cr. App. R. 79; *R. v. Callaghan* [1999] 5 Arch. News 2.

[57] *R. v. Mullen* [1999] 2 Cr.App.R. 143; *R. v. Togher* [2001] 3 All E.R. 463.

[58] See the detailed analysis by A. Clarke, [1999] Crim. L.R. 108.

[59] [1998] 2 Cr. App.R. 79.

[60] This was followed in *R. v. Togher* [2001] 3 All E.R. 463.

[61] See also *R. v. Rajcoomar* [1999] Crim. L.R. 728; *R. v. Thomas* [2000] 1 Cr. App. R. 447; *cf.* H. Blaxland, [1999] 2 Arch. News.

[62] *R. v. A.* [2001] UKHL 25; *R .v. Forbes* [2001] 1 A.C. 473

[63] See *Edwards v. U.K.* (1992) 15 E.H.R.R. 417.

[64] See *R. v. Craven* [2001] Crim. L.R. 464 and commentary.

In addition, some of the rights guaranteed by Article 6 have been accepted as conferring separate guarantees such as the right to a trial within a reasonable time. If these rights are breached, the conviction should be treated as safe if founded on an otherwise procedurally proper trial.[65] The defendant should be granted a "remedy" by way of reduction of sentence, unless the delay was such as to render the trial unfair.

The 1995 version of section 2 and the challenges to trial procedures based on Article 6 arguments have also caused the courts to reconsider the "lurking doubt" test adopted in *R. v. Cooper* (above).[66]

Where fresh evidence is admitted, the question for the court is still whether in the light of the evidence overall, the verdict is unsafe (formerly, unsafe and unsatisfactory[67]). This point was made by the House of Lords in *Stafford v. DPP*.[68] After referring to the concept of the "lurking doubt" mentioned in *R. v. Cooper*[69] Viscount Dilhorne continued, "That this is the effect of section 2(1)(a) is not to be doubted",[70] although he also emphasised that the Court of Appeal should not place any fetter or restriction on its power under section 2. The court was not bound to ask in a case where new evidence was admitted whether that evidence "might ... have led to the jury returning a verdict of not guilty?": if it was satisfied that there was no reasonable doubt about the guilt of the accused the conviction should not be quashed even though the jury might have come to a different view. The House of Lords has confirmed that the "lurking doubt" test and the decision of the House in *Stafford v. DPP* still stand after the Human Rights Act 1998.[71]

This approach to "fresh evidence" cases has been roundly criticised by Lord Devlin[72] on the basis that it is wrong in principle for judges rather than juries to determine whether the appellant is guilty; the proper course of action where the fresh evidence *could* have made a difference to the verdict[73] would be for the court to order a new trial.[74] The first verdict should be regarded as unsatisfactory simply on the ground that it was not given upon the whole of the evidence.[75] Given that the appeal in *Stafford v. DPP* was

---

[65] See *Darmalingum v. The State* [2000] 2 Cr. App. R. 445; *cf. Flowers v. R.* [2000] 1 W.L.R. 2396, *Attorney-General's Reference (No. 2 of 2001)* [2001] 1 W.L.R. 1869.

[66] The courts had originally held that following the 1995 Act, the "lurking doubt" test was no longer appropriate: *R. v. F.* [1999] Crim. L.R. 306 and commentary.

[67] The fresh evidence would not reveal an error of law or constitute a "material irregularity" under s.2(1)(b) and (c) of the Criminal Appeal Act 1968 as originally drafted.

[68] [1974] A.C. 878. Followed in *R. v. Callaghan* (1988) 88 Cr.App.R. 40 (the first reference to the Court of Appeal in the Birmingham pub bombing case); *R. v. Byrne* (1988) 88 Cr.App.R. 33.

[69] Above.

[70] [1974] A.C. p. 892.

[71] The House of Lords in *R. v. Pendleton* [2002] 1 W.L.R. 72 ruled that the Court of Appeal should be careful to avoid trying to stand in the shoes of the jury, but that it is useful for the Court of Appeal to ask whether if the new evidence had been given at trial, it might reasonably have affected the decision of the jury. See also *R. v. Hakala* [2002] Crim. L.R. (July).

[72] *The Judge* (1979), pp. 133–135, 148–176.

[73] This was in effect the same test as that for applying the proviso: see *Stirland v. DPP* (1944) 30 Cr.App.R. 40 at 46–47.

[74] See below, para. 18-015. Indeed, until 1989 the court could only order a new trial in fresh evidence cases.

[75] See counsel's argument in *Stafford v. DPP* [1974] A.C. 878 at 884C. See also *R. v. Craven* [2001] Crim. L.R. 464.

dismissed, the appellants were thereafter imprisoned on the basis of the verdict of the judges.

Given that the matter is to be tested by reference to the views of the appeal court judges rather than the views of a hypothetical jury, a further question arises whether that is so in all fresh evidence cases. In particular, should the judges determine issues as to whether the oral testimony of a new or re-examined witness is credible?[76] In a number of cases the court has ordered a new trial,[77] but in *R. v. Cooper and McMahon*[78] the court determined such a question itself. The case is one of the most publicised examples of a miscarriage of justice, and came before the Court of Appeal on no less than five occasions. Three men, Cooper, McMahon and Murphy, were convicted of the murder of a Luton subpostmaster during an unsuccessful robbery. They were identified by a professional criminal, Mathews, who admitted taking part in the robbery but denied involvement in the murder. He turned Queen's evidence and the men were convicted solely on his testimony. They appealed without success to the Court of Appeal. Mathews subsequently received part of the reward offered by the Post Office. In 1973 Murphy's conviction was quashed by the Court of Appeal following the discovery of a fresh alibi witness. This naturally threw doubt on Mathews' identification of Cooper and McMahon and the Home Secretary referred the case to the Court of Appeal on three further occasions. On the first of these in 1975, the court refused to permit Mathews to be recalled for further cross-examination, indicated that the jury "could" have acquitted Murphy and convicted the others, and dismissed the appeal. The court refused leave to appeal to the House of Lords, reaffirming that in the light of *Stafford v. DPP*[79] it was "not a necessary function of this Court, when considering fresh evidence, to evaluate the effect which it would have on the jury at the trial".[80] On the second, in 1976, Mathews was recalled and cross-examined: the judges concluded from their observations that he was telling the truth on the "vital part of his story" although other parts were discredited (a "cock and bull story"). This self-evidently surprising result did not inspire confidence in trial (or at least partial trial) by judges alone. The final reference by the Home Secretary (of the case of McMahon alone) was unsuccessful on the ground that the fresh alibi evidence sought to be tendered was not likely to be credible, and even if believed would be insufficient to afford a ground for allowing the appeal.[81] In 1980, following the publication of a book on the case edited by Ludovic Kennedy (*Wicked Beyond Belief*), the Home Secretary, William Whitelaw, ordered the release of Cooper and McMahon[82]: the case was "wholly exceptional" and there was a "widely felt sense of unease about it" which he shared. He was not to be taken as criticising his predecessors, who had "acted with scrupulous regard to the constitutional conventions in referring each piece of alleged new evidence to the Court of Appeal and in acting in accordance with the

---

[76] The test for admissibility is merely whether the fresh evidence is capable of belief: see above, para 18-012.

[77] See Devlin (1979), pp. 165–166.

[78] See Devlin (1979), pp. 166–173; L. Kennedy (ed) *Wicked Beyond Belief* (1980).

[79] [1974] A.C. 878.

[80] (1975) 61 Cr.App.R. 215.

[81] *R. v. McMahon* (1978) 68 Cr.App.R. 18: criticised in Kennedy (1980), pp. 132–135.

[82] Written Answer, H. C. Deb. Vol. 988, cols. 719–720, July 18, 1980.

court's judgment. Any general departure from that rule would clearly be disastrous." His action was not to be taken as a precedent.

The RCCJ[83] endorsed Lord Devlin's criticism insofar as it concerned a decision by the court to hear and evaluate itself the fresh evidence and despite it to reject the appeal. In their view, the proper approach once the court has decided to receive fresh evidence that is relevant and capable of belief, and which could have affected the outcome of the case, is that it should quash the conviction and order a retrial. However, if a retrial was not practicable or desirable, the court should decide the matter itself in accordance with *Stafford*, and not simply allow the appeal automatically. The Criminal Appeal Act 1995 did not address this question.

A further problem in determining the safety of a conviction is that the Court of Appeal is now faced with an increasing number of appeals from convictions of many years standing. The Court has decided that in conducting the appeal, the present law of evidence and procedure should be applied to the case (including major changes in suspect protection such as PACE) but that the substantive criminal law should remain as at the time of the conviction.[84] This presents problems where the law has made radical changes regarding, *e.g.* identification evidence, disclosure, character evidence, etc. It also creates anomalies because changes in legal attitude to offences are ignored whilst changes to procedure are taken into account. As Sir John Smith has pointed out, there is a danger that the courts will be swamped with applications from cases in which convictions were perfectly proper at the time.[85] The Court of Appeal has resisted some attempts to challenge convictions on this basis.[86]

The *Auld Report* has recommended that when hearing appeals on a reference from the Criminal Cases Review Commission, the Court of Appeal should apply the law in force at the time of conviction/sentence.[87]

The Human Rights Act introduced further difficulties with arguments arising as to its potential retrospectivity.[88] The House of Lords has confirmed that the Human Rights Act does not permit an appellant to make a retrospective challenge to a decision which was lawfully correct at the time but which would be regarded as breaking the 1998 Act.[89] In addition the Human Rights Act 1998 raised the question of whether the Court of Appeal

---

[83] Cm. 2263, p. 175.

[84] See *R. v. O'Brien* [2000] Crim. L.R. 676; *R. v. Bentley* [1999] Crim. L.R. 330; *R. v. King* [2000] Crim. L.R. 835.

[85] See commentary on *R. v. Bentley* [1999] Crim. L.R. 330 at 331 and *R. v. Johnson* [2001] Crim L.R. 125.

[86] See for example Rose L.J. expressing surprise that a case had been referred by the CCRC without new evidence, on the basis of changes to the law relating to legal advice in police stations: *R. v. Gerald* [1999] Crim. L.R. 315.

[87] Chap. 12, para. 106.

[88] See K. Kerrigan [2000] Crim. L.R. 71.

[89] *R. v. Lambert* [2001] 3 W.L.R. 206. The majority held that an appellant could not rely on the provisions of Sched. 1 of the the Human Rights Act 1998 in respect of a conviction before the Act came into force. In *R. v. Kansal (No.2)* [2001] UKHL 6, the House confirmed this approach although doubting the reasoning in *Lambert*, which had been 'decided only months before. The House of Lords in *Kansal (No. 2)* held that the Human Rights Act 1998 would not apply to an appellant who had been tried before the Act came into force, even if the appeal was occurring after the Act was in force. See also *R. v. Benjafield* [2002] UKHL 2 in which the House of Lords confirmed that the Human Rights Act 1998 would not apply to an appeal against a confiscation order imposed before October 2, 2000.

can remedy defects in the trial procedure. Since Article 6 of the ECHR applies to the whole of the criminal proceedings, it is accepted that in some circumstances the Court of Appeal's scrutiny of a piece of evidence will be sufficient to cure a defect at trial.[90] The Court usually gives reason for its decision, bit it can decline to do so where the public interest demands secrecy.[90a]

As alternatives to quashing a conviction, other possibilities that may be open to the Court of Appeal are the substitution of a conviction for an alternative offence, where the jury would have found the defendant guilty of that offence and it appears to the court that the jury must have been satisfied of facts which proved him or her guilty of it,[91] and the substitution of a finding of insanity or of unfitness to plead.[92]

Ultimately, the Court of Appeal's task is a difficult one in which it must strive to direct the law and offer coherent precedent for the trial courts whilst at the same time being prepared to rectify errors in the trial process without jeopardising the finality of the system.[93]

18–015 (4) *New Trials.* Where the Court of Appeal allows an appeal against conviction, it may order that the appellant be retried where it appears that this is required by the interests of justice.[94] The appellant may only be retried for the offence in respect of which the appeal was allowed, an offence of which he or she could have been convicted at the original trial on an indictment for that offence or an offence charged in an alternative count of the indictment at the trial on which the jury were discharged from giving a verdict.[95]

Prior to the amendment made by section 43 of the Criminal Justice Act 1988, the Court of Appeal could only order a retrial where fresh evidence

---

[90] See, *e.g. Edwards v. U.K.* (1992) 15 E.H.R.R. 417; *cf. Condron v. U.K.* (2000) 31 E.H.R.R.

[90a] *R. v. Doubtfire* [2001] 2 Cr. App. R. 209 (secrecy of information involved).

[91] Criminal Appeal Act 1968, s.3. The sentence may not be higher than that originally passed; *Archbold* (2002) para. 7–106. The power is a discretionary one: *R. v. Peterson* [1997] Crim. L.R. 339. The court may substitute a conviction for manslaughter on the grounds of diminished responsibility on an appeal against a conviction for murder, even where the defence was not raised before the jury: *R. v. Weekes* [1999] 2 Cr. App. R. 520. No substitution can occur where the appeal arises from a guilty plea: *R. v. Horsman* [1997] 2 Cr. App. R. 418; *R. v. Greene* [1997] Crim. L.R. 659. This power has produced particular difficulties in the wake of the House of Lords' decision in *R. v. Preddy* [1996] 3 W.L.R. 255. See especially *R. v. Graham* [1997] Crim. L.R. 340. It is not sufficient that the Court of Appeal is of the opinion that the defendant is guilty, on the facts found by the jury, of another equally serious offence, and on that basis that his original conviction can be upheld: *R. v. Graham* [1997] Crim. L.R. 340. The imposition of an alternative offence is not incompatible with Article 6 of the ECHR: *Pelissier v. France* (2000) 30 E.H.R.R. 715.

[92] Criminal Appeal Act 1968, s.6, Sched. 1.

[93] See K. Malleson, "Appeals Against Conviction and the Principle of Finality" in Field and Thomas (eds), *Justice and Efficiency? The Royal Commission on Criminal Justice* (1994). For criticism of the judiciary sitting in the Court of Appeal as to their awareness of the scope of their powers, see K. Malleson, *Review of the Appeal Process* (Research Study 17, 1993). For an analysis of the Court of Appeal's work in terms of due process and crime control modes (as used in Chaps.13 and 17 evaluations of the trial process) see S. Greer, "Miscarriages of Criminal Justice Reconsidered" (1994) 57 M.L.R. 58.

[94] 1968 Act, s.7(l), as amended by the Criminal Justice Act 1988, s.43(2). See Pattenden (1990), pp. 366–370. For the procedure on retrial see s.8 and Sched. 1. Any sentence passed after a retrial may not be longer than the original one.

[95] *ibid.*, s.7(2). For the analogous power to award a *venire de novo*, see below, para. 18-020. This can only be done where the original trial is a nullity.

was received under section 23 of the Criminal Appeal Act 1968.[96] This limitation was cogently criticised, and the case for its removal powerful.[97] In particular, in a number of cases where (1) the appellant appeared to have a good argument in law but little or none on the merits, but (2) the case was not suitable for an application of the proviso,[98] the Court of Appeal or House of Lords succumbed to the temptation to "bend" the law to enable the appeal to be dismissed. Justice appeared to be done in the case itself but at the expense of the development of the law in a consistent, coherent and principled way.[99] Unfortunately, the change can still be criticised as not going far enough,[1] in that the power does not extend to ordering a retrial for an offence which arises out of the same facts, but which is different from those charged in the original indictment. Such a power might well be necessary where there is a flaw in the indictment which is not so serious as to render the trial a nullity (in which case a *venire de novo* may be ordered). This could arise where the defendant is convicted of the wrong or a non-existent offence,[2] and the indictment contains no suitable alternative count. The omission was drawn to the Government's attention, but the position was defended on the basis that

> "It is one thing to legislate for the differing interpretations of the law by higher and lower courts, but quite another to build into the law the assumption that the prosecution will occasionally blunder. And in addition there might be difficulties in principle in conferring on the Court of Appeal what might appear to be a prosecutorial function if it was to have a role in specifying the charges on which a retrial could be based."[3]

A wider retrial power exists in Scotland.[4]

In ordering a retrial, considerations must include the question whether the accused can have a fair trial given the delay since the original trial[5] and to the danger that adverse publicity following the original conviction will render a fair retrial impossible.[6]

Where a retrial is ordered, arrangements must normally take place within two months.[7] Thereafter, if the prosecution wishes to proceed, it must apply to the Court of Appeal for leave; conversely, the defendant may apply to the Court of Appeal to set aside the retrial order and enter a verdict of acquittal of the offence for which he or she was ordered to be retried. On either application, the court may grant leave, but may only do so if it is satisfied that the prosecution has acted with due expedition, and that there is a good

---

[96] See above, para. 18-012.

[97] See the first edition of this book at pp. 712–714.

[98] See above.

[99] J. R. Spencer, "Criminal Law and Criminal Appeals" [1982] Crim.L.R. 260.

[1] J. R. Spencer, "Retrials and Tribulations" (1988) 138 N.L.J. 315.

[2] *e.g.* "anal rape": *R. v. Gaston* (1981) 73 Cr.App.R. 164, see now Criminal Justice and Public Order Act 1994, s.142.

[3] Home Office letter in response to Spencer: (1988) 138 N.L.J. 641.

[4] Criminal Procedure (Scotland) Act 1995, s.185.

[5] *R. v. Graham* [1997] 1 Cr. App. R. 302.

[6] *R. v. Stone* [2001] Crim. L.R. 465 (Subsequent retrial and reconvention for murder).

[7] As amended See *Archbold* (2002) para. 7–114. In *R. v. Kimber* [2001] Crim. L.R. 897, it was held that there could be an extension in exceptional cases.

and sufficient cause for a retrial in spite of the lapse of time since the retrial order was made.

There are many well established categories on which appeals are based.[8]

(ii) Appeals against sentence and reviews of sentencing

18–016 A person who has been convicted of an offence on indictment may appeal to the Court of Appeal (Criminal Division) against any sentence[9] passed on him or her for the offence, except where the sentence is fixed by law.[10] Leave to appeal must be obtained from the Court of Appeal, or the judge who passed the sentence must certify that the case is fit for appeal,[11] and the procedure is essentially the same as in appeals against conviction. The court, if it considers that the appellant should be sentenced differently, may quash any sentence or order which is the subject of the appeal and substitute any other sentence or order that it thinks appropriate, provided that it would have been within the jurisdiction of the court below. The appellant may not, however, be dealt with more severely than by the court below,[12] except that the court may bring a suspended sentence into effect.[13]

The court will interfere with an exercise of discretion as to sentence where the sentence is not justified by law, where matters are improperly taken into account or improperly ignored, where fresh matters are to be taken into account, or where the sentence is manifestly excessive or wrong in principle. One of the accepted functions of the Court of Appeal is that of laying down guidelines for sentencing.[14]

The court has the same powers to deal with sentences imposed in cases

---

[8] The most common grounds of appeal are examined in detail in *Archbold* (2002) Chap. 7.

[9] This includes any order made by the court when dealing with an offender including a hospital order under the Mental Health Act 1983, a recommendation for deportation, a confiscation order under the Drug Trafficking Act 1994 (other than one made by the High Court) or Part VI of the Criminal Justice Act 1988 (or variations thereof), a probation order or an absolute or conditional discharge: Criminal Appeal Act 1968, s.50, as amended. Apart from the orders expressly mentioned in s.50, the section covers such matters as driving disqualifications, costs orders, compensation orders: see *R. v. Hoyden* [1975] 1 W.L.R. 852. It also includes binding-over orders contingent on a conviction: *R. v. Williams (Carl)* [1982] 1 W.L.R. 1398, but not a recommendation as to the minimum period that a person convicted of murder should serve (Murder (Abolition of Death Penalty) Act 1965, s.l(2)): *R. v. Aitken* [1966] 1 W.L.R. 1076; *R. v. Bowden and Begley* (1983) 77 Cr. App. R. 66; or an order to contribute toward legal aid costs: *R. v. Hoyden* [1975] 1 W.L.R. 852; *R. v. Raeburn* (1981) 74 Cr.App.R. 21.

[10] Criminal Appeal Act 1968, s.9(1). Sentences incompatible with the ECHR are not fixed by law for these purposes: *R. v. Lichniak; R. v. Pyrah, The Times,* May 16, 2001. He or she may also appeal against any sentence passed for a summary offence dealt with by the Crown Court under s.41 of the Criminal Justice Act 1988 or a summary offence "sent" with an indictable offence to the Crown Court under the Crime and Disorder Act 1998, s.51. (above, para. 14-043); 1968 Act, s.9(2), inserted by the 1988 Act. Sched. 15, para. 2l (as amended).

[11] 1968 Act, s.11 as amended by the Criminal Justice Acts 1982, s.29(2)(a), and 1988, Sched. 15, para. 23, and the Power of Criminal Courts (Sentencing) Act 2000, s.165.

[12] *ibid.* A hospital order with an indefinite restriction order was held not to be more severe than a sentence of three years' imprisonment in *R. v. Bennett* [1968] 1 W.L.R. 980. The court may add a recommendation for deportation.

[13] 1968 Act, s.11(4), substituted by the Criminal Justice Act 1988, Sched. 15, para. 24.

[14] See generally, *R. v. Newsome and Browne* [1970] 2 Q.B. 711. For a comparison with Scots law see G. Maher, [1998] Crim. L.R. 854, explaining that the Scottish Court has emphasised that it will not use the scheme to introduce guidelines or set minimum standards for sentencing.

where a person convicted after summary trial is committed to the Crown Court for sentence,[15] or where a person previously made the subject of a conditional discharge, a community order, or suspended sentence is further dealt with by the Crown Court for the offence.[16] However, an appeal in such a case only lies if the sentence of imprisonment or detention in a young offender institution is for six months or more,[17] or the sentence is outside the power of the court which convicted him or her, or the court recommends deportation, orders disqualification from driving, activates a suspended sentence, makes a banning order or makes a declaration of relevance under the Football Spectators Act 1989.[18]

Part IV of the Criminal Justice Act 1988[19] introduced a new procedure whereby the Attorney-General may refer certain sentences[20] to the Court of Appeal (Criminal Division). It is available in respect of cases of a description specified by statutory instrument made by the Secretary of State, or in which sentence is passed on a person for an offence triable only on indictment or for an offence of a description specified by statutory instrument.[21] The power may be exercised where "it appears to the Attorney-General that the sentencing of a person in a proceeding in the Crown Court has been unduly lenient". Without prejudice to the generality of this, the condition may be satisfied if it appears that the judge erred in law as to his or her powers of sentencing.[22] The Attorney-General must apply for leave to refer a case within 28 days of the passing of the sentence.[23] The Court's power to grant leave to the Attorney-General is unfettered by the comments of the trial judge in sentencing, but leave may be declined if the prosecution have made comments in the course of plea bargaining giving rise to a legitimate expectation as to sentence.[23a] The Court of Appeal may

---

[15] Not in cases where the defendant appeals to the Crown Court.

[16] 1968 Act, s.10, as amended by the Criminal Justice Acts 1982, Sched. 14, para. 23, 1988, Sched. 15, para. 22; and 1991, Sched 11, para. 3, and by the Powers of Criminal Courts (Sentencing) Act 2000, s.165.

[17] Two sentences are treated as a single sentence if they are passed on the same day or expressed by the court to be a single sentence, or are consecutive sentences.

[18] 1968 Act, s.10(3), as amended.

[19] ss. 35, 36: in force from February 1, 1989. See also Sched. 3 and the Criminal Appeal (Reviews of Sentencing) Rules 1989 (S.I. 1989 No. 19). See the notes by I. Leigh in *Current Law Statutes Annotated 1988*; A. Green, 1990) 43 C.L.P. 55; and R. Henham, [1994] Crim L.R. 499.

[20] The term has the same meaning as in the Criminal Appeal Act 1968, except that it does not include an interim hospital order under Part III of the Mental Health Act 1983: 1988 Act, s.35(6). It includes a deferred sentence: *Attorney-General's Reference (No. 22 of 1992)* [1994] 1 All E.R. 105.

[21] 1968 Act, s.35(3)–(5), as amended by the Criminal Justice and Public Order Act 1994, Sched 9, para. 34. The Criminal Justice Act 1988 (Review of Sentencing) Order 1994 (S.I. 1994 No.119) extended the procedure to cover offences of indecent assault, threats to kill, cruelty to a person under 16, and attempts to commit or inciting the commission of those offences. Criminal Justice Act 1988 (Reviews of Sentencing) Order 1995 (S.I. 1995 No. 10) extended the procedure to cases of complex fraud, and Criminal Justice Act 1988 (Reviews of Sentencing) Order 2000 (S.I. 2000 No.1924) applies the procedure to smuggling offences, unlawful sexual intercourse with a girl under 16, and indecency with children and attempts to commit or inciting the commission of the offences. For an argument that the scheme should extend to eitherway offences see S. Shute, (1994) 57 M.L.R. 745.

[22] 1988 Act, ss.36(1)(a), (2), as amended.

[23] See Criminal Justice Act 1988, Sched.3, para.1.

[23a] Attorney-General's Reference Nos 86 and 87 of 1999 [2001] 1 Cr. App.R. (S) 141; *Attorney-General's Reference No. 44 of 2000 [2001] 1 Cr. App.R. (S) 416.*

quash any sentence passed on the defendant, and in place of it pass such sentence (including a heavier sentence[24]) as it thinks appropriate and as the court below had power to pass when dealing with him or her. The Court considers the reference on the facts proved at trial or admitted.[25] When the Court of Appeal has concluded its review, the Attorney-General or the defendant may refer a point of law to the House of Lords. The Court of Appeal must certify that it is a point of law of general public importance, and the leave of either the Court of Appeal or the House of Lords is necessary.

The government had previously proposed a procedure analogous to the Attorney-General's reference procedure, in which the Court of Appeal would have had power to give guidance as to sentencing principles but no power to vary the sentence in question. This had been included in the Prosecution of Offences Bill 1985, but had been defeated in the House of Lords.[26] The present procedure gives the Court of Appeal power to increase or otherwise vary the sentence in question. The Home Secretary indicated that he did not expect the procedure to be employed frequently, suggesting a dozen cases a year as the probable number of such references.[27] The arguments in favour of the new procedure were marshalled by J. R. Spencer,[28] who wrote that under-sentencing: (i) blunts the deterrent effect of the criminal law; (ii) causes outrage to the victim; (iii) is demoralising to the police; (iv) causes injustice to those who were appropriately sentenced; (v) undermines public confidence in the administration of justice and the authority of the courts; (vi) may cause public danger; and (vii) hinders development of a rational sentencing policy by the Court of Appeal. The main[29] contrary argument is that the procedure offends the principle against double jeopardy, in particular the need "to prevent the state ... abusing its power and control over the prosecution process in order to harass and oppress an individual or minority".[30] While it is "virtually unthinkable" that the government would seek to abuse its powers in this way, the risk should nevertheless be recognised.[31] One weakness in the new procedure is that no provision is made for the comprehensive review of sentences: the possible, undesirable, consequence is that it will be sentences that happen to attract adverse comment in the media that will be referred.[32]

The Court of Appeal has stated that an application will not be granted unless there was some error of principle in the judge's sentence and that

---

[24] *Attorney-General's Reference (No. 4 of 1989)* [1990] 1 W.L.R. 41.

[25] *Attorney General's Reference (No. 95 of 1998), The Times*, April 21, 1999. The increase of sentence will not necessarily breach Article 6 of the ECHR: *De Salvador Torres v. Spain* (1996) 23 E.H.R.R. 601.

[26] See J. R. Spencer, (1985) 149 J.P.N. 262.

[27] Standing Committee H, February 23, 1988, col. 219, cited by Leigh, *op. cit*. The decision is, however, the Attorney-General's and not the Home Secretary's.

[28] "Do We need a Prosecution Appeal Against Sentence?" [1987] Crim.L.R. 724.

[29] Others are summarised, and dismissed by Spencer, *ibid.* pp. 729–736.

[30] S. Seabrooke, "Two-timing the Double Jeopardy Principle" [1988] Crim.L.R. 103 at 104. Spencer takes a narrower view of the double jeopardy principle: [1987] Crim.L.R. 724 at 735, as meaning (1) that it is wrong to punish a person twice for the same offence; and (2) that a person must not be put in peril of conviction twice.

[31] Seabrooke, [1988] Crim.L.R, 103.

[32] Spencer, [1987] Crim.L.R. 724 at 730; A. Heaton-Armstrong, (1988) 152 J.P. 278. See e.g. *Attorney-General's References (No.s 4 and 7 of 2002* [2002] EWCA Crim. 127, reviewing sentences for mobile phone thefts.

public confidence would be damaged if the sentence was not altered.[33]

It is open to the Court of Appeal to increase the sentence even if it is in accord with the tariff for the offence.[34]

Shute has examined the use of the reference procedure from 1989–1997.[35] His research reveals that between 1989 and the end of 1997, 367 sentences were reviewed as unduly lenient. The most common offences appealed were robbery and offences of causing grievous bodily harm. The majority of the referrals are from circuit judges (71 per cent) with assistant recorders (6.5 per cent), High Court judges (7.5 per cent) and full recorders (15 per cent) significantly lower. The success rate for the Attorney-General remained high and pretty constant for each group (over 80 per cent), except High Court judges (61 per cent). Twelve per cent of all cases reviewed were tried at the Old Bailey. The research also revealed a number of problems of misallocation of cases to judges not authorised for that class of offence. The *Auld Report* recommends that there should be less "tinkering" with sentences by the Court of Appeal.[36]

The Law Commission provisionally proposed that the prosecution should be permitted to appeal against certain "terminating" rulings of a trial judge (*i.e.* those which bring the case to an end such as a stay for abuse of process).[37] The Commission aims to construct rights of appeal which will not jeopardise the fairness of the proceedings to the accused, and would therefore be compatible with the ECHR.[38] In its Report *Double Jeopardy and Prosecution Appeals*,[39] the Law Commission also proposes that the Court of Appeal should be empowered to set aside acquittals for murder where reliable and compelling new evidence of guilt comes to light and it is in the interests of justice to quash the acquittal.[40] The Commission did not recommend any prosecution power to appeal against a jury acquittal, even if a judicial misdirection led to the acquittal, however, the government is anxious to consider new prosecution rights of appeal.[41] The *Auld Report*, recommends that where a jury's verdict reveals that it is perverse, it should be appeallable by the defence or prosecution.[42]

---

[33] *Attorney-General's Reference (No. 5 of 1989) (R. v. HW-Trevor)* (1990) 90 Cr.App. R. 358 (custodial sentence substituted for a fine for causing death by reckless driving); *Attorney-General's Reference (No.4 of 1989)* [1990] 1 W.L.R. 41. The first was *Attorney-General's Reference (No. 1 of 1989)* (1989) 90 Cr.App.R. 141. which set guidelines for sentencing for incest.

[34] *Attorney-General's Reference (No. 33 of 1996)* [1997] 2 Cr. App. R. (S) 10.

[35] S. Shute, [1999] Crim. L.R. 603.

[36] Chap. 12, para. 101.

[37] See Law Commission Consultation Paper No. 158, *Prosecution Appeals Against Judges Rulings* (2000).

[38] See R. Pattenden, [2000] Crim. L.R. 971.

[39] (2001), Report No. 267.

[40] See I.H. Dennis, [2000] Crim. L.R. 933, on the Consultation Paper. The Auld Report criticised the Law Commission's restriction of the power to cases of murder, but supported the proposal in principle, subject to the consent of the DPP being sought in such cases: Chap. 12, para. 60–63.

[41] See Home Office *Criminal Justice: the Way Ahead* (2001), para. 3.53–3.56.

[42] Chap. 12, para. 67.

(iii) Appeals against findings of insanity

18–017   A person in whose case a verdict of not guilty by reasons of insanity[43] is returned may appeal to the Court of Appeal on the same grounds as against a conviction.[44] The powers of the court are similar. However it may dismiss the appeal if none of the grounds for allowing it relates to the question of the appellant's insanity under the *M'Naghten* rules and, but for that insanity, the proper verdict would have been that he was guilty of some other offence.[45] In appropriate cases, the court may substitute a conviction for an offence, or a verdict of acquittal[46]: in the former case it has power to pass an appropriate sentence or make a hospital or other order, in the latter it may order that the appellant be admitted to hospital for assessment.[47]

Similar provisions govern appeals against findings that a person is under a disability and did the act or made the omission charged against him.[48] If the court allows an appeal against a finding of disability, the appellant may then be tried for the offence, and the court may order that pending the trial the appellant may be kept in custody, released on bail or detained under the Mental Health Act 1983. If, otherwise, the court allows an appeal against a finding that the appellant did the act or made the omission, the court must direct a verdict of acquittal to be recorded.

(iv) Appeals against conviction on special verdict

If the Court of Appeal considers that the trial judge has drawn an incorrect conclusion from a special verdict entered by a jury, it may substitute the correct conclusion, and pass any sentence that may be authorised by law.[49]

(v) References by the Criminal Cases Review Commission

18–018   Where a person was (1) convicted on indictment or (2) tried on indictment and found not guilty by reason of insanity or (3) found by a jury to be under a disability, the Home Secretary formerly had power to refer the case to the Court of Appeal.[50] Two kinds of reference were possible. The first was a reference of the whole case, in which event the reference was treated as an appeal.[51] The court was not limited to the grounds mentioned in the Home Secretary's letter of reference.[52] A further appeal could then lie to the House of Lords. The other possibility was that a particular point might be referred

---

[43] "Insanity" here means insanity under the *M'Naghten* rules, which do not cover all cases of mental disorder and do cover some situations where there is no mental disorder: see generally J. C. Smith, *Criminal Law* (10th ed., 2002), pp. 213–229

[44] 1968 Act, ss.12, 13, as amended by the Criminal Appeal Act 1995, s.2. See above, para. 18-013

[45] *ibid.* s.13(3).

[46] *ibid.* s.13(4).

[47] *ibid.* ss.14, 14A, as substituted by the Criminal Procedure (Insanity and Unfitness to Plead) Act 1991, s.4, and Sched. 1 to the 1991 Act.

[48] *ibid.* ss.15, 16, as amended by the 1991 Act, Sched. 3, paras. 2, 3.

[49] 1968 Act, s.5.

[50] 1968 Act, s.17.

[51] *ibid.* s.17(1)(a).

[52] *R. v. Chard* [1984] A.C. 279; followed in *R. v. Callaghan* [1988] 1 W.L.R. 1.

for the opinion of the court.[53] The court gave what was essentially only an advisory opinion, with any further action to be taken by the Home Secretary.[54] This form of reference was uncommon.[55]

The Home Secretary preferred to refer a case to the Court of Appeal rather than to recommend the exercise of the prerogative to grant a pardon or remit a sentence[56]: it was thought that persistent use of the power to recommend a pardon would undermine the distinction between the functions of the executive and of the judiciary.[57] Indeed it was, in part, dissatisfaction with the review by the Home Office of criminal convictions that led to the establishment of the Court of Criminal Appeal. The Home Secretary's approach was summarised in a memorandum to the Home Affairs Committee[58]:

"In considering convictions on indictment, the Home Secretary ...

(a) will not normally intervene where normal avenues of appeal to the Court of Appeal have not been exhausted;

(b) will, where the normal avenues are not available and intervention seems justified, consider using his power of reference to enable the Court to hear the case;

(c) will consider recommending the exercise of the Royal Prerogative where intervention seems justified but for some reason (e.g. lapse of time, inadmissibility as evidence of salient new facts) a resort to the judicial appeal process would not be appropriate."

However, the Home Secretary would not intervene on the basis of evidence already considered by the courts. A case would only be referred where there was some new evidence or new consideration of substance which had not been before the courts and which appeared to cast doubt on the safety of the conviction.[59] Moreover, if a case was referred to the Court of Appeal and the conviction was upheld, the Home Secretary would only intervene thereafter if the case was wholly exceptional.[60]

A further point is that it is only the Court of Appeal that can quash a conviction: a pardon does not have that effect.[61] Thus, in a number of cases the reference procedure was used to secure the formal quashing of a

---

[53] 1968 Act, s.17(l)(b).

[54] See *Thomas (Arthur) v. The Queen* [1980] A.C. 125, where the Privy Council held that advice given to the Governor-General under an identically worded provision was not binding on him, and could not be the subject of an appeal to the Privy Council.

[55] See, *e.g. R. v. O'Neill* (1948) 33 Cr. App.R. 19; *R. v. McCartan* (1958) 42 Cr. App. R. 262; *R. v. McMahan* (1978) 68 Cr. App. R. 18.

[56] See below, para. 18-070.

[57] 1981–82 H.C. 421, 6th Report on *Miscarriages of Justice*, p. 2.

[58] *ibid.*

[59] *ibid.* In a number of cases the courts rejected applications for judicial review of decisions not to make s.17 references, holding that this policy was not applied inflexibly: *R. v. Secretary of State for the Home Department, ex p. Pegg (Kenneth Stephen)* [1991] C.O.D. 47; *R. v. Secretary of State for the Home Department, ex p. McCallion* [1993] C.O.D. 148.

[60] *e.g. R. v. Cooper and McMahon*, above, para. 18-014. The previous Home Secretaries had firmly taken the view that they should not override the court's decision: see L. Kennedy; (ed.), *Wicked Beyond Belief* (1980), pp. 130, 159–160, 169.

[61] *R. v. Foster* [1985] Q.B. 115: see above, para 18-012, below, para. 18-070.

conviction[62] or a sentence[63] that fell outside the powers of the trial court, often for reasons of some technicality. Indeed, it was uncommon for the Court of Appeal to quash a conviction, following a reference, on the basis of its doubts about the merits of the conviction.[64] "Judicial distaste for the whole reference procedure has verged at times upon open hostility."[65] A decision of the Home Secretary to refuse to refer a case to the Court of Appeal could be challenged on an application for judicial review; such challenges were generally unsuccessful.[66] However, in *R. v. Secretary of State for the Home Department, ex p. Hickey (No. 2)*[67] the Divisional Court held that where the Secretary of State ordered inquiries to be made following receipt of a petition, he was obliged as a matter of fairness to disclose the outcome of those inquiries to the petitioner before deciding whether to refer a case under section 17.

The exercise of the section 17 reference power, particularly in the context of the high profile miscarriage of justice cases, generated much controversy.[68] The RCCJ found that the power was not often exercised,[69] noting the self-imposed limitations adopted by the Home Office. It concluded that the Home Secretary's role was "incompatible with the proper separation of powers as between the courts and the executive" and recommended the establishment of a new independent Criminal Cases Review Authority to consider alleged miscarriages of justice, to supervise further inquiries (if needed) and to refer cases to the Court of Appeal.[70] This recommendation was implemented by Part II (ss.8–25) of the Criminal Appeal Act 1995.

The 1995 Act establishes the Criminal Cases Review Commission as a

---

[62] *R. v. Davies* (1981) 76 Cr. App. R. 120 (following D's extradition, a new count was added to the indictment with D.'s agreement, but contrary to the Extradition Act 1870, s.19).

[63] *e.g. R. v. Bardoe* [1969] 1 W.L.R. 398 (youth of 17 wrongly sentenced to life imprisonment); *R. v. McKenna* (1985) 7 Cr. App. R.(S.) 348; *R. v. Seafietd, The Times*, May 17, 1988 (suspended sentence supervision order wrongly attached to six-month and three-month sentences, neither being a sentence of "more than six months").

[64] Widely publicised rejections of appeals included the Cooper and McMahon case, above, para.18-014; the Birmingham pub bombing case (*R. v. Callaghan* (1988) 88 Cr. App. R. 40; C. Mullin, *Error of Judgment* (rev. ed., 1990); the Carl Bridgwater murder case (see P. Foot, *Murder at the Farm* (1988)). By contrast, the Court of Appeal allowed an appeal in case of the Guildford Four (*R. v. Richardson, The Times*, October 20, 1989) although here the prosecution felt itself unable to support the convictions (see G. McKee and R. Franey, *Time Bomb* (1988); S. Edwards (1989) 139 NLJ 1449). It also ultimately allowed an appeal in the case of the Birmingham Six: *R. v. Mcllkenny* [1992] 2 All E. R. 417 and the Maguire Seven: *R. v. Maguire* [1992] 2 All E.R. 433. See more generally C. Walker, and K. Starmer, (eds), *Miscarriages of Justice* (1999); M. Wasik, T. Gibbons, and M. Redmayne, *Criminal Justice: Text and Materials* (1999), pp.563–576.

[65] P. O'Connor, [1990] Crim. L.R. 615 at 617.

[66] *R. v. Secretary of State for the Home Department, ex p. Cleeland* (unreported, October 8, 1987); *R. v. Same, ex p. Ewing* (unreported, July 28, 1988): *R. v. Same, ex p. Garner* [1989] C.O.D. 461; the cases cited in above, *R. v. Secretary of State for the Home Department, ex p. Ram* [1995] C.O.D. 250.

[67] [1995] 1 W.L.R. 734.

[68] For an examination of miscarriages of justice throughout the century and a theoretical analysis of the reforms introduced to address miscarriages see R. Nobles and D. Schiff, *Understanding Miscarriages of Justice* (2000). For an examination of the history of appeals see R. Pattenden, *English Criminal Appeals, 1844–1994: Appeals Against Conviction and Sentence in England and Wales* (1996).

[69] 36 cases (48 appellants) between 1981 and 1988, 28 (49 appellants) between 1989 and 1992. The Home Office received between 700 and 800 "petitions" each year: Cm. 2263, p. 181.

[70] *ibid.* pp. 182–187. See K. Malleson, (1994) 21 J.L.S. 151.

body corporate, independent of the Crown, with not fewer than 11 members appointed by the Queen on the recommendation of the Prime Minister. Members may be full-time or part-time and are appointed for five years (renewable to a maximum of 10 years). At least one-third of the members must be legally qualified, and at least two-thirds must be persons who appear to the Prime Minister to have knowledge or experience of any aspect of the criminal justice system (of whom one must have knowledge, etc., of the Northern Ireland system).[71] Where a person has been convicted of an offence on indictment, the Commission may at any time refer the conviction to the Court of Appeal and (whether or not they refer the conviction) any sentence (not fixed by law) imposed in relation to the conviction. The reference is to be treated as an appeal under sections 1 or 9 of the 1968 Act.[72] On a reference, the Commission may give notice that any other conviction on the indictment in question is to be treated as also referred. The Commission also has power to refer a verdict of not guilty by reason of insanity, and findings that a person is under a disability and did the act or made the omission charged; these are to be treated as appeals under sections 12 and 15 of the 1968 Act, respectively.[73] The Criminal Cases (Insanity) Act 1999 also allows the Commission to refer cases of "guilty but insane".[74] The Commission also has power to refer summary convictions and sentences to the Crown Court.[75] References may not be made unless

"(a) the Commission consider that there is a real possibility that the conviction, verdict, finding or sentence would not be upheld were the reference to be made,

(b) the Commission so consider—

(i) in the case of a conviction, verdict or finding, because of any argument, or evidence, not raised in the proceedings which led to it or on any appeal or application for leave to appeal against it, or

(ii) in the case of a sentence, because of an argument on a point of law, or information, not so raised, and

(c) an appeal against the conviction, verdict, finding or sentence has been determined or leave to appeal against it has been refused."[76]

However this is not to prevent the making of a reference

"if it appears to the Commission that there are exceptional circumstances which justify making it".[77]

Notwithstanding the view of the RCCJ that the approach of the Home

---

[71] 1995 Act, s.8 and Sched. 1. See also Criminal Appeal Act 1995 (Commencement No.4 and Transitional Provisions) Order 1997 (S.I. 1997 No.), and H.O. Circular 13/1997.

[72] Above, para. 18-011.

[73] 1994 Act, s.9 and (on ss.12, 15 of the 1968 Act) see above, para. 18-017

[74] A verdict abolished by the Criminal Procedure (Insanity) Act 1964.

[75] *ibid.* s.11. The Crown Court may grant bail to a person whose conviction or sentence is referred.

[76] *ibid.* s.13(1).

[77] *ibid.* s.13(2). *R. v. Gerald* [1999] Crim. L.R. 315.

Office was unduly restrictive,[78] these provisions appear to enshrine the previous policy. The Commission should only refer a case if it considers that there is a "real possibility" that the conviction will not be upheld because of new evidence or information or an argument not advanced at trial. The case should also only be referred if an appeal has been unsuccessful or an application to appeal refused.[79] A "real possibility" has been interpreted as meaning that there has to be a "reasonable prospect" of a conviction not being upheld. Lord Bingham described it as "imprecise, but plainly denotes ... more than an outside chance or a bare probability".[80] The Commission received two referrals from the Court of Appeal in its first year and one each year since.

Reference to the Court of Appeal from the CCRC are to be treated as ordinary appeals except that the Court is not bound by its previous determinations on the merits of an appeal.[80a]

Other points to note are that references may be made with or without an application having been made by the person to whom it relates; the Commission must take account of any application or representations made to it by or on behalf of the person concerned, any other representations made to it and any other matters which appear to it to be relevant; the Commission may refer a particular point to the Court of Appeal for its opinion; where a reference is treated as an appeal, the appeal may be on any ground whether or not related to the Commission's reason for making the reference; where an application is made for a reference, the Commission must give reasons to the applicant for deciding not to make one.[81] The Commission is entitled to make evaluative judgments when referring a case and making its report under section 15 to the Court.[82] The Commission may be directed to make an investigation by the Court of Appeal and may be asked by the Home Secretary to consider a matter arising in the consideration of whether to recommend the exercise of the prerogative of mercy.[83] The Commission has powers to obtain documents and to require the appointment of investigating officers from a police force or (if appropriate) another public body, who must undertake such inquiries as the Commission may from time to time reasonably direct. There is also a general power to take any steps which they consider appropriate for assisting them in the exercise of any of their functions, including undertaking or arranging for others to undertake inquiries, and obtaining, or arranging for others to obtain, statements, opinions and reports.[84]

The Commission has been generally well received.[85] Initial fears about the Commission's independence and ability to investigate cases have not

---

[78] Above.

[79] *R. v. Criminal Cases Review Commission, ex p. Pearson* [2000] 1 Cr. App.R. 141.

[80] *ibid.*

[80a] *R. v. Thomas* [2002] EWCA Crim. 941.

[81] 1995 Act, s.14.

[82] *R. v. Coles and Bradley* [1999] 8 Archbold News 3.

[83] *ibid.* ss.15, 16. The Commission statement is conclusive of the matter referred. The Commission may also give a reasoned opinion to the Home Secretary that he or she should consider whether to recommend exercise of the prerogative of mercy.

[84] *ibid.* ss.17–22. For restrictions on the disclosure of information by members or employees of the Commission, see ss.23–25.

[85] See K. Malleson, [1995] Crim.L.R. 929 at 930–931, noting, however, that an increase in workload was also anticipated.

materialised, but concerns regarding its workload have been a persistent problem. The number of cases referred to the Commission means that even on its own estimates, it is barely able to deal with the new cases referred each year, leaving several hundred in the backlog.[86] The Commission stands to suffer from its own success: the more appeals referred by the Commission to the appeal court, and the more that lead to a conviction being quashed, the more likely there will be an increase in the number of applications made by defendants.[87]

In 1999 the Home Affairs Committee published a Report[88] which recognised that the Commission's own projections regarding its workload and the need for more case workers needed to be reviewed. The Committee was "impressed by the overwhelmingly positive tone of the opinions on the Commission's work" from lawyers (para. 18). The Home Affairs Committee commented on the scope for greater efficiency in the Commission and recommended that it ought to be capable of processing cases with greater speed.[89] The Commission noted the concern in its *Annual Report* 1998–99 when there were 1,133 cases awaiting review.[90] In 2001 the Commission's *Annual Report*[91] revealed that at the end of March 2001 there were 580 cases waiting to be reviewed, which compared with a peak figure of over 1,200 at May 31, 1999. During the 12 months up to March 31, 2001, 799 applications for a review of convictions or sentence were received. The Commission reviewed a total of 1,109 cases during the year. Of these, 44 cases were referred to the Court of Appeal.[92] James, Walker and Taylor[93] examined the work of the CCRC and commented on the Home Affairs Select Committee recommendations. As the authors observe, there is a danger that unless it is adequately funded, the Commission will succumb to the pressures of workload and backlog, resulting in a less thorough examination of cases than exists at present.

The process for assessment of a case is as follows.[94] A caseworker first examines whether a case is eligible for review. This involves assessing the scope of the Commission's jurisdiction, and ensuring that normal appeals processes have been exhausted. This process is greatly assisted where the application is based on legal advice, as is now occurring in a greater proportion of applications.[95] The Commission then reviews the eligible cases to identify those that offer little or no new evidence or which can be reviewed easily. A decision is made whether to pursue the case. Few cases

---

[86] See, *e.g. CCRC Annual Report*, p.21. Available from www.ccrc.gov.uk.
[87] The Commission continues to bid for further funding to increase its workforce in order to meet the demand. See *Annual Report (2001)*.
[88] Home Affairs Select Committee Report, *The Work of the Criminal Cases Review Commission* (1999).
[89] The Home Affairs Select Committee Report was particularly concerned about the failure of the Commission to keep pace with applications (para. 6), and about the delay in processing applications (para. 17).
[90] The CCRC publishes its annual statistics providing a detailed breakdown of the number of cases referred to it, reviewed and its decisions.
[91] Available from *www.ccrc.gov.uk*.
[92] For results in individual cases see *www.ccrc.gov.uk/latestnews/*.
[93] A. James, N. Taylor and C. Walker, [2000] Crim. L.R. 140.
[94] For an accessible account of the Commission's procedure see J. MacKeith, (1999) 67(2) Medico-Legal Journal 47. See also L. Jason-Lloyd, (2000) 164 J.P.N. 791; B. Capon, (1998) 162 J.P.N. 659; S. O'Doherty, (1999) 163 J.P.N. 844.
[95] From around one in ten in 1997 to 30% in 2000.

are investigated in full; many are rejected after an initial review by a caseworker and consultation with a single commissioner. This shift in procedure to avoid full investigation in every case was forced upon the Commission by demands of efficiency and the increasing backlog of work. It was inevitable that such reorganisation would be necessary following the Home Affairs Committee's report, concluding that such improvement was a "priority".[96]

In cases that are investigated, the Commission gather evidence, interviews witnesses, seeks expert advice, (particularly forensic advice), liases with other agencies (especially the Court Service, Prison Service, CPS, police, Customs and Excise, etc). An investigating officer is appointed in the rare cases in which the inquiry requires such (on approval of three Commission members).[97] Of the cases so far referred the most common bases for referral are a failing in the prosecution (*e.g.* breach of identification rules) followed by failings in scientific evidence (*e.g.* DNA) and by non-disclosure of evidence.[98] (The Auld Report recommended that the Court of Appeal should be empowered to instruct the Commission to investigate and report on a matter already on appeal to assist the court in resolving the appeal.[99]) Once the investigation has occurred, a commissioner decides whether refer a case to the Court of Appeal or not.[1]

The applicant is kept informed of the progress of the case and of the decision and the reasons for that decision. A decision of the Commission not to refer a case because the matters relied on had been considered by the court already should not be challenged by way of judicial review except in rare cases. The judicial review procedure should be used only to ensure that the Commission has acted in a lawful manner and not to invite the courts to act as an appellate body in respect of the Commission's decision.[2]

Recent concerns have been raised regarding the Commission's prioritising of cases. It has been questioned whether it would be more desirable to devote resources to those more recent alleged miscarriages where the applicants are still detained, rather than review the admittedly serious, but not pressing, cases of miscarriages where offenders were hanged.[3] The Commission operates a policy of ranking in terms of date-order received as well as in terms of ease of completion: "in-custody" cases are generally assigned priority over at-liberty cases".[4] The Home Affairs select Committee recommended that the Commission divert some resources away from high-priority cases to ensure that a short review of cases could help reduce the backlog.[5] Moreover, the Commission was to "fence" a small proportion of

---

[96] (para. 36). See also paras 42–58.
[97] These are relatively rare: in 1998–9 there were five appointed. The Home Affairs Committee suggested further monitoring of the use of police investigations by the Commission, but recognised that these have proved satisfactory: para. 68.
[98] *Annual Report 2000*, p.1.
[99] Chap. 12, para. 104.
[1] In complex cases this requires a committee of at least three Commission members.
[2] *R. v. CCRC, ex p. Pearson* [1999] Crim. L.R. 732; *Mills and Poole v. CCRC* (unreported) January 3, 2002.
[3] See, *e.g. Derek Bentley* [1999] Crim. L.R. 330; Mahmood Mattan (1998) conviction quashed after he hanged in 1952. Not all such appeals from capital cases are successful: see *R.v. Hanratty*, May 10, 2002, CA, on which see D. Mason (2002)
[4] *Annual Report 2000*, 152 N.L.J. 777. p.22.
[5] *op cit*. para. 39.

resources to deal with "at-liberty cases".[6] The Commission reports that the average time taken to complete a full review of an application is three years.[7]

In a detailed review of the CCRC, Nobles and Schiff[8] note that it has been more pro-active than the previous Home Office system for reviewing miscarriages. As at May 31, 2001, the Commission had received 4,135 applications, with 542 cases open, 474 actively being worked on, 3,119 completed, 133 referrals, 70 having been heard by the Court of Appeal with 53 quashed, 16 upheld and one reserved.[9] Nobles and Schiff highlight the fact that despite its success, the Commission cannot escape a position of deference to the Court of Appeal so long as its objective is to investigate cases with a view to referring them to the Court of Appeal. In part this stems from the Commission being compelled to second guess, by use of the "real possibility" test, whether the Court of Appeal would allow the appeal.[10] Similarly, Duff,[11] examining the English and Scottish Commissions, concludes that the Commissions are less effective than they should be because they are bound to show deference to the Court of Appeal on this basis.

(vi) Attorney-General's references[12]

Section 36 of the Criminal Justice Act 1972 introduced a procedure whereby **18–019** the Attorney-General may refer a point of law to the Court of Appeal where the defendant in a trial on indictment has been acquitted. The point must actually have arisen in the case. The court gives its opinion and may thereafter refer the point to the House of Lords. The Attorney-General may appear in person or be represented by counsel: the acquitted person may be represented by counsel, or with leave may appear in person.[13]

The reference has no effect on the trial or the acquittal. No mention must be made in the reference of the proper name of any person or place which is likely to lead to the identification of the acquitted person.[14] His or her identity must not be disclosed during the proceedings except with consent.

The aim of this procedure is to ensure that an erroneous direction by a trial judge on the law is corrected at the earliest opportunity and without the need for legislation. Whereas the defendant may appeal where such a

---

[6] *p cit.* para. 40.

[7] *Annual Report 2001*, p.21

[8] R. Nobles and D. Schiff, "The Criminal Cases Review Commission: Reporting Success?" [2001] 64 M.L.R. 280.

[9] *www.ccrc.gov.uk.*

[10] On "real possibility" as the appropriate test, for criticism of the use of this test see Nobles and Schiff, [2001] 64 M.L.R. 280 at p.284. See also Home Affairs Committee Report, paras 20–24, recommending a review of the test after the Commission has been in operation for five years.

[11] [2001] Crim. L.R. 341.

[12] See J. Jaconelli, [1981] Crim.L.R. 543.

[13] In practice, however, the defendant is normally not represented and counsel for the Attorney-General is opposed by counsel appearing as an advocate to the court, instructed by the Treasury Solicitor. In *Attorney-General's References (Nos. 1 and 2 of 1979)* [1980] Q. B. 180, the Law Commission, who had instigated the references in order to secure clarification of the law concerning conditional intention to steal, submitted a memorandum for the assistance of the court.

[14] Criminal Appeal (Reference of Points of Law) Rules 1973 (S. I. 1973 No. 1114), r.3.

direction leads to an erroneous conviction, the prosecution has (as yet) no right to appeal against an erroneous acquittal in a trial on indictment. The sanctity of an acquittal by a jury is maintained by the provisions designed to secure that the reference procedure cannot operate to the detriment of the person acquitted.

In general, judges have resisted the introduction of procedures whereby matters may be referred to them for an advisory opinion.[15] One of the grounds for refusing in the exercise of their discretion to grant a declaration on a disputed matter of law is that the dispute is hypothetical rather than real.[16] However, the opinions under the reference procedure relate to a real case, and, moreover, one in which an opinion has already been expressed by the trial judge. The exact status of the opinions as precedent is, however, uncertain: as they have no actual effect on the outcome of the case as far as the defendant is concerned, it is arguable that they are not binding, either on trial judges or on the Court of Appeal itself; however, they are obviously of strong persuasive force.

The reference procedure has been characterised as "problematic"[17] in view of the doubts as to precedental status and the fact that the defendant often has little interest in contesting the case.[18] Nevertheless, the procedure has been of value in providing authoritative guidance in a number of areas of criminal law, most notably that of conditional intention to steal, where the Court of Appeal's decision on a reference put an end to a line of argument that had led to a large number of undeserved acquittals.[19] One further difficulty with the reference procedure is that it applies only on acquittals, and as such, a reference cannot be taken against a stay of proceedings for abuse of process.[20]

(vii) Venire de novo

18–020 Where there has been a "mistrial", in the sense either that the trial has never been validly commenced or the jury has not validly returned a verdict, the Court of Appeal may order the issue of a writ of *venire de novo* for a "new" trial: the first "trial" is treated as a nullity.[21] This may be done, for

---

[15] There was weighty judicial opposition to clause 4 of the Rating and Valuation Bill 1928, which would have enabled the Minister of Health to seek advisory opinions from the High Court on questions of rating law: the clause was dropped: see Lord Hewart, *The New Despotism* (1929) Chap. 7; E. C. S. Wade, (1930) 46 L.Q.R. 169 and (1931) 47 L.Q.R. 58; C. K. Allen, (1931) 47 L.Q.R. 43 at 60. But note the introductory appeal procedure discussed above, para. 14-081.

[16] *e.g. Blackburn v. Att.-Gen.* [1971] 1 W.L.R. 1037, where the court declined to make a declaration on the hypothetical question whether by signing the Treaty of Rome, Her Majesty's Government would irreversibly surrender in part the sovereignty of Parliament.

[17] J. Jaconelli, *op. cit.*

[18] The Supreme Court of the United States refuses to consider "moot" points even where they arise out of real and not hypothetical situations.

[19] *Attorney-General's References (Nos. 1 and 2 of 1979)* [1980] Q.B. 180. See *R. v. Bayley and Easterbrook* [1980] Crim.L.R. 503.

[20] The solution in such cases is to ask the judge to lift the stay, with the CPS guaranteeing to offer no evidence so that an acquittal can be recorded; see, *e.g. Attorney-General's Reference (No.3 of 2000)* [2001] UKHL 53.

[21] This jurisdiction, formerly exercised by the Court for Crown Cases Reserved, was preserved for the Court of Criminal Appeal (*Crane v. DPP* [1921] 2 A.C. 299) and is now exercised by the Court of Appeal under the Supreme Court Act 1981, s.53(2).

example,[22] where proceedings have not been properly instituted,[23] where the court is not properly constituted,[24] where the defendants although separately indicted are tried together,[25] where there is an equivocal plea of guilty which should not have been accepted as such,[26] where the jury is not properly constituted,[27] where the jury is improperly discharged before giving a verdict,[28] or the verdict is ambiguous.[29] It is open to the Court of Appeal simply to quash a conviction without ordering a retrial.[30] Moreover, there may be a rule that the court may not order a *venire de novo* where the "mistrial" led to an acquittal.[31]

In *R. v. Rose*[32] the House of Lords emphasised that the power to order a *venire de novo* was not available where there was an irregularity in the course of the trial occurring between the time that it had been validly commenced and the discharge of the jury after returning a verdict. Here, the judge had applied improper pressure on the jury to reach a verdict by imposing a time limit: the House held that the Court of Appeal had no alternative but to quash the conviction under section 2 of the Criminal Appeal Act 1968, and had no jurisdiction to order a *venire de novo*.[33]

The court of trial may direct a *venire de novo* where the jury is discharged before giving a verdict, for example where they fail to agree or there is an irregularity in the conduct of proceedings.[34]

---

[22] See R. B. Cooke, (1955) 71 L.Q.R. 100 (now Lord Cooke of Thorndon); M. Knight, *Criminal Appeals* (1970), pp. 216–219.

[23] *R. v. Angel* (1968) 52 CrApp.R. 280: the consent of the DPP was necessary but had not been obtained *R. v. Newland* [1988] Q.B. 402: the indictment was a nullity as it joined disparate offences (*cf. R. v. O'Reilly* (1989) 90 Cr.App.R. 40).

[24] *R. v. Cronin* (1940) 27 Cr.App.R. 179: trial presided over by a person unqualified to act as a deputy recorder.

[25] *Crane v. DPP* above.

[26] See above, para. 18-005. see, *e.g. R. v. Baker* (1912) 7 CrApp.R. 217 at 252.

[27] *e.g.* where a juror was personated by his bailiff, who was neither on the jury panel nor qualified to be so: *R. v. Wakefield* (1918) 13 Cr.App.R. 56 or where the defendant is denied his right of challenge: *R. v. Williams* (1925) 19 Cr.App.R. 67; *R. v. Gash* (1967) 51 Cr.App.R. 37.

[28] *R. v. Hancock* (1931) 100 L.J.K.B. 419: the defendant changed his pleas from not guilty to guilty, but the jury did not formally return a guilty verdict; *cf. R. v. Poole* [2002] Crim. L.R. 242.

[29] *R. v. Lewis* (1988) 87 Cr.App.R. 270: the way the verdicts were taken left it unclear whether they were unanimous or majority.

[30] See, *e.g. R. v. Golathan* (1915) 11 CrApp.R. 79; *R. v. Lewis* (1988) 87 Cr.App.R. 270. It is not clear whether it is open to the prosecution to recommence proceedings: if the court is simply regarded as holding the decision of the "first" trial to be a nullity, it seems that there could be such proceedings; if, however, the conviction is quashed under the Criminal Appeal Act 1968, s.2, the position is as if there had been a judgment and verdict of acquittal and fresh proceedings could be met by a plea of *autrefois acquit*.

[31] *R. v. Middlesex Quarter Sessions, ex p. DPP* [1952] 2 Q.B. 758. An alternative ground for the decision was that the irregularity was not such as to cause a mistrial. There may be exceptions to the supposed rule where the defendant is party to the irregularity or is tried by a court with no jurisdiction over charges of the kind in question: R. B. Cooke, (1955) 71 L.Q.R. 100 at 116.

[32] [1982] A.C. 822; see also *R. v. O'Donnell* [1996] 1 Cr. App. R. 286.

[33] The position is the same where the defendant changes his or her plea to guilty in reliance on the judge's ruling on a point of law that is subsequently shown to be erroneous: *R. v. Hunt* [1986] Q.B. 125 at 132 (an appeal was allowed by the House of Lords, but this point was not dealt with: [1987] A.C. 352.)

[34] See R. B. Cooke, *op. cit.* pp. 120–125; Juries Act 1974, s.21(4).

(b) Appeals from the Court of Appeal (Criminal Division) to the House of Lords

18–021   An appeal lies from the Court of Appeal (Criminal Division) to the House of Lords at the instance of either the defendant or the prosecutor.[35] The Court of Appeal must certify that a point of law of general public importance is involved.[36] In addition, leave must be obtained from either the Court of Appeal or the House of Lords and this can only be granted where it appears that the point is "one which ought to be considered by the House".[37] If leave is granted, the House may in its discretion allow a point to be argued that is not connected with the point certified.[38]

An application for leave to appeal is normally made immediately after the Court of Appeal's decision, but may be made in writing within 14 days.[39] The point is normally formulated by counsel for the applicant, sometimes with the assistance of counsel for the other side. If a certificate is refused the matter may not be taken any further: the refusal is not itself a decision that may be subject to appeal.[40] Reasons are not normally given for refusing a certificate.[41] Where a certificate is granted, the application for leave should be made first to the Court of Appeal, and only if leave then is refused by that court, to the House of Lords, within 14 days.[42] The Court of Appeal may grant bail[43] and legal aid.[44]

Where the prosecutor is granted leave to appeal or gives notice of intention to apply for leave, and but for the decision of the Court of Appeal the defendant would be liable to be detained, the Court of Appeal may make an order for his or her detention or direct that he or she is not to be released except on bail so long as the appeal is pending.[45] An order under the Mental Health Act 1983 may be continued.[46] A defendant who is detained may apply to the Court of Appeal or House of Lords to be present at the hearing

---

[35]   Criminal Appeal Act 1968, s.33(1). Where a point of law is referred to the Court of Appeal by the Attorney-General under the Criminal Justice Act 1972, s.36 (see above) the court may thereafter refer the point to the House of Lords. If the Court of Appeal had certified a point but refused leave, and then failed to inform the prosecution — thereby rendering it impossible for the prosecution to petition the House of Lords for leave within 14 days—the Court of Appeal could relist the matter: *R. v. Cadman-Smith* [2001] Crim. L.R. 644.

[36]   The RCCJ recommended that this requirement be dropped: Cm. 2263, p. 178.

[37]   1968 Act, s.33(2).

[38]   *Att.-Gen. for Northern Ireland v. Gallagher* [1963] A.C.349. Where, however, the certificate relates to conviction only the House will not deal with matters of sentence: *Jones v. DPP* [1962] A.C. 635.

[39]   Criminal Appeal Act 1968, s.34. The time limit may be extended for applications by the defence only. There is no power to extend prosecution time limits: *R. v. Weir* [2001] 1 W.L.R. 421. *Auld* recommends that there should be: Chap. 12, para. 117.

[40]   *cf.* in relation to appeals to the House of Lords from the Divisional Court, *Gelberg v. Miller* [1961] 1 W.L.R. 459, above,

[41]   *R. v. Jones* (1975) 61 Cr.App.R. 120; *R. v. Cooper, R. v. McMahon* (1975) 61 Cr.App.R. 215.

[42]   Criminal Appeal Act 1968, s.34. The time limit may be extended for defendants.

[43]   *ibid.* s.36.

[44]   See further *Report of the Appeal Committee of the House of Lords upon a Reference thereto by the Clerk of the Parliaments Regarding Criminal Legal Aid Taxation* [1999] 1 W.L.R. 1860.

[45]   Criminal Appeal Act 1968, s.37(2). The order ceases to have effect if leave is refused, or the application for leave is not made within the due time, or the appeal is determined, or the liability for detention otherwise ceases, as the case may be: *ibid.* ss.34(3), 37(3).

[46]   *ibid.* s.37(4)(4A).

of the appeal of preliminary or incidental matters.[47] If no order for continued detention is made, or the defendant is released or discharged before the appeal is disposed of, the defendant cannot be detained again as the result of the decision of the House of Lords on the appeal.[48]

The rules governing petitions to the House of Lords for leave to appeal and petitions of appeal are prescribed by the House of Lords Directions as to Procedure applicable to Criminal Appeals.[49] The former are heard by an Appeal Committee, the latter by the House itself or an Appellate Committee.[50] If leave is granted by the Court of Appeal there is no statutory time limit for lodging the petition of appeal although the Procedure Directions state that this must be done within three months: if leave is granted by an Appeal Committee, the committee may set a time limit.[51] Statement(s) of facts and issues, an Appendix of Documents and cases must be lodged on a similar basis to that for civil appeals.[52] If any of the parties intend to invite the House to depart from one of its own previous decisions, this intention must be clearly stated.

The House in disposing of an appeal may exercise any of the powers of the Court of Appeal or remit the case to that court.[53] Any sentence substituted by the House of Lords runs from the time when the other sentence would have begun to run, unless the House otherwise directs.[54] Any time spent on bail pending hearing of the appeal does not count towards the sentence.[55]

Until 1960, an appeal could only be taken from the Court of Criminal Appeal to the House of Lords if the Attorney-General granted a *fiat* or certificate that a point of law of exceptional public importance was involved and that it was in the public interest that a further appeal be brought.[56] Between 1907 and 1960 there were 23 successful applications for a *fiat*. The exercise of the Attorney-General's discretion to grant or refuse a *fiat* was in

---

[47] *ibid.* s.38.

[48] *ibid.* s.37(5). See *DPP v. Merriman* [1973] A.C. 584 at 606; *U.S. Government v. McCaffery* [1984] 1 W.L.R. 867, 873; *R. v. Hollinshead* [1985] A.C. 975 at 998–999, per Lord Roskill, who stated that an order should be made unless there were strong reasons for not so doing.

[49] The House of Lords has issued directions as to the appropriate procedure to be adopted: see *House of Lords — Practice Directions applicable to Criminal Appeals* (1997), *Archbold* (2002), para. 7–250; these and subsequent directions are available from the House of Lords website *www.parliament.the-stationery-office.co.uk/pa/ld/ldjudinf.htm*. See also *Practice Direction (House of Lords: Criminal Appeals)* (2001) 145 S.J. For consideration of whether the House of Lords procedure on refusing leave to appeal without giving reasons is compatible with the ECHR see Emmerson and Ashworth, (2001), p.521 and *Webb v. U.K.* (1997) 24 E.H.R.R. CD 73.

[50] See above, para. 2-072.

[51] House of Lords Directions as to Procedure applicable to Criminal Appeals 1992, Dirs 8, 9; *Practice Direction (House of Lords: Procedure Amendments)* [1996] 1 W.L.R. 450.

[52] See below, para. 18-039.

[53] Criminal Appeal Act 1968, s.35(3). Where the House of Lords hears an appeal, but it turns out that points not disposed of by the Court of Appeal are relevant to whether a conviction should stand, the House may remit the matter to the Court of Appeal or itself exercise the powers of the Court of Appeal in relation to those points: *R. v. Mandair* [1995] 1 A.C. 208, H.L. The Court of Appeal may not otherwise itself relist the case to consider the unresolved grounds: *R. v. Berry (No.2)* [1991] 1 W.L.R. 125 and *R. v. Berry (No.3)* [1995] 1 W.L.R. 7, CA.

[54] *ibid.* s.43(2).

[55] *ibid.* s.43(1).

[56] See "Appeals to the House of Lords" [1957] Crim.L.R. 566.

certain instances highly controversial. The Administration of Justice Act 1960[57] introduced the present arrangements which, *inter alia*, brought an end to the involvement of the Attorney-General. The number of criminal appeals to the House of Lords has, accordingly, increased. However, it has been debated whether, on balance, the increased involvement of the House in criminal law matters has proved beneficial. In his commentary on *R. v. Caldwell*,[58] Professor J. C. Smith noted that the "House of Lords has a dismal record in criminal cases. All too often their Lordships' decisions have to be reversed by legislation."[59] His criticisms were echoed by Professor Glanville Williams,[60] who remarked that the average age of Law Lords is higher than that of members of the Court of Appeal, and that "old men" are "often fixed in their opinions" and "tend to ignore the opinions of others". He noted that a further drawback was the breadth of the House's jurisdiction: "It is particularly inapt that a Chancery judge should have the casting vote in the House of Lords in a criminal case, as Lord Cross did in *Hyam*."[61]

After a survey of the record of the House in criminal cases between 1960 and 1984, Professor A. T. H. Smith concluded that appeals by the Crown in such cases should be abolished, and replaced by the Attorney-General's reference procedure. Decisions from the Divisional Court could go to the Court of Appeal (Criminal Division), but no further.[62]

3. Appeals in Civil Cases

18–022   In this section we consider appeals in civil cases originating in the county court or the High Court. Appeals in civil cases originating in the magistrates' court or Crown Court have already been discussed.[63]

(a) Appeals in the county court, High Court and Court of Appeal

The structure of appeals in civil cases originating in the county court or High Court has been remodelled as part of the Woolf reforms.[64] The aim has been to enable appeals to be directed to the most appropriate level, to require permission for most appeals, to restrict second and further appeals, and to reduce the proportion of appeals dealt with by re-hearing rather than review. A single structure has been created covering appeals to and within county courts, the High Court and the Court of Appeal. Amendments to the legislative structure were made by the Access to Justice Act 1999[65] and the

---

[57] See D. G. T. Williams, [1961] Crim.L.R. 87.
[58] [1982] A.C. 341.
[59] [1981] Crim.L.R. 393.
[60] *ibid.* pp. 581–582.
[61] [1975] A.C. 55.
[62] "Criminal Appeals in the House of Lords" (1984) 47 M.L.R. 133.
[63] See above, paras 18-005–18-009.
[64] See *Access to Justice* (HMSO, 1996), Chap. 14; *Report of the Review of the Court of Appeal (Civil Division)* (Bowman Report) (1997) (LCD website). The changes have been described as "the most significant changes in the arrangements for appeals in civil proceedings in this country for 125 years": Brooke L.J. in *Tanfern Ltd, v. Cameron MacDonald (Practice Note)* [2000] 1 W.L.R. 1311. See generally N. Andrews, [2000] C.L.J. 464.
[65] ss. 54–57.

main provisions are now to be found in CPR Part 52 and the associated Practice Direction. Appeal proceedings are subject to the "overriding objective" in CPR r.1.1 "of enabling the court to deal with cases justly."

(i) When is an appeal available?

It is provided generally that, subject to an order made by the Lord Chancellor,[66] any party to any proceedings dissatisfied with the determination of the judge or jury may appeal to the Court of Appeal;[67] and that the Court of Appeal has jurisdiction to hear and determine appeals from any judgment or order of the High Court.[68] However, in a number of situations, appeals to the Court of Appeal are expressly excluded: **18–023**

- in respect of questions of fact arising in certain actions by a landlord for possession of the premises;[69]
- where the parties have agreed in writing that the judge's decision shall be final;[70]
- from any judgment of the High Court in any criminal cause or matter;[71]
- from any order of the High Court or any other court or tribunal allowing an extension of time for appealing from a judgment or order;[72]
- from any decision expressed by statute to be final;[73]
- from a decree absolute of nullity of marriage, by a party who, having had time and opportunity to appeal from the decree nisi, has not done so;[74]
- from a divorce order;[75]
- from any decision of the High Court under Part I of the Arbitration Act 1996, except as provided by that Act;[76]
- from a judgment or order of the High Court sitting as a Prize Court;[77]
- from an order refusing leave to a vexatious litigant to institute or continue legal proceedings.[78]

In some circumstances, an appeal lies directly from the High Court to the House of Lords.[79]

The Court of Appeal also has a residual jurisdiction to reopen proceedings in order to avoid real injustice in exceptional circumstances

---

[66] Under s.56(1) of the Access to Justice Act 1999, which enables the Lord Chancellor to provide that appeals which would otherwise lie to a county court, the High Court or the Court of Appeal shall lie instead to another of those courts.

[67] County Courts Act 1984, s,77(1), as amended.

[68] Supreme Court Act 1981, s. 16(1), as amended.

[69] County Courts Act 1984, s.77(6) (excluding the appeal under s.77(1)).

[70] 1984 Act, s.79(1).

[71] Supreme Court Act 1981, s.18(1)(a). Here, the appeal lies to the House of Lords under the Administration of Justice Act 1960: see above 18-009.

[72] s. 18(1)(b). An appeal lies from a refusal to make such an order: *cf. Rickards v. Rickards* [1990] Fam. 194.

[73] s.18(1)(c).

[74] s.18(a)(d), as amended by the Family Law Act 1996, Sched. 10.

[75] s.18(1)(d), inserted by the Family Law Act 1996, Sched. 8, para. 30.

[76] s.18(1)(g), substituted by the 1996 Act, Sched. 3, para. 37.

[77] *ibid.* s.16(2). An appeal lies to the Privy Council.

[78] *ibid.* s.42(4).

[79] See below, para. 18-038.

where there is no other effective remedy; this may include cases where an order has been procured by fraud or evidence has arisen that suggests that there is a real possibility that the trial judge was biased.[80]

(ii) When is permission required?

18–024   The Access to Justice Act 1999 introduced a general provision whereby rules of court may provide that any right of appeal to a county court, the High Court or the Court of Appeal (other than a right of appeal in a criminal cause or matter) may be exercised only with permission.[81] No appeal can be made against a decision of a court under this provision to give or refuse permission, although this does not affect any right under rules of court to make a further application for permission.[82] CPR, r.52.3 provides that an appellant or respondent requires permission to appeal where the appeal is from the decision of a judge in the county court or the High Court, except where the appeal is against a committal order, a refusal to grant habeas corpus or a secure accommodation order made under section 25 of the Children Act 1989, or as provided by Practice Direction 52. The Practice Direction provides that the permission of the Court of Appeal or, where the lower court's rules allow, the lower court is required for all appeals except as provided for by statute or CPR, r.52.3.[83] These general provisions are not to be construed as introducing a general requirement for permission to appeal across specific statutory appeals which are not otherwise subject to any restriction.[84]

(iii) Routes of appeal

18–025   These are now prescribed by an order made by the Lord Chancellor[85]:

(1) an appeal from the decision[86] of a District judge or deputy District judge of a county court lies to a Circuit judge[87];

(2) subject to (1), an appeal from a decision of a county court lies to the High Court[88];

---

[80] *James v. Williams* [2001] C.P. Rep. 42; *Taylor v. Lawrence* [2002] EWCA Civ 90. The permission of the Court of Appeal is necessary for a case to be reopened.

[81] Access to Justice Act 1999. s.54(1)(2).

[82] *ibid.* s.54(4).

[83] para. 4.2.

[84] *Colley v. Council for Licensed Conveyancers* [2001] EWCA Civ 1137 (statutory right of appeal under the Administration of Justice Act 1985, s.26(7)).

[85] Access to Justice Act 1999 (Destination of Appeals) Order 2000 (S.I. 2000 No. 1071), made under the 1999 Act, s.56(1) and (3).

[86] This includes any judgment, order or direction of the High Court or a county court: para. 1(2)(a).

[87] S.I. 2000 No. 1071, art.3(2).

[88] *ibid.* art. 3(l). Until 1934 the appeal lay first to a Divisional Court and thereafter to the Court of Appeal. In bankruptcy cases an appeal lies to a Divisional Court of the Chancery Division; an appeal lies from that Court to the Court of Appeal and the latter's decision is final: Insolvency Act 1986, s.375(2), as amended by the 1999 Act, Sched. 15.

(3)   an appeal from a registrar, master, District judge of the High Court or deputy lies to a High Court judge.[89]

(1) to (3) are subject to the following:

(4)   an appeal lies to the Court of Appeal where the decision to be appealed is a final decision[90] on a claim allocated to the multi-track or made in specialist proceedings[91]; and

(5)   where an appeal is made to a county court or the High Court (other than from a decision of a court officer authorised to assess costs) and on hearing the appeal the court makes a decision, an appeal lies only to the Court of Appeal.[92]

Family proceedings and appeals against a decision of an authorised court officer in detailed costs assessment proceedings are subject to different arrangements.[93] Where a decision in a multi-track case or specialist proceedings is not a final decision,[94] the route of appeal depends on the type of judge who made the order, the appeal lying to the next judge in the hierarchy.[95] The same applies to decisions in claims allocated to the small claims track and fast track, and to claims under the CPR, Part 8 procedure.

Where in any proceedings in a county court or the High Court a person appeals, or seeks permission to appeal, to a court other than the Court of Appeal or the House of Lords, the Master of the Rolls, or the court from which or to which the appeal is to be made, or from which permission to appeal is sought, may direct that the appeal shall be heard instead by the Court of Appeal.[96] Furthermore, where a relevant court (i.e. the court from or to which an appeal is made or from which permission to appeal is sought) considers that an appeal which is to be heard by a county court or the High Court would raise an important point of principle or practice, or there is some other compelling reason for the Court of Appeal to hear it, the

---

[89]   *ibid.* art. 2.
[90]   *i.e.* a decision of a court that would finally determine (subject to any possible appeal or detailed assessment of costs) the entire proceedings (or part of a hearing or trial which has been split into parts) whichever way the court decided the issues before it: *ibid.* para. 1 (2)(c), (3). It does not include a decision only on the detailed assessment of costs: *Dooley v. Parker* [2002] EWCA Civ 96.
[91]   *ibid.* art. 4, as amended by S.I. 2002 No. 439, art. 12. Specialist proceedings are admiralty and arbitration proceedings, commercial and mercantile actions, Patents Court and Technology and Construction Court business and proceedings under the Companies Acts.
[92]   *ibid.* art.5.
[93]   In family proceedings, appeals lie from a District judge in the county court to a Circuit judge; District judge in the Principal Registry to a High Court judge of the Family Division; Circuit judge or High Court judge to Court of Appeal. Appeals from an authorised Court officer lie to a costs judge (taxing master) or a District judge of the High Court (CPR, r.47.21–47.26).
[94]   *e.g.* a case management decision, an order striking out proceedings or an order giving summary judgment under CPR. Part 24.
[95]   Practice Direction 52, para. 2A1: District judge of a county court to Circuit judge; Master, District judge of the High Court or Circuit judge to High Court judge; High Court judge to Court of Appeal.
[96]   Access to Justice Act 1999, s.57.

relevant court may order the appeal to be transferred to the Court of Appeal, the Master of the Rolls or the Court of Appeal may remit it.[97]

(iv) Grounds of appeal and the powers of the appeal court

18–026   Every appeal is limited to a review of the decision of the lower court unless a practice direction makes different provision for a particular category of appeal; or the court considers that in the circumstances of an individual appeal it would be in the interests of justice to hold a re-hearing.[98] Unless it orders otherwise, the appeal court will not receive oral evidence or evidence which was not before the lower court.[99] The appeal court will allow an appeal where the decision of the lower court was (a) wrong; or (b) unjust because of a serious procedural irregularity or other irregularity in the proceedings of the lower court. It may draw any inference of fact which it considers justified on the evidence.[1]

A decision will be wrong where the court erred in law or fact or there was an error in the exercise of discretion sufficient for the appeal court to intervene.[2] On the last of these the principle stated by Lord Fraser of Tullybelton in *G v. G(Minors: Custody Appeal)*[3] has been held[4] to be relevant:

"... the appellate court should only interfere when it considers that the judge of first instance has not merely preferred an imperfect solution which is different from an alternative imperfect solution which the Court of Appeal might or would have adopted, but has exceeded the generous ambit within which a reasonable disagreement is possible."

[97] CPR, r.52.14. This power should be used sparingly and if the lower court is in doubt the matter can be referred to the Master of the Rolls: *Clark (Inspector of Taxes) v. Perks* [2001] 1 W.L.R. 17.

[98] The hearing is a re-hearing if the appeal is from the decision of a Minister, person or other body and that Minister, etc., did not hold a hearing to come to that decision or held a hearing but the procedure adopted did not provide for the consideration of evidence: Practice Direction 52, para. 9.1.

[99] Where the court at first instance has failed to provide reasons for its decision, an appellate court should not accede to a request for a re-hearing unless the lower court had refused to provide reasons when asked to do so or there was good reason for not asking it to do so: *Secretary of State for Trade and Industry v. Lewis,* [2001] 2 B.C.L.C. 597 August 16,2001; as a general rule, appeals should proceed by way of review and there are no set criteria for determining when proceeding by way of re-hearing is appropriate, the court having a wide discretion according to the circumstances of the case: *Audergon v. La Baguette Ltd.* [2002] EWCA Civ 10.

[1] Prior to the changes, the tests for accepting fresh evidence were set out in *Ladd v. Marshall* [1954] 1 W.L.R. 1489: (1) the evidence could not have been obtained with reasonable diligence for use at the trial; (2) the evidence must be such that, if given, it would probably have an important influence on the result of the case, though it need not be decisive; (3) the evidence must be such as is presumably to be believed; it must be apparently credible, though it need not be incontrovertible. These tests remain of persuasive authority when the court exercises its discretion under the new rules: *Hertfordshire Investements Ltd, v. Bubb* [2000] 1 W.L.R. 2318; *Hamilton v. Al Fayed* (unreported, December 21, 2000); *Gillingham v. Gillingham* [2001] EWCA Civ 906; but the application of the principles in a particular case may require modification in the light of the overriding objective.

[2] CPR, r.52.11.

[3] *White Book 2001*, para. 52.11.7.

[4] [1985] 1 W.L.R. 647 at 652.

This approach will not, however, apply where the appeal is by way of re-hearing as there the discretion will be exercised afresh. Ground (b) may apply where the decision is not itself "wrong".[5]

On an appeal, the appeal court has all the powers of the lower court, unless restricted by statutory provisions, and has express power (a) to affirm, set aside or vary any order or judgment; (b) refer any claim or issue for determination by the lower court; (c) order a new trial or hearing; (d) make orders for the payment of interest; and (e) make a cost order. In an appeal from a claim tried with a jury, the Court of Appeal may (a) make an order for damages; or (b) vary an award of damages made by the jury.[6]

A judge must give sufficient reasons for his or her decision to enable the parties and any appellate tribunal readily to analyse the reasoning that was essential to that decision.[7] For example, if the expert evidence of one witness is preferred to that of another, the judge must explain why.[8] However, it is not necessary to deal with every argument presented by counsel.[9]

(v) Second appeals

Where an appeal is made to the county court or the High Court in relation to any matter (other than a criminal cause or matter), no appeal may be made to the Court of Appeal from that decision unless the Court of Appeal considers that the appeal would raise an important point of principle or practice, or there is some other compelling reason for the Court of Appeal to hear it.[10]   **18–027**

(vi) Applications for permission to appeal

An application for permission to appeal may be made (a) to the lower court at the hearing at which the decision to be appealed was made; or (b) to the appeal court in an appeal notice. There is no requirement to raise the matter with the lower court. Where the lower court refuses permission, a further application for permission may be made to the appeal court. Applications arc normally dealt with on paper. If that court refuses permission without a hearing the applicant may within seven days request the decision to be reconsidered at a hearing.[11] Permission will only be given where (a) the court   **18–028**

---

[5] By Brooke L.J. in *Tanfern Ltd v. Carmeron MacDonald* [2000] 1 W.L.R. 1311, para. [32].
[6] CPR, r. 52.10.
[7] *English v. Emery Reimbold & Strick Ltd and other cases* [2002] EWCA Civ 605. If a well founded application for permission to appeal on the ground of inadequate reasons is made to the trial judge, the judge should consider whether additional reasons should be given; if it is made to the appeal court, it should consider adjourning the application and remitting the case to the trial judge: *ibid.*
[8] *Flannery v. Halifax Estate Agencies Ltd* [2000] 1 W.L.R. 377.
[9] *Eagil Trust Co. Ltd, v. Pigott-Brown* [1985] 3 All E.R. 119 at 121, *per* Griffiths L.J.; approved in *English* at para. [17], subject to the general principle set out above.
[10] Access to Justice Act 1999, s.55.
[11] The respondent may be notified of the date of the hearing and is entitled to attend or submit written representations (which should be addressed to the application of the relevant test for granting permission to appeal or to any material inaccuracy in the papers before the court); if the application is unsuccessful there is a discretion to award the respondent costs, although costs of appearance at the hearing will not be ordered where written submissions would have been sufficient: see *Jolly v. Jay* [2002] EWCA Civ 277.

considers that the appeal would have a real prospect of success[12]; or (b) there is some other compelling reason why the appeal should be heard.[13] An order giving permission may (a) limit the issues to be heard; and (b) be made subject to conditions.[14] Reasons must be given for refusing permission.[15] If permission is refused, no further appeal is available.[16] Permission to appeal will be granted more sparingly in respect of case management decisions[17] and second appeals. Where an appellant or respondent seeks permission from the appeal court it must be requested in the appellant's or respondent's notice as the case may be.

(vii) The appeal process

18–029 The appellant must file an "appellant's notice" setting out the grounds of appeal at the appeal court within (a) such period as may be directed by the lower court; or (b) where there is no such direction, 14 days after the date of the decision that the appellant wishes to appeal. Unless the appeal court orders otherwise, an appellant's notice must be served on each respondent[18] as soon as practicable and in any event not later than seven days, after it is filed.[19] If the appellant is represented, a skeleton argument must accompany or be included in the appellant's notice; if that is impracticable it must be lodged and served within 14 days of filing the notice. An appellant who is not represented is encouraged to lodge a skeleton argument but is not required to do so.[20]

---

[12] *i.e.* a realistic as opposed to a fanciful prospect of success: Lord Woolf M.R. in *Swain v. Hillman* [2001] 1 All E.R. 91, cited by Brooke L.J. in *Tanfern*, above, para. [21].

[13] The *White Book 2001*, para. 52.3.16, suggests that this should be interpreted as requiring the test in (a) to be applied more charitably in the case of appeals to the Court of Appeal where, for example, an important question of law or general policy is at stake; in the case of junior appellate courts only (a) should be applied.

[14] CPR, r.52.3(2)–(7). If limited or conditional permission is granted by an appellate judge after a hearing, the issue cannot be re-opened at the full hearing: *Fieldman v. Markovitch, The Times,* July 31, 2001.

[15] *Hyams v. Plender* [2001] 1 W.L.R. 32, para. [17].

[16] Access to Justice Act 1999, s.54(4); *Rineker v. University College London* [2001] 1 W.L.R. 13 (Court of Appeal has no jurisdiction to entertain interim appeal against refusal of High Court judge to grant permission to appeal against an order of a costs judge).

[17] Practice Direction 52, paras 4.4, 4.5 (specifying as relevant considerations the significance of the issue, the practical consequence of an appeal and whether it would be more convenient to determine the issue at or after trial).

[18] *i.e.* a person other than the appellant who was a party to the proceedings in the lower court and who is affected by the appeal; and a person who is permitted by the appeal court to be a party to the appeal: CPR, r.52.1(3)(e).

[19] CPR, r.52.4. Form Nl61 is to be used. Specified documents, and any others which the appellant reasonably considers necessary to enable the appeal court to reach its decision must also be filed then, or reasons given why they are not currently available (Practice Direction 52, paras 5.6–5.8). A more limited set is needed for the small claims track (*ibid.* para. 5.8A–5.8D). If permission has been given by the lower court or is not required, the documents must also be served on the respondents at this stage (*ibid.*, para. 5.24); if permission is obtained from the appeal court, they must be served within seven days of receiving the order granting permission (*ibid.* para.6.2).

[20] Practice Direction 52, para. 5.9. Such skeleton arguments should contain a numbered list of points stated in no more than a few sentences which should both define and confine the areas of controversy; each point should be followed by references to any documentation on which the appellant proposes to rely. Other information needed may include glossaries, a chronology of relevant events and authorities on points of law: Practice Direction 52, paras 5.10, 5.11.

Unless the court otherwise directs, a respondent need not take any action when served with an appellant's notice until notified that permission to appeal has been granted.[21] A respondent may file and serve a respondent's notice; and must file a notice if seeking permission from the appeal court to appeal or wishing to ask that court to uphold the order for reasons different from or additional to those of the lower court. The notice must be filed within (a) such period as may be directed by the lower court; or (b) where there is no such direction, 14 days after the date he or she is served with the appellant's notice, or notification that the appeal court has given the appellant permission to appeal or notification that the application for permission to appeal and the appeal itself are to be heard. Unless the appeal court otherwise orders, a respondent's notice must be served on the appellant and any other respondent (a) as soon as practicable and, in any event, not later than seven days after it is filed.[22] Similar requirements apply to respondent's notices as for appellant's notices. The respondent must supply a skeleton argument in all cases where he or she proposes to address arguments to the court, or may do so in the case of the small claims track.[23]

The appeal court may extend or shorten time.[24] Unless the appeal court or the lower court orders otherwise, or the appeal is from the Immigration Appeal Tribunal, an appeal does not operate as a stay of any order or decision of the lower court.[25] An appeal notice may not be amended without the permission of the appeal court.[26] The appeal court has power, where there is a compelling reason, to strike out the whole or part of an appeal notice, to set aside permission to appeal in whole or in part, or to impose or vary conditions upon which an appeal may be brought.[27]

If permission is granted, the appeal court will send the parties notification of the date of the hearing or the period of time (the "listing window") during which the appeal is likely to be heard and, in the Court of Appeal, the "hear by date", a copy of any order giving permission to appeal and any other directions given by the court.[28] The appellant will also be sent an Appeal Questionnaire, to be returned within 14 days. This will include, if the appellant is legally represented, the advocate's time estimate for the hearing and confirmation of other matters.[29]

(viii) Who may exercise the powers of the Court of Appeal

A court officer assigned to the Civil Appeals Office who is a barrister or solicitor may, with the consent of the Master of the Rolls, exercise the jurisdiction of the Court of Appeal with regard to: matters incidental to any proceedings in the Court of Appeal, any other matter where there is no

18–030

---

[21] *ibid.* para. 5.22.

[22] CPR, r.52.5. Form N162 is to be used.

[23] Practice Direction 52, paras 7.6, 7.7, 7.7A. It should, where appropriate, answer the arguments set out in the appellant's skeleton argument: *ibid.*, para. 7.8.

[24] CPR, r.3.1(2)(a) and 52.6. An appeal may lie, with permission, against a decision that time should not be extended: *Foenander v. Bond Lewis & Co.* [2001] 2 All E.R. 1019.

[25] CPR, r.52.7.

[26] CPR, r.52.8.

[27] CPR, r.52.9.

[28] Practice Direction 52, para. 6.3.

[29] *ibid.*, para. 6.5.

substantial dispute between the parties, and the dismissal of any appeal or application for non-compliance with an order, rule or practice direction. However, such an officer may not decide an application for permission to appeal, bail pending on appeal, an injunction, or (normally) a stay of proceedings. A party may request any decision of a court officer to be reviewed by the Court of Appeal.[30]

(ix) Effect of new authorities and legislation

18–031   The court should take account of any new authorities and of any relevant, retrospective legislation. For example, in *Attorney-General v. Vernazza*,[31] Mr Vemazza was declared to be a vexatious litigant and prohibited by the High Court from *instituting* legal proceedings without leave. By the time his appeal was heard by the Court of Appeal, the High Court had been given a new statutory power to prohibit vexatious litigants from *continuing existing* proceedings without leave. The House of Lords held that the new legislation, as it affected procedural and not substantive rights, was retrospective, should have been applied to Mr Vernazza by the Court of Appeal, and should be applied to him now. Where there are new authorities or legislative provisions which are relevant to a decision of the High Court, leave to appeal out of time will be granted if it is just to do so.[32]

Similarly, the court should take account of any material changes in the facts since the trial. For example, in *Murphy v. Stone-Wallwork (Charlton) Ltd*.[33] an action was brought by an employee against his employers for breach of statutory duty. The judge and the Court of Appeal assessed the damages on the assumption that the plaintiff would continue to be employed by the defendants on lighter work. A fortnight after the decision in the Court of Appeal, the plaintiff was dismissed because of his incapacity. The House of Lords[34] held that even though it did not appear that the employers had acted in bad faith or oppressively, evidence of the change of circumstances was admissible, as the basis on which the case had been conducted on both sides had been suddenly and materially falsified. It should, however, be noted that the change occurred within the time limit for appealing: it is unlikely that a leave to appeal out of time would be granted in such circumstances, in view of the need for finality in litigation, unless, perhaps, there was bad faith or oppression. A more restrictive approach is adopted in respect of the admission of fresh evidence.[35]

---

[30] CPR, r.52.16.

[31] [1960] A.C. 965.

[32] *In Re Earl of Berkeley, Borrer v. Berkeley* [1945] Ch. 1; *Anns v. Walcroft Property Co. Ltd.* [1976] Q.B. 882; *Property and Reversionary Investment Corporation Ltd v. Templar* [1977] 1 W.L.R. 1223.

[33] [1969] 1 W.L.R. 1023. See also *Mulholland v. Mitchell* [1971] A.C. 666; *Hughes v. Smith, The Times*, April 21, 1989. Evidence concerning post-hearing developments is "readily admitted" in cases concerning the welfare of children: *G v. G (Minors: Custody Appeal)* [1985] 1 W.L.R. 647 at 654, *per* Lord Eraser. See, *e.g. M v. M (Minor: Custody Appeal)* [1987] 1 W.L.R. 404; *A. v. A. (Custody Appeal: Role of Appellate Court))* [1988] 1 F.L.R. 193; *Re A (A Minor) (Abduction)* [1989] 1 F.L.R. 365.

[34] The same principle would have applied by the Court of Appeal if the change had occurred after the trial.

[35] See above, para. 18-026.

The Court of Appeal similarly adopts a restrictive approach to points not taken at the trial and presented for the first time in the Court of Appeal. The court will not decide in favour of an appellant on a new point unless it is satisfied beyond doubt (1) that it has before it all the facts bearing upon the new contention as completely as if it had been raised at the trial, and (2) that no evidence could have been adduced at the trial which by any possibility could prevent the point from succeeding.[36] Accordingly it may permit a new question to be raised on the construction and application of a regulation where the facts are not disputed.[37]

(x) Decision-making in the Court of Appeal

The approach of the Court of Appeal varies according to whether the appeal concerns (1) questions of fact; (2) awards of damages; (3) exercises of judicial discretion; (4) questions of law; and (5) a new trial. The principles set out in this section were developed before the recent changes to appeals. It remains to be seen how far they may be modified in applying the new formulation of the grounds of appeal.[38]

18–032

(1) *Questions of fact.* In the vast majority of cases, the trial will have been conducted by a judge sitting without a jury. The findings of fact will be set out in the judgment. On an appeal, a distinction will be drawn by the Court of Appeal between findings of "primary fact" and inferences of fact drawn from those primary facts (sometimes termed "secondary facts").[39] The Court of Appeal is most reluctant to disturb findings of primary fact where they are based on the testimony of witnesses who have been seen by the judge, and who, in accordance with the practice of the Court of Appeal, will not be seen in person on the appeal.[40] The judge's findings will normally have been based, at least in part, on his or her observations of manner and demeanour, and this advantage is denied to the Court of Appeal. In exceptional cases, the court may find that the trial judge has "failed to use or has palpably misused his advantage".[41] The judge's impression of the witnesses' demeanour "should be carefully checked by a critical examination of the whole of the evidence".[42] A judgment:

18–033

> " ... may be demonstrated ... to be affected by material inconsistencies and inaccuracies or [the trial judge] may be shown to have failed to

---

[36] See Lord Herschell in *The Tasmania* (1890) 15 App.Cas. at 225 and Jessell M.R. in *Ex p. Firth, re Cowburn* (1882) 19 Ch.D. 419, 429; *Ashcroft v. Mersey Regional Health Authority* [1985] 2 All E.R. 96; *Transcontainer Express Ltd v. Custodian Security Ltd* [1988] 1 Lloyd's L.R. 128.

[37] *Donaghey v. P. O'Brien & Co.* [1966] 1 W.L.R. 1170 at 1180; on appeal: *Donaghey v. Boulton & Paul Ltd* [1968] A.C. 1 at 14, 23, 31; *cf. Jones v. Department of Employment* [1989] Q.B. 1 (Court of Appeal willing to entertain a new argument on a point of law on an appeal against striking out, where the facts are assumed).

[38] Above, para. 18-026.

[39] See above, paras 1-011–1-013.

[40] *SS. Hontestroom (Owners) v. SS. Sagaporack (Owners)* [1927] A.C. 37; *Powell v. Streatham Manor Nursing Home* [1935] A.C. 243; *Watt or Thomas v. Thomas* [1947] A.C. 484.

[41] *per* Lord Summer in *SS. Hontestroom v. SS. Sagaporack*, above, at 47.

[42] *per* Lord Greene M.R. in *Yuill v. Yuill* [1945] P. 15 at 22.

appreciate the weight or bearing of circumstances admitted or proved or otherwise to have gone plainly wrong".[43]

The court is a little less reluctant to interfere with findings based upon expert evidence.[44]

On the other hand, the Court of Appeal is much more willing to draw inferences from the primary facts different from those drawn by the trial judge, provided that it is in as good a position as the judge to draw such inferences.[45] Overall, in considering how reluctant an appellate court should be "to interfere with the judge's evaluation of, and conclusion, on the primary facts ... there is no single standard which is appropriate to every case. The most important variables include the nature of the evaluation required, the standing and experience of the fact-finding judge or tribunal, and the extent to which the judge or tribunal had to assess oral evidence."[46]

The role of the Court of Appeal in appeals on questions of fact was considered in *Whitehouse v. Jordan*.[47] The trial judge held a senior hospital registrar to have been negligent in the course of delivering a baby by pulling too hard and too long on obstetric forceps, causing brain damage. This finding was based on a combination of expert evidence, a report by the consultant professor who was the registrar's head of department, and the testimony of the mother. This finding was reversed by the Court of Appeal (Lord Denning M.R. and Lawton L.J., Donaldson L.J. dissenting). The majority held that the expert evidence against the registrar was defective in certain respects, and could not stand up against the expert evidence in his favour; that the judge had acted incorrectly in interpreting a crucial word in the report in its dictionary sense rather than in that now stated by the professor to be the sense intended; and that as the judge had disbelieved most of the mother's evidence, he ought not to have relied upon any of it. The mother had testified that force had been applied to the extent that her hips had been lifted off the table. The judge accepted that this could not literally have been true, but held that it showed that she "could" have been pulled towards the bottom of the delivery bed. On this last point, Lawton L.J. said that this was one of the rare cases where the appeal court was entitled to disregard the trial judge's assessment of the reliability of a witness. He had "palpably misused his advantage" in seeing the witness by turning her account of what had happened, which physically could not have taken place, into one which could. The House of Lords unanimously endorsed the conclusion of the majority of the Court of Appeal. They stressed the point that apart from the mother's testimony, the issues concerned inferences from the primary facts in the sense of the evaluation of

---

[43] *per* Lord Macmillan in *Watt or Thomas v. Thomas* [1947] A.C. 484 at 491.

[44] *Joyce v. Yeomans* [1981] 1 W.L.R. 549 (medical witnesses).

[45] *Benmax v. Austin Motor Co. Ltd* [1955] A.C. 370; *Biogen Inc v. Medeva plc.* [1997] R.P.C. 1 at 45, *per* Lord Goff: "It would ... be wrong to treat *Benmax* as authorising or requiring an appellate court to undertake a *de novo* evaluation of the facts in all cases in which no question of the credibility of witnesses is involved. Where the application of a legal standard such as negligence ... involves no question of principle but is simply a matter of degree, an appellate court should be very cautious in differing from the judge's evaluation."

[46] *per* Robert Walker L.J. in *Bessant v. South Cone Incorporated* [2002] EWCA Civ 763 para. [12] (should be a real but not the highest degree of reluctance to interfere with decision of hearing officer in complex patents case).

[47] [1981] 1 W.L.R. 246.

testimony accepted to have been honestly given.[48] As to the mother's testimony, the House agreed unanimously that the judge's "reconstruction" of it should be disregarded.

Where the trial is conducted with a jury, the powers of the Court of Appeal are more limited. A verdict will be set aside if the evidence was such that no jury properly directed could reasonably have returned it.[49]

(2) *Awards of damages.* The Court of Appeal will not vary an award of **18–034** damages merely because the judges sitting on the appeal would have awarded a different figure. It will only do so:

" ... if satisfied that the judge has acted on a wrong principle of law or has misapprehended the facts, or has, for those or other reasons, made a wholly erroneous estimate of the damage suffered".[50]

In practice, the Court of Appeal is much more likely to interfere with an award of damages than a finding of fact, especially where, as with large personal injuries awards, complex calculations are necessary.

Where damages were assessed by a jury, the Court of Appeal was only prepared to interfere with an award where it was "so excessive or so inadequate that no 12 reasonable jurors could reasonably have awarded it".[51] The consequence of this cautious approach was that awards of significantly different amounts in similar cases were permitted to stand. This was one of the factors in the move away from trial by jury in civil cases.[52] In *Ward v. James,*[53] Lord Denning M.R. said[54]:

"In future this court will not feel the same hesitation as it formerly did in upsetting an award of damages by a jury. If it is out of all proportion to the circumstances of the case (that is, if it is far too high or far too low), this court will set it aside."

This approach appears to bring the position closer to that applied to awards by judges. In *Sutcliffe v. Pressdram Ltd*[55] the Court of Appeal set aside a libel award of £600,000 to the wife of the so-called "Yorkshire Ripper". The traditional approach was followed, and it was not regarded as having been changed by *Ward v. James.*[56]

The Court of Appeal may substitute an award of damages for that made by a judge. If the award was made by a jury the position formerly was that the Court of Appeal could only vary an award with the consent of the parties[57]: otherwise it had to order a new trial, which could be by judge

[48] See Lord Wilberforce, *ibid.* pp. 249–250; Lord Fraser of Tullybelton, *ibid.,* p.263.
[49] See below, para. 18-037.
[50] *per* Morris L.J. in *Scott v. Musial* [1959] 2 Q.B.
[51] *ibid.* pp. 437–438.
[52] See above, para. 15-007.
[53] [1966] 1 Q.B. 273.
[54] *ibid.,* p. 301.
[55] [1991] 1 Q.B. 153.
[56] *op. cit.* n. 54. A majority of the Court of Appeal regarded the jury in the *Sutcliffe* case as having wrongly included an award of exemplary damages. Mrs Sutcliffe settled the case for £60,000.
[57] RSC Ord. 59, r. 11(4).

alone. However, there is now power to make rules of court enabling the Court of Appeal in specified cases to substitute an award for that made by the jury.[58] Accordingly, it was provided that in any case where the Court of Appeal has power to order a new trial on the ground that damages awarded by a jury are excessive or inadequate, the court may instead of so ordering substitute such sum as appears to it to be proper.[59]

18–035   (3) *Exercises of discretion.* On many matters, a decision may be left to an exercise of the judge's discretion. Where the matter is then taken to the Court of Appeal, that court will only interfere with the judge's exercise of discretion if he or she has erred in law, applied an incorrect principle, misapprehended the facts, taken irrelevant matters into consideration or ignored relevant considerations, or if the court is satisfied that the decision was wrong.[60] This is not regarded as enabling the Court of Appeal to interfere merely because the judges sitting on the appeal would have exercised the discretion differently.[61] An example is *Charles Osenton & Co. v. Johnston,*[62] where the House of Lords reversed an order for trial by an official referee on the ground that the judge had not given sufficient weight to the point that the professional reputation of surveyors was at stake.

In addition, modern statutes commonly leave decisions on substantive as distinct from procedural matters to the discretion of judges. Examples include awards under the Inheritance (Provision for Family and Dependants) Act 1975, financial provision after divorce and decisions concerning custody of and access to children. The same principles have been applied to the role of the Court of Appeal here,[63] and it has been stressed that the court should be particularly unwilling to interfere where the exercise of discretion is based on the impression made by a person in the witness box.[64]

However, in custody cases there has been a difference between: (1) those who take the view that the appellate court should only interfere where the judge has erred in law, taken some irrelevant matter into account or failed to take some relevant matter into account, or where the decision is "plainly wrong" in the sense that no reasonable judge could have so decided[65]; and (2) those who take the view that, in addition, the appellate court may

---

[58]   Courts and Legal Services Act 1990, s.8.

[59]   Ord. 59, r.11(4), as substituted by S.I. 1990 No. 2599; see now CPR, r.52.10(3). See *Rantzen v. Mirror Group Newspapers Ltd* [1994] Q.B. 670, where the CA reduced a libel award from £250,000 to £110,000, the court noting that it should scrutinise large awards of damages more closely than hitherto in the context of the protection of freedom of expression by Art. 10, ECHR; *John v. Mirror Group Newspapers Ltd.* [1997] Q.B. 586, where the CA reduced an award of £350,000 to £75,000, and held that in future juries could be referred by way of comparison to the conventional compensation scales in personal injury cases, as well as previous libel awards, and both judge and counsel could indicate to the jury the level of award they thought appropriate; *Kiam II v. MGN Ltd.* [2002] EWCA Civ 43.

[60]   *Evans v. Bartlam* [1937] A.C. 473. This is regarded as broader than the tests applied by the court in reviewing exercises of administrative discretion under the principles stated in the *Wednesbury* case (see below, para. 18–050): *Tsai v. Woodworth, The Times,* November 30, 1983.

[61]   *per* Viscount Simon L.C. in *Charles Osenton & Co. v. Johnston* [1942] A.C. 130 at 138.

[62]   *ibid.*

[63]   See, *e.g. In re Thornley, Deed.* [1969] 1 W.L.R. 1037; *Preston v. Preston* [1982] Fam. 17.

[64]   *B v. W (Wardship: Appeal)* [1979] 1 W.L.R. 1041.

[65]   Stamp L.J. dissenting, in *Re F (A Minor) (Wardship: Appeal)* [1976] Fam. 238 at 249–255; Sir John Arnold P. in *Clode v. Clode* (1982) 3 F.L.R. 360 at 363.

interfere on the ground that the judge's decision is "plainly wrong" as a consequence of erring in the course of balancing the relevant factors.[66] The House of Lords in *G v. G (Minors: Custody Appeal)*[67] clearly endorsed the second school of thought. It expressly rejected as too narrow the "no reasonable judge" formulation: this was based on the "*Wednesbury* unreasonableness" principle[68] applicable to judicial control over the decision of an administrative body, and was not the appropriate test here. The distinction between the tests was admittedly "a fine one". Furthermore, it was clear that even under the less restricted approach approved by the House of Lords, the Court of Appeal would only exceptionally interfere with a decision where it could not point to an error of law or to a particular factor that should (or should not) have been taken into account: *i.e.* only in a case where the judge had "exceeded the generous ambit within which a reasonable disagreement is possible".[69]

A further point made by the House of Lords in *G v. G (Minors: Custody Appeal)*[70] was that the principles set out are generally applicable to all judicial exercises of discretion: appeals concerning the welfare of children do not form a special category.[71] The principles have subsequently been cited in connection with financial provision after divorce,[72] the award of costs[73] and the grant of injunctions,[74] and have been held to be relevant under the CPR.[75] The adherents of both schools were agreed that the Court of Appeal may not interfere merely because the members of that court would have exercised the discretion differently.[76]

If an appellate court wishes to vary a discretionary order, it may either substitute an appropriate order, remit the case to the judge (or to another judge) or, in exceptional cases, hear evidence in order to resolve any doubts.[77]

(4) *Questions of law.* Here, the Court of Appeal may simply substitute its opinion for that of the court below.   **18–036**

---

[66] *Re O (Infants) (Wardship: Appeal)* [1971] Ch. 748; Browne and Bridge L.JJ. in *Re F (A Minor) (Wardship: Appeal)* [1976] Fam. 238; *B v. W (Wardship: Appeal)* [1979] 1 W.L.R. 1041; *D v. M (Minor: Custody Appeal)* [1983] Fam. 33.

[67] [1985] 1 W.L.R. 647. See J. Eekelaar, (1985) 48 M.L.R. 704; C. Forder and R. Ward, "Child Custody Appeals: the Search for Principle" [1987] C.L.J. 489; S. P. de Cruz, (1986) 130 S.J. 563.

[68] Below, para. 18-050.

[69] [1985] 1 W.L.R. 647 at 656, *per* Lord Bridge.

[70] *per* Lord Fraser at 652, based on Asquith L.J. in *Bellenden (formerly Satterthwaite) v. Satterthwaite* [1948] 1 All E.R. 343 at 345. The point that this formulation should not apply where there is an error of law or principle is emphasised by Eekelaar, and by Forder and Ward, *op. cit.* n.68 above. Most of the post-*G v. G* cases in which an appeal has been allowed have been characterised as involving errors of principle, rather than errors in balancing the relevant factors.

[71] *ibid.*, at 651, *per* Lord Fraser.

[72] *Morris v. Morris* [1985] 1 F.L.R. 1176; *Mason v. Mason* [1986] 2 F.L.R. 212; *Allen v. Allen* [1986] 2 F.L.R. 265; *Whiting v. Whiting* [1988] 1 W.L.R. 565.

[73] *Hawkins v. Dhawan* [1987] 2 E.O.L.R. 157.

[74] *Att.-Gen. v. Guardian Newspapers Ltd* [1987] 1 W.L.R. 1248.

[75] See above, para. 18-026.

[76] *Re F (A Minor)*, n. 67 above, at 250 (Stamp L.J.); 257–258 (Browne L.J.); *Clarke-Hunt v. Newcombe* (1983) 4 F.L.R. 482 at 486–487 (Cumming-Bruce L.J.).

[77] *per* Lord Scarman in *B. v. W.*, n. 67 above, at p. 1055, in relation to custody orders.

18–037   (5) *New trial.* Section 17 of the Supreme Court Act 1981 provides that applications for a new trial of any matter tried in the High Court must normally be directed to the Court of Appeal. However, rules of court may prescribe cases or classes of cases where applications are to be made to the High Court: such cases can only be those where trial was by a judge alone and no error of the court at the trial is alleged.[78]

Where a case is tried by judge alone, the proper course for a dissatisfied party is normally[79] to appeal. On an appeal, the Court of Appeal may, as we have noted, correct any error of fact or law and may vary the judgment. However, in some cases it may be appropriate for the Court of Appeal to order a new trial.[80] This may be so where, for example, the essence of the complaint is that there has not been a fair trial. For example, a party may be "taken by surprise" where a case is called on for hearing unexpectedly, or develops in a wholly unexpected manner. Similarly, a new trial may be ordered where fresh evidence is discovered,[81] or a witness confesses that his or her evidence was false,[82] or in cases of misconduct by the judge[83] or counsel.

Where a case is tried by a judge sitting with a jury, the proper course for a party dissatisfied is again to appeal and, where appropriate, apply for a new trial.[84] The grounds for such applications mentioned above in relation to trial by judge alone will also be relevant here. In addition, there are a number of grounds related particularly to jury trial, including misdirection of the jury, the improper admission or rejection of evidence, and claims that there was no evidence to go to the jury, that the verdict was against the weight of evidence or that the damages are excessive or inadequate.[85] There will, however, be no new trial if the court is satisfied that the jury, if rightly directed, would still have returned the same verdict.[86]

A verdict supported by no evidence is regarded as erroneous in law: if it is claimed, however, that a verdict is against the weight of evidence, it will only be set aside if it was perverse in the sense that it was one that no reasonable jury could have found.[87]

A new trial may be ordered on one particular aspect of a case, without affecting the other aspects. For example, there may be a new trial on a question of damages without prejudice to a finding of liability.

---

[78] *e.g.* where judgment has been obtained in the absence of a party. CPR, r.39.3(3),(5).
[79] *i.e.* unless an application must be made to the High Court: n. 79 above.
[80] Jurisdiction to do so is conferred by CPR, r.52.10(2)(c).
[81] See above, para. 18-026. *Meek v. Fleming* [1961] 2 Q.B. 366 (court misled by concealment of material evidence).
[82] *Piotrowska v. Piotrowski* [1958] 1 W.L.R. 798.
[83] *Jones v. National Coal Board* [1957] 2 Q.B. 55, above, para. 4-028, n.44.
[84] Under the CPR, applications for a new trial appear to have been subsumed into appeals See, *e.g. McPhilemy v. Times Newspapers Ltd.* [2001] EWCA Civ 871. For the purposes of the rules requiring permission to be obtained, a right of appeal includes a right to apply for a new trial or to set aside a verdict, finding or judgment in any matter in the High Court tried by a jury: Access to Justice Act 1999, s.54(6).
[85] See above, para. 18-034.
[86] *Rowell v. Pratt* [1938] A.C. 101, 116.
[87] *Metropolitan Ry. Co. v. Wright* (1886) 11 App. Cas. at 152; *Mechanical Inventions Co. Ltd v. Austin* [1935] A.C. 346; *Grobbelaar v. News Group Newspapers Ltd.* [2001] 2 All E.R. 437. If it is obvious that no verdict for the plaintiff on all the available evidence could be supported, the court may save the waste of time in ordering a new trial by ordering judgment to be entered for the defendant: *Mechanical Inventions Co. Ltd. v. Austin, ibid; Grobbelaar, ibid.*

(b) Appeals from the High Court to the House of Lords

In certain circumstances an appeal in a civil case may be taken directly from **18–038** the High Court (whether a single judge or a Divisional Court) to the House of Lords, "leap-frogging" the Court of Appeal. The conditions are prescribed by Part II of the Administration of Justice Act 1969.[88]

Any of the parties to civil proceedings[89] in the High Court may apply to the trial judge[90] for a certificate to the effect that he is satisfied:

(1) that the "relevant conditions" are fulfilled in relation to his decision in the proceedings;

(2) that a sufficient case for a "leap-frog" appeal has been made out to justify an application for leave to appeal; and

(3) that all the parties consent to the grant of a certificate.[91]

Where apart from the provisions of Part II of the 1969 Act no appeal would lie to the Court of Appeal without the leave of the trial judge or the Court of Appeal, the judge is not to grant a certificate unless it appears to the judge that apart from those provisions "it would be a proper case for granting leave".[92] The "relevant conditions" are:

(1) that a point of law of general public importance is involved in the decision; and

(2) that the point of law either—

"(a) relates wholly or mainly to the construction of an enactment or of a statutory instrument, and has been fully argued in the proceedings and fully considered in the judgment of the judge in the proceedings, or

(b) is one in respect of which the judge is bound by a decision of the Court of Appeal or of the House of Lords in previous proceedings, and was fully considered in the judgments given by the Court of Appeal or the House of Lords (as the case may be) in those previous proceedings."[93]

No certificate can be granted if by virtue of any enactment no appeal would lie from the High Court to the Court of Appeal or from the Court of Appeal to the House of Lords, or if the decision or order of the judge was made in the exercise of jurisdiction to punish for contempt of court.[94]

Otherwise, the judge has a discretion whether to grant a certificate,[95] and

---

[88] This possibility was recommended by the Evershed Committee on Supreme Court Practice and Procedure, Final Report (Cmd. 8878, 1953), paras. 483–503. The Law Lords at the time were not in favour of the proposal, but attitudes had changed by the late 1960s. See L. Blom-Cooper and G. Drewry, *Final Appeal* (1972), pp. 149–151.

[89] *i.e.* "proceedings other than proceedings in a criminal cause or matter": Administration of Justice Act 1969, s.12(8).

[90] Or Divisional Court, as the case may be: *ibid.*

[91] 1969 Act, s.12(1).

[92] *ibid.* s.15(3).

[93] *ibid.* s.12(3).

[94] *ibid.* s.15(1),(2),(4).

[95] *I.R.C. v. Church Commissioners for England* [1975] 1 W.L.R. 1383.

no appeal lies from a grant or refusal.[96] The application for a certificate should normally be made at the hearing but may be made within 14 days.[97]

If a certificate is granted any party may apply within one month to the House of Lords for leave to appeal directly.[98] No hearing is held. The House may grant leave "if ... it appears ... to be expedient to do so", whereupon no appeal will lie to the Court of Appeal.[99] Moreover, no appeal will lie to the Court of Appeal once a certificate is granted until either the time for an application for leave has expired or, where an application is made, until it has been determined by the House.[1]

The "leap-frog" procedure is used in comparatively few cases,[2] although it does enable there to be a significant saving in time and expense if a case is destined for the House of Lords. One of the problems is that it may be difficult for a trial judge to perceive that a case is so destined: it may only become so in the light of the decision in the Court of Appeal.[3]

(c) Appeals from the Court of Appeal to the House of Lords

18–039   An appeal lies from any judgment or order of the Court of Appeal to the House of Lords, provided that leave is obtained from either court.[4] No appeal lies from a decision of the Court of Appeal to refuse leave for an appeal to itself; such a refusal does not constitute a "judgment or order".[5] An application for leave is made first to the Court of Appeal, normally immediately after judgment. It is only if leave is refused that a petition for leave may be made to the House.

Among grounds commonly given by the Court of Appeal for refusing leave to appeal are that the point concerns an interlocutory matter, the point is one of fact rather than law, the subject matter is trivial, the matter has become of academic interest only to one or both of the parties[6] and that the Court of Appeal was unanimous and not divided. On the other hand, leave is normally granted in revenue cases.[7]

Petitions to the House of Lords for leave are heard by an Appeal Committee of three Law Lords,[8] and must be lodged within one month from

---

[96] 1969 Act, s. 12(5).
[97] *ibid.* s.12(4).
[98] The House may grant an extension of time: *ibid.* s.13(1).
[99] *ibid.* s.13(2).
[1] *ibid.* s.13(5).
[2] The early practice is reviewed by G. Drewry in "Leapfrogging—And a Lord Justices' Eye View of the Final Appeal" (1973) 89 L.Q.R. 260. A recent example is *Alconbury*, above para. 8-021.
[3] *e.g.* as in *Cassell & Co. Ltd v. Broome* [1972] A.C. 1027: see above, para. 1-015. The Lord Chancellor suggested that in view of the doubts raised about the direction in *Rookes v. Barnard* [1964] A.C. 1129, the proper course would have been to wait for a case in which the point was directly raised and suggest that the parties take *that* case directly to the House of Lords: *ibid.* p. 1053.
[4] Appellate Jurisdiction Act 1876, s.3; Administration of Justice (Appeals) Act 1934, s.1.
[5] *Lane v. Esdaile* [1891] A.C. 210; *Whitehouse v. The Board of Control* [1960] 1 W.L.R. 1093; *R. v. Secretary of State for Trade and Industry, ex p. Eastaway* [2000] 1 W.L.R. 2222. *cf. Geogas S.A. v. Trammo Gas* [1991] 1 W.L.R. 776 (no appeal against grant of leave by CA).
[6] *cf. Ainsbury v. Millington* [1987] 1 W.L.R. 379, where the House refused to hear arguments on this ground in a case in which leave had been granted.
[7] See L. Blom-Cooper and G. Drewry, *Final Appeal* (1972), pp. 146–149.
[8] See above, para. 2-073. and L. Blom-Cooper and G. Drewry, *Final Appeal* (1972), Chap. VII.

the date of the order of which complaint is made.[9] The committee considers the petition, and if all three members are unanimously of the opinion that it is not admissible it is dismissed without a hearing. If a petition is admissible, the Appeal Committee considers whether leave should be given. The test applied is whether a petition raises "an arguable point of law of general public importance which ought to be considered by the House at that time, bearing in mind that the cause will already have been the subject of judicial decision". If it is unanimously of the opinion that leave should be refused, it is dismissed without a hearing. If the Appeal Committee takes the provisional view that leave should be given, or given on terms, the respondents are invited to lodge objections. If having considered those objections, the Appeal Committee's opinion remains the same, leave is granted without a further hearing. In any case in which the members are not unanimous, the petition is referred for an oral hearing by the committee.[10] The parties may appear in person or may be represented by solicitors (known as "agents" on appeals to the House) or counsel. In the case of "leap-frog" appeals from the High Court[11] the petition for leave must be lodged within one month from the date on which the necessary certificate was granted: the time can be extended. The petition is considered by the Appeal Committee without a hearing.[12] No reasons are normally given for refusing leave. Conditions may be attached to a grant of leave: this is commonly done on appeals by the Inland Revenue in tax cases, where leave is only granted if the Revenue undertake to pay the costs of the appeal for the respondent in any event. If a condition is imposed by the Court of Appeal, the applicant may treat this as a refusal and apply for leave to the House of Lords.

Where an application for leave to appeal has been refused, it is nevertheless possible, in exceptional cases, for a fresh application to be made and granted.[13]

An appeal must be lodged in the House of Lords within three months of the date of the order appealed from, unless the House or the court below otherwise orders, or a different period is fixed by statute.[14] Leave to appeal out of time may be obtained. Unless a certificate of public funding or legal aid certificate has been granted, or the appellant is in an appeal under the Child Abduction and Custody Act 1985 or a Minister or government department, or the respondent agrees to waive the requirement, the appellant must give security for costs in the sum of £25,000.[15]

The appeal is normally considered by an Appellate Committee of five Law Lords.[16] The parties may appear in person or be represented by counsel. Wherever possible, a "statement of the facts and issues involved in the

---

[9] House of Lords Practice Directions applicable to Civil Appeals (June 2001 ed.), Dir. 2.
[10] *ibid.* Dir. 4.
[11] See above, para. 18-038.
[12] Practice Directions applicable to Civil Appeals, Dir. 6.
[13] See *Buttes Gas v. Hammer* [1982] A.C. 888 (leave to appeal from [1975] Q.B. 557 in the light of related proceedings: but note the criticisms of F. A. Mann, (1983) 2 C.J.Q. 320 at 325–326); *R. v. Home Secretary, ex p. Khera* [1984] A.C. 74, (the House of Lords invited the appellant to re-apply for leave following their Lordships' decision to review *R. v. Home Secretary, ex p. Zamir* [1980] A.C. 930).
[14] Practice Directions applicable to Civil Appeals, Dir. 7.
[15] *ibid.* Dir. 10.
[16] See above, para. 2-073.

appeal" should be agreed by the parties; otherwise, each must submit their own. An appendix of documents should also be prepared. The statement and appendix must be lodged within six weeks of the presentation of the appeal. The parties must also each lodge a "case", "being a succinct statement of [their] argument in the Appeal", in the form of the heads of argument counsel proposes to submit.[17] All members of the Appellate Committee will have read the statement(s) and case and the judgments in the court below in advance of the hearing.

The House has noted and deprecated a tendency to expand the written cases to incorporate and develop in them detailed written arguments, supported by lengthy citations and references to numerous authorities:

> " ... much on the same lines as the written 'briefs' submitted by the parties in appeals to appellate courts in the United States, which have resulted in oral argument playing a relatively insignificant role in the decision-making process adopted by appellate courts in that country".[18]

The pre-reading was, it was emphasised, not intended to reduce the part played by oral argument in the decision-making process. Cases should include the *heads* of argument on each issue, and only *key* authorities should be mentioned.

It has, however, been doubted whether all members of the Committee do always read all the papers in advance, and whether all the members always come to a hearing without at least a provisional conclusion in mind.[19] It would obviously be undesirable for preconceived opinions to be based on limited information. Indeed, it has been suggested that changes in the practice of both the Court of Appeal[20] and the House of Lords may inevitably transform the nature of oral argument:

> " ... which is bound to lose its force where it is no longer a dialogue in the traditional sense, but an attempt to dislodge or fortify an existing impression, however provisional it may be said to be ....
> [T]he introduction of radical changes under the heading of practice and procedure is outside the province of judges."[21]

The respective approaches of the House to question of fact, discretion and law are similar to that taken by the Court of Appeal.[22] The House "may determine what of right, and according to the law and custom of this realm, ought to be done" in relation to the appeal. Where the House reverses or varies an order of the court below, or orders anything to be done by the

---

[17] See above, para. 2-073. Practice Directions applicable to Civil Appeals, Dir. 15.
[18] *M.V. Yorke Motors v. Edwards* [1982] 1 W.L.R. 444 at 446–448; reaffirmed in *G v. G (Minors: Custody Appeal)* [1985] 1 W.L.R. 647. These principles now apply to the statement(s) of facts and issues: Dir. 11.
[19] F.A. Mann, (1983) 2 C.J.Q. 320 at 327–328, 334–335.
[20] See above, paras 2-071, 18-029.
[21] F. A. Mann, above.
[22] See above, paras 18-0322–18-037.

court below, the order of the House of Lords must be made an order of the High Court[23]: the House itself has no machinery for enforcement.

The House also has inherent jurisdiction to correct any injustice caused by an earlier order of the House, although it will not reopen any appeal save in circumstances where, through no fault of a party, he or she has been subjected to an unfair procedure. There is no question of an order being reopened just because it is thought that the first decision is wrong.[24]

4. APPEALS IN ADMINISTRATIVE LAW MATTERS

(a) Introduction

No neat classification is possible of the vast range of functions performed by **18–040** administrative authorities. Neither is it possible to discern any clear pattern in the availability of rights of appeal from administrative decisions.[25]

The Franks Committee[26] noted that:

" ... over most of the field of public administration no formal procedure is provided for objecting or deciding on objections. ... Of course the aggrieved individual can always complain to the appropriate administrative authority, to his Member of Parliament, to a representative organisation or to the press. But there is no formal procedure on which he can insist. ... It may be thought that in these cases the individual is less protected against unfair or wrong decisions [than where there is provision for a formal procedure involving a tribunal or inquiry]."[27]

Such decisions were outside the committee's terms of reference, although it did express "much sympathy" with the proposal by Professor W. A. Robson that there should be a general administrative appeal tribunal, with jurisdiction to hear not only appeals from tribunals and from Ministers after a public inquiry, "but also appeals against harsh or unfair administrative decisions in that considerable field of administration in which no special tribunal or enquiry procedure is provided".[28] The committee, however, felt that it had to consider the proposal in relation to its limited terms of reference, and that, viewed from that standpoint, the proposal was to be rejected.

Since then, the problem noted by the Franks Committee has been partly met by the establishment of "Ombudsmen" of various kinds. The Parliamentary Commissioner for Administration and Local Commissioners

---

[23] See Practice Direction 40B, para. 13.

[24] *R. v. Bow Street Metropolitan Stipendiary Magistrate, ex p. Pinochet Ugarte (No. 2)* [1999] 1 All E.R. 577, *per* Lord Browne-Wilkinson at pp. 585–586.

[25] See S.A. de Smith and R. Brazier, *Constitutional and Administrative Law* (8th ed., 1998), pp. 513–514; *Law Commission Report, Administrative Law: Judicial Review and Statutory Appeals* (Law Com. No. 226), Part XII.

[26] See above, para. 2-008.

[27] Cmnd. 218, pp. 2–3.

[28] Cmnd. 218, p. 28.

have power to investigate complaints that there has been injustice consequent on "maladministration" in central and local government.[29] The concept of "maladministration" covers such matters as corruption, bias, unfair discrimination, giving misleading advice, failure to explain the reasons for a decision, losing correspondence and unreasonable delay. The relevant defects are mostly procedural, although where a decision is "thoroughly bad in quality" maladministration may be inferred, and in certain circumstances authorities may be required to reconsider a rule that has caused hardship. The commissioners may not, however, question the merits of a discretionary decision taken without maladministration,[30] and may not entertain a complaint in respect of which there is a right of appeal to a tribunal or a remedy by way of proceedings in a court of law, unless it is not reasonable to expect the complainant to utilise those possibilities.[31]

As to the availability of statutory appeals against administrative decisions, the late Professor de Smith noted[32] that there is in general no appeal against discretionary decisions of central government involving questions of national policy or the allocation of scarce resources, against decisions of public corporations or against most discretionary decisions of local authorities on the allocation of limited resources.

However, in certain other areas of public administration, particularly where no sensitive issue of policy is involved, where questions of law may loom large or where a decision has a significant impact on individual rights of liberty or property there may be provision for an appeal.

(b) Particular areas

(i) Regulatory functions

18–041 Many activities are subjected to state regulation for such purposes as the protection of public health and welfare. Certain activities are prohibited by law. Others are permitted provided that those who participate in them register with a public authority.[33] Yet others require a specific permission or licence from a public authority: the ease with which a licence may be obtained, and the grounds upon which a licence may be refused are almost infinitely variable.

Control may also be exerted by procedures for inspection. For example, health and safety inspectors may inspect factory premises, offer advice on safety matters, issue notices requiring the cessation of dangerous activities, and, in the last resort, bring criminal proceedings for breaches of the law.

Decisions made in the course of regulatory procedures of this kind are commonly subject to a statutory right of appeal to a tribunal,[34] the Crown

---

[29] See generally, de Smith and Brazier (1998), Chap 30; Sir William Wade and C.F. Forsyth, *Administrative Law* (8th ed., 2000), pp. 87–112, 137–138; P. P. Craig, *Administrative Law* (4th ed. 1999). pp. 230–248. There is also an office of National Health Service Commissioner (held by the PCA) and there are separate Commissioners in Northern Ireland.

[30] Parliamentary Commissioner Act 1967, s.12(3); Local Government Act 1974, s.34(3).

[31] *ibid.* ss.5(2) and 26(6) respectively.

[32] de Smith and Brazier (1998), pp. 513–514.

[33] Registration requirements may also be imposed to raise revenue.

[34] *e.g.* appeals to an Employment Tribunal against an improvement or prohibition notice served by a health and safety inspector.

Court,[35] a county court[36] or, most commonly, a magistrates' court.[37]

In a small number of cases, such as decisions of the Director-General of Fair Trading concerning consumer credit licensing and the supervision of estate agency work, an appeal lies to a Minister, in these examples the Secretary of State for Trade and Industry, who appoints a panel of independent persons to hear such appeals.[38]

It is normal for it to be possible on such appeals to challenge a decision on the merits as well as on any point of law. This may be so even where it is expressly stated that the decision is "at the discretion" of the authority in question. For example, a grant of a permit for amusements with prizes,[39] is "at the discretion of the local authority."[40] An appeal lies to the Crown Court. In *Sagnata Ltd v. Norwich Corporation*,[41] the Court of Appeal held that the recorder at quarter sessions (now the Crown Court) had been correct to go into the merits of a refusal of a permit afresh on appeal, although this did not mean that he "ought not to pay great attention to the fact that the duly constituted and elected local authority have come to an opinion on the matter, and ought not lightly to reverse their opinion."[42]

(ii) Welfare benefits

Another important sphere of state activity is that of the provision of many kinds of welfare benefits. Here, it is common for rights of appeal to be granted to a tribunal.[43]   **18–042**

(iii) Tribunals

Where a decision-making function has been entrusted to a tribunal, it is normal for there to be a further appeal on points of law, either to a special appellate tribunal such as the Social Security Commissioners or the   **18–043**

---

[35] *e.g.* decisions of a chief officer of police in relation to firearms certificates and the registration of firearms; refusal of a permit for the commercial provision of amusements with prizes; and many decisions of justices of the peace in administrative matters: see D. Price, *Appeals* (1982), pp. 37–40.

[36] *e.g.* a person aggrieved by a notice requiring him or her to carry out works of repair, by a demand for the recovery of expenses where the authority has acted in default or by a demolition or closing order: Housing Act 1985, ss.191, 269, and Sched. 10, para. 6: Price (1982), pp. 46–49.

[37] *e.g.* revocation of a pilot's licence; refusal of a pet shop licence; refusal of registration of a nursery, child minder, or nursing home: Price (1982), pp. 53–60.

[38] From November 2, 2000, the Secretary of State has automatically accepted the panel's recommendation, unless they have reached a conclusion that is wrong in law; panel members can now only be removed from office on the ground of misbehaviour or incapacity; the changes reflecting implementation of the ECHR: *Changes to Appeals System under the Consumer Credit Act and the Estate Agents Act* (DTI Statement, November 2, 2000).

[39] *e.g.* fruit machines.

[40] Lotteries and Amusements Act 1976, Sched. 3. para. 7(1)(a).

[41] [1971] 2 Q.B. 614.

[42] *per* Lord Goddard C.J. in *Stepney Borough Council v. Joffe* [1949] 1 K.B. 599 at 603, endorsed by Edmund Davies L.J. in *Sagnata, ibid.* at 637. See also *Darlington Borough Council v. Paul Wakefield* (1988) 153 J.P. 481.

[43] See above, paras 2-034–2-038.

Employment Appeal Tribunal,[44] to the High Court or to the Court of Appeal.[45] For example, the Tribunals and Inquiries Act 1992 provides[46] for a right of appeal on a point of law to the High Court from the decisions of over 10 tribunals,[47] and there are several others for which similar provision is made by specific statutes. Appeals from tribunals to the High Court on points of law may be required to be made by means of a case stated procedure. Most lie to the Queen's Bench Division, but some, such as those against decisions of the Commons Commissioners and the Special and General Commissioners of Income Tax, lie to the Chancery Division. Appeals are generally heard by a single judge.[48] The Leggatt Review of Tribunal has recommended, the creation of a series of intermediate appellate tribunals.[49]

(iv) Land use

Given the traditional concern of the law for the protection of property rights it is perhaps not surprising that statutory rights to appeal figure prominedy in respect of governmental decisions that infringe or affect property rights. Two kinds of procedure require special mention here. First, planning permission is generally necessary for "the carrying out of building, engineering, mining or other operations in, on, over or under land" or "the making of any material change in the use" of buildings or land.[50] Applications for permission are made to the local planning authority and an appeal on merits, fact or law lies against a refusal to the Secretary of State.[51] An appeal may involve a hearing by way of a public local inquiry conducted by an inspector appointed by the Secretary of State, unless the appellant wishes simply to make written representations. The inspector may make the decision personally, except in the 30 per cent or so of larger-scale applications, where the decision is taken by the Secretary of State. An appeal thereafter lies on a point of law to the Queen's Bench Division.[52]

Secondly, there are many powers which authorise the compulsory acquisition of land. The typical procedure provides for a compulsory purchase order to be made by a local authority, subject to confirmation by a Minister. If there are objections, a hearing before an inspector must be held on behalf of the Minister. If the Minister confirms the order, the typical

---

[44] See above, para. 2-033.

[45] *e.g.* from the Lands Tribunal and the Foreign Compensation Commission.

[46] s.11. The appeal must be brought by a "party" to proceedings: *i.e.* a litigant and not merely a beneficiary of the litigation: *S. (a minor) v. Special Educational Needs Tribunal* [1996] 1 W.L.R. 382.

[47] *e.g.* Employment Tribunals (for certain matters), Rent Assessment Committees and Pension Appeal Tribunals.

[48] See RSC, Ord. 94, rr 8,9. (CPR Sched. 1).

[49] Above para. 2-010.

[50] Town and Country Planning Act 1990, s.55.

[51] Successively, the Secretary of State for the Environment, the Secretary of State for Transport, Local Government and the Regions and, from May 2002, the Deputy Prime Minister.

[52] Similar arrangements apply in respect of enforcement notices issued following a breach of planning control. As to compliance with Article 6(1) of the ECHR see above, para. 8–021.

provision[53] governing further appeals enables a person aggrieved by the order to apply within six weeks to the High Court for the order to be quashed on the ground either:

(1) that it is "not within the powers of the Act"; or

(2) that the applicant has been substantially prejudiced by failure to comply with a requirement of the Act.

The order may not otherwise be challenged: thus the person aggrieved may not, for example, seek to challenge an order by applying for judicial review[54] whether within the six week period or not.[55]

The first limb of the grounds of challenge purports to approximate to judicial review under the *ultra vires* doctrine,[56] although it has been given a wider interpretation by the courts. The correct approach was stated as follows by Lord Denning M.R. in *Ashbridge Investments Ltd v. Minister of Housing and Local Government*[57]:

"The court can only interfere on the ground that the Minister has gone outside the powers of the Act or that any requirement of the Act has not been complied with. Under this section it seems to me that the court can interfere with the Minister's decision if he has acted on no evidence; or if he has come to a conclusion to which on the evidence he could not reasonably come; or if he has given a wrong interpretation to the words of the statute; or if he has taken into consideration matters which he ought not to have taken into account, or vice versa; or has otherwise gone wrong in law. It is identical with the position when the court has power to interfere with the decision of a lower tribunal which has erred in point of law."

This would appear to extend the grounds of challenge to include errors of law not of a kind to cause the authority to act *ultra vires*.

(v) Appeals from Ministers

In a small number of situations where Ministers have to determine questions which may have a significant legal content, there is a further right of appeal on a point of law (or analogous grounds) to the High Court. These include the procedures mentioned in the previous section, decisions of the Secretary of State for Trade and Industry on appeals from the Director-General of Fair Trading, and deportation decisions.[58]

18–044

---

[53] *e.g.* Acquisition of Land Act 1981, ss.23–25; Housing Act 1985, Sched. 22, para. 7; Town and Country Planning Act 1990, ss.287, 288. See RSC, Ord. 94, rr. 1–3, 12, 13.

[54] See below, paras 18-046–18-059.

[55] See *Smith v. East Elloe R.D.C.* [1956] A.C. 736; *R. v. Secretary of State for the Environment, ex p. Ostler* [1977] Q.B. 122.

[56] See below, paras 18-047–18-050.

[57] [1965] 1 W.L.R. 1320 at 1326. Applied by the Court of Appeal in *Coleen Properties Ltd v. Minister of Housing and Local Government* [1971] 1 W.L.R. 433, and subsequent cases.

[58] See below.

(vi) Immigration

18–045   The impact on individual liberty of decisions to refuse entry to or to deport persons who have no legal right to enter or remain in the United Kingdom is such that a special appellate structure has been established.[59] The decisions of immigration officers or the Home Secretary, whether discretionary or not, may normally be the subject of an appeal to an Immigration Adjudicator, and then to the Immigration Appeal Tribunal.[60] An appeal then lies, with leave, on a point of law, to the Court of Appeal.[61]

D. APPLICATIONS FOR JUDICIAL REVIEW

18–046   An appeal will only lie if expressly provided by statute. Apart from, but parallel to, any appellate structure is the control exercised by the High Court over the decisions of any statutory authority[62] with a limited jurisdiction or area of power. This "judicial" control is exercised on the basis of two doctrines. By far the more significant is the *ultra vires* doctrine. The other is the power of the High Court to quash any decision within the reach of the prerogative order of certiorari if an error of law is apparent on the face of the decision-making body's record of proceedings: for this purpose it is immaterial whether the error of law is such as to cause the body to act *ultra vires*.[63] There is not the space here to give more than a very brief account of the *ultra vires* doctrine, and the procedures for seeking judicial review.[64]

1. The Ultra Vires Doctrine

18–047   Public authorities are normally given a circumscribed area of authority by Parliament. The function of the courts is to ensure that such authorities, whether inferior courts, tribunals, ministers or local authorities, do not exceed any of the limits expressly set by Parliament, and that they perform

---

[59] Immigration and Asylum Act 1999, Part IV.

[60] In specified cases involving national security an appeal lies to the Special Immigration Appeals Commission under the Special Immigration Appeals Commission Act 1997, as amended.

[61] 1999 Act, Sched. 4, para. 23.

[62] Or bodies established under the royal prerogative: *R. v. Criminal Injuries Compensation Board, ex p. Lain* [1967] 2 Q.B. 864; or otherwise performing public functions: *R. v. Panel on Take-Overs and Mergers, ex p. Datafin plc.* [1987] Q.B. 815.

[63] *R. v. Northumberland Compensation Appeal Tribunal, ex p. Shaw* [1952] 1 K.B. 338. This doctrine is in practice obsolete.

[64] The leading works include de Smith, Woolf and Jowell, *Judicial Review of Administrative Action* (5th ed. 1995); Sir William Wade and C. F. Forsyth, *Administrative Law* (8th ed., 2000); P. P. Craig, *Administrative Law* (8th ed., 1999); J. Goudie and M. Supperstone (eds), *Judicial Review* (2nd ed., 1997). For a briefer account see S. A. de Smith and R. Brazier. *Constitutional and Administrative Law* (4th, ed., 1998), Chaps 26, 27. On the application for judicial review, see R.J. Gordon, *Judicial Review and Crown Office Practice* (1998); C. Lewis, *Judicial Remedies in Public Law* (2nd ed., 2001); M. Fordham, *Judicial Review Handbook* (3rd ed., 2001).

any statutory duties. If that were all to be done, the *ultra vires* doctrine would simply be an exercise in statutory interpretation, and more or less straightforward as the case might be. However, the courts have in addition read certain implied limitations into governmental powers aimed at ensuring that those powers are not abused, and that decision-making processes are fair procedurally. It is assumed that these limitations are to be observed unless Parliament expressly provides otherwise.

If express or implied limits are exceeded, the body in question is said to have acted "*ultra vires*", *i.e.* beyond its powers: if they are not, the body has acted "*intra vires*". Where a decision is judicial rather than administrative[65] the term "jurisdiction" is used rather than "power", but the difference is one of terminology rather than substance. For convenience of exposition a number of different *ultra vires* situations are commonly distinguished.

The principles of judicial review are applied to bodies exercising public functions even where there is no statutory background. The theoretical foundations for judicial intervention here cannot be the *ultra vires* doctrine as such. It is then argued, first, that the substantive principles of judicial review as applied in such cases are the product of the common law (which is relatively uncontroversial) and, second, that this is also true when those principles are applied in areas with a statutory background (which is hotly contested).[66] The *ultra vires* theory may be easier to reconcile with parliamentary sovereignty and seems to have significant, although not universal, judicial support.[67] However, both theories recognise that the principles of judicial review may be modified or excluded from operation where Parliament legislates with the necessary specific intent to do so.

(a) Straightforward situations

In some cases a question may arise whether a particular activity falls within the scope of existing statutory authority. For example, in *Attorney-General v. Fulham Corporation*[68] the establishment of a municipal laundry was held not to be within the corporation's statutory powers to provide wash-houses. The courts, however, accept that authority may be "reasonably implied" from the express provisions of a statute,[69] and, furthermore, that matters "reasonably incidental" to activities expressly or impliedly authorised will also be held to be *intra vires*.[70]   **18–048**

(b) Jurisdiction over fact and law

In many situations, a body may only act where it is first established that a given state of affairs exists. For example, a court or tribunal may only have   **18–049**

---

[65] These categories represent each end of a spectrum rather than two discrete categories.

[66] See, *e.g.* C. Forsyth (ed.), *Judical Review and the Constitution* (2000); M. Elliott, *The Constitutional Foundations of Judicial Review* (2001) (setting out a modified *ultra vires* theory), critically reviewed by P.P. Craig and N. Bamforth, [2001] P.L. 763 (exponents of the common law theory).

[67] Lord Irvine, [1999] E.H.R.L.R. 350 at 368; Lord Steyn's exposition of the principle of legality in the context of statutory interpretation, *contra*: Lord Woolf M.R. [1995] P.L. 65; Sir John Laws, [1995] P.L. 72 at 79.

[68] [1921] 1 Ch. 440.

[69] *Baroness Wenlock v. River Dee Co.* (1885) 10 App.Cas.354 at 362.

[70] *Att.-Gen. v. Great Eastern Railway Co.* (1880) 5 App.Cas.473 at 478.

jurisdiction over a certain geographical area; a rent tribunal may only have jurisdiction in respect of "leases" of "furnished" premises; there may be a monetary limit to jurisdiction. In these examples, the "preliminary", "collateral" or "threshold" question is clearly distinguishable from the "main" question the court or tribunal has to determine. Moreover, the former is determinable at the commencement of that body's hearing. The superior courts have taken the view that inferior courts and tribunals may not extend their jurisdiction by erroneous determinations of these "preliminary", "collateral" or "jurisdictional" issues, whether or not the error is one of fact or law.[71] If challenged, decisions on these points will be redetermined by the High Court on an application for judicial review.

In other cases, however, the distinction between "preliminary" and "main" questions is less easy to draw. This is particularly so where it is alleged that a tribunal with jurisdiction at the commencement of an inquiry has "wandered outside its designated territory" by misconstruing the statute which gives it power to act. This area of administrative law has been the subject of much sophisticated analysis: it has, however, been doubted whether there is any clear cut or convincing test to distinguish "jurisdictional" questions from others. It may be that in the last resort the classification applied by a reviewing court turns more on whether that court wishes to intervene than on the application of any clear principle.

The decision of the House of Lords in *Anisminic Ltd v. Foreign Compensation Commission*[72] was widely regarded as broadening significantly the range of errors of law that would be regarded as causing a tribunal to exceed its jurisdiction.

In *Pearlman v. Keepers and Governors of Harrow School*[73] Lord Denning M.R. said that the traditional distinction between jurisdictional and non-jurisdictional errors should be discarded and replaced by a rule that all errors of law, as distinct from errors of fact, should be regarded as jurisditional. This view has been broadly endorsed by certain members of the House of Lords, but not in respect of courts whose decisions are in law "final".[74]

(c) Discretion

18–050   The courts under the *ultra vires* doctrine ensure that bodies entrusted with a discretion do not fetter it unlawfully by developing rigid rules which preclude a genuine consideration of each case on its merits or by entering contracts or other agreements incompatible with a proper exercise of discretion. Similarly, a body may not be estopped from exercising a statutory discretion and may not delegate the exercise of a discretion without express or implied statutory authority.

Furthermore, an administrative body may not "abuse" its discretion by exercising powers in bad faith or for an improper purpose, by taking account of irrelevant considerations or ignoring relevant considerations, or

---

[71] See, *e.g. R. v. City of London, etc. Rent Tribunal, ex p. Honig* [1951] 1 K.B. 641.
[72] [1969] 2 A.C. 147.
[73] [1979] Q.B. 56.
[74] *In Re Racal Communications Ltd* [1981] A.C. 374, *per* Lord Diplock and Lord Keith; *R. v. Hull University Visitor, ex p. Page* [1993] A.C. 682.

by making a decision that is so unreasonable that no reasonable authority could make it.[75] This last principle, sometimes termed one of "irrationality".[76] In recent years, this has been applied flexibly according to context so that

> "the more substantial the interference with human rights, the more the court will require by way of justification before it is satisfied that the decision is reasonable"

in this sense.[77] Conversely,

> "the greater the policy content of a decision, and the more remote the subject matter of a decision from ordinary judicial experience, the more hesitant the court must necessarily be in holding a decision to be irrational".[78]

(d) Natural justice

There are two basic principles of natural justice. The first, the *nemo judex in sua causa* rule, provides that no person should be a judge in his or her own cause. It is applied to judicial or quasi-judicial decision and may extend beyond.[79] The rule is breached where the adjudicator has a direct financial interest[80] or is a party or associated with a party[81], or where there is a real possibility of bias.[82]

18–051

The other, the *audi alteram partem* rule, applies to a wider range of decision-making functions and requires prior notice to be given of a decision adverse to individual interests together with an opportunity to make representations. The detailed content of this rule varies from the rigorous procedural standards expected of courts to the minimal standards of "fairness" required in respect of purely administrative decisions: the content in any given case will depend on the court's appraisal of what is appropriate in the circumstances.[83]

---

[75] These principles were expounded by Lord Greene M. R. in *Associated Provincial Picture Houses Ltd v. Wednesbury Corporation* [1948] 1 K.B. 223.

[76] Lord Diplock in *Council of Civil Service Unions v. Minister for Civil Service* [1985] A.C. 374 at 410–414.

[77] Submission of David Pannick Q.C., approved by the Court of Appeal in *R. v. Ministry of Defence, ex p. Smith* [1996] 2 W.L.R. 305 at 336, 346.

[78] Sir Thomas Bingham M.R. in *ibid.* at 337–338.

[79] See Sedley J. in *R. v. Secretary of State for the Environment, ex p. Kirkstall Valley Campaign Ltd.* [1996] 3 All E.R. 304.

[80] *e.g. Dimes v. Grand Junction Canal Proprietors* (1852) 3 H.L.Cas. 759 (decision of Lord Cottenham L.C. set aside by the House of Lords on the ground that he held shares in the plaintiff company).

[81] *R. v. Bow Street Magistrate, ex p. Pinochet Ugarte (No. 2)* [2000] 1 A.C. 119, above, 4-036.

[82] See above, para. 4-036.

[83] See, *e.g. Ridge v. Baldwin* [1964] A.C. 40 (dismissal of a chief constable without prior notice and a proper hearing held to be void); *R. v. Commission for Racial Equality, ex p. Cottrell and Rothon* [1980] 1 W.L.R. 1580 at 1586–87 (emphasising the variable content of the *audi alteram partem* rule and the duty to act fairly); *R. v. Secretary of State for the Home Department, ex p. Doody* [1994] 1 A.C. 531 (fairness may require reasons to be given for a decision).

(e) Procedural ultra vires

18–052 The procedure to be adopted for a particular decision-making process may be expressly prescribed by statute or statutory instrument. However, the consequences of failure to observe a particular step are not commonly spelled out. The courts have traditionally drawn a distinction between *mandatory* and *directory* requirements: failure to observe a mandatory step renders the ultimate decision *ultra vires*; failure to observe a directory step does not have this effect, although in some cases "substantial compliance" may be necessary. Important safeguards such as an obligation to consult[84] or to inform a person of rights of appeal[85] are normally held to be mandatory: trivial typographical errors which do not mislead[86] are normally regarded as directory matters, although the distinction is not always easy to draw.[87] In more recent cases, the courts have emphasised that these issues do not turn simply on a generic analysis of the nature of different kinds of requirement but on the examination of the facts and context of the particular case. Key questions are (1) is substantial compliance sufficient and has there been substantial compliance? (2) is the non-compliance capable of being waived? (3) if it is not capable of being waived or has not been waived, what have the consequences of non-compliance been?[88] In most cases, the courts will only quash a decision where the applicant has been prejudiced; however, there remain some situations where this may happen without evidence of prejudice.

2. The Methods of Obtaining Judicial Review

(a) Introduction

18–053 Judicial review of judicial and administrative decisions and delegated legislation may be sought "directly" or "collaterally". A direct challenge may be made either:

(1) by a claim for judicial review" in the Queen's Bench Division where the court may award one or more of a number of remedies: namely, certiorari (a quashing order), mandamus (a mandatory order), prohibition (a prohibiting order),[89] an injunction, a declaration and damages; or

(2) in an ordinary claim in the Queen's Bench or Chancery Divisions for an injunction, a declaration, or damages.

---

[84] *Agricultural etc. Training Board v. Aylesbury Mushrooms Ltd* [1972] 1 W.L.R. 190.

[85] *London & Clydeside Ltd v. Aberdeen District Council* [1980] 1 W.L.R. 182.

[86] *e.g. R. v. Dacorum Gaming Licensing Committee* [1971] 3 All E.R. 666.

[87] Lord Hailsham in the *London & Clydeside* case, *op. cit.* n. 86 at 183; his Lordship also suggested *obiter* that the courts should adopt a more flexible approach to this issue: this view is beginning to find favour: see, *e.g.* the Court of Appeal in *R. v. Lambeth Borough Council, ex p. Sharp* [1987] J.P.L. 440.

[88] *R. v. Immigration Appeal Tribunal, ex p. Jeyeanthan* [2000] 1 W.L.R. 354.

[89] The English labels have been introduced as part of the drive against the use of latin terms as part of the Woolf reforms; whether this break with history will add to the general public's understanding of judicial review remedies is doubtful.

A challenge is made collaterally where the argument that an act or decision, such as a byelaw, is *ultra vires* is raised as a defence to enforcement proceedings or prosecution.[90]

A new, unified, procedure for an application for judicial review was introduced in 1978.[91] It was remodelled as part of the Woolf reforms and is now governed by the CPR, Part 54[92] In 1982, the House of Lords held that as a general rule it would be contrary to public policy and an abuse of the process of the court for a plaintiff complaining of a public authority's infringement of his or her "public law rights" to seek redress by an ordinary action rather than an application for judicial review.[93] Private law claims against public authorities, such as actions for damages, might still be brought by ordinary proceedings.[94] The distinction between public law and private law matters was, however, very difficult to draw. After some hesitation,[95] it was held that the principle of *O'Reilly v. Mackman*[96] did not prevent a defendant in criminal proceedings for breach of a byelaw raising the validity of the byelaw collaterally by way of defence at the trial.[97] Similarly, in a civil case, matters of *vires* could be raised in defence of private law rights, where those rights were not dependent upon a public law decision.[98] These difficulties have now been much diminished by the reduction in the differences between ordinary procedure and judicial review procedure under the Civil Procedure Rules.[99]

(b) Procedure on applications for judicial review

The procedure on applications for judicial review is prescribed by section 31 of the Supreme Court Act 1981 and CPR, Part 54. A "claim for judicial review" is a claim to review the lawfulness of an enactment, or of "a decision, action or failure to act in relation to a public function". The "judicial review procedure" is the procedure under CPR, Part 8, modified by Part 54.[1] The judicial review procedure *must* be used in a claim for judicial

18–054

---

[90] See, *e.g. Kruse v. Johnson* [1898] 2 Q.B. 91.

[91] RSC, Ord. 53; Supreme Court Act 1981, s.31.

[92] Introduced following Sir Jeffrey Bowman's *Review of the Crown Office* (2000), with effect from October 2, 2000 (also implementation date for the Human Rights Act 1998).

[93] *O'Reilly v. Mackman* [1983] 2 A.C. 237.

[94] *Davy v. Spelthorne Borough Council* [1984] A.C. 262.

[95] *Quietlynn Ltd v. Plymouth City Council* [1988] Q.B. 114, D.C. (pet.dis. [1987] 1 W.L.R. 1090, HL).

[96] *op. cit.* n. 94

[97] *R. v. Reading Crown Court, ex p. Hutchinson* [1988] Q.B. 384, DC (pet.dis. [1988] 1 W.L.R. 308). The challenge was ultimately successful: *DPP v. Hutchinson* [1990] 2 A.C. 783.

[98] *Wandsworth London Borough Council v. Winder* [1985] A.C 461 (council tenant entitled to raise in defence to an action for arrears of rent that the council's decision to raise the rent was an *ultra vires* abuse of discretion under the *Wednesbury* principles: the argument ultimately failed: *Wandsworth London Borough Council v. Winder (No. 2)* (1988) 20 H.L.R. 400). In *Roy v. Kensington and Chelsea and Westminster Family Practitioner Committee* [1992] 1 A.C. 624, the House of Lords held that a doctor was entitled to enforce his private law rights to remuneration (whether contractual or statutory) by an ordinary action. In *Mercury Communications Ltd. v. Director General of Telecommunications* [1996] 1 W.L.R. 48, Lord Slynn emphasised that flexibility should be retained in determining the limits of "public law" and "private law".

[99] Lord Woolf C.J. in *Clark v. University of Lincolnshire and Humberside* [2000] 1 W.L.R. 1988.

[1] CPR, r.54.1.

review where the claimant is seeking a mandatory, prohibiting or quashing order or an injunction under section 30 of the Supreme Court Act 1981 restraining a person from acting in any office in which he or she is not entitled to act.[2] The judicial review procedure *may* be used in a claim for judicial review where the claimant is seeking a declaration or injunction (other than under section 30 of the 1981 Act), although it must be used if a declaration or injunction is sought in addition to one of the remedies listed in rule 54.2.[3] The court may grant the declaration or injunction claimed if it considers that it would be just and convenient to do so, having regard to the nature of the matters in respect of which, and the persons and bodies against whom, mandatory, prohibiting and quashing orders may be granted, and all the circumstances of the case.[4] On a claim for judicial review the claimant may seek any of the remedies mentioned above in respect of the same matter; he or she may also claim and be awarded damages if there is a good cause of action, although this procedure may not be used to seek damages alone.[5]

The procedure is in two stages. The claimant must first obtain permission from a High Court judge by filing a claim form in the Administrative Court Office, which must be served on the defendant and other interested parties. The application for permission is dealt with on paper, although if permission is refused (or granted on terms) the claimant may request an oral hearing.[6] The court itself may adjourn a permission application into open court.[7] The test for the grant of permission is whether the claimant has a reasonable or arguable case to put forward.[8] If permission is refused after a hearing, the person seeking permission may in a civil case[9] apply to the Court of Appeal within seven days for permission to appeal. On such an application, the Court of Appeal may, instead of giving permission to appeal, give permission to apply for judicial review, and the case then proceeds in the High Court unless the Court of Appeal otherwise orders.[10] If the Court of Appeal refuses permission to appeal, there is no further appeal to the House of Lords,[11] although if the Court of Appeal does grant permission to appeal, but then refuses permission to apply for judicial review, an appeal does lie to the House of Lords.[12]

The claim form must state the remedy or remedies sought and include or

---

[2] Supreme Court Act 1981, s.31(l); CPR, r.54.2.

[3] CPR, r.54.3(l).

[4] 1981 Act, s.31(2).

[5] CPR, r.54.3(2), 54.6; Supreme Court Act 1981, s.31(4).

[6] *ibid*. r.54.12(3).

[7] *White Book 2001*, para. 54.4.3. A respondent who chooses to attend is unlikely to be awarded costs notwithstanding that the application for permission is rejected: Practice Direction 54, paras 8.4–8.6.

[8] *per* Lord Diplock in *IRC v. National Federation of Self-Employed and Small Businesses Ltd.* [1982] A.C. 617 at 644. Permission may be refused in the exercise of the court's discretion.

[9] There is no further appeal in a criminal case (Supreme Court Act 1981, s.18(1)(a)), but the High Court may chose to grant permission, dismiss the substantive application, and certify that a question of general public importance arises, leaving the claimant to seek leave to appeal from the House of Lords: *White Book 2001*, para. 54.12.4.

[10] CPR, r. 52.15.

[11] *Re Poh* [1983] 1 W.L.R. 2; *R. v. Secretary of State for Trade and Industry, ex p. Eastaway* [2000] 1 W.L.R. 2222.

[12] *R. v. London Borough of Hammersmith and Fulham. ex p. Burkett* [2002] UKHL 23.

be accompanied by a detailed statement of the claimant's grounds for bringing the claim, a statement of the facts relied on, and other specified documents.[13] Any person who wishes to take part in the judicial review must file an acknowledgement of service within 21 days.[14] The court may not grant permission unless it considers that the applicant has a "sufficient interest" in the matter (*locus standi* or standing): it is not necessary, however, for it to be shown that his or her legal rights are affected, and a broad rather than narrow approach is normally adopted.[15]

Once permission is granted, the case normally proceeds to a hearing in the Administrative Court, although it may with the consent of the parties be determined without a hearing.[16] A defendant and any other person served with a claim form who wishes to contest the claim or support it on additional grounds must file and serve detailed grounds and any written evidence within 35 days.[17] Furthermore, any person may apply for permission to file evidence or make representations at the hearing.[18] Evidence is normally presented in written form; cross-examination of a witness may exceptionally be permitted.[19] Interim remedies may be granted and (again exceptionally) disclosure of documents.[20]

The claim form must be filed promptly and in any event not later than three months after the grounds to make the claim first arose. The time limit may not be extended by agreement. These rules do not apply when any other enactment specifies a shorter time limit.[21] The time limit may be extended by the court.[22] Where the High Court considers there has been undue delay in making a claim for judicial review, the court may refuse to grant permission on any relief sought if it considers that granting the relief sought would be likely to cause substantial hardship to, or substantially prejudice the rights of, any person, or would be detrimental to good administration.[23] A remedy

---

[13] CPR, r.54.6(1), 54.6(5).

[14] Practice Direction 54, paras 5.6, 5.7.

[15] *IRC v. National Federation of Self Employed and Small Businesses Ltd.* [1982] A.C. 617; *R. v. H.M. Inspectorate of Pollution, ex p. Greenpeace (No. 2)* [1994] 4 All E.R. 329; *R. v. Secretary of State for Foreign Affairs, ex p. World Development Movement Ltd.* [1995] 1 W.L.R. 386.

[16] CPR, r.54.18.

[17] CPR, r.54.14.

[18] CPR, r.54.17.

[19] CPR, r.54.16. This disapplies CPR 4.8.6, but it is thought the court retains an inherent jurisdiction to order cross-examination in an appropriate case.

[20] CPR, Part 25 and r.31.6.

[21] CPR, r.54.5. A claim is not necessarily made promptly when it is brought within three months: *R. v. Greenwich Borough Council, ex p. Cedar Transport Group Ltd.* [1983] R.A. 173. There is, however, no standard expectation that challenges to grants of planning permission be brought within six weeks, mirroring the time limit available for appeals against refusal of planning permission: *R. v. Hammersmith and Fulham London Borough Council, ex p. Burkett* [2002] UKHL 23.

[22] CPR, r.3.1(2)(a).

[23] Supreme Court Act 1981, s.31(6). In *R. v. Diary Produce Quota Tribunal For England and Wales, ex p. Caswell* [1990] 2 A.C. 738, the House of Lords held that where an application was not brought promptly or within three months within RSC, Ord. 53, r.4, there was "undue delay" even if an extension of time had been granted, and so s.31(6) was brought into play. A decision to extend time cannot itself be reopened at the substantive hearing, although s.31(6) may be applied: *R. v. Criminal Injuries Compensation Board, ex p. A* [1999] 2 A.C. 330 (in respect of Ord. 53); *R. v. Lichfield District Council, ex p. Lichfield Securities Ltd.* [2001] EWCA Civ 3014.

may also be refused in the exercise of the court's discretion on other grounds.[24]

Where substantive judicial review proceedings are determined (one way or the other) by the High Court or the Court of Appeal, further appeals lie as in other cases.

(c) The remedies

(i) Mandamus (mandatory order)

18–055   The prerogative[25] order of mandamus[26] (now a mandatory order) lies to compel performance of a public (not necessarily statutory) duty. For example, it may be granted where a tribunal wrongfully declines to hear a matter that does in fact lie within its jurisdiction, or, where there has been an ultra vires abuse of discretion, to ensure that the matter is reconsidered according to law.[27]

(ii) Prohibition (prohibitory order) and certiorari (quashing order)

18–056   The prerogative orders of prohibition and certiorari[28] are similar in scope. Prohibition lies to restrain a tribunal or other authority where it is about to act ultra vires or to complete an ultra vires act already begun. Certiorari lies to quash[29] a decision already made where:

(1) it is ultra vires; or

(2) it has been obtained by fraud[30]; or

(3) there is an error of law apparent on the face of the record of proceedings.

These orders were formerly confined to decisions in respect of which there was a duty to act judicially, but they may now be sought in respect of any judicial or administrative[31] (but not legislative) act.

(iii) Declarations and injunctions

18–057   A person may obtain a declaration on a disputed matter of law, or an injunction, whereby a party to an action is required to do or refrain from doing a particular thing.[32] These were in origin private law remedies but are today frequently sought in respect of the decisions of public authorities.

---

[24] e.g. where the applicant is actuated by improper motives or there is another equally convenient and beneficial remedy.

[25] So called because the writ replaced by the modern order was thought to be especially associated with the Crown.

[26] Normally pronounced "mandaymus".

[27] e.g. Padfield v. Minister of Agriculture [1968] A.C. 997.

[28] Normally pronounced "sersheeorair'eye".

[29] Not "squash," "quosh" or "gnash" (cf. R. v. Pressick [1978] Crim.L.R. 377).

[30] See R. v. Wolverhamptom Crown Court, ex p. Crofts [1983] 1 W.L.R. 204.

[31] R. v. Hillingdon London Borough Council, ex p. Royco Homes Ltd [1974] Q.B. 720.

[32] See Zanir and Woolf, The Declaratory Judgment. (3rd ed., 2002)

(iv) Habeas corpus[33]

The prerogative writ of *habeas corpus ad subjiciendum* lies to secure a   **18–058**
person's release from wrongful imprisonment. An *ex parte* application for a
writ must be made to a single judge of any Division of the High Court,[34] or
to a Divisional Court of the Queen's Bench Division if the court so directs,
and takes precedence over other business. In an emergency, an application
may be made to a judge out of court, for example, at home at night. If prima
facie grounds are shown by an affidavit by or on behalf of the prisoner the
matter is normally adjourned for a full hearing. In exceptional cases the writ
may be issued forthwith to the custodian, requiring that the prisoner be
produced to the court at the time specified for the full hearing. It either
event, the burden of justifying the detention lies on the custodian: if he or
she fails, the prisoner's release is ordered.

The grounds for granting a writ of habeas corpus are essentially the same
as for an application for judicial review. An appeal lies in civil cases as of
right to the Court of Appeal and then with leave to the House of Lords. In
criminal cases an appeal lies from the High Court to the House of Lords,
with the leave of either.[35] An appeal may be taken from a refusal to
discharge the prisoner or grant an order of release: in the latter event the
person's right to remain at large cannot be affected by the outcome of the
appeal.[36] After a refusal to grant habeas corpus no further application may
be made on the same grounds and evidence.[37]

An application for habeas corpus is the standard method of challenging
extradition decisions.

(d) Relationship between claims for judicial review and appeals

The remedies available on a claim for judicial review are discretionary, and   **18–059**
will not be awarded if there is some equally convenient and beneficial
remedy such as a right of appeal. However, an appeal to a Minister against a
planning condition will not, for example, be regarded as convenient as
certiorari where the issue is purely one of law.[38] Indeed, it has sometimes
been stated that a claim for judicial review must be made where a challenge
is based on the *ultra vires* doctrine, rather than exercising a right to appeal
on a point of law.[39]

Conversely, a claim for judicial review will be less appropriate than an

---

[33] See R. J. Sharpe, *The Law of Habeas Corpus* (2nd ed., 1989); de Smith, Woolf and Jowell, *Judicial Review of Administrative Action* (5th ed., 1995), pp. 672–681; RSC Ord. 54.

[34] An application by a parent or guardian in respect of the custody, care or control of a child lies to the Family Division: RSC, Ord. 54, r. 11.

[35] *ibid.* ss.1, 15(3).

[36] *ibid.* s.15(1)(4), as amended by the Access to Justice Act 1999, s.65(2)(a). In criminal cases an order may be made providing for the continued detention as amended by *ibid.* of the defendant or directing that he or she shall not be released except on bail: *ibid.* s.5.

[37] *ibid.* s.14(2).

[38] *R. v. Hillingdon London Borough Council, ex p. Royco Homes Ltd* [1974] Q.B. 720.

[39] *Metropolitan Properties Co. v. Lannon* [1968] 1 W.L.R. 815; *Chapman v. Earl* [1968] 1 W.L.R. 1315; *Henry Moss Ltd v. Customs and Excise Commissioners* [1981] 2 All E.R. 86 at 90 (*per* Lord Denning M.R.), criticised by A. W. Bradley [1981] P.L. 476; *contra, Elliott v. Brighton Borough Council* (1980) 79 L.G.R. 506.

appeal by case stated where complicated findings of fact are involved,[40] and will not be entertained in respect of points arising in the course of trials or committal proceedings[41]: such proceedings must be concluded before any challenge can take place, whether by appeal or application for judicial review.

Statutory provisions may purport to exclude or restrict judicial review. For example, the Crown Court is made amenable to the supervisory jurisdiction of the High Court in respect of matters other than those relating to trial on indictment.[42]

A claim for judicial review may be made to challenge a sentence or order on the ground that it is harsh or oppressive.[43]

E. REFERENCES TO THE EUROPEAN COURT OF JUSTICE[44]

18–060 One of the major functions of the Court of Justice of the European Communities[45] is that of ensuring consistency in the decision-making of national courts[46] in community law matters. The governing provision in the E.C. Treaty is Article 234 (ex 177) E.C.:

"(1) The Court of Justice shall have jurisdiction to give preliminary rulings concerning:

(a) the interpretation of this Treaty;

(b) the validity and interpretation of acts of the institutions of the Community and of the European Central Bank;

(c) the interpretation of the statutes of bodies established by an act of the Council, where those statutes so provide.

---

[40] *R. v. Crown Court at Ipswich, ex p. Baldwin* [1981] 1 All E.R. 596.

[41] *R. v. Wells Street Stipendiary Magistrate, ex p. Seillon* [1978] 1 W.L.R. 1002 (committal proceedings); *R. v. Rochford JJ., ex p. Buck* (1978) 68 Cr.App.R. 114. (summary trial).

[42] Supreme Court Act 1981, s.29(3); *R. v. Sheffield Crown Court, ex p. Brownlow* [1980] Q.B. 530 (jury vetting order held to relate to trial on indictment); J. Kodwo Bentil, (1988) 152 J.P.N. 323.

[43] *R. v. St Albans Crown Court, ex p. Cinnamond* [1981] Q.B. 480; *R. v. Tottenham JJ., ex p. Joshi* [1982] 1 W.L.R. 631. It has been suggested that *Cinnamond* was wrongly decided (Watkins L.J. in *Arthur v. Stringer* (1986) 84 Cr.App.R. 361 at 368), or should at least be confined to cases where the sentence is "truly astonishing" (Watkins L.J. in *R. v. Crown Court at Croydon, ex p. Miller* (1986) 85 Cr.App.R. 152 (decided before *Arthur v. Stringer*)). The court may, however, refuse in the exercise of its discretion to entertain an application for judicial review if a right to appeal against sentence has not been exercised: *R. v. Battle Magistrates' Court, ex p. Shepherd* (1983) 5 Cr.App.R. (S.) 124.

[44] D. W. K. Anderson, *References to the European Court* (1995); L. Collins, *European Community Law in the United Kingdom* (4th ed., 1990), Chap. 3; T. C. Hartley, *The Foundations of European Community Law* (4th ed., 1998), Chap. 9; L. N. Brown and T. Kennedy, *The Court of Justice of the European Communities* (5th ed.), Chap. 10; H. G. Schermers, *et al.* (eds.), *Article 177 EEC: Experiences and Problems* (1987); A. Arnull, "The Use and Abuse of Article 177 EEC" (1989) 52 M.L.R. 622, "References to the European Court" (1990) 15 E.L. Rev. 375, and (1993) 18 E.L. Rev. 129; C. Barnard and E. Sharpston, (1997) 34 CML Rev 113; D. O'Keefe, (1998) 23 E.L. Rev. 509.

[45] See above, papas 2-075–2-081.

[46] The equivalent provision in the Euratom Treaty (Art. 150) is virtually identical.

(2) Where such a question is raised before any court or tribunal of a Member State, that court or tribunal may, if it considers that a decision on the question is necessary to enable it to give judgment, request the Court of Justice to give a ruling thereon.

(3) Where any such question is raised in a case pending before a court or tribunal of a Member State, against whose decisions there is no judicial remedy under national law, that court or tribunal shall bring the matter before the Court of Justice."

The equivalent provision in the European Coal and Steel Community Treaty (Art. 41) is more narrowly drawn:

"The Court shall have sole jurisdiction to give preliminary rulings on the validity of acts of the High Authority and of the Council where such validity is in issue in proceedings brought before a national court or tribunal."

Thus it would appear that only questions of *validity* can be referred. However, the Court has held that it does have jurisdiction to give preliminary rulings on the interpretation of the ECSC Treaty and of acts of the Commission and the Council adopted under it.[47] It should be noted, moreover, that within these narrower limits the jurisdiction of the court is exclusive: the label "preliminary" ruling is in this context misleading.

It should be noted that the reference procedure is not strictly an appeal: the decision to refer is taken by the national court and not a party and the court will only rule on the point of Community law raised and remit the case to the national court to apply the law to the facts of the case. The remainder of this discussion will relate to the E.C. Treaty and Euratom. We now examine the elementsof Article 234 (ex 177) E.C. in more detail.

1. THE MATTERS THAT MAY BE REFERRED

The Court may give rulings concerning (1) the interpretation of Treaty provisions[48]; and (2) the interpretation and validity of acts of the Community institutions (certainly the Council[49] and Commission and **18–061**

---

[47] Case C–221/88. *Busoni* [1990] E.C.R. I-495.

[48] Art. 177(l)(a) (now Art. 234(1)(a)) E.C. covers the E.C. Treaty and all Treaties amending or supplementing it: subsidiary conventions are not covered: Case 44/84. *Hurd v. Jones (Inspector of Taxes)* [1986] E.C.R. 29 (agreement between the Member States setting up European Schools in Community Countries not within Art. 177): see L.N. Brown, (1986) 23 C.M.L. Rev. 895; Case 152/83. *Demouche v. Fonds de Garantie Automobile* [1987] E.C.R. 3833 (agreement between national bureaux of motor vehicle insurers not within Art. 177, notwithstanding that it implemented a Council Directive). The Court may also interpret the final provisions of the Maastricht Treaty Arts 46 to 53, and those parts that amend other treaties (Art. 46 of the E.U. Treaty);' see further below.

[49] The Court has asserted jurisdiction under Art. 177 to interpret agreements between the Community and non-Member States, concluded on behalf of the Community by the Council: Case 181/73. *Haegeman v. Belgium* [1974] E.C.R. 449 (Association Agreement between the EEC and Greece); or even agreements involving Member States to which the Community is not formally a party: Cases 267–269/81. *SPI* [1983] E.C.R. 801 (General Agreement on Tariffs and Trade). For criticism, see Hartley (1998). pp. 262–265.

probably the Parliament and the Court itself[50]). Where, however, the act of the Council in question is the "statute" regulating the operation of an institution or body established by the Council, the court may only give a ruling if the statute so provides,[51] and the ruling may only concern interpretation, not validity.[52] The task of "interpretation" is taken to include that of determining whether a provision is directly effective.[53] A question of validity *must* be referred as the European Court has the exclusive jurisdiction to rule on such a question.[54]

An additional jurisdiction to give preliminary rulings has been conferred on the Court by Article 68 (ex 73p) E.C. in respect of Title IV (ex Title IIIa) of the E.C. Treaty (visas, asylum, immigration and other policies related to free movement of persons).[55] Questions on the interpretation of Title IV or on the validity or interpretation of acts of Community institutions based on Title IV raised in a case pending before a final court or tribunal within Article 234(3) (ex 177(3)) E.C. can be referred by that court on the same basis as for other references. Lower courts cannot refer these matters. Furthermore, the Court of Justice is expressly excluded from ruling on any measure or decision taken pursuant to Article 62(1) relating to the maintenance of law and order and the safeguarding of internal security.[56] Finally, the Council, Commission or a Member State may request the Court to give a ruling on a question of interpretation of Title IV or the acts of Community institutions based on Title IV. Such a ruling is not to apply to judgments of courts or tribunals of the Member States which have become *res judicata*. These provisions do not, however, apply to the U.K. or Ireland.[57]

A further jurisdiction to give preliminary rulings arises in respect of Title VI of the Treaty of European Union (third pillar of the Treaty, narrowed by the Treaty of Amsterdam to cover only criminal issues). This, however, only arises where a Member State accepts that jurisdiction. The ruling may be on the validity and interpretation of framework decisions and decisions on the interpretation of conventions established under Title VI, and on the validity and interpretation of the measures implementing them.[58]

---

[50] Although a preliminary ruling is not itself an act that can be questioned on an application for a further preliminary ruling: Case 69/85. *Wunsche Handelsgesellschaft v. Germany* [1986] E.C.R. 947: see G. Bebr, (1987) 24 C.M.L. Rev. 719; this does not prevent the national court making a subsequent reference in the same proceedings: *ibid.*; Case 14/86. *Pretore di Salo v. Persons Unknown* [1989] 1 C.M.L.R. 71.

[51] Under Art. 150, Euratom, rulings concerning "statutes" may be given "save" where those statutes provide otherwise.

[52] Article 234(1)(a) (ex Art. 177(1)(c)) E.C.

[53] See above, paras 5-040–5-042.

[54] This is expressly provided by Art. 41, ECSC, and the same position has been reached as regards the E.C. by the Court in Cases 314/85 *Firma Foto Frost v. Haupzollant Lübeck-Ost* [1988] 3 C.M.L.R. 57, applied in *R. v. Ministry of Agriculture, Fisheries and Food, ex p. FEDESA* [1988] 3 C.M.LR. 661.

[55] Articles 61–69 (ex 73i–73q) E.C. This was added by the Treaty of Amsterdam and contains material transferred from the Justice and Home Affairs Cooperation pillar of the E.U.

[56] "This seems an extraordinary departure from the rule of law": Weatherill and Beaumont (1999), p. 658.

[57] Protocol on the position of the United Kingdom and Ireland annexed by the Treaty of Amsterdam to the Treaty on European Union and the E.C. Treaty.

[58] Article 35(l)–(4) (ex K.7) of the E.U. Treaty. There is also a jurisdiction under Title VII (provisions on closer co-operation of Member States that wish to use E.U. mechanisms to do so): Article 46(C) of the E.U. Treaty.

2. "Any Court or Tribunal"

Article 234(2) (ex 177(2)) E.C. provides that "any court or tribunal" may **18–062** refer a question if the conditions stated are applicable. In the United Kingdom, procedural rules have been made governing references from the High Court and the Court of Appeal (Civil Division),[59] the Court of Appeal (Criminal Division),[60] the Crown Court[61] and county courts.[62] However, it is clear that magistrates' courts[63] and statutory tribunals[64] have power to refer matters to the Court of Justice even though no procedural rules have been made. The meaning of the expression "court or tribunal" will in the last resort be determined by the Court of Justice, and the title of an institution and its status in national law is not decisive.[65] It seems that any institution which exercises judicial or quasi-judicial functions and which has at least "a measure of official recognition"[66] will be included, and not, therefore, bodies whose functions are advisory,[67] investigatory, conciliatory, legislative or executive,[68] and not arbitrators[69] or (probably) domestic tribunals which exercise jurisdiction solely by virtue of a contractual arrangement between the parties.[70] The Court takes account of a number of factors

"such as whether the body is established by law, whether it is permanent, whether its jurisdiction is compulsory, whether its

---

[59] RSC, Ord. 114 (CPR, Sched. 1).
[60] Criminal Appeal (References to the European Court) Rules 1972 (S.I. 1972 No. 1786).
[61] Crown Court Rules 1982 (S.I. 1982 No. 1109), r.29.
[62] CCR, Ord. 19. r.15 (CPR, Sched. 2).
[63] See, *e.g. R. v. Plymouth JJ., ex p. Rogers* [1982] Q.B. 863.
[64] By 1989 references had been made by the Employment Appeal Tribunal, a National Insurance Commissioner, Social Security Commissioners, Special Income Tax Commissioners, Value Added Tax Tribunals and a Northern Ireland industrial tribunal.
[65] See W. Alexander and E. Grabandt, (1982) 19 C.M.L.Rev. 413; Case 61/65 *Vaassen* [1966] E.C.R. 261; Case 36/73 *Nederlandse Spoorwegen* [1973] E.C.R. 1299; Case 138/80 *Borker* [1980] E.C.R. 1975; Case 246/80 *Broekmeulen* [1981] E.C.R. 2311; Case 102/81 *Nordsee v. Reederei Mond* [1982] E.C.R. 1095.
[66] *e.g.* supervision or regulation by a Minister: *Vaassen* and *Broekmeulen*, above.
[67] The fact that functions are technically advisory will not prevent the institution from being regarded as a "court or tribunal" if in reality it operates as a judicial body; accordingly, the Dutch *Road van State* (Council of State), in practice the supreme administrative court, has been held to be within Article 177: *Nederlandse Spoorwegen*, n. 66 above. By contrast, the *commissione consultiva per la infrazioni valutarie* (Consultative Commission for Currency Offences), which gives reasoned opinions to the Italian Treasury on sanctions to be imposed for foreign exchange violations, was held not to fall within Art. 177 in Case 318/85 *Criminal Proceedings Against Undterweger* [1986] E.C.R. 955: its opinions were not binding on the Treasury Minister.
[68] *e.g.* the professional association of the Paris Bar: *Borker*, n. 66 above.; or the Luxembourg Director of Taxation: Case C–24/92 *Corbiau v. Administration des Contributions* [1993] E.C.R. I-1227 (although entertaining a complaint against tax authorities, the Director was not an independent third party).
[69] *Nordsee*, n. 66 above: See G. Bebr, (1985) 22 C.M.L.Rev. 489; C. M. Schmitthoff, (1987) 24 C.M.L. Rev. 143.
[70] Hartley (1998), pp. 268–270.

procedure is *inter partes*, whether it applies rules of law and whether it is independent".[71]

Where a court or tribunal performs both judicial and non-judicial functions in respect of particular proceedings, (*e.g.* as examining magistrate and public prosecutor), the Court of Justice will accept a reference from it in the first of those capacities.[72] The expression "court or tribunal of a Member State" extends to the courts of dependent territories to which at least the general institutional provisions (and possibly any provisions) of the E.C. Treaty apply.[73]

3. THE POWER TO REFER

18–063 Where any "question" within the scope of the preliminary rulings procedure is "raised before" any national court or tribunal that body may, "if it considers that a decision on the question is necessary to enable it to give judgment", refer the question to the European Court.

(a) "Question ... raised before"

18–064 The question can be raised by a party or by the court itself.[74] Moreover, it is immaterial that the parties take the same position on the point of Community law.[75] The question for reference will be formulated by the national court, although the Court of Justice will confine itself to ruling on matters of *interpretation* and *validity*: it will not rule on the *application* of Community law to the facts or the compatibility of national law with Community law even if requested to do so. The Court will reformulate questions put too widely, and may even formulate the question for itself if the national court fails to do so.[76]

(b) "A decision on the question is necessary to enable it to give judgment"

18–065 This wording makes it clear that the material issue is whether a *decision* on

---

[71] Case C–54/96, *Dorsch Consult Ingenieurgesellschaft mbH v. Bundesbaugesellschaft Berlin mbH* [1997] E.C.R. I–4961, para. 23 (holding that the German Federal Public Procurement Awards Supervisory Board, which made binding decisions, although not after *inter partes* hearings, on appeals from lower bodies concerning public procurement procedures, was able to make a reference); *cf.* Case C–516/99 *Schmid*, Judgment of May 30, 2002 (appeal chamber of regional finance authority held to be insufficiently independent to be a court or tribunal); Case C–182/00 *Lutz GmbH*, Judgment of January 15, 2002 (Austrian commercial court exercising function of maintaining a register of companies not dealing with a dispute and so not exercising a judicial function or a court or tribunal).

[72] Case 14/86 *Pretore di Salo v. Persons Unknown* [1987] E.C.R. 2545.

[73] Case C–355/89 *Barr and Montrose Holdings* [1991] E.C.R. I–3479 (courts of the Isle of Man).

[74] See, *e.g.* RSC, Ord. 114, r.2(l).

[75] Advocate General Slynn in Case 244/80 *Foglia v. Novello (No. 2)* [1981] E.C.R. 3045 at 3071–3072.

[76] This was done in Case 6/64 *Costa v. E.N.E.L.* [1964] E.C.R. 585; however, the Court may be unable to do so: Case 14/86 *Pretore di Salo v. Persons Unknown* [1987] E.C.R. 2545, where the Court could not make anything of a very general question posed by the Italian court.

the point of Community law is necessary and not whether a *reference* is necessary. The Court of Justice will not normally review the decision of the national court that a reference should be made,[77] although in exceptional circumstances it may decline to accept a reference on the ground that the matter has not arisen in real, genuine, litigation: it is not willing to render advisory opinions, of academic interest only, on "general or hypothetical questions".[78] Accordingly, the Court has now said that the national court should state in its order for reference the reasons for which it considers it necessary to obtain a preliminary ruling, unless these can be clearly deduced from the file on the case,[79] and some explanation of the reasons for the choice of the Community provisions of which it requests an interpretation and their relationship to the applicable national law.[80] Furthermore, the Court will not rule on questions clearly irrelevant to the issues before the national court.[81]

Essentially, the decision to refer is for the national court or tribunal. However, in the *Rheinmuhlen* cases the Court of Justice held that: (1) "a rule of national law whereby a court is bound on points of law by the rulings of a superior court cannot deprive the inferior courts of their power to refer ... questions" to the Court,[82] but that (2) Article 177 does not preclude a decision of an inferior court to refer a question "from remaining subject to the remedies normally available under national law".[83] This suggests that any attempt to fetter the discretion of a court under Article 234(2) (ex 177(2)) will be contrary to Community law. Nevertheless, in *Bulmer v. Bollinger*[84] Lord Denning M.R. laid down certain "guidelines", which have been relied upon in a number of cases since, but which have also, in some respects, been the subject of widespread criticism, not least on the basis that they may constitute "fetters" which are contrary to Community law.[85] His Lordship set out the guidelines in two groups: (1) guidelines as to whether a decision is "necessary"; and (2) guidelines as to the exercise of the

---

[77] *ibid.*; Cases 98, 162 and 258/85 *Bertini v. Regione Lazio* [1986] E.C.R. 1885.

[78] Case 104/79, *Foglia v. Novello (No. 1)* [1980] E.C.R. 745; Case 244/80 *Foglia v. Novello (No. 2)* [1981] E.C.R. 3045: see A. Barav, (1980) 5 E.L. Rev. 443, G. Bebr, (1980) 17 C.M.L.Rev. 525 (*Foglia No. 1*); D. Wyatt, (1981) 6 E.L. Rev. 449, G. Bebr, (1982) 19 C.M.L.Rev. 421 (*Foglia No. 2*). It should be noted that this litigation was between private parties in Italy but was in reality directed at the alleged incompatibility of a French law with Community law. *cf.* Cases 98, 162 and 258/85 *Bertini*, above.

[79] *Foglia v. Novello (No. 2)*, above, at 3062.

[80] Case C–167/94R *Grau Gomis* [1995] E.C.R. I-1023. The Court has issued *Guidance on references by National Courts for Preliminary Rulings* [1997] 1 C.M.L.R. 78.

[81] Case C–83/91 *Meilicke* [1992] E.C.R. 1–4871 and Case 343/90, *Lourenço Dias v. Director da Alfândega do Porto* [1992] E.C.R. I–4673 see T. Kennedy, (1993) 18 E.L. Rev. 121.

[82] Case 166/73, *Rheinmühlen-Düsseldorf v. EVSt (No. 1)* [1974] E.C.R. 33: the lower court was, under German law, bound on points of law by decisions of a superior court; the Court of Justice held that this could not take away the lower court's power to refer under Art. 177(2). See also Case 106/77, *Italian Minister for Finance v. Simmenthal (No. 2)* [1978] E.C.R. 629.

[83] Case 166/73, *ibid. (No. 2)* [1974] E.C.R. 139. The court rejected the suggestion by A. G. Warner that the existence of a right to appeal against an order referring a question to the Court was contrary to Community law: see [1974] E.C.R. 33 at 43–44.

[84] [1974] Ch. 401 at 422–425.

[85] See, *e.g.* F. G. Jacobs, (1974) 90 L.Q.R. 486; J.D.B. Mitchell, (1974) 11 C.M.L.Rev. 351; E. Freeman, [1975] C.L.P. 176; Collins (1990), pp. 176–183. In *Bulmer v. Bollinger*, Stephenson L.J. (with whom Stamp L.J. agreed) stated that judges should "bear in mind" the considerations set out by Lord Denning M.R. ([1974] Ch. 401 at 430) but was also conscious of the requirement that the discretion must not be fettered (*ibid.* at 431).

"discretion" to refer. He regarded the question of "necessity" as a condition precedent to the exercise of the discretion and, presumably, as raising matters of law or jurisdiction rather than discretion.[86] However, it seems that his Lordship erroneously thought that it was the *reference* that had to be "necessary," whereas Article 234(2)(ex 177(2)) makes it clear that the significant point is whether a *decision* by the national court on the point is "necessary".[87] Accordingly, two of the matters mentioned by Lord Denning M.R. in relation to "necessity" should have been placed with the other group: the presentation here has been revised accordingly.

(i) Jurisdiction to refer: is a decision "necessary"?

18-066 (1) "*The point must be conclusive*" and (2) "*find the facts first*". According to Lord Denning M.R. the point must be conclusive in the sense that a decision one way must lead to judgment for one party and a decision the other way to judgment for the other. Where the point would only be conclusive if decided one way, and the trial would have to go its full course in respect of the contested issues of fact or of English law if decided the other, then, according to Lord Denning M.R., a reference might be "desirable" or "convenient" but could not be "necessary". Moreover, "[a]s a rule you cannot tell whether it is necessary to decide a point until all the facts are ascertained. So in general it is best to decide the facts first."[88]

It seems to be generally agreed that this is too narrow, and that the correct view is that it may be appropriate to refer a point where there are still matters outstanding which will have to be determined should the decision of the Court of Justice go one way rather than another.[89] This broader view has been adopted by Ormrod L.J. in the Court of Appeal,[90] by the Divisional Court[91] and by Bingham J. in the High Court.[92] These cases suggest, however, that while there is jurisdiction to refer at an early stage, the facts should normally be found first.[93] A difficulty here is that it may not be clear which facts are relevant for the purposes of Community law until after the reference has been made. On the other hand, it has also been

---

[86] Collins (1990), p. 179.

[87] *ibid.* p. 177.

[88] [1974] Ch. 401 at 422, 423.

[89] RSC, Ord. 114, r.2(l) provides that an order for reference may be made at any stage.

[90] *Polydor Ltd v. Harlequin Record Shops Ltd* [1980] 2 C.M.L.R. 413 at 428: "necessary" to mean "reasonably necessary" and not "unavoidable".

[91] *R. v. Plymouth JJ., ex p. Rogers* [1982] Q.B. 863 at 867–870.

[92] *Customs and Excise Commissioners v. ApS Samex* [1983] 1 All E.R. 1042 at 1054.

[93] Templeman L.J. in *Polydor, op. cit.* n.91 at *op. cit.* n.92 426; Lord Lane C.J. in *R. v. Plymouth JJ.*, n. above, at p. 182; Bingham J. in *Samex*, at 1056c. See also Lord Diplock in *R. v. Henn and Darby* [1981] A.C. 850 *ibid.* at 904. In *R. v. Plymouth JJ.* and *Samex* the matters outstanding were not significant in extent; a reference was, however, made at an early stage by Taylor J., with the agreement of both sides, in *R. v. Ministry of Agriculture, Fisheries and Food, ex p. Agegate Ltd* [1987] 3 C.M.L.R. 939, and by Henry J. in *R. v. Ministry of Agriculture, Fisheries and Food, ex p. FEDESA* [1988] 3 C.M.L.R. 661; a reference was made notwithstanding that there was an unresolved conflict on some factual matters, and over the objections of one party, by the Court of Appeal in *R. v. Pharmaceutical Society of Great Britain, ex p. Association of Pharmaceutical Importers* [1987] C.M.L.R. 951.

stressed by English courts that it may be impossible to formulate the questions to be referred until after a case has been argued.[94]

A further point is that it is not necessary that the whole of a case be affected by Community law for a decision to be necessary: it is sufficient if a particular aspect, such as the measure of damages or the terms of a court order should be so affected.

The move away from Lord Denning M.R.'s attempt to formulate a narrow, clear-cut rule in this context means that the matter is so much one for the appreciation of the court itself that it would be artificial to seek to perpetuate the supposed distinction between "necessity" and "discretion": the approach of an appellate court is in practice likely to be similar in each case.

(ii) Exercise of the discretion to refer

(1) *Previous ruling. In Da Costa v. Nederlandse Belastringadministratie*[95] the Court of Justice stated that where it has given a ruling on a particular question of interpretation, and the same question arises in a subsequent case before a national court of last resort, the earlier ruling may "deprive the obligation [under Art. 177(3)] of its purpose and thus empty it of its substance".[96] There would thus be no *obligation* to refer, although the Court also stressed that a national court still had a *discretion* to refer the question. In *Bulmer v. Bollinger*[97] Lord Denning M.R. noted that the Court of Justice was not bound by its own previous decisions and said that an English court should only refer a case in such circumstances if it thinks the earlier ruling to be wrong or if there are new factors which ought to be brought to the notice of the Court of Justice.

(2) *Acte clair.* It has been a matter of much controversy whether a national court, whether a court of last resort or not, may decline to refer a question to the Court of Justice on the ground that, notwithstanding the absence of any prior ruling on the point by the Court of Justice, the point is clear and so no "question" arises. Commentators, both academic and judicial, have argued against the *acte clair* doctrine on the basis that there is a real risk that the national courts of different countries may each regard a question as "clear" but in fact decide it differently.[98] Conversely, national courts in several Member States have endorsed and relied upon the doctrine. In

18–067

---

[94] *Church of Scientology v. Customs and Excise Commissioners* [1981] 1 All E.R. 1035 at 1039 (Brightman L.J.); *Lord Bethell v. SABENA* [1983] 3 C.M.L.R. 1 (Parker J.).

[95] Cases 28, 29 and 30/62, [1963] E.C.R. 31.

[96] *ibid.* at 38. The same effect may be produced where previous decisions of the court have already dealt with the point of law in question "irrespective of the nature of the proceedings which led to those decisions, even though the questions at issue are not strictly identical": Case 283/81 *CILFIT v. Ministry of Health* [1982] E.C.R. 3415 at 3429. The point is even stronger where "the question raised is substantially the same as a question which has already been the subject of a preliminary ruling in the same national proceedings": Case C–337/95 *Parfums Christian Dior* [1997] I-E.C.R. 6013, para. 25.

[97] [1974] Ch. 401 at 422.

[98] See, *e.g.* Judge Pescatore in M. E. Bathhurst *et al.* (eds), *Legal Problems of an Enlarged European Community* (1972), pp. 27–46 (but *cf.* M. Lagrange, (1971) 8 C.M.L.Rev. 313); A. G. Capotorti in Case 283/81 at *CILFIT v. Ministry of Health* [1982] E.C.R. 3415; G. Bebr, (1981) 18 C.M.L.Rev. 475 at 484–489.

Bulmer v. Bollinger[99] Lord Denning M.R. stated that there was no need to refer a question if the point is considered to be "reasonably clear and free from doubt".[1] Rather to everyone's surprise, in *CILFIT v. Ministry of Health*[2] the Court of Justice approved the doctrine, although not in nearly so broad a formulation as Lord Denning's: thus, there is no *obligation* to refer if:

" ... the correct application of Community law is so obvious as to leave no scope for any reasonable doubt. The existence of such a possibility must be assessed in the light of the specific characteristics of Community law, the particular difficulties to which its interpretation gives rise and the risk of divergences in judicial decisions within the Community."

In practice in United Kingdom courts the *acte clair* issue has arisen in courts other than of last resort, which accordingly have a discretion to refer.[3] There appears to have been a variation in approach depending on the context. Thus, the unwillingess of judges to refer possible defences arising under Community law to actions for breach of intellectual property rights has been contrasted with an apparent willingness to refer questions concerning equal pay and sex discrimination in employment law.[4] Points regarded by judges as clear turn out on closer examination by commentators to be at least arguable. The dangers of a reluctance to refer questions have been stressed by the House of Lords in *R. v. Henn and Darby*,[5] where Lord Diplock noted the different approaches to statutory interpretation adopted respectively by the Court of Justice and English courts[6] and the point that each of the (then) six texts of Community law was of equal authority. His Lordship said that English judges should not be "too ready to hold that because the meaning of the English text ... seems plain to them no question of interpretation can be involved".[7] However, where the point was one "to which an established body of case law plainly applies" an English court

---

[99] [1974] Ch. 401. See also the decision of the Conseil d'Etat in *Cohn-Bendit* [1980] 1 C.M.L.R. 543; G. Bebr, (1983) 20 C.M.L.Rev. 439.

[1] *ibid.* p. 423.

[2] [1982] E.C.R. 3415, para. 21. See D. Wyatt, (1983) 8 E.L.Rev. 179; N. P. Gravells, (1983) 99 L.Q.R. 518; H. Rasmussen, (1984) 9 E.L. Rev. 242.

[3] But *cf. S.A. Magnavision v. General Optical Council (No.2)* [1987] 2 C.M.L.R. 262, below, p. 986.

[4] A. Arnull, "Article 177 and the Retreat from Van Duyn" (1983) 8 E.L. Rev. 365. See also A. Dashwood and A. Amull, "English Courts and Article 177 of the EEC Treaty" (1984) 4 Y.E.L. 255; L. W. Gormley, "The Application of Community Law in the United Kingdom, 1976–1985" (1986) 23 C.M.L.Rev 287 at 288–303.

[5] [1981] A.C. 850.

[6] See above, pp.

[7] [1981] A.C. 850 at 906. See also Lord Diplock's speech in *Garland v. British Rail Engineering Ltd* [1983] 2 A.C. 751; *cf.* Bingham J. in *Customs and Excise Commissioners v. Ap S Samex* [1983] 1 All E.R. 1042: on three of four points the judge held clear views, but accepted that each was not so clear as to be *acte clair*; the Court of Appeal in *R. v. Pharmaceutical Society of Great Britain, ex p. Association of Pharmaceutical Importers* [1987] 3 C.M.L.R. 951, *per* Kerr L.J. at 969–970; and McCullough J. in *R. v. Dairy Produce Quota Tribunal, ex p. Hall & Sons (Dairy Farmers) Ltd* [1988] 1 C.M.L.R. 592 (discussed by Amull, (1989) 52 M.L.R. 622 at 628–631).

might properly take the view that no real question of interpretation was involved.[8]

Lord Diplock's views were echoed by Sir Thomas Bingham M.R. in *R. v. International Stock Exchange of the U.K. and the Republic of Ireland Ltd, ex p. Else (1982) Ltd*[9]:

> "I understand the correct approach in principle of a national court (other than a final court of appeal) to be quite clear: if the facts have been found and the Community law issue is critical to the court's final decision, the appropriate course is ordinarily to refer the issue to the Court of Justice unless the national court can with complete confidence resolve the issue itself. In considering whether it can with complete confidence resolve the issue itself the national court must be fully mindful of the differences between national and Community legislation, of the pitfalls which face a national court venturing into what may be an unfamiliar field, of the need for uniform interpretation throughout the Community and of the great advantage enjoyed by the Court of Justice in construing Community instruments. If the national court has any real doubts, it should ordinarily[10] refer."

While this should "no more be read as a statute than Lord Denning's original guidelines"[11] this does reflect a "*communitaire* approach consistent with the spirit of judicial co-operation that is needed if the Article 234 (ex 177) E.C. system is to do its job of ensuring uniform interpretation of Community law throughout the Community".[12]

More recently, however, the Court of Appeal[13] has expressed caution, picking up on concerns expressed by A.G. Jacobs as to the caseload of the Court of Justice. A.G. Jacobs suggested that references under Article 234(2) (ex 177(2)) E.C.

> "will be most appropriate where the question is one of general importance and where the ruling is likely to promote the uniform application of the law throughout the European Union. A reference will be least appropriate where there is an established body of case law which could readily be transposed to the facts of the instant case; or where the question turns on a narrow point considered in the light of a

[8] [1981] A.C. 850 at 906. Lord Diplock thought that the interpretation of Art. 30 was clear in this sense, but as the Court of Appeal had taken a different view, the point was referred to the Court of Justice. See also *R. v. Secretary of State for Social Services, ex p. Bomore Medical Supplies Ltd* [1986] 1 C.M.L.R. 228 (and other cases, discussed by Arnull, (1989) 52 M.L.R. 622 at 631–636).

[9] [1993] Q.B.534 at 545: see Walsh, (1993) 56 M.L.R. 881 and E. Szyszczak, (1995) 20 E.L.Rev. 214. Applied by Leggatt L.J. in *R. v. Secretary of State for the National Heritage, ex p. Continental Television BV* [1993] 2 C.M.L.R. 333 at 346.

[10] Not *necessarily*: see *R. v. Ministry of Agriculture, Fisheries and Food, ex p. Portman Agrochemicals Ltd* [1994] 3 C.M.L.R. 18, where while the judge did have doubts as to the meaning of Community law, the issue would become academic by the time the response to an Art.177 reference would be received.

[11] S. Weatherill and P. Beaumont, *EU Law* (3rd ed., 1999), p. 336.

[12] *ibid.*

[13] *Trinity Mirror plc v. Commissioners of Customs and Excise* [2001] EWCA Civ 65; followed in *Littlewoods Organisation plc v. Commissioners of Customs and Excise* [2001] EWCA Civ 1542.

very specific set of facts and the ruling is unlikely to have any application beyond the instant case."[14]

The Court of Appeal held that the court should bear these observations in mind and that there was no "real doubt" on the substantive point in issue.[15] Even in cases arising under Article 234(3) (ex 177(2) E.C.,[16] the Court's body of case law had developed to the extent that, particularly in technical fields such as customs and VAT, it

"now provides sufficient guidance to enable national courts and tribunals – and in particular specialised courts and tribunals — to decide many cases for themselves without the need for a reference".[17]

(3) *Other points.* Other factors identified by Lord Denning M.R. in *Bulmer v. Bollinger*[18] as relevant to the exercise of a court's discretion included: (1) the time to get a ruling; (2) the need not to overload the Court of Justice; (3) the need to formulate the question clearly, which was another reason for finding the facts first; (4) "Unless the point is really difficult and important, it would seem better for the English judge to decide it himself"; (5) expense; and (6) the wishes of the parties:

"If both parties want the point to be referred to the European Court, the English court should have regard to their wishes, but it should not give them undue weight. The English court should hesitate before making a reference against the wishes of one of the parties, seeing the expense and delay which it involves."

The tenor of Lord Denning's judgment was obviously restrictive: references should only be made in exceptional cases, and (possibly) only by the House of Lords. The possibility that the guidelines may, to an extent, conflict with Community law has already been noted.[19] However, the breadth of the discretion to refer has also been noted:

"The matters referred to by Lord Denning are specifically stated only to be guidelines and, as Lord Denning himself said, when referring to the guidelines laid down by the House of Lords in *The Nema*,[20] with reference to applications for leave to appeal in matters of arbitration, 'guidelines may be stepped over, and are flexible'. I take it that he would apply the same standard to his own guidelines. At all events, it is perfectly clear that, where a discretion is conferred upon the court, that discretion cannot be fettered."[21]

---

[14] Case C–338/95 *Wiener S.I. GmbH v. Hauptzollamt Emmerich* [1997] E.C.R. I–6495, para. 20 of A.G. Jacobs' opinion.
[15] para. 52.
[16] Below, para. 18-068.
[17] para. 61 of A.G. Jacob's opinion.
[18] [1974] Ch. 401 at 423–425.
[19] See above, para. 18-065.
[20] [1980] 2 Lloyd's Rep. 83.
[21] *per* Parker J. in *Lord Bethell v. SABENA* [1983] 3 C.M.L.R. 1 at 4. *Cf.* Sir Thomas Bingham in *ex p. Else (1982) Ltd*, n.10 above.

One point not stressed expressly in *Bulmer v. Bollinger*[22] is whether references should normally only be made by appellate courts. It has since been suggested that references should only exceptionally be made by trial judges in the Crown Court[23] and by magistrates' courts.[24] It is, however, often argued that an early reference may save time and expense.

4. THE OBLIGATION TO REFER

Article 234(3) (ex 177(3)) E.C. provides that where a decision on a question **18–068** of Community law is necessary to enable a court or tribunal to give judgment in a pending case, and that court or tribunal is one "against whose decisions there is no judicial remedy under national law", an *obligation* to refer arises. The points discussed above concerning "necessity", previous rulings and the *acte clair* doctrine[25] are equally applicable here: indeed the decision in *CILFIT v. Ministry of Health*[26] arose in respect of Article 177(3).

In addition, there is the question as to which courts are covered by Article 234(3) (ex 177 (3)) E.C. The wording of the paragraph suggests that it applies only to courts from which an appeal never lies.[27] The view more widely favoured, however, is that it applies to any court from which an appeal or other "judicial remedy" does not lie in the case in question.[28] One difficulty that has not been settled is whether the remedy has to be available as of right. In *Hagen v. Fratelli D. & G. Moretti S.N.C.*[29] Buckley L.J. stated that the "ultimate court of appeal" in this country "is either [the Court of Appeal] if leave to appeal to the House of Lords is not obtainable, or the House of Lords".[30] It is not clear whether "obtainable" means "obtainable ever" or "obtainable in the particular case" but the latter interpretation seems more likely. In *S.A. Magnavision NV v. General Optical Council (No. 2)*,[31] it was argued that once the Divisional Court, on an appeal by case stated from a magistrates' court in a criminal matter, had refused to certify a point of law of general public importance, it fell within Article 177(3). The

---

[22] [1974] Ch. 401.
[23] *R. v. Henn and Darby* [1981] A.C. 850 at 906: Lord Diplock regarded this as equivalent to referring before the facts are found. The Crown Court is presumably not so inhibited when dealing with an appeal from the magistrates in a summary criminal case: *cf. Charles Robertson (Developments) Ltd v. Caradon District Council* [1988] 1 C.M.L.R. 293.
[24] *R. v. Plymouth JJ., ex p. Rogers* [1982] Q.B. 863 at 870–871.
[25] *e.g. Three Rivers District Council v. Governor of the Bank of England* [2000] 2 W.L.R. 1220.
[26] Above, para. 18-067.
[27] This was stated to be the correct view by Lord Denning M.R. *obiter* in *Bulmer v. Bollinger* [1974] Ch. 401: the other members of the Court of Appeal expressed no view on the matter.
[28] See the Court of Justice, *obiter*, in Case 6/64, *Costa v. E.N.E.L.* [1964] E.C.R. 585 at 592 and Case C–99/000 *Lyckeskog*, Judgment of June 4, 2002 (Swedish court from which appeal could lie to supreme court if that court declared it admissible if important for guidance or there were special grounds, held not to be a final court or tribunal).
[29] [1980] 3 C.M.L.R. 253.
[30] *ibid.* p. 255, *cf.* Kerr L. J. (for a unanimous Court of Appeal) in *R. v. Pharmaneutical Society of Great Britain, ex p. Association of Pharmaceutical Importers* [1987] 3 C.M.L.R. 951 at 969: "A court or tribunal below the House of Lords can only fall within [Art. 177(2)] where there is no possibility of any further appeal from it." In *Chiron Corp. v. Murex Diagnostics (No. 3)* [1995] F.S.R. 309 the Court of Appeal held that an application to the House of Lords for leave to appeal constituted a "judicial remedy" for the purposes of Art. 177.
[31] [1987] 2 C.M.L.R. 262.

refusal of the certificate would block any further appeal (to the House of Lords) and could not itself be challenged on appeal.[32] The Divisional Court sidestepped the argument, holding (1) that as it had already dismissed the appeal, it was *functus officio*,[33] notwithstanding that the order had not yet been drawn up and (2) that in any event the point of Community law was clear and the *acte clair* doctrine applicable. It is also uncertain whether the availability of the remedy of certiorari (now quashing on order), which may only be sought if leave to apply is obtained, counts as a "judicial remedy".[34]

The fact that an interlocutory order may not be the subject of an appeal does not render it final for the purposes of Article 234(3) (ex 177(3)) E.C. provided that the decision is subject to review in the main or subsequent proceedings from which a reference may be made.[35]

5. PROCEDURE

18–069   As mentioned above, procedural rules have been made for county courts, the Crown Court, the High Court and the Court of Appeal.[36] All references from these courts must be channelled through the Senior Master of the Queen's Bench Division.

An appeal lies against a decision or refusal to refer in the ordinary way.[37] Notice of appeal must be served within 14 days and the order is not transmitted until this time limit has expired, and, if an appeal is lodged, until after it has been disposed of.[38–39]

F. THE ROYAL PREROGATIVE OF MERCY[40]

"Mercy is not the subject of legal rights. It begins where legal rights end."[41]

---

[32] See above, para. 18-009.

[33] "having performed his function": *i.e.* the function of the judge is exhausted: D. M. Walker. *The Oxford Companion to Law* (1980), p. 508. *cf. Chiron Corp. v. Murex Diagnostics*, n. 31 above.

[34] It was so held by Mr J. G. Monroe in *Re a Holiday in Italy* [1975] 1 C.M.L.R 184 (decision of a National Insurance Commissioner) but see F. G. Jacobs, (1977) 2 E.L. Rev. 119.

[35] Case 107/76 *Hoffman-La Roche v. Cemrafarm* [1977] E.C.R. 957: see F. G. Jacobs, (1977) 2 E.L. Rev. 354; Cases 35 and 36/82, *Morson v. Netherlands: Jhanjan v. Netherlands* [1982] E.C.R. 3723: see N. P. Gravells. (1983) 8 E.L. Rev. 250.

[36] See above, para. 18–062.

[37] See *R. v. International Stock Exchange of the UK. and the Republic of Ireland Ltd, ex p. Else (1982) Ltd.* [1993] Q.B. 534, where the Court of Appeal set aside a reference by the High Court.

[38–39] RSC, Ord. 114, rr.4, 5, 6. (C.P.R. Sched. 1).

[40] See generally P. Taylor, *Taylor on Appeals* (2001), Chap. 13; N. Walker, *Aggravation, Mitigation and Mercy in English Criminal Justice* (1999), Chap. 14; N. Taylor and J. Wood, "Victims of Miscarriages of Justice" in C. Walker and K. Starmer (eds.), *Miscarriages of Justice: A Review of Justice in Error* (1999); on the history, particularly during the transition when the death penalty was being abolished, see R.F.V. Heuston, *Essays in Constitutional Law* (2nd ed. 1964), p.7.

[41] *per* Lord Diplock in *de Freitas v. Benny* [1976] A.C. 239 at 247.

The Crown has retained certain of its prerogative powers as "fountain of   **18–070**
justice" in the field of the administration of justice. One such area is the
prerogative of mercy exercised by the Crown on the advice of the Home
Secretary.[42] This may take one of three forms[43]:

"(i) *A Free Pardon*, the effect of which is that a conviction is to be
disregarded, so that, so far as is possible, the person is relieved of all
penalties and other consequences of the conviction; or

(ii) *A Conditional Pardon*, which excuses or varies the consequences of the
conviction subject to conditions—this power was used primarily to
commute a sentence of death to one of life imprisonment[44] or

(iii) *Remission* of all or part of the penalty imposed by the Court."

The power to recommend special remission is normally used for reasons
unconnected with the merits of the conviction, for example, to reward
assistance to the prison authorities[45] or to release a dying prisoner.
Occasionally it may be used where new information casts doubt on the

---

[42] Section 9 of the Criminal Law Act 1967 deems a pardon signed by the Home Secretary to be
"of like effect" as a pardon under the great seal. There may be a pardon by Act of
Parliament: see *R.v. Crosby* (1695) 12 St. Tr. 1291; *R.v. Rookwood* (1696) 13 St. Tr. 139 at
186.

[43] "*Sixth Report from the Home Affairs Committee of the House of Commons* (1981–82, H.C.
421). Home Office Memorandum, p. 1. The Criminal Cases Review Commission (previously
the Home Secretary) may refer cases to the Court of Appeal (Criminal Division): see above,
para. 18-018. The following summary is based on this Memorandum. See also the
comprehensive survey by A. T. H. Smith, [1983] P.L. 398, and the works cited therein; C. H.
Rolph, *The Queen's Pardon* (1978): C. H. W. Gane, 1980 J.R. 18.

[44] On the Privy Council's approach to the exercise of the prerogative of mercy and the right of
appeal on capital cases from territories over which it has jurisdiction, see *Linsberth Logan v
The Queen* [1996] 2 W.L.R. 711 (emphasising the distinction between appeal and prerogative
processes). The Privy Council has held that the exercise of the prerogative of mercy is not
sufficient mechanism in itself to legitimate the otherwise cruel and unusual punishment of
imposing mandatory death penalties in murder cases: *The Queen v. Hughes* [2002] UKPC 12;
see also *Reyes v. The Queen* [2002] UKPC 11. The Privy Council has also emphasised that
although there is there is no legal rights to mercy, the exercise of the prerogative must be
conducted according to procedures which are fair, proper and amenable to judicial review,
and which comply with State's international obligations. The condemned person therefore
has a right information about the procedure: *Lewis v. Attorney-General of Jamaica* [2001] 2
A.C. 50.

[45] Jack Straw, then Home Secretary, granted remission of the remainder of the sentences of
imprisonment of two prisoners who saved the life of a prison worker who was attacked by a
wild boar when working at the prison farm: *The Times* June 19, 2001. See also reward of a
prisoner who saved a suicidal cellmate, leading to a challenge over whether the remission led
to his being recategorised as a short term prisoner (and therefore eligible for earlier release):
R. (on the application of Ghartley v. Home Secretary [2001] EWHC Admin 199. More
controversially, early release under the Good Friday Agreement was granted to a number of
convicted terrorists, including those serving sentences for murder. In total, 428 prisoners
were freed early: *The Times*, July 29, 2000. See also Lord Laird's question on the procedure
adopted in the grant of the prerogative in these cases: *Hansard*, H.L., April 17, 2002, col.
WA164. Mr Charles Clarke MP, Minister for the Home Office confirmed that the use of the
royal prerogative was a "very rare" occurrence, to be used in "exceptional circumstances".
The Minister reported that he had commissioned a review of the exercise of the power. See
Hansard, H.C., May 8, 2001, col. 82W.

rightness of a conviction but the case is not suitable for reference to the Court of Appeal.[46]

The fact that an offender is terminally ill is not seen by the courts as a reason to interfere with an otherwise appropriate sentence.[47]

A free pardon[48] is "normally only recommended when there are not merely doubts about the defendant's guilt but convincing grounds for thinking that he was innocent"; and this means "morally as well as technically innocent. This "clean hands" doctrine implies that the Home Secretary must be satisfied ... that in the incident in question the defendant had no intention of committing an offence and did not in fact commit one."[49]

In practice the prerogative is more freely used in respect of cases tried summarily than tried on indictment.

A person who is acquitted on a criminal charge or whose conviction is quashed on appeal normally has no legal right to compensation.[50] However, for many years it has been the normal practice of the Home Secretary to offer *ex gratia* compensation where a person is granted a free pardon, or, following the emergence of new evidence, has had his or her conviction quashed on appeal out of time or after the Home Secretary has referred the case to the Court of Appeal.[51] A payment may also be made where there has been misconduct or default by the police or some other agency of the criminal justice system and in other, exceptional, cases. Payments are not, however, made simply because there has been an acquittal or a quashed

---

[46] *Home Office Memorandum*, pp. 2–3.

[47] *R.v. Bernard* [1997] 1 Cr. App. R.(S.) 135; [1996] Crim. L.R. 673 and commentary.

[48] There is much confusion over the exact implications of a "free pardon": see A. T. H. Smith, *op. cit.*, pp. 417–422. It seems to depend on the exact terms of the pardon in question. The terminology is clearly inappropriate where a person has been pronounced to be innocent. In New Zealand it has been held to be technically no more than an indication that the person concerned was wrongfully convicted: *Re Royal Commission on Thomas* [1980] 1 N.Z.L.R. 602, and in *R. v. Foster* [1985] Q.B. 115, the Court of Appeal (Criminal Division) held that the effect of a free pardon was to remove from the subject of the pardon all pain, penalties and punishments ensuing from the conviction but not to eliminate the conviction. (The court proceeded to quash the conviction: see A. Wolfgarten and A. N. Khan, (1986) 130 S.J. 157.) Compare the current Home Office view, above. On the difficulties in taking account of pardoned convictions when considering sentencing for a subsequent offence where there is an increased sentence for repeated offending, see *Archbold* (2002), para. 4–163. See also *R. v. Bolton JJ., ex p. Scally* [1991] 1 QB 537 at 546.

[49] *ibid.* p. 3. In *R. v. Secretary of State for the Home Department, exp.Bentley* [1993] 4 All E.R. 442. the Divisional Court invited the Home Secretary to reconsider his decision not to recommend a posthumous free pardon for Derek Bentley, who was hanged in 1953 for the murder of a police officer; his decision was flawed in that he had failed to consider the possibility of a posthumous conditional pardon reflecting not that B was "morally and technically innocent" (the criteria for a full (or free) pardon, which in the Home Secretary's view were not fulfilled), but simply that B ought to have been reprieved. Michael Howard, then Home Secretary, recommended the grant of a pardon and eventually the Court of Appeal overturned the conviction criticising heavily Lord Goddard's actions as trial judge in the case: [1999] Crim. L.R. 330.

[50] It is difficult to establish a cause of action for malicious prosecution: it is necessary to prove, *inter alia*, that the prosecution lacked reasonable and probable cause and that the defendant acted maliciously: W. V. H. Rogers, *Winfield and Jolowicz on Tort* (15th ed., 1998), pp.678–688.)

[51] See especially N. Taylor and J. Wood (1999) *op. cit.*, discussing the costs — financial, psychological and physical — to the wrongly convicted and their families. As an example, see the discussion in P. Foot, *Murder at the Farm* (1998) (the Carl Bridgewater case). See also R. Brandon and C. Davies, *Wrongful Imprisonment* (1973).

conviction.[52] The amount of compensation is fixed on the recommendation of an independent assessor (in practice the chairman of the Criminal Injuries Compensation whose advice is always accepted).[53] The assessor takes account of pecuniary losses, damage to character or reputation and physical hardship. The offer is made without admission of liability, and while the claimant is free to accept or refuse, if he or she accepts any legal claim must be waived.[54]

In 1985, the Home Secretary stated that he would pay compensation

(1) wherever that was required by the United Kingdom's international obligations; the provision in point was Article 14.6 of the International Covenant on Civil and Political Rights, which provides:

> "When a person has by a final decision been convicted of a criminal offence and when subsequently his conviction has been reversed or he has been pardoned on the ground that a new or newly discovered fact shows conclusively that there has been a miscarriage of justice, the person who has suffered punishment as a result of such conviction shall be compensated according to law, unless it is proved that the nondisclosure of the unknown fact in time is wholly or partly attributable to him."[55]

He remained willing to pay compensation in two further situations:

(2) to people who did not fall within the terms of the preceding paragraph but who had spent time in custody following a wrongful conviction or charge, where he was satisfied that it had resulted from serious default on the part of a member of a police force or of some other public authority;

(3) in other, exceptional, circumstances; in particular where facts emerged at trial or on appeal within time that completely exonerated the accused person (and not merely where the prosecution had been unable to sustain the burden of proof beyond reasonable doubt). The Home Secretary also stated that he would regard any recommendation as to amount made by the

---

[52] There is no legitimate expectation created by the existence of the scheme: *R (on the application of Mullen) v. Home Secretary* February 21 2002. on the exercise of ex gratia payments and their ECHR compatibility; see also *Secretary of State for Home Department, ex p. Chahal* [1999] E.H.R.L.R, (payments only in case of fault in administration not incompatible). The ECtHR does not *require* a financial remedy: *Masson and Van Zon v Netherlands* [1996] 22 E.H.R.R. 491.

[53] The procedure was set out in H.C. Deb, July 29, 1976. written answers, cols, 328–330.

[54] Between 1972 and 1981 there were 47 *ex gratia* payments: 16 of £10,000 or more and three of £20,000 or more: *Home Office Memorandum.* Appendix A(4). In 1983, £77,000 was paid to a man convicted of murder in 1973 on the basis of evidence of a Home Office scientist subsequently discredited. In 1984 Patrick Meehan accepted an offer of £50,500 after seven years in prison: he had previously rejected an offer of £7,500 and the amount was reassessed by an Edinburgh advocate: *Daily Telegraph*, February 2, 1984.

[55] It is essential that there is a discovery of new facts: *R. v. Secretary of State for the Home Department, ex p. Bateman* [1995] 7 Admin. L.R. 175. it is not a "new fact" simply to show that the court made an error in the exercise of its discretion or in application of the law. See *R. (on the application of Conlon) v. Secretary of State for the Home Office* December 11 2000.

assessor as binding upon him.[56] The *ex gratia scheme* was considered by the Divisional Court in *R. v. Secretary of State for the Home Department, ex p. Garner*.[57] The Court held that "exceptional circumstances" included cases where it could be shown that the applicant had been completely exonerated of the crime for which he was convicted or there had been judicial error or misconduct that was so great as to give rise to exceptional circumstances.[58]

A further step was taken by section 133 of the Criminal Justice Act 1988, which enacted a statutory right to compensation in situation (1) above. The right follows the terms of Article 14.6, except that it must be shown "beyond reasonable doubt" (not "conclusively") that there has been a miscarriage of justice. The compensation is paid to the accused person or, if he or she is dead, to the personal representatives. Whether there is a right to compensation is determined by the Secretary of State; the amount by an assessor appointed under Schedule 12 to the 1988 Act.[59] The assessor must in particular have regard to the seriousness of the offence and the severity of the punishment, the conduct of the investigation and prosecution and any other conviction of the person and any punishment resulting from them.[60] There must be a "quashing" of the conviction for the purposes of section 133. Thus, where a claimant was successful on his third appeal against a murder conviction to the extent only that the Court of Appeal substituted a conviction for a lesser offence, there could be no compensation order.[61] The Divisional Court has recently reviewed the scope of the provision, and concluded that the section requires proof of more than a quashed conviction and a "newly discovered fact". There had to be proof beyond reasonable doubt that there had been a miscarriage of justice. "In short, a miscarriage of justice in the context of section 133 means, in my judgment, the wrongful conviction of an innocent accused. Compensation goes only to those

---

[56] Vol. 87, H. C. Deb, November 29, 1985, written answers, cols.691–692: see P. Ashman, (1986) 136 N.L.J. 497.

[57] April 19 1999.

[58] In general, errors of the judiciary (including magistrates) will not suffice: *R. v. Secretary of State for the Home Department, ex p. Bateman*, May 5, 1993; *R. (on the application of Conlon) v. Secretary of State for the Home Department* December 11, 2000. See also *R. v. Secretary of State for the Home Department, ex p. Howse* [1993] C.O.D. 494; *R. v. Secretary of State for the Home Department, ex p. Harrison* [1988] 3 All E.R. 86.

[59] An assessor must be a lawyer who possesses a seven-year general qualification under the Courts and Legal Services Act 1990, s.71, or an advocate or solicitor in Scotland or a Northern Ireland barrister or solicitor of seven years standing, a person who holds or has held judicial office in any part of the United Kingdom, or the chairman or a member of the Criminal Injuries Compensation Board: Criminal Justice Act 1988, Sched. 6, para. 2, as amended by the 1990 Act, Sched. 10, para. 72(1).

[60] 1988 Act, s.133,(4A), added by the Criminal Appeal Act 1995, s.28. A company cannot recover under s. 133: *R. v. Secretary of State for the Home Department, ex p. Atlantic Commercial UK Ltd The Times*, March 10, 1997.

[61] *R. v. Secretary of State for the Home Department ex p. Christofides* [2002] May 14. It was also noted that the Secretary of State's scheme of compensation did not have to parallel the ECHR jurisprudence regarding just satisfaction.

ultimately proved innocent, not to all those whose convictions are adjudged unsafe."[62]

Cases for the exercise of the prerogative of mercy and requests for compensation are considered by the Home Office's Criminal Department.[63] The reievant papers are scrutinised, and, if it is thought to be necessary, further inquiries are commissioned.

The working of the system has been considered in reports by the Home Affairs Committee and JUSTICE.[64] The Home Affairs Committee thought that cases should continue to be processed by the Home Office, but noted that decisions were often presented in such a way as to seem arbitrary: delays should be explained and reasons given for a refusal to take action normally given. However, there should be an independent review body to advise the Home Secretary on the exercise of the prerogative of mercy. This body should be able to take into account a wider range of matters than those currently considered by the Home Office, including evidence which was known to counsel or the police but not put before the jury, for example for tactical reasons that turn out to have been misguided. It should also be able to advise the exercise of the royal prerogative where its investigation has shown the verdict to be unsafe and unsatisfactory: it should not be necessary for the convicted person to prove his or her innocence. The committee were impressed by Sir David Napley's statement that he was unable from his own experience to recall "a single case where the Home Office has, as a result of its own investigations, felt able to recommend a pardon or any other recognition that a conviction was necessarily wrongful". On the other hand officials had expressed disquiet about certain cases where the courts had refused to interfere with a verdict.[65]

The government rejected most of the Committee's proposals, apart from those concerning matters of presentation.[66] The Home Secretary indicated that he would in future be prepared to exercise his power of reference more readily and the Lord Chief Justice that there was scope for the Court of Appeal to be more ready to exercise its powers to receive evidence or order a retrial.

The JUSTICE Committee considered the issue of compensation. It thought that persons given a free pardon and those whose convictions are quashed after a reference by the Home Secretary should have a *right* to compensation. Other persons whose convictions are quashed on appeal should be entitled to apply for compensation although that compensation

---

[62] *per* Simon Brown L.J. in *R (on the application of Mullen) v. Secretary of State* February 21, 2002. The conviction of M was quashed following a decision that the proceedings should have been stayed as an abuse of process owing to the police methods in securing his extradition to the U.K. The court went on: "the quashing of the claimant's conviction in this case was a vindication of the rule of law, not the righting of a mistaken verdict".

[63] See the Devlin Report, *Evidence of Identification in Criminal Cases* (1975–76 H.C. 338), pp. 55–56. 142–145: *Home Office Memorandum*, pp. 4–5. For further information see the website of the Justice and Victims Unit at the Home Office *www.homeoffice. gov.uk.*

[64] 1981–82 H.C. 421; JUSTICE Report, *Compensation for Wrongful Imprisonment* (1982): JUSTICE Report, *Miscarriages of Justice* (1989). See also the JUSTICE Report. *Home Office Reviews of Criminal Convictions* (1968); B. Woffinden, *Miscarriages of Justice* (1987); and, on the compensation issue G.H.L. Fridman, (1963) 26 M.L.R. 481; C. Shelboum, [1978] Crim. L.R. 22.

[65] 1981–82 H.C. 421, p. x.

[66] *Government Reply to the Sixth Report from the Home Affairs Committee Session, 1981–82* H.C. 421 (Cmnd. 8856, 1983).

could be refused or reduced in the light of the claimant's conduct or if the conviction was quashed on a technicality. In certain circumstances compensation should be paid to persons committed for trial in custody and acquitted or discharged, and persons who have had part of their sentence remitted. Claims should be dealt with by an Imprisonment Compensation Board established on the lines of the Criminal Injuries Compensation Board. The recent reforms constitute only a partial move in this direction.[67]

JUSTICE returned to these matters in its 1989 Report on *Miscarriages of Justice*. It summarised its own case work in connection with alleged miscarriages of justice, and examined the reasons why such miscarriages occur. Many of its recommendations concern the investigation, trial and appeal stages of the criminal process. As regards the post-appeal stage, it took the view that the government's response to the Home Affairs Committee's report had not met the criticisms, and that there had been no discernible change in the practice of the Home Office and the Court of Appeal since then.

The changes introduced by the Criminal Appeal Act 1995[68] do not affect directly the exercise of the royal prerogative of mercy. However, the RCCJ was of the view that it would normally only be appropriate to exercise the prerogative, in a miscarriage of justice case where that was shown by evidence that would be inadmissible in court.[69] The CCRC has express power to give assistance to the Secretary of State in connection with the prerogative of mercy,[70] and the investigation of cases is supervised by them rather than the Home Office. Although administered by the Home Secretary, the schemes of compensation have been held to be compatible with the ECHR requirement of an independent and impartial tribunal under Article 6 because the Home Secretary's decision is subject to judicial review.[71]

---

[67] JUSTICE described the details of the scheme as "disappointing": 31st Annual Report of JUSTICE, pp. 27–28.

[68] Above, para. 18-018.

[69] Cm. 2263, p. 184.

[70] Above, para. 18-018.

[71] See *Mullen* (above). On the ECHR obligations to provide remedies and their application in domestic law, see Chap. 8 above, and the Human Rights Act 1998, s.7. See generally Emmerson and Ashworth (2001), Chap. 3, Part G. See also Protocol 7 of Article 3 (not yet incorporated in English law). On remedies for violations of ECHR rights under the Human Rights Act 1998 see [1998] E.H.R.L.R. 691.

INDEX

1341

Summary:

- less serious
- trial only by judge
- lawyer can appear as agent
- usually not arrested; rather, given notice to appear in court.

Indictable:

- More serious
- trial by judge & jury
- has to show up in court
- arrested if power have reasonable grounds to believe that person has committed indictable offence.